# CRIME IN THE UNITED STATES

## 2011

## FIFTH EDITION

# CRIME IN THE UNITED STATES

## 2011

## FIFTH EDITION

Bernan Press

Published in the United States of America
by Bernan Press, a wholly owned subsidiary of
The Rowman & Littlefield Publishing Group, Inc.
4501 Forbes Boulevard, Suite 200
Lanham, Maryland 20706

Bernan Press
800-865-3457
info@bernan.com
www.bernan.com



ISBN: 978-1-59888-482-1
eISBN: 978-1-59888-483-8

∞™ The paper used in this publication meets the minimum requirements of American National Standard for Information Sciences—Permanence of Paper for Printed Library Materials, ANSI/NISO Z39.48-1992.
Manufactured in the United States of America.

# CONTENTS

## SECTION I:

# SUMMARY OF THE UNIFORM CRIME REPORTING (UCR) PROGRAM

# SUMMARY OF THE UNIFORM CRIME REPORTING (UCR) PROGRAM

Bernan Press is proud to present its fifh edition of *Crime in the United States*. This title was formerly published by the Federal Bureau of Investigation (FBI), but is no longer available in printed form from the government. This edition contains final data from 2009, the latest data that are currently available.

This section examines the best way of using the publication's data and discusses the history of the UCR Program, which collects the data used in *Crime in the United States*.

## About the UCR Program

The UCR Program's primary objective is to generate reliable information for use in law enforcement administration, operation, and management; however, over the course of the program, its data have become one of the country's leading social indicators.

The UCR Program is a nationwide, cooperative statistical effort of nearly 18,000 city, university and college, county, state, tribal, and federal law enforcement agencies voluntarily reporting data on crimes brought to their attention. Since 1930, the FBI has administered the UCR Program and continued to assess and monitor the nature and type of crime in the Nation. The program's primary objective is to generate reliable information for use in law enforcement administration, operation, and management; however, its data have over the years become one of the country's leading social indicators. Criminologists, sociologists, legislators, municipal planners, the media, and other students of criminal justice use the data for varied research and planning purposes. In 2009, law enforcement agencies active in the UCR Program represented more than 295 million United States inhabitants—96.3 percent of the total population. The coverage amounted to 97.1 percent of the population in Metropolitan Statistical Areas, 90.9 percent of the population in cities outside metropolitan areas, and 93.0 percent of the population in nonmetropolitan counties.

## Note for Users

It is important for UCR data users to remember that the FBI's primary objective is to generate a reliable set of crime statistics for use in law enforcement administration, operation, and management. The FBI does not provide a ranking of agencies; instead, it provides alphabetical tabulations of states, metropolitan statistical areas, cities with over 10,000 inhabitants, suburban and rural counties, and colleges and universities. Law enforcement officials use these data for their designed purposes. Additionally, the public relies on these data for information about the fluctuations in levels of crime from year to year, while criminologists, sociologists, legislators, city planners, media outlets, and other students of criminal justice use them for a variety of research and planning purposes. Since crime is a sociological phenomenon influenced by a variety of factors, the FBI discourages data users from ranking agencies and using the data as a measurement of the effectiveness of law enforcement.

To ensure that data are uniformly reported, the FBI provides contributing law enforcement agencies with a handbook that explains how to classify and score offenses and provides uniform crime offense definitions. Acknowledging that offense definitions may vary from state to state, the FBI cautions agencies to report offenses according to the guidelines provided in the handbook, rather than by local or state statutes. Most agencies make a good faith effort to comply with established guidelines.

The UCR Program publishes the statistics most commonly requested by data users. More information regarding the availability of UCR Program data is available by telephone at (304) 625-4995, by fax at (304) 625-5394, or by e-mail at <cjis_comm@leo.gov>. E-mail data requests cannot be processed without the requester's full name, mailing address, and contact telephone number.

### *Variables Affecting Crime*

Until data users examine all the variables that affect crime in a town, city, county, state, region, or college or university, they can make no meaningful comparisons.

### *Caution Against Ranking*

In each edition of *Crime in the United States*, many entities—including news media, tourism agencies, and other organizations with an interest in crime in the nation—use reported figures to compile rankings of cities and counties. However, these rankings are merely a quick choice made by that data user; they provide no insight into the many variables that mold the crime in a particular town, city, county, state, or region. Consequently, these rankings may lead to simplistic and/or incomplete analyses, which can create misleading perceptions and thus adversely affect cities and counties, along with their residents.

### *Considering Other Characteristics of a Jurisdiction*

To assess criminality and law enforcement's response from jurisdiction to jurisdiction, data users must consider many variables, some of which (despite having significant impact on crime) are not readily measurable or applicable among all locales. Geographic and demographic factors specific to each jurisdiction must be considered and applied in order to make an accurate and complete assessment of crime in that jurisdiction. Several sources of information are available to help the researcher explore the variables that affect crime in a particular locale. U.S. Census Bureau data, for example, can help the user better understand the makeup of a locale's population. The transience of the population, its racial and ethnic makeup, and its composition by age and gender, educational levels, and prevalent family structures are all key factors in assessing and understanding crime.

Local chambers of commerce, planning offices, and similar entities provide information regarding the economic and cultural makeup of cities and counties. Understanding a jurisdiction's industrial/economic base, its dependence upon neighboring jurisdictions, its transportation system, its economic dependence on nonresidents (such as tourists and convention attendees), and its proximity to military installations, correctional institutions, and other types of facilities all contribute to accurately gauging and interpreting the crime known to and reported by law enforcement.

The strength (including personnel and other resources) and aggressiveness of a jurisdiction's law enforcement agency are also key factors in understanding the nature and extent of crime occurring in that area. Although information pertaining to the number of sworn and civilian employees can be found in this publication, it cannot be used alone as an assessment of the emphasis that a community places on enforcing the law. For example, one city may report more crime than another comparable city because its law enforcement agency identifies more offenses. Attitudes of citizens toward crime and their crime reporting practices—especially for minor offenses—also have an impact on the volume of crimes known to police.

### *Make Valid Assessments of Crime*

It is essential for all data users to become as well educated as possible about understanding and quantifying the nature and extent of crime in the United States and in the more than 17,000 jurisdictions represented by law enforcement contributors to the UCR Program. Valid assessments are possible only with careful study and analysis of the various unique conditions that affect each local law enforcement jurisdiction.

Some factors that are known to affect the volume and type of crime occurring from place to place are:

- Population density and degree of urbanization
- Variations in composition of population, particularly in the concentration of youth
- Stability of the population with respect to residents' mobility, commuting patterns, and transient factors
- Modes of transportation and highway systems
- Economic conditions, including median income, poverty level, and job availability
- Cultural factors and educational, recreational, and religious characteristics
- Family conditions, with respect to divorce and family cohesiveness
- Climate
- Effective strength of law enforcement agencies
- Administrative and investigative emphases of law enforcement
- Policies of other components of the criminal justice system (i.e., prosecutorial, judicial, correctional, and probational policies)
- Residents' attitudes toward crime
- Crime reporting practices of residents

Although many of the listed factors equally affect the crime of a particular area, the UCR Program makes no attempt to relate them to the data presented. **The data user is therefore cautioned against comparing statistical data of individual reporting units from cities, counties, metropolitan areas, states, or colleges or universities solely on the basis on their population coverage or student enrollment.** Until data users examine all the variables that affect crime in a town, city, county, state, region, or college or university, they can make no meaningful comparisons.

## Historical Background

Since 1930, the FBI has administered the UCR Program; the agency continues to assess and monitor the nature and type of crime in the nation. Data users look to the UCR Program for various research and planning purposes.

Recognizing a need for national crime statistics, the IACP formed the Committee on Uniform Crime Records in the 1920s to develop a system of uniform crime statistics. After studying state criminal codes and making an evaluation of the recordkeeping practices in use, the Committee completed a plan for crime reporting that became the foundation of the UCR Program in 1929. The plan included standardized offense definitions for seven main offense classifications known as Part I crimes to gauge fluctuations in the overall volume and rate of crime. Developers also instituted the Hierarchy Rule as the main reporting procedure for what is now known as the Summary Reporting System of the UCR Program.

Seven main offense classifications, known as Part I crimes, were chosen to gauge the state of crime in the nation. These seven offense classifications included the violent crimes of murder and nonnegligent manslaughter, forcible rape, robbery, and aggravated assault; also included were the property crimes of burglary, larceny-theft, and motor vehicle theft. By congressional mandate, arson was added as the eighth Part I offense category. Data collection for arson began in 1979. Agencies classify and score offenses according to a Hierarchy Rule (with the exception of justifiable homicide, motor vehicle theft, and arson) and report their data to the FBI. More information about the Hierarchy Rule is presented in Appendix I.

During the early planning of the program, it was recognized that the differences among criminal codes precluded a mere aggregation of state statistics to arrive at a national total. Also, because of the variances in punishment for the same offenses in different states, no distinction between felony and misdemeanor crimes was possible. To avoid these problems and provide nationwide uniformity in crime reporting, standardized offense definitions were developed. Law enforcement agencies use these to submit data without regard for local statutes. The definitions used by the program can be found in Appendix II.

In January 1930, 400 cities (representing 20 million inhabitants in 43 states) began participating in the UCR Program. Congress enacted Title 28, Section 534, of the United States Code that same year, which authorized the attorney general to gather crime information. The attorney general, in turn, designated the FBI to serve as the national clearinghouse for the collected crime data. Since then, data based on uniform classifications and procedures for reporting have been obtained annually from the nation's law enforcement agencies.

## Advisory Groups

Providing vital links between local law enforcement and the FBI for the UCR Program are the Criminal Justice Information Systems Committees of the IACP and the National Sheriffs' Association (NSA). The IACP represents the thousands of police departments nationwide, as it has since the program began. The NSA encourages sheriffs throughout the country to participate fully in the program. Both committees serve the program in advisory capacities.

In 1988, a Data Providers' Advisory Policy Board was established. This board operated until 1993, when it combined with the National Crime Information Center Advisory Policy Board to form a single Advisory Policy Board (APB) to address all FBI criminal justice information services. The current APB works to ensure continuing emphasis on UCR-related issues. The Association of State Uniform Crime Reporting Programs (ASUCRP) focuses on UCR issues within individual state law enforcement associations and also promotes interest in the UCR Program. These organizations foster widespread and responsible use of uniform crime statistics and lend assistance to data contributors.

## Redesign of UCR

Although UCR data collection was originally conceived as a tool for law enforcement administration, the data were widely used by other entities involved in various forms of social planning by the 1980s. Recognizing the need for more detailed crime statistics, law enforcement called for a thorough evaluative study to modernize the UCR Program. The FBI formulated a comprehensive three-phase redesign effort. The Bureau of Justice Statistics (BJS) agency in the Department of Justice responsible for funding criminal justice information projects, agreed to underwrite the first two phases. These phases were conducted by an independent contractor and structured to determine what, if any, changes should be made to the current program. The third phase would involve implementation of the changes identified.

During the first phase, which began in 1982, the historical evolution of the UCR Program was examined. All aspects of the program, including its objectives and intended user audience, data items, reporting mechanisms, quality control issues, publications and user services, and relationships with other criminal justice data systems, were studied.

Early in 1984, a conference on the future of UCR Program launched the second phase of the study that examined the program's potential and concluded with a set of recommended changes. Phase two ended in early 1985 with the production of a report, *Blueprint for the Future of the Uniform Crime Reporting Program.* The study's Steering Committee reviewed the draft report at a March 1985 meeting and made various recommendations for revision. The committee members, however, endorsed the report's concepts.

In April 1985, the phase two recommendations were presented at the eighth National UCR Conference. Various considerations for the final report were set forth, and the overall concept for the revised UCR Program was unanimously approved. The joint IACP/NSA Committee on UCR also issued a resolution endorsing the *Blueprint.*

The final report, the *Blueprint for the Future of the Uniform Crime Reporting Program,* was released in the summer of 1985. It specifically outlined recommendations for an expanded, improved UCR Program to meet future informational needs. There were three recommended areas of enhancement to the UCR Program:

- Offenses and arrests would be reported using an incident-based system.
- Data would be collected on two levels. Agencies in level one would report important details about those offenses comprising the Part I crimes, their victims, and arrestees. Level two would consist of law enforcement agencies covering populations of more than 100,000 and a sampling of smaller agencies that would collect expanded detail on all significant offenses.
- A quality assurance program would be introduced.

To begin implementation, the FBI awarded a contract to develop new offense definitions and data elements for the redesigned system. The work involved (a) revising the definitions of certain Part I offenses, (b) identifying additional significant offenses to be reported, (c) refining definitions for both, and (d) developing data elements (incident details) for all UCR Program offenses in order to fulfill the requirements of incident-based reporting versus the current summary system.

Concurrent with the preparation of the data elements, the FBI studied the various state systems to select an experimental site for implementing the redesigned program. In view of its long-standing incident-based program and well-established staff dedicated solely to UCR, the South Carolina Law Enforcement Division (SLED) was chosen. The SLED agreed to adapt its existing system to meet the requirements of the redesigned program and to collect data on both offenses and arrests relating to the newly defined offenses.

Following the completion of the pilot project conducted by the SLED, the FBI produced a draft of guidelines for an enhanced UCR Program. Law enforcement executives from around the country were then invited to a conference where the guidelines were presented for final review.

During the conference, three overall recommendations were passed without dissent: the establishment of a new, incident-based national crime reporting system; the FBI as the managing agency for the program; and the creation of an Advisory Policy Board composed of law enforcement executives to assist in directing and implementing the new program.

Information about the redesigned UCR Program, call the National Incident-Based Reporting System, or NIBRS, is contained in several documents. The *Data Collection Guidelines* publication (August 2000) contains a system overview and descriptions of the offense codes, reports, data elements, and data values used in the system. The *Error Message Manual* (December 1999) contains designations of mandatory and optional data elements, data element edits, and error messages. The *Data Submission Specifications* publication is for the use of local and state systems personnel who are responsible for preparing magnetic media for submission to the FBI. The document is available on the FBI's Web site at <www.fbi.gov/ucr/ucr .htm>. Another publication, *Handbook for Acquiring a Records Management System (RMS) that is Compatible with NIBRS,* is also available on that site.

A NIBRS edition of the *UCR Handbook* was published in 1992 to assist law enforcement agency data contributors implementing the NIBRS within their departments. This document is geared toward familiarizing local and state law enforcement personnel with the definitions, policies, and procedures of the NIBRS. It does not contain the technical coding and data transmission requirements presented in the other NIBRS publications.

The NIBRS collects data on each single incident and arrest within 22 crime categories. For each offense known to police within these categories, incident, victim, property, offender, and arrestee information are gathered when available. The goal of the redesign is to modernize crime information by collecting data currently maintained law enforcement records, making the enhanced UCR Program a by-product of current records systems while maintaining the integrity of the program's long-running statistical series.

The FBI began accepting NIBRS data from a handful of agencies in January 1989. As more contributing law enforcement agencies become educated about the rich data available through incident-based reporting and as resources permit, more agencies are implementing the NIBRS. Based on 2008 data submissions, approximately 39 percent of reporting agencies are certified for NIBRS participation. These agencies include one individual agency each in Alabama, Georgia, Illinois, and the District of Columbia, as well as the state UCR Programs of the following 31 states: Arizona, Arkansas, Colorado, Connecticut, Delaware, Idaho, Iowa, Kansas, Kentucky, Louisiana, Maine, Massachusetts, Michigan, Missouri, Montana, Nebraska, New Hampshire, North Dakota, Ohio, Oregon, Rhode Island, South Carolina, South Dakota, Tennessee, Texas, Utah, Vermont, Virginia, Washington, West Virginia, and Wisconsin. Among those that submit NIBRS data, 13 states (Delaware, Idaho, Iowa, Michigan, Montana, New Hampshire, Rhode Island, South Carolina, South Dakota, Tennessee, Vermont, Virginia, and West Virginia) submit all their data via the NIBRS. Nine state UCR Programs are in various stages of testing the NIBRS. Six other state agencies are planning and developing the NIBRS.

## Suspension of the Crime Index and Modified Crime Index

In June 2004, the CJIS APB approved discontinuing the use of the Crime Index in the UCR Program and its publications and directed the FBI to publish a violent crime total and a property crime total. The Crime Index, first published in Crime in the United States in 1960, was the title used for a simple aggregation of the seven main offense classifications (Part I offenses) in the Summary Reporting System. The Modified Crime Index was the number of Crime Index offenses plus arson.

For several years the CJIS Division studied the appropriateness and usefulness of these indices and brought the matter before many advisory groups including the UCR Subcommittee of the CJIS APB, the ASUCRP, and a meeting of leading criminologists and sociologists hosted by the BJS. In short, the Crime Index and the Modified Crime Index were not true indicators of the degrees of criminality because they were always driven upward by the offense with the highest number, typically larceny-theft. The sheer volume of those offenses overshadowed more serious but less frequently committed offenses, creating a bias against a jurisdiction with a high number of larceny-thefts but a low number of other serious crimes such as murder and forcible rape.

## Recent Development in UCR Program

In response to federal legislation outlined in the USA Patriot Improvement and Reauthorization Act of 2005, the UCR Program began accepting cargo theft data from local, state, tribal, and federal agencies on January 1, 2010. Congress commissioned the FBI to begin capturing crime data on human trafficking in the William Wilberforce Trafficking Victims Protection Reauthorization Act of 2008. The Matthew Shepard and James Byrd, Jr. Hate Crime Prevention Act of 2009 requires the collection of data on crimes motivated by "gender and gender identity" bias, as well as "crimes committed by, and crimes directed against, juveniles." The national UCR Program staff is developing collection strategies to meet both of these most recent mandates.

In addition, to meet a directive of the U.S. Government's Office of Management and Budget, the national UCR Program will expand race categories from four (White, Black, American Indian or Alaska Native, and Asian or Other Pacific Islander) to five (White, Black, American Indian or Alaska Native, Asian, and Native Hawaiian or Other Pacific Islander). The ethnicity categories will change from "Hispanic" to "Hispanic or Latino Origin" and from "Non-Hispanic" to "Not of Hispanic or Latino Origin."

## Expanded Offense Tables

The FBI collects the number of offenses for the crimes of murder, forcible rape, robbery, aggravated assault, burglary, larceny-theft, motor vehicle theft, and arson through the Uniform Crime Reporting Program. In addition to the number of offenses known to the police, the FBI also collects additional data about these offenses, such as the locations of robberies, time of day of burglaries, and other analyses about the offenses. These expanded data also include trends (2-, 5-, and 10-year comparisons) in both crime volume and crime rate per 100,000 inhabitants. Expanded homicide data, (supplemental details about murders such as the age, sex, and race of both the victim and the offender, the weapon used in the homicide, the circumstances surrounding the offense, and the relationship of the victim to the offender) are also available.

Expanded offense data, including expanded homicide data, are information collected beyond the reports of the number of crimes known. As a result, law enforcement agencies can report an offense without providing the supplemental data about that offense. These additional tables can be found at <http://www2.fbi.gov/ucr/cius2009/offenses/expanded_information/index.html>.

## About the Editor

Sarah E. Baltic, associate editor with Bernan Press, received her bachelor's degree in magazine journalism from Syracuse University's S.I. Newhouse School of Public Communications and is a former magazine editor with Voice of Youth Advocates. Additionally, Ms. Baltic has worked in the publications field as a book acquisitions editor and a freelance magazine writer and editor. She has also served as the editor of *Employment, Hours, and Earnings*, and *The Almanac of American Education*, and has assisted with the *Social Security Handbook* (Large Print Edition), *The United States Government Internet Manual*, and is currently working on *The Almanac of the Unelected*; all published by Bernan Press.

# SECTION II:
# OFFENSES KNOWN TO POLICE

## VIOLENT CRIME

- Murder
- Forcible Rape
- Robbery
- Aggravated Assault

## PROPERTY CRIME

- Burglary
- Larceny-Theft
- Motor Vehicle Theft
- Arson

# VIOLENT CRIME

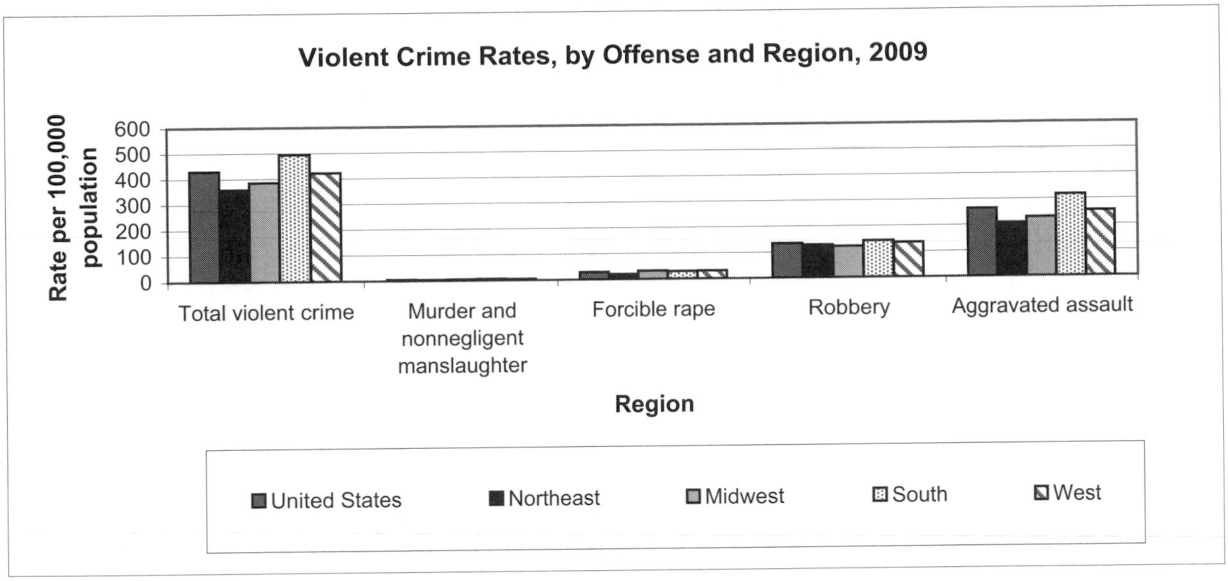


## Definition

Violent crime consists of four offenses: murder and nonnegligent manslaughter, forcible rape, robbery, and aggravated assault. According to the Uniform Crime Reporting (UCR) Program, run by the Federal Bureau of Investigation (FBI), violent crimes involve either the use of force or the threat of force.

## Data Collection

The data presented in *Crime in the United States* reflect the Hierarchy Rule, which counts only the most serious offense in a multiple-offense criminal incident. In descending order of severity, the violent crimes are murder and nonnegligent manslaughter, forcible rape, robbery, and aggravated assault; these are followed by the property crimes of burglary, larceny-theft, and motor vehicle theft. More information on the expanded violent crime tables (which are available online but not included in this publication) can be found in Section I.

## National Volume, Trends, and Rate

In 2009, an estimated 1,318,398 violent crimes occurred in the United States, showing a decrease of 5.3 percent from the 2008 estimate. There were an estimated 429.4 violent crimes per 100,000 inhabitants in 2009. Aggravated assaults accounted for 61.2 percent of violent crimes, the highest number of violent crimes reported to law enforcement. Robbery made up 31.0 percent of violent crimes, forcible rape accounted for 6.7 percent, and murder accounted for 1.2 percent of estimated violent crimes in 2009. (Table 1)

All violent crimes decreased in 2009 compared to the 2008 estimates. Murder decreased by 7.3 percent; forcible rape declined 2.6 percent; aggravated assault fell 4.2 percent; and robbery decreased 8.0 percent. The 2009 murder rate, 5.0 offenses per 100,000 inhabitants, was an 8.1 percent decrease when compared with the rate for 2008. (Tables 1 and 1A)

The UCR Program reports data in 2-year, 5-year, and 10-year increments to formulate trend information. The 2009 estimated violent crime total was 5.2 percent below the 2005 level and 7.5 percent below the 2000 level. The 5-year and 10-year trend data showed that the violent crime rate decreased 8.4 percent between 2005 and 2009 and decreased 15.2 percent between 2000 and 2009. The rate of violent crime declined in 2009 to 429.4 per 100,000, a decrease of 6.1 percent when compared with 2008 data. (Tables 1 and 1A)

In 2009, offenders used firearms in 67.1 percent of the nation's murders, 42.6 percent of robberies, and 20.9 percent of aggravated assaults. Although the largest percent of murders and robberies were committed with firearms, weapons such as clubs and blunt objects accounted for the majority (33.5 percent) of aggravated assaults. (Weapon data are not collected for forcible rape offenses.) (Expanded Homicide Table 7, Robbery Table 3, and Aggravated Assault Table)

## Regional Offense Trends and Rate

The UCR Program divides the United States into four regions: the Northeast, the South, the Midwest, and the West. (More details concerning geographic regions are provided in Appendix III.) The population distribution of the regions can be found in Table 3, and the estimated volume and rate of violent crime by region are provided in Table 4.

### *The Northeast*

The Northeast accounted for an estimated 18.0 percent of the nation's population in 2009 and an estimated 15.0 percent of its violent crimes. (Table 3) The estimated number of violent crimes remained relatively unchanged in 2009 when compared with the estimate from 2008. Murder decreased 8.7 percent in the Northeast, which was the largest decrease in all the regions. Forcible rapes decreased 1.9 percent and aggravated assaults dropped 0.5 percent from 2008. In 2009, there were an estimated 358.3 violent crimes per 100,000 inhabitants. (Table 4)

### *The Midwest*

With an estimated 21.8 percent of the total population of the United States, the Midwest accounted for 19.6 percent of the nation's estimated number of violent crimes in 2009. (Table 3) The region had a 4.3 percent decrease in violent crime from 2008 to 2009. The estimated number of aggravated assaults declined 3.8 percent, the estimated number of robberies decreased 4.9 percent, the number of murders declined 5.4 percent, and the estimated number of forcible rapes fell 5.1 percent from 2008 to 2009. The rate of violent crime per 100,000 inhabitants in the Midwest declined 4.6 percent from 2008 to 2009. (Table 4)

### *The South*

The South, the nation's most populous region, accounted for a 36.9 percent of the nation's population in 2009. Almost 43 percent (42.5) of violent crimes in 2009 occurred in the South. (Table 3) While the estimated number of violent crimes decreased in three of the four regions, the largest decrease (6.6 percent) occurred in the South. The estimated number of forcible rapes fell 1.9 percent in the South. Robberies had the largest decline (9.9 percent) of the four offenses, followed by murders (7.6 percent) and aggravated assaults (5.4 percent). While all four regions experienced declines in the estimated number of aggravated assaults, the greatest decrease was in the South. The estimated rate of violent crime in the South was 494.3 incidents per 100,000 inhabitants in 2009. (Table 4)

### *The West*

With 23.3 percent of the nation's population in 2009, the West accounted for an estimated 22.9 percent of the nation's violent crime. (Table 3) Violent crime in the West decreased 5.3 percent from 2008 to 2009. All four violent offense categories decreased in number from 2008 to 2009: murder declined 7.6 percent, aggravated assault fell 4.5 percent, robbery decreased by 7.4 percent, and forcible rape dropped 1.6 percent. The region's violent crime rate in 2009 was 422.4 per 100,000 population, a 6.4 percent decrease from the 2008 rate. (Table 4)

## Community Types

The UCR Program aggregates crime data into three community types: metropolitan statistical areas (MSAs), cities outside MSAs, and nonmetropolitan counties outside MSAs. Appendix III provides additional information regarding community types. In 2009, 83.6 percent of the nation's population lived in MSAs. Residents of cities outside MSAs accounted for 6.5 percent of the country's population, while 9.8 percent of the population lived in nonmetropolitan counties. (Table 2)

Approximately 84 percent of the estimated number of violent crimes in the United States occurred in MSAs, 5.6 percent occurred in cities outside MSAs, and 4.4 percent occurred in nonmetropolitan counties. By community type, the violent crime rates were estimated at 458.7 incidents per 100,000 inhabitants in MSAs, 396.4 incidents per 100,000 inhabitants in cities outside MSAs, and 202.4 incidents per 100,000 inhabitants in nonmetropolitan counties. (Table 2)

## Population Groups: Trends and Rates

In the UCR Program, data are also aggregated into population groups; these groups are described in more detail in Appendix III. The nation's cities had an overall decrease of 5.5 percent in the estimated number of violent crimes from 2008 to 2009. By city population group, cities with 500,000 to 999,999 inhabitants had the largest percentage decline in the estimated number of violent crimes (7.4 percent). (Table 12)

The law enforcement agencies in the nation's cities collectively reported a rate of 518.4 violent crimes per 100,000 inhabitants in 2009. Law enforcement agencies in cities subset of 500,000 to 999,999 inhabitants reported the highest violent crime rate, with 877.8 violent crimes per 100,000 inhabitants; the violent crime rate for all cities with 250,000 or more inhabitants was 801.6 per 100,000 inhabitants. Agencies in cities with 10,000 to 24,999 inhabitants reported the lowest violent crime rate (307.0 incidents per 100,000 inhabitants). Law enforcement agencies in the nation's metropolitan counties reported a collective violent crime rate of 307.6 per 100,000 inhabitants, while agencies in nonmetropolitan counties reported a collective rate of 208.4 violent crimes per 100,000 inhabitants. (Table 16)

# MURDER

## Definition

The UCR Program defines murder and nonnegligent manslaughter as the willful (nonnegligent) killing of one human being by another. The classification of this offense is based solely on police investigation, rather than on the determination of a court, medical examiner, coroner, jury, or other judicial body. The UCR Program does not include the following situations under this offense classification: deaths caused by negligence, suicide, or accident; justifiable homicides; and attempts to murder or assaults to murder, which are considered aggravated assaults.

## Data Collection/Supplementary Homicide Reports (SHR)

The UCR Program's *Supplementary Homicide Report* (SHR) provides information about murder victims and offenders by age, sex, and race; the types of weapons used in the murders; the relationships of the victims to the offenders; and the circumstances surrounding the incident. Law enforcement agencies are asked to complete an SHR for each murder reported to the UCR Program. Data from SHRs can be viewed in the Expanded Homicide Data section, found on the FBI Web site: <http://www2.fbi.gov/ucr/cius2009/offenses/expanded_information/homicide.html>. Of the estimated 15,241 murders that were committed in the United States in 2009, law enforcement agencies contributed data to the UCR Program through SHRs for 13,636 murders. More information on these reports and the expanded homicide tables can be found in Section I. Highlights from these tables have been included below.

## National Volume, Trends, and Rates

An estimated 15,241 persons were murdered nationwide in 2009. This number was a 7.3 percent decrease from the 2008 estimate, a 9.0 percent increase from the 2005 figure, and a 2.2 percent increase from the 2000 estimate. The 2009 murder rate, 5.0 offenses per 100,000 inhabitants, was an 8.1 percent decrease when compared with the rate for 2008. Murder accounted for 1.2 percent of the overall estimated number of violent crimes in 2009. (Table 1)

## Regional Offense Trends and Rates

The UCR Program divides the United States into four regions: the Northeast, the South, the Midwest, and the West. (More details concerning geographic regions are provided in Appendix III.) In 2009, more than 44 percent of murders were reported in the South, the most populous region. The West reported 21.3 percent of murders, 20.0 percent reported in the Midwest, and 13.9 percent reported in the Northeast. In 2009, the estimated number of murders decreased in all four regions, with the largest decrease, 8.7 percent, occurring in the Northeast.

### *The Northeast*

In 2009, the Northeast accounted for an estimated 18.0 percent of the nation's population and 13.9 percent of its estimated number of murders. With an estimated 2,111 murders, the Northeast saw an 8.7 percent decrease compared with the 2008 figure. The offense rate for the Northeast was 3.8 murders per 100,000 inhabitants, down from 4.2 murders per 100,000 inhabitants in 2008. (Tables 3 and 4)

### *The Midwest*

The Midwest accounted for an estimated 21.8 percent of the nation's total population and 20.0 percent of the country's estimated number of murders in 2009. There were an estimated 3,054 murders in the Midwest in 2009, a 5.4 percent decrease from the estimated figure for 2008. The Midwest experienced a rate of 4.6 murders per 100,000 inhabitants in 2009, slightly lower than in 2008. (Tables 3 and 4)

### *The South*

The South accounted for an estimated 36.9 percent of the nation's population in 2009 and 44.8 percent of the nation's murders, the highest proportion among the four regions. The estimated 6,835 murders represented a 7.6 percent decrease in the estimated number of murders from 2008 to 2009. The region's estimated rate of 6.0 murders per 100,000 inhabitants represented a decrease of 8.6 percent from the estimated rate for 2008. (Tables 3 and 4)

### *The West*

The West accounted for an estimated 23.3 percent of the nation's population and 21.3 percent of the estimated number of murders in 2009. The region's population grew 1.2 percent from 2008 to 2009. The West experienced an estimated 3,241 murders, a 7.6 percent decrease from the 2008 estimate. The region's murder rate was 4.5 per 100,000 inhabitants, an 8.7 percent decrease from the 2008 rate. (Tables 3 and 4)

## Community Types

The UCR Program aggregates data for three community types: metropolitan statistical areas (MSAs), cities outside MSAs, and nonmetropolitan counties outside MSAs. (See Appendix III for definitions.) In 2009, MSAs accounted for 83.6 percent of the nation's population and 88.0 percent of the estimated total number of murders. With 13,408 estimated homicides, MSAs experienced a rate of 5.2 murders per 100,000 inhabitants in 2009. Cities outside MSAs accounted for 6.5 percent of the U.S. population and (with an estimated 798 murders) accounted for 9.8 percent of the estimated murders in the nation. The murder rate for cities outside MSAs was 4.0 per 100,000 inhabitants. In 2009, 9.9 percent of the nation's population lived in nonmetropolitan counties outside MSAs. An estimated 1,035 murders took place in these counties, accounting for 6.8 percent of the nation's estimated total. (Table 2)

## Population Groups: Trends and Rates

The UCR Program uses the following population group designations in its data presentations: cities (grouped according to population size) and counties (classified as either metropolitan or nonmetropolitan). A breakdown of these classifications is provided in Appendix III.

From 2008 to 2009, the nation's cities experienced a 7.3 percent decrease in homicides. The only city group to experience an increase (1.8 percent) was those with populations between 25,000 and 49,999. The city group with the largest decrease (11.3 percent) was those with 1,000,000 or more inhabitants. Metropolitan counties experienced a decrease in homicides of 8.6 percent from 2008 to 2009, while nonmetropolitan counties experienced a decrease of 0.3 percent. (Table 12)

In 2009, cities collectively had a rate of 5.9 murders per 100,000 inhabitants. Cities with 500,000 to 999,999 inhabitants had the highest murder rate (11.4 murders per 100,000 inhabitants). Cities with 10,000 to 24,999 inhabitants had the lowest murder rates, with 2.7 murders per 100,000 inhabitants. The homicide rates for metropolitan and nonmetropolitan counties were both 3.6 per 100,000 inhabitants. Suburban areas had a homicide rate of 3.0 per 100,000 inhabitants. (Table 16)

## Supplementary Homicide Reports Data

### *Victims/Offenders*

Based on 2009 supplemental homicide data (where the ages, sexes, or races of the murder victims were *known*), 88.7 percent of victims were over 18 years of age, 24.2 percent were under age 22, 9.9 percent were under 18 years of age, and the age of 1.4 percent of the victims was unknown. Of the 13,618 murder victims in 2009 for whom gender was known, 77.0 percent were male. Concerning murder victims for whom race was known, 48.7 percent were white, 48.6 percent were black, and 2.7 percent were from other races. Race was unknown for 152 victims. (Expanded Homicide Tables 1 and 2) For murders where the gender of the offender was known, 89.7 percent were males. Of the offenders for whom race was known, 51.6 percent were Black, 46.3 percent were White, and 2.1 percent were from other races. (Based on Expanded Homicide Data Table 3)

### *Victim-Offender Relationships*

For incidents in which the victim-offender relationship was known, 24.2 percent of victims were slain by family members, 21.9 percent were murdered by strangers, and 53.8 percent were killed by acquaintances (neighbor, friend, boyfriend, etc.). Among female victims for whom relationships with their offenders were known, 34.6 percent were murdered by their husbands or boyfriends. (Based on Expanded Homicide Data Tables 2 and 10)

### *Circumstances/Weapons*

Concerning the known circumstances surrounding murders, 41.2 percent of victims were murdered during arguments (including romantic triangles) in 2009. Felony circumstances (rape, robbery, burglary, etc.) accounted for 22.9 percent of murders. Circumstances were unknown for

35.4 percent of reported homicides. (Based on Expanded Homicide Data Table 12) Of the homicides for which the type of weapon was specified, 71.8 percent involved the use of firearms. Of the identified firearms used, handguns comprised 88.2 percent. (Based on Expanded Homicide Data Table 8)

## Justifiable Homicide

Certain willful killings must be reported as justifiable, or excusable, homicide. In the UCR Program, justifiable homicide is defined as, and is limited to, the following:

- The killing of a felon by a peace officer in the line of duty.
- The killing of a felon, during the commission of a felony, by a private citizen.

Because these killings are determined by law enforcement investigation to be justifiable, they are tabulated separately from murder and nonnegligent manslaughter. Law enforcement reported 667 justifiable homicides in 2009. Of those, law enforcement officers justifiably killed 406 individuals, and private citizens justifiably killed 261 individuals. (Based on Expanded Homicide Data Tables 14 and 15)

# FORCIBLE RAPE

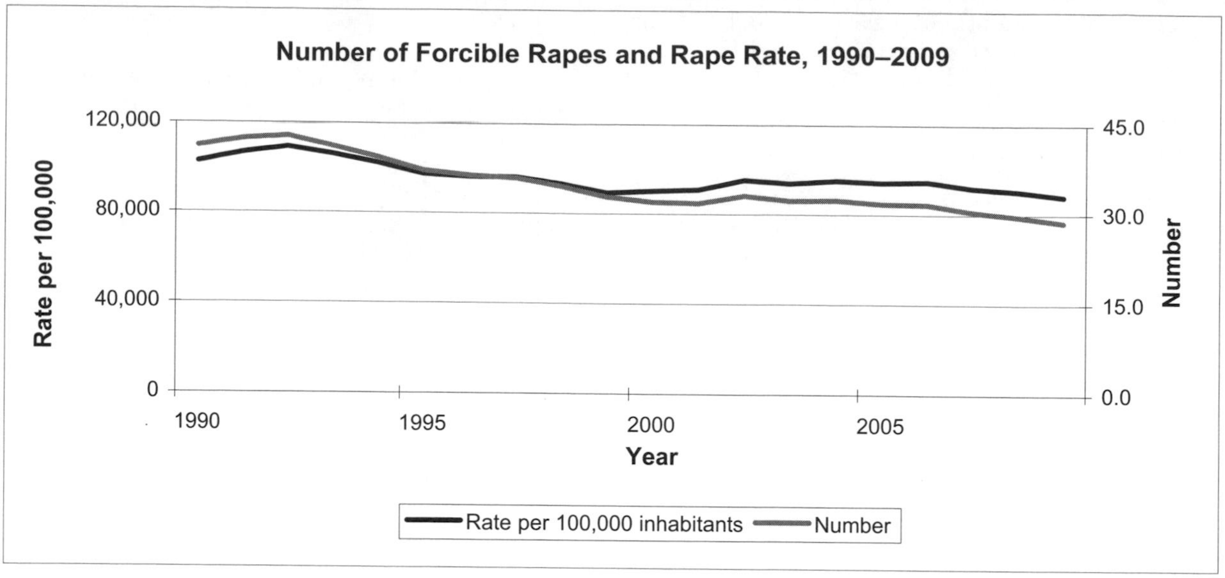


## Definition

Forcible rape is the carnal knowledge of a female forcibly and against her will. Assaults and attempts to commit rape by force or threat of force are included; however, statutory rape (without force) and other sex offenses are excluded.

## Data Collection

The UCR Program counts one offense for each female victim of a forcible rape, attempted forcible rape, or assault with intent to rape, regardless of the victim's age. A rape by force involving a female victim and a familial offender is counted as a forcible rape not an act of incest. The Program collects only arrest statistics concerning all other crimes of a sexual nature. The offense of statutory rape, in which no force is used but the female victim is under the age of consent, is included in the arrest total for the sex offenses category. Sexual attacks on males are counted as aggravated assaults or sex offenses, depending on the circumstances and the extent of any injuries.

For this overview only, the FBI deviated from standard procedure and manually calculated the 2008 and 2009 rates of females raped based on the national female population provided by the U.S. Census Bureau.

## National Volume, Trends, and Rates

In 2009, the estimated number of forcible rapes (88,097)—the lowest figure in the last 20 years—decreased 2.6 percent from the 2008 estimate. The estimated volume of rapes in 2009 was 6.6 percent lower than in 2005 and was 2.3 percent below the 2000 level. (Tables 1 and 1A)

In preparing rate tables, the UCR Program's computer system automatically calculates offense rates per 100,000 inhabitants for all Part I crimes, which include murder and nonnegligent manslaughter, forcible rape, robbery, aggravated assault, burglary, larceny-theft, motor vehicle theft, and arson. (See Appendix II for more information.) Thus, the rate data are based upon the total U.S. population. However, for this overview, the 2009 rate of female rapes has been recalculated based upon the national female population provided by the Census Bureau. The recalculation resulted in a rate of 56.6 offenses per 100,000 females, a 3.4 percent decrease when compared with the 2008 estimated rate of 58.6.

Of the forcible rapes known to law enforcement agencies in 2009, rapes by force made up 93 percent of reported rape offenses, and assaults to rape attempts accounted for 7.0 percent of reported rape offenses. (Tables 1 and 19)

## Regional Offense Trends and Rates

The UCR Program divides the United States into four regions: the Northeast, the South, the Midwest, and the West. (More details concerning geographic regions are provided in Appendix III.) Regional analysis offers estimates of the volume of female rapes, the percent change from the previous year's estimate, and the rate of rape per 100,000 female inhabitants in each region. (Tables 3 and 4)

### *The Northeast*

The Northeast made up 18.0 percent of the U.S. population in 2009 and experienced a 0.4 percent increase in population from 2008 to 2009. In 2009, an estimated 10,871 forcible rapes of females—12.3 percent of the national total—occurred in the Northeast. This was a decrease of 1.9 percent from the 2008 estimated figure. (Tables 3 and 4)

### *The Midwest*

The Midwest, which accounted for 21.8 percent of the U.S. population in 2009, experienced a 0.4 percent increase in population from 2008 to 2009. Almost one-quarter (24.7 percent) of all forcible rapes in the nation occurred in the Midwest in 2009. The 2009 estimate (21,795 forcible rapes) represented a decline of 5.1 percent from the 2008 estimate. (Tables 3 and 4)

### *The South*

The South, the nation's most populous region, accounted for an estimated 36.9 percent of the nation's population in 2009 (and experienced a population growth of 1.2 percent from 2008 to 2009); the region also accounted for an estimated 38.4 percent of the nation's estimated number of forcible rapes. There were an estimated 33,796 female victims of forcible rape in the South in 2009, down 1.9 percent from 34,436 in 2008. (Tables 3 and 4)

### *The West*

The West, which experienced a population growth of 1.2 percent from 2008 to 2009, accounted for 23.3 percent of the nation's population in 2009. The region also accounted for 24.6 percent of the nation's total number of estimated forcible rapes with an estimated 21,689 offenses. The West saw a 1.6 percent decline in forcible rapes from 2008 to 2009. (Tables 3 and 4)

## Community Types

Using the U.S. Office of Management and Budget's designations, the UCR Program aggregates crime data by type of community in which the offenses occur: metropolitan statistical areas (MSAs), cities outside MSAs, and nonmetropolitan counties outside MSAs. (Appendix III provides more detailed information about community types.)

### *MSAs*

In 2009, MSAs accounted for 83.6 percent of the nation's population and 82.2 percent of the nation's estimated number of forcible rapes. An estimated 72,413 females were forcibly raped in metropolitan areas. (Table 2)

### *Cities Outside MSAs*

Cities outside MSAs are mostly incorporated areas served by city law enforcement agencies. Although accounting for only 6.5 percent of the U.S. population in 2009, cities outside MSAs accounted for 9.4 percent of the nation's estimated forcible rapes (8,259 offenses). (Table 2)

### *Nonmetropolitan Counties*

In 2009, approximately 9.8 percent of the nation's population lived in nonmetropolitan counties outside MSAs (counties made up of mostly nonincorporated areas served by noncity law enforcement agencies). Collectively, these areas had an estimated 7,425 forcible rapes, representing 8.4 percent of the nation's estimated total. (Table 2)

# ROBBERY

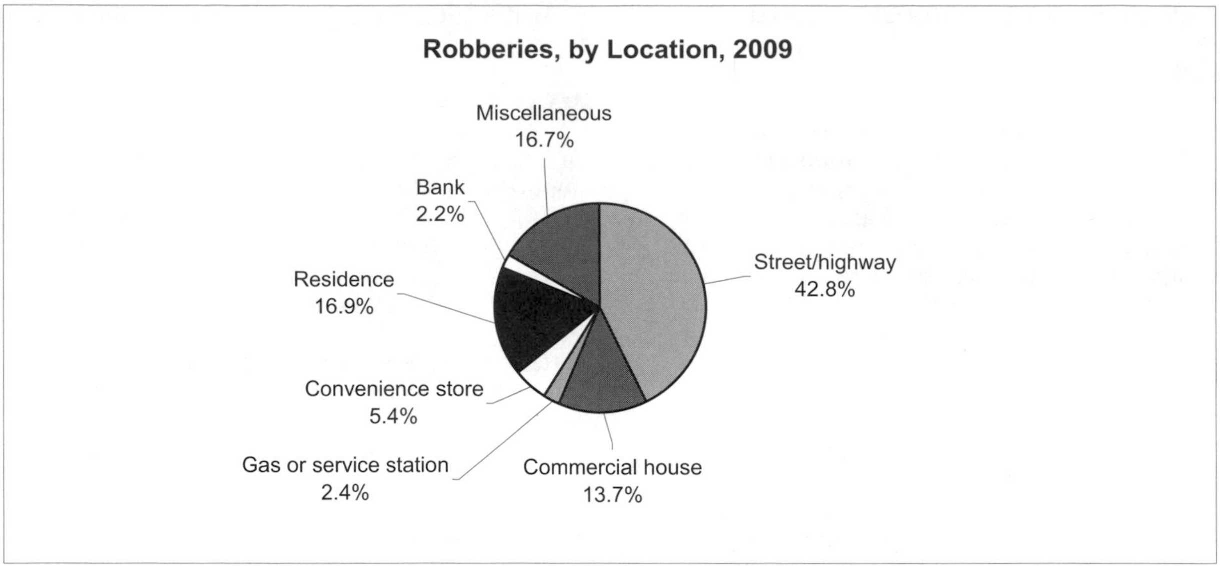


## Definition

The UCR Program defines robbery as the taking or attempting to take anything of value from the care, custody, or control of a person or persons by force or threat of force or violence and/or by putting the victim in fear.

## National Volume, Trends, and Rates

In 2009, the estimated robbery total (408,217) decreased 8.0 percent from the 2008 estimate. The 5-year robbery trend (2005 data compared with 2009 data) showed an increase of 2.2 percent. The 2009 estimated robbery rate (133.0 per 100,000 inhabitants) showed a decrease of 8.8 percent when compared with the 2008 rate. (Tables 1 and 1A)

## Regional Offense Trends and Rates

The UCR Program divides the United States into four regions: the Northeast, the South, the Midwest, and the West. (More details concerning geographic regions are provided in Appendix III.)

### *The Northeast*

The Northeast, with an estimated 18.0 percent of the nation's population in 2009, accounted for 17.3 percent of its estimated number of robberies. (Table 3) The estimated number of robberies decreased 7.5 percent from 2008. The rate for this region was 127.4 robberies per 100,000 inhabitants down from 138.4 robberies per 100,000 inhabitants in 2008. (Table 4)

### *The Midwest*

The Midwest accounted for 21.8 percent of the total population of the United States, and 19.8 percent of its estimated number of robberies, in 2009. (Table 3) There were an estimated 80,724 robberies in the Midwest in 2009, a 4.9 percent decrease from the estimated figure from 2008. The region's robbery rate was 120.8 robberies per 100,000 inhabitants in 2009, the lowest rate among the four regions. (Table 4)

### *The South*

The South, the nation's most highly populated region, experienced a 1.2 percent growth in population from 2008 to 2009; in 2009, it accounted for an estimated 36.9 percent of the nation's population and 39.4 percent of the nation's estimated number of robberies. (Table 3) There were an estimated 160,880 robberies in 2009, representing a 9.9 percent decrease from the 2008 figure, the greatest decline in all four regions. The region experienced the highest rate of robberies per 100,000 inhabitants (142.0), an 11.0 percent drop from the 2008 rate. (Table 4)

### *The West*

The West, was home to an estimated 23.3 percent of the nation's population and accounted for 23.6 percent of the nation's estimated number of robberies in 2009. (Table 3) The estimated number of robberies (96,156) in the region in 2009 represented a 7.4 percent decrease from the 2008 figure. The rate of robberies per 100,000 inhabitants in the West was 134.4, an 8.6 percent decrease from the 2008 rate. This was the second highest rate among the four regions. (Table 4)

## Community Types

The UCR Program aggregates data for three community types: metropolitan statistical areas (MSAs), cities outside MSAs, and nonmetropolitan counties outside MSAs. MSAs include a central city or urbanized area with at least 50,000 inhabitants, as well as the county that contains the principal city and other adjacent counties that have, as defined by the U.S. Office of Management and Budget, a high degree of social and economic integration as measured through commuting. Cities outside MSAs are mostly incorporated areas, and nonmetropolitan counties are made up of mostly unincorporated areas served by noncity law enforcement.

In 2009, MSAs were home to an estimated 83.6 percent of the nation's population, and 95.7 percent of the nation's estimated number of robberies took place in these areas. Robberies in MSAs occurred at a rate of 152.1 per 100,000 inhabitants. Cities outside MSAs accounted for 6.5 percent of the U.S. population and accounted for 3.1 percent of the estimated number of robberies in the nation. The robbery rate for cities outside MSAs was 63.1 per 100,000 inhabitants. Nonmetropolitan counties made up 9.8 percent of the nation's estimated population and 1.2 percent of the nation's estimated robberies, at a rate of 16.9 robberies per 100,000 inhabitants. (Table 2)

## Population Groups: Trends and Rates

The national UCR Program aggregates data by various population groups, which include cities, metropolitan counties, and nonmetropolitan counties. A definition of these groups can be found in Appendix III. The number of robberies in cities as a whole decreased 8.0 percent. Among the population groups labeled *city*, those cities with 100,000 to 249,999 inhabitants had the greatest decrease in the number of robberies (10.2 percent). Nonmetropolitan counties had a 2.3 percent decrease in the estimated number of robberies, and metropolitan counties showed an 8.5 percent decrease. The number of robberies in suburban areas fell 7.1 percent. (Table 12)

Among the population groups, the nation's cities collectively had a rate of 179.0 robberies per 100,000 inhabitants. Of the population groups and subsets designated *city*, those with 500,000 to 999,999 inhabitants had the highest rate (334.4 per 100,000 inhabitants), while those with fewer than 10,000 inhabitants had the lowest rate (54.2 per 100,000 inhabitants) of robberies. Of the two county groups, metropolitan counties had a rate of 71.7 robberies per 100,000 inhabitants, while nonmetropolitan counties had a rate of 17.2 robberies per 100,000 inhabitants. Suburban areas had a robbery rate of 72.4 (Table 16)

## Offense Analysis

The UCR Program collects supplemental data about robberies to document the use of weapons, the dollar loss associated with the offense, and the location types.

### *Robbery by Weapon*

Firearms were used in 42.6 percent of robberies in 2009. Strong-arm robberies accounted for 41.1 percent of the total. Offenders used knives or cutting instruments in 7.7 percent of these crimes. In the remainder of the robberies, the offenders used other types of weapons. (Table 19)

### *Loss by Dollar Value*

Based on the supplemental reports from law enforcement agencies, robberies cost victims, collectively, an estimated $508 million in 2009. (Tables 1 and 23) The average loss per robbery was $1,244. Average dollar losses were the highest for banks, which suffered an average loss of $4,029 per offense. Gas and service stations lost an average of $863 per offense. Commercial houses, which include supermarkets, department stores, and restaurants, had average losses of $1,772. An average of $1,683 was taken from residences. An average of $704 was lost in each offense against convenience stores. (Table 23)

### *Robbery Trends by Location*

Among the location types, gas or service station robberies had the greatest percentage decrease from 2008 to 2009, declining 12.9 percent. Robberies that occurred at residences decreased 4.2 percent. The number of robberies that occurred at convenience stores fell 9.7 percent, robberies on streets and highways decreased 8.4 percent, robberies at commercial houses decreased 8.2 percent, and robberies at banks decreased 2.3 percent. (Table 23)

By location type, the greatest proportion of robberies in 2009 occurred on streets and highways (42.8 percent). Robbers targeted commercial houses in 13.7 percent of offenses and residences in 16.9 percent of offenses. Convenience stores accounted for 5.4 percent of robberies, followed by gas and service stations (2.4 percent) and banks (2.4 percent). (Table 23)

# AGGRAVATED ASSAULT

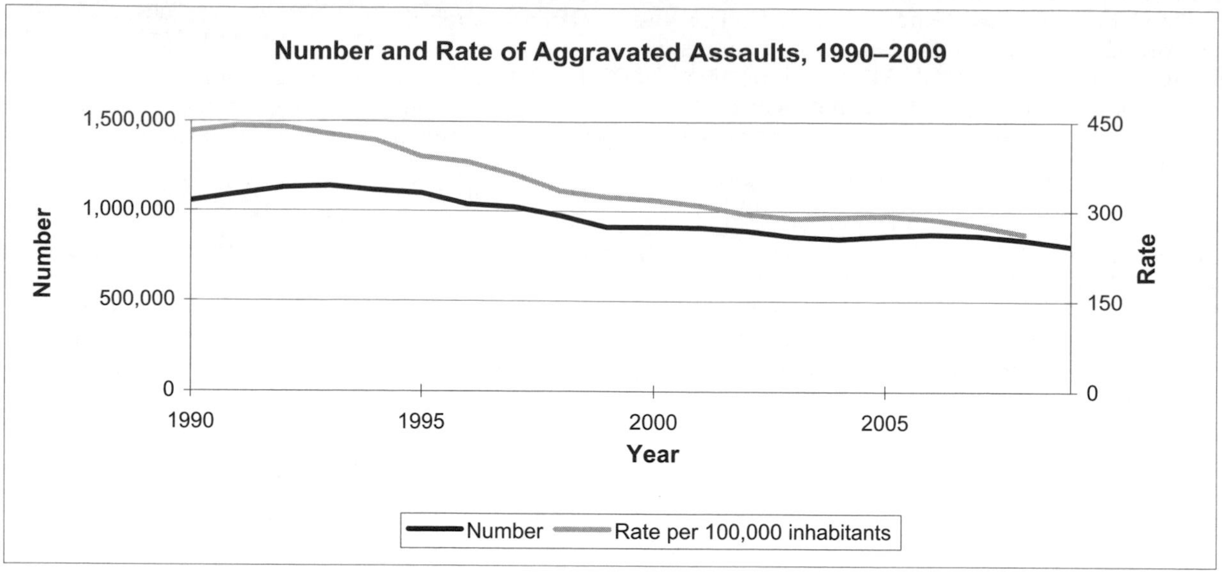


## Definition

The UCR Program defines aggravated assault as an unlawful attack by one person upon another for the purpose of inflicting severe or aggravated bodily injury. This type of assault is usually accompanied by the use of a weapon or by other means likely to produce death or great bodily harm. Attempted aggravated assaults that involve the display or threat of a gun, knife, or other weapon are included in this crime category because serious personal injury would likely result if these assaults were completed. When aggravated assault and larceny-theft occur together, the offense falls under the category of robbery.

## National Volume, Trends, and Rates

In 2009, estimated occurrences of aggravated assaults totaled 806,843, a 4.2 percent decrease from the 2008 figure. According to 2- and 10-year trend data, the estimated number of aggravated assaults in 2009 declined 4.2 percent and 11.5 percent, respectively, when compared with the estimates for 2008 and 2000. The 2009 data also show a decrease for the fourth consecutive year in the rate of aggravated assault per 100,000 U.S. inhabitants. This rate, estimated at 262.8, represents a 5.0 percent decrease from the 2008 rate. However, it also represents a 9.6 percent decrease from the 2005 (5-year trend) rate and an 18.9 percent decrease from the 2000 (10-year trend) rate. (Tables 1 and 1A)

Among the four types of violent crime offenses (murder, forcible rape, robbery, and aggravated assault), aggravated assault typically has the highest rate of occurrence. This trend continued in 2009 with aggravated assault accounting for 61.2 percent of all violent crime. (Table 1)

## Regional Offense Trends and Rates

The UCR Program divides the United States into four regions: the Northeast, the South, the Midwest, and the West. (More details concerning geographic regions are provided in Appendix III.) All four regions experienced decreases in the number of aggravated assaults from 2008 to 2009. (Table 4)

### *The Northeast*

The region with the smallest proportion of the nation's population (an estimated 18.0 percent in 2009) also accounted for the smallest proportion of the nation's estimated number of aggravated assaults (14.2 percent). (Table 3) Occurrences of aggravated assault decreased 0.5 percent from 2008 to 2009, down to an estimated 114,691. The region also had the lowest aggravated assault rate in the nation, at 207.5 incidents per 100,000 inhabitants, a 0.9 percent decline from the 2008 rate. (Table 4)

### *The Midwest*

With 21.8 percent of the nation's total population in 2009—and with a 0.4 percent growth in population from 2008 to 2009—the Midwest accounted for approximately 18.9 percent of the nation's estimated number of aggravated assaults. (Table 3) Occurrences of this offense decreased 3.8 percent from the estimated total for 2008, declining to an estimated 152,254 incidents. The region's aggravated assault rate, at 227.8 incidents per 100,000 inhabitants, represented a 4.1 percent decrease from the 2008 rate. (Table 4)

### *The South*

The South, the nation's most highly populated region, accounted for an estimated 36.9 percent of the nation's population in 2009 and the largest amount of the nation's estimated number of aggravated assaults (44.5 percent). (Table 3) From 2008 to 2009, the estimated number of aggravated assaults decreased 5.4 percent, falling to a total of 358,672 incidents. The rate of aggravated assaults declined to 316.5 per 100,000 inhabitants. (Table 4)

### *The West*

In 2009, the West was home to an estimated 23.3 percent of the nation's population and experienced a 1.2 percent growth in population from 2008 to 2009. The region accounted for 22.5 percent of the nation's estimated number of aggravated assaults. (Table 3) From 2008 to 2009, the estimated number of offenses decreased 4.5 percent to 181,226 incidents. The rate, estimated at 253.2 offenses per 100,000 inhabitants, fell 5.6 percent from 2008. (Table 4)

## Community Types

The UCR Program aggregates data for three community types: metropolitan statistical areas (MSAs), cities outside MSAs, and nonmetropolitan counties outside MSAs. MSAs include a central city or urbanized area with at least 50,000 inhabitants, as well as the county that contains the principal city and other adjacent counties that have a high degree of social and economic integration as measured through commuting. Cities outside MSAs are mostly incorporated areas, and nonmetropolitan counties are made up of mostly unincorporated areas. (For additional information about community types, see Appendix III.)

In 2009, 83.6 percent of the nation's population lived in MSAs, where the rate of aggravated assault was an estimated 273.2 per 100,000 inhabitants. Cities outside MSAs (with 6.5 percent of the U.S. population) had the highest rate of aggravated assault at 288.2 offenses per 100,000 inhabitants. Nonmetropolitan counties accounted for 9.8 percent of the U.S. population and had an offense rate of 157.6 aggravated assaults per 100,000 inhabitants. (Table 2)

From 2008 to 2009, the number of aggravated assaults fell for all cities. Cities with 500,000 to 999,999 inhabitants experienced the greatest decrease (6.3 percent), followed by cities with 250,000 to 499,999, which fell 6.0 percent. In metropolitan counties, the number of aggravated assaults declined 4.5 percent; in nonmetropolitan counties, this number decreased 3.6 percent. Aggravated assaults in suburban areas declined 3.9 percent from 2008 to 2009. (Table 12)

Based on reports from agencies submitting 12 months of complete data for 2009, aggravated assault occurred at an estimated rate of 268.3 offenses per 100,000 inhabitants nationwide. The collective rate for cities was 302.2 aggravated assaults per 100,000 inhabitants. Among city population groups, rates ranged from a high of 493.0 offenses per 100,000 inhabitants (in cities with 500,000 to 999,999 inhabitants) to a low of 202.0 offenses per 100,000 inhabitants (in cities with 10,000 to 24,999 inhabitants). The aggravated assault rate was 209.7 in metropolitan counties and 162.6 in nonmetropolitan counties. (Table 16)

## Offense Analysis

### *Aggravated Assault by Weapon*

Of the aggravated assault offenses for which law enforcement agencies provided expanded data in 2009, 33.5 percent were committed with blunt objects or other dangerous weapons; 26.9 percent involved personal weapons such as hands, fists, and feet; 20.9 percent were committed with firearms; and 18.7 percent involved knives or other cutting instruments. (Table 19)

# PROPERTY CRIME

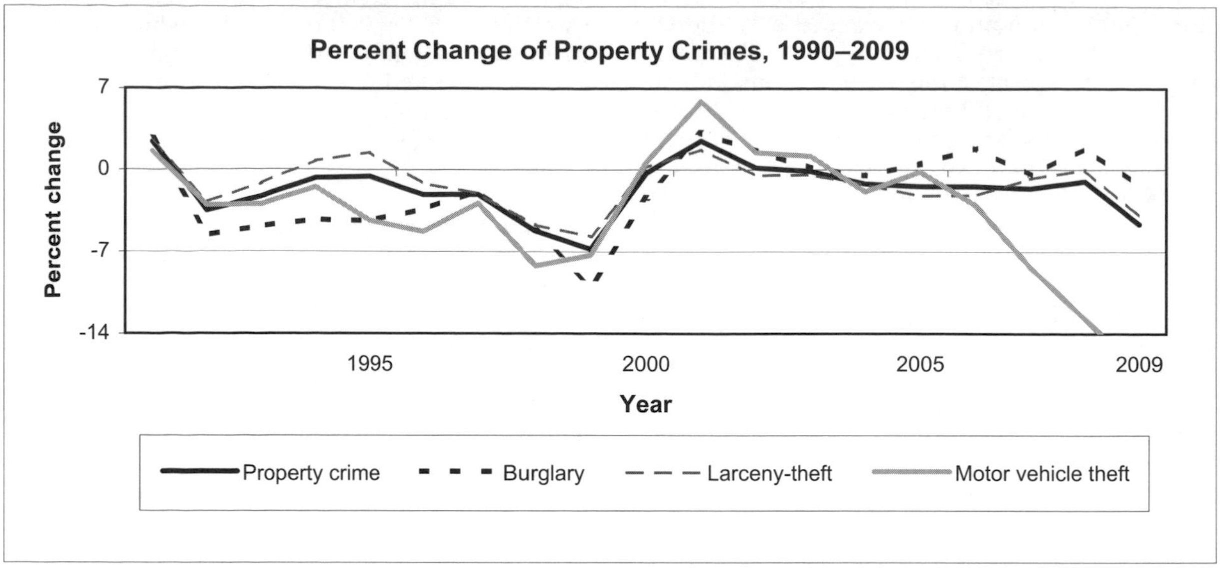


## Definition

The Uniform Crime Reporting (UCR) Program's definition of property crime includes the offenses of burglary, larceny-theft, motor vehicle theft, and arson. The object of theft-type offenses is the taking of money or property without the use of force or threat of force against the victims. Property crime includes arson because the offense involves the destruction of property; however, arson victims may be subjected to force. Because of limited participation and the varying collection procedures conducted by local law enforcement agencies, only limited data are available for arson. Arson statistics are included in the trend, clearance, and arrest tables in *Crime in the United States*, but they are not included in any estimated volume data. More information on the expanded arson tables (which are available online but not included in this publication) can be found in Section I.

## Data Collection

The data presented in *Crime in the United States* reflect the Hierarchy Rule, which counts only the most serious offense in a multiple-offense criminal incident. In descending order of severity, the violent crimes are murder and nonnegligent manslaughter, forcible rape, robbery, aggravated assault; these are followed by the property crimes of burglary, larceny-theft, and motor vehicle theft. The Hierarchy Rule does not apply to the offense of arson.

## National Volume, Trends, and Rates

An estimated 9,320,971 property crimes were committed in the United States in 2009, representing a 4.6 percent decrease from the 2008 (2-year trend) estimate, a 8.4 percent decrease from the 2005 (5-year trend) estimate, and an 8.5 percent decrease from the 2000 (10-year trend) estimate. (Tables 1 and 1A)

From 2008 to 2009, motor vehicle theft fell by 17.1 percent. Larceny-theft (4.0 percent) and burglary (1.3 percent) both showed decreases from their 2008 estimates as well as from both the 2005 and 2000 estimates. (Tables 1 and 1A)

The estimated property crime rate per 100,000 inhabitants in 2009 was 3,036.1, a 5.5 percent decrease from the 2008 rate, an 11.5 percent decrease from the 2005 rate, and a 16.1 percent decrease from the 2000 rate. The number of burglaries grew 7.2 percent from 2000 to 2009, but the burglary rate per 100,000 population fell 1.7 percent. The motor vehicle theft rates per 100,000 residents fell from 412.2 in 2000 to 258.8 in 2009. (Tables 1 and 1A)

## Regional Offense Trends and Rates

The UCR Program separates the United States into four regions: the Northeast, the Midwest, the South, and the West. (Geographic breakdowns can be found in Appendix III.) Property crime data collected by the UCR Program and aggregated by region reflected the following results.

### *The Northeast*

The Northeast region accounted for 18.0 percent of the nation's population and experienced a 0.4 percent increase in population from 2008 to 2009. The region also accounted for 12.6 percent of the nation's estimated number of property crimes in 2009. (Table 3) Law enforcement in the Northeast saw a 5.2 percent decrease in the estimated number of property crimes from 2008 to 2009. The property crime rate for the Northeast, estimated at 2,123.2 incidents per 100,000 inhabitants, was 5.5 percent lower than the 2008 rate. (Table 4)

### *The Midwest*

The Midwest, with 21.8 percent of the U.S. population in 2009 and a 0.4 percent growth in population from 2008 to 2009, accounted for 19.6 percent of the nation's estimated number of property crimes. (Table 3) Law enforcement in the Midwest saw a 5.4 percent decrease in the estimated number of property crimes from 2008 to 2009. The rate of property crime in the Midwest in 2009, estimated at 2,901.4 incidents per 100,000 inhabitants, represented a 5.7 percent decrease from the 2008 rate. (Table 4)

### *The South*

The South, the nation's most populous region, accounted for 36.9 percent of the U.S. population in 2009 and experienced a 1.2 percent growth in population from 2008 to 2009. The region also accounted for an estimated 43.2 percent of the nation's property crimes. (Table 3) The South experienced a 0.6 percent increase in its estimated number of property crimes from 2007 to 2008. The 2008 property crime rate, an estimated 3,780.8 incidents per 100,000 inhabitants, was 0.6 percent lower than the 2007 rate. (Table 4)

### *The West*

In 2008, the West accounted for 23.3 percent of the nation's population; the region experienced a 1.2 percent growth in population from 2008 to 2009. The West also accounted for 22.7 percent of the nation's estimated number of property crimes. (Table 3) From 2008 to 2009, the estimated number of property crimes in this region decreased 6.1 percent. The estimated property crime rate in the West in 2009, 2,962.5 incidents per 100,000 inhabitants, was 7.2 percent lower than the 2008 rate. (Table 4)

## Community Types

The UCR Program aggregates data by three community types: metropolitan statistical areas (MSAs), cities outside metropolitan areas, and nonmetropolitan counties. (Additional in-depth information regarding community types can be found in Appendix III.) In 2009, 83.6 percent of the U.S. population lived in MSAs. The property crime rate for MSAs was 3,160.2 per 100,000 inhabitants. Cities outside metropolitan areas, which accounted for 6.5 percent of the total population in 2009, had a property crime rate of 3,658.5 per 100,000 inhabitants. Nonmetropolitan counties, with 9.8 percent of the nation's population in 2009, had a property crime rate of 1,569.8 per 100,000 inhabitants. (Table 2)

## Population Groups: Trends and Rates

The UCR Program organizes the agencies that contribute data into population groups, which include cities, metropolitan counties, and nonmetropolitan counties. (Appendix III provides further details about these groups.) From 2008 to 2009, law enforcement in the nation's cities collectively reported a 4.3 percent decrease in the number of property crimes. All city groups experienced decreases in the number of property crimes; cities with 1,000,000 inhabitants or more had the largest declines at 6.9 percent. Metropolitan counties experienced a decrease of 5.9 percent from 2008 to 2009 and property crime decreased in nonmetropolitan counties by 6.3 percent. (Table 12)

The nation's cities collectively had a property crime rate of 3,566.7 incidents per 100,000 inhabitants in 2009. Nonmetropolitan counties had a rate of 1,591.5 incidents per 100,000 inhabitants, and metropolitan counties had a rate of 2,276.8 incidents per 100,000 inhabitants. (Table 16)

## Offense Analysis

The estimated dollar loss attributing to property crimes, not including arson, in 2009 was $15.2 billion. Among the individual property crime categories, the dollar losses were an estimated $4.6 billion for burglary, $5.5 billion for larceny-theft, and $ 5.2 billion for motor vehicle theft. (Tables 1 and 23) Arson had an average dollar loss of $17,411. Arsons of industrial/manufacturing structures resulted in the highest average dollar losses with an average loss of $93,287. (Expanded Arson Table 2) In 2009, the average dollar value per motor vehicle stolen in the United States was $6,505. The average dollar value of property taken during burglaries was $2,096; during robberies, $1,244; and during larceny-thefts, $864. The average dollar loss per arson offense was $17,411.

# BURGLARY

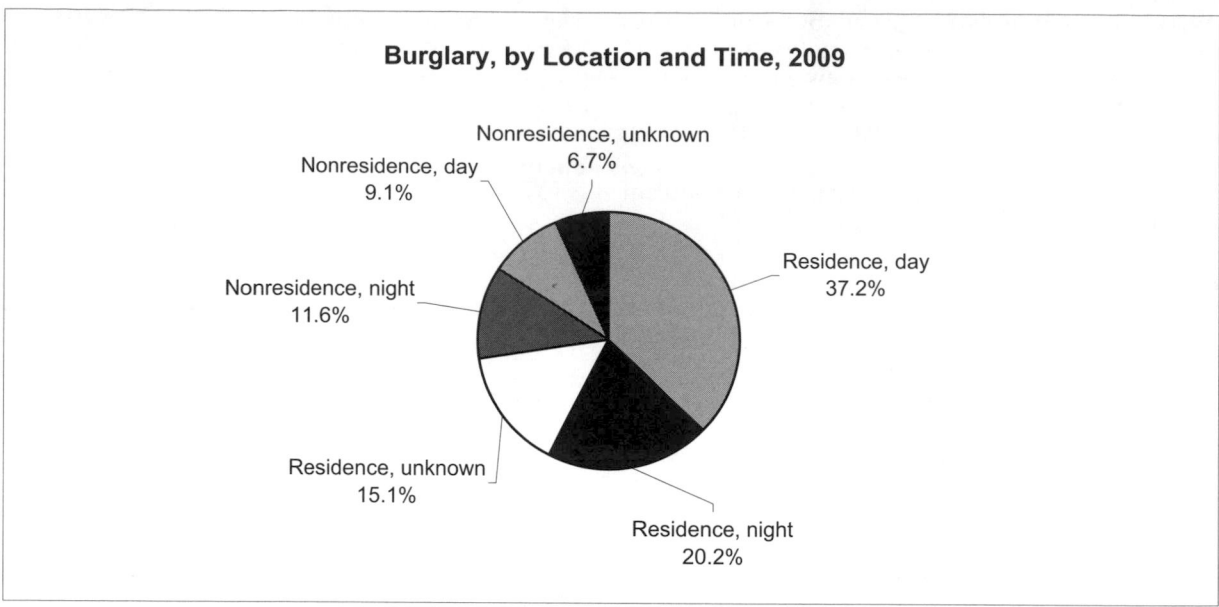

Burglary, by Location and Time, 2009

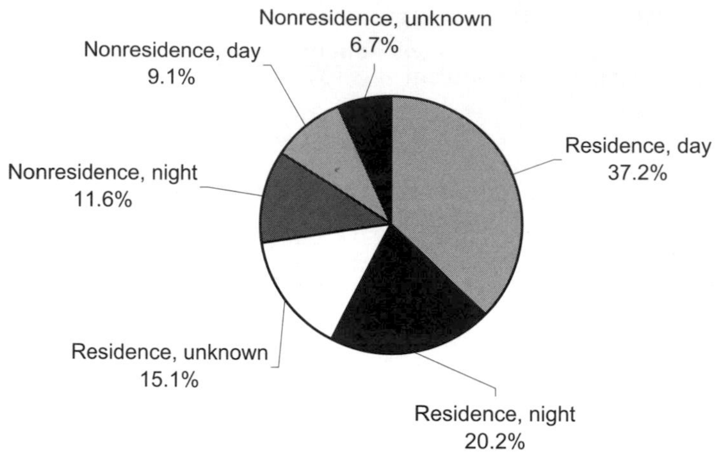


## Definition

The UCR Program defines burglary as the unlawful entry of a structure to commit a felony or theft. To classify an offense as a burglary, the use of force to gain entry need not have occurred. The program has three subclassifications for burglary: forcible entry, unlawful entry where no force is used, and attempted forcible entry. The UCR definition of "structure" includes, but is not limited to, apartments, barns, house trailers or houseboats (when used as permanent dwellings), offices, railroad cars (but not automobiles), stables, and vessels (i.e., ships).

## National Volume, Trends, and Rate

In 2009, there were an estimated 2,199,125 burglaries—a decrease of 1.3 percent when compared with 2008 data. There was an increase of 2.0 percent in the number of burglaries in 2009 when compared with the 2005 estimate and an increase of 7.2 percent when compared with the 2000 estimate. Burglary accounted for 23.6 percent of the estimated number of property crimes committed in 2009. The burglary rate for the United States in 2009 was 716.3 incidents per 100,000 inhabitants, a 2.2 percent decrease from the 2008 rate. (Tables 1 and 1A)

## Regional Offense Trends and Rates

The UCR Program divides the United States into four regions: the Northeast, the Midwest, the South, and the West. (Details regarding these regions can be found in Appendix III.) An analysis of burglary data by region showed the following details.

### *The Northeast*

In 2009, 18.0 percent of the nation's population lived in the Northeast, which experienced a 0.4 percent increase in population from 2008 to 2009. This region accounted for 10.3 percent of the estimated total number of burglary offenses in the nation in 2009. The region's burglary rate, an estimated 407.9 offenses per 100,000 inhabitants, represented a decrease of 4.9 percent from the 2008 rate. The Northeast had the lowest burglary rate of the four regions. (Tables 3 and 4)

### *The Midwest*

The Midwest accounted for 21.8 percent of the nation's population in 2009 and experienced a 0.4 percent growth in population from 2008 to 2009. This region accounted for 20.6 percent of the nation's estimated number of burglaries. The estimated number of burglaries in this region decreased 0.6 percent from 2008 to 2009. The Midwest had a burglary rate of 676.3 offenses per 100,000 inhabitants, a 1.0 percent decrease from the 2008 rate. (Tables 3 and 4)

### *The South*

The South, the nation's most highly populated region, had the most burglaries in 2009 (an estimated 1,055,109). With 36.9 percent of the nation's population (and having experienced a 1.2 percent growth in population from 2008 to 2009), this region accounted for 48.0 percent of all burglaries in the United States. The estimated rate of burglary in the South was 931.1 incidents per 100,000 inhabitants, a 1.1 percent decrease from the 2008 rate. (Tables 3 and 4)

### *The West*

The West accounted for 23.3 percent of the nation's population in 2009 and experienced a 1.2 percent growth in population from 2008 to 2009. In 2009, this region accounted for an estimated 21.2 percent of the nation's burglaries. The region's burglary rate was 651.8, a 4.6 percent decrease from the 2008 rate. The total number of burglaries (466,490) represented a 3.4 percent decrease from the 2008 figure. (Tables 3 and 4)

## Community Types

The UCR Program aggregates data by three community types: metropolitan statistical areas (MSAs), cities outside MSAs, and nonmetropolitan counties. (See Appendix III for more information regarding community types.) In 2009, 83.6 percent of the U.S. population lived in MSAs, and an estimated 84.9 percent of all burglaries occurred in this type of community. Inhabitants of cities outside MSAs accounted for 6.5 percent of the total population in 2009 and 7.5 percent of the estimated number of burglaries; nonmetropolitan counties, with 9.8 percent of the U.S. population, accounted for 7.6 percent of all burglaries. The burglary rates per 100,000 inhabitants were 727.3 in MSAs, 822.6 in cities outside MSAs, and 552.8 in nonmetropolitan counties. (Table 2)

## Population Groups: Trends and Rates

In addition to analyzing data by region and community type, the UCR Program aggregates crime statistics by population groups. Cities are categorized into six groups based on the number of inhabitants; counties are categorized into two groups, metropolitan and nonmetropolitan. (Appendix III offers further details regarding these population groups.)

An examination of data from law enforcement agencies that provided statistics for at least six common months in 2008 and 2009 showed that the nation's cities experienced a collective 1.7 percent decrease in burglaries from 2008 to 2009. Burglaries decreased the most in cities with a population of 1,000,000 and over. The volume of burglaries decreased 1.3 percent in metropolitan counties, and 1.9 percent in suburban areas, but increased 0.8 percent in nonmetropolitan counties. (Table 12)

The UCR Program calculates burglary rates for population groups from the information provided by participating agencies that submitted all 12 months of offense data for the year. In 2009, the nation's cities had 785.4 offenses per 100,000 inhabitants. Cities with 500,000 to 999,999 population had the highest burglary rate at 1,166.4 incidents per 100,000 inhabitants. Cities with 10,000 to 24,999 inhabitants had the lowest burglary rate—631.2 incidents per 100,000 inhabitants. Metropolitan counties had a rate of 619.6 per 100,000 inhabitants, and nonmetropolitan counties had a rate of 560.0 per 100,000 inhabitants. (Table 16)

## Offense Analysis

The UCR Program requests that participating law enforcement agencies provide details regarding the nature of burglaries in their jurisdictions, such as type of entry, type of structure, time of day, and dollar loss associated with each offense.

Of all burglaries, 61.0 percent involved forcible entry, 32.6 percent were unlawful entries (without force), and the remainder (6.5 percent) were forcible entry attempts. (Table 19)

Victims of burglary offenses suffered an estimated $4.6 billion in lost property in 2009; overall, the average dollar loss per burglary offense was $2,096.

As in the past, burglars targeted residences more often than nonresidential structures. In 2009, burglaries of residential properties accounted for 72.6 percent of all burglary offenses. Law enforcement agencies were unable to determine the time of day for 21.9 percent of all reported burglaries. However, of the burglaries for which time of day could be established, most burglaries of residences (64.8 percent) occurred during the day, while most burglaries of nonresidential structures (55.9 percent) occurred at night. (Table 23)

## LARCENY-THEFT

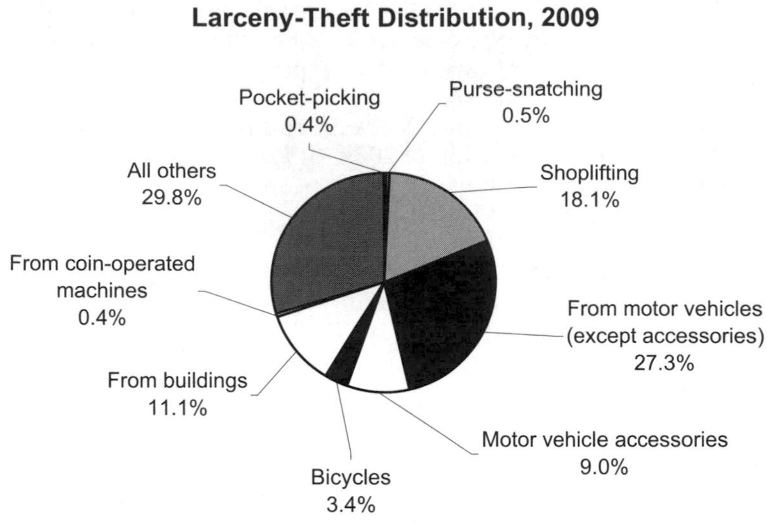


### Definition

The UCR Program defines larceny-theft as the unlawful taking, carrying, leading, or riding away of property from the possession or constructive possession of another. Examples are thefts of bicycles, motor vehicle parts and accessories, shoplifting, pocket picking, or the stealing of any property or article not taken by force and violence or by fraud. Attempted larcenies are included. Embezzlement, confidence games, forgery, check fraud, etc., are excluded from this category.

### National Volume, Trends, and Rates

There were an estimated 6.6 million (6,327,230) larceny-thefts nationwide in 2009. Larceny-thefts accounted for an estimated 67.9 percent of property crimes in 2009. There was a 4.0 percent decrease in the estimated number of larceny-thefts in 2009 compared with the 2008 estimate. The 2009 figure showed a 9.2 percent decline compared with the 2000 estimate. The trend data also showed decreases in the larceny-theft rates per 100,000 inhabitants during these periods. The rate of larceny-thefts declined 4.8 percent from 2008 to 2009, and the rate declined 16.8 percent from 2000 to 2009. (Table 1)

### Regional Offense Trends and Rates

The UCR Program defines four regions within the United States: the Northeast, the Midwest, the South, and the West. (See Appendix III for a geographical description of each region.) Larceny-theft decreased in all four regions; the Midwest and the West saw the largest declines, 5.3 percent and 4.6 percent, respectively, while the Northeast and South dropped 4.1 and 2.9 percent, respectively. (Tables 3 and 4) The following paragraphs provide a region overview of larceny-theft.

#### *The Northeast*

The Northeast was the region with the smallest proportion (18.0 percent) of the U.S. population in 2009. The region's population grew by 0.4 percent from 2008 to 2009. The region also experienced the fewest larceny-thefts in the country, accounting for only 13.7 percent of all larceny-thefts. (Table 3) The estimated number of offenses in 2009—868,864—represented a 4.1 percent decline from 2008, and the estimated rate—1571.6 incidents per 100,000 inhabitants—represented a 4.4 percent decline. (Table 4)

#### *The Midwest*

With 21.8 percent of the U.S. population in 2009, and a 0.4 percent growth in population from 2008 to 2009, the Midwest accounted for an estimated 21.2 percent of the nation's larceny-thefts. (Table 3) The estimated number of offenses (1,344,420) declined 5.3 percent compared with the 2008 data, and the estimated rate of occurrences (2,011.5 incidents per 100,000 inhabitants) declined 5.6 percent. (Table 4)

#### *The South*

With more than one-third of the U.S. population in 2009 (36.9 percent), the South experienced a 1.2 percent growth in population from 2008 to 2009. The region had the nation's highest proportion of larceny-theft offenses: an estimated 43.2 percent. (Table 3) Estimated offenses in this region totaled 2,732,182, a 2.9 percent decrease from the 2008 estimate. The South's larceny-theft rate—estimated at 2,411.1 offenses per 100,000 inhabitants—decreased 4.0 percent from the 2008 estimate. (Table 4)

#### *The West*

In 2009, an estimated 23.3 percent of the U.S. population lived in the West, which experienced a 1.2 percent growth in population from 2008 to 2009. This region was also where 21.8 percent of the nation's estimated number of larceny-thefts took place. (Table 3) Occurrences of larceny-theft declined 4.6 percent from 2008 to 2009, dropping to an estimated total of 1,381,764 offenses. The region's larceny-theft rate, estimated at 1,930.7 offenses per 100,000 inhabitants, declined 5.8 percent from the 2008 rate. (Table 4)

### Community Types

The UCR Program aggregates data for three community types: metropolitan statistical areas (MSAs), cities outside MSAs, and nonmetropolitan counties outside MSAs. MSAs include a central city or urbanized area with at least 50,000 inhabitants, as well as the county that contains the principal city and other adjacent counties that share a high degree of social and economic integration as measured through commuting. Cities outside MSAs are mostly incorporated areas, and nonmetropolitan counties are composed of unincorporated areas. (See Appendix III for more information regarding community types.)

In 2009, MSAs were home to an estimated 83.6 percent of the nation's population and experienced 87.1 percent of the nation's larceny-theft incidents. Cities outside MSAs accounted for 6.5 percent of the U.S. population and 8.5 percent of larceny-theft offenses. Nonmetropolitan counties, which were home to 9.8 percent of the nation's population, accounted for 4.4 percent of the estimated number of larceny-theft offenses. (Table 2)

### Population Groups: Trends and Rates

In cities, collectively, occurrences of larceny-theft declined 3.2 percent between 2008 and 2009. Cities with 1,000,000 or more inhabitants experienced the greatest decrease (4.6 percent), followed by cities with 10,000 to 24,999 inhabitants (3.9 percent). In both metropolitan and nonmetropolitan counties larceny-theft decreased, by 5.9 and 9.1 percent, respectively. (Table 12)

Based on reports of larceny-theft offenses from U.S. law enforcement agencies that submitted 12 months of complete data for 2009, this offense occurred at a rate of 2,094.6 offenses per 100,000 inhabitants. The collective rate for cities was 2,466.8 offenses per 100,000 inhabitants. Among city population groups, cities with 500,000 to 999,000 inhabitants had the highest larceny-theft rate, 3,150.4 incidents per 100,000 inhabitants. Cities with over 1,000,000 inhabitants had the lowest rate, at 2,146.9. In metropolitan counties, the rate was 1,457.5 incidents per 100,000 inhabitants; in nonmetropolitan counties, the rate was 923.0 incidents per 100,000 inhabitants. (Table 16)

### Offense Analysis

#### *Distribution*

Thefts from motor vehicles accounted for the majority of larceny-theft offenses in 2009 (36.3 percent). Table 23 provides a further breakdown of larceny-theft offenses, including shoplifting, thefts from buildings, thefts of motor vehicle accessories, thefts of bicycles, thefts from coin-operated machines, purse snatching, and pocket picking. The "all other" category, which includes the less-defined types of larceny-theft, accounted for 29.8 percent of all offenses.

#### *Loss by Dollar Value*

Larceny-theft offenses cost victims an estimated $5.5 billion dollars in 2009, down from $6.1 billion in 2008. (Tables 1 and 23) The average value of property stolen was $864 per offense. Larceny-theft from buildings had the highest average dollar loss per offense at $1,234. Thefts from motor vehicles had an average dollar loss of $742 per offense; thefts of motor vehicle accessories, $530; purse snatching, $445; pocket picking, $504; thefts from coin-operated machines, $364; thefts of bicycles, $318; and shoplifting, $181. (Table 23)

Offenses in which the stolen property was valued at more than $200 accounted for 44.7 percent of all larceny-thefts. Table 23 provides further analysis, including the average dollar value per offense, of all offenses in the overall category of property crime.

# MOTOR VEHICLE THEFT

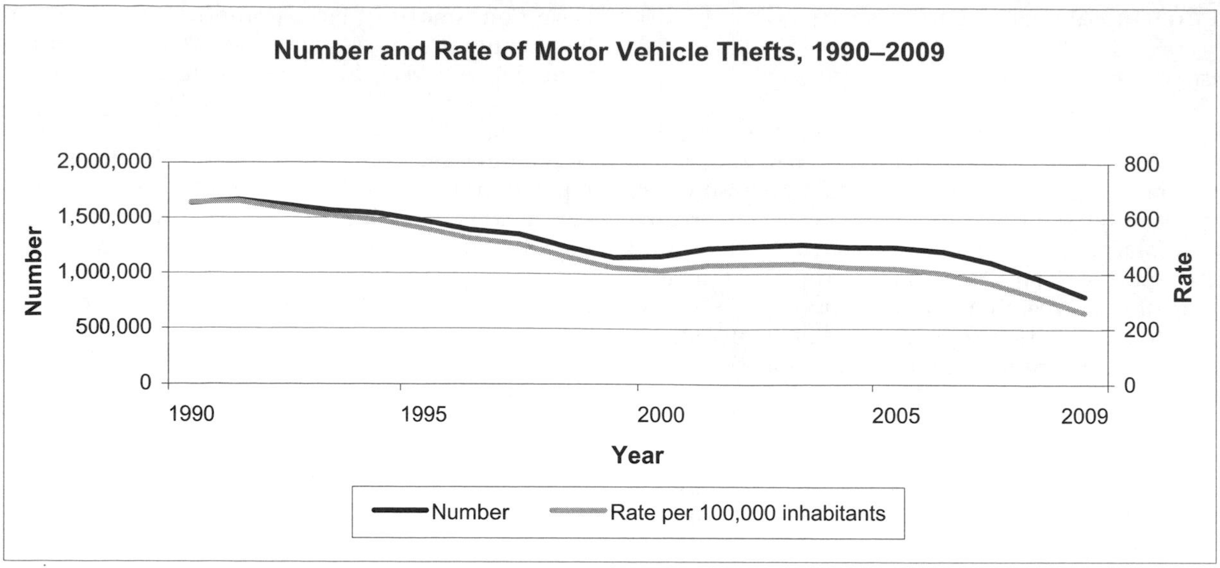


## Definition

The UCR Program defines motor vehicle theft as the theft or attempted theft of a motor vehicle. The offense includes the stealing of automobiles, trucks, buses, motorcycles, snowmobiles, etc. The taking of a motor vehicle for temporary use by a person or persons with lawful access is excluded.

## National Volume, Trends, and Rates

In 2009, an estimated 794,616 motor vehicle thefts took place in the United States. The estimated number of motor vehicle thefts declined 17.1 percent when compared with data from 2008, 35.7 percent when compared with 2005 figures, and 31.5 percent when compared with 2000 figures. (Table 1)

The estimated rate of motor vehicle theft in 2009 was 258.8 incidents per 100,000 inhabitants. In the 2-year, 5-year, and 10-year trend data, this rate showed decline: the 2009 rate was 17.8 percent lower than the 2008 rate, 37.9 percent lower than the 2005 rate, and 27.2 percent lower than the 2000 rate. (Table 1)

## Regional Offense Trends and Rates

In order to analyze crime by geographic area, the UCR Program divides the United States into four regions: the Northeast, the Midwest, the South, and the West. (Appendix III provides a map delineating the regions.) This section provides a regional overview of motor vehicle theft.

### *The Northeast*

The Northeast accounted for an estimated 18.0 percent of the nation's population in 2009 and experienced a 0.4 percent increase in population from 2008 to 2009. The region also accounted for an estimated 10.0 percent of its motor vehicle thefts. (Table 3) An estimated 79,396 motor vehicle thefts occurred in the Northeast in 2009, representing a 17.1 percent decrease from the 2008 estimate. The estimated rate of 143.6 motor vehicle thefts per 100,000 inhabitants in the Northeast in 2009 represented a 17.5 percent decline from the 2008 rate. (Table 4)

### *The Midwest*

An estimated 21.8 percent of the country's population resided in the Midwest in 2009, and the region experienced a 0.4 growth in population from 2008 to 2009. The region accounted for 18.0 percent of the nation's motor vehicle thefts. (Table 3) The Midwest had an estimated 142,740 motor vehicle thefts in 2009, an 18.4 percent decrease from the previous year's total. This was the largest decline among the regions. The motor vehicle theft rate was estimated at 213.6 motor vehicles stolen per 100,000 inhabitants, an 18.7 percent decrease from the 2008 rate. (Table 4)

### *The South*

The South, the nation's most populous region, was home to an estimated 36.9 percent of the U.S. population in 2009 and experienced a 1.2 percent growth in population from 2008 to 2009. This region accounted for 37.8 percent of the nation's motor vehicle thefts. (Table 3) The estimated 300,530 motor vehicle thefts in the South decreased 16.9 percent from the 2008 estimate. Motor vehicles in the South were stolen at an estimated rate of 265.2 per 100,000 inhabitants in 2009, a rate that was 17.8 percent lower than the 2008 rate. (Table 4)

### *The West*

With approximately 23.3 percent of the U.S. population in 2009, the West experienced a 1.2 percent growth in population from 2008 to 2009. This region accounted for 34.2 percent of all motor vehicle thefts in the nation in 2009. (Table 3) An estimated 271,950 motor vehicle thefts occurred in this region. This number represented a 16.7 percent decrease from the previous year's estimate. The motor vehicle theft rate for the West was also lower in 2009 than in 2008; the 2009 rate of 380.0 motor vehicles stolen per 100,000 inhabitants was 17.7 percent lower than the 2008 rate. (Table 4)

## Community Types

The UCR Program aggregates data by three community types: metropolitan statistical areas (MSAs), cities outside MSAs, and nonmetropolitan counties. MSAs are areas that include a principal city or urbanized area with at least 50,000 inhabitants and the county that contains the principal city and other adjacent counties that have, as defined by the U.S. Office of Management and Budget, a high degree of economic and social integration.

In 2009, the vast majority (83.6 percent) of the U.S. population resided in MSAs, where approximately 92.4 percent of motor vehicle thefts occurred. For 2009, the UCR Program estimated an overall rate of 286.0 motor vehicles stolen per 100,000 MSA inhabitants. Cities outside MSAs accounted for 3.6 percent of motor vehicle thefts, and nonmetropolitan counties accounted for 4.0 percent of motor vehicle thefts. The UCR Program estimated a 2009 rate of 142.6 motor vehicles stolen for every 100,000 inhabitants in cities outside MSAs and a rate of 105.3 motor vehicles stolen per 100,000 inhabitants in nonmetropolitan counties. (Table 2)

## Population Groups: Trends and Rates

The UCR Program aggregates data by various population groups, which include cities, metropolitan counties, and nonmetropolitan counties. (A definition of these groups can be found in Appendix III.)

In cities, collectively, the number of motor vehicle thefts decreased 17.2 percent from 2008 to 2009. The number of motor vehicle thefts decreased for all city groups. Cities with 1,000,000 and more inhabitants experienced the greatest decline—20.1 percent. Both metropolitan and nonmetropolitan counties experienced decreases, at 17.5 percent and 15.1 percent, respectively. (Table 12)

In 2009, cities had a collective motor vehicle theft rate of 314.5 per 100,000 inhabitants. Among the population groups, cities with 500,000 to 999,999 inhabitants experienced the highest rate of motor vehicle thefts with 577.2 motor vehicle thefts per 100,000 inhabitants. Conversely, the nation's smallest cities, those with populations under 10,000, had the lowest rate of motor vehicle theft with 144.2 incidents per 100,000 in population. Within the county groups, metropolitan counties had a rate of 199.6 motor vehicles stolen per 100,000 inhabitants, while nonmetropolitan counties had a rate of 107.9 incidents per 100,000 inhabitants. (Table 16)

## Offense Analysis

Based on the reports of law enforcement agencies, the UCR Program estimated the combined value of motor vehicles stolen nationwide in 2009 at approximately $5.2 billion. (Tables 1 and 23) In 2009, the average dollar value per motor vehicle stolen in the United States was $6,505. Automobiles were, by far, the most frequently stolen vehicle, accounting for 72.1 percent of all vehicles stolen. Trucks and buses accounted for 17.2 percent of stolen vehicles, and other vehicles accounted for 10.8 percent of stolen vehicles. (Expanded Motor Vehicle Theft Table)

By type of vehicle, automobiles were stolen at a rate of 195.0 cars per 100,000 inhabitants in 2009. Trucks and buses were stolen at a rate of 46.4 vehicles per 100,000 in population, and other types of vehicles were stolen at a rate of 29.1 vehicles per 100,000 inhabitants. (Table 19)

# ARSON

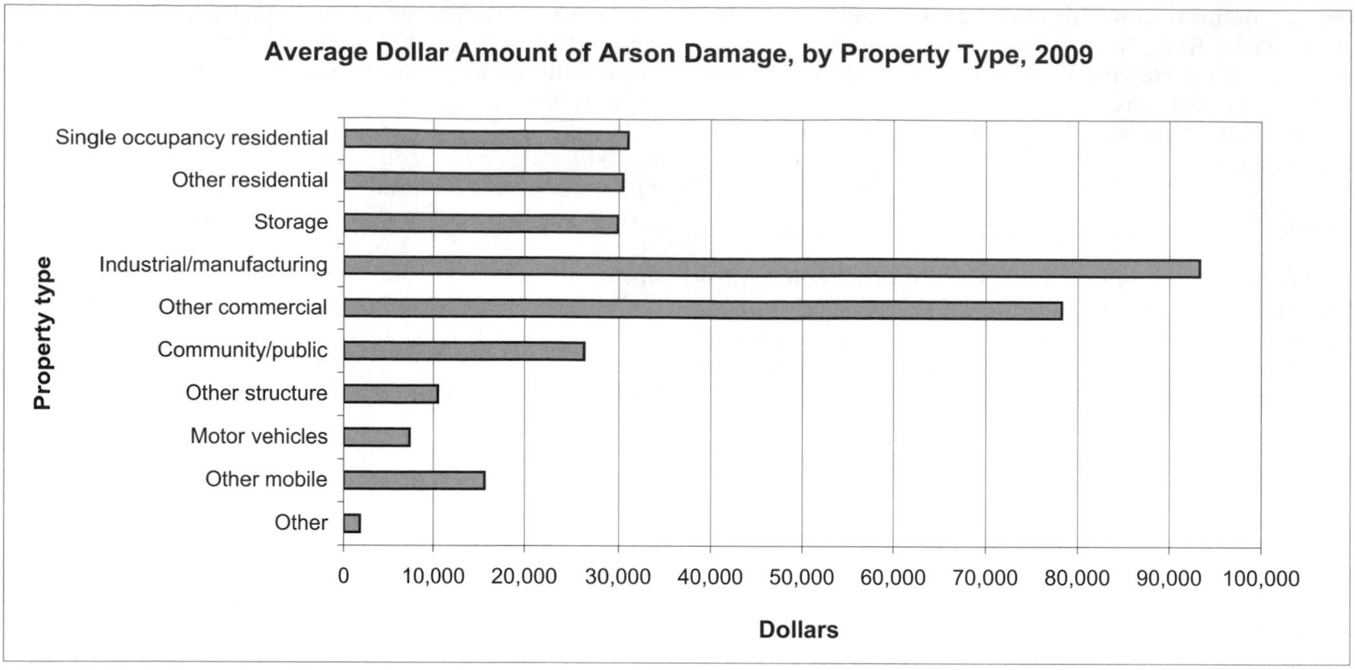


## Definition

The UCR Program defines arson as any willful or malicious burning or attempt to burn (with or without intent to defraud) a dwelling house, public building, motor vehicle, aircraft, personal property of another, etc.

## Data Collection

Only fires that investigators determined were willfully set (not fires labeled as "suspicious" or "of unknown origin") are included in this arson data collection. Points to consider regarding arson statistics include:

National offense rates per 100,000 inhabitants (found in Tables 1, 2, and 4) do not include arson data; the FBI presents rates for arson separately. Arson rates are calculated based upon data received from all law enforcement agencies that provide the UCR Program with data for 12 complete months.

Arson data collection does not include estimates for arson, because the degree of reporting arson offenses varies from agency to agency. Because of this unevenness of reporting, arson offenses are excluded from Tables 1 through 7, all of which contain offense estimations.

The number of arsons reported by individual law enforcement agencies is available in Tables 8 through 11. Arson trend data (which indicate year-to-year changes) can be found in Tables 12 through 15, and arson clearance data (crimes solved) can be found in Tables 25 through 28.

## National Coverage

In 2009, 14,957 agencies (providing 1 to 12 months of data) reported 58,871 arson offenses. Of those agencies, 14,693 provided expanded offense data about 51,389 arsons. (Unpublished Expanded Arson Table 1; see Section I for more information)

## Population Groups: Trends and Rates

The number of arsons reported in 2009 decreased 10.8 percent from the 2008 figure. Law enforcement agencies in the nation's cities collectively reported a 10.5 percent decline in the number of arsons from the 2008 figure. The number of arsons declined for all population groups. Among the population groups labeled *city,* the subsets with 250,000 to 499,999 inhabitants and 10,000 to 24,999 inhabitants had the largest year-to-year decrease in reported arsons, 13.8 percent. Agencies in the nation's metropolitan counties reported a 6.3 percent decrease in the number of arsons, and those in nonmetropolitan counties reported an 11.6 percent decline. (Table 12)

Arson rates were based on information received from 12,395 agencies that provided 12 months of complete arson data to the UCR Program. An examination of data indicated that in 2009, the highest rate among city groups—34.8 arsons per 100,000 inhabitants—was reported in cities with 250,000 or more inhabitants. Among cities with 250,000 or more inhabitants, those with a population of 250,000 to 499,999 had the highest rate at 38.6 per 100,000 inhabitants. Cities with 10,000 to 24,999 inhabitants had the lowest rate of arson at 14.9 per 100,000 inhabitants. Metropolitan counties had 17.3 arsons per 100,000 inhabitants, and nonmetropolitan counties had 13.8 arsons per 100,000 inhabitants, the lowest of all the population groups. (Expanded Arson Table 1)

## Offense Analysis

The UCR Program breaks down arson offenses into three property categories: structural, mobile, and other. In addition, the structural property type is broken down into seven types of structures, and the mobile property type consists of two subgroupings. The program also collects information on the estimated dollar value of the damaged property.

## Property Type

The total number of arsons decreased in 2009. Arsons for the structural property type decreased 9.1 percent, mobile property type dropped 12.6 percent, and other arsons fell 11.8 percent from 2008 to 2009. (Table 15)

### *Distribution by Property Type*

Arsons involving structures (residential, storage, public, etc.) accounted for 44.5 percent of the total number of arson offenses; arsons involving mobile property accounted for 28.4 percent; and other types of property (such as crops, timber, fences, etc.) accounted for 27.1 percent of reported arsons. Of the arsons involving structures, 63.4 percent involved residential properties. Of the residential arsons, three-fourths were single-occupancy residences. Approximately 17 percent of structures were not in use when the arson occurred. Mobile arsons accounted for 28.4 percent of all arsons. Within this category, 95 percent of offenses involved the burning of motor vehicles. Other types of property, such as crops, timber, fences, etc., accounted for 27.1 percent of reported arson offenses. (Expanded Arson Table 2)

### *Dollar Loss*

In monetary terms, the average dollar loss in 2009 for arson was $17,411. The average dollar loss for a structural arson was $33,118. Within the structural arson category, the industrial/manufacturing subcategory had the highest average dollar loss at $93,287. Within that same category, single-occupancy dwellings had an average dollar loss of $31,000. Mobile property had an average dollar loss of $7,715. Other property types had an average dollar loss of $1,791. (Expanded Arson Table 2)

## Table 1. Crime in the United States, by Volume and Rate per 100,000 Inhabitants, 1990–2009

(Number, rate per 100,000 population, percent.)

| Year | Population[1] | Violent crime | | Murder and nonnegligent manslaughter | | Forcible rape | | Robbery | | Aggravated assault | |
|---|---|---|---|---|---|---|---|---|---|---|---|
| | | Number | Rate | Number | Rate | Number | Rate | Number | Rate | Number | Rate |
| 1990 | 249,464,396 | 1,820,127 | 729.6 | 23,438 | 9.4 | 102,555 | 41.1 | 639,271 | 256.3 | 1,054,863 | 422.9 |
| 1991 | 252,153,092 | 1,911,767 | 758.2 | 24,703 | 9.8 | 106,593 | 42.3 | 687,732 | 272.7 | 1,092,739 | 433.4 |
| 1992 | 255,029,699 | 1,932,274 | 757.7 | 23,760 | 9.3 | 109,062 | 42.8 | 672,478 | 263.7 | 1,126,974 | 441.9 |
| 1993 | 257,782,608 | 1,926,017 | 747.1 | 24,526 | 9.5 | 106,014 | 41.1 | 659,870 | 256.0 | 1,135,607 | 440.5 |
| 1994 | 260,327,021 | 1,857,670 | 713.6 | 23,326 | 9.0 | 102,216 | 39.3 | 618,949 | 237.8 | 1,113,179 | 427.6 |
| 1995 | 262,803,276 | 1,798,792 | 684.5 | 21,606 | 8.2 | 97,470 | 37.1 | 580,509 | 220.9 | 1,099,207 | 418.3 |
| 1996 | 265,228,572 | 1,688,540 | 636.6 | 19,645 | 7.4 | 96,252 | 36.3 | 535,594 | 201.9 | 1,037,049 | 391.0 |
| 1997 | 267,783,607 | 1,636,096 | 611.0 | 18,208 | 6.8 | 96,153 | 35.9 | 498,534 | 186.2 | 1,023,201 | 382.1 |
| 1998 | 270,248,003 | 1,533,887 | 567.6 | 16,974 | 6.3 | 93,144 | 34.5 | 447,186 | 165.5 | 976,583 | 361.4 |
| 1999 | 272,690,813 | 1,426,044 | 523.0 | 15,522 | 5.7 | 89,411 | 32.8 | 409,371 | 150.1 | 911,740 | 334.3 |
| 2000 | 281,421,906 | 1,425,486 | 506.5 | 15,586 | 5.5 | 90,178 | 32.0 | 408,016 | 145.0 | 911,706 | 324.0 |
| 2001[2] | 285,317,559 | 1,439,480 | 504.5 | 16,037 | 5.6 | 90,863 | 31.8 | 423,557 | 148.5 | 909,023 | 318.6 |
| 2002 | 287,973,924 | 1,423,677 | 494.4 | 16,229 | 5.6 | 95,235 | 33.1 | 420,806 | 146.1 | 891,407 | 309.5 |
| 2003 | 290,788,976 | 1,383,676 | 475.8 | 16,528 | 5.7 | 93,883 | 32.3 | 414,235 | 142.5 | 859,030 | 295.4 |
| 2004 | 293,656,842 | 1,360,088 | 463.2 | 16,148 | 5.5 | 95,089 | 32.4 | 401,470 | 136.7 | 847,381 | 288.6 |
| 2005 | 296,507,061 | 1,390,745 | 469.0 | 16,740 | 5.6 | 94,347 | 31.8 | 417,438 | 140.8 | 862,220 | 290.8 |
| 2006 | 298,754,819 | 1,435,951 | 480.6 | 17,318 | 5.8 | 94,782 | 31.7 | 449,803 | 150.6 | 874,048 | 292.6 |
| 2007 | 301,290,332 | 1,421,990 | 472.0 | 17,157 | 5.7 | 91,874 | 30.5 | 447,155 | 148.4 | 865,804 | 287.4 |
| 2008 | 304,374,846 | 1,392,629 | 457.5 | 16,442 | 5.4 | 90,479 | 29.7 | 443,574 | 145.7 | 842,134 | 276.7 |
| 2009 | 307,006,550 | 1,318,398 | 429.4 | 15,241 | 5.0 | 88,097 | 28.7 | 408,217 | 133.0 | 806,843 | 262.8 |

| Year | Property crime | | Burglary | | Larceny-theft | | Motor vehicle theft | |
|---|---|---|---|---|---|---|---|---|
| | Number | Rate | Number | Rate | Number | Rate | Number | Rate |
| 1990 | 12,655,486 | 5,073.1 | 3,073,909 | 1,232.2 | 7,945,670 | 3,185.1 | 1,635,907 | 655.8 |
| 1991 | 12,961,116 | 5,140.2 | 3,157,150 | 1,252.1 | 8,142,228 | 3,229.1 | 1,661,738 | 659.0 |
| 1992 | 12,505,917 | 4,903.7 | 2,979,884 | 1,168.4 | 7,915,199 | 3,103.6 | 1,610,834 | 631.6 |
| 1993 | 12,218,777 | 4,740.0 | 2,834,808 | 1,099.7 | 7,820,909 | 3,033.9 | 1,563,060 | 606.3 |
| 1994 | 12,131,873 | 4,660.2 | 2,712,774 | 1,042.1 | 7,879,812 | 3,026.9 | 1,539,287 | 591.3 |
| 1995 | 12,063,935 | 4,590.5 | 2,593,784 | 987.0 | 7,997,710 | 3,043.2 | 1,472,441 | 560.3 |
| 1996 | 11,805,323 | 4,451.0 | 2,506,400 | 945.0 | 7,904,685 | 2,980.3 | 1,394,238 | 525.7 |
| 1997 | 11,558,475 | 4,316.3 | 2,460,526 | 918.8 | 7,743,760 | 2,891.8 | 1,354,189 | 505.7 |
| 1998 | 10,951,827 | 4,052.5 | 2,332,735 | 863.2 | 7,376,311 | 2,729.5 | 1,242,781 | 459.9 |
| 1999 | 10,208,334 | 3,743.6 | 2,100,739 | 770.4 | 6,955,520 | 2,550.7 | 1,152,075 | 422.5 |
| 2000 | 10,182,584 | 3,618.3 | 2,050,992 | 728.8 | 6,971,590 | 2,477.3 | 1,160,002 | 412.2 |
| 2001[2] | 10,437,189 | 3,658.1 | 2,116,531 | 741.8 | 7,092,267 | 2,485.7 | 1,228,391 | 430.5 |
| 2002 | 10,455,277 | 3,630.6 | 2,151,252 | 747.0 | 7,057,379 | 2,450.7 | 1,246,646 | 432.9 |
| 2003 | 10,442,862 | 3,591.2 | 2,154,834 | 741.0 | 7,026,802 | 2,416.5 | 1,261,226 | 433.7 |
| 2004 | 10,319,386 | 3,514.1 | 2,144,446 | 730.3 | 6,937,089 | 2,362.3 | 1,237,851 | 421.5 |
| 2005 | 10,174,754 | 3,431.5 | 2,155,448 | 726.9 | 6,783,447 | 2,287.8 | 1,235,859 | 416.8 |
| 2006 | 10,031,359 | 3,357.7 | 2,196,304 | 735.2 | 6,636,615 | 2,221.4 | 1,198,440 | 401.1 |
| 2007 | 9,872,815 | 3,276.8 | 2,187,277 | 726.0 | 6,587,040 | 2,186.3 | 1,098,498 | 364.6 |
| 2008 | 9,775,149 | 3,211.5 | 2,228,474 | 732.1 | 6,588,046 | 2,164.5 | 958,629 | 315.0 |
| 2009 | 9,320,971 | 3,036.1 | 2,199,125 | 716.3 | 6,327,230 | 2,060.9 | 794,616 | 258.8 |

[1] Populations are U.S. Census Bureau provisional estimates as of July 1 for each year except 1990 and 2000, which are decennial census counts.
[2] The murder and nonnegligent homicides that occurred as a result of the events of September 11, 2001, are not included in this table.

## Table 1A. Crime in the United States, Percent Change in Volume and Rate per 100,000 Inhabitants for 2 Years, 5 Years, and 10 Years

(Percent change.)

| Year | Violent crime | | Murder and nonnegligent manslaughter | | Forcible rape | | Robbery | | Aggravated assault | |
|---|---|---|---|---|---|---|---|---|---|---|
| | Number | Rate | Number | Rate | Number | Rate | Number | Rate | Number | Rate |
| 2008–2009 | -5.3 | -6.1 | -7.3 | -8.1 | -2.6 | -3.5 | -8.0 | -8.8 | -4.2 | -5.0 |
| 2005–2009 | -5.2 | -8.4 | -9.0 | -12.1 | -6.6 | -9.8 | -2.2 | -5.6 | -6.4 | -9.6 |
| 2000–2009 | -7.5 | -15.2 | -2.2 | -10.4 | -2.3 | -10.4 | * | -8.3 | -11.5 | -18.9 |

| Year | Property crime | | Burglary | | Larceny-theft | | Motor vehicle theft | |
|---|---|---|---|---|---|---|---|---|
| | Number | Rate | Number | Rate | Number | Rate | Number | Rate |
| 2008–2009 | -4.6 | -5.5 | -1.3 | -2.2 | -4.0 | -4.8 | -17.1 | -17.8 |
| 2005–2009 | -8.4 | -11.5 | +2.0 | -1.5 | -6.7 | -9.9 | -35.7 | -37.9 |
| 2000–2009 | -8.5 | -16.1 | +7.2 | -1.7 | -9.2 | -16.8 | -31.5 | -37.2 |

* Less than one-tenth of 1 percent.

## Table 2. Crime in the United States, by Community Type, 2009

(Number, percent, rate per 100,000 population.)

| Area | Population[1] | Violent crime | Murder and non-negligent manslaughter | Forcible rape | Robbery | Aggravated assault | Property crime | Burglary | Larceny-theft | Motor vehicle theft |
|---|---|---|---|---|---|---|---|---|---|---|
| **United States Total** | 307,006,550 | 1,318,398 | 15,241 | 88,097 | 408,217 | 806,843 | 9,320,971 | 2,199,125 | 6,327,230 | 794,616 |
| Rate per 100,000 inhabitants | | 429.4 | 5.0 | 28.7 | 133.0 | 262.8 | 3,036.1 | 716.3 | 2,060.9 | 258.8 |
| **Metropolitan Statistical Areas** | 256,734,191 | | | | | | | | | |
| Area actually reporting[2] | 97.1% | 1,109,526 | 12,616 | 67,096 | 366,691 | 663,123 | 7,737,397 | 1,784,613 | 5,247,592 | 705,192 |
| Estimated total | 100.0% | 1,177,758 | 13,408 | 72,413 | 390,483 | 701,454 | 8,113,233 | 1,867,157 | 5,511,868 | 734,208 |
| Rate per 100,000 inhabitants | | 458.7 | 5.2 | 28.2 | 152.1 | 273.2 | 3,160.2 | 727.3 | 2,146.9 | 286.0 |
| **Cities Outside Metropolitan Areas** | 20,040,075 | | | | | | | | | |
| Area actually reporting[2] | 90.9% | 73,338 | 741 | 7,394 | 11,542 | 53,661 | 665,369 | 149,740 | 489,037 | 26,592 |
| Estimated total | 100.0% | 79,446 | 798 | 8,259 | 12,639 | 57,750 | 733,161 | 164,859 | 539,720 | 28,582 |
| Rate per 100,000 inhabitants | | 396.4 | 4.0 | 41.2 | 63.1 | 288.2 | 3,658.5 | 822.6 | 2,693.2 | 142.6 |
| **Nonmetropolitan Counties** | 30,232,284 | | | | | | | | | |
| Area actually reporting[2] | 93.0% | 57,997 | 961 | 6,665 | 4,794 | 45,577 | 445,641 | 156,246 | 259,148 | 30,247 |
| Estimated total | 100.0% | 61,194 | 1,035 | 7,425 | 5,095 | 47,639 | 474,577 | 167,109 | 275,642 | 31,826 |
| Rate per 100,000 inhabitants | | 202.4 | 3.4 | 24.6 | 16.9 | 157.6 | 1,569.8 | 552.8 | 911.7 | 105.3 |

[1] Population figures are U.S. Census Bureau provisional estimates as of July 1, 2009.
[2] The percentage reported under "Area actually reporting" is based on the population covered by agencies providing 3 months or more of crime reports to the FBI.

## Table 3. Crime in the United States, Population and Offense Distribution, by Region, 2009

(Percent distribution.)

| Region | Population | Violent crime | Murder and non-negligent manslaughter | Forcible rape | Robbery | Aggravated assault | Property crime | Burglary | Larceny-theft | Motor vehicle theft |
|---|---|---|---|---|---|---|---|---|---|---|
| **United States Total[1]** | 100.0 | 100.0 | 100.0 | 100.0 | 100.0 | 100.0 | 100.0 | 100.0 | 100.0 | 100.0 |
| Northeast | 18.0 | 15.0 | 13.9 | 12.3 | 17.3 | 14.2 | 12.6 | 10.3 | 13.7 | 10.0 |
| Midwest | 21.8 | 19.6 | 20.0 | 24.7 | 19.8 | 18.9 | 20.8 | 20.6 | 21.2 | 18.0 |
| South | 36.9 | 42.5 | 44.8 | 38.4 | 39.4 | 44.5 | 43.9 | 48.0 | 43.2 | 37.8 |
| West | 23.3 | 22.9 | 21.3 | 24.6 | 23.6 | 22.5 | 22.7 | 21.2 | 21.8 | 34.2 |

[1] Because of rounding, the percentages may not add to 100.0.

## Table 4. Crime, by Region, Geographic Division, and State, 2008–2009

(Number, rate per 100,000 population, percent.)

| Area | Population[1] | Violent crime | | Murder and non-negligent manslaughter | | Forcible rape | | Robbery | |
|---|---|---|---|---|---|---|---|---|---|
| | | Number | Rate | Number | Rate | Number | Rate | Number | Rate |
| **UNITED STATES TOTAL[2,3,4,5]** | | | | | | | | | |
| 2008 | 304,374,846 | 1,392,629 | 457.5 | 16,442 | 5.4 | 90,479 | 29.7 | 443,574 | 145.7 |
| 2009 | 307,006,550 | 1,318,398 | 429.4 | 15,241 | 5.0 | 88,097 | 28.7 | 408,217 | 133.0 |
| Percent change | | -5.3 | -6.1 | -7.3 | -8.1 | -2.6 | -3.5 | -8.0 | -8.8 |
| **Northeast** | | | | | | | | | |
| 2008 | 55,060,196 | 204,781 | 371.9 | 2,311 | 4.2 | 11,025 | 20.0 | 76,207 | 138.4 |
| 2009 | 55,283,679 | 198,076 | 358.3 | 2,111 | 3.8 | 10,817 | 19.6 | 70,457 | 127.4 |
| Percent change | | -3.3 | -3.7 | -8.7 | -9.0 | -1.9 | -2.3 | -7.5 | -7.9 |
| New England | | | | | | | | | |
| 2008 | 14,362,641 | 47,834 | 333.0 | 392 | 2.7 | 3,618 | 25.2 | 12,844 | 89.4 |
| 2009 | 14,429,720 | 47,814 | 331.4 | 353 | 2.4 | 3,539 | 24.5 | 13,168 | 91.3 |
| Percent change | | * | -0.5 | -9.9 | -10.4 | -2.2 | -2.6 | +2.5 | +2.0 |
| Connecticut | | | | | | | | | |
| 2008 | 3,502,932 | 10,737 | 306.5 | 132 | 3.8 | 680 | 19.4 | 4,043 | 115.4 |
| 2009 | 3,518,288 | 10,508 | 298.7 | 107 | 3.0 | 651 | 18.5 | 3,990 | 113.4 |
| Percent change | | -2.1 | -2.6 | -18.9 | -19.3 | -4.3 | -4.7 | -1.3 | -1.7 |
| Maine | | | | | | | | | |
| 2008 | 1,319,691 | 1,572 | 119.1 | 31 | 2.3 | 379 | 28.7 | 333 | 25.2 |
| 2009 | 1,318,301 | 1,579 | 119.8 | 26 | 2.0 | 376 | 28.5 | 399 | 30.3 |
| Percent change | | +0.4 | +0.6 | -16.1 | -16.0 | -0.8 | -0.7 | +19.8 | +19.9 |
| Massachusetts | | | | | | | | | |
| 2008 | 6,543,595 | 29,888 | 456.8 | 167 | 2.6 | 1,744 | 26.7 | 7,071 | 108.1 |
| 2009 | 6,593,587 | 30,136 | 457.1 | 172 | 2.6 | 1,701 | 25.8 | 7,427 | 112.6 |
| Percent change | | +0.8 | +0.1 | +3.0 | +2.2 | -2.5 | -3.2 | +5.0 | +4.2 |
| New Hampshire | | | | | | | | | |
| 2008 | 1,321,872 | 2,127 | 160.9 | 14 | 1.1 | 400 | 30.3 | 424 | 32.1 |
| 2009 | 1,324,575 | 2,114 | 159.6 | 10 | 0.8 | 400 | 30.2 | 455 | 34.4 |
| Percent change | | -0.6 | -0.8 | -28.6 | -28.7 | 0.0 | -0.2 | +7.3 | +7.1 |
| Rhode Island | | | | | | | | | |
| 2008 | 1,053,502 | 2,656 | 252.1 | 31 | 2.9 | 282 | 26.8 | 880 | 83.5 |
| 2009 | 1,053,209 | 2,660 | 252.6 | 31 | 2.9 | 287 | 27.3 | 786 | 74.6 |
| Percent change | | +0.2 | +0.2 | 0.0 | * | +1.8 | +1.8 | -10.7 | -10.7 |
| Vermont | | | | | | | | | |
| 2008 | 621,049 | 854 | 137.5 | 17 | 2.7 | 133 | 21.4 | 93 | 15.0 |
| 2009 | 621,760 | 817 | 131.4 | 7 | 1.1 | 124 | 19.9 | 111 | 17.9 |
| Percent change | | -4.3 | -4.4 | -58.8 | -58.9 | -6.8 | -6.9 | +19.4 | +19.2 |
| Middle Atlantic | | | | | | | | | |
| 2008 | 40,697,555 | 156,947 | 385.6 | 1,919 | 4.7 | 7,407 | 18.2 | 63,363 | 155.7 |
| 2009 | 40,853,959 | 150,262 | 367.8 | 1,758 | 4.3 | 7,278 | 17.8 | 57,289 | 140.2 |
| Percent change | | -4.3 | -4.6 | -8.4 | -8.7 | -1.7 | -2.1 | -9.6 | -9.9 |
| New Jersey | | | | | | | | | |
| 2008 | 8,663,398 | 28,351 | 327.3 | 376 | 4.3 | 1,122 | 13.0 | 12,701 | 146.6 |
| 2009 | 8,707,739 | 27,121 | 311.5 | 319 | 3.7 | 1,041 | 12.0 | 11,639 | 133.7 |
| Percent change | | -4.3 | -4.8 | -15.2 | -15.6 | -7.2 | -7.7 | -8.4 | -8.8 |
| New York | | | | | | | | | |
| 2008 | 19,467,789 | 77,546 | 398.3 | 836 | 4.3 | 2,799 | 14.4 | 31,789 | 163.3 |
| 2009 | 19,541,453 | 75,176 | 384.7 | 778 | 4.0 | 2,586 | 13.2 | 28,136 | 144.0 |
| Percent change | | -3.1 | -3.4 | -6.9 | -7.3 | -7.6 | -8.0 | -11.5 | -11.8 |
| Pennsylvania | | | | | | | | | |
| 2008 | 12,566,368 | 51,050 | 406.2 | 707 | 5.6 | 3,486 | 27.7 | 18,873 | 150.2 |
| 2009 | 12,604,767 | 47,965 | 380.5 | 661 | 5.2 | 3,651 | 29.0 | 17,514 | 138.9 |
| Percent change | | -6.0 | -6.3 | -6.5 | -6.8 | +4.7 | +4.4 | -7.2 | -7.5 |
| **Midwest[2,3,4]** | | | | | | | | | |
| 2008 | 66,595,597 | 269,278 | 404.3 | 3,229 | 4.8 | 22,974 | 34.5 | 84,869 | 127.4 |
| 2009 | 66,836,911 | 257,827 | 385.8 | 3,054 | 4.6 | 21,795 | 32.6 | 80,724 | 120.8 |
| Percent change | | -4.3 | -4.6 | -5.4 | -5.8 | -5.1 | -5.5 | -4.9 | -5.2 |
| East North Central[2,3,4] | | | | | | | | | |
| 2008 | 46,389,431 | 196,585 | 423.8 | 2,363 | 5.1 | 15,940 | 34.4 | 68,859 | 148.4 |
| 2009 | 46,500,668 | 188,001 | 404.3 | 2,373 | 5.1 | 15,185 | 32.7 | 65,237 | 140.3 |
| Percent change | | -4.4 | -4.6 | +0.4 | +0.2 | -4.7 | -5.0 | -5.3 | -5.5 |
| Illinois[2,3] | | | | | | | | | |
| 2008 | 12,842,954 | 67,840 | 528.2 | 790 | 6.2 | 4,104 | 32.0 | 24,067 | 187.4 |
| 2009 | 12,910,409 | 64,185 | 497.2 | 773 | 6.0 | 3,901 | 30.2 | 22,923 | 177.6 |
| Percent change | | -5.4 | -5.9 | -2.2 | -2.7 | -4.9 | -5.4 | -4.8 | -5.3 |
| Indiana | | | | | | | | | |
| 2008 | 6,388,309 | 21,520 | 336.9 | 322 | 5.0 | 1,708 | 26.7 | 7,591 | 118.8 |
| 2009 | 6,423,113 | 21,404 | 333.2 | 310 | 4.8 | 1,640 | 25.5 | 7,352 | 114.5 |
| Percent change | | -0.5 | -1.1 | -3.7 | -4.2 | -4.0 | -4.5 | -3.1 | -3.7 |

[1] Populations are U.S. Census Bureau provisional estimates as of July 1, 2009, and July 1, 2008.
[2] Limited data for 2008 and 2009 were available for Illinois.
[3] The data collection methodology for the offense of forcible rape used by the Illinois and the Minnesota state UCR Programs (with the exception of Rockford, IL, and Minneapolis and St. Paul, MN) does not comply with national UCR guidelines. Consequently, their state figures for forcible rape (with the exception of Rockford, IL, and Minneapolis and St. Paul, MN) have been estimated for inclusion in this table.
[4] Because of changes in the state's reporting practices, figures are not comparable to previous years' data.
[5] Includes offenses reported by the Zoological Police and the Metro Transit Police.
* Less than one-tenth of 1 percent.

## Table 4. Crime, by Region, Geographic Division, and State, 2008–2009—*Continued*

(Number, rate per 100,000 population, percent.)

| Area | Aggravated assault | | Property crime | | Burglary | | Larceny-theft | | Motor vehicle theft | |
|---|---|---|---|---|---|---|---|---|---|---|
| | Number | Rate | Number | Rate | Number | Rate | Number | Rate | Number | Rate |
| **UNITED STATES TOTAL[2,3,4,5]** | | | | | | | | | | |
| 2008 | 842,134 | 276.7 | 9,775,149 | 3,211.5 | 2,228,474 | 732.1 | 6,588,046 | 2,164.5 | 958,629 | 315.0 |
| 2009 | 806,843 | 262.8 | 9,320,971 | 3,036.1 | 2,199,125 | 716.3 | 6,327,230 | 2,060.9 | 794,616 | 258.8 |
| Percent change | -4.2 | -5.0 | -4.6 | -5.5 | -1.3 | -2.2 | -4.0 | -4.8 | -17.1 | -17.8 |
| **Northeast** | | | | | | | | | | |
| 2008 | 115,238 | 209.3 | 1,237,593 | 2,247.7 | 236,165 | 428.9 | 905,623 | 1,644.8 | 95,805 | 174.0 |
| 2009 | 114,691 | 207.5 | 1,173,756 | 2,123.2 | 225,496 | 407.9 | 868,864 | 1,571.6 | 79,396 | 143.6 |
| Percent change | -0.5 | -0.9 | -5.2 | -5.5 | -4.5 | -4.9 | -4.1 | -4.4 | -17.1 | -17.5 |
| New England | | | | | | | | | | |
| 2008 | 30,980 | 215.7 | 349,578 | 2,433.9 | 71,539 | 498.1 | 249,999 | 1,740.6 | 28,040 | 195.2 |
| 2009 | 30,754 | 213.1 | 336,832 | 2,334.3 | 70,595 | 489.2 | 242,040 | 1,677.4 | 24,197 | 167.7 |
| Percent change | -0.7 | -1.2 | -3.6 | -4.1 | -1.3 | -1.8 | -3.2 | -3.6 | -13.7 | -14.1 |
| Connecticut | | | | | | | | | | |
| 2008 | 5,882 | 167.9 | 87,210 | 2,489.6 | 15,107 | 431.3 | 63,212 | 1,804.5 | 8,891 | 253.8 |
| 2009 | 5,760 | 163.7 | 82,181 | 2,335.8 | 15,073 | 428.4 | 59,632 | 1,694.9 | 7,476 | 212.5 |
| Percent change | -2.1 | -2.5 | -5.8 | -6.2 | -0.2 | -0.7 | -5.7 | -6.1 | -15.9 | -16.3 |
| Maine | | | | | | | | | | |
| 2008 | 829 | 62.8 | 32,433 | 2,457.6 | 6,559 | 497.0 | 24,695 | 1,871.3 | 1,179 | 89.3 |
| 2009 | 778 | 59.0 | 31,685 | 2,403.5 | 6,728 | 510.4 | 23,936 | 1,815.7 | 1,021 | 77.4 |
| Percent change | -6.2 | -6.1 | -2.3 | -2.2 | +2.6 | +2.7 | -3.1 | -3.0 | -13.4 | -13.3 |
| Massachusetts | | | | | | | | | | |
| 2008 | 20,906 | 319.5 | 156,083 | 2,385.3 | 36,260 | 554.1 | 107,048 | 1,635.9 | 12,775 | 195.2 |
| 2009 | 20,836 | 316.0 | 151,914 | 2,304.0 | 34,665 | 525.7 | 105,514 | 1,600.3 | 11,735 | 178.0 |
| Percent change | -0.3 | -1.1 | -2.7 | -3.4 | -4.4 | -5.1 | -1.4 | -2.2 | -8.1 | -8.8 |
| New Hampshire | | | | | | | | | | |
| 2008 | 1,289 | 97.5 | 28,054 | 2,122.3 | 4,332 | 327.7 | 22,316 | 1,688.2 | 1,406 | 106.4 |
| 2009 | 1,249 | 94.3 | 28,624 | 2,161.0 | 4,928 | 372.0 | 22,572 | 1,704.1 | 1,124 | 84.9 |
| Percent change | -3.1 | -3.3 | +2.0 | +1.8 | +13.8 | +13.5 | +1.1 | +0.9 | -20.1 | -20.2 |
| Rhode Island | | | | | | | | | | |
| 2008 | 1,463 | 138.9 | 29,895 | 2,837.7 | 5,766 | 547.3 | 20,926 | 1,986.3 | 3,203 | 304.0 |
| 2009 | 1,556 | 147.7 | 27,497 | 2,610.8 | 5,749 | 545.9 | 19,355 | 1,837.7 | 2,393 | 227.2 |
| Percent change | +6.4 | +6.4 | -8.0 | -8.0 | -0.3 | -0.3 | -7.5 | -7.5 | -25.3 | -25.3 |
| Vermont | | | | | | | | | | |
| 2008 | 611 | 98.4 | 15,903 | 2,560.7 | 3,515 | 566.0 | 11,802 | 1,900.3 | 586 | 94.4 |
| 2009 | 575 | 92.5 | 14,931 | 2,401.4 | 3,452 | 555.2 | 11,031 | 1,774.2 | 448 | 72.1 |
| Percent change | -5.9 | -6.0 | -6.1 | -6.2 | -1.8 | -1.9 | -6.5 | -6.6 | -23.5 | -23.6 |
| Middle Atlantic | | | | | | | | | | |
| 2008 | 84,258 | 207.0 | 888,015 | 2,182.0 | 164,626 | 404.5 | 655,624 | 1,611.0 | 67,765 | 166.5 |
| 2009 | 83,937 | 205.5 | 836,924 | 2,048.6 | 154,901 | 379.2 | 626,824 | 1,534.3 | 55,199 | 135.1 |
| Percent change | -0.4 | -0.8 | -5.8 | -6.1 | -5.9 | -6.3 | -4.4 | -4.8 | -18.5 | -18.9 |
| New Jersey | | | | | | | | | | |
| 2008 | 14,152 | 163.4 | 199,127 | 2,298.5 | 40,402 | 466.4 | 138,545 | 1,599.2 | 20,180 | 232.9 |
| 2009 | 14,122 | 162.2 | 181,097 | 2,079.7 | 37,262 | 427.9 | 128,327 | 1,473.7 | 15,508 | 178.1 |
| Percent change | -0.2 | -0.7 | -9.1 | -9.5 | -7.8 | -8.2 | -7.4 | -7.8 | -23.2 | -23.5 |
| New York | | | | | | | | | | |
| 2008 | 42,122 | 216.4 | 388,585 | 1,996.0 | 65,537 | 336.6 | 297,952 | 1,530.5 | 25,096 | 128.9 |
| 2009 | 43,676 | 223.5 | 378,315 | 1,936.0 | 62,842 | 321.6 | 293,603 | 1,502.5 | 21,870 | 111.9 |
| Percent change | +3.7 | +3.3 | -2.6 | -3.0 | -4.1 | -4.5 | -1.5 | -1.8 | -12.9 | -13.2 |
| Pennsylvania | | | | | | | | | | |
| 2008 | 27,984 | 222.7 | 300,303 | 2,389.7 | 58,687 | 467.0 | 219,127 | 1,743.8 | 22,489 | 179.0 |
| 2009 | 26,139 | 207.4 | 277,512 | 2,201.6 | 54,797 | 434.7 | 204,894 | 1,625.5 | 17,821 | 141.4 |
| Percent change | -6.6 | -6.9 | -7.6 | -7.9 | -6.6 | -6.9 | -6.5 | -6.8 | -20.8 | -21.0 |
| **Midwest[2,3,4]** | | | | | | | | | | |
| 2008 | 158,206 | 237.6 | 2,049,232 | 3,077.1 | 454,838 | 683.0 | 1,419,458 | 2,131.5 | 174,936 | 262.7 |
| 2009 | 152,254 | 227.8 | 1,939,190 | 2,901.4 | 452,030 | 676.3 | 1,344,420 | 2,011.5 | 142,740 | 213.6 |
| Percent change | -3.8 | -4.1 | -5.4 | -5.7 | -0.6 | -1.0 | -5.3 | -5.6 | -18.4 | -18.7 |
| East North Central[2,3,4] | | | | | | | | | | |
| 2008 | 109,423 | 235.9 | 1,437,000 | 3,097.7 | 332,630 | 717.0 | 978,143 | 2,108.5 | 126,227 | 272.1 |
| 2009 | 105,206 | 226.2 | 1,361,464 | 2,927.8 | 333,528 | 717.3 | 926,182 | 1,991.8 | 101,754 | 218.8 |
| Percent change | -3.9 | -4.1 | -5.3 | -5.5 | +0.3 | * | -5.3 | -5.5 | -19.4 | -19.6 |
| Illinois[2,3] | | | | | | | | | | |
| 2008 | 38,879 | 302.7 | 381,247 | 2,968.5 | 78,968 | 614.9 | 269,553 | 2,098.8 | 32,726 | 254.8 |
| 2009 | 36,588 | 283.4 | 353,347 | 2,736.9 | 77,850 | 603.0 | 248,821 | 1,927.3 | 26,676 | 206.6 |
| Percent change | -5.9 | -6.4 | -7.3 | -7.8 | -1.4 | -1.9 | -7.7 | -8.2 | -18.5 | -18.9 |
| Indiana | | | | | | | | | | |
| 2008 | 11,899 | 186.3 | 212,959 | 3,333.6 | 48,905 | 765.5 | 146,545 | 2,294.0 | 17,509 | 274.1 |
| 2009 | 12,102 | 188.4 | 200,160 | 3,116.2 | 48,910 | 761.5 | 137,371 | 2,138.7 | 13,879 | 216.1 |
| Percent change | +1.7 | +1.2 | -6.0 | -6.5 | * | -0.5 | -6.3 | -6.8 | -20.7 | -21.2 |

[2] Limited data for 2008 and 2009 were available for Illinois.

[3] The data collection methodology for the offense of forcible rape used by the Illinois and the Minnesota state UCR Programs (with the exception of Rockford, IL, and Minneapolis and St. Paul, MN) does not comply with national UCR guidelines. Consequently, their state figures for forcible rape (with the exception of Rockford, IL, and Minneapolis and St. Paul, MN) have been estimated for inclusion in this table.

[4] Because of changes in the state's reporting practices, figures are not comparable to previous years' data.

[5] Includes offenses reported by the Zoological Police and the Metro Transit Police.

* Less than one-tenth of 1 percent.

**Table 4. Crime, by Region, Geographic Division, and State, 2008–2009**—*Continued*

(Number, rate per 100,000 population, percent.)

| Area | Population[1] | Violent crime | | Murder and non-negligent manslaughter | | Forcible rape | | Robbery | |
|---|---|---|---|---|---|---|---|---|---|
| | | Number | Rate | Number | Rate | Number | Rate | Number | Rate |
| Michigan[4] | | | | | | | | | |
| 2008 | 10,002,486 | 51,384 | 513.7 | 554 | 5.5 | 4,486 | 44.8 | 13,234 | 132.3 |
| 2009 | 9,969,727 | 49,547 | 497.0 | 627 | 6.3 | 4,514 | 45.3 | 12,330 | 123.7 |
| Percent change | | -3.6 | -3.3 | +13.2 | +13.5 | +0.6 | +1.0 | -6.8 | -6.5 |
| Ohio | | | | | | | | | |
| 2008 | 11,528,072 | 40,342 | 349.9 | 551 | 4.8 | 4,514 | 39.2 | 18,804 | 163.1 |
| 2009 | 11,542,645 | 38,332 | 332.1 | 519 | 4.5 | 4,022 | 34.8 | 17,782 | 154.1 |
| Percent change | | -5.0 | -5.1 | -5.8 | -5.9 | -10.9 | -11.0 | -5.4 | -5.6 |
| Wisconsin | | | | | | | | | |
| 2008 | 5,627,610 | 15,499 | 275.4 | 146 | 2.6 | 1,128 | 20.0 | 5,163 | 91.7 |
| 2009 | 5,654,774 | 14,533 | 257.0 | 144 | 2.5 | 1,108 | 19.6 | 4,850 | 85.8 |
| Percent change | | -6.2 | -6.7 | -1.4 | -1.8 | -1.8 | -2.2 | -6.1 | -6.5 |
| West North Central[3] | | | | | | | | | |
| 2008 | 20,206,166 | 72,693 | 359.8 | 866 | 4.3 | 7,034 | 34.8 | 16,010 | 79.2 |
| 2009 | 20,336,243 | 69,826 | 343.4 | 681 | 3.3 | 6,610 | 32.5 | 15,487 | 76.2 |
| Percent change | | -3.9 | -4.6 | -21.4 | -21.9 | -6.0 | -6.6 | -3.3 | -3.9 |
| Iowa | | | | | | | | | |
| 2008 | 2,993,987 | 8,651 | 288.9 | 77 | 2.6 | 937 | 31.3 | 1,249 | 41.7 |
| 2009 | 3,007,856 | 8,397 | 279.2 | 34 | 1.1 | 853 | 28.4 | 1,195 | 39.7 |
| Percent change | | -2.9 | -3.4 | -55.8 | -56.0 | -9.0 | -9.4 | -4.3 | -4.8 |
| Kansas | | | | | | | | | |
| 2008 | 2,797,375 | 11,586 | 414.2 | 113 | 4.0 | 1,230 | 44.0 | 1,682 | 60.1 |
| 2009 | 2,818,747 | 11,278 | 400.1 | 119 | 4.2 | 1,096 | 38.9 | 1,786 | 63.4 |
| Percent change | | -2.7 | -3.4 | +5.3 | +4.5 | -10.9 | -11.6 | +6.2 | +5.4 |
| Minnesota[3] | | | | | | | | | |
| 2008 | 5,230,567 | 13,771 | 263.3 | 109 | 2.1 | 1,805 | 34.5 | 4,179 | 79.9 |
| 2009 | 5,266,214 | 12,842 | 243.9 | 74 | 1.4 | 1,789 | 34.0 | 3,619 | 68.7 |
| Percent change | | -6.7 | -7.4 | -32.1 | -32.6 | -0.9 | -1.6 | -13.4 | -14.0 |
| Missouri | | | | | | | | | |
| 2008 | 5,956,335 | 29,711 | 498.8 | 456 | 7.7 | 1,614 | 27.1 | 7,396 | 124.2 |
| 2009 | 5,987,580 | 29,444 | 491.8 | 383 | 6.4 | 1,607 | 26.8 | 7,452 | 124.5 |
| Percent change | | -0.9 | -1.4 | -16.0 | -16.4 | -0.4 | -1.0 | +0.8 | +0.2 |
| Nebraska | | | | | | | | | |
| 2008 | 1,781,949 | 5,537 | 310.7 | 69 | 3.9 | 600 | 33.7 | 1,297 | 72.8 |
| 2009 | 1,796,619 | 5,059 | 281.6 | 40 | 2.2 | 595 | 33.1 | 1,219 | 67.8 |
| Percent change | | -8.6 | -9.4 | -42.0 | -42.5 | -0.8 | -1.6 | -6.0 | -6.8 |
| North Dakota | | | | | | | | | |
| 2008 | 641,421 | 1,216 | 189.6 | 5 | 0.8 | 286 | 44.6 | 73 | 11.4 |
| 2009 | 646,844 | 1,298 | 200.7 | 10 | 1.5 | 225 | 34.8 | 105 | 16.2 |
| Percent change | | +6.7 | +5.8 | +100.0 | +98.3 | -21.3 | -22.0 | +43.8 | +42.6 |
| South Dakota | | | | | | | | | |
| 2008 | 804,532 | 2,221 | 276.1 | 37 | 4.6 | 562 | 69.9 | 134 | 16.7 |
| 2009 | 812,383 | 1,508 | 185.6 | 21 | 2.6 | 445 | 54.8 | 111 | 13.7 |
| Percent change | | -32.1 | -32.8 | -43.2 | -43.8 | -20.8 | -21.6 | -17.2 | -18.0 |
| **South[4, 5]** | | | | | | | | | |
| 2008 | 112,021,022 | 599,458 | 535.1 | 7,396 | 6.6 | 34,436 | 30.7 | 178,626 | 159.5 |
| 2009 | 113,317,879 | 560,183 | 494.3 | 6,835 | 6.0 | 33,796 | 29.8 | 160,880 | 142.0 |
| Percent change | | -6.6 | -7.6 | -7.6 | -8.6 | -1.9 | -3.0 | -9.9 | -11.0 |
| South Atlantic[5] | | | | | | | | | |
| 2008 | 58,607,367 | 324,739 | 554.1 | 3,904 | 6.7 | 16,159 | 27.6 | 102,895 | 175.6 |
| 2009 | 59,195,930 | 294,550 | 497.6 | 3,418 | 5.8 | 15,308 | 25.9 | 88,315 | 149.2 |
| Percent change | | -9.3 | -10.2 | -12.4 | -13.3 | -5.3 | -6.2 | -14.2 | -15.0 |
| Delaware | | | | | | | | | |
| 2008 | 876,211 | 6,187 | 706.1 | 57 | 6.5 | 371 | 42.3 | 1,847 | 210.8 |
| 2009 | 885,122 | 5,635 | 636.6 | 41 | 4.6 | 338 | 38.2 | 1,671 | 188.8 |
| Percent change | | -8.9 | -9.8 | -28.1 | -28.8 | -8.9 | -9.8 | -9.5 | -10.4 |
| District of Columbia[5] | | | | | | | | | |
| 2008 | 590,074 | 8,509 | 1,442.0 | 186 | 31.5 | 186 | 31.5 | 4,430 | 750.8 |
| 2009 | 599,657 | 8,071 | 1,345.9 | 144 | 24.0 | 150 | 25.0 | 4,389 | 731.9 |
| Percent change | | -5.1 | -6.7 | -22.6 | -23.8 | -19.4 | -20.6 | -0.9 | -2.5 |
| Florida | | | | | | | | | |
| 2008 | 18,423,878 | 126,260 | 685.3 | 1,169 | 6.3 | 5,972 | 32.4 | 36,269 | 196.9 |
| 2009 | 18,537,969 | 113,541 | 612.5 | 1,017 | 5.5 | 5,501 | 29.7 | 30,911 | 166.7 |
| Percent change | | -10.1 | -10.6 | -13.0 | -13.5 | -7.9 | -8.5 | -14.8 | -15.3 |
| Georgia | | | | | | | | | |
| 2008 | 9,697,838 | 47,461 | 489.4 | 650 | 6.7 | 2,344 | 24.2 | 17,862 | 184.2 |
| 2009 | 9,829,211 | 41,880 | 426.1 | 566 | 5.8 | 2,301 | 23.4 | 14,603 | 148.6 |
| Percent change | | -11.8 | -12.9 | -12.9 | -14.1 | -1.8 | -3.1 | -18.2 | -19.3 |

[1] Populations are U.S. Census Bureau provisional estimates as of July 1, 2009, and July 1, 2008.

[3] The data collection methodology for the offense of forcible rape used by the Illinois and the Minnesota state UCR Programs (with the exception of Rockford, IL, and Minneapolis and St. Paul, MN) does not comply with national UCR guidelines. Consequently, their state figures for forcible rape (with the exception of Rockford, IL, and Minneapolis and St. Paul, MN) have been estimated for inclusion in this table.

[4] Because of changes in the state's reporting practices, figures are not comparable to previous years' data.

[5] Includes offenses reported by the Zoological Police and the Metro Transit Police.

**Table 4. Crime, by Region, Geographic Division, and State, 2008–2009—*Continued***

(Number, rate per 100,000 population, percent.)

| Area | Aggravated assault | | Property crime | | Burglary | | Larceny-theft | | Motor vehicle theft | |
|---|---|---|---|---|---|---|---|---|---|---|
| | Number | Rate | Number | Rate | Number | Rate | Number | Rate | Number | Rate |
| Michigan[4] | | | | | | | | | | |
| 2008 | 33,110 | 331.0 | 294,669 | 2,946.0 | 74,686 | 746.7 | 184,268 | 1,842.2 | 35,715 | 357.1 |
| 2009 | 32,076 | 321.7 | 282,918 | 2,837.8 | 75,815 | 760.5 | 177,720 | 1,782.6 | 29,383 | 294.7 |
| Percent change | -3.1 | -2.8 | -4.0 | -3.7 | +1.5 | +1.8 | -3.6 | -3.2 | -17.7 | -17.5 |
| Ohio | | | | | | | | | | |
| 2008 | 16,473 | 142.9 | 392,729 | 3,406.7 | 102,616 | 890.1 | 261,375 | 2,267.3 | 28,738 | 249.3 |
| 2009 | 16,009 | 138.7 | 377,553 | 3,270.9 | 104,213 | 902.9 | 250,450 | 2,169.8 | 22,890 | 198.3 |
| Percent change | -2.8 | -2.9 | -3.9 | -4.0 | +1.6 | +1.4 | -4.2 | -4.3 | -20.3 | -20.4 |
| Wisconsin | | | | | | | | | | |
| 2008 | 9,062 | 161.0 | 155,396 | 2,761.3 | 27,455 | 487.9 | 116,402 | 2,068.4 | 11,539 | 205.0 |
| 2009 | 8,431 | 149.1 | 147,486 | 2,608.2 | 26,740 | 472.9 | 111,820 | 1,977.4 | 8,926 | 157.8 |
| Percent change | -7.0 | -7.4 | -5.1 | -5.5 | -2.6 | -3.1 | -3.9 | -4.4 | -22.6 | -23.0 |
| West North Central[3] | | | | | | | | | | |
| 2008 | 48,783 | 241.4 | 612,232 | 3,029.9 | 122,208 | 604.8 | 441,315 | 2,184.1 | 48,709 | 241.1 |
| 2009 | 47,048 | 231.4 | 577,726 | 2,840.9 | 118,502 | 582.7 | 418,238 | 2,056.6 | 40,986 | 201.5 |
| Percent change | -3.6 | -4.2 | -5.6 | -6.2 | -3.0 | -3.7 | -5.2 | -5.8 | -15.9 | -16.4 |
| Iowa | | | | | | | | | | |
| 2008 | 6,388 | 213.4 | 73,276 | 2,447.4 | 16,598 | 554.4 | 52,302 | 1,746.9 | 4,376 | 146.2 |
| 2009 | 6,315 | 210.0 | 69,441 | 2,308.7 | 16,224 | 539.4 | 49,329 | 1,640.0 | 3,888 | 129.3 |
| Percent change | -1.1 | -1.6 | -5.2 | -5.7 | -2.3 | -2.7 | -5.7 | -6.1 | -11.2 | -11.6 |
| Kansas | | | | | | | | | | |
| 2008 | 8,561 | 306.0 | 95,189 | 3,402.8 | 19,743 | 705.8 | 68,028 | 2,431.9 | 7,418 | 265.2 |
| 2009 | 8,277 | 293.6 | 90,420 | 3,207.8 | 19,469 | 690.7 | 64,997 | 2,305.9 | 5,954 | 211.2 |
| Percent change | -3.3 | -4.1 | -5.0 | -5.7 | -1.4 | -2.1 | -4.5 | -5.2 | -19.7 | -20.3 |
| Minnesota[3] | | | | | | | | | | |
| 2008 | 7,678 | 146.8 | 149,205 | 2,852.6 | 26,483 | 506.3 | 112,579 | 2,152.3 | 10,143 | 193.9 |
| 2009 | 7,360 | 139.8 | 139,083 | 2,641.0 | 25,488 | 484.0 | 105,076 | 1,995.3 | 8,519 | 161.8 |
| Percent change | -4.1 | -4.8 | -6.8 | -7.4 | -3.8 | -4.4 | -6.7 | -7.3 | -16.0 | -16.6 |
| Missouri | | | | | | | | | | |
| 2008 | 20,245 | 339.9 | 216,575 | 3,636.0 | 45,772 | 768.5 | 150,041 | 2,519.0 | 20,762 | 348.6 |
| 2009 | 20,002 | 334.1 | 202,698 | 3,385.3 | 43,787 | 731.3 | 141,432 | 2,362.1 | 17,479 | 291.9 |
| Percent change | -1.2 | -1.7 | -6.4 | -6.9 | -4.3 | -4.8 | -5.7 | -6.2 | -15.8 | -16.3 |
| Nebraska | | | | | | | | | | |
| 2008 | 3,571 | 200.4 | 51,333 | 2,880.7 | 8,717 | 489.2 | 38,393 | 2,154.6 | 4,223 | 237.0 |
| 2009 | 3,205 | 178.4 | 49,614 | 2,761.5 | 8,701 | 484.3 | 37,432 | 2,083.5 | 3,481 | 193.8 |
| Percent change | -10.2 | -11.0 | -3.3 | -4.1 | -0.2 | -1.0 | -2.5 | -3.3 | -17.6 | -18.2 |
| North Dakota | | | | | | | | | | |
| 2008 | 852 | 132.8 | 12,934 | 2,016.5 | 2,304 | 359.2 | 9,728 | 1,516.6 | 902 | 140.6 |
| 2009 | 958 | 148.1 | 12,502 | 1,932.8 | 2,354 | 363.9 | 9,296 | 1,437.1 | 852 | 131.7 |
| Percent change | +12.4 | +11.5 | -3.3 | -4.2 | +2.2 | +1.3 | -4.4 | -5.2 | -5.5 | -6.3 |
| South Dakota | | | | | | | | | | |
| 2008 | 1,488 | 185.0 | 13,720 | 1,705.3 | 2,591 | 322.1 | 10,244 | 1,273.3 | 885 | 110.0 |
| 2009 | 931 | 114.6 | 13,968 | 1,719.4 | 2,479 | 305.2 | 10,676 | 1,314.2 | 813 | 100.1 |
| Percent change | -37.4 | -38.0 | +1.8 | +0.8 | -4.3 | -5.2 | +4.2 | +3.2 | -8.1 | -9.0 |
| **South[4,5]** | | | | | | | | | | |
| 2008 | 379,000 | 338.3 | 4,230,765 | 3,776.8 | 1,054,614 | 941.4 | 2,814,655 | 2,512.6 | 361,496 | 322.7 |
| 2009 | 358,672 | 316.5 | 4,087,821 | 3,607.4 | 1,055,109 | 931.1 | 2,732,182 | 2,411.1 | 300,530 | 265.2 |
| Percent change | -5.4 | -6.4 | -3.4 | -4.5 | * | -1.1 | -2.9 | -4.0 | -16.9 | -17.8 |
| South Atlantic[5] | | | | | | | | | | |
| 2008 | 201,781 | 344.3 | 2,211,418 | 3,773.3 | 539,145 | 919.9 | 1,473,880 | 2,514.8 | 198,393 | 338.5 |
| 2009 | 187,509 | 316.8 | 2,071,837 | 3,500.0 | 524,545 | 886.1 | 1,389,080 | 2,346.6 | 158,212 | 267.3 |
| Percent change | -7.1 | -8.0 | -6.3 | -7.2 | -2.7 | -3.7 | -5.8 | -6.7 | -20.3 | -21.0 |
| Delaware | | | | | | | | | | |
| 2008 | 3,912 | 446.5 | 31,385 | 3,581.9 | 6,783 | 774.1 | 22,045 | 2,515.9 | 2,557 | 291.8 |
| 2009 | 3,585 | 405.0 | 29,648 | 3,349.6 | 6,932 | 783.2 | 20,809 | 2,351.0 | 1,907 | 215.5 |
| Percent change | -8.4 | -9.3 | -5.5 | -6.5 | +2.2 | +1.2 | -5.6 | -6.6 | -25.4 | -26.2 |
| District of Columbia[5] | | | | | | | | | | |
| 2008 | 3,707 | 628.2 | 30,211 | 5,119.9 | 3,788 | 642.0 | 19,958 | 3,382.3 | 6,465 | 1,095.6 |
| 2009 | 3,388 | 565.0 | 28,456 | 4,745.4 | 3,696 | 616.4 | 19,228 | 3,206.5 | 5,532 | 922.5 |
| Percent change | -8.6 | -10.1 | -5.8 | -7.3 | -2.4 | -4.0 | -3.7 | -5.2 | -14.4 | -15.8 |
| Florida | | | | | | | | | | |
| 2008 | 82,850 | 449.7 | 758,906 | 4,119.1 | 188,475 | 1,023.0 | 506,914 | 2,751.4 | 63,517 | 344.8 |
| 2009 | 76,112 | 410.6 | 712,010 | 3,840.8 | 181,884 | 981.1 | 479,867 | 2,588.6 | 50,259 | 271.1 |
| Percent change | -8.1 | -8.7 | -6.2 | -6.8 | -3.5 | -4.1 | -5.3 | -5.9 | -20.9 | -21.4 |
| Georgia | | | | | | | | | | |
| 2008 | 26,605 | 274.3 | 387,099 | 3,991.6 | 100,662 | 1,038.0 | 246,844 | 2,545.4 | 39,593 | 408.3 |
| 2009 | 24,410 | 248.3 | 360,400 | 3,666.6 | 98,362 | 1,000.7 | 228,893 | 2,328.7 | 33,145 | 337.2 |
| Percent change | -8.3 | -9.5 | -6.9 | -8.1 | -2.3 | -3.6 | -7.3 | -8.5 | -16.3 | -17.4 |

[3] The data collection methodology for the offense of forcible rape used by the Illinois and the Minnesota state UCR Programs (with the exception of Rockford, IL, and Minneapolis and St. Paul, MN) does not comply with national UCR guidelines. Consequently, their state figures for forcible rape (with the exception of Rockford, IL, and Minneapolis and St. Paul, MN) have been estimated for inclusion in this table.

[4] Because of changes in the state's reporting practices, figures are not comparable to previous years' data.

[5] Includes offenses reported by the Zoological Police and the Metro Transit Police.

* Less than one-tenth of 1 percent.

## Table 4. Crime, by Region, Geographic Division, and State, 2008–2009—*Continued*

(Number, rate per 100,000 population, percent.)

| Area | Population[1] | Violent crime | | Murder and non-negligent manslaughter | | Forcible rape | | Robbery | |
|---|---|---|---|---|---|---|---|---|---|
| | | Number | Rate | Number | Rate | Number | Rate | Number | Rate |
| Maryland | | | | | | | | | |
| 2008 | 5,658,655 | 35,385 | 625.3 | 493 | 8.7 | 1,127 | 19.9 | 13,201 | 233.3 |
| 2009 | 5,699,478 | 33,623 | 589.9 | 438 | 7.7 | 1,156 | 20.3 | 12,007 | 210.7 |
| Percent change | | -5.0 | -5.7 | -11.2 | -11.8 | +2.6 | +1.8 | -9.0 | -9.7 |
| North Carolina | | | | | | | | | |
| 2008 | 9,247,134 | 43,120 | 466.3 | 605 | 6.5 | 2,290 | 24.8 | 14,321 | 154.9 |
| 2009 | 9,380,884 | 37,929 | 404.3 | 494 | 5.3 | 2,306 | 24.6 | 11,825 | 126.1 |
| Percent change | | -12.0 | -13.3 | -18.3 | -19.5 | +0.7 | -0.7 | -17.4 | -18.6 |
| South Carolina | | | | | | | | | |
| 2008 | 4,503,280 | 32,752 | 727.3 | 307 | 6.8 | 1,683 | 37.4 | 6,596 | 146.5 |
| 2009 | 4,561,242 | 30,596 | 670.8 | 287 | 6.3 | 1,612 | 35.3 | 5,735 | 125.7 |
| Percent change | | -6.6 | -7.8 | -6.5 | -7.7 | -4.2 | -5.4 | -13.1 | -14.2 |
| Virginia | | | | | | | | | |
| 2008 | 7,795,424 | 20,038 | 257.0 | 370 | 4.7 | 1,794 | 23.0 | 7,470 | 95.8 |
| 2009 | 7,882,590 | 17,879 | 226.8 | 347 | 4.4 | 1,511 | 19.2 | 6,257 | 79.4 |
| Percent change | | -10.8 | -11.8 | -6.2 | -7.3 | -15.8 | -16.7 | -16.2 | -17.2 |
| West Virginia | | | | | | | | | |
| 2008 | 1,814,873 | 5,027 | 277.0 | 67 | 3.7 | 392 | 21.6 | 899 | 49.5 |
| 2009 | 1,819,777 | 5,396 | 296.5 | 84 | 4.6 | 433 | 23.8 | 917 | 50.4 |
| Percent change | | +7.3 | +7.1 | +25.4 | +25.0 | +10.5 | +10.2 | +2.0 | +1.7 |
| East South Central[4] | | | | | | | | | |
| 2008 | 18,146,063 | 87,844 | 484.1 | 1,205 | 6.6 | 6,079 | 33.5 | 25,305 | 139.5 |
| 2009 | 18,271,071 | 82,683 | 452.5 | 1,152 | 6.3 | 5,945 | 32.5 | 22,500 | 123.1 |
| Percent change | | -5.9 | -6.5 | -4.4 | -5.1 | -2.2 | -2.9 | -11.1 | -11.7 |
| Alabama | | | | | | | | | |
| 2008 | 4,677,464 | 21,109 | 451.3 | 357 | 7.6 | 1,618 | 34.6 | 7,344 | 157.0 |
| 2009 | 4,708,708 | 21,179 | 449.8 | 323 | 6.9 | 1,504 | 31.9 | 6,259 | 132.9 |
| Percent change | | +0.3 | -0.3 | -9.5 | -10.1 | -7.0 | -7.7 | -14.8 | -15.3 |
| Kentucky[4] | | | | | | | | | |
| 2008 | 4,287,931 | 12,815 | 298.9 | 202 | 4.7 | 1,449 | 33.8 | 4,060 | 94.7 |
| 2009 | 4,314,113 | 11,159 | 258.7 | 178 | 4.1 | 1,509 | 35.0 | 3,629 | 84.1 |
| Percent change | | -12.9 | -13.5 | -11.9 | -12.4 | +4.1 | +3.5 | -10.6 | -11.2 |
| Mississippi | | | | | | | | | |
| 2008 | 2,940,212 | 8,952 | 304.5 | 234 | 8.0 | 927 | 31.5 | 3,092 | 105.2 |
| 2009 | 2,951,996 | 8,304 | 281.3 | 190 | 6.4 | 939 | 31.8 | 2,965 | 100.4 |
| Percent change | | -7.2 | -7.6 | -18.8 | -19.1 | +1.3 | +0.9 | -4.1 | -4.5 |
| Tennessee | | | | | | | | | |
| 2008 | 6,240,456 | 44,968 | 720.6 | 412 | 6.6 | 2,085 | 33.4 | 10,809 | 173.2 |
| 2009 | 6,296,254 | 42,041 | 667.7 | 461 | 7.3 | 1,993 | 31.7 | 9,647 | 153.2 |
| Percent change | | -6.5 | -7.3 | +11.9 | +10.9 | -4.4 | -5.3 | -10.8 | -11.5 |
| West South Central | | | | | | | | | |
| 2008 | 35,267,592 | 186,875 | 529.9 | 2,287 | 6.5 | 12,198 | 34.6 | 50,426 | 143.0 |
| 2009 | 35,850,878 | 182,950 | 510.3 | 2,265 | 6.3 | 12,543 | 35.0 | 50,065 | 139.6 |
| Percent change | | -2.1 | -3.7 | -1.0 | -2.6 | +2.8 | +1.2 | -0.7 | -2.3 |
| Arkansas | | | | | | | | | |
| 2008 | 2,867,764 | 14,472 | 504.6 | 164 | 5.7 | 1,425 | 49.7 | 2,756 | 96.1 |
| 2009 | 2,889,450 | 14,959 | 517.7 | 179 | 6.2 | 1,368 | 47.3 | 2,582 | 89.4 |
| Percent change | | +3.4 | +2.6 | +9.1 | +8.3 | -4.0 | -4.7 | -6.3 | -7.0 |
| Louisiana | | | | | | | | | |
| 2008 | 4,451,513 | 29,576 | 664.4 | 541 | 12.2 | 1,253 | 28.1 | 6,250 | 140.4 |
| 2009 | 4,492,076 | 27,849 | 620.0 | 530 | 11.8 | 1,359 | 30.3 | 6,105 | 135.9 |
| Percent change | | -5.8 | -6.7 | -2.0 | -2.9 | +8.5 | +7.5 | -2.3 | -3.2 |
| Oklahoma | | | | | | | | | |
| 2008 | 3,644,025 | 19,241 | 528.0 | 212 | 5.8 | 1,465 | 40.2 | 3,681 | 101.0 |
| 2009 | 3,687,050 | 18,474 | 501.1 | 228 | 6.2 | 1,529 | 41.5 | 3,343 | 90.7 |
| Percent change | | -4.0 | -5.1 | +7.5 | +6.3 | +4.4 | +3.2 | -9.2 | -10.2 |
| Texas | | | | | | | | | |
| 2008 | 24,304,290 | 123,586 | 508.5 | 1,370 | 5.6 | 8,055 | 33.1 | 37,739 | 155.3 |
| 2009 | 24,782,302 | 121,668 | 490.9 | 1,328 | 5.4 | 8,287 | 33.4 | 38,035 | 153.5 |
| Percent change | | -1.6 | -3.5 | -3.1 | -4.9 | +2.9 | +0.9 | +0.8 | -1.2 |
| **West** | | | | | | | | | |
| 2008 | 70,698,031 | 319,112 | 451.4 | 3,506 | 5.0 | 22,044 | 31.2 | 103,872 | 146.9 |
| 2009 | 71,568,081 | 302,312 | 422.4 | 3,241 | 4.5 | 21,689 | 30.3 | 96,156 | 134.4 |
| Percent change | | -5.3 | -6.4 | -7.6 | -8.7 | -1.6 | -2.8 | -7.4 | -8.6 |
| Mountain | | | | | | | | | |
| 2008 | 21,792,990 | 94,368 | 433.0 | 1,033 | 4.7 | 8,528 | 39.1 | 23,705 | 108.8 |
| 2009 | 22,122,914 | 88,073 | 398.1 | 961 | 4.3 | 8,365 | 37.8 | 21,214 | 95.9 |
| Percent change | | -6.7 | -8.1 | -7.0 | -8.4 | -1.9 | -3.4 | -10.5 | -11.8 |

[1] Populations are U.S. Census Bureau provisional estimates as of July 1, 2009, and July 1, 2008.

[4] Because of changes in the state's reporting practices, figures are not comparable to previous years' data.

**Table 4. Crime, by Region, Geographic Division, and State, 2008–2009**—*Continued*

(Number, rate per 100,000 population, percent.)

| Area | Aggravated assault | | Property crime | | Burglary | | Larceny-theft | | Motor vehicle theft | |
|---|---|---|---|---|---|---|---|---|---|---|
| | Number | Rate | Number | Rate | Number | Rate | Number | Rate | Number | Rate |
| Maryland | | | | | | | | | | |
| 2008 | 20,564 | 363.4 | 198,079 | 3,500.5 | 38,828 | 686.2 | 133,922 | 2,366.7 | 25,329 | 447.6 |
| 2009 | 20,022 | 351.3 | 182,422 | 3,200.7 | 37,032 | 649.7 | 125,771 | 2,206.7 | 19,619 | 344.2 |
| Percent change | -2.6 | -3.3 | -7.9 | -8.6 | -4.6 | -5.3 | -6.1 | -6.8 | -22.5 | -23.1 |
| North Carolina | | | | | | | | | | |
| 2008 | 25,904 | 280.1 | 372,690 | 4,030.3 | 111,541 | 1,206.2 | 234,425 | 2,535.1 | 26,724 | 289.0 |
| 2009 | 23,304 | 248.4 | 344,098 | 3,668.1 | 107,830 | 1,149.5 | 216,244 | 2,305.2 | 20,024 | 213.5 |
| Percent change | -10.0 | -11.3 | -7.7 | -9.0 | -3.3 | -4.7 | -7.8 | -9.1 | -25.1 | -26.1 |
| South Carolina | | | | | | | | | | |
| 2008 | 24,166 | 536.6 | 189,999 | 4,219.1 | 45,970 | 1,020.8 | 126,360 | 2,806.0 | 17,669 | 392.4 |
| 2009 | 22,962 | 503.4 | 177,369 | 3,888.6 | 45,282 | 992.8 | 118,521 | 2,598.4 | 13,566 | 297.4 |
| Percent change | -5.0 | -6.2 | -6.6 | -7.8 | -1.5 | -2.7 | -6.2 | -7.4 | -23.2 | -24.2 |
| Virginia | | | | | | | | | | |
| 2008 | 10,404 | 133.5 | 196,700 | 2,523.3 | 32,184 | 412.9 | 151,171 | 1,939.2 | 13,345 | 171.2 |
| 2009 | 9,764 | 123.9 | 191,453 | 2,428.8 | 31,576 | 400.6 | 148,458 | 1,883.4 | 11,419 | 144.9 |
| Percent change | -6.2 | -7.2 | -2.7 | -3.7 | -1.9 | -3.0 | -1.8 | -2.9 | -14.4 | -15.4 |
| West Virginia | | | | | | | | | | |
| 2008 | 3,669 | 202.2 | 46,349 | 2,553.8 | 10,914 | 601.4 | 32,241 | 1,776.5 | 3,194 | 176.0 |
| 2009 | 3,962 | 217.7 | 45,981 | 2,526.7 | 11,951 | 656.7 | 31,289 | 1,719.4 | 2,741 | 150.6 |
| Percent change | +8.0 | +7.7 | -0.8 | -1.1 | +9.5 | +9.2 | -3.0 | -3.2 | -14.2 | -14.4 |
| East South Central[4] | | | | | | | | | | |
| 2008 | 55,255 | 304.5 | 642,625 | 3,541.4 | 170,989 | 942.3 | 424,916 | 2,341.6 | 46,720 | 257.5 |
| 2009 | 53,086 | 290.5 | 609,576 | 3,336.3 | 171,346 | 937.8 | 400,695 | 2,193.1 | 37,535 | 205.4 |
| Percent change | -3.9 | -4.6 | -5.1 | -5.8 | +0.2 | -0.5 | -5.7 | -6.3 | -19.7 | -20.2 |
| Alabama | | | | | | | | | | |
| 2008 | 11,790 | 252.1 | 190,292 | 4,068.3 | 50,379 | 1,077.1 | 126,461 | 2,703.6 | 13,452 | 287.6 |
| 2009 | 13,093 | 278.1 | 177,629 | 3,772.4 | 48,837 | 1,037.2 | 117,711 | 2,499.9 | 11,081 | 235.3 |
| Percent change | +11.1 | +10.3 | -6.7 | -7.3 | -3.1 | -3.7 | -6.9 | -7.5 | -17.6 | -18.2 |
| Kentucky[4] | | | | | | | | | | |
| 2008 | 7,104 | 165.7 | 114,291 | 2,665.4 | 29,535 | 688.8 | 77,093 | 1,797.9 | 7,663 | 178.7 |
| 2009 | 5,843 | 135.4 | 108,401 | 2,512.7 | 29,701 | 688.5 | 72,620 | 1,683.3 | 6,080 | 140.9 |
| Percent change | -17.8 | -18.2 | -5.2 | -5.7 | +0.6 | * | -5.8 | -6.4 | -20.7 | -21.1 |
| Mississippi | | | | | | | | | | |
| 2008 | 4,699 | 159.8 | 86,445 | 2,940.1 | 25,810 | 877.8 | 54,282 | 1,846.2 | 6,353 | 216.1 |
| 2009 | 4,210 | 142.6 | 87,181 | 2,953.3 | 29,162 | 987.9 | 52,618 | 1,782.5 | 5,401 | 183.0 |
| Percent change | -10.4 | -10.8 | +0.9 | +0.4 | +13.0 | +12.5 | -3.1 | -3.5 | -15.0 | -15.3 |
| Tennessee | | | | | | | | | | |
| 2008 | 31,662 | 507.4 | 251,597 | 4,031.7 | 65,265 | 1,045.8 | 167,080 | 2,677.4 | 19,252 | 308.5 |
| 2009 | 29,940 | 475.5 | 236,365 | 3,754.1 | 63,646 | 1,010.9 | 157,746 | 2,505.4 | 14,973 | 237.8 |
| Percent change | -5.4 | -6.3 | -6.1 | -6.9 | -2.5 | -3.3 | -5.6 | -6.4 | -22.2 | -22.9 |
| West South Central | | | | | | | | | | |
| 2008 | 121,964 | 345.8 | 1,376,722 | 3,903.6 | 344,480 | 976.8 | 915,859 | 2,596.9 | 116,383 | 330.0 |
| 2009 | 118,077 | 329.4 | 1,406,408 | 3,922.9 | 359,218 | 1,002.0 | 942,407 | 2,628.7 | 104,783 | 292.3 |
| Percent change | -3.2 | -4.8 | +2.2 | +0.5 | +4.3 | +2.6 | +2.9 | +1.2 | -10.0 | -11.4 |
| Arkansas | | | | | | | | | | |
| 2008 | 10,127 | 353.1 | 109,752 | 3,827.1 | 33,772 | 1,177.6 | 69,482 | 2,422.9 | 6,498 | 226.6 |
| 2009 | 10,830 | 374.8 | 109,038 | 3,773.7 | 34,764 | 1,203.1 | 68,171 | 2,359.3 | 6,103 | 211.2 |
| Percent change | +6.9 | +6.1 | -0.7 | -1.4 | +2.9 | +2.2 | -1.9 | -2.6 | -6.1 | -6.8 |
| Louisiana | | | | | | | | | | |
| 2008 | 21,532 | 483.7 | 171,147 | 3,844.7 | 45,513 | 1,022.4 | 112,062 | 2,517.4 | 13,572 | 304.9 |
| 2009 | 19,855 | 442.0 | 170,456 | 3,794.6 | 46,246 | 1,029.5 | 112,493 | 2,504.3 | 11,717 | 260.8 |
| Percent change | -7.8 | -8.6 | -0.4 | -1.3 | +1.6 | +0.7 | +0.4 | -0.5 | -13.7 | -14.4 |
| Oklahoma | | | | | | | | | | |
| 2008 | 13,883 | 381.0 | 125,903 | 3,455.1 | 35,141 | 964.3 | 79,833 | 2,190.8 | 10,929 | 299.9 |
| 2009 | 13,374 | 362.7 | 131,769 | 3,573.8 | 37,975 | 1,030.0 | 83,390 | 2,261.7 | 10,404 | 282.2 |
| Percent change | -3.7 | -4.8 | +4.7 | +3.4 | +8.1 | +6.8 | +4.5 | +3.2 | -4.8 | -5.9 |
| Texas | | | | | | | | | | |
| 2008 | 76,422 | 314.4 | 969,920 | 3,990.7 | 230,054 | 946.6 | 654,482 | 2,692.9 | 85,384 | 351.3 |
| 2009 | 74,018 | 298.7 | 995,145 | 4,015.5 | 240,233 | 969.4 | 678,353 | 2,737.2 | 76,559 | 308.9 |
| Percent change | -3.1 | -5.0 | +2.6 | +0.6 | +4.4 | +2.4 | +3.6 | +1.6 | -10.3 | -12.1 |
| **West** | | | | | | | | | | |
| 2008 | 189,690 | 268.3 | 2,257,559 | 3,193.2 | 482,857 | 683.0 | 1,448,310 | 2,048.6 | 326,392 | 461.7 |
| 2009 | 181,226 | 253.2 | 2,120,204 | 2,962.5 | 466,490 | 651.8 | 1,381,764 | 1,930.7 | 271,950 | 380.0 |
| Percent change | -4.5 | -5.6 | -6.1 | -7.2 | -3.4 | -4.6 | -4.6 | -5.8 | -16.7 | -17.7 |
| Mountain | | | | | | | | | | |
| 2008 | 61,102 | 280.4 | 737,825 | 3,385.6 | 158,688 | 728.2 | 492,131 | 2,258.2 | 87,006 | 399.2 |
| 2009 | 57,533 | 260.1 | 684,715 | 3,095.0 | 151,410 | 684.4 | 465,433 | 2,103.9 | 67,872 | 306.8 |
| Percent change | -5.8 | -7.2 | -7.2 | -8.6 | -4.6 | -6.0 | -5.4 | -6.8 | -22.0 | -23.2 |

[4] Because of changes in the state's reporting practices, figures are not comparable to previous years' data.
* Less than one-tenth of 1 percent.

## Table 4. Crime, by Region, Geographic Division, and State, 2008–2009—*Continued*

(Number, rate per 100,000 population, percent.)

| Area | Population[1] | Violent crime | | Murder and non-negligent manslaughter | | Forcible rape | | Robbery | |
|---|---|---|---|---|---|---|---|---|---|
| | | Number | Rate | Number | Rate | Number | Rate | Number | Rate |
| Arizona | | | | | | | | | |
| 2008 | 6,499,377 | 31,274 | 481.2 | 454 | 7.0 | 2,193 | 33.7 | 9,757 | 150.1 |
| 2009 | 6,595,778 | 26,929 | 408.3 | 354 | 5.4 | 2,110 | 32.0 | 8,099 | 122.8 |
| Percent change | | -13.9 | -15.2 | -22.0 | -23.2 | -3.8 | -5.2 | -17.0 | -18.2 |
| Colorado | | | | | | | | | |
| 2008 | 4,935,213 | 17,129 | 347.1 | 156 | 3.2 | 2,094 | 42.4 | 3,369 | 68.3 |
| 2009 | 5,024,748 | 16,976 | 337.8 | 175 | 3.5 | 2,242 | 44.6 | 3,387 | 67.4 |
| Percent change | | -0.9 | -2.7 | +12.2 | +10.2 | +7.1 | +5.2 | +0.5 | -1.3 |
| Idaho | | | | | | | | | |
| 2008 | 1,527,506 | 3,678 | 240.8 | 23 | 1.5 | 577 | 37.8 | 241 | 15.8 |
| 2009 | 1,545,801 | 3,530 | 228.4 | 22 | 1.4 | 552 | 35.7 | 245 | 15.8 |
| Percent change | | -4.0 | -5.2 | -4.3 | -5.5 | -4.3 | -5.5 | +1.7 | +0.5 |
| Montana | | | | | | | | | |
| 2008 | 968,035 | 2,918 | 301.4 | 33 | 3.4 | 346 | 35.7 | 203 | 21.0 |
| 2009 | 974,989 | 2,473 | 253.6 | 28 | 2.9 | 294 | 30.2 | 216 | 22.2 |
| Percent change | | -15.3 | -15.9 | -15.2 | -15.8 | -15.0 | -15.6 | +6.4 | +5.6 |
| Nevada | | | | | | | | | |
| 2008 | 2,615,772 | 18,917 | 723.2 | 165 | 6.3 | 1,104 | 42.2 | 6,475 | 247.5 |
| 2009 | 2,643,085 | 18,559 | 702.2 | 157 | 5.9 | 1,021 | 38.6 | 6,021 | 227.8 |
| Percent change | | -1.9 | -2.9 | -4.8 | -5.8 | -7.5 | -8.5 | -7.0 | -8.0 |
| New Mexico | | | | | | | | | |
| 2008 | 1,986,763 | 13,010 | 654.8 | 150 | 7.5 | 1,114 | 56.1 | 2,152 | 108.3 |
| 2009 | 2,009,671 | 12,440 | 619.0 | 175 | 8.7 | 1,057 | 52.6 | 1,870 | 93.1 |
| Percent change | | -4.4 | -5.5 | +16.7 | +15.3 | -5.1 | -6.2 | -13.1 | -14.1 |
| Utah | | | | | | | | | |
| 2008 | 2,727,343 | 6,130 | 224.8 | 40 | 1.5 | 916 | 33.6 | 1,422 | 52.1 |
| 2009 | 2,784,572 | 5,924 | 212.7 | 37 | 1.3 | 905 | 32.5 | 1,299 | 46.6 |
| Percent change | | -3.4 | -5.3 | -7.5 | -9.4 | -1.2 | -3.2 | -8.6 | -10.5 |
| Wyoming | | | | | | | | | |
| 2008 | 532,981 | 1,312 | 246.2 | 12 | 2.3 | 184 | 34.5 | 86 | 16.1 |
| 2009 | 544,270 | 1,242 | 228.2 | 13 | 2.4 | 184 | 33.8 | 77 | 14.1 |
| Percent change | | -5.3 | -7.3 | +8.3 | +6.1 | 0.0 | -2.1 | -10.5 | -12.3 |
| Pacific | | | | | | | | | |
| 2008 | 48,905,041 | 224,744 | 459.6 | 2,473 | 5.1 | 13,516 | 27.6 | 80,167 | 163.9 |
| 2009 | 49,445,167 | 214,239 | 433.3 | 2,280 | 4.6 | 13,324 | 26.9 | 74,942 | 151.6 |
| Percent change | | -4.7 | -5.7 | -7.8 | -8.8 | -1.4 | -2.5 | -6.5 | -7.5 |
| Alaska | | | | | | | | | |
| 2008 | 688,125 | 4,479 | 650.9 | 27 | 3.9 | 445 | 64.7 | 644 | 93.6 |
| 2009 | 698,473 | 4,421 | 633.0 | 22 | 3.1 | 512 | 73.3 | 655 | 93.8 |
| Percent change | | -1.3 | -2.8 | -18.5 | -19.7 | +15.1 | +13.4 | +1.7 | +0.2 |
| California | | | | | | | | | |
| 2008 | 36,580,371 | 185,173 | 506.2 | 2,142 | 5.9 | 8,903 | 24.3 | 69,385 | 189.7 |
| 2009 | 36,961,664 | 174,459 | 472.0 | 1,972 | 5.3 | 8,713 | 23.6 | 64,093 | 173.4 |
| Percent change | | -5.8 | -6.8 | -7.9 | -8.9 | -2.1 | -3.1 | -7.6 | -8.6 |
| Hawaii | | | | | | | | | |
| 2008 | 1,287,481 | 3,510 | 272.6 | 26 | 2.0 | 363 | 28.2 | 1,085 | 84.3 |
| 2009 | 1,295,178 | 3,559 | 274.8 | 22 | 1.7 | 392 | 30.3 | 1,034 | 79.8 |
| Percent change | | +1.4 | +0.8 | -15.4 | -15.9 | +8.0 | +7.3 | -4.7 | -5.3 |
| Oregon | | | | | | | | | |
| 2008 | 3,782,991 | 9,843 | 260.2 | 85 | 2.2 | 1,178 | 31.1 | 2,656 | 70.2 |
| 2009 | 3,825,657 | 9,744 | 254.7 | 85 | 2.2 | 1,168 | 30.5 | 2,461 | 64.3 |
| Percent change | | -1.0 | -2.1 | 0.0 | -1.1 | -0.8 | -2.0 | -7.3 | -8.4 |
| Washington | | | | | | | | | |
| 2008 | 6,566,073 | 21,739 | 331.1 | 193 | 2.9 | 2,627 | 40.0 | 6,397 | 97.4 |
| 2009 | 6,664,195 | 22,056 | 331.0 | 179 | 2.7 | 2,539 | 38.1 | 6,699 | 100.5 |
| Percent change | | +1.5 | * | -7.3 | -8.6 | -3.3 | -4.8 | +4.7 | +3.2 |
| Puerto Rico | | | | | | | | | |
| 2008 | 3,954,553 | 9,484 | 239.8 | 807 | 20.4 | 95 | 2.4 | 5,467 | 138.2 |
| 2009 | 3,967,288 | 10,492 | 264.5 | 894 | 22.5 | 65 | 1.6 | 6,093 | 153.6 |
| Percent change | | +10.6 | +10.3 | +10.8 | +10.4 | -31.6 | -31.8 | +11.5 | +11.1 |

[1] Populations are U.S. Census Bureau provisional estimates as of July 1, 2009, and July 1, 2008.
* Less than one-tenth of 1 percent.

## Table 4. Crime, by Region, Geographic Division, and State, 2008–2009—*Continued*

(Number, rate per 100,000 population, percent.)

| Area | Aggravated assault | | Property crime | | Burglary | | Larceny-theft | | Motor vehicle theft | |
|---|---|---|---|---|---|---|---|---|---|---|
| | Number | Rate | Number | Rate | Number | Rate | Number | Rate | Number | Rate |
| Arizona | | | | | | | | | | |
| 2008 | 18,870 | 290.3 | 265,682 | 4,087.8 | 58,125 | 894.3 | 169,346 | 2,605.6 | 38,211 | 587.9 |
| 2009 | 16,366 | 248.1 | 234,582 | 3,556.5 | 53,412 | 809.8 | 155,184 | 2,352.8 | 25,986 | 394.0 |
| Percent change | -13.3 | -14.5 | -11.7 | -13.0 | -8.1 | -9.5 | -8.4 | -9.7 | -32.0 | -33.0 |
| Colorado | | | | | | | | | | |
| 2008 | 11,510 | 233.2 | 141,107 | 2,859.2 | 28,222 | 571.8 | 99,468 | 2,015.5 | 13,417 | 271.9 |
| 2009 | 11,172 | 222.3 | 133,968 | 2,666.2 | 26,649 | 530.4 | 94,861 | 1,887.9 | 12,458 | 247.9 |
| Percent change | -2.9 | -4.7 | -5.1 | -6.8 | -5.6 | -7.3 | -4.6 | -6.3 | -7.1 | -8.8 |
| Idaho | | | | | | | | | | |
| 2008 | 2,837 | 185.7 | 32,252 | 2,111.4 | 6,805 | 445.5 | 23,772 | 1,556.3 | 1,675 | 109.7 |
| 2009 | 2,711 | 175.4 | 30,741 | 1,988.7 | 6,558 | 424.2 | 22,741 | 1,471.1 | 1,442 | 93.3 |
| Percent change | -4.4 | -5.6 | -4.7 | -5.8 | -3.6 | -4.8 | -4.3 | -5.5 | -13.9 | -14.9 |
| Montana | | | | | | | | | | |
| 2008 | 2,336 | 241.3 | 26,323 | 2,719.2 | 3,654 | 377.5 | 20,898 | 2,158.8 | 1,771 | 182.9 |
| 2009 | 1,935 | 198.5 | 24,024 | 2,464.0 | 3,386 | 347.3 | 19,182 | 1,967.4 | 1,456 | 149.3 |
| Percent change | -17.2 | -17.8 | -8.7 | -9.4 | -7.3 | -8.0 | -8.2 | -8.9 | -17.8 | -18.4 |
| Nevada | | | | | | | | | | |
| 2008 | 11,173 | 427.1 | 89,873 | 3,435.8 | 24,208 | 925.5 | 49,747 | 1,901.8 | 15,918 | 608.5 |
| 2009 | 11,360 | 429.8 | 80,763 | 3,055.6 | 21,994 | 832.1 | 46,390 | 1,755.1 | 12,379 | 468.4 |
| Percent change | +1.7 | +0.6 | -10.1 | -11.1 | -9.1 | -10.1 | -6.7 | -7.7 | -22.2 | -23.0 |
| New Mexico | | | | | | | | | | |
| 2008 | 9,594 | 482.9 | 75,750 | 3,812.7 | 20,720 | 1,042.9 | 47,004 | 2,365.9 | 8,026 | 404.0 |
| 2009 | 9,338 | 464.7 | 75,078 | 3,735.8 | 22,022 | 1,095.8 | 46,580 | 2,317.8 | 6,476 | 322.2 |
| Percent change | -2.7 | -3.8 | -0.9 | -2.0 | +6.3 | +5.1 | -0.9 | -2.0 | -19.3 | -20.2 |
| Utah | | | | | | | | | | |
| 2008 | 3,752 | 137.6 | 92,327 | 3,385.2 | 14,754 | 541.0 | 70,308 | 2,577.9 | 7,265 | 266.4 |
| 2009 | 3,683 | 132.3 | 91,205 | 3,275.4 | 15,159 | 544.4 | 69,142 | 2,483.0 | 6,904 | 247.9 |
| Percent change | -1.8 | -3.9 | -1.2 | -3.2 | +2.7 | +0.6 | -1.7 | -3.7 | -5.0 | -6.9 |
| Wyoming | | | | | | | | | | |
| 2008 | 1,030 | 193.3 | 14,511 | 2,722.6 | 2,200 | 412.8 | 11,588 | 2,174.2 | 723 | 135.7 |
| 2009 | 968 | 177.9 | 14,354 | 2,637.3 | 2,230 | 409.7 | 11,353 | 2,085.9 | 771 | 141.7 |
| Percent change | -6.0 | -8.0 | -1.1 | -3.1 | +1.4 | -0.7 | -2.0 | -4.1 | +6.6 | +4.4 |
| Pacific | | | | | | | | | | |
| 2008 | 128,588 | 262.9 | 1,519,734 | 3,107.5 | 324,169 | 662.9 | 956,179 | 1,955.2 | 239,386 | 489.5 |
| 2009 | 123,693 | 250.2 | 1,435,489 | 2,903.2 | 315,080 | 637.2 | 916,331 | 1,853.2 | 204,078 | 412.7 |
| Percent change | -3.8 | -4.9 | -5.5 | -6.6 | -2.8 | -3.9 | -4.2 | -5.2 | -14.7 | -15.7 |
| Alaska | | | | | | | | | | |
| 2008 | 3,363 | 488.7 | 20,097 | 2,920.5 | 3,232 | 469.7 | 15,235 | 2,214.0 | 1,630 | 236.9 |
| 2009 | 3,232 | 462.7 | 20,577 | 2,946.0 | 3,597 | 515.0 | 15,291 | 2,189.2 | 1,689 | 241.8 |
| Percent change | -3.9 | -5.3 | +2.4 | +0.9 | +11.3 | +9.6 | +0.4 | -1.1 | +3.6 | +2.1 |
| California | | | | | | | | | | |
| 2008 | 104,743 | 286.3 | 1,080,766 | 2,954.5 | 237,724 | 649.9 | 650,513 | 1,778.3 | 192,529 | 526.3 |
| 2009 | 99,681 | 269.7 | 1,009,614 | 2,731.5 | 230,137 | 622.6 | 615,456 | 1,665.1 | 164,021 | 443.8 |
| Percent change | -4.8 | -5.8 | -6.6 | -7.5 | -3.2 | -4.2 | -5.4 | -6.4 | -14.8 | -15.7 |
| Hawaii | | | | | | | | | | |
| 2008 | 2,036 | 158.1 | 45,944 | 3,568.5 | 9,404 | 730.4 | 31,424 | 2,440.7 | 5,116 | 397.4 |
| 2009 | 2,111 | 163.0 | 47,419 | 3,661.2 | 9,178 | 708.6 | 33,422 | 2,580.5 | 4,819 | 372.1 |
| Percent change | +3.7 | +3.1 | +3.2 | +2.6 | -2.4 | -3.0 | +6.4 | +5.7 | -5.8 | -6.4 |
| Oregon | | | | | | | | | | |
| 2008 | 5,924 | 156.6 | 125,042 | 3,305.4 | 21,053 | 556.5 | 92,623 | 2,448.4 | 11,366 | 300.5 |
| 2009 | 6,030 | 157.6 | 113,511 | 2,967.1 | 19,377 | 506.5 | 84,265 | 2,202.6 | 9,869 | 258.0 |
| Percent change | +1.8 | +0.7 | -9.2 | -10.2 | -8.0 | -9.0 | -9.0 | -10.0 | -13.2 | -14.1 |
| Washington | | | | | | | | | | |
| 2008 | 12,522 | 190.7 | 247,885 | 3,775.2 | 52,756 | 803.5 | 166,384 | 2,534.0 | 28,745 | 437.8 |
| 2009 | 12,639 | 189.7 | 244,368 | 3,666.9 | 52,791 | 792.2 | 167,897 | 2,519.4 | 23,680 | 355.3 |
| Percent change | +0.9 | -0.6 | -1.4 | -2.9 | +0.1 | -1.4 | +0.9 | -0.6 | -17.6 | -18.8 |
| Puerto Rico | | | | | | | | | | |
| 2008 | 3,115 | 78.8 | 59,254 | 1,498.4 | 19,138 | 483.9 | 33,113 | 837.3 | 7,003 | 177.1 |
| 2009 | 3,440 | 86.7 | 55,937 | 1,410.0 | 18,521 | 466.8 | 30,584 | 770.9 | 6,832 | 172.2 |
| Percent change | +10.4 | +10.1 | -5.6 | -5.9 | -3.2 | -3.5 | -7.6 | -7.9 | -2.4 | -2.8 |

## Table 5. Crime, by State and Area, 2009

(Number, percent, rate per 100,000 population.)

| Area | Population | Violent crime | Murder and non-negligent man-slaughter | Forcible rape | Robbery | Aggravated assault | Property crime | Burglary | Larceny-theft | Motor vehicle theft |
|---|---|---|---|---|---|---|---|---|---|---|
| **ALABAMA** | | | | | | | | | | |
| **Metropolitan statistical area** | 3,365,303 | | | | | | | | | |
| Area actually reporting | 98.4% | 16,313 | 244 | 1,104 | 5,586 | 9,379 | 139,955 | 39,097 | 91,697 | 9,161 |
| Estimated total | 100.0% | 16,512 | 247 | 1,116 | 5,642 | 9,507 | 141,768 | 39,611 | 92,882 | 9,275 |
| **Cities outside metropolitan areas** | 607,223 | | | | | | | | | |
| Area actually reporting | 99.1% | 3,319 | 46 | 255 | 534 | 2,484 | 26,142 | 5,709 | 19,277 | 1,156 |
| Estimated total | 100.0% | 3,348 | 46 | 257 | 539 | 2,506 | 26,375 | 5,760 | 19,449 | 1,166 |
| **Nonmetropolitan counties** | 736,182 | | | | | | | | | |
| Area actually reporting | 99.0% | 1,306 | 30 | 130 | 77 | 1,069 | 9,389 | 3,431 | 5,325 | 633 |
| Estimated total | 100.0% | 1,319 | 30 | 131 | 78 | 1,080 | 9,486 | 3,466 | 5,380 | 640 |
| **State total** | 4,708,708 | 21,179 | 323 | 1,504 | 6,259 | 13,093 | 177,629 | 48,837 | 117,711 | 11,081 |
| Rate per 100,000 inhabitants | | 449.8 | 6.9 | 31.9 | 132.9 | 278.1 | 3,772.4 | 1,037.2 | 2,499.9 | 235.3 |
| **ALASKA** | | | | | | | | | | |
| **Metropolitan statistical area** | 343,318 | | | | | | | | | |
| Area actually reporting | 100.0% | 2,892 | 14 | 351 | 590 | 1,937 | 12,805 | 1,932 | 9,854 | 1,019 |
| **Cities outside metropolitan areas** | 122,142 | | | | | | | | | |
| Area actually reporting | 92.8% | 622 | 2 | 88 | 36 | 496 | 4,107 | 612 | 3,208 | 287 |
| Estimated total | 100.0% | 670 | 2 | 95 | 39 | 534 | 4,424 | 659 | 3,456 | 309 |
| **Nonmetropolitan counties** | 233,013 | | | | | | | | | |
| Area actually reporting | 100.0% | 859 | 6 | 66 | 26 | 761 | 3,348 | 1,006 | 1,981 | 361 |
| **State total** | 698,473 | 4,421 | 22 | 512 | 655 | 3,232 | 20,577 | 3,597 | 15,291 | 1,689 |
| Rate per 100,000 inhabitants | | 633.0 | 3.1 | 73.3 | 93.8 | 462.7 | 2,946.0 | 515.0 | 2,189.2 | 241.8 |
| **ARIZONA** | | | | | | | | | | |
| **Metropolitan statistical area** | 6,125,527 | | | | | | | | | |
| Area actually reporting | 99.3% | 23,912 | 311 | 1,574 | 7,910 | 14,117 | 219,512 | 49,028 | 146,173 | 24,311 |
| Estimated total | 100.0% | 24,004 | 312 | 1,581 | 7,933 | 14,178 | 220,736 | 49,303 | 147,028 | 24,405 |
| **Cities outside metropolitan areas** | 204,955 | | | | | | | | | |
| Area actually reporting | 97.3% | 2,136 | 33 | 486 | 120 | 1,497 | 10,287 | 2,682 | 6,446 | 1,159 |
| Estimated total | 100.0% | 2,196 | 34 | 500 | 123 | 1,539 | 10,578 | 2,758 | 6,628 | 1,192 |
| **Nonmetropolitan counties** | 265,296 | | | | | | | | | |
| Area actually reporting | 100.0% | 729 | 8 | 29 | 43 | 649 | 3,268 | 1,351 | 1,528 | 389 |
| **State total** | 6,595,778 | 26,929 | 354 | 2,110 | 8,099 | 16,366 | 234,582 | 53,412 | 155,184 | 25,986 |
| Rate per 100,000 inhabitants | | 408.3 | 5.4 | 32.0 | 122.8 | 248.1 | 3,556.5 | 809.8 | 2,352.8 | 394.0 |
| **ARKANSAS** | | | | | | | | | | |
| **Metropolitan statistical area** | 1,737,722 | | | | | | | | | |
| Area actually reporting | 93.7% | 10,485 | 94 | 889 | 2,099 | 7,403 | 73,301 | 21,827 | 47,122 | 4,352 |
| Estimated total | 100.0% | 10,875 | 98 | 929 | 2,121 | 7,727 | 75,801 | 22,888 | 48,366 | 4,547 |
| **Cities outside metropolitan areas** | 502,577 | | | | | | | | | |
| Area actually reporting | 98.1% | 2,669 | 41 | 245 | 383 | 2,000 | 22,683 | 7,814 | 14,023 | 846 |
| Estimated total | 100.0% | 2,721 | 42 | 250 | 390 | 2,039 | 23,123 | 7,966 | 14,295 | 862 |
| **Nonmetropolitan counties** | 649,151 | | | | | | | | | |
| Area actually reporting | 92.7% | 1,263 | 36 | 175 | 66 | 986 | 9,371 | 3,623 | 5,105 | 643 |
| Estimated total | 100.0% | 1,363 | 39 | 189 | 71 | 1,064 | 10,114 | 3,910 | 5,510 | 694 |
| **State total** | 2,889,450 | 14,959 | 179 | 1,368 | 2,582 | 10,830 | 109,038 | 34,764 | 68,171 | 6,103 |
| Rate per 100,000 inhabitants | | 517.7 | 6.2 | 47.3 | 89.4 | 374.8 | 3,773.7 | 1,203.1 | 2,359.3 | 211.2 |
| **CALIFORNIA** | | | | | | | | | | |
| **Metropolitan statistical area** | 36,127,220 | | | | | | | | | |
| Area actually reporting | 100.0% | 171,240 | 1,941 | 8,412 | 63,726 | 97,161 | 992,141 | 224,746 | 605,031 | 162,364 |
| **Cities outside metropolitan areas** | 267,466 | | | | | | | | | |
| Area actually reporting | 100.0% | 1,320 | 6 | 108 | 213 | 993 | 9,033 | 2,400 | 5,989 | 644 |
| **Nonmetropolitan counties** | 566,978 | | | | | | | | | |
| Area actually reporting | 100.0% | 1,899 | 25 | 193 | 154 | 1,527 | 8,440 | 2,991 | 4,436 | 1,013 |
| **State total** | 36,961,664 | 174,459 | 1,972 | 8,713 | 64,093 | 99,681 | 1,009,614 | 230,137 | 615,456 | 164,021 |
| Rate per 100,000 inhabitants | | 472.0 | 5.3 | 23.6 | 173.4 | 269.7 | 2,731.5 | 622.6 | 1,665.1 | 443.8 |
| **COLORADO** | | | | | | | | | | |
| **Metropolitan statistical area** | 4,337,573 | | | | | | | | | |
| Area actually reporting | 99.7% | 15,261 | 157 | 2,030 | 3,285 | 9,789 | 119,558 | 24,124 | 83,645 | 11,789 |
| Estimated total | 100.0% | 15,291 | 157 | 2,034 | 3,291 | 9,809 | 119,895 | 24,177 | 83,899 | 11,819 |
| **Cities outside metropolitan areas** | 314,714 | | | | | | | | | |
| Area actually reporting | 92.2% | 1,037 | 12 | 140 | 71 | 814 | 9,883 | 1,551 | 7,975 | 357 |
| Estimated total | 100.0% | 1,125 | 13 | 152 | 77 | 883 | 10,722 | 1,683 | 8,652 | 387 |
| **Nonmetropolitan counties** | 372,461 | | | | | | | | | |
| Area actually reporting | 88.7% | 497 | 4 | 50 | 17 | 426 | 2,974 | 700 | 2,050 | 224 |
| Estimated total | 100.0% | 560 | 5 | 56 | 19 | 480 | 3,351 | 789 | 2,310 | 252 |
| **State total** | 5,024,748 | 16,976 | 175 | 2,242 | 3,387 | 11,172 | 133,968 | 26,649 | 94,861 | 12,458 |
| Rate per 100,000 inhabitants | | 337.8 | 3.5 | 44.6 | 67.4 | 222.3 | 2,666.2 | 530.4 | 1,887.9 | 247.9 |

## Table 5. Crime, by State and Area, 2009—*Continued*

(Number, percent, rate per 100,000 population.)

| Area | Population | Violent crime | Murder and non-negligent man-slaughter | Forcible rape | Robbery | Aggravated assault | Property crime | Burglary | Larceny-theft | Motor vehicle theft |
|---|---|---|---|---|---|---|---|---|---|---|
| **CONNECTICUT** | | | | | | | | | | |
| **Metropolitan statistical area** | 2,818,870 | | | | | | | | | |
| Area actually reporting | 100.0% | 9,907 | 98 | 548 | 3,878 | 5,383 | 74,554 | 13,089 | 54,562 | 6,903 |
| **Cities outside metropolitan areas** | 157,654 | | | | | | | | | |
| Area actually reporting | 100.0% | 255 | 1 | 40 | 63 | 151 | 2,853 | 582 | 2,142 | 129 |
| **Nonmetropolitan counties** | 541,764 | | | | | | | | | |
| Area actually reporting | 100.0% | 346 | 8 | 63 | 49 | 226 | 4,774 | 1,402 | 2,928 | 444 |
| **State total** | 3,518,288 | 10,508 | 107 | 651 | 3,990 | 5,760 | 82,181 | 15,073 | 59,632 | 7,476 |
| Rate per 100,000 inhabitants | | 298.7 | 3.0 | 18.5 | 113.4 | 163.7 | 2,335.8 | 428.4 | 1,694.9 | 212.5 |
| **DELAWARE** | | | | | | | | | | |
| **Metropolitan statistical area** | 692,991 | | | | | | | | | |
| Area actually reporting | 100.0% | 4,546 | 37 | 228 | 1,457 | 2,824 | 23,385 | 5,071 | 16,660 | 1,654 |
| **Cities outside metropolitan areas** | 43,137 | | | | | | | | | |
| Area actually reporting | 98.2% | 399 | 1 | 40 | 110 | 248 | 2,392 | 517 | 1,810 | 65 |
| Estimated total | 100.0% | 407 | 1 | 41 | 112 | 253 | 2,437 | 527 | 1,844 | 66 |
| **Nonmetropolitan counties** | 148,994 | | | | | | | | | |
| Area actually reporting | 100.0% | 682 | 3 | 69 | 102 | 508 | 3,826 | 1,334 | 2,305 | 187 |
| **State total** | 885,122 | 5,635 | 41 | 338 | 1,671 | 3,585 | 29,648 | 6,932 | 20,809 | 1,907 |
| Rate per 100,000 inhabitants | | 636.6 | 4.6 | 38.2 | 188.8 | 405.0 | 3,349.6 | 783.2 | 2,351.0 | 215.5 |
| **DISTRICT OF COLUMBIA**[1] | | | | | | | | | | |
| **Metropolitan statistical area** | 599,657 | | | | | | | | | |
| Area actually reporting | 100.0% | 8,071 | 144 | 150 | 4,389 | 3,388 | 28,456 | 3,696 | 19,228 | 5,532 |
| **Cities outside metropolitan areas** | None | | | | | | | | | |
| **Nonmetropolitan counties** | None | | | | | | | | | |
| Total | 599,657 | 8,071 | 144 | 150 | 4,389 | 3,388 | 28,456 | 3,696 | 19,228 | 5,532 |
| Rate per 100,000 inhabitants | | 1,345.9 | 24.0 | 25.0 | 731.9 | 565.0 | 4,745.4 | 616.4 | 3,206.5 | 922.5 |
| **FLORIDA** | | | | | | | | | | |
| **Metropolitan statistical area** | 17,451,538 | | | | | | | | | |
| Area actually reporting | 99.9% | 107,889 | 967 | 5,139 | 30,193 | 71,590 | 681,390 | 171,407 | 461,293 | 48,690 |
| Estimated total | 100.0% | 107,967 | 967 | 5,143 | 30,217 | 71,640 | 681,988 | 171,541 | 461,716 | 48,731 |
| **Cities outside metropolitan areas** | 184,846 | | | | | | | | | |
| Area actually reporting | 99.1% | 1,594 | 13 | 96 | 332 | 1,153 | 9,016 | 2,462 | 6,159 | 395 |
| Estimated total | 100.0% | 1,608 | 13 | 97 | 335 | 1,163 | 9,098 | 2,484 | 6,215 | 399 |
| **Nonmetropolitan counties** | 901,585 | | | | | | | | | |
| Area actually reporting | 99.1% | 3,932 | 37 | 259 | 356 | 3,280 | 20,738 | 7,789 | 11,830 | 1,119 |
| Estimated total | 100.0% | 3,966 | 37 | 261 | 359 | 3,309 | 20,924 | 7,859 | 11,936 | 1,129 |
| **State total** | 18,537,969 | 113,541 | 1,017 | 5,501 | 30,911 | 76,112 | 712,010 | 181,884 | 479,867 | 50,259 |
| Rate per 100,000 inhabitants | | 612.5 | 5.5 | 29.7 | 166.7 | 410.6 | 3,840.8 | 981.1 | 2,588.6 | 271.1 |
| **GEORGIA** | | | | | | | | | | |
| **Metropolitan statistical area** | 8,020,064 | | | | | | | | | |
| Area actually reporting | 99.5% | 34,705 | 488 | 1,882 | 13,314 | 19,021 | 301,213 | 82,261 | 188,558 | 30,394 |
| Estimated total | 100.0% | 34,856 | 489 | 1,891 | 13,365 | 19,111 | 302,613 | 82,601 | 189,500 | 30,512 |
| **Cities outside metropolitan areas** | 680,207 | | | | | | | | | |
| Area actually reporting | 86.3% | 3,778 | 34 | 187 | 881 | 2,676 | 29,474 | 7,062 | 21,465 | 947 |
| Estimated total | 100.0% | 4,372 | 39 | 217 | 1,019 | 3,097 | 34,106 | 8,171 | 24,839 | 1,096 |
| **Nonmetropolitan counties** | 1,128,940 | | | | | | | | | |
| Area actually reporting | 94.5% | 2,505 | 36 | 182 | 207 | 2,080 | 22,373 | 7,171 | 13,750 | 1,452 |
| Estimated total | 100.0% | 2,652 | 38 | 193 | 219 | 2,202 | 23,681 | 7,590 | 14,554 | 1,537 |
| **State total** | 9,829,211 | 41,880 | 566 | 2,301 | 14,603 | 24,410 | 360,400 | 98,362 | 228,893 | 33,145 |
| Rate per 100,000 inhabitants | | 426.1 | 5.8 | 23.4 | 148.6 | 248.3 | 3,666.6 | 1,000.7 | 2,328.7 | 337.2 |
| **HAWAII** | | | | | | | | | | |
| **Metropolitan statistical area** | 907,124 | | | | | | | | | |
| Area actually reporting | 100.0% | 2,537 | 14 | 243 | 869 | 1,411 | 33,375 | 5,999 | 23,647 | 3,729 |
| **Cities outside metropolitan areas** | None | | | | | | | | | |
| **Nonmetropolitan counties** | 388,054 | | | | | | | | | |
| Area actually reporting | 100.0% | 1,022 | 8 | 149 | 165 | 700 | 14,044 | 3,179 | 9,775 | 1,090 |
| **State total** | 1,295,178 | 3,559 | 22 | 392 | 1,034 | 2,111 | 47,419 | 9,178 | 33,422 | 4,819 |
| Rate per 100,000 inhabitants | | 274.8 | 1.7 | 30.3 | 79.8 | 163.0 | 3,661.2 | 708.6 | 2,580.5 | 372.1 |

[1] Includes offenses reported by the Zoological Police and the Metro Transit Police.

## Table 5. Crime, by State and Area, 2009—*Continued*

(Number, percent, rate per 100,000 population.)

| Area | Population | Violent crime | Murder and non-negligent man-slaughter | Forcible rape | Robbery | Aggravated assault | Property crime | Burglary | Larceny-theft | Motor vehicle theft |
|---|---|---|---|---|---|---|---|---|---|---|
| **IDAHO** | | | | | | | | | | |
| **Metropolitan statistical area** | 1,019,745 | | | | | | | | | |
| Area actually reporting | 99.3% | 2,553 | 16 | 390 | 211 | 1,936 | 22,323 | 4,604 | 16,723 | 996 |
| Estimated total | 100.0% | 2,566 | 16 | 392 | 212 | 1,946 | 22,418 | 4,631 | 16,786 | 1,001 |
| **Cities outside metropolitan areas** | 240,694 | | | | | | | | | |
| Area actually reporting | 99.3% | 519 | 2 | 86 | 18 | 413 | 5,221 | 1,044 | 3,952 | 225 |
| Estimated total | 100.0% | 523 | 2 | 87 | 18 | 416 | 5,255 | 1,051 | 3,978 | 226 |
| **Nonmetropolitan counties** | 285,362 | | | | | | | | | |
| Area actually reporting | 100.0% | 441 | 4 | 73 | 15 | 349 | 3,068 | 876 | 1,977 | 215 |
| **State total** | 1,545,801 | 3,530 | 22 | 552 | 245 | 2,711 | 30,741 | 6,558 | 22,741 | 1,442 |
| Rate per 100,000 inhabitants | | 228.4 | 1.4 | 35.7 | 15.8 | 175.4 | 1,988.7 | 424.2 | 1,471.1 | 93.3 |
| **ILLINOIS**[2, 3] | | | | | | | | | | |
| **State total** | 12,910,409 | 64,185 | 773 | 3,901 | 22,923 | 36,588 | 353,347 | 77,850 | 248,821 | 26,676 |
| Rate per 100,000 inhabitants | | 497.2 | 6.0 | 30.2 | 177.6 | 283.4 | 2,736.9 | 603.0 | 1,927.3 | 206.6 |
| **INDIANA** | | | | | | | | | | |
| **Metropolitan statistical area** | 5,034,111 | | | | | | | | | |
| Area actually reporting | 90.0% | 18,722 | 261 | 1,324 | 6,888 | 10,249 | 159,046 | 39,778 | 107,640 | 11,628 |
| Estimated total | 100.0% | 19,389 | 270 | 1,391 | 7,028 | 10,700 | 168,565 | 41,843 | 114,506 | 12,216 |
| **Cities outside metropolitan areas** | 504,766 | | | | | | | | | |
| Area actually reporting | 82.5% | 893 | 7 | 118 | 203 | 565 | 15,794 | 2,907 | 12,125 | 762 |
| Estimated total | 100.0% | 1,083 | 9 | 143 | 246 | 685 | 19,152 | 3,525 | 14,703 | 924 |
| **Nonmetropolitan counties** | 884,236 | | | | | | | | | |
| Area actually reporting | 77.5% | 722 | 24 | 82 | 60 | 556 | 9,643 | 2,745 | 6,325 | 573 |
| Estimated total | 100.0% | 932 | 31 | 106 | 78 | 717 | 12,443 | 3,542 | 8,162 | 739 |
| **State total** | 6,423,113 | 21,404 | 310 | 1,640 | 7,352 | 12,102 | 200,160 | 48,910 | 137,371 | 13,879 |
| Rate per 100,000 inhabitants | | 333.2 | 4.8 | 25.5 | 114.5 | 188.4 | 3,116.2 | 761.5 | 2,138.7 | 216.1 |
| **IOWA** | | | | | | | | | | |
| **Metropolitan statistical area** | 1,704,661 | | | | | | | | | |
| Area actually reporting | 99.3% | 5,798 | 22 | 626 | 1,050 | 4,100 | 48,263 | 10,449 | 35,062 | 2,752 |
| Estimated total | 100.0% | 5,822 | 22 | 629 | 1,053 | 4,118 | 48,510 | 10,495 | 35,255 | 2,760 |
| **Cities outside metropolitan areas** | 584,432 | | | | | | | | | |
| Area actually reporting | 94.4% | 1,826 | 8 | 145 | 126 | 1,547 | 15,275 | 3,635 | 10,938 | 702 |
| Estimated total | 100.0% | 1,933 | 8 | 154 | 133 | 1,638 | 16,174 | 3,849 | 11,582 | 743 |
| **Nonmetropolitan counties** | 718,763 | | | | | | | | | |
| Area actually reporting | 98.6% | 633 | 4 | 69 | 9 | 551 | 4,689 | 1,853 | 2,456 | 380 |
| Estimated total | 100.0% | 642 | 4 | 70 | 9 | 559 | 4,757 | 1,880 | 2,492 | 385 |
| **State total** | 3,007,856 | 8,397 | 34 | 853 | 1,195 | 6,315 | 69,441 | 16,224 | 49,329 | 3,888 |
| Rate per 100,000 inhabitants | | 279.2 | 1.1 | 28.4 | 39.7 | 210.0 | 2,308.7 | 539.4 | 1,640.0 | 129.3 |
| **KANSAS** | | | | | | | | | | |
| **Metropolitan statistical area** | 1,927,388 | | | | | | | | | |
| Area actually reporting | 99.4% | 8,417 | 93 | 772 | 1,590 | 5,962 | 65,554 | 13,682 | 47,007 | 4,865 |
| Estimated total | 100.0% | 8,445 | 93 | 775 | 1,593 | 5,984 | 65,820 | 13,729 | 47,212 | 4,879 |
| **Cities outside metropolitan areas** | 564,427 | | | | | | | | | |
| Area actually reporting | 96.2% | 2,080 | 20 | 249 | 175 | 1,636 | 19,342 | 3,988 | 14,578 | 776 |
| Estimated total | 100.0% | 2,163 | 21 | 259 | 182 | 1,701 | 20,110 | 4,146 | 15,157 | 807 |
| **Nonmetropolitan counties** | 326,932 | | | | | | | | | |
| Area actually reporting | 95.1% | 637 | 5 | 59 | 10 | 563 | 4,271 | 1,516 | 2,500 | 255 |
| Estimated total | 100.0% | 670 | 5 | 62 | 11 | 592 | 4,490 | 1,594 | 2,628 | 268 |
| **State total** | 2,818,747 | 11,278 | 119 | 1,096 | 1,786 | 8,277 | 90,420 | 19,469 | 64,997 | 5,954 |
| Rate per 100,000 inhabitants | | 400.1 | 4.2 | 38.9 | 63.4 | 293.6 | 3,207.8 | 690.7 | 2,305.9 | 211.2 |
| **KENTUCKY** | | | | | | | | | | |
| **Metropolitan statistical area** | 2,487,317 | | | | | | | | | |
| Area actually reporting | 98.6% | 8,372 | 100 | 744 | 3,059 | 4,469 | 74,701 | 18,564 | 52,082 | 4,055 |
| Estimated total | 100.0% | 8,468 | 100 | 756 | 3,093 | 4,519 | 75,844 | 18,816 | 52,919 | 4,109 |
| **Cities outside metropolitan areas** | 526,584 | | | | | | | | | |
| Area actually reporting | 95.7% | 1,026 | 12 | 187 | 320 | 507 | 15,817 | 3,523 | 11,685 | 609 |
| Estimated total | 100.0% | 1,072 | 13 | 195 | 334 | 530 | 16,532 | 3,682 | 12,213 | 637 |
| **Nonmetropolitan counties** | 1,300,212 | | | | | | | | | |
| Area actually reporting | 89.8% | 1,453 | 58 | 501 | 181 | 713 | 14,388 | 6,467 | 6,723 | 1,198 |
| Estimated total | 100.0% | 1,619 | 65 | 558 | 202 | 794 | 16,025 | 7,203 | 7,488 | 1,334 |
| **State total** | 4,314,113 | 11,159 | 178 | 1,509 | 3,629 | 5,843 | 108,401 | 29,701 | 72,620 | 6,080 |
| Rate per 100,000 inhabitants | | 258.7 | 4.1 | 35.0 | 84.1 | 135.4 | 2,512.7 | 688.5 | 1,683.3 | 140.9 |

[2] Limited data for 2008 were available for Illinois.

[3] The data collection methodology for the offense of forcible rape used by the Illinois and the Minnesota state UCR Programs (with the exception of Rockford, IL, and Minneapolis and St. Paul, MN) does not comply with national UCR guidelines. Consequently, their state figures for forcible rape (with the exception of Rockford, IL, and Minneapolis and St. Paul, MN) have been estimated for inclusion in this table. "Table 8. Offenses Known to Law Enforcement, by State and City" provides the reported female forcible rape crime figure.

## Table 5. Crime, by State and Area, 2009—*Continued*

(Number, percent, rate per 100,000 population.)

| Area | Population | Violent crime | Murder and non-negligent man-slaughter | Forcible rape | Robbery | Aggravated assault | Property crime | Burglary | Larceny-theft | Motor vehicle theft |
|---|---|---|---|---|---|---|---|---|---|---|
| **LOUISIANA** | | | | | | | | | | |
| **Metropolitan statistical area** | 3,349,906 | | | | | | | | | |
| Area actually reporting | 98.2% | 20,338 | 460 | 947 | 5,166 | 13,765 | 128,333 | 33,181 | 85,319 | 9,833 |
| Estimated total | 100.0% | 20,754 | 464 | 960 | 5,217 | 14,113 | 131,226 | 33,750 | 87,533 | 9,943 |
| **Cities outside metropolitan areas** | 390,156 | | | | | | | | | |
| Area actually reporting | 74.6% | 2,616 | 20 | 129 | 410 | 2,057 | 16,493 | 5,072 | 10,827 | 594 |
| Estimated total | 100.0% | 3,506 | 27 | 173 | 549 | 2,757 | 22,106 | 6,798 | 14,512 | 796 |
| **Nonmetropolitan counties** | 752,014 | | | | | | | | | |
| Area actually reporting | 100.0% | 3,589 | 39 | 226 | 339 | 2,985 | 17,124 | 5,698 | 10,448 | 978 |
| **State total** | 4,492,076 | 27,849 | 530 | 1,359 | 6,105 | 19,855 | 170,456 | 46,246 | 112,493 | 11,717 |
| Rate per 100,000 inhabitants | | 620.0 | 11.8 | 30.3 | 135.9 | 442.0 | 3,794.6 | 1,029.5 | 2,504.3 | 260.8 |
| **MAINE** | | | | | | | | | | |
| **Metropolitan statistical area** | 771,644 | | | | | | | | | |
| Area actually reporting | 100.0% | 979 | 17 | 196 | 345 | 421 | 20,075 | 3,987 | 15,463 | 625 |
| **Cities outside metropolitan areas** | 275,182 | | | | | | | | | |
| Area actually reporting | 100.0% | 418 | 7 | 117 | 38 | 256 | 7,868 | 1,404 | 6,250 | 214 |
| **Nonmetropolitan counties** | 271,475 | | | | | | | | | |
| Area actually reporting | 100.0% | 182 | 2 | 63 | 16 | 101 | 3,742 | 1,337 | 2,223 | 182 |
| **State total** | 1,318,301 | 1,579 | 26 | 376 | 399 | 778 | 31,685 | 6,728 | 23,936 | 1,021 |
| Rate per 100,000 inhabitants | | 119.8 | 2.0 | 28.5 | 30.3 | 59.0 | 2,403.5 | 510.4 | 1,815.7 | 77.4 |
| **MARYLAND** | | | | | | | | | | |
| **Metropolitan statistical area** | 5,392,905 | | | | | | | | | |
| Area actually reporting | 100.0% | 32,495 | 435 | 1,094 | 11,833 | 19,133 | 174,270 | 35,034 | 119,917 | 19,319 |
| **Cities outside metropolitan areas** | 79,700 | | | | | | | | | |
| Area actually reporting | 100.0% | 472 | 0 | 23 | 108 | 341 | 3,932 | 800 | 3,046 | 86 |
| **Nonmetropolitan counties** | 226,873 | | | | | | | | | |
| Area actually reporting | 100.0% | 656 | 3 | 39 | 66 | 548 | 4,220 | 1,198 | 2,808 | 214 |
| **State total** | 5,699,478 | 33,623 | 438 | 1,156 | 12,007 | 20,022 | 182,422 | 37,032 | 125,771 | 19,619 |
| Rate per 100,000 inhabitants | | 589.9 | 7.7 | 20.3 | 210.7 | 351.3 | 3,200.7 | 649.7 | 2,206.7 | 344.2 |
| **MASSACHUSETTS** | | | | | | | | | | |
| **Metropolitan statistical area** | 6,566,452 | | | | | | | | | |
| Area actually reporting | 98.8% | 29,791 | 170 | 1,675 | 7,377 | 20,569 | 149,468 | 34,078 | 103,791 | 11,599 |
| Estimated total | 100.0% | 30,044 | 171 | 1,693 | 7,425 | 20,755 | 151,047 | 34,460 | 104,883 | 11,704 |
| **Cities outside metropolitan areas** | 26,963 | | | | | | | | | |
| Area actually reporting | 86.0% | 80 | 1 | 7 | 2 | 70 | 746 | 176 | 543 | 27 |
| Estimated total | 100.0% | 92 | 1 | 8 | 2 | 81 | 867 | 205 | 631 | 31 |
| **Nonmetropolitan counties** | 172 | | | | | | | | | |
| Area actually reporting | 100.0% | 0 | 0 | 0 | 0 | 0 | 0 | 0 | 0 | 0 |
| **State total** | 6,593,587 | 30,136 | 172 | 1,701 | 7,427 | 20,836 | 151,914 | 34,665 | 105,514 | 11,735 |
| Rate per 100,000 inhabitants | | 457.1 | 2.6 | 25.8 | 112.6 | 316.0 | 2,304.0 | 525.7 | 1,600.3 | 178.0 |
| **MICHIGAN**[4] | | | | | | | | | | |
| **Metropolitan statistical area** | 8,130,632 | | | | | | | | | |
| Area actually reporting | 99.4% | 45,446 | 593 | 3,347 | 12,109 | 29,397 | 244,407 | 66,436 | 150,033 | 27,938 |
| Estimated total | 100.0% | 45,597 | 593 | 3,364 | 12,144 | 29,496 | 245,798 | 66,721 | 151,027 | 28,050 |
| **Cities outside metropolitan areas** | 633,364 | | | | | | | | | |
| Area actually reporting | 90.5% | 1,434 | 6 | 368 | 115 | 945 | 17,068 | 2,768 | 13,883 | 417 |
| Estimated total | 100.0% | 1,555 | 7 | 400 | 122 | 1,026 | 18,584 | 3,003 | 15,125 | 456 |
| **Nonmetropolitan counties** | 1,205,731 | | | | | | | | | |
| Area actually reporting | 96.3% | 2,307 | 26 | 722 | 62 | 1,497 | 17,855 | 5,867 | 11,143 | 845 |
| Estimated total | 100.0% | 2,395 | 27 | 750 | 64 | 1,554 | 18,536 | 6,091 | 11,568 | 877 |
| **State total** | 9,969,727 | 49,547 | 627 | 4,514 | 12,330 | 32,076 | 282,918 | 75,815 | 177,720 | 29,383 |
| Rate per 100,000 inhabitants | | 497.0 | 6.3 | 45.3 | 123.7 | 321.7 | 2,837.8 | 760.5 | 1,782.6 | 294.7 |

[4] Because of changes in the state's reporting practices, figures are not comparable to previous years' data.

## Table 5. Crime, by State and Area, 2009—*Continued*

(Number, percent, rate per 100,000 population.)

| Area | Population | Violent crime | Murder and non-negligent man-slaughter | Forcible rape | Robbery | Aggravated assault | Property crime | Burglary | Larceny-theft | Motor vehicle theft |
|---|---|---|---|---|---|---|---|---|---|---|
| **MINNESOTA**[3] | | | | | | | | | | |
| **Metropolitan statistical area** | 3,947,216 | | | | | | | | | |
| Area actually reporting | 99.7% | | 63 | | 3,512 | 5,989 | 115,539 | 20,655 | 87,486 | 7,398 |
| Estimated total | 100.0% | | 63 | | 3,516 | 5,996 | 115,837 | 20,698 | 87,728 | 7,411 |
| **Cities outside metropolitan areas** | 498,584 | | | | | | | | | |
| Area actually reporting | 98.4% | | 2 | | 86 | 820 | 13,953 | 2,017 | 11,434 | 502 |
| Estimated total | 100.0% | | 2 | | 87 | 833 | 14,174 | 2,049 | 11,615 | 510 |
| **Nonmetropolitan counties** | 820,414 | | | | | | | | | |
| Area actually reporting | 97.4% | | 9 | | 16 | 517 | 8,834 | 2,669 | 5,583 | 582 |
| Estimated total | 100.0% | | 9 | | 16 | 531 | 9,072 | 2,741 | 5,733 | 598 |
| **State total** | 5,266,214 | 12,842 | 74 | 1,789 | 3,619 | 7,360 | 139,083 | 25,488 | 105,076 | 8,519 |
| Rate per 100,000 inhabitants | | 243.9 | 1.4 | 34.0 | 68.7 | 139.8 | 2,641.0 | 484.0 | 1,995.3 | 161.8 |
| **MISSISSIPPI** | | | | | | | | | | |
| **Metropolitan statistical area** | 1,308,437 | | | | | | | | | |
| Area actually reporting | 90.9% | 3,727 | 78 | 400 | 1,678 | 1,571 | 44,345 | 13,327 | 27,658 | 3,360 |
| Estimated total | 100.0% | 3,935 | 81 | 434 | 1,723 | 1,697 | 46,970 | 14,125 | 29,307 | 3,538 |
| **Cities outside metropolitan areas** | 596,602 | | | | | | | | | |
| Area actually reporting | 84.1% | 2,172 | 37 | 240 | 782 | 1,113 | 22,196 | 7,482 | 13,858 | 856 |
| Estimated total | 100.0% | 2,584 | 44 | 286 | 930 | 1,324 | 26,405 | 8,901 | 16,486 | 1,018 |
| **Nonmetropolitan counties** | 1,046,957 | | | | | | | | | |
| Area actually reporting | 58.1% | 1,037 | 38 | 127 | 181 | 691 | 8,023 | 3,566 | 3,966 | 491 |
| Estimated total | 100.0% | 1,785 | 65 | 219 | 312 | 1,189 | 13,806 | 6,136 | 6,825 | 845 |
| **State total** | 2,951,996 | 8,304 | 190 | 939 | 2,965 | 4,210 | 87,181 | 29,162 | 52,618 | 5,401 |
| Rate per 100,000 inhabitants | | 281.3 | 6.4 | 31.8 | 100.4 | 142.6 | 2,953.3 | 987.9 | 1,782.5 | 183.0 |
| **MISSOURI** | | | | | | | | | | |
| **Metropolitan statistical area** | 4,504,484 | | | | | | | | | |
| Area actually reporting | 99.5% | 25,031 | 335 | 1,321 | 7,109 | 16,266 | 166,799 | 35,249 | 115,775 | 15,775 |
| Estimated total | 100.0% | 25,104 | 336 | 1,326 | 7,126 | 16,316 | 167,573 | 35,384 | 116,360 | 15,829 |
| **Cities outside metropolitan areas** | 643,622 | | | | | | | | | |
| Area actually reporting | 98.1% | 2,543 | 24 | 171 | 275 | 2,073 | 23,790 | 4,280 | 18,730 | 780 |
| Estimated total | 100.0% | 2,592 | 24 | 174 | 280 | 2,114 | 24,258 | 4,364 | 19,099 | 795 |
| **Nonmetropolitan counties** | 839,474 | | | | | | | | | |
| Area actually reporting | 100.0% | 1,748 | 23 | 107 | 46 | 1,572 | 10,867 | 4,039 | 5,973 | 855 |
| **State total** | 5,987,580 | 29,444 | 383 | 1,607 | 7,452 | 20,002 | 202,698 | 43,787 | 141,432 | 17,479 |
| Rate per 100,000 inhabitants | | 491.8 | 6.4 | 26.8 | 124.5 | 334.1 | 3,385.3 | 731.3 | 2,362.1 | 291.9 |
| **MONTANA** | | | | | | | | | | |
| **Metropolitan statistical area** | 344,222 | | | | | | | | | |
| Area actually reporting | 100.0% | 859 | 11 | 88 | 151 | 609 | 11,129 | 1,646 | 8,892 | 591 |
| **Cities outside metropolitan areas** | 214,560 | | | | | | | | | |
| Area actually reporting | 98.9% | 621 | 8 | 92 | 35 | 486 | 6,757 | 736 | 5,623 | 398 |
| Estimated total | 100.0% | 627 | 8 | 93 | 35 | 491 | 6,831 | 744 | 5,685 | 402 |
| **Nonmetropolitan counties** | 416,207 | | | | | | | | | |
| Area actually reporting | 98.2% | 969 | 9 | 111 | 29 | 820 | 5,955 | 978 | 4,522 | 455 |
| Estimated total | 100.0% | 987 | 9 | 113 | 30 | 835 | 6,064 | 996 | 4,605 | 463 |
| **State total** | 974,989 | 2,473 | 28 | 294 | 216 | 1,935 | 24,024 | 3,386 | 19,182 | 1,456 |
| Rate per 100,000 inhabitants | | 253.6 | 2.9 | 30.2 | 22.2 | 198.5 | 2,464.0 | 347.3 | 1,967.4 | 149.3 |
| **NEBRASKA** | | | | | | | | | | |
| **Metropolitan statistical area** | 1,053,696 | | | | | | | | | |
| Area actually reporting | 99.3% | 3,952 | 36 | 394 | 1,131 | 2,391 | 34,111 | 5,926 | 25,403 | 2,782 |
| Estimated total | 100.0% | 3,960 | 36 | 397 | 1,132 | 2,395 | 34,286 | 5,950 | 25,544 | 2,792 |
| **Cities outside metropolitan areas** | 387,558 | | | | | | | | | |
| Area actually reporting | 94.0% | 797 | 4 | 147 | 72 | 574 | 11,372 | 1,744 | 9,155 | 473 |
| Estimated total | 100.0% | 848 | 4 | 156 | 77 | 611 | 12,096 | 1,855 | 9,738 | 503 |
| **Nonmetropolitan counties** | 355,365 | | | | | | | | | |
| Area actually reporting | 80.8% | 203 | 0 | 34 | 8 | 161 | 2,612 | 724 | 1,738 | 150 |
| Estimated total | 100.0% | 251 | 0 | 42 | 10 | 199 | 3,232 | 896 | 2,150 | 186 |
| **State total** | 1,796,619 | 5,059 | 40 | 595 | 1,219 | 3,205 | 49,614 | 8,701 | 37,432 | 3,481 |
| Rate per 100,000 inhabitants | | 281.6 | 2.2 | 33.1 | 67.8 | 178.4 | 2,761.5 | 484.3 | 2,083.5 | 193.8 |
| **NEVADA** | | | | | | | | | | |
| **Metropolitan statistical area** | 2,376,643 | | | | | | | | | |
| Area actually reporting | 100.0% | 17,785 | 151 | 939 | 5,960 | 10,735 | 76,237 | 20,640 | 43,585 | 12,012 |
| **Cities outside metropolitan areas** | 46,868 | | | | | | | | | |
| Area actually reporting | 100.0% | 224 | 1 | 31 | 20 | 172 | 1,490 | 446 | 949 | 95 |
| **Nonmetropolitan counties** | 219,574 | | | | | | | | | |
| Area actually reporting | 100.0% | 550 | 5 | 51 | 41 | 453 | 3,036 | 908 | 1,856 | 272 |
| **State total** | 2,643,085 | 18,559 | 157 | 1,021 | 6,021 | 11,360 | 80,763 | 21,994 | 46,390 | 12,379 |
| Rate per 100,000 inhabitants | | 702.2 | 5.9 | 38.6 | 227.8 | 429.8 | 3,055.6 | 832.1 | 1,755.1 | 468.4 |

[3] The data collection methodology for the offense of forcible rape used by the Illinois and the Minnesota state UCR Programs (with the exception of Rockford, IL, and Minneapolis and St. Paul, MN) does not comply with national UCR guidelines. Consequently, their state figures for forcible rape (with the exception of Rockford, IL, and Minneapolis and St. Paul, MN) have been estimated for inclusion in this table. "Table 8. Offenses Known to Law Enforcement, by State and City" provides the reported female forcible rape crime figure.

**Table 5. Crime, by State and Area, 2009—*Continued***

(Number, percent, rate per 100,000 population.)

| Area | Population | Violent crime | Murder and non-negligent man-slaughter | Forcible rape | Robbery | Aggravated assault | Property crime | Burglary | Larceny-theft | Motor vehicle theft |
|---|---|---|---|---|---|---|---|---|---|---|
| **NEW HAMPSHIRE** | | | | | | | | | | |
| **Metropolitan statistical area** | 826,814 | | | | | | | | | |
| Area actually reporting | 91.6% | 1,337 | 9 | 206 | 315 | 807 | 16,401 | 2,773 | 12,955 | 673 |
| Estimated total | 100.0% | 1,392 | 9 | 216 | 324 | 843 | 17,332 | 2,921 | 13,700 | 711 |
| **Cities outside metropolitan areas** | 446,945 | | | | | | | | | |
| Area actually reporting | 89.8% | 603 | 1 | 152 | 116 | 334 | 9,875 | 1,675 | 7,844 | 356 |
| Estimated total | 100.0% | 671 | 1 | 169 | 129 | 372 | 10,993 | 1,865 | 8,732 | 396 |
| **Nonmetropolitan counties** | 50,816 | | | | | | | | | |
| Area actually reporting | 2.9% | 15 | 0 | 5 | 0 | 10 | 71 | 16 | 48 | 7 |
| Estimated total | 100.0% | 51 | 0 | 15 | 2 | 34 | 299 | 142 | 140 | 17 |
| **State total** | 1,324,575 | 2,114 | 10 | 400 | 455 | 1,249 | 28,624 | 4,928 | 22,572 | 1,124 |
| Rate per 100,000 inhabitants | | 159.6 | 0.8 | 30.2 | 34.4 | 94.3 | 2,161.0 | 372.0 | 1,704.1 | 84.9 |
| **NEW JERSEY** | | | | | | | | | | |
| **Metropolitan statistical area** | 8,707,739 | | | | | | | | | |
| Area actually reporting | 99.9% | 27,112 | 319 | 1,041 | 11,635 | 14,117 | 181,025 | 37,248 | 128,274 | 15,503 |
| Estimated total | 100.0% | 27,121 | 319 | 1,041 | 11,639 | 14,122 | 181,097 | 37,262 | 128,327 | 15,508 |
| **Cities outside metropolitan areas** | None | | | | | | | | | |
| **Nonmetropolitan counties** | None | | | | | | | | | |
| **State total** | 8,707,739 | 27,121 | 319 | 1,041 | 11,639 | 14,122 | 181,097 | 37,262 | 128,327 | 15,508 |
| Rate per 100,000 inhabitants | | 311.5 | 3.7 | 12.0 | 133.7 | 162.2 | 2,079.7 | 427.9 | 1,473.7 | 178.1 |
| **NEW MEXICO** | | | | | | | | | | |
| **Metropolitan statistical area** | 1,337,330 | | | | | | | | | |
| Area actually reporting | 98.0% | 7,880 | 92 | 657 | 1,529 | 5,602 | 51,896 | 14,358 | 32,306 | 5,232 |
| Estimated total | 100.0% | 8,019 | 93 | 667 | 1,542 | 5,717 | 52,811 | 14,581 | 32,931 | 5,299 |
| **Cities outside metropolitan areas** | 382,883 | | | | | | | | | |
| Area actually reporting | 96.5% | 3,355 | 58 | 270 | 256 | 2,771 | 16,882 | 5,056 | 11,108 | 718 |
| Estimated total | 100.0% | 3,477 | 60 | 280 | 265 | 2,872 | 17,496 | 5,240 | 11,512 | 744 |
| **Nonmetropolitan counties** | 289,458 | | | | | | | | | |
| Area actually reporting | 72.5% | 685 | 16 | 80 | 46 | 543 | 3,458 | 1,595 | 1,549 | 314 |
| Estimated total | 100.0% | 944 | 22 | 110 | 63 | 749 | 4,771 | 2,201 | 2,137 | 433 |
| **State total** | 2,009,671 | 12,440 | 175 | 1,057 | 1,870 | 9,338 | 75,078 | 22,022 | 46,580 | 6,476 |
| Rate per 100,000 inhabitants | | 619.0 | 8.7 | 52.6 | 93.1 | 464.7 | 3,735.8 | 1,095.8 | 2,317.8 | 322.2 |
| **NEW YORK** | | | | | | | | | | |
| **Metropolitan statistical area** | 17,999,657 | | | | | | | | | |
| Area actually reporting | 99.8% | 72,234 | 761 | 2,173 | 27,822 | 41,478 | 348,884 | 56,201 | 271,492 | 21,191 |
| Estimated total | 100.0% | 72,315 | 761 | 2,176 | 27,851 | 41,527 | 349,799 | 56,330 | 272,244 | 21,225 |
| **Cities outside metropolitan areas** | 565,896 | | | | | | | | | |
| Area actually reporting | 98.0% | 1,497 | 5 | 167 | 201 | 1,124 | 15,352 | 2,764 | 12,285 | 303 |
| Estimated total | 100.0% | 1,527 | 5 | 170 | 205 | 1,147 | 15,666 | 2,821 | 12,536 | 309 |
| **Nonmetropolitan counties** | 975,900 | | | | | | | | | |
| Area actually reporting | 100.0% | 1,334 | 12 | 240 | 80 | 1,002 | 12,850 | 3,691 | 8,823 | 336 |
| **State total** | 19,541,453 | 75,176 | 778 | 2,586 | 28,136 | 43,676 | 378,315 | 62,842 | 293,603 | 21,870 |
| Rate per 100,000 inhabitants | | 384.7 | 4.0 | 13.2 | 144.0 | 223.5 | 1,936.0 | 321.6 | 1,502.5 | 111.9 |
| **NORTH CAROLINA** | | | | | | | | | | |
| **Metropolitan statistical area** | 6,620,271 | | | | | | | | | |
| Area actually reporting | 99.0% | 27,801 | 329 | 1,678 | 9,529 | 16,265 | 249,646 | 73,918 | 160,567 | 15,161 |
| Estimated total | 100.0% | 28,030 | 330 | 1,693 | 9,592 | 16,415 | 252,558 | 74,593 | 162,684 | 15,281 |
| **Cities outside metropolitan areas** | 845,543 | | | | | | | | | |
| Area actually reporting | 93.6% | 5,062 | 79 | 254 | 1,452 | 3,277 | 44,867 | 12,534 | 30,527 | 1,806 |
| Estimated total | 100.0% | 5,396 | 84 | 270 | 1,547 | 3,495 | 47,849 | 13,368 | 32,556 | 1,925 |
| **Nonmetropolitan counties** | 1,915,070 | | | | | | | | | |
| Area actually reporting | 95.8% | 4,315 | 77 | 329 | 657 | 3,252 | 41,867 | 19,040 | 20,127 | 2,700 |
| Estimated total | 100.0% | 4,503 | 80 | 343 | 686 | 3,394 | 43,691 | 19,869 | 21,004 | 2,818 |
| **State total** | 9,380,884 | 37,929 | 494 | 2,306 | 11,825 | 23,304 | 344,098 | 107,830 | 216,244 | 20,024 |
| Rate per 100,000 inhabitants | | 404.3 | 5.3 | 24.6 | 126.1 | 248.4 | 3,668.1 | 1,149.5 | 2,305.2 | 213.5 |
| **NORTH DAKOTA** | | | | | | | | | | |
| **Metropolitan statistical area** | 317,071 | | | | | | | | | |
| Area actually reporting | 100.0% | 755 | 5 | 135 | 81 | 534 | 8,096 | 1,515 | 6,039 | 542 |
| **Cities outside metropolitan areas** | 138,126 | | | | | | | | | |
| Area actually reporting | 93.9% | 414 | 3 | 61 | 16 | 334 | 2,989 | 509 | 2,309 | 171 |
| Estimated total | 100.0% | 441 | 3 | 65 | 17 | 356 | 3,184 | 542 | 2,460 | 182 |
| **Nonmetropolitan counties** | 191,647 | | | | | | | | | |
| Area actually reporting | 89.3% | 91 | 2 | 22 | 6 | 61 | 1,091 | 265 | 712 | 114 |
| Estimated total | 100.0% | 102 | 2 | 25 | 7 | 68 | 1,222 | 297 | 797 | 128 |
| **State total** | 646,844 | 1,298 | 10 | 225 | 105 | 958 | 12,502 | 2,354 | 9,296 | 852 |
| Rate per 100,000 inhabitants | | 200.7 | 1.5 | 34.8 | 16.2 | 148.1 | 1,932.8 | 363.9 | 1,437.1 | 131.7 |

## Table 5. Crime, by State and Area, 2009—*Continued*

(Number, percent, rate per 100,000 population.)

| Area | Population | Violent crime | Murder and non-negligent man-slaughter | Forcible rape | Robbery | Aggravated assault | Property crime | Burglary | Larceny-theft | Motor vehicle theft |
|---|---|---|---|---|---|---|---|---|---|---|
| **OHIO** | | | | | | | | | | |
| **Metropolitan statistical area** | 9,318,858 | | | | | | | | | |
| Area actually reporting | 93.5% | 34,336 | 475 | 3,348 | 16,710 | 13,803 | 307,483 | 87,427 | 199,609 | 20,447 |
| Estimated total | 100.0% | 35,321 | 486 | 3,497 | 17,100 | 14,238 | 323,805 | 90,795 | 211,907 | 21,103 |
| **Cities outside metropolitan areas** | 922,840 | | | | | | | | | |
| Area actually reporting | 80.6% | 1,511 | 12 | 242 | 447 | 810 | 28,311 | 5,615 | 22,055 | 641 |
| Estimated total | 100.0% | 1,873 | 15 | 300 | 554 | 1,004 | 35,109 | 6,963 | 27,351 | 795 |
| **Nonmetropolitan counties** | 1,300,947 | | | | | | | | | |
| Area actually reporting | 90.6% | 1,031 | 16 | 204 | 116 | 695 | 16,894 | 5,851 | 10,144 | 899 |
| Estimated total | 100.0% | 1,138 | 18 | 225 | 128 | 767 | 18,639 | 6,455 | 11,192 | 992 |
| **State total** | 11,542,645 | 38,332 | 519 | 4,022 | 17,782 | 16,009 | 377,553 | 104,213 | 250,450 | 22,890 |
| Rate per 100,000 inhabitants | | 332.1 | 4.5 | 34.8 | 154.1 | 138.7 | 3,270.9 | 902.9 | 2,169.8 | 198.3 |
| **OKLAHOMA** | | | | | | | | | | |
| **Metropolitan statistical area** | 2,358,425 | | | | | | | | | |
| Area actually reporting | 99.9% | 13,844 | 177 | 1,021 | 2,972 | 9,674 | 96,210 | 27,743 | 60,095 | 8,372 |
| **Cities outside metropolitan areas** | 100.0% | 13,846 | 177 | 1,021 | 2,972 | 9,676 | 96,238 | 27,750 | 60,114 | 8,374 |
| Area actually reporting | 715,224 | | | | | | | | | |
| Estimated total | 99.6% | 3,406 | 32 | 372 | 338 | 2,664 | 27,285 | 7,036 | 18,987 | 1,262 |
| **Nonmetropolitan counties** | 100.0% | 3,420 | 32 | 374 | 339 | 2,675 | 27,398 | 7,065 | 19,066 | 1,267 |
| Area actually reporting | 613,401 | | | | | | | | | |
| Estimated total | 100.0% | 1,208 | 19 | 134 | 32 | 1,023 | 8,133 | 3,160 | 4,210 | 763 |
| **State total** | 3,687,050 | 18,474 | 228 | 1,529 | 3,343 | 13,374 | 131,769 | 37,975 | 83,390 | 10,404 |
| Rate per 100,000 inhabitants | | 501.1 | 6.2 | 41.5 | 90.7 | 362.7 | 3,573.8 | 1,030.0 | 2,261.7 | 282.2 |
| **OREGON** | | | | | | | | | | |
| **Metropolitan statistical area** | 2,984,822 | | | | | | | | | |
| Area actually reporting | 100.0% | 7,792 | 55 | 929 | 2,208 | 4,600 | 92,270 | 14,992 | 68,694 | 8,584 |
| **Cities outside metropolitan areas** | 396,094 | | | | | | | | | |
| Area actually reporting | 96.7% | 783 | 11 | 117 | 191 | 464 | 14,120 | 2,310 | 11,141 | 669 |
| Estimated total | 100.0% | 809 | 11 | 121 | 197 | 480 | 14,599 | 2,388 | 11,519 | 692 |
| **Nonmetropolitan counties** | 444,741 | | | | | | | | | |
| Area actually reporting | 100.0% | 1,143 | 19 | 118 | 56 | 950 | 6,642 | 1,997 | 4,052 | 593 |
| **State total** | 3,825,657 | 9,744 | 85 | 1,168 | 2,461 | 6,030 | 113,511 | 19,377 | 84,265 | 9,869 |
| Rate per 100,000 inhabitants | | 254.7 | 2.2 | 30.5 | 64.3 | 157.6 | 2,967.1 | 506.5 | 2,202.6 | 258.0 |
| **PENNSYLVANIA** | | | | | | | | | | |
| **Metropolitan statistical area** | 10,616,700 | | | | | | | | | |
| Area actually reporting | 99.5% | 43,862 | 612 | 2,975 | 17,025 | 23,250 | 242,769 | 46,520 | 179,685 | 16,564 |
| Estimated total | 100.0% | 43,975 | 613 | 2,981 | 17,056 | 23,325 | 243,797 | 46,683 | 180,506 | 16,608 |
| **Cities outside metropolitan areas** | 927,270 | | | | | | | | | |
| Area actually reporting | 96.3% | 2,316 | 15 | 223 | 312 | 1,766 | 18,972 | 3,452 | 15,033 | 487 |
| Estimated total | 100.0% | 2,407 | 16 | 232 | 324 | 1,835 | 19,709 | 3,586 | 15,617 | 506 |
| **Nonmetropolitan counties** | 1,060,797 | | | | | | | | | |
| Area actually reporting | 100.0% | 1,583 | 32 | 438 | 134 | 979 | 14,006 | 4,528 | 8,771 | 707 |
| **State total** | 12,604,767 | 47,965 | 661 | 3,651 | 17,514 | 26,139 | 277,512 | 54,797 | 204,894 | 17,821 |
| Rate per 100,000 inhabitants | | 380.5 | 5.2 | 29.0 | 138.9 | 207.4 | 2,201.6 | 434.7 | 1,625.5 | 141.4 |
| **PUERTO RICO** | | | | | | | | | | |
| **Metropolitan statistical area** | 3,118,752 | | | | | | | | | |
| Area actually reporting | 100.0% | 8,861 | 784 | 44 | 5,551 | 2,482 | 46,401 | 14,094 | 25,970 | 6,337 |
| **Cities outside metropolitan areas** | 848,536 | | | | | | | | | |
| Area actually reporting | 100.0% | 1,631 | 110 | 21 | 542 | 958 | 9,536 | 4,427 | 4,614 | 495 |
| **Total** | 3,967,288 | 10,492 | 894 | 65 | 6,093 | 3,440 | 55,937 | 18,521 | 30,584 | 6,832 |
| Rate per 100,000 inhabitants | | 264.5 | 22.5 | 1.6 | 153.6 | 86.7 | 1,410.0 | 466.8 | 770.9 | 172.2 |
| **RHODE ISLAND** | | | | | | | | | | |
| **Metropolitan statistical area** | 1,053,209 | | | | | | | | | |
| Area actually reporting | 100.0% | 2,647 | 30 | 282 | 786 | 1,549 | 27,470 | 5,749 | 19,339 | 2,382 |
| **Cities outside metropolitan areas** | None | | | | | | | | | |
| **Nonmetropolitan counties** | None | | | | | | | | | |
| Area actually reporting | 100.0% | 13 | 1 | 5 | 0 | 7 | 27 | 0 | 16 | 11 |
| **State total** | 1,053,209 | 2,660 | 31 | 287 | 786 | 1,556 | 27,497 | 5,749 | 19,355 | 2,393 |
| Rate per 100,000 inhabitants | | 252.6 | 2.9 | 27.3 | 74.6 | 147.7 | 2,610.8 | 545.9 | 1,837.7 | 227.2 |

## Table 5. Crime, by State and Area, 2009—*Continued*

(Number, percent, rate per 100,000 population.)

| Area | Population | Violent crime | Murder and non-negligent man-slaughter | Forcible rape | Robbery | Aggravated assault | Property crime | Burglary | Larceny-theft | Motor vehicle theft |
|---|---|---|---|---|---|---|---|---|---|---|
| **SOUTH CAROLINA** | | | | | | | | | | |
| **Metropolitan statistical area** | 3,488,626 | | | | | | | | | |
| Area actually reporting | 99.9% | 22,767 | 199 | 1,217 | 4,576 | 16,775 | 135,306 | 33,019 | 91,490 | 10,797 |
| Estimated total | 100.0% | 22,782 | 199 | 1,217 | 4,578 | 16,788 | 135,422 | 33,043 | 91,576 | 10,803 |
| **Cities outside metropolitan areas** | 279,964 | | | | | | | | | |
| Area actually reporting | 97.9% | 3,079 | 28 | 141 | 596 | 2,314 | 15,476 | 3,815 | 10,997 | 664 |
| Estimated total | 100.0% | 3,147 | 29 | 144 | 609 | 2,365 | 15,816 | 3,899 | 11,238 | 679 |
| **Nonmetropolitan counties** | 792,652 | | | | | | | | | |
| Area actually reporting | 100.0% | 4,667 | 59 | 251 | 548 | 3,809 | 26,131 | 8,340 | 15,707 | 2,084 |
| **State total** | 4,561,242 | 30,596 | 287 | 1,612 | 5,735 | 22,962 | 177,369 | 45,282 | 118,521 | 13,566 |
| Rate per 100,000 inhabitants | | 670.8 | 6.3 | 35.3 | 125.7 | 503.4 | 3,888.6 | 992.8 | 2,598.4 | 297.4 |
| **SOUTH DAKOTA** | | | | | | | | | | |
| **Metropolitan statistical area** | 377,499 | | | | | | | | | |
| Area actually reporting | 98.4% | 895 | 3 | 282 | 90 | 520 | 8,927 | 1,497 | 6,936 | 494 |
| Estimated total | 100.0% | 899 | 3 | 283 | 90 | 523 | 9,012 | 1,509 | 7,006 | 497 |
| **Cities outside metropolitan areas** | 206,711 | | | | | | | | | |
| Area actually reporting | 89.4% | 403 | 9 | 106 | 14 | 274 | 3,467 | 574 | 2,692 | 201 |
| Estimated total | 100.0% | 451 | 10 | 119 | 16 | 306 | 3,877 | 642 | 3,010 | 225 |
| **Nonmetropolitan counties** | 228,173 | | | | | | | | | |
| Area actually reporting | 78.5% | 124 | 6 | 34 | 4 | 80 | 846 | 257 | 518 | 71 |
| Estimated total | 100.0% | 158 | 8 | 43 | 5 | 102 | 1,079 | 328 | 660 | 91 |
| **State total** | 812,383 | 1,508 | 21 | 445 | 111 | 931 | 13,968 | 2,479 | 10,676 | 813 |
| Rate per 100,000 inhabitants | | 185.6 | 2.6 | 54.8 | 13.7 | 114.6 | 1,719.4 | 305.2 | 1,314.2 | 100.1 |
| **TENNESSEE** | | | | | | | | | | |
| **Metropolitan statistical area** | 4,621,940 | | | | | | | | | |
| Area actually reporting | 100.0% | 34,718 | 364 | 1,599 | 8,924 | 23,831 | 185,290 | 48,653 | 124,504 | 12,133 |
| **Cities outside metropolitan areas** | 610,990 | | | | | | | | | |
| Area actually reporting | 100.0% | 3,957 | 37 | 202 | 550 | 3,168 | 28,719 | 6,550 | 21,003 | 1,166 |
| **Nonmetropolitan counties** | 1,063,324 | | | | | | | | | |
| Area actually reporting | 100.0% | 3,366 | 60 | 192 | 173 | 2,941 | 22,356 | 8,443 | 12,239 | 1,674 |
| **State total** | 6,296,254 | 42,041 | 461 | 1,993 | 9,647 | 29,940 | 236,365 | 63,646 | 157,746 | 14,973 |
| Rate per 100,000 inhabitants | | 667.7 | 7.3 | 31.7 | 153.2 | 475.5 | 3,754.1 | 1,010.9 | 2,505.4 | 237.8 |
| **TEXAS** | | | | | | | | | | |
| **Metropolitan statistical area** | 21,787,209 | | | | | | | | | |
| Area actually reporting | 99.9% | 111,793 | 1,194 | 7,275 | 36,958 | 66,366 | 919,563 | 216,655 | 629,987 | 72,921 |
| Estimated total | 100.0% | 111,809 | 1,194 | 7,276 | 36,962 | 66,377 | 919,761 | 216,697 | 630,130 | 72,934 |
| **Cities outside metropolitan areas** | 1,388,267 | | | | | | | | | |
| Area actually reporting | 99.3% | 6,550 | 54 | 637 | 872 | 4,987 | 51,273 | 13,515 | 35,794 | 1,964 |
| Estimated total | 100.0% | 6,574 | 54 | 640 | 874 | 5,006 | 51,451 | 13,569 | 35,917 | 1,965 |
| **Nonmetropolitan counties** | 1,606,826 | | | | | | | | | |
| Area actually reporting | 100.0% | 3,285 | 80 | 371 | 199 | 2,635 | 23,933 | 9,967 | 12,306 | 1,660 |
| **State total** | 24,782,302 | 121,668 | 1,328 | 8,287 | 38,035 | 74,018 | 995,145 | 240,233 | 678,353 | 76,559 |
| Rate per 100,000 inhabitants | | 490.9 | 5.4 | 33.4 | 153.5 | 298.7 | 4,015.5 | 969.4 | 2,737.2 | 308.9 |
| **UTAH** | | | | | | | | | | |
| **Metropolitan statistical area** | 2,483,636 | | | | | | | | | |
| Area actually reporting | 99.9% | 5,497 | 34 | 791 | 1,272 | 3,400 | 84,557 | 13,749 | 64,190 | 6,618 |
| Estimated total | 100.0% | 5,501 | 34 | 792 | 1,273 | 3,402 | 84,620 | 13,759 | 64,238 | 6,623 |
| **Cities outside metropolitan areas** | 148,931 | | | | | | | | | |
| Area actually reporting | 88.2% | 210 | 1 | 53 | 16 | 140 | 3,752 | 635 | 2,960 | 157 |
| Estimated total | 100.0% | 238 | 1 | 60 | 18 | 159 | 4,254 | 720 | 3,356 | 178 |
| **Nonmetropolitan counties** | 152,005 | | | | | | | | | |
| Area actually reporting | 88.2% | 164 | 2 | 47 | 7 | 108 | 2,056 | 600 | 1,365 | 91 |
| Estimated total | 100.0% | 185 | 2 | 53 | 8 | 122 | 2,331 | 680 | 1,548 | 103 |
| **State total** | 2,784,572 | 5,924 | 37 | 905 | 1,299 | 3,683 | 91,205 | 15,159 | 69,142 | 6,904 |
| Rate per 100,000 inhabitants | | 212.7 | 1.3 | 32.5 | 46.6 | 132.3 | 3,275.4 | 544.4 | 2,483.0 | 247.9 |
| **VERMONT** | | | | | | | | | | |
| **Metropolitan statistical area** | 209,200 | | | | | | | | | |
| Area actually reporting | 100.0% | 332 | 1 | 58 | 39 | 234 | 6,417 | 1,148 | 5,102 | 167 |
| **Cities outside metropolitan areas** | 204,883 | | | | | | | | | |
| Area actually reporting | 100.0% | 310 | 1 | 32 | 54 | 223 | 5,196 | 1,012 | 4,065 | 119 |
| **Nonmetropolitan counties** | 207,677 | | | | | | | | | |
| Area actually reporting | 98.0% | 172 | 5 | 33 | 18 | 116 | 3,253 | 1,267 | 1,827 | 159 |
| Estimated total | 100.0% | 175 | 5 | 34 | 18 | 118 | 3,318 | 1,292 | 1,864 | 162 |
| **State total** | 621,760 | 817 | 7 | 124 | 111 | 575 | 14,931 | 3,452 | 11,031 | 448 |
| Rate per 100,000 inhabitants | | 131.4 | 1.1 | 19.9 | 17.9 | 92.5 | 2,401.4 | 555.2 | 1,774.2 | 72.1 |

## Table 5. Crime, by State and Area, 2009—*Continued*

(Number, percent, rate per 100,000 population.)

| Area | Population | Violent crime | Murder and non-negligent man-slaughter | Forcible rape | Robbery | Aggravated assault | Property crime | Burglary | Larceny-theft | Motor vehicle theft |
|---|---|---|---|---|---|---|---|---|---|---|
| **VIRGINIA** | | | | | | | | | | |
| **Metropolitan statistical area** | 6,766,343 | | | | | | | | | |
| Area actually reporting | 100.0% | 16,118 | 291 | 1,299 | 5,935 | 8,593 | 172,200 | 27,276 | 134,541 | 10,383 |
| **Cities outside metropolitan areas** | 270,931 | | | | | | | | | |
| Area actually reporting | 100.0% | 649 | 11 | 67 | 151 | 420 | 8,367 | 1,245 | 6,831 | 291 |
| **Nonmetropolitan counties** | 845,316 | | | | | | | | | |
| Area actually reporting | 100.0% | 1,112 | 45 | 145 | 171 | 751 | 10,886 | 3,055 | 7,086 | 745 |
| **State total** | 7,882,590 | 17,879 | 347 | 1,511 | 6,257 | 9,764 | 191,453 | 31,576 | 148,458 | 11,419 |
| Rate per 100,000 inhabitants | | 226.8 | 4.4 | 19.2 | 79.4 | 123.9 | 2,428.8 | 400.6 | 1,883.4 | 144.9 |
| **WASHINGTON** | | | | | | | | | | |
| **Metropolitan statistical area** | 5,846,504 | | | | | | | | | |
| Area actually reporting | 100.0% | 20,173 | 149 | 2,156 | 6,402 | 11,466 | 218,919 | 46,062 | 151,070 | 21,787 |
| **Cities outside metropolitan areas** | 332,214 | | | | | | | | | |
| Area actually reporting | 97.3% | 1,134 | 13 | 241 | 214 | 666 | 15,604 | 3,343 | 11,179 | 1,082 |
| Estimated total | 100.0% | 1,166 | 13 | 248 | 220 | 685 | 16,042 | 3,437 | 11,493 | 1,112 |
| **Nonmetropolitan counties** | 485,477 | | | | | | | | | |
| Area actually reporting | 100.0% | 717 | 17 | 135 | 77 | 488 | 9,407 | 3,292 | 5,334 | 781 |
| **State total** | 6,664,195 | 22,056 | 179 | 2,539 | 6,699 | 12,639 | 244,368 | 52,791 | 167,897 | 23,680 |
| Rate per 100,000 inhabitants | | 331.0 | 2.7 | 38.1 | 100.5 | 189.7 | 3,666.9 | 792.2 | 2,519.4 | 355.3 |
| **WEST VIRGINIA** | | | | | | | | | | |
| **Metropolitan statistical area** | 1,012,423 | | | | | | | | | |
| Area actually reporting | 93.0% | 3,057 | 38 | 231 | 628 | 2,160 | 26,871 | 7,044 | 18,181 | 1,646 |
| Estimated total | 100.0% | 3,238 | 41 | 241 | 659 | 2,297 | 28,989 | 7,547 | 19,689 | 1,753 |
| **Cities outside metropolitan areas** | 221,473 | | | | | | | | | |
| Area actually reporting | 77.6% | 662 | 11 | 67 | 118 | 466 | 6,079 | 1,217 | 4,625 | 237 |
| Estimated total | 100.0% | 852 | 14 | 86 | 152 | 600 | 7,833 | 1,568 | 5,960 | 305 |
| **Nonmetropolitan counties** | 585,881 | | | | | | | | | |
| Area actually reporting | 91.7% | 1,197 | 27 | 97 | 97 | 976 | 8,396 | 2,600 | 5,170 | 626 |
| Estimated total | 100.0% | 1,306 | 29 | 106 | 106 | 1,065 | 9,159 | 2,836 | 5,640 | 683 |
| **State total** | 1,819,777 | 5,396 | 84 | 433 | 917 | 3,962 | 45,981 | 11,951 | 31,289 | 2,741 |
| Rate per 100,000 inhabitants | | 296.5 | 4.6 | 23.8 | 50.4 | 217.7 | 2,526.7 | 656.7 | 1,719.4 | 150.6 |
| **WISCONSIN** | | | | | | | | | | |
| **Metropolitan statistical area** | 4,126,916 | | | | | | | | | |
| Area actually reporting | 99.8% | 12,646 | 125 | 870 | 4,744 | 6,907 | 117,114 | 20,657 | 88,594 | 7,863 |
| Estimated total | 100.0% | 12,656 | 125 | 871 | 4,747 | 6,913 | 117,290 | 20,680 | 88,742 | 7,868 |
| **Cities outside metropolitan areas** | 627,299 | | | | | | | | | |
| Area actually reporting | 98.4% | 1,031 | 8 | 119 | 75 | 829 | 19,183 | 2,531 | 16,180 | 472 |
| Estimated total | 100.0% | 1,047 | 8 | 121 | 76 | 842 | 19,487 | 2,571 | 16,437 | 479 |
| **Nonmetropolitan counties** | 900,559 | | | | | | | | | |
| Area actually reporting | 100.0% | 830 | 11 | 116 | 27 | 676 | 10,709 | 3,489 | 6,641 | 579 |
| **State total** | 5,654,774 | 14,533 | 144 | 1,108 | 4,850 | 8,431 | 147,486 | 26,740 | 111,820 | 8,926 |
| Rate per 100,000 inhabitants | | 257.0 | 2.5 | 19.6 | 85.8 | 149.1 | 2,608.2 | 472.9 | 1,977.4 | 157.8 |
| **WYOMING** | | | | | | | | | | |
| **Metropolitan statistical area** | 164,211 | | | | | | | | | |
| Area actually reporting | 100.0% | 343 | 4 | 66 | 46 | 227 | 5,838 | 896 | 4,636 | 306 |
| **Cities outside metropolitan areas** | 224,827 | | | | | | | | | |
| Area actually reporting | 97.9% | 648 | 4 | 76 | 25 | 543 | 6,616 | 939 | 5,352 | 325 |
| Estimated total | 100.0% | 663 | 4 | 78 | 26 | 555 | 6,759 | 959 | 5,468 | 332 |
| **Nonmetropolitan counties** | 155,232 | | | | | | | | | |
| Area actually reporting | 100.0% | 236 | 5 | 40 | 5 | 186 | 1,757 | 375 | 1,249 | 133 |
| **State total** | 544,270 | 1,242 | 13 | 184 | 77 | 968 | 14,354 | 2,230 | 11,353 | 771 |
| Rate per 100,000 inhabitants | | 228.2 | 2.4 | 33.8 | 14.1 | 177.9 | 2,637.3 | 409.7 | 2,085.9 | 141.7 |

## Table 6. Crime, by Metropolitan Statistical Area, 2009

(Number, percent, rate per 100,000 population.)

| Area | Population | Violent crime | Murder and non-negligent man-slaughter | Forcible rape | Robbery | Aggravated assault | Property crime | Burglary | Larceny-theft | Motor vehicle theft |
|---|---|---|---|---|---|---|---|---|---|---|
| **Abilene, TX M.S.A.** | **159,632** | | | | | | | | | |
| Includes Callahan, Jones, and Taylor Counties | | | | | | | | | | |
| City of Abilene | 116,557 | 658 | 7 | 114 | 137 | 400 | 4,830 | 1,301 | 3,267 | 262 |
| Total area actually reporting | 100.0% | 741 | 7 | 134 | 146 | 454 | 5,607 | 1,488 | 3,816 | 303 |
| Rate per 100,000 inhabitants | | 464.2 | 4.4 | 83.9 | 91.5 | 284.4 | 3,512.5 | 932.1 | 2,390.5 | 189.8 |
| **Akron, OH M.S.A.** | **700,932** | | | | | | | | | |
| Includes Portage and Summit Counties | | | | | | | | | | |
| City of Akron | 206,497 | 1,916 | 20 | 189 | 727 | 980 | 10,485 | 3,759 | 5,763 | 963 |
| Total area actually reporting | 92.6% | 2,414 | 27 | 298 | 880 | 1,209 | 21,455 | 5,805 | 14,302 | 1,348 |
| Estimated total | 100.0% | 2,503 | 28 | 311 | 916 | 1,248 | 22,909 | 6,095 | 15,408 | 1,406 |
| Rate per 100,000 inhabitants | | 357.1 | 4.0 | 44.4 | 130.7 | 178.0 | 3,268.4 | 869.6 | 2,198.2 | 200.6 |
| **Albany, GA M.S.A.** | **165,165** | | | | | | | | | |
| Includes Baker, Dougherty, Lee, Terrell, and Worth Counties | | | | | | | | | | |
| City of Albany | 75,734 | 812 | 8 | 47 | 221 | 536 | 4,788 | 1,451 | 3,048 | 289 |
| Total area actually reporting | 97.4% | 941 | 9 | 65 | 245 | 622 | 6,994 | 2,137 | 4,438 | 419 |
| Estimated total | 100.0% | 957 | 9 | 66 | 251 | 631 | 7,140 | 2,176 | 4,532 | 432 |
| Rate per 100,000 inhabitants | | 579.4 | 5.4 | 40.0 | 152.0 | 382.0 | 4,322.9 | 1,317.5 | 2,743.9 | 261.6 |
| **Albany-Schenectady-Troy, NY M.S.A.** | **856,725** | | | | | | | | | |
| Includes Albany, Rensselaer, Saratoga, Schenectady, and Schoharie Counties | | | | | | | | | | |
| City of Albany | 93,445 | 1,007 | 9 | 49 | 327 | 622 | 4,264 | 876 | 3,149 | 239 |
| City of Schenectady | 61,087 | 592 | 7 | 31 | 243 | 311 | 3,336 | 822 | 2,299 | 215 |
| City of Troy | 47,268 | 350 | 3 | 17 | 155 | 175 | 2,340 | 608 | 1,612 | 120 |
| Total area actually reporting | 100.0% | 2,655 | 24 | 162 | 885 | 1,584 | 21,873 | 4,093 | 16,919 | 861 |
| Rate per 100,000 inhabitants | | 309.9 | 2.8 | 18.9 | 103.3 | 184.9 | 2,553.1 | 477.7 | 1,974.8 | 100.5 |
| **Albuquerque, NM M.S.A.** | 862,190 | | | | | | | | | |
| Includes Bernalillo, Sandoval, Torrance, and Valencia Counties | | | | | | | | | | |
| City of Albuquerque | 530,636 | 4,082 | 56 | 326 | 1,103 | 2,597 | 29,140 | 6,376 | 19,365 | 3,399 |
| Total area actually reporting | 97.2% | 5,498 | 67 | 412 | 1,255 | 3,764 | 36,529 | 9,055 | 23,195 | 4,279 |
| Estimated Total | 100.0% | 5,625 | 68 | 421 | 1,267 | 3,869 | 37,368 | 9,260 | 23,768 | 4,340 |
| Rate per 100,000 inhabitants | | 652.4 | 7.9 | 48.8 | 147.0 | 448.7 | 4,334.1 | 1,074.0 | 2,756.7 | 503.4 |
| **Alexandria, LA M.S.A.** | **817,689** | | | | | | | | | |
| Includes Grant and Rapides Parishes | | | | | | | | | | |
| City of Alexandria | 107,326 | 749 | 13 | 72 | 474 | 190 | 5,270 | 1,414 | 3,385 | 471 |
| Total area actually reporting | 72,349 | 219 | 1 | 16 | 96 | 106 | 1,932 | 365 | 1,443 | 124 |
| Estimated total | 100.0% | 1,992 | 24 | 165 | 798 | 1,005 | 19,065 | 3,489 | 14,517 | 1,059 |
| Rate per 100,000 inhabitants | | 243.6 | 2.9 | 20.2 | 97.6 | 122.9 | 2,331.6 | 426.7 | 1,775.4 | 129.5 |
| **Allentown-Bethlehem-Easton, PA-NJ M.S.A.** | **817,689** | | | | | | | | | |
| Includes Warren County, NJ and Carbon, Lehigh, and Northampton Counties, PA | | | | | | | | | | |
| City of Allentown, PA | 107,326 | 749 | 13 | 72 | 474 | 190 | 5,270 | 1,414 | 3,385 | 471 |
| City of Bethlehem, PA | 72,349 | 219 | 1 | 16 | 96 | 106 | 1,932 | 365 | 1,443 | 124 |
| Total area actually reporting | 100.0% | 1,992 | 24 | 165 | 798 | 1,005 | 19,065 | 3,489 | 14,517 | 1,059 |
| Rate per 100,000 inhabitants | | 243.6 | 2.9 | 20.2 | 97.6 | 122.9 | 2,331.6 | 426.7 | 1,775.4 | 129.5 |
| **Altoona, PA M.S.A.** | **125,069** | | | | | | | | | |
| Includes Blair County | | | | | | | | | | |
| City of Altoona | 45,793 | 169 | 1 | 20 | 43 | 105 | 974 | 260 | 657 | 57 |
| Total area actually reporting | 100.0% | 349 | 3 | 39 | 58 | 249 | 2,368 | 444 | 1,812 | 112 |
| Rate per 100,000 inhabitants | | 279.0 | 2.4 | 31.2 | 46.4 | 199.1 | 1,893.4 | 355.0 | 1,448.8 | 89.6 |
| **Amarillo, TX M.S.A.** | **246,040** | | | | | | | | | |
| Includes Armstrong, Carson, Potter, and Randall Counties | | | | | | | | | | |
| City of Amarillo | 188,767 | 1,580 | 10 | 99 | 352 | 1,119 | 11,039 | 2,561 | 7,768 | 710 |
| Total area actually reporting | 100.0% | 1,661 | 13 | 108 | 358 | 1,182 | 11,864 | 2,801 | 8,307 | 756 |
| Rate per 100,000 inhabitants | | 675.1 | 5.3 | 43.9 | 145.5 | 480.4 | 4,822.0 | 1,138.4 | 3,376.3 | 307.3 |
| **Ames, IA M.S.A.** | **87,399** | | | | | | | | | |
| Includes Story County | | | | | | | | | | |
| City of Ames | 57,173 | 177 | 0 | 23 | 15 | 139 | 1,613 | 279 | 1,285 | 49 |
| Total area actually reporting | 100.0% | 228 | 0 | 32 | 20 | 176 | 2,280 | 430 | 1,786 | 64 |
| Rate per 100,000 inhabitants | | 260.9 | 0.0 | 36.6 | 22.9 | 201.4 | 2,608.7 | 492.0 | 2,043.5 | 73.2 |

## Table 6. Crime, by Metropolitan Statistical Area, 2009—*Continued*

(Number, percent, rate per 100,000 population.)

| Area | Population | Violent crime | Murder and non-negligent man-slaughter | Forcible rape | Robbery | Aggravated assault | Property crime | Burglary | Larceny-theft | Motor vehicle theft |
|---|---|---|---|---|---|---|---|---|---|---|
| **Anchorage, AK M.S.A.** | **305,284** | | | | | | | | | |
| Includes Anchorage Municipality and Matanuska-Susitna Borough | | | | | | | | | | |
| City of Anchorage | 283,300 | 2,488 | 14 | 282 | 534 | 1,658 | 10,316 | 1,613 | 7,835 | 868 |
| Total area actually reporting | 100.0% | 2,606 | 14 | 289 | 543 | 1,760 | 11,210 | 1,724 | 8,570 | 916 |
| Rate per 100,000 inhabitants | | 853.6 | 4.6 | 94.7 | 177.9 | 576.5 | 3,672.0 | 564.7 | 2,807.2 | 300.0 |
| **Anderson, IN M.S.A.** | **131,524** | | | | | | | | | |
| Includes Madison County | | | | | | | | | | |
| City of Anderson | 57,020 | 170 | 1 | 34 | 64 | 71 | 3,085 | 722 | 2,148 | 215 |
| Total area actually reporting | 100.0% | 204 | 1 | 38 | 78 | 87 | 4,649 | 1,147 | 3,220 | 282 |
| Rate per 100,000 inhabitants | | 155.1 | 0.8 | 28.9 | 59.3 | 66.1 | 3,534.7 | 872.1 | 2,448.2 | 214.4 |
| **Anderson, SC M.S.A.** | **185,794** | | | | | | | | | |
| Includes Anderson County | | | | | | | | | | |
| City of Anderson | 27,144 | 205 | 1 | 8 | 57 | 139 | 1,879 | 408 | 1,361 | 110 |
| Total area actually reporting | 99.5% | 1,209 | 9 | 68 | 184 | 948 | 7,816 | 2,112 | 5,054 | 650 |
| Estimated total | 100.0% | 1,214 | 9 | 68 | 185 | 952 | 7,856 | 2,120 | 5,084 | 652 |
| Rate per 100,000 inhabitants | | 653.4 | 4.8 | 36.6 | 99.6 | 512.4 | 4,228.3 | 1,141.0 | 2,736.4 | 350.9 |
| **Ann Arbor, MI M.S.A.**[1] | **348,606** | | | | | | | | | |
| Includes Washtenaw County[1] | | | | | | | | | | |
| City of Ann Arbor[1] | 114,367 | 270 | 1 | 29 | 63 | 177 | 2,950 | 609 | 2,216 | 125 |
| Total area actually reporting | 100.0% | 1,122 | 6 | 158 | 223 | 735 | 9,348 | 2,400 | 6,400 | 548 |
| Rate per 100,000 inhabitants | | 321.9 | 1.7 | 45.3 | 64.0 | 210.8 | 2,681.5 | 688.5 | 1,835.9 | 157.2 |
| **Anniston-Oxford, AL M.S.A.** | **114,155** | | | | | | | | | |
| Includes Calhoun County | | | | | | | | | | |
| City of Anniston | 23,598 | 584 | 5 | 27 | 113 | 439 | 4,603 | 2,379 | 966 | 1,258 |
| City of Oxford | 18,038 | 117 | 0 | 8 | 32 | 77 | 1,237 | 215 | 964 | 58 |
| Total area actually reporting | 100.0% | 829 | 6 | 63 | 172 | 588 | 5,466 | 1,832 | 3,365 | 269 |
| Rate per 100,000 inhabitants | | 726.2 | 5.3 | 55.2 | 150.7 | 515.1 | 4,788.2 | 1,604.8 | 2,947.7 | 235.6 |
| **Appleton, WI M.S.A.** | **221,608** | | | | | | | | | |
| Includes Calumet and Outagamie Counties | | | | | | | | | | |
| City of Appleton | 70,294 | 165 | 1 | 21 | 18 | 125 | 1,884 | 327 | 1,521 | 36 |
| Total area actually reporting | 98.7% | 253 | 3 | 38 | 28 | 184 | 4,377 | 619 | 3,621 | 137 |
| Estimated total | 100.0% | 256 | 3 | 38 | 29 | 186 | 4,447 | 628 | 3,680 | 139 |
| Rate per 100,000 inhabitants | | 115.5 | 1.4 | 17.1 | 13.1 | 83.9 | 2,006.7 | 283.4 | 1,660.6 | 62.7 |
| **Asheville, NC M.S.A.** | **413,556** | | | | | | | | | |
| Includes Buncombe, Haywood, Henderson, and Madison Counties | | | | | | | | | | |
| City of Asheville | 74,923 | 415 | 2 | 24 | 178 | 211 | 3,701 | 821 | 2,576 | 304 |
| Total area actually reporting | 99.5% | 940 | 11 | 91 | 260 | 578 | 10,068 | 3,059 | 6,276 | 733 |
| Estimated total | 100.0% | 948 | 11 | 92 | 262 | 583 | 10,164 | 3,081 | 6,346 | 737 |
| Rate per 100,000 inhabitants | | 229.2 | 2.7 | 22.2 | 63.4 | 141.0 | 2,457.7 | 745.0 | 1,534.5 | 178.2 |
| **Athens-Clarke County, GA M.S.A.** | **191,096** | | | | | | | | | |
| Includes Clarke, Madison, Oconee, and Oglethorpe Counties | | | | | | | | | | |
| City of Athens-Clarke County | 114,540 | 472 | 10 | 42 | 155 | 265 | 5,644 | 1,917 | 3,453 | 274 |
| Total area actually reporting | 98.7% | 720 | 11 | 53 | 170 | 486 | 7,562 | 2,346 | 4,852 | 364 |
| Estimated total | 100.0% | 732 | 11 | 54 | 174 | 493 | 7,671 | 2,369 | 4,930 | 372 |
| Rate per 100,000 inhabitants | | 383.1 | 5.8 | 28.3 | 91.1 | 258.0 | 4,014.2 | 1,239.7 | 2,579.9 | 194.7 |
| **Atlanta-Sandy Springs-Marietta, GA M.S.A.** | **5,494,398** | | | | | | | | | |
| Includes Barrow, Bartow, Butts, Carroll, Cherokee, Clayton, Cobb, Coweta, Dawson, DeKalb, Douglas, Fayette, Forsyth, Fulton, Gwinnett, Haralson, Heard, Henry, Jasper, Lamar, Meriwether, Newton, Paulding, Pickens, Pike, Rockdale, Spalding, and Walton Counties | | | | | | | | | | |
| City of Atlanta | 552,901 | 6,359 | 80 | 135 | 2,725 | 3,419 | 34,349 | 9,112 | 19,511 | 5,726 |
| City of Sandy Springs | 82,435 | 189 | 4 | 19 | 124 | 42 | 2,975 | 848 | 1,865 | 262 |
| City of Marietta | 68,037 | 433 | 2 | 17 | 194 | 220 | 2,530 | 610 | 1,725 | 195 |
| Total area actually reporting | 99.9% | 24,131 | 325 | 1,168 | 9,669 | 12,969 | 194,248 | 54,131 | 118,083 | 22,034 |
| Estimated total | 100.0% | 24,161 | 325 | 1,170 | 9,678 | 12,988 | 194,529 | 54,190 | 118,285 | 22,054 |
| Rate per 100,000 inhabitants | | 439.7 | 5.9 | 21.3 | 176.1 | 236.4 | 3,540.5 | 986.3 | 2,152.8 | 401.4 |

[1] The FBI determined that the agency's data were overreported. Consequently, affected data are not included in this table.

## Table 6. Crime, by Metropolitan Statistical Area, 2009—*Continued*

(Number, percent, rate per 100,000 population.)

| Area | Population | Violent crime | Murder and non-negligent man-slaughter | Forcible rape | Robbery | Aggravated assault | Property crime | Burglary | Larceny-theft | Motor vehicle theft |
|---|---|---|---|---|---|---|---|---|---|---|
| **Atlantic City-Hammonton, NJ M.S.A.** | **272,593** | | | | | | | | | |
| Includes Atlantic County | | | | | | | | | | |
| City of Atlantic City | 39,295 | 825 | 10 | 32 | 404 | 379 | 2,500 | 379 | 1,987 | 134 |
| City of Hammonton | 13,517 | 27 | 0 | 0 | 5 | 22 | 168 | 54 | 104 | 10 |
| Total area actually reporting | 100.0% | 1,465 | 24 | 60 | 625 | 756 | 9,298 | 1,776 | 7,148 | 374 |
| Rate per 100,000 inhabitants | | 537.4 | 8.8 | 22.0 | 229.3 | 277.3 | 3,410.9 | 651.5 | 2,622.2 | 137.2 |
| **Auburn-Opelika, AL M.S.A.**[2] | **135,710** | | | | | | | | | |
| Includes Lee County | | | | | | | | | | |
| City of Auburn[2] | 57,342 | 139 | 3 | 8 | 43 | 85 | | | 1,779 | 38 |
| City of Opelika[2] | 27,087 | | 3 | 22 | 83 | | | 389 | 1,213 | |
| Total area actually reporting | 100.0% | | 9 | 55 | 148 | | | | 3,929 | |
| Rate per 100,000 inhabitants | | | 6.6 | 40.5 | 109.1 | | | | 2,895.1 | |
| **Augusta-Richmond County, GA-SC M.S.A.** | **537,765** | | | | | | | | | |
| Includes Burke, Columbia, McDuffie, and Richmond Counties, GA and Aiken and Edgefield Counties, SC | | | | | | | | | | |
| Total area actually reporting | 99.8% | 2,227 | 42 | 212 | 1,010 | 963 | 24,936 | 6,679 | 15,855 | 2,402 |
| Estimated total | 100.0% | 2,232 | 42 | 212 | 1,012 | 966 | 24,987 | 6,690 | 15,891 | 2,406 |
| Rate per 100,000 inhabitants | | 415.1 | 7.8 | 39.4 | 188.2 | 179.6 | 4,646.5 | 1,244.0 | 2,955.0 | 447.4 |
| **Austin-Round Rock-San Marcos, TX M.S.A.** | **1,705,541** | | | | | | | | | |
| Includes Bastrop, Caldwell, Hays, Travis, and Williamson Counties | | | | | | | | | | |
| City of Austin | 768,970 | 4,024 | 22 | 265 | 1,415 | 2,322 | 48,026 | 8,753 | 37,054 | 2,219 |
| City of Round Rock | 110,531 | 128 | 1 | 23 | 32 | 72 | 2,772 | 412 | 2,255 | 105 |
| City of San Marcos | 55,187 | 182 | 1 | 3 | 46 | 132 | 1,702 | 300 | 1,317 | 85 |
| Total area actually reporting | 100.0% | 6,074 | 41 | 455 | 1,670 | 3,908 | 68,644 | 13,403 | 52,199 | 3,042 |
| Rate per 100,000 inhabitants | | 356.1 | 2.4 | 26.7 | 97.9 | 229.1 | 4,024.8 | 785.9 | 3,060.6 | 178.4 |
| **Bakersfield-Delano, CA M.S.A.** | **814,516** | | | | | | | | | |
| Includes Kern County | | | | | | | | | | |
| City of Bakersfield | 330,897 | 2,099 | 27 | 49 | 704 | 1,319 | 15,605 | 3,888 | 9,341 | 2,376 |
| City of Delano | 54,801 | 238 | 2 | 3 | 46 | 187 | 1,895 | 886 | 527 | 482 |
| Total area actually reporting | 100.0% | 4,892 | 75 | 205 | 1,331 | 3,281 | 31,445 | 9,413 | 17,034 | 4,998 |
| Rate per 100,000 inhabitants | | 600.6 | 9.2 | 25.2 | 163.4 | 402.8 | 3,860.6 | 1,155.7 | 2,091.3 | 613.6 |
| **Baltimore-Towson, MD M.S.A.** | **2,693,099** | | | | | | | | | |
| Includes Anne Arundel, Baltimore, Carroll, Harford, Howard, and Queen Anne's Counties and Baltimore City | | | | | | | | | | |
| City of Baltimore | 638,755 | 9,664 | 238 | 158 | 3,707 | 5,561 | 29,163 | 7,798 | 16,741 | 4,624 |
| Total area actually reporting | 100.0% | 19,456 | 298 | 552 | 6,492 | 12,114 | 88,764 | 18,191 | 61,555 | 9,018 |
| Rate per 100,000 inhabitants | | 722.4 | 11.1 | 20.5 | 241.1 | 449.8 | 3,296.0 | 675.5 | 2,285.7 | 334.9 |
| **Bangor, ME M.S.A.** | **148,774** | | | | | | | | | |
| Includes Penobscot County | | | | | | | | | | |
| City of Bangor | 31,789 | 65 | 1 | 10 | 35 | 19 | 2,210 | 284 | 1,884 | 42 |
| Total area actually reporting | 100.0% | 124 | 4 | 21 | 56 | 43 | 5,027 | 946 | 3,954 | 127 |
| Rate per 100,000 inhabitants | | 83.3 | 2.7 | 14.1 | 37.6 | 28.9 | 3,379.0 | 635.9 | 2,657.7 | 85.4 |
| **Barnstable Town, MA M.S.A.** | **224,302** | | | | | | | | | |
| Includes Barnstable County | | | | | | | | | | |
| City of Barnstable | 48,042 | 369 | 2 | 23 | 52 | 292 | 1,324 | 480 | 791 | 53 |
| Total area actually reporting | 100.0% | 1,044 | 4 | 76 | 139 | 825 | 7,006 | 2,704 | 4,088 | 214 |
| Rate per 100,000 inhabitants | | 465.4 | 1.8 | 33.9 | 62.0 | 367.8 | 3,123.5 | 1,205.5 | 1,822.5 | 95.4 |
| **Baton Rouge, LA M.S.A.** | **787,715** | | | | | | | | | |
| Includes Ascension, East Baton Rouge, East Feliciana, Iberville, Livingston, Pointe Coupee, St. Helena, West Baton Rouge, and West Feliciana Parishes | | | | | | | | | | |
| City of Baton Rouge | 223,187 | 2,823 | 75 | 55 | 1,135 | 1,558 | 13,656 | 4,268 | 8,459 | 929 |
| Total area actually reporting | 98.3% | 5,398 | 109 | 157 | 1,577 | 3,555 | 33,045 | 8,791 | 22,294 | 1,960 |
| Estimated total | 100.0% | 5,493 | 110 | 160 | 1,589 | 3,634 | 33,701 | 8,920 | 22,796 | 1,985 |
| Rate per 100,000 inhabitants | | 697.3 | 14.0 | 20.3 | 201.7 | 461.3 | 4,278.3 | 1,132.4 | 2,893.9 | 252.0 |
| **Battle Creek, MI M.S.A.**[1] | **135,076** | | | | | | | | | |
| Includes Calhoun County[1] | | | | | | | | | | |
| City of Battle Creek[1] | 61,139 | 636 | 8 | 53 | 137 | 438 | 3,263 | 1,166 | 1,964 | 133 |
| Total area actually reporting | 100.0% | 927 | 14 | 87 | 169 | 657 | 5,343 | 1,666 | 3,478 | 199 |
| Rate per 100,000 inhabitants | | 686.3 | 10.4 | 64.4 | 125.1 | 486.4 | 3,955.6 | 1,233.4 | 2,574.8 | 147.3 |

[1] The FBI determined that the agency's data were overreported. Consequently, affected data are not included in this table.

[2] Because of changes in the state/local agency's reporting practices, figures are not comparable to previous years' data.

## Table 6. Crime, by Metropolitan Statistical Area, 2009—*Continued*

(Number, percent, rate per 100,000 population.)

| Area | Population | Violent crime | Murder and non-negligent man-slaughter | Forcible rape | Robbery | Aggravated assault | Property crime | Burglary | Larceny-theft | Motor vehicle theft |
|---|---|---|---|---|---|---|---|---|---|---|
| **Bay City, MI M.S.A.[1]** | **106,777** | | | | | | | | | |
| Includes Bay County[1] | | | | | | | | | | |
| City of Bay City[1] | 33,572 | 218 | 2 | 33 | 43 | 140 | 1,067 | 294 | 733 | 40 |
| Total area actually reporting | 100.0% | 337 | 3 | 73 | 58 | 203 | 2,595 | 601 | 1,887 | 107 |
| Rate per 100,000 inhabitants | | 315.6 | 2.8 | 68.4 | 54.3 | 190.1 | 2,430.3 | 562.9 | 1,767.2 | 100.2 |
| **Beaumont-Port Arthur, TX M.S.A.** | **377,984** | | | | | | | | | |
| Includes Hardin, Jefferson, and Orange Counties | | | | | | | | | | |
| City of Beaumont | 110,237 | 1,002 | 5 | 73 | 332 | 592 | 6,331 | 1,665 | 4,385 | 281 |
| City of Port Arthur | 55,725 | 433 | 7 | 31 | 165 | 230 | 2,644 | 980 | 1,471 | 193 |
| Total area actually reporting | 100.0% | 2,021 | 19 | 165 | 639 | 1,198 | 14,918 | 4,363 | 9,658 | 897 |
| Rate per 100,000 inhabitants | | 534.7 | 5.0 | 43.7 | 169.1 | 316.9 | 3,946.7 | 1,154.3 | 2,555.1 | 237.3 |
| **Bellingham, WA M.S.A.** | **201,195** | | | | | | | | | |
| Includes Whatcom County | | | | | | | | | | |
| City of Bellingham | 80,243 | 171 | 2 | 37 | 48 | 84 | 4,341 | 651 | 3,547 | 143 |
| Total area actually reporting | 100.0% | 443 | 8 | 76 | 90 | 269 | 6,989 | 1,400 | 5,323 | 266 |
| Rate per 100,000 inhabitants | | 220.2 | 4.0 | 37.8 | 44.7 | 133.7 | 3,473.7 | 695.8 | 2,645.7 | 132.2 |
| **Bend, OR M.S.A.** | **163,637** | | | | | | | | | |
| Includes Deschutes County | | | | | | | | | | |
| City of Bend | 80,550 | 150 | 0 | 14 | 19 | 117 | 2,036 | 316 | 1,642 | 78 |
| Total area actually reporting | 100.0% | 346 | 2 | 38 | 32 | 274 | 4,089 | 770 | 3,149 | 170 |
| Rate per 100,000 inhabitants | | 211.4 | 1.2 | 23.2 | 19.6 | 167.4 | 2,498.8 | 470.6 | 1,924.4 | 103.9 |
| **Billings, MT M.S.A.** | **153,443** | | | | | | | | | |
| Includes Carbon and Yellowstone Counties | | | | | | | | | | |
| City of Billings | 105,427 | 259 | 2 | 28 | 71 | 158 | 4,597 | 752 | 3,592 | 253 |
| Total area actually reporting | 100.0% | 355 | 3 | 34 | 76 | 242 | 5,662 | 956 | 4,387 | 319 |
| Rate per 100,000 inhabitants | | 231.4 | 2.0 | 22.2 | 49.5 | 157.7 | 3,690.0 | 623.0 | 2,859.0 | 207.9 |
| **Binghamton, NY M.S.A.** | **244,367** | | | | | | | | | |
| Includes Broome and Tioga Counties | | | | | | | | | | |
| City of Binghamton | 44,455 | 215 | 14 | 11 | 56 | 134 | 2,074 | 286 | 1,744 | 44 |
| Total area actually reporting | 100.0% | 481 | 17 | 46 | 93 | 325 | 6,166 | 944 | 5,100 | 122 |
| Rate per 100,000 inhabitants | | 196.8 | 7.0 | 18.8 | 38.1 | 133.0 | 2,523.3 | 386.3 | 2,087.0 | 49.9 |
| **Birmingham-Hoover, AL M.S.A.** | **1,130,745** | | | | | | | | | |
| Includes Bibb, Blount, Chilton, Jefferson, St. Clair, Shelby, and Walker Counties | | | | | | | | | | |
| City of Birmingham | 227,373 | 2,812 | 65 | 198 | 1,150 | 1,399 | 18,159 | 5,019 | 11,546 | 1,594 |
| City of Hoover | 71,919 | 88 | 2 | 9 | 44 | 33 | 2,288 | 439 | 1,762 | 87 |
| Total area actually reporting | 97.7% | 5,922 | 103 | 427 | 2,144 | 3,248 | 50,124 | 13,657 | 33,003 | 3,464 |
| Estimated total | 100.0% | 6,045 | 105 | 433 | 2,186 | 3,321 | 51,286 | 13,947 | 33,805 | 3,534 |
| Rate per 100,000 inhabitants | | 534.6 | 9.3 | 38.3 | 193.3 | 293.7 | 4,535.6 | 1,233.4 | 2,989.6 | 312.5 |
| **Bismarck, ND M.S.A.** | **106,952** | | | | | | | | | |
| Includes Burleigh and Morton Counties | | | | | | | | | | |
| City of Bismarck | 60,923 | 157 | 2 | 17 | 12 | 126 | 1,583 | 204 | 1,277 | 102 |
| Total area actually reporting | 100.0% | 221 | 3 | 36 | 13 | 169 | 2,239 | 308 | 1,771 | 160 |
| Rate per 100,000 inhabitants | | 206.6 | 2.8 | 33.7 | 12.2 | 158.0 | 2,093.5 | 288.0 | 1,655.9 | 149.6 |
| **Blacksburg-Christiansburg-Radford, VA M.S.A.** | **159,705** | | | | | | | | | |
| Includes Giles, Montgomery, and Pulaski Counties and Radford City | | | | | | | | | | |
| City of Blacksburg | 42,047 | 50 | 0 | 15 | 11 | 24 | 700 | 165 | 507 | 28 |
| City of Christiansburg | 19,755 | 35 | 2 | 9 | 7 | 17 | 722 | 107 | 600 | 15 |
| City of Radford | 16,216 | 80 | 1 | 15 | 8 | 56 | 514 | 167 | 335 | 12 |
| Total area actually reporting | 100.0% | 319 | 8 | 65 | 53 | 193 | 4,142 | 901 | 3,114 | 127 |
| Rate per 100,000 inhabitants | | 199.7 | 5.0 | 40.7 | 33.2 | 120.8 | 2,593.5 | 564.2 | 1,949.8 | 79.5 |
| **Bloomington, IN M.S.A.** | **185,191** | | | | | | | | | |
| Includes Greene, Monroe, and Owen Counties | | | | | | | | | | |
| City of Bloomington | 71,845 | 366 | 3 | 44 | 74 | 245 | 3,215 | 883 | 2,185 | 147 |
| Total area actually reporting | 83.5% | 472 | 3 | 54 | 85 | 330 | 4,804 | 1,386 | 3,163 | 255 |
| Estimated total | 100.0% | 512 | 3 | 58 | 93 | 358 | 5,383 | 1,511 | 3,582 | 290 |
| Rate per 100,000 inhabitants | | 276.5 | 1.6 | 31.3 | 50.2 | 193.3 | 2,906.7 | 815.9 | 1,934.2 | 156.6 |

[1] The FBI determined that the agency's data were overreported. Consequently, affected data are not included in this table.

## Table 6. Crime, by Metropolitan Statistical Area, 2009—*Continued*

(Number, percent, rate per 100,000 population.)

| Area | Population | Violent crime | Murder and non-negligent man-slaughter | Forcible rape | Robbery | Aggravated assault | Property crime | Burglary | Larceny-theft | Motor vehicle theft |
|---|---|---|---|---|---|---|---|---|---|---|
| **Boise City-Nampa, ID M.S.A.** | **614,020** | | | | | | | | | |
| Includes Ada, Boise, Canyon, Gem, and Owyhee Counties | | | | | | | | | | |
| City of Boise | 206,437 | 538 | 7 | 70 | 62 | 399 | 5,757 | 1,046 | 4,537 | 174 |
| City of Nampa | 83,875 | 274 | 0 | 39 | 21 | 214 | 1,996 | 470 | 1,423 | 103 |
| Total area actually reporting | 98.8% | 1,427 | 10 | 213 | 126 | 1,078 | 12,113 | 2,618 | 9,005 | 490 |
| Estimated total | 100.0% | 1,440 | 10 | 215 | 127 | 1,088 | 12,208 | 2,645 | 9,068 | 495 |
| Rate per 100,000 inhabitants | | 234.5 | 1.6 | 35.0 | 20.7 | 177.2 | 1,988.2 | 430.8 | 1,476.8 | 80.6 |
| **Boston-Cambridge-Quincy, MA-NH M.S.A.** | **4,586,485** | | | | | | | | | |
| Includes the Metropolitan Divisions of Boston-Quincy, MA; Cambridge-Newton-Framingham, MA; and Peabody, MA and Rockingham County-Strafford County, NH | | | | | | | | | | |
| City of Boston, MA | 624,222 | 6,192 | 50 | 269 | 2,277 | 3,596 | 20,749 | 2,955 | 15,507 | 2,287 |
| City of Cambridge, MA | 102,866 | 497 | 2 | 21 | 179 | 295 | 3,149 | 434 | 2,524 | 191 |
| City of Quincy, MA | 96,580 | 384 | 5 | 20 | 96 | 263 | 1,759 | 478 | 1,145 | 136 |
| City of Newton, MA | 84,427 | 94 | 1 | 9 | 18 | 66 | 971 | 187 | 753 | 31 |
| City of Framingham, MA | 65,478 | 204 | 2 | 8 | 33 | 161 | 1,443 | 253 | 1,058 | 132 |
| City of Waltham, MA | 61,357 | 115 | 0 | 8 | 24 | 83 | 878 | 166 | 653 | 59 |
| City of Peabody, MA | 52,483 | 124 | 0 | 6 | 27 | 91 | 1,337 | 161 | 1,087 | 89 |
| Total area actually reporting | 98.6% | 18,250 | 111 | 983 | 5,094 | 12,062 | 97,494 | 19,006 | 70,699 | 7,789 |
| Estimated total | 100.0% | 18,357 | 111 | 996 | 5,113 | 12,137 | 98,609 | 19,216 | 71,548 | 7,845 |
| Rate per 100,000 inhabitants | | 400.2 | 2.4 | 21.7 | 111.5 | 264.6 | 2,150.0 | 419.0 | 1,560.0 | 171.0 |
| **Boston-Quincy, MA M.D.** | **1,912,393** | | | | | | | | | |
| Includes Norfolk, Plymouth, and Suffolk Counties | | | | | | | | | | |
| Total area actually reporting | 99.1% | 11,015 | 75 | 534 | 3,522 | 6,884 | 45,722 | 8,402 | 33,260 | 4,060 |
| Estimated total | 100.0% | 11,068 | 75 | 538 | 3,532 | 6,923 | 46,053 | 8,482 | 33,489 | 4,082 |
| Rate per 100,000 inhabitants | | 578.8 | 3.9 | 28.1 | 184.7 | 362.0 | 2,408.1 | 443.5 | 1,751.2 | 213.4 |
| **Cambridge-Newton-Framingham, MA M.D.** | **1,504,293** | | | | | | | | | |
| Includes Middlesex County | | | | | | | | | | |
| Total area actually reporting | 99.8% | 4,210 | 18 | 228 | 943 | 3,021 | 28,247 | 5,887 | 20,384 | 1,976 |
| Estimated total | 100.0% | 4,221 | 18 | 229 | 945 | 3,029 | 28,315 | 5,903 | 20,431 | 1,981 |
| Rate per 100,000 inhabitants | | 280.6 | 1.2 | 15.2 | 62.8 | 201.4 | 1,882.3 | 392.4 | 1,358.2 | 131.7 |
| **Peabody, MA M.D.** | **747,294** | | | | | | | | | |
| Includes Essex County | | | | | | | | | | |
| Total area actually reporting | 100.0% | 2,572 | 15 | 134 | 549 | 1,874 | 16,109 | 3,550 | 11,111 | 1,448 |
| Rate per 100,000 inhabitants | | 344.2 | 2.0 | 17.9 | 73.5 | 250.8 | 2,155.6 | 475.0 | 1,486.8 | 193.8 |
| **Rockingham County-Strafford County, NH M.D.** | **422,505** | | | | | | | | | |
| Includes Rockingham and Strafford Counties | | | | | | | | | | |
| Total area actually reporting | 89.2% | 453 | 3 | 87 | 80 | 283 | 7,416 | 1,167 | 5,944 | 305 |
| Estimated total | 100.0% | 496 | 3 | 95 | 87 | 311 | 8,132 | 1,281 | 6,517 | 334 |
| Rate per 100,000 inhabitants | | 117.4 | 0.7 | 22.5 | 20.6 | 73.6 | 1,924.7 | 303.2 | 1,542.5 | 79.1 |
| **Boulder, CO M.S.A.** | **296,153** | | | | | | | | | |
| Includes Boulder County | | | | | | | | | | |
| City of Boulder | 100,035 | 245 | 5 | 32 | 51 | 157 | 2,776 | 564 | 2,093 | 119 |
| Total area actually reporting | 100.0% | 719 | 7 | 67 | 117 | 528 | 7,134 | 1,367 | 5,447 | 320 |
| Rate per 100,000 inhabitants | | 242.8 | 2.4 | 22.6 | 39.5 | 178.3 | 2,408.9 | 461.6 | 1,839.3 | 108.1 |
| **Bowling Green, KY M.S.A.**[1] | **119,746** | | | | | | | | | |
| Includes Edmonson and Warren Counties[1] | | | | | | | | | | |
| City of Bowling Green[1] | 55,754 | 230 | 3 | 51 | 72 | 104 | 3,088 | 543 | 2,400 | 145 |
| Total area actually reporting | 99.3% | 259 | 3 | 58 | 72 | 126 | 3,894 | 842 | 2,870 | 182 |
| Estimated total | 100.0% | 261 | 3 | 58 | 73 | 127 | 3,922 | 848 | 2,891 | 183 |
| Rate per 100,000 inhabitants | | 218.0 | 2.5 | 48.4 | 61.0 | 106.1 | 3,275.3 | 708.2 | 2,414.3 | 152.8 |
| **Bremerton-Silverdale, WA M.S.A.** | **242,027** | | | | | | | | | |
| Includes Kitsap County | | | | | | | | | | |
| City of Bremerton | 35,888 | 250 | 0 | 46 | 46 | 158 | 1,696 | 362 | 1,222 | 112 |
| Total area actually reporting | 100.0% | 1,069 | 4 | 169 | 107 | 789 | 6,156 | 1,499 | 4,309 | 348 |
| Rate per 100,000 inhabitants | | 441.7 | 1.7 | 69.8 | 44.2 | 326.0 | 2,543.5 | 619.4 | 1,780.4 | 143.8 |

[1] The FBI determined that the agency's data were overreported. Consequently, affected data are not included in this table.

## Table 6. Crime, by Metropolitan Statistical Area, 2009—*Continued*

(Number, percent, rate per 100,000 population.)

| Area | Population | Violent crime | Murder and non-negligent man-slaughter | Forcible rape | Robbery | Aggravated assault | Property crime | Burglary | Larceny-theft | Motor vehicle theft |
|---|---|---|---|---|---|---|---|---|---|---|
| **Bridgeport-Stamford-Norwalk, CT M.S.A.** | **878,051** | | | | | | | | | |
| Includes Fairfield County | | | | | | | | | | |
| City of Bridgeport | 136,049 | 1,527 | 12 | 58 | 680 | 777 | 5,615 | 1,276 | 3,375 | 964 |
| City of Stamford | 119,507 | 353 | 2 | 31 | 151 | 169 | 2,143 | 370 | 1,600 | 173 |
| City of Norwalk | 83,198 | 425 | 1 | 10 | 157 | 257 | 1,786 | 314 | 1,269 | 203 |
| City of Danbury | 79,729 | 130 | 2 | 25 | 50 | 53 | 1,536 | 219 | 1,219 | 98 |
| City of Stratford | 48,726 | 162 | 0 | 11 | 74 | 77 | 1,425 | 215 | 1,057 | 153 |
| Total area actually reporting | 100.0% | 2,792 | 18 | 154 | 1,181 | 1,439 | 17,241 | 3,217 | 12,144 | 1,880 |
| Rate per 100,000 inhabitants | | 318.0 | 2.0 | 17.5 | 134.5 | 163.9 | 1,963.6 | 366.4 | 1,383.1 | 214.1 |
| **Brownsville-Harlingen, TX M.S.A.** | **399,958** | | | | | | | | | |
| Includes Cameron County | | | | | | | | | | |
| City of Brownsville | 179,491 | 454 | 4 | 26 | 152 | 272 | 9,778 | 1,576 | 7,865 | 337 |
| City of Harlingen | 65,552 | 300 | 1 | 32 | 70 | 197 | 4,433 | 799 | 3,435 | 199 |
| Total area actually reporting | 100.0% | 1,337 | 8 | 95 | 297 | 937 | 19,074 | 3,736 | 14,544 | 794 |
| Rate per 100,000 inhabitants | | 334.3 | 2.0 | 23.8 | 74.3 | 234.3 | 4,769.0 | 934.1 | 3,636.4 | 198.5 |
| **Brunswick, GA M.S.A.** | **103,525** | | | | | | | | | |
| Includes Brantley, Glynn, and McIntosh Counties | | | | | | | | | | |
| City of Brunswick | 16,348 | 349 | 2 | 10 | 71 | 266 | 1,414 | 375 | 968 | 71 |
| Total area actually reporting | 97.3% | 774 | 16 | 37 | 149 | 572 | 4,759 | 1,291 | 3,257 | 211 |
| Estimated total | 100.0% | 801 | 16 | 37 | 152 | 596 | 4,819 | 1,318 | 3,290 | 211 |
| Rate per 100,000 inhabitants | | 773.7 | 15.5 | 35.7 | 146.8 | 575.7 | 4,654.9 | 1,273.1 | 3,178.0 | 203.8 |
| **Buffalo-Niagara Falls, NY M.S.A.** | **1,119,104** | | | | | | | | | |
| Includes Erie and Niagara Counties | | | | | | | | | | |
| City of Buffalo | 268,655 | 3,920 | 60 | 141 | 1,636 | 2,083 | 14,481 | 3,954 | 8,947 | 1,580 |
| City of Cheektowaga Town | 77,772 | 210 | 0 | 15 | 81 | 114 | 2,570 | 334 | 2,134 | 102 |
| City of Tonawanda | 14,683 | 37 | 0 | 4 | 9 | 24 | 400 | 53 | 336 | 11 |
| City of Niagara Falls | 50,909 | 609 | 6 | 28 | 166 | 409 | 2,810 | 805 | 1,877 | 128 |
| Total area actually reporting | 100.0% | 5,759 | 75 | 260 | 2,155 | 3,269 | 33,998 | 7,608 | 24,108 | 2,282 |
| Rate per 100,000 inhabitants | | 514.6 | 6.7 | 23.2 | 192.6 | 292.1 | 3,038.0 | 679.8 | 2,154.2 | 203.9 |
| **Burlington, NC M.S.A.** | **150,252** | | | | | | | | | |
| Includes Alamance County | | | | | | | | | | |
| City of Burlington | 51,440 | 401 | 1 | 26 | 115 | 259 | 3,364 | 794 | 2,425 | 145 |
| Total area actually reporting | 98.7% | 670 | 4 | 48 | 161 | 457 | 5,712 | 1,600 | 3,841 | 271 |
| Estimated total | 100.0% | 677 | 4 | 48 | 163 | 462 | 5,802 | 1,621 | 3,906 | 275 |
| Rate per 100,000 inhabitants | | 450.6 | 2.7 | 31.9 | 108.5 | 307.5 | 3,861.5 | 1,078.9 | 2,599.6 | 183.0 |
| **Burlington-South Burlington, VT M.S.A.** | **209,200** | | | | | | | | | |
| Includes Chittenden, Franklin, and Grand Isle Counties | | | | | | | | | | |
| City of Burlington | 38,794 | 118 | 0 | 12 | 14 | 92 | 1,760 | 235 | 1,493 | 32 |
| City of South Burlington | 17,893 | 28 | 0 | 7 | 1 | 20 | 612 | 59 | 541 | 12 |
| Total area actually reporting | 100.0% | 332 | 1 | 58 | 39 | 234 | 6,417 | 1,148 | 5,102 | 167 |
| Rate per 100,000 inhabitants | | 158.7 | 0.5 | 27.7 | 18.6 | 111.9 | 3,067.4 | 548.8 | 2,438.8 | 79.8 |
| **Cape Coral-Fort Myers, FL M.S.A.** | **607,216** | | | | | | | | | |
| Includes Lee County | | | | | | | | | | |
| City of Cape Coral | 164,344 | 332 | 3 | 16 | 92 | 221 | 4,233 | 1,267 | 2,792 | 174 |
| City of Fort Myers | 67,031 | 819 | 17 | 23 | 226 | 553 | 2,831 | 710 | 1,821 | 300 |
| Total area actually reporting | 100.0% | 2,561 | 40 | 121 | 725 | 1,675 | 17,940 | 5,858 | 10,844 | 1,238 |
| Rate per 100,000 inhabitants | | 421.8 | 6.6 | 19.9 | 119.4 | 275.8 | 2,954.5 | 964.7 | 1,785.9 | 203.9 |
| **Cape Girardeau-Jackson, MO-IL M.S.A.** | **93,713** | | | | | | | | | |
| Includes Alexander County, IL and Bollinger and Cape Girardeau Counties, MO | | | | | | | | | | |
| City of Cape Girardeau, MO | 37,588 | 178 | 2 | 17 | 51 | 108 | 2,141 | 363 | 1,740 | 38 |
| City of Jackson, MO | 13,956 | 22 | 0 | 3 | 1 | 18 | 405 | 68 | 323 | 14 |
| Total area actually reporting | 91.5% | 352 | 2 | 28 | 54 | 268 | 2,882 | 560 | 2,259 | 63 |
| Estimated total | 100.0% | 363 | 2 | 28 | 56 | 277 | 3,016 | 591 | 2,356 | 69 |
| Rate per 100,000 inhabitants | | 387.4 | 2.1 | 29.9 | 59.8 | 295.6 | 3,218.3 | 630.6 | 2,514.1 | 73.6 |
| **Carson City, NV M.S.A.** | **54,462** | | | | | | | | | |
| Includes Carson City | | | | | | | | | | |
| Total area actually reporting | 100.0% | 180 | 0 | 1 | 26 | 153 | 1,151 | 268 | 797 | 86 |
| Rate per 100,000 inhabitants | | 330.5 | 0.0 | 1.8 | 47.7 | 280.9 | 2,113.4 | 492.1 | 1,463.4 | 157.9 |

## Table 6. Crime, by Metropolitan Statistical Area, 2009—*Continued*

(Number, percent, rate per 100,000 population.)

| Area | Population | Violent crime | Murder and non-negligent man-slaughter | Forcible rape | Robbery | Aggravated assault | Property crime | Burglary | Larceny-theft | Motor vehicle theft |
|---|---|---|---|---|---|---|---|---|---|---|
| **Casper, WY M.S.A.** | **74,856** | | | | | | | | | |
| Includes Natrona County | | | | | | | | | | |
| City of Casper | 54,550 | 107 | 0 | 20 | 12 | 75 | 2,504 | 411 | 1,970 | 123 |
| Total area actually reporting | 100.0% | 163 | 0 | 26 | 16 | 121 | 2,954 | 562 | 2,232 | 160 |
| Rate per 100,000 inhabitants | | 217.8 | 0.0 | 34.7 | 21.4 | 161.6 | 3,946.2 | 750.8 | 2,981.7 | 213.7 |
| **Cedar Rapids, IA M.S.A.** | **257,120** | | | | | | | | | |
| Includes Benton, Jones, and Linn Counties | | | | | | | | | | |
| City of Cedar Rapids | 128,779 | 403 | 1 | 43 | 107 | 252 | 5,588 | 1,279 | 4,068 | 241 |
| Total area actually reporting | 96.3% | 513 | 1 | 64 | 119 | 329 | 7,034 | 1,660 | 5,052 | 322 |
| Estimated total | 100.0% | 531 | 1 | 66 | 121 | 343 | 7,226 | 1,696 | 5,202 | 328 |
| Rate per 100,000 inhabitants | | 206.5 | 0.4 | 25.7 | 47.1 | 133.4 | 2,810.4 | 659.6 | 2,023.2 | 127.6 |
| **Charleston, WV M.S.A.** | **303,984** | | | | | | | | | |
| Includes Boone, Clay, Kanawha, Lincoln, and Putnam Counties | | | | | | | | | | |
| City of Charleston | 49,976 | 535 | 5 | 18 | 128 | 384 | 2,625 | 636 | 1,813 | 176 |
| Total area actually reporting | 85.1% | 1,217 | 24 | 61 | 226 | 906 | 8,501 | 2,372 | 5,508 | 621 |
| Estimated total | 100.0% | 1,330 | 26 | 68 | 243 | 993 | 9,660 | 2,675 | 6,295 | 690 |
| Rate per 100,000 inhabitants | | 437.5 | 8.6 | 22.4 | 79.9 | 326.7 | 3,177.8 | 880.0 | 2,070.8 | 227.0 |
| **Charleston-North Charleston-Summerville, SC M.S.A.**[3] | **659,704** | | | | | | | | | |
| Includes Berkeley, Charleston, and Dorchester Counties | | | | | | | | | | |
| City of Charleston | 113,681 | 595 | 9 | 31 | 218 | 337 | 3,991 | 566 | 3,152 | 273 |
| City of North Charleston | 95,982 | 993 | 10 | 55 | 376 | 552 | 6,140 | 1,024 | 4,510 | 606 |
| City of Summerville[3] | 47,507 | 138 | 6 | 10 | 47 | 75 | | | 1,336 | 82 |
| Total area actually reporting | 99.9% | 4,064 | 36 | 218 | 1,058 | 2,752 | | | 17,092 | 2,067 |
| Estimated total | 100.0% | 4,066 | 36 | 218 | 1,058 | 2,754 | | | 17,103 | 2,068 |
| Rate per 100,000 inhabitants | | 616.3 | 5.5 | 33.0 | 160.4 | 417.5 | | | 2,592.5 | 313.5 |
| **Charlotte-Gastonia-Rock Hill, NC-SC M.S.A.** | **1,752,202** | | | | | | | | | |
| Includes Anson, Cabarrus, Gaston, Mecklenburg, and Union Counties, NC and York County, SC | | | | | | | | | | |
| City of Charlotte-Mecklenburg, NC | 777,708 | 5,625 | 58 | 303 | 2,346 | 2,918 | 38,533 | 9,817 | 25,379 | 3,337 |
| City of Gastonia, NC | 73,060 | 600 | 5 | 30 | 220 | 345 | 4,581 | 1,059 | 3,187 | 335 |
| City of Rock Hill, SC | 69,506 | 708 | 5 | 27 | 82 | 594 | 2,930 | 578 | 2,138 | 214 |
| City of Concord, NC | 67,478 | 190 | 6 | 16 | 69 | 99 | 3,270 | 527 | 2,517 | 226 |
| Total area actually reporting | 97.5% | 9,105 | 97 | 488 | 3,074 | 5,446 | 66,463 | 16,957 | 44,361 | 5,145 |
| Estimated total | 100.0% | 9,255 | 98 | 498 | 3,115 | 5,544 | 68,374 | 17,400 | 45,750 | 5,224 |
| Rate per 100,000 inhabitants | | 528.2 | 5.6 | 28.4 | 177.8 | 316.4 | 3,902.2 | 993.0 | 2,611.0 | 298.1 |
| **Charlottesville, VA M.S.A.** | **197,483** | | | | | | | | | |
| Includes Albemarle, Fluvanna, Greene, and Nelson Counties and Charlottesville City | | | | | | | | | | |
| City of Charlottesville | 41,798 | 247 | 0 | 35 | 88 | 124 | 2,070 | 184 | 1,763 | 123 |
| Total area actually reporting | 100.0% | 426 | 1 | 68 | 124 | 233 | 5,185 | 649 | 4,241 | 295 |
| Rate per 100,000 inhabitants | | 215.7 | 0.5 | 34.4 | 62.8 | 118.0 | 2,625.5 | 328.6 | 2,147.5 | 149.4 |
| **Chattanooga, TN-GA M.S.A.** | **523,787** | | | | | | | | | |
| Includes Catoosa, Dade, and Walker Counties, GA and Hamilton, Marion, and Sequatchie Counties, TN | | | | | | | | | | |
| City of Chattanooga, TN | 172,536 | 1,792 | 17 | 53 | 535 | 1,187 | 12,849 | 2,987 | 8,949 | 913 |
| Total area actually reporting | 100.0% | 3,090 | 24 | 130 | 635 | 2,301 | 22,502 | 5,356 | 15,614 | 1,532 |
| Rate per 100,000 inhabitants | | 589.9 | 4.6 | 24.8 | 121.2 | 439.3 | 4,296.0 | 1,022.6 | 2,981.0 | 292.5 |
| **Cheyenne, WY M.S.A.** | **89,355** | | | | | | | | | |
| Includes Laramie County | | | | | | | | | | |
| City of Cheyenne | 57,317 | 125 | 4 | 28 | 28 | 65 | 2,365 | 226 | 2,028 | 111 |
| Total area actually reporting | 100.0% | 180 | 4 | 40 | 30 | 106 | 2,884 | 334 | 2,404 | 146 |
| Rate per 100,000 inhabitants | | 201.4 | 4.5 | 44.8 | 33.6 | 118.6 | 3,227.6 | 373.8 | 2,690.4 | 163.4 |
| **Chico, CA M.S.A.** | **221,473** | | | | | | | | | |
| Includes Butte County | | | | | | | | | | |
| City of Chico | 84,724 | 310 | 3 | 42 | 124 | 141 | 2,352 | 685 | 1,359 | 308 |
| Total area actually reporting | 100.0% | 932 | 10 | 87 | 187 | 648 | 6,338 | 1,733 | 3,765 | 840 |
| Rate per 100,000 inhabitants | | 420.8 | 4.5 | 39.3 | 84.4 | 292.6 | 2,861.7 | 782.5 | 1,700.0 | 379.3 |

## Table 6. Crime, by Metropolitan Statistical Area, 2009—*Continued*

(Number, percent, rate per 100,000 population.)

| Area | Population | Violent crime | Murder and non-negligent man-slaughter | Forcible rape | Robbery | Aggravated assault | Property crime | Burglary | Larceny-theft | Motor vehicle theft |
|---|---|---|---|---|---|---|---|---|---|---|
| **Cincinnati-Middletown, OH-KY-IN M.S.A.[1]** | **2,178,158** | | | | | | | | | |
| Includes Dearborn, Franklin, and Ohio Counties, IN; Boone, Bracken, Campbell, Gallatin, Grant, Kenton, and Pendleton Counties, KY;[1] and Brown, Butler, Clermont, Hamilton, and Warren Counties, OH | | | | | | | | | | |
| City of Cincinnati, OH | 333,568 | 3,976 | 55 | 235 | 2,272 | 1,414 | 20,357 | 6,287 | 12,513 | 1,557 |
| City of Middletown, OH | 51,401 | 364 | 2 | 46 | 119 | 197 | 4,297 | 1,091 | 2,999 | 207 |
| Total area actually reporting | 95.5% | 7,272 | 87 | 696 | 3,514 | 2,975 | 69,303 | 16,552 | 49,259 | 3,492 |
| Estimated total | 100.0% | 7,444 | 89 | 720 | 3,580 | 3,055 | 71,996 | 17,088 | 51,302 | 3,606 |
| Rate per 100,000 inhabitants | | 341.8 | 4.1 | 33.1 | 164.4 | 140.3 | 3,305.4 | 784.5 | 2,355.3 | 165.6 |
| **Clarksville, TN-KY M.S.A.[1]** | **265,303** | | | | | | | | | |
| Includes Christian and Trigg Counties, KY[1] and Montgomery and Stewart Counties, TN | | | | | | | | | | |
| City of Clarksville, TN | 121,661 | 805 | 16 | 55 | 105 | 629 | 4,551 | 1,569 | 2,767 | 215 |
| Total area actually reporting | 99.3% | 1,161 | 20 | 96 | 188 | 857 | 7,911 | 2,716 | 4,805 | 390 |
| Estimated total | 100.0% | 1,167 | 20 | 97 | 190 | 860 | 7,981 | 2,731 | 4,857 | 393 |
| Rate per 100,000 inhabitants | | 439.9 | 7.5 | 36.6 | 71.6 | 324.2 | 3,008.3 | 1,029.4 | 1,830.7 | 148.1 |
| **Cleveland, TN M.S.A.** | **113,409** | | | | | | | | | |
| Includes Bradley and Polk Counties | | | | | | | | | | |
| City of Cleveland | 40,024 | 391 | 3 | 13 | 43 | 332 | 2,111 | 422 | 1,615 | 74 |
| Total area actually reporting | 100.0% | 735 | 3 | 28 | 50 | 654 | 3,385 | 818 | 2,380 | 187 |
| Rate per 100,000 inhabitants | | 648.1 | 2.6 | 24.7 | 44.1 | 576.7 | 2,984.8 | 721.3 | 2,098.6 | 164.9 |
| **Cleveland-Elyria-Mentor, OH M.S.A.** | **2,093,232** | | | | | | | | | |
| Includes Cuyahoga, Geauga, Lake, Lorain, and Medina Counties | | | | | | | | | | |
| City of Cleveland | 429,238 | 5,990 | 86 | 373 | 3,555 | 1,976 | 24,128 | 9,226 | 10,871 | 4,031 |
| City of Elyria | 54,857 | 220 | 3 | 24 | 87 | 106 | 2,380 | 691 | 1,605 | 84 |
| City of Mentor | 51,993 | 45 | 0 | 10 | 19 | 16 | 1,191 | 117 | 1,026 | 48 |
| Total area actually reporting | 84.0% | 8,456 | 116 | 640 | 4,589 | 3,111 | 50,766 | 15,805 | 29,430 | 5,531 |
| Estimated total | 100.0% | 8,973 | 122 | 720 | 4,791 | 3,340 | 59,408 | 17,642 | 35,887 | 5,879 |
| Rate per 100,000 inhabitants | | 428.7 | 5.8 | 34.4 | 228.9 | 159.6 | 2,838.1 | 842.8 | 1,714.4 | 280.9 |
| **Coeur d'Alene, ID M.S.A.** | **140,410** | | | | | | | | | |
| Includes Kootenai County | | | | | | | | | | |
| City of Coeur d'Alene | 44,406 | 286 | 1 | 41 | 32 | 212 | 1,737 | 348 | 1,284 | 105 |
| Total area actually reporting | 100.0% | 482 | 2 | 82 | 48 | 350 | 3,713 | 896 | 2,616 | 201 |
| Rate per 100,000 inhabitants | | 343.3 | 1.4 | 58.4 | 34.2 | 249.3 | 2,644.4 | 638.1 | 1,863.1 | 143.2 |
| **College Station-Bryan, TX M.S.A.** | **210,281** | | | | | | | | | |
| Includes Brazos, Burleson, and Robertson Counties | | | | | | | | | | |
| City of College Station | 86,072 | 170 | 3 | 43 | 24 | 100 | 3,267 | 613 | 2,580 | 74 |
| City of Bryan | 73,111 | 567 | 1 | 33 | 128 | 405 | 4,134 | 1,140 | 2,809 | 185 |
| Total area actually reporting | 100.0% | 894 | 5 | 91 | 171 | 627 | 9,158 | 2,312 | 6,493 | 353 |
| Rate per 100,000 inhabitants | | 425.1 | 2.4 | 43.3 | 81.3 | 298.2 | 4,355.1 | 1,099.5 | 3,087.8 | 167.9 |
| **Colorado Springs, CO M.S.A.** | **628,075** | | | | | | | | | |
| Includes El Paso and Teller Counties | | | | | | | | | | |
| City of Colorado Springs | 401,626 | 1,968 | 15 | 344 | 525 | 1,084 | 14,723 | 3,305 | 10,357 | 1,061 |
| Total area actually reporting | 99.9% | 2,835 | 21 | 421 | 561 | 1,832 | 17,783 | 4,120 | 12,330 | 1,333 |
| Estimated total | 100.0% | 2,837 | 21 | 421 | 561 | 1,834 | 17,809 | 4,124 | 12,350 | 1,335 |
| Rate per 100,000 inhabitants | | 451.7 | 3.3 | 67.0 | 89.3 | 292.0 | 2,835.5 | 656.6 | 1,966.3 | 212.6 |
| **Columbia, MO M.S.A.** | **166,465** | | | | | | | | | |
| Includes Boone and Howard Counties | | | | | | | | | | |
| City of Columbia | 102,588 | 501 | 3 | 32 | 157 | 309 | 3,906 | 692 | 3,082 | 132 |
| Total area actually reporting | 99.5% | 667 | 3 | 38 | 174 | 452 | 5,219 | 943 | 4,086 | 190 |
| Estimated total | 100.0% | 670 | 3 | 38 | 175 | 454 | 5,248 | 948 | 4,108 | 192 |
| Rate per 100,000 inhabitants | | 402.5 | 1.8 | 22.8 | 105.1 | 272.7 | 3,152.6 | 569.5 | 2,467.8 | 115.3 |
| **Columbia, SC M.S.A.** | **741,623** | | | | | | | | | |
| Includes Calhoun, Fairfield, Kershaw, Lexington, Richland, and Saluda Counties | | | | | | | | | | |
| City of Columbia | 127,884 | 1,338 | 13 | 68 | 379 | 878 | 7,689 | 1,678 | 5,321 | 690 |
| Total area actually reporting | 99.9% | 5,641 | 47 | 288 | 1,042 | 4,264 | 29,593 | 7,115 | 19,883 | 2,595 |
| Estimated total | 100.0% | 5,643 | 47 | 288 | 1,042 | 4,266 | 29,611 | 7,119 | 19,896 | 2,596 |
| Rate per 100,000 inhabitants | | 760.9 | 6.3 | 38.8 | 140.5 | 575.2 | 3,992.7 | 959.9 | 2,682.8 | 350.0 |

[1] The FBI determined that the agency's data were overreported. Consequently, affected data are not included in this table.

## Table 6. Crime, by Metropolitan Statistical Area, 2009—*Continued*

(Number, percent, rate per 100,000 population.)

| Area | Population | Violent crime | Murder and non-negligent man-slaughter | Forcible rape | Robbery | Aggravated assault | Property crime | Burglary | Larceny-theft | Motor vehicle theft |
|---|---|---|---|---|---|---|---|---|---|---|
| **Columbus, GA-AL M.S.A.** | **287,607** | | | | | | | | | |
| Includes Russell County, AL and Chattahoochee, Harris, Marion, and Muscogee Counties, GA | | | | | | | | | | |
| City of Columbus, GA | 186,224 | 1,153 | 13 | 47 | 574 | 519 | 14,684 | 3,792 | 9,374 | 1,518 |
| Total area actually reporting | 95.1% | 1,454 | 15 | 63 | 669 | 707 | 17,285 | 4,686 | 10,883 | 1,716 |
| Estimated total | 100.0% | 1,500 | 16 | 66 | 686 | 732 | 17,709 | 4,812 | 11,136 | 1,761 |
| Rate per 100,000 inhabitants | | 521.5 | 5.6 | 22.9 | 238.5 | 254.5 | 6,157.4 | 1,673.1 | 3,872.0 | 612.3 |
| **Columbus, IN M.S.A.** | **75,902** | | | | | | | | | |
| Includes Bartholomew County | | | | | | | | | | |
| City of Columbus | 40,087 | 53 | 0 | 4 | 24 | 25 | 2,184 | 244 | 1,768 | 172 |
| Total area actually reporting | 99.5% | 81 | 0 | 7 | 27 | 47 | 2,600 | 338 | 2,068 | 194 |
| Estimated total | 100.0% | 82 | 0 | 7 | 27 | 48 | 2,612 | 340 | 2,077 | 195 |
| Rate per 100,000 inhabitants | | 108.0 | 0.0 | 9.2 | 35.6 | 63.2 | 3,441.3 | 447.9 | 2,736.4 | 256.9 |
| **Columbus, OH M.S.A.** | **1,797,471** | | | | | | | | | |
| Includes Delaware, Fairfield, Franklin, Licking, Madison, Morrow, Pickaway, and Union Counties | | | | | | | | | | |
| City of Columbus | 759,391 | 5,340 | 83 | 574 | 3,395 | 1,288 | 48,813 | 14,583 | 30,044 | 4,186 |
| Total area actually reporting | 98.1% | 6,598 | 102 | 823 | 3,936 | 1,737 | 76,158 | 20,732 | 50,335 | 5,091 |
| Estimated total | 100.0% | 6,658 | 103 | 832 | 3,960 | 1,763 | 77,126 | 20,925 | 51,071 | 5,130 |
| Rate per 100,000 inhabitants | | 370.4 | 5.7 | 46.3 | 220.3 | 98.1 | 4,290.8 | 1,164.1 | 2,841.3 | 285.4 |
| **Corpus Christi, TX M.S.A.** | **417,198** | | | | | | | | | |
| Includes Aransas, Nueces, and San Patricio Counties | | | | | | | | | | |
| City of Corpus Christi | 287,277 | 2,363 | 12 | 212 | 459 | 1,680 | 16,095 | 2,973 | 12,525 | 597 |
| Total area actually reporting | 100.0% | 2,739 | 15 | 252 | 508 | 1,964 | 20,873 | 4,402 | 15,713 | 758 |
| Rate per 100,000 inhabitants | | 656.5 | 3.6 | 60.4 | 121.8 | 470.8 | 5,003.1 | 1,055.1 | 3,766.3 | 181.7 |
| **Corvallis, OR M.S.A.** | **82,116** | | | | | | | | | |
| Includes Benton County | | | | | | | | | | |
| City of Corvallis | 51,302 | 66 | 1 | 10 | 19 | 36 | 1,706 | 249 | 1,396 | 61 |
| Total area actually reporting | 100.0% | 103 | 1 | 15 | 25 | 62 | 2,292 | 383 | 1,822 | 87 |
| Rate per 100,000 inhabitants | | 125.4 | 1.2 | 18.3 | 30.4 | 75.5 | 2,791.2 | 466.4 | 2,218.8 | 105.9 |
| **Crestview-Fort Walton Beach-Destin, FL M.S.A.** | **179,103** | | | | | | | | | |
| Includes Okaloosa County | | | | | | | | | | |
| City of Crestview | 20,023 | 115 | 1 | 15 | 27 | 72 | 702 | 127 | 547 | 28 |
| City of Fort Walton Beach | 18,759 | 95 | 1 | 13 | 31 | 50 | 768 | 140 | 579 | 49 |
| Total area actually reporting | 100.0% | 528 | 5 | 60 | 138 | 325 | 5,176 | 1,038 | 3,876 | 262 |
| Rate per 100,000 inhabitants | | 294.8 | 2.8 | 33.5 | 77.1 | 181.5 | 2,890.0 | 579.6 | 2,164.1 | 146.3 |
| **Cumberland, MD-WV M.S.A.** | **99,133** | | | | | | | | | |
| Includes Allegany County, MD and Mineral County, WV | | | | | | | | | | |
| City of Cumberland, MD | 20,372 | 202 | 1 | 15 | 20 | 166 | 1,318 | 380 | 916 | 22 |
| Total area actually reporting | 98.4% | 451 | 2 | 29 | 46 | 374 | 2,698 | 751 | 1,883 | 64 |
| Estimated total | 100.0% | 455 | 2 | 29 | 47 | 377 | 2,756 | 763 | 1,927 | 66 |
| Rate per 100,000 inhabitants | | 459.0 | 2.0 | 29.3 | 47.4 | 380.3 | 2,780.1 | 769.7 | 1,943.9 | 66.6 |
| **Dallas-Fort Worth-Arlington, TX M.S.A.** | **6,449,790** | | | | | | | | | |
| Includes the Metropolitan Divisions of Dallas-Plano-Irving and Fort Worth-Arlington | | | | | | | | | | |
| City of Dallas | 1,290,266 | 10,221 | 166 | 485 | 5,501 | 4,069 | 71,364 | 19,428 | 41,481 | 10,455 |
| City of Fort Worth | 723,456 | 4,232 | 44 | 370 | 1,449 | 2,369 | 35,884 | 10,188 | 23,564 | 2,132 |
| City of Arlington | 379,104 | 2,330 | 12 | 152 | 672 | 1,494 | 20,516 | 4,891 | 14,186 | 1,439 |
| City of Plano | 272,747 | 464 | 4 | 45 | 143 | 272 | 7,993 | 1,477 | 6,047 | 469 |
| City of Irving | 202,447 | 604 | 4 | 34 | 214 | 352 | 8,427 | 1,913 | 5,730 | 784 |
| City of Carrollton | 127,432 | 250 | 4 | 16 | 124 | 106 | 4,061 | 1,085 | 2,633 | 343 |
| City of Denton | 124,308 | 306 | 2 | 71 | 79 | 154 | 3,271 | 681 | 2,403 | 187 |
| City of McKinney | 132,146 | 245 | 0 | 47 | 56 | 142 | 3,339 | 711 | 2,518 | 110 |
| City of Richardson | 102,675 | 230 | 0 | 12 | 109 | 109 | 3,575 | 919 | 2,372 | 284 |
| Total area actually reporting | 99.9% | 26,494 | 310 | 1,944 | 10,361 | 13,879 | 252,343 | 63,685 | 165,112 | 23,546 |
| Estimated total | 100.0% | 26,495 | 310 | 1,944 | 10,361 | 13,880 | 252,361 | 63,689 | 165,125 | 23,547 |
| Rate per 100,000 inhabitants | | 410.8 | 4.8 | 30.1 | 160.6 | 215.2 | 3,912.7 | 987.5 | 2,560.2 | 365.1 |

## Table 6. Crime, by Metropolitan Statistical Area, 2009—*Continued*

(Number, percent, rate per 100,000 population.)

| Area | Population | Violent crime | Murder and non-negligent man-slaughter | Forcible rape | Robbery | Aggravated assault | Property crime | Burglary | Larceny-theft | Motor vehicle theft |
|---|---|---|---|---|---|---|---|---|---|---|
| **Dallas-Plano-Irving, TX M.D.** | **4,330,070** | | | | | | | | | |
| Includes Collin, Dallas, Delta, Denton, Ellis, Hunt, Kaufman, and Rockwall Counties | | | | | | | | | | |
| Total area actually reporting | 99.9% | 17,354 | 235 | 1,178 | 7,727 | 8,214 | 165,359 | 41,801 | 105,469 | 18,089 |
| Estimated total | 100.0% | 17,355 | 235 | 1,178 | 7,727 | 8,215 | 165,377 | 41,805 | 105,482 | 18,090 |
| Rate per 100,000 inhabitants | | 400.8 | 5.4 | 27.2 | 178.4 | 189.7 | 3,819.3 | 965.5 | 2,436.0 | 417.8 |
| **Fort Worth-Arlington, TX M.D.** | **2,119,720** | | | | | | | | | |
| Includes Johnson, Parker, Tarrant, and Wise Counties | | | | | | | | | | |
| Total area actually reporting | 100.0% | 9,140 | 75 | 766 | 2,634 | 5,665 | 86,984 | 21,884 | 59,643 | 5,457 |
| Rate per 100,000 inhabitants | | 431.2 | 3.5 | 36.1 | 124.3 | 267.3 | 4,103.6 | 1,032.4 | 2,813.7 | 257.4 |
| **Dalton, GA M.S.A.** | **135,102** | | | | | | | | | |
| Includes Murray and Whitfield Counties | | | | | | | | | | |
| City of Dalton | 34,299 | 118 | 1 | 15 | 16 | 86 | 1,232 | 228 | 958 | 46 |
| Total area actually reporting | 97.4% | 380 | 2 | 31 | 33 | 314 | 3,752 | 772 | 2,807 | 173 |
| Estimated total | 100.0% | 396 | 2 | 32 | 38 | 324 | 3,900 | 803 | 2,913 | 184 |
| Rate per 100,000 inhabitants | | 293.1 | 1.5 | 23.7 | 28.1 | 239.8 | 2,886.7 | 594.4 | 2,156.1 | 136.2 |
| **Danville, IL M.S.A.**[4] | **80,017** | | | | | | | | | |
| Includes Vermilion County[4] | | | | | | | | | | |
| City of Danville[4] | 32,076 | | 4 | | 108 | 219 | 2,211 | 791 | 1,338 | 82 |
| Total area actually reporting | 98.9% | | 6 | | 114 | 298 | 3,134 | 1,097 | 1,917 | 120 |
| Estimated total | 100.0% | | 6 | | 115 | 299 | 3,155 | 1,101 | 1,933 | 121 |
| Rate per 100,000 inhabitants | | | 7.5 | | 143.7 | 373.7 | 3,942.9 | 1,376.0 | 2,415.7 | 151.2 |
| **Danville, VA M.S.A.** | **105,723** | | | | | | | | | |
| Includes Pittsylvania County and Danville City | | | | | | | | | | |
| City of Danville | 44,442 | 174 | 8 | 7 | 80 | 79 | 2,308 | 515 | 1,724 | 69 |
| Total area actually reporting | 100.0% | 235 | 9 | 13 | 93 | 120 | 2,936 | 725 | 2,107 | 104 |
| Rate per 100,000 inhabitants | | 222.3 | 8.5 | 12.3 | 88.0 | 113.5 | 2,777.1 | 685.8 | 1,992.9 | 98.4 |
| **Dayton, OH M.S.A.** | **837,876** | | | | | | | | | |
| Includes Greene, Miami, Montgomery, and Preble Counties | | | | | | | | | | |
| City of Dayton | 152,965 | 1,542 | 39 | 91 | 770 | 642 | 8,949 | 3,244 | 4,932 | 773 |
| Total area actually reporting | 97.2% | 2,753 | 47 | 307 | 1,212 | 1,187 | 27,893 | 7,526 | 18,721 | 1,646 |
| Estimated total | 100.0% | 2,793 | 47 | 313 | 1,228 | 1,205 | 28,562 | 7,659 | 19,230 | 1,673 |
| Rate per 100,000 inhabitants | | 333.3 | 5.6 | 37.4 | 146.6 | 143.8 | 3,408.9 | 914.1 | 2,295.1 | 199.7 |
| **Decatur, AL M.S.A.**[3] | **151,260** | | | | | | | | | |
| Includes Lawrence[3] and Morgan Counties | | | | | | | | | | |
| City of Decatur | 56,290 | 223 | 0 | 28 | 78 | 117 | 3,234 | 743 | 2,398 | 93 |
| Total area actually reporting | 100.0% | | 2 | 35 | 86 | | 4,817 | 1,178 | 3,486 | 153 |
| Rate per 100,000 inhabitants | | | 1.3 | 23.1 | 56.9 | | 3,184.6 | 778.8 | 2,304.6 | 101.2 |
| **Decatur, IL M.S.A.**[4] | **107,232** | | | | | | | | | |
| Includes Macon County[4] | | | | | | | | | | |
| City of Decatur[4] | 75,651 | | 3 | | 149 | 415 | 3,079 | 1,344 | 1,580 | 155 |
| Total area actually reporting | 91.7% | | 3 | | 151 | 448 | 3,460 | 1,465 | 1,827 | 168 |
| Estimated total | 100.0% | | 3 | | 157 | 459 | 3,669 | 1,503 | 1,989 | 177 |
| Rate per 100,000 inhabitants | | | 2.8 | | 146.4 | 428.0 | 3,421.6 | 1,401.6 | 1,854.9 | 165.1 |
| **Deltona-Daytona Beach-Ormond Beach, FL M.S.A.** | **499,859** | | | | | | | | | |
| Includes Volusia County | | | | | | | | | | |
| City of Daytona Beach | 64,257 | 975 | 9 | 38 | 290 | 638 | 4,694 | 1,023 | 3,148 | 523 |
| City of Ormond Beach | 38,153 | 133 | 0 | 8 | 28 | 97 | 1,170 | 336 | 788 | 46 |
| Total area actually reporting | 100.0% | 2,762 | 19 | 138 | 702 | 1,903 | 18,359 | 4,858 | 12,075 | 1,426 |
| Rate per 100,000 inhabitants | | 552.6 | 3.8 | 27.6 | 140.4 | 380.7 | 3,672.8 | 971.9 | 2,415.7 | 285.3 |
| **Denver-Aurora-Broomfield, CO M.S.A.** | **2,550,871** | | | | | | | | | |
| Includes Adams, Arapahoe, Broomfield, Clear Creek, Denver, Douglas, Elbert, Gilpin, Jefferson, and Park Counties | | | | | | | | | | |
| City of Denver | 604,680 | 3,493 | 39 | 343 | 946 | 2,165 | 20,879 | 4,763 | 12,628 | 3,488 |
| City of Aurora | 324,014 | 1,524 | 22 | 216 | 553 | 733 | 10,037 | 2,051 | 6,820 | 1,166 |
| City of Broomfield | 56,991 | 42 | 3 | 5 | 11 | 23 | 1,115 | 112 | 946 | 57 |
| Total area actually reporting | 99.9% | 8,843 | 100 | 1,224 | 2,172 | 5,347 | 71,309 | 13,634 | 49,046 | 8,629 |
| Estimated total | 100.0% | 8,848 | 100 | 1,225 | 2,173 | 5,350 | 71,361 | 13,642 | 49,085 | 8,634 |
| Rate per 100,000 inhabitants | | 346.9 | 3.9 | 48.0 | 85.2 | 209.7 | 2,797.5 | 534.8 | 1,924.2 | 338.5 |

[3] The FBI determined that the agency's data were underreported. Consequently, affected data are not included in this table.

[4] It was determined that the agency did not follow national Uniform Crime Reporting (UCR) Program guidelines for reporting an offense. Consequently, this figure is not included in this table.

## Table 6. Crime, by Metropolitan Statistical Area, 2009—*Continued*

(Number, percent, rate per 100,000 population.)

| Area | Population | Violent crime | Murder and non-negligent man-slaughter | Forcible rape | Robbery | Aggravated assault | Property crime | Burglary | Larceny-theft | Motor vehicle theft |
|---|---|---|---|---|---|---|---|---|---|---|
| **Des Moines-West Des Moines, IA M.S.A.[1]** | **564,422** | | | | | | | | | |
| Includes Dallas, Guthrie, Madison, Polk, and Warren Counties | | | | | | | | | | |
| City of Des Moines[1] | 196,794 | 1,067 | 6 | 153 | 244 | 664 | 8,688 | 1,830 | 6,146 | 712 |
| City of West Des Moines | 56,400 | 73 | 0 | 18 | 6 | 49 | 1,772 | 196 | 1,536 | 40 |
| Total area actually reporting | 100.0% | 1,554 | 7 | 236 | 294 | 1,017 | 15,592 | 3,084 | 11,527 | 981 |
| Rate per 100,000 inhabitants | | 275.3 | 1.2 | 41.8 | 52.1 | 180.2 | 2,762.5 | 546.4 | 2,042.3 | 173.8 |
| **Detroit-Warren-Livonia, MI M.S.A.[1]** | **4,404,383** | | | | | | | | | |
| Includes the Metropolitan Divisions of Detroit-Livonia-Dearborn and Warren-Troy-Farmington Hills | | | | | | | | | | |
| City of Detroit | 908,441 | 17,868 | 365 | 335 | 5,913 | 11,255 | 50,578 | 18,993 | 18,574 | 13,011 |
| City of Warren[1] | 133,485 | 778 | 4 | 67 | 209 | 498 | 3,785 | 887 | 1,897 | 1,001 |
| City of Livonia | 90,232 | 176 | 3 | 16 | 40 | 117 | 2,232 | 341 | 1,580 | 311 |
| City of Dearborn | 85,305 | 339 | 3 | 16 | 112 | 208 | 4,255 | 712 | 2,961 | 582 |
| City of Troy | 80,182 | 79 | 0 | 17 | 13 | 49 | 1,880 | 231 | 1,564 | 85 |
| City of Farmington Hills | 78,140 | 108 | 1 | 10 | 20 | 77 | 1,520 | 256 | 1,134 | 130 |
| City of Southfield | 75,074 | 409 | 2 | 32 | 129 | 246 | 3,082 | 653 | 1,960 | 469 |
| City of Pontiac | 65,924 | 1,212 | 10 | 57 | 343 | 802 | 2,312 | 1,026 | 959 | 327 |
| City of Taylor | 60,054 | 403 | 0 | 31 | 104 | 268 | 2,594 | 566 | 1,762 | 266 |
| City of Novi | 54,842 | 52 | 0 | 1 | 10 | 41 | 1,103 | 137 | 925 | 41 |
| Total area actually reporting | 99.5% | 28,867 | 447 | 1,405 | 8,545 | 18,470 | 134,697 | 36,698 | 75,485 | 22,514 |
| Estimated total | 100.0% | 28,929 | 447 | 1,412 | 8,559 | 18,511 | 135,260 | 36,813 | 75,888 | 22,559 |
| Rate per 100,000 inhabitants | | 656.8 | 10.1 | 32.1 | 194.3 | 420.3 | 3,071.0 | 835.8 | 1,723.0 | 512.2 |
| **Detroit-Livonia-Dearborn, MI M.D.** | **1,930,388** | | | | | | | | | |
| Includes Wayne County | | | | | | | | | | |
| Total area actually reporting | 99.1% | 21,946 | 398 | 670 | 7,035 | 13,843 | 82,773 | 25,775 | 39,620 | 17,378 |
| Estimated total | 100.0% | 22,002 | 398 | 676 | 7,048 | 13,880 | 83,282 | 25,879 | 39,984 | 17,419 |
| Rate per 100,000 inhabitants | | 1,139.8 | 20.6 | 35.0 | 365.1 | 719.0 | 4,314.3 | 1,340.6 | 2,071.3 | 902.4 |
| **Warren-Troy-Farmington Hills, MI M.D.[1]** | **2,473,995** | | | | | | | | | |
| Includes Lapeer, Livingston, Macomb, Oakland, and St. Clair Counties | | | | | | | | | | |
| Total area actually reporting | 99.9% | 6,921 | 49 | 735 | 1,510 | 4,627 | 51,924 | 10,923 | 35,865 | 5,136 |
| Estimated total | 100.0% | 6,927 | 49 | 736 | 1,511 | 4,631 | 51,978 | 10,934 | 35,904 | 5,140 |
| Rate per 100,000 inhabitants | | 280.0 | 2.0 | 29.7 | 61.1 | 187.2 | 2,101.0 | 442.0 | 1,451.3 | 207.8 |
| **Dothan, AL M.S.A.[2,3]** | **142,752** | | | | | | | | | |
| Includes Geneva,[2,3] Henry, and Houston Counties | | | | | | | | | | |
| City of Dothan[3] | 66,476 | | 1 | 32 | 165 | | 3,211 | 801 | 2,275 | 135 |
| Total area actually reporting | 81.1% | | 2 | 39 | 170 | | | | 2,752 | 181 |
| Estimated total | 100.0% | | 3 | 45 | 183 | | | | 3,117 | 223 |
| Rate per 100,000 inhabitants | | | 2.1 | 31.5 | 128.2 | | | | 2,183.5 | 156.2 |
| **Dover, DE M.S.A.** | **159,218** | | | | | | | | | |
| Includes Kent County | | | | | | | | | | |
| City of Dover | 36,571 | 288 | 2 | 21 | 69 | 196 | 1,916 | 158 | 1,669 | 89 |
| Total area actually reporting | 100.0% | 1,007 | 4 | 81 | 189 | 733 | 5,658 | 1,354 | 4,055 | 249 |
| Rate per 100,000 inhabitants | | 632.5 | 2.5 | 50.9 | 118.7 | 460.4 | 3,553.6 | 850.4 | 2,546.8 | 156.4 |
| **Dubuque, IA M.S.A.** | **92,984** | | | | | | | | | |
| Includes Dubuque County | | | | | | | | | | |
| City of Dubuque | 57,192 | 294 | 2 | 15 | 17 | 260 | 1,883 | 483 | 1,323 | 77 |
| Total area actually reporting | 100.0% | 360 | 2 | 18 | 17 | 323 | 2,182 | 595 | 1,493 | 94 |
| Rate per 100,000 inhabitants | | 387.2 | 2.2 | 19.4 | 18.3 | 347.4 | 2,346.6 | 639.9 | 1,605.7 | 101.1 |
| **Duluth, MN-WI M.S.A.[4]** | **274,899** | | | | | | | | | |
| Includes Carlton and St. Louis Counties, MN[4] and Douglas County, WI | | | | | | | | | | |
| City of Duluth, MN[4] | 84,071 | | 3 | | 122 | 201 | 4,253 | 632 | 3,431 | 190 |
| Total area actually reporting | 98.9% | | 5 | | 161 | 383 | 9,280 | 1,623 | 7,225 | 432 |
| Estimated total | 100.0% | | 5 | | 162 | 385 | 9,365 | 1,635 | 7,294 | 436 |
| Rate per 100,000 inhabitants | | | 1.8 | | 58.9 | 140.1 | 3,406.7 | 594.8 | 2,653.3 | 158.6 |

[1] The FBI determined that the agency's data were overreported. Consequently, affected data are not included in this table.
[2] Because of changes in the state/local agency's reporting practices, figures are not comparable to previous years' data.
[3] The FBI determined that the agency's data were underreported. Consequently, affected data are not included in this table.
[4] It was determined that the agency did not follow national Uniform Crime Reporting (UCR) Program guidelines for reporting an offense. Consequently, this figure is not included in this table.

## Table 6. Crime, by Metropolitan Statistical Area, 2009—*Continued*

(Number, percent, rate per 100,000 population.)

| Area | Population | Violent crime | Murder and non-negligent man-slaughter | Forcible rape | Robbery | Aggravated assault | Property crime | Burglary | Larceny-theft | Motor vehicle theft |
|---|---|---|---|---|---|---|---|---|---|---|
| **Durham-Chapel Hill, NC M.S.A.** | **498,273** | | | | | | | | | |
| Includes Chatham, Durham, Orange, and Person Counties | | | | | | | | | | |
| City of Durham | 227,492 | 1,591 | 21 | 63 | 710 | 797 | 11,763 | 3,643 | 7,366 | 754 |
| City of Chapel Hill | 53,069 | 130 | 0 | 14 | 48 | 68 | 1,727 | 427 | 1,225 | 75 |
| Total area actually reporting | 100.0% | 2,206 | 29 | 120 | 875 | 1,182 | 19,994 | 6,215 | 12,696 | 1,083 |
| Rate per 100,000 inhabitants | | 442.7 | 5.8 | 24.1 | 175.6 | 237.2 | 4,012.7 | 1,247.3 | 2,548.0 | 217.4 |
| **Eau Claire, WI M.S.A.** | **159,822** | | | | | | | | | |
| Includes Chippewa and Eau Claire Counties | | | | | | | | | | |
| City of Eau Claire | 65,802 | 119 | 0 | 28 | 15 | 76 | 1,717 | 248 | 1,402 | 67 |
| Total area actually reporting | 100.0% | 193 | 1 | 39 | 21 | 132 | 3,249 | 546 | 2,575 | 128 |
| Rate per 100,000 inhabitants | | 120.8 | 0.6 | 24.4 | 13.1 | 82.6 | 2,032.9 | 341.6 | 1,611.2 | 80.1 |
| **El Centro, CA M.S.A.**[3,5] | **165,988** | | | | | | | | | |
| Includes Imperial County[3,5] | | | | | | | | | | |
| City of El Centro | 40,337 | 177 | 1 | 7 | 36 | 133 | 2,257 | 570 | 1,436 | 251 |
| Total area actually reporting | 100.0% | | 3 | 18 | 99 | | | 1,758 | | 940 |
| Rate per 100,000 inhabitants | | | 1.8 | 10.8 | 59.6 | | | 1,059.1 | | 566.3 |
| **Elizabethtown, KY M.S.A.**[1] | **112,967** | | | | | | | | | |
| Includes Hardin and Larue Counties[1] | | | | | | | | | | |
| City of Elizabethtown[1] | 24,321 | 52 | 1 | 5 | 25 | 21 | 1,058 | 152 | 878 | 28 |
| Total area actually reporting | 100.0% | 341 | 2 | 25 | 38 | 276 | 2,054 | 443 | 1,556 | 55 |
| Rate per 100,000 inhabitants | | 301.9 | 1.8 | 22.1 | 33.6 | 244.3 | 1,818.2 | 392.1 | 1,377.4 | 48.7 |
| **Elkhart-Goshen, IN M.S.A.** | **201,289** | | | | | | | | | |
| Includes Elkhart County | | | | | | | | | | |
| City of Elkhart | 52,661 | 159 | 8 | 22 | 118 | 11 | 2,534 | 639 | 1,730 | 165 |
| City of Goshen | 32,952 | 36 | 0 | 13 | 14 | 9 | 1,032 | 186 | 803 | 43 |
| Total area actually reporting | 100.0% | 260 | 8 | 55 | 155 | 42 | 5,343 | 1,340 | 3,657 | 346 |
| Rate per 100,000 inhabitants | | 129.2 | 4.0 | 27.3 | 77.0 | 20.9 | 2,654.4 | 665.7 | 1,816.8 | 171.9 |
| **Elmira, NY M.S.A.** | **87,431** | | | | | | | | | |
| Includes Chemung County | | | | | | | | | | |
| City of Elmira | 29,090 | 93 | 4 | 3 | 25 | 61 | 1,053 | 212 | 823 | 18 |
| Total area actually reporting | 100.0% | 161 | 4 | 13 | 29 | 115 | 1,962 | 384 | 1,533 | 45 |
| Rate per 100,000 inhabitants | | 184.1 | 4.6 | 14.9 | 33.2 | 131.5 | 2,244.1 | 439.2 | 1,753.4 | 51.5 |
| **El Paso, TX M.S.A.** | **749,958** | | | | | | | | | |
| Includes El Paso County | | | | | | | | | | |
| City of El Paso | 618,812 | 2,830 | 12 | 182 | 452 | 2,184 | 18,528 | 1,991 | 14,647 | 1,890 |
| Total area actually reporting | 100.0% | 3,303 | 16 | 231 | 511 | 2,545 | 21,909 | 2,793 | 16,977 | 2,139 |
| Rate per 100,000 inhabitants | | 440.4 | 2.1 | 30.8 | 68.1 | 339.4 | 2,921.4 | 372.4 | 2,263.7 | 285.2 |
| **Erie, PA M.S.A.** | **279,714** | | | | | | | | | |
| Includes Erie County | | | | | | | | | | |
| City of Erie | 103,837 | 472 | 4 | 83 | 121 | 264 | 3,018 | 1,013 | 1,853 | 152 |
| Total area actually reporting | 100.0% | 694 | 10 | 121 | 161 | 402 | 6,663 | 1,738 | 4,705 | 220 |
| Rate per 100,000 inhabitants | | 248.1 | 3.6 | 43.3 | 57.6 | 143.7 | 2,382.1 | 621.3 | 1,682.1 | 78.7 |
| **Eugene-Springfield, OR M.S.A.** | **348,528** | | | | | | | | | |
| Includes Lane County | | | | | | | | | | |
| City of Eugene | 151,383 | 470 | 1 | 73 | 201 | 195 | 8,627 | 1,868 | 5,871 | 888 |
| City of Springfield | 57,653 | 238 | 1 | 10 | 44 | 183 | 2,828 | 497 | 2,026 | 305 |
| Total area actually reporting | 100.0% | 1,057 | 4 | 114 | 271 | 668 | 14,238 | 3,211 | 9,574 | 1,453 |
| Rate per 100,000 inhabitants | | 303.3 | 1.1 | 32.7 | 77.8 | 191.7 | 4,085.2 | 921.3 | 2,747.0 | 416.9 |
| **Evansville, IN-KY M.S.A.**[1] | **351,684** | | | | | | | | | |
| Includes Gibson, Posey, Vanderburgh, and Warrick Counties, IN and Henderson and Webster Counties, KY[1] | | | | | | | | | | |
| City of Evansville, IN | 115,770 | 432 | 3 | 60 | 136 | 233 | 5,376 | 1,110 | 4,038 | 228 |
| Total area actually reporting | 89.4% | 761 | 6 | 96 | 178 | 481 | 8,729 | 1,670 | 6,714 | 345 |
| Estimated total | 100.0% | 827 | 7 | 102 | 195 | 523 | 9,606 | 1,842 | 7,365 | 399 |
| Rate per 100,000 inhabitants | | 235.2 | 2.0 | 29.0 | 55.4 | 148.7 | 2,731.4 | 523.8 | 2,094.2 | 113.5 |

[1] The FBI determined that the agency's data were overreported. Consequently, affected data are not included in this table.
[3] The FBI determined that the agency's data were underreported. Consequently, affected data are not included in this table.
[5] The data collection methodology for the offense of forcible rape used by the Minnesota state UCR Program (with the exception of Minneapolis and St. Paul, MN) does not comply with national UCR Program guidelines. Consequently, their figures for forcible rape and violent crime (of which forcible rape is a part) are not published in this table.

## Table 6. Crime, by Metropolitan Statistical Area, 2009—*Continued*

(Number, percent, rate per 100,000 population.)

| Area | Population | Violent crime | Murder and non-negligent man-slaughter | Forcible rape | Robbery | Aggravated assault | Property crime | Burglary | Larceny-theft | Motor vehicle theft |
|---|---|---|---|---|---|---|---|---|---|---|
| **Fairbanks, AK M.S.A.** | **38,034** | | | | | | | | | |
| Includes Fairbanks North Star Borough | | | | | | | | | | |
| City of Fairbanks | 35,735 | 268 | 0 | 59 | 46 | 163 | 1,395 | 191 | 1,113 | 91 |
| Total area actually reporting | 100.0% | 286 | 0 | 62 | 47 | 177 | 1,595 | 208 | 1,284 | 103 |
| Rate per 100,000 inhabitants | | 752.0 | 0.0 | 163.0 | 123.6 | 465.4 | 4,193.6 | 546.9 | 3,375.9 | 270.8 |
| **Fargo, ND-MN M.S.A.[4]** | **199,348** | | | | | | | | | |
| Includes Clay County, MN[4] and Cass County, ND | | | | | | | | | | |
| City of Fargo, ND | 93,830 | 303 | 2 | 54 | 34 | 213 | 3,187 | 639 | 2,302 | 246 |
| Total area actually reporting | 100.0% | | 2 | | 45 | 291 | 5,111 | 1,012 | 3,762 | 337 |
| Rate per 100,000 inhabitants | | | 1.0 | | 22.6 | 146.0 | 2,563.9 | 507.7 | 1,887.2 | 169.1 |
| **Farmington, NM M.S.A.** | **123,809** | | | | | | | | | |
| Includes San Juan County | | | | | | | | | | |
| City of Farmington | 43,131 | 536 | 2 | 85 | 33 | 416 | 1,709 | 359 | 1,236 | 114 |
| Total area actually reporting | 100.0% | 919 | 3 | 141 | 45 | 730 | 3,032 | 701 | 2,072 | 259 |
| Rate per 100,000 inhabitants | | 742.3 | 2.4 | 113.9 | 36.3 | 589.6 | 2,448.9 | 566.2 | 1,673.5 | 209.2 |
| **Fayetteville, NC M.S.A.** | **358,986** | | | | | | | | | |
| Includes Cumberland and Hoke Counties | | | | | | | | | | |
| City of Fayetteville | 173,995 | 1,268 | 21 | 94 | 491 | 662 | 13,506 | 4,289 | 8,455 | 762 |
| Total area actually reporting | 100.0% | 1,998 | 35 | 123 | 674 | 1,166 | 20,655 | 6,919 | 12,562 | 1,174 |
| Rate per 100,000 inhabitants | | 556.6 | 9.7 | 34.3 | 187.8 | 324.8 | 5,753.7 | 1,927.4 | 3,499.3 | 327.0 |
| **Fayetteville-Springdale-Rogers, AR-MO M.S.A.** | **457,820** | | | | | | | | | |
| Includes Benton, Madison, and Washington Counties, AR and McDonald County, MO | | | | | | | | | | |
| City of Fayetteville, AR | 75,120 | 325 | 2 | 48 | 38 | 237 | 2,908 | 483 | 2,306 | 119 |
| City of Springdale, AR | 70,935 | 288 | 0 | 56 | 25 | 207 | 2,413 | 486 | 1,828 | 99 |
| City of Rogers, AR | 58,992 | 183 | 2 | 52 | 17 | 112 | 2,160 | 399 | 1,684 | 77 |
| City of Bentonville, AR | 37,816 | 44 | 0 | 6 | 4 | 34 | 724 | 89 | 618 | 17 |
| Total area actually reporting | 99.3% | 1,385 | 8 | 244 | 100 | 1,033 | 11,265 | 2,573 | 8,184 | 508 |
| Estimated total | 100.0% | 1,400 | 8 | 245 | 102 | 1,045 | 11,376 | 2,610 | 8,253 | 513 |
| Rate per 100,000 inhabitants | | 305.8 | 1.7 | 53.5 | 22.3 | 228.3 | 2,484.8 | 570.1 | 1,802.7 | 112.1 |
| **Flagstaff, AZ M.S.A.** | **128,458** | | | | | | | | | |
| Includes Coconino County | | | | | | | | | | |
| City of Flagstaff | 61,072 | 282 | 4 | 43 | 53 | 182 | 3,118 | 303 | 2,725 | 90 |
| Total area actually reporting | 94.6% | 409 | 6 | 61 | 57 | 285 | 4,183 | 557 | 3,502 | 124 |
| Estimated total | 100.0% | 425 | 6 | 62 | 61 | 296 | 4,396 | 605 | 3,651 | 140 |
| Rate per 100,000 inhabitants | | 330.8 | 4.7 | 48.3 | 47.5 | 230.4 | 3,422.1 | 471.0 | 2,842.2 | 109.0 |
| **Flint, MI M.S.A.[1]** | **426,176** | | | | | | | | | |
| Includes Genesee County[1] | | | | | | | | | | |
| City of Flint[1] | 111,657 | 2,244 | 36 | 91 | 590 | 1,527 | 6,397 | 3,057 | 2,664 | 676 |
| Total area actually reporting | 99.7% | 3,285 | 44 | 235 | 845 | 2,161 | 16,219 | 5,769 | 9,252 | 1,198 |
| Estimated total | 100.0% | 3,288 | 44 | 235 | 846 | 2,163 | 16,252 | 5,776 | 9,275 | 1,201 |
| Rate per 100,000 inhabitants | | 771.5 | 10.3 | 55.1 | 198.5 | 507.5 | 3,813.4 | 1,355.3 | 2,176.3 | 281.8 |
| **Florence, SC M.S.A.** | **201,707** | | | | | | | | | |
| Includes Darlington and Florence Counties | | | | | | | | | | |
| City of Florence | 31,642 | 370 | 5 | 14 | 92 | 259 | 3,071 | 549 | 2,378 | 144 |
| Total area actually reporting | 100.0% | 1,558 | 20 | 81 | 292 | 1,165 | 10,312 | 2,782 | 6,860 | 670 |
| Rate per 100,000 inhabitants | | 772.4 | 9.9 | 40.2 | 144.8 | 577.6 | 5,112.4 | 1,379.2 | 3,401.0 | 332.2 |
| **Florence-Muscle Shoals, AL M.S.A.** | **144,517** | | | | | | | | | |
| Includes Colbert and Lauderdale Counties | | | | | | | | | | |
| City of Florence | 38,055 | 130 | 3 | 14 | 50 | 63 | 1,637 | 415 | 1,184 | 38 |
| City of Muscle Shoals | 13,125 | 66 | 0 | 4 | 12 | 50 | 541 | 93 | 430 | 18 |
| Total area actually reporting | 100.0% | 432 | 7 | 34 | 90 | 301 | 4,455 | 1,203 | 3,116 | 136 |
| Rate per 100,000 inhabitants | | 298.9 | 4.8 | 23.5 | 62.3 | 208.3 | 3,082.7 | 832.4 | 2,156.1 | 94.1 |
| **Fond du Lac, WI M.S.A.** | **99,634** | | | | | | | | | |
| Includes Fond du Lac County | | | | | | | | | | |
| City of Fond du Lac | 42,001 | 114 | 1 | 22 | 7 | 84 | 1,142 | 99 | 1,010 | 33 |
| Total area actually reporting | 100.0% | 162 | 2 | 29 | 7 | 124 | 1,773 | 235 | 1,486 | 52 |
| Rate per 100,000 inhabitants | | 162.6 | 2.0 | 29.1 | 7.0 | 124.5 | 1,779.5 | 235.9 | 1,491.5 | 52.2 |

[1] The FBI determined that the agency's data were overreported. Consequently, affected data are not included in this table.
[4] It was determined that the agency did not follow national Uniform Crime Reporting (UCR) Program guidelines for reporting an offense. Consequently, this figure is not included in this table.

## Table 6. Crime, by Metropolitan Statistical Area, 2009—*Continued*

(Number, percent, rate per 100,000 population.)

| Area | Population | Violent crime | Murder and non-negligent man-slaughter | Forcible rape | Robbery | Aggravated assault | Property crime | Burglary | Larceny-theft | Motor vehicle theft |
|---|---|---|---|---|---|---|---|---|---|---|
| **Fort Collins-Loveland, CO M.S.A.** | **298,107** | | | | | | | | | |
| Includes Larimer County | | | | | | | | | | |
| City of Fort Collins | 138,487 | 535 | 2 | 87 | 68 | 378 | 4,586 | 752 | 3,604 | 230 |
| City of Loveland | 67,324 | 147 | 4 | 14 | 30 | 99 | 1,985 | 318 | 1,601 | 66 |
| Total area actually reporting | 100.0% | 807 | 6 | 143 | 107 | 551 | 8,266 | 1,356 | 6,513 | 397 |
| Rate per 100,000 inhabitants | | 270.7 | 2.0 | 48.0 | 35.9 | 184.8 | 2,772.8 | 454.9 | 2,184.8 | 133.2 |
| **Fort Smith, AR-OK M.S.A.** | **294,314** | | | | | | | | | |
| Includes Crawford, Franklin, and Sebastian Counties, AR and Le Flore and Sequoyah Counties, OK | | | | | | | | | | |
| City of Fort Smith, AR | 85,175 | 712 | 3 | 62 | 144 | 503 | 4,992 | 1,119 | 3,670 | 203 |
| Total area actually reporting | 89.0% | 1,159 | 9 | 99 | 165 | 886 | 8,680 | 2,241 | 6,072 | 367 |
| Estimated total | 100.0% | 1,270 | 10 | 110 | 170 | 980 | 9,398 | 2,549 | 6,423 | 426 |
| Rate per 100,000 inhabitants | | 431.5 | 3.4 | 37.4 | 57.8 | 333.0 | 3,193.2 | 866.1 | 2,182.4 | 144.7 |
| **Fort Wayne, IN M.S.A.** | **414,144** | | | | | | | | | |
| Includes Allen, Wells, and Whitley Counties | | | | | | | | | | |
| City of Fort Wayne | 251,584 | 876 | 18 | 75 | 485 | 298 | 9,379 | 2,269 | 6,683 | 427 |
| Total area actually reporting | 100.0% | 1,020 | 22 | 98 | 512 | 388 | 11,577 | 2,739 | 8,289 | 549 |
| Rate per 100,000 inhabitants | | 246.3 | 5.3 | 23.7 | 123.6 | 93.7 | 2,795.4 | 661.4 | 2,001.5 | 132.6 |
| **Fresno, CA M.S.A.** | **918,710** | | | | | | | | | |
| Includes Fresno County | | | | | | | | | | |
| City of Fresno | 481,370 | 2,933 | 42 | 86 | 1,085 | 1,720 | 21,030 | 4,423 | 13,359 | 3,248 |
| Total area actually reporting | 100.0% | 4,694 | 69 | 178 | 1,453 | 2,994 | 35,152 | 7,912 | 21,749 | 5,491 |
| Rate per 100,000 inhabitants | | 510.9 | 7.5 | 19.4 | 158.2 | 325.9 | 3,826.2 | 861.2 | 2,367.3 | 597.7 |
| **Gadsden, AL M.S.A.** | **103,760** | | | | | | | | | |
| Includes Etowah County | | | | | | | | | | |
| City of Gadsden | 36,595 | 261 | 2 | 41 | 105 | 113 | 2,563 | 609 | 1,807 | 147 |
| Total area actually reporting | 100.0% | 367 | 3 | 57 | 113 | 194 | 3,734 | 868 | 2,660 | 206 |
| Rate per 100,000 inhabitants | | 353.7 | 2.9 | 54.9 | 108.9 | 187.0 | 3,598.7 | 836.5 | 2,563.6 | 198.5 |
| **Gainesville, FL M.S.A.** | **259,242** | | | | | | | | | |
| Includes Alachua and Gilchrist Counties | | | | | | | | | | |
| City of Gainesville | 115,265 | 1,156 | 3 | 95 | 239 | 819 | 6,384 | 1,487 | 4,457 | 440 |
| Total area actually reporting | 99.7% | 2,048 | 7 | 149 | 376 | 1,516 | 11,071 | 2,971 | 7,391 | 709 |
| Estimated total | 100.0% | 2,052 | 7 | 149 | 377 | 1,519 | 11,105 | 2,979 | 7,415 | 711 |
| Rate per 100,000 inhabitants | | 791.5 | 2.7 | 57.5 | 145.4 | 585.9 | 4,283.6 | 1,149.1 | 2,860.3 | 274.3 |
| **Gainesville, GA M.S.A.** | **189,639** | | | | | | | | | |
| Includes Hall County | | | | | | | | | | |
| City of Gainesville | 36,896 | 125 | 3 | 15 | 33 | 74 | 1,695 | 349 | 1,255 | 91 |
| Total area actually reporting | 100.0% | 342 | 5 | 39 | 68 | 230 | 4,515 | 1,196 | 2,992 | 327 |
| Rate per 100,000 inhabitants | | 180.3 | 2.6 | 20.6 | 35.9 | 121.3 | 2,380.8 | 630.7 | 1,577.7 | 172.4 |
| **Glens Falls, NY M.S.A.** | **129,238** | | | | | | | | | |
| Includes Warren and Washington Counties | | | | | | | | | | |
| City of Glens Falls | 13,828 | 19 | 0 | 0 | 5 | 14 | 425 | 35 | 383 | 7 |
| Total area actually reporting | 100.0% | 137 | 0 | 15 | 11 | 111 | 2,073 | 336 | 1,682 | 55 |
| Rate per 100,000 inhabitants | | 106.0 | 0.0 | 11.6 | 8.5 | 85.9 | 1,604.0 | 260.0 | 1,301.5 | 42.6 |
| **Goldsboro, NC M.S.A.** | **113,890** | | | | | | | | | |
| Includes Wayne County | | | | | | | | | | |
| City of Goldsboro | 37,421 | 323 | 8 | 9 | 92 | 214 | 2,657 | 730 | 1,789 | 138 |
| Total area actually reporting | 97.4% | 504 | 14 | 11 | 129 | 350 | 4,871 | 1,658 | 2,923 | 290 |
| Estimated total | 100.0% | 515 | 14 | 12 | 132 | 357 | 5,001 | 1,688 | 3,018 | 295 |
| Rate per 100,000 inhabitants | | 452.2 | 12.3 | 10.5 | 115.9 | 313.5 | 4,391.1 | 1,482.1 | 2,649.9 | 259.0 |
| **Grand Forks, ND-MN M.S.A.**[4] | **97,848** | | | | | | | | | |
| Includes Polk County, MN[4] and Grand Forks County, ND | | | | | | | | | | |
| City of Grand Forks, ND | 51,553 | 141 | 0 | 29 | 27 | 85 | 1,515 | 261 | 1,185 | 69 |
| Total area actually reporting | 100.0% | | 0 | | 33 | 139 | 2,298 | 438 | 1,750 | 110 |
| Rate per 100,000 inhabitants | | | 0.0 | | 33.7 | 142.1 | 2,348.5 | 447.6 | 1,788.5 | 112.4 |
| **Grand Junction, CO M.S.A.** | **146,602** | | | | | | | | | |
| Includes Mesa County | | | | | | | | | | |
| City of Grand Junction | 50,195 | 230 | 0 | 39 | 49 | 142 | 2,638 | 377 | 2,120 | 141 |
| Total area actually reporting | 97.7% | 431 | 2 | 73 | 68 | 288 | 4,411 | 807 | 3,317 | 287 |
| Estimated total | 100.0% | 440 | 2 | 74 | 70 | 294 | 4,511 | 823 | 3,392 | 296 |
| Rate per 100,000 inhabitants | | 300.1 | 1.4 | 50.5 | 47.7 | 200.5 | 3,077.0 | 561.4 | 2,313.7 | 201.9 |

[4] It was determined that the agency did not follow national Uniform Crime Reporting (UCR) Program guidelines for reporting an offense. Consequently, this figure is not included in this table.

## Table 6. Crime, by Metropolitan Statistical Area, 2009—*Continued*

(Number, percent, rate per 100,000 population.)

| Area | Population | Violent crime | Murder and non-negligent man-slaughter | Forcible rape | Robbery | Aggravated assault | Property crime | Burglary | Larceny-theft | Motor vehicle theft |
|---|---|---|---|---|---|---|---|---|---|---|
| **Grand Rapids-Wyoming, MI M.S.A.[1]** | **777,531** | | | | | | | | | |
| Includes Barry, Ionia, Kent, and Newaygo Counties[1] | | | | | | | | | | |
| City of Grand Rapids[1] | 192,901 | 1,604 | 9 | 78 | 581 | 936 | 8,835 | 2,454 | 6,010 | 371 |
| City of Wyoming[1] | 70,565 | 299 | 1 | 40 | 67 | 191 | 1,658 | 423 | 1,098 | 137 |
| Total area actually reporting | 99.6% | 2,945 | 13 | 350 | 794 | 1,788 | 21,685 | 5,379 | 15,373 | 933 |
| Estimated total | 100.0% | 2,954 | 13 | 351 | 796 | 1,794 | 21,771 | 5,397 | 15,434 | 940 |
| Rate per 100,000 inhabitants | | 379.9 | 1.7 | 45.1 | 102.4 | 230.7 | 2,800.0 | 694.1 | 1,985.0 | 120.9 |
| **Great Falls, MT M.S.A.** | **82,193** | | | | | | | | | |
| Includes Cascade County | | | | | | | | | | |
| City of Great Falls | 59,499 | 183 | 6 | 14 | 40 | 123 | 2,419 | 252 | 2,064 | 103 |
| Total area actually reporting | 100.0% | 230 | 7 | 16 | 41 | 166 | 2,702 | 299 | 2,270 | 133 |
| Rate per 100,000 inhabitants | | 279.8 | 8.5 | 19.5 | 49.9 | 202.0 | 3,287.4 | 363.8 | 2,761.8 | 161.8 |
| **Greeley, CO M.S.A.** | **259,011** | | | | | | | | | |
| Includes Weld County | | | | | | | | | | |
| City of Greeley | 93,070 | 441 | 3 | 40 | 69 | 329 | 3,130 | 585 | 2,373 | 172 |
| Total area actually reporting | 98.0% | 697 | 7 | 71 | 89 | 530 | 5,945 | 1,282 | 4,230 | 433 |
| Estimated total | 100.0% | 711 | 7 | 73 | 92 | 539 | 6,104 | 1,307 | 4,350 | 447 |
| Rate per 100,000 inhabitants | | 274.5 | 2.7 | 28.2 | 35.5 | 208.1 | 2,356.7 | 504.6 | 1,679.5 | 172.6 |
| **Green Bay, WI M.S.A.** | **305,045** | | | | | | | | | |
| Includes Brown, Kewaunee, and Oconto Counties | | | | | | | | | | |
| City of Green Bay | 100,836 | 473 | 1 | 66 | 87 | 319 | 2,742 | 637 | 1,980 | 125 |
| Total area actually reporting | 100.0% | 577 | 5 | 103 | 96 | 373 | 5,921 | 1,233 | 4,436 | 252 |
| Rate per 100,000 inhabitants | | 189.2 | 1.6 | 33.8 | 31.5 | 122.3 | 1,941.0 | 404.2 | 1,454.2 | 82.6 |
| **Greensboro-High Point, NC M.S.A.** | **713,890** | | | | | | | | | |
| Includes Guilford, Randolph, and Rockingham Counties | | | | | | | | | | |
| City of Greensboro | 253,191 | 1,940 | 24 | 76 | 908 | 932 | 15,303 | 4,789 | 9,668 | 846 |
| City of High Point | 101,969 | 667 | 3 | 32 | 269 | 363 | 5,241 | 1,440 | 3,561 | 240 |
| Total area actually reporting | 99.9% | 3,420 | 35 | 151 | 1,377 | 1,857 | 30,796 | 9,444 | 19,783 | 1,569 |
| Estimated total | 100.0% | 3,421 | 35 | 151 | 1,377 | 1,858 | 30,807 | 9,447 | 19,791 | 1,569 |
| Rate per 100,000 inhabitants | | 479.2 | 4.9 | 21.2 | 192.9 | 260.3 | 4,315.4 | 1,323.3 | 2,772.3 | 219.8 |
| **Gulfport-Biloxi, MS M.S.A.** | **233,616** | | | | | | | | | |
| Includes Hancock, Harrison, and Stone Counties | | | | | | | | | | |
| City of Gulfport | 69,926 | 149 | 4 | 18 | 91 | 36 | 3,687 | 990 | 2,547 | 150 |
| City of Biloxi | 45,160 | 252 | 5 | 3 | 127 | 117 | 2,583 | 1,020 | 1,427 | 136 |
| Total area actually reporting | 81.5% | 494 | 11 | 41 | 254 | 188 | 9,339 | 2,688 | 6,201 | 450 |
| Estimated total | 100.0% | 565 | 12 | 53 | 269 | 231 | 10,207 | 2,964 | 6,730 | 513 |
| Rate per 100,000 inhabitants | | 241.8 | 5.1 | 22.7 | 115.1 | 98.9 | 4,369.1 | 1,268.7 | 2,880.8 | 219.6 |
| **Hagerstown-Martinsburg, MD-WV M.S.A.** | **269,769** | | | | | | | | | |
| Includes Washington County, MD and Berkeley and Morgan Counties, WV | | | | | | | | | | |
| City of Hagerstown, MD | 40,062 | 191 | 0 | 3 | 73 | 115 | 1,398 | 239 | 1,041 | 118 |
| City of Martinsburg, WV | 17,275 | 81 | 0 | 4 | 25 | 52 | 1,177 | 127 | 1,009 | 41 |
| Total area actually reporting | 99.7% | 640 | 3 | 50 | 148 | 439 | 6,053 | 1,367 | 4,306 | 380 |
| Estimated total | 100.0% | 641 | 3 | 50 | 148 | 440 | 6,078 | 1,372 | 4,325 | 381 |
| Rate per 100,000 inhabitants | | 237.6 | 1.1 | 18.5 | 54.9 | 163.1 | 2,253.0 | 508.6 | 1,603.2 | 141.2 |
| **Harrisburg-Carlisle, PA M.S.A.** | **534,951** | | | | | | | | | |
| Includes Cumberland, Dauphin, and Perry Counties | | | | | | | | | | |
| City of Harrisburg | 46,961 | 831 | 16 | 50 | 510 | 255 | 2,163 | 474 | 1,513 | 176 |
| City of Carlisle | 18,406 | 42 | 1 | 10 | 17 | 14 | 541 | 76 | 462 | 3 |
| Total area actually reporting | 99.7% | 1,723 | 26 | 168 | 710 | 819 | 11,448 | 1,941 | 9,070 | 437 |
| Estimated total | 100.0% | 1,726 | 26 | 168 | 711 | 821 | 11,474 | 1,945 | 9,091 | 438 |
| Rate per 100,000 inhabitants | | 322.6 | 4.9 | 31.4 | 132.9 | 153.5 | 2,144.9 | 363.6 | 1,699.4 | 81.9 |
| **Harrisonburg, VA M.S.A.** | **120,036** | | | | | | | | | |
| Includes Rockingham County and Harrisonburg City | | | | | | | | | | |
| City of Harrisonburg | 44,597 | 134 | 0 | 10 | 27 | 97 | 1,236 | 187 | 996 | 53 |
| Total area actually reporting | 100.0% | 184 | 2 | 27 | 35 | 120 | 1,823 | 298 | 1,435 | 90 |
| Rate per 100,000 inhabitants | | 153.3 | 1.7 | 22.5 | 29.2 | 100.0 | 1,518.7 | 248.3 | 1,195.5 | 75.0 |

[1] The FBI determined that the agency's data were overreported. Consequently, affected data are not included in this table.

## Table 6. Crime, by Metropolitan Statistical Area, 2009—*Continued*

(Number, percent, rate per 100,000 population.)

| Area | Population | Violent crime | Murder and non-negligent man-slaughter | Forcible rape | Robbery | Aggravated assault | Property crime | Burglary | Larceny-theft | Motor vehicle theft |
|---|---|---|---|---|---|---|---|---|---|---|
| **Hartford-West Hartford-East Hartford, CT M.S.A.** | **1,007,503** | | | | | | | | | |
| Includes Hartford, Middlesex, and Tolland Counties | | | | | | | | | | |
| City of Hartford | 124,049 | 1,603 | 33 | 49 | 600 | 921 | 6,189 | 1,135 | 4,061 | 993 |
| City of West Hartford | 60,430 | 84 | 1 | 6 | 40 | 37 | 1,708 | 292 | 1,323 | 93 |
| City of East Hartford | 48,459 | 180 | 2 | 13 | 78 | 87 | 1,670 | 328 | 1,173 | 169 |
| City of Middletown | 48,299 | 60 | 1 | 0 | 32 | 27 | 1,492 | 214 | 1,186 | 92 |
| Total area actually reporting | 100.0% | 2,965 | 46 | 193 | 1,145 | 1,581 | 27,761 | 5,044 | 20,281 | 2,436 |
| Rate per 100,000 inhabitants | | 294.3 | 4.6 | 19.2 | 113.6 | 156.9 | 2,755.4 | 500.6 | 2,013.0 | 241.8 |
| **Hattiesburg, MS M.S.A.[1,2]** | **142,822** | | | | | | | | | |
| Includes Forrest,[1] Lamar,[2] and Perry Counties | | | | | | | | | | |
| City of Hattiesburg | 52,716 | 136 | 5 | 19 | 66 | 46 | 2,408 | 460 | 1,857 | 91 |
| Total area actually reporting | 91.4% | 243 | 10 | 55 | 81 | 97 | | 895 | | 136 |
| Estimated total | 100.0% | 262 | 10 | 59 | 84 | 109 | | 969 | | 154 |
| Rate per 100,000 inhabitants | | 183.4 | 7.0 | 41.3 | 58.8 | 76.3 | | 678.5 | | 107.8 |
| **Hickory-Lenoir-Morganton, NC M.S.A.** | **365,928** | | | | | | | | | |
| Includes Alexander, Burke, Caldwell, and Catawba Counties | | | | | | | | | | |
| City of Hickory | 41,718 | 338 | 5 | 14 | 118 | 201 | 2,833 | 670 | 2,020 | 143 |
| City of Lenoir | 17,869 | 70 | 2 | 2 | 22 | 44 | 907 | 225 | 626 | 56 |
| City of Morganton | 17,169 | 47 | 0 | 3 | 13 | 31 | 533 | 135 | 378 | 20 |
| Total area actually reporting | 99.6% | 995 | 17 | 58 | 241 | 679 | 12,196 | 4,059 | 7,472 | 665 |
| Estimated total | 100.0% | 999 | 17 | 58 | 242 | 682 | 12,262 | 4,074 | 7,520 | 668 |
| Rate per 100,000 inhabitants | | 273.0 | 4.6 | 15.9 | 66.1 | 186.4 | 3,350.9 | 1,113.3 | 2,055.0 | 182.5 |
| **Hinesville-Fort Stewart, GA M.S.A.** | **69,456** | | | | | | | | | |
| Includes Liberty and Long Counties | | | | | | | | | | |
| City of Hinesville | 30,130 | 191 | 2 | 14 | 67 | 108 | 1,790 | 606 | 1,108 | 76 |
| Total area actually reporting | 100.0% | 325 | 2 | 34 | 95 | 194 | 2,657 | 1,001 | 1,520 | 136 |
| Rate per 100,000 inhabitants | | 467.9 | 2.9 | 49.0 | 136.8 | 279.3 | 3,825.4 | 1,441.2 | 2,188.4 | 195.8 |
| **Holland-Grand Haven, MI M.S.A.[1]** | **261,736** | | | | | | | | | |
| Includes Ottawa County[1] | | | | | | | | | | |
| City of Holland[1] | 26,688 | 96 | 0 | 20 | 15 | 61 | 890 | 177 | 700 | 13 |
| City of Grand Haven[1] | 10,548 | 33 | 0 | 7 | 2 | 24 | 340 | 33 | 300 | 7 |
| Total area actually reporting | 97.3% | 433 | 4 | 122 | 39 | 268 | 4,371 | 982 | 3,271 | 118 |
| Estimated total | 100.0% | 454 | 4 | 124 | 44 | 282 | 4,568 | 1,022 | 3,412 | 134 |
| Rate per 100,000 inhabitants | | 173.5 | 1.5 | 47.4 | 16.8 | 107.7 | 1,745.3 | 390.5 | 1,303.6 | 51.2 |
| **Honolulu, HI M.S.A.** | **907,124** | | | | | | | | | |
| Includes Honolulu County | | | | | | | | | | |
| City of Honolulu | 907,124 | 2,537 | 14 | 243 | 869 | 1,411 | 33,375 | 5,999 | 23,647 | 3,729 |
| Total area actually reporting | 100.0% | 2,537 | 14 | 243 | 869 | 1,411 | 33,375 | 5,999 | 23,647 | 3,729 |
| Rate per 100,000 inhabitants | | 279.7 | 1.5 | 26.8 | 95.8 | 155.5 | 3,679.2 | 661.3 | 2,606.8 | 411.1 |
| **Hot Springs, AR M.S.A.** | **98,925** | | | | | | | | | |
| Includes Garland County | | | | | | | | | | |
| City of Hot Springs | 39,864 | 478 | 5 | 21 | 121 | 331 | 3,723 | 889 | 2,644 | 190 |
| Total area actually reporting | 100.0% | 625 | 10 | 42 | 141 | 432 | 6,206 | 2,119 | 3,702 | 385 |
| Rate per 100,000 inhabitants | | 631.8 | 10.1 | 42.5 | 142.5 | 436.7 | 6,273.4 | 2,142.0 | 3,742.2 | 389.2 |
| **Houma-Bayou Cane-Thibodaux, LA M.S.A.** | **203,180** | | | | | | | | | |
| Includes Lafourche and Terrebonne Parishes | | | | | | | | | | |
| City of Houma | 32,477 | 339 | 10 | 16 | 125 | 188 | 1,387 | 311 | 1,011 | 65 |
| City of Thibodaux | 14,012 | 99 | 0 | 4 | 32 | 63 | 698 | 112 | 566 | 20 |
| Total area actually reporting | 100.0% | 896 | 14 | 55 | 251 | 576 | 6,648 | 1,239 | 5,018 | 391 |
| Rate per 100,000 inhabitants | | 441.0 | 6.9 | 27.1 | 123.5 | 283.5 | 3,272.0 | 609.8 | 2,469.7 | 192.4 |
| **Houston-Sugar Land-Baytown, TX M.S.A.** | **5,858,967** | | | | | | | | | |
| Includes Austin, Brazoria, Chambers, Fort Bend, Galveston, Harris, Liberty, Montgomery, San Jacinto, and Waller Counties | | | | | | | | | | |
| City of Houston | 2,273,771 | 25,593 | 287 | 823 | 11,367 | 13,116 | 120,933 | 29,279 | 77,058 | 14,596 |
| City of Sugar Land | 82,696 | 113 | 0 | 6 | 61 | 46 | 1,854 | 270 | 1,506 | 78 |
| City of Baytown | 70,764 | 330 | 2 | 34 | 114 | 180 | 4,001 | 831 | 2,889 | 281 |
| City of Galveston | 57,040 | 412 | 6 | 64 | 121 | 221 | 3,272 | 954 | 2,069 | 249 |
| City of Conroe | 57,685 | 253 | 1 | 26 | 99 | 127 | 2,616 | 610 | 1,858 | 148 |
| Total area actually reporting | 99.9% | 41,408 | 462 | 1,715 | 16,180 | 23,051 | 241,419 | 60,686 | 155,828 | 24,905 |
| Estimated total | 100.0% | 41,409 | 462 | 1,715 | 16,180 | 23,052 | 241,437 | 60,690 | 155,841 | 24,906 |
| Rate per 100,000 inhabitants | | 706.8 | 7.9 | 29.3 | 276.2 | 393.4 | 4,120.8 | 1,035.8 | 2,659.9 | 425.1 |

[1] The FBI determined that the agency's data were overreported. Consequently, affected data are not included in this table.

[2] Because of changes in the state/local agency's reporting practices, figures are not comparable to previous years' data.

## Table 6. Crime, by Metropolitan Statistical Area, 2009—*Continued*

(Number, percent, rate per 100,000 population.)

| Area | Population | Violent crime | Murder and non-negligent man-slaughter | Forcible rape | Robbery | Aggravated assault | Property crime | Burglary | Larceny-theft | Motor vehicle theft |
|---|---|---|---|---|---|---|---|---|---|---|
| **Huntsville, AL M.S.A.** | **403,661** | | | | | | | | | |
| Includes Limestone and Madison Counties | | | | | | | | | | |
| City of Huntsville | 178,601 | 1,164 | 13 | 89 | 433 | 629 | 9,790 | 2,520 | 6,375 | 895 |
| Total area actually reporting | 100.0% | 1,637 | 21 | 128 | 551 | 937 | 14,572 | 3,841 | 9,537 | 1,194 |
| Rate per 100,000 inhabitants | | 405.5 | 5.2 | 31.7 | 136.5 | 232.1 | 3,610.0 | 951.5 | 2,362.6 | 295.8 |
| **Idaho Falls, ID M.S.A.** | **125,056** | | | | | | | | | |
| Includes Bonneville and Jefferson Counties | | | | | | | | | | |
| City of Idaho Falls | 54,702 | 202 | 2 | 25 | 16 | 159 | 1,624 | 283 | 1,263 | 78 |
| Total area actually reporting | 100.0% | 368 | 2 | 45 | 18 | 303 | 2,691 | 507 | 2,029 | 155 |
| Rate per 100,000 inhabitants | | 294.3 | 1.6 | 36.0 | 14.4 | 242.3 | 2,151.8 | 405.4 | 1,622.5 | 123.9 |
| **Indianapolis-Carmel, IN M.S.A.** | **1,742,101** | | | | | | | | | |
| Includes Boone, Brown, Hamilton, Hancock, Hendricks, Johnson, Marion, Morgan, Putnam, and Shelby Counties | | | | | | | | | | |
| City of Indianapolis | 813,471 | 9,760 | 100 | 460 | 3,929 | 5,271 | 47,419 | 15,217 | 27,717 | 4,485 |
| City of Carmel | 68,424 | 22 | 0 | 2 | 5 | 15 | 897 | 165 | 701 | 31 |
| Total area actually reporting | 84.6% | 10,575 | 105 | 534 | 4,086 | 5,850 | 61,511 | 17,194 | 39,198 | 5,119 |
| Estimated total | 100.0% | 10,938 | 111 | 570 | 4,163 | 6,094 | 66,672 | 18,298 | 42,936 | 5,438 |
| Rate per 100,000 inhabitants | | 627.9 | 6.4 | 32.7 | 239.0 | 349.8 | 3,827.1 | 1,050.3 | 2,464.6 | 312.2 |
| **Iowa City, IA M.S.A.** | **151,283** | | | | | | | | | |
| Includes Johnson and Washington Counties | | | | | | | | | | |
| City of Iowa City | 68,427 | 245 | 1 | 24 | 50 | 170 | 1,549 | 280 | 1,192 | 77 |
| Total area actually reporting | 100.0% | 442 | 2 | 50 | 69 | 321 | 2,901 | 587 | 2,186 | 128 |
| Rate per 100,000 inhabitants | | 292.2 | 1.3 | 33.1 | 45.6 | 212.2 | 1,917.6 | 388.0 | 1,445.0 | 84.6 |
| **Ithaca, NY M.S.A.**[3] | **101,616** | | | | | | | | | |
| Includes Tompkins County[3] | | | | | | | | | | |
| City of Ithaca | 29,862 | 67 | 0 | 2 | 26 | 39 | 1,185 | 140 | 1,021 | 24 |
| Total area actually reporting | 100.0% | | 3 | 12 | 34 | | 2,358 | 362 | 1,962 | 34 |
| Rate per 100,000 inhabitants | | | 3.0 | 11.8 | 33.5 | | 2,320.5 | 356.2 | 1,930.8 | 33.5 |
| **Jackson, MI M.S.A.**[1] | **159,695** | | | | | | | | | |
| Includes Jackson County[1] | | | | | | | | | | |
| City of Jackson[1] | 33,228 | 366 | 2 | 58 | 70 | 236 | 1,769 | 384 | 1,309 | 76 |
| Total area actually reporting | 98.6% | 671 | 8 | 104 | 105 | 454 | 4,092 | 892 | 3,002 | 198 |
| Estimated total | 100.0% | 678 | 8 | 105 | 107 | 458 | 4,154 | 905 | 3,046 | 203 |
| Rate per 100,000 inhabitants | | 424.6 | 5.0 | 65.8 | 67.0 | 286.8 | 2,601.2 | 566.7 | 1,907.4 | 127.1 |
| **Jackson, MS M.S.A.** | **542,259** | | | | | | | | | |
| Includes Copiah, Hinds, Madison, Rankin, and Simpson Counties | | | | | | | | | | |
| City of Jackson | 172,799 | 1,515 | 37 | 124 | 958 | 396 | 13,182 | 4,569 | 6,994 | 1,619 |
| Total area actually reporting | 88.5% | 2,005 | 42 | 200 | 1,066 | 697 | 19,551 | 6,330 | 11,206 | 2,015 |
| Estimated total | 100.0% | 2,120 | 44 | 218 | 1,092 | 766 | 21,030 | 6,764 | 12,157 | 2,109 |
| Rate per 100,000 inhabitants | | 391.0 | 8.1 | 40.2 | 201.4 | 141.3 | 3,878.2 | 1,247.4 | 2,241.9 | 388.9 |
| **Jackson, TN M.S.A.** | **113,615** | | | | | | | | | |
| Includes Chester and Madison Counties | | | | | | | | | | |
| City of Jackson | 63,530 | 606 | 14 | 24 | 184 | 384 | 4,413 | 1,123 | 2,994 | 296 |
| Total area actually reporting | 100.0% | 813 | 15 | 35 | 194 | 569 | 5,693 | 1,509 | 3,798 | 386 |
| Rate per 100,000 inhabitants | | 715.6 | 13.2 | 30.8 | 170.8 | 500.8 | 5,010.8 | 1,328.2 | 3,342.9 | 339.7 |
| **Jacksonville, FL M.S.A.** | **1,324,985** | | | | | | | | | |
| Includes Baker, Clay, Duval, Nassau, and St. Johns Counties | | | | | | | | | | |
| City of Jacksonville | 810,064 | 6,772 | 99 | 218 | 2,359 | 4,096 | 41,781 | 11,306 | 27,754 | 2,721 |
| Total area actually reporting | 100.0% | 9,218 | 120 | 331 | 2,729 | 6,038 | 57,086 | 14,747 | 38,889 | 3,450 |
| Rate per 100,000 inhabitants | | 695.7 | 9.1 | 25.0 | 206.0 | 455.7 | 4,308.4 | 1,113.0 | 2,935.1 | 260.4 |
| **Jacksonville, NC M.S.A.** | **168,113** | | | | | | | | | |
| Includes Onslow County | | | | | | | | | | |
| City of Jacksonville | 77,508 | 241 | 8 | 38 | 50 | 145 | 2,598 | 618 | 1,869 | 111 |
| Total area actually reporting | 100.0% | 561 | 11 | 96 | 99 | 355 | 6,079 | 1,983 | 3,849 | 247 |
| Rate per 100,000 inhabitants | | 333.7 | 6.5 | 57.1 | 58.9 | 211.2 | 3,616.0 | 1,179.6 | 2,289.5 | 146.9 |

[1] The FBI determined that the agency's data were overreported. Consequently, affected data are not included in this table.

## Table 6. Crime, by Metropolitan Statistical Area, 2009—*Continued*

(Number, percent, rate per 100,000 population.)

| Area | Population | Violent crime | Murder and non-negligent man-slaughter | Forcible rape | Robbery | Aggravated assault | Property crime | Burglary | Larceny-theft | Motor vehicle theft |
|---|---|---|---|---|---|---|---|---|---|---|
| **Janesville, WI M.S.A.** | **161,011** | | | | | | | | | |
| Includes Rock County | | | | | | | | | | |
| City of Janesville | 62,761 | 153 | 1 | 18 | 40 | 94 | 2,245 | 332 | 1,839 | 74 |
| Total area actually reporting | 100.0% | 398 | 6 | 40 | 108 | 244 | 4,606 | 862 | 3,564 | 180 |
| Rate per 100,000 inhabitants | | 247.2 | 3.7 | 24.8 | 67.1 | 151.5 | 2,860.7 | 535.4 | 2,213.5 | 111.8 |
| **Jefferson City, MO M.S.A.** | **147,055** | | | | | | | | | |
| Includes Callaway, Cole, Moniteau, and Osage Counties | | | | | | | | | | |
| City of Jefferson City | 40,829 | 237 | 2 | 5 | 41 | 189 | 1,409 | 218 | 1,157 | 34 |
| Total area actually reporting | 100.0% | 462 | 5 | 30 | 65 | 362 | 3,250 | 667 | 2,461 | 122 |
| Rate per 100,000 inhabitants | | 314.2 | 3.4 | 20.4 | 44.2 | 246.2 | 2,210.1 | 453.6 | 1,673.5 | 83.0 |
| **Johnson City, TN M.S.A.** | **198,071** | | | | | | | | | |
| Includes Carter, Unicoi, and Washington Counties | | | | | | | | | | |
| City of Johnson City | 62,689 | 278 | 7 | 15 | 62 | 194 | 2,656 | 515 | 2,036 | 105 |
| Total area actually reporting | 100.0% | 679 | 11 | 40 | 89 | 539 | 5,551 | 1,443 | 3,856 | 252 |
| Rate per 100,000 inhabitants | | 342.8 | 5.6 | 20.2 | 44.9 | 272.1 | 2,802.5 | 728.5 | 1,946.8 | 127.2 |
| **Jonesboro, AR M.S.A.** | **118,932** | | | | | | | | | |
| Includes Craighead and Poinsett Counties | | | | | | | | | | |
| City of Jonesboro | 64,944 | 296 | 1 | 27 | 74 | 194 | 3,097 | 1,221 | 1,772 | 104 |
| Total area actually reporting | 98.8% | 458 | 3 | 47 | 82 | 326 | 4,519 | 1,808 | 2,569 | 142 |
| Estimated total | 100.0% | 465 | 3 | 48 | 83 | 331 | 4,569 | 1,825 | 2,600 | 144 |
| Rate per 100,000 inhabitants | | 391.0 | 2.5 | 40.4 | 69.8 | 278.3 | 3,841.7 | 1,534.5 | 2,186.1 | 121.1 |
| **Kalamazoo-Portage, MI M.S.A.**[1] | **323,342** | | | | | | | | | |
| Includes Kalamazoo and Van Buren Counties[1] | | | | | | | | | | |
| City of Kalamazoo[1] | 71,664 | 702 | 2 | 71 | 204 | 425 | 4,326 | 1,430 | 2,632 | 264 |
| City of Portage[1] | 46,269 | 140 | 2 | 24 | 24 | 90 | 1,953 | 248 | 1,653 | 52 |
| Total area actually reporting | 99.0% | 1,407 | 12 | 200 | 294 | 901 | 11,370 | 3,104 | 7,733 | 533 |
| Estimated total | 100.0% | 1,417 | 12 | 201 | 296 | 908 | 11,462 | 3,123 | 7,799 | 540 |
| Rate per 100,000 inhabitants | | 438.2 | 3.7 | 62.2 | 91.5 | 280.8 | 3,544.9 | 965.9 | 2,412.0 | 167.0 |
| **Kansas City, MO-KS M.S.A.**[5] | **2,060,705** | | | | | | | | | |
| Includes Franklin, Johnson, Leavenworth, Linn, Miami, and Wyandotte Counties, KS and Bates, Caldwell, Cass,[5] Clay, Clinton, Jackson, Lafayette, Platte, and Ray Counties, MO | | | | | | | | | | |
| City of Kansas City, MO | 484,684 | 6,303 | 100 | 276 | 1,970 | 3,957 | 26,695 | 7,231 | 15,937 | 3,527 |
| City of Overland Park, KS | 173,688 | 308 | 3 | 28 | 51 | 226 | 4,507 | 534 | 3,628 | 345 |
| City of Kansas City, KS | 142,102 | 940 | 35 | 80 | 318 | 507 | 7,742 | 1,918 | 4,744 | 1,080 |
| Total area actually reporting | 99.0% | 10,983 | 162 | 696 | 2,990 | 7,135 | | | 48,224 | 7,482 |
| Estimated total | 100.0% | 11,044 | 163 | 700 | 3,004 | 7,177 | | | 48,714 | 7,527 |
| Rate per 100,000 inhabitants | | 535.9 | 7.9 | 34.0 | 145.8 | 348.3 | | | 2,363.9 | 365.3 |
| **Kennewick-Pasco-Richland, WA M.S.A.** | **242,824** | | | | | | | | | |
| Includes Benton and Franklin Counties | | | | | | | | | | |
| City of Kennewick | 64,009 | 244 | 0 | 37 | 33 | 174 | 2,312 | 352 | 1,812 | 148 |
| City of Pasco | 58,316 | 218 | 1 | 29 | 45 | 143 | 1,561 | 315 | 1,079 | 167 |
| City of Richland | 47,040 | 92 | 0 | 22 | 12 | 58 | 1,095 | 160 | 873 | 62 |
| Total area actually reporting | 100.0% | 659 | 1 | 108 | 100 | 450 | 6,012 | 1,134 | 4,429 | 449 |
| Rate per 100,000 inhabitants | | 271.4 | 0.4 | 44.5 | 41.2 | 185.3 | 2,475.9 | 467.0 | 1,824.0 | 184.9 |
| **Killeen-Temple-Fort Hood, TX M.S.A.** | **385,136** | | | | | | | | | |
| Includes Bell, Coryell, and Lampasas Counties | | | | | | | | | | |
| City of Killeen | 120,670 | 750 | 5 | 69 | 179 | 497 | 5,513 | 1,735 | 3,566 | 212 |
| City of Temple | 60,243 | 178 | 3 | 22 | 66 | 87 | 2,219 | 507 | 1,623 | 89 |
| Total area actually reporting | 100.0% | 1,308 | 13 | 161 | 306 | 828 | 12,103 | 3,441 | 8,230 | 432 |
| Rate per 100,000 inhabitants | | 339.6 | 3.4 | 41.8 | 79.5 | 215.0 | 3,142.5 | 893.5 | 2,136.9 | 112.2 |
| **Kingsport-Bristol-Bristol, TN-VA M.S.A.** | **306,401** | | | | | | | | | |
| Includes Hawkins and Sullivan Counties, TN and Scott and Washington Counties and Bristol City, VA | | | | | | | | | | |
| City of Kingsport, TN | 44,402 | 400 | 4 | 25 | 56 | 315 | 2,896 | 474 | 2,328 | 94 |
| City of Bristol, TN | 25,859 | 104 | 0 | 15 | 13 | 76 | 1,215 | 188 | 960 | 67 |
| City of Bristol, VA | 17,502 | 54 | 0 | 5 | 11 | 38 | 627 | 108 | 492 | 27 |
| Total area actually reporting | 100.0% | 1,158 | 10 | 96 | 128 | 924 | 10,384 | 2,624 | 7,299 | 461 |
| Rate per 100,000 inhabitants | | 377.9 | 3.3 | 31.3 | 41.8 | 301.6 | 3,389.0 | 856.4 | 2,382.2 | 150.5 |

[1] The FBI determined that the agency's data were overreported. Consequently, affected data are not included in this table.

[5] The data collection methodology for the offense of forcible rape used by the Minnesota state UCR Program (with the exception of Minneapolis and St. Paul, MN) does not comply with national UCR Program guidelines. Consequently, their figures for forcible rape and violent crime (of which forcible rape is a part) are not published in this table.

## Table 6. Crime, by Metropolitan Statistical Area, 2009—*Continued*

(Number, percent, rate per 100,000 population.)

| Area | Population | Violent crime | Murder and non-negligent man-slaughter | Forcible rape | Robbery | Aggravated assault | Property crime | Burglary | Larceny-theft | Motor vehicle theft |
|---|---|---|---|---|---|---|---|---|---|---|
| **Kingston, NY M.S.A.** | **182,041** | | | | | | | | | |
| Includes Ulster County | | | | | | | | | | |
| City of Kingston | 22,333 | 97 | 0 | 2 | 69 | 26 | 662 | 122 | 510 | 30 |
| Total area actually reporting | 100.0% | 445 | 1 | 27 | 98 | 319 | 3,440 | 705 | 2,618 | 117 |
| Rate per 100,000 inhabitants | | 244.5 | 0.5 | 14.8 | 53.8 | 175.2 | 1,889.7 | 387.3 | 1,438.1 | 64.3 |
| **Knoxville, TN M.S.A.** | **702,038** | | | | | | | | | |
| Includes Anderson, Blount, Knox, Loudon, and Union Counties | | | | | | | | | | |
| City of Knoxville | 185,850 | 1,966 | 22 | 147 | 660 | 1,137 | 11,821 | 2,589 | 8,553 | 679 |
| Total area actually reporting | 100.0% | 3,471 | 31 | 238 | 929 | 2,273 | 24,783 | 6,724 | 16,623 | 1,436 |
| Rate per 100,000 inhabitants | | 494.4 | 4.4 | 33.9 | 132.3 | 323.8 | 3,530.2 | 957.8 | 2,367.8 | 204.5 |
| **Kokomo, IN M.S.A.** | **99,224** | | | | | | | | | |
| Includes Howard and Tipton Counties | | | | | | | | | | |
| City of Kokomo | 45,562 | 139 | 1 | 19 | 41 | 78 | 2,500 | 482 | 1,955 | 63 |
| Total area actually reporting | 100.0% | 199 | 1 | 23 | 43 | 132 | 3,314 | 753 | 2,466 | 95 |
| Rate per 100,000 inhabitants | | 200.6 | 1.0 | 23.2 | 43.3 | 133.0 | 3,339.9 | 758.9 | 2,485.3 | 95.7 |
| **La Crosse, WI-MN M.S.A.**[4] | **132,407** | | | | | | | | | |
| Includes Houston County, MN[4] and La Crosse County, WI | | | | | | | | | | |
| City of La Crosse, WI | 50,791 | 189 | 1 | 24 | 31 | 133 | 1,837 | 349 | 1,412 | 76 |
| Total area actually reporting | 97.0% | | 1 | | 36 | 185 | 3,244 | 575 | 2,557 | 112 |
| Estimated total | 100.0% | | 1 | | 38 | 188 | 3,362 | 592 | 2,653 | 117 |
| Rate per 100,000 inhabitants | | | 0.8 | | 28.7 | 142.0 | 2,539.1 | 447.1 | 2,003.7 | 88.4 |
| **Lafayette, IN M.S.A.** | **194,848** | | | | | | | | | |
| Includes Benton, Carroll, and Tippecanoe Counties | | | | | | | | | | |
| City of Lafayette | 64,370 | 341 | 0 | 24 | 66 | 251 | 3,121 | 645 | 2,285 | 191 |
| Total area actually reporting | 96.6% | 465 | 0 | 44 | 86 | 335 | 5,448 | 1,059 | 4,095 | 294 |
| Estimated total | 100.0% | 471 | 0 | 45 | 87 | 339 | 5,536 | 1,083 | 4,154 | 299 |
| Rate per 100,000 inhabitants | | 241.7 | 0.0 | 23.1 | 44.7 | 174.0 | 2,841.2 | 555.8 | 2,131.9 | 153.5 |
| **Lafayette, LA M.S.A.** | **263,042** | | | | | | | | | |
| Includes Lafayette and St. Martin Parishes | | | | | | | | | | |
| City of Lafayette | 113,868 | 1,115 | 7 | 46 | 286 | 776 | 7,451 | 1,407 | 5,612 | 432 |
| Total area actually reporting | 90.6% | 1,847 | 13 | 83 | 370 | 1,381 | 10,774 | 2,179 | 8,011 | 584 |
| Estimated total | 100.0% | 2,020 | 14 | 89 | 391 | 1,526 | 11,979 | 2,416 | 8,933 | 630 |
| Rate per 100,000 inhabitants | | 767.9 | 5.3 | 33.8 | 148.6 | 580.1 | 4,554.0 | 918.5 | 3,396.0 | 239.5 |
| **Lake Charles, LA M.S.A.** | **194,066** | | | | | | | | | |
| Includes Calcasieu and Cameron Parishes | | | | | | | | | | |
| City of Lake Charles | 70,975 | 623 | 10 | 46 | 199 | 368 | 3,446 | 2,158 | 1,081 | 207 |
| Total area actually reporting | 100.0% | 1,452 | 19 | 132 | 271 | 1,030 | 9,073 | 3,960 | 4,537 | 576 |
| Rate per 100,000 inhabitants | | 748.2 | 9.8 | 68.0 | 139.6 | 530.7 | 4,675.2 | 2,040.5 | 2,337.9 | 296.8 |
| **Lake Havasu City-Kingman, AZ M.S.A.** | **199,041** | | | | | | | | | |
| Includes Mohave County | | | | | | | | | | |
| City of Lake Havasu City | 58,406 | 106 | 3 | 19 | 12 | 72 | 1,362 | 323 | 955 | 84 |
| City of Kingman | 28,700 | 90 | 3 | 10 | 12 | 65 | 1,799 | 347 | 1,348 | 104 |
| Total area actually reporting | 100.0% | 456 | 8 | 34 | 69 | 345 | 6,747 | 1,667 | 4,641 | 439 |
| Rate per 100,000 inhabitants | | 229.1 | 4.0 | 17.1 | 34.7 | 173.3 | 3,389.8 | 837.5 | 2,331.7 | 220.6 |
| **Lakeland-Winter Haven, FL M.S.A.** | **587,062** | | | | | | | | | |
| Includes Polk County | | | | | | | | | | |
| City of Lakeland | 94,322 | 487 | 5 | 33 | 169 | 280 | 5,030 | 1,247 | 3,515 | 268 |
| City of Winter Haven | 34,103 | 289 | 3 | 27 | 92 | 167 | 1,966 | 475 | 1,388 | 103 |
| Total area actually reporting | 98.9% | 2,698 | 25 | 184 | 593 | 1,896 | 21,608 | 6,781 | 13,720 | 1,107 |
| Estimated total | 100.0% | 2,734 | 25 | 186 | 604 | 1,919 | 21,882 | 6,842 | 13,914 | 1,126 |
| Rate per 100,000 inhabitants | | 465.7 | 4.3 | 31.7 | 102.9 | 326.9 | 3,727.4 | 1,165.5 | 2,370.1 | 191.8 |
| **Lancaster, PA M.S.A.** | **507,174** | | | | | | | | | |
| Includes Lancaster County | | | | | | | | | | |
| City of Lancaster | 54,441 | 461 | 9 | 30 | 241 | 181 | 2,858 | 550 | 2,154 | 154 |
| Total area actually reporting | 100.0% | 842 | 12 | 91 | 348 | 391 | 9,932 | 1,726 | 7,773 | 433 |
| Rate per 100,000 inhabitants | | 166.0 | 2.4 | 17.9 | 68.6 | 77.1 | 1,958.3 | 340.3 | 1,532.6 | 85.4 |

[4] It was determined that the agency did not follow national Uniform Crime Reporting (UCR) Program guidelines for reporting an offense. Consequently, this figure is not included in this table.

## Table 6. Crime, by Metropolitan Statistical Area, 2009—*Continued*

(Number, percent, rate per 100,000 population.)

| Area | Population | Violent crime | Murder and non-negligent man-slaughter | Forcible rape | Robbery | Aggravated assault | Property crime | Burglary | Larceny-theft | Motor vehicle theft |
|---|---|---|---|---|---|---|---|---|---|---|
| **Lansing-East Lansing, MI M.S.A.[1]** | **452,842** | | | | | | | | | |
| Includes Clinton, Eaton, and Ingham Counties[1] | | | | | | | | | | |
| City of Lansing[1] | 113,392 | 1,200 | 11 | 89 | 255 | 845 | 3,882 | 1,340 | 2,341 | 201 |
| City of East Lansing[1] | 45,779 | 160 | 0 | 18 | 31 | 111 | 1,099 | 272 | 798 | 29 |
| Total area actually reporting | 97.6% | 1,815 | 12 | 213 | 356 | 1,234 | 11,582 | 2,861 | 8,279 | 442 |
| Estimated total | 100.0% | 1,849 | 12 | 217 | 364 | 1,256 | 11,892 | 2,924 | 8,501 | 467 |
| Rate per 100,000 inhabitants | | 408.3 | 2.6 | 47.9 | 80.4 | 277.4 | 2,626.1 | 645.7 | 1,877.3 | 103.1 |
| **Laredo, TX M.S.A.** | **242,446** | | | | | | | | | |
| Includes Webb County | | | | | | | | | | |
| City of Laredo | 226,944 | 1,294 | 17 | 73 | 309 | 895 | 13,725 | 2,164 | 10,077 | 1,484 |
| Total area actually reporting | 100.0% | 1,395 | 17 | 77 | 310 | 991 | 14,116 | 2,282 | 10,310 | 1,524 |
| Rate per 100,000 inhabitants | | 575.4 | 7.0 | 31.8 | 127.9 | 408.8 | 5,822.3 | 941.2 | 4,252.5 | 628.6 |
| **Las Cruces, NM M.S.A.** | **205,347** | | | | | | | | | |
| Includes Dona Ana County | | | | | | | | | | |
| City of Las Cruces | 94,024 | 464 | 4 | 23 | 96 | 341 | 4,591 | 964 | 3,387 | 240 |
| Total area actually reporting | 98.9% | 831 | 7 | 66 | 113 | 645 | 6,584 | 1,561 | 4,623 | 400 |
| Estimated total | 100.0% | 843 | 7 | 67 | 114 | 655 | 6,660 | 1,579 | 4,675 | 406 |
| Rate per 100,000 inhabitants | | 410.5 | 3.4 | 32.6 | 55.5 | 319.0 | 3,243.3 | 768.9 | 2,276.6 | 197.7 |
| **Las Vegas-Paradise, NV M.S.A.** | **1,903,935** | | | | | | | | | |
| Includes Clark County | | | | | | | | | | |
| City of Las Vegas Metropolitan Police Department | 1,377,282 | 13,039 | 111 | 698 | 4,495 | 7,735 | 47,668 | 13,512 | 25,229 | 8,927 |
| Total area actually reporting | 100.0% | 15,439 | 133 | 810 | 5,399 | 9,097 | 61,525 | 17,163 | 33,570 | 10,792 |
| Rate per 100,000 inhabitants | | 810.9 | 7.0 | 42.5 | 283.6 | 477.8 | 3,231.5 | 901.4 | 1,763.2 | 566.8 |
| **Lawrence, KS M.S.A.** | **116,602** | | | | | | | | | |
| Includes Douglas County | | | | | | | | | | |
| City of Lawrence | 91,703 | 424 | 0 | 57 | 76 | 291 | 4,390 | 683 | 3,551 | 156 |
| Total area actually reporting | 100.0% | 485 | 0 | 66 | 87 | 332 | 5,081 | 845 | 4,064 | 172 |
| Rate per 100,000 inhabitants | | 415.9 | 0.0 | 56.6 | 74.6 | 284.7 | 4,357.6 | 724.7 | 3,485.4 | 147.5 |
| **Lawton, OK M.S.A.[1]** | **112,142** | | | | | | | | | |
| Includes Comanche County[1] | | | | | | | | | | |
| City of Lawton | 89,835 | 1,098 | 9 | 81 | 181 | 827 | 4,922 | 1,448 | 3,240 | 234 |
| Total area actually reporting | 100.0% | 1,142 | 9 | 86 | 182 | 865 | 5,322 | 1,602 | 3,441 | 279 |
| Rate per 100,000 inhabitants | | 1,018.4 | 8.0 | 76.7 | 162.3 | 771.3 | 4,745.8 | 1,428.5 | 3,068.4 | 248.8 |
| **Lebanon, PA M.S.A.** | **130,248** | | | | | | | | | |
| Includes Lebanon County | | | | | | | | | | |
| City of Lebanon | 24,061 | 95 | 2 | 7 | 36 | 50 | 726 | 132 | 556 | 38 |
| Total area actually reporting | 100.0% | 221 | 8 | 15 | 43 | 155 | 2,198 | 422 | 1,701 | 75 |
| Rate per 100,000 inhabitants | | 169.7 | 6.1 | 11.5 | 33.0 | 119.0 | 1,687.5 | 324.0 | 1,306.0 | 57.6 |
| **Lewiston, ID-WA M.S.A.** | **60,637** | | | | | | | | | |
| Includes Nez Perce County, ID and Asotin County, WA | | | | | | | | | | |
| City of Lewiston, ID | 31,864 | 46 | 1 | 16 | 5 | 24 | 1,192 | 216 | 917 | 59 |
| Total area actually reporting | 100.0% | 97 | 1 | 19 | 12 | 65 | 1,833 | 332 | 1,406 | 95 |
| Rate per 100,000 inhabitants | | 160.0 | 1.6 | 31.3 | 19.8 | 107.2 | 3,022.9 | 547.5 | 2,318.7 | 156.7 |
| **Lewiston-Auburn, ME M.S.A.** | **107,004** | | | | | | | | | |
| Includes Androscoggin County | | | | | | | | | | |
| City of Lewiston | 35,074 | 93 | 0 | 21 | 38 | 34 | 1,106 | 216 | 865 | 25 |
| City of Auburn | 23,176 | 33 | 0 | 7 | 13 | 13 | 849 | 134 | 694 | 21 |
| Total area actually reporting | 100.0% | 162 | 0 | 37 | 58 | 67 | 2,502 | 493 | 1,936 | 73 |
| Rate per 100,000 inhabitants | | 151.4 | 0.0 | 34.6 | 54.2 | 62.6 | 2,338.2 | 460.7 | 1,809.3 | 68.2 |
| **Lexington-Fayette, KY M.S.A.[1]** | **470,843** | | | | | | | | | |
| Includes Bourbon, Clark, Fayette, Jessamine, Scott, and Woodford Counties[1] | | | | | | | | | | |
| City of Lexington[1] | 296,406 | 1,760 | 13 | 107 | 578 | 1,062 | 10,124 | 2,427 | 7,154 | 543 |
| Total area actually reporting | 99.7% | 2,068 | 14 | 141 | 656 | 1,257 | 15,920 | 3,632 | 11,544 | 744 |
| Estimated total | 100.0% | 2,073 | 14 | 142 | 658 | 1,259 | 15,971 | 3,643 | 11,582 | 746 |
| Rate per 100,000 inhabitants | | 440.3 | 3.0 | 30.2 | 139.7 | 267.4 | 3,392.0 | 773.7 | 2,459.8 | 158.4 |
| **Lima, OH M.S.A.** | **105,110** | | | | | | | | | |
| Includes Allen County | | | | | | | | | | |
| City of Lima | 37,437 | 469 | 5 | 61 | 144 | 259 | 2,526 | 883 | 1,484 | 159 |
| Total area actually reporting | 91.2% | 543 | 6 | 73 | 161 | 303 | 4,246 | 1,333 | 2,677 | 236 |
| Estimated total | 100.0% | 558 | 6 | 75 | 167 | 310 | 4,506 | 1,385 | 2,875 | 246 |
| Rate per 100,000 inhabitants | | 530.9 | 5.7 | 71.4 | 158.9 | 294.9 | 4,286.9 | 1,317.7 | 2,735.2 | 234.0 |

[1] The FBI determined that the agency's data were overreported. Consequently, affected data are not included in this table.

## Table 6. Crime, by Metropolitan Statistical Area, 2009—*Continued*

(Number, percent, rate per 100,000 population.)

| Area | Population | Violent crime | Murder and non-negligent man-slaughter | Forcible rape | Robbery | Aggravated assault | Property crime | Burglary | Larceny-theft | Motor vehicle theft |
|---|---|---|---|---|---|---|---|---|---|---|
| **Lincoln, NE M.S.A.** | **299,461** | | | | | | | | | |
| Includes Lancaster and Seward Counties | | | | | | | | | | |
| City of Lincoln | 254,438 | 4,730 | 126 | 197 | 838 | 3,569 | 10,007 | 1,618 | 8,095 | 294 |
| Total area actually reporting | 100.0% | 1,200 | 4 | 137 | 199 | 860 | 10,645 | 1,739 | 8,594 | 312 |
| Rate per 100,000 inhabitants | | 400.7 | 1.3 | 45.7 | 66.5 | 287.2 | 3,554.7 | 580.7 | 2,869.8 | 104.2 |
| **Little Rock-North Little Rock-Conway, AR M.S.A.[1]** | **685,389** | | | | | | | | | |
| Includes Faulkner, Grant, Lonoke, Perry, Pulaski, and Saline Counties | | | | | | | | | | |
| City of Little Rock[1] | 190,205 | 2,795 | 32 | 171 | 799 | 1,793 | 15,828 | 4,412 | 10,253 | 1,163 |
| City of North Little Rock | 59,320 | 788 | 11 | 20 | 242 | 515 | 6,000 | 1,629 | 4,009 | 362 |
| City of Conway | 59,343 | 269 | 2 | 28 | 57 | 182 | 2,575 | 444 | 1,999 | 132 |
| Total area actually reporting | 91.6% | 5,208 | 49 | 344 | 1,229 | 3,586 | 34,903 | 9,831 | 22,787 | 2,285 |
| Estimated total | 100.0% | 5,410 | 51 | 365 | 1,240 | 3,754 | 36,186 | 10,384 | 23,413 | 2,389 |
| Rate per 100,000 inhabitants | | 789.3 | 7.4 | 53.3 | 180.9 | 547.7 | 5,279.6 | 1,515.1 | 3,416.0 | 348.6 |
| **Logan, UT-ID M.S.A.** | **127,116** | | | | | | | | | |
| Includes Franklin County, ID and Cache County, UT | | | | | | | | | | |
| City of Logan, UT | 49,105 | 45 | 0 | 11 | 1 | 33 | 770 | 137 | 602 | 31 |
| Total area actually reporting | 100.0% | 98 | 0 | 30 | 2 | 66 | 1,924 | 314 | 1,537 | 73 |
| Rate per 100,000 inhabitants | | 77.1 | 0.0 | 23.6 | 1.6 | 51.9 | 1,513.6 | 247.0 | 1,209.1 | 57.4 |
| **Longview, TX M.S.A.** | **206,197** | | | | | | | | | |
| Includes Gregg, Rusk, and Upshur Counties | | | | | | | | | | |
| City of Longview | 75,890 | 692 | 11 | 27 | 181 | 473 | 5,372 | 1,189 | 3,754 | 429 |
| Total area actually reporting | 99.4% | 1,153 | 17 | 85 | 251 | 800 | 9,590 | 2,298 | 6,457 | 835 |
| Estimated total | 100.0% | 1,156 | 17 | 85 | 252 | 802 | 9,631 | 2,307 | 6,486 | 838 |
| Rate per 100,000 inhabitants | | 560.6 | 8.2 | 41.2 | 122.2 | 388.9 | 4,670.8 | 1,118.8 | 3,145.5 | 406.4 |
| **Longview, WA M.S.A.** | **102,816** | | | | | | | | | |
| Includes Cowlitz County | | | | | | | | | | |
| City of Longview | 36,778 | 114 | 1 | 31 | 29 | 53 | 2,040 | 385 | 1,438 | 217 |
| Total area actually reporting | 100.0% | 218 | 1 | 56 | 40 | 121 | 3,893 | 818 | 2,686 | 389 |
| Rate per 100,000 inhabitants | | 212.0 | 1.0 | 54.5 | 38.9 | 117.7 | 3,786.4 | 795.6 | 2,612.4 | 378.3 |
| **Los Angeles-Long Beach-Santa Ana, CA M.S.A.** | **12,881,669** | | | | | | | | | |
| Includes the Metropolitan Divisions of Los Angeles-Long Beach-Glendale and Santa Ana-Anaheim-Irvine | | | | | | | | | | |
| City of Los Angeles | 3,848,776 | 22,250 | 312 | 841 | 11,106 | 9,991 | 85,251 | 16,550 | 51,742 | 16,959 |
| City of Long Beach | 463,969 | 3,161 | 40 | 131 | 1,381 | 1,609 | 12,643 | 3,116 | 7,166 | 2,361 |
| City of Santa Ana | 339,196 | 1,726 | 25 | 77 | 869 | 755 | 6,798 | 1,160 | 4,165 | 1,473 |
| City of Anaheim | 335,970 | 1,184 | 9 | 72 | 504 | 599 | 7,993 | 1,457 | 5,591 | 945 |
| City of Irvine | 215,673 | 153 | 3 | 28 | 55 | 67 | 2,996 | 481 | 2,365 | 150 |
| City of Glendale | 197,384 | 302 | 3 | 15 | 126 | 158 | 3,755 | 635 | 2,723 | 397 |
| City of Pomona | 153,217 | 968 | 17 | 46 | 344 | 561 | 4,134 | 854 | 2,273 | 1,007 |
| City of Pasadena | 144,063 | 483 | 5 | 25 | 182 | 271 | 4,158 | 824 | 3,023 | 311 |
| City of Torrance | 141,109 | 259 | 1 | 25 | 139 | 94 | 2,874 | 442 | 2,034 | 398 |
| City of Orange | 137,132 | 160 | 2 | 11 | 68 | 79 | 2,625 | 431 | 1,959 | 235 |
| City of Fullerton | 132,478 | 526 | 2 | 44 | 189 | 291 | 3,824 | 779 | 2,684 | 361 |
| City of Costa Mesa | 110,150 | 304 | 1 | 27 | 114 | 162 | 3,321 | 516 | 2,557 | 248 |
| City of Burbank | 103,248 | 253 | 1 | 22 | 93 | 137 | 2,663 | 499 | 1,829 | 335 |
| City of Compton | 93,872 | 1,457 | 36 | 36 | 509 | 876 | 3,051 | 768 | 1,355 | 928 |
| City of Carson | 92,635 | 500 | 5 | 14 | 164 | 317 | 2,331 | 475 | 1,389 | 467 |
| City of Santa Monica | 88,038 | 393 | 3 | 14 | 162 | 214 | 3,354 | 512 | 2,578 | 264 |
| City of Newport Beach | 79,912 | 125 | 0 | 4 | 32 | 89 | 2,239 | 512 | 1,600 | 127 |
| City of Tustin | 72,286 | 92 | 0 | 4 | 57 | 31 | 1,379 | 209 | 1,039 | 131 |
| City of Montebello | 61,870 | 196 | 1 | 5 | 112 | 78 | 1,762 | 540 | 782 | 440 |
| City of Monterey Park | 61,353 | 146 | 1 | 4 | 95 | 46 | 966 | 249 | 524 | 193 |
| City of Gardena | 58,623 | 381 | 6 | 11 | 216 | 148 | 1,546 | 390 | 830 | 326 |
| City of Arcadia | 56,596 | 115 | 0 | 5 | 50 | 60 | 1,633 | 329 | 1,172 | 132 |
| City of Paramount | 55,220 | 389 | 4 | 11 | 193 | 181 | 1,656 | 310 | 721 | 625 |
| City of Fountain Valley | 55,570 | 116 | 0 | 4 | 33 | 79 | 1,170 | 237 | 873 | 60 |
| City of Cerritos | 51,299 | 81 | 2 | 4 | 50 | 25 | 1,762 | 254 | 1,291 | 217 |
| Total area actually reporting | 100.0% | 62,176 | 768 | 2,570 | 27,456 | 31,382 | 302,654 | 61,496 | 188,100 | 53,058 |
| Rate per 100,000 inhabitants | | 482.7 | 6.0 | 20.0 | 213.1 | 243.6 | 2,349.5 | 477.4 | 1,460.2 | 411.9 |

[1] The FBI determined that the agency's data were overreported. Consequently, affected data are not included in this table.

## Table 6. Crime, by Metropolitan Statistical Area, 2009—*Continued*

(Number, percent, rate per 100,000 population.)

| Area | Population | Violent crime | Murder and non-negligent man-slaughter | Forcible rape | Robbery | Aggravated assault | Property crime | Burglary | Larceny-theft | Motor vehicle theft |
|---|---|---|---|---|---|---|---|---|---|---|
| **Los Angeles-Long Beach-Glendale, CA M.D.** | **9,863,786** | | | | | | | | | |
| Includes Los Angeles County | | | | | | | | | | |
| Total area actually reporting | 100.0% | 54,747 | 699 | 2,114 | 24,528 | 27,406 | 241,960 | 50,558 | 144,589 | 46,813 |
| Rate per 100,000 inhabitants | | 555.0 | 7.1 | 21.4 | 248.7 | 277.8 | 2,453.0 | 512.6 | 1,465.9 | 474.6 |
| Santa Ana-Anaheim-Irvine, CA M.D. | **3,017,883** | | | | | | | | | |
| Includes Orange County | | | | | | | | | | |
| Total area actually reporting | 100.0% | 7,429 | 69 | 456 | 2,928 | 3,976 | 60,694 | 10,938 | 43,511 | 6,245 |
| Rate per 100,000 inhabitants | | 246.2 | 2.3 | 15.1 | 97.0 | 131.7 | 2,011.1 | 362.4 | 1,441.8 | 206.9 |
| **Louisville/Jefferson County, KY-IN M.S.A.**[1] | **1,256,252** | | | | | | | | | |
| Includes Clark, Floyd, Harrison, and Washington Counties, IN and Bullitt, Henry, Jefferson, Meade, Nelson, Oldham, Shelby, Spencer, and Trimble Counties, KY[1] | | | | | | | | | | |
| City of Louisville Metro, KY[1] | 631,260 | 3,769 | 62 | 230 | 1,570 | 1,907 | 26,907 | 7,085 | 18,094 | 1,728 |
| Total area actually reporting | 96.6% | 4,574 | 69 | 353 | 1,856 | 2,296 | 40,764 | 10,508 | 27,708 | 2,548 |
| Estimated total | 100.0% | 4,653 | 69 | 361 | 1,879 | 2,344 | 41,798 | 10,733 | 28,460 | 2,605 |
| Rate per 100,000 inhabitants | | 370.4 | 5.5 | 28.7 | 149.6 | 186.6 | 3,327.2 | 854.4 | 2,265.5 | 207.4 |
| **Lubbock, TX M.S.A.** | **273,291** | | | | | | | | | |
| Includes Crosby and Lubbock Counties | | | | | | | | | | |
| City of Lubbock | 222,884 | 2,079 | 13 | 93 | 311 | 1,662 | 13,010 | 3,730 | 8,754 | 526 |
| Total area actually reporting | 100.0% | 2,315 | 14 | 118 | 325 | 1,858 | 14,456 | 4,263 | 9,583 | 610 |
| Rate per 100,000 inhabitants | | 847.1 | 5.1 | 43.2 | 118.9 | 679.9 | 5,289.6 | 1,559.9 | 3,506.5 | 223.2 |
| **Lynchburg, VA M.S.A.** | **248,706** | | | | | | | | | |
| Includes Amherst, Appomattox, Bedford, and Campbell Counties and Bedford and Lynchburg Cities | | | | | | | | | | |
| City of Lynchburg | 73,735 | 339 | 0 | 21 | 80 | 238 | 2,218 | 372 | 1,735 | 111 |
| Total area actually reporting | 100.0% | 671 | 5 | 64 | 111 | 491 | 4,687 | 886 | 3,525 | 276 |
| Rate per 100,000 inhabitants | | 269.8 | 2.0 | 25.7 | 44.6 | 197.4 | 1,884.6 | 356.2 | 1,417.3 | 111.0 |
| **Macon, GA M.S.A.** | **230,750** | | | | | | | | | |
| Includes Bibb, Crawford, Jones, Monroe, and Twiggs Counties | | | | | | | | | | |
| City of Macon | 92,299 | 704 | 18 | 28 | 342 | 316 | 7,118 | 1,814 | 4,679 | 625 |
| Total area actually reporting | 99.4% | 1,010 | 23 | 51 | 404 | 532 | 11,347 | 3,012 | 7,367 | 968 |
| Estimated total | 100.0% | 1,016 | 23 | 51 | 406 | 536 | 11,404 | 3,024 | 7,408 | 972 |
| Rate per 100,000 inhabitants | | 440.3 | 10.0 | 22.1 | 175.9 | 232.3 | 4,942.1 | 1,310.5 | 3,210.4 | 421.2 |
| **Madera-Chowchilla, CA M.S.A.** | **150,856** | | | | | | | | | |
| Includes Madera County | | | | | | | | | | |
| City of Madera | 58,372 | 408 | 1 | 15 | 133 | 259 | 1,300 | 459 | 614 | 227 |
| City of Chowchilla | 19,817 | 47 | 0 | 1 | 2 | 44 | 389 | 200 | 157 | 32 |
| Total area actually reporting | 100.0% | 685 | 3 | 36 | 162 | 484 | 3,170 | 1,166 | 1,484 | 520 |
| Rate per 100,000 inhabitants | | 454.1 | 2.0 | 23.9 | 107.4 | 320.8 | 2,101.3 | 772.9 | 983.7 | 344.7 |
| **Madison, WI M.S.A.** | **568,019** | | | | | | | | | |
| Includes Columbia, Dane, and Iowa Counties | | | | | | | | | | |
| City of Madison | 234,461 | 853 | 4 | 28 | 364 | 457 | 7,884 | 1,523 | 6,015 | 346 |
| Total area actually reporting | 100.0% | 1,296 | 11 | 86 | 469 | 730 | 14,903 | 2,553 | 11,782 | 568 |
| Rate per 100,000 inhabitants | | 228.2 | 1.9 | 15.1 | 82.6 | 128.5 | 2,623.7 | 449.5 | 2,074.2 | 100.0 |
| **Manchester-Nashua, NH M.S.A.** | **404,309** | | | | | | | | | |
| Includes Hillsborough County | | | | | | | | | | |
| City of Manchester | 108,671 | 537 | 2 | 71 | 171 | 293 | 3,714 | 760 | 2,791 | 163 |
| City of Nashua | 86,554 | 176 | 1 | 25 | 38 | 112 | 2,443 | 379 | 1,962 | 102 |
| Total area actually reporting | 94.1% | 884 | 6 | 119 | 235 | 524 | 8,985 | 1,606 | 7,011 | 368 |
| Estimated total | 100.0% | 896 | 6 | 121 | 237 | 532 | 9,200 | 1,640 | 7,183 | 377 |
| Rate per 100,000 inhabitants | | 221.6 | 1.5 | 29.9 | 58.6 | 131.6 | 2,275.5 | 405.6 | 1,776.6 | 93.2 |
| **Manhattan, KS M.S.A.** | **123,597** | | | | | | | | | |
| Includes Geary, Pottawatomie, and Riley Counties | | | | | | | | | | |
| Total area actually reporting | 100.0% | 428 | 4 | 68 | 48 | 308 | 2,763 | 536 | 2,148 | 79 |
| Rate per 100,000 inhabitants | | 346.3 | 3.2 | 55.0 | 38.8 | 249.2 | 2,235.5 | 433.7 | 1,737.9 | 63.9 |

[1] The FBI determined that the agency's data were overreported. Consequently, affected data are not included in this table.

## Table 6. Crime, by Metropolitan Statistical Area, 2009—*Continued*

(Number, percent, rate per 100,000 population.)

| Area | Population | Violent crime | Murder and non-negligent man-slaughter | Forcible rape | Robbery | Aggravated assault | Property crime | Burglary | Larceny-theft | Motor vehicle theft |
|---|---|---|---|---|---|---|---|---|---|---|
| **Mankato-North Mankato, MN M.S.A.[4]** | **93,372** | | | | | | | | | |
| Includes Blue Earth and Nicollet Counties[4] | | | | | | | | | | |
| City of Mankato[4] | 36,676 | | 0 | | 13 | 56 | 1,840 | 292 | 1,487 | 61 |
| City of North Mankato[4] | 12,605 | | 0 | | 0 | 1 | 259 | 22 | 229 | 8 |
| Total area actually reporting | 100.0% | | 1 | | 16 | 88 | 2,758 | 475 | 2,180 | 103 |
| Rate per 100,000 inhabitants | | | 1.1 | | 17.1 | 94.2 | 2,953.8 | 508.7 | 2,334.7 | 110.3 |
| **Mansfield, OH M.S.A.** | **124,956** | | | | | | | | | |
| Includes Richland County | | | | | | | | | | |
| City of Mansfield | 49,349 | 166 | 2 | 29 | 63 | 72 | 2,711 | 942 | 1,710 | 59 |
| Total area actually reporting | 99.2% | 241 | 3 | 44 | 80 | 114 | 4,902 | 1,487 | 3,320 | 95 |
| Estimated total | 100.0% | 243 | 3 | 44 | 81 | 115 | 4,929 | 1,492 | 3,341 | 96 |
| Rate per 100,000 inhabitants | | 194.5 | 2.4 | 35.2 | 64.8 | 92.0 | 3,944.6 | 1,194.0 | 2,673.7 | 76.8 |
| **McAllen-Edinburg-Mission, TX M.S.A.** | **746,767** | | | | | | | | | |
| Includes Hidalgo County | | | | | | | | | | |
| City of McAllen | 132,598 | 348 | 4 | 20 | 132 | 192 | 8,020 | 796 | 6,783 | 441 |
| City of Edinburg | 74,611 | 267 | 3 | 20 | 69 | 175 | 4,669 | 820 | 3,596 | 253 |
| City of Mission | 69,997 | 124 | 1 | 7 | 41 | 75 | 3,425 | 570 | 2,538 | 317 |
| City of Pharr | 67,628 | 302 | 2 | 23 | 84 | 193 | 3,958 | 842 | 2,773 | 343 |
| Total area actually reporting | 100.0% | 3,036 | 40 | 212 | 691 | 2,093 | 37,311 | 7,935 | 26,750 | 2,626 |
| Rate per 100,000 inhabitants | | 406.6 | 5.4 | 28.4 | 92.5 | 280.3 | 4,996.3 | 1,062.6 | 3,582.1 | 351.6 |
| **Medford, OR M.S.A.** | **203,007** | | | | | | | | | |
| Includes Jackson County | | | | | | | | | | |
| City of Medford | 74,042 | 227 | 2 | 30 | 24 | 171 | 2,961 | 324 | 2,539 | 98 |
| Total area actually reporting | 100.0% | 396 | 2 | 55 | 34 | 305 | 5,065 | 638 | 4,239 | 188 |
| Rate per 100,000 inhabitants | | 195.1 | 1.0 | 27.1 | 16.7 | 150.2 | 2,495.0 | 314.3 | 2,088.1 | 92.6 |
| **Memphis, TN-MS-AR M.S.A.** | **1,299,027** | | | | | | | | | |
| Includes Crittenden County, AR; DeSoto, Marshall, Tate, and Tunica Counties; MS, and Fayette, Shelby, and Tipton Counties, TN | | | | | | | | | | |
| City of Memphis | 667,421 | 12,055 | 132 | 382 | 4,139 | 7,402 | 47,195 | 13,943 | 29,059 | 4,193 |
| Total area actually reporting | 99.9% | 14,895 | 157 | 553 | 4,574 | 9,611 | 65,829 | 19,394 | 41,056 | 5,379 |
| Estimated total | 100.0% | 14,898 | 157 | 553 | 4,575 | 9,613 | 65,884 | 19,408 | 41,094 | 5,382 |
| Rate per 100,000 inhabitants | | 1,146.9 | 12.1 | 42.6 | 352.2 | 740.0 | 5,071.8 | 1,494.0 | 3,163.4 | 414.3 |
| **Merced, CA M.S.A.** | **249,432** | | | | | | | | | |
| Includes Merced County | | | | | | | | | | |
| City of Merced | 78,693 | 733 | 7 | 27 | 158 | 541 | 2,850 | 679 | 1,906 | 265 |
| Total area actually reporting | 100.0% | 1,658 | 26 | 78 | 276 | 1,278 | 8,310 | 2,318 | 5,089 | 903 |
| Rate per 100,000 inhabitants | | 664.7 | 10.4 | 31.3 | 110.7 | 512.4 | 3,331.6 | 929.3 | 2,040.2 | 362.0 |
| **Miami-Fort Lauderdale-Pompano Beach, FL M.S.A.** | **5,501,220** | | | | | | | | | |
| Includes the Metropolitan Divisions of Fort Lauderdale-Pompano Beach-Deerfield Beach, Miami-Miami Beach-Kendall, and West Palm Beach-Boca Raton-Boynton Beach | | | | | | | | | | |
| City of Miami | 419,205 | 4,983 | 59 | 65 | 2,094 | 2,765 | 20,778 | 4,856 | 13,386 | 2,536 |
| City of Fort Lauderdale | 182,942 | 1,481 | 13 | 56 | 685 | 727 | 10,374 | 2,907 | 6,780 | 687 |
| City of Pompano Beach | 101,840 | 1,029 | 8 | 57 | 348 | 616 | 5,066 | 971 | 3,698 | 397 |
| City of West Palm Beach | 100,763 | 905 | 19 | 42 | 376 | 468 | 5,365 | 1,291 | 3,645 | 429 |
| City of Miami Beach | 84,260 | 906 | 7 | 41 | 421 | 437 | 8,439 | 1,207 | 6,567 | 665 |
| City of Boca Raton | 85,956 | 217 | 2 | 24 | 78 | 113 | 3,087 | 554 | 2,375 | 158 |
| City of Deerfield Beach | 74,509 | 468 | 2 | 23 | 145 | 298 | 2,408 | 501 | 1,745 | 162 |
| City of Boynton Beach | 69,211 | 648 | 2 | 8 | 182 | 456 | 3,607 | 837 | 2,610 | 160 |
| City of Delray Beach | 64,522 | 606 | 3 | 29 | 218 | 356 | 3,430 | 771 | 2,448 | 211 |
| City of Homestead | 62,037 | 901 | 3 | 26 | 294 | 578 | 3,288 | 1,095 | 1,945 | 248 |
| Total area actually reporting | 100.0% | 37,403 | 377 | 1,404 | 13,095 | 22,527 | 244,389 | 54,500 | 169,207 | 20,682 |
| Rate per 100,000 inhabitants | | 679.9 | 6.9 | 25.5 | 238.0 | 409.5 | 4,442.5 | 990.7 | 3,075.8 | 376.0 |
| **Fort Lauderdale-Pompano Beach-Deerfield Beach, FL M.D.** | **1,749,470** | | | | | | | | | |
| Includes Broward County | | | | | | | | | | |
| Total area actually reporting | 100.0% | 9,562 | 76 | 439 | 3,374 | 5,673 | 69,568 | 15,952 | 48,487 | 5,129 |
| Rate per 100,000 inhabitants | | 546.6 | 4.3 | 25.1 | 192.9 | 324.3 | 3,976.5 | 911.8 | 2,771.5 | 293.2 |

[4] It was determined that the agency did not follow national Uniform Crime Reporting (UCR) Program guidelines for reporting an offense. Consequently, this figure is not included in this table.

## Table 6. Crime, by Metropolitan Statistical Area, 2009—*Continued*

(Number, percent, rate per 100,000 population.)

| Area | Population | Violent crime | Murder and non-negligent man-slaughter | Forcible rape | Robbery | Aggravated assault | Property crime | Burglary | Larceny-theft | Motor vehicle theft |
|---|---|---|---|---|---|---|---|---|---|---|
| **Miami-Miami Beach-Kendall, FL M.D.** | **2,482,417** | | | | | | | | | |
| Includes Miami-Dade County | | | | | | | | | | |
| Total area actually reporting | 100.0% | 19,797 | 215 | 577 | 7,054 | 11,951 | 122,854 | 25,345 | 85,359 | 12,150 |
| Rate per 100,000 inhabitants | | 797.5 | 8.7 | 23.2 | 284.2 | 481.4 | 4,949.0 | 1,021.0 | 3,438.5 | 489.4 |
| **West Palm Beach-Boca Raton-Boynton Beach, FL M.D.** | **1,269,333** | | | | | | | | | |
| Includes Palm Beach County | | | | | | | | | | |
| Total area actually reporting | 100.0% | 8,044 | 86 | 388 | 2,667 | 4,903 | 51,967 | 13,203 | 35,361 | 3,403 |
| Rate per 100,000 inhabitants | | 633.7 | 6.8 | 30.6 | 210.1 | 386.3 | 4,094.0 | 1,040.2 | 2,785.8 | 268.1 |
| **Michigan City-La Porte, IN M.S.A.** | **111,155** | | | | | | | | | |
| Includes La Porte County | | | | | | | | | | |
| City of Michigan City | 32,355 | 121 | 0 | 13 | 61 | 47 | 1,740 | 371 | 1,259 | 110 |
| City of La Porte | 21,128 | 46 | 0 | 7 | 15 | 24 | 1,232 | 197 | 990 | 45 |
| Total area actually reporting | 96.8% | 203 | 3 | 26 | 86 | 88 | 3,924 | 910 | 2,805 | 209 |
| Estimated total | 100.0% | 213 | 3 | 27 | 89 | 94 | 4,045 | 929 | 2,899 | 217 |
| Rate per 100,000 inhabitants | | 191.6 | 2.7 | 24.3 | 80.1 | 84.6 | 3,639.1 | 835.8 | 2,608.1 | 195.2 |
| **Midland, TX M.S.A.** | **131,294** | | | | | | | | | |
| Includes Midland County | | | | | | | | | | |
| City of Midland | 107,554 | 425 | 3 | 51 | 85 | 286 | 3,909 | 905 | 2,834 | 170 |
| Total area actually reporting | 100.0% | 468 | 3 | 52 | 89 | 324 | 4,559 | 1,116 | 3,228 | 215 |
| Rate per 100,000 inhabitants | | 356.5 | 2.3 | 39.6 | 67.8 | 246.8 | 3,472.4 | 850.0 | 2,458.6 | 163.8 |
| **Milwaukee-Waukesha-West Allis, WI M.S.A.** | **1,553,875** | | | | | | | | | |
| Includes Milwaukee, Ozaukee, Washington, and Waukesha Counties | | | | | | | | | | |
| City of Milwaukee | 604,673 | 6,584 | 72 | 204 | 3,122 | 3,186 | 34,791 | 6,534 | 23,397 | 4,860 |
| City of Waukesha | 68,248 | 109 | 2 | 15 | 27 | 65 | 1,163 | 251 | 871 | 41 |
| City of West Allis | 59,240 | 206 | 2 | 7 | 98 | 99 | 3,082 | 537 | 2,356 | 189 |
| Total area actually reporting | 99.7% | 7,672 | 81 | 301 | 3,468 | 3,822 | 56,272 | 9,377 | 41,273 | 5,622 |
| Estimated total | 100.0% | 7,679 | 81 | 302 | 3,470 | 3,826 | 56,378 | 9,391 | 41,362 | 5,625 |
| Rate per 100,000 inhabitants | | 494.2 | 5.2 | 19.4 | 223.3 | 246.2 | 3,628.2 | 604.4 | 2,661.9 | 362.0 |
| **Minneapolis-St. Paul-Bloomington, MN-WI M.S.A.**[4] | **3,266,869** | | | | | | | | | |
| Includes Anoka, Carver, Chisago, Dakota, Hennepin, Isanti, Ramsey, Scott, Sherburne, Washington, and Wright Counties, MN[4] and Pierce and St. Croix Counties, WI | | | | | | | | | | |
| City of Minneapolis, MN | 382,618 | 4,242 | 18 | 413 | 1,663 | 2,148 | 17,859 | 4,741 | 11,320 | 1,798 |
| City of St. Paul, MN | 280,194 | 2,137 | 13 | 165 | 694 | 1,265 | 11,431 | 2,929 | 6,713 | 1,789 |
| City of Bloomington, MN[4] | 80,864 | | 2 | | 49 | 66 | 3,235 | 277 | 2,846 | 112 |
| City of Plymouth, MN[4] | 72,121 | | 0 | | 13 | 31 | 1,408 | 303 | 1,053 | 52 |
| City of Eagan, MN[4] | 64,014 | | 1 | | 16 | 22 | 1,582 | 218 | 1,323 | 41 |
| City of Eden Prairie, MN[4] | 61,893 | | 0 | | 10 | 34 | 1,166 | 165 | 977 | 24 |
| City of Minnetonka, MN[4] | 49,968 | | 1 | | 10 | 12 | 1,086 | 177 | 885 | 24 |
| Total area actually reporting | 100.0% | | 55 | | 3,250 | 5,150 | 97,445 | 17,723 | 73,085 | 6,637 |
| Rate per 100,000 inhabitants | | | 1.7 | | 99.5 | 157.6 | 2,982.8 | 542.5 | 2,237.2 | 203.2 |
| **Missoula, MT M.S.A.** | **108,586** | | | | | | | | | |
| Includes Missoula County | | | | | | | | | | |
| City of Missoula | 69,479 | 193 | 1 | 28 | 30 | 134 | 2,102 | 277 | 1,729 | 96 |
| Total area actually reporting | 100.0% | 274 | 1 | 38 | 34 | 201 | 2,765 | 391 | 2,235 | 139 |
| Rate per 100,000 inhabitants | | 252.3 | 0.9 | 35.0 | 31.3 | 185.1 | 2,546.4 | 360.1 | 2,058.3 | 128.0 |
| **Mobile, AL M.S.A.**[6] | **408,816** | | | | | | | | | |
| Includes Mobile County | | | | | | | | | | |
| City of Mobile[6] | 246,171 | 1,994 | 24 | 37 | 857 | 1,076 | 14,123 | 3,716 | 9,457 | 950 |
| Total area actually reporting | 100.0% | 2,963 | 36 | 64 | 1,211 | 1,652 | 20,066 | 5,872 | 12,598 | 1,596 |
| Rate per 100,000 inhabitants | | 724.8 | 8.8 | 15.7 | 296.2 | 404.1 | 4,908.3 | 1,436.3 | 3,081.6 | 390.4 |
| **Modesto, CA M.S.A.** | **516,191** | | | | | | | | | |
| Includes Stanislaus County | | | | | | | | | | |
| City of Modesto | 204,474 | 1,419 | 21 | 55 | 369 | 974 | 10,269 | 2,291 | 6,637 | 1,341 |
| Total area actually reporting | 100.0% | 2,721 | 46 | 122 | 706 | 1,847 | 21,577 | 5,748 | 12,428 | 3,401 |
| Rate per 100,000 inhabitants | | 527.1 | 8.9 | 23.6 | 136.8 | 357.8 | 4,180.0 | 1,113.5 | 2,407.6 | 658.9 |

[4] It was determined that the agency did not follow national Uniform Crime Reporting (UCR) Program guidelines for reporting an offense. Consequently, this figure is not included in this table.
[6] The population for the city of Mobile, Alabama, includes 61,856 inhabitants from the jurisdiction of the Mobile County Sheriff's Department.

## Table 6. Crime, by Metropolitan Statistical Area, 2009—*Continued*

(Number, percent, rate per 100,000 population.)

| Area | Population | Violent crime | Murder and non-negligent man-slaughter | Forcible rape | Robbery | Aggravated assault | Property crime | Burglary | Larceny-theft | Motor vehicle theft |
|---|---|---|---|---|---|---|---|---|---|---|
| **Monroe, MI M.S.A.[1]** | **153,073** | | | | | | | | | |
| Includes Monroe County[1] | | | | | | | | | | |
| City of Monroe[1] | 21,301 | 63 | 0 | 8 | 12 | 43 | 674 | 142 | 506 | 26 |
| Total area actually reporting | 100.0% | 340 | 5 | 82 | 54 | 199 | 3,656 | 876 | 2,568 | 212 |
| Rate per 100,000 inhabitants | | 222.1 | 3.3 | 53.6 | 35.3 | 130.0 | 2,388.4 | 572.3 | 1,677.6 | 138.5 |
| **Montgomery, AL M.S.A.** | **369,848** | | | | | | | | | |
| Includes Autauga, Elmore, Lowndes, and Montgomery Counties | | | | | | | | | | |
| City of Montgomery | 202,818 | 871 | 31 | 85 | 453 | 302 | 11,065 | 3,092 | 7,113 | 860 |
| Total area actually reporting | 100.0% | 1,374 | 39 | 128 | 535 | 672 | 15,513 | 4,294 | 10,113 | 1,106 |
| Rate per 100,000 inhabitants | | 371.5 | 10.5 | 34.6 | 144.7 | 181.7 | 4,194.4 | 1,161.0 | 2,734.4 | 299.0 |
| **Morgantown, WV M.S.A.** | **119,585** | | | | | | | | | |
| Includes Monongalia and Preston Counties | | | | | | | | | | |
| City of Morgantown | 29,989 | 130 | 1 | 10 | 23 | 96 | 818 | 196 | 604 | 18 |
| Total area actually reporting | 93.1% | 388 | 1 | 20 | 48 | 319 | 2,525 | 612 | 1,793 | 120 |
| Estimated total | 100.0% | 411 | 2 | 21 | 53 | 335 | 2,831 | 676 | 2,023 | 132 |
| Rate per 100,000 inhabitants | | 343.7 | 1.7 | 17.6 | 44.3 | 280.1 | 2,367.4 | 565.3 | 1,691.7 | 110.4 |
| **Morristown, TN M.S.A.** | **137,792** | | | | | | | | | |
| Includes Grainger, Hamblen, and Jefferson Counties | | | | | | | | | | |
| City of Morristown | 27,775 | 215 | 1 | 18 | 36 | 160 | 1,804 | 163 | 1,580 | 61 |
| Total area actually reporting | 100.0% | 483 | 3 | 37 | 82 | 361 | 4,442 | 1,015 | 3,223 | 204 |
| Rate per 100,000 inhabitants | | 350.5 | 2.2 | 26.9 | 59.5 | 262.0 | 3,223.7 | 736.6 | 2,339.0 | 148.0 |
| **Mount Vernon-Anacortes, WA M.S.A.** | **120,438** | | | | | | | | | |
| Includes Skagit County | | | | | | | | | | |
| City of Mount Vernon | 32,096 | 88 | 2 | 20 | 33 | 33 | 2,124 | 275 | 1,769 | 80 |
| City of Anacortes | 17,063 | 22 | 0 | 1 | 7 | 14 | 459 | 109 | 328 | 22 |
| Total area actually reporting | 100.0% | 231 | 3 | 51 | 54 | 123 | 5,469 | 1,012 | 4,191 | 266 |
| Rate per 100,000 inhabitants | | 191.8 | 2.5 | 42.3 | 44.8 | 102.1 | 4,540.9 | 840.3 | 3,479.8 | 220.9 |
| **Muncie, IN M.S.A.** | **114,435** | | | | | | | | | |
| Includes Delaware County | | | | | | | | | | |
| City of Muncie | 64,639 | 387 | 6 | 44 | 123 | 214 | 2,535 | 606 | 1,804 | 125 |
| Total area actually reporting | 100.0% | 434 | 6 | 54 | 134 | 240 | 3,363 | 783 | 2,394 | 186 |
| Rate per 100,000 inhabitants | | 379.3 | 5.2 | 47.2 | 117.1 | 209.7 | 2,938.8 | 684.2 | 2,092.0 | 162.5 |
| **Muskegon-Norton Shores, MI M.S.A.[1]** | **174,071** | | | | | | | | | |
| Includes Muskegon County[1] | | | | | | | | | | |
| City of Muskegon[1] | 39,327 | 312 | 1 | 24 | 97 | 190 | 2,307 | 544 | 1,656 | 107 |
| City of Norton Shores[1] | 23,389 | 41 | 0 | 8 | 8 | 25 | 847 | 138 | 684 | 25 |
| Total area actually reporting | 100.0% | 734 | 6 | 85 | 196 | 447 | 7,258 | 1,455 | 5,437 | 366 |
| Rate per 100,000 inhabitants | | 421.7 | 3.4 | 48.8 | 112.6 | 256.8 | 4,169.6 | 835.9 | 3,123.4 | 210.3 |
| **Napa, CA M.S.A.** | **133,996** | | | | | | | | | |
| Includes Napa County | | | | | | | | | | |
| City of Napa | 74,736 | 272 | 0 | 21 | 60 | 191 | 1,909 | 413 | 1,330 | 166 |
| Total area actually reporting | 100.0% | 393 | 1 | 34 | 93 | 265 | 3,116 | 716 | 2,091 | 309 |
| Rate per 100,000 inhabitants | | 293.3 | 0.7 | 25.4 | 69.4 | 197.8 | 2,325.4 | 534.3 | 1,560.5 | 230.6 |
| **Naples-Marco Island, FL M.S.A.** | **320,093** | | | | | | | | | |
| Includes Collier County | | | | | | | | | | |
| City of Naples | 21,587 | 40 | 0 | 2 | 11 | 27 | 732 | 78 | 646 | 8 |
| City of Marco Island | 15,713 | 10 | 0 | 0 | 0 | 10 | 155 | 18 | 132 | 5 |
| Total area actually reporting | 100.0% | 1,050 | 14 | 51 | 199 | 786 | 5,861 | 1,287 | 4,346 | 228 |
| Rate per 100,000 inhabitants | | 328.0 | 4.4 | 15.9 | 62.2 | 245.6 | 1,831.0 | 402.1 | 1,357.7 | 71.2 |
| **Nashville-Davidson Murfreesboro Franklin, TN M.S.A.** | **1,584,715** | | | | | | | | | |
| Includes Cannon, Cheatham, Davidson, Dickson, Hickman, Macon, Robertson, Rutherford, Smith, Sumner, Trousdale, Williamson, and Wilson Counties | | | | | | | | | | |
| City of Nashville | 610,176 | 6,959 | 77 | 262 | 1,971 | 4,649 | 29,156 | 6,318 | 21,113 | 1,725 |
| City of Murfreesboro | 105,910 | 697 | 5 | 46 | 187 | 459 | 4,851 | 1,346 | 3,321 | 184 |
| City of Franklin | 60,074 | 110 | 2 | 9 | 12 | 87 | 1,059 | 181 | 839 | 39 |
| Total area actually reporting | 100.0% | 10,450 | 110 | 518 | 2,460 | 7,362 | 53,143 | 12,282 | 37,855 | 3,006 |
| Rate per 100,000 inhabitants | | 659.4 | 6.9 | 32.7 | 155.2 | 464.6 | 3,353.5 | 775.0 | 2,388.8 | 189.7 |

[1] The FBI determined that the agency's data were overreported. Consequently, affected data are not included in this table.

**Table 6. Crime, by Metropolitan Statistical Area, 2009**—*Continued*

(Number, percent, rate per 100,000 population.)

| Area | Population | Violent crime | Murder and non-negligent man-slaughter | Forcible rape | Robbery | Aggravated assault | Property crime | Burglary | Larceny-theft | Motor vehicle theft |
|---|---|---|---|---|---|---|---|---|---|---|
| **New Haven-Milford, CT M.S.A.** | **794,705** | | | | | | | | | |
| Includes New Haven County | | | | | | | | | | |
| City of New Haven | 123,659 | 2,183 | 12 | 59 | 906 | 1,206 | 7,043 | 1,430 | 4,533 | 1,080 |
| City of Milford | 56,310 | 83 | 1 | 6 | 31 | 45 | 1,857 | 163 | 1,598 | 96 |
| Total area actually reporting | 100.0% | 3,572 | 30 | 143 | 1,423 | 1,976 | 25,974 | 4,220 | 19,329 | 2,425 |
| Rate per 100,000 inhabitants | | 449.5 | 3.8 | 18.0 | 179.1 | 248.6 | 3,268.4 | 531.0 | 2,432.2 | 305.1 |
| **New Orleans-Metairie-Kenner, LA M.S.A.[5]** | **1,179,206** | | | | | | | | | |
| Includes Jefferson, Orleans, Plaquemines, St. Bernard,[5] St. Charles, St. John the Baptist, and St. Tammany Parishes | | | | | | | | | | |
| City of New Orleans | 336,425 | 2,614 | 174 | 98 | 932 | 1,410 | 12,940 | 3,821 | 6,507 | 2,612 |
| City of Kenner | 66,592 | 296 | 10 | 16 | 116 | 154 | 2,662 | 461 | 2,054 | 147 |
| Total area actually reporting | 100.0% | 6,458 | 252 | 282 | 1,808 | 4,116 | | | 26,369 | |
| Rate per 100,000 inhabitants | | 547.7 | 21.4 | 23.9 | 153.3 | 349.0 | | | 2,236.2 | |
| **New York-Northern New Jersey-Long Island, NY-NJ-PA M.S.A.** | **19,075,412** | | | | | | | | | |
| Includes the Metropolitan Divisions of Edison-New Brunswick, NJ; Nassau-Suffolk, NY; Newark-Union, NJ-PA; and New York-White Plains-Wayne, NY-NJ | | | | | | | | | | |
| City of New York, NY | 8,400,907 | 46,357 | 471 | 832 | 18,597 | 26,457 | 142,000 | 18,780 | 112,526 | 10,694 |
| City of Newark, NJ | 279,203 | 2,597 | 80 | 68 | 1,319 | 1,130 | 8,822 | 1,947 | 3,781 | 3,094 |
| City of Edison Township, NJ | 99,356 | 264 | 1 | 4 | 97 | 162 | 2,192 | 423 | 1,585 | 184 |
| City of White Plains, NY | 57,810 | 117 | 0 | 1 | 38 | 78 | 1,087 | 40 | 1,012 | 35 |
| City of Wayne Township, NJ | 53,891 | 57 | 1 | 7 | 27 | 22 | 1,316 | 134 | 1,132 | 50 |
| City of Union Township, NJ | 53,579 | 133 | 1 | 4 | 65 | 63 | 1,030 | 159 | 776 | 95 |
| City of New Brunswick, NJ | 51,474 | 389 | 5 | 21 | 152 | 211 | 1,754 | 510 | 1,124 | 120 |
| Total area actually reporting | 99.9% | 72,799 | 778 | 1,771 | 30,255 | 39,995 | 333,411 | 53,240 | 253,104 | 27,067 |
| Estimated total | 100.0% | 72,842 | 778 | 1,773 | 30,270 | 40,021 | 333,906 | 53,310 | 253,510 | 27,086 |
| Rate per 100,000 inhabitants | | 381.9 | 4.1 | 9.3 | 158.7 | 209.8 | 1,750.5 | 279.5 | 1,329.0 | 142.0 |
| **Edison-New Brunswick, NJ M.D.** | **2,340,627** | | | | | | | | | |
| Includes Middlesex, Monmouth, Ocean, and Somerset Counties | | | | | | | | | | |
| Total area actually reporting | 100.0% | 3,831 | 30 | 205 | 1,399 | 2,197 | 43,410 | 8,351 | 33,156 | 1,903 |
| Rate per 100,000 inhabitants | | 163.7 | 1.3 | 8.8 | 59.8 | 93.9 | 1,854.6 | 356.8 | 1,416.5 | 81.3 |
| **Nassau-Suffolk, NY M.D.** | **2,874,918** | | | | | | | | | |
| Includes Nassau and Suffolk Counties | | | | | | | | | | |
| Total area actually reporting | 99.2% | 5,189 | 63 | 179 | 2,243 | 2,704 | 48,599 | 7,057 | 38,340 | 3,202 |
| Estimated total | 100.0% | 5,229 | 63 | 181 | 2,257 | 2,728 | 49,052 | 7,121 | 38,712 | 3,219 |
| Rate per 100,000 inhabitants | | 181.9 | 2.2 | 6.3 | 78.5 | 94.9 | 1,706.2 | 247.7 | 1,346.5 | 112.0 |
| Newark-Union, NJ-PA M.D. | **2,122,829** | | | | | | | | | |
| Includes Essex, Hunterdon, Morris, Sussex, and Union Counties, NJ and Pike County, PA | | | | | | | | | | |
| Total area actually reporting | 100.0% | 8,103 | 134 | 293 | 4,024 | 3,652 | 41,895 | 8,937 | 26,238 | 6,720 |
| Rate per 100,000 inhabitants | | 381.7 | 6.3 | 13.8 | 189.6 | 172.0 | 1,973.5 | 421.0 | 1,236.0 | 316.6 |
| New York-White Plains-Wayne, NY-NJ M.D. | **11,737,038** | | | | | | | | | |
| Includes Bergen, Hudson, and Passaic Counties, NJ and Bronx, Kings, New York, Putnam, Queens, Richmond, Rockland, and Westchester Counties, NY | | | | | | | | | | |
| Total area actually reporting | 99.9% | 55,676 | 551 | 1,094 | 22,589 | 31,442 | 199,507 | 28,895 | 155,370 | 15,242 |
| Estimated total | 100.0% | 55,679 | 551 | 1,094 | 22,590 | 31,444 | 199,549 | 28,901 | 155,404 | 15,244 |
| Rate per 100,000 inhabitants | | 474.4 | 4.7 | 9.3 | 192.5 | 267.9 | 1,700.2 | 246.2 | 1,324.0 | 129.9 |
| **Niles-Benton Harbor, MI M.S.A.[1]** | **158,501** | | | | | | | | | |
| Includes Berrien County[1] | | | | | | | | | | |
| City of Niles[1] | 11,159 | 65 | 1 | 12 | 15 | 37 | 388 | 66 | 304 | 18 |
| City of Benton Harbor[1] | 10,760 | 135 | 0 | 8 | 15 | 112 | 247 | 109 | 127 | 11 |
| Total area actually reporting | 98.9% | 627 | 3 | 114 | 96 | 414 | 4,740 | 983 | 3,588 | 169 |
| Estimated total | 100.0% | 632 | 3 | 115 | 97 | 417 | 4,788 | 993 | 3,622 | 173 |
| Rate per 100,000 inhabitants | | 398.7 | 1.9 | 72.6 | 61.2 | 263.1 | 3,020.8 | 626.5 | 2,285.2 | 109.1 |
| North Port-Bradenton-Sarasota, FL M.S.A. | **693,167** | | | | | | | | | |
| Includes Manatee and Sarasota Counties | | | | | | | | | | |
| City of North Port | 60,512 | 186 | 1 | 13 | 20 | 152 | 1,491 | 415 | 1,043 | 33 |
| City of Bradenton | 53,951 | 422 | 4 | 12 | 136 | 270 | 2,292 | 537 | 1,605 | 150 |
| City of Sarasota | 52,308 | 540 | 7 | 27 | 174 | 332 | 3,225 | 758 | 2,320 | 147 |
| City of Venice | 21,236 | 47 | 0 | 11 | 4 | 32 | 650 | 140 | 492 | 18 |
| Total area actually reporting | 100.0% | 4,053 | 42 | 182 | 947 | 2,882 | 27,159 | 6,706 | 19,190 | 1,263 |
| Rate per 100,000 inhabitants | | 584.7 | 6.1 | 26.3 | 136.6 | 415.8 | 3,918.1 | 967.4 | 2,768.5 | 182.2 |

[1] The FBI determined that the agency's data were overreported. Consequently, affected data are not included in this table.

[5] The data collection methodology for the offense of forcible rape used by the Minnesota state UCR Program (with the exception of Minneapolis and St. Paul, MN) does not comply with national UCR Program guidelines. Consequently, their figures for forcible rape and violent crime (of which forcible rape is a part) are not published in this table.

## Table 6. Crime, by Metropolitan Statistical Area, 2009—*Continued*

(Number, percent, rate per 100,000 population.)

| Area | Population | Violent crime | Murder and non-negligent man-slaughter | Forcible rape | Robbery | Aggravated assault | Property crime | Burglary | Larceny-theft | Motor vehicle theft |
|---|---|---|---|---|---|---|---|---|---|---|
| **Norwich-New London, CT M.S.A.** | **138,611** | | | | | | | | | |
| Includes New London County | | | | | | | | | | |
| City of Norwich | 36,418 | 165 | 2 | 25 | 44 | 94 | 1,079 | 215 | 797 | 67 |
| City of New London | 25,859 | 265 | 2 | 17 | 56 | 190 | 897 | 216 | 624 | 57 |
| Total area actually reporting | 100.0% | 578 | 4 | 58 | 129 | 387 | 3,578 | 608 | 2,808 | 162 |
| Rate per 100,000 inhabitants | | 417.0 | 2.9 | 41.8 | 93.1 | 279.2 | 2,581.3 | 438.6 | 2,025.8 | 116.9 |
| **Ocala, FL M.S.A.** | **335,426** | | | | | | | | | |
| Includes Marion County | | | | | | | | | | |
| City of Ocala | 55,847 | 495 | 3 | 41 | 160 | 291 | 3,216 | 678 | 2,438 | 100 |
| Total area actually reporting | 100.0% | 1,911 | 12 | 164 | 266 | 1,469 | 8,480 | 2,384 | 5,724 | 372 |
| Rate per 100,000 inhabitants | | 569.7 | 3.6 | 48.9 | 79.3 | 438.0 | 2,528.1 | 710.7 | 1,706.5 | 110.9 |
| **Ocean City, NJ M.S.A.** | **95,099** | | | | | | | | | |
| Includes Cape May County | | | | | | | | | | |
| City of Ocean City | 14,686 | 25 | 0 | 3 | 6 | 16 | 851 | 178 | 668 | 5 |
| Total area actually reporting | 97.4% | 260 | 1 | 26 | 67 | 166 | 4,198 | 1,036 | 3,084 | 78 |
| Estimated total | 100.0% | 266 | 1 | 26 | 70 | 169 | 4,244 | 1,045 | 3,118 | 81 |
| Rate per 100,000 inhabitants | | 279.7 | 1.1 | 27.3 | 73.6 | 177.7 | 4,462.7 | 1,098.9 | 3,278.7 | 85.2 |
| **Odessa, TX M.S.A.** | **133,400** | | | | | | | | | |
| Includes Ector County | | | | | | | | | | |
| City of Odessa | 99,770 | 787 | 5 | 36 | 189 | 557 | 4,109 | 1,084 | 2,834 | 191 |
| Total area actually reporting | 100.0% | 894 | 7 | 36 | 216 | 635 | 5,663 | 1,611 | 3,724 | 328 |
| Rate per 100,000 inhabitants | | 670.2 | 5.2 | 27.0 | 161.9 | 476.0 | 4,245.1 | 1,207.6 | 2,791.6 | 245.9 |
| **Ogden-Clearfield, UT M.S.A.** | **539,260** | | | | | | | | | |
| Includes Davis, Morgan, and Weber Counties | | | | | | | | | | |
| City of Ogden | 83,016 | 391 | 4 | 31 | 107 | 249 | 4,040 | 771 | 2,955 | 314 |
| City of Clearfield | 27,913 | 49 | 0 | 10 | 8 | 31 | 860 | 112 | 713 | 35 |
| Total area actually reporting | 100.0% | 882 | 7 | 142 | 200 | 533 | 14,639 | 2,371 | 11,512 | 756 |
| Rate per 100,000 inhabitants | | 163.6 | 1.3 | 26.3 | 37.1 | 98.8 | 2,714.6 | 439.7 | 2,134.8 | 140.2 |
| **Oklahoma City, OK M.S.A.[1,3]** | **1,226,361** | | | | | | | | | |
| Includes Canadian,[3] Cleveland, Grady,[1] Lincoln,[1] Logan, McClain,[1] and Oklahoma Counties | | | | | | | | | | |
| City of Oklahoma City | 556,939 | 5,181 | 65 | 294 | 1,249 | 3,573 | 33,964 | 10,594 | 19,544 | 3,826 |
| Total area actually reporting | 100.0% | | 83 | 501 | 1,528 | | 54,709 | 15,948 | 33,670 | 5,091 |
| Rate per 100,000 inhabitants | | | 6.8 | 40.9 | 124.6 | | 4,461.1 | 1,300.4 | 2,745.5 | 415.1 |
| **Olympia, WA M.S.A.** | **251,133** | | | | | | | | | |
| Includes Thurston County | | | | | | | | | | |
| City of Olympia | 45,603 | 122 | 1 | 30 | 24 | 67 | 2,115 | 382 | 1,556 | 177 |
| Total area actually reporting | 100.0% | 616 | 5 | 99 | 110 | 402 | 7,452 | 1,634 | 5,291 | 527 |
| Rate per 100,000 inhabitants | | 245.3 | 2.0 | 39.4 | 43.8 | 160.1 | 2,967.4 | 650.7 | 2,106.9 | 209.8 |
| **Omaha-Council Bluffs, NE-IA M.S.A.** | **847,725** | | | | | | | | | |
| Includes Harrison, Mills, and Pottawattamie Counties, IA and Cass, Douglas, Sarpy, Saunders, and Washington Counties, NE | | | | | | | | | | |
| City of Omaha, NE | 443,037 | 2,363 | 30 | 192 | 892 | 1,249 | 18,291 | 3,228 | 12,938 | 2,125 |
| City of Council Bluffs, IA | 59,669 | 527 | 2 | 66 | 97 | 362 | 4,405 | 818 | 3,129 | 458 |
| Total area actually reporting | 98.8% | 3,325 | 33 | 328 | 1,033 | 1,931 | 28,289 | 5,199 | 20,088 | 3,002 |
| Estimated total | 100.0% | 3,339 | 33 | 332 | 1,035 | 1,939 | 28,519 | 5,233 | 20,272 | 3,014 |
| Rate per 100,000 inhabitants | | 393.9 | 3.9 | 39.2 | 122.1 | 228.7 | 3,364.2 | 617.3 | 2,391.3 | 355.5 |
| **Orlando-Kissimmee-Sanford, FL M.S.A.** | **2,087,292** | | | | | | | | | |
| Includes Lake, Orange, Osceola, and Seminole Counties | | | | | | | | | | |
| City of Orlando | 235,109 | 2,814 | 28 | 117 | 767 | 1,902 | 17,357 | 3,770 | 12,332 | 1,255 |
| City of Kissimmee | 63,986 | 555 | 4 | 17 | 129 | 405 | 2,928 | 877 | 1,892 | 159 |
| City of Sanford | 52,118 | 377 | 3 | 26 | 199 | 149 | 3,334 | 798 | 2,284 | 252 |
| Total area actually reporting | 100.0% | 14,253 | 111 | 731 | 3,538 | 9,873 | 83,452 | 22,784 | 54,647 | 6,021 |
| Rate per 100,000 inhabitants | | 682.8 | 5.3 | 35.0 | 169.5 | 473.0 | 3,998.1 | 1,091.6 | 2,618.1 | 288.5 |

[1] The FBI determined that the agency's data were overreported. Consequently, affected data are not included in this table.
[3] The FBI determined that the agency's data were underreported. Consequently, affected data are not included in this table.

## Table 6. Crime, by Metropolitan Statistical Area, 2009—*Continued*

(Number, percent, rate per 100,000 population.)

| Area | Population | Violent crime | Murder and non-negligent man-slaughter | Forcible rape | Robbery | Aggravated assault | Property crime | Burglary | Larceny-theft | Motor vehicle theft |
|---|---|---|---|---|---|---|---|---|---|---|
| **Oshkosh-Neenah, WI M.S.A.** | **162,596** | | | | | | | | | |
| Includes Winnebago County | | | | | | | | | | |
| City of Oshkosh | 63,700 | 250 | 0 | 13 | 42 | 195 | 2,112 | 357 | 1,672 | 83 |
| City of Neenah | 25,105 | 31 | 0 | 3 | 1 | 27 | 521 | 101 | 410 | 10 |
| Total area actually reporting | 100.0% | 383 | 0 | 25 | 47 | 311 | 3,895 | 778 | 2,996 | 121 |
| Rate per 100,000 inhabitants | | 235.6 | 0.0 | 15.4 | 28.9 | 191.3 | 2,395.5 | 478.5 | 1,842.6 | 74.4 |
| **Owensboro, KY M.S.A.**[1] | **113,253** | | | | | | | | | |
| Includes Daviess, Hancock, and McLean Counties[1] | | | | | | | | | | |
| City of Owensboro[1] | 55,651 | 119 | 1 | 36 | 34 | 48 | 2,340 | 417 | 1,841 | 82 |
| Total area actually reporting | 92.3% | 145 | 2 | 40 | 38 | 65 | 3,030 | 606 | 2,303 | 121 |
| Estimated total | 100.0% | 157 | 2 | 42 | 42 | 71 | 3,186 | 648 | 2,409 | 129 |
| Rate per 100,000 inhabitants | | 138.6 | 1.8 | 37.1 | 37.1 | 62.7 | 2,813.2 | 572.2 | 2,127.1 | 113.9 |
| **Oxnard-Thousand Oaks-Ventura, CA M.S.A.** | **799,696** | | | | | | | | | |
| Includes Ventura County | | | | | | | | | | |
| City of Oxnard | 187,357 | 771 | 13 | 24 | 384 | 350 | 4,087 | 704 | 2,929 | 454 |
| City of Thousand Oaks | 123,735 | 163 | 2 | 19 | 40 | 102 | 1,793 | 323 | 1,386 | 84 |
| City of Ventura | 103,997 | 368 | 5 | 18 | 125 | 220 | 3,068 | 615 | 2,276 | 177 |
| City of Camarillo | 64,011 | 80 | 0 | 8 | 28 | 44 | 951 | 167 | 729 | 55 |
| Total area actually reporting | 100.0% | 2,021 | 29 | 116 | 757 | 1,119 | 15,329 | 2,954 | 11,221 | 1,154 |
| Rate per 100,000 inhabitants | | 252.7 | 3.6 | 14.5 | 94.7 | 139.9 | 1,916.9 | 369.4 | 1,403.2 | 144.3 |
| **Palm Bay-Melbourne-Titusville, FL M.S.A.** | **538,696** | | | | | | | | | |
| Includes Brevard County | | | | | | | | | | |
| City of Palm Bay | 103,475 | 532 | 5 | 26 | 72 | 429 | 2,426 | 664 | 1,602 | 160 |
| City of Melbourne | 77,854 | 906 | 6 | 24 | 192 | 684 | 3,980 | 737 | 3,058 | 185 |
| City of Titusville | 45,197 | 266 | 4 | 25 | 55 | 182 | 1,735 | 439 | 1,109 | 187 |
| Total area actually reporting | 100.0% | 3,617 | 26 | 174 | 598 | 2,819 | 17,975 | 4,137 | 12,873 | 965 |
| Rate per 100,000 inhabitants | | 671.4 | 4.8 | 32.3 | 111.0 | 523.3 | 3,336.8 | 768.0 | 2,389.7 | 179.1 |
| **Palm Coast, FL M.S.A.** | **96,615** | | | | | | | | | |
| Includes Flagler County | | | | | | | | | | |
| Total area actually reporting | 100.0% | 296 | 3 | 22 | 48 | 223 | 2,291 | 592 | 1,589 | 110 |
| Rate per 100,000 inhabitants | | 306.4 | 3.1 | 22.8 | 49.7 | 230.8 | 2,371.3 | 612.7 | 1,644.7 | 113.9 |
| **Panama City-Lynn Haven-Panama City Beach, FL M.S.A.** | **164,328** | | | | | | | | | |
| Includes Bay County | | | | | | | | | | |
| City of Panama City | 36,619 | 369 | 3 | 6 | 89 | 271 | 2,308 | 459 | 1,726 | 123 |
| City of Lynn Haven | 15,606 | 68 | 0 | 4 | 11 | 53 | 518 | 158 | 356 | 4 |
| City of Panama City Beach | 15,758 | 83 | 0 | 15 | 13 | 55 | 1,116 | 210 | 902 | 4 |
| Total area actually reporting | 100.0% | 990 | 9 | 83 | 170 | 728 | 7,164 | 1,725 | 5,108 | 331 |
| Rate per 100,000 inhabitants | | 602.5 | 5.5 | 50.5 | 103.5 | 443.0 | 4,359.6 | 1,049.7 | 3,108.4 | 201.4 |
| **Pascagoula, MS M.S.A.** | **153,415** | | | | | | | | | |
| Includes George and Jackson Counties | | | | | | | | | | |
| City of Pascagoula | 23,346 | 74 | 1 | 6 | 45 | 22 | 1,429 | 297 | 1,033 | 99 |
| Total area actually reporting | 100.0% | 416 | 7 | 62 | 121 | 226 | 5,307 | 1,845 | 3,158 | 304 |
| Rate per 100,000 inhabitants | | 271.2 | 4.6 | 40.4 | 78.9 | 147.3 | 3,459.2 | 1,202.6 | 2,058.5 | 198.2 |
| **Pensacola-Ferry Pass-Brent, FL M.S.A.** | **453,889** | | | | | | | | | |
| Includes Escambia and Santa Rosa Counties | | | | | | | | | | |
| City of Pensacola | 53,570 | 471 | 3 | 25 | 99 | 344 | 2,767 | 626 | 2,026 | 115 |
| Total area actually reporting | 100.0% | 2,968 | 18 | 226 | 657 | 2,067 | 14,731 | 3,745 | 10,136 | 850 |
| Rate per 100,000 inhabitants | | 653.9 | 4.0 | 49.8 | 144.7 | 455.4 | 3,245.5 | 825.1 | 2,233.1 | 187.3 |
| **Philadelphia-Camden-Wilmington, PA-NJ-DE-MD M.S.A.** | **5,970,355** | | | | | | | | | |
| Includes the Metropolitan Divisions of Camden, NJ; Philadelphia, PA; and Wilmington, DE-MD-NJ | | | | | | | | | | |
| City of Philadelphia, PA | 1,547,605 | 19,163 | 302 | 896 | 9,037 | 8,928 | 55,888 | 10,969 | 37,941 | 6,978 |
| City of Camden, NJ | 78,980 | 1,880 | 34 | 60 | 766 | 1,020 | 3,935 | 1,035 | 2,251 | 649 |
| City of Wilmington, DE | 72,580 | 1,342 | 17 | 39 | 524 | 762 | 3,631 | 856 | 2,259 | 516 |
| Total area actually reporting | 99.8% | 34,335 | 436 | 1,909 | 14,047 | 17,943 | 157,209 | 29,972 | 114,225 | 13,012 |
| Estimated total | 100.0% | 34,364 | 436 | 1,911 | 14,055 | 17,962 | 157,469 | 30,014 | 114,431 | 13,024 |
| Rate per 100,000 inhabitants | | 575.6 | 7.3 | 32.0 | 235.4 | 300.9 | 2,637.5 | 502.7 | 1,916.7 | 218.1 |

[1] The FBI determined that the agency's data were overreported. Consequently, affected data are not included in this table.

## Table 6. Crime, by Metropolitan Statistical Area, 2009—*Continued*

(Number, percent, rate per 100,000 population.)

| Area | Population | Violent crime | Murder and non-negligent man-slaughter | Forcible rape | Robbery | Aggravated assault | Property crime | Burglary | Larceny-theft | Motor vehicle theft |
|---|---|---|---|---|---|---|---|---|---|---|
| **Camden, NJ M.D.** | **1,257,180** | | | | | | | | | |
| Includes Burlington, Camden, and Gloucester Counties | | | | | | | | | | |
| Total area actually reporting | 99.9% | 4,471 | 50 | 210 | 1,661 | 2,550 | 30,890 | 6,584 | 22,308 | 1,998 |
| Estimated total | 100.0% | 4,474 | 50 | 210 | 1,662 | 2,552 | 30,916 | 6,589 | 22,327 | 2,000 |
| Rate per 100,000 inhabitants | | 355.9 | 4.0 | 16.7 | 132.2 | 203.0 | 2,459.2 | 524.1 | 1,776.0 | 159.1 |
| **Philadelphia, PA M.D.** | **4,011,029** | | | | | | | | | |
| Includes Bucks, Chester, Delaware, Montgomery, and Philadelphia Counties | | | | | | | | | | |
| Total area actually reporting | 99.7% | 25,424 | 351 | 1,521 | 10,917 | 12,635 | 103,439 | 18,291 | 75,863 | 9,285 |
| Estimated total | 100.0% | 25,450 | 351 | 1,523 | 10,924 | 12,652 | 103,673 | 18,328 | 76,050 | 9,295 |
| Rate per 100,000 inhabitants | | 634.5 | 8.8 | 38.0 | 272.3 | 315.4 | 2,584.7 | 456.9 | 1,896.0 | 231.7 |
| **Wilmington, DE-MD-NJ M.D.** | **702,146** | | | | | | | | | |
| Includes New Castle County, DE; Cecil County, MD; and Salem County, NJ | | | | | | | | | | |
| Total area actually reporting | 100.0% | 4,440 | 35 | 178 | 1,469 | 2,758 | 22,880 | 5,097 | 16,054 | 1,729 |
| Rate per 100,000 inhabitants | | 632.3 | 5.0 | 25.4 | 209.2 | 392.8 | 3,258.6 | 725.9 | 2,286.4 | 246.2 |
| **Phoenix-Mesa-Glendale, AZ M.S.A.** | **4,362,725** | | | | | | | | | |
| Includes Maricopa and Pinal Counties | | | | | | | | | | |
| City of Phoenix | 1,597,397 | 8,730 | 122 | 522 | 3,757 | 4,329 | 65,617 | 16,281 | 39,643 | 9,693 |
| City of Mesa | 470,833 | 2,000 | 14 | 123 | 611 | 1,252 | 16,079 | 3,076 | 11,700 | 1,303 |
| City of Glendale | 255,080 | 1,147 | 18 | 54 | 420 | 655 | 12,489 | 2,551 | 8,214 | 1,724 |
| City of Scottsdale | 239,115 | 410 | 10 | 19 | 129 | 252 | 6,798 | 1,337 | 5,155 | 306 |
| City of Tempe | 177,486 | 922 | 2 | 66 | 306 | 548 | 8,986 | 1,478 | 6,692 | 816 |
| Total area actually reporting | 99.8% | 17,159 | 230 | 1,109 | 6,082 | 9,738 | 156,953 | 36,145 | 102,600 | 18,208 |
| Estimated total | 100.0% | 17,174 | 230 | 1,110 | 6,086 | 9,748 | 157,161 | 36,192 | 102,745 | 18,224 |
| Rate per 100,000 inhabitants | | 393.7 | 5.3 | 25.4 | 139.5 | 223.4 | 3,602.4 | 829.6 | 2,355.1 | 417.7 |
| **Pine Bluff, AR M.S.A.** | **100,339** | | | | | | | | | |
| Includes Cleveland, Jefferson, and Lincoln Counties | | | | | | | | | | |
| City of Pine Bluff | 49,915 | 721 | 12 | 50 | 207 | 452 | 4,159 | 1,606 | 2,185 | 368 |
| Total area actually reporting | 97.8% | 842 | 14 | 63 | 217 | 548 | 5,025 | 2,004 | 2,554 | 467 |
| Estimated total | 100.0% | 852 | 14 | 64 | 218 | 556 | 5,103 | 2,030 | 2,603 | 470 |
| Rate per 100,000 inhabitants | | 849.1 | 14.0 | 63.8 | 217.3 | 554.1 | 5,085.8 | 2,023.1 | 2,594.2 | 468.4 |
| **Pittsburgh, PA M.S.A.** | **2,348,787** | | | | | | | | | |
| Includes Allegheny, Armstrong, Beaver, Butler, Fayette, Washington, and Westmoreland Counties | | | | | | | | | | |
| City of Pittsburgh | 312,232 | 3,087 | 39 | 116 | 1,367 | 1,565 | 11,775 | 2,811 | 8,134 | 830 |
| Total area actually reporting | 99.0% | 8,001 | 110 | 429 | 2,553 | 4,909 | 47,532 | 10,395 | 34,564 | 2,573 |
| Estimated total | 100.0% | 8,053 | 111 | 432 | 2,567 | 4,943 | 47,997 | 10,469 | 34,935 | 2,593 |
| Rate per 100,000 inhabitants | | 342.9 | 4.7 | 18.4 | 109.3 | 210.4 | 2,043.5 | 445.7 | 1,487.4 | 110.4 |
| **Pittsfield, MA M.S.A.** | **131,299** | | | | | | | | | |
| Includes Berkshire County | | | | | | | | | | |
| City of Pittsfield | 43,050 | 284 | 2 | 34 | 23 | 225 | 1,004 | 319 | 636 | 49 |
| Total area actually reporting | 96.2% | 540 | 2 | 51 | 33 | 454 | 2,828 | 929 | 1,808 | 91 |
| Estimated total | 100.0% | 556 | 2 | 52 | 36 | 466 | 2,928 | 953 | 1,877 | 98 |
| Rate per 100,000 inhabitants | | 423.5 | 1.5 | 39.6 | 27.4 | 354.9 | 2,230.0 | 725.8 | 1,429.6 | 74.6 |
| **Pocatello, ID M.S.A.** | **88,737** | | | | | | | | | |
| Includes Bannock and Power Counties | | | | | | | | | | |
| City of Pocatello | 55,272 | 170 | 1 | 29 | 11 | 129 | 1,622 | 260 | 1,296 | 66 |
| Total area actually reporting | 100.0% | 219 | 1 | 34 | 14 | 170 | 2,419 | 331 | 2,004 | 84 |
| Rate per 100,000 inhabitants | | 246.8 | 1.1 | 38.3 | 15.8 | 191.6 | 2,726.0 | 373.0 | 2,258.4 | 94.7 |
| **Portland-South Portland-Biddeford, ME M.S.A.** | **515,866** | | | | | | | | | |
| Includes Cumberland, Sagadahoc, and York Counties | | | | | | | | | | |
| City of Portland | 62,382 | 234 | 4 | 27 | 120 | 83 | 2,806 | 546 | 2,153 | 107 |
| City of South Portland | 23,852 | 62 | 0 | 3 | 13 | 46 | 1,062 | 96 | 929 | 37 |
| City of Biddeford | 21,479 | 57 | 2 | 11 | 20 | 24 | 1,030 | 156 | 856 | 18 |
| Total area actually reporting | 100.0% | 693 | 13 | 138 | 231 | 311 | 12,546 | 2,548 | 9,573 | 425 |
| Rate per 100,000 inhabitants | | 134.3 | 2.5 | 26.8 | 44.8 | 60.3 | 2,432.0 | 493.9 | 1,855.7 | 82.4 |

## Table 6. Crime, by Metropolitan Statistical Area, 2009—*Continued*

(Number, percent, rate per 100,000 population.)

| Area | Population | Violent crime | Murder and non-negligent man-slaughter | Forcible rape | Robbery | Aggravated assault | Property crime | Burglary | Larceny-theft | Motor vehicle theft |
|---|---|---|---|---|---|---|---|---|---|---|
| **Portland-Vancouver-Hillsboro, OR-WA M.S.A.** | **2,239,268** | | | | | | | | | |
| Includes Clackamas, Columbia, Multnomah, Washington, and Yamhill Counties, OR and Clark and Skamania Counties, WA | | | | | | | | | | |
| City of Portland, OR | 560,908 | 3,105 | 19 | 252 | 1,037 | 1,797 | 26,495 | 3,696 | 19,624 | 3,175 |
| City of Vancouver, WA | 165,147 | 656 | 6 | 117 | 158 | 375 | 5,944 | 886 | 4,159 | 899 |
| City of Hillsboro, OR | 96,563 | 147 | 4 | 31 | 60 | 52 | 1,886 | 235 | 1,527 | 124 |
| City of Beaverton, OR | 93,221 | 190 | 3 | 23 | 47 | 117 | 1,592 | 226 | 1,230 | 136 |
| Total area actually reporting | 100.0% | 6,012 | 48 | 821 | 1,895 | 3,248 | 65,588 | 9,709 | 48,986 | 6,893 |
| Rate per 100,000 inhabitants | | 268.5 | 2.1 | 36.7 | 84.6 | 145.0 | 2,929.0 | 433.6 | 2,187.6 | 307.8 |
| **Port St. Lucie, FL M.S.A.** | **410,941** | | | | | | | | | |
| Includes Martin and St. Lucie Counties | | | | | | | | | | |
| City of Port St. Lucie | 164,069 | 421 | 1 | 51 | 60 | 309 | 3,552 | 1,102 | 2,389 | 61 |
| Total area actually reporting | 100.0% | 1,701 | 17 | 114 | 394 | 1,176 | 11,559 | 3,363 | 7,770 | 426 |
| Rate per 100,000 inhabitants | | 413.9 | 4.1 | 27.7 | 95.9 | 286.2 | 2,812.8 | 818.4 | 1,890.8 | 103.7 |
| **Poughkeepsie-Newburgh-Middletown, NY M.S.A.** | **677,974** | | | | | | | | | |
| Includes Dutchess and Orange Counties | | | | | | | | | | |
| City of Poughkeepsie | 29,599 | 410 | 3 | 11 | 200 | 196 | 1,022 | 274 | 683 | 65 |
| City of Newburgh | 28,071 | 466 | 4 | 8 | 187 | 267 | 1,065 | 316 | 661 | 88 |
| City of Middletown | 25,921 | 155 | 1 | 8 | 57 | 89 | 1,024 | 204 | 794 | 26 |
| Total area actually reporting | 98.2% | 1,843 | 13 | 82 | 599 | 1,149 | 13,036 | 1,971 | 10,641 | 424 |
| Estimated total | 100.0% | 1,865 | 13 | 83 | 607 | 1,162 | 13,279 | 2,005 | 10,841 | 433 |
| Rate per 100,000 inhabitants | | 275.1 | 1.9 | 12.2 | 89.5 | 171.4 | 1,958.6 | 295.7 | 1,599.0 | 63.9 |
| **Prescott, AZ M.S.A.** | **218,897** | | | | | | | | | |
| Includes Yavapai County | | | | | | | | | | |
| City of Prescott | 43,748 | 147 | 2 | 8 | 27 | 110 | 1,238 | 266 | 941 | 31 |
| Total area actually reporting | 100.0% | 697 | 3 | 37 | 49 | 608 | 4,550 | 1,135 | 3,184 | 231 |
| Rate per 100,000 inhabitants | | 318.4 | 1.4 | 16.9 | 22.4 | 277.8 | 2,078.6 | 518.5 | 1,454.6 | 105.5 |
| **Providence-New Bedford-Fall River, RI-MA M.S.A.** | **1,607,064** | | | | | | | | | |
| Includes Bristol County, MA and Bristol, Kent, Newport, Providence, and Washington Counties, RI | | | | | | | | | | |
| City of Providence, RI | 171,664 | 1,182 | 23 | 50 | 395 | 714 | 7,990 | 1,825 | 5,088 | 1,077 |
| City of New Bedford, MA | 92,621 | 1,184 | 9 | 66 | 340 | 769 | 3,235 | 1,144 | 1,806 | 285 |
| City of Fall River, MA | 91,901 | 1,086 | 4 | 46 | 273 | 763 | 3,312 | 775 | 2,144 | 393 |
| City of Warwick, RI | 84,488 | 121 | 0 | 26 | 38 | 57 | 2,725 | 361 | 2,242 | 122 |
| City of Cranston, RI | 80,223 | 120 | 2 | 20 | 37 | 61 | 2,077 | 415 | 1,466 | 196 |
| Total area actually reporting | 100.0% | 6,020 | 47 | 449 | 1,587 | 3,937 | 41,086 | 9,487 | 28,179 | 3,420 |
| Rate per 100,000 inhabitants | | 374.6 | 2.9 | 27.9 | 98.8 | 245.0 | 2,556.6 | 590.3 | 1,753.4 | 212.8 |
| **Provo-Orem, UT M.S.A.** | **559,579** | | | | | | | | | |
| Includes Juab and Utah Counties | | | | | | | | | | |
| City of Provo | 119,472 | 167 | 1 | 35 | 32 | 99 | 2,919 | 407 | 2,367 | 145 |
| City of Orem | 93,785 | 50 | 1 | 14 | 22 | 13 | 2,520 | 220 | 2,184 | 116 |
| Total area actually reporting | 100.0% | 427 | 4 | 109 | 85 | 229 | 12,273 | 1,777 | 9,943 | 553 |
| Rate per 100,000 inhabitants | | 76.3 | 0.7 | 19.5 | 15.2 | 40.9 | 2,193.3 | 317.6 | 1,776.9 | 98.8 |
| **Pueblo, CO M.S.A.** | **158,754** | | | | | | | | | |
| Includes Pueblo County | | | | | | | | | | |
| City of Pueblo | 105,271 | 897 | 13 | 31 | 165 | 688 | 3,392 | 1,311 | 1,736 | 345 |
| Total area actually reporting | 100.0% | 929 | 14 | 31 | 171 | 713 | 4,710 | 1,558 | 2,762 | 390 |
| Rate per 100,000 inhabitants | | 585.2 | 8.8 | 19.5 | 107.7 | 449.1 | 2,966.9 | 981.4 | 1,739.8 | 245.7 |
| **Punta Gorda, FL M.S.A.** | **149,640** | | | | | | | | | |
| Includes Charlotte County | | | | | | | | | | |
| City of Punta Gorda | 16,567 | 33 | 1 | 0 | 3 | 29 | 329 | 121 | 203 | 5 |
| Total area actually reporting | 100.0% | 472 | 3 | 18 | 62 | 389 | 4,151 | 1,068 | 2,906 | 177 |
| Rate per 100,000 inhabitants | | 315.4 | 2.0 | 12.0 | 41.4 | 260.0 | 2,774.0 | 713.7 | 1,942.0 | 118.3 |
| **Racine, WI M.S.A.** | **200,613** | | | | | | | | | |
| Includes Racine County | | | | | | | | | | |
| City of Racine | 82,232 | 448 | 3 | 35 | 228 | 182 | 3,521 | 1,108 | 2,266 | 147 |
| Total area actually reporting | 100.0% | 591 | 5 | 41 | 267 | 278 | 5,642 | 1,468 | 3,936 | 238 |
| Rate per 100,000 inhabitants | | 294.6 | 2.5 | 20.4 | 133.1 | 138.6 | 2,812.4 | 731.8 | 1,962.0 | 118.6 |

## Table 6. Crime, by Metropolitan Statistical Area, 2009—*Continued*

(Number, percent, rate per 100,000 population.)

| Area | Population | Violent crime | Murder and non-negligent man-slaughter | Forcible rape | Robbery | Aggravated assault | Property crime | Burglary | Larceny-theft | Motor vehicle theft |
|---|---|---|---|---|---|---|---|---|---|---|
| **Raleigh-Cary, NC M.S.A.** | **1,127,897** | | | | | | | | | |
| Includes Franklin, Johnston, and Wake Counties | | | | | | | | | | |
| City of Raleigh | 406,005 | 2,001 | 14 | 99 | 832 | 1,056 | 13,817 | 3,187 | 9,834 | 796 |
| City of Cary | 133,757 | 132 | 0 | 12 | 48 | 72 | 2,005 | 469 | 1,454 | 82 |
| Total area actually reporting | 99.6% | 3,121 | 26 | 192 | 1,122 | 1,781 | 29,504 | 7,776 | 19,958 | 1,770 |
| Estimated total | 100.0% | 3,138 | 26 | 193 | 1,127 | 1,792 | 29,720 | 7,826 | 20,115 | 1,779 |
| Rate per 100,000 inhabitants | | 278.2 | 2.3 | 17.1 | 99.9 | 158.9 | 2,635.0 | 693.9 | 1,783.4 | 157.7 |
| **Rapid City, SD M.S.A.** | **123,903** | | | | | | | | | |
| Includes Meade and Pennington Counties | | | | | | | | | | |
| City of Rapid City | 66,170 | 307 | 2 | 97 | 41 | 167 | 2,829 | 433 | 2,264 | 132 |
| Total area actually reporting | 100.0% | 386 | 2 | 131 | 42 | 211 | 3,474 | 540 | 2,775 | 159 |
| Rate per 100,000 inhabitants | | 311.5 | 1.6 | 105.7 | 33.9 | 170.3 | 2,803.8 | 435.8 | 2,239.7 | 128.3 |
| **Reading, PA M.S.A.** | **407,999** | | | | | | | | | |
| Includes Berks County | | | | | | | | | | |
| City of Reading | 80,418 | 766 | 12 | 22 | 369 | 363 | 3,788 | 1,321 | 1,872 | 595 |
| Total area actually reporting | 100.0% | 1,254 | 16 | 54 | 461 | 723 | 9,607 | 2,153 | 6,488 | 966 |
| Rate per 100,000 inhabitants | | 307.4 | 3.9 | 13.2 | 113.0 | 177.2 | 2,354.7 | 527.7 | 1,590.2 | 236.8 |
| **Redding, CA M.S.A.** | **181,512** | | | | | | | | | |
| Includes Shasta County | | | | | | | | | | |
| City of Redding | 91,242 | 688 | 2 | 64 | 83 | 539 | 2,979 | 783 | 1,992 | 204 |
| Total area actually reporting | 100.0% | 1,280 | 3 | 111 | 130 | 1,036 | 4,640 | 1,462 | 2,839 | 339 |
| Rate per 100,000 inhabitants | | 705.2 | 1.7 | 61.2 | 71.6 | 570.8 | 2,556.3 | 805.5 | 1,564.1 | 186.8 |
| **Reno-Sparks, NV M.S.A.** | **418,246** | | | | | | | | | |
| Includes Storey and Washoe Counties | | | | | | | | | | |
| City of Reno | 221,010 | 1,473 | 9 | 84 | 409 | 971 | 8,810 | 1,848 | 6,209 | 753 |
| City of Sparks | 91,421 | 399 | 5 | 40 | 112 | 242 | 3,105 | 850 | 2,007 | 248 |
| Total area actually reporting | 100.0% | 2,166 | 18 | 128 | 535 | 1,485 | 13,561 | 3,209 | 9,218 | 1,134 |
| Rate per 100,000 inhabitants | | 517.9 | 4.3 | 30.6 | 127.9 | 355.1 | 3,242.4 | 767.3 | 2,204.0 | 271.1 |
| **Richmond, VA M.S.A.** | **1,245,391** | | | | | | | | | |
| Includes Amelia, Caroline, Charles City, Chesterfield, Cumberland, Dinwiddie, Goochland, Hanover, Henrico, King and Queen, King William, Louisa, New Kent, Powhatan, Prince George, and Sussex Counties and Colonial Heights, Hopewell, Petersburg, and Richmond Cities | | | | | | | | | | |
| City of Richmond | 203,233 | 1,631 | 37 | 35 | 850 | 709 | 8,349 | 1,555 | 5,822 | 972 |
| Total area actually reporting | 100.0% | 3,652 | 72 | 201 | 1,639 | 1,740 | 33,864 | 6,838 | 24,453 | 2,573 |
| Rate per 100,000 inhabitants | | 293.2 | 5.8 | 16.1 | 131.6 | 139.7 | 2,719.1 | 549.1 | 1,963.5 | 206.6 |
| **Riverside-San Bernardino-Ontario, CA M.S.A.** | **4,208,217** | | | | | | | | | |
| Includes Riverside and San Bernardino Counties | | | | | | | | | | |
| City of Riverside | 299,871 | 1,535 | 15 | 98 | 667 | 755 | 9,590 | 2,020 | 6,239 | 1,331 |
| City of San Bernardino | 199,683 | 1,908 | 32 | 61 | 677 | 1,138 | 9,245 | 2,349 | 4,775 | 2,121 |
| City of Ontario | 173,212 | 732 | 5 | 49 | 286 | 392 | 5,146 | 986 | 3,207 | 953 |
| City of Victorville | 117,150 | 783 | 10 | 48 | 289 | 436 | 3,939 | 1,253 | 2,219 | 467 |
| City of Temecula | 100,922 | 126 | 1 | 14 | 59 | 52 | 2,370 | 576 | 1,574 | 220 |
| City of Chino | 84,626 | 169 | 1 | 15 | 69 | 84 | 2,122 | 543 | 1,346 | 233 |
| City of Hemet | 72,417 | 374 | 7 | 17 | 122 | 228 | 2,841 | 865 | 1,655 | 321 |
| City of Redlands | 70,360 | 233 | 2 | 13 | 101 | 117 | 2,473 | 634 | 1,544 | 295 |
| City of Colton | 50,803 | 222 | 5 | 8 | 94 | 115 | 1,702 | 437 | 988 | 277 |
| City of Palm Desert | 51,630 | 44 | 1 | 5 | 30 | 8 | 1,927 | 705 | 1,114 | 108 |
| Total area actually reporting | 100.0% | 17,416 | 214 | 928 | 5,675 | 10,599 | 119,210 | 32,847 | 67,830 | 18,533 |
| Rate per 100,000 inhabitants | | 413.9 | 5.1 | 22.1 | 134.9 | 251.9 | 2,832.8 | 780.5 | 1,611.8 | 440.4 |
| **Roanoke, VA M.S.A.** | **300,340** | | | | | | | | | |
| Includes Botetourt, Craig, Franklin, and Roanoke Counties and Roanoke and Salem Cities | | | | | | | | | | |
| City of Roanoke | 93,110 | 639 | 9 | 26 | 184 | 420 | 4,975 | 913 | 3,774 | 288 |
| Total area actually reporting | 100.0% | 899 | 12 | 67 | 225 | 595 | 8,464 | 1,544 | 6,475 | 445 |
| Rate per 100,000 inhabitants | | 299.3 | 4.0 | 22.3 | 74.9 | 198.1 | 2,818.1 | 514.1 | 2,155.9 | 148.2 |
| **Rochester, MN M.S.A.**[4] | **185,487** | | | | | | | | | |
| Includes Dodge, Olmsted, and Wabasha Counties[4] | | | | | | | | | | |
| City of Rochester[4] | 101,884 | | 1 | | 58 | 142 | 2,845 | 398 | 2,343 | 104 |
| Total area actually reporting | 98.3% | | 1 | | 60 | 195 | 3,772 | 594 | 3,021 | 157 |
| Estimated total | 100.0% | | 1 | | 61 | 197 | 3,867 | 608 | 3,098 | 161 |
| Rate per 100,000 inhabitants | | | 0.5 | | 32.9 | 106.2 | 2,084.8 | 327.8 | 1,670.2 | 86.8 |

[4] It was determined that the agency did not follow national Uniform Crime Reporting (UCR) Program guidelines for reporting an offense. Consequently, this figure is not included in this table.

## Table 6. Crime, by Metropolitan Statistical Area, 2009—*Continued*

(Number, percent, rate per 100,000 population.)

| Area | Population | Violent crime | Murder and non-negligent man-slaughter | Forcible rape | Robbery | Aggravated assault | Property crime | Burglary | Larceny-theft | Motor vehicle theft |
|---|---|---|---|---|---|---|---|---|---|---|
| **Rochester, NY M.S.A.** | **1,032,945** | | | | | | | | | |
| Includes Livingston, Monroe, Ontario, Orleans, and Wayne Counties | | | | | | | | | | |
| City of Rochester | 205,537 | 2,042 | 28 | 97 | 846 | 1,071 | 10,991 | 2,899 | 7,130 | 962 |
| Total area actually reporting | 100.0% | 3,022 | 37 | 240 | 1,083 | 1,662 | 28,608 | 5,703 | 21,420 | 1,485 |
| Rate per 100,000 inhabitants | | 292.6 | 3.6 | 23.2 | 104.8 | 160.9 | 2,769.6 | 552.1 | 2,073.7 | 143.8 |
| **Rocky Mount, NC M.S.A.** | **146,985** | | | | | | | | | |
| Includes Edgecombe and Nash Counties | | | | | | | | | | |
| City of Rocky Mount | 57,121 | 731 | 7 | 30 | 267 | 427 | 4,234 | 1,345 | 2,704 | 185 |
| Total area actually reporting | 100.0% | 986 | 11 | 50 | 323 | 602 | 6,365 | 2,285 | 3,775 | 305 |
| Rate per 100,000 inhabitants | | 670.8 | 7.5 | 34.0 | 219.8 | 409.6 | 4,330.4 | 1,554.6 | 2,568.3 | 207.5 |
| **Rome, GA M.S.A.** | **96,145** | | | | | | | | | |
| Includes Floyd County | | | | | | | | | | |
| City of Rome | 36,091 | 211 | 1 | 22 | 85 | 103 | 1,876 | 455 | 1,341 | 80 |
| Total area actually reporting | 100.0% | 426 | 3 | 26 | 95 | 302 | 3,093 | 787 | 2,122 | 184 |
| Rate per 100,000 inhabitants | | 443.1 | 3.1 | 27.0 | 98.8 | 314.1 | 3,217.0 | 818.6 | 2,207.1 | 191.4 |
| **Sacramento Arden-Arcade Roseville, CA M.S.A.** | **2,139,517** | | | | | | | | | |
| Includes El Dorado, Placer, Sacramento, and Yolo Counties | | | | | | | | | | |
| City of Sacramento | 470,308 | 4,165 | 30 | 179 | 1,606 | 2,350 | 21,001 | 5,135 | 11,720 | 4,146 |
| City of Roseville | 116,846 | 323 | 2 | 14 | 92 | 215 | 3,869 | 525 | 3,020 | 324 |
| City of Folsom | 69,728 | 108 | 2 | 13 | 28 | 65 | 1,504 | 272 | 1,164 | 68 |
| City of Woodland | 55,138 | 158 | 2 | 10 | 33 | 113 | 1,537 | 384 | 978 | 175 |
| Total area actually reporting | 100.0% | 10,880 | 86 | 627 | 3,680 | 6,487 | 68,361 | 16,421 | 41,868 | 10,072 |
| Rate per 100,000 inhabitants | | 508.5 | 4.0 | 29.3 | 172.0 | 303.2 | 3,195.2 | 767.5 | 1,956.9 | 470.8 |
| **Saginaw-Saginaw Township North, MI M.S.A.[1]** | **198,943** | | | | | | | | | |
| Includes Saginaw County[1] | | | | | | | | | | |
| City of Saginaw[1] | 54,997 | 1,393 | 11 | 37 | 256 | 1,089 | 2,553 | 1,501 | 899 | 153 |
| Total area actually reporting | 100.0% | 1,852 | 14 | 91 | 327 | 1,420 | 6,181 | 2,474 | 3,391 | 316 |
| Rate per 100,000 inhabitants | | 930.9 | 7.0 | 45.7 | 164.4 | 713.8 | 3,106.9 | 1,243.6 | 1,704.5 | 158.8 |
| **Salem, OR M.S.A.** | **396,094** | | | | | | | | | |
| Includes Marion and Polk Counties | | | | | | | | | | |
| City of Salem | 155,329 | 576 | 5 | 71 | 121 | 379 | 6,213 | 967 | 4,617 | 629 |
| Total area actually reporting | 100.0% | 934 | 7 | 124 | 187 | 616 | 12,257 | 2,163 | 8,818 | 1,276 |
| Rate per 100,000 inhabitants | | 235.8 | 1.8 | 31.3 | 47.2 | 155.5 | 3,094.5 | 546.1 | 2,226.2 | 322.1 |
| **Salinas, CA M.S.A.** | **407,403** | | | | | | | | | |
| Includes Monterey County | | | | | | | | | | |
| City of Salinas | 143,660 | 1,133 | 29 | 47 | 379 | 678 | 4,966 | 1,382 | 2,463 | 1,121 |
| Total area actually reporting | 100.0% | 2,118 | 51 | 125 | 657 | 1,285 | 11,204 | 3,151 | 6,245 | 1,808 |
| Rate per 100,000 inhabitants | | 519.9 | 12.5 | 30.7 | 161.3 | 315.4 | 2,750.1 | 773.4 | 1,532.9 | 443.8 |
| **Salisbury, MD M.S.A.** | **122,004** | | | | | | | | | |
| Includes Somerset and Wicomico Counties | | | | | | | | | | |
| City of Salisbury | 28,800 | 643 | 2 | 20 | 198 | 423 | 2,609 | 727 | 1,778 | 104 |
| Total area actually reporting | 100.0% | 1,027 | 7 | 39 | 274 | 707 | 4,970 | 1,553 | 3,236 | 181 |
| Rate per 100,000 inhabitants | | 841.8 | 5.7 | 32.0 | 224.6 | 579.5 | 4,073.6 | 1,272.9 | 2,652.4 | 148.4 |
| **Salt Lake City, UT M.S.A.** | **1,126,937** | | | | | | | | | |
| Includes Salt Lake, Summit, and Tooele Counties | | | | | | | | | | |
| City of Salt Lake City | 180,724 | 1,276 | 3 | 100 | 411 | 762 | 14,503 | 2,173 | 10,888 | 1,442 |
| Total area actually reporting | 99.8% | 3,915 | 21 | 480 | 967 | 2,447 | 53,378 | 8,790 | 39,476 | 5,112 |
| Estimated total | 100.0% | 3,919 | 21 | 481 | 968 | 2,449 | 53,441 | 8,800 | 39,524 | 5,117 |
| Rate per 100,000 inhabitants | | 347.8 | 1.9 | 42.7 | 85.9 | 217.3 | 4,742.1 | 780.9 | 3,507.2 | 454.1 |
| **San Angelo, TX M.S.A.** | **110,104** | | | | | | | | | |
| Includes Irion and Tom Green Counties | | | | | | | | | | |
| City of San Angelo | 92,269 | 368 | 8 | 65 | 45 | 250 | 4,247 | 996 | 3,092 | 159 |
| Total area actually reporting | 100.0% | 406 | 9 | 79 | 46 | 272 | 4,625 | 1,111 | 3,347 | 167 |
| Rate per 100,000 inhabitants | | 368.7 | 8.2 | 71.8 | 41.8 | 247.0 | 4,200.6 | 1,009.0 | 3,039.9 | 151.7 |

[1] The FBI determined that the agency's data were overreported. Consequently, affected data are not included in this table.

**Table 6. Crime, by Metropolitan Statistical Area, 2009—*Continued***

(Number, percent, rate per 100,000 population.)

| Area | Population | Violent crime | Murder and non-negligent man-slaughter | Forcible rape | Robbery | Aggravated assault | Property crime | Burglary | Larceny-theft | Motor vehicle theft |
|---|---|---|---|---|---|---|---|---|---|---|
| **San Antonio-New Braunfels, TX M.S.A.** | **2,072,016** | | | | | | | | | |
| Includes Atascosa, Bandera, Bexar, Comal, Guadalupe, Kendall, Medina, and Wilson Counties | | | | | | | | | | |
| City of San Antonio | 1,373,936 | 7,844 | 99 | 628 | 2,683 | 4,434 | 91,651 | 18,164 | 67,684 | 5,803 |
| City of New Braunfels | 55,584 | 142 | 0 | 14 | 39 | 89 | 2,149 | 366 | 1,691 | 92 |
| Total area actually reporting | 99.9% | 9,727 | 130 | 869 | 3,031 | 5,697 | 113,579 | 23,593 | 83,102 | 6,884 |
| Estimated total | 100.0% | 9,731 | 130 | 869 | 3,032 | 5,700 | 113,628 | 23,603 | 83,138 | 6,887 |
| Rate per 100,000 inhabitants | | 469.6 | 6.3 | 41.9 | 146.3 | 275.1 | 5,483.9 | 1,139.1 | 4,012.4 | 332.4 |
| **San Diego-Carlsbad-San Marcos, CA M.S.A.** | **3,010,824** | | | | | | | | | |
| Includes San Diego County | | | | | | | | | | |
| City of San Diego | 1,314,773 | 5,931 | 41 | 318 | 1,905 | 3,667 | 32,246 | 6,693 | 18,057 | 7,496 |
| City of Carlsbad | 98,482 | 287 | 5 | 26 | 53 | 203 | 1,908 | 446 | 1,327 | 135 |
| City of San Marcos | 82,258 | 226 | 2 | 16 | 68 | 140 | 1,416 | 307 | 901 | 208 |
| City of National City | 59,230 | 426 | 2 | 14 | 194 | 216 | 1,923 | 308 | 1,051 | 564 |
| Total area actually reporting | 100.0% | 12,775 | 75 | 746 | 4,033 | 7,921 | 69,738 | 14,522 | 41,278 | 13,938 |
| Rate per 100,000 inhabitants | | 424.3 | 2.5 | 24.8 | 134.0 | 263.1 | 2,316.2 | 482.3 | 1,371.0 | 462.9 |
| **Sandusky, OH M.S.A.** | **77,014** | | | | | | | | | |
| Includes Erie County | | | | | | | | | | |
| City of Sandusky | 25,461 | 127 | 0 | 12 | 31 | 84 | 1,237 | 295 | 922 | 20 |
| Total area actually reporting | 98.7% | 188 | 2 | 17 | 46 | 123 | 2,326 | 539 | 1,733 | 54 |
| Estimated total | 100.0% | 190 | 2 | 17 | 47 | 124 | 2,355 | 545 | 1,755 | 55 |
| Rate per 100,000 inhabitants | | 246.7 | 2.6 | 22.1 | 61.0 | 161.0 | 3,057.9 | 707.7 | 2,278.8 | 71.4 |
| **San Francisco-Oakland-Fremont, CA M.S.A.** | **4,275,475** | | | | | | | | | |
| Includes the Metropolitan Divisions of Oakland-Fremont-Hayward and San Francisco-San Mateo-Redwood City | | | | | | | | | | |
| City of San Francisco | 809,755 | 5,957 | 45 | 179 | 3,423 | 2,310 | 34,509 | 5,197 | 24,399 | 4,913 |
| City of Oakland | 404,553 | 6,793 | 104 | 326 | 2,898 | 3,465 | 20,173 | 4,798 | 8,833 | 6,542 |
| City of Fremont | 202,714 | 490 | 2 | 34 | 217 | 237 | 4,978 | 1,190 | 3,237 | 551 |
| City of Hayward | 142,227 | 741 | 7 | 29 | 446 | 259 | 4,405 | 979 | 1,974 | 1,452 |
| City of Berkeley | 101,190 | 615 | 6 | 27 | 444 | 138 | 6,467 | 1,079 | 4,661 | 727 |
| City of San Mateo | 92,208 | 338 | 2 | 16 | 110 | 210 | 2,172 | 274 | 1,720 | 178 |
| City of San Leandro | 77,676 | 409 | 2 | 22 | 261 | 124 | 3,445 | 547 | 1,966 | 932 |
| City of Redwood City | 73,905 | 232 | 1 | 20 | 89 | 122 | 1,860 | 437 | 1,199 | 224 |
| City of Pleasanton | 67,116 | 73 | 0 | 4 | 20 | 49 | 1,284 | 136 | 1,053 | 95 |
| City of Walnut Creek | 63,356 | 131 | 1 | 4 | 41 | 85 | 2,647 | 504 | 1,940 | 203 |
| City of South San Francisco | 62,716 | 196 | 0 | 9 | 72 | 115 | 1,468 | 400 | 790 | 278 |
| City of San Rafael | 55,544 | 204 | 1 | 14 | 77 | 112 | 1,705 | 333 | 1,086 | 286 |
| Total area actually reporting | 100.0% | 24,072 | 292 | 1,098 | 11,305 | 11,377 | 143,999 | 28,386 | 88,827 | 26,786 |
| Rate per 100,000 inhabitants | | 563.0 | 6.8 | 25.7 | 264.4 | 266.1 | 3,368.0 | 663.9 | 2,077.6 | 626.5 |
| **Oakland-Fremont-Hayward, CA M.D.** | **2,506,947** | | | | | | | | | |
| Includes Alameda and Contra Costa Counties | | | | | | | | | | |
| Total area actually reporting | 100.0% | 15,446 | 227 | 753 | 6,948 | 7,518 | 87,413 | 18,839 | 49,314 | 19,260 |
| Rate per 100,000 inhabitants | | 616.1 | 9.1 | 30.0 | 277.1 | 299.9 | 3,486.8 | 751.5 | 1,967.1 | 768.3 |
| **San Francisco-San Mateo-Redwood City, CA M.D.** | **1,768,528** | | | | | | | | | |
| Includes Marin, San Francisco, and San Mateo Counties | | | | | | | | | | |
| Total area actually reporting | 100.0% | 8,626 | 65 | 345 | 4,357 | 3,859 | 56,586 | 9,547 | 39,513 | 7,526 |
| Rate per 100,000 inhabitants | | 487.8 | 3.7 | 19.5 | 246.4 | 218.2 | 3,199.6 | 539.8 | 2,234.2 | 425.6 |
| **San Jose-Sunnyvale-Santa Clara, CA M.S.A.** | **1,821,945** | | | | | | | | | |
| Includes San Benito and Santa Clara Counties | | | | | | | | | | |
| City of San Jose | 954,009 | 3,439 | 28 | 258 | 1,025 | 2,128 | 22,755 | 3,741 | 13,635 | 5,379 |
| City of Sunnyvale | 132,144 | 169 | 1 | 11 | 71 | 86 | 2,769 | 431 | 2,026 | 312 |
| City of Santa Clara | 111,106 | 168 | 6 | 20 | 63 | 79 | 3,028 | 428 | 2,182 | 418 |
| City of Mountain View | 71,423 | 180 | 0 | 14 | 47 | 119 | 1,972 | 253 | 1,554 | 165 |
| City of Milpitas | 68,047 | 132 | 2 | 6 | 59 | 65 | 2,050 | 274 | 1,561 | 215 |
| City of Palo Alto | 59,490 | 108 | 1 | 9 | 29 | 69 | 1,666 | 267 | 1,350 | 49 |
| City of Cupertino | 53,760 | 37 | 1 | 4 | 11 | 21 | 1,045 | 191 | 799 | 55 |
| Total area actually reporting | 100.0% | 5,259 | 46 | 396 | 1,553 | 3,264 | 43,862 | 7,539 | 28,838 | 7,485 |
| Rate per 100,000 inhabitants | | 288.6 | 2.5 | 21.7 | 85.2 | 179.1 | 2,407.4 | 413.8 | 1,582.8 | 410.8 |

## Table 6. Crime, by Metropolitan Statistical Area, 2009—*Continued*

(Number, percent, rate per 100,000 population.)

| Area | Population | Violent crime | Murder and non-negligent man-slaughter | Forcible rape | Robbery | Aggravated assault | Property crime | Burglary | Larceny-theft | Motor vehicle theft |
|---|---|---|---|---|---|---|---|---|---|---|
| **San Luis Obispo-Paso Robles, CA M.S.A.** | **266,382** | | | | | | | | | |
| Includes San Luis Obispo County | | | | | | | | | | |
| City of San Luis Obispo | 43,565 | 140 | 0 | 30 | 39 | 71 | 1,632 | 324 | 1,240 | 68 |
| City of Paso Robles | 29,204 | 93 | 0 | 15 | 11 | 67 | 927 | 267 | 595 | 65 |
| Total area actually reporting | 100.0% | 694 | 4 | 89 | 106 | 495 | 5,977 | 1,433 | 4,169 | 375 |
| Rate per 100,000 inhabitants | | 260.5 | 1.5 | 33.4 | 39.8 | 185.8 | 2,243.8 | 537.9 | 1,565.0 | 140.8 |
| **Santa Barbara-Santa Maria-Goleta, CA M.S.A.** | **404,613** | | | | | | | | | |
| Includes Santa Barbara County | | | | | | | | | | |
| City of Santa Barbara | 85,715 | 428 | 3 | 29 | 109 | 287 | 2,885 | 610 | 2,176 | 99 |
| City of Santa Maria | 87,381 | 735 | 5 | 42 | 73 | 615 | 1,826 | 554 | 864 | 408 |
| City of Goleta | 29,471 | 51 | 0 | 1 | 10 | 40 | 409 | 121 | 280 | 8 |
| Total area actually reporting | 100.0% | 1,897 | 11 | 123 | 262 | 1,501 | 8,909 | 2,290 | 5,937 | 682 |
| Rate per 100,000 inhabitants | | 468.8 | 2.7 | 30.4 | 64.8 | 371.0 | 2,201.9 | 566.0 | 1,467.3 | 168.6 |
| **Santa Cruz-Watsonville, CA M.S.A.** | **251,964** | | | | | | | | | |
| Includes Santa Cruz County | | | | | | | | | | |
| City of Santa Cruz | 56,155 | 453 | 4 | 36 | 91 | 322 | 3,116 | 466 | 2,467 | 183 |
| City of Watsonville | 50,898 | 350 | 4 | 17 | 86 | 243 | 1,825 | 285 | 1,259 | 281 |
| Total area actually reporting | 100.0% | 1,215 | 10 | 79 | 222 | 904 | 9,059 | 1,732 | 6,480 | 847 |
| Rate per 100,000 inhabitants | | 482.2 | 4.0 | 31.4 | 88.1 | 358.8 | 3,595.4 | 687.4 | 2,571.8 | 336.2 |
| **Santa Fe, NM M.S.A.** | **145,984** | | | | | | | | | |
| Includes Santa Fe County | | | | | | | | | | |
| City of Santa Fe | 72,845 | 309 | 13 | 15 | 88 | 193 | 4,273 | 2,217 | 1,854 | 202 |
| Total area actually reporting | 100.0% | 632 | 15 | 38 | 116 | 463 | 5,751 | 3,041 | 2,416 | 294 |
| Rate per 100,000 inhabitants | | 432.9 | 10.3 | 26.0 | 79.5 | 317.2 | 3,939.5 | 2,083.1 | 1,655.0 | 201.4 |
| **Santa Rosa-Petaluma, CA M.S.A.** | **465,831** | | | | | | | | | |
| Includes Sonoma County | | | | | | | | | | |
| City of Santa Rosa | 156,541 | 803 | 2 | 75 | 180 | 546 | 4,265 | 710 | 3,165 | 390 |
| City of Petaluma | 54,649 | 168 | 0 | 17 | 29 | 122 | 852 | 152 | 625 | 75 |
| Total area actually reporting | 100.0% | 1,917 | 9 | 163 | 318 | 1,427 | 9,450 | 1,993 | 6,671 | 786 |
| Rate per 100,000 inhabitants | | 411.5 | 1.9 | 35.0 | 68.3 | 306.3 | 2,028.6 | 427.8 | 1,432.1 | 168.7 |
| **Savannah, GA M.S.A.** | **337,908** | | | | | | | | | |
| Includes Bryan, Chatham, and Effingham Counties | | | | | | | | | | |
| City of Savannah-Chatham Metropolitan | 212,711 | 1,128 | 30 | 46 | 642 | 410 | 10,654 | 2,652 | 6,867 | 1,135 |
| Total area actually reporting | 100.0% | 1,448 | 31 | 76 | 711 | 630 | 14,210 | 3,590 | 9,222 | 1,398 |
| Rate per 100,000 inhabitants | | 428.5 | 9.2 | 22.5 | 210.4 | 186.4 | 4,205.3 | 1,062.4 | 2,729.1 | 413.7 |
| **Scranton Wilkes-Barre, PA M.S.A.** | **549,402** | | | | | | | | | |
| Includes Lackawanna, Luzerne, and Wyoming Counties | | | | | | | | | | |
| City of Scranton | 71,843 | 284 | 1 | 35 | 108 | 140 | 2,622 | 640 | 1,836 | 146 |
| City of Wilkes-Barre | 40,710 | 171 | 10 | 7 | 88 | 66 | 1,497 | 284 | 1,119 | 94 |
| Total area actually reporting | 98.1% | 1,422 | 26 | 119 | 310 | 967 | 12,023 | 2,395 | 8,999 | 629 |
| Estimated total | 100.0% | 1,444 | 26 | 120 | 316 | 982 | 12,229 | 2,428 | 9,163 | 638 |
| Rate per 100,000 inhabitants | | 262.8 | 4.7 | 21.8 | 57.5 | 178.7 | 2,225.9 | 441.9 | 1,667.8 | 116.1 |
| **Seattle-Tacoma-Bellevue, WA M.S.A.** | **3,398,863** | | | | | | | | | |
| Includes the Metropolitan Divisions of Seattle-Bellevue-Everett and Tacoma | | | | | | | | | | |
| City of Seattle | 602,531 | 3,861 | 22 | 102 | 1,792 | 1,945 | 35,090 | 6,709 | 25,095 | 3,286 |
| City of Tacoma | 197,557 | 1,944 | 8 | 143 | 648 | 1,145 | 13,977 | 2,905 | 9,395 | 1,677 |
| City of Bellevue | 125,054 | 162 | 2 | 25 | 61 | 74 | 3,950 | 621 | 3,150 | 179 |
| City of Everett | 98,431 | 610 | 2 | 51 | 263 | 294 | 6,948 | 1,099 | 5,070 | 779 |
| City of Kent | 84,363 | 507 | 1 | 82 | 180 | 244 | 3,820 | 828 | 2,381 | 611 |
| City of Renton | 63,599 | 314 | 2 | 32 | 152 | 128 | 4,322 | 800 | 3,041 | 481 |
| City of Auburn | 56,934 | 274 | 4 | 13 | 92 | 165 | 3,321 | 590 | 2,362 | 369 |
| Total area actually reporting | 100.0% | 13,061 | 89 | 1,090 | 4,863 | 7,019 | 137,001 | 28,673 | 94,210 | 14,118 |
| Rate per 100,000 inhabitants | | 384.3 | 2.6 | 32.1 | 143.1 | 206.5 | 4,030.8 | 843.6 | 2,771.8 | 415.4 |
| **Seattle-Bellevue-Everett, WA M.D.** | **2,598,918** | | | | | | | | | |
| Includes King and Snohomish Counties | | | | | | | | | | |
| Total area actually reporting | 100.0% | 8,833 | 60 | 743 | 3,626 | 4,404 | 102,225 | 20,746 | 71,217 | 10,262 |
| Rate per 100,000 inhabitants | | 339.9 | 2.3 | 28.6 | 139.5 | 169.5 | 3,933.4 | 798.3 | 2,740.3 | 394.9 |
| **Tacoma, WA M.D.** | **799,945** | | | | | | | | | |
| Includes Pierce County | | | | | | | | | | |
| Total area actually reporting | 100.0% | 4,228 | 29 | 347 | 1,237 | 2,615 | 34,776 | 7,927 | 22,993 | 3,856 |
| Rate per 100,000 inhabitants | | 528.5 | 3.6 | 43.4 | 154.6 | 326.9 | 4,347.3 | 990.9 | 2,874.3 | 482.0 |

## Table 6. Crime, by Metropolitan Statistical Area, 2009—*Continued*

(Number, percent, rate per 100,000 population.)

| Area | Population | Violent crime | Murder and non-negligent man-slaughter | Forcible rape | Robbery | Aggravated assault | Property crime | Burglary | Larceny-theft | Motor vehicle theft |
|---|---|---|---|---|---|---|---|---|---|---|
| **Sebastian-Vero Beach, FL M.S.A.** | **133,420** | | | | | | | | | |
| Includes Indian River County | | | | | | | | | | |
| City of Sebastian | 20,777 | 40 | 1 | 5 | 3 | 31 | 655 | 188 | 452 | 15 |
| City of Vero Beach | 16,908 | 89 | 1 | 1 | 25 | 62 | 557 | 125 | 413 | 19 |
| Total area actually reporting | 100.0% | 450 | 7 | 16 | 80 | 347 | 4,034 | 1,034 | 2,849 | 151 |
| Rate per 100,000 inhabitants | | 337.3 | 5.2 | 12.0 | 60.0 | 260.1 | 3,023.5 | 775.0 | 2,135.4 | 113.2 |
| **Sheboygan, WI M.S.A.** | **114,705** | | | | | | | | | |
| Includes Sheboygan County | | | | | | | | | | |
| City of Sheboygan | 47,578 | 99 | 2 | 18 | 28 | 51 | 1,900 | 312 | 1,539 | 49 |
| Total area actually reporting | 100.0% | 159 | 2 | 26 | 32 | 99 | 2,941 | 477 | 2,396 | 68 |
| Rate per 100,000 inhabitants | | 138.6 | 1.7 | 22.7 | 27.9 | 86.3 | 2,564.0 | 415.8 | 2,088.8 | 59.3 |
| **Sherman-Denison, TX M.S.A.** | **119,831** | | | | | | | | | |
| Includes Grayson County | | | | | | | | | | |
| City of Sherman | 38,414 | 187 | 1 | 2 | 29 | 155 | 1,596 | 329 | 1,216 | 51 |
| City of Denison | 24,142 | 92 | 1 | 3 | 28 | 60 | 1,178 | 253 | 865 | 60 |
| Total area actually reporting | 100.0% | 340 | 4 | 10 | 67 | 259 | 3,884 | 939 | 2,765 | 180 |
| Rate per 100,000 inhabitants | | 283.7 | 3.3 | 8.3 | 55.9 | 216.1 | 3,241.2 | 783.6 | 2,307.4 | 150.2 |
| **Shreveport-Bossier City, LA M.S.A.**[2] | **393,564** | | | | | | | | | |
| Includes Bossier, Caddo, and De Soto Parishes | | | | | | | | | | |
| City of Shreveport | 199,629 | 1,776 | 31 | 124 | 485 | 1,136 | 10,425 | 2,730 | 7,054 | 641 |
| City of Bossier City[2] | 63,077 | | 3 | | 59 | | 2,646 | 478 | 1,994 | 174 |
| Total area actually reporting | 97.5% | | 36 | | 562 | | 15,172 | 3,733 | 10,494 | 945 |
| Estimated total | 100.0% | | 37 | | 570 | | 15,645 | 3,826 | 10,856 | 963 |
| Rate per 100,000 inhabitants | | | 9.4 | | 144.8 | | 3,975.2 | 972.1 | 2,758.4 | 244.7 |
| **Sioux City, IA-NE-SD M.S.A.** | **143,132** | | | | | | | | | |
| Includes Woodbury County, IA; Dakota and Dixon Counties, NE; and Union County, SD | | | | | | | | | | |
| City of Sioux City, IA | 82,573 | 342 | 3 | 25 | 43 | 271 | 2,833 | 625 | 2,037 | 171 |
| Total area actually reporting | 96.8% | 404 | 4 | 33 | 43 | 324 | 3,467 | 747 | 2,518 | 202 |
| Estimated total | 100.0% | 407 | 4 | 34 | 43 | 326 | 3,530 | 756 | 2,570 | 204 |
| Rate per 100,000 inhabitants | | 284.4 | 2.8 | 23.8 | 30.0 | 227.8 | 2,466.3 | 528.2 | 1,795.5 | 142.5 |
| **Sioux Falls, SD M.S.A.** | **239,252** | | | | | | | | | |
| Includes Lincoln, McCook, Minnehaha, and Turner Counties | | | | | | | | | | |
| City of Sioux Falls | 158,672 | 454 | 1 | 133 | 47 | 273 | 4,609 | 748 | 3,584 | 277 |
| Total area actually reporting | 99.3% | 506 | 1 | 149 | 48 | 308 | 5,370 | 946 | 4,092 | 332 |
| Estimated total | 100.0% | 507 | 1 | 149 | 48 | 309 | 5,392 | 949 | 4,110 | 333 |
| Rate per 100,000 inhabitants | | 211.9 | 0.4 | 62.3 | 20.1 | 129.2 | 2,253.7 | 396.7 | 1,717.9 | 139.2 |
| **South Bend-Mishawaka, IN-MI M.S.A.**[1] | **317,097** | | | | | | | | | |
| Includes St. Joseph County, IN and Cass County, MI[1] | | | | | | | | | | |
| City of South Bend, IN | 103,326 | 769 | 14 | 56 | 346 | 353 | 6,113 | 2,086 | 3,702 | 325 |
| City of Mishawaka, IN | 50,378 | 182 | 1 | 15 | 72 | 94 | 3,275 | 459 | 2,629 | 187 |
| Total area actually reporting | 99.8% | 1,175 | 19 | 109 | 455 | 592 | 12,954 | 3,458 | 8,798 | 698 |
| Estimated total | 100.0% | 1,176 | 19 | 109 | 455 | 593 | 12,974 | 3,461 | 8,814 | 699 |
| Rate per 100,000 inhabitants | | 370.9 | 6.0 | 34.4 | 143.5 | 187.0 | 4,091.5 | 1,091.5 | 2,779.6 | 220.4 |
| **Spartanburg, SC M.S.A.** | **285,421** | | | | | | | | | |
| Includes Spartanburg County | | | | | | | | | | |
| City of Spartanburg | 39,561 | 800 | 4 | 19 | 175 | 602 | 3,381 | 764 | 2,390 | 227 |
| Total area actually reporting | 99.8% | 1,740 | 13 | 101 | 351 | 1,275 | 10,846 | 2,734 | 7,322 | 790 |
| Estimated total | 100.0% | 1,744 | 13 | 101 | 352 | 1,278 | 10,871 | 2,739 | 7,341 | 791 |
| Rate per 100,000 inhabitants | | 611.0 | 4.6 | 35.4 | 123.3 | 447.8 | 3,808.8 | 959.6 | 2,572.0 | 277.1 |
| **Spokane, WA M.S.A.** | **470,570** | | | | | | | | | |
| Includes Spokane County | | | | | | | | | | |
| City of Spokane | 202,932 | 1,270 | 7 | 75 | 443 | 745 | 13,166 | 2,565 | 8,864 | 1,737 |
| Total area actually reporting | 100.0% | 1,775 | 10 | 116 | 538 | 1,111 | 20,070 | 4,071 | 13,739 | 2,260 |
| Rate per 100,000 inhabitants | | 377.2 | 2.1 | 24.7 | 114.3 | 236.1 | 4,265.0 | 865.1 | 2,919.7 | 480.3 |
| **Springfield, MA M.S.A.** | **697,676** | | | | | | | | | |
| Includes Franklin, Hampden, and Hampshire Counties | | | | | | | | | | |
| City of Springfield | 153,533 | 1,929 | 16 | 116 | 581 | 1,216 | 7,518 | 2,068 | 4,615 | 835 |
| Total area actually reporting | 93.6% | 3,563 | 23 | 302 | 798 | 2,440 | 19,035 | 4,926 | 12,562 | 1,547 |
| Estimated total | 100.0% | 3,706 | 24 | 312 | 825 | 2,545 | 19,930 | 5,143 | 13,181 | 1,606 |
| Rate per 100,000 inhabitants | | 531.2 | 3.4 | 44.7 | 118.2 | 364.8 | 2,856.6 | 737.2 | 1,889.3 | 230.2 |

[1] The FBI determined that the agency's data were overreported. Consequently, affected data are not included in this table.

[2] Because of changes in the state/local agency's reporting practices, figures are not comparable to previous years' data.

## Table 6. Crime, by Metropolitan Statistical Area, 2009—*Continued*

(Number, percent, rate per 100,000 population.)

| Area | Population | Violent crime | Murder and non-negligent man-slaughter | Forcible rape | Robbery | Aggravated assault | Property crime | Burglary | Larceny-theft | Motor vehicle theft |
|---|---|---|---|---|---|---|---|---|---|---|
| **Springfield, MO M.S.A.[1]** | **433,099** | | | | | | | | | |
| Includes Christian, Dallas, Greene, Polk, and Webster[1] Counties | | | | | | | | | | |
| City of Springfield | 156,659 | 1,197 | 6 | 112 | 299 | 780 | 14,012 | 2,314 | 10,859 | 839 |
| Total area actually reporting | 100.0% | 1,833 | 8 | 154 | 339 | 1,332 | 19,056 | 3,697 | 14,275 | 1,084 |
| Rate per 100,000 inhabitants | | 423.2 | 1.8 | 35.6 | 78.3 | 307.6 | 4,399.9 | 853.6 | 3,296.0 | 250.3 |
| **Springfield, OH M.S.A.** | **139,752** | | | | | | | | | |
| Includes Clark County | | | | | | | | | | |
| City of Springfield | 61,881 | 467 | 4 | 43 | 214 | 206 | 4,512 | 1,287 | 2,977 | 248 |
| Total area actually reporting | 99.8% | 489 | 4 | 49 | 223 | 213 | 5,650 | 1,554 | 3,820 | 276 |
| Estimated total | 100.0% | 489 | 4 | 49 | 223 | 213 | 5,658 | 1,556 | 3,826 | 276 |
| Rate per 100,000 inhabitants | | 349.9 | 2.9 | 35.1 | 159.6 | 152.4 | 4,048.6 | 1,113.4 | 2,737.7 | 197.5 |
| **Springfield, OH M.S.A.** | **146,172** | | | | | | | | | |
| Includes Centre County | | | | | | | | | | |
| City of State College | 53,587 | 75 | 0 | 2 | 14 | 59 | 1,000 | 117 | 871 | 12 |
| Total area actually reporting | 100.0% | 183 | 2 | 25 | 25 | 131 | 2,677 | 382 | 2,246 | 49 |
| Rate per 100,000 inhabitants | | 125.2 | 1.4 | 17.1 | 17.1 | 89.6 | 1,831.4 | 261.3 | 1,536.5 | 33.5 |
| **St. Cloud, MN M.S.A.[4]** | **189,562** | | | | | | | | | |
| Includes Benton and Stearns Counties[4] | | | | | | | | | | |
| City of St. Cloud[4] | 67,804 | | 1 | | 41 | 143 | 2,768 | 348 | 2,328 | 92 |
| Total area actually reporting | 100.0% | | 2 | | 43 | 214 | 4,374 | 574 | 3,656 | 144 |
| Rate per 100,000 inhabitants | | | 1.1 | | 22.7 | 112.9 | 2,307.4 | 302.8 | 1,928.7 | 76.0 |
| **St. George, UT M.S.A.** | **143,274** | | | | | | | | | |
| Includes Washington County | | | | | | | | | | |
| City of St. George | 75,391 | 92 | 0 | 13 | 13 | 66 | 1,540 | 322 | 1,143 | 75 |
| Total area actually reporting | 100.0% | 184 | 2 | 30 | 18 | 134 | 2,458 | 518 | 1,812 | 128 |
| Rate per 100,000 inhabitants | | 128.4 | 1.4 | 20.9 | 12.6 | 93.5 | 1,715.6 | 361.5 | 1,264.7 | 89.3 |
| **St. Joseph, MO-KS M.S.A.** | **126,650** | | | | | | | | | |
| Includes Doniphan County, KS and Andrew, Buchanan, and De Kalb Counties, MO | | | | | | | | | | |
| City of St. Joseph, MO | 76,436 | 441 | 3 | 12 | 109 | 317 | 3,794 | 970 | 2,639 | 185 |
| Total area actually reporting | 99.2% | 516 | 4 | 17 | 114 | 381 | 4,678 | 1,247 | 3,201 | 230 |
| Estimated total | 100.0% | 518 | 4 | 17 | 114 | 383 | 4,702 | 1,251 | 3,220 | 231 |
| Rate per 100,000 inhabitants | | 409.0 | 3.2 | 13.4 | 90.0 | 302.4 | 3,712.6 | 987.8 | 2,542.4 | 182.4 |
| **St. Louis, MO-IL M.S.A.[4]** | **2,829,698** | | | | | | | | | |
| Includes Bond, Calhoun, Clinton, Jersey, Macoupin, Madison, Monroe, and St. Clair Counties, IL[4] and Franklin, Jefferson, Lincoln, St. Charles, St. Louis, Warren, and Washington Counties and St. Louis City, MO | | | | | | | | | | |
| City of St. Louis, MO | 355,208 | 7,353 | 143 | 250 | 2,721 | 4,239 | 29,595 | 6,834 | 17,799 | 4,962 |
| City of St. Charles, MO | 64,807 | 159 | 0 | 9 | 31 | 119 | 2,085 | 270 | 1,739 | 76 |
| Total area actually reporting | 76.7% | | 192 | | 3,845 | 7,624 | 76,024 | 14,840 | 52,914 | 8,270 |
| Estimated total | 100.0% | | 210 | | 4,182 | 8,410 | 89,656 | 17,541 | 63,245 | 8,870 |
| Rate per 100,000 inhabitants | | | 7.4 | | 147.8 | 297.2 | 3,168.4 | 619.9 | 2,235.0 | 313.5 |
| **Stockton, CA M.S.A.** | **682,784** | | | | | | | | | |
| Includes San Joaquin County | | | | | | | | | | |
| City of Stockton | 292,212 | 3,703 | 33 | 82 | 1,259 | 2,329 | 15,427 | 3,980 | 9,274 | 2,173 |
| Total area actually reporting | 100.0% | 5,531 | 51 | 148 | 1,759 | 3,573 | 28,772 | 7,521 | 17,260 | 3,991 |
| Rate per 100,000 inhabitants | | 810.1 | 7.5 | 21.7 | 257.6 | 523.3 | 4,213.9 | 1,101.5 | 2,527.9 | 584.5 |
| **Sumter, SC M.S.A.[1]** | **104,675** | | | | | | | | | |
| Includes Sumter County[1] | | | | | | | | | | |
| City of Sumter | 38,399 | 486 | 8 | 8 | 102 | 368 | 2,731 | 829 | 1,735 | 167 |
| Total area actually reporting | 100.0% | 695 | 12 | 17 | 140 | 526 | 3,433 | 1,250 | 1,943 | 240 |
| Rate per 100,000 inhabitants | | 664.0 | 11.5 | 16.2 | 133.7 | 502.5 | 3,279.7 | 1,194.2 | 1,856.2 | 229.3 |
| **Syracuse, NY M.S.A.** | **642,939** | | | | | | | | | |
| Includes Madison, Onondaga, and Oswego Counties | | | | | | | | | | |
| City of Syracuse | 137,208 | 1,343 | 18 | 70 | 403 | 852 | 5,779 | 1,946 | 3,495 | 338 |
| Total area actually reporting | 99.3% | 1,917 | 21 | 140 | 535 | 1,221 | 15,858 | 3,922 | 11,317 | 619 |
| Estimated total | 100.0% | 1,925 | 21 | 140 | 538 | 1,226 | 15,945 | 3,934 | 11,389 | 622 |
| Rate per 100,000 inhabitants | | 299.4 | 3.3 | 21.8 | 83.7 | 190.7 | 2,480.0 | 611.9 | 1,771.4 | 96.7 |

[1] The FBI determined that the agency's data were overreported. Consequently, affected data are not included in this table.
[4] It was determined that the agency did not follow national Uniform Crime Reporting (UCR) Program guidelines for reporting an offense. Consequently, this figure is not included in this table.

## Table 6. Crime, by Metropolitan Statistical Area, 2009—*Continued*

(Number, percent, rate per 100,000 population.)

| Area | Population | Violent crime | Murder and non-negligent man-slaughter | Forcible rape | Robbery | Aggravated assault | Property crime | Burglary | Larceny-theft | Motor vehicle theft |
|---|---|---|---|---|---|---|---|---|---|---|
| **Tallahassee, FL M.S.A.** | **358,382** | | | | | | | | | |
| Includes Gadsden, Jefferson, Leon, and Wakulla Counties | | | | | | | | | | |
| City of Tallahassee | 174,183 | 1,647 | 6 | 120 | 474 | 1,047 | 8,438 | 3,125 | 4,975 | 338 |
| Total area actually reporting | 98.1% | 2,710 | 13 | 165 | 586 | 1,946 | 12,582 | 4,741 | 7,354 | 487 |
| Estimated total | 100.0% | 2,748 | 13 | 167 | 598 | 1,970 | 12,872 | 4,806 | 7,559 | 507 |
| Rate per 100,000 inhabitants | | 766.8 | 3.6 | 46.6 | 166.9 | 549.7 | 3,591.7 | 1,341.0 | 2,109.2 | 141.5 |
| **Tampa-St. Petersburg-Clearwater, FL M.S.A.** | **2,750,962** | | | | | | | | | |
| Includes Hernando, Hillsborough, Pasco, and Pinellas Counties | | | | | | | | | | |
| City of Tampa | 345,233 | 2,597 | 20 | 80 | 909 | 1,588 | 12,960 | 3,501 | 8,098 | 1,361 |
| City of St. Petersburg | 244,933 | 3,334 | 11 | 112 | 907 | 2,304 | 17,198 | 4,366 | 10,575 | 2,257 |
| City of Clearwater | 105,383 | 924 | 3 | 43 | 275 | 603 | 4,720 | 802 | 3,617 | 301 |
| City of Largo | 72,567 | 517 | 1 | 46 | 133 | 337 | 3,175 | 519 | 2,477 | 179 |
| Total area actually reporting | 100.0% | 16,200 | 99 | 806 | 4,290 | 11,005 | 106,322 | 27,088 | 70,799 | 8,435 |
| Rate per 100,000 inhabitants | | 588.9 | 3.6 | 29.3 | 155.9 | 400.0 | 3,864.9 | 984.7 | 2,573.6 | 306.6 |
| **Texarkana, TX-Texarkana, AR M.S.A.** | **136,443** | | | | | | | | | |
| Includes Miller County, AR and Bowie County, TX | | | | | | | | | | |
| City of Texarkana, TX | 36,812 | 555 | 10 | 28 | 145 | 372 | 2,544 | 735 | 1,667 | 142 |
| City of Texarkana, AR | 30,348 | 269 | 2 | 25 | 66 | 176 | 1,894 | 476 | 1,261 | 157 |
| Total area actually reporting | 90.2% | 982 | 14 | 68 | 225 | 675 | 5,470 | 1,635 | 3,469 | 366 |
| Estimated total | 100.0% | 1,029 | 15 | 73 | 227 | 714 | 5,758 | 1,762 | 3,606 | 390 |
| Rate per 100,000 inhabitants | | 754.2 | 11.0 | 53.5 | 166.4 | 523.3 | 4,220.1 | 1,291.4 | 2,642.9 | 285.8 |
| **Toledo, OH M.S.A.**[5] | **649,954** | | | | | | | | | |
| Includes Fulton, Lucas, Ottawa, and Wood Counties | | | | | | | | | | |
| City of Toledo[5] | 291,066 | 3,251 | 33 | 165 | 1,222 | 1,831 | | 8,064 | | 1,337 |
| Total area actually reporting | 95.1% | 3,568 | 34 | 220 | 1,304 | 2,010 | | 9,799 | | 1,633 |
| Estimated total | 100.0% | 3,623 | 35 | 228 | 1,326 | 2,034 | | 9,977 | | 1,669 |
| Rate per 100,000 inhabitants | | 557.4 | 5.4 | 35.1 | 204.0 | 312.9 | | 1,535.0 | | 256.8 |
| **Topeka, KS M.S.A.** | **230,405** | | | | | | | | | |
| Includes Jackson, Jefferson, Osage, Shawnee, and Wabaunsee Counties | | | | | | | | | | |
| City of Topeka | 123,449 | 715 | 10 | 44 | 301 | 360 | 6,702 | 1,663 | 4,632 | 407 |
| Total area actually reporting | 97.4% | 944 | 20 | 63 | 316 | 545 | 8,949 | 2,260 | 6,187 | 502 |
| Estimated total | 100.0% | 960 | 20 | 65 | 318 | 557 | 9,096 | 2,286 | 6,300 | 510 |
| Rate per 100,000 inhabitants | | 416.7 | 8.7 | 28.2 | 138.0 | 241.7 | 3,947.8 | 992.2 | 2,734.3 | 221.3 |
| **Trenton-Ewing, NJ M.S.A.** | **366,219** | | | | | | | | | |
| Includes Mercer County | | | | | | | | | | |
| City of Trenton | 82,609 | 1,154 | 17 | 26 | 512 | 599 | 2,624 | 824 | 1,399 | 401 |
| City of Ewing Township | 36,098 | 108 | 0 | 2 | 33 | 73 | 664 | 142 | 478 | 44 |
| Total area actually reporting | 100.0% | 1,677 | 17 | 63 | 699 | 898 | 7,701 | 1,663 | 5,404 | 634 |
| Rate per 100,000 inhabitants | | 457.9 | 4.6 | 17.2 | 190.9 | 245.2 | 2,102.8 | 454.1 | 1,475.6 | 173.1 |
| **Tucson, AZ M.S.A.**[5] | **1,020,210** | | | | | | | | | |
| Includes Pima County | | | | | | | | | | |
| City of Tucson[5] | 547,981 | 3,560 | 35 | 204 | 1,246 | 2,075 | | 5,062 | | 3,564 |
| Total area actually reporting | 100.0% | 4,481 | 55 | 301 | 1,559 | 2,566 | | 7,998 | | 4,872 |
| Rate per 100,000 inhabitants | | 439.2 | 5.4 | 29.5 | 152.8 | 251.5 | | 784.0 | | 477.5 |
| **Tulsa, OK M.S.A.** | **928,117** | | | | | | | | | |
| Includes Creek, Okmulgee, Osage, Pawnee, Rogers, Tulsa, and Wagoner Counties | | | | | | | | | | |
| City of Tulsa | 384,851 | 4,295 | 68 | 254 | 1,117 | 2,856 | 23,220 | 6,626 | 14,521 | 2,073 |
| Total area actually reporting | 100.0% | 5,768 | 80 | 416 | 1,248 | 4,024 | 34,358 | 9,629 | 21,828 | 2,901 |
| Rate per 100,000 inhabitants | | 621.5 | 8.6 | 44.8 | 134.5 | 433.6 | 3,701.9 | 1,037.5 | 2,351.9 | 312.6 |
| **Tuscaloosa, AL M.S.A.** | **209,255** | | | | | | | | | |
| Includes Greene, Hale, and Tuscaloosa Counties | | | | | | | | | | |
| City of Tuscaloosa | 91,688 | 418 | 5 | 28 | 195 | 190 | 5,082 | 1,507 | 3,355 | 220 |
| Total area actually reporting | 99.7% | 989 | 14 | 60 | 282 | 633 | 9,519 | 2,844 | 6,136 | 539 |
| Estimated total | 100.0% | 992 | 14 | 60 | 283 | 635 | 9,546 | 2,851 | 6,154 | 541 |
| Rate per 100,000 inhabitants | | 474.1 | 6.7 | 28.7 | 135.2 | 303.5 | 4,561.9 | 1,362.5 | 2,940.9 | 258.5 |

[5] The data collection methodology for the offense of forcible rape used by the Minnesota state UCR Program (with the exception of Minneapolis and St. Paul, MN) does not comply with national UCR Program guidelines. Consequently, their figures for forcible rape and violent crime (of which forcible rape is a part) are not published in this table.

## Table 6. Crime, by Metropolitan Statistical Area, 2009—*Continued*

(Number, percent, rate per 100,000 population.)

| Area | Population | Violent crime | Murder and non-negligent man-slaughter | Forcible rape | Robbery | Aggravated assault | Property crime | Burglary | Larceny-theft | Motor vehicle theft |
|---|---|---|---|---|---|---|---|---|---|---|
| **Tyler, TX M.S.A.** | **204,582** | | | | | | | | | |
| Includes Smith County | | | | | | | | | | |
| City of Tyler | 99,279 | 525 | 3 | 55 | 88 | 379 | 5,835 | 1,044 | 4,549 | 242 |
| Total area actually reporting | 99.0% | 872 | 5 | 105 | 114 | 648 | 8,231 | 1,817 | 5,991 | 423 |
| Estimated total | 100.0% | 879 | 5 | 106 | 116 | 652 | 8,303 | 1,832 | 6,043 | 428 |
| Rate per 100,000 inhabitants | | 429.7 | 2.4 | 51.8 | 56.7 | 318.7 | 4,058.5 | 895.5 | 2,953.8 | 209.2 |
| **Utica-Rome, NY M.S.A.** | **293,084** | | | | | | | | | |
| Includes Herkimer and Oneida Counties | | | | | | | | | | |
| City of Utica | 57,831 | 475 | 5 | 18 | 148 | 304 | 2,582 | 505 | 2,000 | 77 |
| City of Rome | 33,543 | 30 | 0 | 3 | 14 | 13 | 700 | 157 | 516 | 27 |
| Total area actually reporting | 98.5% | 804 | 8 | 61 | 193 | 542 | 7,097 | 1,323 | 5,622 | 152 |
| Estimated total | 100.0% | 812 | 8 | 61 | 196 | 547 | 7,187 | 1,336 | 5,696 | 155 |
| Rate per 100,000 inhabitants | | 277.1 | 2.7 | 20.8 | 66.9 | 186.6 | 2,452.2 | 455.8 | 1,943.5 | 52.9 |
| **Valdosta, GA M.S.A.** | **134,375** | | | | | | | | | |
| Includes Brooks, Echols, Lanier, and Lowndes Counties | | | | | | | | | | |
| City of Valdosta | 49,041 | 249 | 9 | 36 | 85 | 119 | 2,862 | 729 | 2,012 | 121 |
| Total area actually reporting | 96.8% | 570 | 11 | 51 | 137 | 371 | 4,884 | 1,323 | 3,298 | 263 |
| Estimated total | 100.0% | 590 | 11 | 52 | 143 | 384 | 5,068 | 1,362 | 3,430 | 276 |
| Rate per 100,000 inhabitants | | 439.1 | 8.2 | 38.7 | 106.4 | 285.8 | 3,771.5 | 1,013.6 | 2,552.6 | 205.4 |
| **Vallejo-Fairfield, CA M.S.A.** | **407,294** | | | | | | | | | |
| Includes Solano County | | | | | | | | | | |
| City of Vallejo | 114,443 | 998 | 10 | 42 | 439 | 507 | 5,478 | 2,358 | 1,854 | 1,266 |
| City of Fairfield | 104,478 | 437 | 6 | 23 | 193 | 215 | 3,246 | 779 | 2,077 | 390 |
| Total area actually reporting | 100.0% | 2,064 | 20 | 112 | 810 | 1,122 | 13,270 | 4,168 | 7,018 | 2,084 |
| Rate per 100,000 inhabitants | | 506.8 | 4.9 | 27.5 | 198.9 | 275.5 | 3,258.1 | 1,023.3 | 1,723.1 | 511.7 |
| **Victoria, TX M.S.A.** | **114,735** | | | | | | | | | |
| Includes Calhoun, Goliad, and Victoria Counties | | | | | | | | | | |
| City of Victoria | 62,788 | 431 | 1 | 48 | 80 | 302 | 4,175 | 1,044 | 3,023 | 108 |
| Total area actually reporting | 100.0% | 639 | 3 | 66 | 87 | 483 | 5,337 | 1,344 | 3,831 | 162 |
| Rate per 100,000 inhabitants | | 556.9 | 2.6 | 57.5 | 75.8 | 421.0 | 4,651.6 | 1,171.4 | 3,339.0 | 141.2 |
| **Vineland-Millville-Bridgeton, NJ M.S.A.** | **157,963** | | | | | | | | | |
| Includes Cumberland County | | | | | | | | | | |
| City of Vineland | 59,121 | 276 | 3 | 14 | 120 | 139 | 2,316 | 537 | 1,708 | 71 |
| City of Millville | 29,175 | 203 | 2 | 8 | 70 | 123 | 1,256 | 364 | 840 | 52 |
| City of Bridgeton | 24,980 | 283 | 1 | 5 | 109 | 168 | 908 | 265 | 589 | 54 |
| Total area actually reporting | 100.0% | 859 | 8 | 29 | 311 | 511 | 5,260 | 1,429 | 3,604 | 227 |
| Rate per 100,000 inhabitants | | 543.8 | 5.1 | 18.4 | 196.9 | 323.5 | 3,329.9 | 904.6 | 2,281.5 | 143.7 |
| **Visalia-Porterville, CA M.S.A.** | **431,712** | | | | | | | | | |
| Includes Tulare County | | | | | | | | | | |
| City of Visalia | 124,263 | 648 | 9 | 53 | 185 | 401 | 5,135 | 1,261 | 3,346 | 528 |
| City of Porterville | 52,555 | 264 | 1 | 17 | 64 | 182 | 1,656 | 372 | 1,045 | 239 |
| Total area actually reporting | 100.0% | 2,230 | 31 | 132 | 488 | 1,579 | 15,681 | 4,139 | 9,326 | 2,216 |
| Rate per 100,000 inhabitants | | 516.5 | 7.2 | 30.6 | 113.0 | 365.8 | 3,632.3 | 958.7 | 2,160.2 | 513.3 |
| **Waco, TX M.S.A.** | **232,320** | | | | | | | | | |
| Includes McLennan County | | | | | | | | | | |
| City of Waco | 125,098 | 883 | 9 | 49 | 228 | 597 | 7,110 | 1,897 | 4,879 | 334 |
| Total area actually reporting | 100.0% | 1,263 | 13 | 123 | 260 | 867 | 10,408 | 2,538 | 7,393 | 477 |
| Rate per 100,000 inhabitants | | 543.6 | 5.6 | 52.9 | 111.9 | 373.2 | 4,480.0 | 1,092.5 | 3,182.2 | 205.3 |
| **Warner Robins, GA M.S.A.** | **135,248** | | | | | | | | | |
| Includes Houston County | | | | | | | | | | |
| City of Warner Robins | 62,269 | 367 | 3 | 13 | 110 | 241 | 3,486 | 815 | 2,530 | 141 |
| Total area actually reporting | 100.0% | 509 | 4 | 21 | 125 | 359 | 5,212 | 1,139 | 3,846 | 227 |
| Rate per 100,000 inhabitants | | 376.3 | 3.0 | 15.5 | 92.4 | 265.4 | 3,853.7 | 842.2 | 2,843.7 | 167.8 |
| **Washington-Arlington-Alexandria, DC-VA-MD-WV M.S.A.** | **5,452,184** | | | | | | | | | |
| Includes the Metropolitan Divisions of Bethesda-Rockville-Frederick, MD and Washington-Arlington-Alexandria, DC-VA-MD-WV | | | | | | | | | | |
| City of Washington, D.C. | 599,657 | 7,586 | 143 | 150 | 3,998 | 3,295 | 27,007 | 3,696 | 18,012 | 5,299 |
| City of Alexandria, VA | 146,145 | 287 | 5 | 12 | 141 | 129 | 3,296 | 347 | 2,613 | 336 |
| City of Frederick, MD | 59,936 | 514 | 1 | 18 | 150 | 345 | 1,786 | 299 | 1,386 | 101 |
| Total area actually reporting | 100.0% | 21,942 | 325 | 908 | 10,331 | 10,378 | 148,521 | 21,514 | 108,922 | 18,085 |
| Rate per 100,000 inhabitants | | 402.4 | 6.0 | 16.7 | 189.5 | 190.3 | 2,724.1 | 394.6 | 1,997.8 | 331.7 |

## Table 6. Crime, by Metropolitan Statistical Area, 2009—*Continued*

(Number, percent, rate per 100,000 population.)

| Area | Population | Violent crime | Murder and non-negligent man-slaughter | Forcible rape | Robbery | Aggravated assault | Property crime | Burglary | Larceny-theft | Motor vehicle theft |
|---|---|---|---|---|---|---|---|---|---|---|
| **Bethesda-Rockville-Frederick, MD M.D.** | **1,194,257** | | | | | | | | | |
| Includes Frederick and Montgomery Counties | | | | | | | | | | |
| Total area actually reporting | 100.0% | 2,955 | 22 | 163 | 1,241 | 1,529 | 28,016 | 3,829 | 22,188 | 1,999 |
| Rate per 100,000 inhabitants | | 247.4 | 1.8 | 13.6 | 103.9 | 128.0 | 2,345.9 | 320.6 | 1,857.9 | 167.4 |
| **Washington-Arlington-Alexandria, DC-VA-MD-WV M.D.** | **4,257,927** | | | | | | | | | |
| Includes District of Columbia; Calvert, Charles, and Prince George's Counties, MD; Arlington, Clarke, Fairfax, Fauquier, Loudoun, Prince William, Spotsylvania, Stafford, and Warren Counties and Alexandria, Fairfax, Falls Church, Fredericksburg, Manassas, and Manassas Park Cities, VA; and Jefferson County, WV | | | | | | | | | | |
| Total area actually reporting | 100.0% | 18,987 | 303 | 745 | 9,090 | 8,849 | 120,505 | 17,685 | 86,734 | 16,086 |
| Rate per 100,000 inhabitants | | 445.9 | 7.1 | 17.5 | 213.5 | 207.8 | 2,830.1 | 415.3 | 2,037.0 | 377.8 |
| **Waterloo-Cedar Falls, IA M.S.A.** | **164,044** | | | | | | | | | |
| Includes Black Hawk, Bremer, and Grundy Counties | | | | | | | | | | |
| City of Waterloo | 66,436 | 599 | 2 | 30 | 140 | 427 | 2,694 | 787 | 1,761 | 146 |
| City of Cedar Falls | 38,271 | 131 | 0 | 21 | 9 | 101 | 653 | 111 | 519 | 23 |
| Total area actually reporting | 100.0% | 922 | 2 | 70 | 156 | 694 | 4,055 | 1,077 | 2,776 | 202 |
| Rate per 100,000 inhabitants | | 562.0 | 1.2 | 42.7 | 95.1 | 423.1 | 2,471.9 | 656.5 | 1,692.2 | 123.1 |
| **Wausau, WI M.S.A.**[1] | **131,469** | | | | | | | | | |
| Includes Marathon County[1] | | | | | | | | | | |
| City of Wausau | 37,459 | 128 | 2 | 18 | 10 | 98 | 995 | 257 | 705 | 33 |
| Total area actually reporting | 100.0% | 206 | 2 | 39 | 17 | 148 | 2,247 | 515 | 1,670 | 62 |
| Rate per 100,000 inhabitants | | 156.7 | 1.5 | 29.7 | 12.9 | 112.6 | 1,709.1 | 391.7 | 1,270.3 | 47.2 |
| **Wenatchee-East Wenatchee, WA M.S.A.** | **109,866** | | | | | | | | | |
| Includes Chelan and Douglas Counties | | | | | | | | | | |
| City of Wenatchee | 30,051 | 98 | 1 | 14 | 17 | 66 | 1,203 | 182 | 954 | 67 |
| City of East Wenatchee | 12,355 | 23 | 0 | 3 | 5 | 15 | 622 | 82 | 517 | 23 |
| Total area actually reporting | 100.0% | 215 | 2 | 36 | 31 | 146 | 3,288 | 599 | 2,535 | 154 |
| Rate per 100,000 inhabitants | | 195.7 | 1.8 | 32.8 | 28.2 | 132.9 | 2,992.7 | 545.2 | 2,307.4 | 140.2 |
| **Wheeling, WV-OH M.S.A.** | **144,342** | | | | | | | | | |
| Includes Belmont County, OH and Marshall and Ohio Counties, WV | | | | | | | | | | |
| City of Wheeling, WV | 28,660 | 143 | 1 | 22 | 36 | 84 | 1,006 | 200 | 752 | 54 |
| Total area actually reporting | 93.1% | 298 | 4 | 45 | 48 | 201 | 2,504 | 573 | 1,794 | 137 |
| Estimated total | 100.0% | 319 | 4 | 48 | 54 | 213 | 2,817 | 637 | 2,030 | 150 |
| Rate per 100,000 inhabitants | | 221.0 | 2.8 | 33.3 | 37.4 | 147.6 | 1,951.6 | 441.3 | 1,406.4 | 103.9 |
| **Wichita, KS M.S.A.** | **608,013** | | | | | | | | | |
| Includes Butler, Harvey, Sedgwick, and Sumner Counties | | | | | | | | | | |
| City of Wichita | 367,635 | 3,245 | 25 | 254 | 527 | 2,439 | 19,597 | 4,045 | 13,886 | 1,666 |
| Total area actually reporting | 99.4% | 3,896 | 26 | 317 | 577 | 2,976 | 24,965 | 5,435 | 17,568 | 1,962 |
| Estimated total | 100.0% | 3,905 | 26 | 318 | 578 | 2,983 | 25,048 | 5,450 | 17,632 | 1,966 |
| Rate per 100,000 inhabitants | | 642.3 | 4.3 | 52.3 | 95.1 | 490.6 | 4,119.6 | 896.4 | 2,899.9 | 323.3 |
| **Wichita Falls, TX M.S.A.** | **147,018** | | | | | | | | | |
| Includes Archer, Clay, and Wichita Counties | | | | | | | | | | |
| City of Wichita Falls | 100,884 | 520 | 11 | 46 | 157 | 306 | 5,618 | 1,277 | 4,011 | 330 |
| Total area actually reporting | 100.0% | 592 | 11 | 49 | 165 | 367 | 6,316 | 1,539 | 4,421 | 356 |
| Rate per 100,000 inhabitants | | 402.7 | 7.5 | 33.3 | 112.2 | 249.6 | 4,296.1 | 1,046.8 | 3,007.1 | 242.1 |
| **Williamsport, PA M.S.A.** | **116,606** | | | | | | | | | |
| Includes Lycoming County | | | | | | | | | | |
| City of Williamsport | 29,329 | 118 | 2 | 14 | 63 | 39 | 1,119 | 191 | 876 | 52 |
| Total area actually reporting | 97.9% | 222 | 2 | 43 | 71 | 106 | 2,167 | 446 | 1,638 | 83 |
| Estimated total | 100.0% | 226 | 2 | 43 | 72 | 109 | 2,213 | 453 | 1,675 | 85 |
| Rate per 100,000 inhabitants | | 193.8 | 1.7 | 36.9 | 61.7 | 93.5 | 1,897.8 | 388.5 | 1,436.5 | 72.9 |
| **Wilmington, NC M.S.A.**[2,3] | **356,659** | | | | | | | | | |
| Includes Brunswick, New Hanover, and Pender[2,3] Counties | | | | | | | | | | |
| City of Wilmington | 101,438 | 814 | 4 | 50 | 306 | 454 | 6,236 | 1,626 | 4,119 | 491 |
| Total area actually reporting | 98.3% | | 9 | 107 | 409 | | | 4,315 | 9,140 | |
| Estimated total | 100.0% | | 9 | 108 | 415 | | | 4,378 | 9,336 | |
| Rate per 100,000 inhabitants | | | 2.5 | 30.3 | 116.4 | | | 1,227.5 | 2,617.6 | |

[1] The FBI determined that the agency's data were overreported. Consequently, affected data are not included in this table.
[2] Because of changes in the state/local agency's reporting practices, figures are not comparable to previous years' data.
[3] The FBI determined that the agency's data were underreported. Consequently, affected data are not included in this table.

## Table 6. Crime, by Metropolitan Statistical Area, 2009—*Continued*

(Number, percent, rate per 100,000 population.)

| Area | Population | Violent crime | Murder and non-negligent man-slaughter | Forcible rape | Robbery | Aggravated assault | Property crime | Burglary | Larceny-theft | Motor vehicle theft |
|---|---|---|---|---|---|---|---|---|---|---|
| **Winchester, VA-WV M.S.A.** | **125,112** | | | | | | | | | |
| Includes Frederick County and Winchester City, VA and Hampshire County, WV | | | | | | | | | | |
| City of Winchester, VA | 26,252 | 84 | 0 | 9 | 40 | 35 | 1,166 | 150 | 977 | 39 |
| Total area actually reporting | 98.3% | 222 | 3 | 51 | 65 | 103 | 2,913 | 567 | 2,200 | 146 |
| Estimated total | 100.0% | 227 | 3 | 51 | 66 | 107 | 2,994 | 584 | 2,261 | 149 |
| Rate per 100,000 inhabitants | | 181.4 | 2.4 | 40.8 | 52.8 | 85.5 | 2,393.1 | 466.8 | 1,807.2 | 119.1 |
| **Winston-Salem, NC M.S.A.** | **474,159** | | | | | | | | | |
| Includes Davie, Forsyth, Stokes, and Yadkin Counties | | | | | | | | | | |
| City of Winston-Salem | 230,978 | 1,739 | 15 | 110 | 575 | 1,039 | 13,788 | 4,532 | 8,429 | 827 |
| Total area actually reporting | 99.4% | 2,411 | 22 | 161 | 657 | 1,571 | 20,778 | 6,493 | 13,098 | 1,187 |
| Estimated total | 100.0% | 2,421 | 22 | 162 | 660 | 1,577 | 20,900 | 6,521 | 13,187 | 1,192 |
| Rate per 100,000 inhabitants | | 510.6 | 4.6 | 34.2 | 139.2 | 332.6 | 4,407.8 | 1,375.3 | 2,781.1 | 251.4 |
| **Worcester, MA M.S.A.** | **795,340** | | | | | | | | | |
| Includes Worcester County | | | | | | | | | | |
| City of Worcester | 178,474 | 1,790 | 7 | 25 | 414 | 1,344 | 6,691 | 1,485 | 4,522 | 684 |
| Total area actually reporting | 98.8% | 3,474 | 16 | 183 | 592 | 2,683 | 16,905 | 3,942 | 11,738 | 1,225 |
| Estimated total | 100.0% | 3,504 | 16 | 185 | 598 | 2,705 | 17,090 | 3,987 | 11,866 | 1,237 |
| Rate per 100,000 inhabitants | | 440.6 | 2.0 | 23.3 | 75.2 | 340.1 | 2,148.8 | 501.3 | 1,491.9 | 155.5 |
| **York-Hanover, PA M.S.A.** | **430,605** | | | | | | | | | |
| Includes York County | | | | | | | | | | |
| City of York | 39,970 | 504 | 10 | 52 | 325 | 117 | 1,957 | 415 | 1,333 | 209 |
| City of Hanover | 15,076 | 30 | 0 | 6 | 9 | 15 | 662 | 67 | 583 | 12 |
| Total area actually reporting | 100.0% | 1,018 | 18 | 118 | 464 | 418 | 8,906 | 1,467 | 6,987 | 452 |
| Rate per 100,000 inhabitants | | 236.4 | 4.2 | 27.4 | 107.8 | 97.1 | 2,068.3 | 340.7 | 1,622.6 | 105.0 |
| **Youngstown-Warren-Boardman, OH-PA M.S.A.** | **563,698** | | | | | | | | | |
| Includes Mahoning and Trumbull Counties, OH and Mercer County, PA | | | | | | | | | | |
| City of Youngstown, OH | 72,008 | 856 | 22 | 41 | 317 | 476 | 4,273 | 2,086 | 1,745 | 442 |
| City of Warren, OH | 43,331 | 309 | 7 | 18 | 137 | 147 | 2,015 | 765 | 1,084 | 166 |
| City of Boardman, OH | 38,827 | 48 | 0 | 4 | 35 | 9 | 1,779 | 256 | 1,452 | 71 |
| Total area actually reporting | 98.1% | 1,852 | 32 | 142 | 649 | 1,029 | 18,147 | 5,618 | 11,401 | 1,128 |
| Estimated total | 100.0% | 1,870 | 32 | 145 | 656 | 1,037 | 18,446 | 5,678 | 11,628 | 1,140 |
| Rate per 100,000 inhabitants | | 331.7 | 5.7 | 25.7 | 116.4 | 184.0 | 3,272.3 | 1,007.3 | 2,062.8 | 202.2 |
| **Yuba City, CA M.S.A.** | **167,852** | | | | | | | | | |
| Includes Sutter and Yuba Counties | | | | | | | | | | |
| City of Yuba City | 62,495 | 196 | 1 | 16 | 44 | 135 | 1,555 | 289 | 1,130 | 136 |
| Total area actually reporting | 100.0% | 595 | 4 | 48 | 100 | 443 | 3,617 | 899 | 2,309 | 409 |
| Rate per 100,000 inhabitants | | 354.5 | 2.4 | 28.6 | 59.6 | 263.9 | 2,154.9 | 535.6 | 1,375.6 | 243.7 |
| **Yuma, AZ M.S.A.** | **196,196** | | | | | | | | | |
| Includes Yuma County | | | | | | | | | | |
| City of Yuma | 91,433 | 570 | 2 | 24 | 86 | 458 | 3,471 | 1,082 | 2,075 | 314 |
| Total area actually reporting | 86.6% | 710 | 9 | 32 | 94 | 575 | 4,530 | 1,526 | 2,567 | 437 |
| Estimated total | 100.0% | 771 | 10 | 37 | 109 | 615 | 5,333 | 1,706 | 3,128 | 499 |
| Rate per 100,000 inhabitants | | 393.0 | 5.1 | 18.9 | 55.6 | 313.5 | 2,718.2 | 869.5 | 1,594.3 | 254.3 |
| **Aguadilla-Isabela-San Sebastian, Puerto Rico M.S.A.** | **342,495** | | | | | | | | | |
| Includes Aguada, Aguadilla, Anasco, Isabela, Lares, Moca, Rincon, and San Sebastian Municipios | | | | | | | | | | |
| Total area actually reporting | 100.0% | 332 | 13 | 1 | 158 | 160 | 3,077 | 1,457 | 1,425 | 195 |
| Rate per 100,000 inhabitants | | 96.9 | 3.8 | 0.3 | 46.1 | 46.7 | 898.4 | 425.4 | 416.1 | 56.9 |
| **Fajardo, Puerto Rico M.S.A.** | **80,707** | | | | | | | | | |
| Includes Ceiba, Fajardo, and Luquillo Municipios | | | | | | | | | | |
| Total area actually reporting | 100.0% | 206 | 23 | 4 | 79 | 100 | 1,102 | 509 | 546 | 47 |
| Rate per 100,000 inhabitants | | 255.2 | 28.5 | 5.0 | 97.9 | 123.9 | 1,365.4 | 630.7 | 676.5 | 58.2 |
| **Guayama, Puerto Rico M.S.A.** | **84,284** | | | | | | | | | |
| Includes Arroyo, Guayama, and Patillas Municipios | | | | | | | | | | |
| Total area actually reporting | 100.0% | 195 | 14 | 0 | 56 | 125 | 892 | 429 | 435 | 28 |
| Rate per 100,000 inhabitants | | 231.4 | 16.6 | 0.0 | 66.4 | 148.3 | 1,058.3 | 509.0 | 516.1 | 33.2 |

## Table 6. Crime, by Metropolitan Statistical Area, 2009—*Continued*

(Number, percent, rate per 100,000 population.)

| Area | Population | Violent crime | Murder and non-negligent man-slaughter | Forcible rape | Robbery | Aggravated assault | Property crime | Burglary | Larceny-theft | Motor vehicle theft |
|---|---|---|---|---|---|---|---|---|---|---|
| **Mayaguez, Puerto Rico M.S.A.** | **109,842** | | | | | | | | | |
| Includes Hormigueros and Mayaguez Municipios | | | | | | | | | | |
| Total area actually reporting | 100.0% | 260 | 19 | 1 | 152 | 88 | 2,587 | 868 | 1,551 | 168 |
| Rate per 100,000 inhabitants | | 236.7 | 17.3 | 0.9 | 138.4 | 80.1 | 2,355.2 | 790.2 | 1,412.0 | 152.9 |
| **Ponce, Puerto Rico M.S.A.** | **262,414** | | | | | | | | | |
| Includes Juana Diaz, Ponce, and Villalba Municipios | | | | | | | | | | |
| Total area actually reporting | 100.0% | 905 | 102 | 17 | 411 | 375 | 3,777 | 1,111 | 2,414 | 252 |
| Rate per 100,000 inhabitants | | 344.9 | 38.9 | 6.5 | 156.6 | 142.9 | 1,439.3 | 423.4 | 919.9 | 96.0 |
| **San German-Cabo Rojo, Puerto Rico M.S.A.** | **148,559** | | | | | | | | | |
| Includes Cabo Rojo, Lajas, Sabana Grande, and San German Municipios | | | | | | | | | | |
| Total area actually reporting | 100.0% | 93 | 3 | 1 | 49 | 40 | 799 | 406 | 348 | 45 |
| Rate per 100,000 inhabitants | | 62.6 | 2.0 | 0.7 | 33.0 | 26.9 | 537.8 | 273.3 | 234.3 | 30.3 |
| **San Juan-Caguas-Guaynabo, Puerto Rico M.S.A.** | **2,617,089** | | | | | | | | | |
| Includes Aguas Buenas, Aibonito, Arecibo, Barceloneta, Barranquitas, Bayamon, Caguas, Camuy, Canovanas, Carolina, Catano, Cayey, Ciales, Cidra, Comerio, Corozal, Dorado, Florida, Guaynabo, Gurabo, Hatillo, Humacao, Juncos, Las Piedras, Loiza, Manati, Maunabo, Morovis, Naguabo, Naranjito, Orocovis, Quebradillas, Rio Grande, San Juan, San Lorenzo, Toa Alta, Toa Baja, Trujillo Alto, Vega Alta, Vega Baja, and Yabucoa Municipios | | | | | | | | | | |
| Total area actually reporting | 100.0% | 7,906 | 681 | 28 | 4,972 | 2,225 | 39,841 | 12,085 | 21,841 | 5,915 |
| Rate per 100,000 inhabitants | | 302.1 | 26.0 | 1.1 | 190.0 | 85.0 | 1,522.3 | 461.8 | 834.6 | 226.0 |
| **Yauco, Puerto Rico M.S.A.** | **125,266** | | | | | | | | | |
| Includes Guanica, Guayanilla, Penuelas, and Yauco Municipios | | | | | | | | | | |
| Total area actually reporting | 100.0% | 203 | 21 | 5 | 74 | 103 | 978 | 436 | 488 | 54 |
| Rate per 100,000 inhabitants | | 162.1 | 16.8 | 4.0 | 59.1 | 82.2 | 780.7 | 348.1 | 389.6 | 43.1 |

## Table 7. Offense Analysis, 2005–2009

(Number.)

| Classification | 2005 | 2006[1] | 2007[1] | 2008[1] | 2009 |
|---|---|---|---|---|---|
| **Murder** | 16,740 | 17,318 | 17,157 | 16,442 | 15,241 |
| **Forcible rape** | 94,347 | 94,782 | 91,874 | 90,479 | 88,097 |
| **Robbery:**[2] | 417,438 | 449,803 | 447,155 | 443,574 | 408,217 |
| By location: | | | | | |
| Street/highway | 184,188 | 200,310 | 195,660 | 191,054 | 174,661 |
| Commercial house | 59,694 | 61,342 | 62,309 | 61,208 | 55,908 |
| Gas or service station | 11,889 | 12,140 | 11,820 | 11,469 | 9,868 |
| Convenience store | 23,822 | 25,054 | 25,047 | 24,395 | 21,955 |
| Residence | 59,207 | 64,367 | 67,815 | 72,218 | 69,191 |
| Bank | 8,766 | 9,643 | 9,294 | 8,996 | 8,818 |
| Miscellaneous | 69,871 | 76,947 | 75,209 | 74,223 | 67,816 |
| **Burglary:**[2] | 2,155,448 | 2,196,304 | 2,187,277 | 2,228,474 | 2,199,125 |
| By location: | | | | | |
| Residence (dwelling): | 1,417,440 | 1,453,870 | 1,484,423 | 1,567,391 | 1,596,008 |
| Residence night | 402,881 | 413,925 | 423,430 | 438,242 | 445,136 |
| Residence day | 669,579 | 709,230 | 741,413 | 807,467 | 818,167 |
| Residence unknown | 344,980 | 330,715 | 319,581 | 321,683 | 332,706 |
| Nonresidence (store, office, etc.): | 738,008 | 742,434 | 702,854 | 661,083 | 603,117 |
| Nonresidence night | 305,729 | 308,842 | 294,565 | 276,692 | 254,662 |
| Nonresidence day | 221,183 | 235,806 | 227,940 | 223,261 | 200,542 |
| Nonresidence unknown | 211,096 | 197,786 | 180,350 | 161,129 | 147,913 |
| **Larceny-theft (except motor vehicle theft):**[2] | 6,783,447 | 6,636,615 | 6,587,040 | 6,588,046 | 6,327,230 |
| By type: | | | | | |
| Pocket-picking | 29,221 | 28,899 | 27,485 | 27,148 | 26,585 |
| Purse-snatching | 42,040 | 40,176 | 38,165 | 33,323 | 30,441 |
| Shoplifting | 940,411 | 876,545 | 981,731 | 1,067,954 | 1,147,436 |
| From motor vehicles (except accessories) | 1,752,280 | 1,760,284 | 1,711,779 | 1,715,224 | 1,724,622 |
| Motor vehicle accessories | 693,225 | 641,540 | 600,747 | 643,144 | 572,288 |
| Bicycles | 248,792 | 232,274 | 224,976 | 221,908 | 211,998 |
| From buildings | 852,462 | 833,473 | 791,341 | 753,661 | 702,977 |
| From coin-operated machines | 40,885 | 35,422 | 31,124 | 26,907 | 26,041 |
| All others | 2,184,131 | 2,188,003 | 2,179,692 | 2,098,778 | 1,884,844 |
| By value: | | | | | |
| Over $200 | 2,715,997 | 2,817,907 | 2,892,235 | 2,966,660 | 2,828,993 |
| $50 to $200 | 1,522,810 | 1,481,301 | 1,475,214 | 1,465,411 | 1,441,444 |
| Under $50 | 2,544,640 | 2,337,408 | 2,219,591 | 2,155,975 | 2,056,793 |
| **Motor vehicle theft** | 1,235,859 | 1,198,440 | 1,098,498 | 958,629 | 794,616 |

[1] The crime figures have been adjusted.

[2] Because of rounding, the number of offenses may not add to the total.

## Table 8. Offenses Known to Law Enforcement, by State and City, 2009

(Number.)

| State/city | Population | Violent crime | Murder and non-negligent man-slaughter | Forcible rape | Robbery | Aggravated assault | Property crime | Burglary | Larceny-theft | Motor vehicle theft | Arson[1] |
|---|---|---|---|---|---|---|---|---|---|---|---|
| **ALABAMA** | | | | | | | | | | | |
| Abbeville | 2,932 | 9 | 0 | 1 | 0 | 8 | 53 | 18 | 33 | 2 | |
| Adamsville | 4,704 | 25 | 0 | 1 | 17 | 7 | 342 | 33 | 291 | 18 | |
| Addison | 710 | 5 | 0 | 1 | 0 | 4 | 29 | 4 | 22 | 3 | |
| Alabaster | 30,002 | 41 | 0 | 2 | 12 | 27 | 635 | 82 | 522 | 31 | |
| Albertville | 20,078 | 82 | 0 | 11 | 12 | 59 | 928 | 233 | 659 | 36 | |
| Alexander City | 15,057 | 132 | 2 | 10 | 31 | 89 | 843 | 180 | 631 | 32 | |
| Aliceville[2] | 2,456 | 22 | 0 | 0 | 3 | 19 | | 7 | | 4 | |
| Andalusia | 8,994 | 54 | 1 | 5 | 7 | 41 | 484 | 61 | 408 | 15 | |
| Anniston | 23,598 | 584 | 5 | 27 | 113 | 439 | 2,379 | 966 | 1,258 | 155 | |
| Ardmore | 1,275 | 0 | 0 | 0 | 0 | 0 | 13 | 2 | 11 | 0 | |
| Ashford | 2,087 | 5 | 0 | 0 | 0 | 5 | 47 | 16 | 28 | 3 | |
| Ashland | 1,873 | 5 | 0 | 0 | 0 | 5 | 32 | 5 | 27 | 0 | |
| Ashville | 2,599 | 8 | 0 | 0 | 0 | 8 | 57 | 15 | 37 | 5 | |
| Athens | 24,261 | 32 | 0 | 3 | 18 | 11 | 802 | 132 | 630 | 40 | |
| Attalla | 6,514 | 57 | 1 | 4 | 3 | 49 | 253 | 42 | 204 | 7 | |
| Auburn[2] | 57,342 | 139 | 3 | 8 | 43 | 85 | | | 1,779 | 38 | |
| Autaugaville | 875 | 0 | 0 | 0 | 0 | 0 | 20 | 12 | 6 | 2 | 0 |
| Baker Hill | 313 | 0 | 0 | 0 | 0 | 0 | 1 | 0 | 1 | 0 | |
| Bear Creek | 995 | 8 | 0 | 0 | 0 | 8 | 38 | 9 | 25 | 4 | |
| Berry | 1,184 | 0 | 0 | 0 | 0 | 0 | 3 | 1 | 1 | 1 | |
| Bessemer | 28,372 | 568 | 10 | 24 | 209 | 325 | 3,813 | 1,170 | 2,416 | 227 | |
| Birmingham | 227,373 | 2,812 | 65 | 198 | 1,150 | 1,399 | 18,159 | 5,019 | 11,546 | 1,594 | 135 |
| Blountsville | 2,010 | 9 | 0 | 0 | 2 | 7 | 31 | 10 | 17 | 4 | |
| Boaz | 8,418 | 39 | 0 | 6 | 13 | 20 | 568 | 117 | 439 | 12 | |
| Brantley | 910 | 3 | 0 | 0 | 0 | 3 | 9 | 1 | 8 | 0 | |
| Brent | 4,381 | 5 | 0 | 1 | 0 | 4 | 48 | 9 | 39 | 0 | |
| Bridgeport | 2,627 | 1 | 0 | 0 | 0 | 1 | 50 | 15 | 30 | 5 | |
| Brilliant | 717 | 2 | 0 | 0 | 0 | 2 | 16 | 2 | 13 | 1 | |
| Brundidge | 2,262 | 14 | 0 | 3 | 3 | 8 | 78 | 22 | 52 | 4 | |
| Butler | 1,687 | 9 | 0 | 0 | 1 | 8 | 38 | 14 | 22 | 2 | |
| Camden | 2,225 | 1 | 0 | 0 | 0 | 1 | 6 | 6 | 0 | 0 | |
| Camp Hill | 1,200 | 7 | 0 | 0 | 2 | 5 | 19 | 3 | 16 | 0 | |
| Carrollton | 923 | 6 | 0 | 1 | 0 | 5 | 14 | 4 | 10 | 0 | |
| Cedar Bluff | 1,672 | 22 | 0 | 1 | 0 | 21 | 70 | 23 | 45 | 2 | |
| Centreville | 2,563 | 4 | 0 | 0 | 1 | 3 | 12 | 2 | 9 | 1 | |
| Chatom | 1,161 | 6 | 0 | 1 | 0 | 5 | 23 | 4 | 19 | 0 | |
| Cherokee | 1,160 | 2 | 0 | 1 | 0 | 1 | 26 | 10 | 16 | 0 | |
| Childersburg | 4,991 | 28 | 0 | 1 | 8 | 19 | 210 | 60 | 142 | 8 | |
| Citronelle | 3,744 | 6 | 1 | 0 | 1 | 4 | 32 | 11 | 19 | 2 | |
| Clanton | 8,943 | 45 | 0 | 3 | 11 | 31 | 565 | 107 | 441 | 17 | |
| Clayhatchee | 492 | 0 | 0 | 0 | 0 | 0 | 7 | 1 | 5 | 1 | 0 |
| Clayton | 1,367 | 6 | 0 | 0 | 1 | 5 | 60 | 24 | 34 | 2 | |
| Cleveland | 1,432 | 1 | 0 | 0 | 0 | 1 | 14 | 5 | 4 | 5 | |
| Clio | 2,211 | 0 | 0 | 0 | 0 | 0 | 1 | 0 | 1 | 0 | 0 |
| Coffeeville | 342 | 0 | 0 | 0 | 0 | 0 | 2 | 1 | 1 | 0 | |
| Collinsville | 1,698 | 3 | 0 | 1 | 0 | 2 | 28 | 5 | 20 | 3 | |
| Coosada | 1,676 | 2 | 0 | 0 | 0 | 2 | 27 | 8 | 19 | 0 | |
| Cordova | 2,270 | 37 | 2 | 2 | 3 | 30 | 139 | 26 | 105 | 8 | |
| Cottonwood | 1,206 | 4 | 0 | 0 | 0 | 4 | 23 | 11 | 11 | 1 | |
| Courtland | 763 | 0 | 0 | 0 | 0 | 0 | 9 | 4 | 2 | 3 | |
| Creola | 2,086 | 8 | 0 | 2 | 1 | 5 | 77 | 20 | 53 | 4 | |
| Crossville | 1,515 | 0 | 0 | 0 | 0 | 0 | 1 | 1 | 0 | 0 | |
| Cullman | 15,412 | 13 | 0 | 1 | 2 | 10 | 791 | 74 | 694 | 23 | |
| Dadeville[2] | 3,231 | 72 | 0 | 1 | 4 | 67 | | | 84 | 7 | |
| Daleville | 4,535 | 32 | 0 | 4 | 0 | 28 | 169 | 39 | 119 | 11 | |
| Daphne | 19,368 | 42 | 4 | 1 | 20 | 17 | 459 | 75 | 366 | 18 | |
| Dauphin Island | 1,610 | 5 | 0 | 0 | 0 | 5 | 73 | 20 | 49 | 4 | |
| Decatur | 56,290 | 223 | 0 | 28 | 78 | 117 | 3,234 | 743 | 2,398 | 93 | |
| Demopolis | 7,297 | 78 | 0 | 5 | 16 | 57 | 424 | 71 | 345 | 8 | |
| Dora | 2,424 | 6 | 0 | 0 | 4 | 2 | 70 | 23 | 39 | 8 | |
| Dothan[3] | 67,496 | | 1 | 32 | 168 | | 3,260 | 813 | 2,310 | 137 | |
| Double Springs | 969 | 1 | 0 | 0 | 0 | 1 | 25 | 0 | 24 | 1 | |
| Douglas | 601 | 12 | 0 | 0 | 0 | 12 | 43 | 14 | 25 | 4 | |
| Dozier | 396 | 1 | 0 | 1 | 0 | 0 | 8 | 0 | 8 | 0 | 0 |
| East Brewton | 2,482 | 12 | 0 | 0 | 0 | 12 | 90 | 17 | 69 | 4 | |
| Eclectic | 1,159 | 10 | 0 | 0 | 2 | 8 | 53 | 12 | 39 | 2 | |
| Elba | 4,163 | 8 | 0 | 2 | 1 | 5 | 191 | 62 | 125 | 4 | |
| Elberta | 1,474 | 13 | 0 | 2 | 1 | 10 | 77 | 24 | 45 | 8 | |
| Enterprise | 25,868 | 106 | 3 | 14 | 20 | 69 | 403 | 149 | 225 | 29 | |

[1] The FBI does not publish arson data unless it receives data from either the agency or the state for all 12 months of the calendar year.
[2] The FBI determined that the agency's data were underreported. Consequently, those data are not included in this table.
[3] The FBI determined that the agency's data were overreported. Consequently, those data are not included in this table.

## Table 8. Offenses Known to Law Enforcement, by State and City, 2009—*Continued*

(Number.)

| State/city | Population | Violent crime | Murder and non-negligent man-slaughter | Forcible rape | Robbery | Aggravated assault | Property crime | Burglary | Larceny-theft | Motor vehicle theft | Arson[1] |
|---|---|---|---|---|---|---|---|---|---|---|---|
| **ALABAMA**—*Continued* | | | | | | | | | | | |
| Eufaula | 14,564 | 36 | 0 | 4 | 11 | 21 | 527 | 69 | 443 | 15 | |
| Excel | 605 | 2 | 0 | 0 | 0 | 2 | 23 | 2 | 21 | 0 | |
| Fairfield | 11,212 | 102 | 0 | 5 | 50 | 47 | 1,229 | 373 | 771 | 85 | 3 |
| Fairhope | 17,723 | 7 | 2 | 1 | 3 | 1 | 532 | 124 | 403 | 5 | |
| Falkville | 1,165 | 2 | 0 | 0 | 0 | 2 | 36 | 10 | 23 | 3 | |
| Fayette | 4,766 | 10 | 0 | 3 | 1 | 6 | 167 | 33 | 121 | 13 | |
| Flomaton | 1,532 | 13 | 0 | 1 | 1 | 11 | 41 | 4 | 35 | 2 | |
| Florala[3] | 1,877 | | 0 | 0 | 0 | | 73 | 7 | 62 | 4 | |
| Florence | 38,055 | 130 | 3 | 14 | 50 | 63 | 1,637 | 415 | 1,184 | 38 | 7 |
| Foley | 14,566 | 63 | 1 | 3 | 16 | 43 | 575 | 82 | 475 | 18 | |
| Fort Payne | 14,189 | 38 | 1 | 4 | 4 | 29 | 519 | 89 | 394 | 36 | |
| Frisco City | 1,332 | 0 | 0 | 0 | 0 | 0 | 22 | 8 | 14 | 0 | |
| Gadsden | 36,595 | 261 | 2 | 41 | 105 | 113 | 2,563 | 609 | 1,807 | 147 | 10 |
| Gantt | 237 | 1 | 0 | 1 | 0 | 0 | 4 | 0 | 4 | 0 | |
| Gardendale | 13,880 | 21 | 0 | 4 | 8 | 9 | 570 | 98 | 447 | 25 | |
| Geneva[2] | 4,448 | 15 | 0 | 0 | 1 | 14 | | | | 7 | |
| Georgiana | 1,549 | 21 | 0 | 0 | 1 | 20 | 45 | 16 | 29 | 0 | |
| Geraldine | 845 | 5 | 0 | 0 | 0 | 5 | 23 | 2 | 20 | 1 | |
| Glencoe | 5,399 | 4 | 0 | 1 | 0 | 3 | 70 | 22 | 41 | 7 | |
| Goodwater | 1,510 | 5 | 1 | 0 | 3 | 1 | 71 | 15 | 49 | 7 | |
| Gordo | 1,545 | 2 | 0 | 1 | 0 | 1 | 29 | 17 | 11 | 1 | |
| Grant | 713 | 2 | 0 | 0 | 0 | 2 | 21 | 9 | 9 | 3 | |
| Greenville | 6,999 | 28 | 0 | 4 | 5 | 19 | 275 | 49 | 218 | 8 | |
| Grove Hill | 1,332 | 14 | 0 | 1 | 1 | 12 | 26 | 10 | 14 | 2 | |
| Guin | 2,169 | 3 | 0 | 0 | 2 | 1 | 38 | 2 | 35 | 1 | |
| Gulf Shores | 10,947 | 22 | 0 | 8 | 3 | 11 | 570 | 51 | 511 | 8 | 0 |
| Guntersville | 8,510 | 41 | 5 | 1 | 9 | 26 | 756 | 140 | 583 | 33 | |
| Gurley | 846 | 2 | 0 | 0 | 1 | 1 | 4 | 0 | 4 | 0 | |
| Hackleburg | 1,440 | 7 | 0 | 0 | 0 | 7 | 36 | 5 | 28 | 3 | |
| Hamilton | 6,350 | 10 | 0 | 2 | 1 | 7 | 173 | 34 | 128 | 11 | |
| Hammondville | 547 | 0 | 0 | 0 | 0 | 0 | 14 | 3 | 9 | 2 | |
| Harpersville | 1,728 | 1 | 0 | 0 | 0 | 1 | 10 | 0 | 8 | 2 | |
| Hartford | 2,432 | 16 | 0 | 0 | 0 | 16 | 71 | 13 | 55 | 3 | |
| Hartselle | 14,070 | 17 | 1 | 4 | 2 | 10 | 543 | 88 | 429 | 26 | |
| Hayneville | 1,117 | 5 | 0 | 0 | 1 | 4 | 73 | 52 | 21 | 0 | |
| Headland | 4,053 | 16 | 0 | 1 | 2 | 13 | 133 | 39 | 87 | 7 | |
| Helena[2] | 15,192 | 13 | 0 | 1 | 2 | 10 | | 17 | | 0 | |
| Henagar | 2,597 | 6 | 0 | 0 | 0 | 6 | 54 | 22 | 32 | 0 | |
| Hillsboro | 589 | 2 | 0 | 0 | 0 | 2 | 3 | 0 | 2 | 1 | |
| Hokes Bluff | 4,485 | 3 | 0 | 0 | 1 | 2 | 42 | 0 | 41 | 1 | |
| Hollywood | 921 | 0 | 0 | 0 | 0 | 0 | 10 | 0 | 9 | 1 | |
| Homewood | 23,708 | 117 | 1 | 4 | 90 | 22 | 1,594 | 339 | 1,168 | 87 | |
| Hoover | 71,919 | 88 | 2 | 9 | 44 | 33 | 2,288 | 439 | 1,762 | 87 | 1 |
| Huntsville | 178,601 | 1,164 | 13 | 89 | 433 | 629 | 9,790 | 2,520 | 6,375 | 895 | |
| Hurtsboro | 541 | 0 | 0 | 0 | 0 | 0 | 22 | 12 | 9 | 1 | |
| Ider | 721 | 1 | 0 | 0 | 0 | 1 | 20 | 5 | 15 | 0 | |
| Jackson | 5,069 | 25 | 0 | 5 | 3 | 17 | 175 | 54 | 105 | 16 | |
| Jacksonville | 10,276 | 47 | 0 | 3 | 17 | 27 | 630 | 262 | 334 | 34 | |
| Jasper | 14,129 | 69 | 0 | 11 | 26 | 32 | 1,400 | 181 | 1,147 | 72 | |
| Jemison | 3,008 | 17 | 0 | 2 | 0 | 15 | 116 | 23 | 86 | 7 | |
| Killen | 1,145 | 11 | 0 | 0 | 4 | 7 | 62 | 22 | 37 | 3 | |
| Kimberly | 2,887 | 1 | 0 | 0 | 0 | 1 | 44 | 9 | 31 | 4 | |
| Kinston | 615 | 2 | 0 | 0 | 0 | 2 | 8 | 5 | 3 | 0 | |
| Lafayette | 2,858 | 34 | 0 | 1 | 5 | 28 | 179 | 47 | 125 | 7 | 0 |
| Leeds | 11,398 | 68 | 0 | 3 | 38 | 27 | 694 | 172 | 488 | 34 | |
| Leesburg | 823 | 8 | 0 | 0 | 0 | 8 | 53 | 17 | 35 | 1 | |
| Leighton | 827 | 0 | 0 | 0 | 0 | 0 | 13 | 5 | 8 | 0 | |
| Level Plains | 1,507 | 12 | 0 | 1 | 1 | 10 | 46 | 10 | 35 | 1 | |
| Lexington | 843 | 1 | 0 | 0 | 0 | 1 | 21 | 4 | 16 | 1 | |
| Lincoln | 5,963 | 23 | 0 | 5 | 7 | 11 | 331 | 86 | 217 | 28 | |
| Linden | 2,237 | 11 | 0 | 1 | 1 | 9 | 39 | 8 | 26 | 5 | |
| Littleville | 1,043 | 0 | 0 | 0 | 0 | 0 | 23 | 3 | 17 | 3 | |
| Lockhart | 538 | 2 | 0 | 0 | 0 | 2 | 5 | 0 | 4 | 1 | |
| Louisville | 560 | 1 | 0 | 1 | 0 | 0 | 7 | 2 | 4 | 1 | |
| Luverne | 2,768 | 8 | 0 | 0 | 1 | 7 | 93 | 14 | 75 | 4 | |
| Lynn | 711 | 0 | 0 | 0 | 0 | 0 | 9 | 3 | 6 | 0 | |
| Madison | 39,880 | 59 | 3 | 3 | 17 | 36 | 877 | 176 | 669 | 32 | 1 |
| Maplesville | 692 | 3 | 0 | 1 | 2 | 0 | 29 | 4 | 25 | 0 | |
| Marion | 3,270 | 34 | 0 | 1 | 1 | 32 | 182 | 64 | 108 | 10 | |
| McIntosh | 233 | 0 | 0 | 0 | 0 | 0 | 20 | 3 | 16 | 1 | |

[1] The FBI does not publish arson data unless it receives data from either the agency or the state for all 12 months of the calendar year.
[2] The FBI determined that the agency's data were underreported. Consequently, those data are not included in this table.
[3] The FBI determined that the agency's data were overreported. Consequently, those data are not included in this table.

**Table 8. Offenses Known to Law Enforcement, by State and City, 2009—*Continued***

(Number.)

| State/city | Population | Violent crime | Murder and non-negligent man-slaughter | Forcible rape | Robbery | Aggravated assault | Property crime | Burglary | Larceny-theft | Motor vehicle theft | Arson[1] |
|---|---|---|---|---|---|---|---|---|---|---|---|
| **ALABAMA**—*Continued* | | | | | | | | | | | |
| McKenzie | 602 | 1 | 0 | 0 | 0 | 1 | 7 | 2 | 4 | 1 | |
| Mentone | 485 | 0 | 0 | 0 | 0 | 0 | 9 | 6 | 3 | 0 | |
| Midland City | 1,904 | 13 | 1 | 1 | 1 | 10 | 19 | 8 | 10 | 1 | |
| Millbrook | 17,383 | 9 | 1 | 2 | 4 | 2 | 504 | 128 | 374 | 2 | |
| Millry | 590 | 0 | 0 | 0 | 0 | 0 | 6 | 2 | 3 | 1 | |
| Mobile[4] | 246,171 | 1,994 | 24 | 37 | 857 | 1,076 | 14,123 | 3,716 | 9,457 | 950 | 91 |
| Montevallo | 6,469 | 8 | 0 | 0 | 2 | 6 | 181 | 53 | 124 | 4 | |
| Montgomery | 202,818 | 871 | 31 | 85 | 453 | 302 | 11,065 | 3,092 | 7,113 | 860 | |
| Moody | 14,175 | 10 | 3 | 3 | 0 | 4 | 471 | 104 | 324 | 43 | |
| Morris | 1,894 | 1 | 0 | 0 | 0 | 1 | 18 | 1 | 14 | 3 | |
| Mosses | 1,033 | 2 | 1 | 0 | 0 | 1 | 9 | 7 | 1 | 1 | |
| Moulton | 3,267 | 12 | 0 | 0 | 0 | 12 | 101 | 12 | 87 | 2 | |
| Moundville | 2,696 | 10 | 0 | 0 | 1 | 9 | 95 | 21 | 66 | 8 | |
| Mount Vernon | 812 | 15 | 0 | 0 | 0 | 15 | 54 | 24 | 25 | 5 | |
| Muscle Shoals | 13,125 | 66 | 0 | 4 | 12 | 50 | 541 | 93 | 430 | 18 | 0 |
| Napier Field | 395 | 6 | 0 | 1 | 0 | 5 | 17 | 7 | 9 | 1 | |
| New Brockton | 1,233 | 0 | 0 | 0 | 0 | 0 | 18 | 7 | 11 | 0 | |
| New Hope | 2,778 | 4 | 0 | 0 | 1 | 3 | 46 | 10 | 32 | 4 | |
| New Site | 829 | 1 | 0 | 0 | 0 | 1 | 2 | 0 | 1 | 1 | |
| Newton | 1,647 | 2 | 0 | 0 | 0 | 2 | 38 | 8 | 30 | 0 | |
| Newville | 542 | 0 | 0 | 0 | 0 | 0 | 10 | 3 | 7 | 0 | |
| North Courtland | 798 | 2 | 0 | 0 | 0 | 2 | 12 | 6 | 6 | 0 | |
| Northport | 23,498 | 130 | 2 | 7 | 29 | 92 | 1,188 | 272 | 856 | 60 | 1 |
| Notasulga | 838 | 5 | 0 | 0 | 0 | 5 | 21 | 8 | 13 | 0 | |
| Oakman | 925 | 1 | 0 | 0 | 0 | 1 | 19 | 7 | 11 | 1 | |
| Odenville | 2,291 | 3 | 0 | 0 | 1 | 2 | 62 | 12 | 45 | 5 | 0 |
| Ohatchee | 1,247 | 2 | 1 | 0 | 0 | 1 | 7 | 4 | 3 | 0 | |
| Opelika[2] | 27,087 | | 3 | 22 | 83 | | | 389 | 1,213 | | |
| Opp | 6,555 | 27 | 0 | 7 | 2 | 18 | 175 | 34 | 141 | 0 | |
| Orange Beach | 6,563 | 17 | 0 | 6 | 3 | 8 | 293 | 43 | 245 | 5 | |
| Oxford | 20,808 | 135 | 0 | 9 | 37 | 89 | 1,427 | 248 | 1,112 | 67 | |
| Ozark | 14,670 | 108 | 1 | 8 | 24 | 75 | 686 | 204 | 459 | 23 | |
| Parrish | 1,244 | 7 | 0 | 0 | 1 | 6 | 55 | 13 | 42 | 0 | |
| Pelham | 22,172 | 16 | 1 | 2 | 7 | 6 | 495 | 71 | 390 | 34 | |
| Pell City | 13,252 | 70 | 1 | 7 | 3 | 59 | 629 | 97 | 518 | 14 | |
| Phenix City[3] | 31,438 | 162 | 1 | 5 | 80 | 76 | | | 904 | 171 | |
| Phil Campbell | 1,048 | 1 | 0 | 0 | 1 | 0 | 31 | 5 | 24 | 2 | |
| Pickensville | 627 | 1 | 0 | 0 | 1 | 0 | 4 | 3 | 0 | 1 | |
| Piedmont | 4,952 | 24 | 0 | 2 | 2 | 20 | 192 | 41 | 138 | 13 | |
| Pine Hill | 907 | 12 | 1 | 0 | 0 | 11 | 35 | 10 | 24 | 1 | |
| Pisgah | 695 | 0 | 0 | 0 | 0 | 0 | 0 | 0 | 0 | 0 | |
| Powell | 983 | 1 | 0 | 0 | 0 | 1 | 11 | 1 | 10 | 0 | |
| Prattville[5] | 33,279 | | 0 | 6 | 27 | | | | 720 | 57 | |
| Priceville | 2,981 | 1 | 0 | 0 | 1 | 0 | 48 | 7 | 39 | 2 | |
| Prichard | 27,560 | 586 | 4 | 3 | 281 | 298 | 2,303 | 983 | 981 | 339 | |
| Ragland | 2,161 | 13 | 0 | 0 | 0 | 13 | 38 | 0 | 33 | 5 | |
| Rainbow City | 9,425 | 3 | 0 | 0 | 0 | 3 | 251 | 29 | 207 | 15 | |
| Rainsville | 5,046 | 6 | 0 | 0 | 0 | 6 | 87 | 13 | 71 | 3 | |
| Ranburne | 487 | 3 | 0 | 0 | 0 | 3 | 16 | 1 | 14 | 1 | |
| Red Bay | 3,288 | 10 | 0 | 1 | 1 | 8 | 45 | 8 | 34 | 3 | |
| Red Level | 547 | 0 | 0 | 0 | 0 | 0 | 3 | 1 | 1 | 1 | |
| Reform | 1,771 | 11 | 0 | 0 | 4 | 7 | 64 | 22 | 42 | 0 | |
| Riverside | 2,084 | 22 | 0 | 0 | 0 | 22 | 11 | 0 | 11 | 0 | |
| Robertsdale | 5,111 | 16 | 0 | 5 | 3 | 8 | 277 | 56 | 212 | 9 | |
| Rockford | 393 | 0 | 0 | 0 | 0 | 0 | 1 | 0 | 1 | 0 | |
| Rogersville | 1,205 | 0 | 0 | 0 | 0 | 0 | 13 | 2 | 7 | 4 | |
| Samson | 2,025 | 6 | 0 | 0 | 0 | 6 | 32 | 8 | 24 | 0 | |
| Sardis City | 2,206 | 3 | 0 | 0 | 1 | 2 | 76 | 17 | 54 | 5 | |
| Satsuma | 6,042 | 21 | 1 | 0 | 0 | 20 | 148 | 37 | 96 | 15 | |
| Scottsboro | 15,015 | 34 | 2 | 1 | 4 | 27 | 594 | 36 | 540 | 18 | |
| Section | 758 | 0 | 0 | 0 | 0 | 0 | 1 | 0 | 1 | 0 | |
| Sheffield | 9,072 | 28 | 0 | 3 | 10 | 15 | 381 | 93 | 279 | 9 | |
| Shorter | 377 | 3 | 1 | 0 | 1 | 1 | 33 | 6 | 21 | 6 | |
| Silas | 470 | 0 | 0 | 0 | 0 | 0 | 2 | 0 | 2 | 0 | |
| Silverhill | 707 | 2 | 0 | 0 | 0 | 2 | 43 | 14 | 26 | 3 | |
| Sipsey | 542 | 3 | 0 | 0 | 0 | 3 | 21 | 1 | 19 | 1 | |
| Skyline | 834 | 0 | 0 | 0 | 0 | 0 | 4 | 0 | 3 | 1 | |
| Slocomb | 2,046 | 6 | 0 | 0 | 1 | 5 | 23 | 7 | 15 | 1 | |

[1] The FBI does not publish arson data unless it receives data from either the agency or the state for all 12 months of the calendar year.
[2] The FBI determined that the agency's data were underreported. Consequently, those data are not included in this table.
[3] The FBI determined that the agency's data were overreported. Consequently, those data are not included in this table.
[4] The population for the city of Mobile, Alabama, includes 55,995 inhabitants from the jurisdiction of the Mobile County Sheriff's Department.
[5] The FBI determined that the agency did not follow national Uniform Crime Reporting (UCR) Program guidelines for reporting an offense. Consequently, this figure is not included in this table.

## Table 8. Offenses Known to Law Enforcement, by State and City, 2009—*Continued*

(Number.)

| State/city | Population | Violent crime | Murder and non-negligent man-slaughter | Forcible rape | Robbery | Aggravated assault | Property crime | Burglary | Larceny-theft | Motor vehicle theft | Arson[1] |
|---|---|---|---|---|---|---|---|---|---|---|---|
| **ALABAMA**—*Continued* | | | | | | | | | | | |
| Snead | 860 | 2 | 0 | 0 | 0 | 2 | 14 | 5 | 9 | 0 | |
| Southside | 8,572 | 21 | 0 | 3 | 0 | 18 | 94 | 13 | 80 | 1 | |
| Spanish Fort | 5,809 | 9 | 0 | 1 | 2 | 6 | 219 | 11 | 206 | 2 | |
| Springville | 3,814 | 3 | 0 | 0 | 0 | 3 | 94 | 20 | 71 | 3 | |
| Steele | 1,235 | 1 | 0 | 0 | 0 | 1 | 12 | 1 | 11 | 0 | |
| Stevenson | 2,015 | 8 | 0 | 0 | 0 | 8 | 40 | 5 | 35 | 0 | |
| St. Florian | 492 | 1 | 0 | 0 | 0 | 1 | 4 | 4 | 0 | 0 | |
| Sulligent | 1,949 | 5 | 0 | 0 | 0 | 5 | 35 | 6 | 26 | 3 | |
| Sumiton | 2,554 | 7 | 0 | 1 | 4 | 2 | 339 | 48 | 265 | 26 | |
| Summerdale | 756 | 5 | 0 | 3 | 0 | 2 | 45 | 13 | 31 | 1 | |
| Sylacauga | 12,844 | 78 | 1 | 11 | 16 | 50 | 781 | 229 | 542 | 10 | |
| Sylvania | 1,276 | 0 | 0 | 0 | 0 | 0 | 11 | 0 | 11 | 0 | |
| Talladega | 16,902 | 123 | 3 | 18 | 16 | 86 | 1,283 | 426 | 788 | 69 | |
| Tarrant | 6,445 | 80 | 1 | 3 | 35 | 41 | 586 | 213 | 342 | 31 | |
| Taylor | 2,004 | 1 | 0 | 0 | 0 | 1 | 7 | 2 | 3 | 2 | |
| Thomasville | 4,460 | 56 | 0 | 1 | 2 | 53 | 158 | 47 | 103 | 8 | |
| Thorsby | 2,097 | 3 | 0 | 2 | 0 | 1 | 26 | 6 | 18 | 2 | |
| Town Creek | 1,208 | 2 | 0 | 0 | 0 | 2 | 32 | 11 | 19 | 2 | |
| Triana | 493 | 0 | 0 | 0 | 0 | 0 | 11 | 3 | 6 | 2 | |
| Trinity | 2,003 | 1 | 0 | 0 | 0 | 1 | 24 | 4 | 18 | 2 | |
| Troy | 15,278 | 77 | 0 | 7 | 42 | 28 | 860 | 263 | 566 | 31 | |
| Trussville | 19,596 | 27 | 0 | 1 | 16 | 10 | 927 | 104 | 784 | 39 | |
| Tuscaloosa | 91,688 | 418 | 5 | 28 | 195 | 190 | 5,082 | 1,507 | 3,355 | 220 | |
| Tuscumbia | 8,346 | 13 | 0 | 1 | 7 | 5 | 302 | 78 | 218 | 6 | |
| Tuskegee | 11,281 | 159 | 5 | 4 | 13 | 137 | 770 | 190 | 541 | 39 | |
| Union Springs | 4,682 | 19 | 1 | 0 | 6 | 12 | 142 | 45 | 93 | 4 | |
| Uniontown | 1,397 | 11 | 0 | 0 | 1 | 10 | 46 | 10 | 31 | 5 | |
| Valley | 10,017 | 44 | 0 | 1 | 7 | 36 | 397 | 88 | 274 | 35 | |
| Valley Head | 654 | 1 | 0 | 0 | 0 | 1 | 16 | 5 | 10 | 1 | |
| Vance | 1,018 | 9 | 0 | 0 | 0 | 9 | 38 | 10 | 26 | 2 | |
| Vernon | 1,867 | 1 | 0 | 0 | 0 | 1 | 2 | 0 | 1 | 1 | |
| Vestavia Hills | 30,906 | 23 | 0 | 2 | 10 | 11 | 386 | 155 | 212 | 19 | |
| Warrior | 3,100 | 2 | 0 | 0 | 2 | 0 | 47 | 12 | 30 | 5 | |
| Weaver | 2,738 | 5 | 0 | 0 | 0 | 5 | 46 | 20 | 24 | 2 | |
| Webb | 1,375 | 2 | 0 | 0 | 0 | 2 | 12 | 2 | 9 | 1 | |
| Wedowee | 825 | 14 | 0 | 0 | 0 | 14 | 17 | 3 | 13 | 1 | |
| West Blocton | 1,433 | 2 | 0 | 0 | 0 | 2 | 7 | 1 | 6 | 0 | |
| Wetumpka | 7,964 | 42 | 2 | 1 | 10 | 29 | 368 | 74 | 283 | 11 | |
| Winfield | 4,626 | 18 | 0 | 0 | 0 | 18 | 146 | 33 | 102 | 11 | |
| Woodstock | 1,029 | 23 | 0 | 0 | 0 | 23 | 110 | 14 | 88 | 8 | |
| York | 2,481 | 27 | 0 | 0 | 4 | 23 | 102 | 22 | 69 | 11 | |
| Houston | 2,153 | 3 | 0 | 0 | 0 | 3 | 29 | 9 | 17 | 3 | 0 |
| **ALASKA** | | | | | | | | | | | |
| Anchorage | 283,300 | 2,488 | 14 | 282 | 534 | 1,658 | 10,316 | 1,613 | 7,835 | 868 | 111 |
| Bethel | 6,584 | 52 | 1 | 8 | 3 | 40 | 161 | 50 | 43 | 68 | 3 |
| Bristol Bay Borough | 933 | 7 | 0 | 0 | 2 | 5 | 43 | 11 | 18 | 14 | 1 |
| Cordova | 2,219 | 19 | 0 | 0 | 0 | 19 | 18 | 1 | 11 | 6 | 0 |
| Craig | 1,150 | 13 | 0 | 0 | 0 | 13 | 25 | 2 | 23 | 0 | 0 |
| Dillingham | 2,465 | 35 | 0 | 12 | 1 | 22 | 54 | 2 | 39 | 13 | 0 |
| Fairbanks | 35,735 | 268 | 0 | 59 | 46 | 163 | 1,395 | 191 | 1,113 | 91 | 11 |
| Haines | 2,273 | 10 | 0 | 0 | 0 | 10 | 48 | 18 | 29 | 1 | 0 |
| Homer | 5,921 | 54 | 0 | 0 | 0 | 54 | 178 | 20 | 149 | 9 | 1 |
| Houston | 2,298 | 5 | 0 | 1 | 0 | 4 | 27 | 8 | 14 | 5 | 0 |
| Juneau | 31,024 | 141 | 0 | 25 | 18 | 98 | 1,446 | 266 | 1,142 | 38 | 5 |
| Kenai | 7,836 | 32 | 0 | 1 | 2 | 29 | 324 | 42 | 267 | 15 | 2 |
| Ketchikan | 7,215 | 30 | 0 | 8 | 3 | 19 | 473 | 54 | 395 | 24 | 2 |
| Kodiak | 6,212 | 31 | 0 | 2 | 2 | 27 | 204 | 32 | 139 | 33 | 1 |
| Kotzebue | 3,187 | 17 | 0 | 9 | 0 | 8 | 55 | 9 | 36 | 10 | 1 |
| North Pole | 2,299 | 13 | 0 | 2 | 1 | 10 | 92 | 12 | 75 | 5 | 0 |
| North Slope Borough | 6,581 | 73 | 1 | 11 | 1 | 60 | 94 | 23 | 63 | 8 | 4 |
| Palmer | 8,706 | 27 | 0 | 3 | 0 | 24 | 249 | 48 | 195 | 6 | 1 |
| Petersburg | 2,784 | 28 | 0 | 0 | 0 | 28 | 110 | 9 | 100 | 1 | 0 |
| Seward | 3,161 | 7 | 0 | 0 | 1 | 6 | 103 | 7 | 91 | 5 | 0 |
| Sitka | 8,896 | 18 | 0 | 7 | 2 | 9 | 269 | 18 | 229 | 22 | 1 |
| Skagway | 895 | 1 | 0 | 0 | 0 | 1 | 24 | 8 | 16 | 0 | 0 |
| Soldotna | 4,461 | 20 | 0 | 3 | 1 | 16 | 263 | 15 | 244 | 4 | 1 |
| St. Paul | 405 | 0 | 0 | 0 | 0 | 0 | 1 | 0 | 1 | 0 | 0 |
| Unalaska | 3,462 | 12 | 0 | 1 | 0 | 11 | 51 | 11 | 36 | 4 | 0 |

[1] The FBI does not publish arson data unless it receives data from either the agency or the state for all 12 months of the calendar year.

## Table 8. Offenses Known to Law Enforcement, by State and City, 2009—*Continued*

(Number.)

| State/city | Population | Violent crime | Murder and non-negligent man-slaughter | Forcible rape | Robbery | Aggravated assault | Property crime | Burglary | Larceny-theft | Motor vehicle theft | Arson[1] |
|---|---|---|---|---|---|---|---|---|---|---|---|
| **ALASKA**—*Continued* | | | | | | | | | | | |
| Valdez | 3,758 | 19 | 0 | 1 | 0 | 18 | 103 | 8 | 86 | 9 | 0 |
| Wasilla | 10,980 | 75 | 0 | 3 | 8 | 64 | 416 | 49 | 341 | 26 | 0 |
| Wrangell | 1,958 | 3 | 0 | 0 | 0 | 3 | 56 | 6 | 47 | 3 | 0 |
| **ARIZONA** | | | | | | | | | | | |
| Apache Junction | 32,869 | 104 | 0 | 8 | 15 | 81 | 1,200 | 296 | 780 | 124 | 11 |
| Avondale | 88,773 | 351 | 5 | 23 | 111 | 212 | 4,389 | 1,012 | 2,831 | 546 | 18 |
| Bisbee | 5,965 | 66 | 0 | 0 | 0 | 66 | 208 | 32 | 176 | 0 | 0 |
| Buckeye | 56,780 | 69 | 1 | 6 | 15 | 47 | 1,268 | 361 | 794 | 113 | 3 |
| Bullhead City | 41,721 | 65 | 1 | 1 | 27 | 36 | 1,577 | 324 | 1,166 | 87 | 10 |
| Camp Verde | 11,012 | 23 | 0 | 1 | 0 | 22 | 243 | 47 | 178 | 18 | 3 |
| Casa Grande | 43,254 | 254 | 4 | 6 | 60 | 184 | 2,806 | 677 | 1,901 | 228 | 19 |
| Chandler | 256,091 | 740 | 5 | 46 | 205 | 484 | 7,458 | 1,376 | 5,599 | 483 | 62 |
| Clarkdale | 4,374 | 9 | 0 | 0 | 0 | 9 | 54 | 24 | 28 | 2 | 0 |
| Clifton | 2,438 | 8 | 0 | 0 | 0 | 8 | 48 | 25 | 19 | 4 | 0 |
| Colorado City | 4,934 | 3 | 0 | 0 | 0 | 3 | 14 | 4 | 10 | 0 | 0 |
| Coolidge | 10,540 | 61 | 2 | 3 | 10 | 46 | 548 | 136 | 365 | 47 | 12 |
| Cottonwood | 11,664 | 42 | 0 | 1 | 4 | 37 | 375 | 45 | 312 | 18 | 4 |
| Douglas | 17,622 | 41 | 0 | 5 | 8 | 28 | 593 | 81 | 457 | 55 | 0 |
| Eagar | 4,541 | 8 | 0 | 0 | 0 | 8 | 81 | 19 | 57 | 5 | 0 |
| El Mirage | 28,196 | 87 | 0 | 4 | 24 | 59 | 919 | 226 | 621 | 72 | 12 |
| Eloy | 13,049 | 106 | 0 | 21 | 15 | 70 | 590 | 217 | 328 | 45 | 19 |
| Flagstaff | 61,072 | 282 | 4 | 43 | 53 | 182 | 3,118 | 303 | 2,725 | 90 | 17 |
| Florence | 21,229 | 28 | 0 | 1 | 4 | 23 | 266 | 72 | 174 | 20 | 0 |
| Fredonia | 1,135 | 1 | 0 | 0 | 0 | 1 | 6 | 2 | 4 | 0 | 0 |
| Gilbert | 231,799 | 194 | 4 | 22 | 59 | 109 | 4,571 | 1,010 | 3,337 | 224 | 28 |
| Glendale | 255,080 | 1,147 | 18 | 54 | 420 | 655 | 12,489 | 2,551 | 8,214 | 1,724 | 82 |
| Goodyear | 67,390 | 134 | 0 | 14 | 28 | 92 | 2,079 | 952 | 842 | 285 | 18 |
| Holbrook | 5,094 | 4 | 1 | 0 | 3 | 0 | 381 | 106 | 254 | 21 | 0 |
| Huachuca City | 1,988 | 4 | 0 | 0 | 0 | 4 | 35 | 9 | 20 | 6 | 1 |
| Jerome | 356 | 2 | 0 | 0 | 0 | 2 | 31 | 10 | 21 | 0 | 0 |
| Kingman | 28,700 | 90 | 3 | 10 | 12 | 65 | 1,799 | 347 | 1,348 | 104 | 5 |
| Lake Havasu City | 58,406 | 106 | 3 | 19 | 12 | 72 | 1,362 | 323 | 955 | 84 | 5 |
| Mammoth | 2,682 | 6 | 0 | 0 | 0 | 6 | 38 | 15 | 20 | 3 | 1 |
| Marana | 38,028 | 46 | 0 | 4 | 22 | 20 | 1,011 | 141 | 781 | 89 | 7 |
| Maricopa | 52,200 | 52 | 0 | 9 | 4 | 39 | 896 | 195 | 638 | 63 | 1 |
| Mesa | 470,833 | 2,000 | 14 | 123 | 611 | 1,252 | 16,079 | 3,076 | 11,700 | 1,303 | 85 |
| Miami | 1,762 | 27 | 0 | 3 | 1 | 23 | 71 | 30 | 38 | 3 | 5 |
| Nogales | 19,433 | 69 | 0 | 1 | 8 | 60 | 720 | 139 | 456 | 125 | 0 |
| Oro Valley | 44,854 | 21 | 0 | 2 | 3 | 16 | 691 | 122 | 536 | 33 | 4 |
| Paradise Valley | 15,141 | 14 | 0 | 1 | 7 | 6 | 327 | 227 | 85 | 15 | 0 |
| Parker | 3,180 | 22 | 0 | 0 | 3 | 19 | 244 | 57 | 168 | 19 | 1 |
| Peoria | 164,366 | 321 | 8 | 53 | 89 | 171 | 4,872 | 1,120 | 3,303 | 449 | 8 |
| Phoenix | 1,597,397 | 8,730 | 122 | 522 | 3,757 | 4,329 | 65,617 | 16,281 | 39,643 | 9,693 | 436 |
| Pima | 2,173 | 7 | 0 | 1 | 0 | 6 | 78 | 26 | 47 | 5 | 0 |
| Pinetop-Lakeside | 4,654 | 26 | 1 | 0 | 1 | 24 | 226 | 62 | 158 | 6 | 3 |
| Prescott | 43,748 | 147 | 2 | 8 | 27 | 110 | 1,238 | 266 | 941 | 31 | 8 |
| Prescott Valley | 40,539 | 127 | 0 | 7 | 10 | 110 | 692 | 159 | 509 | 24 | 4 |
| Quartzsite | 3,497 | 1 | 0 | 0 | 0 | 1 | 71 | 1 | 67 | 3 | 1 |
| Safford[5] | 9,894 | | 0 | 2 | 4 | | 569 | 167 | 382 | 20 | 5 |
| Sahuarita | 28,201 | 14 | 0 | 2 | 2 | 10 | 333 | 53 | 257 | 23 | 1 |
| Scottsdale | 239,115 | 410 | 10 | 19 | 129 | 252 | 6,798 | 1,337 | 5,155 | 306 | 31 |
| Sedona | 11,759 | 27 | 0 | 6 | 1 | 20 | 246 | 65 | 177 | 4 | 2 |
| Show Low | 12,929 | 99 | 3 | 4 | 1 | 91 | 451 | 131 | 305 | 15 | 2 |
| Sierra Vista | 43,956 | 111 | 1 | 13 | 23 | 74 | 1,397 | 174 | 1,159 | 64 | 8 |
| Snowflake-Taylor | 10,084 | 39 | 0 | 0 | 1 | 38 | 186 | 58 | 109 | 19 | 2 |
| Somerton | 13,041 | 19 | 1 | 0 | 2 | 16 | 208 | 43 | 135 | 30 | 4 |
| South Tucson | 6,071 | 178 | 2 | 8 | 83 | 85 | 921 | 116 | 736 | 69 | 0 |
| Springerville | 1,994 | 12 | 0 | 1 | 0 | 11 | 34 | 5 | 28 | 1 | 0 |
| Surprise | 104,692 | 111 | 1 | 9 | 37 | 64 | 2,405 | 532 | 1,706 | 167 | 24 |
| Tempe | 177,486 | 922 | 2 | 66 | 306 | 548 | 8,986 | 1,478 | 6,692 | 816 | 68 |
| Thatcher | 5,122 | 0 | 0 | 0 | 0 | 0 | 105 | 19 | 85 | 1 | 0 |
| Tolleson | 7,498 | 47 | 0 | 5 | 10 | 32 | 808 | 210 | 535 | 63 | 1 |
| Tombstone | 1,573 | 12 | 0 | 2 | 0 | 10 | 76 | 20 | 50 | 6 | 0 |
| Tucson[5] | 547,981 | 3,560 | 35 | 204 | 1,246 | 2,075 | | 5,062 | | 3,564 | 225 |
| Wellton | 1,916 | 1 | 0 | 0 | 1 | 0 | 20 | 6 | 11 | 3 | 0 |
| Wickenburg | 6,707 | 17 | 0 | 4 | 0 | 13 | 156 | 33 | 102 | 21 | 0 |
| Willcox | 3,807 | 9 | 0 | 0 | 1 | 8 | 222 | 40 | 174 | 8 | 1 |
| Williams | 3,361 | 20 | 0 | 1 | 1 | 18 | 140 | 25 | 114 | 1 | 1 |

[1] The FBI does not publish arson data unless it receives data from either the agency or the state for all 12 months of the calendar year.
[5] The FBI determined that the agency did not follow national Uniform Crime Reporting (UCR) Program guidelines for reporting an offense. Consequently, this figure is not included in this table.

## Table 8. Offenses Known to Law Enforcement, by State and City, 2009—*Continued*

(Number.)

| State/city | Population | Violent crime | Murder and non-negligent man-slaughter | Forcible rape | Robbery | Aggravated assault | Property crime | Burglary | Larceny-theft | Motor vehicle theft | Arson[1] |
|---|---|---|---|---|---|---|---|---|---|---|---|
| **ARIZONA**—*Continued* | | | | | | | | | | | |
| Winslow | 9,903 | 103 | 1 | 3 | 17 | 82 | 619 | 73 | 525 | 21 | 2 |
| Youngtown | 5,177 | 11 | 1 | 0 | 2 | 8 | 101 | 28 | 55 | 18 | 1 |
| Yuma | 91,433 | 570 | 2 | 24 | 86 | 458 | 3,471 | 1,082 | 2,075 | 314 | 32 |
| **ARKANSAS** | | | | | | | | | | | |
| Alma | 5,219 | 11 | 0 | 1 | 0 | 10 | 218 | 65 | 146 | 7 | 0 |
| Arkadelphia | 11,158 | 42 | 0 | 4 | 8 | 30 | 429 | 153 | 259 | 17 | 3 |
| Arkansas City | 510 | 0 | 0 | 0 | 0 | 0 | 14 | 4 | 10 | 0 | 0 |
| Ashdown | 4,405 | 7 | 0 | 2 | 1 | 4 | 170 | 38 | 120 | 12 | 0 |
| Ash Flat | 1,106 | 2 | 0 | 1 | 0 | 1 | 30 | 16 | 14 | 0 | 0 |
| Atkins | 2,968 | 1 | 0 | 1 | 0 | 0 | 66 | 25 | 39 | 2 | 0 |
| Augusta | 2,210 | 8 | 0 | 0 | 1 | 7 | 40 | 5 | 35 | 0 | 2 |
| Austin | 2,054 | 1 | 0 | 0 | 0 | 1 | 19 | 9 | 8 | 2 | 0 |
| Bald Knob | 3,443 | 9 | 0 | 1 | 0 | 8 | 108 | 41 | 59 | 8 | 1 |
| Barling | 4,507 | 14 | 0 | 0 | 1 | 13 | 74 | 14 | 53 | 7 | 0 |
| Bay | 2,055 | 1 | 0 | 1 | 0 | 0 | 24 | 15 | 9 | 0 | 0 |
| Bearden | 977 | 5 | 1 | 0 | 0 | 4 | 30 | 16 | 13 | 1 | 0 |
| Beebe | 7,096 | 58 | 3 | 6 | 1 | 48 | 310 | 135 | 155 | 20 | 1 |
| Bella Vista | 27,167 | 16 | 0 | 4 | 0 | 12 | 208 | 121 | 81 | 6 | 2 |
| Benton | 30,276 | 86 | 0 | 11 | 15 | 60 | 1,276 | 212 | 988 | 76 | 2 |
| Bentonville | 37,816 | 44 | 0 | 6 | 4 | 34 | 724 | 89 | 618 | 17 | 4 |
| Berryville | 5,335 | 19 | 1 | 3 | 4 | 11 | 305 | 116 | 182 | 7 | 0 |
| Blytheville | 15,889 | 178 | 6 | 20 | 44 | 108 | 1,329 | 476 | 788 | 65 | 9 |
| Booneville | 4,083 | 19 | 0 | 1 | 1 | 17 | 167 | 39 | 125 | 3 | 1 |
| Bryant | 15,573 | 57 | 0 | 13 | 8 | 36 | 758 | 179 | 552 | 27 | 1 |
| Bull Shoals | 2,155 | 8 | 0 | 0 | 0 | 8 | 30 | 13 | 17 | 0 | 2 |
| Cabot | 24,766 | 81 | 0 | 12 | 6 | 63 | 810 | 329 | 461 | 20 | 0 |
| Caddo Valley | 649 | 0 | 0 | 0 | 0 | 0 | 22 | 8 | 14 | 0 | 0 |
| Camden | 11,349 | 82 | 1 | 10 | 19 | 52 | 613 | 158 | 434 | 21 | 1 |
| Cammack Village | 776 | 2 | 0 | 1 | 0 | 1 | 9 | 8 | 1 | 0 | 0 |
| Carlisle | 2,420 | 1 | 0 | 0 | 0 | 1 | 67 | 28 | 34 | 5 | 0 |
| Cave City | 2,057 | 2 | 1 | 0 | 0 | 1 | 35 | 6 | 27 | 2 | 0 |
| Cave Springs | 1,782 | 2 | 0 | 0 | 0 | 2 | 22 | 3 | 19 | 0 | 0 |
| Centerton | 9,911 | 11 | 0 | 6 | 0 | 5 | 81 | 35 | 45 | 1 | 0 |
| Charleston | 3,035 | 3 | 0 | 1 | 0 | 2 | 14 | 3 | 11 | 0 | 0 |
| Cherokee Village | 4,792 | 5 | 0 | 2 | 0 | 3 | 151 | 45 | 100 | 6 | 1 |
| Clarksville | 8,679 | 11 | 0 | 5 | 0 | 6 | 374 | 61 | 305 | 8 | 0 |
| Clinton | 2,482 | 2 | 0 | 1 | 0 | 1 | 87 | 10 | 73 | 4 | 0 |
| Conway | 59,343 | 269 | 2 | 28 | 57 | 182 | 2,575 | 444 | 1,999 | 132 | 4 |
| Corning | 3,270 | 7 | 0 | 1 | 1 | 5 | 55 | 30 | 20 | 5 | 2 |
| Cotter | 1,098 | 1 | 0 | 0 | 0 | 1 | 35 | 15 | 19 | 1 | 0 |
| Crossett | 5,459 | 23 | 0 | 4 | 2 | 17 | 252 | 70 | 177 | 5 | 2 |
| Danville | 2,486 | 5 | 0 | 1 | 0 | 4 | 18 | 11 | 6 | 1 | 0 |
| Dardanelle | 4,458 | 22 | 0 | 1 | 1 | 20 | 236 | 117 | 113 | 6 | 2 |
| Decatur | 1,990 | 5 | 0 | 0 | 0 | 5 | 35 | 18 | 16 | 1 | 0 |
| De Queen | 5,970 | 18 | 0 | 1 | 0 | 17 | 263 | 96 | 158 | 9 | 0 |
| Des Arc | 1,685 | 4 | 0 | 1 | 1 | 2 | 13 | 4 | 9 | 0 | 0 |
| De Witt | 3,223 | 21 | 0 | 2 | 6 | 13 | 144 | 56 | 79 | 9 | 1 |
| Diaz | 1,143 | 3 | 0 | 0 | 0 | 3 | 10 | 5 | 4 | 1 | 0 |
| Dierks | 1,216 | 2 | 0 | 0 | 0 | 2 | 6 | 0 | 5 | 1 | 0 |
| Dover | 1,407 | 0 | 0 | 0 | 0 | 0 | 37 | 22 | 14 | 1 | 0 |
| Dumas | 4,560 | 16 | 0 | 1 | 9 | 6 | 142 | 48 | 90 | 4 | 1 |
| Earle | 2,704 | 3 | 0 | 1 | 2 | 0 | 78 | 55 | 23 | 0 | 1 |
| El Dorado | 19,741 | 214 | 2 | 2 | 38 | 172 | 1,394 | 731 | 598 | 65 | 2 |
| Elkins | 2,730 | 1 | 0 | 1 | 0 | 0 | 10 | 2 | 8 | 0 | 0 |
| Etowah | 339 | 0 | 0 | 0 | 0 | 0 | 8 | 5 | 3 | 0 | 0 |
| Eudora | 2,292 | 6 | 0 | 0 | 0 | 6 | 47 | 10 | 37 | 0 | 0 |
| Eureka Springs | 2,361 | 9 | 3 | 1 | 0 | 5 | 107 | 36 | 68 | 3 | 0 |
| Fairfield Bay | 2,500 | 4 | 0 | 0 | 0 | 4 | 31 | 7 | 24 | 0 | 0 |
| Farmington | 4,802 | 8 | 0 | 2 | 1 | 5 | 122 | 30 | 87 | 5 | 0 |
| Fayetteville | 75,120 | 325 | 2 | 48 | 38 | 237 | 2,908 | 483 | 2,306 | 119 | 11 |
| Flippin | 1,384 | 6 | 0 | 2 | 0 | 4 | 61 | 18 | 43 | 0 | 1 |
| Fordyce | 4,171 | 18 | 0 | 0 | 3 | 15 | 135 | 58 | 70 | 7 | 1 |
| Forrest City | 13,123 | 101 | 4 | 5 | 34 | 58 | 1,152 | 218 | 895 | 39 | 6 |
| Fort Smith | 85,175 | 712 | 3 | 62 | 144 | 503 | 4,992 | 1,119 | 3,670 | 203 | 9 |
| Gassville | 2,203 | 3 | 0 | 1 | 0 | 2 | 36 | 10 | 26 | 0 | 0 |
| Gentry | 3,041 | 11 | 0 | 6 | 2 | 3 | 31 | 17 | 12 | 2 | 1 |
| Glenwood | 1,985 | 4 | 0 | 0 | 0 | 4 | 36 | 23 | 13 | 0 | 0 |
| Gosnell | 3,541 | 34 | 0 | 2 | 0 | 32 | 81 | 34 | 41 | 6 | 1 |
| Gravette | 2,653 | 6 | 0 | 0 | 1 | 5 | 18 | 5 | 13 | 0 | 0 |
| Greenbrier | 4,642 | 6 | 0 | 0 | 0 | 6 | 4 | 1 | 3 | 0 | 0 |

[1] The FBI does not publish arson data unless it receives data from either the agency or the state for all 12 months of the calendar year.

## Table 8. Offenses Known to Law Enforcement, by State and City, 2009—*Continued*

(Number.)

| State/city | Population | Violent crime | Murder and non-negligent man-slaughter | Forcible rape | Robbery | Aggravated assault | Property crime | Burglary | Larceny-theft | Motor vehicle theft | Arson[1] |
|---|---|---|---|---|---|---|---|---|---|---|---|
| **ARKANSAS**—*Continued* | | | | | | | | | | | |
| Green Forest | 3,081 | 24 | 0 | 4 | 1 | 19 | 104 | 41 | 58 | 5 | 2 |
| Greenland | 1,282 | 2 | 0 | 1 | 0 | 1 | 21 | 9 | 12 | 0 | 0 |
| Greenwood | 8,814 | 22 | 0 | 2 | 0 | 20 | 100 | 51 | 46 | 3 | 0 |
| Greers Ferry | 967 | 1 | 0 | 0 | 0 | 1 | 12 | 1 | 11 | 0 | 0 |
| Gurdon | 2,286 | 15 | 0 | 1 | 2 | 12 | 63 | 24 | 37 | 2 | 1 |
| Guy | 566 | 0 | 0 | 0 | 0 | 0 | 9 | 3 | 5 | 1 | 0 |
| Hamburg | 2,689 | 16 | 0 | 6 | 1 | 9 | 79 | 28 | 51 | 0 | 0 |
| Hampton | 1,457 | 1 | 0 | 1 | 0 | 0 | 24 | 15 | 9 | 0 | 0 |
| Harrisburg | 2,109 | 17 | 0 | 0 | 1 | 16 | 131 | 47 | 81 | 3 | 0 |
| Harrison | 13,312 | 89 | 1 | 19 | 6 | 63 | 677 | 238 | 409 | 30 | 3 |
| Hazen | 1,441 | 2 | 0 | 2 | 0 | 0 | 28 | 10 | 18 | 0 | 0 |
| Heber Springs | 7,279 | 23 | 0 | 6 | 1 | 16 | 312 | 138 | 171 | 3 | 0 |
| Helena-West Helena | 11,921 | 211 | 1 | 5 | 31 | 174 | 767 | 412 | 340 | 15 | 6 |
| Highfill | 785 | 1 | 0 | 0 | 0 | 1 | 6 | 1 | 5 | 0 | 0 |
| Highland | 1,096 | 3 | 0 | 1 | 0 | 2 | 19 | 9 | 9 | 1 | 0 |
| Hope | 10,354 | 71 | 0 | 1 | 16 | 54 | 574 | 174 | 379 | 21 | 1 |
| Horseshoe Bend | 2,213 | 1 | 0 | 0 | 1 | 0 | 34 | 10 | 23 | 1 | 1 |
| Hot Springs | 39,864 | 478 | 5 | 21 | 121 | 331 | 3,723 | 889 | 2,644 | 190 | 3 |
| Hoxie | 2,630 | 4 | 0 | 1 | 0 | 3 | 11 | 6 | 5 | 0 | 0 |
| Jacksonville | 31,483 | 235 | 0 | 17 | 38 | 180 | 1,473 | 369 | 1,036 | 68 | 10 |
| Jonesboro | 64,944 | 296 | 1 | 27 | 74 | 194 | 3,097 | 1,221 | 1,772 | 104 | 10 |
| Judsonia | 2,202 | 2 | 2 | 0 | 0 | 0 | 30 | 11 | 18 | 1 | 1 |
| Kensett | 1,852 | 4 | 0 | 0 | 1 | 3 | 45 | 18 | 20 | 7 | 0 |
| Lake City | 2,147 | 2 | 0 | 0 | 0 | 2 | 12 | 6 | 5 | 1 | 0 |
| Lakeview | 857 | 2 | 0 | 0 | 0 | 2 | 12 | 3 | 9 | 0 | 0 |
| Lake Village | 2,342 | 92 | 0 | 0 | 4 | 88 | 92 | 56 | 36 | 0 | 4 |
| Leachville | 1,834 | 5 | 0 | 2 | 0 | 3 | 14 | 1 | 12 | 1 | 0 |
| Lepanto | 2,007 | 3 | 0 | 1 | 0 | 2 | 53 | 24 | 29 | 0 | 0 |
| Lincoln | 2,118 | 10 | 0 | 2 | 0 | 8 | 27 | 18 | 7 | 2 | 0 |
| Little Flock | 3,210 | 2 | 0 | 1 | 0 | 1 | 14 | 5 | 6 | 3 | 0 |
| Little Rock[6] | 190,205 | 2,795 | 32 | 171 | 799 | 1,793 | 15,828 | 4,412 | 10,253 | 1,163 | 105 |
| Lonoke | 4,636 | 28 | 0 | 2 | 2 | 24 | 209 | 66 | 140 | 3 | 0 |
| Lowell | 7,397 | 17 | 0 | 5 | 1 | 11 | 211 | 117 | 90 | 4 | 1 |
| Luxora | 1,209 | 1 | 0 | 0 | 0 | 1 | 5 | 1 | 4 | 0 | 0 |
| Magnolia | 11,011 | 84 | 4 | 2 | 23 | 55 | 472 | 224 | 237 | 11 | 12 |
| Marianna | 4,319 | 26 | 3 | 1 | 5 | 17 | 159 | 62 | 97 | 0 | 3 |
| Marion | 12,641 | 68 | 0 | 4 | 6 | 58 | 397 | 189 | 190 | 18 | 1 |
| Marked Tree | 2,615 | 0 | 0 | 0 | 0 | 0 | 57 | 8 | 49 | 0 | 0 |
| Marmaduke | 1,175 | 4 | 0 | 0 | 0 | 4 | 46 | 15 | 30 | 1 | 3 |
| Marvell | 1,102 | 5 | 0 | 1 | 1 | 3 | 47 | 14 | 31 | 2 | 0 |
| Maumelle | 16,958 | 14 | 0 | 1 | 3 | 10 | 362 | 221 | 129 | 12 | 3 |
| Mayflower | 2,310 | 3 | 0 | 0 | 0 | 3 | 82 | 20 | 57 | 5 | 1 |
| McGehee | 3,888 | 49 | 0 | 1 | 3 | 45 | 141 | 38 | 97 | 6 | 3 |
| McRae | 712 | 0 | 0 | 0 | 0 | 0 | 18 | 8 | 10 | 0 | 0 |
| Mena | 5,626 | 22 | 0 | 2 | 1 | 19 | 209 | 51 | 153 | 5 | 1 |
| Monette | 1,234 | 2 | 0 | 0 | 0 | 2 | 12 | 5 | 7 | 0 | 1 |
| Monticello | 9,281 | 50 | 0 | 4 | 5 | 41 | 390 | 114 | 257 | 19 | 0 |
| Morrilton | 6,584 | 32 | 0 | 3 | 8 | 21 | 459 | 76 | 365 | 18 | 3 |
| Mountain Home | 12,767 | 11 | 0 | 4 | 1 | 6 | 536 | 51 | 469 | 16 | 0 |
| Mountain View | 3,133 | 13 | 0 | 3 | 0 | 10 | 56 | 11 | 43 | 2 | 0 |
| Mulberry | 1,730 | 7 | 0 | 1 | 0 | 6 | 15 | 6 | 9 | 0 | 0 |
| Murfreesboro | 1,629 | 4 | 0 | 0 | 0 | 4 | 37 | 11 | 25 | 1 | 0 |
| Nashville | 4,806 | 25 | 2 | 2 | 2 | 19 | 265 | 85 | 177 | 3 | 1 |
| Newport | 7,364 | 56 | 0 | 3 | 7 | 46 | 454 | 127 | 317 | 10 | 1 |
| North Little Rock | 59,320 | 788 | 11 | 20 | 242 | 515 | 6,000 | 1,629 | 4,009 | 362 | 18 |
| Ola | 1,242 | 0 | 0 | 0 | 0 | 0 | 8 | 7 | 1 | 0 | 0 |
| Osceola | 7,816 | 150 | 1 | 8 | 9 | 132 | 502 | 176 | 302 | 24 | 6 |
| Ozark | 3,587 | 15 | 0 | 1 | 2 | 12 | 123 | 32 | 89 | 2 | 0 |
| Paragould | 25,113 | 86 | 0 | 18 | 11 | 57 | 1,835 | 644 | 1,125 | 66 | 4 |
| Paris | 3,602 | 17 | 0 | 2 | 2 | 13 | 123 | 34 | 85 | 4 | 0 |
| Pea Ridge | 4,924 | 10 | 0 | 1 | 0 | 9 | 68 | 33 | 31 | 4 | 0 |
| Perryville | 1,440 | 14 | 0 | 2 | 0 | 12 | 44 | 17 | 27 | 0 | 0 |
| Piggott | 3,440 | 6 | 0 | 1 | 0 | 5 | 45 | 21 | 20 | 4 | 0 |
| Pine Bluff | 49,915 | 721 | 12 | 50 | 207 | 452 | 4,159 | 1,606 | 2,185 | 368 | 29 |
| Plainview | 778 | 6 | 0 | 0 | 0 | 6 | 9 | 7 | 2 | 0 | 0 |
| Plummerville | 865 | 3 | 0 | 1 | 1 | 1 | 10 | 4 | 5 | 1 | 0 |
| Pocahontas | 6,736 | 3 | 0 | 2 | 0 | 1 | 61 | 10 | 49 | 2 | 0 |
| Pottsville | 2,902 | 3 | 0 | 0 | 0 | 3 | 33 | 18 | 13 | 2 | 0 |
| Prairie Grove | 3,809 | 5 | 0 | 2 | 1 | 2 | 52 | 7 | 45 | 0 | 1 |
| Prescott | 4,439 | 13 | 1 | 1 | 0 | 11 | 133 | 52 | 79 | 2 | 1 |

[1] The FBI does not publish arson data unless it receives data from either the agency or the state for all 12 months of the calendar year.

[6] Because of changes in the state/local agency's reporting practices, figures are not comparable to previous years' data.

## Table 8. Offenses Known to Law Enforcement, by State and City, 2009—*Continued*

(Number.)

| State/city | Population | Violent crime | Murder and non-negligent man-slaughter | Forcible rape | Robbery | Aggravated assault | Property crime | Burglary | Larceny-theft | Motor vehicle theft | Arson[1] |
|---|---|---|---|---|---|---|---|---|---|---|---|
| **ARKANSAS**—*Continued* | | | | | | | | | | | |
| Quitman | 738 | 0 | 0 | 0 | 0 | 0 | 19 | 7 | 12 | 0 | 0 |
| Redfield | 1,171 | 1 | 0 | 0 | 0 | 1 | 15 | 5 | 7 | 3 | 0 |
| Rison | 1,282 | 0 | 0 | 0 | 0 | 0 | 20 | 11 | 9 | 0 | 0 |
| Rogers | 58,992 | 183 | 2 | 52 | 17 | 112 | 2,160 | 399 | 1,684 | 77 | 3 |
| Rose Bud | 460 | 1 | 0 | 0 | 0 | 1 | 10 | 2 | 8 | 0 | 0 |
| Russellville | 28,035 | 113 | 1 | 17 | 11 | 84 | 1,471 | 292 | 1,102 | 77 | 3 |
| Salem | 1,613 | 1 | 0 | 0 | 0 | 1 | 25 | 9 | 14 | 2 | 0 |
| Searcy | 22,647 | 70 | 0 | 7 | 14 | 49 | 1,203 | 426 | 737 | 40 | 6 |
| Sheridan | 4,640 | 14 | 0 | 3 | 2 | 9 | 121 | 52 | 64 | 5 | 0 |
| Sherwood | 24,888 | 148 | 1 | 6 | 21 | 120 | 1,096 | 239 | 782 | 75 | 2 |
| Siloam Springs | 15,325 | 22 | 0 | 5 | 4 | 13 | 275 | 64 | 199 | 12 | 0 |
| Springdale | 70,935 | 288 | 0 | 56 | 25 | 207 | 2,413 | 486 | 1,828 | 99 | 11 |
| Stamps | 1,888 | 1 | 0 | 0 | 0 | 1 | 83 | 60 | 22 | 1 | 0 |
| Star City | 2,203 | 7 | 0 | 0 | 1 | 6 | 33 | 11 | 22 | 0 | 1 |
| Stuttgart | 8,891 | 33 | 0 | 4 | 4 | 25 | 484 | 152 | 309 | 23 | 2 |
| Texarkana | 30,348 | 269 | 2 | 25 | 66 | 176 | 1,894 | 476 | 1,261 | 157 | 9 |
| Trumann | 6,781 | 43 | 0 | 9 | 3 | 31 | 463 | 152 | 301 | 10 | 6 |
| Vilonia | 3,685 | 8 | 0 | 1 | 0 | 7 | 86 | 25 | 61 | 0 | 0 |
| Waldron | 3,574 | 12 | 0 | 2 | 0 | 10 | 111 | 69 | 40 | 2 | 1 |
| Walnut Ridge | 4,636 | 11 | 0 | 2 | 0 | 9 | 77 | 30 | 45 | 2 | 2 |
| Ward | 4,086 | 22 | 0 | 1 | 1 | 20 | 117 | 38 | 78 | 1 | 0 |
| Warren | 6,079 | 17 | 0 | 5 | 2 | 10 | 182 | 130 | 46 | 6 | 1 |
| Weiner | 719 | 1 | 0 | 0 | 0 | 1 | 9 | 6 | 3 | 0 | 0 |
| West Fork | 2,355 | 3 | 0 | 2 | 0 | 1 | 38 | 21 | 16 | 1 | 1 |
| West Memphis | 26,995 | 703 | 4 | 30 | 102 | 567 | 2,265 | 1,077 | 1,042 | 146 | 7 |
| White Hall | 5,158 | 6 | 0 | 0 | 0 | 6 | 101 | 9 | 80 | 12 | 0 |
| Wynne | 8,419 | 38 | 1 | 6 | 4 | 27 | 488 | 240 | 243 | 5 | 0 |
| **CALIFORNIA** | | | | | | | | | | | |
| Adelanto | 30,045 | 272 | 2 | 8 | 40 | 222 | 797 | 346 | 324 | 127 | 13 |
| Agoura Hills | 22,469 | 27 | 0 | 2 | 6 | 19 | 308 | 105 | 192 | 11 | 6 |
| Alameda | 70,372 | 199 | 4 | 13 | 87 | 95 | 1,955 | 325 | 1,390 | 240 | 12 |
| Albany | 15,950 | 45 | 0 | 1 | 36 | 8 | 600 | 112 | 381 | 107 | 17 |
| Alhambra | 85,956 | 248 | 0 | 15 | 133 | 100 | 1,874 | 360 | 1,209 | 305 | 4 |
| Aliso Viejo | 41,740 | 37 | 0 | 4 | 15 | 18 | 438 | 57 | 367 | 14 | 9 |
| Alturas | 2,778 | 2 | 0 | 0 | 0 | 2 | 56 | 11 | 39 | 6 | 1 |
| American Canyon | 17,259 | 59 | 0 | 2 | 31 | 26 | 516 | 107 | 354 | 55 | 2 |
| Anaheim | 335,970 | 1,184 | 9 | 72 | 504 | 599 | 7,993 | 1,457 | 5,591 | 945 | 37 |
| Anderson | 10,718 | 79 | 0 | 11 | 12 | 56 | 507 | 137 | 343 | 27 | 1 |
| Antioch | 101,243 | 897 | 5 | 40 | 315 | 537 | 2,653 | 824 | 1,082 | 747 | 40 |
| Apple Valley | 72,200 | 266 | 1 | 20 | 54 | 191 | 1,764 | 557 | 1,003 | 204 | 10 |
| Arcadia | 56,596 | 115 | 0 | 5 | 50 | 60 | 1,633 | 329 | 1,172 | 132 | 3 |
| Arcata | 17,093 | 50 | 0 | 8 | 10 | 32 | 655 | 126 | 490 | 39 | 2 |
| Arroyo Grande | 17,323 | 24 | 0 | 4 | 9 | 11 | 368 | 83 | 269 | 16 | 5 |
| Artesia | 16,226 | 49 | 0 | 2 | 20 | 27 | 288 | 73 | 163 | 52 | 3 |
| Arvin | 15,320 | 158 | 2 | 1 | 21 | 134 | 639 | 244 | 306 | 89 | 14 |
| Atascadero | 28,675 | 65 | 1 | 11 | 10 | 43 | 532 | 121 | 380 | 31 | 10 |
| Atherton | 7,430 | 21 | 0 | 0 | 4 | 17 | 204 | 42 | 153 | 9 | 0 |
| Atwater | 26,966 | 138 | 2 | 8 | 21 | 107 | 1,338 | 414 | 822 | 102 | 15 |
| Auburn | 13,306 | 53 | 0 | 4 | 8 | 41 | 284 | 52 | 191 | 41 | 4 |
| Avalon | 3,098 | 26 | 0 | 0 | 2 | 24 | 89 | 21 | 52 | 16 | 2 |
| Avenal | 17,451 | 71 | 1 | 4 | 7 | 59 | 224 | 133 | 79 | 12 | 5 |
| Azusa | 47,078 | 245 | 1 | 10 | 78 | 156 | 1,222 | 281 | 751 | 190 | 2 |
| Bakersfield | 330,897 | 2,099 | 27 | 49 | 704 | 1,319 | 15,605 | 3,888 | 9,341 | 2,376 | 127 |
| Baldwin Park | 77,539 | 295 | 4 | 9 | 112 | 170 | 1,661 | 365 | 760 | 536 | 16 |
| Banning | 29,568 | 161 | 0 | 12 | 29 | 120 | 570 | 232 | 255 | 83 | 0 |
| Barstow | 24,822 | 248 | 3 | 16 | 66 | 163 | 903 | 299 | 423 | 181 | 9 |
| Bear Valley | 4,618 | 3 | 0 | 0 | 0 | 3 | 83 | 12 | 70 | 1 | 0 |
| Beaumont | 36,800 | 85 | 0 | 9 | 15 | 61 | 897 | 190 | 630 | 77 | 1 |
| Bell | 36,651 | 186 | 1 | 8 | 89 | 88 | 546 | 115 | 280 | 151 | 0 |
| Bellflower | 73,038 | 558 | 3 | 16 | 243 | 296 | 1,843 | 406 | 825 | 612 | 13 |
| Bell Gardens | 44,756 | 204 | 4 | 6 | 112 | 82 | 829 | 184 | 320 | 325 | 2 |
| Belmont | 24,742 | 20 | 1 | 2 | 5 | 12 | 439 | 56 | 338 | 45 | 5 |
| Belvedere | 2,052 | 0 | 0 | 0 | 0 | 0 | 27 | 7 | 19 | 1 | 0 |
| Benicia | 26,089 | 48 | 0 | 5 | 20 | 23 | 417 | 140 | 230 | 47 | 8 |
| Berkeley | 101,190 | 615 | 6 | 27 | 444 | 138 | 6,467 | 1,079 | 4,661 | 727 | 21 |
| Beverly Hills | 34,506 | 81 | 0 | 4 | 45 | 32 | 1,230 | 295 | 895 | 40 | 4 |
| Big Bear Lake | 6,210 | 41 | 0 | 4 | 2 | 35 | 373 | 150 | 208 | 15 | 3 |
| Biggs | 1,823 | 19 | 0 | 0 | 0 | 19 | 39 | 16 | 18 | 5 | 0 |
| Bishop | 3,393 | 20 | 0 | 3 | 1 | 16 | 109 | 19 | 86 | 4 | 0 |
| Blythe | 21,841 | 69 | 1 | 1 | 18 | 49 | 630 | 237 | 366 | 27 | 29 |

[1] The FBI does not publish arson data unless it receives data from either the agency or the state for all 12 months of the calendar year.

## Table 8. Offenses Known to Law Enforcement, by State and City, 2009—*Continued*

(Number.)

| State/city | Population | Violent crime | Murder and non-negligent man-slaughter | Forcible rape | Robbery | Aggravated assault | Property crime | Burglary | Larceny-theft | Motor vehicle theft | Arson[1] |
|---|---|---|---|---|---|---|---|---|---|---|---|
| **CALIFORNIA**—*Continued* | | | | | | | | | | | |
| Bradbury | 1,088 | 0 | 0 | 0 | 0 | 0 | 10 | 4 | 6 | 0 | 0 |
| Brawley | 22,810 | 66 | 0 | 5 | 21 | 40 | 999 | 388 | 508 | 103 | 8 |
| Brea | 38,637 | 68 | 1 | 2 | 40 | 25 | 1,394 | 161 | 1,153 | 80 | 4 |
| Brentwood | 53,494 | 119 | 1 | 5 | 46 | 67 | 928 | 193 | 640 | 95 | 15 |
| Brisbane | 3,686 | 16 | 0 | 1 | 2 | 13 | 121 | 22 | 85 | 14 | 0 |
| Broadmoor | 4,393 | 16 | 0 | 0 | 7 | 9 | 78 | 23 | 41 | 14 | 1 |
| Buellton | 4,346 | 15 | 0 | 3 | 2 | 10 | 64 | 8 | 51 | 5 | 0 |
| Buena Park | 79,525 | 247 | 2 | 12 | 127 | 106 | 1,982 | 441 | 1,145 | 396 | 20 |
| Burbank | 103,248 | 253 | 1 | 22 | 93 | 137 | 2,663 | 499 | 1,829 | 335 | 18 |
| Burlingame | 27,656 | 65 | 0 | 5 | 21 | 39 | 757 | 126 | 555 | 76 | 9 |
| Calabasas | 22,359 | 20 | 0 | 1 | 6 | 13 | 291 | 83 | 193 | 15 | 3 |
| Calexico | 39,820 | 63 | 0 | 2 | 23 | 38 | 1,380 | 385 | 580 | 415 | 7 |
| California City | 15,492 | 60 | 1 | 4 | 13 | 42 | 471 | 166 | 276 | 29 | 0 |
| Calimesa | 7,497 | 24 | 0 | 1 | 9 | 14 | 169 | 48 | 103 | 18 | 2 |
| Calipatria | 7,623 | 13 | 0 | 0 | 0 | 13 | 32 | 15 | 15 | 2 | 0 |
| Calistoga | 5,178 | 12 | 1 | 1 | 1 | 9 | 109 | 25 | 78 | 6 | 1 |
| Camarillo | 64,011 | 80 | 0 | 8 | 28 | 44 | 951 | 167 | 729 | 55 | 6 |
| Campbell | 38,584 | 116 | 0 | 13 | 25 | 78 | 1,425 | 248 | 1,038 | 139 | 14 |
| Canyon Lake | 11,387 | 12 | 0 | 0 | 1 | 11 | 132 | 46 | 70 | 16 | 0 |
| Capitola | 9,565 | 107 | 0 | 4 | 4 | 99 | 623 | 71 | 534 | 18 | 7 |
| Carlsbad | 98,482 | 287 | 5 | 26 | 53 | 203 | 1,908 | 446 | 1,327 | 135 | 12 |
| Carmel | 3,864 | 14 | 0 | 0 | 3 | 11 | 116 | 36 | 77 | 3 | 0 |
| Carpinteria | 13,595 | 26 | 0 | 3 | 2 | 21 | 189 | 41 | 144 | 4 | 0 |
| Carson | 92,635 | 500 | 5 | 14 | 164 | 317 | 2,331 | 475 | 1,389 | 467 | 27 |
| Cathedral City | 53,236 | 203 | 3 | 15 | 62 | 123 | 1,221 | 430 | 596 | 195 | 6 |
| Ceres | 43,669 | 145 | 2 | 7 | 53 | 83 | 1,768 | 376 | 1,006 | 386 | 14 |
| Cerritos | 51,299 | 81 | 2 | 4 | 50 | 25 | 1,762 | 254 | 1,291 | 217 | 6 |
| Chico | 84,724 | 310 | 3 | 42 | 124 | 141 | 2,352 | 685 | 1,359 | 308 | 34 |
| Chino | 84,626 | 169 | 1 | 15 | 69 | 84 | 2,122 | 543 | 1,346 | 233 | 21 |
| Chino Hills | 74,650 | 101 | 3 | 2 | 22 | 74 | 1,111 | 251 | 753 | 107 | 3 |
| Chowchilla | 19,817 | 47 | 0 | 1 | 2 | 44 | 389 | 200 | 157 | 32 | 16 |
| Chula Vista | 224,841 | 747 | 4 | 49 | 335 | 359 | 5,263 | 912 | 3,048 | 1,303 | 27 |
| Citrus Heights | 84,333 | 415 | 0 | 26 | 128 | 261 | 3,627 | 702 | 2,447 | 478 | 17 |
| City of Angels | 3,804 | 16 | 0 | 2 | 0 | 14 | 84 | 37 | 44 | 3 | 0 |
| Claremont | 35,628 | 74 | 2 | 7 | 31 | 34 | 802 | 225 | 538 | 39 | 3 |
| Clayton | 11,333 | 7 | 1 | 2 | 2 | 2 | 179 | 27 | 140 | 12 | 1 |
| Clearlake | 15,261 | 78 | 2 | 13 | 21 | 42 | 557 | 166 | 307 | 84 | 4 |
| Cloverdale | 8,304 | 16 | 0 | 1 | 2 | 13 | 177 | 44 | 125 | 8 | 4 |
| Clovis | 95,229 | 141 | 1 | 23 | 54 | 63 | 3,289 | 705 | 2,254 | 330 | 10 |
| Coachella | 41,863 | 255 | 4 | 9 | 64 | 178 | 1,354 | 479 | 578 | 297 | 10 |
| Coalinga | 19,308 | 105 | 0 | 6 | 8 | 91 | 418 | 136 | 259 | 23 | 19 |
| Colma | 1,452 | 11 | 0 | 0 | 7 | 4 | 212 | 8 | 193 | 11 | 0 |
| Colton | 50,803 | 222 | 5 | 8 | 94 | 115 | 1,702 | 437 | 988 | 277 | 11 |
| Colusa | 5,946 | 13 | 0 | 4 | 3 | 6 | 160 | 63 | 90 | 7 | 0 |
| Commerce | 13,529 | 190 | 2 | 2 | 68 | 118 | 1,020 | 138 | 597 | 285 | 12 |
| Compton | 93,872 | 1,457 | 36 | 36 | 509 | 876 | 3,051 | 768 | 1,355 | 928 | 91 |
| Concord | 121,042 | 397 | 2 | 19 | 212 | 164 | 3,870 | 808 | 2,202 | 860 | 13 |
| Corcoran | 25,474 | 40 | 0 | 2 | 6 | 32 | 286 | 91 | 157 | 38 | 3 |
| Corning | 7,253 | 51 | 1 | 2 | 8 | 40 | 279 | 55 | 202 | 22 | 5 |
| Corona | 152,438 | 214 | 8 | 12 | 117 | 77 | 3,810 | 612 | 2,632 | 566 | 13 |
| Coronado | 22,482 | 28 | 0 | 2 | 4 | 22 | 522 | 65 | 418 | 39 | 4 |
| Costa Mesa | 110,150 | 304 | 1 | 27 | 114 | 162 | 3,321 | 516 | 2,557 | 248 | 14 |
| Cotati | 7,248 | 32 | 0 | 2 | 4 | 26 | 157 | 39 | 104 | 14 | 1 |
| Covina | 46,946 | 169 | 4 | 12 | 68 | 85 | 1,691 | 340 | 1,160 | 191 | 15 |
| Crescent City | 7,889 | 31 | 0 | 5 | 6 | 20 | 302 | 84 | 199 | 19 | 0 |
| Cudahy | 24,337 | 150 | 2 | 4 | 66 | 78 | 500 | 55 | 276 | 169 | 2 |
| Culver City | 38,545 | 186 | 1 | 5 | 125 | 55 | 1,398 | 225 | 1,048 | 125 | 1 |
| Cupertino | 53,760 | 37 | 1 | 4 | 11 | 21 | 1,045 | 191 | 799 | 55 | 14 |
| Cypress | 47,181 | 89 | 1 | 9 | 35 | 44 | 750 | 102 | 558 | 90 | 8 |
| Daly City | 101,284 | 240 | 1 | 18 | 102 | 119 | 1,753 | 317 | 1,126 | 310 | 13 |
| Dana Point | 35,756 | 47 | 0 | 3 | 13 | 31 | 672 | 113 | 516 | 43 | 7 |
| Danville | 41,118 | 19 | 1 | 3 | 6 | 9 | 572 | 94 | 442 | 36 | 0 |
| Davis | 62,994 | 151 | 0 | 23 | 57 | 71 | 1,644 | 412 | 1,126 | 106 | 19 |
| Delano | 54,801 | 238 | 2 | 3 | 46 | 187 | 1,895 | 886 | 527 | 482 | 77 |
| Del Mar | 4,453 | 20 | 0 | 1 | 5 | 14 | 195 | 38 | 141 | 16 | 1 |
| Del Rey Oaks | 1,516 | 2 | 0 | 0 | 1 | 1 | 59 | 10 | 48 | 1 | 0 |
| Desert Hot Springs | 25,577 | 326 | 8 | 8 | 85 | 225 | 1,511 | 549 | 594 | 368 | 20 |
| Diamond Bar | 57,330 | 86 | 0 | 4 | 40 | 42 | 894 | 244 | 564 | 86 | 1 |
| Dinuba | 20,682 | 144 | 1 | 10 | 27 | 106 | 923 | 350 | 436 | 137 | 8 |
| Dixon | 17,562 | 58 | 0 | 8 | 15 | 35 | 581 | 59 | 472 | 50 | 5 |
| Dorris | 825 | 4 | 0 | 0 | 0 | 4 | 15 | 5 | 10 | 0 | 0 |

[1] The FBI does not publish arson data unless it receives data from either the agency or the state for all 12 months of the calendar year.

## Table 8. Offenses Known to Law Enforcement, by State and City, 2009—*Continued*

(Number.)

| State/city | Population | Violent crime | Murder and non-negligent man-slaughter | Forcible rape | Robbery | Aggravated assault | Property crime | Burglary | Larceny-theft | Motor vehicle theft | Arson[1] |
|---|---|---|---|---|---|---|---|---|---|---|---|
| **CALIFORNIA**—*Continued* | | | | | | | | | | | |
| Dos Palos | 5,015 | 36 | 0 | 1 | 5 | 30 | 109 | 43 | 57 | 9 | 0 |
| Downey | 107,598 | 444 | 4 | 18 | 234 | 188 | 3,575 | 524 | 2,105 | 946 | 0 |
| Duarte | 21,873 | 80 | 1 | 4 | 21 | 54 | 478 | 133 | 277 | 68 | 3 |
| Dublin | 46,157 | 73 | 1 | 6 | 21 | 45 | 822 | 172 | 593 | 57 | 1 |
| Dunsmuir | 1,788 | 5 | 0 | 1 | 0 | 4 | 64 | 15 | 46 | 3 | 1 |
| East Palo Alto | 34,005 | 396 | 8 | 17 | 157 | 214 | 915 | 415 | 298 | 202 | 0 |
| El Cajon | 92,466 | 461 | 2 | 29 | 226 | 204 | 2,609 | 487 | 1,562 | 560 | 17 |
| El Centro | 40,337 | 177 | 1 | 7 | 36 | 133 | 2,257 | 570 | 1,436 | 251 | 9 |
| El Cerrito | 22,116 | 156 | 0 | 6 | 78 | 72 | 929 | 215 | 611 | 103 | 14 |
| Elk Grove | 140,576 | 608 | 4 | 15 | 152 | 437 | 3,443 | 859 | 2,152 | 432 | 11 |
| El Monte | 122,428 | 716 | 3 | 14 | 304 | 395 | 2,810 | 644 | 1,407 | 759 | 9 |
| El Segundo | 16,235 | 36 | 0 | 4 | 17 | 15 | 719 | 208 | 462 | 49 | 1 |
| Emeryville | 9,929 | 160 | 2 | 3 | 67 | 88 | 914 | 109 | 718 | 87 | 1 |
| Encinitas | 60,625 | 167 | 0 | 15 | 28 | 124 | 1,079 | 279 | 684 | 116 | 3 |
| Escalon | 7,414 | 20 | 0 | 1 | 2 | 17 | 223 | 61 | 142 | 20 | 0 |
| Escondido | 137,432 | 629 | 4 | 42 | 249 | 334 | 3,880 | 779 | 2,402 | 699 | 23 |
| Etna | 768 | 0 | 0 | 0 | 0 | 0 | 6 | 3 | 3 | 0 | 0 |
| Eureka | 25,216 | 148 | 1 | 7 | 59 | 81 | 1,395 | 480 | 750 | 165 | 22 |
| Exeter | 10,054 | 32 | 0 | 6 | 11 | 15 | 356 | 120 | 202 | 34 | 1 |
| Fairfax | 7,038 | 17 | 0 | 2 | 2 | 13 | 178 | 35 | 139 | 4 | 6 |
| Fairfield | 104,478 | 437 | 6 | 23 | 193 | 215 | 3,246 | 779 | 2,077 | 390 | 22 |
| Farmersville | 10,214 | 97 | 0 | 2 | 11 | 84 | 196 | 59 | 102 | 35 | 1 |
| Ferndale | 1,384 | 0 | 0 | 0 | 0 | 0 | 7 | 1 | 5 | 1 | 0 |
| Fillmore | 15,206 | 32 | 0 | 2 | 12 | 18 | 235 | 51 | 171 | 13 | 0 |
| Firebaugh | 7,032 | 19 | 0 | 2 | 6 | 11 | 210 | 33 | 152 | 25 | 0 |
| Folsom | 69,728 | 108 | 2 | 13 | 28 | 65 | 1,504 | 272 | 1,164 | 68 | 27 |
| Fontana | 190,303 | 859 | 6 | 46 | 299 | 508 | 4,391 | 1,060 | 2,430 | 901 | 10 |
| Fort Bragg | 6,581 | 50 | 0 | 2 | 1 | 47 | 201 | 50 | 143 | 8 | 3 |
| Fort Jones | 646 | 1 | 0 | 0 | 0 | 1 | 12 | 5 | 7 | 0 | 1 |
| Fortuna | 11,424 | 58 | 0 | 5 | 6 | 47 | 345 | 56 | 264 | 25 | 3 |
| Foster City | 29,123 | 11 | 0 | 2 | 4 | 5 | 495 | 129 | 333 | 33 | 6 |
| Fountain Valley | 55,570 | 116 | 0 | 4 | 33 | 79 | 1,170 | 237 | 873 | 60 | 6 |
| Fowler | 5,769 | 8 | 0 | 1 | 1 | 6 | 145 | 39 | 81 | 25 | 0 |
| Fremont | 202,714 | 490 | 2 | 34 | 217 | 237 | 4,978 | 1,190 | 3,237 | 551 | 19 |
| Fresno | 481,370 | 2,933 | 42 | 86 | 1,085 | 1,720 | 21,030 | 4,423 | 13,359 | 3,248 | 155 |
| Fullerton | 132,478 | 526 | 2 | 44 | 189 | 291 | 3,824 | 779 | 2,684 | 361 | 16 |
| Galt | 24,554 | 58 | 2 | 8 | 14 | 34 | 632 | 186 | 357 | 89 | 6 |
| Gardena | 58,623 | 381 | 6 | 11 | 216 | 148 | 1,546 | 390 | 830 | 326 | 7 |
| Garden Grove | 165,837 | 541 | 6 | 34 | 167 | 334 | 3,306 | 687 | 2,145 | 474 | 21 |
| Gilroy | 50,946 | 177 | 1 | 4 | 59 | 113 | 1,562 | 280 | 1,097 | 185 | 8 |
| Glendale | 197,384 | 302 | 3 | 15 | 126 | 158 | 3,755 | 635 | 2,723 | 397 | 12 |
| Glendora | 49,400 | 58 | 1 | 7 | 28 | 22 | 1,279 | 178 | 1,026 | 75 | 1 |
| Goleta | 29,471 | 51 | 0 | 1 | 10 | 40 | 409 | 121 | 280 | 8 | 5 |
| Gonzales | 8,637 | 34 | 0 | 1 | 7 | 26 | 168 | 48 | 101 | 19 | 0 |
| Grand Terrace | 12,266 | 24 | 1 | 0 | 11 | 12 | 230 | 61 | 129 | 40 | 7 |
| Grass Valley | 12,271 | 73 | 0 | 9 | 7 | 57 | 467 | 80 | 360 | 27 | 3 |
| Greenfield | 15,511 | 147 | 6 | 3 | 58 | 80 | 360 | 106 | 205 | 49 | 4 |
| Gridley | 6,589 | 80 | 0 | 2 | 2 | 76 | 247 | 93 | 133 | 21 | 1 |
| Grover Beach | 13,135 | 52 | 0 | 3 | 7 | 42 | 344 | 99 | 215 | 30 | 2 |
| Guadalupe | 6,708 | 20 | 0 | 3 | 3 | 14 | 77 | 18 | 54 | 5 | 5 |
| Gustine | 5,133 | 12 | 2 | 0 | 2 | 8 | 167 | 50 | 101 | 16 | 2 |
| Half Moon Bay | 12,514 | 19 | 0 | 3 | 2 | 14 | 215 | 31 | 179 | 5 | 2 |
| Hawaiian Gardens[2] | 15,276 | 79 | 0 | 4 | 35 | 40 | | 34 | 146 | | 3 |
| Hawthorne | 84,314 | 700 | 4 | 34 | 354 | 308 | 2,104 | 654 | 1,062 | 388 | 12 |
| Hayward | 142,227 | 741 | 7 | 29 | 446 | 259 | 4,405 | 979 | 1,974 | 1,452 | 51 |
| Healdsburg | 10,968 | 16 | 0 | 2 | 2 | 12 | 286 | 58 | 216 | 12 | 0 |
| Hemet | 72,417 | 374 | 7 | 17 | 122 | 228 | 2,841 | 865 | 1,655 | 321 | 13 |
| Hercules | 25,120 | 49 | 2 | 2 | 15 | 30 | 419 | 125 | 219 | 75 | 2 |
| Hermosa Beach | 19,431 | 83 | 0 | 9 | 30 | 44 | 715 | 148 | 524 | 43 | 2 |
| Hesperia | 88,904 | 290 | 3 | 23 | 84 | 180 | 1,673 | 476 | 907 | 290 | 20 |
| Hidden Hills | 2,037 | 2 | 0 | 0 | 0 | 2 | 19 | 6 | 12 | 1 | 0 |
| Highland | 51,847 | 260 | 7 | 13 | 87 | 153 | 1,268 | 426 | 572 | 270 | 14 |
| Hillsborough | 10,846 | 2 | 0 | 0 | 2 | 0 | 82 | 34 | 45 | 3 | 0 |
| Hollister | 34,883 | 179 | 0 | 5 | 46 | 128 | 806 | 345 | 378 | 83 | 6 |
| Holtville | 5,392 | 6 | 0 | 1 | 2 | 3 | 117 | 55 | 41 | 21 | 0 |
| Hughson | 6,647 | 12 | 0 | 0 | 2 | 10 | 113 | 35 | 68 | 10 | 0 |
| Huntington Beach | 192,911 | 377 | 1 | 30 | 128 | 218 | 4,571 | 704 | 3,571 | 296 | 44 |
| Huntington Park | 60,840 | 546 | 5 | 14 | 381 | 146 | 2,309 | 248 | 1,246 | 815 | 12 |
| Huron | 7,764 | 69 | 0 | 0 | 14 | 55 | 126 | 44 | 73 | 9 | 9 |
| Imperial | 14,565 | 11 | 0 | 0 | 5 | 6 | 81 | 12 | 50 | 19 | 1 |

[1] The FBI does not publish arson data unless it receives data from either the agency or the state for all 12 months of the calendar year.

[2] The FBI determined that the agency's data were underreported. Consequently, those data are not included in this table.

**Table 8. Offenses Known to Law Enforcement, by State and City, 2009—*Continued***

(Number.)

| State/city | Population | Violent crime | Murder and non-negligent man-slaughter | Forcible rape | Robbery | Aggravated assault | Property crime | Burglary | Larceny-theft | Motor vehicle theft | Arson[1] |
|---|---|---|---|---|---|---|---|---|---|---|---|
| **CALIFORNIA**—*Continued* | | | | | | | | | | | |
| Imperial Beach | 26,490 | 213 | 2 | 9 | 46 | 156 | 555 | 125 | 237 | 193 | 4 |
| Indian Wells | 5,323 | 3 | 0 | 0 | 2 | 1 | 170 | 58 | 105 | 7 | 0 |
| Indio | 89,459 | 428 | 5 | 28 | 112 | 283 | 2,821 | 927 | 1,408 | 486 | 9 |
| Industry | 930 | 83 | 0 | 2 | 47 | 34 | 1,405 | 209 | 984 | 212 | 8 |
| Inglewood | 112,712 | 1,039 | 27 | 32 | 485 | 495 | 3,030 | 685 | 1,615 | 730 | 17 |
| Ione | 7,518 | 13 | 0 | 0 | 1 | 12 | 132 | 52 | 77 | 3 | 0 |
| Irvine | 215,673 | 153 | 3 | 28 | 55 | 67 | 2,996 | 481 | 2,365 | 150 | 32 |
| Irwindale | 1,438 | 22 | 0 | 1 | 8 | 13 | 218 | 51 | 119 | 48 | 2 |
| Isleton | 839 | 6 | 0 | 0 | 0 | 6 | 9 | 3 | 5 | 1 | 0 |
| Jackson | 4,359 | 20 | 0 | 3 | 2 | 15 | 160 | 53 | 99 | 8 | 2 |
| Kensington | 5,387 | 3 | 0 | 0 | 1 | 2 | 96 | 34 | 54 | 8 | 0 |
| Kerman | 13,285 | 31 | 2 | 3 | 7 | 19 | 523 | 103 | 341 | 79 | 2 |
| King City | 11,683 | 68 | 4 | 8 | 16 | 40 | 294 | 94 | 152 | 48 | 3 |
| Kingsburg | 11,276 | 26 | 0 | 0 | 4 | 22 | 403 | 62 | 257 | 84 | 2 |
| La Canada Flintridge | 20,706 | 21 | 1 | 1 | 9 | 10 | 385 | 102 | 266 | 17 | 9 |
| Lafayette | 25,128 | 25 | 0 | 3 | 8 | 14 | 503 | 129 | 344 | 30 | 0 |
| Laguna Beach | 24,019 | 86 | 1 | 11 | 9 | 65 | 524 | 115 | 389 | 20 | 4 |
| Laguna Hills | 31,816 | 39 | 0 | 1 | 16 | 22 | 604 | 85 | 485 | 34 | 7 |
| Laguna Niguel | 64,649 | 48 | 0 | 2 | 12 | 34 | 654 | 110 | 520 | 24 | 15 |
| Laguna Woods | 18,246 | 10 | 1 | 1 | 3 | 5 | 107 | 15 | 81 | 11 | 0 |
| La Habra | 59,120 | 200 | 3 | 12 | 66 | 119 | 1,236 | 264 | 873 | 99 | 5 |
| La Habra Heights | 5,911 | 5 | 0 | 1 | 2 | 2 | 61 | 29 | 30 | 2 | 2 |
| Lake Elsinore | 54,235 | 137 | 1 | 10 | 37 | 89 | 1,653 | 386 | 979 | 288 | 1 |
| Lake Forest | 75,509 | 109 | 0 | 3 | 30 | 76 | 964 | 179 | 721 | 64 | 11 |
| Lakeport | 5,171 | 28 | 0 | 4 | 5 | 19 | 252 | 60 | 180 | 12 | 0 |
| Lake Shastina | 2,390 | 4 | 0 | 0 | 0 | 4 | 0 | 0 | 0 | 0 | 0 |
| Lakewood | 78,334 | 366 | 1 | 20 | 173 | 172 | 2,117 | 316 | 1,401 | 400 | 12 |
| La Mesa | 54,663 | 225 | 0 | 11 | 112 | 102 | 1,782 | 355 | 1,188 | 239 | 9 |
| La Mirada | 50,139 | 80 | 1 | 4 | 22 | 53 | 671 | 173 | 393 | 105 | 3 |
| Lancaster | 148,742 | 976 | 10 | 60 | 322 | 584 | 3,507 | 1,206 | 1,829 | 472 | 50 |
| La Palma | 15,619 | 20 | 1 | 0 | 6 | 13 | 208 | 59 | 124 | 25 | 2 |
| La Puente | 40,589 | 181 | 3 | 8 | 69 | 101 | 614 | 156 | 294 | 164 | 15 |
| La Quinta | 46,805 | 123 | 1 | 8 | 22 | 92 | 1,573 | 537 | 958 | 78 | 4 |
| La Verne | 33,842 | 55 | 0 | 3 | 27 | 25 | 697 | 146 | 511 | 40 | 2 |
| Lawndale | 31,301 | 173 | 1 | 5 | 82 | 85 | 490 | 158 | 205 | 127 | 6 |
| Lemon Grove | 23,997 | 203 | 0 | 14 | 74 | 115 | 475 | 166 | 200 | 109 | 4 |
| Lincoln | 50,654 | 48 | 0 | 5 | 12 | 31 | 415 | 140 | 236 | 39 | 10 |
| Lindsay | 10,587 | 58 | 0 | 3 | 5 | 50 | 400 | 136 | 189 | 75 | 2 |
| Livermore | 80,915 | 161 | 3 | 26 | 55 | 77 | 1,727 | 393 | 1,191 | 143 | 14 |
| Livingston | 13,764 | 92 | 1 | 9 | 13 | 69 | 393 | 195 | 155 | 43 | 1 |
| Lodi | 61,748 | 262 | 1 | 11 | 110 | 140 | 2,384 | 793 | 1,211 | 380 | 17 |
| Loma Linda | 21,878 | 47 | 1 | 8 | 13 | 25 | 626 | 145 | 351 | 130 | 2 |
| Lomita | 20,164 | 100 | 0 | 3 | 24 | 73 | 380 | 98 | 230 | 52 | 4 |
| Lompoc | 41,085 | 358 | 3 | 17 | 41 | 297 | 955 | 225 | 683 | 47 | 24 |
| Long Beach | 463,969 | 3,161 | 40 | 131 | 1,381 | 1,609 | 12,643 | 3,116 | 7,166 | 2,361 | 107 |
| Los Alamitos | 11,668 | 32 | 1 | 2 | 13 | 16 | 278 | 56 | 195 | 27 | 8 |
| Los Altos | 28,380 | 6 | 0 | 0 | 5 | 1 | 315 | 108 | 194 | 13 | 2 |
| Los Altos Hills | 8,632 | 3 | 0 | 0 | 0 | 3 | 39 | 14 | 24 | 1 | 0 |
| Los Angeles | 3,848,776 | 24,070 | 312 | 903 | 12,217 | 10,638 | 94,240 | 18,435 | 57,414 | 18,391 | 1,561 |
| Los Banos | 36,097 | 156 | 0 | 7 | 23 | 126 | 1,075 | 243 | 721 | 111 | 2 |
| Los Gatos | 29,388 | 28 | 0 | 1 | 9 | 18 | 622 | 107 | 467 | 48 | 6 |
| Lynwood | 70,032 | 644 | 2 | 11 | 242 | 389 | 1,414 | 298 | 455 | 661 | 19 |
| Madera | 58,372 | 408 | 1 | 15 | 133 | 259 | 1,300 | 459 | 614 | 227 | 0 |
| Malibu | 13,058 | 25 | 0 | 0 | 3 | 22 | 279 | 61 | 198 | 20 | 2 |
| Mammoth Lakes | 7,433 | 39 | 0 | 2 | 2 | 35 | 329 | 96 | 223 | 10 | 1 |
| Manhattan Beach | 36,907 | 59 | 0 | 8 | 27 | 24 | 931 | 157 | 718 | 56 | 4 |
| Manteca | 66,908 | 182 | 2 | 11 | 85 | 84 | 1,974 | 405 | 1,221 | 348 | 16 |
| Marina | 17,837 | 48 | 0 | 5 | 15 | 28 | 472 | 152 | 276 | 44 | 1 |
| Martinez | 35,059 | 77 | 0 | 7 | 18 | 52 | 1,079 | 232 | 670 | 177 | 0 |
| Marysville | 11,638 | 84 | 1 | 7 | 17 | 59 | 474 | 124 | 286 | 64 | 4 |
| Maywood | 28,234 | 151 | 2 | 8 | 67 | 74 | 467 | 76 | 208 | 183 | 3 |
| Menifee | 68,083 | 70 | 0 | 6 | 30 | 34 | 1,444 | 393 | 805 | 246 | 0 |
| Menlo Park | 30,011 | 69 | 1 | 7 | 31 | 30 | 670 | 137 | 484 | 49 | 2 |
| Merced | 78,693 | 733 | 7 | 27 | 158 | 541 | 2,850 | 679 | 1,906 | 265 | 57 |
| Millbrae | 20,811 | 35 | 0 | 7 | 9 | 19 | 319 | 81 | 194 | 44 | 3 |
| Mill Valley | 13,230 | 7 | 0 | 0 | 3 | 4 | 228 | 73 | 149 | 6 | 1 |
| Milpitas | 68,047 | 132 | 2 | 6 | 59 | 65 | 2,050 | 274 | 1,561 | 215 | 19 |
| Mission Viejo | 94,552 | 95 | 0 | 5 | 38 | 52 | 1,164 | 221 | 899 | 44 | 18 |
| Modesto | 204,474 | 1,419 | 21 | 55 | 369 | 974 | 10,269 | 2,291 | 6,637 | 1,341 | 97 |

[1] The FBI does not publish arson data unless it receives data from either the agency or the state for all 12 months of the calendar year.

## Table 8. Offenses Known to Law Enforcement, by State and City, 2009—*Continued*

(Number.)

| State/city | Population | Violent crime | Murder and non-negligent man-slaughter | Forcible rape | Robbery | Aggravated assault | Property crime | Burglary | Larceny-theft | Motor vehicle theft | Arson[1] |
|---|---|---|---|---|---|---|---|---|---|---|---|
| **CALIFORNIA**—*Continued* | | | | | | | | | | | |
| Monrovia | 37,723 | 107 | 2 | 4 | 45 | 56 | 1,068 | 141 | 792 | 135 | 1 |
| Montague | 1,454 | 11 | 0 | 2 | 0 | 9 | 24 | 9 | 13 | 2 | 0 |
| Montclair | 36,819 | 204 | 4 | 12 | 90 | 98 | 2,110 | 250 | 1,479 | 381 | 5 |
| Montebello | 61,870 | 196 | 1 | 5 | 112 | 78 | 1,762 | 540 | 782 | 440 | 25 |
| Monterey | 27,554 | 188 | 1 | 15 | 49 | 123 | 999 | 187 | 766 | 46 | 6 |
| Monterey Park | 61,353 | 146 | 1 | 4 | 95 | 46 | 966 | 249 | 524 | 193 | 2 |
| Monte Sereno | 3,615 | 1 | 0 | 0 | 1 | 0 | 30 | 19 | 10 | 1 | 2 |
| Moorpark | 36,919 | 57 | 0 | 1 | 25 | 31 | 493 | 119 | 352 | 22 | 3 |
| Moraga | 17,131 | 12 | 0 | 4 | 2 | 6 | 179 | 34 | 140 | 5 | 1 |
| Moreno Valley | 197,114 | 921 | 6 | 30 | 467 | 418 | 5,958 | 2,020 | 3,086 | 852 | 16 |
| Morgan Hill | 38,568 | 89 | 1 | 13 | 25 | 50 | 639 | 141 | 427 | 71 | 15 |
| Morro Bay | 10,327 | 20 | 0 | 2 | 2 | 16 | 163 | 35 | 124 | 4 | 2 |
| Mountain View | 71,423 | 180 | 0 | 14 | 47 | 119 | 1,972 | 253 | 1,554 | 165 | 3 |
| Mount Shasta | 3,528 | 8 | 0 | 2 | 1 | 5 | 77 | 29 | 42 | 6 | 1 |
| Murrieta | 105,238 | 118 | 0 | 17 | 34 | 67 | 1,509 | 471 | 884 | 154 | 3 |
| Napa | 74,736 | 272 | 0 | 21 | 60 | 191 | 1,909 | 413 | 1,330 | 166 | 8 |
| National City | 59,230 | 426 | 2 | 14 | 194 | 216 | 1,923 | 308 | 1,051 | 564 | 7 |
| Needles | 5,289 | 37 | 0 | 2 | 14 | 21 | 238 | 70 | 133 | 35 | 1 |
| Nevada City | 2,920 | 24 | 0 | 1 | 0 | 23 | 69 | 21 | 44 | 4 | 0 |
| Newark | 41,685 | 202 | 1 | 15 | 73 | 113 | 1,695 | 328 | 1,183 | 184 | 5 |
| Newman | 10,646 | 27 | 0 | 0 | 2 | 25 | 351 | 100 | 206 | 45 | 2 |
| Newport Beach | 79,912 | 125 | 0 | 4 | 32 | 89 | 2,239 | 512 | 1,600 | 127 | 6 |
| Norco | 26,933 | 54 | 0 | 3 | 14 | 37 | 686 | 159 | 451 | 76 | 3 |
| Norwalk | 102,807 | 456 | 13 | 16 | 178 | 249 | 2,151 | 396 | 1,146 | 609 | 23 |
| Novato | 53,374 | 103 | 1 | 12 | 21 | 69 | 1,088 | 197 | 780 | 111 | 13 |
| Oakdale | 20,902 | 65 | 0 | 6 | 7 | 52 | 739 | 265 | 411 | 63 | 2 |
| Oakland | 404,553 | 6,793 | 104 | 326 | 2,898 | 3,465 | 20,173 | 4,798 | 8,833 | 6,542 | 223 |
| Oakley | 32,818 | 71 | 0 | 9 | 22 | 40 | 619 | 156 | 306 | 157 | 6 |
| Oceanside | 170,579 | 749 | 4 | 62 | 221 | 462 | 3,995 | 768 | 2,786 | 441 | 24 |
| Ojai | 7,765 | 17 | 0 | 3 | 3 | 11 | 197 | 38 | 157 | 2 | 2 |
| Ontario | 173,212 | 732 | 5 | 49 | 286 | 392 | 5,146 | 986 | 3,207 | 953 | 47 |
| Orange | 137,132 | 160 | 2 | 11 | 68 | 79 | 2,625 | 431 | 1,959 | 235 | 16 |
| Orinda | 18,536 | 13 | 0 | 1 | 7 | 5 | 249 | 82 | 151 | 16 | 1 |
| Orland | 7,281 | 25 | 0 | 0 | 4 | 21 | 191 | 62 | 106 | 23 | 0 |
| Oroville | 14,765 | 285 | 0 | 16 | 20 | 249 | 1,126 | 244 | 703 | 179 | 20 |
| Oxnard | 187,357 | 771 | 13 | 24 | 384 | 350 | 4,087 | 704 | 2,929 | 454 | 10 |
| Pacifica | 37,668 | 54 | 0 | 3 | 10 | 41 | 729 | 96 | 567 | 66 | 6 |
| Pacific Grove | 14,502 | 23 | 1 | 6 | 3 | 13 | 449 | 120 | 315 | 14 | 2 |
| Palmdale | 146,377 | 818 | 8 | 41 | 264 | 505 | 3,598 | 1,080 | 2,031 | 487 | 28 |
| Palm Desert | 51,630 | 44 | 1 | 5 | 30 | 8 | 1,927 | 705 | 1,114 | 108 | 5 |
| Palm Springs | 48,537 | 297 | 1 | 16 | 117 | 163 | 2,361 | 750 | 1,382 | 229 | 26 |
| Palo Alto | 59,490 | 108 | 1 | 9 | 29 | 69 | 1,666 | 267 | 1,350 | 49 | 33 |
| Palos Verdes Estates | 13,610 | 7 | 0 | 0 | 2 | 5 | 96 | 43 | 49 | 4 | 0 |
| Paradise | 26,471 | 90 | 1 | 13 | 10 | 66 | 759 | 165 | 539 | 55 | 5 |
| Paramount | 55,220 | 389 | 4 | 11 | 193 | 181 | 1,656 | 310 | 721 | 625 | 13 |
| Parlier | 13,500 | 116 | 1 | 5 | 23 | 87 | 458 | 155 | 224 | 79 | 15 |
| Pasadena | 144,063 | 483 | 5 | 25 | 182 | 271 | 4,158 | 824 | 3,023 | 311 | 23 |
| Paso Robles | 29,204 | 93 | 0 | 15 | 11 | 67 | 927 | 267 | 595 | 65 | 5 |
| Patterson | 20,085 | 46 | 0 | 3 | 17 | 26 | 638 | 218 | 326 | 94 | 9 |
| Perris | 58,362 | 188 | 4 | 8 | 94 | 82 | 1,883 | 556 | 933 | 394 | 3 |
| Petaluma | 54,649 | 168 | 0 | 17 | 29 | 122 | 852 | 152 | 625 | 75 | 15 |
| Pico Rivera | 63,098 | 215 | 6 | 15 | 84 | 110 | 1,375 | 199 | 824 | 352 | 6 |
| Piedmont | 10,427 | 9 | 0 | 1 | 7 | 1 | 248 | 47 | 158 | 43 | 0 |
| Pinole | 18,766 | 94 | 1 | 1 | 49 | 43 | 718 | 154 | 462 | 102 | 3 |
| Pismo Beach | 8,573 | 15 | 0 | 2 | 5 | 8 | 392 | 75 | 306 | 11 | 0 |
| Pittsburg | 64,989 | 151 | 8 | 3 | 94 | 46 | 2,097 | 493 | 1,082 | 522 | 5 |
| Placentia | 50,041 | 94 | 1 | 5 | 23 | 65 | 967 | 188 | 703 | 76 | 6 |
| Placerville | 10,025 | 65 | 0 | 4 | 7 | 54 | 212 | 48 | 143 | 21 | 4 |
| Pleasant Hill | 32,841 | 104 | 1 | 7 | 46 | 50 | 1,486 | 238 | 1,096 | 152 | 11 |
| Pleasanton | 67,116 | 73 | 0 | 4 | 20 | 49 | 1,284 | 136 | 1,053 | 95 | 5 |
| Pomona | 153,217 | 968 | 17 | 46 | 344 | 561 | 4,134 | 854 | 2,273 | 1,007 | 39 |
| Porterville | 52,555 | 264 | 1 | 17 | 64 | 182 | 1,656 | 372 | 1,045 | 239 | 2 |
| Port Hueneme | 21,440 | 81 | 1 | 7 | 23 | 50 | 352 | 90 | 223 | 39 | 6 |
| Poway | 48,931 | 119 | 0 | 5 | 26 | 88 | 694 | 169 | 453 | 72 | 1 |
| Rancho Cordova | 63,303 | 391 | 3 | 30 | 145 | 213 | 1,928 | 527 | 1,011 | 390 | 1 |
| Rancho Cucamonga | 176,676 | 342 | 1 | 20 | 123 | 198 | 3,765 | 860 | 2,445 | 460 | 19 |
| Rancho Mirage | 17,137 | 17 | 0 | 1 | 13 | 3 | 604 | 204 | 361 | 39 | 0 |
| Rancho Palos Verdes | 41,093 | 42 | 0 | 2 | 8 | 32 | 386 | 115 | 247 | 24 | 3 |
| Rancho Santa Margarita | 49,854 | 23 | 0 | 2 | 6 | 15 | 405 | 71 | 319 | 15 | 11 |
| Red Bluff | 14,111 | 124 | 0 | 6 | 15 | 103 | 680 | 168 | 480 | 32 | 8 |
| Redding | 91,242 | 688 | 2 | 64 | 83 | 539 | 2,979 | 783 | 1,992 | 204 | 17 |

[1] The FBI does not publish arson data unless it receives data from either the agency or the state for all 12 months of the calendar year.

## Table 8. Offenses Known to Law Enforcement, by State and City, 2009—*Continued*

(Number.)

| State/city | Population | Violent crime | Murder and non-negligent man-slaughter | Forcible rape | Robbery | Aggravated assault | Property crime | Burglary | Larceny-theft | Motor vehicle theft | Arson[1] |
|---|---|---|---|---|---|---|---|---|---|---|---|
| **CALIFORNIA**—*Continued* | | | | | | | | | | | |
| Redlands | 70,360 | 233 | 2 | 13 | 101 | 117 | 2,473 | 634 | 1,544 | 295 | 16 |
| Redondo Beach | 67,268 | 199 | 0 | 7 | 90 | 102 | 1,568 | 297 | 1,143 | 128 | 1 |
| Redwood City | 73,905 | 232 | 1 | 20 | 89 | 122 | 1,860 | 437 | 1,199 | 224 | 9 |
| Reedley | 23,744 | 144 | 5 | 9 | 27 | 103 | 622 | 118 | 368 | 136 | 4 |
| Rialto | 99,386 | 542 | 6 | 28 | 225 | 283 | 2,862 | 801 | 1,391 | 670 | 15 |
| Richmond | 102,566 | 1,095 | 47 | 44 | 407 | 597 | 4,440 | 1,486 | 1,533 | 1,421 | 42 |
| Ridgecrest | 25,719 | 166 | 0 | 15 | 10 | 141 | 548 | 170 | 335 | 43 | 23 |
| Rio Dell | 3,184 | 9 | 0 | 1 | 1 | 7 | 97 | 20 | 71 | 6 | 5 |
| Rio Vista | 8,256 | 50 | 0 | 0 | 1 | 49 | 200 | 65 | 125 | 10 | 2 |
| Ripon | 15,039 | 32 | 0 | 4 | 7 | 21 | 312 | 38 | 233 | 41 | 2 |
| Riverbank | 21,226 | 57 | 3 | 1 | 11 | 42 | 577 | 172 | 332 | 73 | 4 |
| Riverside | 299,871 | 1,535 | 15 | 98 | 667 | 755 | 9,590 | 2,020 | 6,239 | 1,331 | 79 |
| Rocklin | 54,919 | 71 | 0 | 11 | 17 | 43 | 1,021 | 221 | 735 | 65 | 5 |
| Rohnert Park | 40,401 | 201 | 0 | 8 | 27 | 166 | 905 | 155 | 698 | 52 | 13 |
| Rolling Hills | 1,912 | 2 | 0 | 0 | 0 | 2 | 9 | 1 | 7 | 1 | 0 |
| Rolling Hills Estates | 7,879 | 14 | 1 | 1 | 5 | 7 | 156 | 43 | 110 | 3 | 1 |
| Rosemead | 54,501 | 246 | 2 | 13 | 114 | 117 | 1,085 | 283 | 571 | 231 | 4 |
| Roseville | 116,846 | 323 | 2 | 14 | 92 | 215 | 3,869 | 525 | 3,020 | 324 | 9 |
| Ross | 2,272 | 0 | 0 | 0 | 0 | 0 | 19 | 9 | 8 | 2 | 0 |
| Sacramento | 470,308 | 4,165 | 30 | 179 | 1,606 | 2,350 | 21,001 | 5,135 | 11,720 | 4,146 | 168 |
| Salinas | 143,660 | 1,133 | 29 | 47 | 379 | 678 | 4,966 | 1,382 | 2,463 | 1,121 | 46 |
| San Anselmo | 11,943 | 15 | 0 | 4 | 2 | 9 | 256 | 59 | 191 | 6 | 2 |
| San Bernardino | 199,683 | 1,908 | 32 | 61 | 677 | 1,138 | 9,245 | 2,349 | 4,775 | 2,121 | 89 |
| San Bruno | 40,333 | 99 | 0 | 8 | 42 | 49 | 907 | 109 | 629 | 169 | 10 |
| San Carlos | 27,187 | 25 | 0 | 2 | 12 | 11 | 578 | 113 | 436 | 29 | 4 |
| San Clemente | 62,821 | 69 | 1 | 8 | 28 | 32 | 866 | 168 | 644 | 54 | 11 |
| Sand City | 375 | 4 | 0 | 0 | 4 | 0 | 115 | 3 | 105 | 7 | 0 |
| San Diego | 1,314,773 | 5,931 | 41 | 318 | 1,905 | 3,667 | 32,246 | 6,693 | 18,057 | 7,496 | 186 |
| San Dimas | 35,043 | 104 | 1 | 9 | 33 | 61 | 789 | 167 | 573 | 49 | 0 |
| San Fernando | 23,856 | 90 | 0 | 6 | 38 | 46 | 382 | 82 | 198 | 102 | 1 |
| San Francisco | 809,755 | 5,957 | 45 | 179 | 3,423 | 2,310 | 34,509 | 5,197 | 24,399 | 4,913 | 198 |
| San Gabriel | 40,507 | 151 | 1 | 3 | 71 | 76 | 557 | 149 | 346 | 62 | 4 |
| Sanger | 26,285 | 125 | 0 | 8 | 18 | 99 | 778 | 165 | 517 | 96 | 5 |
| San Jacinto | 39,848 | 161 | 3 | 9 | 53 | 96 | 1,382 | 489 | 707 | 186 | 5 |
| San Jose | 954,009 | 3,439 | 28 | 258 | 1,025 | 2,128 | 22,755 | 3,741 | 13,635 | 5,379 | 243 |
| San Juan Capistrano | 34,896 | 63 | 0 | 1 | 15 | 47 | 538 | 101 | 391 | 46 | 5 |
| San Leandro | 77,676 | 409 | 2 | 22 | 261 | 124 | 3,445 | 547 | 1,966 | 932 | 12 |
| San Luis Obispo | 43,565 | 140 | 0 | 30 | 39 | 71 | 1,632 | 324 | 1,240 | 68 | 50 |
| San Marcos | 82,258 | 226 | 2 | 16 | 68 | 140 | 1,416 | 307 | 901 | 208 | 4 |
| San Marino | 12,792 | 9 | 0 | 2 | 3 | 4 | 157 | 44 | 109 | 4 | 0 |
| San Mateo | 92,208 | 338 | 2 | 16 | 110 | 210 | 2,172 | 274 | 1,720 | 178 | 19 |
| San Pablo | 30,783 | 287 | 8 | 7 | 134 | 138 | 1,319 | 366 | 511 | 442 | 16 |
| San Rafael | 55,544 | 204 | 1 | 14 | 77 | 112 | 1,705 | 333 | 1,086 | 286 | 8 |
| San Ramon | 49,660 | 46 | 0 | 1 | 17 | 28 | 987 | 156 | 769 | 62 | 14 |
| Santa Ana | 339,196 | 1,726 | 25 | 77 | 869 | 755 | 6,798 | 1,160 | 4,165 | 1,473 | 94 |
| Santa Barbara | 85,715 | 428 | 3 | 29 | 109 | 287 | 2,885 | 610 | 2,176 | 99 | 14 |
| Santa Clara | 111,106 | 168 | 6 | 20 | 63 | 79 | 3,028 | 428 | 2,182 | 418 | 13 |
| Santa Clarita | 171,112 | 427 | 5 | 20 | 129 | 273 | 3,067 | 705 | 2,035 | 327 | 38 |
| Santa Cruz | 56,155 | 453 | 4 | 36 | 91 | 322 | 3,116 | 466 | 2,467 | 183 | 23 |
| Santa Fe Springs | 17,239 | 131 | 5 | 7 | 53 | 66 | 1,102 | 166 | 729 | 207 | 6 |
| Santa Maria | 87,381 | 735 | 5 | 42 | 73 | 615 | 1,826 | 554 | 864 | 408 | 12 |
| Santa Monica | 88,038 | 393 | 3 | 14 | 162 | 214 | 3,354 | 512 | 2,578 | 264 | 26 |
| Santa Paula | 28,603 | 108 | 0 | 4 | 40 | 64 | 637 | 114 | 450 | 73 | 2 |
| Santa Rosa | 156,541 | 803 | 2 | 75 | 180 | 546 | 4,265 | 710 | 3,165 | 390 | 14 |
| Santee | 53,957 | 172 | 0 | 12 | 37 | 123 | 993 | 193 | 684 | 116 | 5 |
| Saratoga | 30,486 | 17 | 1 | 1 | 3 | 12 | 263 | 97 | 156 | 10 | 8 |
| Sausalito | 7,139 | 11 | 1 | 1 | 0 | 9 | 174 | 47 | 121 | 6 | 0 |
| Scotts Valley | 11,098 | 9 | 0 | 2 | 1 | 6 | 286 | 59 | 219 | 8 | 0 |
| Seal Beach | 24,121 | 51 | 0 | 1 | 10 | 40 | 504 | 133 | 338 | 33 | 2 |
| Seaside | 33,875 | 167 | 1 | 13 | 48 | 105 | 714 | 172 | 467 | 75 | 11 |
| Sebastopol | 7,487 | 15 | 0 | 1 | 4 | 10 | 200 | 68 | 121 | 11 | 2 |
| Selma | 23,181 | 101 | 1 | 6 | 45 | 49 | 998 | 187 | 567 | 244 | 18 |
| Shafter | 16,174 | 73 | 3 | 5 | 18 | 47 | 662 | 241 | 317 | 104 | 18 |
| Sierra Madre | 10,860 | 10 | 0 | 0 | 0 | 10 | 140 | 46 | 87 | 7 | 0 |
| Signal Hill | 11,062 | 53 | 2 | 6 | 19 | 26 | 425 | 96 | 271 | 58 | 3 |
| Simi Valley | 121,538 | 155 | 2 | 10 | 51 | 92 | 1,997 | 375 | 1,508 | 114 | 16 |
| Solana Beach | 12,807 | 33 | 0 | 2 | 11 | 20 | 232 | 48 | 162 | 22 | 1 |
| Soledad | 28,748 | 80 | 1 | 0 | 20 | 59 | 313 | 145 | 137 | 31 | 5 |
| Solvang | 5,127 | 8 | 0 | 0 | 0 | 8 | 69 | 23 | 46 | 0 | 0 |
| Sonoma | 9,955 | 25 | 0 | 2 | 5 | 18 | 228 | 63 | 148 | 17 | 3 |

[1] The FBI does not publish arson data unless it receives data from either the agency or the state for all 12 months of the calendar year.

## Table 8. Offenses Known to Law Enforcement, by State and City, 2009—*Continued*

(Number.)

| State/city | Population | Violent crime | Murder and non-negligent man-slaughter | Forcible rape | Robbery | Aggravated assault | Property crime | Burglary | Larceny-theft | Motor vehicle theft | Arson[1] |
|---|---|---|---|---|---|---|---|---|---|---|---|
| **CALIFORNIA**—*Continued* | | | | | | | | | | | |
| Sonora | 4,573 | 50 | 0 | 7 | 7 | 36 | 457 | 56 | 388 | 13 | 2 |
| South El Monte | 21,422 | 150 | 0 | 6 | 69 | 75 | 610 | 124 | 355 | 131 | 9 |
| South Gate | 96,651 | 566 | 10 | 19 | 360 | 177 | 2,571 | 377 | 1,070 | 1,124 | 38 |
| South Lake Tahoe | 23,300 | 143 | 0 | 13 | 30 | 100 | 422 | 169 | 237 | 16 | 1 |
| South Pasadena | 24,462 | 30 | 1 | 3 | 20 | 6 | 470 | 141 | 265 | 64 | 5 |
| South San Francisco | 62,716 | 196 | 0 | 9 | 72 | 115 | 1,468 | 400 | 790 | 278 | 29 |
| Stallion Springs | 1,661 | 7 | 0 | 0 | 0 | 7 | 21 | 3 | 15 | 3 | 0 |
| Stanton | 37,583 | 135 | 3 | 5 | 56 | 71 | 617 | 120 | 376 | 121 | 1 |
| St. Helena | 5,803 | 4 | 0 | 0 | 0 | 4 | 77 | 24 | 49 | 4 | 0 |
| Stockton | 292,212 | 3,703 | 33 | 82 | 1,259 | 2,329 | 15,427 | 3,980 | 9,274 | 2,173 | 33 |
| Suisun City | 27,056 | 109 | 1 | 12 | 30 | 66 | 706 | 150 | 466 | 90 | 6 |
| Sunnyvale | 132,144 | 169 | 1 | 11 | 71 | 86 | 2,769 | 431 | 2,026 | 312 | 21 |
| Susanville | 17,308 | 70 | 1 | 3 | 8 | 58 | 230 | 65 | 154 | 11 | 8 |
| Sutter Creek | 2,770 | 14 | 0 | 1 | 3 | 10 | 54 | 14 | 35 | 5 | 0 |
| Taft | 9,184 | 47 | 0 | 1 | 6 | 40 | 278 | 60 | 197 | 21 | 0 |
| Tehachapi | 11,807 | 39 | 1 | 2 | 1 | 35 | 340 | 116 | 203 | 21 | 0 |
| Temecula | 100,922 | 126 | 1 | 14 | 59 | 52 | 2,370 | 576 | 1,574 | 220 | 4 |
| Temple City | 38,909 | 56 | 0 | 0 | 20 | 36 | 456 | 176 | 194 | 86 | 0 |
| Thousand Oaks | 123,735 | 163 | 2 | 19 | 40 | 102 | 1,793 | 323 | 1,386 | 84 | 26 |
| Tiburon | 8,675 | 5 | 1 | 0 | 0 | 4 | 109 | 10 | 92 | 7 | 1 |
| Torrance | 141,109 | 259 | 1 | 25 | 139 | 94 | 2,874 | 442 | 2,034 | 398 | 11 |
| Tracy | 82,019 | 153 | 5 | 4 | 80 | 64 | 2,507 | 476 | 1,719 | 312 | 18 |
| Trinidad | 309 | 0 | 0 | 0 | 0 | 0 | 23 | 4 | 19 | 0 | 0 |
| Truckee | 16,447 | 24 | 1 | 3 | 2 | 18 | 217 | 58 | 151 | 8 | 3 |
| Tulare | 58,006 | 405 | 4 | 9 | 84 | 308 | 2,679 | 569 | 1,733 | 377 | 34 |
| Tulelake | 952 | 2 | 0 | 0 | 1 | 1 | 14 | 3 | 9 | 2 | 0 |
| Turlock | 69,859 | 409 | 6 | 22 | 117 | 264 | 2,934 | 805 | 1,604 | 525 | 46 |
| Tustin | 72,286 | 92 | 0 | 4 | 57 | 31 | 1,379 | 209 | 1,039 | 131 | 8 |
| Twentynine Palms | 34,083 | 114 | 0 | 5 | 9 | 100 | 572 | 211 | 311 | 50 | 12 |
| Twin Cities | 20,918 | 41 | 0 | 2 | 7 | 32 | 644 | 162 | 403 | 79 | 5 |
| Ukiah | 14,896 | 117 | 0 | 5 | 16 | 96 | 447 | 151 | 270 | 26 | 5 |
| Union City | 72,666 | 384 | 2 | 15 | 174 | 193 | 2,115 | 502 | 1,258 | 355 | 25 |
| Vacaville | 92,538 | 274 | 1 | 15 | 96 | 162 | 2,122 | 398 | 1,567 | 157 | 9 |
| Vallejo | 114,443 | 998 | 10 | 42 | 439 | 507 | 5,478 | 2,358 | 1,854 | 1,266 | 48 |
| Ventura | 103,997 | 368 | 5 | 18 | 125 | 220 | 3,068 | 615 | 2,276 | 177 | 23 |
| Vernon | 90 | 49 | 2 | 0 | 35 | 12 | 298 | 33 | 175 | 90 | 1 |
| Victorville | 117,150 | 783 | 10 | 48 | 289 | 436 | 3,939 | 1,253 | 2,219 | 467 | 35 |
| Villa Park | 5,968 | 2 | 0 | 1 | 1 | 0 | 98 | 22 | 75 | 1 | 0 |
| Visalia | 124,263 | 648 | 9 | 53 | 185 | 401 | 5,135 | 1,261 | 3,346 | 528 | 13 |
| Vista | 91,252 | 490 | 0 | 29 | 145 | 316 | 2,238 | 519 | 1,341 | 378 | 13 |
| Walnut | 30,819 | 43 | 0 | 3 | 21 | 19 | 456 | 122 | 299 | 35 | 1 |
| Walnut Creek | 63,356 | 131 | 1 | 4 | 41 | 85 | 2,647 | 504 | 1,940 | 203 | 12 |
| Waterford | 9,124 | 32 | 0 | 1 | 5 | 26 | 219 | 62 | 137 | 20 | 1 |
| Watsonville | 50,898 | 350 | 4 | 17 | 86 | 243 | 1,825 | 285 | 1,259 | 281 | 15 |
| Weed | 3,031 | 29 | 0 | 2 | 4 | 23 | 135 | 46 | 77 | 12 | 0 |
| West Covina | 105,846 | 315 | 8 | 14 | 152 | 141 | 3,282 | 470 | 2,199 | 613 | 5 |
| West Hollywood | 36,020 | 326 | 0 | 10 | 115 | 201 | 1,559 | 286 | 1,142 | 131 | 7 |
| Westlake Village | 8,479 | 5 | 0 | 0 | 3 | 2 | 142 | 33 | 103 | 6 | 0 |
| Westminster | 89,057 | 265 | 0 | 14 | 93 | 158 | 2,331 | 406 | 1,701 | 224 | 9 |
| Westmorland | 2,207 | 1 | 0 | 0 | 0 | 1 | 21 | 10 | 6 | 5 | 0 |
| West Sacramento | 49,646 | 189 | 4 | 23 | 73 | 89 | 1,272 | 325 | 742 | 205 | 24 |
| Wheatland | 3,771 | 4 | 0 | 0 | 0 | 4 | 57 | 17 | 39 | 1 | 0 |
| Whittier | 82,096 | 337 | 3 | 16 | 94 | 224 | 2,105 | 400 | 1,435 | 270 | 4 |
| Wildomar | 31,496 | 87 | 1 | 11 | 30 | 45 | 859 | 237 | 484 | 138 | 2 |
| Williams | 4,900 | 8 | 0 | 1 | 2 | 5 | 62 | 33 | 24 | 5 | 3 |
| Willits | 4,960 | 25 | 0 | 1 | 8 | 16 | 92 | 29 | 46 | 17 | 2 |
| Willows | 6,272 | 19 | 0 | 1 | 3 | 15 | 242 | 60 | 170 | 12 | 0 |
| Windsor | 25,634 | 80 | 1 | 8 | 11 | 60 | 352 | 86 | 247 | 19 | 3 |
| Winters | 7,074 | 10 | 1 | 1 | 1 | 7 | 184 | 37 | 133 | 14 | 1 |
| Woodlake | 7,506 | 26 | 0 | 1 | 6 | 19 | 207 | 48 | 114 | 45 | 2 |
| Woodland | 55,138 | 158 | 2 | 10 | 33 | 113 | 1,537 | 384 | 978 | 175 | 20 |
| Yorba Linda | 66,498 | 51 | 1 | 2 | 14 | 34 | 967 | 199 | 714 | 54 | 7 |
| Yountville | 3,265 | 4 | 0 | 2 | 0 | 2 | 43 | 11 | 31 | 1 | 0 |
| Yreka | 7,379 | 55 | 0 | 2 | 4 | 49 | 224 | 48 | 162 | 14 | 0 |
| Yuba City | 62,495 | 196 | 1 | 16 | 44 | 135 | 1,555 | 289 | 1,130 | 136 | 10 |
| Yucaipa | 50,782 | 128 | 4 | 13 | 19 | 92 | 1,030 | 247 | 640 | 143 | 22 |
| Yucca Valley | 20,798 | 83 | 1 | 7 | 12 | 63 | 570 | 187 | 329 | 54 | 6 |
| **COLORADO** | | | | | | | | | | | |
| Alamosa | 8,781 | 32 | 2 | 6 | 2 | 22 | 496 | 65 | 418 | 13 | 5 |
| Arvada | 107,943 | 190 | 2 | 30 | 36 | 122 | 2,696 | 402 | 2,057 | 237 | 17 |
| Aspen | 5,897 | 24 | 0 | 4 | 1 | 19 | 306 | 53 | 248 | 5 | 0 |

[1] The FBI does not publish arson data unless it receives data from either the agency or the state for all 12 months of the calendar year.

**Table 8. Offenses Known to Law Enforcement, by State and City, 2009—*Continued***

(Number.)

| State/city | Population | Violent crime | Murder and non-negligent man-slaughter | Forcible rape | Robbery | Aggravated assault | Property crime | Burglary | Larceny-theft | Motor vehicle theft | Arson[1] |
|---|---|---|---|---|---|---|---|---|---|---|---|
| **COLORADO**—*Continued* | | | | | | | | | | | |
| Ault | 1,444 | 4 | 0 | 0 | 0 | 4 | 31 | 17 | 14 | 0 | 0 |
| Aurora | 324,014 | 1,524 | 22 | 216 | 553 | 733 | 10,037 | 2,051 | 6,820 | 1,166 | 96 |
| Avon | 6,691 | 8 | 0 | 2 | 1 | 5 | 194 | 37 | 151 | 6 | 0 |
| Basalt | 3,304 | 1 | 0 | 0 | 1 | 0 | 93 | 17 | 73 | 3 | 0 |
| Bayfield | 2,079 | 1 | 0 | 0 | 1 | 0 | 11 | 4 | 5 | 2 | 0 |
| Berthoud | 5,477 | 5 | 0 | 0 | 1 | 4 | 65 | 16 | 44 | 5 | 3 |
| Black Hawk | 104 | 4 | 0 | 0 | 0 | 4 | 148 | 2 | 143 | 3 | 0 |
| Boulder | 100,035 | 245 | 5 | 32 | 51 | 157 | 2,776 | 564 | 2,093 | 119 | 41 |
| Bow Mar | 808 | 0 | 0 | 0 | 0 | 0 | 12 | 9 | 3 | 0 | 0 |
| Breckenridge | 3,493 | 2 | 0 | 0 | 0 | 2 | 330 | 44 | 283 | 3 | 0 |
| Brighton | 32,770 | 87 | 0 | 11 | 15 | 61 | 1,156 | 171 | 900 | 85 | 19 |
| Broomfield | 56,991 | 42 | 3 | 5 | 11 | 23 | 1,115 | 112 | 946 | 57 | 13 |
| Brush | 5,356 | 4 | 0 | 0 | 3 | 1 | 57 | 18 | 37 | 2 | 0 |
| Buena Vista | 2,127 | 1 | 0 | 0 | 0 | 1 | 16 | 2 | 13 | 1 | 0 |
| Burlington | 3,900 | 7 | 0 | 0 | 0 | 7 | 86 | 16 | 67 | 3 | 0 |
| Campo | 125 | 0 | 0 | 0 | 0 | 0 | 1 | 0 | 1 | 0 | 0 |
| Canon City | 15,925 | 82 | 0 | 33 | 4 | 45 | 461 | 57 | 390 | 14 | 1 |
| Castle Rock | 48,287 | 21 | 0 | 3 | 2 | 16 | 455 | 95 | 339 | 21 | 2 |
| Cedaredge | 2,300 | 3 | 0 | 1 | 1 | 1 | 43 | 8 | 30 | 5 | 0 |
| Centennial | 99,385 | 148 | 1 | 21 | 23 | 103 | 1,401 | 269 | 1,053 | 79 | 19 |
| Center | 2,389 | 5 | 0 | 0 | 0 | 5 | 29 | 9 | 19 | 1 | 1 |
| Central City | 572 | 1 | 0 | 0 | 0 | 1 | 34 | 1 | 29 | 4 | 0 |
| Cherry Hills Village | 6,397 | 1 | 1 | 0 | 0 | 0 | 73 | 26 | 47 | 0 | 0 |
| Colorado Springs | 401,626 | 1,968 | 15 | 344 | 525 | 1,084 | 14,723 | 3,305 | 10,357 | 1,061 | 101 |
| Columbine Valley | 1,341 | 0 | 0 | 0 | 0 | 0 | 15 | 8 | 7 | 0 | 0 |
| Commerce City | 45,914 | 126 | 1 | 21 | 17 | 87 | 1,243 | 255 | 814 | 174 | 6 |
| Cortez | 8,680 | 28 | 1 | 0 | 5 | 22 | 388 | 16 | 360 | 12 | 2 |
| Craig | 9,250 | 29 | 0 | 4 | 0 | 25 | 294 | 62 | 225 | 7 | 2 |
| Crested Butte | 1,665 | 0 | 0 | 0 | 0 | 0 | 25 | 0 | 23 | 2 | 0 |
| Cripple Creek | 1,001 | 7 | 0 | 0 | 3 | 4 | 58 | 10 | 47 | 1 | 2 |
| Dacono | 4,179 | 10 | 0 | 0 | 1 | 9 | 46 | 19 | 24 | 3 | 0 |
| De Beque | 528 | 1 | 0 | 0 | 0 | 1 | 25 | 3 | 20 | 2 | 0 |
| Del Norte | 1,576 | 0 | 0 | 0 | 0 | 0 | 22 | 9 | 11 | 2 | 0 |
| Delta | 9,162 | 44 | 0 | 13 | 2 | 29 | 387 | 70 | 304 | 13 | 5 |
| Denver | 604,680 | 3,493 | 39 | 343 | 946 | 2,165 | 20,879 | 4,763 | 12,628 | 3,488 | 136 |
| Dillon | 809 | 2 | 0 | 0 | 0 | 2 | 50 | 4 | 44 | 2 | 0 |
| Durango | 16,644 | 161 | 0 | 4 | 13 | 144 | 753 | 92 | 620 | 41 | 3 |
| Eagle | 6,349 | 12 | 0 | 0 | 0 | 12 | 79 | 14 | 63 | 2 | 0 |
| Eaton | 4,415 | 2 | 0 | 0 | 0 | 2 | 12 | 2 | 9 | 1 | 0 |
| Edgewater | 5,101 | 20 | 1 | 2 | 9 | 8 | 415 | 53 | 338 | 24 | 3 |
| Elizabeth | 1,434 | 1 | 0 | 1 | 0 | 0 | 34 | 11 | 23 | 0 | 3 |
| Englewood | 32,750 | 210 | 3 | 16 | 28 | 163 | 1,881 | 226 | 1,425 | 230 | 14 |
| Erie | 18,195 | 6 | 0 | 0 | 2 | 4 | 147 | 23 | 114 | 10 | 2 |
| Estes Park | 6,539 | 7 | 0 | 1 | 0 | 6 | 70 | 6 | 63 | 1 | 1 |
| Evans | 20,145 | 40 | 1 | 3 | 4 | 32 | 420 | 110 | 274 | 36 | 20 |
| Federal Heights | 11,695 | 57 | 0 | 10 | 8 | 39 | 616 | 91 | 456 | 69 | 0 |
| Firestone | 9,408 | 10 | 2 | 3 | 1 | 4 | 213 | 46 | 151 | 16 | 1 |
| Florence | 3,618 | 12 | 0 | 3 | 0 | 9 | 88 | 11 | 74 | 3 | 1 |
| Fort Collins | 138,487 | 535 | 2 | 87 | 68 | 378 | 4,586 | 752 | 3,604 | 230 | 17 |
| Fort Lupton | 7,668 | 20 | 0 | 0 | 1 | 19 | 192 | 24 | 160 | 8 | 4 |
| Fort Morgan | 10,485 | 25 | 0 | 2 | 7 | 16 | 264 | 43 | 208 | 13 | 1 |
| Fountain | 20,205 | 20 | 1 | 10 | 6 | 3 | 532 | 106 | 394 | 32 | 2 |
| Fowler | 1,082 | 0 | 0 | 0 | 0 | 0 | 15 | 0 | 13 | 2 | 0 |
| Fraser/Winter Park | 1,809 | 20 | 0 | 0 | 0 | 20 | 66 | 13 | 49 | 4 | 0 |
| Frederick | 9,190 | 8 | 0 | 1 | 1 | 6 | 108 | 36 | 67 | 5 | 0 |
| Frisco | 2,727 | 1 | 0 | 1 | 0 | 0 | 57 | 9 | 46 | 2 | 3 |
| Fruita | 7,501 | 15 | 0 | 6 | 3 | 6 | 281 | 60 | 213 | 8 | 1 |
| Glendale | 4,830 | 54 | 0 | 4 | 14 | 36 | 338 | 26 | 278 | 34 | 1 |
| Glenwood Springs | 9,198 | 47 | 0 | 3 | 4 | 40 | 532 | 59 | 459 | 14 | 1 |
| Golden | 17,334 | 42 | 1 | 2 | 2 | 37 | 452 | 66 | 366 | 20 | 5 |
| Granby | 1,658 | 8 | 0 | 0 | 0 | 8 | 51 | 4 | 47 | 0 | 0 |
| Grand Junction | 50,195 | 230 | 0 | 39 | 49 | 142 | 2,638 | 377 | 2,120 | 141 | 22 |
| Greeley | 93,070 | 441 | 3 | 40 | 69 | 329 | 3,130 | 585 | 2,373 | 172 | 35 |
| Green Mountain Falls | 806 | 10 | 0 | 0 | 0 | 10 | 20 | 9 | 7 | 4 | 0 |
| Greenwood Village | 14,552 | 34 | 4 | 0 | 9 | 21 | 584 | 95 | 450 | 39 | 6 |
| Gunnison | 5,468 | 26 | 0 | 2 | 2 | 22 | 434 | 39 | 384 | 11 | 1 |
| Haxtun | 963 | 1 | 0 | 0 | 0 | 1 | 4 | 0 | 4 | 0 | 0 |
| Hayden | 1,573 | 4 | 0 | 1 | 0 | 3 | 30 | 9 | 20 | 1 | 0 |
| Holyoke | 2,220 | 2 | 0 | 0 | 0 | 2 | 30 | 3 | 24 | 3 | 0 |
| Hotchkiss | 1,093 | 6 | 0 | 5 | 0 | 1 | 30 | 4 | 26 | 0 | 1 |
| Idaho Springs | 1,715 | 7 | 0 | 0 | 0 | 7 | 54 | 12 | 38 | 4 | 2 |

[1] The FBI does not publish arson data unless it receives data from either the agency or the state for all 12 months of the calendar year.

**Table 8. Offenses Known to Law Enforcement, by State and City, 2009**—*Continued*

(Number.)

| State/city | Population | Violent crime | Murder and non-negligent man-slaughter | Forcible rape | Robbery | Aggravated assault | Property crime | Burglary | Larceny-theft | Motor vehicle theft | Arson[1] |
|---|---|---|---|---|---|---|---|---|---|---|---|
| **COLORADO**—*Continued* | | | | | | | | | | | |
| Ignacio | 761 | 4 | 0 | 3 | 0 | 1 | 4 | 1 | 2 | 1 | 0 |
| Johnstown | 10,116 | 8 | 0 | 1 | 1 | 6 | 129 | 27 | 93 | 9 | 10 |
| Kersey | 1,467 | 3 | 0 | 1 | 1 | 1 | 36 | 9 | 23 | 4 | 0 |
| Kiowa | 596 | 6 | 0 | 0 | 1 | 5 | 19 | 11 | 8 | 0 | 0 |
| Kremmling | 1,523 | 8 | 0 | 0 | 0 | 8 | 16 | 3 | 12 | 1 | 0 |
| Lafayette | 25,267 | 50 | 1 | 8 | 10 | 31 | 428 | 80 | 328 | 20 | 4 |
| La Junta | 6,992 | 24 | 0 | 4 | 1 | 19 | 266 | 69 | 189 | 8 | 5 |
| Lakeside | 19 | 1 | 0 | 0 | 0 | 1 | 10 | 0 | 10 | 0 | 0 |
| Lakewood | 140,618 | 689 | 5 | 84 | 171 | 429 | 6,314 | 901 | 4,788 | 625 | 22 |
| La Salle | 2,001 | 5 | 0 | 1 | 0 | 4 | 35 | 10 | 21 | 4 | 0 |
| Las Animas | 2,305 | 4 | 0 | 0 | 1 | 3 | 35 | 4 | 28 | 3 | 0 |
| La Veta | 878 | 0 | 0 | 0 | 0 | 0 | 0 | 0 | 0 | 0 | 0 |
| Leadville | 2,736 | 8 | 0 | 0 | 1 | 7 | 52 | 9 | 40 | 3 | 0 |
| Limon | 1,719 | 5 | 0 | 2 | 0 | 3 | 10 | 0 | 9 | 1 | 0 |
| Littleton | 40,815 | 63 | 0 | 5 | 18 | 40 | 1,249 | 215 | 933 | 101 | 4 |
| Lone Tree | 9,668 | 10 | 0 | 1 | 6 | 3 | 522 | 31 | 466 | 25 | 1 |
| Longmont | 87,611 | 330 | 1 | 16 | 44 | 269 | 2,388 | 415 | 1,844 | 129 | 40 |
| Louisville | 19,147 | 16 | 0 | 0 | 4 | 12 | 262 | 60 | 196 | 6 | 3 |
| Loveland | 67,324 | 147 | 4 | 14 | 30 | 99 | 1,985 | 318 | 1,601 | 66 | 38 |
| Mancos | 1,278 | 9 | 0 | 0 | 0 | 9 | 20 | 6 | 10 | 4 | 0 |
| Manitou Springs | 5,182 | 22 | 0 | 2 | 1 | 19 | 188 | 17 | 162 | 9 | 2 |
| Meeker | 2,405 | 25 | 0 | 0 | 0 | 25 | 33 | 10 | 23 | 0 | 2 |
| Milliken | 6,670 | 4 | 0 | 2 | 0 | 2 | 60 | 14 | 41 | 5 | 1 |
| Minturn | 1,198 | 0 | 0 | 0 | 0 | 0 | 13 | 4 | 9 | 0 | 0 |
| Monte Vista | 3,950 | 20 | 0 | 0 | 0 | 20 | 96 | 25 | 71 | 0 | 0 |
| Montrose | 18,651 | 65 | 1 | 4 | 8 | 52 | 893 | 119 | 756 | 18 | 4 |
| Monument | 2,673 | 9 | 0 | 0 | 2 | 7 | 131 | 18 | 109 | 4 | 1 |
| Morrison | 413 | 0 | 0 | 0 | 0 | 0 | 1 | 0 | 1 | 0 | 0 |
| Mountain View | 515 | 0 | 0 | 0 | 0 | 0 | 8 | 3 | 5 | 0 | 0 |
| Mount Crested Butte | 864 | 6 | 0 | 1 | 0 | 5 | 39 | 6 | 30 | 3 | 0 |
| Nederland | 1,366 | 1 | 0 | 0 | 0 | 1 | 22 | 0 | 22 | 0 | 0 |
| New Castle | 4,065 | 7 | 0 | 1 | 0 | 6 | 70 | 14 | 52 | 4 | 1 |
| Northglenn | 33,849 | 108 | 2 | 24 | 10 | 72 | 1,306 | 191 | 943 | 172 | 9 |
| Olathe | 1,758 | 2 | 0 | 1 | 0 | 1 | 22 | 2 | 17 | 3 | 0 |
| Ouray | 946 | 1 | 0 | 0 | 0 | 1 | 25 | 4 | 21 | 0 | 0 |
| Pagosa Springs | 1,762 | 11 | 0 | 1 | 0 | 10 | 88 | 11 | 72 | 5 | 0 |
| Paonia | 1,645 | 4 | 0 | 0 | 0 | 4 | 50 | 8 | 39 | 3 | 0 |
| Parachute | 1,326 | 3 | 0 | 1 | 0 | 2 | 27 | 9 | 16 | 2 | 1 |
| Parker | 46,676 | 39 | 0 | 10 | 7 | 22 | 529 | 91 | 410 | 28 | 10 |
| Platteville | 2,664 | 4 | 0 | 1 | 0 | 3 | 40 | 10 | 26 | 4 | 0 |
| Pueblo | 105,271 | 897 | 13 | 31 | 165 | 688 | 3,392 | 1,311 | 1,736 | 345 | 44 |
| Rangely | 2,143 | 4 | 1 | 0 | 0 | 3 | 21 | 0 | 15 | 6 | 0 |
| Rocky Ford | 3,916 | 8 | 0 | 0 | 2 | 6 | 88 | 46 | 38 | 4 | 1 |
| Salida | 5,375 | 4 | 0 | 0 | 0 | 4 | 196 | 25 | 164 | 7 | 3 |
| Sheridan | 5,398 | 20 | 1 | 2 | 6 | 11 | 319 | 33 | 237 | 49 | 3 |
| Silt | 2,791 | 2 | 0 | 1 | 0 | 1 | 56 | 12 | 43 | 1 | 0 |
| Silverthorne | 4,074 | 8 | 0 | 3 | 0 | 5 | 143 | 7 | 132 | 4 | 1 |
| Snowmass Village | 1,923 | 2 | 0 | 0 | 0 | 2 | 61 | 2 | 59 | 0 | 0 |
| Springfield | 1,265 | 16 | 0 | 1 | 0 | 15 | 0 | 0 | 0 | 0 | 0 |
| Steamboat Springs | 9,560 | 32 | 2 | 7 | 2 | 21 | 396 | 59 | 315 | 22 | 1 |
| Sterling | 12,800 | 49 | 0 | 5 | 1 | 43 | 335 | 74 | 249 | 12 | 6 |
| Telluride | 2,377 | 6 | 0 | 0 | 1 | 5 | 107 | 14 | 87 | 6 | 0 |
| Thornton | 117,415 | 296 | 1 | 66 | 61 | 168 | 3,832 | 683 | 2,729 | 420 | 17 |
| Trinidad | 9,125 | 32 | 2 | 3 | 5 | 22 | 220 | 56 | 154 | 10 | 3 |
| Vail | 4,783 | 20 | 1 | 4 | 1 | 14 | 370 | 36 | 324 | 10 | 0 |
| Victor | 402 | 1 | 0 | 0 | 0 | 1 | 2 | 0 | 2 | 0 | 0 |
| Walsh | 629 | 0 | 0 | 0 | 0 | 0 | 4 | 1 | 3 | 0 | 0 |
| Westminster | 107,705 | 240 | 2 | 27 | 42 | 169 | 3,446 | 481 | 2,511 | 454 | 10 |
| Wheat Ridge | 30,683 | 152 | 1 | 18 | 32 | 101 | 1,222 | 217 | 890 | 115 | 6 |
| Wiggins | 956 | 0 | 0 | 0 | 0 | 0 | 2 | 1 | 0 | 1 | 0 |
| Windsor | 19,217 | 9 | 0 | 1 | 3 | 5 | 318 | 68 | 236 | 14 | 10 |
| Woodland Park | 6,490 | 8 | 0 | 1 | 2 | 5 | 89 | 19 | 69 | 1 | 1 |
| Wray | 2,100 | 0 | 0 | 0 | 0 | 0 | 6 | 0 | 6 | 0 | 0 |
| Yuma | 3,261 | 1 | 0 | 1 | 0 | 0 | 28 | 2 | 25 | 1 | 0 |
| **CONNECTICUT** | | | | | | | | | | | |
| Ansonia | 18,496 | 36 | 2 | 4 | 22 | 8 | 352 | 36 | 278 | 38 | 0 |
| Avon | 17,495 | 8 | 0 | 3 | 3 | 2 | 172 | 28 | 138 | 6 | 0 |
| Berlin | 20,610 | 12 | 0 | 1 | 5 | 6 | 306 | 62 | 231 | 13 | 0 |
| Bethel | 18,476 | 1 | 0 | 0 | 1 | 0 | 214 | 36 | 171 | 7 | 0 |
| Bloomfield | 20,856 | 47 | 1 | 12 | 12 | 22 | 499 | 101 | 367 | 31 | 1 |
| Branford | 28,999 | 24 | 1 | 0 | 9 | 14 | 671 | 82 | 558 | 31 | 1 |

[1] The FBI does not publish arson data unless it receives data from either the agency or the state for all 12 months of the calendar year.

## Table 8. Offenses Known to Law Enforcement, by State and City, 2009—*Continued*

(Number.)

| State/city | Population | Violent crime | Murder and non-negligent man-slaughter | Forcible rape | Robbery | Aggravated assault | Property crime | Burglary | Larceny-theft | Motor vehicle theft | Arson[1] |
|---|---|---|---|---|---|---|---|---|---|---|---|
| **CONNECTICUT**—*Continued* | | | | | | | | | | | |
| Bridgeport | 136,049 | 1,527 | 12 | 58 | 680 | 777 | 5,615 | 1,276 | 3,375 | 964 | 42 |
| Bristol | 60,998 | 182 | 1 | 26 | 32 | 123 | 1,104 | 250 | 777 | 77 | 0 |
| Brookfield | 16,766 | 5 | 0 | 0 | 2 | 3 | 168 | 24 | 138 | 6 | 1 |
| Canton | 10,253 | 1 | 0 | 0 | 1 | 0 | 86 | 8 | 72 | 6 | 0 |
| Cheshire | 29,120 | 13 | 0 | 0 | 1 | 12 | 293 | 59 | 226 | 8 | 1 |
| Clinton | 13,602 | 16 | 1 | 3 | 3 | 9 | 304 | 51 | 252 | 1 | 0 |
| Coventry | 12,286 | 20 | 0 | 4 | 1 | 15 | 161 | 56 | 99 | 6 | 0 |
| Cromwell | 13,676 | 14 | 0 | 2 | 6 | 6 | 378 | 50 | 310 | 18 | 1 |
| Danbury | 79,729 | 130 | 2 | 25 | 50 | 53 | 1,536 | 219 | 1,219 | 98 | 6 |
| Darien | 20,237 | 14 | 0 | 0 | 4 | 10 | 130 | 17 | 111 | 2 | 0 |
| Derby | 12,392 | 26 | 1 | 4 | 11 | 10 | 386 | 105 | 258 | 23 | 0 |
| East Hampton | 12,887 | 1 | 0 | 0 | 1 | 0 | 102 | 24 | 78 | 0 | 1 |
| East Hartford | 48,459 | 180 | 2 | 13 | 78 | 87 | 1,670 | 328 | 1,173 | 169 | 10 |
| East Haven | 28,633 | 35 | 0 | 3 | 18 | 14 | 718 | 147 | 500 | 71 | 0 |
| Easton | 7,344 | 2 | 0 | 0 | 0 | 2 | 62 | 27 | 32 | 3 | 0 |
| East Windsor | 10,936 | 12 | 0 | 2 | 3 | 7 | 406 | 64 | 298 | 44 | 1 |
| Enfield | 44,857 | 48 | 0 | 0 | 20 | 28 | 932 | 176 | 710 | 46 | 6 |
| Fairfield | 57,341 | 37 | 0 | 2 | 9 | 26 | 1,110 | 218 | 838 | 54 | 0 |
| Farmington | 25,278 | 17 | 0 | 5 | 9 | 3 | 690 | 52 | 610 | 28 | 0 |
| Glastonbury | 33,411 | 23 | 0 | 3 | 9 | 11 | 355 | 84 | 263 | 8 | 0 |
| Granby | 11,315 | 3 | 0 | 2 | 0 | 1 | 137 | 22 | 106 | 9 | 1 |
| Greenwich | 62,018 | 23 | 1 | 2 | 7 | 13 | 514 | 72 | 404 | 38 | 5 |
| Groton | 9,319 | 27 | 0 | 5 | 5 | 17 | 171 | 27 | 138 | 6 | 1 |
| Groton Long Point | 682 | 0 | 0 | 0 | 0 | 0 | 7 | 2 | 5 | 0 | 0 |
| Groton Town | 29,105 | 31 | 0 | 4 | 10 | 17 | 542 | 68 | 461 | 13 | 3 |
| Guilford | 22,506 | 20 | 0 | 5 | 4 | 11 | 372 | 69 | 288 | 15 | 1 |
| Hamden | 57,975 | 97 | 0 | 10 | 54 | 33 | 1,162 | 123 | 941 | 98 | 2 |
| Hartford | 124,049 | 1,603 | 33 | 49 | 600 | 921 | 6,189 | 1,135 | 4,061 | 993 | 84 |
| Madison | 18,900 | 6 | 0 | 0 | 0 | 6 | 179 | 46 | 131 | 2 | 1 |
| Manchester | 56,566 | 137 | 0 | 12 | 55 | 70 | 2,040 | 297 | 1,636 | 107 | 9 |
| Meriden | 59,289 | 176 | 3 | 12 | 88 | 73 | 2,092 | 393 | 1,574 | 125 | 8 |
| Middlebury | 7,447 | 3 | 0 | 1 | 0 | 2 | 53 | 6 | 42 | 5 | 0 |
| Middletown | 48,299 | 60 | 1 | 0 | 32 | 27 | 1,492 | 214 | 1,186 | 92 | 4 |
| Milford | 56,310 | 83 | 1 | 6 | 31 | 45 | 1,857 | 163 | 1,598 | 96 | 1 |
| Monroe | 19,366 | 7 | 0 | 2 | 1 | 4 | 163 | 47 | 109 | 7 | 1 |
| Naugatuck | 32,033 | 30 | 1 | 9 | 11 | 9 | 561 | 69 | 463 | 29 | 0 |
| New Britain | 70,368 | 294 | 1 | 6 | 154 | 133 | 3,275 | 812 | 2,076 | 387 | 1 |
| New Canaan | 19,965 | 3 | 0 | 2 | 0 | 1 | 152 | 16 | 121 | 15 | 0 |
| New Haven | 123,659 | 2,183 | 12 | 59 | 906 | 1,206 | 7,043 | 1,430 | 4,533 | 1,080 | 16 |
| Newington | 29,739 | 27 | 1 | 8 | 16 | 2 | 848 | 127 | 676 | 45 | 2 |
| New London | 25,859 | 265 | 2 | 17 | 56 | 190 | 897 | 216 | 624 | 57 | 8 |
| New Milford | 28,471 | 18 | 1 | 3 | 6 | 8 | 344 | 64 | 263 | 17 | 1 |
| Newtown | 26,924 | 8 | 0 | 1 | 1 | 6 | 182 | 42 | 135 | 5 | 0 |
| North Branford | 14,426 | 5 | 0 | 0 | 2 | 3 | 247 | 46 | 183 | 18 | 2 |
| North Haven | 24,060 | 12 | 1 | 0 | 9 | 2 | 527 | 93 | 408 | 26 | 0 |
| Norwalk | 83,198 | 425 | 1 | 10 | 157 | 257 | 1,786 | 314 | 1,269 | 203 | 8 |
| Norwich | 36,418 | 165 | 2 | 25 | 44 | 94 | 1,079 | 215 | 797 | 67 | 6 |
| Old Saybrook | 10,537 | 6 | 0 | 0 | 2 | 4 | 228 | 25 | 194 | 9 | 0 |
| Orange | 13,843 | 10 | 0 | 0 | 10 | 0 | 447 | 50 | 387 | 10 | 0 |
| Plainfield | 15,519 | 7 | 0 | 0 | 2 | 5 | 97 | 46 | 47 | 4 | 0 |
| Plainville | 17,221 | 12 | 1 | 2 | 6 | 3 | 666 | 89 | 540 | 37 | 1 |
| Plymouth | 12,003 | 5 | 0 | 0 | 2 | 3 | 190 | 44 | 138 | 8 | 0 |
| Portland | 9,642 | 10 | 0 | 0 | 3 | 7 | 82 | 13 | 63 | 6 | 0 |
| Putnam | 9,342 | 28 | 0 | 7 | 5 | 16 | 167 | 33 | 126 | 8 | 1 |
| Redding | 8,855 | 1 | 0 | 0 | 0 | 1 | 48 | 9 | 38 | 1 | 0 |
| Ridgefield | 24,046 | 4 | 0 | 0 | 0 | 4 | 67 | 7 | 60 | 0 | 0 |
| Rocky Hill | 18,948 | 11 | 0 | 1 | 7 | 3 | 307 | 48 | 248 | 11 | 2 |
| Seymour | 16,340 | 17 | 0 | 7 | 3 | 7 | 225 | 66 | 149 | 10 | 0 |
| Shelton | 40,195 | 31 | 0 | 2 | 18 | 11 | 495 | 97 | 346 | 52 | 0 |
| Simsbury | 23,654 | 3 | 0 | 0 | 1 | 2 | 201 | 36 | 156 | 9 | 0 |
| Southington | 42,523 | 23 | 0 | 4 | 11 | 8 | 759 | 107 | 612 | 40 | 9 |
| South Windsor | 26,139 | 9 | 0 | 3 | 2 | 4 | 429 | 62 | 353 | 14 | 1 |
| Stamford | 119,507 | 353 | 2 | 31 | 151 | 169 | 2,143 | 370 | 1,600 | 173 | 8 |
| Stonington | 18,420 | 11 | 0 | 4 | 4 | 3 | 258 | 28 | 223 | 7 | 0 |
| Stratford | 48,726 | 162 | 0 | 11 | 74 | 77 | 1,425 | 215 | 1,057 | 153 | 8 |
| Suffield | 15,317 | 13 | 0 | 1 | 7 | 5 | 162 | 88 | 63 | 11 | 0 |
| Thomaston | 7,792 | 2 | 0 | 0 | 0 | 2 | 121 | 24 | 87 | 10 | 0 |
| Torrington | 35,321 | 70 | 0 | 14 | 8 | 48 | 765 | 119 | 618 | 28 | 0 |
| Trumbull | 34,731 | 23 | 0 | 5 | 13 | 5 | 798 | 108 | 610 | 80 | 1 |
| Vernon | 30,038 | 31 | 1 | 5 | 9 | 16 | 376 | 105 | 244 | 27 | 7 |
| Wallingford | 45,059 | 22 | 0 | 7 | 4 | 11 | 775 | 90 | 646 | 39 | 5 |

[1] The FBI does not publish arson data unless it receives data from either the agency or the state for all 12 months of the calendar year.

## Table 8. Offenses Known to Law Enforcement, by State and City, 2009—*Continued*

(Number.)

| State/city | Population | Violent crime | Murder and non-negligent man-slaughter | Forcible rape | Robbery | Aggravated assault | Property crime | Burglary | Larceny-theft | Motor vehicle theft | Arson[1] |
|---|---|---|---|---|---|---|---|---|---|---|---|
| **CONNECTICUT**—*Continued* | | | | | | | | | | | |
| Waterbury | 107,007 | 375 | 6 | 15 | 174 | 180 | 5,635 | 749 | 4,422 | 464 | 0 |
| Waterford | 18,808 | 51 | 0 | 3 | 10 | 38 | 602 | 51 | 542 | 9 | 0 |
| Watertown | 22,139 | 36 | 0 | 6 | 5 | 25 | 361 | 65 | 288 | 8 | 0 |
| West Hartford | 60,430 | 84 | 1 | 6 | 40 | 37 | 1,708 | 292 | 1,323 | 93 | 2 |
| West Haven | 52,425 | 380 | 1 | 0 | 57 | 322 | 1,532 | 241 | 1,092 | 199 | 12 |
| Weston | 10,196 | 2 | 0 | 0 | 0 | 2 | 61 | 6 | 53 | 2 | 1 |
| Westport | 26,681 | 23 | 0 | 1 | 7 | 15 | 337 | 56 | 270 | 11 | 2 |
| Wethersfield | 25,656 | 20 | 0 | 5 | 8 | 7 | 476 | 74 | 369 | 33 | 1 |
| Willimantic | 16,346 | 65 | 0 | 6 | 31 | 28 | 526 | 124 | 365 | 37 | 2 |
| Wilton | 17,701 | 3 | 0 | 0 | 2 | 1 | 104 | 15 | 87 | 2 | 0 |
| Winchester | 10,721 | 23 | 0 | 4 | 3 | 16 | 214 | 60 | 146 | 8 | 1 |
| Windsor | 28,915 | 16 | 0 | 7 | 6 | 3 | 578 | 86 | 464 | 28 | 0 |
| Windsor Locks | 12,543 | 11 | 1 | 4 | 1 | 5 | 288 | 56 | 205 | 27 | 2 |
| Wolcott | 16,571 | 5 | 0 | 0 | 1 | 4 | 263 | 41 | 202 | 20 | 1 |
| Woodbridge | 9,215 | 9 | 0 | 0 | 6 | 3 | 142 | 37 | 101 | 4 | 0 |
| **DELAWARE** | | | | | | | | | | | |
| Bethany Beach | 971 | 4 | 0 | 3 | 0 | 1 | 158 | 8 | 150 | 0 | 0 |
| Blades | 1,166 | 6 | 0 | 0 | 0 | 6 | 11 | 4 | 7 | 0 | 0 |
| Bridgeville | 1,645 | 4 | 0 | 1 | 0 | 3 | 72 | 7 | 64 | 1 | 0 |
| Camden | 2,621 | 21 | 0 | 1 | 7 | 13 | 299 | 15 | 281 | 3 | 0 |
| Cheswold | 479 | 4 | 0 | 1 | 0 | 3 | 15 | 6 | 9 | 0 | 0 |
| Clayton | 1,501 | 9 | 0 | 3 | 0 | 6 | 41 | 10 | 29 | 2 | 0 |
| Dagsboro | 585 | 2 | 0 | 0 | 1 | 1 | 24 | 7 | 17 | 0 | 0 |
| Delaware City | 1,523 | 5 | 0 | 1 | 1 | 3 | 29 | 11 | 17 | 1 | 1 |
| Delmar | 1,528 | 12 | 0 | 1 | 6 | 5 | 54 | 9 | 44 | 1 | 1 |
| Dewey Beach | 320 | 22 | 0 | 2 | 3 | 17 | 69 | 15 | 51 | 3 | 0 |
| Dover | 36,571 | 288 | 2 | 21 | 69 | 196 | 1,916 | 158 | 1,669 | 89 | 16 |
| Ellendale | 357 | 1 | 0 | 0 | 0 | 1 | 1 | 0 | 1 | 0 | 0 |
| Elsmere | 5,676 | 34 | 0 | 0 | 10 | 24 | 164 | 40 | 104 | 20 | 0 |
| Felton | 916 | 2 | 0 | 0 | 0 | 2 | 7 | 2 | 5 | 0 | 0 |
| Fenwick Island | 369 | 0 | 0 | 0 | 0 | 0 | 17 | 8 | 8 | 1 | 0 |
| Georgetown | 5,277 | 58 | 0 | 9 | 19 | 30 | 258 | 71 | 174 | 13 | 0 |
| Greenwood | 914 | 1 | 0 | 0 | 1 | 0 | 21 | 2 | 17 | 2 | 0 |
| Harrington | 3,466 | 40 | 0 | 2 | 7 | 31 | 232 | 101 | 125 | 6 | 0 |
| Laurel | 4,009 | 59 | 0 | 4 | 19 | 36 | 209 | 68 | 139 | 2 | 1 |
| Lewes | 3,150 | 9 | 0 | 0 | 0 | 9 | 90 | 22 | 64 | 4 | 0 |
| Middletown | 13,093 | 74 | 0 | 9 | 22 | 43 | 420 | 68 | 341 | 11 | 0 |
| Milford | 8,704 | 121 | 1 | 15 | 31 | 74 | 649 | 110 | 524 | 15 | 0 |
| Millsboro | 2,724 | 31 | 0 | 4 | 6 | 21 | 135 | 27 | 105 | 3 | 0 |
| Milton | 1,848 | 12 | 0 | 2 | 3 | 7 | 95 | 45 | 44 | 6 | 1 |
| Newark | 29,983 | 125 | 1 | 7 | 47 | 70 | 958 | 163 | 755 | 40 | 9 |
| New Castle | 4,976 | 24 | 0 | 3 | 5 | 16 | 226 | 34 | 181 | 11 | 0 |
| Newport | 1,104 | 16 | 0 | 1 | 1 | 14 | 56 | 25 | 28 | 3 | 0 |
| Ocean View | 1,149 | 2 | 0 | 0 | 0 | 2 | 39 | 18 | 21 | 0 | 1 |
| Rehoboth Beach | 1,597 | 21 | 0 | 0 | 3 | 18 | 209 | 25 | 179 | 5 | 0 |
| Seaford | 7,310 | 73 | 0 | 5 | 26 | 42 | 426 | 76 | 341 | 9 | 0 |
| Selbyville | 1,871 | 11 | 0 | 0 | 5 | 6 | 100 | 26 | 68 | 6 | 0 |
| Smyrna | 8,981 | 54 | 0 | 5 | 13 | 36 | 291 | 66 | 216 | 9 | 0 |
| South Bethany | 530 | 0 | 0 | 0 | 0 | 0 | 28 | 15 | 13 | 0 | 0 |
| Wilmington | 72,580 | 1,342 | 17 | 39 | 524 | 762 | 3,631 | 856 | 2,259 | 516 | 8 |
| Wyoming | 1,443 | 3 | 0 | 1 | 1 | 1 | 28 | 13 | 15 | 0 | 0 |
| **DISTRICT OF COLUMBIA** | | | | | | | | | | | |
| Washington | 599,657 | 7,586 | 143 | 150 | 3,998 | 3,295 | 27,007 | 3,696 | 18,012 | 5,299 | 55 |
| **FLORIDA** | | | | | | | | | | | |
| Alachua | 9,669 | 55 | 0 | 1 | 16 | 38 | 346 | 89 | 244 | 13 | 1 |
| Altamonte Springs | 39,797 | 184 | 1 | 18 | 43 | 122 | 1,551 | 294 | 1,158 | 99 | 7 |
| Altha | 521 | 1 | 0 | 0 | 0 | 1 | 7 | 1 | 6 | 0 | 0 |
| Apalachicola | 2,197 | 4 | 0 | 0 | 0 | 4 | 37 | 9 | 25 | 3 | 0 |
| Apopka | 39,308 | 263 | 1 | 10 | 84 | 168 | 1,527 | 353 | 1,097 | 77 | 7 |
| Arcadia | 6,788 | 105 | 0 | 4 | 23 | 78 | 310 | 95 | 202 | 13 | 1 |
| Astatula | 1,887 | 3 | 0 | 0 | 0 | 3 | 3 | 1 | 2 | 0 | 1 |
| Atlantic Beach | 13,124 | 83 | 0 | 5 | 14 | 64 | 449 | 88 | 344 | 17 | 0 |
| Atlantis | 2,074 | 7 | 0 | 0 | 1 | 6 | 8 | 3 | 5 | 0 | 0 |
| Auburndale | 14,619 | 92 | 1 | 9 | 30 | 52 | 786 | 238 | 524 | 24 | 2 |
| Aventura | 29,743 | 68 | 0 | 3 | 31 | 34 | 2,127 | 138 | 1,931 | 58 | 5 |
| Avon Park | 9,090 | 75 | 0 | 4 | 23 | 48 | 491 | 155 | 309 | 27 | 2 |
| Bal Harbour Village | 3,099 | 2 | 0 | 0 | 0 | 2 | 68 | 5 | 61 | 2 | 0 |
| Bartow | 17,069 | 140 | 0 | 8 | 37 | 95 | 1,149 | 305 | 813 | 31 | 1 |
| Bay Harbor Islands | 4,912 | 5 | 0 | 1 | 1 | 3 | 70 | 23 | 40 | 7 | 1 |
| Belleair | 4,073 | 2 | 0 | 0 | 2 | 0 | 103 | 21 | 79 | 3 | 3 |

[1] The FBI does not publish arson data unless it receives data from either the agency or the state for all 12 months of the calendar year.

# Table 8. Offenses Known to Law Enforcement, by State and City, 2009—*Continued*

(Number.)

| State/city | Population | Violent crime | Murder and non-negligent man-slaughter | Forcible rape | Robbery | Aggravated assault | Property crime | Burglary | Larceny-theft | Motor vehicle theft | Arson[1] |
|---|---|---|---|---|---|---|---|---|---|---|---|
| **FLORIDA**—*Continued* | | | | | | | | | | | |
| Belleair Beach | 1,581 | 0 | 0 | 0 | 0 | 0 | 47 | 14 | 33 | 0 | 0 |
| Belleair Bluffs | 2,155 | 5 | 0 | 0 | 3 | 2 | 65 | 12 | 51 | 2 | 0 |
| Belle Glade | 16,642 | 415 | 3 | 10 | 116 | 286 | 1,476 | 420 | 974 | 82 | 7 |
| Belle Isle | 6,553 | 10 | 0 | 3 | 0 | 7 | 125 | 50 | 66 | 9 | 0 |
| Belleview | 4,538 | 20 | 0 | 3 | 3 | 14 | 237 | 68 | 165 | 4 | 1 |
| Biscayne Park | 2,930 | 9 | 0 | 0 | 3 | 6 | 65 | 27 | 34 | 4 | 0 |
| Blountstown | 2,517 | 4 | 0 | 0 | 0 | 4 | 29 | 4 | 25 | 0 | 0 |
| Boca Raton | 85,956 | 217 | 2 | 24 | 78 | 113 | 3,087 | 554 | 2,375 | 158 | 3 |
| Bonifay | 2,772 | 4 | 0 | 2 | 1 | 1 | 22 | 15 | 6 | 1 | 0 |
| Bowling Green | 2,958 | 15 | 0 | 1 | 2 | 12 | 73 | 17 | 47 | 9 | 0 |
| Boynton Beach | 69,211 | 648 | 2 | 8 | 182 | 456 | 3,607 | 837 | 2,610 | 160 | 4 |
| Bradenton | 53,951 | 422 | 4 | 12 | 136 | 270 | 2,292 | 537 | 1,605 | 150 | 3 |
| Bradenton Beach | 1,560 | 3 | 0 | 1 | 0 | 2 | 108 | 17 | 89 | 2 | 0 |
| Brooksville | 8,375 | 57 | 1 | 3 | 11 | 42 | 350 | 70 | 265 | 15 | 1 |
| Bunnell | 3,281 | 63 | 0 | 0 | 9 | 54 | 151 | 35 | 97 | 19 | 0 |
| Bushnell | 2,301 | 6 | 0 | 2 | 0 | 4 | 128 | 29 | 93 | 6 | 0 |
| Cape Coral | 164,344 | 332 | 3 | 16 | 92 | 221 | 4,233 | 1,267 | 2,792 | 174 | 10 |
| Carrabelle | 1,222 | 7 | 0 | 0 | 0 | 7 | 23 | 14 | 8 | 1 | 0 |
| Casselberry | 24,782 | 156 | 2 | 12 | 42 | 100 | 1,086 | 195 | 817 | 74 | 1 |
| Cedar Key | 999 | 0 | 0 | 0 | 0 | 0 | 16 | 3 | 13 | 0 | 0 |
| Center Hill | 1,124 | 0 | 0 | 0 | 0 | 0 | 20 | 5 | 12 | 3 | 0 |
| Chattahoochee | 3,746 | 22 | 0 | 1 | 2 | 19 | 62 | 20 | 34 | 8 | 0 |
| Chiefland | 2,149 | 17 | 0 | 0 | 0 | 17 | 138 | 51 | 83 | 4 | 0 |
| Chipley | 3,800 | 17 | 0 | 3 | 1 | 13 | 46 | 7 | 37 | 2 | 0 |
| Clearwater | 105,383 | 924 | 3 | 43 | 275 | 603 | 4,720 | 802 | 3,617 | 301 | 17 |
| Clermont | 13,484 | 106 | 1 | 6 | 29 | 70 | 903 | 209 | 662 | 32 | 1 |
| Clewiston | 7,248 | 52 | 0 | 3 | 11 | 38 | 326 | 107 | 204 | 15 | 2 |
| Cocoa | 16,418 | 616 | 5 | 20 | 83 | 508 | 1,329 | 456 | 821 | 52 | 5 |
| Cocoa Beach | 11,860 | 80 | 0 | 7 | 16 | 57 | 855 | 88 | 739 | 28 | 2 |
| Coconut Creek | 50,385 | 72 | 2 | 3 | 13 | 54 | 1,509 | 299 | 1,128 | 82 | 3 |
| Cooper City | 29,392 | 64 | 0 | 3 | 14 | 47 | 665 | 123 | 525 | 17 | 3 |
| Coral Gables | 42,784 | 100 | 1 | 3 | 37 | 59 | 2,100 | 462 | 1,538 | 100 | 0 |
| Coral Springs | 125,656 | 338 | 2 | 4 | 90 | 242 | 2,918 | 541 | 2,222 | 155 | 3 |
| Crescent City | 1,817 | 12 | 0 | 0 | 4 | 8 | 58 | 22 | 35 | 1 | 1 |
| Crestview | 20,023 | 115 | 1 | 15 | 27 | 72 | 702 | 127 | 547 | 28 | 3 |
| Cross City | 1,824 | 5 | 0 | 0 | 0 | 5 | 63 | 17 | 46 | 0 | 2 |
| Crystal River | 3,559 | 39 | 0 | 2 | 4 | 33 | 234 | 44 | 184 | 6 | 0 |
| Cutler Bay | 28,935 | 199 | 5 | 8 | 57 | 129 | 2,095 | 340 | 1,626 | 129 | 0 |
| Dade City | 7,321 | 59 | 0 | 0 | 10 | 49 | 373 | 141 | 221 | 11 | 1 |
| Dania | 28,065 | 279 | 3 | 12 | 100 | 164 | 1,511 | 321 | 1,024 | 166 | 3 |
| Davenport | 2,646 | 1 | 0 | 0 | 0 | 1 | 77 | 26 | 42 | 9 | 0 |
| Davie | 90,147 | 437 | 4 | 21 | 91 | 321 | 3,869 | 686 | 2,828 | 355 | 20 |
| Daytona Beach | 64,257 | 975 | 9 | 38 | 290 | 638 | 4,694 | 1,023 | 3,148 | 523 | 12 |
| Daytona Beach Shores | 5,225 | 29 | 0 | 1 | 5 | 23 | 206 | 85 | 106 | 15 | 0 |
| Deerfield Beach | 74,509 | 468 | 2 | 23 | 145 | 298 | 2,408 | 501 | 1,745 | 162 | 3 |
| De Funiak Springs | 5,008 | 77 | 1 | 4 | 5 | 67 | 241 | 109 | 122 | 10 | 1 |
| Deland | 28,009 | 225 | 0 | 4 | 66 | 155 | 1,373 | 504 | 800 | 69 | 6 |
| Delray Beach | 64,522 | 606 | 3 | 29 | 218 | 356 | 3,430 | 771 | 2,448 | 211 | 8 |
| Doral | 32,209 | 84 | 1 | 5 | 17 | 61 | 2,588 | 328 | 2,077 | 183 | 2 |
| Dunedin | 35,963 | 122 | 0 | 8 | 27 | 87 | 1,209 | 191 | 980 | 38 | 3 |
| Dunnellon | 2,021 | 10 | 0 | 0 | 0 | 10 | 88 | 32 | 56 | 0 | 0 |
| Eatonville | 2,354 | 64 | 0 | 6 | 16 | 42 | 127 | 66 | 46 | 15 | 1 |
| Edgewater | 21,714 | 60 | 1 | 4 | 9 | 46 | 591 | 186 | 366 | 39 | 4 |
| Edgewood | 2,101 | 3 | 0 | 0 | 1 | 2 | 86 | 24 | 57 | 5 | 0 |
| El Portal | 2,297 | 14 | 0 | 0 | 7 | 7 | 93 | 54 | 33 | 6 | 0 |
| Eustis | 19,500 | 68 | 0 | 3 | 20 | 45 | 577 | 115 | 423 | 39 | 5 |
| Fellsmere | 5,054 | 17 | 2 | 0 | 6 | 9 | 69 | 18 | 42 | 9 | 0 |
| Fernandina Beach | 11,714 | 56 | 0 | 4 | 22 | 30 | 458 | 108 | 340 | 10 | 0 |
| Flagler Beach | 5,963 | 17 | 0 | 0 | 1 | 16 | 113 | 32 | 74 | 7 | 0 |
| Florida City | 10,204 | 364 | 1 | 4 | 133 | 226 | 1,443 | 365 | 1,017 | 61 | 3 |
| Fort Lauderdale | 182,942 | 1,481 | 13 | 56 | 685 | 727 | 10,374 | 2,907 | 6,780 | 687 | 39 |
| Fort Myers | 67,031 | 819 | 17 | 23 | 226 | 553 | 2,831 | 710 | 1,821 | 300 | 9 |
| Fort Pierce | 41,114 | 519 | 8 | 23 | 134 | 354 | 2,508 | 722 | 1,653 | 133 | 8 |
| Fort Walton Beach | 18,759 | 95 | 1 | 13 | 31 | 50 | 768 | 140 | 579 | 49 | 5 |
| Fruitland Park | 4,413 | 9 | 2 | 3 | 1 | 3 | 121 | 27 | 84 | 10 | 0 |
| Gainesville | 115,265 | 1,156 | 3 | 95 | 239 | 819 | 6,384 | 1,487 | 4,457 | 440 | 42 |
| Golden Beach | 870 | 0 | 0 | 0 | 0 | 0 | 19 | 6 | 11 | 2 | 0 |
| Graceville | 2,428 | 2 | 0 | 0 | 0 | 2 | 46 | 15 | 29 | 2 | 0 |
| Greenacres City | 32,649 | 226 | 0 | 18 | 67 | 141 | 1,175 | 307 | 792 | 76 | 2 |
| Green Cove Springs | 6,693 | 81 | 0 | 6 | 9 | 66 | 359 | 88 | 256 | 15 | 10 |

[1] The FBI does not publish arson data unless it receives data from either the agency or the state for all 12 months of the calendar year.

## Table 8. Offenses Known to Law Enforcement, by State and City, 2009—*Continued*

(Number.)

| State/city | Population | Violent crime | Murder and non-negligent man-slaughter | Forcible rape | Robbery | Aggravated assault | Property crime | Burglary | Larceny-theft | Motor vehicle theft | Arson[1] |
|---|---|---|---|---|---|---|---|---|---|---|---|
| **FLORIDA**—*Continued* | | | | | | | | | | | |
| Greensboro | 598 | 3 | 0 | 0 | 2 | 1 | 13 | 3 | 10 | 0 | 0 |
| Gretna | 1,603 | 31 | 0 | 0 | 2 | 29 | 21 | 10 | 10 | 1 | 0 |
| Groveland | 8,445 | 18 | 0 | 0 | 2 | 16 | 142 | 44 | 89 | 9 | 2 |
| Gulf Breeze | 6,689 | 9 | 0 | 2 | 0 | 7 | 131 | 16 | 114 | 1 | 1 |
| Gulfport | 12,286 | 56 | 1 | 0 | 23 | 32 | 624 | 165 | 380 | 79 | 2 |
| Gulf Stream | 737 | 0 | 0 | 0 | 0 | 0 | 18 | 1 | 15 | 2 | 0 |
| Haines City | 19,610 | 99 | 0 | 3 | 38 | 58 | 845 | 251 | 556 | 38 | 0 |
| Hallandale | 38,644 | 364 | 2 | 15 | 87 | 260 | 1,642 | 388 | 1,131 | 123 | 5 |
| Hampton | 460 | 0 | 0 | 0 | 0 | 0 | 4 | 4 | 0 | 0 | 0 |
| Havana | 1,689 | 13 | 0 | 1 | 4 | 8 | 52 | 13 | 38 | 1 | 0 |
| Hialeah | 208,874 | 925 | 8 | 32 | 309 | 576 | 8,213 | 1,093 | 5,957 | 1,163 | 20 |
| Hialeah Gardens | 19,667 | 58 | 1 | 1 | 27 | 29 | 884 | 137 | 627 | 120 | 1 |
| Highland Beach | 3,988 | 0 | 0 | 0 | 0 | 0 | 32 | 7 | 23 | 2 | 0 |
| High Springs | 4,696 | 27 | 0 | 1 | 3 | 23 | 141 | 27 | 110 | 4 | 1 |
| Hillsboro Beach | 2,252 | 4 | 0 | 1 | 0 | 3 | 30 | 6 | 23 | 1 | 0 |
| Holly Hill | 13,321 | 116 | 1 | 5 | 28 | 82 | 593 | 184 | 344 | 65 | 1 |
| Hollywood | 141,597 | 696 | 7 | 40 | 317 | 332 | 6,841 | 1,687 | 4,481 | 673 | 14 |
| Holmes Beach | 5,023 | 9 | 0 | 0 | 1 | 8 | 252 | 72 | 178 | 2 | 0 |
| Homestead | 62,037 | 901 | 3 | 26 | 294 | 578 | 3,288 | 1,095 | 1,945 | 248 | 5 |
| Howey-in-the-Hills | 1,282 | 0 | 0 | 0 | 0 | 0 | 10 | 5 | 5 | 0 | 0 |
| Hypoluxo | 2,592 | 1 | 0 | 0 | 0 | 1 | 34 | 8 | 25 | 1 | 0 |
| Indialantic | 2,930 | 13 | 0 | 1 | 3 | 9 | 131 | 20 | 108 | 3 | 0 |
| Indian Creek Village | 37 | 0 | 0 | 0 | 0 | 0 | 1 | 0 | 1 | 0 | 0 |
| Indian Harbour Beach | 8,328 | 14 | 0 | 2 | 7 | 5 | 189 | 28 | 151 | 10 | 1 |
| Indian River Shores | 3,387 | 0 | 0 | 0 | 0 | 0 | 24 | 7 | 15 | 2 | 0 |
| Indian Rocks Beach | 5,143 | 16 | 0 | 1 | 1 | 14 | 170 | 26 | 139 | 5 | 0 |
| Indian Shores | 4,235 | 6 | 0 | 2 | 0 | 4 | 97 | 14 | 81 | 2 | 0 |
| Inglis | 1,652 | 11 | 0 | 0 | 0 | 11 | 32 | 7 | 22 | 3 | 0 |
| Interlachen | 1,508 | 8 | 0 | 0 | 1 | 7 | 91 | 23 | 64 | 4 | 0 |
| Jacksonville | 810,064 | 6,772 | 99 | 218 | 2,359 | 4,096 | 41,781 | 11,306 | 27,754 | 2,721 | 103 |
| Jacksonville Beach | 21,750 | 226 | 1 | 14 | 69 | 142 | 1,415 | 186 | 1,156 | 73 | 8 |
| Jasper | 2,047 | 11 | 0 | 1 | 0 | 10 | 85 | 34 | 46 | 5 | 1 |
| Jennings | 844 | 8 | 0 | 0 | 2 | 6 | 11 | 5 | 6 | 0 | 0 |
| Juno Beach | 3,338 | 5 | 0 | 0 | 2 | 3 | 86 | 16 | 70 | 0 | 0 |
| Jupiter | 51,514 | 137 | 5 | 13 | 39 | 80 | 1,385 | 284 | 1,054 | 47 | 5 |
| Jupiter Inlet Colony | 387 | 0 | 0 | 0 | 0 | 0 | 5 | 1 | 4 | 0 | 0 |
| Jupiter Island | 672 | 1 | 0 | 0 | 1 | 0 | 16 | 7 | 7 | 2 | 0 |
| Kenneth City | 4,285 | 29 | 0 | 0 | 4 | 25 | 233 | 41 | 188 | 4 | 0 |
| Key Biscayne | 9,655 | 6 | 0 | 0 | 0 | 6 | 207 | 9 | 193 | 5 | 0 |
| Key Colony Beach | 757 | 1 | 0 | 0 | 1 | 0 | 21 | 4 | 17 | 0 | 0 |
| Key West | 22,049 | 195 | 1 | 20 | 68 | 106 | 1,830 | 408 | 1,288 | 134 | 1 |
| Kissimmee | 63,986 | 555 | 4 | 17 | 129 | 405 | 2,928 | 877 | 1,892 | 159 | 11 |
| Lady Lake | 15,282 | 33 | 0 | 4 | 4 | 25 | 289 | 46 | 226 | 17 | 2 |
| Lake Alfred | 4,560 | 4 | 0 | 0 | 2 | 2 | 117 | 23 | 85 | 9 | 2 |
| Lake City | 12,709 | 161 | 3 | 3 | 32 | 123 | 978 | 251 | 703 | 24 | 3 |
| Lake Clarke Shores | 3,313 | 6 | 0 | 0 | 0 | 6 | 68 | 27 | 38 | 3 | 0 |
| Lake Hamilton | 1,450 | 5 | 0 | 0 | 1 | 4 | 117 | 52 | 56 | 9 | 2 |
| Lake Helen | 2,784 | 11 | 0 | 0 | 1 | 10 | 59 | 16 | 39 | 4 | 0 |
| Lakeland | 94,322 | 487 | 5 | 33 | 169 | 280 | 5,030 | 1,247 | 3,515 | 268 | 10 |
| Lake Mary | 15,604 | 30 | 0 | 2 | 3 | 25 | 306 | 75 | 220 | 11 | 2 |
| Lake Park | 8,664 | 109 | 0 | 4 | 58 | 47 | 866 | 99 | 729 | 38 | 3 |
| Lake Placid | 1,897 | 6 | 0 | 0 | 1 | 5 | 69 | 12 | 55 | 2 | 0 |
| Lake Wales | 14,875 | 68 | 0 | 0 | 29 | 39 | 872 | 189 | 667 | 16 | 1 |
| Lake Worth | 35,500 | 527 | 9 | 25 | 224 | 269 | 2,059 | 775 | 1,148 | 136 | 3 |
| Lantana | 10,150 | 57 | 0 | 3 | 22 | 32 | 602 | 147 | 416 | 39 | 2 |
| Largo | 72,567 | 517 | 1 | 46 | 133 | 337 | 3,175 | 519 | 2,477 | 179 | 10 |
| Lauderdale-by-the-Sea | 5,825 | 22 | 0 | 1 | 5 | 16 | 194 | 30 | 157 | 7 | 2 |
| Lauderdale Lakes | 32,087 | 403 | 4 | 14 | 145 | 240 | 1,750 | 401 | 1,240 | 109 | 7 |
| Lauderhill | 67,005 | 525 | 4 | 22 | 164 | 335 | 2,402 | 843 | 1,330 | 229 | 15 |
| Lawtey | 705 | 1 | 0 | 0 | 0 | 1 | 29 | 14 | 15 | 0 | 0 |
| Leesburg | 22,836 | 221 | 1 | 21 | 45 | 154 | 1,272 | 280 | 936 | 56 | 1 |
| Lighthouse Point | 11,107 | 24 | 0 | 0 | 11 | 13 | 327 | 44 | 277 | 6 | 0 |
| Live Oak | 7,298 | 103 | 0 | 3 | 50 | 50 | 299 | 149 | 141 | 9 | 0 |
| Longboat Key | 7,277 | 2 | 0 | 0 | 0 | 2 | 170 | 18 | 149 | 3 | 1 |
| Longwood | 13,453 | 89 | 0 | 6 | 16 | 67 | 554 | 185 | 350 | 19 | 3 |
| Lynn Haven | 15,606 | 68 | 0 | 4 | 11 | 53 | 518 | 158 | 356 | 4 | 0 |
| Madeira Beach | 4,320 | 23 | 0 | 2 | 5 | 16 | 337 | 45 | 280 | 12 | 0 |
| Madison | 3,036 | 56 | 1 | 6 | 14 | 35 | 212 | 47 | 160 | 5 | 0 |
| Maitland | 14,984 | 35 | 0 | 4 | 9 | 22 | 496 | 177 | 282 | 37 | 0 |
| Manalapan | 341 | 2 | 0 | 0 | 0 | 2 | 19 | 0 | 19 | 0 | 0 |

[1] The FBI does not publish arson data unless it receives data from either the agency or the state for all 12 months of the calendar year.

## Table 8. Offenses Known to Law Enforcement, by State and City, 2009—*Continued*

(Number.)

| State/city | Population | Violent crime | Murder and non-negligent man-slaughter | Forcible rape | Robbery | Aggravated assault | Property crime | Burglary | Larceny-theft | Motor vehicle theft | Arson[1] |
|---|---|---|---|---|---|---|---|---|---|---|---|
| **FLORIDA**—*Continued* | | | | | | | | | | | |
| Mangonia Park | 1,224 | 62 | 2 | 2 | 20 | 38 | 251 | 46 | 176 | 29 | 0 |
| Marco Island | 15,713 | 10 | 0 | 0 | 0 | 10 | 155 | 18 | 132 | 5 | 1 |
| Margate | 54,032 | 215 | 0 | 6 | 50 | 159 | 1,123 | 301 | 753 | 69 | 5 |
| Marianna[6] | 6,290 | 22 | 0 | 7 | 0 | 15 | 253 | 80 | 169 | 4 | 0 |
| Mascotte | 6,032 | 28 | 2 | 3 | 3 | 20 | 102 | 31 | 63 | 8 | 0 |
| Medley | 1,017 | 4 | 0 | 0 | 1 | 3 | 365 | 40 | 261 | 64 | 0 |
| Melbourne | 77,854 | 906 | 6 | 24 | 192 | 684 | 3,980 | 737 | 3,058 | 185 | 7 |
| Melbourne Beach | 3,130 | 0 | 0 | 0 | 0 | 0 | 38 | 0 | 37 | 1 | 0 |
| Melbourne Village | 667 | 0 | 0 | 0 | 0 | 0 | 12 | 3 | 9 | 0 | 0 |
| Mexico Beach | 1,298 | 11 | 0 | 0 | 0 | 11 | 54 | 21 | 31 | 2 | 0 |
| Miami | 419,205 | 4,983 | 59 | 65 | 2,094 | 2,765 | 20,778 | 4,856 | 13,386 | 2,536 | 116 |
| Miami Beach | 84,260 | 906 | 7 | 41 | 421 | 437 | 8,439 | 1,207 | 6,567 | 665 | 11 |
| Miami Gardens | 110,346 | 1,069 | 24 | 28 | 351 | 666 | 6,231 | 1,663 | 3,921 | 647 | 18 |
| Miami Lakes | 21,626 | 61 | 0 | 2 | 24 | 35 | 902 | 140 | 656 | 106 | 0 |
| Miami Shores | 9,464 | 50 | 0 | 3 | 35 | 12 | 658 | 145 | 484 | 29 | 1 |
| Miami Springs | 12,412 | 35 | 0 | 0 | 16 | 19 | 491 | 120 | 335 | 36 | 2 |
| Milton | 8,789 | 17 | 0 | 1 | 4 | 12 | 349 | 49 | 289 | 11 | 3 |
| Minneola | 9,509 | 8 | 0 | 1 | 3 | 4 | 177 | 46 | 114 | 17 | 0 |
| Miramar | 108,375 | 524 | 7 | 35 | 174 | 308 | 3,591 | 1,020 | 2,227 | 344 | 16 |
| Monticello | 2,541 | 30 | 0 | 0 | 4 | 26 | 58 | 53 | 3 | 2 | 0 |
| Mount Dora | 13,226 | 71 | 3 | 2 | 20 | 46 | 514 | 82 | 419 | 13 | 3 |
| Naples | 21,587 | 40 | 0 | 2 | 11 | 27 | 732 | 78 | 646 | 8 | 0 |
| Neptune Beach | 6,731 | 31 | 1 | 0 | 10 | 20 | 302 | 27 | 262 | 13 | 0 |
| New Port Richey | 17,766 | 158 | 1 | 11 | 42 | 104 | 1,004 | 277 | 693 | 34 | 2 |
| New Smyrna Beach | 23,656 | 98 | 1 | 4 | 31 | 62 | 937 | 180 | 708 | 49 | 4 |
| Niceville | 12,368 | 17 | 0 | 2 | 4 | 11 | 184 | 31 | 143 | 10 | 0 |
| North Bay Village | 8,024 | 9 | 0 | 0 | 2 | 7 | 235 | 119 | 92 | 24 | 0 |
| North Lauderdale | 41,730 | 263 | 0 | 11 | 77 | 175 | 1,246 | 466 | 716 | 64 | 4 |
| North Miami | 55,495 | 645 | 9 | 28 | 298 | 310 | 3,692 | 823 | 2,534 | 335 | 13 |
| North Miami Beach | 41,324 | 401 | 1 | 27 | 169 | 204 | 2,242 | 697 | 1,358 | 187 | 14 |
| North Palm Beach | 12,155 | 38 | 0 | 0 | 16 | 22 | 293 | 85 | 194 | 14 | 1 |
| North Port | 60,512 | 186 | 1 | 13 | 20 | 152 | 1,491 | 415 | 1,043 | 33 | 3 |
| North Redington Beach | 1,475 | 5 | 0 | 0 | 0 | 5 | 34 | 12 | 20 | 2 | 0 |
| Oak Hill | 1,611 | 8 | 0 | 2 | 1 | 5 | 43 | 15 | 22 | 6 | 0 |
| Oakland | 1,167 | 8 | 0 | 0 | 1 | 7 | 44 | 10 | 27 | 7 | 0 |
| Oakland Park | 42,250 | 399 | 3 | 24 | 150 | 222 | 2,286 | 535 | 1,589 | 162 | 5 |
| Ocala | 55,847 | 495 | 3 | 41 | 160 | 291 | 3,216 | 678 | 2,438 | 100 | 9 |
| Ocean Ridge | 1,639 | 3 | 0 | 0 | 0 | 3 | 53 | 12 | 40 | 1 | 0 |
| Ocoee | 33,251 | 190 | 2 | 3 | 54 | 131 | 1,614 | 279 | 1,190 | 145 | 10 |
| Okeechobee | 6,060 | 20 | 1 | 0 | 7 | 12 | 376 | 63 | 296 | 17 | 0 |
| Oldsmar | 13,538 | 32 | 0 | 5 | 4 | 23 | 532 | 97 | 414 | 21 | 3 |
| Opa Locka | 16,775 | 372 | 3 | 3 | 132 | 234 | 1,388 | 772 | 476 | 140 | 0 |
| Orange City | 10,033 | 91 | 0 | 1 | 22 | 68 | 882 | 124 | 729 | 29 | 1 |
| Orange Park | 9,038 | 49 | 1 | 2 | 11 | 35 | 248 | 49 | 184 | 15 | 0 |
| Orlando | 235,109 | 2,814 | 28 | 117 | 767 | 1,902 | 17,357 | 3,770 | 12,332 | 1,255 | 63 |
| Ormond Beach | 38,153 | 133 | 0 | 8 | 28 | 97 | 1,170 | 336 | 788 | 46 | 0 |
| Oviedo | 33,382 | 73 | 0 | 5 | 7 | 61 | 567 | 99 | 456 | 12 | 4 |
| Pahokee | 6,650 | 104 | 0 | 6 | 12 | 86 | 189 | 60 | 112 | 17 | 4 |
| Palatka | 10,902 | 182 | 2 | 5 | 39 | 136 | 808 | 159 | 620 | 29 | 4 |
| Palm Bay | 103,475 | 532 | 5 | 26 | 72 | 429 | 2,426 | 664 | 1,602 | 160 | 13 |
| Palm Beach | 9,519 | 8 | 0 | 1 | 3 | 4 | 140 | 15 | 123 | 2 | 0 |
| Palm Beach Gardens | 50,937 | 100 | 4 | 5 | 30 | 61 | 1,658 | 293 | 1,302 | 63 | 1 |
| Palm Beach Shores | 1,569 | 3 | 0 | 0 | 1 | 2 | 46 | 14 | 28 | 4 | 0 |
| Palmetto | 14,453 | 247 | 0 | 6 | 82 | 159 | 580 | 220 | 326 | 34 | 8 |
| Palmetto Bay | 22,543 | 58 | 1 | 3 | 15 | 39 | 954 | 143 | 754 | 57 | 1 |
| Palm Springs | 16,514 | 120 | 1 | 4 | 64 | 51 | 940 | 273 | 578 | 89 | 1 |
| Panama City | 36,619 | 369 | 3 | 6 | 89 | 271 | 2,308 | 459 | 1,726 | 123 | 9 |
| Panama City Beach | 15,758 | 83 | 0 | 15 | 13 | 55 | 1,116 | 210 | 902 | 4 | 3 |
| Parker | 4,532 | 19 | 0 | 2 | 3 | 14 | 212 | 42 | 154 | 16 | 3 |
| Parkland | 23,993 | 25 | 0 | 1 | 6 | 18 | 295 | 50 | 238 | 7 | 0 |
| Pembroke Park | 4,739 | 38 | 0 | 4 | 10 | 24 | 331 | 79 | 212 | 40 | 0 |
| Pembroke Pines | 145,514 | 300 | 4 | 10 | 101 | 185 | 5,386 | 1,091 | 3,954 | 341 | 3 |
| Pensacola | 53,570 | 471 | 3 | 25 | 99 | 344 | 2,767 | 626 | 2,026 | 115 | 6 |
| Perry | 6,780 | 149 | 3 | 12 | 11 | 123 | 278 | 89 | 176 | 13 | 1 |
| Pinellas Park | 47,173 | 280 | 1 | 25 | 75 | 179 | 2,931 | 532 | 2,245 | 154 | 17 |
| Plantation | 83,544 | 372 | 3 | 13 | 172 | 184 | 3,638 | 674 | 2,729 | 235 | 4 |
| Plant City | 33,048 | 304 | 2 | 6 | 106 | 190 | 2,039 | 409 | 1,372 | 258 | 9 |
| Pompano Beach | 101,840 | 1,029 | 8 | 57 | 348 | 616 | 5,066 | 971 | 3,698 | 397 | 18 |
| Ponce Inlet | 3,217 | 4 | 0 | 0 | 1 | 3 | 53 | 9 | 38 | 6 | 0 |
| Port Orange | 55,604 | 85 | 0 | 1 | 23 | 61 | 1,300 | 258 | 978 | 64 | 4 |
| Port Richey | 3,458 | 18 | 0 | 1 | 7 | 10 | 228 | 43 | 178 | 7 | 0 |

[1] The FBI does not publish arson data unless it receives data from either the agency or the state for all 12 months of the calendar year.
[6] Because of changes in the state/local agency's reporting practices, figures are not comparable to previous years' data.

**Table 8. Offenses Known to Law Enforcement, by State and City, 2009**—*Continued*

(Number.)

| State/city | Population | Violent crime | Murder and non-negligent man-slaughter | Forcible rape | Robbery | Aggravated assault | Property crime | Burglary | Larceny-theft | Motor vehicle theft | Arson[1] |
|---|---|---|---|---|---|---|---|---|---|---|---|
| **FLORIDA**—*Continued* | | | | | | | | | | | |
| Port St. Joe | 3,537 | 9 | 0 | 0 | 0 | 9 | 17 | 3 | 14 | 0 | 0 |
| Port St. Lucie | 164,069 | 421 | 1 | 51 | 60 | 309 | 3,552 | 1,102 | 2,389 | 61 | 8 |
| Punta Gorda | 16,567 | 33 | 1 | 0 | 3 | 29 | 329 | 121 | 203 | 5 | 1 |
| Redington Beaches | 1,476 | 7 | 0 | 2 | 0 | 5 | 39 | 11 | 26 | 2 | 1 |
| Riviera Beach | 37,247 | 677 | 9 | 16 | 214 | 438 | 2,248 | 807 | 1,224 | 217 | 14 |
| Rockledge | 25,289 | 79 | 2 | 1 | 25 | 51 | 785 | 185 | 564 | 36 | 4 |
| Royal Palm Beach | 31,468 | 121 | 0 | 7 | 41 | 73 | 1,386 | 272 | 1,057 | 57 | 4 |
| Safety Harbor | 17,060 | 48 | 0 | 7 | 10 | 31 | 399 | 106 | 286 | 7 | 1 |
| Sanford | 52,118 | 377 | 3 | 26 | 199 | 149 | 3,334 | 798 | 2,284 | 252 | 1 |
| Sanibel | 5,601 | 3 | 0 | 0 | 0 | 3 | 111 | 14 | 94 | 3 | 0 |
| Sarasota | 52,308 | 540 | 7 | 27 | 174 | 332 | 3,225 | 758 | 2,320 | 147 | 12 |
| Satellite Beach | 11,774 | 19 | 0 | 0 | 5 | 14 | 245 | 55 | 188 | 2 | 0 |
| Sea Ranch Lakes | 734 | 2 | 0 | 0 | 2 | 0 | 27 | 4 | 22 | 1 | 0 |
| Sebastian | 20,777 | 40 | 1 | 5 | 3 | 31 | 655 | 188 | 452 | 15 | 2 |
| Sebring | 10,796 | 63 | 1 | 5 | 19 | 38 | 518 | 161 | 348 | 9 | 3 |
| Seminole | 19,047 | 82 | 0 | 4 | 17 | 61 | 747 | 96 | 631 | 20 | 3 |
| Sewall's Point | 2,010 | 0 | 0 | 0 | 0 | 0 | 23 | 4 | 19 | 0 | 0 |
| Shalimar | 699 | 0 | 0 | 0 | 0 | 0 | 8 | 6 | 1 | 1 | 0 |
| Sneads | 1,942 | 4 | 0 | 0 | 2 | 2 | 31 | 15 | 9 | 7 | 0 |
| South Bay | 4,584 | 62 | 3 | 4 | 4 | 51 | 132 | 44 | 76 | 12 | 1 |
| South Daytona | 13,662 | 63 | 0 | 2 | 14 | 47 | 441 | 108 | 295 | 38 | 3 |
| South Miami | 10,708 | 104 | 4 | 2 | 42 | 56 | 920 | 140 | 737 | 43 | 0 |
| South Palm Beach | 1,461 | 1 | 0 | 0 | 1 | 0 | 14 | 4 | 8 | 2 | 0 |
| South Pasadena | 5,523 | 12 | 0 | 2 | 3 | 7 | 164 | 21 | 138 | 5 | 0 |
| Southwest Ranches | 7,222 | 14 | 0 | 1 | 5 | 8 | 210 | 45 | 136 | 29 | 4 |
| Springfield | 8,792 | 47 | 0 | 2 | 7 | 38 | 225 | 84 | 126 | 15 | 0 |
| Starke | 6,011 | 33 | 0 | 1 | 4 | 28 | 176 | 15 | 150 | 11 | 0 |
| St. Augustine | 12,476 | 111 | 0 | 9 | 10 | 92 | 772 | 127 | 597 | 48 | 1 |
| St. Augustine Beach | 6,400 | 12 | 0 | 1 | 2 | 9 | 234 | 44 | 183 | 7 | 0 |
| St. Cloud | 29,604 | 152 | 0 | 7 | 22 | 123 | 902 | 267 | 612 | 23 | 4 |
| St. Pete Beach | 9,925 | 39 | 0 | 3 | 6 | 30 | 580 | 208 | 359 | 13 | 0 |
| St. Petersburg | 244,933 | 3,334 | 11 | 112 | 907 | 2,304 | 17,198 | 4,366 | 10,575 | 2,257 | 100 |
| Stuart | 16,000 | 70 | 3 | 2 | 22 | 43 | 750 | 120 | 611 | 19 | 2 |
| Sunny Isles Beach | 16,438 | 29 | 0 | 2 | 6 | 21 | 507 | 87 | 400 | 20 | 0 |
| Sunrise | 88,936 | 292 | 4 | 14 | 113 | 161 | 3,963 | 742 | 3,004 | 217 | 8 |
| Surfside | 4,480 | 27 | 0 | 0 | 1 | 26 | 175 | 26 | 142 | 7 | 1 |
| Sweetwater | 12,952 | 34 | 0 | 3 | 9 | 22 | 230 | 46 | 106 | 78 | 0 |
| Tallahassee | 174,183 | 1,647 | 6 | 120 | 474 | 1,047 | 8,438 | 3,125 | 4,975 | 338 | 32 |
| Tamarac | 59,280 | 227 | 0 | 14 | 91 | 122 | 1,354 | 337 | 912 | 105 | 0 |
| Tampa | 345,233 | 2,597 | 20 | 80 | 909 | 1,588 | 12,960 | 3,501 | 8,098 | 1,361 | 150 |
| Tarpon Springs | 23,628 | 189 | 0 | 10 | 40 | 139 | 731 | 157 | 541 | 33 | 5 |
| Tavares | 14,227 | 44 | 1 | 2 | 8 | 33 | 234 | 41 | 168 | 25 | 0 |
| Temple Terrace | 22,713 | 124 | 0 | 4 | 51 | 69 | 877 | 328 | 498 | 51 | 0 |
| Tequesta | 5,757 | 6 | 0 | 2 | 1 | 3 | 61 | 13 | 47 | 1 | 0 |
| Titusville | 45,197 | 266 | 4 | 25 | 55 | 182 | 1,735 | 439 | 1,109 | 187 | 12 |
| Treasure Island | 7,454 | 22 | 1 | 9 | 3 | 9 | 322 | 53 | 259 | 10 | 0 |
| Trenton | 1,889 | 4 | 0 | 0 | 2 | 2 | 67 | 19 | 43 | 5 | 0 |
| Umatilla | 3,107 | 28 | 0 | 0 | 5 | 23 | 86 | 3 | 81 | 2 | 0 |
| Valparaiso | 5,991 | 10 | 0 | 2 | 0 | 8 | 34 | 11 | 21 | 2 | 0 |
| Venice | 21,236 | 47 | 0 | 11 | 4 | 32 | 650 | 140 | 492 | 18 | 1 |
| Vero Beach | 16,908 | 89 | 1 | 1 | 25 | 62 | 557 | 125 | 413 | 19 | 0 |
| Village of Pinecrest | 18,565 | 28 | 0 | 0 | 13 | 15 | 640 | 79 | 538 | 23 | 0 |
| Virginia Gardens | 2,150 | 1 | 0 | 0 | 0 | 1 | 31 | 7 | 18 | 6 | 0 |
| Wauchula | 4,522 | 15 | 0 | 1 | 2 | 12 | 217 | 80 | 131 | 6 | 0 |
| Webster | 924 | 7 | 0 | 0 | 0 | 7 | 33 | 13 | 19 | 1 | 0 |
| Welaka | 818 | 0 | 0 | 0 | 0 | 0 | 2 | 0 | 2 | 0 | 0 |
| Wellington | 56,588 | 134 | 0 | 11 | 41 | 82 | 1,901 | 399 | 1,412 | 90 | 4 |
| West Melbourne | 16,034 | 48 | 0 | 1 | 14 | 33 | 595 | 210 | 357 | 28 | 1 |
| West Miami | 5,497 | 19 | 0 | 0 | 5 | 14 | 174 | 53 | 93 | 28 | 0 |
| Weston | 63,564 | 38 | 0 | 2 | 7 | 29 | 948 | 133 | 779 | 36 | 1 |
| West Palm Beach | 100,763 | 905 | 19 | 42 | 376 | 468 | 5,365 | 1,291 | 3,645 | 429 | 11 |
| West Park | 14,417 | 116 | 0 | 2 | 41 | 73 | 590 | 214 | 322 | 54 | 4 |
| White Springs | 830 | 6 | 0 | 0 | 0 | 6 | 23 | 4 | 18 | 1 | 0 |
| Wildwood | 3,809 | 29 | 0 | 6 | 3 | 20 | 187 | 61 | 121 | 5 | 1 |
| Williston | 2,979 | 50 | 0 | 1 | 1 | 48 | 88 | 22 | 64 | 2 | 1 |
| Wilton Manors | 12,603 | 58 | 1 | 1 | 29 | 27 | 728 | 217 | 473 | 38 | 1 |
| Windermere | 2,582 | 1 | 0 | 0 | 0 | 1 | 30 | 1 | 29 | 0 | 0 |
| Winter Garden | 31,554 | 172 | 1 | 4 | 46 | 121 | 1,174 | 203 | 890 | 81 | 4 |
| Winter Haven | 34,103 | 289 | 3 | 27 | 92 | 167 | 1,966 | 475 | 1,388 | 103 | 20 |
| Winter Park | 27,917 | 78 | 0 | 2 | 33 | 43 | 1,082 | 282 | 755 | 45 | 2 |
| Winter Springs | 32,846 | 62 | 0 | 8 | 9 | 45 | 541 | 129 | 379 | 33 | 0 |

[1] The FBI does not publish arson data unless it receives data from either the agency or the state for all 12 months of the calendar year.

**Table 8. Offenses Known to Law Enforcement, by State and City, 2009—*Continued***

(Number.)

| State/city | Population | Violent crime | Murder and non-negligent man-slaughter | Forcible rape | Robbery | Aggravated assault | Property crime | Burglary | Larceny-theft | Motor vehicle theft | Arson[1] |
|---|---|---|---|---|---|---|---|---|---|---|---|
| **FLORIDA**—*Continued* | | | | | | | | | | | |
| Zephyrhills | 13,377 | 63 | 0 | 10 | 19 | 34 | 819 | 190 | 602 | 27 | 1 |
| Zolfo Springs | 1,708 | 2 | 0 | 0 | 1 | 1 | 40 | 20 | 19 | 1 | 0 |
| **GEORGIA** | | | | | | | | | | | |
| Abbeville | 2,802 | 4 | 0 | 0 | 0 | 4 | 9 | 5 | 3 | 1 | 0 |
| Acworth | 20,193 | 93 | 1 | 0 | 3 | 89 | 550 | 64 | 463 | 23 | |
| Adairsville | 3,280 | 9 | 0 | 0 | 3 | 6 | 222 | 52 | 165 | 5 | 0 |
| Adel | 5,405 | 16 | 1 | 1 | 2 | 12 | 268 | 108 | 154 | 6 | 0 |
| Alamo | 2,722 | 8 | 0 | 0 | 1 | 7 | 23 | 4 | 19 | 0 | 0 |
| Albany | 75,734 | 812 | 8 | 47 | 221 | 536 | 4,788 | 1,451 | 3,048 | 289 | 14 |
| Alpharetta | 50,279 | 51 | 0 | 2 | 21 | 28 | 1,600 | 267 | 1,301 | 32 | 0 |
| Alto | 915 | 3 | 0 | 0 | 0 | 3 | 8 | 5 | 3 | 0 | |
| Americus | 16,467 | 199 | 2 | 1 | 28 | 168 | 1,135 | 425 | 663 | 47 | |
| Aragon | 1,083 | 0 | 0 | 0 | 0 | 0 | 32 | 0 | 32 | 0 | 0 |
| Arcade | 1,981 | 12 | 0 | 1 | 0 | 11 | 24 | 3 | 20 | 1 | |
| Arlington | 1,491 | 4 | 0 | 0 | 0 | 4 | 37 | 25 | 12 | 0 | 0 |
| Athens-Clarke County | 114,540 | 472 | 10 | 42 | 155 | 265 | 5,644 | 1,917 | 3,453 | 274 | 21 |
| Atlanta | 552,901 | 6,359 | 80 | 135 | 2,725 | 3,419 | 34,349 | 9,112 | 19,511 | 5,726 | 157 |
| Attapulgus | 468 | 0 | 0 | 0 | 0 | 0 | 0 | 0 | 0 | 0 | 0 |
| Auburn | 7,563 | 9 | 0 | 4 | 0 | 5 | 81 | 30 | 46 | 5 | 0 |
| Austell | 7,267 | 53 | 1 | 2 | 6 | 44 | 270 | 66 | 174 | 30 | |
| Avondale Estates | 2,854 | 2 | 1 | 0 | 1 | 0 | 82 | 18 | 56 | 8 | 0 |
| Bainbridge | 12,380 | 82 | 0 | 3 | 25 | 54 | 642 | 131 | 500 | 11 | |
| Baldwin | 3,028 | 0 | 0 | 0 | 0 | 0 | 50 | 4 | 43 | 3 | 0 |
| Ball Ground | 972 | 0 | 0 | 0 | 0 | 0 | 18 | 2 | 14 | 2 | 0 |
| Barnesville | 6,001 | 83 | 0 | 3 | 9 | 71 | 238 | 71 | 160 | 7 | 0 |
| Baxley | 4,575 | 25 | 2 | 0 | 6 | 17 | 208 | 58 | 146 | 4 | 0 |
| Berlin | 618 | 1 | 0 | 0 | 0 | 1 | 0 | 0 | 0 | 0 | 0 |
| Blackshear | 3,528 | 8 | 0 | 0 | 5 | 3 | 204 | 45 | 147 | 12 | 2 |
| Blairsville | 727 | 0 | 0 | 0 | 0 | 0 | 0 | 0 | 0 | 0 | 0 |
| Blakely | 5,212 | 22 | 1 | 1 | 7 | 13 | 103 | 39 | 64 | 0 | |
| Bloomingdale | 2,627 | 0 | 0 | 0 | 0 | 0 | 65 | 23 | 36 | 6 | 0 |
| Blythe | 827 | 0 | 0 | 0 | 0 | 0 | 15 | 5 | 8 | 2 | 0 |
| Bowdon | 2,066 | 0 | 0 | 0 | 0 | 0 | 56 | 9 | 47 | 0 | 0 |
| Braselton | 5,647 | 4 | 0 | 0 | 1 | 3 | 182 | 49 | 127 | 6 | 0 |
| Bremen | 5,842 | 39 | 0 | 1 | 6 | 32 | 341 | 67 | 246 | 28 | |
| Brooklet | 1,363 | 4 | 0 | 0 | 2 | 2 | 27 | 5 | 19 | 3 | 0 |
| Brunswick | 16,348 | 349 | 2 | 10 | 71 | 266 | 1,414 | 375 | 968 | 71 | 2 |
| Buchanan | 1,054 | 2 | 0 | 0 | 0 | 2 | 50 | 8 | 39 | 3 | |
| Buena Vista | 1,639 | 14 | 0 | 0 | 2 | 12 | 81 | 29 | 52 | 0 | |
| Butler | 1,808 | 12 | 0 | 1 | 1 | 10 | 25 | 12 | 12 | 1 | 0 |
| Byron | 4,515 | 32 | 1 | 0 | 0 | 31 | 190 | 34 | 147 | 9 | 0 |
| Cairo | 9,871 | 33 | 0 | 5 | 17 | 11 | 262 | 67 | 180 | 15 | 0 |
| Calhoun | 15,295 | 37 | 2 | 3 | 9 | 23 | 853 | 178 | 657 | 18 | 0 |
| Camilla | 5,658 | 103 | 0 | 2 | 6 | 95 | 270 | 57 | 212 | 1 | 1 |
| Canton | 25,370 | 28 | 1 | 3 | 8 | 16 | 486 | 63 | 406 | 17 | 0 |
| Carrollton | 23,679 | 308 | 2 | 11 | 25 | 270 | 1,292 | 229 | 998 | 65 | |
| Cartersville | 19,325 | 57 | 2 | 6 | 17 | 32 | 879 | 145 | 682 | 52 | 2 |
| Cedartown | 10,177 | 24 | 1 | 7 | 9 | 7 | 334 | 90 | 227 | 17 | 1 |
| Centerville | 7,502 | 15 | 1 | 1 | 2 | 11 | 325 | 50 | 261 | 14 | 4 |
| Chamblee | 11,410 | 91 | 1 | 2 | 59 | 29 | 789 | 112 | 605 | 72 | 3 |
| Chatsworth | 4,193 | 18 | 0 | 0 | 1 | 17 | 128 | 24 | 98 | 6 | 1 |
| Chickamauga | 2,608 | 18 | 0 | 0 | 1 | 17 | 100 | 24 | 73 | 3 | 0 |
| Clarkston | 7,871 | 61 | 1 | 3 | 33 | 24 | 281 | 99 | 152 | 30 | 0 |
| Claxton | 2,422 | 13 | 0 | 0 | 4 | 9 | 110 | 29 | 79 | 2 | 0 |
| Cleveland | 2,732 | 31 | 0 | 0 | 2 | 29 | 178 | 70 | 98 | 10 | 0 |
| Climax | 290 | 0 | 0 | 0 | 0 | 0 | 0 | 0 | 0 | 0 | 0 |
| Cochran | 5,302 | 22 | 1 | 2 | 6 | 13 | 237 | 49 | 183 | 5 | 2 |
| College Park | 19,936 | 300 | 3 | 14 | 151 | 132 | 2,049 | 590 | 1,198 | 261 | 8 |
| Colquitt | 1,911 | 5 | 0 | 1 | 0 | 4 | 52 | 12 | 39 | 1 | |
| Columbus | 186,224 | 1,153 | 13 | 47 | 574 | 519 | 14,684 | 3,792 | 9,374 | 1,518 | 49 |
| Commerce | 6,508 | 28 | 1 | 1 | 5 | 21 | 182 | 53 | 124 | 5 | 4 |
| Conyers | 13,798 | 75 | 0 | 6 | 38 | 31 | 988 | 174 | 749 | 65 | 4 |
| Coolidge | 559 | 1 | 0 | 1 | 0 | 0 | 4 | 2 | 1 | 1 | 0 |
| Cordele | 11,507 | 156 | 2 | 13 | 57 | 84 | 938 | 241 | 669 | 28 | 1 |
| Covington | 15,385 | 64 | 0 | 5 | 26 | 33 | 811 | 201 | 579 | 31 | 0 |
| Cumming | 5,909 | 12 | 0 | 3 | 7 | 2 | 330 | 42 | 275 | 13 | 0 |
| Cuthbert | 3,387 | 10 | 0 | 0 | 2 | 8 | 55 | 22 | 32 | 1 | |
| Dalton | 34,299 | 118 | 1 | 15 | 16 | 86 | 1,232 | 228 | 958 | 46 | |
| Danielsville | 452 | 1 | 0 | 0 | 0 | 1 | 36 | 13 | 23 | 0 | 0 |
| Davisboro | 1,879 | 0 | 0 | 0 | 0 | 0 | 12 | 3 | 9 | 0 | 0 |
| Decatur | 19,071 | 63 | 1 | 4 | 26 | 32 | 772 | 168 | 529 | 75 | |

[1] The FBI does not publish arson data unless it receives data from either the agency or the state for all 12 months of the calendar year.

## Table 8. Offenses Known to Law Enforcement, by State and City, 2009—*Continued*

(Number.)

| State/city | Population | Violent crime | Murder and non-negligent man-slaughter | Forcible rape | Robbery | Aggravated assault | Property crime | Burglary | Larceny-theft | Motor vehicle theft | Arson[1] |
|---|---|---|---|---|---|---|---|---|---|---|---|
| **GEORGIA**—*Continued* | | | | | | | | | | | |
| Donalsonville | 2,684 | 8 | 0 | 0 | 2 | 6 | 89 | 17 | 70 | 2 | 0 |
| Doraville | 10,308 | 77 | 2 | 1 | 31 | 43 | 405 | 111 | 242 | 52 | 0 |
| Douglas | 11,477 | 129 | 0 | 7 | 30 | 92 | 1,210 | 258 | 909 | 43 | 2 |
| Douglasville | 32,586 | 189 | 0 | 4 | 44 | 141 | 1,757 | 220 | 1,440 | 97 | 2 |
| Dublin | 17,666 | 131 | 1 | 12 | 28 | 90 | 1,302 | 310 | 966 | 26 | 0 |
| Duluth | 26,495 | 63 | 0 | 2 | 16 | 45 | 949 | 130 | 792 | 27 | 1 |
| East Ellijay | 705 | 5 | 0 | 1 | 1 | 3 | 124 | 4 | 120 | 0 | 0 |
| East Point | 43,753 | 433 | 6 | 21 | 253 | 153 | 3,377 | 1,113 | 1,827 | 437 | |
| Eatonton | 6,331 | 32 | 0 | 0 | 3 | 29 | 143 | 17 | 126 | 0 | 0 |
| Edison | 1,241 | 2 | 1 | 0 | 0 | 1 | 14 | 6 | 8 | 0 | 0 |
| Elberton | 4,524 | 44 | 0 | 2 | 7 | 35 | 507 | 125 | 373 | 9 | 0 |
| Ellaville | 1,861 | 7 | 0 | 0 | 0 | 7 | 14 | 1 | 12 | 1 | 0 |
| Ellijay | 1,587 | 0 | 0 | 0 | 0 | 0 | 0 | 0 | 0 | 0 | 0 |
| Emerson | 1,473 | 4 | 0 | 0 | 2 | 2 | 60 | 12 | 31 | 17 | 2 |
| Ephesus | 386 | 0 | 0 | 0 | 0 | 0 | 0 | 0 | 0 | 0 | 0 |
| Eton | 481 | 2 | 0 | 0 | 1 | 1 | 27 | 4 | 23 | 0 | 0 |
| Fairburn | 11,750 | 34 | 0 | 3 | 14 | 17 | 577 | 187 | 333 | 57 | 2 |
| Fairmount | 813 | 2 | 0 | 1 | 0 | 1 | 9 | 2 | 7 | 0 | 0 |
| Flowery Branch | 4,318 | 0 | 0 | 0 | 0 | 0 | 42 | 15 | 26 | 1 | |
| Folkston | 3,230 | 8 | 0 | 0 | 2 | 6 | 117 | 23 | 89 | 5 | 0 |
| Forest Park | 21,760 | 171 | 0 | 9 | 92 | 70 | 1,188 | 336 | 691 | 161 | |
| Forsyth | 5,148 | 24 | 0 | 1 | 4 | 19 | 225 | 41 | 174 | 10 | 0 |
| Fort Gaines | 991 | 0 | 0 | 0 | 0 | 0 | 0 | 0 | 0 | 0 | 0 |
| Fort Oglethorpe | 10,000 | 32 | 0 | 2 | 9 | 21 | 802 | 83 | 696 | 23 | 0 |
| Fort Valley | 8,178 | 89 | 1 | 4 | 9 | 75 | 576 | 169 | 400 | 7 | 0 |
| Franklin | 883 | 12 | 0 | 1 | 1 | 10 | 48 | 8 | 39 | 1 | 0 |
| Franklin Springs | 803 | 0 | 0 | 0 | 0 | 0 | 10 | 0 | 10 | 0 | 0 |
| Gainesville | 36,896 | 125 | 3 | 15 | 33 | 74 | 1,695 | 349 | 1,255 | 91 | 4 |
| Garden City | 9,329 | 151 | 1 | 6 | 24 | 120 | 450 | 106 | 264 | 80 | 1 |
| Glennville | 5,464 | 10 | 0 | 1 | 1 | 8 | 196 | 45 | 146 | 5 | 1 |
| Glenwood | 897 | 0 | 0 | 0 | 0 | 0 | 0 | 0 | 0 | 0 | 0 |
| Gordon | 2,103 | 2 | 0 | 0 | 2 | 0 | 40 | 8 | 29 | 3 | 2 |
| Greensboro | 3,281 | 36 | 0 | 2 | 6 | 28 | 168 | 42 | 115 | 11 | |
| Greenville | 921 | 4 | 0 | 0 | 0 | 4 | 38 | 5 | 30 | 3 | 0 |
| Griffin | 23,795 | 181 | 1 | 14 | 64 | 102 | 1,444 | 248 | 1,155 | 41 | 8 |
| Guyton | 2,006 | 4 | 0 | 1 | 0 | 3 | 20 | 8 | 10 | 2 | 0 |
| Hagan | 1,073 | 0 | 0 | 0 | 0 | 0 | 3 | 3 | 0 | 0 | 0 |
| Hahira | 2,579 | 5 | 0 | 0 | 3 | 2 | 45 | 7 | 37 | 1 | 0 |
| Hampton | 5,464 | 26 | 0 | 2 | 1 | 23 | 144 | 43 | 87 | 14 | 1 |
| Hapeville | 5,964 | 35 | 0 | 1 | 21 | 13 | 369 | 90 | 197 | 82 | 0 |
| Harlem[2] | 2,071 | 2 | 0 | 0 | 0 | 2 | | 20 | | 1 | 0 |
| Hartwell | 4,306 | 31 | 0 | 1 | 13 | 17 | 267 | 35 | 229 | 3 | 0 |
| Hazlehurst | 3,898 | 10 | 0 | 0 | 4 | 6 | 306 | 50 | 252 | 4 | |
| Helen | 903 | 13 | 0 | 0 | 1 | 12 | 57 | 7 | 49 | 1 | 0 |
| Helena | 2,466 | 6 | 1 | 0 | 0 | 5 | 18 | 17 | 1 | 0 | |
| Hephzibah | 4,610 | 17 | 0 | 1 | 4 | 12 | 153 | 44 | 93 | 16 | 0 |
| Hiawassee | 862 | 6 | 0 | 0 | 0 | 6 | 32 | 6 | 26 | 0 | 0 |
| Hinesville | 30,130 | 191 | 2 | 14 | 67 | 108 | 1,790 | 606 | 1,108 | 76 | 5 |
| Hiram | 2,129 | 32 | 0 | 1 | 6 | 25 | 436 | 36 | 388 | 12 | 1 |
| Hoboken | 528 | 1 | 0 | 0 | 0 | 1 | 3 | 0 | 3 | 0 | 0 |
| Holly Springs | 9,753 | 5 | 1 | 0 | 0 | 4 | 125 | 34 | 88 | 3 | 0 |
| Irwinton | 583 | 0 | 0 | 0 | 0 | 0 | 1 | 0 | 1 | 0 | 0 |
| Ivey | 1,064 | 0 | 0 | 0 | 0 | 0 | 2 | 0 | 0 | 2 | 0 |
| Jackson | 4,556 | 4 | 0 | 0 | 2 | 2 | 123 | 26 | 89 | 8 | 0 |
| Jefferson | 8,531 | 26 | 0 | 4 | 5 | 17 | 174 | 45 | 115 | 14 | |
| Jesup | 10,600 | 31 | 0 | 1 | 16 | 14 | 577 | 151 | 409 | 17 | 0 |
| Johns Creek | 59,305 | 52 | 0 | 4 | 27 | 21 | 773 | 197 | 551 | 25 | 5 |
| Jonesboro | 4,167 | 45 | 0 | 0 | 8 | 37 | 147 | 37 | 95 | 15 | 0 |
| Kennesaw | 33,060 | 30 | 0 | 3 | 8 | 19 | 609 | 107 | 469 | 33 | 0 |
| Keysville | 246 | 0 | 0 | 0 | 0 | 0 | 1 | 0 | 1 | 0 | 0 |
| Kingsland | 14,049 | 97 | 1 | 7 | 12 | 77 | 492 | 106 | 371 | 15 | 0 |
| Kingston | 670 | 3 | 0 | 0 | 1 | 2 | 5 | 1 | 3 | 1 | 0 |
| Lafayette | 7,632 | 42 | 2 | 3 | 10 | 27 | 379 | 82 | 284 | 13 | 1 |
| Lagrange | 28,634 | 157 | 5 | 12 | 73 | 67 | 1,779 | 398 | 1,300 | 81 | 8 |
| Lake City | 2,661 | 13 | 0 | 0 | 9 | 4 | 218 | 28 | 152 | 38 | |
| Lavonia | 2,102 | 5 | 0 | 0 | 2 | 3 | 92 | 14 | 77 | 1 | |
| Lawrenceville | 30,046 | 87 | 0 | 7 | 45 | 35 | 1,188 | 265 | 852 | 71 | 0 |
| Leesburg | 2,987 | 15 | 0 | 11 | 4 | 0 | 93 | 22 | 69 | 2 | |
| Lilburn | 11,625 | 51 | 0 | 4 | 31 | 16 | 543 | 127 | 381 | 35 | 2 |
| Lincolnton | 1,523 | 24 | 0 | 0 | 0 | 24 | 43 | 11 | 30 | 2 | 0 |
| Locust Grove | 5,151 | 7 | 0 | 0 | 4 | 3 | 303 | 44 | 248 | 11 | 0 |

[1] The FBI does not publish arson data unless it receives data from either the agency or the state for all 12 months of the calendar year.
[2] The FBI determined that the agency's data were underreported. Consequently, those data are not included in this table.

**Table 8. Offenses Known to Law Enforcement, by State and City, 2009**—*Continued*

(Number.)

| State/city | Population | Violent crime | Murder and non-negligent man-slaughter | Forcible rape | Robbery | Aggravated assault | Property crime | Burglary | Larceny-theft | Motor vehicle theft | Arson[1] |
|---|---|---|---|---|---|---|---|---|---|---|---|
| **GEORGIA**—*Continued* | | | | | | | | | | | |
| Loganville | 11,291 | 20 | 1 | 4 | 6 | 9 | 334 | 50 | 266 | 18 | 2 |
| Lookout Mountain | 1,515 | 0 | 0 | 0 | 0 | 0 | 4 | 3 | 1 | 0 | 0 |
| Ludowici | 1,568 | 10 | 0 | 0 | 1 | 9 | 74 | 32 | 37 | 5 | |
| Lumber City | 1,175 | 6 | 0 | 1 | 0 | 5 | 17 | 1 | 15 | 1 | 0 |
| Lumpkin | 1,205 | 13 | 0 | 0 | 3 | 10 | 21 | 11 | 10 | 0 | 0 |
| Macon | 92,299 | 704 | 18 | 28 | 342 | 316 | 7,118 | 1,814 | 4,679 | 625 | 80 |
| Madison | 3,959 | 12 | 0 | 0 | 2 | 10 | 180 | 47 | 126 | 7 | 0 |
| Manchester | 3,755 | 16 | 0 | 2 | 1 | 13 | 245 | 70 | 163 | 12 | 0 |
| Marietta | 68,037 | 433 | 2 | 17 | 194 | 220 | 2,530 | 610 | 1,725 | 195 | |
| McCaysville | 977 | 1 | 0 | 0 | 0 | 1 | 6 | 3 | 3 | 0 | 0 |
| McDonough | 21,635 | 166 | 1 | 4 | 15 | 146 | 713 | 124 | 544 | 45 | 2 |
| McIntyre | 712 | 2 | 0 | 0 | 0 | 2 | 31 | 7 | 22 | 2 | 0 |
| McRae | 4,647 | 29 | 0 | 0 | 1 | 28 | 115 | 39 | 69 | 7 | 0 |
| Midville | 451 | 1 | 0 | 0 | 0 | 1 | 0 | 0 | 0 | 0 | 0 |
| Midway | 1,034 | 13 | 0 | 0 | 2 | 11 | 55 | 23 | 31 | 1 | 0 |
| Milledgeville | 20,922 | 80 | 2 | 6 | 19 | 53 | 1,001 | 258 | 719 | 24 | 3 |
| Millen | 3,445 | 44 | 0 | 0 | 6 | 38 | 81 | 24 | 54 | 3 | 0 |
| Milton | 15,134 | 12 | 0 | 1 | 6 | 5 | 390 | 92 | 274 | 24 | 2 |
| Molena | 473 | 0 | 0 | 0 | 0 | 0 | 0 | 0 | 0 | 0 | 0 |
| Monroe | 13,607 | 76 | 1 | 7 | 18 | 50 | 594 | 172 | 400 | 22 | 2 |
| Montezuma | 3,839 | 25 | 0 | 1 | 3 | 21 | 142 | 44 | 90 | 8 | 1 |
| Morrow | 5,575 | 41 | 0 | 1 | 29 | 11 | 1,040 | 69 | 909 | 62 | 1 |
| Moultrie | 15,515 | 126 | 1 | 7 | 54 | 64 | 1,323 | 320 | 970 | 33 | 8 |
| Mountain City | 737 | 1 | 0 | 0 | 0 | 1 | 9 | 2 | 7 | 0 | 0 |
| Mount Airy | 1,209 | 2 | 0 | 0 | 0 | 2 | 19 | 6 | 12 | 1 | |
| Mount Zion | 1,612 | 1 | 0 | 0 | 0 | 1 | 7 | 2 | 5 | 0 | 0 |
| Nashville | 4,884 | 22 | 0 | 2 | 4 | 16 | 198 | 81 | 112 | 5 | 1 |
| Newnan | 32,645 | 149 | 2 | 2 | 30 | 115 | 1,058 | 213 | 791 | 54 | 3 |
| Newton | 794 | 0 | 0 | 0 | 0 | 0 | 6 | 6 | 0 | 0 | 0 |
| Nicholls | 2,846 | 1 | 0 | 0 | 0 | 1 | 40 | 7 | 31 | 2 | 0 |
| Norcross | 11,031 | 88 | 1 | 0 | 48 | 39 | 472 | 148 | 258 | 66 | 3 |
| Oakwood | 4,531 | 16 | 0 | 0 | 3 | 13 | 161 | 29 | 122 | 10 | |
| Oxford | 2,631 | 3 | 0 | 1 | 1 | 1 | 39 | 11 | 24 | 4 | 0 |
| Palmetto | 5,242 | 31 | 0 | 0 | 1 | 30 | 133 | 59 | 63 | 11 | |
| Patterson | 687 | 6 | 0 | 0 | 0 | 6 | 14 | 7 | 7 | 0 | 0 |
| Peachtree City | 35,147 | 18 | 0 | 4 | 4 | 10 | 643 | 44 | 513 | 86 | 0 |
| Pearson | 1,966 | 16 | 0 | 1 | 2 | 13 | 121 | 19 | 101 | 1 | 0 |
| Pembroke | 2,565 | 19 | 0 | 2 | 3 | 14 | 113 | 39 | 70 | 4 | |
| Perry | 13,358 | 52 | 0 | 1 | 9 | 42 | 391 | 59 | 311 | 21 | |
| Pine Mountain | 1,323 | 5 | 0 | 0 | 1 | 4 | 56 | 10 | 45 | 1 | |
| Pineview | 516 | 1 | 0 | 0 | 0 | 1 | 1 | 1 | 0 | 0 | 0 |
| Pooler | 16,223 | 28 | 0 | 3 | 9 | 16 | 625 | 101 | 479 | 45 | |
| Portal | 609 | 0 | 0 | 0 | 0 | 0 | 0 | 0 | 0 | 0 | 0 |
| Porterdale | 1,909 | 8 | 0 | 1 | 1 | 6 | 40 | 30 | 8 | 2 | 0 |
| Port Wentworth | 4,744 | 4 | 0 | 0 | 3 | 1 | 138 | 32 | 89 | 17 | 2 |
| Powder Springs | 15,947 | 41 | 0 | 2 | 14 | 25 | 367 | 131 | 210 | 26 | 0 |
| Quitman | 4,616 | 105 | 1 | 3 | 15 | 86 | 255 | 81 | 162 | 12 | 0 |
| Ray City | 803 | 3 | 0 | 0 | 0 | 3 | 28 | 7 | 21 | 0 | 0 |
| Richmond Hill | 11,096 | 10 | 0 | 2 | 6 | 2 | 354 | 58 | 279 | 17 | 0 |
| Rincon | 8,424 | 3 | 0 | 1 | 1 | 1 | 210 | 55 | 146 | 9 | 1 |
| Ringgold | 2,822 | 5 | 0 | 0 | 3 | 2 | 196 | 20 | 165 | 11 | 0 |
| Riverdale | 15,619 | 122 | 1 | 9 | 49 | 63 | 971 | 330 | 528 | 113 | 1 |
| Roberta | 748 | 3 | 0 | 0 | 2 | 1 | 56 | 12 | 42 | 2 | 3 |
| Rockmart | 4,622 | 20 | 0 | 2 | 3 | 15 | 169 | 37 | 117 | 15 | 0 |
| Rome | 36,091 | 211 | 1 | 22 | 85 | 103 | 1,876 | 455 | 1,341 | 80 | 15 |
| Rossville | 3,392 | 23 | 0 | 0 | 3 | 20 | 226 | 70 | 147 | 9 | |
| Roswell | 88,371 | 163 | 5 | 11 | 73 | 74 | 2,349 | 584 | 1,642 | 123 | 1 |
| Royston | 2,762 | 0 | 0 | 0 | 0 | 0 | 45 | 0 | 45 | 0 | 0 |
| Sandersville | 6,224 | 23 | 0 | 1 | 14 | 8 | 344 | 111 | 213 | 20 | 0 |
| Sandy Springs | 82,435 | 189 | 4 | 19 | 124 | 42 | 2,975 | 848 | 1,865 | 262 | |
| Savannah-Chatham Metropolitan | 212,711 | 1,128 | 30 | 46 | 642 | 410 | 10,654 | 2,652 | 6,867 | 1,135 | 50 |
| Screven | 796 | 0 | 0 | 0 | 0 | 0 | 12 | 3 | 5 | 4 | 0 |
| Senoia | 3,793 | 6 | 0 | 0 | 1 | 5 | 52 | 8 | 42 | 2 | 0 |
| Shiloh | 434 | 0 | 0 | 0 | 0 | 0 | 4 | 4 | 0 | 0 | 0 |
| Sky Valley | 217 | 0 | 0 | 0 | 0 | 0 | 2 | 1 | 1 | 0 | 0 |
| Smyrna | 50,485 | 293 | 4 | 6 | 71 | 212 | 1,834 | 563 | 1,114 | 157 | 0 |
| Snellville | 20,464 | 58 | 2 | 4 | 9 | 43 | 806 | 81 | 675 | 50 | |
| Social Circle | 4,940 | 6 | 0 | 1 | 0 | 5 | 94 | 34 | 55 | 5 | |
| Sparta | 1,240 | 14 | 0 | 0 | 1 | 13 | 56 | 25 | 30 | 1 | |
| Springfield | 2,158 | 8 | 0 | 2 | 1 | 5 | 84 | 25 | 53 | 6 | 0 |
| Statesboro | 27,682 | 327 | 1 | 13 | 62 | 251 | 1,536 | 380 | 1,100 | 56 | 2 |

[1] The FBI does not publish arson data unless it receives data from either the agency or the state for all 12 months of the calendar year.

## Table 8. Offenses Known to Law Enforcement, by State and City, 2009—*Continued*

(Number.)

| State/city | Population | Violent crime | Murder and non-negligent man-slaughter | Forcible rape | Robbery | Aggravated assault | Property crime | Burglary | Larceny-theft | Motor vehicle theft | Arson[1] |
|---|---|---|---|---|---|---|---|---|---|---|---|
| **GEORGIA**—*Continued* | | | | | | | | | | | |
| Statham | 3,039 | 27 | 0 | 1 | 2 | 24 | 158 | 37 | 107 | 14 | |
| St. Marys | 16,997 | 92 | 0 | 1 | 12 | 79 | 514 | 115 | 368 | 31 | 5 |
| Stone Mountain | 7,706 | 19 | 0 | 3 | 4 | 12 | 228 | 84 | 60 | 84 | |
| Suwanee | 17,197 | 22 | 0 | 3 | 8 | 11 | 409 | 70 | 309 | 30 | 1 |
| Sylvania | 2,494 | 10 | 0 | 1 | 3 | 6 | 151 | 26 | 118 | 7 | 0 |
| Talbotton | 964 | 3 | 0 | 0 | 0 | 3 | 21 | 6 | 15 | 0 | 0 |
| Tallapoosa | 3,151 | 4 | 0 | 0 | 1 | 3 | 133 | 25 | 91 | 17 | 1 |
| Temple | 4,801 | 26 | 0 | 1 | 1 | 24 | 126 | 22 | 95 | 9 | 0 |
| Tennille | 1,462 | 20 | 0 | 1 | 1 | 18 | 56 | 19 | 37 | 0 | 0 |
| Thomaston | 9,166 | 56 | 0 | 4 | 12 | 40 | 444 | 113 | 318 | 13 | |
| Thomasville | 19,416 | 70 | 0 | 7 | 36 | 27 | 1,025 | 259 | 727 | 39 | 6 |
| Thunderbolt | 2,627 | 13 | 0 | 1 | 7 | 5 | 103 | 32 | 63 | 8 | 1 |
| Tifton | 17,469 | 176 | 1 | 5 | 63 | 107 | 1,305 | 295 | 973 | 37 | 4 |
| Tignall | 611 | 1 | 0 | 0 | 0 | 1 | 10 | 6 | 4 | 0 | 0 |
| Toccoa | 9,130 | 39 | 1 | 2 | 11 | 25 | 351 | 51 | 294 | 6 | |
| Trenton | 2,425 | 3 | 0 | 1 | 0 | 2 | 55 | 8 | 38 | 9 | 0 |
| Tybee Island | 3,914 | 8 | 0 | 2 | 0 | 6 | 77 | 10 | 66 | 1 | 0 |
| Tyrone | 6,857 | 4 | 0 | 0 | 2 | 2 | 106 | 23 | 76 | 7 | 0 |
| Union City | 17,627 | 267 | 1 | 3 | 56 | 207 | 1,412 | 381 | 842 | 189 | |
| Union Point | 1,519 | 4 | 0 | 3 | 1 | 0 | 65 | 17 | 44 | 4 | 0 |
| Valdosta | 49,041 | 249 | 9 | 36 | 85 | 119 | 2,862 | 729 | 2,012 | 121 | 10 |
| Vidalia | 11,449 | 111 | 1 | 1 | 52 | 57 | 754 | 157 | 541 | 56 | |
| Villa Rica | 14,456 | 146 | 1 | 5 | 13 | 127 | 636 | 82 | 523 | 31 | |
| Warner Robins | 62,769 | 370 | 3 | 13 | 111 | 243 | 3,514 | 822 | 2,550 | 142 | 17 |
| Washington | 4,037 | 62 | 0 | 2 | 4 | 56 | 115 | 22 | 92 | 1 | 0 |
| Watkinsville | 2,983 | 2 | 0 | 0 | 1 | 1 | 56 | 8 | 47 | 1 | 0 |
| Waverly Hall | 789 | 1 | 0 | 0 | 0 | 1 | 4 | 3 | 1 | 0 | 0 |
| Waycross[6] | 14,712 | 86 | 2 | 3 | 47 | 34 | 1,189 | 217 | 944 | 28 | 3 |
| Waynesboro | 5,881 | 52 | 0 | 0 | 19 | 33 | 507 | 134 | 334 | 39 | 1 |
| West Point | 3,356 | 56 | 0 | 1 | 13 | 42 | 285 | 69 | 196 | 20 | 0 |
| Whigham | 602 | 0 | 0 | 0 | 0 | 0 | 0 | 0 | 0 | 0 | 0 |
| Willacoochee | 1,539 | 1 | 0 | 0 | 0 | 1 | 12 | 1 | 10 | 1 | 0 |
| Winder | 14,549 | 65 | 0 | 7 | 14 | 44 | 845 | 180 | 633 | 32 | 2 |
| Woodbury | 1,060 | 4 | 0 | 0 | 2 | 2 | 34 | 15 | 15 | 4 | 1 |
| Woodstock | 25,117 | 26 | 0 | 5 | 10 | 11 | 569 | 81 | 488 | 0 | 0 |
| Wrens | 2,205 | 13 | 0 | 0 | 3 | 10 | 142 | 36 | 101 | 5 | 0 |
| Zebulon | 1,257 | 5 | 0 | 0 | 0 | 5 | 41 | 6 | 34 | 1 | |
| **HAWAII** | | | | | | | | | | | |
| Honolulu | 907,124 | 2,537 | 14 | 243 | 869 | 1,411 | 33,375 | 5,999 | 23,647 | 3,729 | 413 |
| **IDAHO** | | | | | | | | | | | |
| Aberdeen | 1,740 | 2 | 0 | 0 | 1 | 1 | 9 | 4 | 4 | 1 | 0 |
| American Falls | 4,067 | 6 | 0 | 1 | 0 | 5 | 113 | 20 | 92 | 1 | 0 |
| Bellevue | 2,200 | 9 | 0 | 0 | 0 | 9 | 34 | 15 | 18 | 1 | 1 |
| Blackfoot | 11,072 | 36 | 1 | 5 | 1 | 29 | 383 | 54 | 312 | 17 | 3 |
| Boise | 206,437 | 538 | 7 | 70 | 62 | 399 | 5,757 | 1,046 | 4,537 | 174 | 55 |
| Bonners Ferry | 2,592 | 3 | 0 | 0 | 0 | 3 | 43 | 15 | 27 | 1 | 1 |
| Buhl | 4,088 | 15 | 0 | 5 | 0 | 10 | 99 | 23 | 68 | 8 | 0 |
| Caldwell | 44,391 | 167 | 2 | 14 | 13 | 138 | 1,125 | 201 | 838 | 86 | 7 |
| Cascade | 989 | 2 | 0 | 0 | 1 | 1 | 7 | 5 | 2 | 0 | 2 |
| Challis | 895 | 2 | 0 | 1 | 0 | 1 | 5 | 2 | 2 | 1 | 0 |
| Chubbuck | 12,087 | 32 | 0 | 1 | 2 | 29 | 507 | 27 | 467 | 13 | 0 |
| Coeur d'alene | 44,406 | 286 | 1 | 41 | 32 | 212 | 1,737 | 348 | 1,284 | 105 | 24 |
| Cottonwood | 1,053 | 5 | 0 | 0 | 0 | 5 | 8 | 3 | 5 | 0 | 0 |
| Emmett | 6,437 | 38 | 0 | 13 | 0 | 25 | 112 | 21 | 87 | 4 | 2 |
| Filer | 2,189 | 2 | 0 | 0 | 0 | 2 | 14 | 2 | 11 | 1 | 0 |
| Fruitland | 4,836 | 15 | 0 | 2 | 1 | 12 | 76 | 28 | 42 | 6 | 0 |
| Garden City | 11,833 | 58 | 1 | 10 | 4 | 43 | 388 | 115 | 259 | 14 | 4 |
| Gooding | 3,180 | 3 | 0 | 0 | 0 | 3 | 34 | 6 | 28 | 0 | 1 |
| Grangeville | 3,099 | 4 | 0 | 1 | 0 | 3 | 98 | 30 | 65 | 3 | 1 |
| Hagerman | 795 | 0 | 0 | 0 | 0 | 0 | 1 | 0 | 0 | 1 | 0 |
| Hailey | 8,081 | 21 | 0 | 1 | 0 | 20 | 69 | 30 | 37 | 2 | 1 |
| Heyburn | 2,674 | 3 | 0 | 1 | 0 | 2 | 28 | 12 | 13 | 3 | 0 |
| Homedale | 2,464 | 2 | 0 | 0 | 0 | 2 | 57 | 13 | 44 | 0 | 0 |
| Idaho Falls | 54,702 | 202 | 2 | 25 | 16 | 159 | 1,624 | 283 | 1,263 | 78 | 8 |
| Jerome | 9,280 | 25 | 0 | 2 | 1 | 22 | 256 | 41 | 188 | 27 | 2 |
| Kamiah | 1,081 | 7 | 0 | 0 | 0 | 7 | 23 | 5 | 16 | 2 | 0 |
| Kellogg | 2,208 | 3 | 0 | 1 | 0 | 2 | 51 | 9 | 37 | 5 | 1 |
| Ketchum | 3,302 | 5 | 0 | 0 | 0 | 5 | 66 | 12 | 52 | 2 | 0 |
| Kimberly | 3,213 | 6 | 0 | 2 | 0 | 4 | 60 | 13 | 40 | 7 | 1 |
| Lewiston | 31,864 | 46 | 1 | 16 | 5 | 24 | 1,192 | 216 | 917 | 59 | 2 |
| McCall | 2,656 | 12 | 0 | 5 | 0 | 7 | 122 | 23 | 98 | 1 | 1 |

[1] The FBI does not publish arson data unless it receives data from either the agency or the state for all 12 months of the calendar year.

[6] Because of changes in the state/local agency's reporting practices, figures are not comparable to previous years' data.

## Table 8. Offenses Known to Law Enforcement, by State and City, 2009—*Continued*

(Number.)

| State/city | Population | Violent crime | Murder and non-negligent man-slaughter | Forcible rape | Robbery | Aggravated assault | Property crime | Burglary | Larceny-theft | Motor vehicle theft | Arson[1] |
|---|---|---|---|---|---|---|---|---|---|---|---|
| **IDAHO**—*Continued* | | | | | | | | | | | |
| Meridian | 71,581 | 115 | 0 | 21 | 14 | 80 | 1,011 | 227 | 764 | 20 | 8 |
| Montpelier | 2,313 | 8 | 0 | 2 | 0 | 6 | 62 | 9 | 50 | 3 | 0 |
| Moscow | 24,604 | 25 | 1 | 12 | 1 | 11 | 549 | 79 | 452 | 18 | 2 |
| Mountain Home | 12,482 | 38 | 0 | 10 | 1 | 27 | 336 | 47 | 281 | 8 | 2 |
| Nampa | 83,875 | 274 | 0 | 39 | 21 | 214 | 1,996 | 470 | 1,423 | 103 | 15 |
| Orofino | 3,024 | 9 | 0 | 0 | 0 | 9 | 100 | 40 | 55 | 5 | 2 |
| Osburn | 1,373 | 0 | 0 | 0 | 0 | 0 | 23 | 8 | 13 | 2 | 0 |
| Parma | 1,881 | 0 | 0 | 0 | 0 | 0 | 33 | 13 | 18 | 2 | 0 |
| Payette | 7,682 | 25 | 0 | 1 | 1 | 23 | 229 | 72 | 151 | 6 | 2 |
| Pinehurst | 1,582 | 0 | 0 | 0 | 0 | 0 | 16 | 6 | 8 | 2 | 0 |
| Pocatello | 55,272 | 170 | 1 | 29 | 11 | 129 | 1,622 | 260 | 1,296 | 66 | 11 |
| Ponderay | 702 | 0 | 0 | 0 | 0 | 0 | 50 | 7 | 42 | 1 | 0 |
| Post Falls | 27,603 | 58 | 1 | 13 | 7 | 37 | 685 | 109 | 542 | 34 | 6 |
| Preston | 5,101 | 2 | 0 | 0 | 0 | 2 | 67 | 9 | 57 | 1 | 1 |
| Priest River | 1,930 | 6 | 0 | 1 | 0 | 5 | 45 | 15 | 26 | 4 | 1 |
| Rathdrum | 7,086 | 9 | 0 | 3 | 0 | 6 | 150 | 38 | 101 | 11 | 0 |
| Rexburg | 30,020 | 5 | 0 | 0 | 0 | 5 | 232 | 28 | 201 | 3 | 0 |
| Rigby | 3,438 | 14 | 0 | 0 | 0 | 14 | 112 | 10 | 97 | 5 | 0 |
| Rupert | 5,025 | 16 | 0 | 3 | 0 | 13 | 136 | 18 | 109 | 9 | 0 |
| Salmon | 2,975 | 11 | 0 | 0 | 1 | 10 | 36 | 10 | 23 | 3 | 0 |
| Sandpoint | 8,519 | 14 | 0 | 3 | 3 | 8 | 209 | 59 | 143 | 7 | 2 |
| Shelley | 4,304 | 1 | 0 | 0 | 0 | 1 | 78 | 7 | 70 | 1 | 0 |
| Soda Springs | 3,040 | 2 | 0 | 0 | 0 | 2 | 28 | 7 | 21 | 0 | 0 |
| Spirit Lake | 1,772 | 4 | 0 | 0 | 0 | 4 | 27 | 5 | 20 | 2 | 0 |
| St. Anthony | 3,409 | 7 | 0 | 1 | 0 | 6 | 56 | 0 | 54 | 2 | 0 |
| St. Maries | 2,642 | 9 | 0 | 1 | 0 | 8 | 30 | 7 | 18 | 5 | 1 |
| Sun Valley | 1,470 | 3 | 0 | 0 | 0 | 3 | 18 | 3 | 15 | 0 | 0 |
| Twin Falls | 43,095 | 153 | 0 | 24 | 5 | 124 | 1,374 | 230 | 1,102 | 42 | 12 |
| Weiser | 5,275 | 1 | 0 | 1 | 0 | 0 | 103 | 52 | 38 | 13 | 1 |
| Wendell | 2,423 | 6 | 0 | 1 | 1 | 4 | 25 | 8 | 15 | 2 | 0 |
| Wilder | 1,474 | 4 | 0 | 0 | 0 | 4 | 20 | 4 | 15 | 1 | 1 |
| **ILLINOIS**[6] | | | | | | | | | | | |
| Addison | 36,968 | | 4 | | 15 | 29 | 799 | 126 | 624 | 49 | 0 |
| Arcola | 2,776 | | 0 | | 0 | 5 | 7 | 0 | 6 | 1 | 0 |
| Arlington Heights | 73,061 | | 2 | | 14 | 38 | 1,265 | 171 | 1,070 | 24 | 5 |
| Aurora | 175,135 | | 5 | | 138 | 531 | 4,222 | 755 | 3,272 | 195 | 21 |
| Aviston | 1,784 | | 0 | | 0 | 0 | 7 | 3 | 4 | 0 | 0 |
| Bartlett | 42,856 | | 0 | | 8 | 9 | 486 | 53 | 422 | 11 | 0 |
| Belgium | 460 | | 0 | | 0 | 0 | 5 | 1 | 3 | 1 | 0 |
| Bellwood | 18,810 | | 4 | | 42 | 68 | 389 | 124 | 224 | 41 | 6 |
| Berkeley | 4,878 | | 0 | | 1 | 7 | 130 | 28 | 98 | 4 | 0 |
| Bloomington | 73,897 | | 2 | | 54 | 291 | 1,891 | 431 | 1,382 | 78 | 19 |
| Blue Island | 22,203 | | 0 | | 60 | 57 | 819 | 281 | 431 | 107 | 3 |
| Broadview | 7,558 | | 2 | | 23 | 16 | 368 | 77 | 251 | 40 | 0 |
| Burbank | 27,529 | | 0 | | 18 | 40 | 658 | 100 | 532 | 26 | 2 |
| Calumet Park | 7,924 | | 2 | | 55 | 19 | 424 | 70 | 309 | 45 | 2 |
| Cambridge | 2,084 | | 0 | | 0 | 0 | 11 | 1 | 9 | 1 | 0 |
| Carlyle | 3,375 | | 0 | | 1 | 2 | 66 | 9 | 56 | 1 | 0 |
| Catlin | 2,111 | | 0 | | 0 | 1 | 18 | 6 | 12 | 0 | 0 |
| Chester | 7,775 | | 0 | | 0 | 17 | 68 | 25 | 40 | 3 | 0 |
| Chicago | 2,848,431 | | 458 | | 15,877 | 15,727 | 120,407 | 26,494 | 78,444 | 15,469 | 610 |
| Cortland | 4,489 | | 0 | | 0 | 3 | 43 | 6 | 33 | 4 | 2 |
| Country Club Hills | 16,783 | | 5 | | 24 | 26 | 638 | 145 | 475 | 18 | 4 |
| Countryside | 5,766 | | 1 | | 4 | 11 | 299 | 18 | 266 | 15 | 0 |
| Danville | 32,076 | | 4 | | 108 | 219 | 2,211 | 791 | 1,338 | 82 | 12 |
| Decatur | 75,651 | | 3 | | 149 | 415 | 3,079 | 1,344 | 1,580 | 155 | 39 |
| Deerfield | 19,797 | | 0 | | 1 | 4 | 190 | 24 | 164 | 2 | 0 |
| Deer Park | 3,373 | | 0 | | 0 | 1 | 66 | 8 | 56 | 2 | 0 |
| De Kalb | 46,253 | | 0 | | 39 | 77 | 1,419 | 213 | 1,171 | 35 | 7 |
| Dixon | 14,931 | | 1 | | 1 | 13 | 569 | 64 | 495 | 10 | 0 |
| East Hazel Crest | 1,528 | | 0 | | 4 | 4 | 101 | 37 | 58 | 6 | 0 |
| East Peoria | 22,769 | | 0 | | 9 | 71 | 703 | 258 | 431 | 14 | 2 |
| Effingham | 12,498 | | 0 | | 2 | 30 | 362 | 48 | 305 | 9 | 2 |
| Elgin | 107,686 | | 3 | | 79 | 167 | 2,244 | 445 | 1,683 | 116 | 13 |
| Fairmount | 624 | | 0 | | 0 | 0 | 0 | 0 | 0 | 0 | 0 |
| Fithian | 550 | | 0 | | 0 | 0 | 0 | 0 | 0 | 0 | 0 |
| Flora | 4,742 | | 0 | | 0 | 9 | 106 | 4 | 99 | 3 | 0 |
| Flossmoor | 9,305 | | 0 | | 4 | 4 | 141 | 37 | 101 | 3 | 0 |
| Freeport | 24,424 | | 0 | | 15 | 40 | 1,156 | 324 | 817 | 15 | 4 |
| Geneseo | 6,430 | | 0 | | 0 | 14 | 99 | 15 | 82 | 2 | 0 |

[1] The FBI does not publish arson data unless it receives data from either the agency or the state for all 12 months of the calendar year.
[6] Because of changes in the state/local agency's reporting practices, figures are not comparable to previous years' data.

# Table 8. Offenses Known to Law Enforcement, by State and City, 2009—*Continued*

(Number.)

| State/city | Population | Violent crime | Murder and non-negligent man-slaughter | Forcible rape | Robbery | Aggravated assault | Property crime | Burglary | Larceny-theft | Motor vehicle theft | Arson[1] |
|---|---|---|---|---|---|---|---|---|---|---|---|
| **ILLINOIS**—*Continued* | | | | | | | | | | | |
| Georgetown | 3,421 | | 0 | | 1 | 6 | 38 | 16 | 22 | 0 | 0 |
| Grayville | 1,570 | | 1 | | 0 | 13 | 25 | 1 | 24 | 0 | 0 |
| Hanover | 786 | | 0 | | 0 | 6 | 18 | 5 | 12 | 1 | 1 |
| Hanover Park | 36,617 | | 4 | | 17 | 48 | 570 | 95 | 443 | 32 | 1 |
| Harwood Heights | 8,031 | | 0 | | 3 | 2 | 243 | 34 | 191 | 18 | 0 |
| Henning | 228 | | 0 | | 0 | 0 | 0 | 0 | 0 | 0 | 0 |
| Hickory Hills | 13,263 | | 1 | | 6 | 6 | 237 | 42 | 184 | 11 | 1 |
| Hinsdale | 18,553 | | 0 | | 4 | 1 | 271 | 39 | 228 | 4 | 1 |
| Homewood | 18,361 | | 0 | | 19 | 11 | 646 | 95 | 532 | 19 | 4 |
| Hoopeston | 5,621 | | 1 | | 0 | 20 | 202 | 50 | 145 | 7 | 0 |
| Indianola | 220 | | 0 | | 0 | 0 | 0 | 0 | 0 | 0 | 0 |
| Johnsburg | 6,894 | | 0 | | 0 | 6 | 103 | 20 | 81 | 2 | 1 |
| Joliet | 151,103 | | 12 | | 142 | 316 | 3,878 | 899 | 2,853 | 126 | 29 |
| Kankakee | 26,615 | | 2 | | 98 | 103 | 1,095 | 271 | 761 | 63 | 10 |
| Kenilworth | 2,387 | | 0 | | 0 | 0 | 34 | 4 | 30 | 0 | 0 |
| Kewanee | 12,229 | | 0 | | 2 | 40 | 673 | 101 | 552 | 20 | 2 |
| Kildeer | 4,196 | | 0 | | 0 | 0 | 42 | 4 | 37 | 1 | 0 |
| Kingston | 1,069 | | 0 | | 0 | 0 | 5 | 1 | 4 | 0 | 0 |
| La Grange Park | 12,311 | | 1 | | 1 | 1 | 103 | 19 | 79 | 5 | 0 |
| Lake Zurich | 20,835 | | 0 | | 3 | 6 | 377 | 35 | 337 | 5 | 4 |
| La Salle | 9,480 | | 0 | | 2 | 18 | 260 | 77 | 179 | 4 | 0 |
| Le Roy | 3,548 | | 0 | | 0 | 6 | 54 | 18 | 34 | 2 | 4 |
| Lincolnshire | 8,196 | | 1 | | 2 | 1 | 100 | 19 | 76 | 5 | 0 |
| Litchfield | 6,613 | | 0 | | 0 | 22 | 200 | 28 | 167 | 5 | 1 |
| Lombard | 42,905 | | 0 | | 11 | 33 | 1,148 | 81 | 1,044 | 23 | 4 |
| Marion | 17,524 | | 2 | | 8 | 62 | 421 | 178 | 211 | 32 | 6 |
| Maryville | 7,747 | | 1 | | 2 | 4 | 94 | 12 | 76 | 6 | 0 |
| McHenry | 27,489 | | 0 | | 4 | 36 | 483 | 58 | 419 | 6 | 1 |
| Melrose Park | 21,712 | | 1 | | 20 | 21 | 691 | 111 | 492 | 88 | 3 |
| Midlothian | 13,583 | | 2 | | 15 | 12 | 429 | 135 | 261 | 33 | 1 |
| Minooka | 11,738 | | 0 | | 2 | 13 | 225 | 18 | 205 | 2 | 1 |
| Morris | 14,027 | | 0 | | 3 | 21 | 607 | 54 | 538 | 15 | 2 |
| Morton | 16,105 | | 0 | | 1 | 8 | 193 | 40 | 152 | 1 | 3 |
| Mount Carroll | 1,641 | | 0 | | 0 | 2 | 21 | 5 | 16 | 0 | 0 |
| Mount Morris | 3,083 | | 0 | | 0 | 0 | 52 | 4 | 48 | 0 | 0 |
| Naperville | 144,731 | | 0 | | 22 | 78 | 2,404 | 296 | 2,047 | 61 | 7 |
| Northfield | 5,418 | | 0 | | 0 | 5 | 107 | 18 | 85 | 4 | 0 |
| Oak Forest | 27,699 | | 2 | | 12 | 24 | 471 | 103 | 347 | 21 | 4 |
| Oak Lawn | 53,028 | | 3 | | 29 | 37 | 1,139 | 180 | 897 | 62 | 7 |
| Oak Park | 53,286 | | 1 | | 147 | 37 | 1,983 | 577 | 1,324 | 82 | 6 |
| Oakwood | 1,418 | | 0 | | 0 | 1 | 19 | 4 | 14 | 1 | 0 |
| Orion | 1,685 | | 0 | | 0 | 0 | 6 | 0 | 5 | 1 | 0 |
| Orland Park | 55,990 | | 1 | | 8 | 16 | 1,300 | 62 | 1,221 | 17 | 3 |
| Palos Hills | 16,844 | | 0 | | 2 | 6 | 208 | 18 | 179 | 11 | 0 |
| Park Ridge | 36,835 | | 0 | | 5 | 8 | 563 | 124 | 424 | 15 | 4 |
| Pawnee | 2,534 | | 0 | | 0 | 4 | 22 | 1 | 21 | 0 | 0 |
| Peoria | 114,241 | | 16 | | 409 | 554 | 5,333 | 1,606 | 3,378 | 349 | 59 |
| Peotone | 4,406 | | 0 | | 0 | 3 | 28 | 6 | 20 | 2 | 0 |
| Potomac | 653 | | 0 | | 0 | 0 | 4 | 2 | 2 | 0 | 0 |
| Quincy | 39,906 | | 0 | | 24 | 161 | 1,442 | 234 | 1,183 | 25 | 3 |
| Rankin | 581 | | 0 | | 0 | 0 | 0 | 0 | 0 | 0 | 0 |
| Rantoul | 12,109 | | 0 | | 17 | 94 | 330 | 130 | 184 | 16 | 9 |
| Richton Park | 12,873 | | 1 | | 13 | 6 | 363 | 106 | 228 | 29 | 1 |
| River Forest | 11,128 | | 0 | | 9 | 5 | 334 | 74 | 252 | 8 | 3 |
| Riverside | 8,207 | | 0 | | 5 | 4 | 190 | 21 | 162 | 7 | 0 |
| Rock Falls | 9,277 | | 0 | | 1 | 14 | 141 | 60 | 71 | 10 | 1 |
| Rockford | 157,943 | 2,061 | 21 | 112 | 596 | 1,332 | 8,606 | 2,459 | 5,697 | 450 | 39 |
| Rock Island | 37,976 | | 1 | | 81 | 268 | 1,680 | 385 | 1,172 | 123 | 14 |
| Romeoville | 40,465 | | 1 | | 11 | 58 | 922 | 148 | 753 | 21 | 2 |
| Rosemont | 3,898 | | 0 | | 2 | 3 | 224 | 22 | 186 | 16 | 0 |
| Rossville | 1,147 | | 0 | | 0 | 0 | 3 | 1 | 1 | 1 | 0 |
| Round Lake Beach | 28,054 | | 0 | | 5 | 28 | 826 | 96 | 721 | 9 | 3 |
| Salem | 7,398 | | 0 | | 1 | 9 | 448 | 75 | 353 | 20 | 0 |
| Sidell | 589 | | 0 | | 0 | 0 | 5 | 2 | 3 | 0 | 0 |
| South Holland | 20,969 | | 1 | | 34 | 10 | 554 | 183 | 325 | 46 | 2 |
| Springfield | 117,973 | | 12 | | 268 | 1,076 | 7,181 | 1,711 | 5,206 | 264 | 43 |
| Tilton | 2,759 | | 0 | | 0 | 4 | 58 | 9 | 46 | 3 | 0 |
| West Chicago | 26,756 | | 1 | | 5 | 19 | 417 | 74 | 310 | 33 | 8 |
| West Dundee | 8,293 | | 0 | | 0 | 0 | 273 | 9 | 263 | 1 | 0 |
| Western Springs | 12,705 | | 0 | | 1 | 0 | 102 | 22 | 78 | 2 | 2 |

[1] The FBI does not publish arson data unless it receives data from either the agency or the state for all 12 months of the calendar year.

## Table 8. Offenses Known to Law Enforcement, by State and City, 2009—*Continued*

(Number.)

| State/city | Population | Violent crime | Murder and non-negligent man-slaughter | Forcible rape | Robbery | Aggravated assault | Property crime | Burglary | Larceny-theft | Motor vehicle theft | Arson[1] |
|---|---|---|---|---|---|---|---|---|---|---|---|
| **ILLINOIS**—*Continued* | | | | | | | | | | | |
| Westmont | 24,985 | | 1 | | 9 | 11 | 458 | 80 | 356 | 22 | 0 |
| Westville | 2,983 | | 0 | | 1 | 9 | 61 | 15 | 44 | 2 | 0 |
| Willowbrook | 8,710 | | 0 | | 4 | 5 | 197 | 27 | 160 | 10 | 0 |
| Winthrop Harbor | 7,263 | | 0 | | 2 | 4 | 160 | 16 | 141 | 3 | 0 |
| **INDIANA** | | | | | | | | | | | |
| Albion | 2,337 | 1 | 0 | 0 | 0 | 1 | 0 | 0 | 0 | 0 | 0 |
| Alexandria | 5,811 | 5 | 0 | 2 | 1 | 2 | 263 | 72 | 183 | 8 | 4 |
| Anderson | 57,020 | 170 | 1 | 34 | 64 | 71 | 3,085 | 722 | 2,148 | 215 | 23 |
| Angola | 7,936 | 7 | 0 | 2 | 0 | 5 | 447 | 29 | 404 | 14 | 2 |
| Auburn | 13,128 | 18 | 0 | 5 | 5 | 8 | 352 | 54 | 290 | 8 | 0 |
| Austin | 4,587 | 72 | 1 | 0 | 5 | 66 | 188 | 51 | 118 | 19 | 0 |
| Avon | 12,722 | 37 | 1 | 1 | 6 | 29 | 509 | 51 | 443 | 15 | 1 |
| Bargersville | 2,770 | 4 | 0 | 0 | 0 | 4 | 2 | 2 | 0 | 0 | 0 |
| Batesville | 6,477 | 40 | 2 | 1 | 2 | 35 | 122 | 20 | 102 | 0 | 0 |
| Bedford | 13,458 | 27 | 2 | 4 | 6 | 15 | 474 | 46 | 405 | 23 | 0 |
| Beech Grove | 14,257 | 42 | 1 | 4 | 24 | 13 | 492 | 98 | 359 | 35 | 0 |
| Berne | 4,389 | 1 | 0 | 1 | 0 | 0 | 61 | 11 | 45 | 5 | 0 |
| Bloomington | 71,845 | 366 | 3 | 44 | 74 | 245 | 3,215 | 883 | 2,185 | 147 | 23 |
| Bluffton | 9,293 | 3 | 0 | 1 | 1 | 1 | 239 | 39 | 196 | 4 | 0 |
| Boonville | 6,736 | 2 | 0 | 0 | 0 | 2 | 179 | 6 | 159 | 14 | 0 |
| Brazil | 8,296 | 10 | 0 | 0 | 1 | 9 | 174 | 30 | 141 | 3 | 0 |
| Bremen | 4,660 | 0 | 0 | 0 | 0 | 0 | 64 | 12 | 48 | 4 | 0 |
| Brownsburg | 20,651 | 29 | 0 | 1 | 3 | 25 | 258 | 51 | 195 | 12 | 1 |
| Burns Harbor | 1,148 | 0 | 0 | 0 | 0 | 0 | 29 | 5 | 19 | 5 | 0 |
| Carmel | 68,424 | 22 | 0 | 2 | 5 | 15 | 897 | 165 | 701 | 31 | 2 |
| Cedar Lake | 11,188 | 5 | 0 | 3 | 0 | 2 | 427 | 71 | 341 | 15 | 3 |
| Charlestown | 7,359 | 2 | 0 | 0 | 0 | 2 | 274 | 81 | 190 | 3 | 0 |
| Chesterfield | 2,733 | 8 | 0 | 0 | 0 | 8 | 62 | 12 | 47 | 3 | 0 |
| Chesterton | 12,968 | 9 | 0 | 0 | 1 | 8 | 235 | 45 | 184 | 6 | 0 |
| Clarks Hill | 689 | 1 | 0 | 0 | 0 | 1 | 2 | 0 | 2 | 0 | 0 |
| Clarksville | 21,921 | 90 | 0 | 11 | 21 | 58 | 1,638 | 238 | 1,291 | 109 | 3 |
| Clinton | 4,766 | 9 | 0 | 0 | 0 | 9 | 66 | 10 | 54 | 2 | 2 |
| Columbia City | 8,386 | 7 | 0 | 2 | 2 | 3 | 150 | 22 | 120 | 8 | 0 |
| Columbus | 40,087 | 53 | 0 | 4 | 24 | 25 | 2,184 | 244 | 1,768 | 172 | 11 |
| Corydon | 2,787 | 3 | 0 | 0 | 1 | 2 | 47 | 16 | 28 | 3 | 0 |
| Crawfordsville | 15,036 | 30 | 1 | 7 | 3 | 19 | 703 | 193 | 490 | 20 | 1 |
| Crown Point | 24,942 | 14 | 1 | 2 | 5 | 6 | 508 | 54 | 415 | 39 | 1 |
| Culver | 1,502 | 10 | 0 | 0 | 0 | 10 | 57 | 10 | 41 | 6 | 0 |
| Danville | 8,319 | 6 | 0 | 4 | 0 | 2 | 118 | 15 | 96 | 7 | 0 |
| Decatur | 9,576 | 7 | 1 | 0 | 0 | 6 | 68 | 8 | 52 | 8 | 4 |
| Delphi | 2,844 | 3 | 0 | 2 | 0 | 1 | 116 | 13 | 96 | 7 | 0 |
| Dyer | 16,148 | 12 | 0 | 0 | 8 | 4 | 329 | 29 | 266 | 34 | 0 |
| East Chicago | 29,728 | 249 | 12 | 14 | 141 | 82 | 1,830 | 430 | 1,189 | 211 | 10 |
| Elkhart | 52,661 | 159 | 8 | 22 | 118 | 11 | 2,534 | 639 | 1,730 | 165 | 22 |
| Ellettsville | 6,107 | 44 | 0 | 1 | 4 | 39 | 157 | 42 | 109 | 6 | 0 |
| Elwood | 8,956 | 8 | 0 | 0 | 8 | 0 | 644 | 182 | 442 | 20 | 2 |
| Evansville | 115,770 | 432 | 3 | 60 | 136 | 233 | 5,376 | 1,110 | 4,038 | 228 | 69 |
| Fairmount | 2,701 | 4 | 0 | 0 | 3 | 1 | 48 | 6 | 42 | 0 | 3 |
| Fishers | 73,538 | 14 | 0 | 0 | 13 | 1 | 701 | 85 | 592 | 24 | 1 |
| Fort Wayne | 251,584 | 876 | 18 | 75 | 485 | 298 | 9,379 | 2,269 | 6,683 | 427 | 45 |
| Fowler | 2,177 | 1 | 0 | 0 | 0 | 1 | 7 | 0 | 5 | 2 | 0 |
| Franklin | 23,704 | 80 | 0 | 7 | 8 | 65 | 823 | 85 | 728 | 10 | 1 |
| Gary | 95,219 | 661 | 49 | 47 | 289 | 276 | 3,408 | 1,493 | 1,069 | 846 | 69 |
| Gas City | 5,658 | 7 | 0 | 0 | 0 | 7 | 140 | 15 | 118 | 7 | 0 |
| Goshen | 32,952 | 36 | 0 | 13 | 14 | 9 | 1,032 | 186 | 803 | 43 | 8 |
| Greendale | 4,372 | 5 | 0 | 1 | 1 | 3 | 26 | 14 | 12 | 0 | 0 |
| Greenfield | 19,262 | 17 | 0 | 5 | 3 | 9 | 398 | 42 | 330 | 26 | 5 |
| Greenwood | 49,136 | 189 | 0 | 2 | 15 | 172 | 1,896 | 154 | 1,672 | 70 | 8 |
| Griffith | 16,205 | 34 | 3 | 2 | 17 | 12 | 581 | 70 | 454 | 57 | 2 |
| Hagerstown | 1,613 | 3 | 0 | 1 | 2 | 0 | 40 | 15 | 25 | 0 | 0 |
| Hammond | 76,085 | 741 | 11 | 30 | 233 | 467 | 3,754 | 938 | 2,314 | 502 | 36 |
| Hartford City | 6,239 | 11 | 0 | 3 | 2 | 6 | 184 | 33 | 147 | 4 | 0 |
| Hebron | 3,707 | 1 | 0 | 0 | 0 | 1 | 9 | 3 | 3 | 3 | 0 |
| Highland | 22,544 | 33 | 1 | 3 | 17 | 12 | 893 | 101 | 737 | 55 | 2 |
| Hobart | 28,173 | 53 | 1 | 3 | 19 | 30 | 1,375 | 162 | 1,126 | 87 | 9 |
| Huntingburg | 6,147 | 0 | 0 | 0 | 0 | 0 | 126 | 33 | 87 | 6 | 0 |
| Huntington | 16,424 | 25 | 0 | 7 | 4 | 14 | 362 | 77 | 274 | 11 | 1 |
| Indianapolis | 813,471 | 9,760 | 100 | 460 | 3,929 | 5,271 | 47,419 | 15,217 | 27,717 | 4,485 | 346 |
| Jasper | 14,224 | 4 | 0 | 1 | 0 | 3 | 168 | 38 | 123 | 7 | 0 |
| Kokomo | 45,562 | 139 | 1 | 19 | 41 | 78 | 2,500 | 482 | 1,955 | 63 | 2 |
| Lafayette | 64,370 | 341 | 0 | 24 | 66 | 251 | 3,121 | 645 | 2,285 | 191 | 10 |

[1] The FBI does not publish arson data unless it receives data from either the agency or the state for all 12 months of the calendar year.

## Table 8. Offenses Known to Law Enforcement, by State and City, 2009—*Continued*

(Number.)

| State/city | Population | Violent crime | Murder and non-negligent man-slaughter | Forcible rape | Robbery | Aggravated assault | Property crime | Burglary | Larceny-theft | Motor vehicle theft | Arson[1] |
|---|---|---|---|---|---|---|---|---|---|---|---|
| **INDIANA**—*Continued* | | | | | | | | | | | |
| La Porte | 21,128 | 46 | 0 | 7 | 15 | 24 | 1,232 | 197 | 990 | 45 | 7 |
| Ligonier | 4,551 | 0 | 0 | 0 | 0 | 0 | 34 | 6 | 22 | 6 | 0 |
| Logansport | 18,551 | 15 | 0 | 4 | 3 | 8 | 701 | 89 | 579 | 33 | 2 |
| Long Beach | 1,546 | 0 | 0 | 0 | 0 | 0 | 3 | 3 | 0 | 0 | 0 |
| Loogootee | 2,568 | 1 | 0 | 0 | 1 | 0 | 20 | 8 | 10 | 2 | 0 |
| Lowell | 8,504 | 18 | 1 | 0 | 2 | 15 | 159 | 19 | 136 | 4 | 0 |
| Marion | 29,987 | 85 | 0 | 19 | 52 | 14 | 1,549 | 252 | 1,163 | 134 | 15 |
| Martinsville | 11,812 | 24 | 0 | 6 | 6 | 12 | 859 | 74 | 752 | 33 | 1 |
| Merrillville | 33,349 | 44 | 0 | 3 | 28 | 13 | 909 | 146 | 664 | 99 | 3 |
| Michigan City | 32,355 | 121 | 0 | 13 | 61 | 47 | 1,740 | 371 | 1,259 | 110 | 6 |
| Mishawaka | 50,378 | 182 | 1 | 15 | 72 | 94 | 3,275 | 459 | 2,629 | 187 | 16 |
| Monticello | 5,249 | 3 | 0 | 0 | 2 | 1 | 183 | 24 | 148 | 11 | 2 |
| Mooresville | 12,037 | 16 | 0 | 2 | 2 | 12 | 349 | 23 | 305 | 21 | 0 |
| Muncie | 64,639 | 387 | 6 | 44 | 123 | 214 | 2,535 | 606 | 1,804 | 125 | 36 |
| Munster | 22,173 | 15 | 0 | 1 | 12 | 2 | 692 | 62 | 593 | 37 | 1 |
| Nappanee | 7,196 | 3 | 0 | 0 | 0 | 3 | 114 | 10 | 102 | 2 | 1 |
| New Albany | 37,237 | 123 | 1 | 8 | 49 | 65 | 2,159 | 421 | 1,616 | 122 | 24 |
| New Castle | 18,236 | 8 | 0 | 2 | 3 | 3 | 1,130 | 216 | 881 | 33 | 3 |
| New Haven | 13,729 | 23 | 0 | 2 | 11 | 10 | 367 | 57 | 280 | 30 | 0 |
| New Whiteland | 5,961 | 22 | 0 | 0 | 1 | 21 | 118 | 10 | 104 | 4 | 0 |
| Noblesville | 43,820 | 49 | 0 | 14 | 14 | 21 | 1,006 | 113 | 849 | 44 | 3 |
| North Liberty | 1,397 | 2 | 0 | 0 | 0 | 2 | 20 | 4 | 16 | 0 | 0 |
| North Manchester | 5,784 | 14 | 0 | 6 | 1 | 7 | 127 | 26 | 98 | 3 | 0 |
| North Vernon | 6,269 | 14 | 0 | 8 | 1 | 5 | 245 | 31 | 209 | 5 | 0 |
| Oakland City | 2,505 | 5 | 0 | 0 | 1 | 4 | 60 | 16 | 42 | 2 | 0 |
| Peru | 12,225 | 25 | 0 | 1 | 4 | 20 | 189 | 48 | 128 | 13 | 5 |
| Plainfield | 28,811 | 38 | 0 | 8 | 3 | 27 | 805 | 95 | 658 | 52 | 0 |
| Plymouth | 11,170 | 15 | 0 | 2 | 6 | 7 | 481 | 35 | 424 | 22 | 1 |
| Portage | 37,373 | 182 | 1 | 10 | 10 | 161 | 1,304 | 222 | 1,028 | 54 | 5 |
| Portland | 6,131 | 3 | 0 | 1 | 2 | 0 | 263 | 21 | 241 | 1 | 1 |
| Rensselaer | 6,285 | 27 | 0 | 3 | 2 | 22 | 246 | 27 | 212 | 7 | 0 |
| Richmond | 36,479 | 142 | 0 | 8 | 45 | 89 | 1,669 | 462 | 1,068 | 139 | 28 |
| Rushville | 6,011 | 13 | 0 | 0 | 2 | 11 | 272 | 61 | 208 | 3 | 0 |
| Salem | 6,538 | 8 | 0 | 0 | 2 | 6 | 3 | 3 | 0 | 0 | 0 |
| Schererville | 29,361 | 21 | 0 | 1 | 13 | 7 | 797 | 82 | 655 | 60 | 0 |
| Scottsburg | 5,896 | 47 | 0 | 2 | 7 | 38 | 365 | 54 | 304 | 7 | 0 |
| Seymour | 19,342 | 91 | 0 | 5 | 8 | 78 | 1,036 | 184 | 807 | 45 | 5 |
| Shelbyville[2] | 18,568 | 6 | 0 | 0 | 0 | 6 | | | 931 | | 0 |
| South Bend | 103,326 | 769 | 14 | 56 | 346 | 353 | 6,113 | 2,086 | 3,702 | 325 | 43 |
| South Whitley | 1,852 | 1 | 0 | 0 | 0 | 1 | 9 | 2 | 7 | 0 | 0 |
| Speedway | 12,567 | 29 | 0 | 0 | 25 | 4 | 494 | 74 | 371 | 49 | 3 |
| St. John | 13,616 | 2 | 0 | 1 | 1 | 0 | 153 | 16 | 125 | 12 | 0 |
| Tell City | 7,493 | 6 | 0 | 4 | 0 | 2 | 163 | 29 | 128 | 6 | 1 |
| Terre Haute | 60,065 | 135 | 1 | 26 | 57 | 51 | 4,187 | 1,114 | 2,722 | 351 | 43 |
| Tipton | 4,968 | 1 | 0 | 1 | 0 | 0 | 209 | 34 | 169 | 6 | 0 |
| Valparaiso | 30,680 | 98 | 1 | 3 | 7 | 87 | 753 | 121 | 595 | 37 | 3 |
| Vincennes | 17,902 | 25 | 0 | 3 | 11 | 11 | 1,267 | 296 | 916 | 55 | 1 |
| Wabash | 10,718 | 9 | 0 | 0 | 7 | 2 | 179 | 50 | 124 | 5 | 1 |
| Walkerton | 2,164 | 4 | 0 | 0 | 0 | 4 | 75 | 24 | 46 | 5 | 1 |
| Warsaw | 13,733 | 16 | 0 | 7 | 9 | 0 | 639 | 58 | 557 | 24 | 11 |
| Washington | 11,400 | 17 | 0 | 8 | 2 | 7 | 663 | 125 | 505 | 33 | 0 |
| Waterloo | 2,160 | 11 | 0 | 0 | 1 | 10 | 55 | 18 | 36 | 1 | 0 |
| Westfield | 21,946 | 26 | 0 | 2 | 7 | 17 | 505 | 56 | 428 | 21 | 4 |
| West Lafayette | 31,092 | 63 | 0 | 7 | 11 | 45 | 498 | 80 | 397 | 21 | 5 |
| Westville | 5,179 | 4 | 0 | 1 | 0 | 3 | 62 | 16 | 40 | 6 | 0 |
| Whitestown | 709 | 2 | 1 | 0 | 0 | 1 | 54 | 11 | 39 | 4 | 0 |
| Whiting | 4,712 | 6 | 1 | 0 | 4 | 1 | 218 | 21 | 176 | 21 | 1 |
| Winchester | 4,562 | 13 | 0 | 0 | 0 | 13 | 320 | 60 | 255 | 5 | 0 |
| Winona Lake | 4,327 | 8 | 0 | 0 | 0 | 8 | 43 | 1 | 41 | 1 | 1 |
| Zionsville | 14,065 | 14 | 0 | 0 | 3 | 11 | 130 | 22 | 102 | 6 | 2 |
| **IOWA** | | | | | | | | | | | |
| Adel | 4,553 | 9 | 0 | 1 | 0 | 8 | 101 | 21 | 77 | 3 | 1 |
| Albia | 3,537 | 11 | 0 | 0 | 0 | 11 | 47 | 16 | 28 | 3 | 0 |
| Algona | 5,285 | 14 | 0 | 0 | 0 | 14 | 36 | 7 | 29 | 0 | 0 |
| Altoona | 14,297 | 22 | 0 | 2 | 6 | 14 | 417 | 59 | 342 | 16 | 1 |
| Ames | 57,173 | 177 | 0 | 23 | 15 | 139 | 1,613 | 279 | 1,285 | 49 | 3 |
| Anamosa | 5,764 | 6 | 0 | 0 | 0 | 6 | 162 | 26 | 131 | 5 | 1 |
| Ankeny | 44,339 | 46 | 0 | 13 | 10 | 23 | 694 | 101 | 580 | 13 | 26 |
| Atlantic | 6,726 | 6 | 0 | 2 | 0 | 4 | 170 | 21 | 139 | 10 | 0 |
| Audubon | 2,082 | 0 | 0 | 0 | 0 | 0 | 36 | 9 | 25 | 2 | 0 |

[1] The FBI does not publish arson data unless it receives data from either the agency or the state for all 12 months of the calendar year.
[2] The FBI determined that the agency's data were underreported. Consequently, those data are not included in this table.

## Table 8. Offenses Known to Law Enforcement, by State and City, 2009—*Continued*

(Number.)

| State/city | Population | Violent crime | Murder and non-negligent man-slaughter | Forcible rape | Robbery | Aggravated assault | Property crime | Burglary | Larceny-theft | Motor vehicle theft | Arson[1] |
|---|---|---|---|---|---|---|---|---|---|---|---|
| **IOWA**—*Continued* | | | | | | | | | | | |
| Bettendorf | 32,734 | 37 | 0 | 4 | 7 | 26 | 599 | 107 | 470 | 22 | 4 |
| Boone | 12,592 | 47 | 0 | 3 | 0 | 44 | 214 | 71 | 130 | 13 | 4 |
| Burlington | 25,172 | 170 | 1 | 10 | 25 | 134 | 985 | 287 | 652 | 46 | 15 |
| Camanche | 4,288 | 1 | 0 | 0 | 0 | 1 | 49 | 7 | 35 | 7 | 0 |
| Carlisle | 3,708 | 5 | 0 | 2 | 0 | 3 | 61 | 28 | 30 | 3 | 0 |
| Carroll | 9,974 | 6 | 0 | 2 | 0 | 4 | 158 | 23 | 125 | 10 | 0 |
| Cedar Falls | 38,271 | 131 | 0 | 21 | 9 | 101 | 653 | 111 | 519 | 23 | 7 |
| Cedar Rapids | 128,779 | 403 | 1 | 43 | 107 | 252 | 5,588 | 1,279 | 4,068 | 241 | 12 |
| Centerville | 5,393 | 22 | 0 | 4 | 0 | 18 | 280 | 82 | 182 | 16 | 3 |
| Chariton | 4,401 | 21 | 0 | 0 | 1 | 20 | 147 | 53 | 89 | 5 | 0 |
| Charles City | 7,435 | 10 | 1 | 0 | 1 | 8 | 139 | 33 | 105 | 1 | 4 |
| Cherokee | 4,629 | 28 | 0 | 0 | 0 | 28 | 66 | 17 | 47 | 2 | 0 |
| Clarinda | 5,474 | 10 | 0 | 2 | 0 | 8 | 152 | 46 | 97 | 9 | 1 |
| Clarion | 2,692 | 4 | 0 | 1 | 0 | 3 | 58 | 13 | 44 | 1 | 1 |
| Clinton | 26,266 | 162 | 2 | 14 | 20 | 126 | 1,073 | 236 | 781 | 56 | 17 |
| Clive | 15,522 | 29 | 0 | 4 | 3 | 22 | 439 | 66 | 363 | 10 | 4 |
| Coralville | 18,884 | 35 | 0 | 4 | 13 | 18 | 583 | 66 | 500 | 17 | 4 |
| Council Bluffs | 59,669 | 527 | 2 | 66 | 97 | 362 | 4,405 | 818 | 3,129 | 458 | 45 |
| Cresco | 3,712 | 2 | 0 | 1 | 0 | 1 | 93 | 26 | 62 | 5 | 2 |
| Creston | 7,597 | 22 | 0 | 1 | 2 | 19 | 260 | 42 | 206 | 12 | 2 |
| Davenport | 101,116 | 739 | 3 | 47 | 221 | 468 | 5,155 | 1,097 | 3,866 | 192 | 22 |
| Decorah | 7,877 | 8 | 0 | 0 | 0 | 8 | 115 | 13 | 99 | 3 | 0 |
| Denison | 7,167 | 8 | 0 | 0 | 1 | 7 | 87 | 12 | 72 | 3 | 0 |
| Des Moines[6] | 196,794 | 1,067 | 6 | 153 | 244 | 664 | 8,688 | 1,830 | 6,146 | 712 | 55 |
| De Witt | 5,286 | 9 | 0 | 0 | 0 | 9 | 86 | 32 | 49 | 5 | 1 |
| Dubuque | 57,192 | 294 | 2 | 15 | 17 | 260 | 1,883 | 483 | 1,323 | 77 | 32 |
| Dyersville | 4,222 | 1 | 0 | 0 | 0 | 1 | 44 | 11 | 33 | 0 | 0 |
| Eagle Grove | 3,269 | 8 | 0 | 1 | 0 | 7 | 55 | 20 | 33 | 2 | 1 |
| Eldora | 2,703 | 6 | 0 | 1 | 0 | 5 | 34 | 11 | 20 | 3 | 0 |
| Eldridge | 4,962 | 5 | 0 | 0 | 1 | 4 | 65 | 21 | 40 | 4 | 0 |
| Emmetsburg | 3,586 | 4 | 0 | 1 | 0 | 3 | 15 | 2 | 13 | 0 | 0 |
| Estherville | 6,255 | 15 | 0 | 0 | 0 | 15 | 100 | 29 | 71 | 0 | 0 |
| Evansdale | 5,121 | 14 | 0 | 1 | 2 | 11 | 112 | 46 | 58 | 8 | 1 |
| Fairfield | 9,177 | 13 | 0 | 4 | 0 | 9 | 280 | 63 | 206 | 11 | 3 |
| Forest City | 4,066 | 6 | 0 | 0 | 0 | 6 | 28 | 17 | 11 | 0 | 0 |
| Fort Dodge | 25,058 | 197 | 3 | 0 | 37 | 157 | 1,298 | 351 | 862 | 85 | 13 |
| Fort Madison | 10,818 | 69 | 1 | 12 | 1 | 55 | 348 | 83 | 249 | 16 | 5 |
| Glenwood | 5,675 | 9 | 0 | 2 | 0 | 7 | 85 | 28 | 52 | 5 | 2 |
| Grinnell | 9,174 | 20 | 0 | 3 | 0 | 17 | 278 | 101 | 175 | 2 | 0 |
| Grundy Center | 2,510 | 2 | 0 | 0 | 0 | 2 | 10 | 0 | 9 | 1 | 0 |
| Hampton | 4,126 | 2 | 0 | 0 | 0 | 2 | 22 | 4 | 18 | 0 | 0 |
| Hawarden | 2,396 | 2 | 0 | 0 | 0 | 2 | 28 | 9 | 15 | 4 | 0 |
| Humboldt | 4,170 | 1 | 0 | 0 | 0 | 1 | 56 | 22 | 32 | 2 | 0 |
| Independence | 6,125 | 8 | 0 | 0 | 2 | 6 | 135 | 28 | 96 | 11 | 2 |
| Indianola | 14,500 | 25 | 0 | 7 | 1 | 17 | 340 | 37 | 288 | 15 | 5 |
| Iowa City | 68,427 | 245 | 1 | 24 | 50 | 170 | 1,549 | 280 | 1,192 | 77 | 4 |
| Iowa Falls | 4,940 | 4 | 0 | 0 | 0 | 4 | 122 | 15 | 104 | 3 | 1 |
| Jefferson | 4,095 | 2 | 0 | 0 | 0 | 2 | 33 | 17 | 15 | 1 | 0 |
| Johnston | 16,725 | 9 | 0 | 3 | 2 | 4 | 202 | 34 | 161 | 7 | 0 |
| Le Mars | 9,114 | 10 | 0 | 4 | 0 | 6 | 200 | 31 | 159 | 10 | 2 |
| Manchester | 4,834 | 31 | 0 | 3 | 0 | 28 | 59 | 17 | 35 | 7 | 2 |
| Maquoketa | 5,882 | 17 | 0 | 4 | 1 | 12 | 205 | 63 | 137 | 5 | 0 |
| Marion | 33,590 | 52 | 0 | 8 | 10 | 34 | 560 | 138 | 394 | 28 | 6 |
| Marshalltown | 25,833 | 126 | 0 | 1 | 6 | 119 | 1,256 | 318 | 867 | 71 | 11 |
| Mason City | 27,142 | 37 | 0 | 12 | 4 | 21 | 1,135 | 203 | 896 | 36 | 4 |
| Monticello | 3,652 | 3 | 0 | 0 | 0 | 3 | 56 | 13 | 37 | 6 | 0 |
| Mount Pleasant | 8,780 | 29 | 0 | 1 | 1 | 27 | 224 | 55 | 157 | 12 | 3 |
| Mount Vernon | 4,196 | 5 | 0 | 1 | 1 | 3 | 64 | 4 | 59 | 1 | 0 |
| Muscatine | 22,480 | 131 | 0 | 23 | 3 | 105 | 598 | 103 | 468 | 27 | 2 |
| Newton | 14,981 | 18 | 0 | 0 | 2 | 16 | 450 | 97 | 329 | 24 | 2 |
| North Liberty | 12,569 | 31 | 0 | 3 | 3 | 25 | 87 | 29 | 49 | 9 | 0 |
| Norwalk | 9,048 | 8 | 0 | 2 | 0 | 6 | 95 | 11 | 81 | 3 | 1 |
| Oelwein | 6,019 | 17 | 0 | 2 | 0 | 15 | 146 | 44 | 95 | 7 | 1 |
| Ogden | 1,968 | 5 | 0 | 0 | 0 | 5 | 28 | 9 | 19 | 0 | 0 |
| Osage | 3,424 | 3 | 0 | 0 | 0 | 3 | 39 | 7 | 30 | 2 | 0 |
| Osceola | 4,708 | 5 | 0 | 0 | 1 | 4 | 121 | 30 | 86 | 5 | 1 |
| Oskaloosa | 11,077 | 24 | 0 | 6 | 2 | 16 | 284 | 56 | 211 | 17 | 1 |
| Ottumwa | 24,276 | 158 | 0 | 8 | 7 | 143 | 1,003 | 210 | 747 | 46 | 12 |
| Pella | 10,238 | 23 | 0 | 0 | 1 | 22 | 126 | 16 | 106 | 4 | 2 |
| Perry | 9,809 | 42 | 0 | 0 | 0 | 42 | 178 | 27 | 148 | 3 | 2 |

[1] The FBI does not publish arson data unless it receives data from either the agency or the state for all 12 months of the calendar year.
[6] Because of changes in the state/local agency's reporting practices, figures are not comparable to previous years' data.

**Table 8. Offenses Known to Law Enforcement, by State and City, 2009**—*Continued*

(Number.)

| State/city | Population | Violent crime | Murder and non-negligent man-slaughter | Forcible rape | Robbery | Aggravated assault | Property crime | Burglary | Larceny-theft | Motor vehicle theft | Arson[1] |
|---|---|---|---|---|---|---|---|---|---|---|---|
| **IOWA**—*Continued* | | | | | | | | | | | |
| Pleasant Hill | 8,873 | 16 | 0 | 3 | 2 | 11 | 129 | 58 | 59 | 12 | 0 |
| Polk City | 3,314 | 2 | 0 | 0 | 0 | 2 | 31 | 13 | 17 | 1 | 0 |
| Prairie City | 1,444 | 0 | 0 | 0 | 0 | 0 | 16 | 11 | 5 | 0 | 0 |
| Red Oak | 5,627 | 7 | 0 | 1 | 0 | 6 | 173 | 61 | 108 | 4 | 2 |
| Sergeant Bluff | 4,093 | 7 | 0 | 0 | 0 | 7 | 38 | 5 | 32 | 1 | 2 |
| Sheldon | 4,740 | 8 | 0 | 0 | 0 | 8 | 81 | 35 | 43 | 3 | 0 |
| Shenandoah | 4,884 | 4 | 0 | 0 | 0 | 4 | 98 | 12 | 81 | 5 | 3 |
| Sioux City | 82,573 | 342 | 3 | 25 | 43 | 271 | 2,833 | 625 | 2,037 | 171 | 19 |
| Spencer | 10,949 | 2 | 0 | 0 | 2 | 0 | 294 | 91 | 202 | 1 | 2 |
| Spirit Lake | 4,742 | 1 | 0 | 0 | 0 | 1 | 113 | 10 | 103 | 0 | 1 |
| State Center | 1,340 | 0 | 0 | 0 | 0 | 0 | 14 | 1 | 13 | 0 | 1 |
| Storm Lake | 9,542 | 33 | 0 | 2 | 1 | 30 | 304 | 62 | 236 | 6 | 8 |
| Story City | 3,406 | 5 | 0 | 1 | 0 | 4 | 41 | 10 | 29 | 2 | 0 |
| Tipton | 2,997 | 2 | 0 | 2 | 0 | 0 | 35 | 4 | 28 | 3 | 0 |
| Urbandale | 39,518 | 48 | 0 | 7 | 7 | 34 | 809 | 143 | 639 | 27 | 3 |
| Vinton | 5,078 | 6 | 0 | 1 | 0 | 5 | 73 | 17 | 55 | 1 | 1 |
| Washington | 7,276 | 42 | 0 | 4 | 1 | 37 | 113 | 55 | 54 | 4 | 1 |
| Waterloo | 66,436 | 599 | 2 | 30 | 140 | 427 | 2,694 | 787 | 1,761 | 146 | 29 |
| Waukee | 13,558 | 18 | 0 | 2 | 0 | 16 | 239 | 107 | 130 | 2 | 1 |
| Waverly | 9,334 | 101 | 0 | 3 | 0 | 98 | 161 | 23 | 130 | 8 | 2 |
| Webster City | 7,672 | 37 | 0 | 2 | 3 | 32 | 233 | 55 | 167 | 11 | 2 |
| West Burlington | 3,298 | 10 | 0 | 0 | 1 | 9 | 162 | 12 | 150 | 0 | 0 |
| West Des Moines | 56,400 | 73 | 0 | 18 | 6 | 49 | 1,772 | 196 | 1,536 | 40 | 9 |
| West Liberty | 3,685 | 2 | 0 | 0 | 0 | 2 | 62 | 19 | 39 | 4 | 0 |
| West Union | 2,416 | 4 | 0 | 0 | 0 | 4 | 40 | 25 | 13 | 2 | 0 |
| Williamsburg | 2,831 | 3 | 0 | 0 | 0 | 3 | 22 | 4 | 16 | 2 | 0 |
| Windsor Heights | 4,616 | 16 | 0 | 1 | 3 | 12 | 229 | 20 | 200 | 9 | 0 |
| Winterset | 4,825 | 5 | 1 | 1 | 0 | 3 | 102 | 13 | 89 | 0 | 0 |
| **KANSAS** | | | | | | | | | | | |
| Abilene | 6,383 | 16 | 0 | 5 | 0 | 11 | 289 | 33 | 246 | 10 | 4 |
| Andover | 10,792 | 14 | 0 | 1 | 2 | 11 | 354 | 54 | 283 | 17 | 0 |
| Arma | 1,511 | 3 | 0 | 1 | 0 | 2 | 41 | 23 | 17 | 1 | 0 |
| Atchison | 10,378 | 47 | 0 | 4 | 2 | 41 | 422 | 98 | 310 | 14 | 4 |
| Auburn | 1,155 | 0 | 0 | 0 | 0 | 0 | 0 | 0 | 0 | 0 | 0 |
| Baldwin City | 4,416 | 1 | 0 | 0 | 0 | 1 | 108 | 18 | 87 | 3 | 1 |
| Basehor | 4,525 | 2 | 0 | 0 | 0 | 2 | 30 | 10 | 20 | 0 | 1 |
| Burlington | 2,667 | 6 | 0 | 0 | 0 | 6 | 32 | 6 | 25 | 1 | 0 |
| Burns | 259 | 0 | 0 | 0 | 0 | 0 | 0 | 0 | 0 | 0 | 0 |
| Bushton | 282 | 0 | 0 | 0 | 0 | 0 | 0 | 0 | 0 | 0 | 0 |
| Chanute | 8,784 | 27 | 1 | 3 | 1 | 22 | 259 | 44 | 209 | 6 | 0 |
| Chetopa | 1,228 | 2 | 0 | 1 | 0 | 1 | 14 | 5 | 9 | 0 | 0 |
| Clay Center | 4,430 | 23 | 0 | 1 | 1 | 21 | 65 | 14 | 47 | 4 | 0 |
| Clearwater | 2,427 | 1 | 0 | 0 | 0 | 1 | 63 | 26 | 36 | 1 | 1 |
| Colony | 375 | 0 | 0 | 0 | 0 | 0 | 0 | 0 | 0 | 0 | 0 |
| Columbus | 3,163 | 8 | 0 | 0 | 0 | 8 | 53 | 8 | 41 | 4 | 1 |
| Colwich | 1,426 | 0 | 0 | 0 | 0 | 0 | 14 | 1 | 12 | 1 | 0 |
| Concordia | 5,158 | 18 | 1 | 5 | 0 | 12 | 190 | 22 | 160 | 8 | 1 |
| Ellinwood | 2,022 | 2 | 0 | 0 | 0 | 2 | 38 | 11 | 24 | 3 | 0 |
| Elwood | 1,118 | 14 | 0 | 0 | 0 | 14 | 39 | 13 | 23 | 3 | 0 |
| Emporia | 26,330 | 81 | 3 | 13 | 5 | 60 | 1,298 | 282 | 979 | 37 | 2 |
| Eskridge | 562 | 0 | 0 | 0 | 0 | 0 | 3 | 3 | 0 | 0 | 0 |
| Eudora | 6,482 | 10 | 0 | 3 | 0 | 7 | 127 | 38 | 87 | 2 | 3 |
| Fairway | 3,831 | 2 | 1 | 0 | 0 | 1 | 30 | 4 | 24 | 2 | 0 |
| Fredonia | 2,372 | 5 | 0 | 0 | 0 | 5 | 57 | 14 | 41 | 2 | 2 |
| Garnett | 3,207 | 26 | 0 | 0 | 1 | 25 | 71 | 24 | 44 | 3 | 0 |
| Girard | 2,712 | 6 | 0 | 0 | 0 | 6 | 51 | 14 | 35 | 2 | 0 |
| Goddard | 4,140 | 4 | 0 | 1 | 0 | 3 | 82 | 23 | 56 | 3 | 1 |
| Grandview Plaza | 1,425 | 13 | 0 | 1 | 0 | 12 | 30 | 10 | 20 | 0 | 0 |
| Hays | 20,405 | 61 | 0 | 5 | 2 | 54 | 502 | 52 | 426 | 24 | 4 |
| Herington | 2,439 | 5 | 0 | 1 | 0 | 4 | 50 | 11 | 36 | 3 | 1 |
| Hiawatha | 3,143 | 3 | 0 | 0 | 0 | 3 | 70 | 9 | 57 | 4 | 1 |
| Hillsboro | 2,615 | 3 | 0 | 1 | 0 | 2 | 46 | 17 | 26 | 3 | 0 |
| Hoisington | 2,875 | 8 | 0 | 3 | 0 | 5 | 23 | 5 | 18 | 0 | 2 |
| Holcomb | 1,992 | 0 | 0 | 0 | 0 | 0 | 23 | 7 | 16 | 0 | 0 |
| Independence | 9,182 | 37 | 1 | 8 | 3 | 25 | 455 | 92 | 349 | 14 | 3 |
| Iola | 5,727 | 22 | 0 | 5 | 0 | 17 | 235 | 42 | 186 | 7 | 6 |
| Kansas City | 142,102 | 940 | 35 | 80 | 318 | 507 | 7,742 | 1,918 | 4,744 | 1,080 | |
| La Cygne | 1,106 | 2 | 0 | 0 | 0 | 2 | 27 | 9 | 18 | 0 | 1 |
| Lawrence | 91,703 | 424 | 0 | 57 | 76 | 291 | 4,390 | 683 | 3,551 | 156 | 20 |
| Leawood | 31,765 | 24 | 0 | 4 | 2 | 18 | 453 | 69 | 372 | 12 | 0 |

[1] The FBI does not publish arson data unless it receives data from either the agency or the state for all 12 months of the calendar year.

**Table 8. Offenses Known to Law Enforcement, by State and City, 2009**—*Continued*

(Number.)

| State/city | Population | Violent crime | Murder and non-negligent man-slaughter | Forcible rape | Robbery | Aggravated assault | Property crime | Burglary | Larceny-theft | Motor vehicle theft | Arson[1] |
|---|---|---|---|---|---|---|---|---|---|---|---|
| **KANSAS**—*Continued* | | | | | | | | | | | |
| Lenexa | 47,601 | 91 | 0 | 12 | 21 | 58 | 1,025 | 122 | 833 | 70 | 5 |
| Lindsborg | 3,236 | 2 | 0 | 1 | 1 | 0 | 67 | 20 | 46 | 1 | 1 |
| Linn Valley | 587 | 1 | 0 | 0 | 0 | 1 | 9 | 5 | 2 | 2 | 0 |
| Maize | 3,200 | 5 | 0 | 2 | 0 | 3 | 57 | 13 | 41 | 3 | 0 |
| Marion | 1,856 | 4 | 0 | 1 | 0 | 3 | 42 | 23 | 15 | 4 | 1 |
| Marysville | 3,101 | 6 | 0 | 0 | 0 | 6 | 24 | 10 | 14 | 0 | 1 |
| McLouth | 828 | 0 | 0 | 0 | 0 | 0 | 18 | 6 | 12 | 0 | 0 |
| McPherson | 13,353 | 29 | 0 | 7 | 2 | 20 | 300 | 57 | 228 | 15 | 1 |
| Merriam | 10,793 | 70 | 0 | 12 | 9 | 49 | 540 | 78 | 408 | 54 | 1 |
| Mission | 9,738 | 27 | 0 | 1 | 10 | 16 | 405 | 53 | 292 | 60 | 2 |
| Moran | 518 | 0 | 0 | 0 | 0 | 0 | 0 | 0 | 0 | 0 | 0 |
| Neodesha | 2,611 | 4 | 0 | 1 | 1 | 2 | 41 | 15 | 23 | 3 | 0 |
| Nickerson | 1,139 | 1 | 0 | 0 | 0 | 1 | 22 | 1 | 20 | 1 | 0 |
| Norton | 2,614 | 1 | 0 | 0 | 0 | 1 | 50 | 12 | 36 | 2 | 4 |
| Oakley | 1,812 | 7 | 0 | 3 | 0 | 4 | 44 | 9 | 34 | 1 | 0 |
| Oberlin | 1,623 | 3 | 0 | 0 | 0 | 3 | 10 | 3 | 5 | 2 | 0 |
| Olathe[6] | 123,321 | 264 | 0 | 48 | 44 | 172 | 2,609 | 321 | 2,126 | 162 | 23 |
| Oskaloosa | 1,146 | 0 | 0 | 0 | 0 | 0 | 0 | 0 | 0 | 0 | 0 |
| Overland Park | 173,688 | 308 | 3 | 28 | 51 | 226 | 4,507 | 534 | 3,628 | 345 | 21 |
| Park City | 7,984 | 14 | 0 | 1 | 2 | 11 | 188 | 38 | 142 | 8 | 1 |
| Pittsburg | 19,693 | 114 | 0 | 11 | 9 | 94 | 1,329 | 246 | 1,026 | 57 | 16 |
| Prairie Village | 21,416 | 20 | 0 | 1 | 7 | 12 | 340 | 104 | 216 | 20 | 2 |
| Rose Hill | 4,103 | 4 | 0 | 0 | 0 | 4 | 73 | 10 | 61 | 2 | 1 |
| Russell | 4,168 | 25 | 0 | 0 | 0 | 25 | 83 | 26 | 50 | 7 | 1 |
| Salina | 46,561 | 151 | 5 | 27 | 30 | 89 | 2,672 | 435 | 2,138 | 99 | 23 |
| Shawnee | 62,508 | 106 | 1 | 18 | 23 | 64 | 1,199 | 176 | 925 | 98 | 22 |
| Spring Hill | 5,578 | 9 | 0 | 0 | 1 | 8 | 98 | 14 | 81 | 3 | 2 |
| Sterling | 2,520 | 5 | 0 | 2 | 0 | 3 | 48 | 10 | 35 | 3 | 0 |
| Topeka | 123,449 | 715 | 10 | 44 | 301 | 360 | 6,702 | 1,663 | 4,632 | 407 | 9 |
| Ulysses | 5,515 | 10 | 0 | 1 | 0 | 9 | 59 | 9 | 47 | 3 | 0 |
| Wa Keeney | 1,692 | 0 | 0 | 0 | 0 | 0 | 17 | 4 | 13 | 0 | 0 |
| Wamego | 4,317 | 9 | 0 | 0 | 0 | 9 | 50 | 9 | 41 | 0 | 0 |
| Wathena | 1,291 | 2 | 0 | 0 | 0 | 2 | 34 | 14 | 20 | 0 | 0 |
| Wellsville | 1,751 | 1 | 0 | 0 | 0 | 1 | 50 | 22 | 28 | 0 | 2 |
| Westwood | 1,838 | 2 | 0 | 0 | 0 | 2 | 42 | 5 | 37 | 0 | 0 |
| Wichita | 367,635 | 3,245 | 25 | 254 | 527 | 2,439 | 19,597 | 4,045 | 13,886 | 1,666 | 180 |
| Yates Center | 1,354 | 2 | 0 | 0 | 0 | 2 | 21 | 7 | 13 | 1 | 0 |
| **KENTUCKY[6]** | | | | | | | | | | | |
| Albany | 2,321 | 0 | 0 | 0 | 0 | 0 | 8 | 1 | 7 | 0 | 0 |
| Alexandria | 8,605 | 9 | 0 | 1 | 4 | 4 | 219 | 28 | 183 | 8 | 1 |
| Anchorage | 3,417 | 1 | 0 | 0 | 0 | 1 | 34 | 9 | 25 | 0 | 0 |
| Ashland | 21,276 | 81 | 0 | 16 | 35 | 30 | 1,389 | 424 | 921 | 44 | 4 |
| Auburn | 1,506 | 1 | 0 | 1 | 0 | 0 | 23 | 7 | 16 | 0 | 1 |
| Audubon Park | 1,676 | 5 | 0 | 0 | 5 | 0 | 85 | 16 | 59 | 10 | 0 |
| Barbourville | 3,614 | 4 | 0 | 2 | 1 | 1 | 34 | 4 | 25 | 5 | 0 |
| Bardstown | 11,292 | 23 | 0 | 6 | 7 | 10 | 329 | 83 | 233 | 13 | 1 |
| Bardwell | 772 | 0 | 0 | 0 | 0 | 0 | 3 | 2 | 1 | 0 | 0 |
| Beattyville | 1,113 | 0 | 0 | 0 | 0 | 0 | 4 | 2 | 2 | 0 | 0 |
| Beaver Dam | 3,144 | 3 | 0 | 0 | 0 | 3 | 15 | 1 | 10 | 4 | 2 |
| Bellevue | 5,788 | 14 | 0 | 2 | 7 | 5 | 361 | 37 | 306 | 18 | 0 |
| Benham | 524 | 1 | 0 | 1 | 0 | 0 | 2 | 1 | 1 | 0 | 0 |
| Benton | 4,370 | 2 | 0 | 0 | 2 | 0 | 128 | 26 | 100 | 2 | 0 |
| Berea | 14,825 | 17 | 1 | 4 | 8 | 4 | 433 | 115 | 305 | 13 | 1 |
| Bowling Green | 55,754 | 230 | 3 | 51 | 72 | 104 | 3,088 | 543 | 2,400 | 145 | 2 |
| Bradfordsville | 324 | 0 | 0 | 0 | 0 | 0 | 0 | 0 | 0 | 0 | 0 |
| Brandenburg | 2,196 | 0 | 0 | 0 | 0 | 0 | 61 | 13 | 48 | 0 | 0 |
| Brownsville | 1,049 | 1 | 0 | 0 | 0 | 1 | 6 | 2 | 4 | 0 | 0 |
| Burnside | 697 | 1 | 0 | 0 | 1 | 0 | 35 | 13 | 19 | 3 | 0 |
| Cadiz | 2,592 | 4 | 0 | 1 | 0 | 3 | 78 | 14 | 62 | 2 | 1 |
| Calhoun | 783 | 0 | 0 | 0 | 0 | 0 | 0 | 0 | 0 | 0 | 0 |
| Calvert City | 2,769 | 0 | 0 | 0 | 0 | 0 | 54 | 17 | 35 | 2 | 0 |
| Campbellsville | 11,072 | 20 | 0 | 2 | 9 | 9 | 298 | 80 | 204 | 14 | 1 |
| Catlettsburg | 1,928 | 8 | 0 | 2 | 4 | 2 | 115 | 18 | 96 | 1 | 1 |
| Cave City | 2,014 | 3 | 0 | 2 | 0 | 1 | 42 | 20 | 21 | 1 | 0 |
| Central City | 5,678 | 5 | 0 | 1 | 1 | 3 | 66 | 9 | 52 | 5 | 0 |
| Clarkson | 843 | 0 | 0 | 0 | 0 | 0 | 15 | 9 | 6 | 0 | 0 |
| Clay City | 1,364 | 2 | 0 | 0 | 1 | 1 | 26 | 8 | 18 | 0 | 0 |
| Clinton | 1,321 | 2 | 0 | 0 | 0 | 2 | 7 | 6 | 1 | 0 | 0 |
| Cloverport | 1,232 | 0 | 0 | 0 | 0 | 0 | 2 | 2 | 0 | 0 | 0 |

[1] The FBI does not publish arson data unless it receives data from either the agency or the state for all 12 months of the calendar year.
[6] Because of changes in the state/local agency's reporting practices, figures are not comparable to previous years' data.

## Table 8. Offenses Known to Law Enforcement, by State and City, 2009—*Continued*

(Number.)

| State/city | Population | Violent crime | Murder and non-negligent man-slaughter | Forcible rape | Robbery | Aggravated assault | Property crime | Burglary | Larceny-theft | Motor vehicle theft | Arson[1] |
|---|---|---|---|---|---|---|---|---|---|---|---|
| **KENTUCKY**—*Continued* | | | | | | | | | | | |
| Coal Run Village | 625 | 0 | 0 | 0 | 0 | 0 | 8 | 1 | 7 | 0 | 0 |
| Cold Spring | 6,072 | 6 | 0 | 1 | 4 | 1 | 151 | 13 | 136 | 2 | 0 |
| Columbia | 4,296 | 1 | 0 | 0 | 1 | 0 | 10 | 3 | 6 | 1 | 0 |
| Corbin | 8,376 | 20 | 1 | 2 | 9 | 8 | 363 | 70 | 283 | 10 | 8 |
| Covington | 43,215 | 354 | 1 | 39 | 180 | 134 | 2,267 | 624 | 1,464 | 179 | 31 |
| Cumberland | 2,327 | 2 | 0 | 1 | 1 | 0 | 16 | 12 | 2 | 2 | 0 |
| Cynthiana | 6,277 | 15 | 0 | 1 | 5 | 9 | 358 | 85 | 263 | 10 | 0 |
| Danville | 15,530 | 40 | 0 | 5 | 13 | 22 | 557 | 136 | 408 | 13 | 5 |
| Dawson Springs | 2,895 | 3 | 0 | 0 | 1 | 2 | 39 | 19 | 19 | 1 | 0 |
| Dayton | 5,400 | 18 | 1 | 1 | 7 | 9 | 175 | 49 | 123 | 3 | 1 |
| Dry Ridge | 2,245 | 1 | 0 | 0 | 1 | 0 | 10 | 3 | 5 | 2 | 0 |
| Earlington | 1,563 | 1 | 0 | 0 | 1 | 0 | 7 | 1 | 6 | 0 | 0 |
| Eddyville | 2,423 | 0 | 0 | 0 | 0 | 0 | 46 | 6 | 39 | 1 | 0 |
| Edgewood | 8,858 | 4 | 0 | 1 | 2 | 1 | 142 | 22 | 113 | 7 | 0 |
| Edmonton | 1,650 | 0 | 0 | 0 | 0 | 0 | 10 | 5 | 5 | 0 | 0 |
| Elizabethtown | 24,321 | 52 | 1 | 5 | 25 | 21 | 1,058 | 152 | 878 | 28 | 6 |
| Elkton | 1,981 | 1 | 0 | 0 | 0 | 1 | 25 | 7 | 13 | 5 | 1 |
| Elsmere | 7,908 | 11 | 0 | 5 | 5 | 1 | 122 | 40 | 75 | 7 | 1 |
| Eminence | 2,213 | 4 | 0 | 1 | 0 | 3 | 21 | 9 | 9 | 3 | 0 |
| Erlanger | 21,299 | 27 | 0 | 8 | 13 | 6 | 502 | 102 | 376 | 24 | 2 |
| Evarts | 1,019 | 6 | 1 | 1 | 1 | 3 | 15 | 7 | 8 | 0 | 1 |
| Falmouth | 2,058 | 4 | 0 | 1 | 0 | 3 | 88 | 20 | 65 | 3 | 0 |
| Ferguson | 943 | 0 | 0 | 0 | 0 | 0 | 1 | 1 | 0 | 0 | 0 |
| Flatwoods | 7,663 | 8 | 0 | 0 | 5 | 3 | 135 | 64 | 66 | 5 | 0 |
| Flemingsburg | 2,682 | 1 | 0 | 0 | 0 | 1 | 66 | 21 | 39 | 6 | 0 |
| Florence | 28,232 | 207 | 0 | 8 | 46 | 153 | 1,478 | 134 | 1,278 | 66 | 9 |
| Fort Mitchell | 7,507 | 3 | 0 | 1 | 1 | 1 | 180 | 24 | 147 | 9 | 0 |
| Fort Thomas | 15,089 | 3 | 0 | 0 | 1 | 2 | 204 | 44 | 149 | 11 | 0 |
| Fort Wright | 5,425 | 14 | 0 | 1 | 11 | 2 | 340 | 39 | 292 | 9 | 1 |
| Frankfort | 27,272 | 82 | 0 | 7 | 29 | 46 | 999 | 186 | 753 | 60 | 4 |
| Franklin | 7,981 | 14 | 0 | 3 | 4 | 7 | 355 | 74 | 261 | 20 | 1 |
| Fulton | 2,406 | 7 | 0 | 3 | 2 | 2 | 91 | 27 | 60 | 4 | 0 |
| Gamaliel | 426 | 0 | 0 | 0 | 0 | 0 | 1 | 1 | 0 | 0 | 0 |
| Georgetown | 21,962 | 111 | 0 | 3 | 12 | 96 | 974 | 124 | 814 | 36 | 0 |
| Glasgow | 14,440 | 27 | 0 | 7 | 5 | 15 | 305 | 80 | 216 | 9 | 11 |
| Graymoor-Devondale | 3,215 | 1 | 0 | 0 | 1 | 0 | 95 | 32 | 55 | 8 | 0 |
| Grayson | 3,996 | 8 | 0 | 0 | 6 | 2 | 80 | 20 | 57 | 3 | 2 |
| Greensburg | 2,416 | 1 | 0 | 0 | 0 | 1 | 29 | 11 | 17 | 1 | 0 |
| Greenup | 1,184 | 0 | 0 | 0 | 0 | 0 | 1 | 0 | 1 | 0 | 0 |
| Greenville | 4,218 | 4 | 0 | 1 | 0 | 3 | 12 | 8 | 4 | 0 | 0 |
| Guthrie | 1,453 | 3 | 0 | 1 | 0 | 2 | 13 | 5 | 6 | 2 | 0 |
| Hardinsburg | 2,443 | 2 | 0 | 0 | 0 | 2 | 13 | 3 | 9 | 1 | 0 |
| Harlan | 1,843 | 6 | 0 | 1 | 2 | 3 | 57 | 8 | 46 | 3 | 1 |
| Harrodsburg | 8,195 | 19 | 1 | 7 | 5 | 6 | 130 | 51 | 68 | 11 | 1 |
| Hartford | 2,677 | 1 | 0 | 0 | 0 | 1 | 15 | 6 | 8 | 1 | 1 |
| Hazard | 4,789 | 15 | 0 | 4 | 5 | 6 | 269 | 37 | 221 | 11 | 4 |
| Henderson | 27,984 | 49 | 1 | 10 | 23 | 15 | 1,046 | 174 | 838 | 34 | 2 |
| Heritage Creek | 1,831 | 0 | 0 | 0 | 0 | 0 | 7 | 7 | 0 | 0 | 0 |
| Highland Heights Southgate | 8,948 | 57 | 0 | 2 | 3 | 52 | 130 | 26 | 98 | 6 | 0 |
| Hillview | 7,630 | 13 | 0 | 1 | 4 | 8 | 219 | 54 | 149 | 16 | 2 |
| Hodgenville | 2,762 | 0 | 0 | 0 | 0 | 0 | 24 | 11 | 13 | 0 | 0 |
| Hopkinsville | 32,294 | 103 | 2 | 16 | 43 | 42 | 1,292 | 388 | 849 | 55 | 10 |
| Horse Cave | 2,334 | 0 | 0 | 0 | 0 | 0 | 7 | 4 | 3 | 0 | 0 |
| Independence | 22,572 | 23 | 0 | 7 | 5 | 11 | 311 | 85 | 210 | 16 | 3 |
| Indian Hills | 3,552 | 0 | 0 | 0 | 0 | 0 | 35 | 12 | 22 | 1 | 0 |
| Inez | 431 | 1 | 0 | 0 | 0 | 1 | 2 | 0 | 2 | 0 | 0 |
| Irvine | 2,648 | 7 | 0 | 1 | 2 | 4 | 60 | 24 | 35 | 1 | 0 |
| Irvington | 1,417 | 2 | 0 | 0 | 0 | 2 | 5 | 2 | 3 | 0 | 0 |
| Jackson | 2,387 | 2 | 0 | 0 | 1 | 1 | 43 | 13 | 29 | 1 | 0 |
| Jamestown | 1,750 | 0 | 0 | 0 | 0 | 0 | 18 | 10 | 7 | 1 | 0 |
| Jeffersontown | 26,199 | 64 | 0 | 11 | 35 | 18 | 635 | 122 | 464 | 49 | 0 |
| Jenkins | 2,228 | 1 | 0 | 0 | 1 | 0 | 9 | 1 | 7 | 1 | 0 |
| Junction City | 2,212 | 0 | 0 | 0 | 0 | 0 | 3 | 0 | 2 | 1 | 0 |
| La Grange | 6,354 | 13 | 1 | 4 | 4 | 4 | 173 | 23 | 141 | 9 | 0 |
| Lakeside Park-Crestview Hills | 6,470 | 1 | 0 | 0 | 1 | 0 | 165 | 21 | 141 | 3 | 0 |
| Lancaster | 4,473 | 7 | 0 | 0 | 1 | 6 | 110 | 32 | 76 | 2 | 1 |
| Lawrenceburg | 10,071 | 11 | 0 | 1 | 1 | 9 | 79 | 19 | 55 | 5 | 0 |
| Lebanon | 5,993 | 17 | 1 | 2 | 2 | 12 | 178 | 85 | 86 | 7 | 1 |
| Leitchfield | 6,572 | 13 | 0 | 3 | 1 | 9 | 163 | 47 | 108 | 8 | 0 |
| Lewisburg | 913 | 0 | 0 | 0 | 0 | 0 | 10 | 2 | 8 | 0 | 0 |

[1] The FBI does not publish arson data unless it receives data from either the agency or the state for all 12 months of the calendar year.

## Table 8. Offenses Known to Law Enforcement, by State and City, 2009—*Continued*

(Number.)

| State/city | Population | Violent crime | Murder and non-negligent man-slaughter | Forcible rape | Robbery | Aggravated assault | Property crime | Burglary | Larceny-theft | Motor vehicle theft | Arson[1] |
|---|---|---|---|---|---|---|---|---|---|---|---|
| **KENTUCKY**—*Continued* | | | | | | | | | | | |
| Lexington | 296,406 | 1,760 | 13 | 107 | 578 | 1,062 | 10,124 | 2,427 | 7,154 | 543 | 29 |
| Liberty | 1,898 | 2 | 0 | 0 | 0 | 2 | 15 | 6 | 7 | 2 | 0 |
| London | 8,020 | 9 | 0 | 1 | 2 | 6 | 400 | 52 | 328 | 20 | 0 |
| Louisa | 2,096 | 6 | 0 | 1 | 3 | 2 | 60 | 18 | 41 | 1 | 0 |
| Louisville Metro | 631,260 | 3,769 | 62 | 230 | 1,570 | 1,907 | 26,907 | 7,085 | 18,094 | 1,728 | 239 |
| Ludlow | 4,856 | 5 | 0 | 1 | 3 | 1 | 175 | 51 | 114 | 10 | 0 |
| Lynch | 812 | 1 | 0 | 1 | 0 | 0 | 3 | 1 | 2 | 0 | 0 |
| Lynnview | 1,044 | 3 | 0 | 0 | 2 | 1 | 7 | 3 | 4 | 0 | 0 |
| Madisonville | 19,083 | 69 | 1 | 19 | 13 | 36 | 593 | 150 | 419 | 24 | 0 |
| Manchester | 1,939 | 2 | 0 | 0 | 1 | 1 | 55 | 11 | 37 | 7 | 0 |
| Marion | 3,091 | 5 | 0 | 1 | 0 | 4 | 52 | 12 | 37 | 3 | 1 |
| Mayfield | 10,167 | 28 | 0 | 4 | 4 | 20 | 272 | 76 | 184 | 12 | 2 |
| Maysville | 9,277 | 15 | 0 | 4 | 6 | 5 | 484 | 144 | 329 | 11 | 1 |
| Meadow Vale | 859 | 0 | 0 | 0 | 0 | 0 | 12 | 2 | 9 | 1 | 0 |
| Middlesboro | 9,881 | 24 | 0 | 4 | 10 | 10 | 572 | 74 | 496 | 2 | 1 |
| Monticello | 6,182 | 7 | 0 | 1 | 4 | 2 | 160 | 54 | 100 | 6 | 2 |
| Morehead | 7,718 | 13 | 0 | 1 | 9 | 3 | 218 | 36 | 175 | 7 | 1 |
| Morganfield | 3,274 | 3 | 0 | 0 | 0 | 3 | 113 | 20 | 89 | 4 | 0 |
| Morgantown | 2,566 | 2 | 0 | 1 | 0 | 1 | 9 | 3 | 5 | 1 | 0 |
| Mortons Gap | 935 | 0 | 0 | 0 | 0 | 0 | 0 | 0 | 0 | 0 | 0 |
| Mount Sterling | 7,026 | 27 | 1 | 0 | 5 | 21 | 451 | 86 | 355 | 10 | 0 |
| Mount Vernon | 2,612 | 8 | 0 | 0 | 4 | 4 | 38 | 14 | 22 | 2 | 0 |
| Mount Washington | 12,414 | 6 | 0 | 1 | 1 | 4 | 188 | 62 | 109 | 17 | 1 |
| Munfordville | 1,616 | 9 | 0 | 8 | 0 | 1 | 17 | 6 | 10 | 1 | 0 |
| Murray | 16,709 | 26 | 0 | 9 | 7 | 10 | 636 | 174 | 434 | 28 | 0 |
| New Castle | 908 | 0 | 0 | 0 | 0 | 0 | 0 | 0 | 0 | 0 | 0 |
| Nicholasville | 27,162 | 65 | 0 | 6 | 28 | 31 | 1,259 | 253 | 967 | 39 | 6 |
| Nortonville | 1,231 | 0 | 0 | 0 | 0 | 0 | 8 | 2 | 6 | 0 | 0 |
| Oak Grove | 9,480 | 32 | 0 | 5 | 21 | 6 | 349 | 163 | 163 | 23 | 1 |
| Olive Hill | 1,820 | 0 | 0 | 0 | 0 | 0 | 30 | 6 | 21 | 3 | 0 |
| Owensboro | 55,651 | 119 | 1 | 36 | 34 | 48 | 2,340 | 417 | 1,841 | 82 | 3 |
| Owenton | 1,486 | 1 | 0 | 0 | 0 | 1 | 5 | 2 | 1 | 2 | 0 |
| Owingsville | 1,684 | 0 | 0 | 0 | 0 | 0 | 57 | 11 | 45 | 1 | 0 |
| Paducah | 25,439 | 107 | 4 | 20 | 49 | 34 | 1,473 | 225 | 1,179 | 69 | 7 |
| Paintsville | 4,226 | 6 | 0 | 0 | 2 | 4 | 86 | 12 | 63 | 11 | 0 |
| Park Hills | 2,762 | 0 | 0 | 0 | 0 | 0 | 14 | 8 | 5 | 1 | 0 |
| Pewee Valley | 1,625 | 0 | 0 | 0 | 0 | 0 | 2 | 0 | 2 | 0 | 0 |
| Pikeville | 6,406 | 11 | 0 | 2 | 1 | 8 | 433 | 28 | 396 | 9 | 1 |
| Pioneer Village | 2,732 | 1 | 0 | 1 | 0 | 0 | 2 | 1 | 1 | 0 | 0 |
| Prestonsburg | 3,861 | 5 | 0 | 2 | 2 | 1 | 106 | 27 | 70 | 9 | 0 |
| Princeton | 6,384 | 21 | 0 | 4 | 6 | 11 | 165 | 38 | 120 | 7 | 1 |
| Providence | 3,399 | 4 | 0 | 0 | 0 | 4 | 73 | 19 | 50 | 4 | 0 |
| Raceland | 2,630 | 1 | 0 | 0 | 0 | 1 | 62 | 21 | 40 | 1 | 0 |
| Radcliff | 22,008 | 281 | 1 | 19 | 12 | 249 | 729 | 165 | 546 | 18 | 7 |
| Richmond | 33,546 | 91 | 0 | 17 | 34 | 40 | 1,562 | 337 | 1,171 | 54 | 3 |
| Russell | 3,584 | 6 | 0 | 0 | 4 | 2 | 98 | 20 | 77 | 1 | 0 |
| Russell Springs | 2,345 | 0 | 0 | 0 | 0 | 0 | 96 | 25 | 69 | 2 | 0 |
| Russellville | 7,281 | 18 | 0 | 3 | 4 | 11 | 227 | 59 | 159 | 9 | 0 |
| Sadieville | 326 | 0 | 0 | 0 | 0 | 0 | 1 | 0 | 1 | 0 | 0 |
| Salyersville | 1,566 | 0 | 0 | 0 | 0 | 0 | 11 | 4 | 7 | 0 | 0 |
| Science Hill | 674 | 0 | 0 | 0 | 0 | 0 | 4 | 2 | 2 | 0 | 0 |
| Scottsville | 4,610 | 0 | 0 | 0 | 0 | 0 | 13 | 7 | 6 | 0 | 0 |
| Shelbyville | 11,422 | 28 | 1 | 7 | 9 | 11 | 359 | 78 | 266 | 15 | 1 |
| Shepherdsville | 9,293 | 24 | 0 | 7 | 5 | 12 | 439 | 87 | 333 | 19 | 1 |
| Shively | 16,816 | 81 | 0 | 3 | 56 | 22 | 730 | 227 | 424 | 79 | 2 |
| Silver Grove | 1,147 | 3 | 0 | 1 | 1 | 1 | 21 | 8 | 12 | 1 | 0 |
| Somerset | 12,570 | 38 | 1 | 8 | 13 | 16 | 522 | 71 | 438 | 13 | 3 |
| Springfield | 2,894 | 11 | 0 | 2 | 1 | 8 | 21 | 8 | 10 | 3 | 0 |
| Stamping Ground | 691 | 0 | 0 | 0 | 0 | 0 | 3 | 1 | 2 | 0 | 0 |
| Stanford | 3,396 | 4 | 0 | 0 | 2 | 2 | 19 | 9 | 9 | 1 | 0 |
| Stanton | 3,162 | 3 | 0 | 1 | 1 | 1 | 70 | 22 | 46 | 2 | 0 |
| St. Matthews | 18,871 | 27 | 0 | 4 | 20 | 3 | 776 | 114 | 638 | 24 | 0 |
| Strathmoor Village | 697 | 0 | 0 | 0 | 0 | 0 | 14 | 2 | 12 | 0 | 0 |
| Sturgis | 1,912 | 1 | 0 | 1 | 0 | 0 | 21 | 10 | 10 | 1 | 0 |
| Taylorsville | 1,258 | 1 | 0 | 0 | 1 | 0 | 30 | 4 | 25 | 1 | 0 |
| Tompkinsville | 2,604 | 1 | 0 | 0 | 0 | 1 | 7 | 4 | 1 | 2 | 0 |
| Trenton | 428 | 0 | 0 | 0 | 0 | 0 | 3 | 2 | 1 | 0 | 0 |
| Uniontown | 1,015 | 0 | 0 | 0 | 0 | 0 | 6 | 3 | 3 | 0 | 0 |
| Vanceburg | 1,693 | 2 | 0 | 0 | 1 | 1 | 10 | 4 | 5 | 1 | 0 |
| Versailles | 7,817 | 25 | 0 | 7 | 3 | 15 | 576 | 164 | 387 | 25 | 0 |
| Vine Grove | 4,386 | 4 | 0 | 0 | 1 | 3 | 119 | 69 | 48 | 2 | 0 |

[1] The FBI does not publish arson data unless it receives data from either the agency or the state for all 12 months of the calendar year.

## Table 8. Offenses Known to Law Enforcement, by State and City, 2009—*Continued*

(Number.)

| State/city | Population | Violent crime | Murder and non-negligent man-slaughter | Forcible rape | Robbery | Aggravated assault | Property crime | Burglary | Larceny-theft | Motor vehicle theft | Arson[1] |
|---|---|---|---|---|---|---|---|---|---|---|---|
| **KENTUCKY**—*Continued* | | | | | | | | | | | |
| Warsaw | 1,788 | 1 | 0 | 1 | 0 | 0 | 20 | 8 | 12 | 0 | 0 |
| West Liberty | 3,289 | 4 | 0 | 1 | 1 | 2 | 63 | 13 | 47 | 3 | 2 |
| West Point | 961 | 0 | 0 | 0 | 0 | 0 | 7 | 3 | 3 | 1 | 1 |
| Williamsburg | 5,230 | 12 | 0 | 1 | 5 | 6 | 119 | 41 | 73 | 5 | 0 |
| Williamstown | 3,565 | 1 | 0 | 0 | 1 | 0 | 82 | 19 | 54 | 9 | 0 |
| Wilmore | 6,016 | 4 | 0 | 1 | 0 | 3 | 150 | 16 | 124 | 10 | 0 |
| Winchester | 16,583 | 29 | 0 | 3 | 15 | 11 | 743 | 160 | 561 | 22 | 4 |
| Worthington | 1,677 | 0 | 0 | 0 | 0 | 0 | 3 | 3 | 0 | 0 | 0 |
| **LOUISIANA** | | | | | | | | | | | |
| Addis | 3,652 | 4 | 0 | 0 | 0 | 4 | 1 | 0 | 1 | 0 | 0 |
| Alexandria | 48,886 | 586 | 6 | 17 | 176 | 387 | 4,117 | 1,133 | 2,862 | 122 | |
| Amite | 4,343 | 75 | 1 | 3 | 5 | 66 | 520 | 151 | 357 | 12 | 3 |
| Baker | 13,315 | 41 | 1 | 3 | 4 | 33 | 495 | 113 | 362 | 20 | 2 |
| Basile | 2,372 | 1 | 0 | 0 | 0 | 1 | 13 | 2 | 10 | 1 | 0 |
| Baton Rouge | 223,187 | 2,823 | 75 | 55 | 1,135 | 1,558 | 13,656 | 4,268 | 8,459 | 929 | 207 |
| Bernice | 1,626 | 6 | 0 | 0 | 0 | 6 | 10 | 3 | 7 | 0 | 0 |
| Bogalusa | 12,531 | 170 | 3 | 9 | 44 | 114 | 833 | 322 | 472 | 39 | 5 |
| Bossier City[2] | 63,077 | | 3 | | 59 | | 2,646 | 478 | 1,994 | 174 | 2 |
| Broussard | 7,973 | 42 | 2 | 2 | 10 | 28 | 590 | 172 | 418 | 0 | 0 |
| Brusly | 2,176 | 0 | 0 | 0 | 0 | 0 | 0 | 0 | 0 | 0 | 0 |
| Clarence | 498 | 0 | 0 | 0 | 0 | 0 | 0 | 0 | 0 | 0 | 0 |
| Clinton | 1,880 | 27 | 1 | 0 | 0 | 26 | 36 | 8 | 26 | 2 | 0 |
| Coushatta | 2,067 | 21 | 0 | 0 | 2 | 19 | 76 | 34 | 42 | 0 | 0 |
| Covington | 9,218 | 51 | 0 | 3 | 8 | 40 | 258 | 52 | 196 | 10 | 0 |
| Crowley | 13,865 | 88 | 2 | 5 | 24 | 57 | 583 | 173 | 395 | 15 | 0 |
| Cullen | 1,365 | 26 | 0 | 0 | 4 | 22 | 19 | 8 | 10 | 1 | 0 |
| Denham Springs | 10,398 | 66 | 0 | 3 | 21 | 42 | 849 | 149 | 668 | 32 | 0 |
| De Quincy | 3,206 | 13 | 0 | 0 | 4 | 9 | 143 | 48 | 91 | 4 | 0 |
| De Ridder | 10,043 | 64 | 0 | 0 | 2 | 62 | 223 | 54 | 166 | 3 | |
| Erath | 2,173 | 11 | 0 | 0 | 0 | 11 | 19 | 2 | 15 | 2 | 0 |
| Eunice | 11,501 | 67 | 1 | 7 | 5 | 54 | 676 | 192 | 460 | 24 | |
| Farmerville | 3,615 | 35 | 0 | 0 | 5 | 30 | 210 | 69 | 138 | 3 | 0 |
| Ferriday | 3,556 | 32 | 0 | 1 | 5 | 26 | 94 | 42 | 50 | 2 | 0 |
| Franklin | 7,613 | 65 | 0 | 2 | 8 | 55 | 456 | 99 | 354 | 3 | 2 |
| Franklinton | 3,759 | 37 | 1 | 1 | 3 | 32 | 243 | 50 | 187 | 6 | 1 |
| French Settlement | 1,070 | 0 | 0 | 0 | 0 | 0 | 18 | 3 | 14 | 1 | 0 |
| Golden Meadow | 2,102 | 12 | 0 | 0 | 1 | 11 | 55 | 18 | 33 | 4 | 0 |
| Gonzales | 9,531 | 19 | 2 | 2 | 2 | 13 | 423 | 4 | 393 | 26 | |
| Gramercy | 3,278 | 39 | 0 | 0 | 3 | 36 | 120 | 24 | 86 | 10 | 0 |
| Gretna | 16,299 | 140 | 2 | 9 | 48 | 81 | 790 | 178 | 537 | 75 | 0 |
| Hammond | 20,056 | 442 | 1 | 12 | 95 | 334 | 2,546 | 1,116 | 1,267 | 163 | |
| Harahan | 9,249 | 19 | 1 | 0 | 4 | 14 | 175 | 28 | 141 | 6 | 0 |
| Hodge | 473 | 3 | 0 | 0 | 0 | 3 | 0 | 0 | 0 | 0 | 0 |
| Houma | 32,477 | 339 | 10 | 16 | 125 | 188 | 1,387 | 311 | 1,011 | 65 | |
| Independence | 1,803 | 4 | 0 | 2 | 0 | 2 | 35 | 8 | 23 | 4 | 0 |
| Iowa | 2,616 | 11 | 0 | 0 | 1 | 10 | 117 | 29 | 84 | 4 | 0 |
| Jeanerette | 5,871 | 12 | 0 | 0 | 2 | 10 | 135 | 47 | 77 | 11 | 0 |
| Jennings | 10,483 | 67 | 0 | 7 | 12 | 48 | 366 | 76 | 272 | 18 | 1 |
| Kenner | 66,592 | 296 | 10 | 16 | 116 | 154 | 2,662 | 461 | 2,054 | 147 | 23 |
| Kentwood[6] | 2,283 | 27 | 0 | 1 | 4 | 22 | 163 | 26 | 128 | 9 | |
| Lafayette | 113,868 | 1,115 | 7 | 46 | 286 | 776 | 7,451 | 1,407 | 5,612 | 432 | 25 |
| Lake Arthur | 2,866 | 5 | 1 | 1 | 0 | 3 | 94 | 27 | 67 | 0 | 0 |
| Lake Charles | 70,975 | 623 | 10 | 46 | 199 | 368 | 3,446 | 2,158 | 1,081 | 207 | |
| Lake Providence | 4,151 | 49 | 0 | 1 | 5 | 43 | 41 | 24 | 17 | 0 | 1 |
| Leesville | 5,600 | 37 | 0 | 3 | 6 | 28 | 429 | 41 | 383 | 5 | 0 |
| Lutcher | 3,437 | 20 | 0 | 0 | 6 | 14 | 37 | 22 | 14 | 1 | 0 |
| Mamou | 3,399 | 16 | 0 | 1 | 2 | 13 | 106 | 14 | 82 | 10 | 0 |
| Mandeville | 12,645 | 42 | 0 | 2 | 9 | 31 | 303 | 39 | 254 | 10 | 0 |
| Mansfield | 5,386 | 204 | 0 | 3 | 5 | 196 | 292 | 72 | 211 | 9 | 0 |
| Many | 2,739 | 17 | 0 | 0 | 1 | 16 | 144 | 25 | 117 | 2 | 0 |
| Marion | 744 | 1 | 0 | 0 | 0 | 1 | 39 | 7 | 32 | 0 | 0 |
| Marksvllle | 5,692 | 94 | 0 | 3 | 5 | 86 | 408 | 102 | 293 | 13 | 0 |
| Minden | 12,926 | 28 | 0 | 3 | 6 | 19 | 249 | 66 | 168 | 15 | 0 |
| Morgan City | 11,497 | 94 | 0 | 9 | 26 | 59 | 643 | 189 | 432 | 22 | 0 |
| Napoleonville | 654 | 1 | 0 | 0 | 0 | 1 | 0 | 0 | 0 | 0 | 0 |
| New Orleans | 336,425 | 2,614 | 174 | 98 | 932 | 1,410 | 12,940 | 3,821 | 6,507 | 2,612 | |
| Oil City | 1,189 | 6 | 0 | 0 | 1 | 5 | 16 | 2 | 12 | 2 | 0 |
| Olla | 1,348 | 2 | 0 | 0 | 0 | 2 | 39 | 5 | 34 | 0 | 0 |
| Pearl River | 2,230 | 18 | 0 | 1 | 1 | 16 | 105 | 21 | 80 | 4 | 0 |
| Plaquemine | 6,718 | 81 | 1 | 3 | 0 | 77 | 388 | 49 | 324 | 15 | 0 |

[1] The FBI does not publish arson data unless it receives data from either the agency or the state for all 12 months of the calendar year.
[2] The FBI determined that the agency's data were underreported. Consequently, those data are not included in this table.
[6] Because of changes in the state/local agency's reporting practices, figures are not comparable to previous years' data.

**Table 8. Offenses Known to Law Enforcement, by State and City, 2009**—*Continued*

(Number.)

| State/city | Population | Violent crime | Murder and non-negligent man-slaughter | Forcible rape | Robbery | Aggravated assault | Property crime | Burglary | Larceny-theft | Motor vehicle theft | Arson[1] |
|---|---|---|---|---|---|---|---|---|---|---|---|
| **LOUISIANA**—*Continued* | | | | | | | | | | | |
| Ponchatoula | 6,449 | 69 | 0 | 4 | 9 | 56 | 519 | 189 | 300 | 30 | 0 |
| Port Allen | 4,955 | 32 | 2 | 0 | 10 | 20 | 169 | 51 | 111 | 7 | 1 |
| Port Vincent | 534 | 19 | 0 | 0 | 0 | 19 | 37 | 8 | 25 | 4 | 0 |
| Rayville | 3,993 | 32 | 0 | 2 | 2 | 28 | 353 | 57 | 289 | 7 | 1 |
| Ruston | 21,181 | 107 | 1 | 7 | 21 | 78 | 1,034 | 325 | 688 | 21 | 1 |
| Shreveport | 199,629 | 1,776 | 31 | 124 | 485 | 1,136 | 10,425 | 2,730 | 7,054 | 641 | 108 |
| Slidell | 27,355 | 141 | 1 | 12 | 26 | 102 | 1,637 | 211 | 1,351 | 75 | 1 |
| Springhill | 5,082 | 25 | 1 | 0 | 3 | 21 | 165 | 44 | 121 | 0 | 0 |
| Sterlington | 1,415 | 5 | 0 | 0 | 0 | 5 | 19 | 5 | 14 | 0 | 1 |
| St. Gabriel | 5,555 | 43 | 0 | 3 | 0 | 40 | 70 | 23 | 47 | 0 | 0 |
| Stonewall | 1,937 | 1 | 0 | 0 | 0 | 1 | 22 | 9 | 10 | 3 | 0 |
| Sulphur | 19,341 | 269 | 1 | 3 | 15 | 250 | 1,151 | 325 | 801 | 25 | 0 |
| Tallulah | 7,504 | 57 | 2 | 4 | 8 | 43 | 142 | 57 | 83 | 2 | 0 |
| Thibodaux | 14,012 | 99 | 0 | 4 | 32 | 63 | 698 | 112 | 566 | 20 | 1 |
| Vidalia | 4,098 | 31 | 0 | 1 | 1 | 29 | 185 | 32 | 151 | 2 | 0 |
| Vinton | 3,247 | 5 | 0 | 0 | 0 | 5 | 143 | 38 | 99 | 6 | 0 |
| Walker | 6,427 | 74 | 0 | 0 | 7 | 67 | 396 | 55 | 332 | 9 | 2 |
| Westlake | 4,566 | 6 | 0 | 0 | 0 | 6 | 123 | 36 | 82 | 5 | 0 |
| West Monroe | 12,863 | 47 | 0 | 2 | 11 | 34 | 1,077 | 156 | 883 | 38 | 2 |
| Westwego | 10,033 | 31 | 1 | 1 | 3 | 26 | 209 | 52 | 142 | 15 | 2 |
| Winnfield | 5,031 | 8 | 0 | 1 | 0 | 7 | 144 | 31 | 113 | 0 | 0 |
| Wisner | 1,019 | 4 | 0 | 1 | 0 | 3 | 5 | 4 | 0 | 1 | 0 |
| Zachary | 14,625 | 36 | 0 | 1 | 0 | 35 | 211 | 32 | 171 | 8 | 0 |
| **MAINE** | | | | | | | | | | | |
| Ashland | 1,441 | 0 | 0 | 0 | 0 | 0 | 8 | 6 | 1 | 1 | 0 |
| Auburn | 23,176 | 33 | 0 | 7 | 13 | 13 | 849 | 134 | 694 | 21 | 4 |
| Augusta | 18,252 | 53 | 0 | 11 | 12 | 30 | 1,071 | 167 | 872 | 32 | 6 |
| Baileyville | 1,540 | 3 | 0 | 1 | 0 | 2 | 46 | 8 | 35 | 3 | 0 |
| Bangor | 31,789 | 65 | 1 | 10 | 35 | 19 | 2,210 | 284 | 1,884 | 42 | 1 |
| Bar Harbor | 5,163 | 1 | 0 | 0 | 0 | 1 | 29 | 9 | 19 | 1 | 0 |
| Bath | 8,847 | 8 | 0 | 5 | 3 | 0 | 296 | 33 | 255 | 8 | 6 |
| Belfast | 6,754 | 9 | 0 | 6 | 2 | 1 | 200 | 45 | 146 | 9 | 0 |
| Berwick | 7,681 | 8 | 0 | 3 | 2 | 3 | 117 | 23 | 87 | 7 | 7 |
| Bethel | 2,687 | 2 | 1 | 0 | 0 | 1 | 96 | 10 | 84 | 2 | 0 |
| Biddeford | 21,479 | 57 | 2 | 11 | 20 | 24 | 1,030 | 156 | 856 | 18 | 12 |
| Boothbay Harbor | 2,242 | 2 | 0 | 0 | 0 | 2 | 92 | 8 | 82 | 2 | 0 |
| Brewer | 9,041 | 9 | 0 | 0 | 6 | 3 | 365 | 36 | 324 | 5 | 0 |
| Bridgton | 5,507 | 2 | 0 | 0 | 0 | 2 | 76 | 17 | 58 | 1 | 1 |
| Brownville | 1,292 | 5 | 0 | 0 | 0 | 5 | 49 | 11 | 38 | 0 | 0 |
| Brunswick | 21,781 | 24 | 0 | 6 | 6 | 12 | 450 | 69 | 377 | 4 | 1 |
| Bucksport | 4,892 | 12 | 0 | 0 | 0 | 12 | 102 | 27 | 73 | 2 | 1 |
| Buxton | 8,138 | 2 | 0 | 0 | 0 | 2 | 63 | 14 | 46 | 3 | 0 |
| Calais | 3,157 | 27 | 0 | 0 | 0 | 27 | 178 | 17 | 161 | 0 | 0 |
| Camden | 5,216 | 6 | 0 | 2 | 2 | 2 | 96 | 21 | 72 | 3 | 2 |
| Cape Elizabeth | 8,769 | 1 | 0 | 0 | 0 | 1 | 75 | 10 | 63 | 2 | 0 |
| Caribou | 8,070 | 5 | 0 | 0 | 1 | 4 | 140 | 18 | 117 | 5 | 1 |
| Carrabassett Valley | 479 | 0 | 0 | 0 | 0 | 0 | 71 | 3 | 65 | 3 | 0 |
| Clinton | 3,312 | 2 | 0 | 2 | 0 | 0 | 51 | 20 | 30 | 1 | 0 |
| Cumberland | 7,639 | 4 | 0 | 3 | 0 | 1 | 36 | 13 | 21 | 2 | 0 |
| Damariscotta | 1,900 | 5 | 0 | 4 | 0 | 1 | 43 | 9 | 34 | 0 | 0 |
| Dexter | 3,666 | 5 | 0 | 1 | 1 | 3 | 177 | 50 | 124 | 3 | 0 |
| Dixfield | 2,532 | 2 | 0 | 1 | 0 | 1 | 44 | 14 | 30 | 0 | 0 |
| Dover-Foxcroft | 4,221 | 10 | 0 | 3 | 0 | 7 | 115 | 18 | 93 | 4 | 1 |
| East Millinocket | 3,157 | 1 | 0 | 0 | 0 | 1 | 16 | 4 | 12 | 0 | 0 |
| Eastport | 1,525 | 0 | 0 | 0 | 0 | 0 | 14 | 6 | 8 | 0 | 0 |
| Eliot | 6,339 | 3 | 0 | 2 | 0 | 1 | 54 | 18 | 34 | 2 | 0 |
| Ellsworth | 7,177 | 3 | 0 | 1 | 0 | 2 | 315 | 39 | 263 | 13 | 0 |
| Fairfield | 6,718 | 7 | 0 | 3 | 1 | 3 | 194 | 42 | 145 | 7 | 2 |
| Falmouth | 10,768 | 3 | 0 | 0 | 2 | 1 | 168 | 32 | 131 | 5 | 0 |
| Farmington | 7,561 | 11 | 0 | 5 | 1 | 5 | 256 | 18 | 234 | 4 | 0 |
| Fort Fairfield | 3,437 | 6 | 0 | 0 | 0 | 6 | 38 | 6 | 31 | 1 | 0 |
| Fort Kent | 4,177 | 6 | 0 | 0 | 0 | 6 | 23 | 1 | 22 | 0 | 0 |
| Freeport | 8,239 | 4 | 0 | 1 | 0 | 3 | 121 | 17 | 104 | 0 | 0 |
| Fryeburg | 3,363 | 13 | 0 | 0 | 0 | 13 | 38 | 18 | 17 | 3 | 0 |
| Gardiner | 6,090 | 10 | 0 | 5 | 3 | 2 | 128 | 26 | 102 | 0 | 3 |
| Gorham | 15,725 | 12 | 1 | 4 | 1 | 6 | 226 | 94 | 126 | 6 | 3 |
| Gouldsboro | 1,999 | 0 | 0 | 0 | 0 | 0 | 13 | 8 | 4 | 1 | 0 |
| Greenville | 1,722 | 2 | 0 | 0 | 0 | 2 | 66 | 24 | 41 | 1 | 0 |
| Hallowell | 2,434 | 0 | 0 | 0 | 0 | 0 | 52 | 20 | 31 | 1 | 1 |
| Hampden | 6,984 | 1 | 0 | 1 | 0 | 0 | 94 | 15 | 77 | 2 | 0 |

[1] The FBI does not publish arson data unless it receives data from either the agency or the state for all 12 months of the calendar year.

## Table 8. Offenses Known to Law Enforcement, by State and City, 2009—*Continued*

(Number.)

| State/city | Population | Violent crime | Murder and non-negligent man-slaughter | Forcible rape | Robbery | Aggravated assault | Property crime | Burglary | Larceny-theft | Motor vehicle theft | Arson[1] |
|---|---|---|---|---|---|---|---|---|---|---|---|
| **LOUISIANA**—*Continued* | | | | | | | | | | | |
| Holden | 3,006 | 1 | 0 | 0 | 0 | 1 | 55 | 20 | 34 | 1 | 1 |
| Houlton | 6,109 | 5 | 0 | 1 | 1 | 3 | 184 | 34 | 144 | 6 | 0 |
| Jay | 4,749 | 2 | 0 | 1 | 0 | 1 | 84 | 20 | 58 | 6 | 0 |
| Kennebunk | 11,551 | 3 | 0 | 1 | 1 | 1 | 149 | 42 | 104 | 3 | 1 |
| Kennebunkport | 4,012 | 2 | 0 | 2 | 0 | 0 | 57 | 8 | 49 | 0 | 0 |
| Kittery | 10,524 | 3 | 0 | 2 | 0 | 1 | 171 | 15 | 149 | 7 | 1 |
| Lewiston | 35,074 | 93 | 0 | 21 | 38 | 34 | 1,106 | 216 | 865 | 25 | 6 |
| Limestone | 2,252 | 2 | 1 | 0 | 0 | 1 | 28 | 5 | 22 | 1 | 0 |
| Lincoln | 5,263 | 6 | 0 | 2 | 2 | 2 | 209 | 62 | 144 | 3 | 1 |
| Lincolnville | 2,202 | 1 | 0 | 0 | 0 | 1 | 17 | 6 | 11 | 0 | 0 |
| Lisbon | 9,343 | 5 | 0 | 3 | 2 | 0 | 104 | 17 | 82 | 5 | 0 |
| Livermore Falls | 3,124 | 3 | 0 | 1 | 0 | 2 | 53 | 13 | 37 | 3 | 1 |
| Machias | 2,112 | 4 | 0 | 2 | 0 | 2 | 30 | 12 | 18 | 0 | 0 |
| Madawaska | 4,315 | 1 | 0 | 0 | 0 | 1 | 40 | 2 | 38 | 0 | 0 |
| Madison | 4,575 | 4 | 0 | 2 | 0 | 2 | 127 | 26 | 99 | 2 | 0 |
| Mechanic Falls | 3,242 | 0 | 0 | 0 | 0 | 0 | 34 | 3 | 31 | 0 | 0 |
| Mexico | 2,856 | 5 | 0 | 2 | 1 | 2 | 121 | 28 | 91 | 2 | 0 |
| Milbridge | 1,312 | 0 | 0 | 0 | 0 | 0 | 6 | 2 | 4 | 0 | 0 |
| Millinocket | 4,871 | 3 | 0 | 1 | 2 | 0 | 102 | 33 | 61 | 8 | 0 |
| Milo | 2,313 | 17 | 0 | 0 | 0 | 17 | 61 | 25 | 32 | 4 | 1 |
| Monmouth | 3,862 | 1 | 1 | 0 | 0 | 0 | 70 | 21 | 45 | 4 | 1 |
| Mount Desert | 2,169 | 0 | 0 | 0 | 0 | 0 | 25 | 7 | 18 | 0 | 0 |
| Newport | 3,114 | 4 | 1 | 0 | 0 | 3 | 114 | 17 | 96 | 1 | 0 |
| North Berwick | 4,891 | 0 | 0 | 0 | 0 | 0 | 35 | 7 | 27 | 1 | 1 |
| Norway | 4,779 | 7 | 0 | 2 | 0 | 5 | 92 | 12 | 75 | 5 | 0 |
| Oakland | 6,209 | 7 | 0 | 3 | 3 | 1 | 152 | 30 | 117 | 5 | 0 |
| Ogunquit | 1,266 | 2 | 0 | 0 | 0 | 2 | 39 | 11 | 28 | 0 | 0 |
| Old Orchard Beach | 9,451 | 19 | 1 | 7 | 6 | 5 | 322 | 58 | 252 | 12 | 4 |
| Old Town | 7,689 | 5 | 0 | 1 | 3 | 1 | 207 | 35 | 170 | 2 | 3 |
| Orono | 9,708 | 2 | 0 | 0 | 2 | 0 | 179 | 20 | 155 | 4 | 1 |
| Oxford | 3,922 | 3 | 0 | 2 | 0 | 1 | 147 | 24 | 121 | 2 | 0 |
| Paris | 4,980 | 2 | 0 | 1 | 1 | 0 | 81 | 17 | 61 | 3 | 0 |
| Phippsburg | 2,167 | 0 | 0 | 0 | 0 | 0 | 23 | 10 | 11 | 2 | 0 |
| Pittsfield | 4,217 | 2 | 0 | 1 | 0 | 1 | 74 | 11 | 58 | 5 | 0 |
| Portland | 62,382 | 234 | 4 | 27 | 120 | 83 | 2,806 | 546 | 2,153 | 107 | 21 |
| Presque Isle | 8,996 | 6 | 0 | 4 | 0 | 2 | 372 | 66 | 304 | 2 | 2 |
| Rangeley | 1,188 | 1 | 0 | 1 | 0 | 0 | 25 | 11 | 13 | 1 | 0 |
| Richmond | 3,429 | 0 | 0 | 0 | 0 | 0 | 24 | 9 | 12 | 3 | 0 |
| Rockland | 7,417 | 4 | 0 | 2 | 0 | 2 | 420 | 31 | 382 | 7 | 0 |
| Rockport | 3,553 | 0 | 0 | 0 | 0 | 0 | 34 | 8 | 25 | 1 | 0 |
| Rumford | 6,293 | 11 | 2 | 7 | 1 | 1 | 189 | 39 | 144 | 6 | 1 |
| Sabattus | 4,666 | 1 | 0 | 0 | 0 | 1 | 54 | 28 | 25 | 1 | 0 |
| Saco | 18,262 | 25 | 1 | 11 | 7 | 6 | 524 | 92 | 413 | 19 | 3 |
| Sanford | 21,183 | 59 | 0 | 20 | 14 | 25 | 687 | 132 | 523 | 32 | 5 |
| Scarborough | 19,281 | 9 | 0 | 0 | 7 | 2 | 358 | 49 | 296 | 13 | 3 |
| Searsport | 2,577 | 4 | 0 | 0 | 0 | 4 | 60 | 12 | 42 | 6 | 0 |
| Skowhegan | 8,664 | 19 | 1 | 10 | 2 | 6 | 327 | 57 | 265 | 5 | 3 |
| South Berwick | 7,205 | 0 | 0 | 0 | 0 | 0 | 67 | 15 | 50 | 2 | 0 |
| South Portland | 23,852 | 62 | 0 | 3 | 13 | 46 | 1,062 | 96 | 929 | 37 | 2 |
| Southwest Harbor | 1,939 | 0 | 0 | 0 | 0 | 0 | 73 | 13 | 59 | 1 | 0 |
| Swan's Island | 300 | 0 | 0 | 0 | 0 | 0 | 0 | 0 | 0 | 0 | 0 |
| Thomaston | 3,646 | 0 | 0 | 0 | 0 | 0 | 55 | 7 | 43 | 5 | 1 |
| Topsham | 9,909 | 0 | 0 | 0 | 0 | 0 | 203 | 29 | 165 | 9 | 0 |
| Van Buren | 2,463 | 2 | 0 | 0 | 1 | 1 | 13 | 6 | 3 | 4 | 0 |
| Veazie | 1,908 | 1 | 0 | 0 | 1 | 0 | 36 | 9 | 27 | 0 | 0 |
| Waldoboro | 5,015 | 7 | 1 | 1 | 1 | 4 | 112 | 24 | 84 | 4 | 2 |
| Washburn | 1,571 | 0 | 0 | 0 | 0 | 0 | 32 | 7 | 25 | 0 | 0 |
| Waterville | 16,063 | 26 | 0 | 10 | 3 | 13 | 758 | 90 | 660 | 8 | 9 |
| Wells | 9,944 | 11 | 1 | 3 | 1 | 6 | 153 | 28 | 119 | 6 | 1 |
| Westbrook | 16,579 | 33 | 1 | 8 | 13 | 11 | 635 | 100 | 510 | 25 | 5 |
| Wilton | 4,176 | 20 | 0 | 9 | 0 | 11 | 139 | 42 | 92 | 5 | 0 |
| Windham | 16,927 | 10 | 0 | 5 | 1 | 4 | 453 | 80 | 364 | 9 | 1 |
| Winslow | 7,856 | 12 | 0 | 9 | 1 | 2 | 135 | 28 | 101 | 6 | 0 |
| Winter Harbor | 960 | 0 | 0 | 0 | 0 | 0 | 2 | 0 | 2 | 0 | 0 |
| Winthrop | 6,451 | 2 | 0 | 1 | 0 | 1 | 77 | 29 | 43 | 5 | 1 |
| Wiscasset | 3,768 | 0 | 0 | 0 | 0 | 0 | 59 | 16 | 41 | 2 | 1 |
| Yarmouth | 8,069 | 2 | 0 | 1 | 1 | 0 | 100 | 28 | 70 | 2 | 1 |
| York | 14,195 | 6 | 0 | 1 | 2 | 3 | 224 | 30 | 192 | 2 | 1 |
| **MARYLAND** | | | | | | | | | | | |
| Aberdeen | 14,003 | 89 | 1 | 7 | 36 | 45 | 567 | 64 | 471 | 32 | 1 |
| Annapolis | 36,586 | 243 | 4 | 9 | 82 | 148 | 980 | 199 | 702 | 79 | 3 |
| Baltimore | 638,755 | 9,664 | 238 | 158 | 3,707 | 5,561 | 29,163 | 7,798 | 16,741 | 4,624 | 347 |

[1] The FBI does not publish arson data unless it receives data from either the agency or the state for all 12 months of the calendar year.

## Table 8. Offenses Known to Law Enforcement, by State and City, 2009—*Continued*

(Number.)

| State/city | Population | Violent crime | Murder and non-negligent man-slaughter | Forcible rape | Robbery | Aggravated assault | Property crime | Burglary | Larceny-theft | Motor vehicle theft | Arson[1] |
|---|---|---|---|---|---|---|---|---|---|---|---|
| **MARYLAND**—*Continued* | | | | | | | | | | | |
| Baltimore City Sheriff | | 0 | 0 | 0 | 0 | 0 | 0 | 0 | 0 | 0 | 0 |
| Bel Air | 9,824 | 63 | 0 | 3 | 11 | 49 | 457 | 42 | 406 | 9 | 2 |
| Berlin | 4,111 | 16 | 0 | 0 | 3 | 13 | 116 | 24 | 92 | 0 | 0 |
| Berwyn Heights | 2,929 | 8 | 0 | 0 | 7 | 1 | 91 | 22 | 60 | 9 | 0 |
| Bladensburg | 7,557 | 89 | 1 | 2 | 48 | 38 | 486 | 101 | 262 | 123 | 0 |
| Boonsboro | 3,463 | 0 | 0 | 0 | 0 | 0 | 24 | 8 | 16 | 0 | 0 |
| Bowie | 52,577 | 124 | 0 | 4 | 65 | 55 | 1,102 | 254 | 742 | 106 | 3 |
| Brunswick | 5,262 | 17 | 0 | 0 | 1 | 16 | 99 | 23 | 70 | 6 | 1 |
| Cambridge | 11,840 | 128 | 0 | 10 | 25 | 93 | 500 | 113 | 374 | 13 | 4 |
| Capitol Heights | 4,094 | 15 | 0 | 0 | 6 | 9 | 38 | 8 | 14 | 16 | 0 |
| Centreville | 3,681 | 2 | 0 | 0 | 1 | 1 | 50 | 9 | 41 | 0 | 0 |
| Chestertown | 4,915 | 42 | 0 | 0 | 9 | 33 | 159 | 47 | 105 | 7 | 2 |
| Cheverly | 6,365 | 34 | 2 | 0 | 19 | 13 | 196 | 64 | 96 | 36 | 0 |
| Chevy Chase Village | 2,116 | 0 | 0 | 0 | 0 | 0 | 103 | 5 | 95 | 3 | 0 |
| Colmar Manor | 1,256 | 11 | 0 | 0 | 6 | 5 | 37 | 4 | 28 | 5 | 0 |
| Cottage City | 1,120 | 10 | 0 | 0 | 5 | 5 | 72 | 21 | 45 | 6 | 0 |
| Crisfield | 2,751 | 11 | 0 | 0 | 2 | 9 | 79 | 13 | 63 | 3 | 0 |
| Cumberland | 20,372 | 202 | 1 | 15 | 20 | 166 | 1,318 | 380 | 916 | 22 | 12 |
| Delmar | 3,576 | 18 | 0 | 1 | 4 | 13 | 83 | 24 | 58 | 1 | 1 |
| Denton | 4,147 | 20 | 0 | 2 | 5 | 13 | 240 | 64 | 173 | 3 | 2 |
| District Heights | 6,026 | 32 | 1 | 0 | 11 | 20 | 183 | 39 | 106 | 38 | 0 |
| Easton | 15,030 | 61 | 0 | 3 | 22 | 36 | 587 | 109 | 473 | 5 | 1 |
| Edmonston | 1,328 | 8 | 0 | 0 | 4 | 4 | 47 | 4 | 35 | 8 | 0 |
| Elkton | 15,202 | 371 | 1 | 7 | 90 | 273 | 1,270 | 250 | 942 | 78 | 7 |
| Fairmount Heights | 1,493 | 1 | 0 | 0 | 1 | 0 | 5 | 1 | 3 | 1 | 0 |
| Federalsburg | 2,627 | 26 | 0 | 3 | 6 | 17 | 137 | 31 | 100 | 6 | 0 |
| Forest Heights | 2,550 | 9 | 0 | 0 | 5 | 4 | 42 | 26 | 10 | 6 | 0 |
| Frederick | 59,936 | 514 | 1 | 18 | 150 | 345 | 1,786 | 299 | 1,386 | 101 | 16 |
| Frostburg | 7,669 | 15 | 0 | 0 | 3 | 12 | 191 | 51 | 133 | 7 | 0 |
| Fruitland | 4,511 | 44 | 0 | 1 | 9 | 34 | 250 | 29 | 218 | 3 | 0 |
| Glenarden | 6,304 | 18 | 0 | 0 | 8 | 10 | 119 | 33 | 72 | 14 | 4 |
| Greenbelt | 21,087 | 202 | 0 | 8 | 127 | 67 | 1,199 | 212 | 822 | 165 | 0 |
| Greensboro | 2,043 | 9 | 0 | 0 | 1 | 8 | 70 | 16 | 47 | 7 | 2 |
| Hagerstown | 40,062 | 191 | 0 | 3 | 73 | 115 | 1,398 | 239 | 1,041 | 118 | 17 |
| Hampstead | 5,501 | 7 | 0 | 0 | 0 | 7 | 97 | 10 | 85 | 2 | 1 |
| Hancock | 1,743 | 17 | 2 | 1 | 0 | 14 | 41 | 5 | 32 | 4 | 1 |
| Havre de Grace | 13,289 | 78 | 0 | 4 | 16 | 58 | 350 | 50 | 285 | 15 | 2 |
| Hurlock | 2,069 | 6 | 0 | 0 | 1 | 5 | 83 | 23 | 57 | 3 | 0 |
| Hyattsville | 15,346 | 126 | 0 | 0 | 86 | 40 | 1,517 | 142 | 1,249 | 126 | 0 |
| Landover Hills | 1,512 | 5 | 0 | 0 | 1 | 4 | 20 | 6 | 13 | 1 | 0 |
| La Plata | 9,170 | 34 | 0 | 0 | 6 | 28 | 326 | 30 | 279 | 17 | 0 |
| Laurel | 22,463 | 169 | 1 | 1 | 74 | 93 | 1,161 | 171 | 771 | 219 | 5 |
| Lonaconing | 1,117 | 0 | 0 | 0 | 0 | 0 | 3 | 0 | 3 | 0 | 2 |
| Luke | 72 | 0 | 0 | 0 | 0 | 0 | 0 | 0 | 0 | 0 | 0 |
| Manchester | 3,567 | 3 | 0 | 0 | 0 | 3 | 37 | 10 | 26 | 1 | 0 |
| Morningside | 1,305 | 9 | 0 | 1 | 1 | 7 | 33 | 10 | 16 | 7 | 0 |
| Mount Rainier | 8,303 | 79 | 0 | 1 | 69 | 9 | 312 | 57 | 181 | 74 | 2 |
| New Carrollton | 12,445 | 60 | 1 | 3 | 39 | 17 | 441 | 87 | 301 | 53 | 0 |
| North East | 2,872 | 14 | 0 | 0 | 5 | 9 | 171 | 24 | 134 | 13 | 5 |
| Oakland | 1,832 | 0 | 0 | 0 | 0 | 0 | 57 | 12 | 45 | 0 | 0 |
| Ocean City | 7,026 | 88 | 0 | 2 | 23 | 63 | 1,295 | 213 | 1,052 | 30 | 1 |
| Oxford | 699 | 1 | 0 | 0 | 0 | 1 | 2 | 1 | 1 | 0 | 0 |
| Perryville | 3,816 | 10 | 0 | 2 | 2 | 6 | 225 | 34 | 186 | 5 | 3 |
| Pocomoke City | 3,854 | 28 | 0 | 1 | 7 | 20 | 216 | 45 | 169 | 2 | 0 |
| Port Deposit | 704 | 0 | 0 | 0 | 0 | 0 | 11 | 1 | 9 | 1 | 0 |
| Preston | 685 | 1 | 0 | 0 | 0 | 1 | 9 | 3 | 6 | 0 | 0 |
| Princess Anne | 3,104 | 41 | 1 | 4 | 17 | 19 | 202 | 84 | 117 | 1 | 2 |
| Ridgely | 1,536 | 29 | 0 | 1 | 3 | 25 | 88 | 31 | 55 | 2 | 2 |
| Rising Sun | 1,815 | 3 | 0 | 0 | 0 | 3 | 67 | 8 | 59 | 0 | 1 |
| Riverdale Park | 6,413 | 58 | 0 | 0 | 36 | 22 | 247 | 55 | 124 | 68 | 0 |
| Rock Hall | 1,496 | 0 | 0 | 0 | 0 | 0 | 29 | 6 | 23 | 0 | 0 |
| Salisbury | 28,800 | 643 | 2 | 20 | 198 | 423 | 2,609 | 727 | 1,778 | 104 | 20 |
| Seat Pleasant | 4,822 | 35 | 1 | 0 | 15 | 19 | 159 | 38 | 95 | 26 | 0 |
| Smithsburg | 3,002 | 2 | 0 | 0 | 0 | 2 | 9 | 5 | 4 | 0 | 0 |
| Snow Hill | 2,305 | 7 | 0 | 0 | 1 | 6 | 51 | 17 | 34 | 0 | 1 |
| St. Michaels | 1,054 | 2 | 0 | 0 | 0 | 2 | 56 | 6 | 48 | 2 | 0 |
| Sykesville | 4,444 | 3 | 0 | 0 | 1 | 2 | 56 | 8 | 43 | 5 | 4 |
| Takoma Park | 17,741 | 104 | 0 | 5 | 54 | 45 | 659 | 112 | 470 | 77 | 5 |
| Taneytown | 5,455 | 2 | 0 | 0 | 0 | 2 | 113 | 15 | 97 | 1 | 2 |
| Thurmont | 6,082 | 9 | 0 | 1 | 1 | 7 | 75 | 15 | 55 | 5 | 0 |
| Trappe | 1,136 | 0 | 0 | 0 | 0 | 0 | 11 | 0 | 9 | 2 | 0 |

[1] The FBI does not publish arson data unless it receives data from either the agency or the state for all 12 months of the calendar year.

## Table 8. Offenses Known to Law Enforcement, by State and City, 2009—*Continued*

(Number.)

| State/city | Population | Violent crime | Murder and non-negligent man-slaughter | Forcible rape | Robbery | Aggravated assault | Property crime | Burglary | Larceny-theft | Motor vehicle theft | Arson[1] |
|---|---|---|---|---|---|---|---|---|---|---|---|
| **MARYLAND**—*Continued* | | | | | | | | | | | |
| University Park | 2,278 | 6 | 0 | 0 | 4 | 2 | 74 | 17 | 53 | 4 | 0 |
| Upper Marlboro | 658 | 2 | 0 | 0 | 1 | 1 | 31 | 6 | 19 | 6 | 0 |
| Westernport | 1,929 | 2 | 0 | 1 | 0 | 1 | 26 | 9 | 16 | 1 | 1 |
| Westminster | 17,787 | 123 | 0 | 0 | 11 | 112 | 743 | 93 | 633 | 17 | 9 |
| **MASSACHUSETTS** | | | | | | | | | | | |
| Abington | 16,732 | 58 | 0 | 3 | 18 | 37 | 373 | 124 | 236 | 13 | 0 |
| Acton | 21,104 | 14 | 0 | 2 | 1 | 11 | 167 | 31 | 131 | 5 | 0 |
| Acushnet | 10,606 | 12 | 0 | 0 | 1 | 11 | 118 | 55 | 60 | 3 | 0 |
| Adams | 8,232 | 43 | 0 | 11 | 1 | 31 | 232 | 62 | 163 | 7 | 4 |
| Agawam | 28,781 | 61 | 0 | 4 | 9 | 48 | 283 | 69 | 181 | 33 | 2 |
| Amesbury | 16,623 | 28 | 0 | 2 | 0 | 26 | 278 | 39 | 223 | 16 | 0 |
| Amherst | 36,845 | 71 | 0 | 17 | 5 | 49 | 532 | 242 | 264 | 26 | 1 |
| Andover | 33,853 | 19 | 0 | 3 | 4 | 12 | 421 | 59 | 349 | 13 | 5 |
| Aquinnah | 358 | 0 | 0 | 0 | 0 | 0 | 13 | 0 | 13 | 0 | 0 |
| Arlington | 41,598 | 73 | 0 | 3 | 11 | 59 | 535 | 119 | 390 | 26 | 9 |
| Ashburnham | 6,054 | 11 | 0 | 1 | 1 | 9 | 58 | 16 | 39 | 3 | 5 |
| Ashland | 16,164 | 17 | 0 | 4 | 0 | 13 | 166 | 44 | 115 | 7 | 4 |
| Athol | 11,724 | 48 | 0 | 6 | 4 | 38 | 317 | 125 | 184 | 8 | 3 |
| Attleboro | 43,772 | 127 | 1 | 5 | 21 | 100 | 751 | 147 | 551 | 53 | 5 |
| Auburn[5] | 16,420 | | 0 | 5 | 8 | | 601 | 65 | 518 | 18 | 3 |
| Avon | 4,354 | 11 | 0 | 2 | 4 | 5 | 133 | 20 | 108 | 5 | 0 |
| Ayer | 7,488 | 25 | 0 | 2 | 2 | 21 | 168 | 72 | 89 | 7 | 3 |
| Barnstable | 48,042 | 369 | 2 | 23 | 52 | 292 | 1,324 | 480 | 791 | 53 | 5 |
| Barre | 5,496 | 11 | 0 | 2 | 0 | 9 | 56 | 17 | 35 | 4 | 2 |
| Becket | 1,822 | 2 | 0 | 1 | 0 | 1 | 41 | 21 | 20 | 0 | 0 |
| Bedford | 13,411 | 8 | 0 | 3 | 0 | 5 | 117 | 16 | 97 | 4 | 1 |
| Belchertown | 14,383 | 31 | 0 | 1 | 4 | 26 | 176 | 30 | 135 | 11 | 1 |
| Bellingham | 16,235 | 29 | 0 | 4 | 5 | 20 | 225 | 34 | 176 | 15 | 2 |
| Belmont | 23,597 | 28 | 0 | 6 | 3 | 19 | 289 | 98 | 166 | 25 | 2 |
| Berkley | 6,601 | 21 | 0 | 1 | 0 | 20 | 82 | 41 | 33 | 8 | 1 |
| Berlin | 2,760 | 0 | 0 | 0 | 0 | 0 | 22 | 0 | 22 | 0 | 0 |
| Bernardston | 2,258 | 2 | 0 | 0 | 0 | 2 | 25 | 8 | 15 | 2 | 0 |
| Beverly | 39,919 | 97 | 0 | 10 | 12 | 75 | 619 | 114 | 474 | 31 | 1 |
| Billerica[5] | 43,058 | | 0 | 9 | 4 | | 567 | 112 | 437 | 18 | 1 |
| Blackstone | 9,126 | 11 | 0 | 1 | 1 | 9 | 108 | 20 | 85 | 3 | 3 |
| Bolton | 4,556 | 5 | 0 | 2 | 1 | 2 | 40 | 11 | 27 | 2 | 0 |
| Boston | 624,222 | 6,192 | 50 | 269 | 2,277 | 3,596 | 20,749 | 2,955 | 15,507 | 2,287 | |
| Bourne | 19,133 | 107 | 1 | 5 | 12 | 89 | 713 | 288 | 398 | 27 | 5 |
| Boxford | 8,187 | 1 | 0 | 0 | 0 | 1 | 29 | 1 | 28 | 0 | 0 |
| Boylston | 4,330 | 0 | 0 | 0 | 0 | 0 | 30 | 7 | 22 | 1 | 0 |
| Braintree | 35,047 | 82 | 2 | 7 | 15 | 58 | 962 | 103 | 815 | 44 | 2 |
| Brewster | 10,054 | 18 | 0 | 0 | 1 | 17 | 254 | 79 | 168 | 7 | 0 |
| Brimfield | 3,796 | 0 | 0 | 0 | 0 | 0 | 12 | 3 | 8 | 1 | 0 |
| Brockton | 96,471 | 1,194 | 9 | 53 | 262 | 870 | 3,207 | 772 | 2,042 | 393 | 42 |
| Brookline[5] | 55,400 | | 0 | 4 | 30 | | 763 | 103 | 636 | 24 | 3 |
| Burlington | 25,695 | 54 | 0 | 3 | 12 | 39 | 703 | 133 | 558 | 12 | 3 |
| Cambridge | 102,866 | 497 | 2 | 21 | 179 | 295 | 3,149 | 434 | 2,524 | 191 | 6 |
| Canton | 22,407 | 45 | 0 | 2 | 5 | 38 | 222 | 44 | 163 | 15 | 0 |
| Carver | 11,691 | 24 | 0 | 4 | 3 | 17 | 122 | 51 | 58 | 13 | 1 |
| Charlemont | 1,383 | 1 | 0 | 0 | 0 | 1 | 6 | 0 | 6 | 0 | 0 |
| Charlton | 12,835 | 15 | 0 | 2 | 3 | 10 | 157 | 55 | 86 | 16 | 0 |
| Chatham | 6,765 | 9 | 0 | 0 | 0 | 9 | 170 | 35 | 135 | 0 | 0 |
| Chelmsford | 34,695 | 38 | 0 | 0 | 5 | 33 | 584 | 82 | 475 | 27 | 0 |
| Chelsea | 39,883 | 663 | 0 | 24 | 256 | 383 | 1,532 | 436 | 858 | 238 | 7 |
| Cheshire | 3,322 | 0 | 0 | 0 | 0 | 0 | 37 | 7 | 29 | 1 | 0 |
| Chesterfield | 1,308 | 0 | 0 | 0 | 0 | 0 | 3 | 3 | 0 | 0 | 0 |
| Chicopee | 54,589 | 283 | 0 | 23 | 50 | 210 | 1,684 | 450 | 1,119 | 115 | 9 |
| Chilmark | 986 | 0 | 0 | 0 | 0 | 0 | 15 | 5 | 10 | 0 | 0 |
| Clinton | 14,206 | 8 | 0 | 0 | 0 | 8 | 48 | 7 | 35 | 6 | 0 |
| Cohasset | 7,286 | 9 | 0 | 0 | 0 | 9 | 86 | 22 | 61 | 3 | 1 |
| Concord | 17,804 | 9 | 0 | 0 | 1 | 8 | 208 | 33 | 173 | 2 | 1 |
| Cummington | 994 | 0 | 0 | 0 | 0 | 0 | 2 | 0 | 2 | 0 | 0 |
| Dalton | 6,616 | 19 | 0 | 1 | 1 | 17 | 79 | 29 | 49 | 1 | 0 |
| Danvers | 27,289 | 51 | 0 | 4 | 8 | 39 | 851 | 50 | 772 | 29 | 3 |
| Dartmouth | 34,879 | 88 | 0 | 4 | 13 | 71 | 1,074 | 146 | 890 | 38 | 6 |
| Dedham | 24,605 | 40 | 0 | 2 | 15 | 23 | 580 | 51 | 499 | 30 | 0 |
| Deerfield | 4,780 | 17 | 0 | 2 | 0 | 15 | 109 | 38 | 71 | 0 | 0 |
| Dennis | 15,475 | 86 | 0 | 9 | 15 | 62 | 629 | 240 | 379 | 10 | 4 |
| Dighton | 6,905 | 11 | 0 | 1 | 0 | 10 | 41 | 24 | 15 | 2 | 0 |
| Douglas | 8,093 | 20 | 0 | 2 | 0 | 18 | 41 | 18 | 22 | 1 | 0 |

[1] The FBI does not publish arson data unless it receives data from either the agency or the state for all 12 months of the calendar year.
[5] The FBI determined that the agency did not follow national Uniform Crime Reporting (UCR) Program guidelines for reporting an offense. Consequently, this figure is not included in this table.

## Table 8. Offenses Known to Law Enforcement, by State and City, 2009—*Continued*

(Number.)

| State/city | Population | Violent crime | Murder and non-negligent man-slaughter | Forcible rape | Robbery | Aggravated assault | Property crime | Burglary | Larceny-theft | Motor vehicle theft | Arson[1] |
|---|---|---|---|---|---|---|---|---|---|---|---|
| **MASSACHUSETTS**—*Continued* | | | | | | | | | | | |
| Dover | 5,724 | 1 | 0 | 1 | 0 | 0 | 42 | 12 | 29 | 1 | 0 |
| Dracut | 30,048 | 24 | 0 | 4 | 9 | 11 | 261 | 32 | 193 | 36 | 0 |
| Dudley | 11,264 | 25 | 0 | 1 | 0 | 24 | 46 | 25 | 18 | 3 | 4 |
| Duxbury | 14,588 | 11 | 0 | 0 | 0 | 11 | 130 | 30 | 98 | 2 | 1 |
| East Bridgewater | 14,108 | 25 | 0 | 4 | 5 | 16 | 266 | 50 | 202 | 14 | 4 |
| East Brookfield | 2,080 | 5 | 0 | 1 | 0 | 4 | 32 | 8 | 23 | 1 | 1 |
| Eastham | 5,464 | 7 | 0 | 0 | 1 | 6 | 104 | 31 | 70 | 3 | 0 |
| Easthampton | 16,401 | 41 | 0 | 6 | 2 | 33 | 188 | 65 | 105 | 18 | 4 |
| East Longmeadow | 15,595 | 28 | 0 | 1 | 3 | 24 | 420 | 91 | 307 | 22 | 0 |
| Easton | 23,337 | 42 | 0 | 2 | 8 | 32 | 240 | 65 | 165 | 10 | 2 |
| Egremont | 1,365 | 2 | 0 | 0 | 0 | 2 | 19 | 3 | 16 | 0 | 0 |
| Erving | 1,563 | 5 | 0 | 3 | 0 | 2 | 58 | 41 | 17 | 0 | 0 |
| Essex | 3,369 | 5 | 0 | 0 | 1 | 4 | 52 | 25 | 27 | 0 | |
| Everett | 37,724 | 203 | 1 | 7 | 81 | 114 | 1,121 | 288 | 687 | 146 | 1 |
| Fairhaven | 16,318 | 53 | 0 | 2 | 9 | 42 | 413 | 96 | 306 | 11 | 2 |
| Fall River | 91,901 | 1,086 | 4 | 46 | 273 | 763 | 3,312 | 775 | 2,144 | 393 | 44 |
| Falmouth | 33,451 | 152 | 0 | 14 | 22 | 116 | 1,318 | 767 | 499 | 52 | 1 |
| Fitchburg | 40,678 | 288 | 5 | 30 | 49 | 204 | 1,193 | 364 | 740 | 89 | 12 |
| Framingham | 65,478 | 204 | 2 | 8 | 33 | 161 | 1,443 | 253 | 1,058 | 132 | |
| Franklin | 32,114 | 11 | 0 | 3 | 4 | 4 | 165 | 18 | 140 | 7 | 0 |
| Freetown | 9,103 | 36 | 0 | 2 | 2 | 32 | 153 | 48 | 90 | 15 | 8 |
| Gardner | 20,741 | 111 | 0 | 13 | 14 | 84 | 524 | 171 | 327 | 26 | 3 |
| Gill | 1,396 | 0 | 0 | 0 | 0 | 0 | 25 | 10 | 13 | 2 | 0 |
| Gloucester | 30,675 | 31 | 0 | 2 | 8 | 21 | 629 | 93 | 531 | 5 | 1 |
| Goshen | 980 | 0 | 0 | 0 | 0 | 0 | 5 | 1 | 3 | 1 | 0 |
| Grafton | 18,005 | 16 | 0 | 3 | 1 | 12 | 99 | 40 | 53 | 6 | 0 |
| Granby | 6,432 | 9 | 0 | 3 | 0 | 6 | 55 | 12 | 42 | 1 | 0 |
| Granville | 1,721 | 0 | 0 | 0 | 0 | 0 | 9 | 2 | 7 | 0 | 0 |
| Great Barrington | 7,431 | 7 | 0 | 0 | 1 | 6 | 175 | 50 | 121 | 4 | 1 |
| Greenfield | 17,840 | 91 | 0 | 10 | 3 | 78 | 525 | 224 | 282 | 19 | 6 |
| Groton | 10,936 | 1 | 0 | 0 | 1 | 0 | 31 | 6 | 25 | 0 | 0 |
| Groveland | 7,127 | 8 | 0 | 0 | 0 | 8 | 44 | 0 | 42 | 2 | 0 |
| Hadley | 4,884 | 12 | 0 | 1 | 3 | 8 | 211 | 52 | 151 | 8 | 0 |
| Halifax | 7,788 | 15 | 0 | 1 | 1 | 13 | 102 | 40 | 46 | 16 | 0 |
| Hamilton | 8,270 | 6 | 0 | 0 | 0 | 6 | 45 | 3 | 39 | 3 | 0 |
| Hampden | 5,401 | 9 | 0 | 1 | 1 | 7 | 40 | 10 | 27 | 3 | 1 |
| Hanover | 14,185 | 4 | 0 | 0 | 1 | 3 | 402 | 45 | 352 | 5 | 1 |
| Hanson[5] | 10,096 | | 1 | 0 | 4 | | 136 | 27 | 94 | 15 | 0 |
| Hardwick | 2,673 | 7 | 0 | 0 | 1 | 6 | 37 | 8 | 27 | 2 | 4 |
| Harvard | 6,046 | 2 | 0 | 1 | 0 | 1 | 46 | 17 | 29 | 0 | 2 |
| Harwich | 12,436 | 20 | 0 | 1 | 3 | 16 | 271 | 120 | 146 | 5 | 1 |
| Hatfield | 3,326 | 0 | 0 | 0 | 0 | 0 | 6 | 6 | 0 | 0 | 0 |
| Haverhill | 60,738 | 329 | 1 | 19 | 50 | 259 | 1,475 | 700 | 632 | 143 | 12 |
| Hingham | 22,919 | 11 | 0 | 0 | 2 | 9 | 270 | 35 | 228 | 7 | 0 |
| Hinsdale | 1,966 | 6 | 0 | 0 | 0 | 6 | 3 | 1 | 1 | 1 | 0 |
| Holbrook | 10,817 | 52 | 0 | 3 | 13 | 36 | 271 | 85 | 175 | 11 | 0 |
| Holden | 16,819 | 9 | 0 | 1 | 0 | 8 | 107 | 16 | 85 | 6 | 0 |
| Holliston | 14,160 | 5 | 0 | 1 | 0 | 4 | 62 | 12 | 47 | 3 | 1 |
| Holyoke | 40,322 | 397 | 3 | 38 | 68 | 288 | 2,643 | 514 | 1,897 | 232 | 12 |
| Hopkinton | 14,633 | 4 | 0 | 0 | 1 | 3 | 102 | 8 | 91 | 3 | 0 |
| Hubbardston | 4,565 | 11 | 0 | 0 | 0 | 11 | 31 | 10 | 19 | 2 | 1 |
| Hudson | 20,060 | 2 | 0 | 1 | 1 | 0 | 249 | 38 | 194 | 17 | 0 |
| Hull | 11,159 | 29 | 0 | 6 | 2 | 21 | 169 | 58 | 100 | 11 | 2 |
| Ipswich | 13,435 | 7 | 0 | 1 | 1 | 5 | 111 | 28 | 82 | 1 | 0 |
| Kingston | 12,511 | 50 | 0 | 7 | 8 | 35 | 387 | 52 | 325 | 10 | 3 |
| Lakeville | 10,769 | 16 | 0 | 0 | 1 | 15 | 178 | 111 | 62 | 5 | 3 |
| Lancaster | 7,183 | 5 | 1 | 0 | 0 | 4 | 51 | 12 | 32 | 7 | 1 |
| Lanesboro | 2,910 | 3 | 0 | 0 | 0 | 3 | 27 | 8 | 18 | 1 | 1 |
| Lawrence | 70,670 | 503 | 9 | 15 | 175 | 304 | 2,157 | 566 | 1,173 | 418 | |
| Lee | 5,843 | 7 | 0 | 0 | 1 | 6 | 114 | 29 | 82 | 3 | 0 |
| Leicester | 11,124 | 28 | 0 | 4 | 3 | 21 | 238 | 37 | 194 | 7 | 2 |
| Lenox | 5,160 | 10 | 0 | 0 | 0 | 10 | 142 | 48 | 92 | 2 | 1 |
| Leominster | 41,401 | 265 | 2 | 21 | 29 | 213 | 1,325 | 235 | 1,006 | 84 | 9 |
| Lexington | 30,771 | 13 | 0 | 0 | 1 | 12 | 220 | 26 | 192 | 2 | 1 |
| Lincoln | 8,103 | 4 | 0 | 1 | 0 | 3 | 37 | 8 | 26 | 3 | 0 |
| Littleton | 8,906 | 17 | 0 | 2 | 1 | 14 | 83 | 24 | 55 | 4 | 0 |
| Longmeadow | 15,506 | 5 | 0 | 0 | 1 | 4 | 206 | 34 | 163 | 9 | 2 |
| Ludlow | 22,870 | 20 | 1 | 1 | 7 | 11 | 297 | 63 | 215 | 19 | 1 |
| Lunenburg | 10,087 | 29 | 0 | 2 | 0 | 27 | 157 | 38 | 117 | 2 | 0 |
| Lynn | 91,149 | 819 | 4 | 31 | 178 | 606 | 2,884 | 771 | 1,687 | 426 | 13 |

[1] The FBI does not publish arson data unless it receives data from either the agency or the state for all 12 months of the calendar year.

[5] The FBI determined that the agency did not follow national Uniform Crime Reporting (UCR) Program guidelines for reporting an offense. Consequently, this figure is not included in this table.

# Table 8. Offenses Known to Law Enforcement, by State and City, 2009—*Continued*

(Number.)

| State/city | Population | Violent crime | Murder and non-negligent man-slaughter | Forcible rape | Robbery | Aggravated assault | Property crime | Burglary | Larceny-theft | Motor vehicle theft | Arson[1] |
|---|---|---|---|---|---|---|---|---|---|---|---|
| **MASSACHUSETTS**—*Continued* | | | | | | | | | | | |
| Lynnfield | 11,500 | 6 | 0 | 0 | 2 | 4 | 183 | 15 | 165 | 3 | 1 |
| Malden | 56,455 | 286 | 1 | 7 | 92 | 186 | 1,437 | 374 | 921 | 142 | 3 |
| Mansfield | 23,347 | 67 | 1 | 2 | 7 | 57 | 308 | 73 | 214 | 21 | 0 |
| Marblehead | 20,240 | 31 | 0 | 9 | 2 | 20 | 274 | 34 | 223 | 17 | 0 |
| Marion | 5,271 | 12 | 0 | 0 | 1 | 11 | 85 | 23 | 57 | 5 | 1 |
| Marlborough | 38,821 | 180 | 0 | 11 | 20 | 149 | 773 | 118 | 589 | 66 | 5 |
| Marshfield | 24,811 | 40 | 0 | 3 | 3 | 34 | 330 | 64 | 240 | 26 | 1 |
| Mashpee | 14,481 | 47 | 0 | 3 | 5 | 39 | 444 | 127 | 303 | 14 | 3 |
| Mattapoisett | 6,523 | 13 | 1 | 1 | 1 | 10 | 89 | 14 | 73 | 2 | 0 |
| Medfield | 12,457 | 7 | 0 | 1 | 1 | 5 | 65 | 6 | 59 | 0 | 2 |
| Medford | 56,380 | 59 | 0 | 2 | 43 | 14 | 1,198 | 232 | 879 | 87 | |
| Melrose | 27,134 | 36 | 0 | 2 | 11 | 23 | 318 | 102 | 193 | 23 | 1 |
| Mendon | 5,866 | 8 | 0 | 0 | 0 | 8 | 62 | 22 | 35 | 5 | 2 |
| Merrimac | 6,538 | 11 | 0 | 2 | 1 | 8 | 30 | 3 | 23 | 4 | 1 |
| Methuen | 44,527 | 94 | 0 | 2 | 26 | 66 | 1,020 | 159 | 795 | 66 | 4 |
| Middleboro | 21,585 | 97 | 0 | 7 | 13 | 77 | 476 | 136 | 288 | 52 | 3 |
| Middleton | 9,662 | 13 | 0 | 1 | 0 | 12 | 107 | 0 | 102 | 5 | 0 |
| Milford | 27,526 | 60 | 0 | 5 | 6 | 49 | 309 | 40 | 252 | 17 | 4 |
| Millbury | 13,652 | 33 | 1 | 5 | 0 | 27 | 412 | 73 | 323 | 16 | 3 |
| Millville | 2,878 | 5 | 0 | 1 | 0 | 4 | 56 | 11 | 39 | 6 | 2 |
| Milton | 26,719 | 17 | 2 | 0 | 7 | 8 | 251 | 43 | 198 | 10 | |
| Monson | 8,974 | 16 | 0 | 0 | 1 | 15 | 138 | 61 | 67 | 10 | 0 |
| Monterey | 973 | 3 | 0 | 0 | 0 | 3 | 4 | 1 | 3 | 0 | 0 |
| Nahant | 3,548 | 6 | 0 | 0 | 0 | 6 | 34 | 10 | 23 | 1 | 0 |
| Nantucket | 11,380 | 58 | 1 | 3 | 1 | 53 | 400 | 95 | 288 | 17 | 0 |
| Natick | 32,418 | 54 | 0 | 1 | 6 | 47 | 895 | 69 | 803 | 23 | 2 |
| Needham | 28,683 | 11 | 0 | 0 | 4 | 7 | 284 | 51 | 221 | 12 | 1 |
| New Bedford | 92,621 | 1,184 | 9 | 66 | 340 | 769 | 3,235 | 1,144 | 1,806 | 285 | 38 |
| Newbury | 7,035 | 8 | 0 | 1 | 0 | 7 | 41 | 10 | 28 | 3 | 1 |
| Newburyport | 17,343 | 15 | 0 | 0 | 3 | 12 | 274 | 45 | 207 | 22 | 2 |
| New Salem | 1,009 | 1 | 0 | 0 | 0 | 1 | 6 | 2 | 4 | 0 | 1 |
| Newton | 84,427 | 94 | 1 | 9 | 18 | 66 | 971 | 187 | 753 | 31 | 3 |
| Norfolk | 10,837 | 2 | 0 | 2 | 0 | 0 | 83 | 51 | 30 | 2 | 0 |
| North Adams | 13,927 | 114 | 0 | 1 | 4 | 109 | 521 | 207 | 302 | 12 | 2 |
| Northampton | 28,921 | 96 | 3 | 19 | 10 | 64 | 845 | 146 | 670 | 29 | 24 |
| North Andover | 28,116 | 8 | 0 | 1 | 2 | 5 | 318 | 36 | 272 | 10 | 0 |
| North Attleboro | 28,346 | 30 | 0 | 7 | 5 | 18 | 636 | 85 | 540 | 11 | 1 |
| Northborough | 14,792 | 9 | 0 | 1 | 0 | 8 | 117 | 13 | 99 | 5 | 0 |
| Northbridge | 14,634 | 41 | 0 | 6 | 4 | 31 | 317 | 77 | 229 | 11 | 2 |
| North Brookfield[5] | 4,870 | | 0 | 0 | 0 | | 52 | 26 | 24 | 2 | 1 |
| Northfield | 3,022 | 2 | 0 | 0 | 0 | 2 | 35 | 14 | 21 | 0 | 0 |
| North Reading | 14,249 | 20 | 0 | 1 | 1 | 18 | 120 | 25 | 90 | 5 | 0 |
| Norton | 19,610 | 4 | 0 | 0 | 1 | 3 | 89 | 35 | 50 | 4 | 0 |
| Norwell | 10,418 | 11 | 0 | 0 | 2 | 9 | 145 | 51 | 89 | 5 | 0 |
| Norwood | 28,569 | 27 | 0 | 2 | 14 | 11 | 522 | 83 | 398 | 41 | 6 |
| Orange | 7,915 | 26 | 0 | 2 | 3 | 21 | 161 | 56 | 101 | 4 | 2 |
| Orleans | 6,337 | 20 | 0 | 3 | 1 | 16 | 194 | 47 | 146 | 1 | 0 |
| Oxford | 13,773 | 39 | 0 | 0 | 8 | 31 | 178 | 38 | 125 | 15 | 0 |
| Palmer | 13,086 | 39 | 0 | 5 | 3 | 31 | 188 | 64 | 107 | 17 | 4 |
| Paxton | 4,580 | 1 | 0 | 0 | 0 | 1 | 22 | 6 | 15 | 1 | 0 |
| Peabody | 52,483 | 124 | 0 | 6 | 27 | 91 | 1,337 | 161 | 1,087 | 89 | 1 |
| Pelham | 1,433 | 0 | 0 | 0 | 0 | 0 | 11 | 7 | 4 | 0 | 0 |
| Pembroke | 18,967 | 31 | 0 | 2 | 8 | 21 | 190 | 55 | 123 | 12 | 0 |
| Pepperell | 11,608 | 17 | 0 | 3 | 0 | 14 | 158 | 32 | 117 | 9 | 0 |
| Pittsfield | 43,050 | 284 | 2 | 34 | 23 | 225 | 1,004 | 319 | 636 | 49 | 10 |
| Plainville | 8,522 | 12 | 1 | 1 | 1 | 9 | 95 | 21 | 71 | 3 | 0 |
| Plymouth | 56,084 | 163 | 2 | 7 | 12 | 142 | 1,026 | 185 | 819 | 22 | 1 |
| Plympton | 2,812 | 9 | 0 | 0 | 0 | 9 | 28 | 6 | 20 | 2 | 0 |
| Princeton | 3,536 | 1 | 0 | 0 | 0 | 1 | 32 | 15 | 17 | 0 | 0 |
| Quincy | 96,580 | 384 | 5 | 20 | 96 | 263 | 1,759 | 478 | 1,145 | 136 | 10 |
| Randolph | 30,549 | 137 | 0 | 11 | 17 | 109 | 780 | 132 | 597 | 51 | 4 |
| Raynham | 14,068 | 31 | 0 | 2 | 12 | 17 | 393 | 70 | 304 | 19 | 0 |
| Reading | 23,398 | 11 | 0 | 1 | 1 | 9 | 203 | 29 | 165 | 9 | 0 |
| Rehoboth | 11,795 | 28 | 0 | 0 | 3 | 25 | 171 | 74 | 85 | 12 | 2 |
| Revere | 58,290 | 233 | 0 | 14 | 82 | 137 | 1,406 | 278 | 938 | 190 | 6 |
| Rochester | 5,346 | 10 | 0 | 1 | 1 | 8 | 54 | 20 | 28 | 6 | 1 |
| Rockland | 17,941 | 61 | 0 | 7 | 13 | 41 | 375 | 81 | 273 | 21 | |
| Rockport | 7,709 | 6 | 0 | 0 | 0 | 6 | 11 | 3 | 6 | 2 | 0 |
| Royalston | 1,406 | 4 | 0 | 0 | 0 | 4 | 12 | 8 | 4 | 0 | 0 |
| Rutland | 8,109 | 15 | 0 | 4 | 1 | 10 | 55 | 27 | 23 | 5 | 1 |

[1] The FBI does not publish arson data unless it receives data from either the agency or the state for all 12 months of the calendar year.
[5] The FBI determined that the agency did not follow national Uniform Crime Reporting (UCR) Program guidelines for reporting an offense. Consequently, this figure is not included in this table.

**Table 8. Offenses Known to Law Enforcement, by State and City, 2009—*Continued***

(Number.)

| State/city | Population | Violent crime | Murder and non-negligent man-slaughter | Forcible rape | Robbery | Aggravated assault | Property crime | Burglary | Larceny-theft | Motor vehicle theft | Arson[1] |
|---|---|---|---|---|---|---|---|---|---|---|---|
| **MASSACHUSETTS**—*Continued* | | | | | | | | | | | |
| Salisbury | 8,715 | 36 | 0 | 1 | 2 | 33 | 194 | 92 | 97 | 5 | 0 |
| Sandwich | 20,349 | 63 | 0 | 8 | 6 | 49 | 349 | 82 | 260 | 7 | 4 |
| Saugus | 27,663 | 132 | 0 | 9 | 22 | 101 | 1,138 | 265 | 815 | 58 | 2 |
| Savoy | 730 | 0 | 0 | 0 | 0 | 0 | 0 | 0 | 0 | 0 | 0 |
| Scituate | 18,032 | 25 | 0 | 0 | 2 | 23 | 244 | 66 | 159 | 19 | 4 |
| Sharon | 17,256 | 10 | 0 | 0 | 1 | 9 | 112 | 23 | 83 | 6 | 1 |
| Shelburne | 2,056 | 4 | 0 | 0 | 0 | 4 | 17 | 1 | 14 | 2 | 1 |
| Sherborn | 4,281 | 2 | 0 | 0 | 0 | 2 | 29 | 12 | 15 | 2 | 0 |
| Shirley | 7,853 | 7 | 0 | 0 | 0 | 7 | 55 | 22 | 29 | 4 | 0 |
| Shrewsbury | 33,957 | 6 | 0 | 2 | 2 | 2 | 346 | 48 | 283 | 15 | 0 |
| Somerville | 75,112 | 312 | 3 | 7 | 104 | 198 | 1,955 | 494 | 1,301 | 160 | 4 |
| Southampton | 6,160 | 16 | 0 | 0 | 1 | 15 | 52 | 11 | 39 | 2 | 0 |
| Southborough | 9,640 | 4 | 0 | 0 | 3 | 1 | 48 | 20 | 23 | 5 | 0 |
| Southbridge | 17,012 | 75 | 0 | 7 | 7 | 61 | 363 | 150 | 195 | 18 | 6 |
| South Hadley | 17,267 | 29 | 0 | 1 | 5 | 23 | 253 | 66 | 168 | 19 | 1 |
| Southwick | 9,651 | 12 | 0 | 0 | 0 | 12 | 133 | 51 | 73 | 9 | 0 |
| Springfield | 153,533 | 1,929 | 16 | 116 | 581 | 1,216 | 7,518 | 2,068 | 4,615 | 835 | 50 |
| Sterling | 8,009 | 7 | 0 | 3 | 0 | 4 | 91 | 48 | 38 | 5 | 3 |
| Stockbridge | 2,251 | 4 | 0 | 0 | 0 | 4 | 118 | 68 | 48 | 2 | 0 |
| Stow | 6,473 | 2 | 0 | 1 | 0 | 1 | 19 | 5 | 13 | 1 | 0 |
| Sturbridge | 9,335 | 20 | 0 | 3 | 1 | 16 | 153 | 39 | 112 | 2 | 1 |
| Sudbury | 17,445 | 8 | 0 | 1 | 1 | 6 | 84 | 18 | 63 | 3 | 0 |
| Sutton | 9,175 | 10 | 0 | 0 | 3 | 7 | 76 | 23 | 46 | 7 | 0 |
| Swampscott | 14,111 | 21 | 0 | 1 | 4 | 16 | 279 | 34 | 235 | 10 | 0 |
| Swansea | 16,479 | 50 | 0 | 1 | 6 | 43 | 314 | 63 | 231 | 20 | 0 |
| Taunton | 56,446 | 344 | 2 | 16 | 80 | 246 | 1,183 | 523 | 586 | 74 | 5 |
| Templeton | 7,970 | 20 | 0 | 0 | 2 | 18 | 103 | 39 | 57 | 7 | 0 |
| Tewksbury | 30,133 | 82 | 0 | 12 | 8 | 62 | 557 | 96 | 431 | 30 | 2 |
| Tisbury | 3,841 | 13 | 0 | 3 | 1 | 9 | 136 | 19 | 115 | 2 | 0 |
| Townsend | 9,534 | 5 | 0 | 1 | 0 | 4 | 124 | 77 | 38 | 9 | 1 |
| Truro | 2,149 | 1 | 0 | 0 | 0 | 1 | 25 | 10 | 15 | 0 | 0 |
| Tyngsboro | 12,133 | 20 | 0 | 1 | 1 | 18 | 167 | 39 | 118 | 10 | 0 |
| Upton | 6,678 | 3 | 0 | 0 | 0 | 3 | 47 | 7 | 38 | 2 | 1 |
| Wakefield | 25,057 | 57 | 1 | 9 | 4 | 43 | 275 | 51 | 207 | 17 | 2 |
| Wales | 1,885 | 0 | 0 | 0 | 0 | 0 | 5 | 1 | 4 | 0 | 1 |
| Walpole | 23,483 | 23 | 0 | 5 | 7 | 11 | 415 | 36 | 370 | 9 | 1 |
| Waltham | 61,357 | 115 | 0 | 8 | 24 | 83 | 878 | 166 | 653 | 59 | 7 |
| Ware | 10,165 | 45 | 0 | 2 | 8 | 35 | 170 | 44 | 113 | 13 | 0 |
| Wareham | 21,432 | 146 | 1 | 12 | 30 | 103 | 681 | 212 | 432 | 37 | 4 |
| Warren | 5,146 | 33 | 0 | 1 | 1 | 31 | 76 | 25 | 50 | 1 | 0 |
| Watertown | 32,944 | 38 | 0 | 2 | 7 | 29 | 630 | 89 | 509 | 32 | 0 |
| Wayland | 13,195 | 4 | 0 | 0 | 3 | 1 | 33 | 6 | 23 | 4 | 0 |
| Wellesley | 27,407 | 29 | 0 | 3 | 3 | 23 | 223 | 54 | 165 | 4 | 0 |
| Wellfleet | 2,758 | 3 | 0 | 0 | 0 | 3 | 68 | 34 | 32 | 2 | 0 |
| Wenham | 4,665 | 3 | 0 | 1 | 1 | 1 | 20 | 6 | 14 | 0 | 1 |
| Westborough | 18,647 | 24 | 0 | 1 | 0 | 23 | 266 | 61 | 184 | 21 | 2 |
| West Boylston | 8,364 | 9 | 0 | 0 | 3 | 6 | 160 | 20 | 137 | 3 | 0 |
| West Brookfield | 3,856 | 5 | 0 | 0 | 0 | 5 | 31 | 6 | 24 | 1 | 0 |
| Westfield | 41,474 | 91 | 0 | 20 | 15 | 56 | 692 | 157 | 496 | 39 | 3 |
| Westford | 22,239 | 30 | 0 | 2 | 1 | 27 | 196 | 47 | 144 | 5 | 0 |
| Westhampton | 1,634 | 1 | 0 | 0 | 0 | 1 | 7 | 4 | 3 | 0 | 0 |
| Westminster | 7,502 | 19 | 0 | 3 | 0 | 16 | 116 | 13 | 98 | 5 | 2 |
| West Newbury | 4,336 | 17 | 0 | 0 | 0 | 17 | 33 | 4 | 26 | 3 | 0 |
| Weston | 11,897 | 6 | 1 | 1 | 0 | 4 | 71 | 14 | 53 | 4 | 0 |
| Westport | 15,445 | 44 | 0 | 2 | 6 | 36 | 213 | 89 | 101 | 23 | 0 |
| West Tisbury | 2,668 | 4 | 0 | 1 | 0 | 3 | 44 | 11 | 32 | 1 | 0 |
| Westwood | 14,219 | 17 | 0 | 1 | 2 | 14 | 160 | 21 | 124 | 15 | 0 |
| Weymouth | 54,031 | 171 | 1 | 17 | 41 | 112 | 872 | 192 | 623 | 57 | 4 |
| Whately | 1,571 | 1 | 0 | 0 | 0 | 1 | 22 | 5 | 17 | 0 | 0 |
| Whitman | 14,564 | 52 | 0 | 1 | 8 | 43 | 339 | 58 | 269 | 12 | 1 |
| Wilbraham | 14,311 | 20 | 0 | 0 | 3 | 17 | 194 | 29 | 153 | 12 | 0 |
| Williamstown | 8,157 | 17 | 0 | 3 | 0 | 14 | 206 | 29 | 174 | 3 | 2 |
| Wilmington | 22,035 | 40 | 0 | 2 | 4 | 34 | 291 | 76 | 206 | 9 | 1 |
| Winchendon | 10,268 | 38 | 0 | 6 | 2 | 30 | 306 | 28 | 267 | 11 | 1 |
| Winchester | 21,486 | 8 | 0 | 0 | 3 | 5 | 257 | 46 | 205 | 6 | 0 |
| Woburn | 37,555 | 57 | 0 | 7 | 14 | 36 | 700 | 122 | 541 | 37 | 3 |
| Worcester | 178,474 | 1,790 | 7 | 25 | 414 | 1,344 | 6,691 | 1,485 | 4,522 | 684 | 12 |
| Wrentham | 11,360 | 2 | 0 | 1 | 0 | 1 | 188 | 54 | 128 | 6 | 1 |
| Yarmouth | 24,010 | 127 | 1 | 9 | 21 | 96 | 962 | 349 | 581 | 32 | 8 |

[1] The FBI does not publish arson data unless it receives data from either the agency or the state for all 12 months of the calendar year.

## Table 8. Offenses Known to Law Enforcement, by State and City, 2009—*Continued*

(Number.)

| State/city | Population | Violent crime | Murder and non-negligent man-slaughter | Forcible rape | Robbery | Aggravated assault | Property crime | Burglary | Larceny-theft | Motor vehicle theft | Arson[1] |
|---|---|---|---|---|---|---|---|---|---|---|---|
| **MICHIGAN[6]** | | | | | | | | | | | |
| Adrian | 21,295 | 124 | 0 | 32 | 16 | 76 | 683 | 150 | 505 | 28 | 3 |
| Adrian Township | 7,422 | 0 | 0 | 0 | 0 | 0 | 14 | 2 | 12 | 0 | 0 |
| Albion | 9,100 | 66 | 2 | 5 | 13 | 46 | 339 | 102 | 226 | 11 | 4 |
| Algonac | 4,532 | 8 | 0 | 0 | 1 | 7 | 36 | 11 | 24 | 1 | 0 |
| Allegan | 4,826 | 69 | 0 | 7 | 0 | 62 | 100 | 14 | 81 | 5 | 0 |
| Allen Park | 25,658 | 45 | 0 | 2 | 13 | 30 | 664 | 119 | 452 | 93 | 8 |
| Alma | 9,215 | 23 | 0 | 13 | 1 | 9 | 84 | 35 | 48 | 1 | 4 |
| Almont | 2,737 | 11 | 0 | 1 | 0 | 10 | 109 | 25 | 80 | 4 | 2 |
| Alpena | 10,378 | 59 | 2 | 12 | 2 | 43 | 348 | 65 | 277 | 6 | 5 |
| Ann Arbor | 114,367 | 270 | 1 | 29 | 63 | 177 | 2,950 | 609 | 2,216 | 125 | 14 |
| Argentine Township | 7,099 | 22 | 0 | 1 | 0 | 21 | 64 | 28 | 34 | 2 | 1 |
| Armada | 1,661 | 2 | 0 | 0 | 1 | 1 | 11 | 2 | 8 | 1 | 0 |
| Auburn | 2,034 | 0 | 0 | 0 | 0 | 0 | 19 | 0 | 19 | 0 | 0 |
| Auburn Hills | 21,021 | 75 | 0 | 3 | 16 | 56 | 872 | 98 | 726 | 48 | 5 |
| Bad Axe | 3,029 | 3 | 0 | 1 | 1 | 1 | 157 | 15 | 139 | 3 | 0 |
| Bangor | 1,828 | 3 | 0 | 0 | 0 | 3 | 95 | 14 | 80 | 1 | 1 |
| Barry Township | 3,537 | 0 | 0 | 0 | 0 | 0 | 12 | 4 | 8 | 0 | 0 |
| Bath Township | 11,886 | 5 | 0 | 0 | 2 | 3 | 132 | 38 | 91 | 3 | 1 |
| Battle Creek | 61,139 | 636 | 8 | 53 | 137 | 438 | 3,263 | 1,166 | 1,964 | 133 | 26 |
| Bay City | 33,572 | 218 | 2 | 33 | 43 | 140 | 1,067 | 294 | 733 | 40 | 11 |
| Beaverton | 1,054 | 1 | 0 | 1 | 0 | 0 | 21 | 1 | 19 | 1 | 0 |
| Belding | 5,672 | 30 | 0 | 9 | 1 | 20 | 303 | 52 | 245 | 6 | 0 |
| Bellaire | 1,118 | 1 | 0 | 0 | 0 | 1 | 17 | 2 | 15 | 0 | 0 |
| Belleville | 3,510 | 5 | 0 | 0 | 2 | 3 | 118 | 27 | 86 | 5 | 1 |
| Benton Harbor | 10,760 | 135 | 0 | 8 | 15 | 112 | 247 | 109 | 127 | 11 | 4 |
| Benton Township | 15,043 | 164 | 0 | 17 | 46 | 101 | 1,315 | 206 | 1,054 | 55 | 3 |
| Berkley | 14,708 | 13 | 0 | 1 | 1 | 11 | 233 | 30 | 186 | 17 | 2 |
| Berrien Springs-Oronoko Township | 9,534 | 16 | 0 | 8 | 1 | 7 | 258 | 39 | 212 | 7 | 4 |
| Beverly Hills | 9,805 | 3 | 0 | 0 | 2 | 1 | 127 | 17 | 106 | 4 | 0 |
| Big Rapids | 10,194 | 28 | 0 | 7 | 6 | 15 | 360 | 80 | 273 | 7 | 3 |
| Birch Run | 1,636 | 4 | 0 | 2 | 0 | 2 | 108 | 5 | 99 | 4 | 0 |
| Birmingham | 18,895 | 18 | 0 | 1 | 4 | 13 | 390 | 70 | 300 | 20 | 1 |
| Blackman Township | 24,512 | 50 | 2 | 11 | 17 | 20 | 660 | 73 | 564 | 23 | 2 |
| Blissfield | 3,164 | 0 | 0 | 0 | 0 | 0 | 102 | 8 | 91 | 3 | 0 |
| Bloomfield Hills | 3,755 | 3 | 0 | 1 | 0 | 2 | 61 | 13 | 42 | 6 | 0 |
| Bloomfield Township | 40,699 | 29 | 0 | 3 | 11 | 15 | 638 | 118 | 487 | 33 | 1 |
| Boyne City | 3,103 | 5 | 0 | 1 | 1 | 3 | 129 | 17 | 110 | 2 | 0 |
| Breckenridge | 1,278 | 0 | 0 | 0 | 0 | 0 | 24 | 5 | 18 | 1 | 0 |
| Bridgeport Township | 10,727 | 62 | 0 | 5 | 7 | 50 | 351 | 141 | 189 | 21 | 2 |
| Bridgman | 2,396 | 4 | 0 | 2 | 0 | 2 | 80 | 15 | 62 | 3 | 0 |
| Brighton | 7,256 | 8 | 0 | 2 | 0 | 6 | 165 | 17 | 147 | 1 | 5 |
| Bronson | 2,258 | 4 | 0 | 0 | 0 | 4 | 64 | 15 | 48 | 1 | 0 |
| Brown City | 1,243 | 1 | 0 | 1 | 0 | 0 | 23 | 5 | 18 | 0 | 0 |
| Brownstown Township | 29,045 | 62 | 1 | 12 | 12 | 37 | 549 | 172 | 321 | 56 | 5 |
| Buchanan | 4,320 | 29 | 0 | 9 | 1 | 19 | 182 | 26 | 150 | 6 | 1 |
| Buena Vista Township | 9,253 | 93 | 0 | 4 | 20 | 69 | 499 | 253 | 205 | 41 | 12 |
| Burr Oak | 745 | 0 | 0 | 0 | 0 | 0 | 16 | 4 | 12 | 0 | 0 |
| Burton | 29,788 | 145 | 2 | 18 | 51 | 74 | 1,607 | 389 | 1,132 | 86 | 5 |
| Cadillac | 10,271 | 54 | 0 | 8 | 7 | 39 | 589 | 104 | 475 | 10 | 2 |
| Calumet | 795 | 1 | 0 | 0 | 0 | 1 | 28 | 7 | 20 | 1 | 0 |
| Cambridge Township | 5,865 | 0 | 0 | 0 | 0 | 0 | 5 | 1 | 4 | 0 | 0 |
| Camp Grayling | 0 | 0 | 0 | 0 | 0 | 0 | 0 | 0 | 0 | 0 | 0 |
| Canton Township | 82,634 | 138 | 1 | 21 | 26 | 90 | 1,506 | 294 | 1,120 | 92 | 9 |
| Capac | 2,089 | 1 | 0 | 0 | 0 | 1 | 34 | 8 | 25 | 1 | 0 |
| Carleton | 2,572 | 6 | 0 | 1 | 0 | 5 | 44 | 7 | 34 | 3 | 5 |
| Caro | 3,994 | 18 | 0 | 5 | 2 | 11 | 214 | 26 | 186 | 2 | 1 |
| Carrollton Township | 5,904 | 15 | 0 | 1 | 2 | 12 | 183 | 79 | 99 | 5 | 0 |
| Caseville | 829 | 2 | 0 | 1 | 0 | 1 | 33 | 3 | 30 | 0 | 0 |
| Cassopolis | 1,924 | 1 | 0 | 0 | 0 | 1 | 13 | 0 | 12 | 1 | 0 |
| Cedar Springs | 3,259 | 12 | 0 | 4 | 2 | 6 | 106 | 16 | 87 | 3 | 0 |
| Center Line | 8,093 | 37 | 0 | 4 | 12 | 21 | 245 | 23 | 173 | 49 | 1 |
| Central Lake | 962 | 0 | 0 | 0 | 0 | 0 | 12 | 0 | 11 | 1 | 0 |
| Charlevoix | 2,622 | 3 | 0 | 1 | 0 | 2 | 82 | 12 | 70 | 0 | 1 |
| Charlotte | 8,996 | 26 | 0 | 11 | 1 | 14 | 272 | 26 | 234 | 12 | 2 |
| Cheboygan | 4,904 | 4 | 0 | 2 | 0 | 2 | 170 | 24 | 146 | 0 | 0 |
| Chelsea | 5,075 | 7 | 0 | 3 | 1 | 3 | 98 | 26 | 70 | 2 | 1 |
| Chesaning | 2,324 | 3 | 0 | 0 | 0 | 3 | 25 | 7 | 18 | 0 | 0 |
| Chesterfield Township | 45,432 | 139 | 2 | 10 | 13 | 114 | 1,302 | 218 | 1,022 | 62 | 7 |
| Chikaming Township | 3,653 | 3 | 0 | 1 | 0 | 2 | 72 | 23 | 49 | 0 | 0 |

[1] The FBI does not publish arson data unless it receives data from either the agency or the state for all 12 months of the calendar year.
[6] Because of changes in the state/local agency's reporting practices, figures are not comparable to previous years' data.

## Table 8. Offenses Known to Law Enforcement, by State and City, 2009—*Continued*

(Number.)

| State/city | Population | Violent crime | Murder and non-negligent man-slaughter | Forcible rape | Robbery | Aggravated assault | Property crime | Burglary | Larceny-theft | Motor vehicle theft | Arson[1] |
|---|---|---|---|---|---|---|---|---|---|---|---|
| **MICHIGAN**—*Continued* | | | | | | | | | | | |
| Chocolay Township | 6,040 | 0 | 0 | 0 | 0 | 0 | 43 | 2 | 40 | 1 | 0 |
| Clare | 3,080 | 2 | 0 | 0 | 1 | 1 | 122 | 12 | 108 | 2 | 0 |
| Clarkston | 908 | 0 | 0 | 0 | 0 | 0 | 7 | 0 | 7 | 0 | 0 |
| Clawson | 12,097 | 10 | 0 | 1 | 4 | 5 | 113 | 20 | 83 | 10 | 2 |
| Clayton Township | 7,750 | 7 | 0 | 1 | 1 | 5 | 94 | 39 | 55 | 0 | 0 |
| Clay Township | 9,458 | 10 | 0 | 4 | 2 | 4 | 133 | 38 | 94 | 1 | 0 |
| Clinton | 2,400 | 3 | 0 | 2 | 0 | 1 | 40 | 11 | 28 | 1 | 0 |
| Clinton Township | 95,956 | 277 | 1 | 24 | 50 | 202 | 2,303 | 518 | 1,553 | 232 | 15 |
| Clio | 2,490 | 11 | 0 | 1 | 0 | 10 | 77 | 13 | 64 | 0 | 0 |
| Coldwater | 10,527 | 30 | 0 | 8 | 1 | 21 | 359 | 47 | 304 | 8 | 0 |
| Coleman | 1,221 | 8 | 0 | 2 | 0 | 6 | 46 | 12 | 34 | 0 | 0 |
| Coloma Township | 6,503 | 9 | 0 | 1 | 0 | 8 | 110 | 26 | 84 | 0 | 0 |
| Colon | 1,160 | 0 | 0 | 0 | 0 | 0 | 20 | 0 | 18 | 2 | 0 |
| Columbia Township | 7,552 | 8 | 0 | 1 | 1 | 6 | 141 | 14 | 118 | 9 | 1 |
| Corunna | 3,273 | 13 | 0 | 1 | 1 | 11 | 88 | 17 | 68 | 3 | 0 |
| Covert Township | 3,049 | 15 | 0 | 4 | 0 | 11 | 73 | 22 | 49 | 2 | 3 |
| Croswell | 2,455 | 7 | 1 | 2 | 0 | 4 | 93 | 15 | 76 | 2 | 1 |
| Crystal Falls | 1,574 | 0 | 0 | 0 | 0 | 0 | 22 | 4 | 17 | 1 | 0 |
| Davison | 5,093 | 9 | 0 | 1 | 0 | 8 | 74 | 15 | 57 | 2 | 1 |
| Davison Township | 18,561 | 41 | 0 | 10 | 5 | 26 | 358 | 101 | 237 | 20 | 2 |
| Dearborn | 85,305 | 339 | 3 | 16 | 112 | 208 | 4,255 | 712 | 2,961 | 582 | 23 |
| Dearborn Heights | 51,308 | 250 | 0 | 9 | 71 | 170 | 1,464 | 453 | 783 | 228 | 7 |
| Decatur | 1,765 | 12 | 0 | 1 | 1 | 10 | 156 | 15 | 137 | 4 | 1 |
| Denton Township | 5,375 | 2 | 0 | 0 | 0 | 2 | 105 | 23 | 79 | 3 | 0 |
| Detroit | 908,441 | 17,868 | 365 | 335 | 5,913 | 11,255 | 50,578 | 18,993 | 18,574 | 13,011 | 624 |
| Dewitt | 4,399 | 6 | 0 | 2 | 0 | 4 | 33 | 4 | 29 | 0 | 0 |
| Dewitt Township | 13,188 | 29 | 0 | 4 | 4 | 21 | 171 | 55 | 106 | 10 | 0 |
| Dowagiac | 5,670 | 20 | 0 | 4 | 2 | 14 | 295 | 32 | 253 | 10 | 2 |
| Dryden Township | 4,591 | 1 | 0 | 0 | 0 | 1 | 43 | 13 | 27 | 3 | 0 |
| Durand | 3,718 | 5 | 0 | 3 | 0 | 2 | 82 | 21 | 59 | 2 | 0 |
| East Grand Rapids | 10,435 | 7 | 0 | 2 | 1 | 4 | 211 | 39 | 168 | 4 | 1 |
| East Jordan | 2,206 | 13 | 0 | 8 | 0 | 5 | 103 | 12 | 89 | 2 | 1 |
| East Lansing | 45,779 | 160 | 0 | 18 | 31 | 111 | 1,099 | 272 | 798 | 29 | 39 |
| Eastpointe | 32,331 | 268 | 2 | 16 | 84 | 166 | 1,025 | 223 | 507 | 295 | 12 |
| East Tawas | 2,699 | 15 | 0 | 4 | 3 | 8 | 146 | 37 | 107 | 2 | 0 |
| Eaton Rapids | 5,236 | 18 | 0 | 3 | 0 | 15 | 120 | 9 | 108 | 3 | 3 |
| Eau Claire | 620 | 0 | 0 | 0 | 0 | 0 | 17 | 2 | 15 | 0 | 0 |
| Elk Rapids | 1,669 | 6 | 0 | 0 | 0 | 6 | 59 | 7 | 51 | 1 | 0 |
| Elkton | 747 | 1 | 0 | 0 | 0 | 1 | 23 | 6 | 17 | 0 | 0 |
| Elsie | 971 | 1 | 0 | 0 | 0 | 1 | 16 | 3 | 12 | 1 | 0 |
| Emmett Township | 11,791 | 55 | 0 | 3 | 11 | 41 | 636 | 96 | 534 | 6 | 1 |
| Erie Township | 4,654 | 1 | 0 | 0 | 0 | 1 | 43 | 13 | 26 | 4 | 0 |
| Escanaba | 12,117 | 35 | 0 | 9 | 3 | 23 | 669 | 106 | 549 | 14 | 2 |
| Essexville | 3,465 | 4 | 0 | 1 | 1 | 2 | 106 | 16 | 88 | 2 | 0 |
| Evart | 1,659 | 5 | 0 | 2 | 0 | 3 | 19 | 3 | 16 | 0 | 0 |
| Fairgrove | 587 | 0 | 0 | 0 | 0 | 0 | 8 | 1 | 7 | 0 | 0 |
| Farmington | 9,778 | 13 | 0 | 0 | 2 | 11 | 215 | 29 | 171 | 15 | 1 |
| Farmington Hills | 78,140 | 108 | 1 | 10 | 20 | 77 | 1,520 | 256 | 1,134 | 130 | 8 |
| Fenton | 11,796 | 29 | 0 | 2 | 8 | 19 | 327 | 48 | 260 | 19 | 1 |
| Ferndale | 21,008 | 91 | 1 | 8 | 25 | 57 | 674 | 151 | 413 | 110 | 9 |
| Flat Rock | 8,797 | 24 | 1 | 1 | 4 | 18 | 216 | 37 | 152 | 27 | 0 |
| Flint | 111,657 | 2,244 | 36 | 91 | 590 | 1,527 | 6,397 | 3,057 | 2,664 | 676 | 173 |
| Flint Township | 31,391 | 215 | 2 | 19 | 79 | 115 | 2,160 | 454 | 1,591 | 115 | 10 |
| Flushing | 7,759 | 8 | 0 | 4 | 1 | 3 | 133 | 17 | 110 | 6 | 1 |
| Flushing Township | 10,078 | 9 | 0 | 3 | 0 | 6 | 101 | 38 | 57 | 6 | 0 |
| Forsyth Township | 4,894 | 13 | 0 | 5 | 0 | 8 | 66 | 10 | 48 | 8 | 0 |
| Fowlerville | 3,113 | 7 | 0 | 2 | 0 | 5 | 100 | 8 | 91 | 1 | 0 |
| Frankenmuth | 4,631 | 3 | 0 | 3 | 0 | 0 | 87 | 17 | 69 | 1 | 0 |
| Frankfort | 1,444 | 3 | 1 | 0 | 0 | 2 | 41 | 7 | 32 | 2 | 0 |
| Franklin | 2,912 | 0 | 0 | 0 | 0 | 0 | 52 | 11 | 41 | 0 | 0 |
| Fraser | 14,861 | 40 | 0 | 6 | 5 | 29 | 407 | 52 | 327 | 28 | 2 |
| Fremont | 4,182 | 10 | 0 | 2 | 0 | 8 | 168 | 19 | 146 | 3 | 1 |
| Frost Township | 1,109 | 0 | 0 | 0 | 0 | 0 | 18 | 11 | 7 | 0 | 0 |
| Fruitport | 1,075 | 23 | 0 | 3 | 6 | 14 | 568 | 39 | 511 | 18 | 2 |
| Gagetown | 364 | 0 | 0 | 0 | 0 | 0 | 2 | 2 | 0 | 0 | 0 |
| Galien | 550 | 0 | 0 | 0 | 0 | 0 | 0 | 0 | 0 | 0 | 0 |
| Garden City | 26,398 | 95 | 0 | 9 | 34 | 52 | 761 | 144 | 527 | 90 | 8 |
| Gaylord | 3,580 | 8 | 0 | 3 | 1 | 4 | 249 | 41 | 205 | 3 | 0 |
| Genesee Township | 22,926 | 103 | 1 | 12 | 16 | 74 | 691 | 303 | 342 | 46 | 4 |
| Gerrish Township | 3,075 | 4 | 0 | 1 | 0 | 3 | 27 | 1 | 26 | 0 | 0 |

[1] The FBI does not publish arson data unless it receives data from either the agency or the state for all 12 months of the calendar year.

## Table 8. Offenses Known to Law Enforcement, by State and City, 2009—*Continued*

(Number.)

| State/city | Population | Violent crime | Murder and non-negligent man-slaughter | Forcible rape | Robbery | Aggravated assault | Property crime | Burglary | Larceny-theft | Motor vehicle theft | Arson[1] |
|---|---|---|---|---|---|---|---|---|---|---|---|
| **MICHIGAN**—*Continued* | | | | | | | | | | | |
| Gibraltar | 4,893 | 12 | 0 | 1 | 3 | 8 | 111 | 12 | 84 | 15 | 1 |
| Gladstone | 5,068 | 7 | 0 | 4 | 0 | 3 | 96 | 18 | 78 | 0 | 0 |
| Gladwin | 2,891 | 15 | 0 | 2 | 0 | 13 | 133 | 25 | 108 | 0 | 1 |
| Grand Beach | 242 | 0 | 0 | 0 | 0 | 0 | 4 | 1 | 3 | 0 | 0 |
| Grand Blanc | 7,479 | 20 | 0 | 3 | 6 | 11 | 226 | 50 | 169 | 7 | 2 |
| Grand Blanc Township | 35,451 | 83 | 2 | 5 | 10 | 66 | 854 | 239 | 584 | 31 | 6 |
| Grand Haven | 10,548 | 33 | 0 | 7 | 2 | 24 | 340 | 33 | 300 | 7 | 1 |
| Grand Ledge | 7,653 | 5 | 0 | 0 | 0 | 5 | 177 | 19 | 155 | 3 | 0 |
| Grand Rapids | 192,901 | 1,604 | 9 | 78 | 581 | 936 | 8,835 | 2,454 | 6,010 | 371 | 76 |
| Grandville | 16,763 | 47 | 0 | 11 | 11 | 25 | 828 | 76 | 733 | 19 | 2 |
| Grayling | 1,822 | 3 | 0 | 0 | 0 | 3 | 74 | 8 | 66 | 0 | 0 |
| Green Oak Township | 17,836 | 25 | 0 | 4 | 3 | 18 | 329 | 63 | 255 | 11 | 0 |
| Greenville | 8,165 | 26 | 0 | 8 | 3 | 15 | 535 | 61 | 465 | 9 | 0 |
| Grosse Ile Township | 9,776 | 1 | 0 | 0 | 1 | 0 | 55 | 3 | 49 | 3 | 0 |
| Grosse Pointe | 4,926 | 8 | 0 | 1 | 1 | 6 | 88 | 5 | 70 | 13 | 0 |
| Grosse Pointe Farms | 8,495 | 6 | 0 | 0 | 1 | 5 | 130 | 11 | 88 | 31 | 1 |
| Grosse Pointe Park | 10,802 | 15 | 0 | 1 | 6 | 8 | 287 | 18 | 227 | 42 | 0 |
| Grosse Pointe Shores | 2,476 | 0 | 0 | 0 | 0 | 0 | 0 | 0 | 0 | 0 | 0 |
| Grosse Pointe Woods | 14,954 | 23 | 0 | 0 | 8 | 15 | 289 | 25 | 237 | 27 | 0 |
| Hamburg Township | 21,772 | 8 | 0 | 1 | 0 | 7 | 102 | 24 | 77 | 1 | 2 |
| Hampton Township | 9,679 | 21 | 0 | 10 | 1 | 10 | 404 | 75 | 322 | 7 | 1 |
| Hamtramck | 20,255 | 378 | 1 | 12 | 137 | 228 | 1,152 | 435 | 356 | 361 | 23 |
| Hancock | 4,141 | 2 | 0 | 1 | 0 | 1 | 81 | 25 | 54 | 2 | 1 |
| Harbor Beach | 1,595 | 2 | 0 | 0 | 0 | 2 | 32 | 7 | 25 | 0 | 1 |
| Harbor Springs | 1,545 | 0 | 0 | 0 | 0 | 0 | 49 | 4 | 45 | 0 | 0 |
| Harper Woods | 12,411 | 136 | 0 | 8 | 56 | 72 | 1,211 | 144 | 723 | 344 | 3 |
| Hart | 1,911 | 8 | 0 | 0 | 1 | 7 | 116 | 8 | 107 | 1 | 0 |
| Hartford | 2,451 | 6 | 0 | 2 | 1 | 3 | 73 | 22 | 50 | 1 | 0 |
| Hastings | 6,832 | 19 | 0 | 5 | 1 | 13 | 185 | 22 | 154 | 9 | 2 |
| Hazel Park | 17,851 | 98 | 0 | 7 | 30 | 61 | 507 | 132 | 240 | 135 | 7 |
| Hillsdale | 7,710 | 8 | 0 | 2 | 3 | 3 | 226 | 42 | 177 | 7 | 2 |
| Holland | 33,970 | 122 | 0 | 26 | 19 | 77 | 1,132 | 225 | 890 | 17 | 6 |
| Holly | 6,283 | 18 | 0 | 4 | 2 | 12 | 134 | 30 | 97 | 7 | 0 |
| Homer | 1,736 | 13 | 0 | 0 | 1 | 12 | 21 | 7 | 14 | 0 | 0 |
| Houghton | 6,852 | 12 | 0 | 2 | 0 | 10 | 122 | 4 | 113 | 5 | 2 |
| Howell | 9,733 | 37 | 0 | 6 | 1 | 30 | 289 | 44 | 236 | 9 | 1 |
| Hudson | 2,294 | 2 | 0 | 1 | 0 | 1 | 107 | 14 | 84 | 9 | 0 |
| Huntington Woods | 5,776 | 4 | 0 | 0 | 0 | 4 | 86 | 7 | 74 | 5 | 0 |
| Huron Township | 16,133 | 38 | 0 | 7 | 4 | 27 | 405 | 98 | 276 | 31 | 2 |
| Imlay City | 3,667 | 8 | 0 | 2 | 0 | 6 | 98 | 16 | 77 | 5 | 0 |
| Inkster | 26,261 | 451 | 9 | 23 | 90 | 329 | 903 | 366 | 404 | 133 | 18 |
| Ionia | 12,713 | 24 | 0 | 9 | 1 | 14 | 245 | 38 | 202 | 5 | 0 |
| Iron River | 2,964 | 5 | 0 | 3 | 0 | 2 | 83 | 21 | 56 | 6 | 4 |
| Ishpeming | 6,459 | 7 | 0 | 0 | 2 | 5 | 115 | 20 | 90 | 5 | 1 |
| Ishpeming Township | 3,615 | 0 | 0 | 0 | 0 | 0 | 10 | 1 | 9 | 0 | 0 |
| Ithaca | 3,008 | 2 | 0 | 1 | 0 | 1 | 65 | 6 | 59 | 0 | 0 |
| Jackson | 33,228 | 366 | 2 | 58 | 70 | 236 | 1,769 | 384 | 1,309 | 76 | 18 |
| Jonesville | 2,216 | 10 | 0 | 2 | 0 | 8 | 72 | 7 | 64 | 1 | 0 |
| Kalamazoo | 71,664 | 702 | 2 | 71 | 204 | 425 | 4,326 | 1,430 | 2,632 | 264 | 30 |
| Kalamazoo Township | 22,008 | 88 | 1 | 12 | 16 | 59 | 536 | 213 | 293 | 30 | 1 |
| Kalkaska | 2,164 | 2 | 0 | 0 | 0 | 2 | 107 | 11 | 89 | 7 | 1 |
| Keego Harbor | 2,846 | 3 | 0 | 1 | 0 | 2 | 33 | 8 | 23 | 2 | 0 |
| Kentwood | 47,646 | 185 | 0 | 7 | 52 | 126 | 1,606 | 369 | 1,144 | 93 | 9 |
| Kingsford | 5,270 | 7 | 0 | 7 | 0 | 0 | 59 | 5 | 54 | 0 | 0 |
| Kinross Township | 8,869 | 2 | 0 | 0 | 0 | 2 | 35 | 5 | 29 | 1 | 0 |
| Laingsburg | 1,251 | 0 | 0 | 0 | 0 | 0 | 28 | 8 | 20 | 0 | 0 |
| Lake Angelus | 311 | 0 | 0 | 0 | 0 | 0 | 4 | 0 | 4 | 0 | 0 |
| Lake Linden | 1,044 | 0 | 0 | 0 | 0 | 0 | 4 | 1 | 2 | 1 | 0 |
| Lake Odessa | 2,209 | 3 | 0 | 2 | 0 | 1 | 17 | 2 | 14 | 1 | 0 |
| Lake Orion | 2,712 | 7 | 0 | 1 | 0 | 6 | 85 | 10 | 73 | 2 | 2 |
| Lakeview | 1,089 | 1 | 0 | 0 | 0 | 1 | 41 | 15 | 26 | 0 | 0 |
| Lansing | 113,392 | 1,200 | 11 | 89 | 255 | 845 | 3,882 | 1,340 | 2,341 | 201 | 33 |
| Lapeer | 9,007 | 28 | 0 | 5 | 4 | 19 | 392 | 42 | 343 | 7 | 0 |
| Lapeer Township | 5,012 | 1 | 0 | 0 | 0 | 1 | 17 | 2 | 11 | 4 | 0 |
| Lathrup Village | 4,042 | 25 | 0 | 1 | 6 | 18 | 107 | 20 | 76 | 11 | 1 |
| Laurium | 1,991 | 1 | 0 | 1 | 0 | 0 | 30 | 4 | 26 | 0 | 0 |
| Lawton | 1,794 | 2 | 0 | 0 | 0 | 2 | 56 | 9 | 41 | 6 | 1 |
| Lennon | 488 | 1 | 0 | 0 | 0 | 1 | 11 | 4 | 6 | 1 | 0 |
| Leoni Township | 13,505 | 8 | 0 | 0 | 1 | 7 | 188 | 46 | 123 | 19 | 1 |
| Leslie | 2,302 | 1 | 0 | 0 | 1 | 0 | 40 | 7 | 29 | 4 | 0 |

[1] The FBI does not publish arson data unless it receives data from either the agency or the state for all 12 months of the calendar year.

## Table 8. Offenses Known to Law Enforcement, by State and City, 2009—*Continued*

(Number.)

| State/city | Population | Violent crime | Murder and non-negligent man-slaughter | Forcible rape | Robbery | Aggravated assault | Property crime | Burglary | Larceny-theft | Motor vehicle theft | Arson[1] |
|---|---|---|---|---|---|---|---|---|---|---|---|
| **MICHIGAN**—*Continued* | | | | | | | | | | | |
| Lexington | 1,040 | 2 | 0 | 0 | 0 | 2 | 20 | 5 | 13 | 2 | 0 |
| Lincoln Park | 34,832 | 111 | 0 | 10 | 41 | 60 | 1,643 | 389 | 1,052 | 202 | 12 |
| Lincoln Township | 14,342 | 4 | 0 | 2 | 0 | 2 | 245 | 32 | 212 | 1 | 3 |
| Linden | 3,417 | 1 | 0 | 0 | 1 | 0 | 42 | 3 | 39 | 0 | 0 |
| Litchfield | 1,385 | 0 | 0 | 0 | 0 | 0 | 39 | 21 | 18 | 0 | 0 |
| Livonia | 90,232 | 176 | 3 | 16 | 40 | 117 | 2,232 | 341 | 1,580 | 311 | 13 |
| Lowell | 4,167 | 11 | 0 | 2 | 0 | 9 | 52 | 14 | 30 | 8 | 1 |
| Ludington | 8,319 | 35 | 0 | 11 | 4 | 20 | 280 | 45 | 230 | 5 | 2 |
| Luna Pier | 1,524 | 2 | 0 | 1 | 0 | 1 | 39 | 10 | 29 | 0 | 0 |
| Mackinac Island | 456 | 10 | 0 | 4 | 0 | 6 | 371 | 6 | 363 | 2 | 0 |
| Mackinaw City | 838 | 0 | 0 | 0 | 0 | 0 | 47 | 1 | 45 | 1 | 0 |
| Madison Heights | 29,367 | 84 | 0 | 10 | 25 | 49 | 877 | 143 | 607 | 127 | 6 |
| Madison Township | 8,155 | 0 | 0 | 0 | 0 | 0 | 47 | 6 | 41 | 0 | 0 |
| Mancelona | 1,349 | 1 | 0 | 0 | 0 | 1 | 28 | 7 | 20 | 1 | 0 |
| Manistee | 6,058 | 1 | 0 | 0 | 0 | 1 | 136 | 23 | 108 | 5 | 0 |
| Manistique | 3,034 | 14 | 0 | 10 | 0 | 4 | 106 | 14 | 85 | 7 | 1 |
| Manton | 1,161 | 0 | 0 | 0 | 0 | 0 | 14 | 2 | 11 | 1 | 0 |
| Marine City | 4,349 | 8 | 1 | 0 | 0 | 7 | 137 | 26 | 111 | 0 | 1 |
| Marion | 798 | 1 | 0 | 0 | 0 | 1 | 21 | 5 | 16 | 0 | 0 |
| Marlette | 1,971 | 16 | 0 | 3 | 0 | 13 | 56 | 10 | 44 | 2 | 0 |
| Marquette | 20,943 | 25 | 0 | 9 | 2 | 14 | 442 | 60 | 371 | 11 | 1 |
| Marshall | 7,085 | 17 | 3 | 2 | 0 | 12 | 183 | 21 | 157 | 5 | 1 |
| Marysville | 9,972 | 11 | 0 | 5 | 0 | 6 | 232 | 37 | 188 | 7 | 1 |
| Mason | 8,204 | 10 | 0 | 0 | 2 | 8 | 185 | 14 | 165 | 6 | 1 |
| Mattawan | 2,830 | 0 | 0 | 0 | 0 | 0 | 72 | 3 | 69 | 0 | 0 |
| Melvindale | 9,715 | 38 | 1 | 2 | 11 | 24 | 321 | 61 | 226 | 34 | 5 |
| Memphis | 1,108 | 3 | 0 | 1 | 0 | 2 | 14 | 4 | 10 | 0 | 0 |
| Mendon | 906 | 0 | 0 | 0 | 0 | 0 | 8 | 1 | 7 | 0 | 0 |
| Meridian Township | 38,414 | 85 | 0 | 6 | 21 | 58 | 1,244 | 182 | 1,039 | 23 | 10 |
| Metamora Township | 4,625 | 5 | 0 | 1 | 0 | 4 | 55 | 12 | 37 | 6 | 0 |
| Michiana | 192 | 0 | 0 | 0 | 0 | 0 | 6 | 6 | 0 | 0 | 0 |
| Midland | 40,821 | 62 | 1 | 15 | 7 | 39 | 787 | 97 | 669 | 21 | 3 |
| Milan | 5,762 | 17 | 0 | 2 | 0 | 15 | 152 | 26 | 124 | 2 | 2 |
| Milford | 16,661 | 7 | 1 | 1 | 0 | 5 | 123 | 35 | 81 | 7 | 3 |
| Monroe | 21,301 | 63 | 0 | 8 | 12 | 43 | 674 | 142 | 506 | 26 | 5 |
| Morenci | 2,245 | 3 | 0 | 0 | 0 | 3 | 71 | 11 | 60 | 0 | 1 |
| Morrice | 871 | 0 | 0 | 0 | 0 | 0 | 23 | 4 | 19 | 0 | 0 |
| Mount Morris | 3,166 | 30 | 0 | 5 | 7 | 18 | 131 | 41 | 83 | 7 | 3 |
| Mount Morris Township | 22,058 | 145 | 1 | 11 | 52 | 81 | 935 | 404 | 448 | 83 | 14 |
| Mount Pleasant | 26,765 | 47 | 0 | 4 | 2 | 41 | 642 | 106 | 513 | 23 | 10 |
| Mundy Township | 14,141 | 26 | 0 | 5 | 4 | 17 | 416 | 89 | 315 | 12 | 3 |
| Munising | 2,289 | 2 | 0 | 0 | 1 | 1 | 9 | 2 | 7 | 0 | 0 |
| Muskegon | 39,327 | 312 | 1 | 24 | 97 | 190 | 2,307 | 544 | 1,656 | 107 | 9 |
| Muskegon Heights | 11,578 | 226 | 3 | 23 | 64 | 136 | 1,074 | 377 | 601 | 96 | 10 |
| Muskegon Township | 18,354 | 42 | 1 | 3 | 12 | 26 | 914 | 88 | 793 | 33 | 3 |
| Napoleon Township | 6,959 | 18 | 0 | 2 | 0 | 16 | 86 | 20 | 61 | 5 | 3 |
| Nashville | 1,651 | 3 | 0 | 0 | 0 | 3 | 65 | 8 | 55 | 2 | 0 |
| Negaunee | 4,444 | 6 | 0 | 2 | 2 | 2 | 109 | 12 | 88 | 9 | 0 |
| Newaygo | 1,621 | 7 | 0 | 3 | 0 | 4 | 81 | 8 | 72 | 1 | 1 |
| New Baltimore | 11,869 | 19 | 0 | 3 | 3 | 13 | 202 | 32 | 154 | 16 | 1 |
| New Buffalo | 2,449 | 1 | 0 | 0 | 1 | 0 | 92 | 25 | 63 | 4 | 1 |
| New Haven | 5,425 | 11 | 0 | 1 | 1 | 9 | 20 | 2 | 16 | 2 | 1 |
| Niles | 11,159 | 65 | 1 | 12 | 15 | 37 | 388 | 66 | 304 | 18 | 3 |
| Northfield Township | 8,505 | 19 | 0 | 7 | 1 | 11 | 185 | 61 | 112 | 12 | 0 |
| North Muskegon | 3,902 | 2 | 0 | 0 | 1 | 1 | 129 | 3 | 123 | 3 | 0 |
| Northville | 5,947 | 3 | 0 | 0 | 0 | 3 | 103 | 13 | 88 | 2 | 1 |
| Northville Township | 25,266 | 23 | 0 | 3 | 3 | 17 | 491 | 80 | 399 | 12 | 0 |
| Norton Shores | 23,389 | 41 | 0 | 8 | 8 | 25 | 847 | 138 | 684 | 25 | 2 |
| Novi | 54,842 | 52 | 0 | 1 | 10 | 41 | 1,103 | 137 | 925 | 41 | 0 |
| Oak Park | 30,350 | 148 | 0 | 8 | 46 | 94 | 1,002 | 327 | 502 | 173 | 4 |
| Ontwa Township-Edwardsburg | 5,872 | 9 | 0 | 3 | 1 | 5 | 160 | 31 | 117 | 12 | 3 |
| Orchard Lake | 2,207 | 7 | 0 | 0 | 0 | 7 | 30 | 3 | 27 | 0 | 0 |
| Oscoda Township | 6,764 | 32 | 0 | 10 | 1 | 21 | 261 | 86 | 166 | 9 | 1 |
| Otsego | 3,807 | 7 | 0 | 2 | 1 | 4 | 77 | 16 | 59 | 2 | 0 |
| Ovid | 1,387 | 1 | 0 | 0 | 0 | 1 | 21 | 6 | 13 | 2 | 0 |
| Owosso | 14,885 | 75 | 1 | 17 | 9 | 48 | 702 | 117 | 575 | 10 | 2 |
| Oxford | 3,524 | 6 | 0 | 2 | 1 | 3 | 37 | 7 | 29 | 1 | 0 |
| Parchment | 1,795 | 9 | 0 | 1 | 0 | 8 | 78 | 8 | 66 | 4 | 1 |
| Parma-Sandstone | 6,782 | 15 | 0 | 0 | 0 | 15 | 31 | 9 | 20 | 2 | 0 |
| Paw Paw | 3,206 | 11 | 0 | 2 | 0 | 9 | 155 | 30 | 123 | 2 | 2 |

[1] The FBI does not publish arson data unless it receives data from either the agency or the state for all 12 months of the calendar year.

## Table 8. Offenses Known to Law Enforcement, by State and City, 2009—*Continued*

(Number.)

| State/city | Population | Violent crime | Murder and non-negligent man-slaughter | Forcible rape | Robbery | Aggravated assault | Property crime | Burglary | Larceny-theft | Motor vehicle theft | Arson[1] |
|---|---|---|---|---|---|---|---|---|---|---|---|
| **MICHIGAN**—*Continued* | | | | | | | | | | | |
| Peck | 558 | 0 | 0 | 0 | 0 | 0 | 10 | 1 | 8 | 1 | 0 |
| Pentwater | 940 | 1 | 0 | 0 | 0 | 1 | 24 | 0 | 24 | 0 | 0 |
| Perry | 2,016 | 1 | 0 | 0 | 0 | 1 | 19 | 4 | 15 | 0 | 0 |
| Petoskey | 6,022 | 10 | 0 | 0 | 0 | 10 | 126 | 14 | 111 | 1 | 0 |
| Pinckney | 2,449 | 11 | 0 | 2 | 0 | 9 | 87 | 10 | 76 | 1 | 2 |
| Pittsfield Township | 34,699 | 78 | 1 | 16 | 14 | 47 | 1,218 | 211 | 932 | 75 | 4 |
| Plainwell | 3,840 | 13 | 0 | 2 | 2 | 9 | 99 | 5 | 91 | 3 | 0 |
| Pleasant Ridge | 2,456 | 0 | 0 | 0 | 0 | 0 | 20 | 6 | 11 | 3 | 0 |
| Plymouth | 8,430 | 23 | 0 | 1 | 4 | 18 | 197 | 29 | 152 | 16 | 3 |
| Plymouth Township | 25,071 | 22 | 0 | 3 | 9 | 10 | 445 | 77 | 344 | 24 | 2 |
| Pontiac | 65,924 | 1,212 | 10 | 57 | 343 | 802 | 2,312 | 1,026 | 959 | 327 | 27 |
| Portage | 46,269 | 140 | 2 | 24 | 24 | 90 | 1,953 | 248 | 1,653 | 52 | 4 |
| Port Austin | 643 | 1 | 0 | 1 | 0 | 0 | 31 | 6 | 24 | 1 | 0 |
| Port Huron | 30,718 | 214 | 2 | 16 | 55 | 141 | 1,356 | 315 | 974 | 67 | 11 |
| Portland | 3,672 | 6 | 0 | 1 | 0 | 5 | 87 | 13 | 72 | 2 | 1 |
| Potterville | 2,144 | 7 | 0 | 1 | 0 | 6 | 49 | 9 | 37 | 3 | 0 |
| Prairieville Township | 3,512 | 0 | 0 | 0 | 0 | 0 | 23 | 8 | 15 | 0 | 0 |
| Raisin Township | 7,368 | 2 | 0 | 0 | 0 | 2 | 29 | 4 | 22 | 3 | 0 |
| Reading | 1,064 | 0 | 0 | 0 | 0 | 0 | 12 | 1 | 11 | 0 | 0 |
| Redford Township | 45,291 | 207 | 1 | 9 | 92 | 105 | 1,686 | 444 | 949 | 293 | 18 |
| Reed City | 2,319 | 5 | 0 | 5 | 0 | 0 | 37 | 3 | 32 | 2 | 1 |
| Richfield Township, Genesee County | 8,570 | 8 | 0 | 4 | 0 | 4 | 138 | 85 | 46 | 7 | 3 |
| Richfield Township, Roscommon County | 4,072 | 1 | 0 | 0 | 0 | 1 | 33 | 6 | 26 | 1 | 0 |
| Richland | 771 | 0 | 0 | 0 | 0 | 0 | 10 | 2 | 8 | 0 | 0 |
| Richland Township, Saginaw County | 4,214 | 2 | 0 | 0 | 0 | 2 | 34 | 10 | 24 | 0 | 0 |
| Richmond | 5,684 | 41 | 0 | 5 | 3 | 33 | 105 | 13 | 90 | 2 | 3 |
| Riverview | 11,665 | 13 | 0 | 2 | 6 | 5 | 167 | 25 | 119 | 23 | 0 |
| Rochester | 11,057 | 14 | 0 | 1 | 2 | 11 | 191 | 29 | 158 | 4 | 5 |
| Rockford | 5,503 | 8 | 0 | 2 | 1 | 5 | 139 | 12 | 126 | 1 | 0 |
| Rockwood | 3,127 | 7 | 0 | 0 | 0 | 7 | 58 | 13 | 37 | 8 | 0 |
| Rogers City | 3,002 | 6 | 0 | 2 | 0 | 4 | 58 | 6 | 52 | 0 | 0 |
| Romeo | 3,739 | 15 | 0 | 2 | 1 | 12 | 50 | 6 | 41 | 3 | 1 |
| Romulus | 22,957 | 158 | 3 | 18 | 40 | 97 | 1,144 | 324 | 661 | 159 | 2 |
| Roosevelt Park | 3,756 | 6 | 0 | 1 | 1 | 4 | 220 | 18 | 199 | 3 | 0 |
| Roseville | 46,642 | 241 | 0 | 26 | 50 | 165 | 1,924 | 320 | 1,377 | 227 | 26 |
| Rothbury | 435 | 1 | 0 | 0 | 0 | 1 | 24 | 2 | 22 | 0 | 0 |
| Royal Oak | 56,800 | 99 | 0 | 24 | 17 | 58 | 909 | 162 | 651 | 96 | 6 |
| Saginaw | 54,997 | 1,393 | 11 | 37 | 256 | 1,089 | 2,553 | 1,501 | 899 | 153 | 155 |
| Saginaw Township | 38,436 | 106 | 1 | 8 | 28 | 69 | 1,035 | 144 | 860 | 31 | 5 |
| Saline | 8,977 | 14 | 0 | 4 | 2 | 8 | 145 | 23 | 115 | 7 | 5 |
| Sand Lake | 517 | 0 | 0 | 0 | 0 | 0 | 13 | 2 | 11 | 0 | 0 |
| Sandusky | 2,593 | 20 | 0 | 3 | 1 | 16 | 123 | 12 | 109 | 2 | 1 |
| Saugatuck-Douglas | 2,171 | 4 | 0 | 0 | 0 | 4 | 79 | 8 | 69 | 2 | 1 |
| Sault Ste. Marie | 14,063 | 47 | 0 | 19 | 3 | 25 | 560 | 69 | 471 | 20 | 2 |
| Schoolcraft | 1,504 | 1 | 0 | 0 | 0 | 1 | 33 | 9 | 24 | 0 | 0 |
| Shelby Township | 72,094 | 93 | 0 | 19 | 14 | 60 | 1,007 | 185 | 739 | 83 | 5 |
| Somerset Township | 4,703 | 1 | 0 | 1 | 0 | 0 | 60 | 2 | 57 | 1 | 0 |
| Southfield | 75,074 | 409 | 2 | 32 | 129 | 246 | 3,082 | 653 | 1,960 | 469 | 12 |
| Southgate | 27,455 | 79 | 0 | 3 | 19 | 57 | 1,011 | 111 | 818 | 82 | 11 |
| South Haven | 5,151 | 22 | 1 | 4 | 3 | 14 | 284 | 37 | 245 | 2 | 1 |
| South Lyon | 11,052 | 11 | 0 | 0 | 0 | 11 | 154 | 23 | 127 | 4 | 1 |
| South Rockwood | 1,705 | 0 | 0 | 0 | 0 | 0 | 23 | 6 | 17 | 0 | 0 |
| Sparta | 4,041 | 10 | 0 | 3 | 2 | 5 | 186 | 18 | 166 | 2 | 0 |
| Spaulding Township | 2,168 | 5 | 0 | 0 | 0 | 5 | 8 | 4 | 3 | 1 | 0 |
| Spring Arbor Township | 8,409 | 3 | 0 | 0 | 0 | 3 | 51 | 15 | 34 | 2 | 0 |
| Springfield | 5,020 | 28 | 0 | 2 | 0 | 26 | 172 | 37 | 124 | 11 | 0 |
| Spring Lake-Ferrysburg | 5,464 | 3 | 0 | 3 | 0 | 0 | 65 | 8 | 55 | 2 | 0 |
| Standish | 1,972 | 1 | 0 | 0 | 0 | 1 | 17 | 2 | 15 | 0 | 0 |
| St. Charles | 1,999 | 3 | 0 | 0 | 0 | 3 | 52 | 11 | 39 | 2 | 0 |
| St. Clair | 5,760 | 8 | 0 | 0 | 0 | 8 | 134 | 24 | 109 | 1 | 2 |
| St. Clair Shores | 60,076 | 124 | 2 | 22 | 19 | 81 | 1,068 | 203 | 758 | 107 | 9 |
| Stephenson | 796 | 0 | 0 | 0 | 0 | 0 | 2 | 0 | 2 | 0 | 0 |
| Sterling Heights | 127,440 | 214 | 2 | 27 | 35 | 150 | 2,611 | 365 | 2,061 | 185 | 10 |
| St. Ignace | 2,301 | 5 | 0 | 1 | 0 | 4 | 61 | 6 | 51 | 4 | 0 |
| St. Johns | 7,225 | 12 | 0 | 2 | 4 | 6 | 155 | 27 | 123 | 5 | 2 |
| St. Joseph | 8,423 | 21 | 0 | 1 | 2 | 18 | 306 | 55 | 250 | 1 | 3 |
| St. Joseph Township | 9,580 | 22 | 1 | 7 | 2 | 12 | 182 | 40 | 136 | 6 | 2 |
| St. Louis | 7,008 | 6 | 0 | 2 | 0 | 4 | 71 | 11 | 59 | 1 | 1 |
| Stockbridge | 1,275 | 9 | 0 | 1 | 0 | 8 | 74 | 19 | 54 | 1 | 1 |
| Sturgis | 10,866 | 55 | 0 | 16 | 1 | 38 | 375 | 92 | 266 | 17 | 0 |
| Summit Township | 21,642 | 52 | 1 | 0 | 6 | 45 | 312 | 81 | 220 | 11 | 4 |

[1] The FBI does not publish arson data unless it receives data from either the agency or the state for all 12 months of the calendar year.

**Table 8. Offenses Known to Law Enforcement, by State and City, 2009**—*Continued*

(Number.)

| State/city | Population | Violent crime | Murder and non-negligent man-slaughter | Forcible rape | Robbery | Aggravated assault | Property crime | Burglary | Larceny-theft | Motor vehicle theft | Arson[1] |
|---|---|---|---|---|---|---|---|---|---|---|---|
| **MICHIGAN**—*Continued* | | | | | | | | | | | |
| Sumpter Township | 11,114 | 20 | 0 | 3 | 2 | 15 | 201 | 62 | 118 | 21 | 5 |
| Suttons Bay | 576 | 2 | 0 | 0 | 2 | 0 | 8 | 0 | 8 | 0 | 0 |
| Swartz Creek | 5,235 | 4 | 0 | 1 | 0 | 3 | 146 | 30 | 111 | 5 | 0 |
| Sylvan Lake | 1,629 | 4 | 0 | 0 | 2 | 2 | 13 | 2 | 11 | 0 | 0 |
| Taylor | 60,054 | 403 | 0 | 31 | 104 | 268 | 2,594 | 566 | 1,762 | 266 | 27 |
| Tecumseh | 8,602 | 8 | 0 | 0 | 0 | 8 | 140 | 29 | 109 | 2 | 1 |
| Thetford Township | 7,784 | 3 | 0 | 0 | 0 | 3 | 49 | 22 | 25 | 2 | 0 |
| Thomas Township | 12,252 | 13 | 0 | 1 | 1 | 11 | 286 | 23 | 259 | 4 | 1 |
| Three Rivers | 7,136 | 50 | 0 | 1 | 7 | 42 | 385 | 106 | 266 | 13 | 5 |
| Tittabawassee Township | 8,833 | 14 | 0 | 2 | 2 | 10 | 125 | 20 | 105 | 0 | 1 |
| Traverse City | 14,385 | 32 | 0 | 8 | 5 | 19 | 514 | 65 | 441 | 8 | 1 |
| Trenton | 17,792 | 18 | 0 | 1 | 2 | 15 | 255 | 34 | 201 | 20 | 1 |
| Troy | 80,182 | 79 | 0 | 17 | 13 | 49 | 1,880 | 231 | 1,564 | 85 | 3 |
| Tuscarora Township | 3,014 | 5 | 0 | 2 | 0 | 3 | 122 | 10 | 112 | 0 | 1 |
| Ubly | 761 | 0 | 0 | 0 | 0 | 0 | 20 | 0 | 20 | 0 | 0 |
| Unadilla Township | 3,443 | 5 | 0 | 0 | 0 | 5 | 50 | 16 | 34 | 0 | 0 |
| Union City | 1,705 | 3 | 0 | 0 | 1 | 2 | 84 | 22 | 59 | 3 | 0 |
| Utica | 4,961 | 10 | 0 | 3 | 0 | 7 | 222 | 27 | 183 | 12 | 1 |
| Van Buren Township | 26,513 | 80 | 2 | 17 | 20 | 41 | 803 | 202 | 503 | 98 | 2 |
| Vernon | 784 | 1 | 0 | 1 | 0 | 0 | 7 | 2 | 5 | 0 | 0 |
| Vicksburg | 2,181 | 1 | 0 | 0 | 0 | 1 | 16 | 1 | 15 | 0 | 1 |
| Walker | 23,918 | 37 | 0 | 8 | 7 | 22 | 864 | 103 | 738 | 23 | 9 |
| Walled Lake | 6,895 | 18 | 0 | 1 | 0 | 17 | 148 | 32 | 109 | 7 | 0 |
| Warren[6] | 133,485 | 778 | 4 | 67 | 209 | 498 | 3,785 | 887 | 1,897 | 1,001 | 36 |
| Waterford Township | 70,403 | 217 | 0 | 25 | 66 | 126 | 1,728 | 422 | 1,219 | 87 | 11 |
| Waterloo Township | 2,958 | 1 | 0 | 0 | 0 | 1 | 15 | 6 | 9 | 0 | 0 |
| Watervliet | 1,726 | 5 | 0 | 0 | 0 | 5 | 41 | 8 | 32 | 1 | 0 |
| Wayland | 3,794 | 3 | 0 | 3 | 0 | 0 | 50 | 6 | 42 | 2 | 0 |
| Wayne | 16,990 | 121 | 1 | 7 | 25 | 88 | 650 | 174 | 402 | 74 | 3 |
| West Bloomfield Township | 63,728 | 50 | 0 | 10 | 8 | 32 | 750 | 179 | 554 | 17 | 2 |
| West Branch | 1,803 | 3 | 0 | 1 | 0 | 2 | 81 | 7 | 71 | 3 | 0 |
| Westland | 78,149 | 387 | 2 | 39 | 98 | 248 | 2,489 | 611 | 1,566 | 312 | 31 |
| White Cloud | 1,387 | 8 | 0 | 1 | 0 | 7 | 124 | 21 | 103 | 0 | 0 |
| Whitehall | 2,794 | 5 | 0 | 1 | 1 | 3 | 85 | 5 | 77 | 3 | 0 |
| White Lake Township | 30,102 | 40 | 0 | 6 | 6 | 28 | 567 | 91 | 449 | 27 | 4 |
| White Pigeon | 1,552 | 3 | 0 | 2 | 0 | 1 | 42 | 9 | 31 | 2 | 0 |
| Williamston | 3,799 | 4 | 0 | 1 | 0 | 3 | 52 | 14 | 36 | 2 | 0 |
| Wixom | 13,431 | 25 | 1 | 8 | 10 | 6 | 372 | 66 | 269 | 37 | 1 |
| Wolverine Lake | 4,292 | 3 | 0 | 0 | 0 | 3 | 73 | 10 | 60 | 3 | 0 |
| Woodhaven | 12,643 | 15 | 0 | 2 | 8 | 5 | 365 | 33 | 301 | 31 | 1 |
| Wyandotte | 24,399 | 64 | 1 | 3 | 13 | 47 | 690 | 119 | 490 | 81 | 2 |
| Wyoming | 70,565 | 299 | 1 | 40 | 67 | 191 | 1,658 | 423 | 1,098 | 137 | 10 |
| Ypsilanti | 21,369 | 198 | 1 | 24 | 41 | 132 | 841 | 294 | 482 | 65 | 12 |
| Zeeland | 5,410 | 6 | 0 | 1 | 0 | 5 | 82 | 20 | 59 | 3 | 0 |
| Zilwaukee | 1,636 | 0 | 0 | 0 | 0 | 0 | 15 | 8 | 7 | 0 | 0 |
| **MINNESOTA[7]** | | | | | | | | | | | |
| Albert Lea | 17,279 | | 1 | | 4 | 24 | 386 | 33 | 335 | 18 | 0 |
| Alexandria | 11,409 | | 0 | | 4 | 13 | 332 | 24 | 297 | 11 | 0 |
| Annandale | 3,150 | | 0 | | 0 | 2 | 126 | 9 | 114 | 3 | 0 |
| Anoka | 17,203 | | 0 | | 12 | 21 | 745 | 103 | 609 | 33 | 6 |
| Appleton | 3,011 | | 0 | | 0 | 3 | 55 | 16 | 37 | 2 | 0 |
| Apple Valley | 50,480 | | 1 | | 14 | 17 | 1,313 | 180 | 1,107 | 26 | 8 |
| Aurora | 1,735 | | 0 | | 0 | 0 | 0 | 0 | 0 | 0 | 0 |
| Austin | 22,721 | | 0 | | 6 | 31 | 812 | 137 | 645 | 30 | 2 |
| Avon | 1,324 | | 0 | | 0 | 2 | 12 | 2 | 9 | 1 | 0 |
| Babbitt | 1,578 | | 0 | | 0 | 0 | 0 | 0 | 0 | 0 | 0 |
| Baxter | 8,625 | | 0 | | 0 | 4 | 344 | 8 | 334 | 2 | 0 |
| Bayport | 3,305 | | 0 | | 0 | 1 | 54 | 8 | 43 | 3 | 0 |
| Becker | 4,381 | | 0 | | 0 | 0 | 1 | 0 | 1 | 0 | 0 |
| Belgrade | 710 | | 0 | | 0 | 0 | 0 | 0 | 0 | 0 | 0 |
| Belle Plaine | 7,067 | | 0 | | 0 | 8 | 112 | 18 | 88 | 6 | 3 |
| Bemidji | 13,694 | | 0 | | 8 | 58 | 1,001 | 80 | 893 | 28 | 2 |
| Benson | 3,014 | | 0 | | 0 | 4 | 51 | 5 | 41 | 5 | 1 |
| Big Lake | 10,282 | | 0 | | 1 | 6 | 196 | 19 | 175 | 2 | 1 |
| Biwabik | 976 | | 0 | | 0 | 0 | 0 | 0 | 0 | 0 | 0 |
| Blackduck | 768 | | 0 | | 0 | 1 | 16 | 3 | 12 | 1 | 0 |
| Blaine | 56,228 | | 1 | | 20 | 26 | 2,108 | 228 | 1,788 | 92 | 11 |
| Bloomington | 80,864 | | 2 | | 49 | 66 | 3,235 | 277 | 2,846 | 112 | 14 |
| Blue Earth | 3,209 | | 0 | | 0 | 1 | 56 | 8 | 47 | 1 | 0 |
| Brainerd | 13,694 | | 0 | | 4 | 41 | 519 | 83 | 419 | 17 | 4 |

[1] The FBI does not publish arson data unless it receives data from either the agency or the state for all 12 months of the calendar year.
[6] Because of changes in the state/local agency's reporting practices, figures are not comparable to previous years' data.
[7] The data collection methodology for the offense of forcible rape used by the Illinois and the Minnesota state UCR Programs (with the exception of Rockford, Illinois, and Minneapolis and St. Paul, Minnesota) does not comply with national UCR Program guidelines. Consequently, their figures for forcible rape and violent crime (of which forcible rape is a part) are not published in this table.

## Table 8. Offenses Known to Law Enforcement, by State and City, 2009—*Continued*

(Number.)

| State/city | Population | Violent crime | Murder and non-negligent man-slaughter | Forcible rape | Robbery | Aggravated assault | Property crime | Burglary | Larceny-theft | Motor vehicle theft | Arson[1] |
|---|---|---|---|---|---|---|---|---|---|---|---|
| **MINNESOTA**—*Continued* | | | | | | | | | | | |
| Breckenridge | 3,159 | | 0 | | 0 | 0 | 59 | 15 | 42 | 2 | 0 |
| Brooklyn Center | 27,217 | | 0 | | 75 | 70 | 1,704 | 258 | 1,314 | 132 | 4 |
| Brooklyn Park | 71,740 | | 0 | | 109 | 147 | 2,885 | 571 | 2,134 | 180 | 11 |
| Browns Valley | 594 | | 0 | | 0 | 0 | 0 | 0 | 0 | 0 | 0 |
| Brownton | 782 | | 0 | | 0 | 1 | 4 | 2 | 2 | 0 | 0 |
| Buffalo | 14,741 | | 0 | | 1 | 5 | 367 | 23 | 335 | 9 | 3 |
| Burnsville | 59,015 | | 2 | | 33 | 18 | 1,935 | 297 | 1,563 | 75 | 7 |
| Cambridge | 7,965 | | 0 | | 2 | 5 | 269 | 29 | 234 | 6 | 2 |
| Cannon Falls | 4,049 | | 0 | | 1 | 1 | 186 | 24 | 160 | 2 | 3 |
| Centennial Lakes | 11,262 | | 1 | | 1 | 12 | 159 | 31 | 124 | 4 | 1 |
| Champlin | 23,640 | | 0 | | 4 | 16 | 479 | 70 | 401 | 8 | 0 |
| Chaska | 24,939 | | 0 | | 0 | 13 | 386 | 39 | 340 | 7 | 6 |
| Cloquet | 11,407 | | 0 | | 5 | 15 | 500 | 55 | 425 | 20 | 0 |
| Cold Spring | 3,802 | | 0 | | 0 | 2 | 68 | 21 | 47 | 0 | 0 |
| Columbia Heights | 18,176 | | 0 | | 23 | 30 | 725 | 165 | 515 | 45 | 4 |
| Coon Rapids | 61,844 | | 1 | | 30 | 65 | 2,628 | 251 | 2,307 | 70 | 7 |
| Corcoran | 5,629 | | 0 | | 0 | 6 | 66 | 20 | 43 | 3 | 0 |
| Cottage Grove | 33,969 | | 0 | | 9 | 20 | 645 | 74 | 545 | 26 | 2 |
| Crookston | 7,744 | | 0 | | 0 | 11 | 29 | 11 | 15 | 3 | 0 |
| Crosby | 2,237 | | 0 | | 0 | 4 | 78 | 11 | 67 | 0 | 0 |
| Crystal | 21,600 | | 0 | | 22 | 20 | 808 | 158 | 602 | 48 | 4 |
| Dawson | 1,339 | | 0 | | 0 | 0 | 18 | 4 | 14 | 0 | 0 |
| Dayton | 4,635 | | 0 | | 0 | 2 | 42 | 13 | 22 | 7 | 0 |
| Deephaven-Woodland | 4,235 | | 0 | | 0 | 0 | 24 | 8 | 16 | 0 | 1 |
| Detroit Lakes | 8,209 | | 0 | | 1 | 7 | 355 | 19 | 331 | 5 | 0 |
| Dilworth | 3,757 | | 0 | | 0 | 2 | 96 | 5 | 90 | 1 | 0 |
| Duluth | 84,071 | | 3 | | 122 | 201 | 4,253 | 632 | 3,431 | 190 | 34 |
| Eagan | 64,014 | | 1 | | 16 | 22 | 1,582 | 218 | 1,323 | 41 | 10 |
| Eagle Lake | 2,340 | | 0 | | 0 | 2 | 23 | 9 | 13 | 1 | 0 |
| East Grand Forks | 7,839 | | 0 | | 3 | 6 | 244 | 39 | 191 | 14 | 0 |
| Eden Prairie | 61,893 | | 0 | | 10 | 34 | 1,166 | 165 | 977 | 24 | 3 |
| Edina | 45,414 | | 0 | | 14 | 10 | 933 | 139 | 778 | 16 | 3 |
| Elk River | 24,061 | | 0 | | 4 | 11 | 656 | 71 | 565 | 20 | 1 |
| Elmore | 648 | | 0 | | 0 | 3 | 7 | 2 | 5 | 0 | 0 |
| Ely | 3,447 | | 0 | | 0 | 0 | 72 | 5 | 56 | 11 | 0 |
| Eveleth | 3,553 | | 0 | | 0 | 8 | 113 | 23 | 84 | 6 | 1 |
| Fairmont | 10,148 | | 0 | | 2 | 8 | 288 | 29 | 254 | 5 | 0 |
| Falcon Heights | 5,648 | | 0 | | 1 | 0 | 88 | 26 | 60 | 2 | 0 |
| Faribault | 22,129 | | 0 | | 16 | 52 | 698 | 154 | 518 | 26 | 8 |
| Farmington | 19,945 | | 0 | | 5 | 5 | 246 | 39 | 202 | 5 | 2 |
| Fergus Falls | 13,631 | | 0 | | 0 | 23 | 417 | 77 | 331 | 9 | 6 |
| Floodwood | 494 | | 0 | | 0 | 1 | 21 | 1 | 20 | 0 | 0 |
| Forest Lake | 17,727 | | 0 | | 1 | 6 | 518 | 63 | 431 | 24 | 1 |
| Gilbert | 1,745 | | 0 | | 1 | 1 | 31 | 7 | 23 | 1 | 0 |
| Glencoe | 5,560 | | 0 | | 0 | 4 | 134 | 17 | 114 | 3 | 1 |
| Glenwood | 2,518 | | 0 | | 0 | 0 | 26 | 3 | 22 | 1 | 0 |
| Golden Valley | 20,345 | | 0 | | 14 | 17 | 623 | 138 | 441 | 44 | 9 |
| Goodview | 3,577 | | 0 | | 0 | 3 | 67 | 18 | 46 | 3 | 0 |
| Granite Falls | 2,885 | | 0 | | 0 | 3 | 31 | 4 | 26 | 1 | 0 |
| Hallock | 1,003 | | 0 | | 0 | 0 | 0 | 0 | 0 | 0 | 0 |
| Hastings | 22,600 | | 0 | | 2 | 11 | 607 | 84 | 504 | 19 | 0 |
| Hermantown | 9,518 | | 0 | | 1 | 2 | 275 | 25 | 238 | 12 | 0 |
| Hibbing | 16,115 | | 0 | | 2 | 15 | 344 | 37 | 289 | 18 | 1 |
| Hilltop | 674 | | 0 | | 1 | 6 | 90 | 19 | 66 | 5 | 1 |
| Hokah | 556 | | 0 | | 0 | 0 | 19 | 9 | 10 | 0 | 1 |
| Hopkins | 16,915 | | 1 | | 16 | 18 | 433 | 107 | 279 | 47 | 6 |
| Houston | 949 | | 0 | | 0 | 2 | 31 | 20 | 10 | 1 | 0 |
| Hoyt Lakes | 1,943 | | 0 | | 0 | 0 | 0 | 0 | 0 | 0 | 0 |
| Hutchinson | 13,995 | | 0 | | 0 | 16 | 415 | 47 | 358 | 10 | 3 |
| Inver Grove Heights | 33,800 | | 0 | | 13 | 14 | 880 | 129 | 688 | 63 | 14 |
| Jackson | 3,285 | | 0 | | 0 | 3 | 80 | 17 | 62 | 1 | 0 |
| Janesville | 2,255 | | 0 | | 0 | 1 | 26 | 7 | 19 | 0 | 0 |
| Jordan | 5,642 | | 0 | | 0 | 6 | 82 | 4 | 74 | 4 | 0 |
| Kasson | 5,697 | | 0 | | 0 | 0 | 35 | 5 | 30 | 0 | 0 |
| Kimball | 710 | | 0 | | 0 | 1 | 8 | 3 | 4 | 1 | 0 |
| Lake City | 5,310 | | 0 | | 0 | 2 | 84 | 13 | 69 | 2 | 0 |
| Lake Crystal | 2,619 | | 0 | | 0 | 2 | 56 | 10 | 42 | 4 | 1 |
| Lakefield | 1,603 | | 0 | | 0 | 1 | 7 | 1 | 6 | 0 | 0 |
| Lakes Area | 8,373 | | 0 | | 0 | 6 | 151 | 20 | 126 | 5 | 1 |
| Lakeville | 55,921 | | 0 | | 7 | 10 | 983 | 169 | 788 | 26 | 4 |
| Lauderdale | 2,193 | | 1 | | 0 | 0 | 63 | 27 | 33 | 3 | 0 |

[1] The FBI does not publish arson data unless it receives data from either the agency or the state for all 12 months of the calendar year.

## Table 8. Offenses Known to Law Enforcement, by State and City, 2009—*Continued*

(Number.)

| State/city | Population | Violent crime | Murder and non-negligent man-slaughter | Forcible rape | Robbery | Aggravated assault | Property crime | Burglary | Larceny-theft | Motor vehicle theft | Arson[1] |
|---|---|---|---|---|---|---|---|---|---|---|---|
| **MINNESOTA**—*Continued* | | | | | | | | | | | |
| Lester Prairie | 1,795 | | 0 | | 0 | 4 | 28 | 5 | 22 | 1 | 0 |
| Le Sueur | 4,286 | | 0 | | 0 | 0 | 87 | 8 | 78 | 1 | 0 |
| Lewiston | 1,479 | | 0 | | 0 | 0 | 1 | 1 | 0 | 0 | 0 |
| Lino Lakes | 20,565 | | 0 | | 1 | 11 | 203 | 30 | 165 | 8 | 3 |
| Litchfield | 6,557 | | 0 | | 0 | 2 | 104 | 17 | 83 | 4 | 1 |
| Little Falls | 8,105 | | 0 | | 0 | 2 | 181 | 2 | 171 | 8 | 0 |
| Long Prairie | 2,785 | | 0 | | 0 | 5 | 83 | 4 | 75 | 4 | 0 |
| Madison | 1,542 | | 0 | | 0 | 0 | 9 | 0 | 9 | 0 | 0 |
| Mankato | 36,676 | | 0 | | 13 | 56 | 1,840 | 292 | 1,487 | 61 | 5 |
| Maple Grove | 62,801 | | 1 | | 10 | 22 | 1,316 | 172 | 1,123 | 21 | 1 |
| Mapleton | 1,656 | | 0 | | 0 | 0 | 19 | 4 | 14 | 1 | 0 |
| Maplewood | 36,165 | | 0 | | 28 | 45 | 2,407 | 270 | 1,961 | 176 | 9 |
| Marshall | 12,634 | | 0 | | 2 | 26 | 395 | 81 | 302 | 12 | 0 |
| Medina | 5,209 | | 0 | | 0 | 0 | 115 | 20 | 94 | 1 | 0 |
| Melrose | 3,150 | | 0 | | 0 | 3 | 29 | 5 | 24 | 0 | 0 |
| Mendota Heights | 11,610 | | 0 | | 0 | 7 | 262 | 56 | 201 | 5 | 0 |
| Milaca | 3,052 | | 0 | | 0 | 3 | 96 | 3 | 92 | 1 | 0 |
| Minneapolis | 382,618 | 4,242 | 18 | 413 | 1,663 | 2,148 | 17,859 | 4,741 | 11,320 | 1,798 | 143 |
| Minnetonka | 49,968 | | 1 | | 10 | 12 | 1,086 | 177 | 885 | 24 | 9 |
| Minnetrista | 8,588 | | 0 | | 0 | 5 | 90 | 12 | 72 | 6 | 0 |
| Montevideo | 5,203 | | 0 | | 0 | 8 | 123 | 17 | 102 | 4 | 0 |
| Montgomery | 3,323 | | 0 | | 0 | 7 | 89 | 12 | 76 | 1 | 0 |
| Moorhead | 36,429 | | 0 | | 5 | 26 | 913 | 115 | 761 | 37 | 1 |
| Moose Lake | 2,404 | | 0 | | 0 | 1 | 99 | 4 | 95 | 0 | 0 |
| Mora | 3,438 | | 0 | | 0 | 17 | 113 | 12 | 98 | 3 | 0 |
| Morris | 4,975 | | 0 | | 0 | 8 | 129 | 15 | 108 | 6 | 0 |
| Mound | 9,558 | | 0 | | 1 | 6 | 143 | 29 | 103 | 11 | 2 |
| Mounds View | 11,925 | | 0 | | 5 | 21 | 429 | 68 | 316 | 45 | 3 |
| Mountain Lake | 1,912 | | 0 | | 0 | 1 | 9 | 0 | 6 | 3 | 0 |
| New Brighton | 21,494 | | 0 | | 7 | 10 | 543 | 107 | 403 | 33 | 5 |
| New Hope | 20,381 | | 0 | | 9 | 30 | 566 | 88 | 449 | 29 | 9 |
| Newport | 3,459 | | 0 | | 2 | 5 | 146 | 34 | 97 | 15 | 0 |
| New Prague | 7,001 | | 0 | | 0 | 7 | 141 | 12 | 125 | 4 | 0 |
| New Richland | 1,152 | | 0 | | 0 | 0 | 0 | 0 | 0 | 0 | 0 |
| New Ulm | 12,989 | | 0 | | 0 | 12 | 271 | 83 | 179 | 9 | 1 |
| North Branch | 10,705 | | 0 | | 1 | 2 | 352 | 30 | 314 | 8 | 0 |
| Northfield | 19,919 | | 0 | | 1 | 13 | 399 | 42 | 350 | 7 | 12 |
| North Mankato | 12,605 | | 0 | | 0 | 1 | 259 | 22 | 229 | 8 | 3 |
| North Oaks | 4,785 | | 0 | | 0 | 1 | 33 | 6 | 25 | 2 | 0 |
| North St. Paul | 11,177 | | 1 | | 5 | 4 | 362 | 53 | 273 | 36 | 0 |
| Oakdale | 27,068 | | 0 | | 8 | 26 | 1,253 | 118 | 1,073 | 62 | 5 |
| Oak Park Heights | 4,802 | | 0 | | 1 | 6 | 276 | 14 | 256 | 6 | 1 |
| Olivia | 2,340 | | 0 | | 0 | 1 | 49 | 14 | 35 | 0 | 0 |
| Orono | 12,002 | | 0 | | 1 | 3 | 134 | 32 | 97 | 5 | 0 |
| Osakis | 1,573 | | 0 | | 1 | 1 | 23 | 4 | 16 | 3 | 0 |
| Osseo | 2,565 | | 0 | | 0 | 1 | 11 | 1 | 10 | 0 | 0 |
| Owatonna | 25,119 | | 0 | | 4 | 21 | 502 | 83 | 401 | 18 | 2 |
| Park Rapids | 3,673 | | 0 | | 1 | 7 | 245 | 36 | 200 | 9 | 0 |
| Paynesville | 2,260 | | 0 | | 0 | 0 | 80 | 20 | 59 | 1 | 1 |
| Plymouth | 72,121 | | 0 | | 13 | 31 | 1,408 | 303 | 1,053 | 52 | 10 |
| Princeton | 4,858 | | 0 | | 0 | 6 | 145 | 14 | 127 | 4 | 1 |
| Prior Lake | 24,870 | | 0 | | 2 | 20 | 490 | 93 | 385 | 12 | 1 |
| Proctor | 2,838 | | 0 | | 0 | 2 | 130 | 16 | 110 | 4 | 0 |
| Ramsey | 24,391 | | 0 | | 2 | 8 | 643 | 90 | 528 | 25 | 11 |
| Red Wing | 15,643 | | 0 | | 4 | 19 | 478 | 113 | 348 | 17 | 1 |
| Redwood Falls | 5,035 | | 0 | | 1 | 16 | 175 | 36 | 134 | 5 | 1 |
| Richfield | 32,547 | | 2 | | 38 | 29 | 964 | 158 | 762 | 44 | 8 |
| Richmond | 1,274 | | 0 | | 0 | 0 | 1 | 1 | 0 | 0 | 0 |
| Robbinsdale | 13,452 | | 0 | | 16 | 14 | 489 | 139 | 325 | 25 | 2 |
| Rochester | 101,884 | | 1 | | 58 | 142 | 2,845 | 398 | 2,343 | 104 | 26 |
| Rogers | 8,111 | | 0 | | 0 | 3 | 78 | 1 | 77 | 0 | 0 |
| Roseau | 2,759 | | 0 | | 0 | 1 | 51 | 3 | 48 | 0 | 0 |
| Rosemount | 22,061 | | 0 | | 3 | 4 | 402 | 56 | 340 | 6 | 1 |
| Roseville | 32,719 | | 0 | | 16 | 35 | 1,542 | 147 | 1,292 | 103 | 4 |
| Sartell | 14,467 | | 0 | | 0 | 2 | 196 | 15 | 178 | 3 | 0 |
| Sauk Centre | 3,946 | | 0 | | 0 | 5 | 113 | 7 | 105 | 1 | 0 |
| Sauk Rapids | 12,197 | | 0 | | 1 | 8 | 88 | 13 | 68 | 7 | 0 |
| Savage | 28,473 | | 0 | | 9 | 31 | 750 | 134 | 597 | 19 | 4 |
| Shakopee | 35,231 | | 0 | | 10 | 50 | 1,007 | 173 | 805 | 29 | 6 |
| Silver Lake | 802 | | 0 | | 0 | 0 | 9 | 3 | 4 | 2 | 0 |
| Slayton | 1,810 | | 0 | | 0 | 1 | 29 | 13 | 16 | 0 | 0 |

[1] The FBI does not publish arson data unless it receives data from either the agency or the state for all 12 months of the calendar year.

## Table 8. Offenses Known to Law Enforcement, by State and City, 2009—*Continued*

(Number.)

| State/city | Population | Violent crime | Murder and non-negligent man-slaughter | Forcible rape | Robbery | Aggravated assault | Property crime | Burglary | Larceny-theft | Motor vehicle theft | Arson[1] |
|---|---|---|---|---|---|---|---|---|---|---|---|
| **MINNESOTA**—*Continued* | | | | | | | | | | | |
| South Eastern Faribault County | 1,091 | | 0 | | 0 | 0 | 0 | 0 | 0 | 0 | 0 |
| South Lake Minnetonka | 12,071 | | 0 | | 2 | 9 | 151 | 27 | 114 | 10 | 1 |
| South St. Paul | 19,485 | | 1 | | 12 | 14 | 653 | 137 | 468 | 48 | 2 |
| Springfield | 2,141 | | 0 | | 0 | 0 | 0 | 0 | 0 | 0 | 0 |
| Spring Lake Park | 6,426 | | 0 | | 11 | 21 | 356 | 65 | 271 | 20 | 0 |
| St. Anthony | 8,459 | | 0 | | 5 | 3 | 328 | 66 | 253 | 9 | 1 |
| Staples | 3,006 | | 0 | | 0 | 1 | 105 | 5 | 97 | 3 | 0 |
| St. Charles | 3,606 | | 0 | | 0 | 1 | 35 | 9 | 25 | 1 | 0 |
| St. Cloud | 67,804 | | 1 | | 41 | 143 | 2,768 | 348 | 2,328 | 92 | 24 |
| St. Francis | 7,568 | | 0 | | 0 | 8 | 184 | 22 | 159 | 3 | 3 |
| Stillwater | 18,168 | | 2 | | 3 | 7 | 447 | 51 | 383 | 13 | 2 |
| St. James | 4,241 | | 0 | | 0 | 5 | 121 | 24 | 92 | 5 | 1 |
| St. Louis Park | 45,613 | | 0 | | 30 | 22 | 1,455 | 239 | 1,166 | 50 | 8 |
| St. Paul | 280,194 | 2,137 | 13 | 165 | 694 | 1,265 | 11,431 | 2,929 | 6,713 | 1,789 | 145 |
| St. Paul Park[2] | 5,256 | | 0 | | 3 | 7 | | 49 | | 10 | 1 |
| St. Peter | 11,103 | | 1 | | 2 | 13 | 289 | 50 | 237 | 2 | 0 |
| Thief River Falls | 8,482 | | 0 | | 2 | 7 | 202 | 24 | 168 | 10 | 0 |
| Two Harbors | 3,252 | | 0 | | 0 | 4 | 60 | 9 | 47 | 4 | 1 |
| Virginia | 8,409 | | 1 | | 2 | 36 | 442 | 65 | 370 | 7 | 3 |
| Wabasha | 2,511 | | 0 | | 0 | 0 | 74 | 9 | 61 | 4 | 0 |
| Wadena | 3,947 | | 0 | | 1 | 8 | 110 | 8 | 100 | 2 | 0 |
| Waite Park | 6,809 | | 0 | | 5 | 15 | 567 | 28 | 525 | 14 | 0 |
| Warroad | 1,650 | | 0 | | 0 | 1 | 43 | 8 | 35 | 0 | 0 |
| Waseca | 9,416 | | 0 | | 1 | 9 | 223 | 22 | 184 | 17 | 0 |
| Wayzata | 3,859 | | 0 | | 0 | 1 | 110 | 10 | 95 | 5 | 0 |
| Wells | 2,319 | | 0 | | 0 | 1 | 39 | 11 | 27 | 1 | 0 |
| West Hennepin | 5,550 | | 0 | | 0 | 1 | 64 | 9 | 53 | 2 | 0 |
| West St. Paul | 18,871 | | 0 | | 26 | 20 | 1,210 | 107 | 1,048 | 55 | 1 |
| Wheaton | 1,402 | | 1 | | 0 | 1 | 33 | 10 | 19 | 4 | 0 |
| White Bear Lake | 24,068 | | 0 | | 9 | 16 | 915 | 179 | 681 | 55 | 17 |
| Willmar | 17,698 | | 0 | | 4 | 32 | 716 | 66 | 629 | 21 | 1 |
| Windom | 4,165 | | 0 | | 0 | 5 | 119 | 18 | 99 | 2 | 2 |
| Winnebago | 1,319 | | 0 | | 0 | 1 | 39 | 13 | 24 | 2 | 0 |
| Winona | 26,752 | | 0 | | 9 | 27 | 489 | 57 | 410 | 22 | 2 |
| Winsted | 2,455 | | 0 | | 0 | 9 | 37 | 7 | 29 | 1 | 0 |
| Woodbury | 57,259 | | 0 | | 7 | 22 | 1,397 | 266 | 1,078 | 53 | 4 |
| Worthington | 11,013 | | 0 | | 7 | 17 | 361 | 97 | 253 | 11 | 1 |
| Wyoming | 3,889 | | 0 | | 1 | 3 | 142 | 9 | 131 | 2 | 0 |
| Zumbrota | 3,104 | | 0 | | 0 | 0 | 54 | 5 | 44 | 5 | 0 |
| **MISSISSIPPI** | | | | | | | | | | | |
| Aberdeen | 6,054 | 29 | 0 | 1 | 13 | 15 | 194 | 65 | 126 | 3 | 0 |
| Amory | 7,226 | 13 | 0 | 0 | 4 | 9 | 354 | 78 | 267 | 9 | 2 |
| Batesville[3] | 7,928 | 24 | 0 | 7 | 10 | 7 | | | 391 | 12 | 0 |
| Bay St. Louis | 7,774 | 14 | 1 | 3 | 6 | 4 | 416 | 84 | 317 | 15 | 0 |
| Belzoni | 2,407 | 10 | 1 | 2 | 2 | 5 | 23 | 4 | 19 | 0 | 0 |
| Biloxi | 45,160 | 252 | 5 | 3 | 127 | 117 | 2,583 | 1,020 | 1,427 | 136 | 1 |
| Booneville | 8,763 | 7 | 0 | 0 | 3 | 4 | 247 | 77 | 170 | 0 | 0 |
| Brandon | 22,716 | 12 | 1 | 5 | 3 | 3 | 201 | 69 | 123 | 9 | 0 |
| Brookhaven | 13,334 | 19 | 0 | 1 | 12 | 6 | 254 | 69 | 170 | 15 | 0 |
| Byhalia | 1,313 | 4 | 0 | 0 | 0 | 4 | 39 | 14 | 19 | 6 | 0 |
| Canton | 12,476 | 85 | 0 | 9 | 27 | 49 | 517 | 317 | 187 | 13 | 0 |
| Carthage | 4,836 | 5 | 0 | 1 | 1 | 3 | 94 | 59 | 31 | 4 | 0 |
| Charleston | 1,850 | 72 | 1 | 1 | 45 | 25 | 75 | 31 | 44 | 0 | 1 |
| Clarksdale | 17,741 | 129 | 4 | 18 | 57 | 50 | 996 | 621 | 334 | 41 | 9 |
| Cleveland | 12,057 | 50 | 1 | 5 | 19 | 25 | 898 | 150 | 731 | 17 | 3 |
| Collins | 2,774 | 10 | 0 | 1 | 5 | 4 | 141 | 26 | 106 | 9 | 0 |
| Columbus | 23,577 | 81 | 1 | 9 | 37 | 34 | 1,164 | 276 | 836 | 52 | 4 |
| Crystal Springs | 5,959 | 17 | 0 | 1 | 2 | 14 | 183 | 88 | 85 | 10 | 1 |
| D'Iberville | 7,934 | 34 | 0 | 9 | 12 | 13 | 688 | 102 | 570 | 16 | 2 |
| Drew | 2,146 | 17 | 0 | 5 | 4 | 8 | 65 | 43 | 19 | 3 | 16 |
| Edwards | 1,286 | 4 | 0 | 2 | 0 | 2 | 5 | 3 | 2 | 0 | 0 |
| Eupora | 2,201 | 7 | 0 | 1 | 0 | 6 | 51 | 25 | 24 | 2 | 1 |
| Florence[6] | 3,612 | 1 | 0 | 0 | 0 | 1 | 50 | 13 | 34 | 3 | 0 |
| Flowood | 7,182 | 38 | 0 | 4 | 3 | 31 | 499 | 114 | 365 | 20 | 0 |
| Fulton | 4,093 | 6 | 0 | 0 | 2 | 4 | 66 | 28 | 35 | 3 | 0 |
| Gautier | 16,248 | 60 | 0 | 7 | 13 | 40 | 721 | 214 | 467 | 40 | 3 |
| Gloster | 1,021 | 1 | 0 | 1 | 0 | 0 | 5 | 5 | 0 | 0 | 0 |
| Greenville | 35,187 | 65 | 8 | 7 | 45 | 5 | 2,036 | 896 | 1,045 | 95 | 75 |
| Greenwood | 15,842 | 124 | 2 | 17 | 32 | 73 | 988 | 409 | 553 | 26 | 0 |
| Grenada | 14,647 | 93 | 3 | 0 | 22 | 68 | 640 | 212 | 408 | 20 | 0 |
| Gulfport | 69,926 | 149 | 4 | 18 | 91 | 36 | 3,687 | 990 | 2,547 | 150 | 16 |

[1] The FBI does not publish arson data unless it receives data from either the agency or the state for all 12 months of the calendar year.
[2] The FBI determined that the agency's data were underreported. Consequently, those data are not included in this table.
[3] The FBI determined that the agency's data were overreported. Consequently, those data are not included in this table.
[6] Because of changes in the state/local agency's reporting practices, figures are not comparable to previous years' data.

## Table 8. Offenses Known to Law Enforcement, by State and City, 2009—*Continued*

(Number.)

| State/city | Population | Violent crime | Murder and non-negligent man-slaughter | Forcible rape | Robbery | Aggravated assault | Property crime | Burglary | Larceny-theft | Motor vehicle theft | Arson[1] |
|---|---|---|---|---|---|---|---|---|---|---|---|
| **MISSISSIPPI**—*Continued* | | | | | | | | | | | |
| Hattiesburg | 52,716 | 136 | 5 | 19 | 66 | 46 | 2,408 | 460 | 1,857 | 91 | 4 |
| Heidelberg | 809 | 0 | 0 | 0 | 0 | 0 | 30 | 7 | 22 | 1 | 0 |
| Hernando | 12,913 | 12 | 0 | 2 | 1 | 9 | 314 | 79 | 223 | 12 | 1 |
| Holly Springs | 7,997 | 110 | 1 | 1 | 20 | 88 | 360 | 159 | 177 | 24 | 0 |
| Horn Lake | 25,238 | 34 | 1 | 0 | 17 | 16 | 737 | 143 | 555 | 39 | 1 |
| Itta Bena | 1,844 | 1 | 0 | 0 | 0 | 1 | 137 | 78 | 54 | 5 | 0 |
| Iuka | 2,926 | 5 | 0 | 0 | 2 | 3 | 83 | 34 | 46 | 3 | 0 |
| Jackson | 172,799 | 1,515 | 37 | 124 | 958 | 396 | 13,182 | 4,569 | 6,994 | 1,619 | 113 |
| Kosciusko | 7,371 | 18 | 0 | 1 | 3 | 14 | 173 | 80 | 92 | 1 | 0 |
| Laurel | 18,741 | 134 | 3 | 13 | 82 | 36 | 1,011 | 310 | 670 | 31 | 6 |
| Leakesville | 1,025 | 0 | 0 | 0 | 0 | 0 | 0 | 0 | 0 | 0 | 0 |
| Leland | 4,720 | 18 | 0 | 0 | 3 | 15 | 128 | 48 | 78 | 2 | 0 |
| Long Beach | 11,879 | 6 | 0 | 1 | 3 | 2 | 304 | 52 | 241 | 11 | 0 |
| Louisville | 6,561 | 13 | 0 | 2 | 6 | 5 | 63 | 53 | 10 | 0 | 0 |
| Lucedale | 3,152 | 17 | 0 | 0 | 5 | 12 | 84 | 17 | 63 | 4 | 0 |
| Macon | 2,718 | 22 | 0 | 0 | 2 | 20 | 90 | 17 | 73 | 0 | 0 |
| Madison | 18,040 | 13 | 0 | 2 | 1 | 10 | 273 | 13 | 253 | 7 | 0 |
| Magnolia | 2,090 | 5 | 0 | 0 | 1 | 4 | 33 | 20 | 12 | 1 | 0 |
| McComb | 13,726 | 64 | 2 | 1 | 43 | 18 | 793 | 201 | 547 | 45 | 0 |
| Meridian | 38,054 | 250 | 3 | 40 | 107 | 100 | 2,269 | 1,038 | 1,104 | 127 | 20 |
| Morton | 3,432 | 9 | 0 | 0 | 4 | 5 | 31 | 5 | 17 | 9 | 2 |
| Natchez | 16,209 | 47 | 2 | 10 | 21 | 14 | 611 | 218 | 370 | 23 | 1 |
| New Albany | 8,234 | 6 | 0 | 1 | 2 | 3 | 108 | 24 | 78 | 6 | 1 |
| Ocean Springs | 17,140 | 21 | 1 | 1 | 8 | 11 | 639 | 239 | 366 | 34 | 1 |
| Olive Branch | 33,284 | 90 | 1 | 17 | 29 | 43 | 1,046 | 226 | 743 | 77 | 5 |
| Oxford | 17,719 | 12 | 0 | 3 | 4 | 5 | 385 | 83 | 286 | 16 | 0 |
| Pascagoula | 23,346 | 74 | 1 | 6 | 45 | 22 | 1,429 | 297 | 1,033 | 99 | 4 |
| Pass Christian | 3,864 | 5 | 0 | 0 | 2 | 3 | 147 | 36 | 105 | 6 | 0 |
| Pearl | 24,592 | 70 | 1 | 7 | 7 | 55 | 771 | 275 | 448 | 48 | 1 |
| Petal | 10,659 | 9 | 2 | 0 | 2 | 5 | 71 | 44 | 24 | 3 | 1 |
| Philadelphia | 8,046 | 51 | 0 | 5 | 14 | 32 | 329 | 116 | 204 | 9 | 0 |
| Picayune | 11,937 | 47 | 0 | 9 | 18 | 20 | 380 | 138 | 228 | 14 | 4 |
| Poplarville | 3,054 | 13 | 0 | 0 | 6 | 7 | 54 | 26 | 27 | 1 | 0 |
| Port Gibson | 1,650 | 2 | 0 | 0 | 1 | 1 | 9 | 0 | 9 | 0 | 0 |
| Purvis | 2,706 | 0 | 0 | 0 | 0 | 0 | 1 | 0 | 1 | 0 | 0 |
| Ridgeland | 21,644 | 35 | 0 | 2 | 15 | 18 | 728 | 57 | 644 | 27 | 0 |
| Ripley | 5,664 | 9 | 0 | 1 | 2 | 6 | 95 | 30 | 60 | 5 | 0 |
| Roxie | 556 | 0 | 0 | 0 | 0 | 0 | 0 | 0 | 0 | 0 | 0 |
| Shaw | 2,116 | 6 | 0 | 0 | 1 | 5 | 106 | 51 | 53 | 2 | 0 |
| Southaven | 46,093 | 84 | 1 | 8 | 40 | 35 | 2,184 | 338 | 1,739 | 107 | 2 |
| Starkville | 24,444 | 64 | 0 | 6 | 18 | 40 | 728 | 157 | 558 | 13 | 2 |
| Summit | 1,627 | 2 | 0 | 0 | 0 | 2 | 46 | 17 | 29 | 0 | 0 |
| Tupelo | 36,453 | 87 | 0 | 25 | 25 | 37 | 1,864 | 382 | 1,404 | 78 | 0 |
| Vicksburg | 24,827 | 187 | 3 | 26 | 49 | 109 | 1,870 | 480 | 1,294 | 96 | 10 |
| Waveland | 5,091 | 10 | 0 | 2 | 2 | 6 | 341 | 45 | 285 | 11 | 0 |
| West Point | 11,203 | 30 | 0 | 4 | 10 | 16 | 269 | 62 | 206 | 1 | 0 |
| Winona | 4,434 | 9 | 0 | 0 | 3 | 6 | 27 | 10 | 13 | 4 | 0 |
| Yazoo City | 11,346 | 62 | 1 | 6 | 25 | 30 | 460 | 238 | 191 | 31 | 0 |
| **MISSOURI** | | | | | | | | | | | |
| Adrian | 1,912 | 5 | 0 | 0 | 0 | 5 | 34 | 5 | 26 | 3 | 0 |
| Advance | 1,212 | 1 | 0 | 1 | 0 | 0 | 16 | 3 | 11 | 2 | 0 |
| Anderson | 2,061 | 5 | 0 | 0 | 0 | 5 | 54 | 11 | 35 | 8 | 1 |
| Appleton City | 1,257 | 1 | 0 | 0 | 0 | 1 | 16 | 8 | 7 | 1 | 0 |
| Arbyrd | 485 | 2 | 0 | 0 | 0 | 2 | 2 | 1 | 1 | 0 | 0 |
| Archie | 1,008 | 2 | 0 | 1 | 0 | 1 | 15 | 1 | 11 | 3 | 0 |
| Arnold | 20,676 | 53 | 0 | 4 | 3 | 46 | 916 | 60 | 837 | 19 | 0 |
| Ash Grove | 1,540 | 0 | 0 | 0 | 0 | 0 | 20 | 10 | 9 | 1 | 1 |
| Ashland | 2,185 | 5 | 0 | 1 | 1 | 3 | 56 | 9 | 44 | 3 | 0 |
| Aurora | 7,529 | 61 | 0 | 2 | 8 | 51 | 446 | 107 | 311 | 28 | 2 |
| Auxvasse | 999 | 1 | 0 | 0 | 0 | 1 | 28 | 3 | 25 | 0 | 0 |
| Ava | 3,164 | 11 | 0 | 0 | 0 | 11 | 82 | 17 | 61 | 4 | 1 |
| Ballwin | 29,897 | 17 | 0 | 2 | 2 | 13 | 331 | 62 | 262 | 7 | 0 |
| Bates City | 268 | 2 | 0 | 0 | 0 | 2 | 17 | 7 | 9 | 1 | 0 |
| Battlefield | 4,521 | 0 | 0 | 0 | 0 | 0 | 77 | 18 | 59 | 0 | 0 |
| Bella Villa | 631 | 1 | 0 | 0 | 0 | 1 | 6 | 0 | 6 | 0 | 0 |
| Belle | 1,386 | 3 | 0 | 0 | 0 | 3 | 10 | 0 | 10 | 0 | 0 |
| Bellefontaine Neighbors | 10,152 | 65 | 0 | 4 | 20 | 41 | 397 | 147 | 178 | 72 | 7 |
| Bellerive | 252 | 2 | 0 | 0 | 0 | 2 | 0 | 0 | 0 | 0 | 0 |
| Bellflower | 385 | 1 | 0 | 0 | 0 | 1 | 2 | 0 | 2 | 0 | 0 |
| Bel-Nor | 1,469 | 2 | 0 | 1 | 1 | 0 | 24 | 15 | 9 | 0 | 0 |
| Bel-Ridge | 2,879 | 62 | 0 | 1 | 11 | 50 | 153 | 68 | 63 | 22 | 1 |

[1] The FBI does not publish arson data unless it receives data from either the agency or the state for all 12 months of the calendar year.

**Table 8. Offenses Known to Law Enforcement, by State and City, 2009**—*Continued*

(Number.)

| State/city | Population | Violent crime | Murder and non-negligent man-slaughter | Forcible rape | Robbery | Aggravated assault | Property crime | Burglary | Larceny-theft | Motor vehicle theft | Arson[1] |
|---|---|---|---|---|---|---|---|---|---|---|---|
| **MISSOURI**—*Continued* | | | | | | | | | | | |
| Belton | 24,908 | 52 | 1 | 7 | 12 | 32 | 587 | 92 | 454 | 41 | 5 |
| Berkeley | 9,316 | 133 | 3 | 9 | 45 | 76 | 477 | 203 | 213 | 61 | 4 |
| Bernie | 1,789 | 5 | 0 | 1 | 0 | 4 | 30 | 4 | 23 | 3 | 0 |
| Bethany | 3,066 | 14 | 0 | 0 | 0 | 14 | 57 | 22 | 32 | 3 | 1 |
| Beverly Hills | 553 | 0 | 0 | 0 | 0 | 0 | 0 | 0 | 0 | 0 | 0 |
| Billings | 1,120 | 4 | 0 | 1 | 0 | 3 | 19 | 0 | 16 | 3 | 0 |
| Birch Tree | 623 | 1 | 0 | 0 | 0 | 1 | 3 | 2 | 1 | 0 | 0 |
| Birmingham | 223 | 2 | 0 | 0 | 0 | 2 | 2 | 2 | 0 | 0 | 0 |
| Bismarck | 1,545 | 0 | 0 | 0 | 0 | 0 | 4 | 1 | 0 | 3 | 2 |
| Bloomfield | 1,861 | 5 | 0 | 0 | 0 | 5 | 17 | 1 | 15 | 1 | 1 |
| Blue Springs | 56,567 | 119 | 0 | 19 | 32 | 68 | 1,739 | 352 | 1,223 | 164 | 3 |
| Bolivar | 11,240 | 114 | 1 | 0 | 8 | 105 | 338 | 74 | 258 | 6 | 4 |
| Bonne Terre | 7,307 | 11 | 0 | 0 | 1 | 10 | 56 | 20 | 23 | 13 | 0 |
| Boonville | 8,841 | 24 | 0 | 1 | 0 | 23 | 251 | 21 | 223 | 7 | 0 |
| Bourbon | 1,533 | 8 | 0 | 0 | 0 | 8 | 26 | 0 | 25 | 1 | 0 |
| Bowling Green | 5,300 | 5 | 0 | 1 | 2 | 2 | 100 | 20 | 79 | 1 | 0 |
| Branson | 7,734 | 112 | 0 | 1 | 9 | 102 | 928 | 116 | 797 | 15 | 1 |
| Branson West | 520 | 0 | 0 | 0 | 0 | 0 | 50 | 0 | 50 | 0 | 0 |
| Braymer | 948 | 1 | 0 | 0 | 0 | 1 | 10 | 2 | 7 | 1 | 0 |
| Breckenridge Hills | 4,444 | 21 | 0 | 4 | 8 | 9 | 204 | 53 | 138 | 13 | 2 |
| Brentwood | 7,129 | 7 | 0 | 0 | 3 | 4 | 221 | 17 | 201 | 3 | 0 |
| Bridgeton | 14,972 | 73 | 0 | 2 | 21 | 50 | 996 | 81 | 836 | 79 | 1 |
| Brookfield | 4,275 | 8 | 0 | 0 | 0 | 8 | 96 | 27 | 62 | 7 | 1 |
| Brunswick | 846 | 1 | 0 | 0 | 0 | 1 | 7 | 6 | 1 | 0 | 0 |
| Bucklin | 469 | 0 | 0 | 0 | 0 | 0 | 3 | 2 | 1 | 0 | 0 |
| Buckner | 2,796 | 6 | 0 | 0 | 0 | 6 | 91 | 19 | 70 | 2 | 0 |
| Buffalo | 3,348 | 8 | 0 | 0 | 1 | 7 | 162 | 35 | 124 | 3 | 3 |
| Butler | 4,314 | 6 | 0 | 0 | 0 | 6 | 165 | 18 | 142 | 5 | 0 |
| Butterfield Village | 422 | 2 | 0 | 1 | 0 | 1 | 2 | 1 | 1 | 0 | 0 |
| Cabool | 2,138 | 1 | 0 | 0 | 0 | 1 | 43 | 23 | 16 | 4 | 1 |
| California | 4,165 | 15 | 0 | 0 | 1 | 14 | 61 | 13 | 46 | 2 | 0 |
| Calverton Park | 1,265 | 3 | 0 | 0 | 1 | 2 | 26 | 10 | 15 | 1 | 0 |
| Camden Point | 545 | 0 | 0 | 0 | 0 | 0 | 0 | 0 | 0 | 0 | 0 |
| Camdenton | 3,569 | 6 | 0 | 0 | 1 | 5 | 132 | 15 | 114 | 3 | 0 |
| Cameron | 9,226 | 28 | 0 | 1 | 2 | 25 | 215 | 44 | 165 | 6 | 2 |
| Campbell | 1,832 | 1 | 1 | 0 | 0 | 0 | 53 | 9 | 43 | 1 | 0 |
| Canton | 2,459 | 7 | 0 | 1 | 0 | 6 | 57 | 8 | 49 | 0 | 0 |
| Cape Girardeau | 37,588 | 178 | 2 | 17 | 51 | 108 | 2,141 | 363 | 1,740 | 38 | 9 |
| Cardwell | 716 | 3 | 0 | 1 | 1 | 1 | 2 | 0 | 2 | 0 | 0 |
| Carl Junction | 7,588 | 7 | 0 | 2 | 0 | 5 | 164 | 30 | 131 | 3 | 2 |
| Carrollton | 3,830 | 4 | 0 | 0 | 1 | 3 | 72 | 16 | 54 | 2 | 1 |
| Carterville | 1,985 | 2 | 0 | 0 | 0 | 2 | 10 | 3 | 6 | 1 | 0 |
| Carthage | 14,054 | 49 | 0 | 7 | 4 | 38 | 486 | 95 | 378 | 13 | 2 |
| Caruthersville | 6,082 | 63 | 0 | 1 | 5 | 57 | 213 | 93 | 108 | 12 | 2 |
| Cassville | 3,337 | 10 | 0 | 1 | 0 | 9 | 216 | 33 | 175 | 8 | 0 |
| Center | 641 | 0 | 0 | 0 | 0 | 0 | 12 | 1 | 11 | 0 | 0 |
| Centralia | 3,658 | 11 | 0 | 2 | 0 | 9 | 117 | 18 | 91 | 8 | 0 |
| Chaffee | 2,940 | 7 | 0 | 0 | 0 | 7 | 72 | 13 | 59 | 0 | 0 |
| Charlack | 1,336 | 3 | 0 | 0 | 1 | 2 | 43 | 7 | 32 | 4 | 0 |
| Charleston | 5,160 | 35 | 0 | 1 | 7 | 27 | 139 | 31 | 103 | 5 | 0 |
| Chesterfield | 45,977 | 27 | 1 | 1 | 6 | 19 | 913 | 86 | 814 | 13 | 4 |
| Clarkton | 1,228 | 3 | 0 | 0 | 0 | 3 | 21 | 9 | 12 | 0 | 1 |
| Claycomo | 1,316 | 6 | 0 | 1 | 2 | 3 | 44 | 6 | 31 | 7 | 1 |
| Clayton | 16,105 | 18 | 0 | 0 | 10 | 8 | 296 | 67 | 218 | 11 | 0 |
| Cleveland | 689 | 0 | 0 | 0 | 0 | 0 | 5 | 0 | 4 | 1 | 0 |
| Clever | 1,720 | 1 | 0 | 0 | 0 | 1 | 7 | 1 | 3 | 3 | 0 |
| Clinton | 9,387 | 28 | 0 | 4 | 4 | 20 | 379 | 85 | 273 | 21 | 0 |
| Cole Camp | 1,143 | 6 | 3 | 0 | 0 | 3 | 10 | 1 | 8 | 1 | 0 |
| Columbia | 102,588 | 501 | 3 | 32 | 157 | 309 | 3,906 | 692 | 3,082 | 132 | 11 |
| Concordia | 2,386 | 1 | 0 | 0 | 0 | 1 | 53 | 8 | 41 | 4 | 0 |
| Conway | 784 | 4 | 0 | 0 | 1 | 3 | 14 | 5 | 9 | 0 | 0 |
| Cool Valley | 996 | 9 | 0 | 0 | 4 | 5 | 74 | 15 | 53 | 6 | 0 |
| Cooter | 411 | 0 | 0 | 0 | 0 | 0 | 0 | 0 | 0 | 0 | 0 |
| Cottleville | 3,331 | 3 | 0 | 1 | 1 | 1 | 53 | 2 | 51 | 0 | 0 |
| Country Club Hills | 1,269 | 1 | 0 | 0 | 0 | 1 | 66 | 16 | 42 | 8 | 0 |
| Country Club Village | 2,447 | 1 | 0 | 0 | 0 | 1 | 24 | 6 | 17 | 1 | 0 |
| Crane | 1,372 | 5 | 0 | 0 | 0 | 5 | 23 | 7 | 15 | 1 | 0 |
| Creighton | 348 | 0 | 0 | 0 | 0 | 0 | 0 | 0 | 0 | 0 | 0 |
| Crestwood | 11,358 | 22 | 0 | 1 | 4 | 17 | 399 | 24 | 372 | 3 | 1 |
| Creve Coeur | 16,881 | 13 | 0 | 1 | 7 | 5 | 325 | 36 | 274 | 15 | 1 |
| Crocker | 995 | 3 | 0 | 0 | 0 | 3 | 40 | 5 | 34 | 1 | 0 |

[1] The FBI does not publish arson data unless it receives data from either the agency or the state for all 12 months of the calendar year.

**Table 8. Offenses Known to Law Enforcement, by State and City, 2009**—*Continued*

(Number.)

| State/city | Population | Violent crime | Murder and non-negligent man-slaughter | Forcible rape | Robbery | Aggravated assault | Property crime | Burglary | Larceny-theft | Motor vehicle theft | Arson[1] |
|---|---|---|---|---|---|---|---|---|---|---|---|
| **MISSOURI**—*Continued* | | | | | | | | | | | |
| Crystal City | 4,568 | 10 | 0 | 3 | 2 | 5 | 142 | 13 | 121 | 8 | 0 |
| Cuba | 3,592 | 15 | 0 | 1 | 2 | 12 | 159 | 30 | 124 | 5 | 2 |
| Deepwater | 488 | 1 | 0 | 0 | 0 | 1 | 15 | 3 | 12 | 0 | 1 |
| Dellwood | 4,864 | 32 | 0 | 0 | 12 | 20 | 167 | 70 | 71 | 26 | 1 |
| Delta | 543 | 0 | 0 | 0 | 0 | 0 | 0 | 0 | 0 | 0 | 0 |
| Desloge | 5,228 | 15 | 0 | 0 | 5 | 10 | 255 | 15 | 231 | 9 | 1 |
| De Soto | 6,479 | 35 | 0 | 1 | 3 | 31 | 232 | 20 | 199 | 13 | 1 |
| Des Peres | 8,604 | 12 | 0 | 1 | 9 | 2 | 438 | 19 | 418 | 1 | 0 |
| Dexter | 7,674 | 18 | 0 | 0 | 0 | 18 | 261 | 53 | 200 | 8 | 0 |
| Diamond | 905 | 0 | 0 | 0 | 0 | 0 | 1 | 0 | 1 | 0 | 0 |
| Dixon | 1,530 | 1 | 1 | 0 | 0 | 0 | 53 | 6 | 47 | 0 | 0 |
| Doniphan | 1,883 | 6 | 1 | 0 | 0 | 5 | 122 | 14 | 107 | 1 | 0 |
| Doolittle | 654 | 2 | 0 | 0 | 0 | 2 | 11 | 6 | 4 | 1 | 0 |
| Drexel | 1,097 | 1 | 0 | 0 | 0 | 1 | 36 | 13 | 22 | 1 | 0 |
| Duenweg | 1,260 | 1 | 0 | 0 | 0 | 1 | 58 | 4 | 53 | 1 | 0 |
| Duquesne | 1,758 | 9 | 0 | 0 | 1 | 8 | 59 | 21 | 31 | 7 | 0 |
| East Prairie | 3,053 | 15 | 0 | 0 | 0 | 15 | 138 | 19 | 114 | 5 | 1 |
| Edina | 1,111 | 1 | 0 | 0 | 0 | 1 | 2 | 2 | 0 | 0 | 0 |
| Edmundson | 775 | 8 | 0 | 0 | 4 | 4 | 59 | 10 | 43 | 6 | 2 |
| Eldon | 4,996 | 15 | 0 | 3 | 0 | 12 | 170 | 32 | 131 | 7 | 0 |
| El Dorado Springs | 3,672 | 29 | 0 | 2 | 1 | 26 | 136 | 30 | 99 | 7 | 4 |
| Ellington | 977 | 6 | 0 | 1 | 0 | 5 | 25 | 6 | 17 | 2 | 0 |
| Ellisville | 9,224 | 10 | 0 | 1 | 2 | 7 | 152 | 16 | 118 | 18 | 0 |
| Elsberry | 2,707 | 4 | 0 | 0 | 0 | 4 | 35 | 11 | 24 | 0 | 1 |
| Eminence | 555 | 0 | 0 | 0 | 0 | 0 | 1 | 0 | 1 | 0 | 0 |
| Eureka | 9,505 | 16 | 0 | 2 | 0 | 14 | 240 | 26 | 204 | 10 | 1 |
| Everton | 303 | 0 | 0 | 0 | 0 | 0 | 4 | 2 | 2 | 0 | 0 |
| Excelsior Springs | 12,132 | 62 | 0 | 5 | 6 | 51 | 342 | 87 | 238 | 17 | 2 |
| Exeter | 753 | 0 | 0 | 0 | 0 | 0 | 0 | 0 | 0 | 0 | 0 |
| Fair Grove | 1,443 | 1 | 0 | 1 | 0 | 0 | 18 | 7 | 10 | 1 | 0 |
| Fair Play | 459 | 0 | 0 | 0 | 0 | 0 | 8 | 2 | 4 | 2 | 0 |
| Farber | 392 | 0 | 0 | 0 | 0 | 0 | 0 | 0 | 0 | 0 | 0 |
| Farmington | 16,351 | 42 | 0 | 7 | 3 | 32 | 586 | 41 | 536 | 9 | 0 |
| Fayette | 2,685 | 1 | 0 | 0 | 0 | 1 | 18 | 8 | 7 | 3 | 0 |
| Ferguson | 20,814 | 113 | 3 | 3 | 52 | 55 | 1,171 | 302 | 702 | 167 | 2 |
| Ferrelview | 576 | 1 | 0 | 1 | 0 | 0 | 9 | 2 | 7 | 0 | 0 |
| Festus | 11,417 | 43 | 0 | 4 | 6 | 33 | 234 | 37 | 185 | 12 | 6 |
| Fleming | 116 | 0 | 0 | 0 | 0 | 0 | 0 | 0 | 0 | 0 | 0 |
| Flordell Hills | 854 | 11 | 0 | 2 | 2 | 7 | 43 | 18 | 14 | 11 | 0 |
| Florissant | 50,205 | 129 | 1 | 9 | 62 | 57 | 1,438 | 297 | 1,004 | 137 | 1 |
| Foley | 215 | 0 | 0 | 0 | 0 | 0 | 0 | 0 | 0 | 0 | 0 |
| Fordland | 771 | 1 | 0 | 0 | 0 | 1 | 3 | 1 | 2 | 0 | 0 |
| Foristell | 330 | 0 | 0 | 0 | 0 | 0 | 25 | 1 | 23 | 1 | 0 |
| Forsyth | 1,725 | 2 | 0 | 1 | 0 | 1 | 63 | 16 | 45 | 2 | 1 |
| Fredericktown | 4,177 | 32 | 2 | 5 | 0 | 25 | 90 | 16 | 72 | 2 | 1 |
| Freeman | 607 | 0 | 0 | 0 | 0 | 0 | 0 | 0 | 0 | 0 | 0 |
| Frontenac | 3,842 | 4 | 0 | 0 | 1 | 3 | 53 | 6 | 43 | 4 | 0 |
| Fulton | 12,771 | 45 | 0 | 2 | 9 | 34 | 466 | 80 | 368 | 18 | 6 |
| Gallatin | 1,724 | 1 | 0 | 0 | 0 | 1 | 11 | 1 | 9 | 1 | 0 |
| Garden City | 1,669 | 0 | 0 | 0 | 0 | 0 | 28 | 8 | 17 | 3 | 0 |
| Gerald | 1,254 | 2 | 0 | 0 | 0 | 2 | 25 | 6 | 19 | 0 | 0 |
| Gideon | 945 | 0 | 0 | 0 | 0 | 0 | 1 | 0 | 1 | 0 | 0 |
| Gladstone | 28,454 | 70 | 3 | 2 | 27 | 38 | 782 | 149 | 549 | 84 | 11 |
| Glasgow | 1,193 | 3 | 0 | 2 | 0 | 1 | 8 | 2 | 6 | 0 | 0 |
| Glendale | 5,461 | 3 | 0 | 0 | 2 | 1 | 36 | 4 | 32 | 0 | 0 |
| Glen Echo Park | 157 | 1 | 0 | 0 | 0 | 1 | 5 | 4 | 1 | 0 | 0 |
| Goodman | 1,262 | 2 | 0 | 0 | 0 | 2 | 10 | 3 | 6 | 1 | 0 |
| Gower | 1,435 | 0 | 0 | 0 | 0 | 0 | 25 | 6 | 17 | 2 | 0 |
| Granby | 2,243 | 3 | 0 | 0 | 0 | 3 | 21 | 4 | 16 | 1 | 2 |
| Grandview | 23,939 | 181 | 1 | 7 | 60 | 113 | 1,120 | 308 | 685 | 127 | 3 |
| Greendale | 687 | 0 | 0 | 0 | 0 | 0 | 4 | 3 | 1 | 0 | 0 |
| Greenfield | 1,220 | 1 | 0 | 0 | 0 | 1 | 19 | 5 | 9 | 5 | 0 |
| Greenville | 430 | 1 | 0 | 0 | 0 | 1 | 11 | 1 | 8 | 2 | 0 |
| Greenwood | 4,728 | 0 | 0 | 0 | 0 | 0 | 56 | 11 | 43 | 2 | 0 |
| Hallsville | 956 | 2 | 0 | 0 | 0 | 2 | 25 | 7 | 16 | 2 | 0 |
| Hamilton | 1,781 | 5 | 0 | 1 | 0 | 4 | 34 | 4 | 26 | 4 | 2 |
| Hannibal | 17,396 | 107 | 2 | 14 | 24 | 67 | 1,305 | 177 | 1,100 | 28 | 3 |
| Hardin | 550 | 2 | 0 | 0 | 0 | 2 | 6 | 2 | 4 | 0 | 0 |
| Harrisonville | 9,837 | 24 | 0 | 0 | 4 | 20 | 383 | 63 | 308 | 12 | 2 |
| Hartville | 604 | 6 | 0 | 0 | 0 | 6 | 22 | 5 | 17 | 0 | 0 |
| Hawk Point | 590 | 1 | 0 | 0 | 0 | 1 | 9 | 3 | 6 | 0 | 0 |

[1] The FBI does not publish arson data unless it receives data from either the agency or the state for all 12 months of the calendar year.

## Table 8. Offenses Known to Law Enforcement, by State and City, 2009—*Continued*

(Number.)

| State/city | Population | Violent crime | Murder and non-negligent man-slaughter | Forcible rape | Robbery | Aggravated assault | Property crime | Burglary | Larceny-theft | Motor vehicle theft | Arson[1] |
|---|---|---|---|---|---|---|---|---|---|---|---|
| **MISSOURI**—*Continued* | | | | | | | | | | | |
| Hayti | 2,933 | 10 | 0 | 0 | 4 | 6 | 150 | 25 | 121 | 4 | 0 |
| Hazelwood | 25,254 | 91 | 3 | 6 | 28 | 54 | 1,129 | 164 | 889 | 76 | 1 |
| Henrietta | 429 | 0 | 0 | 0 | 0 | 0 | 2 | 0 | 2 | 0 | 0 |
| Herculaneum[6] | 3,675 | 8 | 0 | 1 | 0 | 7 | 69 | 13 | 54 | 2 | 1 |
| Hermann | 2,720 | 11 | 0 | 0 | 0 | 11 | 75 | 12 | 62 | 1 | 0 |
| Higginsville | 4,558 | 7 | 0 | 0 | 0 | 7 | 118 | 20 | 94 | 4 | 1 |
| High Hill | 210 | 0 | 0 | 0 | 0 | 0 | 2 | 1 | 1 | 0 | 0 |
| Highlandville | 915 | 0 | 0 | 0 | 0 | 0 | 3 | 0 | 2 | 1 | 0 |
| Hillsboro | 2,111 | 14 | 0 | 2 | 0 | 12 | 108 | 18 | 87 | 3 | 1 |
| Hillsdale | 1,401 | 36 | 1 | 1 | 12 | 22 | 56 | 29 | 14 | 13 | 0 |
| Holcomb | 668 | 0 | 0 | 0 | 0 | 0 | 0 | 0 | 0 | 0 | 0 |
| Holden | 2,546 | 18 | 0 | 1 | 2 | 15 | 89 | 19 | 66 | 4 | 0 |
| Hollister | 4,054 | 53 | 0 | 3 | 2 | 48 | 144 | 31 | 113 | 0 | 0 |
| Holt | 477 | 1 | 0 | 0 | 0 | 1 | 2 | 1 | 1 | 0 | 0 |
| Holts Summit | 3,833 | 15 | 0 | 3 | 2 | 10 | 90 | 18 | 71 | 1 | 0 |
| Hornersville | 653 | 1 | 1 | 0 | 0 | 0 | 0 | 0 | 0 | 0 | 0 |
| Houston | 2,043 | 0 | 0 | 0 | 0 | 0 | 68 | 15 | 51 | 2 | 1 |
| Humansville | 1,025 | 4 | 0 | 1 | 0 | 3 | 9 | 1 | 5 | 3 | 0 |
| Huntsville | 1,645 | 0 | 0 | 0 | 0 | 0 | 4 | 0 | 3 | 1 | 0 |
| Hurley | 150 | 0 | 0 | 0 | 0 | 0 | 0 | 0 | 0 | 0 | 0 |
| Iberia | 682 | 6 | 0 | 2 | 0 | 4 | 4 | 3 | 0 | 1 | 0 |
| Independence | 122,174 | 749 | 3 | 51 | 167 | 528 | 7,165 | 1,328 | 5,134 | 703 | 29 |
| Iron Mountain Lake | 700 | 1 | 0 | 0 | 0 | 1 | 10 | 5 | 5 | 0 | 0 |
| Ironton | 1,310 | 0 | 0 | 0 | 0 | 0 | 28 | 7 | 18 | 3 | 0 |
| Jackson | 13,956 | 22 | 0 | 3 | 1 | 18 | 405 | 68 | 323 | 14 | 0 |
| Jasper | 1,073 | 0 | 0 | 0 | 0 | 0 | 13 | 4 | 9 | 0 | 1 |
| Jefferson City | 40,829 | 237 | 2 | 5 | 41 | 189 | 1,409 | 218 | 1,157 | 34 | 31 |
| Jennings | 14,536 | 220 | 3 | 8 | 51 | 158 | 1,090 | 340 | 575 | 175 | 4 |
| Jonesburg | 729 | 3 | 0 | 1 | 0 | 2 | 28 | 12 | 14 | 2 | 0 |
| Kansas City | 484,684 | 6,303 | 100 | 276 | 1,970 | 3,957 | 26,695 | 7,231 | 15,937 | 3,527 | 297 |
| Kearney | 9,018 | 9 | 0 | 2 | 0 | 7 | 130 | 17 | 110 | 3 | 1 |
| Kennett | 10,649 | 43 | 0 | 7 | 8 | 28 | 555 | 129 | 410 | 16 | 1 |
| Kimberling City | 2,466 | 3 | 0 | 0 | 0 | 3 | 51 | 12 | 37 | 2 | 0 |
| Kimmswick | 111 | 0 | 0 | 0 | 0 | 0 | 0 | 0 | 0 | 0 | 0 |
| King City | 879 | 0 | 0 | 0 | 0 | 0 | 2 | 1 | 1 | 0 | 0 |
| Kirksville | 17,376 | 56 | 0 | 1 | 4 | 51 | 524 | 63 | 450 | 11 | 3 |
| Kirkwood | 26,698 | 32 | 0 | 0 | 11 | 21 | 780 | 95 | 657 | 28 | 14 |
| Knob Noster | 3,349 | 6 | 0 | 0 | 0 | 6 | 127 | 36 | 90 | 1 | 0 |
| Ladue | 8,169 | 10 | 0 | 1 | 1 | 8 | 109 | 11 | 96 | 2 | 0 |
| La Grange | 918 | 3 | 2 | 0 | 0 | 1 | 0 | 0 | 0 | 0 | 0 |
| Lake Lafayette | 369 | 6 | 0 | 0 | 0 | 6 | 8 | 4 | 3 | 1 | 1 |
| Lake Lotawana | 1,963 | 0 | 0 | 0 | 0 | 0 | 27 | 5 | 19 | 3 | 0 |
| Lake Ozark | 2,093 | 7 | 0 | 0 | 0 | 7 | 68 | 7 | 60 | 1 | 0 |
| Lakeshire | 1,276 | 3 | 0 | 0 | 1 | 2 | 13 | 10 | 1 | 2 | 0 |
| Lake St. Louis | 14,686 | 8 | 0 | 1 | 0 | 7 | 310 | 33 | 269 | 8 | 3 |
| Lake Tapawingo | 780 | 1 | 0 | 0 | 0 | 1 | 14 | 2 | 11 | 1 | 1 |
| Lake Waukomis | 897 | 0 | 0 | 0 | 0 | 0 | 2 | 0 | 1 | 1 | 0 |
| Lake Winnebago | 1,168 | 0 | 0 | 0 | 0 | 0 | 6 | 0 | 4 | 2 | 0 |
| Lamar | 4,478 | 17 | 0 | 9 | 0 | 8 | 118 | 15 | 102 | 1 | 1 |
| La Monte | 1,101 | 1 | 0 | 0 | 0 | 1 | 19 | 4 | 15 | 0 | 5 |
| Lanagan | 432 | 0 | 0 | 0 | 0 | 0 | 3 | 1 | 2 | 0 | 1 |
| La Plata | 1,470 | 0 | 0 | 0 | 0 | 0 | 4 | 2 | 2 | 0 | 0 |
| Lathrop | 2,357 | 5 | 0 | 0 | 1 | 4 | 24 | 11 | 13 | 0 | 1 |
| Laurie | 740 | 2 | 0 | 0 | 0 | 2 | 57 | 8 | 49 | 0 | 0 |
| Lawson | 2,340 | 7 | 0 | 0 | 0 | 7 | 71 | 27 | 41 | 3 | 1 |
| Leadington | 420 | 0 | 0 | 0 | 0 | 0 | 3 | 1 | 1 | 1 | 0 |
| Lebanon | 14,574 | 62 | 1 | 6 | 3 | 52 | 758 | 98 | 638 | 22 | 3 |
| Lee's Summit | 85,792 | 106 | 1 | 16 | 34 | 55 | 2,179 | 378 | 1,665 | 136 | 8 |
| Leeton | 626 | 0 | 0 | 0 | 0 | 0 | 14 | 2 | 12 | 0 | 0 |
| Lexington | 4,528 | 12 | 0 | 2 | 1 | 9 | 134 | 27 | 102 | 5 | 0 |
| Liberal | 773 | 1 | 0 | 0 | 0 | 1 | 11 | 6 | 5 | 0 | 0 |
| Liberty | 31,073 | 38 | 0 | 6 | 3 | 29 | 542 | 87 | 413 | 42 | 7 |
| Licking | 3,023 | 3 | 0 | 0 | 0 | 3 | 55 | 9 | 46 | 0 | 1 |
| Lincoln | 1,087 | 2 | 0 | 1 | 0 | 1 | 21 | 4 | 15 | 2 | 0 |
| Linn | 1,434 | 0 | 0 | 0 | 0 | 0 | 21 | 6 | 13 | 2 | 0 |
| Linn Creek | 312 | 0 | 0 | 0 | 0 | 0 | 6 | 4 | 1 | 1 | 0 |
| Lockwood | 910 | 1 | 0 | 0 | 0 | 1 | 4 | 1 | 3 | 0 | 0 |
| Lone Jack | 977 | 1 | 0 | 0 | 0 | 1 | 15 | 4 | 10 | 1 | 0 |
| Louisiana | 3,759 | 12 | 0 | 0 | 0 | 12 | 23 | 4 | 18 | 1 | 0 |
| Lowry City | 723 | 7 | 0 | 0 | 0 | 7 | 13 | 7 | 6 | 0 | 0 |

[1] The FBI does not publish arson data unless it receives data from either the agency or the state for all 12 months of the calendar year.

[6] Because of changes in the state/local agency's reporting practices, figures are not comparable to previous years' data.

## Table 8. Offenses Known to Law Enforcement, by State and City, 2009—*Continued*

(Number.)

| State/city | Population | Violent crime | Murder and non-negligent man-slaughter | Forcible rape | Robbery | Aggravated assault | Property crime | Burglary | Larceny-theft | Motor vehicle theft | Arson[1] |
|---|---|---|---|---|---|---|---|---|---|---|---|
| **MISSOURI**—*Continued* | | | | | | | | | | | |
| Macon | 5,484 | 14 | 0 | 1 | 0 | 13 | 171 | 27 | 140 | 4 | 1 |
| Malden | 4,448 | 14 | 0 | 0 | 0 | 14 | 66 | 25 | 36 | 5 | 1 |
| Manchester | 18,504 | 12 | 1 | 1 | 3 | 7 | 333 | 36 | 277 | 20 | 0 |
| Mansfield | 1,363 | 0 | 0 | 0 | 0 | 0 | 29 | 8 | 20 | 1 | 0 |
| Maplewood | 8,563 | 34 | 0 | 2 | 14 | 18 | 482 | 63 | 379 | 40 | 2 |
| Marble Hill | 1,479 | 9 | 0 | 2 | 0 | 7 | 30 | 8 | 22 | 0 | 0 |
| Marceline[5] | 2,280 | | 0 | 0 | 0 | | 39 | 12 | 22 | 5 | 0 |
| Marionville | 2,183 | 4 | 1 | 0 | 0 | 3 | 72 | 16 | 52 | 4 | 1 |
| Marquand | 267 | 0 | 0 | 0 | 0 | 0 | 0 | 0 | 0 | 0 | 0 |
| Marshall | 12,055 | 19 | 0 | 2 | 1 | 16 | 364 | 94 | 264 | 6 | 1 |
| Marshfield | 7,463 | 7 | 0 | 1 | 3 | 3 | 179 | 29 | 146 | 4 | 0 |
| Marthasville | 866 | 0 | 0 | 0 | 0 | 0 | 2 | 0 | 0 | 2 | 0 |
| Martinsburg | 327 | 0 | 0 | 0 | 0 | 0 | 4 | 2 | 1 | 1 | 0 |
| Maryland Heights | 25,815 | 36 | 0 | 2 | 14 | 20 | 740 | 104 | 591 | 45 | 5 |
| Maryville | 10,815 | 26 | 0 | 0 | 0 | 26 | 218 | 35 | 169 | 14 | 0 |
| Matthews | 526 | 1 | 0 | 0 | 0 | 1 | 10 | 4 | 3 | 3 | 0 |
| Maysville | 1,131 | 1 | 0 | 1 | 0 | 0 | 5 | 0 | 5 | 0 | 0 |
| Memphis | 1,949 | 12 | 0 | 2 | 0 | 10 | 15 | 9 | 6 | 0 | 0 |
| Mexico | 11,050 | 10 | 0 | 3 | 3 | 4 | 245 | 50 | 191 | 4 | 0 |
| Milan | 1,754 | 6 | 0 | 1 | 0 | 5 | 27 | 9 | 16 | 2 | 0 |
| Miller | 801 | 2 | 0 | 0 | 0 | 2 | 20 | 6 | 13 | 1 | 1 |
| Miner | 1,343 | 6 | 0 | 1 | 0 | 5 | 29 | 0 | 28 | 1 | 0 |
| Moberly | 14,282 | 31 | 0 | 4 | 12 | 15 | 571 | 107 | 445 | 19 | 1 |
| Moline Acres | 2,502 | 22 | 0 | 0 | 7 | 15 | 171 | 24 | 130 | 17 | 0 |
| Monett | 9,082 | 17 | 1 | 1 | 2 | 13 | 342 | 75 | 253 | 14 | 3 |
| Monroe City | 2,460 | 19 | 0 | 2 | 0 | 17 | 63 | 10 | 51 | 2 | 0 |
| Montgomery City | 2,490 | 1 | 0 | 0 | 1 | 0 | 44 | 11 | 31 | 2 | 0 |
| Morehouse | 910 | 1 | 0 | 1 | 0 | 0 | 5 | 4 | 1 | 0 | 2 |
| Moscow Mills | 2,553 | 5 | 0 | 1 | 0 | 4 | 59 | 19 | 36 | 4 | 1 |
| Mound City | 1,062 | 1 | 0 | 0 | 0 | 1 | 15 | 2 | 8 | 5 | 0 |
| Mountain Grove | 4,694 | 21 | 0 | 2 | 2 | 17 | 109 | 35 | 64 | 10 | 0 |
| Mountain View[5] | 2,623 | | 0 | 0 | 3 | | 123 | 19 | 97 | 7 | 0 |
| Mount Vernon | 4,666 | 15 | 0 | 0 | 0 | 15 | 183 | 19 | 152 | 12 | 2 |
| Napoleon | 195 | 0 | 0 | 0 | 0 | 0 | 1 | 0 | 1 | 0 | 0 |
| Naylor | 595 | 0 | 0 | 0 | 0 | 0 | 0 | 0 | 0 | 0 | 0 |
| Neosho | 11,398 | 22 | 0 | 3 | 5 | 14 | 527 | 58 | 457 | 12 | 6 |
| Nevada | 8,299 | 44 | 2 | 3 | 4 | 35 | 568 | 73 | 474 | 21 | 3 |
| New Bloomfield | 750 | 1 | 0 | 0 | 0 | 1 | 8 | 3 | 5 | 0 | 0 |
| Newburg | 465 | 0 | 0 | 0 | 0 | 0 | 26 | 8 | 18 | 0 | 0 |
| New Florence | 750 | 0 | 0 | 0 | 0 | 0 | 23 | 10 | 12 | 1 | 0 |
| New Franklin | 1,108 | 0 | 0 | 0 | 0 | 0 | 9 | 4 | 4 | 1 | 0 |
| New Haven | 2,045 | 6 | 0 | 0 | 0 | 6 | 35 | 13 | 21 | 1 | 0 |
| New London | 1,010 | 2 | 0 | 0 | 1 | 1 | 23 | 6 | 17 | 0 | 1 |
| New Madrid | 2,980 | 0 | 0 | 0 | 0 | 0 | 38 | 3 | 35 | 0 | 0 |
| New Melle | 281 | 1 | 0 | 0 | 0 | 1 | 0 | 0 | 0 | 0 | 0 |
| Niangua | 499 | 1 | 0 | 0 | 0 | 1 | 1 | 0 | 0 | 1 | 0 |
| Nixa | 19,782 | 24 | 0 | 6 | 2 | 16 | 287 | 60 | 219 | 8 | 5 |
| Noel | 1,624 | 13 | 1 | 0 | 0 | 12 | 38 | 9 | 24 | 5 | 0 |
| Normandy | 4,866 | 40 | 0 | 0 | 12 | 28 | 147 | 48 | 58 | 41 | 0 |
| North Kansas City | 5,876 | 21 | 0 | 1 | 11 | 9 | 286 | 41 | 209 | 36 | 0 |
| Northmoor | 399 | 5 | 0 | 0 | 0 | 5 | 17 | 3 | 8 | 6 | 0 |
| Northwoods | 4,276 | 21 | 0 | 1 | 7 | 13 | 148 | 43 | 67 | 38 | 1 |
| Norwood | 581 | 1 | 0 | 0 | 0 | 1 | 0 | 0 | 0 | 0 | 0 |
| Oakland | 1,557 | 1 | 0 | 0 | 0 | 1 | 15 | 5 | 10 | 0 | 0 |
| Oakview Village | 397 | 4 | 0 | 0 | 0 | 4 | 10 | 0 | 9 | 1 | 0 |
| Odessa | 4,725 | 4 | 1 | 1 | 0 | 2 | 100 | 28 | 69 | 3 | 0 |
| O'Fallon | 80,528 | 65 | 1 | 3 | 11 | 50 | 1,323 | 144 | 1,154 | 25 | 5 |
| Old Monroe | 313 | 0 | 0 | 0 | 0 | 0 | 1 | 0 | 1 | 0 | 0 |
| Olivette | 7,449 | 11 | 1 | 1 | 2 | 7 | 184 | 46 | 133 | 5 | 2 |
| Oran | 1,247 | 3 | 0 | 0 | 0 | 3 | 18 | 1 | 17 | 0 | 0 |
| Orrick | 815 | 1 | 0 | 0 | 0 | 1 | 33 | 6 | 26 | 1 | 0 |
| Osage Beach | 4,845 | 29 | 0 | 1 | 2 | 26 | 265 | 19 | 241 | 5 | 0 |
| Osceola | 780 | 1 | 0 | 0 | 0 | 1 | 12 | 5 | 7 | 0 | 0 |
| Overland | 15,507 | 53 | 0 | 4 | 15 | 34 | 650 | 99 | 517 | 34 | 0 |
| Owensville | 2,583 | 10 | 0 | 0 | 0 | 10 | 112 | 15 | 94 | 3 | 1 |
| Ozark | 19,259 | 28 | 0 | 0 | 7 | 21 | 512 | 71 | 427 | 14 | 2 |
| Pacific | 7,345 | 30 | 1 | 4 | 3 | 22 | 207 | 30 | 170 | 7 | 0 |
| Pagedale | 3,379 | 34 | 1 | 3 | 13 | 17 | 172 | 38 | 108 | 26 | 1 |
| Palmyra | 3,410 | 2 | 0 | 0 | 0 | 2 | 45 | 6 | 39 | 0 | 3 |
| Parkville | 5,417 | 5 | 0 | 0 | 0 | 5 | 182 | 13 | 164 | 5 | 0 |
| Parma | 731 | 6 | 0 | 0 | 0 | 6 | 38 | 31 | 7 | 0 | 0 |

[1] The FBI does not publish arson data unless it receives data from either the agency or the state for all 12 months of the calendar year.

[5] The FBI determined that the agency did not follow national Uniform Crime Reporting (UCR) Program guidelines for reporting an offense. Consequently, this figure is not included in this table.

## Table 8. Offenses Known to Law Enforcement, by State and City, 2009—*Continued*

(Number.)

| State/city | Population | Violent crime | Murder and non-negligent man-slaughter | Forcible rape | Robbery | Aggravated assault | Property crime | Burglary | Larceny-theft | Motor vehicle theft | Arson[1] |
|---|---|---|---|---|---|---|---|---|---|---|---|
| **MISSOURI**—*Continued* | | | | | | | | | | | |
| Pasadena Park | 454 | 1 | 0 | 0 | 0 | 1 | 2 | 2 | 0 | 0 | 0 |
| Peculiar | 4,928 | 5 | 0 | 3 | 0 | 2 | 108 | 35 | 68 | 5 | 1 |
| Perryville | 8,222 | 15 | 0 | 4 | 1 | 10 | 246 | 43 | 198 | 5 | 2 |
| Pevely | 6,098 | 7 | 0 | 0 | 0 | 7 | 146 | 20 | 121 | 5 | 0 |
| Piedmont | 1,905 | 1 | 0 | 0 | 0 | 1 | 78 | 19 | 57 | 2 | 0 |
| Pierce City | 1,473 | 0 | 0 | 0 | 0 | 0 | 46 | 10 | 32 | 4 | 0 |
| Pilot Grove | 746 | 0 | 0 | 0 | 0 | 0 | 20 | 2 | 17 | 1 | 0 |
| Pine Lawn | 3,964 | 59 | 0 | 5 | 23 | 31 | 163 | 69 | 60 | 34 | 1 |
| Pineville | 865 | 0 | 0 | 0 | 0 | 0 | 0 | 0 | 0 | 0 | 0 |
| Platte City | 4,920 | 5 | 0 | 0 | 2 | 3 | 95 | 12 | 76 | 7 | 1 |
| Platte Woods | 455 | 1 | 0 | 0 | 0 | 1 | 6 | 2 | 2 | 2 | 0 |
| Plattsburg | 2,424 | 2 | 0 | 1 | 0 | 1 | 47 | 8 | 34 | 5 | 0 |
| Pleasant Hill | 7,374 | 5 | 0 | 1 | 1 | 3 | 134 | 18 | 102 | 14 | 0 |
| Pleasant Hope | 604 | 0 | 0 | 0 | 0 | 0 | 18 | 0 | 18 | 0 | 0 |
| Pleasant Valley | 3,548 | 5 | 0 | 0 | 0 | 5 | 52 | 11 | 35 | 6 | 1 |
| Polo | 603 | 0 | 0 | 0 | 0 | 0 | 5 | 1 | 4 | 0 | 0 |
| Poplar Bluff | 17,109 | 129 | 0 | 8 | 34 | 87 | 1,277 | 271 | 980 | 26 | 6 |
| Potosi | 2,702 | 9 | 0 | 0 | 1 | 8 | 122 | 16 | 104 | 2 | 0 |
| Purdy | 1,164 | 3 | 0 | 1 | 0 | 2 | 13 | 3 | 10 | 0 | 0 |
| Puxico | 1,138 | 8 | 0 | 1 | 0 | 7 | 11 | 6 | 3 | 2 | 1 |
| Queen City | 608 | 0 | 0 | 0 | 0 | 0 | 1 | 1 | 0 | 0 | 0 |
| Qulin | 480 | 0 | 0 | 0 | 0 | 0 | 2 | 0 | 2 | 0 | 0 |
| Randolph | 51 | 1 | 0 | 0 | 1 | 0 | 7 | 3 | 3 | 1 | 0 |
| Raymore | 18,620 | 14 | 0 | 4 | 4 | 6 | 492 | 42 | 434 | 16 | 4 |
| Raytown | 27,966 | 96 | 6 | 5 | 57 | 28 | 1,138 | 379 | 637 | 122 | 5 |
| Reeds Spring | 786 | 0 | 0 | 0 | 0 | 0 | 10 | 1 | 8 | 1 | 0 |
| Republic | 14,380 | 54 | 0 | 6 | 2 | 46 | 395 | 67 | 319 | 9 | 1 |
| Rich Hill | 1,497 | 0 | 0 | 0 | 0 | 0 | 34 | 9 | 24 | 1 | 1 |
| Richland | 1,778 | 7 | 0 | 0 | 0 | 7 | 70 | 11 | 59 | 0 | 0 |
| Richmond | 5,865 | 10 | 0 | 1 | 0 | 9 | 184 | 22 | 159 | 3 | 2 |
| Richmond Heights | 9,040 | 21 | 1 | 5 | 1 | 14 | 737 | 44 | 654 | 39 | 1 |
| Riverside | 2,987 | 11 | 0 | 4 | 3 | 4 | 204 | 21 | 173 | 10 | 0 |
| Riverview | 2,895 | 45 | 0 | 0 | 11 | 34 | 150 | 52 | 69 | 29 | 2 |
| Rockaway Beach | 597 | 0 | 0 | 0 | 0 | 0 | 15 | 7 | 8 | 0 | 1 |
| Rock Hill | 4,561 | 11 | 0 | 0 | 7 | 4 | 70 | 9 | 55 | 6 | 0 |
| Rock Port | 1,284 | 0 | 0 | 0 | 0 | 0 | 10 | 2 | 8 | 0 | 0 |
| Rogersville | 3,278 | 4 | 0 | 1 | 0 | 3 | 96 | 18 | 72 | 6 | 0 |
| Rolla | 18,669 | 66 | 0 | 2 | 11 | 53 | 842 | 137 | 665 | 40 | 2 |
| Salem | 4,873 | 14 | 0 | 1 | 0 | 13 | 205 | 17 | 187 | 1 | 1 |
| Salisbury | 1,541 | 1 | 0 | 1 | 0 | 0 | 27 | 8 | 18 | 1 | 0 |
| Sarcoxie | 1,379 | 2 | 0 | 0 | 0 | 2 | 4 | 2 | 2 | 0 | 0 |
| Savannah | 5,107 | 2 | 0 | 1 | 0 | 1 | 91 | 22 | 63 | 6 | 2 |
| Scott City | 4,533 | 8 | 0 | 3 | 0 | 5 | 64 | 2 | 59 | 3 | 1 |
| Sedalia | 21,065 | 173 | 1 | 6 | 24 | 142 | 1,390 | 283 | 1,056 | 51 | 7 |
| Seligman | 950 | 0 | 0 | 0 | 0 | 0 | 0 | 0 | 0 | 0 | 0 |
| Senath | 1,579 | 7 | 0 | 0 | 0 | 7 | 11 | 1 | 10 | 0 | 0 |
| Seneca | 2,282 | 1 | 0 | 0 | 1 | 0 | 67 | 17 | 47 | 3 | 0 |
| Seymour | 2,101 | 10 | 0 | 1 | 0 | 9 | 44 | 11 | 31 | 2 | 0 |
| Shelbina | 1,778 | 4 | 0 | 1 | 0 | 3 | 19 | 8 | 11 | 0 | 0 |
| Shrewsbury | 6,192 | 8 | 0 | 0 | 5 | 3 | 107 | 12 | 82 | 13 | 2 |
| Sikeston | 17,063 | 292 | 3 | 10 | 37 | 242 | 870 | 184 | 644 | 42 | 6 |
| Silex | 249 | 0 | 0 | 0 | 0 | 0 | 0 | 0 | 0 | 0 | 0 |
| Slater | 1,881 | 2 | 0 | 0 | 0 | 2 | 45 | 4 | 38 | 3 | 0 |
| Smithville | 8,416 | 12 | 0 | 0 | 1 | 11 | 90 | 22 | 64 | 4 | 0 |
| Southwest City | 930 | 6 | 0 | 0 | 1 | 5 | 24 | 3 | 21 | 0 | 0 |
| Sparta | 1,204 | 5 | 0 | 1 | 0 | 4 | 18 | 5 | 13 | 0 | 0 |
| Springfield | 156,659 | 1,197 | 6 | 112 | 299 | 780 | 14,012 | 2,314 | 10,859 | 839 | 80 |
| St. Ann | 12,678 | 72 | 0 | 1 | 15 | 56 | 473 | 68 | 360 | 45 | 0 |
| St. Charles | 64,807 | 159 | 0 | 9 | 31 | 119 | 2,085 | 270 | 1,739 | 76 | 6 |
| St. Clair | 4,475 | 34 | 0 | 2 | 2 | 30 | 332 | 37 | 279 | 16 | 3 |
| Steele[3] | 2,076 | | 0 | 1 | 3 | | 134 | 41 | 89 | 4 | 1 |
| Steelville | 1,500 | 2 | 0 | 1 | 1 | 0 | 54 | 18 | 32 | 4 | 0 |
| Ste. Genevieve | 4,407 | 2 | 0 | 0 | 0 | 2 | 66 | 9 | 55 | 2 | 1 |
| Stewartsville | 740 | 0 | 0 | 0 | 0 | 0 | 4 | 0 | 4 | 0 | 0 |
| St. James | 4,045 | 3 | 0 | 0 | 1 | 2 | 250 | 32 | 213 | 5 | 0 |
| St. John | 6,330 | 34 | 1 | 0 | 6 | 27 | 198 | 41 | 140 | 17 | 3 |
| St. Joseph | 76,436 | 441 | 3 | 12 | 109 | 317 | 3,794 | 970 | 2,639 | 185 | 20 |
| St. Louis | 355,208 | 7,353 | 143 | 250 | 2,721 | 4,239 | 29,595 | 6,834 | 17,799 | 4,962 | 256 |
| St. Marys | 380 | 1 | 0 | 0 | 0 | 1 | 4 | 0 | 4 | 0 | 0 |
| Stover | 1,051 | 5 | 0 | 1 | 0 | 4 | 52 | 18 | 33 | 1 | 0 |

[1] The FBI does not publish arson data unless it receives data from either the agency or the state for all 12 months of the calendar year.
[3] The FBI determined that the agency's data were overreported. Consequently, those data are not included in this table.

## Table 8. Offenses Known to Law Enforcement, by State and City, 2009—*Continued*

(Number.)

| State/city | Population | Violent crime | Murder and non-negligent man-slaughter | Forcible rape | Robbery | Aggravated assault | Property crime | Burglary | Larceny-theft | Motor vehicle theft | Arson[1] |
|---|---|---|---|---|---|---|---|---|---|---|---|
| **MISSOURI**—*Continued* | | | | | | | | | | | |
| Strafford | 2,218 | 1 | 0 | 0 | 0 | 1 | 121 | 18 | 99 | 4 | 0 |
| Strasburg | 136 | 0 | 0 | 0 | 0 | 0 | 1 | 1 | 0 | 0 | 0 |
| St. Robert | 3,525 | 45 | 0 | 4 | 10 | 31 | 331 | 50 | 269 | 12 | 1 |
| Sugar Creek | 3,498 | 23 | 0 | 1 | 2 | 20 | 146 | 35 | 98 | 13 | 0 |
| Sullivan | 6,769 | 10 | 0 | 1 | 1 | 8 | 278 | 41 | 228 | 9 | 0 |
| Summersville | 555 | 0 | 0 | 0 | 0 | 0 | 4 | 2 | 0 | 2 | 0 |
| Sunset Hills | 8,181 | 24 | 0 | 3 | 2 | 19 | 200 | 36 | 149 | 15 | 1 |
| Sweet Springs | 1,505 | 6 | 0 | 0 | 0 | 6 | 50 | 7 | 42 | 1 | 0 |
| Tarkio | 1,793 | 1 | 0 | 0 | 0 | 1 | 31 | 4 | 27 | 0 | 0 |
| Thayer | 2,145 | 8 | 0 | 0 | 0 | 8 | 34 | 8 | 25 | 1 | 2 |
| Theodosia | 250 | 0 | 0 | 0 | 0 | 0 | 6 | 6 | 0 | 0 | 0 |
| Tipton | 3,284 | 2 | 0 | 1 | 0 | 1 | 23 | 4 | 13 | 6 | 0 |
| Town and Country | 10,692 | 7 | 0 | 0 | 3 | 4 | 158 | 14 | 144 | 0 | 1 |
| Tracy | 209 | 0 | 0 | 0 | 0 | 0 | 3 | 0 | 3 | 0 | 0 |
| Trenton | 6,030 | 9 | 0 | 0 | 1 | 8 | 196 | 54 | 132 | 10 | 1 |
| Trimble | 478 | 0 | 0 | 0 | 0 | 0 | 2 | 0 | 2 | 0 | 0 |
| Troy | 13,093 | 17 | 0 | 0 | 0 | 17 | 306 | 31 | 265 | 10 | 0 |
| Truesdale | 701 | 5 | 0 | 0 | 1 | 4 | 24 | 5 | 19 | 0 | 2 |
| Union[6] | 9,932 | 19 | 1 | 1 | 1 | 16 | 500 | 38 | 452 | 10 | 1 |
| University City | 36,135 | 273 | 2 | 5 | 93 | 173 | 1,723 | 357 | 1,203 | 163 | 22 |
| Uplands Park | 435 | 0 | 0 | 0 | 0 | 0 | 13 | 3 | 4 | 6 | 0 |
| Urbana | 436 | 0 | 0 | 0 | 0 | 0 | 1 | 1 | 0 | 0 | 0 |
| Van Buren | 812 | 0 | 0 | 0 | 0 | 0 | 3 | 1 | 2 | 0 | 0 |
| Vandalia | 4,404 | 5 | 0 | 1 | 0 | 4 | 67 | 13 | 49 | 5 | 0 |
| Velda City | 1,485 | 9 | 0 | 0 | 0 | 9 | 36 | 16 | 10 | 10 | 0 |
| Velda Village Hills | 1,029 | 1 | 0 | 0 | 0 | 1 | 3 | 0 | 3 | 0 | 0 |
| Verona | 725 | 0 | 0 | 0 | 0 | 0 | 1 | 1 | 0 | 0 | 0 |
| Versailles | 2,732 | 1 | 0 | 0 | 0 | 1 | 59 | 5 | 54 | 0 | 0 |
| Viburnum | 778 | 1 | 0 | 0 | 0 | 1 | 13 | 8 | 4 | 1 | 0 |
| Vienna | 639 | 2 | 0 | 0 | 0 | 2 | 21 | 4 | 16 | 1 | 0 |
| Vinita Park | 1,769 | 17 | 0 | 0 | 2 | 15 | 80 | 23 | 53 | 4 | 1 |
| Walnut Grove | 671 | 0 | 0 | 0 | 0 | 0 | 7 | 4 | 1 | 2 | 0 |
| Warrensburg | 19,351 | 23 | 1 | 1 | 3 | 18 | 654 | 102 | 536 | 16 | 1 |
| Warrenton | 7,664 | 63 | 0 | 0 | 3 | 60 | 556 | 31 | 519 | 6 | 0 |
| Warsaw[6] | 2,236 | 27 | 0 | 2 | 4 | 21 | 140 | 47 | 87 | 6 | 1 |
| Warson Woods | 1,853 | 1 | 0 | 0 | 1 | 0 | 28 | 1 | 27 | 0 | 0 |
| Washburn | 485 | 1 | 0 | 0 | 0 | 1 | 0 | 0 | 0 | 0 | 0 |
| Washington | 14,516 | 21 | 0 | 2 | 2 | 17 | 457 | 61 | 381 | 15 | 1 |
| Waynesville | 4,006 | 23 | 0 | 4 | 2 | 17 | 168 | 24 | 138 | 6 | 0 |
| Weatherby Lake | 1,862 | 2 | 0 | 0 | 0 | 2 | 20 | 3 | 16 | 1 | 0 |
| Webb City | 11,734 | 4 | 0 | 2 | 1 | 1 | 506 | 60 | 421 | 25 | 0 |
| Webster Groves | 22,237 | 20 | 0 | 2 | 9 | 9 | 238 | 46 | 174 | 18 | 1 |
| Wellsville | 1,314 | 2 | 0 | 2 | 0 | 0 | 16 | 8 | 8 | 0 | 0 |
| Wentzville | 27,090 | 35 | 1 | 6 | 7 | 21 | 485 | 62 | 417 | 6 | 3 |
| Weston | 1,666 | 1 | 0 | 1 | 0 | 0 | 48 | 21 | 26 | 1 | 0 |
| West Plains | 12,175 | 67 | 0 | 4 | 8 | 55 | 899 | 147 | 725 | 27 | 0 |
| Wheaton | 752 | 0 | 0 | 0 | 0 | 0 | 1 | 0 | 1 | 0 | 0 |
| Willard | 3,350 | 8 | 1 | 0 | 1 | 6 | 133 | 28 | 101 | 4 | 0 |
| Willow Springs | 2,158 | 3 | 1 | 0 | 0 | 2 | 59 | 11 | 45 | 3 | 0 |
| Winfield | 1,199 | 2 | 0 | 0 | 0 | 2 | 16 | 3 | 13 | 0 | 0 |
| Winona | 1,330 | 7 | 0 | 0 | 0 | 7 | 47 | 16 | 29 | 2 | 0 |
| Wood Heights | 749 | 0 | 0 | 0 | 0 | 0 | 20 | 20 | 0 | 0 | 0 |
| Woodson Terrace | 3,986 | 24 | 0 | 1 | 6 | 17 | 176 | 43 | 102 | 31 | 1 |
| Wright City | 3,168 | 7 | 0 | 0 | 1 | 6 | 76 | 16 | 57 | 3 | 0 |
| **MONTANA** | | | | | | | | | | | |
| Baker | 1,629 | 2 | 0 | 0 | 0 | 2 | 10 | 2 | 8 | 0 | 0 |
| Belgrade | 8,485 | 24 | 0 | 6 | 1 | 17 | 151 | 13 | 129 | 9 | 1 |
| Billings | 105,427 | 259 | 2 | 28 | 71 | 158 | 4,597 | 752 | 3,592 | 253 | 13 |
| Boulder | 1,458 | 3 | 0 | 0 | 0 | 3 | 7 | 1 | 5 | 1 | 0 |
| Bozeman | 40,910 | 59 | 1 | 13 | 6 | 39 | 1,245 | 141 | 1,029 | 75 | 14 |
| Bridger | 723 | 0 | 0 | 0 | 0 | 0 | 10 | 3 | 7 | 0 | 0 |
| Colstrip | 2,345 | 8 | 2 | 0 | 0 | 6 | 41 | 5 | 33 | 3 | 0 |
| Columbia Falls | 5,441 | 22 | 0 | 1 | 3 | 18 | 238 | 8 | 216 | 14 | 2 |
| Columbus | 1,982 | 1 | 0 | 0 | 0 | 1 | 23 | 3 | 20 | 0 | 1 |
| Conrad | 2,477 | 8 | 0 | 1 | 0 | 7 | 29 | 0 | 28 | 1 | 0 |
| Cut Bank | 3,106 | 22 | 0 | 4 | 0 | 18 | 103 | 5 | 90 | 8 | 3 |
| Dillon | 4,186 | 7 | 0 | 0 | 0 | 7 | 94 | 9 | 81 | 4 | 0 |
| East Helena | 2,173 | 3 | 0 | 1 | 0 | 2 | 24 | 9 | 13 | 2 | 0 |
| Ennis | 1,081 | 2 | 0 | 1 | 0 | 1 | 4 | 3 | 1 | 0 | 0 |
| Eureka | 1,013 | 4 | 0 | 0 | 0 | 4 | 22 | 5 | 17 | 0 | 0 |
| Fort Benton | 1,445 | 4 | 1 | 0 | 0 | 3 | 30 | 1 | 27 | 2 | 0 |

[1] The FBI does not publish arson data unless it receives data from either the agency or the state for all 12 months of the calendar year.

[6] Because of changes in the state/local agency's reporting practices, figures are not comparable to previous years' data.

**Table 8. Offenses Known to Law Enforcement, by State and City, 2009—*Continued***

(Number.)

| State/city | Population | Violent crime | Murder and non-negligent man-slaughter | Forcible rape | Robbery | Aggravated assault | Property crime | Burglary | Larceny-theft | Motor vehicle theft | Arson[1] |
|---|---|---|---|---|---|---|---|---|---|---|---|
| **MONTANA**—*Continued* | | | | | | | | | | | |
| Glasgow | 2,888 | 6 | 1 | 0 | 0 | 5 | 62 | 9 | 47 | 6 | 1 |
| Glendive | 4,555 | 6 | 0 | 3 | 1 | 2 | 163 | 18 | 135 | 10 | 0 |
| Great Falls | 59,499 | 183 | 6 | 14 | 40 | 123 | 2,419 | 252 | 2,064 | 103 | 14 |
| Hamilton | 4,951 | 15 | 0 | 4 | 0 | 11 | 182 | 18 | 157 | 7 | 2 |
| Havre | 9,572 | 78 | 0 | 9 | 3 | 66 | 433 | 40 | 362 | 31 | 5 |
| Helena | 29,718 | 92 | 1 | 17 | 11 | 63 | 874 | 117 | 707 | 50 | 10 |
| Hot Springs | 568 | 0 | 0 | 0 | 0 | 0 | 17 | 5 | 12 | 0 | 0 |
| Joliet | 631 | 0 | 0 | 0 | 0 | 0 | 7 | 1 | 5 | 1 | 0 |
| Kalispell | 21,986 | 73 | 1 | 7 | 6 | 59 | 1,132 | 107 | 980 | 45 | 1 |
| Laurel | 6,645 | 17 | 0 | 2 | 0 | 15 | 204 | 20 | 179 | 5 | 0 |
| Lewistown | 5,915 | 13 | 0 | 2 | 0 | 11 | 82 | 9 | 69 | 4 | 0 |
| Libby | 2,925 | 8 | 0 | 0 | 1 | 7 | 49 | 2 | 47 | 0 | 0 |
| Livingston | 7,550 | 22 | 0 | 2 | 1 | 19 | 131 | 17 | 108 | 6 | 0 |
| Manhattan | 1,649 | 0 | 0 | 0 | 0 | 0 | 19 | 1 | 18 | 0 | 0 |
| Miles City | 8,062 | 12 | 0 | 2 | 0 | 10 | 285 | 16 | 260 | 9 | 2 |
| Missoula | 69,479 | 193 | 1 | 28 | 30 | 134 | 2,102 | 277 | 1,729 | 96 | 9 |
| Plains | 1,257 | 1 | 0 | 0 | 0 | 1 | 16 | 2 | 14 | 0 | 0 |
| Polson | 5,356 | 12 | 0 | 3 | 0 | 9 | 247 | 18 | 219 | 10 | 1 |
| Poplar | 861 | 6 | 0 | 0 | 0 | 6 | 4 | 1 | 3 | 0 | 0 |
| Red Lodge | 2,481 | 7 | 0 | 0 | 0 | 7 | 88 | 12 | 76 | 0 | 0 |
| Ronan City | 2,030 | 14 | 1 | 1 | 0 | 12 | 79 | 10 | 66 | 3 | 1 |
| Sidney | 4,759 | 12 | 0 | 4 | 0 | 8 | 93 | 6 | 76 | 11 | 0 |
| Stevensville | 2,036 | 11 | 0 | 2 | 0 | 9 | 59 | 7 | 48 | 4 | 0 |
| St. Ignatius | 816 | 3 | 0 | 0 | 0 | 3 | 20 | 4 | 15 | 1 | 0 |
| Thompson Falls | 1,435 | 6 | 0 | 2 | 0 | 4 | 32 | 8 | 21 | 3 | 1 |
| Three Forks | 1,951 | 3 | 0 | 0 | 0 | 3 | 26 | 1 | 23 | 2 | 1 |
| Troy | 987 | 2 | 0 | 1 | 0 | 1 | 23 | 4 | 19 | 0 | 0 |
| West Yellowstone | 1,554 | 1 | 0 | 0 | 0 | 1 | 2 | 0 | 1 | 1 | 0 |
| Whitefish | 8,625 | 11 | 0 | 1 | 1 | 9 | 305 | 24 | 275 | 6 | 1 |
| Wolf Point | 2,492 | 20 | 0 | 0 | 0 | 20 | 124 | 29 | 84 | 11 | 0 |
| **NEBRASKA** | | | | | | | | | | | |
| Alliance | 8,024 | 26 | 0 | 0 | 5 | 21 | 146 | 24 | 114 | 8 | 1 |
| Ashland | 2,597 | 1 | 1 | 0 | 0 | 0 | 11 | 4 | 6 | 1 | 0 |
| Auburn | 3,340 | 2 | 0 | 0 | 0 | 2 | 82 | 4 | 70 | 8 | 0 |
| Aurora | 4,195 | 4 | 0 | 1 | 0 | 3 | 29 | 19 | 10 | 0 | 0 |
| Bayard | 1,104 | 2 | 0 | 0 | 0 | 2 | 17 | 6 | 11 | 0 | 0 |
| Beatrice | 12,793 | 36 | 0 | 12 | 2 | 22 | 541 | 112 | 423 | 6 | 5 |
| Bellevue | 50,311 | 63 | 0 | 25 | 13 | 25 | 1,327 | 203 | 1,023 | 101 | 11 |
| Bennington | 1,011 | 0 | 0 | 0 | 0 | 0 | 9 | 5 | 4 | 0 | 0 |
| Blair | 7,820 | 2 | 0 | 2 | 0 | 0 | 121 | 12 | 101 | 8 | 0 |
| Bridgeport | 1,433 | 1 | 0 | 0 | 0 | 1 | 31 | 7 | 22 | 2 | 0 |
| Broken Bow | 3,119 | 8 | 0 | 7 | 0 | 1 | 47 | 6 | 40 | 1 | 0 |
| Central City | 2,810 | 1 | 0 | 0 | 0 | 1 | 65 | 11 | 49 | 5 | 0 |
| Chadron | 5,409 | 17 | 0 | 4 | 4 | 9 | 126 | 18 | 100 | 8 | 0 |
| Columbus | 21,652 | 15 | 0 | 3 | 2 | 10 | 425 | 61 | 341 | 23 | 1 |
| Cozad | 4,222 | 9 | 0 | 4 | 0 | 5 | 53 | 16 | 34 | 3 | 0 |
| Crete | 6,258 | 14 | 0 | 4 | 0 | 10 | 175 | 32 | 137 | 6 | 3 |
| David City | 2,460 | 2 | 0 | 0 | 0 | 2 | 17 | 4 | 13 | 0 | 0 |
| Falls City | 3,952 | 2 | 0 | 0 | 0 | 2 | 75 | 32 | 38 | 5 | 0 |
| Fremont | 25,220 | 33 | 0 | 11 | 4 | 18 | 833 | 117 | 685 | 31 | 0 |
| Gering | 7,672 | 6 | 0 | 0 | 0 | 6 | 172 | 34 | 129 | 9 | 0 |
| Gothenburg | 3,695 | 2 | 0 | 1 | 0 | 1 | 63 | 5 | 57 | 1 | 0 |
| Grand Island | 46,083 | 224 | 1 | 22 | 31 | 170 | 2,264 | 376 | 1,779 | 109 | 14 |
| Hastings | 25,476 | 52 | 0 | 16 | 5 | 31 | 805 | 97 | 665 | 43 | 3 |
| Holdrege | 5,122 | 3 | 0 | 1 | 0 | 2 | 114 | 13 | 95 | 6 | 0 |
| Imperial | 1,740 | 5 | 0 | 1 | 0 | 4 | 9 | 3 | 4 | 2 | 1 |
| Kearney | 30,759 | 63 | 0 | 14 | 3 | 46 | 1,019 | 151 | 834 | 34 | 14 |
| La Vista | 17,293 | 9 | 0 | 4 | 1 | 4 | 345 | 44 | 276 | 25 | 4 |
| Lexington | 10,138 | 21 | 0 | 6 | 3 | 12 | 380 | 53 | 311 | 16 | 4 |
| Lincoln | 254,438 | 1,165 | 4 | 126 | 197 | 838 | 10,007 | 1,618 | 8,095 | 294 | |
| Lyons | 847 | 1 | 0 | 0 | 0 | 1 | 2 | 0 | 2 | 0 | 0 |
| Madison | 2,168 | 5 | 0 | 1 | 0 | 4 | 25 | 1 | 22 | 2 | 0 |
| McCook | 7,377 | 2 | 0 | 1 | 0 | 1 | 202 | 21 | 172 | 9 | 0 |
| Milford | 2,037 | 1 | 0 | 0 | 0 | 1 | 32 | 11 | 18 | 3 | 0 |
| Minden | 2,782 | 1 | 0 | 1 | 0 | 0 | 53 | 10 | 42 | 1 | 0 |
| Nebraska City | 7,011 | 3 | 1 | 0 | 0 | 2 | 172 | 31 | 135 | 6 | 1 |
| Norfolk | 22,892 | 34 | 0 | 14 | 4 | 16 | 692 | 70 | 591 | 31 | 5 |
| Ogallala | 4,361 | 3 | 0 | 1 | 0 | 2 | 139 | 11 | 127 | 1 | 0 |
| Omaha | 443,037 | 2,363 | 30 | 192 | 892 | 1,249 | 18,291 | 3,228 | 12,938 | 2,125 | 131 |
| O'Neill | 3,267 | 0 | 0 | 0 | 0 | 0 | 15 | 3 | 12 | 0 | 1 |
| Papillion | 24,390 | 19 | 0 | 8 | 3 | 8 | 397 | 34 | 348 | 15 | 2 |

[1] The FBI does not publish arson data unless it receives data from either the agency or the state for all 12 months of the calendar year.

**Table 8. Offenses Known to Law Enforcement, by State and City, 2009—*Continued***

(Number.)

| State/city | Population | Violent crime | Murder and non-negligent man-slaughter | Forcible rape | Robbery | Aggravated assault | Property crime | Burglary | Larceny-theft | Motor vehicle theft | Arson[1] |
|---|---|---|---|---|---|---|---|---|---|---|---|
| **NEBRASKA**—*Continued* | | | | | | | | | | | |
| Plainview | 1,185 | 1 | 0 | 0 | 0 | 1 | 9 | 0 | 9 | 0 | 0 |
| Ralston | 6,077 | 13 | 0 | 0 | 7 | 6 | 147 | 24 | 114 | 9 | 3 |
| Scottsbluff | 14,773 | 53 | 2 | 8 | 6 | 37 | 784 | 102 | 653 | 29 | 8 |
| Scribner | 952 | 1 | 0 | 0 | 0 | 1 | 1 | 0 | 1 | 0 | 0 |
| Seward | 6,883 | 7 | 0 | 3 | 1 | 3 | 77 | 8 | 69 | 0 | 0 |
| Sidney | 6,514 | 4 | 0 | 0 | 0 | 4 | 96 | 5 | 87 | 4 | 0 |
| South Sioux City | 11,933 | 16 | 1 | 2 | 0 | 13 | 284 | 33 | 238 | 13 | 0 |
| Superior | 1,767 | 0 | 0 | 0 | 0 | 0 | 4 | 0 | 4 | 0 | 0 |
| Tecumseh | 1,563 | 1 | 0 | 0 | 1 | 0 | 19 | 6 | 11 | 2 | 0 |
| Valentine | 2,568 | 6 | 0 | 1 | 0 | 5 | 37 | 4 | 27 | 6 | 0 |
| Valley | 1,937 | 4 | 0 | 0 | 0 | 4 | 46 | 15 | 30 | 1 | 0 |
| Wahoo | 3,968 | 4 | 0 | 1 | 1 | 2 | 72 | 6 | 59 | 7 | 2 |
| Wayne | 5,268 | 4 | 0 | 4 | 0 | 0 | 89 | 18 | 71 | 0 | 0 |
| West Point | 3,322 | 0 | 0 | 0 | 0 | 0 | 19 | 3 | 15 | 1 | 0 |
| Wilber | 1,725 | 1 | 0 | 0 | 0 | 1 | 36 | 16 | 20 | 0 | 0 |
| Wymore | 1,580 | 2 | 0 | 1 | 0 | 1 | 36 | 5 | 31 | 0 | 0 |
| York | 7,847 | 3 | 0 | 0 | 0 | 3 | 208 | 31 | 174 | 3 | 2 |
| **NEVADA** | | | | | | | | | | | |
| Boulder City | 14,686 | 14 | 1 | 0 | 2 | 11 | 119 | 50 | 61 | 8 | 2 |
| Carlin | 2,075 | 11 | 0 | 1 | 0 | 10 | 40 | 17 | 13 | 10 | 0 |
| Elko | 17,177 | 88 | 0 | 18 | 10 | 60 | 665 | 181 | 435 | 49 | 4 |
| Fallon | 8,589 | 29 | 0 | 1 | 3 | 25 | 340 | 64 | 268 | 8 | 1 |
| Henderson | 261,883 | 612 | 4 | 56 | 257 | 295 | 5,171 | 1,411 | 3,141 | 619 | 72 |
| Las Vegas Metropolitan Police Department | 1,377,282 | 13,039 | 111 | 698 | 4,495 | 7,735 | 47,668 | 13,512 | 25,229 | 8,927 | 271 |
| Lovelock | 1,840 | 8 | 0 | 1 | 0 | 7 | 58 | 23 | 34 | 1 | 0 |
| Mesquite | 17,453 | 12 | 0 | 0 | 8 | 4 | 243 | 50 | 177 | 16 | 1 |
| North Las Vegas | 232,631 | 1,668 | 17 | 51 | 587 | 1,013 | 6,515 | 1,913 | 3,436 | 1,166 | 20 |
| Reno | 221,010 | 1,473 | 9 | 84 | 409 | 971 | 8,810 | 1,848 | 6,209 | 753 | 33 |
| Sparks | 91,421 | 399 | 5 | 40 | 112 | 242 | 3,105 | 850 | 2,007 | 248 | 24 |
| West Wendover | 5,025 | 29 | 0 | 9 | 5 | 15 | 152 | 57 | 88 | 7 | 3 |
| Winnemucca | 8,202 | 28 | 1 | 1 | 2 | 24 | 161 | 52 | 93 | 16 | 1 |
| Yerington | 3,960 | 14 | 0 | 0 | 0 | 14 | 59 | 47 | 12 | 0 | 0 |
| **NEW HAMPSHIRE** | | | | | | | | | | | |
| Alexandria | 1,561 | 2 | 0 | 1 | 0 | 1 | 30 | 15 | 15 | 0 | 0 |
| Alstead | 2,115 | 1 | 0 | 1 | 0 | 0 | 19 | 8 | 10 | 1 | 0 |
| Alton | 5,148 | 1 | 0 | 0 | 1 | 0 | 73 | 28 | 36 | 9 | 3 |
| Amherst | 11,914 | 11 | 0 | 0 | 1 | 10 | 197 | 26 | 169 | 2 | 0 |
| Antrim | 2,640 | 1 | 0 | 1 | 0 | 0 | 54 | 9 | 43 | 2 | 0 |
| Ashland | 2,102 | 2 | 0 | 1 | 1 | 0 | 118 | 6 | 107 | 5 | 0 |
| Auburn | 5,216 | 3 | 0 | 0 | 1 | 2 | 44 | 12 | 32 | 0 | 5 |
| Barnstead | 4,678 | 13 | 0 | 7 | 1 | 5 | 66 | 25 | 37 | 4 | 1 |
| Barrington | 8,580 | 4 | 0 | 0 | 1 | 3 | 125 | 23 | 98 | 4 | 0 |
| Bartlett | 2,934 | 2 | 0 | 1 | 0 | 1 | 59 | 23 | 35 | 1 | 0 |
| Bedford | 21,438 | 20 | 0 | 3 | 6 | 11 | 392 | 60 | 322 | 10 | 3 |
| Belmont | 7,181 | 5 | 0 | 1 | 1 | 3 | 183 | 28 | 146 | 9 | 0 |
| Bennington | 1,470 | 2 | 0 | 1 | 0 | 1 | 36 | 2 | 31 | 3 | 0 |
| Berlin | 9,474 | 16 | 0 | 5 | 1 | 10 | 134 | 31 | 95 | 8 | 11 |
| Bethlehem | 2,490 | 1 | 0 | 0 | 0 | 1 | 75 | 20 | 52 | 3 | 1 |
| Boscawen | 3,984 | 4 | 0 | 0 | 0 | 4 | 48 | 9 | 37 | 2 | 0 |
| Bow | 8,186 | 3 | 0 | 0 | 1 | 2 | 109 | 16 | 86 | 7 | 0 |
| Bradford | 1,545 | 0 | 0 | 0 | 0 | 0 | 17 | 6 | 9 | 2 | 0 |
| Brentwood | 4,057 | 3 | 0 | 0 | 0 | 3 | 56 | 8 | 40 | 8 | 1 |
| Bristol | 3,133 | 5 | 0 | 1 | 1 | 3 | 74 | 14 | 58 | 2 | 0 |
| Campton | 3,039 | 5 | 0 | 0 | 2 | 3 | 71 | 17 | 50 | 4 | 2 |
| Candia | 4,205 | 5 | 0 | 0 | 0 | 5 | 58 | 15 | 42 | 1 | 0 |
| Canterbury | 2,334 | 0 | 0 | 0 | 0 | 0 | 16 | 3 | 12 | 1 | 0 |
| Carroll | 750 | 0 | 0 | 0 | 0 | 0 | 67 | 24 | 41 | 2 | 0 |
| Center Harbor | 1,118 | 0 | 0 | 0 | 0 | 0 | 28 | 5 | 23 | 0 | 0 |
| Charlestown | 4,849 | 2 | 0 | 1 | 0 | 1 | 39 | 15 | 22 | 2 | 0 |
| Chester | 4,831 | 3 | 0 | 0 | 0 | 3 | 54 | 24 | 26 | 4 | 3 |
| Claremont | 12,940 | 46 | 0 | 9 | 9 | 28 | 466 | 60 | 392 | 14 | 3 |
| Colebrook | 2,344 | 4 | 0 | 2 | 0 | 2 | 60 | 9 | 49 | 2 | 0 |
| Concord | 42,427 | 95 | 0 | 12 | 33 | 50 | 1,279 | 158 | 1,100 | 21 | 8 |
| Conway | 9,240 | 24 | 0 | 5 | 4 | 15 | 424 | 64 | 348 | 12 | 8 |
| Dalton | 880 | 2 | 0 | 0 | 1 | 1 | 19 | 11 | 7 | 1 | 0 |
| Danville | 4,375 | 2 | 0 | 1 | 0 | 1 | 57 | 18 | 36 | 3 | 0 |
| Deerfield | 4,261 | 1 | 0 | 1 | 0 | 0 | 46 | 7 | 37 | 2 | 0 |
| Deering | 2,066 | 6 | 0 | 0 | 0 | 6 | 31 | 9 | 19 | 3 | 1 |
| Derry | 34,189 | 59 | 1 | 5 | 11 | 42 | 739 | 140 | 550 | 49 | 21 |
| Dover | 28,794 | 21 | 0 | 5 | 9 | 7 | 540 | 45 | 482 | 13 | 2 |
| Dublin | 1,598 | 0 | 0 | 0 | 0 | 0 | 24 | 5 | 17 | 2 | 0 |

[1] The FBI does not publish arson data unless it receives data from either the agency or the state for all 12 months of the calendar year.

## Table 8. Offenses Known to Law Enforcement, by State and City, 2009—*Continued*

(Number.)

| State/city | Population | Violent crime | Murder and non-negligent man-slaughter | Forcible rape | Robbery | Aggravated assault | Property crime | Burglary | Larceny-theft | Motor vehicle theft | Arson[1] |
|---|---|---|---|---|---|---|---|---|---|---|---|
| **NEW HAMPSHIRE**—*Continued* | | | | | | | | | | | |
| Dunbarton | 2,684 | 0 | 0 | 0 | 0 | 0 | 26 | 12 | 13 | 1 | 0 |
| Durham | 13,782 | 14 | 0 | 2 | 1 | 11 | 114 | 24 | 88 | 2 | 0 |
| Enfield | 4,872 | 6 | 0 | 2 | 0 | 4 | 43 | 9 | 34 | 0 | 0 |
| Epping | 6,341 | 7 | 0 | 3 | 1 | 3 | 153 | 21 | 122 | 10 | 0 |
| Epsom | 4,643 | 5 | 0 | 0 | 0 | 5 | 53 | 10 | 40 | 3 | 0 |
| Exeter | 14,838 | 8 | 0 | 5 | 0 | 3 | 153 | 21 | 125 | 7 | 1 |
| Farmington | 6,821 | 10 | 0 | 5 | 0 | 5 | 127 | 36 | 81 | 10 | 4 |
| Fitzwilliam | 2,315 | 1 | 0 | 0 | 0 | 1 | 31 | 10 | 15 | 6 | 0 |
| Franconia | 1,059 | 0 | 0 | 0 | 0 | 0 | 20 | 5 | 14 | 1 | 0 |
| Freedom | 1,448 | 0 | 0 | 0 | 0 | 0 | 23 | 6 | 17 | 0 | 0 |
| Fremont | 4,204 | 3 | 0 | 0 | 0 | 3 | 47 | 4 | 39 | 4 | 3 |
| Gilford | 7,526 | 10 | 0 | 3 | 3 | 4 | 240 | 29 | 201 | 10 | 1 |
| Gilmanton | 3,565 | 0 | 0 | 0 | 0 | 0 | 42 | 18 | 24 | 0 | 1 |
| Goffstown | 17,634 | 10 | 0 | 0 | 3 | 7 | 302 | 42 | 253 | 7 | 2 |
| Gorham | 2,787 | 0 | 0 | 0 | 0 | 0 | 37 | 7 | 28 | 2 | 0 |
| Grantham | 2,558 | 1 | 0 | 0 | 0 | 1 | 23 | 1 | 22 | 0 | 0 |
| Greenland | 3,444 | 1 | 0 | 0 | 1 | 0 | 42 | 5 | 37 | 0 | 1 |
| Hampstead | 9,026 | 3 | 0 | 1 | 1 | 1 | 131 | 26 | 101 | 4 | 0 |
| Hampton | 15,412 | 22 | 0 | 7 | 6 | 9 | 432 | 69 | 341 | 22 | 1 |
| Hancock | 1,807 | 0 | 0 | 0 | 0 | 0 | 18 | 7 | 11 | 0 | 0 |
| Hanover | 11,093 | 7 | 0 | 4 | 1 | 2 | 202 | 16 | 184 | 2 | 3 |
| Haverhill | 4,694 | 15 | 0 | 3 | 0 | 12 | 141 | 34 | 101 | 6 | 0 |
| Henniker | 5,125 | 3 | 0 | 1 | 0 | 2 | 129 | 22 | 105 | 2 | 1 |
| Hill | 1,124 | 0 | 0 | 0 | 0 | 0 | 0 | 0 | 0 | 0 | 0 |
| Hillsborough | 5,618 | 6 | 0 | 2 | 0 | 4 | 160 | 22 | 132 | 6 | 3 |
| Hinsdale | 4,178 | 8 | 0 | 2 | 1 | 5 | 122 | 25 | 96 | 1 | 0 |
| Hooksett | 14,027 | 10 | 0 | 2 | 3 | 5 | 371 | 52 | 312 | 7 | 4 |
| Hopkinton | 5,616 | 1 | 0 | 0 | 0 | 1 | 35 | 11 | 24 | 0 | 0 |
| Hudson | 24,978 | 41 | 0 | 7 | 5 | 29 | 403 | 63 | 316 | 24 | 3 |
| Jaffrey | 5,686 | 4 | 0 | 0 | 0 | 4 | 74 | 20 | 53 | 1 | 1 |
| Keene | 22,376 | 49 | 0 | 12 | 17 | 20 | 814 | 96 | 684 | 34 | 6 |
| Kingston | 6,250 | 5 | 0 | 0 | 0 | 5 | 59 | 14 | 39 | 6 | 2 |
| Laconia | 17,127 | 63 | 0 | 14 | 14 | 35 | 703 | 110 | 562 | 31 | 3 |
| Lancaster | 3,246 | 5 | 0 | 2 | 0 | 3 | 137 | 31 | 100 | 6 | 0 |
| Lebanon | 12,832 | 28 | 0 | 11 | 2 | 15 | 448 | 31 | 410 | 7 | 2 |
| Lee | 4,495 | 3 | 0 | 0 | 1 | 2 | 41 | 4 | 36 | 1 | 0 |
| Lincoln | 1,358 | 7 | 0 | 4 | 1 | 2 | 93 | 5 | 88 | 0 | 0 |
| Lisbon | 1,668 | 1 | 0 | 0 | 0 | 1 | 21 | 5 | 16 | 0 | 0 |
| Litchfield | 8,884 | 4 | 0 | 3 | 0 | 1 | 110 | 18 | 88 | 4 | 0 |
| Littleton | 6,221 | 10 | 0 | 3 | 3 | 4 | 163 | 46 | 104 | 13 | 0 |
| Londonderry | 25,205 | 22 | 1 | 2 | 3 | 16 | 353 | 65 | 266 | 22 | 3 |
| Loudon | 5,168 | 5 | 0 | 4 | 0 | 1 | 130 | 19 | 106 | 5 | 0 |
| Madison | 2,339 | 5 | 0 | 1 | 0 | 4 | 47 | 19 | 27 | 1 | 0 |
| Manchester | 108,671 | 537 | 2 | 71 | 171 | 293 | 3,714 | 760 | 2,791 | 163 | 42 |
| Marlborough | 2,077 | 3 | 0 | 3 | 0 | 0 | 39 | 5 | 32 | 2 | 0 |
| Meredith | 6,700 | 2 | 0 | 0 | 1 | 1 | 169 | 19 | 146 | 4 | 0 |
| Merrimack | 26,594 | 2 | 1 | 0 | 1 | 0 | 287 | 40 | 239 | 8 | 2 |
| Middleton | 1,872 | 1 | 0 | 0 | 0 | 1 | 10 | 3 | 7 | 0 | 1 |
| Milford | 15,133 | 30 | 0 | 1 | 4 | 25 | 267 | 35 | 225 | 7 | 4 |
| Milton | 4,655 | 13 | 0 | 3 | 1 | 9 | 119 | 38 | 75 | 6 | 3 |
| Mont Vernon | 2,404 | 2 | 1 | 0 | 0 | 1 | 13 | 4 | 9 | 0 | 1 |
| Moultonborough | 5,041 | 4 | 0 | 0 | 0 | 4 | 67 | 17 | 48 | 2 | 2 |
| Nashua | 86,554 | 176 | 1 | 25 | 38 | 112 | 2,443 | 379 | 1,962 | 102 | 14 |
| New Boston | 5,186 | 1 | 0 | 0 | 0 | 1 | 37 | 12 | 21 | 4 | 0 |
| Newbury | 2,134 | 0 | 0 | 0 | 0 | 0 | 29 | 6 | 22 | 1 | 0 |
| New Durham | 2,590 | 6 | 0 | 1 | 0 | 5 | 36 | 10 | 21 | 5 | 1 |
| Newfields | 1,635 | 0 | 0 | 0 | 0 | 0 | 22 | 3 | 18 | 1 | 0 |
| New Hampton | 2,280 | 2 | 0 | 0 | 0 | 2 | 56 | 13 | 32 | 11 | 1 |
| Newington | 805 | 0 | 0 | 0 | 0 | 0 | 254 | 2 | 249 | 3 | 1 |
| New Ipswich | 5,430 | 2 | 0 | 1 | 0 | 1 | 62 | 13 | 46 | 3 | 4 |
| New London | 4,509 | 0 | 0 | 0 | 0 | 0 | 38 | 6 | 31 | 1 | 0 |
| Newmarket | 9,602 | 10 | 0 | 4 | 0 | 6 | 56 | 8 | 45 | 3 | 0 |
| Newport | 6,550 | 9 | 0 | 6 | 0 | 3 | 263 | 57 | 189 | 17 | 0 |
| Newton | 4,594 | 2 | 0 | 2 | 0 | 0 | 41 | 9 | 28 | 4 | 0 |
| Northfield | 5,187 | 5 | 0 | 2 | 0 | 3 | 115 | 32 | 80 | 3 | 1 |
| North Hampton | 4,536 | 2 | 0 | 0 | 0 | 2 | 83 | 27 | 53 | 3 | 0 |
| Northumberland | 2,302 | 6 | 0 | 1 | 0 | 5 | 47 | 12 | 30 | 5 | 0 |
| Northwood | 4,192 | 6 | 0 | 2 | 0 | 4 | 112 | 43 | 68 | 1 | 1 |
| Nottingham | 4,628 | 1 | 0 | 0 | 0 | 1 | 42 | 7 | 33 | 2 | 0 |
| Orford | 1,054 | 1 | 0 | 0 | 0 | 1 | 4 | 2 | 2 | 0 | 0 |

[1] The FBI does not publish arson data unless it receives data from either the agency or the state for all 12 months of the calendar year.

## Table 8. Offenses Known to Law Enforcement, by State and City, 2009—*Continued*

(Number.)

| State/city | Population | Violent crime | Murder and non-negligent man-slaughter | Forcible rape | Robbery | Aggravated assault | Property crime | Burglary | Larceny-theft | Motor vehicle theft | Arson[1] |
|---|---|---|---|---|---|---|---|---|---|---|---|
| **NEW HAMPSHIRE**—*Continued* | | | | | | | | | | | |
| Ossipee | 4,733 | 6 | 0 | 1 | 1 | 4 | 115 | 41 | 69 | 5 | 1 |
| Pelham | 12,770 | 8 | 0 | 1 | 3 | 4 | 191 | 49 | 133 | 9 | 3 |
| Pembroke | 7,379 | 13 | 0 | 3 | 2 | 8 | 124 | 17 | 104 | 3 | 0 |
| Peterborough | 6,218 | 5 | 1 | 0 | 1 | 3 | 119 | 26 | 90 | 3 | 1 |
| Pittsfield | 4,409 | 12 | 0 | 3 | 1 | 8 | 65 | 12 | 52 | 1 | 0 |
| Plaistow | 7,607 | 5 | 0 | 1 | 1 | 3 | 182 | 12 | 160 | 10 | 1 |
| Plymouth | 6,444 | 17 | 0 | 3 | 2 | 12 | 266 | 33 | 223 | 10 | 10 |
| Portsmouth | 20,401 | 39 | 0 | 5 | 12 | 22 | 642 | 77 | 549 | 16 | 1 |
| Raymond | 10,296 | 15 | 0 | 8 | 1 | 6 | 182 | 24 | 152 | 6 | 1 |
| Rindge | 6,669 | 6 | 0 | 2 | 0 | 4 | 118 | 16 | 99 | 3 | 4 |
| Rochester | 30,889 | 65 | 0 | 11 | 15 | 39 | 944 | 123 | 790 | 31 | 5 |
| Rollinsford | 2,642 | 3 | 0 | 1 | 0 | 2 | 27 | 9 | 18 | 0 | 0 |
| Rye | 5,140 | 5 | 0 | 0 | 0 | 5 | 67 | 3 | 63 | 1 | 0 |
| Sandown | 5,948 | 4 | 0 | 0 | 0 | 4 | 64 | 20 | 41 | 3 | 1 |
| Sandwich | 1,319 | 0 | 0 | 0 | 0 | 0 | 31 | 5 | 26 | 0 | 2 |
| Seabrook | 8,551 | 11 | 0 | 0 | 1 | 10 | 394 | 55 | 322 | 17 | 0 |
| Somersworth | 12,020 | 36 | 1 | 2 | 7 | 26 | 367 | 53 | 303 | 11 | 6 |
| South Hampton | 879 | 0 | 0 | 0 | 0 | 0 | 3 | 0 | 3 | 0 | 0 |
| Strafford | 4,115 | 1 | 0 | 0 | 1 | 0 | 57 | 18 | 39 | 0 | 0 |
| Stratham | 7,394 | 1 | 0 | 0 | 0 | 1 | 51 | 5 | 45 | 1 | 0 |
| Sugar Hill | 618 | 0 | 0 | 0 | 0 | 0 | 3 | 1 | 2 | 0 | 0 |
| Sunapee | 3,396 | 2 | 0 | 0 | 0 | 2 | 2 | 1 | 1 | 0 | 1 |
| Thornton | 2,166 | 3 | 0 | 2 | 0 | 1 | 17 | 1 | 12 | 4 | 0 |
| Tilton | 3,604 | 3 | 0 | 0 | 2 | 1 | 156 | 14 | 136 | 6 | 1 |
| Troy | 2,073 | 0 | 0 | 0 | 0 | 0 | 35 | 17 | 15 | 3 | 0 |
| Wakefield | 5,485 | 6 | 0 | 0 | 2 | 4 | 123 | 26 | 87 | 10 | 1 |
| Walpole | 3,684 | 2 | 0 | 1 | 1 | 0 | 38 | 7 | 29 | 2 | 0 |
| Warner | 2,967 | 1 | 0 | 0 | 0 | 1 | 14 | 5 | 9 | 0 | 0 |
| Washington | 1,097 | 2 | 0 | 1 | 0 | 1 | 12 | 4 | 8 | 0 | 0 |
| Waterville Valley | 271 | 0 | 0 | 0 | 0 | 0 | 61 | 2 | 58 | 1 | 0 |
| Weare | 9,242 | 15 | 0 | 3 | 0 | 12 | 62 | 15 | 43 | 4 | 1 |
| Webster | 1,902 | 1 | 0 | 1 | 0 | 0 | 14 | 8 | 6 | 0 | 0 |
| Wilton | 3,940 | 5 | 0 | 0 | 2 | 3 | 87 | 15 | 68 | 4 | 0 |
| Winchester | 4,301 | 15 | 0 | 7 | 3 | 5 | 83 | 22 | 57 | 4 | 0 |
| Windham | 13,528 | 15 | 0 | 8 | 3 | 4 | 126 | 32 | 88 | 6 | 4 |
| Wolfeboro | 6,578 | 4 | 1 | 0 | 0 | 3 | 86 | 21 | 62 | 3 | 1 |
| Woodstock | 1,168 | 1 | 0 | 1 | 0 | 0 | 19 | 4 | 13 | 2 | 0 |
| **NEW JERSEY** | | | | | | | | | | | |
| Aberdeen Township | 18,493 | 20 | 1 | 1 | 6 | 12 | 260 | 40 | 204 | 16 | 1 |
| Absecon | 8,478 | 22 | 0 | 1 | 9 | 12 | 224 | 64 | 157 | 3 | 1 |
| Allendale | 6,587 | 5 | 0 | 3 | 0 | 2 | 66 | 16 | 49 | 1 | 0 |
| Allenhurst | 697 | 0 | 0 | 0 | 0 | 0 | 35 | 8 | 27 | 0 | 0 |
| Allentown | 1,840 | 1 | 0 | 0 | 0 | 1 | 30 | 3 | 25 | 2 | 0 |
| Alpha | 2,376 | 8 | 0 | 0 | 2 | 6 | 11 | 1 | 8 | 2 | 0 |
| Alpine | 2,514 | 1 | 0 | 0 | 0 | 1 | 8 | 1 | 6 | 1 | 0 |
| Andover Township | 6,585 | 8 | 0 | 0 | 1 | 7 | 34 | 10 | 23 | 1 | 0 |
| Asbury Park | 16,499 | 353 | 2 | 6 | 178 | 167 | 1,016 | 298 | 644 | 74 | 5 |
| Atlantic City | 39,295 | 825 | 10 | 32 | 404 | 379 | 2,500 | 379 | 1,987 | 134 | 10 |
| Atlantic Highlands | 4,589 | 5 | 0 | 0 | 1 | 4 | 104 | 26 | 76 | 2 | 0 |
| Audubon | 8,852 | 7 | 0 | 2 | 4 | 1 | 302 | 25 | 270 | 7 | 1 |
| Audubon Park | 1,053 | 3 | 0 | 0 | 2 | 1 | 26 | 5 | 19 | 2 | 1 |
| Avalon | 2,087 | 2 | 0 | 0 | 1 | 1 | 247 | 52 | 195 | 0 | 0 |
| Avon-by-the-Sea | 2,196 | 0 | 0 | 0 | 0 | 0 | 58 | 11 | 45 | 2 | 0 |
| Barnegat Light | 846 | 0 | 0 | 0 | 0 | 0 | 15 | 5 | 10 | 0 | 0 |
| Barnegat Township | 23,196 | 24 | 0 | 2 | 5 | 17 | 230 | 79 | 147 | 4 | 2 |
| Barrington | 6,924 | 7 | 0 | 2 | 3 | 2 | 96 | 17 | 76 | 3 | 2 |
| Bay Head | 1,268 | 1 | 0 | 0 | 0 | 1 | 73 | 12 | 58 | 3 | 0 |
| Bayonne | 56,982 | 185 | 0 | 7 | 86 | 92 | 875 | 209 | 584 | 82 | 2 |
| Beach Haven | 1,404 | 1 | 0 | 0 | 0 | 1 | 121 | 6 | 115 | 0 | 0 |
| Beachwood | 10,886 | 10 | 0 | 3 | 2 | 5 | 229 | 29 | 192 | 8 | 3 |
| Bedminster Township | 8,356 | 1 | 0 | 0 | 1 | 0 | 47 | 11 | 33 | 3 | 0 |
| Belleville | 33,610 | 84 | 1 | 0 | 49 | 34 | 718 | 168 | 405 | 145 | 7 |
| Bellmawr | 11,168 | 13 | 0 | 0 | 4 | 9 | 226 | 52 | 161 | 13 | 0 |
| Belmar | 5,891 | 26 | 0 | 4 | 6 | 16 | 287 | 60 | 222 | 5 | 0 |
| Belvidere | 2,622 | 1 | 0 | 0 | 0 | 1 | 17 | 2 | 14 | 1 | 0 |
| Bergenfield | 25,542 | 20 | 0 | 0 | 6 | 14 | 167 | 51 | 110 | 6 | 1 |
| Berkeley Heights Township | 13,335 | 3 | 0 | 0 | 1 | 2 | 90 | 21 | 65 | 4 | 0 |
| Berkeley Township | 43,044 | 33 | 0 | 2 | 7 | 24 | 643 | 153 | 482 | 8 | 3 |
| Berlin | 8,142 | 12 | 0 | 0 | 4 | 8 | 182 | 34 | 140 | 8 | 1 |
| Berlin Township | 5,429 | 5 | 0 | 0 | 0 | 5 | 187 | 24 | 155 | 8 | 1 |
| Bernards Township | 26,681 | 2 | 0 | 0 | 0 | 2 | 151 | 29 | 115 | 7 | 1 |

[1] The FBI does not publish arson data unless it receives data from either the agency or the state for all 12 months of the calendar year.

## Table 8. Offenses Known to Law Enforcement, by State and City, 2009—*Continued*

(Number.)

| State/city | Population | Violent crime | Murder and non-negligent man-slaughter | Forcible rape | Robbery | Aggravated assault | Property crime | Burglary | Larceny-theft | Motor vehicle theft | Arson[1] |
|---|---|---|---|---|---|---|---|---|---|---|---|
| **NEW JERSEY**—*Continued* | | | | | | | | | | | |
| Bernardsville | 7,799 | 2 | 0 | 0 | 0 | 2 | 28 | 4 | 24 | 0 | 0 |
| Beverly | 2,553 | 15 | 0 | 1 | 6 | 8 | 67 | 21 | 43 | 3 | 2 |
| Blairstown Township | 5,961 | 12 | 0 | 2 | 0 | 10 | 48 | 16 | 29 | 3 | 0 |
| Bloomfield | 43,489 | 107 | 0 | 6 | 69 | 32 | 997 | 136 | 718 | 143 | 0 |
| Bloomingdale | 7,436 | 2 | 1 | 0 | 0 | 1 | 54 | 12 | 40 | 2 | 0 |
| Bogota | 7,881 | 19 | 0 | 0 | 3 | 16 | 68 | 10 | 54 | 4 | 0 |
| Boonton | 8,467 | 15 | 0 | 1 | 5 | 9 | 144 | 19 | 124 | 1 | 1 |
| Boonton Township | 4,509 | 0 | 0 | 0 | 0 | 0 | 25 | 5 | 20 | 0 | 0 |
| Bordentown | 3,801 | 4 | 0 | 1 | 2 | 1 | 39 | 6 | 31 | 2 | 0 |
| Bordentown Township | 10,301 | 11 | 0 | 0 | 6 | 5 | 134 | 29 | 101 | 4 | 0 |
| Bound Brook | 10,398 | 24 | 0 | 3 | 12 | 9 | 208 | 52 | 150 | 6 | 0 |
| Bradley Beach | 4,849 | 6 | 0 | 0 | 2 | 4 | 173 | 28 | 142 | 3 | 0 |
| Branchburg Township | 15,087 | 2 | 0 | 1 | 0 | 1 | 103 | 12 | 83 | 8 | 0 |
| Brick Township | 78,666 | 124 | 1 | 8 | 37 | 78 | 1,382 | 315 | 1,025 | 42 | 9 |
| Bridgeton | 24,980 | 283 | 1 | 5 | 109 | 168 | 908 | 265 | 589 | 54 | 14 |
| Bridgewater Township | 44,519 | 20 | 1 | 1 | 5 | 13 | 765 | 72 | 663 | 30 | 0 |
| Brielle | 4,879 | 2 | 0 | 0 | 0 | 2 | 61 | 19 | 42 | 0 | 0 |
| Brigantine | 12,654 | 10 | 0 | 2 | 2 | 6 | 203 | 44 | 158 | 1 | 1 |
| Brooklawn | 2,253 | 15 | 0 | 2 | 6 | 7 | 300 | 28 | 265 | 7 | 0 |
| Buena | 3,693 | 8 | 0 | 0 | 2 | 6 | 96 | 35 | 54 | 7 | 4 |
| Burlington | 9,360 | 51 | 0 | 1 | 16 | 34 | 164 | 63 | 93 | 8 | 5 |
| Burlington Township | 21,413 | 35 | 0 | 0 | 22 | 13 | 430 | 48 | 366 | 16 | 0 |
| Butler | 8,188 | 11 | 0 | 2 | 1 | 8 | 89 | 15 | 71 | 3 | 0 |
| Byram Township | 8,479 | 2 | 0 | 0 | 0 | 2 | 53 | 11 | 39 | 3 | 0 |
| Caldwell | 7,085 | 6 | 1 | 1 | 0 | 4 | 31 | 7 | 24 | 0 | 0 |
| Califon | 1,026 | 1 | 0 | 0 | 0 | 1 | 7 | 4 | 2 | 1 | 0 |
| Camden | 78,980 | 1,880 | 34 | 60 | 766 | 1,020 | 3,935 | 1,035 | 2,251 | 649 | 137 |
| Cape May | 3,650 | 1 | 0 | 0 | 0 | 1 | 207 | 14 | 193 | 0 | 0 |
| Cape May Point | 221 | 0 | 0 | 0 | 0 | 0 | 27 | 5 | 22 | 0 | 0 |
| Carlstadt | 6,030 | 8 | 0 | 1 | 1 | 6 | 154 | 20 | 117 | 17 | 0 |
| Carney's Point Township | 8,002 | 15 | 0 | 1 | 6 | 8 | 146 | 38 | 97 | 11 | 5 |
| Carteret | 23,669 | 48 | 0 | 2 | 20 | 26 | 302 | 77 | 202 | 23 | 1 |
| Cedar Grove Township | 12,685 | 9 | 0 | 0 | 2 | 7 | 131 | 30 | 99 | 2 | 1 |
| Chatham | 8,187 | 3 | 1 | 0 | 0 | 2 | 61 | 12 | 43 | 6 | 0 |
| Chatham Township | 10,167 | 1 | 0 | 0 | 0 | 1 | 51 | 7 | 44 | 0 | 0 |
| Cherry Hill Township | 70,953 | 99 | 1 | 1 | 54 | 43 | 2,165 | 331 | 1,735 | 99 | 2 |
| Chesilhurst | 1,959 | 8 | 0 | 0 | 3 | 5 | 47 | 13 | 30 | 4 | 0 |
| Chester | 1,682 | 3 | 0 | 1 | 1 | 1 | 23 | 5 | 18 | 0 | 0 |
| Chesterfield Township | 7,609 | 0 | 0 | 0 | 0 | 0 | 25 | 6 | 19 | 0 | 0 |
| Chester Township | 7,812 | 3 | 0 | 0 | 0 | 3 | 38 | 7 | 30 | 1 | 0 |
| Cinnaminson Township | 15,448 | 14 | 0 | 0 | 5 | 9 | 376 | 67 | 298 | 11 | 2 |
| Clark Township | 14,330 | 2 | 0 | 0 | 0 | 2 | 132 | 11 | 117 | 4 | 0 |
| Clayton | 7,601 | 9 | 0 | 0 | 1 | 8 | 193 | 44 | 144 | 5 | 1 |
| Clementon | 4,876 | 37 | 0 | 1 | 10 | 26 | 275 | 51 | 217 | 7 | 0 |
| Cliffside Park | 22,848 | 35 | 0 | 0 | 12 | 23 | 236 | 49 | 177 | 10 | 0 |
| Clifton | 78,124 | 197 | 0 | 10 | 101 | 86 | 1,693 | 294 | 1,219 | 180 | 8 |
| Clinton | 2,534 | 1 | 0 | 0 | 0 | 1 | 24 | 10 | 14 | 0 | 0 |
| Clinton Township | 13,913 | 4 | 0 | 0 | 0 | 4 | 66 | 14 | 47 | 5 | 0 |
| Closter | 8,689 | 2 | 0 | 0 | 0 | 2 | 52 | 11 | 41 | 0 | 0 |
| Collingswood | 13,764 | 30 | 0 | 1 | 14 | 15 | 518 | 134 | 359 | 25 | 1 |
| Colts Neck Township | 10,119 | 4 | 0 | 2 | 0 | 2 | 81 | 26 | 54 | 1 | 0 |
| Cranbury Township | 4,013 | 4 | 0 | 0 | 1 | 3 | 35 | 3 | 31 | 1 | 0 |
| Cranford Township | 21,820 | 12 | 0 | 3 | 6 | 3 | 212 | 48 | 157 | 7 | 0 |
| Cresskill | 8,716 | 0 | 0 | 0 | 0 | 0 | 42 | 18 | 24 | 0 | 0 |
| Deal | 1,042 | 1 | 0 | 0 | 0 | 1 | 47 | 21 | 25 | 1 | 0 |
| Delanco Township | 4,848 | 8 | 0 | 2 | 4 | 2 | 58 | 18 | 40 | 0 | 1 |
| Delaware Township | 4,691 | 0 | 0 | 0 | 0 | 0 | 34 | 9 | 21 | 4 | 1 |
| Delran Township | 16,936 | 20 | 0 | 2 | 4 | 14 | 233 | 38 | 178 | 17 | 0 |
| Demarest | 5,162 | 0 | 0 | 0 | 0 | 0 | 31 | 10 | 19 | 2 | 0 |
| Denville Township | 16,558 | 7 | 0 | 0 | 1 | 6 | 122 | 24 | 92 | 6 | 1 |
| Deptford Township | 31,090 | 133 | 1 | 1 | 43 | 88 | 1,492 | 209 | 1,228 | 55 | 10 |
| Dover | 17,827 | 43 | 0 | 6 | 19 | 18 | 358 | 93 | 239 | 26 | 1 |
| Dumont | 16,910 | 17 | 0 | 0 | 6 | 11 | 125 | 12 | 111 | 2 | 0 |
| Dunellen | 7,011 | 7 | 0 | 1 | 2 | 4 | 135 | 28 | 102 | 5 | 0 |
| Eastampton Township | 6,578 | 4 | 0 | 1 | 0 | 3 | 96 | 23 | 72 | 1 | 1 |
| East Brunswick Township | 47,323 | 50 | 1 | 6 | 21 | 22 | 941 | 125 | 789 | 27 | 6 |
| East Greenwich Township | 8,105 | 4 | 0 | 0 | 0 | 4 | 124 | 33 | 89 | 2 | 1 |
| East Hanover Township | 11,395 | 5 | 0 | 0 | 3 | 2 | 164 | 17 | 141 | 6 | 0 |
| East Newark | 2,113 | 2 | 0 | 0 | 0 | 2 | 28 | 7 | 18 | 3 | 0 |
| East Orange | 64,924 | 504 | 11 | 22 | 224 | 247 | 1,247 | 388 | 632 | 227 | 22 |
| East Rutherford | 10,248 | 7 | 0 | 0 | 0 | 7 | 233 | 14 | 188 | 31 | 1 |

[1] The FBI does not publish arson data unless it receives data from either the agency or the state for all 12 months of the calendar year.

## Table 8. Offenses Known to Law Enforcement, by State and City, 2009—*Continued*

(Number.)

| State/city | Population | Violent crime | Murder and non-negligent man-slaughter | Forcible rape | Robbery | Aggravated assault | Property crime | Burglary | Larceny-theft | Motor vehicle theft | Arson[1] |
|---|---|---|---|---|---|---|---|---|---|---|---|
| **NEW JERSEY**—*Continued* | | | | | | | | | | | |
| East Windsor Township | 26,965 | 23 | 0 | 1 | 5 | 17 | 269 | 26 | 233 | 10 | 0 |
| Eatontown | 14,212 | 34 | 0 | 1 | 14 | 19 | 674 | 66 | 589 | 19 | 3 |
| Edgewater | 9,846 | 23 | 0 | 0 | 7 | 16 | 238 | 36 | 185 | 17 | 0 |
| Edgewater Park Township | 7,674 | 12 | 0 | 0 | 7 | 5 | 192 | 41 | 137 | 14 | 1 |
| Edison Township | 99,356 | 264 | 1 | 4 | 97 | 162 | 2,192 | 423 | 1,585 | 184 | 8 |
| Egg Harbor City | 4,362 | 12 | 1 | 0 | 4 | 7 | 107 | 16 | 84 | 7 | 2 |
| Egg Harbor Township | 41,005 | 101 | 3 | 8 | 36 | 54 | 976 | 184 | 748 | 44 | 13 |
| Elizabeth | 124,910 | 1,288 | 5 | 44 | 761 | 478 | 5,113 | 1,002 | 3,164 | 947 | 17 |
| Elk Township | 4,001 | 8 | 0 | 1 | 0 | 7 | 85 | 24 | 56 | 5 | 1 |
| Elmer | 1,341 | 0 | 0 | 0 | 0 | 0 | 18 | 5 | 13 | 0 | 0 |
| Elmwood Park | 18,602 | 22 | 1 | 0 | 10 | 11 | 398 | 69 | 300 | 29 | 2 |
| Elsinboro Township | 1,046 | 3 | 0 | 0 | 0 | 3 | 16 | 6 | 10 | 0 | 0 |
| Emerson | 7,370 | 3 | 0 | 0 | 2 | 1 | 79 | 7 | 71 | 1 | 0 |
| Englewood | 29,463 | 67 | 0 | 4 | 27 | 36 | 433 | 129 | 271 | 33 | 1 |
| Englewood Cliffs | 5,858 | 2 | 0 | 0 | 1 | 1 | 86 | 19 | 62 | 5 | 0 |
| Englishtown | 1,934 | 1 | 0 | 0 | 0 | 1 | 20 | 4 | 16 | 0 | 0 |
| Essex Fells | 2,102 | 0 | 0 | 0 | 0 | 0 | 8 | 2 | 6 | 0 | 0 |
| Evesham Township | 45,633 | 38 | 0 | 8 | 15 | 15 | 616 | 80 | 521 | 15 | 3 |
| Ewing Township | 36,098 | 108 | 0 | 2 | 33 | 73 | 664 | 142 | 478 | 44 | 4 |
| Fairfield Township, Essex County | 7,529 | 11 | 1 | 1 | 1 | 8 | 262 | 37 | 203 | 22 | 0 |
| Fair Haven | 5,905 | 1 | 0 | 0 | 0 | 1 | 31 | 4 | 27 | 0 | 0 |
| Fair Lawn | 30,400 | 30 | 0 | 1 | 6 | 23 | 360 | 35 | 309 | 16 | 6 |
| Fairview | 13,571 | 37 | 0 | 1 | 18 | 18 | 229 | 56 | 163 | 10 | 0 |
| Fanwood | 7,078 | 3 | 0 | 0 | 1 | 2 | 87 | 15 | 66 | 6 | 0 |
| Far Hills | 903 | 0 | 0 | 0 | 0 | 0 | 4 | 0 | 4 | 0 | 0 |
| Flemington | 4,285 | 14 | 0 | 2 | 4 | 8 | 120 | 26 | 90 | 4 | 0 |
| Florence Township | 11,458 | 9 | 0 | 0 | 7 | 2 | 94 | 27 | 65 | 2 | 0 |
| Florham Park | 12,605 | 2 | 0 | 1 | 0 | 1 | 90 | 7 | 72 | 11 | 0 |
| Fort Lee | 36,342 | 15 | 0 | 1 | 7 | 7 | 341 | 63 | 266 | 12 | 1 |
| Franklin | 5,068 | 5 | 0 | 0 | 0 | 5 | 101 | 13 | 86 | 2 | 0 |
| Franklin Lakes | 11,757 | 5 | 0 | 0 | 0 | 5 | 88 | 26 | 60 | 2 | 0 |
| Franklin Township, Gloucester County | 17,499 | 25 | 0 | 1 | 5 | 19 | 337 | 101 | 220 | 16 | 1 |
| Franklin Township, Hunterdon County | 3,254 | 0 | 0 | 0 | 0 | 0 | 36 | 6 | 30 | 0 | 1 |
| Franklin Township, Somerset County | 60,364 | 79 | 0 | 2 | 43 | 34 | 909 | 303 | 533 | 73 | 3 |
| Freehold | 11,474 | 41 | 0 | 2 | 19 | 20 | 245 | 30 | 210 | 5 | 1 |
| Freehold Township | 35,099 | 39 | 0 | 7 | 17 | 15 | 950 | 100 | 838 | 12 | 2 |
| Frenchtown | 1,450 | 0 | 0 | 0 | 0 | 0 | 20 | 6 | 13 | 1 | 0 |
| Galloway Township | 37,051 | 70 | 0 | 6 | 22 | 42 | 653 | 153 | 460 | 40 | 7 |
| Garfield | 28,882 | 53 | 1 | 1 | 19 | 32 | 396 | 106 | 241 | 49 | 1 |
| Garwood | 4,438 | 3 | 0 | 0 | 1 | 2 | 32 | 7 | 25 | 0 | 0 |
| Gibbsboro | 2,434 | 8 | 0 | 0 | 1 | 7 | 52 | 19 | 29 | 4 | 0 |
| Glassboro | 19,829 | 67 | 0 | 4 | 24 | 39 | 436 | 133 | 283 | 20 | 5 |
| Glen Ridge | 6,599 | 5 | 0 | 1 | 3 | 1 | 153 | 54 | 93 | 6 | 0 |
| Glen Rock | 11,086 | 1 | 0 | 0 | 0 | 1 | 76 | 14 | 62 | 0 | 1 |
| Gloucester City | 11,508 | 32 | 0 | 2 | 13 | 17 | 313 | 55 | 223 | 35 | 3 |
| Gloucester Township | 64,909 | 268 | 1 | 4 | 89 | 174 | 1,487 | 400 | 1,007 | 80 | 13 |
| Green Brook Township | 7,034 | 4 | 0 | 1 | 1 | 2 | 155 | 29 | 112 | 14 | 0 |
| Greenwich Township, Gloucester County | 4,997 | 6 | 0 | 0 | 2 | 4 | 150 | 38 | 104 | 8 | 0 |
| Greenwich Township, Warren County | 5,195 | 4 | 0 | 0 | 4 | 0 | 98 | 7 | 90 | 1 | 0 |
| Guttenberg | 10,493 | 39 | 0 | 0 | 13 | 26 | 103 | 26 | 67 | 10 | 0 |
| Hackensack | 42,801 | 142 | 1 | 1 | 39 | 101 | 1,105 | 104 | 908 | 93 | 4 |
| Hackettstown | 9,565 | 11 | 0 | 0 | 0 | 11 | 150 | 27 | 122 | 1 | 0 |
| Haddonfield | 11,420 | 6 | 0 | 0 | 3 | 3 | 172 | 21 | 147 | 4 | 1 |
| Haddon Heights | 7,596 | 3 | 0 | 0 | 0 | 3 | 113 | 19 | 88 | 6 | 0 |
| Haddon Township | 14,293 | 22 | 0 | 1 | 15 | 6 | 328 | 62 | 259 | 7 | 1 |
| Haledon | 8,546 | 10 | 0 | 1 | 7 | 2 | 181 | 47 | 103 | 31 | 1 |
| Hamburg | 3,504 | 1 | 0 | 0 | 0 | 1 | 42 | 8 | 32 | 2 | 0 |
| Hamilton Township, Atlantic County | 24,863 | 71 | 3 | 2 | 13 | 53 | 1,214 | 173 | 1,001 | 40 | 7 |
| Hamilton Township, Mercer County | 90,491 | 205 | 0 | 10 | 107 | 88 | 1,693 | 320 | 1,275 | 98 | 6 |
| Hammonton | 13,517 | 27 | 0 | 0 | 5 | 22 | 168 | 54 | 104 | 10 | 0 |
| Hanover Township | 13,736 | 14 | 0 | 0 | 7 | 7 | 160 | 18 | 131 | 11 | 1 |
| Harding Township | 3,332 | 2 | 0 | 0 | 0 | 2 | 19 | 2 | 17 | 0 | 4 |
| Hardyston Township | 8,559 | 8 | 0 | 3 | 0 | 5 | 93 | 35 | 54 | 4 | 1 |
| Harrington Park | 4,883 | 0 | 0 | 0 | 0 | 0 | 13 | 2 | 11 | 0 | 0 |
| Harrison | 15,296 | 50 | 0 | 1 | 26 | 23 | 249 | 72 | 132 | 45 | 0 |
| Harrison Township | 12,916 | 8 | 0 | 1 | 1 | 6 | 157 | 24 | 131 | 2 | 3 |
| Harvey Cedars | 397 | 2 | 0 | 0 | 0 | 2 | 35 | 11 | 24 | 0 | 0 |
| Hasbrouck Heights | 11,383 | 4 | 0 | 0 | 3 | 1 | 76 | 14 | 61 | 1 | 1 |
| Haworth | 3,416 | 0 | 0 | 0 | 0 | 0 | 12 | 7 | 5 | 0 | 0 |
| Hawthorne | 17,972 | 13 | 0 | 0 | 3 | 10 | 250 | 42 | 196 | 12 | 0 |
| Hazlet Township | 20,893 | 6 | 0 | 0 | 4 | 2 | 310 | 30 | 272 | 8 | 2 |

[1] The FBI does not publish arson data unless it receives data from either the agency or the state for all 12 months of the calendar year.

## Table 8. Offenses Known to Law Enforcement, by State and City, 2009—*Continued*

(Number.)

| State/city | Population | Violent crime | Murder and non-negligent man-slaughter | Forcible rape | Robbery | Aggravated assault | Property crime | Burglary | Larceny-theft | Motor vehicle theft | Arson[1] |
|---|---|---|---|---|---|---|---|---|---|---|---|
| **NEW JERSEY**—*Continued* | | | | | | | | | | | |
| Helmetta | 2,031 | 0 | 0 | 0 | 0 | 0 | 12 | 4 | 8 | 0 | 1 |
| High Bridge | 3,662 | 3 | 0 | 1 | 0 | 2 | 52 | 14 | 37 | 1 | 3 |
| Highland Park | 14,271 | 11 | 0 | 1 | 6 | 4 | 206 | 31 | 166 | 9 | 0 |
| Highlands | 5,292 | 9 | 0 | 3 | 0 | 6 | 31 | 7 | 24 | 0 | 0 |
| Hightstown | 5,303 | 8 | 0 | 2 | 1 | 5 | 69 | 21 | 47 | 1 | 0 |
| Hillsborough Township | 39,265 | 16 | 0 | 5 | 4 | 7 | 266 | 55 | 206 | 5 | 1 |
| Hillsdale | 9,822 | 5 | 0 | 0 | 1 | 4 | 57 | 13 | 43 | 1 | 0 |
| Hillside Township | 21,108 | 104 | 0 | 12 | 57 | 35 | 592 | 183 | 303 | 106 | 0 |
| Hi-Nella | 995 | 7 | 0 | 0 | 1 | 6 | 32 | 12 | 19 | 1 | 2 |
| Hoboken | 40,792 | 142 | 0 | 3 | 56 | 83 | 1,052 | 243 | 717 | 92 | 8 |
| Ho-Ho-Kus | 3,995 | 1 | 0 | 0 | 1 | 0 | 14 | 6 | 8 | 0 | 0 |
| Holland Township | 5,226 | 0 | 0 | 0 | 0 | 0 | 19 | 7 | 12 | 0 | 0 |
| Holmdel Township | 17,009 | 22 | 0 | 2 | 2 | 18 | 256 | 31 | 222 | 3 | 2 |
| Hopatcong | 15,447 | 7 | 0 | 1 | 0 | 6 | 127 | 28 | 97 | 2 | 0 |
| Hopewell | 1,983 | 0 | 0 | 0 | 0 | 0 | 21 | 5 | 15 | 1 | 0 |
| Hopewell Township | 17,941 | 4 | 0 | 0 | 1 | 3 | 120 | 28 | 85 | 7 | 0 |
| Howell Township | 51,596 | 62 | 0 | 4 | 19 | 39 | 701 | 163 | 517 | 21 | 3 |
| Independence Township | 5,705 | 4 | 0 | 0 | 0 | 4 | 33 | 6 | 26 | 1 | 0 |
| Interlaken | 874 | 0 | 0 | 0 | 0 | 0 | 11 | 1 | 10 | 0 | 0 |
| Irvington | 55,838 | 1,016 | 17 | 21 | 479 | 499 | 2,383 | 621 | 1,102 | 660 | 12 |
| Island Heights | 1,884 | 1 | 0 | 0 | 0 | 1 | 23 | 3 | 19 | 1 | 1 |
| Jackson Township | 53,734 | 34 | 0 | 4 | 12 | 18 | 620 | 148 | 437 | 35 | 20 |
| Jamesburg | 6,401 | 7 | 0 | 0 | 4 | 3 | 40 | 15 | 21 | 4 | 0 |
| Jefferson Township | 21,903 | 19 | 0 | 0 | 1 | 18 | 257 | 83 | 170 | 4 | 1 |
| Jersey City | 240,858 | 1,791 | 28 | 49 | 871 | 843 | 5,984 | 1,400 | 3,744 | 840 | 59 |
| Keansburg | 10,527 | 44 | 0 | 3 | 9 | 32 | 272 | 54 | 208 | 10 | 2 |
| Kearny | 36,352 | 91 | 1 | 5 | 38 | 47 | 1,051 | 134 | 805 | 112 | 9 |
| Kenilworth | 7,612 | 7 | 0 | 0 | 4 | 3 | 156 | 20 | 114 | 22 | 0 |
| Keyport | 7,464 | 5 | 0 | 0 | 0 | 5 | 76 | 9 | 66 | 1 | 1 |
| Kinnelon | 9,606 | 0 | 0 | 0 | 0 | 0 | 57 | 14 | 43 | 0 | 0 |
| Lacey Township | 26,491 | 27 | 0 | 1 | 8 | 18 | 705 | 100 | 590 | 15 | 5 |
| Lake Como | 1,769 | 9 | 0 | 0 | 0 | 9 | 26 | 2 | 21 | 3 | 0 |
| Lakehurst | 2,714 | 6 | 0 | 1 | 1 | 4 | 50 | 5 | 45 | 0 | 0 |
| Lakewood Township[2] | 72,206 | 142 | 1 | 7 | 58 | 76 | | | 693 | 38 | 5 |
| Lambertville | 3,727 | 3 | 0 | 0 | 1 | 2 | 48 | 4 | 40 | 4 | 0 |
| Laurel Springs | 1,896 | 12 | 0 | 0 | 1 | 11 | 57 | 15 | 40 | 2 | 0 |
| Lavallette | 2,764 | 4 | 0 | 0 | 0 | 4 | 102 | 26 | 76 | 0 | 0 |
| Lawnside | 2,858 | 27 | 2 | 1 | 5 | 19 | 73 | 9 | 51 | 13 | 1 |
| Lawrence Township, Mercer County | 31,913 | 51 | 0 | 10 | 19 | 22 | 782 | 95 | 656 | 31 | 14 |
| Lebanon Township | 6,208 | 4 | 0 | 0 | 0 | 4 | 48 | 12 | 35 | 1 | 0 |
| Leonia | 8,563 | 10 | 0 | 1 | 3 | 6 | 109 | 37 | 69 | 3 | 0 |
| Lincoln Park | 10,604 | 4 | 0 | 0 | 0 | 4 | 60 | 7 | 50 | 3 | 0 |
| Linden | 39,131 | 114 | 0 | 6 | 62 | 46 | 1,186 | 193 | 855 | 138 | 6 |
| Lindenwold | 17,496 | 164 | 0 | 9 | 68 | 87 | 655 | 223 | 350 | 82 | 9 |
| Linwood | 7,220 | 13 | 1 | 1 | 4 | 7 | 113 | 39 | 74 | 0 | 0 |
| Little Egg Harbor Township | 21,291 | 44 | 1 | 11 | 3 | 29 | 418 | 66 | 342 | 10 | 5 |
| Little Falls Township | 11,625 | 7 | 0 | 0 | 1 | 6 | 218 | 29 | 163 | 26 | 0 |
| Little Ferry | 10,442 | 12 | 1 | 1 | 3 | 7 | 109 | 28 | 73 | 8 | 0 |
| Little Silver | 6,111 | 5 | 0 | 0 | 0 | 5 | 88 | 14 | 73 | 1 | 0 |
| Livingston Township | 27,722 | 16 | 0 | 1 | 7 | 8 | 379 | 34 | 339 | 6 | 3 |
| Loch Arbour | 273 | 1 | 0 | 0 | 0 | 1 | 7 | 2 | 5 | 0 | 0 |
| Lodi | 23,754 | 44 | 0 | 0 | 7 | 37 | 320 | 67 | 228 | 25 | 0 |
| Logan Township | 6,270 | 8 | 1 | 0 | 2 | 5 | 125 | 24 | 94 | 7 | 0 |
| Long Beach Township | 3,571 | 6 | 0 | 0 | 0 | 6 | 133 | 22 | 110 | 1 | 1 |
| Long Branch | 32,758 | 129 | 2 | 1 | 60 | 66 | 857 | 170 | 652 | 35 | 1 |
| Long Hill Township | 8,593 | 1 | 0 | 0 | 0 | 1 | 86 | 10 | 73 | 3 | 1 |
| Longport | 1,092 | 0 | 0 | 0 | 0 | 0 | 25 | 4 | 21 | 0 | 0 |
| Lopatcong Township | 8,748 | 6 | 0 | 0 | 2 | 4 | 108 | 13 | 94 | 1 | 0 |
| Lower Alloways Creek Township | 1,888 | 0 | 0 | 0 | 0 | 0 | 14 | 2 | 12 | 0 | 0 |
| Lower Township | 20,060 | 38 | 0 | 5 | 7 | 26 | 432 | 107 | 317 | 8 | 8 |
| Lumberton Township | 12,174 | 18 | 0 | 1 | 7 | 10 | 339 | 43 | 287 | 9 | 2 |
| Lyndhurst Township | 19,286 | 11 | 0 | 0 | 6 | 5 | 302 | 29 | 254 | 19 | 2 |
| Madison | 16,073 | 14 | 0 | 1 | 4 | 9 | 131 | 18 | 106 | 7 | 1 |
| Magnolia | 4,321 | 23 | 0 | 2 | 8 | 13 | 94 | 27 | 60 | 7 | 0 |
| Mahwah Township | 24,180 | 6 | 0 | 0 | 1 | 5 | 147 | 16 | 126 | 5 | 0 |
| Manalapan Township | 39,615 | 22 | 0 | 2 | 9 | 11 | 387 | 90 | 272 | 25 | 2 |
| Manasquan | 6,243 | 7 | 0 | 1 | 0 | 6 | 128 | 18 | 110 | 0 | 0 |
| Manchester Township | 41,921 | 17 | 0 | 0 | 6 | 11 | 383 | 92 | 282 | 9 | 4 |
| Mansfield Township, Burlington County | 8,373 | 7 | 3 | 0 | 1 | 3 | 129 | 16 | 106 | 7 | 0 |
| Mansfield Township, Warren County | 8,123 | 16 | 2 | 1 | 1 | 12 | 122 | 16 | 102 | 4 | 1 |
| Mantoloking | 455 | 0 | 0 | 0 | 0 | 0 | 19 | 1 | 18 | 0 | 0 |

[1] The FBI does not publish arson data unless it receives data from either the agency or the state for all 12 months of the calendar year.
[2] The FBI determined that the agency's data were underreported. Consequently, those data are not included in this table.

**Table 8. Offenses Known to Law Enforcement, by State and City, 2009**—*Continued*

(Number.)

| State/city | Population | Violent crime | Murder and non-negligent man-slaughter | Forcible rape | Robbery | Aggravated assault | Property crime | Burglary | Larceny-theft | Motor vehicle theft | Arson[1] |
|---|---|---|---|---|---|---|---|---|---|---|---|
| **NEW JERSEY**—*Continued* | | | | | | | | | | | |
| Mantua Township | 15,285 | 22 | 0 | 2 | 13 | 7 | 264 | 45 | 214 | 5 | 3 |
| Manville | 10,863 | 6 | 0 | 0 | 2 | 4 | 228 | 22 | 188 | 18 | 2 |
| Maple Shade Township | 19,165 | 24 | 0 | 6 | 5 | 13 | 467 | 82 | 351 | 34 | 0 |
| Maplewood Township | 21,795 | 57 | 0 | 4 | 27 | 26 | 406 | 67 | 299 | 40 | 2 |
| Margate City | 8,536 | 5 | 0 | 1 | 1 | 3 | 250 | 54 | 191 | 5 | 0 |
| Marlboro Township | 41,009 | 27 | 0 | 2 | 9 | 16 | 360 | 90 | 248 | 22 | 0 |
| Matawan | 8,735 | 14 | 0 | 0 | 1 | 13 | 122 | 49 | 65 | 8 | 0 |
| Maywood | 9,104 | 5 | 0 | 0 | 1 | 4 | 80 | 26 | 48 | 6 | 0 |
| Medford Lakes | 4,097 | 0 | 0 | 0 | 0 | 0 | 65 | 9 | 56 | 0 | 0 |
| Medford Township | 22,872 | 5 | 0 | 0 | 0 | 5 | 282 | 65 | 212 | 5 | 3 |
| Mendham | 5,048 | 1 | 0 | 0 | 0 | 1 | 21 | 3 | 17 | 1 | 0 |
| Mendham Township | 5,513 | 1 | 0 | 0 | 0 | 1 | 32 | 2 | 30 | 0 | 0 |
| Merchantville | 3,760 | 4 | 0 | 0 | 1 | 3 | 74 | 18 | 55 | 1 | 0 |
| Metuchen | 13,121 | 12 | 0 | 0 | 4 | 8 | 240 | 47 | 183 | 10 | 0 |
| Middlesex | 13,634 | 15 | 0 | 2 | 3 | 10 | 105 | 23 | 78 | 4 | 1 |
| Middle Township | 16,263 | 65 | 0 | 10 | 10 | 45 | 607 | 155 | 431 | 21 | 3 |
| Middletown Township | 66,565 | 50 | 0 | 5 | 11 | 34 | 768 | 148 | 599 | 21 | 0 |
| Midland Park | 6,743 | 2 | 0 | 0 | 2 | 0 | 68 | 9 | 59 | 0 | 1 |
| Millburn Township | 18,418 | 22 | 0 | 0 | 6 | 16 | 510 | 66 | 434 | 10 | 1 |
| Milltown | 6,959 | 9 | 0 | 2 | 3 | 4 | 120 | 12 | 105 | 3 | 1 |
| Millville | 29,175 | 203 | 2 | 8 | 70 | 123 | 1,256 | 364 | 840 | 52 | 5 |
| Mine Hill Township | 3,577 | 0 | 0 | 0 | 0 | 0 | 23 | 10 | 13 | 0 | 0 |
| Monmouth Beach | 3,566 | 2 | 0 | 0 | 0 | 2 | 42 | 4 | 37 | 1 | 0 |
| Monroe Township, Gloucester County | 33,420 | 58 | 0 | 4 | 16 | 38 | 789 | 204 | 551 | 34 | 1 |
| Monroe Township, Middlesex County | 38,264 | 13 | 0 | 0 | 1 | 12 | 245 | 43 | 190 | 12 | 1 |
| Montclair | 36,788 | 89 | 0 | 1 | 48 | 40 | 535 | 157 | 352 | 26 | 6 |
| Montgomery Township[2] | 23,524 | 1 | 0 | 0 | 0 | 1 | | | 125 | 6 | 2 |
| Montvale | 7,625 | 2 | 0 | 0 | 1 | 1 | 55 | 6 | 44 | 5 | 0 |
| Montville Township | 21,078 | 8 | 0 | 2 | 1 | 5 | 159 | 30 | 125 | 4 | 1 |
| Moonachie | 2,722 | 4 | 0 | 0 | 0 | 4 | 64 | 16 | 40 | 8 | 0 |
| Moorestown Township | 19,559 | 18 | 0 | 2 | 10 | 6 | 596 | 61 | 519 | 16 | 0 |
| Morris Plains | 6,050 | 3 | 0 | 0 | 1 | 2 | 101 | 6 | 94 | 1 | 0 |
| Morristown | 19,351 | 80 | 0 | 2 | 30 | 48 | 475 | 79 | 378 | 18 | 1 |
| Morris Township | 21,214 | 19 | 1 | 3 | 2 | 13 | 147 | 38 | 96 | 13 | 0 |
| Mountain Lakes | 4,276 | 2 | 0 | 0 | 1 | 1 | 63 | 2 | 61 | 0 | 0 |
| Mountainside | 6,545 | 5 | 0 | 0 | 4 | 1 | 53 | 9 | 41 | 3 | 0 |
| Mount Arlington | 5,968 | 1 | 0 | 0 | 0 | 1 | 62 | 11 | 50 | 1 | 0 |
| Mount Ephraim | 4,381 | 6 | 0 | 2 | 3 | 1 | 113 | 21 | 86 | 6 | 0 |
| Mount Holly Township | 10,195 | 39 | 0 | 0 | 19 | 20 | 271 | 31 | 231 | 9 | 1 |
| Mount Laurel Township | 39,071 | 34 | 0 | 9 | 13 | 12 | 729 | 109 | 600 | 20 | 2 |
| Mount Olive Township | 25,989 | 14 | 0 | 3 | 1 | 10 | 284 | 38 | 235 | 11 | 1 |
| Mullica Township | 6,032 | 13 | 0 | 1 | 1 | 11 | 88 | 28 | 49 | 11 | 0 |
| National Park | 3,230 | 13 | 0 | 2 | 1 | 10 | 68 | 15 | 49 | 4 | 0 |
| Neptune City | 5,100 | 15 | 1 | 0 | 7 | 7 | 175 | 26 | 146 | 3 | 0 |
| Neptune Township | 28,484 | 191 | 2 | 8 | 72 | 109 | 1,713 | 380 | 1,273 | 60 | 6 |
| Netcong | 3,221 | 2 | 0 | 1 | 0 | 1 | 69 | 19 | 50 | 0 | 0 |
| Newark | 279,203 | 2,597 | 80 | 68 | 1,319 | 1,130 | 8,822 | 1,947 | 3,781 | 3,094 | 85 |
| New Brunswick | 51,474 | 389 | 5 | 21 | 152 | 211 | 1,754 | 510 | 1,124 | 120 | 8 |
| Newfield | 1,675 | 0 | 0 | 0 | 0 | 0 | 20 | 8 | 11 | 1 | 0 |
| New Hanover Township | 9,442 | 0 | 0 | 0 | 0 | 0 | 7 | 3 | 4 | 0 | 2 |
| New Milford | 15,898 | 3 | 0 | 0 | 0 | 3 | 121 | 24 | 95 | 2 | 0 |
| New Providence | 11,904 | 2 | 0 | 0 | 1 | 1 | 82 | 4 | 76 | 2 | 0 |
| Newton | 8,079 | 10 | 1 | 0 | 3 | 6 | 145 | 18 | 126 | 1 | 0 |
| North Arlington | 14,648 | 12 | 0 | 1 | 4 | 7 | 180 | 35 | 125 | 20 | 0 |
| North Bergen Township | 54,948 | 107 | 0 | 5 | 45 | 57 | 865 | 155 | 582 | 128 | 5 |
| North Brunswick Township | 39,904 | 79 | 1 | 3 | 33 | 42 | 796 | 151 | 561 | 84 | 0 |
| North Caldwell | 7,016 | 2 | 0 | 1 | 0 | 1 | 30 | 14 | 16 | 0 | 0 |
| Northfield | 7,903 | 9 | 1 | 0 | 5 | 3 | 114 | 32 | 80 | 2 | 0 |
| North Haledon | 9,021 | 1 | 0 | 0 | 0 | 1 | 48 | 13 | 33 | 2 | 0 |
| North Hanover Township | 7,335 | 10 | 0 | 0 | 2 | 8 | 87 | 22 | 63 | 2 | 0 |
| North Plainfield | 21,077 | 78 | 0 | 4 | 30 | 44 | 499 | 91 | 382 | 26 | 0 |
| Northvale | 4,748 | 3 | 0 | 0 | 1 | 2 | 48 | 0 | 48 | 0 | 0 |
| North Wildwood | 4,786 | 17 | 0 | 2 | 3 | 12 | 302 | 52 | 240 | 10 | 0 |
| Norwood | 6,256 | 1 | 0 | 0 | 0 | 1 | 24 | 10 | 13 | 1 | 0 |
| Nutley Township | 26,033 | 25 | 0 | 2 | 7 | 16 | 361 | 86 | 239 | 36 | 3 |
| Oakland | 13,400 | 5 | 0 | 0 | 1 | 4 | 112 | 17 | 91 | 4 | 1 |
| Oaklyn | 4,014 | 8 | 0 | 0 | 3 | 5 | 93 | 22 | 68 | 3 | 1 |
| Ocean City | 14,686 | 25 | 0 | 3 | 6 | 16 | 851 | 178 | 668 | 5 | 2 |
| Ocean Gate | 2,143 | 2 | 0 | 0 | 1 | 1 | 43 | 9 | 33 | 1 | 0 |
| Oceanport | 5,723 | 3 | 0 | 0 | 2 | 1 | 73 | 21 | 50 | 2 | 3 |
| Ocean Township, Monmouth County | 28,360 | 61 | 0 | 4 | 28 | 29 | 855 | 134 | 705 | 16 | 3 |

[1] The FBI does not publish arson data unless it receives data from either the agency or the state for all 12 months of the calendar year.

[2] The FBI determined that the agency's data were underreported. Consequently, those data are not included in this table.

# Table 8. Offenses Known to Law Enforcement, by State and City, 2009—*Continued*

(Number.)

| State/city | Population | Violent crime | Murder and non-negligent man-slaughter | Forcible rape | Robbery | Aggravated assault | Property crime | Burglary | Larceny-theft | Motor vehicle theft | Arson[1] |
|---|---|---|---|---|---|---|---|---|---|---|---|
| **NEW JERSEY**—*Continued* | | | | | | | | | | | |
| Ocean Township, Ocean County | 9,329 | 1 | 0 | 0 | 0 | 1 | 115 | 13 | 97 | 5 | 0 |
| Ogdensburg | 2,535 | 1 | 0 | 0 | 0 | 1 | 15 | 5 | 10 | 0 | 0 |
| Old Bridge Township | 66,460 | 41 | 0 | 6 | 13 | 22 | 860 | 156 | 649 | 55 | 1 |
| Old Tappan | 6,091 | 1 | 0 | 0 | 0 | 1 | 22 | 1 | 21 | 0 | 1 |
| Oradell | 7,751 | 3 | 0 | 0 | 1 | 2 | 65 | 12 | 52 | 1 | 0 |
| Orange | 30,873 | 358 | 4 | 10 | 193 | 151 | 992 | 348 | 447 | 197 | 2 |
| Oxford Township | 2,603 | 0 | 0 | 0 | 0 | 0 | 7 | 4 | 3 | 0 | 0 |
| Palisades Park | 19,639 | 20 | 0 | 0 | 10 | 10 | 170 | 30 | 130 | 10 | 0 |
| Palmyra | 7,374 | 16 | 0 | 2 | 4 | 10 | 191 | 32 | 141 | 18 | 0 |
| Paramus | 26,168 | 88 | 0 | 0 | 45 | 43 | 1,847 | 119 | 1,692 | 36 | 5 |
| Park Ridge | 8,940 | 3 | 0 | 1 | 0 | 2 | 29 | 7 | 21 | 1 | 0 |
| Parsippany-Troy Hills Township | 50,095 | 27 | 0 | 1 | 8 | 18 | 695 | 232 | 437 | 26 | 0 |
| Passaic | 66,773 | 516 | 3 | 2 | 246 | 265 | 1,580 | 306 | 1,124 | 150 | 2 |
| Paterson | 144,943 | 1,318 | 15 | 28 | 631 | 644 | 3,836 | 1,241 | 1,966 | 629 | 15 |
| Paulsboro | 6,066 | 35 | 0 | 0 | 20 | 15 | 242 | 63 | 175 | 4 | 0 |
| Peapack and Gladstone | 2,572 | 0 | 0 | 0 | 0 | 0 | 13 | 3 | 10 | 0 | 0 |
| Pemberton | 1,583 | 1 | 0 | 1 | 0 | 0 | 21 | 3 | 18 | 0 | 0 |
| Pemberton Township | 27,914 | 53 | 1 | 4 | 16 | 32 | 583 | 165 | 380 | 38 | 2 |
| Pennington | 2,651 | 0 | 0 | 0 | 0 | 0 | 17 | 3 | 13 | 1 | 1 |
| Pennsauken Township | 34,905 | 114 | 0 | 13 | 51 | 50 | 1,183 | 242 | 811 | 130 | 5 |
| Penns Grove | 4,668 | 28 | 0 | 2 | 12 | 14 | 184 | 57 | 120 | 7 | 1 |
| Pennsville Township | 13,365 | 23 | 0 | 1 | 4 | 18 | 424 | 82 | 332 | 10 | 3 |
| Pequannock Township | 17,003 | 4 | 0 | 0 | 0 | 4 | 137 | 35 | 99 | 3 | 0 |
| Perth Amboy | 48,897 | 164 | 1 | 3 | 81 | 79 | 1,057 | 207 | 736 | 114 | 7 |
| Phillipsburg | 14,459 | 47 | 0 | 8 | 18 | 21 | 408 | 76 | 320 | 12 | 2 |
| Pine Beach | 2,093 | 0 | 0 | 0 | 0 | 0 | 24 | 3 | 21 | 0 | 0 |
| Pine Hill | 11,358 | 36 | 0 | 0 | 9 | 27 | 264 | 70 | 175 | 19 | 2 |
| Pine Valley | 25 | 0 | 0 | 0 | 0 | 0 | 1 | 1 | 0 | 0 | 0 |
| Piscataway Township | 52,605 | 54 | 3 | 0 | 17 | 34 | 487 | 120 | 334 | 33 | 2 |
| Pitman | 9,193 | 3 | 0 | 0 | 2 | 1 | 131 | 23 | 99 | 9 | 3 |
| Plainfield | 45,939 | 474 | 2 | 8 | 254 | 210 | 1,299 | 334 | 846 | 119 | 2 |
| Plainsboro Township | 21,243 | 11 | 0 | 1 | 2 | 8 | 171 | 17 | 146 | 8 | 0 |
| Pleasantville | 18,838 | 171 | 4 | 5 | 82 | 80 | 579 | 181 | 360 | 38 | 4 |
| Plumsted Township | 8,318 | 8 | 0 | 3 | 1 | 4 | 53 | 12 | 37 | 4 | 1 |
| Pohatcong Township | 3,321 | 12 | 0 | 0 | 2 | 10 | 84 | 8 | 76 | 0 | 0 |
| Point Pleasant | 20,232 | 12 | 0 | 0 | 2 | 10 | 339 | 31 | 300 | 8 | 0 |
| Point Pleasant Beach | 5,430 | 6 | 0 | 0 | 2 | 4 | 275 | 29 | 241 | 5 | 0 |
| Pompton Lakes | 11,075 | 20 | 1 | 1 | 3 | 15 | 134 | 30 | 98 | 6 | 0 |
| Princeton | 13,373 | 19 | 0 | 1 | 8 | 10 | 342 | 73 | 264 | 5 | 2 |
| Princeton Township | 17,517 | 15 | 0 | 0 | 4 | 11 | 149 | 31 | 117 | 1 | 1 |
| Prospect Park | 5,574 | 25 | 0 | 0 | 9 | 16 | 97 | 22 | 67 | 8 | 1 |
| Rahway | 28,869 | 89 | 1 | 2 | 52 | 34 | 585 | 145 | 386 | 54 | 1 |
| Ramsey | 14,620 | 10 | 0 | 1 | 3 | 6 | 135 | 13 | 119 | 3 | 0 |
| Randolph Township | 25,226 | 5 | 0 | 1 | 3 | 1 | 179 | 23 | 149 | 7 | 0 |
| Raritan | 7,413 | 6 | 0 | 2 | 1 | 3 | 176 | 20 | 153 | 3 | 0 |
| Raritan Township | 22,637 | 6 | 0 | 1 | 2 | 3 | 205 | 21 | 180 | 4 | 0 |
| Readington Township | 16,053 | 6 | 0 | 0 | 2 | 4 | 107 | 28 | 75 | 4 | 1 |
| Red Bank | 11,866 | 30 | 2 | 1 | 10 | 17 | 227 | 22 | 200 | 5 | 2 |
| Ridgefield | 10,852 | 3 | 0 | 0 | 1 | 2 | 91 | 23 | 57 | 11 | 0 |
| Ridgefield Park | 12,316 | 19 | 0 | 0 | 3 | 16 | 148 | 25 | 114 | 9 | 0 |
| Ridgewood | 24,080 | 10 | 0 | 2 | 3 | 5 | 196 | 43 | 146 | 7 | 3 |
| Ringwood | 12,711 | 8 | 0 | 1 | 2 | 5 | 66 | 6 | 60 | 0 | 0 |
| Riverdale | 2,902 | 1 | 0 | 0 | 0 | 1 | 101 | 3 | 95 | 3 | 0 |
| River Edge | 10,644 | 3 | 0 | 0 | 0 | 3 | 73 | 26 | 47 | 0 | 0 |
| Riverside Township | 7,671 | 11 | 0 | 1 | 3 | 7 | 83 | 24 | 54 | 5 | 1 |
| Riverton | 2,613 | 3 | 0 | 2 | 1 | 0 | 69 | 15 | 53 | 1 | 0 |
| River Vale Township | 9,634 | 3 | 0 | 0 | 0 | 3 | 35 | 15 | 17 | 3 | 0 |
| Robbinsville Township | 12,314 | 7 | 0 | 3 | 1 | 3 | 102 | 16 | 85 | 1 | 0 |
| Rochelle Park Township | 6,144 | 1 | 0 | 0 | 0 | 1 | 72 | 17 | 52 | 3 | 1 |
| Rockaway | 6,241 | 3 | 0 | 0 | 1 | 2 | 65 | 13 | 50 | 2 | 0 |
| Rockaway Township | 25,828 | 19 | 0 | 2 | 4 | 13 | 447 | 43 | 398 | 6 | 1 |
| Rockleigh | 388 | 0 | 0 | 0 | 0 | 0 | 2 | 0 | 2 | 0 | 0 |
| Roseland | 5,358 | 1 | 0 | 0 | 0 | 1 | 29 | 3 | 25 | 1 | 0 |
| Roselle | 20,523 | 83 | 1 | 2 | 48 | 32 | 451 | 113 | 256 | 82 | 2 |
| Roselle Park | 12,750 | 20 | 0 | 1 | 7 | 12 | 114 | 29 | 74 | 11 | 1 |
| Roxbury Township | 23,311 | 17 | 0 | 3 | 3 | 11 | 299 | 56 | 230 | 13 | 0 |
| Rumson | 7,276 | 1 | 0 | 0 | 0 | 1 | 67 | 23 | 43 | 1 | 1 |
| Runnemede | 8,398 | 18 | 0 | 3 | 5 | 10 | 290 | 50 | 227 | 13 | 1 |
| Rutherford | 17,384 | 7 | 0 | 0 | 1 | 6 | 298 | 39 | 240 | 19 | 3 |
| Saddle Brook Township | 14,019 | 14 | 0 | 0 | 4 | 10 | 308 | 48 | 245 | 15 | 0 |
| Saddle River | 3,858 | 0 | 0 | 0 | 0 | 0 | 18 | 5 | 13 | 0 | 0 |

[1] The FBI does not publish arson data unless it receives data from either the agency or the state for all 12 months of the calendar year.

**Table 8. Offenses Known to Law Enforcement, by State and City, 2009—*Continued***

(Number.)

| State/city | Population | Violent crime | Murder and non-negligent man-slaughter | Forcible rape | Robbery | Aggravated assault | Property crime | Burglary | Larceny-theft | Motor vehicle theft | Arson[1] |
|---|---|---|---|---|---|---|---|---|---|---|---|
| **NEW JERSEY**—*Continued* | | | | | | | | | | | |
| Salem | 5,641 | 50 | 0 | 3 | 18 | 29 | 244 | 76 | 151 | 17 | 1 |
| Sayreville | 42,401 | 75 | 1 | 2 | 21 | 51 | 652 | 106 | 504 | 42 | 1 |
| Scotch Plains Township | 22,907 | 12 | 0 | 0 | 6 | 6 | 257 | 58 | 192 | 7 | 0 |
| Sea Bright | 1,802 | 1 | 0 | 0 | 0 | 1 | 31 | 2 | 29 | 0 | 0 |
| Sea Girt | 2,061 | 5 | 0 | 0 | 0 | 5 | 37 | 7 | 30 | 0 | 0 |
| Sea Isle City | 2,915 | 10 | 0 | 1 | 0 | 9 | 278 | 90 | 186 | 2 | 1 |
| Seaside Heights | 3,364 | 38 | 0 | 4 | 9 | 25 | 275 | 47 | 217 | 11 | 0 |
| Seaside Park | 2,317 | 2 | 0 | 0 | 0 | 2 | 74 | 7 | 65 | 2 | 0 |
| Secaucus | 15,312 | 15 | 0 | 0 | 4 | 11 | 551 | 36 | 473 | 42 | 0 |
| Ship Bottom | 1,456 | 3 | 0 | 0 | 0 | 3 | 60 | 6 | 54 | 0 | 0 |
| Shrewsbury | 3,798 | 7 | 0 | 0 | 5 | 2 | 82 | 14 | 65 | 3 | 0 |
| Somerdale | 5,074 | 15 | 0 | 1 | 4 | 10 | 113 | 37 | 68 | 8 | 2 |
| Somers Point | 11,316 | 36 | 0 | 0 | 8 | 28 | 409 | 83 | 320 | 6 | 4 |
| Somerville | 12,672 | 16 | 0 | 2 | 10 | 4 | 173 | 35 | 131 | 7 | 2 |
| South Amboy | 7,761 | 12 | 0 | 0 | 3 | 9 | 106 | 15 | 84 | 7 | 0 |
| South Bound Brook | 5,191 | 1 | 0 | 0 | 0 | 1 | 35 | 12 | 22 | 1 | 0 |
| South Brunswick Township | 41,448 | 24 | 0 | 1 | 10 | 13 | 405 | 78 | 306 | 21 | 1 |
| South Hackensack Township | 2,262 | 13 | 0 | 4 | 6 | 3 | 47 | 6 | 38 | 3 | 0 |
| South Harrison Township | 3,223 | 2 | 0 | 1 | 0 | 1 | 26 | 11 | 14 | 1 | 0 |
| South Orange | 15,767 | 43 | 1 | 0 | 26 | 16 | 459 | 73 | 331 | 55 | 0 |
| South Plainfield | 22,710 | 23 | 0 | 1 | 11 | 11 | 454 | 50 | 386 | 18 | 4 |
| South River | 15,715 | 38 | 0 | 3 | 6 | 29 | 224 | 40 | 171 | 13 | 2 |
| South Toms River | 3,718 | 9 | 0 | 1 | 2 | 6 | 98 | 20 | 75 | 3 | 1 |
| Sparta Township | 19,336 | 4 | 0 | 0 | 0 | 4 | 118 | 14 | 104 | 0 | 0 |
| Spotswood | 8,173 | 5 | 0 | 0 | 3 | 2 | 98 | 8 | 87 | 3 | 2 |
| Springfield | 14,873 | 10 | 0 | 0 | 8 | 2 | 268 | 34 | 218 | 16 | 1 |
| Springfield Township | 3,492 | 2 | 0 | 0 | 0 | 2 | 52 | 26 | 23 | 3 | 0 |
| Spring Lake | 3,514 | 2 | 0 | 0 | 0 | 2 | 82 | 16 | 66 | 0 | 2 |
| Spring Lake Heights | 5,122 | 3 | 0 | 0 | 0 | 3 | 24 | 2 | 19 | 3 | 2 |
| Stafford Township | 26,985 | 20 | 0 | 0 | 0 | 20 | 484 | 50 | 428 | 6 | 1 |
| Stanhope | 3,559 | 4 | 1 | 0 | 1 | 2 | 28 | 5 | 23 | 0 | 0 |
| Stillwater Township | 4,294 | 1 | 0 | 0 | 0 | 1 | 43 | 15 | 27 | 1 | 0 |
| Stone Harbor | 1,000 | 0 | 0 | 0 | 0 | 0 | 125 | 19 | 105 | 1 | 0 |
| Stratford | 7,026 | 14 | 0 | 0 | 3 | 11 | 145 | 44 | 92 | 9 | 0 |
| Summit | 20,494 | 10 | 0 | 1 | 3 | 6 | 278 | 33 | 240 | 5 | 0 |
| Surf City | 1,571 | 0 | 0 | 0 | 0 | 0 | 45 | 6 | 39 | 0 | 0 |
| Tavistock | 31 | 0 | 0 | 0 | 0 | 0 | 0 | 0 | 0 | 0 | 0 |
| Teaneck Township | 37,985 | 63 | 0 | 3 | 20 | 40 | 551 | 117 | 399 | 35 | 8 |
| Tenafly | 14,759 | 0 | 0 | 0 | 0 | 0 | 78 | 21 | 54 | 3 | 0 |
| Teterboro | 17 | 0 | 0 | 0 | 0 | 0 | 21 | 3 | 15 | 3 | 0 |
| Tewksbury Township | 6,088 | 1 | 0 | 0 | 0 | 1 | 22 | 4 | 18 | 0 | 0 |
| Tinton Falls | 20,069 | 12 | 0 | 1 | 7 | 4 | 366 | 36 | 320 | 10 | 1 |
| Toms River Township | 96,614 | 111 | 2 | 4 | 43 | 62 | 2,467 | 485 | 1,944 | 38 | 12 |
| Totowa | 10,705 | 11 | 0 | 2 | 5 | 4 | 330 | 34 | 266 | 30 | 1 |
| Trenton | 82,609 | 1,154 | 17 | 26 | 512 | 599 | 2,624 | 824 | 1,399 | 401 | 23 |
| Tuckerton | 3,918 | 6 | 0 | 0 | 0 | 6 | 44 | 14 | 29 | 1 | 0 |
| Union Beach | 6,615 | 6 | 0 | 1 | 2 | 3 | 72 | 20 | 51 | 1 | 1 |
| Union City | 61,665 | 291 | 1 | 0 | 119 | 171 | 1,398 | 279 | 962 | 157 | 3 |
| Union Township | 53,579 | 133 | 1 | 4 | 65 | 63 | 1,030 | 159 | 776 | 95 | 1 |
| Upper Saddle River | 8,537 | 0 | 0 | 0 | 0 | 0 | 30 | 6 | 22 | 2 | 1 |
| Ventnor City | 12,111 | 27 | 0 | 0 | 14 | 13 | 389 | 120 | 262 | 7 | 0 |
| Vernon Township | 24,870 | 9 | 0 | 2 | 1 | 6 | 482 | 62 | 414 | 6 | 5 |
| Verona | 12,384 | 8 | 1 | 0 | 2 | 5 | 105 | 27 | 76 | 2 | 0 |
| Vineland | 59,121 | 276 | 3 | 14 | 120 | 139 | 2,316 | 537 | 1,708 | 71 | 16 |
| Voorhees Township | 31,686 | 58 | 0 | 9 | 14 | 35 | 706 | 118 | 561 | 27 | 5 |
| Waldwick | 9,511 | 4 | 0 | 0 | 2 | 2 | 59 | 6 | 53 | 0 | 1 |
| Wallington | 11,265 | 11 | 0 | 0 | 9 | 2 | 179 | 42 | 117 | 20 | 0 |
| Wall Township | 26,265 | 25 | 0 | 2 | 3 | 20 | 509 | 117 | 379 | 13 | 0 |
| Wanaque | 12,433 | 4 | 0 | 0 | 2 | 2 | 140 | 6 | 132 | 2 | 0 |
| Warren Township | 16,150 | 2 | 0 | 0 | 0 | 2 | 87 | 23 | 61 | 3 | 0 |
| Washington Township, Bergen County | 9,615 | 2 | 0 | 0 | 1 | 1 | 39 | 17 | 22 | 0 | 0 |
| Washington Township, Gloucester County | 51,757 | 97 | 0 | 5 | 32 | 60 | 1,086 | 189 | 842 | 55 | 8 |
| Washington Township, Morris County | 18,468 | 7 | 0 | 0 | 0 | 7 | 94 | 27 | 64 | 3 | 0 |
| Washington Township, Warren County | 6,935 | 3 | 0 | 0 | 0 | 3 | 50 | 18 | 30 | 2 | 0 |
| Watchung | 6,720 | 3 | 0 | 0 | 2 | 1 | 342 | 13 | 327 | 2 | 0 |
| Waterford Township | 10,674 | 12 | 0 | 3 | 3 | 6 | 143 | 46 | 87 | 10 | 3 |
| Wayne Township | 53,891 | 57 | 1 | 7 | 27 | 22 | 1,316 | 134 | 1,132 | 50 | 0 |
| Weehawken Township | 12,252 | 25 | 0 | 0 | 15 | 10 | 342 | 47 | 263 | 32 | 0 |
| Wenonah | 2,360 | 0 | 0 | 0 | 0 | 0 | 19 | 4 | 14 | 1 | 0 |
| Westampton Township | 8,799 | 13 | 0 | 2 | 6 | 5 | 190 | 29 | 152 | 9 | 0 |
| West Amwell Township | 2,970 | 5 | 0 | 0 | 0 | 5 | 29 | 8 | 20 | 1 | 0 |

[1] The FBI does not publish arson data unless it receives data from either the agency or the state for all 12 months of the calendar year.

## Table 8. Offenses Known to Law Enforcement, by State and City, 2009—*Continued*

(Number.)

| State/city | Population | Violent crime | Murder and non-negligent man-slaughter | Forcible rape | Robbery | Aggravated assault | Property crime | Burglary | Larceny-theft | Motor vehicle theft | Arson[1] |
|---|---|---|---|---|---|---|---|---|---|---|---|
| **NEW JERSEY**—*Continued* | | | | | | | | | | | |
| West Caldwell Township | 10,358 | 7 | 0 | 0 | 3 | 4 | 72 | 8 | 62 | 2 | 1 |
| West Cape May | 968 | 0 | 0 | 0 | 0 | 0 | 33 | 6 | 27 | 0 | 0 |
| West Deptford Township | 22,326 | 44 | 0 | 2 | 11 | 31 | 483 | 99 | 351 | 33 | 2 |
| Westfield | 29,426 | 11 | 0 | 1 | 6 | 4 | 276 | 58 | 211 | 7 | 2 |
| West Long Branch | 8,346 | 10 | 0 | 0 | 4 | 6 | 219 | 21 | 193 | 5 | 1 |
| West Milford Township | 27,879 | 26 | 1 | 1 | 4 | 20 | 350 | 96 | 242 | 12 | 2 |
| West New York | 46,528 | 180 | 0 | 3 | 91 | 86 | 715 | 178 | 442 | 95 | 5 |
| West Orange | 42,357 | 70 | 0 | 1 | 40 | 29 | 713 | 156 | 504 | 53 | 4 |
| Westville | 4,464 | 24 | 0 | 2 | 4 | 18 | 138 | 37 | 92 | 9 | 2 |
| West Wildwood | 395 | 0 | 0 | 0 | 0 | 0 | 40 | 17 | 22 | 1 | 0 |
| West Windsor Township | 27,061 | 12 | 0 | 1 | 8 | 3 | 536 | 64 | 448 | 24 | 0 |
| Westwood | 10,666 | 10 | 0 | 0 | 2 | 8 | 61 | 14 | 45 | 2 | 0 |
| Wharton | 6,060 | 1 | 0 | 0 | 1 | 0 | 122 | 18 | 102 | 2 | 1 |
| Wildwood | 5,242 | 59 | 1 | 3 | 33 | 22 | 490 | 162 | 317 | 11 | 2 |
| Wildwood Crest | 3,987 | 5 | 0 | 1 | 1 | 3 | 141 | 36 | 105 | 0 | 1 |
| Willingboro Township | 36,977 | 118 | 2 | 7 | 57 | 52 | 708 | 169 | 484 | 55 | 8 |
| Winfield Township | 1,435 | 0 | 0 | 0 | 0 | 0 | 16 | 3 | 12 | 1 | 0 |
| Winslow Township | 39,975 | 186 | 1 | 3 | 32 | 150 | 755 | 256 | 451 | 48 | 4 |
| Woodbridge Township | 98,013 | 139 | 1 | 7 | 61 | 70 | 2,377 | 278 | 1,919 | 180 | 18 |
| Woodbury | 10,467 | 52 | 0 | 1 | 19 | 32 | 505 | 97 | 396 | 12 | 2 |
| Woodbury Heights | 3,059 | 6 | 0 | 0 | 4 | 2 | 90 | 23 | 66 | 1 | 2 |
| Woodcliff Lake | 5,962 | 2 | 0 | 0 | 0 | 2 | 41 | 8 | 30 | 3 | 0 |
| Woodland Park | 12,014 | 23 | 0 | 5 | 6 | 12 | 228 | 50 | 159 | 19 | 2 |
| Woodlynne | 2,676 | 26 | 1 | 3 | 14 | 8 | 119 | 28 | 85 | 6 | 0 |
| Wood-Ridge | 7,432 | 0 | 0 | 0 | 0 | 0 | 55 | 12 | 42 | 1 | 0 |
| Woodstown | 3,385 | 1 | 0 | 0 | 0 | 1 | 40 | 10 | 30 | 0 | 0 |
| Woolwich Township | 12,624 | 5 | 0 | 0 | 2 | 3 | 99 | 23 | 76 | 0 | 0 |
| Wyckoff Township | 16,938 | 10 | 0 | 0 | 1 | 9 | 101 | 27 | 73 | 1 | 3 |
| **NEW MEXICO** | | | | | | | | | | | |
| Alamogordo | 35,823 | 132 | 4 | 21 | 8 | 99 | 995 | 171 | 798 | 26 | 5 |
| Albuquerque | 530,636 | 4,082 | 56 | 326 | 1,103 | 2,597 | 29,140 | 6,376 | 19,365 | 3,399 | 98 |
| Angel Fire | 974 | 2 | 0 | 0 | 0 | 2 | 38 | 31 | 7 | 0 | 0 |
| Aztec | 6,977 | 33 | 0 | 2 | 6 | 25 | 235 | 55 | 164 | 16 | 6 |
| Bayard | 2,386 | 7 | 0 | 0 | 1 | 6 | 14 | 3 | 11 | 0 | 0 |
| Belen | 7,342 | 64 | 1 | 3 | 8 | 52 | 571 | 187 | 329 | 55 | 4 |
| Bloomfield | 7,292 | 67 | 0 | 11 | 4 | 52 | 228 | 46 | 167 | 15 | 0 |
| Bosque Farms | 4,073 | 2 | 0 | 0 | 0 | 2 | 40 | 16 | 18 | 6 | 0 |
| Carlsbad | 25,638 | 154 | 2 | 25 | 13 | 114 | 1,315 | 370 | 900 | 45 | 5 |
| Carrizozo | 1,048 | 6 | 0 | 0 | 0 | 6 | 18 | 9 | 9 | 0 | 1 |
| Clovis | 32,332 | 277 | 2 | 25 | 33 | 217 | 2,109 | 736 | 1,309 | 64 | 38 |
| Corrales | 7,848 | 6 | 0 | 0 | 1 | 5 | 84 | 40 | 44 | 0 | 0 |
| Cuba | 1,498 | 17 | 0 | 0 | 0 | 17 | 25 | 9 | 13 | 3 | 0 |
| Edgewood | 2,858 | 11 | 0 | 1 | 1 | 9 | 56 | 14 | 38 | 4 | 0 |
| Espanola | 9,690 | 255 | 3 | 3 | 17 | 232 | 837 | 290 | 505 | 42 | 5 |
| Estancia | 1,571 | 1 | 0 | 0 | 0 | 1 | 64 | 23 | 38 | 3 | 0 |
| Eunice | 2,798 | 12 | 0 | 1 | 2 | 9 | 54 | 25 | 26 | 3 | 2 |
| Farmington | 43,131 | 536 | 2 | 85 | 33 | 416 | 1,709 | 359 | 1,236 | 114 | 12 |
| Gallup | 19,916 | 379 | 2 | 34 | 46 | 297 | 1,304 | 206 | 982 | 116 | 5 |
| Grants[5] | 8,877 | | 0 | 5 | 8 | | 251 | 123 | 97 | 31 | 2 |
| Hobbs | 30,710 | 179 | 5 | 16 | 20 | 138 | 1,692 | 397 | 1,235 | 60 | 1 |
| Jal | 2,052 | 0 | 0 | 0 | 0 | 0 | 20 | 10 | 9 | 1 | 0 |
| Las Cruces | 94,024 | 464 | 4 | 23 | 96 | 341 | 4,591 | 964 | 3,387 | 240 | 9 |
| Las Vegas | 13,737 | 155 | 3 | 11 | 20 | 121 | 510 | 204 | 276 | 30 | 5 |
| Logan | 992 | 4 | 0 | 0 | 0 | 4 | 44 | 21 | 22 | 1 | 0 |
| Lordsburg | 2,765 | 1 | 0 | 1 | 0 | 0 | 3 | 2 | 0 | 1 | 0 |
| Lovington | 10,040 | 46 | 1 | 8 | 5 | 32 | 394 | 208 | 174 | 12 | 0 |
| Milan | 2,577 | 20 | 0 | 1 | 0 | 19 | 79 | 29 | 46 | 4 | 0 |
| Moriarty | 1,962 | 10 | 0 | 3 | 1 | 6 | 97 | 36 | 52 | 9 | 0 |
| Portales | 12,343 | 101 | 1 | 5 | 3 | 92 | 301 | 114 | 178 | 9 | 1 |
| Raton | 6,381 | 56 | 0 | 2 | 3 | 51 | 150 | 63 | 84 | 3 | 2 |
| Red River | 519 | 2 | 0 | 0 | 0 | 2 | 20 | 6 | 9 | 5 | 0 |
| Rio Rancho | 83,417 | 233 | 1 | 24 | 30 | 178 | 1,774 | 430 | 1,209 | 135 | 11 |
| Ruidoso | 9,233 | 16 | 0 | 8 | 1 | 7 | 286 | 107 | 170 | 9 | 0 |
| Ruidoso Downs | 2,638 | 1 | 0 | 0 | 0 | 1 | 122 | 39 | 76 | 7 | 1 |
| Santa Clara | 1,847 | 0 | 0 | 0 | 0 | 0 | 18 | 9 | 9 | 0 | 2 |
| Santa Fe | 72,845 | 309 | 13 | 15 | 88 | 193 | 4,273 | 2,217 | 1,854 | 202 | 9 |
| Santa Rosa | 2,630 | 40 | 0 | 1 | 0 | 39 | 54 | 20 | 32 | 2 | 0 |
| Silver City | 10,310 | 88 | 0 | 7 | 4 | 77 | 596 | 179 | 391 | 26 | 7 |
| Socorro[3] | 9,004 | | 1 | 4 | 3 | | 394 | 104 | 279 | 11 | 1 |
| Sunland Park | 14,574 | 14 | 0 | 3 | 0 | 11 | 278 | 79 | 180 | 19 | 0 |
| Taos | 5,646 | 45 | 0 | 5 | 5 | 35 | 380 | 104 | 257 | 19 | 0 |

[1] The FBI does not publish arson data unless it receives data from either the agency or the state for all 12 months of the calendar year.
[3] The FBI determined that the agency's data were overreported. Consequently, those data are not included in this table.
[5] The FBI determined that the agency did not follow national Uniform Crime Reporting (UCR) Program guidelines for reporting an offense. Consequently, this figure is not included in this table.

**Table 8. Offenses Known to Law Enforcement, by State and City, 2009—*Continued***

(Number.)

| State/city | Population | Violent crime | Murder and non-negligent man-slaughter | Forcible rape | Robbery | Aggravated assault | Property crime | Burglary | Larceny-theft | Motor vehicle theft | Arson[1] |
|---|---|---|---|---|---|---|---|---|---|---|---|
| **NEW MEXICO**—*Continued* | | | | | | | | | | | |
| Taos Ski Valley | 58 | 0 | 0 | 0 | 0 | 0 | 17 | 8 | 9 | 0 | 0 |
| Tatum | 764 | 0 | 0 | 0 | 0 | 0 | 70 | 4 | 66 | 0 | 0 |
| Texico | 979 | 0 | 0 | 0 | 0 | 0 | 10 | 4 | 6 | 0 | 0 |
| Truth or Consequences | 6,732 | 54 | 1 | 4 | 1 | 48 | 228 | 59 | 159 | 10 | 0 |
| Tucumcari | 5,198 | 74 | 1 | 3 | 4 | 66 | 346 | 147 | 191 | 8 | 0 |
| Tularosa | 3,018 | 8 | 1 | 0 | 1 | 6 | 69 | 21 | 47 | 1 | 0 |
| **NEW YORK** | | | | | | | | | | | |
| Adams Village | 1,665 | 0 | 0 | 0 | 0 | 0 | 17 | 2 | 15 | 0 | 0 |
| Addison Town and Village | 2,498 | 6 | 0 | 1 | 0 | 5 | 17 | 1 | 14 | 2 | 0 |
| Akron Village | 2,955 | 4 | 0 | 0 | 0 | 4 | 41 | 4 | 37 | 0 | 0 |
| Albany | 93,445 | 1,007 | 9 | 49 | 327 | 622 | 4,264 | 876 | 3,149 | 239 | 9 |
| Albion Village | 5,505 | 29 | 0 | 2 | 5 | 22 | 420 | 96 | 306 | 18 | 2 |
| Alexandria Bay Village | 1,118 | 0 | 0 | 0 | 0 | 0 | 23 | 6 | 17 | 0 | 0 |
| Alfred Village | 4,943 | 1 | 0 | 0 | 0 | 1 | 41 | 8 | 30 | 3 | 0 |
| Allegany Village | 1,747 | 3 | 0 | 0 | 1 | 2 | 20 | 1 | 19 | 0 | 0 |
| Altamont Village | 1,695 | 0 | 0 | 0 | 0 | 0 | 13 | 1 | 11 | 1 | 0 |
| Amherst Town | 110,399 | 129 | 1 | 7 | 46 | 75 | 2,130 | 238 | 1,844 | 48 | 2 |
| Amity Town and Belmont Village | 2,158 | 5 | 0 | 0 | 0 | 5 | 1 | 1 | 0 | 0 | 0 |
| Amityville Village | 9,974 | 19 | 0 | 0 | 7 | 12 | 189 | 24 | 154 | 11 | 0 |
| Amsterdam | 17,448 | 95 | 0 | 0 | 0 | 95 | 167 | 51 | 113 | 3 | 1 |
| Arcade Village | 1,874 | 0 | 0 | 0 | 0 | 0 | 56 | 14 | 42 | 0 | 0 |
| Ardsley Village | 4,910 | 1 | 0 | 0 | 1 | 0 | 36 | 9 | 26 | 1 | 0 |
| Asharoken Village | 664 | 0 | 0 | 0 | 0 | 0 | 1 | 1 | 0 | 0 | 0 |
| Attica Village | 2,393 | 2 | 0 | 2 | 0 | 0 | 15 | 0 | 15 | 0 | 0 |
| Auburn | 26,991 | 127 | 1 | 15 | 24 | 87 | 929 | 214 | 698 | 17 | 4 |
| Avon Village | 2,904 | 1 | 0 | 0 | 0 | 1 | 33 | 3 | 28 | 2 | 0 |
| Bainbridge Village | 1,318 | 0 | 0 | 0 | 0 | 0 | 13 | 4 | 8 | 1 | 0 |
| Baldwinsville Village | 7,266 | 8 | 0 | 0 | 1 | 7 | 172 | 30 | 138 | 4 | 0 |
| Ballston Spa Village | 5,453 | 4 | 0 | 0 | 0 | 4 | 133 | 22 | 103 | 8 | 1 |
| Batavia | 15,092 | 37 | 0 | 7 | 7 | 23 | 550 | 85 | 456 | 9 | 3 |
| Bath Village | 5,409 | 9 | 0 | 1 | 2 | 6 | 140 | 25 | 114 | 1 | 0 |
| Beacon | 14,545 | 74 | 0 | 0 | 17 | 57 | 304 | 83 | 199 | 22 | 4 |
| Bedford Town | 18,627 | 5 | 0 | 0 | 2 | 3 | 115 | 20 | 94 | 1 | 0 |
| Bethlehem Town | 33,286 | 30 | 0 | 2 | 6 | 22 | 541 | 81 | 451 | 9 | 1 |
| Binghamton | 44,455 | 215 | 14 | 11 | 56 | 134 | 2,074 | 286 | 1,744 | 44 | 4 |
| Bolivar Village | 1,107 | 1 | 0 | 0 | 0 | 1 | 4 | 0 | 4 | 0 | 0 |
| Bolton Town | 2,158 | 2 | 0 | 0 | 0 | 2 | 16 | 3 | 13 | 0 | 0 |
| Boonville Village | 2,032 | 0 | 0 | 0 | 0 | 0 | 17 | 2 | 15 | 0 | 0 |
| Brant Town | 1,814 | 1 | 0 | 0 | 0 | 1 | 23 | 5 | 18 | 0 | 0 |
| Brewster | 2,106 | 7 | 0 | 0 | 0 | 7 | 16 | 6 | 7 | 3 | 0 |
| Briarcliff Manor Village | 8,018 | 0 | 0 | 0 | 0 | 0 | 28 | 1 | 27 | 0 | 0 |
| Brighton Town | 34,275 | 42 | 0 | 3 | 12 | 27 | 1,205 | 173 | 1,001 | 31 | 1 |
| Brockport Village | 8,370 | 20 | 2 | 3 | 3 | 12 | 169 | 50 | 113 | 6 | 1 |
| Bronxville Village | 6,513 | 1 | 0 | 0 | 1 | 0 | 69 | 10 | 55 | 4 | 0 |
| Buffalo | 268,655 | 3,920 | 60 | 141 | 1,636 | 2,083 | 14,481 | 3,954 | 8,947 | 1,580 | 101 |
| Caledonia Village | 2,124 | 2 | 0 | 0 | 0 | 2 | 6 | 2 | 4 | 0 | 0 |
| Cambridge Village | 1,808 | 4 | 0 | 1 | 0 | 3 | 47 | 12 | 33 | 2 | 0 |
| Camden Village | 2,244 | 4 | 0 | 0 | 0 | 4 | 75 | 13 | 60 | 2 | 0 |
| Camillus Town and Village | 23,316 | 10 | 0 | 0 | 3 | 7 | 305 | 42 | 257 | 6 | 5 |
| Canandaigua | 11,145 | 34 | 0 | 6 | 5 | 23 | 292 | 30 | 255 | 7 | 0 |
| Canisteo Village | 2,209 | 6 | 0 | 0 | 0 | 6 | 46 | 9 | 34 | 3 | 0 |
| Canton Village[2] | 6,090 | 3 | 0 | 0 | 2 | 1 | | 1 | | 1 | 0 |
| Cape Vincent Village | 785 | 0 | 0 | 0 | 0 | 0 | 17 | 2 | 15 | 0 | 0 |
| Carmel Town | 34,492 | 17 | 0 | 0 | 2 | 15 | 289 | 46 | 229 | 14 | 1 |
| Carroll Town | 3,442 | 2 | 0 | 0 | 0 | 2 | 10 | 3 | 7 | 0 | 0 |
| Carthage Village | 3,748 | 2 | 0 | 0 | 0 | 2 | 67 | 18 | 48 | 1 | 0 |
| Catskill Village | 4,193 | 18 | 0 | 2 | 1 | 15 | 171 | 13 | 157 | 1 | 0 |
| Cattaraugus Village | 975 | 0 | 0 | 0 | 0 | 0 | 2 | 2 | 0 | 0 | 0 |
| Cayuga Heights Village | 3,663 | 3 | 1 | 0 | 1 | 1 | 19 | 3 | 15 | 1 | 0 |
| Cazenovia Village | 2,948 | 2 | 0 | 1 | 0 | 1 | 35 | 1 | 34 | 0 | 0 |
| Central Square Village | 1,725 | 0 | 0 | 0 | 0 | 0 | 26 | 4 | 22 | 0 | 0 |
| Centre Island Village | 445 | 0 | 0 | 0 | 0 | 0 | 0 | 0 | 0 | 0 | 0 |
| Chatham Village | 1,674 | 16 | 0 | 1 | 1 | 14 | 74 | 24 | 48 | 2 | 0 |
| Cheektowaga Town | 77,772 | 210 | 0 | 15 | 81 | 114 | 2,570 | 334 | 2,134 | 102 | 10 |
| Chester Town | 10,047 | 3 | 0 | 0 | 0 | 3 | 19 | 3 | 16 | 0 | 1 |
| Chester Village | 3,584 | 5 | 0 | 1 | 1 | 3 | 153 | 4 | 148 | 1 | 1 |
| Chittenango Village | 4,888 | 4 | 0 | 0 | 1 | 3 | 99 | 10 | 89 | 0 | 0 |
| Cicero Town | 28,354 | 18 | 0 | 0 | 5 | 13 | 561 | 68 | 478 | 15 | 3 |
| Clarkstown Town | 78,899 | 92 | 1 | 3 | 25 | 63 | 1,898 | 136 | 1,710 | 52 | 5 |
| Clayton Village | 1,879 | 1 | 0 | 0 | 0 | 1 | 12 | 1 | 11 | 0 | 0 |
| Clifton Springs Village | 2,132 | 1 | 0 | 1 | 0 | 0 | 22 | 1 | 21 | 0 | 0 |

[1] The FBI does not publish arson data unless it receives data from either the agency or the state for all 12 months of the calendar year.
[2] The FBI determined that the agency's data were underreported. Consequently, those data are not included in this table.

## Table 8. Offenses Known to Law Enforcement, by State and City, 2009—*Continued*

(Number.)

| State/city | Population | Violent crime | Murder and non-negligent man-slaughter | Forcible rape | Robbery | Aggravated assault | Property crime | Burglary | Larceny-theft | Motor vehicle theft | Arson[1] |
|---|---|---|---|---|---|---|---|---|---|---|---|
| **NEW YORK**—*Continued* | | | | | | | | | | | |
| Clyde Village | 2,082 | 5 | 0 | 0 | 1 | 4 | 57 | 19 | 38 | 0 | 0 |
| Cobleskill Village | 4,601 | 2 | 0 | 0 | 1 | 1 | 223 | 30 | 192 | 1 | 0 |
| Coeymans Town | 7,993 | 31 | 1 | 1 | 2 | 27 | 67 | 20 | 45 | 2 | 1 |
| Cohoes | 14,973 | 51 | 0 | 4 | 12 | 35 | 337 | 93 | 226 | 18 | 1 |
| Colchester Town | 2,030 | 0 | 0 | 0 | 0 | 0 | 7 | 5 | 2 | 0 | 0 |
| Colonie Town | 78,003 | 61 | 0 | 1 | 29 | 31 | 2,284 | 205 | 2,037 | 42 | 13 |
| Cooperstown Village | 1,884 | 1 | 0 | 1 | 0 | 0 | 43 | 7 | 36 | 0 | 0 |
| Copake Town | 3,254 | 0 | 0 | 0 | 0 | 0 | 16 | 3 | 13 | 0 | 0 |
| Corning | 10,222 | 58 | 0 | 6 | 5 | 47 | 356 | 69 | 284 | 3 | 5 |
| Cornwall Town | 9,815 | 0 | 0 | 0 | 0 | 0 | 70 | 8 | 62 | 0 | 1 |
| Cortland | 18,404 | 82 | 0 | 8 | 12 | 62 | 367 | 108 | 242 | 17 | 6 |
| Coxsackie Village | 2,745 | 4 | 0 | 0 | 0 | 4 | 50 | 14 | 34 | 2 | 0 |
| Crawford Town | 9,581 | 2 | 0 | 0 | 1 | 1 | 92 | 7 | 83 | 2 | 0 |
| Cuba Town | 3,316 | 2 | 0 | 0 | 0 | 2 | 58 | 13 | 43 | 2 | 0 |
| Deerpark Town[2] | 8,501 | 2 | 0 | 0 | 1 | 1 | | 13 | | 2 | 0 |
| Delhi Village | 2,846 | 1 | 0 | 0 | 1 | 0 | 43 | 9 | 34 | 0 | 1 |
| Depew Village | 15,173 | 25 | 0 | 4 | 7 | 14 | 377 | 53 | 319 | 5 | 3 |
| Deposit Village | 1,581 | 3 | 0 | 0 | 1 | 2 | 24 | 10 | 11 | 3 | 0 |
| Dewitt Town | 21,451 | 25 | 0 | 1 | 11 | 13 | 588 | 73 | 497 | 18 | 2 |
| Dobbs Ferry Village | 11,187 | 5 | 0 | 0 | 2 | 3 | 176 | 26 | 144 | 6 | 3 |
| Dolgeville Village | 2,001 | 1 | 0 | 0 | 0 | 1 | 45 | 10 | 35 | 0 | 0 |
| Dryden Village | 1,819 | 7 | 0 | 0 | 0 | 7 | 99 | 12 | 87 | 0 | 1 |
| Dunkirk | 11,978 | 27 | 0 | 4 | 11 | 12 | 346 | 79 | 261 | 6 | 1 |
| Durham Town | 2,685 | 0 | 0 | 0 | 0 | 0 | 3 | 1 | 2 | 0 | 0 |
| East Aurora-Aurora Town | 13,451 | 4 | 0 | 0 | 0 | 4 | 155 | 26 | 121 | 8 | 0 |
| Eastchester Town | 18,698 | 10 | 0 | 0 | 3 | 7 | 224 | 19 | 200 | 5 | 0 |
| East Fishkill Town | 29,193 | 182 | 1 | 1 | 2 | 178 | 246 | 20 | 214 | 12 | 0 |
| East Greenbush Town | 17,066 | 35 | 0 | 1 | 8 | 26 | 405 | 35 | 355 | 15 | 0 |
| East Hampton Town | 19,964 | 28 | 0 | 1 | 2 | 25 | 411 | 74 | 327 | 10 | 2 |
| East Hampton Village | 1,400 | 9 | 0 | 0 | 1 | 8 | 107 | 11 | 94 | 2 | |
| East Rochester Village | 6,229 | 13 | 0 | 1 | 4 | 8 | 131 | 27 | 97 | 7 | 1 |
| East Syracuse Village | 2,950 | 3 | 0 | 0 | 0 | 3 | 174 | 23 | 144 | 7 | 2 |
| Eden Town | 7,700 | 2 | 0 | 0 | 0 | 2 | 47 | 7 | 36 | 4 | 0 |
| Ellenville Village | 3,889 | 26 | 0 | 0 | 2 | 24 | 111 | 25 | 85 | 1 | 3 |
| Ellicott Town | 5,219 | 5 | 0 | 1 | 1 | 3 | 199 | 30 | 164 | 5 | 0 |
| Ellicottville | 1,910 | 0 | 0 | 0 | 0 | 0 | 126 | 5 | 121 | 0 | 0 |
| Elmira | 29,090 | 93 | 4 | 3 | 25 | 61 | 1,053 | 212 | 823 | 18 | 3 |
| Elmira Heights Village | 3,869 | 0 | 0 | 0 | 0 | 0 | 95 | 20 | 73 | 2 | 0 |
| Elmira Town | 5,833 | 0 | 0 | 0 | 0 | 0 | 14 | 4 | 10 | 0 | 0 |
| Elmsford Village | 4,765 | 7 | 0 | 1 | 1 | 5 | 71 | 19 | 43 | 9 | 0 |
| Endicott Village | 12,346 | 53 | 1 | 5 | 10 | 37 | 490 | 93 | 392 | 5 | 2 |
| Evans Town | 16,756 | 20 | 0 | 1 | 3 | 16 | 312 | 47 | 246 | 19 | 3 |
| Fairport Village | 5,444 | 4 | 0 | 0 | 2 | 2 | 61 | 18 | 42 | 1 | 0 |
| Fallsburg Town | 12,385 | 22 | 0 | 3 | 2 | 17 | 232 | 93 | 136 | 3 | 0 |
| Floral Park Village | 15,832 | 13 | 0 | 0 | 10 | 3 | 72 | 13 | 51 | 8 | 1 |
| Florida Village | 2,831 | 4 | 0 | 0 | 0 | 4 | 24 | 3 | 20 | 1 | 0 |
| Fort Edward Village | 3,013 | 4 | 0 | 0 | 0 | 4 | 12 | 5 | 6 | 1 | 0 |
| Frankfort Town | 4,829 | 2 | 0 | 0 | 0 | 2 | 29 | 13 | 15 | 1 | 0 |
| Frankfort Village | 2,343 | 1 | 0 | 0 | 0 | 1 | 10 | 0 | 10 | 0 | 0 |
| Franklinville Village | 1,688 | 0 | 0 | 0 | 0 | 0 | 26 | 3 | 23 | 0 | 0 |
| Fredonia Village | 11,107 | 11 | 0 | 0 | 2 | 9 | 368 | 28 | 336 | 4 | 0 |
| Freeport Village | 43,890 | 196 | 5 | 4 | 115 | 72 | 1,048 | 129 | 794 | 125 | 2 |
| Fulton City | 11,151 | 17 | 0 | 2 | 3 | 12 | 511 | 75 | 426 | 10 | 2 |
| Garden City Village | 22,342 | 13 | 1 | 0 | 6 | 6 | 366 | 25 | 335 | 6 | 0 |
| Gates Town | 28,590 | 66 | 0 | 12 | 18 | 36 | 1,094 | 106 | 939 | 49 | 3 |
| Geddes Town | 10,367 | 3 | 0 | 0 | 2 | 1 | 198 | 28 | 159 | 11 | 0 |
| Geneseo Village | 7,715 | 2 | 0 | 0 | 1 | 1 | 121 | 9 | 110 | 2 | 1 |
| Geneva | 13,177 | 43 | 2 | 1 | 20 | 20 | 329 | 69 | 256 | 4 | 1 |
| Germantown Town | 1,964 | 0 | 0 | 0 | 0 | 0 | 0 | 0 | 0 | 0 | 0 |
| Glen Cove | 26,920 | 31 | 0 | 0 | 14 | 17 | 257 | 38 | 207 | 12 | 3 |
| Glen Park Village | 500 | 1 | 0 | 0 | 0 | 1 | 3 | 0 | 3 | 0 | 0 |
| Glens Falls | 13,828 | 19 | 0 | 0 | 5 | 14 | 425 | 35 | 383 | 7 | 3 |
| Glenville Town | 21,971 | 5 | 0 | 3 | 0 | 2 | 322 | 37 | 277 | 8 | 0 |
| Gloversville | 14,948 | 71 | 1 | 11 | 9 | 50 | 603 | 100 | 484 | 19 | 2 |
| Goshen Town | 8,491 | 3 | 0 | 0 | 0 | 3 | 86 | 16 | 66 | 4 | 0 |
| Goshen Village | 5,573 | 8 | 0 | 0 | 1 | 7 | 84 | 13 | 70 | 1 | 0 |
| Gowanda Village | 2,578 | 6 | 0 | 0 | 0 | 6 | 72 | 12 | 60 | 0 | 1 |
| Granville Village | 2,530 | 3 | 0 | 2 | 0 | 1 | 51 | 14 | 37 | 0 | 0 |
| Great Neck Estates Village | 2,770 | 1 | 0 | 0 | 1 | 0 | 4 | 0 | 4 | 0 | 0 |
| Greece Town | 93,274 | 98 | 1 | 13 | 41 | 43 | 2,612 | 345 | 2,190 | 77 | 2 |
| Greene Village | 1,640 | 0 | 0 | 0 | 0 | 0 | 0 | 0 | 0 | 0 | 0 |

[1] The FBI does not publish arson data unless it receives data from either the agency or the state for all 12 months of the calendar year.
[2] The FBI determined that the agency's data were underreported. Consequently, those data are not included in this table.

## Table 8. Offenses Known to Law Enforcement, by State and City, 2009—*Continued*

(Number.)

| State/city | Population | Violent crime | Murder and non-negligent man-slaughter | Forcible rape | Robbery | Aggravated assault | Property crime | Burglary | Larceny-theft | Motor vehicle theft | Arson[1] |
|---|---|---|---|---|---|---|---|---|---|---|---|
| **NEW YORK**—*Continued* | | | | | | | | | | | |
| Green Island Village | 2,565 | 8 | 0 | 0 | 1 | 7 | 101 | 13 | 88 | 0 | 1 |
| Greenport Town | 4,145 | 0 | 0 | 0 | 0 | 0 | 93 | 8 | 83 | 2 | 0 |
| Greenwich Village | 1,819 | 0 | 0 | 0 | 0 | 0 | 29 | 5 | 22 | 2 | 0 |
| Greenwood Lake Village | 3,417 | 4 | 0 | 0 | 0 | 4 | 37 | 6 | 28 | 3 | 0 |
| Groton Village | 2,394 | 4 | 0 | 0 | 2 | 2 | 40 | 9 | 31 | 0 | 0 |
| Guilderland Town | 33,161 | 19 | 0 | 3 | 8 | 8 | 717 | 48 | 658 | 11 | 2 |
| Hamburg Town | 44,012 | 39 | 0 | 2 | 9 | 28 | 1,019 | 152 | 838 | 29 | 3 |
| Hamburg Village | 9,327 | 9 | 0 | 0 | 2 | 7 | 199 | 39 | 155 | 5 | 0 |
| Hamilton Village | 3,818 | 1 | 0 | 0 | 1 | 0 | 33 | 9 | 24 | 0 | 0 |
| Hancock Village | 1,078 | 6 | 0 | 0 | 0 | 6 | 12 | 8 | 4 | 0 | 0 |
| Harriman Village | 2,247 | 0 | 0 | 0 | 0 | 0 | 16 | 5 | 11 | 0 | 0 |
| Harrison Town | 26,953 | 12 | 0 | 0 | 1 | 11 | 289 | 51 | 219 | 19 | 0 |
| Hastings-on-Hudson Village | 7,939 | 16 | 0 | 0 | 2 | 14 | 140 | 17 | 120 | 3 | 4 |
| Haverstraw Town | 37,449 | 67 | 0 | 4 | 32 | 31 | 510 | 89 | 407 | 14 | 6 |
| Hempstead Village | 53,996 | 482 | 6 | 9 | 254 | 213 | 1,074 | 199 | 646 | 229 | 10 |
| Herkimer Village | 6,915 | 78 | 0 | 9 | 7 | 62 | 455 | 45 | 409 | 1 | 0 |
| Highland Falls Village | 3,706 | 5 | 0 | 0 | 2 | 3 | 22 | 5 | 17 | 0 | 0 |
| Highlands Town | 9,170 | 0 | 0 | 0 | 0 | 0 | 6 | 2 | 3 | 1 | 0 |
| Holley Village | 1,674 | 1 | 0 | 1 | 0 | 0 | 49 | 5 | 43 | 1 | 0 |
| Homer Village | 3,232 | 0 | 0 | 0 | 0 | 0 | 65 | 6 | 59 | 0 | 0 |
| Hornell | 8,454 | 11 | 0 | 2 | 1 | 8 | 153 | 15 | 134 | 4 | 0 |
| Horseheads Village | 6,221 | 13 | 0 | 1 | 1 | 11 | 141 | 22 | 111 | 8 | 0 |
| Hudson | 6,864 | 36 | 0 | 4 | 3 | 29 | 208 | 41 | 165 | 2 | 0 |
| Hudson Falls Village | 6,615 | 3 | 0 | 0 | 0 | 3 | 89 | 10 | 76 | 3 | 0 |
| Hunter Town | 2,690 | 3 | 0 | 0 | 0 | 3 | 9 | 3 | 6 | 0 | 0 |
| Huntington Bay Village | 1,515 | 0 | 0 | 0 | 0 | 0 | 5 | 2 | 2 | 1 | 0 |
| Hyde Park Town | 20,207 | 13 | 0 | 0 | 4 | 9 | 270 | 42 | 222 | 6 | 0 |
| Ilion Village | 7,953 | 26 | 0 | 2 | 5 | 19 | 193 | 21 | 171 | 1 | 2 |
| Independence Town | 1,034 | 0 | 0 | 0 | 0 | 0 | 10 | 1 | 7 | 2 | 0 |
| Inlet Town | 376 | 0 | 0 | 0 | 0 | 0 | 15 | 4 | 11 | 0 | 0 |
| Irondequoit Town | 49,755 | 67 | 0 | 6 | 24 | 37 | 1,526 | 213 | 1,258 | 55 | 1 |
| Irvington Village | 6,669 | 1 | 0 | 0 | 0 | 1 | 27 | 6 | 21 | 0 | 0 |
| Ithaca | 29,862 | 67 | 0 | 2 | 26 | 39 | 1,185 | 140 | 1,021 | 24 | 1 |
| Jamestown | 29,204 | 152 | 1 | 20 | 26 | 105 | 1,100 | 266 | 814 | 20 | 10 |
| Johnson City Village | 14,646 | 62 | 1 | 7 | 11 | 43 | 882 | 82 | 789 | 11 | 2 |
| Johnstown | 8,421 | 7 | 0 | 1 | 1 | 5 | 225 | 22 | 197 | 6 | 0 |
| Kenmore Village | 14,856 | 30 | 0 | 2 | 14 | 14 | 297 | 54 | 229 | 14 | 1 |
| Kensington Village | 1,203 | 0 | 0 | 0 | 0 | 0 | 0 | 0 | 0 | 0 | 0 |
| Kent Town | 14,190 | 4 | 0 | 1 | 1 | 2 | 88 | 21 | 66 | 1 | 0 |
| Kings Point Village | 5,430 | 0 | 0 | 0 | 0 | 0 | 16 | 3 | 12 | 1 | 0 |
| Kingston | 22,333 | 97 | 0 | 2 | 69 | 26 | 662 | 122 | 510 | 30 | 7 |
| Kirkland Town | 8,344 | 1 | 0 | 0 | 0 | 1 | 104 | 18 | 83 | 3 | 0 |
| Lackawanna | 17,435 | 89 | 0 | 1 | 18 | 70 | 463 | 104 | 344 | 15 | 0 |
| Lake Placid Village | 2,763 | 1 | 0 | 1 | 0 | 0 | 67 | 14 | 50 | 3 | 0 |
| Lake Success Village | 2,898 | 1 | 0 | 0 | 0 | 1 | 44 | 5 | 37 | 2 | 0 |
| Lakewood-Busti | 7,355 | 0 | 0 | 0 | 0 | 0 | 242 | 8 | 229 | 5 | 0 |
| Lancaster Town | 23,502 | 27 | 0 | 0 | 7 | 20 | 592 | 94 | 484 | 14 | 4 |
| Larchmont Village | 6,575 | 1 | 0 | 0 | 0 | 1 | 135 | 17 | 115 | 3 | 0 |
| Le Roy Village | 4,109 | 4 | 0 | 0 | 2 | 2 | 62 | 5 | 53 | 4 | 0 |
| Lewisboro Town | 12,530 | 0 | 0 | 0 | 0 | 0 | 77 | 8 | 69 | 0 | 0 |
| Lewiston Town and Village | 16,737 | 2 | 0 | 0 | 0 | 2 | 165 | 20 | 137 | 8 | 0 |
| Liberty Village | 3,844 | 7 | 0 | 2 | 0 | 5 | 175 | 41 | 129 | 5 | 0 |
| Little Falls | 4,833 | 38 | 0 | 0 | 5 | 33 | 168 | 31 | 135 | 2 | 8 |
| Liverpool Village | 2,326 | 4 | 0 | 0 | 1 | 3 | 49 | 6 | 43 | 0 | 0 |
| Lloyd Harbor Village | 3,748 | 0 | 0 | 0 | 0 | 0 | 19 | 0 | 18 | 1 | 0 |
| Lloyd Town | 10,808 | 10 | 0 | 2 | 3 | 5 | 143 | 19 | 117 | 7 | 0 |
| Lockport | 20,461 | 58 | 1 | 1 | 22 | 34 | 779 | 170 | 565 | 44 | 5 |
| Long Beach | 35,722 | 26 | 0 | 2 | 6 | 18 | 232 | 21 | 207 | 4 | 0 |
| Lowville Village | 3,133 | 4 | 0 | 2 | 0 | 2 | 107 | 12 | 89 | 6 | 0 |
| Lynbrook Village | 19,844 | 22 | 0 | 3 | 10 | 9 | 175 | 18 | 144 | 13 | 0 |
| Lyons Village | 3,391 | 21 | 0 | 1 | 5 | 15 | 143 | 31 | 107 | 5 | 1 |
| Macedon Town and Village | 8,845 | 2 | 0 | 1 | 0 | 1 | 89 | 14 | 74 | 1 | 0 |
| Malone Village | 5,764 | 8 | 0 | 0 | 0 | 8 | 198 | 26 | 172 | 0 | 0 |
| Malverne Village | 8,873 | 2 | 0 | 0 | 1 | 1 | 46 | 9 | 34 | 3 | 0 |
| Mamaroneck Town | 11,538 | 1 | 0 | 0 | 1 | 0 | 155 | 21 | 126 | 8 | 0 |
| Mamaroneck Village | 18,404 | 17 | 0 | 0 | 6 | 11 | 212 | 37 | 160 | 15 | 0 |
| Manchester Village | 1,410 | 0 | 0 | 0 | 0 | 0 | 1 | 0 | 1 | 0 | 0 |
| Manlius Town | 24,850 | 24 | 0 | 4 | 7 | 13 | 481 | 64 | 411 | 6 | 3 |
| Marcellus Village | 1,813 | 0 | 0 | 0 | 0 | 0 | 13 | 1 | 12 | 0 | 0 |
| Marlborough Town | 8,301 | 9 | 0 | 1 | 2 | 6 | 137 | 27 | 100 | 10 | 0 |
| Massena Village | 10,470 | 21 | 0 | 7 | 4 | 10 | 135 | 33 | 102 | 0 | 0 |

[1] The FBI does not publish arson data unless it receives data from either the agency or the state for all 12 months of the calendar year.

## Table 8. Offenses Known to Law Enforcement, by State and City, 2009—*Continued*

(Number.)

| State/city | Population | Violent crime | Murder and non-negligent man-slaughter | Forcible rape | Robbery | Aggravated assault | Property crime | Burglary | Larceny-theft | Motor vehicle theft | Arson[1] |
|---|---|---|---|---|---|---|---|---|---|---|---|
| **NEW YORK**—*Continued* | | | | | | | | | | | |
| Maybrook Village | 4,110 | 0 | 0 | 0 | 0 | 0 | 34 | 10 | 23 | 1 | 0 |
| McGraw Village | 949 | 0 | 0 | 0 | 0 | 0 | 0 | 0 | 0 | 0 | 0 |
| Mechanicville | 4,839 | 8 | 0 | 2 | 3 | 3 | 99 | 23 | 73 | 3 | 0 |
| Medina Village | 6,007 | 14 | 0 | 3 | 3 | 8 | 258 | 82 | 171 | 5 | 0 |
| Menands Village | 3,783 | 9 | 0 | 0 | 3 | 6 | 157 | 18 | 129 | 10 | 1 |
| Middleport Village | 1,765 | 0 | 0 | 0 | 0 | 0 | 28 | 4 | 23 | 1 | 0 |
| Middletown | 25,921 | 155 | 1 | 8 | 57 | 89 | 1,024 | 204 | 794 | 26 | 0 |
| Millbrook Village | 1,517 | 0 | 0 | 0 | 0 | 0 | 0 | 0 | 0 | 0 | 0 |
| Monroe Village | 8,207 | 24 | 0 | 0 | 2 | 22 | 231 | 22 | 203 | 6 | 0 |
| Montgomery Village | 4,878 | 0 | 0 | 0 | 0 | 0 | 18 | 0 | 18 | 0 | 0 |
| Monticello Village | 6,487 | 49 | 1 | 3 | 16 | 29 | 192 | 35 | 154 | 3 | 1 |
| Moravia Village | 1,286 | 0 | 0 | 0 | 0 | 0 | 16 | 2 | 14 | 0 | 0 |
| Moriah Town | 3,432 | 2 | 0 | 0 | 0 | 2 | 1 | 0 | 1 | 0 | 0 |
| Mount Hope Town | 7,568 | 3 | 0 | 0 | 0 | 3 | 35 | 11 | 21 | 3 | 0 |
| Mount Kisco Village[3] | 10,434 | 40 | 0 | 0 | 18 | 22 | | | 161 | 7 | 1 |
| Mount Morris Village | 2,852 | 7 | 1 | 0 | 1 | 5 | 62 | 5 | 53 | 4 | 0 |
| Mount Pleasant Town | 26,437 | 9 | 0 | 1 | 1 | 7 | 236 | 39 | 188 | 9 | 0 |
| Mount Vernon | 68,677 | 664 | 10 | 10 | 274 | 370 | 1,643 | 342 | 1,140 | 161 | |
| Nassau Village | 1,111 | 3 | 0 | 0 | 0 | 3 | 12 | 1 | 11 | 0 | 0 |
| Newark Village | 9,033 | 19 | 0 | 3 | 3 | 13 | 368 | 51 | 308 | 9 | 1 |
| New Berlin Town | 1,698 | 3 | 0 | 0 | 1 | 2 | 26 | 4 | 22 | 0 | 0 |
| Newburgh | 28,071 | 466 | 4 | 8 | 187 | 267 | 1,065 | 316 | 661 | 88 | 10 |
| Newburgh Town | 31,394 | 41 | 3 | 4 | 14 | 20 | 1,161 | 99 | 1,033 | 29 | 0 |
| New Castle Town | 17,750 | 0 | 0 | 0 | 0 | 0 | 100 | 7 | 90 | 3 | 0 |
| New Hartford Town and Village | 19,145 | 5 | 0 | 2 | 1 | 2 | 894 | 34 | 856 | 4 | 0 |
| New Paltz Town and Village | 13,854 | 62 | 0 | 4 | 8 | 50 | 328 | 44 | 279 | 5 | 0 |
| New Rochelle | 74,320 | 204 | 2 | 3 | 80 | 119 | 1,309 | 198 | 1,018 | 93 | 3 |
| New Windsor Town | 25,407 | 29 | 0 | 5 | 6 | 18 | 515 | 63 | 436 | 16 | 1 |
| New York | 8,400,907 | 46,357 | 471 | 832 | 18,597 | 26,457 | 142,000 | 18,780 | 112,526 | 10,694 | |
| New York Mills Village | 3,303 | 1 | 0 | 0 | 0 | 1 | 41 | 10 | 31 | 0 | 0 |
| Niagara Falls | 50,909 | 609 | 6 | 28 | 166 | 409 | 2,810 | 805 | 1,877 | 128 | 37 |
| Niagara Town | 8,344 | 19 | 0 | 0 | 4 | 15 | 379 | 47 | 322 | 10 | 2 |
| Niskayuna Town | 21,920 | 17 | 0 | 1 | 7 | 9 | 409 | 28 | 377 | 4 | 0 |
| Nissequogue Village | 1,611 | 0 | 0 | 0 | 0 | 0 | 7 | 0 | 7 | 0 | 0 |
| North Castle Town | 12,293 | 4 | 0 | 0 | 1 | 3 | 104 | 22 | 80 | 2 | 0 |
| North Greenbush Town | 11,954 | 13 | 0 | 0 | 4 | 9 | 240 | 34 | 201 | 5 | 0 |
| Northport Village | 7,683 | 4 | 0 | 1 | 3 | 0 | 66 | 7 | 57 | 2 | 0 |
| North Syracuse Village | 6,537 | 6 | 0 | 0 | 1 | 5 | 61 | 10 | 50 | 1 | |
| North Tonawanda | 31,012 | 51 | 0 | 5 | 14 | 32 | 610 | 189 | 403 | 18 | 3 |
| Northville Village | 1,155 | 0 | 0 | 0 | 0 | 0 | 8 | 1 | 7 | 0 | 0 |
| Norwich | 6,954 | 12 | 0 | 5 | 4 | 3 | 308 | 50 | 252 | 6 | 0 |
| Ocean Beach Village | 148 | 1 | 0 | 0 | 0 | 1 | 66 | 4 | 62 | 0 | 0 |
| Ogdensburg | 10,993 | 22 | 0 | 3 | 1 | 18 | 415 | 74 | 331 | 10 | 0 |
| Ogden Town | 19,377 | 14 | 0 | 0 | 5 | 9 | 355 | 36 | 301 | 18 | 2 |
| Old Brookville Village | 2,330 | 0 | 0 | 0 | 0 | 0 | 78 | 12 | 66 | 0 | 1 |
| Old Westbury Village | 5,430 | 3 | 0 | 0 | 0 | 3 | 27 | 5 | 20 | 2 | 0 |
| Olean | 14,025 | 78 | 0 | 4 | 6 | 68 | 545 | 42 | 500 | 3 | 2 |
| Oneida | 10,695 | 13 | 0 | 1 | 3 | 9 | 409 | 40 | 367 | 2 | 0 |
| Oneonta City | 13,205 | 63 | 0 | 4 | 5 | 54 | 334 | 104 | 226 | 4 | 4 |
| Orangetown Town | 36,108 | 38 | 0 | 0 | 13 | 25 | 578 | 48 | 510 | 20 | 0 |
| Orchard Park Town | 28,626 | 31 | 2 | 5 | 6 | 18 | 420 | 49 | 358 | 13 | 1 |
| Oriskany Village | 1,398 | 1 | 0 | 0 | 1 | 0 | 26 | 6 | 20 | 0 | 0 |
| Ossining Town | 5,731 | 0 | 0 | 0 | 0 | 0 | 31 | 4 | 26 | 1 | 0 |
| Ossining Village | 23,773 | 33 | 0 | 1 | 15 | 17 | 285 | 77 | 194 | 14 | 1 |
| Oswego City | 17,271 | 60 | 0 | 4 | 13 | 43 | 494 | 95 | 386 | 13 | 4 |
| Owego Village | 3,687 | 3 | 0 | 0 | 0 | 3 | 24 | 8 | 16 | 0 | 0 |
| Oxford Village | 1,529 | 0 | 0 | 0 | 0 | 0 | 26 | 7 | 19 | 0 | 0 |
| Oyster Bay Cove Village | 2,303 | 0 | 0 | 0 | 0 | 0 | 7 | 4 | 3 | 0 | 0 |
| Painted Post Village | 1,772 | 2 | 0 | 0 | 0 | 2 | 89 | 3 | 86 | 0 | 0 |
| Palmyra Village | 3,403 | 2 | 0 | 0 | 0 | 2 | 42 | 4 | 36 | 2 | 0 |
| Peekskill | 24,711 | 34 | 0 | 2 | 12 | 20 | 225 | 43 | 177 | 5 | 0 |
| Pelham Village | 6,438 | 12 | 0 | 1 | 10 | 1 | 98 | 15 | 76 | 7 | 0 |
| Penn Yan Village | 5,157 | 5 | 0 | 2 | 1 | 2 | 134 | 18 | 116 | 0 | 1 |
| Perry Village | 3,638 | 7 | 0 | 1 | 0 | 6 | 86 | 14 | 72 | 0 | 0 |
| Phelps Village | 1,896 | 0 | 0 | 0 | 0 | 0 | 3 | 0 | 3 | 0 | 0 |
| Philmont Village | 1,354 | 2 | 0 | 0 | 0 | 2 | 6 | 0 | 6 | 0 | 0 |
| Piermont Village | 2,562 | 0 | 0 | 0 | 0 | 0 | 42 | 3 | 38 | 1 | 0 |
| Pine Plains Town | 2,704 | 0 | 0 | 0 | 0 | 0 | 7 | 0 | 7 | 0 | 0 |
| Plattekill Town | 10,897 | 11 | 0 | 0 | 1 | 10 | 115 | 35 | 79 | 1 | 1 |
| Plattsburgh City | 19,457 | 38 | 0 | 6 | 9 | 23 | 513 | 82 | 417 | 14 | 4 |
| Pleasantville Village | 7,142 | 0 | 0 | 0 | 0 | 0 | 0 | 0 | 0 | 0 | 0 |

[1] The FBI does not publish arson data unless it receives data from either the agency or the state for all 12 months of the calendar year.
[3] The FBI determined that the agency's data were overreported. Consequently, those data are not included in this table.

**Table 8. Offenses Known to Law Enforcement, by State and City, 2009—*Continued***

(Number.)

| State/city | Population | Violent crime | Murder and non-negligent man-slaughter | Forcible rape | Robbery | Aggravated assault | Property crime | Burglary | Larceny-theft | Motor vehicle theft | Arson[1] |
|---|---|---|---|---|---|---|---|---|---|---|---|
| **NEW YORK**—*Continued* | | | | | | | | | | | |
| Port Byron Village | 1,226 | 4 | 0 | 1 | 0 | 3 | 0 | 0 | 0 | 0 | 0 |
| Port Chester Village | 28,202 | 72 | 0 | 3 | 40 | 29 | 658 | 73 | 540 | 45 | 1 |
| Port Dickinson Village | 1,584 | 2 | 0 | 0 | 1 | 1 | 14 | 3 | 11 | 0 | 0 |
| Port Jervis | 9,139 | 30 | 0 | 3 | 8 | 19 | 291 | 57 | 228 | 6 | 0 |
| Portville Village | 943 | 0 | 0 | 0 | 0 | 0 | 0 | 0 | 0 | 0 | 0 |
| Potsdam Village | 9,877 | 20 | 0 | 3 | 1 | 16 | 220 | 43 | 171 | 6 | 0 |
| Poughkeepsie | 29,599 | 410 | 3 | 11 | 200 | 196 | 1,022 | 274 | 683 | 65 | 4 |
| Poughkeepsie Town | 43,027 | 49 | 0 | 2 | 19 | 28 | 1,430 | 93 | 1,333 | 4 | 2 |
| Pound Ridge Town | 4,960 | 1 | 0 | 1 | 0 | 0 | 40 | 7 | 30 | 3 | 0 |
| Pulaski Village | 2,270 | 6 | 0 | 0 | 2 | 4 | 50 | 10 | 38 | 2 | 0 |
| Quogue Village | 1,172 | 0 | 0 | 0 | 0 | 0 | 32 | 6 | 23 | 3 | 0 |
| Ramapo Town | 76,611 | 63 | 1 | 4 | 13 | 45 | 669 | 94 | 542 | 33 | 5 |
| Red Hook Village | 1,890 | 1 | 0 | 0 | 0 | 1 | 9 | 1 | 7 | 1 | 0 |
| Rensselaer City | 7,906 | 20 | 0 | 4 | 7 | 9 | 244 | 54 | 176 | 14 | 0 |
| Rhinebeck Village | 3,046 | 2 | 0 | 0 | 0 | 2 | 49 | 10 | 39 | 0 | 1 |
| Riverhead Town | 36,318 | 101 | 1 | 7 | 44 | 49 | 1,011 | 157 | 825 | 29 | 0 |
| Rochester | 205,537 | 2,042 | 28 | 97 | 846 | 1,071 | 10,991 | 2,899 | 7,130 | 962 | 186 |
| Rockville Centre Village | 24,396 | 20 | 0 | 1 | 13 | 6 | 320 | 63 | 237 | 20 | 1 |
| Rome | 33,543 | 30 | 0 | 3 | 14 | 13 | 700 | 157 | 516 | 27 | 5 |
| Rosendale Town | 6,232 | 1 | 0 | 0 | 0 | 1 | 22 | 3 | 17 | 2 | 0 |
| Rotterdam Town | 30,223 | 23 | 0 | 4 | 4 | 15 | 829 | 95 | 710 | 24 | 8 |
| Rouses Point Village | 2,325 | 1 | 0 | 0 | 0 | 1 | 27 | 2 | 25 | 0 | 0 |
| Rye | 15,070 | 3 | 0 | 0 | 2 | 1 | 215 | 38 | 168 | 9 | 0 |
| Rye Brook Village | 9,672 | 1 | 1 | 0 | 0 | 0 | 78 | 6 | 69 | 3 | 0 |
| Sackets Harbor Village | 1,429 | 0 | 0 | 0 | 0 | 0 | 7 | 1 | 6 | 0 | 0 |
| Sag Harbor Village | 2,439 | 7 | 0 | 0 | 0 | 7 | 53 | 7 | 45 | 1 | 0 |
| Salamanca | 5,540 | 18 | 0 | 3 | 3 | 12 | 230 | 45 | 182 | 3 | 2 |
| Sands Point Village | 2,929 | 0 | 0 | 0 | 0 | 0 | 15 | 1 | 14 | 0 | 0 |
| Saranac Lake Village | 4,783 | 8 | 0 | 1 | 2 | 5 | 187 | 37 | 146 | 4 | 0 |
| Saratoga Springs | 29,125 | 22 | 0 | 1 | 9 | 12 | 579 | 81 | 485 | 13 | 2 |
| Saugerties Town | 15,844 | 6 | 0 | 0 | 2 | 4 | 188 | 43 | 136 | 9 | 2 |
| Saugerties Village | 3,852 | 7 | 0 | 0 | 1 | 6 | 113 | 18 | 92 | 3 | 0 |
| Scarsdale Village | 17,677 | 6 | 0 | 0 | 3 | 3 | 215 | 24 | 185 | 6 | 0 |
| Schenectady | 61,087 | 592 | 7 | 31 | 243 | 311 | 3,336 | 822 | 2,299 | 215 | 35 |
| Schodack Town | 11,533 | 11 | 0 | 1 | 0 | 10 | 86 | 27 | 56 | 3 | 0 |
| Schoharie Village | 999 | 1 | 0 | 1 | 0 | 0 | 24 | 6 | 18 | 0 | 0 |
| Scotia Village | 8,043 | 11 | 0 | 1 | 3 | 7 | 198 | 22 | 171 | 5 | 1 |
| Seneca Falls Village | 6,604 | 6 | 0 | 0 | 3 | 3 | 58 | 10 | 44 | 4 | 0 |
| Shandaken Town | 3,045 | 2 | 0 | 0 | 0 | 2 | 70 | 26 | 44 | 0 | 0 |
| Shawangunk Town | 12,786 | 13 | 0 | 0 | 0 | 13 | 97 | 21 | 75 | 1 | 1 |
| Shelter Island Town | 2,569 | 0 | 0 | 0 | 0 | 0 | 51 | 17 | 34 | 0 | 0 |
| Sherburne Village | 1,408 | 0 | 0 | 0 | 0 | 0 | 56 | 6 | 50 | 0 | 0 |
| Sherrill | 3,111 | 1 | 0 | 0 | 0 | 1 | 23 | 5 | 18 | 0 | 0 |
| Shortsville Village | 1,313 | 0 | 0 | 0 | 0 | 0 | 1 | 0 | 1 | 0 | 0 |
| Sidney Village | 3,654 | 12 | 0 | 1 | 0 | 11 | 167 | 23 | 141 | 3 | 0 |
| Silver Creek Village | 2,789 | 9 | 0 | 1 | 1 | 7 | 31 | 1 | 30 | 0 | 0 |
| Skaneateles Village | 2,531 | 2 | 0 | 0 | 0 | 2 | 8 | 1 | 7 | 0 | 0 |
| Sleepy Hollow Village[3] | 10,331 | 1 | 0 | 0 | 0 | 1 | | 19 | | 2 | 1 |
| Sodus Point Village | 1,102 | 0 | 0 | 0 | 0 | 0 | 1 | 0 | 1 | 0 | 0 |
| Sodus Village | 1,598 | 2 | 0 | 0 | 1 | 1 | 42 | 7 | 35 | 0 | 0 |
| Solvay Village | 6,372 | 13 | 0 | 1 | 4 | 8 | 204 | 54 | 141 | 9 | 1 |
| Southampton Town | 53,044 | 79 | 0 | 6 | 27 | 46 | 1,037 | 244 | 732 | 61 | 8 |
| Southampton Village | 4,363 | 2 | 0 | 0 | 0 | 2 | 179 | 26 | 151 | 2 | 0 |
| South Glens Falls Village | 3,383 | 12 | 0 | 1 | 0 | 11 | 102 | 31 | 70 | 1 | 0 |
| South Nyack Village | 3,361 | 8 | 0 | 1 | 1 | 6 | 45 | 9 | 35 | 1 | 0 |
| Spring Valley Village | 26,340 | 168 | 0 | 5 | 56 | 107 | 463 | 80 | 361 | 22 | 4 |
| Stillwater Town | 6,591 | 0 | 0 | 0 | 0 | 0 | 22 | 3 | 19 | 0 | 0 |
| St. Johnsville Village | 1,600 | 1 | 0 | 0 | 0 | 1 | 8 | 0 | 7 | 1 | 0 |
| Stockport Town | 2,797 | 0 | 0 | 0 | 0 | 0 | 5 | 2 | 3 | 0 | 0 |
| Stony Point Town | 15,229 | 9 | 0 | 0 | 0 | 9 | 145 | 25 | 118 | 2 | 0 |
| Suffern Village | 11,099 | 10 | 0 | 0 | 7 | 3 | 70 | 10 | 55 | 5 | 0 |
| Syracuse | 137,208 | 1,343 | 18 | 70 | 403 | 852 | 5,779 | 1,946 | 3,495 | 338 | 40 |
| Tarrytown Village | 11,019 | 8 | 0 | 1 | 5 | 2 | 96 | 12 | 80 | 4 | 0 |
| Ticonderoga Town | 4,941 | 11 | 0 | 2 | 1 | 8 | 71 | 19 | 49 | 3 | 1 |
| Tonawanda | 14,683 | 37 | 0 | 4 | 9 | 24 | 400 | 53 | 336 | 11 | 1 |
| Tonawanda Town | 56,203 | 119 | 3 | 10 | 37 | 69 | 1,107 | 216 | 847 | 44 | 4 |
| Troy | 47,268 | 350 | 3 | 17 | 155 | 175 | 2,340 | 608 | 1,612 | 120 | 17 |
| Trumansburg Village | 1,593 | 6 | 0 | 1 | 1 | 4 | 43 | 9 | 33 | 1 | 0 |
| Tuckahoe Village | 6,247 | 2 | 0 | 0 | 1 | 1 | 31 | 2 | 25 | 4 | 1 |
| Tupper Lake Village | 3,812 | 11 | 0 | 1 | 0 | 10 | 123 | 12 | 106 | 5 | 0 |
| Tuxedo Park Village | 718 | 0 | 0 | 0 | 0 | 0 | 0 | 0 | 0 | 0 | 0 |

[1] The FBI does not publish arson data unless it receives data from either the agency or the state for all 12 months of the calendar year.

[3] The FBI determined that the agency's data were overreported. Consequently, those data are not included in this table.

## Table 8. Offenses Known to Law Enforcement, by State and City, 2009—*Continued*

(Number.)

| State/city | Population | Violent crime | Murder and non-negligent man-slaughter | Forcible rape | Robbery | Aggravated assault | Property crime | Burglary | Larceny-theft | Motor vehicle theft | Arson[1] |
|---|---|---|---|---|---|---|---|---|---|---|---|
| **NEW YORK**—*Continued* | | | | | | | | | | | |
| Tuxedo Town | 2,990 | 3 | 0 | 0 | 0 | 3 | 1 | 0 | 1 | 0 | 0 |
| Ulster Town | 12,674 | 8 | 0 | 1 | 2 | 5 | 440 | 37 | 388 | 15 | 2 |
| Utica | 57,831 | 475 | 5 | 18 | 148 | 304 | 2,582 | 505 | 2,000 | 77 | 8 |
| Vernon Village | 1,145 | 1 | 0 | 0 | 0 | 1 | 17 | 3 | 14 | 0 | 0 |
| Vestal Town | 27,332 | 15 | 0 | 2 | 3 | 10 | 503 | 35 | 463 | 5 | 1 |
| Walden Village | 7,055 | 27 | 0 | 5 | 2 | 20 | 93 | 11 | 76 | 6 | 0 |
| Wallkill Town | 27,760 | 34 | 0 | 2 | 22 | 10 | 942 | 55 | 856 | 31 | 3 |
| Walton Village | 2,823 | 7 | 0 | 0 | 1 | 6 | 61 | 16 | 44 | 1 | 1 |
| Wappingers Falls Village | 5,748 | 11 | 0 | 0 | 4 | 7 | 138 | 27 | 106 | 5 | 0 |
| Warsaw Village | 3,602 | 3 | 0 | 1 | 0 | 2 | 77 | 13 | 64 | 0 | 0 |
| Warwick Town | 20,040 | 6 | 0 | 0 | 2 | 4 | 181 | 33 | 147 | 1 | 0 |
| Washingtonville Village | 6,167 | 6 | 0 | 0 | 4 | 2 | 110 | 2 | 106 | 2 | 0 |
| Waterford Town and Village | 8,534 | 5 | 0 | 2 | 2 | 1 | 87 | 5 | 80 | 2 | 0 |
| Waterloo Village | 4,975 | 11 | 0 | 1 | 2 | 8 | 194 | 15 | 178 | 1 | 0 |
| Watertown | 27,387 | 118 | 1 | 12 | 19 | 86 | 1,319 | 217 | 1,068 | 34 | 11 |
| Watervliet | 9,718 | 40 | 1 | 3 | 9 | 27 | 320 | 57 | 249 | 14 | 0 |
| Watkins Glen Village | 2,015 | 2 | 0 | 2 | 0 | 0 | 80 | 14 | 64 | 2 | 0 |
| Waverly Village | 4,272 | 6 | 0 | 1 | 0 | 5 | 112 | 23 | 89 | 0 | 0 |
| Wayland Village | 1,778 | 0 | 0 | 0 | 0 | 0 | 22 | 3 | 19 | 0 | 0 |
| Webster Town and Village | 42,179 | 8 | 0 | 0 | 4 | 4 | 579 | 87 | 476 | 16 | 1 |
| Weedsport Village | 1,904 | 1 | 0 | 0 | 0 | 1 | 24 | 1 | 23 | 0 | 0 |
| Wellsville Village | 4,868 | 37 | 0 | 0 | 0 | 37 | 125 | 32 | 93 | 0 | 1 |
| West Carthage Village | 2,175 | 5 | 0 | 3 | 0 | 2 | 7 | 1 | 6 | 0 | 0 |
| Westfield Village | 3,349 | 5 | 0 | 0 | 1 | 4 | 59 | 14 | 45 | 0 | 0 |
| Westhampton Beach Village | 2,023 | 3 | 0 | 0 | 0 | 3 | 45 | 3 | 39 | 3 | 0 |
| West Seneca Town | 43,574 | 53 | 0 | 4 | 22 | 27 | 901 | 129 | 731 | 41 | 0 |
| Whitehall Village | 2,557 | 2 | 0 | 0 | 2 | 0 | 44 | 13 | 30 | 1 | 1 |
| White Plains | 57,810 | 117 | 0 | 1 | 38 | 78 | 1,087 | 40 | 1,012 | 35 | 2 |
| Whitesboro Village | 3,742 | 10 | 0 | 0 | 0 | 10 | 51 | 11 | 38 | 2 | 0 |
| Whitestown Town | 9,219 | 2 | 0 | 0 | 1 | 1 | 97 | 11 | 85 | 1 | 0 |
| Windham Town | 1,911 | 0 | 0 | 0 | 0 | 0 | 56 | 13 | 41 | 2 | 0 |
| Wolcott Village | 1,585 | 0 | 0 | 0 | 0 | 0 | 1 | 0 | 1 | 0 | 0 |
| Woodbury Town | 10,301 | 6 | 0 | 1 | 3 | 2 | 434 | 16 | 408 | 10 | 0 |
| Woodstock Town | 6,139 | 3 | 0 | 0 | 0 | 3 | 87 | 24 | 59 | 4 | 0 |
| Yonkers | 202,192 | 965 | 8 | 36 | 475 | 446 | 3,145 | 620 | 2,182 | 343 | 35 |
| Yorktown Town | 37,955 | 27 | 0 | 3 | 5 | 19 | 450 | 43 | 404 | 3 | 0 |
| Yorkville Village | 2,548 | 5 | 0 | 0 | 1 | 4 | 58 | 8 | 48 | 2 | 0 |
| Youngstown Village | 1,855 | 0 | 0 | 0 | 0 | 0 | 9 | 3 | 6 | 0 | 0 |
| **NORTH CAROLINA** | | | | | | | | | | | |
| Aberdeen | 5,936 | 24 | 0 | 2 | 9 | 13 | 378 | 88 | 268 | 22 | 1 |
| Ahoskie | 4,232 | 42 | 2 | 4 | 13 | 23 | 322 | 114 | 199 | 9 | 3 |
| Albemarle | 15,471 | 99 | 4 | 6 | 26 | 63 | 1,022 | 253 | 691 | 78 | 8 |
| Andrews | 1,700 | 10 | 0 | 3 | 2 | 5 | 49 | 11 | 36 | 2 | 0 |
| Angier | 4,467 | 22 | 0 | 0 | 2 | 20 | 186 | 72 | 101 | 13 | 0 |
| Apex | 34,766 | 50 | 0 | 3 | 7 | 40 | 398 | 87 | 293 | 18 | 3 |
| Archdale | 9,358 | 17 | 0 | 0 | 9 | 8 | 311 | 86 | 199 | 26 | 4 |
| Asheboro | 24,891 | 90 | 0 | 13 | 43 | 34 | 1,608 | 372 | 1,163 | 73 | 1 |
| Asheville | 74,923 | 415 | 2 | 24 | 178 | 211 | 3,701 | 821 | 2,576 | 304 | 25 |
| Atlantic Beach | 1,817 | 24 | 1 | 2 | 0 | 21 | 193 | 54 | 132 | 7 | 1 |
| Aulander | 835 | 1 | 0 | 0 | 0 | 1 | 17 | 9 | 7 | 1 | 0 |
| Ayden | 5,041 | 22 | 0 | 1 | 9 | 12 | 253 | 71 | 180 | 2 | 0 |
| Bailey | 685 | 2 | 0 | 0 | 0 | 2 | 23 | 7 | 14 | 2 | 0 |
| Banner Elk | 905 | 1 | 1 | 0 | 0 | 0 | 25 | 12 | 12 | 1 | 0 |
| Beaufort | 4,236 | 13 | 0 | 3 | 3 | 7 | 196 | 44 | 147 | 5 | 0 |
| Beech Mountain | 341 | 0 | 0 | 0 | 0 | 0 | 36 | 9 | 25 | 2 | 0 |
| Belhaven | 2,043 | 13 | 0 | 0 | 3 | 10 | 64 | 19 | 44 | 1 | 0 |
| Belmont | 9,433 | 34 | 0 | 1 | 6 | 27 | 442 | 53 | 371 | 18 | 4 |
| Benson | 3,554 | 36 | 0 | 1 | 14 | 21 | 228 | 91 | 113 | 24 | 1 |
| Bethel | 1,741 | 8 | 0 | 0 | 2 | 6 | 50 | 1 | 46 | 3 | 1 |
| Beulaville | 1,147 | 3 | 0 | 1 | 1 | 1 | 39 | 6 | 31 | 2 | 0 |
| Biltmore Forest | 1,573 | 1 | 0 | 0 | 0 | 1 | 21 | 4 | 17 | 0 | 0 |
| Biscoe | 1,671 | 5 | 1 | 0 | 3 | 1 | 153 | 11 | 136 | 6 | 0 |
| Black Mountain | 7,915 | 11 | 0 | 1 | 5 | 5 | 170 | 84 | 79 | 7 | 0 |
| Bladenboro | 1,668 | 5 | 0 | 0 | 2 | 3 | 132 | 29 | 99 | 4 | 1 |
| Blowing Rock | 1,497 | 0 | 0 | 0 | 0 | 0 | 74 | 22 | 51 | 1 | 0 |
| Boiling Spring Lakes | 4,920 | 7 | 0 | 1 | 0 | 6 | 83 | 24 | 53 | 6 | 1 |
| Boiling Springs | 3,883 | 6 | 0 | 0 | 0 | 6 | 72 | 14 | 56 | 2 | 0 |
| Boone | 13,995 | 32 | 0 | 4 | 6 | 22 | 553 | 93 | 441 | 19 | 1 |
| Brevard | 6,708 | 25 | 1 | 3 | 1 | 20 | 208 | 65 | 136 | 7 | 2 |
| Broadway | 1,167 | 9 | 0 | 0 | 6 | 3 | 35 | 10 | 23 | 2 | 1 |
| Bryson City | 1,370 | 33 | 0 | 2 | 0 | 31 | 126 | 1 | 118 | 7 | 1 |

[1] The FBI does not publish arson data unless it receives data from either the agency or the state for all 12 months of the calendar year.

**Table 8. Offenses Known to Law Enforcement, by State and City, 2009**—*Continued*

(Number.)

| State/city | Population | Violent crime | Murder and non-negligent man-slaughter | Forcible rape | Robbery | Aggravated assault | Property crime | Burglary | Larceny-theft | Motor vehicle theft | Arson[1] |
|---|---|---|---|---|---|---|---|---|---|---|---|
| **NORTH CAROLINA**—*Continued* | | | | | | | | | | | |
| Bunn | 415 | 4 | 0 | 0 | 2 | 2 | 28 | 6 | 22 | 0 | 0 |
| Burgaw | 4,377 | 11 | 0 | 0 | 1 | 10 | 114 | 30 | 80 | 4 | 1 |
| Burlington | 51,440 | 401 | 1 | 26 | 115 | 259 | 3,364 | 794 | 2,425 | 145 | 9 |
| Burnsville | 1,639 | 12 | 0 | 1 | 0 | 11 | 91 | 15 | 75 | 1 | 0 |
| Candor | 839 | 1 | 0 | 0 | 1 | 0 | 20 | 6 | 14 | 0 | 0 |
| Canton | 3,852 | 17 | 0 | 0 | 1 | 16 | 221 | 57 | 151 | 13 | 2 |
| Cape Carteret | 1,407 | 2 | 0 | 0 | 0 | 2 | 31 | 8 | 19 | 4 | 1 |
| Carolina Beach | 5,955 | 22 | 0 | 0 | 4 | 18 | 374 | 70 | 289 | 15 | 1 |
| Carrboro | 18,213 | 64 | 0 | 3 | 18 | 43 | 731 | 229 | 480 | 22 | 4 |
| Carthage | 2,039 | 3 | 0 | 0 | 3 | 0 | 72 | 20 | 45 | 7 | 1 |
| Cary | 133,757 | 132 | 0 | 12 | 48 | 72 | 2,005 | 469 | 1,454 | 82 | 10 |
| Catawba | 817 | 1 | 0 | 0 | 0 | 1 | 16 | 2 | 14 | 0 | 0 |
| Chadbourn | 2,053 | 17 | 1 | 0 | 7 | 9 | 213 | 87 | 116 | 10 | 4 |
| Chapel Hill | 53,069 | 130 | 0 | 14 | 48 | 68 | 1,727 | 427 | 1,225 | 75 | 1 |
| Charlotte-Mecklenburg | 777,708 | 5,625 | 58 | 303 | 2,346 | 2,918 | 38,533 | 9,817 | 25,379 | 3,337 | 249 |
| Cherryville | 5,651 | 26 | 0 | 0 | 2 | 24 | 255 | 54 | 195 | 6 | 2 |
| China Grove | 3,755 | 13 | 0 | 1 | 7 | 5 | 104 | 20 | 82 | 2 | 0 |
| Claremont | 1,153 | 6 | 0 | 1 | 1 | 4 | 68 | 19 | 45 | 4 | 0 |
| Clayton | 16,952 | 40 | 0 | 1 | 16 | 23 | 371 | 101 | 257 | 13 | 8 |
| Cleveland | 841 | 3 | 0 | 0 | 0 | 3 | 45 | 19 | 24 | 2 | 0 |
| Clinton | 8,896 | 67 | 1 | 4 | 23 | 39 | 474 | 138 | 315 | 21 | 1 |
| Coats | 2,166 | 9 | 1 | 1 | 1 | 6 | 85 | 29 | 51 | 5 | 1 |
| Columbus | 973 | 8 | 0 | 1 | 3 | 4 | 58 | 14 | 42 | 2 | 0 |
| Concord | 67,478 | 190 | 6 | 16 | 69 | 99 | 3,270 | 527 | 2,517 | 226 | 6 |
| Conover | 7,348 | 19 | 0 | 1 | 5 | 13 | 486 | 86 | 378 | 22 | 0 |
| Cornelius[3] | 26,027 | 47 | 2 | 4 | 14 | 27 | | 109 | | 29 | 2 |
| Cramerton | 3,162 | 8 | 0 | 0 | 0 | 8 | 89 | 29 | 57 | 3 | 0 |
| Creedmoor | 3,859 | 13 | 0 | 1 | 1 | 11 | 121 | 27 | 93 | 1 | 0 |
| Dallas | 3,813 | 29 | 0 | 2 | 3 | 24 | 161 | 44 | 109 | 8 | 1 |
| Davidson | 10,716 | 14 | 0 | 1 | 2 | 11 | 134 | 27 | 97 | 10 | 0 |
| Dobson | 1,457 | 3 | 0 | 0 | 0 | 3 | 61 | 17 | 43 | 1 | 0 |
| Duck | 497 | 4 | 0 | 1 | 0 | 3 | 116 | 48 | 66 | 2 | 0 |
| Dunn | 10,115 | 90 | 1 | 4 | 23 | 62 | 753 | 162 | 537 | 54 | 4 |
| Durham | 227,492 | 1,591 | 21 | 63 | 710 | 797 | 11,763 | 3,643 | 7,366 | 754 | 32 |
| East Spencer | 1,795 | 9 | 0 | 0 | 5 | 4 | 43 | 15 | 21 | 7 | 0 |
| Eden | 15,426 | 88 | 1 | 5 | 27 | 55 | 721 | 205 | 482 | 34 | 1 |
| Edenton | 4,964 | 37 | 0 | 0 | 12 | 25 | 172 | 53 | 110 | 9 | 0 |
| Elizabeth City | 20,363 | 129 | 0 | 9 | 34 | 86 | 787 | 196 | 562 | 29 | 2 |
| Elkin | 4,104 | 24 | 0 | 4 | 0 | 20 | 246 | 47 | 189 | 10 | 1 |
| Elon | 7,092 | 9 | 0 | 4 | 1 | 4 | 111 | 35 | 74 | 2 | 2 |
| Emerald Isle | 3,659 | 10 | 0 | 1 | 0 | 9 | 241 | 106 | 133 | 2 | 1 |
| Enfield | 2,337 | 46 | 2 | 2 | 7 | 35 | 147 | 73 | 70 | 4 | 0 |
| Erwin | 4,866 | 17 | 0 | 0 | 2 | 15 | 176 | 40 | 129 | 7 | 3 |
| Fairmont[2] | 2,734 | 23 | 1 | 1 | 12 | 9 | | 54 | | 7 | 0 |
| Farmville | 4,637 | 35 | 0 | 1 | 8 | 26 | 219 | 68 | 138 | 13 | 0 |
| Fayetteville | 173,995 | 1,268 | 21 | 94 | 491 | 662 | 13,506 | 4,289 | 8,455 | 762 | 40 |
| Fletcher | 4,770 | 7 | 0 | 0 | 2 | 5 | 141 | 31 | 108 | 2 | 1 |
| Forest City | 7,117 | 35 | 0 | 4 | 10 | 21 | 576 | 127 | 435 | 14 | 5 |
| Franklin | 3,982 | 15 | 0 | 1 | 0 | 14 | 185 | 55 | 123 | 7 | 1 |
| Franklinton | 2,013 | 12 | 0 | 0 | 4 | 8 | 77 | 18 | 56 | 3 | 0 |
| Fuquay-Varina | 18,457 | 70 | 1 | 3 | 15 | 51 | 598 | 147 | 419 | 32 | 0 |
| Garner | 28,268 | 62 | 0 | 1 | 33 | 28 | 1,088 | 204 | 842 | 42 | 3 |
| Garysburg | 1,121 | 8 | 0 | 0 | 1 | 7 | 34 | 19 | 15 | 0 | 0 |
| Gastonia | 73,060 | 600 | 5 | 30 | 220 | 345 | 4,581 | 1,059 | 3,187 | 335 | 39 |
| Gibsonville | 4,757 | 9 | 0 | 0 | 3 | 6 | 124 | 45 | 73 | 6 | 3 |
| Goldsboro | 37,421 | 323 | 8 | 9 | 92 | 214 | 2,657 | 730 | 1,789 | 138 | 3 |
| Graham | 14,684 | 86 | 0 | 6 | 22 | 58 | 670 | 213 | 437 | 20 | 1 |
| Granite Falls | 4,606 | 8 | 1 | 0 | 5 | 2 | 252 | 37 | 206 | 9 | 0 |
| Granite Quarry | 2,278 | 5 | 0 | 0 | 1 | 4 | 82 | 30 | 45 | 7 | 0 |
| Greensboro | 253,191 | 1,940 | 24 | 76 | 908 | 932 | 15,303 | 4,789 | 9,668 | 846 | 108 |
| Grifton | 2,238 | 9 | 2 | 1 | 1 | 5 | 61 | 7 | 51 | 3 | 0 |
| Hamlet | 5,764 | 46 | 0 | 2 | 21 | 23 | 472 | 202 | 252 | 18 | 6 |
| Henderson | 15,795 | 177 | 2 | 1 | 79 | 95 | 1,533 | 515 | 965 | 53 | 9 |
| Hendersonville | 12,077 | 64 | 0 | 6 | 13 | 45 | 733 | 95 | 580 | 58 | 2 |
| Hertford | 2,198 | 12 | 1 | 1 | 2 | 8 | 112 | 40 | 67 | 5 | 0 |
| Hickory | 41,718 | 338 | 5 | 14 | 118 | 201 | 2,833 | 670 | 2,020 | 143 | 21 |
| Highlands | 955 | 6 | 0 | 2 | 0 | 4 | 47 | 13 | 34 | 0 | 0 |
| High Point | 103,675 | 678 | 3 | 33 | 273 | 369 | 5,326 | 1,463 | 3,619 | 244 | 32 |
| Hillsborough | 5,669 | 33 | 0 | 5 | 14 | 14 | 434 | 117 | 302 | 15 | 1 |
| Holden Beach | 857 | 0 | 0 | 0 | 0 | 0 | 68 | 24 | 43 | 1 | 0 |
| Holly Ridge | 917 | 10 | 0 | 1 | 0 | 9 | 57 | 20 | 36 | 1 | 0 |

[1] The FBI does not publish arson data unless it receives data from either the agency or the state for all 12 months of the calendar year.
[2] The FBI determined that the agency's data were underreported. Consequently, those data are not included in this table.
[3] The FBI determined that the agency's data were overreported. Consequently, those data are not included in this table.

## Table 8. Offenses Known to Law Enforcement, by State and City, 2009—*Continued*

(Number.)

| State/city | Population | Violent crime | Murder and non-negligent man-slaughter | Forcible rape | Robbery | Aggravated assault | Property crime | Burglary | Larceny-theft | Motor vehicle theft | Arson[1] |
|---|---|---|---|---|---|---|---|---|---|---|---|
| **NORTH CAROLINA**—*Continued* | | | | | | | | | | | |
| Holly Springs | 22,639 | 13 | 0 | 0 | 2 | 11 | 342 | 67 | 270 | 5 | 1 |
| Hudson | 3,042 | 6 | 0 | 0 | 2 | 4 | 119 | 23 | 89 | 7 | 0 |
| Huntersville | 46,695 | 68 | 0 | 4 | 19 | 45 | 1,000 | 156 | 806 | 38 | 6 |
| Jacksonville | 77,508 | 241 | 8 | 38 | 50 | 145 | 2,598 | 618 | 1,869 | 111 | 5 |
| Jefferson | 1,344 | 1 | 0 | 0 | 0 | 1 | 40 | 11 | 26 | 3 | 0 |
| Jonesville | 2,271 | 10 | 0 | 3 | 0 | 7 | 128 | 27 | 97 | 4 | 0 |
| Kannapolis | 43,166 | 135 | 5 | 12 | 48 | 70 | 1,160 | 360 | 709 | 91 | 10 |
| Kenansville | 1,186 | 1 | 0 | 0 | 0 | 1 | 29 | 5 | 23 | 1 | 1 |
| Kernersville | 22,822 | 92 | 0 | 7 | 19 | 66 | 1,184 | 216 | 919 | 49 | 2 |
| Kill Devil Hills | 6,726 | 54 | 0 | 1 | 6 | 47 | 566 | 146 | 407 | 13 | 1 |
| King | 7,011 | 16 | 0 | 2 | 2 | 12 | 204 | 49 | 146 | 9 | 1 |
| Kings Mountain | 11,275 | 35 | 0 | 2 | 17 | 16 | 394 | 96 | 292 | 6 | 3 |
| Kinston | 22,203 | 264 | 0 | 11 | 60 | 193 | 1,560 | 486 | 999 | 75 | 6 |
| Knightdale | 8,419 | 14 | 0 | 3 | 5 | 6 | 406 | 67 | 324 | 15 | 1 |
| Lake Lure | 1,010 | 0 | 0 | 0 | 0 | 0 | 47 | 20 | 26 | 1 | 0 |
| Lake Royale | 0 | 1 | 0 | 0 | 0 | 1 | 84 | 35 | 43 | 6 | 0 |
| Landis | 3,133 | 6 | 0 | 1 | 3 | 2 | 71 | 18 | 50 | 3 | 0 |
| Laurel Park | 2,178 | 0 | 0 | 0 | 0 | 0 | 17 | 3 | 14 | 0 | 0 |
| Laurinburg | 15,506 | 120 | 5 | 8 | 34 | 73 | 1,026 | 354 | 626 | 46 | 9 |
| Leland | 5,216 | 21 | 0 | 2 | 5 | 14 | 256 | 94 | 157 | 5 | 0 |
| Lenoir | 17,869 | 70 | 2 | 2 | 22 | 44 | 907 | 225 | 626 | 56 | 4 |
| Lexington | 20,450 | 110 | 0 | 2 | 40 | 68 | 787 | 235 | 508 | 44 | 3 |
| Liberty | 2,739 | 6 | 0 | 0 | 2 | 4 | 27 | 9 | 18 | 0 | 0 |
| Lillington | 3,327 | 9 | 0 | 1 | 2 | 6 | 135 | 32 | 97 | 6 | 2 |
| Lincolnton | 10,944 | 45 | 0 | 0 | 11 | 34 | 655 | 164 | 478 | 13 | 4 |
| Long View | 4,967 | 25 | 0 | 3 | 7 | 15 | 310 | 161 | 122 | 27 | 1 |
| Louisburg | 3,856 | 15 | 0 | 0 | 5 | 10 | 170 | 44 | 114 | 12 | 1 |
| Lumberton | 22,111 | 382 | 8 | 8 | 151 | 215 | 2,940 | 770 | 2,002 | 168 | 11 |
| Madison | 2,255 | 68 | 0 | 0 | 1 | 67 | 184 | 40 | 144 | 0 | 0 |
| Maggie Valley | 814 | 3 | 0 | 0 | 1 | 2 | 111 | 12 | 97 | 2 | 0 |
| Maiden | 3,523 | 6 | 0 | 1 | 3 | 2 | 122 | 49 | 68 | 5 | 0 |
| Manteo | 1,331 | 2 | 0 | 0 | 0 | 2 | 84 | 9 | 74 | 1 | 0 |
| Marion | 5,168 | 32 | 0 | 1 | 8 | 23 | 455 | 131 | 300 | 24 | 8 |
| Marshville | 3,317 | 14 | 1 | 1 | 4 | 8 | 96 | 29 | 60 | 7 | 0 |
| Matthews | 27,359 | 61 | 0 | 1 | 31 | 29 | 1,044 | 147 | 835 | 62 | 6 |
| Maxton | 2,699 | 56 | 1 | 0 | 23 | 32 | 153 | 79 | 70 | 4 | 1 |
| Mayodan | 2,595 | 22 | 0 | 0 | 1 | 21 | 157 | 16 | 138 | 3 | 0 |
| Maysville | 955 | 2 | 0 | 0 | 1 | 1 | 11 | 4 | 6 | 1 | 0 |
| McAdenville | 669 | 2 | 0 | 0 | 1 | 1 | 20 | 7 | 11 | 2 | 0 |
| Middlesex | 860 | 1 | 0 | 0 | 0 | 1 | 27 | 7 | 18 | 2 | 0 |
| Mint Hill | 20,740 | 43 | 0 | 4 | 19 | 20 | 495 | 309 | 154 | 32 | 6 |
| Mocksville | 4,686 | 25 | 0 | 1 | 7 | 17 | 264 | 54 | 199 | 11 | 3 |
| Mooresville | 22,247 | 99 | 1 | 8 | 35 | 55 | 1,414 | 246 | 1,111 | 57 | 8 |
| Morehead City | 9,715 | 50 | 0 | 3 | 8 | 39 | 606 | 105 | 492 | 9 | 2 |
| Morganton | 17,169 | 47 | 0 | 3 | 13 | 31 | 533 | 135 | 378 | 20 | 2 |
| Morrisville | 15,207 | 4 | 0 | 0 | 3 | 1 | 376 | 63 | 299 | 14 | 2 |
| Mount Airy | 9,487 | 59 | 5 | 3 | 11 | 40 | 542 | 114 | 392 | 36 | 2 |
| Mount Gilead | 1,396 | 8 | 0 | 0 | 2 | 6 | 51 | 12 | 37 | 2 | 0 |
| Mount Holly | 10,130 | 45 | 0 | 5 | 8 | 32 | 336 | 100 | 211 | 25 | 0 |
| Mount Olive | 4,371 | 34 | 3 | 0 | 8 | 23 | 301 | 71 | 223 | 7 | 0 |
| Murfreesboro | 2,372 | 8 | 1 | 0 | 2 | 5 | 100 | 10 | 86 | 4 | 0 |
| Murphy | 1,558 | 19 | 0 | 0 | 0 | 19 | 145 | 13 | 130 | 2 | 0 |
| Nags Head | 3,051 | 9 | 0 | 1 | 1 | 7 | 357 | 163 | 191 | 3 | 1 |
| Newland | 650 | 0 | 0 | 0 | 0 | 0 | 18 | 5 | 13 | 0 | 0 |
| Newport | 4,419 | 7 | 0 | 0 | 1 | 6 | 89 | 39 | 48 | 2 | 0 |
| Newton | 13,449 | 29 | 0 | 1 | 17 | 11 | 616 | 196 | 383 | 37 | 1 |
| North Topsail Beach | 969 | 1 | 0 | 1 | 0 | 0 | 11 | 7 | 3 | 1 | 0 |
| North Wilkesboro | 4,158 | 15 | 0 | 3 | 3 | 9 | 210 | 56 | 146 | 8 | 1 |
| Norwood | 2,403 | 4 | 0 | 0 | 1 | 3 | 95 | 38 | 53 | 4 | 4 |
| Oak Island | 8,375 | 31 | 0 | 3 | 4 | 24 | 284 | 80 | 196 | 8 | 1 |
| Ocean Isle Beach | 539 | 1 | 0 | 0 | 1 | 0 | 113 | 68 | 39 | 6 | 0 |
| Oxford | 8,667 | 120 | 1 | 5 | 19 | 95 | 612 | 212 | 384 | 16 | 3 |
| Pembroke | 2,763 | 29 | 0 | 0 | 12 | 17 | 273 | 124 | 142 | 7 | 5 |
| Pilot Mountain | 1,271 | 7 | 0 | 2 | 1 | 4 | 160 | 45 | 110 | 5 | 0 |
| Pinebluff | 1,422 | 1 | 0 | 0 | 0 | 1 | 29 | 21 | 8 | 0 | 0 |
| Pinehurst | 12,649 | 1 | 0 | 0 | 0 | 1 | 104 | 5 | 96 | 3 | 1 |
| Pine Knoll Shores | 1,550 | 0 | 0 | 0 | 0 | 0 | 39 | 9 | 30 | 0 | 0 |
| Pinetops | 1,251 | 7 | 0 | 0 | 2 | 5 | 67 | 24 | 42 | 1 | 0 |
| Pineville | 6,878 | 70 | 0 | 4 | 36 | 30 | 1,081 | 122 | 904 | 55 | 7 |
| Pittsboro | 2,664 | 10 | 0 | 1 | 1 | 8 | 99 | 24 | 68 | 7 | 1 |
| Plymouth | 3,834 | 77 | 0 | 0 | 13 | 64 | 245 | 79 | 163 | 3 | 2 |

[1] The FBI does not publish arson data unless it receives data from either the agency or the state for all 12 months of the calendar year.

**Table 8. Offenses Known to Law Enforcement, by State and City, 2009**—*Continued*

(Number.)

| State/city | Population | Violent crime | Murder and non-negligent man-slaughter | Forcible rape | Robbery | Aggravated assault | Property crime | Burglary | Larceny-theft | Motor vehicle theft | Arson[1] |
|---|---|---|---|---|---|---|---|---|---|---|---|
| **NORTH CAROLINA**—*Continued* | | | | | | | | | | | |
| Raeford | 3,534 | 28 | 0 | 0 | 12 | 16 | 255 | 72 | 171 | 12 | 3 |
| Raleigh | 406,005 | 2,001 | 14 | 99 | 832 | 1,056 | 13,817 | 3,187 | 9,834 | 796 | 66 |
| Ramseur | 1,769 | 5 | 0 | 0 | 0 | 5 | 91 | 50 | 41 | 0 | 0 |
| Randleman | 3,696 | 12 | 0 | 1 | 1 | 10 | 350 | 69 | 274 | 7 | 0 |
| Red Springs | 3,530 | 48 | 1 | 3 | 17 | 27 | 356 | 148 | 188 | 20 | 4 |
| Reidsville | 14,899 | 78 | 0 | 8 | 16 | 54 | 916 | 242 | 639 | 35 | 14 |
| Richlands | 934 | 3 | 0 | 0 | 1 | 2 | 35 | 9 | 25 | 1 | 0 |
| Roanoke Rapids | 16,339 | 84 | 5 | 7 | 27 | 45 | 973 | 284 | 639 | 50 | 2 |
| Robbins | 1,228 | 3 | 1 | 2 | 0 | 0 | 26 | 9 | 17 | 0 | 2 |
| Robersonville | 1,535 | 19 | 2 | 1 | 6 | 10 | 78 | 30 | 43 | 5 | 0 |
| Rockingham | 8,810 | 61 | 1 | 4 | 29 | 27 | 966 | 187 | 760 | 19 | 4 |
| Rockwell | 2,017 | 3 | 0 | 0 | 0 | 3 | 72 | 17 | 51 | 4 | 0 |
| Rocky Mount | 57,121 | 731 | 7 | 30 | 267 | 427 | 4,234 | 1,345 | 2,704 | 185 | 36 |
| Rolesville | 3,220 | 6 | 1 | 1 | 1 | 3 | 84 | 19 | 60 | 5 | 0 |
| Rowland | 1,160 | 6 | 0 | 0 | 5 | 1 | 52 | 22 | 24 | 6 | 1 |
| Roxboro | 8,663 | 85 | 0 | 3 | 17 | 65 | 535 | 165 | 353 | 17 | 1 |
| Rutherfordton | 4,031 | 9 | 0 | 1 | 6 | 2 | 114 | 17 | 90 | 7 | 1 |
| Salisbury | 29,008 | 267 | 5 | 12 | 112 | 138 | 1,954 | 416 | 1,433 | 105 | 12 |
| Sanford | 30,020 | 112 | 6 | 3 | 46 | 57 | 1,128 | 320 | 758 | 50 | 5 |
| Scotland Neck | 2,150 | 37 | 0 | 1 | 8 | 28 | 139 | 57 | 77 | 5 | 1 |
| Selma | 7,049 | 51 | 0 | 3 | 9 | 39 | 494 | 235 | 223 | 36 | 1 |
| Shallotte | 2,218 | 13 | 0 | 2 | 6 | 5 | 237 | 79 | 152 | 6 | 1 |
| Sharpsburg | 2,403 | 12 | 1 | 0 | 5 | 6 | 76 | 39 | 35 | 2 | 0 |
| Shelby | 21,515 | 141 | 3 | 8 | 41 | 89 | 1,078 | 339 | 717 | 22 | 6 |
| Siler City | 8,744 | 31 | 0 | 1 | 13 | 17 | 343 | 77 | 251 | 15 | 2 |
| Smithfield | 13,199 | 94 | 0 | 7 | 23 | 64 | 1,012 | 280 | 690 | 42 | 0 |
| Southern Pines | 12,865 | 85 | 3 | 4 | 24 | 54 | 684 | 179 | 481 | 24 | 9 |
| Southern Shores | 2,631 | 1 | 0 | 0 | 0 | 1 | 97 | 52 | 43 | 2 | 0 |
| Southport | 3,165 | 12 | 1 | 1 | 5 | 5 | 140 | 27 | 107 | 6 | 1 |
| Sparta | 1,770 | 4 | 0 | 0 | 0 | 4 | 51 | 6 | 42 | 3 | 1 |
| Spencer | 3,394 | 26 | 0 | 1 | 8 | 17 | 209 | 107 | 100 | 2 | 3 |
| Spring Hope | 1,291 | 4 | 0 | 0 | 1 | 3 | 47 | 11 | 34 | 2 | 0 |
| Stallings | 9,186 | 16 | 1 | 3 | 4 | 8 | 290 | 59 | 220 | 11 | 4 |
| Stanley | 3,201 | 6 | 0 | 0 | 2 | 4 | 111 | 30 | 80 | 1 | 0 |
| Star | 791 | 5 | 0 | 1 | 0 | 4 | 20 | 4 | 13 | 3 | 0 |
| Statesville | 26,763 | 266 | 0 | 15 | 78 | 173 | 1,246 | 456 | 739 | 51 | 12 |
| Stoneville | 971 | 6 | 0 | 0 | 1 | 5 | 42 | 16 | 25 | 1 | 0 |
| St. Pauls | 2,044 | 8 | 0 | 0 | 1 | 7 | 107 | 32 | 73 | 2 | 1 |
| Sunset Beach | 2,663 | 3 | 0 | 1 | 1 | 1 | 102 | 69 | 33 | 0 | 0 |
| Surf City | 2,132 | 10 | 0 | 0 | 1 | 9 | 139 | 63 | 75 | 1 | 0 |
| Swansboro | 1,988 | 3 | 0 | 0 | 1 | 2 | 87 | 16 | 66 | 5 | 1 |
| Sylva | 2,437 | 35 | 0 | 0 | 7 | 28 | 238 | 45 | 181 | 12 | 0 |
| Tabor City | 2,764 | 32 | 1 | 1 | 6 | 24 | 248 | 17 | 223 | 8 | 3 |
| Tarboro | 10,155 | 67 | 0 | 2 | 16 | 49 | 400 | 108 | 273 | 19 | 3 |
| Taylorsville | 1,858 | 8 | 1 | 1 | 3 | 3 | 184 | 34 | 143 | 7 | 1 |
| Thomasville | 26,759 | 150 | 0 | 6 | 43 | 101 | 1,266 | 321 | 907 | 38 | 5 |
| Trent Woods | 3,960 | 1 | 0 | 0 | 0 | 1 | 42 | 8 | 34 | 0 | 0 |
| Troutman | 1,841 | 4 | 0 | 2 | 1 | 1 | 86 | 19 | 65 | 2 | 0 |
| Troy | 3,403 | 14 | 0 | 3 | 3 | 8 | 156 | 31 | 118 | 7 | 2 |
| Tryon | 1,702 | 1 | 0 | 0 | 0 | 1 | 56 | 37 | 16 | 3 | 0 |
| Valdese | 4,542 | 0 | 0 | 0 | 0 | 0 | 72 | 26 | 42 | 4 | 0 |
| Vass | 803 | 0 | 0 | 0 | 0 | 0 | 33 | 5 | 27 | 1 | 0 |
| Wake Forest | 29,368 | 34 | 1 | 0 | 10 | 23 | 728 | 108 | 609 | 11 | 1 |
| Wallace | 3,619 | 18 | 2 | 2 | 10 | 4 | 135 | 42 | 84 | 9 | 4 |
| Walnut Cove | 1,611 | 2 | 0 | 0 | 0 | 2 | 25 | 3 | 18 | 4 | 0 |
| Warsaw | 3,192 | 6 | 0 | 0 | 1 | 5 | 180 | 44 | 130 | 6 | 0 |
| Washington | 10,157 | 76 | 0 | 3 | 16 | 57 | 613 | 130 | 470 | 13 | 2 |
| Waynesville | 9,915 | 27 | 0 | 5 | 6 | 16 | 317 | 113 | 192 | 12 | 1 |
| Weaverville | 3,102 | 5 | 0 | 1 | 0 | 4 | 93 | 3 | 88 | 2 | 0 |
| Weldon[2] | 1,656 | 10 | 0 | 0 | 8 | 2 | | 12 | | 0 | 0 |
| Wendell | 5,414 | 12 | 0 | 1 | 3 | 8 | 136 | 40 | 90 | 6 | 0 |
| West Jefferson | 1,118 | 1 | 0 | 0 | 0 | 1 | 56 | 8 | 44 | 4 | 0 |
| Whispering Pines | 2,157 | 0 | 0 | 0 | 0 | 0 | 23 | 9 | 14 | 0 | 0 |
| Whitakers | 770 | 5 | 0 | 0 | 0 | 5 | 32 | 17 | 14 | 1 | 0 |
| White Lake | 515 | 4 | 0 | 0 | 0 | 4 | 85 | 15 | 69 | 1 | 0 |
| Whiteville | 5,242 | 63 | 1 | 1 | 15 | 46 | 533 | 107 | 385 | 41 | 2 |
| Wilkesboro | 3,134 | 18 | 0 | 1 | 7 | 10 | 385 | 77 | 299 | 9 | 1 |
| Williamston | 5,323 | 60 | 1 | 1 | 15 | 43 | 376 | 117 | 239 | 20 | 2 |
| Wilmington | 101,438 | 814 | 4 | 50 | 306 | 454 | 6,236 | 1,626 | 4,119 | 491 | 25 |
| Wilson | 48,807 | 227 | 1 | 6 | 71 | 149 | 2,143 | 637 | 1,425 | 81 | 8 |
| Wilson's Mills | 1,634 | 10 | 0 | 0 | 0 | 10 | 58 | 37 | 17 | 4 | 0 |

[1] The FBI does not publish arson data unless it receives data from either the agency or the state for all 12 months of the calendar year.
[2] The FBI determined that the agency's data were underreported. Consequently, those data are not included in this table.

## Table 8. Offenses Known to Law Enforcement, by State and City, 2009—*Continued*

(Number.)

| State/city | Population | Violent crime | Murder and non-negligent man-slaughter | Forcible rape | Robbery | Aggravated assault | Property crime | Burglary | Larceny-theft | Motor vehicle theft | Arson[1] |
|---|---|---|---|---|---|---|---|---|---|---|---|
| **NORTH CAROLINA**—*Continued* | | | | | | | | | | | |
| Windsor | 3,093 | 7 | 0 | 0 | 2 | 5 | 47 | 18 | 27 | 2 | 0 |
| Wingate | 4,097 | 3 | 0 | 0 | 2 | 1 | 96 | 40 | 52 | 4 | 0 |
| Winston-Salem | 230,978 | 1,739 | 15 | 110 | 575 | 1,039 | 13,788 | 4,532 | 8,429 | 827 | 88 |
| Winterville | 4,812 | 33 | 0 | 1 | 7 | 25 | 194 | 52 | 128 | 14 | 2 |
| Wrightsville Beach | 2,654 | 21 | 0 | 6 | 2 | 13 | 243 | 48 | 191 | 4 | 0 |
| Yadkinville | 2,865 | 11 | 0 | 0 | 1 | 10 | 153 | 29 | 120 | 4 | 0 |
| Youngsville | 786 | 1 | 0 | 0 | 1 | 0 | 47 | 12 | 35 | 0 | 0 |
| **NORTH DAKOTA** | | | | | | | | | | | |
| Beulah | 2,834 | 6 | 0 | 4 | 0 | 2 | 44 | 6 | 37 | 1 | 0 |
| Bismarck | 60,923 | 157 | 2 | 17 | 12 | 126 | 1,583 | 204 | 1,277 | 102 | 4 |
| Cando | 989 | 0 | 0 | 0 | 0 | 0 | 10 | 1 | 9 | 0 | 0 |
| Carrington | 2,052 | 0 | 0 | 0 | 0 | 0 | 4 | 0 | 3 | 1 | 0 |
| Cavalier | 1,301 | 0 | 0 | 0 | 0 | 0 | 30 | 10 | 17 | 3 | 0 |
| Devils Lake | 6,654 | 29 | 0 | 1 | 0 | 28 | 296 | 39 | 243 | 14 | 1 |
| Dickinson | 16,043 | 30 | 2 | 0 | 2 | 26 | 301 | 34 | 252 | 15 | 0 |
| Elgin | 532 | 0 | 0 | 0 | 0 | 0 | 3 | 0 | 2 | 1 | 0 |
| Ellendale | 1,446 | 1 | 0 | 0 | 0 | 1 | 15 | 11 | 4 | 0 | 1 |
| Emerado | 473 | 2 | 0 | 0 | 0 | 2 | 4 | 1 | 3 | 0 | 0 |
| Fargo | 93,830 | 303 | 2 | 54 | 34 | 213 | 3,187 | 639 | 2,302 | 246 | 19 |
| Fessenden | 488 | 0 | 0 | 0 | 0 | 0 | 0 | 0 | 0 | 0 | 0 |
| Grafton | 3,924 | 4 | 0 | 2 | 1 | 1 | 114 | 24 | 82 | 8 | 0 |
| Grand Forks | 51,553 | 141 | 0 | 29 | 27 | 85 | 1,515 | 261 | 1,185 | 69 | 2 |
| Harvey | 1,583 | 4 | 0 | 2 | 0 | 2 | 34 | 4 | 29 | 1 | 0 |
| Hillsboro | 1,459 | 0 | 0 | 0 | 0 | 0 | 5 | 1 | 3 | 1 | 0 |
| Jamestown | 14,535 | 19 | 0 | 7 | 1 | 11 | 303 | 53 | 226 | 24 | 2 |
| Larimore | 1,300 | 3 | 0 | 0 | 0 | 3 | 20 | 7 | 13 | 0 | 0 |
| Lincoln | 2,875 | 2 | 0 | 0 | 0 | 2 | 22 | 7 | 11 | 4 | 0 |
| Lisbon | 2,170 | 2 | 0 | 0 | 1 | 1 | 34 | 20 | 12 | 2 | 0 |
| Mandan | 18,244 | 45 | 0 | 16 | 1 | 28 | 368 | 47 | 288 | 33 | 1 |
| Mayville | 1,751 | 0 | 0 | 0 | 0 | 0 | 8 | 3 | 3 | 2 | 0 |
| Minot | 35,293 | 108 | 0 | 13 | 5 | 90 | 643 | 102 | 489 | 52 | 10 |
| Northwood | 924 | 0 | 0 | 0 | 0 | 0 | 14 | 4 | 9 | 1 | 0 |
| Oakes | 1,740 | 1 | 0 | 0 | 0 | 1 | 4 | 0 | 3 | 1 | 0 |
| Rolla | 1,420 | 0 | 0 | 0 | 0 | 0 | 36 | 8 | 28 | 0 | 0 |
| Rugby | 2,538 | 5 | 0 | 2 | 1 | 2 | 42 | 8 | 31 | 3 | 0 |
| Steele | 639 | 2 | 0 | 1 | 0 | 1 | 5 | 1 | 3 | 1 | 0 |
| St. John | 354 | 0 | 0 | 0 | 0 | 0 | 2 | 1 | 1 | 0 | 0 |
| Thompson | 954 | 0 | 0 | 0 | 0 | 0 | 4 | 2 | 2 | 0 | 0 |
| Valley City | 6,172 | 4 | 0 | 1 | 0 | 3 | 56 | 14 | 38 | 4 | 0 |
| Wahpeton | 7,484 | 11 | 0 | 2 | 0 | 9 | 163 | 16 | 142 | 5 | 0 |
| Watford City | 1,382 | 0 | 0 | 0 | 0 | 0 | 2 | 1 | 1 | 0 | 0 |
| West Fargo | 24,862 | 63 | 0 | 12 | 5 | 46 | 548 | 180 | 339 | 29 | 5 |
| Williston | 12,662 | 36 | 0 | 15 | 4 | 17 | 330 | 36 | 268 | 26 | 3 |
| **OHIO** | | | | | | | | | | | |
| Aberdeen | 1,499 | 4 | 0 | 1 | 2 | 1 | 106 | 30 | 71 | 5 | 0 |
| Ada | 6,109 | 1 | 0 | 1 | 0 | 0 | 73 | 29 | 44 | 0 | 0 |
| Akron | 206,497 | 1,916 | 20 | 189 | 727 | 980 | 10,485 | 3,759 | 5,763 | 963 | 107 |
| Alliance | 22,402 | 75 | 1 | 19 | 26 | 29 | 869 | 194 | 649 | 26 | 16 |
| Amberley Village | 3,573 | 5 | 0 | 1 | 2 | 2 | 33 | 9 | 22 | 2 | 0 |
| Amelia | 3,648 | 0 | 0 | 0 | 0 | 0 | 100 | 16 | 84 | 0 | 0 |
| Amherst | 11,718 | 9 | 1 | 2 | 4 | 2 | 226 | 36 | 183 | 7 | 1 |
| Arcanum | 1,953 | 0 | 0 | 0 | 0 | 0 | 22 | 2 | 20 | 0 | 0 |
| Archbold | 4,450 | 7 | 0 | 2 | 0 | 5 | 94 | 17 | 76 | 1 | 0 |
| Ashland | 21,916 | 14 | 0 | 3 | 4 | 7 | 521 | 72 | 439 | 10 | 0 |
| Ashville | 3,300 | 4 | 0 | 0 | 2 | 2 | 103 | 14 | 86 | 3 | 0 |
| Athens | 22,173 | 33 | 0 | 2 | 4 | 27 | 458 | 76 | 374 | 8 | 3 |
| Aurora | 14,651 | 3 | 0 | 1 | 1 | 1 | 223 | 21 | 191 | 11 | 0 |
| Austintown | 34,821 | 17 | 0 | 0 | 16 | 1 | 1,420 | 253 | 1,107 | 60 | 0 |
| Bainbridge Township | 11,175 | 11 | 1 | 0 | 0 | 10 | 233 | 21 | 212 | 0 | 1 |
| Barberton | 26,436 | 70 | 1 | 14 | 26 | 29 | 1,217 | 230 | 947 | 40 | 21 |
| Barnesville | 4,024 | 2 | 0 | 2 | 0 | 0 | 9 | 2 | 7 | 0 | 0 |
| Batavia | 1,757 | 3 | 0 | 2 | 1 | 0 | 94 | 15 | 78 | 1 | 1 |
| Bath Township, Summit County | 10,247 | 3 | 0 | 1 | 2 | 0 | 179 | 35 | 141 | 3 | 0 |
| Bay Village | 14,454 | 4 | 0 | 1 | 0 | 3 | 14 | 4 | 10 | 0 | 0 |
| Beavercreek | 40,119 | 38 | 0 | 11 | 11 | 16 | 1,109 | 101 | 980 | 28 | 4 |
| Beaver Township | 6,045 | 0 | 0 | 0 | 0 | 0 | 186 | 69 | 113 | 4 | 0 |
| Bedford | 12,836 | 28 | 0 | 1 | 14 | 13 | 569 | 54 | 444 | 71 | 1 |
| Bedford Heights | 10,393 | 20 | 1 | 1 | 14 | 4 | 245 | 58 | 134 | 53 | 0 |
| Bellaire | 4,528 | 8 | 1 | 1 | 0 | 6 | 82 | 20 | 60 | 2 | 0 |
| Bellbrook | 7,000 | 3 | 0 | 1 | 1 | 1 | 65 | 11 | 54 | 0 | 0 |
| Bellefontaine | 12,622 | 39 | 1 | 6 | 8 | 24 | 720 | 76 | 636 | 8 | 0 |

[1] The FBI does not publish arson data unless it receives data from either the agency or the state for all 12 months of the calendar year.

## Table 8. Offenses Known to Law Enforcement, by State and City, 2009—*Continued*

(Number.)

| State/city | Population | Violent crime | Murder and non-negligent man-slaughter | Forcible rape | Robbery | Aggravated assault | Property crime | Burglary | Larceny-theft | Motor vehicle theft | Arson[1] |
|---|---|---|---|---|---|---|---|---|---|---|---|
| **OHIO**—*Continued* | | | | | | | | | | | |
| Bellville | 1,694 | 3 | 0 | 0 | 1 | 2 | 77 | 7 | 70 | 0 | 0 |
| Belpre | 6,515 | 15 | 0 | 4 | 3 | 8 | 118 | 24 | 89 | 5 | 0 |
| Berea | 17,883 | 17 | 0 | 1 | 4 | 12 | 363 | 50 | 306 | 7 | 2 |
| Bethesda | 1,350 | 0 | 0 | 0 | 0 | 0 | 10 | 7 | 2 | 1 | 0 |
| Bexley | 12,435 | 21 | 1 | 3 | 11 | 6 | 396 | 106 | 278 | 12 | 0 |
| Blanchester | 4,306 | 2 | 0 | 0 | 2 | 0 | 67 | 11 | 56 | 0 | 1 |
| Blue Ash | 12,812 | 13 | 0 | 4 | 8 | 1 | 322 | 37 | 279 | 6 | 1 |
| Bluffton | 3,949 | 5 | 0 | 1 | 0 | 4 | 52 | 18 | 31 | 3 | 0 |
| Boardman | 38,827 | 48 | 0 | 4 | 35 | 9 | 1,779 | 256 | 1,452 | 71 | 11 |
| Bowling Green | 29,536 | 41 | 0 | 1 | 9 | 31 | 735 | 99 | 621 | 15 | 0 |
| Brecksville | 12,792 | 9 | 3 | 3 | 2 | 1 | 55 | 14 | 41 | 0 | 0 |
| Bridgeport | 2,031 | 6 | 0 | 3 | 0 | 3 | 20 | 3 | 17 | 0 | 0 |
| Broadview Heights | 17,422 | 11 | 0 | 0 | 0 | 11 | 60 | 24 | 35 | 1 | 0 |
| Brookfield Township | 9,360 | 15 | 0 | 0 | 3 | 12 | 301 | 88 | 194 | 19 | 2 |
| Brooklyn | 10,290 | 35 | 1 | 1 | 17 | 16 | 503 | 60 | 398 | 45 | 3 |
| Brooklyn Heights | 1,443 | 1 | 0 | 0 | 0 | 1 | 32 | 8 | 22 | 2 | 0 |
| Brook Park | 18,987 | 20 | 0 | 5 | 4 | 11 | 176 | 31 | 139 | 6 | 0 |
| Brookville | 5,430 | 9 | 0 | 1 | 2 | 6 | 88 | 22 | 63 | 3 | 0 |
| Brunswick Hills Township | 7,486 | 3 | 0 | 0 | 0 | 3 | 64 | 14 | 49 | 1 | 0 |
| Buckeye Lake | 3,041 | 27 | 0 | 3 | 1 | 23 | 119 | 18 | 97 | 4 | 0 |
| Butler Township | 8,101 | 18 | 0 | 0 | 7 | 11 | 296 | 20 | 261 | 15 | 0 |
| Cadiz | 3,281 | 5 | 0 | 3 | 0 | 2 | 115 | 48 | 64 | 3 | 3 |
| Cambridge | 11,156 | 70 | 0 | 2 | 15 | 53 | 520 | 193 | 294 | 33 | 1 |
| Campbell | 8,333 | 23 | 0 | 4 | 12 | 7 | 276 | 158 | 97 | 21 | 0 |
| Canal Fulton | 5,016 | 2 | 0 | 0 | 0 | 2 | 117 | 20 | 97 | 0 | 1 |
| Canfield | 6,805 | 3 | 0 | 0 | 0 | 3 | 89 | 9 | 78 | 2 | 0 |
| Canton | 78,085 | 683 | 13 | 67 | 324 | 279 | 4,241 | 1,369 | 2,627 | 245 | 41 |
| Cardington | 2,008 | 1 | 0 | 0 | 0 | 1 | 32 | 15 | 16 | 1 | 0 |
| Carrollton | 3,209 | 14 | 0 | 1 | 0 | 13 | 3 | 2 | 0 | 1 | 0 |
| Celina | 10,242 | 20 | 0 | 8 | 4 | 8 | 427 | 46 | 372 | 9 | 11 |
| Centerville | 22,891 | 15 | 0 | 1 | 5 | 9 | 420 | 54 | 354 | 12 | 8 |
| Champion Township | 9,145 | 9 | 0 | 1 | 1 | 7 | 169 | 33 | 128 | 8 | 1 |
| Chardon | 5,213 | 10 | 0 | 0 | 0 | 10 | 70 | 7 | 63 | 0 | 0 |
| Cheviot | 8,322 | 10 | 0 | 1 | 5 | 4 | 260 | 49 | 201 | 10 | 2 |
| Chillicothe | 22,312 | 271 | 0 | 5 | 46 | 220 | 2,206 | 407 | 1,762 | 37 | 12 |
| Cincinnati | 333,568 | 3,976 | 55 | 235 | 2,272 | 1,414 | 20,357 | 6,287 | 12,513 | 1,557 | 224 |
| Circleville | 13,701 | 39 | 0 | 6 | 22 | 11 | 1,067 | 202 | 841 | 24 | 2 |
| Clayton | 12,858 | 13 | 0 | 3 | 4 | 6 | 204 | 47 | 141 | 16 | 1 |
| Clay Township, Ottawa County | 2,722 | 1 | 0 | 1 | 0 | 0 | 32 | 13 | 17 | 2 | 0 |
| Clearcreek Township | 12,850 | 2 | 0 | 0 | 0 | 2 | 106 | 29 | 76 | 1 | 0 |
| Cleveland | 429,238 | 5,990 | 86 | 373 | 3,555 | 1,976 | 24,128 | 9,226 | 10,871 | 4,031 | 401 |
| Cleveland Heights | 45,320 | 84 | 3 | 2 | 70 | 9 | 646 | 118 | 418 | 110 | 0 |
| Cleves | 2,678 | 1 | 0 | 1 | 0 | 0 | 63 | 16 | 45 | 2 | 4 |
| Clinton Township | 4,019 | 38 | 0 | 3 | 20 | 15 | 393 | 77 | 292 | 24 | 0 |
| Clyde | 6,120 | 5 | 0 | 0 | 2 | 3 | 220 | 41 | 164 | 15 | 0 |
| Coitsville Township | 1,619 | 6 | 0 | 0 | 0 | 6 | 59 | 28 | 27 | 4 | 0 |
| Columbus | 759,391 | 5,340 | 83 | 574 | 3,395 | 1,288 | 48,813 | 14,583 | 30,044 | 4,186 | 432 |
| Conneaut | 12,342 | 29 | 1 | 3 | 6 | 19 | 326 | 81 | 228 | 17 | 1 |
| Cortland | 6,319 | 2 | 0 | 0 | 2 | 0 | 84 | 22 | 62 | 0 | 3 |
| Covington | 2,623 | 1 | 0 | 0 | 0 | 1 | 38 | 10 | 28 | 0 | 0 |
| Creston | 2,109 | 1 | 0 | 0 | 0 | 1 | 85 | 5 | 78 | 2 | 0 |
| Cridersville | 1,696 | 2 | 0 | 0 | 1 | 1 | 17 | 3 | 14 | 0 | 0 |
| Cross Creek Township | 5,469 | 1 | 0 | 0 | 0 | 1 | 21 | 9 | 12 | 0 | 0 |
| Cuyahoga Falls | 51,281 | 76 | 0 | 17 | 20 | 39 | 1,432 | 235 | 1,145 | 52 | 5 |
| Danville | 1,070 | 0 | 0 | 0 | 0 | 0 | 18 | 6 | 12 | 0 | 0 |
| Dayton | 152,965 | 1,542 | 39 | 91 | 770 | 642 | 8,949 | 3,244 | 4,932 | 773 | 173 |
| Deer Park | 5,725 | 11 | 0 | 1 | 5 | 5 | 131 | 21 | 105 | 5 | 1 |
| Defiance | 16,006 | 19 | 0 | 11 | 4 | 4 | 630 | 60 | 563 | 7 | 3 |
| Delaware | 34,734 | 82 | 0 | 26 | 19 | 37 | 869 | 173 | 667 | 29 | 9 |
| Delhi Township | 31,419 | 31 | 1 | 6 | 11 | 13 | 503 | 97 | 392 | 14 | 4 |
| Delphos | 6,704 | 4 | 0 | 1 | 0 | 3 | 195 | 54 | 135 | 6 | 1 |
| Delta | 2,897 | 0 | 0 | 0 | 0 | 0 | 116 | 26 | 88 | 2 | 0 |
| Dover | 12,487 | 5 | 0 | 1 | 3 | 1 | 111 | 25 | 80 | 6 | 0 |
| Dublin | 39,390 | 14 | 0 | 2 | 7 | 5 | 809 | 124 | 661 | 24 | 5 |
| Eastlake | 19,443 | 11 | 1 | 0 | 6 | 4 | 440 | 23 | 404 | 13 | 0 |
| Eaton | 7,983 | 14 | 0 | 1 | 2 | 11 | 345 | 53 | 289 | 3 | 0 |
| Elida | 1,897 | 2 | 0 | 0 | 0 | 2 | 8 | 3 | 5 | 0 | 0 |
| Elmwood Place | 2,461 | 5 | 0 | 1 | 4 | 0 | 34 | 11 | 21 | 2 | 0 |
| Elyria | 54,857 | 220 | 3 | 24 | 87 | 106 | 2,380 | 691 | 1,605 | 84 | 5 |
| Englewood | 12,734 | 15 | 0 | 4 | 6 | 5 | 383 | 19 | 353 | 11 | 1 |
| Euclid | 46,871 | 195 | 6 | 19 | 95 | 75 | 1,223 | 510 | 672 | 41 | 6 |

[1] The FBI does not publish arson data unless it receives data from either the agency or the state for all 12 months of the calendar year.

## Table 8. Offenses Known to Law Enforcement, by State and City, 2009—*Continued*

(Number.)

| State/city | Population | Violent crime | Murder and non-negligent man-slaughter | Forcible rape | Robbery | Aggravated assault | Property crime | Burglary | Larceny-theft | Motor vehicle theft | Arson[1] |
|---|---|---|---|---|---|---|---|---|---|---|---|
| **OHIO**—*Continued* | | | | | | | | | | | |
| Evendale | 2,942 | 4 | 2 | 0 | 2 | 0 | 222 | 3 | 216 | 3 | 0 |
| Fairborn | 32,451 | 79 | 0 | 24 | 26 | 29 | 1,175 | 289 | 836 | 50 | 5 |
| Fairfield | 42,414 | 123 | 1 | 6 | 37 | 79 | 1,501 | 257 | 1,181 | 63 | 4 |
| Fairfield Township | 17,487 | 35 | 0 | 3 | 11 | 21 | 696 | 95 | 582 | 19 | 2 |
| Fairlawn | 7,000 | 21 | 0 | 0 | 6 | 15 | 396 | 23 | 364 | 9 | 0 |
| Fairport Harbor | 3,214 | 9 | 0 | 2 | 1 | 6 | 161 | 40 | 116 | 5 | 2 |
| Findlay | 36,751 | 67 | 0 | 17 | 18 | 32 | 1,535 | 296 | 1,205 | 34 | 0 |
| Fort Recovery | 1,338 | 0 | 0 | 0 | 0 | 0 | 26 | 7 | 18 | 1 | 0 |
| Fredericktown | 2,480 | 1 | 0 | 0 | 0 | 1 | 63 | 16 | 46 | 1 | 1 |
| Fremont | 16,556 | 31 | 0 | 0 | 13 | 18 | 975 | 137 | 811 | 27 | 1 |
| Gahanna | 34,028 | 18 | 1 | 4 | 10 | 3 | 906 | 147 | 729 | 30 | 8 |
| Galion | 10,644 | 16 | 0 | 2 | 5 | 9 | 473 | 114 | 354 | 5 | 1 |
| Gallipolis | 4,189 | 11 | 0 | 1 | 6 | 4 | 398 | 48 | 342 | 8 | 0 |
| Garfield Heights | 27,424 | 131 | 0 | 14 | 43 | 74 | 813 | 297 | 515 | 1 | 7 |
| Gates Mills | 2,254 | 1 | 0 | 0 | 0 | 1 | 13 | 4 | 9 | 0 | 0 |
| Geneva-on-the-Lake | 1,478 | 0 | 0 | 0 | 0 | 0 | 11 | 2 | 9 | 0 | 0 |
| Genoa | 2,270 | 0 | 0 | 0 | 0 | 0 | 66 | 15 | 49 | 2 | 0 |
| Georgetown | 3,405 | 3 | 0 | 2 | 1 | 0 | 166 | 45 | 121 | 0 | 1 |
| Germantown | 5,031 | 7 | 0 | 1 | 0 | 6 | 87 | 15 | 72 | 0 | 2 |
| German Township, Montgomery County | 3,290 | 1 | 0 | 0 | 0 | 1 | 64 | 21 | 42 | 1 | 0 |
| Gibsonburg | 2,430 | 1 | 0 | 0 | 0 | 1 | 125 | 19 | 106 | 0 | 0 |
| Girard | 9,982 | 38 | 0 | 2 | 7 | 29 | 426 | 118 | 273 | 35 | 4 |
| Gnadenhutten | 1,283 | 1 | 0 | 0 | 0 | 1 | 15 | 2 | 13 | 0 | 0 |
| Goshen Township, Clermont County | 16,564 | 9 | 0 | 5 | 1 | 3 | 388 | 108 | 271 | 9 | 2 |
| Goshen Township, Mahoning County | 3,429 | 4 | 0 | 0 | 0 | 4 | 133 | 43 | 84 | 6 | 0 |
| Grandview Heights | 6,265 | 4 | 0 | 0 | 3 | 1 | 219 | 55 | 159 | 5 | 1 |
| Granville | 5,414 | 3 | 0 | 0 | 0 | 3 | 63 | 3 | 60 | 0 | 1 |
| Greenhills | 3,810 | 1 | 0 | 0 | 0 | 1 | 48 | 11 | 36 | 1 | 0 |
| Greenville | 12,908 | 46 | 2 | 7 | 8 | 29 | 672 | 140 | 499 | 33 | 8 |
| Grove City | 34,598 | 42 | 1 | 4 | 30 | 7 | 1,401 | 201 | 1,158 | 42 | 4 |
| Groveport | 5,409 | 6 | 0 | 0 | 2 | 4 | 206 | 61 | 136 | 9 | 2 |
| Hamilton | 62,690 | 408 | 2 | 54 | 188 | 164 | 4,061 | 1,022 | 2,797 | 242 | 31 |
| Harrison | 9,628 | 5 | 0 | 2 | 1 | 2 | 288 | 15 | 272 | 1 | 2 |
| Hartville | 2,598 | 4 | 0 | 0 | 2 | 2 | 47 | 19 | 25 | 3 | 0 |
| Heath | 8,938 | 14 | 1 | 5 | 6 | 2 | 526 | 45 | 477 | 4 | 4 |
| Hebron | 2,161 | 1 | 0 | 0 | 1 | 0 | 33 | 7 | 26 | 0 | 0 |
| Hicksville | 3,383 | 2 | 0 | 1 | 0 | 1 | 75 | 8 | 67 | 0 | 2 |
| Highland Heights | 8,580 | 2 | 0 | 0 | 2 | 0 | 65 | 7 | 54 | 4 | 0 |
| Highland Hills | 1,366 | 0 | 0 | 0 | 0 | 0 | 3 | 0 | 3 | 0 | 0 |
| Hilliard | 28,326 | 33 | 0 | 4 | 22 | 7 | 930 | 154 | 739 | 37 | 10 |
| Hillsboro | 6,688 | 8 | 0 | 2 | 6 | 0 | 441 | 61 | 377 | 3 | 0 |
| Holland | 1,329 | 8 | 0 | 0 | 7 | 1 | 180 | 5 | 170 | 5 | 0 |
| Howland Township | 16,245 | 28 | 0 | 4 | 12 | 12 | 650 | 144 | 488 | 18 | 3 |
| Hubbard | 7,625 | 9 | 0 | 0 | 2 | 7 | 103 | 14 | 86 | 3 | 0 |
| Hubbard Township | 5,649 | 7 | 0 | 2 | 1 | 4 | 192 | 52 | 126 | 14 | 1 |
| Huber Heights | 37,027 | 84 | 0 | 12 | 46 | 26 | 1,451 | 252 | 1,144 | 55 | 24 |
| Hudson | 23,098 | 2 | 0 | 1 | 1 | 0 | 239 | 62 | 170 | 7 | 2 |
| Huron | 7,285 | 29 | 0 | 2 | 7 | 20 | 122 | 23 | 94 | 5 | 0 |
| Independence | 6,733 | 8 | 0 | 1 | 1 | 6 | 152 | 14 | 134 | 4 | 0 |
| Indian Hill | 6,047 | 2 | 0 | 2 | 0 | 0 | 49 | 5 | 44 | 0 | 1 |
| Ironton | 11,307 | 5 | 0 | 1 | 3 | 1 | 174 | 60 | 106 | 8 | 0 |
| Jackson | 6,135 | 6 | 0 | 2 | 1 | 3 | 411 | 55 | 352 | 4 | 1 |
| Jackson Township, Mahoning County | 2,257 | 1 | 0 | 0 | 0 | 1 | 66 | 12 | 49 | 5 | 1 |
| Jackson Township, Montgomery County | 3,844 | 1 | 0 | 1 | 0 | 0 | 38 | 19 | 15 | 4 | 0 |
| Jackson Township, Stark County | 40,989 | 62 | 2 | 13 | 27 | 20 | 1,315 | 179 | 1,097 | 39 | 4 |
| Jamestown | 1,855 | 3 | 0 | 1 | 0 | 2 | 96 | 27 | 68 | 1 | 0 |
| Jefferson | 3,399 | 4 | 0 | 0 | 0 | 4 | 58 | 11 | 47 | 0 | 0 |
| Junction City | 843 | 0 | 0 | 0 | 0 | 0 | 29 | 10 | 19 | 0 | 0 |
| Kent | 27,964 | 66 | 1 | 12 | 15 | 38 | 588 | 129 | 431 | 28 | 32 |
| Kenton | 8,021 | 7 | 0 | 2 | 4 | 1 | 697 | 180 | 506 | 11 | 2 |
| Kettering | 53,288 | 69 | 0 | 24 | 28 | 17 | 1,459 | 344 | 1,039 | 76 | 13 |
| Kirtland | 7,439 | 0 | 0 | 0 | 0 | 0 | 54 | 10 | 41 | 3 | 0 |
| Kirtland Hills | 812 | 0 | 0 | 0 | 0 | 0 | 3 | 1 | 2 | 0 | 0 |
| Lake Township | 7,446 | 6 | 0 | 4 | 1 | 1 | 155 | 38 | 113 | 4 | 0 |
| Lakewood | 50,098 | 91 | 1 | 7 | 33 | 50 | 740 | 156 | 554 | 30 | 4 |
| Lancaster | 37,143 | 113 | 3 | 26 | 52 | 32 | 2,161 | 413 | 1,694 | 54 | 13 |
| Lawrence Township | 8,483 | 1 | 0 | 1 | 0 | 0 | 90 | 33 | 55 | 2 | 3 |
| Lebanon | 20,944 | 27 | 3 | 7 | 10 | 7 | 426 | 62 | 347 | 17 | 5 |
| Lexington | 4,086 | 1 | 0 | 0 | 0 | 1 | 102 | 10 | 92 | 0 | 0 |
| Liberty Township | 11,749 | 14 | 0 | 0 | 8 | 6 | 210 | 33 | 168 | 9 | 0 |
| Lima | 37,437 | 469 | 5 | 61 | 144 | 259 | 2,526 | 883 | 1,484 | 159 | 30 |

[1] The FBI does not publish arson data unless it receives data from either the agency or the state for all 12 months of the calendar year.

## Table 8. Offenses Known to Law Enforcement, by State and City, 2009—*Continued*

(Number.)

| State/city | Population | Violent crime | Murder and non-negligent man-slaughter | Forcible rape | Robbery | Aggravated assault | Property crime | Burglary | Larceny-theft | Motor vehicle theft | Arson[1] |
|---|---|---|---|---|---|---|---|---|---|---|---|
| **OHIO**—*Continued* | | | | | | | | | | | |
| Liverpool Township | 4,129 | 2 | 0 | 1 | 0 | 1 | 70 | 17 | 47 | 6 | 0 |
| Lockland | 3,450 | 18 | 0 | 2 | 8 | 8 | 163 | 60 | 82 | 21 | 4 |
| Logan | 7,489 | 7 | 0 | 3 | 1 | 3 | 335 | 51 | 274 | 10 | 1 |
| London | 9,679 | 6 | 0 | 3 | 1 | 2 | 275 | 43 | 223 | 9 | 0 |
| Lorain | 70,410 | 394 | 5 | 36 | 178 | 175 | 2,930 | 1,037 | 1,768 | 125 | 42 |
| Lordstown | 3,509 | 1 | 0 | 0 | 0 | 1 | 87 | 19 | 66 | 2 | 0 |
| Loudonville | 3,083 | 0 | 0 | 0 | 0 | 0 | 77 | 11 | 65 | 1 | 1 |
| Louisville | 9,516 | 5 | 0 | 1 | 3 | 1 | 174 | 34 | 138 | 2 | 2 |
| Lyndhurst | 13,702 | 2 | 0 | 1 | 0 | 1 | 0 | 0 | 0 | 0 | 0 |
| Madeira | 8,521 | 2 | 0 | 0 | 1 | 1 | 109 | 13 | 93 | 3 | 0 |
| Madison | 3,124 | 2 | 0 | 0 | 1 | 1 | 34 | 6 | 26 | 2 | 1 |
| Madison Township, Franklin County | 18,389 | 7 | 0 | 0 | 3 | 4 | 181 | 69 | 96 | 16 | 0 |
| Madison Township, Lake County | 17,005 | 37 | 0 | 6 | 1 | 30 | 385 | 65 | 303 | 17 | 1 |
| Manchester | 2,099 | 4 | 0 | 0 | 0 | 4 | 12 | 6 | 6 | 0 | 0 |
| Mansfield | 49,349 | 166 | 2 | 29 | 63 | 72 | 2,711 | 942 | 1,710 | 59 | 27 |
| Maple Heights | 23,411 | 105 | 1 | 7 | 66 | 31 | 558 | 249 | 207 | 102 | 5 |
| Mariemont | 3,161 | 2 | 0 | 0 | 2 | 0 | 74 | 4 | 69 | 1 | 0 |
| Marietta | 14,272 | 26 | 0 | 10 | 9 | 7 | 451 | 88 | 348 | 15 | 1 |
| Marion | 35,683 | 57 | 1 | 8 | 30 | 18 | 1,605 | 461 | 1,113 | 31 | 7 |
| Martins Ferry | 6,609 | 2 | 0 | 0 | 0 | 2 | 33 | 4 | 25 | 4 | 0 |
| Marysville | 18,447 | 16 | 0 | 7 | 6 | 3 | 512 | 64 | 445 | 3 | 2 |
| Mason | 30,624 | 13 | 0 | 1 | 5 | 7 | 475 | 49 | 413 | 13 | 3 |
| Maumee | 13,729 | 11 | 0 | 4 | 3 | 4 | 538 | 81 | 444 | 13 | 2 |
| Mayfield Heights | 17,568 | 15 | 0 | 2 | 8 | 5 | 279 | 34 | 229 | 16 | 2 |
| Mayfield Village | 3,089 | 4 | 0 | 0 | 1 | 3 | 62 | 11 | 50 | 1 | 0 |
| McArthur | 2,036 | 7 | 0 | 1 | 3 | 3 | 77 | 21 | 54 | 2 | 1 |
| Medina Township | 9,023 | 5 | 0 | 2 | 1 | 2 | 115 | 16 | 92 | 7 | 0 |
| Mentor | 51,993 | 45 | 0 | 10 | 19 | 16 | 1,191 | 117 | 1,026 | 48 | 16 |
| Mentor-on-the-Lake | 8,306 | 6 | 0 | 1 | 2 | 3 | 83 | 18 | 64 | 1 | 0 |
| Miamisburg | 19,819 | 35 | 1 | 9 | 8 | 17 | 571 | 91 | 449 | 31 | 0 |
| Miami Township, Clermont County | 40,027 | 26 | 1 | 5 | 10 | 10 | 854 | 115 | 723 | 16 | 9 |
| Miami Township, Montgomery County | 25,016 | 44 | 0 | 6 | 19 | 19 | 1,054 | 153 | 867 | 34 | 5 |
| Middlefield | 2,392 | 2 | 0 | 1 | 0 | 1 | 38 | 0 | 38 | 0 | 0 |
| Middletown | 51,401 | 364 | 2 | 46 | 119 | 197 | 4,297 | 1,091 | 2,999 | 207 | 4 |
| Milford | 6,334 | 15 | 0 | 1 | 3 | 11 | 380 | 44 | 329 | 7 | 0 |
| Millersburg | 3,636 | 3 | 0 | 2 | 0 | 1 | 97 | 15 | 81 | 1 | 0 |
| Milton Township | 2,827 | 8 | 0 | 0 | 0 | 8 | 45 | 17 | 26 | 2 | 3 |
| Minerva | 3,903 | 11 | 0 | 1 | 1 | 9 | 107 | 15 | 90 | 2 | 0 |
| Mingo Junction | 3,288 | 30 | 0 | 0 | 0 | 30 | 59 | 26 | 31 | 2 | 0 |
| Monroe | 15,319 | 36 | 0 | 3 | 5 | 28 | 658 | 112 | 534 | 12 | 0 |
| Montgomery | 10,497 | 1 | 0 | 0 | 0 | 1 | 205 | 20 | 173 | 12 | 3 |
| Montpelier | 3,983 | 14 | 0 | 3 | 1 | 10 | 161 | 33 | 124 | 4 | 1 |
| Montville Township | 6,517 | 1 | 0 | 1 | 0 | 0 | 63 | 12 | 50 | 1 | 0 |
| Moraine | 6,421 | 33 | 0 | 8 | 12 | 13 | 609 | 90 | 504 | 15 | 3 |
| Mount Healthy | 6,044 | 16 | 0 | 4 | 12 | 0 | 278 | 91 | 179 | 8 | 0 |
| Mount Orab | 2,781 | 1 | 0 | 1 | 0 | 0 | 59 | 7 | 52 | 0 | 0 |
| Mount Sterling | 1,827 | 0 | 0 | 0 | 0 | 0 | 26 | 3 | 23 | 0 | 0 |
| Munroe Falls | 5,149 | 2 | 0 | 1 | 0 | 1 | 45 | 5 | 39 | 1 | 0 |
| Napoleon | 8,764 | 18 | 0 | 7 | 2 | 9 | 387 | 68 | 310 | 9 | 2 |
| Navarre | 1,892 | 3 | 0 | 0 | 1 | 2 | 21 | 6 | 11 | 4 | 1 |
| Nelsonville | 5,390 | 11 | 0 | 5 | 4 | 2 | 315 | 92 | 215 | 8 | 0 |
| New Albany | 7,546 | 0 | 0 | 0 | 0 | 0 | 47 | 13 | 34 | 0 | 0 |
| Newark | 47,338 | 90 | 2 | 35 | 20 | 33 | 2,088 | 437 | 1,589 | 62 | 36 |
| New Boston | 2,151 | 7 | 0 | 2 | 4 | 1 | 293 | 68 | 217 | 8 | 0 |
| New Franklin | 14,986 | 3 | 0 | 0 | 2 | 1 | 151 | 60 | 85 | 6 | 1 |
| New Lebanon | 4,085 | 6 | 0 | 1 | 3 | 2 | 134 | 38 | 85 | 11 | 0 |
| New Lexington | 4,569 | 1 | 0 | 0 | 1 | 0 | 77 | 22 | 55 | 0 | 0 |
| New London | 2,586 | 0 | 0 | 0 | 0 | 0 | 10 | 3 | 7 | 0 | 0 |
| New Middletown | 1,539 | 0 | 0 | 0 | 0 | 0 | 12 | 2 | 9 | 1 | 0 |
| New Philadelphia | 17,342 | 9 | 0 | 3 | 5 | 1 | 146 | 7 | 138 | 1 | 1 |
| New Richmond | 2,544 | 3 | 0 | 0 | 0 | 3 | 73 | 14 | 57 | 2 | 0 |
| Newton Falls | 4,603 | 4 | 0 | 2 | 1 | 1 | 30 | 8 | 22 | 0 | 0 |
| Newtown | 4,148 | 0 | 0 | 0 | 0 | 0 | 33 | 4 | 28 | 1 | 0 |
| New Washington | 903 | 1 | 0 | 0 | 0 | 1 | 16 | 6 | 10 | 0 | 0 |
| Niles | 19,095 | 53 | 0 | 7 | 23 | 23 | 1,193 | 261 | 873 | 59 | 3 |
| North Canton | 16,929 | 14 | 0 | 2 | 3 | 9 | 279 | 53 | 225 | 1 | 2 |
| North Olmsted | 31,025 | 18 | 0 | 3 | 8 | 7 | 358 | 67 | 282 | 9 | 6 |
| North Ridgeville | 28,875 | 15 | 0 | 3 | 6 | 6 | 310 | 75 | 222 | 13 | 1 |
| Northwood | 5,524 | 13 | 0 | 3 | 4 | 6 | 266 | 44 | 213 | 9 | 0 |
| Norton | 11,465 | 4 | 0 | 1 | 2 | 1 | 27 | 6 | 19 | 2 | 0 |

[1] The FBI does not publish arson data unless it receives data from either the agency or the state for all 12 months of the calendar year.

**Table 8. Offenses Known to Law Enforcement, by State and City, 2009—*Continued***

(Number.)

| State/city | Population | Violent crime | Murder and non-negligent man-slaughter | Forcible rape | Robbery | Aggravated assault | Property crime | Burglary | Larceny-theft | Motor vehicle theft | Arson[1] |
|---|---|---|---|---|---|---|---|---|---|---|---|
| **OHIO**—*Continued* | | | | | | | | | | | |
| Norwalk | 16,652 | 10 | 0 | 6 | 3 | 1 | 420 | 85 | 327 | 8 | 1 |
| Norwood | 20,207 | 86 | 0 | 7 | 67 | 12 | 1,230 | 254 | 905 | 71 | 0 |
| Oberlin | 8,404 | 18 | 0 | 3 | 6 | 9 | 203 | 37 | 164 | 2 | 2 |
| Olmsted Falls | 8,183 | 10 | 0 | 2 | 1 | 7 | 75 | 17 | 57 | 1 | 1 |
| Ontario | 5,193 | 12 | 1 | 1 | 6 | 4 | 619 | 31 | 578 | 10 | 0 |
| Orange Village | 3,249 | 0 | 0 | 0 | 0 | 0 | 27 | 5 | 16 | 6 | 0 |
| Oregon | 18,872 | 45 | 0 | 4 | 17 | 24 | 789 | 140 | 626 | 23 | 1 |
| Orrville | 8,367 | 16 | 0 | 5 | 10 | 1 | 137 | 41 | 93 | 3 | 1 |
| Ottawa Hills | 4,597 | 2 | 0 | 0 | 0 | 2 | 54 | 15 | 39 | 0 | 1 |
| Oxford | 22,995 | 76 | 0 | 14 | 5 | 57 | 601 | 118 | 459 | 24 | 6 |
| Painesville | 18,569 | 31 | 0 | 5 | 14 | 12 | 340 | 105 | 220 | 15 | 0 |
| Parma Heights | 19,559 | 27 | 0 | 5 | 4 | 18 | 362 | 83 | 250 | 29 | 1 |
| Pataskala | 12,967 | 6 | 1 | 0 | 3 | 2 | 238 | 47 | 186 | 5 | 2 |
| Paulding | 3,331 | 1 | 0 | 1 | 0 | 0 | 16 | 4 | 12 | 0 | 0 |
| Pepper Pike | 5,681 | 1 | 0 | 0 | 1 | 0 | 34 | 8 | 24 | 2 | 2 |
| Perkins Township | 12,820 | 7 | 0 | 1 | 3 | 3 | 269 | 8 | 261 | 0 | 0 |
| Perrysburg | 17,051 | 11 | 0 | 5 | 3 | 3 | 469 | 81 | 367 | 21 | 0 |
| Perry Township, Allen County | 3,580 | 8 | 0 | 0 | 0 | 8 | 68 | 17 | 50 | 1 | 0 |
| Perry Township, Franklin County | 3,653 | 1 | 0 | 0 | 0 | 1 | 40 | 7 | 31 | 2 | 2 |
| Perry Township, Montgomery County | 3,829 | 4 | 0 | 3 | 0 | 1 | 44 | 22 | 21 | 1 | 0 |
| Perry Township, Stark County | 28,005 | 54 | 1 | 0 | 15 | 38 | 677 | 163 | 470 | 44 | 9 |
| Pickerington | 18,672 | 23 | 0 | 4 | 12 | 7 | 367 | 42 | 314 | 11 | 6 |
| Pierce Township | 11,177 | 11 | 0 | 1 | 5 | 5 | 257 | 52 | 203 | 2 | 0 |
| Piqua | 20,559 | 28 | 0 | 11 | 13 | 4 | 1,015 | 162 | 835 | 18 | 2 |
| Plain City | 3,629 | 2 | 0 | 0 | 1 | 1 | 23 | 2 | 20 | 1 | 0 |
| Poland Township | 11,014 | 1 | 1 | 0 | 0 | 0 | 75 | 30 | 44 | 1 | 0 |
| Poland Village | 2,640 | 0 | 0 | 0 | 0 | 0 | 26 | 5 | 21 | 0 | 0 |
| Port Clinton | 6,108 | 10 | 0 | 3 | 2 | 5 | 247 | 40 | 199 | 8 | 1 |
| Portsmouth | 20,235 | 133 | 3 | 11 | 85 | 34 | 2,073 | 516 | 1,507 | 50 | 1 |
| Powell | 13,869 | 3 | 0 | 0 | 0 | 3 | 77 | 18 | 59 | 0 | 0 |
| Ravenna | 11,335 | 44 | 0 | 8 | 6 | 30 | 483 | 53 | 415 | 15 | 3 |
| Reading | 10,446 | 26 | 0 | 5 | 16 | 5 | 388 | 67 | 290 | 31 | 2 |
| Reminderville | 2,799 | 0 | 0 | 0 | 0 | 0 | 10 | 2 | 8 | 0 | 0 |
| Reynoldsburg | 33,825 | 73 | 0 | 10 | 42 | 21 | 1,202 | 278 | 881 | 43 | 9 |
| Richfield | 3,598 | 1 | 0 | 0 | 1 | 0 | 31 | 8 | 21 | 2 | 0 |
| Richmond Heights | 10,093 | 16 | 0 | 0 | 10 | 6 | 305 | 33 | 253 | 19 | 0 |
| Rittman | 6,260 | 3 | 0 | 0 | 3 | 0 | 112 | 17 | 89 | 6 | 0 |
| Riverside | 25,147 | 65 | 0 | 8 | 22 | 35 | 834 | 207 | 568 | 59 | 10 |
| Rossford | 6,401 | 1 | 0 | 1 | 0 | 0 | 192 | 31 | 156 | 5 | 1 |
| Russells Point | 1,509 | 0 | 0 | 0 | 0 | 0 | 38 | 11 | 26 | 1 | 2 |
| Russell Township | 5,575 | 0 | 0 | 0 | 0 | 0 | 10 | 4 | 5 | 1 | 0 |
| Sabina | 2,783 | 2 | 0 | 0 | 1 | 1 | 50 | 7 | 43 | 0 | 0 |
| Salem | 11,709 | 1 | 0 | 0 | 0 | 1 | 65 | 5 | 54 | 6 | 0 |
| Saline Township | 1,331 | 8 | 0 | 0 | 1 | 7 | 24 | 7 | 10 | 7 | 1 |
| Sandusky | 25,461 | 127 | 0 | 12 | 31 | 84 | 1,237 | 295 | 922 | 20 | 9 |
| Sebring | 4,484 | 3 | 0 | 3 | 0 | 0 | 58 | 18 | 38 | 2 | 0 |
| Seven Hills | 11,565 | 2 | 0 | 0 | 0 | 2 | 21 | 11 | 10 | 0 | 0 |
| Seville | 2,419 | 1 | 0 | 0 | 0 | 1 | 34 | 8 | 26 | 0 | 0 |
| Shaker Heights | 26,159 | 68 | 0 | 5 | 51 | 12 | 506 | 156 | 318 | 32 | 2 |
| Sharon Township | 2,373 | 0 | 0 | 0 | 0 | 0 | 42 | 14 | 27 | 1 | 1 |
| Sharonville | 13,334 | 23 | 1 | 5 | 15 | 2 | 552 | 76 | 461 | 15 | 1 |
| Sheffield Lake | 8,858 | 0 | 0 | 0 | 0 | 0 | 195 | 42 | 150 | 3 | 3 |
| Shelby | 9,256 | 4 | 0 | 0 | 2 | 2 | 300 | 57 | 239 | 4 | 0 |
| Sidney | 19,899 | 40 | 1 | 16 | 13 | 10 | 1,123 | 227 | 881 | 15 | 18 |
| Smith Township | 4,792 | 8 | 0 | 2 | 2 | 4 | 46 | 22 | 22 | 2 | 0 |
| Smithville | 1,294 | 2 | 0 | 1 | 1 | 0 | 52 | 7 | 45 | 0 | 0 |
| Solon | 21,870 | 9 | 0 | 2 | 2 | 5 | 208 | 28 | 179 | 1 | 2 |
| South Bloomfield | 1,700 | 0 | 0 | 0 | 0 | 0 | 54 | 16 | 36 | 2 | 0 |
| South Charleston | 1,766 | 0 | 0 | 0 | 0 | 0 | 24 | 8 | 16 | 0 | 1 |
| South Euclid | 20,970 | 34 | 0 | 8 | 19 | 7 | 446 | 116 | 292 | 38 | 2 |
| South Russell | 3,902 | 0 | 0 | 0 | 0 | 0 | 11 | 1 | 10 | 0 | 0 |
| South Solon | 385 | 0 | 0 | 0 | 0 | 0 | 0 | 0 | 0 | 0 | 0 |
| Spencerville | 2,152 | 0 | 0 | 0 | 0 | 0 | 49 | 10 | 38 | 1 | 0 |
| Springdale | 10,370 | 33 | 0 | 1 | 30 | 2 | 752 | 90 | 640 | 22 | 0 |
| Springfield | 61,881 | 467 | 4 | 43 | 214 | 206 | 4,512 | 1,287 | 2,977 | 248 | 29 |
| Springfield Township, Hamilton County | 40,051 | 60 | 1 | 5 | 42 | 12 | 788 | 195 | 553 | 40 | 6 |
| Springfield Township, Mahoning County | 5,956 | 0 | 0 | 0 | 0 | 0 | 101 | 36 | 63 | 2 | 0 |
| Springfield Township, Summit County | 15,263 | 35 | 0 | 6 | 14 | 15 | 934 | 129 | 775 | 30 | 3 |
| St. Bernard | 4,596 | 5 | 1 | 1 | 3 | 0 | 128 | 33 | 88 | 7 | 0 |
| St. Clair Township | 7,596 | 1 | 0 | 0 | 1 | 0 | 71 | 0 | 71 | 0 | 0 |
| Stow | 34,067 | 25 | 0 | 7 | 11 | 7 | 751 | 130 | 610 | 11 | 5 |

[1] The FBI does not publish arson data unless it receives data from either the agency or the state for all 12 months of the calendar year.

## Table 8. Offenses Known to Law Enforcement, by State and City, 2009—*Continued*

(Number.)

| State/city | Population | Violent crime | Murder and non-negligent man-slaughter | Forcible rape | Robbery | Aggravated assault | Property crime | Burglary | Larceny-theft | Motor vehicle theft | Arson[1] |
|---|---|---|---|---|---|---|---|---|---|---|---|
| **OHIO**—*Continued* | | | | | | | | | | | |
| St. Paris | 1,960 | 1 | 0 | 1 | 0 | 0 | 44 | 4 | 40 | 0 | 0 |
| Strasburg | 2,719 | 5 | 0 | 3 | 1 | 1 | 54 | 12 | 41 | 1 | 0 |
| Streetsboro | 14,749 | 7 | 0 | 0 | 2 | 5 | 113 | 6 | 104 | 3 | 0 |
| Strongsville | 42,478 | 15 | 0 | 1 | 8 | 6 | 770 | 87 | 655 | 28 | 2 |
| Sugarcreek Township | 7,005 | 5 | 0 | 2 | 1 | 2 | 291 | 49 | 233 | 9 | 0 |
| Swanton | 3,676 | 3 | 0 | 0 | 1 | 2 | 82 | 14 | 66 | 2 | 1 |
| Sylvania Township | 26,142 | 19 | 0 | 0 | 12 | 7 | 726 | 108 | 594 | 24 | 0 |
| Tallmadge | 17,390 | 31 | 0 | 5 | 11 | 15 | 562 | 117 | 425 | 20 | 2 |
| Tipp City | 9,255 | 4 | 0 | 1 | 2 | 1 | 160 | 23 | 137 | 0 | 2 |
| Toledo[5] | 291,066 | 3,251 | 33 | 165 | 1,222 | 1,831 | | 8,064 | | 1,337 | 510 |
| Trotwood | 25,894 | 100 | 0 | 11 | 48 | 41 | 1,023 | 392 | 531 | 100 | 17 |
| Twinsburg | 17,432 | 5 | 1 | 0 | 1 | 3 | 130 | 19 | 100 | 11 | 2 |
| Uhrichsville | 5,501 | 6 | 0 | 3 | 1 | 2 | 197 | 37 | 140 | 20 | 1 |
| Union | 6,361 | 7 | 0 | 2 | 0 | 5 | 62 | 6 | 54 | 2 | 0 |
| University Heights | 12,353 | 20 | 0 | 5 | 11 | 4 | 248 | 46 | 196 | 6 | 0 |
| Upper Arlington | 31,686 | 7 | 0 | 0 | 3 | 4 | 403 | 67 | 328 | 8 | 3 |
| Urbana | 11,424 | 12 | 0 | 2 | 1 | 9 | 361 | 52 | 303 | 6 | 1 |
| Utica | 2,101 | 1 | 0 | 0 | 1 | 0 | 45 | 18 | 27 | 0 | 1 |
| Vandalia | 14,070 | 15 | 0 | 6 | 5 | 4 | 290 | 55 | 212 | 23 | 3 |
| Van Wert | 10,139 | 25 | 0 | 5 | 3 | 17 | 486 | 97 | 385 | 4 | 5 |
| Vermilion | 10,735 | 11 | 1 | 0 | 8 | 2 | 309 | 104 | 194 | 11 | 2 |
| Village of Leesburg | 1,307 | 0 | 0 | 0 | 0 | 0 | 60 | 21 | 39 | 0 | 1 |
| Wadsworth | 20,943 | 13 | 0 | 8 | 2 | 3 | 451 | 73 | 370 | 8 | 0 |
| Waite Hill | 567 | 0 | 0 | 0 | 0 | 0 | 2 | 2 | 0 | 0 | 0 |
| Walton Hills | 2,265 | 1 | 0 | 0 | 0 | 1 | 23 | 4 | 16 | 3 | 0 |
| Wapakoneta | 9,427 | 7 | 0 | 2 | 0 | 5 | 181 | 30 | 149 | 2 | 1 |
| Warren | 43,331 | 309 | 7 | 18 | 137 | 147 | 2,015 | 765 | 1,084 | 166 | 5 |
| Warrensville Heights | 13,465 | 47 | 0 | 5 | 31 | 11 | 476 | 201 | 208 | 67 | 1 |
| Warren Township | 5,968 | 9 | 0 | 1 | 0 | 8 | 79 | 20 | 54 | 5 | 0 |
| Washington Court House | 13,659 | 21 | 1 | 5 | 6 | 9 | 449 | 100 | 334 | 15 | 0 |
| Wauseon | 7,261 | 7 | 1 | 1 | 2 | 3 | 216 | 26 | 187 | 3 | 1 |
| Waverly | 4,437 | 0 | 0 | 0 | 0 | 0 | 78 | 3 | 75 | 0 | 0 |
| Waynesburg | 965 | 3 | 0 | 0 | 1 | 2 | 19 | 5 | 14 | 0 | 0 |
| Wellston | 5,923 | 2 | 0 | 0 | 1 | 1 | 30 | 6 | 24 | 0 | 0 |
| Wells Township | 2,817 | 0 | 0 | 0 | 0 | 0 | 54 | 16 | 36 | 2 | 0 |
| West Alexandria | 1,289 | 2 | 0 | 1 | 1 | 0 | 30 | 5 | 25 | 0 | 0 |
| West Carrollton | 12,652 | 30 | 0 | 5 | 19 | 6 | 465 | 118 | 304 | 43 | 4 |
| West Chester Township | 56,060 | 73 | 2 | 29 | 13 | 29 | 1,580 | 300 | 1,254 | 26 | 9 |
| Westerville | 36,319 | 44 | 2 | 9 | 14 | 19 | 863 | 126 | 731 | 6 | 11 |
| West Jefferson | 4,252 | 3 | 0 | 2 | 0 | 1 | 123 | 30 | 87 | 6 | 1 |
| West Liberty | 1,720 | 1 | 0 | 0 | 0 | 1 | 20 | 7 | 12 | 1 | 0 |
| West Salem | 1,460 | 0 | 0 | 0 | 0 | 0 | 29 | 7 | 20 | 2 | 0 |
| West Union | 3,102 | 7 | 0 | 0 | 0 | 7 | 168 | 48 | 116 | 4 | 0 |
| Whitehall | 18,071 | 171 | 4 | 17 | 113 | 37 | 1,614 | 330 | 1,217 | 67 | 0 |
| Willard | 6,640 | 5 | 0 | 0 | 3 | 2 | 254 | 19 | 223 | 12 | 3 |
| Williamsburg | 2,385 | 3 | 0 | 1 | 0 | 2 | 116 | 23 | 92 | 1 | 2 |
| Willoughby | 22,555 | 12 | 0 | 3 | 2 | 7 | 378 | 65 | 298 | 15 | 2 |
| Willoughby Hills | 8,535 | 9 | 0 | 3 | 4 | 2 | 131 | 32 | 83 | 16 | 2 |
| Willowick | 13,661 | 14 | 0 | 4 | 3 | 7 | 138 | 25 | 102 | 11 | 0 |
| Wilmington | 12,680 | 20 | 0 | 3 | 10 | 7 | 634 | 74 | 554 | 6 | 2 |
| Wintersville | 3,873 | 0 | 0 | 0 | 0 | 0 | 75 | 11 | 64 | 0 | 0 |
| Woodlawn | 2,628 | 17 | 0 | 1 | 8 | 8 | 130 | 18 | 100 | 12 | 1 |
| Woodsfield | 2,406 | 9 | 0 | 6 | 0 | 3 | 18 | 6 | 12 | 0 | 0 |
| Wooster | 26,318 | 58 | 0 | 13 | 24 | 21 | 1,230 | 226 | 986 | 18 | 15 |
| Worthington | 13,230 | 20 | 0 | 1 | 5 | 14 | 326 | 65 | 259 | 2 | 3 |
| Wyoming | 8,364 | 3 | 0 | 0 | 3 | 0 | 122 | 26 | 94 | 2 | 1 |
| Xenia | 27,718 | 35 | 0 | 5 | 18 | 12 | 1,164 | 199 | 938 | 27 | 4 |
| Yellow Springs | 3,391 | 5 | 0 | 0 | 1 | 4 | 81 | 14 | 66 | 1 | 0 |
| Youngstown | 72,008 | 856 | 22 | 41 | 317 | 476 | 4,273 | 2,086 | 1,745 | 442 | 251 |
| Zanesville | 25,080 | 130 | 1 | 18 | 50 | 61 | 1,665 | 338 | 1,290 | 37 | 14 |
| **OKLAHOMA** | | | | | | | | | | | |
| Achille[6] | 537 | 2 | 0 | 0 | 0 | 2 | 9 | 5 | 3 | 1 | 0 |
| Ada | 16,807 | 140 | 0 | 12 | 6 | 122 | 825 | 233 | 544 | 48 | 3 |
| Allen[6] | 998 | 0 | 0 | 0 | 0 | 0 | 13 | 2 | 9 | 2 | 0 |
| Altus | 18,664 | 45 | 2 | 5 | 14 | 24 | 639 | 221 | 410 | 8 | 9 |
| Alva[6] | 4,805 | 4 | 0 | 1 | 0 | 3 | 115 | 19 | 89 | 7 | 0 |
| Anadarko | 6,289 | 20 | 1 | 1 | 1 | 17 | 286 | 72 | 201 | 13 | 4 |
| Antlers[6] | 2,478 | 12 | 0 | 1 | 0 | 11 | 68 | 16 | 48 | 4 | 0 |
| Apache[6] | 1,528 | 4 | 0 | 0 | 0 | 4 | 22 | 4 | 15 | 3 | 0 |
| Ardmore | 24,933 | 326 | 0 | 14 | 26 | 286 | 1,495 | 351 | 1,080 | 64 | 4 |
| Arkoma[6] | 2,175 | 3 | 0 | 0 | 0 | 3 | 21 | 5 | 13 | 3 | 0 |

[1] The FBI does not publish arson data unless it receives data from either the agency or the state for all 12 months of the calendar year.
[5] The FBI determined that the agency did not follow national Uniform Crime Reporting (UCR) Program guidelines for reporting an offense. Consequently, this figure is not included in this table.
[6] Because of changes in the state/local agency's reporting practices, figures are not comparable to previous years' data.

## Table 8. Offenses Known to Law Enforcement, by State and City, 2009—*Continued*

(Number.)

| State/city | Population | Violent crime | Murder and non-negligent man-slaughter | Forcible rape | Robbery | Aggravated assault | Property crime | Burglary | Larceny-theft | Motor vehicle theft | Arson[1] |
|---|---|---|---|---|---|---|---|---|---|---|---|
| **OKLAHOMA**—*Continued* | | | | | | | | | | | |
| Atoka[6] | 3,115 | 5 | 0 | 2 | 0 | 3 | 102 | 33 | 61 | 8 | 0 |
| Bartlesville | 36,045 | 114 | 1 | 13 | 13 | 87 | 1,238 | 224 | 963 | 51 | 8 |
| Beaver | 1,352 | 4 | 0 | 2 | 0 | 2 | 13 | 7 | 6 | 0 | 0 |
| Beggs[6] | 1,354 | 5 | 0 | 1 | 1 | 3 | 39 | 18 | 16 | 5 | 0 |
| Bethany | 19,667 | 71 | 1 | 12 | 21 | 37 | 669 | 204 | 415 | 50 | 1 |
| Bixby | 21,681 | 21 | 0 | 2 | 3 | 16 | 360 | 108 | 224 | 28 | 3 |
| Blackwell[6] | 7,092 | 24 | 0 | 6 | 1 | 17 | 147 | 31 | 99 | 17 | 1 |
| Blanchard | 6,825 | 11 | 0 | 4 | 0 | 7 | 120 | 33 | 71 | 16 | 0 |
| Boise City[6] | 1,158 | 0 | 0 | 0 | 0 | 0 | 12 | 3 | 8 | 1 | 0 |
| Boley[6] | 1,083 | 0 | 0 | 0 | 0 | 0 | 2 | 0 | 1 | 1 | 0 |
| Bristow | 4,395 | 26 | 0 | 1 | 3 | 22 | 147 | 36 | 98 | 13 | 0 |
| Broken Arrow | 94,415 | 180 | 2 | 29 | 37 | 112 | 2,017 | 423 | 1,486 | 108 | 15 |
| Broken Bow | 4,136 | 41 | 0 | 6 | 3 | 32 | 306 | 119 | 167 | 20 | 3 |
| Caddo[6] | 994 | 3 | 0 | 0 | 0 | 3 | 4 | 0 | 0 | 4 | 0 |
| Calera | 1,841 | 18 | 2 | 1 | 1 | 14 | 40 | 17 | 21 | 2 | 0 |
| Calumet[6] | 532 | 3 | 0 | 1 | 1 | 1 | 13 | 2 | 10 | 1 | 0 |
| Caney[6] | 214 | 0 | 0 | 0 | 0 | 0 | 6 | 1 | 5 | 0 | 0 |
| Carnegie | 1,534 | 9 | 0 | 0 | 0 | 9 | 22 | 16 | 5 | 1 | 0 |
| Catoosa[3] | 6,748 | | 0 | 7 | 2 | | 188 | 56 | 113 | 19 | 3 |
| Chandler[6] | 2,820 | 5 | 0 | 0 | 0 | 5 | 85 | 13 | 70 | 2 | 0 |
| Checotah[6] | 3,468 | 8 | 0 | 2 | 3 | 3 | 124 | 8 | 107 | 9 | 1 |
| Chelsea[6] | 2,237 | 7 | 0 | 0 | 1 | 6 | 12 | 3 | 7 | 2 | 0 |
| Cherokee[6] | 1,418 | 0 | 0 | 0 | 0 | 0 | 13 | 8 | 5 | 0 | 1 |
| Chickasha | 17,195 | 87 | 0 | 12 | 10 | 65 | 968 | 254 | 651 | 63 | 6 |
| Choctaw | 11,579 | 5 | 0 | 0 | 1 | 4 | 172 | 62 | 102 | 8 | 0 |
| Chouteau[6] | 2,021 | 5 | 0 | 0 | 0 | 5 | 67 | 10 | 54 | 3 | 1 |
| Claremore | 17,635 | 26 | 0 | 9 | 0 | 17 | 588 | 132 | 424 | 32 | 3 |
| Clayton[6] | 728 | 2 | 0 | 0 | 0 | 2 | 14 | 8 | 4 | 2 | 0 |
| Cleveland[6] | 3,123 | 11 | 0 | 0 | 0 | 11 | 81 | 21 | 57 | 3 | 2 |
| Clinton | 8,761 | 50 | 1 | 14 | 6 | 29 | 197 | 55 | 137 | 5 | 1 |
| Coalgate[6] | 1,861 | 0 | 0 | 0 | 0 | 0 | 6 | 1 | 3 | 2 | 1 |
| Colbert | 1,129 | 1 | 0 | 1 | 0 | 0 | 30 | 16 | 14 | 0 | 0 |
| Collinsville | 5,150 | 10 | 0 | 2 | 1 | 7 | 73 | 22 | 49 | 2 | 0 |
| Comanche[6] | 1,519 | 8 | 0 | 2 | 0 | 6 | 56 | 26 | 27 | 3 | 2 |
| Cordell | 2,936 | 22 | 0 | 1 | 0 | 21 | 45 | 2 | 43 | 0 | 0 |
| Coweta[6] | 9,282 | 19 | 0 | 3 | 0 | 16 | 177 | 28 | 135 | 14 | 2 |
| Crescent | 1,415 | 6 | 0 | 0 | 0 | 6 | 17 | 3 | 12 | 2 | 0 |
| Cushing[6] | 8,818 | 15 | 3 | 2 | 0 | 10 | 215 | 26 | 180 | 9 | 1 |
| Davenport[6] | 873 | 0 | 0 | 0 | 0 | 0 | 7 | 2 | 5 | 0 | 0 |
| Davis | 2,640 | 2 | 0 | 0 | 0 | 2 | 80 | 33 | 45 | 2 | 1 |
| Del City | 22,060 | 157 | 5 | 4 | 36 | 112 | 1,438 | 414 | 914 | 110 | 7 |
| Dewar[6] | 896 | 3 | 0 | 0 | 0 | 3 | 20 | 12 | 8 | 0 | 0 |
| Dewey | 3,324 | 9 | 0 | 0 | 0 | 9 | 139 | 44 | 95 | 0 | 2 |
| Dibble[6] | 648 | 2 | 0 | 0 | 0 | 2 | 10 | 5 | 3 | 2 | 0 |
| Drumright[6] | 2,881 | 3 | 0 | 0 | 0 | 3 | 65 | 27 | 33 | 5 | 0 |
| Duncan | 22,630 | 70 | 0 | 13 | 8 | 49 | 1,027 | 243 | 744 | 40 | 2 |
| Durant | 16,726 | 67 | 2 | 15 | 9 | 41 | 744 | 192 | 519 | 33 | 1 |
| Edmond | 80,889 | 87 | 2 | 16 | 18 | 51 | 1,762 | 373 | 1,319 | 70 | 11 |
| Elk City | 11,408 | 32 | 1 | 2 | 1 | 28 | 223 | 57 | 157 | 9 | 5 |
| El Reno | 16,583 | 72 | 5 | 10 | 11 | 46 | 508 | 142 | 339 | 27 | 8 |
| Enid | 47,448 | 251 | 2 | 39 | 32 | 178 | 2,439 | 556 | 1,792 | 91 | 10 |
| Eufaula | 2,767 | 7 | 0 | 1 | 0 | 6 | 124 | 41 | 68 | 15 | 0 |
| Fairfax[6] | 1,443 | 1 | 0 | 0 | 0 | 1 | 21 | 7 | 12 | 2 | 0 |
| Fairview[6] | 2,503 | 4 | 0 | 2 | 0 | 2 | 116 | 27 | 85 | 4 | 0 |
| Fletcher[6] | 1,084 | 0 | 0 | 0 | 0 | 0 | 11 | 0 | 10 | 1 | 0 |
| Forest Park[6] | 1,190 | 1 | 0 | 0 | 0 | 1 | 14 | 3 | 11 | 0 | 0 |
| Fort Gibson[6] | 4,404 | 7 | 0 | 2 | 0 | 5 | 97 | 34 | 54 | 9 | 0 |
| Frederick[6] | 3,794 | 28 | 1 | 0 | 2 | 25 | 101 | 44 | 53 | 4 | 4 |
| Geary[6] | 1,234 | 3 | 0 | 1 | 1 | 1 | 48 | 19 | 27 | 2 | 1 |
| Glenpool | 10,097 | 35 | 0 | 2 | 3 | 30 | 210 | 46 | 150 | 14 | 0 |
| Goodwell | 1,182 | 0 | 0 | 0 | 0 | 0 | 17 | 3 | 14 | 0 | 0 |
| Grandfield[6] | 925 | 5 | 0 | 1 | 0 | 4 | 3 | 2 | 1 | 0 | 0 |
| Grove | 6,476 | 20 | 0 | 0 | 1 | 19 | 161 | 24 | 135 | 2 | 1 |
| Guthrie | 11,175 | 23 | 0 | 2 | 4 | 17 | 294 | 59 | 228 | 7 | 3 |
| Guymon | 10,721 | 37 | 0 | 3 | 4 | 30 | 291 | 89 | 190 | 12 | 4 |
| Haileyville[6] | 905 | 5 | 0 | 0 | 0 | 5 | 11 | 6 | 5 | 0 | 0 |
| Harrah | 5,259 | 9 | 0 | 1 | 0 | 8 | 113 | 27 | 79 | 7 | 0 |
| Hartshorne[6] | 2,077 | 2 | 0 | 0 | 0 | 2 | 46 | 16 | 23 | 7 | 0 |
| Haskell[6] | 1,989 | 2 | 0 | 0 | 1 | 1 | 6 | 1 | 4 | 1 | 0 |
| Healdton[6] | 2,782 | 3 | 0 | 0 | 0 | 3 | 30 | 14 | 11 | 5 | 1 |

[1] The FBI does not publish arson data unless it receives data from either the agency or the state for all 12 months of the calendar year.
[3] The FBI determined that the agency's data were overreported. Consequently, those data are not included in this table.
[6] Because of changes in the state/local agency's reporting practices, figures are not comparable to previous years' data.

## Table 8. Offenses Known to Law Enforcement, by State and City, 2009—*Continued*

(Number.)

| State/city | Population | Violent crime | Murder and non-negligent man-slaughter | Forcible rape | Robbery | Aggravated assault | Property crime | Burglary | Larceny-theft | Motor vehicle theft | Arson[1] |
|---|---|---|---|---|---|---|---|---|---|---|---|
| **OKLAHOMA**—*Continued* | | | | | | | | | | | |
| Heavener | 3,236 | 14 | 0 | 2 | 1 | 11 | 54 | 21 | 31 | 2 | 0 |
| Henryetta | 6,016 | 21 | 1 | 6 | 2 | 12 | 153 | 41 | 101 | 11 | 0 |
| Hinton[6] | 2,129 | 3 | 0 | 0 | 0 | 3 | 13 | 3 | 7 | 3 | 1 |
| Hobart | 3,595 | 16 | 0 | 2 | 1 | 13 | 71 | 25 | 44 | 2 | 2 |
| Holdenville[6] | 5,388 | 10 | 0 | 0 | 1 | 9 | 144 | 30 | 104 | 10 | 2 |
| Hollis | 1,931 | 3 | 0 | 0 | 0 | 3 | 48 | 23 | 25 | 0 | 0 |
| Hominy | 3,613 | 14 | 0 | 0 | 1 | 13 | 27 | 8 | 13 | 6 | 0 |
| Hooker[6] | 1,715 | 0 | 0 | 0 | 0 | 0 | 11 | 4 | 6 | 1 | 0 |
| Howe[6] | 718 | 1 | 0 | 1 | 0 | 0 | 2 | 0 | 1 | 1 | 0 |
| Hugo[6] | 5,371 | 13 | 0 | 1 | 2 | 10 | 222 | 93 | 122 | 7 | 3 |
| Hulbert[6] | 539 | 0 | 0 | 0 | 0 | 0 | 7 | 0 | 5 | 2 | 0 |
| Hydro[6] | 1,004 | 0 | 0 | 0 | 0 | 0 | 23 | 9 | 11 | 3 | 1 |
| Idabel | 6,831 | 51 | 2 | 7 | 7 | 35 | 206 | 43 | 153 | 10 | 2 |
| Jay | 3,057 | 12 | 0 | 2 | 0 | 10 | 37 | 9 | 28 | 0 | 1 |
| Jenks | 16,438 | 23 | 0 | 5 | 3 | 15 | 328 | 89 | 227 | 12 | 3 |
| Jones[6] | 2,723 | 4 | 0 | 0 | 2 | 2 | 32 | 18 | 11 | 3 | 0 |
| Kaw City[6] | 367 | 0 | 0 | 0 | 0 | 0 | 1 | 0 | 1 | 0 | 0 |
| Kiefer[6] | 1,646 | 3 | 0 | 0 | 0 | 3 | 13 | 5 | 5 | 3 | 0 |
| Kingfisher[6] | 4,357 | 1 | 0 | 0 | 0 | 1 | 70 | 12 | 56 | 2 | 0 |
| Kingston[6] | 1,599 | 1 | 0 | 0 | 0 | 1 | 5 | 2 | 2 | 1 | 0 |
| Krebs[6] | 2,139 | 6 | 0 | 1 | 2 | 3 | 36 | 10 | 22 | 4 | 2 |
| Lawton | 89,835 | 1,098 | 9 | 81 | 181 | 827 | 4,922 | 1,448 | 3,240 | 234 | 30 |
| Lexington | 2,117 | 10 | 0 | 0 | 0 | 10 | 48 | 13 | 31 | 4 | 4 |
| Lindsay[6] | 2,913 | 3 | 0 | 1 | 0 | 2 | 76 | 18 | 44 | 14 | 1 |
| Locust Grove[6] | 1,596 | 2 | 0 | 1 | 0 | 1 | 40 | 8 | 28 | 4 | 0 |
| Lone Grove[6] | 5,356 | 8 | 0 | 1 | 1 | 6 | 117 | 39 | 70 | 8 | 1 |
| Luther[6] | 1,147 | 1 | 0 | 0 | 0 | 1 | 14 | 5 | 8 | 1 | 1 |
| Madill[6] | 3,808 | 14 | 0 | 2 | 2 | 10 | 141 | 55 | 78 | 8 | 0 |
| Mangum | 2,689 | 4 | 0 | 3 | 0 | 1 | 44 | 14 | 29 | 1 | 0 |
| Mannford | 2,878 | 4 | 0 | 0 | 0 | 4 | 31 | 11 | 19 | 1 | 0 |
| Marietta[6] | 2,540 | 10 | 0 | 0 | 0 | 10 | 50 | 6 | 40 | 4 | 0 |
| Marlow | 4,601 | 19 | 0 | 1 | 0 | 18 | 152 | 34 | 111 | 7 | 0 |
| Maysville[6] | 1,300 | 1 | 0 | 0 | 0 | 1 | 21 | 2 | 16 | 3 | 0 |
| McAlester | 18,459 | 57 | 0 | 6 | 12 | 39 | 854 | 157 | 659 | 38 | 1 |
| McLoud[6] | 4,448 | 12 | 0 | 0 | 2 | 10 | 43 | 11 | 29 | 3 | 0 |
| Medicine Park[6] | 379 | 0 | 0 | 0 | 0 | 0 | 4 | 2 | 2 | 0 | 0 |
| Meeker[6] | 982 | 1 | 0 | 0 | 0 | 1 | 29 | 11 | 15 | 3 | 0 |
| Miami | 12,953 | 60 | 0 | 5 | 3 | 52 | 578 | 110 | 438 | 30 | 8 |
| Midwest City | 56,631 | 184 | 2 | 24 | 45 | 113 | 2,574 | 878 | 1,553 | 143 | 5 |
| Minco[6] | 1,817 | 0 | 0 | 0 | 0 | 0 | 15 | 6 | 6 | 3 | 0 |
| Moore | 54,059 | 83 | 1 | 17 | 18 | 47 | 2,413 | 560 | 1,682 | 171 | 3 |
| Mooreland | 1,256 | 5 | 1 | 0 | 1 | 3 | 31 | 11 | 20 | 0 | 0 |
| Morris[6] | 1,311 | 0 | 0 | 0 | 0 | 0 | 7 | 3 | 4 | 0 | 0 |
| Mountain View | 777 | 5 | 0 | 0 | 0 | 5 | 4 | 0 | 4 | 0 | 0 |
| Muldrow | 3,158 | 5 | 0 | 1 | 1 | 3 | 61 | 16 | 44 | 1 | 1 |
| Muskogee[6] | 40,197 | 472 | 0 | 24 | 65 | 383 | 2,068 | 711 | 1,283 | 74 | 19 |
| Mustang | 18,314 | 49 | 0 | 4 | 0 | 45 | 490 | 108 | 355 | 27 | 3 |
| Newcastle | 7,474 | 5 | 0 | 0 | 0 | 5 | 232 | 46 | 163 | 23 | 0 |
| Newkirk[6] | 2,112 | 3 | 0 | 0 | 1 | 2 | 56 | 19 | 35 | 2 | 0 |
| Nichols Hills | 4,031 | 2 | 1 | 0 | 1 | 0 | 84 | 18 | 59 | 7 | 0 |
| Nicoma Park[6] | 2,398 | 5 | 0 | 0 | 0 | 5 | 33 | 12 | 18 | 3 | 0 |
| Noble | 5,875 | 23 | 0 | 5 | 0 | 18 | 113 | 33 | 73 | 7 | 0 |
| Norman | 108,152 | 162 | 0 | 44 | 47 | 71 | 3,783 | 765 | 2,874 | 144 | 6 |
| Nowata | 3,997 | 24 | 0 | 2 | 0 | 22 | 76 | 9 | 66 | 1 | 1 |
| Oilton[6] | 1,125 | 4 | 0 | 0 | 0 | 4 | 16 | 5 | 8 | 3 | 0 |
| Okemah[6] | 2,897 | 6 | 1 | 1 | 0 | 4 | 90 | 17 | 72 | 1 | 3 |
| Oklahoma City | 556,939 | 5,181 | 65 | 294 | 1,249 | 3,573 | 33,964 | 10,594 | 19,544 | 3,826 | 121 |
| Okmulgee | 12,595 | 95 | 1 | 7 | 15 | 72 | 468 | 141 | 308 | 19 | 12 |
| Oologah | 1,158 | 0 | 0 | 0 | 0 | 0 | 16 | 4 | 9 | 3 | 0 |
| Owasso | 28,631 | 77 | 0 | 4 | 5 | 68 | 662 | 131 | 485 | 46 | 2 |
| Pauls Valley | 6,106 | 29 | 0 | 4 | 3 | 22 | 502 | 144 | 341 | 17 | 1 |
| Pawhuska | 3,403 | 68 | 0 | 3 | 0 | 65 | 98 | 45 | 37 | 16 | 0 |
| Pawnee[6] | 2,140 | 2 | 0 | 1 | 0 | 1 | 13 | 5 | 4 | 4 | 0 |
| Perkins[6] | 2,412 | 6 | 0 | 0 | 0 | 6 | 42 | 7 | 32 | 3 | 0 |
| Perry | 5,041 | 12 | 0 | 1 | 1 | 10 | 91 | 16 | 62 | 13 | 1 |
| Piedmont | 5,756 | 2 | 0 | 1 | 0 | 1 | 56 | 12 | 43 | 1 | 0 |
| Pocola[6] | 4,518 | 6 | 0 | 0 | 1 | 5 | 70 | 31 | 30 | 9 | 0 |
| Ponca City | 24,359 | 173 | 2 | 20 | 21 | 130 | 1,226 | 297 | 888 | 41 | 8 |
| Porum[6] | 736 | 0 | 0 | 0 | 0 | 0 | 7 | 3 | 3 | 1 | 0 |
| Poteau | 8,287 | 42 | 0 | 5 | 2 | 35 | 278 | 34 | 215 | 29 | 0 |
| Prague[6] | 2,126 | 5 | 0 | 1 | 0 | 4 | 54 | 15 | 35 | 4 | 0 |

[1] The FBI does not publish arson data unless it receives data from either the agency or the state for all 12 months of the calendar year.

[6] Because of changes in the state/local agency's reporting practices, figures are not comparable to previous years' data.

## Table 8. Offenses Known to Law Enforcement, by State and City, 2009—*Continued*

(Number.)

| State/city | Population | Violent crime | Murder and non-negligent man-slaughter | Forcible rape | Robbery | Aggravated assault | Property crime | Burglary | Larceny-theft | Motor vehicle theft | Arson[1] |
|---|---|---|---|---|---|---|---|---|---|---|---|
| **OKLAHOMA**—*Continued* | | | | | | | | | | | |
| Pryor[3] | 9,345 | | 0 | 5 | 3 | | 324 | 91 | 212 | 21 | 0 |
| Purcell | 6,194 | 17 | 0 | 4 | 2 | 11 | 267 | 34 | 225 | 8 | 3 |
| Ringling[6] | 1,035 | 1 | 0 | 1 | 0 | 0 | 8 | 4 | 3 | 1 | 0 |
| Roland[6] | 3,453 | 4 | 0 | 0 | 1 | 3 | 88 | 21 | 66 | 1 | 0 |
| Rush Springs[6] | 1,352 | 3 | 0 | 0 | 0 | 3 | 13 | 4 | 7 | 2 | 0 |
| Sallisaw | 8,823 | 17 | 0 | 1 | 4 | 12 | 308 | 60 | 236 | 12 | 4 |
| Sand Springs | 18,602 | 43 | 1 | 11 | 10 | 21 | 682 | 116 | 522 | 44 | 0 |
| Sapulpa | 21,288 | 39 | 0 | 5 | 8 | 26 | 712 | 125 | 546 | 41 | 3 |
| Sayre | 4,413 | 2 | 0 | 0 | 0 | 2 | 65 | 28 | 31 | 6 | 2 |
| Seminole | 6,797 | 47 | 3 | 1 | 5 | 38 | 397 | 144 | 231 | 22 | 0 |
| Shawnee | 30,724 | 229 | 1 | 22 | 28 | 178 | 1,845 | 477 | 1,240 | 128 | 3 |
| Skiatook | 6,973 | 88 | 0 | 12 | 0 | 76 | 217 | 62 | 145 | 10 | 2 |
| Snyder[6] | 1,365 | 4 | 0 | 0 | 0 | 4 | 11 | 2 | 6 | 3 | 0 |
| South Coffeyville | 787 | 6 | 0 | 0 | 0 | 6 | 8 | 3 | 4 | 1 | 0 |
| Spencer[6] | 4,056 | 8 | 0 | 0 | 1 | 7 | 109 | 60 | 33 | 16 | 0 |
| Spiro[6] | 2,334 | 5 | 0 | 1 | 0 | 4 | 36 | 9 | 21 | 6 | 0 |
| Stigler[6] | 2,876 | 9 | 2 | 0 | 0 | 7 | 91 | 18 | 67 | 6 | 0 |
| Stillwater | 48,690 | 115 | 0 | 18 | 15 | 82 | 1,472 | 289 | 1,140 | 43 | 9 |
| Stilwell[6] | 3,519 | 5 | 0 | 0 | 1 | 4 | 43 | 7 | 35 | 1 | 0 |
| Stonewall[6] | 496 | 0 | 0 | 0 | 0 | 0 | 15 | 10 | 5 | 0 | 0 |
| Stratford[6] | 1,491 | 3 | 0 | 0 | 1 | 2 | 51 | 22 | 25 | 4 | 0 |
| Stringtown[6] | 424 | 2 | 0 | 0 | 0 | 2 | 13 | 8 | 5 | 0 | 0 |
| Stroud[6] | 2,721 | 4 | 0 | 0 | 3 | 1 | 76 | 15 | 52 | 9 | 1 |
| Sulphur | 4,844 | 5 | 0 | 1 | 1 | 3 | 81 | 34 | 46 | 1 | 0 |
| Tahlequah[6] | 16,865 | 38 | 1 | 14 | 2 | 21 | 637 | 122 | 485 | 30 | 5 |
| Talihina[6] | 1,237 | 8 | 0 | 1 | 2 | 5 | 60 | 22 | 37 | 1 | 0 |
| Tecumseh | 6,732 | 18 | 1 | 6 | 2 | 9 | 215 | 77 | 128 | 10 | 0 |
| The Village | 9,728 | 27 | 0 | 2 | 7 | 18 | 331 | 93 | 215 | 23 | 1 |
| Tishomingo[6] | 3,151 | 18 | 0 | 3 | 0 | 15 | 88 | 45 | 36 | 7 | 1 |
| Tonkawa | 3,121 | 19 | 0 | 7 | 2 | 10 | 87 | 21 | 60 | 6 | 1 |
| Tryon[6] | 448 | 3 | 0 | 0 | 0 | 3 | 9 | 4 | 4 | 1 | 0 |
| Tulsa | 384,851 | 4,295 | 68 | 254 | 1,117 | 2,856 | 23,220 | 6,626 | 14,521 | 2,073 | 202 |
| Tushka[6] | 373 | 0 | 0 | 0 | 0 | 0 | 2 | 0 | 2 | 0 | 0 |
| Tuttle | 6,265 | 9 | 0 | 0 | 0 | 9 | 102 | 38 | 57 | 7 | 2 |
| Valliant[6] | 740 | 5 | 0 | 1 | 0 | 4 | 23 | 5 | 16 | 2 | 0 |
| Verdigris[6] | 3,126 | 2 | 0 | 1 | 0 | 1 | 24 | 4 | 16 | 4 | 0 |
| Vian[6] | 1,447 | 2 | 0 | 0 | 0 | 2 | 18 | 6 | 10 | 2 | 0 |
| Vinita | 6,052 | 21 | 0 | 1 | 0 | 20 | 152 | 32 | 114 | 6 | 1 |
| Wagoner[3] | 8,122 | | 0 | 2 | 3 | | 412 | 88 | 307 | 17 | 2 |
| Walters[6] | 2,408 | 4 | 0 | 0 | 0 | 4 | 34 | 6 | 28 | 0 | 0 |
| Warner[6] | 1,449 | 4 | 0 | 0 | 0 | 4 | 3 | 2 | 1 | 0 | 0 |
| Warr Acres | 9,394 | 86 | 0 | 7 | 23 | 56 | 534 | 179 | 303 | 52 | 4 |
| Washington[6] | 555 | 1 | 0 | 0 | 0 | 1 | 4 | 3 | 1 | 0 | 0 |
| Watonga[6] | 5,818 | 7 | 0 | 2 | 1 | 4 | 71 | 17 | 53 | 1 | 0 |
| Waukomis[6] | 1,209 | 3 | 0 | 1 | 0 | 2 | 18 | 6 | 10 | 2 | 0 |
| Waurika | 1,802 | 12 | 0 | 0 | 1 | 11 | 12 | 2 | 8 | 2 | 0 |
| Waynoka[6] | 892 | 3 | 0 | 2 | 0 | 1 | 19 | 10 | 9 | 0 | 0 |
| Weatherford[3] | 10,224 | | 0 | 7 | 3 | | 378 | 75 | 288 | 15 | 1 |
| Weleetka[6] | 917 | 5 | 0 | 0 | 1 | 4 | 37 | 8 | 25 | 4 | 1 |
| Westville[6] | 1,643 | 12 | 0 | 1 | 1 | 10 | 54 | 14 | 35 | 5 | 3 |
| Wetumka[6] | 1,400 | 5 | 0 | 1 | 1 | 3 | 20 | 9 | 10 | 1 | 0 |
| Wewoka | 3,289 | 6 | 1 | 0 | 0 | 5 | 110 | 35 | 71 | 4 | 0 |
| Wilburton[6] | 2,885 | 4 | 0 | 0 | 0 | 4 | 63 | 18 | 43 | 2 | 0 |
| Wilson[3] | 1,640 | | 0 | 2 | 0 | | 37 | 12 | 20 | 5 | 2 |
| Woodward | 12,355 | 39 | 0 | 17 | 7 | 15 | 591 | 178 | 396 | 17 | 0 |
| Wright City[6] | 785 | 1 | 0 | 1 | 0 | 0 | 20 | 2 | 15 | 3 | 0 |
| Wynnewood[6] | 2,280 | 4 | 0 | 0 | 0 | 4 | 32 | 1 | 28 | 3 | 2 |
| Yale[6] | 1,359 | 1 | 0 | 0 | 0 | 1 | 4 | 0 | 4 | 0 | 1 |
| Yukon | 23,058 | 20 | 0 | 2 | 6 | 12 | 627 | 115 | 486 | 26 | 3 |
| **OREGON** | | | | | | | | | | | |
| Albany | 48,933 | 69 | 0 | 10 | 35 | 24 | 1,860 | 155 | 1,629 | 76 | 16 |
| Amity | 1,466 | 0 | 0 | 0 | 0 | 0 | 25 | 7 | 17 | 1 | 1 |
| Ashland | 21,611 | 18 | 0 | 6 | 3 | 9 | 548 | 61 | 474 | 13 | 4 |
| Astoria | 9,859 | 27 | 1 | 7 | 6 | 13 | 536 | 100 | 415 | 21 | 5 |
| Aumsville | 3,673 | 6 | 0 | 2 | 0 | 4 | 47 | 8 | 37 | 2 | 1 |
| Aurora | 1,053 | 1 | 0 | 0 | 0 | 1 | 13 | 1 | 11 | 1 | 1 |
| Baker City | 9,367 | 3 | 0 | 0 | 0 | 3 | 123 | 25 | 91 | 7 | 2 |
| Bandon | 3,299 | 1 | 0 | 0 | 1 | 0 | 113 | 21 | 88 | 4 | 0 |
| Banks | 1,643 | 2 | 0 | 0 | 0 | 2 | 18 | 5 | 13 | 0 | 1 |
| Beaverton | 93,221 | 189 | 2 | 23 | 47 | 117 | 1,592 | 226 | 1,230 | 136 | 23 |
| Bend | 80,550 | 150 | 0 | 14 | 19 | 117 | 2,036 | 316 | 1,642 | 78 | 16 |

[1] The FBI does not publish arson data unless it receives data from either the agency or the state for all 12 months of the calendar year.
[3] The FBI determined that the agency's data were overreported. Consequently, those data are not included in this table.
[6] Because of changes in the state/local agency's reporting practices, figures are not comparable to previous years' data.

## Table 8. Offenses Known to Law Enforcement, by State and City, 2009—*Continued*

(Number.)

| State/city | Population | Violent crime | Murder and non-negligent man-slaughter | Forcible rape | Robbery | Aggravated assault | Property crime | Burglary | Larceny-theft | Motor vehicle theft | Arson[1] |
|---|---|---|---|---|---|---|---|---|---|---|---|
| **OREGON**—*Continued* | | | | | | | | | | | |
| Black Butte | 0 | 0 | 0 | 0 | 0 | 0 | 3 | 0 | 3 | 0 | 0 |
| Boardman | 2,919 | 9 | 0 | 0 | 0 | 9 | 73 | 16 | 54 | 3 | 0 |
| Burns | 2,622 | 2 | 0 | 0 | 0 | 2 | 81 | 23 | 54 | 4 | 1 |
| Canby | 15,982 | 19 | 0 | 5 | 4 | 10 | 423 | 42 | 366 | 15 | 2 |
| Cannon Beach | 1,741 | 3 | 0 | 0 | 1 | 2 | 44 | 12 | 32 | 0 | 2 |
| Carlton | 1,699 | 0 | 0 | 0 | 0 | 0 | 29 | 6 | 23 | 0 | 0 |
| Central Point | 16,971 | 5 | 0 | 2 | 2 | 1 | 295 | 41 | 246 | 8 | 1 |
| Clatskanie | 1,650 | 2 | 0 | 1 | 0 | 1 | 46 | 10 | 35 | 1 | 0 |
| Coburg | 1,080 | 1 | 0 | 0 | 1 | 0 | 22 | 6 | 14 | 2 | 1 |
| Columbia City | 2,013 | 1 | 0 | 1 | 0 | 0 | 10 | 1 | 8 | 1 | 0 |
| Condon | 659 | 1 | 0 | 0 | 0 | 1 | 1 | 0 | 0 | 1 | 0 |
| Coos Bay | 15,703 | 37 | 0 | 7 | 6 | 24 | 660 | 107 | 509 | 44 | 6 |
| Coquille | 4,110 | 0 | 0 | 0 | 0 | 0 | 54 | 19 | 34 | 1 | 0 |
| Cornelius | 11,676 | 15 | 1 | 0 | 1 | 13 | 259 | 63 | 180 | 16 | 2 |
| Corvallis | 51,302 | 66 | 1 | 10 | 19 | 36 | 1,706 | 249 | 1,396 | 61 | 8 |
| Cottage Grove | 9,200 | 13 | 0 | 1 | 7 | 5 | 587 | 83 | 469 | 35 | 10 |
| Creswell | 5,243 | 27 | 1 | 2 | 2 | 22 | 189 | 66 | 115 | 8 | 1 |
| Dallas | 16,317 | 29 | 0 | 8 | 2 | 19 | 295 | 43 | 235 | 17 | 5 |
| Eagle Point | 8,787 | 2 | 0 | 1 | 0 | 1 | 161 | 12 | 146 | 3 | 3 |
| Enterprise | 1,691 | 0 | 0 | 0 | 0 | 0 | 24 | 4 | 20 | 0 | 0 |
| Estacada | 2,580 | 7 | 0 | 2 | 1 | 4 | 74 | 26 | 45 | 3 | 0 |
| Eugene | 151,383 | 470 | 1 | 73 | 201 | 195 | 8,627 | 1,868 | 5,871 | 888 | 70 |
| Fairview | 10,080 | 15 | 0 | 3 | 5 | 7 | 325 | 47 | 244 | 34 | 1 |
| Florence | 8,867 | 5 | 0 | 1 | 0 | 4 | 303 | 49 | 239 | 15 | 0 |
| Forest Grove | 21,333 | 37 | 2 | 1 | 12 | 22 | 717 | 112 | 588 | 17 | 3 |
| Gaston | 805 | 0 | 0 | 0 | 0 | 0 | 7 | 1 | 6 | 0 | 0 |
| Gearhart | 1,202 | 0 | 0 | 0 | 0 | 0 | 8 | 4 | 4 | 0 | 0 |
| Gervais | 2,453 | 7 | 0 | 0 | 1 | 6 | 85 | 14 | 49 | 22 | 0 |
| Gladstone | 12,152 | 38 | 0 | 6 | 2 | 30 | 333 | 63 | 244 | 26 | 8 |
| Gold Beach | 1,815 | 2 | 0 | 0 | 0 | 2 | 28 | 5 | 20 | 3 | 0 |
| Gresham | 102,463 | 382 | 0 | 37 | 153 | 192 | 3,988 | 572 | 2,747 | 669 | 25 |
| Hermiston | 15,544 | 50 | 0 | 3 | 11 | 36 | 655 | 108 | 500 | 47 | 2 |
| Hillsboro | 96,563 | 147 | 4 | 31 | 60 | 52 | 1,886 | 235 | 1,527 | 124 | 13 |
| Hines | 1,384 | 0 | 0 | 0 | 0 | 0 | 22 | 4 | 18 | 0 | 0 |
| Hood River | 6,967 | 2 | 0 | 0 | 0 | 2 | 179 | 24 | 145 | 10 | 0 |
| Hubbard | 2,850 | 0 | 0 | 0 | 0 | 0 | 38 | 4 | 32 | 2 | 0 |
| Independence | 9,822 | 25 | 0 | 4 | 1 | 20 | 212 | 28 | 178 | 6 | 7 |
| Jacksonville | 2,177 | 0 | 0 | 0 | 0 | 0 | 35 | 10 | 25 | 0 | 0 |
| John Day | 1,482 | 1 | 0 | 0 | 0 | 1 | 32 | 7 | 24 | 1 | 0 |
| Junction City | 5,657 | 4 | 0 | 1 | 2 | 1 | 73 | 10 | 63 | 0 | 0 |
| Keizer | 36,275 | 63 | 1 | 7 | 5 | 50 | 736 | 94 | 585 | 57 | 5 |
| King City | 2,989 | 3 | 0 | 2 | 1 | 0 | 54 | 7 | 45 | 2 | 0 |
| Klamath Falls | 20,358 | 95 | 1 | 15 | 23 | 56 | 715 | 134 | 542 | 39 | 6 |
| La Grande | 12,697 | 17 | 0 | 3 | 0 | 14 | 396 | 72 | 312 | 12 | 4 |
| Lake Oswego | 37,100 | 23 | 0 | 3 | 6 | 14 | 491 | 75 | 407 | 9 | 15 |
| Lakeview | 2,423 | 9 | 0 | 0 | 0 | 9 | 47 | 12 | 34 | 1 | 0 |
| Lebanon | 15,665 | 30 | 0 | 3 | 5 | 22 | 562 | 91 | 453 | 18 | 4 |
| Lincoln City | 8,121 | 34 | 0 | 6 | 6 | 22 | 359 | 81 | 263 | 15 | 1 |
| Madras | 6,093 | 21 | 1 | 2 | 8 | 10 | 310 | 52 | 233 | 25 | 1 |
| Malin | 616 | 0 | 0 | 0 | 0 | 0 | 2 | 2 | 0 | 0 | 0 |
| Manzanita | 624 | 0 | 0 | 0 | 0 | 0 | 8 | 1 | 7 | 0 | 0 |
| McMinnville | 31,730 | 59 | 1 | 13 | 17 | 28 | 818 | 125 | 663 | 30 | 5 |
| Medford | 74,042 | 227 | 2 | 30 | 24 | 171 | 2,961 | 324 | 2,539 | 98 | 47 |
| Milton-Freewater | 6,415 | 14 | 1 | 1 | 1 | 11 | 184 | 51 | 120 | 13 | 1 |
| Milwaukie | 20,732 | 28 | 0 | 7 | 5 | 16 | 466 | 69 | 356 | 41 | 2 |
| Molalla | 7,451 | 9 | 0 | 2 | 1 | 6 | 221 | 27 | 178 | 16 | 1 |
| Monmouth | 9,836 | 15 | 0 | 0 | 0 | 15 | 209 | 49 | 155 | 5 | 1 |
| Mount Angel | 3,511 | 5 | 0 | 0 | 1 | 4 | 51 | 7 | 39 | 5 | 0 |
| Myrtle Creek | 3,489 | 2 | 0 | 1 | 0 | 1 | 65 | 3 | 59 | 3 | 1 |
| Newberg-Dundee | 26,669 | 18 | 0 | 7 | 1 | 10 | 453 | 41 | 396 | 16 | 2 |
| Newport | 9,993 | 35 | 0 | 7 | 4 | 24 | 437 | 62 | 351 | 24 | 3 |
| North Bend | 9,648 | 3 | 0 | 0 | 2 | 1 | 392 | 65 | 307 | 20 | 3 |
| North Plains | 1,930 | 0 | 0 | 0 | 0 | 0 | 8 | 2 | 6 | 0 | 0 |
| Oakridge | 3,195 | 2 | 0 | 2 | 0 | 0 | 96 | 27 | 61 | 8 | 0 |
| Ontario[6] | 10,986 | 47 | 2 | 7 | 9 | 29 | 624 | 86 | 527 | 11 | 2 |
| Oregon City | 31,976 | 46 | 0 | 10 | 18 | 18 | 829 | 93 | 679 | 57 | 1 |
| Pendleton | 16,378 | 51 | 1 | 8 | 12 | 30 | 629 | 116 | 477 | 36 | 2 |
| Philomath | 4,558 | 6 | 0 | 1 | 1 | 4 | 113 | 35 | 75 | 3 | 2 |
| Phoenix | 4,429 | 5 | 0 | 0 | 0 | 5 | 72 | 9 | 61 | 2 | 0 |
| Pilot Rock | 1,512 | 2 | 0 | 0 | 1 | 1 | 19 | 2 | 15 | 2 | 0 |
| Portland | 560,908 | 3,105 | 19 | 252 | 1,037 | 1,797 | 26,495 | 3,696 | 19,624 | 3,175 | 269 |

[1] The FBI does not publish arson data unless it receives data from either the agency or the state for all 12 months of the calendar year.

[6] Because of changes in the state/local agency's reporting practices, figures are not comparable to previous years' data.

## Table 8. Offenses Known to Law Enforcement, by State and City, 2009—*Continued*

(Number.)

| State/city | Population | Violent crime | Murder and non-negligent man-slaughter | Forcible rape | Robbery | Aggravated assault | Property crime | Burglary | Larceny-theft | Motor vehicle theft | Arson[1] |
|---|---|---|---|---|---|---|---|---|---|---|---|
| **OREGON**—*Continued* | | | | | | | | | | | |
| Prineville | 10,293 | 30 | 1 | 2 | 0 | 27 | 337 | 55 | 275 | 7 | 7 |
| Rainier | 1,820 | 4 | 0 | 0 | 0 | 4 | 40 | 9 | 24 | 7 | 2 |
| Redmond | 25,856 | 73 | 0 | 16 | 8 | 49 | 1,107 | 175 | 883 | 49 | 16 |
| Reedsport | 4,195 | 0 | 0 | 0 | 0 | 0 | 96 | 23 | 71 | 2 | 1 |
| Rockaway Beach | 1,378 | 2 | 0 | 0 | 0 | 2 | 45 | 26 | 17 | 2 | 0 |
| Rogue River | 1,942 | 3 | 0 | 2 | 1 | 0 | 51 | 12 | 38 | 1 | 3 |
| Roseburg | 20,741 | 36 | 0 | 14 | 13 | 9 | 733 | 84 | 609 | 40 | 7 |
| Salem | 155,329 | 576 | 5 | 71 | 121 | 379 | 6,213 | 967 | 4,617 | 629 | 35 |
| Sandy | 9,282 | 20 | 0 | 3 | 10 | 7 | 250 | 24 | 211 | 15 | 1 |
| Scappoose | 6,543 | 4 | 0 | 2 | 0 | 2 | 90 | 14 | 71 | 5 | 3 |
| Seaside | 6,300 | 22 | 0 | 0 | 11 | 11 | 560 | 93 | 451 | 16 | 5 |
| Shady Cove | 2,647 | 0 | 0 | 0 | 0 | 0 | 20 | 6 | 12 | 2 | 1 |
| Sherwood | 18,111 | 11 | 0 | 2 | 4 | 5 | 223 | 27 | 195 | 1 | 1 |
| Silverton | 9,895 | 13 | 0 | 4 | 3 | 6 | 134 | 20 | 103 | 11 | 1 |
| Springfield | 57,653 | 238 | 1 | 10 | 44 | 183 | 2,828 | 497 | 2,026 | 305 | 26 |
| Stayton | 7,375 | 12 | 0 | 1 | 2 | 9 | 325 | 64 | 245 | 16 | 7 |
| St. Helens | 12,804 | 10 | 1 | 4 | 0 | 5 | 289 | 37 | 234 | 18 | 5 |
| Sunriver | 0 | 2 | 0 | 0 | 0 | 2 | 66 | 10 | 52 | 4 | 0 |
| Sutherlin | 7,154 | 12 | 0 | 3 | 0 | 9 | 145 | 25 | 108 | 12 | 3 |
| Sweet Home | 9,039 | 6 | 0 | 1 | 2 | 3 | 310 | 44 | 257 | 9 | 2 |
| Talent | 6,287 | 4 | 0 | 3 | 0 | 1 | 138 | 18 | 118 | 2 | 2 |
| The Dalles | 11,874 | 14 | 0 | 3 | 3 | 8 | 610 | 151 | 431 | 28 | 0 |
| Tigard | 49,422 | 63 | 0 | 12 | 37 | 14 | 1,684 | 173 | 1,454 | 57 | 8 |
| Tillamook | 4,414 | 6 | 2 | 1 | 0 | 3 | 227 | 36 | 186 | 5 | 2 |
| Toledo | 3,278 | 4 | 1 | 0 | 1 | 2 | 94 | 11 | 80 | 3 | 2 |
| Troutdale | 15,630 | 17 | 0 | 3 | 9 | 5 | 463 | 62 | 368 | 33 | 3 |
| Tualatin | 26,903 | 58 | 1 | 17 | 17 | 23 | 873 | 69 | 762 | 42 | 0 |
| Turner | 1,784 | 8 | 0 | 1 | 0 | 7 | 49 | 10 | 37 | 2 | 1 |
| Umatilla | 6,443 | 12 | 0 | 1 | 0 | 11 | 69 | 8 | 51 | 10 | 1 |
| Veneta | 4,489 | 41 | 0 | 4 | 2 | 35 | 212 | 58 | 132 | 22 | 5 |
| Vernonia | 2,280 | 0 | 0 | 0 | 0 | 0 | 33 | 13 | 19 | 1 | 1 |
| Warrenton | 4,489 | 0 | 0 | 0 | 0 | 0 | 136 | 24 | 105 | 7 | 6 |
| West Linn | 25,568 | 12 | 0 | 3 | 3 | 6 | 271 | 23 | 237 | 11 | 3 |
| Weston | 690 | 1 | 0 | 0 | 0 | 1 | 20 | 4 | 14 | 2 | 0 |
| Wilsonville | 19,666 | 14 | 0 | 2 | 6 | 6 | 587 | 55 | 489 | 43 | 5 |
| Winston | 5,622 | 6 | 0 | 1 | 1 | 4 | 110 | 26 | 77 | 7 | 15 |
| Woodburn | 23,103 | 59 | 0 | 6 | 24 | 29 | 997 | 139 | 702 | 156 | 6 |
| Yamhill | 928 | 1 | 0 | 1 | 0 | 0 | 13 | 2 | 11 | 0 | 0 |
| **PENNSYLVANIA** | | | | | | | | | | | |
| Abington Township | 53,761 | 78 | 2 | 1 | 36 | 39 | 1,405 | 163 | 1,213 | 29 | 5 |
| Adamstown | 1,572 | 1 | 0 | 0 | 1 | 0 | 28 | 2 | 26 | 0 | 0 |
| Adams Township, Butler County | 9,823 | 11 | 0 | 1 | 0 | 10 | 51 | 4 | 46 | 1 | 0 |
| Adams Township, Cambria County | 6,008 | 1 | 0 | 0 | 0 | 1 | 38 | 3 | 32 | 3 | 0 |
| Akron | 4,014 | 0 | 0 | 0 | 0 | 0 | 46 | 10 | 35 | 1 | 0 |
| Albion | 1,490 | 2 | 0 | 0 | 0 | 2 | 13 | 4 | 9 | 0 | 0 |
| Alburtis | 2,425 | 2 | 0 | 0 | 0 | 2 | 30 | 8 | 21 | 1 | 0 |
| Aldan | 4,229 | 12 | 1 | 1 | 2 | 8 | 94 | 10 | 80 | 4 | 0 |
| Aleppo Township | 1,271 | 0 | 0 | 0 | 0 | 0 | 12 | 2 | 10 | 0 | 0 |
| Aliquippa | 10,525 | 65 | 5 | 5 | 12 | 43 | 170 | 38 | 113 | 19 | 0 |
| Allegheny Township, Blair County | 6,845 | 52 | 0 | 2 | 2 | 48 | 124 | 17 | 106 | 1 | 2 |
| Allegheny Township, Westmoreland County | 8,199 | 4 | 0 | 0 | 1 | 3 | 76 | 3 | 70 | 3 | 0 |
| Allentown | 107,326 | 749 | 13 | 72 | 474 | 190 | 5,270 | 1,414 | 3,385 | 471 | 26 |
| Altoona | 45,793 | 169 | 1 | 20 | 43 | 105 | 974 | 260 | 657 | 57 | 13 |
| Ambler | 6,171 | 10 | 0 | 0 | 6 | 4 | 147 | 5 | 139 | 3 | 1 |
| Ambridge | 6,949 | 77 | 0 | 4 | 15 | 58 | 250 | 47 | 198 | 5 | 3 |
| Amity Township | 12,149 | 7 | 0 | 1 | 1 | 5 | 134 | 17 | 107 | 10 | 2 |
| Annville Township | 4,786 | 9 | 1 | 0 | 0 | 8 | 65 | 9 | 56 | 0 | 0 |
| Apollo | 1,619 | 4 | 0 | 0 | 0 | 4 | 1 | 1 | 0 | 0 | 0 |
| Arnold | 5,165 | 29 | 1 | 2 | 13 | 13 | 115 | 41 | 59 | 15 | 2 |
| Ashland | 3,080 | 12 | 0 | 0 | 3 | 9 | 69 | 15 | 54 | 0 | 1 |
| Ashley | 2,642 | 1 | 0 | 0 | 0 | 1 | 20 | 9 | 7 | 4 | 0 |
| Ashville | 256 | 0 | 0 | 0 | 0 | 0 | 0 | 0 | 0 | 0 | 0 |
| Aspinwall | 2,678 | 2 | 0 | 0 | 1 | 1 | 42 | 5 | 35 | 2 | 0 |
| Aston Township | 16,886 | 18 | 0 | 1 | 9 | 8 | 307 | 28 | 265 | 14 | 0 |
| Atglen | 1,383 | 1 | 0 | 1 | 0 | 0 | 7 | 1 | 5 | 1 | 0 |
| Athens | 3,188 | 8 | 0 | 0 | 0 | 8 | 58 | 12 | 46 | 0 | 0 |
| Auburn | 795 | 0 | 0 | 0 | 0 | 0 | 7 | 1 | 5 | 1 | 1 |
| Avalon | 4,763 | 9 | 0 | 0 | 4 | 5 | 80 | 14 | 54 | 12 | 1 |
| Avoca | 2,637 | 7 | 0 | 0 | 1 | 6 | 36 | 13 | 20 | 3 | 1 |
| Avondale | 1,083 | 0 | 0 | 0 | 0 | 0 | 0 | 0 | 0 | 0 | 0 |

[1] The FBI does not publish arson data unless it receives data from either the agency or the state for all 12 months of the calendar year.

## Table 8. Offenses Known to Law Enforcement, by State and City, 2009—*Continued*

(Number.)

| State/city | Population | Violent crime | Murder and non-negligent man-slaughter | Forcible rape | Robbery | Aggravated assault | Property crime | Burglary | Larceny-theft | Motor vehicle theft | Arson[1] |
|---|---|---|---|---|---|---|---|---|---|---|---|
| **PENNSYLVANIA**—*Continued* | | | | | | | | | | | |
| Avonmore Boro | 754 | 0 | 0 | 0 | 0 | 0 | 0 | 0 | 0 | 0 | 0 |
| Baden | 3,978 | 6 | 0 | 0 | 1 | 5 | 56 | 2 | 53 | 1 | 0 |
| Baldwin Borough | 18,414 | 20 | 0 | 2 | 8 | 10 | 147 | 27 | 109 | 11 | 0 |
| Baldwin Township | 2,016 | 3 | 0 | 0 | 0 | 3 | 14 | 3 | 10 | 1 | 0 |
| Bally | 1,098 | 0 | 0 | 0 | 0 | 0 | 1 | 0 | 0 | 1 | 0 |
| Bangor | 5,249 | 13 | 0 | 0 | 1 | 12 | 113 | 11 | 100 | 2 | 0 |
| Barrett Township | 4,278 | 6 | 0 | 1 | 1 | 4 | 45 | 15 | 29 | 1 | 0 |
| Beaver | 4,330 | 5 | 0 | 0 | 2 | 3 | 102 | 17 | 84 | 1 | 0 |
| Beaver Falls | 8,967 | 58 | 0 | 0 | 21 | 37 | 376 | 45 | 311 | 20 | 2 |
| Beaver Meadows | 944 | 1 | 0 | 0 | 0 | 1 | 9 | 0 | 8 | 1 | 0 |
| Bedford | 2,984 | 4 | 0 | 0 | 1 | 3 | 38 | 8 | 30 | 0 | 0 |
| Bedminster Township | 6,273 | 2 | 0 | 0 | 0 | 2 | 47 | 3 | 44 | 0 | 0 |
| Bell Acres | 1,384 | 0 | 0 | 0 | 0 | 0 | 2 | 0 | 2 | 0 | 0 |
| Bellefonte | 6,125 | 3 | 0 | 1 | 0 | 2 | 71 | 3 | 67 | 1 | |
| Bellevue | 7,899 | 31 | 1 | 3 | 17 | 10 | 230 | 53 | 152 | 25 | |
| Bellwood | 1,854 | 3 | 0 | 0 | 0 | 3 | 6 | 1 | 5 | 0 | 0 |
| Ben Avon | 1,730 | 2 | 0 | 0 | 0 | 2 | 14 | 3 | 11 | 0 | 0 |
| Ben Avon Heights | 356 | 0 | 0 | 0 | 0 | 0 | 4 | 1 | 3 | 0 | 0 |
| Bendersville | 604 | 0 | 0 | 0 | 0 | 0 | 0 | 0 | 0 | 0 | 0 |
| Bensalem Township | 58,284 | 105 | 0 | 6 | 67 | 32 | 2,258 | 340 | 1,790 | 128 | 35 |
| Berks-Lehigh Regional | 30,216 | 15 | 0 | 3 | 5 | 7 | 336 | 52 | 266 | 18 | 2 |
| Berlin | 2,059 | 2 | 0 | 1 | 0 | 1 | 25 | 3 | 21 | 1 | 0 |
| Bern Township | 7,231 | 21 | 0 | 1 | 0 | 20 | 83 | 24 | 55 | 4 | 2 |
| Bernville | 878 | 0 | 0 | 0 | 0 | 0 | 0 | 0 | 0 | 0 | 0 |
| Berwick | 10,160 | 37 | 0 | 10 | 2 | 25 | 412 | 61 | 341 | 10 | 2 |
| Bessemer | 1,088 | 0 | 0 | 0 | 0 | 0 | 2 | 0 | 2 | 0 | 0 |
| Bethel Park | 31,354 | 63 | 1 | 4 | 7 | 51 | 291 | 35 | 249 | 7 | 5 |
| Bethel Township, Armstrong County | 1,198 | 0 | 0 | 0 | 0 | 0 | 0 | 0 | 0 | 0 | 0 |
| Bethel Township, Berks County | 4,521 | 0 | 0 | 0 | 0 | 0 | 28 | 4 | 24 | 0 | 0 |
| Bethel Township, Delaware County | 11,954 | 3 | 0 | 0 | 0 | 3 | 93 | 14 | 76 | 3 | 0 |
| Bethlehem | 72,349 | 219 | 1 | 16 | 96 | 106 | 1,932 | 365 | 1,443 | 124 | 13 |
| Bethlehem Township | 23,846 | 26 | 0 | 0 | 8 | 18 | 519 | 55 | 454 | 10 | 1 |
| Biglerville | 1,151 | 1 | 0 | 0 | 0 | 1 | 25 | 1 | 24 | 0 | |
| Birdsboro | 5,178 | 10 | 0 | 1 | 1 | 8 | 86 | 17 | 60 | 9 | 0 |
| Birmingham Township | 4,257 | 1 | 0 | 0 | 0 | 1 | 19 | 4 | 14 | 1 | 0 |
| Blacklick Township | 2,053 | 0 | 0 | 0 | 0 | 0 | 6 | 3 | 3 | 0 | 0 |
| Blair Township | 4,712 | 3 | 0 | 0 | 0 | 3 | 54 | 9 | 41 | 4 | 1 |
| Blakely | 6,718 | 1 | 0 | 0 | 1 | 0 | 91 | 11 | 78 | 2 | 1 |
| Blawnox | 1,424 | 1 | 0 | 0 | 0 | 1 | 7 | 2 | 5 | 0 | 0 |
| Bloomsburg Town | 12,821 | 25 | 1 | 5 | 4 | 15 | 334 | 38 | 289 | 7 | 1 |
| Blythe Township | 905 | 1 | 0 | 0 | 0 | 1 | 0 | 0 | 0 | 0 | 0 |
| Bolivar | 460 | 0 | 0 | 0 | 0 | 0 | 0 | 0 | 0 | 0 | 0 |
| Boswell | 1,241 | 0 | 0 | 0 | 0 | 0 | 0 | 0 | 0 | 0 | 0 |
| Boyertown | 3,917 | 6 | 0 | 0 | 1 | 5 | 101 | 13 | 84 | 4 | 1 |
| Brackenridge | 3,195 | 15 | 0 | 2 | 6 | 7 | 102 | 13 | 87 | 2 | 0 |
| Braddock Hills | 1,809 | 4 | 0 | 0 | 1 | 3 | 21 | 1 | 19 | 1 | 0 |
| Bradford | 8,312 | 45 | 0 | 9 | 1 | 35 | 259 | 18 | 233 | 8 | 1 |
| Brecknock Township, Berks County | 4,949 | 3 | 0 | 0 | 0 | 3 | 31 | 2 | 25 | 4 | 0 |
| Briar Creek Township | 3,102 | 0 | 0 | 0 | 0 | 0 | 34 | 11 | 23 | 0 | 1 |
| Bridgeport | 4,347 | 11 | 1 | 2 | 1 | 7 | 110 | 24 | 79 | 7 | 1 |
| Bridgeville | 4,828 | 6 | 0 | 1 | 1 | 4 | 69 | 15 | 51 | 3 | 1 |
| Brighton Township | 7,929 | 11 | 0 | 0 | 0 | 11 | 45 | 3 | 41 | 1 | 0 |
| Bristol | 9,602 | 30 | 0 | 0 | 13 | 17 | 364 | 42 | 308 | 14 | 1 |
| Bristol Township | 53,660 | 127 | 1 | 17 | 61 | 48 | 1,548 | 254 | 1,151 | 143 | 7 |
| Brockway | 2,044 | 3 | 0 | 1 | 0 | 2 | 15 | 1 | 14 | 0 | 0 |
| Brookhaven | 7,876 | 16 | 0 | 0 | 10 | 6 | 269 | 23 | 237 | 9 | 15 |
| Brookville | 3,968 | 7 | 0 | 3 | 0 | 4 | 64 | 3 | 58 | 3 | 0 |
| Brownsville | 2,613 | 12 | 0 | 0 | 3 | 9 | 46 | 12 | 29 | 5 | 0 |
| Bryn Athyn | 1,324 | 0 | 0 | 0 | 0 | 0 | 14 | 2 | 12 | 0 | 0 |
| Buckingham Township | 19,847 | 7 | 0 | 0 | 1 | 6 | 160 | 17 | 143 | 0 | 0 |
| Bushkill Township | 8,361 | 9 | 0 | 0 | 0 | 9 | 51 | 7 | 39 | 5 | 0 |
| Butler | 13,809 | 100 | 0 | 0 | 25 | 75 | 587 | 111 | 463 | 13 | 6 |
| Butler Township, Butler County | 16,514 | 17 | 1 | 0 | 3 | 13 | 492 | 43 | 443 | 6 | 2 |
| Butler Township, Schuylkill County | 6,120 | 2 | 0 | 0 | 1 | 1 | 35 | 11 | 23 | 1 | 0 |
| Caernarvon Township, Berks County | 3,601 | 9 | 0 | 1 | 0 | 8 | 70 | 5 | 63 | 2 | 1 |
| California | 6,384 | 14 | 0 | 2 | 2 | 10 | 106 | 27 | 79 | 0 | 0 |
| Caln Township | 12,217 | 41 | 0 | 3 | 17 | 21 | 304 | 51 | 244 | 9 | 2 |
| Cambria Township | 6,164 | 1 | 0 | 0 | 1 | 0 | 100 | 16 | 78 | 6 | 0 |
| Cambridge Springs | 2,665 | 1 | 0 | 0 | 0 | 1 | 7 | 1 | 6 | 0 | 0 |
| Camp Hill | 7,351 | 8 | 0 | 1 | 4 | 3 | 115 | 5 | 107 | 3 | 0 |
| Canonsburg[2] | 8,730 | 17 | 0 | 0 | 0 | 17 | | | | 2 | 0 |

[1] The FBI does not publish arson data unless it receives data from either the agency or the state for all 12 months of the calendar year.
[2] The FBI determined that the agency's data were underreported. Consequently, those data are not included in this table.

## Table 8. Offenses Known to Law Enforcement, by State and City, 2009—*Continued*

(Number.)

| State/city | Population | Violent crime | Murder and non-negligent man-slaughter | Forcible rape | Robbery | Aggravated assault | Property crime | Burglary | Larceny-theft | Motor vehicle theft | Arson[1] |
|---|---|---|---|---|---|---|---|---|---|---|---|
| **PENNSYLVANIA**—*Continued* | | | | | | | | | | | |
| Canton | 1,683 | 8 | 0 | 0 | 0 | 8 | 19 | 6 | 12 | 1 | 0 |
| Carbondale | 9,147 | 17 | 0 | 0 | 2 | 15 | 148 | 36 | 98 | 14 | 0 |
| Carlisle | 18,406 | 42 | 1 | 10 | 17 | 14 | 541 | 76 | 462 | 3 | 2 |
| Carmichaels | 517 | 0 | 0 | 0 | 0 | 0 | 4 | 1 | 3 | 0 | 0 |
| Carnegie | 7,871 | 15 | 0 | 0 | 9 | 6 | 249 | 28 | 209 | 12 | 2 |
| Carrolltown | 950 | 1 | 0 | 1 | 0 | 0 | 14 | 2 | 12 | 0 | 0 |
| Carroll Township, Washington County | 5,449 | 14 | 0 | 0 | 0 | 14 | 38 | 5 | 32 | 1 | 0 |
| Carroll Township, York County | 5,855 | 5 | 0 | 2 | 0 | 3 | 108 | 29 | 75 | 4 | 1 |
| Carroll Valley | 3,558 | 1 | 0 | 0 | 1 | 0 | 75 | 2 | 72 | 1 | 0 |
| Castle Shannon | 7,974 | 7 | 0 | 1 | 1 | 5 | 115 | 24 | 88 | 3 | 0 |
| Catasauqua | 6,555 | 23 | 0 | 0 | 7 | 16 | 164 | 12 | 133 | 19 | 0 |
| Catawissa | 1,533 | 1 | 0 | 0 | 0 | 1 | 39 | 3 | 36 | 0 | 0 |
| Cecil Township | 10,600 | 6 | 0 | 0 | 2 | 4 | 35 | 15 | 20 | 0 | 0 |
| Center Township | 11,666 | 31 | 2 | 0 | 5 | 24 | 389 | 32 | 354 | 3 | 2 |
| Centerville | 3,192 | 2 | 0 | 1 | 1 | 0 | 22 | 3 | 19 | 0 | 0 |
| Chalfont | 4,191 | 1 | 0 | 0 | 0 | 1 | 20 | 0 | 19 | 1 | 0 |
| Charleroi | 5,673 | 43 | 0 | 1 | 9 | 33 | 202 | 26 | 175 | 1 | 2 |
| Chartiers Township | 7,455 | 8 | 0 | 1 | 1 | 6 | 64 | 11 | 50 | 3 | 0 |
| Cheltenham Township | 35,760 | 88 | 0 | 6 | 61 | 21 | 912 | 205 | 667 | 40 | 1 |
| Cherry Tree | 411 | 0 | 0 | 0 | 0 | 0 | 0 | 0 | 0 | 0 | 0 |
| Chester | 36,529 | 967 | 14 | 25 | 194 | 734 | 1,299 | 488 | 632 | 179 | 40 |
| Chester Township | 4,431 | 77 | 0 | 4 | 13 | 60 | 126 | 46 | 75 | 5 | 2 |
| Cheswick | 1,725 | 1 | 0 | 0 | 0 | 1 | 5 | 0 | 5 | 0 | 0 |
| Chippewa Township | 9,789 | 1 | 0 | 0 | 1 | 0 | 191 | 13 | 172 | 6 | 0 |
| Christiana | 1,109 | 0 | 0 | 0 | 0 | 0 | 17 | 2 | 15 | 0 | 0 |
| Churchill | 3,222 | 46 | 0 | 0 | 1 | 45 | 44 | 11 | 32 | 1 | 0 |
| Clarion | 5,170 | 2 | 0 | 1 | 0 | 1 | 70 | 10 | 59 | 1 | 0 |
| Clarks Summit | 6,490 | 3 | 0 | 0 | 1 | 2 | 55 | 12 | 42 | 1 | 0 |
| Claysville | 670 | 1 | 0 | 0 | 1 | 0 | 10 | 2 | 8 | 0 | 0 |
| Clay Township | 5,965 | 1 | 0 | 0 | 0 | 1 | 70 | 13 | 53 | 4 | 1 |
| Clearfield | 6,124 | 21 | 0 | 3 | 4 | 14 | 356 | 22 | 329 | 5 | 0 |
| Cleona | 2,118 | 1 | 0 | 0 | 0 | 1 | 16 | 2 | 14 | 0 | 0 |
| Clifton Heights | 6,516 | 51 | 0 | 1 | 3 | 47 | 204 | 16 | 175 | 13 | 1 |
| Coaldale | 2,104 | 0 | 0 | 0 | 0 | 0 | 10 | 1 | 9 | 0 | 0 |
| Coal Township | 10,194 | 49 | 0 | 2 | 1 | 46 | 181 | 18 | 157 | 6 | 7 |
| Coatesville | 11,711 | 176 | 0 | 4 | 88 | 84 | 390 | 97 | 255 | 38 | 27 |
| Cochranton | 1,057 | 1 | 0 | 0 | 0 | 1 | 9 | 1 | 8 | 0 | 0 |
| Colebrookdale District | 6,413 | 1 | 0 | 1 | 0 | 0 | 140 | 4 | 130 | 6 | 0 |
| Collegeville | 5,066 | 6 | 0 | 1 | 5 | 0 | 76 | 6 | 68 | 2 | 2 |
| Collier Township | 6,582 | 18 | 3 | 1 | 3 | 11 | 243 | 18 | 200 | 25 | 2 |
| Collingdale | 8,334 | 83 | 0 | 1 | 16 | 66 | 224 | 26 | 174 | 24 | 3 |
| Colonial Regional | 20,125 | 8 | 0 | 1 | 5 | 2 | 582 | 39 | 537 | 6 | 1 |
| Columbia | 10,001 | 22 | 0 | 1 | 10 | 11 | 247 | 56 | 180 | 11 | 0 |
| Conemaugh Township, Cambria County | 2,441 | 3 | 0 | 0 | 1 | 2 | 11 | 3 | 6 | 2 | 0 |
| Conemaugh Township, Somerset County | 7,194 | 6 | 1 | 1 | 1 | 3 | 41 | 4 | 36 | 1 | 0 |
| Conewago Township, Adams County | 6,130 | 3 | 0 | 1 | 1 | 1 | 125 | 4 | 115 | 6 | 0 |
| Conewango Township | 3,518 | 10 | 0 | 3 | 0 | 7 | 134 | 20 | 112 | 2 | 0 |
| Conneaut Lake Regional | 3,488 | 2 | 0 | 0 | 1 | 1 | 35 | 8 | 27 | 0 | 0 |
| Connellsville | 8,404 | 20 | 1 | 4 | 6 | 9 | 409 | 92 | 299 | 18 | 0 |
| Conoy Township | 3,348 | 3 | 1 | 0 | 0 | 2 | 46 | 10 | 33 | 3 | 1 |
| Conshohocken | 8,509 | 11 | 0 | 0 | 1 | 10 | 166 | 31 | 125 | 10 | 1 |
| Conyngham | 1,823 | 0 | 0 | 0 | 0 | 0 | 0 | 0 | 0 | 0 | 0 |
| Coopersburg[2] | 2,560 | 4 | 0 | 0 | 0 | 4 | | 0 | | 0 | 0 |
| Coplay | 3,365 | 7 | 0 | 0 | 0 | 7 | 55 | 9 | 45 | 1 | 0 |
| Coraopolis | 5,552 | 48 | 0 | 1 | 1 | 46 | 103 | 18 | 81 | 4 | 0 |
| Corry | 6,253 | 23 | 0 | 2 | 0 | 21 | 107 | 10 | 94 | 3 | 0 |
| Coudersport | 2,346 | 0 | 0 | 0 | 0 | 0 | 3 | 1 | 2 | 0 | 0 |
| Covington Township | 2,203 | 3 | 0 | 0 | 1 | 2 | 72 | 7 | 62 | 3 | 0 |
| Crafton | 6,473 | 20 | 0 | 0 | 5 | 15 | 148 | 23 | 116 | 9 | 0 |
| Cranberry Township | 27,605 | 30 | 0 | 4 | 6 | 20 | 364 | 31 | 330 | 3 | 1 |
| Crescent Township | 2,790 | 10 | 0 | 1 | 0 | 9 | 37 | 14 | 22 | 1 | 0 |
| Cresson | 1,466 | 2 | 0 | 0 | 0 | 2 | 46 | 5 | 41 | 0 | 0 |
| Cresson Township | 4,539 | 2 | 1 | 0 | 0 | 1 | 40 | 8 | 32 | 0 | 1 |
| Croyle Township | 2,221 | 0 | 0 | 0 | 0 | 0 | 24 | 0 | 22 | 2 | 0 |
| Cumberland Township, Adams Township | 6,357 | 1 | 0 | 0 | 0 | 1 | 23 | 6 | 14 | 3 | 0 |
| Cumru Township | 17,607 | 10 | 0 | 0 | 4 | 6 | 377 | 50 | 303 | 24 | 4 |
| Curwensville | 2,443 | 1 | 0 | 0 | 0 | 1 | 27 | 3 | 24 | 0 | 1 |
| Dale | 1,343 | 1 | 0 | 0 | 0 | 1 | 12 | 3 | 8 | 1 | 0 |
| Dallas | 2,467 | 2 | 0 | 0 | 1 | 1 | 31 | 7 | 24 | 0 | 0 |
| Dallas Township | 8,908 | 5 | 0 | 2 | 0 | 3 | 48 | 9 | 36 | 3 | 7 |
| Dalton | 1,217 | 8 | 0 | 1 | 0 | 7 | 18 | 5 | 10 | 3 | 0 |

[1] The FBI does not publish arson data unless it receives data from either the agency or the state for all 12 months of the calendar year.
[2] The FBI determined that the agency's data were underreported. Consequently, those data are not included in this table.

**Table 8. Offenses Known to Law Enforcement, by State and City, 2009—*Continued***

(Number.)

| State/city | Population | Violent crime | Murder and non-negligent man-slaughter | Forcible rape | Robbery | Aggravated assault | Property crime | Burglary | Larceny-theft | Motor vehicle theft | Arson[1] |
|---|---|---|---|---|---|---|---|---|---|---|---|
| **PENNSYLVANIA**—*Continued* | | | | | | | | | | | |
| Danville | 4,403 | 23 | 0 | 3 | 1 | 19 | 82 | 4 | 75 | 3 | 0 |
| Darby | 9,861 | 398 | 3 | 11 | 78 | 306 | 441 | 174 | 231 | 36 | 3 |
| Darby Township | 9,509 | 60 | 0 | 2 | 18 | 40 | 303 | 47 | 235 | 21 | 3 |
| Darlington Township | 1,999 | 0 | 0 | 0 | 0 | 0 | 0 | 0 | 0 | 0 | 0 |
| Decatur Township | 4,736 | 2 | 0 | 0 | 0 | 2 | 53 | 12 | 40 | 1 | 0 |
| Delaware Water Gap | 796 | 0 | 0 | 0 | 0 | 0 | 0 | 0 | 0 | 0 | 0 |
| Delmont | 2,409 | 2 | 0 | 0 | 0 | 2 | 56 | 15 | 41 | 0 | 0 |
| Denver | 3,684 | 2 | 0 | 1 | 1 | 0 | 73 | 14 | 55 | 4 | 0 |
| Derry | 2,753 | 8 | 0 | 0 | 1 | 7 | 19 | 3 | 16 | 0 | 0 |
| Derry Township, Dauphin County | 22,091 | 52 | 0 | 6 | 5 | 41 | 741 | 70 | 656 | 15 | 3 |
| Donegal Township | 2,601 | 2 | 0 | 1 | 0 | 1 | 16 | 2 | 12 | 2 | 1 |
| Donora | 5,221 | 13 | 0 | 2 | 2 | 9 | 61 | 18 | 40 | 3 | 2 |
| Dormont | 8,330 | 33 | 0 | 1 | 6 | 26 | 120 | 23 | 88 | 9 | 0 |
| Douglass Township, Berks County | 3,503 | 3 | 0 | 0 | 0 | 3 | 28 | 9 | 17 | 2 | 0 |
| Douglass Township, Montgomery County | 10,259 | 17 | 0 | 1 | 3 | 13 | 141 | 20 | 113 | 8 | 0 |
| Downingtown | 7,974 | 47 | 0 | 0 | 19 | 28 | 276 | 38 | 224 | 14 | 2 |
| Doylestown | 8,100 | 12 | 0 | 1 | 5 | 6 | 209 | 19 | 183 | 7 | |
| Doylestown Township | 18,705 | 9 | 0 | 1 | 3 | 5 | 319 | 18 | 289 | 12 | 1 |
| Dublin Borough | 2,146 | 2 | 0 | 0 | 0 | 2 | 3 | 0 | 3 | 0 | 0 |
| Du Bois | 7,598 | 25 | 0 | 2 | 0 | 23 | 280 | 20 | 252 | 8 | 0 |
| Duboistown | 1,186 | 0 | 0 | 0 | 0 | 0 | 0 | 0 | 0 | 0 | 0 |
| Duncansville | 1,159 | 0 | 0 | 0 | 0 | 0 | 15 | 0 | 15 | 0 | 0 |
| Dunmore | 13,942 | 15 | 0 | 2 | 1 | 12 | 197 | 42 | 133 | 22 | 0 |
| Dunnstable Township | 990 | 1 | 0 | 1 | 0 | 0 | 0 | 0 | 0 | 0 | 0 |
| Duquesne | 6,616 | 75 | 3 | 4 | 32 | 36 | 268 | 98 | 144 | 26 | 9 |
| Duryea | 4,305 | 6 | 0 | 0 | 0 | 6 | 86 | 22 | 62 | 2 | 1 |
| Earl Township | 7,202 | 3 | 1 | 1 | 0 | 1 | 55 | 20 | 34 | 1 | 1 |
| East Bangor | 1,129 | 0 | 0 | 0 | 0 | 0 | 2 | 0 | 2 | 0 | 0 |
| East Bethlehem Township | 2,332 | 12 | 0 | 0 | 0 | 12 | 35 | 8 | 25 | 2 | 0 |
| East Brandywine Township | 6,792 | 10 | 0 | 1 | 0 | 9 | 95 | 2 | 92 | 1 | 0 |
| East Buffalo Township | 5,916 | 6 | 0 | 1 | 0 | 5 | 32 | 5 | 26 | 1 | 0 |
| East Cocalico Township | 10,509 | 1 | 0 | 0 | 0 | 1 | 148 | 25 | 119 | 4 | 0 |
| East Conemaugh | 1,150 | 0 | 0 | 0 | 0 | 0 | 7 | 3 | 3 | 1 | 0 |
| East Coventry Township | 6,853 | 6 | 0 | 0 | 0 | 6 | 48 | 15 | 30 | 3 | 0 |
| East Deer Township | 1,318 | 6 | 0 | 0 | 0 | 6 | 26 | 5 | 19 | 2 | 0 |
| East Earl Township | 6,669 | 5 | 0 | 1 | 1 | 3 | 86 | 16 | 64 | 6 | 0 |
| Eastern Adams Regional | 9,948 | 6 | 1 | 3 | 0 | 2 | 143 | 19 | 118 | 6 | |
| Eastern Pike Regional | 5,535 | 13 | 0 | 2 | 1 | 10 | 241 | 20 | 215 | 6 | 0 |
| East Fallowfield Township | 7,817 | 6 | 0 | 0 | 2 | 4 | 72 | 22 | 48 | 2 | 2 |
| East Hempfield Township | 23,680 | 23 | 0 | 5 | 8 | 10 | 554 | 53 | 490 | 11 | 0 |
| East Lampeter Township | 15,147 | 18 | 0 | 4 | 6 | 8 | 801 | 54 | 740 | 7 | 4 |
| East Marlborough Township | 8,219 | 0 | 0 | 0 | 0 | 0 | 17 | 1 | 16 | 0 | 0 |
| East McKeesport | 2,772 | 11 | 0 | 0 | 2 | 9 | 43 | 11 | 28 | 4 | 0 |
| East Norriton Township | 13,627 | 15 | 0 | 0 | 13 | 2 | 246 | 18 | 219 | 9 | 0 |
| East Norwegian Township | 828 | 0 | 0 | 0 | 0 | 0 | 0 | 0 | 0 | 0 | 0 |
| Easton | 26,065 | 137 | 1 | 15 | 66 | 55 | 744 | 111 | 601 | 32 | 10 |
| East Pennsboro Township | 19,992 | 16 | 0 | 5 | 8 | 3 | 337 | 60 | 272 | 5 | 0 |
| East Penn Township | 2,750 | 4 | 0 | 1 | 0 | 3 | 22 | 7 | 12 | 3 | 0 |
| East Petersburg | 4,336 | 3 | 0 | 0 | 1 | 2 | 52 | 8 | 44 | 0 | 0 |
| East Pikeland Township | 6,940 | 8 | 0 | 0 | 3 | 5 | 50 | 12 | 36 | 2 | 1 |
| East Rochester | 558 | 5 | 1 | 0 | 3 | 1 | 62 | 2 | 56 | 4 | 0 |
| Easttown Township | 10,549 | 4 | 0 | 0 | 0 | 4 | 79 | 18 | 60 | 1 | 0 |
| East Union Township | 1,423 | 0 | 0 | 0 | 0 | 0 | 0 | 0 | 0 | 0 | 0 |
| East Vincent Township | 6,589 | 5 | 0 | 0 | 1 | 4 | 50 | 14 | 35 | 1 | 1 |
| East Washington | 1,847 | 8 | 0 | 1 | 0 | 7 | 33 | 10 | 21 | 2 | 0 |
| East Whiteland Township | 10,790 | 15 | 0 | 0 | 3 | 12 | 96 | 9 | 82 | 5 | 0 |
| Ebensburg | 2,907 | 14 | 0 | 0 | 2 | 12 | 55 | 12 | 41 | 2 | 1 |
| Economy | 9,112 | 5 | 1 | 1 | 1 | 2 | 51 | 7 | 44 | 0 | 0 |
| Eddystone | 2,330 | 23 | 0 | 0 | 3 | 20 | 296 | 21 | 269 | 6 | 0 |
| Edgewood | 2,987 | 8 | 0 | 0 | 7 | 1 | 319 | 18 | 298 | 3 | 0 |
| Edgeworth | 1,575 | 0 | 0 | 0 | 0 | 0 | 0 | 0 | 0 | 0 | 0 |
| Edinboro | 6,625 | 8 | 0 | 2 | 1 | 5 | 121 | 17 | 104 | 0 | 0 |
| Edwardsville | 4,625 | 30 | 0 | 1 | 5 | 24 | 123 | 9 | 107 | 7 | 2 |
| Elizabethtown | 12,090 | 9 | 0 | 3 | 3 | 3 | 156 | 24 | 122 | 10 | 1 |
| Elizabeth Township | 12,752 | 19 | 0 | 0 | 1 | 18 | 134 | 28 | 96 | 10 | 0 |
| Elkland | 1,651 | 1 | 0 | 0 | 0 | 1 | 14 | 1 | 10 | 3 | 0 |
| Ellwood City | 7,889 | 41 | 0 | 1 | 14 | 26 | 319 | 74 | 244 | 1 | 2 |
| Emlenton Borough | 728 | 0 | 0 | 0 | 0 | 0 | 8 | 0 | 8 | 0 | 0 |
| Emmaus | 11,354 | 9 | 0 | 1 | 5 | 3 | 258 | 46 | 205 | 7 | 0 |
| Emsworth | 2,354 | 1 | 0 | 0 | 0 | 1 | 28 | 2 | 25 | 1 | 0 |
| Ephrata Township | 9,666 | 4 | 0 | 0 | 0 | 4 | 196 | 23 | 167 | 6 | 0 |

[1] The FBI does not publish arson data unless it receives data from either the agency or the state for all 12 months of the calendar year.

## Table 8. Offenses Known to Law Enforcement, by State and City, 2009—*Continued*

(Number.)

| State/city | Population | Violent crime | Murder and non-negligent man-slaughter | Forcible rape | Robbery | Aggravated assault | Property crime | Burglary | Larceny-theft | Motor vehicle theft | Arson[1] |
|---|---|---|---|---|---|---|---|---|---|---|---|
| **PENNSYLVANIA**—*Continued* | | | | | | | | | | | |
| Erie | 103,837 | 472 | 4 | 83 | 121 | 264 | 3,018 | 1,013 | 1,853 | 152 | 20 |
| Everett | 1,843 | 5 | 0 | 0 | 0 | 5 | 20 | 6 | 12 | 2 | 0 |
| Everson | 781 | 0 | 0 | 0 | 0 | 0 | 0 | 0 | 0 | 0 | 0 |
| Exeter | 5,899 | 12 | 1 | 0 | 1 | 10 | 93 | 12 | 77 | 4 | 2 |
| Exeter Township, Berks County | 27,355 | 18 | 0 | 3 | 5 | 10 | 445 | 60 | 362 | 23 | 11 |
| Exeter Township, Luzerne County | 2,519 | 2 | 0 | 0 | 0 | 2 | 11 | 1 | 10 | 0 | 0 |
| Fairfield | 512 | 0 | 0 | 0 | 0 | 0 | 7 | 1 | 5 | 1 | 0 |
| Fairview Township, Luzerne County | 4,301 | 1 | 0 | 0 | 1 | 0 | 44 | 5 | 39 | 0 | 0 |
| Fairview Township, York County | 17,114 | 20 | 1 | 0 | 2 | 17 | 286 | 35 | 246 | 5 | 0 |
| Falls Township, Bucks County | 33,445 | 45 | 0 | 7 | 23 | 15 | 829 | 83 | 684 | 62 | 5 |
| Falls Township, Wyoming County | 1,955 | 2 | 0 | 0 | 0 | 2 | 11 | 1 | 10 | 0 | 0 |
| Fawn Township | 2,291 | 1 | 0 | 0 | 0 | 1 | 35 | 12 | 19 | 4 | 0 |
| Ferguson Township | 16,747 | 10 | 0 | 3 | 2 | 5 | 214 | 23 | 184 | 7 | 2 |
| Ferndale | 1,635 | 8 | 0 | 1 | 0 | 7 | 2 | 0 | 2 | 0 | 0 |
| Findlay Township | 5,045 | 7 | 0 | 1 | 0 | 6 | 60 | 7 | 53 | 0 | 0 |
| Fleetwood | 3,996 | 4 | 0 | 0 | 1 | 3 | 97 | 9 | 84 | 4 | 0 |
| Folcroft | 6,806 | 30 | 0 | 2 | 10 | 18 | 114 | 25 | 73 | 16 | 0 |
| Ford City | 3,150 | 5 | 0 | 1 | 1 | 3 | 40 | 9 | 29 | 2 | 0 |
| Forest City | 1,712 | 3 | 0 | 0 | 0 | 3 | 39 | 14 | 24 | 1 | 0 |
| Forest Hills | 6,179 | 7 | 1 | 0 | 2 | 4 | 79 | 14 | 64 | 1 | 0 |
| Forks Township | 15,173 | 6 | 0 | 2 | 0 | 4 | 168 | 13 | 150 | 5 | 0 |
| Forty Fort | 4,209 | 5 | 0 | 1 | 1 | 3 | 110 | 17 | 88 | 5 | 0 |
| Forward Township | 3,458 | 2 | 0 | 0 | 0 | 2 | 32 | 7 | 25 | 0 | 0 |
| Foster Township | 4,204 | 4 | 0 | 1 | 0 | 3 | 56 | 4 | 51 | 1 | 0 |
| Fountain Hill | 4,571 | 12 | 0 | 1 | 2 | 9 | 157 | 25 | 128 | 4 | 0 |
| Fox Chapel | 5,107 | 0 | 0 | 0 | 0 | 0 | 6 | 0 | 6 | 0 | 0 |
| Frackville | 4,098 | 2 | 0 | 0 | 2 | 0 | 3 | 3 | 0 | 0 | 0 |
| Franconia Township | 12,920 | 4 | 0 | 2 | 0 | 2 | 117 | 15 | 99 | 3 | 1 |
| Franklin | 6,608 | 25 | 0 | 5 | 5 | 15 | 176 | 27 | 144 | 5 | 0 |
| Franklin Park | 12,264 | 6 | 0 | 1 | 0 | 5 | 52 | 9 | 43 | 0 | 1 |
| Frazer Township | 1,196 | 0 | 0 | 0 | 0 | 0 | 90 | 2 | 87 | 1 | 0 |
| Freedom | 1,578 | 7 | 1 | 2 | 2 | 2 | 49 | 7 | 38 | 4 | 0 |
| Freedom Township | 3,171 | 0 | 0 | 0 | 0 | 0 | 37 | 1 | 32 | 4 | 0 |
| Freemansburg | 2,037 | 1 | 0 | 1 | 0 | 0 | 49 | 12 | 35 | 2 | 0 |
| Freeport | 1,794 | 4 | 0 | 0 | 0 | 4 | 25 | 9 | 15 | 1 | 0 |
| Gaines Township | 564 | 0 | 0 | 0 | 0 | 0 | 1 | 1 | 0 | 0 | 0 |
| Galeton | 1,196 | 0 | 0 | 0 | 0 | 0 | 14 | 8 | 6 | 0 | 0 |
| Gallitzin | 1,855 | 2 | 0 | 0 | 1 | 1 | 24 | 5 | 19 | 0 | 0 |
| Gallitzin Township | 1,295 | 1 | 0 | 0 | 0 | 1 | 0 | 0 | 0 | 0 | 0 |
| Geistown | 2,331 | 3 | 0 | 0 | 1 | 2 | 39 | 6 | 28 | 5 | 0 |
| Gettysburg | 8,103 | 32 | 1 | 2 | 10 | 19 | 171 | 33 | 134 | 4 | 4 |
| Girard | 2,904 | 6 | 0 | 0 | 0 | 6 | 43 | 9 | 34 | 0 | 0 |
| Glassport | 4,503 | 20 | 1 | 0 | 3 | 16 | 89 | 31 | 57 | 1 | 7 |
| Glenolden | 7,174 | 14 | 0 | 0 | 6 | 8 | 159 | 15 | 135 | 9 | 1 |
| Granville Township | 4,953 | 3 | 0 | 1 | 0 | 2 | 97 | 13 | 82 | 2 | 0 |
| Greencastle | 4,092 | 5 | 0 | 0 | 1 | 4 | 57 | 12 | 44 | 1 | |
| Greenfield Township, Blair County | 3,709 | 8 | 0 | 2 | 0 | 6 | 123 | 15 | 104 | 4 | 0 |
| Greensburg | 15,183 | 32 | 0 | 2 | 8 | 22 | 419 | 64 | 346 | 9 | 1 |
| Green Tree | 4,295 | 9 | 0 | 0 | 1 | 8 | 84 | 10 | 74 | 0 | 0 |
| Greenville | 6,077 | 15 | 0 | 3 | 1 | 11 | 170 | 41 | 123 | 6 | 3 |
| Greenwood Township | 2,059 | 0 | 0 | 0 | 0 | 0 | 0 | 0 | 0 | 0 | 0 |
| Grove City | 7,684 | 14 | 0 | 1 | 5 | 8 | 117 | 20 | 97 | 0 | 0 |
| Halifax | 829 | 1 | 0 | 0 | 0 | 1 | 8 | 0 | 7 | 1 | 0 |
| Hamburg | 4,222 | 7 | 0 | 1 | 1 | 5 | 75 | 13 | 59 | 3 | 0 |
| Hamiltonban Township | 2,777 | 0 | 0 | 0 | 0 | 0 | 5 | 3 | 2 | 0 | 0 |
| Hampden Township | 27,352 | 6 | 0 | 1 | 3 | 2 | 302 | 46 | 253 | 3 | 1 |
| Hampton Township | 17,183 | 11 | 0 | 1 | 1 | 9 | 144 | 17 | 120 | 7 | 0 |
| Hanover | 15,076 | 30 | 0 | 6 | 9 | 15 | 662 | 67 | 583 | 12 | 2 |
| Hanover Township, Luzerne County | 10,931 | 16 | 0 | 3 | 6 | 7 | 126 | 19 | 99 | 8 | |
| Hanover Township, Washington County | 2,711 | 12 | 0 | 0 | 1 | 11 | 27 | 14 | 11 | 2 | 0 |
| Harmar Township | 3,015 | 7 | 0 | 0 | 2 | 5 | 84 | 7 | 72 | 5 | 0 |
| Harmony Township | 3,029 | 8 | 0 | 1 | 1 | 6 | 62 | 5 | 56 | 1 | 0 |
| Harrisburg | 46,961 | 831 | 16 | 50 | 510 | 255 | 2,163 | 474 | 1,513 | 176 | 25 |
| Harrison Township | 9,922 | 6 | 1 | 1 | 1 | 3 | 81 | 19 | 55 | 7 | 0 |
| Harrisville | 875 | 1 | 0 | 0 | 0 | 1 | 5 | 1 | 4 | 0 | 0 |
| Harveys Lake | 2,936 | 0 | 0 | 0 | 0 | 0 | 16 | 2 | 13 | 1 | 0 |
| Hastings | 1,285 | 1 | 0 | 1 | 0 | 0 | 27 | 9 | 18 | 0 | 0 |
| Hatboro | 7,096 | 10 | 0 | 0 | 2 | 8 | 103 | 23 | 76 | 4 | 0 |
| Hatfield Township | 20,037 | 22 | 0 | 3 | 5 | 14 | 366 | 43 | 314 | 9 | 4 |
| Haverford Township | 47,827 | 27 | 1 | 1 | 11 | 14 | 637 | 105 | 517 | 15 | 1 |
| Hawley | 1,298 | 1 | 0 | 0 | 0 | 1 | 5 | 1 | 3 | 1 | 0 |

[1] The FBI does not publish arson data unless it receives data from either the agency or the state for all 12 months of the calendar year.

## Table 8. Offenses Known to Law Enforcement, by State and City, 2009—*Continued*

(Number.)

| State/city | Population | Violent crime | Murder and non-negligent man-slaughter | Forcible rape | Robbery | Aggravated assault | Property crime | Burglary | Larceny-theft | Motor vehicle theft | Arson[1] |
|---|---|---|---|---|---|---|---|---|---|---|---|
| **PENNSYLVANIA**—*Continued* | | | | | | | | | | | |
| Hazleton | 21,569 | 81 | 2 | 9 | 19 | 51 | 463 | 133 | 270 | 60 | 5 |
| Heidelberg | 1,135 | 2 | 0 | 0 | 1 | 1 | 2 | 2 | 0 | 0 | 0 |
| Heidelberg Township, Berks County | 1,768 | 3 | 0 | 0 | 0 | 3 | 6 | 0 | 6 | 0 | 0 |
| Heidelberg Township, Lebanon County | 4,192 | 1 | 0 | 1 | 0 | 0 | 26 | 5 | 21 | 0 | 0 |
| Hellam Township | 9,149 | 27 | 0 | 3 | 2 | 22 | 82 | 8 | 67 | 7 | 0 |
| Hellertown | 5,666 | 17 | 0 | 1 | 0 | 16 | 100 | 10 | 88 | 2 | 4 |
| Hemlock Township | 2,273 | 1 | 0 | 0 | 0 | 1 | 158 | 7 | 150 | 1 | 2 |
| Hempfield Township, Mercer County | 3,833 | 5 | 0 | 0 | 0 | 5 | 107 | 17 | 86 | 4 | 1 |
| Hermitage | 16,340 | 26 | 0 | 3 | 7 | 16 | 585 | 68 | 510 | 7 | 0 |
| Highland Township | 1,213 | 0 | 0 | 0 | 0 | 0 | 2 | 2 | 0 | 0 | 0 |
| Highspire | 2,594 | 12 | 0 | 2 | 1 | 9 | 56 | 10 | 43 | 3 | 2 |
| Hilltown Township | 13,602 | 4 | 0 | 0 | 1 | 3 | 194 | 15 | 171 | 8 | 0 |
| Hollidaysburg | 5,477 | 5 | 0 | 0 | 0 | 5 | 96 | 10 | 86 | 0 | 1 |
| Homer City | 1,697 | 4 | 0 | 0 | 0 | 4 | 16 | 3 | 13 | 0 | 0 |
| Homestead | 3,483 | 51 | 0 | 7 | 28 | 16 | 271 | 76 | 172 | 23 | 0 |
| Honesdale | 4,702 | 7 | 0 | 0 | 0 | 7 | 121 | 20 | 101 | 0 | 0 |
| Hooversville | 701 | 0 | 0 | 0 | 0 | 0 | 9 | 3 | 6 | 0 | 0 |
| Hop Bottom Borough | 301 | 0 | 0 | 0 | 0 | 0 | 0 | 0 | 0 | 0 | 0 |
| Hopewell Township | 12,297 | 3 | 0 | 2 | 0 | 1 | 257 | 49 | 199 | 9 | 0 |
| Horsham Township | 24,765 | 13 | 1 | 1 | 4 | 7 | 335 | 41 | 280 | 14 | 1 |
| Houston | 1,238 | 1 | 0 | 0 | 0 | 1 | 8 | 1 | 7 | 0 | 0 |
| Hughesville | 2,028 | 1 | 0 | 0 | 0 | 1 | 35 | 7 | 27 | 1 | 0 |
| Hummelstown | 4,432 | 12 | 0 | 1 | 1 | 10 | 86 | 12 | 73 | 1 | 0 |
| Huntingdon | 6,742 | 6 | 0 | 0 | 0 | 6 | 65 | 2 | 63 | 0 | 1 |
| Independence Township, Beaver County | 2,666 | 2 | 0 | 1 | 0 | 1 | 24 | 7 | 13 | 4 | 1 |
| Indiana[3] | 14,727 | | 0 | 4 | 6 | | 351 | 38 | 311 | 2 | 7 |
| Indiana Township | 7,059 | 2 | 0 | 0 | 0 | 2 | 40 | 6 | 34 | 0 | 2 |
| Ingram | 3,336 | 9 | 0 | 0 | 2 | 7 | 44 | 8 | 32 | 4 | 0 |
| Irwin | 4,017 | 7 | 0 | 2 | 2 | 3 | 80 | 21 | 57 | 2 | 2 |
| Ivyland | 853 | 2 | 0 | 0 | 1 | 1 | 17 | 4 | 13 | 0 | 0 |
| Jackson Township, Butler County | 3,720 | 7 | 0 | 0 | 1 | 6 | 55 | 8 | 47 | 0 | 1 |
| Jackson Township, Cambria County | 4,669 | 3 | 0 | 1 | 2 | 0 | 46 | 12 | 29 | 5 | 1 |
| Jackson Township, Luzerne County | 4,801 | 3 | 0 | 0 | 0 | 3 | 12 | 9 | 1 | 2 | 0 |
| Jamestown | 571 | 0 | 0 | 0 | 0 | 0 | 11 | 1 | 9 | 1 | 0 |
| Jeannette | 9,777 | 69 | 0 | 1 | 5 | 63 | 159 | 37 | 122 | 0 | 3 |
| Jefferson Hills Borough | 9,660 | 9 | 0 | 0 | 1 | 8 | 57 | 12 | 40 | 5 | 0 |
| Jefferson Township, Mercer County | 2,293 | 0 | 0 | 0 | 0 | 0 | 16 | 7 | 8 | 1 | 0 |
| Jenkins Township | 4,893 | 5 | 0 | 0 | 0 | 5 | 90 | 22 | 65 | 3 | 0 |
| Jenkintown | 4,280 | 4 | 0 | 0 | 3 | 1 | 15 | 5 | 10 | 0 | 0 |
| Jermyn | 2,225 | 33 | 0 | 2 | 4 | 27 | 65 | 29 | 35 | 1 | 0 |
| Jersey Shore | 4,282 | 18 | 0 | 1 | 0 | 17 | 83 | 13 | 66 | 4 | 0 |
| Jim Thorpe | 4,870 | 22 | 0 | 1 | 0 | 21 | 112 | 11 | 95 | 6 | 0 |
| Johnsonburg | 2,645 | 10 | 0 | 1 | 0 | 9 | 64 | 22 | 42 | 0 | 1 |
| Juniata Valley Regional | 2,685 | 0 | 0 | 0 | 0 | 0 | 3 | 1 | 2 | 0 | 0 |
| Kane | 3,729 | 6 | 0 | 2 | 0 | 4 | 9 | 1 | 8 | 0 | 0 |
| Kennett Square | 5,269 | 13 | 0 | 0 | 6 | 7 | 125 | 21 | 90 | 14 | 0 |
| Kidder Township | 1,477 | 8 | 0 | 0 | 1 | 7 | 122 | 19 | 99 | 4 | 0 |
| Kilbuck Township | 652 | 0 | 0 | 0 | 0 | 0 | 3 | 0 | 3 | 0 | 0 |
| Kingston | 12,850 | 26 | 0 | 3 | 12 | 11 | 345 | 52 | 282 | 11 | 0 |
| Kingston Township | 7,038 | 14 | 0 | 1 | 1 | 12 | 54 | 10 | 40 | 4 | 0 |
| Kiskiminetas Township | 4,768 | 12 | 0 | 0 | 0 | 12 | 81 | 19 | 60 | 2 | 0 |
| Kittanning | 4,312 | 18 | 0 | 0 | 2 | 16 | 40 | 8 | 31 | 1 | 0 |
| Kline Township | 1,484 | 2 | 0 | 1 | 0 | 1 | 35 | 4 | 31 | 0 | 0 |
| Kulpmont | 2,740 | 0 | 0 | 0 | 0 | 0 | 58 | 16 | 41 | 1 | 0 |
| Kutztown | 5,107 | 15 | 0 | 3 | 6 | 6 | 170 | 38 | 129 | 3 | 0 |
| Laflin Borough | 1,485 | 3 | 0 | 0 | 0 | 3 | 25 | 2 | 21 | 2 | 0 |
| Lake City | 2,880 | 6 | 0 | 0 | 0 | 6 | 39 | 8 | 31 | 0 | 0 |
| Lamar Township | 2,403 | 0 | 0 | 0 | 0 | 0 | 16 | 3 | 11 | 2 | 0 |
| Lancaster | 54,441 | 461 | 9 | 30 | 241 | 181 | 2,858 | 550 | 2,154 | 154 | 34 |
| Lancaster Township, Butler County | 2,578 | 4 | 0 | 0 | 0 | 4 | 15 | 0 | 9 | 6 | 0 |
| Lancaster Township, Lancaster County | 14,607 | 28 | 1 | 2 | 7 | 18 | 417 | 79 | 316 | 22 | 4 |
| Lanesboro | 547 | 0 | 0 | 0 | 0 | 0 | 1 | 0 | 1 | 0 | 0 |
| Langhorne Borough | 1,944 | 3 | 0 | 0 | 0 | 3 | 5 | 0 | 5 | 0 | 0 |
| Lansdale | 15,466 | 34 | 0 | 7 | 10 | 17 | 366 | 52 | 303 | 11 | 8 |
| Lansdowne | 10,595 | 38 | 0 | 4 | 17 | 17 | 267 | 77 | 181 | 9 | 0 |
| Larksville | 4,408 | 6 | 0 | 0 | 1 | 5 | 91 | 15 | 68 | 8 | 0 |
| Latimore Township | 2,867 | 0 | 0 | 0 | 0 | 0 | 22 | 1 | 20 | 1 | 0 |
| Latrobe | 8,281 | 22 | 0 | 0 | 1 | 21 | 233 | 33 | 197 | 3 | 2 |
| Laureldale | 3,734 | 2 | 0 | 0 | 1 | 1 | 63 | 7 | 48 | 8 | 0 |
| Lawrence Park Township | 3,650 | 9 | 0 | 2 | 0 | 7 | 62 | 12 | 50 | 0 | 0 |
| Lawrence Township, Clearfield County | 7,436 | 56 | 0 | 1 | 3 | 52 | 286 | 21 | 254 | 11 | 1 |

[1] The FBI does not publish arson data unless it receives data from either the agency or the state for all 12 months of the calendar year.

## Table 8. Offenses Known to Law Enforcement, by State and City, 2009—*Continued*

(Number.)

| State/city | Population | Violent crime | Murder and non-negligent man-slaughter | Forcible rape | Robbery | Aggravated assault | Property crime | Burglary | Larceny-theft | Motor vehicle theft | Arson[1] |
|---|---|---|---|---|---|---|---|---|---|---|---|
| **PENNSYLVANIA**—*Continued* | | | | | | | | | | | |
| Lawrence Township, Tioga County | 1,680 | 9 | 0 | 1 | 0 | 8 | 0 | 0 | 0 | 0 | 0 |
| Lebanon | 24,061 | 95 | 2 | 7 | 36 | 50 | 726 | 132 | 556 | 38 | 0 |
| Leechburg | 2,194 | 5 | 0 | 1 | 0 | 4 | 13 | 7 | 5 | 1 | 0 |
| Leetsdale | 1,105 | 0 | 0 | 0 | 0 | 0 | 0 | 0 | 0 | 0 | 0 |
| Leet Township | 1,485 | 0 | 0 | 0 | 0 | 0 | 0 | 0 | 0 | 0 | 0 |
| Lehighton | 5,417 | 10 | 0 | 1 | 4 | 5 | 226 | 39 | 169 | 18 | 0 |
| Lehigh Township, Northampton County | 10,926 | 9 | 0 | 0 | 2 | 7 | 142 | 30 | 106 | 6 | 0 |
| Lehman Township | 3,324 | 0 | 0 | 0 | 0 | 0 | 6 | 3 | 3 | 0 | 0 |
| Lewisburg | 5,435 | 20 | 0 | 0 | 3 | 17 | 75 | 8 | 67 | 0 | 0 |
| Liberty | 2,412 | 1 | 0 | 0 | 0 | 1 | 24 | 4 | 13 | 7 | 0 |
| Liberty Township, Adams County | 1,303 | 1 | 0 | 0 | 0 | 1 | 29 | 4 | 23 | 2 | 0 |
| Ligonier | 1,589 | 2 | 0 | 0 | 0 | 2 | 18 | 0 | 16 | 2 | 0 |
| Ligonier Township | 6,709 | 3 | 0 | 0 | 0 | 3 | 45 | 8 | 36 | 1 | 1 |
| Lincoln | 1,110 | 2 | 0 | 0 | 0 | 2 | 11 | 7 | 4 | 0 | 0 |
| Linesville | 1,084 | 0 | 0 | 0 | 0 | 0 | 0 | 0 | 0 | 0 | 0 |
| Lititz | 9,034 | 4 | 0 | 0 | 0 | 4 | 127 | 20 | 101 | 6 | |
| Littlestown | 4,134 | 17 | 0 | 4 | 1 | 12 | 94 | 15 | 77 | 2 | 0 |
| Lock Haven | 8,477 | 21 | 0 | 7 | 1 | 13 | 287 | 46 | 240 | 1 | 0 |
| Logan Township | 12,185 | 46 | 0 | 1 | 5 | 40 | 340 | 32 | 303 | 5 | 1 |
| Loretto | 1,356 | 0 | 0 | 0 | 0 | 0 | 0 | 0 | 0 | 0 | 0 |
| Lower Allen Township | 17,471 | 8 | 0 | 2 | 2 | 4 | 297 | 12 | 282 | 3 | 2 |
| Lower Burrell | 12,032 | 17 | 0 | 3 | 2 | 12 | 114 | 26 | 84 | 4 | 0 |
| Lower Chichester Township | 3,424 | 33 | 0 | 2 | 4 | 27 | 124 | 23 | 91 | 10 | 1 |
| Lower Frederick Township | 4,813 | 2 | 0 | 0 | 0 | 2 | 23 | 5 | 18 | 0 | 0 |
| Lower Gwynedd Township | 11,433 | 11 | 0 | 0 | 0 | 11 | 175 | 24 | 145 | 6 | 0 |
| Lower Heidelberg Township | 5,470 | 1 | 0 | 0 | 0 | 1 | 23 | 7 | 16 | 0 | 0 |
| Lower Makefield Township | 32,111 | 10 | 0 | 0 | 4 | 6 | 397 | 38 | 344 | 15 | 1 |
| Lower Merion Township | 57,033 | 32 | 0 | 3 | 22 | 7 | 876 | 133 | 705 | 38 | 1 |
| Lower Moreland Township | 12,807 | 6 | 0 | 2 | 2 | 2 | 238 | 79 | 150 | 9 | 3 |
| Lower Paxton Township | 45,534 | 90 | 0 | 8 | 25 | 57 | 1,109 | 165 | 904 | 40 | 7 |
| Lower Pottsgrove Township | 12,266 | 17 | 0 | 2 | 1 | 14 | 278 | 33 | 230 | 15 | 2 |
| Lower Providence Township | 26,271 | 48 | 0 | 5 | 2 | 41 | 289 | 49 | 232 | 8 | 2 |
| Lower Salford Township | 14,683 | 7 | 0 | 0 | 2 | 5 | 71 | 9 | 60 | 2 | 11 |
| Lower Saucon Township | 11,435 | 20 | 0 | 0 | 1 | 19 | 102 | 16 | 80 | 6 | 1 |
| Lower Southampton Township | 18,954 | 66 | 0 | 3 | 9 | 54 | 422 | 80 | 325 | 17 | 4 |
| Lower Swatara Township | 8,563 | 4 | 0 | 2 | 0 | 2 | 77 | 16 | 60 | 1 | 1 |
| Lower Windsor Township | 7,875 | 10 | 0 | 0 | 0 | 10 | 113 | 27 | 80 | 6 | 0 |
| Luzerne Township | 6,753 | 1 | 0 | 0 | 0 | 1 | 17 | 5 | 10 | 2 | 0 |
| Lykens | 1,839 | 1 | 0 | 0 | 0 | 1 | 4 | 3 | 1 | 0 | 0 |
| Macungie | 3,131 | 2 | 0 | 0 | 0 | 2 | 13 | 2 | 10 | 1 | 0 |
| Madison Township | 1,594 | 0 | 0 | 0 | 0 | 0 | 0 | 0 | 0 | 0 | 0 |
| Mahanoy City | 4,347 | 5 | 0 | 3 | 0 | 2 | 37 | 8 | 29 | 0 | 0 |
| Mahanoy Township | 3,780 | 1 | 0 | 0 | 0 | 1 | 2 | 0 | 2 | 0 | 0 |
| Mahoning Township, Montour County | 4,238 | 31 | 0 | 0 | 0 | 31 | 23 | 4 | 18 | 1 | 0 |
| Malvern | 3,102 | 5 | 0 | 0 | 0 | 5 | 16 | 3 | 12 | 1 | 0 |
| Manheim | 4,631 | 10 | 0 | 0 | 5 | 5 | 104 | 17 | 84 | 3 | 0 |
| Manheim Township | 36,582 | 49 | 0 | 0 | 14 | 35 | 678 | 61 | 597 | 20 | |
| Manor | 2,927 | 4 | 0 | 0 | 0 | 4 | 13 | 7 | 5 | 1 | 0 |
| Manor Township, Armstrong County | 3,917 | 0 | 0 | 0 | 0 | 0 | 0 | 0 | 0 | 0 | 0 |
| Manor Township, Lancaster County | 19,812 | 11 | 0 | 1 | 9 | 1 | 131 | 23 | 104 | 4 | 0 |
| Mansfield | 3,152 | 5 | 0 | 0 | 1 | 4 | 8 | 0 | 8 | 0 | 0 |
| Marietta | 2,583 | 1 | 0 | 1 | 0 | 0 | 82 | 25 | 53 | 4 | 0 |
| Marion Township, Beaver County | 880 | 0 | 0 | 0 | 0 | 0 | 1 | 0 | 1 | 0 | 0 |
| Marion Township, Berks County | 1,782 | 0 | 0 | 0 | 0 | 0 | 9 | 3 | 5 | 1 | 0 |
| Marlborough Township | 3,283 | 3 | 0 | 1 | 2 | 0 | 50 | 12 | 36 | 2 | 0 |
| Marple Township | 23,407 | 10 | 0 | 2 | 2 | 6 | 335 | 26 | 306 | 3 | 0 |
| Mars | 1,643 | 1 | 0 | 0 | 0 | 1 | 9 | 0 | 9 | 0 | 0 |
| Martinsburg | 2,109 | 0 | 0 | 0 | 0 | 0 | 39 | 5 | 34 | 0 | 0 |
| Marysville | 2,439 | 1 | 0 | 0 | 0 | 1 | 32 | 4 | 26 | 2 | 1 |
| Masontown | 3,371 | 9 | 0 | 0 | 4 | 5 | 91 | 25 | 59 | 7 | 1 |
| Mayfield | 1,698 | 0 | 0 | 0 | 0 | 0 | 2 | 1 | 1 | 0 | 0 |
| McAdoo | 2,069 | 3 | 0 | 1 | 0 | 2 | 33 | 5 | 25 | 3 | 0 |
| McCandless | 27,119 | 10 | 1 | 0 | 3 | 6 | 316 | 30 | 276 | 10 | 1 |
| McDonald Borough | 2,103 | 10 | 0 | 1 | 0 | 9 | 62 | 8 | 53 | 1 | 0 |
| McKeesport | 21,932 | 344 | 8 | 6 | 55 | 275 | 994 | 402 | 520 | 72 | 17 |
| McKees Rocks | 5,956 | 87 | 1 | 5 | 45 | 36 | 346 | 106 | 206 | 34 | 0 |
| McSherrystown | 2,803 | 9 | 0 | 1 | 0 | 8 | 63 | 6 | 55 | 2 | 1 |
| Mechanicsburg | 8,688 | 54 | 0 | 0 | 4 | 50 | 214 | 27 | 184 | 3 | 4 |
| Media | 5,381 | 25 | 0 | 0 | 4 | 21 | 73 | 23 | 49 | 1 | 0 |
| Mercer | 2,188 | 7 | 0 | 0 | 0 | 7 | 46 | 22 | 23 | 1 | 0 |
| Mercersburg | 1,589 | 0 | 0 | 0 | 0 | 0 | 28 | 5 | 20 | 3 | 1 |

[1] The FBI does not publish arson data unless it receives data from either the agency or the state for all 12 months of the calendar year.

**Table 8. Offenses Known to Law Enforcement, by State and City, 2009**—*Continued*

(Number.)

| State/city | Population | Violent crime | Murder and non-negligent man-slaughter | Forcible rape | Robbery | Aggravated assault | Property crime | Burglary | Larceny-theft | Motor vehicle theft | Arson[1] |
|---|---|---|---|---|---|---|---|---|---|---|---|
| **PENNSYLVANIA**—*Continued* | | | | | | | | | | | |
| Meshoppen | 424 | 0 | 0 | 0 | 0 | 0 | 0 | 0 | 0 | 0 | 0 |
| Meyersdale | 2,252 | 2 | 0 | 0 | 0 | 2 | 34 | 6 | 28 | 0 | 0 |
| Middleburg | 1,321 | 0 | 0 | 0 | 0 | 0 | 37 | 8 | 28 | 1 | 0 |
| Middlesex Township, Butler County | 5,438 | 2 | 0 | 0 | 0 | 2 | 44 | 12 | 30 | 2 | 1 |
| Middlesex Township, Cumberland County | 6,920 | 10 | 0 | 2 | 5 | 3 | 211 | 19 | 180 | 12 | 1 |
| Middletown | 8,799 | 24 | 1 | 9 | 4 | 10 | 135 | 25 | 107 | 3 | 2 |
| Middletown Township | 46,978 | 52 | 0 | 3 | 14 | 35 | 1,474 | 172 | 1,252 | 50 | 6 |
| Midland | 2,817 | 28 | 0 | 0 | 2 | 26 | 135 | 28 | 101 | 6 | 0 |
| Mifflin | 603 | 0 | 0 | 0 | 0 | 0 | 0 | 0 | 0 | 0 | 0 |
| Mifflinburg | 3,509 | 2 | 0 | 0 | 0 | 2 | 79 | 9 | 70 | 0 | 2 |
| Mifflin County Regional | 26,265 | 48 | 0 | 3 | 1 | 44 | 760 | 92 | 636 | 32 | 3 |
| Mifflin Township | 2,249 | 0 | 0 | 0 | 0 | 0 | 0 | 0 | 0 | 0 | 0 |
| Milford | 2,904 | 1 | 0 | 0 | 1 | 0 | 40 | 2 | 38 | 0 | 0 |
| Millbourne | 901 | 7 | 0 | 0 | 4 | 3 | 36 | 5 | 28 | 3 | 0 |
| Millcreek Township, Lebanon County | 3,210 | 3 | 0 | 0 | 0 | 3 | 31 | 3 | 27 | 1 | 0 |
| Millersburg | 2,449 | 7 | 0 | 0 | 0 | 7 | 41 | 6 | 35 | 0 | 0 |
| Millersville | 7,296 | 10 | 0 | 4 | 0 | 6 | 84 | 8 | 75 | 1 | 2 |
| Mill Hall | 1,469 | 0 | 0 | 0 | 0 | 0 | 0 | 0 | 0 | 0 | 0 |
| Millvale | 3,618 | 0 | 0 | 0 | 0 | 0 | 27 | 14 | 9 | 4 | 0 |
| Millville | 940 | 0 | 0 | 0 | 0 | 0 | 0 | 0 | 0 | 0 | 0 |
| Milton | 6,331 | 25 | 0 | 3 | 2 | 20 | 123 | 24 | 98 | 1 | 4 |
| Minersville | 4,187 | 4 | 0 | 0 | 0 | 4 | 61 | 2 | 58 | 1 | 0 |
| Mohnton | 3,081 | 1 | 0 | 0 | 0 | 1 | 17 | 4 | 12 | 1 | 0 |
| Monaca | 5,694 | 11 | 0 | 0 | 3 | 8 | 141 | 28 | 103 | 10 | 0 |
| Monessen | 7,958 | 46 | 0 | 3 | 10 | 33 | 232 | 54 | 168 | 10 | 3 |
| Monongahela | 4,387 | 28 | 0 | 1 | 7 | 20 | 125 | 26 | 93 | 6 | 0 |
| Monroeville | 27,462 | 82 | 0 | 2 | 16 | 64 | 501 | 47 | 422 | 32 | 1 |
| Montgomery | 5,184 | 1 | 0 | 0 | 0 | 1 | 24 | 6 | 17 | 1 | 0 |
| Montgomery Township | 24,360 | 15 | 1 | 0 | 8 | 6 | 524 | 22 | 499 | 3 | 1 |
| Montoursville | 4,536 | 1 | 0 | 0 | 0 | 1 | 70 | 1 | 66 | 3 | |
| Moon Township | 22,923 | 12 | 0 | 0 | 3 | 9 | 265 | 46 | 204 | 15 | 0 |
| Moosic | 5,779 | 33 | 0 | 3 | 0 | 30 | 261 | 33 | 217 | 11 | 2 |
| Morris-Cooper Regional | 5,625 | 1 | 0 | 0 | 0 | 1 | 0 | 0 | 0 | 0 | 0 |
| Morrisville | 9,547 | 17 | 0 | 0 | 3 | 14 | 228 | 57 | 142 | 29 | 1 |
| Morton | 2,625 | 10 | 0 | 1 | 0 | 9 | 114 | 15 | 96 | 3 | 0 |
| Moscow | 1,945 | 5 | 0 | 0 | 0 | 5 | 29 | 2 | 27 | 0 | 0 |
| Mount Carmel | 5,836 | 21 | 0 | 2 | 2 | 17 | 109 | 27 | 79 | 3 | 0 |
| Mount Carmel Township | 2,568 | 2 | 0 | 0 | 0 | 2 | 22 | 4 | 16 | 2 | 0 |
| Mount Gretna Borough | 233 | 0 | 0 | 0 | 0 | 0 | 0 | 0 | 0 | 0 | 0 |
| Mount Holly Springs | 1,907 | 4 | 0 | 0 | 0 | 4 | 48 | 10 | 36 | 2 | 0 |
| Mount Jewett | 987 | 17 | 0 | 0 | 0 | 17 | 68 | 6 | 61 | 1 | 0 |
| Mount Joy | 7,304 | 8 | 0 | 0 | 1 | 7 | 135 | 22 | 109 | 4 | 0 |
| Mount Lebanon | 30,106 | 23 | 0 | 0 | 7 | 16 | 222 | 30 | 191 | 1 | 5 |
| Mount Oliver | 3,621 | 53 | 0 | 4 | 28 | 21 | 168 | 49 | 95 | 24 | 0 |
| Mount Pleasant | 4,344 | 6 | 0 | 1 | 2 | 3 | 113 | 15 | 98 | 0 | 1 |
| Mount Pleasant Township | 3,633 | 4 | 0 | 0 | 0 | 4 | 31 | 9 | 21 | 1 | 1 |
| Mount Union | 2,327 | 3 | 0 | 0 | 0 | 3 | 75 | 6 | 66 | 3 | 0 |
| Muhlenberg Township | 18,767 | 34 | 0 | 0 | 23 | 11 | 706 | 53 | 603 | 50 | 0 |
| Munhall | 11,090 | 19 | 0 | 0 | 6 | 13 | 171 | 60 | 104 | 7 | 1 |
| Murrysville | 19,563 | 0 | 0 | 0 | 0 | 0 | 142 | 31 | 110 | 1 | 0 |
| Myerstown | 3,115 | 2 | 0 | 0 | 0 | 2 | 64 | 8 | 54 | 2 | 0 |
| Nanticoke | 10,122 | 74 | 1 | 5 | 7 | 61 | 470 | 138 | 312 | 20 | 3 |
| Narberth | 4,019 | 6 | 0 | 0 | 2 | 4 | 56 | 20 | 36 | 0 | 0 |
| Nelson Township | 562 | 1 | 0 | 0 | 0 | 1 | 1 | 0 | 1 | 0 | 0 |
| Nescopeck | 1,417 | 0 | 0 | 0 | 0 | 0 | 2 | 1 | 0 | 1 | 0 |
| Neshannock Township | 9,290 | 2 | 0 | 0 | 0 | 2 | 142 | 26 | 114 | 2 | 0 |
| Nether Providence Township | 13,123 | 21 | 0 | 1 | 0 | 20 | 154 | 32 | 119 | 3 | 0 |
| Neville Township | 1,114 | 1 | 0 | 0 | 0 | 1 | 40 | 5 | 34 | 1 | 0 |
| New Berlin | 815 | 1 | 0 | 0 | 0 | 1 | 3 | 0 | 3 | 0 | 0 |
| Newberry Township | 15,577 | 17 | 0 | 6 | 3 | 8 | 326 | 60 | 259 | 7 | 1 |
| New Brighton | 9,252 | 47 | 0 | 1 | 13 | 33 | 458 | 76 | 375 | 7 | 1 |
| New Britain | 2,255 | 9 | 0 | 1 | 0 | 8 | 23 | 2 | 21 | 0 | 0 |
| New Britain Township | 10,981 | 2 | 0 | 0 | 0 | 2 | 117 | 17 | 98 | 2 | 0 |
| New Castle Township | 393 | 0 | 0 | 0 | 0 | 0 | 27 | 0 | 27 | 0 | 0 |
| New Garden Township | 12,073 | 7 | 0 | 0 | 5 | 2 | 172 | 27 | 133 | 12 | 5 |
| New Hanover Township | 9,694 | 8 | 0 | 2 | 0 | 6 | 89 | 11 | 70 | 8 | 0 |
| New Holland | 5,158 | 4 | 0 | 1 | 2 | 1 | 136 | 23 | 113 | 0 | 0 |
| New Kensington | 13,561 | 52 | 0 | 11 | 17 | 24 | 464 | 117 | 320 | 27 | 3 |
| Newport | 1,459 | 12 | 0 | 0 | 0 | 12 | 39 | 7 | 30 | 2 | 0 |
| New Sewickley Township | 7,591 | 16 | 0 | 3 | 0 | 13 | 102 | 22 | 77 | 3 | 1 |
| Newton Township | 2,774 | 1 | 0 | 0 | 0 | 1 | 12 | 3 | 9 | 0 | 0 |

[1] The FBI does not publish arson data unless it receives data from either the agency or the state for all 12 months of the calendar year.

## Table 8. Offenses Known to Law Enforcement, by State and City, 2009—*Continued*

(Number.)

| State/city | Population | Violent crime | Murder and non-negligent man-slaughter | Forcible rape | Robbery | Aggravated assault | Property crime | Burglary | Larceny-theft | Motor vehicle theft | Arson[1] |
|---|---|---|---|---|---|---|---|---|---|---|---|
| **PENNSYLVANIA**—*Continued* | | | | | | | | | | | |
| Newtown | 2,384 | 0 | 0 | 0 | 0 | 0 | 18 | 0 | 18 | 0 | 0 |
| Newtown Township, Bucks County | 19,327 | 14 | 0 | 1 | 0 | 13 | 246 | 20 | 223 | 3 | 1 |
| Newtown Township, Delaware County | 11,796 | 10 | 0 | 1 | 0 | 9 | 107 | 13 | 85 | 9 | 0 |
| Newville | 1,296 | 13 | 0 | 0 | 0 | 13 | 42 | 2 | 39 | 1 | 0 |
| Norristown | 31,909 | 370 | 10 | 18 | 197 | 145 | 985 | 205 | 646 | 134 | 7 |
| Northampton | 9,892 | 11 | 0 | 0 | 7 | 4 | 173 | 36 | 135 | 2 | 0 |
| Northampton Township | 40,813 | 19 | 1 | 1 | 3 | 14 | 367 | 63 | 294 | 10 | |
| North Belle Vernon | 1,933 | 12 | 0 | 2 | 1 | 9 | 76 | 15 | 59 | 2 | 0 |
| North Catasauqua | 2,837 | 2 | 0 | 0 | 0 | 2 | 50 | 6 | 38 | 6 | 0 |
| North Charleroi | 1,304 | 2 | 0 | 0 | 2 | 0 | 13 | 3 | 7 | 3 | 0 |
| North Cornwall Township | 6,589 | 15 | 0 | 0 | 1 | 14 | 108 | 9 | 93 | 6 | 2 |
| North Coventry Township | 7,747 | 4 | 0 | 2 | 0 | 2 | 260 | 24 | 227 | 9 | 0 |
| North East, Erie County | 4,146 | 8 | 0 | 4 | 2 | 2 | 161 | 27 | 134 | 0 | 1 |
| Northeastern Regional | 11,264 | 15 | 0 | 3 | 0 | 12 | 162 | 33 | 116 | 13 | 0 |
| Northern Berks Regional | 12,590 | 10 | 0 | 0 | 3 | 7 | 200 | 31 | 151 | 18 | 3 |
| Northern Cambria Borough | 3,877 | 8 | 0 | 2 | 1 | 5 | 104 | 36 | 63 | 5 | 0 |
| Northern Regional | 28,544 | 6 | 0 | 1 | 2 | 3 | 313 | 26 | 278 | 9 | 0 |
| Northern York Regional | 66,764 | 54 | 0 | 4 | 16 | 34 | 987 | 136 | 808 | 43 | 6 |
| North Franklin Township | 4,619 | 20 | 0 | 0 | 3 | 17 | 108 | 5 | 102 | 1 | 0 |
| North Huntingdon Township | 29,516 | 14 | 0 | 0 | 6 | 8 | 438 | 53 | 364 | 21 | 1 |
| North Lebanon Township | 10,987 | 12 | 1 | 0 | 1 | 10 | 264 | 52 | 208 | 4 | 0 |
| North Londonderry Township | 7,012 | 2 | 0 | 0 | 1 | 1 | 138 | 22 | 113 | 3 | 1 |
| North Middleton Township | 11,066 | 7 | 0 | 2 | 3 | 2 | 56 | 6 | 43 | 7 | 0 |
| North Sewickley Township | 5,615 | 5 | 0 | 0 | 1 | 4 | 92 | 18 | 69 | 5 | 0 |
| North Strabane Township | 12,647 | 9 | 0 | 0 | 2 | 7 | 172 | 23 | 146 | 3 | 1 |
| Northumberland | 3,491 | 2 | 0 | 0 | 0 | 2 | 103 | 32 | 69 | 2 | 0 |
| North Union Township | 1,257 | 1 | 0 | 0 | 0 | 1 | 1 | 1 | 0 | 0 | 0 |
| North Versailles Township | 12,112 | 87 | 0 | 3 | 8 | 76 | 269 | 52 | 207 | 10 | 0 |
| North Wales | 3,213 | 0 | 0 | 0 | 0 | 0 | 47 | 4 | 40 | 3 | 1 |
| Northwest Lancaster County Regional | 18,094 | 8 | 0 | 5 | 1 | 2 | 140 | 3 | 135 | 2 | 0 |
| Northwest Lawrence County Regional | 6,627 | 11 | 0 | 2 | 1 | 8 | 64 | 33 | 28 | 3 | 1 |
| Norwood | 5,752 | 16 | 0 | 0 | 2 | 14 | 114 | 13 | 96 | 5 | 0 |
| Oakland | 567 | 1 | 0 | 0 | 0 | 1 | 1 | 0 | 1 | 0 | 0 |
| Oakmont | 6,373 | 19 | 0 | 0 | 4 | 15 | 169 | 44 | 123 | 2 | 0 |
| O'Hara Township | 9,578 | 3 | 0 | 0 | 1 | 2 | 77 | 17 | 57 | 3 | 0 |
| Ohio Township | 4,166 | 2 | 0 | 0 | 0 | 2 | 61 | 2 | 58 | 1 | 0 |
| Ohioville | 3,599 | 6 | 0 | 0 | 0 | 6 | 49 | 13 | 30 | 6 | 0 |
| Oil City | 10,504 | 23 | 0 | 8 | 5 | 10 | 187 | 22 | 160 | 5 | 0 |
| Old Forge | 8,497 | 17 | 0 | 0 | 0 | 17 | 43 | 4 | 39 | 0 | 1 |
| Old Lycoming Township | 5,248 | 6 | 0 | 2 | 0 | 4 | 74 | 7 | 67 | 0 | 0 |
| Oliver Township | 2,064 | 3 | 0 | 0 | 0 | 3 | 7 | 1 | 6 | 0 | 0 |
| Olyphant | 4,953 | 8 | 0 | 0 | 0 | 8 | 51 | 11 | 38 | 2 | 0 |
| Orangeville Area | 1,637 | 1 | 0 | 0 | 0 | 1 | 23 | 5 | 17 | 1 | 0 |
| Orwigsburg | 2,966 | 2 | 0 | 0 | 0 | 2 | 25 | 6 | 19 | 0 | 0 |
| Oxford | 4,696 | 23 | 0 | 3 | 3 | 17 | 160 | 12 | 140 | 8 | 1 |
| Paint Township | 3,133 | 11 | 1 | 0 | 1 | 9 | 4 | 0 | 4 | 0 | 0 |
| Palmerton | 5,205 | 11 | 0 | 3 | 2 | 6 | 125 | 4 | 113 | 8 | 0 |
| Palmer Township | 20,742 | 16 | 1 | 2 | 8 | 5 | 446 | 41 | 388 | 17 | 3 |
| Palmyra | 6,987 | 10 | 0 | 0 | 2 | 8 | 136 | 15 | 117 | 4 | 0 |
| Parkesburg | 3,436 | 21 | 0 | 8 | 2 | 11 | 52 | 15 | 34 | 3 | 0 |
| Patterson Area | 3,539 | 0 | 0 | 0 | 0 | 0 | 60 | 15 | 40 | 5 | 0 |
| Patton | 1,830 | 0 | 0 | 0 | 0 | 0 | 9 | 1 | 8 | 0 | 0 |
| Patton Township | 13,425 | 8 | 0 | 3 | 2 | 3 | 223 | 22 | 199 | 2 | 0 |
| Paxtang | 1,477 | 3 | 0 | 0 | 0 | 3 | 32 | 2 | 25 | 5 | 1 |
| Pen Argyl | 3,629 | 3 | 0 | 0 | 0 | 3 | 57 | 7 | 44 | 6 | 1 |
| Penn Hills | 43,755 | 188 | 4 | 11 | 73 | 100 | 1,024 | 414 | 560 | 50 | 14 |
| Pennridge Regional | 10,633 | 16 | 0 | 3 | 0 | 13 | 127 | 25 | 100 | 2 | 0 |
| Penn Township, Butler County | 5,142 | 0 | 0 | 0 | 0 | 0 | 35 | 6 | 26 | 3 | 0 |
| Penn Township, Lancaster County | 8,688 | 16 | 0 | 0 | 0 | 16 | 132 | 11 | 84 | 37 | 1 |
| Penn Township, York County | 15,959 | 30 | 0 | 2 | 3 | 25 | 222 | 29 | 185 | 8 | 1 |
| Pequea Township | 4,542 | 8 | 0 | 2 | 0 | 6 | 50 | 7 | 40 | 3 | 2 |
| Perkasie | 8,614 | 14 | 0 | 1 | 2 | 11 | 193 | 23 | 170 | 0 | 0 |
| Perryopolis | 1,707 | 0 | 0 | 0 | 0 | 0 | 39 | 9 | 30 | 0 | 0 |
| Peters Township | 20,540 | 6 | 0 | 0 | 1 | 5 | 120 | 25 | 93 | 2 | 0 |
| Philadelphia | 1,547,605 | 19,163 | 302 | 896 | 9,037 | 8,928 | 55,888 | 10,969 | 37,941 | 6,978 | |
| Pine Creek Township | 3,199 | 5 | 0 | 0 | 0 | 5 | 20 | 3 | 17 | 0 | 0 |
| Pine Grove | 2,031 | 4 | 0 | 0 | 0 | 4 | 5 | 0 | 4 | 1 | 0 |
| Pitcairn | 3,308 | 15 | 1 | 3 | 6 | 5 | 70 | 25 | 42 | 3 | 0 |
| Pittsburgh | 312,232 | 3,087 | 39 | 116 | 1,367 | 1,565 | 11,775 | 2,811 | 8,134 | 830 | 146 |
| Plainfield Township | 6,235 | 1 | 0 | 0 | 0 | 1 | 48 | 13 | 35 | 0 | 0 |
| Plains Township | 10,364 | 16 | 1 | 2 | 2 | 11 | 159 | 38 | 116 | 5 | 1 |

[1] The FBI does not publish arson data unless it receives data from either the agency or the state for all 12 months of the calendar year.

## Table 8. Offenses Known to Law Enforcement, by State and City, 2009—*Continued*

(Number.)

| State/city | Population | Violent crime | Murder and non-negligent man-slaughter | Forcible rape | Robbery | Aggravated assault | Property crime | Burglary | Larceny-theft | Motor vehicle theft | Arson[1] |
|---|---|---|---|---|---|---|---|---|---|---|---|
| **PENNSYLVANIA**—*Continued* | | | | | | | | | | | |
| Pleasant Hills | 7,684 | 1 | 0 | 0 | 1 | 0 | 110 | 15 | 86 | 9 | 0 |
| Plum | 26,118 | 28 | 0 | 1 | 5 | 22 | 121 | 47 | 73 | 1 | 1 |
| Plumstead Township | 11,811 | 4 | 1 | 0 | 0 | 3 | 127 | 10 | 106 | 11 | 4 |
| Plymouth Township, Montgomery County | 16,350 | 41 | 0 | 4 | 23 | 14 | 541 | 58 | 469 | 14 | 0 |
| Pocono Mountain Regional | 35,793 | 64 | 1 | 8 | 22 | 33 | 1,002 | 468 | 509 | 25 | 11 |
| Pocono Township | 11,295 | 26 | 0 | 3 | 7 | 16 | 395 | 55 | 321 | 19 | 2 |
| Point Marion | 1,238 | 12 | 0 | 0 | 0 | 12 | 28 | 9 | 19 | 0 | 0 |
| Point Township | 3,885 | 6 | 0 | 0 | 0 | 6 | 36 | 11 | 20 | 5 | 0 |
| Portage | 2,555 | 12 | 0 | 0 | 0 | 12 | 46 | 7 | 35 | 4 | 2 |
| Port Allegany | 2,173 | 3 | 0 | 0 | 0 | 3 | 10 | 0 | 10 | 0 | 0 |
| Port Carbon | 1,733 | 1 | 0 | 0 | 1 | 0 | 5 | 0 | 4 | 1 | 0 |
| Porter Township | 1,591 | 6 | 0 | 0 | 0 | 6 | 27 | 6 | 20 | 1 | 0 |
| Port Vue | 3,804 | 6 | 0 | 1 | 1 | 4 | 46 | 12 | 30 | 4 | 0 |
| Pottstown | 21,226 | 179 | 0 | 10 | 64 | 105 | 1,011 | 165 | 773 | 73 | 10 |
| Pottsville | 14,288 | 51 | 1 | 3 | 8 | 39 | 224 | 26 | 191 | 7 | 1 |
| Punxsutawney | 5,910 | 46 | 0 | 4 | 3 | 39 | 98 | 25 | 72 | 1 | 1 |
| Pymatuning Township | 3,530 | 6 | 0 | 2 | 3 | 1 | 110 | 16 | 87 | 7 | 0 |
| Quakertown | 8,612 | 37 | 0 | 3 | 4 | 30 | 287 | 30 | 251 | 6 | 3 |
| Quarryville | 2,163 | 6 | 0 | 0 | 1 | 5 | 48 | 14 | 31 | 3 | 0 |
| Raccoon Township | 3,199 | 4 | 0 | 0 | 0 | 4 | 28 | 4 | 23 | 1 | 0 |
| Radnor Township | 30,958 | 20 | 0 | 2 | 3 | 15 | 333 | 34 | 291 | 8 | 0 |
| Rankin | 2,087 | 12 | 0 | 1 | 0 | 11 | 10 | 6 | 1 | 3 | 0 |
| Reading | 80,418 | 766 | 12 | 22 | 369 | 363 | 3,788 | 1,321 | 1,872 | 595 | 30 |
| Resa Regional | 2,536 | 8 | 0 | 0 | 1 | 7 | 16 | 8 | 8 | 0 | 0 |
| Reserve Township | 3,497 | 4 | 0 | 0 | 0 | 4 | 36 | 9 | 26 | 1 | 0 |
| Reynoldsville | 2,535 | 5 | 0 | 2 | 0 | 3 | 18 | 5 | 13 | 0 | 0 |
| Rice Township | 3,055 | 3 | 0 | 0 | 0 | 3 | 3 | 0 | 3 | 0 | 0 |
| Richland | 1,490 | 0 | 0 | 0 | 0 | 0 | 0 | 0 | 0 | 0 | 0 |
| Richland Township, Bucks County | 12,914 | 3 | 0 | 3 | 0 | 0 | 303 | 30 | 266 | 7 | 0 |
| Richland Township, Cambria County | 12,275 | 15 | 0 | 1 | 8 | 6 | 543 | 31 | 504 | 8 | 0 |
| Ridgway | 4,046 | 4 | 0 | 1 | 0 | 3 | 117 | 23 | 92 | 2 | 5 |
| Ridley Park | 6,956 | 19 | 0 | 1 | 5 | 13 | 82 | 15 | 64 | 3 | 0 |
| Ridley Township | 29,767 | 54 | 1 | 3 | 19 | 31 | 564 | 99 | 438 | 27 | 4 |
| Ringtown | 756 | 0 | 0 | 0 | 0 | 0 | 6 | 1 | 5 | 0 | 0 |
| Roaring Brook Township | 1,804 | 2 | 0 | 0 | 0 | 2 | 8 | 1 | 6 | 1 | 0 |
| Roaring Spring | 2,235 | 0 | 0 | 0 | 0 | 0 | 66 | 5 | 60 | 1 | 0 |
| Robesonia | 2,050 | 0 | 0 | 0 | 0 | 0 | 20 | 5 | 15 | 0 | 0 |
| Robeson Township | 7,682 | 5 | 0 | 0 | 2 | 3 | 58 | 16 | 32 | 10 | 0 |
| Robinson Township, Allegheny County | 13,534 | 18 | 0 | 2 | 3 | 13 | 293 | 28 | 260 | 5 | 0 |
| Rochester | 3,626 | 24 | 0 | 1 | 7 | 16 | 345 | 69 | 261 | 15 | 0 |
| Rochester Township | 2,846 | 5 | 0 | 0 | 0 | 5 | 71 | 12 | 55 | 4 | 0 |
| Rockledge | 2,467 | 4 | 0 | 0 | 2 | 2 | 38 | 8 | 30 | 0 | 1 |
| Roseto | 1,642 | 1 | 0 | 0 | 0 | 1 | 8 | 1 | 6 | 1 | 0 |
| Rosslyn Farms | 419 | 0 | 0 | 0 | 0 | 0 | 0 | 0 | 0 | 0 | 0 |
| Ross Township | 30,340 | 23 | 0 | 1 | 10 | 12 | 948 | 91 | 843 | 14 | |
| Rostraver Township | 11,621 | 12 | 1 | 1 | 6 | 4 | 373 | 39 | 328 | 6 | 1 |
| Royalton | 944 | 1 | 0 | 0 | 0 | 1 | 11 | 2 | 8 | 1 | 0 |
| Royersford | 4,368 | 14 | 0 | 4 | 2 | 8 | 106 | 23 | 77 | 6 | 0 |
| Rush Township | 3,724 | 0 | 0 | 0 | 0 | 0 | 150 | 17 | 133 | 0 | 2 |
| Ryan Township | 2,544 | 0 | 0 | 0 | 0 | 0 | 3 | 2 | 1 | 0 | 0 |
| Rye Township | 2,548 | 0 | 0 | 0 | 0 | 0 | 6 | 1 | 5 | 0 | 0 |
| Sadsbury Township, Chester County | 3,393 | 1 | 0 | 0 | 0 | 1 | 1 | 1 | 0 | 0 | 0 |
| Salisbury Township | 14,068 | 6 | 0 | 0 | 1 | 5 | 271 | 40 | 221 | 10 | 0 |
| Saltsburg | 876 | 2 | 0 | 0 | 0 | 2 | 24 | 2 | 21 | 1 | 0 |
| Sandy Lake | 686 | 1 | 0 | 0 | 0 | 1 | 4 | 2 | 2 | 0 | 0 |
| Sandy Township | 11,577 | 15 | 0 | 3 | 0 | 12 | 315 | 52 | 241 | 22 | 2 |
| Sankertown | 649 | 0 | 0 | 0 | 0 | 0 | 3 | 0 | 3 | 0 | 0 |
| Saxonburg | 1,589 | 2 | 0 | 0 | 0 | 2 | 6 | 1 | 5 | 0 | 0 |
| Saxton | 758 | 0 | 0 | 0 | 0 | 0 | 0 | 0 | 0 | 0 | 0 |
| Sayre | 5,401 | 3 | 0 | 0 | 0 | 3 | 138 | 18 | 119 | 1 | 1 |
| Schuylkill Haven | 5,121 | 8 | 0 | 0 | 0 | 8 | 81 | 11 | 69 | 1 | 2 |
| Schuylkill Township, Chester County | 7,779 | 10 | 0 | 1 | 0 | 9 | 75 | 15 | 58 | 2 | 0 |
| Scottdale | 4,372 | 20 | 0 | 1 | 2 | 17 | 128 | 12 | 115 | 1 | 0 |
| Scott Township, Allegheny County | 15,732 | 24 | 0 | 0 | 8 | 16 | 274 | 48 | 223 | 3 | 1 |
| Scott Township, Columbia County | 5,062 | 0 | 0 | 0 | 0 | 0 | 45 | 1 | 44 | 0 | 0 |
| Scott Township, Lackawanna County | 4,892 | 8 | 0 | 0 | 2 | 6 | 16 | 7 | 9 | 0 | 1 |
| Scranton | 71,843 | 284 | 1 | 35 | 108 | 140 | 2,622 | 640 | 1,836 | 146 | 13 |
| Selinsgrove | 5,341 | 117 | 0 | 6 | 1 | 110 | 226 | 46 | 176 | 4 | 5 |
| Seward | 448 | 0 | 0 | 0 | 0 | 0 | 0 | 0 | 0 | 0 | 0 |
| Sewickley Heights | 912 | 0 | 0 | 0 | 0 | 0 | 3 | 1 | 2 | 0 | 0 |
| Shamokin | 7,301 | 17 | 0 | 1 | 1 | 15 | 110 | 20 | 84 | 6 | 4 |

[1] The FBI does not publish arson data unless it receives data from either the agency or the state for all 12 months of the calendar year.

## Table 8. Offenses Known to Law Enforcement, by State and City, 2009—*Continued*

(Number.)

| State/city | Population | Violent crime | Murder and non-negligent man-slaughter | Forcible rape | Robbery | Aggravated assault | Property crime | Burglary | Larceny-theft | Motor vehicle theft | Arson[1] |
|---|---|---|---|---|---|---|---|---|---|---|---|
| **PENNSYLVANIA**—*Continued* | | | | | | | | | | | |
| Shamokin Dam | 1,432 | 3 | 0 | 0 | 0 | 3 | 38 | 3 | 34 | 1 | 0 |
| Sharon | 14,721 | 143 | 2 | 3 | 32 | 106 | 516 | 146 | 340 | 30 | 1 |
| Sharon Hill | 5,291 | 39 | 1 | 1 | 8 | 29 | 147 | 14 | 122 | 11 | 0 |
| Sharpsburg | 3,229 | 18 | 0 | 0 | 1 | 17 | 98 | 33 | 50 | 15 | 0 |
| Sharpsville | 4,059 | 15 | 0 | 0 | 0 | 15 | 82 | 3 | 78 | 1 | 0 |
| Shenango Township, Lawrence County | 7,614 | 9 | 0 | 0 | 1 | 8 | 149 | 31 | 113 | 5 | 1 |
| Shillington | 4,990 | 1 | 0 | 1 | 0 | 0 | 105 | 4 | 89 | 12 | 0 |
| Shippensburg | 5,577 | 3 | 0 | 0 | 2 | 1 | 59 | 10 | 47 | 2 | |
| Shippingport | 217 | 0 | 0 | 0 | 0 | 0 | 2 | 1 | 1 | 0 | 0 |
| Shiremanstown | 1,458 | 4 | 0 | 0 | 1 | 3 | 3 | 1 | 2 | 0 | 0 |
| Shohola Township | 2,469 | 0 | 0 | 0 | 0 | 0 | 22 | 13 | 9 | 0 | 0 |
| Silver Lake Township | 1,723 | 2 | 0 | 0 | 0 | 2 | 8 | 2 | 4 | 2 | 0 |
| Sinking Spring | 3,726 | 5 | 0 | 2 | 3 | 0 | 80 | 20 | 53 | 7 | 0 |
| Slatington | 4,401 | 23 | 0 | 3 | 3 | 17 | 80 | 8 | 72 | 0 | 0 |
| Slippery Rock | 3,069 | 3 | 0 | 0 | 0 | 3 | 39 | 3 | 36 | 0 | 0 |
| Smethport | 1,551 | 0 | 0 | 0 | 0 | 0 | 30 | 9 | 21 | 0 | 0 |
| Smith Township | 4,467 | 0 | 0 | 0 | 0 | 0 | 0 | 0 | 0 | 0 | 0 |
| Solebury Township | 8,889 | 8 | 1 | 0 | 1 | 6 | 76 | 14 | 60 | 2 | 0 |
| Somerset | 6,316 | 17 | 0 | 2 | 7 | 8 | 184 | 29 | 142 | 13 | 3 |
| Souderton | 6,533 | 5 | 0 | 1 | 2 | 2 | 98 | 10 | 82 | 6 | 3 |
| South Abington Township | 9,663 | 8 | 0 | 1 | 0 | 7 | 97 | 14 | 81 | 2 | 0 |
| South Beaver Township | 2,827 | 6 | 0 | 0 | 0 | 6 | 26 | 7 | 19 | 0 | 0 |
| South Buffalo Township | 2,797 | 1 | 0 | 0 | 0 | 1 | 22 | 3 | 19 | 0 | 0 |
| South Centre Township | 1,903 | 9 | 0 | 0 | 0 | 9 | 57 | 5 | 52 | 0 | 0 |
| South Coatesville | 1,067 | 6 | 0 | 0 | 0 | 6 | 26 | 6 | 16 | 4 | 0 |
| South Connellsville Borough | 2,137 | 0 | 0 | 0 | 0 | 0 | 10 | 2 | 8 | 0 | 0 |
| Southern Regional Lancaster County | 3,842 | 1 | 0 | 0 | 0 | 1 | 33 | 11 | 22 | 0 | 1 |
| Southern Regional York County | 10,027 | 13 | 0 | 3 | 4 | 6 | 206 | 31 | 174 | 1 | 1 |
| South Fayette Township | 13,304 | 9 | 0 | 1 | 1 | 7 | 71 | 15 | 54 | 2 | |
| South Fork | 1,017 | 0 | 0 | 0 | 0 | 0 | 1 | 0 | 1 | 0 | 0 |
| South Greensburg | 2,210 | 4 | 0 | 0 | 1 | 3 | 39 | 12 | 25 | 2 | 0 |
| South Heidelberg Township | 7,409 | 6 | 0 | 2 | 1 | 3 | 63 | 7 | 56 | 0 | 0 |
| South Heights | 487 | 0 | 0 | 0 | 0 | 0 | 0 | 0 | 0 | 0 | 0 |
| South Lebanon Township | 8,732 | 3 | 0 | 0 | 0 | 3 | 96 | 25 | 71 | 0 | 0 |
| South Londonderry Township | 7,503 | 2 | 0 | 0 | 0 | 2 | 48 | 7 | 40 | 1 | 0 |
| South Park Township | 13,823 | 5 | 0 | 1 | 1 | 3 | 39 | 13 | 21 | 5 | 0 |
| South Strabane Township | 8,807 | 16 | 0 | 0 | 7 | 9 | 359 | 16 | 337 | 6 | 1 |
| South Waverly | 962 | 0 | 0 | 0 | 0 | 0 | 29 | 5 | 24 | 0 | 0 |
| Southwestern Regional | 18,230 | 18 | 0 | 7 | 3 | 8 | 162 | 33 | 126 | 3 | 2 |
| Southwest Greensburg | 2,181 | 4 | 0 | 0 | 1 | 3 | 57 | 4 | 52 | 1 | 0 |
| Southwest Mercer County Regional | 11,096 | 34 | 0 | 2 | 10 | 22 | 274 | 54 | 199 | 21 | |
| Southwest Regional | 2,842 | 4 | 0 | 0 | 0 | 4 | 15 | 5 | 10 | 0 | 1 |
| South Williamsport | 5,976 | 5 | 0 | 0 | 1 | 4 | 91 | 8 | 82 | 1 | 2 |
| Spring City | 3,383 | 4 | 0 | 0 | 0 | 4 | 113 | 14 | 92 | 7 | 0 |
| Springettsbury Township | 24,940 | 34 | 1 | 4 | 23 | 6 | 942 | 44 | 884 | 14 | 5 |
| Springfield Township, Bucks County | 5,079 | 2 | 0 | 0 | 1 | 1 | 56 | 21 | 33 | 2 | 1 |
| Springfield Township, Delaware County | 22,682 | 21 | 0 | 3 | 9 | 9 | 712 | 42 | 658 | 12 | 3 |
| Springfield Township, Montgomery County | 18,778 | 22 | 1 | 1 | 4 | 16 | 228 | 29 | 193 | 6 | 0 |
| Spring Garden Township | 12,154 | 31 | 2 | 0 | 14 | 15 | 415 | 83 | 312 | 20 | 2 |
| Spring Township, Berks County | 26,803 | 15 | 2 | 0 | 6 | 7 | 321 | 42 | 264 | 15 | 2 |
| Spring Township, Centre County | 7,083 | 2 | 0 | 0 | 0 | 2 | 96 | 15 | 74 | 7 | 0 |
| Spring Township, Snyder County | 1,547 | 0 | 0 | 0 | 0 | 0 | 6 | 1 | 3 | 2 | 0 |
| State College | 53,587 | 75 | 0 | 2 | 14 | 59 | 1,000 | 117 | 871 | 12 | 12 |
| St. Clair Boro | 2,960 | 0 | 0 | 0 | 0 | 0 | 51 | 2 | 49 | 0 | 1 |
| St. Clair Township | 1,329 | 2 | 0 | 0 | 0 | 2 | 0 | 0 | 0 | 0 | 0 |
| Steelton | 5,571 | 34 | 2 | 5 | 16 | 11 | 253 | 64 | 172 | 17 | 1 |
| Stewartstown | 2,024 | 1 | 0 | 0 | 0 | 1 | 44 | 10 | 33 | 1 | 0 |
| St. Marys City | 13,296 | 18 | 0 | 4 | 3 | 11 | 189 | 30 | 152 | 7 | 0 |
| Stockertown | 761 | 3 | 0 | 0 | 0 | 3 | 6 | 0 | 6 | 0 | 0 |
| Stoneboro | 1,006 | 1 | 0 | 0 | 0 | 1 | 9 | 2 | 4 | 3 | 0 |
| Stonycreek Township | 2,874 | 2 | 0 | 0 | 0 | 2 | 55 | 15 | 37 | 3 | 0 |
| Stowe Township[2] | 6,032 | 18 | 2 | 2 | 4 | 10 | | | | 5 | 0 |
| Strasburg | 2,774 | 1 | 0 | 0 | 0 | 1 | 28 | 5 | 23 | 0 | 0 |
| Stroud Area Regional | 34,763 | 103 | 2 | 16 | 47 | 38 | 1,435 | 156 | 1,254 | 25 | 11 |
| Sugarloaf Township, Luzerne County | 4,086 | 6 | 0 | 0 | 0 | 6 | 195 | 8 | 186 | 1 | 0 |
| Summerhill Township | 2,565 | 1 | 0 | 0 | 0 | 1 | 43 | 5 | 32 | 6 | 0 |
| Summit Hill | 2,954 | 0 | 0 | 0 | 0 | 0 | 6 | 1 | 5 | 0 | 1 |
| Summit Township | 2,234 | 4 | 0 | 0 | 0 | 4 | 8 | 0 | 7 | 1 | 0 |
| Sunbury | 9,737 | 96 | 0 | 9 | 4 | 83 | 297 | 66 | 223 | 8 | 2 |
| Susquehanna Depot | 1,547 | 4 | 0 | 1 | 0 | 3 | 2 | 1 | 1 | 0 | 0 |
| Susquehanna Regional | 7,177 | 5 | 0 | 2 | 1 | 2 | 99 | 18 | 78 | 3 | 0 |

[1] The FBI does not publish arson data unless it receives data from either the agency or the state for all 12 months of the calendar year.
[2] The FBI determined that the agency's data were underreported. Consequently, those data are not included in this table.

## Table 8. Offenses Known to Law Enforcement, by State and City, 2009—*Continued*

(Number.)

| State/city | Population | Violent crime | Murder and non-negligent man-slaughter | Forcible rape | Robbery | Aggravated assault | Property crime | Burglary | Larceny-theft | Motor vehicle theft | Arson[1] |
|---|---|---|---|---|---|---|---|---|---|---|---|
| **PENNSYLVANIA**—*Continued* | | | | | | | | | | | |
| Susquehanna Township, Dauphin County | 23,181 | 42 | 1 | 2 | 24 | 15 | 407 | 67 | 333 | 7 | 4 |
| Sutersville | 582 | 0 | 0 | 0 | 0 | 0 | 0 | 0 | 0 | 0 | 0 |
| Swarthmore | 6,082 | 7 | 0 | 0 | 2 | 5 | 84 | 9 | 74 | 1 | 0 |
| Swatara Township | 22,426 | 153 | 1 | 0 | 33 | 119 | 682 | 90 | 579 | 13 | 5 |
| Swissvale | 8,674 | 120 | 0 | 0 | 29 | 91 | 259 | 58 | 184 | 17 | 2 |
| Swoyersville | 7,534 | 21 | 0 | 2 | 1 | 18 | 152 | 42 | 105 | 5 | 0 |
| Tamaqua | 6,521 | 10 | 0 | 4 | 1 | 5 | 218 | 18 | 197 | 3 | 1 |
| Tarentum | 4,487 | 15 | 0 | 3 | 3 | 9 | 118 | 22 | 91 | 5 | 0 |
| Tatamy | 1,097 | 0 | 0 | 0 | 0 | 0 | 6 | 0 | 6 | 0 | 0 |
| Taylor | 6,118 | 10 | 0 | 1 | 0 | 9 | 130 | 22 | 106 | 2 | 0 |
| Telford | 4,590 | 25 | 1 | 4 | 0 | 20 | 60 | 9 | 47 | 4 | 2 |
| Terre Hill | 1,264 | 0 | 0 | 0 | 0 | 0 | 6 | 0 | 6 | 0 | 0 |
| Throop | 4,057 | 22 | 1 | 0 | 0 | 21 | 66 | 18 | 47 | 1 | 1 |
| Tidioute | 710 | 0 | 0 | 0 | 0 | 0 | 5 | 0 | 5 | 0 | 0 |
| Tinicum Township, Bucks County | 4,201 | 2 | 0 | 1 | 0 | 1 | 37 | 10 | 27 | 0 | 0 |
| Tinicum Township, Delaware County | 4,178 | 11 | 0 | 1 | 2 | 8 | 179 | 23 | 145 | 11 | 1 |
| Titusville | 5,735 | 4 | 0 | 0 | 0 | 4 | 162 | 18 | 143 | 1 | 0 |
| Towamencin Township | 17,619 | 16 | 0 | 1 | 2 | 13 | 216 | 20 | 193 | 3 | 3 |
| Towanda | 2,805 | 7 | 0 | 4 | 0 | 3 | 70 | 11 | 56 | 3 | 1 |
| Trafford | 2,987 | 11 | 0 | 1 | 1 | 9 | 35 | 5 | 30 | 0 | 0 |
| Tredyffrin Township | 28,915 | 15 | 0 | 3 | 4 | 8 | 299 | 44 | 250 | 5 | 2 |
| Troy | 1,451 | 0 | 0 | 0 | 0 | 0 | 39 | 8 | 29 | 2 | 0 |
| Tullytown | 1,948 | 5 | 0 | 0 | 1 | 4 | 131 | 9 | 119 | 3 | 0 |
| Tulpehocken Township | 3,570 | 1 | 0 | 0 | 0 | 1 | 13 | 1 | 11 | 1 | 0 |
| Tunkhannock | 1,759 | 7 | 0 | 0 | 1 | 6 | 19 | 4 | 13 | 2 | 2 |
| Tunkhannock Township, Wyoming County | 4,284 | 2 | 0 | 0 | 0 | 2 | 73 | 3 | 63 | 7 | 0 |
| Tyrone | 5,163 | 14 | 0 | 3 | 4 | 7 | 157 | 20 | 136 | 1 | 3 |
| Union City | 3,257 | 4 | 0 | 1 | 0 | 3 | 43 | 2 | 41 | 0 | 0 |
| Union Dale | 338 | 0 | 0 | 0 | 0 | 0 | 0 | 0 | 0 | 0 | 0 |
| Uniontown | 11,603 | 69 | 0 | 5 | 44 | 20 | 586 | 171 | 355 | 60 | 1 |
| Union Township, Lawrence County | 4,992 | 7 | 0 | 0 | 2 | 5 | 135 | 15 | 115 | 5 | 1 |
| Union Township, Schuylkill County | 1,335 | 0 | 0 | 0 | 0 | 0 | 0 | 0 | 0 | 0 | 0 |
| Upland | 2,852 | 51 | 0 | 4 | 9 | 38 | 100 | 25 | 66 | 9 | 2 |
| Upper Allen Township | 18,353 | 1 | 0 | 1 | 0 | 0 | 168 | 43 | 122 | 3 | 0 |
| Upper Burrell Township | 2,113 | 1 | 0 | 1 | 0 | 0 | 13 | 2 | 11 | 0 | 0 |
| Upper Chichester Township | 17,621 | 63 | 0 | 6 | 15 | 42 | 508 | 67 | 413 | 28 | 2 |
| Upper Darby Township | 78,088 | 499 | 1 | 18 | 270 | 210 | 2,154 | 278 | 1,748 | 128 | 7 |
| Upper Dublin Township | 25,904 | 44 | 0 | 3 | 2 | 39 | 337 | 64 | 257 | 16 | 4 |
| Upper Gwynedd Township | 16,234 | 19 | 2 | 1 | 4 | 12 | 147 | 37 | 105 | 5 | 2 |
| Upper Leacock Township | 8,617 | 3 | 0 | 1 | 1 | 1 | 126 | 33 | 83 | 10 | 1 |
| Upper Makefield Township | 8,630 | 5 | 0 | 0 | 0 | 5 | 79 | 14 | 64 | 1 | 0 |
| Upper Merion Township | 26,410 | 24 | 0 | 3 | 14 | 7 | 1,421 | 58 | 1,318 | 45 | 0 |
| Upper Moreland Township | 24,093 | 21 | 0 | 4 | 7 | 10 | 453 | 68 | 373 | 12 | 1 |
| Upper Nazareth Township | 6,026 | 6 | 0 | 0 | 0 | 6 | 78 | 3 | 75 | 0 | 0 |
| Upper Perkiomen | 6,372 | 13 | 0 | 1 | 2 | 10 | 119 | 18 | 93 | 8 | 3 |
| Upper Pottsgrove Township | 5,330 | 7 | 0 | 0 | 2 | 5 | 51 | 10 | 39 | 2 | 0 |
| Upper Providence Township, Delaware County | 11,131 | 3 | 0 | 0 | 0 | 3 | 24 | 10 | 13 | 1 | 0 |
| Upper Providence Township, Montgomery County | 20,048 | 4 | 0 | 0 | 2 | 2 | 268 | 31 | 231 | 6 | 0 |
| Upper Saucon Township | 15,182 | 3 | 0 | 2 | 0 | 1 | 192 | 32 | 159 | 1 | 0 |
| Upper Southampton Township | 15,192 | 22 | 0 | 1 | 3 | 18 | 240 | 56 | 175 | 9 | 0 |
| Upper St. Clair Township | 18,723 | 6 | 0 | 0 | 0 | 6 | 96 | 10 | 83 | 3 | 0 |
| Upper Uwchlan Township | 11,728 | 4 | 0 | 0 | 0 | 4 | 66 | 10 | 53 | 3 | 0 |
| Upper Yoder Township | 5,455 | 2 | 0 | 0 | 0 | 2 | 35 | 10 | 25 | 0 | 0 |
| Uwchlan Township | 18,869 | 23 | 0 | 3 | 3 | 17 | 221 | 28 | 189 | 4 | 3 |
| Valley Township | 6,869 | 20 | 0 | 0 | 4 | 16 | 20 | 2 | 18 | 0 | 0 |
| Vandergrift | 4,950 | 7 | 0 | 0 | 2 | 5 | 17 | 6 | 10 | 1 | 1 |
| Vandling | 696 | 0 | 0 | 0 | 0 | 0 | 9 | 6 | 3 | 0 | 1 |
| Vernon Township | 5,413 | 6 | 0 | 0 | 2 | 4 | 106 | 6 | 100 | 0 | 0 |
| Verona | 2,813 | 20 | 0 | 2 | 6 | 12 | 101 | 23 | 78 | 0 | 0 |
| Vintondale | 472 | 0 | 0 | 0 | 0 | 0 | 0 | 0 | 0 | 0 | 0 |
| Walker Township | 976 | 0 | 0 | 0 | 0 | 0 | 3 | 1 | 2 | 0 | 0 |
| Warminster Township | 33,914 | 35 | 0 | 8 | 16 | 11 | 634 | 97 | 520 | 17 | |
| Warren | 9,316 | 132 | 2 | 2 | 3 | 125 | 156 | 25 | 129 | 2 | 4 |
| Warrington Township | 23,417 | 29 | 0 | 3 | 5 | 21 | 261 | 33 | 216 | 12 | 4 |
| Warwick Township, Lancaster County | 17,426 | 5 | 0 | 1 | 0 | 4 | 76 | 11 | 63 | 2 | 0 |
| Washington, Washington County | 14,709 | 109 | 2 | 15 | 36 | 56 | 552 | 142 | 370 | 40 | 3 |
| Washington Township, Fayette County | 4,126 | 11 | 0 | 0 | 1 | 10 | 62 | 16 | 45 | 1 | 0 |
| Washington Township, Franklin County | 12,201 | 13 | 0 | 1 | 4 | 8 | 259 | 40 | 213 | 6 | 4 |
| Washington Township, Northampton County | 4,932 | 9 | 0 | 0 | 0 | 9 | 67 | 19 | 47 | 1 | 0 |
| Washington Township, Westmoreland County | 7,347 | 7 | 0 | 0 | 0 | 7 | 71 | 18 | 51 | 2 | 0 |
| Watsontown | 2,086 | 22 | 0 | 2 | 0 | 20 | 49 | 6 | 43 | 0 | 0 |

[1] The FBI does not publish arson data unless it receives data from either the agency or the state for all 12 months of the calendar year.

## Table 8. Offenses Known to Law Enforcement, by State and City, 2009—*Continued*

(Number.)

| State/city | Population | Violent crime | Murder and non-negligent man-slaughter | Forcible rape | Robbery | Aggravated assault | Property crime | Burglary | Larceny-theft | Motor vehicle theft | Arson[1] |
|---|---|---|---|---|---|---|---|---|---|---|---|
| **PENNSYLVANIA**—*Continued* | | | | | | | | | | | |
| Waymart | 3,467 | 2 | 0 | 0 | 0 | 2 | 7 | 3 | 4 | 0 | 0 |
| Waynesboro | 9,985 | 23 | 0 | 6 | 7 | 10 | 229 | 33 | 190 | 6 | 2 |
| Waynesburg | 4,144 | 5 | 0 | 0 | 1 | 4 | 129 | 28 | 96 | 5 | 1 |
| Weatherly | 2,586 | 9 | 0 | 0 | 1 | 8 | 57 | 17 | 38 | 2 | 0 |
| Wellsboro | 3,233 | 1 | 0 | 0 | 1 | 0 | 55 | 4 | 50 | 1 | 1 |
| Wernersville | 2,478 | 0 | 0 | 0 | 0 | 0 | 37 | 7 | 27 | 3 | 0 |
| Wesleyville | 3,267 | 5 | 0 | 0 | 1 | 4 | 138 | 12 | 125 | 1 | 0 |
| West Brandywine Township | 7,936 | 5 | 0 | 0 | 0 | 5 | 76 | 16 | 55 | 5 | 1 |
| West Brownsville | 1,015 | 1 | 0 | 0 | 0 | 1 | 3 | 1 | 2 | 0 | 0 |
| West Caln Township | 8,477 | 6 | 0 | 0 | 1 | 5 | 68 | 14 | 52 | 2 | 0 |
| West Carroll Township | 1,335 | 1 | 0 | 0 | 0 | 1 | 11 | 6 | 5 | 0 | 0 |
| West Chester | 18,366 | 74 | 1 | 13 | 27 | 33 | 518 | 92 | 385 | 41 | 0 |
| West Cocalico Township | 7,184 | 2 | 0 | 0 | 0 | 2 | 76 | 18 | 55 | 3 | 2 |
| West Cornwall Township | 2,005 | 2 | 0 | 0 | 0 | 2 | 3 | 1 | 2 | 0 | 0 |
| West Deer Township | 11,974 | 2 | 0 | 0 | 1 | 1 | 73 | 27 | 43 | 3 | 0 |
| West Fallowfield Town | 2,603 | 0 | 0 | 0 | 0 | 0 | 13 | 3 | 10 | 0 | 0 |
| Westfield | 1,108 | 0 | 0 | 0 | 0 | 0 | 8 | 2 | 6 | 0 | 0 |
| West Goshen Township | 21,262 | 21 | 0 | 3 | 7 | 11 | 456 | 43 | 398 | 15 | 4 |
| West Grove Borough | 2,773 | 0 | 0 | 0 | 0 | 0 | 22 | 3 | 17 | 2 | 0 |
| West Hazleton | 3,278 | 15 | 0 | 1 | 5 | 9 | 185 | 50 | 123 | 12 | 2 |
| West Hempfield Township | 16,179 | 6 | 0 | 0 | 1 | 5 | 263 | 21 | 230 | 12 | 1 |
| West Hills Regional | 10,568 | 5 | 0 | 0 | 1 | 4 | 201 | 27 | 170 | 4 | 4 |
| West Kittanning | 1,129 | 0 | 0 | 0 | 0 | 0 | 0 | 0 | 0 | 0 | 0 |
| West Lampeter Township | 15,819 | 7 | 0 | 0 | 3 | 4 | 168 | 27 | 137 | 4 | 2 |
| West Lebanon Township | 843 | 4 | 0 | 0 | 1 | 3 | 84 | 3 | 80 | 1 | 0 |
| West Manchester Township | 18,393 | 30 | 0 | 2 | 14 | 14 | 779 | 76 | 687 | 16 | 0 |
| West Manheim Township | 7,762 | 2 | 0 | 1 | 0 | 1 | 52 | 9 | 38 | 5 | 1 |
| West Mayfield Borough | 1,068 | 3 | 0 | 0 | 0 | 3 | 7 | 3 | 4 | 0 | 0 |
| West Mead Township | 5,047 | 1 | 1 | 0 | 0 | 0 | 0 | 0 | 0 | 0 | 0 |
| West Mifflin | 20,484 | 49 | 0 | 3 | 20 | 26 | 383 | 90 | 271 | 22 | 2 |
| West Newton | 2,824 | 9 | 0 | 1 | 1 | 7 | 72 | 13 | 57 | 2 | 1 |
| West Norriton Township | 14,488 | 24 | 0 | 3 | 7 | 14 | 291 | 28 | 256 | 7 | 1 |
| West Nottingham Township | 2,806 | 0 | 0 | 0 | 0 | 0 | 3 | 1 | 2 | 0 | 0 |
| West Penn Township | 4,343 | 5 | 0 | 0 | 0 | 5 | 32 | 31 | 0 | 1 | 0 |
| West Pikeland Township | 4,089 | 8 | 0 | 0 | 2 | 6 | 32 | 3 | 28 | 1 | 0 |
| West Pike Run | 1,829 | 0 | 0 | 0 | 0 | 0 | 7 | 1 | 6 | 0 | 0 |
| West Pittston | 4,901 | 3 | 0 | 0 | 2 | 1 | 97 | 17 | 79 | 1 | 0 |
| West Pottsgrove Township | 3,755 | 10 | 0 | 1 | 5 | 4 | 146 | 16 | 120 | 10 | 0 |
| West Reading | 4,025 | 29 | 0 | 0 | 6 | 23 | 259 | 26 | 218 | 15 | 0 |
| West Sadsbury Township | 2,510 | 6 | 0 | 0 | 1 | 5 | 85 | 0 | 84 | 1 | 0 |
| West Salem Township | 3,324 | 6 | 0 | 0 | 0 | 6 | 26 | 10 | 16 | 0 | 0 |
| West Shore Regional | 6,568 | 38 | 0 | 1 | 10 | 27 | 45 | 33 | 3 | 9 | 1 |
| Westtown-East Goshen | 31,830 | 24 | 0 | 2 | 1 | 21 | 303 | 50 | 244 | 9 | 0 |
| West View | 6,615 | 3 | 0 | 1 | 0 | 2 | 172 | 15 | 154 | 3 | 0 |
| West Vincent Township | 5,082 | 0 | 0 | 0 | 0 | 0 | 24 | 2 | 21 | 1 | 1 |
| West Whiteland Township | 18,397 | 14 | 0 | 2 | 8 | 4 | 447 | 24 | 409 | 14 | 1 |
| West Wyoming | 2,668 | 1 | 0 | 0 | 1 | 0 | 22 | 5 | 16 | 1 | 0 |
| West York | 4,183 | 15 | 0 | 0 | 5 | 10 | 83 | 17 | 64 | 2 | 0 |
| Whitaker Borough | 1,204 | 5 | 0 | 1 | 4 | 0 | 22 | 5 | 14 | 3 | 0 |
| Whitehall | 13,293 | 8 | 0 | 2 | 0 | 6 | 47 | 9 | 36 | 2 | 0 |
| Whitehall Township | 27,053 | 44 | 0 | 1 | 30 | 13 | 1,324 | 112 | 1,166 | 46 | |
| White Haven Borough | 1,135 | 3 | 0 | 0 | 1 | 2 | 11 | 1 | 9 | 1 | 0 |
| Whitemarsh Township | 17,840 | 9 | 0 | 2 | 0 | 7 | 212 | 31 | 175 | 6 | 0 |
| White Oak | 7,958 | 10 | 0 | 1 | 4 | 5 | 137 | 24 | 105 | 8 | 0 |
| White Township | 1,298 | 6 | 0 | 0 | 1 | 5 | 28 | 8 | 13 | 7 | 0 |
| Whitpain Township | 18,829 | 23 | 0 | 1 | 7 | 15 | 185 | 28 | 150 | 7 | 0 |
| Wiconisco Township | 1,100 | 0 | 0 | 0 | 0 | 0 | 4 | 1 | 3 | 0 | 1 |
| Wilkes-Barre | 40,710 | 171 | 10 | 7 | 88 | 66 | 1,497 | 284 | 1,119 | 94 | 6 |
| Wilkes-Barre Township | 3,045 | 10 | 0 | 0 | 7 | 3 | 666 | 18 | 641 | 7 | 0 |
| Wilkinsburg | 17,351 | 212 | 8 | 7 | 85 | 112 | 653 | 300 | 291 | 62 | 5 |
| Williamsburg | 1,238 | 0 | 0 | 0 | 0 | 0 | 20 | 0 | 20 | 0 | 0 |
| Williamsport | 29,329 | 118 | 2 | 14 | 63 | 39 | 1,119 | 191 | 876 | 52 | |
| Willistown Township | 10,838 | 5 | 0 | 0 | 0 | 5 | 90 | 19 | 71 | 0 | 0 |
| Windber | 3,973 | 13 | 1 | 0 | 2 | 10 | 50 | 11 | 38 | 1 | 1 |
| Wind Gap | 2,782 | 6 | 0 | 0 | 0 | 6 | 57 | 3 | 45 | 9 | 0 |
| Womelsdorf | 2,811 | 2 | 0 | 1 | 0 | 1 | 25 | 11 | 12 | 2 | 1 |
| Woodward Township | 2,266 | 0 | 0 | 0 | 0 | 0 | 0 | 0 | 0 | 0 | 0 |
| Wrightsville | 2,234 | 5 | 0 | 0 | 3 | 2 | 29 | 5 | 24 | 0 | 0 |
| Wyoming | 2,972 | 2 | 0 | 0 | 1 | 1 | 107 | 13 | 82 | 12 | 0 |
| Wyomissing | 10,396 | 9 | 0 | 0 | 6 | 3 | 556 | 34 | 507 | 15 | 1 |

[1] The FBI does not publish arson data unless it receives data from either the agency or the state for all 12 months of the calendar year.

**Table 8. Offenses Known to Law Enforcement, by State and City, 2009**—*Continued*

(Number.)

| State/city | Population | Violent crime | Murder and non-negligent man-slaughter | Forcible rape | Robbery | Aggravated assault | Property crime | Burglary | Larceny-theft | Motor vehicle theft | Arson[1] |
|---|---|---|---|---|---|---|---|---|---|---|---|
| **PENNSYLVANIA**—*Continued* | | | | | | | | | | | |
| Yardley | 2,491 | 0 | 0 | 0 | 0 | 0 | 11 | 3 | 8 | 0 | 0 |
| Yeadon | 11,325 | 59 | 0 | 5 | 35 | 19 | 323 | 94 | 191 | 38 | 0 |
| York | 39,970 | 504 | 10 | 52 | 325 | 117 | 1,957 | 415 | 1,333 | 209 | 8 |
| York Area Regional | 58,530 | 96 | 2 | 12 | 23 | 59 | 682 | 136 | 515 | 31 | 2 |
| Youngsville | 1,649 | 4 | 0 | 0 | 0 | 4 | 14 | 3 | 11 | 0 | 0 |
| Zelienople | 3,902 | 9 | 0 | 1 | 0 | 8 | 115 | 6 | 106 | 3 | 0 |
| Zerbe Township | 1,863 | 0 | 0 | 0 | 0 | 0 | 0 | 0 | 0 | 0 | 0 |
| **RHODE ISLAND** | | | | | | | | | | | |
| Barrington | 16,353 | 2 | 0 | 0 | 0 | 2 | 214 | 38 | 172 | 4 | 0 |
| Bristol | 22,510 | 15 | 0 | 3 | 3 | 9 | 367 | 60 | 298 | 9 | 2 |
| Burrillville | 16,590 | 16 | 0 | 3 | 0 | 13 | 151 | 45 | 100 | 6 | 1 |
| Central Falls | 18,696 | 102 | 0 | 9 | 30 | 63 | 435 | 129 | 232 | 74 | 6 |
| Charlestown | 8,067 | 7 | 0 | 0 | 1 | 6 | 142 | 31 | 109 | 2 | 1 |
| Coventry | 34,837 | 27 | 0 | 6 | 3 | 18 | 591 | 112 | 445 | 34 | 10 |
| Cranston | 80,223 | 120 | 2 | 20 | 37 | 61 | 2,077 | 415 | 1,466 | 196 | 15 |
| Cumberland | 34,546 | 22 | 1 | 3 | 5 | 13 | 451 | 68 | 361 | 22 | 5 |
| East Greenwich | 13,357 | 10 | 0 | 3 | 3 | 4 | 147 | 23 | 118 | 6 | 1 |
| East Providence | 48,557 | 67 | 0 | 7 | 21 | 39 | 749 | 134 | 550 | 65 | 16 |
| Foster | 4,537 | 4 | 0 | 0 | 0 | 4 | 33 | 20 | 12 | 1 | 0 |
| Glocester | 10,583 | 4 | 0 | 2 | 1 | 1 | 60 | 11 | 48 | 1 | 1 |
| Hopkinton | 7,988 | 5 | 0 | 1 | 1 | 3 | 109 | 40 | 56 | 13 | 1 |
| Jamestown | 5,467 | 3 | 0 | 2 | 0 | 1 | 101 | 13 | 84 | 4 | 1 |
| Johnston | 28,617 | 34 | 0 | 6 | 5 | 23 | 608 | 121 | 442 | 45 | 4 |
| Lincoln | 22,156 | 21 | 0 | 2 | 7 | 12 | 451 | 66 | 356 | 29 | 3 |
| Little Compton | 3,513 | 2 | 0 | 0 | 0 | 2 | 58 | 15 | 43 | 0 | 0 |
| Middletown | 16,009 | 8 | 0 | 2 | 1 | 5 | 368 | 52 | 296 | 20 | 1 |
| Narragansett | 16,476 | 16 | 0 | 4 | 2 | 10 | 342 | 80 | 253 | 9 | 2 |
| Newport | 23,260 | 121 | 0 | 10 | 28 | 83 | 1,004 | 205 | 760 | 39 | 13 |
| New Shoreham | 1,036 | 0 | 0 | 0 | 0 | 0 | 54 | 13 | 36 | 5 | 0 |
| North Kingstown | 26,615 | 31 | 1 | 5 | 4 | 21 | 458 | 90 | 348 | 20 | 5 |
| North Providence | 32,794 | 51 | 0 | 11 | 14 | 26 | 548 | 128 | 368 | 52 | 5 |
| North Smithfield | 11,640 | 7 | 0 | 2 | 4 | 1 | 115 | 24 | 80 | 11 | 0 |
| Pawtucket | 71,787 | 297 | 1 | 25 | 115 | 156 | 2,279 | 604 | 1,458 | 217 | 27 |
| Portsmouth | 16,913 | 14 | 0 | 5 | 3 | 6 | 299 | 42 | 238 | 19 | 3 |
| Providence | 171,664 | 1,182 | 23 | 50 | 395 | 714 | 7,990 | 1,825 | 5,088 | 1,077 | 43 |
| Richmond | 7,657 | 2 | 0 | 0 | 0 | 2 | 104 | 29 | 70 | 5 | 0 |
| Scituate | 10,894 | 1 | 0 | 0 | 0 | 1 | 77 | 18 | 57 | 2 | 0 |
| Smithfield | 21,289 | 14 | 0 | 3 | 2 | 9 | 290 | 29 | 248 | 13 | 3 |
| South Kingstown | 29,270 | 11 | 0 | 3 | 1 | 7 | 323 | 69 | 241 | 13 | 4 |
| Tiverton | 14,944 | 14 | 0 | 2 | 2 | 10 | 306 | 80 | 200 | 26 | 1 |
| Warren | 10,990 | 19 | 0 | 3 | 2 | 14 | 194 | 40 | 147 | 7 | 3 |
| Warwick | 84,488 | 121 | 0 | 26 | 38 | 57 | 2,725 | 361 | 2,242 | 122 | 18 |
| Westerly | 23,466 | 27 | 0 | 8 | 2 | 17 | 481 | 86 | 389 | 6 | 3 |
| West Greenwich | 6,540 | 3 | 0 | 0 | 1 | 2 | 106 | 24 | 80 | 2 | 3 |
| West Warwick | 29,282 | 65 | 0 | 17 | 19 | 29 | 594 | 131 | 426 | 37 | 5 |
| Woonsocket | 43,366 | 149 | 2 | 27 | 31 | 89 | 1,368 | 350 | 908 | 110 | 21 |
| **SOUTH CAROLINA** | | | | | | | | | | | |
| Abbeville | 5,514 | 92 | 0 | 0 | 4 | 88 | 192 | 38 | 149 | 5 | 1 |
| Aiken | 29,829 | 128 | 1 | 8 | 45 | 74 | 1,216 | 212 | 953 | 51 | 0 |
| Allendale | 3,617 | 79 | 0 | 1 | 10 | 68 | 181 | 94 | 80 | 7 | 0 |
| Anderson | 27,144 | 205 | 1 | 8 | 57 | 139 | 1,879 | 408 | 1,361 | 110 | 8 |
| Andrews | 2,968 | 29 | 0 | 2 | 9 | 18 | 188 | 39 | 140 | 9 | 0 |
| Aynor | 642 | 14 | 0 | 0 | 0 | 14 | 27 | 6 | 21 | 0 | 0 |
| Bamberg | 3,401 | 27 | 0 | 1 | 3 | 23 | 199 | 60 | 132 | 7 | 2 |
| Barnwell | 4,766 | 49 | 0 | 3 | 9 | 37 | 297 | 109 | 182 | 6 | 2 |
| Batesburg-Leesville | 5,584 | 31 | 1 | 1 | 2 | 27 | 284 | 73 | 189 | 22 | 0 |
| Beaufort | 11,663 | 124 | 1 | 10 | 28 | 85 | 695 | 150 | 524 | 21 | 0 |
| Belton | 4,691 | 14 | 0 | 1 | 4 | 9 | 153 | 24 | 119 | 10 | 1 |
| Bennettsville | 8,956 | 123 | 1 | 7 | 19 | 96 | 499 | 118 | 367 | 14 | 3 |
| Bishopville | 3,880 | 27 | 0 | 2 | 3 | 22 | 203 | 63 | 135 | 5 | 5 |
| Blacksburg | 1,905 | 17 | 1 | 1 | 2 | 13 | 121 | 35 | 81 | 5 | 0 |
| Blackville | 2,823 | 35 | 1 | 0 | 2 | 32 | 99 | 30 | 63 | 6 | 0 |
| Bluffton | 12,557 | 46 | 0 | 0 | 13 | 33 | 393 | 60 | 311 | 22 | 4 |
| Burnettown | 2,669 | 7 | 0 | 0 | 3 | 4 | 39 | 11 | 26 | 2 | 0 |
| Calhoun Falls | 2,170 | 11 | 0 | 1 | 1 | 9 | 57 | 14 | 42 | 1 | 1 |
| Camden | 7,072 | 83 | 2 | 4 | 14 | 63 | 460 | 128 | 307 | 25 | 0 |
| Cayce | 12,700 | 119 | 1 | 3 | 15 | 100 | 763 | 189 | 518 | 56 | 3 |
| Central | 4,154 | 19 | 0 | 2 | 5 | 12 | 227 | 31 | 179 | 17 | 2 |
| Chapin | 718 | 2 | 0 | 0 | 0 | 2 | 36 | 5 | 30 | 1 | 0 |
| Charleston | 113,681 | 595 | 9 | 31 | 218 | 337 | 3,991 | 566 | 3,152 | 273 | 11 |
| Cheraw | 5,411 | 54 | 0 | 3 | 13 | 38 | 386 | 67 | 303 | 16 | 1 |

[1] The FBI does not publish arson data unless it receives data from either the agency or the state for all 12 months of the calendar year.

## Table 8. Offenses Known to Law Enforcement, by State and City, 2009—*Continued*

(Number.)

| State/city | Population | Violent crime | Murder and non-negligent man-slaughter | Forcible rape | Robbery | Aggravated assault | Property crime | Burglary | Larceny-theft | Motor vehicle theft | Arson[1] |
|---|---|---|---|---|---|---|---|---|---|---|---|
| **SOUTH CAROLINA**—*Continued* | | | | | | | | | | | |
| Chesnee | 1,084 | 16 | 0 | 1 | 3 | 12 | 59 | 14 | 40 | 5 | 0 |
| Chester | 5,999 | 161 | 0 | 5 | 31 | 125 | 310 | 78 | 213 | 19 | 1 |
| Chesterfield | 1,313 | 6 | 0 | 0 | 3 | 3 | 46 | 13 | 32 | 1 | 0 |
| Clemson | 13,147 | 33 | 1 | 0 | 7 | 25 | 339 | 67 | 221 | 51 | 0 |
| Clinton | 8,865 | 66 | 1 | 5 | 5 | 55 | 475 | 102 | 347 | 26 | 2 |
| Clio | 715 | 1 | 0 | 0 | 0 | 1 | 34 | 17 | 13 | 4 | 0 |
| Clover | 5,032 | 140 | 0 | 1 | 4 | 135 | 187 | 38 | 144 | 5 | 1 |
| Columbia | 127,884 | 1,338 | 13 | 68 | 379 | 878 | 7,689 | 1,678 | 5,321 | 690 | 11 |
| Conway | 16,295 | 192 | 0 | 2 | 42 | 148 | 1,112 | 278 | 775 | 59 | 3 |
| Cottageville | 674 | 5 | 1 | 0 | 3 | 1 | 23 | 6 | 16 | 1 | 1 |
| Coward | 679 | 8 | 1 | 1 | 0 | 6 | 21 | 10 | 10 | 1 | 0 |
| Cowpens | 2,428 | 18 | 0 | 0 | 2 | 16 | 140 | 40 | 93 | 7 | 0 |
| Darlington | 6,645 | 103 | 0 | 4 | 15 | 84 | 582 | 125 | 440 | 17 | 0 |
| Denmark | 2,972 | 32 | 0 | 5 | 4 | 23 | 105 | 34 | 64 | 7 | 3 |
| Dillon | 6,350 | 197 | 0 | 8 | 34 | 155 | 850 | 250 | 567 | 33 | 2 |
| Due West | 1,274 | 0 | 0 | 0 | 0 | 0 | 21 | 11 | 10 | 0 | 0 |
| Duncan | 3,141 | 17 | 0 | 3 | 3 | 11 | 116 | 23 | 83 | 10 | 0 |
| Edgefield | 4,415 | 13 | 0 | 3 | 3 | 7 | 63 | 13 | 46 | 4 | 0 |
| Edisto Beach | 726 | 0 | 0 | 0 | 0 | 0 | 38 | 4 | 32 | 2 | 0 |
| Elgin | 1,294 | 7 | 0 | 1 | 0 | 6 | 67 | 5 | 58 | 4 | 0 |
| Fairfax | 3,154 | 25 | 1 | 0 | 3 | 21 | 89 | 32 | 52 | 5 | 1 |
| Florence | 31,642 | 370 | 5 | 14 | 92 | 259 | 3,071 | 549 | 2,378 | 144 | 5 |
| Folly Beach | 2,445 | 22 | 0 | 3 | 4 | 15 | 225 | 40 | 174 | 11 | 1 |
| Forest Acres | 9,859 | 101 | 0 | 3 | 26 | 72 | 574 | 123 | 426 | 25 | 3 |
| Fort Lawn | 804 | 9 | 1 | 1 | 1 | 6 | 37 | 11 | 26 | 0 | 0 |
| Fort Mill | 10,316 | 106 | 0 | 3 | 5 | 98 | 266 | 39 | 216 | 11 | 2 |
| Fountain Inn | 7,944 | 32 | 0 | 1 | 4 | 27 | 141 | 26 | 105 | 10 | 0 |
| Gaffney | 13,223 | 125 | 4 | 12 | 31 | 78 | 339 | 89 | 223 | 27 | 2 |
| Georgetown | 8,450 | 106 | 1 | 8 | 22 | 75 | 657 | 102 | 522 | 33 | 0 |
| Goose Creek | 38,770 | 110 | 0 | 8 | 36 | 66 | 865 | 170 | 654 | 41 | 13 |
| Great Falls | 2,027 | 42 | 0 | 2 | 5 | 35 | 102 | 38 | 57 | 7 | 2 |
| Greenville | 60,355 | 638 | 1 | 28 | 160 | 449 | 3,674 | 622 | 2,790 | 262 | 9 |
| Greenwood | 22,551 | 325 | 1 | 15 | 57 | 252 | 1,796 | 460 | 1,279 | 57 | 5 |
| Hampton | 2,745 | 21 | 0 | 1 | 4 | 16 | 143 | 35 | 104 | 4 | 1 |
| Hanahan | 16,460 | 72 | 0 | 8 | 22 | 42 | 510 | 90 | 382 | 38 | 2 |
| Hardeeville | 2,918 | 47 | 0 | 2 | 9 | 36 | 186 | 27 | 144 | 15 | 1 |
| Harleyville | 690 | 9 | 0 | 0 | 1 | 8 | 49 | 10 | 34 | 5 | 0 |
| Hemingway | 493 | 3 | 0 | 0 | 2 | 1 | 33 | 10 | 21 | 2 | 0 |
| Holly Hill | 1,337 | 11 | 0 | 0 | 8 | 3 | 85 | 22 | 57 | 6 | 0 |
| Honea Path | 3,691 | 48 | 0 | 2 | 7 | 39 | 201 | 59 | 128 | 14 | 2 |
| Inman | 2,107 | 16 | 0 | 0 | 3 | 13 | 91 | 24 | 56 | 11 | 0 |
| Irmo | 11,738 | 53 | 0 | 3 | 8 | 42 | 311 | 66 | 236 | 9 | 1 |
| Isle of Palms | 4,690 | 6 | 0 | 1 | 1 | 4 | 201 | 49 | 148 | 4 | 0 |
| Iva | 1,205 | 0 | 0 | 0 | 0 | 0 | 7 | 0 | 6 | 1 | 0 |
| Jackson | 1,650 | 8 | 0 | 1 | 2 | 5 | 27 | 4 | 23 | 0 | 1 |
| Johnsonville | 1,496 | 7 | 0 | 0 | 0 | 7 | 74 | 39 | 33 | 2 | 1 |
| Johnston | 2,330 | 25 | 1 | 2 | 1 | 21 | 100 | 35 | 60 | 5 | 0 |
| Jonesville | 893 | 5 | 0 | 0 | 1 | 4 | 31 | 15 | 15 | 1 | 0 |
| Kingstree | 3,211 | 45 | 0 | 1 | 11 | 33 | 278 | 117 | 155 | 6 | 2 |
| Lake City | 6,687 | 103 | 1 | 5 | 17 | 80 | 477 | 124 | 330 | 23 | 6 |
| Lake View | 781 | 4 | 0 | 0 | 0 | 4 | 40 | 26 | 14 | 0 | 0 |
| Lamar | 988 | 8 | 0 | 0 | 0 | 8 | 40 | 7 | 28 | 5 | 0 |
| Lancaster | 10,193 | 165 | 3 | 3 | 27 | 132 | 607 | 133 | 452 | 22 | 1 |
| Landrum | 2,630 | 3 | 0 | 0 | 0 | 3 | 98 | 29 | 68 | 1 | 0 |
| Latta | 1,485 | 36 | 0 | 2 | 5 | 29 | 101 | 12 | 83 | 6 | 0 |
| Laurens | 9,582 | 151 | 1 | 1 | 29 | 120 | 567 | 139 | 410 | 18 | 1 |
| Lexington | 16,628 | 47 | 0 | 5 | 8 | 34 | 612 | 51 | 543 | 18 | 1 |
| Liberty | 3,070 | 12 | 0 | 0 | 1 | 11 | 135 | 21 | 106 | 8 | 0 |
| Lyman | 2,890 | 14 | 0 | 3 | 1 | 10 | 102 | 21 | 79 | 2 | 0 |
| Lynchburg | 549 | 1 | 0 | 0 | 1 | 0 | 33 | 10 | 22 | 1 | 1 |
| Manning[3] | 3,935 | 52 | 0 | 4 | 11 | 37 | | 68 | 262 | | 1 |
| Marion | 6,775 | 124 | 0 | 4 | 25 | 95 | 606 | 166 | 406 | 34 | 5 |
| Mauldin | 22,602 | 49 | 0 | 2 | 5 | 42 | 428 | 74 | 320 | 34 | 0 |
| McColl | 2,288 | 25 | 0 | 1 | 4 | 20 | 126 | 37 | 85 | 4 | 2 |
| McCormick | 2,660 | 22 | 0 | 0 | 3 | 19 | 76 | 20 | 49 | 7 | 0 |
| Moncks Corner | 7,160 | 54 | 2 | 5 | 19 | 28 | 430 | 75 | 329 | 26 | 1 |
| Mount Pleasant | 67,641 | 139 | 0 | 3 | 23 | 113 | 1,375 | 204 | 1,116 | 55 | 6 |
| Mullins | 4,683 | 62 | 0 | 2 | 18 | 42 | 382 | 109 | 256 | 17 | 2 |
| Myrtle Beach | 31,465 | 375 | 4 | 29 | 154 | 188 | 3,984 | 664 | 3,056 | 264 | 3 |
| Newberry | 10,952 | 59 | 1 | 5 | 11 | 42 | 348 | 62 | 281 | 5 | 2 |

[1] The FBI does not publish arson data unless it receives data from either the agency or the state for all 12 months of the calendar year.

**Table 8. Offenses Known to Law Enforcement, by State and City, 2009—*Continued***

(Number.)

| State/city | Population | Violent crime | Murder and non-negligent man-slaughter | Forcible rape | Robbery | Aggravated assault | Property crime | Burglary | Larceny-theft | Motor vehicle theft | Arson[1] |
|---|---|---|---|---|---|---|---|---|---|---|---|
| **SOUTH CAROLINA**—*Continued* | | | | | | | | | | | |
| New Ellenton | 2,224 | 21 | 0 | 1 | 3 | 17 | 52 | 22 | 26 | 4 | 0 |
| Ninety Six | 1,920 | 5 | 0 | 0 | 0 | 5 | 67 | 17 | 47 | 3 | 0 |
| North | 772 | 4 | 0 | 0 | 2 | 2 | 33 | 11 | 20 | 2 | 0 |
| North Augusta | 21,066 | 92 | 0 | 7 | 49 | 36 | 1,026 | 219 | 720 | 87 | 0 |
| North Charleston | 95,982 | 993 | 10 | 55 | 376 | 552 | 6,140 | 1,024 | 4,510 | 606 | 22 |
| Orangeburg | 13,278 | 79 | 1 | 9 | 34 | 35 | 841 | 232 | 544 | 65 | 2 |
| Pacolet | 2,834 | 14 | 0 | 0 | 3 | 11 | 61 | 9 | 46 | 6 | 1 |
| Pageland | 2,512 | 32 | 1 | 0 | 2 | 29 | 228 | 53 | 171 | 4 | 1 |
| Pamplico | 1,156 | 2 | 0 | 0 | 0 | 2 | 15 | 5 | 9 | 1 | 0 |
| Pelion | 597 | 1 | 0 | 0 | 0 | 1 | 26 | 3 | 22 | 1 | 0 |
| Pickens | 3,024 | 6 | 0 | 2 | 0 | 4 | 129 | 17 | 107 | 5 | 0 |
| Pine Ridge | 2,007 | 4 | 0 | 0 | 1 | 3 | 22 | 7 | 14 | 1 | 0 |
| Port Royal | 11,282 | 20 | 0 | 2 | 4 | 14 | 219 | 53 | 145 | 21 | 1 |
| Prosperity | 1,065 | 0 | 0 | 0 | 0 | 0 | 40 | 10 | 27 | 3 | 0 |
| Ridgeland | 2,586 | 26 | 0 | 0 | 11 | 15 | 203 | 30 | 162 | 11 | 1 |
| Rock Hill | 69,506 | 708 | 5 | 27 | 82 | 594 | 2,930 | 578 | 2,138 | 214 | 10 |
| Salley | 414 | 0 | 0 | 0 | 0 | 0 | 11 | 2 | 9 | 0 | 0 |
| Saluda | 2,894 | 63 | 0 | 2 | 3 | 58 | 72 | 12 | 58 | 2 | 0 |
| Santee | 715 | 26 | 0 | 0 | 7 | 19 | 84 | 20 | 59 | 5 | 0 |
| Scranton | 1,039 | 5 | 0 | 0 | 1 | 4 | 22 | 7 | 15 | 0 | 1 |
| Simpsonville | 17,433 | 83 | 1 | 5 | 12 | 65 | 657 | 124 | 512 | 21 | 3 |
| Society Hill | 683 | 3 | 0 | 0 | 0 | 3 | 28 | 16 | 10 | 2 | 0 |
| South Congaree | 2,379 | 2 | 0 | 1 | 0 | 1 | 54 | 19 | 29 | 6 | 0 |
| Spartanburg | 39,561 | 800 | 4 | 19 | 175 | 602 | 3,381 | 764 | 2,390 | 227 | 36 |
| Springdale | 2,946 | 18 | 0 | 1 | 2 | 15 | 95 | 14 | 75 | 6 | 3 |
| St. George | 2,127 | 34 | 0 | 1 | 11 | 22 | 137 | 33 | 95 | 9 | 0 |
| St. Matthews | 1,931 | 40 | 0 | 0 | 1 | 39 | 82 | 15 | 62 | 5 | 0 |
| St. Stephen | 1,778 | 4 | 0 | 0 | 1 | 3 | 55 | 18 | 34 | 3 | 0 |
| Sullivans Island | 1,866 | 1 | 0 | 0 | 0 | 1 | 34 | 11 | 23 | 0 | 0 |
| Summerton | 1,025 | 18 | 0 | 2 | 4 | 12 | 52 | 12 | 38 | 2 | 0 |
| Summerville[3] | 47,507 | 138 | 6 | 10 | 47 | 75 | | | 1,336 | 82 | 0 |
| Sumter | 38,399 | 486 | 8 | 8 | 102 | 368 | 2,731 | 829 | 1,735 | 167 | 11 |
| Surfside Beach | 4,823 | 22 | 0 | 0 | 7 | 15 | 321 | 68 | 212 | 41 | 0 |
| Swansea | 805 | 7 | 0 | 0 | 0 | 7 | 56 | 8 | 46 | 2 | 0 |
| Tega Cay | 5,103 | 12 | 0 | 1 | 0 | 11 | 140 | 25 | 113 | 2 | 0 |
| Timmonsville | 2,380 | 36 | 1 | 2 | 4 | 29 | 155 | 48 | 95 | 12 | 2 |
| Travelers Rest | 4,574 | 19 | 0 | 0 | 4 | 15 | 220 | 27 | 185 | 8 | 0 |
| Turbeville | 705 | 3 | 0 | 0 | 0 | 3 | 14 | 4 | 8 | 2 | 0 |
| Union | 7,960 | 133 | 0 | 4 | 23 | 106 | 473 | 108 | 351 | 14 | 4 |
| Wagener | 876 | 3 | 0 | 0 | 0 | 3 | 41 | 10 | 28 | 3 | 0 |
| Walhalla | 3,551 | 22 | 0 | 4 | 1 | 17 | 106 | 23 | 79 | 4 | 1 |
| Walterboro | 5,825 | 118 | 4 | 5 | 15 | 94 | 637 | 113 | 500 | 24 | 0 |
| Wellford | 2,479 | 12 | 0 | 2 | 5 | 5 | 64 | 22 | 39 | 3 | 0 |
| West Columbia | 13,982 | 189 | 0 | 5 | 50 | 134 | 1,048 | 152 | 848 | 48 | 2 |
| Westminster | 2,654 | 18 | 0 | 0 | 2 | 16 | 94 | 12 | 78 | 4 | 0 |
| West Union | 301 | 5 | 0 | 0 | 3 | 2 | 22 | 1 | 20 | 1 | 0 |
| Whitmire | 1,530 | 7 | 0 | 0 | 1 | 6 | 35 | 8 | 26 | 1 | 0 |
| Williamston | 3,983 | 21 | 0 | 0 | 3 | 18 | 124 | 18 | 98 | 8 | 1 |
| Williston | 3,178 | 21 | 0 | 1 | 6 | 14 | 103 | 25 | 76 | 2 | 1 |
| Winnsboro | 3,562 | 41 | 1 | 4 | 1 | 35 | 269 | 25 | 243 | 1 | 4 |
| Woodruff | 4,089 | 22 | 0 | 2 | 6 | 14 | 131 | 23 | 103 | 5 | 0 |
| Yemassee | 866 | 1 | 0 | 0 | 0 | 1 | 39 | 8 | 27 | 4 | 1 |
| York | 8,083 | 83 | 0 | 3 | 11 | 69 | 449 | 82 | 352 | 15 | 1 |
| **SOUTH DAKOTA** | | | | | | | | | | | |
| Aberdeen | 24,441 | 45 | 1 | 21 | 1 | 22 | 545 | 108 | 412 | 25 | 1 |
| Armour | 642 | 0 | 0 | 0 | 0 | 0 | 0 | 0 | 0 | 0 | 0 |
| Avon | 511 | 0 | 0 | 0 | 0 | 0 | 0 | 0 | 0 | 0 | 0 |
| Belle Fourche | 5,001 | 4 | 0 | 2 | 0 | 2 | 30 | 5 | 20 | 5 | 0 |
| Bonesteel | 251 | 0 | 0 | 0 | 0 | 0 | 0 | 0 | 0 | 0 | 0 |
| Box Elder | 3,601 | 8 | 0 | 0 | 1 | 7 | 58 | 9 | 45 | 4 | 0 |
| Brandon | 9,195 | 0 | 0 | 0 | 0 | 0 | 22 | 0 | 22 | 0 | 0 |
| Brookings | 19,986 | 3 | 0 | 0 | 0 | 3 | 41 | 3 | 31 | 7 | 0 |
| Burke | 561 | 0 | 0 | 0 | 0 | 0 | 0 | 0 | 0 | 0 | 0 |
| Canton | 3,680 | 4 | 0 | 1 | 0 | 3 | 42 | 12 | 27 | 3 | 0 |
| Centerville | 837 | 0 | 0 | 0 | 0 | 0 | 3 | 1 | 2 | 0 | 0 |
| Chamberlain | 2,255 | 2 | 0 | 0 | 1 | 1 | 17 | 3 | 11 | 3 | 0 |
| Colman | 546 | 0 | 0 | 0 | 0 | 0 | 2 | 1 | 0 | 1 | 0 |
| Corsica | 563 | 0 | 0 | 0 | 0 | 0 | 2 | 0 | 1 | 1 | 0 |
| Deadwood | 1,273 | 4 | 0 | 1 | 0 | 3 | 40 | 2 | 37 | 1 | 0 |
| Delmont | 210 | 0 | 0 | 0 | 0 | 0 | 0 | 0 | 0 | 0 | 0 |
| Eagle Butte | 927 | 0 | 0 | 0 | 0 | 0 | 7 | 2 | 5 | 0 | 0 |

[1] The FBI does not publish arson data unless it receives data from either the agency or the state for all 12 months of the calendar year.
[3] The FBI determined that the agency's data were overreported. Consequently, those data are not included in this table.

## Table 8. Offenses Known to Law Enforcement, by State and City, 2009—*Continued*

(Number.)

| State/city | Population | Violent crime | Murder and non-negligent man-slaughter | Forcible rape | Robbery | Aggravated assault | Property crime | Burglary | Larceny-theft | Motor vehicle theft | Arson[1] |
|---|---|---|---|---|---|---|---|---|---|---|---|
| **SOUTH DAKOTA**—*Continued* | | | | | | | | | | | |
| Estelline | 665 | 0 | 0 | 0 | 0 | 0 | 5 | 1 | 4 | 0 | 0 |
| Eureka | 921 | 0 | 0 | 0 | 0 | 0 | 0 | 0 | 0 | 0 | 0 |
| Faith | 436 | 0 | 0 | 0 | 0 | 0 | 1 | 0 | 1 | 0 | 0 |
| Flandreau | 2,206 | 4 | 0 | 0 | 0 | 4 | 24 | 7 | 16 | 1 | 0 |
| Freeman | 1,181 | 0 | 0 | 0 | 0 | 0 | 0 | 0 | 0 | 0 | 0 |
| Gettysburg | 1,031 | 0 | 0 | 0 | 0 | 0 | 3 | 0 | 2 | 1 | 0 |
| Hermosa | 354 | 0 | 0 | 0 | 0 | 0 | 0 | 0 | 0 | 0 | 0 |
| Hot Springs | 4,015 | 5 | 0 | 0 | 0 | 5 | 35 | 9 | 24 | 2 | 0 |
| Hoven | 384 | 0 | 0 | 0 | 0 | 0 | 0 | 0 | 0 | 0 | 0 |
| Irene | 401 | 0 | 0 | 0 | 0 | 0 | 0 | 0 | 0 | 0 | 0 |
| Jefferson | 600 | 0 | 0 | 0 | 0 | 0 | 2 | 1 | 1 | 0 | 0 |
| Kadoka | 628 | 0 | 0 | 0 | 0 | 0 | 2 | 1 | 0 | 1 | 0 |
| Kimball | 687 | 0 | 0 | 0 | 0 | 0 | 3 | 3 | 0 | 0 | 0 |
| Lead | 2,878 | 2 | 0 | 0 | 0 | 2 | 25 | 4 | 20 | 1 | 0 |
| Lemmon | 1,164 | 0 | 0 | 0 | 0 | 0 | 9 | 3 | 5 | 1 | 0 |
| Lennox | 2,453 | 0 | 0 | 0 | 0 | 0 | 15 | 3 | 11 | 1 | 0 |
| Leola | 383 | 0 | 0 | 0 | 0 | 0 | 0 | 0 | 0 | 0 | 0 |
| Madison | 6,478 | 9 | 0 | 3 | 2 | 4 | 102 | 14 | 85 | 3 | 0 |
| Martin | 986 | 1 | 0 | 1 | 0 | 0 | 5 | 2 | 3 | 0 | 0 |
| McIntosh | 204 | 0 | 0 | 0 | 0 | 0 | 0 | 0 | 0 | 0 | 0 |
| Menno | 648 | 0 | 0 | 0 | 0 | 0 | 0 | 0 | 0 | 0 | 0 |
| Miller | 1,321 | 0 | 0 | 0 | 0 | 0 | 10 | 1 | 9 | 0 | 0 |
| Mitchell | 14,769 | 38 | 0 | 9 | 0 | 29 | 424 | 59 | 351 | 14 | 2 |
| Mobridge | 3,113 | 10 | 0 | 1 | 1 | 8 | 80 | 7 | 70 | 3 | 0 |
| North Sioux City | 2,547 | 0 | 0 | 0 | 0 | 0 | 29 | 1 | 26 | 2 | 0 |
| Parkston | 1,467 | 0 | 0 | 0 | 0 | 0 | 6 | 2 | 4 | 0 | 0 |
| Pierre | 13,901 | 27 | 0 | 12 | 2 | 13 | 509 | 77 | 404 | 28 | 1 |
| Rapid City | 66,170 | 307 | 2 | 97 | 41 | 167 | 2,829 | 433 | 2,264 | 132 | 21 |
| Rosholt | 427 | 0 | 0 | 0 | 0 | 0 | 0 | 0 | 0 | 0 | 0 |
| Scotland | 780 | 0 | 0 | 0 | 0 | 0 | 0 | 0 | 0 | 0 | 0 |
| Selby | 638 | 1 | 0 | 0 | 0 | 1 | 0 | 0 | 0 | 0 | 0 |
| Sioux Falls | 158,672 | 454 | 1 | 133 | 47 | 273 | 4,609 | 748 | 3,584 | 277 | 24 |
| Sisseton | 2,437 | 16 | 0 | 3 | 1 | 12 | 47 | 10 | 35 | 2 | 0 |
| Spearfish | 10,171 | 20 | 0 | 11 | 0 | 9 | 293 | 52 | 231 | 10 | 0 |
| Springfield | 1,479 | 0 | 0 | 0 | 0 | 0 | 0 | 0 | 0 | 0 | 1 |
| Sturgis | 5,899 | 3 | 0 | 0 | 0 | 3 | 196 | 22 | 168 | 6 | 0 |
| Summerset | 442 | 1 | 0 | 1 | 0 | 0 | 16 | 0 | 16 | 0 | 0 |
| Tea | 4,073 | 5 | 0 | 2 | 0 | 3 | 100 | 19 | 79 | 2 | 0 |
| Tripp | 623 | 0 | 0 | 0 | 0 | 0 | 2 | 1 | 1 | 0 | 0 |
| Tyndall | 1,088 | 0 | 0 | 0 | 0 | 0 | 0 | 0 | 0 | 0 | 0 |
| Vermillion | 10,523 | 2 | 0 | 0 | 0 | 2 | 152 | 9 | 143 | 0 | 1 |
| Viborg | 768 | 0 | 0 | 0 | 0 | 0 | 4 | 4 | 0 | 0 | 3 |
| Wagner | 1,538 | 1 | 0 | 0 | 0 | 1 | 5 | 3 | 2 | 0 | 0 |
| Watertown | 20,515 | 48 | 1 | 16 | 4 | 27 | 512 | 74 | 408 | 30 | 3 |
| Whitewood | 850 | 3 | 0 | 1 | 0 | 2 | 1 | 1 | 0 | 0 | 0 |
| Wilmot | 511 | 0 | 0 | 0 | 0 | 0 | 0 | 0 | 0 | 0 | 0 |
| Winner | 2,705 | 5 | 0 | 0 | 0 | 5 | 13 | 3 | 8 | 2 | 0 |
| Yankton | 13,831 | 11 | 0 | 4 | 0 | 7 | 358 | 41 | 309 | 8 | 1 |
| **TENNESSEE** | | | | | | | | | | | |
| Adamsville | 2,138 | 3 | 0 | 1 | 0 | 2 | 38 | 9 | 26 | 3 | 1 |
| Alcoa | 8,681 | 81 | 1 | 2 | 13 | 65 | 520 | 69 | 427 | 24 | 1 |
| Alexandria | 879 | 3 | 0 | 0 | 0 | 3 | 22 | 10 | 11 | 1 | 0 |
| Algood | 3,430 | 8 | 0 | 4 | 0 | 4 | 140 | 12 | 126 | 2 | 0 |
| Ardmore | 1,172 | 9 | 0 | 0 | 3 | 6 | 25 | 9 | 16 | 0 | 0 |
| Ashland City | 4,695 | 32 | 0 | 1 | 2 | 29 | 253 | 45 | 196 | 12 | 0 |
| Athens | 14,388 | 231 | 2 | 14 | 25 | 190 | 1,118 | 249 | 814 | 55 | 5 |
| Atoka | 7,900 | 13 | 0 | 0 | 2 | 11 | 138 | 17 | 116 | 5 | 1 |
| Baileyton | 491 | 2 | 0 | 0 | 2 | 0 | 13 | 2 | 11 | 0 | 0 |
| Baneberry | 488 | 0 | 0 | 0 | 0 | 0 | 1 | 1 | 0 | 0 | 0 |
| Bartlett | 47,881 | 130 | 2 | 5 | 23 | 100 | 971 | 159 | 773 | 39 | 2 |
| Baxter | 1,422 | 6 | 0 | 0 | 0 | 6 | 48 | 18 | 26 | 4 | 0 |
| Bean Station | 3,072 | 14 | 0 | 1 | 5 | 8 | 209 | 56 | 138 | 15 | 1 |
| Belle Meade | 3,513 | 1 | 0 | 0 | 1 | 0 | 29 | 7 | 22 | 0 | 0 |
| Bells | 2,247 | 15 | 1 | 0 | 2 | 12 | 55 | 27 | 26 | 2 | 3 |
| Benton | 1,189 | 3 | 0 | 0 | 0 | 3 | 47 | 4 | 40 | 3 | 0 |
| Berry Hill | 822 | 6 | 0 | 0 | 3 | 3 | 90 | 6 | 80 | 4 | 0 |
| Bethel Springs | 777 | 2 | 0 | 0 | 1 | 1 | 20 | 8 | 11 | 1 | 0 |
| Big Sandy | 508 | 5 | 1 | 0 | 0 | 4 | 10 | 3 | 6 | 1 | 0 |
| Blaine | 1,770 | 3 | 0 | 0 | 2 | 1 | 23 | 11 | 12 | 0 | 3 |
| Bluff City | 1,664 | 7 | 0 | 0 | 0 | 7 | 29 | 6 | 20 | 3 | 0 |
| Bolivar | 5,627 | 61 | 0 | 3 | 6 | 52 | 286 | 77 | 198 | 11 | 1 |

[1] The FBI does not publish arson data unless it receives data from either the agency or the state for all 12 months of the calendar year.

## Table 8. Offenses Known to Law Enforcement, by State and City, 2009—*Continued*

(Number.)

| State/city | Population | Violent crime | Murder and non-negligent man-slaughter | Forcible rape | Robbery | Aggravated assault | Property crime | Burglary | Larceny-theft | Motor vehicle theft | Arson[1] |
|---|---|---|---|---|---|---|---|---|---|---|---|
| **TENNESSEE**—*Continued* | | | | | | | | | | | |
| Bradford | 1,063 | 4 | 0 | 0 | 0 | 4 | 15 | 1 | 13 | 1 | 1 |
| Brentwood | 37,479 | 21 | 0 | 0 | 5 | 16 | 490 | 81 | 398 | 11 | 4 |
| Brighton | 2,736 | 6 | 0 | 0 | 1 | 5 | 37 | 9 | 24 | 4 | 0 |
| Bristol | 25,859 | 104 | 0 | 15 | 13 | 76 | 1,215 | 188 | 960 | 67 | 5 |
| Brownsville | 10,267 | 182 | 2 | 11 | 16 | 153 | 640 | 236 | 378 | 26 | 3 |
| Bruceton | 1,439 | 7 | 0 | 0 | 0 | 7 | 23 | 7 | 13 | 3 | 0 |
| Burns | 1,401 | 1 | 0 | 1 | 0 | 0 | 9 | 3 | 4 | 2 | 0 |
| Calhoun | 526 | 1 | 0 | 0 | 1 | 0 | 4 | 2 | 2 | 0 | 0 |
| Camden | 3,640 | 4 | 0 | 0 | 0 | 4 | 166 | 31 | 132 | 3 | 0 |
| Carthage | 2,234 | 13 | 0 | 0 | 1 | 12 | 81 | 21 | 57 | 3 | 1 |
| Caryville | 2,400 | 25 | 0 | 0 | 3 | 22 | 73 | 17 | 48 | 8 | 2 |
| Celina | 1,332 | 4 | 0 | 0 | 0 | 4 | 21 | 9 | 11 | 1 | 0 |
| Centerville | 3,994 | 9 | 0 | 2 | 0 | 7 | 116 | 33 | 78 | 5 | 1 |
| Chapel Hill | 1,363 | 4 | 0 | 0 | 1 | 3 | 17 | 5 | 11 | 1 | 0 |
| Charleston | 668 | 3 | 0 | 0 | 0 | 3 | 12 | 8 | 3 | 1 | 0 |
| Chattanooga | 172,536 | 1,792 | 17 | 53 | 535 | 1,187 | 12,849 | 2,987 | 8,949 | 913 | 13 |
| Church Hill | 6,864 | 7 | 0 | 0 | 3 | 4 | 167 | 58 | 106 | 3 | 0 |
| Clarksburg | 369 | 0 | 0 | 0 | 0 | 0 | 2 | 0 | 2 | 0 | 0 |
| Clarksville | 121,661 | 805 | 16 | 55 | 105 | 629 | 4,551 | 1,569 | 2,767 | 215 | 29 |
| Cleveland | 40,024 | 391 | 3 | 13 | 43 | 332 | 2,111 | 422 | 1,615 | 74 | 3 |
| Clifton | 2,694 | 5 | 0 | 0 | 0 | 5 | 19 | 4 | 14 | 1 | 0 |
| Clinton | 9,646 | 43 | 0 | 0 | 8 | 35 | 476 | 108 | 343 | 25 | 0 |
| Collegedale | 8,106 | 5 | 0 | 1 | 1 | 3 | 159 | 27 | 128 | 4 | 0 |
| Collierville | 39,973 | 82 | 0 | 2 | 5 | 75 | 724 | 91 | 614 | 19 | 2 |
| Collinwood | 1,011 | 2 | 0 | 0 | 0 | 2 | 5 | 3 | 2 | 0 | 0 |
| Columbia | 34,529 | 382 | 3 | 17 | 70 | 292 | 1,651 | 393 | 1,210 | 48 | 7 |
| Cookeville | 29,609 | 152 | 1 | 17 | 40 | 94 | 1,678 | 389 | 1,239 | 50 | 3 |
| Coopertown | 3,428 | 3 | 0 | 0 | 0 | 3 | 32 | 13 | 15 | 4 | 1 |
| Copperhill | 435 | 3 | 0 | 0 | 0 | 3 | 6 | 0 | 5 | 1 | 0 |
| Cornersville | 965 | 1 | 0 | 0 | 0 | 1 | 3 | 1 | 2 | 0 | 0 |
| Covington | 9,339 | 82 | 1 | 0 | 15 | 66 | 464 | 118 | 332 | 14 | 1 |
| Cowan | 1,710 | 6 | 0 | 0 | 0 | 6 | 41 | 7 | 33 | 1 | 0 |
| Cross Plains | 1,671 | 1 | 0 | 0 | 0 | 1 | 21 | 7 | 12 | 2 | 0 |
| Crossville | 11,908 | 110 | 1 | 4 | 15 | 90 | 1,178 | 222 | 894 | 62 | 0 |
| Crump | 1,463 | 4 | 0 | 0 | 0 | 4 | 79 | 22 | 55 | 2 | 0 |
| Cumberland City | 328 | 2 | 0 | 0 | 0 | 2 | 14 | 8 | 6 | 0 | 0 |
| Cumberland Gap | 208 | 0 | 0 | 0 | 0 | 0 | 5 | 2 | 3 | 0 | 0 |
| Dandridge | 2,760 | 9 | 0 | 0 | 1 | 8 | 77 | 16 | 56 | 5 | 2 |
| Dayton | 6,799 | 22 | 1 | 0 | 3 | 18 | 298 | 54 | 232 | 12 | 0 |
| Decatur | 1,485 | 0 | 0 | 0 | 0 | 0 | 58 | 15 | 38 | 5 | 0 |
| Decherd | 2,112 | 6 | 0 | 0 | 0 | 6 | 49 | 21 | 28 | 0 | 1 |
| Dickson | 14,095 | 90 | 0 | 9 | 15 | 66 | 830 | 96 | 675 | 59 | 6 |
| Dover | 1,633 | 4 | 0 | 1 | 0 | 3 | 25 | 3 | 19 | 3 | 0 |
| Dresden | 2,816 | 11 | 0 | 1 | 2 | 8 | 116 | 15 | 101 | 0 | 0 |
| Dunlap | 5,521 | 42 | 0 | 4 | 3 | 35 | 165 | 42 | 109 | 14 | 1 |
| Dyer | 2,415 | 5 | 0 | 0 | 0 | 5 | 27 | 11 | 16 | 0 | 0 |
| Dyersburg | 17,088 | 179 | 2 | 16 | 37 | 124 | 1,402 | 370 | 970 | 62 | 3 |
| East Ridge | 19,546 | 191 | 0 | 6 | 27 | 158 | 1,255 | 294 | 894 | 67 | 6 |
| Elizabethton | 13,944 | 58 | 0 | 7 | 11 | 40 | 732 | 120 | 589 | 23 | 3 |
| Elkton | 593 | 0 | 0 | 0 | 0 | 0 | 7 | 0 | 7 | 0 | 0 |
| Englewood | 1,768 | 4 | 0 | 0 | 0 | 4 | 27 | 9 | 17 | 1 | 0 |
| Erin | 1,458 | 13 | 0 | 0 | 0 | 13 | 31 | 11 | 20 | 0 | 0 |
| Erwin | 5,798 | 6 | 0 | 0 | 1 | 5 | 76 | 15 | 54 | 7 | 2 |
| Estill Springs | 2,263 | 1 | 0 | 0 | 0 | 1 | 31 | 11 | 20 | 0 | 0 |
| Ethridge | 555 | 3 | 0 | 0 | 0 | 3 | 11 | 2 | 8 | 1 | 0 |
| Etowah | 3,787 | 27 | 0 | 1 | 1 | 25 | 102 | 23 | 77 | 2 | 0 |
| Fairview | 8,094 | 12 | 0 | 3 | 1 | 8 | 109 | 34 | 63 | 12 | 0 |
| Fayetteville | 7,184 | 41 | 1 | 1 | 3 | 36 | 352 | 51 | 284 | 17 | 1 |
| Franklin | 60,074 | 110 | 2 | 9 | 12 | 87 | 1,059 | 181 | 839 | 39 | 2 |
| Friendship | 592 | 2 | 0 | 0 | 1 | 1 | 10 | 1 | 7 | 2 | 0 |
| Gadsden | 531 | 1 | 0 | 0 | 0 | 1 | 3 | 0 | 3 | 0 | 0 |
| Gainesboro | 841 | 2 | 0 | 0 | 1 | 1 | 30 | 9 | 20 | 1 | 0 |
| Gallatin | 30,102 | 129 | 0 | 11 | 22 | 96 | 601 | 80 | 506 | 15 | 3 |
| Gallaway | 694 | 4 | 0 | 1 | 0 | 3 | 29 | 7 | 18 | 4 | 0 |
| Gates | 846 | 3 | 1 | 0 | 0 | 2 | 24 | 8 | 14 | 2 | 0 |
| Gatlinburg | 5,862 | 35 | 1 | 2 | 5 | 27 | 434 | 147 | 277 | 10 | 0 |
| Germantown | 41,419 | 27 | 1 | 1 | 10 | 15 | 425 | 73 | 341 | 11 | 5 |
| Gibson | 400 | 1 | 0 | 1 | 0 | 0 | 12 | 2 | 10 | 0 | 0 |
| Gleason | 1,395 | 6 | 0 | 1 | 0 | 5 | 33 | 8 | 23 | 2 | 0 |
| Goodlettsville | 17,481 | 82 | 0 | 5 | 18 | 59 | 1,123 | 155 | 933 | 35 | 1 |
| Gordonsville | 1,319 | 5 | 0 | 0 | 0 | 5 | 40 | 3 | 35 | 2 | 0 |

[1] The FBI does not publish arson data unless it receives data from either the agency or the state for all 12 months of the calendar year.

**Table 8. Offenses Known to Law Enforcement, by State and City, 2009**—*Continued*

(Number.)

| State/city | Population | Violent crime | Murder and non-negligent man-slaughter | Forcible rape | Robbery | Aggravated assault | Property crime | Burglary | Larceny-theft | Motor vehicle theft | Arson[1] |
|---|---|---|---|---|---|---|---|---|---|---|---|
| **TENNESSEE**—*Continued* | | | | | | | | | | | |
| Grand Junction | 304 | 5 | 0 | 0 | 2 | 3 | 15 | 2 | 13 | 0 | 0 |
| Graysville | 1,430 | 11 | 0 | 0 | 0 | 11 | 20 | 1 | 17 | 2 | 0 |
| Greenbrier | 6,752 | 21 | 0 | 1 | 1 | 19 | 111 | 29 | 75 | 7 | 2 |
| Greeneville | 15,446 | 65 | 1 | 7 | 26 | 31 | 815 | 131 | 646 | 38 | 1 |
| Greenfield | 2,022 | 2 | 0 | 0 | 1 | 1 | 27 | 8 | 18 | 1 | 0 |
| Halls | 2,178 | 9 | 0 | 0 | 2 | 7 | 38 | 6 | 31 | 1 | 0 |
| Harriman | 6,646 | 46 | 0 | 2 | 11 | 33 | 310 | 79 | 215 | 16 | 4 |
| Henderson | 6,483 | 49 | 0 | 1 | 4 | 44 | 216 | 44 | 164 | 8 | 0 |
| Hendersonville | 48,513 | 144 | 0 | 8 | 20 | 116 | 1,250 | 205 | 984 | 61 | 5 |
| Henning | 1,270 | 10 | 0 | 0 | 1 | 9 | 28 | 12 | 16 | 0 | 0 |
| Henry | 549 | 0 | 0 | 0 | 0 | 0 | 6 | 2 | 4 | 0 | 0 |
| Hohenwald | 3,803 | 19 | 0 | 0 | 0 | 19 | 115 | 24 | 84 | 7 | 4 |
| Hollow Rock | 930 | 0 | 0 | 0 | 0 | 0 | 6 | 2 | 3 | 1 | 0 |
| Hornbeak | 414 | 0 | 0 | 0 | 0 | 0 | 3 | 0 | 3 | 0 | 0 |
| Humboldt | 9,126 | 96 | 1 | 1 | 18 | 76 | 476 | 117 | 347 | 12 | 10 |
| Huntingdon | 4,101 | 23 | 1 | 0 | 1 | 21 | 120 | 17 | 99 | 4 | 0 |
| Huntland | 861 | 0 | 0 | 0 | 0 | 0 | 10 | 2 | 8 | 0 | 0 |
| Jacksboro | 2,127 | 8 | 0 | 0 | 1 | 7 | 352 | 18 | 328 | 6 | 0 |
| Jackson | 63,530 | 606 | 14 | 24 | 184 | 384 | 4,413 | 1,123 | 2,994 | 296 | 14 |
| Jamestown | 1,927 | 8 | 0 | 0 | 0 | 8 | 143 | 22 | 120 | 1 | 0 |
| Jasper | 3,113 | 8 | 0 | 0 | 0 | 8 | 101 | 9 | 83 | 9 | 0 |
| Jefferson City | 8,188 | 26 | 0 | 3 | 7 | 16 | 404 | 77 | 308 | 19 | 1 |
| Jellico | 2,532 | 15 | 0 | 0 | 1 | 14 | 118 | 20 | 96 | 2 | 0 |
| Johnson City | 62,689 | 278 | 7 | 15 | 62 | 194 | 2,656 | 515 | 2,036 | 105 | 10 |
| Jonesborough | 5,351 | 12 | 0 | 1 | 0 | 11 | 104 | 24 | 78 | 2 | 0 |
| Kenton | 1,289 | 0 | 0 | 0 | 0 | 0 | 21 | 10 | 11 | 0 | 0 |
| Kimball | 1,411 | 1 | 0 | 0 | 0 | 1 | 56 | 4 | 50 | 2 | 0 |
| Kingsport | 44,402 | 400 | 4 | 25 | 56 | 315 | 2,896 | 474 | 2,328 | 94 | 18 |
| Kingston | 5,641 | 5 | 1 | 0 | 1 | 3 | 79 | 20 | 56 | 3 | 0 |
| Kingston Springs | 2,972 | 1 | 0 | 0 | 0 | 1 | 37 | 4 | 33 | 0 | 0 |
| Knoxville | 185,850 | 1,966 | 22 | 147 | 660 | 1,137 | 11,821 | 2,589 | 8,553 | 679 | 72 |
| Lafayette | 4,482 | 8 | 0 | 0 | 1 | 7 | 109 | 20 | 86 | 3 | 0 |
| La Follette | 8,218 | 97 | 0 | 3 | 12 | 82 | 686 | 193 | 461 | 32 | 5 |
| La Grange | 143 | 0 | 0 | 0 | 0 | 0 | 1 | 0 | 0 | 1 | 0 |
| Lakewood | 2,624 | 17 | 0 | 0 | 1 | 16 | 91 | 28 | 59 | 4 | 0 |
| La Vergne | 31,620 | 133 | 0 | 11 | 16 | 106 | 818 | 260 | 502 | 56 | 3 |
| Lawrenceburg | 10,779 | 130 | 1 | 7 | 5 | 117 | 643 | 120 | 488 | 35 | 3 |
| Lebanon | 25,161 | 171 | 0 | 11 | 35 | 125 | 1,103 | 188 | 859 | 56 | 1 |
| Lenoir City | 8,147 | 108 | 0 | 3 | 10 | 95 | 394 | 110 | 258 | 26 | 3 |
| Lewisburg | 11,048 | 71 | 0 | 4 | 8 | 59 | 299 | 70 | 217 | 12 | 0 |
| Lexington | 7,908 | 69 | 0 | 2 | 7 | 60 | 437 | 79 | 340 | 18 | 1 |
| Livingston | 3,574 | 20 | 0 | 0 | 0 | 20 | 113 | 38 | 72 | 3 | 0 |
| Lookout Mountain | 1,853 | 0 | 0 | 0 | 0 | 0 | 12 | 6 | 6 | 0 | 0 |
| Loretto | 1,710 | 12 | 0 | 0 | 1 | 11 | 27 | 3 | 24 | 0 | 0 |
| Loudon | 4,959 | 9 | 1 | 0 | 0 | 8 | 104 | 12 | 90 | 2 | 0 |
| Lynnville | 337 | 0 | 0 | 0 | 0 | 0 | 0 | 0 | 0 | 0 | 0 |
| Madisonville | 4,800 | 31 | 0 | 0 | 4 | 27 | 253 | 45 | 192 | 16 | 2 |
| Manchester | 10,188 | 103 | 0 | 2 | 5 | 96 | 567 | 82 | 462 | 23 | 0 |
| Martin | 10,172 | 42 | 0 | 3 | 5 | 34 | 393 | 68 | 317 | 8 | 1 |
| Maryville | 27,641 | 51 | 0 | 0 | 12 | 39 | 730 | 130 | 571 | 29 | 3 |
| Mason | 1,248 | 14 | 0 | 0 | 0 | 14 | 35 | 15 | 17 | 3 | 1 |
| Maury City | 689 | 0 | 0 | 0 | 0 | 0 | 9 | 3 | 5 | 1 | 0 |
| Maynardville | 1,923 | 13 | 0 | 1 | 1 | 11 | 140 | 22 | 105 | 13 | 0 |
| McEwen | 1,671 | 3 | 0 | 0 | 1 | 2 | 22 | 12 | 9 | 1 | 0 |
| McKenzie | 5,362 | 19 | 0 | 1 | 4 | 14 | 155 | 54 | 95 | 6 | 0 |
| McMinnville | 13,318 | 83 | 3 | 5 | 9 | 66 | 649 | 124 | 487 | 38 | 3 |
| Medina | 2,342 | 9 | 0 | 0 | 0 | 9 | 46 | 7 | 38 | 1 | 0 |
| Memphis | 667,421 | 12,055 | 132 | 382 | 4,139 | 7,402 | 47,195 | 13,943 | 29,059 | 4,193 | 333 |
| Middleton | 609 | 8 | 0 | 1 | 0 | 7 | 14 | 6 | 8 | 0 | 0 |
| Milan | 7,939 | 62 | 0 | 1 | 4 | 57 | 309 | 71 | 226 | 12 | 2 |
| Millersville | 6,387 | 22 | 0 | 0 | 3 | 19 | 173 | 48 | 117 | 8 | 7 |
| Millington | 10,137 | 108 | 0 | 6 | 11 | 91 | 510 | 113 | 372 | 25 | 1 |
| Minor Hill | 450 | 1 | 0 | 0 | 0 | 1 | 21 | 8 | 11 | 2 | 0 |
| Monteagle | 1,197 | 3 | 0 | 0 | 2 | 1 | 13 | 3 | 6 | 4 | 0 |
| Monterey | 2,943 | 6 | 0 | 0 | 0 | 6 | 66 | 24 | 37 | 5 | 1 |
| Morristown | 27,775 | 215 | 1 | 18 | 36 | 160 | 1,804 | 163 | 1,580 | 61 | 5 |
| Moscow | 558 | 1 | 0 | 0 | 1 | 0 | 13 | 6 | 5 | 2 | 0 |
| Mountain City | 2,398 | 7 | 0 | 0 | 0 | 7 | 36 | 17 | 18 | 1 | 0 |
| Mount Carmel | 5,538 | 12 | 0 | 0 | 2 | 10 | 70 | 19 | 47 | 4 | 0 |
| Mount Juliet | 22,778 | 53 | 0 | 3 | 4 | 46 | 463 | 88 | 362 | 13 | 0 |
| Mount Pleasant | 4,438 | 22 | 0 | 0 | 6 | 16 | 162 | 21 | 135 | 6 | 0 |

[1] The FBI does not publish arson data unless it receives data from either the agency or the state for all 12 months of the calendar year.

## Table 8. Offenses Known to Law Enforcement, by State and City, 2009—*Continued*

(Number.)

| State/city | Population | Violent crime | Murder and non-negligent man-slaughter | Forcible rape | Robbery | Aggravated assault | Property crime | Burglary | Larceny-theft | Motor vehicle theft | Arson[1] |
|---|---|---|---|---|---|---|---|---|---|---|---|
| **TENNESSEE**—*Continued* | | | | | | | | | | | |
| Munford | 6,851 | 15 | 1 | 6 | 1 | 7 | 137 | 26 | 104 | 7 | 0 |
| Murfreesboro | 105,910 | 697 | 5 | 46 | 187 | 459 | 4,851 | 1,346 | 3,321 | 184 | 13 |
| Nashville | 610,176 | 6,959 | 77 | 262 | 1,971 | 4,649 | 29,156 | 6,318 | 21,113 | 1,725 | 70 |
| New Hope | 1,049 | 0 | 0 | 0 | 0 | 0 | 1 | 0 | 1 | 0 | 0 |
| New Johnsonville | 1,959 | 2 | 1 | 0 | 0 | 1 | 16 | 5 | 11 | 0 | 0 |
| New Market | 1,330 | 0 | 0 | 0 | 0 | 0 | 6 | 1 | 5 | 0 | 0 |
| Newport | 7,539 | 86 | 0 | 2 | 18 | 66 | 769 | 147 | 594 | 28 | 2 |
| New Tazewell | 2,883 | 7 | 0 | 1 | 3 | 3 | 58 | 8 | 48 | 2 | 0 |
| Niota | 802 | 0 | 0 | 0 | 0 | 0 | 5 | 3 | 2 | 0 | 0 |
| Nolensville | 2,713 | 2 | 0 | 1 | 0 | 1 | 117 | 46 | 67 | 4 | 1 |
| Norris | 1,481 | 0 | 0 | 0 | 0 | 0 | 13 | 3 | 8 | 2 | 0 |
| Oakland | 5,792 | 2 | 0 | 0 | 0 | 2 | 16 | 0 | 14 | 2 | 0 |
| Oak Ridge | 27,718 | 120 | 0 | 16 | 36 | 68 | 1,360 | 407 | 894 | 59 | 6 |
| Obion | 1,063 | 1 | 0 | 0 | 0 | 1 | 15 | 5 | 10 | 0 | 0 |
| Oliver Springs | 3,329 | 9 | 0 | 0 | 1 | 8 | 110 | 11 | 81 | 18 | 1 |
| Oneida | 3,861 | 14 | 0 | 0 | 0 | 14 | 205 | 44 | 154 | 7 | 0 |
| Parsons | 2,338 | 2 | 0 | 0 | 0 | 2 | 43 | 12 | 31 | 0 | 0 |
| Petersburg | 606 | 4 | 0 | 0 | 0 | 4 | 11 | 4 | 5 | 2 | 0 |
| Pigeon Forge | 6,318 | 45 | 0 | 7 | 11 | 27 | 811 | 251 | 503 | 57 | 3 |
| Pikeville | 1,907 | 4 | 0 | 0 | 0 | 4 | 27 | 4 | 22 | 1 | 0 |
| Piperton | 1,297 | 3 | 0 | 0 | 0 | 3 | 25 | 9 | 9 | 7 | 0 |
| Pittman Center | 697 | 0 | 0 | 0 | 0 | 0 | 14 | 7 | 7 | 0 | 0 |
| Pleasant View | 4,232 | 7 | 0 | 0 | 5 | 2 | 51 | 17 | 34 | 0 | 0 |
| Powells Crossroads | 1,267 | 0 | 0 | 0 | 0 | 0 | 1 | 0 | 1 | 0 | 0 |
| Pulaski | 7,835 | 40 | 0 | 5 | 7 | 28 | 376 | 82 | 287 | 7 | 0 |
| Puryear | 676 | 2 | 0 | 0 | 0 | 2 | 10 | 2 | 8 | 0 | 0 |
| Red Bank | 11,488 | 74 | 0 | 7 | 3 | 64 | 554 | 113 | 397 | 44 | 3 |
| Red Boiling Springs | 1,116 | 7 | 0 | 0 | 0 | 7 | 32 | 8 | 18 | 6 | 0 |
| Ridgely | 1,496 | 4 | 0 | 0 | 1 | 3 | 42 | 16 | 24 | 2 | 0 |
| Ridgetop | 1,758 | 9 | 0 | 2 | 0 | 7 | 22 | 6 | 14 | 2 | 0 |
| Ripley | 7,616 | 110 | 0 | 0 | 14 | 96 | 527 | 193 | 306 | 28 | 3 |
| Rockwood | 5,553 | 17 | 0 | 1 | 4 | 12 | 373 | 95 | 269 | 9 | 0 |
| Rogersville | 4,357 | 24 | 0 | 0 | 3 | 21 | 362 | 79 | 275 | 8 | 1 |
| Rossville | 582 | 1 | 0 | 0 | 1 | 0 | 4 | 2 | 2 | 0 | 0 |
| Rutherford | 1,253 | 1 | 0 | 0 | 0 | 1 | 15 | 5 | 10 | 0 | 0 |
| Rutledge | 1,295 | 3 | 0 | 1 | 0 | 2 | 28 | 4 | 20 | 4 | 0 |
| Samburg | 248 | 0 | 0 | 0 | 0 | 0 | 7 | 2 | 5 | 0 | 0 |
| Savannah | 7,354 | 53 | 1 | 3 | 7 | 42 | 570 | 122 | 423 | 25 | 0 |
| Scotts Hill | 925 | 5 | 0 | 0 | 0 | 5 | 10 | 2 | 8 | 0 | 0 |
| Selmer | 4,716 | 19 | 1 | 4 | 1 | 13 | 230 | 44 | 184 | 2 | 0 |
| Sevierville | 17,489 | 69 | 1 | 7 | 18 | 43 | 1,215 | 202 | 946 | 67 | 1 |
| Sewanee | 2,613 | 0 | 0 | 0 | 0 | 0 | 115 | 31 | 83 | 1 | 1 |
| Sharon | 908 | 5 | 1 | 0 | 0 | 4 | 31 | 7 | 24 | 0 | 0 |
| Shelbyville | 20,078 | 114 | 2 | 14 | 13 | 85 | 545 | 124 | 397 | 24 | 0 |
| Signal Mountain | 7,075 | 6 | 0 | 0 | 2 | 4 | 64 | 10 | 54 | 0 | 0 |
| Smithville | 4,435 | 33 | 0 | 0 | 8 | 25 | 239 | 49 | 181 | 9 | 5 |
| Sneedville | 1,308 | 4 | 0 | 0 | 1 | 3 | 48 | 15 | 33 | 0 | 0 |
| Soddy-Daisy | 12,624 | 51 | 0 | 5 | 9 | 37 | 512 | 102 | 380 | 30 | 2 |
| Somerville | 2,966 | 33 | 0 | 0 | 2 | 31 | 106 | 19 | 85 | 2 | 0 |
| South Carthage | 1,363 | 0 | 0 | 0 | 0 | 0 | 36 | 6 | 29 | 1 | 0 |
| South Fulton | 2,389 | 6 | 0 | 0 | 1 | 5 | 73 | 30 | 42 | 1 | 0 |
| South Pittsburg | 3,125 | 16 | 0 | 1 | 0 | 15 | 89 | 16 | 68 | 5 | 0 |
| Sparta | 4,976 | 27 | 2 | 1 | 8 | 16 | 468 | 125 | 326 | 17 | 4 |
| Spencer | 1,696 | 2 | 0 | 1 | 0 | 1 | 26 | 6 | 19 | 1 | 0 |
| Spring City | 2,021 | 4 | 0 | 0 | 1 | 3 | 44 | 5 | 35 | 4 | 2 |
| Springfield | 17,608 | 212 | 1 | 16 | 53 | 142 | 771 | 137 | 596 | 38 | 10 |
| Spring Hill | 29,870 | 45 | 0 | 7 | 0 | 38 | 392 | 67 | 311 | 14 | 2 |
| St. Joseph | 859 | 1 | 0 | 0 | 0 | 1 | 14 | 6 | 7 | 1 | 0 |
| Surgoinsville | 1,830 | 0 | 0 | 0 | 0 | 0 | 12 | 4 | 8 | 0 | 1 |
| Sweetwater | 6,758 | 43 | 0 | 1 | 4 | 38 | 216 | 59 | 136 | 21 | 3 |
| Tazewell | 2,221 | 18 | 1 | 1 | 0 | 16 | 96 | 26 | 66 | 4 | 0 |
| Tellico Plains | 976 | 7 | 0 | 1 | 0 | 6 | 39 | 8 | 28 | 3 | 0 |
| Tiptonville | 3,978 | 24 | 0 | 0 | 0 | 24 | 34 | 7 | 27 | 0 | 0 |
| Toone | 349 | 0 | 0 | 0 | 0 | 0 | 2 | 0 | 1 | 1 | 0 |
| Townsend | 275 | 2 | 0 | 0 | 0 | 2 | 8 | 6 | 1 | 1 | 0 |
| Tracy City | 1,649 | 25 | 0 | 0 | 2 | 23 | 69 | 35 | 28 | 6 | 0 |
| Trenton | 4,499 | 38 | 1 | 0 | 2 | 35 | 180 | 35 | 144 | 1 | 1 |
| Trezevant | 878 | 0 | 0 | 0 | 0 | 0 | 21 | 8 | 13 | 0 | 0 |
| Trimble | 717 | 2 | 0 | 0 | 0 | 2 | 5 | 1 | 3 | 1 | 0 |
| Troy | 1,201 | 1 | 0 | 1 | 0 | 0 | 20 | 2 | 18 | 0 | 0 |
| Tullahoma | 18,636 | 144 | 0 | 7 | 19 | 118 | 790 | 149 | 610 | 31 | 3 |

[1] The FBI does not publish arson data unless it receives data from either the agency or the state for all 12 months of the calendar year.

## Table 8. Offenses Known to Law Enforcement, by State and City, 2009—*Continued*

(Number.)

| State/city | Population | Violent crime | Murder and non-negligent man-slaughter | Forcible rape | Robbery | Aggravated assault | Property crime | Burglary | Larceny-theft | Motor vehicle theft | Arson[1] |
|---|---|---|---|---|---|---|---|---|---|---|---|
| **TENNESSEE**—*Continued* | | | | | | | | | | | |
| Tusculum | 2,309 | 2 | 0 | 0 | 0 | 2 | 36 | 12 | 24 | 0 | 0 |
| Union City | 10,533 | 69 | 1 | 3 | 17 | 48 | 552 | 108 | 427 | 17 | 4 |
| Vonore | 1,533 | 6 | 0 | 0 | 1 | 5 | 98 | 12 | 86 | 0 | 1 |
| Wartburg | 932 | 1 | 0 | 0 | 1 | 0 | 12 | 1 | 10 | 1 | 0 |
| Wartrace | 593 | 4 | 0 | 0 | 0 | 4 | 10 | 3 | 7 | 0 | 0 |
| Watertown | 1,425 | 5 | 0 | 0 | 0 | 5 | 17 | 7 | 10 | 0 | 0 |
| Waverly | 4,201 | 9 | 0 | 0 | 0 | 9 | 87 | 10 | 71 | 6 | 0 |
| Waynesboro | 2,130 | 9 | 0 | 0 | 0 | 9 | 33 | 12 | 20 | 1 | 1 |
| Westmoreland | 2,199 | 8 | 0 | 0 | 0 | 8 | 37 | 12 | 20 | 5 | 0 |
| White Bluff | 2,556 | 4 | 0 | 0 | 2 | 2 | 31 | 8 | 21 | 2 | 0 |
| White House | 10,385 | 13 | 0 | 2 | 1 | 10 | 191 | 49 | 131 | 11 | 1 |
| White Pine | 2,159 | 9 | 0 | 1 | 2 | 6 | 101 | 12 | 83 | 6 | 0 |
| Whiteville | 4,456 | 14 | 0 | 0 | 1 | 13 | 79 | 25 | 51 | 3 | 1 |
| Whitwell | 1,597 | 11 | 0 | 0 | 2 | 9 | 84 | 19 | 54 | 11 | 1 |
| Winchester | 7,919 | 40 | 0 | 1 | 4 | 35 | 302 | 64 | 228 | 10 | 2 |
| Winfield | 1,002 | 6 | 0 | 0 | 0 | 6 | 27 | 7 | 16 | 4 | 0 |
| Woodbury | 2,630 | 5 | 0 | 1 | 1 | 3 | 72 | 23 | 40 | 9 | 0 |
| **TEXAS** | | | | | | | | | | | |
| Abernathy | 2,721 | 7 | 0 | 1 | 1 | 5 | 22 | 8 | 13 | 1 | 0 |
| Abilene | 116,557 | 658 | 7 | 114 | 137 | 400 | 4,830 | 1,301 | 3,267 | 262 | 30 |
| Addison | 15,063 | 90 | 1 | 7 | 35 | 47 | 1,019 | 142 | 742 | 135 | 2 |
| Alamo | 16,810 | 133 | 1 | 15 | 24 | 93 | 1,444 | 264 | 1,057 | 123 | 5 |
| Alamo Heights | 7,378 | 7 | 0 | 0 | 1 | 6 | 269 | 40 | 222 | 7 | 1 |
| Alice | 19,886 | 186 | 0 | 7 | 13 | 166 | 1,406 | 436 | 913 | 57 | 21 |
| Allen | 86,901 | 78 | 2 | 14 | 15 | 47 | 1,535 | 273 | 1,198 | 64 | 0 |
| Alpine | 6,322 | 16 | 0 | 5 | 1 | 10 | 90 | 31 | 56 | 3 | 0 |
| Alto | 1,175 | 5 | 0 | 1 | 0 | 4 | 46 | 21 | 24 | 1 | 0 |
| Alton | 11,945 | 34 | 0 | 0 | 10 | 24 | 416 | 148 | 206 | 62 | 2 |
| Alvarado | 4,290 | 6 | 0 | 1 | 3 | 2 | 154 | 38 | 104 | 12 | 0 |
| Alvin | 23,013 | 53 | 2 | 5 | 14 | 32 | 692 | 153 | 492 | 47 | 4 |
| Amarillo | 188,767 | 1,580 | 10 | 99 | 352 | 1,119 | 11,039 | 2,561 | 7,768 | 710 | 76 |
| Andrews | 10,209 | 79 | 1 | 10 | 0 | 68 | 350 | 93 | 243 | 14 | 3 |
| Angleton | 18,665 | 104 | 0 | 21 | 8 | 75 | 577 | 153 | 401 | 23 | 3 |
| Anna | 1,906 | 7 | 0 | 5 | 1 | 1 | 114 | 39 | 67 | 8 | 1 |
| Anson | 2,252 | 3 | 0 | 0 | 1 | 2 | 32 | 5 | 26 | 1 | 0 |
| Anthony | 4,401 | 20 | 0 | 0 | 4 | 16 | 197 | 10 | 180 | 7 | 0 |
| Aransas Pass | 8,885 | 30 | 0 | 6 | 10 | 14 | 611 | 166 | 418 | 27 | 1 |
| Arcola | 1,251 | 10 | 0 | 1 | 4 | 5 | 38 | 8 | 22 | 8 | 0 |
| Argyle | 3,681 | 1 | 0 | 0 | 0 | 1 | 24 | 5 | 15 | 4 | 0 |
| Arlington | 379,104 | 2,330 | 12 | 152 | 672 | 1,494 | 20,516 | 4,891 | 14,186 | 1,439 | 49 |
| Arp | 969 | 3 | 0 | 0 | 1 | 2 | 9 | 1 | 8 | 0 | 0 |
| Athens | 12,402 | 74 | 0 | 13 | 25 | 36 | 529 | 148 | 352 | 29 | 1 |
| Atlanta | 5,444 | 38 | 0 | 3 | 4 | 31 | 238 | 64 | 164 | 10 | 0 |
| Austin | 768,970 | 4,024 | 22 | 265 | 1,415 | 2,322 | 48,026 | 8,753 | 37,054 | 2,219 | 96 |
| Azle | 11,555 | 35 | 0 | 5 | 5 | 25 | 452 | 89 | 345 | 18 | 9 |
| Baird | 1,677 | 4 | 0 | 2 | 0 | 2 | 14 | 2 | 12 | 0 | 0 |
| Balch Springs | 20,052 | 155 | 0 | 21 | 44 | 90 | 1,686 | 254 | 1,296 | 136 | 0 |
| Balcones Heights | 2,981 | 39 | 0 | 1 | 12 | 26 | 453 | 42 | 385 | 26 | 1 |
| Ballinger | 3,672 | 5 | 0 | 1 | 0 | 4 | 81 | 20 | 58 | 3 | 1 |
| Bangs | 1,561 | 4 | 0 | 1 | 0 | 3 | 11 | 4 | 7 | 0 | 0 |
| Bastrop | 8,792 | 18 | 0 | 3 | 5 | 10 | 431 | 42 | 377 | 12 | 2 |
| Bay City | 17,811 | 65 | 1 | 10 | 28 | 26 | 902 | 217 | 680 | 5 | 4 |
| Bayou Vista | 1,691 | 0 | 0 | 0 | 0 | 0 | 6 | 2 | 4 | 0 | 1 |
| Baytown | 70,764 | 330 | 2 | 34 | 114 | 180 | 4,001 | 831 | 2,889 | 281 | 32 |
| Beaumont | 110,237 | 1,002 | 5 | 73 | 332 | 592 | 6,331 | 1,665 | 4,385 | 281 | 35 |
| Bedford | 49,375 | 190 | 0 | 13 | 36 | 141 | 1,769 | 392 | 1,271 | 106 | 5 |
| Bee Cave | 2,996 | 15 | 0 | 1 | 6 | 8 | 182 | 19 | 159 | 4 | 1 |
| Beeville | 12,642 | 77 | 0 | 16 | 8 | 53 | 426 | 102 | 314 | 10 | 0 |
| Bellaire | 18,492 | 33 | 0 | 0 | 22 | 11 | 365 | 72 | 277 | 16 | 1 |
| Bellmead | 9,610 | 141 | 0 | 16 | 16 | 109 | 1,105 | 91 | 982 | 32 | 3 |
| Bellville | 4,486 | 11 | 0 | 2 | 0 | 9 | 102 | 15 | 83 | 4 | 0 |
| Belton | 18,130 | 35 | 0 | 0 | 9 | 26 | 726 | 154 | 564 | 8 | 3 |
| Benbrook | 23,280 | 33 | 1 | 3 | 12 | 17 | 488 | 127 | 337 | 24 | 5 |
| Bertram | 1,444 | 5 | 0 | 2 | 1 | 2 | 14 | 3 | 9 | 2 | 2 |
| Beverly Hills | 2,040 | 6 | 0 | 0 | 0 | 6 | 46 | 22 | 23 | 1 | 0 |
| Big Sandy | 1,368 | 2 | 0 | 0 | 1 | 1 | 17 | 5 | 12 | 0 | 0 |
| Big Spring | 24,181 | 182 | 2 | 22 | 40 | 118 | 1,725 | 349 | 1,317 | 59 | 24 |
| Bishop | 3,122 | 3 | 0 | 0 | 0 | 3 | 108 | 30 | 75 | 3 | 0 |
| Blanco | 1,562 | 7 | 0 | 0 | 1 | 6 | 52 | 17 | 33 | 2 | 1 |
| Bloomburg | 359 | 0 | 0 | 0 | 0 | 0 | 0 | 0 | 0 | 0 | 0 |
| Blue Mound | 2,362 | 3 | 0 | 0 | 2 | 1 | 57 | 30 | 22 | 5 | 2 |

[1] The FBI does not publish arson data unless it receives data from either the agency or the state for all 12 months of the calendar year.

## Table 8. Offenses Known to Law Enforcement, by State and City, 2009—*Continued*

(Number.)

| State/city | Population | Violent crime | Murder and non-negligent man-slaughter | Forcible rape | Robbery | Aggravated assault | Property crime | Burglary | Larceny-theft | Motor vehicle theft | Arson[1] |
|---|---|---|---|---|---|---|---|---|---|---|---|
| **TEXAS**—*Continued* | | | | | | | | | | | |
| Boerne | 10,835 | 13 | 0 | 1 | 3 | 9 | 301 | 42 | 253 | 6 | 0 |
| Bogata | 1,219 | 3 | 0 | 0 | 0 | 3 | 24 | 10 | 11 | 3 | 0 |
| Bonham | 10,735 | 23 | 0 | 5 | 0 | 18 | 353 | 85 | 257 | 11 | 5 |
| Borger | 12,516 | 206 | 0 | 22 | 9 | 175 | 683 | 168 | 488 | 27 | 2 |
| Bowie | 5,601 | 11 | 0 | 0 | 3 | 8 | 306 | 67 | 227 | 12 | 1 |
| Brady | 5,306 | 11 | 0 | 0 | 2 | 9 | 146 | 30 | 113 | 3 | 0 |
| Brazoria | 2,970 | 24 | 0 | 3 | 3 | 18 | 102 | 18 | 80 | 4 | 0 |
| Breckenridge | 5,610 | 7 | 0 | 0 | 1 | 6 | 109 | 34 | 72 | 3 | 1 |
| Bremond | 853 | 4 | 0 | 0 | 1 | 3 | 16 | 11 | 5 | 0 | 0 |
| Brenham | 15,415 | 104 | 0 | 1 | 12 | 91 | 618 | 175 | 409 | 34 | 0 |
| Bridge City | 8,587 | 9 | 0 | 0 | 0 | 9 | 151 | 39 | 93 | 19 | 0 |
| Bridgeport | 6,231 | 9 | 1 | 1 | 3 | 4 | 113 | 26 | 80 | 7 | 0 |
| Brookshire | 4,009 | 22 | 2 | 3 | 5 | 12 | 189 | 60 | 118 | 11 | 0 |
| Brookside Village | 1,987 | 3 | 0 | 0 | 0 | 3 | 23 | 8 | 14 | 1 | 0 |
| Brownfield | 8,893 | 19 | 1 | 0 | 6 | 12 | 171 | 60 | 104 | 7 | 1 |
| Brownsville | 179,491 | 454 | 4 | 26 | 152 | 272 | 9,778 | 1,576 | 7,865 | 337 | 31 |
| Brownwood | 19,115 | 88 | 2 | 0 | 7 | 79 | 814 | 175 | 615 | 24 | 3 |
| Bruceville-Eddy | 1,544 | 4 | 0 | 2 | 0 | 2 | 68 | 30 | 36 | 2 | 0 |
| Bryan | 73,111 | 567 | 1 | 33 | 128 | 405 | 4,134 | 1,140 | 2,809 | 185 | 27 |
| Bullard | 1,909 | 5 | 0 | 2 | 2 | 1 | 67 | 13 | 52 | 2 | 0 |
| Bulverde | 4,704 | 5 | 0 | 1 | 0 | 4 | 82 | 10 | 72 | 0 | 0 |
| Burkburnett | 10,361 | 18 | 0 | 1 | 2 | 15 | 152 | 81 | 71 | 0 | 1 |
| Burleson | 36,807 | 69 | 1 | 8 | 12 | 48 | 1,127 | 181 | 898 | 48 | 8 |
| Burnet | 6,105 | 12 | 0 | 0 | 1 | 11 | 84 | 11 | 70 | 3 | 2 |
| Cactus | 2,612 | 21 | 0 | 0 | 2 | 19 | 40 | 16 | 14 | 10 | 0 |
| Caddo Mills | 1,210 | 12 | 0 | 0 | 1 | 11 | 49 | 27 | 20 | 2 | 0 |
| Caldwell | 3,744 | 3 | 0 | 0 | 2 | 1 | 27 | 8 | 16 | 3 | 0 |
| Calvert | 1,351 | 13 | 0 | 2 | 3 | 8 | 70 | 35 | 29 | 6 | 0 |
| Cameron | 5,750 | 12 | 0 | 0 | 1 | 11 | 189 | 32 | 152 | 5 | 2 |
| Canton | 3,703 | 15 | 0 | 0 | 1 | 14 | 150 | 21 | 124 | 5 | 0 |
| Canyon | 14,781 | 13 | 1 | 2 | 1 | 9 | 136 | 19 | 113 | 4 | 0 |
| Carrollton | 127,432 | 250 | 4 | 16 | 124 | 106 | 4,061 | 1,085 | 2,633 | 343 | 17 |
| Carthage | 6,632 | 23 | 0 | 0 | 3 | 20 | 154 | 42 | 97 | 15 | 0 |
| Castle Hills | 4,206 | 8 | 0 | 0 | 6 | 2 | 311 | 54 | 245 | 12 | 0 |
| Castroville | 3,104 | 13 | 0 | 1 | 2 | 10 | 70 | 16 | 51 | 3 | 0 |
| Cedar Hill | 46,480 | 121 | 1 | 7 | 49 | 64 | 1,693 | 436 | 1,156 | 101 | 1 |
| Cedar Park | 68,464 | 70 | 4 | 13 | 12 | 41 | 982 | 160 | 795 | 27 | 3 |
| Celina | 6,017 | 13 | 0 | 1 | 0 | 12 | 68 | 23 | 43 | 2 | 0 |
| Center | 5,754 | 60 | 1 | 8 | 16 | 35 | 344 | 89 | 245 | 10 | 0 |
| Childress | 6,484 | 22 | 0 | 0 | 6 | 16 | 96 | 52 | 38 | 6 | 0 |
| Chillicothe | 676 | 2 | 0 | 1 | 0 | 1 | 5 | 4 | 1 | 0 | 0 |
| Cibolo | 17,291 | 18 | 1 | 2 | 3 | 12 | 180 | 36 | 130 | 14 | 2 |
| Cisco | 3,711 | 7 | 0 | 0 | 2 | 5 | 51 | 19 | 32 | 0 | 0 |
| Clarksville | 3,436 | 1 | 0 | 0 | 1 | 0 | 45 | 17 | 28 | 0 | 0 |
| Cleburne | 30,287 | 196 | 0 | 44 | 24 | 128 | 1,303 | 210 | 1,033 | 60 | 4 |
| Cleveland | 7,979 | 72 | 0 | 5 | 17 | 50 | 696 | 89 | 562 | 45 | 5 |
| Clifton | 3,567 | 3 | 1 | 0 | 1 | 1 | 31 | 10 | 20 | 1 | 0 |
| Clint | 971 | 1 | 0 | 0 | 0 | 1 | 19 | 10 | 7 | 2 | 0 |
| Clute | 10,803 | 46 | 0 | 4 | 17 | 25 | 378 | 101 | 254 | 23 | 1 |
| Clyde | 3,833 | 8 | 0 | 1 | 1 | 6 | 87 | 22 | 61 | 4 | 0 |
| Cockrell Hill | 4,254 | 19 | 0 | 2 | 11 | 6 | 143 | 35 | 92 | 16 | 0 |
| Coffee City | 209 | 0 | 0 | 0 | 0 | 0 | 7 | 2 | 5 | 0 | 0 |
| Coleman | 4,648 | 1 | 0 | 0 | 0 | 1 | 172 | 84 | 80 | 8 | 3 |
| College Station | 86,072 | 170 | 3 | 43 | 24 | 100 | 3,267 | 613 | 2,580 | 74 | 6 |
| Colleyville | 25,006 | 2 | 0 | 1 | 1 | 0 | 281 | 74 | 206 | 1 | 1 |
| Collinsville | 1,524 | 2 | 0 | 1 | 0 | 1 | 27 | 7 | 19 | 1 | 0 |
| Colorado City | 3,851 | 14 | 0 | 8 | 0 | 6 | 158 | 24 | 131 | 3 | 2 |
| Columbus | 3,886 | 43 | 0 | 4 | 5 | 34 | 99 | 20 | 79 | 0 | 0 |
| Comanche | 4,173 | 15 | 0 | 5 | 1 | 9 | 157 | 39 | 117 | 1 | 0 |
| Combes | 2,850 | 10 | 0 | 0 | 1 | 9 | 55 | 13 | 38 | 4 | 1 |
| Commerce | 9,427 | 32 | 0 | 4 | 10 | 18 | 323 | 115 | 191 | 17 | 2 |
| Conroe | 57,685 | 253 | 1 | 26 | 99 | 127 | 2,616 | 610 | 1,858 | 148 | 3 |
| Converse | 18,353 | 34 | 0 | 2 | 17 | 15 | 466 | 98 | 351 | 17 | 1 |
| Coppell | 39,465 | 43 | 1 | 2 | 10 | 30 | 660 | 154 | 462 | 44 | 1 |
| Copperas Cove | 30,793 | 110 | 0 | 2 | 18 | 90 | 962 | 261 | 679 | 22 | 18 |
| Corinth | 22,152 | 29 | 0 | 2 | 2 | 25 | 304 | 74 | 205 | 25 | 0 |
| Corpus Christi | 287,507 | 2,365 | 12 | 212 | 459 | 1,682 | 16,112 | 2,976 | 12,538 | 598 | 83 |
| Corrigan | 1,887 | 12 | 0 | 2 | 0 | 10 | 30 | 9 | 21 | 0 | 0 |
| Corsicana | 26,678 | 101 | 1 | 11 | 24 | 65 | 1,233 | 309 | 841 | 83 | 3 |
| Cottonwood Shores | 1,221 | 0 | 0 | 0 | 0 | 0 | 2 | 2 | 0 | 0 | 0 |
| Crandall | 3,983 | 12 | 0 | 0 | 2 | 10 | 67 | 17 | 43 | 7 | 0 |

[1] The FBI does not publish arson data unless it receives data from either the agency or the state for all 12 months of the calendar year.

## Table 8. Offenses Known to Law Enforcement, by State and City, 2009—*Continued*

(Number.)

| State/city | Population | Violent crime | Murder and non-negligent man-slaughter | Forcible rape | Robbery | Aggravated assault | Property crime | Burglary | Larceny-theft | Motor vehicle theft | Arson[1] |
|---|---|---|---|---|---|---|---|---|---|---|---|
| **TEXAS**—*Continued* | | | | | | | | | | | |
| Crane | 3,199 | 5 | 0 | 1 | 0 | 4 | 28 | 7 | 20 | 1 | 0 |
| Crockett | 6,782 | 15 | 0 | 1 | 2 | 12 | 276 | 73 | 192 | 11 | 0 |
| Crowell | 935 | 0 | 0 | 0 | 0 | 0 | 1 | 0 | 1 | 0 | 0 |
| Crowley | 13,077 | 26 | 0 | 6 | 9 | 11 | 318 | 74 | 244 | 0 | 0 |
| Crystal City | 7,159 | 41 | 3 | 0 | 0 | 38 | 83 | 39 | 43 | 1 | 2 |
| Cuero | 6,401 | 13 | 0 | 3 | 1 | 9 | 106 | 39 | 61 | 6 | 2 |
| Daingerfield | 2,446 | 11 | 0 | 1 | 3 | 7 | 100 | 41 | 58 | 1 | 0 |
| Dalhart | 7,008 | 17 | 1 | 2 | 0 | 14 | 147 | 43 | 100 | 4 | 2 |
| Dallas | 1,290,266 | 10,221 | 166 | 485 | 5,501 | 4,069 | 71,364 | 19,428 | 41,481 | 10,455 | 758 |
| Dalworthington Gardens | 2,437 | 5 | 0 | 0 | 0 | 5 | 67 | 18 | 43 | 6 | 1 |
| Danbury | 1,692 | 0 | 0 | 0 | 0 | 0 | 5 | 4 | 1 | 0 | 0 |
| Dayton | 7,461 | 19 | 0 | 3 | 6 | 10 | 215 | 68 | 136 | 11 | 0 |
| Decatur | 6,575 | 19 | 0 | 8 | 1 | 10 | 256 | 33 | 212 | 11 | 0 |
| Deer Park | 31,164 | 79 | 0 | 11 | 8 | 60 | 837 | 150 | 621 | 66 | 4 |
| De Kalb | 1,804 | 4 | 0 | 0 | 0 | 4 | 47 | 24 | 20 | 3 | 0 |
| De Leon | 2,325 | 3 | 0 | 0 | 0 | 3 | 39 | 17 | 21 | 1 | 0 |
| Del Rio | 36,996 | 89 | 2 | 0 | 8 | 79 | 780 | 156 | 581 | 43 | 8 |
| Denison | 24,142 | 92 | 1 | 3 | 28 | 60 | 1,178 | 253 | 865 | 60 | 3 |
| Denton | 124,308 | 306 | 2 | 71 | 79 | 154 | 3,271 | 681 | 2,403 | 187 | 18 |
| Denver City | 4,085 | 4 | 1 | 1 | 0 | 2 | 59 | 36 | 18 | 5 | 0 |
| DeSoto | 48,798 | 178 | 2 | 8 | 81 | 87 | 1,742 | 604 | 1,010 | 128 | 5 |
| Devine | 4,589 | 13 | 0 | 3 | 3 | 7 | 79 | 25 | 50 | 4 | 0 |
| Diboll | 5,545 | 10 | 0 | 3 | 0 | 7 | 139 | 39 | 96 | 4 | 0 |
| Dickinson | 17,975 | 64 | 1 | 12 | 16 | 35 | 698 | 239 | 419 | 40 | 1 |
| Dilley | 3,597 | 9 | 0 | 0 | 1 | 8 | 29 | 16 | 10 | 3 | 1 |
| Dimmitt | 3,636 | 5 | 0 | 0 | 0 | 5 | 113 | 36 | 73 | 4 | 1 |
| Donna | 17,323 | 134 | 0 | 1 | 22 | 111 | 1,188 | 252 | 856 | 80 | 5 |
| Double Oak | 3,426 | 3 | 0 | 0 | 0 | 3 | 16 | 7 | 8 | 1 | 0 |
| Driscoll | 800 | 0 | 0 | 0 | 0 | 0 | 17 | 3 | 14 | 0 | 0 |
| Dublin | 3,808 | 1 | 0 | 0 | 0 | 1 | 41 | 4 | 35 | 2 | 0 |
| Dumas | 13,933 | 51 | 1 | 12 | 1 | 37 | 411 | 60 | 339 | 12 | 2 |
| Duncanville | 36,115 | 183 | 3 | 13 | 94 | 73 | 1,633 | 450 | 1,010 | 173 | 5 |
| Eagle Lake | 3,681 | 14 | 1 | 1 | 1 | 11 | 49 | 21 | 28 | 0 | 0 |
| Eagle Pass | 27,147 | 41 | 0 | 0 | 4 | 37 | 1,078 | 253 | 801 | 24 | 1 |
| Early | 2,774 | 1 | 0 | 0 | 0 | 1 | 65 | 8 | 57 | 0 | 1 |
| Eastland | 3,888 | 14 | 0 | 1 | 3 | 10 | 138 | 30 | 102 | 6 | 1 |
| East Mountain | 633 | 3 | 0 | 0 | 0 | 3 | 14 | 6 | 6 | 2 | 0 |
| Edcouch | 4,771 | 15 | 0 | 0 | 2 | 13 | 129 | 45 | 76 | 8 | 1 |
| Eden | 2,362 | 1 | 0 | 0 | 0 | 1 | 41 | 10 | 31 | 0 | 0 |
| Edgewood | 1,452 | 8 | 0 | 0 | 0 | 8 | 24 | 9 | 14 | 1 | 1 |
| Edinburg | 74,611 | 267 | 3 | 20 | 69 | 175 | 4,669 | 820 | 3,596 | 253 | 26 |
| Edna | 5,792 | 17 | 1 | 6 | 1 | 9 | 132 | 40 | 89 | 3 | 0 |
| El Campo | 10,735 | 50 | 0 | 10 | 4 | 36 | 318 | 69 | 237 | 12 | 4 |
| Electra | 2,867 | 6 | 0 | 0 | 1 | 5 | 72 | 21 | 43 | 8 | 1 |
| Elgin | 10,524 | 20 | 0 | 2 | 8 | 10 | 321 | 70 | 238 | 13 | 2 |
| El Paso | 618,812 | 2,830 | 12 | 182 | 452 | 2,184 | 18,528 | 1,991 | 14,647 | 1,890 | 110 |
| Elsa | 6,744 | 34 | 0 | 1 | 5 | 28 | 445 | 91 | 332 | 22 | 3 |
| Ennis | 19,887 | 91 | 2 | 7 | 22 | 60 | 890 | 185 | 662 | 43 | 0 |
| Euless | 53,339 | 108 | 3 | 15 | 40 | 50 | 1,884 | 471 | 1,257 | 156 | 6 |
| Everman | 5,767 | 17 | 0 | 1 | 5 | 11 | 188 | 47 | 122 | 19 | 2 |
| Fairfield | 3,677 | 6 | 1 | 0 | 0 | 5 | 43 | 6 | 30 | 7 | 0 |
| Fair Oaks Ranch | 6,565 | 5 | 0 | 0 | 0 | 5 | 51 | 35 | 15 | 1 | 0 |
| Falfurrias | 4,906 | 35 | 0 | 0 | 3 | 32 | 254 | 117 | 137 | 0 | 13 |
| Farmers Branch | 26,344 | 71 | 1 | 6 | 41 | 23 | 1,538 | 285 | 1,085 | 168 | 5 |
| Farmersville | 3,516 | 1 | 0 | 0 | 0 | 1 | 51 | 18 | 33 | 0 | 0 |
| Farwell | 1,240 | 4 | 0 | 0 | 0 | 4 | 27 | 6 | 21 | 0 | 0 |
| Ferris | 2,611 | 9 | 2 | 3 | 0 | 4 | 84 | 29 | 48 | 7 | 2 |
| Flatonia | 1,437 | 2 | 0 | 0 | 0 | 2 | 17 | 1 | 16 | 0 | 2 |
| Florence | 1,140 | 1 | 0 | 0 | 0 | 1 | 7 | 0 | 6 | 1 | 0 |
| Floresville | 7,859 | 8 | 0 | 0 | 1 | 7 | 214 | 55 | 154 | 5 | 0 |
| Flower Mound | 71,605 | 47 | 1 | 10 | 3 | 33 | 566 | 121 | 425 | 20 | 4 |
| Floydada | 2,999 | 17 | 0 | 1 | 0 | 16 | 102 | 41 | 59 | 2 | 0 |
| Forest Hill | 13,961 | 114 | 1 | 5 | 27 | 81 | 565 | 171 | 348 | 46 | 0 |
| Forney | 16,977 | 24 | 1 | 4 | 5 | 14 | 349 | 108 | 225 | 16 | 3 |
| Fort Stockton | 7,498 | 52 | 0 | 1 | 4 | 47 | 389 | 90 | 290 | 9 | 0 |
| Fort Worth | 723,456 | 4,232 | 44 | 370 | 1,449 | 2,369 | 35,884 | 10,188 | 23,564 | 2,132 | 210 |
| Frankston | 1,237 | 1 | 0 | 0 | 1 | 0 | 39 | 15 | 22 | 2 | 0 |
| Fredericksburg | 11,339 | 7 | 0 | 0 | 2 | 5 | 205 | 20 | 181 | 4 | 0 |
| Freeport | 12,471 | 28 | 0 | 1 | 4 | 23 | 483 | 150 | 315 | 18 | 2 |
| Freer | 2,906 | 14 | 0 | 0 | 0 | 14 | 57 | 21 | 34 | 2 | 2 |
| Friendswood | 34,558 | 27 | 0 | 5 | 7 | 15 | 447 | 111 | 316 | 20 | 5 |

[1] The FBI does not publish arson data unless it receives data from either the agency or the state for all 12 months of the calendar year.

## Table 8. Offenses Known to Law Enforcement, by State and City, 2009—*Continued*

(Number.)

| State/city | Population | Violent crime | Murder and non-negligent man-slaughter | Forcible rape | Robbery | Aggravated assault | Property crime | Burglary | Larceny-theft | Motor vehicle theft | Arson[1] |
|---|---|---|---|---|---|---|---|---|---|---|---|
| **TEXAS**—*Continued* | | | | | | | | | | | |
| Friona | 3,489 | 7 | 0 | 0 | 0 | 7 | 34 | 14 | 16 | 4 | 0 |
| Frisco | 108,244 | 108 | 2 | 15 | 13 | 78 | 2,058 | 357 | 1,627 | 74 | 2 |
| Gainesville | 16,547 | 90 | 0 | 7 | 12 | 71 | 823 | 237 | 552 | 34 | 3 |
| Galena Park | 10,166 | 31 | 1 | 2 | 15 | 13 | 285 | 107 | 155 | 23 | 1 |
| Galveston | 57,040 | 412 | 6 | 64 | 121 | 221 | 3,272 | 954 | 2,069 | 249 | 169 |
| Ganado | 1,833 | 1 | 0 | 0 | 0 | 1 | 4 | 3 | 0 | 1 | 0 |
| Garland | 218,872 | 608 | 7 | 54 | 304 | 243 | 9,098 | 2,206 | 6,139 | 753 | 53 |
| Gatesville | 15,198 | 20 | 0 | 3 | 1 | 16 | 245 | 70 | 162 | 13 | 3 |
| Georgetown | 52,555 | 53 | 0 | 8 | 10 | 35 | 805 | 134 | 617 | 54 | 3 |
| Giddings | 5,455 | 43 | 0 | 6 | 2 | 35 | 189 | 44 | 143 | 2 | 0 |
| Gilmer | 5,300 | 41 | 0 | 4 | 6 | 31 | 277 | 38 | 223 | 16 | 0 |
| Gladewater | 6,298 | 52 | 1 | 8 | 14 | 29 | 384 | 97 | 264 | 23 | 8 |
| Glenn Heights | 11,594 | 33 | 0 | 1 | 11 | 21 | 235 | 106 | 111 | 18 | 2 |
| Godley | 1,021 | 3 | 0 | 0 | 0 | 3 | 25 | 2 | 23 | 0 | 0 |
| Gonzales | 7,305 | 97 | 0 | 5 | 5 | 87 | 326 | 76 | 242 | 8 | 0 |
| Gorman | 1,230 | 4 | 0 | 0 | 0 | 4 | 10 | 4 | 5 | 1 | 0 |
| Graham | 8,455 | 18 | 0 | 3 | 1 | 14 | 244 | 70 | 159 | 15 | 1 |
| Granbury | 8,931 | 23 | 0 | 4 | 2 | 17 | 410 | 40 | 359 | 11 | 1 |
| Grand Prairie | 164,766 | 524 | 7 | 52 | 194 | 271 | 7,948 | 2,082 | 4,743 | 1,123 | 29 |
| Grand Saline | 3,187 | 4 | 0 | 0 | 2 | 2 | 51 | 10 | 41 | 0 | 0 |
| Granger | 1,371 | 5 | 0 | 0 | 0 | 5 | 23 | 10 | 13 | 0 | 0 |
| Granite Shoals | 2,877 | 11 | 0 | 0 | 0 | 11 | 68 | 37 | 29 | 2 | 1 |
| Grapeland | 1,373 | 10 | 0 | 0 | 0 | 10 | 29 | 12 | 15 | 2 | 0 |
| Grapevine | 51,427 | 82 | 0 | 8 | 12 | 62 | 1,709 | 206 | 1,378 | 125 | 11 |
| Greenville | 25,865 | 194 | 1 | 10 | 43 | 140 | 1,213 | 270 | 891 | 52 | 2 |
| Gregory | 2,188 | 1 | 0 | 0 | 1 | 0 | 25 | 12 | 11 | 2 | 0 |
| Groesbeck | 4,279 | 9 | 0 | 1 | 3 | 5 | 91 | 32 | 51 | 8 | 1 |
| Groves | 14,255 | 53 | 1 | 1 | 18 | 33 | 475 | 139 | 305 | 31 | 1 |
| Gun Barrel City | 6,057 | 26 | 0 | 10 | 2 | 14 | 262 | 49 | 209 | 4 | 0 |
| Hale Center | 2,102 | 4 | 0 | 0 | 0 | 4 | 24 | 6 | 18 | 0 | 0 |
| Hallettsville | 2,480 | 6 | 0 | 1 | 1 | 4 | 65 | 10 | 55 | 0 | 0 |
| Hallsville | 3,037 | 0 | 0 | 0 | 0 | 0 | 53 | 14 | 37 | 2 | 0 |
| Haltom City | 40,303 | 139 | 0 | 5 | 39 | 95 | 1,916 | 478 | 1,264 | 174 | 7 |
| Hamlin | 1,870 | 2 | 0 | 0 | 0 | 2 | 10 | 5 | 5 | 0 | 0 |
| Harker Heights | 26,468 | 56 | 0 | 16 | 17 | 23 | 771 | 204 | 558 | 9 | 0 |
| Harlingen | 65,552 | 300 | 1 | 32 | 70 | 197 | 4,433 | 799 | 3,435 | 199 | 33 |
| Haskell | 2,577 | 6 | 0 | 0 | 0 | 6 | 86 | 32 | 54 | 0 | 1 |
| Hawk Cove | 618 | 3 | 0 | 0 | 1 | 2 | 5 | 2 | 2 | 1 | 0 |
| Hawkins | 1,547 | 6 | 0 | 0 | 0 | 6 | 37 | 14 | 21 | 2 | 0 |
| Hawley | 569 | 0 | 0 | 0 | 0 | 0 | 11 | 2 | 8 | 1 | 0 |
| Hearne | 4,566 | 37 | 1 | 3 | 6 | 27 | 122 | 54 | 64 | 4 | 3 |
| Heath | 8,267 | 21 | 0 | 3 | 0 | 18 | 84 | 13 | 70 | 1 | 0 |
| Hedwig Village | 2,345 | 7 | 0 | 0 | 7 | 0 | 152 | 20 | 124 | 8 | 0 |
| Helotes | 8,176 | 2 | 0 | 1 | 1 | 0 | 69 | 18 | 51 | 0 | 1 |
| Hemphill | 1,018 | 5 | 0 | 3 | 0 | 2 | 18 | 3 | 13 | 2 | 0 |
| Hempstead | 7,763 | 30 | 0 | 0 | 10 | 20 | 266 | 117 | 129 | 20 | 5 |
| Henderson | 11,675 | 86 | 0 | 5 | 16 | 65 | 640 | 115 | 487 | 38 | 1 |
| Hereford | 14,495 | 72 | 1 | 0 | 11 | 60 | 464 | 133 | 313 | 18 | 3 |
| Hewitt | 13,853 | 14 | 0 | 5 | 1 | 8 | 201 | 37 | 152 | 12 | 0 |
| Hickory Creek | 4,032 | 2 | 0 | 0 | 1 | 1 | 91 | 12 | 68 | 11 | 0 |
| Hidalgo | 12,590 | 11 | 0 | 0 | 2 | 9 | 151 | 32 | 85 | 34 | 0 |
| Highland Park | 9,222 | 9 | 0 | 0 | 5 | 4 | 250 | 59 | 176 | 15 | 0 |
| Highland Village | 17,317 | 6 | 0 | 2 | 0 | 4 | 105 | 7 | 92 | 6 | 0 |
| Hill Country Village | 1,124 | 1 | 1 | 0 | 0 | 0 | 42 | 7 | 32 | 3 | 0 |
| Hillsboro | 9,002 | 28 | 0 | 4 | 11 | 13 | 277 | 57 | 210 | 10 | 0 |
| Hitchcock | 7,289 | 30 | 0 | 4 | 9 | 17 | 202 | 63 | 113 | 26 | 1 |
| Holland | 1,144 | 2 | 0 | 0 | 1 | 1 | 11 | 7 | 3 | 1 | 0 |
| Holliday | 1,809 | 0 | 0 | 0 | 0 | 0 | 11 | 10 | 1 | 0 | 0 |
| Hollywood Park | 3,345 | 5 | 0 | 2 | 1 | 2 | 102 | 18 | 78 | 6 | 0 |
| Hondo | 9,121 | 51 | 0 | 6 | 3 | 42 | 311 | 59 | 246 | 6 | 5 |
| Hooks | 2,953 | 9 | 0 | 2 | 0 | 7 | 34 | 15 | 18 | 1 | 1 |
| Horizon City | 14,408 | 16 | 0 | 0 | 6 | 10 | 253 | 109 | 121 | 23 | 2 |
| Horseshoe Bay | 2,487 | 3 | 0 | 0 | 0 | 3 | 46 | 16 | 27 | 3 | 1 |
| Houston | 2,273,771 | 25,593 | 287 | 823 | 11,367 | 13,116 | 120,933 | 29,279 | 77,058 | 14,596 | 959 |
| Howe | 2,717 | 4 | 0 | 0 | 0 | 4 | 28 | 9 | 19 | 0 | 2 |
| Hubbard | 1,770 | 2 | 0 | 0 | 0 | 2 | 4 | 2 | 2 | 0 | 0 |
| Hudson | 4,358 | 17 | 0 | 3 | 0 | 14 | 96 | 50 | 44 | 2 | 0 |
| Hudson Oaks | 2,123 | 6 | 0 | 0 | 2 | 4 | 75 | 6 | 67 | 2 | 0 |
| Humble | 14,934 | 171 | 1 | 17 | 92 | 61 | 2,038 | 212 | 1,684 | 142 | 4 |
| Huntington | 2,110 | 4 | 0 | 1 | 0 | 3 | 31 | 4 | 25 | 2 | 0 |
| Huntsville | 38,875 | 188 | 3 | 12 | 49 | 124 | 1,407 | 289 | 1,066 | 52 | 4 |

[1] The FBI does not publish arson data unless it receives data from either the agency or the state for all 12 months of the calendar year.

## Table 8. Offenses Known to Law Enforcement, by State and City, 2009—*Continued*

(Number.)

| State/city | Population | Violent crime | Murder and non-negligent man-slaughter | Forcible rape | Robbery | Aggravated assault | Property crime | Burglary | Larceny-theft | Motor vehicle theft | Arson[1] |
|---|---|---|---|---|---|---|---|---|---|---|---|
| **TEXAS**—*Continued* | | | | | | | | | | | |
| Hurst | 38,801 | 191 | 1 | 13 | 43 | 134 | 2,338 | 318 | 1,931 | 89 | 2 |
| Hutchins | 3,129 | 16 | 0 | 2 | 5 | 9 | 228 | 25 | 165 | 38 | 0 |
| Hutto | 17,482 | 29 | 0 | 1 | 1 | 27 | 137 | 28 | 105 | 4 | 0 |
| Idalou | 2,114 | 3 | 0 | 2 | 0 | 1 | 23 | 11 | 10 | 2 | 0 |
| Ingleside | 9,004 | 16 | 0 | 6 | 2 | 8 | 244 | 74 | 157 | 13 | 0 |
| Ingram | 1,928 | 11 | 0 | 7 | 1 | 3 | 62 | 14 | 44 | 4 | 0 |
| Iowa Park | 6,256 | 8 | 0 | 1 | 0 | 7 | 82 | 15 | 60 | 7 | 1 |
| Irving | 202,447 | 604 | 4 | 34 | 214 | 352 | 8,427 | 1,913 | 5,730 | 784 | 35 |
| Italy | 2,161 | 9 | 0 | 0 | 1 | 8 | 49 | 15 | 32 | 2 | 1 |
| Itasca | 1,717 | 1 | 0 | 0 | 0 | 1 | 13 | 5 | 8 | 0 | 1 |
| Jacinto City | 9,883 | 35 | 0 | 0 | 15 | 20 | 328 | 89 | 205 | 34 | 0 |
| Jacksboro | 4,488 | 1 | 0 | 0 | 0 | 1 | 76 | 17 | 52 | 7 | 0 |
| Jacksonville | 14,424 | 120 | 1 | 19 | 22 | 78 | 858 | 294 | 534 | 30 | 6 |
| Jamaica Beach | 1,103 | 2 | 0 | 0 | 1 | 1 | 20 | 7 | 12 | 1 | 0 |
| Jarrell | 1,462 | 1 | 0 | 0 | 0 | 1 | 37 | 15 | 19 | 3 | 0 |
| Jasper | 7,319 | 29 | 0 | 4 | 4 | 21 | 341 | 60 | 270 | 11 | 1 |
| Jefferson | 1,908 | 4 | 0 | 0 | 0 | 4 | 76 | 19 | 55 | 2 | 2 |
| Jersey Village | 7,324 | 20 | 0 | 0 | 4 | 16 | 318 | 64 | 224 | 30 | 0 |
| Johnson City | 1,606 | 0 | 0 | 0 | 0 | 0 | 32 | 6 | 26 | 0 | 0 |
| Jones Creek | 2,100 | 2 | 0 | 1 | 0 | 1 | 13 | 4 | 6 | 3 | 0 |
| Jonestown | 2,533 | 16 | 0 | 4 | 0 | 12 | 44 | 8 | 35 | 1 | 1 |
| Joshua | 5,967 | 13 | 0 | 1 | 4 | 8 | 56 | 15 | 33 | 8 | 2 |
| Jourdanton | 4,382 | 2 | 0 | 1 | 0 | 1 | 32 | 14 | 17 | 1 | 1 |
| Junction | 2,546 | 11 | 0 | 1 | 1 | 9 | 72 | 19 | 51 | 2 | 1 |
| Karnes City | 3,326 | 10 | 0 | 3 | 0 | 7 | 81 | 22 | 58 | 1 | 0 |
| Katy | 14,166 | 49 | 1 | 0 | 21 | 27 | 648 | 56 | 566 | 26 | 0 |
| Kaufman | 9,073 | 15 | 0 | 0 | 4 | 11 | 170 | 42 | 120 | 8 | 3 |
| Keene | 6,452 | 2 | 0 | 0 | 2 | 0 | 112 | 41 | 70 | 1 | 0 |
| Keller | 40,421 | 27 | 0 | 0 | 4 | 23 | 504 | 115 | 377 | 12 | 2 |
| Kemah | 2,518 | 6 | 0 | 0 | 5 | 1 | 98 | 4 | 88 | 6 | 0 |
| Kemp | 1,355 | 0 | 0 | 0 | 0 | 0 | 20 | 7 | 13 | 0 | 0 |
| Kempner | 1,199 | 0 | 0 | 0 | 0 | 0 | 0 | 0 | 0 | 0 | 0 |
| Kenedy | 3,288 | 11 | 0 | 2 | 2 | 7 | 108 | 51 | 57 | 0 | 0 |
| Kennedale | 7,252 | 29 | 3 | 0 | 6 | 20 | 251 | 78 | 143 | 30 | 4 |
| Kerens | 1,824 | 2 | 1 | 1 | 0 | 0 | 35 | 18 | 15 | 2 | 0 |
| Kermit | 5,189 | 14 | 0 | 0 | 1 | 13 | 75 | 27 | 46 | 2 | 0 |
| Kerrville | 23,091 | 52 | 2 | 4 | 11 | 35 | 873 | 134 | 710 | 29 | 3 |
| Kilgore | 12,094 | 43 | 0 | 5 | 11 | 27 | 809 | 121 | 642 | 46 | 0 |
| Killeen | 120,670 | 750 | 5 | 69 | 179 | 497 | 5,513 | 1,735 | 3,566 | 212 | 39 |
| Kingsville | 24,612 | 214 | 0 | 16 | 16 | 182 | 1,303 | 445 | 809 | 49 | 6 |
| Kirby | 8,599 | 14 | 0 | 0 | 6 | 8 | 163 | 52 | 98 | 13 | 4 |
| Kirbyville | 1,931 | 8 | 1 | 0 | 0 | 7 | 35 | 17 | 18 | 0 | 0 |
| Kountze | 2,177 | 16 | 0 | 1 | 4 | 11 | 59 | 32 | 22 | 5 | 0 |
| Kress | 761 | 0 | 0 | 0 | 0 | 0 | 6 | 2 | 4 | 0 | 0 |
| Kyle | 30,846 | 17 | 0 | 1 | 1 | 15 | 342 | 52 | 280 | 10 | 0 |
| Lacy-Lakeview | 5,896 | 41 | 2 | 8 | 3 | 28 | 239 | 65 | 161 | 13 | 0 |
| La Feria | 7,042 | 7 | 0 | 0 | 3 | 4 | 334 | 64 | 267 | 3 | 0 |
| Lago Vista | 6,506 | 6 | 0 | 0 | 0 | 6 | 105 | 13 | 85 | 7 | 1 |
| La Grange | 4,733 | 3 | 0 | 0 | 1 | 2 | 49 | 8 | 39 | 2 | 0 |
| La Grulla | 1,867 | 7 | 0 | 0 | 1 | 6 | 18 | 5 | 6 | 7 | 0 |
| Laguna Vista | 4,291 | 5 | 0 | 2 | 0 | 3 | 74 | 22 | 49 | 3 | 0 |
| La Joya | 4,983 | 5 | 0 | 1 | 4 | 0 | 38 | 15 | 22 | 1 | 0 |
| Lake Dallas | 8,011 | 31 | 0 | 13 | 4 | 14 | 197 | 46 | 130 | 21 | 0 |
| Lake Jackson | 27,531 | 40 | 0 | 5 | 13 | 22 | 745 | 119 | 602 | 24 | 1 |
| Lakeside | 1,359 | 0 | 0 | 0 | 0 | 0 | 17 | 6 | 10 | 1 | 0 |
| Lakeview | 6,477 | 1 | 0 | 0 | 0 | 1 | 91 | 23 | 62 | 6 | 1 |
| Lakeway | 11,587 | 14 | 0 | 2 | 2 | 10 | 180 | 32 | 139 | 9 | 0 |
| Lake Worth | 4,832 | 20 | 0 | 0 | 4 | 16 | 468 | 75 | 379 | 14 | 0 |
| La Marque | 14,297 | 151 | 4 | 16 | 39 | 92 | 672 | 240 | 386 | 46 | 11 |
| Lamesa | 8,772 | 36 | 1 | 2 | 0 | 33 | 334 | 111 | 204 | 19 | 5 |
| Lampasas | 8,107 | 20 | 0 | 2 | 3 | 15 | 191 | 39 | 145 | 7 | 5 |
| La Porte | 34,535 | 68 | 0 | 7 | 10 | 51 | 678 | 110 | 515 | 53 | 3 |
| Laredo | 226,944 | 1,294 | 17 | 73 | 309 | 895 | 13,725 | 2,164 | 10,077 | 1,484 | 32 |
| La Vernia | 1,252 | 0 | 0 | 0 | 0 | 0 | 35 | 6 | 28 | 1 | 0 |
| La Villa | 1,447 | 13 | 0 | 0 | 3 | 10 | 81 | 21 | 55 | 5 | 2 |
| Lavon | 426 | 3 | 0 | 0 | 0 | 3 | 37 | 12 | 24 | 1 | 0 |
| League City | 74,801 | 122 | 2 | 20 | 32 | 68 | 2,086 | 456 | 1,568 | 62 | 7 |
| Leander | 28,646 | 25 | 0 | 0 | 3 | 22 | 284 | 40 | 231 | 13 | 5 |
| Leon Valley | 10,390 | 41 | 0 | 4 | 11 | 26 | 765 | 118 | 591 | 56 | 0 |
| Levelland | 12,410 | 70 | 1 | 14 | 8 | 47 | 493 | 153 | 325 | 15 | 8 |
| Lewisville | 104,601 | 197 | 3 | 21 | 75 | 98 | 3,619 | 657 | 2,526 | 436 | 5 |

[1] The FBI does not publish arson data unless it receives data from either the agency or the state for all 12 months of the calendar year.

## Table 8. Offenses Known to Law Enforcement, by State and City, 2009—*Continued*

(Number.)

| State/city | Population | Violent crime | Murder and non-negligent man-slaughter | Forcible rape | Robbery | Aggravated assault | Property crime | Burglary | Larceny-theft | Motor vehicle theft | Arson[1] |
|---|---|---|---|---|---|---|---|---|---|---|---|
| **TEXAS**—*Continued* | | | | | | | | | | | |
| Lexington | 1,241 | 1 | 0 | 0 | 0 | 1 | 33 | 0 | 31 | 2 | 0 |
| Liberty | 8,362 | 51 | 2 | 0 | 4 | 45 | 420 | 93 | 291 | 36 | 0 |
| Lindale | 4,910 | 15 | 0 | 0 | 2 | 13 | 192 | 30 | 152 | 10 | 0 |
| Linden | 2,116 | 14 | 0 | 1 | 1 | 12 | 63 | 18 | 40 | 5 | 0 |
| Little Elm | 30,392 | 22 | 1 | 0 | 3 | 18 | 253 | 37 | 202 | 14 | 0 |
| Littlefield | 5,871 | 25 | 0 | 1 | 1 | 23 | 206 | 63 | 135 | 8 | 0 |
| Live Oak | 13,677 | 31 | 0 | 9 | 8 | 14 | 627 | 70 | 510 | 47 | 1 |
| Livingston | 6,280 | 50 | 1 | 16 | 8 | 25 | 347 | 56 | 269 | 22 | 2 |
| Llano | 3,226 | 3 | 0 | 1 | 0 | 2 | 112 | 16 | 95 | 1 | 0 |
| Lockhart | 13,891 | 77 | 0 | 1 | 3 | 73 | 352 | 99 | 238 | 15 | 2 |
| Lockney | 1,631 | 3 | 0 | 0 | 0 | 3 | 44 | 18 | 23 | 3 | 0 |
| Lone Star | 1,584 | 4 | 0 | 0 | 2 | 2 | 61 | 23 | 34 | 4 | 0 |
| Longview | 77,663 | 708 | 11 | 28 | 185 | 484 | 5,498 | 1,217 | 3,842 | 439 | 37 |
| Lorena | 1,698 | 1 | 0 | 0 | 0 | 1 | 43 | 5 | 36 | 2 | 0 |
| Lorenzo | 1,166 | 1 | 0 | 0 | 0 | 1 | 7 | 4 | 3 | 0 | 0 |
| Los Fresnos | 5,657 | 15 | 0 | 2 | 1 | 12 | 129 | 40 | 83 | 6 | 0 |
| Lott | 670 | 5 | 0 | 0 | 0 | 5 | 21 | 7 | 12 | 2 | 2 |
| Lubbock | 222,884 | 2,079 | 13 | 93 | 311 | 1,662 | 13,010 | 3,730 | 8,754 | 526 | 69 |
| Lufkin | 34,668 | 167 | 1 | 13 | 50 | 103 | 2,563 | 626 | 1,874 | 63 | 2 |
| Luling | 5,499 | 49 | 0 | 3 | 7 | 39 | 228 | 69 | 143 | 16 | 1 |
| Lumberton | 10,530 | 12 | 0 | 0 | 0 | 12 | 262 | 63 | 183 | 16 | 1 |
| Lytle | 2,869 | 2 | 0 | 0 | 0 | 2 | 111 | 12 | 95 | 4 | 0 |
| Madisonville | 4,396 | 48 | 0 | 5 | 26 | 17 | 224 | 60 | 154 | 10 | 0 |
| Magnolia | 1,267 | 4 | 0 | 2 | 1 | 1 | 39 | 7 | 29 | 3 | 0 |
| Malakoff | 2,333 | 7 | 0 | 0 | 1 | 6 | 52 | 13 | 35 | 4 | 0 |
| Manor | 3,928 | 10 | 0 | 2 | 2 | 6 | 122 | 30 | 87 | 5 | 0 |
| Mansfield | 48,710 | 113 | 3 | 12 | 33 | 65 | 1,162 | 218 | 868 | 76 | 2 |
| Manvel | 6,570 | 14 | 0 | 1 | 2 | 11 | 80 | 34 | 41 | 5 | 4 |
| Marble Falls | 7,785 | 14 | 0 | 5 | 0 | 9 | 377 | 39 | 324 | 14 | 2 |
| Marlin | 5,736 | 28 | 0 | 1 | 2 | 25 | 95 | 47 | 46 | 2 | 1 |
| Marshall | 23,791 | 174 | 3 | 17 | 28 | 126 | 1,155 | 350 | 740 | 65 | 4 |
| Mart | 2,433 | 6 | 0 | 1 | 0 | 5 | 34 | 5 | 29 | 0 | 0 |
| Martindale | 1,171 | 3 | 0 | 0 | 0 | 3 | 19 | 5 | 12 | 2 | 0 |
| Mathis | 5,286 | 35 | 0 | 3 | 4 | 28 | 228 | 78 | 146 | 4 | 4 |
| McAllen | 132,598 | 348 | 4 | 20 | 132 | 192 | 8,020 | 796 | 6,783 | 441 | 5 |
| McGregor | 4,909 | 14 | 0 | 1 | 0 | 13 | 117 | 31 | 85 | 1 | 0 |
| McKinney | 132,146 | 245 | 0 | 47 | 56 | 142 | 3,339 | 711 | 2,518 | 110 | 28 |
| Meadows Place | 6,624 | 8 | 0 | 0 | 6 | 2 | 138 | 29 | 96 | 13 | 0 |
| Melissa | 4,859 | 4 | 0 | 0 | 0 | 4 | 79 | 20 | 57 | 2 | 1 |
| Memorial Villages | 12,024 | 7 | 0 | 0 | 4 | 3 | 99 | 23 | 73 | 3 | 0 |
| Memphis | 2,169 | 4 | 0 | 0 | 0 | 4 | 19 | 9 | 9 | 1 | 0 |
| Mercedes | 15,261 | 84 | 1 | 6 | 7 | 70 | 825 | 169 | 580 | 76 | 3 |
| Meridian | 1,495 | 1 | 0 | 0 | 1 | 0 | 8 | 2 | 6 | 0 | 0 |
| Merkel | 2,612 | 6 | 0 | 0 | 1 | 5 | 32 | 10 | 20 | 2 | 0 |
| Mesquite | 132,941 | 534 | 5 | 17 | 220 | 292 | 6,739 | 1,390 | 4,661 | 688 | 6 |
| Mexia | 6,545 | 53 | 0 | 5 | 12 | 36 | 461 | 96 | 351 | 14 | 4 |
| Midland | 107,933 | 426 | 3 | 51 | 85 | 287 | 3,925 | 909 | 2,845 | 171 | 4 |
| Midlothian | 17,718 | 48 | 1 | 7 | 2 | 38 | 403 | 121 | 261 | 21 | 0 |
| Milford | 754 | 1 | 0 | 0 | 0 | 1 | 12 | 4 | 8 | 0 | 0 |
| Mineola | 5,253 | 13 | 0 | 0 | 1 | 12 | 153 | 42 | 110 | 1 | 1 |
| Mineral Wells | 16,872 | 83 | 0 | 25 | 8 | 50 | 891 | 178 | 664 | 49 | 1 |
| Mission | 69,997 | 124 | 1 | 7 | 41 | 75 | 3,425 | 570 | 2,538 | 317 | 7 |
| Missouri City | 77,543 | 123 | 1 | 15 | 46 | 61 | 1,300 | 366 | 877 | 57 | 9 |
| Monahans | 6,489 | 46 | 0 | 1 | 1 | 44 | 240 | 94 | 141 | 5 | 2 |
| Mont Belvieu | 2,737 | 6 | 0 | 2 | 1 | 3 | 107 | 21 | 72 | 14 | 0 |
| Montgomery | 609 | 4 | 0 | 0 | 0 | 4 | 12 | 1 | 9 | 2 | 0 |
| Morgans Point Resort | 4,603 | 2 | 0 | 2 | 0 | 0 | 57 | 11 | 45 | 1 | 0 |
| Mount Pleasant | 15,111 | 64 | 0 | 0 | 14 | 50 | 672 | 137 | 507 | 28 | 2 |
| Muleshoe | 4,234 | 15 | 0 | 2 | 1 | 12 | 111 | 48 | 62 | 1 | 0 |
| Munday | 1,178 | 4 | 0 | 0 | 1 | 3 | 17 | 3 | 14 | 0 | 0 |
| Murphy | 17,459 | 10 | 0 | 2 | 2 | 6 | 143 | 25 | 113 | 5 | 1 |
| Mustang Ridge | 950 | 1 | 0 | 0 | 0 | 1 | 10 | 7 | 3 | 0 | 0 |
| Nacogdoches | 32,459 | 185 | 4 | 29 | 36 | 116 | 1,401 | 321 | 1,019 | 61 | 10 |
| Nash | 2,430 | 3 | 0 | 0 | 2 | 1 | 57 | 23 | 34 | 0 | 0 |
| Nassau Bay | 4,026 | 5 | 0 | 3 | 0 | 2 | 126 | 23 | 97 | 6 | 1 |
| Navasota | 7,647 | 46 | 1 | 5 | 9 | 31 | 267 | 74 | 181 | 12 | 3 |
| Nederland | 15,959 | 51 | 0 | 7 | 16 | 28 | 639 | 137 | 476 | 26 | 1 |
| Needville | 3,564 | 5 | 0 | 0 | 1 | 4 | 12 | 4 | 8 | 0 | 0 |
| New Boston | 4,642 | 21 | 1 | 1 | 1 | 18 | 203 | 58 | 135 | 10 | 1 |
| New Braunfels | 55,584 | 142 | 0 | 14 | 39 | 89 | 2,149 | 366 | 1,691 | 92 | 13 |
| New Deal | 753 | 0 | 0 | 0 | 0 | 0 | 8 | 2 | 6 | 0 | 0 |

[1] The FBI does not publish arson data unless it receives data from either the agency or the state for all 12 months of the calendar year.

## Table 8. Offenses Known to Law Enforcement, by State and City, 2009—*Continued*

(Number.)

| State/city | Population | Violent crime | Murder and non-negligent man-slaughter | Forcible rape | Robbery | Aggravated assault | Property crime | Burglary | Larceny-theft | Motor vehicle theft | Arson[1] |
|---|---|---|---|---|---|---|---|---|---|---|---|
| **TEXAS**—*Continued* | | | | | | | | | | | |
| Nixon | 2,188 | 8 | 0 | 0 | 1 | 7 | 23 | 11 | 12 | 0 | 1 |
| Nocona | 3,241 | 3 | 0 | 1 | 0 | 2 | 24 | 11 | 13 | 0 | 0 |
| Nolanville | 3,015 | 13 | 0 | 0 | 0 | 13 | 71 | 16 | 53 | 2 | 0 |
| Northlake | 2,260 | 1 | 0 | 0 | 0 | 1 | 43 | 7 | 34 | 2 | 0 |
| North Richland Hills | 66,181 | 178 | 2 | 25 | 38 | 113 | 2,041 | 423 | 1,506 | 112 | 0 |
| Oak Ridge | 249 | 1 | 0 | 0 | 0 | 1 | 10 | 4 | 6 | 0 | 0 |
| Oak Ridge North | 3,446 | 6 | 0 | 1 | 1 | 4 | 102 | 28 | 63 | 11 | 0 |
| Odessa | 99,770 | 787 | 5 | 36 | 189 | 557 | 4,109 | 1,084 | 2,834 | 191 | 30 |
| Olmos Park | 2,309 | 1 | 0 | 0 | 1 | 0 | 94 | 17 | 74 | 3 | 0 |
| Olney | 3,220 | 4 | 0 | 1 | 0 | 3 | 93 | 34 | 56 | 3 | 1 |
| Olton | 2,137 | 6 | 0 | 0 | 0 | 6 | 22 | 8 | 14 | 0 | 1 |
| Onalaska | 1,452 | 0 | 0 | 0 | 0 | 0 | 1 | 0 | 1 | 0 | 0 |
| Orange | 19,366 | 161 | 2 | 23 | 57 | 79 | 1,139 | 437 | 619 | 83 | 13 |
| Orange Grove | 1,417 | 0 | 0 | 0 | 0 | 0 | 12 | 5 | 7 | 0 | 0 |
| Overton | 2,381 | 8 | 0 | 0 | 1 | 7 | 61 | 16 | 43 | 2 | 2 |
| Ovilla | 4,026 | 4 | 0 | 0 | 1 | 3 | 20 | 9 | 9 | 2 | 0 |
| Oyster Creek | 1,244 | 11 | 0 | 0 | 0 | 11 | 43 | 18 | 22 | 3 | 0 |
| Paducah | 1,234 | 1 | 0 | 0 | 0 | 1 | 11 | 7 | 4 | 0 | 0 |
| Palacios | 5,058 | 7 | 0 | 0 | 2 | 5 | 188 | 83 | 101 | 4 | 7 |
| Palestine | 18,477 | 167 | 3 | 21 | 29 | 114 | 924 | 377 | 508 | 39 | 6 |
| Palmer | 2,316 | 2 | 0 | 0 | 0 | 2 | 33 | 10 | 22 | 1 | 3 |
| Palmhurst | 5,002 | 9 | 0 | 0 | 3 | 6 | 216 | 15 | 196 | 5 | 0 |
| Palmview | 5,537 | 12 | 0 | 0 | 6 | 6 | 374 | 44 | 320 | 10 | 0 |
| Pampa | 17,345 | 119 | 0 | 0 | 10 | 109 | 850 | 242 | 574 | 34 | 4 |
| Panhandle | 2,474 | 3 | 0 | 0 | 0 | 3 | 25 | 4 | 20 | 1 | 0 |
| Pantego | 2,388 | 11 | 0 | 1 | 6 | 4 | 135 | 28 | 101 | 6 | 0 |
| Paris | 26,080 | 169 | 0 | 7 | 34 | 128 | 1,724 | 355 | 1,334 | 35 | 13 |
| Parker | 3,066 | 0 | 0 | 0 | 0 | 0 | 24 | 3 | 20 | 1 | 0 |
| Pasadena | 146,963 | 706 | 8 | 56 | 184 | 458 | 5,610 | 1,213 | 3,955 | 442 | 17 |
| Pearland | 88,528 | 130 | 1 | 20 | 40 | 69 | 2,006 | 387 | 1,514 | 105 | 5 |
| Pearsall | 7,663 | 27 | 0 | 1 | 2 | 24 | 193 | 79 | 109 | 5 | 2 |
| Pecos | 7,643 | 26 | 0 | 4 | 5 | 17 | 199 | 51 | 136 | 12 | 0 |
| Pelican Bay | 1,626 | 6 | 0 | 0 | 0 | 6 | 41 | 15 | 23 | 3 | 1 |
| Penitas | 1,183 | 3 | 0 | 0 | 1 | 2 | 42 | 13 | 22 | 7 | 1 |
| Perryton | 8,365 | 14 | 1 | 0 | 0 | 13 | 111 | 39 | 64 | 8 | 0 |
| Pflugerville | 42,395 | 69 | 0 | 16 | 11 | 42 | 875 | 185 | 648 | 42 | 9 |
| Pharr | 67,628 | 302 | 2 | 23 | 84 | 193 | 3,958 | 842 | 2,773 | 343 | 4 |
| Pilot Point | 4,513 | 5 | 0 | 1 | 0 | 4 | 34 | 17 | 15 | 2 | 0 |
| Pinehurst | 2,151 | 6 | 0 | 0 | 1 | 5 | 127 | 27 | 99 | 1 | 0 |
| Pittsburg | 4,703 | 28 | 0 | 5 | 7 | 16 | 136 | 33 | 98 | 5 | 1 |
| Plainview | 21,227 | 83 | 0 | 8 | 12 | 63 | 1,085 | 269 | 780 | 36 | 4 |
| Plano | 272,747 | 464 | 4 | 45 | 143 | 272 | 7,993 | 1,477 | 6,047 | 469 | 19 |
| Pleasanton | 9,844 | 42 | 1 | 15 | 3 | 23 | 373 | 85 | 268 | 20 | 1 |
| Point Comfort | 706 | 1 | 0 | 0 | 0 | 1 | 15 | 3 | 11 | 1 | 0 |
| Ponder | 1,427 | 0 | 0 | 0 | 0 | 0 | 7 | 1 | 6 | 0 | 0 |
| Port Aransas | 3,896 | 25 | 0 | 2 | 3 | 20 | 338 | 72 | 254 | 12 | 1 |
| Port Arthur | 55,725 | 433 | 7 | 31 | 165 | 230 | 2,644 | 980 | 1,471 | 193 | 56 |
| Port Isabel | 5,322 | 23 | 0 | 4 | 4 | 15 | 326 | 55 | 267 | 4 | 1 |
| Portland | 16,675 | 18 | 0 | 8 | 2 | 8 | 479 | 45 | 422 | 12 | 3 |
| Port Lavaca | 11,375 | 64 | 1 | 3 | 1 | 59 | 289 | 61 | 213 | 15 | 0 |
| Port Neches | 12,501 | 16 | 0 | 0 | 3 | 13 | 340 | 75 | 257 | 8 | 0 |
| Poteet | 3,677 | 14 | 0 | 0 | 1 | 13 | 101 | 21 | 79 | 1 | 0 |
| Pottsboro | 2,162 | 1 | 0 | 0 | 0 | 1 | 64 | 27 | 34 | 3 | 0 |
| Premont | 2,791 | 11 | 0 | 0 | 2 | 9 | 60 | 28 | 27 | 5 | 1 |
| Presidio | 4,753 | 6 | 0 | 0 | 0 | 6 | 39 | 13 | 23 | 3 | 1 |
| Primera | 4,319 | 2 | 0 | 0 | 0 | 2 | 50 | 20 | 26 | 4 | 0 |
| Princeton | 6,519 | 18 | 0 | 10 | 0 | 8 | 125 | 32 | 91 | 2 | 1 |
| Progreso | 5,588 | 17 | 1 | 0 | 2 | 14 | 123 | 16 | 99 | 8 | 1 |
| Prosper | 8,005 | 2 | 0 | 0 | 0 | 2 | 92 | 33 | 57 | 2 | 0 |
| Queen City | 1,541 | 11 | 0 | 1 | 0 | 10 | 40 | 18 | 19 | 3 | 0 |
| Quinlan | 1,438 | 3 | 0 | 0 | 0 | 3 | 49 | 14 | 34 | 1 | 1 |
| Quitman | 2,254 | 21 | 0 | 0 | 0 | 21 | 72 | 13 | 54 | 5 | 0 |
| Ralls | 1,946 | 5 | 0 | 0 | 0 | 5 | 43 | 16 | 24 | 3 | 0 |
| Rancho Viejo | 1,854 | 6 | 0 | 0 | 0 | 6 | 33 | 12 | 16 | 5 | 0 |
| Ranger | 2,557 | 12 | 0 | 1 | 0 | 11 | 68 | 23 | 44 | 1 | 0 |
| Ransom Canyon | 1,125 | 0 | 0 | 0 | 0 | 0 | 7 | 0 | 7 | 0 | 0 |
| Raymondville | 9,502 | 243 | 0 | 0 | 11 | 232 | 589 | 220 | 364 | 5 | 11 |
| Red Oak | 9,852 | 8 | 0 | 1 | 3 | 4 | 237 | 78 | 146 | 13 | 1 |
| Refugio | 2,694 | 5 | 0 | 0 | 0 | 5 | 23 | 4 | 18 | 1 | 0 |
| Reno | 3,121 | 4 | 0 | 2 | 0 | 2 | 40 | 11 | 29 | 0 | 0 |
| Richardson | 102,675 | 230 | 0 | 12 | 109 | 109 | 3,575 | 919 | 2,372 | 284 | 3 |

[1] The FBI does not publish arson data unless it receives data from either the agency or the state for all 12 months of the calendar year.

## Table 8. Offenses Known to Law Enforcement, by State and City, 2009—*Continued*

(Number.)

| State/city | Population | Violent crime | Murder and non-negligent man-slaughter | Forcible rape | Robbery | Aggravated assault | Property crime | Burglary | Larceny-theft | Motor vehicle theft | Arson[1] |
|---|---|---|---|---|---|---|---|---|---|---|---|
| **TEXAS**—*Continued* | | | | | | | | | | | |
| Richland Hills | 8,090 | 11 | 0 | 0 | 5 | 6 | 358 | 82 | 236 | 40 | 0 |
| Richmond | 13,706 | 60 | 2 | 9 | 11 | 38 | 327 | 87 | 219 | 21 | 3 |
| Richwood | 3,502 | 1 | 0 | 0 | 1 | 0 | 57 | 5 | 49 | 3 | 0 |
| Riesel | 1,016 | 2 | 0 | 0 | 1 | 1 | 20 | 4 | 14 | 2 | 0 |
| Rio Grande City | 14,167 | 45 | 2 | 9 | 2 | 32 | 621 | 157 | 394 | 70 | 6 |
| Rising Star | 826 | 4 | 0 | 3 | 0 | 1 | 0 | 0 | 0 | 0 | 0 |
| River Oaks | 6,961 | 10 | 0 | 4 | 3 | 3 | 148 | 42 | 98 | 8 | 0 |
| Roanoke | 4,429 | 11 | 0 | 0 | 3 | 8 | 140 | 24 | 113 | 3 | 0 |
| Robinson | 10,642 | 15 | 0 | 1 | 2 | 12 | 206 | 22 | 175 | 9 | 0 |
| Robstown | 12,106 | 22 | 0 | 0 | 12 | 10 | 537 | 209 | 311 | 17 | 0 |
| Rockdale | 5,983 | 12 | 0 | 0 | 2 | 10 | 163 | 29 | 127 | 7 | 0 |
| Rockport | 10,026 | 18 | 0 | 2 | 2 | 14 | 522 | 147 | 365 | 10 | 1 |
| Rockwall | 37,856 | 46 | 0 | 11 | 6 | 29 | 1,047 | 122 | 817 | 108 | 0 |
| Rollingwood | 1,438 | 0 | 0 | 0 | 0 | 0 | 22 | 7 | 14 | 1 | 1 |
| Roma | 11,441 | 35 | 0 | 10 | 4 | 21 | 207 | 47 | 120 | 40 | 0 |
| Roman Forest | 4,219 | 1 | 0 | 0 | 0 | 1 | 13 | 5 | 6 | 2 | 0 |
| Roscoe | 1,260 | 1 | 0 | 0 | 0 | 1 | 1 | 1 | 0 | 0 | 0 |
| Rosebud | 1,320 | 3 | 0 | 0 | 0 | 3 | 9 | 2 | 7 | 0 | 2 |
| Rose City | 502 | 3 | 0 | 0 | 1 | 2 | 5 | 3 | 2 | 0 | 2 |
| Rosenberg | 34,838 | 65 | 2 | 7 | 17 | 39 | 673 | 199 | 441 | 33 | 3 |
| Round Rock | 110,531 | 128 | 1 | 23 | 32 | 72 | 2,772 | 412 | 2,255 | 105 | 7 |
| Rowlett | 57,119 | 61 | 0 | 14 | 5 | 42 | 1,083 | 265 | 768 | 50 | 0 |
| Royse City | 10,277 | 23 | 0 | 3 | 1 | 19 | 172 | 21 | 143 | 8 | 1 |
| Runaway Bay | 1,463 | 0 | 0 | 0 | 0 | 0 | 8 | 8 | 0 | 0 | 0 |
| Rusk | 5,330 | 10 | 0 | 1 | 2 | 7 | 130 | 32 | 89 | 9 | 0 |
| Sabinal | 1,625 | 4 | 0 | 0 | 0 | 4 | 26 | 7 | 16 | 3 | 1 |
| Sachse | 19,996 | 13 | 0 | 2 | 5 | 6 | 220 | 60 | 153 | 7 | 0 |
| Saginaw | 21,388 | 51 | 0 | 3 | 10 | 38 | 598 | 102 | 472 | 24 | 8 |
| Salado | 2,071 | 0 | 0 | 0 | 0 | 0 | 20 | 5 | 13 | 2 | 0 |
| San Angelo | 92,269 | 368 | 8 | 65 | 45 | 250 | 4,247 | 996 | 3,092 | 159 | 15 |
| San Antonio | 1,373,936 | 7,844 | 99 | 628 | 2,683 | 4,434 | 91,651 | 18,164 | 67,684 | 5,803 | 416 |
| San Augustine | 2,333 | 10 | 0 | 0 | 0 | 10 | 57 | 14 | 41 | 2 | 0 |
| San Benito | 25,176 | 64 | 1 | 5 | 17 | 41 | 1,183 | 261 | 878 | 44 | 3 |
| San Diego | 4,401 | 26 | 0 | 0 | 2 | 24 | 147 | 73 | 72 | 2 | 3 |
| San Felipe | 985 | 4 | 0 | 0 | 2 | 2 | 12 | 8 | 3 | 1 | 0 |
| Sanger | 8,209 | 18 | 0 | 3 | 4 | 11 | 149 | 34 | 111 | 4 | 0 |
| San Juan | 34,896 | 181 | 0 | 16 | 33 | 132 | 1,779 | 378 | 1,303 | 98 | 1 |
| San Marcos | 55,187 | 182 | 1 | 3 | 46 | 132 | 1,702 | 300 | 1,317 | 85 | 3 |
| San Saba | 2,481 | 2 | 0 | 0 | 0 | 2 | 27 | 7 | 17 | 3 | 0 |
| Sansom Park Village | 4,198 | 26 | 0 | 3 | 3 | 20 | 133 | 43 | 83 | 7 | 0 |
| Santa Anna | 1,010 | 5 | 0 | 0 | 1 | 4 | 15 | 5 | 9 | 1 | 3 |
| Santa Fe | 10,578 | 31 | 1 | 3 | 4 | 23 | 298 | 109 | 168 | 21 | 0 |
| Santa Rosa | 3,163 | 14 | 0 | 0 | 1 | 13 | 64 | 12 | 49 | 3 | 0 |
| Schertz | 31,984 | 86 | 2 | 17 | 11 | 56 | 630 | 103 | 486 | 41 | 2 |
| Schulenburg | 2,690 | 15 | 0 | 1 | 2 | 12 | 60 | 12 | 48 | 0 | 1 |
| Seabrook | 11,777 | 14 | 1 | 2 | 4 | 7 | 242 | 61 | 169 | 12 | 1 |
| Seadrift | 1,442 | 2 | 0 | 0 | 0 | 2 | 29 | 7 | 21 | 1 | 1 |
| Seagoville | 12,133 | 33 | 2 | 1 | 10 | 20 | 603 | 132 | 417 | 54 | 0 |
| Seagraves | 2,351 | 4 | 0 | 1 | 0 | 3 | 34 | 16 | 16 | 2 | 1 |
| Sealy | 6,383 | 42 | 0 | 0 | 5 | 37 | 145 | 45 | 94 | 6 | 0 |
| Seguin | 26,705 | 123 | 2 | 17 | 34 | 70 | 1,325 | 265 | 1,026 | 34 | 8 |
| Selma | 5,626 | 6 | 0 | 0 | 1 | 5 | 223 | 19 | 198 | 6 | 0 |
| Seminole | 6,149 | 5 | 0 | 1 | 0 | 4 | 102 | 14 | 84 | 4 | 0 |
| Seven Points | 1,328 | 7 | 0 | 4 | 1 | 2 | 61 | 10 | 41 | 10 | 0 |
| Seymour | 2,590 | 13 | 0 | 0 | 2 | 11 | 33 | 12 | 15 | 6 | 0 |
| Shallowater | 2,312 | 0 | 0 | 0 | 0 | 0 | 23 | 8 | 14 | 1 | 0 |
| Shamrock | 1,786 | 5 | 0 | 2 | 2 | 1 | 11 | 2 | 7 | 2 | 0 |
| Shavano Park | 3,332 | 0 | 0 | 0 | 0 | 0 | 60 | 4 | 56 | 0 | 0 |
| Shenandoah | 2,066 | 4 | 0 | 0 | 2 | 2 | 227 | 11 | 207 | 9 | 0 |
| Sherman | 38,414 | 187 | 1 | 2 | 29 | 155 | 1,596 | 329 | 1,216 | 51 | 2 |
| Silsbee | 6,923 | 28 | 0 | 0 | 9 | 19 | 160 | 48 | 104 | 8 | 0 |
| Sinton | 5,321 | 25 | 1 | 1 | 4 | 19 | 146 | 52 | 91 | 3 | 0 |
| Slaton | 5,770 | 39 | 0 | 6 | 0 | 33 | 153 | 40 | 104 | 9 | 2 |
| Smithville | 4,534 | 11 | 0 | 2 | 1 | 8 | 85 | 12 | 69 | 4 | 0 |
| Snyder | 10,376 | 128 | 1 | 15 | 4 | 108 | 420 | 109 | 297 | 14 | 2 |
| Socorro | 32,522 | 104 | 0 | 3 | 16 | 85 | 707 | 200 | 442 | 65 | 1 |
| Somerset | 1,874 | 5 | 0 | 1 | 0 | 4 | 51 | 14 | 35 | 2 | 0 |
| Somerville | 1,683 | 5 | 0 | 0 | 1 | 4 | 40 | 16 | 20 | 4 | 0 |
| Sonora | 3,054 | 5 | 0 | 1 | 0 | 4 | 31 | 7 | 22 | 2 | 0 |
| Sour Lake | 1,744 | 2 | 0 | 0 | 0 | 2 | 48 | 13 | 32 | 3 | 0 |
| South Houston | 16,410 | 105 | 3 | 4 | 54 | 44 | 763 | 163 | 504 | 96 | 0 |

[1] The FBI does not publish arson data unless it receives data from either the agency or the state for all 12 months of the calendar year.

**Table 8. Offenses Known to Law Enforcement, by State and City, 2009**—*Continued*

(Number.)

| State/city | Population | Violent crime | Murder and non-negligent man-slaughter | Forcible rape | Robbery | Aggravated assault | Property crime | Burglary | Larceny-theft | Motor vehicle theft | Arson[1] |
|---|---|---|---|---|---|---|---|---|---|---|---|
| **TEXAS**—*Continued* | | | | | | | | | | | |
| Southlake | 27,189 | 13 | 0 | 0 | 3 | 10 | 512 | 99 | 401 | 12 | 1 |
| South Padre Island | 2,884 | 70 | 0 | 7 | 12 | 51 | 715 | 78 | 622 | 15 | 0 |
| Southside Place | 1,680 | 2 | 0 | 0 | 1 | 1 | 7 | 3 | 3 | 1 | 0 |
| Spearman | 2,937 | 9 | 0 | 2 | 1 | 6 | 60 | 6 | 53 | 1 | 0 |
| Springtown | 3,274 | 15 | 0 | 1 | 1 | 13 | 71 | 26 | 43 | 2 | 0 |
| Spring Valley | 3,910 | 6 | 0 | 0 | 5 | 1 | 97 | 12 | 84 | 1 | 0 |
| Spur | 923 | 3 | 0 | 0 | 0 | 3 | 5 | 4 | 1 | 0 | 0 |
| Stafford | 19,990 | 78 | 2 | 9 | 31 | 36 | 849 | 189 | 591 | 69 | 2 |
| Stamford | 3,060 | 12 | 0 | 1 | 0 | 11 | 134 | 42 | 89 | 3 | 0 |
| Stanton | 2,193 | 1 | 0 | 0 | 1 | 0 | 33 | 6 | 25 | 2 | 0 |
| Stephenville | 17,151 | 53 | 0 | 12 | 7 | 34 | 584 | 82 | 488 | 14 | 3 |
| Stratford | 1,905 | 3 | 0 | 0 | 0 | 3 | 15 | 2 | 11 | 2 | 0 |
| Sudan | 973 | 1 | 0 | 1 | 0 | 0 | 8 | 0 | 8 | 0 | 0 |
| Sugar Land | 82,696 | 113 | 0 | 6 | 61 | 46 | 1,854 | 270 | 1,506 | 78 | 0 |
| Sullivan City | 4,485 | 3 | 0 | 0 | 0 | 3 | 50 | 29 | 15 | 6 | 0 |
| Sulphur Springs | 15,564 | 39 | 1 | 4 | 8 | 26 | 296 | 73 | 212 | 11 | 1 |
| Sunrise Beach Village | 758 | 0 | 0 | 0 | 0 | 0 | 53 | 39 | 13 | 1 | 0 |
| Sunset Valley | 903 | 3 | 0 | 0 | 2 | 1 | 161 | 9 | 144 | 8 | 0 |
| Surfside Beach | 896 | 7 | 0 | 0 | 1 | 6 | 28 | 12 | 14 | 2 | 0 |
| Sweeny | 3,612 | 8 | 0 | 0 | 1 | 7 | 72 | 19 | 47 | 6 | 1 |
| Sweetwater | 10,581 | 176 | 0 | 17 | 15 | 144 | 514 | 121 | 369 | 24 | 1 |
| Taft | 3,331 | 20 | 0 | 0 | 0 | 20 | 95 | 47 | 44 | 4 | 0 |
| Tahoka | 2,479 | 1 | 0 | 1 | 0 | 0 | 41 | 11 | 28 | 2 | 1 |
| Tatum | 1,215 | 7 | 0 | 0 | 0 | 7 | 16 | 6 | 8 | 2 | 0 |
| Taylor | 16,394 | 10 | 1 | 0 | 7 | 2 | 409 | 109 | 293 | 7 | 8 |
| Teague | 4,754 | 28 | 0 | 0 | 1 | 27 | 107 | 46 | 47 | 14 | 0 |
| Terrell | 20,300 | 128 | 0 | 12 | 31 | 85 | 1,001 | 303 | 621 | 77 | 2 |
| Terrell Hills | 5,266 | 3 | 0 | 0 | 1 | 2 | 118 | 22 | 92 | 4 | 0 |
| Texarkana | 36,812 | 555 | 10 | 28 | 145 | 372 | 2,544 | 735 | 1,667 | 142 | 22 |
| Texas City | 44,807 | 251 | 3 | 6 | 103 | 139 | 1,901 | 484 | 1,315 | 102 | 3 |
| The Colony | 44,448 | 53 | 0 | 11 | 7 | 35 | 693 | 212 | 437 | 44 | 8 |
| Thorndale | 1,313 | 6 | 0 | 0 | 1 | 5 | 7 | 4 | 3 | 0 | 0 |
| Thrall | 939 | 0 | 0 | 0 | 0 | 0 | 6 | 2 | 3 | 1 | 0 |
| Three Rivers | 1,655 | 7 | 0 | 2 | 0 | 5 | 43 | 22 | 15 | 6 | 0 |
| Tioga | 947 | 1 | 0 | 1 | 0 | 0 | 23 | 2 | 17 | 4 | 3 |
| Tolar | 704 | 0 | 0 | 0 | 0 | 0 | 5 | 5 | 0 | 0 | 0 |
| Tomball | 10,345 | 33 | 0 | 4 | 7 | 22 | 448 | 68 | 348 | 32 | 1 |
| Tool | 2,457 | 15 | 0 | 1 | 0 | 14 | 97 | 40 | 53 | 4 | 0 |
| Trinity | 2,725 | 27 | 0 | 1 | 3 | 23 | 209 | 55 | 135 | 19 | 1 |
| Trophy Club | 8,276 | 6 | 0 | 0 | 0 | 6 | 83 | 14 | 66 | 3 | 0 |
| Troy | 1,428 | 1 | 0 | 1 | 0 | 0 | 25 | 10 | 10 | 5 | 0 |
| Tulia | 4,535 | 17 | 0 | 3 | 1 | 13 | 97 | 37 | 54 | 6 | 0 |
| Tye | 1,138 | 3 | 0 | 0 | 2 | 1 | 19 | 3 | 14 | 2 | 0 |
| Tyler | 99,279 | 525 | 3 | 55 | 88 | 379 | 5,835 | 1,044 | 4,549 | 242 | 17 |
| Universal City | 18,821 | 51 | 0 | 1 | 10 | 40 | 470 | 126 | 321 | 23 | 4 |
| University Park | 25,026 | 12 | 0 | 1 | 8 | 3 | 416 | 63 | 332 | 21 | 0 |
| Uvalde | 16,171 | 69 | 0 | 0 | 7 | 62 | 722 | 241 | 477 | 4 | 5 |
| Valley View | 793 | 2 | 0 | 0 | 1 | 1 | 4 | 4 | 0 | 0 | 0 |
| Van | 2,603 | 22 | 0 | 2 | 0 | 20 | 53 | 20 | 31 | 2 | 1 |
| Van Alstyne | 3,013 | 8 | 0 | 0 | 0 | 8 | 41 | 13 | 27 | 1 | 0 |
| Vernon | 10,849 | 44 | 1 | 5 | 2 | 36 | 352 | 64 | 272 | 16 | 9 |
| Victoria | 62,788 | 431 | 1 | 48 | 80 | 302 | 4,175 | 1,044 | 3,023 | 108 | 15 |
| Vidor | 11,023 | 39 | 0 | 3 | 5 | 31 | 441 | 97 | 314 | 30 | 1 |
| Waco | 125,098 | 883 | 9 | 49 | 228 | 597 | 7,110 | 1,897 | 4,879 | 334 | 21 |
| Waelder | 997 | 5 | 0 | 1 | 1 | 3 | 12 | 7 | 5 | 0 | 0 |
| Wake Village | 5,659 | 0 | 0 | 0 | 0 | 0 | 69 | 23 | 42 | 4 | 1 |
| Waller | 2,051 | 20 | 0 | 3 | 4 | 13 | 79 | 23 | 51 | 5 | 0 |
| Wallis | 1,343 | 5 | 0 | 0 | 1 | 4 | 17 | 5 | 8 | 4 | 0 |
| Watauga | 24,235 | 102 | 0 | 0 | 11 | 91 | 587 | 173 | 374 | 40 | 0 |
| Waxahachie | 29,576 | 106 | 1 | 8 | 22 | 75 | 992 | 193 | 729 | 70 | 9 |
| Weatherford | 27,667 | 43 | 0 | 6 | 10 | 27 | 844 | 128 | 684 | 32 | 3 |
| Webster | 10,868 | 46 | 0 | 6 | 16 | 24 | 797 | 103 | 625 | 69 | 0 |
| Weimar | 2,021 | 4 | 0 | 1 | 3 | 0 | 33 | 16 | 16 | 1 | 0 |
| Wells | 799 | 8 | 0 | 0 | 0 | 8 | 21 | 7 | 12 | 2 | 0 |
| Weslaco | 33,998 | 222 | 4 | 21 | 38 | 159 | 2,485 | 556 | 1,745 | 184 | 6 |
| West | 2,688 | 0 | 0 | 0 | 0 | 0 | 38 | 8 | 30 | 0 | 0 |
| West Columbia | 4,175 | 28 | 0 | 2 | 0 | 26 | 63 | 21 | 38 | 4 | 1 |
| West Lake Hills | 3,160 | 9 | 0 | 1 | 2 | 6 | 87 | 17 | 70 | 0 | 0 |
| West Orange | 3,803 | 12 | 0 | 3 | 3 | 6 | 370 | 52 | 313 | 5 | 0 |
| Westover Hills | 730 | 0 | 0 | 0 | 0 | 0 | 23 | 7 | 14 | 2 | 0 |
| West Tawakoni | 1,760 | 5 | 0 | 0 | 1 | 4 | 50 | 17 | 29 | 4 | 0 |

[1] The FBI does not publish arson data unless it receives data from either the agency or the state for all 12 months of the calendar year.

## Table 8. Offenses Known to Law Enforcement, by State and City, 2009—*Continued*

(Number.)

| State/city | Population | Violent crime | Murder and non-negligent man-slaughter | Forcible rape | Robbery | Aggravated assault | Property crime | Burglary | Larceny-theft | Motor vehicle theft | Arson[1] |
|---|---|---|---|---|---|---|---|---|---|---|---|
| **TEXAS**—*Continued* | | | | | | | | | | | |
| West University Place | 15,736 | 4 | 0 | 0 | 4 | 0 | 195 | 45 | 148 | 2 | 0 |
| Westworth | 3,141 | 5 | 0 | 0 | 4 | 1 | 108 | 29 | 79 | 0 | 2 |
| Wharton | 9,137 | 68 | 1 | 8 | 19 | 40 | 475 | 107 | 360 | 8 | 5 |
| Whitehouse | 7,957 | 10 | 0 | 2 | 0 | 8 | 100 | 18 | 73 | 9 | 0 |
| White Oak | 6,377 | 3 | 0 | 1 | 0 | 2 | 141 | 30 | 91 | 20 | 0 |
| Whitesboro | 4,056 | 7 | 0 | 0 | 3 | 4 | 113 | 18 | 92 | 3 | 0 |
| White Settlement | 16,471 | 45 | 0 | 0 | 10 | 35 | 655 | 190 | 430 | 35 | 2 |
| Whitney | 2,076 | 3 | 0 | 0 | 1 | 2 | 68 | 24 | 39 | 5 | 0 |
| Wichita Falls | 100,884 | 520 | 11 | 46 | 157 | 306 | 5,618 | 1,277 | 4,011 | 330 | 16 |
| Willis | 4,325 | 48 | 1 | 2 | 11 | 34 | 156 | 63 | 82 | 11 | 0 |
| Willow Park | 4,755 | 2 | 0 | 0 | 0 | 2 | 56 | 22 | 33 | 1 | 0 |
| Wills Point | 3,839 | 6 | 0 | 0 | 0 | 6 | 51 | 24 | 23 | 4 | 0 |
| Wilmer | 3,594 | 7 | 0 | 0 | 0 | 7 | 84 | 26 | 48 | 10 | 1 |
| Windcrest | 5,386 | 16 | 1 | 2 | 11 | 2 | 394 | 43 | 332 | 19 | 1 |
| Wink | 907 | 0 | 0 | 0 | 0 | 0 | 8 | 1 | 5 | 2 | 0 |
| Winnsboro | 3,969 | 20 | 1 | 0 | 1 | 18 | 49 | 26 | 22 | 1 | 0 |
| Winters | 2,535 | 7 | 0 | 2 | 1 | 4 | 41 | 28 | 13 | 0 | 0 |
| Wolfe City | 1,640 | 4 | 0 | 0 | 0 | 4 | 20 | 10 | 10 | 0 | 0 |
| Wolfforth | 3,619 | 7 | 0 | 1 | 3 | 3 | 53 | 22 | 28 | 3 | 0 |
| Woodville | 2,266 | 8 | 0 | 5 | 1 | 2 | 29 | 9 | 20 | 0 | 0 |
| Woodway | 8,823 | 21 | 0 | 5 | 1 | 15 | 148 | 15 | 128 | 5 | 1 |
| Wortham | 1,090 | 8 | 0 | 0 | 2 | 6 | 32 | 5 | 21 | 6 | 4 |
| Wylie | 41,824 | 26 | 1 | 6 | 4 | 15 | 696 | 191 | 478 | 27 | 1 |
| Yoakum | 5,443 | 13 | 1 | 0 | 6 | 6 | 226 | 104 | 118 | 4 | 0 |
| Yorktown | 2,145 | 5 | 0 | 3 | 0 | 2 | 30 | 14 | 13 | 3 | 1 |
| **UTAH** | | | | | | | | | | | |
| American Fork/Cedar Hills | 38,183 | 34 | 0 | 8 | 10 | 16 | 1,174 | 162 | 969 | 43 | 1 |
| Big Water | 403 | 4 | 0 | 0 | 0 | 4 | 0 | 0 | 0 | 0 | 0 |
| Blanding | 3,280 | 14 | 0 | 0 | 0 | 14 | 60 | 13 | 46 | 1 | 0 |
| Bountiful | 44,591 | 56 | 0 | 15 | 10 | 31 | 1,147 | 156 | 954 | 37 | 2 |
| Brian Head | 127 | 0 | 0 | 0 | 0 | 0 | 30 | 6 | 24 | 0 | 0 |
| Brigham City | 18,750 | 47 | 0 | 14 | 5 | 28 | 496 | 81 | 400 | 15 | 0 |
| Cedar City | 29,568 | 41 | 1 | 18 | 7 | 15 | 746 | 105 | 610 | 31 | 2 |
| Centerville | 15,763 | 10 | 0 | 0 | 1 | 9 | 387 | 41 | 328 | 18 | 0 |
| Clearfield | 27,913 | 49 | 0 | 10 | 8 | 31 | 860 | 112 | 713 | 35 | 7 |
| Clinton | 20,745 | 19 | 0 | 7 | 4 | 8 | 335 | 47 | 272 | 16 | 1 |
| Cottonwood Heights | 35,258 | 54 | 1 | 5 | 15 | 33 | 1,134 | 227 | 837 | 70 | 3 |
| Draper | 44,537 | 46 | 1 | 10 | 4 | 31 | 970 | 231 | 670 | 69 | 7 |
| Enoch | 5,263 | 3 | 0 | 0 | 0 | 3 | 46 | 20 | 25 | 1 | 0 |
| Farmington | 17,788 | 3 | 0 | 3 | 0 | 0 | 166 | 29 | 127 | 10 | 0 |
| Grantsville | 9,402 | 6 | 0 | 1 | 0 | 5 | 116 | 24 | 80 | 12 | 1 |
| Harrisville | 6,367 | 18 | 0 | 2 | 12 | 4 | 313 | 27 | 277 | 9 | 0 |
| Heber | 10,068 | 2 | 0 | 1 | 1 | 0 | 75 | 11 | 61 | 3 | 0 |
| Helper | 1,852 | 1 | 0 | 0 | 0 | 1 | 24 | 3 | 18 | 3 | 2 |
| Hildale | 1,967 | 3 | 0 | 0 | 0 | 3 | 4 | 2 | 2 | 0 | 0 |
| Hurricane | 13,961 | 28 | 0 | 5 | 0 | 23 | 307 | 62 | 223 | 22 | 1 |
| Ivins | 8,294 | 4 | 0 | 2 | 0 | 2 | 54 | 15 | 37 | 2 | 1 |
| Kanab | 3,786 | 9 | 0 | 1 | 0 | 8 | 133 | 23 | 107 | 3 | 1 |
| Kaysville | 26,363 | 18 | 0 | 8 | 3 | 7 | 426 | 73 | 331 | 22 | 0 |
| La Verkin | 4,602 | 5 | 0 | 1 | 0 | 4 | 51 | 15 | 32 | 4 | 0 |
| Layton | 65,947 | 115 | 0 | 21 | 23 | 71 | 1,953 | 240 | 1,647 | 66 | 4 |
| Leeds | 774 | 0 | 0 | 0 | 0 | 0 | 3 | 0 | 2 | 1 | 0 |
| Lehi | 51,307 | 26 | 0 | 11 | 0 | 15 | 871 | 169 | 648 | 54 | 2 |
| Lindon | 10,666 | 10 | 0 | 2 | 3 | 5 | 306 | 39 | 252 | 15 | 1 |
| Logan | 49,105 | 45 | 0 | 11 | 1 | 33 | 770 | 137 | 602 | 31 | 5 |
| Lone Peak | 27,542 | 12 | 0 | 5 | 1 | 6 | 343 | 100 | 230 | 13 | 4 |
| Mapleton | 8,183 | 1 | 0 | 0 | 0 | 1 | 92 | 10 | 80 | 2 | 0 |
| Midvale | 28,099 | 103 | 0 | 14 | 22 | 67 | 1,640 | 361 | 1,070 | 209 | 5 |
| Moab | 5,130 | 14 | 0 | 1 | 1 | 12 | 261 | 34 | 218 | 9 | 0 |
| Monticello | 2,015 | 2 | 0 | 1 | 0 | 1 | 21 | 8 | 13 | 0 | 1 |
| Mount Pleasant | 2,811 | 4 | 0 | 1 | 0 | 3 | 80 | 23 | 44 | 13 | 0 |
| Murray | 46,026 | 187 | 0 | 29 | 53 | 105 | 3,669 | 552 | 2,766 | 351 | 6 |
| Naples | 1,735 | 1 | 0 | 0 | 0 | 1 | 50 | 8 | 38 | 4 | 0 |
| Nephi | 5,459 | 6 | 0 | 1 | 0 | 5 | 151 | 44 | 97 | 10 | 2 |
| North Ogden | 17,897 | 8 | 1 | 4 | 1 | 2 | 267 | 46 | 216 | 5 | 0 |
| North Park | 12,739 | 13 | 0 | 10 | 0 | 3 | 274 | 37 | 226 | 11 | 3 |
| North Salt Lake | 14,026 | 5 | 0 | 2 | 0 | 3 | 350 | 114 | 194 | 42 | 0 |
| Ogden | 83,016 | 391 | 4 | 31 | 107 | 249 | 4,040 | 771 | 2,955 | 314 | 23 |
| Orem | 93,785 | 50 | 1 | 14 | 22 | 13 | 2,520 | 220 | 2,184 | 116 | 1 |
| Park City | 7,998 | 21 | 0 | 0 | 5 | 16 | 512 | 52 | 447 | 13 | 0 |
| Parowan | 2,615 | 3 | 0 | 1 | 0 | 2 | 14 | 4 | 9 | 1 | 0 |

[1] The FBI does not publish arson data unless it receives data from either the agency or the state for all 12 months of the calendar year.

## Table 8. Offenses Known to Law Enforcement, by State and City, 2009—*Continued*

(Number.)

| State/city | Population | Violent crime | Murder and non-negligent man-slaughter | Forcible rape | Robbery | Aggravated assault | Property crime | Burglary | Larceny-theft | Motor vehicle theft | Arson[1] |
|---|---|---|---|---|---|---|---|---|---|---|---|
| **UTAH**—*Continued* | | | | | | | | | | | |
| Payson | 17,890 | 15 | 0 | 4 | 3 | 8 | 577 | 90 | 465 | 22 | 0 |
| Perry | 4,080 | 0 | 0 | 0 | 0 | 0 | 63 | 6 | 54 | 3 | 0 |
| Pleasant Grove | 35,016 | 19 | 1 | 7 | 2 | 9 | 571 | 107 | 438 | 26 | 1 |
| Pleasant View | 7,183 | 2 | 0 | 2 | 0 | 0 | 103 | 13 | 86 | 4 | 0 |
| Price | 7,957 | 12 | 0 | 3 | 1 | 8 | 380 | 60 | 308 | 12 | 0 |
| Provo | 119,472 | 167 | 1 | 35 | 32 | 99 | 2,919 | 407 | 2,367 | 145 | 14 |
| Richfield | 7,220 | 3 | 0 | 2 | 0 | 1 | 262 | 42 | 211 | 9 | 0 |
| Riverdale | 8,135 | 23 | 0 | 3 | 8 | 12 | 560 | 27 | 516 | 17 | 2 |
| Roosevelt | 5,088 | 7 | 0 | 2 | 0 | 5 | 202 | 45 | 154 | 3 | 1 |
| Roy | 35,761 | 29 | 2 | 11 | 7 | 9 | 975 | 181 | 766 | 28 | 6 |
| Salem | 6,635 | 4 | 0 | 3 | 0 | 1 | 75 | 11 | 60 | 4 | 0 |
| Salina | 2,403 | 3 | 0 | 0 | 0 | 3 | 119 | 29 | 87 | 3 | 0 |
| Salt Lake City | 180,724 | 1,276 | 3 | 100 | 411 | 762 | 14,503 | 2,173 | 10,888 | 1,442 | 55 |
| Sandy | 97,031 | 167 | 2 | 22 | 23 | 120 | 3,456 | 565 | 2,685 | 206 | 13 |
| Santaquin/Genola | 9,990 | 3 | 0 | 0 | 0 | 3 | 125 | 30 | 88 | 7 | 0 |
| Saratoga Springs | 21,450 | 2 | 0 | 1 | 0 | 1 | 224 | 54 | 164 | 6 | 0 |
| Smithfield | 9,770 | 6 | 0 | 0 | 0 | 6 | 143 | 41 | 97 | 5 | 0 |
| South Jordan | 54,042 | 39 | 1 | 6 | 8 | 24 | 1,184 | 224 | 896 | 64 | 2 |
| South Ogden | 15,989 | 38 | 0 | 4 | 6 | 28 | 384 | 76 | 294 | 14 | 4 |
| South Salt Lake | 21,448 | 197 | 1 | 44 | 55 | 97 | 1,813 | 295 | 1,247 | 271 | 7 |
| Spanish Fork | 32,882 | 8 | 0 | 4 | 2 | 2 | 651 | 109 | 517 | 25 | 0 |
| Springville | 29,395 | 41 | 1 | 5 | 7 | 28 | 839 | 113 | 695 | 31 | 2 |
| St. George | 75,391 | 92 | 0 | 13 | 13 | 66 | 1,540 | 322 | 1,143 | 75 | 12 |
| Stockton | 588 | 0 | 0 | 0 | 0 | 0 | 2 | 0 | 2 | 0 | 0 |
| Sunset | 4,892 | 4 | 0 | 1 | 1 | 2 | 130 | 26 | 100 | 4 | 0 |
| Syracuse | 24,168 | 18 | 0 | 4 | 0 | 14 | 312 | 50 | 258 | 4 | 5 |
| Taylorsville City | 58,472 | 190 | 1 | 25 | 51 | 113 | 3,220 | 491 | 2,429 | 300 | 17 |
| Tooele | 30,851 | 76 | 0 | 19 | 10 | 47 | 1,085 | 223 | 810 | 52 | 10 |
| Tremonton | 6,891 | 4 | 0 | 3 | 1 | 0 | 174 | 35 | 135 | 4 | 0 |
| Vernal | 8,769 | 14 | 0 | 4 | 0 | 10 | 382 | 44 | 318 | 20 | 2 |
| Washington | 19,183 | 33 | 0 | 3 | 5 | 25 | 367 | 66 | 285 | 16 | 1 |
| Wellington | 1,553 | 1 | 0 | 0 | 0 | 1 | 29 | 12 | 15 | 2 | 0 |
| West Bountiful | 5,402 | 2 | 0 | 1 | 0 | 1 | 210 | 18 | 181 | 11 | 0 |
| West Jordan | 107,113 | 165 | 4 | 24 | 36 | 101 | 3,617 | 532 | 2,807 | 278 | 16 |
| West Valley | 124,472 | 564 | 4 | 87 | 155 | 318 | 6,263 | 1,068 | 4,377 | 818 | 15 |
| Woods Cross | 8,946 | 12 | 0 | 4 | 3 | 5 | 233 | 36 | 177 | 20 | 1 |
| **VERMONT** | | | | | | | | | | | |
| Barre | 8,790 | 7 | 0 | 1 | 0 | 6 | 230 | 34 | 196 | 0 | 1 |
| Barre Town | 8,049 | 0 | 0 | 0 | 0 | 0 | 137 | 30 | 102 | 5 | 0 |
| Bennington | 15,026 | 45 | 0 | 5 | 5 | 35 | 477 | 77 | 377 | 23 | 1 |
| Berlin | 2,818 | 1 | 0 | 0 | 0 | 1 | 40 | 2 | 38 | 0 | 0 |
| Brandon | 3,860 | 3 | 0 | 0 | 1 | 2 | 56 | 15 | 41 | 0 | 0 |
| Brattleboro | 11,438 | 35 | 1 | 3 | 6 | 25 | 574 | 152 | 408 | 14 | 1 |
| Bristol | 3,736 | 0 | 0 | 0 | 0 | 0 | 0 | 0 | 0 | 0 | 0 |
| Burlington | 38,794 | 118 | 0 | 12 | 14 | 92 | 1,760 | 235 | 1,493 | 32 | 2 |
| Castleton | 4,647 | 1 | 0 | 0 | 0 | 1 | 23 | 10 | 12 | 1 | 0 |
| Chester | 2,995 | 1 | 0 | 0 | 0 | 1 | 55 | 20 | 34 | 1 | 0 |
| Colchester | 17,274 | 19 | 0 | 1 | 5 | 13 | 554 | 103 | 436 | 15 | 2 |
| Dover | 1,434 | 0 | 0 | 0 | 0 | 0 | 126 | 13 | 112 | 1 | 0 |
| Essex | 19,759 | 16 | 1 | 6 | 1 | 8 | 393 | 74 | 310 | 9 | 2 |
| Fair Haven | 2,923 | 2 | 0 | 0 | 0 | 2 | 100 | 21 | 75 | 4 | 0 |
| Hardwick | 3,209 | 6 | 0 | 0 | 0 | 6 | 100 | 39 | 60 | 1 | 0 |
| Hartford | 10,730 | 5 | 0 | 0 | 0 | 5 | 175 | 42 | 127 | 6 | 0 |
| Hinesburg | 4,660 | 0 | 0 | 0 | 0 | 0 | 80 | 11 | 66 | 3 | 0 |
| Ludlow | 2,659 | 1 | 0 | 0 | 1 | 0 | 74 | 17 | 57 | 0 | 0 |
| Manchester | 4,279 | 2 | 0 | 0 | 1 | 1 | 97 | 13 | 81 | 3 | 0 |
| Middlebury | 8,281 | 13 | 0 | 5 | 2 | 6 | 263 | 19 | 243 | 1 | 1 |
| Milton | 10,853 | 7 | 0 | 1 | 2 | 4 | 278 | 52 | 223 | 3 | 3 |
| Montpelier | 7,731 | 13 | 0 | 2 | 1 | 10 | 352 | 40 | 307 | 5 | 0 |
| Morristown | 5,606 | 6 | 0 | 0 | 1 | 5 | 123 | 17 | 102 | 4 | 0 |
| Mount Tabor | 197 | 0 | 0 | 0 | 0 | 0 | 0 | 0 | 0 | 0 | 0 |
| Newport | 5,163 | 5 | 0 | 1 | 2 | 2 | 157 | 35 | 121 | 1 | 0 |
| Northfield | 5,735 | 8 | 0 | 3 | 2 | 3 | 101 | 28 | 71 | 2 | 0 |
| Norwich | 3,519 | 2 | 0 | 0 | 0 | 2 | 20 | 8 | 12 | 0 | 0 |
| Randolph | 5,057 | 6 | 0 | 0 | 0 | 6 | 31 | 6 | 25 | 0 | 0 |
| Richmond | 4,167 | 5 | 0 | 1 | 0 | 4 | 21 | 10 | 9 | 2 | 0 |
| Royalton | 2,421 | 0 | 0 | 0 | 0 | 0 | 0 | 0 | 0 | 0 | 0 |
| Rutland | 16,688 | 74 | 0 | 6 | 23 | 45 | 916 | 156 | 734 | 26 | 6 |
| Rutland Town | 4,076 | 0 | 0 | 0 | 0 | 0 | 0 | 0 | 0 | 0 | 0 |
| Shelburne | 7,161 | 3 | 0 | 0 | 0 | 3 | 78 | 25 | 49 | 4 | 0 |
| South Burlington | 17,893 | 28 | 0 | 7 | 1 | 20 | 612 | 59 | 541 | 12 | 1 |

[1] The FBI does not publish arson data unless it receives data from either the agency or the state for all 12 months of the calendar year.

## Table 8. Offenses Known to Law Enforcement, by State and City, 2009—*Continued*

(Number.)

| State/city | Population | Violent crime | Murder and non-negligent man-slaughter | Forcible rape | Robbery | Aggravated assault | Property crime | Burglary | Larceny-theft | Motor vehicle theft | Arson[1] |
|---|---|---|---|---|---|---|---|---|---|---|---|
| **VERMONT**—*Continued* | | | | | | | | | | | |
| Springfield | 8,551 | 31 | 0 | 2 | 3 | 26 | 212 | 56 | 149 | 7 | 5 |
| St. Albans | 7,207 | 29 | 0 | 3 | 3 | 23 | 441 | 68 | 369 | 4 | 4 |
| St. Johnsbury | 7,404 | 6 | 0 | 2 | 2 | 2 | 121 | 43 | 77 | 1 | 1 |
| Stowe | 4,984 | 1 | 0 | 0 | 0 | 1 | 174 | 19 | 153 | 2 | 1 |
| Swanton | 6,451 | 3 | 0 | 0 | 1 | 2 | 90 | 15 | 73 | 2 | 0 |
| Vergennes | 2,658 | 2 | 0 | 1 | 0 | 1 | 17 | 2 | 15 | 0 | 0 |
| Waterbury | 5,399 | 7 | 0 | 0 | 1 | 6 | 59 | 9 | 50 | 0 | 0 |
| Weathersfield | 2,836 | 0 | 0 | 0 | 0 | 0 | 25 | 10 | 14 | 1 | 0 |
| Williston | 8,515 | 11 | 0 | 0 | 2 | 9 | 317 | 23 | 290 | 4 | 0 |
| Wilmington | 2,351 | 2 | 0 | 0 | 0 | 2 | 43 | 9 | 33 | 1 | 0 |
| Windsor | 3,585 | 8 | 0 | 0 | 0 | 8 | 56 | 17 | 37 | 2 | 1 |
| Winhall | 796 | 0 | 0 | 0 | 0 | 0 | 74 | 8 | 65 | 1 | 0 |
| Winooski | 6,401 | 20 | 0 | 1 | 4 | 15 | 346 | 74 | 265 | 7 | 4 |
| Woodstock | 3,122 | 1 | 0 | 0 | 1 | 0 | 31 | 7 | 21 | 3 | 0 |
| **VIRGINIA** | | | | | | | | | | | |
| Abingdon | 8,034 | 14 | 0 | 2 | 1 | 11 | 299 | 28 | 262 | 9 | 0 |
| Alexandria | 146,145 | 287 | 5 | 12 | 141 | 129 | 3,296 | 347 | 2,613 | 336 | 3 |
| Altavista | 3,362 | 12 | 0 | 1 | 2 | 9 | 103 | 22 | 75 | 6 | 1 |
| Amherst | 2,216 | 1 | 0 | 0 | 1 | 0 | 25 | 5 | 20 | 0 | 0 |
| Appalachia | 1,729 | 1 | 0 | 1 | 0 | 0 | 66 | 8 | 55 | 3 | 1 |
| Ashland | 7,152 | 29 | 0 | 0 | 10 | 19 | 273 | 21 | 234 | 18 | 0 |
| Bedford | 6,335 | 20 | 0 | 4 | 5 | 11 | 206 | 26 | 170 | 10 | 0 |
| Berryville | 3,187 | 4 | 1 | 0 | 0 | 3 | 80 | 9 | 71 | 0 | 0 |
| Big Stone Gap | 5,652 | 9 | 0 | 1 | 1 | 7 | 176 | 19 | 150 | 7 | 0 |
| Blacksburg | 42,047 | 50 | 0 | 15 | 11 | 24 | 700 | 165 | 507 | 28 | 2 |
| Blackstone | 3,568 | 14 | 0 | 0 | 5 | 9 | 135 | 21 | 107 | 7 | 1 |
| Bluefield | 5,122 | 7 | 0 | 1 | 2 | 4 | 246 | 27 | 214 | 5 | 1 |
| Bowling Green | 1,031 | 0 | 0 | 0 | 0 | 0 | 0 | 0 | 0 | 0 | 0 |
| Boykins | 599 | 0 | 0 | 0 | 0 | 0 | 5 | 2 | 3 | 0 | 0 |
| Bridgewater | 5,458 | 2 | 0 | 0 | 0 | 2 | 26 | 9 | 15 | 2 | 0 |
| Bristol | 17,502 | 54 | 0 | 5 | 11 | 38 | 627 | 108 | 492 | 27 | 5 |
| Broadway | 3,335 | 1 | 0 | 0 | 0 | 1 | 10 | 1 | 6 | 3 | 0 |
| Brookneal | 1,248 | 2 | 0 | 1 | 0 | 1 | 13 | 2 | 10 | 1 | 0 |
| Buena Vista | 6,509 | 9 | 0 | 0 | 2 | 7 | 102 | 1 | 99 | 2 | 2 |
| Burkeville | 470 | 2 | 0 | 0 | 1 | 1 | 13 | 2 | 10 | 1 | 0 |
| Cape Charles | 1,510 | 0 | 0 | 0 | 0 | 0 | 13 | 3 | 10 | 0 | 0 |
| Cedar Bluff | 1,039 | 1 | 0 | 1 | 0 | 0 | 11 | 3 | 7 | 1 | 0 |
| Charlottesville | 41,798 | 247 | 0 | 35 | 88 | 124 | 2,070 | 184 | 1,763 | 123 | 9 |
| Chase City | 2,307 | 5 | 0 | 0 | 1 | 4 | 66 | 8 | 56 | 2 | 1 |
| Chatham | 1,543 | 0 | 0 | 0 | 0 | 0 | 12 | 0 | 12 | 0 | 0 |
| Chesapeake | 223,261 | 831 | 12 | 42 | 229 | 548 | 7,731 | 1,317 | 5,985 | 429 | 30 |
| Chilhowie | 1,737 | 0 | 0 | 0 | 0 | 0 | 25 | 6 | 17 | 2 | 0 |
| Chincoteague | 4,293 | 3 | 0 | 0 | 0 | 3 | 85 | 18 | 55 | 12 | 0 |
| Christiansburg | 19,775 | 35 | 2 | 9 | 7 | 17 | 722 | 107 | 600 | 15 | 5 |
| Clarksville | 1,251 | 4 | 0 | 0 | 3 | 1 | 25 | 0 | 25 | 0 | 0 |
| Clifton Forge | 3,895 | 8 | 0 | 1 | 1 | 6 | 88 | 21 | 66 | 1 | 1 |
| Clintwood | 1,517 | 3 | 0 | 0 | 0 | 3 | 35 | 9 | 25 | 1 | 0 |
| Coeburn | 1,974 | 4 | 0 | 1 | 1 | 2 | 63 | 11 | 50 | 2 | 1 |
| Colonial Beach | 3,859 | 4 | 0 | 1 | 1 | 2 | 71 | 16 | 51 | 4 | 0 |
| Colonial Heights | 17,932 | 48 | 0 | 2 | 22 | 24 | 842 | 65 | 743 | 34 | 7 |
| Covington | 6,124 | 20 | 1 | 6 | 2 | 11 | 173 | 30 | 137 | 6 | 8 |
| Crewe | 2,274 | 6 | 0 | 1 | 4 | 1 | 64 | 10 | 51 | 3 | 0 |
| Culpeper | 14,562 | 70 | 0 | 6 | 16 | 48 | 460 | 35 | 415 | 10 | 1 |
| Damascus | 1,081 | 3 | 0 | 2 | 0 | 1 | 25 | 1 | 24 | 0 | 0 |
| Danville | 44,442 | 174 | 8 | 7 | 80 | 79 | 2,308 | 515 | 1,724 | 69 | 13 |
| Dayton | 1,354 | 0 | 0 | 0 | 0 | 0 | 21 | 3 | 18 | 0 | 0 |
| Dublin | 2,180 | 3 | 0 | 0 | 2 | 1 | 75 | 22 | 51 | 2 | 0 |
| Dumfries | 4,792 | 23 | 0 | 2 | 15 | 6 | 170 | 35 | 115 | 20 | 0 |
| Edinburg | 903 | 1 | 0 | 1 | 0 | 0 | 8 | 3 | 5 | 0 | 0 |
| Elkton | 2,625 | 0 | 0 | 0 | 0 | 0 | 33 | 4 | 28 | 1 | 0 |
| Emporia | 5,662 | 43 | 0 | 5 | 10 | 28 | 337 | 62 | 260 | 15 | 2 |
| Exmore | 1,341 | 3 | 0 | 0 | 1 | 2 | 44 | 8 | 34 | 2 | 0 |
| Fairfax City | 24,194 | 27 | 0 | 1 | 15 | 11 | 621 | 35 | 564 | 22 | 6 |
| Falls Church | 11,301 | 16 | 0 | 3 | 6 | 7 | 315 | 18 | 279 | 18 | 5 |
| Farmville | 7,462 | 16 | 4 | 1 | 1 | 10 | 173 | 15 | 155 | 3 | 0 |
| Franklin | 8,980 | 31 | 1 | 2 | 14 | 14 | 355 | 64 | 280 | 11 | 6 |
| Fredericksburg | 23,326 | 114 | 2 | 6 | 22 | 84 | 1,094 | 93 | 975 | 26 | 4 |
| Fries | 546 | 0 | 0 | 0 | 0 | 0 | 0 | 0 | 0 | 0 | 0 |
| Front Royal | 14,731 | 33 | 0 | 7 | 11 | 15 | 600 | 56 | 520 | 24 | 0 |
| Galax | 6,828 | 28 | 1 | 0 | 4 | 23 | 301 | 37 | 258 | 6 | 2 |
| Gate City | 2,037 | 3 | 0 | 1 | 0 | 2 | 37 | 7 | 27 | 3 | 0 |

[1] The FBI does not publish arson data unless it receives data from either the agency or the state for all 12 months of the calendar year.

**Table 8. Offenses Known to Law Enforcement, by State and City, 2009**—*Continued*

(Number.)

| State/city | Population | Violent crime | Murder and non-negligent man-slaughter | Forcible rape | Robbery | Aggravated assault | Property crime | Burglary | Larceny-theft | Motor vehicle theft | Arson[1] |
|---|---|---|---|---|---|---|---|---|---|---|---|
| **VIRGINIA**—*Continued* | | | | | | | | | | | |
| Glade Spring | 1,538 | 1 | 0 | 0 | 1 | 0 | 1 | 0 | 1 | 0 | 0 |
| Glasgow | 1,003 | 0 | 0 | 0 | 0 | 0 | 4 | 0 | 4 | 0 | 0 |
| Glen Lyn | 164 | 0 | 0 | 0 | 0 | 0 | 2 | 1 | 0 | 1 | 1 |
| Gordonsville | 1,720 | 2 | 0 | 0 | 0 | 2 | 21 | 3 | 17 | 1 | 0 |
| Gretna | 1,185 | 3 | 0 | 0 | 0 | 3 | 22 | 7 | 14 | 1 | 0 |
| Grottoes | 2,192 | 1 | 0 | 0 | 0 | 1 | 31 | 2 | 29 | 0 | 0 |
| Grundy | 947 | 0 | 0 | 0 | 0 | 0 | 5 | 1 | 4 | 0 | 0 |
| Halifax | 1,280 | 1 | 1 | 0 | 0 | 0 | 31 | 6 | 22 | 3 | 1 |
| Hampton | 145,932 | 454 | 11 | 27 | 195 | 221 | 5,226 | 835 | 4,001 | 390 | 31 |
| Harrisonburg | 44,597 | 134 | 0 | 10 | 27 | 97 | 1,236 | 187 | 996 | 53 | 5 |
| Haymarket | 1,268 | 1 | 0 | 0 | 0 | 1 | 24 | 2 | 22 | 0 | 0 |
| Haysi | 308 | 0 | 0 | 0 | 0 | 0 | 3 | 1 | 2 | 0 | 0 |
| Herndon | 22,078 | 48 | 1 | 9 | 15 | 23 | 395 | 27 | 344 | 24 | 0 |
| Hillsville | 2,630 | 9 | 0 | 1 | 2 | 6 | 89 | 38 | 49 | 2 | 0 |
| Honaker | 1,438 | 1 | 0 | 0 | 0 | 1 | 22 | 2 | 20 | 0 | 0 |
| Hopewell | 23,324 | 207 | 4 | 13 | 70 | 120 | 833 | 263 | 501 | 69 | 11 |
| Hurt | 1,208 | 0 | 0 | 0 | 0 | 0 | 14 | 3 | 11 | 0 | 0 |
| Jonesville | 964 | 0 | 0 | 0 | 0 | 0 | 28 | 3 | 25 | 0 | 1 |
| Kenbridge | 1,273 | 7 | 0 | 1 | 0 | 6 | 5 | 2 | 2 | 1 | 0 |
| Kilmarnock | 1,287 | 2 | 0 | 1 | 0 | 1 | 26 | 9 | 15 | 2 | 0 |
| La Crosse | 586 | 0 | 0 | 0 | 0 | 0 | 19 | 4 | 5 | 10 | 0 |
| Lawrenceville | 1,342 | 1 | 0 | 0 | 1 | 0 | 51 | 35 | 16 | 0 | 1 |
| Lebanon | 3,186 | 6 | 0 | 0 | 2 | 4 | 104 | 7 | 94 | 3 | 0 |
| Leesburg | 41,092 | 62 | 2 | 8 | 19 | 33 | 732 | 44 | 664 | 24 | 4 |
| Lexington | 7,049 | 1 | 0 | 0 | 0 | 1 | 60 | 6 | 51 | 3 | 2 |
| Louisa | 1,583 | 1 | 0 | 1 | 0 | 0 | 22 | 3 | 17 | 2 | 0 |
| Luray | 4,840 | 3 | 0 | 0 | 2 | 1 | 140 | 16 | 115 | 9 | 1 |
| Lynchburg | 73,735 | 339 | 0 | 21 | 80 | 238 | 2,218 | 372 | 1,735 | 111 | 14 |
| Manassas | 35,321 | 173 | 2 | 10 | 56 | 105 | 1,083 | 152 | 831 | 100 | 8 |
| Manassas Park | 11,477 | 11 | 0 | 0 | 5 | 6 | 213 | 15 | 179 | 19 | 1 |
| Marion | 5,965 | 24 | 0 | 1 | 2 | 21 | 248 | 14 | 227 | 7 | 0 |
| Martinsville | 14,509 | 39 | 0 | 2 | 9 | 28 | 499 | 90 | 388 | 21 | 8 |
| Middleburg | 979 | 0 | 0 | 0 | 0 | 0 | 16 | 0 | 15 | 1 | 0 |
| Middletown | 1,154 | 3 | 0 | 2 | 1 | 0 | 23 | 4 | 19 | 0 | 1 |
| Mount Jackson | 2,014 | 0 | 0 | 0 | 0 | 0 | 50 | 9 | 35 | 6 | 0 |
| Narrows | 2,151 | 5 | 0 | 2 | 0 | 3 | 11 | 5 | 5 | 1 | 1 |
| New Market | 1,865 | 1 | 0 | 0 | 0 | 1 | 13 | 6 | 5 | 2 | 0 |
| Norfolk | 235,097 | 1,542 | 34 | 102 | 630 | 776 | 12,940 | 2,078 | 9,912 | 950 | 42 |
| Norton | 3,697 | 8 | 0 | 1 | 2 | 5 | 285 | 18 | 265 | 2 | 1 |
| Occoquan | 824 | 0 | 0 | 0 | 0 | 0 | 2 | 0 | 2 | 0 | 0 |
| Onancock | 1,375 | 1 | 0 | 0 | 0 | 1 | 34 | 7 | 26 | 1 | 0 |
| Onley | 468 | 2 | 0 | 0 | 0 | 2 | 15 | 3 | 12 | 0 | 0 |
| Orange | 4,688 | 5 | 0 | 2 | 1 | 2 | 106 | 13 | 86 | 7 | 1 |
| Parksley | 785 | 2 | 0 | 0 | 2 | 0 | 19 | 1 | 18 | 0 | 0 |
| Pearisburg | 2,767 | 3 | 0 | 0 | 1 | 2 | 71 | 7 | 62 | 2 | 1 |
| Pembroke | 1,166 | 2 | 0 | 0 | 0 | 2 | 25 | 10 | 15 | 0 | 0 |
| Pennington Gap | 1,721 | 0 | 0 | 0 | 0 | 0 | 7 | 3 | 4 | 0 | 0 |
| Petersburg | 32,966 | 307 | 6 | 12 | 121 | 168 | 2,192 | 673 | 1,272 | 247 | 0 |
| Pocahontas | 417 | 0 | 0 | 0 | 0 | 0 | 0 | 0 | 0 | 0 | 0 |
| Poquoson | 11,902 | 28 | 0 | 4 | 1 | 23 | 165 | 24 | 131 | 10 | 4 |
| Portsmouth | 100,970 | 707 | 17 | 20 | 351 | 319 | 5,643 | 1,184 | 4,163 | 296 | 14 |
| Pound | 1,070 | 6 | 0 | 0 | 1 | 5 | 36 | 8 | 27 | 1 | 0 |
| Pulaski | 8,932 | 30 | 2 | 3 | 9 | 16 | 400 | 79 | 305 | 16 | 1 |
| Purcellville | 5,338 | 6 | 0 | 0 | 1 | 5 | 69 | 8 | 56 | 5 | 1 |
| Quantico | 614 | 0 | 0 | 0 | 0 | 0 | 2 | 0 | 2 | 0 | 0 |
| Radford | 16,216 | 80 | 1 | 15 | 8 | 56 | 514 | 167 | 335 | 12 | 5 |
| Remington | 678 | 0 | 0 | 0 | 0 | 0 | 6 | 2 | 4 | 0 | 0 |
| Rich Creek | 682 | 2 | 0 | 2 | 0 | 0 | 14 | 0 | 13 | 1 | 0 |
| Richlands | 3,983 | 12 | 1 | 0 | 2 | 9 | 224 | 64 | 155 | 5 | 0 |
| Richmond | 203,233 | 1,631 | 37 | 35 | 850 | 709 | 8,349 | 1,555 | 5,822 | 972 | 60 |
| Roanoke | 93,110 | 639 | 9 | 26 | 184 | 420 | 4,975 | 913 | 3,774 | 288 | 45 |
| Rocky Mount | 4,536 | 9 | 0 | 1 | 1 | 7 | 201 | 14 | 183 | 4 | 0 |
| Rural Retreat | 1,346 | 1 | 0 | 0 | 1 | 0 | 5 | 0 | 5 | 0 | 0 |
| Salem | 25,616 | 32 | 0 | 5 | 8 | 19 | 782 | 88 | 657 | 37 | 4 |
| Saltville | 2,207 | 3 | 0 | 0 | 0 | 3 | 44 | 9 | 35 | 0 | 0 |
| Shenandoah | 1,856 | 3 | 0 | 0 | 0 | 3 | 46 | 8 | 37 | 1 | 2 |
| Smithfield | 7,115 | 8 | 1 | 0 | 4 | 3 | 218 | 27 | 180 | 11 | 0 |
| South Boston | 7,822 | 38 | 0 | 8 | 7 | 23 | 464 | 116 | 341 | 7 | 5 |
| South Hill | 4,558 | 15 | 0 | 2 | 5 | 8 | 247 | 21 | 220 | 6 | 1 |
| Stanley | 1,562 | 1 | 0 | 0 | 1 | 0 | 50 | 1 | 47 | 2 | 1 |
| Staunton | 24,072 | 31 | 2 | 2 | 7 | 20 | 546 | 60 | 466 | 20 | 5 |

[1] The FBI does not publish arson data unless it receives data from either the agency or the state for all 12 months of the calendar year.

**Table 8. Offenses Known to Law Enforcement, by State and City, 2009—*Continued***

(Number.)

| State/city | Population | Violent crime | Murder and non-negligent man-slaughter | Forcible rape | Robbery | Aggravated assault | Property crime | Burglary | Larceny-theft | Motor vehicle theft | Arson[1] |
|---|---|---|---|---|---|---|---|---|---|---|---|
| **VIRGINIA**—*Continued* | | | | | | | | | | | |
| Stephens City | 1,505 | 0 | 0 | 0 | 0 | 0 | 58 | 9 | 43 | 6 | 1 |
| St. Paul | 963 | 0 | 0 | 0 | 0 | 0 | 30 | 4 | 26 | 0 | 0 |
| Strasburg | 4,405 | 8 | 0 | 1 | 0 | 7 | 124 | 12 | 110 | 2 | 0 |
| Suffolk | 84,929 | 289 | 6 | 33 | 81 | 169 | 2,200 | 465 | 1,641 | 94 | 41 |
| Tappahannock | 2,202 | 9 | 0 | 1 | 0 | 8 | 131 | 17 | 109 | 5 | 0 |
| Tazewell | 4,247 | 5 | 0 | 0 | 1 | 4 | 91 | 18 | 71 | 2 | 1 |
| Timberville | 1,714 | 5 | 0 | 2 | 1 | 2 | 17 | 4 | 13 | 0 | 1 |
| Victoria | 1,722 | 9 | 0 | 1 | 3 | 5 | 25 | 2 | 21 | 2 | 0 |
| Vienna | 14,946 | 10 | 2 | 0 | 4 | 4 | 301 | 27 | 267 | 7 | 0 |
| Vinton | 7,879 | 20 | 0 | 3 | 3 | 14 | 272 | 41 | 222 | 9 | 3 |
| Virginia Beach | 436,175 | 910 | 18 | 70 | 452 | 370 | 13,359 | 2,043 | 10,751 | 565 | 107 |
| Warrenton | 9,235 | 25 | 1 | 3 | 6 | 15 | 253 | 27 | 221 | 5 | 0 |
| Warsaw | 1,350 | 0 | 0 | 0 | 0 | 0 | 10 | 1 | 9 | 0 | 0 |
| Waverly | 2,142 | 6 | 0 | 0 | 3 | 3 | 18 | 3 | 13 | 2 | 0 |
| Waynesboro | 22,313 | 67 | 0 | 9 | 21 | 37 | 793 | 119 | 646 | 28 | 4 |
| Weber City | 1,322 | 0 | 0 | 0 | 0 | 0 | 29 | 2 | 27 | 0 | 0 |
| West Point | 3,177 | 2 | 0 | 1 | 1 | 0 | 38 | 9 | 26 | 3 | 0 |
| White Stone | 336 | 0 | 0 | 0 | 0 | 0 | 0 | 0 | 0 | 0 | 0 |
| Williamsburg | 12,584 | 24 | 1 | 0 | 8 | 15 | 213 | 11 | 192 | 10 | 0 |
| Winchester | 26,252 | 84 | 0 | 9 | 40 | 35 | 1,166 | 150 | 977 | 39 | 4 |
| Wise | 3,226 | 3 | 0 | 0 | 0 | 3 | 101 | 11 | 84 | 6 | 1 |
| Woodstock | 4,315 | 8 | 0 | 2 | 2 | 4 | 74 | 1 | 65 | 8 | 0 |
| Wytheville | 8,336 | 17 | 0 | 0 | 7 | 10 | 218 | 13 | 198 | 7 | 1 |
| **WASHINGTON** | | | | | | | | | | | |
| Aberdeen | 16,000 | 68 | 0 | 6 | 28 | 34 | 1,010 | 198 | 734 | 78 | 5 |
| Airway Heights | 5,384 | 12 | 0 | 0 | 2 | 10 | 132 | 35 | 83 | 14 | 0 |
| Algona | 2,763 | 12 | 0 | 3 | 0 | 9 | 24 | 3 | 16 | 5 | 0 |
| Anacortes | 17,063 | 22 | 0 | 1 | 7 | 14 | 459 | 109 | 328 | 22 | 2 |
| Arlington | 17,413 | 31 | 1 | 3 | 15 | 12 | 608 | 94 | 429 | 85 | 0 |
| Asotin | 1,133 | 17 | 0 | 0 | 1 | 16 | 15 | 6 | 8 | 1 | 0 |
| Auburn | 56,934 | 274 | 4 | 13 | 92 | 165 | 3,321 | 590 | 2,362 | 369 | 18 |
| Bainbridge Island | 22,061 | 31 | 0 | 4 | 4 | 23 | 302 | 80 | 210 | 12 | 2 |
| Battle Ground | 17,865 | 62 | 1 | 24 | 7 | 30 | 484 | 59 | 392 | 33 | 3 |
| Bellevue | 125,054 | 162 | 2 | 25 | 61 | 74 | 3,950 | 621 | 3,150 | 179 | 16 |
| Bellingham | 80,243 | 171 | 2 | 37 | 48 | 84 | 4,341 | 651 | 3,547 | 143 | 17 |
| Bingen | 681 | 2 | 0 | 0 | 0 | 2 | 41 | 22 | 13 | 6 | 0 |
| Black Diamond | 4,007 | 10 | 0 | 1 | 0 | 9 | 56 | 15 | 35 | 6 | 0 |
| Blaine | 5,128 | 6 | 0 | 2 | 2 | 2 | 177 | 29 | 144 | 4 | 2 |
| Bonney Lake | 17,461 | 26 | 0 | 4 | 8 | 14 | 394 | 71 | 297 | 26 | 0 |
| Bothell | 32,517 | 33 | 0 | 3 | 17 | 13 | 884 | 169 | 649 | 66 | 6 |
| Bremerton | 35,888 | 250 | 0 | 46 | 46 | 158 | 1,696 | 362 | 1,222 | 112 | 22 |
| Brewster | 2,076 | 8 | 0 | 2 | 1 | 5 | 115 | 36 | 69 | 10 | 1 |
| Brier | 6,340 | 3 | 0 | 1 | 0 | 2 | 86 | 22 | 62 | 2 | 4 |
| Buckley | 5,514 | 7 | 0 | 0 | 1 | 6 | 126 | 33 | 89 | 4 | 3 |
| Burien | 31,263 | 167 | 2 | 13 | 62 | 90 | 1,536 | 352 | 957 | 227 | 13 |
| Burlington | 8,920 | 12 | 0 | 4 | 4 | 4 | 1,157 | 118 | 988 | 51 | 10 |
| Camas | 18,618 | 14 | 0 | 7 | 3 | 4 | 348 | 61 | 274 | 13 | 4 |
| Carnation | 1,806 | 0 | 0 | 0 | 0 | 0 | 29 | 2 | 25 | 2 | 1 |
| Castle Rock | 2,120 | 6 | 0 | 0 | 0 | 6 | 78 | 13 | 60 | 5 | 1 |
| Centralia | 15,811 | 82 | 0 | 17 | 14 | 51 | 767 | 151 | 550 | 66 | 15 |
| Chehalis | 7,397 | 11 | 0 | 3 | 2 | 6 | 570 | 65 | 474 | 31 | 2 |
| Cheney | 10,572 | 24 | 0 | 6 | 4 | 14 | 311 | 57 | 242 | 12 | 1 |
| Chewelah | 2,313 | 7 | 0 | 1 | 1 | 5 | 81 | 30 | 48 | 3 | 0 |
| Clarkston | 7,194 | 20 | 0 | 2 | 5 | 13 | 346 | 55 | 271 | 20 | 0 |
| Cle Elum | 3,514 | 3 | 0 | 1 | 0 | 2 | 150 | 32 | 106 | 12 | 0 |
| Clyde Hill | 2,708 | 4 | 0 | 0 | 0 | 4 | 31 | 3 | 23 | 5 | 0 |
| Colfax | 2,744 | 0 | 0 | 0 | 0 | 0 | 11 | 1 | 9 | 1 | 2 |
| College Place | 9,106 | 2 | 0 | 1 | 0 | 1 | 247 | 48 | 195 | 4 | 0 |
| Colville | 4,919 | 3 | 0 | 0 | 1 | 2 | 157 | 18 | 136 | 3 | 0 |
| Connell | 3,214 | 1 | 0 | 0 | 0 | 1 | 24 | 2 | 22 | 0 | 0 |
| Cosmopolis | 1,669 | 1 | 0 | 1 | 0 | 0 | 31 | 10 | 16 | 5 | 0 |
| Coulee Dam | 1,051 | 3 | 0 | 1 | 1 | 1 | 33 | 15 | 16 | 2 | 0 |
| Coupeville | 1,907 | 7 | 0 | 1 | 0 | 6 | 80 | 36 | 41 | 3 | 0 |
| Covington | 18,619 | 37 | 0 | 4 | 15 | 18 | 641 | 134 | 467 | 40 | 1 |
| Des Moines | 28,667 | 113 | 0 | 18 | 48 | 47 | 915 | 229 | 525 | 161 | 8 |
| Dupont | 7,799 | 7 | 0 | 1 | 2 | 4 | 69 | 15 | 50 | 4 | 0 |
| Duvall | 6,150 | 3 | 0 | 3 | 0 | 0 | 50 | 15 | 35 | 0 | 0 |
| East Wenatchee | 12,355 | 23 | 0 | 3 | 5 | 15 | 622 | 82 | 517 | 23 | 2 |
| Eatonville | 2,512 | 3 | 0 | 1 | 0 | 2 | 52 | 14 | 37 | 1 | 2 |
| Edgewood | 9,778 | 17 | 0 | 1 | 5 | 11 | 249 | 91 | 145 | 13 | 1 |
| Edmonds | 40,227 | 73 | 1 | 4 | 27 | 41 | 931 | 213 | 666 | 52 | 11 |

[1] The FBI does not publish arson data unless it receives data from either the agency or the state for all 12 months of the calendar year.

**Table 8. Offenses Known to Law Enforcement, by State and City, 2009—*Continued***

(Number.)

| State/city | Population | Violent crime | Murder and non-negligent man-slaughter | Forcible rape | Robbery | Aggravated assault | Property crime | Burglary | Larceny-theft | Motor vehicle theft | Arson[1] |
|---|---|---|---|---|---|---|---|---|---|---|---|
| **WASHINGTON**—*Continued* | | | | | | | | | | | |
| Ellensburg | 17,331 | 50 | 0 | 12 | 10 | 28 | 975 | 202 | 742 | 31 | 3 |
| Elma | 3,114 | 11 | 0 | 2 | 3 | 6 | 169 | 38 | 113 | 18 | 0 |
| Enumclaw | 10,640 | 9 | 0 | 2 | 1 | 6 | 267 | 42 | 213 | 12 | 2 |
| Ephrata | 7,399 | 20 | 1 | 0 | 8 | 11 | 530 | 124 | 382 | 24 | 2 |
| Everett | 98,431 | 610 | 2 | 51 | 263 | 294 | 6,948 | 1,099 | 5,070 | 779 | 15 |
| Everson | 2,210 | 5 | 0 | 0 | 1 | 4 | 70 | 16 | 51 | 3 | 0 |
| Federal Way | 84,219 | 369 | 5 | 51 | 198 | 115 | 4,533 | 741 | 3,231 | 561 | 13 |
| Ferndale | 11,669 | 19 | 2 | 1 | 6 | 10 | 323 | 60 | 251 | 12 | 1 |
| Fife | 8,622 | 42 | 0 | 4 | 11 | 27 | 591 | 115 | 395 | 81 | 0 |
| Fircrest | 6,251 | 18 | 0 | 2 | 2 | 14 | 117 | 34 | 76 | 7 | 0 |
| Forks | 3,276 | 26 | 2 | 5 | 2 | 17 | 92 | 23 | 68 | 1 | 0 |
| Gig Harbor | 7,059 | 19 | 0 | 5 | 7 | 7 | 403 | 54 | 333 | 16 | 1 |
| Goldendale | 3,733 | 6 | 0 | 0 | 0 | 6 | 171 | 37 | 126 | 8 | 2 |
| Grand Coulee | 1,924 | 10 | 0 | 1 | 0 | 9 | 58 | 19 | 39 | 0 | 0 |
| Grandview | 9,498 | 13 | 1 | 1 | 1 | 10 | 422 | 154 | 211 | 57 | 0 |
| Granger | 3,019 | 12 | 1 | 3 | 1 | 7 | 158 | 48 | 84 | 26 | 1 |
| Granite Falls | 3,180 | 8 | 0 | 0 | 2 | 6 | 124 | 27 | 92 | 5 | 1 |
| Hoquiam | 8,823 | 24 | 0 | 5 | 11 | 8 | 469 | 111 | 332 | 26 | 7 |
| Ilwaco | 991 | 2 | 0 | 0 | 0 | 2 | 29 | 11 | 15 | 3 | 1 |
| Issaquah | 25,019 | 19 | 0 | 4 | 9 | 6 | 633 | 51 | 531 | 51 | 1 |
| Kalama | 2,295 | 1 | 0 | 0 | 0 | 1 | 50 | 7 | 39 | 4 | 1 |
| Kelso | 12,226 | 46 | 0 | 10 | 5 | 31 | 896 | 147 | 670 | 79 | 3 |
| Kenmore | 20,568 | 22 | 0 | 1 | 3 | 18 | 404 | 131 | 229 | 44 | 5 |
| Kennewick | 64,009 | 244 | 0 | 37 | 33 | 174 | 2,312 | 352 | 1,812 | 148 | 41 |
| Kent | 84,363 | 507 | 1 | 82 | 180 | 244 | 3,820 | 828 | 2,381 | 611 | 15 |
| Kettle Falls | 1,430 | 3 | 0 | 0 | 0 | 3 | 62 | 10 | 51 | 1 | 0 |
| Kirkland | 47,565 | 59 | 0 | 8 | 22 | 29 | 1,640 | 256 | 1,286 | 98 | 9 |
| Kittitas | 1,246 | 1 | 0 | 0 | 0 | 1 | 29 | 9 | 20 | 0 | 0 |
| La Center | 2,660 | 0 | 0 | 0 | 0 | 0 | 37 | 5 | 26 | 6 | 0 |
| Lacey | 41,915 | 95 | 0 | 13 | 22 | 60 | 1,506 | 217 | 1,183 | 106 | 3 |
| Lake Forest Park | 12,394 | 9 | 0 | 2 | 2 | 5 | 238 | 78 | 143 | 17 | 0 |
| Lake Stevens | 13,758 | 25 | 0 | 3 | 10 | 12 | 455 | 76 | 344 | 35 | 8 |
| Lakewood | 56,824 | 565 | 2 | 50 | 171 | 342 | 3,040 | 588 | 2,196 | 256 | 17 |
| Langley | 1,085 | 2 | 0 | 0 | 2 | 0 | 41 | 11 | 30 | 0 | 1 |
| Liberty Lake | 7,592 | 3 | 0 | 1 | 0 | 2 | 65 | 13 | 50 | 2 | 0 |
| Long Beach | 1,361 | 3 | 2 | 0 | 0 | 1 | 77 | 18 | 57 | 2 | 0 |
| Longview | 36,778 | 114 | 1 | 31 | 29 | 53 | 2,040 | 385 | 1,438 | 217 | 17 |
| Lynden | 12,022 | 12 | 0 | 1 | 2 | 9 | 175 | 36 | 139 | 0 | 0 |
| Lynnwood | 33,544 | 108 | 0 | 9 | 53 | 46 | 2,266 | 230 | 1,887 | 149 | 8 |
| Maple Valley | 20,700 | 24 | 0 | 2 | 6 | 16 | 436 | 129 | 278 | 29 | 6 |
| Marysville | 35,110 | 89 | 1 | 9 | 34 | 45 | 1,485 | 245 | 1,093 | 147 | 7 |
| McCleary | 1,616 | 5 | 0 | 0 | 0 | 5 | 38 | 12 | 20 | 6 | 0 |
| Medina | 3,634 | 0 | 0 | 0 | 0 | 0 | 69 | 11 | 53 | 5 | 0 |
| Mercer Island | 24,411 | 11 | 0 | 2 | 2 | 7 | 411 | 74 | 323 | 14 | 5 |
| Mill Creek | 17,270 | 30 | 0 | 3 | 11 | 16 | 505 | 108 | 372 | 25 | 3 |
| Milton | 6,901 | 25 | 0 | 0 | 11 | 14 | 287 | 68 | 198 | 21 | 3 |
| Monroe | 17,458 | 59 | 0 | 11 | 10 | 38 | 529 | 81 | 386 | 62 | 4 |
| Montesano | 3,633 | 3 | 0 | 0 | 0 | 3 | 80 | 19 | 58 | 3 | 6 |
| Morton | 1,090 | 3 | 0 | 2 | 0 | 1 | 66 | 11 | 55 | 0 | 0 |
| Moses Lake | 19,214 | 98 | 0 | 23 | 21 | 54 | 1,490 | 275 | 1,116 | 99 | 6 |
| Mountlake Terrace | 19,853 | 43 | 0 | 10 | 14 | 19 | 509 | 98 | 368 | 43 | 12 |
| Mount Vernon | 32,096 | 88 | 2 | 20 | 33 | 33 | 2,124 | 275 | 1,769 | 80 | 11 |
| Moxee | 2,601 | 3 | 0 | 0 | 2 | 1 | 21 | 8 | 11 | 2 | 0 |
| Mukilteo | 21,057 | 21 | 0 | 6 | 6 | 9 | 552 | 134 | 386 | 32 | 7 |
| Newcastle | 10,138 | 3 | 0 | 0 | 0 | 3 | 224 | 54 | 147 | 23 | |
| Normandy Park | 6,225 | 2 | 0 | 0 | 1 | 1 | 139 | 47 | 88 | 4 | 0 |
| North Bend | 4,618 | 10 | 0 | 0 | 4 | 6 | 232 | 47 | 170 | 15 | |
| Oak Harbor | 23,098 | 56 | 0 | 8 | 6 | 42 | 576 | 120 | 438 | 18 | 8 |
| Oakville | 727 | 0 | 0 | 0 | 0 | 0 | 10 | 3 | 6 | 1 | 0 |
| Ocean Shores | 5,180 | 10 | 0 | 3 | 2 | 5 | 156 | 50 | 102 | 4 | 0 |
| Odessa | 913 | 3 | 0 | 0 | 0 | 3 | 26 | 14 | 11 | 1 | 0 |
| Olympia | 45,603 | 122 | 1 | 30 | 24 | 67 | 2,115 | 382 | 1,556 | 177 | 10 |
| Omak | 4,697 | 13 | 0 | 3 | 3 | 7 | 194 | 36 | 150 | 8 | 0 |
| Oroville | 1,653 | 7 | 0 | 3 | 1 | 3 | 69 | 21 | 42 | 6 | 0 |
| Othello | 6,662 | 33 | 0 | 2 | 12 | 19 | 465 | 72 | 353 | 40 | 4 |
| Pacific | 6,102 | 13 | 0 | 3 | 0 | 10 | 146 | 51 | 72 | 23 | 1 |
| Palouse | 926 | 0 | 0 | 0 | 0 | 0 | 9 | 4 | 5 | 0 | 0 |
| Pasco | 58,316 | 218 | 1 | 29 | 45 | 143 | 1,561 | 315 | 1,079 | 167 | 24 |
| Pe Ell | 681 | 6 | 0 | 0 | 0 | 6 | 18 | 6 | 10 | 2 | 0 |
| Port Angeles | 19,044 | 80 | 1 | 25 | 15 | 39 | 802 | 152 | 616 | 34 | 8 |
| Port Orchard | 7,973 | 52 | 0 | 5 | 3 | 44 | 560 | 113 | 429 | 18 | 4 |

[1] The FBI does not publish arson data unless it receives data from either the agency or the state for all 12 months of the calendar year.

## Table 8. Offenses Known to Law Enforcement, by State and City, 2009—*Continued*

(Number.)

| State/city | Population | Violent crime | Murder and non-negligent man-slaughter | Forcible rape | Robbery | Aggravated assault | Property crime | Burglary | Larceny-theft | Motor vehicle theft | Arson[1] |
|---|---|---|---|---|---|---|---|---|---|---|---|
| **WASHINGTON**—*Continued* | | | | | | | | | | | |
| Port Townsend | 9,223 | 16 | 0 | 0 | 4 | 12 | 327 | 74 | 243 | 10 | 0 |
| Poulsbo | 8,271 | 44 | 0 | 8 | 5 | 31 | 315 | 54 | 260 | 1 | 2 |
| Prosser | 5,148 | 6 | 0 | 3 | 1 | 2 | 143 | 31 | 102 | 10 | 2 |
| Pullman | 27,141 | 39 | 0 | 7 | 2 | 30 | 430 | 96 | 320 | 14 | 2 |
| Puyallup | 36,659 | 151 | 0 | 20 | 50 | 81 | 2,980 | 420 | 2,238 | 322 | 15 |
| Quincy | 5,977 | 24 | 1 | 4 | 5 | 14 | 296 | 84 | 190 | 22 | 0 |
| Rainier | 1,664 | 6 | 0 | 0 | 0 | 6 | 32 | 12 | 19 | 1 | 0 |
| Raymond | 2,853 | 9 | 0 | 1 | 0 | 8 | 80 | 35 | 42 | 3 | 0 |
| Reardan | 596 | 0 | 0 | 0 | 0 | 0 | 3 | 1 | 2 | 0 | 0 |
| Redmond | 50,009 | 58 | 0 | 9 | 23 | 26 | 1,653 | 206 | 1,382 | 65 | 3 |
| Renton | 63,599 | 314 | 2 | 32 | 152 | 128 | 4,322 | 800 | 3,041 | 481 | 7 |
| Republic | 939 | 3 | 0 | 1 | 0 | 2 | 7 | 3 | 4 | 0 | 0 |
| Richland | 47,040 | 92 | 0 | 22 | 12 | 58 | 1,095 | 160 | 873 | 62 | 5 |
| Ridgefield | 4,681 | 2 | 0 | 0 | 1 | 1 | 59 | 10 | 47 | 2 | 0 |
| Ritzville | 1,736 | 0 | 0 | 0 | 0 | 0 | 61 | 16 | 42 | 3 | 1 |
| Roy | 809 | 3 | 0 | 0 | 0 | 3 | 22 | 6 | 13 | 3 | 0 |
| Royal City | 1,981 | 9 | 0 | 1 | 0 | 8 | 74 | 27 | 40 | 7 | 0 |
| Ruston | 733 | 8 | 0 | 1 | 2 | 5 | 32 | 5 | 22 | 5 | 0 |
| Sammamish | 40,837 | 11 | 0 | 5 | 2 | 4 | 349 | 69 | 263 | 17 | 6 |
| SeaTac | 25,886 | 134 | 2 | 20 | 49 | 63 | 1,455 | 338 | 847 | 270 | 13 |
| Seattle | 602,531 | 3,861 | 22 | 102 | 1,792 | 1,945 | 35,090 | 6,709 | 25,095 | 3,286 | 156 |
| Sedro Woolley | 11,114 | 10 | 0 | 2 | 5 | 3 | 496 | 109 | 354 | 33 | 2 |
| Selah | 7,215 | 2 | 0 | 0 | 1 | 1 | 179 | 31 | 129 | 19 | 0 |
| Sequim | 5,979 | 20 | 0 | 2 | 4 | 14 | 254 | 45 | 201 | 8 | 2 |
| Shelton | 9,372 | 63 | 0 | 17 | 7 | 39 | 843 | 135 | 633 | 75 | 0 |
| Shoreline | 51,877 | 92 | 0 | 13 | 34 | 45 | 1,606 | 395 | 1,104 | 107 | 18 |
| Snohomish | 8,794 | 35 | 0 | 5 | 13 | 17 | 431 | 77 | 325 | 29 | 6 |
| Snoqualmie | 9,772 | 8 | 0 | 1 | 0 | 7 | 147 | 11 | 126 | 10 | 7 |
| Soap Lake | 1,838 | 2 | 0 | 0 | 1 | 1 | 56 | 28 | 25 | 3 | 0 |
| South Bend | 1,783 | 1 | 0 | 0 | 0 | 1 | 41 | 6 | 35 | 0 | 0 |
| Spokane | 202,932 | 1,270 | 7 | 75 | 443 | 745 | 13,166 | 2,565 | 8,864 | 1,737 | 74 |
| Spokane Valley | 86,756 | 265 | 1 | 19 | 63 | 182 | 3,262 | 616 | 2,393 | 253 | 17 |
| Stanwood | 6,340 | 13 | 0 | 1 | 1 | 11 | 306 | 47 | 242 | 17 | 1 |
| Steilacoom | 6,061 | 15 | 0 | 2 | 1 | 12 | 73 | 22 | 44 | 7 | 1 |
| Sultan | 4,334 | 24 | 1 | 3 | 3 | 17 | 174 | 46 | 104 | 24 | 2 |
| Sumas | 1,265 | 5 | 0 | 2 | 1 | 2 | 47 | 11 | 35 | 1 | 0 |
| Sumner | 9,832 | 46 | 1 | 2 | 10 | 33 | 464 | 98 | 312 | 54 | 3 |
| Sunnyside | 15,040 | 33 | 1 | 2 | 12 | 18 | 855 | 255 | 461 | 139 | 8 |
| Tacoma | 197,557 | 1,944 | 8 | 143 | 648 | 1,145 | 13,977 | 2,905 | 9,395 | 1,677 | 76 |
| Tenino | 2,241 | 7 | 0 | 1 | 0 | 6 | 67 | 22 | 43 | 2 | 3 |
| Toledo | 681 | 1 | 0 | 0 | 0 | 1 | 9 | 4 | 3 | 2 | 0 |
| Tonasket | 942 | 1 | 0 | 0 | 0 | 1 | 51 | 9 | 40 | 2 | 0 |
| Toppenish | 9,185 | 57 | 3 | 6 | 28 | 20 | 572 | 122 | 366 | 84 | 6 |
| Tukwila | 17,084 | 165 | 1 | 19 | 88 | 57 | 3,267 | 327 | 2,584 | 356 | 11 |
| Tumwater | 14,235 | 58 | 0 | 18 | 11 | 29 | 508 | 131 | 341 | 36 | 1 |
| Twisp | 896 | 4 | 1 | 1 | 0 | 2 | 30 | 16 | 14 | 0 | 0 |
| Union Gap | 5,707 | 16 | 0 | 3 | 8 | 5 | 653 | 79 | 524 | 50 | 2 |
| University Place | 30,385 | 104 | 1 | 12 | 35 | 56 | 932 | 311 | 559 | 62 | 5 |
| Vancouver | 165,147 | 656 | 6 | 117 | 158 | 375 | 5,944 | 886 | 4,159 | 899 | 49 |
| Walla Walla | 30,658 | 110 | 0 | 34 | 16 | 60 | 1,421 | 302 | 1,065 | 54 | 11 |
| Wapato | 4,537 | 36 | 0 | 4 | 12 | 20 | 337 | 95 | 193 | 49 | 4 |
| Washougal | 14,182 | 23 | 0 | 5 | 4 | 14 | 237 | 37 | 177 | 23 | 4 |
| Wenatchee | 30,051 | 98 | 1 | 14 | 17 | 66 | 1,203 | 182 | 954 | 67 | 8 |
| Westport | 2,631 | 6 | 0 | 3 | 1 | 2 | 108 | 21 | 85 | 2 | 1 |
| West Richland | 11,162 | 8 | 0 | 1 | 0 | 7 | 181 | 26 | 144 | 11 | 1 |
| White Salmon | 2,434 | 0 | 0 | 0 | 0 | 0 | 84 | 44 | 32 | 8 | 0 |
| Winlock | 1,254 | 3 | 0 | 2 | 1 | 0 | 33 | 11 | 19 | 3 | 0 |
| Winthrop | 392 | 1 | 0 | 0 | 0 | 1 | 15 | 4 | 10 | 1 | 0 |
| Woodinville | 11,417 | 8 | 0 | 2 | 1 | 5 | 448 | 105 | 312 | 31 | 2 |
| Woodland | 4,952 | 15 | 0 | 6 | 2 | 7 | 175 | 31 | 122 | 22 | 7 |
| Woodway | 1,157 | 0 | 0 | 0 | 0 | 0 | 14 | 8 | 6 | 0 | 0 |
| Yarrow Point | 1,081 | 1 | 0 | 0 | 0 | 1 | 10 | 2 | 6 | 2 | 0 |
| Yelm | 6,182 | 20 | 1 | 3 | 10 | 6 | 226 | 32 | 173 | 21 | 0 |
| Zillah | 2,735 | 5 | 0 | 2 | 2 | 1 | 137 | 29 | 88 | 20 | 1 |
| **WEST VIRGINIA** | | | | | | | | | | | |
| Barboursville | 3,428 | 3 | 0 | 0 | 1 | 2 | 482 | 39 | 437 | 6 | 1 |
| Beckley | 16,777 | 188 | 2 | 18 | 38 | 130 | 1,356 | 243 | 1,056 | 57 | 4 |
| Benwood | 1,416 | 0 | 0 | 0 | 0 | 0 | 10 | 0 | 10 | 0 | 0 |
| Bluefield | 11,056 | 56 | 2 | 6 | 10 | 38 | 302 | 120 | 167 | 15 | 2 |
| Bridgeport | 7,982 | 13 | 0 | 0 | 4 | 9 | 308 | 35 | 269 | 4 | 2 |
| Buckhannon | 5,476 | 5 | 1 | 2 | 0 | 2 | 74 | 24 | 42 | 8 | 2 |
| Chapmanville | 1,108 | 2 | 0 | 0 | 0 | 2 | 54 | 5 | 48 | 1 | 1 |

[1] The FBI does not publish arson data unless it receives data from either the agency or the state for all 12 months of the calendar year.

## Table 8. Offenses Known to Law Enforcement, by State and City, 2009—*Continued*

(Number.)

| State/city | Population | Violent crime | Murder and non-negligent man-slaughter | Forcible rape | Robbery | Aggravated assault | Property crime | Burglary | Larceny-theft | Motor vehicle theft | Arson[1] |
|---|---|---|---|---|---|---|---|---|---|---|---|
| **WEST VIRGINIA**—*Continued* | | | | | | | | | | | |
| Charleston | 49,976 | 535 | 5 | 18 | 128 | 384 | 2,625 | 636 | 1,813 | 176 | 16 |
| Charles Town | 5,005 | 8 | 0 | 0 | 1 | 7 | 111 | 23 | 80 | 8 | 0 |
| Clarksburg | 16,409 | 107 | 0 | 12 | 17 | 78 | 875 | 127 | 718 | 30 | 14 |
| Clearview | 544 | 0 | 0 | 0 | 0 | 0 | 0 | 0 | 0 | 0 | 0 |
| Dunbar | 7,614 | 19 | 0 | 1 | 6 | 12 | 199 | 52 | 127 | 20 | 5 |
| Elkins | 6,972 | 24 | 0 | 1 | 3 | 20 | 244 | 54 | 181 | 9 | 3 |
| Fairmont | 18,997 | 65 | 2 | 21 | 14 | 28 | 537 | 181 | 332 | 24 | 9 |
| Follansbee | 2,829 | 5 | 0 | 0 | 0 | 5 | 26 | 8 | 18 | 0 | 1 |
| Glen Dale | 1,380 | 0 | 0 | 0 | 0 | 0 | 52 | 9 | 42 | 1 | 1 |
| Glenville | 1,447 | 0 | 0 | 0 | 0 | 0 | 20 | 3 | 15 | 2 | 2 |
| Granville | 816 | 14 | 0 | 0 | 0 | 14 | 75 | 6 | 69 | 0 | 1 |
| Harpers Ferry/Bolivar | 1,369 | 2 | 0 | 0 | 1 | 1 | 11 | 1 | 9 | 1 | 0 |
| Hurricane | 6,435 | 15 | 0 | 5 | 3 | 7 | 195 | 15 | 170 | 10 | 1 |
| Kenova | 3,245 | 9 | 0 | 1 | 4 | 4 | 198 | 48 | 146 | 4 | 0 |
| Keyser | 5,217 | 9 | 0 | 2 | 4 | 3 | 159 | 48 | 108 | 3 | 0 |
| Lewisburg | 3,524 | 1 | 0 | 0 | 0 | 1 | 84 | 3 | 81 | 0 | 0 |
| Logan | 1,488 | 20 | 0 | 0 | 7 | 13 | 287 | 24 | 258 | 5 | 2 |
| Martinsburg | 17,275 | 81 | 0 | 4 | 25 | 52 | 1,177 | 127 | 1,009 | 41 | 6 |
| Matoaka | 304 | 0 | 0 | 0 | 0 | 0 | 0 | 0 | 0 | 0 | 0 |
| Montgomery | 1,920 | 2 | 0 | 0 | 2 | 0 | 48 | 11 | 35 | 2 | 0 |
| Moorefield | 2,444 | 6 | 1 | 1 | 0 | 4 | 86 | 14 | 68 | 4 | 1 |
| Morgantown | 29,989 | 130 | 1 | 10 | 23 | 96 | 818 | 196 | 604 | 18 | 5 |
| Moundsville | 9,019 | 17 | 0 | 1 | 2 | 14 | 282 | 65 | 209 | 8 | 6 |
| Nitro | 6,770 | 14 | 1 | 1 | 3 | 9 | 235 | 40 | 184 | 11 | 0 |
| Nutter Fort | 1,628 | 10 | 0 | 0 | 2 | 8 | 56 | 8 | 44 | 4 | 1 |
| Oceana | 1,397 | 9 | 0 | 1 | 1 | 7 | 62 | 6 | 54 | 2 | 0 |
| Paden City | 2,572 | 0 | 0 | 0 | 0 | 0 | 2 | 0 | 2 | 0 | 0 |
| Point Pleasant | 4,432 | 18 | 0 | 1 | 5 | 12 | 175 | 38 | 127 | 10 | 0 |
| Princeton | 6,248 | 48 | 1 | 2 | 11 | 34 | 429 | 84 | 324 | 21 | 2 |
| Ranson | 4,838 | 3 | 0 | 2 | 0 | 1 | 146 | 23 | 114 | 9 | 4 |
| Ravenswood | 3,925 | 7 | 0 | 0 | 0 | 7 | 44 | 16 | 24 | 4 | 0 |
| Ripley | 3,239 | 4 | 0 | 0 | 2 | 2 | 80 | 8 | 70 | 2 | 0 |
| Ronceverte | 1,598 | 4 | 0 | 0 | 0 | 4 | 16 | 3 | 13 | 0 | 0 |
| Salem | 2,046 | 6 | 0 | 0 | 0 | 6 | 27 | 8 | 19 | 0 | 1 |
| Shinnston | 2,238 | 6 | 0 | 0 | 1 | 5 | 19 | 2 | 16 | 1 | 0 |
| South Charleston | 12,326 | 69 | 4 | 2 | 13 | 50 | 490 | 78 | 387 | 25 | 6 |
| Spencer | 2,136 | 7 | 0 | 0 | 0 | 7 | 65 | 10 | 52 | 3 | 0 |
| St. Albans | 10,938 | 33 | 1 | 0 | 6 | 26 | 452 | 92 | 334 | 26 | 3 |
| Summersville | 3,305 | 7 | 0 | 0 | 0 | 7 | 227 | 11 | 210 | 6 | 0 |
| Wardensville | 259 | 0 | 0 | 0 | 0 | 0 | 0 | 0 | 0 | 0 | 0 |
| Weirton | 18,577 | 23 | 0 | 2 | 6 | 15 | 239 | 25 | 207 | 7 | 0 |
| Wellsburg | 2,561 | 6 | 0 | 0 | 2 | 4 | 44 | 14 | 27 | 3 | 1 |
| West Logan | 386 | 0 | 0 | 0 | 0 | 0 | 0 | 0 | 0 | 0 | 0 |
| Weston | 4,261 | 0 | 0 | 0 | 0 | 0 | 18 | 0 | 16 | 2 | 0 |
| West Union | 774 | 0 | 0 | 0 | 0 | 0 | 4 | 1 | 3 | 0 | 0 |
| Wheeling | 28,660 | 143 | 1 | 22 | 36 | 84 | 1,006 | 200 | 752 | 54 | 4 |
| White Sulphur Springs | 2,275 | 3 | 0 | 0 | 0 | 3 | 0 | 0 | 0 | 0 | 0 |
| Williamson | 3,018 | 10 | 0 | 1 | 1 | 8 | 49 | 22 | 23 | 4 | 0 |
| **WISCONSIN** | | | | | | | | | | | |
| Adams | 1,734 | 5 | 0 | 0 | 1 | 4 | 89 | 18 | 66 | 5 | 1 |
| Albany | 1,108 | 7 | 0 | 0 | 1 | 6 | 25 | 3 | 21 | 1 | 0 |
| Algoma | 3,091 | 4 | 0 | 3 | 1 | 0 | 87 | 2 | 83 | 2 | 0 |
| Altoona | 6,759 | 6 | 1 | 2 | 0 | 3 | 107 | 17 | 82 | 8 | 0 |
| Amery | 2,770 | 5 | 0 | 0 | 0 | 5 | 53 | 8 | 43 | 2 | 0 |
| Antigo | 7,849 | 14 | 0 | 0 | 1 | 13 | 471 | 57 | 405 | 9 | 0 |
| Appleton | 70,294 | 165 | 1 | 21 | 18 | 125 | 1,884 | 327 | 1,521 | 36 | 9 |
| Arcadia | 2,312 | 2 | 0 | 0 | 1 | 1 | 40 | 11 | 28 | 1 | 0 |
| Ashland | 8,066 | 29 | 0 | 4 | 2 | 23 | 479 | 73 | 389 | 17 | 4 |
| Ashwaubenon | 17,197 | 21 | 0 | 9 | 1 | 11 | 577 | 60 | 502 | 15 | 1 |
| Athens | 1,029 | 1 | 0 | 0 | 0 | 1 | 9 | 0 | 9 | 0 | 0 |
| Avoca | 563 | 2 | 0 | 0 | 0 | 2 | 14 | 9 | 4 | 1 | 0 |
| Bangor | 1,405 | 0 | 0 | 0 | 0 | 0 | 16 | 3 | 13 | 0 | 0 |
| Baraboo[6] | 11,302 | 39 | 0 | 0 | 1 | 38 | 498 | 46 | 440 | 12 | 0 |
| Barron | 3,104 | 5 | 0 | 4 | 0 | 1 | 41 | 7 | 28 | 6 | 0 |
| Bayfield | 566 | 0 | 0 | 0 | 0 | 0 | 26 | 3 | 22 | 1 | 0 |
| Beaver Dam | 15,116 | 3 | 0 | 0 | 0 | 3 | 553 | 74 | 477 | 2 | 0 |
| Belleville | 2,306 | 5 | 0 | 1 | 0 | 4 | 25 | 2 | 21 | 2 | 0 |
| Beloit | 36,197 | 171 | 5 | 13 | 57 | 96 | 1,389 | 279 | 1,040 | 70 | 3 |
| Beloit Town | 7,555 | 12 | 0 | 1 | 5 | 6 | 174 | 40 | 123 | 11 | 0 |
| Berlin | 4,965 | 4 | 0 | 0 | 0 | 4 | 175 | 20 | 155 | 0 | 0 |
| Big Bend | 1,334 | 1 | 0 | 0 | 0 | 1 | 37 | 7 | 28 | 2 | 0 |
| Black River Falls | 3,382 | 2 | 0 | 0 | 0 | 2 | 148 | 33 | 111 | 4 | 0 |

[1] The FBI does not publish arson data unless it receives data from either the agency or the state for all 12 months of the calendar year.

## Table 8. Offenses Known to Law Enforcement, by State and City, 2009—*Continued*

(Number.)

| State/city | Population | Violent crime | Murder and non-negligent man-slaughter | Forcible rape | Robbery | Aggravated assault | Property crime | Burglary | Larceny-theft | Motor vehicle theft | Arson[1] |
|---|---|---|---|---|---|---|---|---|---|---|---|
| **WISCONSIN**—*Continued* | | | | | | | | | | | |
| Blair | 1,243 | 1 | 0 | 0 | 0 | 1 | 24 | 4 | 17 | 3 | 0 |
| Bloomer | 3,294 | 3 | 0 | 1 | 0 | 2 | 78 | 8 | 69 | 1 | 0 |
| Bloomfield | 5,087 | 11 | 0 | 1 | 1 | 9 | 104 | 24 | 77 | 3 | 1 |
| Brillion | 2,857 | 2 | 0 | 0 | 0 | 2 | 23 | 2 | 20 | 1 | 0 |
| Brodhead | 3,118 | 2 | 0 | 0 | 0 | 2 | 80 | 1 | 75 | 4 | 0 |
| Brookfield | 39,049 | 29 | 0 | 0 | 9 | 20 | 1,261 | 93 | 1,145 | 23 | 2 |
| Brown Deer | 11,671 | 32 | 0 | 1 | 4 | 27 | 434 | 34 | 388 | 12 | 0 |
| Burlington | 11,030 | 6 | 0 | 1 | 5 | 0 | 314 | 23 | 282 | 9 | 0 |
| Burlington Town | 6,671 | 2 | 0 | 0 | 1 | 1 | 47 | 12 | 34 | 1 | 0 |
| Butler | 1,759 | 9 | 0 | 1 | 3 | 5 | 43 | 9 | 25 | 9 | 0 |
| Caledonia | 24,291 | 43 | 0 | 0 | 7 | 36 | 350 | 115 | 220 | 15 | 1 |
| Campbellsport | 1,943 | 0 | 0 | 0 | 0 | 0 | 21 | 6 | 14 | 1 | 0 |
| Campbell Township | 4,551 | 12 | 0 | 2 | 0 | 10 | 75 | 15 | 58 | 2 | 0 |
| Cashton | 1,060 | 0 | 0 | 0 | 0 | 0 | 0 | 0 | 0 | 0 | 0 |
| Cedarburg | 11,092 | 1 | 0 | 0 | 1 | 0 | 133 | 5 | 128 | 0 | 1 |
| Chenequa | 591 | 0 | 0 | 0 | 0 | 0 | 4 | 0 | 4 | 0 | 0 |
| Chetek | 2,135 | 2 | 0 | 0 | 0 | 2 | 33 | 3 | 29 | 1 | 0 |
| Chilton | 3,563 | 3 | 0 | 1 | 0 | 2 | 74 | 4 | 65 | 5 | 0 |
| Chippewa Falls | 12,897 | 24 | 0 | 0 | 2 | 22 | 309 | 56 | 236 | 17 | 6 |
| Cleveland | 1,408 | 0 | 0 | 0 | 0 | 0 | 10 | 1 | 9 | 0 | 0 |
| Clinton | 3,298 | 3 | 0 | 0 | 1 | 2 | 34 | 2 | 32 | 0 | 0 |
| Clintonville | 4,235 | 2 | 0 | 0 | 0 | 2 | 245 | 14 | 226 | 5 | 0 |
| Colby-Abbotsford | 3,540 | 3 | 0 | 0 | 1 | 2 | 70 | 9 | 59 | 2 | 0 |
| Columbus | 5,162 | 12 | 0 | 0 | 0 | 12 | 102 | 8 | 94 | 0 | 0 |
| Combined Locks | 3,348 | 1 | 0 | 0 | 0 | 1 | 20 | 3 | 17 | 0 | 0 |
| Coon Valley | 747 | 0 | 0 | 0 | 0 | 0 | 4 | 3 | 1 | 0 | 0 |
| Cornell | 1,377 | 0 | 0 | 0 | 0 | 0 | 24 | 7 | 17 | 0 | 0 |
| Cottage Grove[6] | 6,445 | 9 | 0 | 0 | 2 | 7 | 206 | 25 | 175 | 6 | 0 |
| Crandon | 1,801 | 2 | 0 | 1 | 0 | 1 | 50 | 15 | 34 | 1 | 0 |
| Cross Plains | 3,603 | 1 | 0 | 0 | 0 | 1 | 77 | 2 | 74 | 1 | 0 |
| Cuba City | 2,035 | 1 | 0 | 0 | 0 | 1 | 27 | 1 | 26 | 0 | 0 |
| Cudahy | 18,856 | 68 | 0 | 3 | 8 | 57 | 671 | 124 | 502 | 45 | 3 |
| Cumberland | 2,231 | 0 | 0 | 0 | 0 | 0 | 21 | 2 | 19 | 0 | 0 |
| Dane | 1,026 | 0 | 0 | 0 | 0 | 0 | 0 | 0 | 0 | 0 | 0 |
| Darien | 1,708 | 0 | 0 | 0 | 0 | 0 | 40 | 6 | 33 | 1 | 0 |
| Darlington | 2,191 | 4 | 0 | 2 | 0 | 2 | 57 | 3 | 50 | 4 | 0 |
| DeForest | 9,006 | 7 | 0 | 2 | 1 | 4 | 160 | 25 | 132 | 3 | 1 |
| Delafield | 6,821 | 5 | 0 | 0 | 0 | 5 | 118 | 6 | 111 | 1 | 0 |
| Delavan | 8,555 | 25 | 0 | 1 | 4 | 20 | 302 | 42 | 253 | 7 | 1 |
| Delavan Town | 4,521 | 2 | 0 | 2 | 0 | 0 | 73 | 18 | 49 | 6 | 1 |
| Denmark | 2,138 | 0 | 0 | 0 | 0 | 0 | 11 | 4 | 7 | 0 | 0 |
| De Pere | 25,288 | 15 | 0 | 5 | 3 | 7 | 360 | 70 | 275 | 15 | 1 |
| Dodgeville | 5,063 | 1 | 0 | 0 | 0 | 1 | 67 | 10 | 57 | 0 | 0 |
| Durand | 1,847 | 1 | 0 | 0 | 0 | 1 | 8 | 2 | 6 | 0 | 0 |
| Eagle River | 1,754 | 2 | 0 | 0 | 0 | 2 | 125 | 7 | 116 | 2 | 0 |
| Eagle Village[6] | 1,836 | 10 | 0 | 0 | 0 | 10 | 10 | 3 | 7 | 0 | 0 |
| East Troy | 4,591 | 3 | 0 | 3 | 0 | 0 | 96 | 4 | 91 | 1 | 7 |
| Eau Claire | 65,802 | 119 | 0 | 28 | 15 | 76 | 1,717 | 248 | 1,402 | 67 | 7 |
| Edgar | 1,339 | 0 | 0 | 0 | 0 | 0 | 6 | 0 | 5 | 1 | 0 |
| Edgerton | 5,374 | 3 | 0 | 0 | 2 | 1 | 93 | 32 | 58 | 3 | 0 |
| Eleva | 637 | 0 | 0 | 0 | 0 | 0 | 15 | 1 | 12 | 2 | 0 |
| Elkhart Lake | 1,186 | 0 | 0 | 0 | 0 | 0 | 28 | 2 | 26 | 0 | 0 |
| Elkhorn | 9,480 | 13 | 0 | 4 | 2 | 7 | 223 | 40 | 182 | 1 | 5 |
| Elk Mound | 814 | 2 | 0 | 0 | 1 | 1 | 14 | 1 | 13 | 0 | 0 |
| Ellsworth | 3,119 | 1 | 0 | 1 | 0 | 0 | 85 | 9 | 72 | 4 | 0 |
| Elm Grove | 6,118 | 0 | 0 | 0 | 0 | 0 | 69 | 12 | 57 | 0 | 0 |
| Elroy | 1,471 | 0 | 0 | 0 | 0 | 0 | 16 | 4 | 12 | 0 | 0 |
| Everest | 15,718 | 28 | 0 | 5 | 3 | 20 | 382 | 62 | 309 | 11 | 0 |
| Fall Creek | 1,280 | 0 | 0 | 0 | 0 | 0 | 7 | 0 | 7 | 0 | 0 |
| Fennimore | 2,306 | 1 | 0 | 0 | 1 | 0 | 68 | 12 | 56 | 0 | 0 |
| Fitchburg | 23,668 | 60 | 2 | 2 | 24 | 32 | 619 | 65 | 522 | 32 | 2 |
| Fond du Lac | 42,001 | 114 | 1 | 22 | 7 | 84 | 1,142 | 99 | 1,010 | 33 | 7 |
| Fontana | 1,957 | 3 | 0 | 0 | 0 | 3 | 30 | 3 | 27 | 0 | 0 |
| Fort Atkinson | 11,923 | 38 | 0 | 0 | 3 | 35 | 223 | 15 | 201 | 7 | 3 |
| Fountain City | 993 | 1 | 0 | 0 | 0 | 1 | 4 | 0 | 3 | 1 | 0 |
| Fox Lake | 1,461 | 3 | 0 | 0 | 0 | 3 | 14 | 1 | 13 | 0 | 0 |
| Fox Point | 6,797 | 2 | 0 | 1 | 1 | 0 | 75 | 9 | 65 | 1 | 0 |
| Fox Valley Metro | 17,428 | 9 | 0 | 2 | 1 | 6 | 327 | 38 | 283 | 6 | 4 |
| Franklin | 36,217 | 38 | 0 | 8 | 3 | 27 | 651 | 130 | 501 | 20 | 4 |
| Freedom | 5,994 | 0 | 0 | 0 | 0 | 0 | 15 | 4 | 10 | 1 | 0 |
| Germantown | 19,740 | 15 | 1 | 4 | 2 | 8 | 352 | 31 | 309 | 12 | 2 |

[1] The FBI does not publish arson data unless it receives data from either the agency or the state for all 12 months of the calendar year.

[6] Because of changes in the state/local agency's reporting practices, figures are not comparable to previous years' data.

## Table 8. Offenses Known to Law Enforcement, by State and City, 2009—*Continued*

(Number.)

| State/city | Population | Violent crime | Murder and non-negligent man-slaughter | Forcible rape | Robbery | Aggravated assault | Property crime | Burglary | Larceny-theft | Motor vehicle theft | Arson[1] |
|---|---|---|---|---|---|---|---|---|---|---|---|
| **WISCONSIN**—*Continued* | | | | | | | | | | | |
| Glendale | 12,956 | 23 | 0 | 2 | 18 | 3 | 831 | 36 | 767 | 28 | 0 |
| Grafton | 11,728 | 4 | 0 | 2 | 1 | 1 | 237 | 4 | 230 | 3 | 2 |
| Grand Chute | 21,079 | 21 | 1 | 2 | 6 | 12 | 990 | 49 | 909 | 32 | 0 |
| Grand Rapids | 7,347 | 0 | 0 | 0 | 0 | 0 | 76 | 25 | 50 | 1 | 0 |
| Grantsburg | 1,354 | 1 | 0 | 0 | 0 | 1 | 46 | 3 | 42 | 1 | 0 |
| Green Bay | 100,836 | 473 | 1 | 66 | 87 | 319 | 2,742 | 637 | 1,980 | 125 | 28 |
| Greendale | 13,937 | 8 | 0 | 0 | 2 | 6 | 612 | 18 | 585 | 9 | 0 |
| Greenfield | 36,148 | 51 | 0 | 3 | 26 | 22 | 1,293 | 195 | 1,038 | 60 | 0 |
| Green Lake | 1,092 | 1 | 0 | 0 | 0 | 1 | 25 | 1 | 24 | 0 | 0 |
| Hales Corners | 7,556 | 7 | 0 | 0 | 3 | 4 | 157 | 17 | 139 | 1 | 0 |
| Hartford | 14,207 | 8 | 0 | 0 | 2 | 6 | 326 | 27 | 288 | 11 | 0 |
| Hartland | 8,774 | 7 | 0 | 0 | 0 | 7 | 116 | 18 | 94 | 4 | 0 |
| Hayward | 2,365 | 9 | 0 | 1 | 1 | 7 | 201 | 22 | 170 | 9 | 1 |
| Hazel Green | 1,176 | 0 | 0 | 0 | 0 | 0 | 1 | 1 | 0 | 0 | 0 |
| Highland | 795 | 0 | 0 | 0 | 0 | 0 | 6 | 1 | 5 | 0 | 0 |
| Hobart-Lawrence | 9,229 | 0 | 0 | 0 | 0 | 0 | 40 | 10 | 29 | 1 | 0 |
| Holmen | 8,769 | 10 | 0 | 1 | 0 | 9 | 183 | 32 | 144 | 7 | 1 |
| Horicon | 3,466 | 3 | 1 | 1 | 0 | 1 | 49 | 3 | 45 | 1 | 0 |
| Hudson | 12,623 | 24 | 1 | 3 | 4 | 16 | 591 | 76 | 501 | 14 | 0 |
| Hurley | 1,514 | 6 | 0 | 0 | 0 | 6 | 63 | 7 | 53 | 3 | 0 |
| Independence | 1,208 | 1 | 0 | 0 | 0 | 1 | 18 | 3 | 13 | 2 | 0 |
| Iron Ridge | 975 | 0 | 0 | 0 | 0 | 0 | 20 | 4 | 16 | 0 | 0 |
| Jackson | 6,978 | 7 | 0 | 0 | 0 | 7 | 40 | 8 | 29 | 3 | 0 |
| Janesville | 62,761 | 153 | 1 | 18 | 40 | 94 | 2,245 | 332 | 1,839 | 74 | 9 |
| Jefferson | 7,874 | 18 | 2 | 5 | 0 | 11 | 287 | 17 | 267 | 3 | 0 |
| Juneau | 2,615 | 1 | 0 | 0 | 0 | 1 | 75 | 2 | 72 | 1 | 0 |
| Kaukauna | 15,695 | 5 | 0 | 3 | 0 | 2 | 196 | 16 | 172 | 8 | 0 |
| Kenosha | 97,657 | 270 | 4 | 36 | 102 | 128 | 3,017 | 593 | 2,296 | 128 | 12 |
| Kewaskum | 3,999 | 4 | 0 | 0 | 1 | 3 | 41 | 6 | 33 | 2 | 0 |
| Kewaunee | 2,748 | 1 | 0 | 0 | 0 | 1 | 25 | 4 | 21 | 0 | 0 |
| Kiel | 3,600 | 6 | 0 | 0 | 0 | 6 | 56 | 5 | 50 | 1 | 0 |
| Kohler | 1,951 | 0 | 0 | 0 | 0 | 0 | 62 | 0 | 62 | 0 | 0 |
| Kronenwetter | 7,118 | 5 | 0 | 3 | 0 | 2 | 60 | 30 | 28 | 2 | 0 |
| La Crosse | 50,791 | 189 | 1 | 24 | 31 | 133 | 1,837 | 349 | 1,412 | 76 | 12 |
| Ladysmith | 3,279 | 0 | 0 | 0 | 0 | 0 | 142 | 15 | 125 | 2 | 0 |
| Lake Delton | 3,311 | 16 | 0 | 5 | 1 | 10 | 598 | 25 | 569 | 4 | 0 |
| Lake Geneva | 8,437 | 12 | 0 | 0 | 2 | 10 | 411 | 11 | 393 | 7 | 0 |
| Lake Hallie | 4,455 | 14 | 0 | 0 | 2 | 12 | 254 | 45 | 201 | 8 | 0 |
| Lake Mills | 5,639 | 9 | 0 | 0 | 0 | 9 | 93 | 15 | 74 | 4 | 1 |
| Lancaster | 3,904 | 0 | 0 | 0 | 0 | 0 | 50 | 22 | 28 | 0 | 0 |
| Lodi | 3,021 | 3 | 0 | 1 | 0 | 2 | 77 | 6 | 68 | 3 | 0 |
| Luxemburg | 2,271 | 1 | 0 | 0 | 0 | 1 | 24 | 6 | 17 | 1 | 0 |
| Madison | 234,461 | 853 | 4 | 28 | 364 | 457 | 7,884 | 1,523 | 6,015 | 346 | 87 |
| Manitowoc | 33,056 | 47 | 0 | 1 | 6 | 40 | 655 | 87 | 553 | 15 | 2 |
| Maple Bluff | 1,354 | 1 | 0 | 0 | 1 | 0 | 22 | 6 | 16 | 0 | 0 |
| Marathon City | 1,527 | 9 | 0 | 0 | 0 | 9 | 11 | 3 | 8 | 0 | 0 |
| Marinette | 10,699 | 13 | 0 | 1 | 4 | 8 | 463 | 73 | 373 | 17 | 1 |
| Marion | 1,163 | 0 | 0 | 0 | 0 | 0 | 14 | 3 | 11 | 0 | 0 |
| Markesan | 1,270 | 0 | 0 | 0 | 0 | 0 | 24 | 7 | 17 | 0 | 0 |
| Marshall Village | 3,778 | 4 | 0 | 0 | 0 | 4 | 43 | 11 | 32 | 0 | 0 |
| Marshfield | 18,205 | 6 | 0 | 0 | 1 | 5 | 518 | 79 | 432 | 7 | 3 |
| Mauston | 4,491 | 22 | 0 | 2 | 0 | 20 | 177 | 33 | 139 | 5 | 1 |
| Mayville | 5,107 | 5 | 0 | 1 | 0 | 4 | 105 | 8 | 97 | 0 | 0 |
| McFarland | 7,923 | 2 | 1 | 0 | 0 | 1 | 162 | 13 | 146 | 3 | 0 |
| Medford | 4,085 | 6 | 0 | 2 | 0 | 4 | 166 | 12 | 152 | 2 | 0 |
| Menasha | 16,651 | 51 | 0 | 5 | 3 | 43 | 538 | 108 | 422 | 8 | 2 |
| Menomonee Falls | 34,822 | 16 | 1 | 1 | 7 | 7 | 362 | 31 | 322 | 9 | 0 |
| Menomonie | 15,652 | 11 | 3 | 0 | 1 | 7 | 361 | 70 | 284 | 7 | 2 |
| Mequon | 23,688 | 7 | 0 | 1 | 1 | 5 | 157 | 33 | 120 | 4 | 0 |
| Merrill | 9,617 | 39 | 0 | 2 | 5 | 32 | 341 | 47 | 284 | 10 | 0 |
| Middleton | 16,284 | 16 | 0 | 2 | 8 | 6 | 374 | 59 | 305 | 10 | 2 |
| Milwaukee | 604,673 | 6,584 | 72 | 204 | 3,122 | 3,186 | 34,791 | 6,534 | 23,397 | 4,860 | 355 |
| Mineral Point | 2,446 | 6 | 0 | 2 | 0 | 4 | 40 | 4 | 33 | 3 | 0 |
| Minocqua | 4,749 | 1 | 0 | 0 | 0 | 1 | 263 | 22 | 236 | 5 | 1 |
| Mishicot | 1,380 | 0 | 0 | 0 | 0 | 0 | 7 | 2 | 5 | 0 | 0 |
| Monona | 7,814 | 12 | 0 | 2 | 5 | 5 | 453 | 20 | 426 | 7 | 0 |
| Monroe | 10,442 | 20 | 0 | 1 | 0 | 19 | 298 | 34 | 255 | 9 | 6 |
| Montello | 1,466 | 3 | 0 | 1 | 0 | 2 | 42 | 12 | 30 | 0 | 0 |
| Mosinee | 3,962 | 1 | 0 | 0 | 0 | 1 | 112 | 23 | 85 | 4 | 0 |
| Mount Horeb | 6,799 | 1 | 0 | 0 | 1 | 0 | 147 | 12 | 133 | 2 | 1 |
| Mount Pleasant | 26,985 | 68 | 1 | 4 | 18 | 45 | 695 | 87 | 591 | 17 | 3 |
| Mukwonago | 7,341 | 5 | 0 | 1 | 2 | 2 | 184 | 19 | 160 | 5 | 0 |

[1] The FBI does not publish arson data unless it receives data from either the agency or the state for all 12 months of the calendar year.

## Table 8. Offenses Known to Law Enforcement, by State and City, 2009—*Continued*

(Number.)

| State/city | Population | Violent crime | Murder and non-negligent man-slaughter | Forcible rape | Robbery | Aggravated assault | Property crime | Burglary | Larceny-theft | Motor vehicle theft | Arson[1] |
|---|---|---|---|---|---|---|---|---|---|---|---|
| **WISCONSIN**—*Continued* | | | | | | | | | | | |
| Muskego | 23,440 | 10 | 0 | 3 | 5 | 2 | 236 | 60 | 173 | 3 | 1 |
| Neenah | 25,105 | 31 | 0 | 3 | 1 | 27 | 521 | 101 | 410 | 10 | 1 |
| Neillsville | 2,576 | 1 | 1 | 0 | 0 | 0 | 114 | 31 | 83 | 0 | 0 |
| Neshkoro | 438 | 0 | 0 | 0 | 0 | 0 | 11 | 1 | 10 | 0 | 0 |
| New Berlin | 38,686 | 26 | 0 | 1 | 6 | 19 | 556 | 99 | 447 | 10 | 4 |
| New Glarus | 2,065 | 0 | 0 | 0 | 0 | 0 | 75 | 5 | 66 | 4 | 0 |
| New Holstein | 3,150 | 3 | 0 | 0 | 0 | 3 | 83 | 15 | 68 | 0 | 0 |
| New Lisbon | 2,553 | 5 | 0 | 0 | 0 | 5 | 8 | 1 | 7 | 0 | 0 |
| New London | 6,702 | 5 | 0 | 2 | 1 | 2 | 184 | 9 | 174 | 1 | 0 |
| New Richmond | 8,486 | 1 | 0 | 0 | 1 | 0 | 279 | 35 | 240 | 4 | 1 |
| Niagara | 1,720 | 0 | 0 | 0 | 0 | 0 | 53 | 20 | 32 | 1 | 0 |
| North Fond du Lac | 5,271 | 5 | 0 | 1 | 0 | 4 | 109 | 9 | 95 | 5 | 0 |
| North Hudson | 3,869 | 0 | 0 | 0 | 0 | 0 | 24 | 0 | 24 | 0 | 0 |
| North Prairie | 2,111 | 1 | 0 | 0 | 0 | 1 | 9 | 1 | 7 | 1 | 0 |
| Oak Creek | 34,069 | 27 | 0 | 6 | 5 | 16 | 1,122 | 94 | 985 | 43 | 1 |
| Oconomowoc | 14,359 | 9 | 1 | 4 | 1 | 3 | 184 | 23 | 157 | 4 | 0 |
| Oconomowoc Town | 8,251 | 3 | 0 | 1 | 1 | 1 | 48 | 17 | 29 | 2 | 0 |
| Oconto | 4,278 | 3 | 0 | 0 | 0 | 3 | 222 | 35 | 180 | 7 | 1 |
| Oconto Falls | 2,582 | 2 | 0 | 0 | 0 | 2 | 79 | 9 | 66 | 4 | 1 |
| Omro | 3,446 | 7 | 0 | 0 | 0 | 7 | 16 | 16 | 0 | 0 | 0 |
| Onalaska | 16,998 | 19 | 0 | 1 | 4 | 14 | 550 | 62 | 482 | 6 | 0 |
| Oregon | 9,594 | 8 | 0 | 2 | 2 | 4 | 184 | 26 | 154 | 4 | 0 |
| Osceola | 2,754 | 10 | 0 | 0 | 0 | 10 | 59 | 5 | 53 | 1 | 0 |
| Oshkosh | 63,700 | 250 | 0 | 13 | 42 | 195 | 2,112 | 357 | 1,672 | 83 | 5 |
| Osseo | 1,624 | 3 | 0 | 0 | 1 | 2 | 53 | 3 | 48 | 2 | 0 |
| Oxford | 942 | 0 | 0 | 0 | 0 | 0 | 20 | 5 | 15 | 0 | 0 |
| Park Falls | 2,210 | 0 | 0 | 0 | 0 | 0 | 34 | 1 | 32 | 1 | 0 |
| Pepin | 912 | 1 | 0 | 1 | 0 | 0 | 27 | 9 | 17 | 1 | 0 |
| Peshtigo | 3,200 | 8 | 0 | 0 | 0 | 8 | 43 | 11 | 31 | 1 | 0 |
| Pewaukee | 12,631 | 6 | 0 | 0 | 0 | 6 | 114 | 11 | 96 | 7 | 0 |
| Pewaukee Village | 8,874 | 7 | 0 | 0 | 1 | 6 | 155 | 16 | 139 | 0 | 0 |
| Phillips | 1,377 | 2 | 0 | 0 | 0 | 2 | 62 | 12 | 48 | 2 | 1 |
| Plainfield | 883 | 0 | 0 | 0 | 0 | 0 | 16 | 7 | 8 | 1 | 0 |
| Platteville | 10,330 | 5 | 0 | 3 | 0 | 2 | 153 | 19 | 126 | 8 | 0 |
| Pleasant Prairie | 20,297 | 16 | 0 | 1 | 4 | 11 | 406 | 30 | 369 | 7 | 2 |
| Plover | 11,852 | 13 | 0 | 0 | 0 | 13 | 225 | 23 | 198 | 4 | 0 |
| Plymouth | 8,276 | 14 | 0 | 2 | 1 | 11 | 220 | 32 | 188 | 0 | 0 |
| Portage[6] | 9,939 | 40 | 0 | 10 | 1 | 29 | 286 | 16 | 263 | 7 | 0 |
| Port Washington | 11,247 | 3 | 0 | 2 | 0 | 1 | 163 | 10 | 148 | 5 | 1 |
| Poynette | 2,577 | 0 | 0 | 0 | 0 | 0 | 31 | 7 | 24 | 0 | 0 |
| Prescott | 4,039 | 5 | 0 | 1 | 0 | 4 | 163 | 14 | 145 | 4 | 0 |
| Pulaski | 3,602 | 4 | 0 | 3 | 1 | 0 | 56 | 8 | 47 | 1 | 1 |
| Racine | 82,232 | 448 | 3 | 35 | 228 | 182 | 3,521 | 1,108 | 2,266 | 147 | 22 |
| Reedsburg | 8,758 | 12 | 0 | 3 | 1 | 8 | 154 | 10 | 141 | 3 | 0 |
| Rhinelander | 7,602 | 7 | 0 | 1 | 0 | 6 | 340 | 36 | 296 | 8 | 1 |
| Rice Lake | 8,247 | 21 | 0 | 1 | 4 | 16 | 368 | 30 | 320 | 18 | 3 |
| Richland Center | 5,040 | 6 | 0 | 4 | 0 | 2 | 124 | 9 | 114 | 1 | 1 |
| Ripon | 7,392 | 7 | 0 | 0 | 0 | 7 | 123 | 12 | 109 | 2 | 0 |
| River Falls | 14,549 | 35 | 0 | 5 | 4 | 26 | 374 | 50 | 317 | 7 | 1 |
| River Hills | 1,660 | 1 | 0 | 0 | 0 | 1 | 8 | 3 | 4 | 1 | 0 |
| Rome Town | 2,997 | 2 | 0 | 0 | 0 | 2 | 45 | 7 | 36 | 2 | 0 |
| Rothschild | 5,052 | 1 | 0 | 0 | 1 | 0 | 148 | 16 | 131 | 1 | 0 |
| Sauk Prairie | 4,050 | 1 | 0 | 1 | 0 | 0 | 340 | 44 | 289 | 7 | 0 |
| Saukville | 4,301 | 4 | 0 | 2 | 0 | 2 | 93 | 5 | 84 | 4 | 0 |
| Seymour | 3,490 | 5 | 0 | 1 | 1 | 3 | 39 | 6 | 32 | 1 | 0 |
| Shawano | 8,706 | 27 | 0 | 3 | 2 | 22 | 389 | 35 | 340 | 14 | 1 |
| Sheboygan | 47,578 | 99 | 2 | 18 | 28 | 51 | 1,900 | 312 | 1,539 | 49 | 7 |
| Sheboygan Falls | 8,025 | 2 | 0 | 0 | 0 | 2 | 129 | 10 | 117 | 2 | 0 |
| Shiocton | 913 | 2 | 0 | 0 | 0 | 2 | 13 | 0 | 11 | 2 | 0 |
| Shorewood | 13,173 | 11 | 0 | 3 | 5 | 3 | 454 | 43 | 401 | 10 | 5 |
| Shorewood Hills | 1,675 | 4 | 0 | 0 | 4 | 0 | 89 | 1 | 88 | 0 | 0 |
| Silver Lake | 2,543 | 8 | 0 | 1 | 0 | 7 | 23 | 3 | 20 | 0 | 1 |
| Siren | 998 | 3 | 0 | 0 | 0 | 3 | 44 | 3 | 38 | 3 | 0 |
| Slinger | 4,757 | 4 | 0 | 1 | 0 | 3 | 115 | 12 | 97 | 6 | 0 |
| Somerset | 2,836 | 0 | 0 | 0 | 0 | 0 | 42 | 4 | 36 | 2 | 0 |
| South Milwaukee | 21,122 | 27 | 0 | 5 | 19 | 3 | 500 | 96 | 383 | 21 | 1 |
| Spencer | 1,792 | 1 | 0 | 0 | 0 | 1 | 29 | 6 | 23 | 0 | 0 |
| Spooner | 2,653 | 1 | 0 | 1 | 0 | 0 | 82 | 9 | 72 | 1 | 0 |
| Spring Green | 1,503 | 0 | 0 | 0 | 0 | 0 | 31 | 4 | 27 | 0 | 0 |
| Stanley | 3,567 | 0 | 0 | 0 | 0 | 0 | 98 | 7 | 91 | 0 | 0 |
| St. Croix Falls | 2,163 | 1 | 0 | 0 | 0 | 1 | 84 | 4 | 77 | 3 | 0 |

[1] The FBI does not publish arson data unless it receives data from either the agency or the state for all 12 months of the calendar year.

[6] Because of changes in the state/local agency's reporting practices, figures are not comparable to previous years' data.

## Table 8. Offenses Known to Law Enforcement, by State and City, 2009—*Continued*

(Number.)

| State/city | Population | Violent crime | Murder and non-negligent man-slaughter | Forcible rape | Robbery | Aggravated assault | Property crime | Burglary | Larceny-theft | Motor vehicle theft | Arson[1] |
|---|---|---|---|---|---|---|---|---|---|---|---|
| **WISCONSIN**—*Continued* | | | | | | | | | | | |
| Stevens Point | 25,320 | 34 | 0 | 4 | 0 | 30 | 706 | 68 | 625 | 13 | 2 |
| St. Francis | 9,862 | 14 | 0 | 1 | 3 | 10 | 271 | 33 | 227 | 11 | 3 |
| Stoughton | 13,013 | 10 | 0 | 0 | 3 | 7 | 214 | 32 | 177 | 5 | 2 |
| Strum | 1,022 | 0 | 0 | 0 | 0 | 0 | 14 | 0 | 14 | 0 | 0 |
| Sturgeon Bay | 8,721 | 7 | 0 | 0 | 0 | 7 | 134 | 13 | 116 | 5 | 1 |
| Sturtevant | 7,120 | 6 | 1 | 0 | 0 | 5 | 78 | 14 | 62 | 2 | 0 |
| Summit | 5,055 | 2 | 0 | 0 | 0 | 2 | 22 | 5 | 17 | 0 | 0 |
| Sun Prairie | 29,324 | 41 | 1 | 2 | 10 | 28 | 738 | 78 | 640 | 20 | 8 |
| Superior | 26,098 | 72 | 0 | 7 | 19 | 46 | 1,396 | 201 | 1,147 | 48 | 7 |
| Theresa | 1,249 | 4 | 0 | 2 | 0 | 2 | 34 | 4 | 30 | 0 | 0 |
| Thiensville | 3,013 | 3 | 0 | 0 | 0 | 3 | 36 | 4 | 29 | 3 | 0 |
| Three Lakes | 2,251 | 1 | 0 | 1 | 0 | 0 | 38 | 6 | 31 | 1 | 0 |
| Tomah | 8,692 | 24 | 0 | 6 | 0 | 18 | 297 | 42 | 253 | 2 | 2 |
| Tomahawk | 3,684 | 10 | 0 | 2 | 0 | 8 | 127 | 15 | 111 | 1 | 0 |
| Town of East Troy | 3,970 | 1 | 0 | 0 | 0 | 1 | 28 | 5 | 23 | 0 | 0 |
| Town of Madison | 6,309 | 39 | 0 | 11 | 19 | 9 | 199 | 35 | 137 | 27 | 2 |
| Town of Menasha | 16,005 | 14 | 0 | 1 | 0 | 13 | 283 | 78 | 194 | 11 | 0 |
| Trempealeau | 1,529 | 0 | 0 | 0 | 0 | 0 | 8 | 3 | 5 | 0 | 0 |
| Twin Lakes | 5,809 | 5 | 0 | 1 | 0 | 4 | 135 | 23 | 107 | 5 | 0 |
| Two Rivers | 11,716 | 21 | 0 | 7 | 1 | 13 | 132 | 14 | 114 | 4 | 0 |
| Verona | 12,056 | 16 | 0 | 3 | 3 | 10 | 195 | 18 | 177 | 0 | 0 |
| Viroqua | 4,437 | 4 | 0 | 2 | 0 | 2 | 103 | 4 | 94 | 5 | 0 |
| Walworth | 2,738 | 8 | 0 | 0 | 0 | 8 | 33 | 6 | 27 | 0 | 0 |
| Washburn[6] | 2,155 | 2 | 0 | 1 | 0 | 1 | 41 | 2 | 38 | 1 | 0 |
| Waterloo | 3,273 | 4 | 0 | 1 | 0 | 3 | 49 | 8 | 40 | 1 | 0 |
| Watertown | 23,066 | 90 | 0 | 7 | 8 | 75 | 426 | 79 | 341 | 6 | 14 |
| Waukesha | 68,248 | 109 | 2 | 15 | 27 | 65 | 1,163 | 251 | 871 | 41 | 10 |
| Waunakee | 11,569 | 12 | 0 | 1 | 1 | 10 | 112 | 33 | 75 | 4 | 0 |
| Waupaca | 5,837 | 17 | 0 | 0 | 0 | 17 | 206 | 32 | 172 | 2 | 1 |
| Waupun | 10,441 | 13 | 1 | 5 | 1 | 6 | 268 | 74 | 193 | 1 | 0 |
| Wausau | 37,459 | 128 | 2 | 18 | 10 | 98 | 995 | 257 | 705 | 33 | 16 |
| Wautoma | 2,122 | 9 | 0 | 0 | 0 | 9 | 55 | 7 | 45 | 3 | 0 |
| Wauwatosa | 44,777 | 88 | 1 | 2 | 54 | 31 | 1,820 | 255 | 1,516 | 49 | 0 |
| West Allis | 59,240 | 206 | 2 | 7 | 98 | 99 | 3,082 | 537 | 2,356 | 189 | 19 |
| West Bend | 30,070 | 34 | 1 | 1 | 7 | 25 | 804 | 39 | 754 | 11 | 4 |
| Westfield | 1,174 | 4 | 0 | 1 | 0 | 3 | 17 | 2 | 14 | 1 | 0 |
| West Salem | 4,829 | 1 | 0 | 1 | 0 | 0 | 98 | 12 | 84 | 2 | 0 |
| Whitefish Bay | 13,527 | 2 | 0 | 0 | 2 | 0 | 214 | 11 | 200 | 3 | 0 |
| Whitehall | 1,593 | 0 | 0 | 0 | 0 | 0 | 42 | 2 | 40 | 0 | 0 |
| Whitewater | 14,380 | 18 | 0 | 2 | 3 | 13 | 363 | 57 | 299 | 7 | 0 |
| Williams Bay | 2,734 | 2 | 0 | 1 | 1 | 0 | 31 | 3 | 28 | 0 | 0 |
| Winneconne | 2,469 | 3 | 0 | 0 | 0 | 3 | 36 | 8 | 28 | 0 | 1 |
| Wisconsin Dells | 2,474 | 35 | 0 | 2 | 3 | 30 | 314 | 20 | 292 | 2 | 0 |
| Wisconsin Rapids | 17,020 | 14 | 0 | 4 | 6 | 4 | 956 | 225 | 712 | 19 | 1 |
| Woodruff | 1,895 | 1 | 0 | 0 | 0 | 1 | 42 | 4 | 37 | 1 | 0 |
| **WYOMING** | | | | | | | | | | | |
| Afton | 1,866 | 3 | 0 | 0 | 0 | 3 | 30 | 7 | 23 | 0 | 0 |
| Alpine | 845 | 2 | 0 | 0 | 0 | 2 | 12 | 5 | 7 | 0 | 0 |
| Basin | 1,243 | 1 | 0 | 0 | 0 | 1 | 13 | 2 | 11 | 0 | 0 |
| Buffalo | 4,945 | 12 | 0 | 0 | 0 | 12 | 96 | 20 | 66 | 10 | 0 |
| Casper | 54,550 | 107 | 0 | 20 | 12 | 75 | 2,504 | 411 | 1,970 | 123 | 11 |
| Cheyenne | 57,317 | 125 | 4 | 28 | 28 | 65 | 2,365 | 226 | 2,028 | 111 | 11 |
| Cody | 9,358 | 23 | 0 | 6 | 0 | 17 | 240 | 32 | 201 | 7 | 3 |
| Diamondville | 657 | 0 | 0 | 0 | 0 | 0 | 7 | 0 | 7 | 0 | 0 |
| Douglas | 6,049 | 11 | 0 | 0 | 0 | 11 | 175 | 18 | 151 | 6 | 2 |
| Evanston | 11,823 | 11 | 0 | 3 | 0 | 8 | 329 | 29 | 281 | 19 | 0 |
| Evansville | 2,408 | 17 | 0 | 0 | 2 | 15 | 67 | 15 | 48 | 4 | 0 |
| Gillette | 27,709 | 33 | 0 | 6 | 3 | 24 | 871 | 120 | 710 | 41 | 12 |
| Glenrock | 2,443 | 9 | 0 | 4 | 0 | 5 | 44 | 8 | 34 | 2 | 0 |
| Green River | 12,194 | 82 | 0 | 1 | 5 | 76 | 308 | 49 | 253 | 6 | 0 |
| Greybull | 1,732 | 11 | 0 | 1 | 0 | 10 | 14 | 7 | 6 | 1 | 0 |
| Guernsey | 1,065 | 0 | 0 | 0 | 0 | 0 | 7 | 3 | 4 | 0 | 0 |
| Hanna | 866 | 1 | 0 | 0 | 0 | 1 | 1 | 0 | 1 | 0 | 0 |
| Jackson | 9,937 | 35 | 0 | 6 | 3 | 26 | 310 | 40 | 258 | 12 | 5 |
| Kemmerer | 2,449 | 6 | 0 | 0 | 0 | 6 | 35 | 5 | 30 | 0 | 0 |
| Lander | 7,304 | 7 | 0 | 2 | 0 | 5 | 228 | 22 | 204 | 2 | 0 |
| Laramie | 27,730 | 26 | 0 | 6 | 1 | 19 | 670 | 109 | 522 | 39 | 1 |
| Lovell | 2,268 | 4 | 0 | 1 | 0 | 3 | 67 | 11 | 54 | 2 | 0 |
| Lusk | 1,485 | 7 | 0 | 0 | 0 | 7 | 11 | 4 | 7 | 0 | 0 |
| Mills | 3,177 | 23 | 0 | 2 | 2 | 19 | 123 | 32 | 78 | 13 | 0 |
| Moorcroft | 900 | 3 | 0 | 1 | 0 | 2 | 20 | 5 | 13 | 2 | 0 |
| Newcastle | 3,406 | 5 | 0 | 1 | 0 | 4 | 142 | 17 | 117 | 8 | 0 |

[1] The FBI does not publish arson data unless it receives data from either the agency or the state for all 12 months of the calendar year.

[6] Because of changes in the state/local agency's reporting practices, figures are not comparable to previous years' data.

## Table 8. Offenses Known to Law Enforcement, by State and City, 2009—*Continued*

(Number.)

| State/city | Population | Violent crime | Murder and non-negligent man-slaughter | Forcible rape | Robbery | Aggravated assault | Property crime | Burglary | Larceny-theft | Motor vehicle theft | Arson[1] |
|---|---|---|---|---|---|---|---|---|---|---|---|
| **WYOMING**—*Continued* | | | | | | | | | | | |
| Pine Bluffs | 1,155 | 7 | 0 | 0 | 0 | 7 | 15 | 5 | 8 | 2 | 0 |
| Powell | 5,540 | 23 | 0 | 8 | 2 | 13 | 195 | 23 | 168 | 4 | 1 |
| Rawlins | 8,716 | 23 | 0 | 1 | 2 | 20 | 310 | 36 | 254 | 20 | 1 |
| Riverton | 10,123 | 31 | 1 | 2 | 2 | 26 | 540 | 45 | 474 | 21 | 1 |
| Rock Springs | 20,391 | 96 | 0 | 9 | 6 | 81 | 758 | 78 | 644 | 36 | 1 |
| Saratoga | 1,763 | 3 | 0 | 0 | 0 | 3 | 21 | 9 | 9 | 3 | 0 |
| Sheridan | 17,350 | 43 | 1 | 3 | 1 | 38 | 488 | 107 | 356 | 25 | 2 |
| Sundance | 1,264 | 0 | 0 | 0 | 0 | 0 | 14 | 5 | 9 | 0 | 0 |
| Thermopolis | 2,951 | 10 | 0 | 0 | 0 | 10 | 38 | 6 | 30 | 2 | 0 |
| Torrington | 5,486 | 11 | 0 | 2 | 0 | 9 | 138 | 29 | 102 | 7 | 0 |
| Wheatland | 3,273 | 4 | 0 | 0 | 0 | 4 | 114 | 26 | 85 | 3 | 0 |
| Worland | 4,926 | 2 | 0 | 0 | 0 | 2 | 28 | 0 | 27 | 1 | 0 |

[1] The FBI does not publish arson data unless it receives data from either the agency or the state for all 12 months of the calendar year.

## Table 9. Offenses Known to Law Enforcement, by State and University and College, 2009

(Number.)

| State and University/College | Campus | Student enrollment[1] | Violent crime | Murder and nonnegligent manslaughter | Forcible rape | Robbery | Aggravated assault | Property crime | Burglary | Larceny-theft | Motor vehicle theft | Arson[2] |
|---|---|---|---|---|---|---|---|---|---|---|---|---|
| **ALABAMA** | | | | | | | | | | | | |
| Alabama A&M University | | 5,124 | 4 | 0 | 1 | 1 | 2 | 86 | 32 | 51 | 3 | |
| Alabama State University | | 5,695 | 9 | 0 | 1 | 4 | 4 | 133 | 33 | 95 | 5 | |
| Calhoun Community College[3] | | | 0 | 0 | 0 | 0 | 0 | 14 | 0 | 14 | 0 | |
| Jacksonville State University | | 9,481 | 2 | 0 | 0 | 0 | 2 | 111 | 8 | 103 | 0 | |
| Troy University | | 28,303 | 2 | 0 | 1 | 0 | 1 | 124 | 17 | 104 | 3 | |
| University of Alabama: | Huntsville | 7,431 | 1 | 0 | 1 | 0 | 0 | 86 | 4 | 80 | 2 | |
| | Tuscaloosa | 27,014 | 10 | 0 | 1 | 7 | 2 | 479 | 99 | 378 | 2 | 0 |
| University of Montevallo | | 3,023 | 1 | 0 | 0 | 1 | 0 | 35 | 9 | 26 | 0 | |
| University of North Alabama | | 7,203 | 3 | 0 | 0 | 0 | 3 | 113 | 42 | 69 | 2 | |
| University of South Alabama | | 14,064 | 14 | 0 | 1 | 4 | 9 | 277 | 45 | 218 | 14 | |
| University of West Alabama | | 4,888 | 2 | 0 | 0 | 0 | 2 | 18 | 4 | 14 | 0 | |
| **ALASKA** | | | | | | | | | | | | |
| University of Alaska: | Anchorage | 16,649 | 2 | 0 | 0 | 0 | 2 | 126 | 5 | 115 | 6 | 0 |
| | Fairbanks | 8,575 | 2 | 0 | 1 | 0 | 1 | 89 | 5 | 80 | 4 | 1 |
| **ARIZONA** | | | | | | | | | | | | |
| Arizona State University | Main Campus | 67,082 | 34 | 0 | 1 | 5 | 28 | 1,179 | 128 | 1,016 | 35 | 3 |
| Central Arizona College | | 5,865 | 4 | 0 | 0 | 0 | 4 | 49 | 22 | 25 | 2 | 1 |
| Northern Arizona University | | 22,502 | 21 | 0 | 3 | 0 | 18 | 283 | 28 | 255 | 0 | 9 |
| Pima Community College | | 34,136 | 6 | 0 | 2 | 2 | 2 | 194 | 6 | 167 | 21 | 0 |
| University of Arizona | | 38,057 | 20 | 0 | 5 | 6 | 9 | 1,080 | 49 | 1,006 | 25 | 0 |
| Yavapai College | | 9,033 | 1 | 0 | 0 | 0 | 1 | 28 | 10 | 18 | 0 | 0 |
| **ARKANSAS** | | | | | | | | | | | | |
| Arkansas State University | Jonesboro | 11,490 | 8 | 0 | 2 | 2 | 4 | 197 | 89 | 107 | 1 | 0 |
| Arkansas Tech University | | 7,492 | 2 | 0 | 2 | 0 | 0 | 91 | 22 | 68 | 1 | 0 |
| Henderson State University | | 3,652 | 0 | 0 | 0 | 0 | 0 | 67 | 28 | 37 | 2 | 0 |
| University of Arkansas: | Fayetteville | 19,194 | 7 | 0 | 5 | 1 | 1 | 277 | 64 | 192 | 21 | 0 |
| | Little Rock | 11,965 | 9 | 0 | 0 | 5 | 4 | 164 | 62 | 100 | 2 | 0 |
| | Medical Sciences | 2,652 | 17 | 0 | 0 | 1 | 16 | 252 | 4 | 239 | 9 | 2 |
| University of Central Arkansas | | 12,974 | 3 | 0 | 1 | 0 | 2 | 162 | 83 | 78 | 1 | 0 |
| **CALIFORNIA** | | | | | | | | | | | | |
| Allan Hancock College | | 11,552 | 0 | 0 | 0 | 0 | 0 | 55 | 5 | 49 | 1 | 0 |
| California State Polytechnic University: | Pomona | 21,190 | 6 | 0 | 1 | 4 | 1 | 202 | 13 | 171 | 18 | 0 |
| | San Luis Obispo | 19,471 | 2 | 0 | 1 | 0 | 1 | 181 | 8 | 170 | 3 | 4 |
| California State University: | Bakersfield | 7,684 | 0 | 0 | 0 | 0 | 0 | 92 | 29 | 59 | 4 | 0 |
| | Channel Islands | 3,783 | 0 | 0 | 0 | 0 | 0 | 41 | 4 | 37 | 0 | 0 |
| | Chico | 17,132 | 6 | 0 | 1 | 3 | 2 | 239 | 22 | 215 | 2 | 2 |
| | Dominguez Hills | 12,851 | 12 | 0 | 2 | 5 | 5 | 165 | 57 | 100 | 8 | 1 |
| | East Bay | 14,167 | 2 | 0 | 0 | 2 | 0 | 156 | 18 | 126 | 12 | 0 |
| | Fresno | 22,613 | 9 | 0 | 3 | 3 | 3 | 361 | 66 | 274 | 21 | 6 |
| | Fullerton | 36,996 | 6 | 0 | 0 | 1 | 5 | 293 | 77 | 193 | 23 | 0 |
| | Long Beach | 37,891 | 2 | 0 | 1 | 1 | 0 | 213 | 15 | 170 | 28 | 0 |
| | Los Angeles | 20,743 | 6 | 0 | 2 | 2 | 2 | 244 | 43 | 194 | 7 | 0 |
| | Monterey Bay | 4,340 | 6 | 0 | 1 | 0 | 5 | 80 | 21 | 55 | 4 | 0 |
| | Northridge | 36,208 | 7 | 0 | 2 | 1 | 4 | 351 | 14 | 327 | 10 | 2 |
| | Sacramento | 29,011 | 3 | 0 | 0 | 0 | 3 | 228 | 24 | 188 | 16 | 0 |
| | San Bernardino | 17,646 | 10 | 0 | 1 | 1 | 8 | 145 | 16 | 106 | 23 | 0 |
| | San Jose[3] | | 21 | 0 | 3 | 3 | 15 | 408 | 53 | 342 | 13 | 1 |
| | San Marcos | 9,148 | 2 | 0 | 0 | 1 | 1 | 88 | 21 | 64 | 3 | 0 |
| | Stanislaus | 8,601 | 1 | 0 | 0 | 0 | 1 | 55 | 5 | 44 | 6 | 0 |
| College of the Sequoias | | 13,449 | 2 | 0 | 0 | 2 | 0 | 100 | 37 | 60 | 3 | 0 |
| Contra Costa Community College | | 7,580 | 20 | 0 | 1 | 10 | 9 | 237 | 7 | 207 | 23 | 0 |
| Cuesta College | | 11,341 | 0 | 0 | 0 | 0 | 0 | 29 | 1 | 28 | 0 | 0 |
| El Camino College | | 27,098 | 6 | 0 | 1 | 3 | 2 | 181 | 10 | 151 | 20 | 0 |
| Foothill-De Anza College | | 45,541 | 0 | 0 | 0 | 0 | 0 | 92 | 24 | 64 | 4 | 0 |
| Fresno Community College | | 24,783 | 9 | 0 | 1 | 3 | 5 | 213 | 16 | 183 | 14 | 4 |
| Humboldt State University | | 7,800 | 2 | 0 | 0 | 2 | 0 | 111 | 7 | 104 | 0 | 1 |
| Marin Community College | | 6,047 | 0 | 0 | 0 | 0 | 0 | 34 | 2 | 31 | 1 | 0 |
| Pasadena Community College | | 26,713 | 5 | 0 | 0 | 1 | 4 | 182 | 3 | 171 | 8 | 0 |
| Reedley Community College | | 14,223 | 3 | 0 | 2 | 0 | 1 | 55 | 4 | 47 | 4 | 1 |
| Riverside Community College | | 36,146 | 8 | 0 | 0 | 2 | 6 | 121 | 17 | 101 | 3 | 1 |
| San Bernardino Community College | | 14,136 | 5 | 0 | 0 | 1 | 4 | 129 | 24 | 92 | 13 | 0 |

*Note*: Caution should be exercised in making any intercampus comparisons or ranking schools because university/college crime statistics are affected by a variety of factors. These include demographic characteristics of the surrounding community, ratio of male to female students, number of on-campus residents, accessibility of the campus to outside visitors, size of enrollment, etc.

[1] The student enrollment figures provided by the United States Department of Education are for the 2008 school year, the most recent available. The enrollment figures include full-time and part-time students.

[2] The FBI does not publish arson data unless it receives data from either the agency or the state for all 12 months of the calendar year.

[3] Student enrollment figures were not available.

## Table 9. Offenses Known to Law Enforcement, by State and University and College, 2009—*Continued*

(Number.)

| State and University/College | Campus | Student enrollment[1] | Violent crime | Murder and nonnegligent manslaughter | Forcible rape | Robbery | Aggravated assault | Property crime | Burglary | Larceny-theft | Motor vehicle theft | Arson[2] |
|---|---|---|---|---|---|---|---|---|---|---|---|---|
| San Diego State University | | 34,889 | 25 | 0 | 1 | 12 | 12 | 537 | 85 | 394 | 58 | 3 |
| San Francisco State University | | 30,014 | 17 | 0 | 0 | 16 | 1 | 292 | 26 | 253 | 13 | 0 |
| San Jose/Evergreen Community College | | 22,826 | 0 | 0 | 0 | 0 | 0 | 81 | 3 | 69 | 9 | 0 |
| Santa Rosa Junior College | | 20,298 | 5 | 0 | 1 | 3 | 1 | 109 | 9 | 96 | 4 | 0 |
| Solano Community College | | 11,055 | 0 | 0 | 0 | 0 | 0 | 79 | 1 | 70 | 8 | 0 |
| Sonoma State University | | 8,921 | 1 | 0 | 0 | 0 | 1 | 103 | 9 | 90 | 4 | 0 |
| University of California: | Berkeley | 35,396 | 39 | 0 | 1 | 17 | 21 | 855 | 59 | 778 | 18 | 12 |
| | Davis | 30,568 | 7 | 0 | 5 | 1 | 1 | 728 | 76 | 645 | 7 | 7 |
| | Hastings College of Law | 1,306 | 5 | 0 | 0 | 3 | 2 | 22 | 14 | 7 | 1 | 0 |
| | Irvine | 26,984 | 13 | 1 | 2 | 1 | 9 | 516 | 40 | 471 | 5 | 2 |
| | Los Angeles | 38,220 | 60 | 0 | 15 | 14 | 31 | 1,130 | 192 | 911 | 27 | 3 |
| | Medical Center, Sacramento[3] | | 4 | 0 | 0 | 3 | 1 | 174 | 24 | 145 | 5 | 0 |
| | Merced | 2,718 | 0 | 0 | 0 | 0 | 0 | 35 | 3 | 32 | 0 | 0 |
| | Riverside | 18,079 | 7 | 0 | 2 | 4 | 1 | 393 | 37 | 349 | 7 | 0 |
| | San Diego | 27,520 | 5 | 0 | 1 | 2 | 2 | 580 | 50 | 491 | 39 | 3 |
| | San Francisco | 2,998 | 13 | 0 | 0 | 3 | 10 | 381 | 34 | 338 | 9 | 0 |
| | Santa Barbara | 21,868 | 9 | 0 | 0 | 1 | 8 | 581 | 37 | 541 | 3 | 2 |
| | Santa Cruz | 16,615 | 5 | 0 | 2 | 0 | 3 | 295 | 45 | 247 | 3 | 1 |
| Ventura County Community College District | | 14,207 | 0 | 0 | 0 | 0 | 0 | 131 | 0 | 131 | 0 | 0 |
| West Valley-Mission College | | 22,159 | 3 | 0 | 0 | 1 | 2 | 99 | 7 | 88 | 4 | 0 |
| **COLORADO** | | | | | | | | | | | | |
| Adams State College | | 2,920 | 11 | 0 | 2 | 0 | 9 | 51 | 21 | 30 | 0 | 0 |
| Arapahoe Community College | | 7,204 | 0 | 0 | 0 | 0 | 0 | 24 | 0 | 22 | 2 | 0 |
| Auraria Higher Education Center[3] | | | 6 | 0 | 0 | 2 | 4 | 174 | 4 | 164 | 6 | 0 |
| Colorado School of Mines | | 4,704 | 1 | 0 | 0 | 0 | 1 | 71 | 3 | 67 | 1 | 1 |
| Colorado State University: | Fort Collins | 28,882 | 10 | 0 | 5 | 1 | 4 | 435 | 20 | 403 | 12 | 12 |
| | Pueblo | 6,759 | 0 | 0 | 0 | 0 | 0 | 52 | 6 | 46 | 0 | 0 |
| Fort Lewis College | | 3,740 | 1 | 0 | 1 | 0 | 0 | 70 | 10 | 58 | 2 | 2 |
| Pikes Peak Community College | | 11,873 | 1 | 0 | 0 | 0 | 1 | 51 | 5 | 44 | 2 | 0 |
| Red Rocks Community College | | 7,667 | 2 | 0 | 0 | 0 | 2 | 24 | 0 | 23 | 1 | 0 |
| University of Colorado: | Boulder | 32,469 | 11 | 0 | 4 | 1 | 6 | 531 | 41 | 489 | 1 | 2 |
| | Colorado Springs | 9,373 | 0 | 0 | 0 | 0 | 0 | 58 | 10 | 48 | 0 | 0 |
| | Denver | 21,903 | 0 | 0 | 0 | 0 | 0 | 70 | 5 | 62 | 3 | 0 |
| | Health Sciences Center[3] | | 0 | 0 | 0 | 0 | 0 | 11 | 5 | 6 | 0 | 0 |
| University of Northern Colorado | | 12,498 | 2 | 0 | 1 | 0 | 1 | 219 | 23 | 195 | 1 | 0 |
| **CONNECTICUT** | | | | | | | | | | | | |
| Central Connecticut State University | | 12,233 | 2 | 0 | 0 | 1 | 1 | 100 | 3 | 94 | 3 | 1 |
| Eastern Connecticut State University | | 5,427 | 1 | 0 | 0 | 1 | 0 | 68 | 3 | 64 | 1 | 0 |
| Southern Connecticut State University | | 11,769 | 2 | 0 | 1 | 0 | 1 | 53 | 4 | 44 | 5 | 0 |
| University of Connecticut: | Health Center[3] | | 1 | 0 | 1 | 0 | 0 | 27 | 4 | 23 | 0 | 0 |
| | Storrs, Avery Point, and Hartford[3] | | 8 | 1 | 3 | 1 | 3 | 224 | 15 | 207 | 2 | 6 |
| Western Connecticut State University | | 6,462 | 4 | 0 | 1 | 2 | 1 | 67 | 26 | 37 | 4 | 0 |
| Yale University | | 10,192 | 3 | 1 | 0 | 2 | 0 | 389 | 75 | 305 | 9 | 1 |
| **DELAWARE** | | | | | | | | | | | | |
| Delaware State University | | 3,534 | 9 | 0 | 3 | 1 | 5 | 54 | 24 | 29 | 1 | 0 |
| University of Delaware | | 20,500 | 6 | 0 | 1 | 3 | 2 | 305 | 25 | 273 | 7 | 2 |
| **FLORIDA** | | | | | | | | | | | | |
| Florida A&M University | | 11,857 | 15 | 0 | 5 | 7 | 3 | 259 | 33 | 223 | 3 | 0 |
| Florida Atlantic University | | 26,839 | 3 | 0 | 2 | 0 | 1 | 262 | 32 | 218 | 12 | 1 |
| Florida Gulf Coast University | | 10,204 | 2 | 0 | 1 | 0 | 1 | 63 | 3 | 59 | 1 | 0 |
| Florida International University | | 38,759 | 8 | 0 | 1 | 5 | 2 | 543 | 96 | 402 | 45 | 1 |
| Florida State University: | Panama City[3] | | 0 | 0 | 0 | 0 | 0 | 8 | 0 | 8 | 0 | 0 |
| | Tallahassee | 38,682 | 32 | 0 | 2 | 12 | 18 | 543 | 79 | 453 | 11 | 2 |
| New College of Florida | | 785 | 1 | 0 | 1 | 0 | 0 | 33 | 5 | 28 | 0 | 3 |
| Pensacola Junior College | | 10,665 | 4 | 0 | 1 | 2 | 1 | 50 | 8 | 42 | 0 | 0 |
| Santa Fe College | | 14,796 | 0 | 0 | 0 | 0 | 0 | 66 | 4 | 62 | 0 | 0 |
| Tallahassee Community College | | 14,005 | 5 | 0 | 0 | 1 | 4 | 81 | 5 | 76 | 0 | 0 |

*Note*: Caution should be exercised in making any intercampus comparisons or ranking schools because university/college crime statistics are affected by a variety of factors. These include demographic characteristics of the surrounding community, ratio of male to female students, number of on-campus residents, accessibility of the campus to outside visitors, size of enrollment, etc.

[1] The student enrollment figures provided by the United States Department of Education are for the 2008 school year, the most recent available. The enrollment figures include full-time and part-time students.

[2] The FBI does not publish arson data unless it receives data from either the agency or the state for all 12 months of the calendar year.

[3] Student enrollment figures were not available.

## Table 9. Offenses Known to Law Enforcement, by State and University and College, 2009—*Continued*

(Number.)

| State and University/College | Campus | Student enroll-ment[1] | Violent crime | Murder and non-negligent man-slaughter | Forcible rape | Robbery | Aggra-vated assault | Property crime | Burglary | Larceny-theft | Motor vehicle theft | Arson[2] |
|---|---|---|---|---|---|---|---|---|---|---|---|---|
| University of Central Florida | | 50,121 | 19 | 0 | 3 | 5 | 11 | 485 | 66 | 383 | 36 | 0 |
| University of Florida | | 51,474 | 13 | 0 | 3 | 3 | 7 | 546 | 31 | 486 | 29 | 0 |
| University of North Florida | | 15,280 | 1 | 0 | 0 | 0 | 1 | 193 | 15 | 175 | 3 | 0 |
| University of South Florida: | St. Petersburg[3] | | 1 | 0 | 0 | 1 | 0 | 40 | 3 | 35 | 2 | 0 |
| | Tampa | 46,189 | 4 | 0 | 1 | 1 | 2 | 310 | 40 | 251 | 19 | 2 |
| University of West Florida | | 10,491 | 0 | 0 | 0 | 0 | 0 | 114 | 20 | 88 | 6 | 1 |
| **GEORGIA** | | | | | | | | | | | | |
| Abraham Baldwin Agricultural College | | 3,600 | 4 | 0 | 1 | 1 | 2 | 58 | 19 | 37 | 2 | 0 |
| Albany State University | | 4,176 | 1 | 0 | 0 | 1 | 0 | 63 | 11 | 51 | 1 | 0 |
| Armstrong Atlantic State University | | 7,067 | 1 | 0 | 0 | 0 | 1 | 44 | 6 | 36 | 2 | 0 |
| Augusta State University | | 6,689 | 0 | 0 | 0 | 0 | 0 | 52 | 0 | 52 | 0 | 0 |
| Berry College | | 1,795 | 0 | 0 | 0 | 0 | 0 | 23 | 7 | 16 | 0 | 0 |
| Clark Atlanta University | | 4,068 | 16 | 0 | 5 | 9 | 2 | 199 | 44 | 148 | 7 | 0 |
| Coastal Georgia Community College[3] | | | 0 | 0 | 0 | 0 | 0 | 23 | 3 | 20 | 0 | 1 |
| Columbus State University | | 7,951 | 3 | 0 | 0 | 3 | 0 | 109 | 9 | 97 | 3 | 1 |
| Dalton State College | | 4,957 | 0 | 0 | 0 | 0 | 0 | 20 | 0 | 20 | 0 | 0 |
| Emory University | | 12,755 | 5 | 0 | 5 | 0 | 0 | 429 | 45 | 364 | 20 | 0 |
| Fort Valley State University[4] | | 3,106 | 21 | 0 | 3 | 5 | 13 | | 86 | | 0 | |
| Georgia College and State University | | 6,506 | 0 | 0 | 0 | 0 | 0 | 3 | 1 | 2 | 0 | 0 |
| Georgia Institute of Technology | | 19,413 | 9 | 0 | 2 | 4 | 3 | 631 | 60 | 532 | 39 | 0 |
| Georgia Military College[3] | | | 2 | 0 | 0 | 0 | 2 | 6 | 0 | 6 | 0 | 0 |
| Georgia Perimeter College | | 22,808 | 2 | 0 | 0 | 1 | 1 | 169 | 2 | 160 | 7 | |
| Georgia Southern University | | 17,764 | 2 | 0 | 1 | 1 | 0 | 341 | 21 | 317 | 3 | 0 |
| Georgia Southwestern State University | | 2,717 | 1 | 0 | 0 | 0 | 1 | 36 | 3 | 32 | 1 | |
| Georgia State University | | 28,229 | 21 | 0 | 3 | 14 | 4 | 368 | 11 | 337 | 20 | 0 |
| Gordon College | | 3,855 | 1 | 0 | 1 | 0 | 0 | 59 | 15 | 44 | 0 | 0 |
| Kennesaw State University | | 21,449 | 5 | 0 | 4 | 0 | 1 | 158 | 22 | 134 | 2 | |
| Medical College of Georgia | | 2,443 | 0 | 0 | 0 | 0 | 0 | 92 | 0 | 88 | 4 | 0 |
| Mercer University | | 7,622 | 2 | 0 | 0 | 0 | 2 | 74 | 5 | 69 | 0 | 0 |
| Middle Georgia College | | 3,434 | 3 | 0 | 0 | 0 | 3 | 28 | 1 | 26 | 1 | 0 |
| Morehouse College | | 2,781 | 14 | 0 | 0 | 9 | 5 | 136 | 26 | 110 | 0 | 0 |
| North Georgia College and State University | | 5,500 | 0 | 0 | 0 | 0 | 0 | 35 | 0 | 35 | 0 | |
| Savannah State University | | 3,453 | 12 | 0 | 1 | 6 | 5 | 302 | 72 | 220 | 10 | 10 |
| Southern Polytechnic State University | | 4,818 | 0 | 0 | 0 | 0 | 0 | 51 | 5 | 42 | 4 | 0 |
| South Georgia College | | 1,880 | 1 | 0 | 1 | 0 | 0 | 11 | 1 | 10 | 0 | 0 |
| University of Georgia | | 34,180 | 7 | 0 | 2 | 3 | 2 | 403 | 80 | 321 | 2 | 2 |
| Valdosta State University | | 11,490 | 3 | 0 | 1 | 1 | 1 | 214 | 5 | 205 | 4 | 4 |
| Wesleyan College | | 739 | 0 | 0 | 0 | 0 | 0 | 11 | 4 | 7 | 0 | 0 |
| Young Harris College | | 654 | 1 | 0 | 1 | 0 | 0 | 18 | 4 | 14 | 0 | 0 |
| **ILLINOIS[5]** | | | | | | | | | | | | |
| Joliet Junior College | | 14,088 | | 0 | | 0 | 0 | 85 | 8 | 76 | 1 | 0 |
| **INDIANA** | | | | | | | | | | | | |
| Ball State University | | 20,243 | 18 | 0 | 2 | 7 | 9 | 302 | 51 | 249 | 2 | 2 |
| Indiana State University | | 10,457 | 11 | 0 | 0 | 1 | 10 | 185 | 9 | 172 | 4 | 0 |
| Indiana University: | Bloomington | 40,354 | 0 | 0 | 0 | 0 | 0 | 383 | 33 | 338 | 12 | 0 |
| | Gary | 4,794 | 0 | 0 | 0 | 0 | 0 | 47 | 1 | 44 | 2 | 0 |
| | Indianapolis[3] | | 10 | 0 | 1 | 4 | 5 | 364 | 64 | 287 | 13 | 1 |
| | New Albany | 6,482 | 3 | 0 | 0 | 1 | 2 | 31 | 4 | 27 | 0 | 0 |
| Marian University | | 2,143 | 0 | 0 | 0 | 0 | 0 | 22 | 0 | 22 | 0 | 0 |
| Purdue University | | 41,433 | 12 | 0 | 3 | 4 | 5 | 540 | 40 | 495 | 5 | 1 |
| **IOWA** | | | | | | | | | | | | |
| Iowa State University | | 26,856 | 7 | 0 | 2 | 1 | 4 | 327 | 35 | 289 | 3 | 4 |
| University of Iowa | | 29,152 | 5 | 0 | 1 | 0 | 4 | 205 | 20 | 185 | 0 | 0 |
| University of Northern Iowa | | 12,998 | 6 | 0 | 5 | 0 | 1 | 94 | 5 | 87 | 2 | 0 |
| **KANSAS** | | | | | | | | | | | | |
| Emporia State University | | 6,404 | 1 | 0 | 1 | 0 | 0 | 42 | 10 | 31 | 1 | 0 |
| Fort Hays State University | | 10,107 | 0 | 0 | 0 | 0 | 0 | 67 | 5 | 62 | 0 | 0 |
| Kansas State University | | 23,520 | 6 | 0 | 2 | 0 | 4 | 156 | 20 | 135 | 1 | 0 |
| Pittsburg State University | | 7,127 | 4 | 0 | 0 | 0 | 4 | 88 | 8 | 80 | 0 | 0 |
| Wichita State University | | 14,405 | 3 | 0 | 2 | 1 | 0 | 123 | 4 | 118 | 1 | 0 |
| **KENTUCKY[6]** | | | | | | | | | | | | |
| Eastern Kentucky University | | 16,031 | 7 | 0 | 3 | 3 | 1 | 252 | 64 | 186 | 2 | 0 |
| Kentucky State University | | 2,659 | 2 | 0 | 0 | 1 | 1 | 141 | 37 | 103 | 1 | 0 |
| Morehead State University | | 8,832 | 2 | 0 | 1 | 0 | 1 | 73 | 12 | 61 | 0 | 1 |
| Murray State University | | 10,014 | 3 | 0 | 1 | 0 | 2 | 130 | 15 | 112 | 3 | 5 |
| Northern Kentucky University | | 15,082 | 0 | 0 | 0 | 0 | 0 | 147 | 33 | 114 | 0 | 0 |
| University of Kentucky | | 26,054 | 13 | 0 | 1 | 6 | 6 | 539 | 26 | 502 | 11 | 0 |
| University of Louisville | | 20,834 | 17 | 0 | 0 | 15 | 2 | 286 | 29 | 252 | 5 | 1 |
| Western Kentucky University | | 19,742 | 5 | 0 | 2 | 0 | 3 | 269 | 68 | 196 | 5 | 0 |

*Note*: Caution should be exercised in making any intercampus comparisons or ranking schools because university/college crime statistics are affected by a variety of factors. These include demographic characteristics of the surrounding community, ratio of male to female students, number of on-campus residents, accessibility of the campus to outside visitors, size of enrollment, etc.

[1] The student enrollment figures provided by the United States Department of Education are for the 2008 school year, the most recent available. The enrollment figures include full-time and part-time students.

[2] The FBI does not publish arson data unless it receives data from either the agency or the state for all 12 months of the calendar year.

[3] Student enrollment figures were not available.

[4] The FBI determined that the agency's data were underreported. Consequently, those data are not included in this table.

[5] The data collection methodology for the offense of forcible rape used by the Illinois and the Minnesota state Uniform Crime Reporting (UCR) programs does not comply with national UCR Program guidelines. Consequently, their figures for forcible rape and violent crime (of which forcible rape is a part) are not published in this table.

[6] Because of changes in the state/local agency's reporting practices, figures are not comparable to previous years' data.

**Table 9. Offenses Known to Law Enforcement, by State and University and College, 2009—*Continued***

(Number.)

| State and University/College | Campus | Student enrollment[1] | Violent crime | Murder and nonnegligent manslaughter | Forcible rape | Robbery | Aggravated assault | Property crime | Burglary | Larceny-theft | Motor vehicle theft | Arson[2] |
|---|---|---|---|---|---|---|---|---|---|---|---|---|
| **LOUISIANA** | | | | | | | | | | | | |
| Delgado Community College | | 14,450 | 0 | 0 | 0 | 0 | 0 | 23 | 6 | 17 | 0 | 0 |
| Grambling State University | | 5,253 | 8 | 0 | 0 | 5 | 3 | 151 | 47 | 98 | 6 | 0 |
| Louisiana State University: | Baton Rouge[3] | | 39 | 0 | 1 | 13 | 25 | 543 | 101 | 428 | 14 | 2 |
| | Eunice | 3,031 | 0 | 0 | 0 | 0 | 0 | 0 | 0 | 0 | 0 | 0 |
| | Health Sciences Center, New Orleans | 2,431 | 0 | 0 | 0 | 0 | 0 | 0 | 0 | 0 | 0 | 0 |
| Louisiana Tech University | | 10,917 | 2 | 0 | 0 | 1 | 1 | 119 | 17 | 99 | 3 | 1 |
| McNeese State University | | 8,283 | 2 | 0 | 1 | 1 | 0 | 76 | 6 | 68 | 2 | 0 |
| Nicholls State University | | 6,916 | 1 | 0 | 0 | 0 | 1 | 36 | 5 | 31 | 0 | 0 |
| Northwestern State University | | 9,111 | 0 | 0 | 0 | 0 | 0 | 64 | 33 | 31 | 0 | 0 |
| Southeastern Louisiana University | | 15,215 | 2 | 0 | 0 | 1 | 1 | 113 | 7 | 104 | 2 | 1 |
| Southern University and A&M College: | Baton Rouge | 7,669 | 13 | 0 | 0 | 3 | 10 | 157 | 23 | 129 | 5 | 1 |
| | Shreveport | 2,429 | 5 | 0 | 0 | 0 | 5 | 18 | 4 | 14 | 0 | 0 |
| Tulane University | | 10,737 | 2 | 0 | 1 | 0 | 1 | 175 | 48 | 123 | 4 | 2 |
| University of Louisiana | Monroe | 8,754 | 3 | 0 | 0 | 0 | 3 | 104 | 6 | 96 | 2 | 0 |
| University of New Orleans | | 11,428 | 8 | 0 | 0 | 6 | 2 | 89 | 6 | 82 | 1 | 0 |
| **MAINE** | | | | | | | | | | | | |
| University of Maine: | Farmington | 2,174 | 2 | 0 | 2 | 0 | 0 | 32 | 4 | 28 | 0 | 1 |
| | Orono | 11,818 | 1 | 0 | 1 | 0 | 0 | 275 | 7 | 266 | 2 | 21 |
| University of Southern Maine | | 10,009 | 1 | 0 | 1 | 0 | 0 | 84 | 4 | 79 | 1 | 0 |
| **MARYLAND** | | | | | | | | | | | | |
| Bowie State University | | 5,483 | 11 | 0 | 2 | 0 | 9 | 61 | 27 | 33 | 1 | 0 |
| Coppin State University | | 4,051 | 5 | 0 | 0 | 1 | 4 | 57 | 10 | 46 | 1 | 0 |
| Frostburg State University | | 5,215 | 11 | 0 | 0 | 1 | 10 | 59 | 19 | 40 | 0 | 0 |
| Morgan State University | | 7,005 | 24 | 0 | 0 | 15 | 9 | 183 | 48 | 130 | 5 | 0 |
| Salisbury University | | 7,868 | 7 | 0 | 0 | 1 | 6 | 125 | 28 | 97 | 0 | 0 |
| St. Mary's College | | 2,068 | 0 | 0 | 0 | 0 | 0 | 53 | 3 | 50 | 0 | 0 |
| Towson University | | 21,111 | 0 | 0 | 0 | 0 | 0 | 156 | 25 | 129 | 2 | 1 |
| University of Baltimore | | 5,843 | 0 | 0 | 0 | 0 | 0 | 74 | 0 | 74 | 0 | 0 |
| University of Maryland: | Baltimore City | 6,156 | 7 | 0 | 0 | 3 | 4 | 86 | 0 | 85 | 1 | 0 |
| | Baltimore County | 12,268 | 3 | 0 | 1 | 0 | 2 | 122 | 6 | 115 | 1 | 2 |
| | College Park | 37,000 | 16 | 0 | 0 | 7 | 9 | 491 | 88 | 365 | 38 | 3 |
| | Eastern Shore | 4,290 | 9 | 0 | 1 | 4 | 4 | 139 | 58 | 78 | 3 | 1 |
| **MASSACHUSETTS** | | | | | | | | | | | | |
| Amherst College | | 1,697 | 3 | 0 | 0 | 0 | 3 | 78 | 2 | 76 | 0 | 0 |
| Assumption College | | 2,876 | 3 | 0 | 0 | 0 | 3 | 45 | 5 | 40 | 0 | 0 |
| Bentley College | | 5,693 | 9 | 0 | 2 | 0 | 7 | 56 | 16 | 40 | 0 | 2 |
| Boston College | | 14,836 | 10 | 0 | 6 | 0 | 4 | 168 | 35 | 131 | 2 | 0 |
| Boston University | | 31,766 | 11 | 0 | 1 | 7 | 3 | 402 | 66 | 332 | 4 | 0 |
| Brandeis University | | 5,327 | 3 | 0 | 1 | 0 | 2 | 53 | 7 | 46 | 0 | 0 |
| Bridgewater State College | | 10,269 | 5 | 0 | 0 | 0 | 5 | 71 | 15 | 54 | 2 | 1 |
| Bristol Community College | | 8,100 | 0 | 0 | 0 | 0 | 0 | 11 | 0 | 11 | 0 | 0 |
| Clark University | | 3,330 | 9 | 0 | 0 | 5 | 4 | 53 | 15 | 37 | 1 | 0 |
| Dean College | | 1,341 | 1 | 0 | 1 | 0 | 0 | 50 | 30 | 20 | 0 | |
| Emerson College | | 4,536 | 7 | 0 | 2 | 1 | 4 | 57 | 11 | 46 | 0 | 0 |
| Fitchburg State College | | 6,761 | 13 | 0 | 0 | 2 | 11 | 46 | 2 | 41 | 3 | 0 |
| Framingham State College | | 6,086 | 2 | 0 | 0 | 1 | 1 | 28 | 11 | 17 | 0 | 0 |
| Harvard University | | 26,496 | 10 | 1 | 2 | 3 | 4 | 505 | 273 | 228 | 4 | 0 |
| Holyoke Community College | | 6,592 | 7 | 0 | 0 | 1 | 6 | 47 | 6 | 40 | 1 | |
| Lasell College | | 1,488 | 5 | 0 | 0 | 0 | 5 | 49 | 12 | 37 | 0 | 0 |
| Massachusetts College of Art | | 2,340 | 0 | 0 | 0 | 0 | 0 | 43 | 5 | 38 | 0 | 0 |
| Massachusetts College of Liberal Arts | | 1,942 | 8 | 0 | 0 | 2 | 6 | 42 | 15 | 27 | 0 | 0 |
| Merrimack College | | 2,143 | 4 | 0 | 0 | 0 | 4 | 37 | 3 | 34 | 0 | 0 |
| Mount Holyoke College | | 2,241 | 2 | 0 | 2 | 0 | 0 | 93 | 5 | 87 | 1 | 0 |
| Northeastern University | | 25,837 | 16 | 0 | 0 | 12 | 4 | 380 | 17 | 363 | 0 | 0 |
| North Shore Community College | | 7,224 | 2 | 0 | 0 | 0 | 2 | 28 | 1 | 26 | 1 | 0 |
| Salem State College | | 10,157 | 0 | 0 | 0 | 0 | 0 | 83 | 18 | 65 | 0 | 0 |
| Smith College | | 3,101 | 2 | 0 | 2 | 0 | 0 | 87 | 12 | 72 | 3 | 0 |
| Springfield College | | 4,806 | 9 | 0 | 1 | 3 | 5 | 77 | 13 | 61 | 3 | 0 |
| University of Massachusetts: | Amherst | 26,359 | 11 | 0 | 6 | 1 | 4 | 271 | 40 | 227 | 4 | 0 |
| | Dartmouth | 9,155 | 25 | 0 | 3 | 1 | 21 | 154 | 40 | 114 | 0 | |
| | Harbor Campus, Boston | 14,117 | 0 | 0 | 0 | 0 | 0 | 93 | 26 | 67 | 0 | 0 |

*Note*: Caution should be exercised in making any intercampus comparisons or ranking schools because university/college crime statistics are affected by a variety of factors. These include demographic characteristics of the surrounding community, ratio of male to female students, number of on-campus residents, accessibility of the campus to outside visitors, size of enrollment, etc.

[1] The student enrollment figures provided by the United States Department of Education are for the 2008 school year, the most recent available. The enrollment figures include full-time and part-time students.

[2] The FBI does not publish arson data unless it receives data from either the agency or the state for all 12 months of the calendar year.

[3] Student enrollment figures were not available.

## Table 9. Offenses Known to Law Enforcement, by State and University and College, 2009—*Continued*

(Number.)

| State and University/College | Campus | Student enroll-ment[1] | Violent crime | Murder and non-negligent man-slaughter | Forcible rape | Robbery | Aggra-vated assault | Property crime | Burglary | Larceny-theft | Motor vehicle theft | Arson[2] |
|---|---|---|---|---|---|---|---|---|---|---|---|---|
| Wellesley College | | 2,498 | 0 | 0 | 0 | 0 | 0 | 62 | 11 | 50 | 1 | 0 |
| Western New England College | | 3,722 | 3 | 0 | 1 | 0 | 2 | 57 | 2 | 54 | 1 | 0 |
| Westfield State College | | 5,548 | 1 | 0 | 1 | 0 | 0 | 65 | 6 | 59 | 0 | 1 |
| Worcester Polytechnic Institute | | 4,556 | 1 | 0 | 0 | 1 | 0 | 47 | 2 | 45 | 0 | 0 |
| **MICHIGAN[6]** | | | | | | | | | | | | |
| Central Michigan University | | 27,225 | 4 | 0 | 4 | 0 | 0 | 223 | 20 | 202 | 1 | 4 |
| Delta College | | 10,899 | 0 | 0 | 0 | 0 | 0 | 54 | 3 | 51 | 0 | 1 |
| Eastern Michigan University | | 22,032 | 9 | 0 | 1 | 3 | 5 | 219 | 40 | 175 | 4 | 4 |
| Ferris State University | | 13,532 | 9 | 0 | 3 | 1 | 5 | 129 | 18 | 110 | 1 | 1 |
| Grand Rapids Community College | | 15,403 | 4 | 0 | 0 | 2 | 2 | 205 | 1 | 204 | 0 | 1 |
| Grand Valley State University | | 23,892 | 3 | 0 | 0 | 0 | 3 | 74 | 1 | 73 | 0 | 0 |
| Lansing Community College | | 19,445 | 1 | 0 | 0 | 1 | 0 | 108 | 2 | 106 | 0 | 0 |
| Macomb Community College | | 22,985 | 1 | 0 | 0 | 1 | 0 | 85 | 1 | 78 | 6 | 0 |
| Michigan State University | | 46,510 | 15 | 0 | 3 | 2 | 10 | 911 | 116 | 786 | 9 | 6 |
| Michigan Technological University | | 7,009 | 2 | 0 | 2 | 0 | 0 | 96 | 2 | 93 | 1 | 0 |
| Mott Community College | | 10,813 | 2 | 0 | 0 | 2 | 0 | 109 | 6 | 103 | 0 | 1 |
| Northern Michigan University | | 9,347 | 5 | 0 | 2 | 0 | 3 | 128 | 69 | 56 | 3 | 0 |
| Oakland Community College | | 24,957 | 4 | 0 | 0 | 2 | 2 | 58 | 0 | 55 | 3 | 0 |
| Oakland University | | 18,175 | 3 | 0 | 1 | 0 | 2 | 88 | 8 | 79 | 1 | 0 |
| Saginaw Valley State University | | 9,837 | 3 | 0 | 1 | 1 | 1 | 98 | 21 | 77 | 0 | 0 |
| University of Michigan: | Ann Arbor | 41,028 | 6 | 0 | 0 | 0 | 6 | 763 | 13 | 742 | 8 | 10 |
| | Dearborn | 8,311 | 0 | 0 | 0 | 0 | 0 | 68 | 0 | 57 | 11 | 0 |
| | Flint | 7,260 | 4 | 0 | 0 | 3 | 1 | 131 | 9 | 117 | 5 | 0 |
| **MINNESOTA[5]** | | | | | | | | | | | | |
| University of Minnesota: | Duluth | 11,366 | | 0 | | 0 | 1 | 66 | 4 | 62 | 0 | 1 |
| | Morris | 1,607 | | 0 | | 0 | 0 | 17 | 1 | 16 | 0 | 0 |
| | Twin Cities | 51,140 | | 0 | | 5 | 2 | 658 | 51 | 592 | 15 | 1 |
| **MISSISSIPPI** | | | | | | | | | | | | |
| Coahoma Community College | | 2,263 | 3 | 0 | 0 | 0 | 3 | 21 | 19 | 1 | 1 | 0 |
| Jackson State University | | 8,377 | 11 | 0 | 1 | 3 | 7 | 219 | 23 | 191 | 5 | 0 |
| Mississippi State University | | 17,824 | 3 | 0 | 0 | 1 | 2 | 176 | 1 | 171 | 4 | 0 |
| Northeast Mississippi Community College | | 3,190 | 1 | 0 | 0 | 0 | 1 | 116 | 12 | 103 | 1 | 0 |
| University of Mississippi: | Medical Center | 2,266 | 0 | 0 | 0 | 0 | 0 | 163 | 6 | 151 | 6 | 0 |
| | Oxford | 15,289 | 1 | 0 | 1 | 0 | 0 | 209 | 29 | 178 | 2 | 0 |
| **MISSOURI** | | | | | | | | | | | | |
| Lincoln University | | 3,109 | 22 | 0 | 0 | 3 | 19 | 54 | 15 | 38 | 1 | 1 |
| Mineral Area College | | 3,238 | 0 | 0 | 0 | 0 | 0 | 10 | 3 | 7 | 0 | 0 |
| Missouri Southern State University | | 5,264 | 2 | 0 | 1 | 0 | 1 | 48 | 9 | 39 | 0 | 0 |
| Missouri University of Science and Technology | | 6,367 | 0 | 0 | 0 | 0 | 0 | 50 | 5 | 45 | 0 | 0 |
| Missouri Western State University | | 5,508 | 0 | 0 | 0 | 0 | 0 | 74 | 7 | 67 | 0 | 0 |
| Northwest Missouri State University | | 6,687 | 5 | 0 | 5 | 0 | 0 | 61 | 11 | 48 | 2 | 1 |
| Southeast Missouri State University | | 10,736 | 2 | 0 | 0 | 1 | 1 | 41 | 8 | 33 | 0 | 0 |
| St. Louis Community College: | Florissant Valley | 6,514 | 1 | 0 | 1 | 0 | 0 | 88 | 0 | 86 | 2 | 0 |
| | Meramec | 10,209 | 0 | 0 | 0 | 0 | 0 | 26 | 2 | 24 | 0 | 0 |
| Truman State University | | 5,880 | 0 | 0 | 0 | 0 | 0 | 76 | 4 | 71 | 1 | 0 |
| University of Central Missouri | | 11,063 | 2 | 0 | 0 | 1 | 1 | 140 | 38 | 100 | 2 | 1 |
| University of Missouri: | Columbia | 30,130 | 15 | 0 | 0 | 3 | 12 | 354 | 35 | 318 | 1 | 1 |
| | Kansas City | 14,481 | 4 | 0 | 0 | 3 | 1 | 172 | 35 | 136 | 1 | 0 |
| | St. Louis | 15,741 | 12 | 0 | 0 | 1 | 11 | 113 | 12 | 99 | 2 | 0 |
| Washington University | | 13,339 | 3 | 0 | 1 | 0 | 2 | 193 | 7 | 180 | 6 | 0 |
| **MONTANA** | | | | | | | | | | | | |
| Montana State University | | 11,976 | 0 | 0 | 0 | 0 | 0 | 157 | 6 | 149 | 2 | 3 |
| University of Montana | | 14,207 | 5 | 0 | 1 | 2 | 2 | 157 | 4 | 151 | 2 | 1 |
| **NEBRASKA** | | | | | | | | | | | | |
| University of Nebraska: | Kearney | 6,543 | 0 | 0 | 0 | 0 | 0 | 42 | 5 | 37 | 0 | 0 |
| | Lincoln | 23,573 | 4 | 0 | 0 | 0 | 4 | 228 | 15 | 212 | 1 | 0 |
| **NEVADA** | | | | | | | | | | | | |
| Truckee Meadows Community College | | 12,492 | 2 | 0 | 0 | 1 | 1 | 25 | 12 | 13 | 0 | 0 |
| University of Nevada | Las Vegas | 28,600 | 7 | 0 | 1 | 2 | 4 | 199 | 30 | 151 | 18 | 1 |
| **NEW HAMPSHIRE** | | | | | | | | | | | | |
| University of New Hampshire | | 14,898 | 8 | 0 | 2 | 2 | 4 | 164 | 5 | 156 | 3 | 3 |
| **NEW JERSEY** | | | | | | | | | | | | |
| Brookdale Community College | | 14,642 | 0 | 0 | 0 | 0 | 0 | 42 | 0 | 42 | 0 | 0 |
| Essex County College | | 12,318 | 1 | 0 | 0 | 1 | 0 | 68 | 0 | 66 | 2 | 0 |
| Kean University | | 14,203 | 1 | 0 | 0 | 1 | 0 | 151 | 68 | 82 | 1 | 1 |
| Middlesex County College | | 12,381 | 0 | 0 | 0 | 0 | 0 | 50 | 1 | 49 | 0 | 2 |
| Monmouth University | | 6,442 | 0 | 0 | 0 | 0 | 0 | 69 | 10 | 55 | 4 | 0 |
| Montclair State University | | 17,475 | 9 | 0 | 2 | 1 | 6 | 235 | 13 | 222 | 0 | 0 |
| New Jersey Institute of Technology | | 8,398 | 14 | 0 | 1 | 11 | 2 | 146 | 5 | 130 | 11 | 0 |

*Note*: Caution should be exercised in making any intercampus comparisons or ranking schools because university/college crime statistics are affected by a variety of factors. These include demographic characteristics of the surrounding community, ratio of male to female students, number of on-campus residents, accessibility of the campus to outside visitors, size of enrollment, etc.

[1] The student enrollment figures provided by the United States Department of Education are for the 2008 school year, the most recent available. The enrollment figures include full-time and part-time students.

[2] The FBI does not publish arson data unless it receives data from either the agency or the state for all 12 months of the calendar year.

[5] The data collection methodology for the offense of forcible rape used by the Illinois and the Minnesota state Uniform Crime Reporting (UCR) programs does not comply with national UCR Program guidelines. Consequently, their figures for forcible rape and violent crime (of which forcible rape is a part) are not published in this table.

[6] Because of changes in the state/local agency's reporting practices, figures are not comparable to previous years' data.

**Table 9. Offenses Known to Law Enforcement, by State and University and College, 2009—*Continued***

(Number.)

| State and University/College | Campus | Student enroll-ment[1] | Violent crime | Murder and non-negligent man-slaughter | Forcible rape | Robbery | Aggra-vated assault | Property crime | Burglary | Larceny-theft | Motor vehicle theft | Arson[2] |
|---|---|---|---|---|---|---|---|---|---|---|---|---|
| Richard Stockton College of New Jersey | | 7,307 | 3 | 0 | 0 | 0 | 3 | 99 | 12 | 87 | 0 | 0 |
| Rowan University | | 10,270 | 3 | 0 | 0 | 1 | 2 | 122 | 10 | 110 | 2 | 0 |
| Rutgers University: | Camden | 5,398 | 5 | 0 | 0 | 1 | 4 | 117 | 12 | 104 | 1 | 2 |
| | Newark | 11,032 | 7 | 0 | 1 | 6 | 0 | 125 | 5 | 109 | 11 | 1 |
| | New Brunswick | 36,041 | 17 | 0 | 2 | 3 | 12 | 483 | 60 | 414 | 9 | 0 |
| Stevens Institute of Technology | | 5,595 | 1 | 0 | 0 | 0 | 1 | 20 | 0 | 20 | 0 | 0 |
| The College of New Jersey | | 6,949 | 0 | 0 | 0 | 0 | 0 | 77 | 5 | 69 | 3 | 0 |
| University of Medicine and Dentistry: | Camden[3] | | 0 | 0 | 0 | 0 | 0 | 1 | 0 | 1 | 0 | 0 |
| | Newark | 5,906 | 22 | 0 | 0 | 13 | 9 | 193 | 5 | 180 | 8 | 0 |
| | New Brunswick[3] | | 0 | 0 | 0 | 0 | 0 | 53 | 1 | 51 | 1 | 0 |
| William Paterson University | | 10,256 | 0 | 0 | 0 | 0 | 0 | 83 | 11 | 68 | 4 | 0 |
| **NEW MEXICO** | | | | | | | | | | | | |
| Eastern New Mexico University | | 4,294 | 4 | 0 | 0 | 0 | 4 | 63 | 12 | 49 | 2 | 0 |
| New Mexico State University | | 17,239 | 28 | 0 | 0 | 1 | 27 | 364 | 46 | 303 | 15 | 0 |
| University of New Mexico | | 25,754 | 18 | 0 | 2 | 5 | 11 | 630 | 59 | 537 | 34 | 3 |
| **NEW YORK** | | | | | | | | | | | | |
| Cornell University | | 20,273 | 1 | 0 | 0 | 0 | 1 | 245 | 17 | 228 | 0 | 0 |
| Ithaca College | | 6,448 | 1 | 0 | 1 | 0 | 0 | 94 | 9 | 84 | 1 | 5 |
| Rensselaer Polytechnic Institute | | 6,777 | 4 | 0 | 0 | 3 | 1 | 104 | 1 | 103 | 0 | 0 |
| State University of New York: | Buffalo[3] | | 9 | 0 | 2 | 6 | 1 | 445 | 65 | 368 | 12 | 1 |
| | Maritime College | 1,630 | 0 | 0 | 0 | 0 | 0 | 42 | 11 | 31 | 0 | 1 |
| | Stony Brook[3] | | 13 | 0 | 2 | 2 | 9 | 675 | 137 | 531 | 7 | 10 |
| | Upstate Medical Center[3] | | 2 | 0 | 0 | 0 | 2 | 118 | 2 | 115 | 1 | 0 |
| State University of New York Agricultural and Technical College: | Alfred | 3,276 | 2 | 0 | 1 | 0 | 1 | 72 | 11 | 60 | 1 | 0 |
| | Canton | 2,970 | 1 | 0 | 1 | 0 | 0 | 48 | 2 | 46 | 0 | 0 |
| | Cobleskill | 2,615 | 2 | 0 | 0 | 0 | 2 | 88 | 30 | 58 | 0 | 0 |
| | Farmingdale[3] | | 0 | 0 | 0 | 0 | 0 | 17 | 2 | 15 | 0 | 0 |
| | Morrisville[3] | | 2 | 0 | 0 | 2 | 0 | 98 | 32 | 65 | 1 | 0 |
| State University of New York College: | Brockport | 8,275 | 4 | 0 | 0 | 0 | 4 | 72 | 8 | 64 | 0 | 0 |
| | Buffalo | 11,234 | 10 | 0 | 4 | 1 | 5 | 208 | 47 | 156 | 5 | 0 |
| | Cortland | 7,234 | 0 | 0 | 0 | 0 | 0 | 82 | 18 | 64 | 0 | 0 |
| | Environmental Science and Forestry | 2,523 | 0 | 0 | 0 | 0 | 0 | 14 | 1 | 13 | 0 | 0 |
| | Geneseo[3] | | 2 | 0 | 1 | 0 | 1 | 118 | 9 | 109 | 0 | 0 |
| | New Paltz | 8,205 | 7 | 0 | 1 | 1 | 5 | 102 | 12 | 90 | 0 | 0 |
| | Old Westbury | 3,505 | 3 | 0 | 0 | 1 | 2 | 70 | 10 | 60 | 0 | 0 |
| | Oneonta | 5,757 | 1 | 0 | 0 | 1 | 0 | 64 | 9 | 55 | 0 | 0 |
| | Optometry | 303 | 0 | 0 | 0 | 0 | 0 | 2 | 0 | 2 | 0 | 0 |
| | Oswego | 8,909 | 0 | 0 | 0 | 0 | 0 | 133 | 47 | 86 | 0 | 1 |
| | Plattsburgh | 6,358 | 1 | 0 | 0 | 0 | 1 | 110 | 25 | 85 | 0 | 0 |
| | Potsdam | 4,325 | 2 | 0 | 2 | 0 | 0 | 80 | 22 | 58 | 0 | 0 |
| | Purchase | 4,251 | 5 | 0 | 2 | 2 | 1 | 138 | 36 | 102 | 0 | 4 |
| | Utica-Rome[3] | | 0 | 0 | 0 | 0 | 0 | 28 | 2 | 26 | 0 | 0 |
| United States Merchant Marine Academy | | 986 | 0 | 0 | 0 | 0 | 0 | 13 | 5 | 8 | 0 | 0 |
| **NORTH CAROLINA** | | | | | | | | | | | | |
| Appalachian State University | | 16,610 | 4 | 0 | 3 | 0 | 1 | 177 | 13 | 163 | 1 | 0 |
| Duke University | | 14,060 | 23 | 0 | 4 | 6 | 13 | 777 | 47 | 718 | 12 | 1 |
| East Carolina University | | 27,677 | 8 | 0 | 5 | 0 | 3 | 233 | 10 | 219 | 4 | 1 |
| Elizabeth City State University | | 3,104 | 2 | 0 | 0 | 1 | 1 | 63 | 22 | 41 | 0 | 0 |
| Elon University | | 5,628 | 0 | 0 | 0 | 0 | 0 | 54 | 20 | 34 | 0 | 0 |
| Fayetteville State University | | 6,217 | 5 | 0 | 0 | 4 | 1 | 148 | 32 | 108 | 8 | 0 |
| North Carolina Agricultural and Technical State University | | 10,388 | 6 | 0 | 1 | 4 | 1 | 166 | 44 | 115 | 7 | 1 |
| North Carolina Central University | | 8,035 | 9 | 0 | 2 | 3 | 4 | 208 | 40 | 161 | 7 | 0 |
| North Carolina School of the Arts | | 879 | 1 | 0 | 0 | 0 | 1 | 33 | 3 | 27 | 3 | 0 |
| North Carolina State University | Raleigh | 32,872 | 11 | 0 | 2 | 5 | 4 | 407 | 28 | 372 | 7 | 1 |
| University of North Carolina: | Asheville | 3,629 | 0 | 0 | 0 | 0 | 0 | 44 | 1 | 43 | 0 | 0 |
| | Chapel Hill | 28,567 | 6 | 0 | 1 | 1 | 4 | 281 | 10 | 268 | 3 | 0 |
| | Greensboro | 19,976 | 1 | 0 | 0 | 0 | 1 | 186 | 9 | 170 | 7 | 0 |
| | Pembroke | 6,303 | 0 | 0 | 0 | 0 | 0 | 60 | 8 | 51 | 1 | 0 |
| | Wilmington | 12,643 | 3 | 0 | 2 | 1 | 0 | 261 | 29 | 230 | 2 | 0 |

*Note*: Caution should be exercised in making any intercampus comparisons or ranking schools because university/college crime statistics are affected by a variety of factors. These include demographic characteristics of the surrounding community, ratio of male to female students, number of on-campus residents, accessibility of the campus to outside visitors, size of enrollment, etc.

[1] The student enrollment figures provided by the United States Department of Education are for the 2008 school year, the most recent available. The enrollment figures include full-time and part-time students.

[2] The FBI does not publish arson data unless it receives data from either the agency or the state for all 12 months of the calendar year.

[3] Student enrollment figures were not available.

**Table 9. Offenses Known to Law Enforcement, by State and University and College, 2009—*Continued***

(Number.)

| State and University/College | Campus | Student enroll-ment[1] | Violent crime | Murder and non-negligent man-slaughter | Forcible rape | Robbery | Aggra-vated assault | Property crime | Burglary | Larceny-theft | Motor vehicle theft | Arson[2] |
|---|---|---|---|---|---|---|---|---|---|---|---|---|
| Wake Forest University | | 6,862 | 5 | 0 | 3 | 1 | 1 | 205 | 41 | 160 | 4 | 1 |
| Western Carolina University | | 9,050 | 2 | 0 | 1 | 0 | 1 | 124 | 11 | 112 | 1 | 0 |
| Winston-Salem State University | | 6,442 | 5 | 0 | 0 | 4 | 1 | 135 | 7 | 118 | 10 | 0 |
| **NORTH DAKOTA** | | | | | | | | | | | | |
| North Dakota State College of Science | | 2,707 | 1 | 0 | 0 | 0 | 1 | 26 | 6 | 18 | 2 | 0 |
| North Dakota State University | | 13,230 | 0 | 0 | 0 | 0 | 0 | 121 | 10 | 107 | 4 | 0 |
| University of North Dakota | | 12,748 | 5 | 0 | 1 | 1 | 3 | 144 | 17 | 127 | 0 | 1 |
| **OHIO** | | | | | | | | | | | | |
| Bowling Green State University | | 17,874 | 2 | 0 | 2 | 0 | 0 | 232 | 38 | 194 | 0 | 2 |
| Cleveland State University | | 15,139 | 4 | 0 | 0 | 4 | 0 | 56 | 1 | 53 | 2 | 0 |
| Cuyahoga Community College | | 23,234 | 2 | 0 | 0 | 2 | 0 | 147 | 1 | 145 | 1 | 0 |
| Kent State University | | 22,944 | 4 | 0 | 0 | 4 | 0 | 190 | 15 | 172 | 3 | 0 |
| Lakeland Community College | | 9,017 | 0 | 0 | 0 | 0 | 0 | 41 | 0 | 40 | 1 | 0 |
| Miami University | | 17,191 | 10 | 0 | 3 | 4 | 3 | 194 | 16 | 178 | 0 | 0 |
| Notre Dame College | | 1,637 | 1 | 0 | 1 | 0 | 0 | 44 | 9 | 35 | 0 | 0 |
| Ohio State University | Columbus | 53,715 | 20 | 0 | 4 | 11 | 5 | 1,017 | 211 | 797 | 9 | 11 |
| Ohio University | | 21,369 | 7 | 0 | 6 | 1 | 0 | 234 | 42 | 192 | 0 | 0 |
| Sinclair Community College | | 19,466 | 0 | 0 | 0 | 0 | 0 | 31 | 0 | 31 | 0 | 0 |
| University of Akron | | 24,119 | 2 | 0 | 0 | 2 | 0 | 421 | 11 | 397 | 13 | 1 |
| University of Cincinnati | | 29,617 | 16 | 0 | 1 | 10 | 5 | 546 | 37 | 504 | 5 | 1 |
| University of Rio Grande | | 1,967 | 0 | 0 | 0 | 0 | 0 | 24 | 0 | 24 | 0 | 0 |
| University of Toledo | | 22,336 | 8 | 0 | 1 | 4 | 3 | 551 | 117 | 433 | 1 | 0 |
| Wright State University | | 16,672 | 5 | 0 | 4 | 1 | 0 | 190 | 35 | 152 | 3 | 0 |
| Youngstown State University | | 13,704 | 3 | 0 | 3 | 0 | 0 | 164 | 13 | 149 | 2 | 0 |
| **OKLAHOMA** | | | | | | | | | | | | |
| Cameron University | | 5,449 | 2 | 0 | 0 | 0 | 2 | 46 | 27 | 18 | 1 | 0 |
| Murray State College[6] | | 2,379 | 0 | 0 | 0 | 0 | 0 | 5 | 2 | 3 | 0 | 0 |
| Northeastern Oklahoma A&M College | | 1,807 | 1 | 0 | 0 | 0 | 1 | 65 | 31 | 33 | 1 | 0 |
| Northeastern State University: | Broken Arrow[3,6] | | 0 | 0 | 0 | 0 | 0 | 3 | 0 | 3 | 0 | 0 |
| | Tahlequah[3,6] | | 2 | 0 | 1 | 0 | 1 | 67 | 14 | 49 | 4 | 0 |
| Oklahoma State University: | Main Campus | 22,995 | 4 | 0 | 3 | 1 | 0 | 278 | 67 | 207 | 4 | 0 |
| | Okmulgee[3,6] | | 1 | 0 | 0 | 0 | 1 | 10 | 2 | 7 | 1 | 0 |
| | Tulsa[3] | | 0 | 0 | 0 | 0 | 0 | 10 | 4 | 6 | 0 | 0 |
| Rogers State University | | 3,913 | 0 | 0 | 0 | 0 | 0 | 29 | 5 | 24 | 0 | 0 |
| Seminole State College[6] | | 2,031 | 1 | 0 | 1 | 0 | 0 | 9 | 0 | 9 | 0 | 0 |
| Southeastern Oklahoma State University[6] | | 3,866 | 1 | 0 | 0 | 0 | 1 | 40 | 17 | 23 | 0 | 0 |
| Southwestern Oklahoma State University[6] | | 4,850 | 0 | 0 | 0 | 0 | 0 | 39 | 6 | 32 | 1 | 0 |
| Tulsa Community College[6] | | 18,325 | 0 | 0 | 0 | 0 | 0 | 38 | 1 | 37 | 0 | 0 |
| University of Central Oklahoma | | 15,724 | 2 | 0 | 1 | 1 | 0 | 157 | 19 | 136 | 2 | 0 |
| University of Oklahoma: | Health Sciences Center[6] | 3,926 | 7 | 0 | 0 | 2 | 5 | 157 | 4 | 144 | 9 | 0 |
| | Norman | 26,140 | 5 | 0 | 1 | 1 | 3 | 354 | 41 | 306 | 7 | 5 |
| **PENNSYLVANIA** | | | | | | | | | | | | |
| California University | | 8,519 | 0 | 0 | 0 | 0 | 0 | 30 | 1 | 29 | 0 | 0 |
| Cheyney University | | 1,488 | 9 | 0 | 1 | 0 | 8 | 94 | 52 | 40 | 2 | 1 |
| Clarion University | | 7,100 | 6 | 0 | 1 | 0 | 5 | 43 | 5 | 38 | 0 | 0 |
| Dickinson College | | 2,388 | 4 | 0 | 3 | 0 | 1 | 59 | 6 | 53 | 0 | 0 |
| East Stroudsburg University | | 7,234 | 13 | 0 | 0 | 1 | 12 | 99 | 48 | 51 | 0 | 0 |
| Edinboro University | | 7,671 | 6 | 0 | 1 | 0 | 5 | 94 | 12 | 82 | 0 | 0 |
| Elizabethtown College | | 2,311 | 2 | 0 | 1 | 0 | 1 | 23 | 0 | 23 | 0 | 0 |
| Indiana University | | 14,310 | 6 | 0 | 4 | 1 | 1 | 90 | 3 | 87 | 0 | 0 |
| Kutztown University | | 10,393 | 0 | 0 | 0 | 0 | 0 | 82 | 1 | 81 | 0 | |
| Lehigh University | | 6,994 | 4 | 0 | 1 | 2 | 1 | 108 | 9 | 98 | 1 | 0 |
| Lock Haven University | | 5,266 | 0 | 0 | 0 | 0 | 0 | 54 | 8 | 46 | 0 | 0 |
| Millersville University | | 8,320 | 2 | 0 | 0 | 0 | 2 | 42 | 7 | 35 | 0 | 0 |
| Moravian College | | 2,040 | 1 | 0 | 1 | 0 | 0 | 44 | 2 | 42 | 0 | 0 |
| Pennsylvania State University: | Altoona | 4,013 | 0 | 0 | 0 | 0 | 0 | 32 | 1 | 31 | 0 | 2 |
| | Behrend | 4,334 | 0 | 0 | 0 | 0 | 0 | 23 | 0 | 23 | 0 | 0 |
| | Berks | 2,800 | 0 | 0 | 0 | 0 | 0 | 29 | 4 | 25 | 0 | 0 |
| | Harrisburg | 3,936 | 0 | 0 | 0 | 0 | 0 | 14 | 0 | 14 | 0 | 0 |
| | Hazelton | 1,228 | 0 | 0 | 0 | 0 | 0 | 20 | 1 | 19 | 0 | 0 |
| | McKeesport[3] | | 2 | 0 | 0 | 0 | 2 | 28 | 3 | 25 | 0 | 0 |
| | Mont Alto | 1,189 | 0 | 0 | 0 | 0 | 0 | 14 | 1 | 13 | 0 | 0 |
| | University Park | 44,406 | 25 | 0 | 2 | 0 | 23 | 489 | 46 | 439 | 4 | 13 |
| Shippensburg University | | 7,942 | 7 | 0 | 1 | 4 | 2 | 54 | 15 | 39 | 0 | 0 |
| Slippery Rock University | | 8,458 | 2 | 0 | 0 | 0 | 2 | 42 | 6 | 36 | 0 | 0 |

*Note*: Caution should be exercised in making any intercampus comparisons or ranking schools because university/college crime statistics are affected by a variety of factors. These include demographic characteristics of the surrounding community, ratio of male to female students, number of on-campus residents, accessibility of the campus to outside visitors, size of enrollment, etc.

[1] The student enrollment figures provided by the United States Department of Education are for the 2008 school year, the most recent available. The enrollment figures include full-time and part-time students.

[2] The FBI does not publish arson data unless it receives data from either the agency or the state for all 12 months of the calendar year.

[3] Student enrollment figures were not available.

[6] Because of changes in the state/local agency's reporting practices, figures are not comparable to previous years' data.

## Table 9. Offenses Known to Law Enforcement, by State and University and College, 2009—*Continued*

(Number.)

| State and University/College | Campus | Student enroll-ment[1] | Violent crime | Murder and non-negligent man-slaughter | Forcible rape | Robbery | Aggra-vated assault | Property crime | Burglary | Larceny-theft | Motor vehicle theft | Arson[2] |
|---|---|---|---|---|---|---|---|---|---|---|---|---|
| University of Pittsburgh: | Bradford | 1,502 | 1 | 0 | 0 | 0 | 1 | 20 | 7 | 13 | 0 | 0 |
| | Pittsburgh | 27,562 | 16 | 0 | 0 | 9 | 7 | 361 | 23 | 338 | 0 | 0 |
| West Chester University | | 13,619 | 6 | 0 | 4 | 0 | 2 | 98 | 27 | 69 | 2 | 0 |
| **RHODE ISLAND** | | | | | | | | | | | | |
| Brown University | | 8,318 | 1 | 0 | 1 | 0 | 0 | 171 | 65 | 106 | 0 | 1 |
| University of Rhode Island | | 15,904 | 4 | 0 | 1 | 2 | 1 | 224 | 19 | 193 | 12 | 1 |
| **SOUTH CAROLINA** | | | | | | | | | | | | |
| Benedict College | | 2,883 | 8 | 0 | 2 | 4 | 2 | 300 | 161 | 136 | 3 | 2 |
| Bob Jones University | | 4,141 | 0 | 0 | 0 | 0 | 0 | 63 | 20 | 43 | 0 | 0 |
| Clemson University | | 18,317 | 4 | 0 | 2 | 1 | 1 | 260 | 63 | 184 | 13 | 1 |
| Coastal Carolina University | | 8,154 | 6 | 0 | 1 | 0 | 5 | 184 | 21 | 159 | 4 | 1 |
| College of Charleston | | 11,367 | 3 | 0 | 3 | 0 | 0 | 135 | 11 | 124 | 0 | 0 |
| Francis Marion University | | 4,020 | 0 | 0 | 0 | 0 | 0 | 66 | 4 | 61 | 1 | 1 |
| Greenville Technical College | | 14,414 | 5 | 0 | 1 | 0 | 4 | 113 | 2 | 111 | 0 | 0 |
| Medical University of South Carolina | | 2,528 | 3 | 0 | 0 | 0 | 3 | 201 | 7 | 193 | 1 | 0 |
| South Carolina State University | | 4,888 | 20 | 0 | 1 | 14 | 5 | 196 | 67 | 122 | 7 | 0 |
| The Citadel | | 3,328 | 5 | 0 | 0 | 5 | 0 | 36 | 8 | 28 | 0 | 0 |
| University of South Carolina: | Aiken | 3,232 | 0 | 0 | 0 | 0 | 0 | 26 | 1 | 25 | 0 | 0 |
| | Columbia | 27,488 | 5 | 0 | 0 | 2 | 3 | 358 | 116 | 221 | 21 | 0 |
| Winthrop University | | 6,249 | 1 | 0 | 1 | 0 | 0 | 55 | 6 | 46 | 3 | 0 |
| **SOUTH DAKOTA** | | | | | | | | | | | | |
| South Dakota State University | | 11,995 | 0 | 0 | 0 | 0 | 0 | 30 | 1 | 29 | 0 | 1 |
| **TENNESSEE** | | | | | | | | | | | | |
| Austin Peay State University | | 9,401 | 4 | 0 | 0 | 0 | 4 | 134 | 38 | 94 | 2 | 1 |
| Christian Brothers University | | 1,869 | 0 | 0 | 0 | 0 | 0 | 15 | 0 | 14 | 1 | 0 |
| East Tennessee State University | | 13,646 | 8 | 0 | 5 | 1 | 2 | 152 | 28 | 122 | 2 | 1 |
| Middle Tennessee State University | | 23,872 | 6 | 0 | 3 | 1 | 2 | 308 | 41 | 260 | 7 | 0 |
| Northeast State Technical Community College | | 5,470 | 0 | 0 | 0 | 0 | 0 | 23 | 0 | 23 | 0 | 0 |
| Southwest Tennessee Community College | | 11,427 | 2 | 0 | 0 | 0 | 2 | 23 | 0 | 23 | 0 | 0 |
| Tennessee State University | | 8,254 | 11 | 2 | 0 | 6 | 3 | 178 | 18 | 155 | 5 | 1 |
| Tennessee Technological University | | 10,793 | 4 | 0 | 0 | 2 | 2 | 105 | 24 | 80 | 1 | 2 |
| University of Memphis | | 20,220 | 5 | 0 | 1 | 1 | 3 | 187 | 50 | 135 | 2 | 2 |
| University of Tennessee: | Chattanooga | 9,807 | 7 | 0 | 3 | 1 | 3 | 183 | 14 | 164 | 5 | 0 |
| | Knoxville | 30,410 | 6 | 0 | 3 | 2 | 1 | 420 | 18 | 391 | 11 | 1 |
| | Martin | 7,574 | 0 | 0 | 0 | 0 | 0 | 49 | 4 | 45 | 0 | 0 |
| | Memphis[3] | | 3 | 0 | 0 | 0 | 3 | 59 | 6 | 52 | 1 | 0 |
| Vanderbilt University | | 12,093 | 9 | 0 | 0 | 2 | 7 | 637 | 36 | 597 | 4 | 0 |
| Volunteer State Community College | | 7,241 | 0 | 0 | 0 | 0 | 0 | 25 | 0 | 25 | 0 | 0 |
| Walters State Community College | | 5,918 | 0 | 0 | 0 | 0 | 0 | 10 | 0 | 10 | 0 | 0 |
| **TEXAS** | | | | | | | | | | | | |
| Abilene Christian University | | 4,669 | 2 | 0 | 0 | 0 | 2 | 109 | 1 | 105 | 3 | 0 |
| Alamo Community College District[3] | | | 12 | 0 | 0 | 5 | 7 | 455 | 17 | 409 | 29 | 0 |
| Alvin Community College | | 4,402 | 0 | 0 | 0 | 0 | 0 | 5 | 0 | 5 | 0 | 0 |
| Amarillo College | | 10,224 | 0 | 0 | 0 | 0 | 0 | 57 | 4 | 53 | 0 | 0 |
| Angelo State University | | 6,155 | 1 | 0 | 0 | 0 | 1 | 68 | 7 | 61 | 0 | 0 |
| Austin College | | 1,298 | 0 | 0 | 0 | 0 | 0 | 19 | 3 | 16 | 0 | 0 |
| Baylor Health Care System[3] | | | 3 | 0 | 0 | 3 | 0 | 437 | 15 | 407 | 15 | 0 |
| Baylor University | Waco | 14,541 | 1 | 0 | 0 | 0 | 1 | 190 | 11 | 176 | 3 | 1 |
| Blinn College | | 15,608 | 7 | 0 | 0 | 1 | 6 | 94 | 37 | 56 | 1 | 0 |
| Brookhaven College | | 11,173 | 1 | 0 | 0 | 0 | 1 | 45 | 0 | 43 | 2 | 0 |
| Central Texas College | | 24,498 | 0 | 0 | 0 | 0 | 0 | 12 | 1 | 11 | 0 | 0 |
| College of the Mainland | | 3,561 | 0 | 0 | 0 | 0 | 0 | 48 | 6 | 41 | 1 | 0 |
| Eastfield College | | 10,501 | 0 | 0 | 0 | 0 | 0 | 46 | 18 | 15 | 13 | 0 |
| El Paso Community College | | 25,818 | 0 | 0 | 0 | 0 | 0 | 162 | 1 | 158 | 3 | 0 |
| Grayson County College | | 3,676 | 0 | 0 | 0 | 0 | 0 | 16 | 1 | 15 | 0 | 0 |
| Hardin-Simmons University | | 2,387 | 1 | 0 | 0 | 1 | 0 | 27 | 4 | 23 | 0 | 0 |
| Houston Baptist University | | 2,564 | 0 | 0 | 0 | 0 | 0 | 25 | 5 | 20 | 0 | 0 |
| Lamar University | Beaumont | 13,465 | 5 | 0 | 1 | 2 | 2 | 167 | 11 | 153 | 3 | 0 |
| Laredo Community College | | 8,256 | 2 | 0 | 0 | 1 | 1 | 19 | 1 | 14 | 4 | 0 |
| McLennan Community College | | 7,884 | 0 | 0 | 0 | 0 | 0 | 21 | 0 | 21 | 0 | 0 |
| Midwestern State University | | 6,093 | 1 | 0 | 0 | 0 | 1 | 40 | 8 | 30 | 2 | 0 |
| Mountain View College | | 7,126 | 0 | 0 | 0 | 0 | 0 | 49 | 0 | 29 | 20 | 0 |
| North Lake College | | 10,174 | 0 | 0 | 0 | 0 | 0 | 49 | 4 | 45 | 0 | 0 |
| Paris Junior College | | 4,733 | 4 | 0 | 0 | 1 | 3 | 42 | 13 | 29 | 0 | 0 |
| Prairie View A&M University | | 8,203 | 9 | 0 | 2 | 2 | 5 | 157 | 47 | 99 | 11 | 0 |
| Rice University | | 5,357 | 9 | 0 | 2 | 0 | 7 | 234 | 38 | 196 | 0 | 0 |
| Richland College | | 15,917 | 0 | 0 | 0 | 0 | 0 | 103 | 4 | 90 | 9 | 0 |
| Southern Methodist University | | 10,965 | 9 | 0 | 4 | 3 | 2 | 201 | 33 | 156 | 12 | 0 |
| South Plains College | | 9,111 | 0 | 0 | 0 | 0 | 0 | 24 | 3 | 21 | 0 | 1 |
| Southwestern University | | 1,270 | 0 | 0 | 0 | 0 | 0 | 12 | 1 | 9 | 2 | 0 |

*Note*: Caution should be exercised in making any intercampus comparisons or ranking schools because university/college crime statistics are affected by a variety of factors. These include demographic characteristics of the surrounding community, ratio of male to female students, number of on-campus residents, accessibility of the campus to outside visitors, size of enrollment, etc.

[1] The student enrollment figures provided by the United States Department of Education are for the 2008 school year, the most recent available. The enrollment figures include full-time and part-time students.

[2] The FBI does not publish arson data unless it receives data from either the agency or the state for all 12 months of the calendar year.

[3] Student enrollment figures were not available.

## Table 9. Offenses Known to Law Enforcement, by State and University and College, 2009—*Continued*

(Number.)

| State and University/College | Campus | Student enroll-ment[1] | Violent crime | Murder and non-negligent man-slaughter | Forcible rape | Robbery | Aggra-vated assault | Property crime | Burglary | Larceny-theft | Motor vehicle theft | Arson[2] |
|---|---|---|---|---|---|---|---|---|---|---|---|---|
| Stephen F. Austin State University | | 12,000 | 9 | 0 | 3 | 2 | 4 | 224 | 35 | 182 | 7 | 1 |
| St. Mary's University | | 3,889 | 2 | 0 | 1 | 1 | 0 | 57 | 4 | 52 | 1 | 0 |
| Sul Ross State University | | 2,772 | 0 | 0 | 0 | 0 | 0 | 57 | 23 | 30 | 4 | 0 |
| Tarleton State University | | 9,633 | 0 | 0 | 0 | 0 | 0 | 44 | 7 | 37 | 0 | 0 |
| Texas A&M International University | | 5,856 | 0 | 0 | 0 | 0 | 0 | 58 | 4 | 51 | 3 | 0 |
| Texas A&M University: | College Station | 48,039 | 1 | 0 | 0 | 1 | 0 | 598 | 30 | 565 | 3 | 0 |
| | Commerce | 8,725 | 1 | 0 | 0 | 0 | 1 | 79 | 15 | 64 | 0 | 0 |
| | Corpus Christi | 9,007 | 2 | 0 | 1 | 1 | 0 | 71 | 3 | 67 | 1 | 0 |
| | Galveston | 1,612 | 0 | 0 | 0 | 0 | 0 | 41 | 1 | 40 | 0 | 0 |
| | Kingsville | 7,133 | 6 | 0 | 0 | 2 | 4 | 111 | 36 | 74 | 1 | 0 |
| Texas Christian University | | 8,696 | 5 | 0 | 2 | 0 | 3 | 198 | 8 | 184 | 6 | 0 |
| Texas Southern University | | 9,102 | 22 | 0 | 1 | 14 | 7 | 347 | 81 | 254 | 12 | 0 |
| Texas State Technical College: | Harlingen | 5,466 | 2 | 0 | 0 | 1 | 1 | 34 | 1 | 33 | 0 | 0 |
| | Marshall | 946 | 1 | 0 | 0 | 0 | 1 | 19 | 13 | 6 | 0 | 0 |
| | Waco | 5,093 | 10 | 0 | 1 | 2 | 7 | 109 | 26 | 80 | 3 | 0 |
| Texas State University | San Marcos | 29,105 | 6 | 0 | 0 | 0 | 6 | 312 | 49 | 261 | 2 | 2 |
| Texas Tech University | Lubbock | 28,422 | 3 | 0 | 1 | 1 | 1 | 322 | 26 | 295 | 1 | 0 |
| Texas Woman's University | | 12,465 | 1 | 0 | 0 | 0 | 1 | 37 | 3 | 32 | 2 | 0 |
| Trinity University | | 2,703 | 0 | 0 | 0 | 0 | 0 | 121 | 23 | 92 | 6 | 2 |
| Tyler Junior College | | 9,928 | 0 | 0 | 0 | 0 | 0 | 125 | 9 | 116 | 0 | 1 |
| University of Houston: | Central Campus | 36,104 | 22 | 1 | 1 | 13 | 7 | 451 | 27 | 411 | 13 | 0 |
| | Clearlake | 7,658 | 1 | 0 | 0 | 1 | 0 | 19 | 0 | 19 | 0 | 0 |
| | Downtown Campus | 12,283 | 4 | 0 | 0 | 3 | 1 | 83 | 1 | 80 | 2 | 0 |
| University of Mary Hardin-Baylor | | 2,648 | 0 | 0 | 0 | 0 | 0 | 46 | 8 | 38 | 0 | 0 |
| University of North Texas: | Denton | 34,830 | 3 | 0 | 0 | 0 | 3 | 195 | 29 | 162 | 4 | 0 |
| | Health Science Center | 1,225 | 0 | 0 | 0 | 0 | 0 | 26 | 1 | 23 | 2 | 0 |
| University of Texas: | Arlington | 25,084 | 9 | 0 | 3 | 6 | 0 | 266 | 37 | 222 | 7 | 0 |
| | Austin | 49,984 | 6 | 0 | 0 | 3 | 3 | 595 | 40 | 551 | 4 | 1 |
| | Brownsville | 17,189 | 1 | 0 | 0 | 0 | 1 | 49 | 0 | 43 | 6 | 0 |
| | Dallas | 14,913 | 4 | 0 | 1 | 0 | 3 | 102 | 23 | 74 | 5 | 0 |
| | El Paso | 20,458 | 6 | 0 | 0 | 1 | 5 | 175 | 38 | 132 | 5 | 0 |
| | Health Science Center, San Antonio | 3,093 | 1 | 0 | 0 | 1 | 0 | 97 | 0 | 97 | 0 | 0 |
| | Health Science Center, Tyler[3] | | 0 | 0 | 0 | 0 | 0 | 17 | 0 | 17 | 0 | 0 |
| | Houston[3] | | 0 | 0 | 0 | 0 | 0 | 334 | 20 | 307 | 7 | 0 |
| | Medical Branch | 2,338 | 3 | 0 | 0 | 1 | 2 | 98 | 1 | 97 | 0 | 0 |
| | Pan American | 17,534 | 0 | 0 | 0 | 0 | 0 | 166 | 21 | 135 | 10 | 0 |
| | Permian Basin | 3,496 | 2 | 0 | 1 | 1 | 0 | 42 | 8 | 33 | 1 | 0 |
| | San Antonio | 28,413 | 2 | 0 | 0 | 0 | 2 | 203 | 12 | 190 | 1 | 0 |
| | Southwestern Medical School | 2,461 | 1 | 0 | 0 | 1 | 0 | 192 | 7 | 166 | 19 | 0 |
| | Tyler | 6,117 | 2 | 0 | 1 | 0 | 1 | 34 | 10 | 24 | 0 | 0 |
| Western Texas College | | 2,090 | 1 | 0 | 0 | 0 | 1 | 12 | 2 | 10 | 0 | 0 |
| West Texas A&M University | | 7,535 | 1 | 0 | 1 | 0 | 0 | 53 | 12 | 41 | 0 | 0 |
| **UTAH** | | | | | | | | | | | | |
| Brigham Young University | | 34,244 | 2 | 0 | 0 | 1 | 1 | 283 | 11 | 270 | 2 | 0 |
| College of Eastern Utah | | 1,438 | 0 | 0 | 0 | 0 | 0 | 12 | 1 | 11 | 0 | 0 |
| Southern Utah University | | 7,516 | 0 | 0 | 0 | 0 | 0 | 63 | 12 | 48 | 3 | 0 |
| University of Utah | | 28,211 | 7 | 0 | 2 | 0 | 5 | 604 | 38 | 540 | 26 | 0 |
| Utah State University | | 15,099 | 2 | 0 | 2 | 0 | 0 | 141 | 12 | 128 | 1 | 0 |
| Utah Valley University | | 26,696 | 3 | 0 | 1 | 1 | 1 | 70 | 3 | 65 | 2 | 0 |
| Weber State University | | 21,388 | 0 | 0 | 0 | 0 | 0 | 66 | 10 | 56 | 0 | 0 |
| **VERMONT** | | | | | | | | | | | | |
| University of Vermont | | 12,800 | 3 | 0 | 0 | 0 | 3 | 254 | 23 | 231 | 0 | 3 |

*Note*: Caution should be exercised in making any intercampus comparisons or ranking schools because university/college crime statistics are affected by a variety of factors. These include demographic characteristics of the surrounding community, ratio of male to female students, number of on-campus residents, accessibility of the campus to outside visitors, size of enrollment, etc.

[1] The student enrollment figures provided by the United States Department of Education are for the 2008 school year, the most recent available. The enrollment figures include full-time and part-time students.

[2] The FBI does not publish arson data unless it receives data from either the agency or the state for all 12 months of the calendar year.

[3] Student enrollment figures were not available.

## Table 9. Offenses Known to Law Enforcement, by State and University and College, 2009—*Continued*

(Number.)

| State and University/College | Campus | Student enroll-ment[1] | Violent crime | Murder and non-negligent man-slaughter | Forcible rape | Robbery | Aggra-vated assault | Property crime | Burglary | Larceny-theft | Motor vehicle theft | Arson[2] |
|---|---|---|---|---|---|---|---|---|---|---|---|---|
| **VIRGINIA** | | | | | | | | | | | | |
| Christopher Newport University | | 4,904 | 3 | 0 | 1 | 0 | 2 | 104 | 1 | 103 | 0 | 2 |
| College of William and Mary | | 7,892 | 10 | 0 | 3 | 1 | 6 | 258 | 17 | 241 | 0 | 1 |
| Emory and Henry College | | 1,015 | 1 | 0 | 0 | 0 | 1 | 2 | 1 | 1 | 0 | 0 |
| Ferrum College | | 1,397 | 5 | 0 | 0 | 1 | 4 | 27 | 3 | 24 | 0 | 0 |
| George Mason University | | 30,613 | 3 | 0 | 1 | 1 | 1 | 253 | 6 | 242 | 5 | 1 |
| Hampton University | | 5,427 | 3 | 0 | 1 | 2 | 0 | 109 | 37 | 71 | 1 | 0 |
| James Madison University | | 18,454 | 7 | 0 | 2 | 0 | 5 | 199 | 12 | 186 | 1 | 0 |
| Longwood University | | 4,727 | 3 | 0 | 2 | 0 | 1 | 58 | 10 | 46 | 2 | 0 |
| Norfolk State University | | 6,325 | 10 | 0 | 2 | 2 | 6 | 150 | 50 | 96 | 4 | 4 |
| Northern Virginia Community College | | 42,663 | 4 | 0 | 0 | 0 | 4 | 184 | 1 | 181 | 2 | 0 |
| Old Dominion University | | 23,086 | 12 | 0 | 2 | 1 | 9 | 244 | 21 | 218 | 5 | 0 |
| Radford University | | 9,157 | 4 | 0 | 1 | 0 | 3 | 102 | 5 | 97 | 0 | 0 |
| Thomas Nelson Community College | | 10,557 | 1 | 0 | 0 | 1 | 0 | 13 | 0 | 13 | 0 | 0 |
| University of Richmond | | 4,249 | 3 | 0 | 1 | 0 | 2 | 131 | 14 | 99 | 18 | 0 |
| University of Virginia | | 24,541 | 10 | 0 | 2 | 2 | 6 | 386 | 77 | 300 | 9 | 2 |
| University of Virginia's College at Wise | | 1,964 | 0 | 0 | 0 | 0 | 0 | 1 | 0 | 1 | 0 | 0 |
| Virginia Commonwealth University | | 32,044 | 10 | 0 | 1 | 5 | 4 | 581 | 11 | 551 | 19 | 2 |
| Virginia Military Institute | | 1,428 | 1 | 0 | 1 | 0 | 0 | 30 | 15 | 15 | 0 | 0 |
| Virginia Polytechnic Institute and State University | | 30,739 | 2 | 1 | 1 | 0 | 0 | 212 | 34 | 173 | 5 | 3 |
| Virginia State University | | 5,042 | 11 | 0 | 0 | 6 | 5 | 178 | 3 | 171 | 4 | 0 |
| Virginia Western Community College | | 8,532 | 0 | 0 | 0 | 0 | 0 | 6 | 0 | 6 | 0 | 0 |
| **WASHINGTON** | | | | | | | | | | | | |
| Central Washington University | | 10,662 | 6 | 0 | 2 | 0 | 4 | 126 | 16 | 106 | 4 | 0 |
| Eastern Washington University | | 10,809 | 3 | 0 | 1 | 1 | 1 | 102 | 8 | 94 | 0 | 0 |
| Evergreen State College | | 4,696 | 0 | 0 | 0 | 0 | 0 | 116 | 11 | 105 | 0 | 1 |
| University of Washington | | 39,675 | 17 | 0 | 0 | 10 | 7 | 563 | 82 | 471 | 10 | 2 |
| Washington State University: | Pullman | 25,352 | 11 | 0 | 7 | 0 | 4 | 161 | 20 | 138 | 3 | 1 |
| | Vancouver[3] | | 0 | 0 | 0 | 0 | 0 | 28 | 1 | 26 | 1 | 1 |
| Western Washington University | | 14,620 | 2 | 0 | 0 | 1 | 1 | 181 | 20 | 159 | 2 | 1 |
| **WEST VIRGINIA** | | | | | | | | | | | | |
| Fairmont State University | | 4,547 | 0 | 0 | 0 | 0 | 0 | 18 | 3 | 15 | 0 | 0 |
| Marshall University | | 13,573 | 6 | 0 | 0 | 3 | 3 | 146 | 8 | 138 | 0 | 0 |
| Shepherd University | | 4,185 | 2 | 0 | 0 | 0 | 2 | 57 | 4 | 50 | 3 | 0 |
| West Virginia State University | | 3,003 | 0 | 0 | 0 | 0 | 0 | 28 | 6 | 21 | 1 | 0 |
| West Virginia Tech | | 1,224 | 4 | 0 | 1 | 0 | 3 | 29 | 4 | 25 | 0 | 0 |
| West Virginia University | | 28,840 | 40 | 0 | 1 | 3 | 36 | 164 | 9 | 150 | 5 | 1 |
| **WISCONSIN** | | | | | | | | | | | | |
| University of Wisconsin: | Eau Claire | 11,140 | 0 | 0 | 0 | 0 | 0 | 77 | 0 | 77 | 0 | 0 |
| | Green Bay | 6,286 | 0 | 0 | 0 | 0 | 0 | 37 | 0 | 36 | 1 | 0 |
| | La Crosse | 9,880 | 2 | 0 | 1 | 0 | 1 | 73 | 4 | 69 | 0 | 0 |
| | Madison | 41,620 | 12 | 0 | 2 | 3 | 7 | 433 | 70 | 357 | 6 | 1 |
| | Milwaukee | 29,215 | 5 | 0 | 4 | 0 | 1 | 237 | 23 | 210 | 4 | 0 |
| | Oshkosh | 12,753 | 1 | 0 | 1 | 0 | 0 | 59 | 4 | 55 | 0 | 2 |
| | Parkside | 5,167 | 0 | 0 | 0 | 0 | 0 | 54 | 1 | 53 | 0 | 0 |
| | Platteville | 7,512 | 2 | 0 | 1 | 0 | 1 | 63 | 8 | 54 | 1 | 2 |
| | Stevens Point | 9,163 | 0 | 0 | 0 | 0 | 0 | 117 | 9 | 108 | 0 | 1 |
| | Stout | 8,839 | 2 | 0 | 0 | 0 | 2 | 140 | 20 | 120 | 0 | 0 |
| | Superior | 2,689 | 0 | 0 | 0 | 0 | 0 | 25 | 4 | 21 | 0 | 0 |
| | Whitewater | 10,962 | 2 | 0 | 0 | 0 | 2 | 117 | 16 | 101 | 0 | 0 |
| **WYOMING** | | | | | | | | | | | | |
| Sheridan College | | 4,130 | 0 | 0 | 0 | 0 | 0 | 1 | 0 | 1 | 0 | 0 |
| University of Wyoming | | 12,067 | 0 | 0 | 0 | 0 | 0 | 162 | 5 | 157 | 0 | 0 |

*Note*: Caution should be exercised in making any intercampus comparisons or ranking schools because university/college crime statistics are affected by a variety of factors. These include demographic characteristics of the surrounding community, ratio of male to female students, number of on-campus residents, accessibility of the campus to outside visitors, size of enrollment, etc.

[1] The student enrollment figures provided by the United States Department of Education are for the 2008 school year, the most recent available. The enrollment figures include full-time and part-time students.

[2] The FBI does not publish arson data unless it receives data from either the agency or the state for all 12 months of the calendar year.

[3] Student enrollment figures were not available.

## Table 10. Offenses Known to Law Enforcement, by State Metropolitan and Nonmetropolitan Counties, 2009

(Number.)

| State/County | Violent crime | Murder and non-negligent man-slaughter | Forcible rape | Robbery | Aggravated assault | Property crime | Burglary | Larceny-theft | Motor vehicle theft | Arson[1] |
|---|---|---|---|---|---|---|---|---|---|---|
| **ALABAMA - Metropolitan Counties** | | | | | | | | | | |
| Bibb | 20 | 1 | 2 | 2 | 15 | 131 | 64 | 57 | 10 | |
| Calhoun | 48 | 0 | 23 | 8 | 17 | 862 | 316 | 539 | 7 | |
| Chilton | 455 | 0 | 19 | 3 | 433 | 581 | 182 | 397 | 2 | |
| Etowah | 11 | 0 | 7 | 2 | 2 | 335 | 125 | 188 | 22 | |
| Geneva[2,3] | | 0 | 3 | 0 | | | | 116 | 9 | |
| Hale | 63 | 1 | 1 | 9 | 52 | 220 | 111 | 98 | 11 | |
| Henry | 36 | 1 | 2 | 1 | 32 | 103 | 41 | 52 | 10 | |
| Jefferson | 505 | 5 | 46 | 210 | 244 | 6,131 | 2,334 | 3,260 | 537 | 22 |
| Lauderdale | 35 | 3 | 9 | 2 | 21 | 798 | 300 | 460 | 38 | |
| Lawrence[2] | | 1 | 3 | 3 | | 387 | 74 | 298 | 15 | |
| Lee | 95 | 3 | 25 | 15 | 52 | 1,662 | 717 | 860 | 85 | |
| Limestone | 47 | 2 | 9 | 10 | 26 | 639 | 208 | 395 | 36 | |
| Lowndes | 54 | 1 | 2 | 8 | 43 | 352 | 172 | 176 | 4 | |
| Madison | 323 | 3 | 22 | 70 | 228 | 2,198 | 750 | 1,268 | 180 | |
| Montgomery | 76 | 0 | 5 | 9 | 62 | 673 | 222 | 369 | 82 | |
| Russell | 110 | 1 | 9 | 11 | 89 | 348 | 164 | 166 | 18 | |
| Shelby | 92 | 1 | 23 | 9 | 59 | 1,070 | 417 | 587 | 66 | |
| St. Clair | 24 | 1 | 4 | 4 | 15 | 331 | 139 | 174 | 18 | |
| Tuscaloosa | 230 | 4 | 23 | 28 | 175 | 1,798 | 556 | 1,049 | 193 | |
| Walker | 22 | 0 | 5 | 8 | 9 | 504 | 127 | 324 | 53 | |
| **ALABAMA - Nonmetropolitan Counties** | | | | | | | | | | |
| Baldwin | 101 | 1 | 4 | 8 | 88 | 665 | 261 | 362 | 42 | |
| Barbour[2] | 17 | 0 | 5 | 0 | 12 | | 40 | | 6 | |
| Bullock | 28 | 1 | 0 | 0 | 27 | 105 | 56 | 49 | 0 | |
| Butler | 37 | 0 | 3 | 0 | 34 | 215 | 94 | 111 | 10 | |
| Cherokee | 15 | 0 | 2 | 0 | 13 | 79 | 14 | 56 | 9 | |
| Choctaw | 5 | 0 | 0 | 0 | 5 | 31 | 17 | 14 | 0 | |
| Clarke | 44 | 3 | 5 | 0 | 36 | 52 | 45 | 5 | 2 | |
| Cleburne | 29 | 2 | 4 | 0 | 23 | 267 | 100 | 153 | 14 | |
| Coffee | 21 | 0 | 2 | 3 | 16 | 166 | 56 | 90 | 20 | |
| Conecuh | 36 | 1 | 3 | 4 | 28 | 91 | 17 | 68 | 6 | |
| Coosa | 17 | 0 | 0 | 3 | 14 | 252 | 118 | 127 | 7 | |
| Covington | 34 | 6 | 2 | 1 | 25 | 158 | 63 | 93 | 2 | |
| Crenshaw | 24 | 0 | 2 | 3 | 19 | 186 | 67 | 104 | 15 | |
| Cullman | 117 | 3 | 13 | 2 | 99 | 1,098 | 334 | 709 | 55 | |
| Dale | 43 | 3 | 14 | 0 | 26 | 130 | 44 | 82 | 4 | |
| Dallas | 70 | 0 | 11 | 8 | 51 | 535 | 154 | 330 | 51 | |
| Fayette[3] | 9 | 0 | 2 | 0 | 7 | | | 48 | 9 | |
| Franklin | 26 | 1 | 2 | 4 | 19 | 159 | 54 | 98 | 7 | |
| Jackson | 112 | 1 | 11 | 6 | 94 | 358 | 108 | 209 | 41 | |
| Lamar | 2 | 0 | 0 | 0 | 2 | 8 | 0 | 8 | 0 | |
| Marengo | 34 | 1 | 1 | 2 | 30 | 121 | 43 | 63 | 15 | |
| Marion | 4 | 0 | 0 | 0 | 4 | 24 | 11 | 13 | 0 | |
| Marshall | 73 | 1 | 9 | 2 | 61 | 636 | 219 | 360 | 57 | |
| Monroe | 29 | 3 | 1 | 1 | 24 | 98 | 52 | 43 | 3 | |
| Perry | 4 | 0 | 0 | 1 | 3 | 98 | 34 | 50 | 14 | |
| Pickens | 8 | 0 | 1 | 0 | 7 | 94 | 59 | 32 | 3 | |
| Pike | 5 | 0 | 0 | 2 | 3 | 105 | 47 | 52 | 6 | |
| Randolph | 25 | 0 | 1 | 0 | 24 | 279 | 75 | 200 | 4 | |
| Talladega[2] | 49 | 2 | 6 | 11 | 30 | | 359 | 564 | | |
| Tallapoosa | 22 | 0 | 0 | 2 | 20 | 207 | 63 | 130 | 14 | |
| Washington | 34 | 0 | 4 | 0 | 30 | 103 | 25 | 67 | 11 | |
| Wilcox | 27 | 0 | 0 | 1 | 26 | 126 | 53 | 60 | 13 | |
| Winston | 18 | 0 | 2 | 1 | 15 | 263 | 91 | 164 | 8 | |
| **ARIZONA - Metropolitan Counties** | | | | | | | | | | |
| Coconino | 77 | 2 | 12 | 3 | 60 | 565 | 180 | 353 | 32 | 4 |
| Maricopa | 992 | 25 | 39 | 118 | 810 | 6,264 | 1,841 | 3,658 | 765 | 204 |
| Mohave | 192 | 1 | 4 | 18 | 169 | 1,995 | 669 | 1,162 | 164 | 18 |
| Pima | 635 | 18 | 74 | 195 | 348 | 11,706 | 2,443 | 8,237 | 1,026 | 133 |
| Pinal | 214 | 8 | 50 | 41 | 115 | 3,814 | 740 | 2,494 | 580 | 18 |
| Yavapai | 279 | 1 | 16 | 6 | 256 | 1,419 | 468 | 837 | 114 | 5 |
| Yuma | 104 | 6 | 8 | 4 | 86 | 797 | 389 | 320 | 88 | 11 |
| **ARIZONA - Nonmetropolitan Counties** | | | | | | | | | | |
| Apache | 32 | 2 | 7 | 0 | 23 | 189 | 109 | 75 | 5 | 0 |
| Cochise | 472 | 3 | 14 | 23 | 432 | 973 | 402 | 451 | 120 | 11 |
| Gila | 60 | 0 | 2 | 3 | 55 | 331 | 46 | 250 | 35 | 1 |
| Graham[2] | | 0 | 0 | 1 | | 289 | 105 | 152 | 32 | 23 |
| La Paz | 38 | 0 | 0 | 4 | 34 | 382 | 99 | 249 | 34 | 10 |
| Navajo | 50 | 1 | 6 | 3 | 40 | 668 | 406 | 192 | 70 | 6 |
| Santa Cruz | 18 | 2 | 0 | 9 | 7 | 391 | 168 | 130 | 93 | 1 |

[1] The FBI does not publish arson data unless it receives data from either the agency or the state for all 12 months of the calendar year.
[2] The FBI determined that the agency's data were overreported. Consequently, affected data are not included in this table.
[3] The FBI determined that the agency's data were underreported. Consequently, affected data are not included in this table.

**Table 10. Offenses Known to Law Enforcement, by State Metropolitan and Nonmetropolitan Counties, 2009**—*Continued*

(Number.)

| State/County | Violent crime | Murder and non-negligent man-slaughter | Forcible rape | Robbery | Aggravated assault | Property crime | Burglary | Larceny-theft | Motor vehicle theft | Arson[1] |
|---|---|---|---|---|---|---|---|---|---|---|
| **ARKANSAS - Metropolitan Counties** | | | | | | | | | | |
| Benton | 158 | 2 | 16 | 2 | 138 | 481 | 226 | 238 | 17 | 9 |
| Cleveland | 8 | 0 | 0 | 0 | 8 | 86 | 40 | 34 | 12 | 0 |
| Craighead | 32 | 0 | 5 | 1 | 26 | 360 | 160 | 184 | 16 | 7 |
| Crittenden | 75 | 1 | 9 | 6 | 59 | 329 | 108 | 193 | 28 | 4 |
| Faulkner | 58 | 0 | 14 | 1 | 43 | 855 | 260 | 494 | 101 | 14 |
| Franklin | 29 | 0 | 2 | 0 | 27 | 175 | 63 | 103 | 9 | 0 |
| Garland | 147 | 5 | 21 | 20 | 101 | 2,483 | 1,230 | 1,058 | 195 | 27 |
| Grant | 30 | 0 | 2 | 0 | 28 | 208 | 85 | 113 | 10 | 2 |
| Jefferson | 81 | 1 | 12 | 6 | 62 | 467 | 238 | 159 | 70 | 4 |
| Lincoln | 14 | 1 | 1 | 1 | 11 | 99 | 69 | 28 | 2 | 0 |
| Lonoke | 144 | 0 | 19 | 2 | 123 | 537 | 242 | 246 | 49 | 5 |
| Madison | 31 | 1 | 7 | 0 | 23 | 73 | 37 | 33 | 3 | 7 |
| Perry | 21 | 0 | 3 | 0 | 18 | 65 | 58 | 7 | 0 | 0 |
| Poinsett | 50 | 2 | 2 | 0 | 46 | 74 | 64 | 3 | 7 | 1 |
| Pulaski | 354 | 3 | 16 | 26 | 309 | 1,692 | 725 | 813 | 154 | 11 |
| Sebastian | 49 | 0 | 4 | 2 | 43 | 373 | 120 | 243 | 10 | 2 |
| Washington | 142 | 0 | 15 | 0 | 127 | 551 | 193 | 294 | 64 | 11 |
| **ARKANSAS - Nonmetropolitan Counties** | | | | | | | | | | |
| Arkansas | 8 | 0 | 1 | 2 | 5 | 83 | 35 | 35 | 13 | 0 |
| Ashley | 20 | 0 | 1 | 1 | 18 | 194 | 74 | 105 | 15 | 3 |
| Baxter | 42 | 1 | 7 | 3 | 31 | 641 | 86 | 522 | 33 | 3 |
| Boone | 31 | 1 | 8 | 0 | 22 | 189 | 61 | 128 | 0 | 4 |
| Bradley | 5 | 0 | 0 | 0 | 5 | 34 | 17 | 15 | 2 | 0 |
| Calhoun | 3 | 0 | 0 | 0 | 3 | 17 | 3 | 14 | 0 | 0 |
| Carroll | 26 | 2 | 0 | 0 | 24 | 190 | 54 | 118 | 18 | 3 |
| Chicot | 4 | 1 | 1 | 0 | 2 | 61 | 22 | 36 | 3 | 1 |
| Clark | 27 | 1 | 4 | 2 | 20 | 120 | 52 | 63 | 5 | 2 |
| Clay | 10 | 0 | 3 | 0 | 7 | 99 | 46 | 51 | 2 | 1 |
| Cleburne | 34 | 0 | 5 | 1 | 28 | 357 | 171 | 163 | 23 | 3 |
| Columbia | 45 | 3 | 1 | 1 | 40 | 158 | 50 | 89 | 19 | 2 |
| Conway | 22 | 3 | 3 | 1 | 15 | 249 | 62 | 174 | 13 | 14 |
| Cross | 57 | 1 | 4 | 0 | 52 | 174 | 37 | 131 | 6 | 0 |
| Dallas | 8 | 0 | 0 | 4 | 4 | 39 | 24 | 14 | 1 | 3 |
| Drew | 33 | 1 | 6 | 1 | 25 | 139 | 56 | 56 | 27 | 4 |
| Fulton | 29 | 2 | 0 | 1 | 26 | 71 | 41 | 29 | 1 | 2 |
| Greene | 19 | 1 | 5 | 0 | 13 | 142 | 67 | 64 | 11 | 3 |
| Hempstead | 28 | 0 | 7 | 0 | 21 | 174 | 57 | 87 | 30 | 1 |
| Howard | 19 | 0 | 1 | 0 | 18 | 80 | 38 | 42 | 0 | 0 |
| Independence | 218 | 1 | 18 | 14 | 185 | 1,332 | 579 | 656 | 97 | 17 |
| Izard | 4 | 0 | 2 | 0 | 2 | 76 | 33 | 39 | 4 | 3 |
| Jackson | 22 | 0 | 3 | 2 | 17 | 171 | 81 | 77 | 13 | 3 |
| Johnson | 34 | 2 | 6 | 0 | 26 | 152 | 119 | 33 | 0 | 2 |
| Lawrence | 13 | 1 | 1 | 0 | 11 | 155 | 76 | 79 | 0 | 1 |
| Lee | 15 | 0 | 1 | 1 | 13 | 67 | 42 | 17 | 8 | 0 |
| Little River | 9 | 1 | 1 | 0 | 7 | 67 | 27 | 37 | 3 | 0 |
| Logan | 14 | 0 | 1 | 0 | 13 | 230 | 96 | 114 | 20 | 4 |
| Marion | 26 | 0 | 5 | 0 | 21 | 185 | 72 | 110 | 3 | 5 |
| Mississippi | 34 | 0 | 9 | 3 | 22 | 317 | 83 | 199 | 35 | 8 |
| Monroe | 2 | 0 | 0 | 0 | 2 | 42 | 35 | 7 | 0 | 1 |
| Montgomery | 5 | 1 | 0 | 0 | 4 | 20 | 11 | 9 | 0 | 0 |
| Nevada | 1 | 0 | 1 | 0 | 0 | 28 | 20 | 7 | 1 | 0 |
| Newton | 25 | 1 | 3 | 0 | 21 | 126 | 46 | 76 | 4 | 5 |
| Ouachita | 15 | 0 | 0 | 2 | 13 | 86 | 56 | 30 | 0 | 2 |
| Pike | 3 | 0 | 0 | 0 | 3 | 42 | 20 | 19 | 3 | 0 |
| Polk | 35 | 3 | 6 | 4 | 22 | 171 | 76 | 91 | 4 | 2 |
| Prairie | 4 | 1 | 0 | 1 | 2 | 69 | 30 | 29 | 10 | 1 |
| Randolph | 4 | 1 | 3 | 0 | 0 | 80 | 61 | 19 | 0 | 0 |
| Scott | 10 | 2 | 2 | 1 | 5 | 84 | 37 | 43 | 4 | 1 |
| Searcy | 14 | 0 | 1 | 0 | 13 | 40 | 18 | 20 | 2 | 3 |
| St. Francis | 33 | 0 | 2 | 9 | 22 | 411 | 160 | 251 | 0 | 6 |
| Stone | 11 | 1 | 4 | 0 | 6 | 98 | 42 | 50 | 6 | 0 |
| Union | 39 | 2 | 5 | 4 | 28 | 464 | 116 | 307 | 41 | 2 |
| Van Buren | 36 | 0 | 4 | 0 | 32 | 138 | 27 | 96 | 15 | 3 |
| White | 51 | 2 | 21 | 1 | 27 | 736 | 308 | 325 | 103 | 2 |
| Yell | 45 | 0 | 6 | 3 | 36 | 110 | 73 | 32 | 5 | 2 |
| **CALIFORNIA - Metropolitan Counties** | | | | | | | | | | |
| Alameda | 637 | 3 | 28 | 260 | 346 | 2,503 | 553 | 1,157 | 793 | 33 |
| Butte | 134 | 6 | 12 | 27 | 89 | 1,244 | 508 | 729 | 7 | 19 |
| Contra Costa | 428 | 11 | 29 | 161 | 227 | 2,792 | 989 | 1,785 | 18 | 13 |
| El Dorado | 312 | 3 | 33 | 34 | 242 | 1,862 | 715 | 1,129 | 18 | 12 |

[1] The FBI does not publish arson data unless it receives data from either the agency or the state for all 12 months of the calendar year.

## Table 10. Offenses Known to Law Enforcement, by State Metropolitan and Nonmetropolitan Counties, 2009—*Continued*

(Number.)

| State/County | Violent crime | Murder and non-negligent man-slaughter | Forcible rape | Robbery | Aggravated assault | Property crime | Burglary | Larceny-theft | Motor vehicle theft | Arson[1] |
|---|---|---|---|---|---|---|---|---|---|---|
| Fresno | 774 | 16 | 23 | 143 | 592 | 5,087 | 1,630 | 2,604 | 853 | 238 |
| Imperial[2,4] | | 2 | 3 | 12 | | | 295 | | 13 | 19 |
| Kern | 2,001 | 39 | 125 | 512 | 1,325 | 10,458 | 3,596 | 5,360 | 1,502 | 330 |
| Kings | 211 | 3 | 11 | 20 | 177 | 493 | 197 | 267 | 29 | 10 |
| Los Angeles | 6,540 | 102 | 209 | 1,895 | 4,334 | 18,043 | 5,033 | 8,645 | 4,365 | 314 |
| Madera | 229 | 2 | 20 | 27 | 180 | 1,191 | 506 | 677 | 8 | 2 |
| Marin | 121 | 0 | 3 | 33 | 85 | 885 | 269 | 613 | 3 | 3 |
| Merced | 490 | 14 | 26 | 54 | 396 | 1,923 | 689 | 1,215 | 19 | 13 |
| Monterey | 203 | 8 | 26 | 54 | 115 | 1,693 | 669 | 1,002 | 22 | 12 |
| Napa | 35 | 0 | 6 | 1 | 28 | 367 | 129 | 237 | 1 | 2 |
| Orange | 219 | 1 | 13 | 38 | 167 | 1,296 | 243 | 940 | 113 | 11 |
| Placer | 315 | 4 | 27 | 26 | 258 | 1,951 | 660 | 1,258 | 33 | 14 |
| Riverside | 1,225 | 23 | 74 | 293 | 835 | 10,554 | 3,057 | 5,718 | 1,779 | 26 |
| Sacramento | 3,183 | 29 | 176 | 1,189 | 1,789 | 15,610 | 4,725 | 10,721 | 164 | 129 |
| San Benito | 67 | 0 | 4 | 8 | 55 | 259 | 100 | 154 | 5 | 2 |
| San Bernardino | 1,165 | 22 | 66 | 192 | 885 | 5,835 | 2,104 | 2,614 | 1,117 | 104 |
| San Diego | 1,592 | 9 | 88 | 276 | 1,219 | 5,956 | 1,693 | 3,204 | 1,059 | 41 |
| San Joaquin | 1,058 | 10 | 34 | 195 | 819 | 4,480 | 1,569 | 2,805 | 106 | 20 |
| San Luis Obispo | 199 | 3 | 21 | 20 | 155 | 1,188 | 416 | 763 | 9 | 8 |
| San Mateo | 194 | 1 | 8 | 40 | 145 | 1,636 | 221 | 1,227 | 188 | 7 |
| Santa Barbara | 246 | 0 | 24 | 21 | 201 | 1,673 | 647 | 1,020 | 6 | 7 |
| Santa Clara | 268 | 3 | 30 | 30 | 205 | 1,716 | 404 | 1,125 | 187 | 3 |
| Santa Cruz | 291 | 2 | 18 | 40 | 231 | 2,479 | 804 | 1,663 | 12 | 21 |
| Shasta | 512 | 1 | 36 | 35 | 440 | 1,034 | 542 | 478 | 14 | 9 |
| Solano | 90 | 2 | 7 | 16 | 65 | 381 | 218 | 157 | 6 | 16 |
| Sonoma | 553 | 6 | 45 | 51 | 451 | 1,537 | 597 | 930 | 10 | 30 |
| Stanislaus | 507 | 14 | 27 | 122 | 344 | 3,360 | 1,418 | 1,644 | 298 | 198 |
| Sutter | 120 | 0 | 8 | 10 | 102 | 527 | 155 | 338 | 34 | 1 |
| Tulare[5] | 553 | 16 | 31 | 93 | 413 | | 1,187 | 1,966 | | 28 |
| Ventura | 189 | 6 | 20 | 26 | 137 | 1,271 | 352 | 836 | 83 | 18 |
| Yolo | 39 | 0 | 6 | 5 | 28 | 344 | 120 | 218 | 6 | 4 |
| Yuba | 190 | 2 | 17 | 29 | 142 | 830 | 314 | 502 | 14 | 17 |
| **CALIFORNIA - Nonmetropolitan Counties** | | | | | | | | | | |
| Alpine | 13 | 0 | 1 | 1 | 11 | 60 | 11 | 49 | 0 | 0 |
| Amador | 60 | 1 | 6 | 4 | 49 | 467 | 218 | 247 | 2 | 0 |
| Calaveras | 68 | 1 | 14 | 14 | 39 | 597 | 247 | 347 | 3 | 8 |
| Colusa | 36 | 1 | 8 | 2 | 25 | 287 | 101 | 178 | 8 | 0 |
| Del Norte | 77 | 1 | 17 | 5 | 54 | 287 | 145 | 140 | 2 | 5 |
| Glenn | 9 | 0 | 1 | 3 | 5 | 117 | 55 | 61 | 1 | 0 |
| Humboldt | 272 | 7 | 12 | 38 | 215 | 1,126 | 342 | 763 | 21 | 17 |
| Inyo | 60 | 2 | 8 | 6 | 44 | 145 | 56 | 88 | 1 | 1 |
| Lake | 170 | 2 | 24 | 17 | 127 | 803 | 383 | 406 | 14 | 5 |
| Lassen | 26 | 0 | 3 | 1 | 22 | 110 | 36 | 74 | 0 | 3 |
| Mariposa | 48 | 0 | 3 | 1 | 44 | 278 | 106 | 171 | 1 | 1 |
| Mendocino | 326 | 5 | 23 | 21 | 277 | 528 | 227 | 297 | 4 | 12 |
| Modoc | 8 | 0 | 1 | 0 | 7 | 64 | 33 | 30 | 1 | 0 |
| Mono | 10 | 0 | 1 | 0 | 9 | 76 | 24 | 52 | 0 | 0 |
| Nevada | 165 | 0 | 23 | 8 | 134 | 638 | 207 | 427 | 4 | 5 |
| Plumas | 121 | 1 | 19 | 5 | 96 | 311 | 120 | 186 | 5 | 2 |
| Sierra | 13 | 0 | 0 | 0 | 13 | 43 | 15 | 28 | 0 | 1 |
| Siskiyou | 63 | 1 | 9 | 6 | 47 | 193 | 93 | 95 | 5 | 0 |
| Tehama | 211 | 2 | 1 | 5 | 203 | 299 | 176 | 123 | 0 | 20 |
| Trinity | 22 | 0 | 0 | 3 | 19 | 126 | 60 | 66 | 0 | 0 |
| Tuolumne | 108 | 1 | 18 | 12 | 77 | 749 | 298 | 445 | 6 | 9 |
| **COLORADO - Metropolitan Counties** | | | | | | | | | | |
| Adams | 407 | 5 | 61 | 54 | 287 | 2,613 | 675 | 1,431 | 507 | 24 |
| Arapahoe | 218 | 0 | 19 | 44 | 155 | 1,348 | 370 | 862 | 116 | 15 |
| Boulder | 65 | 0 | 7 | 6 | 52 | 660 | 197 | 423 | 40 | 15 |
| Clear Creek | 25 | 0 | 2 | 0 | 23 | 71 | 23 | 44 | 4 | 1 |
| Douglas | 295 | 0 | 172 | 31 | 92 | 1,709 | 426 | 1,203 | 80 | 8 |
| Elbert | 4 | 0 | 3 | 0 | 1 | 34 | 9 | 25 | 0 | 0 |
| El Paso | 759 | 5 | 55 | 22 | 677 | 1,824 | 585 | 1,026 | 213 | 29 |
| Gilpin | 18 | 0 | 1 | 1 | 16 | 38 | 5 | 28 | 5 | 0 |
| Jefferson | 176 | 5 | 43 | 13 | 115 | 2,630 | 474 | 1,981 | 175 | 27 |
| Larimer | 102 | 0 | 36 | 7 | 59 | 1,085 | 236 | 768 | 81 | 16 |
| Mesa | 185 | 2 | 28 | 16 | 139 | 1,467 | 367 | 964 | 136 | 8 |
| Park | 8 | 0 | 1 | 0 | 7 | 114 | 41 | 63 | 10 | 2 |
| Pueblo | 32 | 1 | 0 | 6 | 25 | 1,258 | 241 | 972 | 45 | 4 |
| Teller | 22 | 0 | 5 | 0 | 17 | 79 | 23 | 51 | 5 | 2 |
| Weld | 120 | 1 | 16 | 6 | 97 | 871 | 270 | 457 | 144 | 6 |

[1] The FBI does not publish arson data unless it receives data from either the agency or the state for all 12 months of the calendar year.
[2] The FBI determined that the agency's data were overreported. Consequently, affected data are not included in this table.
[4] The FBI determined that the agency did not follow national Uniform Crime Reporting (UCR) Program guidelines for reporting an offense. Consequently, this figure is not included in this table.
[5] The motor vehicle thefts for this county are collected by the Tulare County Highway Patrol. These data can be found in Table 11.

**Table 10. Offenses Known to Law Enforcement, by State Metropolitan and Nonmetropolitan Counties, 2009**—*Continued*

(Number.)

| State/County | Violent crime | Murder and non-negligent man-slaughter | Forcible rape | Robbery | Aggravated assault | Property crime | Burglary | Larceny-theft | Motor vehicle theft | Arson[1] |
|---|---|---|---|---|---|---|---|---|---|---|
| **COLORADO - Nonmetropolitan Counties** | | | | | | | | | | |
| Alamosa | 1 | 0 | 0 | 0 | 1 | 58 | 15 | 43 | 0 | 1 |
| Archuleta | 22 | 1 | 6 | 0 | 15 | 103 | 33 | 64 | 6 | 0 |
| Baca | 5 | 0 | 0 | 0 | 5 | 3 | 0 | 0 | 3 | 0 |
| Bent | 3 | 0 | 1 | 0 | 2 | 20 | 3 | 13 | 4 | 0 |
| Chaffee | 10 | 0 | 0 | 0 | 10 | 81 | 24 | 50 | 7 | 0 |
| Cheyenne | 0 | 0 | 0 | 0 | 0 | 3 | 1 | 1 | 1 | 0 |
| Crowley | 1 | 0 | 0 | 0 | 1 | 0 | 0 | 0 | 0 | 0 |
| Custer | 7 | 0 | 0 | 0 | 7 | 49 | 17 | 26 | 6 | 0 |
| Delta | 36 | 0 | 18 | 2 | 16 | 199 | 32 | 145 | 22 | 1 |
| Dolores | 0 | 0 | 0 | 0 | 0 | 19 | 16 | 2 | 1 | 0 |
| Eagle | 19 | 0 | 0 | 3 | 16 | 434 | 70 | 361 | 3 | 3 |
| Fremont | 68 | 0 | 1 | 2 | 65 | 134 | 52 | 76 | 6 | 1 |
| Grand | 7 | 0 | 0 | 0 | 7 | 156 | 35 | 117 | 4 | 0 |
| Gunnison | 13 | 0 | 0 | 0 | 13 | 32 | 13 | 18 | 1 | 0 |
| Hinsdale | 1 | 0 | 1 | 0 | 0 | 8 | 0 | 7 | 1 | 0 |
| Huerfano | 0 | 0 | 0 | 0 | 0 | 5 | 0 | 5 | 0 | 0 |
| Jackson | 1 | 0 | 0 | 0 | 1 | 17 | 14 | 2 | 1 | 0 |
| Kiowa | 0 | 0 | 0 | 0 | 0 | 0 | 0 | 0 | 0 | 0 |
| Kit Carson | 9 | 0 | 0 | 0 | 9 | 30 | 9 | 21 | 0 | 1 |
| Lake | 5 | 0 | 0 | 0 | 5 | 26 | 7 | 17 | 2 | 0 |
| La Plata | 51 | 0 | 2 | 1 | 48 | 247 | 86 | 142 | 19 | 3 |
| Lincoln | 1 | 0 | 0 | 0 | 1 | 0 | 0 | 0 | 0 | 0 |
| Logan | 4 | 0 | 0 | 0 | 4 | 51 | 5 | 41 | 5 | 0 |
| Mineral | 0 | 0 | 0 | 0 | 0 | 2 | 0 | 2 | 0 | 0 |
| Moffat | 7 | 0 | 0 | 0 | 7 | 31 | 13 | 15 | 3 | 0 |
| Montezuma | 34 | 0 | 0 | 1 | 33 | 185 | 64 | 98 | 23 | 0 |
| Montrose | 36 | 0 | 2 | 0 | 34 | 136 | 25 | 95 | 16 | 1 |
| Morgan | 3 | 0 | 0 | 3 | 0 | 40 | 10 | 28 | 2 | 3 |
| Otero | 15 | 0 | 1 | 0 | 14 | 58 | 16 | 39 | 3 | 0 |
| Ouray | 4 | 0 | 0 | 0 | 4 | 18 | 4 | 13 | 1 | 0 |
| Phillips | 2 | 0 | 1 | 0 | 1 | 3 | 1 | 2 | 0 | 0 |
| Pitkin | 8 | 0 | 2 | 0 | 6 | 79 | 10 | 62 | 7 | 0 |
| Prowers | 2 | 0 | 1 | 0 | 1 | 16 | 3 | 12 | 1 | 0 |
| Rio Blanco | 2 | 0 | 0 | 0 | 2 | 8 | 1 | 6 | 1 | 0 |
| Rio Grande | 16 | 2 | 1 | 0 | 13 | 25 | 9 | 15 | 1 | 0 |
| Routt | 21 | 0 | 0 | 0 | 21 | 99 | 23 | 70 | 6 | 2 |
| Saguache | 12 | 0 | 0 | 0 | 12 | 19 | 5 | 14 | 0 | 2 |
| San Juan | 0 | 0 | 0 | 0 | 0 | 15 | 2 | 13 | 0 | 2 |
| San Miguel | 3 | 0 | 0 | 0 | 3 | 36 | 8 | 24 | 4 | 0 |
| Sedgwick | 4 | 0 | 0 | 0 | 4 | 15 | 6 | 9 | 0 | 0 |
| Summit | 25 | 1 | 8 | 5 | 11 | 376 | 45 | 319 | 12 | 1 |
| Washington | 12 | 0 | 2 | 0 | 10 | 63 | 21 | 34 | 8 | 0 |
| Yuma | 7 | 0 | 3 | 0 | 4 | 21 | 2 | 19 | 0 | 0 |
| **DELAWARE - Metropolitan Counties** | | | | | | | | | | |
| New Castle County Police Department | 1,221 | 8 | 69 | 340 | 804 | 6,506 | 1,864 | 4,089 | 553 | 8 |
| **FLORIDA - Metropolitan Counties** | | | | | | | | | | |
| Alachua | 772 | 2 | 49 | 113 | 608 | 3,311 | 1,220 | 1,891 | 200 | 20 |
| Baker | 63 | 1 | 12 | 8 | 42 | 379 | 68 | 298 | 13 | 1 |
| Bay | 393 | 6 | 54 | 47 | 286 | 2,700 | 738 | 1,795 | 167 | 1 |
| Brevard | 1,044 | 4 | 67 | 126 | 847 | 5,644 | 1,248 | 4,123 | 273 | 15 |
| Broward | 324 | 2 | 22 | 94 | 206 | 1,050 | 221 | 746 | 83 | 4 |
| Charlotte | 439 | 2 | 18 | 59 | 360 | 3,821 | 947 | 2,702 | 172 | 1 |
| Clay | 799 | 12 | 44 | 102 | 641 | 4,127 | 933 | 3,025 | 169 | 44 |
| Collier | 1,000 | 14 | 49 | 188 | 749 | 4,971 | 1,191 | 3,566 | 214 | 17 |
| Escambia | 2,248 | 15 | 167 | 534 | 1,532 | 9,833 | 2,610 | 6,593 | 630 | 48 |
| Flagler | 216 | 3 | 22 | 38 | 153 | 2,028 | 525 | 1,419 | 84 | 6 |
| Gadsden | 364 | 2 | 2 | 17 | 343 | 712 | 379 | 331 | 2 | 0 |
| Gilchrist | 18 | 2 | 0 | 0 | 16 | 207 | 94 | 95 | 18 | 0 |
| Hernando | 550 | 3 | 46 | 69 | 432 | 4,891 | 1,372 | 3,334 | 185 | 7 |
| Hillsborough | 3,893 | 34 | 166 | 978 | 2,715 | 26,637 | 7,515 | 17,141 | 1,981 | 47 |
| Indian River | 304 | 3 | 10 | 46 | 245 | 2,727 | 696 | 1,925 | 106 | 4 |
| Jefferson | 82 | 0 | 6 | 2 | 74 | 152 | 65 | 76 | 11 | 1 |
| Lake | 711 | 2 | 50 | 55 | 604 | 3,351 | 1,141 | 1,981 | 229 | 24 |
| Lee | 1,398 | 20 | 81 | 407 | 890 | 10,549 | 3,862 | 5,931 | 756 | 69 |
| Leon | 339 | 4 | 18 | 47 | 270 | 1,460 | 768 | 607 | 85 | 22 |
| Manatee | 1,874 | 22 | 82 | 396 | 1,374 | 9,969 | 2,459 | 7,027 | 483 | 19 |
| Marion | 1,386 | 9 | 120 | 103 | 1,154 | 4,937 | 1,606 | 3,063 | 268 | 3 |
| Martin | 402 | 5 | 14 | 133 | 250 | 2,925 | 796 | 2,000 | 129 | 15 |
| Miami-Dade | 7,815 | 86 | 273 | 2,314 | 5,142 | 47,849 | 9,283 | 33,643 | 4,923 | 70 |
| Nassau | 357 | 2 | 2 | 13 | 340 | 1,252 | 390 | 776 | 86 | 10 |

[1] The FBI does not publish arson data unless it receives data from either the agency or the state for all 12 months of the calendar year.

## Table 10. Offenses Known to Law Enforcement, by State Metropolitan and Nonmetropolitan Counties, 2009—*Continued*

(Number.)

| State/County | Violent crime | Murder and non-negligent man-slaughter | Forcible rape | Robbery | Aggravated assault | Property crime | Burglary | Larceny-theft | Motor vehicle theft | Arson[1] |
|---|---|---|---|---|---|---|---|---|---|---|
| Okaloosa | 290 | 3 | 28 | 76 | 183 | 3,477 | 723 | 2,582 | 172 | 3 |
| Orange | 5,885 | 44 | 332 | 1,636 | 3,873 | 30,070 | 9,178 | 18,260 | 2,632 | 0 |
| Osceola | 954 | 7 | 20 | 105 | 822 | 6,195 | 2,347 | 3,555 | 293 | 1 |
| Palm Beach | 2,656 | 24 | 151 | 812 | 1,669 | 18,059 | 5,095 | 11,597 | 1,367 | 79 |
| Pasco | 1,443 | 11 | 102 | 338 | 992 | 13,392 | 3,809 | 8,723 | 860 | 92 |
| Pinellas | 1,149 | 9 | 95 | 210 | 835 | 7,725 | 1,868 | 5,404 | 453 | 33 |
| Polk | 1,511 | 16 | 104 | 195 | 1,196 | 10,648 | 3,975 | 6,074 | 599 | 0 |
| Santa Rosa | 211 | 0 | 30 | 17 | 164 | 1,483 | 415 | 983 | 85 | 5 |
| Sarasota | 717 | 8 | 29 | 134 | 546 | 8,370 | 2,065 | 5,922 | 383 | 6 |
| Seminole | 725 | 6 | 31 | 116 | 572 | 3,468 | 987 | 2,238 | 243 | 4 |
| St. Johns | 476 | 3 | 13 | 61 | 399 | 4,106 | 961 | 2,927 | 218 | 3 |
| St. Lucie | 286 | 0 | 24 | 44 | 218 | 1,779 | 611 | 1,086 | 82 | 13 |
| Volusia | 848 | 7 | 68 | 176 | 597 | 5,813 | 1,830 | 3,518 | 465 | 29 |
| Wakulla | 124 | 1 | 10 | 12 | 101 | 714 | 187 | 503 | 24 | 0 |
| **FLORIDA - Nonmetropolitan Counties** | | | | | | | | | | |
| Bradford | 115 | 0 | 10 | 8 | 97 | 428 | 207 | 176 | 45 | 3 |
| Calhoun | 11 | 2 | 1 | 0 | 8 | 65 | 23 | 39 | 3 | 0 |
| Citrus | 497 | 2 | 26 | 42 | 427 | 2,831 | 771 | 1,916 | 144 | 26 |
| Columbia | 179 | 3 | 11 | 18 | 147 | 1,274 | 525 | 670 | 79 | 0 |
| DeSoto | 204 | 0 | 9 | 30 | 165 | 837 | 365 | 444 | 28 | 3 |
| Dixie | 84 | 0 | 10 | 6 | 68 | 527 | 230 | 279 | 18 | 0 |
| Franklin | 65 | 0 | 6 | 2 | 57 | 190 | 56 | 130 | 4 | 3 |
| Glades | 33 | 0 | 2 | 3 | 28 | 217 | 85 | 123 | 9 | 3 |
| Gulf | 69 | 1 | 3 | 1 | 64 | 154 | 44 | 100 | 10 | 0 |
| Hamilton | 56 | 1 | 9 | 7 | 39 | 199 | 68 | 119 | 12 | 0 |
| Hardee | 49 | 0 | 10 | 13 | 26 | 476 | 136 | 312 | 28 | 0 |
| Hendry | 189 | 5 | 4 | 23 | 157 | 1,034 | 586 | 378 | 70 | 6 |
| Highlands | 144 | 3 | 4 | 22 | 115 | 1,805 | 620 | 1,097 | 88 | 9 |
| Holmes | 48 | 0 | 3 | 1 | 44 | 234 | 69 | 139 | 26 | 1 |
| Jackson | 211 | 1 | 15 | 16 | 179 | 586 | 203 | 347 | 36 | 4 |
| Lafayette | 24 | 1 | 1 | 3 | 19 | 76 | 37 | 36 | 3 | 0 |
| Levy | 199 | 1 | 13 | 12 | 173 | 968 | 402 | 503 | 63 | 7 |
| Madison | 113 | 3 | 4 | 17 | 89 | 303 | 128 | 167 | 8 | 2 |
| Monroe | 218 | 2 | 10 | 11 | 195 | 2,174 | 541 | 1,548 | 85 | 0 |
| Okeechobee | 231 | 3 | 14 | 12 | 202 | 993 | 449 | 514 | 30 | 2 |
| Putnam | 617 | 2 | 43 | 80 | 492 | 2,459 | 1,199 | 1,109 | 151 | 4 |
| Sumter | 160 | 1 | 24 | 16 | 119 | 761 | 261 | 467 | 33 | 2 |
| Suwannee | 129 | 0 | 8 | 3 | 118 | 507 | 157 | 294 | 56 | 1 |
| Taylor | 74 | 1 | 6 | 0 | 67 | 249 | 164 | 77 | 8 | 1 |
| Union | 37 | 1 | 4 | 2 | 30 | 122 | 51 | 59 | 12 | 0 |
| Walton | 155 | 4 | 6 | 7 | 138 | 1,082 | 354 | 664 | 64 | 1 |
| Washington | 12 | 0 | 3 | 0 | 9 | 172 | 56 | 111 | 5 | 0 |
| **GEORGIA - Metropolitan Counties** | | | | | | | | | | |
| Augusta-Richmond | 1,039 | 26 | 138 | 696 | 179 | 13,925 | 3,587 | 8,712 | 1,626 | 68 |
| Bartow | 190 | 4 | 19 | 29 | 138 | 2,430 | 691 | 1,520 | 219 | 0 |
| Bibb | 175 | 4 | 14 | 44 | 113 | 2,343 | 675 | 1,464 | 204 | 14 |
| Brantley | 49 | 0 | 9 | 5 | 35 | 236 | 148 | 86 | 2 | 0 |
| Brooks | 68 | 1 | 0 | 0 | 67 | 294 | 106 | 146 | 42 | 4 |
| Butts | 72 | 3 | 12 | 12 | 45 | 522 | 125 | 333 | 64 | 2 |
| Carroll | 361 | 4 | 22 | 26 | 309 | 1,460 | 489 | 833 | 138 | 5 |
| Catoosa | 56 | 1 | 5 | 7 | 43 | 988 | 231 | 643 | 114 | 1 |
| Chatham | 0 | 0 | 0 | 0 | 0 | 0 | 0 | 0 | 0 | 0 |
| Cherokee | 108 | 1 | 3 | 11 | 93 | 1,521 | 436 | 1,014 | 71 | 10 |
| Clarke | 0 | 0 | 0 | 0 | 0 | 0 | 0 | 0 | 0 | 0 |
| Clayton | 0 | 0 | 0 | 0 | 0 | 0 | 0 | 0 | 0 | 0 |
| Clayton County Police Department | 1,145 | 17 | 85 | 485 | 558 | 9,444 | 4,195 | 3,987 | 1,262 | 22 |
| Cobb | 5 | 0 | 0 | 0 | 5 | 0 | 0 | 0 | 0 | 0 |
| Cobb County Police Department | 1,105 | 19 | 92 | 418 | 576 | 11,325 | 3,427 | 6,840 | 1,058 | 52 |
| Columbia | 119 | 4 | 14 | 42 | 59 | 2,269 | 353 | 1,795 | 121 | 6 |
| Coweta | 89 | 3 | 11 | 15 | 60 | 1,542 | 506 | 923 | 113 | 3 |
| Dade | 47 | 0 | 3 | 3 | 41 | 240 | 59 | 154 | 27 | |
| Dawson | 23 | 2 | 2 | 2 | 17 | 415 | 108 | 278 | 29 | 5 |
| DeKalb County Police Department | 3,578 | 60 | 158 | 2,178 | 1,182 | 30,026 | 9,511 | 15,982 | 4,533 | 140 |
| Dougherty | 1 | 0 | 0 | 0 | 1 | 81 | 7 | 66 | 8 | 0 |
| Douglas | 165 | 4 | 10 | 38 | 113 | 2,079 | 606 | 1,296 | 177 | 6 |
| Echols | 8 | 0 | 1 | 1 | 6 | 42 | 15 | 26 | 1 | 1 |
| Fayette | 31 | 1 | 1 | 9 | 20 | 609 | 195 | 377 | 37 | 3 |
| Floyd | 25 | 0 | 0 | 0 | 25 | 17 | 7 | 10 | 0 | |
| Floyd County Police Department | 179 | 2 | 4 | 10 | 163 | 1,160 | 310 | 746 | 104 | |
| Forsyth | 86 | 2 | 17 | 18 | 49 | 1,975 | 512 | 1,369 | 94 | 3 |
| Fulton | 3 | 0 | 0 | 0 | 3 | 18 | 0 | 17 | 1 | 0 |

[1] The FBI does not publish arson data unless it receives data from either the agency or the state for all 12 months of the calendar year.

## Table 10. Offenses Known to Law Enforcement, by State Metropolitan and Nonmetropolitan Counties, 2009—*Continued*

(Number.)

| State/County | Violent crime | Murder and non-negligent man-slaughter | Forcible rape | Robbery | Aggravated assault | Property crime | Burglary | Larceny-theft | Motor vehicle theft | Arson[1] |
|---|---|---|---|---|---|---|---|---|---|---|
| Fulton County Police Department | 653 | 10 | 42 | 280 | 321 | 5,824 | 2,236 | 2,695 | 893 | 13 |
| Glynn | 0 | 0 | 0 | 0 | 0 | 0 | 0 | 0 | 0 | 0 |
| Glynn County Police Department | 313 | 14 | 16 | 67 | 216 | 2,635 | 610 | 1,921 | 104 | 5 |
| Gwinnett County Police Department | 1,978 | 35 | 151 | 1,055 | 737 | 18,068 | 5,484 | 10,741 | 1,843 | 85 |
| Hall | 201 | 2 | 24 | 32 | 143 | 2,617 | 803 | 1,589 | 225 | 11 |
| Haralson | 89 | 0 | 3 | 2 | 84 | 330 | 72 | 238 | 20 | |
| Heard | 19 | 0 | 0 | 2 | 17 | 153 | 46 | 79 | 28 | 0 |
| Henry County Police Department | 248 | 3 | 25 | 85 | 135 | 3,953 | 1,087 | 2,482 | 384 | 14 |
| Jasper | 13 | 0 | 2 | 1 | 10 | 143 | 58 | 76 | 9 | 0 |
| Jones | 28 | 0 | 1 | 6 | 21 | 474 | 147 | 286 | 41 | 2 |
| Lee | 18 | 0 | 1 | 5 | 12 | 456 | 129 | 298 | 29 | 1 |
| Liberty | 75 | 0 | 8 | 18 | 49 | 513 | 218 | 258 | 37 | |
| Madison | 106 | 0 | 5 | 7 | 94 | 510 | 53 | 417 | 40 | 0 |
| McDuffie | 26 | 0 | 0 | 8 | 18 | 322 | 93 | 192 | 37 | 0 |
| McIntosh | 62 | 0 | 2 | 6 | 54 | 448 | 155 | 259 | 34 | 5 |
| Meriwether | 31 | 0 | 3 | 7 | 21 | 351 | 101 | 200 | 50 | 0 |
| Monroe | 13 | 1 | 3 | 5 | 4 | 357 | 137 | 175 | 45 | |
| Murray | 39 | 1 | 5 | 5 | 28 | 699 | 141 | 495 | 63 | 0 |
| Newton | 299 | 7 | 7 | 26 | 259 | 1,934 | 743 | 989 | 202 | |
| Oglethorpe | 50 | 1 | 3 | 4 | 42 | 464 | 145 | 298 | 21 | 1 |
| Paulding | 189 | 0 | 15 | 20 | 154 | 2,400 | 571 | 1,611 | 218 | 23 |
| Pickens | 56 | 0 | 7 | 0 | 49 | 389 | 136 | 230 | 23 | 0 |
| Pike | 9 | 2 | 0 | 2 | 5 | 97 | 33 | 56 | 8 | 0 |
| Rockdale | 295 | 4 | 11 | 46 | 234 | 2,319 | 623 | 1,496 | 200 | 7 |
| Spalding | 117 | 0 | 12 | 25 | 80 | 1,281 | 383 | 749 | 149 | 0 |
| Walker | 254 | 0 | 12 | 5 | 237 | 975 | 352 | 573 | 50 | 0 |
| Walton | 110 | 7 | 3 | 7 | 93 | 885 | 195 | 581 | 109 | 2 |
| Whitfield | 203 | 0 | 11 | 10 | 182 | 1,646 | 375 | 1,213 | 58 | 12 |
| Worth | 5 | 1 | 0 | 2 | 2 | 211 | 69 | 112 | 30 | |
| **GEORGIA - Nonmetropolitan Counties** | | | | | | | | | | |
| Baldwin | 337 | 2 | 6 | 14 | 315 | 860 | 332 | 512 | 16 | 6 |
| Banks | 115 | 0 | 0 | 2 | 113 | 522 | 103 | 364 | 55 | |
| Ben Hill | 18 | 0 | 5 | 1 | 12 | 184 | 78 | 91 | 15 | 0 |
| Berrien | 11 | 1 | 1 | 0 | 9 | 219 | 55 | 157 | 7 | 1 |
| Bleckley[2] | 19 | 0 | 0 | 0 | 19 | | | 82 | 5 | 0 |
| Bulloch | 32 | 0 | 2 | 8 | 22 | 773 | 275 | 430 | 68 | 1 |
| Calhoun | 5 | 1 | 1 | 1 | 2 | 35 | 9 | 18 | 8 | 1 |
| Camden | 43 | 0 | 1 | 3 | 39 | 373 | 96 | 263 | 14 | |
| Candler | 6 | 0 | 1 | 2 | 3 | 100 | 28 | 62 | 10 | 0 |
| Charlton | 9 | 0 | 1 | 1 | 7 | 131 | 47 | 73 | 11 | 1 |
| Chattooga | 38 | 0 | 1 | 1 | 36 | 335 | 103 | 227 | 5 | |
| Clinch | 4 | 0 | 1 | 1 | 2 | 42 | 19 | 21 | 2 | 2 |
| Coffee | 52 | 1 | 8 | 13 | 30 | 694 | 219 | 446 | 29 | |
| Cook | 40 | 1 | 0 | 3 | 36 | 134 | 35 | 87 | 12 | 0 |
| Crisp | 17 | 2 | 0 | 0 | 15 | 383 | 74 | 277 | 32 | 0 |
| Decatur | 44 | 2 | 5 | 5 | 32 | 324 | 115 | 203 | 6 | |
| Dodge | 23 | 2 | 4 | 1 | 16 | 289 | 101 | 164 | 24 | 5 |
| Dooly | 13 | 0 | 1 | 0 | 12 | 64 | 13 | 48 | 3 | |
| Early | 26 | 0 | 5 | 3 | 18 | 132 | 58 | 70 | 4 | 0 |
| Elbert | 35 | 0 | 5 | 3 | 27 | 514 | 155 | 332 | 27 | 0 |
| Emanuel | 17 | 1 | 0 | 0 | 16 | 294 | 176 | 99 | 19 | 0 |
| Fannin | 79 | 1 | 5 | 2 | 71 | 459 | 226 | 197 | 36 | 3 |
| Franklin | 29 | 2 | 3 | 3 | 21 | 377 | 116 | 235 | 26 | |
| Gilmer | 38 | 0 | 2 | 0 | 36 | 424 | 190 | 208 | 26 | 0 |
| Glascock | 1 | 0 | 0 | 0 | 1 | 34 | 2 | 24 | 8 | |
| Gordon[2] | | 1 | 8 | 6 | | 730 | 186 | 537 | 7 | 0 |
| Greene | 11 | 0 | 2 | 1 | 8 | 191 | 54 | 112 | 25 | 0 |
| Habersham | 59 | 0 | 11 | 1 | 47 | 457 | 172 | 251 | 34 | 7 |
| Hart | 46 | 1 | 0 | 4 | 41 | 356 | 127 | 212 | 17 | |
| Irwin | 13 | 0 | 3 | 0 | 10 | 123 | 40 | 75 | 8 | 0 |
| Jackson | 42 | 1 | 5 | 7 | 29 | 887 | 274 | 569 | 44 | |
| Jeff Davis | 39 | 0 | 7 | 0 | 32 | 373 | 50 | 267 | 56 | |
| Jefferson | 26 | 0 | 1 | 8 | 17 | 197 | 89 | 89 | 19 | 0 |
| Johnson | 18 | 0 | 0 | 0 | 18 | 58 | 32 | 17 | 9 | 0 |
| Laurens | 51 | 0 | 2 | 8 | 41 | 634 | 176 | 372 | 86 | 1 |
| Lumpkin | 69 | 1 | 4 | 1 | 63 | 492 | 130 | 337 | 25 | |
| Macon | 0 | 0 | 0 | 0 | 0 | 84 | 40 | 35 | 9 | 0 |
| Morgan | 13 | 0 | 1 | 2 | 10 | 124 | 37 | 69 | 18 | 0 |
| Peach | 21 | 2 | 0 | 4 | 15 | 310 | 105 | 165 | 40 | 0 |
| Pierce | 3 | 0 | 0 | 0 | 3 | 228 | 66 | 138 | 24 | 0 |
| Polk | 0 | 0 | 0 | 0 | 0 | 0 | 0 | 0 | 0 | 0 |

[1] The FBI does not publish arson data unless it receives data from either the agency or the state for all 12 months of the calendar year.

[2] The FBI determined that the agency's data were overreported. Consequently, affected data are not included in this table.

**Table 10. Offenses Known to Law Enforcement, by State Metropolitan and Nonmetropolitan Counties, 2009**—*Continued*

(Number.)

| State/County | Violent crime | Murder and non-negligent man-slaughter | Forcible rape | Robbery | Aggravated assault | Property crime | Burglary | Larceny-theft | Motor vehicle theft | Arson[1] |
|---|---|---|---|---|---|---|---|---|---|---|
| Polk County Police Department | 85 | 0 | 11 | 4 | 70 | 779 | 294 | 413 | 72 | 23 |
| Pulaski | 7 | 1 | 0 | 0 | 6 | 144 | 51 | 93 | 0 | 0 |
| Rabun | 18 | 0 | 1 | 0 | 17 | 182 | 56 | 117 | 9 | |
| Schley | 1 | 0 | 1 | 0 | 0 | 26 | 14 | 11 | 1 | 0 |
| Seminole | 9 | 1 | 0 | 0 | 8 | 104 | 26 | 71 | 7 | 0 |
| Stephens | 29 | 0 | 2 | 6 | 21 | 628 | 137 | 481 | 10 | |
| Stewart | 2 | 0 | 0 | 0 | 2 | 5 | 4 | 0 | 1 | 0 |
| Tattnall | 17 | 1 | 0 | 5 | 11 | 232 | 83 | 127 | 22 | 0 |
| Taylor | 2 | 0 | 0 | 2 | 0 | 134 | 15 | 115 | 4 | |
| Telfair | 12 | 2 | 0 | 3 | 7 | 115 | 46 | 64 | 5 | 1 |
| Thomas | 38 | 0 | 2 | 8 | 28 | 523 | 203 | 269 | 51 | 6 |
| Tift | 116 | 2 | 9 | 22 | 83 | 762 | 213 | 500 | 49 | 4 |
| Toombs | 22 | 0 | 4 | 0 | 18 | 293 | 77 | 185 | 31 | 0 |
| Towns | 9 | 0 | 1 | 1 | 7 | 157 | 72 | 79 | 6 | 2 |
| Treutlen | 3 | 0 | 0 | 0 | 3 | 58 | 21 | 35 | 2 | |
| Troup | 41 | 0 | 1 | 2 | 38 | 696 | 153 | 480 | 63 | |
| Turner | 8 | 0 | 1 | 1 | 6 | 62 | 16 | 43 | 3 | |
| Upson | 23 | 0 | 0 | 4 | 19 | 379 | 105 | 260 | 14 | 1 |
| Washington | 25 | 0 | 2 | 5 | 18 | 219 | 87 | 124 | 8 | 0 |
| White | 9 | 0 | 0 | 1 | 8 | 333 | 148 | 151 | 34 | 1 |
| Wilkes | 4 | 0 | 0 | 1 | 3 | 13 | 4 | 8 | 1 | 0 |
| Wilkinson | 5 | 0 | 0 | 0 | 5 | 73 | 38 | 28 | 7 | 0 |
| **HAWAII - Nonmetropolitan Counties** | | | | | | | | | | |
| Hawaii Police Department[6] | 468 | 5 | 66 | 67 | 330 | 5,743 | 1,415 | 3,855 | 473 | 28 |
| Kauai Police Department | 212 | 1 | 32 | 23 | 156 | 2,683 | 810 | 1,758 | 115 | 8 |
| **IDAHO - Metropolitan Counties** | | | | | | | | | | |
| Ada | 148 | 0 | 31 | 11 | 106 | 917 | 280 | 609 | 28 | 8 |
| Bannock | 5 | 0 | 1 | 1 | 3 | 141 | 20 | 120 | 1 | 0 |
| Bonneville | 120 | 0 | 15 | 2 | 103 | 844 | 188 | 596 | 60 | 6 |
| Canyon | 55 | 0 | 9 | 1 | 45 | 578 | 202 | 326 | 50 | 5 |
| Franklin | 7 | 0 | 0 | 0 | 7 | 48 | 12 | 33 | 3 | 0 |
| Gem | 12 | 0 | 0 | 0 | 12 | 33 | 10 | 20 | 3 | 0 |
| Jefferson | 32 | 0 | 5 | 0 | 27 | 111 | 26 | 73 | 12 | 0 |
| Kootenai | 125 | 0 | 25 | 9 | 91 | 1,114 | 396 | 669 | 49 | 7 |
| Nez Perce | 2 | 0 | 0 | 0 | 2 | 80 | 15 | 62 | 3 | 0 |
| Owyhee | 16 | 0 | 6 | 0 | 10 | 86 | 16 | 65 | 5 | 0 |
| Power | 6 | 0 | 2 | 0 | 4 | 36 | 4 | 29 | 3 | 0 |
| **IDAHO - Nonmetropolitan Counties** | | | | | | | | | | |
| Adams | 4 | 0 | 0 | 0 | 4 | 40 | 6 | 34 | 0 | 0 |
| Bear Lake | 1 | 0 | 0 | 0 | 1 | 13 | 3 | 9 | 1 | 0 |
| Benewah | 29 | 0 | 0 | 0 | 29 | 33 | 9 | 21 | 3 | 0 |
| Bingham | 35 | 1 | 11 | 0 | 23 | 286 | 92 | 177 | 17 | 2 |
| Blaine | 9 | 0 | 2 | 0 | 7 | 45 | 9 | 33 | 3 | 0 |
| Bonner | 20 | 0 | 3 | 1 | 16 | 355 | 104 | 226 | 25 | 4 |
| Boundary | 12 | 0 | 5 | 2 | 5 | 84 | 44 | 36 | 4 | 0 |
| Butte | 9 | 0 | 1 | 0 | 8 | 2 | 1 | 0 | 1 | 0 |
| Camas | 2 | 0 | 1 | 0 | 1 | 10 | 2 | 8 | 0 | 0 |
| Caribou | 0 | 0 | 0 | 0 | 0 | 28 | 6 | 21 | 1 | 0 |
| Cassia | 55 | 1 | 10 | 4 | 40 | 492 | 91 | 367 | 34 | 9 |
| Clark | 4 | 0 | 0 | 0 | 4 | 9 | 2 | 7 | 0 | 0 |
| Clearwater | 17 | 0 | 0 | 0 | 17 | 77 | 11 | 66 | 0 | 0 |
| Custer | 3 | 0 | 0 | 0 | 3 | 3 | 0 | 3 | 0 | 0 |
| Elmore | 16 | 0 | 3 | 2 | 11 | 74 | 20 | 49 | 5 | 0 |
| Fremont | 6 | 0 | 1 | 0 | 5 | 95 | 13 | 78 | 4 | 0 |
| Gooding | 11 | 0 | 0 | 0 | 11 | 37 | 10 | 18 | 9 | 1 |
| Idaho | 10 | 0 | 1 | 0 | 9 | 94 | 35 | 57 | 2 | 1 |
| Jerome | 14 | 0 | 0 | 1 | 13 | 82 | 29 | 43 | 10 | 0 |
| Latah | 12 | 0 | 3 | 0 | 9 | 172 | 61 | 100 | 11 | 1 |
| Lemhi | 1 | 0 | 0 | 0 | 1 | 9 | 7 | 1 | 1 | 1 |
| Lewis | 11 | 0 | 0 | 0 | 11 | 52 | 24 | 26 | 2 | 0 |
| Lincoln | 4 | 0 | 0 | 0 | 4 | 17 | 3 | 7 | 7 | 0 |
| Madison | 7 | 0 | 7 | 0 | 0 | 57 | 6 | 46 | 5 | 0 |
| Minidoka | 19 | 0 | 4 | 2 | 13 | 167 | 34 | 117 | 16 | 1 |
| Oneida | 10 | 0 | 2 | 2 | 6 | 65 | 30 | 30 | 5 | 0 |
| Payette | 17 | 0 | 1 | 0 | 16 | 100 | 42 | 50 | 8 | 0 |
| Shoshone | 25 | 0 | 5 | 0 | 20 | 145 | 31 | 100 | 14 | 1 |
| Teton | 8 | 0 | 0 | 0 | 8 | 98 | 24 | 69 | 5 | 0 |
| Twin Falls | 37 | 0 | 4 | 1 | 32 | 209 | 87 | 107 | 15 | 1 |
| Valley | 9 | 0 | 6 | 0 | 3 | 79 | 27 | 50 | 2 | 0 |
| Washington | 8 | 0 | 1 | 0 | 7 | 31 | 13 | 16 | 2 | 0 |

[1] The FBI does not publish arson data unless it receives data from either the agency or the state for all 12 months of the calendar year.

[6] Because of changes in the state/local agency's reporting practices, figures are not comparable to previous years' data.

**Table 10. Offenses Known to Law Enforcement, by State Metropolitan and Nonmetropolitan Counties, 2009**—*Continued*

(Number.)

| State/County | Violent crime | Murder and non-negligent man-slaughter | Forcible rape | Robbery | Aggravated assault | Property crime | Burglary | Larceny-theft | Motor vehicle theft | Arson[1] |
|---|---|---|---|---|---|---|---|---|---|---|
| **ILLINOIS - Metropolitan Counties[7]** | | | | | | | | | | |
| Bond | | 0 | | 0 | 3 | 105 | 28 | 67 | 10 | 0 |
| Clinton | | 0 | | 0 | 8 | 98 | 6 | 89 | 3 | 0 |
| Grundy | | 0 | | 2 | 6 | 284 | 55 | 218 | 11 | 0 |
| Henry | | 0 | | 0 | 6 | 91 | 11 | 72 | 8 | 0 |
| Macon | | 0 | | 2 | 33 | 381 | 121 | 247 | 13 | 4 |
| Rock Island | | 0 | | 4 | 38 | 329 | 98 | 223 | 8 | 1 |
| Stark | | 0 | | 0 | 8 | 64 | 11 | 51 | 2 | 0 |
| Vermilion | | 1 | | 4 | 38 | 510 | 200 | 287 | 23 | 1 |
| Woodford | | 0 | | 0 | 8 | 157 | 49 | 102 | 6 | 2 |
| **ILLINOIS - Nonmetropolitan Counties[7]** | | | | | | | | | | |
| Iroquois | | 0 | | 0 | 8 | 141 | 66 | 71 | 4 | 0 |
| Jackson | | 0 | | 1 | 30 | 271 | 124 | 135 | 12 | 0 |
| Jefferson | | 0 | | 0 | 63 | 338 | 126 | 187 | 25 | 4 |
| La Salle | | 1 | | 0 | 23 | 477 | 161 | 296 | 20 | 3 |
| Livingston | | 0 | | 0 | 8 | 255 | 37 | 210 | 8 | 1 |
| Marion | | 0 | | 1 | 7 | 236 | 70 | 151 | 15 | 0 |
| Morgan | | 0 | | 0 | 11 | 100 | 41 | 56 | 3 | 1 |
| Moultrie | | 0 | | 0 | 3 | 45 | 18 | 23 | 4 | 0 |
| Ogle | | 0 | | 0 | 18 | 238 | 66 | 155 | 17 | 3 |
| Richland | | 0 | | 0 | 9 | 66 | 26 | 37 | 3 | 0 |
| Union | | 1 | | 0 | 3 | 92 | 22 | 66 | 4 | 0 |
| **INDIANA - Metropolitan Counties** | | | | | | | | | | |
| Allen | 92 | 0 | 16 | 9 | 67 | 1,047 | 239 | 750 | 58 | 2 |
| Bartholomew | 27 | 0 | 3 | 3 | 21 | 413 | 94 | 299 | 20 | 0 |
| Boone | 0 | 0 | 0 | 0 | 0 | 253 | 56 | 189 | 8 | 0 |
| Brown | 2 | 1 | 0 | 1 | 0 | 97 | 37 | 57 | 3 | 7 |
| Clark | 63 | 1 | 7 | 4 | 51 | 676 | 259 | 380 | 37 | 4 |
| Delaware | 24 | 0 | 6 | 4 | 14 | 471 | 115 | 297 | 59 | 2 |
| Elkhart | 62 | 0 | 20 | 23 | 19 | 1,669 | 506 | 1,027 | 136 | 4 |
| Floyd | 4 | 0 | 0 | 0 | 4 | 650 | 135 | 483 | 32 | 0 |
| Gibson | 18 | 1 | 1 | 2 | 14 | 165 | 22 | 139 | 4 | 2 |
| Greene | 4 | 0 | 2 | 0 | 2 | 145 | 59 | 66 | 20 | 0 |
| Hancock | 14 | 0 | 4 | 3 | 7 | 367 | 120 | 216 | 31 | 6 |
| Harrison | 4 | 0 | 0 | 2 | 2 | 445 | 97 | 318 | 30 | 0 |
| Howard | 47 | 0 | 3 | 2 | 42 | 496 | 198 | 279 | 19 | 1 |
| Johnson | 11 | 1 | 3 | 4 | 3 | 655 | 89 | 557 | 9 | 2 |
| Lake | 23 | 1 | 3 | 10 | 9 | 955 | 209 | 656 | 90 | 1 |
| La Porte | 22 | 3 | 3 | 9 | 7 | 746 | 295 | 413 | 38 | 1 |
| Madison | 11 | 0 | 2 | 5 | 4 | 558 | 159 | 366 | 33 | 3 |
| Monroe | 49 | 0 | 6 | 7 | 36 | 879 | 363 | 448 | 68 | 1 |
| Newton | 5 | 1 | 0 | 2 | 2 | 240 | 86 | 137 | 17 | 1 |
| Porter | 59 | 1 | 5 | 1 | 52 | 1,091 | 294 | 737 | 60 | 1 |
| Putnam | 27 | 0 | 1 | 1 | 25 | 238 | 90 | 120 | 28 | 0 |
| Shelby | 33 | 0 | 1 | 2 | 30 | 345 | 120 | 198 | 27 | 1 |
| St. Joseph | 127 | 2 | 10 | 29 | 86 | 2,146 | 572 | 1,480 | 94 | 5 |
| Tippecanoe | 30 | 0 | 7 | 4 | 19 | 974 | 223 | 697 | 54 | 2 |
| Tipton | 7 | 0 | 0 | 0 | 7 | 99 | 38 | 56 | 5 | 0 |
| Vanderburgh | 75 | 0 | 9 | 7 | 59 | 1,031 | 123 | 881 | 27 | 3 |
| Vermillion | 7 | 0 | 0 | 2 | 5 | 41 | 10 | 22 | 9 | 2 |
| Warrick | 133 | 0 | 5 | 5 | 123 | 541 | 100 | 425 | 16 | 4 |
| Wells | 3 | 2 | 0 | 0 | 1 | 124 | 45 | 76 | 3 | 0 |
| Whitley | 7 | 1 | 1 | 3 | 2 | 239 | 63 | 161 | 15 | 0 |
| **INDIANA - Nonmetropolitan Counties** | | | | | | | | | | |
| Blackford | 3 | 0 | 0 | 0 | 3 | 57 | 18 | 35 | 4 | 1 |
| Cass | 10 | 0 | 2 | 1 | 7 | 265 | 58 | 203 | 4 | 0 |
| Clinton | 8 | 0 | 3 | 3 | 2 | 358 | 73 | 267 | 18 | 1 |
| Crawford | 39 | 0 | 0 | 0 | 39 | 108 | 34 | 69 | 5 | 0 |
| Daviess | 12 | 0 | 2 | 1 | 9 | 135 | 21 | 89 | 25 | 0 |
| Grant | 5 | 2 | 2 | 1 | 0 | 317 | 75 | 221 | 21 | 2 |
| Henry | 9 | 0 | 1 | 3 | 5 | 611 | 220 | 361 | 30 | 0 |
| Huntington | 11 | 0 | 1 | 0 | 10 | 162 | 47 | 106 | 9 | 0 |
| Jackson | 18 | 2 | 1 | 0 | 15 | 303 | 84 | 208 | 11 | 0 |
| Jay | 19 | 0 | 1 | 4 | 14 | 137 | 37 | 98 | 2 | 1 |
| Kosciusko | 23 | 0 | 1 | 0 | 22 | 637 | 135 | 467 | 35 | 1 |
| LaGrange | 7 | 0 | 4 | 3 | 0 | 212 | 63 | 139 | 10 | 0 |
| Lawrence | 10 | 2 | 4 | 2 | 2 | 294 | 109 | 161 | 24 | 7 |
| Marshall[4] | 8 | 0 | 4 | 0 | 4 | | 138 | | 13 | 2 |
| Martin | 0 | 0 | 0 | 0 | 0 | 56 | 16 | 33 | 7 | 0 |
| Miami | 9 | 0 | 2 | 2 | 5 | 261 | 106 | 152 | 3 | 2 |
| Montgomery | 52 | 2 | 1 | 6 | 43 | 473 | 193 | 253 | 27 | 0 |

[1] The FBI does not publish arson data unless it receives data from either the agency or the state for all 12 months of the calendar year.

[4] The FBI determined that the agency did not follow national Uniform Crime Reporting (UCR) Program guidelines for reporting an offense. Consequently, this figure is not included in this table.

[7] The data collection methodology for the offense of forcible rape used by the Illinois and the Minnesota state UCR Programs (with the exception of Rockford, Illinois, and Minneapolis and St. Paul, Minnesota) does not comply with national UCR Program guidelines. Consequently, their figures for forcible rape and violent crime (of which forcible rape is a part) are not published in this table.

## Table 10. Offenses Known to Law Enforcement, by State Metropolitan and Nonmetropolitan Counties, 2009—*Continued*

(Number.)

| State/County | Violent crime | Murder and non-negligent man-slaughter | Forcible rape | Robbery | Aggravated assault | Property crime | Burglary | Larceny-theft | Motor vehicle theft | Arson[1] |
|---|---|---|---|---|---|---|---|---|---|---|
| Noble | 6 | 0 | 0 | 0 | 6 | 181 | 89 | 78 | 14 | 1 |
| Parke | 3 | 1 | 1 | 0 | 1 | 123 | 30 | 86 | 7 | 0 |
| Perry | 10 | 0 | 2 | 0 | 8 | 48 | 15 | 28 | 5 | 2 |
| Pulaski[2] | | 0 | 0 | 0 | | 181 | 47 | 113 | 21 | 0 |
| Randolph | 7 | 1 | 2 | 2 | 2 | 258 | 105 | 149 | 4 | 0 |
| Ripley | 13 | 0 | 0 | 0 | 13 | 171 | 36 | 130 | 5 | 0 |
| Starke[6] | 37 | 1 | 10 | 5 | 21 | 628 | 156 | 424 | 48 | 5 |
| Steuben | 15 | 1 | 4 | 1 | 9 | 453 | 112 | 322 | 19 | 1 |
| Wabash | 4 | 3 | 0 | 1 | 0 | 130 | 29 | 100 | 1 | 0 |
| Wayne | 0 | 0 | 0 | 0 | 0 | 277 | 109 | 163 | 5 | 0 |
| White | 0 | 0 | 0 | 0 | 0 | 15 | 15 | 0 | 0 | 0 |
| **IOWA - Metropolitan Counties** | | | | | | | | | | |
| Benton | 5 | 0 | 0 | 1 | 4 | 94 | 37 | 52 | 5 | 1 |
| Black Hawk | 46 | 0 | 7 | 5 | 34 | 175 | 64 | 102 | 9 | 0 |
| Bremer | 20 | 0 | 3 | 0 | 17 | 39 | 15 | 22 | 2 | 0 |
| Dallas | 6 | 0 | 0 | 1 | 5 | 107 | 23 | 77 | 7 | 2 |
| Dubuque | 65 | 0 | 3 | 0 | 62 | 258 | 102 | 139 | 17 | 3 |
| Grundy | 3 | 0 | 0 | 0 | 3 | 117 | 26 | 88 | 3 | 0 |
| Guthrie | 0 | 0 | 0 | 0 | 0 | 64 | 29 | 24 | 11 | 0 |
| Harrison | 3 | 0 | 0 | 0 | 3 | 105 | 49 | 45 | 11 | 1 |
| Johnson | 65 | 1 | 5 | 2 | 57 | 244 | 78 | 155 | 11 | 3 |
| Jones | 2 | 0 | 1 | 0 | 1 | 73 | 20 | 47 | 6 | 1 |
| Linn | 31 | 0 | 10 | 0 | 21 | 331 | 119 | 184 | 28 | 2 |
| Madison | 3 | 0 | 0 | 2 | 1 | 30 | 13 | 15 | 2 | 1 |
| Mills | 23 | 0 | 5 | 0 | 18 | 165 | 41 | 93 | 31 | 3 |
| Polk | 81 | 0 | 13 | 6 | 62 | 680 | 199 | 412 | 69 | 4 |
| Scott | 24 | 0 | 3 | 2 | 19 | 193 | 43 | 138 | 12 | 0 |
| Story | 17 | 0 | 4 | 2 | 11 | 174 | 74 | 93 | 7 | 2 |
| Warren | 24 | 0 | 4 | 1 | 19 | 185 | 56 | 113 | 16 | 5 |
| Washington | 19 | 0 | 9 | 0 | 10 | 120 | 59 | 51 | 10 | 0 |
| Woodbury | 24 | 0 | 1 | 0 | 23 | 110 | 46 | 60 | 4 | 1 |
| **IOWA - Nonmetropolitan Counties** | | | | | | | | | | |
| Adair | 1 | 0 | 0 | 0 | 1 | 54 | 21 | 29 | 4 | 0 |
| Adams | 21 | 0 | 1 | 0 | 20 | 63 | 19 | 36 | 8 | 1 |
| Appanoose | 17 | 1 | 2 | 1 | 13 | 62 | 24 | 28 | 10 | 4 |
| Audubon | 3 | 0 | 0 | 0 | 3 | 21 | 6 | 14 | 1 | 0 |
| Boone | 5 | 0 | 0 | 0 | 5 | 14 | 5 | 8 | 1 | 0 |
| Buchanan | 12 | 0 | 0 | 0 | 12 | 132 | 32 | 87 | 13 | 1 |
| Buena Vista | 7 | 0 | 0 | 0 | 7 | 58 | 21 | 36 | 1 | 1 |
| Butler | 6 | 1 | 0 | 0 | 5 | 26 | 20 | 3 | 3 | 0 |
| Calhoun | 6 | 0 | 0 | 0 | 6 | 60 | 33 | 25 | 2 | 0 |
| Carroll | 4 | 0 | 1 | 0 | 3 | 37 | 10 | 26 | 1 | 0 |
| Cass | 15 | 0 | 0 | 0 | 15 | 79 | 30 | 41 | 8 | 0 |
| Cedar | 10 | 0 | 0 | 1 | 9 | 120 | 19 | 93 | 8 | 5 |
| Cerro Gordo | 1 | 0 | 1 | 0 | 0 | 98 | 32 | 58 | 8 | 0 |
| Cherokee | 3 | 0 | 0 | 0 | 3 | 42 | 13 | 26 | 3 | 0 |
| Clarke | 11 | 0 | 2 | 0 | 9 | 41 | 14 | 23 | 4 | 2 |
| Clay | 9 | 0 | 1 | 1 | 7 | 33 | 15 | 14 | 4 | 0 |
| Clayton | 6 | 0 | 1 | 0 | 5 | 76 | 18 | 50 | 8 | 0 |
| Clinton | 28 | 0 | 3 | 0 | 25 | 153 | 61 | 83 | 9 | 4 |
| Davis | 5 | 0 | 0 | 0 | 5 | 10 | 4 | 3 | 3 | 1 |
| Delaware | 14 | 0 | 0 | 0 | 14 | 24 | 10 | 7 | 7 | 0 |
| Des Moines | 21 | 0 | 0 | 0 | 21 | 102 | 30 | 57 | 15 | 3 |
| Dickinson | 1 | 0 | 0 | 0 | 1 | 24 | 12 | 12 | 0 | 1 |
| Emmet | 7 | 0 | 0 | 0 | 7 | 36 | 22 | 14 | 0 | 0 |
| Fayette | 13 | 0 | 1 | 0 | 12 | 58 | 10 | 41 | 7 | 1 |
| Floyd | 2 | 0 | 1 | 0 | 1 | 19 | 9 | 9 | 1 | 0 |
| Fremont | 13 | 0 | 2 | 0 | 11 | 83 | 35 | 43 | 5 | 2 |
| Hamilton | 9 | 0 | 0 | 0 | 9 | 74 | 36 | 33 | 5 | 0 |
| Hardin | 8 | 0 | 4 | 0 | 4 | 125 | 65 | 52 | 8 | 0 |
| Henry | 32 | 0 | 4 | 0 | 28 | 132 | 57 | 69 | 6 | 2 |
| Howard | 3 | 0 | 1 | 1 | 1 | 68 | 14 | 51 | 3 | 0 |
| Humboldt | 0 | 0 | 0 | 0 | 0 | 44 | 23 | 17 | 4 | 0 |
| Ida | 8 | 0 | 1 | 0 | 7 | 79 | 25 | 44 | 10 | 1 |
| Iowa | 9 | 1 | 0 | 1 | 7 | 60 | 15 | 39 | 6 | 1 |
| Jasper | 15 | 0 | 1 | 0 | 14 | 160 | 103 | 49 | 8 | 1 |
| Jefferson | 9 | 0 | 0 | 1 | 8 | 101 | 36 | 55 | 10 | 1 |
| Kossuth | 7 | 0 | 1 | 0 | 6 | 63 | 29 | 32 | 2 | 0 |
| Lee | 23 | 0 | 0 | 0 | 23 | 85 | 34 | 39 | 12 | 0 |
| Louisa | 6 | 0 | 3 | 0 | 3 | 42 | 0 | 38 | 4 | 0 |
| Lyon | 14 | 0 | 5 | 0 | 9 | 88 | 38 | 45 | 5 | 3 |

[1] The FBI does not publish arson data unless it receives data from either the agency or the state for all 12 months of the calendar year.
[2] The FBI determined that the agency's data were overreported. Consequently, affected data are not included in this table.
[6] Because of changes in the state/local agency's reporting practices, figures are not comparable to previous years' data.

**Table 10. Offenses Known to Law Enforcement, by State Metropolitan and Nonmetropolitan Counties, 2009—*Continued***

(Number.)

| State/County | Violent crime | Murder and non-negligent man-slaughter | Forcible rape | Robbery | Aggravated assault | Property crime | Burglary | Larceny-theft | Motor vehicle theft | Arson[1] |
|---|---|---|---|---|---|---|---|---|---|---|
| Mahaska | 13 | 0 | 0 | 1 | 12 | 69 | 26 | 36 | 7 | 0 |
| Marion | 27 | 0 | 7 | 0 | 20 | 129 | 43 | 64 | 22 | 2 |
| Marshall | 17 | 0 | 1 | 1 | 15 | 142 | 52 | 82 | 8 | 3 |
| Mitchell | 0 | 0 | 0 | 0 | 0 | 12 | 7 | 5 | 0 | 0 |
| Monroe | 4 | 0 | 0 | 0 | 4 | 35 | 16 | 17 | 2 | 0 |
| Muscatine | 18 | 0 | 7 | 0 | 11 | 104 | 47 | 50 | 7 | 2 |
| O'Brien | 11 | 0 | 1 | 0 | 10 | 99 | 31 | 64 | 4 | 0 |
| Osceola | 3 | 0 | 0 | 0 | 3 | 15 | 10 | 3 | 2 | 0 |
| Page | 6 | 0 | 2 | 0 | 4 | 50 | 19 | 29 | 2 | 0 |
| Palo Alto | 5 | 0 | 1 | 0 | 4 | 48 | 27 | 20 | 1 | 6 |
| Pocahontas | 1 | 0 | 1 | 0 | 0 | 27 | 16 | 9 | 2 | 0 |
| Poweshiek | 2 | 0 | 1 | 0 | 1 | 125 | 56 | 57 | 12 | 2 |
| Sac | 5 | 0 | 1 | 1 | 3 | 45 | 16 | 26 | 3 | 0 |
| Shelby | 5 | 0 | 1 | 0 | 4 | 29 | 15 | 11 | 3 | 0 |
| Sioux | 3 | 0 | 0 | 0 | 3 | 57 | 15 | 35 | 7 | 3 |
| Tama | 26 | 0 | 0 | 0 | 26 | 144 | 78 | 58 | 8 | 5 |
| Union | 4 | 0 | 0 | 0 | 4 | 38 | 13 | 19 | 6 | 0 |
| Van Buren | 11 | 1 | 1 | 0 | 9 | 72 | 43 | 24 | 5 | 1 |
| Wapello | 17 | 0 | 0 | 0 | 17 | 116 | 58 | 50 | 8 | 2 |
| Wayne | 1 | 0 | 0 | 0 | 1 | 44 | 19 | 24 | 1 | 0 |
| Webster | 32 | 0 | 0 | 0 | 32 | 264 | 106 | 137 | 21 | 3 |
| Winnebago | 2 | 0 | 0 | 0 | 2 | 22 | 13 | 4 | 5 | 0 |
| Winneshiek | 0 | 0 | 0 | 0 | 0 | 22 | 4 | 18 | 0 | 0 |
| Worth | 5 | 0 | 1 | 0 | 4 | 102 | 39 | 59 | 4 | 1 |
| Wright | 1 | 0 | 0 | 0 | 1 | 51 | 20 | 27 | 4 | 0 |
| **KANSAS - Metropolitan Counties** | | | | | | | | | | |
| Douglas | 33 | 0 | 2 | 3 | 28 | 236 | 72 | 153 | 11 | 4 |
| Geary | 7 | 0 | 0 | 1 | 6 | 30 | 8 | 17 | 5 | 0 |
| Linn | 22 | 0 | 1 | 1 | 20 | 106 | 42 | 57 | 7 | 2 |
| Riley County Police Department | 205 | 4 | 47 | 20 | 134 | 1,571 | 268 | 1,258 | 45 | 10 |
| Shawnee | 89 | 1 | 9 | 10 | 69 | 1,226 | 276 | 906 | 44 | 16 |
| Wabaunsee | 13 | 1 | 0 | 1 | 11 | 67 | 22 | 41 | 4 | 5 |
| Wyandotte | 14 | 0 | 1 | 3 | 10 | 10 | 1 | 9 | 0 | 0 |
| **KANSAS - Nonmetropolitan Counties** | | | | | | | | | | |
| Anderson | 7 | 0 | 0 | 1 | 6 | 53 | 24 | 25 | 4 | 6 |
| Chase | 3 | 0 | 0 | 0 | 3 | 8 | 5 | 3 | 0 | 0 |
| Clark | 2 | 0 | 0 | 0 | 2 | 44 | 18 | 24 | 2 | 0 |
| Clay | 3 | 0 | 0 | 0 | 3 | 22 | 9 | 12 | 1 | 0 |
| Cloud | 20 | 0 | 1 | 0 | 19 | 53 | 23 | 28 | 2 | 1 |
| Coffey | 11 | 0 | 0 | 0 | 11 | 51 | 18 | 32 | 1 | 1 |
| Dickinson | 5 | 0 | 1 | 0 | 4 | 136 | 36 | 92 | 8 | 9 |
| Edwards | 1 | 0 | 1 | 0 | 0 | 18 | 2 | 16 | 0 | 2 |
| Elk | 3 | 0 | 1 | 0 | 2 | 26 | 6 | 20 | 0 | 0 |
| Finney | 35 | 0 | 10 | 1 | 24 | 252 | 96 | 147 | 9 | 3 |
| Ford | 11 | 0 | 0 | 1 | 10 | 101 | 29 | 67 | 5 | 3 |
| Graham | 0 | 0 | 0 | 0 | 0 | 13 | 4 | 9 | 0 | 1 |
| Grant | 0 | 0 | 0 | 0 | 0 | 10 | 1 | 8 | 1 | 0 |
| Gray | 0 | 0 | 0 | 0 | 0 | 23 | 10 | 13 | 0 | 0 |
| Harper | 3 | 0 | 1 | 0 | 2 | 23 | 9 | 10 | 4 | 2 |
| Hodgeman | 4 | 0 | 0 | 0 | 4 | 16 | 8 | 7 | 1 | 0 |
| Kiowa | 3 | 1 | 0 | 0 | 2 | 20 | 5 | 13 | 2 | 0 |
| Lane | 6 | 0 | 0 | 0 | 6 | 11 | 4 | 6 | 1 | 0 |
| Lyon | 10 | 0 | 2 | 1 | 7 | 117 | 20 | 95 | 2 | 7 |
| McPherson | 9 | 2 | 1 | 0 | 6 | 85 | 25 | 54 | 6 | 4 |
| Morris | 5 | 0 | 0 | 0 | 5 | 33 | 12 | 21 | 0 | 5 |
| Norton | 2 | 0 | 1 | 0 | 1 | 16 | 10 | 6 | 0 | 0 |
| Ottawa | 10 | 0 | 0 | 0 | 10 | 55 | 23 | 30 | 2 | 0 |
| Republic | 1 | 0 | 0 | 0 | 1 | 40 | 15 | 21 | 4 | 2 |
| Rice | 3 | 0 | 0 | 0 | 3 | 46 | 24 | 19 | 3 | 1 |
| Rush | 2 | 0 | 0 | 0 | 2 | 21 | 15 | 5 | 1 | 0 |
| Russell | 4 | 0 | 1 | 0 | 3 | 62 | 20 | 39 | 3 | 2 |
| Saline | 25 | 1 | 5 | 0 | 19 | 140 | 52 | 85 | 3 | 6 |
| Seward | 8 | 0 | 2 | 0 | 6 | 35 | 9 | 22 | 4 | 0 |
| Sherman | 2 | 0 | 0 | 0 | 2 | 16 | 7 | 9 | 0 | 0 |
| Smith | 4 | 0 | 0 | 0 | 4 | 33 | 8 | 21 | 4 | 0 |
| Stafford | 3 | 0 | 0 | 0 | 3 | 30 | 14 | 13 | 3 | 1 |
| Thomas | 4 | 0 | 0 | 0 | 4 | 19 | 5 | 13 | 1 | 1 |
| Washington | 2 | 0 | 0 | 0 | 2 | 13 | 5 | 4 | 4 | 1 |
| Wichita | 10 | 0 | 1 | 0 | 9 | 18 | 3 | 15 | 0 | 0 |
| Wilson | 5 | 0 | 0 | 0 | 5 | 48 | 21 | 26 | 1 | 1 |
| Woodson | 8 | 0 | 2 | 0 | 6 | 46 | 12 | 32 | 2 | 7 |

[1] The FBI does not publish arson data unless it receives data from either the agency or the state for all 12 months of the calendar year.

**Table 10. Offenses Known to Law Enforcement, by State Metropolitan and Nonmetropolitan Counties, 2009**—*Continued*

(Number.)

| State/County | Violent crime | Murder and non-negligent man-slaughter | Forcible rape | Robbery | Aggravated assault | Property crime | Burglary | Larceny-theft | Motor vehicle theft | Arson[1] |
|---|---|---|---|---|---|---|---|---|---|---|
| **KENTUCKY - Metropolitan Counties[6]** | | | | | | | | | | |
| Boone | 118 | 3 | 10 | 18 | 87 | 1,225 | 357 | 793 | 75 | 2 |
| Bourbon | 2 | 0 | 1 | 1 | 0 | 67 | 16 | 47 | 4 | 0 |
| Boyd | 26 | 0 | 7 | 7 | 12 | 288 | 124 | 150 | 14 | 2 |
| Bracken | 0 | 0 | 0 | 0 | 0 | 30 | 21 | 7 | 2 | 1 |
| Bullitt | 34 | 0 | 12 | 5 | 17 | 541 | 257 | 253 | 31 | 1 |
| Christian | 26 | 1 | 10 | 4 | 11 | 398 | 181 | 205 | 12 | 2 |
| Clark | 7 | 0 | 2 | 3 | 2 | 313 | 141 | 163 | 9 | 0 |
| Daviess | 26 | 1 | 4 | 4 | 17 | 658 | 176 | 446 | 36 | 0 |
| Edmonson | 6 | 0 | 0 | 0 | 6 | 62 | 38 | 21 | 3 | 0 |
| Gallatin | 2 | 0 | 0 | 1 | 1 | 17 | 10 | 6 | 1 | 0 |
| Grant | 3 | 0 | 0 | 1 | 2 | 170 | 76 | 88 | 6 | 1 |
| Greenup | 3 | 0 | 1 | 0 | 2 | 65 | 46 | 17 | 2 | 0 |
| Hardin | 2 | 0 | 0 | 0 | 2 | 82 | 28 | 51 | 3 | 1 |
| Henderson | 11 | 0 | 3 | 3 | 5 | 192 | 86 | 95 | 11 | 1 |
| Henry | 1 | 0 | 0 | 0 | 1 | 16 | 9 | 6 | 1 | 1 |
| Jessamine | 15 | 0 | 4 | 1 | 10 | 245 | 102 | 135 | 8 | 0 |
| Kenton County Police Department | 19 | 1 | 1 | 0 | 17 | 141 | 42 | 92 | 7 | 11 |
| LaRue | 1 | 0 | 1 | 0 | 0 | 33 | 15 | 15 | 3 | 0 |
| McLean | 0 | 0 | 0 | 0 | 0 | 32 | 13 | 16 | 3 | 0 |
| Meade | 5 | 0 | 2 | 0 | 3 | 117 | 88 | 21 | 8 | 1 |
| Nelson | 16 | 2 | 7 | 2 | 5 | 218 | 113 | 87 | 18 | 0 |
| Oldham | 2 | 0 | 0 | 1 | 1 | 5 | 5 | 0 | 0 | 0 |
| Oldham County Police Department | 24 | 0 | 10 | 5 | 9 | 468 | 175 | 280 | 13 | 1 |
| Pendleton | 4 | 0 | 0 | 0 | 4 | 123 | 51 | 65 | 7 | 0 |
| Scott | 9 | 0 | 0 | 3 | 6 | 283 | 99 | 165 | 19 | 0 |
| Shelby | 16 | 0 | 1 | 1 | 14 | 450 | 146 | 268 | 36 | 4 |
| Spencer | 1 | 1 | 0 | 0 | 0 | 21 | 11 | 10 | 0 | 0 |
| Trigg | 3 | 0 | 0 | 0 | 3 | 81 | 27 | 48 | 6 | 0 |
| Trimble | 0 | 0 | 0 | 0 | 0 | 21 | 8 | 7 | 6 | 0 |
| Warren | 17 | 0 | 5 | 0 | 12 | 469 | 191 | 249 | 29 | 1 |
| Webster | 0 | 0 | 0 | 0 | 0 | 5 | 3 | 1 | 1 | 0 |
| Woodford | 1 | 0 | 0 | 0 | 1 | 35 | 12 | 22 | 1 | 0 |
| **KENTUCKY - Nonmetropolitan Counties[6]** | | | | | | | | | | |
| Adair | 3 | 0 | 0 | 0 | 3 | 17 | 11 | 4 | 2 | 2 |
| Allen | 6 | 0 | 2 | 1 | 3 | 141 | 57 | 74 | 10 | 0 |
| Anderson | 4 | 0 | 1 | 0 | 3 | 77 | 34 | 41 | 2 | 0 |
| Ballard | 13 | 0 | 7 | 0 | 6 | 154 | 43 | 102 | 9 | 3 |
| Barren | 6 | 0 | 2 | 0 | 4 | 153 | 85 | 58 | 10 | 3 |
| Bell | 0 | 0 | 0 | 0 | 0 | 38 | 16 | 18 | 4 | 0 |
| Boyle | 2 | 0 | 1 | 0 | 1 | 81 | 40 | 39 | 2 | 1 |
| Breckinridge | 4 | 0 | 1 | 1 | 2 | 34 | 19 | 11 | 4 | 1 |
| Butler | 1 | 0 | 0 | 0 | 1 | 9 | 5 | 4 | 0 | 0 |
| Caldwell | 1 | 0 | 1 | 0 | 0 | 51 | 24 | 25 | 2 | 0 |
| Calloway | 15 | 1 | 4 | 2 | 8 | 377 | 170 | 189 | 18 | 4 |
| Carlisle | 0 | 0 | 0 | 0 | 0 | 12 | 5 | 6 | 1 | 0 |
| Carter | 2 | 0 | 0 | 1 | 1 | 75 | 34 | 39 | 2 | 0 |
| Casey | 5 | 0 | 0 | 1 | 4 | 89 | 38 | 43 | 8 | 1 |
| Clay | 2 | 0 | 1 | 1 | 0 | 94 | 29 | 35 | 30 | 0 |
| Crittenden | 0 | 0 | 0 | 0 | 0 | 29 | 11 | 18 | 0 | 0 |
| Estill | 5 | 0 | 0 | 2 | 3 | 133 | 46 | 79 | 8 | 1 |
| Fleming | 1 | 0 | 0 | 0 | 1 | 69 | 35 | 31 | 3 | 1 |
| Floyd | 1 | 0 | 0 | 1 | 0 | 139 | 45 | 84 | 10 | 0 |
| Franklin | 11 | 1 | 1 | 3 | 6 | 153 | 64 | 80 | 9 | 0 |
| Fulton | 4 | 0 | 2 | 0 | 2 | 24 | 9 | 13 | 2 | 1 |
| Garrard | 1 | 0 | 0 | 0 | 1 | 74 | 28 | 40 | 6 | 0 |
| Graves | 14 | 0 | 3 | 0 | 11 | 135 | 49 | 72 | 14 | 2 |
| Grayson | 2 | 0 | 0 | 0 | 2 | 93 | 52 | 33 | 8 | 2 |
| Green | 1 | 0 | 0 | 0 | 1 | 6 | 0 | 4 | 2 | 0 |
| Harlan | 14 | 0 | 4 | 1 | 9 | 42 | 13 | 25 | 4 | 3 |
| Harrison | 8 | 0 | 1 | 4 | 3 | 210 | 100 | 92 | 18 | 1 |
| Hart | 2 | 0 | 0 | 0 | 2 | 21 | 16 | 2 | 3 | 0 |
| Hopkins | 15 | 2 | 5 | 1 | 7 | 233 | 103 | 115 | 15 | 0 |
| Jackson | 1 | 0 | 0 | 0 | 1 | 60 | 18 | 34 | 8 | 1 |
| Knott | 0 | 0 | 0 | 0 | 0 | 48 | 14 | 33 | 1 | 0 |
| Knox | 16 | 0 | 2 | 3 | 11 | 242 | 106 | 116 | 20 | 1 |
| Laurel | 12 | 1 | 2 | 1 | 8 | 214 | 82 | 84 | 48 | 0 |
| Lawrence | 2 | 0 | 0 | 1 | 1 | 39 | 26 | 8 | 5 | 0 |
| Lee | 1 | 0 | 0 | 0 | 1 | 1 | 0 | 1 | 0 | 0 |
| Letcher | 3 | 0 | 1 | 0 | 2 | 72 | 36 | 29 | 7 | 1 |
| Lewis | 1 | 0 | 0 | 0 | 1 | 57 | 38 | 13 | 6 | 0 |

[1] The FBI does not publish arson data unless it receives data from either the agency or the state for all 12 months of the calendar year.
[6] Because of changes in the state/local agency's reporting practices, figures are not comparable to previous years' data.

**Table 10. Offenses Known to Law Enforcement, by State Metropolitan and Nonmetropolitan Counties, 2009**—*Continued*

(Number.)

| State/County | Violent crime | Murder and non-negligent man-slaughter | Forcible rape | Robbery | Aggravated assault | Property crime | Burglary | Larceny-theft | Motor vehicle theft | Arson[1] |
|---|---|---|---|---|---|---|---|---|---|---|
| Lincoln | 14 | 1 | 0 | 2 | 11 | 94 | 42 | 31 | 21 | 1 |
| Livingston | 4 | 0 | 1 | 0 | 3 | 112 | 61 | 46 | 5 | 2 |
| Logan | 10 | 1 | 0 | 1 | 8 | 176 | 68 | 98 | 10 | 2 |
| Lyon | 2 | 0 | 0 | 0 | 2 | 87 | 49 | 36 | 2 | 0 |
| Madison | 15 | 1 | 4 | 1 | 9 | 367 | 117 | 231 | 19 | 2 |
| Magoffin | 2 | 0 | 0 | 0 | 2 | 44 | 8 | 30 | 6 | 0 |
| Marion | 0 | 0 | 0 | 0 | 0 | 92 | 41 | 46 | 5 | 0 |
| Marshall | 18 | 0 | 8 | 1 | 9 | 385 | 166 | 202 | 17 | 3 |
| Martin | 6 | 0 | 0 | 0 | 6 | 60 | 19 | 32 | 9 | 0 |
| Mason | 8 | 0 | 1 | 2 | 5 | 142 | 73 | 65 | 4 | 0 |
| McCracken | 43 | 0 | 14 | 9 | 20 | 707 | 225 | 423 | 59 | 4 |
| McCreary | 4 | 1 | 1 | 1 | 1 | 149 | 70 | 71 | 8 | 0 |
| Menifee | 1 | 0 | 0 | 0 | 1 | 35 | 26 | 9 | 0 | 0 |
| Metcalfe | 2 | 0 | 0 | 0 | 2 | 31 | 21 | 9 | 1 | 0 |
| Montgomery | 15 | 1 | 0 | 3 | 11 | 478 | 191 | 270 | 17 | 1 |
| Muhlenberg | 0 | 0 | 0 | 0 | 0 | 15 | 8 | 4 | 3 | 0 |
| Nicholas | 0 | 0 | 0 | 0 | 0 | 4 | 2 | 2 | 0 | 0 |
| Ohio | 4 | 0 | 0 | 0 | 4 | 124 | 47 | 68 | 9 | 1 |
| Owen | 3 | 0 | 0 | 0 | 3 | 68 | 36 | 29 | 3 | 0 |
| Perry | 0 | 0 | 0 | 0 | 0 | 44 | 15 | 24 | 5 | 0 |
| Pike | 1 | 0 | 0 | 1 | 0 | 24 | 9 | 13 | 2 | 0 |
| Powell | 1 | 0 | 0 | 1 | 0 | 50 | 29 | 20 | 1 | 0 |
| Pulaski | 32 | 0 | 11 | 8 | 13 | 542 | 270 | 248 | 24 | 5 |
| Rockcastle | 4 | 0 | 0 | 3 | 1 | 65 | 33 | 22 | 10 | 0 |
| Rowan | 7 | 0 | 0 | 3 | 4 | 24 | 5 | 19 | 0 | 0 |
| Russell | 7 | 0 | 0 | 0 | 7 | 29 | 12 | 17 | 0 | 0 |
| Simpson | 8 | 0 | 0 | 2 | 6 | 142 | 63 | 73 | 6 | 0 |
| Taylor | 8 | 0 | 4 | 1 | 3 | 120 | 54 | 60 | 6 | 0 |
| Todd | 0 | 0 | 0 | 0 | 0 | 2 | 1 | 1 | 0 | 0 |
| Union | 1 | 0 | 0 | 0 | 1 | 76 | 39 | 34 | 3 | 0 |
| Washington | 0 | 0 | 0 | 0 | 0 | 50 | 25 | 22 | 3 | 0 |
| Wayne | 3 | 0 | 1 | 0 | 2 | 90 | 43 | 37 | 10 | 0 |
| **LOUISIANA - Metropolitan Counties** | | | | | | | | | | |
| Ascension | 426 | 5 | 28 | 51 | 342 | 2,651 | 632 | 1,766 | 253 | 9 |
| Bossier | 124 | 1 | 4 | 4 | 115 | 416 | 98 | 286 | 32 | 2 |
| Caddo | 127 | 1 | 15 | 6 | 105 | 898 | 246 | 610 | 42 | 9 |
| Cameron | 17 | 0 | 1 | 1 | 15 | 145 | 27 | 110 | 8 | 1 |
| De Soto | 205 | 0 | 0 | 2 | 203 | 324 | 87 | 201 | 36 | 0 |
| East Baton Rouge | 682 | 11 | 22 | 275 | 374 | 8,356 | 2,170 | 5,851 | 335 | 19 |
| East Feliciana | 10 | 1 | 1 | 1 | 7 | 115 | 53 | 52 | 10 | |
| Grant | 17 | 1 | 0 | 0 | 16 | 307 | 117 | 182 | 8 | 0 |
| Jefferson | 2,346 | 51 | 78 | 522 | 1,695 | 14,602 | 3,343 | 9,976 | 1,283 | 104 |
| Lafayette | 396 | 1 | 29 | 55 | 311 | 1,666 | 426 | 1,119 | 121 | 17 |
| Lafourche | 86 | 2 | 1 | 31 | 52 | 1,630 | 199 | 1,358 | 73 | 0 |
| Livingston | 658 | 6 | 20 | 21 | 611 | 2,782 | 612 | 1,962 | 208 | 10 |
| Ouachita | 225 | 6 | 15 | 39 | 165 | 2,666 | 943 | 1,606 | 117 | 4 |
| Plaquemines | 47 | 1 | 7 | 3 | 36 | 397 | 37 | 351 | 9 | 2 |
| Rapides | 320 | 2 | 21 | 14 | 283 | 1,517 | 334 | 1,041 | 142 | 2 |
| St. Bernard[4] | 62 | 1 | 4 | 24 | 33 | | | 734 | | 7 |
| St. Charles | 157 | 1 | 12 | 23 | 121 | 1,526 | 425 | 1,016 | 85 | 14 |
| St. Helena | 77 | 3 | 3 | 4 | 67 | 256 | 109 | 123 | 24 | 8 |
| St. John The Baptist | 120 | 5 | 5 | 57 | 53 | 1,498 | 289 | 1,058 | 151 | 1 |
| St. Martin | 80 | 2 | 1 | 11 | 66 | 398 | 32 | 363 | 3 | 2 |
| St. Tammany | 358 | 4 | 33 | 26 | 295 | 2,546 | 643 | 1,739 | 164 | 11 |
| Terrebonne | 359 | 2 | 34 | 62 | 261 | 2,842 | 594 | 2,019 | 229 | 11 |
| Union | 43 | 0 | 0 | 0 | 43 | 15 | 5 | 10 | 0 | 0 |
| West Baton Rouge | 67 | 0 | 5 | 11 | 51 | 579 | 80 | 470 | 29 | 0 |
| West Feliciana | 38 | 1 | 4 | 6 | 27 | 151 | 35 | 99 | 17 | 0 |
| **LOUISIANA - Nonmetropolitan Counties** | | | | | | | | | | |
| Assumption | 124 | 0 | 0 | 2 | 122 | 390 | 91 | 276 | 23 | 0 |
| Beauregard | 59 | 2 | 0 | 1 | 56 | 309 | 132 | 143 | 34 | 1 |
| Bienville | 34 | 1 | 0 | 5 | 28 | 126 | 38 | 83 | 5 | 1 |
| Caldwell | 45 | 0 | 0 | 4 | 41 | 375 | 134 | 213 | 28 | 0 |
| Catahoula | 192 | 0 | 6 | 0 | 186 | 237 | 54 | 162 | 21 | 0 |
| Claiborne | 78 | 0 | 10 | 6 | 62 | 282 | 130 | 125 | 27 | 1 |
| Concordia | 60 | 0 | 1 | 4 | 55 | 232 | 113 | 115 | 4 | 0 |
| East Carroll | 20 | 4 | 1 | 4 | 11 | 66 | 21 | 39 | 6 | 1 |
| Franklin | 26 | 0 | 2 | 1 | 23 | 150 | 49 | 85 | 16 | 0 |
| Iberia | 464 | 6 | 29 | 128 | 301 | 2,124 | 780 | 1,239 | 105 | |
| Jackson | 6 | 0 | 0 | 1 | 5 | 143 | 49 | 84 | 10 | 0 |
| Jefferson Davis | 60 | 1 | 5 | 3 | 51 | 388 | 63 | 294 | 31 | 0 |

[1] The FBI does not publish arson data unless it receives data from either the agency or the state for all 12 months of the calendar year.

[4] The FBI determined that the agency did not follow national Uniform Crime Reporting (UCR) Program guidelines for reporting an offense. Consequently, this figure is not included in this table.

## Table 10. Offenses Known to Law Enforcement, by State Metropolitan and Nonmetropolitan Counties, 2009—*Continued*

(Number.)

| State/County | Violent crime | Murder and non-negligent man-slaughter | Forcible rape | Robbery | Aggravated assault | Property crime | Burglary | Larceny-theft | Motor vehicle theft | Arson[1] |
|---|---|---|---|---|---|---|---|---|---|---|
| La Salle | 51 | 0 | 3 | 16 | 32 | 79 | 27 | 47 | 5 | 1 |
| Lincoln[2] | | 1 | 9 | 6 | | 327 | 147 | 168 | 12 | 0 |
| Madison | 33 | 0 | 1 | 3 | 29 | 111 | 31 | 73 | 7 | 1 |
| Morehouse | 34 | 1 | 8 | 1 | 24 | 474 | 66 | 390 | 18 | 0 |
| Natchitoches | 90 | 0 | 1 | 9 | 80 | 474 | 167 | 264 | 43 | 0 |
| Red River | 34 | 0 | 1 | 2 | 31 | 83 | 20 | 56 | 7 | 0 |
| Richland | 18 | 0 | 0 | 0 | 18 | 181 | 61 | 112 | 8 | 0 |
| Sabine | 37 | 1 | 0 | 0 | 36 | 390 | 83 | 279 | 28 | 0 |
| St. James | 159 | 0 | 5 | 4 | 150 | 425 | 113 | 266 | 46 | 2 |
| St. Landry | 138 | 1 | 17 | 9 | 111 | 1,030 | 439 | 484 | 107 | 6 |
| St. Mary | 185 | 2 | 13 | 32 | 138 | 849 | 226 | 587 | 36 | 1 |
| Tangipahoa | 926 | 3 | 15 | 62 | 846 | 4,048 | 1,756 | 2,177 | 115 | 0 |
| Tensas | 11 | 0 | 0 | 0 | 11 | 51 | 21 | 29 | 1 | 2 |
| Vermilion | 67 | 2 | 9 | 3 | 53 | 191 | 37 | 151 | 3 | 0 |
| Vernon | 119 | 1 | 12 | 1 | 105 | 641 | 35 | 565 | 41 | 1 |
| Washington | 141 | 4 | 35 | 21 | 81 | 665 | 208 | 412 | 45 | 0 |
| Webster | 48 | 1 | 11 | 2 | 34 | 224 | 112 | 87 | 25 | 0 |
| West Carroll | 39 | 1 | 0 | 0 | 38 | 250 | 58 | 173 | 19 | 1 |
| Winn | 11 | 1 | 0 | 2 | 8 | 100 | 44 | 47 | 9 | 0 |
| **MAINE - Metropolitan Counties** | | | | | | | | | | |
| Androscoggin | 12 | 0 | 5 | 2 | 5 | 204 | 51 | 144 | 9 | 0 |
| Cumberland | 52 | 0 | 9 | 5 | 38 | 699 | 333 | 338 | 28 | 7 |
| Penobscot | 6 | 0 | 1 | 1 | 4 | 615 | 221 | 364 | 30 | 0 |
| Sagadahoc | 6 | 0 | 1 | 1 | 4 | 149 | 50 | 92 | 7 | 1 |
| York | 19 | 0 | 1 | 5 | 13 | 436 | 134 | 284 | 18 | 0 |
| **MAINE - Nonmetropolitan Counties** | | | | | | | | | | |
| Aroostook | 0 | 0 | 0 | 0 | 0 | 73 | 30 | 40 | 3 | 1 |
| Franklin | 2 | 0 | 0 | 0 | 2 | 67 | 17 | 45 | 5 | 0 |
| Hancock | 7 | 0 | 1 | 1 | 5 | 247 | 58 | 181 | 8 | 0 |
| Kennebec | 22 | 0 | 13 | 4 | 5 | 303 | 86 | 207 | 10 | 1 |
| Knox | 11 | 0 | 0 | 0 | 11 | 209 | 48 | 141 | 20 | 0 |
| Lincoln | 12 | 0 | 12 | 0 | 0 | 218 | 60 | 154 | 4 | 1 |
| Oxford | 25 | 0 | 17 | 1 | 7 | 264 | 106 | 144 | 14 | 0 |
| Piscataquis | 1 | 0 | 0 | 0 | 1 | 111 | 61 | 48 | 2 | 0 |
| Somerset | 13 | 0 | 3 | 4 | 6 | 335 | 156 | 165 | 14 | 1 |
| Waldo | 7 | 0 | 0 | 0 | 7 | 113 | 72 | 34 | 7 | 2 |
| Washington | 24 | 0 | 2 | 0 | 22 | 176 | 62 | 106 | 8 | 0 |
| **MARYLAND - Metropolitan Counties** | | | | | | | | | | |
| Allegany | 0 | 0 | 0 | 0 | 0 | 6 | 0 | 6 | 0 | 0 |
| Allegheny County Bureau of Police | 53 | 0 | 4 | 5 | 44 | 201 | 41 | 156 | 4 | 0 |
| Anne Arundel | 0 | 0 | 0 | 0 | 0 | 0 | 0 | 0 | 0 | 0 |
| Anne Arundel County Police Department | 2,668 | 12 | 86 | 664 | 1,906 | 15,950 | 2,867 | 12,036 | 1,047 | 103 |
| Baltimore County | 0 | 0 | 0 | 0 | 0 | 0 | 0 | 0 | 0 | 0 |
| Baltimore County Police Department | 4,534 | 32 | 152 | 1,471 | 2,879 | 25,944 | 4,282 | 19,258 | 2,404 | 258 |
| Calvert | 249 | 0 | 10 | 27 | 212 | 1,522 | 369 | 1,067 | 86 | 3 |
| Carroll | 73 | 0 | 28 | 3 | 42 | 288 | 60 | 220 | 8 | 0 |
| Cecil | 171 | 1 | 13 | 33 | 124 | 933 | 335 | 537 | 61 | 0 |
| Charles | 666 | 7 | 35 | 179 | 445 | 3,349 | 568 | 2,527 | 254 | 0 |
| Frederick | 189 | 4 | 11 | 13 | 161 | 1,406 | 254 | 1,106 | 46 | 10 |
| Harford | 527 | 3 | 44 | 133 | 347 | 2,839 | 604 | 2,076 | 159 | 5 |
| Howard | 2 | 0 | 0 | 0 | 2 | 0 | 0 | 0 | 0 | 0 |
| Howard County Police Department | 744 | 2 | 43 | 262 | 437 | 6,992 | 1,207 | 5,398 | 387 | 73 |
| Montgomery | 0 | 0 | 0 | 0 | 0 | 0 | 0 | 0 | 0 | 0 |
| Montgomery County Police Department | 2,033 | 13 | 124 | 992 | 904 | 23,099 | 3,011 | 18,356 | 1,732 | 220 |
| Prince George's | 77 | 0 | 0 | 0 | 77 | 0 | 0 | 0 | 0 | 0 |
| Prince George's County Police Department | 5,338 | 86 | 197 | 2,634 | 2,421 | 29,647 | 6,707 | 16,894 | 6,046 | 260 |
| Queen Anne's | 63 | 0 | 11 | 5 | 47 | 693 | 157 | 517 | 19 | 3 |
| Somerset | 5 | 0 | 0 | 0 | 5 | 41 | 7 | 34 | 0 | 0 |
| Washington | 137 | 0 | 19 | 18 | 100 | 1,200 | 317 | 836 | 47 | 0 |
| Wicomico | 124 | 3 | 6 | 23 | 92 | 878 | 337 | 508 | 33 | 5 |
| **MARYLAND - Nonmetropolitan Counties** | | | | | | | | | | |
| Caroline | 17 | 0 | 3 | 3 | 11 | 341 | 153 | 176 | 12 | 1 |
| Dorchester | 32 | 0 | 1 | 0 | 31 | 315 | 89 | 219 | 7 | 1 |
| Garrett | 37 | 0 | 0 | 1 | 36 | 270 | 88 | 173 | 9 | 0 |
| Kent | 17 | 1 | 1 | 2 | 13 | 107 | 57 | 46 | 4 | 0 |
| St. Mary's | 271 | 0 | 18 | 44 | 209 | 1,797 | 397 | 1,303 | 97 | 5 |
| Talbot | 9 | 0 | 1 | 0 | 8 | 220 | 75 | 139 | 6 | 0 |
| Worcester | 78 | 0 | 3 | 4 | 71 | 192 | 51 | 124 | 17 | 1 |
| **MICHIGAN - Metropolitan Counties[6]** | | | | | | | | | | |
| Barry | 38 | 0 | 11 | 4 | 23 | 428 | 113 | 295 | 20 | 6 |
| Bay | 42 | 1 | 5 | 7 | 29 | 595 | 108 | 452 | 35 | 3 |
| Berrien | 85 | 0 | 24 | 9 | 52 | 821 | 208 | 576 | 37 | 5 |

[1] The FBI does not publish arson data unless it receives data from either the agency or the state for all 12 months of the calendar year.
[2] The FBI determined that the agency's data were overreported. Consequently, affected data are not included in this table.
[6] Because of changes in the state/local agency's reporting practices, figures are not comparable to previous years' data.

**Table 10. Offenses Known to Law Enforcement, by State Metropolitan and Nonmetropolitan Counties, 2009**—*Continued*

(Number.)

| State/County | Violent crime | Murder and non-negligent man-slaughter | Forcible rape | Robbery | Aggravated assault | Property crime | Burglary | Larceny-theft | Motor vehicle theft | Arson[1] |
|---|---|---|---|---|---|---|---|---|---|---|
| Calhoun | 69 | 0 | 3 | 7 | 59 | 531 | 156 | 357 | 18 | 7 |
| Cass | 38 | 2 | 14 | 4 | 18 | 691 | 193 | 452 | 46 | 2 |
| Clinton | 10 | 0 | 2 | 1 | 7 | 204 | 55 | 132 | 17 | 1 |
| Eaton | 79 | 1 | 22 | 20 | 36 | 1,426 | 255 | 1,112 | 59 | 9 |
| Genesee | 47 | 0 | 14 | 5 | 28 | 544 | 131 | 386 | 27 | 1 |
| Ingham | 104 | 0 | 27 | 10 | 67 | 975 | 309 | 626 | 40 | 12 |
| Ionia | 36 | 0 | 15 | 1 | 20 | 369 | 160 | 196 | 13 | 10 |
| Jackson | 79 | 3 | 12 | 4 | 60 | 498 | 131 | 335 | 32 | 2 |
| Kalamazoo | 205 | 3 | 38 | 41 | 123 | 2,359 | 644 | 1,614 | 101 | 14 |
| Kent | 352 | 1 | 57 | 58 | 236 | 3,495 | 834 | 2,533 | 128 | 29 |
| Lapeer | 50 | 0 | 12 | 1 | 37 | 509 | 143 | 339 | 27 | 1 |
| Livingston | 35 | 0 | 12 | 4 | 19 | 775 | 190 | 545 | 40 | 8 |
| Macomb | 436 | 6 | 48 | 56 | 326 | 2,476 | 511 | 1,801 | 164 | 21 |
| Monroe | 238 | 5 | 61 | 36 | 136 | 2,567 | 622 | 1,783 | 162 | 27 |
| Muskegon | 32 | 1 | 5 | 3 | 23 | 677 | 134 | 491 | 52 | 3 |
| Newaygo | 52 | 1 | 15 | 0 | 36 | 420 | 188 | 216 | 16 | 1 |
| Oakland | 295 | 3 | 35 | 58 | 199 | 3,596 | 825 | 2,585 | 186 | 69 |
| Ottawa | 286 | 4 | 87 | 22 | 173 | 2,862 | 727 | 2,046 | 89 | 26 |
| Saginaw | 92 | 1 | 9 | 7 | 75 | 488 | 135 | 322 | 31 | 2 |
| St. Clair | 191 | 3 | 46 | 8 | 134 | 1,577 | 388 | 1,082 | 107 | 15 |
| Van Buren | 102 | 0 | 22 | 2 | 78 | 646 | 204 | 410 | 32 | 7 |
| Washtenaw | 451 | 3 | 56 | 98 | 294 | 2,634 | 1,022 | 1,379 | 233 | 28 |
| Wayne | 4 | 0 | 1 | 2 | 1 | 15 | 0 | 9 | 6 | 0 |
| **MICHIGAN - Nonmetropolitan Counties[6]** | | | | | | | | | | |
| Alcona | 14 | 1 | 3 | 0 | 10 | 191 | 69 | 118 | 4 | 1 |
| Alger | 2 | 0 | 0 | 0 | 2 | 3 | 3 | 0 | 0 | 0 |
| Allegan | 90 | 1 | 33 | 3 | 53 | 828 | 333 | 449 | 46 | 5 |
| Alpena | 5 | 0 | 1 | 0 | 4 | 61 | 19 | 41 | 1 | 0 |
| Antrim | 18 | 0 | 6 | 1 | 11 | 342 | 141 | 185 | 16 | 0 |
| Arenac | 21 | 0 | 2 | 1 | 18 | 156 | 47 | 98 | 11 | 0 |
| Benzie | 11 | 1 | 5 | 0 | 5 | 184 | 55 | 122 | 7 | 0 |
| Branch | 26 | 1 | 4 | 1 | 20 | 207 | 40 | 153 | 14 | 1 |
| Charlevoix | 25 | 0 | 10 | 0 | 15 | 153 | 39 | 104 | 10 | 0 |
| Cheboygan | 7 | 0 | 1 | 0 | 6 | 140 | 57 | 81 | 2 | 1 |
| Chippewa | 11 | 0 | 1 | 0 | 10 | 96 | 42 | 54 | 0 | 0 |
| Crawford | 42 | 0 | 4 | 1 | 37 | 194 | 75 | 100 | 19 | 2 |
| Delta | 6 | 0 | 1 | 0 | 5 | 68 | 28 | 32 | 8 | 0 |
| Emmet | 14 | 0 | 3 | 1 | 10 | 177 | 47 | 130 | 0 | 0 |
| Gladwin | 7 | 1 | 2 | 0 | 4 | 161 | 60 | 92 | 9 | 1 |
| Grand Traverse | 124 | 0 | 47 | 3 | 74 | 982 | 185 | 761 | 36 | 13 |
| Gratiot | 14 | 0 | 7 | 2 | 5 | 175 | 55 | 107 | 13 | 1 |
| Hillsdale | 28 | 1 | 2 | 2 | 23 | 226 | 67 | 151 | 8 | 1 |
| Houghton | 1 | 0 | 0 | 0 | 1 | 85 | 16 | 67 | 2 | 0 |
| Huron | 15 | 0 | 1 | 2 | 12 | 159 | 52 | 101 | 6 | 3 |
| Iosco | 1 | 0 | 0 | 0 | 1 | 1 | 0 | 1 | 0 | 0 |
| Iron | 7 | 1 | 2 | 0 | 4 | 47 | 17 | 27 | 3 | 0 |
| Isabella | 37 | 0 | 10 | 0 | 27 | 386 | 104 | 265 | 17 | 3 |
| Kalkaska | 32 | 0 | 2 | 0 | 30 | 333 | 105 | 197 | 31 | 3 |
| Keweenaw | 3 | 0 | 0 | 0 | 3 | 45 | 17 | 28 | 0 | 1 |
| Lake | 27 | 0 | 4 | 0 | 23 | 213 | 108 | 101 | 4 | 2 |
| Leelanau | 12 | 1 | 5 | 0 | 6 | 123 | 33 | 87 | 3 | 0 |
| Lenawee | 54 | 0 | 22 | 3 | 29 | 318 | 106 | 196 | 16 | 9 |
| Luce | 8 | 0 | 2 | 0 | 6 | 76 | 38 | 36 | 2 | 0 |
| Mackinac | 4 | 0 | 0 | 0 | 4 | 60 | 25 | 35 | 0 | 0 |
| Manistee | 7 | 0 | 2 | 0 | 5 | 118 | 28 | 87 | 3 | 0 |
| Marquette | 12 | 0 | 6 | 0 | 6 | 163 | 32 | 121 | 10 | 0 |
| Mason | 29 | 0 | 11 | 2 | 16 | 444 | 73 | 361 | 10 | 2 |
| Mecosta | 162 | 0 | 3 | 1 | 158 | 676 | 192 | 464 | 20 | 7 |
| Menominee | 0 | 0 | 0 | 0 | 0 | 2 | 0 | 2 | 0 | 0 |
| Midland | 62 | 4 | 30 | 2 | 26 | 456 | 124 | 319 | 13 | 8 |
| Missaukee | 0 | 0 | 0 | 0 | 0 | 124 | 35 | 89 | 0 | 0 |
| Montcalm | 51 | 1 | 20 | 4 | 26 | 531 | 192 | 301 | 38 | 4 |
| Montmorency | 10 | 0 | 0 | 0 | 10 | 36 | 19 | 15 | 2 | 0 |
| Oceana | 23 | 0 | 8 | 1 | 14 | 279 | 75 | 192 | 12 | 0 |
| Ogemaw | 23 | 0 | 9 | 0 | 14 | 194 | 78 | 103 | 13 | 2 |
| Ontonagon | 1 | 0 | 1 | 0 | 0 | 19 | 8 | 10 | 1 | 0 |
| Osceola | 33 | 0 | 12 | 0 | 21 | 170 | 59 | 100 | 11 | 1 |
| Otsego | 2 | 0 | 0 | 0 | 2 | 91 | 23 | 63 | 5 | 1 |
| Roscommon | 23 | 1 | 3 | 0 | 19 | 198 | 43 | 146 | 9 | 1 |
| Schoolcraft | 0 | 0 | 0 | 0 | 0 | 4 | 0 | 3 | 1 | 1 |
| Shiawassee | 49 | 1 | 4 | 1 | 43 | 420 | 122 | 278 | 20 | 3 |

[1] The FBI does not publish arson data unless it receives data from either the agency or the state for all 12 months of the calendar year.

[6] Because of changes in the state/local agency's reporting practices, figures are not comparable to previous years' data.

**Table 10. Offenses Known to Law Enforcement, by State Metropolitan and Nonmetropolitan Counties, 2009**—*Continued*

(Number.)

| State/County | Violent crime | Murder and non-negligent man-slaughter | Forcible rape | Robbery | Aggravated assault | Property crime | Burglary | Larceny-theft | Motor vehicle theft | Arson[1] |
|---|---|---|---|---|---|---|---|---|---|---|
| St. Joseph | 54 | 0 | 9 | 0 | 45 | 328 | 91 | 214 | 23 | 6 |
| Tuscola | 21 | 0 | 2 | 0 | 19 | 277 | 105 | 156 | 16 | 1 |
| Wexford | 29 | 0 | 1 | 0 | 28 | 392 | 74 | 304 | 14 | 3 |
| **MINNESOTA - Metropolitan Counties[7]** | | | | | | | | | | |
| Anoka | | 1 | | 5 | 57 | 1,495 | 291 | 1,136 | 68 | 10 |
| Benton | | 0 | | 0 | 11 | 222 | 51 | 156 | 15 | 9 |
| Blue Earth | | 0 | | 1 | 8 | 182 | 66 | 97 | 19 | 0 |
| Carlton | | 1 | | 4 | 9 | 347 | 98 | 230 | 19 | 2 |
| Carver | | 0 | | 3 | 24 | 712 | 120 | 569 | 23 | 2 |
| Chisago | | 0 | | 2 | 13 | 484 | 83 | 367 | 34 | 0 |
| Clay | | 0 | | 1 | 1 | 62 | 16 | 43 | 3 | 0 |
| Dakota | | 1 | | 0 | 15 | 182 | 60 | 111 | 11 | 9 |
| Dodge | | 0 | | 1 | 34 | 269 | 30 | 228 | 11 | 0 |
| Hennepin | | 0 | | 1 | 13 | 156 | 31 | 112 | 13 | 1 |
| Houston | | 0 | | 1 | 1 | 60 | 22 | 36 | 2 | 0 |
| Isanti | | 0 | | 1 | 6 | 356 | 92 | 228 | 36 | 0 |
| Nicollet | | 0 | | 0 | 6 | 90 | 22 | 61 | 7 | 0 |
| Olmsted | | 0 | | 1 | 15 | 405 | 131 | 240 | 34 | 8 |
| Polk | | 0 | | 1 | 19 | 208 | 57 | 144 | 7 | 6 |
| Scott | | 0 | | 0 | 7 | 144 | 34 | 98 | 12 | 1 |
| Sherburne | | 1 | | 0 | 25 | 509 | 127 | 362 | 20 | 3 |
| Stearns | | 1 | | 0 | 27 | 420 | 83 | 321 | 16 | 0 |
| St. Louis | | 0 | | 5 | 37 | 701 | 273 | 354 | 74 | 6 |
| Washington | | 1 | | 3 | 30 | 1,126 | 213 | 866 | 47 | 5 |
| Wright | | 0 | | 7 | 56 | 1,868 | 182 | 1,619 | 67 | 3 |
| **MINNESOTA - Nonmetropolitan Counties[7]** | | | | | | | | | | |
| Aitkin | | 1 | | 0 | 13 | 323 | 121 | 176 | 26 | 0 |
| Becker | | 0 | | 0 | 11 | 135 | 56 | 61 | 18 | 4 |
| Beltrami | | 3 | | 1 | 33 | 450 | 127 | 293 | 30 | 2 |
| Big Stone | | 0 | | 0 | 1 | 39 | 16 | 19 | 4 | 0 |
| Brown | | 0 | | 0 | 0 | 3 | 1 | 2 | 0 | 0 |
| Cass | | 0 | | 2 | 22 | 421 | 132 | 252 | 37 | 0 |
| Chippewa | | 0 | | 0 | 6 | 21 | 1 | 20 | 0 | 0 |
| Clearwater | | 0 | | 0 | 15 | 136 | 32 | 90 | 14 | 4 |
| Cook | | 0 | | 2 | 4 | 133 | 38 | 88 | 7 | 0 |
| Cottonwood | | 0 | | 0 | 5 | 40 | 13 | 25 | 2 | 1 |
| Crow Wing | | 0 | | 0 | 15 | 342 | 89 | 234 | 19 | 1 |
| Douglas | | 0 | | 0 | 7 | 228 | 85 | 140 | 3 | 2 |
| Faribault | | 0 | | 0 | 4 | 63 | 17 | 39 | 7 | 1 |
| Fillmore | | 0 | | 0 | 2 | 91 | 25 | 55 | 11 | 0 |
| Freeborn | | 0 | | 0 | 5 | 108 | 25 | 75 | 8 | 0 |
| Goodhue | | 0 | | 0 | 9 | 253 | 77 | 154 | 22 | 1 |
| Grant | | 0 | | 0 | 4 | 85 | 21 | 60 | 4 | 0 |
| Hubbard | | 0 | | 0 | 11 | 305 | 138 | 156 | 11 | 0 |
| Itasca | | 1 | | 2 | 17 | 353 | 69 | 251 | 33 | 1 |
| Jackson | | 0 | | 0 | 1 | 38 | 1 | 36 | 1 | 0 |
| Kanabec | | 2 | | 0 | 14 | 219 | 79 | 121 | 19 | 8 |
| Kandiyohi | | 0 | | 1 | 13 | 259 | 42 | 201 | 16 | 0 |
| Kittson | | 0 | | 0 | 2 | 37 | 9 | 27 | 1 | 0 |
| Lac Qui Parle | | 0 | | 0 | 1 | 21 | 0 | 20 | 1 | 0 |
| Lake | | 0 | | 0 | 4 | 55 | 28 | 23 | 4 | 0 |
| Lake of the Woods | | 0 | | 0 | 4 | 19 | 5 | 13 | 1 | 0 |
| Le Sueur | | 0 | | 0 | 9 | 116 | 33 | 76 | 7 | 0 |
| Lincoln | | 0 | | 0 | 0 | 6 | 0 | 6 | 0 | 0 |
| Lyon | | 0 | | 0 | 2 | 53 | 23 | 26 | 4 | 1 |
| Mahnomen | | 0 | | 0 | 16 | 61 | 12 | 46 | 3 | 0 |
| Marshall | | 0 | | 0 | 7 | 134 | 27 | 99 | 8 | 1 |
| Martin | | 0 | | 0 | 1 | 43 | 8 | 29 | 6 | 0 |
| McLeod | | 0 | | 0 | 9 | 102 | 47 | 44 | 11 | 1 |
| Meeker | | 0 | | 0 | 4 | 198 | 53 | 137 | 8 | 0 |
| Mille Lacs | | 0 | | 0 | 16 | 370 | 67 | 275 | 28 | 3 |
| Morrison | | 0 | | 1 | 15 | 275 | 55 | 207 | 13 | 1 |
| Mower | | 0 | | 0 | 8 | 135 | 38 | 79 | 18 | 2 |
| Murray | | 0 | | 0 | 3 | 38 | 14 | 24 | 0 | 1 |
| Nobles | | 0 | | 0 | 3 | 98 | 44 | 48 | 6 | 1 |
| Otter Tail | | 0 | | 0 | 7 | 442 | 173 | 248 | 21 | 4 |
| Pennington | | 0 | | 0 | 1 | 38 | 8 | 26 | 4 | 1 |
| Pine | | 0 | | 4 | 32 | 975 | 335 | 581 | 59 | 1 |
| Pipestone | | 0 | | 1 | 0 | 73 | 17 | 53 | 3 | 0 |
| Pope | | 0 | | 0 | 2 | 53 | 12 | 35 | 6 | 1 |
| Red Lake | | 0 | | 0 | 5 | 13 | 2 | 9 | 2 | 0 |

[1] The FBI does not publish arson data unless it receives data from either the agency or the state for all 12 months of the calendar year.

[7] The data collection methodology for the offense of forcible rape used by the Illinois and the Minnesota state UCR Programs (with the exception of Rockford, Illinois, and Minneapolis and St. Paul, Minnesota) does not comply with national UCR Program guidelines. Consequently, their figures for forcible rape and violent crime (of which forcible rape is a part) are not published in this table.

## Table 10. Offenses Known to Law Enforcement, by State Metropolitan and Nonmetropolitan Counties, 2009—*Continued*

(Number.)

| State/County | Violent crime | Murder and non-negligent man-slaughter | Forcible rape | Robbery | Aggravated assault | Property crime | Burglary | Larceny-theft | Motor vehicle theft | Arson[1] |
|---|---|---|---|---|---|---|---|---|---|---|
| Redwood | | 0 | | 0 | 3 | 72 | 12 | 52 | 8 | 0 |
| Renville | | 0 | | 0 | 13 | 103 | 26 | 72 | 5 | 4 |
| Rice | | 0 | | 0 | 10 | 193 | 60 | 113 | 20 | 2 |
| Rock | | 0 | | 0 | 81 | 126 | 45 | 78 | 3 | 0 |
| Roseau | | 0 | | 0 | 4 | 37 | 6 | 31 | 0 | 0 |
| Steele | | 1 | | 1 | 8 | 76 | 16 | 55 | 5 | 1 |
| Stevens | | 0 | | 0 | 2 | 34 | 14 | 19 | 1 | 2 |
| Swift | | 0 | | 0 | 0 | 45 | 20 | 23 | 2 | 0 |
| Todd | | 0 | | 0 | 7 | 162 | 62 | 95 | 5 | 4 |
| Traverse | | 0 | | 0 | 4 | 35 | 14 | 21 | 0 | 1 |
| Wadena | | 0 | | 0 | 5 | 76 | 23 | 50 | 3 | 0 |
| Waseca | | 0 | | 0 | 0 | 95 | 38 | 51 | 6 | 4 |
| Watonwan | | 0 | | 0 | 2 | 58 | 8 | 48 | 2 | 2 |
| Wilkin | | 1 | | 0 | 1 | 67 | 14 | 50 | 3 | 0 |
| Winona | | 0 | | 0 | 5 | 98 | 43 | 48 | 7 | 0 |
| Yellow Medicine | | 0 | | 0 | 4 | 60 | 19 | 38 | 3 | 1 |
| **MISSISSIPPI - Metropolitan Counties** | | | | | | | | | | |
| DeSoto | 62 | 1 | 4 | 9 | 48 | 592 | 209 | 313 | 70 | 4 |
| Forrest[6] | 27 | 2 | 0 | 2 | 23 | 391 | 145 | 236 | 10 | 0 |
| George | 11 | 1 | 0 | 1 | 9 | 98 | 40 | 53 | 5 | 9 |
| Harrison | 24 | 1 | 5 | 11 | 7 | 1,173 | 359 | 709 | 105 | 15 |
| Hinds | 98 | 1 | 19 | 25 | 53 | 1,052 | 314 | 614 | 124 | 0 |
| Jackson | 157 | 4 | 44 | 17 | 92 | 1,676 | 698 | 876 | 102 | 7 |
| Lamar[3] | 71 | 1 | 36 | 11 | 23 | | 246 | | 32 | 0 |
| Madison | 40 | 1 | 4 | 6 | 29 | 471 | 149 | 279 | 43 | 0 |
| Rankin | 35 | 0 | 8 | 6 | 21 | 707 | 168 | 504 | 35 | 1 |
| Tate | 12 | 1 | 0 | 2 | 9 | 232 | 96 | 99 | 37 | 2 |
| Tunica | 90 | 2 | 10 | 27 | 51 | 736 | 135 | 545 | 56 | 5 |
| **MISSISSIPPI - Nonmetropolitan Counties** | | | | | | | | | | |
| Adams | 45 | 1 | 8 | 5 | 31 | 610 | 214 | 353 | 43 | 10 |
| Bolivar | 11 | 7 | 1 | 1 | 2 | 16 | 12 | 4 | 0 | 0 |
| Chickasaw | 27 | 1 | 0 | 5 | 21 | 46 | 22 | 24 | 0 | 0 |
| Choctaw | 16 | 1 | 2 | 0 | 13 | 72 | 36 | 33 | 3 | 0 |
| Claiborne | 72 | 4 | 0 | 5 | 63 | 48 | 24 | 20 | 4 | 0 |
| Franklin | 23 | 0 | 1 | 2 | 20 | 15 | 7 | 7 | 1 | 0 |
| Greene | 11 | 0 | 0 | 0 | 11 | 22 | 9 | 13 | 0 | 2 |
| Grenada | 14 | 3 | 0 | 2 | 9 | 119 | 63 | 46 | 10 | 4 |
| Jefferson | 21 | 0 | 3 | 4 | 14 | 58 | 29 | 26 | 3 | 1 |
| Jones[6] | 93 | 1 | 37 | 17 | 38 | 747 | 278 | 424 | 45 | 2 |
| Kemper | 7 | 1 | 0 | 0 | 6 | 65 | 40 | 21 | 4 | 0 |
| Lauderdale | 36 | 0 | 1 | 11 | 24 | 484 | 234 | 205 | 45 | 4 |
| Lee | 54 | 1 | 8 | 8 | 37 | 703 | 301 | 382 | 20 | 5 |
| Leflore | 111 | 2 | 3 | 5 | 101 | 402 | 182 | 203 | 17 | 1 |
| Lincoln | 16 | 0 | 1 | 1 | 14 | 318 | 104 | 196 | 18 | 3 |
| Lowndes | 59 | 1 | 17 | 5 | 36 | 585 | 198 | 359 | 28 | 3 |
| Oktibbeha | 41 | 1 | 0 | 5 | 35 | 224 | 116 | 90 | 18 | 0 |
| Panola | 65 | 0 | 1 | 7 | 57 | 557 | 311 | 223 | 23 | 0 |
| Pearl River | 44 | 3 | 18 | 9 | 14 | 664 | 294 | 350 | 20 | 2 |
| Pike | 43 | 4 | 4 | 10 | 25 | 427 | 229 | 179 | 19 | |
| Pontotoc | 3 | 1 | 0 | 1 | 1 | 23 | 12 | 11 | 0 | 1 |
| Sunflower | 95 | 3 | 9 | 55 | 28 | 114 | 71 | 23 | 20 | 0 |
| Tippah | 22 | 0 | 2 | 0 | 20 | 14 | 8 | 6 | 0 | 0 |
| Union | 3 | 1 | 1 | 1 | 0 | 210 | 105 | 80 | 25 | 5 |
| Warren | 18 | 0 | 6 | 8 | 4 | 369 | 177 | 145 | 47 | 0 |
| Washington | 22 | 0 | 3 | 3 | 16 | 474 | 156 | 292 | 26 | 1 |
| Winston | 5 | 0 | 0 | 1 | 4 | 17 | 8 | 9 | 0 | 0 |
| **MISSOURI - Metropolitan Counties** | | | | | | | | | | |
| Andrew | 9 | 1 | 0 | 0 | 8 | 93 | 26 | 63 | 4 | 0 |
| Bates | 47 | 0 | 5 | 0 | 42 | 141 | 62 | 76 | 3 | 0 |
| Bollinger | 3 | 0 | 2 | 0 | 1 | 40 | 18 | 19 | 3 | 1 |
| Boone | 124 | 0 | 1 | 13 | 110 | 678 | 155 | 483 | 40 | 7 |
| Buchanan | 13 | 0 | 0 | 3 | 10 | 263 | 116 | 130 | 17 | 4 |
| Caldwell | 14 | 0 | 1 | 0 | 13 | 90 | 42 | 42 | 6 | 0 |
| Callaway | 52 | 0 | 9 | 2 | 41 | 637 | 164 | 438 | 35 | 2 |
| Cape Girardeau | 138 | 0 | 4 | 1 | 133 | 225 | 95 | 122 | 8 | 1 |
| Cass[4] | 38 | 2 | 2 | 1 | 33 | | | 139 | 34 | 1 |
| Christian | 142 | 0 | 3 | 1 | 138 | 271 | 89 | 155 | 27 | 1 |
| Clay | 30 | 0 | 3 | 1 | 26 | 169 | 58 | 93 | 18 | 10 |
| Clinton | 25 | 0 | 2 | 1 | 22 | 112 | 35 | 72 | 5 | 1 |
| Cole | 49 | 2 | 9 | 7 | 31 | 265 | 88 | 171 | 6 | 1 |
| Dallas | 37 | 0 | 2 | 0 | 35 | 167 | 61 | 91 | 15 | 0 |

[1] The FBI does not publish arson data unless it receives data from either the agency or the state for all 12 months of the calendar year.
[3] The FBI determined that the agency's data were underreported. Consequently, affected data are not included in this table.
[4] The FBI determined that the agency did not follow national Uniform Crime Reporting (UCR) Program guidelines for reporting an offense. Consequently, this figure is not included in this table.
[6] Because of changes in the state/local agency's reporting practices, figures are not comparable to previous years' data.

**Table 10. Offenses Known to Law Enforcement, by State Metropolitan and Nonmetropolitan Counties, 2009**—*Continued*

(Number.)

| State/County | Violent crime | Murder and non-negligent man-slaughter | Forcible rape | Robbery | Aggravated assault | Property crime | Burglary | Larceny-theft | Motor vehicle theft | Arson[1] |
|---|---|---|---|---|---|---|---|---|---|---|
| De Kalb | 5 | 0 | 1 | 0 | 4 | 71 | 26 | 41 | 4 | 4 |
| Franklin | 64 | 1 | 4 | 2 | 57 | 608 | 141 | 416 | 51 | 1 |
| Howard | 5 | 0 | 0 | 0 | 5 | 48 | 13 | 35 | 0 | 0 |
| Jackson | 59 | 0 | 5 | 16 | 38 | 531 | 177 | 298 | 56 | 2 |
| Jasper | 158 | 1 | 15 | 2 | 140 | 514 | 182 | 285 | 47 | 7 |
| Jefferson | 431 | 3 | 39 | 17 | 372 | 2,614 | 440 | 1,966 | 208 | 25 |
| Lafayette | 12 | 0 | 0 | 1 | 11 | 146 | 53 | 76 | 17 | 0 |
| Lincoln | 53 | 0 | 0 | 0 | 53 | 218 | 86 | 95 | 37 | 2 |
| McDonald | 49 | 0 | 1 | 2 | 46 | 310 | 63 | 211 | 36 | 4 |
| Moniteau | 11 | 0 | 0 | 0 | 11 | 45 | 25 | 12 | 8 | 1 |
| Newton | 73 | 1 | 7 | 4 | 61 | 636 | 226 | 358 | 52 | 7 |
| Osage | 12 | 1 | 1 | 0 | 10 | 98 | 30 | 61 | 7 | 0 |
| Platte | 39 | 0 | 1 | 2 | 36 | 293 | 55 | 229 | 9 | 2 |
| Polk | 26 | 0 | 0 | 1 | 25 | 302 | 139 | 147 | 16 | 0 |
| Ray | 29 | 1 | 0 | 0 | 28 | 124 | 48 | 66 | 10 | 1 |
| St. Charles | 162 | 2 | 4 | 10 | 146 | 1,073 | 255 | 769 | 49 | 19 |
| St. Louis County Police Department | 1,014 | 13 | 82 | 304 | 615 | 10,018 | 1,972 | 7,173 | 873 | 52 |
| Warren | 30 | 1 | 4 | 1 | 24 | 217 | 69 | 133 | 15 | 3 |
| Washington | 32 | 2 | 2 | 2 | 26 | 211 | 57 | 120 | 34 | 2 |
| Webster[6] | 17 | 0 | 2 | 0 | 15 | 216 | 84 | 118 | 14 | 1 |
| **MISSOURI - Nonmetropolitan Counties** | | | | | | | | | | |
| Adair[6] | 8 | 0 | 0 | 0 | 8 | 111 | 31 | 68 | 12 | 3 |
| Atchison | 0 | 0 | 0 | 0 | 0 | 6 | 3 | 2 | 1 | 0 |
| Audrain | 17 | 1 | 1 | 0 | 15 | 141 | 50 | 87 | 4 | 0 |
| Barry | 108 | 0 | 5 | 2 | 101 | 349 | 139 | 200 | 10 | 3 |
| Benton | 53 | 0 | 0 | 0 | 53 | 149 | 65 | 68 | 16 | 2 |
| Butler | 58 | 0 | 0 | 3 | 55 | 424 | 146 | 259 | 19 | 0 |
| Camden | 25 | 0 | 0 | 2 | 23 | 294 | 106 | 171 | 17 | 1 |
| Carroll | 0 | 0 | 0 | 0 | 0 | 42 | 18 | 24 | 0 | 0 |
| Carter | 5 | 1 | 0 | 0 | 4 | 41 | 18 | 17 | 6 | 1 |
| Cedar | 3 | 0 | 1 | 0 | 2 | 115 | 42 | 66 | 7 | 1 |
| Clark | 11 | 0 | 1 | 0 | 10 | 50 | 27 | 21 | 2 | 5 |
| Cooper | 14 | 0 | 1 | 1 | 12 | 144 | 46 | 89 | 9 | 0 |
| Crawford | 22 | 0 | 0 | 0 | 22 | 219 | 97 | 108 | 14 | 1 |
| Daviess | 7 | 1 | 2 | 1 | 3 | 67 | 35 | 26 | 6 | 0 |
| Dent | 12 | 0 | 5 | 1 | 6 | 145 | 81 | 55 | 9 | 0 |
| Douglas | 42 | 2 | 2 | 0 | 38 | 106 | 56 | 39 | 11 | 2 |
| Dunklin | 32 | 0 | 0 | 0 | 32 | 205 | 54 | 136 | 15 | 6 |
| Gasconade | 14 | 0 | 0 | 1 | 13 | 117 | 49 | 56 | 12 | 1 |
| Gentry | 1 | 0 | 0 | 0 | 1 | 34 | 14 | 18 | 2 | 0 |
| Grundy | 3 | 0 | 0 | 0 | 3 | 34 | 11 | 22 | 1 | 1 |
| Harrison | 2 | 0 | 0 | 0 | 2 | 38 | 14 | 23 | 1 | 2 |
| Henry | 27 | 0 | 1 | 2 | 24 | 212 | 75 | 117 | 20 | 1 |
| Hickory | 1 | 0 | 0 | 0 | 1 | 88 | 49 | 36 | 3 | 0 |
| Holt | 3 | 0 | 0 | 0 | 3 | 81 | 21 | 39 | 21 | 0 |
| Howell[6] | 38 | 2 | 3 | 0 | 33 | 360 | 103 | 226 | 31 | 3 |
| Iron | 9 | 0 | 4 | 0 | 5 | 55 | 26 | 19 | 10 | 0 |
| Johnson | 29 | 1 | 0 | 2 | 26 | 294 | 126 | 150 | 18 | 0 |
| Knox | 5 | 0 | 2 | 0 | 3 | 132 | 36 | 96 | 0 | 0 |
| Lawrence | 50 | 1 | 1 | 1 | 47 | 348 | 113 | 213 | 22 | 2 |
| Lewis | 2 | 0 | 0 | 0 | 2 | 63 | 23 | 36 | 4 | 3 |
| Linn | 6 | 0 | 1 | 0 | 5 | 80 | 45 | 29 | 6 | 0 |
| Livingston | 1 | 0 | 0 | 0 | 1 | 60 | 24 | 28 | 8 | 2 |
| Macon | 15 | 0 | 0 | 0 | 15 | 55 | 38 | 13 | 4 | 0 |
| Madison | 3 | 0 | 0 | 0 | 3 | 30 | 7 | 19 | 4 | 0 |
| Maries | 7 | 0 | 2 | 0 | 5 | 61 | 28 | 26 | 7 | 0 |
| Marion | 9 | 0 | 0 | 0 | 9 | 70 | 21 | 47 | 2 | 0 |
| Mercer | 3 | 0 | 0 | 0 | 3 | 15 | 5 | 10 | 0 | 1 |
| Mississippi | 13 | 0 | 0 | 0 | 13 | 40 | 9 | 24 | 7 | 0 |
| Monroe | 7 | 0 | 0 | 0 | 7 | 71 | 33 | 32 | 6 | 0 |
| Montgomery | 7 | 0 | 0 | 1 | 6 | 71 | 43 | 25 | 3 | 0 |
| Morgan | 41 | 0 | 0 | 0 | 41 | 246 | 114 | 113 | 19 | 0 |
| New Madrid | 19 | 0 | 1 | 0 | 18 | 57 | 18 | 33 | 6 | 2 |
| Nodaway | 10 | 0 | 0 | 0 | 10 | 102 | 44 | 53 | 5 | 1 |
| Oregon[6] | 17 | 0 | 0 | 1 | 16 | 39 | 18 | 20 | 1 | 0 |
| Ozark | 16 | 0 | 2 | 0 | 14 | 103 | 49 | 47 | 7 | 3 |
| Pemiscot | 15 | 1 | 0 | 2 | 12 | 130 | 58 | 67 | 5 | 0 |
| Perry | 7 | 1 | 0 | 0 | 6 | 88 | 27 | 54 | 7 | 1 |
| Phelps | 48 | 0 | 5 | 0 | 43 | 377 | 117 | 240 | 20 | 0 |
| Pike | 23 | 1 | 4 | 0 | 18 | 76 | 43 | 22 | 11 | 4 |
| Pulaski | 96 | 1 | 10 | 5 | 80 | 374 | 149 | 194 | 31 | 2 |

[1] The FBI does not publish arson data unless it receives data from either the agency or the state for all 12 months of the calendar year.
[6] Because of changes in the state/local agency's reporting practices, figures are not comparable to previous years' data.

**Table 10. Offenses Known to Law Enforcement, by State Metropolitan and Nonmetropolitan Counties, 2009—*Continued***

(Number.)

| State/County | Violent crime | Murder and non-negligent man-slaughter | Forcible rape | Robbery | Aggravated assault | Property crime | Burglary | Larceny-theft | Motor vehicle theft | Arson[1] |
|---|---|---|---|---|---|---|---|---|---|---|
| Putnam | 0 | 0 | 0 | 0 | 0 | 10 | 5 | 3 | 2 | 0 |
| Ralls | 19 | 0 | 2 | 1 | 16 | 95 | 25 | 64 | 6 | 0 |
| Randolph | 4 | 0 | 0 | 0 | 4 | 83 | 30 | 52 | 1 | 0 |
| Ripley | 21 | 0 | 1 | 2 | 18 | 168 | 59 | 101 | 8 | 2 |
| Saline | 10 | 0 | 5 | 1 | 4 | 94 | 42 | 48 | 4 | 1 |
| Scotland | 4 | 0 | 0 | 0 | 4 | 30 | 14 | 16 | 0 | 0 |
| Scott | 18 | 0 | 1 | 0 | 17 | 119 | 37 | 75 | 7 | 1 |
| Shannon | 5 | 0 | 0 | 0 | 5 | 47 | 14 | 31 | 2 | 0 |
| Shelby | 3 | 0 | 0 | 0 | 3 | 52 | 17 | 33 | 2 | 1 |
| St. Clair | 9 | 0 | 0 | 0 | 9 | 120 | 52 | 68 | 0 | 0 |
| St. Francois | 61 | 2 | 6 | 1 | 52 | 491 | 158 | 266 | 67 | 4 |
| Stoddard | 24 | 0 | 0 | 0 | 24 | 75 | 37 | 35 | 3 | 0 |
| Stone | 118 | 0 | 7 | 2 | 109 | 474 | 176 | 257 | 41 | 0 |
| Sullivan | 7 | 0 | 1 | 1 | 5 | 63 | 27 | 22 | 14 | 0 |
| Taney | 113 | 0 | 7 | 1 | 105 | 483 | 138 | 316 | 29 | 1 |
| Texas | 26 | 1 | 7 | 1 | 17 | 170 | 71 | 87 | 12 | 2 |
| Vernon | 42 | 1 | 0 | 2 | 39 | 274 | 90 | 158 | 26 | 4 |
| Worth | 4 | 0 | 0 | 0 | 4 | 18 | 9 | 8 | 1 | 0 |
| Wright | 30 | 0 | 1 | 1 | 28 | 83 | 36 | 44 | 3 | 0 |
| **MONTANA - Metropolitan Counties** | | | | | | | | | | |
| Carbon | 17 | 1 | 1 | 0 | 15 | 45 | 10 | 28 | 7 | 0 |
| Cascade | 47 | 1 | 2 | 1 | 43 | 283 | 47 | 206 | 30 | 1 |
| Missoula | 76 | 0 | 9 | 2 | 65 | 506 | 110 | 355 | 41 | 16 |
| Yellowstone | 55 | 0 | 3 | 5 | 47 | 711 | 158 | 500 | 53 | 4 |
| **MONTANA - Nonmetropolitan Counties** | | | | | | | | | | |
| Beaverhead | 7 | 0 | 0 | 0 | 7 | 55 | 7 | 43 | 5 | 0 |
| Big Horn | 40 | 0 | 0 | 1 | 39 | 102 | 5 | 82 | 15 | 2 |
| Blaine | 8 | 0 | 0 | 0 | 8 | 29 | 7 | 19 | 3 | 2 |
| Broadwater | 10 | 0 | 0 | 0 | 10 | 92 | 6 | 70 | 16 | 1 |
| Carter | 1 | 0 | 0 | 0 | 1 | 3 | 1 | 2 | 0 | 0 |
| Chouteau | 5 | 0 | 0 | 0 | 5 | 11 | 2 | 6 | 3 | 0 |
| Custer | 1 | 0 | 0 | 0 | 1 | 51 | 8 | 37 | 6 | 0 |
| Daniels | 3 | 0 | 0 | 0 | 3 | 7 | 1 | 4 | 2 | 0 |
| Dawson | 4 | 0 | 1 | 0 | 3 | 55 | 2 | 53 | 0 | 0 |
| Deer Lodge | 30 | 0 | 1 | 0 | 29 | 135 | 13 | 113 | 9 | 0 |
| Fallon | 1 | 0 | 0 | 0 | 1 | 6 | 0 | 6 | 0 | 0 |
| Fergus | 2 | 0 | 0 | 0 | 2 | 19 | 5 | 12 | 2 | 0 |
| Flathead | 198 | 4 | 19 | 4 | 171 | 1,086 | 170 | 848 | 68 | 7 |
| Gallatin | 42 | 1 | 15 | 0 | 26 | 466 | 82 | 342 | 42 | 1 |
| Garfield | 1 | 0 | 0 | 0 | 1 | 2 | 0 | 1 | 1 | 0 |
| Glacier | 14 | 0 | 0 | 0 | 14 | 14 | 3 | 10 | 1 | 0 |
| Granite | 3 | 0 | 0 | 1 | 2 | 47 | 7 | 39 | 1 | 0 |
| Hill | 37 | 0 | 2 | 3 | 32 | 166 | 20 | 138 | 8 | 3 |
| Jefferson | 15 | 0 | 4 | 0 | 11 | 51 | 9 | 37 | 5 | 0 |
| Judith Basin | 0 | 0 | 0 | 0 | 0 | 9 | 1 | 5 | 3 | 0 |
| Lake | 78 | 0 | 9 | 1 | 68 | 341 | 83 | 239 | 19 | 2 |
| Lewis and Clark | 62 | 1 | 10 | 0 | 51 | 305 | 67 | 208 | 30 | 3 |
| Lincoln | 21 | 0 | 4 | 1 | 16 | 187 | 37 | 139 | 11 | 2 |
| Madison | 4 | 0 | 1 | 0 | 3 | 71 | 21 | 49 | 1 | 0 |
| McCone | 0 | 0 | 0 | 0 | 0 | 20 | 4 | 15 | 1 | 0 |
| Meagher | 2 | 0 | 0 | 0 | 2 | 16 | 0 | 16 | 0 | 0 |
| Mineral | 11 | 0 | 0 | 1 | 10 | 5 | 1 | 2 | 2 | 0 |
| Musselshell | 28 | 1 | 3 | 0 | 24 | 103 | 33 | 65 | 5 | 0 |
| Park | 10 | 0 | 0 | 0 | 10 | 84 | 21 | 55 | 8 | 1 |
| Phillips | 13 | 0 | 1 | 0 | 12 | 40 | 5 | 34 | 1 | 1 |
| Pondera | 1 | 0 | 0 | 0 | 1 | 5 | 0 | 5 | 0 | 0 |
| Powell | 15 | 0 | 1 | 0 | 14 | 110 | 10 | 97 | 3 | 1 |
| Prairie | 0 | 0 | 0 | 0 | 0 | 3 | 1 | 2 | 0 | 0 |
| Ravalli | 51 | 0 | 12 | 1 | 38 | 373 | 59 | 295 | 19 | 3 |
| Richland | 1 | 0 | 1 | 0 | 0 | 12 | 2 | 9 | 1 | 0 |
| Roosevelt | 2 | 0 | 0 | 0 | 2 | 42 | 12 | 24 | 6 | 0 |
| Rosebud | 11 | 0 | 0 | 0 | 11 | 51 | 7 | 40 | 4 | 0 |
| Sanders | 31 | 0 | 3 | 1 | 27 | 100 | 27 | 69 | 4 | 2 |
| Sheridan | 8 | 0 | 1 | 0 | 7 | 55 | 7 | 42 | 6 | 0 |
| Silver Bow | 151 | 1 | 16 | 15 | 119 | 1,361 | 177 | 1,059 | 125 | 16 |
| Stillwater | 16 | 1 | 2 | 0 | 13 | 60 | 20 | 38 | 2 | 2 |
| Sweet Grass | 10 | 0 | 2 | 0 | 8 | 29 | 5 | 22 | 2 | 0 |
| Teton | 7 | 0 | 2 | 0 | 5 | 53 | 3 | 46 | 4 | 0 |
| Toole | 14 | 0 | 1 | 0 | 13 | 92 | 20 | 63 | 9 | 1 |
| Valley | 0 | 0 | 0 | 0 | 0 | 27 | 7 | 18 | 2 | 0 |
| Wibaux | 0 | 0 | 0 | 0 | 0 | 4 | 0 | 4 | 0 | 0 |

[1] The FBI does not publish arson data unless it receives data from either the agency or the state for all 12 months of the calendar year.
[3] The FBI determined that the agency's data were underreported. Consequently, affected data are not included in this table.

## Table 10. Offenses Known to Law Enforcement, by State Metropolitan and Nonmetropolitan Counties, 2009—*Continued*

(Number.)

| State/County | Violent crime | Murder and non-negligent man-slaughter | Forcible rape | Robbery | Aggravated assault | Property crime | Burglary | Larceny-theft | Motor vehicle theft | Arson[1] |
|---|---|---|---|---|---|---|---|---|---|---|
| **NEBRASKA - Metropolitan Counties** | | | | | | | | | | |
| Cass | 20 | 0 | 6 | 0 | 14 | 222 | 56 | 147 | 19 | 1 |
| Dakota | 5 | 0 | 0 | 0 | 5 | 63 | 12 | 44 | 7 | 0 |
| Dixon | 5 | 0 | 3 | 0 | 2 | 50 | 12 | 35 | 3 | 0 |
| Douglas | 201 | 0 | 4 | 12 | 185 | 1,125 | 283 | 781 | 61 | 1 |
| Lancaster | 22 | 0 | 7 | 1 | 14 | 270 | 76 | 183 | 11 | 7 |
| Sarpy | 15 | 0 | 10 | 2 | 3 | 712 | 128 | 524 | 60 | 2 |
| Saunders | 6 | 0 | 0 | 1 | 5 | 62 | 16 | 41 | 5 | 0 |
| **NEBRASKA - Nonmetropolitan Counties** | | | | | | | | | | |
| Adams | 3 | 0 | 2 | 0 | 1 | 109 | 35 | 71 | 3 | 0 |
| Antelope | 1 | 0 | 0 | 0 | 1 | 13 | 5 | 8 | 0 | 1 |
| Arthur | 0 | 0 | 0 | 0 | 0 | 0 | 0 | 0 | 0 | 0 |
| Box Butte | 1 | 0 | 0 | 0 | 1 | 12 | 3 | 7 | 2 | 0 |
| Boyd | 0 | 0 | 0 | 0 | 0 | 12 | 1 | 10 | 1 | 0 |
| Brown | 3 | 0 | 0 | 1 | 2 | 49 | 8 | 39 | 2 | 0 |
| Buffalo | 16 | 0 | 1 | 1 | 14 | 152 | 34 | 110 | 8 | 1 |
| Burt | 3 | 0 | 0 | 0 | 3 | 20 | 7 | 12 | 1 | 0 |
| Butler[2] | 2 | 0 | 0 | 0 | 2 | | | 34 | 0 | 0 |
| Cedar | 0 | 0 | 0 | 0 | 0 | 1 | 0 | 1 | 0 | 0 |
| Chase | 3 | 0 | 1 | 0 | 2 | 28 | 8 | 14 | 6 | 0 |
| Cherry | 4 | 0 | 0 | 0 | 4 | 2 | 1 | 1 | 0 | 0 |
| Colfax | 8 | 0 | 0 | 0 | 8 | 27 | 2 | 20 | 5 | 1 |
| Custer | 5 | 0 | 3 | 0 | 2 | 66 | 16 | 48 | 2 | 2 |
| Dawes | 1 | 0 | 0 | 0 | 1 | 12 | 4 | 8 | 0 | 0 |
| Dawson | 9 | 0 | 2 | 0 | 7 | 92 | 24 | 58 | 10 | 0 |
| Deuel | 0 | 0 | 0 | 0 | 0 | 30 | 6 | 23 | 1 | 0 |
| Dodge | 5 | 0 | 0 | 0 | 5 | 149 | 35 | 106 | 8 | 0 |
| Franklin | 1 | 0 | 0 | 0 | 1 | 13 | 3 | 10 | 0 | 0 |
| Gage | 7 | 0 | 4 | 0 | 3 | 177 | 53 | 116 | 8 | 1 |
| Hall | 18 | 0 | 1 | 1 | 16 | 188 | 57 | 126 | 5 | 1 |
| Hamilton | 1 | 0 | 1 | 0 | 0 | 43 | 11 | 27 | 5 | 0 |
| Harlan | 0 | 0 | 0 | 0 | 0 | 1 | 0 | 1 | 0 | 0 |
| Hitchcock | 2 | 0 | 0 | 0 | 2 | 7 | 2 | 2 | 3 | 0 |
| Hooker | 0 | 0 | 0 | 0 | 0 | 0 | 0 | 0 | 0 | 0 |
| Jefferson | 1 | 0 | 1 | 0 | 0 | 57 | 17 | 36 | 4 | 0 |
| Kearney | 3 | 0 | 1 | 0 | 2 | 59 | 26 | 31 | 2 | 0 |
| Keith | 3 | 0 | 2 | 0 | 1 | 37 | 6 | 29 | 2 | 0 |
| Keya Paha | 0 | 0 | 0 | 0 | 0 | 0 | 0 | 0 | 0 | 0 |
| Kimball | 4 | 0 | 0 | 0 | 4 | 15 | 0 | 11 | 4 | 0 |
| Knox | 2 | 0 | 1 | 0 | 1 | 22 | 3 | 18 | 1 | 3 |
| Madison | 5 | 0 | 0 | 0 | 5 | 84 | 26 | 57 | 1 | 0 |
| Merrick | 6 | 0 | 0 | 0 | 6 | 62 | 20 | 41 | 1 | 0 |
| Morrill | 1 | 0 | 0 | 0 | 1 | 27 | 5 | 21 | 1 | 0 |
| Nance | 1 | 0 | 0 | 0 | 1 | 17 | 6 | 9 | 2 | 1 |
| Nemaha | 7 | 0 | 4 | 1 | 2 | 25 | 10 | 14 | 1 | 1 |
| Pawnee | 0 | 0 | 0 | 0 | 0 | 20 | 4 | 15 | 1 | 0 |
| Perkins | 0 | 0 | 0 | 0 | 0 | 29 | 12 | 15 | 2 | 0 |
| Phelps | 4 | 0 | 1 | 0 | 3 | 23 | 6 | 13 | 4 | 0 |
| Pierce | 3 | 0 | 0 | 0 | 3 | 6 | 3 | 3 | 0 | 0 |
| Platte | 11 | 0 | 6 | 0 | 5 | 108 | 14 | 82 | 12 | 1 |
| Polk | 1 | 0 | 0 | 0 | 1 | 52 | 7 | 43 | 2 | 0 |
| Red Willow | 1 | 0 | 0 | 0 | 1 | 27 | 8 | 15 | 4 | 0 |
| Richardson | 6 | 0 | 0 | 1 | 5 | 56 | 15 | 34 | 7 | 0 |
| Rock | 0 | 0 | 0 | 0 | 0 | 7 | 3 | 2 | 2 | 0 |
| Saline | 5 | 0 | 0 | 1 | 4 | 43 | 21 | 18 | 4 | 1 |
| Scotts Bluff | 7 | 0 | 1 | 0 | 6 | 83 | 23 | 58 | 2 | 0 |
| Sheridan | 1 | 0 | 0 | 0 | 1 | 40 | 14 | 22 | 4 | 0 |
| Stanton | 0 | 0 | 0 | 0 | 0 | 38 | 11 | 27 | 0 | 1 |
| Thayer | 4 | 0 | 0 | 1 | 3 | 66 | 16 | 50 | 0 | 0 |
| Wayne | 0 | 0 | 0 | 0 | 0 | 18 | 2 | 16 | 0 | 0 |
| Webster | 3 | 0 | 0 | 0 | 3 | 46 | 17 | 27 | 2 | 0 |
| Wheeler | 1 | 0 | 1 | 0 | 0 | 1 | 0 | 0 | 1 | 0 |
| York | 1 | 0 | 0 | 0 | 1 | 29 | 6 | 23 | 0 | 0 |
| **NEVADA - Metropolitan Counties** | | | | | | | | | | |
| Carson City | 180 | 0 | 1 | 26 | 153 | 1,151 | 268 | 797 | 86 | 12 |
| Storey | 7 | 1 | 0 | 1 | 5 | 64 | 19 | 42 | 3 | 0 |
| Washoe | 265 | 3 | 0 | 11 | 251 | 1,368 | 445 | 801 | 122 | 2 |
| **NEVADA - Nonmetropolitan Counties** | | | | | | | | | | |
| Churchill | 23 | 0 | 5 | 0 | 18 | 174 | 46 | 113 | 15 | 2 |
| Douglas | 107 | 1 | 10 | 9 | 87 | 706 | 176 | 500 | 30 | 6 |
| Elko | 25 | 0 | 7 | 2 | 16 | 201 | 79 | 98 | 24 | 1 |

[1] The FBI does not publish arson data unless it receives data from either the agency or the state for all 12 months of the calendar year.
[2] The FBI determined that the agency's data were overreported. Consequently, affected data are not included in this table.

**Table 10. Offenses Known to Law Enforcement, by State Metropolitan and Nonmetropolitan Counties, 2009**—*Continued*

(Number.)

| State/County | Violent crime | Murder and non-negligent man-slaughter | Forcible rape | Robbery | Aggravated assault | Property crime | Burglary | Larceny-theft | Motor vehicle theft | Arson[1] |
|---|---|---|---|---|---|---|---|---|---|---|
| Esmeralda | 4 | 0 | 0 | 0 | 4 | 2 | 0 | 2 | 0 | 0 |
| Eureka | 9 | 0 | 1 | 1 | 7 | 25 | 13 | 10 | 2 | 0 |
| Humboldt | 51 | 0 | 0 | 1 | 50 | 41 | 18 | 17 | 6 | 1 |
| Lander | 23 | 0 | 8 | 0 | 15 | 159 | 75 | 66 | 18 | 0 |
| Lincoln | 2 | 0 | 0 | 0 | 2 | 51 | 4 | 38 | 9 | 18 |
| Lyon | 111 | 0 | 2 | 5 | 104 | 634 | 177 | 399 | 58 | 3 |
| Mineral | 32 | 0 | 0 | 0 | 32 | 30 | 14 | 10 | 6 | 1 |
| Pershing | 20 | 0 | 3 | 0 | 17 | 38 | 15 | 22 | 1 | 0 |
| White Pine | 14 | 1 | 1 | 1 | 11 | 117 | 37 | 73 | 7 | 2 |
| **NEW HAMPSHIRE - Metropolitan Counties** | | | | | | | | | | |
| Rockingham | 5 | 0 | 0 | 0 | 5 | 0 | 0 | 0 | 0 | 0 |
| **NEW HAMPSHIRE - Nonmetropolitan Counties** | | | | | | | | | | |
| Carroll | 5 | 0 | 1 | 0 | 4 | 47 | 14 | 26 | 7 | 1 |
| Cheshire | 3 | 0 | 0 | 0 | 3 | 3 | 0 | 3 | 0 | 0 |
| Merrimack | 7 | 0 | 4 | 0 | 3 | 7 | 1 | 6 | 0 | 0 |
| **NEW JERSEY - Metropolitan Counties** | | | | | | | | | | |
| Atlantic | 0 | 0 | 0 | 0 | 0 | 0 | 0 | 0 | 0 | 0 |
| Bergen County Police Department | 0 | 0 | 0 | 0 | 0 | 0 | 0 | 0 | 0 | 0 |
| Burlington | 0 | 0 | 0 | 0 | 0 | 0 | 0 | 0 | 0 | 0 |
| Camden | 0 | 0 | 0 | 0 | 0 | 0 | 0 | 0 | 0 | 0 |
| Cape May | 0 | 0 | 0 | 0 | 0 | 0 | 0 | 0 | 0 | 0 |
| Cumberland | 0 | 0 | 0 | 0 | 0 | 0 | 0 | 0 | 0 | 0 |
| Essex | 0 | 0 | 0 | 0 | 0 | 0 | 0 | 0 | 0 | 0 |
| Gloucester | 0 | 0 | 0 | 0 | 0 | 0 | 0 | 0 | 0 | 0 |
| Hudson | 0 | 0 | 0 | 0 | 0 | 0 | 0 | 0 | 0 | 0 |
| Hunterdon | 0 | 0 | 0 | 0 | 0 | 0 | 0 | 0 | 0 | 0 |
| Middlesex | 0 | 0 | 0 | 0 | 0 | 0 | 0 | 0 | 0 | 0 |
| Monmouth | 0 | 0 | 0 | 0 | 0 | 0 | 0 | 0 | 0 | 0 |
| Morris | 0 | 0 | 0 | 0 | 0 | 0 | 0 | 0 | 0 | 0 |
| Ocean | 0 | 0 | 0 | 0 | 0 | 0 | 0 | 0 | 0 | 0 |
| Passaic | 0 | 0 | 0 | 0 | 0 | 0 | 0 | 0 | 0 | 0 |
| Salem | 0 | 0 | 0 | 0 | 0 | 0 | 0 | 0 | 0 | 0 |
| Somerset | 3 | 0 | 0 | 0 | 3 | 0 | 0 | 0 | 0 | 0 |
| Sussex | 0 | 0 | 0 | 0 | 0 | 0 | 0 | 0 | 0 | 0 |
| Union | 0 | 0 | 0 | 0 | 0 | 0 | 0 | 0 | 0 | 0 |
| Warren | 0 | 0 | 0 | 0 | 0 | 0 | 0 | 0 | 0 | 0 |
| **NEW MEXICO - Metropolitan Counties** | | | | | | | | | | |
| Bernalillo | 813 | 6 | 40 | 94 | 673 | 2,413 | 863 | 1,182 | 368 | 54 |
| Dona Ana | 321 | 3 | 40 | 14 | 264 | 1,344 | 472 | 748 | 124 | 8 |
| Sandoval | 13 | 0 | 0 | 1 | 12 | 169 | 120 | 44 | 5 | 0 |
| San Juan | 283 | 1 | 43 | 2 | 237 | 860 | 241 | 505 | 114 | 3 |
| Santa Fe | 198 | 1 | 20 | 21 | 156 | 1,091 | 701 | 320 | 70 | 12 |
| Torrance | 13 | 0 | 1 | 1 | 11 | 159 | 92 | 38 | 29 | 0 |
| Valencia | 99 | 3 | 11 | 5 | 80 | 1,188 | 744 | 239 | 205 | 37 |
| **NEW MEXICO - Nonmetropolitan Counties** | | | | | | | | | | |
| Chaves | 56 | 3 | 10 | 2 | 41 | 444 | 251 | 164 | 29 | 2 |
| Cibola[4] | | 2 | 1 | 0 | | 98 | 55 | 32 | 11 | 0 |
| Colfax | 4 | 0 | 1 | 0 | 3 | 3 | 1 | 1 | 1 | 0 |
| Eddy[2] | | 1 | 16 | 4 | | 480 | 184 | 262 | 34 | 0 |
| Grant | 7 | 0 | 0 | 1 | 6 | 72 | 51 | 21 | 0 | 0 |
| Lea | 52 | 1 | 9 | 4 | 38 | 328 | 130 | 169 | 29 | 1 |
| Lincoln[4] | | 0 | 1 | 0 | | 115 | 34 | 75 | 6 | 0 |
| Luna | 60 | 0 | 0 | 0 | 60 | 209 | 81 | 102 | 26 | 3 |
| McKinley | 87 | 1 | 10 | 3 | 73 | 233 | 81 | 138 | 14 | 7 |
| Mora | 4 | 0 | 0 | 0 | 4 | 1 | 1 | 0 | 0 | 0 |
| Otero | 137 | 1 | 9 | 2 | 125 | 240 | 101 | 124 | 15 | 0 |
| Quay | 2 | 0 | 0 | 0 | 2 | 26 | 8 | 15 | 3 | 0 |
| Roosevelt | 20 | 0 | 4 | 2 | 14 | 62 | 23 | 33 | 6 | 0 |
| Sierra | 13 | 0 | 0 | 1 | 12 | 59 | 27 | 25 | 7 | 1 |
| **NEW YORK - Metropolitan Counties** | | | | | | | | | | |
| Albany | 24 | 0 | 1 | 1 | 22 | 171 | 30 | 132 | 9 | 1 |
| Broome | 70 | 0 | 9 | 6 | 55 | 1,008 | 187 | 800 | 21 | 1 |
| Chemung | 18 | 0 | 2 | 2 | 14 | 351 | 63 | 274 | 14 | 4 |
| Dutchess | 64 | 0 | 6 | 18 | 40 | 733 | 159 | 547 | 27 | 1 |
| Erie | 121 | 0 | 7 | 10 | 104 | 1,016 | 229 | 749 | 38 | 8 |
| Herkimer | 0 | 0 | 0 | 0 | 0 | 3 | 0 | 3 | 0 | 0 |
| Livingston | 26 | 0 | 6 | 4 | 16 | 412 | 73 | 331 | 8 | 4 |
| Madison | 9 | 0 | 1 | 1 | 7 | 201 | 47 | 143 | 11 | 0 |
| Monroe | 212 | 1 | 28 | 47 | 136 | 4,244 | 595 | 3,529 | 120 | 6 |
| Nassau | 1,640 | 18 | 74 | 754 | 794 | 15,185 | 1,998 | 12,066 | 1,121 | |
| Niagara | 96 | 2 | 12 | 22 | 60 | 1,237 | 322 | 864 | 51 | 3 |

[1] The FBI does not publish arson data unless it receives data from either the agency or the state for all 12 months of the calendar year.
[2] The FBI determined that the agency's data were overreported. Consequently, affected data are not included in this table.
[4] The FBI determined that the agency did not follow national Uniform Crime Reporting (UCR) Program guidelines for reporting an offense. Consequently, this figure is not included in this table.

## Table 10. Offenses Known to Law Enforcement, by State Metropolitan and Nonmetropolitan Counties, 2009—*Continued*

(Number.)

| State/County | Violent crime | Murder and non-negligent man-slaughter | Forcible rape | Robbery | Aggravated assault | Property crime | Burglary | Larceny-theft | Motor vehicle theft | Arson[1] |
|---|---|---|---|---|---|---|---|---|---|---|
| Oneida | 17 | 1 | 4 | 3 | 9 | 473 | 96 | 360 | 17 | 4 |
| Onondaga | 189 | 1 | 17 | 57 | 114 | 2,383 | 531 | 1,790 | 62 | 13 |
| Ontario | 44 | 2 | 12 | 5 | 25 | 897 | 165 | 711 | 21 | 2 |
| Orange | 9 | 0 | 0 | 1 | 8 | 25 | 2 | 21 | 2 | 0 |
| Orleans | 19 | 0 | 3 | 1 | 15 | 404 | 120 | 271 | 13 | 4 |
| Oswego | 47 | 0 | 10 | 4 | 33 | 462 | 126 | 314 | 22 | 3 |
| Putnam | 35 | 0 | 2 | 8 | 25 | 318 | 74 | 233 | 11 | 1 |
| Rockland | 9 | 0 | 0 | 1 | 8 | 46 | 2 | 43 | 1 | 0 |
| Saratoga | 40 | 0 | 5 | 10 | 25 | 1,214 | 209 | 980 | 25 | 4 |
| Schenectady | 2 | 0 | 0 | 1 | 1 | 17 | 1 | 16 | 0 | 0 |
| Schoharie | 5 | 0 | 1 | 1 | 3 | 81 | 30 | 44 | 7 | 0 |
| Suffolk | 151 | 0 | 0 | 0 | 151 | 13 | 0 | 6 | 7 | 0 |
| Suffolk County Police Department | 2,262 | 32 | 63 | 959 | 1,208 | 25,141 | 3,743 | 19,887 | 1,511 | 237 |
| Tioga | 10 | 0 | 1 | 0 | 9 | 235 | 57 | 164 | 14 | 0 |
| Tompkins[2] | | 1 | 1 | 3 | | 407 | 111 | 290 | 6 | 1 |
| Ulster | 55 | 0 | 2 | 4 | 49 | 354 | 72 | 275 | 7 | 0 |
| Warren | 45 | 0 | 5 | 2 | 38 | 768 | 119 | 632 | 17 | 2 |
| Washington | 24 | 0 | 3 | 2 | 19 | 313 | 74 | 222 | 17 | 0 |
| Wayne | 38 | 0 | 3 | 8 | 27 | 433 | 138 | 274 | 21 | 0 |
| Westchester Public Safety | 55 | 0 | 0 | 3 | 52 | 192 | 17 | 168 | 7 | 1 |
| **NEW YORK - Nonmetropolitan Counties** | | | | | | | | | | |
| Allegany | 2 | 0 | 0 | 0 | 2 | 3 | 1 | 2 | 0 | 0 |
| Cattaraugus | 48 | 1 | 8 | 1 | 38 | 458 | 124 | 312 | 22 | 3 |
| Cayuga | 27 | 1 | 2 | 2 | 22 | 301 | 63 | 235 | 3 | 2 |
| Chautauqua | 24 | 0 | 6 | 1 | 17 | 804 | 192 | 594 | 18 | 0 |
| Chenango | 12 | 0 | 2 | 1 | 9 | 299 | 78 | 215 | 6 | 2 |
| Clinton | 3 | 0 | 0 | 0 | 3 | 6 | 1 | 5 | 0 | 0 |
| Columbia | 27 | 0 | 0 | 1 | 26 | 329 | 105 | 220 | 4 | 0 |
| Cortland | 18 | 0 | 4 | 3 | 11 | 316 | 82 | 223 | 11 | 3 |
| Delaware | 9 | 0 | 3 | 0 | 6 | 131 | 42 | 86 | 3 | 8 |
| Essex | 0 | 0 | 0 | 0 | 0 | 0 | 0 | 0 | 0 | 0 |
| Franklin | 0 | 0 | 0 | 0 | 0 | 0 | 0 | 0 | 0 | 0 |
| Fulton | 12 | 0 | 5 | 0 | 7 | 422 | 133 | 268 | 21 | 0 |
| Genesee | 40 | 1 | 6 | 6 | 27 | 691 | 110 | 560 | 21 | 3 |
| Greene | 14 | 0 | 0 | 2 | 12 | 89 | 38 | 44 | 7 | 0 |
| Hamilton | 0 | 0 | 0 | 0 | 0 | 2 | 0 | 2 | 0 | 0 |
| Jefferson | 39 | 2 | 9 | 1 | 27 | 363 | 82 | 276 | 5 | 2 |
| Lewis | 11 | 1 | 2 | 2 | 6 | 187 | 74 | 105 | 8 | 1 |
| Montgomery | 26 | 0 | 0 | 4 | 22 | 315 | 31 | 278 | 6 | 0 |
| Otsego | 28 | 0 | 1 | 2 | 25 | 175 | 79 | 90 | 6 | 2 |
| Schuyler[3] | 9 | 0 | 0 | 1 | 8 | | 14 | | 1 | 0 |
| Seneca | 16 | 0 | 1 | 0 | 15 | 228 | 49 | 171 | 8 | 0 |
| Steuben | 0 | 0 | 0 | 0 | 0 | 77 | 26 | 51 | 0 | 0 |
| St. Lawrence | 30 | 0 | 0 | 0 | 30 | 65 | 18 | 45 | 2 | 2 |
| Sullivan | 32 | 0 | 3 | 3 | 26 | 407 | 111 | 288 | 8 | 4 |
| Wyoming | 12 | 0 | 1 | 1 | 10 | 188 | 53 | 128 | 7 | 1 |
| Yates | 5 | 1 | 0 | 0 | 4 | 181 | 54 | 126 | 1 | 0 |
| **NORTH CAROLINA - Metropolitan Counties** | | | | | | | | | | |
| Alamance | 140 | 3 | 8 | 15 | 114 | 1,095 | 462 | 538 | 95 | 3 |
| Alexander | 54 | 1 | 3 | 7 | 43 | 713 | 286 | 385 | 42 | 6 |
| Anson | 56 | 1 | 4 | 10 | 41 | 683 | 341 | 302 | 40 | 0 |
| Brunswick | 160 | 0 | 17 | 14 | 129 | 2,069 | 923 | 1,011 | 135 | 11 |
| Buncombe | 167 | 5 | 20 | 33 | 109 | 2,197 | 879 | 1,151 | 167 | 8 |
| Burke | 90 | 0 | 10 | 8 | 72 | 1,271 | 565 | 644 | 62 | 1 |
| Cabarrus | 44 | 2 | 1 | 18 | 23 | 957 | 612 | 291 | 54 | 12 |
| Caldwell | 61 | 1 | 7 | 7 | 46 | 1,596 | 670 | 837 | 89 | 11 |
| Catawba | 227 | 6 | 11 | 23 | 187 | 2,076 | 871 | 1,074 | 131 | 13 |
| Chatham | 68 | 1 | 9 | 12 | 46 | 823 | 330 | 452 | 41 | 13 |
| Cumberland | 575 | 13 | 23 | 138 | 401 | 4,262 | 1,480 | 2,484 | 298 | 60 |
| Currituck | 48 | 0 | 3 | 3 | 42 | 640 | 175 | 449 | 16 | 2 |
| Davie | 59 | 0 | 5 | 4 | 50 | 581 | 206 | 336 | 39 | 3 |
| Durham | 45 | 1 | 1 | 20 | 23 | 934 | 409 | 466 | 59 | 1 |
| Edgecombe | 80 | 2 | 9 | 15 | 54 | 616 | 326 | 262 | 28 | 7 |
| Forsyth | 267 | 2 | 17 | 36 | 212 | 2,598 | 711 | 1,769 | 118 | 13 |
| Franklin | 52 | 1 | 5 | 16 | 30 | 987 | 407 | 450 | 130 | 2 |
| Gaston | 10 | 0 | 0 | 0 | 10 | 0 | 0 | 0 | 0 | 0 |
| Guilford | 166 | 1 | 7 | 31 | 127 | 1,930 | 825 | 1,001 | 104 | 19 |
| Haywood | 89 | 1 | 9 | 6 | 73 | 760 | 344 | 384 | 32 | 10 |
| Henderson | 98 | 2 | 19 | 11 | 66 | 1,161 | 460 | 584 | 117 | 5 |
| Hoke | 44 | 1 | 3 | 14 | 26 | 1,016 | 786 | 178 | 52 | 1 |

[1] The FBI does not publish arson data unless it receives data from either the agency or the state for all 12 months of the calendar year.
[2] The FBI determined that the agency's data were overreported. Consequently, affected data are not included in this table.
[3] The FBI determined that the agency's data were underreported. Consequently, affected data are not included in this table.

**Table 10. Offenses Known to Law Enforcement, by State Metropolitan and Nonmetropolitan Counties, 2009—*Continued***

(Number.)

| State/County | Violent crime | Murder and non-negligent man-slaughter | Forcible rape | Robbery | Aggravated assault | Property crime | Burglary | Larceny-theft | Motor vehicle theft | Arson[1] |
|---|---|---|---|---|---|---|---|---|---|---|
| Johnston | 141 | 2 | 28 | 22 | 89 | 2,384 | 942 | 1,228 | 214 | 6 |
| Madison | 9 | 0 | 5 | 2 | 2 | 204 | 98 | 97 | 9 | 4 |
| Nash | 66 | 1 | 6 | 15 | 44 | 694 | 345 | 297 | 52 | 9 |
| New Hanover | 176 | 3 | 13 | 49 | 111 | 2,692 | 705 | 1,911 | 76 | 9 |
| Onslow | 302 | 3 | 56 | 47 | 196 | 3,269 | 1,303 | 1,838 | 128 | 39 |
| Orange | 39 | 3 | 8 | 8 | 20 | 633 | 366 | 236 | 31 | 4 |
| Pender[2,3] | | 1 | 9 | 9 | 365 | | | 433 | | 2 |
| Person | 63 | 3 | 5 | 1 | 54 | 608 | 312 | 274 | 22 | 4 |
| Pitt | 231 | 3 | 13 | 30 | 185 | 1,421 | 592 | 754 | 75 | 9 |
| Randolph | 135 | 5 | 6 | 41 | 83 | 2,114 | 662 | 1,346 | 106 | 8 |
| Rockingham | 108 | 1 | 2 | 22 | 83 | 1,379 | 546 | 756 | 77 | 1 |
| Stokes | 121 | 3 | 4 | 5 | 109 | 892 | 373 | 445 | 74 | 3 |
| Union | 172 | 3 | 15 | 28 | 126 | 2,392 | 865 | 1,418 | 109 | 19 |
| Wake | 202 | 6 | 21 | 33 | 142 | 2,497 | 1,023 | 1,234 | 240 | 17 |
| Wayne | 147 | 3 | 2 | 29 | 113 | 1,915 | 857 | 913 | 145 | 7 |
| Yadkin | 58 | 2 | 9 | 3 | 44 | 587 | 242 | 314 | 31 | 3 |
| **NORTH CAROLINA - Nonmetropolitan Counties** | | | | | | | | | | |
| Ashe | 42 | 0 | 5 | 1 | 36 | 361 | 222 | 118 | 21 | 3 |
| Avery | 20 | 0 | 1 | 4 | 15 | 194 | 81 | 110 | 3 | 2 |
| Beaufort | 116 | 3 | 5 | 18 | 90 | 762 | 346 | 373 | 43 | 7 |
| Bertie | 39 | 4 | 4 | 9 | 22 | 320 | 158 | 149 | 13 | 2 |
| Bladen | 117 | 6 | 0 | 19 | 92 | 1,033 | 386 | 608 | 39 | 16 |
| Camden | 6 | 0 | 0 | 1 | 5 | 74 | 24 | 48 | 2 | 2 |
| Carteret | 60 | 1 | 5 | 3 | 51 | 799 | 292 | 464 | 43 | 1 |
| Cherokee | 21 | 0 | 6 | 1 | 14 | 371 | 83 | 283 | 5 | 4 |
| Chowan | 15 | 1 | 3 | 1 | 10 | 130 | 63 | 63 | 4 | 1 |
| Clay | 18 | 0 | 2 | 1 | 15 | 147 | 61 | 76 | 10 | 1 |
| Cleveland | 38 | 0 | 17 | 19 | 2 | 1,719 | 748 | 880 | 91 | 3 |
| Columbus | 179 | 3 | 2 | 23 | 151 | 1,609 | 778 | 688 | 143 | 5 |
| Craven[3] | | 3 | 4 | 12 | | 1,060 | 468 | 525 | 67 | 4 |
| Dare | 34 | 0 | 4 | 3 | 27 | 794 | 209 | 569 | 16 | 8 |
| Davidson | 136 | 0 | 14 | 29 | 93 | 1,832 | 777 | 921 | 134 | 25 |
| Duplin[3] | 85 | 1 | 7 | 6 | 71 | | 468 | 426 | | 12 |
| Granville | 60 | 0 | 6 | 14 | 40 | 821 | 311 | 462 | 48 | 7 |
| Halifax | 144 | 4 | 5 | 25 | 110 | 984 | 459 | 470 | 55 | 10 |
| Hertford | 42 | 1 | 4 | 11 | 26 | 367 | 210 | 139 | 18 | 1 |
| Jackson | 122 | 0 | 8 | 5 | 109 | 792 | 383 | 356 | 53 | 3 |
| Lee | 26 | 0 | 2 | 5 | 19 | 649 | 262 | 335 | 52 | 4 |
| Lenoir[3] | 162 | 0 | 3 | 8 | 151 | | 355 | | 23 | 5 |
| Lincoln | 53 | 2 | 8 | 12 | 31 | 1,809 | 625 | 1,109 | 75 | 8 |
| Macon | 16 | 0 | 5 | 3 | 8 | 504 | 214 | 262 | 28 | 1 |
| Martin | 69 | 1 | 6 | 7 | 55 | 367 | 189 | 161 | 17 | 2 |
| McDowell | 34 | 3 | 4 | 3 | 24 | 531 | 278 | 214 | 39 | 9 |
| Montgomery | 29 | 4 | 5 | 2 | 18 | 432 | 139 | 275 | 18 | 1 |
| Moore | 75 | 10 | 9 | 9 | 47 | 743 | 366 | 324 | 53 | 18 |
| Northampton | 46 | 1 | 2 | 10 | 33 | 381 | 202 | 148 | 31 | 1 |
| Pamlico | 33 | 0 | 5 | 3 | 25 | 271 | 96 | 165 | 10 | 0 |
| Pasquotank | 42 | 0 | 6 | 6 | 30 | 325 | 121 | 196 | 8 | 4 |
| Perquimans | 2 | 0 | 2 | 0 | 0 | 99 | 63 | 33 | 3 | 2 |
| Polk | 20 | 0 | 3 | 0 | 17 | 235 | 47 | 173 | 15 | 2 |
| Richmond | 141 | 3 | 11 | 38 | 89 | 1,163 | 503 | 583 | 77 | 24 |
| Robeson | 678 | 2 | 18 | 139 | 519 | 4,227 | 2,414 | 1,470 | 343 | 44 |
| Rutherford | 100 | 0 | 13 | 12 | 75 | 1,133 | 479 | 573 | 81 | 17 |
| Sampson | 96 | 1 | 9 | 23 | 63 | 1,256 | 610 | 550 | 96 | 16 |
| Scotland | 83 | 4 | 8 | 14 | 57 | 679 | 382 | 232 | 65 | 8 |
| Stanly | 35 | 1 | 8 | 1 | 25 | 491 | 260 | 217 | 14 | 4 |
| Surry | 122 | 2 | 18 | 9 | 93 | 1,087 | 504 | 477 | 106 | 17 |
| Swain | 53 | 0 | 6 | 1 | 46 | 290 | 102 | 167 | 21 | 4 |
| Tyrrell | 9 | 0 | 2 | 3 | 4 | 55 | 11 | 40 | 4 | 1 |
| Vance | 96 | 3 | 6 | 17 | 70 | 1,300 | 676 | 558 | 66 | 7 |
| Warren | 55 | 1 | 6 | 7 | 41 | 626 | 304 | 286 | 36 | 6 |
| Washington | 42 | 1 | 2 | 2 | 37 | 147 | 67 | 65 | 15 | 1 |
| Wilkes | 133 | 3 | 7 | 16 | 107 | 1,371 | 668 | 604 | 99 | 3 |
| Wilson | 86 | 3 | 3 | 20 | 60 | 720 | 236 | 432 | 52 | 5 |
| Yancey | 11 | 2 | 2 | 0 | 7 | 110 | 64 | 40 | 6 | 0 |
| **NORTH DAKOTA - Metropolitan Counties** | | | | | | | | | | |
| Burleigh | 11 | 1 | 2 | 0 | 8 | 192 | 41 | 136 | 15 | 1 |
| Cass | 5 | 0 | 2 | 0 | 3 | 184 | 47 | 120 | 17 | 6 |
| Grand Forks | 12 | 0 | 1 | 1 | 10 | 116 | 39 | 61 | 16 | 1 |
| Morton | 6 | 0 | 1 | 0 | 5 | 74 | 9 | 59 | 6 | 0 |

[1] The FBI does not publish arson data unless it receives data from either the agency or the state for all 12 months of the calendar year.
[2] The FBI determined that the agency's data were overreported. Consequently, affected data are not included in this table.
[3] The FBI determined that the agency's data were underreported. Consequently, affected data are not included in this table.

## Table 10. Offenses Known to Law Enforcement, by State Metropolitan and Nonmetropolitan Counties, 2009—*Continued*

(Number.)

| State/County | Violent crime | Murder and non-negligent man-slaughter | Forcible rape | Robbery | Aggravated assault | Property crime | Burglary | Larceny-theft | Motor vehicle theft | Arson[1] |
|---|---|---|---|---|---|---|---|---|---|---|
| **NORTH DAKOTA - Nonmetropolitan Counties** | | | | | | | | | | |
| Adams | 2 | 0 | 0 | 0 | 2 | 8 | 5 | 2 | 1 | 0 |
| Barnes | 2 | 0 | 0 | 0 | 2 | 13 | 3 | 8 | 2 | 0 |
| Bottineau | 0 | 0 | 0 | 0 | 0 | 50 | 11 | 35 | 4 | 0 |
| Burke | 0 | 0 | 0 | 0 | 0 | 21 | 4 | 16 | 1 | 0 |
| Cavalier | 3 | 0 | 0 | 0 | 3 | 42 | 7 | 33 | 2 | 1 |
| Dickey | 0 | 0 | 0 | 0 | 0 | 5 | 1 | 3 | 1 | 2 |
| Eddy | 3 | 0 | 0 | 0 | 3 | 5 | 1 | 4 | 0 | 0 |
| Emmons | 0 | 0 | 0 | 0 | 0 | 21 | 10 | 9 | 2 | 1 |
| Grant | 0 | 0 | 0 | 0 | 0 | 7 | 1 | 4 | 2 | 0 |
| Griggs | 0 | 0 | 0 | 0 | 0 | 0 | 0 | 0 | 0 | 0 |
| Hettinger | 0 | 0 | 0 | 0 | 0 | 5 | 0 | 4 | 1 | 0 |
| Kidder | 0 | 0 | 0 | 0 | 0 | 2 | 1 | 1 | 0 | 0 |
| Lamoure | 1 | 0 | 0 | 0 | 1 | 2 | 0 | 0 | 2 | 0 |
| Logan | 0 | 0 | 0 | 0 | 0 | 3 | 1 | 2 | 0 | 0 |
| McHenry | 2 | 1 | 1 | 0 | 0 | 14 | 3 | 10 | 1 | 0 |
| McIntosh | 1 | 0 | 0 | 0 | 1 | 4 | 2 | 1 | 1 | 0 |
| McKenzie | 0 | 0 | 0 | 0 | 0 | 30 | 3 | 25 | 2 | 0 |
| McLean | 6 | 0 | 3 | 0 | 3 | 84 | 21 | 53 | 10 | 1 |
| Mercer | 0 | 0 | 0 | 0 | 0 | 40 | 8 | 30 | 2 | 2 |
| Mountrail | 3 | 0 | 0 | 0 | 3 | 62 | 18 | 36 | 8 | 0 |
| Nelson | 4 | 0 | 0 | 1 | 3 | 21 | 4 | 13 | 4 | 0 |
| Oliver | 0 | 0 | 0 | 0 | 0 | 7 | 1 | 6 | 0 | 0 |
| Pembina | 6 | 1 | 1 | 0 | 4 | 15 | 5 | 9 | 1 | 0 |
| Pierce | 2 | 0 | 0 | 1 | 1 | 12 | 4 | 8 | 0 | 1 |
| Ramsey | 3 | 0 | 0 | 0 | 3 | 20 | 5 | 11 | 4 | 0 |
| Ransom | 2 | 0 | 2 | 0 | 0 | 27 | 13 | 11 | 3 | 0 |
| Renville | 1 | 0 | 0 | 1 | 0 | 13 | 1 | 12 | 0 | 0 |
| Richland | 5 | 0 | 2 | 0 | 3 | 90 | 34 | 53 | 3 | 0 |
| Rolette | 3 | 0 | 0 | 0 | 3 | 8 | 7 | 1 | 0 | 0 |
| Sargent | 3 | 0 | 0 | 0 | 3 | 24 | 2 | 19 | 3 | 1 |
| Sheridan | 1 | 0 | 0 | 0 | 1 | 16 | 5 | 11 | 0 | 0 |
| Slope | 0 | 0 | 0 | 0 | 0 | 4 | 0 | 4 | 0 | 0 |
| Stark | 1 | 0 | 0 | 0 | 1 | 40 | 3 | 34 | 3 | 0 |
| Stutsman | 6 | 0 | 4 | 0 | 2 | 40 | 8 | 29 | 3 | 1 |
| Towner | 0 | 0 | 0 | 0 | 0 | 6 | 2 | 3 | 1 | 0 |
| Traill | 1 | 0 | 0 | 1 | 0 | 28 | 5 | 20 | 3 | 0 |
| Walsh | 2 | 0 | 1 | 0 | 1 | 81 | 17 | 52 | 12 | 2 |
| Ward | 18 | 0 | 6 | 2 | 10 | 147 | 28 | 99 | 20 | 2 |
| Wells | 0 | 0 | 0 | 0 | 0 | 7 | 2 | 5 | 0 | 0 |
| Williams | 10 | 0 | 2 | 0 | 8 | 59 | 19 | 30 | 10 | 0 |
| **OHIO - Metropolitan Counties** | | | | | | | | | | |
| Allen | 53 | 1 | 9 | 16 | 27 | 1,103 | 323 | 724 | 56 | 2 |
| Belmont | 33 | 2 | 14 | 9 | 8 | 494 | 139 | 325 | 30 | 9 |
| Brown | 9 | 0 | 6 | 2 | 1 | 384 | 149 | 217 | 18 | 2 |
| Butler | 67 | 0 | 17 | 9 | 41 | 825 | 226 | 599 | 0 | 7 |
| Carroll | 1 | 0 | 1 | 0 | 0 | 67 | 23 | 43 | 1 | 0 |
| Clark | 20 | 0 | 6 | 7 | 7 | 904 | 225 | 651 | 28 | 7 |
| Clermont | 105 | 0 | 21 | 7 | 77 | 1,633 | 541 | 1,047 | 45 | 11 |
| Delaware | 48 | 1 | 23 | 13 | 11 | 1,015 | 324 | 669 | 22 | 5 |
| Erie | 21 | 2 | 2 | 2 | 15 | 555 | 165 | 366 | 24 | 3 |
| Fulton | 16 | 0 | 2 | 3 | 11 | 324 | 124 | 176 | 24 | 5 |
| Geauga | 7 | 0 | 0 | 0 | 7 | 285 | 113 | 159 | 13 | 0 |
| Greene | 11 | 1 | 2 | 3 | 5 | 401 | 135 | 258 | 8 | 3 |
| Hamilton | 249 | 5 | 46 | 147 | 51 | 7,197 | 1,280 | 5,730 | 187 | 31 |
| Jefferson | 26 | 0 | 2 | 3 | 21 | 366 | 99 | 241 | 26 | 1 |
| Licking | 20 | 2 | 4 | 3 | 11 | 875 | 272 | 522 | 81 | 6 |
| Lorain | 52 | 2 | 13 | 20 | 17 | 840 | 439 | 391 | 10 | 19 |
| Lucas | 93 | 0 | 13 | 13 | 67 | 1,501 | 416 | 981 | 104 | 13 |
| Mahoning | 2 | 0 | 0 | 1 | 1 | 201 | 69 | 120 | 12 | 0 |
| Montgomery | 375 | 6 | 36 | 126 | 207 | 1,900 | 691 | 1,054 | 155 | 21 |
| Morrow | 7 | 0 | 3 | 0 | 4 | 210 | 111 | 92 | 7 | 0 |
| Ottawa | 3 | 0 | 2 | 0 | 1 | 320 | 67 | 234 | 19 | 0 |
| Pickaway | 41 | 0 | 6 | 8 | 27 | 1,095 | 466 | 607 | 22 | 17 |
| Preble | 10 | 0 | 2 | 1 | 7 | 414 | 178 | 205 | 31 | 3 |
| Richland | 55 | 0 | 14 | 8 | 33 | 1,085 | 440 | 623 | 22 | 6 |
| Stark | 93 | 2 | 18 | 46 | 27 | 1,027 | 332 | 629 | 66 | 11 |
| Summit | 37 | 1 | 13 | 15 | 8 | 1,041 | 222 | 775 | 44 | 5 |
| Trumbull | 23 | 0 | 4 | 4 | 15 | 518 | 188 | 300 | 30 | 3 |
| Union | 6 | 0 | 0 | 0 | 6 | 326 | 95 | 216 | 15 | 3 |
| Washington | 37 | 1 | 13 | 5 | 18 | 398 | 145 | 239 | 14 | 0 |
| Wood | 7 | 0 | 5 | 0 | 2 | 465 | 153 | 303 | 9 | 5 |

[1] The FBI does not publish arson data unless it receives data from either the agency or the state for all 12 months of the calendar year.

**Table 10. Offenses Known to Law Enforcement, by State Metropolitan and Nonmetropolitan Counties, 2009—*Continued***

(Number.)

| State/County | Violent crime | Murder and non-negligent man-slaughter | Forcible rape | Robbery | Aggravated assault | Property crime | Burglary | Larceny-theft | Motor vehicle theft | Arson[1] |
|---|---|---|---|---|---|---|---|---|---|---|
| **OHIO - Nonmetropolitan Counties** | | | | | | | | | | |
| Adams | 4 | 0 | 2 | 0 | 2 | 166 | 64 | 94 | 8 | 1 |
| Ashland | 14 | 0 | 3 | 1 | 10 | 287 | 135 | 140 | 12 | 1 |
| Auglaize | 6 | 0 | 5 | 0 | 1 | 249 | 109 | 136 | 4 | 1 |
| Champaign | 40 | 0 | 7 | 1 | 32 | 401 | 107 | 274 | 20 | 1 |
| Clinton | 13 | 0 | 4 | 1 | 8 | 193 | 69 | 110 | 14 | 0 |
| Columbiana | 6 | 0 | 1 | 3 | 2 | 31 | 13 | 13 | 5 | 1 |
| Coshocton | 17 | 0 | 5 | 4 | 8 | 680 | 184 | 470 | 26 | 6 |
| Crawford | 13 | 0 | 2 | 2 | 9 | 232 | 85 | 142 | 5 | 0 |
| Darke | 26 | 1 | 10 | 4 | 11 | 480 | 171 | 288 | 21 | 6 |
| Defiance | 6 | 0 | 3 | 0 | 3 | 165 | 37 | 123 | 5 | 3 |
| Fayette | 17 | 0 | 3 | 5 | 9 | 528 | 129 | 381 | 18 | 6 |
| Gallia | 25 | 3 | 8 | 8 | 6 | 594 | 277 | 293 | 24 | 4 |
| Guernsey | 6 | 1 | 3 | 0 | 2 | 198 | 82 | 109 | 7 | 1 |
| Hancock | 9 | 0 | 1 | 1 | 7 | 246 | 86 | 155 | 5 | 3 |
| Hardin | 9 | 0 | 5 | 1 | 3 | 232 | 87 | 139 | 6 | 1 |
| Harrison | 4 | 0 | 0 | 0 | 4 | 102 | 56 | 40 | 6 | 0 |
| Henry | 12 | 0 | 9 | 2 | 1 | 309 | 95 | 200 | 14 | 3 |
| Highland | 28 | 0 | 2 | 0 | 26 | 535 | 209 | 282 | 44 | 0 |
| Hocking | 2 | 0 | 1 | 1 | 0 | 338 | 163 | 149 | 26 | 0 |
| Holmes | 13 | 0 | 6 | 0 | 7 | 322 | 105 | 201 | 16 | 6 |
| Logan | 22 | 0 | 10 | 0 | 12 | 426 | 139 | 276 | 11 | 4 |
| Marion | 10 | 0 | 2 | 4 | 4 | 644 | 112 | 526 | 6 | 3 |
| Mercer | 13 | 0 | 6 | 0 | 7 | 291 | 53 | 233 | 5 | 2 |
| Monroe | 4 | 0 | 0 | 0 | 4 | 48 | 20 | 26 | 2 | 0 |
| Morgan | 6 | 1 | 3 | 1 | 1 | 188 | 75 | 97 | 16 | 5 |
| Muskingum | 36 | 0 | 16 | 8 | 12 | 1,060 | 265 | 704 | 91 | 4 |
| Paulding | 12 | 0 | 2 | 1 | 9 | 154 | 49 | 105 | 0 | 0 |
| Pike | 9 | 1 | 3 | 2 | 3 | 402 | 146 | 237 | 19 | 9 |
| Putnam | 2 | 0 | 1 | 0 | 1 | 61 | 48 | 13 | 0 | 0 |
| Ross | 39 | 0 | 16 | 12 | 11 | 1,668 | 543 | 1,023 | 102 | 4 |
| Scioto | 62 | 3 | 8 | 25 | 26 | 2,064 | 840 | 1,133 | 91 | 25 |
| Seneca | 1 | 0 | 0 | 0 | 1 | 302 | 137 | 160 | 5 | 1 |
| Shelby | 16 | 0 | 0 | 4 | 12 | 121 | 57 | 56 | 8 | 1 |
| Tuscarawas | 15 | 0 | 3 | 2 | 10 | 298 | 101 | 166 | 31 | 0 |
| Van Wert | 9 | 0 | 2 | 1 | 6 | 179 | 72 | 98 | 9 | 0 |
| Wayne | 27 | 0 | 15 | 2 | 10 | 679 | 316 | 336 | 27 | 10 |
| Williams | 12 | 0 | 9 | 1 | 2 | 230 | 50 | 159 | 21 | 2 |
| Wyandot | 3 | 0 | 0 | 0 | 3 | 13 | 6 | 7 | 0 | 0 |
| **OKLAHOMA - Metropolitan Counties** | | | | | | | | | | |
| Canadian[2] | | 0 | 3 | 5 | | 104 | 58 | 28 | 18 | 1 |
| Cleveland | 60 | 1 | 10 | 3 | 46 | 294 | 114 | 147 | 33 | 4 |
| Comanche[6] | 42 | 0 | 5 | 1 | 36 | 339 | 125 | 171 | 43 | 6 |
| Creek | 54 | 0 | 9 | 3 | 42 | 529 | 227 | 258 | 44 | 9 |
| Grady[6] | 28 | 0 | 6 | 2 | 20 | 366 | 114 | 218 | 34 | 3 |
| Le Flore | 72 | 4 | 0 | 1 | 67 | 396 | 155 | 214 | 27 | 3 |
| Lincoln[6] | 36 | 0 | 4 | 1 | 31 | 250 | 69 | 145 | 36 | 4 |
| McClain[6] | 20 | 0 | 4 | 3 | 13 | 263 | 112 | 121 | 30 | 1 |
| Oklahoma | 20 | 0 | 1 | 2 | 17 | 220 | 79 | 118 | 23 | 0 |
| Okmulgee | 28 | 1 | 3 | 3 | 21 | 177 | 70 | 89 | 18 | 9 |
| Osage | 46 | 1 | 9 | 3 | 33 | 376 | 160 | 195 | 21 | 16 |
| Pawnee | 34 | 1 | 4 | 1 | 28 | 193 | 79 | 98 | 16 | 1 |
| Rogers | 31 | 0 | 3 | 2 | 26 | 437 | 106 | 255 | 76 | 0 |
| Sequoyah | 56 | 1 | 6 | 1 | 48 | 429 | 184 | 238 | 7 | 8 |
| Tulsa | 226 | 0 | 13 | 17 | 196 | 883 | 368 | 407 | 108 | 5 |
| Wagoner | 39 | 2 | 5 | 4 | 28 | 447 | 147 | 252 | 48 | 4 |
| **OKLAHOMA - Nonmetropolitan Counties** | | | | | | | | | | |
| Adair | 49 | 2 | 6 | 1 | 40 | 229 | 104 | 100 | 25 | 5 |
| Alfalfa[6] | 0 | 0 | 0 | 0 | 0 | 36 | 9 | 22 | 5 | 1 |
| Atoka[6] | 15 | 1 | 2 | 0 | 12 | 116 | 38 | 65 | 13 | 0 |
| Beckham | 14 | 0 | 2 | 0 | 12 | 52 | 14 | 31 | 7 | 2 |
| Blaine[6] | 4 | 0 | 0 | 0 | 4 | 37 | 8 | 28 | 1 | 1 |
| Bryan[6] | 61 | 1 | 5 | 2 | 53 | 294 | 114 | 138 | 42 | 3 |
| Caddo | 8 | 0 | 1 | 0 | 7 | 132 | 50 | 69 | 13 | 1 |
| Carter | 64 | 0 | 9 | 3 | 52 | 233 | 90 | 120 | 23 | 4 |
| Cherokee[6] | 81 | 0 | 7 | 0 | 74 | 526 | 212 | 262 | 52 | 4 |
| Choctaw | 20 | 0 | 0 | 0 | 20 | 168 | 78 | 69 | 21 | 3 |
| Cimarron[6] | 0 | 0 | 0 | 0 | 0 | 0 | 0 | 0 | 0 | 0 |
| Coal[6] | 10 | 0 | 1 | 0 | 9 | 81 | 14 | 62 | 5 | 4 |
| Custer | 5 | 0 | 1 | 0 | 4 | 71 | 29 | 42 | 0 | 0 |
| Delaware | 85 | 2 | 30 | 0 | 53 | 418 | 214 | 163 | 41 | 3 |

[1] The FBI does not publish arson data unless it receives data from either the agency or the state for all 12 months of the calendar year.
[2] The FBI determined that the agency's data were overreported. Consequently, affected data are not included in this table.
[6] Because of changes in the state/local agency's reporting practices, figures are not comparable to previous years' data.

## Table 10. Offenses Known to Law Enforcement, by State Metropolitan and Nonmetropolitan Counties, 2009—*Continued*

(Number.)

| State/County | Violent crime | Murder and non-negligent man-slaughter | Forcible rape | Robbery | Aggravated assault | Property crime | Burglary | Larceny-theft | Motor vehicle theft | Arson[1] |
|---|---|---|---|---|---|---|---|---|---|---|
| Dewey | 4 | 0 | 1 | 0 | 3 | 25 | 10 | 13 | 2 | 0 |
| Ellis | 4 | 0 | 2 | 0 | 2 | 41 | 11 | 23 | 7 | 0 |
| Garfield | 4 | 0 | 0 | 0 | 4 | 92 | 33 | 55 | 4 | 7 |
| Garvin | 12 | 1 | 5 | 0 | 6 | 182 | 37 | 130 | 15 | 0 |
| Grant | 7 | 0 | 0 | 0 | 7 | 69 | 15 | 40 | 14 | 0 |
| Greer | 9 | 0 | 1 | 1 | 7 | 22 | 9 | 13 | 0 | 0 |
| Harmon | 1 | 0 | 0 | 0 | 1 | 20 | 12 | 8 | 0 | 0 |
| Harper[6] | 4 | 0 | 0 | 0 | 4 | 17 | 9 | 7 | 1 | 0 |
| Haskell[2] | | 0 | 0 | 1 | | 82 | 25 | 37 | 20 | 2 |
| Hughes | 3 | 0 | 2 | 0 | 1 | 122 | 33 | 69 | 20 | 1 |
| Jackson | 4 | 1 | 0 | 0 | 3 | 51 | 15 | 32 | 4 | 1 |
| Jefferson | 4 | 0 | 0 | 0 | 4 | 26 | 10 | 12 | 4 | 1 |
| Johnston | 20 | 0 | 0 | 0 | 20 | 8 | 4 | 4 | 0 | 0 |
| Kay | 21 | 0 | 3 | 0 | 18 | 95 | 39 | 48 | 8 | 6 |
| Kingfisher | 5 | 0 | 0 | 0 | 5 | 49 | 15 | 26 | 8 | 0 |
| Kiowa | 5 | 0 | 1 | 0 | 4 | 72 | 26 | 40 | 6 | 2 |
| Latimer[6] | 20 | 0 | 1 | 0 | 19 | 108 | 45 | 48 | 15 | 2 |
| Major[6] | 1 | 0 | 0 | 0 | 1 | 36 | 7 | 27 | 2 | 0 |
| Marshall[2] | | 2 | 2 | 1 | | 115 | 36 | 61 | 18 | 1 |
| Mayes | 20 | 0 | 2 | 0 | 18 | 216 | 78 | 116 | 22 | 0 |
| McCurtain | 55 | 1 | 8 | 2 | 44 | 539 | 195 | 311 | 33 | 17 |
| McIntosh | 33 | 1 | 4 | 3 | 25 | 333 | 124 | 192 | 17 | 6 |
| Murray | 18 | 0 | 4 | 1 | 13 | 46 | 20 | 25 | 1 | 0 |
| Muskogee | 54 | 0 | 6 | 2 | 46 | 301 | 133 | 143 | 25 | 17 |
| Noble[6] | 6 | 0 | 0 | 1 | 5 | 79 | 25 | 48 | 6 | 1 |
| Nowata | 16 | 0 | 0 | 0 | 16 | 80 | 32 | 41 | 7 | 2 |
| Okfuskee[6] | 18 | 0 | 3 | 0 | 15 | 77 | 38 | 26 | 13 | 3 |
| Ottawa | 8 | 1 | 1 | 3 | 3 | 116 | 77 | 30 | 9 | 6 |
| Payne | 22 | 0 | 4 | 1 | 17 | 252 | 84 | 150 | 18 | 8 |
| Pittsburg | 45 | 2 | 0 | 0 | 43 | 466 | 216 | 189 | 61 | 7 |
| Pontotoc[2] | | 0 | 0 | 2 | | 230 | 99 | 118 | 13 | 4 |
| Pottawatomie | 54 | 3 | 5 | 3 | 43 | 494 | 194 | 258 | 42 | 1 |
| Pushmataha | 14 | 1 | 0 | 2 | 11 | 147 | 77 | 53 | 17 | 1 |
| Seminole | 21 | 0 | 1 | 0 | 20 | 252 | 87 | 150 | 15 | 5 |
| Texas[6] | 2 | 0 | 0 | 1 | 1 | 40 | 13 | 25 | 2 | 0 |
| Tillman | 1 | 0 | 1 | 0 | 0 | 34 | 13 | 19 | 2 | 0 |
| Washington | 10 | 0 | 3 | 1 | 6 | 155 | 66 | 82 | 7 | 1 |
| Washita[6] | 19 | 0 | 4 | 1 | 14 | 60 | 24 | 31 | 5 | 2 |
| Woods[6] | 10 | 0 | 0 | 0 | 10 | 17 | 5 | 10 | 2 | 0 |
| Woodward | 6 | 0 | 0 | 0 | 6 | 83 | 25 | 53 | 5 | 5 |
| **OREGON - Metropolitan Counties** | | | | | | | | | | |
| Benton | 22 | 0 | 3 | 0 | 19 | 233 | 79 | 141 | 13 | 10 |
| Clackamas | 241 | 3 | 33 | 122 | 83 | 5,443 | 870 | 4,129 | 444 | 13 |
| Columbia | 15 | 0 | 3 | 0 | 12 | 149 | 61 | 61 | 27 | 0 |
| Deschutes | 121 | 2 | 8 | 5 | 106 | 877 | 269 | 569 | 39 | 5 |
| Jackson | 132 | 0 | 11 | 4 | 117 | 784 | 145 | 580 | 59 | 5 |
| Lane | 256 | 1 | 20 | 12 | 223 | 1,301 | 547 | 584 | 170 | 7 |
| Marion | 85 | 1 | 17 | 25 | 42 | 2,492 | 609 | 1,561 | 322 | 4 |
| Multnomah | 45 | 1 | 8 | 11 | 25 | 834 | 131 | 647 | 56 | 2 |
| Polk | 30 | 0 | 3 | 2 | 25 | 361 | 106 | 232 | 23 | 3 |
| Washington | 268 | 4 | 74 | 65 | 125 | 2,700 | 585 | 1,901 | 214 | 40 |
| Yamhill | 28 | 0 | 10 | 4 | 14 | 459 | 119 | 313 | 27 | 7 |
| **OREGON - Nonmetropolitan Counties** | | | | | | | | | | |
| Baker | 1 | 0 | 0 | 0 | 1 | 13 | 7 | 6 | 0 | 0 |
| Clatsop | 11 | 0 | 0 | 3 | 8 | 211 | 69 | 125 | 17 | 2 |
| Coos | 26 | 2 | 1 | 3 | 20 | 368 | 106 | 238 | 24 | 3 |
| Crook | 19 | 0 | 4 | 0 | 15 | 110 | 56 | 52 | 2 | 1 |
| Curry | 15 | 0 | 0 | 0 | 15 | 192 | 55 | 115 | 22 | 3 |
| Douglas | 35 | 1 | 13 | 4 | 17 | 859 | 256 | 538 | 65 | 19 |
| Gilliam | 0 | 0 | 0 | 0 | 0 | 18 | 8 | 7 | 3 | 0 |
| Grant | 0 | 0 | 0 | 0 | 0 | 46 | 9 | 37 | 0 | 1 |
| Harney | 2 | 0 | 1 | 0 | 1 | 23 | 7 | 13 | 3 | 0 |
| Hood River | 10 | 0 | 0 | 3 | 7 | 176 | 35 | 129 | 12 | 2 |
| Jefferson | 7 | 0 | 1 | 1 | 5 | 185 | 59 | 108 | 18 | 2 |
| Josephine | 33 | 0 | 6 | 2 | 25 | 723 | 263 | 372 | 88 | 2 |
| Klamath | 72 | 5 | 11 | 11 | 45 | 556 | 181 | 330 | 45 | 6 |
| Lincoln | 31 | 1 | 4 | 6 | 20 | 382 | 112 | 240 | 30 | 4 |
| Linn | 32 | 0 | 9 | 7 | 16 | 891 | 292 | 547 | 52 | 8 |
| Malheur | 3 | 1 | 2 | 0 | 0 | 147 | 49 | 89 | 9 | 2 |
| Morrow | 16 | 1 | 2 | 0 | 13 | 129 | 26 | 97 | 6 | 2 |
| Sherman | 0 | 0 | 0 | 0 | 0 | 38 | 4 | 31 | 3 | 0 |

[1] The FBI does not publish arson data unless it receives data from either the agency or the state for all 12 months of the calendar year.
[2] The FBI determined that the agency's data were overreported. Consequently, affected data are not included in this table.
[6] Because of changes in the state/local agency's reporting practices, figures are not comparable to previous years' data.

**Table 10. Offenses Known to Law Enforcement, by State Metropolitan and Nonmetropolitan Counties, 2009**—*Continued*

(Number.)

| State/County | Violent crime | Murder and non-negligent man-slaughter | Forcible rape | Robbery | Aggravated assault | Property crime | Burglary | Larceny-theft | Motor vehicle theft | Arson[1] |
|---|---|---|---|---|---|---|---|---|---|---|
| Tillamook | 14 | 0 | 0 | 3 | 11 | 330 | 119 | 189 | 22 | 3 |
| Umatilla | 35 | 1 | 5 | 2 | 27 | 354 | 116 | 184 | 54 | 0 |
| Union | 6 | 3 | 0 | 0 | 3 | 121 | 30 | 87 | 4 | 2 |
| Wallowa | 1 | 0 | 0 | 0 | 1 | 40 | 8 | 32 | 0 | 0 |
| Wasco | 9 | 2 | 0 | 3 | 4 | 160 | 68 | 70 | 22 | 1 |
| **PENNSYLVANIA - Metropolitan Counties** | | | | | | | | | | |
| Allegheny County Police Department | 23 | 0 | 3 | 0 | 20 | 149 | 2 | 138 | 9 | 142 |
| Beaver | 0 | 0 | 0 | 0 | 0 | 2 | 0 | 0 | 2 | 0 |
| Cumberland | 0 | 0 | 0 | 0 | 0 | 0 | 0 | 0 | 0 | 0 |
| Luzerne | 1 | 0 | 1 | 0 | 0 | 7 | 0 | 7 | 0 | 0 |
| Lycoming | 0 | 0 | 0 | 0 | 0 | 0 | 0 | 0 | 0 | 0 |
| Montgomery | 0 | 0 | 0 | 0 | 0 | 0 | 0 | 0 | 0 | 0 |
| Pike | 0 | 0 | 0 | 0 | 0 | 0 | 0 | 0 | 0 | 0 |
| Washington | 0 | 0 | 0 | 0 | 0 | 0 | 0 | 0 | 0 | 0 |
| York | 2 | 0 | 0 | 0 | 2 | 0 | 0 | 0 | 0 | 0 |
| **PENNSYLVANIA - Nonmetropolitan Counties** | | | | | | | | | | |
| Bradford | 0 | 0 | 0 | 0 | 0 | 0 | 0 | 0 | 0 | 0 |
| Clarion | 0 | 0 | 0 | 0 | 0 | 0 | 0 | 0 | 0 | 0 |
| Elk | 0 | 0 | 0 | 0 | 0 | 0 | 0 | 0 | 0 | 0 |
| Franklin | 0 | 0 | 0 | 0 | 0 | 0 | 0 | 0 | 0 | 0 |
| Greene | 0 | 0 | 0 | 0 | 0 | 0 | 0 | 0 | 0 | 0 |
| Jefferson | 0 | 0 | 0 | 0 | 0 | 0 | 0 | 0 | 0 | 0 |
| Snyder | 0 | 0 | 0 | 0 | 0 | 0 | 0 | 0 | 0 | 0 |
| Tioga | 0 | 0 | 0 | 0 | 0 | 0 | 0 | 0 | 0 | 0 |
| **SOUTH CAROLINA - Metropolitan Counties** | | | | | | | | | | |
| Aiken | 482 | 10 | 35 | 118 | 319 | 3,288 | 1,351 | 1,608 | 329 | 5 |
| Anderson | 920 | 8 | 57 | 113 | 742 | 5,430 | 1,603 | 3,322 | 505 | 19 |
| Berkeley | 652 | 5 | 41 | 95 | 511 | 3,297 | 999 | 1,904 | 394 | 11 |
| Calhoun | 71 | 3 | 1 | 6 | 61 | 321 | 108 | 146 | 67 | 5 |
| Charleston | 784 | 2 | 31 | 128 | 623 | 2,394 | 769 | 1,327 | 298 | 7 |
| Darlington | 416 | 7 | 35 | 39 | 335 | 2,171 | 841 | 1,157 | 173 | 20 |
| Dorchester | 434 | 1 | 18 | 71 | 344 | 2,424 | 765 | 1,444 | 215 | 4 |
| Edgefield | 21 | 0 | 0 | 2 | 19 | 417 | 160 | 232 | 25 | 1 |
| Fairfield | 175 | 0 | 3 | 9 | 163 | 511 | 162 | 329 | 20 | 0 |
| Florence | 357 | 3 | 13 | 83 | 258 | 2,679 | 794 | 1,633 | 252 | 7 |
| Greenville | 1,990 | 15 | 121 | 426 | 1,428 | 9,390 | 2,712 | 5,903 | 775 | 28 |
| Horry | 0 | 0 | 0 | 0 | 0 | 33 | 0 | 33 | 0 | 0 |
| Horry County Police Department | 961 | 11 | 39 | 183 | 728 | 7,351 | 1,808 | 4,758 | 785 | 35 |
| Kershaw | 258 | 3 | 17 | 18 | 220 | 1,489 | 457 | 894 | 138 | 12 |
| Laurens[2] | 353 | 5 | 29 | 32 | 287 | | 502 | 664 | | 10 |
| Lexington | 528 | 10 | 52 | 97 | 369 | 4,244 | 982 | 2,898 | 364 | 6 |
| Pickens | 262 | 2 | 35 | 22 | 203 | 1,662 | 420 | 1,106 | 136 | 5 |
| Richland | 2,414 | 12 | 99 | 394 | 1,909 | 9,510 | 2,466 | 6,009 | 1,035 | 31 |
| Saluda | 33 | 1 | 13 | 0 | 19 | 258 | 86 | 149 | 23 | 1 |
| Spartanburg | 776 | 9 | 67 | 143 | 557 | 6,234 | 1,699 | 4,044 | 491 | 44 |
| Sumter[6] | 207 | 4 | 9 | 36 | 158 | 694 | 417 | 204 | 73 | 2 |
| York | 467 | 2 | 28 | 40 | 397 | 2,739 | 734 | 1,806 | 199 | 15 |
| **SOUTH CAROLINA - Nonmetropolitan Counties** | | | | | | | | | | |
| Abbeville | 51 | 0 | 2 | 2 | 47 | 285 | 125 | 149 | 11 | 5 |
| Allendale | 14 | 0 | 0 | 2 | 12 | 76 | 43 | 27 | 6 | 0 |
| Bamberg | 55 | 1 | 3 | 3 | 48 | 248 | 91 | 133 | 24 | 6 |
| Barnwell | 110 | 1 | 2 | 6 | 101 | 433 | 120 | 293 | 20 | 2 |
| Beaufort | 711 | 5 | 38 | 127 | 541 | 4,020 | 1,087 | 2,725 | 208 | 12 |
| Chester[2] | 239 | 2 | 11 | 15 | 211 | | 253 | 674 | | 6 |
| Chesterfield | 168 | 1 | 3 | 7 | 157 | 872 | 272 | 529 | 71 | 5 |
| Clarendon | 202 | 1 | 18 | 22 | 161 | 859 | 285 | 492 | 82 | 2 |
| Colleton | 233 | 8 | 9 | 19 | 197 | 1,289 | 400 | 711 | 178 | 16 |
| Dillon | 281 | 5 | 13 | 24 | 239 | 1,218 | 492 | 655 | 71 | 9 |
| Georgetown | 262 | 3 | 15 | 26 | 218 | 1,434 | 386 | 938 | 110 | 7 |
| Greenwood | 325 | 0 | 10 | 12 | 303 | 1,744 | 395 | 1,265 | 84 | 4 |
| Hampton | 94 | 3 | 6 | 7 | 78 | 304 | 104 | 175 | 25 | 0 |
| Jasper | 121 | 4 | 5 | 20 | 92 | 677 | 209 | 395 | 73 | 4 |
| Lancaster | 202 | 1 | 16 | 38 | 147 | 1,834 | 661 | 1,076 | 97 | 8 |
| Lee | 89 | 2 | 4 | 7 | 76 | 478 | 204 | 228 | 46 | 11 |
| Marion | 115 | 1 | 6 | 10 | 98 | 756 | 266 | 432 | 58 | 6 |
| Marlboro | 150 | 2 | 5 | 8 | 135 | 647 | 220 | 374 | 53 | 6 |
| McCormick | 28 | 0 | 1 | 1 | 26 | 91 | 28 | 44 | 19 | 1 |
| Newberry | 72 | 2 | 6 | 6 | 58 | 441 | 88 | 329 | 24 | 1 |
| Oconee | 315 | 2 | 40 | 20 | 253 | 1,413 | 432 | 902 | 79 | 5 |
| Orangeburg | 467 | 8 | 28 | 105 | 326 | 3,546 | 1,214 | 1,769 | 563 | 6 |
| Union | 95 | 0 | 0 | 12 | 83 | 450 | 142 | 280 | 28 | 0 |
| Williamsburg | 164 | 4 | 8 | 39 | 113 | 816 | 331 | 414 | 71 | 9 |

[1] The FBI does not publish arson data unless it receives data from either the agency or the state for all 12 months of the calendar year.
[2] The FBI determined that the agency's data were overreported. Consequently, affected data are not included in this table.
[6] Because of changes in the state/local agency's reporting practices, figures are not comparable to previous years' data.

## Table 10. Offenses Known to Law Enforcement, by State Metropolitan and Nonmetropolitan Counties, 2009—*Continued*

(Number.)

| State/County | Violent crime | Murder and non-negligent man-slaughter | Forcible rape | Robbery | Aggravated assault | Property crime | Burglary | Larceny-theft | Motor vehicle theft | Arson[1] |
|---|---|---|---|---|---|---|---|---|---|---|
| **SOUTH DAKOTA - Metropolitan Counties** | | | | | | | | | | |
| Lincoln | 5 | 0 | 0 | 0 | 5 | 98 | 27 | 65 | 6 | 1 |
| McCook | 3 | 0 | 0 | 0 | 3 | 46 | 1 | 45 | 0 | 0 |
| Meade | 7 | 0 | 3 | 0 | 4 | 46 | 17 | 24 | 5 | 0 |
| Minnehaha | 30 | 0 | 13 | 1 | 16 | 398 | 118 | 239 | 41 | 2 |
| Pennington | 60 | 0 | 30 | 0 | 30 | 328 | 59 | 257 | 12 | 5 |
| Turner | 5 | 0 | 0 | 0 | 5 | 33 | 13 | 18 | 2 | 0 |
| Union | 3 | 0 | 2 | 0 | 1 | 52 | 9 | 42 | 1 | 0 |
| **SOUTH DAKOTA - Nonmetropolitan Counties** | | | | | | | | | | |
| Aurora | 1 | 0 | 0 | 0 | 1 | 9 | 2 | 7 | 0 | 0 |
| Beadle | 0 | 0 | 0 | 0 | 0 | 22 | 9 | 12 | 1 | 0 |
| Bennett | 4 | 0 | 2 | 0 | 2 | 9 | 1 | 8 | 0 | 0 |
| Bon Homme | 1 | 0 | 1 | 0 | 0 | 1 | 1 | 0 | 0 | 0 |
| Brookings | 1 | 0 | 1 | 0 | 0 | 74 | 21 | 52 | 1 | 0 |
| Brown | 3 | 0 | 0 | 0 | 3 | 40 | 11 | 23 | 6 | 0 |
| Butte | 5 | 0 | 1 | 0 | 4 | 18 | 8 | 5 | 5 | 0 |
| Campbell | 0 | 0 | 0 | 0 | 0 | 8 | 4 | 3 | 1 | 0 |
| Charles Mix | 6 | 1 | 1 | 0 | 4 | 30 | 12 | 11 | 7 | 0 |
| Clay | 1 | 0 | 0 | 0 | 1 | 20 | 3 | 17 | 0 | 0 |
| Codington | 5 | 0 | 4 | 0 | 1 | 50 | 13 | 32 | 5 | 1 |
| Corson | 0 | 0 | 0 | 0 | 0 | 17 | 1 | 12 | 4 | 0 |
| Custer | 8 | 0 | 0 | 1 | 7 | 33 | 13 | 19 | 1 | 0 |
| Davison | 0 | 0 | 0 | 0 | 0 | 3 | 0 | 3 | 0 | 0 |
| Deuel | 5 | 0 | 0 | 0 | 5 | 29 | 8 | 17 | 4 | 0 |
| Dewey | 2 | 0 | 0 | 0 | 2 | 8 | 1 | 5 | 2 | 0 |
| Douglas | 1 | 0 | 0 | 0 | 1 | 2 | 0 | 2 | 0 | 0 |
| Edmunds | 0 | 0 | 0 | 0 | 0 | 1 | 1 | 0 | 0 | 0 |
| Faulk | 1 | 0 | 0 | 0 | 1 | 13 | 6 | 6 | 1 | 0 |
| Hamlin | 8 | 0 | 3 | 0 | 5 | 44 | 10 | 31 | 3 | 0 |
| Hand | 0 | 0 | 0 | 0 | 0 | 0 | 0 | 0 | 0 | 0 |
| Hanson | 1 | 1 | 0 | 0 | 0 | 9 | 5 | 3 | 1 | 0 |
| Harding | 1 | 0 | 0 | 0 | 1 | 0 | 0 | 0 | 0 | 0 |
| Hughes | 3 | 0 | 0 | 0 | 3 | 19 | 10 | 8 | 1 | 0 |
| Hutchinson | 0 | 0 | 0 | 0 | 0 | 0 | 0 | 0 | 0 | 0 |
| Jerauld | 0 | 0 | 0 | 0 | 0 | 5 | 2 | 2 | 1 | 0 |
| Lawrence | 1 | 0 | 0 | 0 | 1 | 43 | 18 | 20 | 5 | 1 |
| Marshall | 5 | 0 | 1 | 0 | 4 | 43 | 13 | 25 | 5 | 0 |
| McPherson | 1 | 0 | 0 | 0 | 1 | 3 | 2 | 1 | 0 | 0 |
| Miner | 1 | 0 | 0 | 0 | 1 | 20 | 15 | 5 | 0 | 0 |
| Moody | 0 | 0 | 0 | 0 | 0 | 15 | 2 | 10 | 3 | 0 |
| Perkins | 0 | 0 | 0 | 0 | 0 | 13 | 5 | 8 | 0 | 0 |
| Potter | 0 | 0 | 0 | 0 | 0 | 1 | 0 | 1 | 0 | 0 |
| Sanborn | 0 | 0 | 0 | 0 | 0 | 7 | 2 | 5 | 0 | 0 |
| Spink | 15 | 0 | 9 | 0 | 6 | 50 | 19 | 30 | 1 | 0 |
| Stanley | 0 | 0 | 0 | 0 | 0 | 68 | 2 | 63 | 3 | 0 |
| Sully | 1 | 1 | 0 | 0 | 0 | 1 | 0 | 1 | 0 | 0 |
| Tripp | 0 | 0 | 0 | 0 | 0 | 7 | 1 | 6 | 0 | 0 |
| Walworth | 1 | 0 | 0 | 0 | 1 | 10 | 3 | 7 | 0 | 0 |
| Yankton | 5 | 0 | 0 | 0 | 5 | 12 | 3 | 8 | 1 | 0 |
| Ziebach | 0 | 0 | 0 | 0 | 0 | 5 | 1 | 2 | 2 | 0 |
| **TENNESSEE - Metropolitan Counties** | | | | | | | | | | |
| Anderson | 115 | 1 | 13 | 4 | 97 | 909 | 438 | 417 | 54 | 8 |
| Blount | 242 | 2 | 31 | 15 | 194 | 1,573 | 647 | 832 | 94 | 7 |
| Bradley | 299 | 0 | 15 | 5 | 279 | 900 | 312 | 525 | 63 | 5 |
| Cannon | 12 | 0 | 0 | 1 | 11 | 180 | 75 | 78 | 27 | 0 |
| Carter | 62 | 1 | 3 | 6 | 52 | 723 | 311 | 371 | 41 | 9 |
| Cheatham | 109 | 2 | 4 | 4 | 99 | 624 | 215 | 342 | 67 | 4 |
| Chester | 33 | 0 | 2 | 0 | 31 | 146 | 39 | 90 | 17 | 0 |
| Dickson | 93 | 2 | 11 | 3 | 77 | 555 | 201 | 303 | 51 | 9 |
| Fayette | 173 | 1 | 7 | 11 | 154 | 571 | 209 | 312 | 50 | 2 |
| Grainger | 21 | 0 | 0 | 3 | 18 | 264 | 99 | 142 | 23 | 0 |
| Hamblen | 90 | 1 | 6 | 15 | 68 | 675 | 240 | 409 | 26 | 5 |
| Hamilton | 272 | 2 | 18 | 9 | 243 | 2,007 | 637 | 1,263 | 107 | 7 |
| Hartsville/Trousdale | 23 | 0 | 1 | 3 | 19 | 165 | 51 | 100 | 14 | 3 |
| Hawkins | 88 | 5 | 3 | 10 | 70 | 1,252 | 475 | 705 | 72 | 4 |
| Hickman | 61 | 1 | 15 | 1 | 44 | 221 | 93 | 96 | 32 | 1 |
| Jefferson | 90 | 1 | 7 | 10 | 72 | 835 | 334 | 456 | 45 | 5 |
| Knox | 584 | 4 | 18 | 150 | 412 | 5,412 | 1,854 | 3,219 | 339 | 33 |
| Loudon | 96 | 0 | 5 | 13 | 78 | 618 | 212 | 361 | 45 | 5 |
| Macon | 50 | 4 | 3 | 0 | 43 | 126 | 43 | 75 | 8 | 0 |
| Madison | 125 | 1 | 8 | 6 | 110 | 915 | 302 | 548 | 65 | 5 |

[1] The FBI does not publish arson data unless it receives data from either the agency or the state for all 12 months of the calendar year.

## Table 10. Offenses Known to Law Enforcement, by State Metropolitan and Nonmetropolitan Counties, 2009—*Continued*

(Number.)

| State/County | Violent crime | Murder and non-negligent man-slaughter | Forcible rape | Robbery | Aggravated assault | Property crime | Burglary | Larceny-theft | Motor vehicle theft | Arson[1] |
|---|---|---|---|---|---|---|---|---|---|---|
| Marion | 91 | 2 | 0 | 1 | 88 | 311 | 94 | 170 | 47 | 2 |
| Montgomery | 138 | 1 | 8 | 12 | 117 | 794 | 237 | 494 | 63 | 4 |
| Polk | 35 | 0 | 0 | 2 | 33 | 307 | 72 | 190 | 45 | 2 |
| Robertson | 88 | 0 | 5 | 1 | 82 | 442 | 180 | 224 | 38 | 2 |
| Rutherford | 203 | 3 | 19 | 16 | 165 | 1,345 | 452 | 799 | 94 | 13 |
| Sequatchie | 41 | 0 | 6 | 0 | 35 | 119 | 49 | 56 | 14 | 2 |
| Shelby | 461 | 6 | 36 | 76 | 343 | 3,466 | 1,270 | 1,958 | 238 | 24 |
| Smith | 18 | 0 | 0 | 0 | 18 | 21 | 7 | 4 | 10 | 0 |
| Stewart | 40 | 0 | 0 | 3 | 37 | 188 | 88 | 91 | 9 | 1 |
| Sullivan | 364 | 0 | 25 | 17 | 322 | 1,833 | 793 | 927 | 113 | 15 |
| Sumner | 151 | 1 | 15 | 4 | 131 | 784 | 255 | 484 | 45 | 13 |
| Tipton | 252 | 0 | 20 | 3 | 229 | 851 | 254 | 500 | 97 | 4 |
| Unicoi | 27 | 0 | 0 | 0 | 27 | 122 | 28 | 85 | 9 | 1 |
| Union | 35 | 0 | 0 | 4 | 31 | 244 | 114 | 110 | 20 | 2 |
| Washington | 228 | 3 | 9 | 8 | 208 | 999 | 405 | 530 | 64 | 6 |
| Williamson | 54 | 0 | 2 | 6 | 46 | 435 | 121 | 294 | 20 | 0 |
| Wilson | 293 | 3 | 17 | 8 | 265 | 1,130 | 397 | 642 | 91 | 1 |
| **TENNESSEE - Nonmetropolitan Counties** | | | | | | | | | | |
| Bedford | 74 | 0 | 7 | 2 | 65 | 286 | 112 | 153 | 21 | 4 |
| Benton | 25 | 0 | 0 | 2 | 23 | 205 | 69 | 113 | 23 | 1 |
| Bledsoe | 13 | 1 | 0 | 1 | 11 | 102 | 50 | 37 | 15 | 1 |
| Campbell | 96 | 0 | 6 | 8 | 82 | 1,031 | 432 | 538 | 61 | 17 |
| Carroll | 31 | 0 | 1 | 1 | 29 | 190 | 81 | 95 | 14 | 1 |
| Claiborne | 119 | 1 | 12 | 15 | 91 | 764 | 366 | 352 | 46 | 11 |
| Clay | 17 | 0 | 1 | 2 | 14 | 102 | 64 | 32 | 6 | 0 |
| Crockett | 13 | 0 | 0 | 1 | 12 | 93 | 32 | 58 | 3 | 0 |
| Cumberland | 87 | 5 | 5 | 6 | 71 | 930 | 489 | 378 | 63 | 3 |
| Decatur | 16 | 1 | 2 | 1 | 12 | 193 | 69 | 115 | 9 | 1 |
| DeKalb | 26 | 1 | 0 | 1 | 24 | 268 | 98 | 152 | 18 | 2 |
| Dyer | 39 | 0 | 1 | 5 | 33 | 336 | 109 | 209 | 18 | 1 |
| Fentress | 69 | 0 | 0 | 2 | 67 | 403 | 210 | 164 | 29 | 3 |
| Franklin | 41 | 1 | 8 | 1 | 31 | 280 | 78 | 179 | 23 | 4 |
| Gibson | 60 | 1 | 2 | 1 | 56 | 337 | 117 | 193 | 27 | 0 |
| Giles | 35 | 3 | 2 | 1 | 29 | 271 | 107 | 146 | 18 | 2 |
| Greene | 167 | 4 | 6 | 17 | 140 | 1,050 | 502 | 475 | 73 | 11 |
| Hancock | 2 | 0 | 0 | 0 | 2 | 117 | 48 | 67 | 2 | 1 |
| Hardeman | 76 | 6 | 5 | 3 | 62 | 322 | 136 | 143 | 43 | 6 |
| Hardin | 98 | 0 | 4 | 3 | 91 | 464 | 172 | 249 | 43 | 3 |
| Haywood | 57 | 0 | 4 | 3 | 50 | 233 | 106 | 104 | 23 | 5 |
| Henderson | 87 | 1 | 7 | 4 | 75 | 356 | 105 | 214 | 37 | 7 |
| Henry | 52 | 1 | 4 | 2 | 45 | 439 | 135 | 289 | 15 | 2 |
| Houston | 28 | 0 | 1 | 1 | 26 | 157 | 65 | 81 | 11 | 1 |
| Humphreys | 17 | 1 | 1 | 0 | 15 | 107 | 50 | 51 | 6 | 0 |
| Jackson | 18 | 2 | 1 | 1 | 14 | 140 | 38 | 93 | 9 | 2 |
| Johnson | 99 | 2 | 2 | 3 | 92 | 235 | 131 | 82 | 22 | 1 |
| Lake | 4 | 0 | 0 | 0 | 4 | 34 | 11 | 21 | 2 | 0 |
| Lauderdale | 43 | 0 | 4 | 2 | 37 | 376 | 184 | 159 | 33 | 0 |
| Lawrence | 88 | 0 | 8 | 4 | 76 | 595 | 233 | 308 | 54 | 7 |
| Lewis | 34 | 1 | 5 | 0 | 28 | 134 | 46 | 78 | 10 | 0 |
| Lincoln | 95 | 6 | 0 | 1 | 88 | 401 | 177 | 203 | 21 | 3 |
| Marshall | 24 | 1 | 0 | 0 | 23 | 154 | 44 | 93 | 17 | 2 |
| Maury | 139 | 1 | 12 | 6 | 120 | 796 | 206 | 525 | 65 | 8 |
| McMinn | 144 | 0 | 6 | 10 | 128 | 909 | 348 | 464 | 97 | 2 |
| McNairy | 48 | 2 | 2 | 4 | 40 | 415 | 135 | 241 | 39 | 5 |
| Meigs | 53 | 1 | 3 | 0 | 49 | 310 | 120 | 154 | 36 | 10 |
| Monroe | 138 | 2 | 9 | 1 | 126 | 492 | 176 | 279 | 37 | 5 |
| Moore | 10 | 0 | 2 | 0 | 8 | 100 | 20 | 77 | 3 | 0 |
| Obion | 26 | 0 | 3 | 2 | 21 | 212 | 35 | 161 | 16 | 2 |
| Overton | 32 | 2 | 0 | 1 | 29 | 268 | 122 | 135 | 11 | 3 |
| Perry | 21 | 0 | 4 | 0 | 17 | 143 | 43 | 98 | 2 | 2 |
| Pickett[4] | | | | 1 | | 53 | 3 | 47 | 3 | 0 |
| Putnam | 85 | 3 | 6 | 7 | 69 | 675 | 194 | 438 | 43 | 2 |
| Rhea | 76 | 0 | 3 | 1 | 72 | 317 | 90 | 200 | 27 | 0 |
| Roane | 44 | 1 | 3 | 4 | 36 | 768 | 169 | 546 | 53 | 0 |
| Scott | 110 | 0 | 10 | 0 | 100 | 510 | 202 | 281 | 27 | 4 |
| Sevier | 128 | 2 | 14 | 10 | 102 | 2,165 | 978 | 1,094 | 93 | 2 |
| Van Buren | 5 | 1 | 0 | 0 | 4 | 51 | 14 | 31 | 6 | 0 |
| Warren | 19 | 2 | 1 | 0 | 16 | 345 | 125 | 172 | 48 | 1 |
| Wayne | 25 | 1 | 1 | 0 | 23 | 101 | 22 | 60 | 19 | 4 |
| Weakley | 39 | 0 | 2 | 5 | 32 | 225 | 91 | 121 | 13 | 2 |
| White | 51 | 0 | 4 | 1 | 46 | 421 | 85 | 303 | 33 | 5 |

[1] The FBI does not publish arson data unless it receives data from either the agency or the state for all 12 months of the calendar year.

[4] The FBI determined that the agency did not follow national Uniform Crime Reporting (UCR) Program guidelines for reporting an offense. Consequently, this figure is not included in this table.

## Table 10. Offenses Known to Law Enforcement, by State Metropolitan and Nonmetropolitan Counties, 2009—*Continued*

(Number.)

| State/County | Violent crime | Murder and non-negligent man-slaughter | Forcible rape | Robbery | Aggravated assault | Property crime | Burglary | Larceny-theft | Motor vehicle theft | Arson[1] |
|---|---|---|---|---|---|---|---|---|---|---|
| **TEXAS - Metropolitan Counties** | | | | | | | | | | |
| Aransas | 30 | 0 | 1 | 0 | 29 | 502 | 207 | 269 | 26 | 0 |
| Archer | 10 | 0 | 1 | 2 | 7 | 81 | 30 | 47 | 4 | 3 |
| Armstrong | 0 | 0 | 0 | 0 | 0 | 18 | 2 | 10 | 6 | 2 |
| Atascosa | 38 | 2 | 2 | 5 | 29 | 313 | 163 | 122 | 28 | 4 |
| Austin | 17 | 1 | 1 | 1 | 14 | 127 | 44 | 69 | 14 | 0 |
| Bandera | 19 | 0 | 0 | 1 | 18 | 189 | 69 | 118 | 2 | 0 |
| Bastrop | 307 | 4 | 21 | 12 | 270 | 927 | 384 | 467 | 76 | 14 |
| Bell | 72 | 4 | 39 | 2 | 27 | 753 | 269 | 442 | 42 | 17 |
| Bexar | 649 | 16 | 95 | 115 | 423 | 6,914 | 2,299 | 4,202 | 413 | 105 |
| Bowie | 121 | 1 | 12 | 11 | 97 | 622 | 281 | 292 | 49 | 10 |
| Brazoria | 166 | 3 | 14 | 32 | 117 | 1,347 | 577 | 683 | 87 | 0 |
| Brazos | 63 | 0 | 2 | 3 | 58 | 466 | 206 | 235 | 25 | 1 |
| Burleson | 23 | 0 | 6 | 1 | 16 | 185 | 107 | 58 | 20 | 5 |
| Caldwell | 39 | 0 | 6 | 0 | 33 | 183 | 73 | 102 | 8 | 1 |
| Calhoun | 27 | 0 | 2 | 1 | 24 | 150 | 53 | 90 | 7 | 1 |
| Callahan | 3 | 0 | 2 | 0 | 1 | 40 | 15 | 22 | 3 | 3 |
| Cameron | 364 | 2 | 17 | 35 | 310 | 1,817 | 783 | 873 | 161 | 14 |
| Carson | 8 | 1 | 2 | 0 | 5 | 21 | 7 | 12 | 2 | 0 |
| Chambers | 84 | 2 | 2 | 3 | 77 | 489 | 160 | 273 | 56 | 2 |
| Clay | 10 | 0 | 0 | 1 | 9 | 113 | 44 | 66 | 3 | 2 |
| Collin | 81 | 1 | 26 | 2 | 52 | 798 | 394 | 335 | 69 | 0 |
| Comal | 158 | 1 | 17 | 11 | 129 | 873 | 290 | 552 | 31 | 9 |
| Coryell | 25 | 1 | 3 | 0 | 21 | 119 | 60 | 52 | 7 | 4 |
| Crosby | 1 | 0 | 0 | 0 | 1 | 3 | 0 | 3 | 0 | 0 |
| Dallas | 53 | 0 | 1 | 7 | 45 | 269 | 60 | 183 | 26 | 14 |
| Delta | 12 | 0 | 0 | 0 | 12 | 105 | 35 | 69 | 1 | 2 |
| Denton | 87 | 1 | 9 | 5 | 72 | 744 | 199 | 501 | 44 | 4 |
| Ector | 76 | 2 | 0 | 26 | 48 | 1,461 | 532 | 790 | 139 | 0 |
| Ellis | 103 | 3 | 8 | 3 | 89 | 840 | 326 | 434 | 80 | 6 |
| El Paso | 271 | 4 | 45 | 30 | 192 | 1,299 | 381 | 776 | 142 | 25 |
| Fort Bend | 1,037 | 8 | 61 | 152 | 816 | 4,769 | 1,769 | 2,714 | 286 | 33 |
| Galveston | 165 | 2 | 21 | 24 | 118 | 1,101 | 424 | 601 | 76 | 5 |
| Goliad | 11 | 0 | 1 | 0 | 10 | 55 | 31 | 21 | 3 | 0 |
| Grayson | 35 | 2 | 3 | 7 | 23 | 772 | 274 | 443 | 55 | 14 |
| Gregg | 102 | 1 | 22 | 10 | 69 | 728 | 201 | 385 | 142 | 5 |
| Guadalupe | 68 | 0 | 0 | 10 | 58 | 772 | 321 | 404 | 47 | 0 |
| Hardin | 38 | 2 | 8 | 0 | 28 | 353 | 102 | 204 | 47 | 2 |
| Harris | 8,439 | 96 | 281 | 2,975 | 5,087 | 54,903 | 15,053 | 33,921 | 5,929 | 435 |
| Hays | 139 | 0 | 29 | 8 | 102 | 1,313 | 371 | 924 | 18 | 0 |
| Hidalgo | 1,085 | 23 | 81 | 203 | 778 | 7,287 | 2,798 | 3,956 | 533 | 161 |
| Hunt | 130 | 1 | 1 | 13 | 115 | 1,088 | 517 | 491 | 80 | 1 |
| Irion | 3 | 0 | 0 | 0 | 3 | 32 | 9 | 23 | 0 | 0 |
| Jefferson | 32 | 0 | 6 | 12 | 14 | 470 | 159 | 250 | 61 | 3 |
| Johnson | 146 | 0 | 0 | 5 | 141 | 1,045 | 323 | 662 | 60 | 10 |
| Jones | 7 | 0 | 1 | 0 | 6 | 75 | 19 | 51 | 5 | 0 |
| Kaufman | 254 | 3 | 6 | 19 | 226 | 1,596 | 619 | 830 | 147 | 12 |
| Kendall | 26 | 0 | 16 | 2 | 8 | 196 | 49 | 133 | 14 | 1 |
| Lampasas | 8 | 0 | 0 | 1 | 7 | 87 | 33 | 49 | 5 | 0 |
| Liberty | 151 | 3 | 4 | 10 | 134 | 1,209 | 486 | 532 | 191 | 18 |
| Lubbock | 176 | 1 | 15 | 10 | 150 | 799 | 402 | 332 | 65 | 6 |
| McLennan | 104 | 2 | 34 | 6 | 62 | 713 | 269 | 386 | 58 | 10 |
| Medina | 41 | 2 | 5 | 4 | 30 | 254 | 120 | 120 | 14 | 1 |
| Midland | 31 | 0 | 0 | 1 | 30 | 527 | 185 | 300 | 42 | 0 |
| Montgomery | 1,045 | 6 | 53 | 175 | 811 | 7,939 | 2,343 | 4,916 | 680 | 38 |
| Nueces | 72 | 2 | 8 | 7 | 55 | 283 | 132 | 144 | 7 | 4 |
| Orange | 103 | 2 | 8 | 11 | 82 | 737 | 284 | 376 | 77 | 1 |
| Parker | 80 | 1 | 2 | 3 | 74 | 1,100 | 416 | 606 | 78 | 0 |
| Potter | 23 | 1 | 1 | 3 | 18 | 183 | 51 | 119 | 13 | 3 |
| Randall | 33 | 0 | 3 | 2 | 28 | 332 | 141 | 171 | 20 | 5 |
| Robertson | 8 | 0 | 2 | 1 | 5 | 233 | 92 | 112 | 29 | 0 |
| Rockwall | 35 | 0 | 5 | 0 | 30 | 242 | 126 | 103 | 13 | 0 |
| Rusk | 58 | 2 | 3 | 4 | 49 | 543 | 239 | 238 | 66 | 4 |
| San Jacinto | 60 | 3 | 0 | 8 | 49 | 686 | 291 | 316 | 79 | 12 |
| San Patricio | 23 | 0 | 1 | 1 | 21 | 345 | 134 | 191 | 20 | 2 |
| Smith | 312 | 2 | 45 | 21 | 244 | 1,852 | 692 | 1,000 | 160 | 26 |
| Tarrant | 99 | 0 | 26 | 18 | 55 | 1,103 | 422 | 616 | 65 | 9 |
| Taylor | 32 | 0 | 13 | 3 | 16 | 189 | 58 | 114 | 17 | 2 |
| Tom Green | 34 | 1 | 14 | 1 | 18 | 278 | 99 | 171 | 8 | 5 |
| Travis | 531 | 6 | 22 | 46 | 457 | 4,211 | 1,398 | 2,615 | 198 | 52 |
| Upshur | 57 | 2 | 10 | 7 | 38 | 594 | 237 | 308 | 49 | 3 |

[1] The FBI does not publish arson data unless it receives data from either the agency or the state for all 12 months of the calendar year.

**Table 10. Offenses Known to Law Enforcement, by State Metropolitan and Nonmetropolitan Counties, 2009—*Continued***

(Number.)

| State/County | Violent crime | Murder and non-negligent man-slaughter | Forcible rape | Robbery | Aggravated assault | Property crime | Burglary | Larceny-theft | Motor vehicle theft | Arson[1] |
|---|---|---|---|---|---|---|---|---|---|---|
| Victoria | 103 | 1 | 12 | 5 | 85 | 624 | 145 | 452 | 27 | 0 |
| Waller | 37 | 0 | 1 | 3 | 33 | 352 | 159 | 170 | 23 | 0 |
| Webb | 96 | 0 | 4 | 0 | 92 | 276 | 105 | 138 | 33 | 0 |
| Wichita | 19 | 0 | 0 | 2 | 17 | 147 | 53 | 92 | 2 | 18 |
| Williamson | 158 | 2 | 24 | 17 | 115 | 1,443 | 378 | 1,003 | 62 | 18 |
| Wilson | 60 | 2 | 4 | 0 | 54 | 320 | 134 | 168 | 18 | 3 |
| Wise | 140 | 0 | 4 | 3 | 133 | 482 | 178 | 295 | 9 | 0 |
| **TEXAS - Nonmetropolitan Counties** | | | | | | | | | | |
| Anderson | 59 | 2 | 2 | 7 | 48 | 422 | 202 | 200 | 20 | 10 |
| Andrews | 11 | 1 | 0 | 0 | 10 | 71 | 23 | 45 | 3 | 1 |
| Angelina | 124 | 4 | 2 | 12 | 106 | 375 | 184 | 163 | 28 | 0 |
| Bailey | 3 | 0 | 1 | 0 | 2 | 21 | 11 | 9 | 1 | 1 |
| Baylor | 1 | 0 | 0 | 0 | 1 | 19 | 11 | 7 | 1 | 0 |
| Bee | 34 | 0 | 6 | 0 | 28 | 139 | 66 | 67 | 6 | 0 |
| Blanco | 20 | 0 | 2 | 2 | 16 | 88 | 42 | 37 | 9 | 2 |
| Borden | 0 | 0 | 0 | 0 | 0 | 6 | 3 | 1 | 2 | 0 |
| Bosque | 6 | 0 | 2 | 0 | 4 | 68 | 16 | 41 | 11 | 0 |
| Brewster | 11 | 0 | 0 | 2 | 9 | 37 | 14 | 19 | 4 | 2 |
| Briscoe | 0 | 0 | 0 | 0 | 0 | 11 | 4 | 6 | 1 | 0 |
| Brooks | 1 | 1 | 0 | 0 | 0 | 4 | 0 | 1 | 3 | 0 |
| Brown | 26 | 0 | 0 | 1 | 25 | 178 | 78 | 96 | 4 | 1 |
| Burnet | 43 | 0 | 4 | 3 | 36 | 322 | 133 | 165 | 24 | 4 |
| Camp | 13 | 0 | 3 | 4 | 6 | 151 | 77 | 65 | 9 | 0 |
| Cass | 31 | 4 | 7 | 2 | 18 | 391 | 183 | 163 | 45 | 1 |
| Castro | 13 | 0 | 0 | 1 | 12 | 80 | 37 | 38 | 5 | 1 |
| Cherokee | 97 | 2 | 12 | 3 | 80 | 460 | 176 | 234 | 50 | 4 |
| Childress | 2 | 0 | 2 | 0 | 0 | 14 | 4 | 9 | 1 | 0 |
| Cochran | 3 | 1 | 0 | 0 | 2 | 67 | 25 | 38 | 4 | 1 |
| Coke | 1 | 0 | 0 | 0 | 1 | 14 | 11 | 3 | 0 | 0 |
| Coleman | 1 | 0 | 1 | 0 | 0 | 26 | 14 | 10 | 2 | 0 |
| Collingsworth | 0 | 0 | 0 | 0 | 0 | 2 | 2 | 0 | 0 | 0 |
| Colorado | 22 | 1 | 4 | 2 | 15 | 142 | 61 | 72 | 9 | 1 |
| Comanche | 6 | 0 | 0 | 0 | 6 | 118 | 42 | 72 | 4 | 2 |
| Concho | 2 | 0 | 0 | 0 | 2 | 17 | 7 | 9 | 1 | 1 |
| Cooke | 25 | 0 | 4 | 4 | 17 | 297 | 151 | 119 | 27 | 6 |
| Cottle | 1 | 0 | 0 | 0 | 1 | 16 | 16 | 0 | 0 | 0 |
| Crane | 1 | 0 | 0 | 0 | 1 | 36 | 13 | 23 | 0 | 0 |
| Culberson | 0 | 0 | 0 | 0 | 0 | 11 | 2 | 9 | 0 | 0 |
| Dallam | 1 | 0 | 0 | 1 | 0 | 17 | 10 | 4 | 3 | 0 |
| Dawson | 2 | 0 | 1 | 0 | 1 | 28 | 9 | 18 | 1 | 1 |
| Deaf Smith | 6 | 0 | 0 | 0 | 6 | 77 | 32 | 39 | 6 | 2 |
| DeWitt | 12 | 1 | 0 | 1 | 10 | 113 | 49 | 62 | 2 | 1 |
| Dickens | 0 | 0 | 0 | 0 | 0 | 0 | 0 | 0 | 0 | 0 |
| Dimmit | 49 | 0 | 3 | 0 | 46 | 167 | 57 | 97 | 13 | 1 |
| Donley | 10 | 0 | 0 | 0 | 10 | 50 | 21 | 26 | 3 | 0 |
| Duval | 10 | 0 | 0 | 0 | 10 | 67 | 36 | 24 | 7 | 0 |
| Eastland | 6 | 0 | 0 | 1 | 5 | 37 | 13 | 22 | 2 | 0 |
| Edwards | 6 | 1 | 1 | 0 | 4 | 38 | 18 | 17 | 3 | 6 |
| Erath | 31 | 0 | 5 | 1 | 25 | 135 | 51 | 71 | 13 | 0 |
| Falls | 15 | 0 | 1 | 2 | 12 | 79 | 32 | 30 | 17 | 1 |
| Fannin | 19 | 0 | 2 | 2 | 15 | 179 | 78 | 86 | 15 | 3 |
| Fayette | 2 | 0 | 0 | 0 | 2 | 154 | 54 | 89 | 11 | 0 |
| Fisher | 6 | 1 | 3 | 0 | 2 | 58 | 28 | 28 | 2 | 1 |
| Floyd | 3 | 0 | 1 | 0 | 2 | 14 | 7 | 6 | 1 | 2 |
| Foard | 2 | 0 | 2 | 0 | 0 | 2 | 0 | 2 | 0 | 0 |
| Franklin | 19 | 1 | 1 | 2 | 15 | 88 | 47 | 36 | 5 | 0 |
| Freestone | 12 | 0 | 0 | 0 | 12 | 152 | 50 | 82 | 20 | 0 |
| Frio | 1 | 0 | 0 | 0 | 1 | 68 | 28 | 38 | 2 | 0 |
| Gaines | 6 | 0 | 0 | 0 | 6 | 63 | 19 | 33 | 11 | 0 |
| Garza | 6 | 0 | 1 | 1 | 4 | 61 | 23 | 34 | 4 | 0 |
| Gillespie | 9 | 0 | 2 | 0 | 7 | 88 | 22 | 63 | 3 | 0 |
| Glasscock | 1 | 0 | 0 | 0 | 1 | 17 | 3 | 13 | 1 | 2 |
| Gonzales | 27 | 1 | 1 | 3 | 22 | 173 | 80 | 78 | 15 | 0 |
| Gray | 8 | 0 | 0 | 1 | 7 | 131 | 51 | 70 | 10 | 0 |
| Grimes | 31 | 1 | 1 | 7 | 22 | 335 | 119 | 190 | 26 | 1 |
| Hale | 3 | 0 | 1 | 0 | 2 | 93 | 42 | 46 | 5 | 0 |
| Hall | 1 | 0 | 0 | 0 | 1 | 14 | 6 | 5 | 3 | 1 |
| Hamilton | 16 | 1 | 1 | 1 | 13 | 95 | 32 | 51 | 12 | 3 |
| Hansford | 1 | 0 | 0 | 0 | 1 | 17 | 3 | 12 | 2 | 1 |
| Hardeman | 13 | 1 | 3 | 2 | 7 | 136 | 60 | 72 | 4 | 1 |
| Harrison | 108 | 4 | 0 | 3 | 101 | 795 | 436 | 326 | 33 | 0 |

[1] The FBI does not publish arson data unless it receives data from either the agency or the state for all 12 months of the calendar year.

**Table 10. Offenses Known to Law Enforcement, by State Metropolitan and Nonmetropolitan Counties, 2009**—*Continued*

(Number.)

| State/County | Violent crime | Murder and non-negligent man-slaughter | Forcible rape | Robbery | Aggravated assault | Property crime | Burglary | Larceny-theft | Motor vehicle theft | Arson[1] |
|---|---|---|---|---|---|---|---|---|---|---|
| Hartley | 2 | 0 | 1 | 0 | 1 | 9 | 2 | 6 | 1 | 1 |
| Haskell | 3 | 0 | 0 | 0 | 3 | 16 | 2 | 11 | 3 | 0 |
| Hemphill | 17 | 0 | 4 | 0 | 13 | 52 | 17 | 32 | 3 | 0 |
| Henderson | 279 | 6 | 37 | 12 | 224 | 1,198 | 475 | 586 | 137 | 5 |
| Hill | 6 | 2 | 3 | 0 | 1 | 346 | 129 | 199 | 18 | 4 |
| Hockley | 10 | 0 | 1 | 0 | 9 | 92 | 41 | 45 | 6 | 1 |
| Hood | 62 | 1 | 5 | 1 | 55 | 685 | 224 | 410 | 51 | 6 |
| Hopkins | 24 | 1 | 8 | 1 | 14 | 200 | 85 | 107 | 8 | 0 |
| Houston | 25 | 0 | 3 | 2 | 20 | 161 | 43 | 102 | 16 | 2 |
| Howard | 9 | 0 | 2 | 1 | 6 | 85 | 45 | 39 | 1 | 0 |
| Hudspeth | 2 | 0 | 0 | 0 | 2 | 22 | 10 | 11 | 1 | 0 |
| Hutchinson | 7 | 0 | 3 | 0 | 4 | 138 | 55 | 72 | 11 | 0 |
| Jack | 5 | 0 | 1 | 0 | 4 | 51 | 27 | 17 | 7 | 0 |
| Jackson | 24 | 0 | 0 | 0 | 24 | 80 | 33 | 44 | 3 | 0 |
| Jasper | 74 | 0 | 8 | 5 | 61 | 288 | 109 | 149 | 30 | 0 |
| Jeff Davis | 6 | 0 | 2 | 2 | 2 | 8 | 3 | 3 | 2 | 0 |
| Jim Hogg | 4 | 0 | 0 | 0 | 4 | 68 | 18 | 45 | 5 | 0 |
| Jim Wells | 81 | 0 | 4 | 5 | 72 | 555 | 309 | 217 | 29 | 2 |
| Karnes | 9 | 0 | 0 | 0 | 9 | 80 | 41 | 32 | 7 | 1 |
| Kenedy | 3 | 0 | 3 | 0 | 0 | 8 | 4 | 3 | 1 | 1 |
| Kent | 5 | 0 | 0 | 0 | 5 | 7 | 3 | 4 | 0 | 1 |
| Kerr | 44 | 0 | 9 | 2 | 33 | 380 | 123 | 244 | 13 | 1 |
| Kimble | 1 | 0 | 0 | 0 | 1 | 6 | 2 | 4 | 0 | 0 |
| King | 0 | 0 | 0 | 0 | 0 | 5 | 0 | 5 | 0 | 0 |
| Kinney | 1 | 0 | 0 | 0 | 1 | 27 | 14 | 8 | 5 | 0 |
| Kleberg | 12 | 0 | 1 | 0 | 11 | 292 | 44 | 248 | 0 | 0 |
| Knox | 2 | 0 | 0 | 0 | 2 | 20 | 10 | 9 | 1 | 0 |
| Lamar | 55 | 0 | 5 | 6 | 44 | 382 | 166 | 194 | 22 | 0 |
| Lamb | 7 | 1 | 0 | 0 | 6 | 87 | 36 | 50 | 1 | 1 |
| La Salle | 3 | 0 | 0 | 0 | 3 | 67 | 16 | 51 | 0 | 1 |
| Lavaca | 8 | 0 | 0 | 0 | 8 | 91 | 58 | 31 | 2 | 0 |
| Lee | 14 | 0 | 2 | 0 | 12 | 85 | 36 | 41 | 8 | 1 |
| Leon | 31 | 0 | 7 | 4 | 20 | 132 | 62 | 55 | 15 | 0 |
| Limestone | 26 | 0 | 20 | 0 | 6 | 305 | 150 | 145 | 10 | 6 |
| Lipscomb | 2 | 0 | 1 | 0 | 1 | 16 | 3 | 11 | 2 | 0 |
| Live Oak | 0 | 0 | 0 | 0 | 0 | 62 | 26 | 32 | 4 | 0 |
| Llano | 14 | 3 | 7 | 1 | 3 | 336 | 121 | 208 | 7 | 0 |
| Loving | 0 | 0 | 0 | 0 | 0 | 11 | 1 | 10 | 0 | 0 |
| Lynn | 0 | 0 | 0 | 0 | 0 | 44 | 20 | 24 | 0 | 0 |
| Madison | 23 | 0 | 0 | 1 | 22 | 113 | 49 | 42 | 22 | 0 |
| Marion | 35 | 0 | 11 | 2 | 22 | 199 | 99 | 85 | 15 | 0 |
| Martin | 2 | 1 | 0 | 0 | 1 | 22 | 12 | 9 | 1 | 1 |
| Mason | 4 | 0 | 2 | 0 | 2 | 60 | 10 | 45 | 5 | 0 |
| Matagorda | 52 | 2 | 2 | 1 | 47 | 270 | 107 | 154 | 9 | 6 |
| Maverick | 69 | 0 | 0 | 3 | 66 | 634 | 253 | 368 | 13 | 0 |
| McCulloch | 6 | 0 | 1 | 0 | 5 | 39 | 15 | 21 | 3 | 0 |
| McMullen | 0 | 0 | 0 | 0 | 0 | 0 | 0 | 0 | 0 | 0 |
| Menard | 6 | 0 | 1 | 1 | 4 | 7 | 3 | 4 | 0 | 0 |
| Milam | 7 | 0 | 1 | 1 | 5 | 176 | 68 | 97 | 11 | 4 |
| Mills | 11 | 0 | 0 | 0 | 11 | 56 | 18 | 34 | 4 | 0 |
| Mitchell | 2 | 2 | 0 | 0 | 0 | 16 | 4 | 11 | 1 | 1 |
| Montague | 20 | 0 | 2 | 0 | 18 | 172 | 68 | 93 | 11 | 3 |
| Moore | 1 | 0 | 1 | 0 | 0 | 68 | 18 | 48 | 2 | 0 |
| Morris | 29 | 1 | 1 | 1 | 26 | 129 | 60 | 59 | 10 | 0 |
| Motley | 2 | 0 | 0 | 0 | 2 | 9 | 3 | 6 | 0 | 0 |
| Nacogdoches | 83 | 1 | 8 | 3 | 71 | 326 | 110 | 194 | 22 | 3 |
| Navarro | 38 | 2 | 3 | 1 | 32 | 574 | 225 | 329 | 20 | 9 |
| Newton | 13 | 2 | 2 | 0 | 9 | 134 | 45 | 87 | 2 | 0 |
| Nolan | 8 | 0 | 0 | 0 | 8 | 58 | 15 | 37 | 6 | 0 |
| Ochiltree | 6 | 0 | 1 | 0 | 5 | 30 | 8 | 17 | 5 | 0 |
| Oldham | 0 | 0 | 0 | 0 | 0 | 21 | 5 | 15 | 1 | 0 |
| Palo Pinto | 19 | 1 | 0 | 0 | 18 | 196 | 100 | 86 | 10 | 3 |
| Panola | 19 | 0 | 2 | 0 | 17 | 232 | 76 | 124 | 32 | 0 |
| Parmer | 2 | 0 | 0 | 0 | 2 | 46 | 29 | 16 | 1 | 2 |
| Pecos | 10 | 0 | 1 | 0 | 9 | 37 | 13 | 21 | 3 | 0 |
| Polk | 63 | 0 | 23 | 4 | 36 | 642 | 275 | 311 | 56 | 3 |
| Presidio | 3 | 0 | 2 | 0 | 1 | 6 | 2 | 4 | 0 | 2 |
| Rains | 10 | 0 | 2 | 0 | 8 | 167 | 72 | 91 | 4 | 0 |
| Reagan | 1 | 0 | 0 | 0 | 1 | 23 | 10 | 13 | 0 | 0 |
| Real | 1 | 0 | 0 | 0 | 1 | 10 | 5 | 4 | 1 | 0 |
| Red River | 48 | 2 | 1 | 4 | 41 | 113 | 53 | 51 | 9 | 2 |

[1] The FBI does not publish arson data unless it receives data from either the agency or the state for all 12 months of the calendar year.

**Table 10. Offenses Known to Law Enforcement, by State Metropolitan and Nonmetropolitan Counties, 2009**—*Continued*

(Number.)

| State/County | Violent crime | Murder and non-negligent man-slaughter | Forcible rape | Robbery | Aggravated assault | Property crime | Burglary | Larceny-theft | Motor vehicle theft | Arson[1] |
|---|---|---|---|---|---|---|---|---|---|---|
| Reeves | 8 | 0 | 1 | 1 | 6 | 61 | 14 | 45 | 2 | 1 |
| Refugio | 8 | 0 | 0 | 0 | 8 | 56 | 24 | 27 | 5 | 1 |
| Roberts | 2 | 0 | 0 | 0 | 2 | 15 | 2 | 13 | 0 | 0 |
| Runnels | 0 | 0 | 0 | 0 | 0 | 21 | 2 | 19 | 0 | 0 |
| Sabine | 7 | 1 | 0 | 0 | 6 | 69 | 34 | 34 | 1 | 1 |
| San Augustine | 14 | 1 | 2 | 0 | 11 | 99 | 38 | 51 | 10 | 0 |
| San Saba | 5 | 1 | 2 | 0 | 2 | 15 | 8 | 4 | 3 | 0 |
| Schleicher | 1 | 0 | 0 | 0 | 1 | 18 | 10 | 8 | 0 | 0 |
| Scurry | 7 | 0 | 2 | 0 | 5 | 58 | 26 | 28 | 4 | 0 |
| Shackelford | 1 | 0 | 0 | 0 | 1 | 54 | 19 | 25 | 10 | 0 |
| Shelby | 46 | 1 | 7 | 5 | 33 | 280 | 105 | 145 | 30 | 5 |
| Sherman | 0 | 0 | 0 | 0 | 0 | 0 | 0 | 0 | 0 | 0 |
| Somervell | 7 | 0 | 0 | 0 | 7 | 137 | 42 | 92 | 3 | 0 |
| Starr | 89 | 0 | 14 | 10 | 65 | 322 | 136 | 162 | 24 | 4 |
| Stephens | 1 | 1 | 0 | 0 | 0 | 27 | 13 | 11 | 3 | 0 |
| Sterling | 0 | 0 | 0 | 0 | 0 | 12 | 5 | 6 | 1 | 0 |
| Stonewall | 3 | 0 | 0 | 0 | 3 | 14 | 6 | 8 | 0 | 9 |
| Sutton | 2 | 0 | 0 | 0 | 2 | 20 | 5 | 13 | 2 | 0 |
| Swisher | 2 | 0 | 0 | 0 | 2 | 34 | 19 | 11 | 4 | 0 |
| Terrell | 1 | 0 | 0 | 0 | 1 | 66 | 46 | 18 | 2 | 0 |
| Terry | 3 | 0 | 0 | 0 | 3 | 39 | 15 | 20 | 4 | 0 |
| Throckmorton | 1 | 0 | 0 | 0 | 1 | 4 | 2 | 1 | 1 | 0 |
| Titus | 24 | 1 | 7 | 2 | 14 | 271 | 105 | 147 | 19 | 4 |
| Trinity | 22 | 0 | 4 | 3 | 15 | 167 | 70 | 88 | 9 | 0 |
| Tyler | 74 | 1 | 6 | 3 | 64 | 367 | 211 | 132 | 24 | 5 |
| Upton | 2 | 0 | 0 | 0 | 2 | 7 | 2 | 5 | 0 | 0 |
| Uvalde | 22 | 1 | 1 | 0 | 20 | 177 | 64 | 100 | 13 | 2 |
| Val Verde | 5 | 0 | 1 | 0 | 4 | 118 | 55 | 59 | 4 | 1 |
| Van Zandt | 68 | 4 | 1 | 9 | 54 | 716 | 288 | 334 | 94 | 8 |
| Walker | 76 | 0 | 19 | 13 | 44 | 457 | 211 | 216 | 30 | 0 |
| Ward | 8 | 0 | 0 | 0 | 8 | 85 | 33 | 51 | 1 | 1 |
| Washington | 34 | 1 | 8 | 3 | 22 | 186 | 107 | 69 | 10 | 0 |
| Wharton | 78 | 1 | 2 | 6 | 69 | 406 | 214 | 171 | 21 | 7 |
| Wheeler | 6 | 0 | 0 | 0 | 6 | 29 | 11 | 14 | 4 | 0 |
| Wilbarger | 1 | 1 | 0 | 0 | 0 | 22 | 8 | 9 | 5 | 7 |
| Willacy | 44 | 2 | 1 | 2 | 39 | 162 | 53 | 96 | 13 | 3 |
| Winkler | 4 | 0 | 0 | 0 | 4 | 45 | 16 | 27 | 2 | 0 |
| Wood | 40 | 2 | 2 | 1 | 35 | 535 | 169 | 336 | 30 | 7 |
| Yoakum | 6 | 0 | 1 | 0 | 5 | 38 | 15 | 21 | 2 | 0 |
| Young | 9 | 1 | 1 | 0 | 7 | 101 | 54 | 41 | 6 | 3 |
| Zapata | 39 | 0 | 2 | 3 | 34 | 272 | 155 | 101 | 16 | 0 |
| Zavala | 32 | 4 | 1 | 3 | 24 | 93 | 34 | 51 | 8 | 4 |
| **UTAH - Metropolitan Counties** | | | | | | | | | | |
| Cache | 23 | 0 | 7 | 1 | 15 | 481 | 66 | 394 | 21 | 0 |
| Davis | 18 | 0 | 3 | 0 | 15 | 285 | 53 | 218 | 14 | 0 |
| Juab | 3 | 0 | 1 | 0 | 2 | 71 | 12 | 56 | 3 | 0 |
| Morgan | 3 | 0 | 1 | 0 | 2 | 48 | 10 | 34 | 4 | 0 |
| Salt Lake | 736 | 3 | 80 | 110 | 543 | 8,175 | 1,562 | 5,783 | 830 | 27 |
| Summit | 16 | 0 | 4 | 2 | 10 | 638 | 105 | 497 | 36 | 0 |
| Tooele | 33 | 0 | 9 | 0 | 24 | 279 | 63 | 178 | 38 | 6 |
| Utah | 17 | 0 | 6 | 0 | 11 | 336 | 68 | 246 | 22 | 0 |
| Washington | 19 | 2 | 6 | 0 | 11 | 132 | 36 | 88 | 8 | 1 |
| Weber | 41 | 0 | 5 | 6 | 30 | 1,088 | 215 | 811 | 62 | 7 |
| **UTAH - Nonmetropolitan Counties** | | | | | | | | | | |
| Beaver | 5 | 0 | 0 | 0 | 5 | 54 | 13 | 37 | 4 | 0 |
| Box Elder | 6 | 0 | 3 | 1 | 2 | 187 | 43 | 137 | 7 | 0 |
| Carbon | 9 | 0 | 6 | 0 | 3 | 159 | 86 | 71 | 2 | 4 |
| Daggett | 0 | 0 | 0 | 0 | 0 | 18 | 5 | 12 | 1 | 0 |
| Duchesne | 12 | 0 | 5 | 0 | 7 | 201 | 69 | 123 | 9 | 0 |
| Emery | 6 | 2 | 1 | 1 | 2 | 108 | 31 | 76 | 1 | 0 |
| Grand | 7 | 0 | 6 | 0 | 1 | 56 | 12 | 41 | 3 | 0 |
| Iron | 22 | 0 | 9 | 2 | 11 | 164 | 65 | 87 | 12 | 3 |
| Kane | 7 | 0 | 1 | 0 | 6 | 55 | 37 | 18 | 0 | 0 |
| Millard | 15 | 0 | 3 | 0 | 12 | 271 | 50 | 210 | 11 | 0 |
| Rich | 0 | 0 | 0 | 0 | 0 | 51 | 18 | 32 | 1 | 0 |
| San Juan | 10 | 0 | 2 | 2 | 6 | 49 | 12 | 36 | 1 | 0 |
| Sevier | 12 | 0 | 3 | 1 | 8 | 143 | 39 | 100 | 4 | 1 |
| Uintah | 33 | 0 | 6 | 1 | 26 | 250 | 61 | 167 | 22 | 2 |
| Wasatch | 9 | 0 | 2 | 0 | 7 | 170 | 45 | 113 | 12 | 0 |
| Wayne | 5 | 0 | 0 | 0 | 5 | 106 | 10 | 95 | 1 | 0 |

[1] The FBI does not publish arson data unless it receives data from either the agency or the state for all 12 months of the calendar year.

**Table 10. Offenses Known to Law Enforcement, by State Metropolitan and Nonmetropolitan Counties, 2009**—*Continued*

(Number.)

| State/County | Violent crime | Murder and non-negligent man-slaughter | Forcible rape | Robbery | Aggravated assault | Property crime | Burglary | Larceny-theft | Motor vehicle theft | Arson[1] |
|---|---|---|---|---|---|---|---|---|---|---|
| **VERMONT - Metropolitan Counties** | | | | | | | | | | |
| Franklin | 13 | 0 | 0 | 1 | 12 | 264 | 72 | 183 | 9 | 0 |
| Grand Isle | 2 | 0 | 0 | 0 | 2 | 105 | 43 | 60 | 2 | 0 |
| **VERMONT - Nonmetropolitan Counties** | | | | | | | | | | |
| Bennington | 0 | 0 | 0 | 0 | 0 | 3 | 0 | 2 | 1 | 1 |
| Caledonia | 0 | 0 | 0 | 0 | 0 | 4 | 3 | 1 | 0 | 0 |
| Lamoille | 10 | 0 | 3 | 1 | 6 | 196 | 39 | 150 | 7 | 1 |
| Orange | 3 | 0 | 0 | 0 | 3 | 47 | 14 | 32 | 1 | 0 |
| Orleans | 1 | 0 | 0 | 0 | 1 | 45 | 18 | 25 | 2 | 0 |
| Rutland | 5 | 0 | 0 | 0 | 5 | 158 | 7 | 151 | 0 | 0 |
| Washington | 1 | 0 | 0 | 0 | 1 | 1 | 0 | 1 | 0 | 0 |
| Windham | 1 | 0 | 0 | 0 | 1 | 5 | 0 | 4 | 1 | 0 |
| Windsor | 0 | 0 | 0 | 0 | 0 | 0 | 0 | 0 | 0 | 0 |
| **VIRGINIA - Metropolitan Counties** | | | | | | | | | | |
| Albemarle County Police Department | 108 | 0 | 18 | 27 | 63 | 2,023 | 246 | 1,652 | 125 | 11 |
| Amelia | 12 | 0 | 1 | 2 | 9 | 147 | 47 | 78 | 22 | 2 |
| Amherst | 35 | 0 | 3 | 8 | 24 | 511 | 81 | 403 | 27 | 3 |
| Appomattox | 16 | 0 | 5 | 0 | 11 | 144 | 40 | 97 | 7 | 0 |
| Arlington County Police Department | 324 | 2 | 16 | 149 | 157 | 4,727 | 320 | 4,120 | 287 | 2 |
| Bedford | 153 | 1 | 14 | 5 | 133 | 704 | 148 | 489 | 67 | 0 |
| Botetourt | 20 | 0 | 7 | 2 | 11 | 349 | 76 | 259 | 14 | 2 |
| Campbell | 83 | 4 | 15 | 10 | 54 | 754 | 189 | 518 | 47 | 8 |
| Caroline | 54 | 0 | 16 | 7 | 31 | 409 | 92 | 300 | 17 | 9 |
| Charles City | 3 | 0 | 1 | 1 | 1 | 51 | 19 | 26 | 6 | 0 |
| Chesterfield County Police Department | 506 | 2 | 44 | 230 | 230 | 7,540 | 1,867 | 5,293 | 380 | 72 |
| Clarke | 11 | 1 | 3 | 1 | 6 | 158 | 25 | 127 | 6 | 2 |
| Craig | 4 | 0 | 0 | 0 | 4 | 12 | 6 | 6 | 0 | 1 |
| Cumberland | 12 | 2 | 3 | 0 | 7 | 59 | 12 | 41 | 6 | 1 |
| Dinwiddie | 51 | 3 | 7 | 11 | 30 | 464 | 126 | 297 | 41 | 1 |
| Fairfax County Police Department | 591 | 10 | 69 | 277 | 235 | 16,809 | 1,287 | 14,668 | 854 | 73 |
| Fauquier | 62 | 2 | 10 | 12 | 38 | 588 | 117 | 440 | 31 | 9 |
| Fluvanna | 19 | 0 | 6 | 3 | 10 | 207 | 38 | 145 | 24 | 3 |
| Franklin | 46 | 2 | 4 | 7 | 33 | 560 | 116 | 408 | 36 | 1 |
| Frederick | 95 | 3 | 32 | 23 | 37 | 1,399 | 301 | 1,010 | 88 | 5 |
| Giles | 6 | 0 | 0 | 2 | 4 | 131 | 23 | 103 | 5 | 3 |
| Gloucester | 35 | 0 | 5 | 8 | 22 | 482 | 49 | 401 | 32 | 3 |
| Goochland | 23 | 2 | 2 | 3 | 16 | 228 | 48 | 166 | 14 | 1 |
| Greene | 27 | 0 | 3 | 1 | 23 | 220 | 40 | 174 | 6 | 3 |
| Hanover | 43 | 0 | 6 | 9 | 28 | 1,051 | 112 | 868 | 71 | 4 |
| Henrico County Police Department | 499 | 12 | 30 | 267 | 190 | 8,417 | 1,477 | 6,501 | 439 | 65 |
| Isle of Wight | 40 | 0 | 4 | 4 | 32 | 465 | 127 | 314 | 24 | 4 |
| James City County Police Department | 71 | 0 | 13 | 15 | 43 | 979 | 149 | 798 | 32 | 8 |
| King and Queen | 9 | 0 | 1 | 0 | 8 | 64 | 28 | 29 | 7 | 2 |
| King William | 5 | 0 | 0 | 1 | 4 | 60 | 16 | 35 | 9 | 1 |
| Loudoun | 251 | 2 | 29 | 35 | 185 | 2,956 | 305 | 2,496 | 155 | 46 |
| Louisa | 33 | 2 | 5 | 0 | 26 | 341 | 89 | 250 | 2 | 2 |
| Mathews | 6 | 1 | 0 | 0 | 5 | 104 | 25 | 73 | 6 | 4 |
| Montgomery | 37 | 2 | 5 | 4 | 26 | 482 | 140 | 325 | 17 | 6 |
| Nelson | 13 | 1 | 4 | 3 | 5 | 273 | 63 | 202 | 8 | 1 |
| New Kent | 19 | 1 | 3 | 3 | 12 | 292 | 62 | 204 | 26 | 5 |
| Pittsylvania | 56 | 1 | 6 | 13 | 36 | 562 | 200 | 340 | 22 | 3 |
| Powhatan | 5 | 0 | 3 | 1 | 1 | 247 | 44 | 188 | 15 | 1 |
| Prince George County Police Department | 38 | 1 | 9 | 14 | 14 | 506 | 116 | 354 | 36 | 1 |
| Prince William County Police Department | 662 | 11 | 45 | 267 | 339 | 7,365 | 1,034 | 5,817 | 514 | 47 |
| Pulaski | 58 | 0 | 11 | 9 | 38 | 664 | 135 | 509 | 20 | 2 |
| Roanoke County Police Department | 122 | 1 | 21 | 19 | 81 | 1,263 | 286 | 924 | 53 | 10 |
| Rockingham | 31 | 2 | 13 | 7 | 9 | 218 | 76 | 136 | 6 | 9 |
| Scott | 36 | 0 | 6 | 10 | 20 | 388 | 117 | 241 | 30 | 4 |
| Spotsylvania | 258 | 4 | 46 | 51 | 157 | 2,346 | 280 | 1,960 | 106 | 9 |
| Stafford | 181 | 8 | 35 | 38 | 100 | 1,764 | 200 | 1,442 | 122 | 17 |
| Surry | 20 | 0 | 3 | 3 | 14 | 70 | 30 | 36 | 4 | 0 |
| Sussex | 21 | 0 | 2 | 2 | 17 | 173 | 49 | 107 | 17 | 4 |
| Warren | 29 | 0 | 6 | 3 | 20 | 280 | 33 | 230 | 17 | 2 |
| Washington | 33 | 1 | 11 | 1 | 20 | 1,081 | 259 | 796 | 26 | 5 |
| York | 84 | 1 | 7 | 19 | 57 | 1,301 | 157 | 1,113 | 31 | 12 |
| **VIRGINIA - Nonmetropolitan Counties** | | | | | | | | | | |
| Accomack | 66 | 1 | 11 | 27 | 27 | 531 | 198 | 300 | 33 | 0 |
| Alleghany | 14 | 0 | 4 | 0 | 10 | 103 | 16 | 81 | 6 | 6 |
| Augusta | 85 | 1 | 8 | 5 | 71 | 739 | 178 | 519 | 42 | 2 |
| Bath | 2 | 2 | 0 | 0 | 0 | 33 | 14 | 16 | 3 | 0 |
| Bland | 1 | 0 | 0 | 0 | 1 | 51 | 14 | 34 | 3 | 1 |

[1] The FBI does not publish arson data unless it receives data from either the agency or the state for all 12 months of the calendar year.

## Table 10. Offenses Known to Law Enforcement, by State Metropolitan and Nonmetropolitan Counties, 2009—*Continued*

(Number.)

| State/County | Violent crime | Murder and non-negligent man-slaughter | Forcible rape | Robbery | Aggravated assault | Property crime | Burglary | Larceny-theft | Motor vehicle theft | Arson[1] |
|---|---|---|---|---|---|---|---|---|---|---|
| Brunswick | 16 | 1 | 3 | 3 | 9 | 113 | 50 | 47 | 16 | 0 |
| Buchanan | 41 | 5 | 4 | 6 | 26 | 463 | 133 | 292 | 38 | 12 |
| Buckingham | 28 | 0 | 2 | 7 | 19 | 253 | 97 | 142 | 14 | 6 |
| Carroll | 16 | 1 | 5 | 2 | 8 | 387 | 143 | 218 | 26 | 2 |
| Charlotte | 28 | 2 | 5 | 3 | 18 | 148 | 47 | 92 | 9 | 2 |
| Culpeper | 24 | 0 | 3 | 1 | 20 | 226 | 66 | 147 | 13 | 1 |
| Dickenson | 14 | 1 | 2 | 2 | 9 | 175 | 47 | 115 | 13 | 3 |
| Essex | 5 | 0 | 1 | 1 | 3 | 81 | 12 | 62 | 7 | 1 |
| Floyd | 7 | 1 | 0 | 0 | 6 | 153 | 42 | 104 | 7 | 1 |
| Grayson | 25 | 0 | 3 | 1 | 21 | 139 | 50 | 75 | 14 | 3 |
| Greensville | 10 | 0 | 4 | 1 | 5 | 142 | 51 | 78 | 13 | 3 |
| Halifax | 33 | 2 | 6 | 7 | 18 | 366 | 117 | 211 | 38 | 2 |
| Henry | 138 | 5 | 5 | 30 | 98 | 1,078 | 311 | 706 | 61 | 14 |
| King George | 23 | 1 | 6 | 2 | 14 | 347 | 49 | 266 | 32 | 5 |
| Lancaster | 15 | 0 | 1 | 2 | 12 | 123 | 45 | 75 | 3 | 0 |
| Lee | 19 | 0 | 2 | 5 | 12 | 181 | 61 | 114 | 6 | 2 |
| Lunenburg | 13 | 1 | 6 | 1 | 5 | 113 | 52 | 48 | 13 | 5 |
| Madison | 18 | 0 | 3 | 0 | 15 | 150 | 20 | 120 | 10 | 2 |
| Mecklenburg | 41 | 3 | 7 | 3 | 28 | 329 | 98 | 202 | 29 | 6 |
| Middlesex | 15 | 0 | 3 | 4 | 8 | 108 | 30 | 70 | 8 | 0 |
| Northampton | 24 | 0 | 2 | 14 | 8 | 207 | 72 | 123 | 12 | 2 |
| Northumberland | 19 | 0 | 2 | 6 | 11 | 131 | 49 | 74 | 8 | 0 |
| Nottoway | 23 | 0 | 2 | 1 | 20 | 63 | 19 | 38 | 6 | 0 |
| Orange | 8 | 0 | 0 | 2 | 6 | 190 | 44 | 127 | 19 | 1 |
| Page | 21 | 0 | 6 | 1 | 14 | 245 | 66 | 160 | 19 | 7 |
| Patrick | 32 | 0 | 2 | 1 | 29 | 296 | 77 | 192 | 27 | 11 |
| Prince Edward | 14 | 2 | 3 | 3 | 6 | 88 | 29 | 52 | 7 | 1 |
| Rappahannock | 3 | 0 | 0 | 0 | 3 | 73 | 21 | 46 | 6 | 1 |
| Richmond | 9 | 0 | 0 | 2 | 7 | 46 | 14 | 25 | 7 | 0 |
| Rockbridge | 21 | 0 | 4 | 8 | 9 | 302 | 67 | 222 | 13 | 2 |
| Russell | 23 | 1 | 5 | 1 | 16 | 269 | 70 | 184 | 15 | 8 |
| Shenandoah | 26 | 1 | 2 | 0 | 23 | 283 | 71 | 204 | 8 | 2 |
| Smyth | 18 | 0 | 4 | 1 | 13 | 337 | 71 | 249 | 17 | 2 |
| Southampton | 30 | 3 | 3 | 7 | 17 | 317 | 112 | 181 | 24 | 3 |
| Tazewell | 40 | 4 | 4 | 8 | 24 | 596 | 126 | 453 | 17 | 1 |
| Westmoreland | 6 | 0 | 0 | 0 | 6 | 105 | 28 | 74 | 3 | 0 |
| Wise | 41 | 0 | 6 | 2 | 33 | 377 | 97 | 245 | 35 | 12 |
| Wythe | 21 | 0 | 0 | 1 | 20 | 172 | 38 | 117 | 17 | 1 |
| **WASHINGTON - Metropolitan Counties** | | | | | | | | | | |
| Asotin | 12 | 0 | 1 | 1 | 10 | 200 | 40 | 148 | 12 | 0 |
| Benton | 74 | 0 | 10 | 6 | 58 | 531 | 192 | 303 | 36 | 0 |
| Chelan | 50 | 1 | 12 | 7 | 30 | 918 | 140 | 740 | 38 | 3 |
| Clark | 276 | 1 | 75 | 62 | 138 | 3,894 | 771 | 2,640 | 483 | 33 |
| Cowlitz | 36 | 0 | 9 | 4 | 23 | 658 | 236 | 360 | 62 | 12 |
| Douglas | 44 | 0 | 7 | 2 | 35 | 539 | 192 | 321 | 26 | 5 |
| Franklin | 16 | 0 | 6 | 3 | 7 | 165 | 56 | 94 | 15 | 1 |
| King | 572 | 6 | 100 | 167 | 299 | 6,446 | 2,305 | 3,386 | 755 | 128 |
| Kitsap | 682 | 4 | 103 | 48 | 527 | 3,229 | 881 | 2,145 | 203 | 38 |
| Pierce | 1,184 | 16 | 97 | 260 | 811 | 10,377 | 2,968 | 6,171 | 1,238 | 44 |
| Skagit | 96 | 1 | 22 | 5 | 68 | 1,143 | 386 | 683 | 74 | 18 |
| Skamania | 23 | 1 | 10 | 1 | 11 | 203 | 48 | 132 | 23 | 3 |
| Spokane | 191 | 2 | 14 | 25 | 150 | 3,003 | 765 | 1,996 | 242 | 9 |
| Thurston | 308 | 3 | 34 | 43 | 228 | 2,862 | 827 | 1,851 | 184 | 29 |
| Whatcom | 120 | 3 | 28 | 16 | 73 | 1,254 | 430 | 737 | 87 | 12 |
| Yakima | 125 | 8 | 24 | 26 | 67 | 2,377 | 1,043 | 987 | 347 | 45 |
| **WASHINGTON - Nonmetropolitan Counties** | | | | | | | | | | |
| Adams | 24 | 1 | 4 | 7 | 12 | 259 | 97 | 130 | 32 | 5 |
| Clallam | 87 | 0 | 21 | 7 | 59 | 603 | 183 | 387 | 33 | 3 |
| Columbia | 2 | 0 | 0 | 0 | 2 | 158 | 26 | 120 | 12 | 0 |
| Ferry | 4 | 0 | 0 | 0 | 4 | 14 | 4 | 10 | 0 | 0 |
| Garfield | 3 | 0 | 0 | 0 | 3 | 56 | 16 | 36 | 4 | 0 |
| Grant | 104 | 9 | 12 | 29 | 54 | 1,404 | 486 | 753 | 165 | 14 |
| Grays Harbor | 33 | 0 | 2 | 7 | 24 | 327 | 104 | 195 | 28 | 2 |
| Island | 33 | 0 | 8 | 3 | 22 | 765 | 287 | 449 | 29 | 3 |
| Jefferson | 39 | 2 | 3 | 1 | 33 | 324 | 83 | 235 | 6 | 5 |
| Kittitas | 16 | 0 | 3 | 2 | 11 | 537 | 157 | 346 | 34 | 6 |
| Klickitat | 7 | 1 | 0 | 0 | 6 | 146 | 104 | 8 | 34 | 3 |
| Lewis | 59 | 1 | 9 | 3 | 46 | 716 | 261 | 413 | 42 | 6 |
| Lincoln | 13 | 0 | 1 | 0 | 12 | 114 | 39 | 68 | 7 | 1 |
| Mason | 133 | 0 | 26 | 10 | 97 | 1,576 | 597 | 793 | 186 | 2 |
| Okanogan | 22 | 2 | 4 | 1 | 15 | 340 | 123 | 189 | 28 | 1 |
| Pacific | 42 | 0 | 9 | 1 | 32 | 303 | 142 | 151 | 10 | 1 |

[1] The FBI does not publish arson data unless it receives data from either the agency or the state for all 12 months of the calendar year.

**Table 10. Offenses Known to Law Enforcement, by State Metropolitan and Nonmetropolitan Counties, 2009**—*Continued*

(Number.)

| State/County | Violent crime | Murder and non-negligent man-slaughter | Forcible rape | Robbery | Aggravated assault | Property crime | Burglary | Larceny-theft | Motor vehicle theft | Arson[1] |
|---|---|---|---|---|---|---|---|---|---|---|
| Pend Oreille | 5 | 0 | 1 | 0 | 4 | 337 | 82 | 234 | 21 | 1 |
| San Juan | 9 | 0 | 2 | 0 | 7 | 272 | 91 | 166 | 15 | 1 |
| Stevens | 47 | 1 | 19 | 4 | 23 | 669 | 229 | 369 | 71 | 2 |
| Wahkiakum | 8 | 0 | 1 | 0 | 7 | 15 | 7 | 7 | 1 | 2 |
| Walla Walla | 24 | 0 | 10 | 1 | 13 | 414 | 158 | 240 | 16 | 0 |
| Whitman | 3 | 0 | 0 | 1 | 2 | 58 | 16 | 35 | 7 | 0 |
| **WEST VIRGINIA - Metropolitan Counties** | | | | | | | | | | |
| Berkeley | 66 | 0 | 12 | 15 | 39 | 1,109 | 324 | 697 | 88 | 15 |
| Boone | 25 | 0 | 1 | 0 | 24 | 69 | 37 | 29 | 3 | 0 |
| Brooke | 6 | 0 | 1 | 1 | 4 | 116 | 57 | 51 | 8 | 3 |
| Cabell | 50 | 0 | 10 | 16 | 24 | 1,005 | 335 | 601 | 69 | 3 |
| Hampshire | 25 | 0 | 0 | 1 | 24 | 136 | 58 | 73 | 5 | 4 |
| Hancock | 6 | 0 | 0 | 0 | 6 | 15 | 4 | 7 | 4 | 0 |
| Jefferson | 43 | 0 | 0 | 10 | 33 | 476 | 128 | 324 | 24 | 4 |
| Kanawha | 291 | 8 | 9 | 41 | 233 | 1,413 | 569 | 730 | 114 | 30 |
| Marshall | 12 | 0 | 0 | 0 | 12 | 222 | 66 | 138 | 18 | 1 |
| Mineral | 89 | 1 | 0 | 2 | 86 | 34 | 7 | 26 | 1 | 0 |
| Monongalia | 71 | 0 | 1 | 2 | 68 | 501 | 81 | 401 | 19 | 4 |
| Morgan | 10 | 0 | 2 | 0 | 8 | 104 | 29 | 66 | 9 | 1 |
| Ohio | 67 | 0 | 1 | 0 | 66 | 125 | 30 | 89 | 6 | 1 |
| Preston | 61 | 0 | 1 | 0 | 60 | 153 | 53 | 86 | 14 | 4 |
| Putnam | 54 | 2 | 6 | 13 | 33 | 756 | 197 | 485 | 74 | 3 |
| Wirt | 2 | 0 | 0 | 0 | 2 | 26 | 12 | 12 | 2 | 6 |
| Wood | 54 | 0 | 1 | 7 | 46 | 545 | 162 | 349 | 34 | 13 |
| **WEST VIRGINIA - Nonmetropolitan Counties** | | | | | | | | | | |
| Barbour | 3 | 0 | 0 | 0 | 3 | 10 | 4 | 6 | 0 | 0 |
| Braxton | 9 | 0 | 0 | 0 | 9 | 56 | 17 | 36 | 3 | 0 |
| Fayette | 68 | 4 | 13 | 6 | 45 | 364 | 153 | 178 | 33 | 8 |
| Grant | 12 | 0 | 0 | 0 | 12 | 50 | 16 | 33 | 1 | 0 |
| Greenbrier | 15 | 0 | 1 | 2 | 12 | 98 | 39 | 55 | 4 | 1 |
| Hardy | 10 | 0 | 0 | 0 | 10 | 39 | 26 | 11 | 2 | 0 |
| Harrison | 64 | 2 | 0 | 6 | 56 | 359 | 111 | 216 | 32 | 3 |
| Jackson | 3 | 0 | 0 | 0 | 3 | 47 | 7 | 30 | 10 | 0 |
| Lewis | 6 | 0 | 0 | 1 | 5 | 13 | 5 | 8 | 0 | 0 |
| Logan | 15 | 0 | 1 | 3 | 11 | 27 | 5 | 20 | 2 | 2 |
| McDowell | 11 | 2 | 0 | 2 | 7 | 71 | 19 | 41 | 11 | 0 |
| Mercer | 90 | 2 | 2 | 16 | 70 | 532 | 229 | 268 | 35 | 4 |
| Mingo | 8 | 1 | 0 | 0 | 7 | 6 | 2 | 2 | 2 | 0 |
| Monroe | 7 | 0 | 0 | 1 | 6 | 41 | 20 | 21 | 0 | 0 |
| Nicholas | 43 | 0 | 2 | 2 | 39 | 451 | 95 | 329 | 27 | 2 |
| Raleigh | 143 | 2 | 10 | 23 | 108 | 1,068 | 389 | 613 | 66 | 17 |
| Randolph | 14 | 0 | 0 | 0 | 14 | 74 | 23 | 49 | 2 | 1 |
| Ritchie | 17 | 0 | 0 | 1 | 16 | 47 | 27 | 15 | 5 | 3 |
| Summers | 12 | 0 | 1 | 1 | 10 | 63 | 24 | 39 | 0 | 0 |
| Upshur | 1 | 0 | 0 | 0 | 1 | 48 | 11 | 32 | 5 | 2 |
| Wyoming | 25 | 1 | 0 | 2 | 22 | 293 | 111 | 156 | 26 | 2 |
| **WISCONSIN - Metropolitan Counties** | | | | | | | | | | |
| Brown | 44 | 1 | 15 | 0 | 28 | 1,080 | 227 | 824 | 29 | 5 |
| Calumet | 10 | 0 | 0 | 1 | 9 | 211 | 68 | 135 | 8 | 0 |
| Chippewa | 10 | 0 | 5 | 1 | 4 | 358 | 89 | 255 | 14 | 0 |
| Columbia | 31 | 1 | 6 | 3 | 21 | 334 | 109 | 211 | 14 | 2 |
| Dane | 47 | 2 | 5 | 10 | 30 | 1,087 | 262 | 773 | 52 | 5 |
| Douglas | 9 | 0 | 5 | 0 | 4 | 257 | 111 | 128 | 18 | 1 |
| Eau Claire | 17 | 0 | 3 | 1 | 13 | 220 | 69 | 138 | 13 | 3 |
| Fond du Lac | 32 | 1 | 4 | 0 | 27 | 296 | 86 | 199 | 11 | 1 |
| Iowa | 8 | 0 | 2 | 1 | 5 | 139 | 43 | 89 | 7 | 5 |
| Kenosha | 41 | 1 | 5 | 14 | 21 | 767 | 192 | 532 | 43 | 6 |
| Kewaunee | 3 | 0 | 2 | 1 | 0 | 121 | 16 | 98 | 7 | 1 |
| La Crosse | 14 | 0 | 1 | 0 | 13 | 220 | 45 | 160 | 15 | 0 |
| Marathon[6] | 31 | 0 | 13 | 3 | 15 | 456 | 112 | 335 | 9 | 0 |
| Milwaukee | 7 | 0 | 1 | 3 | 3 | 12 | 0 | 11 | 1 | 0 |
| Oconto | 6 | 3 | 0 | 2 | 1 | 461 | 145 | 272 | 44 | 1 |
| Outagamie | 24 | 1 | 8 | 1 | 14 | 441 | 82 | 323 | 36 | 0 |
| Ozaukee | 9 | 0 | 0 | 0 | 9 | 133 | 24 | 106 | 3 | 4 |
| Pierce | 4 | 0 | 0 | 0 | 4 | 165 | 40 | 118 | 7 | 0 |
| Racine | 18 | 0 | 1 | 8 | 9 | 637 | 109 | 481 | 47 | 3 |
| Rock | 40 | 0 | 8 | 1 | 31 | 442 | 136 | 289 | 17 | 3 |
| Sheboygan | 44 | 0 | 6 | 3 | 35 | 602 | 121 | 464 | 17 | 1 |
| St. Croix | 18 | 0 | 6 | 1 | 11 | 433 | 86 | 311 | 36 | 1 |
| Washington | 26 | 0 | 3 | 3 | 20 | 646 | 148 | 475 | 23 | 8 |
| Waukesha | 43 | 0 | 5 | 3 | 35 | 609 | 93 | 503 | 13 | 0 |
| Winnebago | 28 | 0 | 2 | 1 | 25 | 344 | 109 | 225 | 10 | 0 |

[1] The FBI does not publish arson data unless it receives data from either the agency or the state for all 12 months of the calendar year.

[6] Because of changes in the state/local agency's reporting practices, figures are not comparable to previous years' data.

## Table 10. Offenses Known to Law Enforcement, by State Metropolitan and Nonmetropolitan Counties, 2009—*Continued*

(Number.)

| State/County | Violent crime | Murder and non-negligent man-slaughter | Forcible rape | Robbery | Aggravated assault | Property crime | Burglary | Larceny-theft | Motor vehicle theft | Arson[1] |
|---|---|---|---|---|---|---|---|---|---|---|
| **WISCONSIN - Nonmetropolitan Counties** | | | | | | | | | | |
| Adams | 38 | 0 | 3 | 0 | 35 | 422 | 181 | 218 | 23 | 0 |
| Ashland | 27 | 0 | 0 | 0 | 27 | 62 | 23 | 35 | 4 | 0 |
| Barron | 2 | 1 | 0 | 0 | 1 | 214 | 75 | 128 | 11 | 5 |
| Bayfield | 35 | 0 | 0 | 3 | 32 | 152 | 55 | 94 | 3 | 1 |
| Buffalo | 0 | 0 | 0 | 0 | 0 | 50 | 16 | 31 | 3 | 0 |
| Burnett | 25 | 0 | 5 | 1 | 19 | 211 | 78 | 115 | 18 | 0 |
| Clark[6] | 54 | 0 | 1 | 0 | 53 | 322 | 93 | 210 | 19 | 5 |
| Dodge | 33 | 0 | 5 | 1 | 27 | 239 | 73 | 154 | 12 | 6 |
| Door | 5 | 0 | 0 | 0 | 5 | 195 | 44 | 143 | 8 | 0 |
| Dunn | 28 | 0 | 3 | 1 | 24 | 166 | 52 | 100 | 14 | 0 |
| Florence | 8 | 0 | 0 | 0 | 8 | 84 | 28 | 52 | 4 | 0 |
| Forest | 2 | 0 | 0 | 1 | 1 | 125 | 38 | 76 | 11 | 0 |
| Grant | 34 | 0 | 1 | 0 | 33 | 290 | 126 | 153 | 11 | 1 |
| Green | 11 | 0 | 5 | 0 | 6 | 169 | 53 | 109 | 7 | 0 |
| Green Lake | 1 | 0 | 0 | 0 | 1 | 76 | 28 | 48 | 0 | 1 |
| Iron | 6 | 0 | 0 | 0 | 6 | 95 | 38 | 57 | 0 | 0 |
| Jackson | 5 | 0 | 3 | 2 | 0 | 270 | 92 | 155 | 23 | 7 |
| Jefferson | 36 | 0 | 7 | 2 | 27 | 365 | 113 | 243 | 9 | 5 |
| Juneau | 22 | 0 | 2 | 0 | 20 | 327 | 124 | 188 | 15 | 0 |
| Lafayette | 4 | 0 | 1 | 0 | 3 | 153 | 40 | 104 | 9 | 1 |
| Langlade | 5 | 0 | 1 | 0 | 4 | 306 | 109 | 189 | 8 | 0 |
| Lincoln | 9 | 0 | 0 | 0 | 9 | 105 | 39 | 59 | 7 | 0 |
| Manitowoc | 21 | 1 | 5 | 0 | 15 | 231 | 74 | 145 | 12 | 2 |
| Marinette | 8 | 0 | 2 | 0 | 6 | 452 | 246 | 191 | 15 | 0 |
| Marquette | 11 | 1 | 2 | 0 | 8 | 186 | 54 | 121 | 11 | 0 |
| Menominee | 1 | 0 | 0 | 0 | 1 | 78 | 39 | 35 | 4 | 1 |
| Monroe | 6 | 1 | 0 | 0 | 5 | 242 | 65 | 164 | 13 | 5 |
| Oneida | 17 | 0 | 2 | 0 | 15 | 263 | 123 | 133 | 7 | 0 |
| Pepin | 8 | 0 | 2 | 0 | 6 | 38 | 26 | 9 | 3 | 0 |
| Polk[4] | 100 | 1 | 14 | 0 | 85 | | | 259 | 37 | 0 |
| Portage | 30 | 3 | 2 | 0 | 25 | 330 | 90 | 232 | 8 | 4 |
| Price | 14 | 0 | 3 | 1 | 10 | 116 | 33 | 79 | 4 | 0 |
| Richland | 3 | 0 | 0 | 1 | 2 | 58 | 27 | 22 | 9 | 0 |
| Rusk | 14 | 0 | 1 | 0 | 13 | 174 | 101 | 62 | 11 | 1 |
| Sauk | 28 | 0 | 4 | 2 | 22 | 632 | 143 | 454 | 35 | 0 |
| Sawyer | 22 | 2 | 2 | 2 | 16 | 289 | 85 | 168 | 36 | 0 |
| Shawano | 12 | 0 | 1 | 3 | 8 | 446 | 137 | 270 | 39 | 1 |
| Taylor | 7 | 1 | 6 | 0 | 0 | 173 | 53 | 111 | 9 | 0 |
| Trempealeau | 10 | 0 | 8 | 0 | 2 | 147 | 46 | 91 | 10 | 0 |
| Vernon | 10 | 0 | 2 | 1 | 7 | 190 | 69 | 115 | 6 | 2 |
| Vilas | 9 | 0 | 5 | 0 | 4 | 210 | 58 | 143 | 9 | 2 |
| Walworth | 11 | 0 | 3 | 4 | 4 | 262 | 47 | 199 | 16 | 1 |
| Washburn | 6 | 0 | 1 | 0 | 5 | 206 | 73 | 127 | 6 | 0 |
| Waupaca | 43 | 0 | 10 | 0 | 33 | 456 | 122 | 304 | 30 | 0 |
| Waushara | 16 | 0 | 0 | 2 | 14 | 371 | 72 | 282 | 17 | 1 |
| Wood | 2 | 0 | 0 | 0 | 2 | 198 | 71 | 118 | 9 | 0 |
| **WYOMING - Metropolitan Counties** | | | | | | | | | | |
| Laramie | 48 | 0 | 12 | 2 | 34 | 504 | 103 | 368 | 33 | 2 |
| Natrona | 16 | 0 | 4 | 0 | 12 | 260 | 104 | 136 | 20 | 3 |
| **WYOMING - Nonmetropolitan Counties** | | | | | | | | | | |
| Albany | 4 | 0 | 0 | 0 | 4 | 68 | 15 | 46 | 7 | 0 |
| Big Horn | 4 | 0 | 1 | 0 | 3 | 26 | 16 | 8 | 2 | 0 |
| Campbell | 43 | 1 | 3 | 2 | 37 | 291 | 57 | 218 | 16 | 0 |
| Carbon | 3 | 0 | 0 | 0 | 3 | 48 | 3 | 35 | 10 | 0 |
| Converse | 13 | 2 | 1 | 0 | 10 | 49 | 11 | 34 | 4 | 0 |
| Crook | 0 | 0 | 0 | 0 | 0 | 61 | 14 | 44 | 3 | 0 |
| Fremont | 27 | 0 | 5 | 1 | 21 | 217 | 69 | 126 | 22 | 4 |
| Goshen | 17 | 0 | 1 | 0 | 16 | 63 | 18 | 41 | 4 | 0 |
| Hot Springs | 1 | 0 | 0 | 0 | 1 | 26 | 5 | 21 | 0 | 0 |
| Johnson | 2 | 1 | 0 | 0 | 1 | 26 | 6 | 15 | 5 | 0 |
| Lincoln | 9 | 1 | 3 | 0 | 5 | 108 | 21 | 80 | 7 | 1 |
| Niobrara | 1 | 0 | 0 | 0 | 1 | 8 | 3 | 5 | 0 | 0 |
| Park | 36 | 0 | 12 | 0 | 24 | 72 | 19 | 51 | 2 | 0 |
| Platte | 5 | 0 | 3 | 0 | 2 | 31 | 6 | 25 | 0 | 0 |
| Sheridan | 15 | 0 | 1 | 0 | 14 | 89 | 22 | 64 | 3 | 0 |
| Sublette | 27 | 0 | 4 | 1 | 22 | 167 | 32 | 125 | 10 | 0 |
| Sweetwater | 18 | 0 | 4 | 1 | 13 | 143 | 31 | 99 | 13 | 0 |
| Teton | 5 | 0 | 1 | 0 | 4 | 150 | 20 | 116 | 14 | 3 |
| Uinta | 2 | 0 | 1 | 0 | 1 | 93 | 5 | 79 | 9 | 0 |
| Washakie | 2 | 0 | 0 | 0 | 2 | 14 | 0 | 14 | 0 | 0 |
| Weston | 2 | 0 | 0 | 0 | 2 | 7 | 2 | 3 | 2 | 0 |

[1] The FBI does not publish arson data unless it receives data from either the agency or the state for all 12 months of the calendar year.
[4] The FBI determined that the agency did not follow national Uniform Crime Reporting (UCR) Program guidelines for reporting an offense. Consequently, this figure is not included in this table.
[6] Because of changes in the state/local agency's reporting practices, figures are not comparable to previous years' data.

## Table 11. Offenses Known to Law Enforcement, by State, Tribal, and Other Agencies, 2009

(Number.)

| State/Other Agency | Unit/Office | Violent crime | Murder and non-negligent man-slaughter | Forcible rape | Robbery | Aggra-vated assault | Property crime | Burglary | Larceny-theft | Motor vehicle theft | Arson[1] |
|---|---|---|---|---|---|---|---|---|---|---|---|
| **ALABAMA—Tribal Agencies** | | | | | | | | | | | |
| Poarch Creek Tribal | | 14 | 0 | 2 | 4 | 8 | 91 | 13 | 71 | 7 | 0 |
| **ALABAMA—Other Agencies** | | | | | | | | | | | |
| 2nd Judicial Circuit Drug Task Force | | 0 | 0 | 0 | 0 | 0 | 0 | 0 | 0 | 0 | |
| 22nd Judicial Circuit Drug Task Force | | 0 | 0 | 0 | 0 | 0 | 0 | 0 | 0 | 0 | |
| 24th Judicial Circuit Drug and Violent Crime Task Force | | 0 | 0 | 0 | 0 | 0 | 0 | 0 | 0 | 0 | |
| Madison-Morgan County Strategic Counterdrug Team | | 0 | 0 | 0 | 0 | 0 | 2 | 0 | 2 | 0 | |
| Marshall County Drug Enforcement Unit | | 0 | 0 | 0 | 0 | 0 | 0 | 0 | 0 | 0 | |
| **ALASKA—State Agencies** | | | | | | | | | | | |
| Alaska State Troopers | | 859 | 6 | 66 | 26 | 761 | 3,348 | 1,006 | 1,981 | 361 | 41 |
| Alcohol Beverage Control Board | | 0 | 0 | 0 | 0 | 0 | 4 | 0 | 4 | 0 | 0 |
| **ALASKA—Other Agencies** | | | | | | | | | | | |
| Anchorage International Airport | | 9 | 0 | 0 | 1 | 8 | 76 | 1 | 70 | 5 | 0 |
| Fairbanks International Airport | | 3 | 0 | 0 | 0 | 3 | 19 | 0 | 16 | 3 | 1 |
| **ARIZONA—State Agencies** | | | | | | | | | | | |
| Arizona Department of Public Safety | | 9 | 0 | 0 | 0 | 9 | 1 | 0 | 1 | 0 | 0 |
| **ARIZONA—Tribal Agencies** | | | | | | | | | | | |
| Cocopah Tribal | | 16 | 0 | 0 | 1 | 15 | 34 | 6 | 26 | 2 | 0 |
| Colorado River Tribal | | 48 | 1 | 1 | 0 | 46 | 44 | 19 | 12 | 13 | 30 |
| Fort Apache Tribal | | 152 | 6 | 65 | 3 | 78 | 8 | 4 | 4 | 0 | 5 |
| Hopi Tribal | | 13 | 3 | 6 | 1 | 3 | 0 | 0 | 0 | 0 | 1 |
| Hualapai Tribal | | 127 | 0 | 2 | 1 | 124 | 31 | 22 | 7 | 2 | 2 |
| Navajo Tribal | | 905 | 15 | 374 | 37 | 479 | 2,866 | 1,132 | 1,032 | 702 | 307 |
| Quechan Tribal | | 5 | 0 | 0 | 0 | 5 | 36 | 14 | 17 | 5 | 4 |
| **ARIZONA—Other Agencies** | | | | | | | | | | | |
| Tucson Airport Authority | | 1 | 0 | 0 | 0 | 1 | 72 | 6 | 44 | 22 | 0 |
| **ARKANSAS—State Agencies** | | | | | | | | | | | |
| State Capitol Police | | 0 | 0 | 0 | 0 | 0 | 22 | 11 | 9 | 2 | 0 |
| **CALIFORNIA—State Agencies** | | | | | | | | | | | |
| Atascadero State Hospital | | 77 | 0 | 0 | 2 | 75 | 21 | 0 | 21 | 0 | 2 |
| California State Fair | | 0 | 0 | 0 | 0 | 0 | 52 | 1 | 50 | 1 | 0 |
| Coalinga State Hospital | | 43 | 0 | 0 | 2 | 41 | 25 | 1 | 24 | 0 | 0 |
| Department of Parks and Recreation: | Angeles | 0 | 0 | 0 | 0 | 0 | 0 | 0 | 0 | 0 | 0 |
| | Bay Area | 1 | 1 | 0 | 0 | 0 | 5 | 1 | 4 | 0 | 0 |
| | Calaveras County | 0 | 0 | 0 | 0 | 0 | 0 | 0 | 0 | 0 | 0 |
| | Capital | 0 | 0 | 0 | 0 | 0 | 6 | 0 | 6 | 0 | 0 |
| | Channel Coast | 0 | 0 | 0 | 0 | 0 | 30 | 1 | 29 | 0 | 0 |
| | Colorado | 0 | 0 | 0 | 0 | 0 | 0 | 0 | 0 | 0 | 0 |
| | Four Rivers District | 1 | 0 | 0 | 0 | 1 | 19 | 2 | 13 | 4 | 0 |
| | Gold Fields District | 3 | 0 | 0 | 3 | 0 | 97 | 3 | 92 | 2 | 3 |
| | Hollister Hills | 0 | 0 | 0 | 0 | 0 | 5 | 0 | 3 | 2 | 0 |
| | Hungry Valley | 0 | 0 | 0 | 0 | 0 | 4 | 1 | 0 | 3 | 0 |
| | Inland Empire | 3 | 0 | 0 | 0 | 3 | 14 | 0 | 14 | 0 | 1 |
| | Marin County | 0 | 0 | 0 | 0 | 0 | 6 | 0 | 2 | 4 | 0 |
| | Mendocino Headquarters | 2 | 0 | 0 | 0 | 2 | 25 | 9 | 16 | 0 | 0 |
| | Monterey County | 0 | 0 | 0 | 0 | 0 | 43 | 1 | 42 | 0 | 0 |
| | North Coast Redwoods | 2 | 0 | 0 | 1 | 1 | 57 | 20 | 31 | 6 | 1 |
| | Northern Buttes | 4 | 0 | 1 | 0 | 3 | 22 | 0 | 20 | 2 | 0 |
| | Oceano Dunes | 3 | 0 | 0 | 1 | 2 | 39 | 2 | 31 | 6 | 0 |
| | Ocotillo Wells | 0 | 0 | 0 | 0 | 0 | 0 | 0 | 0 | 0 | 0 |
| | Orange Coast | 1 | 0 | 0 | 1 | 0 | 66 | 15 | 50 | 1 | 0 |
| | Russian River | 0 | 0 | 0 | 0 | 0 | 44 | 0 | 44 | 0 | 0 |
| | San Diego Coast | 0 | 0 | 0 | 0 | 0 | 47 | 0 | 43 | 4 | 1 |
| | San Joaquin | 3 | 0 | 0 | 2 | 1 | 1 | 1 | 0 | 0 | 0 |
| | San Luis Obispo Coast | 2 | 0 | 0 | 0 | 2 | 15 | 2 | 13 | 0 | 0 |
| | Santa Cruz Mountains | 0 | 0 | 0 | 0 | 0 | 42 | 2 | 40 | 0 | 0 |
| | Sierra | 0 | 0 | 0 | 0 | 0 | 15 | 0 | 14 | 1 | 0 |
| | Silverado | 0 | 0 | 0 | 0 | 0 | 13 | 0 | 13 | 0 | 0 |
| | Twin Cities | 0 | 0 | 0 | 0 | 0 | 1 | 0 | 1 | 0 | 0 |
| Fairview Developmental Center | | 3 | 1 | 0 | 2 | 0 | 16 | 3 | 12 | 1 | 0 |
| Highway Patrol: | Alameda County | 0 | 0 | 0 | 0 | 0 | 211 | 0 | 12 | 199 | 0 |
| | Alpine County | 0 | 0 | 0 | 0 | 0 | 2 | 0 | 0 | 2 | 0 |
| | Amador County | 0 | 0 | 0 | 0 | 0 | 43 | 0 | 1 | 42 | 0 |
| | Butte County | 1 | 0 | 0 | 1 | 0 | 307 | 0 | 46 | 261 | 0 |
| | Calaveras County | 0 | 0 | 0 | 0 | 0 | 107 | 0 | 14 | 93 | 0 |
| | Colusa County | 2 | 0 | 0 | 1 | 1 | 18 | 0 | 1 | 17 | 0 |
| | Contra Costa County | 0 | 0 | 0 | 0 | 0 | 1,089 | 0 | 0 | 1,089 | 0 |
| | Del Norte County | 0 | 0 | 0 | 0 | 0 | 54 | 1 | 1 | 52 | 0 |
| | El Dorado County | 0 | 0 | 0 | 0 | 0 | 154 | 0 | 31 | 123 | 0 |

[1] The FBI does not publish arson data unless it receives data from either the agency or the state for all 12 months of the calendar year.

## Table 11. Offenses Known to Law Enforcement, by State, Tribal, and Other Agencies, 2009—*Continued*

(Number.)

| State/Other Agency | Unit/Office | Violent crime | Murder and non-negligent man-slaughter | Forcible rape | Robbery | Aggra-vated assault | Property crime | Burglary | Larceny-theft | Motor vehicle theft | Arson[1] |
|---|---|---|---|---|---|---|---|---|---|---|---|
| | Fresno County | 3 | 0 | 0 | 0 | 3 | 247 | 0 | 42 | 205 | 0 |
| | Glenn County | 1 | 0 | 0 | 0 | 1 | 16 | 0 | 3 | 13 | 0 |
| | Humboldt County | 0 | 0 | 0 | 0 | 0 | 229 | 1 | 16 | 212 | 0 |
| | Imperial County | 1 | 0 | 0 | 0 | 1 | 122 | 0 | 11 | 111 | 0 |
| | Inyo County | 0 | 0 | 0 | 0 | 0 | 16 | 0 | 3 | 13 | 0 |
| | Kern County | 1 | 0 | 0 | 0 | 1 | 352 | 1 | 28 | 323 | 0 |
| | Kings County | 0 | 0 | 0 | 0 | 0 | 53 | 0 | 0 | 53 | 0 |
| | Lake County | 1 | 0 | 1 | 0 | 0 | 129 | 0 | 18 | 111 | 0 |
| | Lassen County | 0 | 0 | 0 | 0 | 0 | 15 | 0 | 1 | 14 | 0 |
| | Los Angeles County | 12 | 0 | 0 | 0 | 12 | 369 | 13 | 21 | 335 | 0 |
| | Madera County | 1 | 0 | 0 | 0 | 1 | 289 | 0 | 36 | 253 | 0 |
| | Marin County | 0 | 0 | 0 | 0 | 0 | 68 | 0 | 0 | 68 | 0 |
| | Mariposa County | 0 | 0 | 0 | 0 | 0 | 17 | 0 | 2 | 15 | 0 |
| | Mendocino County | 0 | 0 | 0 | 0 | 0 | 67 | 3 | 20 | 44 | 0 |
| | Merced County | 0 | 0 | 0 | 0 | 0 | 400 | 0 | 66 | 334 | 0 |
| | Modoc County | 0 | 0 | 0 | 0 | 0 | 0 | 0 | 0 | 0 | 0 |
| | Mono County | 0 | 0 | 0 | 0 | 0 | 3 | 0 | 0 | 3 | 0 |
| | Monterey County | 1 | 0 | 0 | 0 | 1 | 355 | 1 | 33 | 321 | 0 |
| | Napa County | 1 | 0 | 1 | 0 | 0 | 84 | 0 | 8 | 76 | 0 |
| | Nevada County | 3 | 0 | 0 | 0 | 3 | 68 | 0 | 11 | 57 | 0 |
| | Orange County | 3 | 0 | 0 | 0 | 3 | 17 | 1 | 9 | 7 | 0 |
| | Placer County | 2 | 0 | 0 | 1 | 1 | 262 | 1 | 53 | 208 | 0 |
| | Plumas County | 0 | 0 | 0 | 0 | 0 | 20 | 0 | 6 | 14 | 0 |
| | Riverside County | 6 | 0 | 0 | 0 | 6 | 66 | 11 | 3 | 52 | 0 |
| | Sacramento County | 14 | 0 | 0 | 4 | 10 | 3,722 | 17 | 875 | 2,830 | 0 |
| | San Benito County | 0 | 0 | 0 | 0 | 0 | 39 | 0 | 0 | 39 | 0 |
| | San Bernardino County | 3 | 0 | 0 | 0 | 3 | 40 | 0 | 6 | 34 | 0 |
| | San Diego County | 5 | 0 | 0 | 0 | 5 | 79 | 2 | 8 | 69 | 0 |
| | San Francisco County | 1 | 0 | 0 | 0 | 1 | 22 | 0 | 5 | 17 | 0 |
| | San Joaquin County | 0 | 0 | 0 | 0 | 0 | 872 | 0 | 268 | 604 | 0 |
| | San Luis Obispo County | 2 | 0 | 0 | 0 | 2 | 146 | 0 | 14 | 132 | 0 |
| | San Mateo County | 2 | 0 | 0 | 0 | 2 | 22 | 0 | 0 | 22 | 0 |
| | Santa Barbara County | 1 | 0 | 1 | 0 | 0 | 125 | 1 | 28 | 96 | 0 |
| | Santa Clara County | 0 | 0 | 0 | 0 | 0 | 81 | 0 | 12 | 69 | 0 |
| | Santa Cruz County | 0 | 0 | 0 | 0 | 0 | 393 | 0 | 51 | 342 | 0 |
| | Shasta County | 1 | 0 | 0 | 0 | 1 | 119 | 0 | 25 | 94 | 0 |
| | Sierra County | 0 | 0 | 0 | 0 | 0 | 0 | 0 | 0 | 0 | 0 |
| | Siskiyou County | 1 | 0 | 0 | 0 | 1 | 41 | 0 | 3 | 38 | 0 |
| | Solano County | 0 | 0 | 0 | 0 | 0 | 60 | 0 | 0 | 60 | 0 |
| | Sonoma County | 0 | 0 | 0 | 0 | 0 | 214 | 0 | 44 | 170 | 0 |
| | Stanislaus County | 1 | 0 | 0 | 1 | 0 | 549 | 0 | 9 | 540 | 0 |
| | Sutter County | 0 | 0 | 0 | 0 | 0 | 36 | 0 | 5 | 31 | 0 |
| | Tehama County | 1 | 0 | 0 | 0 | 1 | 86 | 1 | 3 | 82 | 0 |
| | Trinity County | 0 | 0 | 0 | 0 | 0 | 26 | 0 | 0 | 26 | 0 |
| | Tulare County | 1 | 0 | 0 | 0 | 1 | 876 | 0 | 133 | 743 | 0 |
| | Tuolumne County | 0 | 0 | 0 | 0 | 0 | 94 | 0 | 13 | 81 | 0 |
| | Ventura County | 0 | 0 | 0 | 0 | 0 | 42 | 0 | 7 | 35 | 1 |
| | Yolo County | 1 | 0 | 0 | 1 | 0 | 50 | 3 | 1 | 46 | 0 |
| | Yuba County | 0 | 0 | 0 | 0 | 0 | 137 | 0 | 8 | 129 | 0 |
| Lanterman State Hospital | | 1 | 0 | 0 | 0 | 1 | 6 | 1 | 5 | 0 | 0 |
| Napa State Hospital[2] | | | 0 | 1 | 0 | | 11 | 7 | 4 | 0 | 0 |
| Patton State Hospital | | 747 | 0 | 5 | 4 | 738 | 12 | 4 | 8 | 0 | 1 |
| Porterville Developmental Center | | 0 | 0 | 0 | 0 | 0 | 0 | 0 | 0 | 0 | 0 |
| Sonoma Developmental Center | | 2 | 0 | 1 | 0 | 1 | 8 | 3 | 5 | 0 | 0 |
| **CALIFORNIA—Other Agencies** | | | | | | | | | | | |
| East Bay Municipal Utility | | 1 | 0 | 1 | 0 | 0 | 25 | 0 | 24 | 1 | 1 |
| East Bay Regional Parks: | Alameda County | 2 | 0 | 1 | 0 | 1 | 217 | 3 | 206 | 8 | 5 |
| | Contra Costa County | 14 | 0 | 1 | 9 | 4 | 178 | 0 | 172 | 6 | 3 |
| Fontana Unified School District | | 36 | 0 | 3 | 8 | 25 | 95 | 36 | 54 | 5 | 3 |
| Los Angeles County Metropolitan Transportation Authority | | 10 | 0 | 0 | 2 | 8 | 23 | 2 | 21 | 0 | 1 |
| Los Angeles Transportation Services Bureau | | 449 | 0 | 5 | 285 | 159 | 670 | 15 | 529 | 126 | 3 |
| Monterey Peninsula Airport | | 0 | 0 | 0 | 0 | 0 | 8 | 4 | 1 | 3 | 0 |
| Port of San Diego Harbor | | 20 | 0 | 0 | 3 | 17 | 446 | 14 | 432 | 0 | 1 |
| San Bernardino Unified School District | | 98 | 0 | 1 | 85 | 12 | 371 | 180 | 173 | 18 | 9 |
| San Francisco Bay Area Rapid Transit: | Alameda County | 149 | 1 | 0 | 130 | 18 | 1,424 | 4 | 1,198 | 222 | 0 |
| | Contra Costa County | 39 | 0 | 1 | 33 | 5 | 784 | 2 | 651 | 131 | 1 |
| | San Francisco County | 37 | 0 | 0 | 33 | 4 | 166 | 1 | 164 | 1 | 0 |
| | San Mateo County | 10 | 0 | 0 | 6 | 4 | 135 | 0 | 116 | 19 | 0 |

[1] The FBI does not publish arson data unless it receives data from either the agency or the state for all 12 months of the calendar year.

[2] The FBI determined that the agency's data were overreported. Consequently, affected data are not included in this table.

## Table 11. Offenses Known to Law Enforcement, by State, Tribal, and Other Agencies, 2009—*Continued*

(Number.)

| State/Other Agency | Unit/Office | Violent crime | Murder and non-negligent man-slaughter | Forcible rape | Robbery | Aggra-vated assault | Property crime | Burglary | Larceny-theft | Motor vehicle theft | Arson[1] |
|---|---|---|---|---|---|---|---|---|---|---|---|
| Santa Clara Transit District | | 51 | 1 | 0 | 33 | 17 | 94 | 4 | 81 | 9 | 0 |
| Stockton Unified School District | | 119 | 0 | 1 | 21 | 97 | 455 | 107 | 341 | 7 | 15 |
| Twin Rivers Unified School District | | 28 | 0 | 1 | 10 | 17 | 80 | 48 | 30 | 2 | 1 |
| Union Pacific Railroad: | Alameda County | 5 | 0 | 0 | 0 | 5 | 129 | 124 | 5 | 0 | 0 |
| | Amador County | 0 | 0 | 0 | 0 | 0 | 0 | 0 | 0 | 0 | 0 |
| | Butte County | 3 | 0 | 0 | 0 | 3 | 3 | 0 | 3 | 0 | 0 |
| | Calaveras County | 0 | 0 | 0 | 0 | 0 | 0 | 0 | 0 | 0 | 0 |
| | Colusa County | 0 | 0 | 0 | 0 | 0 | 0 | 0 | 0 | 0 | 0 |
| | Contra Costa County | 3 | 0 | 0 | 0 | 3 | 16 | 13 | 3 | 0 | 0 |
| | El Dorado County | 0 | 0 | 0 | 0 | 0 | 0 | 0 | 0 | 0 | 0 |
| | Fresno County | 0 | 0 | 0 | 0 | 0 | 0 | 0 | 0 | 0 | 0 |
| | Glenn County | 0 | 0 | 0 | 0 | 0 | 0 | 0 | 0 | 0 | 0 |
| | Humboldt County | 0 | 0 | 0 | 0 | 0 | 0 | 0 | 0 | 0 | 0 |
| | Imperial County | 0 | 0 | 0 | 0 | 0 | 29 | 28 | 1 | 0 | 0 |
| | Inyo County | 0 | 0 | 0 | 0 | 0 | 0 | 0 | 0 | 0 | 0 |
| | Kern County | 0 | 0 | 0 | 0 | 0 | 1 | 1 | 0 | 0 | 0 |
| | Kings County | 0 | 0 | 0 | 0 | 0 | 0 | 0 | 0 | 0 | 0 |
| | Lassen County | 0 | 0 | 0 | 0 | 0 | 0 | 0 | 0 | 0 | 0 |
| | Los Angeles County | 1 | 0 | 0 | 0 | 1 | 95 | 83 | 12 | 0 | 0 |
| | Madera County | 0 | 0 | 0 | 0 | 0 | 1 | 1 | 0 | 0 | 0 |
| | Marin County | 0 | 0 | 0 | 0 | 0 | 0 | 0 | 0 | 0 | 0 |
| | Mendocino County | 0 | 0 | 0 | 0 | 0 | 0 | 0 | 0 | 0 | 0 |
| | Merced County | 0 | 0 | 0 | 0 | 0 | 1 | 0 | 1 | 0 | 0 |
| | Modoc County | 0 | 0 | 0 | 0 | 0 | 0 | 0 | 0 | 0 | 0 |
| | Monterey County | 0 | 0 | 0 | 0 | 0 | 0 | 0 | 0 | 0 | 0 |
| | Napa County | 0 | 0 | 0 | 0 | 0 | 0 | 0 | 0 | 0 | 0 |
| | Nevada County | 0 | 0 | 0 | 0 | 0 | 0 | 0 | 0 | 0 | 0 |
| | Orange County | 0 | 0 | 0 | 0 | 0 | 0 | 0 | 0 | 0 | 0 |
| | Placer County | 4 | 0 | 0 | 0 | 4 | 13 | 7 | 6 | 0 | 0 |
| | Plumas County | 0 | 0 | 0 | 0 | 0 | 2 | 2 | 0 | 0 | 0 |
| | Riverside County[3] | 5 | 0 | 0 | 0 | 5 | | | 1 | 0 | 0 |
| | Sacramento County | 2 | 0 | 0 | 0 | 2 | 7 | 0 | 7 | 0 | 0 |
| | San Benito County | 0 | 0 | 0 | 0 | 0 | 0 | 0 | 0 | 0 | 0 |
| | San Bernardino County | 2 | 0 | 0 | 0 | 2 | 33 | 21 | 12 | 0 | 0 |
| | San Francisco County | 0 | 0 | 0 | 0 | 0 | 1 | 0 | 1 | 0 | 0 |
| | San Joaquin County[3] | 2 | 0 | 0 | 0 | 2 | | 92 | | 0 | 0 |
| | San Luis Obispo County | 0 | 0 | 0 | 0 | 0 | 0 | 0 | 0 | 0 | 0 |
| | San Mateo County | 0 | 0 | 0 | 0 | 0 | 0 | 0 | 0 | 0 | 0 |
| | Santa Barbara County | 0 | 0 | 0 | 0 | 0 | 1 | 0 | 1 | 0 | 0 |
| | Santa Clara County | 0 | 0 | 0 | 0 | 0 | 2 | 0 | 2 | 0 | 0 |
| | Santa Cruz County | 0 | 0 | 0 | 0 | 0 | 0 | 0 | 0 | 0 | 0 |
| | Shasta County | 0 | 0 | 0 | 0 | 0 | 1 | 0 | 1 | 0 | 0 |
| | Sierra County | 0 | 0 | 0 | 0 | 0 | 0 | 0 | 0 | 0 | 0 |
| | Siskiyou County | 0 | 0 | 0 | 0 | 0 | 1 | 1 | 0 | 0 | 0 |
| | Solano County | 0 | 0 | 0 | 0 | 0 | 0 | 0 | 0 | 0 | 0 |
| | Sonoma County | 0 | 0 | 0 | 0 | 0 | 0 | 0 | 0 | 0 | 0 |
| | Stanislaus County | 0 | 0 | 0 | 0 | 0 | 5 | 1 | 4 | 0 | 0 |
| | Sutter County | 0 | 0 | 0 | 0 | 0 | 0 | 0 | 0 | 0 | 0 |
| | Tehama County | 0 | 0 | 0 | 0 | 0 | 0 | 0 | 0 | 0 | 0 |
| | Trinity County | 0 | 0 | 0 | 0 | 0 | 0 | 0 | 0 | 0 | 0 |
| | Tulare County | 0 | 0 | 0 | 0 | 0 | 0 | 0 | 0 | 0 | 0 |
| | Ventura County | 0 | 0 | 0 | 0 | 0 | 0 | 0 | 0 | 0 | 0 |
| | Yolo County | 1 | 0 | 0 | 0 | 1 | 1 | 0 | 1 | 0 | 0 |
| | Yuba County | 1 | 0 | 0 | 0 | 1 | 1 | 0 | 1 | 0 | 0 |
| **COLORADO—State Agencies** | | | | | | | | | | | |
| Colorado Bureau of Investigation | | 0 | 0 | 0 | 0 | 0 | 1 | 0 | 1 | 0 | 0 |
| Colorado Mental Health Institute | | 0 | 0 | 0 | 0 | 0 | 8 | 0 | 8 | 0 | 0 |
| State Patrol | | 20 | 0 | 0 | 0 | 20 | 54 | 0 | 10 | 44 | 1 |
| **COLORADO—Tribal Agencies** | | | | | | | | | | | |
| Southern Ute Tribal | | 22 | 0 | 5 | 1 | 16 | 37 | 26 | 1 | 10 | 1 |
| Ute Mountain Tribal | | 11 | 1 | 2 | 0 | 8 | 2 | 1 | 0 | 1 | 2 |
| **COLORADO—Other Agencies** | | | | | | | | | | | |
| 22nd Judicial District Drug Task Force | | 0 | 0 | 0 | 0 | 0 | 0 | 0 | 0 | 0 | 0 |
| Delta Montrose Drug Task Force | | 0 | 0 | 0 | 0 | 0 | 0 | 0 | 0 | 0 | 0 |
| Southwest Drug Task Force | | 0 | 0 | 0 | 0 | 0 | 4 | 0 | 4 | 0 | 0 |
| **CONNECTICUT—State Agencies** | | | | | | | | | | | |
| Connecticut State Police | | 346 | 8 | 63 | 49 | 226 | 4,774 | 1,402 | 2,928 | 444 | 87 |
| State Capitol Police | | 0 | 0 | 0 | 0 | 0 | 4 | 0 | 4 | 0 | 0 |
| **CONNECTICUT—Tribal Agencies** | | | | | | | | | | | |
| Mashantucket Pequot Tribal | | 28 | 0 | 0 | 0 | 28 | 22 | 1 | 18 | 3 | 0 |

[1] The FBI does not publish arson data unless it receives data from either the agency or the state for all 12 months of the calendar year.

[3] The FBI determined that the agency's data were underreported. Consequently, affected data are not included in this table.

## Table 11. Offenses Known to Law Enforcement, by State, Tribal, and Other Agencies, 2009—*Continued*

(Number.)

| State/Other Agency | Unit/Office | Violent crime | Murder and non-negligent man-slaughter | Forcible rape | Robbery | Aggra-vated assault | Property crime | Burglary | Larceny-theft | Motor vehicle theft | Arson[1] |
|---|---|---|---|---|---|---|---|---|---|---|---|
| **CONNECTICUT—Other Agencies** | | | | | | | | | | | |
| Metropolitan Transportation Authority | | 4 | 0 | 1 | 2 | 1 | 64 | 0 | 64 | 0 | 0 |
| **DELAWARE—State Agencies** | | | | | | | | | | | |
| Attorney General: | Kent County | 0 | 0 | 0 | 0 | 0 | 0 | 0 | 0 | 0 | 0 |
| | New Castle County | 5 | 0 | 0 | 1 | 4 | 1 | 0 | 1 | 0 | 0 |
| | Sussex County | 0 | 0 | 0 | 0 | 0 | 0 | 0 | 0 | 0 | 0 |
| Division of Alcohol and Tobacco Enforcement | | 0 | 0 | 0 | 0 | 0 | 0 | 0 | 0 | 0 | 0 |
| Environmental Control | | 0 | 0 | 0 | 0 | 0 | 1 | 0 | 1 | 0 | 0 |
| Fish and Wildlife | | 7 | 0 | 0 | 0 | 7 | 29 | 1 | 28 | 0 | 0 |
| Park Rangers | | 0 | 0 | 0 | 0 | 0 | 83 | 27 | 55 | 1 | 0 |
| River and Bay Authority | | 1 | 0 | 0 | 0 | 1 | 19 | 5 | 14 | 0 | 0 |
| State Capitol Police | | 4 | 0 | 0 | 0 | 4 | 20 | 0 | 20 | 0 | 0 |
| State Fire Marshal | | 30 | 0 | 0 | 0 | 30 | 26 | 25 | 1 | 0 | 230 |
| State Police: | Kent County | 487 | 2 | 38 | 78 | 369 | 2,348 | 861 | 1,355 | 132 | 0 |
| | New Castle County | 668 | 7 | 17 | 314 | 330 | 5,404 | 622 | 4,539 | 243 | 5 |
| | Sussex County | 682 | 3 | 69 | 102 | 508 | 3,826 | 1,334 | 2,305 | 187 | 4 |
| **DELAWARE—Other Agencies** | | | | | | | | | | | |
| Amtrak Police | | 0 | 0 | 0 | 0 | 0 | 0 | 0 | 0 | 0 | 0 |
| Drug Enforcement Administration | Wilmington Resident Office | 0 | 0 | 0 | 0 | 0 | 0 | 0 | 0 | 0 | 0 |
| Wilmington Fire Department | | 17 | 0 | 0 | 0 | 17 | 3 | 3 | 0 | 0 | 20 |
| **DISTRICT OF COLUMBIA—Other Agencies** | | | | | | | | | | | |
| Metro Transit Police | | 485 | 1 | 0 | 391 | 93 | 1,449 | 0 | 1,216 | 233 | 0 |
| **FLORIDA—State Agencies** | | | | | | | | | | | |
| Capitol Police | | 0 | 0 | 0 | 0 | 0 | 9 | 0 | 9 | 0 | 0 |
| Department of Environmental Protection, Division of Law Enforcement: | Alachua County | 0 | 0 | 0 | 0 | 0 | 2 | 0 | 2 | 0 | 0 |
| | Bay County | 0 | 0 | 0 | 0 | 0 | 23 | 13 | 10 | 0 | 0 |
| | Bradford County | 0 | 0 | 0 | 0 | 0 | 0 | 0 | 0 | 0 | 0 |
| | Brevard County | 0 | 0 | 0 | 0 | 0 | 10 | 4 | 6 | 0 | 0 |
| | Broward County | 0 | 0 | 0 | 0 | 0 | 16 | 7 | 9 | 0 | 0 |
| | Charlotte County | 0 | 0 | 0 | 0 | 0 | 0 | 0 | 0 | 0 | 0 |
| | Citrus County | 0 | 0 | 0 | 0 | 0 | 2 | 0 | 2 | 0 | 0 |
| | Collier County | 0 | 0 | 0 | 0 | 0 | 2 | 0 | 2 | 0 | 0 |
| | Columbia County | 0 | 0 | 0 | 0 | 0 | 2 | 0 | 1 | 1 | 0 |
| | Duval County | 0 | 0 | 0 | 0 | 0 | 7 | 2 | 5 | 0 | 0 |
| | Escambia County | 0 | 0 | 0 | 0 | 0 | 2 | 1 | 1 | 0 | 0 |
| | Franklin County | 0 | 0 | 0 | 0 | 0 | 0 | 0 | 0 | 0 | 0 |
| | Gadsden County | 0 | 0 | 0 | 0 | 0 | 0 | 0 | 0 | 0 | 0 |
| | Hernando County | 0 | 0 | 0 | 0 | 0 | 2 | 2 | 0 | 0 | 0 |
| | Highlands County | 0 | 0 | 0 | 0 | 0 | 0 | 0 | 0 | 0 | 0 |
| | Hillsborough County | 0 | 0 | 0 | 0 | 0 | 3 | 0 | 3 | 0 | 0 |
| | Indian River County | 0 | 0 | 0 | 0 | 0 | 2 | 0 | 2 | 0 | 0 |
| | Lake County | 0 | 0 | 0 | 0 | 0 | 2 | 0 | 2 | 0 | 0 |
| | Lee County | 0 | 0 | 0 | 0 | 0 | 5 | 1 | 4 | 0 | 0 |
| | Leon County | 0 | 0 | 0 | 0 | 0 | 0 | 0 | 0 | 0 | 0 |
| | Levy County | 0 | 0 | 0 | 0 | 0 | 1 | 1 | 0 | 0 | 0 |
| | Manatee County | 0 | 0 | 0 | 0 | 0 | 0 | 0 | 0 | 0 | 0 |
| | Marion County | 0 | 0 | 0 | 0 | 0 | 2 | 0 | 2 | 0 | 0 |
| | Martin County | 0 | 0 | 0 | 0 | 0 | 2 | 1 | 1 | 0 | 0 |
| | Miami-Dade County | 0 | 0 | 0 | 0 | 0 | 6 | 1 | 5 | 0 | 0 |
| | Monroe County | 0 | 0 | 0 | 0 | 0 | 6 | 1 | 5 | 0 | 0 |
| | Nassau County | 0 | 0 | 0 | 0 | 0 | 3 | 0 | 3 | 0 | 0 |
| | Okaloosa County | 0 | 0 | 0 | 0 | 0 | 3 | 0 | 3 | 0 | 0 |
| | Okeechobee County | 0 | 0 | 0 | 0 | 0 | 0 | 0 | 0 | 0 | 0 |
| | Orange County | 1 | 0 | 0 | 0 | 1 | 6 | 1 | 5 | 0 | 0 |
| | Osceola County | 0 | 0 | 0 | 0 | 0 | 0 | 0 | 0 | 0 | 0 |
| | Palm Beach County | 0 | 0 | 0 | 0 | 0 | 3 | 1 | 1 | 1 | 0 |
| | Pasco County | 0 | 0 | 0 | 0 | 0 | 1 | 1 | 0 | 0 | 0 |
| | Pinellas County | 0 | 0 | 0 | 0 | 0 | 3 | 0 | 3 | 0 | 0 |
| | Polk County | 0 | 0 | 0 | 0 | 0 | 0 | 0 | 0 | 0 | 0 |
| | Putnam County | 0 | 0 | 0 | 0 | 0 | 0 | 0 | 0 | 0 | 0 |
| | Santa Rosa County | 0 | 0 | 0 | 0 | 0 | 0 | 0 | 0 | 0 | 0 |
| | Sarasota County | 0 | 0 | 0 | 0 | 0 | 3 | 0 | 3 | 0 | 0 |
| | Seminole County | 0 | 0 | 0 | 0 | 0 | 3 | 0 | 3 | 0 | 0 |
| | St. Johns County | 0 | 0 | 0 | 0 | 0 | 2 | 1 | 1 | 0 | 0 |
| | St. Lucie County | 1 | 0 | 0 | 0 | 1 | 2 | 0 | 2 | 0 | 0 |
| | Volusia County | 0 | 0 | 0 | 0 | 0 | 22 | 0 | 22 | 0 | 0 |
| | Wakulla County | 0 | 0 | 0 | 0 | 0 | 1 | 1 | 0 | 0 | 0 |
| | Walton County | 0 | 0 | 0 | 0 | 0 | 2 | 0 | 2 | 0 | 0 |
| | Washington County | 0 | 0 | 0 | 0 | 0 | 0 | 0 | 0 | 0 | 0 |

[1] The FBI does not publish arson data unless it receives data from either the agency or the state for all 12 months of the calendar year.

**Table 11. Offenses Known to Law Enforcement, by State, Tribal, and Other Agencies, 2009—*Continued***

(Number.)

| State/Other Agency | Unit/Office | Violent crime | Murder and non-negligent man-slaughter | Forcible rape | Robbery | Aggra-vated assault | Property crime | Burglary | Larceny-theft | Motor vehicle theft | Arson[1] |
|---|---|---|---|---|---|---|---|---|---|---|---|
| Department of Insurance: | Broward County | 0 | 0 | 0 | 0 | 0 | 0 | 0 | 0 | 0 | 0 |
| | Duval County | 0 | 0 | 0 | 0 | 0 | 0 | 0 | 0 | 0 | 0 |
| | Escambia County | 0 | 0 | 0 | 0 | 0 | 0 | 0 | 0 | 0 | 0 |
| | Hillsborough County | 0 | 0 | 0 | 0 | 0 | 0 | 0 | 0 | 0 | 0 |
| | Lee County | 0 | 0 | 0 | 0 | 0 | 0 | 0 | 0 | 0 | 0 |
| | Miami-Dade County | 0 | 0 | 0 | 0 | 0 | 0 | 0 | 0 | 0 | 0 |
| | Orange County | 0 | 0 | 0 | 0 | 0 | 0 | 0 | 0 | 0 | 0 |
| | Palm Beach County | 0 | 0 | 0 | 0 | 0 | 0 | 0 | 0 | 0 | 0 |
| | Pinellas County | 0 | 0 | 0 | 0 | 0 | 0 | 0 | 0 | 0 | 0 |
| Department of Law Enforcement: | Duval County, Jacksonville | 0 | 0 | 0 | 0 | 0 | 0 | 0 | 0 | 0 | 0 |
| | Escambia County, Pensacola | 2 | 0 | 0 | 1 | 1 | 0 | 0 | 0 | 0 | 0 |
| | Hillsborough County, Tampa | 0 | 0 | 0 | 0 | 0 | 0 | 0 | 0 | 0 | 0 |
| | Lee County, Fort Myers | 0 | 0 | 0 | 0 | 0 | 0 | 0 | 0 | 0 | 0 |
| | Leon County, Tallahassee | 1 | 0 | 0 | 0 | 1 | 5 | 0 | 5 | 0 | 0 |
| | Miami-Dade County, Miami | 0 | 0 | 0 | 0 | 0 | 5 | 0 | 5 | 0 | 0 |
| | Orange County, Orlando | 0 | 0 | 0 | 0 | 0 | 0 | 0 | 0 | 0 | 0 |
| Florida Game Commission: | Alachua County | 0 | 0 | 0 | 0 | 0 | 0 | 0 | 0 | 0 | 0 |
| | Baker County | 0 | 0 | 0 | 0 | 0 | 0 | 0 | 0 | 0 | 0 |
| | Bay County | 0 | 0 | 0 | 0 | 0 | 0 | 0 | 0 | 0 | 0 |
| | Bradford County | 0 | 0 | 0 | 0 | 0 | 0 | 0 | 0 | 0 | 0 |
| | Brevard County | 0 | 0 | 0 | 0 | 0 | 0 | 0 | 0 | 0 | 0 |
| | Broward County | 0 | 0 | 0 | 0 | 0 | 0 | 0 | 0 | 0 | 0 |
| | Calhoun County | 0 | 0 | 0 | 0 | 0 | 0 | 0 | 0 | 0 | 0 |
| | Charlotte County | 0 | 0 | 0 | 0 | 0 | 0 | 0 | 0 | 0 | 0 |
| | Citrus County | 0 | 0 | 0 | 0 | 0 | 0 | 0 | 0 | 0 | 0 |
| | Clay County | 0 | 0 | 0 | 0 | 0 | 0 | 0 | 0 | 0 | 0 |
| | Collier County | 0 | 0 | 0 | 0 | 0 | 0 | 0 | 0 | 0 | 0 |
| | Columbia County | 0 | 0 | 0 | 0 | 0 | 0 | 0 | 0 | 0 | 0 |
| | DeSoto County | 0 | 0 | 0 | 0 | 0 | 0 | 0 | 0 | 0 | 0 |
| | Dixie County | 0 | 0 | 0 | 0 | 0 | 0 | 0 | 0 | 0 | 0 |
| | Duval County | 0 | 0 | 0 | 0 | 0 | 0 | 0 | 0 | 0 | 0 |
| | Escambia County | 0 | 0 | 0 | 0 | 0 | 0 | 0 | 0 | 0 | 0 |
| | Flagler County | 0 | 0 | 0 | 0 | 0 | 0 | 0 | 0 | 0 | 0 |
| | Franklin County | 0 | 0 | 0 | 0 | 0 | 0 | 0 | 0 | 0 | 0 |
| | Gadsden County | 0 | 0 | 0 | 0 | 0 | 0 | 0 | 0 | 0 | 0 |
| | Gilchrist County | 0 | 0 | 0 | 0 | 0 | 0 | 0 | 0 | 0 | 0 |
| | Glades County | 0 | 0 | 0 | 0 | 0 | 0 | 0 | 0 | 0 | 0 |
| | Gulf County | 0 | 0 | 0 | 0 | 0 | 0 | 0 | 0 | 0 | 0 |
| | Hamilton County | 0 | 0 | 0 | 0 | 0 | 0 | 0 | 0 | 0 | 0 |
| | Hardee County | 0 | 0 | 0 | 0 | 0 | 0 | 0 | 0 | 0 | 0 |
| | Hendry County | 0 | 0 | 0 | 0 | 0 | 0 | 0 | 0 | 0 | 0 |
| | Hernando County | 0 | 0 | 0 | 0 | 0 | 0 | 0 | 0 | 0 | 0 |
| | Highlands County | 0 | 0 | 0 | 0 | 0 | 0 | 0 | 0 | 0 | 0 |
| | Hillsborough County | 0 | 0 | 0 | 0 | 0 | 0 | 0 | 0 | 0 | 0 |
| | Holmes County | 0 | 0 | 0 | 0 | 0 | 0 | 0 | 0 | 0 | 0 |
| | Indian River County | 0 | 0 | 0 | 0 | 0 | 0 | 0 | 0 | 0 | 0 |
| | Jackson County | 0 | 0 | 0 | 0 | 0 | 0 | 0 | 0 | 0 | 0 |
| | Jefferson County | 0 | 0 | 0 | 0 | 0 | 0 | 0 | 0 | 0 | 0 |
| | Lafayette County | 0 | 0 | 0 | 0 | 0 | 0 | 0 | 0 | 0 | 0 |
| | Lake County | 0 | 0 | 0 | 0 | 0 | 0 | 0 | 0 | 0 | 0 |
| | Lee County | 0 | 0 | 0 | 0 | 0 | 0 | 0 | 0 | 0 | 0 |
| | Leon County | 0 | 0 | 0 | 0 | 0 | 0 | 0 | 0 | 0 | 0 |
| | Levy County | 0 | 0 | 0 | 0 | 0 | 0 | 0 | 0 | 0 | 0 |
| | Liberty County | 0 | 0 | 0 | 0 | 0 | 0 | 0 | 0 | 0 | 0 |
| | Madison County | 0 | 0 | 0 | 0 | 0 | 0 | 0 | 0 | 0 | 0 |
| | Manatee County | 0 | 0 | 0 | 0 | 0 | 0 | 0 | 0 | 0 | 0 |
| | Marion County | 0 | 0 | 0 | 0 | 0 | 0 | 0 | 0 | 0 | 0 |
| | Martin County | 0 | 0 | 0 | 0 | 0 | 0 | 0 | 0 | 0 | 0 |
| | Miami-Dade County | 0 | 0 | 0 | 0 | 0 | 0 | 0 | 0 | 0 | 0 |
| | Monroe County | 0 | 0 | 0 | 0 | 0 | 0 | 0 | 0 | 0 | 0 |
| | Nassau County | 0 | 0 | 0 | 0 | 0 | 0 | 0 | 0 | 0 | 0 |
| | Okaloosa County | 0 | 0 | 0 | 0 | 0 | 0 | 0 | 0 | 0 | 0 |
| | Okeechobee County | 0 | 0 | 0 | 0 | 0 | 0 | 0 | 0 | 0 | 0 |
| | Orange County | 0 | 0 | 0 | 0 | 0 | 0 | 0 | 0 | 0 | 0 |

[1] The FBI does not publish arson data unless it receives data from either the agency or the state for all 12 months of the calendar year.

**Table 11. Offenses Known to Law Enforcement, by State, Tribal, and Other Agencies, 2009—*Continued***

(Number.)

| State/Other Agency | Unit/Office | Violent crime | Murder and non-negligent man-slaughter | Forcible rape | Robbery | Aggra-vated assault | Property crime | Burglary | Larceny-theft | Motor vehicle theft | Arson[1] |
|---|---|---|---|---|---|---|---|---|---|---|---|
| | Osceola County | 0 | 0 | 0 | 0 | 0 | 0 | 0 | 0 | 0 | 0 |
| | Palm Beach County | 0 | 0 | 0 | 0 | 0 | 0 | 0 | 0 | 0 | 0 |
| | Pasco County | 0 | 0 | 0 | 0 | 0 | 0 | 0 | 0 | 0 | 0 |
| | Pinellas County | 0 | 0 | 0 | 0 | 0 | 0 | 0 | 0 | 0 | 0 |
| | Polk County | 0 | 0 | 0 | 0 | 0 | 0 | 0 | 0 | 0 | 0 |
| | Putnam County | 0 | 0 | 0 | 0 | 0 | 0 | 0 | 0 | 0 | 0 |
| | Santa Rosa County | 0 | 0 | 0 | 0 | 0 | 0 | 0 | 0 | 0 | 0 |
| | Sarasota County | 0 | 0 | 0 | 0 | 0 | 0 | 0 | 0 | 0 | 0 |
| | Seminole County | 0 | 0 | 0 | 0 | 0 | 0 | 0 | 0 | 0 | 0 |
| | St. Johns County | 0 | 0 | 0 | 0 | 0 | 0 | 0 | 0 | 0 | 0 |
| | St. Lucie County | 0 | 0 | 0 | 0 | 0 | 0 | 0 | 0 | 0 | 0 |
| | Sumter County | 0 | 0 | 0 | 0 | 0 | 0 | 0 | 0 | 0 | 0 |
| | Suwannee County | 0 | 0 | 0 | 0 | 0 | 0 | 0 | 0 | 0 | 0 |
| | Taylor County | 0 | 0 | 0 | 0 | 0 | 0 | 0 | 0 | 0 | 0 |
| | Union County | 0 | 0 | 0 | 0 | 0 | 0 | 0 | 0 | 0 | 0 |
| | Volusia County | 0 | 0 | 0 | 0 | 0 | 0 | 0 | 0 | 0 | 0 |
| | Wakulla County | 0 | 0 | 0 | 0 | 0 | 0 | 0 | 0 | 0 | 0 |
| | Walton County | 0 | 0 | 0 | 0 | 0 | 0 | 0 | 0 | 0 | 0 |
| | Washington County | 0 | 0 | 0 | 0 | 0 | 0 | 0 | 0 | 0 | 0 |
| Highway Patrol: | Alachua County | 3 | 0 | 0 | 0 | 3 | 1 | 0 | 1 | 0 | 0 |
| | Baker County | 0 | 0 | 0 | 0 | 0 | 0 | 0 | 0 | 0 | 0 |
| | Bay County | 0 | 0 | 0 | 0 | 0 | 0 | 0 | 0 | 0 | 0 |
| | Bradford County | 1 | 0 | 0 | 0 | 1 | 0 | 0 | 0 | 0 | 0 |
| | Brevard County | 0 | 0 | 0 | 0 | 0 | 0 | 0 | 0 | 0 | 0 |
| | Broward County | 27 | 0 | 0 | 0 | 27 | 55 | 0 | 21 | 34 | 0 |
| | Calhoun County | 0 | 0 | 0 | 0 | 0 | 0 | 0 | 0 | 0 | 0 |
| | Charlotte County | 0 | 0 | 0 | 0 | 0 | 1 | 0 | 1 | 0 | 0 |
| | Citrus County | 0 | 0 | 0 | 0 | 0 | 1 | 0 | 1 | 0 | 0 |
| | Clay County | 0 | 0 | 0 | 0 | 0 | 0 | 0 | 0 | 0 | 0 |
| | Collier County | 0 | 0 | 0 | 0 | 0 | 1 | 0 | 0 | 1 | 0 |
| | Columbia County | 1 | 0 | 0 | 1 | 0 | 1 | 0 | 1 | 0 | 0 |
| | DeSoto County | 0 | 0 | 0 | 0 | 0 | 0 | 0 | 0 | 0 | 0 |
| | Dixie County | 0 | 0 | 0 | 0 | 0 | 0 | 0 | 0 | 0 | 0 |
| | Duval County | 7 | 0 | 0 | 0 | 7 | 1 | 0 | 1 | 0 | 0 |
| | Escambia County | 6 | 0 | 0 | 0 | 6 | 2 | 0 | 0 | 2 | 0 |
| | Flagler County | 0 | 0 | 0 | 0 | 0 | 0 | 0 | 0 | 0 | 0 |
| | Franklin County | 0 | 0 | 0 | 0 | 0 | 0 | 0 | 0 | 0 | 0 |
| | Gadsden County | 1 | 0 | 0 | 0 | 1 | 0 | 0 | 0 | 0 | 0 |
| | Gilchrist County | 0 | 0 | 0 | 0 | 0 | 0 | 0 | 0 | 0 | 0 |
| | Glades County | 0 | 0 | 0 | 0 | 0 | 0 | 0 | 0 | 0 | 0 |
| | Gulf County | 0 | 0 | 0 | 0 | 0 | 0 | 0 | 0 | 0 | 0 |
| | Hamilton County | 0 | 0 | 0 | 0 | 0 | 0 | 0 | 0 | 0 | 0 |
| | Hardee County | 0 | 0 | 0 | 0 | 0 | 0 | 0 | 0 | 0 | 0 |
| | Hendry County | 1 | 0 | 0 | 0 | 1 | 0 | 0 | 0 | 0 | 0 |
| | Hernando County | 3 | 0 | 0 | 0 | 3 | 0 | 0 | 0 | 0 | 0 |
| | Highlands County | 1 | 0 | 0 | 0 | 1 | 0 | 0 | 0 | 0 | 0 |
| | Hillsborough County | 11 | 0 | 0 | 0 | 11 | 6 | 0 | 3 | 3 | 0 |
| | Holmes County | 0 | 0 | 0 | 0 | 0 | 0 | 0 | 0 | 0 | 0 |
| | Indian River County | 0 | 0 | 0 | 0 | 0 | 0 | 0 | 0 | 0 | 0 |
| | Jackson County | 2 | 0 | 0 | 0 | 2 | 0 | 0 | 0 | 0 | 0 |
| | Jefferson County | 0 | 0 | 0 | 0 | 0 | 0 | 0 | 0 | 0 | 0 |
| | Lafayette County | 0 | 0 | 0 | 0 | 0 | 0 | 0 | 0 | 0 | 0 |
| | Lake County | 1 | 0 | 0 | 0 | 1 | 2 | 0 | 1 | 1 | 0 |
| | Lee County | 6 | 0 | 0 | 0 | 6 | 0 | 0 | 0 | 0 | 0 |
| | Leon County | 0 | 0 | 0 | 0 | 0 | 2 | 0 | 1 | 1 | 0 |
| | Levy County | 0 | 0 | 0 | 0 | 0 | 0 | 0 | 0 | 0 | 0 |
| | Liberty County | 0 | 0 | 0 | 0 | 0 | 0 | 0 | 0 | 0 | 0 |
| | Madison County | 0 | 0 | 0 | 0 | 0 | 0 | 0 | 0 | 0 | 0 |
| | Manatee County | 2 | 0 | 0 | 0 | 2 | 0 | 0 | 0 | 0 | 0 |
| | Marion County | 0 | 0 | 0 | 0 | 0 | 0 | 0 | 0 | 0 | 0 |
| | Martin County | 0 | 0 | 0 | 0 | 0 | 1 | 0 | 1 | 0 | 0 |
| | Miami-Dade County | 30 | 0 | 0 | 0 | 30 | 52 | 0 | 24 | 28 | 0 |
| | Monroe County | 0 | 0 | 0 | 0 | 0 | 0 | 0 | 0 | 0 | 0 |
| | Nassau County | 0 | 0 | 0 | 0 | 0 | 0 | 0 | 0 | 0 | 0 |
| | Okaloosa County | 1 | 0 | 0 | 0 | 1 | 0 | 0 | 0 | 0 | 0 |
| | Okeechobee County | 0 | 0 | 0 | 0 | 0 | 0 | 0 | 0 | 0 | 0 |
| | Orange County | 1 | 0 | 0 | 0 | 1 | 4 | 0 | 3 | 1 | 0 |
| | Osceola County | 3 | 0 | 0 | 0 | 3 | 5 | 0 | 5 | 0 | 0 |
| | Palm Beach County | 19 | 0 | 0 | 0 | 19 | 49 | 0 | 10 | 39 | 0 |
| | Pasco County | 8 | 0 | 0 | 0 | 8 | 0 | 0 | 0 | 0 | 0 |
| | Pinellas County | 5 | 0 | 0 | 0 | 5 | 2 | 0 | 0 | 2 | 0 |

[1] The FBI does not publish arson data unless it receives data from either the agency or the state for all 12 months of the calendar year.

## Table 11. Offenses Known to Law Enforcement, by State, Tribal, and Other Agencies, 2009—*Continued*

(Number.)

| State/Other Agency | Unit/Office | Violent crime | Murder and non-negligent man-slaughter | Forcible rape | Robbery | Aggra-vated assault | Property crime | Burglary | Larceny-theft | Motor vehicle theft | Arson[1] |
|---|---|---|---|---|---|---|---|---|---|---|---|
| | Polk County | 2 | 0 | 0 | 0 | 2 | 1 | 0 | 0 | 1 | 0 |
| | Putnam County | 0 | 0 | 0 | 0 | 0 | 0 | 0 | 0 | 0 | 0 |
| | Santa Rosa County | 0 | 0 | 0 | 0 | 0 | 0 | 0 | 0 | 0 | 0 |
| | Sarasota County | 2 | 0 | 0 | 0 | 2 | 1 | 0 | 0 | 1 | 0 |
| | Seminole County | 0 | 0 | 0 | 0 | 0 | 0 | 0 | 0 | 0 | 0 |
| | St. Johns County | 1 | 0 | 0 | 0 | 1 | 3 | 0 | 3 | 0 | 0 |
| | St. Lucie County | 1 | 0 | 0 | 0 | 1 | 1 | 0 | 1 | 0 | 0 |
| | Sumter County | 3 | 0 | 0 | 0 | 3 | 0 | 0 | 0 | 0 | 0 |
| | Suwannee County | 0 | 0 | 0 | 0 | 0 | 0 | 0 | 0 | 0 | 0 |
| | Taylor County | 0 | 0 | 0 | 0 | 0 | 0 | 0 | 0 | 0 | 0 |
| | Union County | 0 | 0 | 0 | 0 | 0 | 0 | 0 | 0 | 0 | 0 |
| | Volusia County | 5 | 0 | 0 | 0 | 5 | 1 | 0 | 0 | 1 | 0 |
| | Wakulla County | 1 | 0 | 0 | 0 | 1 | 0 | 0 | 0 | 0 | 0 |
| | Walton County | 0 | 0 | 0 | 0 | 0 | 0 | 0 | 0 | 0 | 0 |
| | Washington County | 0 | 0 | 0 | 0 | 0 | 0 | 0 | 0 | 0 | 0 |
| State Treasurer's Office | Division of Insurance Fraud | 0 | 0 | 0 | 0 | 0 | 0 | 0 | 0 | 0 | 0 |
| **FLORIDA—Tribal Agencies** | | | | | | | | | | | |
| Miccosukee Tribal | | 24 | 0 | 0 | 3 | 21 | 130 | 32 | 91 | 7 | 2 |
| Seminole Tribal | | 110 | 1 | 7 | 34 | 68 | 933 | 68 | 786 | 79 | 0 |
| **FLORIDA—Other Agencies** | | | | | | | | | | | |
| Duval County Schools | | 93 | 0 | 1 | 39 | 53 | 932 | 349 | 560 | 23 | 1 |
| Florida School for the Deaf and Blind | | 0 | 0 | 0 | 0 | 0 | 0 | 0 | 0 | 0 | 0 |
| Fort Lauderdale Airport | | 9 | 0 | 0 | 3 | 6 | 254 | 0 | 233 | 21 | 0 |
| Jacksonville Airport Authority | | 0 | 0 | 0 | 0 | 0 | 63 | 5 | 39 | 19 | 0 |
| Lee County Port Authority | | 1 | 0 | 0 | 0 | 1 | 148 | 1 | 143 | 4 | 0 |
| Melbourne International Airport | | 0 | 0 | 0 | 0 | 0 | 1 | 0 | 1 | 0 | 0 |
| Miami-Dade County Public Schools | | 350 | 1 | 13 | 182 | 154 | 1,956 | 688 | 1,240 | 28 | 17 |
| Palm Beach County School District | | 59 | 0 | 1 | 24 | 34 | 960 | 190 | 768 | 2 | 1 |
| Port Everglades | | 3 | 0 | 0 | 0 | 3 | 38 | 0 | 37 | 1 | 0 |
| Sarasota-Bradenton International Airport | | 1 | 0 | 0 | 0 | 1 | 15 | 0 | 8 | 7 | 0 |
| St. Petersburg-Clearwater International Airport | | 0 | 0 | 0 | 0 | 0 | 0 | 0 | 0 | 0 | 0 |
| Tampa International Airport | | 3 | 0 | 0 | 0 | 3 | 203 | 10 | 176 | 17 | 0 |
| Volusia County Beach Management | | 11 | 0 | 0 | 7 | 4 | 180 | 0 | 173 | 7 | 0 |
| **GEORGIA—State Agencies** | | | | | | | | | | | |
| Atlanta State Farmers Market | | 0 | 0 | 0 | 0 | 0 | 68 | 1 | 50 | 17 | 0 |
| Georgia Department of Public Safety | | 0 | 0 | 0 | 0 | 0 | 69 | 1 | 62 | 6 | |
| Department of Transportation | Office of Investigations | 0 | 0 | 0 | 0 | 0 | 2 | 0 | 2 | 0 | 0 |
| Georgia World Congress | | 7 | 1 | 0 | 0 | 6 | 234 | 3 | 229 | 2 | 0 |
| Ports Authority | Savannah | 1 | 0 | 0 | 0 | 1 | 11 | 0 | 11 | 0 | 0 |
| State Board of Workers Compensation | Fraud Investigation Division | 0 | 0 | 0 | 0 | 0 | 0 | 0 | 0 | 0 | 0 |
| **GEORGIA—Other Agencies** | | | | | | | | | | | |
| Atlanta Public Schools | | 0 | 0 | 0 | 0 | 0 | 0 | 0 | 0 | 0 | 0 |
| Augusta Board of Education | | 1 | 0 | 0 | 0 | 1 | 21 | 0 | 21 | 0 | |
| Bibb County Board of Education | | 16 | 0 | 0 | 1 | 15 | 130 | 20 | 107 | 3 | |
| Chatham County Board of Education | | 8 | 0 | 0 | 3 | 5 | 188 | 41 | 141 | 6 | 0 |
| Cherokee County Marshal | | 0 | 0 | 0 | 0 | 0 | 0 | 0 | 0 | 0 | 0 |
| Cobb County Board of Education | | 11 | 0 | 1 | 2 | 8 | 552 | 21 | 531 | 0 | 2 |
| DeKalb County School System | | 312 | 0 | 2 | 7 | 303 | 569 | 144 | 396 | 29 | 0 |
| Fayette County Marshal | | 0 | 0 | 0 | 0 | 0 | 0 | 0 | 0 | 0 | 0 |
| Fulton County Marshal | | 1 | 0 | 0 | 1 | 0 | 5 | 0 | 5 | 0 | |
| Fulton County School System | | 7 | 0 | 0 | 2 | 5 | 250 | 37 | 203 | 10 | 3 |
| Gwinnett County Public Schools | | 13 | 0 | 1 | 6 | 6 | 309 | 24 | 282 | 3 | 5 |
| Habersham County Public Schools | | 9 | 0 | 4 | 0 | 5 | 15 | 3 | 12 | 0 | 0 |
| Hartsfield-Jackson Atlanta International Airport | | 10 | 0 | 0 | 3 | 7 | 250 | 2 | 216 | 32 | 0 |
| Metropolitan Atlanta Rapid Transit Authority | | 163 | 0 | 1 | 66 | 96 | 275 | 9 | 201 | 65 | 4 |
| Muscogee City Marshal | | 0 | 0 | 0 | 0 | 0 | 0 | 0 | 0 | 0 | 0 |
| Stone Mountain Park | | 1 | 0 | 0 | 0 | 1 | 48 | 0 | 48 | 0 | 0 |
| **IDAHO—State Agencies** | | | | | | | | | | | |
| Idaho State Police | | 16 | 2 | 2 | 0 | 12 | 8 | 0 | 5 | 3 | 0 |
| **ILLINOIS—State Agencies[4]** | | | | | | | | | | | |
| State Fire Marshal | | | 0 | | 0 | 0 | 0 | 0 | 0 | 0 | 352 |
| **INDIANA—State Agencies** | | | | | | | | | | | |
| Indiana State Excise Police | | 1 | 0 | 0 | 0 | 1 | 6 | 1 | 5 | 0 | 0 |
| Northern Indiana Commuter Transportation District | | 1 | 0 | 0 | 1 | 0 | 56 | 1 | 52 | 3 | 0 |
| State Police: | Adams County | 0 | 0 | 0 | 0 | 0 | 1 | 0 | 1 | 0 | 0 |
| | Allen County | 1 | 1 | 0 | 0 | 0 | 0 | 0 | 0 | 0 | 0 |
| | Bartholomew County | 1 | 0 | 0 | 0 | 1 | 3 | 0 | 1 | 2 | 0 |
| | Benton County | 1 | 0 | 0 | 0 | 1 | 3 | 0 | 3 | 0 | 0 |
| | Blackford County | 0 | 0 | 0 | 0 | 0 | 0 | 0 | 0 | 0 | 0 |

[1] The FBI does not publish arson data unless it receives data from either the agency or the state for all 12 months of the calendar year.

[4] The data collection methodology for the offense of forcible rape used by the Illinois and the Minnesota state Uniform Crime Reporting (UCR) Programs does not comply with national UCR Program guidelines. Consequently, their figures for forcible rape and violent crime (of which forcible rape is a part) are not published in this table.

**Table 11. Offenses Known to Law Enforcement, by State, Tribal, and Other Agencies, 2009**—*Continued*

(Number.)

| State/Other Agency | Unit/Office | Violent crime | Murder and non-negligent man-slaughter | Forcible rape | Robbery | Aggra-vated assault | Property crime | Burglary | Larceny-theft | Motor vehicle theft | Arson[1] |
|---|---|---|---|---|---|---|---|---|---|---|---|
| | Boone County | 0 | 0 | 0 | 0 | 0 | 0 | 0 | 0 | 0 | 0 |
| | Brown County | 8 | 0 | 0 | 0 | 8 | 27 | 9 | 17 | 1 | 0 |
| | Carroll County | 2 | 0 | 0 | 0 | 2 | 4 | 0 | 3 | 1 | 0 |
| | Cass County | 21 | 0 | 1 | 0 | 20 | 130 | 18 | 98 | 14 | 0 |
| | Clark County | 1 | 0 | 1 | 0 | 0 | 16 | 2 | 12 | 2 | 0 |
| | Clay County | 0 | 0 | 0 | 0 | 0 | 8 | 1 | 6 | 1 | 2 |
| | Clinton County | 4 | 0 | 1 | 0 | 3 | 18 | 2 | 15 | 1 | 0 |
| | Crawford County | 2 | 0 | 0 | 0 | 2 | 9 | 3 | 5 | 1 | 1 |
| | Daviess County | 0 | 0 | 0 | 0 | 0 | 0 | 0 | 0 | 0 | 0 |
| | Dearborn County | 0 | 0 | 0 | 0 | 0 | 0 | 0 | 0 | 0 | 0 |
| | Decatur County | 3 | 0 | 0 | 0 | 3 | 14 | 3 | 11 | 0 | 0 |
| | De Kalb County | 3 | 1 | 1 | 0 | 1 | 29 | 3 | 26 | 0 | 2 |
| | Delaware County | 5 | 0 | 2 | 0 | 3 | 55 | 11 | 44 | 0 | 0 |
| | Dubois County | 1 | 0 | 1 | 0 | 0 | 20 | 1 | 18 | 1 | 0 |
| | Elkhart County | 0 | 0 | 0 | 0 | 0 | 0 | 0 | 0 | 0 | 1 |
| | Fayette County | 9 | 0 | 1 | 1 | 7 | 37 | 11 | 20 | 6 | 0 |
| | Floyd County | 3 | 0 | 1 | 1 | 1 | 14 | 4 | 7 | 3 | 0 |
| | Fountain County | 0 | 0 | 0 | 0 | 0 | 3 | 0 | 3 | 0 | 0 |
| | Franklin County | 2 | 0 | 0 | 0 | 2 | 3 | 1 | 1 | 1 | 0 |
| | Fulton County | 4 | 0 | 0 | 2 | 2 | 22 | 2 | 20 | 0 | 0 |
| | Gibson County | 6 | 1 | 1 | 1 | 3 | 5 | 0 | 5 | 0 | 0 |
| | Grant County | 4 | 0 | 1 | 0 | 3 | 17 | 10 | 7 | 0 | 0 |
| | Greene County | 3 | 0 | 0 | 0 | 3 | 9 | 2 | 7 | 0 | 0 |
| | Hamilton County | 1 | 0 | 0 | 0 | 1 | 8 | 3 | 5 | 0 | 0 |
| | Hancock County | 13 | 0 | 1 | 0 | 12 | 66 | 19 | 43 | 4 | 1 |
| | Harrison County | 5 | 0 | 3 | 0 | 2 | 17 | 0 | 14 | 3 | 0 |
| | Hendricks County | 0 | 0 | 0 | 0 | 0 | 0 | 0 | 0 | 0 | 0 |
| | Henry County | 2 | 0 | 0 | 0 | 2 | 21 | 7 | 13 | 1 | 0 |
| | Howard County | 5 | 0 | 0 | 0 | 5 | 10 | 1 | 7 | 2 | 0 |
| | Huntington County | 13 | 0 | 1 | 0 | 12 | 97 | 25 | 65 | 7 | 3 |
| | Jackson County | 1 | 0 | 0 | 0 | 1 | 8 | 0 | 6 | 2 | 0 |
| | Jasper County | 4 | 0 | 1 | 1 | 2 | 13 | 3 | 10 | 0 | 0 |
| | Jay County | 0 | 0 | 0 | 0 | 0 | 0 | 0 | 0 | 0 | 0 |
| | Jefferson County | 4 | 0 | 2 | 0 | 2 | 19 | 2 | 14 | 3 | 0 |
| | Jennings County | 2 | 2 | 0 | 0 | 0 | 0 | 0 | 0 | 0 | 0 |
| | Johnson County | 10 | 0 | 3 | 2 | 5 | 22 | 6 | 13 | 3 | 0 |
| | Knox County | 1 | 0 | 1 | 0 | 0 | 16 | 1 | 15 | 0 | 0 |
| | Kosciusko County | 8 | 0 | 3 | 1 | 4 | 21 | 5 | 15 | 1 | 0 |
| | LaGrange County | 17 | 0 | 1 | 0 | 16 | 79 | 3 | 41 | 35 | 0 |
| | Lake County | 1 | 0 | 0 | 0 | 1 | 15 | 1 | 8 | 6 | 0 |
| | La Porte County | 9 | 0 | 2 | 0 | 7 | 17 | 8 | 7 | 2 | 0 |
| | Lawrence County | 13 | 1 | 1 | 0 | 11 | 23 | 1 | 20 | 2 | 0 |
| | Madison County | 2 | 0 | 0 | 0 | 2 | 37 | 0 | 34 | 3 | 0 |
| | Marion County | 3 | 0 | 0 | 1 | 2 | 23 | 4 | 19 | 0 | 0 |
| | Marshall County | 5 | 0 | 2 | 0 | 3 | 9 | 3 | 5 | 1 | 1 |
| | Martin County | 14 | 0 | 0 | 1 | 13 | 43 | 11 | 30 | 2 | 0 |
| | Miami County | 9 | 0 | 3 | 0 | 6 | 16 | 2 | 10 | 4 | 0 |
| | Monroe County | 6 | 0 | 1 | 0 | 5 | 11 | 4 | 7 | 0 | 1 |
| | Montgomery County | 3 | 0 | 0 | 0 | 3 | 22 | 1 | 16 | 5 | 0 |
| | Morgan County | 2 | 0 | 0 | 0 | 2 | 3 | 0 | 3 | 0 | 0 |
| | Newton County | 2 | 0 | 0 | 0 | 2 | 25 | 4 | 20 | 1 | 0 |
| | Noble County | 0 | 0 | 0 | 0 | 0 | 0 | 0 | 0 | 0 | 2 |
| | Ohio County | 6 | 0 | 2 | 0 | 4 | 15 | 3 | 12 | 0 | 0 |
| | Orange County | 7 | 0 | 1 | 0 | 6 | 5 | 0 | 5 | 0 | 0 |
| | Owen County | 0 | 0 | 0 | 0 | 0 | 5 | 0 | 3 | 2 | 0 |
| | Parke County | 4 | 0 | 2 | 0 | 2 | 12 | 4 | 7 | 1 | 0 |
| | Perry County | 7 | 0 | 2 | 1 | 4 | 16 | 1 | 14 | 1 | 0 |
| | Pike County | 8 | 0 | 0 | 0 | 8 | 18 | 0 | 12 | 6 | 1 |
| | Porter County | 11 | 0 | 5 | 1 | 5 | 30 | 7 | 20 | 3 | 0 |
| | Posey County | 1 | 0 | 0 | 0 | 1 | 2 | 1 | 1 | 0 | 3 |
| | Pulaski County | 4 | 0 | 0 | 0 | 4 | 13 | 1 | 12 | 0 | 0 |
| | Putnam County | 2 | 0 | 0 | 0 | 2 | 9 | 2 | 7 | 0 | 0 |
| | Randolph County | 0 | 0 | 0 | 0 | 0 | 0 | 0 | 0 | 0 | 0 |
| | Ripley County | 0 | 0 | 0 | 0 | 0 | 4 | 4 | 0 | 0 | 0 |
| | Rush County | 3 | 0 | 1 | 0 | 2 | 12 | 0 | 12 | 0 | 0 |
| | Scott County | 4 | 4 | 0 | 0 | 0 | 0 | 0 | 0 | 0 | 0 |
| | Shelby County | 7 | 0 | 2 | 1 | 4 | 23 | 11 | 10 | 2 | 0 |
| | Spencer County | 4 | 1 | 1 | 1 | 1 | 4 | 1 | 3 | 0 | 1 |
| | Starke County | 7 | 0 | 0 | 0 | 7 | 18 | 3 | 12 | 3 | 0 |
| | Steuben County | 2 | 0 | 0 | 2 | 0 | 31 | 3 | 23 | 5 | 0 |
| | St. Joseph County | 7 | 0 | 0 | 0 | 7 | 49 | 17 | 32 | 0 | 0 |
| | Sullivan County | 2 | 2 | 0 | 0 | 0 | 0 | 0 | 0 | 0 | 0 |

[1] The FBI does not publish arson data unless it receives data from either the agency or the state for all 12 months of the calendar year.

## Table 11. Offenses Known to Law Enforcement, by State, Tribal, and Other Agencies, 2009—*Continued*

(Number.)

| State/Other Agency | Unit/Office | Violent crime | Murder and non-negligent man-slaughter | Forcible rape | Robbery | Aggra-vated assault | Property crime | Burglary | Larceny-theft | Motor vehicle theft | Arson[1] |
|---|---|---|---|---|---|---|---|---|---|---|---|
| | Switzerland County | 7 | 0 | 0 | 0 | 7 | 51 | 6 | 41 | 4 | 0 |
| | Tippecanoe County | 1 | 0 | 1 | 0 | 0 | 4 | 0 | 3 | 1 | 0 |
| | Tipton County | 0 | 0 | 0 | 0 | 0 | 0 | 0 | 0 | 0 | 0 |
| | Union County | 2 | 0 | 1 | 0 | 1 | 26 | 2 | 21 | 3 | 0 |
| | Vanderburgh County | 2 | 0 | 1 | 0 | 1 | 9 | 0 | 7 | 2 | 0 |
| | Vermillion County | 2 | 0 | 0 | 0 | 2 | 78 | 8 | 56 | 14 | 0 |
| | Vigo County | 6 | 0 | 3 | 1 | 2 | 4 | 0 | 1 | 3 | 4 |
| | Wabash County | 1 | 0 | 0 | 0 | 1 | 2 | 0 | 2 | 0 | 0 |
| | Warren County | 1 | 0 | 0 | 0 | 1 | 16 | 0 | 13 | 3 | 0 |
| | Warrick County | 23 | 0 | 6 | 0 | 17 | 45 | 10 | 33 | 2 | 0 |
| | Washington County | 0 | 0 | 0 | 0 | 0 | 0 | 0 | 0 | 0 | 0 |
| | Wayne County | 1 | 0 | 0 | 0 | 1 | 3 | 0 | 3 | 0 | 0 |
| | Wells County | 7 | 0 | 1 | 1 | 5 | 23 | 3 | 16 | 4 | 0 |
| | White County | 2 | 0 | 1 | 0 | 1 | 13 | 3 | 6 | 4 | 0 |
| | Whitley County | 0 | 0 | 0 | 0 | 0 | 0 | 0 | 0 | 0 | 0 |
| **INDIANA—Other Agencies** | | | | | | | | | | | |
| Indianapolis International Airport | | 6 | 0 | 0 | 0 | 6 | 72 | 3 | 63 | 6 | 1 |
| St. Joseph County Airport Authority | | 0 | 0 | 0 | 0 | 0 | 6 | 0 | 4 | 2 | 0 |
| **KANSAS—State Agencies** | | | | | | | | | | | |
| Kansas Bureau of Investigation | | 0 | 0 | 0 | 0 | 0 | 2 | 1 | 1 | 0 | 0 |
| Kansas Department of Wildlife and Parks | | 2 | 0 | 0 | 0 | 2 | 43 | 3 | 38 | 2 | 0 |
| Kansas Highway Patrol | | 19 | 0 | 0 | 1 | 18 | 40 | 4 | 26 | 10 | 1 |
| Kansas Racing Commission | Security Division | 0 | 0 | 0 | 0 | 0 | 0 | 0 | 0 | 0 | 0 |
| State Fire Marshal | | 0 | 0 | 0 | 0 | 0 | 0 | 0 | 0 | 0 | 0 |
| **KANSAS—Tribal Agencies** | | | | | | | | | | | |
| Kickapoo Tribal | | 0 | 0 | 0 | 0 | 0 | 24 | 5 | 19 | 0 | 0 |
| Potawatomi Tribal | | 1 | 0 | 0 | 0 | 1 | 22 | 4 | 18 | 0 | 2 |
| Sac and Fox Tribal | | 1 | 0 | 1 | 0 | 0 | 28 | 2 | 26 | 0 | 0 |
| **KANSAS—Other Agencies** | | | | | | | | | | | |
| Johnson County Park | | 5 | 0 | 0 | 1 | 4 | 32 | 15 | 15 | 2 | 5 |
| Topeka Fire Department | Arson Investigation | 0 | 0 | 0 | 0 | 0 | 4 | 4 | 0 | 0 | 39 |
| **KENTUCKY—State Agencies[5]** | | | | | | | | | | | |
| Kentucky Fairgrounds Security | | 0 | 0 | 0 | 0 | 0 | 4 | 0 | 2 | 2 | 0 |
| Kentucky Horse Park | | 0 | 0 | 0 | 0 | 0 | 30 | 0 | 30 | 0 | 0 |
| Motor Vehicle Enforcement | | 9 | 0 | 0 | 0 | 9 | 8 | 0 | 8 | 0 | 0 |
| Park Security | | 0 | 0 | 0 | 0 | 0 | 35 | 5 | 30 | 0 | 0 |
| State Police: | Ashland | 44 | 4 | 20 | 10 | 10 | 463 | 264 | 173 | 26 | 10 |
| | Bowling Green | 53 | 5 | 23 | 3 | 22 | 242 | 120 | 101 | 21 | 5 |
| | Campbellsburg | 45 | 1 | 15 | 5 | 24 | 306 | 162 | 117 | 27 | 5 |
| | Cannabis Suppression Section | 0 | 0 | 0 | 0 | 0 | 0 | 0 | 0 | 0 | 0 |
| | Columbia | 66 | 7 | 24 | 3 | 32 | 204 | 116 | 84 | 4 | 26 |
| | Drug Enforcement Area[2] | 0 | 0 | 0 | 0 | 0 | 5 | 1 | 4 | 0 | 0 |
| | Dry Ridge | 63 | 2 | 37 | 4 | 20 | 359 | 190 | 131 | 38 | 14 |
| | Electronic Crimes | 0 | 0 | 0 | 0 | 0 | 0 | 0 | 0 | 0 | 0 |
| | Elizabethtown | 66 | 2 | 30 | 3 | 31 | 259 | 131 | 89 | 39 | 5 |
| | Frankfort | 36 | 0 | 17 | 4 | 15 | 237 | 95 | 122 | 20 | 7 |
| | Harlan | 53 | 2 | 16 | 8 | 27 | 414 | 206 | 192 | 16 | 26 |
| | Hazard | 95 | 9 | 25 | 17 | 44 | 572 | 278 | 215 | 79 | 22 |
| | Henderson | 34 | 0 | 15 | 2 | 17 | 172 | 68 | 97 | 7 | 0 |
| | London | 61 | 5 | 27 | 0 | 29 | 373 | 143 | 167 | 63 | 28 |
| | Madisonville | 27 | 1 | 15 | 0 | 11 | 235 | 129 | 88 | 18 | 7 |
| | Mayfield | 62 | 0 | 26 | 4 | 32 | 232 | 100 | 125 | 7 | 13 |
| | Morehead | 83 | 4 | 37 | 7 | 35 | 746 | 374 | 310 | 62 | 8 |
| | Pikeville | 163 | 1 | 42 | 36 | 84 | 1,081 | 432 | 489 | 160 | 32 |
| | Richmond | 93 | 5 | 45 | 10 | 33 | 471 | 255 | 182 | 34 | 25 |
| | Special Investigations | 0 | 0 | 0 | 0 | 0 | 2 | 0 | 2 | 0 | 0 |
| | West Drug Enforcement Branch | 2 | 0 | 0 | 2 | 0 | 9 | 0 | 9 | 0 | 0 |
| Unlawful Narcotics Investigation | Treatment and Education | 1 | 0 | 0 | 1 | 0 | 3 | 1 | 2 | 0 | 0 |
| **KENTUCKY—Other Agencies[6]** | | | | | | | | | | | |
| Barren County Drug Task Force | | 0 | 0 | 0 | 0 | 0 | 2 | 0 | 2 | 0 | 0 |
| Central Kentucky Area Drug Task Force | | 0 | 0 | 0 | 0 | 0 | 1 | 0 | 1 | 0 | 0 |
| Cincinnati-Northern Kentucky International Airport | | 0 | 0 | 0 | 0 | 0 | 91 | 0 | 86 | 5 | 0 |
| Clark County School System | | 0 | 0 | 0 | 0 | 0 | 13 | 2 | 11 | 0 | 0 |
| Fayette County Schools | | 4 | 0 | 0 | 1 | 3 | 268 | 17 | 250 | 1 | 0 |
| FIVCO Area Drug Task Force | | 0 | 0 | 0 | 0 | 0 | 0 | 0 | 0 | 0 | 0 |
| Graves County Schools | | 0 | 0 | 0 | 0 | 0 | 0 | 0 | 0 | 0 | 0 |
| Greater Hardin County Narcotics Task Force | | 1 | 0 | 0 | 0 | 1 | 2 | 0 | 2 | 0 | 0 |
| Jefferson County Board of Education | | 12 | 0 | 0 | 1 | 11 | 111 | 64 | 47 | 0 | 1 |

[1] The FBI does not publish arson data unless it receives data from either the agency or the state for all 12 months of the calendar year.
[2] The FBI determined that the agency's data were overreported. Consequently, affected data are not included in this table.
[5] Because of changes in the state/local agency's reporting practices, figures are not comparable to previous years' data.

**Table 11. Offenses Known to Law Enforcement, by State, Tribal, and Other Agencies, 2009**—*Continued*

(Number.)

| State/Other Agency | Unit/Office | Violent crime | Murder and non-negligent man-slaughter | Forcible rape | Robbery | Aggra-vated assault | Property crime | Burglary | Larceny-theft | Motor vehicle theft | Arson[1] |
|---|---|---|---|---|---|---|---|---|---|---|---|
| Lake Cumberland Area Drug Enforcement Task Force | | 0 | 0 | 0 | 0 | 0 | 0 | 0 | 0 | 0 | 0 |
| Louisville Regional Airport Authority | | 1 | 0 | 0 | 1 | 0 | 26 | 0 | 9 | 17 | 0 |
| Montgomery County School District | | 1 | 0 | 0 | 0 | 1 | 14 | 1 | 13 | 0 | 1 |
| Ohio County School System | | 1 | 0 | 0 | 0 | 1 | 2 | 0 | 2 | 0 | 0 |
| Pennyrile Narcotics Task Force | | 0 | 0 | 0 | 0 | 0 | 7 | 0 | 7 | 0 | 0 |
| South Central Kentucky Drug Task Force | | 0 | 0 | 0 | 0 | 0 | 12 | 0 | 12 | 0 | 0 |
| **LOUISIANA—State Agencies** | | | | | | | | | | | |
| Department of Public Safety | State Capitol Detail | 8 | 0 | 1 | 1 | 6 | 32 | 3 | 28 | 1 | 0 |
| Tensas Basin Levee District | | 0 | 0 | 0 | 0 | 0 | 5 | 5 | 0 | 0 | 2 |
| **LOUISIANA—Tribal Agencies** | | | | | | | | | | | |
| Chitimacha Tribal | | 2 | 0 | 1 | 0 | 1 | 52 | 2 | 47 | 3 | 0 |
| Coushatta Tribal | | 4 | 0 | 1 | 1 | 2 | 162 | 6 | 150 | 6 | 0 |
| Tunica Biloxi Tribal | | 19 | 0 | 0 | 0 | 19 | 188 | 2 | 186 | 0 | 0 |
| **MAINE—State Agencies** | | | | | | | | | | | |
| Drug Enforcement Agency: | Androscoggin County | 0 | 0 | 0 | 0 | 0 | 0 | 0 | 0 | 0 | 0 |
| | Aroostook County | 0 | 0 | 0 | 0 | 0 | 0 | 0 | 0 | 0 | 0 |
| | Cumberland County | 0 | 0 | 0 | 0 | 0 | 0 | 0 | 0 | 0 | 0 |
| | Franklin County | 0 | 0 | 0 | 0 | 0 | 0 | 0 | 0 | 0 | 0 |
| | Hancock County | 0 | 0 | 0 | 0 | 0 | 0 | 0 | 0 | 0 | 0 |
| | Kennebec County | 0 | 0 | 0 | 0 | 0 | 0 | 0 | 0 | 0 | 0 |
| | Knox County | 0 | 0 | 0 | 0 | 0 | 0 | 0 | 0 | 0 | 0 |
| | Lincoln County | 0 | 0 | 0 | 0 | 0 | 0 | 0 | 0 | 0 | 0 |
| | Oxford County | 0 | 0 | 0 | 0 | 0 | 0 | 0 | 0 | 0 | 0 |
| | Penobscot County | 0 | 0 | 0 | 0 | 0 | 0 | 0 | 0 | 0 | 0 |
| | Piscataquis County | 0 | 0 | 0 | 0 | 0 | 0 | 0 | 0 | 0 | 0 |
| | Sagadahoc County | 0 | 0 | 0 | 0 | 0 | 0 | 0 | 0 | 0 | 0 |
| | Somerset County | 0 | 0 | 0 | 0 | 0 | 0 | 0 | 0 | 0 | 0 |
| | Waldo County | 0 | 0 | 0 | 0 | 0 | 0 | 0 | 0 | 0 | 0 |
| | Washington County | 0 | 0 | 0 | 0 | 0 | 0 | 0 | 0 | 0 | 0 |
| | York County | 0 | 0 | 0 | 0 | 0 | 0 | 0 | 0 | 0 | 0 |
| State Police: | Androscoggin County | 15 | 0 | 0 | 3 | 12 | 98 | 31 | 58 | 9 | 2 |
| | Aroostook County | 10 | 0 | 3 | 1 | 6 | 232 | 69 | 144 | 19 | 2 |
| | Cumberland County | 3 | 0 | 0 | 0 | 3 | 130 | 48 | 72 | 10 | 2 |
| | Franklin County | 3 | 0 | 0 | 0 | 3 | 62 | 24 | 34 | 4 | 2 |
| | Hancock County | 11 | 0 | 3 | 1 | 7 | 201 | 70 | 119 | 12 | 2 |
| | Kennebec County | 7 | 0 | 1 | 2 | 4 | 352 | 115 | 226 | 11 | 8 |
| | Knox County | 1 | 1 | 0 | 0 | 0 | 65 | 14 | 47 | 4 | 2 |
| | Lincoln County | 2 | 0 | 0 | 1 | 1 | 8 | 7 | 1 | 0 | 1 |
| | Oxford County | 9 | 0 | 1 | 0 | 8 | 198 | 89 | 101 | 8 | 5 |
| | Penobscot County | 14 | 2 | 3 | 3 | 6 | 373 | 133 | 216 | 24 | 19 |
| | Piscataquis County | 0 | 0 | 0 | 0 | 0 | 23 | 8 | 11 | 4 | 4 |
| | Sagadahoc County | 0 | 0 | 0 | 0 | 0 | 3 | 1 | 2 | 0 | 1 |
| | Somerset County | 7 | 1 | 3 | 1 | 2 | 217 | 95 | 109 | 13 | 8 |
| | Waldo County | 5 | 0 | 2 | 0 | 3 | 106 | 34 | 65 | 7 | 1 |
| | Washington County | 3 | 0 | 2 | 0 | 1 | 162 | 56 | 101 | 5 | 6 |
| | York County | 4 | 2 | 0 | 0 | 2 | 241 | 97 | 132 | 12 | 8 |
| **MAINE—Tribal Agencies** | | | | | | | | | | | |
| Passamaquoddy Indian Township | | 31 | 0 | 0 | 1 | 30 | 13 | 5 | 6 | 2 | 0 |
| Penobscot Tribal | | 6 | 0 | 0 | 0 | 6 | 34 | 8 | 26 | 0 | 0 |
| **MARYLAND—State Agencies** | | | | | | | | | | | |
| Comptroller of the Treasury | Field Enforcement Division | 0 | 0 | 0 | 0 | 0 | 0 | 0 | 0 | 0 | 0 |
| Department of Public Safety and Correctional Services | Internal Investigations Unit | 121 | 4 | 0 | 0 | 117 | 0 | 0 | 0 | 0 | 0 |
| General Services: | Annapolis, Anne Arundel County | 1 | 0 | 0 | 0 | 1 | 8 | 0 | 8 | 0 | 0 |
| | Baltimore City | 1 | 0 | 0 | 0 | 1 | 25 | 0 | 24 | 1 | 0 |
| Maryland State Police Statewide | | 0 | 0 | 0 | 0 | 0 | 6 | 0 | 3 | 3 | 0 |
| Natural Resources Police | | 9 | 0 | 0 | 1 | 8 | 292 | 29 | 262 | 1 | 69 |
| Springfield Hospital | | 0 | 0 | 0 | 0 | 0 | 24 | 0 | 24 | 0 | 0 |
| State Fire Marshal | | 0 | 0 | 0 | 0 | 0 | 0 | 0 | 0 | 0 | 0 |
| State Police: | Allegany County | 40 | 0 | 5 | 9 | 26 | 473 | 106 | 352 | 15 | 8 |
| | Anne Arundel County | 8 | 0 | 0 | 0 | 8 | 26 | 1 | 17 | 8 | 1 |
| | Baltimore City | 0 | 0 | 0 | 0 | 0 | 1 | 0 | 1 | 0 | 0 |
| | Baltimore County | 18 | 0 | 1 | 0 | 17 | 73 | 3 | 34 | 36 | 0 |
| | Calvert County | 22 | 0 | 1 | 1 | 20 | 316 | 67 | 231 | 18 | 6 |
| | Caroline County | 24 | 1 | 4 | 3 | 16 | 132 | 44 | 76 | 12 | 16 |
| | Carroll County | 182 | 2 | 1 | 32 | 147 | 1,366 | 371 | 927 | 68 | 1 |
| | Cecil County | 177 | 0 | 1 | 25 | 151 | 987 | 325 | 572 | 90 | 31 |

[1] The FBI does not publish arson data unless it receives data from either the agency or the state for all 12 months of the calendar year.

## Table 11. Offenses Known to Law Enforcement, by State, Tribal, and Other Agencies, 2009—*Continued*

(Number.)

| State/Other Agency | Unit/Office | Violent crime | Murder and non-negligent man-slaughter | Forcible rape | Robbery | Aggra-vated assault | Property crime | Burglary | Larceny-theft | Motor vehicle theft | Arson[1] |
|---|---|---|---|---|---|---|---|---|---|---|---|
| | Charles County | 1 | 0 | 0 | 0 | 1 | 57 | 0 | 56 | 1 | 35 |
| | Dorchester County | 17 | 0 | 0 | 2 | 15 | 62 | 28 | 31 | 3 | 7 |
| | Frederick County | 64 | 4 | 3 | 14 | 43 | 578 | 96 | 465 | 17 | 15 |
| | Garrett County | 31 | 0 | 4 | 0 | 27 | 179 | 70 | 104 | 5 | 4 |
| | Harford County[3] | 127 | 0 | 2 | 32 | 93 | | | 244 | 36 | 39 |
| | Howard County | 5 | 0 | 1 | 0 | 4 | 28 | 2 | 20 | 6 | 0 |
| | Kent County | 27 | 0 | 0 | 3 | 24 | 43 | 20 | 21 | 2 | 4 |
| | Montgomery County | 4 | 0 | 0 | 0 | 4 | 13 | 0 | 4 | 9 | 0 |
| | Prince George's County | 5 | 0 | 0 | 2 | 3 | 67 | 1 | 17 | 49 | 0 |
| | Queen Anne's County | 52 | 0 | 1 | 3 | 48 | 174 | 40 | 123 | 11 | 16 |
| | Somerset County | 35 | 0 | 2 | 2 | 31 | 239 | 106 | 128 | 5 | 2 |
| | St. Mary's County | 37 | 0 | 2 | 1 | 34 | 206 | 35 | 153 | 18 | 18 |
| | Talbot County | 13 | 1 | 1 | 1 | 10 | 100 | 38 | 58 | 4 | 3 |
| | Washington County | 48 | 0 | 2 | 5 | 41 | 192 | 51 | 128 | 13 | 18 |
| | Wicomico County | 90 | 1 | 4 | 14 | 71 | 325 | 140 | 157 | 28 | 13 |
| | Worcester County | 46 | 0 | 1 | 2 | 43 | 256 | 53 | 185 | 18 | 1 |
| Transit Administration | | 0 | 0 | 0 | 0 | 0 | 0 | 0 | 0 | 0 | 0 |
| Transportation Authority | | 5 | 0 | 0 | 2 | 3 | 288 | 5 | 254 | 29 | 2 |
| **MARYLAND—Other Agencies** | | | | | | | | | | | |
| Maryland-National Capital Park Police: | Montgomery County | 21 | 0 | 1 | 16 | 4 | 198 | 14 | 181 | 3 | 1 |
| | Prince George's County | 64 | 3 | 2 | 43 | 16 | 265 | 17 | 233 | 15 | 0 |
| **MASSACHUSETTS—State Agencies** | | | | | | | | | | | |
| Division of Law Enforcement | Environmental Police | 7 | 0 | 0 | 1 | 6 | 18 | 7 | 7 | 4 | 0 |
| Massachusetts Bay Transportation Authority: | Bristol County | 1 | 0 | 0 | 0 | 1 | 6 | 0 | 5 | 1 | 0 |
| | Essex County | 1 | 0 | 0 | 0 | 1 | 17 | 0 | 16 | 1 | 0 |
| | Middlesex County | 19 | 0 | 1 | 12 | 6 | 132 | 2 | 124 | 6 | 0 |
| | Norfolk County | 20 | 0 | 0 | 15 | 5 | 90 | 1 | 85 | 4 | 0 |
| | Plymouth County | 1 | 0 | 0 | 1 | 0 | 43 | 2 | 38 | 3 | 0 |
| | Suffolk County | 225 | 0 | 1 | 150 | 74 | 241 | 2 | 237 | 2 | 0 |
| | Worcester County | 0 | 0 | 0 | 0 | 0 | 5 | 0 | 5 | 0 | 0 |
| State Police: | Barnstable County | 6 | 0 | 0 | 0 | 6 | 2 | 0 | 1 | 1 | 0 |
| | Berkshire County | 11 | 0 | 0 | 0 | 11 | 64 | 32 | 27 | 5 | 0 |
| | Bristol County | 25 | 0 | 0 | 0 | 25 | 6 | 0 | 4 | 2 | 0 |
| | Dukes County | 0 | 0 | 0 | 0 | 0 | 0 | 0 | 0 | 0 | 0 |
| | Essex County | 3 | 1 | 0 | 0 | 2 | 3 | 0 | 3 | 0 | 0 |
| | Franklin County | 24 | 0 | 6 | 0 | 18 | 1 | 0 | 1 | 0 | 0 |
| | Hampden County | 20 | 0 | 1 | 2 | 17 | 37 | 5 | 20 | 12 | 1 |
| | Hampshire County | 3 | 0 | 0 | 0 | 3 | 6 | 1 | 4 | 1 | 0 |
| | Middlesex County | 3 | 0 | 0 | 1 | 2 | 8 | 0 | 8 | 0 | 0 |
| | Norfolk County | 2 | 0 | 0 | 0 | 2 | 7 | 0 | 4 | 3 | 0 |
| | Plymouth County | 10 | 0 | 0 | 0 | 10 | 5 | 2 | 2 | 1 | 0 |
| | Worcester County | 32 | 0 | 0 | 0 | 32 | 0 | 0 | 0 | 0 | 0 |
| **MASSACHUSETTS—Other Agencies** | | | | | | | | | | | |
| Beth Israel Deaconess Medical Center | | 4 | 0 | 0 | 0 | 4 | 138 | 5 | 132 | 1 | 0 |
| **MICHIGAN—State Agencies5** | | | | | | | | | | | |
| State Police: | Alcona County | 2 | 0 | 0 | 0 | 2 | 17 | 6 | 11 | 0 | 0 |
| | Alger County | 13 | 0 | 4 | 0 | 9 | 67 | 27 | 37 | 3 | 1 |
| | Allegan County | 56 | 0 | 21 | 1 | 34 | 360 | 105 | 228 | 27 | 0 |
| | Alpena County | 29 | 0 | 10 | 5 | 14 | 211 | 68 | 136 | 7 | 3 |
| | Antrim County | 11 | 0 | 8 | 0 | 3 | 25 | 7 | 18 | 0 | 0 |
| | Arenac County | 14 | 0 | 12 | 0 | 2 | 17 | 9 | 7 | 1 | 0 |
| | Baraga County | 5 | 0 | 1 | 0 | 4 | 34 | 19 | 14 | 1 | 0 |
| | Barry County | 50 | 0 | 20 | 0 | 30 | 278 | 115 | 148 | 15 | 2 |
| | Bay County | 52 | 0 | 24 | 6 | 22 | 329 | 102 | 204 | 23 | 2 |
| | Benzie County | 5 | 0 | 2 | 0 | 3 | 53 | 15 | 38 | 0 | 0 |
| | Berrien County | 64 | 1 | 22 | 4 | 37 | 374 | 96 | 259 | 19 | 2 |
| | Branch County | 35 | 2 | 12 | 0 | 21 | 151 | 50 | 89 | 12 | 3 |
| | Calhoun County | 43 | 1 | 19 | 0 | 23 | 195 | 80 | 100 | 15 | 4 |
| | Cass County | 16 | 0 | 7 | 1 | 8 | 111 | 40 | 55 | 16 | 4 |
| | Charlevoix County | 6 | 0 | 3 | 0 | 3 | 18 | 5 | 12 | 1 | 0 |
| | Cheboygan County | 15 | 0 | 7 | 0 | 8 | 139 | 62 | 70 | 7 | 1 |
| | Chippewa County | 20 | 0 | 9 | 0 | 11 | 178 | 75 | 93 | 10 | 2 |
| | Clare County | 13 | 0 | 6 | 0 | 7 | 73 | 31 | 38 | 4 | 0 |
| | Clinton County | 3 | 0 | 3 | 0 | 0 | 53 | 22 | 29 | 2 | 0 |
| | Crawford County | 9 | 0 | 3 | 0 | 6 | 33 | 17 | 15 | 1 | 1 |
| | Delta County | 5 | 0 | 4 | 0 | 1 | 91 | 39 | 49 | 3 | 0 |
| | Dickinson County | 8 | 0 | 8 | 0 | 0 | 63 | 34 | 26 | 3 | 0 |
| | Eaton County | 14 | 0 | 11 | 1 | 2 | 104 | 34 | 66 | 4 | 1 |
| | Emmet County | 24 | 0 | 9 | 3 | 12 | 173 | 42 | 128 | 3 | 3 |

[1] The FBI does not publish arson data unless it receives data from either the agency or the state for all 12 months of the calendar year.
[3] The FBI determined that the agency's data were underreported. Consequently, affected data are not included in this table.
[5] Because of changes in the state/local agency's reporting practices, figures are not comparable to previous years' data.

## Table 11. Offenses Known to Law Enforcement, by State, Tribal, and Other Agencies, 2009—*Continued*

(Number.)

| State/Other Agency | Unit/Office | Violent crime | Murder and non-negligent man-slaughter | Forcible rape | Robbery | Aggra-vated assault | Property crime | Burglary | Larceny-theft | Motor vehicle theft | Arson[1] |
|---|---|---|---|---|---|---|---|---|---|---|---|
| | Genesee County | 57 | 0 | 21 | 3 | 33 | 272 | 115 | 136 | 21 | 1 |
| | Gladwin County | 11 | 0 | 5 | 0 | 6 | 72 | 37 | 34 | 1 | 0 |
| | Gogebic County | 12 | 0 | 4 | 0 | 8 | 33 | 14 | 16 | 3 | 1 |
| | Grand Traverse County | 27 | 0 | 9 | 0 | 18 | 218 | 56 | 153 | 9 | 0 |
| | Gratiot County | 20 | 0 | 4 | 2 | 14 | 117 | 32 | 79 | 6 | 1 |
| | Hillsdale County | 33 | 0 | 11 | 0 | 22 | 142 | 59 | 76 | 7 | 5 |
| | Houghton County | 16 | 4 | 8 | 0 | 4 | 121 | 51 | 66 | 4 | 3 |
| | Huron County | 12 | 0 | 5 | 0 | 7 | 46 | 16 | 29 | 1 | 1 |
| | Ingham County | 10 | 0 | 7 | 0 | 3 | 78 | 24 | 51 | 3 | 3 |
| | Ionia County | 25 | 0 | 8 | 0 | 17 | 315 | 109 | 187 | 19 | 6 |
| | Iosco County | 21 | 0 | 9 | 1 | 11 | 203 | 100 | 93 | 10 | 6 |
| | Iron County | 10 | 0 | 1 | 0 | 9 | 60 | 29 | 30 | 1 | 1 |
| | Isabella County | 17 | 0 | 11 | 0 | 6 | 206 | 50 | 143 | 13 | 0 |
| | Jackson County | 67 | 0 | 20 | 5 | 42 | 333 | 112 | 202 | 19 | 9 |
| | Kalamazoo County | 7 | 0 | 4 | 0 | 3 | 17 | 3 | 13 | 1 | 1 |
| | Kalkaska County | 13 | 2 | 2 | 0 | 9 | 80 | 26 | 51 | 3 | 0 |
| | Kent County | 13 | 0 | 7 | 0 | 6 | 21 | 2 | 16 | 3 | 2 |
| | Lake County | 19 | 0 | 13 | 0 | 6 | 51 | 19 | 29 | 3 | 1 |
| | Lapeer County | 39 | 0 | 14 | 0 | 25 | 51 | 23 | 25 | 3 | 2 |
| | Leelanau County | 2 | 0 | 2 | 0 | 0 | 13 | 6 | 7 | 0 | 0 |
| | Lenawee County | 38 | 0 | 7 | 2 | 29 | 201 | 67 | 118 | 16 | 3 |
| | Livingston County | 33 | 1 | 12 | 2 | 18 | 422 | 99 | 296 | 27 | 8 |
| | Luce County | 17 | 0 | 11 | 0 | 6 | 76 | 40 | 32 | 4 | 0 |
| | Mackinac County | 9 | 0 | 6 | 0 | 3 | 102 | 53 | 43 | 6 | 0 |
| | Macomb County | 6 | 0 | 1 | 0 | 5 | 53 | 11 | 39 | 3 | 0 |
| | Manistee County | 23 | 0 | 4 | 2 | 17 | 204 | 75 | 125 | 4 | 3 |
| | Marquette County | 50 | 0 | 23 | 3 | 24 | 293 | 107 | 171 | 15 | 4 |
| | Mason County | 8 | 0 | 4 | 0 | 4 | 53 | 15 | 38 | 0 | 0 |
| | Mecosta County | 15 | 0 | 10 | 0 | 5 | 111 | 31 | 74 | 6 | 1 |
| | Menominee County | 9 | 0 | 4 | 0 | 5 | 103 | 52 | 47 | 4 | 0 |
| | Midland County | 9 | 0 | 6 | 0 | 3 | 35 | 9 | 25 | 1 | 1 |
| | Missaukee County | 3 | 0 | 2 | 0 | 1 | 25 | 6 | 16 | 3 | 1 |
| | Monroe County | 24 | 0 | 10 | 6 | 8 | 213 | 67 | 130 | 16 | 8 |
| | Montcalm County | 48 | 0 | 13 | 2 | 33 | 333 | 145 | 167 | 21 | 1 |
| | Montmorency County | 4 | 0 | 2 | 0 | 2 | 33 | 16 | 15 | 2 | 0 |
| | Muskegon County | 44 | 0 | 17 | 3 | 24 | 390 | 99 | 265 | 26 | 4 |
| | Newaygo County | 42 | 0 | 26 | 2 | 14 | 342 | 135 | 180 | 27 | 3 |
| | Oakland County | 63 | 3 | 13 | 11 | 36 | 350 | 154 | 167 | 29 | 5 |
| | Oceana County | 15 | 0 | 6 | 0 | 9 | 99 | 26 | 68 | 5 | 0 |
| | Ogemaw County | 31 | 0 | 7 | 0 | 24 | 151 | 73 | 74 | 4 | 1 |
| | Ontonagon County | 3 | 1 | 2 | 0 | 0 | 32 | 9 | 19 | 4 | 2 |
| | Osceola County | 28 | 0 | 15 | 0 | 13 | 112 | 41 | 66 | 5 | 2 |
| | Oscoda County | 6 | 0 | 1 | 1 | 4 | 17 | 3 | 12 | 2 | 0 |
| | Otsego County | 28 | 0 | 13 | 2 | 13 | 248 | 102 | 138 | 8 | 1 |
| | Ottawa County | 6 | 0 | 4 | 0 | 2 | 58 | 16 | 38 | 4 | 0 |
| | Presque Isle County | 3 | 0 | 2 | 0 | 1 | 20 | 7 | 10 | 3 | 0 |
| | Roscommon County | 11 | 0 | 6 | 2 | 3 | 96 | 25 | 68 | 3 | 0 |
| | Saginaw County | 41 | 1 | 18 | 3 | 19 | 234 | 95 | 117 | 22 | 7 |
| | Sanilac County | 39 | 0 | 16 | 1 | 22 | 159 | 63 | 85 | 11 | 4 |
| | Schoolcraft County | 10 | 0 | 5 | 0 | 5 | 107 | 56 | 48 | 3 | 3 |
| | Shiawassee County | 27 | 0 | 14 | 1 | 12 | 148 | 46 | 90 | 12 | 2 |
| | St. Clair County | 25 | 0 | 8 | 0 | 17 | 323 | 118 | 173 | 32 | 0 |
| | St. Joseph County | 26 | 0 | 11 | 1 | 14 | 214 | 99 | 89 | 26 | 3 |
| | Tuscola County | 30 | 0 | 17 | 1 | 12 | 180 | 77 | 97 | 6 | 1 |
| | Van Buren County | 81 | 3 | 15 | 2 | 61 | 432 | 190 | 211 | 31 | 5 |
| | Washtenaw County | 59 | 0 | 17 | 0 | 42 | 190 | 84 | 90 | 16 | 3 |
| | Wayne County | 66 | 3 | 40 | 2 | 21 | 112 | 5 | 89 | 18 | 0 |
| | Wexford County | 25 | 0 | 8 | 1 | 16 | 171 | 38 | 124 | 9 | 1 |
| **MICHIGAN—Tribal Agencies** | | | | | | | | | | | |
| Bay Mills Tribal | | 0 | 0 | 0 | 0 | 0 | 28 | 7 | 20 | 1 | 0 |
| Hannahville Tribal | | 19 | 0 | 11 | 0 | 8 | 198 | 18 | 179 | 1 | 0 |
| Lac Vieux Desert Tribal | | 2 | 0 | 0 | 0 | 2 | 26 | 5 | 20 | 1 | 1 |
| Little River Band of Ottawa Tribal | | 1 | 0 | 0 | 0 | 1 | 42 | 0 | 39 | 3 | 0 |
| **MICHIGAN—Other Agencies[5]** | | | | | | | | | | | |
| Bishop International Airport | | 1 | 0 | 0 | 0 | 1 | 8 | 0 | 4 | 4 | 0 |
| Capitol Region Airport Authority | | 0 | 0 | 0 | 0 | 0 | 1 | 0 | 1 | 0 | 0 |
| Gerald R. Ford International Airport | | 2 | 0 | 2 | 0 | 0 | 2 | 0 | 0 | 2 | 0 |
| Huron-Clinton Metropolitan Authority: | Hudson Mills Metropark | 0 | 0 | 0 | 0 | 0 | 6 | 0 | 6 | 0 | 0 |
| | Kensington Metropark | 0 | 0 | 0 | 0 | 0 | 17 | 1 | 15 | 1 | 1 |
| | Lower Huron Metropark | 7 | 0 | 1 | 0 | 6 | 32 | 0 | 32 | 0 | 0 |
| | Stony Creek Metropark | 3 | 0 | 0 | 0 | 3 | 49 | 6 | 43 | 0 | 0 |
| Wayne County Airport | | 9 | 0 | 0 | 0 | 9 | 314 | 1 | 222 | 91 | 0 |

[1] The FBI does not publish arson data unless it receives data from either the agency or the state for all 12 months of the calendar year.
[5] Because of changes in the state/local agency's reporting practices, figures are not comparable to previous years' data.

## Table 11. Offenses Known to Law Enforcement, by State, Tribal, and Other Agencies, 2009—*Continued*

(Number.)

| State/Other Agency | Unit/Office | Violent crime | Murder and non-negligent man-slaughter | Forcible rape | Robbery | Aggra-vated assault | Property crime | Burglary | Larceny-theft | Motor vehicle theft | Arson[1] |
|---|---|---|---|---|---|---|---|---|---|---|---|
| **MINNESOTA—State Agencies[4]** | | | | | | | | | | | |
| Capitol Security | St. Paul | | 0 | | 0 | 0 | 30 | 0 | 30 | 0 | 0 |
| Minnesota State Patrol | | | 0 | | 0 | 0 | 0 | 0 | 0 | 0 | 0 |
| State Patrol: | Brainerd | | 0 | | 0 | 1 | 0 | 0 | 0 | 0 | 0 |
| | Detroit Lakes | | 0 | | 0 | 0 | 0 | 0 | 0 | 0 | 0 |
| | Duluth | | 0 | | 0 | 0 | 0 | 0 | 0 | 0 | 0 |
| | Golden Valley | | 0 | | 0 | 0 | 0 | 0 | 0 | 0 | 0 |
| | Mankato | | 0 | | 0 | 0 | 0 | 0 | 0 | 0 | 0 |
| | Marshall | | 0 | | 0 | 0 | 0 | 0 | 0 | 0 | 0 |
| | Oakdale | | 0 | | 0 | 0 | 0 | 0 | 0 | 0 | 0 |
| | Rochester | | 0 | | 0 | 0 | 0 | 0 | 0 | 0 | 0 |
| | St. Cloud | | 0 | | 0 | 0 | 0 | 0 | 0 | 0 | 0 |
| | Thief River Falls | | 0 | | 0 | 0 | 0 | 0 | 0 | 0 | 0 |
| | Virginia | | 0 | | 0 | 0 | 0 | 0 | 0 | 0 | 0 |
| **MINNESOTA—Tribal Agencies** | | | | | | | | | | | |
| Red Lake Tribal | | 191 | 0 | 9 | 2 | 180 | 410 | 86 | 258 | 66 | 23 |
| **MINNESOTA—Other Agencies[4]** | | | | | | | | | | | |
| Minneapolis-St. Paul International Airport | | | 0 | | 0 | 0 | 0 | 0 | 0 | 0 | 0 |
| Three Rivers Park District | | | 0 | | 0 | 0 | 131 | 2 | 127 | 2 | 0 |
| **MISSISSIPPI—State Agencies** | | | | | | | | | | | |
| State Capitol Police | | 0 | 0 | 0 | 0 | 0 | 21 | 8 | 11 | 2 | 0 |
| **MISSISSIPPI—Tribal Agencies** | | | | | | | | | | | |
| Choctaw Tribal | | 175 | 1 | 7 | 0 | 167 | 444 | 170 | 268 | 6 | 1 |
| **MISSOURI—State Agencies** | | | | | | | | | | | |
| Capitol Police | | 0 | 0 | 0 | 0 | 0 | 44 | 0 | 42 | 2 | 0 |
| Department of Conservation | | 0 | 0 | 0 | 0 | 0 | 0 | 0 | 0 | 0 | 0 |
| Division of Alcohol and Tobacco Control | | 0 | 0 | 0 | 0 | 0 | 0 | 0 | 0 | 0 | 0 |
| Gaming Commission | Enforcement Division | 11 | 0 | 0 | 3 | 8 | 174 | 1 | 171 | 2 | 0 |
| State Highway Patrol: | Jefferson City | 3 | 0 | 0 | 0 | 3 | 8 | 1 | 4 | 3 | 0 |
| | Kirkwood | 3 | 1 | 0 | 1 | 1 | 8 | 0 | 4 | 4 | 0 |
| | Lee's Summit | 9 | 0 | 0 | 0 | 9 | 19 | 3 | 7 | 9 | 0 |
| | Macon | 5 | 0 | 1 | 0 | 4 | 6 | 2 | 1 | 3 | 0 |
| | Poplar Bluff | 7 | 0 | 0 | 2 | 5 | 7 | 1 | 1 | 5 | 0 |
| | Rolla | 8 | 2 | 1 | 0 | 5 | 9 | 0 | 0 | 9 | 0 |
| | Springfield | 0 | 0 | 0 | 0 | 0 | 7 | 0 | 5 | 2 | 0 |
| | St. Joseph | 13 | 1 | 0 | 1 | 11 | 22 | 1 | 8 | 13 | 0 |
| | Willow Springs | 0 | 0 | 0 | 0 | 0 | 10 | 2 | 1 | 7 | 0 |
| State Fire Marshal | | 0 | 0 | 0 | 0 | 0 | 0 | 0 | 0 | 0 | 249 |
| State Park Rangers | | 6 | 0 | 1 | 1 | 4 | 115 | 8 | 107 | 0 | 0 |
| State Water Patrol | | 14 | 0 | 0 | 0 | 14 | 181 | 0 | 181 | 0 | 0 |
| **MISSOURI—Other Agencies** | | | | | | | | | | | |
| Bootheel Drug Task Force | | 0 | 0 | 0 | 0 | 0 | 0 | 0 | 0 | 0 | 0 |
| Clay County Drug Task Force | | 0 | 0 | 0 | 0 | 0 | 0 | 0 | 0 | 0 | 0 |
| Clay County Park Authority | | 1 | 0 | 0 | 1 | 0 | 14 | 1 | 12 | 1 | 0 |
| Jackson County Drug Task Force | | 0 | 0 | 0 | 0 | 0 | 0 | 0 | 0 | 0 | 0 |
| Jackson County Park Rangers | | 0 | 0 | 0 | 0 | 0 | 0 | 0 | 0 | 0 | 0 |
| Lambert-St. Louis International Airport | | 11 | 0 | 0 | 0 | 11 | 258 | 0 | 257 | 1 | 0 |
| Platte County Multi-Jurisdictional Enforcement Group | | 0 | 0 | 0 | 0 | 0 | 0 | 0 | 0 | 0 | 0 |
| Springfield-Branson Airport | | 0 | 0 | 0 | 0 | 0 | 10 | 1 | 8 | 1 | 0 |
| St. Charles County Park Rangers | | 0 | 0 | 0 | 0 | 0 | 0 | 0 | 0 | 0 | 0 |
| St. Peters Ranger Division | | 0 | 0 | 0 | 0 | 0 | 50 | 7 | 43 | 0 | 0 |
| **MONTANA—Tribal Agencies** | | | | | | | | | | | |
| Crow Tribal | | 25 | 0 | 5 | 1 | 19 | 120 | 52 | 11 | 57 | 2 |
| **NEBRASKA—State Agencies** | | | | | | | | | | | |
| Nebraska State Patrol | | 3 | 0 | 0 | 0 | 3 | 0 | 0 | 0 | 0 | 0 |
| State Patrol: | Adams County | 0 | 0 | 0 | 0 | 0 | 0 | 0 | 0 | 0 | 0 |
| | Antelope County | 0 | 0 | 0 | 0 | 0 | 0 | 0 | 0 | 0 | 0 |
| | Arthur County | 0 | 0 | 0 | 0 | 0 | 0 | 0 | 0 | 0 | 0 |
| | Banner County | 0 | 0 | 0 | 0 | 0 | 0 | 0 | 0 | 0 | 0 |
| | Blaine County | 0 | 0 | 0 | 0 | 0 | 0 | 0 | 0 | 0 | 0 |
| | Boone County | 0 | 0 | 0 | 0 | 0 | 0 | 0 | 0 | 0 | 0 |
| | Box Butte County | 0 | 0 | 0 | 0 | 0 | 0 | 0 | 0 | 0 | 0 |
| | Boyd County | 0 | 0 | 0 | 0 | 0 | 0 | 0 | 0 | 0 | 0 |
| | Brown County | 0 | 0 | 0 | 0 | 0 | 0 | 0 | 0 | 0 | 0 |
| | Buffalo County | 0 | 0 | 0 | 0 | 0 | 1 | 0 | 1 | 0 | 0 |
| | Burt County | 0 | 0 | 0 | 0 | 0 | 0 | 0 | 0 | 0 | 0 |
| | Butler County | 0 | 0 | 0 | 0 | 0 | 0 | 0 | 0 | 0 | 0 |
| | Cass County | 0 | 0 | 0 | 0 | 0 | 0 | 0 | 0 | 0 | 0 |
| | Cedar County | 0 | 0 | 0 | 0 | 0 | 0 | 0 | 0 | 0 | 0 |
| | Chase County | 0 | 0 | 0 | 0 | 0 | 0 | 0 | 0 | 0 | 0 |

[1] The FBI does not publish arson data unless it receives data from either the agency or the state for all 12 months of the calendar year.

[4] The data collection methodology for the offense of forcible rape used by the Illinois and the Minnesota state Uniform Crime Reporting (UCR) Programs does not comply with national UCR Program guidelines. Consequently, their figures for forcible rape and violent crime (of which forcible rape is a part) are not published in this table.

## Table 11. Offenses Known to Law Enforcement, by State, Tribal, and Other Agencies, 2009—*Continued*

(Number.)

| State/Other Agency | Unit/Office | Violent crime | Murder and non-negligent man-slaughter | Forcible rape | Robbery | Aggra-vated assault | Property crime | Burglary | Larceny-theft | Motor vehicle theft | Arson[1] |
|---|---|---|---|---|---|---|---|---|---|---|---|
| | Cherry County | 0 | 0 | 0 | 0 | 0 | 0 | 0 | 0 | 0 | 0 |
| | Cheyenne County | 0 | 0 | 0 | 0 | 0 | 1 | 0 | 1 | 0 | 0 |
| | Clay County | 0 | 0 | 0 | 0 | 0 | 1 | 1 | 0 | 0 | 0 |
| | Colfax County | 1 | 0 | 0 | 0 | 1 | 0 | 0 | 0 | 0 | 0 |
| | Cuming County | 0 | 0 | 0 | 0 | 0 | 0 | 0 | 0 | 0 | 0 |
| | Custer County | 1 | 0 | 0 | 0 | 1 | 4 | 3 | 1 | 0 | 0 |
| | Dakota County | 2 | 0 | 0 | 0 | 2 | 1 | 1 | 0 | 0 | 0 |
| | Dawes County | 0 | 0 | 0 | 0 | 0 | 0 | 0 | 0 | 0 | 0 |
| | Dawson County | 0 | 0 | 0 | 0 | 0 | 0 | 0 | 0 | 0 | 0 |
| | Deuel County | 0 | 0 | 0 | 0 | 0 | 0 | 0 | 0 | 0 | 0 |
| | Dixon County | 0 | 0 | 0 | 0 | 0 | 0 | 0 | 0 | 0 | 0 |
| | Dodge County | 0 | 0 | 0 | 0 | 0 | 0 | 0 | 0 | 0 | 0 |
| | Douglas County | 0 | 0 | 0 | 0 | 0 | 4 | 0 | 4 | 0 | 0 |
| | Dundy County | 0 | 0 | 0 | 0 | 0 | 0 | 0 | 0 | 0 | 0 |
| | Fillmore County | 0 | 0 | 0 | 0 | 0 | 0 | 0 | 0 | 0 | 0 |
| | Franklin County | 0 | 0 | 0 | 0 | 0 | 0 | 0 | 0 | 0 | 0 |
| | Frontier County | 0 | 0 | 0 | 0 | 0 | 0 | 0 | 0 | 0 | 0 |
| | Furnas County | 0 | 0 | 0 | 0 | 0 | 1 | 1 | 0 | 0 | 0 |
| | Gage County | 0 | 0 | 0 | 0 | 0 | 3 | 0 | 3 | 0 | 0 |
| | Garden County | 0 | 0 | 0 | 0 | 0 | 0 | 0 | 0 | 0 | 0 |
| | Garfield County | 0 | 0 | 0 | 0 | 0 | 0 | 0 | 0 | 0 | 0 |
| | Gosper County | 0 | 0 | 0 | 0 | 0 | 0 | 0 | 0 | 0 | 0 |
| | Grant County | 0 | 0 | 0 | 0 | 0 | 0 | 0 | 0 | 0 | 0 |
| | Greeley County | 0 | 0 | 0 | 0 | 0 | 0 | 0 | 0 | 0 | 0 |
| | Hall County | 0 | 0 | 0 | 0 | 0 | 12 | 3 | 8 | 1 | 0 |
| | Hamilton County | 0 | 0 | 0 | 0 | 0 | 0 | 0 | 0 | 0 | 0 |
| | Harlan County | 2 | 0 | 0 | 0 | 2 | 0 | 0 | 0 | 0 | 0 |
| | Hayes County | 0 | 0 | 0 | 0 | 0 | 0 | 0 | 0 | 0 | 0 |
| | Hitchcock County | 1 | 0 | 0 | 0 | 1 | 1 | 0 | 1 | 0 | 0 |
| | Holt County | 0 | 0 | 0 | 0 | 0 | 0 | 0 | 0 | 0 | 0 |
| | Hooker County | 0 | 0 | 0 | 0 | 0 | 0 | 0 | 0 | 0 | 0 |
| | Howard County | 0 | 0 | 0 | 0 | 0 | 3 | 0 | 3 | 0 | 0 |
| | Jefferson County | 0 | 0 | 0 | 0 | 0 | 1 | 0 | 1 | 0 | 0 |
| | Johnson County | 0 | 0 | 0 | 0 | 0 | 0 | 0 | 0 | 0 | 0 |
| | Kearney County | 0 | 0 | 0 | 0 | 0 | 0 | 0 | 0 | 0 | 0 |
| | Keith County | 1 | 0 | 0 | 0 | 1 | 0 | 0 | 0 | 0 | 0 |
| | Keya Paha County | 0 | 0 | 0 | 0 | 0 | 0 | 0 | 0 | 0 | 0 |
| | Kimball County | 0 | 0 | 0 | 0 | 0 | 2 | 0 | 2 | 0 | 0 |
| | Knox County | 0 | 0 | 0 | 0 | 0 | 0 | 0 | 0 | 0 | 0 |
| | Lancaster County | 1 | 0 | 1 | 0 | 0 | 9 | 1 | 5 | 3 | 0 |
| | Lincoln County | 2 | 0 | 0 | 1 | 1 | 4 | 1 | 1 | 2 | 0 |
| | Logan County | 0 | 0 | 0 | 0 | 0 | 0 | 0 | 0 | 0 | 0 |
| | Loup County | 0 | 0 | 0 | 0 | 0 | 0 | 0 | 0 | 0 | 0 |
| | Madison County | 0 | 0 | 0 | 0 | 0 | 5 | 2 | 3 | 0 | 0 |
| | McPherson County | 0 | 0 | 0 | 0 | 0 | 0 | 0 | 0 | 0 | 0 |
| | Merrick County | 0 | 0 | 0 | 0 | 0 | 0 | 0 | 0 | 0 | 0 |
| | Morrill County | 0 | 0 | 0 | 0 | 0 | 0 | 0 | 0 | 0 | 0 |
| | Nance County | 0 | 0 | 0 | 0 | 0 | 0 | 0 | 0 | 0 | 0 |
| | Nemaha County | 1 | 0 | 1 | 0 | 0 | 3 | 3 | 0 | 0 | 0 |
| | Nuckolls County | 0 | 0 | 0 | 0 | 0 | 0 | 0 | 0 | 0 | 0 |
| | Otoe County | 0 | 0 | 0 | 0 | 0 | 0 | 0 | 0 | 0 | 0 |
| | Pawnee County | 0 | 0 | 0 | 0 | 0 | 0 | 0 | 0 | 0 | 0 |
| | Perkins County | 0 | 0 | 0 | 0 | 0 | 0 | 0 | 0 | 0 | 0 |
| | Phelps County | 0 | 0 | 0 | 0 | 0 | 0 | 0 | 0 | 0 | 0 |
| | Pierce County | 1 | 0 | 0 | 0 | 1 | 3 | 2 | 1 | 0 | 0 |
| | Platte County | 0 | 0 | 0 | 0 | 0 | 0 | 0 | 0 | 0 | 0 |
| | Polk County | 0 | 0 | 0 | 0 | 0 | 0 | 0 | 0 | 0 | 0 |
| | Red Willow County | 0 | 0 | 0 | 0 | 0 | 0 | 0 | 0 | 0 | 0 |
| | Richardson County | 1 | 0 | 0 | 0 | 1 | 2 | 0 | 1 | 1 | 0 |
| | Rock County | 0 | 0 | 0 | 0 | 0 | 0 | 0 | 0 | 0 | 0 |
| | Saline County | 0 | 0 | 0 | 0 | 0 | 0 | 0 | 0 | 0 | 0 |
| | Sarpy County | 0 | 0 | 0 | 0 | 0 | 2 | 1 | 0 | 1 | 0 |
| | Saunders County | 0 | 0 | 0 | 0 | 0 | 0 | 0 | 0 | 0 | 0 |
| | Scotts Bluff County | 0 | 0 | 0 | 0 | 0 | 3 | 0 | 2 | 1 | 0 |
| | Seward County | 0 | 0 | 0 | 0 | 0 | 0 | 0 | 0 | 0 | 0 |
| | Sheridan County | 0 | 0 | 0 | 0 | 0 | 1 | 0 | 1 | 0 | 0 |
| | Sherman County | 1 | 0 | 0 | 0 | 1 | 1 | 0 | 1 | 0 | 0 |
| | Sioux County | 2 | 0 | 0 | 0 | 2 | 2 | 0 | 2 | 0 | 0 |
| | Stanton County | 0 | 0 | 0 | 0 | 0 | 0 | 0 | 0 | 0 | 0 |
| | Thayer County | 0 | 0 | 0 | 0 | 0 | 0 | 0 | 0 | 0 | 0 |
| | Thomas County | 0 | 0 | 0 | 0 | 0 | 1 | 0 | 1 | 0 | 0 |

[1] The FBI does not publish arson data unless it receives data from either the agency or the state for all 12 months of the calendar year.

## Table 11. Offenses Known to Law Enforcement, by State, Tribal, and Other Agencies, 2009—*Continued*

(Number.)

| State/Other Agency | Unit/Office | Violent crime | Murder and non-negligent man-slaughter | Forcible rape | Robbery | Aggra-vated assault | Property crime | Burglary | Larceny-theft | Motor vehicle theft | Arson[1] |
|---|---|---|---|---|---|---|---|---|---|---|---|
| | Thurston County | 0 | 0 | 0 | 0 | 0 | 0 | 0 | 0 | 0 | 0 |
| | Valley County | 0 | 0 | 0 | 0 | 0 | 0 | 0 | 0 | 0 | 0 |
| | Washington County | 0 | 0 | 0 | 0 | 0 | 0 | 0 | 0 | 0 | 0 |
| | Wayne County | 0 | 0 | 0 | 0 | 0 | 0 | 0 | 0 | 0 | 0 |
| | Webster County | 0 | 0 | 0 | 0 | 0 | 0 | 0 | 0 | 0 | 0 |
| | Wheeler County | 0 | 0 | 0 | 0 | 0 | 0 | 0 | 0 | 0 | 0 |
| | York County | 0 | 0 | 0 | 0 | 0 | 1 | 0 | 1 | 0 | 0 |
| **NEBRASKA—Tribal Agencies** | | | | | | | | | | | |
| Winnebago Tribal | | 60 | 0 | 0 | 0 | 60 | 6 | 1 | 0 | 5 | 1 |
| **NEVADA—State Agencies** | | | | | | | | | | | |
| Taxicab Authority[5] | | 4 | 0 | 0 | 3 | 1 | 457 | 8 | 449 | 0 | 0 |
| **NEVADA—Tribal Agencies** | | | | | | | | | | | |
| Eastern Nevada Tribal | | 3 | 0 | 0 | 0 | 3 | 0 | 0 | 0 | 0 | 0 |
| Ely Shoshone Tribal | | 1 | 0 | 0 | 0 | 1 | 7 | 2 | 3 | 2 | 0 |
| Las Vegas Paiute Tribal | | 1 | 0 | 0 | 1 | 0 | 129 | 1 | 125 | 3 | 0 |
| Lovelock Paiute Tribal | | 13 | 0 | 0 | 0 | 13 | 8 | 3 | 3 | 2 | 1 |
| Moapa Tribal | | 4 | 0 | 0 | 0 | 4 | 15 | 8 | 7 | 0 | 1 |
| Pyramid Lake Tribal | | 13 | 0 | 4 | 0 | 9 | 31 | 18 | 8 | 5 | 0 |
| **NEVADA—Other Agencies** | | | | | | | | | | | |
| Clark County School District | | 78 | 0 | 4 | 44 | 30 | 1,009 | 180 | 794 | 35 | 32 |
| Washoe County School District | | 7 | 0 | 0 | 1 | 6 | 158 | 17 | 138 | 3 | 8 |
| **NEW HAMPSHIRE—State Agencies** | | | | | | | | | | | |
| Liquor Commission | | 0 | 0 | 0 | 0 | 0 | 14 | 1 | 13 | 0 | 0 |
| **NEW JERSEY—State Agencies** | | | | | | | | | | | |
| Department of Human Services | | 66 | 0 | 7 | 0 | 59 | 113 | 2 | 111 | 0 | 0 |
| New Jersey Transit Police | | 61 | 0 | 0 | 44 | 17 | 352 | 7 | 336 | 9 | 0 |
| Palisades Interstate Parkway | | 6 | 0 | 0 | 0 | 6 | 0 | 0 | 0 | 0 | 0 |
| Port Authority of New York and New Jersey | | 39 | 0 | 0 | 10 | 29 | 343 | 6 | 318 | 19 | 0 |
| State Police: | Atlantic County | 42 | 1 | 1 | 13 | 27 | 1,091 | 121 | 951 | 19 | 5 |
| | Bergen County | 5 | 0 | 0 | 0 | 5 | 117 | 3 | 108 | 6 | 0 |
| | Burlington County | 41 | 2 | 3 | 2 | 34 | 492 | 148 | 322 | 22 | 8 |
| | Camden County | 2 | 0 | 0 | 0 | 2 | 21 | 0 | 21 | 0 | 0 |
| | Cape May County | 38 | 0 | 1 | 6 | 31 | 418 | 143 | 256 | 19 | 5 |
| | Cumberland County | 97 | 2 | 2 | 12 | 81 | 780 | 263 | 467 | 50 | 10 |
| | Essex County | 17 | 0 | 0 | 6 | 11 | 35 | 1 | 31 | 3 | 1 |
| | Hunterdon County | 15 | 0 | 0 | 2 | 13 | 212 | 66 | 139 | 7 | 2 |
| | Mercer County | 5 | 0 | 0 | 0 | 5 | 123 | 8 | 109 | 6 | 0 |
| | Middlesex County | 11 | 0 | 0 | 2 | 9 | 73 | 2 | 69 | 2 | 0 |
| | Monmouth County | 15 | 0 | 1 | 1 | 13 | 273 | 51 | 210 | 12 | 3 |
| | Morris County | 13 | 0 | 1 | 2 | 10 | 27 | 2 | 20 | 5 | 0 |
| | Ocean County | 11 | 0 | 1 | 1 | 9 | 78 | 9 | 67 | 2 | 2 |
| | Salem County | 35 | 0 | 1 | 6 | 28 | 403 | 127 | 245 | 31 | 11 |
| | Sussex County | 33 | 0 | 1 | 7 | 25 | 474 | 95 | 356 | 23 | 10 |
| | Union County | 4 | 0 | 0 | 1 | 3 | 12 | 1 | 9 | 2 | 0 |
| | Warren County | 17 | 0 | 1 | 2 | 14 | 225 | 72 | 138 | 15 | 4 |
| **NEW JERSEY—Other Agencies** | | | | | | | | | | | |
| Park Police: | Camden County | 5 | 0 | 2 | 1 | 2 | 23 | 4 | 18 | 1 | 0 |
| | Morris County | 0 | 0 | 0 | 0 | 0 | 0 | 0 | 0 | 0 | 0 |
| | Union County | 0 | 0 | 0 | 0 | 0 | 0 | 0 | 0 | 0 | 0 |
| Prosecutor: | Atlantic County | 0 | 0 | 0 | 0 | 0 | 0 | 0 | 0 | 0 | 0 |
| | Bergen County | 0 | 0 | 0 | 0 | 0 | 0 | 0 | 0 | 0 | 0 |
| | Burlington County | 0 | 0 | 0 | 0 | 0 | 0 | 0 | 0 | 0 | 0 |
| | Camden County | 0 | 0 | 0 | 0 | 0 | 0 | 0 | 0 | 0 | 0 |
| | Cape May County | 0 | 0 | 0 | 0 | 0 | 0 | 0 | 0 | 0 | 0 |
| | Cumberland County | 0 | 0 | 0 | 0 | 0 | 0 | 0 | 0 | 0 | 0 |
| | Essex County | 0 | 0 | 0 | 0 | 0 | 0 | 0 | 0 | 0 | 0 |
| | Gloucester County | 0 | 0 | 0 | 0 | 0 | 0 | 0 | 0 | 0 | 0 |
| | Hudson County | 0 | 0 | 0 | 0 | 0 | 0 | 0 | 0 | 0 | 0 |
| | Hunterdon County | 0 | 0 | 0 | 0 | 0 | 0 | 0 | 0 | 0 | 0 |
| | Mercer County | 0 | 0 | 0 | 0 | 0 | 0 | 0 | 0 | 0 | 0 |
| | Middlesex County | 0 | 0 | 0 | 0 | 0 | 0 | 0 | 0 | 0 | 0 |
| | Monmouth County | 0 | 0 | 0 | 0 | 0 | 0 | 0 | 0 | 0 | 0 |
| | Morris County | 0 | 0 | 0 | 0 | 0 | 0 | 0 | 0 | 0 | 0 |
| | Ocean County | 0 | 0 | 0 | 0 | 0 | 0 | 0 | 0 | 0 | 0 |
| | Passaic County | 0 | 0 | 0 | 0 | 0 | 0 | 0 | 0 | 0 | 0 |
| | Somerset County | 0 | 0 | 0 | 0 | 0 | 0 | 0 | 0 | 0 | 0 |
| | Sussex County | 0 | 0 | 0 | 0 | 0 | 0 | 0 | 0 | 0 | 0 |
| | Union County | 0 | 0 | 0 | 0 | 0 | 0 | 0 | 0 | 0 | 0 |
| | Warren County | 0 | 0 | 0 | 0 | 0 | 0 | 0 | 0 | 0 | 0 |
| **NEW MEXICO—State Agencies** | | | | | | | | | | | |
| New Mexico State Police | | 114 | 7 | 19 | 25 | 63 | 878 | 474 | 289 | 115 | 3 |

[1] The FBI does not publish arson data unless it receives data from either the agency or the state for all 12 months of the calendar year.
[5] Because of changes in the state/local agency's reporting practices, figures are not comparable to previous years' data.

## Table 11. Offenses Known to Law Enforcement, by State, Tribal, and Other Agencies, 2009—*Continued*

(Number.)

| State/Other Agency | Unit/Office | Violent crime | Murder and non-negligent man-slaughter | Forcible rape | Robbery | Aggra-vated assault | Property crime | Burglary | Larceny-theft | Motor vehicle theft | Arson[1] |
|---|---|---|---|---|---|---|---|---|---|---|---|
| **NEW MEXICO—Tribal Agencies** | | | | | | | | | | | |
| Acoma Tribal | | 16 | 1 | 0 | 0 | 15 | 16 | 5 | 8 | 3 | 0 |
| Isleta Tribal | | 101 | 0 | 2 | 3 | 96 | 159 | 51 | 86 | 22 | 4 |
| Jemez Tribal | | 19 | 0 | 0 | 0 | 19 | 4 | 2 | 1 | 1 | 1 |
| Jicarilla Tribal | | 74 | 2 | 7 | 0 | 65 | 2 | 0 | 2 | 0 | 1 |
| Laguna Tribal | | 102 | 0 | 6 | 0 | 96 | 66 | 12 | 51 | 3 | 1 |
| Mescalero Tribal | | 319 | 2 | 6 | 1 | 310 | 52 | 44 | 1 | 7 | 59 |
| Northern Pueblos Tribal | | 61 | 11 | 2 | 0 | 48 | 38 | 25 | 10 | 3 | 3 |
| Ohkay Owingeh Tribal | | 10 | 1 | 3 | 0 | 6 | 43 | 13 | 23 | 7 | 2 |
| Pojoaque Tribal | | 45 | 0 | 1 | 1 | 43 | 107 | 31 | 69 | 7 | 0 |
| Ramah Navajo Tribal | | 9 | 0 | 1 | 0 | 8 | 48 | 32 | 12 | 4 | 12 |
| Santa Ana Tribal | | 7 | 0 | 0 | 3 | 4 | 12 | 7 | 0 | 5 | 2 |
| Santa Clara Tribal | | 8 | 0 | 1 | 0 | 7 | 24 | 17 | 7 | 0 | 2 |
| Zuni Tribal | | 44 | 4 | 5 | 1 | 34 | 6 | 5 | 1 | 0 | 0 |
| **NEW YORK—State Agencies** | | | | | | | | | | | |
| State Park: | Allegany Region | 0 | 0 | 0 | 0 | 0 | 16 | 1 | 14 | 1 | 0 |
| | Central Region | 1 | 0 | 0 | 0 | 1 | 32 | 1 | 31 | 0 | 0 |
| | Finger Lakes Region | 0 | 0 | 0 | 0 | 0 | 41 | 5 | 36 | 0 | 0 |
| | Genesee Region | 0 | 0 | 0 | 0 | 0 | 28 | 0 | 28 | 0 | 0 |
| | Long Island Region | 9 | 0 | 1 | 1 | 7 | 167 | 7 | 157 | 3 | 2 |
| | New York City Region | 6 | 0 | 0 | 2 | 4 | 89 | 0 | 89 | 0 | 0 |
| | Niagara Region | 1 | 0 | 0 | 1 | 0 | 25 | 2 | 23 | 0 | 0 |
| | Palisades Region | 2 | 0 | 0 | 0 | 2 | 26 | 1 | 25 | 0 | 1 |
| | Saratoga/Capital Region | 7 | 0 | 0 | 2 | 5 | 47 | 1 | 46 | 0 | 0 |
| | Taconic Region | 1 | 0 | 0 | 1 | 0 | 28 | 5 | 22 | 1 | 0 |
| | Thousand Island Region | 0 | 0 | 0 | 0 | 0 | 26 | 1 | 25 | 0 | 0 |
| State Police: | Albany County | 8 | 1 | 0 | 1 | 6 | 142 | 20 | 122 | 0 | 0 |
| | Allegany County | 76 | 0 | 44 | 3 | 29 | 314 | 131 | 174 | 9 | 1 |
| | Broome County | 33 | 1 | 7 | 6 | 19 | 509 | 110 | 381 | 18 | 0 |
| | Cattaraugus County | 37 | 0 | 10 | 2 | 25 | 233 | 84 | 140 | 9 | 1 |
| | Cayuga County | 27 | 0 | 5 | 2 | 20 | 196 | 45 | 148 | 3 | 0 |
| | Chautauqua County | 21 | 0 | 3 | 2 | 16 | 106 | 41 | 63 | 2 | 1 |
| | Chemung County | 37 | 0 | 7 | 1 | 29 | 308 | 63 | 242 | 3 | 0 |
| | Chenango County | 26 | 0 | 4 | 1 | 21 | 203 | 58 | 140 | 5 | |
| | Clinton County | 90 | 1 | 13 | 3 | 73 | 903 | 278 | 605 | 20 | 1 |
| | Columbia County | 29 | 0 | 3 | 0 | 26 | 316 | 109 | 203 | 4 | 1 |
| | Cortland County | 6 | 0 | 1 | 0 | 5 | 148 | 13 | 134 | 1 | 1 |
| | Delaware County | 35 | 0 | 6 | 3 | 26 | 262 | 83 | 175 | 4 | 0 |
| | Dutchess County | 86 | 0 | 13 | 11 | 62 | 692 | 143 | 531 | 18 | |
| | Erie County | 21 | 0 | 4 | 5 | 12 | 461 | 84 | 366 | 11 | 0 |
| | Essex County | 35 | 0 | 5 | 0 | 30 | 330 | 115 | 209 | 6 | 4 |
| | Franklin County | 38 | 0 | 8 | 2 | 28 | 364 | 155 | 190 | 19 | 7 |
| | Fulton County | 22 | 0 | 3 | 1 | 18 | 156 | 31 | 124 | 1 | 0 |
| | Genesee County | 11 | 0 | 4 | 2 | 5 | 100 | 12 | 85 | 3 | 0 |
| | Greene County[5] | 61 | 1 | 5 | 3 | 52 | 314 | 115 | 190 | 9 | 5 |
| | Hamilton County | 1 | 0 | 0 | 0 | 1 | 29 | 9 | 20 | 0 | 0 |
| | Herkimer County | 22 | 0 | 7 | 0 | 15 | 297 | 116 | 174 | 7 | 3 |
| | Jefferson County | 55 | 1 | 9 | 0 | 45 | 624 | 123 | 489 | 12 | 0 |
| | Lewis County | 8 | 0 | 1 | 0 | 7 | 68 | 34 | 32 | 2 | 0 |
| | Livingston County | 26 | 0 | 4 | 1 | 21 | 73 | 11 | 60 | 2 | 0 |
| | Madison County | 21 | 0 | 7 | 2 | 12 | 295 | 95 | 192 | 8 | 0 |
| | Monroe County | 17 | 0 | 8 | 3 | 6 | 64 | 4 | 60 | 0 | 0 |
| | Montgomery County | 9 | 0 | 0 | 2 | 7 | 78 | 22 | 53 | 3 | 0 |
| | Nassau County | 2 | 0 | 0 | 0 | 2 | 12 | 0 | 11 | 1 | 1 |
| | New York County | 3 | 0 | 1 | 0 | 2 | 107 | 0 | 107 | 0 | 0 |
| | Niagara County | 11 | 0 | 1 | 7 | 3 | 269 | 59 | 206 | 4 | 2 |
| | Oneida County | 83 | 2 | 16 | 7 | 58 | 712 | 206 | 501 | 5 | 4 |
| | Onondaga County | 24 | 1 | 6 | 4 | 13 | 569 | 138 | 420 | 11 | 0 |
| | Ontario County | 17 | 0 | 3 | 3 | 11 | 185 | 35 | 148 | 2 | 0 |
| | Orange County | 58 | 1 | 9 | 7 | 41 | 859 | 86 | 760 | 13 | 0 |
| | Orleans County | 8 | 0 | 5 | 0 | 3 | 62 | 16 | 42 | 4 | 0 |
| | Oswego County | 45 | 1 | 15 | 4 | 25 | 902 | 293 | 581 | 28 | 0 |
| | Otsego County | 47 | 0 | 12 | 10 | 25 | 439 | 120 | 311 | 8 | 0 |
| | Putnam County | 21 | 0 | 3 | 4 | 14 | 158 | 40 | 111 | 7 | |
| | Rensselaer County | 42 | 0 | 6 | 10 | 26 | 509 | 122 | 373 | 14 | 0 |
| | Rockland County | 6 | 0 | 1 | 0 | 5 | 24 | 1 | 22 | 1 | 2 |
| | Saratoga County | 75 | 1 | 13 | 11 | 50 | 474 | 98 | 365 | 11 | 2 |
| | Schenectady County | 3 | 0 | 1 | 0 | 2 | 55 | 7 | 47 | 1 | 0 |
| | Schoharie County | 17 | 1 | 2 | 2 | 12 | 127 | 49 | 77 | 1 | 1 |
| | Schuyler County | 7 | 0 | 2 | 0 | 5 | 39 | 9 | 28 | 2 | 0 |
| | Seneca County | 15 | 0 | 1 | 0 | 14 | 111 | 49 | 56 | 6 | 0 |
| | Steuben County | 41 | 1 | 13 | 3 | 24 | 354 | 128 | 217 | 9 | |

[1] The FBI does not publish arson data unless it receives data from either the agency or the state for all 12 months of the calendar year.

[5] Because of changes in the state/local agency's reporting practices, figures are not comparable to previous years' data.

## Table 11. Offenses Known to Law Enforcement, by State, Tribal, and Other Agencies, 2009—*Continued*

(Number.)

| State/Other Agency | Unit/Office | Violent crime | Murder and non-negligent man-slaughter | Forcible rape | Robbery | Aggra-vated assault | Property crime | Burglary | Larceny-theft | Motor vehicle theft | Arson[1] |
|---|---|---|---|---|---|---|---|---|---|---|---|
| | St. Lawrence County | 94 | 0 | 22 | 3 | 69 | 452 | 203 | 235 | 14 | 11 |
| | Suffolk County | 25 | 0 | 5 | 4 | 16 | 79 | 7 | 72 | 0 | |
| | Sullivan County | 74 | 1 | 11 | 7 | 55 | 345 | 149 | 182 | 14 | 3 |
| | Tioga County | 10 | 0 | 2 | 0 | 8 | 127 | 34 | 90 | 3 | 1 |
| | Tompkins County | 36 | 1 | 7 | 1 | 27 | 226 | 52 | 173 | 1 | 1 |
| | Ulster County | 128 | 1 | 14 | 3 | 110 | 461 | 174 | 265 | 22 | 3 |
| | Warren County | 11 | 0 | 1 | 0 | 10 | 158 | 16 | 141 | 1 | 0 |
| | Washington County[5] | 20 | 0 | 3 | 0 | 17 | 121 | 30 | 87 | 4 | 1 |
| | Wayne County | 47 | 0 | 13 | 7 | 27 | 431 | 128 | 293 | 10 | 2 |
| | Westchester County | 68 | 1 | 8 | 8 | 51 | 661 | 110 | 535 | 16 | |
| | Wyoming County | 23 | 0 | 1 | 0 | 22 | 24 | 7 | 14 | 3 | |
| | Yates County | 1 | 0 | 1 | 0 | 0 | 24 | 6 | 18 | 0 | 0 |
| **NEW YORK—Tribal Agencies** | | | | | | | | | | | |
| Oneida Indian Nation | | 14 | 0 | 0 | 0 | 14 | 370 | 12 | 355 | 3 | 0 |
| St. Regis Tribal | | 8 | 0 | 1 | 1 | 6 | 130 | 40 | 70 | 20 | 8 |
| **NEW YORK—Other Agencies** | | | | | | | | | | | |
| Board of Water: | Delaware County | 0 | 0 | 0 | 0 | 0 | 0 | 0 | 0 | 0 | 0 |
| | Sullivan County | 0 | 0 | 0 | 0 | 0 | 0 | 0 | 0 | 0 | 0 |
| | Ulster County | 0 | 0 | 0 | 0 | 0 | 5 | 1 | 4 | 0 | 0 |
| | Westchester County | 0 | 0 | 0 | 0 | 0 | 19 | 0 | 19 | 0 | 0 |
| Broome County Special Investigations Task Force | | 0 | 0 | 0 | 0 | 0 | 0 | 0 | 0 | 0 | 0 |
| New York City Metropolitan Transportation Authority | | 71 | 0 | 0 | 31 | 40 | 561 | 11 | 543 | 7 | 0 |
| Onondaga County Parks | | 0 | 0 | 0 | 0 | 0 | 32 | 2 | 30 | 0 | 0 |
| Suffolk County Parks | | 1 | 0 | 0 | 0 | 1 | 54 | 1 | 53 | 0 | 0 |
| **NORTH CAROLINA—State Agencies** | | | | | | | | | | | |
| Department of Human Resources | | 9 | 0 | 0 | 0 | 9 | 8 | 0 | 8 | 0 | 0 |
| North Carolina Highway Patrol | | 0 | 0 | 0 | 0 | 0 | 0 | 0 | 0 | 0 | 0 |
| State Capitol Police | | 8 | 0 | 1 | 0 | 7 | 67 | 1 | 64 | 2 | 0 |
| State Park Rangers: | Dismal Swamp | 0 | 0 | 0 | 0 | 0 | 0 | 0 | 0 | 0 | 0 |
| | Elk Knob | 0 | 0 | 0 | 0 | 0 | 0 | 0 | 0 | 0 | 0 |
| | Gorges | 0 | 0 | 0 | 0 | 0 | 0 | 0 | 0 | 0 | 0 |
| | Merchants Millpond | 0 | 0 | 0 | 0 | 0 | 0 | 0 | 0 | 0 | 0 |
| | New River-Mount Jefferson | 0 | 0 | 0 | 0 | 0 | 0 | 0 | 0 | 0 | 0 |
| **NORTH CAROLINA—Tribal Agencies** | | | | | | | | | | | |
| Cherokee Tribal | | 34 | 1 | 8 | 3 | 22 | 197 | 86 | 93 | 18 | 3 |
| **NORTH CAROLINA—Other Agencies** | | | | | | | | | | | |
| Raleigh-Durham International Airport | | 5 | 0 | 0 | 3 | 2 | 113 | 2 | 103 | 8 | 0 |
| WakeMed Campus Police | | 0 | 0 | 0 | 0 | 0 | 61 | 1 | 59 | 1 | |
| **NORTH DAKOTA—Tribal Agencies** | | | | | | | | | | | |
| Fort Totten Tribal | | 66 | 1 | 2 | 0 | 63 | 106 | 14 | 88 | 4 | 2 |
| Turtle Mountain Tribal | | 88 | 0 | 9 | 2 | 77 | 403 | 100 | 301 | 2 | 3 |
| **OHIO—State Agencies** | | | | | | | | | | | |
| Ohio Department of Natural Resources[5] | | 33 | 0 | 6 | 4 | 23 | 397 | 54 | 331 | 12 | 5 |
| Ohio State Highway Patrol | | 371 | 5 | 14 | 6 | 346 | 368 | 13 | 285 | 70 | 2 |
| **OHIO—Other Agencies** | | | | | | | | | | | |
| Cleveland Metropolitan Park District | | 10 | 0 | 4 | 1 | 5 | 141 | 0 | 139 | 2 | 0 |
| Hamilton County Park District | | 1 | 0 | 0 | 1 | 0 | 42 | 2 | 40 | 0 | 0 |
| Lake Metroparks | | 1 | 0 | 0 | 1 | 0 | 22 | 1 | 21 | 0 | 0 |
| Lorain County Metropolitan Park District | | 0 | 0 | 0 | 0 | 0 | 0 | 0 | 0 | 0 | 0 |
| Port Columbus International Airport | | 0 | 0 | 0 | 0 | 0 | 161 | 6 | 136 | 19 | 1 |
| **OKLAHOMA—State Agencies** | | | | | | | | | | | |
| Capitol Park Police | | 0 | 0 | 0 | 0 | 0 | 11 | 0 | 7 | 4 | 0 |
| Grand River Dam Authority[5] | Lake Patrol | 0 | 0 | 0 | 0 | 0 | 7 | 3 | 3 | 1 | 0 |
| **OKLAHOMA—Tribal Agencies** | | | | | | | | | | | |
| Absentee Shawnee Tribal | | 8 | 0 | 0 | 1 | 7 | 54 | 27 | 26 | 1 | 0 |
| Cherokee Tribal | | 28 | 1 | 1 | 0 | 26 | 24 | 16 | 8 | 0 | 3 |
| Choctaw Tribal | | 4 | 0 | 0 | 0 | 4 | 178 | 26 | 146 | 6 | 0 |
| Citizen Potawatomi Tribal | | 15 | 0 | 0 | 1 | 14 | 155 | 22 | 111 | 22 | 1 |
| Kickapoo Tribal | | 4 | 0 | 1 | 0 | 3 | 24 | 9 | 12 | 3 | 1 |
| Miami Tribal | | 4 | 0 | 1 | 2 | 1 | 79 | 8 | 64 | 7 | 3 |
| Pawnee Tribal | | 13 | 2 | 2 | 0 | 9 | 90 | 13 | 68 | 9 | 3 |
| Sac and Fox Tribal | | 1 | 0 | 0 | 0 | 1 | 21 | 6 | 10 | 5 | 1 |
| Seminole Nation Lighthorse | | 0 | 0 | 0 | 0 | 0 | 14 | 2 | 9 | 3 | 0 |
| Wyandotte Tribal | | 1 | 0 | 0 | 0 | 1 | 18 | 8 | 10 | 0 | 1 |
| **OKLAHOMA—Other Agencies** | | | | | | | | | | | |
| Guymon Public Schools[5] | | 1 | 0 | 0 | 0 | 1 | 3 | 0 | 3 | 0 | 0 |
| Jenks Public Schools | | 1 | 0 | 1 | 0 | 0 | 40 | 0 | 40 | 0 | 0 |
| Madill Public Schools[5] | | 1 | 0 | 0 | 0 | 1 | 10 | 4 | 6 | 0 | 0 |

[1] The FBI does not publish arson data unless it receives data from either the agency or the state for all 12 months of the calendar year.

[5] Because of changes in the state/local agency's reporting practices, figures are not comparable to previous years' data.

## Table 11. Offenses Known to Law Enforcement, by State, Tribal, and Other Agencies, 2009—*Continued*

(Number.)

| State/Other Agency | Unit/Office | Violent crime | Murder and non-negligent man-slaughter | Forcible rape | Robbery | Aggra-vated assault | Property crime | Burglary | Larceny-theft | Motor vehicle theft | Arson[1] |
|---|---|---|---|---|---|---|---|---|---|---|---|
| McAlester Public Schools[5] | | 1 | 0 | 0 | 0 | 1 | 9 | 0 | 9 | 0 | 2 |
| Norman Public Schools[5] | | 0 | 0 | 0 | 0 | 0 | 31 | 5 | 26 | 0 | 0 |
| Putnam City Campus[5] | | 5 | 0 | 0 | 0 | 5 | 57 | 1 | 56 | 0 | 3 |
| **OREGON—State Agencies** | | | | | | | | | | | |
| State Police | | 765 | 2 | 59 | 8 | 696 | 533 | 50 | 391 | 92 | 177 |
| **OREGON—Tribal Agencies** | | | | | | | | | | | |
| Burns Paiute Tribal | | 0 | 0 | 0 | 0 | 0 | 0 | 0 | 0 | 0 | 0 |
| **OREGON—Other Agencies** | | | | | | | | | | | |
| Blue Mountain Enforcement Narcotics Team: | Morrow County | 0 | 0 | 0 | 0 | 0 | 1 | 0 | 1 | 0 | 0 |
| | Umatilla County | 0 | 0 | 0 | 0 | 0 | 0 | 0 | 0 | 0 | 0 |
| Port of Portland | | 0 | 0 | 0 | 0 | 0 | 361 | 2 | 339 | 20 | 0 |
| **PENNSYLVANIA—State Agencies** | | | | | | | | | | | |
| Bureau of Narcotics: | Allegheny County | 0 | 0 | 0 | 0 | 0 | 0 | 0 | 0 | 0 | 0 |
| | Bedford County | 0 | 0 | 0 | 0 | 0 | 0 | 0 | 0 | 0 | 0 |
| | Blair County | 0 | 0 | 0 | 0 | 0 | 0 | 0 | 0 | 0 | 0 |
| | Bradford County | 0 | 0 | 0 | 0 | 0 | 0 | 0 | 0 | 0 | 0 |
| | Cambria County | 0 | 0 | 0 | 0 | 0 | 0 | 0 | 0 | 0 | 0 |
| | Cameron County | 0 | 0 | 0 | 0 | 0 | 0 | 0 | 0 | 0 | 0 |
| | Centre County | 0 | 0 | 0 | 0 | 0 | 0 | 0 | 0 | 0 | 0 |
| | Chester County | 0 | 0 | 0 | 0 | 0 | 0 | 0 | 0 | 0 | 0 |
| | Clearfield County | 0 | 0 | 0 | 0 | 0 | 0 | 0 | 0 | 0 | 0 |
| | Clinton County | 0 | 0 | 0 | 0 | 0 | 0 | 0 | 0 | 0 | 0 |
| | Columbia County | 0 | 0 | 0 | 0 | 0 | 0 | 0 | 0 | 0 | 0 |
| | Crawford County | 0 | 0 | 0 | 0 | 0 | 0 | 0 | 0 | 0 | 0 |
| | Delaware County | 0 | 0 | 0 | 0 | 0 | 0 | 0 | 0 | 0 | 0 |
| | Elk County | 0 | 0 | 0 | 0 | 0 | 0 | 0 | 0 | 0 | 0 |
| | Erie County | 0 | 0 | 0 | 0 | 0 | 0 | 0 | 0 | 0 | 0 |
| | Fayette County | 0 | 0 | 0 | 0 | 0 | 0 | 0 | 0 | 0 | 0 |
| | Forest County | 0 | 0 | 0 | 0 | 0 | 0 | 0 | 0 | 0 | 0 |
| | Huntingdon County | 0 | 0 | 0 | 0 | 0 | 0 | 0 | 0 | 0 | 0 |
| | Juniata County | 0 | 0 | 0 | 0 | 0 | 0 | 0 | 0 | 0 | 0 |
| | Lackawanna County | 0 | 0 | 0 | 0 | 0 | 0 | 0 | 0 | 0 | 0 |
| | Luzerne County | 0 | 0 | 0 | 0 | 0 | 0 | 0 | 0 | 0 | 0 |
| | Lycoming County | 0 | 0 | 0 | 0 | 0 | 0 | 0 | 0 | 0 | 0 |
| | McKean County | 0 | 0 | 0 | 0 | 0 | 0 | 0 | 0 | 0 | 0 |
| | Mifflin County | 0 | 0 | 0 | 0 | 0 | 0 | 0 | 0 | 0 | 0 |
| | Montour County | 0 | 0 | 0 | 0 | 0 | 0 | 0 | 0 | 0 | 0 |
| | Northumberland County | 0 | 0 | 0 | 0 | 0 | 0 | 0 | 0 | 0 | 0 |
| | Philadelphia County | 0 | 0 | 0 | 0 | 0 | 0 | 0 | 0 | 0 | 0 |
| | Pike County | 0 | 0 | 0 | 0 | 0 | 0 | 0 | 0 | 0 | 0 |
| | Potter County | 0 | 0 | 0 | 0 | 0 | 0 | 0 | 0 | 0 | 0 |
| | Snyder County | 0 | 0 | 0 | 0 | 0 | 0 | 0 | 0 | 0 | 0 |
| | Somerset County | 0 | 0 | 0 | 0 | 0 | 0 | 0 | 0 | 0 | 0 |
| | Sullivan County | 0 | 0 | 0 | 0 | 0 | 0 | 0 | 0 | 0 | 0 |
| | Susquehanna County | 0 | 0 | 0 | 0 | 0 | 0 | 0 | 0 | 0 | 0 |
| | Tioga County | 0 | 0 | 0 | 0 | 0 | 0 | 0 | 0 | 0 | 0 |
| | Union County | 0 | 0 | 0 | 0 | 0 | 0 | 0 | 0 | 0 | 0 |
| | Venango County | 0 | 0 | 0 | 0 | 0 | 0 | 0 | 0 | 0 | 0 |
| | Warren County | 0 | 0 | 0 | 0 | 0 | 0 | 0 | 0 | 0 | 0 |
| | Washington County | 0 | 0 | 0 | 0 | 0 | 0 | 0 | 0 | 0 | 0 |
| | Wayne County | 0 | 0 | 0 | 0 | 0 | 0 | 0 | 0 | 0 | 0 |
| | Westmoreland County | 0 | 0 | 0 | 0 | 0 | 0 | 0 | 0 | 0 | 0 |
| | Wyoming County | 0 | 0 | 0 | 0 | 0 | 0 | 0 | 0 | 0 | 0 |
| Department of Environmental Resources | | 0 | 0 | 0 | 0 | 0 | 15 | 2 | 13 | 0 | 0 |
| State Capitol Police | | 5 | 0 | 0 | 3 | 2 | 56 | 1 | 54 | 1 | 0 |
| State Park Police: | Pine Grove Furnace | 0 | 0 | 0 | 0 | 0 | 8 | 6 | 2 | 0 | 1 |
| | Pymatuning | 0 | 0 | 0 | 0 | 0 | 26 | 1 | 25 | 0 | 0 |
| State Police, Bureau of Criminal Investigation: | Adams County | 0 | 0 | 0 | 0 | 0 | 0 | 0 | 0 | 0 | 0 |
| | Allegheny County | 0 | 0 | 0 | 0 | 0 | 2 | 1 | 0 | 1 | 0 |
| | Armstrong County | 0 | 0 | 0 | 0 | 0 | 0 | 0 | 0 | 0 | 0 |
| | Beaver County | 0 | 0 | 0 | 0 | 0 | 2 | 0 | 2 | 0 | 0 |
| | Bedford County | 0 | 0 | 0 | 0 | 0 | 0 | 0 | 0 | 0 | 0 |
| | Berks County | 0 | 0 | 0 | 0 | 0 | 2 | 0 | 0 | 2 | 0 |
| | Blair County | 0 | 0 | 0 | 0 | 0 | 0 | 0 | 0 | 0 | 0 |
| | Bradford County | 0 | 0 | 0 | 0 | 0 | 0 | 0 | 0 | 0 | 0 |
| | Bucks County | 0 | 0 | 0 | 0 | 0 | 0 | 0 | 0 | 0 | 0 |
| | Butler County | 0 | 0 | 0 | 0 | 0 | 1 | 0 | 0 | 1 | 0 |
| | Cambria County | 0 | 0 | 0 | 0 | 0 | 2 | 0 | 2 | 0 | 0 |
| | Cameron County | 0 | 0 | 0 | 0 | 0 | 0 | 0 | 0 | 0 | 0 |
| | Carbon County | 0 | 0 | 0 | 0 | 0 | 0 | 0 | 0 | 0 | 0 |

[1] The FBI does not publish arson data unless it receives data from either the agency or the state for all 12 months of the calendar year.

[5] Because of changes in the state/local agency's reporting practices, figures are not comparable to previous years' data.

## Table 11. Offenses Known to Law Enforcement, by State, Tribal, and Other Agencies, 2009—*Continued*

(Number.)

| State/Other Agency | Unit/Office | Violent crime | Murder and non-negligent man-slaughter | Forcible rape | Robbery | Aggra-vated assault | Property crime | Burglary | Larceny-theft | Motor vehicle theft | Arson[1] |
|---|---|---|---|---|---|---|---|---|---|---|---|
| | Centre County | 0 | 0 | 0 | 0 | 0 | 0 | 0 | 0 | 0 | 0 |
| | Chester County | 0 | 0 | 0 | 0 | 0 | 0 | 0 | 0 | 0 | 0 |
| | Clarion County | 0 | 0 | 0 | 0 | 0 | 0 | 0 | 0 | 0 | 0 |
| | Clearfield County | 0 | 0 | 0 | 0 | 0 | 0 | 0 | 0 | 0 | 0 |
| | Clinton County | 0 | 0 | 0 | 0 | 0 | 1 | 0 | 0 | 1 | 0 |
| | Columbia County | 0 | 0 | 0 | 0 | 0 | 0 | 0 | 0 | 0 | 0 |
| | Crawford County | 0 | 0 | 0 | 0 | 0 | 0 | 0 | 0 | 0 | 0 |
| | Cumberland County | 0 | 0 | 0 | 0 | 0 | 1 | 0 | 1 | 0 | 0 |
| | Dauphin County | 0 | 0 | 0 | 0 | 0 | 3 | 0 | 2 | 1 | 0 |
| | Delaware County | 0 | 0 | 0 | 0 | 0 | 0 | 0 | 0 | 0 | 0 |
| | Elk County | 0 | 0 | 0 | 0 | 0 | 0 | 0 | 0 | 0 | 0 |
| | Erie County | 0 | 0 | 0 | 0 | 0 | 0 | 0 | 0 | 0 | 0 |
| | Fayette County | 0 | 0 | 0 | 0 | 0 | 1 | 0 | 1 | 0 | 0 |
| | Forest County | 0 | 0 | 0 | 0 | 0 | 0 | 0 | 0 | 0 | 0 |
| | Franklin County | 0 | 0 | 0 | 0 | 0 | 2 | 0 | 2 | 0 | 0 |
| | Fulton County | 0 | 0 | 0 | 0 | 0 | 0 | 0 | 0 | 0 | 0 |
| | Greene County | 0 | 0 | 0 | 0 | 0 | 0 | 0 | 0 | 0 | 0 |
| | Huntingdon County | 0 | 0 | 0 | 0 | 0 | 0 | 0 | 0 | 0 | 0 |
| | Indiana County | 0 | 0 | 0 | 0 | 0 | 0 | 0 | 0 | 0 | 0 |
| | Jefferson County | 0 | 0 | 0 | 0 | 0 | 0 | 0 | 0 | 0 | 0 |
| | Juniata County | 0 | 0 | 0 | 0 | 0 | 0 | 0 | 0 | 0 | 0 |
| | Lackawanna County | 0 | 0 | 0 | 0 | 0 | 0 | 0 | 0 | 0 | 0 |
| | Lancaster County | 0 | 0 | 0 | 0 | 0 | 0 | 0 | 0 | 0 | 0 |
| | Lawrence County | 0 | 0 | 0 | 0 | 0 | 1 | 0 | 1 | 0 | 0 |
| | Lebanon County | 0 | 0 | 0 | 0 | 0 | 4 | 1 | 3 | 0 | 0 |
| | Lehigh County | 0 | 0 | 0 | 0 | 0 | 0 | 0 | 0 | 0 | 0 |
| | Luzerne County | 0 | 0 | 0 | 0 | 0 | 2 | 0 | 1 | 1 | 0 |
| | Lycoming County | 0 | 0 | 0 | 0 | 0 | 0 | 0 | 0 | 0 | 0 |
| | McKean County | 0 | 0 | 0 | 0 | 0 | 1 | 0 | 1 | 0 | 0 |
| | Mercer County | 0 | 0 | 0 | 0 | 0 | 1 | 0 | 0 | 1 | 0 |
| | Mifflin County | 0 | 0 | 0 | 0 | 0 | 0 | 0 | 0 | 0 | 0 |
| | Monroe County | 0 | 0 | 0 | 0 | 0 | 0 | 0 | 0 | 0 | 0 |
| | Montgomery County | 0 | 0 | 0 | 0 | 0 | 2 | 0 | 0 | 2 | 0 |
| | Montour County | 0 | 0 | 0 | 0 | 0 | 0 | 0 | 0 | 0 | 0 |
| | Northampton County | 0 | 0 | 0 | 0 | 0 | 0 | 0 | 0 | 0 | 0 |
| | Northumberland County | 0 | 0 | 0 | 0 | 0 | 0 | 0 | 0 | 0 | 0 |
| | Perry County | 0 | 0 | 0 | 0 | 0 | 0 | 0 | 0 | 0 | 0 |
| | Philadelphia County | 0 | 0 | 0 | 0 | 0 | 0 | 0 | 0 | 0 | 0 |
| | Pike County | 0 | 0 | 0 | 0 | 0 | 1 | 0 | 0 | 1 | 0 |
| | Potter County | 0 | 0 | 0 | 0 | 0 | 0 | 0 | 0 | 0 | 0 |
| | Schuylkill County | 0 | 0 | 0 | 0 | 0 | 1 | 0 | 1 | 0 | 0 |
| | Snyder County | 0 | 0 | 0 | 0 | 0 | 0 | 0 | 0 | 0 | 0 |
| | Somerset County | 0 | 0 | 0 | 0 | 0 | 0 | 0 | 0 | 0 | 0 |
| | Sullivan County | 0 | 0 | 0 | 0 | 0 | 0 | 0 | 0 | 0 | 0 |
| | Susquehanna County | 0 | 0 | 0 | 0 | 0 | 0 | 0 | 0 | 0 | 0 |
| | Tioga County | 0 | 0 | 0 | 0 | 0 | 0 | 0 | 0 | 0 | 0 |
| | Union County | 0 | 0 | 0 | 0 | 0 | 0 | 0 | 0 | 0 | 0 |
| | Venango County | 0 | 0 | 0 | 0 | 0 | 0 | 0 | 0 | 0 | 0 |
| | Warren County | 0 | 0 | 0 | 0 | 0 | 0 | 0 | 0 | 0 | 0 |
| | Washington County | 0 | 0 | 0 | 0 | 0 | 0 | 0 | 0 | 0 | 0 |
| | Wayne County | 0 | 0 | 0 | 0 | 0 | 0 | 0 | 0 | 0 | 0 |
| | Westmoreland County | 0 | 0 | 0 | 0 | 0 | 0 | 0 | 0 | 0 | 0 |
| | Wyoming County | 0 | 0 | 0 | 0 | 0 | 0 | 0 | 0 | 0 | 0 |
| | York County | 0 | 0 | 0 | 0 | 0 | 1 | 0 | 1 | 0 | 0 |
| State Police: | Adams County | 55 | 0 | 13 | 11 | 31 | 526 | 180 | 314 | 32 | 7 |
| | Allegheny County[2] | 19 | 0 | 2 | 2 | 15 | | 4 | | 6 | 0 |
| | Armstrong County | 42 | 1 | 11 | 7 | 23 | 451 | 139 | 275 | 37 | 8 |
| | Beaver County | 23 | 1 | 1 | 0 | 21 | 160 | 66 | 69 | 25 | 17 |
| | Bedford County | 43 | 1 | 12 | 2 | 28 | 446 | 169 | 259 | 18 | 6 |
| | Berks County | 221 | 2 | 8 | 14 | 197 | 865 | 234 | 565 | 66 | 6 |
| | Blair County | 49 | 2 | 12 | 4 | 31 | 285 | 68 | 182 | 35 | 7 |
| | Bradford County | 45 | 0 | 18 | 1 | 26 | 448 | 148 | 286 | 14 | 5 |
| | Bucks County | 42 | 0 | 6 | 16 | 20 | 551 | 93 | 446 | 12 | 3 |
| | Butler County | 151 | 0 | 11 | 11 | 129 | 777 | 235 | 493 | 49 | 7 |
| | Cambria County | 37 | 0 | 6 | 6 | 25 | 306 | 117 | 174 | 15 | 8 |
| | Cameron County | 4 | 0 | 1 | 0 | 3 | 46 | 17 | 29 | 0 | 0 |
| | Carbon County | 87 | 2 | 1 | 1 | 83 | 328 | 129 | 165 | 34 | 27 |
| | Centre County | 60 | 2 | 14 | 7 | 37 | 584 | 156 | 412 | 16 | 10 |
| | Chester County | 137 | 2 | 9 | 33 | 93 | 1,255 | 390 | 797 | 68 | 26 |
| | Clarion County | 39 | 1 | 15 | 3 | 20 | 461 | 129 | 300 | 32 | 9 |
| | Clearfield County | 45 | 0 | 12 | 4 | 29 | 544 | 179 | 331 | 34 | 16 |

[1] The FBI does not publish arson data unless it receives data from either the agency or the state for all 12 months of the calendar year.

[2] The FBI determined that the agency's data were overreported. Consequently, affected data are not included in this table.

## Table 11. Offenses Known to Law Enforcement, by State, Tribal, and Other Agencies, 2009—*Continued*

(Number.)

| State/Other Agency | Unit/Office | Violent crime | Murder and non-negligent man-slaughter | Forcible rape | Robbery | Aggra-vated assault | Property crime | Burglary | Larceny-theft | Motor vehicle theft | Arson[1] |
|---|---|---|---|---|---|---|---|---|---|---|---|
| | Crawford County | 37 | 0 | 19 | 4 | 14 | 657 | 242 | 378 | 37 | 0 |
| | Delaware County | 73 | 1 | 3 | 21 | 48 | 1,338 | 159 | 1,128 | 51 | 3 |
| | Elizabethville | 60 | 0 | 24 | 7 | 29 | 1,121 | 171 | 911 | 39 | 13 |
| | Elk County | 6 | 0 | 5 | 0 | 1 | 194 | 45 | 132 | 17 | 4 |
| | Erie County | 97 | 3 | 17 | 17 | 60 | 1,718 | 365 | 1,316 | 37 | 5 |
| | Fayette County | 208 | 4 | 31 | 57 | 116 | 1,984 | 664 | 1,162 | 158 | 77 |
| | Franklin County | 62 | 3 | 21 | 14 | 24 | 943 | 245 | 651 | 47 | 10 |
| | Fulton County | 25 | 1 | 2 | 0 | 22 | 171 | 59 | 109 | 3 | 5 |
| | Greene County | 48 | 2 | 8 | 17 | 21 | 446 | 182 | 236 | 28 | 6 |
| | Huntingdon County | 54 | 2 | 13 | 5 | 34 | 341 | 98 | 232 | 11 | 0 |
| | Indiana County | 66 | 2 | 18 | 11 | 35 | 1,183 | 397 | 738 | 48 | 10 |
| | Jefferson County | 60 | 2 | 6 | 2 | 50 | 269 | 86 | 165 | 18 | 5 |
| | Juniata County | 16 | 0 | 4 | 1 | 11 | 243 | 52 | 183 | 8 | 1 |
| | Lackawanna County | 23 | 1 | 5 | 5 | 12 | 178 | 70 | 94 | 14 | 24 |
| | Lancaster County | 73 | 0 | 21 | 23 | 29 | 909 | 313 | 541 | 55 | 15 |
| | Lawrence County | 42 | 1 | 7 | 6 | 28 | 456 | 192 | 234 | 30 | 44 |
| | Lebanon County | 56 | 3 | 7 | 1 | 45 | 351 | 126 | 210 | 15 | 2 |
| | Lehigh County | 50 | 2 | 11 | 7 | 30 | 869 | 206 | 626 | 37 | 13 |
| | Luzerne County | 215 | 8 | 10 | 10 | 187 | 966 | 216 | 699 | 51 | 26 |
| | Lycoming County | 66 | 0 | 26 | 7 | 33 | 644 | 207 | 417 | 20 | 4 |
| | McKean County | 8 | 0 | 4 | 0 | 4 | 114 | 36 | 73 | 5 | 3 |
| | Mercer County | 48 | 0 | 21 | 3 | 24 | 472 | 172 | 285 | 15 | 12 |
| | Mifflin County | 6 | 0 | 0 | 2 | 4 | 102 | 35 | 65 | 2 | 1 |
| | Monroe County[2] | | 7 | 20 | 16 | | 1,331 | 436 | 815 | 80 | 5 |
| | Montour County | 15 | 0 | 1 | 1 | 13 | 59 | 22 | 36 | 1 | 1 |
| | Northampton County | 24 | 0 | 4 | 2 | 18 | 411 | 78 | 315 | 18 | 4 |
| | Northumberland County | 118 | 0 | 9 | 2 | 107 | 264 | 86 | 161 | 17 | 4 |
| | Perry County | 61 | 4 | 17 | 1 | 39 | 764 | 190 | 546 | 28 | 14 |
| | Philadelphia County | 12 | 0 | 0 | 0 | 12 | 7 | 0 | 3 | 4 | 0 |
| | Pike County | 61 | 3 | 21 | 6 | 31 | 631 | 285 | 323 | 23 | 8 |
| | Potter County | 18 | 0 | 4 | 0 | 14 | 223 | 89 | 119 | 15 | 3 |
| | Schuylkill County | 158 | 1 | 25 | 6 | 126 | 737 | 199 | 493 | 45 | 30 |
| | Skippack | 309 | 0 | 263 | 13 | 33 | 417 | 92 | 311 | 14 | 7 |
| | Snyder County | 25 | 1 | 6 | 2 | 16 | 393 | 87 | 291 | 15 | 1 |
| | Somerset County | 38 | 4 | 10 | 3 | 21 | 561 | 143 | 393 | 25 | 12 |
| | Sullivan County | 4 | 0 | 1 | 1 | 2 | 115 | 46 | 67 | 2 | 0 |
| | Susquehanna County | 53 | 2 | 19 | 6 | 26 | 379 | 138 | 218 | 23 | 14 |
| | Tioga County | 23 | 0 | 5 | 1 | 17 | 278 | 88 | 175 | 15 | 5 |
| | Tionesta | 18 | 0 | 0 | 0 | 18 | 108 | 46 | 59 | 3 | 1 |
| | Union County | 19 | 0 | 11 | 2 | 6 | 209 | 67 | 132 | 10 | 5 |
| | Venango County | 33 | 0 | 15 | 6 | 12 | 355 | 120 | 221 | 14 | 7 |
| | Warren County | 31 | 1 | 8 | 0 | 22 | 307 | 117 | 182 | 8 | 1 |
| | Washington County | 107 | 5 | 19 | 28 | 55 | 1,283 | 237 | 970 | 76 | 39 |
| | Wayne County | 43 | 1 | 17 | 3 | 22 | 526 | 191 | 307 | 28 | 14 |
| | Westmoreland County | 142 | 5 | 34 | 32 | 71 | 1,450 | 400 | 945 | 105 | 29 |
| | Wyoming County | 23 | 0 | 7 | 2 | 14 | 204 | 64 | 126 | 14 | 2 |
| | York County | 59 | 2 | 11 | 15 | 31 | 603 | 184 | 375 | 44 | 16 |
| **PENNSYLVANIA—Other Agencies** | | | | | | | | | | | |
| Allegheny County Port Authority | | 113 | 0 | 1 | 39 | 73 | 126 | 3 | 115 | 8 | 0 |
| County Detective: | Berks County[2] | | 0 | 1 | 0 | | 3 | 0 | 3 | 0 | 0 |
| | Bucks County | 4 | 0 | 0 | 0 | 4 | 10 | 0 | 10 | 0 | 0 |
| | Butler County | 0 | 0 | 0 | 0 | 0 | 0 | 0 | 0 | 0 | 0 |
| | Clinton County | 0 | 0 | 0 | 0 | 0 | 0 | 0 | 0 | 0 | 0 |
| | Dauphin County | 33 | 0 | 2 | 0 | 31 | 53 | 0 | 53 | 0 | 1 |
| | Lebanon County | 2 | 1 | 0 | 0 | 1 | 2 | 0 | 2 | 0 | 0 |
| | Lehigh County | 8 | 1 | 0 | 1 | 6 | 25 | 0 | 0 | 25 | 1 |
| | Pike County | 0 | 0 | 0 | 0 | 0 | 2 | 0 | 2 | 0 | 0 |
| | Schuylkill County | 0 | 0 | 0 | 0 | 0 | 3 | 0 | 3 | 0 | 0 |
| | Westmoreland County | 1 | 0 | 0 | 0 | 1 | 94 | 0 | 94 | 0 | 0 |
| | York County | 0 | 0 | 0 | 0 | 0 | 3 | 0 | 2 | 1 | 0 |
| Delaware County District Attorney | Criminal Investigation Division | 27 | 0 | 3 | 0 | 24 | 1 | 0 | 0 | 1 | 0 |
| Delaware County Park | | 10 | 0 | 1 | 0 | 9 | 119 | 1 | 118 | 0 | 0 |
| Easton Area School District | | 2 | 0 | 0 | 0 | 2 | 105 | 0 | 105 | 0 | 0 |
| Fort Cherry School District | | 0 | 0 | 0 | 0 | 0 | 0 | 0 | 0 | 0 | 0 |
| Harrisburg International Airport | | 0 | 0 | 0 | 0 | 0 | 5 | 0 | 2 | 3 | 0 |
| Tyrone Area School District | | 1 | 0 | 0 | 0 | 1 | 0 | 0 | 0 | 0 | 0 |
| Westmoreland County Park | | 0 | 0 | 0 | 0 | 0 | 18 | 0 | 18 | 0 | 0 |
| Wilkes-Barre Area School District | | 0 | 0 | 0 | 0 | 0 | 2 | 0 | 2 | 0 | 0 |

[1] The FBI does not publish arson data unless it receives data from either the agency or the state for all 12 months of the calendar year.
[2] The FBI determined that the agency's data were overreported. Consequently, affected data are not included in this table.

## Table 11. Offenses Known to Law Enforcement, by State, Tribal, and Other Agencies, 2009—*Continued*

(Number.)

| State/Other Agency | Unit/Office | Violent crime | Murder and non-negligent man-slaughter | Forcible rape | Robbery | Aggra-vated assault | Property crime | Burglary | Larceny-theft | Motor vehicle theft | Arson[1] |
|---|---|---|---|---|---|---|---|---|---|---|---|
| **RHODE ISLAND—State Agencies** | | | | | | | | | | | |
| Department of Environmental Management | | 1 | 0 | 0 | 0 | 1 | 46 | 3 | 41 | 2 | 0 |
| Rhode Island State Airport | | 0 | 0 | 0 | 0 | 0 | 31 | 0 | 23 | 8 | 0 |
| Rhode Island State Police Headquarters | | 13 | 1 | 5 | 0 | 7 | 27 | 0 | 16 | 11 | 1 |
| State Police: | Chepachet | 3 | 0 | 2 | 0 | 1 | 21 | 1 | 13 | 7 | 0 |
| | Hope Valley | 3 | 0 | 1 | 0 | 2 | 69 | 29 | 33 | 7 | 1 |
| | Lincoln | 16 | 0 | 5 | 0 | 11 | 66 | 0 | 50 | 16 | 0 |
| | Portsmouth | 0 | 0 | 0 | 0 | 0 | 5 | 0 | 3 | 2 | 0 |
| | Wickford | 5 | 0 | 2 | 3 | 0 | 57 | 11 | 43 | 3 | 0 |
| **RHODE ISLAND—Tribal Agencies** | | | | | | | | | | | |
| Narragansett Tribal | | 0 | 0 | 0 | 0 | 0 | 11 | 0 | 9 | 2 | 0 |
| **SOUTH CAROLINA—State Agencies** | | | | | | | | | | | |
| Bureau of Protective Services | | 2 | 0 | 0 | 0 | 2 | 22 | 1 | 20 | 1 | 0 |
| Department of Mental Health | | 0 | 0 | 0 | 0 | 0 | 22 | 0 | 22 | 0 | 0 |
| Department of Natural Resources: | Abbeville County | 0 | 0 | 0 | 0 | 0 | 0 | 0 | 0 | 0 | 0 |
| | Aiken County | 0 | 0 | 0 | 0 | 0 | 0 | 0 | 0 | 0 | 0 |
| | Allendale County | 0 | 0 | 0 | 0 | 0 | 0 | 0 | 0 | 0 | 0 |
| | Anderson County | 0 | 0 | 0 | 0 | 0 | 0 | 0 | 0 | 0 | 0 |
| | Bamberg County | 0 | 0 | 0 | 0 | 0 | 0 | 0 | 0 | 0 | 0 |
| | Barnwell County | 0 | 0 | 0 | 0 | 0 | 0 | 0 | 0 | 0 | 0 |
| | Beaufort County | 0 | 0 | 0 | 0 | 0 | 0 | 0 | 0 | 0 | 0 |
| | Berkeley County | 0 | 0 | 0 | 0 | 0 | 0 | 0 | 0 | 0 | 0 |
| | Calhoun County | 0 | 0 | 0 | 0 | 0 | 0 | 0 | 0 | 0 | 0 |
| | Charleston County | 0 | 0 | 0 | 0 | 0 | 0 | 0 | 0 | 0 | 0 |
| | Cherokee County | 0 | 0 | 0 | 0 | 0 | 0 | 0 | 0 | 0 | 0 |
| | Chester County | 0 | 0 | 0 | 0 | 0 | 0 | 0 | 0 | 0 | 0 |
| | Chesterfield County | 0 | 0 | 0 | 0 | 0 | 0 | 0 | 0 | 0 | 0 |
| | Clarendon County | 0 | 0 | 0 | 0 | 0 | 0 | 0 | 0 | 0 | 0 |
| | Colleton County | 0 | 0 | 0 | 0 | 0 | 0 | 0 | 0 | 0 | 0 |
| | Darlington County | 0 | 0 | 0 | 0 | 0 | 0 | 0 | 0 | 0 | 0 |
| | Dillon County | 0 | 0 | 0 | 0 | 0 | 0 | 0 | 0 | 0 | 0 |
| | Dorchester County | 0 | 0 | 0 | 0 | 0 | 0 | 0 | 0 | 0 | 0 |
| | Edgefield County | 0 | 0 | 0 | 0 | 0 | 0 | 0 | 0 | 0 | 0 |
| | Fairfield County | 0 | 0 | 0 | 0 | 0 | 0 | 0 | 0 | 0 | 0 |
| | Florence County | 0 | 0 | 0 | 0 | 0 | 0 | 0 | 0 | 0 | 0 |
| | Georgetown County | 0 | 0 | 0 | 0 | 0 | 0 | 0 | 0 | 0 | 0 |
| | Greenville County | 0 | 0 | 0 | 0 | 0 | 0 | 0 | 0 | 0 | 0 |
| | Greenwood County | 0 | 0 | 0 | 0 | 0 | 0 | 0 | 0 | 0 | 0 |
| | Hampton County | 0 | 0 | 0 | 0 | 0 | 0 | 0 | 0 | 0 | 0 |
| | Horry County | 0 | 0 | 0 | 0 | 0 | 0 | 0 | 0 | 0 | 0 |
| | Jasper County | 0 | 0 | 0 | 0 | 0 | 0 | 0 | 0 | 0 | 0 |
| | Kershaw County | 0 | 0 | 0 | 0 | 0 | 0 | 0 | 0 | 0 | 0 |
| | Lancaster County | 0 | 0 | 0 | 0 | 0 | 0 | 0 | 0 | 0 | 0 |
| | Laurens County | 0 | 0 | 0 | 0 | 0 | 0 | 0 | 0 | 0 | 0 |
| | Lee County | 0 | 0 | 0 | 0 | 0 | 0 | 0 | 0 | 0 | 0 |
| | Lexington County | 0 | 0 | 0 | 0 | 0 | 0 | 0 | 0 | 0 | 0 |
| | Marion County | 0 | 0 | 0 | 0 | 0 | 0 | 0 | 0 | 0 | 0 |
| | Marlboro County | 0 | 0 | 0 | 0 | 0 | 0 | 0 | 0 | 0 | 0 |
| | McCormick County | 0 | 0 | 0 | 0 | 0 | 0 | 0 | 0 | 0 | 0 |
| | Newberry County | 0 | 0 | 0 | 0 | 0 | 0 | 0 | 0 | 0 | 0 |
| | Oconee County | 0 | 0 | 0 | 0 | 0 | 0 | 0 | 0 | 0 | 0 |
| | Orangeburg County | 0 | 0 | 0 | 0 | 0 | 0 | 0 | 0 | 0 | 0 |
| | Pickens County | 0 | 0 | 0 | 0 | 0 | 0 | 0 | 0 | 0 | 0 |
| | Richland County | 0 | 0 | 0 | 0 | 0 | 0 | 0 | 0 | 0 | 0 |
| | Saluda County | 0 | 0 | 0 | 0 | 0 | 0 | 0 | 0 | 0 | 0 |
| | Spartanburg County | 0 | 0 | 0 | 0 | 0 | 0 | 0 | 0 | 0 | 0 |
| | Sumter County | 0 | 0 | 0 | 0 | 0 | 0 | 0 | 0 | 0 | 0 |
| | Union County | 0 | 0 | 0 | 0 | 0 | 0 | 0 | 0 | 0 | 0 |
| | Williamsburg County | 0 | 0 | 0 | 0 | 0 | 0 | 0 | 0 | 0 | 0 |
| | York County | 0 | 0 | 0 | 0 | 0 | 0 | 0 | 0 | 0 | 0 |
| Forestry Commission: | Abbeville County | 0 | 0 | 0 | 0 | 0 | 0 | 0 | 0 | 0 | 0 |
| | Aiken County | 0 | 0 | 0 | 0 | 0 | 1 | 0 | 1 | 0 | 1 |
| | Allendale County | 0 | 0 | 0 | 0 | 0 | 0 | 0 | 0 | 0 | 4 |
| | Anderson County | 0 | 0 | 0 | 0 | 0 | 1 | 0 | 1 | 0 | 2 |
| | Bamberg County | 0 | 0 | 0 | 0 | 0 | 2 | 0 | 2 | 0 | 0 |
| | Barnwell County | 0 | 0 | 0 | 0 | 0 | 0 | 0 | 0 | 0 | 3 |
| | Beaufort County | 0 | 0 | 0 | 0 | 0 | 0 | 0 | 0 | 0 | 8 |
| | Berkeley County | 0 | 0 | 0 | 0 | 0 | 0 | 0 | 0 | 0 | 23 |
| | Calhoun County | 0 | 0 | 0 | 0 | 0 | 0 | 0 | 0 | 0 | 0 |
| | Charleston County | 0 | 0 | 0 | 0 | 0 | 0 | 0 | 0 | 0 | 1 |
| | Cherokee County | 0 | 0 | 0 | 0 | 0 | 1 | 0 | 1 | 0 | 0 |
| | Chester County | 0 | 0 | 0 | 0 | 0 | 2 | 0 | 2 | 0 | 0 |

[1] The FBI does not publish arson data unless it receives data from either the agency or the state for all 12 months of the calendar year.

# Table 11. Offenses Known to Law Enforcement, by State, Tribal, and Other Agencies, 2009—*Continued*

(Number.)

| State/Other Agency | Unit/Office | Violent crime | Murder and non-negligent man-slaughter | Forcible rape | Robbery | Aggra-vated assault | Property crime | Burglary | Larceny-theft | Motor vehicle theft | Arson[1] |
|---|---|---|---|---|---|---|---|---|---|---|---|
| | Chesterfield County | 0 | 0 | 0 | 0 | 0 | 6 | 0 | 6 | 0 | 7 |
| | Clarendon County | 0 | 0 | 0 | 0 | 0 | 1 | 0 | 1 | 0 | 5 |
| | Colleton County | 0 | 0 | 0 | 0 | 0 | 1 | 0 | 1 | 0 | 5 |
| | Darlington County | 0 | 0 | 0 | 0 | 0 | 2 | 0 | 2 | 0 | 2 |
| | Dillon County | 0 | 0 | 0 | 0 | 0 | 0 | 0 | 0 | 0 | 0 |
| | Dorchester County | 0 | 0 | 0 | 0 | 0 | 0 | 0 | 0 | 0 | 6 |
| | Edgefield County | 0 | 0 | 0 | 0 | 0 | 3 | 0 | 3 | 0 | 0 |
| | Fairfield County | 0 | 0 | 0 | 0 | 0 | 0 | 0 | 0 | 0 | 0 |
| | Florence County | 0 | 0 | 0 | 0 | 0 | 0 | 0 | 0 | 0 | 1 |
| | Georgetown County | 0 | 0 | 0 | 0 | 0 | 0 | 0 | 0 | 0 | 0 |
| | Greenville County | 0 | 0 | 0 | 0 | 0 | 0 | 0 | 0 | 0 | 1 |
| | Greenwood County | 0 | 0 | 0 | 0 | 0 | 0 | 0 | 0 | 0 | 1 |
| | Hampton County | 0 | 0 | 0 | 0 | 0 | 1 | 0 | 1 | 0 | 5 |
| | Horry County | 0 | 0 | 0 | 0 | 0 | 0 | 0 | 0 | 0 | 20 |
| | Jasper County | 0 | 0 | 0 | 0 | 0 | 0 | 0 | 0 | 0 | 9 |
| | Kershaw County | 0 | 0 | 0 | 0 | 0 | 4 | 0 | 4 | 0 | 2 |
| | Lancaster County | 0 | 0 | 0 | 0 | 0 | 4 | 0 | 4 | 0 | 3 |
| | Laurens County | 0 | 0 | 0 | 0 | 0 | 1 | 0 | 1 | 0 | 0 |
| | Lee County | 0 | 0 | 0 | 0 | 0 | 0 | 0 | 0 | 0 | 0 |
| | Lexington County | 0 | 0 | 0 | 0 | 0 | 3 | 0 | 3 | 0 | 1 |
| | Marion County | 0 | 0 | 0 | 0 | 0 | 2 | 0 | 2 | 0 | 1 |
| | Marlboro County | 0 | 0 | 0 | 0 | 0 | 1 | 0 | 1 | 0 | 0 |
| | McCormick County | 0 | 0 | 0 | 0 | 0 | 0 | 0 | 0 | 0 | 0 |
| | Newberry County | 0 | 0 | 0 | 0 | 0 | 1 | 0 | 1 | 0 | 0 |
| | Oconee County | 0 | 0 | 0 | 0 | 0 | 0 | 0 | 0 | 0 | 1 |
| | Orangeburg County | 0 | 0 | 0 | 0 | 0 | 1 | 0 | 1 | 0 | 8 |
| | Pickens County | 0 | 0 | 0 | 0 | 0 | 0 | 0 | 0 | 0 | 1 |
| | Richland County | 0 | 0 | 0 | 0 | 0 | 2 | 0 | 2 | 0 | 1 |
| | Saluda County | 0 | 0 | 0 | 0 | 0 | 0 | 0 | 0 | 0 | 1 |
| | Spartanburg County | 0 | 0 | 0 | 0 | 0 | 0 | 0 | 0 | 0 | 1 |
| | Sumter County | 0 | 0 | 0 | 0 | 0 | 1 | 0 | 1 | 0 | 3 |
| | Union County | 0 | 0 | 0 | 0 | 0 | 0 | 0 | 0 | 0 | 0 |
| | Williamsburg County | 0 | 0 | 0 | 0 | 0 | 2 | 0 | 2 | 0 | 0 |
| | York County | 0 | 0 | 0 | 0 | 0 | 0 | 0 | 0 | 0 | 0 |
| Highway Patrol: | Abbeville County | 0 | 0 | 0 | 0 | 0 | 0 | 0 | 0 | 0 | 0 |
| | Aiken County | 0 | 0 | 0 | 0 | 0 | 2 | 0 | 0 | 2 | 0 |
| | Allendale County | 0 | 0 | 0 | 0 | 0 | 0 | 0 | 0 | 0 | 0 |
| | Anderson County | 0 | 0 | 0 | 0 | 0 | 2 | 0 | 1 | 1 | 0 |
| | Bamberg County | 0 | 0 | 0 | 0 | 0 | 0 | 0 | 0 | 0 | 0 |
| | Barnwell County | 0 | 0 | 0 | 0 | 0 | 0 | 0 | 0 | 0 | 0 |
| | Beaufort County | 0 | 0 | 0 | 0 | 0 | 0 | 0 | 0 | 0 | 0 |
| | Berkeley County | 0 | 0 | 0 | 0 | 0 | 1 | 0 | 0 | 1 | 0 |
| | Calhoun County | 0 | 0 | 0 | 0 | 0 | 1 | 0 | 1 | 0 | 0 |
| | Charleston County | 0 | 0 | 0 | 0 | 0 | 0 | 0 | 0 | 0 | 0 |
| | Cherokee County | 0 | 0 | 0 | 0 | 0 | 1 | 0 | 0 | 1 | 0 |
| | Chester County | 0 | 0 | 0 | 0 | 0 | 0 | 0 | 0 | 0 | 0 |
| | Chesterfield County | 0 | 0 | 0 | 0 | 0 | 0 | 0 | 0 | 0 | 0 |
| | Clarendon County | 0 | 0 | 0 | 0 | 0 | 0 | 0 | 0 | 0 | 0 |
| | Colleton County | 0 | 0 | 0 | 0 | 0 | 0 | 0 | 0 | 0 | 0 |
| | Darlington County | 0 | 0 | 0 | 0 | 0 | 0 | 0 | 0 | 0 | 0 |
| | Dillon County | 0 | 0 | 0 | 0 | 0 | 0 | 0 | 0 | 0 | 0 |
| | Dorchester County | 1 | 1 | 0 | 0 | 0 | 0 | 0 | 0 | 0 | 0 |
| | Edgefield County | 0 | 0 | 0 | 0 | 0 | 0 | 0 | 0 | 0 | 0 |
| | Fairfield County | 0 | 0 | 0 | 0 | 0 | 0 | 0 | 0 | 0 | 0 |
| | Florence County | 0 | 0 | 0 | 0 | 0 | 0 | 0 | 0 | 0 | 0 |
| | Georgetown County | 0 | 0 | 0 | 0 | 0 | 0 | 0 | 0 | 0 | 0 |
| | Greenville County | 1 | 1 | 0 | 0 | 0 | 2 | 0 | 0 | 2 | 0 |
| | Greenwood County | 0 | 0 | 0 | 0 | 0 | 0 | 0 | 0 | 0 | 0 |
| | Hampton County | 0 | 0 | 0 | 0 | 0 | 0 | 0 | 0 | 0 | 0 |
| | Horry County | 0 | 0 | 0 | 0 | 0 | 1 | 0 | 1 | 0 | 0 |
| | Jasper County | 0 | 0 | 0 | 0 | 0 | 0 | 0 | 0 | 0 | 0 |
| | Kershaw County | 0 | 0 | 0 | 0 | 0 | 0 | 0 | 0 | 0 | 0 |
| | Lancaster County | 0 | 0 | 0 | 0 | 0 | 0 | 0 | 0 | 0 | 0 |
| | Laurens County | 0 | 0 | 0 | 0 | 0 | 1 | 0 | 0 | 1 | 0 |
| | Lee County | 0 | 0 | 0 | 0 | 0 | 1 | 0 | 1 | 0 | 0 |
| | Lexington County | 1 | 0 | 0 | 0 | 1 | 0 | 0 | 0 | 0 | 0 |
| | Marion County | 0 | 0 | 0 | 0 | 0 | 0 | 0 | 0 | 0 | 0 |
| | Marlboro County | 0 | 0 | 0 | 0 | 0 | 0 | 0 | 0 | 0 | 0 |
| | McCormick County | 0 | 0 | 0 | 0 | 0 | 0 | 0 | 0 | 0 | 0 |
| | Newberry County | 0 | 0 | 0 | 0 | 0 | 0 | 0 | 0 | 0 | 0 |
| | Oconee County | 0 | 0 | 0 | 0 | 0 | 1 | 0 | 0 | 1 | 0 |
| | Orangeburg County | 0 | 0 | 0 | 0 | 0 | 1 | 0 | 0 | 1 | 0 |

[1] The FBI does not publish arson data unless it receives data from either the agency or the state for all 12 months of the calendar year.

## Table 11. Offenses Known to Law Enforcement, by State, Tribal, and Other Agencies, 2009—*Continued*

(Number.)

| State/Other Agency | Unit/Office | Violent crime | Murder and non-negligent man-slaughter | Forcible rape | Robbery | Aggra-vated assault | Property crime | Burglary | Larceny-theft | Motor vehicle theft | Arson[1] |
|---|---|---|---|---|---|---|---|---|---|---|---|
| | Pickens County | 0 | 0 | 0 | 0 | 0 | 0 | 0 | 0 | 0 | 0 |
| | Richland County | 0 | 0 | 0 | 0 | 0 | 1 | 0 | 0 | 1 | 0 |
| | Saluda County | 0 | 0 | 0 | 0 | 0 | 0 | 0 | 0 | 0 | 0 |
| | Spartanburg County | 0 | 0 | 0 | 0 | 0 | 0 | 0 | 0 | 0 | 0 |
| | Sumter County | 0 | 0 | 0 | 0 | 0 | 0 | 0 | 0 | 0 | 0 |
| | Union County | 0 | 0 | 0 | 0 | 0 | 0 | 0 | 0 | 0 | 0 |
| | Williamsburg County | 0 | 0 | 0 | 0 | 0 | 0 | 0 | 0 | 0 | 0 |
| | York County | 2 | 0 | 0 | 0 | 2 | 4 | 0 | 3 | 1 | 0 |
| South Carolina Law Enforcement Division Vice: | Abbeville County | 0 | 0 | 0 | 0 | 0 | 0 | 0 | 0 | 0 | 0 |
| | Aiken County | 0 | 0 | 0 | 0 | 0 | 0 | 0 | 0 | 0 | 0 |
| | Allendale County | 0 | 0 | 0 | 0 | 0 | 0 | 0 | 0 | 0 | 0 |
| | Anderson County | 0 | 0 | 0 | 0 | 0 | 0 | 0 | 0 | 0 | 0 |
| | Bamberg County | 0 | 0 | 0 | 0 | 0 | 0 | 0 | 0 | 0 | 0 |
| | Barnwell County | 0 | 0 | 0 | 0 | 0 | 0 | 0 | 0 | 0 | 0 |
| | Beaufort County | 0 | 0 | 0 | 0 | 0 | 0 | 0 | 0 | 0 | 0 |
| | Berkeley County | 0 | 0 | 0 | 0 | 0 | 0 | 0 | 0 | 0 | 0 |
| | Calhoun County | 0 | 0 | 0 | 0 | 0 | 0 | 0 | 0 | 0 | 0 |
| | Charleston County | 0 | 0 | 0 | 0 | 0 | 0 | 0 | 0 | 0 | 0 |
| | Cherokee County | 0 | 0 | 0 | 0 | 0 | 0 | 0 | 0 | 0 | 0 |
| | Chester County | 0 | 0 | 0 | 0 | 0 | 0 | 0 | 0 | 0 | 0 |
| | Chesterfield County | 0 | 0 | 0 | 0 | 0 | 0 | 0 | 0 | 0 | 0 |
| | Clarendon County | 0 | 0 | 0 | 0 | 0 | 0 | 0 | 0 | 0 | 0 |
| | Colleton County | 0 | 0 | 0 | 0 | 0 | 0 | 0 | 0 | 0 | 0 |
| | Darlington County | 0 | 0 | 0 | 0 | 0 | 0 | 0 | 0 | 0 | 0 |
| | Dillon County | 0 | 0 | 0 | 0 | 0 | 0 | 0 | 0 | 0 | 0 |
| | Dorchester County | 0 | 0 | 0 | 0 | 0 | 0 | 0 | 0 | 0 | 0 |
| | Edgefield County | 0 | 0 | 0 | 0 | 0 | 0 | 0 | 0 | 0 | 0 |
| | Fairfield County | 0 | 0 | 0 | 0 | 0 | 0 | 0 | 0 | 0 | 0 |
| | Florence County | 0 | 0 | 0 | 0 | 0 | 0 | 0 | 0 | 0 | 0 |
| | Georgetown County | 0 | 0 | 0 | 0 | 0 | 0 | 0 | 0 | 0 | 0 |
| | Greenville County | 0 | 0 | 0 | 0 | 0 | 0 | 0 | 0 | 0 | 0 |
| | Greenwood County | 0 | 0 | 0 | 0 | 0 | 0 | 0 | 0 | 0 | 0 |
| | Hampton County | 0 | 0 | 0 | 0 | 0 | 0 | 0 | 0 | 0 | 0 |
| | Horry County | 0 | 0 | 0 | 0 | 0 | 0 | 0 | 0 | 0 | 0 |
| | Jasper County | 0 | 0 | 0 | 0 | 0 | 0 | 0 | 0 | 0 | 0 |
| | Kershaw County | 0 | 0 | 0 | 0 | 0 | 0 | 0 | 0 | 0 | 0 |
| | Lancaster County | 0 | 0 | 0 | 0 | 0 | 0 | 0 | 0 | 0 | 0 |
| | Laurens County | 0 | 0 | 0 | 0 | 0 | 0 | 0 | 0 | 0 | 0 |
| | Lee County | 0 | 0 | 0 | 0 | 0 | 0 | 0 | 0 | 0 | 0 |
| | Lexington County | 0 | 0 | 0 | 0 | 0 | 0 | 0 | 0 | 0 | 0 |
| | Marion County | 0 | 0 | 0 | 0 | 0 | 0 | 0 | 0 | 0 | 0 |
| | Marlboro County | 0 | 0 | 0 | 0 | 0 | 0 | 0 | 0 | 0 | 0 |
| | McCormick County | 0 | 0 | 0 | 0 | 0 | 0 | 0 | 0 | 0 | 0 |
| | Newberry County | 0 | 0 | 0 | 0 | 0 | 0 | 0 | 0 | 0 | 0 |
| | Oconee County | 0 | 0 | 0 | 0 | 0 | 0 | 0 | 0 | 0 | 0 |
| | Orangeburg County | 0 | 0 | 0 | 0 | 0 | 0 | 0 | 0 | 0 | 0 |
| | Pickens County | 0 | 0 | 0 | 0 | 0 | 0 | 0 | 0 | 0 | 0 |
| | Richland County | 0 | 0 | 0 | 0 | 0 | 0 | 0 | 0 | 0 | 0 |
| | Saluda County | 0 | 0 | 0 | 0 | 0 | 0 | 0 | 0 | 0 | 0 |
| | Spartanburg County | 0 | 0 | 0 | 0 | 0 | 0 | 0 | 0 | 0 | 0 |
| | Sumter County | 0 | 0 | 0 | 0 | 0 | 0 | 0 | 0 | 0 | 0 |
| | Union County | 0 | 0 | 0 | 0 | 0 | 0 | 0 | 0 | 0 | 0 |
| | Williamsburg County | 0 | 0 | 0 | 0 | 0 | 0 | 0 | 0 | 0 | 0 |
| | York County | 0 | 0 | 0 | 0 | 0 | 0 | 0 | 0 | 0 | 0 |
| State Transport Police: | Aiken County | 0 | 0 | 0 | 0 | 0 | 0 | 0 | 0 | 0 | 0 |
| | Allendale County | 0 | 0 | 0 | 0 | 0 | 0 | 0 | 0 | 0 | 0 |
| | Anderson County | 0 | 0 | 0 | 0 | 0 | 0 | 0 | 0 | 0 | 0 |
| | Bamberg County | 0 | 0 | 0 | 0 | 0 | 0 | 0 | 0 | 0 | 0 |
| | Barnwell County | 0 | 0 | 0 | 0 | 0 | 0 | 0 | 0 | 0 | 0 |
| | Beaufort County | 0 | 0 | 0 | 0 | 0 | 0 | 0 | 0 | 0 | 0 |
| | Berkeley County | 0 | 0 | 0 | 0 | 0 | 0 | 0 | 0 | 0 | 0 |
| | Charleston County | 0 | 0 | 0 | 0 | 0 | 0 | 0 | 0 | 0 | 0 |
| | Cherokee County | 0 | 0 | 0 | 0 | 0 | 0 | 0 | 0 | 0 | 0 |
| | Chesterfield County | 0 | 0 | 0 | 0 | 0 | 0 | 0 | 0 | 0 | 0 |
| | Clarendon County | 0 | 0 | 0 | 0 | 0 | 0 | 0 | 0 | 0 | 0 |
| | Colleton County | 0 | 0 | 0 | 0 | 0 | 0 | 0 | 0 | 0 | 0 |
| | Darlington County | 0 | 0 | 0 | 0 | 0 | 0 | 0 | 0 | 0 | 0 |
| | Dillon County | 0 | 0 | 0 | 0 | 0 | 0 | 0 | 0 | 0 | 0 |
| | Dorchester County | 0 | 0 | 0 | 0 | 0 | 0 | 0 | 0 | 0 | 0 |
| | Edgefield County | 0 | 0 | 0 | 0 | 0 | 0 | 0 | 0 | 0 | 0 |
| | Fairfield County | 0 | 0 | 0 | 0 | 0 | 0 | 0 | 0 | 0 | 0 |

[1] The FBI does not publish arson data unless it receives data from either the agency or the state for all 12 months of the calendar year.

## Table 11. Offenses Known to Law Enforcement, by State, Tribal, and Other Agencies, 2009—*Continued*

(Number.)

| State/Other Agency | Unit/Office | Violent crime | Murder and non-negligent man-slaughter | Forcible rape | Robbery | Aggra-vated assault | Property crime | Burglary | Larceny-theft | Motor vehicle theft | Arson[1] |
|---|---|---|---|---|---|---|---|---|---|---|---|
| | Florence County | 0 | 0 | 0 | 0 | 0 | 0 | 0 | 0 | 0 | 0 |
| | Georgetown County | 0 | 0 | 0 | 0 | 0 | 0 | 0 | 0 | 0 | 0 |
| | Greenville County | 0 | 0 | 0 | 0 | 0 | 0 | 0 | 0 | 0 | 0 |
| | Greenwood County | 0 | 0 | 0 | 0 | 0 | 0 | 0 | 0 | 0 | 0 |
| | Hampton County | 0 | 0 | 0 | 0 | 0 | 0 | 0 | 0 | 0 | 0 |
| | Horry County | 0 | 0 | 0 | 0 | 0 | 0 | 0 | 0 | 0 | 0 |
| | Jasper County | 0 | 0 | 0 | 0 | 0 | 0 | 0 | 0 | 0 | 0 |
| | Kershaw County | 0 | 0 | 0 | 0 | 0 | 0 | 0 | 0 | 0 | 0 |
| | Laurens County | 0 | 0 | 0 | 0 | 0 | 0 | 0 | 0 | 0 | 0 |
| | Lee County | 0 | 0 | 0 | 0 | 0 | 0 | 0 | 0 | 0 | 0 |
| | Lexington County | 0 | 0 | 0 | 0 | 0 | 0 | 0 | 0 | 0 | 0 |
| | Marion County | 0 | 0 | 0 | 0 | 0 | 0 | 0 | 0 | 0 | 0 |
| | Marlboro County | 0 | 0 | 0 | 0 | 0 | 0 | 0 | 0 | 0 | 0 |
| | Newberry County | 0 | 0 | 0 | 0 | 0 | 0 | 0 | 0 | 0 | 0 |
| | Oconee County | 0 | 0 | 0 | 0 | 0 | 0 | 0 | 0 | 0 | 0 |
| | Orangeburg County | 0 | 0 | 0 | 0 | 0 | 0 | 0 | 0 | 0 | 0 |
| | Richland County | 0 | 0 | 0 | 0 | 0 | 0 | 0 | 0 | 0 | 0 |
| | Saluda County | 0 | 0 | 0 | 0 | 0 | 0 | 0 | 0 | 0 | 0 |
| | Spartanburg County | 0 | 0 | 0 | 0 | 0 | 0 | 0 | 0 | 0 | 0 |
| | Sumter County | 0 | 0 | 0 | 0 | 0 | 0 | 0 | 0 | 0 | 0 |
| | Union County | 0 | 0 | 0 | 0 | 0 | 0 | 0 | 0 | 0 | 0 |
| | Williamsburg County | 0 | 0 | 0 | 0 | 0 | 0 | 0 | 0 | 0 | 0 |
| | York County | 0 | 0 | 0 | 0 | 0 | 0 | 0 | 0 | 0 | 0 |
| **SOUTH CAROLINA—Other Agencies** | | | | | | | | | | | |
| Charleston County Aviation Authority | | 0 | 0 | 0 | 0 | 0 | 50 | 0 | 47 | 3 | 0 |
| **SOUTH DAKOTA—State Agencies** | | | | | | | | | | | |
| Division of Criminal Investigation | | 27 | 3 | 9 | 2 | 13 | 20 | 11 | 9 | 0 | 1 |
| **SOUTH DAKOTA—Tribal Agencies** | | | | | | | | | | | |
| Crow Creek Tribal | | 7 | 0 | 3 | 0 | 4 | 27 | 10 | 0 | 17 | 1 |
| Pine Ridge Sioux Tribal | | 135 | 7 | 18 | 2 | 108 | 101 | 55 | 12 | 34 | 9 |
| **TENNESSEE—State Agencies** | | | | | | | | | | | |
| Alcoholic Beverage Commission | | 0 | 0 | 0 | 0 | 0 | 0 | 0 | 0 | 0 | 0 |
| Department of Correction | Internal Affairs | 7 | 3 | 0 | 0 | 4 | 0 | 0 | 0 | 0 | 0 |
| Department of Safety | | 64 | 0 | 0 | 1 | 63 | 32 | 1 | 11 | 20 | 0 |
| State Fire Marshal | | 0 | 0 | 0 | 0 | 0 | 0 | 0 | 0 | 0 | 37 |
| State Park Rangers: | Bicentennial Capitol Mall | 0 | 0 | 0 | 0 | 0 | 0 | 0 | 0 | 0 | 0 |
| | Big Hill Pond | 0 | 0 | 0 | 0 | 0 | 0 | 0 | 0 | 0 | 0 |
| | Big Ridge | 0 | 0 | 0 | 0 | 0 | 1 | 0 | 1 | 0 | 0 |
| | Bledsoe Creek | 0 | 0 | 0 | 0 | 0 | 0 | 0 | 0 | 0 | 0 |
| | Booker T. Washington | 0 | 0 | 0 | 0 | 0 | 0 | 0 | 0 | 0 | 0 |
| | Burgess Falls Natural Area | 0 | 0 | 0 | 0 | 0 | 1 | 0 | 1 | 0 | 0 |
| | Cedars of Lebanon | 0 | 0 | 0 | 0 | 0 | 0 | 0 | 0 | 0 | 0 |
| | Chickasaw | 0 | 0 | 0 | 0 | 0 | 2 | 1 | 1 | 0 | 0 |
| | Cove Lake | 0 | 0 | 0 | 0 | 0 | 0 | 0 | 0 | 0 | 0 |
| | Cumberland Mountain | 0 | 0 | 0 | 0 | 0 | 1 | 0 | 1 | 0 | 0 |
| | Cumberland Trail | 0 | 0 | 0 | 0 | 0 | 1 | 0 | 1 | 0 | 0 |
| | David Crockett | 1 | 0 | 0 | 0 | 1 | 2 | 2 | 0 | 0 | 0 |
| | Davy Crockett Birthplace | 0 | 0 | 0 | 0 | 0 | 0 | 0 | 0 | 0 | 0 |
| | Dunbar Cave Natural Area | 0 | 0 | 0 | 0 | 0 | 0 | 0 | 0 | 0 | 0 |
| | Edgar Evins | 0 | 0 | 0 | 0 | 0 | 2 | 0 | 2 | 0 | 0 |
| | Fall Creek Falls | 0 | 0 | 0 | 0 | 0 | 2 | 0 | 1 | 1 | 0 |
| | Fort Loudon State Historic Park | 0 | 0 | 0 | 0 | 0 | 0 | 0 | 0 | 0 | 0 |
| | Fort Pillow State Historic Park | 0 | 0 | 0 | 0 | 0 | 0 | 0 | 0 | 0 | 0 |
| | Frozen Head Natural Area | 0 | 0 | 0 | 0 | 0 | 2 | 0 | 2 | 0 | 0 |
| | Harpeth Scenic Rivers | 0 | 0 | 0 | 0 | 0 | 1 | 0 | 1 | 0 | 0 |
| | Harrison Bay | 0 | 0 | 0 | 0 | 0 | 2 | 0 | 2 | 0 | 0 |
| | Henry Horton | 0 | 0 | 0 | 0 | 0 | 1 | 0 | 1 | 0 | 0 |
| | Hiwassee/Ocoee State Scenic Rivers | 0 | 0 | 0 | 0 | 0 | 1 | 0 | 1 | 0 | 0 |
| | Indian Mountain | 0 | 0 | 0 | 0 | 0 | 0 | 0 | 0 | 0 | 0 |
| | Johnsonville State Historic Park | 0 | 0 | 0 | 0 | 0 | 0 | 0 | 0 | 0 | 0 |
| | Long Hunter | 0 | 0 | 0 | 0 | 0 | 0 | 0 | 0 | 0 | 0 |
| | Meeman-Shelby Forest | 0 | 0 | 0 | 0 | 0 | 1 | 0 | 1 | 0 | 0 |

[1] The FBI does not publish arson data unless it receives data from either the agency or the state for all 12 months of the calendar year.

## Table 11. Offenses Known to Law Enforcement, by State, Tribal, and Other Agencies, 2009—*Continued*

(Number.)

| State/Other Agency | Unit/Office | Violent crime | Murder and non-negligent man-slaughter | Forcible rape | Robbery | Aggra-vated assault | Property crime | Burglary | Larceny-theft | Motor vehicle theft | Arson[1] |
|---|---|---|---|---|---|---|---|---|---|---|---|
| | Montgomery Bell | 0 | 0 | 0 | 0 | 0 | 3 | 0 | 3 | 0 | 0 |
| | Mousetail Landing | 0 | 0 | 0 | 0 | 0 | 0 | 0 | 0 | 0 | 0 |
| | Natchez Trace | 2 | 0 | 1 | 0 | 1 | 2 | 0 | 0 | 2 | 0 |
| | Nathan Bedford Forrest | 0 | 0 | 0 | 0 | 0 | 0 | 0 | 0 | 0 | 0 |
| | Norris Dam | 0 | 0 | 0 | 0 | 0 | 0 | 0 | 0 | 0 | 0 |
| | Old Stone Fort State Archaeological Park | 0 | 0 | 0 | 0 | 0 | 4 | 0 | 4 | 0 | 0 |
| | Panther Creek | 1 | 0 | 0 | 1 | 0 | 4 | 1 | 3 | 0 | 0 |
| | Paris Landing | 0 | 0 | 0 | 0 | 0 | 4 | 0 | 3 | 1 | 0 |
| | Pickett | 0 | 0 | 0 | 0 | 0 | 0 | 0 | 0 | 0 | 0 |
| | Pickwick Landing | 0 | 0 | 0 | 0 | 0 | 3 | 0 | 2 | 1 | 0 |
| | Pinson Mounds State Archaeological Park | 0 | 0 | 0 | 0 | 0 | 0 | 0 | 0 | 0 | 0 |
| | Radnor Lake Natural Area | 0 | 0 | 0 | 0 | 0 | 0 | 0 | 0 | 0 | 0 |
| | Red Clay State Historic Park | 0 | 0 | 0 | 0 | 0 | 1 | 0 | 1 | 0 | 0 |
| | Reelfoot Lake | 0 | 0 | 0 | 0 | 0 | 0 | 0 | 0 | 0 | 0 |
| | Roan Mountain | 0 | 0 | 0 | 0 | 0 | 0 | 0 | 0 | 0 | 0 |
| | Rock Island | 0 | 0 | 0 | 0 | 0 | 0 | 0 | 0 | 0 | 0 |
| | Sgt. Alvin C. York | 0 | 0 | 0 | 0 | 0 | 0 | 0 | 0 | 0 | 0 |
| | South Cumberland Recreation Area | 0 | 0 | 0 | 0 | 0 | 6 | 0 | 6 | 0 | 0 |
| | Standing Stone | 0 | 0 | 0 | 0 | 0 | 0 | 0 | 0 | 0 | 0 |
| | Sycamore Shoals State Historic Park | 0 | 0 | 0 | 0 | 0 | 0 | 0 | 0 | 0 | 0 |
| | Tim's Ford | 0 | 0 | 0 | 0 | 0 | 4 | 0 | 4 | 0 | 0 |
| | T.O. Fuller | 0 | 0 | 0 | 0 | 0 | 0 | 0 | 0 | 0 | 0 |
| | Warrior's Path | 0 | 0 | 0 | 0 | 0 | 4 | 0 | 4 | 0 | 0 |
| TennCare Office of Inspector General | | 0 | 0 | 0 | 0 | 0 | 0 | 0 | 0 | 0 | 0 |
| Tennessee Bureau of Investigation | | 4 | 2 | 1 | 1 | 0 | 4 | 0 | 4 | 0 | 0 |
| Tennessee Department of Revenue | Special Investigations Unit | 0 | 0 | 0 | 0 | 0 | 0 | 0 | 0 | 0 | 0 |
| Wildlife Resources Agency: | Region 1 | 0 | 0 | 0 | 0 | 0 | 0 | 0 | 0 | 0 | 0 |
| | Region 2 | 1 | 0 | 0 | 0 | 1 | 0 | 0 | 0 | 0 | 0 |
| | Region 3 | 0 | 0 | 0 | 0 | 0 | 0 | 0 | 0 | 0 | 0 |
| | Region 4 | 2 | 0 | 0 | 0 | 2 | 1 | 0 | 1 | 0 | 0 |
| **TENNESSEE—Other Agencies** | | | | | | | | | | | |
| Chattanooga Housing Authority | | 1 | 0 | 0 | 0 | 1 | 7 | 0 | 7 | 0 | 0 |
| Chattanooga Metropolitan Airport | | 0 | 0 | 0 | 0 | 0 | 2 | 0 | 2 | 0 | 0 |
| Dickson Parks and Recreation | | 0 | 0 | 0 | 0 | 0 | 1 | 0 | 1 | 0 | 0 |
| Drug Task Force: | 1st Judicial District | 1 | 0 | 0 | 0 | 1 | 1 | 0 | 1 | 0 | 0 |
| | 2nd Judicial District | 0 | 0 | 0 | 0 | 0 | 0 | 0 | 0 | 0 | 0 |
| | 3rd Judicial District | 0 | 0 | 0 | 0 | 0 | 0 | 0 | 0 | 0 | 0 |
| | 4th Judicial District | 0 | 0 | 0 | 0 | 0 | 1 | 0 | 1 | 0 | 0 |
| | 5th Judicial District | 0 | 0 | 0 | 0 | 0 | 1 | 0 | 1 | 0 | 0 |
| | 8th Judicial District | 0 | 0 | 0 | 0 | 0 | 0 | 0 | 0 | 0 | 0 |
| | 9th Judicial District | 0 | 0 | 0 | 0 | 0 | 0 | 0 | 0 | 0 | 0 |
| | 10th Judicial District | 1 | 0 | 0 | 0 | 1 | 0 | 0 | 0 | 0 | 0 |
| | 12th Judicial District | 0 | 0 | 0 | 0 | 0 | 0 | 0 | 0 | 0 | 0 |
| | 13th Judicial District | 0 | 0 | 0 | 0 | 0 | 0 | 0 | 0 | 0 | 0 |
| | 14th Judicial District | 0 | 0 | 0 | 0 | 0 | 0 | 0 | 0 | 0 | 0 |
| | 15th Judicial District | 0 | 0 | 0 | 0 | 0 | 0 | 0 | 0 | 0 | 0 |
| | 17th Judicial District | 0 | 0 | 0 | 0 | 0 | 0 | 0 | 0 | 0 | 0 |
| | 18th Judicial District | 0 | 0 | 0 | 0 | 0 | 0 | 0 | 0 | 0 | 0 |
| | 19th Judicial District | 0 | 0 | 0 | 0 | 0 | 0 | 0 | 0 | 0 | 0 |
| | 21st Judicial District | 2 | 0 | 0 | 0 | 2 | 0 | 0 | 0 | 0 | 0 |
| | 22nd Judicial District | 0 | 0 | 0 | 0 | 0 | 0 | 0 | 0 | 0 | 0 |
| | 23rd Judicial District | 0 | 0 | 0 | 0 | 0 | 0 | 0 | 0 | 0 | 0 |
| | 24th Judicial District | 0 | 0 | 0 | 0 | 0 | 0 | 0 | 0 | 0 | 0 |
| | 25th Judicial District | 3 | 0 | 0 | 0 | 3 | 1 | 0 | 1 | 0 | 0 |
| | 27th Judicial District | 2 | 0 | 0 | 1 | 1 | 0 | 0 | 0 | 0 | 0 |
| | 31st Judicial District | 0 | 0 | 0 | 0 | 0 | 0 | 0 | 0 | 0 | 0 |
| Knoxville Metropolitan Airport | | 0 | 0 | 0 | 0 | 0 | 19 | 0 | 18 | 1 | 0 |
| Memphis International Airport | | 2 | 0 | 0 | 0 | 2 | 168 | 0 | 163 | 5 | 0 |
| Metropolitan Board of Parks and Recreation | Nashville-Davidson | 0 | 0 | 0 | 0 | 0 | 7 | 0 | 6 | 1 | 0 |
| Nashville International Airport | | 1 | 0 | 0 | 0 | 1 | 8 | 0 | 2 | 6 | 0 |
| Smyrna/Rutherford County Airport Authority | | 0 | 0 | 0 | 0 | 0 | 0 | 0 | 0 | 0 | 0 |

[1] The FBI does not publish arson data unless it receives data from either the agency or the state for all 12 months of the calendar year.

## Table 11. Offenses Known to Law Enforcement, by State, Tribal, and Other Agencies, 2009—*Continued*

(Number.)

| State/Other Agency | Unit/Office | Violent crime | Murder and non-negligent man-slaughter | Forcible rape | Robbery | Aggra-vated assault | Property crime | Burglary | Larceny-theft | Motor vehicle theft | Arson[1] |
|---|---|---|---|---|---|---|---|---|---|---|---|
| Tri-Cities Regional Airport | | 0 | 0 | 0 | 0 | 0 | 0 | 0 | 0 | 0 | 0 |
| West Tennessee Violent Crime Task Force | | 0 | 0 | 0 | 0 | 0 | 1 | 0 | 1 | 0 | 0 |
| **TEXAS—Tribal Agencies** | | | | | | | | | | | |
| Ysleta Del Sur Pueblo Tribal | | 31 | 0 | 0 | 1 | 30 | 46 | 8 | 37 | 1 | 1 |
| **TEXAS—Other Agencies** | | | | | | | | | | | |
| Amarillo International Airport | | 0 | 0 | 0 | 0 | 0 | 0 | 0 | 0 | 0 | 0 |
| Dallas-Fort Worth International Airport | | 6 | 0 | 0 | 3 | 3 | 513 | 8 | 478 | 27 | 0 |
| Hospital District: | Dallas County | 7 | 0 | 0 | 2 | 5 | 454 | 8 | 429 | 17 | 0 |
| | Tarrant County | 4 | 0 | 0 | 3 | 1 | 116 | 3 | 109 | 4 | 0 |
| Houston Metropolitan Transit Authority | | 1 | 0 | 0 | 1 | 0 | 50 | 0 | 43 | 7 | 0 |
| Independent School District: | Aldine | 4 | 0 | 1 | 3 | 0 | 115 | 19 | 89 | 7 | 0 |
| | Alvin | 17 | 0 | 0 | 0 | 17 | 105 | 17 | 86 | 2 | 0 |
| | Angleton | 2 | 0 | 0 | 0 | 2 | 31 | 7 | 24 | 0 | 0 |
| | Austin | 19 | 0 | 2 | 7 | 10 | 770 | 67 | 699 | 4 | 11 |
| | Barbers Hill | 1 | 0 | 0 | 0 | 1 | 2 | 1 | 1 | 0 | 0 |
| | Bay City | 1 | 0 | 0 | 0 | 1 | 52 | 8 | 44 | 0 | 2 |
| | Cedar Hill | 5 | 0 | 0 | 0 | 5 | 46 | 1 | 42 | 3 | 0 |
| | Conroe | 15 | 0 | 0 | 0 | 15 | 174 | 8 | 166 | 0 | 0 |
| | Corpus Christi | 32 | 0 | 0 | 0 | 32 | 222 | 18 | 204 | 0 | 0 |
| | East Central | 0 | 0 | 0 | 0 | 0 | 7 | 4 | 3 | 0 | 0 |
| | Ector County | 41 | 0 | 0 | 3 | 38 | 109 | 2 | 107 | 0 | 3 |
| | El Paso | 18 | 0 | 1 | 1 | 16 | 365 | 32 | 332 | 1 | 0 |
| | Floresville | 0 | 0 | 0 | 0 | 0 | 10 | 2 | 8 | 0 | 0 |
| | Fort Bend | 17 | 0 | 2 | 8 | 7 | 438 | 21 | 415 | 2 | 1 |
| | Humble | 13 | 0 | 0 | 0 | 13 | 120 | 15 | 104 | 1 | 4 |
| | Judson | 3 | 0 | 0 | 3 | 0 | 55 | 0 | 55 | 0 | 1 |
| | Katy | 20 | 0 | 10 | 6 | 4 | 312 | 14 | 298 | 0 | 2 |
| | Killeen | 4 | 0 | 0 | 3 | 1 | 117 | 8 | 108 | 1 | 2 |
| | Klein | 3 | 0 | 0 | 1 | 2 | 212 | 2 | 209 | 1 | 0 |
| | Mexia | 2 | 0 | 0 | 0 | 2 | 12 | 1 | 11 | 0 | 0 |
| | Midland | 0 | 0 | 0 | 0 | 0 | 65 | 11 | 54 | 0 | 0 |
| | North East | 0 | 0 | 0 | 0 | 0 | 352 | 1 | 351 | 0 | 0 |
| | Pasadena | 7 | 0 | 0 | 1 | 6 | 155 | 8 | 144 | 3 | 0 |
| | Pflugerville | 3 | 0 | 0 | 1 | 2 | 122 | 3 | 119 | 0 | 4 |
| | Raymondville | 0 | 0 | 0 | 0 | 0 | 19 | 0 | 19 | 0 | 0 |
| | Rio Grande City | 2 | 0 | 0 | 0 | 2 | 38 | 8 | 29 | 1 | 1 |
| | Socorro | 6 | 0 | 0 | 0 | 6 | 158 | 13 | 145 | 0 | 0 |
| | Spring | 31 | 0 | 0 | 1 | 30 | 135 | 2 | 131 | 2 | 6 |
| | Spring Branch | 2 | 0 | 0 | 1 | 1 | 77 | 16 | 59 | 2 | 0 |
| | Taft | 4 | 0 | 1 | 0 | 3 | 5 | 0 | 5 | 0 | 0 |
| | United | 3 | 0 | 0 | 0 | 3 | 38 | 8 | 30 | 0 | 1 |
| **UTAH—State Agencies** | | | | | | | | | | | |
| Parks and Recreation | | 7 | 0 | 0 | 0 | 7 | 14 | 4 | 10 | 0 | 0 |
| **UTAH—Tribal Agencies** | | | | | | | | | | | |
| Uintah and Ouray Tribal | | 21 | 0 | 1 | 0 | 20 | 24 | 10 | 0 | 14 | 1 |
| **UTAH—Other Agencies** | | | | | | | | | | | |
| Cache-Rich Drug Task Force | | 0 | 0 | 0 | 0 | 0 | 6 | 0 | 6 | 0 | 0 |
| Davis Metropolitan Narcotics Strike Force | | 0 | 0 | 0 | 0 | 0 | 1 | 0 | 1 | 0 | 0 |
| Granite School District | | 9 | 0 | 0 | 0 | 9 | 135 | 22 | 109 | 4 | 7 |
| Utah County Attorney | Investigations Division | 0 | 0 | 0 | 0 | 0 | 0 | 0 | 0 | 0 | 0 |
| Utah County Major Crime Task Force | | 1 | 0 | 0 | 1 | 0 | 0 | 0 | 0 | 0 | 0 |
| Utah Transit Authority | | 26 | 0 | 0 | 7 | 19 | 438 | 0 | 410 | 28 | 0 |
| **VERMONT—State Agencies** | | | | | | | | | | | |
| Attorney General | | 0 | 0 | 0 | 0 | 0 | 0 | 0 | 0 | 0 | 0 |
| Department of Liquor Control | Division of Enforcement and Licensing | 0 | 0 | 0 | 0 | 0 | 0 | 0 | 0 | 0 | 0 |
| Fish and Wildlife Department | Law Enforcement Division | 0 | 0 | 0 | 0 | 0 | 1 | 0 | 1 | 0 | 0 |
| State Police: | Bradford | 15 | 0 | 2 | 0 | 13 | 161 | 73 | 71 | 17 | 0 |
| | Brattleboro | 6 | 0 | 2 | 0 | 4 | 190 | 86 | 93 | 11 | 2 |
| | Derby | 18 | 1 | 1 | 2 | 14 | 286 | 141 | 137 | 8 | 6 |
| | Middlesex | 20 | 1 | 5 | 1 | 13 | 376 | 155 | 219 | 2 | 2 |
| | New Haven | 15 | 1 | 1 | 1 | 12 | 263 | 77 | 168 | 18 | 1 |
| | Rockingham | 12 | 0 | 4 | 2 | 6 | 226 | 112 | 93 | 21 | 0 |
| | Royalton | 10 | 1 | 3 | 1 | 5 | 223 | 106 | 96 | 21 | 0 |
| | Rutland | 26 | 1 | 5 | 6 | 14 | 538 | 231 | 289 | 18 | 1 |
| | Shaftsbury | 12 | 0 | 4 | 0 | 8 | 141 | 52 | 82 | 7 | 3 |
| | St. Albans | 32 | 0 | 18 | 3 | 11 | 492 | 155 | 289 | 48 | 3 |
| | St. Johnsbury | 17 | 0 | 3 | 4 | 10 | 390 | 153 | 213 | 24 | 11 |
| | Williston | 23 | 0 | 8 | 2 | 13 | 332 | 106 | 215 | 11 | 5 |

[1] The FBI does not publish arson data unless it receives data from either the agency or the state for all 12 months of the calendar year.

## Table 11. Offenses Known to Law Enforcement, by State, Tribal, and Other Agencies, 2009—*Continued*

(Number.)

| State/Other Agency | Unit/Office | Violent crime | Murder and non-negligent man-slaughter | Forcible rape | Robbery | Aggra-vated assault | Property crime | Burglary | Larceny-theft | Motor vehicle theft | Arson[1] |
|---|---|---|---|---|---|---|---|---|---|---|---|
| Vermont State Police | | 0 | 0 | 0 | 0 | 0 | 0 | 0 | 0 | 0 | 0 |
| Vermont State Police Headquarters | Bureau of Criminal Investigations | 0 | 0 | 0 | 0 | 0 | 0 | 0 | 0 | 0 | 0 |
| **VIRGINIA—State Agencies** | | | | | | | | | | | |
| Alcoholic Beverage Control Commission | | 0 | 0 | 0 | 0 | 0 | 60 | 0 | 60 | 0 | 0 |
| Department of Conservation and Recreation | | 0 | 0 | 0 | 0 | 0 | 29 | 3 | 26 | 0 | 0 |
| Department of Motor Vehicles | | 0 | 0 | 0 | 0 | 0 | 40 | 0 | 8 | 32 | 0 |
| Southside Virginia Training Center | | 1 | 0 | 0 | 0 | 1 | 18 | 0 | 18 | 0 | 0 |
| State Police: | Accomack County | 3 | 1 | 1 | 0 | 1 | 15 | 3 | 12 | 0 | 0 |
| | Albemarle County | 0 | 0 | 0 | 0 | 0 | 3 | 0 | 3 | 0 | 0 |
| | Alexandria | 1 | 0 | 0 | 0 | 1 | 2 | 0 | 0 | 2 | 0 |
| | Alleghany County | 0 | 0 | 0 | 0 | 0 | 1 | 0 | 1 | 0 | 0 |
| | Amherst County | 1 | 0 | 0 | 0 | 1 | 1 | 0 | 1 | 0 | 0 |
| | Appomattox County | 0 | 0 | 0 | 0 | 0 | 0 | 0 | 0 | 0 | 0 |
| | Augusta County | 0 | 0 | 0 | 0 | 0 | 1 | 0 | 0 | 1 | 2 |
| | Bath County | 0 | 0 | 0 | 0 | 0 | 0 | 0 | 0 | 0 | 0 |
| | Bedford | 0 | 0 | 0 | 0 | 0 | 0 | 0 | 0 | 0 | 0 |
| | Bedford County | 9 | 0 | 0 | 0 | 9 | 5 | 1 | 4 | 0 | 1 |
| | Bland County | 0 | 0 | 0 | 0 | 0 | 7 | 0 | 7 | 0 | 0 |
| | Botetourt County | 0 | 0 | 0 | 0 | 0 | 2 | 0 | 2 | 0 | 2 |
| | Bristol | 1 | 0 | 0 | 0 | 1 | 2 | 0 | 2 | 0 | 0 |
| | Brunswick County | 0 | 0 | 0 | 0 | 0 | 1 | 0 | 0 | 1 | 0 |
| | Buchanan County | 3 | 1 | 1 | 0 | 1 | 30 | 6 | 21 | 3 | 1 |
| | Buena Vista | 0 | 0 | 0 | 0 | 0 | 0 | 0 | 0 | 0 | 0 |
| | Campbell County | 0 | 0 | 0 | 0 | 0 | 3 | 0 | 3 | 0 | 0 |
| | Caroline County | 0 | 0 | 0 | 0 | 0 | 26 | 1 | 17 | 8 | 0 |
| | Carroll County | 1 | 0 | 0 | 0 | 1 | 1 | 0 | 0 | 1 | 0 |
| | Charlotte County | 0 | 0 | 0 | 0 | 0 | 0 | 0 | 0 | 0 | 0 |
| | Chesapeake | 0 | 0 | 0 | 0 | 0 | 2 | 0 | 0 | 2 | 0 |
| | Chesterfield County | 13 | 0 | 0 | 0 | 13 | 8 | 0 | 7 | 1 | 0 |
| | Clarke County | 1 | 0 | 0 | 0 | 1 | 0 | 0 | 0 | 0 | 0 |
| | Clifton Forge | 0 | 0 | 0 | 0 | 0 | 0 | 0 | 0 | 0 | 0 |
| | Colonial Heights | 1 | 0 | 0 | 0 | 1 | 0 | 0 | 0 | 0 | 0 |
| | Covington | 0 | 0 | 0 | 0 | 0 | 2 | 0 | 2 | 0 | 0 |
| | Craig County | 0 | 0 | 0 | 0 | 0 | 0 | 0 | 0 | 0 | 2 |
| | Culpeper County | 1 | 0 | 0 | 0 | 1 | 4 | 0 | 4 | 0 | 0 |
| | Cumberland County | 0 | 0 | 0 | 0 | 0 | 0 | 0 | 0 | 0 | 0 |
| | Danville | 0 | 0 | 0 | 0 | 0 | 0 | 0 | 0 | 0 | 0 |
| | Dickenson County | 0 | 0 | 0 | 0 | 0 | 7 | 2 | 4 | 1 | 3 |
| | Dinwiddie County | 0 | 0 | 0 | 0 | 0 | 0 | 0 | 0 | 0 | 0 |
| | Emporia | 0 | 0 | 0 | 0 | 0 | 1 | 0 | 0 | 1 | 0 |
| | Essex County | 0 | 0 | 0 | 0 | 0 | 1 | 0 | 1 | 0 | 1 |
| | Fairfax County | 9 | 0 | 0 | 0 | 9 | 34 | 0 | 17 | 17 | 0 |
| | Fauquier County | 0 | 0 | 0 | 0 | 0 | 2 | 0 | 2 | 0 | 0 |
| | Floyd County | 0 | 0 | 0 | 0 | 0 | 1 | 0 | 1 | 0 | 0 |
| | Fluvanna County | 0 | 0 | 0 | 0 | 0 | 0 | 0 | 0 | 0 | 0 |
| | Franklin | 0 | 0 | 0 | 0 | 0 | 0 | 0 | 0 | 0 | 0 |
| | Franklin County | 0 | 0 | 0 | 0 | 0 | 12 | 1 | 7 | 4 | 0 |
| | Frederick County | 0 | 0 | 0 | 0 | 0 | 3 | 1 | 1 | 1 | 1 |
| | Fredericksburg | 0 | 0 | 0 | 0 | 0 | 0 | 0 | 0 | 0 | 0 |
| | Galax | 1 | 0 | 0 | 0 | 1 | 0 | 0 | 0 | 0 | 0 |
| | Giles County | 0 | 0 | 0 | 0 | 0 | 5 | 0 | 5 | 0 | 0 |
| | Gloucester County | 0 | 0 | 0 | 0 | 0 | 4 | 0 | 3 | 1 | 0 |
| | Goochland County | 3 | 0 | 0 | 0 | 3 | 4 | 1 | 3 | 0 | 0 |
| | Grayson County | 0 | 0 | 0 | 0 | 0 | 1 | 0 | 1 | 0 | 0 |
| | Greene County | 0 | 0 | 0 | 0 | 0 | 1 | 1 | 0 | 0 | 0 |
| | Greensville County | 7 | 0 | 0 | 0 | 7 | 2 | 0 | 0 | 2 | 0 |
| | Halifax County | 1 | 0 | 0 | 0 | 1 | 5 | 0 | 5 | 0 | 1 |
| | Hampton | 2 | 0 | 0 | 0 | 2 | 2 | 0 | 2 | 0 | 0 |
| | Hanover County | 11 | 0 | 0 | 0 | 11 | 4 | 0 | 1 | 3 | 0 |
| | Harrisonburg | 1 | 0 | 0 | 0 | 1 | 4 | 0 | 3 | 1 | 0 |
| | Henrico County | 4 | 0 | 1 | 0 | 3 | 10 | 1 | 8 | 1 | 0 |
| | Henry County | 1 | 0 | 0 | 0 | 1 | 7 | 0 | 4 | 3 | 0 |
| | Hopewell | 0 | 0 | 0 | 0 | 0 | 0 | 0 | 0 | 0 | 0 |
| | Isle of Wight County | 0 | 0 | 0 | 0 | 0 | 1 | 0 | 0 | 1 | 1 |
| | James City County | 0 | 0 | 0 | 0 | 0 | 0 | 0 | 0 | 0 | 0 |
| | King George County | 1 | 0 | 0 | 0 | 1 | 3 | 0 | 2 | 1 | 0 |
| | King William County | 0 | 0 | 0 | 0 | 0 | 0 | 0 | 0 | 0 | 0 |
| | Lancaster County | 2 | 0 | 1 | 0 | 1 | 4 | 1 | 2 | 1 | 0 |
| | Lee County | 1 | 0 | 0 | 0 | 1 | 2 | 0 | 1 | 1 | 3 |
| | Lexington | 0 | 0 | 0 | 0 | 0 | 0 | 0 | 0 | 0 | 0 |
| | Loudoun County | 1 | 0 | 1 | 0 | 0 | 10 | 0 | 3 | 7 | 0 |

[1] The FBI does not publish arson data unless it receives data from either the agency or the state for all 12 months of the calendar year.

## Table 11. Offenses Known to Law Enforcement, by State, Tribal, and Other Agencies, 2009—*Continued*

(Number.)

| State/Other Agency | Unit/Office | Violent crime | Murder and non-negligent man-slaughter | Forcible rape | Robbery | Aggra-vated assault | Property crime | Burglary | Larceny-theft | Motor vehicle theft | Arson[1] |
|---|---|---|---|---|---|---|---|---|---|---|---|
| | Louisa County | 1 | 0 | 0 | 0 | 1 | 5 | 2 | 1 | 2 | 0 |
| | Lunenburg County | 0 | 0 | 0 | 0 | 0 | 4 | 0 | 3 | 1 | 0 |
| | Lynchburg | 0 | 0 | 0 | 0 | 0 | 0 | 0 | 0 | 0 | 0 |
| | Madison County | 0 | 0 | 0 | 0 | 0 | 0 | 0 | 0 | 0 | 0 |
| | Manassas | 0 | 0 | 0 | 0 | 0 | 0 | 0 | 0 | 0 | 0 |
| | Martinsville | 0 | 0 | 0 | 0 | 0 | 1 | 1 | 0 | 0 | 0 |
| | Mathews County | 0 | 0 | 0 | 0 | 0 | 0 | 0 | 0 | 0 | 0 |
| | Mecklenburg County | 0 | 0 | 0 | 0 | 0 | 3 | 0 | 1 | 2 | 0 |
| | Middlesex County | 1 | 0 | 1 | 0 | 0 | 2 | 0 | 2 | 0 | 0 |
| | Montgomery County | 1 | 0 | 1 | 0 | 0 | 4 | 0 | 3 | 1 | 0 |
| | Nelson County | 2 | 0 | 0 | 0 | 2 | 2 | 0 | 2 | 0 | 0 |
| | New Kent County | 0 | 0 | 0 | 0 | 0 | 3 | 0 | 2 | 1 | 0 |
| | Newport News | 3 | 0 | 0 | 0 | 3 | 5 | 0 | 4 | 1 | 0 |
| | Norfolk | 3 | 0 | 0 | 0 | 3 | 6 | 0 | 3 | 3 | 0 |
| | Northampton County | 0 | 0 | 0 | 0 | 0 | 3 | 3 | 0 | 0 | 0 |
| | Northumberland County | 0 | 0 | 0 | 0 | 0 | 2 | 0 | 2 | 0 | 0 |
| | Orange County | 0 | 0 | 0 | 0 | 0 | 0 | 0 | 0 | 0 | 0 |
| | Page County | 0 | 0 | 0 | 0 | 0 | 1 | 0 | 1 | 0 | 0 |
| | Patrick County | 0 | 0 | 0 | 0 | 0 | 3 | 1 | 1 | 1 | 0 |
| | Petersburg | 1 | 0 | 0 | 0 | 1 | 0 | 0 | 0 | 0 | 0 |
| | Pittsylvania County | 2 | 0 | 0 | 0 | 2 | 18 | 0 | 6 | 12 | 0 |
| | Poquoson | 0 | 0 | 0 | 0 | 0 | 0 | 0 | 0 | 0 | 0 |
| | Portsmouth | 0 | 0 | 0 | 0 | 0 | 3 | 0 | 2 | 1 | 0 |
| | Powhatan County | 10 | 0 | 0 | 0 | 10 | 3 | 0 | 2 | 1 | 0 |
| | Prince Edward County | 0 | 0 | 0 | 0 | 0 | 0 | 0 | 0 | 0 | 0 |
| | Prince George County | 2 | 0 | 0 | 0 | 2 | 0 | 0 | 0 | 0 | 0 |
| | Prince William County | 7 | 0 | 0 | 1 | 6 | 19 | 1 | 7 | 11 | 0 |
| | Pulaski County | 1 | 0 | 0 | 0 | 1 | 7 | 1 | 5 | 1 | 0 |
| | Radford | 0 | 0 | 0 | 0 | 0 | 1 | 0 | 1 | 0 | 0 |
| | Rappahannock County | 0 | 0 | 0 | 0 | 0 | 0 | 0 | 0 | 0 | 0 |
| | Richmond | 11 | 0 | 0 | 0 | 11 | 6 | 0 | 4 | 2 | 0 |
| | Richmond County | 0 | 0 | 0 | 0 | 0 | 0 | 0 | 0 | 0 | 0 |
| | Roanoke | 1 | 0 | 0 | 0 | 1 | 0 | 0 | 0 | 0 | 1 |
| | Roanoke County | 1 | 0 | 0 | 0 | 1 | 2 | 0 | 2 | 0 | 0 |
| | Rockbridge County | 0 | 0 | 0 | 0 | 0 | 10 | 2 | 8 | 0 | 0 |
| | Rockingham County | 2 | 0 | 0 | 0 | 2 | 28 | 0 | 5 | 23 | 0 |
| | Russell County | 2 | 0 | 0 | 0 | 2 | 9 | 2 | 6 | 1 | 0 |
| | Salem | 0 | 0 | 0 | 0 | 0 | 1 | 0 | 1 | 0 | 1 |
| | Scott County | 1 | 0 | 0 | 0 | 1 | 3 | 0 | 3 | 0 | 2 |
| | Shenandoah County | 2 | 0 | 0 | 0 | 2 | 5 | 0 | 3 | 2 | 0 |
| | Smyth County | 1 | 1 | 0 | 0 | 0 | 9 | 3 | 5 | 1 | 1 |
| | Southampton County | 0 | 0 | 0 | 0 | 0 | 1 | 0 | 1 | 0 | 0 |
| | Spotsylvania County | 0 | 0 | 0 | 0 | 0 | 0 | 0 | 0 | 0 | 0 |
| | Stafford County | 1 | 0 | 1 | 0 | 0 | 1 | 0 | 1 | 0 | 0 |
| | Suffolk | 0 | 0 | 0 | 0 | 0 | 0 | 0 | 0 | 0 | 0 |
| | Surry County | 0 | 0 | 0 | 0 | 0 | 2 | 1 | 1 | 0 | 0 |
| | Sussex County | 0 | 0 | 0 | 0 | 0 | 5 | 2 | 1 | 2 | 0 |
| | Tazewell County | 4 | 3 | 0 | 0 | 1 | 53 | 7 | 44 | 2 | 0 |
| | Virginia Beach | 2 | 0 | 0 | 0 | 2 | 4 | 0 | 2 | 2 | 0 |
| | Warren County | 0 | 0 | 0 | 0 | 0 | 2 | 0 | 2 | 0 | 1 |
| | Washington County | 3 | 0 | 1 | 0 | 2 | 5 | 0 | 4 | 1 | 0 |
| | Waynesboro | 0 | 0 | 0 | 0 | 0 | 0 | 0 | 0 | 0 | 0 |
| | Westmoreland County | 0 | 0 | 0 | 0 | 0 | 2 | 0 | 2 | 0 | 1 |
| | Williamsburg | 0 | 0 | 0 | 0 | 0 | 0 | 0 | 0 | 0 | 0 |
| | Winchester | 2 | 0 | 0 | 0 | 2 | 1 | 0 | 1 | 0 | 0 |
| | Wise County | 2 | 1 | 1 | 0 | 0 | 2 | 0 | 2 | 0 | 0 |
| | Wythe County | 1 | 0 | 0 | 0 | 1 | 23 | 0 | 22 | 1 | 0 |
| | York County | 0 | 0 | 0 | 0 | 0 | 0 | 0 | 0 | 0 | 0 |
| Virginia State Capitol | | 0 | 0 | 0 | 0 | 0 | 51 | 1 | 50 | 0 | 0 |
| **VIRGINIA—Other Agencies** | | | | | | | | | | | |
| Norfolk Airport Authority | | 0 | 0 | 0 | 0 | 0 | 38 | 0 | 36 | 2 | 0 |
| Port Authority | Norfolk | 0 | 0 | 0 | 0 | 0 | 4 | 0 | 4 | 0 | 0 |
| Reagan National Airport | | 5 | 0 | 1 | 0 | 4 | 401 | 2 | 336 | 63 | 0 |
| Richmond International Airport | | 0 | 0 | 0 | 0 | 0 | 64 | 1 | 39 | 24 | 0 |
| **WASHINGTON—State Agencies** | | | | | | | | | | | |
| State Insurance Commissioner | Special Investigations Unit | 0 | 0 | 0 | 0 | 0 | 0 | 0 | 0 | 0 | 0 |
| **WASHINGTON—Tribal Agencies** | | | | | | | | | | | |
| Chehalis Tribal | | 2 | 0 | 2 | 0 | 0 | 87 | 16 | 64 | 7 | 0 |
| Colville Tribal | | 10 | 0 | 1 | 2 | 7 | 86 | 13 | 52 | 21 | 3 |
| Lummi Tribal | | 92 | 1 | 5 | 7 | 79 | 345 | 115 | 217 | 13 | 1 |
| Nooksack Tribal | | 11 | 0 | 0 | 6 | 5 | 76 | 32 | 43 | 1 | 0 |

[1] The FBI does not publish arson data unless it receives data from either the agency or the state for all 12 months of the calendar year.

**Table 11. Offenses Known to Law Enforcement, by State, Tribal, and Other Agencies, 2009—*Continued***

(Number.)

| State/Other Agency | Unit/Office | Violent crime | Murder and non-negligent man-slaughter | Forcible rape | Robbery | Aggra-vated assault | Property crime | Burglary | Larceny-theft | Motor vehicle theft | Arson[1] |
|---|---|---|---|---|---|---|---|---|---|---|---|
| Port Gamble S'Klallam Tribal | | 10 | 0 | 3 | 1 | 6 | 54 | 9 | 43 | 2 | 0 |
| Puyallup Tribal | | 40 | 0 | 6 | 22 | 12 | 474 | 29 | 251 | 194 | 2 |
| Spokane Tribal | | 41 | 1 | 3 | 4 | 33 | 27 | 24 | 1 | 2 | 1 |
| Swinomish Tribal | | 3 | 0 | 2 | 0 | 1 | 90 | 15 | 69 | 6 | 0 |
| Yakima Tribal | | 34 | 3 | 18 | 0 | 13 | 394 | 190 | 132 | 72 | 4 |
| **WASHINGTON—Other Agencies** | | | | | | | | | | | |
| Port of Seattle[2,3] | | | 0 | 1 | 1 | | | 21 | 627 | | 2 |
| **WEST VIRGINIA—State Agencies** | | | | | | | | | | | |
| Division of Natural Resources: | Barbour County | 0 | 0 | 0 | 0 | 0 | 0 | 0 | 0 | 0 | 0 |
| | Berkeley County | 0 | 0 | 0 | 0 | 0 | 0 | 0 | 0 | 0 | 0 |
| | Boone County | 0 | 0 | 0 | 0 | 0 | 0 | 0 | 0 | 0 | 0 |
| | Braxton County | 0 | 0 | 0 | 0 | 0 | 0 | 0 | 0 | 0 | 0 |
| | Brooke County | 0 | 0 | 0 | 0 | 0 | 0 | 0 | 0 | 0 | 0 |
| | Cabell County | 0 | 0 | 0 | 0 | 0 | 0 | 0 | 0 | 0 | 0 |
| | Calhoun County | 0 | 0 | 0 | 0 | 0 | 0 | 0 | 0 | 0 | 0 |
| | Clay County | 0 | 0 | 0 | 0 | 0 | 0 | 0 | 0 | 0 | 0 |
| | Doddridge County | 0 | 0 | 0 | 0 | 0 | 0 | 0 | 0 | 0 | 0 |
| | Fayette County | 0 | 0 | 0 | 0 | 0 | 0 | 0 | 0 | 0 | 0 |
| | Gilmer County | 0 | 0 | 0 | 0 | 0 | 0 | 0 | 0 | 0 | 0 |
| | Grant County | 0 | 0 | 0 | 0 | 0 | 0 | 0 | 0 | 0 | 0 |
| | Greenbrier County | 0 | 0 | 0 | 0 | 0 | 0 | 0 | 0 | 0 | 0 |
| | Hampshire County | 0 | 0 | 0 | 0 | 0 | 0 | 0 | 0 | 0 | 0 |
| | Hancock County | 0 | 0 | 0 | 0 | 0 | 0 | 0 | 0 | 0 | 0 |
| | Hardy County | 0 | 0 | 0 | 0 | 0 | 0 | 0 | 0 | 0 | 0 |
| | Harrison County | 0 | 0 | 0 | 0 | 0 | 0 | 0 | 0 | 0 | 0 |
| | Jackson County | 0 | 0 | 0 | 0 | 0 | 0 | 0 | 0 | 0 | 0 |
| | Jefferson County | 0 | 0 | 0 | 0 | 0 | 1 | 1 | 0 | 0 | 0 |
| | Kanawha County | 0 | 0 | 0 | 0 | 0 | 0 | 0 | 0 | 0 | 0 |
| | Lewis County | 0 | 0 | 0 | 0 | 0 | 0 | 0 | 0 | 0 | 0 |
| | Lincoln County | 0 | 0 | 0 | 0 | 0 | 0 | 0 | 0 | 0 | 0 |
| | Logan County | 0 | 0 | 0 | 0 | 0 | 0 | 0 | 0 | 0 | 0 |
| | Marion County | 0 | 0 | 0 | 0 | 0 | 0 | 0 | 0 | 0 | 0 |
| | Marshall County | 0 | 0 | 0 | 0 | 0 | 0 | 0 | 0 | 0 | 0 |
| | Mason County | 0 | 0 | 0 | 0 | 0 | 0 | 0 | 0 | 0 | 0 |
| | McDowell County | 0 | 0 | 0 | 0 | 0 | 0 | 0 | 0 | 0 | 0 |
| | Mercer County | 0 | 0 | 0 | 0 | 0 | 0 | 0 | 0 | 0 | 0 |
| | Mineral County | 0 | 0 | 0 | 0 | 0 | 0 | 0 | 0 | 0 | 0 |
| | Mingo County | 0 | 0 | 0 | 0 | 0 | 0 | 0 | 0 | 0 | 0 |
| | Monongalia County | 0 | 0 | 0 | 0 | 0 | 0 | 0 | 0 | 0 | 0 |
| | Monroe County | 0 | 0 | 0 | 0 | 0 | 0 | 0 | 0 | 0 | 0 |
| | Morgan County | 0 | 0 | 0 | 0 | 0 | 0 | 0 | 0 | 0 | 0 |
| | Nicholas County | 0 | 0 | 0 | 0 | 0 | 0 | 0 | 0 | 0 | 0 |
| | Ohio County | 0 | 0 | 0 | 0 | 0 | 0 | 0 | 0 | 0 | 0 |
| | Pendleton County | 0 | 0 | 0 | 0 | 0 | 0 | 0 | 0 | 0 | 0 |
| | Pleasants County | 0 | 0 | 0 | 0 | 0 | 0 | 0 | 0 | 0 | 0 |
| | Pocahontas County | 0 | 0 | 0 | 0 | 0 | 0 | 0 | 0 | 0 | 0 |
| | Preston County | 0 | 0 | 0 | 0 | 0 | 0 | 0 | 0 | 0 | 0 |
| | Putnam County | 0 | 0 | 0 | 0 | 0 | 0 | 0 | 0 | 0 | 0 |
| | Raleigh County | 0 | 0 | 0 | 0 | 0 | 0 | 0 | 0 | 0 | 0 |
| | Randolph County | 0 | 0 | 0 | 0 | 0 | 0 | 0 | 0 | 0 | 0 |
| | Ritchie County | 0 | 0 | 0 | 0 | 0 | 0 | 0 | 0 | 0 | 0 |
| | Roane County | 0 | 0 | 0 | 0 | 0 | 0 | 0 | 0 | 0 | 0 |
| | Summers County | 0 | 0 | 0 | 0 | 0 | 0 | 0 | 0 | 0 | 0 |
| | Taylor County | 0 | 0 | 0 | 0 | 0 | 0 | 0 | 0 | 0 | 0 |
| | Tucker County | 0 | 0 | 0 | 0 | 0 | 0 | 0 | 0 | 0 | 0 |
| | Tyler County | 0 | 0 | 0 | 0 | 0 | 0 | 0 | 0 | 0 | 0 |
| | Upshur County | 0 | 0 | 0 | 0 | 0 | 0 | 0 | 0 | 0 | 0 |
| | Wayne County | 0 | 0 | 0 | 0 | 0 | 0 | 0 | 0 | 0 | 0 |
| | Webster County | 0 | 0 | 0 | 0 | 0 | 0 | 0 | 0 | 0 | 0 |
| | Wetzel County | 0 | 0 | 0 | 0 | 0 | 0 | 0 | 0 | 0 | 0 |
| | Wirt County | 0 | 0 | 0 | 0 | 0 | 0 | 0 | 0 | 0 | 0 |
| | Wood County | 0 | 0 | 0 | 0 | 0 | 0 | 0 | 0 | 0 | 0 |
| | Wyoming County | 0 | 0 | 0 | 0 | 0 | 0 | 0 | 0 | 0 | 0 |
| State Police: | Beckley | 34 | 0 | 4 | 5 | 25 | 317 | 69 | 222 | 26 | 1 |
| | Berkeley Springs | 13 | 0 | 1 | 1 | 11 | 134 | 57 | 67 | 10 | 0 |
| | Bridgeport | 16 | 0 | 3 | 0 | 13 | 229 | 54 | 149 | 26 | 2 |
| | Buckhannon | 6 | 0 | 3 | 0 | 3 | 110 | 23 | 75 | 12 | 0 |
| | Clay | 11 | 0 | 0 | 0 | 11 | 79 | 35 | 33 | 11 | 2 |
| | Danville | 20 | 0 | 3 | 2 | 15 | 193 | 54 | 123 | 16 | 3 |
| | Elizabeth | 6 | 0 | 0 | 0 | 6 | 42 | 15 | 23 | 4 | 0 |
| | Elkins | 28 | 0 | 1 | 1 | 26 | 293 | 73 | 207 | 13 | 0 |
| | Fairmont | 10 | 0 | 3 | 0 | 7 | 145 | 43 | 94 | 8 | 1 |

[1] The FBI does not publish arson data unless it receives data from either the agency or the state for all 12 months of the calendar year.
[2] The FBI determined that the agency's data were overreported. Consequently, affected data are not included in this table.
[3] The FBI determined that the agency's data were underreported. Consequently, affected data are not included in this table.

## Table 11. Offenses Known to Law Enforcement, by State, Tribal, and Other Agencies, 2009—*Continued*

(Number.)

| State/Other Agency | Unit/Office | Violent crime | Murder and non-negligent man-slaughter | Forcible rape | Robbery | Aggra-vated assault | Property crime | Burglary | Larceny-theft | Motor vehicle theft | Arson[1] |
|---|---|---|---|---|---|---|---|---|---|---|---|
| | Franklin | 8 | 0 | 5 | 1 | 2 | 41 | 17 | 22 | 2 | 1 |
| | Gauley Bridge | 3 | 0 | 1 | 0 | 2 | 18 | 5 | 13 | 0 | 1 |
| | Gilbert | 18 | 0 | 1 | 0 | 17 | 95 | 30 | 58 | 7 | 1 |
| | Glenville | 20 | 0 | 0 | 0 | 20 | 58 | 19 | 37 | 2 | 0 |
| | Grafton | 2 | 0 | 0 | 0 | 2 | 19 | 11 | 5 | 3 | 0 |
| | Grantsville | 10 | 2 | 0 | 2 | 6 | 60 | 23 | 34 | 3 | 1 |
| | Hamlin | 42 | 2 | 8 | 2 | 30 | 348 | 127 | 185 | 36 | 12 |
| | Harrisville | 6 | 0 | 1 | 0 | 5 | 74 | 31 | 36 | 7 | 1 |
| | Hinton | 7 | 0 | 0 | 0 | 7 | 96 | 45 | 49 | 2 | 0 |
| | Hundred | 6 | 0 | 1 | 0 | 5 | 26 | 5 | 18 | 3 | 0 |
| | Huntington | 24 | 0 | 5 | 9 | 10 | 615 | 113 | 467 | 35 | 0 |
| | Jesse | 7 | 0 | 2 | 0 | 5 | 39 | 13 | 24 | 2 | 0 |
| | Kearneysville | 22 | 0 | 0 | 1 | 21 | 262 | 40 | 190 | 32 | 1 |
| | Keyser | 30 | 0 | 2 | 2 | 26 | 221 | 90 | 120 | 11 | 4 |
| | Kingwood | 14 | 0 | 5 | 1 | 8 | 130 | 49 | 63 | 18 | 2 |
| | Lewisburg | 7 | 0 | 1 | 1 | 5 | 102 | 27 | 67 | 8 | 1 |
| | Logan | 119 | 1 | 22 | 4 | 92 | 666 | 206 | 388 | 72 | 12 |
| | Marlington | 16 | 0 | 1 | 0 | 15 | 80 | 27 | 51 | 2 | 1 |
| | Martinsburg | 75 | 1 | 6 | 11 | 57 | 665 | 205 | 410 | 50 | 8 |
| | Moorefield | 16 | 0 | 5 | 0 | 11 | 52 | 20 | 28 | 4 | 1 |
| | Morgantown | 52 | 0 | 2 | 16 | 34 | 663 | 203 | 417 | 43 | 2 |
| | Moundsville | 1 | 0 | 0 | 0 | 1 | 20 | 2 | 14 | 4 | 0 |
| | New Cumberland | 7 | 0 | 2 | 0 | 5 | 18 | 2 | 15 | 1 | 0 |
| | Oak Hill | 7 | 0 | 1 | 0 | 6 | 119 | 32 | 83 | 4 | 1 |
| | Paden City | 2 | 0 | 0 | 0 | 2 | 19 | 9 | 9 | 1 | 1 |
| | Parkersburg | 5 | 0 | 0 | 0 | 5 | 147 | 23 | 112 | 12 | 0 |
| | Parsons | 7 | 0 | 0 | 1 | 6 | 29 | 5 | 22 | 2 | 1 |
| | Petersburg | 10 | 1 | 1 | 0 | 8 | 41 | 19 | 19 | 3 | 1 |
| | Point Pleasant | 5 | 0 | 2 | 0 | 3 | 72 | 32 | 35 | 5 | 0 |
| | Princeton | 47 | 1 | 3 | 11 | 32 | 462 | 126 | 305 | 31 | 1 |
| | Quincy | 15 | 1 | 0 | 1 | 13 | 184 | 43 | 124 | 17 | 4 |
| | Rainelle | 1 | 0 | 0 | 0 | 1 | 58 | 16 | 39 | 3 | 0 |
| | Richwood | 5 | 1 | 0 | 1 | 3 | 32 | 4 | 25 | 3 | 0 |
| | Ripley | 4 | 0 | 1 | 0 | 3 | 79 | 28 | 42 | 9 | 0 |
| | Romney | 13 | 0 | 8 | 0 | 5 | 127 | 44 | 76 | 7 | 0 |
| | South Charleston | 38 | 0 | 2 | 4 | 32 | 695 | 121 | 525 | 49 | 3 |
| | Spencer | 5 | 1 | 1 | 0 | 3 | 48 | 13 | 29 | 6 | 2 |
| | St. Marys | 2 | 0 | 0 | 0 | 2 | 16 | 5 | 11 | 0 | 1 |
| | Summersville | 3 | 1 | 0 | 0 | 2 | 73 | 17 | 52 | 4 | 0 |
| | Sutton | 14 | 1 | 1 | 0 | 12 | 143 | 24 | 108 | 11 | 0 |
| | Union | 8 | 0 | 0 | 0 | 8 | 80 | 38 | 37 | 5 | 0 |
| | Upperglade | 24 | 2 | 0 | 0 | 22 | 57 | 18 | 37 | 2 | 0 |
| | Wayne | 38 | 2 | 3 | 3 | 30 | 438 | 171 | 240 | 27 | 3 |
| | Welch | 33 | 0 | 0 | 2 | 31 | 100 | 20 | 73 | 7 | 0 |
| | Wellsburg | 5 | 0 | 3 | 0 | 2 | 16 | 6 | 10 | 0 | 1 |
| | Weston | 13 | 1 | 0 | 0 | 12 | 85 | 15 | 69 | 1 | 0 |
| | West Union | 9 | 1 | 2 | 0 | 6 | 32 | 11 | 18 | 3 | 0 |
| | Wheeling | 4 | 0 | 1 | 0 | 3 | 56 | 10 | 42 | 4 | 0 |
| | Whitesville | 7 | 0 | 0 | 0 | 7 | 54 | 20 | 31 | 3 | 1 |
| | Williamson | 27 | 0 | 1 | 1 | 25 | 151 | 46 | 83 | 22 | 3 |
| | Winfield | 21 | 0 | 5 | 1 | 15 | 221 | 43 | 153 | 25 | 0 |
| State Police, Bureau of Criminal Investigation: | Bluefield | 2 | 0 | 0 | 0 | 2 | 1 | 0 | 1 | 0 | 0 |
| | Fairmont | 0 | 0 | 0 | 0 | 0 | 0 | 0 | 0 | 0 | 0 |
| State Police, Parkway Authority: | Kanawha County | 0 | 0 | 0 | 0 | 0 | 3 | 1 | 1 | 1 | 0 |
| | Raleigh County | 0 | 0 | 0 | 0 | 0 | 3 | 0 | 3 | 0 | 0 |
| **WEST VIRGINIA—Other Agencies** | | | | | | | | | | | |
| Eastern Panhandle Drug and Violent Crime Task Force | | 0 | 0 | 0 | 0 | 0 | 0 | 0 | 0 | 0 | 0 |
| Greenbrier County Drug and Violent Crime Task Force | | 0 | 0 | 0 | 0 | 0 | 0 | 0 | 0 | 0 | 0 |
| Harrison County Drug and Violent Crime Task Force | | 0 | 0 | 0 | 0 | 0 | 0 | 0 | 0 | 0 | 0 |
| Metropolitan Drug Enforcement Network Team | | 0 | 0 | 0 | 0 | 0 | 0 | 0 | 0 | 0 | 0 |
| Three Rivers Drug and Violent Crime Task Force | | 0 | 0 | 0 | 0 | 0 | 0 | 0 | 0 | 0 | 0 |
| **WISCONSIN—State Agencies** | | | | | | | | | | | |
| Capitol Police | | 0 | 0 | 0 | 0 | 0 | 90 | 2 | 87 | 1 | 0 |
| Department of Natural Resources | | 0 | 0 | 0 | 0 | 0 | 0 | 0 | 0 | 0 | 0 |
| Wisconsin State Patrol | | 0 | 0 | 0 | 0 | 0 | 0 | 0 | 0 | 0 | 0 |

[1] The FBI does not publish arson data unless it receives data from either the agency or the state for all 12 months of the calendar year.

## Table 11. Offenses Known to Law Enforcement, by State, Tribal, and Other Agencies, 2009—*Continued*

(Number.)

| State/Other Agency | Unit/Office | Violent crime | Murder and non-negligent man-slaughter | Forcible rape | Robbery | Aggra-vated assault | Property crime | Burglary | Larceny-theft | Motor vehicle theft | Arson[1] |
|---|---|---|---|---|---|---|---|---|---|---|---|
| **WISCONSIN—Tribal Agencies** | | | | | | | | | | | |
| Lac du Flambeau Tribal | | 13 | 0 | 2 | 1 | 10 | 343 | 61 | 252 | 30 | 0 |
| Menominee Tribal | | 35 | 0 | 2 | 1 | 32 | 147 | 25 | 89 | 33 | 1 |
| Oneida Tribal | | 12 | 0 | 1 | 1 | 10 | 192 | 25 | 158 | 9 | 0 |
| Stockbridge Munsee Tribal | | 2 | 0 | 1 | 0 | 1 | 46 | 19 | 27 | 0 | 0 |
| **WYOMING—Tribal Agencies** | | | | | | | | | | | |
| Wind River Tribal | | 110 | 2 | 13 | 0 | 95 | 179 | 57 | 76 | 46 | 2 |
| **PUERTO RICO AND OTHER OUTLYING AREAS** | | | | | | | | | | | |
| Puerto Rico | | 10,492 | 894 | 65 | 6,093 | 3,440 | 55,937 | 18,521 | 30,584 | 6,832 | |
| **FEDERAL AGENCIES** | | | | | | | | | | | |
| National Institutes of Health | | 0 | 0 | 0 | 0 | 0 | 111 | 0 | 111 | 0 | 0 |
| United States Department of the Interior: | Bureau of Indian Affairs[6] | 5,650 | 139 | 882 | 293 | 4,336 | 16,131 | 4,604 | 9,081 | 2,446 | 856 |
| | Bureau of Land Management | 15 | 6 | 1 | 0 | 8 | 429 | 15 | 386 | 28 | 46 |
| | Bureau of Reclamation | 0 | 0 | 0 | 0 | 0 | 3 | 0 | 3 | 0 | 0 |
| | Fish and Wildlife Service | 20 | 0 | 2 | 2 | 16 | 480 | 103 | 316 | 61 | 76 |
| | National Park Service | 307 | 3 | 34 | 64 | 206 | 2,858 | 397 | 2,395 | 66 | 83 |

[1] The FBI does not publish arson data unless it receives data from either the agency or the state for all 12 months of the calendar year.
[6] Tribal figures represented throughout Table 11 are included in the aggregated totals listed under the Bureau of Indian Affairs data.

## Table 12. Crime Trends, by Population Group, 2008–2009

(Number, percent change.)

| Population group | Violent crime | Murder and non-negligent man-slaughter | Forcible rape | Robbery | Aggra-vated assault | Property crime | Burglary | Larceny-theft | Motor vehicle theft | Arson | Number of agencies | 2009 estimated population |
|---|---|---|---|---|---|---|---|---|---|---|---|---|
| **TOTAL ALL AGENCIES:** | | | | | | | | | | | | |
| 2008 | 1,323,108 | 15,672 | 80,991 | 430,978 | 795,467 | 9,209,011 | 2,099,688 | 6,186,018 | 923,305 | 63,253 | | |
| 2009 | 1,251,617 | 14,558 | 78,560 | 396,500 | 761,999 | 8,777,837 | 2,068,694 | 5,944,792 | 764,351 | 56,445 | 14,443 | 288,077,853 |
| Percent change | -5.4 | -7.1 | -3.0 | -8.0 | -4.2 | -4.7 | -1.5 | -3.9 | -17.2 | -10.8 | | |
| **Total Cities** | | | | | | | | | | | | |
| 2008 | 1,055,968 | 12,187 | 60,005 | 375,436 | 608,340 | 7,176,343 | 1,542,174 | 4,902,538 | 731,631 | 47,006 | | |
| 2009 | 997,762 | 11,301 | 58,113 | 345,402 | 582,946 | 6,866,460 | 1,515,306 | 4,745,702 | 605,452 | 42,076 | 10,396 | 194,716,216 |
| Percent change | -5.5 | -7.3 | -3.2 | -8.0 | -4.2 | -4.3 | -1.7 | -3.2 | -17.2 | -10.5 | | |
| GROUP I (250,000 and over) | | | | | | | | | | | | |
| 2008 | 490,691 | 6,504 | 19,283 | 204,103 | 260,801 | 2,404,343 | 544,134 | 1,511,505 | 348,704 | 17,729 | | |
| 2009 | 458,386 | 5,868 | 19,131 | 186,587 | 246,800 | 2,271,199 | 529,599 | 1,459,242 | 282,358 | 15,836 | 76 | 57,278,467 |
| Percent change | -6.6 | -9.8 | -0.8 | -8.6 | -5.4 | -5.5 | -2.7 | -3.5 | -19.0 | -10.7 | | |
| 1,000,000 and over (Group I subset) | | | | | | | | | | | | |
| 2008 | 205,683 | 2,670 | 6,136 | 93,467 | 103,410 | 904,739 | 186,911 | 582,015 | 135,813 | 5,963 | | |
| 2009 | 193,010 | 2,369 | 6,105 | 85,436 | 99,100 | 842,014 | 178,035 | 555,477 | 108,502 | 5,197 | 10 | 25,873,144 |
| Percent change | -6.2 | -11.3 | -0.5 | -8.6 | -4.2 | -6.9 | -4.7 | -4.6 | -20.1 | -12.8 | | |
| 500,000 to 999,999 (Group I subset) | | | | | | | | | | | | |
| 2008 | 162,951 | 2,169 | 6,763 | 63,608 | 90,411 | 865,023 | 203,807 | 538,607 | 122,609 | 5,903 | | |
| 2009 | 150,834 | 1,960 | 6,698 | 57,457 | 84,719 | 823,712 | 200,426 | 524,104 | 99,182 | 5,585 | 25 | 17,183,941 |
| Percent change | -7.4 | -9.6 | -1.0 | -9.7 | -6.3 | -4.8 | -1.7 | -2.7 | -19.1 | -5.4 | | |
| 250,000 to 499,999 (Group I subset) | | | | | | | | | | | | |
| 2008 | 122,057 | 1,665 | 6,384 | 47,028 | 66,980 | 634,581 | 153,416 | 390,883 | 90,282 | 5,863 | | |
| 2009 | 114,542 | 1,539 | 6,328 | 43,694 | 62,981 | 605,473 | 151,138 | 379,661 | 74,674 | 5,054 | 41 | 14,221,382 |
| Percent change | -6.2 | -7.6 | -0.9 | -7.1 | -6.0 | -4.6 | -1.5 | -2.9 | -17.3 | -13.8 | | |
| GROUP II (100,000 to 249,999) | | | | | | | | | | | | |
| 2008 | 176,518 | 2,082 | 10,452 | 64,473 | 99,511 | 1,245,502 | 279,634 | 833,386 | 132,482 | 7,565 | | |
| 2009 | 166,749 | 1,948 | 10,011 | 57,866 | 96,924 | 1,202,260 | 279,040 | 811,063 | 112,157 | 6,783 | 200 | 29,689,527 |
| Percent change | -5.5 | -6.4 | -4.2 | -10.2 | -2.6 | -3.5 | -0.2 | -2.7 | -15.3 | -10.3 | | |
| GROUP III (50,000 to 99,999) | | | | | | | | | | | | |
| 2008 | 135,570 | 1,368 | 9,125 | 43,996 | 81,081 | 1,077,528 | 226,642 | 749,184 | 101,702 | 7,079 | | |
| 2009 | 129,743 | 1,268 | 8,741 | 41,567 | 78,167 | 1,030,519 | 224,010 | 722,062 | 84,447 | 6,432 | 455 | 31,091,344 |
| Percent change | -4.3 | -7.3 | -4.2 | -5.5 | -3.6 | -4.4 | -1.2 | -3.6 | -17.0 | -9.1 | | |
| GROUP IV (25,000 to 49,999) | | | | | | | | | | | | |
| 2008 | 96,387 | 875 | 7,489 | 28,477 | 59,546 | 868,884 | 176,194 | 630,926 | 61,764 | 5,122 | | |
| 2009 | 91,620 | 891 | 7,099 | 27,269 | 56,361 | 843,186 | 172,545 | 618,552 | 52,089 | 4,747 | 790 | 27,122,788 |
| Percent change | -4.9 | +1.8 | -5.2 | -4.2 | -5.3 | -3.0 | -2.1 | -2.0 | -15.7 | -7.3 | | |
| GROUP V (10,000 to 24,999) | | | | | | | | | | | | |
| 2008 | 84,923 | 732 | 7,060 | 21,722 | 55,409 | 845,403 | 172,481 | 622,213 | 50,709 | 4,526 | | |
| 2009 | 82,550 | 725 | 6,886 | 20,236 | 54,703 | 811,192 | 170,241 | 597,795 | 43,156 | 3,903 | 1,710 | 27,080,564 |
| Percent change | -2.8 | -1.0 | -2.5 | -6.8 | -1.3 | -4.0 | -1.3 | -3.9 | -14.9 | -13.8 | | |
| GROUP VI (under 10,000) | | | | | | | | | | | | |
| 2008 | 71,879 | 626 | 6,596 | 12,665 | 51,992 | 734,683 | 143,089 | 555,324 | 36,270 | 4,985 | | |
| 2009 | 68,714 | 601 | 6,245 | 11,877 | 49,991 | 708,104 | 139,871 | 536,988 | 31,245 | 4,375 | 7,165 | 22,453,526 |
| Percent change | -4.4 | -4.0 | -5.3 | -6.2 | -3.8 | -3.6 | -2.2 | -3.3 | -13.9 | -12.2 | | |
| **Metropolitan Counties** | | | | | | | | | | | | |
| 2008 | 213,362 | 2,621 | 15,370 | 51,048 | 144,323 | 1,596,775 | 415,343 | 1,021,937 | 159,495 | 12,670 | | |
| 2009 | 201,553 | 2,396 | 14,637 | 46,709 | 137,811 | 1,502,971 | 410,086 | 961,317 | 131,568 | 11,016 | 1,675 | 66,809,943 |
| Percent change | -5.5 | -8.6 | -4.8 | -8.5 | -4.5 | -5.9 | -1.3 | -5.9 | -17.5 | -13.1 | | |
| **Nonmetropolitan Counties**[1] | | | | | | | | | | | | |
| 2008 | 53,778 | 864 | 5,616 | 4,494 | 42,804 | 435,893 | 142,171 | 261,543 | 32,179 | 3,577 | | |
| 2009 | 52,302 | 861 | 5,810 | 4,389 | 41,242 | 408,406 | 143,302 | 237,773 | 27,331 | 3,353 | 2,372 | 26,551,694 |
| Percent change | -2.7 | -0.3 | +3.5 | -2.3 | -3.6 | -6.3 | +0.8 | -9.1 | -15.1 | -6.3 | | |
| **SUBURBAN AREAS**[2] | | | | | | | | | | | | |
| 2008 | 364,051 | 3,913 | 27,071 | 92,953 | 240,114 | 3,156,315 | 715,548 | 2,174,851 | 265,916 | 21,263 | | |
| 2009 | 346,156 | 3,613 | 25,573 | 86,325 | 230,645 | 3,004,289 | 701,615 | 2,080,768 | 221,906 | 18,795 | 7,624 | 120,999,345 |
| Percent change | -4.9 | -7.7 | -5.5 | -7.1 | -3.9 | -4.8 | -1.9 | -4.3 | -16.6 | -11.6 | | |

[1] Includes state police agencies that report aggregately for the entire state.

[2] Suburban areas include law enforcement agencies in cities with less than 50,000 inhabitants and county law enforcement agencies that are within a Metropolitan Statistical Area. Suburban areas exclude all metropolitan agencies associated with a principal city. The agencies associated with suburban areas also appear in other groups within this table.

## Table 13. Crime Trends, by Suburban and Nonsuburban Cities[1], by Population Group, 2008–2009

(Number, percent change.)

| Population group | Violent crime | Murder and non-negligent man-slaughter | Forcible rape | Robbery | Aggra-vated assault | Property crime | Burglary | Larceny-theft | Motor vehicle theft | Arson | Number of agencies | 2009 estimated population |
|---|---|---|---|---|---|---|---|---|---|---|---|---|
| **TOTAL SUBURBAN CITIES:** | | | | | | | | | | | | |
| 2008 | 150,689 | 1,292 | 11,701 | 41,905 | 95,791 | 1,559,540 | 300,205 | 1,152,914 | 106,421 | 8,593 | | |
| 2009 | 144,571 | 1,217 | 10,904 | 39,616 | 92,834 | 1,501,318 | 291,529 | 1,119,451 | 90,338 | 7,779 | 5,949 | 54,189,402 |
| Percent change | -4.1 | -5.8 | -6.8 | -5.5 | -3.1 | -3.7 | -2.9 | -2.9 | -15.1 | -9.5 | | |
| GROUP IV (25,000 to 49,999) | | | | | | | | | | | | |
| 2008 | 57,730 | 522 | 4,204 | 18,156 | 34,848 | 560,042 | 109,615 | 405,691 | 44,736 | 3,053 | | |
| 2009 | 55,251 | 494 | 3,926 | 17,290 | 33,541 | 540,299 | 105,866 | 396,668 | 37,765 | 2,902 | 594 | 20,197,988 |
| Percent change | -4.3 | -5.4 | -6.6 | -4.8 | -3.8 | -3.5 | -3.4 | -2.2 | -15.6 | -4.9 | | |
| GROUP V (10,000 to 24,999) | | | | | | | | | | | | |
| 2008 | 53,580 | 466 | 4,147 | 15,207 | 33,760 | 552,170 | 109,268 | 405,096 | 37,806 | 3,018 | | |
| 2009 | 51,510 | 436 | 3,965 | 14,140 | 32,969 | 528,623 | 106,545 | 389,909 | 32,169 | 2,581 | 1,270 | 20,307,949 |
| Percent change | -3.9 | -6.4 | -4.4 | -7.0 | -2.3 | -4.3 | -2.5 | -3.7 | -14.9 | -14.5 | | |
| GROUP VI (under 10,000) | | | | | | | | | | | | |
| 2008 | 39,379 | 304 | 3,350 | 8,542 | 27,183 | 447,328 | 81,322 | 342,127 | 23,879 | 2,522 | | |
| 2009 | 37,810 | 287 | 3,013 | 8,186 | 26,324 | 432,396 | 79,118 | 332,874 | 20,404 | 2,296 | 4,085 | 13,683,465 |
| Percent change | -4.0 | -5.6 | -10.1 | -4.2 | -3.2 | -3.3 | -2.7 | -2.7 | -14.6 | -9.0 | | |
| **TOTAL NONSUBURBAN CITIES:** | | | | | | | | | | | | |
| 2008 | 102,500 | 941 | 9,444 | 20,959 | 71,156 | 889,430 | 191,559 | 655,549 | 42,322 | 6,040 | | |
| 2009 | 98,313 | 1,000 | 9,326 | 19,766 | 68,221 | 861,164 | 191,128 | 633,884 | 36,152 | 5,246 | 3,716 | 22,467,476 |
| Percent change | -4.1 | +6.3 | -1.2 | -5.7 | -4.1 | -3.2 | -0.2 | -3.3 | -14.6 | -13.1 | | |
| GROUP IV (25,000 to 49,999) | | | | | | | | | | | | |
| 2008 | 38,657 | 353 | 3,285 | 10,321 | 24,698 | 308,842 | 66,579 | 225,235 | 17,028 | 2,069 | | |
| 2009 | 36,369 | 397 | 3,173 | 9,979 | 22,820 | 302,887 | 66,679 | 221,884 | 14,324 | 1,845 | 196 | 6,924,800 |
| Percent change | -5.9 | +12.5 | -3.4 | -3.3 | -7.6 | -1.9 | +0.2 | -1.5 | -15.9 | -10.8 | | |
| GROUP V (10,000 to 24,999) | | | | | | | | | | | | |
| 2008 | 31,343 | 266 | 2,913 | 6,515 | 21,649 | 293,233 | 63,213 | 217,117 | 12,903 | 1,508 | | |
| 2009 | 31,040 | 289 | 2,921 | 6,096 | 21,734 | 282,569 | 63,696 | 207,886 | 10,987 | 1,322 | 440 | 6,772,615 |
| Percent change | -1.0 | +8.6 | +0.3 | -6.4 | +0.4 | -3.6 | +0.8 | -4.3 | -14.8 | -12.3 | | |
| GROUP VI (under 10,000) | | | | | | | | | | | | |
| 2008 | 32,500 | 322 | 3,246 | 4,123 | 24,809 | 287,355 | 61,767 | 213,197 | 12,391 | 2,463 | | |
| 2009 | 30,904 | 314 | 3,232 | 3,691 | 23,667 | 275,708 | 60,753 | 204,114 | 10,841 | 2,079 | 3,080 | 8,770,061 |
| Percent change | -4.9 | -2.5 | -0.4 | -10.5 | -4.6 | -4.1 | -1.6 | -4.3 | -12.5 | -15.6 | | |

[1] Suburban cities include law enforcement agencies in cities with less than 50,000 inhabitants that are within a Metropolitan Statistical Area. Suburban cities exclude all metropolitan agencies associated with a principal city. Nonsuburban cities include law enforcement agencies in cities with less than 50,000 inhabitants that are not associated with a Metropolitan Statistical Area.

## Table 14. Crime Trends, by Metropolitan and Nonmetropolitan Counties[1], by Population Group, 2008–2009

(Number, percent change.)

| Population group and range | Violent crime | Murder and non-negligent man-slaughter | Forcible rape | Robbery | Aggra-vated assault | Property crime | Burglary | Larceny-theft | Motor vehicle theft | Arson | Number of agencies | 2009 estimated population |
|---|---|---|---|---|---|---|---|---|---|---|---|---|
| **METROPOLITAN COUNTIES** | | | | | | | | | | | | |
| 100,000 and over | | | | | | | | | | | | |
| 2008 | 151,287 | 1,834 | 9,083 | 43,315 | 97,055 | 1,074,221 | 268,106 | 695,904 | 110,211 | 8,163 | | |
| 2009 | 141,532 | 1,653 | 8,439 | 39,467 | 91,973 | 1,007,023 | 260,384 | 657,021 | 89,618 | 6,906 | 150 | 39,800,231 |
| Percent change | -6.4 | -9.9 | -7.1 | -8.9 | -5.2 | -6.3 | -2.9 | -5.6 | -18.7 | -15.4 | | |
| 25,000 to 99,999 | | | | | | | | | | | | |
| 2008 | 44,877 | 590 | 4,724 | 5,547 | 34,016 | 398,009 | 117,763 | 250,618 | 29,628 | 2,966 | | |
| 2009 | 44,198 | 573 | 4,900 | 5,105 | 33,620 | 377,983 | 118,903 | 234,136 | 24,944 | 2,627 | 430 | 22,403,056 |
| Percent change | -1.5 | -2.9 | +3.7 | -8.0 | -1.2 | -5.0 | +1.0 | -6.6 | -15.8 | -11.4 | | |
| Under 25,000 | | | | | | | | | | | | |
| 2008 | 17,535 | 197 | 1,567 | 2,172 | 13,599 | 122,828 | 29,118 | 74,136 | 19,574 | 1,518 | | |
| 2009 | 16,168 | 170 | 1,554 | 2,119 | 12,325 | 116,237 | 30,197 | 69,102 | 16,938 | 1,476 | 1,088 | 4,449,153 |
| Percent change | -7.8 | -13.7 | -0.8 | -2.4 | -9.4 | -5.4 | +3.7 | -6.8 | -13.5 | -2.8 | | |
| **NONMETROPOLITAN COUNTIES** | | | | | | | | | | | | |
| 25,000 and over | | | | | | | | | | | | |
| 2008 | 23,625 | 339 | 2,315 | 2,316 | 18,655 | 196,010 | 67,041 | 115,085 | 13,884 | 1,345 | | |
| 2009 | 23,465 | 343 | 2,417 | 2,308 | 18,397 | 182,247 | 66,382 | 104,407 | 11,458 | 1,268 | 288 | 11,334,915 |
| Percent change | -0.7 | +1.2 | +4.4 | -0.3 | -1.4 | -7.0 | -1.0 | -9.3 | -17.5 | -5.7 | | |
| 10,000 to 24,999 | | | | | | | | | | | | |
| 2008 | 16,282 | 274 | 1,580 | 1,173 | 13,255 | 132,972 | 43,275 | 80,314 | 9,383 | 1,051 | | |
| 2009 | 15,560 | 310 | 1,715 | 1,089 | 12,446 | 125,580 | 44,409 | 73,156 | 8,015 | 953 | 582 | 9,332,289 |
| Percent change | -4.4 | +13.1 | +8.5 | -7.2 | -6.1 | -5.6 | +2.6 | -8.9 | -14.6 | -9.3 | | |
| Under 10,000 | | | | | | | | | | | | |
| 2008 | 8,751 | 167 | 1,241 | 391 | 6,952 | 63,752 | 19,551 | 38,933 | 5,268 | 755 | | |
| 2009 | 8,446 | 149 | 1,258 | 375 | 6,664 | 60,081 | 20,364 | 34,943 | 4,774 | 798 | 1,344 | 3,867,454 |
| Percent change | -3.5 | -10.8 | +1.4 | -4.1 | -4.1 | -5.8 | +4.2 | -10.2 | -9.4 | +5.7 | | |

[1] Metropolitan counties include sheriffs and county law enforcement agencies associated with a Metropolitan Statistical Area. Nonmetropolitan counties include sheriffs and county law enforcement agencies that are not associated with a Metropolitan Statistical Area. The offenses from state police agencies are not included in this table.

## Table 15. Crime Trends, by Population Group, 2008–2009

(Number, percent change.)

| Population group | Forcible rape | | Robbery | | | | Aggravated assault | | | |
|---|---|---|---|---|---|---|---|---|---|---|
| | Rape by force | Assault to rape-attempts | Firearm | Knife or cutting instrument | Other weapon | Strong-arm | Firearm | Knife or cutting instrument | Other weapon | Hands, fists, feet, etc. |
| **TOTAL ALL AGENCIES:** | | | | | | | | | | |
| 2008 | 73,082 | 5,975 | 164,999 | 29,115 | 33,196 | 152,669 | 156,861 | 138,720 | 245,506 | 194,754 |
| 2009 | 71,161 | 5,415 | 149,493 | 26,817 | 30,388 | 144,085 | 146,650 | 131,393 | 234,966 | 189,462 |
| Percent change | -2.6 | -9.4 | -9.4 | -7.9 | -8.5 | -5.6 | -6.5 | -5.3 | -4.3 | -2.7 |
| **Total Cities** | | | | | | | | | | |
| 2008 | 53,757 | 4,708 | 139,683 | 25,139 | 28,189 | 133,508 | 123,352 | 109,247 | 182,366 | 135,755 |
| 2009 | 52,328 | 4,251 | 126,904 | 23,035 | 25,768 | 125,875 | 114,663 | 103,016 | 175,475 | 132,028 |
| Percent change | -2.7 | -9.7 | -9.1 | -8.4 | -8.6 | -5.7 | -7.0 | -5.7 | -3.8 | -2.7 |
| GROUP I (250,000 and over) | | | | | | | | | | |
| 2008 | 16,367 | 1,889 | 75,443 | 11,836 | 12,457 | 61,502 | 62,971 | 42,254 | 73,529 | 34,501 |
| 2009 | 16,429 | 1,712 | 68,752 | 10,727 | 11,264 | 57,663 | 57,717 | 39,174 | 70,483 | 31,681 |
| Percent change | +0.4 | -9.4 | -8.9 | -9.4 | -9.6 | -6.2 | -8.3 | -7.3 | -4.1 | -8.2 |
| 1,000,000 and over (Group I subset) | | | | | | | | | | |
| 2008 | 4,477 | 769 | 24,427 | 4,793 | 4,269 | 21,139 | 17,617 | 13,163 | 20,691 | 10,076 |
| 2009 | 4,610 | 663 | 23,022 | 4,216 | 3,867 | 19,857 | 15,865 | 12,223 | 20,897 | 7,931 |
| Percent change | +3.0 | -13.8 | -5.8 | -12.0 | -9.4 | -6.1 | -9.9 | -7.1 | +1.0 | -21.3 |
| 500,000 to 999,999 (Group I subset) | | | | | | | | | | |
| 2008 | 6,028 | 598 | 29,584 | 3,998 | 4,723 | 21,277 | 26,062 | 16,922 | 29,869 | 11,875 |
| 2009 | 5,988 | 552 | 26,382 | 3,618 | 4,143 | 19,607 | 23,237 | 15,440 | 28,993 | 11,488 |
| Percent change | -0.7 | -7.7 | -10.8 | -9.5 | -12.3 | -7.8 | -10.8 | -8.8 | -2.9 | -3.3 |
| 250,000 to 499,999 (Group I subset) | | | | | | | | | | |
| 2008 | 5,862 | 522 | 21,432 | 3,045 | 3,465 | 19,086 | 19,292 | 12,169 | 22,969 | 12,550 |
| 2009 | 5,831 | 497 | 19,348 | 2,893 | 3,254 | 18,199 | 18,615 | 11,511 | 20,593 | 12,262 |
| Percent change | -0.5 | -4.8 | -9.7 | -5.0 | -6.1 | -4.6 | -3.5 | -5.4 | -10.3 | -2.3 |
| GROUP II (100,000 to 249,999) | | | | | | | | | | |
| 2008 | 9,287 | 744 | 25,240 | 4,630 | 5,715 | 24,522 | 21,637 | 20,447 | 33,568 | 18,038 |
| 2009 | 8,974 | 596 | 22,024 | 4,276 | 5,094 | 22,470 | 20,131 | 19,975 | 32,248 | 18,285 |
| Percent change | -3.4 | -19.9 | -12.7 | -7.6 | -10.9 | -8.4 | -7.0 | -2.3 | -3.9 | +1.4 |
| GROUP III (50,000 to 99,999) | | | | | | | | | | |
| 2008 | 8,515 | 610 | 15,756 | 3,734 | 4,088 | 19,937 | 14,817 | 16,403 | 26,792 | 21,937 |
| 2009 | 8,135 | 606 | 14,656 | 3,388 | 3,882 | 19,238 | 13,957 | 15,692 | 25,617 | 21,904 |
| Percent change | -4.5 | -0.7 | -7.0 | -9.3 | -5.0 | -3.5 | -5.8 | -4.3 | -4.4 | -0.2 |
| GROUP IV (25,000 to 49,999) | | | | | | | | | | |
| 2008 | 6,996 | 443 | 10,422 | 2,306 | 2,824 | 12,380 | 9,673 | 11,588 | 18,928 | 17,743 |
| 2009 | 6,641 | 413 | 9,930 | 2,166 | 2,648 | 11,957 | 9,088 | 10,558 | 18,014 | 17,331 |
| Percent change | -5.1 | -6.8 | -4.7 | -6.1 | -6.2 | -3.4 | -6.0 | -8.9 | -4.8 | -2.3 |
| GROUP V (10,000 to 24,999) | | | | | | | | | | |
| 2008 | 6,585 | 451 | 8,207 | 1,654 | 2,025 | 9,323 | 8,142 | 10,306 | 16,391 | 19,571 |
| 2009 | 6,407 | 441 | 7,374 | 1,566 | 1,860 | 8,950 | 7,976 | 9,877 | 16,434 | 19,575 |
| Percent change | -2.7 | -2.2 | -10.1 | -5.3 | -8.1 | -4.0 | -2.0 | -4.2 | +0.3 | * |
| GROUP VI (under 10,000) | | | | | | | | | | |
| 2008 | 6,007 | 571 | 4,615 | 979 | 1,080 | 5,844 | 6,112 | 8,249 | 13,158 | 23,965 |
| 2009 | 5,742 | 483 | 4,168 | 912 | 1,020 | 5,597 | 5,794 | 7,740 | 12,679 | 23,252 |
| Percent change | -4.4 | -15.4 | -9.7 | -6.8 | -5.6 | -4.2 | -5.2 | -6.2 | -3.6 | -3.0 |
| **Metropolitan Counties** | | | | | | | | | | |
| 2008 | 14,106 | 926 | 23,508 | 3,634 | 4,396 | 17,480 | 26,318 | 23,517 | 50,989 | 41,841 |
| 2009 | 13,431 | 829 | 20,781 | 3,414 | 4,057 | 16,599 | 24,648 | 22,520 | 47,929 | 41,245 |
| Percent change | -4.8 | -10.5 | -11.6 | -6.1 | -7.7 | -5.0 | -6.3 | -4.2 | -6.0 | -1.4 |
| **Nonmetropolitan Counties** | | | | | | | | | | |
| 2008 | 5,219 | 341 | 1,808 | 342 | 611 | 1,681 | 7,191 | 5,956 | 12,151 | 17,158 |
| 2009 | 5,402 | 335 | 1,808 | 368 | 563 | 1,611 | 7,339 | 5,857 | 11,562 | 16,189 |
| Percent change | +3.5 | -1.8 | 0.0 | +7.6 | -7.9 | -4.2 | +2.1 | -1.7 | -4.8 | -5.6 |
| **SUBURBAN AREAS[1]** | | | | | | | | | | |
| 2008 | 25,008 | 1,708 | 39,117 | 6,789 | 8,225 | 36,144 | 39,591 | 40,103 | 79,747 | 77,524 |
| 2009 | 23,673 | 1,502 | 35,223 | 6,371 | 7,681 | 34,553 | 37,230 | 38,147 | 76,328 | 76,166 |
| Percent change | -5.3 | -12.1 | -10.0 | -6.2 | -6.6 | -4.4 | -6.0 | -4.9 | -4.3 | -1.8 |

[1] Suburban areas include law enforcement agencies in cities with less than 50,000 inhabitants and county law enforcement agencies that are within a Metropolitan Statistical Area. Suburban areas exclude all metropolitan agencies associated with a principal city. The agencies associated with suburban areas also appear in other groups within this table.

* Less than one-tenth of 1 percent.

## Table 15. Crime Trends, by Population Group, 2008–2009—*Continued*

(Number, percent change.)

| Population group | Burglary | | | Motor vehicle theft | | | Arson | | | Number of agencies | 2008 estimated population |
|---|---|---|---|---|---|---|---|---|---|---|---|
| | Forcible entry | Unlawful entry | Attempted forcible entry | Autos | Trucks and buses | Other vehicles | Structure | Mobile | Other | | |
| **TOTAL ALL AGENCIES:** | | | | | | | | | | | |
| 2008 | 1,223,495 | 647,616 | 127,553 | 631,827 | 155,817 | 84,595 | 26,017 | 17,159 | 16,786 | | |
| 2009 | 1,200,235 | 640,593 | 127,113 | 519,117 | 124,129 | 78,144 | 23,643 | 14,992 | 14,802 | 14,266 | 270,511,477 |
| Percent change | -1.9 | -1.1 | -0.3 | -17.8 | -20.3 | -7.6 | -9.1 | -12.6 | -11.8 | | |
| **Total Cities** | | | | | | | | | | | |
| 2008 | 891,503 | 465,594 | 98,171 | 510,322 | 120,773 | 54,093 | 19,741 | 12,197 | 12,335 | | |
| 2009 | 870,396 | 460,709 | 97,388 | 421,498 | 95,658 | 49,521 | 17,922 | 10,507 | 11,013 | 10,250 | 178,919,421 |
| Percent change | -2.4 | -1.0 | -0.8 | -17.4 | -20.8 | -8.5 | -9.2 | -13.9 | -10.7 | | |
| GROUP I (250,000 and over) | | | | | | | | | | | |
| 2008 | 337,845 | 121,419 | 31,130 | 224,425 | 68,258 | 19,104 | 7,051 | 5,965 | 3,352 | | |
| 2009 | 327,880 | 117,940 | 30,707 | 181,542 | 52,750 | 17,279 | 6,416 | 4,989 | 3,197 | 73 | 45,390,374 |
| Percent change | -2.9 | -2.9 | -1.4 | -19.1 | -22.7 | -9.6 | -9.0 | -16.4 | -4.6 | | |
| 1,000,000 and over (Group I subset) | | | | | | | | | | | |
| 2008 | 99,131 | 34,584 | 7,288 | 66,630 | 30,542 | 7,232 | 1,888 | 2,408 | 1,030 | | |
| 2009 | 94,331 | 31,731 | 6,699 | 51,675 | 23,518 | 7,146 | 1,737 | 1,848 | 1,002 | 8 | 14,623,806 |
| Percent change | -4.8 | -8.2 | -8.1 | -22.4 | -23.0 | -1.2 | -8.0 | -23.3 | -2.7 | | |
| 500,000 to 999,999 (Group I subset) | | | | | | | | | | | |
| 2008 | 138,763 | 43,571 | 13,641 | 86,729 | 23,094 | 7,278 | 2,411 | 1,658 | 1,137 | | |
| 2009 | 135,228 | 43,439 | 13,961 | 70,730 | 17,753 | 6,075 | 2,285 | 1,573 | 1,136 | 24 | 16,545,186 |
| Percent change | -2.5 | -0.3 | +2.3 | -18.4 | -23.1 | -16.5 | -5.2 | -5.1 | -0.1 | | |
| 250,000 to 499,999 (Group I subset) | | | | | | | | | | | |
| 2008 | 99,951 | 43,264 | 10,201 | 71,066 | 14,622 | 4,594 | 2,752 | 1,899 | 1,185 | | |
| 2009 | 98,321 | 42,770 | 10,047 | 59,137 | 11,479 | 4,058 | 2,394 | 1,568 | 1,059 | 41 | 14,221,382 |
| Percent change | -1.6 | -1.1 | -1.5 | -16.8 | -21.5 | -11.7 | -13.0 | -17.4 | -10.6 | | |
| GROUP II (100,000 to 249,999) | | | | | | | | | | | |
| 2008 | 156,107 | 84,921 | 18,326 | 95,905 | 20,566 | 9,410 | 3,103 | 1,976 | 1,907 | | |
| 2009 | 155,069 | 84,712 | 18,636 | 80,000 | 17,574 | 9,054 | 2,785 | 1,672 | 1,715 | 189 | 27,923,660 |
| Percent change | -0.7 | -0.2 | +1.7 | -16.6 | -14.5 | -3.8 | -10.2 | -15.4 | -10.1 | | |
| GROUP III (50,000 to 99,999) | | | | | | | | | | | |
| 2008 | 129,528 | 78,224 | 16,025 | 78,414 | 14,377 | 8,309 | 2,983 | 1,740 | 2,146 | | |
| 2009 | 127,127 | 78,250 | 15,810 | 65,103 | 11,083 | 7,761 | 2,704 | 1,598 | 1,896 | 447 | 30,524,767 |
| Percent change | -1.9 | * | -1.3 | -17.0 | -22.9 | -6.6 | -9.4 | -8.2 | -11.6 | | |
| GROUP IV (25,000 to 49,999) | | | | | | | | | | | |
| 2008 | 97,205 | 62,044 | 12,022 | 46,991 | 7,166 | 6,719 | 2,042 | 1,006 | 1,798 | | |
| 2009 | 94,386 | 61,827 | 11,672 | 39,871 | 5,626 | 5,775 | 1,935 | 943 | 1,608 | 768 | 26,380,226 |
| Percent change | -2.9 | -0.3 | -2.9 | -15.2 | -21.5 | -14.0 | -5.2 | -6.3 | -10.6 | | |
| GROUP V (10,000 to 24,999) | | | | | | | | | | | |
| 2008 | 94,540 | 62,989 | 11,463 | 37,878 | 6,295 | 5,545 | 2,138 | 829 | 1,419 | | |
| 2009 | 92,456 | 62,437 | 11,324 | 32,234 | 5,168 | 5,034 | 1,866 | 719 | 1,164 | 1,678 | 26,536,705 |
| Percent change | -2.2 | -0.9 | -1.2 | -14.9 | -17.9 | -9.2 | -12.7 | -13.3 | -18.0 | | |
| GROUP VI (under 10,000) | | | | | | | | | | | |
| 2008 | 76,278 | 55,997 | 9,205 | 26,709 | 4,111 | 5,006 | 2,424 | 681 | 1,713 | | |
| 2009 | 73,478 | 55,543 | 9,239 | 22,748 | 3,457 | 4,618 | 2,216 | 586 | 1,433 | 7,095 | 22,163,689 |
| Percent change | -3.7 | -0.8 | +0.4 | -14.8 | -15.9 | -7.8 | -8.6 | -14.0 | -16.3 | | |
| **Metropolitan Counties** | | | | | | | | | | | |
| 2008 | 244,998 | 134,812 | 23,211 | 102,090 | 29,934 | 23,087 | 4,606 | 4,095 | 3,495 | | |
| 2009 | 242,654 | 131,679 | 23,535 | 81,805 | 24,243 | 21,549 | 4,102 | 3,689 | 2,939 | 1,659 | 65,320,992 |
| Percent change | -1.0 | -2.3 | +1.4 | -19.9 | -19.0 | -6.7 | -10.9 | -9.9 | -15.9 | | |
| **Nonmetropolitan Counties** | | | | | | | | | | | |
| 2008 | 86,994 | 47,210 | 6,171 | 19,415 | 5,110 | 7,415 | 1,670 | 867 | 956 | | |
| 2009 | 87,185 | 48,205 | 6,190 | 15,814 | 4,228 | 7,074 | 1,619 | 796 | 850 | 2,357 | 26,271,064 |
| Percent change | +0.2 | +2.1 | +0.3 | -18.5 | -17.3 | -4.6 | -3.1 | -8.2 | -11.1 | | |
| **SUBURBAN AREAS**[1] | | | | | | | | | | | |
| 2008 | 406,252 | 247,453 | 44,872 | 182,539 | 42,803 | 34,593 | 8,274 | 5,626 | 6,569 | | |
| 2009 | 399,094 | 240,857 | 44,674 | 149,967 | 34,889 | 31,806 | 7,559 | 5,074 | 5,595 | 7,515 | 118,364,849 |
| Percent change | -1.8 | -2.7 | -0.4 | -17.8 | -18.5 | -8.1 | -8.6 | -9.8 | -14.8 | | |

[1] Suburban areas include law enforcement agencies in cities with less than 50,000 inhabitants and county law enforcement agencies that are within a Metropolitan Statistical Area. Suburban areas exclude all metropolitan agencies associated with a principal city. The agencies associated with suburban areas also appear in other groups within this table.

* Less than one-tenth of 1 percent.

# Table 16. Crime Per 100,000 Population, by Population Group, 2009

(Number, rate.)

| Population group | Violent crime | | Murder and nonnegligent manslaughter | | Forcible rape | | Robbery | | Aggravated assault | |
|---|---|---|---|---|---|---|---|---|---|---|
| | Number of offenses known | Rate | Number of offenses known | Rate | Number of offenses known | Rate | Number of offenses known | Rate | Number of offenses known | Rate |
| **TOTAL ALL AGENCIES:** | 1,254,358 | 441.9 | 14,604 | 5.1 | 81,992 | 28.9 | 396,169 | 139.6 | 761,593 | 268.3 |
| **Total Cities** | 999,151 | 518.4 | 11,308 | 5.9 | 60,421 | 31.4 | 345,030 | 179.0 | 582,392 | 302.2 |
| GROUP I (250,000 and over) | 459,141 | 801.6 | 5,868 | 10.2 | 19,886 | 34.7 | 186,587 | 325.8 | 246,800 | 430.9 |
| 1,000,000 and over (Group I subset) | 193,765 | 748.9 | 2,369 | 9.2 | 6,860 | 26.5 | 85,436 | 330.2 | 99,100 | 383.0 |
| 500,000 to 999,999 (Group I subset) | 150,834 | 877.8 | 1,960 | 11.4 | 6,698 | 39.0 | 57,457 | 334.4 | 84,719 | 493.0 |
| 250,000 to 499,999 (Group I subset) | 114,542 | 805.4 | 1,539 | 10.8 | 6,328 | 44.5 | 43,694 | 307.2 | 62,981 | 442.9 |
| GROUP II (100,000 to 249,999) | 166,260 | 563.5 | 1,947 | 6.6 | 10,283 | 34.9 | 57,595 | 195.2 | 96,435 | 326.9 |
| GROUP III (50,000 to 99,999) | 131,238 | 425.8 | 1,278 | 4.1 | 9,152 | 29.7 | 41,808 | 135.7 | 79,000 | 256.3 |
| GROUP IV (25,000 to 49,999) | 91,893 | 343.1 | 879 | 3.3 | 7,405 | 27.6 | 27,192 | 101.5 | 56,417 | 210.7 |
| GROUP V (10,000 to 24,999) | 82,221 | 307.0 | 724 | 2.7 | 7,234 | 27.0 | 20,160 | 75.3 | 54,103 | 202.0 |
| GROUP VI (under 10,000) | 68,398 | 317.3 | 612 | 2.8 | 6,461 | 30.0 | 11,688 | 54.2 | 49,637 | 230.3 |
| **Metropolitan Counties** | 202,235 | 307.6 | 2,393 | 3.6 | 15,207 | 23.1 | 46,772 | 71.1 | 137,863 | 209.7 |
| **Nonmetropolitan Counties**[1] | 52,972 | 208.4 | 903 | 3.6 | 6,364 | 25.0 | 4,367 | 17.2 | 41,338 | 162.6 |
| **SUBURBAN AREAS**[2] | 346,293 | 291.3 | 3,609 | 3.0 | 26,612 | 22.4 | 86,048 | 72.4 | 230,024 | 193.5 |

| Population group | Property crime | | Burglary | | Larceny-theft | | Motor vehicle theft | | Number of agencies | 2009 estimated population |
|---|---|---|---|---|---|---|---|---|---|---|
| | Number of offenses known | Rate | Number of offenses known | Rate | Number of offenses known | Rate | Number of offenses known | Rate | | |
| **TOTAL ALL AGENCIES:** | 8,775,197 | 3,091.2 | 2,063,466 | 726.9 | 5,946,981 | 2,094.9 | 764,750 | 269.4 | 14,065 | 283,878,605 |
| **Total Cities** | 6,873,975 | 3,566.7 | 1,513,658 | 785.4 | 4,754,217 | 2,466.8 | 606,100 | 314.5 | 10,089 | 192,724,603 |
| GROUP I (250,000 and over) | 2,296,396 | 4,009.2 | 529,599 | 924.6 | 1,484,439 | 2,591.6 | 282,358 | 493.0 | 76 | 57,278,467 |
| 1,000,000 and over (Group I subset) | 842,014 | 3,254.4 | 178,035 | 688.1 | 555,477 | 2,146.9 | 108,502 | 419.4 | 10 | 25,873,144 |
| 500,000 to 999,999 (Group I subset) | 840,976 | 4,894.0 | 200,426 | 1,166.4 | 541,368 | 3,150.4 | 99,182 | 577.2 | 25 | 17,183,941 |
| 250,000 to 499,999 (Group I subset) | 613,406 | 4,313.3 | 151,138 | 1,062.8 | 387,594 | 2,725.4 | 74,674 | 525.1 | 41 | 14,221,382 |
| GROUP II (100,000 to 249,999) | 1,199,480 | 4,065.6 | 278,990 | 945.6 | 807,534 | 2,737.1 | 112,956 | 382.9 | 199 | 29,502,852 |
| GROUP III (50,000 to 99,999) | 1,028,226 | 3,336.2 | 225,494 | 731.6 | 717,995 | 2,329.6 | 84,737 | 274.9 | 451 | 30,820,037 |
| GROUP IV (25,000 to 49,999) | 840,153 | 3,137.0 | 172,364 | 643.6 | 615,916 | 2,299.7 | 51,873 | 193.7 | 779 | 26,781,876 |
| GROUP V (10,000 to 24,999) | 809,016 | 3,020.3 | 169,080 | 631.2 | 596,845 | 2,228.2 | 43,091 | 160.9 | 1,691 | 26,785,933 |
| GROUP VI (under 10,000) | 700,704 | 3,250.7 | 138,131 | 640.8 | 531,488 | 2,465.7 | 31,085 | 144.2 | 6,893 | 21,555,438 |
| **Metropolitan Counties** | 1,496,739 | 2,276.8 | 407,333 | 619.6 | 958,169 | 1,457.5 | 131,237 | 199.6 | 1,667 | 65,738,581 |
| **Nonmetropolitan Counties**[1] | 404,483 | 1,591.5 | 142,475 | 560.6 | 234,595 | 923.0 | 27,413 | 107.9 | 2,309 | 25,415,421 |
| **SUBURBAN AREAS**[2] | 2,987,781 | 2,513.2 | 697,060 | 586.3 | 2,069,736 | 1,741.0 | 220,985 | 185.9 | 7,447 | 118,881,839 |

[1] Includes state police agencies that report aggregately for the entire state.

[2] Suburban areas include law enforcement agencies in cities with less than 50,000 inhabitants and county law enforcement agencies that are within a metropolitan statistical area. Suburban areas exclude all metropolitan agencies associated with a principal city. The agencies associated with suburban areas also appear in other groups within this table.

## Table 17. Crime Per 100,000 Population, by Suburban and Nonsuburban Cities[1], by Population Group, 2009

(Number, rate.)

| Population group | Violent crime | | Murder and nonnegligent manslaughter | | Forcible rape | | Robbery | | Aggravated assault | |
|---|---|---|---|---|---|---|---|---|---|---|
| | Number of offenses known | Rate | Number of offenses known | Rate | Number of offenses known | Rate | Number of offenses known | Rate | Number of offenses known | Rate |
| **TOTAL SUBURBAN CITIES:** | 144,047 | 271.1 | 1,216 | 2.3 | 11,394 | 21.4 | 39,276 | 73.9 | 92,161 | 173.4 |
| GROUP IV (25,000 to 49,999) | 55,272 | 277.7 | 495 | 2.5 | 4,119 | 20.7 | 17,142 | 86.1 | 33,516 | 168.4 |
| GROUP V (10,000 to 24,999) | 51,431 | 256.7 | 434 | 2.2 | 4,175 | 20.8 | 14,129 | 70.5 | 32,693 | 163.2 |
| GROUP VI (under 10,000) | 37,344 | 282.9 | 287 | 2.2 | 3,100 | 23.5 | 8,005 | 60.6 | 25,952 | 196.6 |
| **TOTAL NONSUBURBAN CITIES:** | 98,399 | 447.7 | 999 | 4.5 | 9,640 | 43.9 | 19,764 | 89.9 | 67,996 | 309.4 |
| GROUP IV (25,000 to 49,999) | 36,568 | 531.7 | 384 | 5.6 | 3,233 | 47.0 | 10,050 | 146.1 | 22,901 | 333.0 |
| GROUP V (10,000 to 24,999) | 30,780 | 456.0 | 290 | 4.3 | 3,049 | 45.2 | 6,031 | 89.4 | 21,410 | 317.2 |
| GROUP VI (under 10,000) | 31,051 | 371.7 | 325 | 3.9 | 3,358 | 40.2 | 3,683 | 44.1 | 23,685 | 283.5 |

| Population group | Property crime | | Burglary | | Larceny-theft | | Motor vehicle theft | | Number of agencies | 2009 estimated population |
|---|---|---|---|---|---|---|---|---|---|---|
| | Number of offenses known | Rate | Number of offenses known | Rate | Number of offenses known | Rate | Number of offenses known | Rate | | |
| **TOTAL SUBURBAN CITIES:** | 1,491,042 | 2,805.7 | 289,727 | 545.2 | 1,111,567 | 2,091.6 | 89,748 | 168.9 | 5,780 | 53,143,258 |
| GROUP IV (25,000 to 49,999) | 537,537 | 2,700.6 | 105,776 | 531.4 | 394,202 | 1,980.5 | 37,559 | 188.7 | 584 | 19,904,276 |
| GROUP V (10,000 to 24,999) | 525,494 | 2,622.7 | 106,168 | 529.9 | 387,200 | 1,932.5 | 32,126 | 160.3 | 1,252 | 20,036,584 |
| GROUP VI (under 10,000) | 428,011 | 3,241.9 | 77,783 | 589.2 | 330,165 | 2,500.8 | 20,063 | 152.0 | 3,944 | 13,202,398 |
| **TOTAL NONSUBURBAN CITIES:** | 858,831 | 3,907.3 | 189,848 | 863.7 | 632,682 | 2,878.4 | 36,301 | 165.2 | 3,583 | 21,979,989 |
| GROUP IV (25,000 to 49,999) | 302,616 | 4,400.0 | 66,588 | 968.2 | 221,714 | 3,223.7 | 14,314 | 208.1 | 195 | 6,877,600 |
| GROUP V (10,000 to 24,999) | 283,522 | 4,200.7 | 62,912 | 932.1 | 209,645 | 3,106.2 | 10,965 | 162.5 | 439 | 6,749,349 |
| GROUP VI (under 10,000) | 272,693 | 3,264.6 | 60,348 | 722.5 | 201,323 | 2,410.2 | 11,022 | 132.0 | 2,949 | 8,353,040 |

[1] Suburban cities include law enforcement agencies in cities with less than 50,000 inhabitants that are within a metropolitan statistical area. Suburban cities exclude all metropolitan agencies associated with a principal city. Nonsuburban cities include law enforcement agencies in cities with less than 50,000 inhabitants that are not associated with a metropolitan statistical area.

## Table 18. Crime Per 100,000 Population, by Metropolitan and Nonmetropolitan Counties,[1] by Population Group, 2009

(Number, rate.)

| Population group | Violent crime | | Murder and nonnegligent manslaughter | | Forcible rape | | Robbery | | Aggravated assault | |
|---|---|---|---|---|---|---|---|---|---|---|
| | Number of offenses known | Rate | Number of offenses known | Rate | Number of offenses known | Rate | Number of offenses known | Rate | Number of offenses known | Rate |
| **METROPOLITAN COUNTIES** | | | | | | | | | | |
| 100,000 and over | 141,717 | 359.4 | 1,655 | 4.2 | 8,611 | 21.8 | 39,438 | 100.0 | 92,013 | 233.4 |
| 25,000 to 99,999 | 44,649 | 205.0 | 567 | 2.6 | 4,985 | 22.9 | 5,210 | 23.9 | 33,887 | 155.6 |
| Under 25,000 | 16,035 | 353.9 | 172 | 3.8 | 1,651 | 36.4 | 2,156 | 47.6 | 12,056 | 266.1 |
| **NONMETROPOLITAN COUNTIES** | | | | | | | | | | |
| 25,000 and over | 22,857 | 206.6 | 345 | 3.1 | 2,419 | 21.9 | 2,269 | 20.5 | 17,824 | 161.1 |
| 10,000 to 24,999 | 15,051 | 168.0 | 302 | 3.4 | 1,649 | 18.4 | 1,050 | 11.7 | 12,050 | 134.5 |
| Under 10,000 | 8,369 | 230.3 | 149 | 4.1 | 1,321 | 36.3 | 363 | 10.0 | 6,536 | 179.8 |

| Population group | Property crime | | Burglary | | Larceny-theft | | Motor vehicle theft | | Number of agencies | 2009 estimated population |
|---|---|---|---|---|---|---|---|---|---|---|
| | Number of offenses known | Rate | Number of offenses known | Rate | Number of offenses known | Rate | Number of offenses known | Rate | | |
| **METROPOLITAN COUNTIES** | | | | | | | | | | |
| 100,000 and over | 1,004,590 | 2,548.0 | 259,109 | 657.2 | 656,141 | 1,664.2 | 89,340 | 226.6 | 148 | 39,427,006 |
| 25,000 to 99,999 | 374,638 | 1,720.0 | 117,800 | 540.8 | 231,926 | 1,064.8 | 24,912 | 114.4 | 416 | 21,781,217 |
| Under 25,000 | 117,840 | 2,601.1 | 30,473 | 672.6 | 70,346 | 1,552.8 | 17,021 | 375.7 | 1,104 | 4,530,358 |
| **NONMETROPOLITAN COUNTIES** | | | | | | | | | | |
| 25,000 and over | 181,434 | 1,640.2 | 65,856 | 595.4 | 104,027 | 940.4 | 11,551 | 104.4 | 283 | 11,061,471 |
| 10,000 to 24,999 | 121,688 | 1,358.7 | 42,830 | 478.2 | 71,024 | 793.0 | 7,834 | 87.5 | 558 | 8,956,284 |
| Under 10,000 | 58,185 | 1,601.0 | 19,595 | 539.2 | 33,978 | 934.9 | 4,612 | 126.9 | 1,295 | 3,634,310 |

[1] Metropolitan counties include sheriffs and county law enforcement agencies associated with a metropolitan statistical area. Nonmetropolitan counties include sheriffs and county law enforcement agencies that are not associated with a metropolitan statistical area. The offenses from state police agencies are not included in this table.

## Table 19. Crime Per 100,000 Population, Selected Known Offenses, by Population Group, 2009

(Number, rate.)

| Population group | Forcible rape | | Robbery | | | | Aggravated assault | | | |
|---|---|---|---|---|---|---|---|---|---|---|
| | Rape by force | Assault to rape-attempts | Firearm | Knife or cutting instrument | Other weapon | Strong-arm | Firearm | Knife or cutting instrument | Other weapon | Hands, fists, feet, etc. |
| **TOTAL ALL AGENCIES:** | | | | | | | | | | |
| Number of offenses known | 73,009 | 5,460 | 149,335 | 26,831 | 30,388 | 144,115 | 146,773 | 131,547 | 234,973 | 188,668 |
| Rate | 27.3 | 2.0 | 55.9 | 10.0 | 11.4 | 54.0 | 55.0 | 49.3 | 88.0 | 70.7 |
| **Total Cities** | | | | | | | | | | |
| Number of offenses known | 53,125 | 4,297 | 126,619 | 23,039 | 25,762 | 125,920 | 114,636 | 103,086 | 175,596 | 131,626 |
| Rate | 30.0 | 2.4 | 71.4 | 13.0 | 14.5 | 71.0 | 64.7 | 58.1 | 99.0 | 74.2 |
| GROUP I (250,000 and over) | | | | | | | | | | |
| Number of offenses known | 16,429 | 1,712 | 68,752 | 10,727 | 11,264 | 57,663 | 57,717 | 39,174 | 70,483 | 31,681 |
| Rate | 36.2 | 3.8 | 151.5 | 23.6 | 24.8 | 127.0 | 127.2 | 86.3 | 155.3 | 69.8 |
| 1,000,000 and over (Group I subset) | | | | | | | | | | |
| Number of offenses known | 4,610 | 663 | 23,022 | 4,216 | 3,867 | 19,857 | 15,865 | 12,223 | 20,897 | 7,931 |
| Rate | 31.5 | 4.5 | 157.4 | 28.8 | 26.4 | 135.8 | 108.5 | 83.6 | 142.9 | 54.2 |
| 500,000 to 999,999 (Group I subset) | | | | | | | | | | |
| Number of offenses known | 5,988 | 552 | 26,382 | 3,618 | 4,143 | 19,607 | 23,237 | 15,440 | 28,993 | 11,488 |
| Rate | 36.2 | 3.3 | 159.5 | 21.9 | 25.0 | 118.5 | 140.4 | 93.3 | 175.2 | 69.4 |
| 250,000 to 499,999 (Group I subset) | | | | | | | | | | |
| Number of offenses known | 5,831 | 497 | 19,348 | 2,893 | 3,254 | 18,199 | 18,615 | 11,511 | 20,593 | 12,262 |
| Rate | 41.0 | 3.5 | 136.0 | 20.3 | 22.9 | 128.0 | 130.9 | 80.9 | 144.8 | 86.2 |
| GROUP II (100,000 to 249,999) | | | | | | | | | | |
| Number of offenses known | 8,963 | 596 | 21,889 | 4,261 | 5,012 | 22,431 | 20,151 | 19,942 | 31,854 | 18,203 |
| Rate | 32.3 | 2.1 | 78.9 | 15.4 | 18.1 | 80.9 | 72.7 | 71.9 | 114.8 | 65.6 |
| GROUP III (50,000 to 99,999) | | | | | | | | | | |
| Number of offenses known | 8,422 | 616 | 14,713 | 3,420 | 3,929 | 19,345 | 14,190 | 15,875 | 26,055 | 22,046 |
| Rate | 27.7 | 2.0 | 48.3 | 11.2 | 12.9 | 63.6 | 46.6 | 52.2 | 85.6 | 72.4 |
| GROUP IV (25,000 to 49,999) | | | | | | | | | | |
| Number of offenses known | 6,815 | 425 | 9,856 | 2,164 | 2,677 | 12,026 | 9,017 | 10,603 | 18,126 | 17,451 |
| Rate | 26.0 | 1.6 | 37.6 | 8.3 | 10.2 | 45.9 | 34.4 | 40.5 | 69.2 | 66.6 |
| GROUP V (10,000 to 24,999) | | | | | | | | | | |
| Number of offenses known | 6,630 | 449 | 7,371 | 1,560 | 1,870 | 8,872 | 7,820 | 9,795 | 16,337 | 19,352 |
| Rate | 25.2 | 1.7 | 28.1 | 5.9 | 7.1 | 33.8 | 29.8 | 37.3 | 62.2 | 73.7 |
| GROUP VI (under 10,000) | | | | | | | | | | |
| Number of offenses known | 5,866 | 499 | 4,038 | 907 | 1,010 | 5,583 | 5,741 | 7,697 | 12,741 | 22,893 |
| Rate | 27.6 | 2.3 | 19.0 | 4.3 | 4.7 | 26.2 | 27.0 | 36.2 | 59.9 | 107.6 |
| **Metropolitan Counties** | | | | | | | | | | |
| Number of offenses known | 13,988 | 838 | 20,886 | 3,424 | 4,057 | 16,619 | 24,902 | 22,658 | 47,962 | 41,142 |
| Rate | 21.7 | 1.3 | 32.3 | 5.3 | 6.3 | 25.7 | 38.6 | 35.1 | 74.3 | 63.7 |
| **Nonmetropolitan Counties** | | | | | | | | | | |
| Number of offenses known | 5,896 | 325 | 1,830 | 368 | 569 | 1,576 | 7,235 | 5,803 | 11,415 | 15,900 |
| Rate | 23.5 | 1.3 | 7.3 | 1.5 | 2.3 | 6.3 | 28.8 | 23.1 | 45.4 | 63.3 |
| **SUBURBAN AREAS**[1] | | | | | | | | | | |
| Number of offenses known | 24,460 | 1,535 | 35,109 | 6,353 | 7,682 | 34,530 | 37,369 | 38,287 | 76,306 | 75,660 |
| Rate | 21.0 | 1.3 | 30.1 | 5.4 | 6.6 | 29.6 | 32.0 | 32.8 | 65.4 | 64.8 |

[1] Suburban areas include law enforcement agencies in cities with less than 50,000 inhabitants and county law enforcement agencies that are within a metropolitan statistical area. Suburban areas exclude all metropolitan agencies associated with a principal city. The agencies associated with suburban areas also appear in other groups within this table.

## Table 19. Crime Per 100,000 Population, Selected Known Offenses, by Population Group, 2009—*Continued*

(Number, rate.)

| Population group | Burglary | | | Motor vehicle theft | | | Number of agencies | 2009 estimated population |
|---|---|---|---|---|---|---|---|---|
| | Forcible entry | Unlawful entry | Attempted forcible entry | Autos | Trucks and buses | Other vehicles | | |
| **TOTAL ALL AGENCIES:** | | | | | | | | |
| Number of offenses known | 1,199,163 | 640,632 | 126,944 | 520,600 | 123,989 | 77,834 | 13,896 | 267,022,671 |
| Rate | 449.1 | 239.9 | 47.5 | 195.0 | 46.4 | 29.1 | | |
| **Total Cities** | | | | | | | | |
| Number of offenses known | 869,607 | 461,585 | 97,453 | 422,702 | 95,536 | 49,435 | 9,950 | 177,300,290 |
| Rate | 490.5 | 260.3 | 55.0 | 238.4 | 53.9 | 27.9 | | |
| GROUP I (250,000 and over) | | | | | | | | |
| Number of offenses known | 327,880 | 117,940 | 30,707 | 181,542 | 52,750 | 17,279 | 73 | 45,390,374 |
| Rate | 722.4 | 259.8 | 67.7 | 400.0 | 116.2 | 38.1 | | |
| 1,000,000 and over (Group I subset) | | | | | | | | |
| Number of offenses known | 94,331 | 31,731 | 6,699 | 51,675 | 23,518 | 7,146 | 8 | 14,623,806 |
| Rate | 645.1 | 217.0 | 45.8 | 353.4 | 160.8 | 48.9 | | |
| 500,000 to 999,999 (Group I subset) | | | | | | | | |
| Number of offenses known | 135,228 | 43,439 | 13,961 | 70,730 | 17,753 | 6,075 | 24 | 16,545,186 |
| Rate | 817.3 | 262.5 | 84.4 | 427.5 | 107.3 | 36.7 | | |
| 250,000 to 499,999 (Group I subset) | | | | | | | | |
| Number of offenses known | 98,321 | 42,770 | 10,047 | 59,137 | 11,479 | 4,058 | 41 | 14,221,382 |
| Rate | 691.4 | 300.7 | 70.6 | 415.8 | 80.7 | 28.5 | | |
| GROUP II (100,000 to 249,999) | | | | | | | | |
| Number of offenses known | 154,817 | 84,947 | 18,603 | 80,782 | 17,617 | 9,028 | 188 | 27,736,985 |
| Rate | 558.2 | 306.3 | 67.1 | 291.2 | 63.5 | 32.5 | | |
| GROUP III (50,000 to 99,999) | | | | | | | | |
| Number of offenses known | 127,975 | 78,948 | 15,806 | 65,519 | 10,994 | 7,806 | 445 | 30,435,124 |
| Rate | 420.5 | 259.4 | 51.9 | 215.3 | 36.1 | 25.6 | | |
| GROUP IV (25,000 to 49,999) | | | | | | | | |
| Number of offenses known | 94,886 | 62,607 | 11,769 | 39,908 | 5,582 | 5,743 | 762 | 26,193,713 |
| Rate | 362.2 | 239.0 | 44.9 | 152.4 | 21.3 | 21.9 | | |
| GROUP V (10,000 to 24,999) | | | | | | | | |
| Number of offenses known | 91,707 | 62,070 | 11,360 | 32,249 | 5,152 | 5,002 | 1,660 | 26,268,856 |
| Rate | 349.1 | 236.3 | 43.2 | 122.8 | 19.6 | 19.0 | | |
| GROUP VI (under 10,000) | | | | | | | | |
| Number of offenses known | 72,342 | 55,073 | 9,208 | 22,702 | 3,441 | 4,577 | 6,822 | 21,275,238 |
| Rate | 340.0 | 258.9 | 43.3 | 106.7 | 16.2 | 21.5 | | |
| **Metropolitan Counties** | | | | | | | | |
| Number of offenses known | 242,312 | 131,013 | 23,485 | 81,826 | 24,199 | 21,554 | 1,652 | 64,586,131 |
| Rate | 375.2 | 202.9 | 36.4 | 126.7 | 37.5 | 33.4 | | |
| **Nonmetropolitan Counties** | | | | | | | | |
| Number of offenses known | 87,244 | 48,034 | 6,006 | 16,072 | 4,254 | 6,845 | 2,294 | 25,136,250 |
| Rate | 347.1 | 191.1 | 23.9 | 63.9 | 16.9 | 27.2 | | |
| **SUBURBAN AREAS[1]** | | | | | | | | |
| Number of offenses known | 397,690 | 239,777 | 44,679 | 149,610 | 34,816 | 31,741 | 7,345 | 116,691,591 |
| Rate | 340.8 | 205.5 | 38.3 | 128.2 | 29.8 | 27.2 | | |

[1] Suburban areas include law enforcement agencies in cities with less than 50,000 inhabitants and county law enforcement agencies that are within a metropolitan statistical area. Suburban areas exclude all metropolitan agencies associated with a principal city. The agencies associated with suburban areas also appear in other groups within this table.

## Table 20. Murder, by State and Type of Weapon, 2009

(Number.)

| State | Total murders[1] | Total firearms | Handguns | Rifles | Shotguns | Firearms (type unknown) | Knives or cutting instruments | Other weapons | Hands, fists, feet, etc.[2] |
|---|---|---|---|---|---|---|---|---|---|
| Alabama | 318 | 229 | 196 | 1 | 32 | 0 | 29 | 40 | 20 |
| Alaska | 22 | 13 | 1 | 0 | 0 | 12 | 4 | 3 | 2 |
| Arizona | 328 | 197 | 164 | 10 | 10 | 13 | 61 | 53 | 17 |
| Arkansas | 171 | 107 | 54 | 5 | 5 | 43 | 21 | 38 | 5 |
| California | 1,972 | 1,360 | 1,022 | 45 | 49 | 244 | 291 | 214 | 107 |
| Colorado | 167 | 94 | 55 | 6 | 6 | 27 | 23 | 30 | 20 |
| Connecticut | 107 | 70 | 51 | 0 | 2 | 17 | 17 | 14 | 6 |
| Delaware | 41 | 31 | 20 | 2 | 0 | 9 | 6 | 1 | 3 |
| District of Columbia | 144 | 113 | 80 | 1 | 1 | 31 | 17 | 9 | 5 |
| Georgia | 543 | 378 | 323 | 17 | 19 | 19 | 56 | 97 | 12 |
| Hawaii | 21 | 8 | 4 | 2 | 1 | 1 | 3 | 4 | 6 |
| Idaho | 22 | 5 | 3 | 0 | 0 | 2 | 3 | 9 | 5 |
| Illinois[3] | 479 | 386 | 360 | 5 | 8 | 13 | 39 | 48 | 6 |
| Indiana | 293 | 209 | 136 | 8 | 14 | 51 | 34 | 40 | 10 |
| Iowa | 34 | 11 | 3 | 1 | 3 | 4 | 8 | 6 | 9 |
| Kansas | 118 | 85 | 38 | 9 | 0 | 38 | 14 | 11 | 8 |
| Kentucky | 170 | 112 | 90 | 5 | 6 | 11 | 22 | 27 | 9 |
| Louisiana | 486 | 402 | 330 | 20 | 11 | 41 | 32 | 37 | 15 |
| Maine | 26 | 11 | 4 | 0 | 0 | 7 | 6 | 6 | 3 |
| Maryland | 438 | 305 | 297 | 2 | 6 | 0 | 58 | 57 | 18 |
| Massachusetts | 169 | 93 | 47 | 2 | 1 | 43 | 40 | 29 | 7 |
| Michigan | 625 | 437 | 239 | 25 | 19 | 154 | 47 | 112 | 29 |
| Minnesota | 72 | 38 | 35 | 1 | 1 | 1 | 14 | 8 | 12 |
| Mississippi | 151 | 105 | 83 | 9 | 6 | 7 | 22 | 15 | 9 |
| Missouri | 381 | 276 | 170 | 8 | 11 | 87 | 40 | 50 | 15 |
| Montana | 28 | 19 | 9 | 2 | 5 | 3 | 4 | 2 | 3 |
| Nebraska | 40 | 23 | 22 | 1 | 0 | 0 | 8 | 4 | 5 |
| Nevada | 156 | 91 | 66 | 1 | 3 | 21 | 25 | 27 | 13 |
| New Hampshire | 10 | 4 | 1 | 0 | 0 | 3 | 3 | 2 | 1 |
| New Jersey | 319 | 220 | 189 | 3 | 6 | 22 | 44 | 36 | 19 |
| New Mexico | 144 | 78 | 54 | 2 | 3 | 19 | 24 | 29 | 13 |
| New York | 779 | 481 | 117 | 8 | 13 | 343 | 166 | 109 | 23 |
| North Carolina | 480 | 335 | 243 | 17 | 20 | 55 | 49 | 64 | 32 |
| North Dakota | 9 | 3 | 1 | 1 | 1 | 0 | 0 | 3 | 3 |
| Ohio | 502 | 311 | 193 | 2 | 9 | 107 | 52 | 95 | 44 |
| Oklahoma | 225 | 125 | 104 | 10 | 4 | 7 | 45 | 25 | 30 |
| Oregon | 83 | 41 | 9 | 2 | 10 | 20 | 21 | 19 | 2 |
| Pennsylvania | 658 | 468 | 373 | 13 | 11 | 71 | 66 | 100 | 24 |
| Rhode Island | 31 | 18 | 0 | 0 | 0 | 18 | 6 | 5 | 2 |
| South Carolina | 286 | 197 | 115 | 4 | 12 | 66 | 28 | 41 | 20 |
| South Dakota | 11 | 4 | 0 | 1 | 2 | 1 | 5 | 1 | 1 |
| Tennessee | 461 | 295 | 200 | 13 | 22 | 60 | 45 | 92 | 29 |
| Texas | 1,325 | 862 | 661 | 55 | 58 | 88 | 197 | 153 | 113 |
| Utah | 37 | 25 | 15 | 0 | 5 | 5 | 8 | 2 | 2 |
| Vermont | 7 | 0 | 0 | 0 | 0 | 0 | 4 | 1 | 2 |
| Virginia | 347 | 229 | 108 | 8 | 7 | 106 | 41 | 55 | 22 |
| Washington | 169 | 101 | 75 | 16 | 4 | 6 | 35 | 14 | 19 |
| West Virginia | 76 | 38 | 20 | 2 | 3 | 13 | 19 | 13 | 6 |
| Wisconsin | 144 | 95 | 65 | 3 | 9 | 18 | 22 | 13 | 14 |
| Wyoming | 11 | 8 | 7 | 0 | 0 | 1 | 1 | 1 | 1 |

[1] Total number of murders for which supplemental homicide data were received.
[2] Pushed is included in hands, fists, feet, etc.
[3] Limited supplemental homicide data were received.

## Table 21. Robbery, by State and Type of Weapon, 2009

(Number.)

| State | Total robberies[1] | Firearms | Knives or cutting instruments | Other weapons | Strong-arm | Agency count | Population |
|---|---|---|---|---|---|---|---|
| Alabama | 2,462 | 1,384 | 156 | 172 | 750 | 299 | 2,855,069 |
| Alaska | 652 | 169 | 45 | 56 | 382 | 34 | 689,711 |
| Arizona | 8,060 | 3,671 | 787 | 816 | 2,786 | 94 | 6,476,531 |
| Arkansas | 2,508 | 1,211 | 146 | 260 | 891 | 235 | 2,633,889 |
| California | 63,867 | 19,820 | 5,647 | 5,810 | 32,590 | 724 | 36,754,564 |
| Colorado | 3,317 | 1,190 | 332 | 459 | 1,336 | 216 | 4,821,337 |
| Connecticut | 3,990 | 1,445 | 393 | 299 | 1,853 | 103 | 3,518,288 |
| Delaware | 1,669 | 755 | 127 | 136 | 651 | 54 | 884,338 |
| District of Columbia | 4,389 | 1,860 | 221 | 218 | 2,090 | 2 | 599,657 |
| Florida | 30,881 | 13,668 | 1,938 | 2,732 | 12,543 | 593 | 18,514,171 |
| Georgia | 12,333 | 7,582 | 506 | 1,032 | 3,213 | 409 | 7,902,755 |
| Hawaii | 959 | 110 | 91 | 84 | 674 | 3 | 1,150,076 |
| Idaho | 243 | 101 | 15 | 33 | 94 | 105 | 1,522,656 |
| Illinois[2] | 596 | 262 | 40 | 57 | 237 | 1 | 157,943 |
| Indiana | 7,101 | 3,434 | 425 | 567 | 2,675 | 285 | 5,354,545 |
| Iowa | 1,178 | 322 | 114 | 107 | 635 | 193 | 2,752,632 |
| Kansas | 1,454 | 763 | 111 | 108 | 472 | 135 | 1,684,577 |
| Kentucky | 3,517 | 1,523 | 276 | 393 | 1,325 | 331 | 4,037,846 |
| Louisiana | 5,579 | 3,217 | 287 | 365 | 1,710 | 156 | 3,845,020 |
| Maine | 399 | 77 | 50 | 39 | 233 | 167 | 1,318,301 |
| Maryland | 8,257 | 3,810 | 746 | 420 | 3,281 | 152 | 5,034,143 |
| Massachusetts | 7,038 | 1,756 | 1,411 | 755 | 3,116 | 323 | 5,967,910 |
| Michigan | 12,280 | 6,148 | 607 | 1,046 | 4,479 | 583 | 9,733,340 |
| Minnesota | 3,574 | 1,120 | 237 | 574 | 1,643 | 304 | 5,063,535 |
| Mississippi | 2,303 | 1,329 | 129 | 238 | 607 | 114 | 1,862,360 |
| Missouri | 7,291 | 3,859 | 389 | 587 | 2,456 | 569 | 5,590,125 |
| Montana | 215 | 52 | 24 | 53 | 86 | 99 | 965,182 |
| Nebraska | 1,209 | 588 | 91 | 78 | 452 | 214 | 1,614,761 |
| Nevada | 5,996 | 2,286 | 518 | 501 | 2,691 | 38 | 2,593,832 |
| New Hampshire | 431 | 85 | 72 | 66 | 208 | 151 | 1,160,414 |
| New Jersey | 11,573 | 3,598 | 942 | 760 | 6,273 | 567 | 8,596,265 |
| New Mexico | 1,746 | 756 | 186 | 145 | 659 | 77 | 1,702,917 |
| New York | 9,410 | 2,797 | 1,062 | 1,075 | 4,476 | 542 | 10,757,201 |
| North Carolina | 11,165 | 6,130 | 735 | 916 | 3,384 | 360 | 8,345,557 |
| North Dakota | 104 | 24 | 15 | 17 | 48 | 84 | 613,406 |
| Ohio | 16,905 | 6,963 | 796 | 1,586 | 7,560 | 457 | 9,476,128 |
| Oklahoma | 3,320 | 1,580 | 248 | 242 | 1,250 | 305 | 3,530,985 |
| Oregon | 2,413 | 554 | 269 | 217 | 1,373 | 158 | 3,767,402 |
| Pennsylvania | 17,133 | 7,243 | 1,102 | 1,033 | 7,755 | 1,121 | 11,653,125 |
| Rhode Island | 786 | 229 | 107 | 99 | 351 | 49 | 1,053,209 |
| South Carolina | 5,482 | 3,058 | 382 | 476 | 1,566 | 427 | 4,256,280 |
| South Dakota | 107 | 24 | 17 | 8 | 58 | 116 | 706,921 |
| Tennessee | 9,594 | 5,692 | 609 | 738 | 2,555 | 450 | 6,137,723 |
| Texas | 37,955 | 19,036 | 3,020 | 3,106 | 12,793 | 1,008 | 24,686,445 |
| Utah | 1,295 | 413 | 142 | 128 | 612 | 122 | 2,747,172 |
| Vermont | 109 | 36 | 21 | 14 | 38 | 77 | 605,536 |
| Virginia | 5,848 | 3,107 | 407 | 613 | 1,721 | 396 | 7,699,105 |
| Washington | 6,423 | 1,713 | 504 | 591 | 3,615 | 237 | 6,214,402 |
| West Virginia | 644 | 188 | 75 | 95 | 286 | 222 | 1,334,287 |
| Wisconsin | 4,833 | 2,565 | 250 | 464 | 1,554 | 371 | 5,539,597 |
| Wyoming | 76 | 32 | 11 | 4 | 29 | 64 | 539,500 |

[1] The number of robberies for which breakdowns by type of weapon were received from agencies that submitted 12 months of data in 2009.
[2] Limited data were received.

## Table 22. Aggravated Assault, by State and Type of Weapon, 2009

(Number.)

| State | Total aggravated assaults[1] | Firearms | Knives or cutting instruments | Other weapons | Personal weapons | Agency count | Population |
|---|---|---|---|---|---|---|---|
| Alabama | 6,769 | 1,609 | 924 | 1,635 | 2,601 | 299 | 2,855,069 |
| Alaska | 3,194 | 540 | 704 | 855 | 1,095 | 34 | 689,711 |
| Arizona | 15,967 | 4,053 | 2,737 | 5,054 | 4,123 | 94 | 6,476,531 |
| Arkansas | 10,166 | 2,515 | 1,597 | 2,169 | 3,885 | 235 | 2,633,889 |
| California | 99,204 | 17,297 | 16,058 | 35,325 | 30,524 | 724 | 36,754,564 |
| Colorado | 10,857 | 2,059 | 2,326 | 3,011 | 3,461 | 216 | 4,821,337 |
| Connecticut | 5,760 | 772 | 1,215 | 2,079 | 1,694 | 103 | 3,518,288 |
| Delaware | 3,580 | 843 | 798 | 1,564 | 375 | 54 | 884,338 |
| District of Columbia | 3,388 | 728 | 953 | 1,256 | 451 | 2 | 599,657 |
| Florida | 76,023 | 15,015 | 13,439 | 29,167 | 18,402 | 593 | 18,514,171 |
| Georgia | 20,726 | 5,186 | 3,714 | 5,578 | 6,248 | 409 | 7,902,755 |
| Hawaii | 1,897 | 156 | 426 | 648 | 667 | 3 | 1,150,076 |
| Idaho | 2,695 | 401 | 469 | 1,032 | 793 | 105 | 1,522,656 |
| Illinois[2] | 1,332 | 624 | 249 | 319 | 140 | 1 | 157,943 |
| Indiana | 11,027 | 1,723 | 1,544 | 3,448 | 4,312 | 285 | 5,354,545 |
| Iowa | 5,978 | 508 | 1,044 | 1,306 | 3,120 | 193 | 2,752,632 |
| Kansas | 5,236 | 1,820 | 1,051 | 1,393 | 972 | 135 | 1,684,577 |
| Kentucky | 5,641 | 1,017 | 881 | 2,350 | 1,393 | 331 | 4,037,846 |
| Louisiana | 16,963 | 4,308 | 2,634 | 4,409 | 5,612 | 156 | 3,845,020 |
| Maine | 778 | 32 | 146 | 240 | 360 | 167 | 1,318,301 |
| Maryland | 14,343 | 1,838 | 3,178 | 4,986 | 4,341 | 152 | 5,034,143 |
| Massachusetts | 18,895 | 1,940 | 4,408 | 9,715 | 2,832 | 323 | 5,967,910 |
| Michigan | 31,748 | 8,251 | 5,964 | 11,390 | 6,143 | 583 | 9,733,340 |
| Minnesota | 7,138 | 1,175 | 1,420 | 2,037 | 2,506 | 304 | 5,063,535 |
| Mississippi | 2,873 | 822 | 520 | 840 | 691 | 114 | 1,862,360 |
| Missouri | 19,092 | 5,789 | 2,526 | 5,020 | 5,757 | 569 | 5,590,125 |
| Montana | 1,915 | 297 | 260 | 580 | 778 | 99 | 965,182 |
| Nebraska | 3,054 | 490 | 493 | 1,298 | 773 | 214 | 1,614,761 |
| Nevada | 11,255 | 1,707 | 2,009 | 5,680 | 1,859 | 38 | 2,593,832 |
| New Hampshire | 1,151 | 191 | 392 | 306 | 262 | 151 | 1,160,414 |
| New Jersey | 14,020 | 1,969 | 3,095 | 4,476 | 4,480 | 567 | 8,596,265 |
| New Mexico | 8,168 | 1,596 | 1,373 | 2,347 | 2,852 | 77 | 1,702,917 |
| New York | 16,801 | 2,276 | 4,995 | 4,859 | 4,671 | 542 | 10,757,201 |
| North Carolina | 21,025 | 6,110 | 4,288 | 5,816 | 4,811 | 360 | 8,345,557 |
| North Dakota | 931 | 12 | 79 | 151 | 689 | 84 | 613,406 |
| Ohio | 14,592 | 3,510 | 2,934 | 4,525 | 3,623 | 457 | 9,476,128 |
| Oklahoma | 12,744 | 2,449 | 2,098 | 4,583 | 3,614 | 305 | 3,530,985 |
| Oregon | 5,290 | 613 | 976 | 1,925 | 1,776 | 158 | 3,767,402 |
| Pennsylvania | 24,662 | 4,851 | 3,689 | 6,181 | 9,941 | 1,121 | 11,653,125 |
| Rhode Island | 1,556 | 320 | 418 | 605 | 213 | 49 | 1,053,209 |
| South Carolina | 21,682 | 5,685 | 3,908 | 5,988 | 6,101 | 427 | 4,256,280 |
| South Dakota | 865 | 109 | 307 | 264 | 185 | 116 | 706,921 |
| Tennessee | 29,390 | 9,154 | 6,018 | 11,015 | 3,203 | 450 | 6,137,723 |
| Texas | 73,823 | 17,516 | 16,393 | 26,622 | 13,292 | 1,008 | 24,686,445 |
| Utah | 3,648 | 537 | 1,039 | 1,199 | 873 | 122 | 2,747,172 |
| Vermont | 560 | 62 | 116 | 120 | 262 | 77 | 605,536 |
| Virginia | 9,187 | 1,819 | 2,128 | 3,127 | 2,113 | 396 | 7,699,105 |
| Washington | 11,971 | 1,719 | 2,023 | 3,843 | 4,386 | 237 | 6,214,402 |
| West Virginia | 3,239 | 762 | 598 | 849 | 1,030 | 222 | 1,334,287 |
| Wisconsin | 8,206 | 1,900 | 814 | 1,518 | 3,974 | 371 | 5,539,597 |
| Wyoming | 956 | 98 | 179 | 270 | 409 | 64 | 539,500 |

[1] The number of aggravated assaults for which breakdowns by type of weapon were received from agencies that submitted 12 months of data in 2009.

[2] Limited data were received.

## Table 23. Offense Analysis, Number and Percent Change, 2008–2009

(Number, percent, dollars; 14,066 agencies; 2009 estimated population 267,639,320.)

| Classification | Number of offenses 2009 | Percent change from 2008 | Percent distribution[1] | Average value |
|---|---|---|---|---|
| **Murder** | 12,648 | -6.0 | - | |
| **Forcible rape** | 74,223 | -2.8 | - | |
| **Robbery:**[1] | 332,805 | -7.7 | 100.0 | $1,244 |
| By location: | | | | |
| Street/highway | 142,395 | -8.4 | 42.8 | 877 |
| Commercial house | 45,580 | -8.2 | 13.7 | 1,772 |
| Gas or service station | 8,045 | -12.9 | 2.4 | 863 |
| Convenience store | 17,899 | -9.7 | 5.4 | 704 |
| Residence | 56,409 | -4.2 | 16.9 | 1,683 |
| Bank | 7,189 | -2.3 | 2.2 | 4,029 |
| Miscellaneous | 55,288 | -7.9 | 16.6 | 1,175 |
| **Burglary:**[1] | 1,919,612 | -1.4 | 100.0 | 2,096 |
| By location: | | | | |
| Residence (dwelling): | 1,393,152 | +1.8 | 72.6 | 2,163 |
| Residence Night | 388,558 | +2.0 | 20.2 | 1,688 |
| Residence Day | 714,176 | +1.4 | 37.2 | 2,261 |
| Residence Unknown | 290,418 | +2.6 | 15.1 | 2,559 |
| Nonresidence (store, office, etc.): | 526,460 | -9.2 | 27.4 | 1,919 |
| Nonresidence Night | 222,294 | -7.9 | 11.6 | 1,628 |
| Nonresidence Day | 175,053 | -11.0 | 9.1 | 1,869 |
| Nonresidence Unknown | 129,113 | -8.7 | 6.7 | 2,486 |
| **Larceny-theft (except motor vehicle theft):**[1] | 5,462,598 | -3.7 | 100.0 | 864 |
| By type: | | | | |
| Pocket-picking | 22,952 | -2.3 | 0.4 | 504 |
| Purse-snatching | 26,281 | -8.8 | 0.5 | 445 |
| Shoplifting | 990,636 | +7.9 | 18.1 | 181 |
| From motor vehicles (except accessories) | 1,488,948 | +1.2 | 27.3 | 742 |
| Motor vehicle accessories | 494,083 | -10.0 | 9.0 | 530 |
| Bicycles | 183,028 | -4.2 | 3.4 | 318 |
| From buildings | 606,913 | -6.4 | 11.1 | 1,234 |
| From coin-operated machines | 22,482 | -3.2 | 0.4 | 364 |
| All others | 1,627,275 | -10.6 | 29.8 | 1,433 |
| By value: | | | | |
| Over $200 | 2,442,404 | -4.5 | 44.7 | 1,862 |
| $50 to $200 | 1,244,467 | -1.4 | 22.8 | 110 |
| Under $50 | 1,775,727 | -4.1 | 32.5 | 18 |
| **Motor vehicle theft** | 693,428 | -17.0 | - | 6,505 |

[1] Because of rounding, the percentages may not add to 100.0.

## Table 24. Property Stolen and Recovered, by Type and Value, 2009

(Dollars, percent; 13,491 agencies; 2009 estimated population 258,947,325.)

| Type of property | Value of property | | Percent recovered |
|---|---|---|---|
| | Stolen | Recovered | |
| **Total** | $13,328,962,860 | $3,149,325,329 | 23.6 |
| Currency, notes, etc. | 1,168,316,822 | 32,617,615 | 2.8 |
| Jewelry and precious metals | 1,538,739,041 | 72,978,617 | 4.7 |
| Clothing and furs | 337,911,736 | 36,652,477 | 10.8 |
| Locally stolen motor vehicles | 4,552,791,742 | 2,585,224,358 | 56.8 |
| Office equipment | 747,728,241 | 32,473,449 | 4.3 |
| Televisions, radios, stereos, etc. | 1,016,400,720 | 52,344,296 | 5.1 |
| Firearms | 132,431,818 | 11,717,290 | 8.8 |
| Household goods | 280,020,695 | 11,331,940 | 4.0 |
| Consumable goods | 139,885,962 | 15,254,271 | 10.9 |
| Livestock | 19,915,656 | 1,957,658 | 9.8 |
| Miscellaneous | 3,394,820,427 | 296,773,358 | 8.7 |

## SECTION III:

# OFFENSES CLEARED

# OFFENSES CLEARED

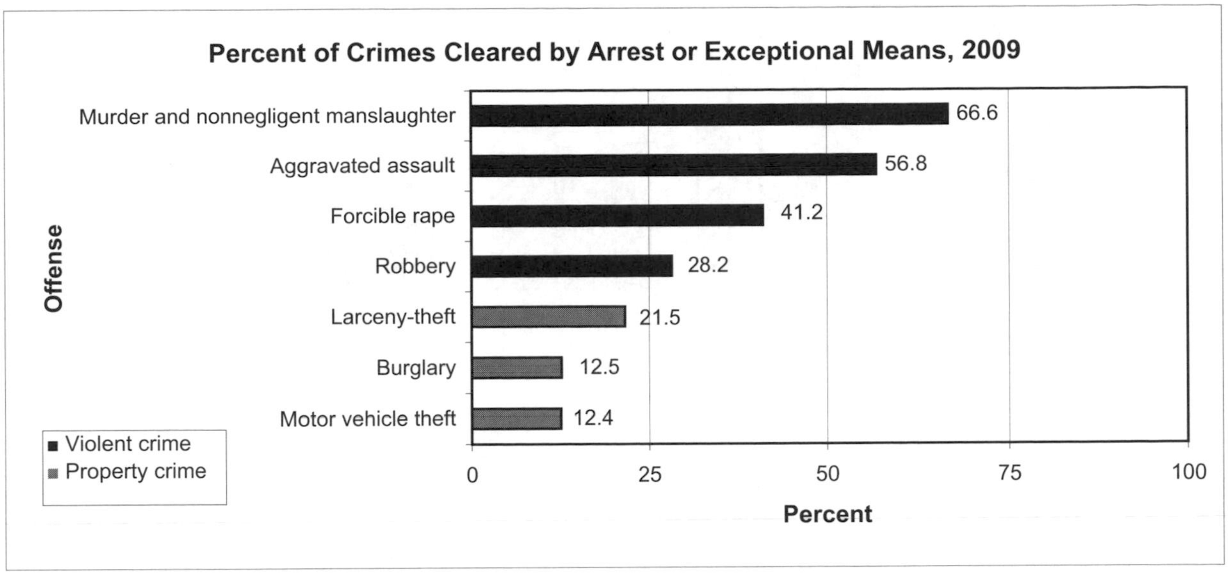


Law enforcement agencies that report crime to the Federal Bureau of Investigation (FBI) can clear, or "close," offenses in one of two ways: by arrest or by exceptional means. However, the administrative closing of a case by a local law enforcement agency does not necessarily mean that the agency can clear an offense for UCR purposes. To clear an offense within the program's guidelines, the reporting agency must adhere to certain criteria, which are outlined in this section. **(*Note:* The UCR Program does not distinguish between offenses cleared by arrest and those cleared by exceptional means in its data presentations. The distinction is made solely for the purpose of a definition and not for data collection and publication.) See Appendix I for information on the UCR Program's statistical methodology.**

## Cleared by Arrest

In the UCR Program, a law enforcement agency reports that an offense is cleared by arrest, or solved for crime reporting purposes, when at least one person is arrested, charged with the commission of the offense, and turned over to the court for prosecution (whether following arrest, court summons, or police notice). To qualify as a clearance, *all* of these conditions must be met.

In its calculations, the UCR Program counts the number of offenses that are cleared, not the number of arrestees. Therefore, the arrest of one person may clear several crimes, and the arrest of many persons may clear only one offense. In addition, some clearances recorded by an agency during a particular calendar year, such as 2009, may pertain to offenses that occurred in previous years.

## Cleared by Exceptional Means

In certain situations, elements beyond law enforcement's control prevent the agency from arresting and formally charging the offender. When this occurs, the agency can clear the offense *exceptionally*. There are four UCR Program requirements that law enforcement must meet in order to clear an offense by exceptional means. The agency must have:

- Identified the offender
- Gathered enough evidence to support an arrest, make a charge, and turn over the offender to the court for prosecution
- Identified the offender's exact location so that the suspect could be taken into custody immediately
- Encountered a circumstance outside the control of law enforcement that prohibits the agency from arresting, charging, and prosecuting the offender

Examples of exceptional clearances include, but are not limited to, the death of the offender (e.g., suicide or justifiably killed by a law enforcement officer or a citizen), the victim's refusal to cooperate with the prosecution after the offender has been identified, or the denial of extradition because the offender committed a crime in another jurisdiction and is being prosecuted for that offense. In the UCR Program, the recovery of property does not clear an offense.

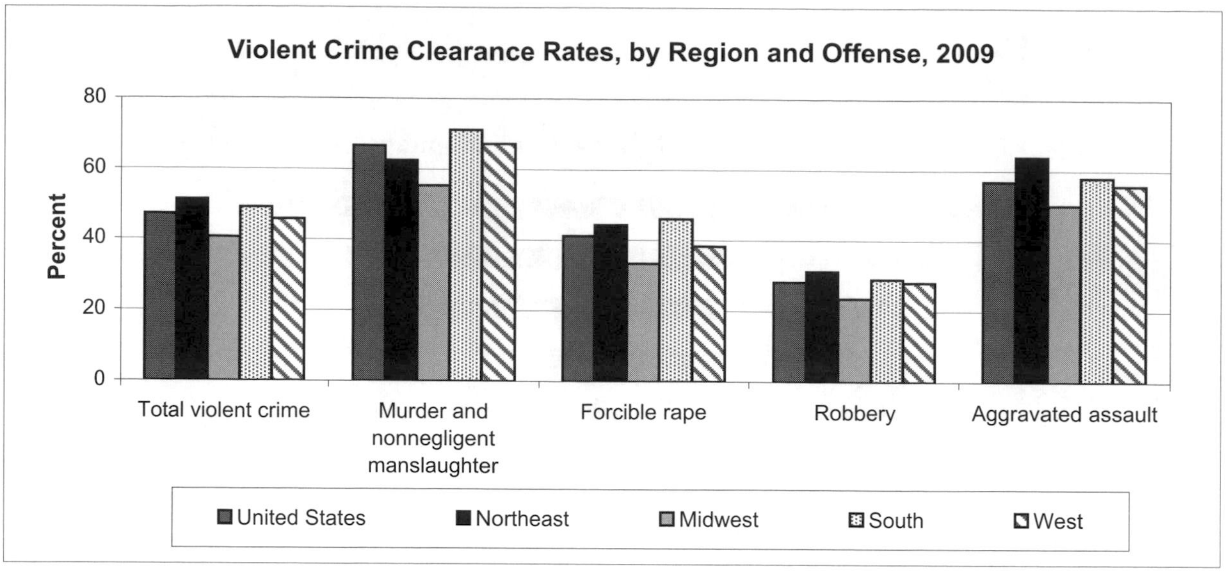


## National Clearances

A review of the data for 2009 revealed law enforcement agencies in the United States cleared 47.1 percent of violent crimes (murder, forcible rape, robbery, and aggravated assault) and 18.6 percent of property crimes (burglary, larceny-theft, and motor vehicle theft) brought to their attention. In addition, law enforcement cleared 34.7 percent of arson offenses, which are reported in a slightly different manner than the other property crimes. (More details concerning this offense are furnished in the arson text in this section.)

As in most years, law enforcement agencies cleared a higher percentage of violent crimes than property crimes in 2009. As a rule, this long-term trend is attributed to the more vigorous investigative efforts put forth for violent crimes. In addition, violent crimes more often involve victims and/or witnesses who are able to identify the perpetrators.

A breakdown of the clearances for violent crimes for 2009 revealed that the nation's law enforcement agencies cleared 66.6 percent of murder offenses, 56.8 percent of aggravated assault offenses, 41.2 percent of forcible rape offenses, and 28.2 percent of robbery offenses. The data for property crimes showed that agencies cleared 21.5 percent of larceny-theft offenses, 12.5 percent of burglary offenses, and 12.4 percent of motor vehicle theft offenses. (Table 25)

Law enforcement agencies throughout the nation collectively cleared 18.6 percent of property crime offenses in 2009, including 12.5 percent of burglary offenses, 21.5 percent of larceny-theft offenses, 12.4 percent of motor vehicle theft offenses, and 18.5 percent of arson offenses. (Table 25)

## Regional Clearances

The UCR Program divides the nation into four regions: the Northeast, the Midwest, the South, and the West. (See Appendix III for further details.) A review of clearance data for 2009 by region showed that agencies in the Northeast cleared the greatest proportion of their violent crime offenses (51.2 percent). Law enforcement agencies in the South cleared 49.0 percent of their violent crimes, while agencies in the West and Midwest cleared 45.7 percent and 40.5 percent, respectively.

For murder and nonnegligent manslaughter, the South cleared 71.1 percent of offenses, followed by the West (67.2 percent), the Northeast (62.5 percent), and the Midwest (55.3 percent each). Forcible rape offenses were cleared 46.0 percent of the time in the South, 44.3 percent of the time in the Northeast, 38.3 percent in the West, and 33.3 percent in the Midwest. For robbery, the Northeast had the highest clearance rate, at 31.2 percent. The Northeast also had the highest proportion of clearances for aggravated assault (63.8 percent). (Table 26)

Clearance data for 2009 showed that, among the regions, law enforcement agencies in the Northeast cleared the highest percentage of their property crimes (21.6 percent). Agencies in the South and Midwest cleared 19.0 percent and 18.5 percent, respectively. Agencies in the West cleared 16.4 percent of their property crimes. (Table 26) Agencies in the Northeast cleared the highest percentage of burglary offenses at 15.5 percent, followed by the South at 13.0 percent, the West at 11.5 percent, and the Midwest at 10.6 percent. For larceny-theft, the Northeast (23.9 percent) was followed by the Midwest (21.8 percent), the South (21.7 percent), and the West (19.7 percent). The Northeast also cleared the highest proportion of motor vehicle thefts at 16.0 percent and the greatest percentage of arson offenses (24.9 percent). (Table 26)

## Clearances by Population Groups

The UCR Program uses the following population group designations in its data presentations: cities (grouped according to population size) and counties (classified as either metropolitan or nonmetropolitan counties).

(A breakdown of these classifications is furnished in Appendix III.)

### *Cities*

In 2009, the clearance data collected showed that law enforcement agencies in the nation's cities cleared 45.1 percent of their violent crime offenses. Among the city population groups, agencies in the smallest cities, those with populations under 10,000 inhabitants, cleared the greatest proportion of their violent crime offenses (56.3 percent), and law enforcement in cities with 1,000,000 and more inhabitants cleared the smallest proportion of their violent crime offenses (38.6 percent).

The clearance data for murder showed that among the city population groups, cities with populations of 10,000 to 24,999 inhabitants cleared the greatest percentage of their murders (73.1 percent). Law enforcement agencies in cities with 250,000 to 499,999 inhabitants cleared the lowest percentage of their murders (59.0 percent). For forcible rape, cities with 1,000,000 or more inhabitants cleared the largest percentage of offenses at 45.6 percent, while cities with 25,000 to 49,999 inhabitants cleared the lowest percentage of offenses at 35.2 percent. Cities with 10,000 to 24,999 inhabitants cleared the greatest percentage of their robbery offenses at 36.1 percent, and cities with 500,000 to 999,999 inhabitants cleared the lowest proportion of their robbery offenses at 22.5 percent. For aggravated assault, cities with under 10,000 inhabitants cleared the highest proportion of offenses (62.9 percent); cities with 1,000,000 and more inhabitants cleared the lowest percentage of offenses (49.1 percent). (Table 25)

In 2009, agencies in the nation's cities collectively cleared 18.7 percent of their property crime offenses. Law enforcement in cities with 10,000 to 24,999 inhabitants cleared the highest proportion of the property crimes (23.4 percent) brought to their attention; cities with 1,000,000 or more inhabitants cleared the smallest proportion of their property crimes (13.3 percent). (Table 25)

Law enforcement agencies in cities cleared 11.9 percent of burglaries, 21.9 percent of larceny-thefts, 11.2 percent of motor vehicle thefts, and 17.7 percent of arsons in 2009. (Table 25) For burglaries, cities with under 10,000 inhabitants cleared the largest percentage of their offenses, at 16.0 percent, while cities with 1,000,000 or more inhabitants cleared the smallest percentage of their offenses, at 8.2 percent. Cities with 10,000 to 24,999 inhabitants cleared the greatest percentage of their larceny-theft offenses (26.2 percent), and cities with 500,000 to 999,999 inhabitants cleared the lowest proportion of larceny-theft offenses (16.2 percent). For motor vehicle theft, cities with under 10,000 inhabitants cleared the highest percentages of their offenses, at 23.9 percent. (Table 25) Cities with 10,000 to 24,999 inhabitants cleared the greatest percentage of their arson offenses, at 25.1 percent.

### *Metropolitan and Nonmetropolitan Counties*

In 2009, law enforcement agencies in metropolitan counties cleared 52.6 percent of their violent crime offenses. Of the violent crimes made known to law enforcement agencies, murder offenses had the highest proportion of clearance (67.9 percent), followed by 60.5 percent of aggravated assaults, 44.8 percent of forcible rapes, and 30.8 percent of robberies being cleared. Law enforcement agencies in metropolitan counties cleared 18.2 percent of their total property crimes, 13.7 percent of burglaries, 20.5 percent of larceny-thefts, 15.2 percent of motor vehicle thefts, and 19.4 percent of their arsons. (Table 25)

Like their counterparts in metropolitan counties, nonmetropolitan counties collectively cleared a greater proportion of their violent crimes than did the nation as a whole in 2009. Nonmetropolitan counties cleared 60.3 percent of their violent crime offenses and 18.3 percent of

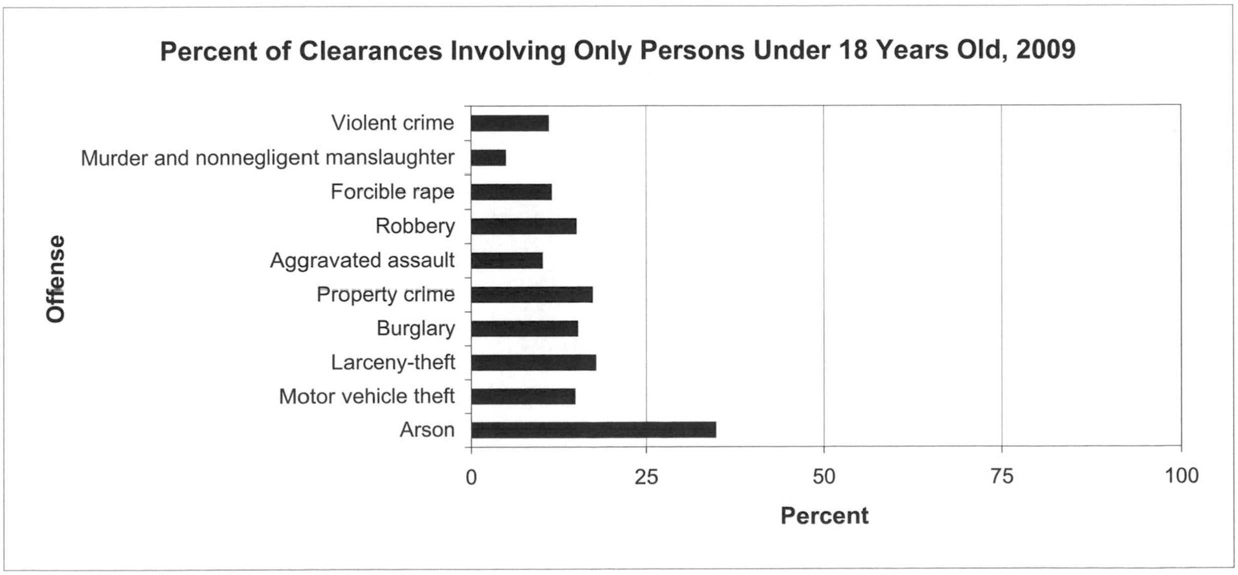

property crimes. Of the violent crimes known to them, law enforcement in nonmetropolitan counties had the highest number of clearances for murder (77.7 percent), with 45.5 percent of forcible rapes, 41.9 percent of robberies, and 64.1 percent of aggravated assaults being cleared. Agencies in nonmetropolitan counties reported clearing 15.8 percent of their burglaries, 19.2 percent of their larceny-thefts, 23.6 percent of their motor vehicle thefts, and 24.6 percent of their arsons. (Table 25)

## Clearances by Classification Group and Type

For forcible rape, by classification group and type, law enforcement agencies cleared 43.1 percent of assault to rape attempts and 40.0 percent of rapes by force in 2009. Cleared robbery offenses included 32.2 percent of offenses involving strong-arm tactics, 31.1 percent of offenses involving knives or other cutting instruments, 22.5 percent of offenses involving firearms, and 28.8 percent of offenses involving other weapons. For aggravated assault, agencies cleared 61.2 percent of offenses involving hands, feet, fists, etc.; 63.4 percent of offenses involving knives or other cutting instruments; 41.2 percent of offenses involving firearms; and 56.9 percent of offenses involving other weapons. (Table 27)

For property crime clearances grouped by classification and type, data showed that the highest percentage of burglary clearances in the nation in 2009 (13.7 percent) were of offenses that involved unlawful entry of structures. Law enforcement agencies cleared 11.7 percent of burglaries involving forcible entry and 10.8 percent of attempted forcible entry offenses. For motor vehicle theft, agencies cleared 12.7 percent of motor vehicle theft offenses involving automobiles and 9.6 percent of motor vehicle theft offenses involving trucks and buses. (Table 27)

In 2009, 22.8 percent of structural arson offenses were cleared by arrest or exceptional means, while 8.8 percent of mobile arson offenses and 20.6 percent of other arson crimes were cleared. (Table 27)

### *Clearances and Juveniles*

When an offender under 18 years of age is cited to appear in juvenile court or before other juvenile authorities, the UCR Program considers the incident for which the juvenile is being held responsible to be cleared by arrest, although a physical arrest may not have occurred. In addition, according to program definitions, clearances that include both adult and juvenile offenders are classified as clearances for crimes committed by adults. Therefore, the juvenile clearance data are limited to those clearances involving juveniles only, and the figures in this publication should not be used to present a definitive picture of juvenile involvement in crime.

Of the clearances for violent crimes that were reported in the nation in 2009, 11.0 percent involved only juveniles, down from 11.9 percent in 2008. In the nation's cities, collectively, 11.2 percent of violent crime clearances involved only juveniles, with juveniles in cities exclusively involved in 5.1 percent of murder clearances, 10.6 percent of forcible rape clearances, 15.0 percent of robbery clearances, and 10.2 percent of aggravated assault clearances. Of the nation's city population groups, cities with 50,000 to 99,999 inhabitants had the highest percentage of overall clearances for violent crime only involving juveniles (12.1 percent); cities with 1,000,000 or more inhabitants had the lowest percentage (8.8 percent). (Table 28)

Law enforcement agencies in metropolitan counties reported that 11.5 percent of their violent crime clearances—including 5.1 percent of their murder clearances, 13.6 percent of their forcible rape clearances, 15.5 percent of their robbery clearances, and 10.7 percent of their aggravated assault clearances—involved only juveniles. Agencies in nonmetropolitan counties reported that 7.6 percent of their clearances for violent crime involved only juveniles, including 2.4 percent of their murder clearances, 14.0 percent of their forcible rape clearances, 6.5 percent of their robbery clearances, and 7.1 percent of their aggravated assault clearances. (Table 28)

In 2009, 17.2 percent of clearances for property crime involved only juveniles. In cities collectively, 17.8 percent of the clearances for property crime, 15.8 percent of clearances for burglary, 18.3 percent of clearances for larceny-theft, 15.1 percent of clearances for motor vehicle theft, and 37.2 percent of clearances for arson involved juveniles only. Among the population groups labeled *city*, the percentages of clearances involving only juveniles for overall property crime ranged from a low of 13.6 percent in cities with populations of 1,000,000 and more inhabitants to a high of 20.1 percent in cities with populations of 100,000 to 249,999.

Metropolitan counties reported 15.1 percent of property crime clearances, 14.0 percent of burglary clearances, 15.6 percent of larceny-theft clearances, 13.9 percent of motor vehicle theft clearances, and 32.0 percent of arson clearances involved persons under 18 years of age. In nonmetropolitan counties, 12.6 percent of property crime clearances, 11.8 percent of burglary clearances, 13.1 percent of larceny-theft clearances, 12.4 percent of motor vehicle theft clearances, and 20.0 percent of arson clearances involved juveniles exclusively. In suburban areas, 38.6 percent of arson clearances involved only juveniles. (Table 28)

Arson offenses had the highest percentage of clearances involving only juveniles—34.7 percent—nationally in 2009. (Table 28) Of clearances for structural arsons, 32.5 percent involved only juveniles. Approximately 14.3 percent of clearances for mobile arsons and 48.5 percent of other property type arsons involved only juveniles. (Expanded Arson Table 2; see Section I for more information)

## Table 25. Number and Percent of Offenses Cleared by Arrest or Exceptional Means, by Population Group, 2009

(Number, percent.)

| Population group | Violent crime | Murder and non-negligent man-slaughter | Forcible rape | Robbery | Aggra-vated assault | Property crime | Burglary | Larceny-theft | Motor vehicle theft | Arson[1] | Number of agencies | 2009 estimated population |
|---|---|---|---|---|---|---|---|---|---|---|---|---|
| **TOTAL ALL AGENCIES:** | | | | | | | | | | | | |
| Offenses known | 1,142,108 | 13,242 | 76,276 | 352,125 | 700,465 | 8,229,516 | 1,957,825 | 5,557,560 | 714,131 | 53,852 | 14,274 | 266,098,836 |
| Percent cleared by arrest | 47.1 | 66.6 | 41.2 | 28.2 | 56.8 | 18.6 | 12.5 | 21.5 | 12.4 | 18.5 | | |
| **Total Cities** | | | | | | | | | | | | |
| Offenses known | 893,944 | 10,026 | 55,544 | 302,854 | 525,520 | 6,384,437 | 1,422,288 | 4,398,412 | 563,737 | 39,818 | 10,328 | 176,953,431 |
| Percent cleared by arrest | 45.1 | 65.3 | 39.8 | 27.6 | 55.4 | 18.7 | 11.9 | 21.9 | 11.2 | 17.7 | | |
| GROUP I (250,000 and over) | | | | | | | | | | | | |
| Offenses known | 375,293 | 4,912 | 17,891 | 150,550 | 201,940 | 1,963,986 | 475,397 | 1,237,912 | 250,677 | 14,840 | 72 | 44,841,811 |
| Percent cleared by arrest | 40.0 | 62.8 | 43.5 | 24.4 | 50.8 | 14.3 | 9.5 | 17.3 | 8.6 | 13.9 | | |
| 1,000,000 and over (Group I subset) | | | | | | | | | | | | |
| Offenses known | 114,591 | 1,440 | 5,273 | 50,962 | 56,916 | 579,607 | 132,761 | 364,507 | 82,339 | 4,587 | 8 | 14,623,806 |
| Percent cleared by arrest | 38.6 | 70.8 | 45.6 | 25.1 | 49.1 | 13.3 | 8.2 | 16.4 | 7.7 | 11.4 | | |
| 500,000 to 999,999 (Group I subset) | | | | | | | | | | | | |
| Offenses known | 148,297 | 1,946 | 6,455 | 56,588 | 83,308 | 790,337 | 194,427 | 500,457 | 95,453 | 5,172 | 24 | 16,276,817 |
| Percent cleared by arrest | 40.5 | 59.8 | 43.1 | 22.5 | 52.1 | 13.6 | 9.2 | 16.2 | 8.7 | 15.2 | | |
| 250,000 to 499,999 (Group I subset) | | | | | | | | | | | | |
| Offenses known | 112,405 | 1,526 | 6,163 | 43,000 | 61,716 | 594,042 | 148,209 | 372,948 | 72,885 | 5,081 | 40 | 13,941,188 |
| Percent cleared by arrest | 40.8 | 59.0 | 42.1 | 26.0 | 50.6 | 16.3 | 11.1 | 19.6 | 9.6 | 14.8 | | |
| GROUP II (100,000 to 249,999) | | | | | | | | | | | | |
| Offenses known | 161,270 | 1,853 | 9,874 | 55,921 | 93,622 | 1,165,153 | 269,953 | 784,051 | 111,149 | 6,574 | 194 | 28,779,842 |
| Percent cleared by arrest | 44.5 | 62.2 | 38.9 | 28.2 | 54.4 | 17.9 | 11.3 | 21.2 | 10.2 | 17.2 | | |
| GROUP III (50,000 to 99,999) | | | | | | | | | | | | |
| Offenses known | 126,490 | 1,197 | 8,585 | 40,110 | 76,598 | 992,763 | 215,528 | 695,647 | 81,588 | 6,223 | 436 | 29,776,055 |
| Percent cleared by arrest | 47.1 | 71.9 | 36.7 | 30.0 | 56.9 | 20.4 | 12.5 | 23.9 | 11.3 | 17.6 | | |
| GROUP IV (25,000 to 49,999) | | | | | | | | | | | | |
| Offenses known | 86,602 | 825 | 6,785 | 25,676 | 53,316 | 800,848 | 163,900 | 587,381 | 49,567 | 4,515 | 746 | 25,666,623 |
| Percent cleared by arrest | 48.6 | 66.8 | 35.2 | 31.6 | 58.2 | 21.8 | 12.4 | 25.2 | 13.3 | 19.9 | | |
| GROUP V (10,000 to 24,999) | | | | | | | | | | | | |
| Offenses known | 79,145 | 684 | 6,722 | 19,109 | 52,630 | 773,613 | 161,949 | 570,470 | 41,194 | 3,760 | 1,628 | 25,757,852 |
| Percent cleared by arrest | 54.2 | 73.1 | 39.4 | 36.1 | 62.5 | 23.4 | 14.8 | 26.2 | 18.2 | 25.1 | | |
| GROUP VI (under 10,000) | | | | | | | | | | | | |
| Offenses known | 65,144 | 555 | 5,687 | 11,488 | 47,414 | 688,074 | 135,561 | 522,951 | 29,562 | 3,906 | 7,252 | 22,131,248 |
| Percent cleared by arrest | 56.3 | 72.3 | 40.6 | 36.0 | 62.9 | 21.4 | 16.0 | 22.7 | 23.3 | 23.6 | | |
| **Metropolitan Counties** | | | | | | | | | | | | |
| Offenses known | 196,862 | 2,337 | 14,645 | 44,988 | 134,892 | 1,449,401 | 395,203 | 930,444 | 123,754 | 10,539 | 1,667 | 64,002,204 |
| Percent cleared by arrest | 52.6 | 67.9 | 44.8 | 30.8 | 60.5 | 18.2 | 13.7 | 20.5 | 15.2 | 19.4 | | |
| **Nonmetropolitan Counties** | | | | | | | | | | | | |
| Offenses known | 51,302 | 879 | 6,087 | 4,283 | 40,053 | 395,678 | 140,334 | 228,704 | 26,640 | 3,495 | 2,279 | 25,143,201 |
| Percent cleared by arrest | 60.3 | 77.7 | 45.5 | 41.9 | 64.1 | 18.3 | 15.8 | 19.2 | 23.6 | 24.6 | | |
| **SUBURBAN AREAS[2]** | | | | | | | | | | | | |
| Offenses known | 336,082 | 3,477 | 25,427 | 82,599 | 224,579 | 2,887,923 | 675,695 | 2,002,073 | 210,155 | 18,054 | 7,540 | 115,777,741 |
| Percent cleared by arrest | 52.8 | 67.9 | 42.5 | 32.1 | 61.3 | 19.9 | 13.9 | 22.4 | 15.3 | 20.8 | | |

[1] Not all agencies submit reports for arson to the FBI. As a result, the number of reports the FBI uses to compute the percent of offenses cleared for arson is less than the number it uses to compute the percent of offenses cleared for all other offenses.

[2] Suburban areas include law enforcement agencies in cities with less than 50,000 inhabitants and county law enforcement agencies that are within a metropolitan statistical area. Suburban areas exclude all metropolitan agencies associated with a principal city. The agencies associated with suburban areas also appear in other groups within this table.

## Table 26. Number and Percent of Offenses Cleared by Arrest or Exceptional Means, by Region and Geographic Division, 2009

(Number, percent.)

| Geographic region/division | Violent crime | Murder and non-negligent man-slaughter | Forcible rape | Robbery | Aggra-vated assault | Property crime | Burglary | Larceny-theft | Motor vehicle theft | Arson[1] | Number of agencies | 2009 estimated population |
|---|---|---|---|---|---|---|---|---|---|---|---|---|
| **TOTAL ALL AGENCIES:** | | | | | | | | | | | | |
| Offenses known | 1,142,108 | 13,242 | 76,276 | 352,125 | 700,465 | 8,229,516 | 1,957,825 | 5,557,560 | 714,131 | 53,852 | 14,274 | 266,098,836 |
| Percent cleared by arrest | 47.1 | 66.6 | 41.2 | 28.2 | 56.8 | 18.6 | 12.5 | 21.5 | 12.4 | 18.5 | | |
| **Northeast** | | | | | | | | | | | | |
| Offenses known | 145,884 | 1,607 | 9,587 | 50,477 | 84,213 | 979,756 | 197,766 | 715,232 | 66,758 | 5,911 | 3,166 | 44,605,809 |
| Percent cleared by arrest | 51.2 | 62.5 | 44.3 | 31.2 | 63.8 | 21.6 | 15.5 | 23.9 | 16.0 | 24.9 | | |
| New England | | | | | | | | | | | | |
| Offenses known | 46,595 | 350 | 3,441 | 12,988 | 29,816 | 328,239 | 68,718 | 235,758 | 23,763 | 1,876 | 896 | 14,001,712 |
| Percent cleared by arrest | 49.2 | 61.1 | 33.9 | 26.2 | 60.8 | 16.9 | 12.9 | 18.7 | 10.5 | 20.2 | | |
| Middle Atlantic | | | | | | | | | | | | |
| Offenses known | 99,289 | 1,257 | 6,146 | 37,489 | 54,397 | 651,517 | 129,048 | 479,474 | 42,995 | 4,035 | 2,270 | 30,604,097 |
| Percent cleared by arrest | 52.1 | 62.9 | 50.1 | 32.9 | 65.4 | 24.0 | 16.9 | 26.4 | 19.1 | 27.0 | | |
| **Midwest** | | | | | | | | | | | | |
| Offenses known | 178,103 | 2,112 | 15,109 | 54,886 | 105,996 | 1,413,869 | 336,042 | 971,695 | 106,132 | 11,518 | 3,503 | 47,539,753 |
| Percent cleared by arrest | 40.5 | 55.3 | 33.3 | 23.5 | 50.1 | 18.5 | 10.6 | 21.8 | 13.0 | 16.4 | | |
| East North Central | | | | | | | | | | | | |
| Offenses known | 118,501 | 1,484 | 10,449 | 40,825 | 65,743 | 899,769 | 232,096 | 597,777 | 69,896 | 7,786 | 1,742 | 29,422,515 |
| Percent cleared by arrest | 36.0 | 50.2 | 31.0 | 22.0 | 45.1 | 16.7 | 9.7 | 20.1 | 11.3 | 15.2 | | |
| West North Central | | | | | | | | | | | | |
| Offenses known | 59,602 | 628 | 4,660 | 14,061 | 40,253 | 514,100 | 103,946 | 373,918 | 36,236 | 3,732 | 1,761 | 18,117,238 |
| Percent cleared by arrest | 49.5 | 67.2 | 38.6 | 27.8 | 58.1 | 21.5 | 12.5 | 24.5 | 16.2 | 18.9 | | |
| **South** | | | | | | | | | | | | |
| Offenses known | 529,435 | 6,429 | 31,569 | 153,267 | 338,170 | 3,843,711 | 982,721 | 2,576,104 | 284,886 | 20,298 | 5,672 | 105,568,056 |
| Percent cleared by arrest | 49.0 | 71.1 | 46.0 | 29.0 | 57.9 | 19.0 | 13.0 | 21.7 | 15.0 | 20.2 | | |
| South Atlantic | | | | | | | | | | | | |
| Offenses known | 279,077 | 3,233 | 14,236 | 83,955 | 177,653 | 1,934,641 | 485,869 | 1,299,821 | 148,951 | 9,592 | 2,760 | 54,839,659 |
| Percent cleared by arrest | 52.0 | 71.9 | 52.5 | 30.4 | 61.8 | 20.7 | 15.2 | 23.3 | 16.1 | 23.1 | | |
| East South Central | | | | | | | | | | | | |
| Offenses known | 73,708 | 986 | 5,179 | 19,936 | 47,607 | 539,333 | 148,167 | 357,996 | 33,170 | 2,582 | 1,208 | 15,990,736 |
| Percent cleared by arrest | 47.6 | 72.6 | 41.3 | 28.4 | 55.8 | 19.9 | 12.4 | 23.3 | 17.4 | 20.3 | | |
| West South Central | | | | | | | | | | | | |
| Offenses known | 176,650 | 2,210 | 12,154 | 49,376 | 112,910 | 1,369,737 | 348,685 | 918,287 | 102,765 | 8,124 | 1,704 | 34,737,661 |
| Percent cleared by arrest | 44.7 | 69.2 | 40.4 | 26.8 | 52.5 | 16.2 | 10.3 | 18.8 | 12.8 | 16.9 | | |
| **West** | | | | | | | | | | | | |
| Offenses known | 288,686 | 3,094 | 20,011 | 93,495 | 172,086 | 1,992,180 | 441,296 | 1,294,529 | 256,355 | 16,125 | 1,933 | 68,385,218 |
| Percent cleared by arrest | 45.7 | 67.2 | 38.3 | 28.1 | 55.7 | 16.4 | 11.5 | 19.7 | 8.2 | 15.5 | | |
| Mountain | | | | | | | | | | | | |
| Offenses known | 82,947 | 882 | 7,513 | 20,932 | 53,620 | 642,960 | 144,478 | 432,605 | 65,877 | 4,465 | 800 | 21,361,759 |
| Percent cleared by arrest | 47.5 | 71.5 | 35.1 | 27.5 | 56.6 | 19.1 | 10.2 | 23.4 | 10.2 | 19.3 | | |
| Pacific | | | | | | | | | | | | |
| Offenses known | 205,739 | 2,212 | 12,498 | 72,563 | 118,466 | 1,349,220 | 296,818 | 861,924 | 190,478 | 11,660 | 1,133 | 47,023,459 |
| Percent cleared by arrest | 44.9 | 65.4 | 40.2 | 28.3 | 55.2 | 15.2 | 12.1 | 17.9 | 7.4 | 14.0 | | |

[1] Not all agencies submit reports for arson to the FBI. As a result, the number of reports the FBI uses to compute the percent of offenses cleared for arson is less than the number it uses to compute the percent of offenses cleared for all other offenses.

## Table 27. Number and Percent of Offenses Cleared by Arrest or Exceptional Means, by Population Group, 2009

(Number, percent.)

| Population group | Forcible rape | | Robbery | | | | Aggravated assault | | | |
|---|---|---|---|---|---|---|---|---|---|---|
| | Rape by force | Assault to rape-attempts | Firearm | Knife or cutting instrument | Other weapon | Strong-arm | Firearm | Knife or cutting instrument | Other weapon | Hands, fists, feet, etc. |
| **TOTAL ALL AGENCIES:** | | | | | | | | | | |
| Offenses known | 65,382 | 4,928 | 134,158 | 24,619 | 27,290 | 129,041 | 130,528 | 116,629 | 203,712 | 166,709 |
| Percent cleared by arrest | 40.0 | 43.1 | 22.5 | 31.1 | 29.8 | 32.2 | 41.2 | 63.4 | 56.9 | 61.2 |
| **Total Cities** | | | | | | | | | | |
| Offenses known | 48,398 | 3,928 | 116,344 | 21,567 | 23,809 | 115,165 | 104,844 | 93,852 | 158,731 | 119,511 |
| Percent cleared by arrest | 38.8 | 42.9 | 22.2 | 30.5 | 29.1 | 31.6 | 38.7 | 62.5 | 55.6 | 60.5 |
| GROUP I (250,000 and over) | | | | | | | | | | |
| Offenses known | 15,720 | 1,650 | 65,437 | 10,322 | 10,771 | 54,951 | 54,622 | 36,815 | 67,311 | 29,182 |
| Percent cleared by arrest | 42.7 | 43.5 | 19.9 | 27.6 | 26.1 | 28.2 | 35.2 | 60.6 | 52.1 | 53.1 |
| 1,000,000 and over (Group I subset) | | | | | | | | | | |
| Offenses known | 4,610 | 663 | 23,022 | 4,216 | 3,867 | 19,857 | 15,865 | 12,223 | 20,897 | 7,931 |
| Percent cleared by arrest | 46.2 | 41.8 | 19.9 | 27.3 | 27.0 | 30.4 | 35.0 | 58.9 | 51.8 | 55.3 |
| 500,000 to 999,999 (Group I subset) | | | | | | | | | | |
| Offenses known | 5,548 | 531 | 24,731 | 3,425 | 3,865 | 18,501 | 21,344 | 14,239 | 27,330 | 10,738 |
| Percent cleared by arrest | 41.4 | 43.3 | 17.8 | 26.5 | 24.8 | 24.8 | 36.1 | 59.4 | 49.7 | 51.2 |
| 250,000 to 499,999 (Group I subset) | | | | | | | | | | |
| Offenses known | 5,562 | 456 | 17,684 | 2,681 | 3,039 | 16,593 | 17,413 | 10,353 | 19,084 | 10,513 |
| Percent cleared by arrest | 41.2 | 46.3 | 22.9 | 29.4 | 26.5 | 29.3 | 34.2 | 64.2 | 55.9 | 53.3 |
| GROUP II (100,000 to 249,999) | | | | | | | | | | |
| Offenses known | 8,242 | 537 | 19,744 | 3,962 | 4,699 | 20,136 | 18,171 | 17,936 | 27,635 | 16,119 |
| Percent cleared by arrest | 37.4 | 39.1 | 22.3 | 32.7 | 30.6 | 32.2 | 37.0 | 62.8 | 54.9 | 62.1 |
| GROUP III (50,000 to 99,999) | | | | | | | | | | |
| Offenses known | 7,427 | 529 | 12,610 | 3,040 | 3,418 | 16,645 | 12,205 | 13,925 | 22,113 | 19,723 |
| Percent cleared by arrest | 35.9 | 42.0 | 24.8 | 28.8 | 30.0 | 33.4 | 41.2 | 62.3 | 58.2 | 60.9 |
| GROUP IV (25,000 to 49,999) | | | | | | | | | | |
| Offenses known | 6,024 | 368 | 8,498 | 1,977 | 2,349 | 10,420 | 7,753 | 9,308 | 15,612 | 15,573 |
| Percent cleared by arrest | 33.9 | 41.6 | 26.3 | 32.5 | 31.5 | 35.1 | 43.3 | 62.3 | 58.1 | 62.0 |
| GROUP V (10,000 to 24,999) | | | | | | | | | | |
| Offenses known | 5,928 | 416 | 6,209 | 1,403 | 1,635 | 7,790 | 6,792 | 8,751 | 14,520 | 17,621 |
| Percent cleared by arrest | 38.7 | 45.2 | 30.3 | 39.6 | 36.9 | 41.0 | 51.8 | 66.8 | 62.7 | 64.8 |
| GROUP VI (under 10,000) | | | | | | | | | | |
| Offenses known | 5,057 | 428 | 3,846 | 863 | 937 | 5,223 | 5,301 | 7,117 | 11,540 | 21,293 |
| Percent cleared by arrest | 39.5 | 45.6 | 29.4 | 42.5 | 34.7 | 39.5 | 52.6 | 67.3 | 60.4 | 64.5 |
| **Metropolitan Counties** | | | | | | | | | | |
| Offenses known | 11,475 | 707 | 16,101 | 2,717 | 2,985 | 12,502 | 18,956 | 17,500 | 34,667 | 32,843 |
| Percent cleared by arrest | 42.7 | 44.7 | 23.1 | 33.7 | 33.6 | 36.2 | 48.1 | 66.6 | 61.0 | 63.0 |
| **Nonmetropolitan Counties** | | | | | | | | | | |
| Offenses known | 5,509 | 293 | 1,713 | 335 | 496 | 1,374 | 6,728 | 5,277 | 10,314 | 14,355 |
| Percent cleared by arrest | 44.7 | 41.0 | 35.7 | 44.8 | 37.3 | 46.2 | 59.8 | 67.6 | 64.0 | 62.8 |
| **SUBURBAN AREAS**[2] | | | | | | | | | | |
| Offenses known | 20,909 | 1,341 | 28,115 | 5,348 | 6,141 | 28,004 | 29,306 | 31,214 | 59,171 | 64,243 |
| Percent cleared by arrest | 40.9 | 43.2 | 24.6 | 35.0 | 33.8 | 37.6 | 48.6 | 66.8 | 61.5 | 64.0 |

[2] Suburban areas include law enforcement agencies in cities with less than 50,000 inhabitants and county law enforcement agencies that are within a Metropolitan Statistical Area. Suburban areas exclude all metropolitan agencies associated with a principal city. The agencies associated with suburban areas also appear in other groups within this table.

## Table 27. Number and Percent of Offenses Cleared by Arrest or Exceptional Means, by Population Group, 2009—*Continued*

(Number, percent.)

| Population group | Burglary | | | Motor vehicle theft | | | Arson[1] | | | Number of agencies | 2009 estimated population |
|---|---|---|---|---|---|---|---|---|---|---|---|
| | Forcible entry | Unlawful entry | Attempted forcible entry | Autos | Trucks and buses | Other vehicles | Structure | Mobile | Other | | |
| **TOTAL ALL AGENCIES:** | | | | | | | | | | | |
| Offenses known | 1,071,265 | 573,780 | 109,942 | 478,283 | 109,074 | 67,697 | 22,026 | 14,272 | 13,715 | 13,664 | 246,214,054 |
| Percent cleared by arrest | 11.7 | 13.7 | 10.8 | 12.7 | 9.6 | 10.7 | 22.8 | 8.8 | 20.6 | | |
| **Total Cities** | | | | | | | | | | | |
| Offenses known | 796,132 | 423,642 | 85,804 | 395,349 | 87,136 | 44,078 | 16,775 | 10,025 | 10,234 | 9,989 | 166,603,985 |
| Percent cleared by arrest | 11.0 | 13.3 | 10.6 | 11.6 | 8.4 | 9.9 | 21.6 | 8.1 | 20.5 | | |
| GROUP I (250,000 and over) | | | | | | | | | | | |
| Offenses known | 307,754 | 111,617 | 28,565 | 173,135 | 50,510 | 15,790 | 6,091 | 4,764 | 2,991 | 68 | 42,628,554 |
| Percent cleared by arrest | 8.8 | 10.9 | 9.7 | 9.1 | 6.1 | 8.5 | 18.5 | 5.8 | 17.3 | | |
| 1,000,000 and over (Group I subset) | | | | | | | | | | | |
| Offenses known | 94,331 | 31,731 | 6,699 | 51,675 | 23,518 | 7,146 | 1,737 | 1,848 | 1,002 | 8 | 14,623,806 |
| Percent cleared by arrest | 7.7 | 9.0 | 11.2 | 9.5 | 4.3 | 5.5 | 17.7 | 5.1 | 12.2 | | |
| 500,000 to 999,999 (Group I subset) | | | | | | | | | | | |
| Offenses known | 122,383 | 40,145 | 12,795 | 66,943 | 16,193 | 4,972 | 2,104 | 1,432 | 942 | 22 | 14,827,998 |
| Percent cleared by arrest | 8.3 | 10.8 | 8.8 | 8.4 | 6.4 | 10.2 | 19.2 | 6.1 | 19.7 | | |
| 250,000 to 499,999 (Group I subset) | | | | | | | | | | | |
| Offenses known | 91,040 | 39,741 | 9,071 | 54,517 | 10,799 | 3,672 | 2,250 | 1,484 | 1,047 | 38 | 13,176,750 |
| Percent cleared by arrest | 10.5 | 12.6 | 9.8 | 9.7 | 9.5 | 12.1 | 18.6 | 6.3 | 20.1 | | |
| GROUP II (100,000 to 249,999) | | | | | | | | | | | |
| Offenses known | 140,839 | 75,945 | 14,994 | 75,842 | 14,881 | 7,899 | 2,599 | 1,571 | 1,710 | 174 | 25,619,584 |
| Percent cleared by arrest | 10.4 | 12.4 | 9.9 | 9.8 | 9.3 | 8.0 | 19.6 | 9.0 | 21.3 | | |
| GROUP III (50,000 to 99,999) | | | | | | | | | | | |
| Offenses known | 111,941 | 70,459 | 13,166 | 59,582 | 9,573 | 6,491 | 2,520 | 1,515 | 1,835 | 405 | 27,740,206 |
| Percent cleared by arrest | 11.5 | 13.9 | 10.8 | 11.3 | 10.0 | 9.9 | 21.7 | 8.7 | 18.7 | | |
| GROUP IV (25,000 to 49,999) | | | | | | | | | | | |
| Offenses known | 84,209 | 56,938 | 10,110 | 36,206 | 4,593 | 5,282 | 1,765 | 902 | 1,542 | 712 | 24,483,825 |
| Percent cleared by arrest | 11.7 | 13.2 | 10.8 | 13.7 | 12.2 | 9.3 | 23.3 | 10.3 | 20.4 | | |
| GROUP V (10,000 to 24,999) | | | | | | | | | | | |
| Offenses known | 82,536 | 56,281 | 10,205 | 29,682 | 4,388 | 4,440 | 1,708 | 687 | 1,130 | 1,555 | 24,581,401 |
| Percent cleared by arrest | 14.6 | 15.5 | 12.6 | 19.3 | 15.9 | 12.4 | 28.5 | 14.1 | 26.6 | | |
| GROUP VI (under 10,000) | | | | | | | | | | | |
| Offenses known | 68,853 | 52,402 | 8,764 | 20,902 | 3,191 | 4,176 | 2,092 | 586 | 1,026 | 7,075 | 21,550,415 |
| Percent cleared by arrest | 15.9 | 16.1 | 12.2 | 24.9 | 21.0 | 16.8 | 26.0 | 13.1 | 25.0 | | |
| **Metropolitan Counties** | | | | | | | | | | | |
| Offenses known | 192,614 | 106,291 | 18,472 | 67,615 | 18,103 | 17,294 | 3,530 | 3,459 | 2,666 | 1,493 | 55,420,041 |
| Percent cleared by arrest | 12.7 | 14.7 | 10.9 | 16.0 | 12.2 | 11.2 | 26.6 | 9.0 | 19.8 | | |
| **Nonmetropolitan Counties** | | | | | | | | | | | |
| Offenses known | 82,519 | 43,847 | 5,666 | 15,319 | 3,835 | 6,325 | 1,721 | 788 | 815 | 2,182 | 24,190,028 |
| Percent cleared by arrest | 15.8 | 15.1 | 12.2 | 26.0 | 24.1 | 15.2 | 27.1 | 15.7 | 24.3 | | |
| **SUBURBAN AREAS[2]** | | | | | | | | | | | |
| Offenses known | 330,998 | 205,296 | 36,948 | 129,654 | 26,977 | 26,428 | 6,716 | 4,795 | 5,139 | 7,148 | 104,830,867 |
| Percent cleared by arrest | 13.0 | 14.9 | 11.3 | 15.9 | 12.7 | 11.4 | 26.6 | 9.7 | 21.6 | | |

[1] Not all agencies submit reports for arson to the FBI. As a result, the number of reports the FBI uses to compute the percent of offenses cleared for arson is less than the number it uses to compute the percent of offenses cleared for all other offenses. Agencies must report arson clearances by detailed property classification as specified on the *Monthly Return of Arson Offenses Known to Law Enforcement* to be included in this table; therefore, clearances in this table may differ from other clearance tables.

[2] Suburban areas include law enforcement agencies in cities with less than 50,000 inhabitants and county law enforcement agencies that are within a Metropolitan Statistical Area. Suburban areas exclude all metropolitan agencies associated with a principal city. The agencies associated with suburban areas also appear in other groups within this table.

## Table 28. Number of Offenses Cleared by Arrest or Exceptional Means and Percent Involving Persons Under 18 Years of Age, by Population Group, 2009

(Number, percent.)

| Population group | Violent crime | Murder and non-negligent man-slaughter | Forcible rape | Robbery | Aggra-vated assault | Property crime | Burglary | Larceny-theft | Motor vehicle theft | Arson[1] | Number of agencies | 2009 estimated population |
|---|---|---|---|---|---|---|---|---|---|---|---|---|
| **TOTAL ALL AGENCIES:** | | | | | | | | | | | | |
| Offenses known | 458,914 | 7,631 | 27,748 | 85,688 | 337,847 | 1,337,882 | 209,717 | 1,051,693 | 76,472 | 9,241 | 13,350 | 469,703,487 |
| Percent under 18 years old | 11.0 | 4.8 | 11.4 | 14.9 | 10.1 | 17.2 | 15.1 | 17.7 | 14.7 | 34.7 | | |
| **Total Cities** | | | | | | | | | | | | |
| Offenses known | 353,891 | 5,761 | 20,081 | 74,119 | 253,930 | 1,072,255 | 149,197 | 866,803 | 56,255 | 6,634 | 9,833 | 391,965,135 |
| Percent under 18 years old | 11.2 | 5.1 | 10.6 | 15.0 | 10.2 | 17.8 | 15.8 | 18.3 | 15.1 | 37.2 | | |
| GROUP I (250,000 and over) | | | | | | | | | | | | |
| Offenses known | 133,484 | 2,716 | 7,293 | 33,422 | 90,053 | 260,657 | 41,475 | 199,217 | 19,965 | 1,958 | 66 | 41,773,817 |
| Percent under 18 years old | 9.9 | 5.2 | 7.9 | 14.1 | 8.7 | 16.0 | 16.0 | 16.2 | 14.3 | 31.3 | | |
| 1,000,000 and over (Group I subset) | | | | | | | | | | | | |
| Offenses known | 44,195 | 1,020 | 2,405 | 12,802 | 27,968 | 76,932 | 10,881 | 59,735 | 6,316 | 523 | 8 | 14,623,806 |
| Percent under 18 years old | 8.8 | 4.2 | 7.2 | 12.3 | 7.5 | 13.6 | 13.5 | 13.8 | 11.1 | 27.5 | | |
| 500,000 to 999,999 (Group I subset) | | | | | | | | | | | | |
| Offenses known | 46,928 | 847 | 2,412 | 10,229 | 33,440 | 94,218 | 15,269 | 71,910 | 7,039 | 709 | 21 | 14,228,341 |
| Percent under 18 years old | 10.3 | 5.7 | 8.1 | 15.2 | 9.1 | 16.3 | 18.4 | 15.9 | 16.2 | 32.0 | | |
| 250,000 to 499,999 (Group I subset) | | | | | | | | | | | | |
| Offenses known | 42,361 | 849 | 2,476 | 10,391 | 28,645 | 89,507 | 15,325 | 67,572 | 6,610 | 726 | 37 | 12,921,670 |
| Percent under 18 years old | 10.7 | 5.8 | 8.2 | 15.4 | 9.3 | 17.8 | 15.4 | 18.6 | 15.3 | 33.2 | | |
| GROUP II (100,000 to 249,999) | | | | | | | | | | | | |
| Offenses known | 60,059 | 978 | 3,220 | 13,430 | 42,431 | 174,640 | 25,039 | 140,362 | 9,239 | 1,011 | 172 | 253,899,946 |
| Percent under 18 years old | 11.8 | 6.0 | 11.4 | 17.3 | 10.2 | 20.1 | 17.2 | 20.8 | 16.9 | 34.0 | | |
| GROUP III (50,000 to 99,999) | | | | | | | | | | | | |
| Offenses known | 52,003 | 751 | 2,850 | 10,365 | 38,037 | 179,396 | 23,599 | 147,759 | 8,038 | 1,045 | 399 | 27,309,526 |
| Percent under 18 years old | 12.1 | 4.7 | 11.5 | 15.8 | 11.3 | 20.0 | 15.4 | 20.9 | 16.2 | 39.6 | | |
| GROUP IV (25,000 to 49,999) | | | | | | | | | | | | |
| Offenses known | 37,450 | 504 | 2,180 | 7,193 | 27,573 | 157,773 | 18,070 | 133,817 | 5,886 | 844 | 697 | 23,975,054 |
| Percent under 18 years old | 12.2 | 4.2 | 12.5 | 15.9 | 11.4 | 18.9 | 15.7 | 19.5 | 16.2 | 43.6 | | |
| GROUP V (10,000 to 24,999) | | | | | | | | | | | | |
| Offenses known | 37,386 | 446 | 2,379 | 5,963 | 28,598 | 162,988 | 21,228 | 135,001 | 6,759 | 882 | 1,512 | 23,868,699 |
| Percent under 18 years old | 11.8 | 4.9 | 12.6 | 12.9 | 11.6 | 17.0 | 15.1 | 17.4 | 13.7 | 43.8 | | |
| GROUP VI (under 10,000) | | | | | | | | | | | | |
| Offenses known | 33,509 | 366 | 2,159 | 3,746 | 27,238 | 136,801 | 19,786 | 110,647 | 6,368 | 894 | 6,987 | 21,138,093 |
| Percent under 18 years old | 11.7 | 4.1 | 13.1 | 13.4 | 11.5 | 15.2 | 15.2 | 15.3 | 14.2 | 38.8 | | |
| **Metropolitan Counties** | | | | | | | | | | | | |
| Offenses known | 77,647 | 1,247 | 5,131 | 10,021 | 61,248 | 200,481 | 40,723 | 145,232 | 14,526 | 1,801 | 1,411 | 54,109,000 |
| Percent under 18 years old | 11.5 | 5.1 | 13.6 | 15.5 | 10.7 | 15.1 | 14.0 | 15.6 | 13.9 | 32.0 | | |
| **Nonmetropolitan Counties** | | | | | | | | | | | | |
| Offenses known | 27,376 | 623 | 2,536 | 1,548 | 22,669 | 65,146 | 19,797 | 39,658 | 5,691 | 806 | 2,106 | 23,629,352 |
| Percent under 18 years old | 7.6 | 2.4 | 14.0 | 6.5 | 7.1 | 12.6 | 11.8 | 13.1 | 12.4 | 20.0 | | |
| **SUBURBAN AREAS[2]** | | | | | | | | | | | | |
| Offenses known | 142,078 | 1,938 | 8,976 | 21,027 | 110,137 | 478,877 | 75,659 | 376,769 | 26,449 | 3,402 | 6,981 | 102,471,266 |
| Percent under 18 years old | 12.2 | 4.9 | 13.6 | 15.4 | 11.6 | 16.4 | 14.7 | 16.9 | 14.0 | 38.6 | | |

[1] Not all agencies submit reports for arson to the FBI. As a result, the number of reports the FBI uses to compute the percent of offenses cleared for arson is less than the number it uses to compute the percent of offenses cleared for all other offenses.

[2] Suburban areas include law enforcement agencies in cities with less than 50,000 inhabitants and county law enforcement agencies that are within a Metropolitan Statistical Area. Suburban areas exclude all metropolitan agencies associated with a principal city. The agencies associated with suburban areas also appear in other groups within this table.

## SECTION IV:

# PERSONS ARRESTED

# PERSONS ARRESTED

Percent Change in the Number of Persons Arrested, by Selected Offense, 2000–2009

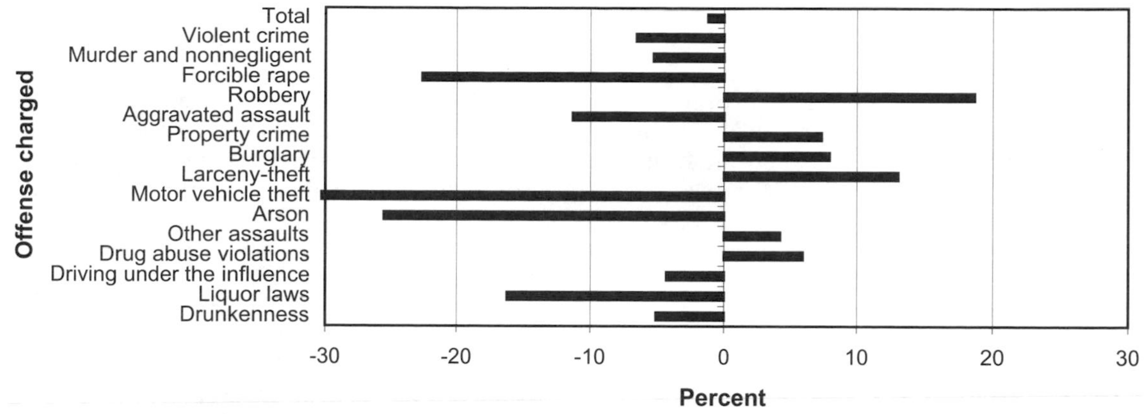


In the Uniform Crime Reporting (UCR) Program, one arrest is counted for each separate instance in which an individual is arrested, cited, or summoned for criminal acts in Part I and Part II crimes. (See Appendix II for additional information concerning Part I and Part II crimes.) One person may be arrested multiple times during the year; as a result, the arrest figures in this section should not be taken as the total number of individuals arrested. Instead, it provides the number of arrest occurrences reported by law enforcement. Information regarding the UCR Program's statistical methodology and table construction can be found in Appendix I.

## National Volume, Trends, and Rates

### *Volume*

The FBI estimated that 13,687,241 arrests occurred in 2009 for all offenses (except traffic violations). Of these arrests, 581,765 were for violent crimes and 1,728,285 were for property crimes. Of the total violent crimes in 2009, aggravated assaults accounted for 72.4 percent, or 421,215 incidents. Robbery had the next highest proportion with 21.8 percent, followed by forcible rape (3.7 percent) and murder and nonnegligent manslaughter (2.1 percent). Of the estimated 1,728,285 arrests for property crimes in 2009, 1,728,285 (77.2 percent) were for larceny-theft, 299,351 (17.3 percent) were for burglary, 81,797 (4.7 percent) were for motor vehicle theft, and 12,204 (0.7 percent) were for arson. (Table 29) The most frequent arrests made in 2009 were for drug abuse violations (estimated at 1,663,582 arrests). These arrests made up 12.6 percent of the total number of all arrests.

A comparison of arrest figures from 2008 to 2009 revealed a 2.4 percent decrease. Arrests for violent crimes decreased 2.3 percent, while arrests for property crimes increased 1.6 percent during the 2-year period. (Table 36) An examination of the 5-year and 10-year arrest trends showed that the total number of arrests in 2009 fell 3.7 percent from the 2005 total. Arrests for violent crimes showed a 4.3 percent decrease from 2005 to 2009 and property crimes showed a 7.0 percent increase. (Table 34) In the 10-year trend data (2000 to 2009), the number of arrests decreased by 1.2 percent. For violent crimes, the number of arrests fell 6.6 percent, while arrests for property crimes increased 7.4 percent. (Tables 32)

The number of adults arrested for violent crime (arrestees age 18 years and over) decreased 1.2 percent from 2008 to 2009, decreased 2.1 percent from 2005 to 2009, but increased 3.4 percent from 2000 to 2009. The number of juveniles arrested for violent crime (arrestees under 18 years of age) decreased 8.9 percent from 2008 to 2009, decreased 12.1 percent from 2005 to 2009, and decreased 20.2 percent from 2000 to 2009. (Tables 32, 34, and 36)

### *Trends*

The trend data for murder showed that the number of arrests for this offense decreased 4.8 percent from 2008 to 2009, decreased 9.2 percent from 2005 to 2009, and decreased 5.3 percent from 2000 to 2009. The number of adults arrested for murder declined 4.3 percent from 2008 to 2009, decreased 9.6 percent from 2005 to 2009, and fell 5.8 percent from 2000 to 2009. The number of juveniles arrested for murder fell 9.0 percent from 2008 to 2009, decreased 4.9 percent from 2005 to 2009, and fell 0.6 percent from 2000 to 2009. (Tables 32, 34, and 36)

For forcible rape, the 2-year trend data showed that arrests decreased 5.7 percent from 2008 to 2009, with adult arrests decreasing 5.4 percent and juvenile arrests dropping 7.0 percent. The 5-year trend data showed that arrests decreased

16.3 percent from 2005 to 2009; adult arrests decreased 15.5 percent and juvenile arrests declined 20.7 percent during this period. The 10-year trend data showed that forcible rape arrests dropped 22.6 percent from 2000 to 2009, with adult arrests falling 20.8 percent and juvenile arrests falling 31.9 percent. (Tables 32, 34, and 36)

For robbery, the 2-year trend data showed that arrests decreased 3.2 percent from 2008 to 2009, with adult arrests falling 0.4 percent and juvenile arrests decreasing 10.7 percent. The 5-year trend data showed that total robbery arrests rose 9.3 percent from 2005 to 2009; adult arrests rose 9.6 percent and juvenile arrests rose 8.3 percent during this period. The 10-year trend data showed that arrests rose 18.7 percent from 2000 to 2009, with adult arrests increasing 19.0 percent and juvenile arrests increasing 18.0 percent. (Tables 32, 34, and 36)

The aggravated assault trend data showed that the number of arrests for this offense fell 1.8 percent from 2008 to 2009, dropped 7.0 percent from 2005 to 2009, and fell 11.3 percent from 2000 to 2009. The number of adults arrested for aggravated assault percent decreased 0.5 percent from 2008 to 2009, declined 4.7 percent from 2005 to 2009, and declined 8.8 percent from 2000 to 2009. The number of juveniles arrested for aggravated assault dropped 10.6 percent from 2008 to 2009, fell 20.9 percent from 2005 to 2009, and dropped 27.2 percent from 2000 to 2009. (Tables 32, 34, and 36)

The 2-year, 5-year, and 10-year trend data showed that the number of arrests for property crime increased 1.6 percent from 2008 to 2009, increased 7.0 percent from 2005 to 2009, and increased 7.4 percent from 2000 to 2009. The number of adults arrested for property crime offenses (arrestees age 18 years and over) increased 3.9 percent from 2008 to 2009, increased 9.8 percent from 2005 to 2009, and increased 12.1 percent from 2000 to 2009. The number of juveniles arrested for property crime (arrestees under 18 years of age) decreased 4.7 percent from 2008 to 2009, decreased 0.7 percent from 2005 to 2009, and decreased 20.3 percent from 2000 to 2009. (Tables 32, 34, and 36)

The trend data for burglary showed that the number of arrests for this offense decreased 3.8 percent from 2008 to 2009, increased 1.8 percent from 2005 to 2009, and increased 8.0 percent from 2000 to 2009. The number of adults arrested for burglary fell 0.9 percent from 2008 to 2009, rose 4.2 percent from 2005 to 2009, and rose 22.8 percent from 2000 to 2009. The number of juveniles arrested for burglary decreased 11.4 percent from 2008 to 2009, decreased 4.9 percent from 2005 to 2009, and fell 20.9 percent from 2000 to 2009. (Tables 32, 34, and 36)

For larceny-theft, the 2-year trend data showed that arrests increased 4.5 percent from 2008 to 2009, with adult arrests increasing 6.7 percent and juvenile arrests decreasing 1.7 percent. The 5-year trend data showed that total larceny-theft arrests increased 15.1 percent from 2005 to 2009; adult arrests increased 18.0 percent and juvenile arrests rose 7.1 percent during this period. The 10-year trend data showed that larceny-theft arrests rose 13.1 percent from 2000 to 2009, with adult arrests increasing 26.6 percent and juvenile arrests falling 15.1 percent. (Tables 32, 34, and 36)

For motor vehicle theft, the 2-year trend data showed that arrests declined 16.9 percent from 2008 to 2009, with adult arrests decreasing 16.0 percent and juvenile arrests decreasing 19.7 percent. The 5-year trend data showed that total motor vehicle theft arrests fell 43.5 percent from 2005 to 2009; adult arrests declined 42.3 percent and juvenile arrests fell 46.7 percent during this period. The 10-year trend data showed that arrests dropped 40.7 percent from 2000 to 2009, with adult arrests falling 30.5 percent and juvenile arrests dropping 59.6 percent. (Tables 32, 34, and 36)

The arson trend data showed that the number of arrests for this offense decreased 15.1 percent from 2008 to 2009, fell 26.6 percent from 2005 to 2009, and fell 25.5 percent from 2000 to 2009. The number of adults arrested for arson fell 12.8 percent from 2008 to 2009, decreased 20.4 percent from 2005 to 2009, and decreased 14.1 percent from 2000 to 2009. The number of juveniles arrested for arson declined by 17.7 percent from 2008 to 2009, dropped 32.8 percent from 2005 to 2009, and dropped 35.3 percent from 2000 to 2009. (Tables 32, 34, and 36)

### *Rates*

The rate of arrests was estimated at 4,478.0 arrests per 100,000 inhabitants in 2009. The arrest rate for violent crime was 191.2 per 100,000 inhabitants, and the arrest rate for property crime was 571.1 per 100,000 inhabitants. Law enforcement agencies throughout the nation reported 4.1 murder arrests, 7.0 forcible rape arrests, 42.0 robbery arrests, and 138.2 aggravated assault arrests per 100,000 inhabitants in 2009. Rates for all violent crimes were down from the 2008 rates. Law enforcement agencies throughout the nation reported 571.1 property crime arrests, 98.1 burglary arrests, 442.3 larceny-theft arrests, 26.8 motor vehicle theft arrests, and 4.0 arson arrests per 100,000 inhabitants in 2009. Rates for all property crimes, except Larceny-theft, were down from the 2008 rates. (Table 30)

## By Age, Sex, and Race

Law enforcement agencies that contributed arrest data to the UCR Program reported information on the age, sex, and race of the persons they arrested. According to the 2009 data, adults accounted for 85.9 percent of arrestees nationally. (Table 38)

A review of arrest data by age from 2008 to 2009 showed that arrests of adults decreased 1.2 percent during this period. Arrests of adults for property crimes increased 3.9 percent, and arrests of adults for violent crimes decreased 0.8 percent over the same time span. The arrest total for juveniles (those under 18 years of age) decreased 8.9 percent from 2008 to 2009. Over the 2-year period, arrests of juveniles for violent crimes fell 10.5 percent; juvenile arrests for property crimes decreased 4.7 percent. (Table 36)

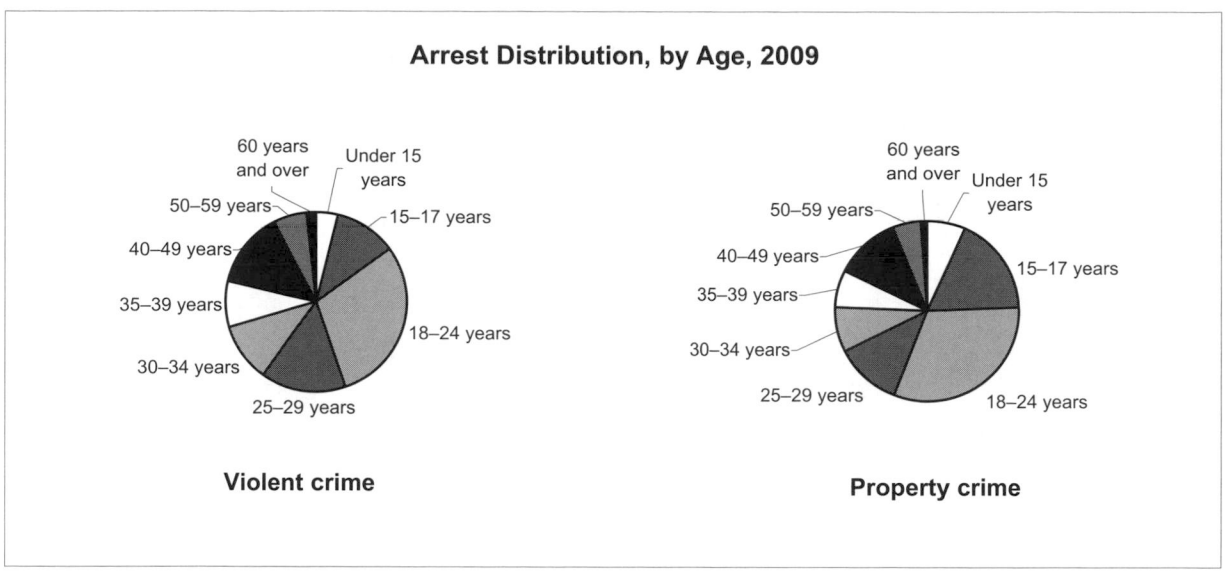

**Arrest Distribution, by Age, 2009**

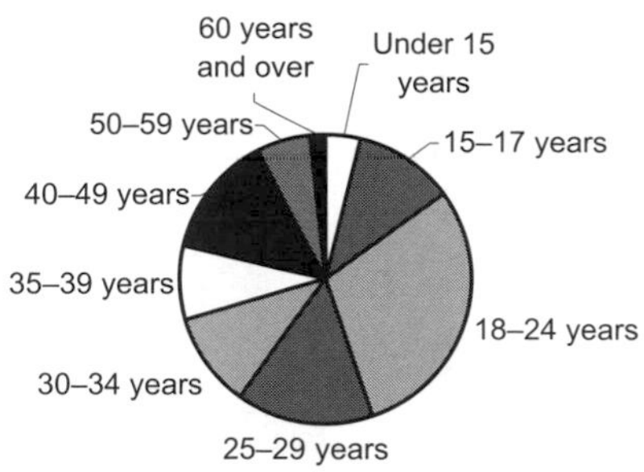


Violent crime

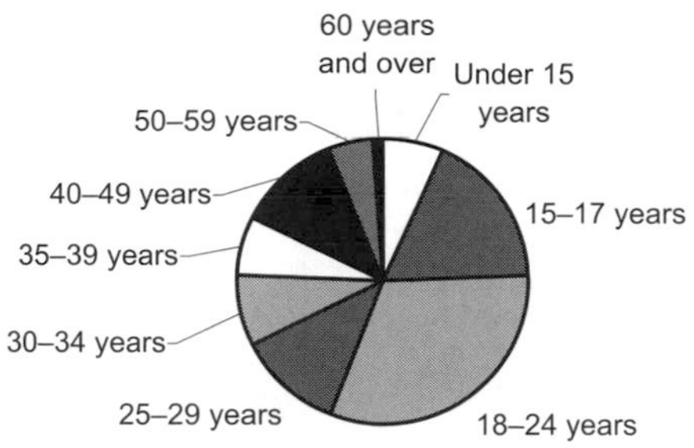


Property crime

By sex, males accounted for 74.7 percent of all persons arrested. Males represented 81.2 percent of arrestees for violent crime, 89.6 percent of arrestees for murder, 98.7 percent of arrestees for forcible rape, 88.2 percent for robbery, and 78.0 percent for aggravated assault. Females accounted for 18.8 percent of violent crime arrestees, 10.4 percent of murder arrestees, 1.3 percent of forcible rape arrestees, 11.8 percent of robbery arrestees, and 22.0 percent of aggravated assault arrestees. (Table 42)

In 2009, most arrestees for property crime (85.9 percent) were over 18 years of age. By sex, males accounted for 65.6 percent of arrestees for property crime, 85.1 percent of arrestees for burglary, 56.3 percent of arrestees for larceny-theft, 82.2 percent of arrestees for motor vehicle theft, and 83.0 percent of arrestees for arson. Females accounted for 37.4 percent of property crime arrestees. Of the four property crimes, larceny-theft had the highest proportion of female arrestees at 43.7 percent. (Tables 38 and 42)

In 2009, 69.1 percent of all persons arrested were White; 28.3 percent were Black; and the remaining 2.6 percent were of other races (American Indian or Alaskan Native and Asian or Pacific Islander). Of all arrestees for violent crimes, 58.7 percent were White, 38.9 percent were Black, and 2.3 percent were of other races. For murder, 48.7 percent of arrestees were White, 49.3 percent were Black, and 2.0 percent were of other races. For forcible rape, 65.1 percent of arrestees were White, 32.5 percent were Black, and 2.4 percent were of other races. For robbery, 42.8 percent of arrestees were White, 55.5 percent of arrestees were Black, and 1.7 percent were of other races. For aggravated assault, 63.5 percent of arrestees were White, 33.9 percent of arrestees were Black, and 2.6 percent were of other races. (Table 43)

Of all arrestees for property crimes, 67.6 percent were White, 29.8 percent were Black, and 2.6 percent were of other races. For burglary, 66.5 percent of arrestees were White, 31.7 percent were Black, and 1.8 percent were of other races. For larceny-theft, 68.1 percent of arrestees were White, 29.0 percent were Black, and 2.8 percent were of other races. For motor vehicle theft, 61.1 percent of arrestees were White, 36.3 percent of arrestees were Black, and 2.6 percent were of other races. For arson, 74.8 percent of arrestees were White, 22.8 percent of arrestees were Black, and 2.4 percent were of other races. (Table 43)

White adults were most commonly arrested for driving under the influence (954,444 arrests) and drug abuse violations (845,974 arrests). Black adults were most frequently arrested for drug abuse violations (437,623 arrests) and other assaults (simple) (332,435 arrests). (Table 43)

## Regional Arrest Rates

The UCR Program divides the United States into four regions: the Northeast, the Midwest, the South, and the West. (Appendix III provides more information about the regions.) Law enforcement agencies in the Northeast had an overall arrest rate of 3,625.2 arrests per 100,000 inhabitants, well below the national rate (4,478.0 arrests per 100,000 inhabitants). In this region, the arrest rate for violent crimes was 168.8 arrests per 100,000 inhabitants, and for property crime, the arrest rate was 467.0 arrests per 100,000 inhabitants. In the Midwest, law enforcement agencies reported an arrest rate of 4,396.6 arrests per 100,000 inhabitants. The arrest rate for violent crimes was 145.7 and the arrest rate for property crime was 581.5. Law enforcement agencies in the South, the nation's most populous region, reported an arrest rate of 5,075.1 per 100,000 inhabitants. Arrests for violent crime occurred at a rate of 182.5 arrests per 100,000 residents, and for property crime, the arrest rate was 652.9 arrests per 100,000 inhabitants. In the Western states, law enforcement agencies reported an overall arrest rate of 4,411.2 arrests per 100,000 inhabitants. The

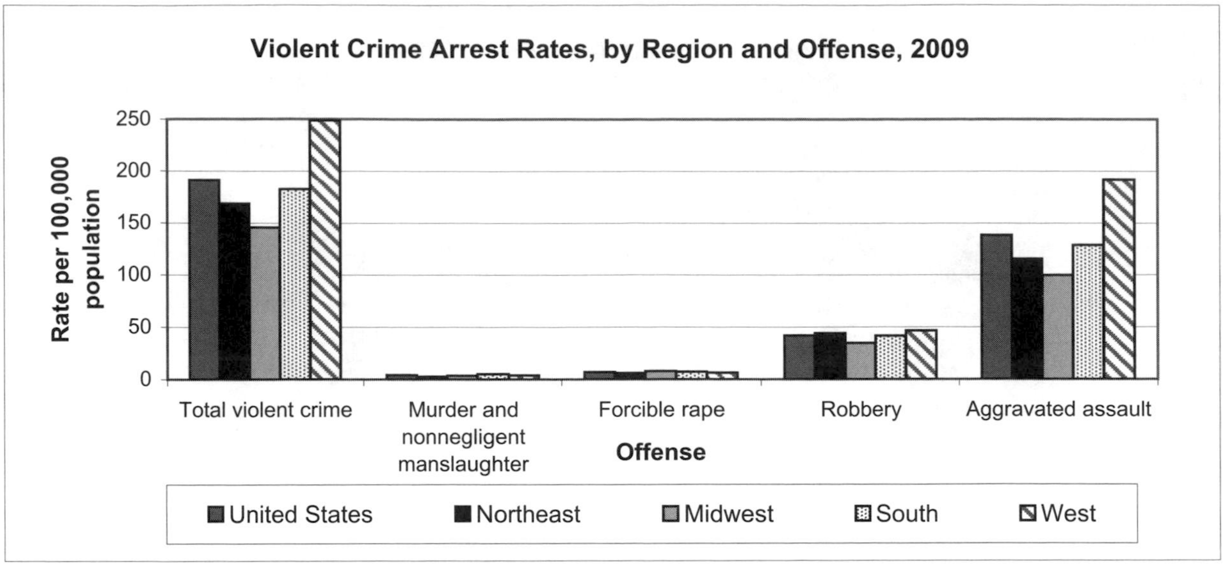


region's violent crime arrest rate was 248.7, while its property crime arrest rate was 538.0. (Table 30)

The regional murder arrest rates were 2.8 in the Northeast, 3.7 in the Midwest, 5.1 in the South, and 4.0 in the West. For forcible rape, the regional arrest rates were 6.2 in the Northeast, 7.8 in the Midwest, 7.2 in the South, and 6.5 in the West. Regional arrest rates for robbery were 44.1 in the Northeast, 34.5 in the Midwest, 41.5 in the South, and 46.5 in the West. For aggravated assault, the regional arrest rates were 115.6 in the Northeast, 99.8 in the Midwest, 128.6 in the South, and 191.7 in the West. (Table 30)

The regional burglary arrest rates were 74.6 in the Northeast, 78.9 in the Midwest, 109.2 in the South, and 114.5 in the West. For larceny-theft, the regional arrest rates were 371.4 in the Northeast, 466.9 in the Midwest, 516.5 in the South, and 385.9 in the West. Regional arrest rates for motor vehicle theft were 17.1 in the Northeast, 32.0 in the Midwest, 23.1 in the South, and 33.5 in the West. For arson, the regional arrest rates were 3.9 in the Northeast, 3.7 in the Midwest, 4.1 in the South, and 4.1 in the West. (Table 30)

By population group, law enforcement agencies in the nation's cities collectively reported 4,872.6 violent crime arrests per 100,000 inhabitants in 2009. In the city population groups, cities with 250,000 or more inhabitants reported the highest violent crime arrest rate (298.4) and cities with 10,000 to 24,999 inhabitants reported the lowest violent crime arrest rate (149.2). Cities reported an overall murder arrest rate of 4.3 per 100,000 inhabitants; cities with 250,000 or more inhabitants had the highest murder arrest rate (7.5) and cities with under 10,000 inhabitants had the lowest murder arrest rate (2.1). The collective city forcible rape arrest rate was 7.3 per 100,000 inhabitants, with the highest rate in cities with 250,000 or more inhabitants (9.7) and the lowest rate in cities with 25,000 to 49,999 inhabitants (6.0). The overall robbery arrest rate for cities was 51.5 per 100,000 inhabitants; cities with 250,000 or more inhabitants had the highest robbery arrest rate (83.2) and cities with under 10,000 inhabitants had the lowest robbery arrest rate (23.5). For aggravated assault, the collective city arrest rate was 151.7 per 100,000 inhabitants, with the greatest arrest rate in cities with 250,000 or more inhabitants (198.0) and the lowest arrest rate in cities with 10,000 to 24,999 inhabitants (111.3). (Table 31)

Agencies in metropolitan counties reported a violent crime arrest rate of 147.8 per 100,000 inhabitants, with arrest rates of 3.5 for murder, 5.6 for forcible rape, 24.9 for robbery, and 113.7 for aggravated assault. Agencies in nonmetropolitan counties reported arrest rates of 113.6 for violent crime, 3.5 for murder, 7.6 for forcible rape, 9.6 for robbery, and 92.8 for aggravated assault. (Table 31)

By population group, law enforcement agencies in the nation's cities collectively reported 675.6 property crime arrests per 100,000 inhabitants in 2009. In the city population groups, cities with 50,000 to 99,999 inhabitants reported the highest property crime arrest rate (706.3) and cities with under 10,000 inhabitants reported the lowest property crime arrest rate (624.5). Cities reported an overall burglary arrest rate of 104.7 per 100,000 inhabitants; cities with 100,000 to 249,999 inhabitants had the highest burglary arrest rate (126.7) and cities with 25,000 to 49,999 inhabitants had the lowest burglary arrest rate (89.5). The collective city larceny-theft arrest rate was 537.4 per 100,000 inhabitants, with the highest rate in cities with 25,000 to 49,999 inhabitants (589.3) and the lowest rate in cities with 250,000 inhabitants or more (488.9). The overall motor vehicle theft arrest rate for cities was 29.3 per 100,000 inhabitants; cities with 250,000 or more inhabitants had the highest motor vehicle theft arrest rate (46.7), and cities with 25,000 to 49,999 inhabitants had the lowest motor vehicle theft arrest rate (18.3). For arson, the collective city arrest rate was 4.2 per 100,000 inhabitants, with the greatest arrest rate in cities with under 10,000 inhabitants (5.6) and the lowest arrest rate in cities with 250,000 or more inhabitants (3.8). (Table 31)

Agencies in metropolitan counties reported a property crime arrest rate of 361.8 per 100,000 inhabitants, with arrest rates of 81.5 for burglary, 254.6 for larceny-theft, 22.1 for motor vehicle theft, and 3.5 for arson. Agencies in nonmetropolitan counties reported arrest rates of 269.0 for property crime, 87.0 for burglary, 160.5 for larceny-theft, 17.9 for motor vehicle theft, and 3.7 for arson. (Table 31)

## Community Types

In 2009, law enforcement agencies in the nation's cities reported that 84.6 percent of arrests in their jurisdictions were of adults and 15.4 percent of arrests were of juveniles. Adults accounted for 84.4 percent of arrestees for violent crimes, while juveniles accounted for 15.6 percent. Adults made up 74.8 percent of the arrestees for property crimes, and juveniles accounted for 25.2 percent. (Table 46) Of all arrests in the nation's cities in 2009, 45.2 percent were of individuals under 25 years of age. (Table 47) In metropolitan counties, 39.7 percent of arrests were of individuals under 25 years of age.(Table 53) In nonmetropolitan counties, 35.9 percent of persons arrested were of individuals under 25 years of age. (Table 59)

Males accounted for 74.4 percent and females accounted for 25.6 percent of arrestees in the nation's cities in 2009. (Table 48) In metropolitan counties, males composed 75.5 percent of arrestees, and in nonmetropolitan counties, males represented 76.5 percent of all arrestees. (Tables 54 and 60)

By race, 66.7 percent of arrestees in the nation's cities in 2009 were White, 30.6 percent were Black, and 2.7 percent were of other races (American Indian or Alaska Native and Asian or Pacific Islander). (Table 49) Whites accounted for 74.4 percent of arrestees in metropolitan counties in 2009, Blacks made up 24.2 percent of arrestees, and persons of other races made up 1.4 percent of the total. (Table 55) In nonmetropolitan counties, Whites made up 81.7 percent of arrestees, Blacks accounted for 13.9 percent of arrestees, and other races made up 4.4 percent of the total. (Table 61)

## Population Groups: Trends and Rates

The national UCR Program aggregates data by various population groups, which include cities, metropolitan counties, and nonmetropolitan counties. Definitions of these groups can be found in Appendix III. The total number of arrests in U.S. cities fell 2.7 percent from 2008 to 2009. The number of arrests for violent crimes declined 2.7 percent and arrests for property crimes increased 2.2 percent during the 2-year time frame. (Table 44)

In 2009, law enforcement agencies in cities collectively recorded an arrest rate of 4,872.6 arrests per 100,000 inhabitants. The nation's smallest cities, those with fewer than 10,000 inhabitants, had the highest arrest rate among the city population groups with 5,744.3 arrests per 100,000 inhabitants. Law enforcement agencies in cities with 25,000 to 49,999 inhabitants recorded the lowest rate, 4,426.8. In the nation's metropolitan counties, law enforcement agencies reported an arrest rate of 3,559.7 per 100,000 inhabitants. Agencies in nonmetropolitan counties reported an arrest rate of 3,648.6. (Table 31)

## Table 29. Estimated Number of Arrests, 2009

(Number.)

| Offense | Arrests |
|---|---|
| **TOTAL**[1] | 13,687,241 |
| | |
| **Violent Crime** | 581,765 |
| Murder and nonnegligent manslaughter | 12,418 |
| Forcible rape | 21,407 |
| Robbery | 126,725 |
| Aggravated assault | 421,215 |
| | |
| **Property Crime** | 1,728,285 |
| Burglary | 299,351 |
| Larceny-theft | 1,334,933 |
| Motor vehicle theft | 81,797 |
| Arson | 12,204 |
| | |
| **Other** | |
| Other assaults | 1,319,458 |
| Forgery and counterfeiting | 85,844 |
| Fraud | 210,255 |
| Embezzlement | 17,920 |
| Stolen property; buying, receiving, possessing | 105,303 |
| Vandalism | 270,439 |
| Weapons; carrying, possessing, etc. | 166,334 |
| Prostitution and commercialized vice | 71,355 |
| Sex offenses (except forcible rape and prostitution) | 77,326 |
| Drug abuse violations | 1,663,582 |
| Gambling | 10,360 |
| Offenses against the family and children | 114,564 |
| Driving under the influence | 1,440,409 |
| Liquor laws | 570,333 |
| Drunkenness | 594,300 |
| Disorderly conduct | 655,322 |
| Vagrancy | 33,388 |
| All other offenses | 3,764,672 |
| Suspicion | 1,975 |
| Curfew and loitering law violations | 112,593 |
| Runaways | 93,434 |

[1] Does not include suspicion.

## Table 30. Number and Rate of Arrests, by Geographic Region, 2009

(Number, rate per 100,000.)

| Offense charged | United States total (12,371 agencies; population 239,839,971) | | Northeast (2,977 agencies; population 44,805,518) | | Midwest (2,975 agencies; population 48,868,101) | | South (4,553 agencies; population 78,247,547) | | West (1,866 agencies; population 67,918,805) | |
|---|---|---|---|---|---|---|---|---|---|---|
| | Total | Rate | Total | Rate | Total | Rate | Total | Rate | Total | Rate |
| **TOTAL**[1] | 10,739,925 | 4,478.0 | 1,624,285 | 3,625.2 | 2,148,525 | 4,396.6 | 3,971,112 | 5,075.1 | 2,996,003 | 4,411.2 |
| **Violent Crime** | 458,576 | 191.2 | 75,614 | 168.8 | 71,225 | 145.7 | 142,797 | 182.5 | 168,940 | 248.7 |
| Murder and nonnegligent manslaughter | 9,775 | 4.1 | 1,268 | 2.8 | 1,791 | 3.7 | 3,984 | 5.1 | 2,732 | 4.0 |
| Forcible rape | 16,727 | 7.0 | 2,799 | 6.2 | 3,828 | 7.8 | 5,670 | 7.2 | 4,430 | 6.5 |
| Robbery | 100,702 | 42.0 | 19,768 | 44.1 | 16,851 | 34.5 | 32,486 | 41.5 | 31,597 | 46.5 |
| Aggravated assault | 331,372 | 138.2 | 51,779 | 115.6 | 48,755 | 99.8 | 100,657 | 128.6 | 130,181 | 191.7 |
| **Property Crime** | 1,369,658 | 571.1 | 209,252 | 467.0 | 284,175 | 581.5 | 510,856 | 652.9 | 365,375 | 538.0 |
| Burglary | 235,226 | 98.1 | 33,427 | 74.6 | 38,563 | 78.9 | 85,458 | 109.2 | 77,778 | 114.5 |
| Larceny-theft | 1,060,754 | 442.3 | 166,398 | 371.4 | 228,173 | 466.9 | 404,112 | 516.5 | 262,071 | 385.9 |
| Motor vehicle theft | 64,169 | 26.8 | 7,668 | 17.1 | 15,653 | 32.0 | 18,079 | 23.1 | 22,769 | 33.5 |
| Arson | 9,509 | 4.0 | 1,759 | 3.9 | 1,786 | 3.7 | 3,207 | 4.1 | 2,757 | 4.1 |
| **Other** | | | | | | | | | | |
| Other assaults | 1,036,754 | 432.3 | 173,018 | 386.2 | 216,558 | 443.1 | 411,223 | 525.5 | 235,955 | 347.4 |
| Forgery and counterfeiting | 67,357 | 28.1 | 9,996 | 22.3 | 10,665 | 21.8 | 29,796 | 38.1 | 16,900 | 24.9 |
| Fraud | 162,243 | 67.6 | 25,808 | 57.6 | 27,824 | 56.9 | 87,005 | 111.2 | 21,606 | 31.8 |
| Embezzlement | 14,097 | 5.9 | 1,341 | 3.0 | 1,987 | 4.1 | 7,682 | 9.8 | 3,087 | 4.5 |
| Stolen property; buying, receiving, possessing | 82,944 | 34.6 | 15,045 | 33.6 | 19,999 | 40.9 | 22,345 | 28.6 | 25,555 | 37.6 |
| Vandalism | 212,981 | 88.8 | 44,581 | 99.5 | 44,952 | 92.0 | 52,840 | 67.5 | 70,608 | 104.0 |
| Weapons; carrying, possessing, etc. | 130,941 | 54.6 | 16,941 | 37.8 | 25,836 | 52.9 | 44,281 | 56.6 | 43,883 | 64.6 |
| Prostitution and commercialized vice | 56,640 | 23.6 | 5,473 | 12.2 | 9,886 | 20.2 | 18,818 | 24.0 | 22,463 | 33.1 |
| Sex offenses (except forcible rape and prostitution) | 60,422 | 25.2 | 10,129 | 22.6 | 11,825 | 24.2 | 15,962 | 20.4 | 22,506 | 33.1 |
| Drug abuse violations | 1,305,191 | 544.2 | 210,868 | 470.6 | 238,502 | 488.1 | 471,426 | 602.5 | 384,395 | 566.0 |
| Gambling | 8,067 | 3.4 | 777 | 1.7 | 3,727 | 7.6 | 2,776 | 3.5 | 787 | 1.2 |
| Offenses against the family and children | 87,889 | 36.6 | 21,006 | 46.9 | 21,035 | 43.0 | 32,271 | 41.2 | 13,577 | 20.0 |
| Driving under the influence | 1,112,384 | 463.8 | 153,696 | 343.0 | 231,656 | 474.0 | 352,010 | 449.9 | 375,022 | 552.2 |
| Liquor laws | 447,496 | 186.6 | 54,296 | 121.2 | 155,168 | 317.5 | 105,453 | 134.8 | 132,579 | 195.2 |
| Drunkenness | 471,727 | 196.7 | 35,073 | 78.3 | 33,333 | 68.2 | 278,005 | 355.3 | 125,316 | 184.5 |
| Disorderly conduct | 518,374 | 216.1 | 127,777 | 285.2 | 157,328 | 321.9 | 155,360 | 198.5 | 77,909 | 114.7 |
| Vagrancy | 26,380 | 11.0 | 3,850 | 8.6 | 4,443 | 9.1 | 9,198 | 11.8 | 8,889 | 13.1 |
| All other offenses (except traffic) | 2,946,277 | 1,228.4 | 395,485 | 882.7 | 545,039 | 1,115.3 | 1,174,948 | 1,501.6 | 830,805 | 1,223.2 |
| Suspicion | 1,517 | 0.6 | 21 | 0.0 | 143 | 0.3 | 1,250 | 1.6 | 103 | 0.2 |
| Curfew and loitering law violations | 89,733 | 37.4 | 28,077 | 62.7 | 15,374 | 31.5 | 20,643 | 26.4 | 25,639 | 37.7 |
| Runaways | 73,794 | 30.8 | 6,182 | 13.8 | 17,988 | 36.8 | 25,417 | 32.5 | 24,207 | 35.6 |

[1] Does not include suspicion.

## Table 31. Number and Rate of Arrests, by Population Group, 2009

(Number, rate per 100,000 population.)

| Offense charged | Total (12,371 agencies; population 239,839,971) | | Cities: Total cities (9,075 cities; population 166,296,396) | | Cities: Group I (66 cities, 250,000 and over; population 45,039,931) | | Cities: Group II (168 cities, 100,000 to 249,999; population 24,893,194) | | Cities: Group III (406 cities, 50,000 to 99,999; population 27,781,644) | |
|---|---|---|---|---|---|---|---|---|---|---|
| | Total | Rate | Total | Rate | Total | Rate | Total | Rate | Total | Rate |
| **TOTAL[1]** | 10,739,925 | 4,478.0 | 8,102,933 | 4,872.6 | 2,289,739 | 5,083.8 | 1,175,989 | 4,724.1 | 1,271,691 | 4,577.5 |
| **Violent Crime** | 458,576 | 191.2 | 357,196 | 214.8 | 134,405 | 298.4 | 59,558 | 239.3 | 57,284 | 206.2 |
| Murder and nonnegligent manslaughter | 9,775 | 4.1 | 7,173 | 4.3 | 3,386 | 7.5 | 1,228 | 4.9 | 925 | 3.3 |
| Forcible rape | 16,727 | 7.0 | 12,163 | 7.3 | 4,360 | 9.7 | 1,735 | 7.0 | 1,750 | 6.3 |
| Robbery | 100,702 | 42.0 | 85,639 | 51.5 | 37,492 | 83.2 | 14,753 | 59.3 | 12,874 | 46.3 |
| Aggravated assault | 331,372 | 138.2 | 252,221 | 151.7 | 89,167 | 198.0 | 41,842 | 168.1 | 41,735 | 150.2 |
| **Property Crime** | 1,369,658 | 571.1 | 1,123,462 | 675.6 | 291,133 | 646.4 | 175,545 | 705.2 | 196,223 | 706.3 |
| Burglary | 235,226 | 98.1 | 174,091 | 104.7 | 48,204 | 107.0 | 31,540 | 126.7 | 30,697 | 110.5 |
| Larceny-theft | 1,060,754 | 442.3 | 893,661 | 537.4 | 220,179 | 488.9 | 135,284 | 543.5 | 158,123 | 569.2 |
| Motor vehicle theft | 64,169 | 26.8 | 48,792 | 29.3 | 21,036 | 46.7 | 7,710 | 31.0 | 6,325 | 22.8 |
| Arson | 9,509 | 4.0 | 6,918 | 4.2 | 1,714 | 3.8 | 1,011 | 4.1 | 1,078 | 3.9 |
| **Other** | | | | | | | | | | |
| Other assaults | 1,036,754 | 432.3 | 790,986 | 475.6 | 228,099 | 506.4 | 126,085 | 506.5 | 121,543 | 437.5 |
| Forgery and counterfeiting | 67,357 | 28.1 | 50,399 | 30.3 | 13,687 | 30.4 | 6,992 | 28.1 | 7,606 | 27.4 |
| Fraud | 162,243 | 67.6 | 99,271 | 59.7 | 18,040 | 40.1 | 11,669 | 46.9 | 14,597 | 52.5 |
| Embezzlement | 14,097 | 5.9 | 10,687 | 6.4 | 2,197 | 4.9 | 1,834 | 7.4 | 2,023 | 7.3 |
| Stolen property; buying, receiving, possessing | 82,944 | 34.6 | 63,739 | 38.3 | 19,903 | 44.2 | 8,957 | 36.0 | 11,095 | 39.9 |
| Vandalism | 212,981 | 88.8 | 167,597 | 100.8 | 45,163 | 100.3 | 24,287 | 97.6 | 27,338 | 98.4 |
| Weapons; carrying, possessing, etc. | 130,941 | 54.6 | 102,869 | 61.9 | 41,459 | 92.0 | 16,243 | 65.3 | 14,959 | 53.8 |
| Prostitution and commercialized vice | 56,640 | 23.6 | 53,421 | 32.1 | 39,206 | 87.0 | 6,919 | 27.8 | 3,683 | 13.3 |
| Sex offenses (except forcible rape and prostitution) | 60,422 | 25.2 | 43,365 | 26.1 | 15,790 | 35.1 | 5,735 | 23.0 | 6,945 | 25.0 |
| Drug abuse violations | 1,305,191 | 544.2 | 985,248 | 592.5 | 347,823 | 772.3 | 147,512 | 592.6 | 149,509 | 538.2 |
| Gambling | 8,067 | 3.4 | 6,558 | 3.9 | 4,967 | 11.0 | 440 | 1.8 | 350 | 1.3 |
| Offenses against the family and children | 87,889 | 36.6 | 43,849 | 26.4 | 6,987 | 15.5 | 6,276 | 25.2 | 7,811 | 28.1 |
| Driving under the influence | 1,112,384 | 463.8 | 690,269 | 415.1 | 154,691 | 343.5 | 83,759 | 336.5 | 102,640 | 369.5 |
| Liquor laws | 447,496 | 186.6 | 357,799 | 215.2 | 62,777 | 139.4 | 38,889 | 156.2 | 55,299 | 199.0 |
| Drunkenness | 471,727 | 196.7 | 405,799 | 244.0 | 100,600 | 223.4 | 64,383 | 258.6 | 67,050 | 241.3 |
| Disorderly conduct | 518,374 | 216.1 | 444,537 | 267.3 | 101,524 | 225.4 | 55,043 | 221.1 | 70,158 | 252.5 |
| Vagrancy | 26,380 | 11.0 | 23,110 | 13.9 | 13,362 | 29.7 | 1,913 | 7.7 | 3,111 | 11.2 |
| All other offenses (except traffic) | 2,946,277 | 1,228.4 | 2,140,195 | 1,287.0 | 584,418 | 1,297.6 | 316,737 | 1,272.4 | 329,676 | 1,186.7 |
| Suspicion | 1,517 | 0.6 | 666 | 0.4 | 7 | 0.0 | 0 | 0.0 | 334 | 1.2 |
| Curfew and loitering law violations | 89,733 | 37.4 | 85,272 | 51.3 | 43,727 | 97.1 | 7,982 | 32.1 | 12,259 | 44.1 |
| Runaways | 73,794 | 30.8 | 57,305 | 34.5 | 19,781 | 43.9 | 9,231 | 37.1 | 10,532 | 37.9 |

[1] Does not include suspicion.

## Table 31. Number and Rate of Arrests, by Population Group, 2009—*Continued*

(Number, rate per 100,000 population.)

| Offense charged | Cities | | | | | | Counties | | | | Suburban areas[2] (6,651 agencies; population 104,853,682) | |
|---|---|---|---|---|---|---|---|---|---|---|---|---|
| | Group IV (701 cities, 25,000 to 49,999; population 24,112,660) | | Group V (1,535 cities, 10,000 to 24,999; population 24,264,715) | | Group VI (6,199 cities, under 10,000; population 20,204,252) | | Metropolitan counties (1,320 agencies; population 52,113,451) | | Nonmetropolitan counties (1,976 agencies; population 21,430,124) | | | |
| | Total | Rate | Total | Rate | Total | Rate | Total | Rate | Total | Rate | Total | Rate |
| **TOTAL**[1] | 1,067,428 | 4,426.8 | 1,137,484 | 4,687.8 | 1,160,602 | 5,744.3 | 1,855,089 | 3,559.7 | 781,903 | 3,648.6 | 4,208,963 | 4,014.1 |
| | | | | | | | | | | | | |
| **Violent Crime** | 38,461 | 159.5 | 36,197 | 149.2 | 31,291 | 154.9 | 77,037 | 147.8 | 24,343 | 113.6 | 153,185 | 146.1 |
| Murder and nonnegligent manslaughter | 652 | 2.7 | 564 | 2.3 | 418 | 2.1 | 1,847 | 3.5 | 755 | 3.5 | 2,913 | 2.8 |
| Forcible rape | 1,440 | 6.0 | 1,480 | 6.1 | 1,398 | 6.9 | 2,938 | 5.6 | 1,626 | 7.6 | 5,798 | 5.5 |
| Robbery | 8,620 | 35.7 | 7,154 | 29.5 | 4,746 | 23.5 | 12,995 | 24.9 | 2,068 | 9.6 | 29,120 | 27.8 |
| Aggravated assault | 27,749 | 115.1 | 26,999 | 111.3 | 24,729 | 122.4 | 59,257 | 113.7 | 19,894 | 92.8 | 115,354 | 110.0 |
| | | | | | | | | | | | | |
| **Property Crime** | 169,052 | 701.1 | 165,326 | 681.3 | 126,183 | 624.5 | 188,542 | 361.8 | 57,654 | 269.0 | 515,589 | 491.7 |
| Burglary | 21,583 | 89.5 | 22,168 | 91.4 | 19,899 | 98.5 | 42,497 | 81.5 | 18,638 | 87.0 | 87,132 | 83.1 |
| Larceny-theft | 142,092 | 589.3 | 137,431 | 566.4 | 100,552 | 497.7 | 132,705 | 254.6 | 34,388 | 160.5 | 403,074 | 384.4 |
| Motor vehicle theft | 4,407 | 18.3 | 4,717 | 19.4 | 4,597 | 22.8 | 11,539 | 22.1 | 3,838 | 17.9 | 21,268 | 20.3 |
| Arson | 970 | 4.0 | 1,010 | 4.2 | 1,135 | 5.6 | 1,801 | 3.5 | 790 | 3.7 | 4,115 | 3.9 |
| | | | | | | | | | | | | |
| **Other** | | | | | | | | | | | | |
| Other assaults | 103,971 | 431.2 | 107,070 | 441.3 | 104,218 | 515.8 | 171,950 | 330.0 | 66,919 | 334.8 | 368,424 | 363.6 |
| Forgery and counterfeiting | 6,905 | 28.6 | 8,016 | 33.0 | 7,193 | 35.6 | 12,624 | 24.2 | 4,282 | 21.4 | 27,345 | 27.0 |
| Fraud | 15,346 | 63.6 | 17,360 | 71.5 | 22,259 | 110.2 | 41,431 | 79.5 | 23,829 | 119.2 | 82,906 | 81.8 |
| Embezzlement | 1,693 | 7.0 | 1,647 | 6.8 | 1,293 | 6.4 | 2,635 | 5.1 | 860 | 4.3 | 6,287 | 6.2 |
| Stolen property; buying, receiving, possessing | 8,662 | 35.9 | 8,479 | 34.9 | 6,643 | 32.9 | 14,497 | 27.8 | 4,422 | 22.1 | 33,541 | 33.1 |
| Vandalism | 23,008 | 95.4 | 23,722 | 97.8 | 24,079 | 119.2 | 32,009 | 61.4 | 12,896 | 64.5 | 84,055 | 83.0 |
| Weapons; carrying, possessing, etc. | 10,474 | 43.4 | 9,863 | 40.6 | 9,871 | 48.9 | 20,980 | 40.3 | 6,625 | 33.1 | 45,035 | 44.4 |
| Prostitution and commercialized vice | 2,407 | 10.0 | 687 | 2.8 | 519 | 2.6 | 3,036 | 5.8 | 208 | 1.0 | 6,505 | 6.4 |
| Sex offenses (except forcible rape and prostitution) | 4,919 | 20.4 | 4,993 | 20.6 | 4,983 | 24.7 | 12,005 | 23.0 | 4,971 | 24.9 | 22,806 | 22.5 |
| Drug abuse violations | 112,285 | 465.7 | 109,104 | 449.6 | 119,015 | 589.1 | 232,252 | 445.7 | 81,704 | 408.8 | 469,767 | 463.6 |
| Gambling | 269 | 1.1 | 218 | 0.9 | 314 | 1.6 | 1,196 | 2.3 | 208 | 1.0 | 1,008 | 1.0 |
| Offenses against the family and children | 7,623 | 31.6 | 7,998 | 33.0 | 7,154 | 35.4 | 31,907 | 61.2 | 12,083 | 60.5 | 48,629 | 48.0 |
| Driving under the influence | 97,103 | 402.7 | 118,312 | 487.6 | 133,764 | 662.1 | 268,019 | 514.3 | 157,703 | 789.0 | 507,664 | 501.0 |
| Liquor laws | 48,655 | 201.8 | 60,980 | 251.3 | 91,199 | 451.4 | 56,920 | 109.2 | 34,571 | 173.0 | 196,121 | 193.6 |
| Drunkenness | 54,784 | 227.2 | 58,146 | 239.6 | 60,836 | 301.1 | 46,045 | 88.4 | 17,838 | 89.2 | 160,349 | 158.2 |
| Disorderly conduct | 58,178 | 241.3 | 72,190 | 297.5 | 87,444 | 432.8 | 50,523 | 96.9 | 22,716 | 113.6 | 205,143 | 202.5 |
| Vagrancy | 1,725 | 7.2 | 1,137 | 4.7 | 1,862 | 9.2 | 2,890 | 5.5 | 253 | 1.3 | 6,112 | 6.0 |
| All other offenses (except traffic) | 287,578 | 1,192.6 | 312,489 | 1,287.8 | 309,297 | 1,530.9 | 571,897 | 1,097.4 | 217,103 | 1,086.2 | 1,207,516 | 1,191.7 |
| Suspicion | 26 | 0.1 | 107 | 0.4 | 192 | 1.0 | 722 | 1.4 | 95 | 0.5 | 592 | 0.6 |
| Curfew and loitering law violations | 7,075 | 29.3 | 7,199 | 29.7 | 7,030 | 34.8 | 3,959 | 7.6 | 462 | 2.3 | 21,747 | 21.5 |
| Runaways | 7,255 | 30.1 | 6,351 | 26.2 | 4,155 | 20.6 | 12,735 | 24.4 | 4,343 | 21.7 | 27,260 | 26.9 |

[1] Does not include suspicion.

[2] Suburban areas include law enforcement agencies in cities with less than 50,000 inhabitants and county law enforcement agencies that are within a metropolitan statistical area. Suburban areas exclude all metropolitan agencies associated with a principal city. The agencies associated with suburban areas also appear in other groups within this table.

## Table 32. Ten-Year Arrest Trends, 2000 and 2009

(Number, percent change; 8,649 agencies; 2009 estimated population 186,864,905; 2000 estimated population 172,176,040.)

| Offense charged | Number of persons arrested | | | | | | | | |
|---|---|---|---|---|---|---|---|---|---|
| | Total all ages | | | Under 18 years of age | | | 18 years of age and over | | |
| | 2000 | 2009 | Percent change | 2000 | 2009 | Percent change | 2000 | 2009 | Percent change |
| **TOTAL**[1] | 8,365,589 | 8,261,590 | -1.2 | 1,455,216 | 1,161,830 | -20.2 | 6,910,373 | 7,099,760 | +2.7 |
| **Violent Crime** | 390,328 | 364,414 | -6.6 | 60,856 | 51,740 | -15.0 | 329,472 | 312,674 | -5.1 |
| Murder and nonnegligent manslaughter | 7,599 | 7,193 | -5.3 | 656 | 652 | -0.6 | 6,943 | 6,541 | -5.8 |
| Forcible rape | 16,308 | 12,617 | -22.6 | 2,674 | 1,820 | -31.9 | 13,634 | 10,797 | -20.8 |
| Robbery | 65,106 | 77,290 | +18.7 | 16,393 | 19,336 | +18.0 | 48,713 | 57,954 | +19.0 |
| Aggravated assault | 301,315 | 267,314 | -11.3 | 41,133 | 29,932 | -27.2 | 260,182 | 237,382 | -8.8 |
| **Property Crime** | 978,552 | 1,050,590 | +7.4 | 324,422 | 258,469 | -20.3 | 654,130 | 792,121 | +21.1 |
| Burglary | 174,741 | 188,781 | +8.0 | 58,963 | 46,637 | -20.9 | 115,778 | 142,144 | +22.8 |
| Larceny-theft | 713,326 | 806,604 | +13.1 | 231,759 | 196,863 | -15.1 | 481,567 | 609,741 | +26.6 |
| Motor vehicle theft | 80,109 | 47,473 | -40.7 | 28,116 | 11,354 | -59.6 | 51,993 | 36,119 | -30.5 |
| Arson | 10,376 | 7,732 | -25.5 | 5,584 | 3,615 | -35.3 | 4,792 | 4,117 | -14.1 |
| **Other** | | | | | | | | | |
| Other assaults | 770,664 | 803,489 | +4.3 | 142,699 | 135,125 | -5.3 | 627,965 | 668,364 | +6.4 |
| Forgery and counterfeiting | 67,233 | 49,992 | -25.6 | 4,144 | 1,277 | -69.2 | 63,089 | 48,715 | -22.8 |
| Fraud | 216,666 | 139,935 | -35.4 | 5,874 | 4,091 | -30.4 | 210,792 | 135,844 | -35.6 |
| Embezzlement | 12,456 | 11,756 | -5.6 | 1,324 | 393 | -70.3 | 11,132 | 11,363 | +2.1 |
| Stolen property; buying, receiving, possessing | 75,471 | 66,304 | -12.1 | 17,991 | 11,990 | -33.4 | 57,480 | 54,314 | -5.5 |
| Vandalism | 169,910 | 162,511 | -4.4 | 71,267 | 55,757 | -21.8 | 98,643 | 106,754 | +8.2 |
| Weapons; carrying, possessing, etc. | 93,638 | 98,222 | +4.9 | 22,383 | 20,696 | -7.5 | 71,255 | 77,526 | +8.8 |
| Prostitution and commercialized vice | 44,665 | 37,396 | -16.3 | 729 | 791 | +8.5 | 43,936 | 36,605 | -16.7 |
| Sex offenses (except forcible rape and prostitution) | 54,150 | 46,628 | -13.9 | 10,848 | 7,799 | -28.1 | 43,302 | 38,829 | -10.3 |
| Drug abuse violations | 939,138 | 995,708 | +6.0 | 121,666 | 103,657 | -14.8 | 817,472 | 892,051 | +9.1 |
| Gambling | 4,568 | 3,359 | -26.5 | 458 | 312 | -31.9 | 4,110 | 3,047 | -25.9 |
| Offenses against the family and children | 86,249 | 70,575 | -18.2 | 4,767 | 2,689 | -43.6 | 81,482 | 67,886 | -16.7 |
| Driving under the influence | 879,666 | 841,869 | -4.3 | 12,683 | 8,085 | -36.3 | 866,983 | 833,784 | -3.8 |
| Liquor laws | 406,772 | 340,842 | -16.2 | 97,338 | 67,859 | -30.3 | 309,434 | 272,983 | -11.8 |
| Drunkenness | 420,017 | 398,412 | -5.1 | 14,252 | 9,837 | -31.0 | 405,765 | 388,575 | -4.2 |
| Disorderly conduct | 369,207 | 354,032 | -4.1 | 98,834 | 92,754 | -6.2 | 270,373 | 261,278 | -3.4 |
| Vagrancy | 16,872 | 16,817 | -0.3 | 1,647 | 1,047 | -36.4 | 15,225 | 15,770 | +3.6 |
| All other offenses (except traffic) | 2,180,750 | 2,277,313 | +4.4 | 252,417 | 196,036 | -22.3 | 1,928,333 | 2,081,277 | +7.9 |
| Suspicion | 3,453 | 1,293 | -62.6 | 749 | 152 | -79.7 | 2,704 | 1,141 | -57.8 |
| Curfew and loitering law violations | 97,353 | 72,203 | -25.8 | 97,353 | 72,203 | -25.8 | - | - | - |
| Runaways | 91,264 | 59,223 | -35.1 | 91,264 | 59,223 | -35.1 | - | - | - |

[1] Does not include suspicion.

# Table 33. Ten-Year Arrest Trends, by Sex, 2000 and 2009

(Number, percent change; 8,649 agencies; 2009 estimated population 186,864,905; 2000 estimated population 172,176,040.)

| Offense charged | Male | | | | | | Female | | | | | |
|---|---|---|---|---|---|---|---|---|---|---|---|---|
| | Total | | | Under 18 | | | Total | | | Under 18 | | |
| | 2000 | 2009 | Percent change | 2000 | 2009 | Percent change | 2000 | 2009 | Percent change | 1998 | 2007 | Percent change |
| **TOTAL**[1] | 6,491,372 | 6,174,287 | -4.9 | 1,047,690 | 807,818 | -22.9 | 1,874,217 | 2,087,303 | +11.4 | 407,526 | 354,012 | -13.1 |
| **Violent Crime** | 321,865 | 295,890 | -8.1 | 49,639 | 42,418 | -14.5 | 68,463 | 68,524 | +0.1 | 11,217 | 9,322 | -16.9 |
| Murder and nonnegligent manslaughter | 6,755 | 6,437 | -4.7 | 576 | 599 | +4.0 | 844 | 756 | -10.4 | 80 | 53 | -33.8 |
| Forcible rape | 16,139 | 12,469 | -22.7 | 2,652 | 1,792 | -32.4 | 169 | 148 | -12.4 | 22 | 28 | +27.3 |
| Robbery | 58,443 | 67,906 | +16.2 | 14,861 | 17,342 | +16.7 | 6,663 | 9,384 | +40.8 | 1,532 | 1,994 | +30.2 |
| Aggravated assault | 240,528 | 209,078 | -13.1 | 31,550 | 22,685 | -28.1 | 60,787 | 58,236 | -4.2 | 9,583 | 7,247 | -24.4 |
| **Property Crime** | 682,562 | 656,186 | -3.9 | 226,346 | 160,299 | -29.2 | 295,990 | 394,404 | +33.2 | 98,076 | 98,170 | +0.1 |
| Burglary | 151,244 | 159,017 | +5.1 | 51,950 | 40,897 | -21.3 | 23,497 | 29,764 | +26.7 | 7,013 | 5,740 | -18.2 |
| Larceny-theft | 454,947 | 451,750 | -0.7 | 146,160 | 106,852 | -26.9 | 258,379 | 354,854 | +37.3 | 85,599 | 90,011 | +5.2 |
| Motor vehicle theft | 67,551 | 38,987 | -42.3 | 23,314 | 9,412 | -59.6 | 12,558 | 8,486 | -32.4 | 4,802 | 1,942 | -59.6 |
| Arson | 8,820 | 6,432 | -27.1 | 4,922 | 3,138 | -36.2 | 1,556 | 1,300 | -16.5 | 662 | 477 | -27.9 |
| **Other** | | | | | | | | | | | | |
| Other assaults | 590,790 | 592,155 | +0.2 | 98,731 | 88,631 | -10.2 | 179,874 | 211,334 | +17.5 | 43,968 | 46,494 | +5.7 |
| Forgery and counterfeiting | 40,765 | 31,152 | -23.6 | 2,746 | 889 | -67.6 | 26,468 | 18,840 | -28.8 | 1,398 | 388 | -72.2 |
| Fraud | 116,447 | 78,550 | -32.5 | 3,871 | 2,637 | -31.9 | 100,219 | 61,385 | -38.7 | 2,003 | 1,454 | -27.4 |
| Embezzlement | 6,207 | 5,743 | -7.5 | 686 | 224 | -67.3 | 6,249 | 6,013 | -3.8 | 638 | 169 | -73.5 |
| Stolen property; buying, receiving, possessing | 62,320 | 52,247 | -16.2 | 15,179 | 9,670 | -36.3 | 13,151 | 14,057 | +6.9 | 2,812 | 2,320 | -17.5 |
| Vandalism | 143,680 | 133,421 | -7.1 | 62,404 | 48,203 | -22.8 | 26,230 | 29,090 | +10.9 | 8,863 | 7,554 | -14.8 |
| Weapons; carrying, possessing, etc. | 86,024 | 90,182 | +4.8 | 20,096 | 18,553 | -7.7 | 7,614 | 8,040 | +5.6 | 2,287 | 2,143 | -6.3 |
| Prostitution and commercialized vice | 18,886 | 11,639 | -38.4 | 332 | 167 | -49.7 | 25,779 | 25,757 | -0.1 | 397 | 624 | +57.2 |
| Sex offenses (except forcible rape and prostitution) | 50,319 | 42,609 | -15.3 | 10,103 | 7,061 | -30.1 | 3,831 | 4,019 | +4.9 | 745 | 738 | -0.9 |
| Drug abuse violations | 771,170 | 806,669 | +4.6 | 102,909 | 86,857 | -15.6 | 167,968 | 189,039 | +12.5 | 18,757 | 16,800 | -10.4 |
| Gambling | 3,984 | 2,877 | -27.8 | 431 | 304 | -29.5 | 584 | 482 | -17.5 | 27 | 8 | -70.4 |
| Offenses against the family and children | 67,421 | 53,001 | -21.4 | 3,029 | 1,701 | -43.8 | 18,828 | 17,574 | -6.7 | 1,738 | 988 | -43.2 |
| Driving under the influence | 734,872 | 651,424 | -11.4 | 10,500 | 6,033 | -42.5 | 144,794 | 190,445 | +31.5 | 2,183 | 2,052 | -6.0 |
| Liquor laws | 311,989 | 244,047 | -21.8 | 66,585 | 41,879 | -37.1 | 94,783 | 96,795 | +2.1 | 30,753 | 25,980 | -15.5 |
| Drunkenness | 363,705 | 331,804 | -8.8 | 11,406 | 7,381 | -35.3 | 56,312 | 66,608 | +18.3 | 2,846 | 2,456 | -13.7 |
| Disorderly conduct | 280,158 | 257,713 | -8.0 | 69,814 | 61,616 | -11.7 | 89,049 | 96,319 | +8.2 | 29,020 | 31,138 | +7.3 |
| Vagrancy | 13,151 | 13,189 | +0.3 | 1,287 | 824 | -36.0 | 3,721 | 3,628 | -2.5 | 360 | 223 | -38.1 |
| All other offenses (except traffic) | 1,720,089 | 1,746,701 | +1.5 | 186,628 | 145,383 | -22.1 | 460,661 | 530,612 | +15.2 | 65,789 | 50,653 | -23.0 |
| Suspicion | 2,757 | 958 | -65.3 | 575 | 119 | -79.3 | 696 | 335 | -51.9 | 174 | 33 | -81.0 |
| Curfew and loitering law violations | 67,275 | 50,288 | -25.3 | 67,275 | 50,288 | -25.3 | 30,078 | 21,915 | -27.1 | 30,078 | 21,915 | -27.1 |
| Runaways | 37,693 | 26,800 | -28.9 | 37,693 | 26,800 | -28.9 | 53,571 | 32,423 | -39.5 | 53,571 | 32,423 | -39.5 |

[1] Does not include suspicion.

## Table 34. Five-Year Arrest Trends, by Age, 2005 and 2009

(Number, percent change; 10,290 agencies; 2009 estimated population 213,631,875; 2005 estimated population 207,132,276.)

| Offense charged | Number of persons arrested | | | | | | | | |
|---|---|---|---|---|---|---|---|---|---|
| | Total all ages | | | Under 18 years of age | | | 18 years of age and over | | |
| | 2005 | 2009 | Percent change | 2005 | 2009 | Percent change | 2005 | 2009 | Percent change |
| TOTAL[1] | 9,715,514 | 9,360,418 | -3.7 | 1,521,673 | 1,337,503 | -12.1 | 8,193,841 | 8,022,915 | -2.1 |
| **Violent Crime** | 414,792 | 396,905 | -4.3 | 66,906 | 59,062 | -11.7 | 347,886 | 337,843 | -2.9 |
| Murder and nonnegligent manslaughter | 9,184 | 8,340 | -9.2 | 844 | 803 | -4.9 | 8,340 | 7,537 | -9.6 |
| Forcible rape | 17,278 | 14,461 | -16.3 | 2,740 | 2,172 | -20.7 | 14,538 | 12,289 | -15.5 |
| Robbery | 79,190 | 86,539 | +9.3 | 20,612 | 22,321 | +8.3 | 58,578 | 64,218 | +9.6 |
| Aggravated assault | 309,140 | 287,565 | -7.0 | 42,710 | 33,766 | -20.9 | 266,430 | 253,799 | -4.7 |
| **Property Crime** | 1,117,653 | 1,195,855 | +7.0 | 298,370 | 296,412 | -0.7 | 819,283 | 899,443 | +9.8 |
| Burglary | 204,628 | 208,262 | +1.8 | 55,002 | 52,299 | -4.9 | 149,626 | 155,963 | +4.2 |
| Larceny-theft | 801,095 | 922,332 | +15.1 | 210,956 | 226,034 | +7.1 | 590,139 | 696,298 | +18.0 |
| Motor vehicle theft | 100,220 | 56,662 | -43.5 | 26,575 | 14,157 | -46.7 | 73,645 | 42,505 | -42.3 |
| Arson | 11,710 | 8,599 | -26.6 | 5,837 | 3,922 | -32.8 | 5,873 | 4,677 | -20.4 |
| **Other** | | | | | | | | | |
| Other assaults | 899,692 | 900,636 | +0.1 | 174,449 | 151,577 | -13.1 | 725,243 | 749,059 | +3.3 |
| Forgery and counterfeiting | 80,968 | 56,241 | -30.5 | 2,951 | 1,431 | -51.5 | 78,017 | 54,810 | -29.7 |
| Fraud | 222,335 | 150,411 | -32.3 | 5,552 | 4,513 | -18.7 | 216,783 | 145,898 | -32.7 |
| Embezzlement | 13,191 | 12,618 | -4.3 | 826 | 431 | -47.8 | 12,365 | 12,187 | -1.4 |
| Stolen property; buying, receiving, possessing | 87,625 | 68,865 | -21.4 | 14,933 | 12,419 | -16.8 | 72,692 | 56,446 | -22.3 |
| Vandalism | 197,697 | 191,200 | -3.3 | 74,503 | 64,484 | -13.4 | 123,194 | 126,716 | +2.9 |
| Weapons; carrying, possessing, etc. | 132,443 | 114,065 | -13.9 | 31,803 | 23,957 | -24.7 | 100,640 | 90,108 | -10.5 |
| Prostitution and commercialized vice | 50,877 | 40,814 | -19.8 | 1,016 | 872 | -14.2 | 49,861 | 39,942 | -19.9 |
| Sex offenses (except forcible rape and prostitution) | 61,253 | 52,322 | -14.6 | 11,719 | 9,260 | -21.0 | 49,534 | 43,062 | -13.1 |
| Drug abuse violations | 1,265,412 | 1,142,407 | -9.7 | 134,623 | 121,424 | -9.8 | 1,130,789 | 1,020,983 | -9.7 |
| Gambling | 7,091 | 6,817 | -3.9 | 1,389 | 1,241 | -10.7 | 5,702 | 5,576 | -2.2 |
| Offenses against the family and children | 90,485 | 80,602 | -10.9 | 3,962 | 3,093 | -21.9 | 86,523 | 77,509 | -10.4 |
| Driving under the influence | 922,736 | 948,672 | +2.8 | 12,201 | 9,306 | -23.7 | 910,535 | 939,366 | +3.2 |
| Liquor laws | 411,258 | 395,282 | -3.9 | 89,728 | 79,688 | -11.2 | 321,530 | 315,594 | -1.8 |
| Drunkenness | 382,632 | 417,579 | +9.1 | 10,809 | 10,065 | -6.9 | 371,823 | 407,514 | +9.6 |
| Disorderly conduct | 469,647 | 447,732 | -4.7 | 142,417 | 115,942 | -18.6 | 327,230 | 331,790 | +1.4 |
| Vagrancy | 23,930 | 20,576 | -14.0 | 1,482 | 1,023 | -31.0 | 22,448 | 19,553 | -12.9 |
| All other offenses (except traffic) | 2,684,127 | 2,577,984 | -4.0 | 262,364 | 228,468 | -12.9 | 2,421,763 | 2,349,516 | -3.0 |
| Suspicion | 2,476 | 1,352 | -45.4 | 328 | 154 | -53.0 | 2,148 | 1,198 | -44.2 |
| Curfew and loitering law violations | 96,932 | 77,679 | -19.9 | 96,932 | 77,679 | -19.9 | - | - | - |
| Runaways | 82,738 | 65,156 | -21.3 | 82,738 | 65,156 | -21.3 | - | - | - |

[1] Does not include suspicion.

## Table 35. Five-Year Arrest Trends, by Age and Sex, 2005 and 2009

(Number, percent change; 9,651 agencies; 2009 estimated population 192,575,487; 2005 estimated population 186,517,601.)

| Offense charged | Male | | | | | | Female | | | | | |
|---|---|---|---|---|---|---|---|---|---|---|---|---|
| | Total | | | Under 18 | | | Total | | | Under 18 | | |
| | 2005 | 2009 | Percent change | 2005 | 2009 | Percent change | 2005 | 2009 | Percent change | 2005 | 2009 | Percent change |
| **TOTAL**[1] | 7,387,112 | 6,999,896 | -5.2 | 1,072,951 | 933,186 | -13.0 | 2,328,402 | 2,360,522 | +1.4 | 448,722 | 404,317 | -9.9 |
| | | | | | | | | | | | | |
| **Violent Crime** | 340,616 | 323,358 | -5.1 | 54,770 | 48,681 | -11.1 | 74,176 | 73,547 | -0.8 | 12,136 | 10,381 | -14.5 |
| Murder and nonnegligent manslaughter | 8,179 | 7,471 | -8.7 | 756 | 747 | -1.2 | 1,005 | 869 | -13.5 | 88 | 56 | -36.4 |
| Forcible rape | 17,066 | 14,289 | -16.3 | 2,684 | 2,134 | -20.5 | 212 | 172 | -18.9 | 56 | 38 | -32.1 |
| Robbery | 70,325 | 76,306 | +8.5 | 18,661 | 20,105 | +7.7 | 8,865 | 10,233 | +15.4 | 1,951 | 2,216 | +13.6 |
| Aggravated assault | 245,046 | 225,292 | -8.1 | 32,669 | 25,695 | -21.3 | 64,094 | 62,273 | -2.8 | 10,041 | 8,071 | -19.6 |
| | | | | | | | | | | | | |
| **Property Crime** | 756,733 | 747,631 | -1.2 | 197,628 | 184,225 | -6.8 | 360,920 | 448,224 | +24.2 | 100,742 | 112,187 | +11.4 |
| Burglary | 174,890 | 176,704 | +1.0 | 48,636 | 46,194 | -5.0 | 29,738 | 31,558 | +6.1 | 6,366 | 6,105 | -4.1 |
| Larceny-theft | 489,368 | 517,082 | +5.7 | 121,909 | 122,850 | +0.8 | 311,727 | 405,250 | +30.0 | 89,047 | 103,184 | +15.9 |
| Motor vehicle theft | 82,705 | 46,703 | -43.5 | 22,048 | 11,775 | -46.6 | 17,515 | 9,959 | -43.1 | 4,527 | 2,382 | -47.4 |
| Arson | 9,770 | 7,142 | -26.9 | 5,035 | 3,406 | -32.4 | 1,940 | 1,457 | -24.9 | 802 | 516 | -35.7 |
| | | | | | | | | | | | | |
| **Other** | | | | | | | | | | | | |
| Other assaults | 677,259 | 665,940 | -1.7 | 116,749 | 99,969 | -14.4 | 222,433 | 234,696 | +5.5 | 57,700 | 51,608 | -10.6 |
| Forgery and counterfeiting | 48,539 | 35,015 | -27.9 | 2,002 | 1,012 | -49.5 | 32,429 | 21,226 | -34.5 | 949 | 419 | -55.8 |
| Fraud | 120,597 | 84,764 | -29.7 | 3,619 | 2,934 | -18.9 | 101,738 | 65,647 | -35.5 | 1,933 | 1,579 | -18.3 |
| Embezzlement | 6,560 | 6,159 | -6.1 | 461 | 239 | -48.2 | 6,631 | 6,459 | -2.6 | 365 | 192 | -47.4 |
| Stolen property; buying, receiving, possessing | 70,996 | 55,717 | -21.5 | 12,626 | 10,406 | -17.6 | 16,629 | 13,148 | -20.9 | 2,307 | 2,013 | -12.7 |
| Vandalism | 163,956 | 156,806 | -4.4 | 64,250 | 55,650 | -13.4 | 33,741 | 34,394 | +1.9 | 10,253 | 8,834 | -13.8 |
| Weapons; carrying, possessing, etc. | 121,704 | 104,946 | -13.8 | 28,398 | 21,500 | -24.3 | 10,739 | 9,119 | -15.1 | 3,405 | 2,457 | -27.8 |
| Prostitution and commercialized vice | 17,924 | 13,105 | -26.9 | 275 | 197 | -28.4 | 32,953 | 27,709 | -15.9 | 741 | 675 | -8.9 |
| Sex offenses (except forcible rape and prostitution) | 56,144 | 47,954 | -14.6 | 10,627 | 8,307 | -21.8 | 5,109 | 4,368 | -14.5 | 1,092 | 953 | -12.7 |
| Drug abuse violations | 1,022,878 | 930,152 | -9.1 | 111,771 | 102,338 | -8.4 | 242,534 | 212,255 | -12.5 | 22,852 | 19,086 | -16.5 |
| Gambling | 6,524 | 6,231 | -4.5 | 1,358 | 1,223 | -9.9 | 567 | 586 | +3.4 | 31 | 18 | -41.9 |
| Offenses against the family and children | 68,478 | 60,511 | -11.6 | 2,415 | 1,976 | -18.2 | 22,007 | 20,091 | -8.7 | 1,547 | 1,117 | -27.8 |
| Driving under the influence | 744,389 | 733,761 | -1.4 | 9,497 | 6,976 | -26.5 | 178,347 | 214,911 | +20.5 | 2,704 | 2,330 | -13.8 |
| Liquor laws | 301,462 | 280,477 | -7.0 | 57,358 | 48,804 | -14.9 | 109,796 | 114,805 | +4.6 | 32,370 | 30,884 | -4.6 |
| Drunkenness | 323,717 | 347,376 | +7.3 | 8,218 | 7,492 | -8.8 | 58,915 | 70,203 | +19.2 | 2,591 | 2,573 | -0.7 |
| Disorderly conduct | 346,952 | 327,950 | -5.5 | 96,322 | 77,679 | -19.4 | 122,695 | 119,782 | -2.4 | 46,095 | 38,263 | -17.0 |
| Vagrancy | 18,620 | 16,445 | -11.7 | 1,160 | 817 | -29.6 | 5,310 | 4,131 | -22.2 | 322 | 206 | -36.0 |
| All other offenses (except traffic) | 2,070,416 | 1,972,015 | -4.8 | 190,799 | 169,178 | -11.3 | 613,711 | 605,969 | -1.3 | 71,565 | 59,290 | -17.2 |
| Suspicion | 2,114 | 971 | -54.1 | 226 | 119 | -47.3 | 362 | 381 | +5.2 | 102 | 35 | -65.7 |
| Curfew and loitering law violations | 67,831 | 54,080 | -20.3 | 67,831 | 54,080 | -20.3 | 29,101 | 23,599 | -18.9 | 29,101 | 23,599 | -18.9 |
| Runaways | 34,817 | 29,503 | -15.3 | 34,817 | 29,503 | -15.3 | 47,921 | 35,653 | -25.6 | 47,921 | 35,653 | -25.6 |

[1] Does not include suspicion.

## Table 36. Current Year Over Previous Year Arrest Trends, 2008–2009

(Number, percent change; 11,310 agencies; 2009 estimated population 224,035,573; 2008 estimated population 222,163,484.)

| Offense charged | Number of persons arrested | | | | | | | | | | | |
|---|---|---|---|---|---|---|---|---|---|---|---|---|
| | Total all ages | | | Under 15 years of age | | | Under 18 years of age | | | 18 years of age and over | | |
| | 2008 | 2009 | Percent change | 2008 | 2009 | Percent change | 2008 | 2009 | Percent change | 2008 | 2009 | Percent change |
| **TOTAL**[1] | 10,151,204 | 9,908,710 | -2.4 | 423,831 | 377,811 | -10.9 | 1,547,360 | 1,409,517 | -8.9 | 8,603,844 | 8,499,193 | -1.2 |
| **Violent Crime** | 436,891 | 426,810 | -2.3 | 18,215 | 15,716 | -13.7 | 68,447 | 61,242 | -10.5 | 368,444 | 365,568 | -0.8 |
| Murder and nonnegligent manslaughter | 9,087 | 8,654 | -4.8 | 67 | 72 | +7.5 | 876 | 797 | -9.0 | 8,211 | 7,857 | -4.3 |
| Forcible rape | 15,997 | 15,093 | -5.7 | 817 | 715 | -12.5 | 2,397 | 2,229 | -7.0 | 13,600 | 12,864 | -5.4 |
| Robbery | 93,575 | 90,620 | -3.2 | 4,807 | 3,995 | -16.9 | 24,840 | 22,175 | -10.7 | 68,735 | 68,445 | -0.4 |
| Aggravated assault | 318,232 | 312,443 | -1.8 | 12,524 | 10,934 | -12.7 | 40,334 | 36,041 | -10.6 | 277,898 | 276,402 | -0.5 |
| **Property Crime** | 1,246,469 | 1,266,859 | +1.6 | 94,585 | 86,223 | -8.8 | 326,367 | 311,060 | -4.7 | 920,102 | 955,799 | +3.9 |
| Burglary | 227,886 | 219,323 | -3.8 | 17,724 | 14,960 | -15.6 | 61,788 | 54,764 | -11.4 | 166,098 | 164,559 | -0.9 |
| Larceny-theft | 938,965 | 981,202 | +4.5 | 70,659 | 66,162 | -6.4 | 242,728 | 238,642 | -1.7 | 696,237 | 742,560 | +6.7 |
| Motor vehicle theft | 69,057 | 57,365 | -16.9 | 3,417 | 2,698 | -21.0 | 16,925 | 13,598 | -19.7 | 52,132 | 43,767 | -16.0 |
| Arson | 10,561 | 8,969 | -15.1 | 2,785 | 2,403 | -13.7 | 4,926 | 4,056 | -17.7 | 5,635 | 4,913 | -12.8 |
| **Other** | | | | | | | | | | | | |
| Other assaults | 938,114 | 946,645 | +0.9 | 63,503 | 58,815 | -7.4 | 168,084 | 158,438 | -5.7 | 770,030 | 788,207 | +2.4 |
| Forgery and counterfeiting | 67,014 | 61,325 | -8.5 | 244 | 208 | -14.8 | 1,964 | 1,568 | -20.2 | 65,050 | 59,757 | -8.1 |
| Fraud | 176,354 | 160,189 | -9.2 | 897 | 793 | -11.6 | 5,584 | 4,783 | -14.3 | 170,770 | 155,406 | -9.0 |
| Embezzlement | 15,856 | 13,215 | -16.7 | 29 | 31 | +6.9 | 952 | 460 | -51.7 | 14,904 | 12,755 | -14.4 |
| Stolen property; buying, receiving, possessing | 83,128 | 77,620 | -6.6 | 3,651 | 3,125 | -14.4 | 15,759 | 14,165 | -10.1 | 67,369 | 63,455 | -5.8 |
| Vandalism | 208,952 | 198,204 | -5.1 | 31,789 | 25,976 | -18.3 | 78,740 | 67,050 | -14.8 | 130,212 | 131,154 | +0.7 |
| Weapons; carrying, possessing, etc. | 127,419 | 118,661 | -6.9 | 9,186 | 7,795 | -15.1 | 28,716 | 24,671 | -14.1 | 98,703 | 93,990 | -4.8 |
| Prostitution and commercialized vice | 46,665 | 44,339 | -5.0 | 115 | 109 | -5.2 | 1,019 | 893 | -12.4 | 45,646 | 43,446 | -4.8 |
| Sex offenses (except forcible rape and prostitution) | 57,289 | 55,634 | -2.9 | 5,064 | 4,833 | -4.6 | 10,591 | 9,955 | -6.0 | 46,698 | 45,679 | -2.2 |
| Drug abuse violations | 1,184,811 | 1,160,203 | -2.1 | 18,801 | 19,426 | +3.3 | 125,238 | 120,625 | -3.7 | 1,059,573 | 1,039,578 | -1.9 |
| Gambling | 3,568 | 4,140 | +16.0 | 75 | 72 | -4.0 | 396 | 449 | +13.4 | 3,172 | 3,691 | +16.4 |
| Offenses against the family and children | 86,274 | 81,665 | -5.3 | 1,219 | 983 | -19.4 | 4,332 | 3,432 | -20.8 | 81,942 | 78,233 | -4.5 |
| Driving under the influence | 1,063,940 | 1,048,934 | -1.4 | 192 | 219 | +14.1 | 11,548 | 10,276 | -11.0 | 1,052,392 | 1,038,658 | -1.3 |
| Liquor laws | 462,298 | 431,028 | -6.8 | 9,026 | 7,815 | -13.4 | 98,441 | 85,992 | -12.6 | 363,857 | 345,036 | -5.2 |
| Drunkenness | 463,495 | 442,830 | -4.5 | 1,276 | 1,219 | -4.5 | 11,851 | 10,534 | -11.1 | 451,644 | 432,296 | -4.3 |
| Disorderly conduct | 492,935 | 474,531 | -3.7 | 50,333 | 44,270 | -12.0 | 136,589 | 122,490 | -10.3 | 356,346 | 352,041 | -1.2 |
| Vagrancy | 23,531 | 23,639 | +0.5 | 901 | 501 | -44.4 | 3,053 | 2,057 | -32.6 | 20,478 | 21,582 | +5.4 |
| All other offenses (except traffic) | 2,786,093 | 2,715,573 | -2.5 | 63,523 | 56,529 | -11.0 | 269,581 | 242,711 | -10.0 | 2,516,512 | 2,472,862 | -1.7 |
| Suspicion | 1,192 | 1,444 | +21.1 | 42 | 44 | +4.8 | 184 | 167 | -9.2 | 1,008 | 1,277 | +26.7 |
| Curfew and loitering law violations | 100,826 | 86,137 | -14.6 | 25,904 | 21,251 | -18.0 | 100,826 | 86,137 | -14.6 | - | - | - |
| Runaways | 79,282 | 70,529 | -11.0 | 25,303 | 21,902 | -13.4 | 79,282 | 70,529 | -11.0 | - | - | - |

[1] Does not include suspicion.

## Table 37. Current Year Over Previous Year Arrest Trends, by Age and Sex, 2008–2009

(Number, percent change; 11,310 agencies; 2009 estimated population 224,035,573; 2008 estimated population 222,163,484.)

| Offense charged | Male | | | | | | Female | | | | | |
|---|---|---|---|---|---|---|---|---|---|---|---|---|
| | Total | | | Under 18 | | | Total | | | Under 18 | | |
| | 2008 | 2009 | Percent change | 2008 | 2009 | Percent change | 2008 | 2009 | Percent change | 2008 | 2009 | Percent change |
| **TOTAL**[1] | 7,640,534 | 7,394,270 | -3.2 | 1,079,484 | 976,538 | -9.5 | 2,510,670 | 2,514,440 | +0.2 | 467,876 | 432,979 | -7.5 |
| **Violent Crime** | 356,112 | 346,382 | -2.7 | 56,424 | 49,957 | -11.5 | 80,779 | 80,428 | -0.4 | 12,023 | 11,285 | -6.1 |
| Murder and nonnegligent manslaughter | 8,113 | 7,723 | -4.8 | 815 | 737 | -9.6 | 974 | 931 | -4.4 | 61 | 60 | -1.6 |
| Forcible rape | 15,808 | 14,906 | -5.7 | 2,359 | 2,189 | -7.2 | 189 | 187 | -1.1 | 38 | 40 | +5.3 |
| Robbery | 82,549 | 79,722 | -3.4 | 22,491 | 19,908 | -11.5 | 11,026 | 10,898 | -1.2 | 2,349 | 2,267 | -3.5 |
| Aggravated assault | 249,642 | 244,031 | -2.2 | 30,759 | 27,123 | -11.8 | 68,590 | 68,412 | -0.3 | 9,575 | 8,918 | -6.9 |
| **Property Crime** | 808,780 | 791,326 | -2.2 | 207,699 | 192,573 | -7.3 | 437,689 | 475,533 | +8.6 | 118,668 | 118,487 | -0.2 |
| Burglary | 194,315 | 186,328 | -4.1 | 54,136 | 48,423 | -10.6 | 33,571 | 32,995 | -1.7 | 7,652 | 6,341 | -17.1 |
| Larceny-theft | 548,430 | 550,408 | +0.4 | 135,022 | 129,359 | -4.2 | 390,535 | 430,794 | +10.3 | 107,706 | 109,283 | +1.5 |
| Motor vehicle theft | 57,144 | 47,126 | -17.5 | 14,220 | 11,264 | -20.8 | 11,913 | 10,239 | -14.1 | 2,705 | 2,334 | -13.7 |
| Arson | 8,891 | 7,464 | -16.0 | 4,321 | 3,527 | -18.4 | 1,670 | 1,505 | -9.9 | 605 | 529 | -12.6 |
| **Other** | | | | | | | | | | | | |
| Other assaults | 696,537 | 699,135 | +0.4 | 110,518 | 103,892 | -6.0 | 241,577 | 247,510 | +2.5 | 57,566 | 54,546 | -5.2 |
| Forgery and counterfeiting | 41,312 | 38,200 | -7.5 | 1,305 | 1,101 | -15.6 | 25,702 | 23,125 | -10.0 | 659 | 467 | -29.1 |
| Fraud | 98,149 | 90,429 | -7.9 | 3,634 | 3,101 | -14.7 | 78,205 | 69,760 | -10.8 | 1,950 | 1,682 | -13.7 |
| Embezzlement | 7,616 | 6,487 | -14.8 | 549 | 259 | -52.8 | 8,240 | 6,728 | -18.3 | 403 | 201 | -50.1 |
| Stolen property; buying, receiving, .possessing | 66,123 | 61,491 | -7.0 | 12,799 | 11,488 | -10.2 | 17,005 | 16,129 | -5.2 | 2,960 | 2,677 | -9.6 |
| Vandalism | 173,154 | 162,543 | -6.1 | 68,134 | 57,864 | -15.1 | 35,798 | 35,661 | -0.4 | 10,606 | 9,186 | -13.4 |
| Weapons; carrying, possessing, etc. | 117,737 | 109,084 | -7.3 | 25,944 | 22,091 | -14.9 | 9,682 | 9,577 | -1.1 | 2,772 | 2,580 | -6.9 |
| Prostitution and commercialized vice | 15,234 | 14,507 | -4.8 | 263 | 203 | -22.8 | 31,431 | 29,832 | -5.1 | 756 | 690 | -8.7 |
| Sex offenses (except forcible rape and prostitution) | 52,437 | 50,862 | -3.0 | 9,570 | 8,913 | -6.9 | 4,852 | 4,772 | -1.6 | 1,021 | 1,042 | +2.1 |
| Drug abuse violations | 961,288 | 941,094 | -2.1 | 104,916 | 101,001 | -3.7 | 223,523 | 219,109 | -2.0 | 20,322 | 19,624 | -3.4 |
| Gambling | 3,091 | 3,548 | +14.8 | 375 | 436 | +16.3 | 477 | 592 | +24.1 | 21 | 13 | -38.1 |
| Offenses against the family and children | 64,462 | 60,878 | -5.6 | 2,759 | 2,194 | -20.5 | 21,812 | 20,787 | -4.7 | 1,573 | 1,238 | -21.3 |
| Driving under the influence | 835,121 | 812,236 | -2.7 | 8,724 | 7,736 | -11.3 | 228,819 | 236,698 | +3.4 | 2,824 | 2,540 | -10.1 |
| Liquor laws | 332,096 | 305,560 | -8.0 | 61,187 | 52,654 | -13.9 | 130,202 | 125,468 | -3.6 | 37,254 | 33,338 | -10.5 |
| Drunkenness | 387,855 | 368,958 | -4.9 | 8,945 | 7,866 | -12.1 | 75,640 | 73,872 | -2.3 | 2,906 | 2,668 | -8.2 |
| Disorderly conduct | 360,391 | 345,338 | -4.2 | 91,385 | 81,531 | -10.8 | 132,544 | 129,193 | -2.5 | 45,204 | 40,959 | -9.4 |
| Vagrancy | 18,151 | 18,552 | +2.2 | 2,179 | 1,479 | -32.1 | 5,380 | 5,087 | -5.4 | 874 | 578 | -33.9 |
| All other offenses (except traffic) | 2,140,820 | 2,076,130 | -3.0 | 198,107 | 178,669 | -9.8 | 645,273 | 639,443 | -0.9 | 71,474 | 64,042 | -10.4 |
| Suspicion | 930 | 1,051 | +13.0 | 139 | 131 | -5.8 | 262 | 393 | +50.0 | 45 | 36 | -20.0 |
| Curfew and loitering law violations | 69,138 | 59,650 | -13.7 | 69,138 | 59,650 | -13.7 | 31,688 | 26,487 | -16.4 | 31,688 | 26,487 | -16.4 |
| Runaways | 34,930 | 31,880 | -8.7 | 34,930 | 31,880 | -8.7 | 44,352 | 38,649 | -12.9 | 44,352 | 38,649 | -12.9 |

[1] Does not include suspicion.

## Table 38. Arrests, Distribution by Age, 2009

(Number, percent; 12,371 agencies; 2009 estimated population 239,839,971.)

| Offense charged | Total all ages | Ages under 15 | Ages under 18 | Ages 18 and over | Under 10 | 10–12 | 13–14 | 15 | 16 | 17 | 18 | 19 | 20 |
|---|---|---|---|---|---|---|---|---|---|---|---|---|---|
| **TOTAL** | 10,741,157 | 403,671 | 1,515,586 | 9,225,571 | 9,737 | 81,927 | 312,007 | 294,866 | 379,225 | 437,824 | 518,358 | 538,242 | 498,582 |
| Total percent distribution[1] | 100.0 | 3.8 | 14.1 | 85.9 | 0.1 | 0.8 | 2.9 | 2.7 | 3.5 | 4.1 | 4.8 | 5.0 | 4.6 |
| **Violent Crime** | 458,291 | 17,400 | 68,074 | 390,217 | 387 | 3,790 | 13,223 | 13,272 | 17,344 | 20,058 | 23,487 | 22,381 | 20,489 |
| Violent crime percent distribution[1] | 100.0 | 3.8 | 14.9 | 85.1 | 0.1 | 0.8 | 2.9 | 2.9 | 3.8 | 4.4 | 5.1 | 4.9 | 4.5 |
| Murder and nonnegligent manslaughter | 9,775 | 87 | 942 | 8,833 | 2 | 11 | 74 | 149 | 290 | 416 | 690 | 626 | 606 |
| Forcible rape | 16,442 | 766 | 2,385 | 14,057 | 10 | 170 | 586 | 460 | 512 | 647 | 819 | 747 | 724 |
| Robbery | 100,702 | 4,601 | 25,280 | 75,422 | 31 | 574 | 3,996 | 5,208 | 7,091 | 8,380 | 9,415 | 8,001 | 6,404 |
| Aggravated assault | 331,372 | 11,946 | 39,467 | 291,905 | 344 | 3,035 | 8,567 | 7,455 | 9,451 | 10,615 | 12,563 | 13,007 | 12,755 |
| **Property Crime** | 1,369,658 | 91,962 | 334,237 | 1,035,421 | 2,027 | 19,362 | 70,573 | 65,290 | 83,760 | 93,225 | 98,194 | 82,946 | 66,097 |
| Property crime percent distribution[1] | 100.0 | 6.7 | 24.4 | 75.6 | 0.1 | 1.4 | 5.2 | 4.8 | 6.1 | 6.8 | 7.2 | 6.1 | 4.8 |
| Burglary | 235,226 | 16,173 | 59,432 | 175,794 | 487 | 3,336 | 12,350 | 11,809 | 14,698 | 16,752 | 19,298 | 16,480 | 12,687 |
| Larceny-theft | 1,060,754 | 70,216 | 254,865 | 805,889 | 1,295 | 14,943 | 53,978 | 49,213 | 63,974 | 71,462 | 73,990 | 62,376 | 50,094 |
| Motor vehicle theft | 64,169 | 3,094 | 15,724 | 48,445 | 27 | 314 | 2,753 | 3,571 | 4,494 | 4,565 | 4,491 | 3,740 | 3,028 |
| Arson | 9,509 | 2,479 | 4,216 | 5,293 | 218 | 769 | 1,492 | 697 | 594 | 446 | 415 | 350 | 288 |
| **Other** | | | | | | | | | | | | | |
| Other assaults | 1,036,754 | 63,405 | 172,984 | 863,770 | 1,718 | 16,207 | 45,480 | 33,705 | 38,243 | 37,631 | 34,663 | 35,305 | 35,583 |
| Forgery and counterfeiting | 67,357 | 220 | 1,691 | 65,666 | 8 | 47 | 165 | 234 | 405 | 832 | 2,050 | 2,865 | 3,146 |
| Fraud | 162,243 | 835 | 5,014 | 157,229 | 35 | 129 | 671 | 775 | 1,306 | 2,098 | 4,020 | 5,138 | 5,821 |
| Embezzlement | 14,097 | 32 | 484 | 13,613 | 0 | 7 | 25 | 33 | 118 | 301 | 700 | 924 | 838 |
| Stolen property; buying, receiving, possessing | 82,944 | 3,250 | 14,875 | 68,069 | 57 | 550 | 2,643 | 3,019 | 3,918 | 4,688 | 5,472 | 5,088 | 4,296 |
| Vandalism | 212,981 | 27,503 | 71,502 | 141,479 | 1,210 | 7,078 | 19,215 | 13,394 | 15,393 | 15,212 | 14,172 | 11,614 | 9,445 |
| Weapons; carrying, possessing, etc. | 130,941 | 8,299 | 26,831 | 104,110 | 404 | 2,127 | 5,768 | 4,812 | 6,154 | 7,566 | 8,801 | 7,856 | 6,907 |
| Prostitution and commercialized vice | 56,640 | 131 | 1,079 | 55,561 | 5 | 15 | 111 | 205 | 277 | 466 | 1,586 | 2,299 | 2,357 |
| Sex offenses (except forcible rape and prostitution) | 60,422 | 5,067 | 10,567 | 49,855 | 209 | 1,377 | 3,481 | 1,785 | 1,757 | 1,958 | 2,384 | 2,367 | 2,111 |
| Drug abuse violations | 1,305,191 | 21,093 | 134,610 | 1,170,581 | 149 | 2,384 | 18,560 | 22,916 | 35,953 | 54,648 | 82,707 | 84,347 | 75,769 |
| Gambling | 8,067 | 156 | 1,395 | 6,672 | 1 | 6 | 149 | 238 | 404 | 597 | 593 | 586 | 540 |
| Offenses against the family and children | 87,889 | 1,027 | 3,612 | 84,277 | 38 | 235 | 754 | 727 | 871 | 987 | 1,697 | 1,772 | 1,968 |
| Driving under the influence | 1,112,384 | 230 | 10,712 | 1,101,672 | 52 | 17 | 161 | 455 | 2,407 | 7,620 | 22,046 | 31,223 | 35,540 |
| Liquor laws | 447,496 | 8,047 | 88,370 | 359,126 | 101 | 622 | 7,324 | 13,009 | 24,825 | 42,489 | 74,907 | 82,717 | 67,585 |
| Drunkenness | 471,727 | 1,278 | 11,102 | 460,625 | 68 | 98 | 1,112 | 1,726 | 2,660 | 5,438 | 12,505 | 14,683 | 14,665 |
| Disorderly conduct | 518,374 | 48,002 | 134,301 | 384,073 | 784 | 11,058 | 36,160 | 28,031 | 30,098 | 28,170 | 24,181 | 21,131 | 19,547 |
| Vagrancy | 26,380 | 521 | 2,151 | 24,229 | 6 | 50 | 465 | 586 | 554 | 490 | 1,379 | 1,137 | 948 |
| All other offenses (except traffic) | 2,946,277 | 60,105 | 258,293 | 2,687,984 | 1,699 | 9,905 | 48,501 | 51,876 | 66,787 | 79,525 | 102,716 | 121,767 | 124,849 |
| Suspicion | 1,517 | 47 | 175 | 1,342 | 8 | 15 | 24 | 27 | 47 | 54 | 98 | 96 | 81 |
| Curfew and loitering law violations | 89,733 | 22,101 | 89,733 | - | 278 | 3,357 | 18,466 | 20,210 | 25,523 | 21,899 | - | - | - |
| Runaways | 73,794 | 22,960 | 73,794 | - | 493 | 3,491 | 18,976 | 18,541 | 20,421 | 11,872 | - | - | - |

[1] Because of rounding, the percentages may not add to 100.0.

## Table 38. Arrests, Distribution by Age, 2009—*Continued*

(Number, percent; 12,371 agencies; 2009 estimated population 239,839,971.)

| Offense charged | 21 | 22 | 23 | 24 | 25–29 | 30–34 | 35–39 | 40–44 | 45–49 | 50–54 | 55–59 | 60–64 | 65 and over |
|---|---|---|---|---|---|---|---|---|---|---|---|---|---|
| **TOTAL** | 447,724 | 411,325 | 387,740 | 365,762 | 1,556,740 | 1,101,739 | 919,270 | 838,012 | 746,658 | 476,548 | 233,305 | 103,601 | 81,965 |
| Total percent distribution[1] | 4.2 | 3.8 | 3.6 | 3.4 | 14.5 | 10.3 | 8.6 | 7.8 | 7.0 | 4.4 | 2.2 | 1.0 | 0.8 |
| | | | | | | | | | | | | | |
| **Violent Crime** | 19,690 | 17,876 | 17,137 | 15,802 | 68,683 | 48,327 | 39,038 | 34,504 | 29,117 | 17,707 | 8,616 | 3,963 | 3,400 |
| Violent crime percent distribution[1] | 4.3 | 3.9 | 3.7 | 3.4 | 15.0 | 10.5 | 8.5 | 7.5 | 6.4 | 3.9 | 1.9 | 0.9 | 0.7 |
| Murder and nonnegligent manslaughter | 586 | 473 | 434 | 422 | 1,649 | 969 | 683 | 534 | 464 | 296 | 164 | 123 | 114 |
| Forcible rape | 706 | 584 | 560 | 470 | 2,248 | 1,880 | 1,633 | 1,352 | 1,018 | 628 | 347 | 196 | 145 |
| Robbery | 5,136 | 4,391 | 3,807 | 3,214 | 12,284 | 7,101 | 5,392 | 4,491 | 3,253 | 1,602 | 621 | 206 | 104 |
| Aggravated assault | 13,262 | 12,428 | 12,336 | 11,696 | 52,502 | 38,377 | 31,330 | 28,127 | 24,382 | 15,181 | 7,484 | 3,438 | 3,037 |
| | | | | | | | | | | | | | |
| **Property Crime** | 55,204 | 46,808 | 42,171 | 38,653 | 159,305 | 110,223 | 93,598 | 86,099 | 73,435 | 44,678 | 21,139 | 9,482 | 7,389 |
| Property crime percent distribution[1] | 4.0 | 3.4 | 3.1 | 2.8 | 11.6 | 8.0 | 6.8 | 6.3 | 5.4 | 3.3 | 1.5 | 0.7 | 0.5 |
| Burglary | 10,625 | 8,755 | 7,775 | 6,887 | 28,472 | 18,309 | 14,694 | 12,950 | 10,144 | 5,394 | 2,140 | 757 | 427 |
| Larceny-theft | 41,695 | 35,452 | 32,013 | 29,616 | 121,573 | 85,344 | 73,676 | 68,801 | 60,038 | 37,666 | 18,305 | 8,463 | 6,787 |
| Motor vehicle theft | 2,650 | 2,363 | 2,189 | 1,969 | 8,482 | 6,011 | 4,750 | 3,899 | 2,761 | 1,319 | 524 | 172 | 97 |
| Arson | 234 | 238 | 194 | 181 | 778 | 559 | 478 | 449 | 492 | 299 | 170 | 90 | 78 |
| | | | | | | | | | | | | | |
| **Other** | | | | | | | | | | | | | |
| Other assaults | 38,431 | 36,892 | 35,835 | 34,868 | 155,281 | 116,378 | 99,132 | 87,375 | 73,669 | 43,323 | 19,983 | 9,223 | 7,829 |
| Forgery and counterfeiting | 2,875 | 2,763 | 2,768 | 2,810 | 13,160 | 10,005 | 7,842 | 6,227 | 4,614 | 2,653 | 1,162 | 460 | 266 |
| Fraud | 5,451 | 5,520 | 5,341 | 5,438 | 27,424 | 23,374 | 21,562 | 18,095 | 13,701 | 8,435 | 4,228 | 2,120 | 1,561 |
| Embezzlement | 790 | 657 | 546 | 581 | 2,225 | 1,592 | 1,479 | 1,166 | 959 | 605 | 321 | 145 | 85 |
| Stolen property; buying, receiving, possessing | 3,729 | 3,295 | 3,094 | 2,708 | 11,893 | 8,388 | 6,591 | 5,759 | 4,092 | 2,203 | 882 | 353 | 226 |
| Vandalism | 9,032 | 7,689 | 6,870 | 6,292 | 24,040 | 15,207 | 11,183 | 9,558 | 8,076 | 4,550 | 2,047 | 928 | 776 |
| Weapons; carrying, possessing, etc. | 6,403 | 5,732 | 5,247 | 4,828 | 19,297 | 11,530 | 7,992 | 6,477 | 5,414 | 3,685 | 1,991 | 1,085 | 865 |
| Prostitution and commercialized vice | 2,230 | 2,267 | 2,179 | 1,923 | 9,031 | 7,124 | 7,307 | 7,019 | 5,264 | 2,832 | 1,155 | 516 | 472 |
| Sex offenses (except forcible rape and prostitution) | 2,033 | 1,787 | 1,608 | 1,541 | 6,607 | 5,476 | 5,401 | 5,288 | 4,867 | 3,396 | 2,104 | 1,319 | 1,566 |
| Drug abuse violations | 66,255 | 59,531 | 55,550 | 51,603 | 211,323 | 136,769 | 102,931 | 89,387 | 76,800 | 46,664 | 20,468 | 7,231 | 3,246 |
| Gambling | 390 | 331 | 263 | 233 | 891 | 505 | 463 | 401 | 463 | 331 | 283 | 188 | 211 |
| Offenses against the family and children | 2,443 | 2,467 | 2,719 | 2,944 | 15,424 | 14,540 | 13,208 | 10,528 | 7,829 | 4,090 | 1,579 | 641 | 428 |
| Driving under the influence | 50,794 | 51,492 | 50,491 | 48,478 | 203,280 | 140,588 | 117,704 | 106,178 | 101,011 | 69,530 | 39,108 | 20,043 | 14,166 |
| Liquor laws | 10,773 | 7,516 | 6,092 | 5,070 | 19,352 | 14,178 | 13,421 | 15,615 | 17,496 | 12,796 | 6,778 | 2,934 | 1,896 |
| Drunkenness | 20,983 | 18,987 | 17,966 | 16,850 | 70,196 | 51,095 | 46,549 | 51,156 | 54,695 | 39,313 | 19,145 | 7,604 | 4,233 |
| Disorderly conduct | 23,272 | 20,431 | 17,972 | 16,037 | 62,804 | 41,509 | 34,145 | 32,592 | 31,878 | 20,609 | 10,121 | 4,388 | 3,456 |
| Vagrancy | 831 | 669 | 630 | 561 | 2,459 | 2,091 | 2,337 | 2,946 | 3,385 | 2,632 | 1,360 | 561 | 303 |
| All other offenses (except traffic) | 126,032 | 118,545 | 113,196 | 108,481 | 473,839 | 342,702 | 287,254 | 261,542 | 229,814 | 146,458 | 70,801 | 30,404 | 29,584 |
| Suspicion | 83 | 70 | 65 | 61 | 226 | 138 | 133 | 100 | 79 | 58 | 34 | 13 | 7 |
| Curfew and loitering law violations | - | - | - | - | - | - | - | - | - | - | - | - | - |
| Runaways | - | - | - | - | - | - | - | - | - | - | - | - | - |

[1] Because of rounding, the percentages may not add to 100.0.

## Table 39. Male Arrests, Distribution by Age, 2009

(Number, percent; 12,371 agencies; 2009 estimated population 239,839,971.)

| Offense charged | Total all ages | Ages under 15 | Ages under 18 | Ages 18 and over | Under 10 | 10–12 | 13–14 | 15 | 16 | 17 | 18 | 19 | 20 |
|---|---|---|---|---|---|---|---|---|---|---|---|---|---|
| **TOTAL** | 8,026,796 | 274,788 | 1,054,659 | 6,972,137 | 7,942 | 58,881 | 207,965 | 198,404 | 263,840 | 317,627 | 388,261 | 403,551 | 374,200 |
| Total percent distribution[1] | 100.0 | 3.4 | 13.1 | 86.9 | 0.1 | 0.7 | 2.6 | 2.5 | 3.3 | 4.0 | 4.8 | 5.0 | 4.7 |
| **Violent Crime** | 372,239 | 13,766 | 55,690 | 316,549 | 340 | 3,084 | 10,342 | 10,636 | 14,293 | 16,995 | 20,004 | 18,776 | 16,842 |
| Violent crime percent distribution[1] | 100.0 | 3.7 | 15.0 | 85.0 | 0.1 | 0.8 | 2.8 | 2.9 | 3.8 | 4.6 | 5.4 | 5.0 | 4.5 |
| Murder and nonnegligent manslaughter | 8,755 | 79 | 873 | 7,882 | 1 | 10 | 68 | 140 | 261 | 393 | 655 | 580 | 562 |
| Forcible rape | 16,234 | 743 | 2,340 | 13,894 | 9 | 163 | 571 | 451 | 505 | 641 | 812 | 738 | 711 |
| Robbery | 88,783 | 4,054 | 22,757 | 66,026 | 31 | 510 | 3,513 | 4,664 | 6,422 | 7,617 | 8,530 | 7,216 | 5,725 |
| Aggravated assault | 258,467 | 8,890 | 29,720 | 228,747 | 299 | 2,401 | 6,190 | 5,381 | 7,105 | 8,344 | 10,007 | 10,242 | 9,844 |
| **Property Crime** | 858,016 | 58,385 | 207,846 | 650,170 | 1,572 | 12,752 | 44,061 | 40,251 | 51,534 | 57,676 | 62,046 | 52,426 | 41,272 |
| Property crime percent distribution[1] | 100.0 | 6.8 | 24.2 | 75.8 | 0.2 | 1.5 | 5.1 | 4.7 | 6.0 | 6.7 | 7.2 | 6.1 | 4.8 |
| Burglary | 200,117 | 14,228 | 52,569 | 147,548 | 429 | 2,941 | 10,858 | 10,353 | 13,107 | 14,881 | 17,055 | 14,421 | 10,923 |
| Larceny-theft | 597,246 | 39,575 | 138,535 | 458,711 | 916 | 8,875 | 29,784 | 26,402 | 34,107 | 38,451 | 40,732 | 34,497 | 27,581 |
| Motor vehicle theft | 52,761 | 2,411 | 13,078 | 39,683 | 24 | 254 | 2,133 | 2,907 | 3,807 | 3,953 | 3,889 | 3,206 | 2,515 |
| Arson | 7,892 | 2,171 | 3,664 | 4,228 | 203 | 682 | 1,286 | 589 | 513 | 391 | 370 | 302 | 253 |
| **Other** | | | | | | | | | | | | | |
| Other assaults | 767,018 | 42,078 | 113,849 | 653,169 | 1,434 | 11,729 | 28,915 | 21,385 | 24,847 | 25,539 | 24,347 | 24,950 | 25,125 |
| Forgery and counterfeiting | 41,932 | 163 | 1,187 | 40,745 | 5 | 36 | 122 | 159 | 300 | 565 | 1,304 | 1,799 | 1,923 |
| Fraud | 92,850 | 542 | 3,252 | 89,598 | 21 | 93 | 428 | 508 | 851 | 1,351 | 2,583 | 3,242 | 3,531 |
| Embezzlement | 6,920 | 23 | 281 | 6,639 | 0 | 6 | 17 | 21 | 64 | 173 | 368 | 436 | 450 |
| Stolen property; buying, receiving, possessing | 65,644 | 2,539 | 12,064 | 53,580 | 44 | 430 | 2,065 | 2,408 | 3,222 | 3,895 | 4,535 | 4,197 | 3,476 |
| Vandalism | 174,477 | 23,689 | 61,720 | 112,757 | 1,091 | 6,065 | 16,533 | 11,633 | 13,314 | 13,084 | 12,089 | 9,656 | 7,717 |
| Weapons; carrying, possessing, etc. | 120,430 | 7,187 | 24,064 | 96,366 | 350 | 1,861 | 4,976 | 4,320 | 5,566 | 6,991 | 8,300 | 7,413 | 6,462 |
| Prostitution and commercialized vice | 17,203 | 49 | 235 | 16,968 | 3 | 14 | 32 | 30 | 57 | 99 | 203 | 367 | 411 |
| Sex offenses (except forcible rape and prostitution) | 55,085 | 4,539 | 9,458 | 45,627 | 183 | 1,241 | 3,115 | 1,565 | 1,578 | 1,776 | 2,135 | 2,101 | 1,870 |
| Drug abuse violations | 1,062,777 | 16,951 | 113,608 | 949,169 | 126 | 1,903 | 14,922 | 19,042 | 30,616 | 46,999 | 70,526 | 71,234 | 63,544 |
| Gambling | 7,163 | 155 | 1,357 | 5,806 | 1 | 6 | 148 | 233 | 391 | 578 | 551 | 532 | 472 |
| Offenses against the family and children | 65,557 | 673 | 2,317 | 63,240 | 26 | 161 | 486 | 405 | 578 | 661 | 1,200 | 1,222 | 1,335 |
| Driving under the influence | 860,689 | 160 | 8,044 | 852,645 | 42 | 11 | 107 | 321 | 1,803 | 5,760 | 16,877 | 24,004 | 27,198 |
| Liquor laws | 319,364 | 4,095 | 54,321 | 265,043 | 75 | 296 | 3,724 | 7,313 | 15,230 | 27,683 | 50,610 | 57,550 | 48,300 |
| Drunkenness | 393,586 | 774 | 8,288 | 385,298 | 55 | 50 | 669 | 1,181 | 2,001 | 4,332 | 10,129 | 11,954 | 12,129 |
| Disorderly conduct | 379,059 | 31,258 | 89,579 | 289,480 | 653 | 7,643 | 22,962 | 18,192 | 20,182 | 19,947 | 17,860 | 15,619 | 14,412 |
| Vagrancy | 20,725 | 357 | 1,550 | 19,175 | 6 | 28 | 323 | 417 | 393 | 383 | 1,086 | 823 | 702 |
| All other offenses (except traffic) | 2,249,656 | 42,510 | 190,500 | 2,059,156 | 1,363 | 7,299 | 33,848 | 36,856 | 49,614 | 61,520 | 81,427 | 95,178 | 96,970 |
| Suspicion | 1,093 | 37 | 136 | 957 | 5 | 14 | 18 | 21 | 37 | 41 | 81 | 72 | 59 |
| Curfew and loitering law violations | 62,229 | 14,659 | 62,229 | - | 205 | 2,315 | 12,139 | 13,552 | 18,063 | 15,955 | - | - | - |
| Runaways | 33,084 | 10,199 | 33,084 | - | 342 | 1,844 | 8,013 | 7,955 | 9,306 | 5,624 | - | - | - |

[1] Because of rounding, the percentages may not add to 100.0.

## Table 39. Male Arrests, Distribution by Age, 2009—*Continued*

(Number, percent; 12,371 agencies; 2009 estimated population 239,839,971.)

| Offense charged | 21 | 22 | 23 | 24 | 25–29 | 30–34 | 35–39 | 40–44 | 45–49 | 50–54 | 55–59 | 60–64 | 65 and over |
|---|---|---|---|---|---|---|---|---|---|---|---|---|---|
| **TOTAL** | 339,290 | 311,789 | 292,731 | 275,913 | 1,175,426 | 826,253 | 678,941 | 622,155 | 567,147 | 377,048 | 190,341 | 85,009 | 64,082 |
| Total percent distribution[1] | 4.2 | 3.9 | 3.6 | 3.4 | 14.6 | 10.3 | 8.5 | 7.8 | 7.1 | 4.7 | 2.4 | 1.1 | 0.8 |
| **Violent Crime** | 16,104 | 14,537 | 13,867 | 12,694 | 55,456 | 38,760 | 30,963 | 27,168 | 23,216 | 14,442 | 7,321 | 3,424 | 2,975 |
| Violent crime percent distribution[1] | 4.3 | 3.9 | 3.7 | 3.4 | 14.9 | 10.4 | 8.3 | 7.3 | 6.2 | 3.9 | 2.0 | 0.9 | 0.8 |
| Murder and nonnegligent manslaughter | 525 | 429 | 398 | 380 | 1,476 | 841 | 601 | 426 | 394 | 250 | 146 | 113 | 106 |
| Forcible rape | 693 | 581 | 552 | 463 | 2,217 | 1,864 | 1,612 | 1,335 | 1,010 | 623 | 342 | 196 | 145 |
| Robbery | 4,555 | 3,848 | 3,306 | 2,785 | 10,575 | 6,073 | 4,581 | 3,806 | 2,792 | 1,402 | 555 | 185 | 92 |
| Aggravated assault | 10,331 | 9,679 | 9,611 | 9,066 | 41,188 | 29,982 | 24,169 | 21,601 | 19,020 | 12,167 | 6,278 | 2,930 | 2,632 |
| **Property Crime** | 34,487 | 29,076 | 25,872 | 23,474 | 97,694 | 67,476 | 58,569 | 55,943 | 48,447 | 29,528 | 13,648 | 5,782 | 4,430 |
| Property crime percent distribution[1] | 4.0 | 3.4 | 3.0 | 2.7 | 11.4 | 7.9 | 6.8 | 6.5 | 5.6 | 3.4 | 1.6 | 0.7 | 0.5 |
| Burglary | 8,996 | 7,443 | 6,516 | 5,756 | 23,410 | 14,798 | 11,851 | 10,661 | 8,432 | 4,554 | 1,780 | 619 | 333 |
| Larceny-theft | 23,065 | 19,503 | 17,406 | 15,978 | 66,994 | 47,442 | 42,536 | 41,791 | 37,385 | 23,630 | 11,276 | 4,938 | 3,957 |
| Motor vehicle theft | 2,224 | 1,935 | 1,786 | 1,594 | 6,686 | 4,801 | 3,812 | 3,166 | 2,273 | 1,107 | 458 | 150 | 81 |
| Arson | 202 | 195 | 164 | 146 | 604 | 435 | 370 | 325 | 357 | 237 | 134 | 75 | 59 |
| **Other** | | | | | | | | | | | | | |
| Other assaults | 27,905 | 26,965 | 26,500 | 26,044 | 118,074 | 89,271 | 75,272 | 66,592 | 57,132 | 34,629 | 16,252 | 7,583 | 6,528 |
| Forgery and counterfeiting | 1,773 | 1,726 | 1,719 | 1,711 | 8,072 | 6,002 | 4,740 | 3,813 | 2,979 | 1,805 | 843 | 323 | 213 |
| Fraud | 3,285 | 3,266 | 3,105 | 3,118 | 15,137 | 12,595 | 11,376 | 10,002 | 8,263 | 5,252 | 2,651 | 1,283 | 909 |
| Embezzlement | 412 | 325 | 268 | 285 | 1,100 | 719 | 700 | 538 | 470 | 284 | 169 | 73 | 42 |
| Stolen property; buying, receiving, possessing | 2,941 | 2,544 | 2,408 | 2,078 | 9,049 | 6,414 | 5,101 | 4,527 | 3,272 | 1,819 | 730 | 296 | 193 |
| Vandalism | 7,286 | 6,128 | 5,508 | 4,985 | 18,895 | 11,856 | 8,460 | 7,305 | 6,210 | 3,606 | 1,666 | 752 | 638 |
| Weapons; carrying, possessing, etc. | 5,981 | 5,342 | 4,869 | 4,483 | 17,888 | 10,608 | 7,264 | 5,820 | 4,885 | 3,390 | 1,833 | 1,020 | 808 |
| Prostitution and commercialized vice | 413 | 536 | 562 | 514 | 2,756 | 2,345 | 2,171 | 2,072 | 1,685 | 1,303 | 762 | 425 | 443 |
| Sex offenses (except forcible rape and prostitution) | 1,840 | 1,602 | 1,440 | 1,365 | 5,937 | 4,950 | 4,901 | 4,866 | 4,525 | 3,243 | 2,020 | 1,282 | 1,550 |
| Drug abuse violations | 54,874 | 49,345 | 45,683 | 42,270 | 171,931 | 109,967 | 79,765 | 67,589 | 58,557 | 37,519 | 17,180 | 6,296 | 2,889 |
| Gambling | 377 | 317 | 250 | 217 | 825 | 451 | 388 | 317 | 361 | 233 | 215 | 134 | 166 |
| Offenses against the family and children | 1,713 | 1,652 | 1,824 | 1,981 | 10,866 | 10,702 | 10,157 | 8,448 | 6,514 | 3,432 | 1,314 | 539 | 341 |
| Driving under the influence | 38,081 | 38,941 | 38,348 | 37,395 | 159,060 | 110,777 | 91,086 | 79,883 | 75,868 | 54,344 | 31,933 | 16,808 | 12,042 |
| Liquor laws | 8,520 | 6,036 | 4,884 | 4,073 | 15,542 | 11,226 | 10,498 | 12,408 | 14,164 | 10,987 | 5,981 | 2,612 | 1,652 |
| Drunkenness | 17,576 | 15,931 | 15,016 | 14,222 | 59,049 | 42,830 | 38,144 | 41,422 | 45,055 | 33,850 | 17,145 | 6,912 | 3,934 |
| Disorderly conduct | 17,724 | 15,651 | 13,600 | 12,126 | 47,297 | 30,936 | 24,608 | 23,945 | 24,310 | 16,468 | 8,399 | 3,685 | 2,840 |
| Vagrancy | 652 | 546 | 497 | 449 | 1,912 | 1,583 | 1,648 | 2,251 | 2,746 | 2,262 | 1,222 | 517 | 279 |
| All other offenses (except traffic) | 97,292 | 91,273 | 86,468 | 82,388 | 358,718 | 256,688 | 213,046 | 197,172 | 178,431 | 118,615 | 59,032 | 25,252 | 21,206 |
| Suspicion | 54 | 50 | 43 | 41 | 168 | 97 | 84 | 74 | 57 | 37 | 25 | 11 | 4 |
| Curfew and loitering law violations | - | - | - | - | - | - | - | - | - | - | - | - | - |
| Runaways | - | - | - | - | - | - | - | - | - | - | - | - | - |

[1] Because of rounding, the percentages may not add to 100.0.

## Table 40. Female Arrests, Distribution by Age, 2009

(Number, percent; 12,371 agencies; 2009 estimated population 239,839,971.)

| Offense charged | Total all ages | Ages under 15 | Ages under 18 | Ages 18 and over | Under 10 | 10–12 | 13–14 | 15 | 16 | 17 | 18 | 19 | 20 |
|---|---|---|---|---|---|---|---|---|---|---|---|---|---|
| **TOTAL** | 2,714,361 | 128,883 | 460,927 | 2,253,434 | 1,795 | 23,046 | 104,042 | 96,462 | 115,385 | 120,197 | 130,097 | 134,691 | 124,382 |
| Total percent distribution[1] | 100.0 | 4.7 | 17.0 | 83.0 | 0.1 | 0.8 | 3.8 | 3.6 | 4.3 | 4.4 | 4.8 | 5.0 | 4.6 |
| | | | | | | | | | | | | | |
| **Violent Crime** | 86,052 | 3,634 | 12,384 | 73,668 | 47 | 706 | 2,881 | 2,636 | 3,051 | 3,063 | 3,483 | 3,605 | 3,647 |
| Violent crime percent distribution[1] | 100.0 | 4.2 | 14.4 | 85.6 | 0.1 | 0.8 | 3.3 | 3.1 | 3.5 | 3.6 | 4.0 | 4.2 | 4.2 |
| Murder and nonnegligent manslaughter | 1,020 | 8 | 69 | 951 | 1 | 1 | 6 | 9 | 29 | 23 | 35 | 46 | 44 |
| Forcible rape | 208 | 23 | 45 | 163 | 1 | 7 | 15 | 9 | 7 | 6 | 7 | 9 | 13 |
| Robbery | 11,919 | 547 | 2,523 | 9,396 | 0 | 64 | 483 | 544 | 669 | 763 | 885 | 785 | 679 |
| Aggravated assault | 72,905 | 3,056 | 9,747 | 63,158 | 45 | 634 | 2,377 | 2,074 | 2,346 | 2,271 | 2,556 | 2,765 | 2,911 |
| | | | | | | | | | | | | | |
| **Property Crime** | 511,642 | 33,577 | 126,391 | 385,251 | 455 | 6,610 | 26,512 | 25,039 | 32,226 | 35,549 | 36,148 | 30,520 | 24,825 |
| Property crime percent distribution[1] | 100.0 | 6.6 | 24.7 | 75.3 | 0.1 | 1.3 | 5.2 | 4.9 | 6.3 | 6.9 | 7.1 | 6.0 | 4.9 |
| Burglary | 35,109 | 1,945 | 6,863 | 28,246 | 58 | 395 | 1,492 | 1,456 | 1,591 | 1,871 | 2,243 | 2,059 | 1,764 |
| Larceny-theft | 463,508 | 30,641 | 116,330 | 347,178 | 379 | 6,068 | 24,194 | 22,811 | 29,867 | 33,011 | 33,258 | 27,879 | 22,513 |
| Motor vehicle theft | 11,408 | 683 | 2,646 | 8,762 | 3 | 60 | 620 | 664 | 687 | 612 | 602 | 534 | 513 |
| Arson | 1,617 | 308 | 552 | 1,065 | 15 | 87 | 206 | 108 | 81 | 55 | 45 | 48 | 35 |
| | | | | | | | | | | | | | |
| **Other** | | | | | | | | | | | | | |
| Other assaults | 269,736 | 21,327 | 59,135 | 210,601 | 284 | 4,478 | 16,565 | 12,320 | 13,396 | 12,092 | 10,316 | 10,355 | 10,458 |
| Forgery and counterfeiting | 25,425 | 57 | 504 | 24,921 | 3 | 11 | 43 | 75 | 105 | 267 | 746 | 1,066 | 1,223 |
| Fraud | 69,393 | 293 | 1,762 | 67,631 | 14 | 36 | 243 | 267 | 455 | 747 | 1,437 | 1,896 | 2,290 |
| Embezzlement | 7,177 | 9 | 203 | 6,974 | 0 | 1 | 8 | 12 | 54 | 128 | 332 | 488 | 388 |
| Stolen property; buying, receiving, possessing | 17,300 | 711 | 2,811 | 14,489 | 13 | 120 | 578 | 611 | 696 | 793 | 937 | 891 | 820 |
| Vandalism | 38,504 | 3,814 | 9,782 | 28,722 | 119 | 1,013 | 2,682 | 1,761 | 2,079 | 2,128 | 2,083 | 1,958 | 1,728 |
| Weapons; carrying, possessing, etc. | 10,511 | 1,112 | 2,767 | 7,744 | 54 | 266 | 792 | 492 | 588 | 575 | 501 | 443 | 445 |
| Prostitution and commercialized vice | 39,437 | 82 | 844 | 38,593 | 2 | 1 | 79 | 175 | 220 | 367 | 1,383 | 1,932 | 1,946 |
| Sex offenses (except forcible rape and prostitution) | 5,337 | 528 | 1,109 | 4,228 | 26 | 136 | 366 | 220 | 179 | 182 | 249 | 266 | 241 |
| Drug abuse violations | 242,414 | 4,142 | 21,002 | 221,412 | 23 | 481 | 3,638 | 3,874 | 5,337 | 7,649 | 12,181 | 13,113 | 12,225 |
| Gambling | 904 | 1 | 38 | 866 | 0 | 0 | 1 | 5 | 13 | 19 | 42 | 54 | 68 |
| Offenses against the family and children | 22,332 | 354 | 1,295 | 21,037 | 12 | 74 | 268 | 322 | 293 | 326 | 497 | 550 | 633 |
| Driving under the influence | 251,695 | 70 | 2,668 | 249,027 | 10 | 6 | 54 | 134 | 604 | 1,860 | 5,169 | 7,219 | 8,342 |
| Liquor laws | 128,132 | 3,952 | 34,049 | 94,083 | 26 | 326 | 3,600 | 5,696 | 9,595 | 14,806 | 24,297 | 25,167 | 19,285 |
| Drunkenness | 78,141 | 504 | 2,814 | 75,327 | 13 | 48 | 443 | 545 | 659 | 1,106 | 2,376 | 2,729 | 2,536 |
| Disorderly conduct | 139,315 | 16,744 | 44,722 | 94,593 | 131 | 3,415 | 13,198 | 9,839 | 9,916 | 8,223 | 6,321 | 5,512 | 5,135 |
| Vagrancy | 5,655 | 164 | 601 | 5,054 | 0 | 22 | 142 | 169 | 161 | 107 | 293 | 314 | 246 |
| All other offenses (except traffic) | 696,621 | 17,595 | 67,793 | 628,828 | 336 | 2,606 | 14,653 | 15,020 | 17,173 | 18,005 | 21,289 | 26,589 | 27,879 |
| Suspicion | 424 | 10 | 39 | 385 | 3 | 1 | 6 | 6 | 10 | 13 | 17 | 24 | 22 |
| Curfew and loitering law violations | 27,504 | 7,442 | 27,504 | - | 73 | 1,042 | 6,327 | 6,658 | 7,460 | 5,944 | - | - | - |
| Runaways | 40,710 | 12,761 | 40,710 | - | 151 | 1,647 | 10,963 | 10,586 | 11,115 | 6,248 | - | - | - |

[1] Because of rounding, the percentages may not add to 100.0.

# Table 40. Female Arrests, Distribution by Age, 2009—*Continued*

(Number, percent; 12,371 agencies; 2009 estimated population 239,839,971.)

| Offense charged | 21 | 22 | 23 | 24 | 25–29 | 30–34 | 35–39 | 40–44 | 45–49 | 50–54 | 55–59 | 60–64 | 65 and over |
|---|---|---|---|---|---|---|---|---|---|---|---|---|---|
| **TOTAL** | 108,434 | 99,536 | 95,009 | 89,849 | 381,314 | 275,486 | 240,329 | 215,857 | 179,511 | 99,500 | 42,964 | 18,592 | 17,883 |
| Total percent distribution[1] | 4.0 | 3.7 | 3.5 | 3.3 | 14.0 | 10.1 | 8.9 | 8.0 | 6.6 | 3.7 | 1.6 | 0.7 | 0.7 |
| **Violent Crime** | 3,586 | 3,339 | 3,270 | 3,108 | 13,227 | 9,567 | 8,075 | 7,336 | 5,901 | 3,265 | 1,295 | 539 | 425 |
| Violent crime percent distribution[1] | 4.2 | 3.9 | 3.8 | 3.6 | 15.4 | 11.1 | 9.4 | 8.5 | 6.9 | 3.8 | 1.5 | 0.6 | 0.5 |
| Murder and nonnegligent manslaughter | 61 | 44 | 36 | 42 | 173 | 128 | 82 | 108 | 70 | 46 | 18 | 10 | 8 |
| Forcible rape | 13 | 3 | 8 | 7 | 31 | 16 | 21 | 17 | 8 | 5 | 5 | 0 | 0 |
| Robbery | 581 | 543 | 501 | 429 | 1,709 | 1,028 | 811 | 685 | 461 | 200 | 66 | 21 | 12 |
| Aggravated assault | 2,931 | 2,749 | 2,725 | 2,630 | 11,314 | 8,395 | 7,161 | 6,526 | 5,362 | 3,014 | 1,206 | 508 | 405 |
| **Property Crime** | 20,717 | 17,732 | 16,299 | 15,179 | 61,611 | 42,747 | 35,029 | 30,156 | 24,988 | 15,150 | 7,491 | 3,700 | 2,959 |
| Property crime percent distribution[1] | 4.0 | 3.5 | 3.2 | 3.0 | 12.0 | 8.4 | 6.8 | 5.9 | 4.9 | 3.0 | 1.5 | 0.7 | 0.6 |
| Burglary | 1,629 | 1,312 | 1,259 | 1,131 | 5,062 | 3,511 | 2,843 | 2,289 | 1,712 | 840 | 360 | 138 | 94 |
| Larceny-theft | 18,630 | 15,949 | 14,607 | 13,638 | 54,579 | 37,902 | 31,140 | 27,010 | 22,653 | 14,036 | 7,029 | 3,525 | 2,830 |
| Motor vehicle theft | 426 | 428 | 403 | 375 | 1,796 | 1,210 | 938 | 733 | 488 | 212 | 66 | 22 | 16 |
| Arson | 32 | 43 | 30 | 35 | 174 | 124 | 108 | 124 | 135 | 62 | 36 | 15 | 19 |
| **Other** | | | | | | | | | | | | | |
| Other assaults | 10,526 | 9,927 | 9,335 | 8,824 | 37,207 | 27,107 | 23,860 | 20,783 | 16,537 | 8,694 | 3,731 | 1,640 | 1,301 |
| Forgery and counterfeiting | 1,102 | 1,037 | 1,049 | 1,099 | 5,088 | 4,003 | 3,102 | 2,414 | 1,635 | 848 | 319 | 137 | 53 |
| Fraud | 2,166 | 2,254 | 2,236 | 2,320 | 12,287 | 10,779 | 10,186 | 8,093 | 5,438 | 3,183 | 1,577 | 837 | 652 |
| Embezzlement | 378 | 332 | 278 | 296 | 1,125 | 873 | 779 | 628 | 489 | 321 | 152 | 72 | 43 |
| Stolen property; buying, receiving, possessing | 788 | 751 | 686 | 630 | 2,844 | 1,974 | 1,490 | 1,232 | 820 | 384 | 152 | 57 | 33 |
| Vandalism | 1,746 | 1,561 | 1,362 | 1,307 | 5,145 | 3,351 | 2,723 | 2,253 | 1,866 | 944 | 381 | 176 | 138 |
| Weapons; carrying, possessing, etc. | 422 | 390 | 378 | 345 | 1,409 | 922 | 728 | 657 | 529 | 295 | 158 | 65 | 57 |
| Prostitution and commercialized vice | 1,817 | 1,731 | 1,617 | 1,409 | 6,275 | 4,779 | 5,136 | 4,947 | 3,579 | 1,529 | 393 | 91 | 29 |
| Sex offenses (except forcible rape and prostitution) | 193 | 185 | 168 | 176 | 670 | 526 | 500 | 422 | 342 | 153 | 84 | 37 | 16 |
| Drug abuse violations | 11,381 | 10,186 | 9,867 | 9,333 | 39,392 | 26,802 | 23,166 | 21,798 | 18,243 | 9,145 | 3,288 | 935 | 357 |
| Gambling | 13 | 14 | 13 | 16 | 66 | 54 | 75 | 84 | 102 | 98 | 68 | 54 | 45 |
| Offenses against the family and children | 730 | 815 | 895 | 963 | 4,558 | 3,838 | 3,051 | 2,080 | 1,315 | 658 | 265 | 102 | 87 |
| Driving under the influence | 12,713 | 12,551 | 12,143 | 11,083 | 44,220 | 29,811 | 26,618 | 26,295 | 25,143 | 15,186 | 7,175 | 3,235 | 2,124 |
| Liquor laws | 2,253 | 1,480 | 1,208 | 997 | 3,810 | 2,952 | 2,923 | 3,207 | 3,332 | 1,809 | 797 | 322 | 244 |
| Drunkenness | 3,407 | 3,056 | 2,950 | 2,628 | 11,147 | 8,265 | 8,405 | 9,734 | 9,640 | 5,463 | 2,000 | 692 | 299 |
| Disorderly conduct | 5,548 | 4,780 | 4,372 | 3,911 | 15,507 | 10,573 | 9,537 | 8,647 | 7,568 | 4,141 | 1,722 | 703 | 616 |
| Vagrancy | 179 | 123 | 133 | 112 | 547 | 508 | 689 | 695 | 639 | 370 | 138 | 44 | 24 |
| All other offenses (except traffic) | 28,740 | 27,272 | 26,728 | 26,093 | 115,121 | 86,014 | 74,208 | 64,370 | 51,383 | 27,843 | 11,769 | 5,152 | 8,378 |
| Suspicion | 29 | 20 | 22 | 20 | 58 | 41 | 49 | 26 | 22 | 21 | 9 | 2 | 3 |
| Curfew and loitering law violations | - | - | - | - | - | - | - | - | - | - | - | - | - |
| Runaways | - | - | - | - | - | - | - | - | - | - | - | - | - |

[1] Because of rounding, the percentages may not add to 100.0.

## Table 41. Arrests of Persons Under 15, 18, 21, and 25 Years of Age, 2009

(Number, percent; 12,371 agencies; 2009 estimated population 239,839,971.)

| Offense charged | Total all ages | Number of persons arrested | | | | Percent of total all ages | | | |
|---|---|---|---|---|---|---|---|---|---|
| | | Under 15 | Under 18 | Under 21 | Under 25 | Under 15 | Under 18 | Under 21 | Under 25 |
| **TOTAL** | 10,741,157 | 403,671 | 1,515,586 | 3,070,768 | 4,683,319 | 3.8 | 14.1 | 28.6 | 43.6 |
| **Violent Crime** | 458,291 | 17,400 | 68,074 | 134,431 | 204,936 | 3.8 | 14.9 | 29.3 | 44.7 |
| Murder and nonnegligent manslaughter | 9,775 | 87 | 942 | 2,864 | 4,779 | 0.9 | 9.6 | 29.3 | 48.9 |
| Forcible rape | 16,442 | 766 | 2,385 | 4,675 | 6,995 | 4.7 | 14.5 | 28.4 | 42.5 |
| Robbery | 100,702 | 4,601 | 25,280 | 49,100 | 65,648 | 4.6 | 25.1 | 48.8 | 65.2 |
| Aggravated assault | 331,372 | 11,946 | 39,467 | 77,792 | 127,514 | 3.6 | 11.9 | 23.5 | 38.5 |
| **Property Crime** | 1,369,658 | 91,962 | 334,237 | 581,474 | 764,310 | 6.7 | 24.4 | 42.5 | 55.8 |
| Burglary | 235,226 | 16,173 | 59,432 | 107,897 | 141,939 | 6.9 | 25.3 | 45.9 | 60.3 |
| Larceny-theft | 1,060,754 | 70,216 | 254,865 | 441,325 | 580,101 | 6.6 | 24.0 | 41.6 | 54.7 |
| Motor vehicle theft | 64,169 | 3,094 | 15,724 | 26,983 | 36,154 | 4.8 | 24.5 | 42.0 | 56.3 |
| Arson | 9,509 | 2,479 | 4,216 | 5,269 | 6,116 | 26.1 | 44.3 | 55.4 | 64.3 |
| **Other** | | | | | | | | | |
| Other assaults | 1,036,754 | 63,405 | 172,984 | 278,535 | 424,561 | 6.1 | 16.7 | 26.9 | 41.0 |
| Forgery and counterfeiting | 67,357 | 220 | 1,691 | 9,752 | 20,968 | 0.3 | 2.5 | 14.5 | 31.1 |
| Fraud | 162,243 | 835 | 5,014 | 19,993 | 41,743 | 0.5 | 3.1 | 12.3 | 25.7 |
| Embezzlement | 14,097 | 32 | 484 | 2,946 | 5,520 | 0.2 | 3.4 | 20.9 | 39.2 |
| Stolen property; buying, receiving, possessing | 82,944 | 3,250 | 14,875 | 29,731 | 42,557 | 3.9 | 17.9 | 35.8 | 51.3 |
| Vandalism | 212,981 | 27,503 | 71,502 | 106,733 | 136,616 | 12.9 | 33.6 | 50.1 | 64.1 |
| Weapons; carrying, possessing, etc. | 130,941 | 8,299 | 26,831 | 50,395 | 72,605 | 6.3 | 20.5 | 38.5 | 55.4 |
| Prostitution and commercialized vice | 56,640 | 131 | 1,079 | 7,321 | 15,920 | 0.2 | 1.9 | 12.9 | 28.1 |
| Sex offenses (except forcible rape and prostitution) | 60,422 | 5,067 | 10,567 | 17,429 | 24,398 | 8.4 | 17.5 | 28.8 | 40.4 |
| Drug abuse violations | 1,305,191 | 21,093 | 134,610 | 377,433 | 610,372 | 1.6 | 10.3 | 28.9 | 46.8 |
| Gambling | 8,067 | 156 | 1,395 | 3,114 | 4,331 | 1.9 | 17.3 | 38.6 | 53.7 |
| Offenses against the family and children | 87,889 | 1,027 | 3,612 | 9,049 | 19,622 | 1.2 | 4.1 | 10.3 | 22.3 |
| Driving under the influence | 1,112,384 | 230 | 10,712 | 99,521 | 300,776 | * | 1.0 | 8.9 | 27.0 |
| Liquor laws | 447,496 | 8,047 | 88,370 | 313,579 | 343,030 | 1.8 | 19.7 | 70.1 | 76.7 |
| Drunkenness | 471,727 | 1,278 | 11,102 | 52,955 | 127,741 | 0.3 | 2.4 | 11.2 | 27.1 |
| Disorderly conduct | 518,374 | 48,002 | 134,301 | 199,160 | 276,872 | 9.3 | 25.9 | 38.4 | 53.4 |
| Vagrancy | 26,380 | 521 | 2,151 | 5,615 | 8,306 | 2.0 | 8.2 | 21.3 | 31.5 |
| All other offenses (except traffic) | 2,946,277 | 60,105 | 258,293 | 607,625 | 1,073,879 | 2.0 | 8.8 | 20.6 | 36.4 |
| Suspicion | 1,517 | 47 | 175 | 450 | 729 | 3.1 | 11.5 | 29.7 | 48.1 |
| Curfew and loitering law violations | 89,733 | 22,101 | 89,733 | 89,733 | 89,733 | 24.6 | 100.0 | 100.0 | 100.0 |
| Runaways | 73,794 | 22,960 | 73,794 | 73,794 | 73,794 | 31.1 | 100.0 | 100.0 | 100.0 |

* Less than one-tenth of 1 percent.

## Table 42. Arrests, Distribution by Sex, 2009

(Number, percent; 12,371 agencies; 2009 estimated population 239,839,971.)

| Offense charged | Number of persons arrested | | | Percent male | Percent female | Percent distribution[1] | | |
|---|---|---|---|---|---|---|---|---|
| | Total | Male | Female | | | Total | Male | Female |
| **TOTAL** | 10,741,157 | 8,026,796 | 2,714,361 | 74.7 | 25.3 | 100.0 | 100.0 | 100.0 |
| **Violent Crime** | 458,291 | 372,239 | 86,052 | 81.2 | 18.8 | 4.3 | 4.6 | 3.2 |
| Murder and nonnegligent manslaughter | 9,775 | 8,755 | 1,020 | 89.6 | 10.4 | 0.1 | 0.1 | * |
| Forcible rape | 16,442 | 16,234 | 208 | 98.7 | 1.3 | 0.2 | 0.2 | * |
| Robbery | 100,702 | 88,783 | 11,919 | 88.2 | 11.8 | 0.9 | 1.1 | 0.4 |
| Aggravated assault | 331,372 | 258,467 | 72,905 | 78.0 | 22.0 | 3.1 | 3.2 | 2.7 |
| **Property Crime** | 1,369,658 | 858,016 | 511,642 | 62.6 | 37.4 | 12.8 | 10.7 | 18.8 |
| Burglary | 235,226 | 200,117 | 35,109 | 85.1 | 14.9 | 2.2 | 2.5 | 1.3 |
| Larceny-theft | 1,060,754 | 597,246 | 463,508 | 56.3 | 43.7 | 9.9 | 7.4 | 17.1 |
| Motor vehicle theft | 64,169 | 52,761 | 11,408 | 82.2 | 17.8 | 0.6 | 0.7 | 0.4 |
| Arson | 9,509 | 7,892 | 1,617 | 83.0 | 17.0 | 0.1 | 0.1 | 0.1 |
| **Other** | | | | | | | | |
| Other assaults | 1,036,754 | 767,018 | 269,736 | 74.0 | 26.0 | 9.7 | 9.6 | 9.9 |
| Forgery and counterfeiting | 67,357 | 41,932 | 25,425 | 62.3 | 37.7 | 0.6 | 0.5 | 0.9 |
| Fraud | 162,243 | 92,850 | 69,393 | 57.2 | 42.8 | 1.5 | 1.2 | 2.6 |
| Embezzlement | 14,097 | 6,920 | 7,177 | 49.1 | 50.9 | 0.1 | 0.1 | 0.3 |
| Stolen property; buying, receiving, possessing | 82,944 | 65,644 | 17,300 | 79.1 | 20.9 | 0.8 | 0.8 | 0.6 |
| Vandalism | 212,981 | 174,477 | 38,504 | 81.9 | 18.1 | 2.0 | 2.2 | 1.4 |
| Weapons; carrying, possessing, etc. | 130,941 | 120,430 | 10,511 | 92.0 | 8.0 | 1.2 | 1.5 | 0.4 |
| Prostitution and commercialized vice | 56,640 | 17,203 | 39,437 | 30.4 | 69.6 | 0.5 | 0.2 | 1.5 |
| Sex offenses (except forcible rape and prostitution) | 60,422 | 55,085 | 5,337 | 91.2 | 8.8 | 0.6 | 0.7 | 0.2 |
| Drug abuse violations | 1,305,191 | 1,062,777 | 242,414 | 81.4 | 18.6 | 12.2 | 13.2 | 8.9 |
| Gambling | 8,067 | 7,163 | 904 | 88.8 | 11.2 | 0.1 | 0.1 | * |
| Offenses against the family and children | 87,889 | 65,557 | 22,332 | 74.6 | 25.4 | 0.8 | 0.8 | 0.8 |
| Driving under the influence | 1,112,384 | 860,689 | 251,695 | 77.4 | 22.6 | 10.4 | 10.7 | 9.3 |
| Liquor laws | 447,496 | 319,364 | 128,132 | 71.4 | 28.6 | 4.2 | 4.0 | 4.7 |
| Drunkenness | 471,727 | 393,586 | 78,141 | 83.4 | 16.6 | 4.4 | 4.9 | 2.9 |
| Disorderly conduct | 518,374 | 379,059 | 139,315 | 73.1 | 26.9 | 4.8 | 4.7 | 5.1 |
| Vagrancy | 26,380 | 20,725 | 5,655 | 78.6 | 21.4 | 0.2 | 0.3 | 0.2 |
| All other offenses (except traffic) | 2,946,277 | 2,249,656 | 696,621 | 76.4 | 23.6 | 27.4 | 28.0 | 25.7 |
| Suspicion | 1,517 | 1,093 | 424 | 72.1 | 27.9 | * | * | * |
| Curfew and loitering law violations | 89,733 | 62,229 | 27,504 | 69.3 | 30.7 | 0.8 | 0.8 | 1.0 |
| Runaways | 73,794 | 33,084 | 40,710 | 44.8 | 55.2 | 0.7 | 0.4 | 1.5 |

[1] Because of rounding, the percentages may not add to 100.0.
* Less than one-tenth of 1 percent.

## Table 43. Arrests, Distribution by Race, 2009

(Number, percent; 12,371 agencies; 2009 estimated population 239,839,971. )

| Offense charged | Total arrests | | | | | Percent distribution[1] | | | | |
|---|---|---|---|---|---|---|---|---|---|---|
| | Total | White | Black | American Indian or Alaskan Native | Asian or Pacific Islander | Total | White | Black | American Indian or Alaskan Native | Asian or Pacific Islander |
| **TOTAL** | 10,690,561 | 7,389,208 | 3,027,153 | 150,544 | 123,656 | 100.0 | 69.1 | 28.3 | 1.4 | 1.2 |
| **Violent Crime** | 456,965 | 268,346 | 177,766 | 5,608 | 5,245 | 100.0 | 58.7 | 38.9 | 1.2 | 1.1 |
| Murder and nonnegligent manslaughter | 9,739 | 4,741 | 4,801 | 100 | 97 | 100.0 | 48.7 | 49.3 | 1.0 | 1.0 |
| Forcible rape | 16,362 | 10,644 | 5,319 | 169 | 230 | 100.0 | 65.1 | 32.5 | 1.0 | 1.4 |
| Robbery | 100,496 | 43,039 | 55,742 | 726 | 989 | 100.0 | 42.8 | 55.5 | 0.7 | 1.0 |
| Aggravated assault | 330,368 | 209,922 | 111,904 | 4,613 | 3,929 | 100.0 | 63.5 | 33.9 | 1.4 | 1.2 |
| **Property Crime** | 1,364,409 | 922,139 | 406,382 | 17,599 | 18,289 | 100.0 | 67.6 | 29.8 | 1.3 | 1.3 |
| Burglary | 234,551 | 155,994 | 74,419 | 2,021 | 2,117 | 100.0 | 66.5 | 31.7 | 0.9 | 0.9 |
| Larceny-theft | 1,056,473 | 719,983 | 306,625 | 14,646 | 15,219 | 100.0 | 68.1 | 29.0 | 1.4 | 1.4 |
| Motor vehicle theft | 63,919 | 39,077 | 23,184 | 817 | 841 | 100.0 | 61.1 | 36.3 | 1.3 | 1.3 |
| Arson | 9,466 | 7,085 | 2,154 | 115 | 112 | 100.0 | 74.8 | 22.8 | 1.2 | 1.2 |
| **Other** | | | | | | | | | | |
| Other assaults | 1,032,502 | 672,865 | 332,435 | 15,127 | 12,075 | 100.0 | 65.2 | 32.2 | 1.5 | 1.2 |
| Forgery and counterfeiting | 67,054 | 44,730 | 21,251 | 345 | 728 | 100.0 | 66.7 | 31.7 | 0.5 | 1.1 |
| Fraud | 161,233 | 108,032 | 50,367 | 1,315 | 1,519 | 100.0 | 67.0 | 31.2 | 0.8 | 0.9 |
| Embezzlement | 13,960 | 9,208 | 4,429 | 75 | 248 | 100.0 | 66.0 | 31.7 | 0.5 | 1.8 |
| Stolen property; buying, receiving, possessing | 82,714 | 51,953 | 29,357 | 662 | 742 | 100.0 | 62.8 | 35.5 | 0.8 | 0.9 |
| Vandalism | 212,173 | 157,723 | 48,746 | 3,352 | 2,352 | 100.0 | 74.3 | 23.0 | 1.6 | 1.1 |
| Weapons; carrying, possessing, etc. | 130,503 | 74,942 | 53,441 | 951 | 1,169 | 100.0 | 57.4 | 41.0 | 0.7 | 0.9 |
| Prostitution and commercialized vice | 56,560 | 31,699 | 23,021 | 427 | 1,413 | 100.0 | 56.0 | 40.7 | 0.8 | 2.5 |
| Sex offenses (except forcible rape and prostitution) | 60,175 | 44,240 | 14,347 | 715 | 873 | 100.0 | 73.5 | 23.8 | 1.2 | 1.5 |
| Drug abuse violations | 1,301,629 | 845,974 | 437,623 | 8,588 | 9,444 | 100.0 | 65.0 | 33.6 | 0.7 | 0.7 |
| Gambling | 8,046 | 2,290 | 5,518 | 27 | 211 | 100.0 | 28.5 | 68.6 | 0.3 | 2.6 |
| Offenses against the family and children | 87,232 | 58,068 | 26,850 | 1,690 | 624 | 100.0 | 66.6 | 30.8 | 1.9 | 0.7 |
| Driving under the influence | 1,105,401 | 954,444 | 121,594 | 14,903 | 14,460 | 100.0 | 86.3 | 11.0 | 1.3 | 1.3 |
| Liquor laws | 444,087 | 373,189 | 50,431 | 14,876 | 5,591 | 100.0 | 84.0 | 11.4 | 3.3 | 1.3 |
| Drunkenness | 469,958 | 387,542 | 71,020 | 8,552 | 2,844 | 100.0 | 82.5 | 15.1 | 1.8 | 0.6 |
| Disorderly conduct | 515,689 | 326,563 | 176,169 | 8,783 | 4,174 | 100.0 | 63.3 | 34.2 | 1.7 | 0.8 |
| Vagrancy | 26,347 | 14,581 | 11,031 | 543 | 192 | 100.0 | 55.3 | 41.9 | 2.1 | 0.7 |
| All other offenses (except traffic) | 2,929,217 | 1,937,221 | 911,670 | 43,880 | 36,446 | 100.0 | 66.1 | 31.1 | 1.5 | 1.2 |
| Suspicion | 1,513 | 677 | 828 | 1 | 7 | 100.0 | 44.7 | 54.7 | 0.1 | 0.5 |
| Curfew and loitering law violations | 89,578 | 54,439 | 33,207 | 872 | 1,060 | 100.0 | 60.8 | 37.1 | 1.0 | 1.2 |
| Runaways | 73,616 | 48,343 | 19,670 | 1,653 | 3,950 | 100.0 | 65.7 | 26.7 | 2.2 | 5.4 |

[1] Because of rounding, the percentages may not add to 100.0.

## Table 43. Arrests, Distribution by Race, 2009—*Continued*

(Number, percent; 12,371 agencies; 2009 estimated population 239,839,971. )

| Offense charged | Arrests under 18 | | | | | Percent distribution[1] | | | | |
|---|---|---|---|---|---|---|---|---|---|---|
| | Total | White | Black | American Indian or Alaskan Native | Asian or Pacific Islander | Total | White | Black | American Indian or Alaskan Native | Asian or Pacific Islander |
| **TOTAL** | 1,508,550 | 993,428 | 472,929 | 18,766 | 23,427 | 100.0 | 65.9 | 31.3 | 1.2 | 1.6 |
| **Violent Crime** | 67,876 | 31,525 | 35,026 | 533 | 792 | 100.0 | 46.4 | 51.6 | 0.8 | 1.2 |
| Murder and nonnegligent manslaughter | 941 | 380 | 546 | 8 | 7 | 100.0 | 40.4 | 58.0 | 0.9 | 0.7 |
| Forcible rape | 2,368 | 1,501 | 818 | 19 | 30 | 100.0 | 63.4 | 34.5 | 0.8 | 1.3 |
| Robbery | 25,226 | 7,854 | 16,968 | 112 | 292 | 100.0 | 31.1 | 67.3 | 0.4 | 1.2 |
| Aggravated assault | 39,341 | 21,790 | 16,694 | 394 | 463 | 100.0 | 55.4 | 42.4 | 1.0 | 1.2 |
| **Property Crime** | 332,571 | 212,448 | 110,382 | 3,949 | 5,792 | 100.0 | 63.9 | 33.2 | 1.2 | 1.7 |
| Burglary | 59,237 | 36,073 | 22,082 | 511 | 571 | 100.0 | 60.9 | 37.3 | 0.9 | 1.0 |
| Larceny-theft | 253,467 | 164,701 | 80,670 | 3,148 | 4,948 | 100.0 | 65.0 | 31.8 | 1.2 | 2.0 |
| Motor vehicle theft | 15,664 | 8,452 | 6,765 | 234 | 213 | 100.0 | 54.0 | 43.2 | 1.5 | 1.4 |
| Arson | 4,203 | 3,222 | 865 | 56 | 60 | 100.0 | 76.7 | 20.6 | 1.3 | 1.4 |
| **Other** | | | | | | | | | | |
| Other assaults | 172,000 | 100,872 | 67,420 | 1,849 | 1,859 | 100.0 | 58.6 | 39.2 | 1.1 | 1.1 |
| Forgery and counterfeiting | 1,687 | 1,120 | 543 | 9 | 15 | 100.0 | 66.4 | 32.2 | 0.5 | 0.9 |
| Fraud | 4,980 | 3,083 | 1,793 | 55 | 49 | 100.0 | 61.9 | 36.0 | 1.1 | 1.0 |
| Embezzlement | 481 | 307 | 160 | 1 | 13 | 100.0 | 63.8 | 33.3 | 0.2 | 2.7 |
| Stolen property; buying, receiving, possessing | 14,831 | 8,104 | 6,461 | 117 | 149 | 100.0 | 54.6 | 43.6 | 0.8 | 1.0 |
| Vandalism | 71,158 | 55,801 | 13,683 | 845 | 829 | 100.0 | 78.4 | 19.2 | 1.2 | 1.2 |
| Weapons; carrying, possessing, etc. | 26,666 | 16,190 | 9,938 | 210 | 328 | 100.0 | 60.7 | 37.3 | 0.8 | 1.2 |
| Prostitution and commercialized vice | 1,072 | 426 | 626 | 4 | 16 | 100.0 | 39.7 | 58.4 | 0.4 | 1.5 |
| Sex offenses (except forcible rape and prostitution) | 10,494 | 7,468 | 2,788 | 89 | 149 | 100.0 | 71.2 | 26.6 | 0.8 | 1.4 |
| Drug abuse violations | 134,207 | 97,232 | 34,295 | 1,212 | 1,468 | 100.0 | 72.4 | 25.6 | 0.9 | 1.1 |
| Gambling | 1,395 | 95 | 1,293 | 0 | 7 | 100.0 | 6.8 | 92.7 | 0.0 | 0.5 |
| Offenses against the family and children | 3,576 | 2,642 | 870 | 48 | 16 | 100.0 | 73.9 | 24.3 | 1.3 | 0.4 |
| Driving under the influence | 10,629 | 9,774 | 541 | 191 | 123 | 100.0 | 92.0 | 5.1 | 1.8 | 1.2 |
| Liquor laws | 87,811 | 78,540 | 5,439 | 2,704 | 1,128 | 100.0 | 89.4 | 6.2 | 3.1 | 1.3 |
| Drunkenness | 11,067 | 9,799 | 966 | 210 | 92 | 100.0 | 88.5 | 8.7 | 1.9 | 0.8 |
| Disorderly conduct | 133,674 | 75,946 | 55,295 | 1,362 | 1,071 | 100.0 | 56.8 | 41.4 | 1.0 | 0.8 |
| Vagrancy | 2,151 | 1,539 | 588 | 9 | 15 | 100.0 | 71.5 | 27.3 | 0.4 | 0.7 |
| All other offenses (except traffic) | 256,855 | 177,661 | 71,845 | 2,844 | 4,505 | 100.0 | 69.2 | 28.0 | 1.1 | 1.8 |
| Suspicion | 175 | 74 | 100 | 0 | 1 | 100.0 | 42.3 | 57.1 | 0.0 | 0.6 |
| Curfew and loitering law violations | 89,578 | 54,439 | 33,207 | 872 | 1,060 | 100.0 | 60.8 | 37.1 | 1.0 | 1.2 |
| Runaways | 73,616 | 48,343 | 19,670 | 1,653 | 3,950 | 100.0 | 65.7 | 26.7 | 2.2 | 5.4 |

[1] Because of rounding, the percentages may not add to 100.0.

## Table 43. Arrests, Distribution by Race, 2009—*Continued*

(Number, percent; 12,371 agencies; 2009 estimated population 239,839,971. )

| Offense charged | Arrests 18 and over | | | | | Percent distribution[1] | | | | |
|---|---|---|---|---|---|---|---|---|---|---|
| | Total | White | Black | American Indian or Alaskan Native | Asian or Pacific Islander | Total | White | Black | American Indian or Alaskan Native | Asian or Pacific Islander |
| **TOTAL** | 9,182,011 | 6,395,780 | 2,554,224 | 131,778 | 100,229 | 100.0 | 69.7 | 27.8 | 1.4 | 1.1 |
| **Violent Crime** | 389,089 | 236,821 | 142,740 | 5,075 | 4,453 | 100.0 | 60.9 | 36.7 | 1.3 | 1.1 |
| Murder and nonnegligent manslaughter | 8,798 | 4,361 | 4,255 | 92 | 90 | 100.0 | 49.6 | 48.4 | 1.0 | 1.0 |
| Forcible rape | 13,994 | 9,143 | 4,501 | 150 | 200 | 100.0 | 65.3 | 32.2 | 1.1 | 1.4 |
| Robbery | 75,270 | 35,185 | 38,774 | 614 | 697 | 100.0 | 46.7 | 51.5 | 0.8 | 0.9 |
| Aggravated assault | 291,027 | 188,132 | 95,210 | 4,219 | 3,466 | 100.0 | 64.6 | 32.7 | 1.4 | 1.2 |
| **Property Crime** | 1,031,838 | 709,691 | 296,000 | 13,650 | 12,497 | 100.0 | 68.8 | 28.7 | 1.3 | 1.2 |
| Burglary | 175,314 | 119,921 | 52,337 | 1,510 | 1,546 | 100.0 | 68.4 | 29.9 | 0.9 | 0.9 |
| Larceny-theft | 803,006 | 555,282 | 225,955 | 11,498 | 10,271 | 100.0 | 69.2 | 28.1 | 1.4 | 1.3 |
| Motor vehicle theft | 48,255 | 30,625 | 16,419 | 583 | 628 | 100.0 | 63.5 | 34.0 | 1.2 | 1.3 |
| Arson | 5,263 | 3,863 | 1,289 | 59 | 52 | 100.0 | 73.4 | 24.5 | 1.1 | 1.0 |
| **Other** | | | | | | | | | | |
| Other assaults | 860,502 | 571,993 | 265,015 | 13,278 | 10,216 | 100.0 | 66.5 | 30.8 | 1.5 | 1.2 |
| Forgery and counterfeiting | 65,367 | 43,610 | 20,708 | 336 | 713 | 100.0 | 66.7 | 31.7 | 0.5 | 1.1 |
| Fraud | 156,253 | 104,949 | 48,574 | 1,260 | 1,470 | 100.0 | 67.2 | 31.1 | 0.8 | 0.9 |
| Embezzlement | 13,479 | 8,901 | 4,269 | 74 | 235 | 100.0 | 66.0 | 31.7 | 0.5 | 1.7 |
| Stolen property; buying, receiving, possessing | 67,883 | 43,849 | 22,896 | 545 | 593 | 100.0 | 64.6 | 33.7 | 0.8 | 0.9 |
| Vandalism | 141,015 | 101,922 | 35,063 | 2,507 | 1,523 | 100.0 | 72.3 | 24.9 | 1.8 | 1.1 |
| Weapons; carrying, possessing, etc. | 103,837 | 58,752 | 43,503 | 741 | 841 | 100.0 | 56.6 | 41.9 | 0.7 | 0.8 |
| Prostitution and commercialized vice | 55,488 | 31,273 | 22,395 | 423 | 1,397 | 100.0 | 56.4 | 40.4 | 0.8 | 2.5 |
| Sex offenses (except forcible rape and prostitution) | 49,681 | 36,772 | 11,559 | 626 | 724 | 100.0 | 74.0 | 23.3 | 1.3 | 1.5 |
| Drug abuse violations | 1,167,422 | 748,742 | 403,328 | 7,376 | 7,976 | 100.0 | 64.1 | 34.5 | 0.6 | 0.7 |
| Gambling | 6,651 | 2,195 | 4,225 | 27 | 204 | 100.0 | 33.0 | 63.5 | 0.4 | 3.1 |
| Offenses against the family and children | 83,656 | 55,426 | 25,980 | 1,642 | 608 | 100.0 | 66.3 | 31.1 | 2.0 | 0.7 |
| Driving under the influence | 1,094,772 | 944,670 | 121,053 | 14,712 | 14,337 | 100.0 | 86.3 | 11.1 | 1.3 | 1.3 |
| Liquor laws | 356,276 | 294,649 | 44,992 | 12,172 | 4,463 | 100.0 | 82.7 | 12.6 | 3.4 | 1.3 |
| Drunkenness | 458,891 | 377,743 | 70,054 | 8,342 | 2,752 | 100.0 | 82.3 | 15.3 | 1.8 | 0.6 |
| Disorderly conduct | 382,015 | 250,617 | 120,874 | 7,421 | 3,103 | 100.0 | 65.6 | 31.6 | 1.9 | 0.8 |
| Vagrancy | 24,196 | 13,042 | 10,443 | 534 | 177 | 100.0 | 53.9 | 43.2 | 2.2 | 0.7 |
| All other offenses (except traffic) | 2,672,362 | 1,759,560 | 839,825 | 41,036 | 31,941 | 100.0 | 65.8 | 31.4 | 1.5 | 1.2 |
| Suspicion | 1,338 | 603 | 728 | 1 | 6 | 100.0 | 45.1 | 54.4 | 0.1 | 0.4 |
| Curfew and loitering law violations | - | - | - | - | - | - | - | - | - | - |
| Runaways | - | - | - | - | - | - | - | - | - | - |

[1] Because of rounding, the percentages may not add to 100.0.

## Table 44. City Arrest Trends, 2008–2009

(Number, percent change; 8,275 agencies; 2009 estimated population 155,344,295; 2008 estimated population 153,870,093.)

| Offense charged | Number of persons arrested | | | | | | | | |
|---|---|---|---|---|---|---|---|---|---|
| | Total all ages | | | Under 18 years of age | | | 18 years of age and over | | |
| | 2008 | 2009 | Percent change | 2008 | 2009 | Percent change | 2008 | 2009 | Percent change |
| **TOTAL**[1] | 7,621,721 | 7,413,679 | -2.7 | 1,274,771 | 1,160,823 | -8.9 | 6,346,950 | 6,252,856 | -1.5 |
| **Violent Crime** | 339,265 | 330,125 | -2.7 | 55,752 | 49,415 | -11.4 | 283,513 | 280,710 | -1.0 |
| Murder and nonnegligent manslaughter | 6,658 | 6,245 | -6.2 | 698 | 635 | -9.0 | 5,960 | 5,610 | -5.9 |
| Forcible rape | 11,576 | 10,889 | -5.9 | 1,783 | 1,594 | -10.6 | 9,793 | 9,295 | -5.1 |
| Robbery | 79,971 | 77,114 | -3.6 | 21,548 | 19,249 | -10.7 | 58,423 | 57,865 | -1.0 |
| Aggravated assault | 241,060 | 235,877 | -2.2 | 31,723 | 27,937 | -11.9 | 209,337 | 207,940 | -0.7 |
| **Property Crime** | 1,019,002 | 1,041,265 | +2.2 | 275,437 | 264,003 | -4.2 | 743,565 | 777,262 | +4.5 |
| Burglary | 168,964 | 162,346 | -3.9 | 47,475 | 42,835 | -9.8 | 121,489 | 119,511 | -1.6 |
| Larceny-theft | 790,389 | 830,021 | +5.0 | 210,965 | 207,556 | -1.6 | 579,424 | 622,465 | +7.4 |
| Motor vehicle theft | 51,781 | 42,333 | -18.2 | 13,069 | 10,394 | -20.5 | 38,712 | 31,939 | -17.5 |
| Arson | 7,868 | 6,565 | -16.6 | 3,928 | 3,218 | -18.1 | 3,940 | 3,347 | -15.1 |
| **Other** | | | | | | | | | |
| Other assaults | 711,914 | 714,460 | +0.4 | 130,630 | 122,578 | -6.2 | 581,284 | 591,882 | +1.8 |
| Forgery and counterfeiting | 51,031 | 46,306 | -9.3 | 1,543 | 1,238 | -19.8 | 49,488 | 45,068 | -8.9 |
| Fraud | 103,280 | 97,198 | -5.9 | 4,415 | 3,779 | -14.4 | 98,865 | 93,419 | -5.5 |
| Embezzlement | 12,302 | 10,105 | -17.9 | 776 | 367 | -52.7 | 11,526 | 9,738 | -15.5 |
| Stolen property; buying, receiving, possessing | 64,997 | 60,436 | -7.0 | 13,494 | 12,149 | -10.0 | 51,503 | 48,287 | -6.2 |
| Vandalism | 165,195 | 155,294 | -6.0 | 64,603 | 54,390 | -15.8 | 100,592 | 100,904 | +0.3 |
| Weapons; carrying, possessing, etc. | 100,178 | 92,769 | -7.4 | 23,444 | 20,259 | -13.6 | 76,734 | 72,510 | -5.5 |
| Prostitution and commercialized vice | 43,446 | 41,267 | -5.0 | 931 | 811 | -12.9 | 42,515 | 40,456 | -4.8 |
| Sex offenses (except forcible rape and prostitution) | 40,669 | 39,610 | -2.6 | 7,542 | 7,134 | -5.4 | 33,127 | 32,476 | -2.0 |
| Drug abuse violations | 894,455 | 863,024 | -3.5 | 99,801 | 95,852 | -4.0 | 794,654 | 767,172 | -3.5 |
| Gambling | 2,952 | 3,123 | +5.8 | 354 | 415 | +17.2 | 2,598 | 2,708 | +4.2 |
| Offenses against the family and children | 39,956 | 40,796 | +2.1 | 2,783 | 2,642 | -5.1 | 37,173 | 38,154 | +2.6 |
| Driving under the influence | 670,055 | 647,773 | -3.3 | 7,910 | 6,994 | -11.6 | 662,145 | 640,779 | -3.2 |
| Liquor laws | 370,021 | 344,087 | -7.0 | 75,529 | 65,715 | -13.0 | 294,492 | 278,372 | -5.5 |
| Drunkenness | 398,014 | 381,503 | -4.1 | 10,311 | 9,158 | -11.2 | 387,703 | 372,345 | -4.0 |
| Disorderly conduct | 420,907 | 405,951 | -3.6 | 118,173 | 105,832 | -10.4 | 302,734 | 300,119 | -0.9 |
| Vagrancy | 21,059 | 20,403 | -3.1 | 2,739 | 1,814 | -33.8 | 18,320 | 18,589 | +1.5 |
| All other offenses (except traffic) | 1,996,755 | 1,942,033 | -2.7 | 222,336 | 200,127 | -10.0 | 1,774,419 | 1,741,906 | -1.8 |
| Suspicion | 886 | 644 | -27.3 | 153 | 83 | -45.8 | 733 | 561 | -23.5 |
| Curfew and loitering law violations | 96,069 | 81,665 | -15.0 | 96,069 | 81,665 | -15.0 | - | - | - |
| Runaways | 60,199 | 54,486 | -9.5 | 60,199 | 54,486 | -9.5 | - | - | - |

[1] Does not include suspicion.

## Table 45. City Arrest Trends, by Age and Sex, 2008–2009

(Number, percent change; 8,275 agencies; 2009 estimated population 155,344,295; 2008 estimated population 153,870,093.)

| Offense charged | Male | | | | | | Female | | | | | |
|---|---|---|---|---|---|---|---|---|---|---|---|---|
| | Total | | | Under 18 | | | Total | | | Under 18 | | |
| | 2008 | 2009 | Percent change | 2008 | 2009 | Percent change | 2008 | 2009 | Percent change | 2008 | 2009 | Percent change |
| **TOTAL**[1] | 5,701,583 | 5,494,797 | -3.6 | 884,010 | 799,180 | -9.6 | 1,920,138 | 1,918,882 | -0.1 | 390,761 | 361,643 | -7.5 |
| **Violent Crime** | 275,423 | 266,937 | -3.1 | 45,976 | 40,374 | -12.2 | 63,842 | 63,188 | -1.0 | 9,776 | 9,041 | -7.5 |
| Murder and nonnegligent manslaughter | 5,966 | 5,602 | -6.1 | 647 | 585 | -9.6 | 692 | 643 | -7.1 | 51 | 50 | -2.0 |
| Forcible rape | 11,449 | 10,759 | -6.0 | 1,754 | 1,568 | -10.6 | 127 | 130 | +2.4 | 29 | 26 | -10.3 |
| Robbery | 70,428 | 67,651 | -3.9 | 19,476 | 17,227 | -11.5 | 9,543 | 9,463 | -0.8 | 2,072 | 2,022 | -2.4 |
| Aggravated assault | 187,580 | 182,925 | -2.5 | 24,099 | 20,994 | -12.9 | 53,480 | 52,952 | -1.0 | 7,624 | 6,943 | -8.9 |
| **Property Crime** | 645,091 | 633,997 | -1.7 | 170,756 | 159,254 | -6.7 | 373,911 | 407,268 | +8.9 | 104,681 | 104,749 | +0.1 |
| Burglary | 143,181 | 137,090 | -4.3 | 41,283 | 37,659 | -8.8 | 25,783 | 25,256 | -2.0 | 6,192 | 5,176 | -16.4 |
| Larceny-theft | 452,441 | 456,752 | +1.0 | 115,012 | 110,192 | -4.2 | 337,948 | 373,269 | +10.5 | 95,953 | 97,364 | +1.5 |
| Motor vehicle theft | 42,810 | 34,687 | -19.0 | 10,992 | 8,603 | -21.7 | 8,971 | 7,646 | -14.8 | 2,077 | 1,791 | -13.8 |
| Arson | 6,659 | 5,468 | -17.9 | 3,469 | 2,800 | -19.3 | 1,209 | 1,097 | -9.3 | 459 | 418 | -8.9 |
| **Other** | | | | | | | | | | | | |
| Other assaults | 528,071 | 527,055 | -0.2 | 85,150 | 79,825 | -6.3 | 183,843 | 187,405 | +1.9 | 45,480 | 42,753 | -6.0 |
| Forgery and counterfeiting | 31,655 | 28,874 | -8.8 | 1,016 | 864 | -15.0 | 19,376 | 17,432 | -10.0 | 527 | 374 | -29.0 |
| Fraud | 60,122 | 57,126 | -5.0 | 2,896 | 2,443 | -15.6 | 43,158 | 40,072 | -7.2 | 1,519 | 1,336 | -12.0 |
| Embezzlement | 5,813 | 4,923 | -15.3 | 447 | 208 | -53.5 | 6,489 | 5,182 | -20.1 | 329 | 159 | -51.7 |
| Stolen property; buying, receiving, possessing | 51,202 | 47,284 | -7.7 | 10,850 | 9,764 | -10.0 | 13,795 | 13,152 | -4.7 | 2,644 | 2,385 | -9.8 |
| Vandalism | 136,785 | 127,288 | -6.9 | 55,938 | 47,005 | -16.0 | 28,410 | 28,006 | -1.4 | 8,665 | 7,385 | -14.8 |
| Weapons; carrying, possessing, etc. | 92,594 | 85,251 | -7.9 | 21,262 | 18,225 | -14.3 | 7,584 | 7,518 | -0.9 | 2,182 | 2,034 | -6.8 |
| Prostitution and commercialized vice | 14,126 | 13,374 | -5.3 | 239 | 175 | -26.8 | 29,320 | 27,893 | -4.9 | 692 | 636 | -8.1 |
| Sex offenses (except forcible rape and prostitution) | 36,710 | 35,851 | -2.3 | 6,732 | 6,359 | -5.5 | 3,959 | 3,759 | -5.1 | 810 | 775 | -4.3 |
| Drug abuse violations | 728,856 | 703,920 | -3.4 | 83,919 | 80,579 | -4.0 | 165,599 | 159,104 | -3.9 | 15,882 | 15,273 | -3.8 |
| Gambling | 2,598 | 2,745 | +5.7 | 337 | 407 | +20.8 | 354 | 378 | +6.8 | 17 | 8 | -52.9 |
| Offenses against the family and children | 26,378 | 27,123 | +2.8 | 1,672 | 1,652 | -1.2 | 13,578 | 13,673 | +0.7 | 1,111 | 990 | -10.9 |
| Driving under the influence | 520,544 | 495,964 | -4.7 | 5,906 | 5,221 | -11.6 | 149,511 | 151,809 | +1.5 | 2,004 | 1,773 | -11.5 |
| Liquor laws | 266,182 | 244,615 | -8.1 | 46,989 | 40,246 | -14.4 | 103,839 | 99,472 | -4.2 | 28,540 | 25,469 | -10.8 |
| Drunkenness | 334,247 | 318,915 | -4.6 | 7,789 | 6,843 | -12.1 | 63,767 | 62,588 | -1.8 | 2,522 | 2,315 | -8.2 |
| Disorderly conduct | 307,347 | 295,566 | -3.8 | 78,918 | 70,183 | -11.1 | 113,560 | 110,385 | -2.8 | 39,255 | 35,649 | -9.2 |
| Vagrancy | 16,385 | 16,361 | -0.1 | 1,955 | 1,315 | -32.7 | 4,674 | 4,042 | -13.5 | 784 | 499 | -36.4 |
| All other offenses (except traffic) | 1,529,191 | 1,480,535 | -3.2 | 163,000 | 147,145 | -9.7 | 467,564 | 461,498 | -1.3 | 59,336 | 52,982 | -10.7 |
| Suspicion | 712 | 481 | -32.4 | 118 | 67 | -43.2 | 174 | 163 | -6.3 | 35 | 16 | -54.3 |
| Curfew and loitering law violations | 66,115 | 56,760 | -14.1 | 66,115 | 56,760 | -14.1 | 29,954 | 24,905 | -16.9 | 29,954 | 24,905 | -16.9 |
| Runaways | 26,148 | 24,333 | -6.9 | 26,148 | 24,333 | -6.9 | 34,051 | 30,153 | -11.4 | 34,051 | 30,153 | -11.4 |

[1] Does not include suspicion.

## Table 46. City Arrests, Distribution by Age, 2009

(Number, percent; 9,075 agencies; 2009 estimated population 166,296,396.)

| Offense charged | Total all ages | Ages under 15 | Ages under 18 | Ages 18 and over | Under 10 | 10–12 | 13–14 | 15 | 16 | 17 | 18 | 19 | 20 |
|---|---|---|---|---|---|---|---|---|---|---|---|---|---|
| **TOTAL** | 8,103,417 | 337,973 | 1,248,979 | 6,854,438 | 7,592 | 68,108 | 262,273 | 246,153 | 312,133 | 352,720 | 405,595 | 417,282 | 381,210 |
| Total percent distribution[1] | 100.0 | 4.2 | 15.4 | 84.6 | 0.1 | 0.8 | 3.2 | 3.0 | 3.9 | 4.4 | 5.0 | 5.1 | 4.7 |
| | | | | | | | | | | | | | |
| **Violent Crime** | 357,014 | 14,064 | 55,530 | 301,484 | 290 | 2,979 | 10,795 | 11,007 | 14,283 | 16,176 | 18,799 | 17,736 | 16,264 |
| Violent crime percent distribution[1] | 100.0 | 3.9 | 15.6 | 84.4 | 0.1 | 0.8 | 3.0 | 3.1 | 4.0 | 4.5 | 5.3 | 5.0 | 4.6 |
| Murder and nonnegligent manslaughter | 7,173 | 60 | 760 | 6,413 | 1 | 7 | 52 | 135 | 229 | 336 | 536 | 504 | 479 |
| Forcible rape | 11,981 | 557 | 1,732 | 10,249 | 9 | 114 | 434 | 340 | 378 | 457 | 570 | 514 | 534 |
| Robbery | 85,639 | 4,134 | 22,019 | 63,620 | 27 | 520 | 3,587 | 4,601 | 6,148 | 7,136 | 7,920 | 6,664 | 5,388 |
| Aggravated assault | 252,221 | 9,313 | 31,019 | 221,202 | 253 | 2,338 | 6,722 | 5,931 | 7,528 | 8,247 | 9,773 | 10,054 | 9,863 |
| | | | | | | | | | | | | | |
| **Property Crime** | 1,123,462 | 79,051 | 282,741 | 840,721 | 1,694 | 16,629 | 60,728 | 55,516 | 70,676 | 77,498 | 80,282 | 67,461 | 53,480 |
| Property crime percent distribution[1] | 100.0 | 7.0 | 25.2 | 74.8 | 0.2 | 1.5 | 5.4 | 4.9 | 6.3 | 6.9 | 7.1 | 6.0 | 4.8 |
| Burglary | 174,091 | 13,043 | 46,267 | 127,824 | 373 | 2,662 | 10,008 | 9,411 | 11,239 | 12,574 | 13,817 | 11,836 | 8,947 |
| Larceny-theft | 893,661 | 61,581 | 220,711 | 672,950 | 1,132 | 13,124 | 47,325 | 42,738 | 55,376 | 61,016 | 62,769 | 52,488 | 42,042 |
| Motor vehicle theft | 48,792 | 2,421 | 12,442 | 36,350 | 19 | 231 | 2,171 | 2,825 | 3,617 | 3,579 | 3,422 | 2,895 | 2,311 |
| Arson | 6,918 | 2,006 | 3,321 | 3,597 | 170 | 612 | 1,224 | 542 | 444 | 329 | 274 | 242 | 180 |
| | | | | | | | | | | | | | |
| **Other** | | | | | | | | | | | | | |
| Other assaults | 790,986 | 49,903 | 134,250 | 656,736 | 1,243 | 12,689 | 35,971 | 26,276 | 29,257 | 28,814 | 26,771 | 27,808 | 27,837 |
| Forgery and counterfeiting | 50,399 | 165 | 1,328 | 49,071 | 5 | 30 | 130 | 184 | 324 | 655 | 1,554 | 2,207 | 2,420 |
| Fraud | 99,271 | 634 | 3,934 | 95,337 | 16 | 100 | 518 | 605 | 1,011 | 1,684 | 3,079 | 3,797 | 4,217 |
| Embezzlement | 10,687 | 28 | 379 | 10,308 | 0 | 7 | 21 | 26 | 91 | 234 | 555 | 739 | 667 |
| Stolen property; buying, receiving, possessing | 63,739 | 2,868 | 12,590 | 51,149 | 51 | 501 | 2,316 | 2,572 | 3,305 | 3,845 | 4,364 | 3,967 | 3,243 |
| Vandalism | 167,597 | 22,883 | 58,139 | 109,458 | 936 | 5,887 | 16,060 | 10,973 | 12,424 | 11,859 | 10,879 | 8,950 | 7,214 |
| Weapons; carrying, possessing, etc. | 102,869 | 6,551 | 22,079 | 80,790 | 254 | 1,603 | 4,694 | 4,049 | 5,145 | 6,334 | 7,199 | 6,478 | 5,595 |
| Prostitution and commercialized vice | 53,421 | 112 | 991 | 52,430 | 5 | 10 | 97 | 185 | 257 | 437 | 1,490 | 2,162 | 2,215 |
| Sex offenses (except forcible rape and prostitution) | 43,365 | 3,562 | 7,527 | 35,838 | 117 | 974 | 2,471 | 1,278 | 1,278 | 1,409 | 1,666 | 1,628 | 1,504 |
| Drug abuse violations | 985,248 | 17,175 | 108,079 | 877,169 | 115 | 1,930 | 15,130 | 18,764 | 29,153 | 42,987 | 63,814 | 64,120 | 56,653 |
| Gambling | 6,558 | 147 | 1,326 | 5,232 | 0 | 6 | 141 | 231 | 384 | 564 | 538 | 486 | 420 |
| Offenses against the family and children | 43,849 | 803 | 2,746 | 41,103 | 29 | 174 | 600 | 553 | 679 | 711 | 1,166 | 1,214 | 1,332 |
| Driving under the influence | 690,269 | 163 | 7,288 | 682,981 | 47 | 10 | 106 | 328 | 1,644 | 5,153 | 14,318 | 20,155 | 22,684 |
| Liquor laws | 357,799 | 6,426 | 67,589 | 290,210 | 89 | 497 | 5,840 | 10,227 | 18,919 | 32,017 | 59,023 | 66,259 | 54,066 |
| Drunkenness | 405,799 | 1,146 | 9,623 | 396,176 | 61 | 86 | 999 | 1,477 | 2,254 | 4,746 | 10,524 | 12,377 | 12,411 |
| Disorderly conduct | 444,537 | 41,937 | 116,047 | 328,490 | 632 | 9,681 | 31,624 | 24,301 | 25,711 | 24,098 | 20,710 | 18,428 | 17,143 |
| Vagrancy | 23,110 | 480 | 1,885 | 21,225 | 5 | 46 | 429 | 529 | 506 | 370 | 1,242 | 1,020 | 845 |
| All other offenses (except traffic) | 2,140,195 | 50,416 | 212,243 | 1,927,952 | 1,311 | 8,181 | 40,924 | 43,534 | 55,013 | 63,280 | 77,563 | 90,229 | 90,952 |
| Suspicion | 666 | 21 | 88 | 578 | 6 | 1 | 14 | 13 | 16 | 38 | 59 | 61 | 48 |
| Curfew and loitering law violations | 85,272 | 21,077 | 85,272 | - | 271 | 3,227 | 17,579 | 19,181 | 24,114 | 20,900 | - | - | - |
| Runaways | 57,305 | 18,361 | 57,305 | - | 415 | 2,860 | 15,086 | 14,344 | 15,689 | 8,911 | - | - | - |

[1] Because of rounding, the percentages may not add to 100.0.

## Table 46. City Arrests, Distribution by Age, 2009—*Continued*

(Number, percent; 9,075 agencies; 2009 estimated population 166,296,396.)

| Offense charged | 21 | 22 | 23 | 24 | 25–29 | 30–34 | 35–39 | 40–44 | 45–49 | 50–54 | 55–59 | 60–64 | 65 and over |
|---|---|---|---|---|---|---|---|---|---|---|---|---|---|
| **TOTAL** | 340,521 | 310,462 | 289,887 | 271,887 | 1,146,722 | 800,328 | 663,299 | 611,623 | 550,868 | 355,733 | 173,163 | 75,237 | 60,621 |
| Total percent distribution[1] | 4.2 | 3.8 | 3.6 | 3.4 | 14.2 | 9.9 | 8.2 | 7.5 | 6.8 | 4.4 | 2.1 | 0.9 | 0.7 |
| **Violent Crime** | 15,605 | 14,155 | 13,496 | 12,441 | 53,548 | 37,206 | 29,559 | 26,062 | 21,943 | 13,175 | 6,375 | 2,809 | 2,311 |
| Violent crime percent distribution[1] | 4.4 | 4.0 | 3.8 | 3.5 | 15.0 | 10.4 | 8.3 | 7.3 | 6.1 | 3.7 | 1.8 | 0.8 | 0.6 |
| Murder and nonnegligent manslaughter | 445 | 349 | 327 | 320 | 1,206 | 701 | 453 | 349 | 309 | 182 | 111 | 78 | 64 |
| Forcible rape | 495 | 445 | 415 | 351 | 1,694 | 1,359 | 1,181 | 990 | 778 | 466 | 240 | 121 | 96 |
| Robbery | 4,324 | 3,662 | 3,162 | 2,689 | 10,303 | 6,000 | 4,608 | 3,859 | 2,834 | 1,385 | 547 | 188 | 87 |
| Aggravated assault | 10,341 | 9,699 | 9,592 | 9,081 | 40,345 | 29,146 | 23,317 | 20,864 | 18,022 | 11,142 | 5,477 | 2,422 | 2,064 |
| **Property Crime** | 44,572 | 37,803 | 34,063 | 31,191 | 127,824 | 88,382 | 75,616 | 70,359 | 60,498 | 37,395 | 17,687 | 7,965 | 6,143 |
| Property crime percent distribution[1] | 4.0 | 3.4 | 3.0 | 2.8 | 11.4 | 7.9 | 6.7 | 6.3 | 5.4 | 3.3 | 1.6 | 0.7 | 0.5 |
| Burglary | 7,634 | 6,240 | 5,625 | 4,949 | 20,343 | 13,133 | 10,834 | 9,788 | 7,829 | 4,249 | 1,699 | 588 | 313 |
| Larceny-theft | 34,794 | 29,586 | 26,664 | 24,635 | 100,567 | 70,448 | 60,952 | 57,314 | 50,313 | 31,977 | 15,493 | 7,197 | 5,711 |
| Motor vehicle theft | 1,980 | 1,818 | 1,641 | 1,483 | 6,395 | 4,432 | 3,501 | 2,935 | 2,005 | 962 | 381 | 119 | 70 |
| Arson | 164 | 159 | 133 | 124 | 519 | 369 | 329 | 322 | 351 | 207 | 114 | 61 | 49 |
| **Other** | | | | | | | | | | | | | |
| Other assaults | 30,334 | 29,318 | 28,169 | 27,486 | 120,486 | 88,594 | 73,677 | 64,223 | 54,118 | 31,902 | 14,456 | 6,417 | 5,140 |
| Forgery and counterfeiting | 2,185 | 2,069 | 2,049 | 2,115 | 9,935 | 7,471 | 5,830 | 4,525 | 3,412 | 1,956 | 825 | 337 | 181 |
| Fraud | 3,738 | 3,701 | 3,461 | 3,519 | 16,732 | 13,508 | 12,305 | 10,316 | 8,010 | 4,706 | 2,287 | 1,133 | 828 |
| Embezzlement | 619 | 524 | 411 | 461 | 1,740 | 1,194 | 1,083 | 851 | 668 | 418 | 216 | 106 | 56 |
| Stolen property; buying, receiving, possessing | 2,882 | 2,535 | 2,330 | 2,043 | 8,772 | 6,243 | 4,840 | 4,279 | 2,985 | 1,632 | 637 | 239 | 158 |
| Vandalism | 7,206 | 6,028 | 5,439 | 4,980 | 18,854 | 11,836 | 8,597 | 7,234 | 6,148 | 3,392 | 1,512 | 648 | 541 |
| Weapons; carrying, possessing, etc. | 5,144 | 4,619 | 4,227 | 3,771 | 15,037 | 8,924 | 5,890 | 4,740 | 3,865 | 2,634 | 1,355 | 734 | 578 |
| Prostitution and commercialized vice | 2,092 | 2,112 | 2,035 | 1,824 | 8,502 | 6,717 | 6,940 | 6,702 | 4,986 | 2,656 | 1,077 | 481 | 439 |
| Sex offenses (except forcible rape and prostitution) | 1,470 | 1,297 | 1,178 | 1,159 | 4,747 | 3,966 | 3,799 | 3,842 | 3,597 | 2,480 | 1,523 | 920 | 1,062 |
| Drug abuse violations | 49,741 | 44,565 | 41,344 | 38,090 | 157,310 | 101,420 | 76,714 | 67,436 | 57,681 | 35,153 | 15,476 | 5,310 | 2,342 |
| Gambling | 372 | 296 | 235 | 214 | 769 | 397 | 316 | 266 | 293 | 213 | 181 | 109 | 127 |
| Offenses against the family and children | 1,572 | 1,526 | 1,628 | 1,690 | 8,222 | 6,737 | 5,678 | 4,238 | 3,154 | 1,672 | 705 | 325 | 244 |
| Driving under the influence | 32,570 | 32,742 | 32,056 | 30,554 | 127,796 | 87,506 | 72,182 | 64,245 | 60,648 | 41,812 | 23,219 | 11,999 | 8,495 |
| Liquor laws | 8,662 | 6,042 | 4,827 | 3,981 | 15,287 | 11,347 | 10,993 | 13,289 | 15,209 | 11,198 | 5,960 | 2,489 | 1,578 |
| Drunkenness | 18,176 | 16,492 | 15,563 | 14,508 | 60,183 | 43,379 | 39,563 | 43,985 | 47,454 | 34,529 | 16,765 | 6,599 | 3,668 |
| Disorderly conduct | 20,525 | 18,002 | 15,615 | 13,982 | 54,287 | 35,216 | 28,568 | 27,087 | 26,719 | 17,357 | 8,443 | 3,655 | 2,753 |
| Vagrancy | 713 | 579 | 542 | 468 | 2,037 | 1,750 | 1,980 | 2,548 | 3,018 | 2,431 | 1,257 | 512 | 283 |
| All other offenses (except traffic) | 92,292 | 86,025 | 81,187 | 77,378 | 334,573 | 238,491 | 199,122 | 185,357 | 166,439 | 109,006 | 53,199 | 22,445 | 23,694 |
| Suspicion | 51 | 32 | 32 | 32 | 81 | 44 | 47 | 39 | 23 | 16 | 8 | 5 | 0 |
| Curfew and loitering law violations | - | - | - | - | - | - | - | - | - | - | - | - | - |
| Runaways | - | - | - | - | - | - | - | - | - | - | - | - | - |

[1] Because of rounding, the percentages may not add to 100.0.

## Table 47. City Arrests of Persons Under 15, 18, 21, and 25 Years of Age, 2009

(Number, percent; 9,075 agencies; 2009 estimated population 166,296,396.)

| Offense charged | Total all ages | Number of persons arrested | | | | Percent of total all ages | | | |
|---|---|---|---|---|---|---|---|---|---|
| | | Under 15 | Under 18 | Under 21 | Under 25 | Under 15 | Under 18 | Under 21 | Under 25 |
| **TOTAL** | 8,103,417 | 337,973 | 1,248,979 | 2,453,066 | 3,665,823 | 4.2 | 15.4 | 30.3 | 45.2 |
| | | | | | | | | | |
| **Violent Crime** | 357,014 | 14,064 | 55,530 | 108,329 | 164,026 | 3.9 | 15.6 | 30.3 | 45.9 |
| Murder and nonnegligent manslaughter | 7,173 | 60 | 760 | 2,279 | 3,720 | 0.8 | 10.6 | 31.8 | 51.9 |
| Forcible rape | 11,981 | 557 | 1,732 | 3,350 | 5,056 | 4.6 | 14.5 | 28.0 | 42.2 |
| Robbery | 85,639 | 4,134 | 22,019 | 41,991 | 55,828 | 4.8 | 25.7 | 49.0 | 65.2 |
| Aggravated assault | 252,221 | 9,313 | 31,019 | 60,709 | 99,422 | 3.7 | 12.3 | 24.1 | 39.4 |
| | | | | | | | | | |
| **Property Crime** | 1,123,462 | 79,051 | 282,741 | 483,964 | 631,593 | 7.0 | 25.2 | 43.1 | 56.2 |
| Burglary | 174,091 | 13,043 | 46,267 | 80,867 | 105,315 | 7.5 | 26.6 | 46.5 | 60.5 |
| Larceny-theft | 893,661 | 61,581 | 220,711 | 378,010 | 493,689 | 6.9 | 24.7 | 42.3 | 55.2 |
| Motor vehicle theft | 48,792 | 2,421 | 12,442 | 21,070 | 27,992 | 5.0 | 25.5 | 43.2 | 57.4 |
| Arson | 6,918 | 2,006 | 3,321 | 4,017 | 4,597 | 29.0 | 48.0 | 58.1 | 66.4 |
| | | | | | | | | | |
| **Other** | | | | | | | | | |
| Other assaults | 790,986 | 49,903 | 134,250 | 216,666 | 331,973 | 6.3 | 17.0 | 27.4 | 42.0 |
| Forgery and counterfeiting | 50,399 | 165 | 1,328 | 7,509 | 15,927 | 0.3 | 2.6 | 14.9 | 31.6 |
| Fraud | 99,271 | 634 | 3,934 | 15,027 | 29,446 | 0.6 | 4.0 | 15.1 | 29.7 |
| Embezzlement | 10,687 | 28 | 379 | 2,340 | 4,355 | 0.3 | 3.5 | 21.9 | 40.8 |
| Stolen property; buying, receiving, possessing | 63,739 | 2,868 | 12,590 | 24,164 | 33,954 | 4.5 | 19.8 | 37.9 | 53.3 |
| Vandalism | 167,597 | 22,883 | 58,139 | 85,182 | 108,835 | 13.7 | 34.7 | 50.8 | 64.9 |
| Weapons; carrying, possessing, etc. | 102,869 | 6,551 | 22,079 | 41,351 | 59,112 | 6.4 | 21.5 | 40.2 | 57.5 |
| Prostitution and commercialized vice | 53,421 | 112 | 991 | 6,858 | 14,921 | 0.2 | 1.9 | 12.8 | 27.9 |
| Sex offenses (except forcible rape and prostitution) | 43,365 | 3,562 | 7,527 | 12,325 | 17,429 | 8.2 | 17.4 | 28.4 | 40.2 |
| Drug abuse violations | 985,248 | 17,175 | 108,079 | 292,666 | 466,406 | 1.7 | 11.0 | 29.7 | 47.3 |
| Gambling | 6,558 | 147 | 1,326 | 2,770 | 3,887 | 2.2 | 20.2 | 42.2 | 59.3 |
| Offenses against the family and children | 43,849 | 803 | 2,746 | 6,458 | 12,874 | 1.8 | 6.3 | 14.7 | 29.4 |
| Driving under the influence | 690,269 | 163 | 7,288 | 64,445 | 192,367 | * | 1.1 | 9.3 | 27.9 |
| Liquor laws | 357,799 | 6,426 | 67,589 | 246,937 | 270,449 | 1.8 | 18.9 | 69.0 | 75.6 |
| Drunkenness | 405,799 | 1,146 | 9,623 | 44,935 | 109,674 | 0.3 | 2.4 | 11.1 | 27.0 |
| Disorderly conduct | 444,537 | 41,937 | 116,047 | 172,328 | 240,452 | 9.4 | 26.1 | 38.8 | 54.1 |
| Vagrancy | 23,110 | 480 | 1,885 | 4,992 | 7,294 | 2.1 | 8.2 | 21.6 | 31.6 |
| All other offenses (except traffic) | 2,140,195 | 50,416 | 212,243 | 470,987 | 807,869 | 2.4 | 9.9 | 22.0 | 37.7 |
| Suspicion | 666 | 21 | 88 | 256 | 403 | 3.2 | 13.2 | 38.4 | 60.5 |
| Curfew and loitering law violations | 85,272 | 21,077 | 85,272 | 85,272 | 85,272 | 24.7 | 100.0 | 100.0 | 100.0 |
| Runaways | 57,305 | 18,361 | 57,305 | 57,305 | 57,305 | 32.0 | 100.0 | 100.0 | 100.0 |

* Less than one-tenth of 1 percent.

## Table 48. City Arrests, Distribution by Sex, 2009

(Number, percent; 9,075 agencies; 2009 estimated population 166,296,396.)

| Offense charged | Number of persons arrested | | | Percent male | Percent female | Percent distribution[1] | | |
|---|---|---|---|---|---|---|---|---|
| | Total | Male | Female | | | Total | Male | Female |
| **TOTAL** | 8,103,417 | 6,027,432 | 2,075,985 | 74.4 | 25.6 | 100.0 | 100.0 | 100.0 |
| **Violent Crime** | 357,014 | 289,066 | 67,948 | 81.0 | 19.0 | 4.4 | 4.8 | 3.3 |
| Murder and nonnegligent manslaughter | 7,173 | 6,462 | 711 | 90.1 | 9.9 | 0.1 | 0.1 | * |
| Forcible rape | 11,981 | 11,840 | 141 | 98.8 | 1.2 | 0.1 | 0.2 | * |
| Robbery | 85,639 | 75,342 | 10,297 | 88.0 | 12.0 | 1.1 | 1.2 | 0.5 |
| Aggravated assault | 252,221 | 195,422 | 56,799 | 77.5 | 22.5 | 3.1 | 3.2 | 2.7 |
| **Property Crime** | 1,123,462 | 688,303 | 435,159 | 61.3 | 38.7 | 13.9 | 11.4 | 21.0 |
| Burglary | 174,091 | 147,597 | 26,494 | 84.8 | 15.2 | 2.1 | 2.4 | 1.3 |
| Larceny-theft | 893,661 | 494,876 | 398,785 | 55.4 | 44.6 | 11.0 | 8.2 | 19.2 |
| Motor vehicle theft | 48,792 | 40,083 | 8,709 | 82.2 | 17.8 | 0.6 | 0.7 | 0.4 |
| Arson | 6,918 | 5,747 | 1,171 | 83.1 | 16.9 | 0.1 | 0.1 | 0.1 |
| **Other** | | | | | | | | |
| Other assaults | 790,986 | 584,761 | 206,225 | 73.9 | 26.1 | 9.8 | 9.7 | 9.9 |
| Forgery and counterfeiting | 50,399 | 31,353 | 19,046 | 62.2 | 37.8 | 0.6 | 0.5 | 0.9 |
| Fraud | 99,271 | 59,170 | 40,101 | 59.6 | 40.4 | 1.2 | 1.0 | 1.9 |
| Embezzlement | 10,687 | 5,177 | 5,510 | 48.4 | 51.6 | 0.1 | 0.1 | 0.3 |
| Stolen property; buying, receiving, possessing | 63,739 | 49,923 | 13,816 | 78.3 | 21.7 | 0.8 | 0.8 | 0.7 |
| Vandalism | 167,597 | 137,321 | 30,276 | 81.9 | 18.1 | 2.1 | 2.3 | 1.5 |
| Weapons; carrying, possessing, etc. | 102,869 | 94,748 | 8,121 | 92.1 | 7.9 | 1.3 | 1.6 | 0.4 |
| Prostitution and commercialized vice | 53,421 | 16,036 | 37,385 | 30.0 | 70.0 | 0.7 | 0.3 | 1.8 |
| Sex offenses (except forcible rape and prostitution) | 43,365 | 39,198 | 4,167 | 90.4 | 9.6 | 0.5 | 0.7 | 0.2 |
| Drug abuse violations | 985,248 | 808,289 | 176,959 | 82.0 | 18.0 | 12.2 | 13.4 | 8.5 |
| Gambling | 6,558 | 6,130 | 428 | 93.5 | 6.5 | 0.1 | 0.1 | * |
| Offenses against the family and children | 43,849 | 29,195 | 14,654 | 66.6 | 33.4 | 0.5 | 0.5 | 0.7 |
| Driving under the influence | 690,269 | 529,912 | 160,357 | 76.8 | 23.2 | 8.5 | 8.8 | 7.7 |
| Liquor laws | 357,799 | 256,325 | 101,474 | 71.6 | 28.4 | 4.4 | 4.3 | 4.9 |
| Drunkenness | 405,799 | 339,531 | 66,268 | 83.7 | 16.3 | 5.0 | 5.6 | 3.2 |
| Disorderly conduct | 444,537 | 325,760 | 118,777 | 73.3 | 26.7 | 5.5 | 5.4 | 5.7 |
| Vagrancy | 23,110 | 18,503 | 4,607 | 80.1 | 19.9 | 0.3 | 0.3 | 0.2 |
| All other offenses (except traffic) | 2,140,195 | 1,633,538 | 506,657 | 76.3 | 23.7 | 26.4 | 27.1 | 24.4 |
| Suspicion | 666 | 497 | 169 | 74.6 | 25.4 | * | * | * |
| Curfew and loitering law violations | 85,272 | 59,333 | 25,939 | 69.6 | 30.4 | 1.1 | 1.0 | 1.2 |
| Runaways | 57,305 | 25,363 | 31,942 | 44.3 | 55.7 | 0.7 | 0.4 | 1.5 |

[1] Because of rounding, the percentages may not add to 100.0.
* Less than one-tenth of 1 percent.

## Table 49. City Arrests, Distribution by Race, 2009

(Number, percent; 9,075 agencies; 2009 estimated population 166,296,396.)

| Offense charged | Total arrests | | | | | Percent distribution[1] | | | | |
|---|---|---|---|---|---|---|---|---|---|---|
| | Total | White | Black | American Indian or Alaskan Native | Asian or Pacific Islander | Total | White | Black | American Indian or Alaskan Native | Asian or Pacific Islander |
| **TOTAL** | 8,069,588 | 5,382,464 | 2,472,370 | 113,265 | 101,489 | 100.0 | 66.7 | 30.6 | 1.4 | 1.3 |
| **Violent Crime** | 356,018 | 199,470 | 148,046 | 3,980 | 4,522 | 100.0 | 56.0 | 41.6 | 1.1 | 1.3 |
| Murder and nonnegligent manslaughter | 7,149 | 3,112 | 3,896 | 65 | 76 | 100.0 | 43.5 | 54.5 | 0.9 | 1.1 |
| Forcible rape | 11,925 | 7,177 | 4,442 | 116 | 190 | 100.0 | 60.2 | 37.2 | 1.0 | 1.6 |
| Robbery | 85,481 | 36,296 | 47,700 | 598 | 887 | 100.0 | 42.5 | 55.8 | 0.7 | 1.0 |
| Aggravated assault | 251,463 | 152,885 | 92,008 | 3,201 | 3,369 | 100.0 | 60.8 | 36.6 | 1.3 | 1.3 |
| **Property Crime** | 1,119,193 | 746,186 | 342,427 | 14,860 | 15,720 | 100.0 | 66.7 | 30.6 | 1.3 | 1.4 |
| Burglary | 173,684 | 109,827 | 60,888 | 1,253 | 1,716 | 100.0 | 63.2 | 35.1 | 0.7 | 1.0 |
| Larceny-theft | 889,995 | 603,735 | 260,103 | 12,952 | 13,205 | 100.0 | 67.8 | 29.2 | 1.5 | 1.5 |
| Motor vehicle theft | 48,625 | 27,653 | 19,696 | 571 | 705 | 100.0 | 56.9 | 40.5 | 1.2 | 1.4 |
| Arson | 6,889 | 4,971 | 1,740 | 84 | 94 | 100.0 | 72.2 | 25.3 | 1.2 | 1.4 |
| **Other** | | | | | | | | | | |
| Other assaults | 787,600 | 489,346 | 276,908 | 11,365 | 9,981 | 100.0 | 62.1 | 35.2 | 1.4 | 1.3 |
| Forgery and counterfeiting | 50,232 | 32,740 | 16,672 | 256 | 564 | 100.0 | 65.2 | 33.2 | 0.5 | 1.1 |
| Fraud | 98,656 | 62,815 | 33,860 | 814 | 1,167 | 100.0 | 63.7 | 34.3 | 0.8 | 1.2 |
| Embezzlement | 10,592 | 6,990 | 3,330 | 53 | 219 | 100.0 | 66.0 | 31.4 | 0.5 | 2.1 |
| Stolen property; buying, receiving, possessing | 63,562 | 37,987 | 24,489 | 454 | 632 | 100.0 | 59.8 | 38.5 | 0.7 | 1.0 |
| Vandalism | 166,968 | 121,327 | 41,046 | 2,585 | 2,010 | 100.0 | 72.7 | 24.6 | 1.5 | 1.2 |
| Weapons; carrying, possessing, etc. | 102,514 | 56,057 | 44,894 | 585 | 978 | 100.0 | 54.7 | 43.8 | 0.6 | 1.0 |
| Prostitution and commercialized vice | 53,355 | 29,616 | 22,080 | 408 | 1,251 | 100.0 | 55.5 | 41.4 | 0.8 | 2.3 |
| Sex offenses (except forcible rape and prostitution) | 43,227 | 30,423 | 11,538 | 541 | 725 | 100.0 | 70.4 | 26.7 | 1.3 | 1.7 |
| Drug abuse violations | 983,034 | 607,678 | 361,976 | 5,981 | 7,399 | 100.0 | 61.8 | 36.8 | 0.6 | 0.8 |
| Gambling | 6,543 | 1,283 | 5,100 | 14 | 146 | 100.0 | 19.6 | 77.9 | 0.2 | 2.2 |
| Offenses against the family and children | 43,600 | 30,068 | 12,184 | 915 | 433 | 100.0 | 69.0 | 27.9 | 2.1 | 1.0 |
| Driving under the influence | 687,408 | 587,190 | 80,171 | 9,381 | 10,666 | 100.0 | 85.4 | 11.7 | 1.4 | 1.6 |
| Liquor laws | 355,286 | 293,778 | 43,956 | 12,985 | 4,567 | 100.0 | 82.7 | 12.4 | 3.7 | 1.3 |
| Drunkenness | 404,246 | 329,309 | 65,113 | 7,278 | 2,546 | 100.0 | 81.5 | 16.1 | 1.8 | 0.6 |
| Disorderly conduct | 442,213 | 274,724 | 156,493 | 7,324 | 3,672 | 100.0 | 62.1 | 35.4 | 1.7 | 0.8 |
| Vagrancy | 23,078 | 12,572 | 9,866 | 517 | 123 | 100.0 | 54.5 | 42.8 | 2.2 | 0.5 |
| All other offenses (except traffic) | 2,129,294 | 1,345,482 | 723,161 | 30,747 | 29,904 | 100.0 | 63.2 | 34.0 | 1.4 | 1.4 |
| Suspicion | 666 | 368 | 293 | 1 | 4 | 100.0 | 55.3 | 44.0 | 0.2 | 0.6 |
| Curfew and loitering law violations | 85,129 | 50,825 | 32,507 | 834 | 963 | 100.0 | 59.7 | 38.2 | 1.0 | 1.1 |
| Runaways | 57,174 | 36,230 | 16,260 | 1,387 | 3,297 | 100.0 | 63.4 | 28.4 | 2.4 | 5.8 |

[1] Because of rounding, the percentages may not add to 100.0.

## Table 49. City Arrests, Distribution by Race, 2009—*Continued*

(Number, percent; 9,075 agencies; 2009 estimated population 166,296,396.)

| Offense charged | Arrests under 18 | | | | | Percent distribution[1] | | | | |
|---|---|---|---|---|---|---|---|---|---|---|
| | Total | White | Black | American Indian or Alaskan Native | Asian or Pacific Islander | Total | White | Black | American Indian or Alaskan Native | Asian or Pacific Islander |
| **TOTAL** | 1,243,191 | 807,748 | 400,250 | 15,146 | 20,047 | 100.0 | 65.0 | 32.2 | 1.2 | 1.6 |
| **Violent Crime** | 55,365 | 25,063 | 29,207 | 413 | 682 | 100.0 | 45.3 | 52.8 | 0.7 | 1.2 |
| Murder and nonnegligent manslaughter | 759 | 282 | 467 | 6 | 4 | 100.0 | 37.2 | 61.5 | 0.8 | 0.5 |
| Forcible rape | 1,718 | 986 | 692 | 16 | 24 | 100.0 | 57.4 | 40.3 | 0.9 | 1.4 |
| Robbery | 21,971 | 6,960 | 14,647 | 98 | 266 | 100.0 | 31.7 | 66.7 | 0.4 | 1.2 |
| Aggravated assault | 30,917 | 16,835 | 13,401 | 293 | 388 | 100.0 | 54.5 | 43.3 | 0.9 | 1.3 |
| **Property Crime** | 281,310 | 179,475 | 93,340 | 3,406 | 5,089 | 100.0 | 63.8 | 33.2 | 1.2 | 1.8 |
| Burglary | 46,142 | 26,920 | 18,408 | 332 | 482 | 100.0 | 58.3 | 39.9 | 0.7 | 1.0 |
| Larceny-theft | 219,458 | 143,835 | 68,397 | 2,838 | 4,388 | 100.0 | 65.5 | 31.2 | 1.3 | 2.0 |
| Motor vehicle theft | 12,400 | 6,226 | 5,821 | 188 | 165 | 100.0 | 50.2 | 46.9 | 1.5 | 1.3 |
| Arson | 3,310 | 2,494 | 714 | 48 | 54 | 100.0 | 75.3 | 21.6 | 1.5 | 1.6 |
| **Other** | | | | | | | | | | |
| Other assaults | 133,434 | 77,184 | 53,306 | 1,387 | 1,557 | 100.0 | 57.8 | 39.9 | 1.0 | 1.2 |
| Forgery and counterfeiting | 1,326 | 881 | 428 | 6 | 11 | 100.0 | 66.4 | 32.3 | 0.5 | 0.8 |
| Fraud | 3,911 | 2,311 | 1,516 | 47 | 37 | 100.0 | 59.1 | 38.8 | 1.2 | 0.9 |
| Embezzlement | 376 | 234 | 130 | 1 | 11 | 100.0 | 62.2 | 34.6 | 0.3 | 2.9 |
| Stolen property; buying, receiving, possessing | 12,552 | 6,598 | 5,727 | 95 | 132 | 100.0 | 52.6 | 45.6 | 0.8 | 1.1 |
| Vandalism | 57,859 | 45,167 | 11,318 | 641 | 733 | 100.0 | 78.1 | 19.6 | 1.1 | 1.3 |
| Weapons; carrying, possessing, etc. | 21,928 | 13,217 | 8,285 | 142 | 284 | 100.0 | 60.3 | 37.8 | 0.6 | 1.3 |
| Prostitution and commercialized vice | 984 | 378 | 587 | 4 | 15 | 100.0 | 38.4 | 59.7 | 0.4 | 1.5 |
| Sex offenses (except forcible rape and prostitution) | 7,480 | 5,135 | 2,157 | 56 | 132 | 100.0 | 68.6 | 28.8 | 0.7 | 1.8 |
| Drug abuse violations | 107,768 | 76,561 | 29,064 | 954 | 1,189 | 100.0 | 71.0 | 27.0 | 0.9 | 1.1 |
| Gambling | 1,326 | 60 | 1,262 | 0 | 4 | 100.0 | 4.5 | 95.2 | 0.0 | 0.3 |
| Offenses against the family and children | 2,719 | 1,921 | 740 | 44 | 14 | 100.0 | 70.7 | 27.2 | 1.6 | 0.5 |
| Driving under the influence | 7,251 | 6,638 | 383 | 135 | 95 | 100.0 | 91.5 | 5.3 | 1.9 | 1.3 |
| Liquor laws | 67,193 | 59,394 | 4,641 | 2,263 | 895 | 100.0 | 88.4 | 6.9 | 3.4 | 1.3 |
| Drunkenness | 9,591 | 8,467 | 876 | 162 | 86 | 100.0 | 88.3 | 9.1 | 1.7 | 0.9 |
| Disorderly conduct | 115,476 | 65,980 | 47,430 | 1,106 | 960 | 100.0 | 57.1 | 41.1 | 1.0 | 0.8 |
| Vagrancy | 1,885 | 1,388 | 477 | 7 | 13 | 100.0 | 73.6 | 25.3 | 0.4 | 0.7 |
| All other offenses (except traffic) | 211,066 | 144,591 | 60,571 | 2,056 | 3,848 | 100.0 | 68.5 | 28.7 | 1.0 | 1.8 |
| Suspicion | 88 | 50 | 38 | 0 | 0 | 100.0 | 56.8 | 43.2 | 0.0 | 0.0 |
| Curfew and loitering law violations | 85,129 | 50,825 | 32,507 | 834 | 963 | 100.0 | 59.7 | 38.2 | 1.0 | 1.1 |
| Runaways | 57,174 | 36,230 | 16,260 | 1,387 | 3,297 | 100.0 | 63.4 | 28.4 | 2.4 | 5.8 |

[1] Because of rounding, the percentages may not add to 100.0.

## Table 49. City Arrests, Distribution by Race, 2009—*Continued*

(Number, percent; 9,075 agencies; 2009 estimated population 166,296,396.)

| Offense charged | Arrests 18 and over | | | | | Percent distribution[1] | | | | |
|---|---|---|---|---|---|---|---|---|---|---|
| | Total | White | Black | American Indian or Alaskan Native | Asian or Pacific Islander | Total | White | Black | American Indian or Alaskan Native | Asian or Pacific Islander |
| **TOTAL** | 6,826,397 | 4,574,716 | 2,072,120 | 98,119 | 81,442 | 100.0 | 67.0 | 30.4 | 1.4 | 1.2 |
| | | | | | | | | | | |
| **Violent Crime** | 300,653 | 174,407 | 118,839 | 3,567 | 3,840 | 100.0 | 58.0 | 39.5 | 1.2 | 1.3 |
| Murder and nonnegligent manslaughter | 6,390 | 2,830 | 3,429 | 59 | 72 | 100.0 | 44.3 | 53.7 | 0.9 | 1.1 |
| Forcible rape | 10,207 | 6,191 | 3,750 | 100 | 166 | 100.0 | 60.7 | 36.7 | 1.0 | 1.6 |
| Robbery | 63,510 | 29,336 | 33,053 | 500 | 621 | 100.0 | 46.2 | 52.0 | 0.8 | 1.0 |
| Aggravated assault | 220,546 | 136,050 | 78,607 | 2,908 | 2,981 | 100.0 | 61.7 | 35.6 | 1.3 | 1.4 |
| | | | | | | | | | | |
| **Property Crime** | 837,883 | 566,711 | 249,087 | 11,454 | 10,631 | 100.0 | 67.6 | 29.7 | 1.4 | 1.3 |
| Burglary | 127,542 | 82,907 | 42,480 | 921 | 1,234 | 100.0 | 65.0 | 33.3 | 0.7 | 1.0 |
| Larceny-theft | 670,537 | 459,900 | 191,706 | 10,114 | 8,817 | 100.0 | 68.6 | 28.6 | 1.5 | 1.3 |
| Motor vehicle theft | 36,225 | 21,427 | 13,875 | 383 | 540 | 100.0 | 59.1 | 38.3 | 1.1 | 1.5 |
| Arson | 3,579 | 2,477 | 1,026 | 36 | 40 | 100.0 | 69.2 | 28.7 | 1.0 | 1.1 |
| | | | | | | | | | | |
| **Other** | | | | | | | | | | |
| Other assaults | 654,166 | 412,162 | 223,602 | 9,978 | 8,424 | 100.0 | 63.0 | 34.2 | 1.5 | 1.3 |
| Forgery and counterfeiting | 48,906 | 31,859 | 16,244 | 250 | 553 | 100.0 | 65.1 | 33.2 | 0.5 | 1.1 |
| Fraud | 94,745 | 60,504 | 32,344 | 767 | 1,130 | 100.0 | 63.9 | 34.1 | 0.8 | 1.2 |
| Embezzlement | 10,216 | 6,756 | 3,200 | 52 | 208 | 100.0 | 66.1 | 31.3 | 0.5 | 2.0 |
| Stolen property; buying, receiving, possessing | 51,010 | 31,389 | 18,762 | 359 | 500 | 100.0 | 61.5 | 36.8 | 0.7 | 1.0 |
| Vandalism | 109,109 | 76,160 | 29,728 | 1,944 | 1,277 | 100.0 | 69.8 | 27.2 | 1.8 | 1.2 |
| Weapons; carrying, possessing, etc. | 80,586 | 42,840 | 36,609 | 443 | 694 | 100.0 | 53.2 | 45.4 | 0.5 | 0.9 |
| Prostitution and commercialized vice | 52,371 | 29,238 | 21,493 | 404 | 1,236 | 100.0 | 55.8 | 41.0 | 0.8 | 2.4 |
| Sex offenses (except forcible rape and prostitution) | 35,747 | 25,288 | 9,381 | 485 | 593 | 100.0 | 70.7 | 26.2 | 1.4 | 1.7 |
| Drug abuse violations | 875,266 | 531,117 | 332,912 | 5,027 | 6,210 | 100.0 | 60.7 | 38.0 | 0.6 | 0.7 |
| Gambling | 5,217 | 1,223 | 3,838 | 14 | 142 | 100.0 | 23.4 | 73.6 | 0.3 | 2.7 |
| Offenses against the family and children | 40,881 | 28,147 | 11,444 | 871 | 419 | 100.0 | 68.9 | 28.0 | 2.1 | 1.0 |
| Driving under the influence | 680,157 | 580,552 | 79,788 | 9,246 | 10,571 | 100.0 | 85.4 | 11.7 | 1.4 | 1.6 |
| Liquor laws | 288,093 | 234,384 | 39,315 | 10,722 | 3,672 | 100.0 | 81.4 | 13.6 | 3.7 | 1.3 |
| Drunkenness | 394,655 | 320,842 | 64,237 | 7,116 | 2,460 | 100.0 | 81.3 | 16.3 | 1.8 | 0.6 |
| Disorderly conduct | 326,737 | 208,744 | 109,063 | 6,218 | 2,712 | 100.0 | 63.9 | 33.4 | 1.9 | 0.8 |
| Vagrancy | 21,193 | 11,184 | 9,389 | 510 | 110 | 100.0 | 52.8 | 44.3 | 2.4 | 0.5 |
| All other offenses (except traffic) | 1,918,228 | 1,200,891 | 662,590 | 28,691 | 26,056 | 100.0 | 62.6 | 34.5 | 1.5 | 1.4 |
| Suspicion | 578 | 318 | 255 | 1 | 4 | 100.0 | 55.0 | 44.1 | 0.2 | 0.7 |
| Curfew and loitering law violations | - | - | - | - | - | - | - | - | - | - |
| Runaways | - | - | - | - | - | - | - | - | - | - |

[1] Because of rounding, the percentages may not add to 100.0.

# Table 50. Metropolitan County Arrest Trends, 2008–2009

(Number, percent change; 1,195 agencies; 2009 estimated population 47,724,783; 2008 estimated population 47,402,595.)

| Offense charged | Number of persons arrested | | | | | | | | |
|---|---|---|---|---|---|---|---|---|---|
| | Total all ages | | | Under 18 years of age | | | 18 years of age and over | | |
| | 2008 | 2009 | Percent change | 2008 | 2009 | Percent change | 2008 | 2009 | Percent change |
| **TOTAL**[1] | 1,768,406 | 1,733,928 | -1.9 | 207,685 | 189,842 | -8.6 | 1,560,721 | 1,544,086 | -1.1 |
| **Violent Crime** | 74,271 | 73,011 | -1.7 | 10,665 | 9,872 | -7.4 | 63,606 | 63,139 | -0.7 |
| Murder and nonnegligent manslaughter | 1,814 | 1,714 | -5.5 | 139 | 124 | -10.8 | 1,675 | 1,590 | -5.1 |
| Forcible rape | 2,985 | 2,778 | -6.9 | 407 | 413 | +1.5 | 2,578 | 2,365 | -8.3 |
| Robbery | 11,855 | 11,617 | -2.0 | 3,114 | 2,715 | -12.8 | 8,741 | 8,902 | +1.8 |
| Aggravated assault | 57,617 | 56,902 | -1.2 | 7,005 | 6,620 | -5.5 | 50,612 | 50,282 | -0.7 |
| **Property Crime** | 171,113 | 170,300 | -0.5 | 40,724 | 37,658 | -7.5 | 130,389 | 132,642 | +1.7 |
| Burglary | 41,059 | 39,236 | -4.4 | 10,585 | 8,667 | -18.1 | 30,474 | 30,569 | +0.3 |
| Larceny-theft | 115,192 | 118,074 | +2.5 | 26,407 | 25,886 | -2.0 | 88,785 | 92,188 | +3.8 |
| Motor vehicle theft | 12,975 | 11,294 | -13.0 | 2,944 | 2,464 | -16.3 | 10,031 | 8,830 | -12.0 |
| Arson | 1,887 | 1,696 | -10.1 | 788 | 641 | -18.7 | 1,099 | 1,055 | -4.0 |
| **Other** | | | | | | | | | |
| Other assaults | 156,262 | 160,477 | +2.7 | 28,683 | 27,599 | -3.8 | 127,579 | 132,878 | +4.2 |
| Forgery and counterfeiting | 11,536 | 11,019 | -4.5 | 320 | 266 | -16.9 | 11,216 | 10,753 | -4.1 |
| Fraud | 46,343 | 39,337 | -15.1 | 839 | 742 | -11.6 | 45,504 | 38,595 | -15.2 |
| Embezzlement | 2,764 | 2,394 | -13.4 | 157 | 82 | -47.8 | 2,607 | 2,312 | -11.3 |
| Stolen property; buying, receiving, possessing | 14,249 | 13,263 | -6.9 | 1,812 | 1,581 | -12.7 | 12,437 | 11,682 | -6.1 |
| Vandalism | 30,406 | 29,857 | -1.8 | 10,569 | 9,186 | -13.1 | 19,837 | 20,671 | +4.2 |
| Weapons; carrying, possessing, etc. | 20,902 | 19,298 | -7.7 | 4,489 | 3,774 | -15.9 | 16,413 | 15,524 | -5.4 |
| Prostitution and commercialized vice | 3,005 | 2,897 | -3.6 | 82 | 77 | -6.1 | 2,923 | 2,820 | -3.5 |
| Sex offenses (except forcible rape and prostitution) | 11,542 | 11,290 | -2.2 | 2,100 | 1,975 | -6.0 | 9,442 | 9,315 | -1.3 |
| Drug abuse violations | 212,689 | 214,519 | +0.9 | 19,982 | 19,480 | -2.5 | 192,707 | 195,039 | +1.2 |
| Gambling | 410 | 758 | +84.9 | 23 | 27 | +17.4 | 387 | 731 | +88.9 |
| Offenses against the family and children | 34,243 | 29,512 | -13.8 | 1,155 | 537 | -53.5 | 33,088 | 28,975 | -12.4 |
| Driving under the influence | 250,611 | 254,494 | +1.5 | 2,097 | 1,769 | -15.6 | 248,514 | 252,725 | +1.7 |
| Liquor laws | 57,586 | 54,625 | -5.1 | 14,678 | 13,210 | -10.0 | 42,908 | 41,415 | -3.5 |
| Drunkenness | 45,546 | 42,643 | -6.4 | 1,021 | 983 | -3.7 | 44,525 | 41,660 | -6.4 |
| Disorderly conduct | 48,891 | 46,544 | -4.8 | 13,743 | 12,433 | -9.5 | 35,148 | 34,111 | -3.0 |
| Vagrancy | 2,233 | 2,876 | +28.8 | 295 | 231 | -21.7 | 1,938 | 2,645 | +36.5 |
| All other offenses (except traffic) | 554,888 | 538,466 | -3.0 | 35,335 | 32,012 | -9.4 | 519,553 | 506,454 | -2.5 |
| Suspicion | 215 | 721 | +235.3 | 17 | 75 | +341.2 | 198 | 646 | +226.3 |
| Curfew and loitering law violations | 4,256 | 3,980 | -6.5 | 4,256 | 3,980 | -6.5 | - | - | - |
| Runaways | 14,660 | 12,368 | -15.6 | 14,660 | 12,368 | -15.6 | - | - | - |

[1] Does not include suspicion.

## Table 51. Metropolitan County Arrest Trends, by Age and Sex, 2008–2009

(Number, percent change; 1,195 agencies; 2009 estimated population 47,724,783; 2008 estimated population 47,402,595.)

| Offense charged | Male | | | | | | Female | | | | | |
|---|---|---|---|---|---|---|---|---|---|---|---|---|
| | Total | | | Under 18 | | | Total | | | Under 18 | | |
| | 2008 | 2009 | Percent change | 2008 | 2009 | Percent change | 2008 | 2009 | Percent change | 2008 | 2009 | Percent change |
| **TOTAL**[1] | 1,355,319 | 1,320,026 | -2.6 | 148,865 | 135,120 | -9.2 | 413,087 | 413,902 | +0.2 | 58,820 | 54,722 | -7.0 |
| **Violent Crime** | 61,198 | 59,855 | -2.2 | 8,770 | 7,987 | -8.9 | 13,073 | 13,156 | +0.6 | 1,895 | 1,885 | -0.5 |
| Murder and nonnegligent manslaughter | 1,605 | 1,520 | -5.3 | 130 | 116 | -10.8 | 209 | 194 | -7.2 | 9 | 8 | -11.1 |
| Forcible rape | 2,946 | 2,740 | -7.0 | 405 | 404 | -0.2 | 39 | 38 | -2.6 | 2 | 9 | +350.0 |
| Robbery | 10,584 | 10,395 | -1.8 | 2,855 | 2,484 | -13.0 | 1,271 | 1,222 | -3.9 | 259 | 231 | -10.8 |
| Aggravated assault | 46,063 | 45,200 | -1.9 | 5,380 | 4,983 | -7.4 | 11,554 | 11,702 | +1.3 | 1,625 | 1,637 | +0.7 |
| **Property Crime** | 120,353 | 116,135 | -3.5 | 28,814 | 26,047 | -9.6 | 50,760 | 54,165 | +6.7 | 11,910 | 11,611 | -2.5 |
| Burglary | 35,498 | 33,831 | -4.7 | 9,483 | 7,804 | -17.7 | 5,561 | 5,405 | -2.8 | 1,102 | 863 | -21.7 |
| Larceny-theft | 72,528 | 71,542 | -1.4 | 16,187 | 15,606 | -3.6 | 42,664 | 46,532 | +9.1 | 10,220 | 10,280 | +0.6 |
| Motor vehicle theft | 10,761 | 9,362 | -13.0 | 2,473 | 2,084 | -15.7 | 2,214 | 1,932 | -12.7 | 471 | 380 | -19.3 |
| Arson | 1,566 | 1,400 | -10.6 | 671 | 553 | -17.6 | 321 | 296 | -7.8 | 117 | 88 | -24.8 |
| **Other** | | | | | | | | | | | | |
| Other assaults | 116,313 | 118,572 | +1.9 | 19,397 | 18,415 | -5.1 | 39,949 | 41,905 | +4.9 | 9,286 | 9,184 | -1.1 |
| Forgery and counterfeiting | 7,166 | 7,016 | -2.1 | 227 | 197 | -13.2 | 4,370 | 4,003 | -8.4 | 93 | 69 | -25.8 |
| Fraud | 24,569 | 21,306 | -13.3 | 521 | 507 | -2.7 | 21,774 | 18,031 | -17.2 | 318 | 235 | -26.1 |
| Embezzlement | 1,440 | 1,227 | -14.8 | 94 | 43 | -54.3 | 1,324 | 1,167 | -11.9 | 63 | 39 | -38.1 |
| Stolen property; buying, receiving, possessing | 11,686 | 10,944 | -6.3 | 1,561 | 1,369 | -12.3 | 2,563 | 2,319 | -9.5 | 251 | 212 | -15.5 |
| Vandalism | 25,264 | 24,495 | -3.0 | 9,132 | 7,849 | -14.0 | 5,142 | 5,362 | +4.3 | 1,437 | 1,337 | -7.0 |
| Weapons; carrying, possessing, etc. | 19,257 | 17,722 | -8.0 | 3,976 | 3,296 | -17.1 | 1,645 | 1,576 | -4.2 | 513 | 478 | -6.8 |
| Prostitution and commercialized vice | 987 | 1,032 | +4.6 | 20 | 24 | +20.0 | 2,018 | 1,865 | -7.6 | 62 | 53 | -14.5 |
| Sex offenses (except forcible rape and prostitution) | 10,913 | 10,575 | -3.1 | 1,952 | 1,795 | -8.0 | 629 | 715 | +13.7 | 148 | 180 | +21.6 |
| Drug abuse violations | 171,242 | 172,071 | +0.5 | 16,668 | 16,193 | -2.8 | 41,447 | 42,448 | +2.4 | 3,314 | 3,287 | -0.8 |
| Gambling | 333 | 578 | +73.6 | 21 | 23 | +9.5 | 77 | 180 | +133.8 | 2 | 4 | +100.0 |
| Offenses against the family and children | 28,383 | 24,699 | -13.0 | 819 | 378 | -53.8 | 5,860 | 4,813 | -17.9 | 336 | 159 | -52.7 |
| Driving under the influence | 199,271 | 199,979 | +0.4 | 1,617 | 1,346 | -16.8 | 51,340 | 54,515 | +6.2 | 480 | 423 | -11.9 |
| Liquor laws | 41,081 | 38,188 | -7.0 | 9,098 | 7,950 | -12.6 | 16,505 | 16,437 | -0.4 | 5,580 | 5,260 | -5.7 |
| Drunkenness | 37,416 | 35,025 | -6.4 | 773 | 724 | -6.3 | 8,130 | 7,618 | -6.3 | 248 | 259 | +4.4 |
| Disorderly conduct | 36,005 | 33,814 | -6.1 | 9,304 | 8,458 | -9.1 | 12,886 | 12,730 | -1.2 | 4,439 | 3,975 | -10.5 |
| Vagrancy | 1,568 | 1,903 | +21.4 | 209 | 157 | -24.9 | 665 | 973 | +46.3 | 86 | 74 | -14.0 |
| All other offenses (except traffic) | 431,443 | 416,451 | -3.5 | 26,461 | 23,923 | -9.6 | 123,445 | 122,015 | -1.2 | 8,874 | 8,089 | -8.8 |
| Suspicion | 147 | 501 | +240.8 | 10 | 56 | +460.0 | 68 | 220 | +223.5 | 7 | 19 | +171.4 |
| Curfew and loitering law violations | 2,705 | 2,607 | -3.6 | 2,705 | 2,607 | -3.6 | 1,551 | 1,373 | -11.5 | 1,551 | 1,373 | -11.5 |
| Runaways | 6,726 | 5,832 | -13.3 | 6,726 | 5,832 | -13.3 | 7,934 | 6,536 | -17.6 | 7,934 | 6,536 | -17.6 |

[1] Does not include suspicion.

## Table 52. Metropolitan County Arrests, Distribution by Age, 2009

(Number, percent; 1,320 agencies; 2009 estimated population 52,113,451.)

| Offense charged | Total all ages | Ages under 15 | Ages under 18 | Ages 18 and over | Under 10 | 10–12 | 13–14 | 15 | 16 | 17 | 18 | 19 | 20 |
|---|---|---|---|---|---|---|---|---|---|---|---|---|---|
| **TOTAL** | 1,855,770 | 51,244 | 204,582 | 1,651,188 | 1,475 | 10,741 | 39,028 | 38,078 | 51,532 | 63,728 | 80,178 | 85,501 | 82,649 |
| Total percent distribution[1] | 100.0 | 2.8 | 11.0 | 89.0 | 0.1 | 0.6 | 2.1 | 2.1 | 2.8 | 3.4 | 4.3 | 4.6 | 4.5 |
| **Violent Crime** | 76,996 | 2,811 | 10,488 | 66,508 | 76 | 675 | 2,060 | 1,928 | 2,577 | 3,172 | 3,740 | 3,644 | 3,257 |
| Violent crime percent distribution[1] | 100.0 | 3.7 | 13.6 | 86.4 | 0.1 | 0.9 | 2.7 | 2.5 | 3.3 | 4.1 | 4.9 | 4.7 | 4.2 |
| Murder and nonnegligent manslaughter | 1,847 | 17 | 134 | 1,713 | 0 | 2 | 15 | 10 | 48 | 59 | 121 | 98 | 98 |
| Forcible rape | 2,897 | 137 | 425 | 2,472 | 0 | 39 | 98 | 72 | 89 | 127 | 160 | 154 | 119 |
| Robbery | 12,995 | 447 | 3,026 | 9,969 | 4 | 51 | 392 | 589 | 868 | 1,122 | 1,323 | 1,162 | 879 |
| Aggravated assault | 59,257 | 2,210 | 6,903 | 52,354 | 72 | 583 | 1,555 | 1,257 | 1,572 | 1,864 | 2,136 | 2,230 | 2,161 |
| **Property Crime** | 188,542 | 10,376 | 41,453 | 147,089 | 234 | 2,159 | 7,983 | 7,949 | 10,575 | 12,553 | 13,492 | 11,753 | 9,490 |
| Property crime percent distribution[1] | 100.0 | 5.5 | 22.0 | 78.0 | 0.1 | 1.1 | 4.2 | 4.2 | 5.6 | 6.7 | 7.2 | 6.2 | 5.0 |
| Burglary | 42,497 | 2,309 | 9,631 | 32,866 | 86 | 490 | 1,733 | 1,806 | 2,551 | 2,965 | 3,673 | 3,151 | 2,529 |
| Larceny-theft | 132,705 | 7,187 | 28,646 | 104,059 | 106 | 1,480 | 5,601 | 5,452 | 7,239 | 8,768 | 8,952 | 7,910 | 6,350 |
| Motor vehicle theft | 11,539 | 500 | 2,508 | 9,031 | 6 | 65 | 429 | 568 | 687 | 753 | 779 | 624 | 539 |
| Arson | 1,801 | 380 | 668 | 1,133 | 36 | 124 | 220 | 123 | 98 | 67 | 88 | 68 | 72 |
| **Other** | | | | | | | | | | | | | |
| Other assaults | 171,950 | 10,685 | 29,999 | 141,951 | 352 | 2,823 | 7,510 | 5,852 | 6,880 | 6,582 | 5,612 | 5,234 | 5,386 |
| Forgery and counterfeiting | 12,624 | 40 | 286 | 12,338 | 1 | 14 | 25 | 34 | 73 | 139 | 385 | 497 | 543 |
| Fraud | 41,431 | 151 | 808 | 40,623 | 10 | 23 | 118 | 127 | 228 | 302 | 651 | 875 | 1,035 |
| Embezzlement | 2,635 | 4 | 88 | 2,547 | 0 | 0 | 4 | 7 | 21 | 56 | 128 | 152 | 144 |
| Stolen property; buying, receiving, possessing | 14,497 | 300 | 1,776 | 12,721 | 4 | 39 | 257 | 348 | 474 | 654 | 842 | 858 | 812 |
| Vandalism | 32,009 | 3,402 | 9,812 | 22,197 | 163 | 863 | 2,376 | 1,778 | 2,195 | 2,437 | 2,320 | 1,840 | 1,552 |
| Weapons; carrying, possessing, etc. | 20,980 | 1,526 | 4,069 | 16,911 | 125 | 448 | 953 | 663 | 841 | 1,039 | 1,289 | 1,105 | 1,018 |
| Prostitution and commercialized vice | 3,036 | 17 | 80 | 2,956 | 0 | 5 | 12 | 16 | 20 | 27 | 92 | 133 | 138 |
| Sex offenses (except forcible rape and prostitution) | 12,005 | 1,095 | 2,115 | 9,890 | 70 | 296 | 729 | 346 | 314 | 360 | 487 | 494 | 414 |
| Drug abuse violations | 232,252 | 3,187 | 21,058 | 211,194 | 22 | 368 | 2,797 | 3,359 | 5,423 | 9,089 | 14,087 | 14,962 | 13,993 |
| Gambling | 1,196 | 7 | 60 | 1,136 | 1 | 0 | 6 | 7 | 19 | 27 | 44 | 81 | 92 |
| Offenses against the family and children | 31,907 | 144 | 578 | 31,329 | 1 | 39 | 104 | 110 | 145 | 179 | 312 | 359 | 419 |
| Driving under the influence | 268,019 | 49 | 1,874 | 266,145 | 3 | 5 | 41 | 73 | 398 | 1,354 | 4,736 | 6,982 | 8,403 |
| Liquor laws | 56,920 | 1,009 | 13,611 | 43,309 | 7 | 82 | 920 | 1,823 | 3,863 | 6,916 | 10,261 | 10,395 | 8,562 |
| Drunkenness | 46,045 | 91 | 1,045 | 45,000 | 5 | 7 | 79 | 186 | 298 | 470 | 1,388 | 1,581 | 1,617 |
| Disorderly conduct | 50,523 | 4,588 | 13,788 | 36,735 | 70 | 1,022 | 3,496 | 2,857 | 3,315 | 3,028 | 2,431 | 1,844 | 1,636 |
| Vagrancy | 2,890 | 31 | 240 | 2,650 | 0 | 2 | 29 | 51 | 46 | 112 | 129 | 104 | 91 |
| All other offenses (except traffic) | 571,897 | 7,267 | 34,584 | 537,313 | 262 | 1,248 | 5,757 | 6,367 | 8,874 | 12,076 | 17,720 | 22,579 | 24,018 |
| Suspicion | 722 | 21 | 76 | 646 | 2 | 9 | 10 | 11 | 31 | 13 | 32 | 29 | 29 |
| Curfew and loitering law violations | 3,959 | 871 | 3,959 | - | 5 | 112 | 754 | 928 | 1,273 | 887 | - | - | - |
| Runaways | 12,735 | 3,572 | 12,735 | - | 62 | 502 | 3,008 | 3,258 | 3,649 | 2,256 | - | - | - |

[1] Because of rounding, the percentages may not add to 100.0.

## Table 52. Metropolitan County Arrests, Distribution by Age, 2009—*Continued*

(Number, percent; 1,320 agencies; 2009 estimated population 52,113,451.)

| Offense charged | 21 | 22 | 23 | 24 | 25–29 | 30–34 | 35–39 | 40–44 | 45–49 | 50–54 | 55–59 | 60–64 | 65 and over |
|---|---|---|---|---|---|---|---|---|---|---|---|---|---|
| **TOTAL** | 76,227 | 71,820 | 69,374 | 66,263 | 287,360 | 209,718 | 177,823 | 157,543 | 134,244 | 81,729 | 39,615 | 18,043 | 13,101 |
| Total percent distribution[1] | 4.1 | 3.9 | 3.7 | 3.6 | 15.5 | 11.3 | 9.6 | 8.5 | 7.2 | 4.4 | 2.1 | 1.0 | 0.7 |
| **Violent Crime** | 3,077 | 2,870 | 2,777 | 2,495 | 11,324 | 8,344 | 7,010 | 6,326 | 5,255 | 3,280 | 1,594 | 781 | 734 |
| Violent crime percent distribution[1] | 4.0 | 3.7 | 3.6 | 3.2 | 14.7 | 10.8 | 9.1 | 8.2 | 6.8 | 4.3 | 2.1 | 1.0 | 1.0 |
| Murder and nonnegligent manslaughter | 103 | 95 | 85 | 63 | 309 | 194 | 162 | 132 | 100 | 62 | 30 | 33 | 28 |
| Forcible rape | 136 | 97 | 98 | 73 | 357 | 338 | 298 | 244 | 160 | 100 | 68 | 43 | 27 |
| Robbery | 685 | 610 | 542 | 425 | 1,616 | 891 | 657 | 556 | 357 | 180 | 58 | 16 | 12 |
| Aggravated assault | 2,153 | 2,068 | 2,052 | 1,934 | 9,042 | 6,921 | 5,893 | 5,394 | 4,638 | 2,938 | 1,438 | 689 | 667 |
| **Property Crime** | 8,102 | 6,773 | 6,066 | 5,568 | 23,286 | 16,381 | 13,696 | 12,087 | 10,053 | 5,695 | 2,599 | 1,128 | 920 |
| Property crime percent distribution[1] | 4.3 | 3.6 | 3.2 | 3.0 | 12.4 | 8.7 | 7.3 | 6.4 | 5.3 | 3.0 | 1.4 | 0.6 | 0.5 |
| Burglary | 2,096 | 1,707 | 1,428 | 1,291 | 5,454 | 3,588 | 2,712 | 2,265 | 1,671 | 820 | 296 | 111 | 74 |
| Larceny-theft | 5,446 | 4,632 | 4,178 | 3,880 | 16,051 | 11,474 | 9,932 | 9,021 | 7,733 | 4,558 | 2,171 | 963 | 808 |
| Motor vehicle theft | 509 | 378 | 415 | 353 | 1,602 | 1,192 | 959 | 708 | 555 | 262 | 99 | 38 | 19 |
| Arson | 51 | 56 | 45 | 44 | 179 | 127 | 93 | 93 | 94 | 55 | 33 | 16 | 19 |
| **Other** | | | | | | | | | | | | | |
| Other assaults | 5,612 | 5,370 | 5,316 | 5,084 | 23,991 | 19,020 | 17,413 | 15,889 | 13,282 | 7,719 | 3,614 | 1,774 | 1,635 |
| Forgery and counterfeiting | 512 | 505 | 545 | 510 | 2,353 | 1,863 | 1,540 | 1,245 | 891 | 541 | 247 | 92 | 69 |
| Fraud | 1,109 | 1,185 | 1,256 | 1,295 | 6,855 | 6,431 | 6,101 | 5,235 | 3,815 | 2,393 | 1,277 | 634 | 476 |
| Embezzlement | 141 | 107 | 104 | 95 | 372 | 295 | 301 | 246 | 216 | 131 | 69 | 29 | 17 |
| Stolen property; buying, receiving, possessing | 648 | 572 | 568 | 505 | 2,371 | 1,573 | 1,326 | 1,145 | 808 | 384 | 183 | 79 | 47 |
| Vandalism | 1,283 | 1,150 | 989 | 890 | 3,615 | 2,334 | 1,794 | 1,615 | 1,317 | 805 | 372 | 175 | 146 |
| Weapons; carrying, possessing, etc. | 966 | 857 | 805 | 789 | 3,144 | 1,813 | 1,475 | 1,174 | 1,023 | 667 | 401 | 216 | 169 |
| Prostitution and commercialized vice | 135 | 146 | 135 | 96 | 502 | 386 | 350 | 294 | 264 | 158 | 65 | 33 | 29 |
| Sex offenses (except forcible rape and prostitution) | 401 | 338 | 309 | 249 | 1,325 | 1,055 | 1,138 | 1,059 | 918 | 662 | 423 | 277 | 341 |
| Drug abuse violations | 12,019 | 10,881 | 10,290 | 9,748 | 38,739 | 25,273 | 18,666 | 15,756 | 13,518 | 8,084 | 3,373 | 1,244 | 561 |
| Gambling | 10 | 25 | 18 | 8 | 84 | 77 | 119 | 107 | 139 | 105 | 86 | 69 | 72 |
| Offenses against the family and children | 592 | 642 | 773 | 873 | 5,065 | 5,676 | 5,519 | 4,712 | 3,518 | 1,827 | 687 | 238 | 117 |
| Driving under the influence | 12,173 | 12,658 | 12,502 | 12,182 | 50,601 | 34,468 | 28,680 | 25,880 | 23,918 | 16,240 | 9,077 | 4,523 | 3,122 |
| Liquor laws | 1,219 | 890 | 784 | 640 | 2,518 | 1,751 | 1,507 | 1,458 | 1,431 | 999 | 467 | 259 | 168 |
| Drunkenness | 1,977 | 1,780 | 1,693 | 1,644 | 7,051 | 5,294 | 4,756 | 4,996 | 5,031 | 3,429 | 1,680 | 714 | 369 |
| Disorderly conduct | 1,873 | 1,612 | 1,586 | 1,365 | 5,697 | 4,043 | 3,642 | 3,545 | 3,402 | 2,101 | 1,079 | 458 | 421 |
| Vagrancy | 109 | 78 | 82 | 81 | 365 | 293 | 327 | 364 | 315 | 169 | 86 | 39 | 18 |
| All other offenses (except traffic) | 24,242 | 23,351 | 22,747 | 22,123 | 97,985 | 73,269 | 62,391 | 54,356 | 45,080 | 26,304 | 12,212 | 5,273 | 3,663 |
| Suspicion | 27 | 30 | 29 | 23 | 117 | 79 | 72 | 54 | 50 | 36 | 24 | 8 | 7 |
| Curfew and loitering law violations | - | - | - | - | - | - | - | - | - | - | - | - | - |
| Runaways | - | - | - | - | - | - | - | - | - | - | - | - | - |

[1] Because of rounding, the percentages may not add to 100.0.

# Table 53. Metropolitan County Arrests of Persons Under 15, 18, 21, and 25 Years of Age, 2009

(Number, percent; 1,320 agencies; 2009 estimated population 52,113,451.)

| Offense charged | Total all ages | Number of persons arrested | | | | Percent of total all ages | | | |
|---|---|---|---|---|---|---|---|---|---|
| | | Under 15 | Under 18 | Under 21 | Under 25 | Under 15 | Under 18 | Under 21 | Under 25 |
| **TOTAL** | 1,855,770 | 51,244 | 204,582 | 452,910 | 736,594 | 2.8 | 11.0 | 24.4 | 39.7 |
| **Violent Crime** | 76,996 | 2,811 | 10,488 | 21,129 | 32,348 | 3.7 | 13.6 | 27.4 | 42.0 |
| Murder and nonnegligent manslaughter | 1,847 | 17 | 134 | 451 | 797 | 0.9 | 7.3 | 24.4 | 43.2 |
| Forcible rape | 2,897 | 137 | 425 | 858 | 1,262 | 4.7 | 14.7 | 29.6 | 43.6 |
| Robbery | 12,995 | 447 | 3,026 | 6,390 | 8,652 | 3.4 | 23.3 | 49.2 | 66.6 |
| Aggravated assault | 59,257 | 2,210 | 6,903 | 13,430 | 21,637 | 3.7 | 11.6 | 22.7 | 36.5 |
| **Property Crime** | 188,542 | 10,376 | 41,453 | 76,188 | 102,697 | 5.5 | 22.0 | 40.4 | 54.5 |
| Burglary | 42,497 | 2,309 | 9,631 | 18,984 | 25,506 | 5.4 | 22.7 | 44.7 | 60.0 |
| Larceny-theft | 132,705 | 7,187 | 28,646 | 51,858 | 69,994 | 5.4 | 21.6 | 39.1 | 52.7 |
| Motor vehicle theft | 11,539 | 500 | 2,508 | 4,450 | 6,105 | 4.3 | 21.7 | 38.6 | 52.9 |
| Arson | 1,801 | 380 | 668 | 896 | 1,092 | 21.1 | 37.1 | 49.8 | 60.6 |
| **Other** | | | | | | | | | |
| Other assaults | 171,950 | 10,685 | 29,999 | 46,231 | 67,613 | 6.2 | 17.4 | 26.9 | 39.3 |
| Forgery and counterfeiting | 12,624 | 40 | 286 | 1,711 | 3,783 | 0.3 | 2.3 | 13.6 | 30.0 |
| Fraud | 41,431 | 151 | 808 | 3,369 | 8,214 | 0.4 | 2.0 | 8.1 | 19.8 |
| Embezzlement | 2,635 | 4 | 88 | 512 | 959 | 0.2 | 3.3 | 19.4 | 36.4 |
| Stolen property; buying, receiving, possessing | 14,497 | 300 | 1,776 | 4,288 | 6,581 | 2.1 | 12.3 | 29.6 | 45.4 |
| Vandalism | 32,009 | 3,402 | 9,812 | 15,524 | 19,836 | 10.6 | 30.7 | 48.5 | 62.0 |
| Weapons; carrying, possessing, etc. | 20,980 | 1,526 | 4,069 | 7,481 | 10,898 | 7.3 | 19.4 | 35.7 | 51.9 |
| Prostitution and commercialized vice | 3,036 | 17 | 80 | 443 | 955 | 0.6 | 2.6 | 14.6 | 31.5 |
| Sex offenses (except forcible rape and prostitution) | 12,005 | 1,095 | 2,115 | 3,510 | 4,807 | 9.1 | 17.6 | 29.2 | 40.0 |
| Drug abuse violations | 232,252 | 3,187 | 21,058 | 64,100 | 107,038 | 1.4 | 9.1 | 27.6 | 46.1 |
| Gambling | 1,196 | 7 | 60 | 277 | 338 | 0.6 | 5.0 | 23.2 | 28.3 |
| Offenses against the family and children | 31,907 | 144 | 578 | 1,668 | 4,548 | 0.5 | 1.8 | 5.2 | 14.3 |
| Driving under the influence | 268,019 | 49 | 1,874 | 21,995 | 71,510 | * | 0.7 | 8.2 | 26.7 |
| Liquor laws | 56,920 | 1,009 | 13,611 | 42,829 | 46,362 | 1.8 | 23.9 | 75.2 | 81.5 |
| Drunkenness | 46,045 | 91 | 1,045 | 5,631 | 12,725 | 0.2 | 2.3 | 12.2 | 27.6 |
| Disorderly conduct | 50,523 | 4,588 | 13,788 | 19,699 | 26,135 | 9.1 | 27.3 | 39.0 | 51.7 |
| Vagrancy | 2,890 | 31 | 240 | 564 | 914 | 1.1 | 8.3 | 19.5 | 31.6 |
| All other offenses (except traffic) | 571,897 | 7,267 | 34,584 | 98,901 | 191,364 | 1.3 | 6.0 | 17.3 | 33.5 |
| Suspicion | 722 | 21 | 76 | 166 | 275 | 2.9 | 10.5 | 23.0 | 38.1 |
| Curfew and loitering law violations | 3,959 | 871 | 3,959 | 3,959 | 3,959 | 22.0 | 100.0 | 100.0 | 100.0 |
| Runaways | 12,735 | 3,572 | 12,735 | 12,735 | 12,735 | 28.0 | 100.0 | 100.0 | 100.0 |

* Less than one-tenth of 1 percent.

## Table 54. Metropolitan County Arrests, Distribution by Sex, 2009

(Number, percent; 1,320 agencies; 2009 estimated population 52,113,451.)

| Offense charged | Number of persons arrested | | | Percent male | Percent female | Percent distribution[1] | | |
|---|---|---|---|---|---|---|---|---|
| | Total | Male | Female | | | Total | Male | Female |
| **TOTAL** | 1,855,770 | 1,401,201 | 454,569 | 75.5 | 24.5 | 100.0 | 100.0 | 100.0 |
| **Violent Crime** | 76,996 | 63,101 | 13,895 | 82.0 | 18.0 | 4.1 | 4.5 | 3.1 |
| Murder and nonnegligent manslaughter | 1,847 | 1,643 | 204 | 89.0 | 11.0 | 0.1 | 0.1 | * |
| Forcible rape | 2,897 | 2,856 | 41 | 98.6 | 1.4 | 0.2 | 0.2 | * |
| Robbery | 12,995 | 11,614 | 1,381 | 89.4 | 10.6 | 0.7 | 0.8 | 0.3 |
| Aggravated assault | 59,257 | 46,988 | 12,269 | 79.3 | 20.7 | 3.2 | 3.4 | 2.7 |
| **Property Crime** | 188,542 | 126,725 | 61,817 | 67.2 | 32.8 | 10.2 | 9.0 | 13.6 |
| Burglary | 42,497 | 36,322 | 6,175 | 85.5 | 14.5 | 2.3 | 2.6 | 1.4 |
| Larceny-theft | 132,705 | 79,410 | 53,295 | 59.8 | 40.2 | 7.2 | 5.7 | 11.7 |
| Motor vehicle theft | 11,539 | 9,510 | 2,029 | 82.4 | 17.6 | 0.6 | 0.7 | 0.4 |
| Arson | 1,801 | 1,483 | 318 | 82.3 | 17.7 | 0.1 | 0.1 | 0.1 |
| **Other** | | | | | | | | |
| Other assaults | 171,950 | 127,101 | 44,849 | 73.9 | 26.1 | 9.3 | 9.1 | 9.9 |
| Forgery and counterfeiting | 12,624 | 8,035 | 4,589 | 63.6 | 36.4 | 0.7 | 0.6 | 1.0 |
| Fraud | 41,431 | 22,537 | 18,894 | 54.4 | 45.6 | 2.2 | 1.6 | 4.2 |
| Embezzlement | 2,635 | 1,369 | 1,266 | 52.0 | 48.0 | 0.1 | 0.1 | 0.3 |
| Stolen property; buying, receiving, possessing | 14,497 | 11,809 | 2,688 | 81.5 | 18.5 | 0.8 | 0.8 | 0.6 |
| Vandalism | 32,009 | 26,124 | 5,885 | 81.6 | 18.4 | 1.7 | 1.9 | 1.3 |
| Weapons; carrying, possessing, etc. | 20,980 | 19,116 | 1,864 | 91.1 | 8.9 | 1.1 | 1.4 | 0.4 |
| Prostitution and commercialized vice | 3,036 | 1,062 | 1,974 | 35.0 | 65.0 | 0.2 | 0.1 | 0.4 |
| Sex offenses (except forcible rape and prostitution) | 12,005 | 11,155 | 850 | 92.9 | 7.1 | 0.6 | 0.8 | 0.2 |
| Drug abuse violations | 232,252 | 185,284 | 46,968 | 79.8 | 20.2 | 12.5 | 13.2 | 10.3 |
| Gambling | 1,196 | 769 | 427 | 64.3 | 35.7 | 0.1 | 0.1 | 0.1 |
| Offenses against the family and children | 31,907 | 26,627 | 5,280 | 83.5 | 16.5 | 1.7 | 1.9 | 1.2 |
| Driving under the influence | 268,019 | 208,257 | 59,762 | 77.7 | 22.3 | 14.4 | 14.9 | 13.1 |
| Liquor laws | 56,920 | 39,904 | 17,016 | 70.1 | 29.9 | 3.1 | 2.8 | 3.7 |
| Drunkenness | 46,045 | 38,112 | 7,933 | 82.8 | 17.2 | 2.5 | 2.7 | 1.7 |
| Disorderly conduct | 50,523 | 36,414 | 14,109 | 72.1 | 27.9 | 2.7 | 2.6 | 3.1 |
| Vagrancy | 2,890 | 1,921 | 969 | 66.5 | 33.5 | 0.2 | 0.1 | 0.2 |
| All other offenses (except traffic) | 571,897 | 436,692 | 135,205 | 76.4 | 23.6 | 30.8 | 31.2 | 29.7 |
| Suspicion | 722 | 502 | 220 | 69.5 | 30.5 | * | * | * |
| Curfew and loitering law violations | 3,959 | 2,607 | 1,352 | 65.8 | 34.2 | 0.2 | 0.2 | 0.3 |
| Runaways | 12,735 | 5,978 | 6,757 | 46.9 | 53.1 | 0.7 | 0.4 | 1.5 |

[1] Because of rounding, the percentages may not add to 100.0.
* Less than one-tenth of 1 percent.

# Table 55. Metropolitan County Arrests, Distribution by Race, 2009

(Number, percent; 1,320 agencies; 2009 estimated population 52,113,451.)

| Offense charged | Total arrests | | | | | Percent distribution[1] | | | | |
|---|---|---|---|---|---|---|---|---|---|---|
| | Total | White | Black | American Indian or Alaskan Native | Asian or Pacific Islander | Total | White | Black | American Indian or Alaskan Native | Asian or Pacific Islander |
| **TOTAL** | 1,847,071 | 1,374,767 | 446,860 | 12,651 | 12,793 | 100.0 | 74.4 | 24.2 | 0.7 | 0.7 |
| **Violent Crime** | 76,840 | 51,217 | 24,616 | 524 | 483 | 100.0 | 66.7 | 32.0 | 0.7 | 0.6 |
| Murder and nonnegligent manslaughter | 1,840 | 1,121 | 694 | 8 | 17 | 100.0 | 60.9 | 37.7 | 0.4 | 0.9 |
| Forcible rape | 2,885 | 2,192 | 652 | 19 | 22 | 100.0 | 76.0 | 22.6 | 0.7 | 0.8 |
| Robbery | 12,952 | 5,657 | 7,182 | 45 | 68 | 100.0 | 43.7 | 55.5 | 0.3 | 0.5 |
| Aggravated assault | 59,163 | 42,247 | 16,088 | 452 | 376 | 100.0 | 71.4 | 27.2 | 0.8 | 0.6 |
| **Property Crime** | 187,979 | 129,342 | 56,010 | 985 | 1,642 | 100.0 | 68.8 | 29.8 | 0.5 | 0.9 |
| Burglary | 42,361 | 31,344 | 10,673 | 141 | 203 | 100.0 | 74.0 | 25.2 | 0.3 | 0.5 |
| Larceny-theft | 132,325 | 88,258 | 41,943 | 747 | 1,377 | 100.0 | 66.7 | 31.7 | 0.6 | 1.0 |
| Motor vehicle theft | 11,501 | 8,300 | 3,070 | 83 | 48 | 100.0 | 72.2 | 26.7 | 0.7 | 0.4 |
| Arson | 1,792 | 1,440 | 324 | 14 | 14 | 100.0 | 80.4 | 18.1 | 0.8 | 0.8 |
| **Other** | | | | | | | | | | |
| Other assaults | 171,520 | 124,944 | 44,285 | 1,102 | 1,189 | 100.0 | 72.8 | 25.8 | 0.6 | 0.7 |
| Forgery and counterfeiting | 12,533 | 8,504 | 3,850 | 36 | 143 | 100.0 | 67.9 | 30.7 | 0.3 | 1.1 |
| Fraud | 41,235 | 28,485 | 12,301 | 200 | 249 | 100.0 | 69.1 | 29.8 | 0.5 | 0.6 |
| Embezzlement | 2,599 | 1,591 | 980 | 9 | 19 | 100.0 | 61.2 | 37.7 | 0.3 | 0.7 |
| Stolen property; buying, receiving, possessing | 14,467 | 10,329 | 3,976 | 71 | 91 | 100.0 | 71.4 | 27.5 | 0.5 | 0.6 |
| Vandalism | 31,949 | 25,145 | 6,366 | 240 | 198 | 100.0 | 78.7 | 19.9 | 0.8 | 0.6 |
| Weapons; carrying, possessing, etc. | 20,931 | 13,543 | 7,123 | 132 | 133 | 100.0 | 64.7 | 34.0 | 0.6 | 0.6 |
| Prostitution and commercialized vice | 3,022 | 1,951 | 908 | 16 | 147 | 100.0 | 64.6 | 30.0 | 0.5 | 4.9 |
| Sex offenses (except forcible rape and prostitution) | 11,933 | 9,501 | 2,281 | 62 | 89 | 100.0 | 79.6 | 19.1 | 0.5 | 0.7 |
| Drug abuse violations | 231,455 | 167,568 | 61,466 | 1,114 | 1,307 | 100.0 | 72.4 | 26.6 | 0.5 | 0.6 |
| Gambling | 1,191 | 745 | 382 | 10 | 54 | 100.0 | 62.6 | 32.1 | 0.8 | 4.5 |
| Offenses against the family and children | 31,576 | 19,421 | 11,833 | 161 | 161 | 100.0 | 61.5 | 37.5 | 0.5 | 0.5 |
| Driving under the influence | 266,838 | 234,414 | 28,368 | 1,725 | 2,331 | 100.0 | 87.8 | 10.6 | 0.6 | 0.9 |
| Liquor laws | 56,539 | 50,218 | 5,059 | 711 | 551 | 100.0 | 88.8 | 8.9 | 1.3 | 1.0 |
| Drunkenness | 45,898 | 40,779 | 4,467 | 404 | 248 | 100.0 | 88.8 | 9.7 | 0.9 | 0.5 |
| Disorderly conduct | 50,319 | 33,942 | 15,751 | 344 | 282 | 100.0 | 67.5 | 31.3 | 0.7 | 0.6 |
| Vagrancy | 2,889 | 1,773 | 1,104 | 7 | 5 | 100.0 | 61.4 | 38.2 | 0.2 | 0.2 |
| All other offenses (except traffic) | 567,979 | 408,578 | 151,438 | 4,639 | 3,324 | 100.0 | 71.9 | 26.7 | 0.8 | 0.6 |
| Suspicion | 719 | 223 | 493 | 0 | 3 | 100.0 | 31.0 | 68.6 | 0.0 | 0.4 |
| Curfew and loitering law violations | 3,950 | 3,213 | 676 | 18 | 43 | 100.0 | 81.3 | 17.1 | 0.5 | 1.1 |
| Runaways | 12,710 | 9,341 | 3,127 | 141 | 101 | 100.0 | 73.5 | 24.6 | 1.1 | 0.8 |

[1] Because of rounding, the percentages may not add to 100.0.

## Table 55. Metropolitan County Arrests, Distribution by Race, 2009—*Continued*

(Number, percent; 1,320 agencies; 2009 estimated population 52,113,451.)

| Offense charged | Arrests under 18 | | | | | Percent distribution[1] | | | | |
|---|---|---|---|---|---|---|---|---|---|---|
| | Total | White | Black | American Indian or Alaskan Native | Asian or Pacific Islander | Total | White | Black | American Indian or Alaskan Native | Asian or Pacific Islander |
| **TOTAL** | 203,903 | 136,687 | 64,398 | 1,309 | 1,509 | 100.0 | 67.0 | 31.6 | 0.6 | 0.7 |
| **Violent Crime** | 10,475 | 5,074 | 5,271 | 48 | 82 | 100.0 | 48.4 | 50.3 | 0.5 | 0.8 |
| Murder and nonnegligent manslaughter | 134 | 67 | 62 | 2 | 3 | 100.0 | 50.0 | 46.3 | 1.5 | 2.2 |
| Forcible rape | 424 | 317 | 102 | 1 | 4 | 100.0 | 74.8 | 24.1 | 0.2 | 0.9 |
| Robbery | 3,020 | 809 | 2,183 | 11 | 17 | 100.0 | 26.8 | 72.3 | 0.4 | 0.6 |
| Aggravated assault | 6,897 | 3,881 | 2,924 | 34 | 58 | 100.0 | 56.3 | 42.4 | 0.5 | 0.8 |
| **Property Crime** | 41,332 | 24,977 | 15,763 | 209 | 383 | 100.0 | 60.4 | 38.1 | 0.5 | 0.9 |
| Burglary | 9,599 | 6,341 | 3,188 | 30 | 40 | 100.0 | 66.1 | 33.2 | 0.3 | 0.4 |
| Larceny-theft | 28,561 | 16,505 | 11,578 | 153 | 325 | 100.0 | 57.8 | 40.5 | 0.5 | 1.1 |
| Motor vehicle theft | 2,505 | 1,598 | 871 | 22 | 14 | 100.0 | 63.8 | 34.8 | 0.9 | 0.6 |
| Arson | 667 | 533 | 126 | 4 | 4 | 100.0 | 79.9 | 18.9 | 0.6 | 0.6 |
| **Other** | | | | | | | | | | |
| Other assaults | 29,910 | 17,407 | 12,167 | 177 | 159 | 100.0 | 58.2 | 40.7 | 0.6 | 0.5 |
| Forgery and counterfeiting | 284 | 179 | 100 | 2 | 3 | 100.0 | 63.0 | 35.2 | 0.7 | 1.1 |
| Fraud | 802 | 539 | 245 | 6 | 12 | 100.0 | 67.2 | 30.5 | 0.7 | 1.5 |
| Embezzlement | 88 | 57 | 29 | 0 | 2 | 100.0 | 64.8 | 33.0 | 0.0 | 2.3 |
| Stolen property; buying, receiving, possessing | 1,774 | 1,110 | 643 | 7 | 14 | 100.0 | 62.6 | 36.2 | 0.4 | 0.8 |
| Vandalism | 9,777 | 7,570 | 2,091 | 66 | 50 | 100.0 | 77.4 | 21.4 | 0.7 | 0.5 |
| Weapons; carrying, possessing, etc. | 4,056 | 2,479 | 1,496 | 41 | 40 | 100.0 | 61.1 | 36.9 | 1.0 | 1.0 |
| Prostitution and commercialized vice | 80 | 41 | 38 | 0 | 1 | 100.0 | 51.3 | 47.5 | 0.0 | 1.3 |
| Sex offenses (except forcible rape and prostitution) | 2,098 | 1,529 | 550 | 13 | 6 | 100.0 | 72.9 | 26.2 | 0.6 | 0.3 |
| Drug abuse violations | 21,004 | 16,042 | 4,663 | 138 | 161 | 100.0 | 76.4 | 22.2 | 0.7 | 0.8 |
| Gambling | 60 | 29 | 29 | 0 | 2 | 100.0 | 48.3 | 48.3 | 0.0 | 3.3 |
| Offenses against the family and children | 575 | 469 | 101 | 3 | 2 | 100.0 | 81.6 | 17.6 | 0.5 | 0.3 |
| Driving under the influence | 1,856 | 1,731 | 92 | 19 | 14 | 100.0 | 93.3 | 5.0 | 1.0 | 0.8 |
| Liquor laws | 13,534 | 12,593 | 655 | 141 | 145 | 100.0 | 93.0 | 4.8 | 1.0 | 1.1 |
| Drunkenness | 1,042 | 944 | 81 | 11 | 6 | 100.0 | 90.6 | 7.8 | 1.1 | 0.6 |
| Disorderly conduct | 13,750 | 7,027 | 6,596 | 67 | 60 | 100.0 | 51.1 | 48.0 | 0.5 | 0.4 |
| Vagrancy | 240 | 129 | 108 | 1 | 2 | 100.0 | 53.8 | 45.0 | 0.4 | 0.8 |
| All other offenses (except traffic) | 34,430 | 24,194 | 9,815 | 201 | 220 | 100.0 | 70.3 | 28.5 | 0.6 | 0.6 |
| Suspicion | 76 | 13 | 62 | 0 | 1 | 100.0 | 17.1 | 81.6 | 0.0 | 1.3 |
| Curfew and loitering law violations | 3,950 | 3,213 | 676 | 18 | 43 | 100.0 | 81.3 | 17.1 | 0.5 | 1.1 |
| Runaways | 12,710 | 9,341 | 3,127 | 141 | 101 | 100.0 | 73.5 | 24.6 | 1.1 | 0.8 |

[1] Because of rounding, the percentages may not add to 100.0.

## Table 55. Metropolitan County Arrests, Distribution by Race, 2009—*Continued*

(Number, percent; 1,320 agencies; 2009 estimated population 52,113,451.)

| Offense charged | Arrests 18 and over | | | | | Percent distribution[1] | | | | |
|---|---|---|---|---|---|---|---|---|---|---|
| | Total | White | Black | American Indian or Alaskan Native | Asian or Pacific Islander | Total | White | Black | American Indian or Alaskan Native | Asian or Pacific Islander |
| **TOTAL** | 1,643,168 | 1,238,080 | 382,462 | 11,342 | 11,284 | 100.0 | 75.3 | 23.3 | 0.7 | 0.7 |
| **Violent Crime** | 66,365 | 46,143 | 19,345 | 476 | 401 | 100.0 | 69.5 | 29.1 | 0.7 | 0.6 |
| Murder and nonnegligent manslaughter | 1,706 | 1,054 | 632 | 6 | 14 | 100.0 | 61.8 | 37.0 | 0.4 | 0.8 |
| Forcible rape | 2,461 | 1,875 | 550 | 18 | 18 | 100.0 | 76.2 | 22.3 | 0.7 | 0.7 |
| Robbery | 9,932 | 4,848 | 4,999 | 34 | 51 | 100.0 | 48.8 | 50.3 | 0.3 | 0.5 |
| Aggravated assault | 52,266 | 38,366 | 13,164 | 418 | 318 | 100.0 | 73.4 | 25.2 | 0.8 | 0.6 |
| **Property Crime** | 146,647 | 104,365 | 40,247 | 776 | 1,259 | 100.0 | 71.2 | 27.4 | 0.5 | 0.9 |
| Burglary | 32,762 | 25,003 | 7,485 | 111 | 163 | 100.0 | 76.3 | 22.8 | 0.3 | 0.5 |
| Larceny-theft | 103,764 | 71,753 | 30,365 | 594 | 1,052 | 100.0 | 69.2 | 29.3 | 0.6 | 1.0 |
| Motor vehicle theft | 8,996 | 6,702 | 2,199 | 61 | 34 | 100.0 | 74.5 | 24.4 | 0.7 | 0.4 |
| Arson | 1,125 | 907 | 198 | 10 | 10 | 100.0 | 80.6 | 17.6 | 0.9 | 0.9 |
| **Other** | | | | | | | | | | |
| Other assaults | 141,610 | 107,537 | 32,118 | 925 | 1,030 | 100.0 | 75.9 | 22.7 | 0.7 | 0.7 |
| Forgery and counterfeiting | 12,249 | 8,325 | 3,750 | 34 | 140 | 100.0 | 68.0 | 30.6 | 0.3 | 1.1 |
| Fraud | 40,433 | 27,946 | 12,056 | 194 | 237 | 100.0 | 69.1 | 29.8 | 0.5 | 0.6 |
| Embezzlement | 2,511 | 1,534 | 951 | 9 | 17 | 100.0 | 61.1 | 37.9 | 0.4 | 0.7 |
| Stolen property; buying, receiving, possessing | 12,693 | 9,219 | 3,333 | 64 | 77 | 100.0 | 72.6 | 26.3 | 0.5 | 0.6 |
| Vandalism | 22,172 | 17,575 | 4,275 | 174 | 148 | 100.0 | 79.3 | 19.3 | 0.8 | 0.7 |
| Weapons; carrying, possessing, etc. | 16,875 | 11,064 | 5,627 | 91 | 93 | 100.0 | 65.6 | 33.3 | 0.5 | 0.6 |
| Prostitution and commercialized vice | 2,942 | 1,910 | 870 | 16 | 146 | 100.0 | 64.9 | 29.6 | 0.5 | 5.0 |
| Sex offenses (except forcible rape and prostitution) | 9,835 | 7,972 | 1,731 | 49 | 83 | 100.0 | 81.1 | 17.6 | 0.5 | 0.8 |
| Drug abuse violations | 210,451 | 151,526 | 56,803 | 976 | 1,146 | 100.0 | 72.0 | 27.0 | 0.5 | 0.5 |
| Gambling | 1,131 | 716 | 353 | 10 | 52 | 100.0 | 63.3 | 31.2 | 0.9 | 4.6 |
| Offenses against the family and children | 31,001 | 18,952 | 11,732 | 158 | 159 | 100.0 | 61.1 | 37.8 | 0.5 | 0.5 |
| Driving under the influence | 264,982 | 232,683 | 28,276 | 1,706 | 2,317 | 100.0 | 87.8 | 10.7 | 0.6 | 0.9 |
| Liquor laws | 43,005 | 37,625 | 4,404 | 570 | 406 | 100.0 | 87.5 | 10.2 | 1.3 | 0.9 |
| Drunkenness | 44,856 | 39,835 | 4,386 | 393 | 242 | 100.0 | 88.8 | 9.8 | 0.9 | 0.5 |
| Disorderly conduct | 36,569 | 26,915 | 9,155 | 277 | 222 | 100.0 | 73.6 | 25.0 | 0.8 | 0.6 |
| Vagrancy | 2,649 | 1,644 | 996 | 6 | 3 | 100.0 | 62.1 | 37.6 | 0.2 | 0.1 |
| All other offenses (except traffic) | 533,549 | 384,384 | 141,623 | 4,438 | 3,104 | 100.0 | 72.0 | 26.5 | 0.8 | 0.6 |
| Suspicion | 643 | 210 | 431 | 0 | 2 | 100.0 | 32.7 | 67.0 | 0.0 | 0.3 |
| Curfew and loitering law violations | - | - | - | - | - | - | - | - | - | - |
| Runaways | - | - | - | - | - | - | - | - | - | - |

[1] Because of rounding, the percentages may not add to 100.0.

## Table 56. Nonmetropolitan County Arrest Trends, 2008–2009

(Number, percent change; 1,840 agencies; 2009 estimated population 20,966,495; 2008 estimated population 20,890,796.)

| Offense charged | Number of persons arrested | | | | | | | | |
|---|---|---|---|---|---|---|---|---|---|
| | Total all ages | | | Under 18 years of age | | | 18 years of age and over | | |
| | 2008 | 2009 | Percent change | 2008 | 2009 | Percent change | 2008 | 2009 | Percent change |
| **TOTAL**[1] | 761,077 | 761,103 | * | 64,904 | 58,852 | -9.3 | 696,173 | 702,251 | +0.9 |
| **Violent Crime** | 23,355 | 23,674 | +1.4 | 2,030 | 1,955 | -3.7 | 21,325 | 21,719 | +1.8 |
| Murder and nonnegligent manslaughter | 615 | 695 | +13.0 | 39 | 38 | -2.6 | 576 | 657 | +14.1 |
| Forcible rape | 1,436 | 1,426 | -0.7 | 207 | 222 | +7.2 | 1,229 | 1,204 | -2.0 |
| Robbery | 1,749 | 1,889 | +8.0 | 178 | 211 | +18.5 | 1,571 | 1,678 | +6.8 |
| Aggravated assault | 19,555 | 19,664 | +0.6 | 1,606 | 1,484 | -7.6 | 17,949 | 18,180 | +1.3 |
| **Property Crime** | 56,354 | 55,294 | -1.9 | 10,206 | 9,399 | -7.9 | 46,148 | 45,895 | -0.5 |
| Burglary | 17,863 | 17,741 | -0.7 | 3,728 | 3,262 | -12.5 | 14,135 | 14,479 | +2.4 |
| Larceny-theft | 33,384 | 33,107 | -0.8 | 5,356 | 5,200 | -2.9 | 28,028 | 27,907 | -0.4 |
| Motor vehicle theft | 4,301 | 3,738 | -13.1 | 912 | 740 | -18.9 | 3,389 | 2,998 | -11.5 |
| Arson | 806 | 708 | -12.2 | 210 | 197 | -6.2 | 596 | 511 | -14.3 |
| **Other** | | | | | | | | | |
| Other assaults | 69,938 | 71,708 | +2.5 | 8,771 | 8,261 | -5.8 | 61,167 | 63,447 | +3.7 |
| Forgery and counterfeiting | 4,447 | 4,000 | -10.1 | 101 | 64 | -36.6 | 4,346 | 3,936 | -9.4 |
| Fraud | 26,731 | 23,654 | -11.5 | 330 | 262 | -20.6 | 26,401 | 23,392 | -11.4 |
| Embezzlement | 790 | 716 | -9.4 | 19 | 11 | -42.1 | 771 | 705 | -8.6 |
| Stolen property; buying, receiving, possessing | 3,882 | 3,921 | +1.0 | 453 | 435 | -4.0 | 3,429 | 3,486 | +1.7 |
| Vandalism | 13,351 | 13,053 | -2.2 | 3,568 | 3,474 | -2.6 | 9,783 | 9,579 | -2.1 |
| Weapons; carrying, possessing, etc. | 6,339 | 6,594 | +4.0 | 783 | 638 | -18.5 | 5,556 | 5,956 | +7.2 |
| Prostitution and commercialized vice | 214 | 175 | -18.2 | 6 | 5 | -16.7 | 208 | 170 | -18.3 |
| Sex offenses (except forcible rape and prostitution) | 5,078 | 4,734 | -6.8 | 949 | 846 | -10.9 | 4,129 | 3,888 | -5.8 |
| Drug abuse violations | 77,667 | 82,660 | +6.4 | 5,455 | 5,293 | -3.0 | 72,212 | 77,367 | +7.1 |
| Gambling | 206 | 259 | +25.7 | 19 | 7 | -63.2 | 187 | 252 | +34.8 |
| Offenses against the family and children | 12,075 | 11,357 | -5.9 | 394 | 253 | -35.8 | 11,681 | 11,104 | -4.9 |
| Driving under the influence | 143,274 | 146,667 | +2.4 | 1,541 | 1,513 | -1.8 | 141,733 | 145,154 | +2.4 |
| Liquor laws | 34,691 | 32,316 | -6.8 | 8,234 | 7,067 | -14.2 | 26,457 | 25,249 | -4.6 |
| Drunkenness | 19,935 | 18,684 | -6.3 | 519 | 393 | -24.3 | 19,416 | 18,291 | -5.8 |
| Disorderly conduct | 23,137 | 22,036 | -4.8 | 4,673 | 4,225 | -9.6 | 18,464 | 17,811 | -3.5 |
| Vagrancy | 239 | 360 | +50.6 | 19 | 12 | -36.8 | 220 | 348 | +58.2 |
| All other offenses (except traffic) | 234,450 | 235,074 | +0.3 | 11,910 | 10,572 | -11.2 | 222,540 | 224,502 | +0.9 |
| Suspicion | 91 | 79 | -13.2 | 14 | 9 | -35.7 | 77 | 70 | -9.1 |
| Curfew and loitering law violations | 501 | 492 | -1.8 | 501 | 492 | -1.8 | - | - | - |
| Runaways | 4,423 | 3,675 | -16.9 | 4,423 | 3,675 | -16.9 | - | - | - |

[1] Does not include suspicion.

* Less than one-tenth of 1 percent.

## Table 57. Nonmetropolitan County Arrest Trends, by Age and Sex, 2008–2009

(Number, percent; 1,840 agencies; 2009 estimated population 20,966,495; 2008 estimated population 20,890,796.)

| Offense charged | Male | | | | | | Female | | | | | |
|---|---|---|---|---|---|---|---|---|---|---|---|---|
| | Total | | | Under 18 | | | Total | | | Under 18 | | |
| | 2008 | 2009 | Percent change | 2008 | 2009 | Percent change | 2008 | 2009 | Percent change | 2008 | 2009 | Percent change |
| **TOTAL[1]** | 583,632 | 579,447 | -0.7 | 46,609 | 42,238 | -9.4 | 177,445 | 181,656 | +2.4 | 18,295 | 16,614 | -9.2 |
| **Violent Crime** | 19,491 | 19,590 | +0.5 | 1,678 | 1,596 | -4.9 | 3,864 | 4,084 | +5.7 | 352 | 359 | +2.0 |
| Murder and nonnegligent manslaughter | 542 | 601 | +10.9 | 38 | 36 | -5.3 | 73 | 94 | +28.8 | 1 | 2 | +100.0 |
| Forcible rape | 1,413 | 1,407 | -0.4 | 200 | 217 | +8.5 | 23 | 19 | -17.4 | 7 | 5 | -28.6 |
| Robbery | 1,537 | 1,676 | +9.0 | 160 | 197 | +23.1 | 212 | 213 | +0.5 | 18 | 14 | -22.2 |
| Aggravated assault | 15,999 | 15,906 | -0.6 | 1,280 | 1,146 | -10.5 | 3,556 | 3,758 | +5.7 | 326 | 338 | +3.7 |
| **Property Crime** | 43,336 | 41,194 | -4.9 | 8,129 | 7,272 | -10.5 | 13,018 | 14,100 | +8.3 | 2,077 | 2,127 | +2.4 |
| Burglary | 15,636 | 15,407 | -1.5 | 3,370 | 2,960 | -12.2 | 2,227 | 2,334 | +4.8 | 358 | 302 | -15.6 |
| Larceny-theft | 23,461 | 22,114 | -5.7 | 3,823 | 3,561 | -6.9 | 9,923 | 10,993 | +10.8 | 1,533 | 1,639 | +6.9 |
| Motor vehicle theft | 3,573 | 3,077 | -13.9 | 755 | 577 | -23.6 | 728 | 661 | -9.2 | 157 | 163 | +3.8 |
| Arson | 666 | 596 | -10.5 | 181 | 174 | -3.9 | 140 | 112 | -20.0 | 29 | 23 | -20.7 |
| **Other** | | | | | | | | | | | | |
| Other assaults | 52,153 | 53,508 | +2.6 | 5,971 | 5,652 | -5.3 | 17,785 | 18,200 | +2.3 | 2,800 | 2,609 | -6.8 |
| Forgery and counterfeiting | 2,491 | 2,310 | -7.3 | 62 | 40 | -35.5 | 1,956 | 1,690 | -13.6 | 39 | 24 | -38.5 |
| Fraud | 13,458 | 11,997 | -10.9 | 217 | 151 | -30.4 | 13,273 | 11,657 | -12.2 | 113 | 111 | -1.8 |
| Embezzlement | 363 | 337 | -7.2 | 8 | 8 | 0.0 | 427 | 379 | -11.2 | 11 | 3 | -72.7 |
| Stolen property; buying, receiving, possessing | 3,235 | 3,263 | +0.9 | 388 | 355 | -8.5 | 647 | 658 | +1.7 | 65 | 80 | +23.1 |
| Vandalism | 11,105 | 10,760 | -3.1 | 3,064 | 3,010 | -1.8 | 2,246 | 2,293 | +2.1 | 504 | 464 | -7.9 |
| Weapons; carrying, possessing, etc. | 5,886 | 6,111 | +3.8 | 706 | 570 | -19.3 | 453 | 483 | +6.6 | 77 | 68 | -11.7 |
| Prostitution and commercialized vice | 121 | 101 | -16.5 | 4 | 4 | 0.0 | 93 | 74 | -20.4 | 2 | 1 | -50.0 |
| Sex offenses (except forcible rape and prostitution) | 4,814 | 4,436 | -7.9 | 886 | 759 | -14.3 | 264 | 298 | +12.9 | 63 | 87 | +38.1 |
| Drug abuse violations | 61,190 | 65,103 | +6.4 | 4,329 | 4,229 | -2.3 | 16,477 | 17,557 | +6.6 | 1,126 | 1,064 | -5.5 |
| Gambling | 160 | 225 | +40.6 | 17 | 6 | -64.7 | 46 | 34 | -26.1 | 2 | 1 | -50.0 |
| Offenses against the family and children | 9,701 | 9,056 | -6.6 | 268 | 164 | -38.8 | 2,374 | 2,301 | -3.1 | 126 | 89 | -29.4 |
| Driving under the influence | 115,306 | 116,293 | +0.9 | 1,201 | 1,169 | -2.7 | 27,968 | 30,374 | +8.6 | 340 | 344 | +1.2 |
| Liquor laws | 24,833 | 22,757 | -8.4 | 5,100 | 4,458 | -12.6 | 9,858 | 9,559 | -3.0 | 3,134 | 2,609 | -16.8 |
| Drunkenness | 16,192 | 15,018 | -7.3 | 383 | 299 | -21.9 | 3,743 | 3,666 | -2.1 | 136 | 94 | -30.9 |
| Disorderly conduct | 17,039 | 15,958 | -6.3 | 3,163 | 2,890 | -8.6 | 6,098 | 6,078 | -0.3 | 1,510 | 1,335 | -11.6 |
| Vagrancy | 198 | 288 | +45.5 | 15 | 7 | -53.3 | 41 | 72 | +75.6 | 4 | 5 | +25.0 |
| All other offenses (except traffic) | 180,186 | 179,144 | -0.6 | 8,646 | 7,601 | -12.1 | 54,264 | 55,930 | +3.1 | 3,264 | 2,971 | -9.0 |
| Suspicion | 71 | 69 | -2.8 | 11 | 8 | -27.3 | 20 | 10 | -50.0 | 3 | 1 | -66.7 |
| Curfew and loitering law violations | 318 | 283 | -11.0 | 318 | 283 | -11.0 | 183 | 209 | +14.2 | 183 | 209 | +14.2 |
| Runaways | 2,056 | 1,715 | -16.6 | 2,056 | 1,715 | -16.6 | 2,367 | 1,960 | -17.2 | 2,367 | 1,960 | -17.2 |

[1] Does not include suspicion.

## Table 58. Nonmetropolitan County Arrests, Distribution by Age, 2009

(Number, percent; 1,976 agencies; 2009 estimated population 21,430,124.)

| Offense charged | Total all ages | Ages under 15 | Ages under 18 | Ages 18 and over | Under 10 | 10–12 | 13–14 | 15 | 16 | 17 | 18 | 19 | 20 |
|---|---|---|---|---|---|---|---|---|---|---|---|---|---|
| **TOTAL** | 781,970 | 14,454 | 62,025 | 719,945 | 670 | 3,078 | 10,706 | 10,635 | 15,560 | 21,376 | 32,585 | 35,459 | 34,723 |
| Total percent distribution[1] | 100.0 | 1.8 | 7.9 | 92.1 | 0.1 | 0.4 | 1.4 | 1.4 | 2.0 | 2.7 | 4.2 | 4.5 | 4.4 |
| | | | | | | | | | | | | | |
| **Violent Crime** | 24,281 | 525 | 2,056 | 22,225 | 21 | 136 | 368 | 337 | 484 | 710 | 948 | 1,001 | 968 |
| Violent crime percent distribution[1] | 100.0 | 2.2 | 8.5 | 91.5 | 0.1 | 0.6 | 1.5 | 1.4 | 2.0 | 2.9 | 3.9 | 4.1 | 4.0 |
| Murder and nonnegligent manslaughter | 755 | 10 | 48 | 707 | 1 | 2 | 7 | 4 | 13 | 21 | 33 | 24 | 29 |
| Forcible rape | 1,564 | 72 | 228 | 1,336 | 1 | 17 | 54 | 48 | 45 | 63 | 89 | 79 | 71 |
| Robbery | 2,068 | 20 | 235 | 1,833 | 0 | 3 | 17 | 18 | 75 | 122 | 172 | 175 | 137 |
| Aggravated assault | 19,894 | 423 | 1,545 | 18,349 | 19 | 114 | 290 | 267 | 351 | 504 | 654 | 723 | 731 |
| | | | | | | | | | | | | | |
| **Property Crime** | 57,654 | 2,535 | 10,043 | 47,611 | 99 | 574 | 1,862 | 1,825 | 2,509 | 3,174 | 4,420 | 3,732 | 3,127 |
| Property crime percent distribution[1] | 100.0 | 4.4 | 17.4 | 82.6 | 0.2 | 1.0 | 3.2 | 3.2 | 4.4 | 5.5 | 7.7 | 6.5 | 5.4 |
| Burglary | 18,638 | 821 | 3,534 | 15,104 | 28 | 184 | 609 | 592 | 908 | 1,213 | 1,808 | 1,493 | 1,211 |
| Larceny-theft | 34,388 | 1,448 | 5,508 | 28,880 | 57 | 339 | 1,052 | 1,023 | 1,359 | 1,678 | 2,269 | 1,978 | 1,702 |
| Motor vehicle theft | 3,838 | 173 | 774 | 3,064 | 2 | 18 | 153 | 178 | 190 | 233 | 290 | 221 | 178 |
| Arson | 790 | 93 | 227 | 563 | 12 | 33 | 48 | 32 | 52 | 50 | 53 | 40 | 36 |
| | | | | | | | | | | | | | |
| **Other** | | | | | | | | | | | | | |
| Other assaults | 73,818 | 2,817 | 8,735 | 65,083 | 123 | 695 | 1,999 | 1,577 | 2,106 | 2,235 | 2,280 | 2,263 | 2,360 |
| Forgery and counterfeiting | 4,334 | 15 | 77 | 4,257 | 2 | 3 | 10 | 16 | 8 | 38 | 111 | 161 | 183 |
| Fraud | 21,541 | 50 | 272 | 21,269 | 9 | 6 | 35 | 43 | 67 | 112 | 290 | 466 | 569 |
| Embezzlement | 775 | 0 | 17 | 758 | 0 | 0 | 0 | 0 | 6 | 11 | 17 | 33 | 27 |
| Stolen property; buying, receiving, possessing | 4,708 | 82 | 509 | 4,199 | 2 | 10 | 70 | 99 | 139 | 189 | 266 | 263 | 241 |
| Vandalism | 13,375 | 1,218 | 3,551 | 9,824 | 111 | 328 | 779 | 643 | 774 | 916 | 973 | 824 | 679 |
| Weapons; carrying, possessing, etc. | 7,092 | 222 | 683 | 6,409 | 25 | 76 | 121 | 100 | 168 | 193 | 313 | 273 | 294 |
| Prostitution and commercialized vice | 183 | 2 | 8 | 175 | 0 | 0 | 2 | 4 | 0 | 2 | 4 | 4 | 4 |
| Sex offenses (except forcible rape and prostitution) | 5,052 | 410 | 925 | 4,127 | 22 | 107 | 281 | 161 | 165 | 189 | 231 | 245 | 193 |
| Drug abuse violations | 87,691 | 731 | 5,473 | 82,218 | 12 | 86 | 633 | 793 | 1,377 | 2,572 | 4,806 | 5,265 | 5,123 |
| Gambling | 313 | 2 | 9 | 304 | 0 | 0 | 2 | 0 | 1 | 6 | 11 | 19 | 28 |
| Offenses against the family and children | 12,133 | 80 | 288 | 11,845 | 8 | 22 | 50 | 64 | 47 | 97 | 219 | 199 | 217 |
| Driving under the influence | 154,096 | 18 | 1,550 | 152,546 | 2 | 2 | 14 | 54 | 365 | 1,113 | 2,992 | 4,086 | 4,453 |
| Liquor laws | 32,777 | 612 | 7,170 | 25,607 | 5 | 43 | 564 | 959 | 2,043 | 3,556 | 5,623 | 6,063 | 4,957 |
| Drunkenness | 19,883 | 41 | 434 | 19,449 | 2 | 5 | 34 | 63 | 108 | 222 | 593 | 725 | 637 |
| Disorderly conduct | 23,314 | 1,477 | 4,466 | 18,848 | 82 | 355 | 1,040 | 873 | 1,072 | 1,044 | 1,040 | 859 | 768 |
| Vagrancy | 380 | 10 | 26 | 354 | 1 | 2 | 7 | 6 | 2 | 8 | 8 | 13 | 12 |
| All other offenses (except traffic) | 234,185 | 2,422 | 11,466 | 222,719 | 126 | 476 | 1,820 | 1,975 | 2,900 | 4,169 | 7,433 | 8,959 | 9,879 |
| Suspicion | 129 | 5 | 11 | 118 | 0 | 5 | 0 | 3 | 0 | 3 | 7 | 6 | 4 |
| Curfew and loitering law violations | 502 | 153 | 502 | - | 2 | 18 | 133 | 101 | 136 | 112 | - | - | - |
| Runaways | 3,754 | 1,027 | 3,754 | - | 16 | 129 | 882 | 939 | 1,083 | 705 | - | - | - |

[1] Because of rounding, the percentages may not add to 100.0.

## Table 58. Nonmetropolitan County Arrests, Distribution by Age, 2009—*Continued*

(Number, percent; 1,976 agencies; 2009 estimated population 21,430,124.)

| Offense charged | 21 | 22 | 23 | 24 | 25–29 | 30–34 | 35–39 | 40–44 | 45–49 | 50–54 | 55–59 | 60–64 | 65 and over |
|---|---|---|---|---|---|---|---|---|---|---|---|---|---|
| **TOTAL** | 30,976 | 29,043 | 28,479 | 27,612 | 122,658 | 91,693 | 78,148 | 68,846 | 61,546 | 39,086 | 20,527 | 10,321 | 8,243 |
| Total percent distribution[1] | 4.0 | 3.7 | 3.6 | 3.5 | 15.7 | 11.7 | 10.0 | 8.8 | 7.9 | 5.0 | 2.6 | 1.3 | 1.1 |
| **Violent Crime** | 1,008 | 851 | 864 | 866 | 3,811 | 2,777 | 2,469 | 2,116 | 1,919 | 1,252 | 647 | 373 | 355 |
| Violent crime percent distribution[1] | 4.2 | 3.5 | 3.6 | 3.6 | 15.7 | 11.4 | 10.2 | 8.7 | 7.9 | 5.2 | 2.7 | 1.5 | 1.5 |
| Murder and nonnegligent manslaughter | 38 | 29 | 22 | 39 | 134 | 74 | 68 | 53 | 55 | 52 | 23 | 12 | 22 |
| Forcible rape | 75 | 42 | 47 | 46 | 197 | 183 | 154 | 118 | 80 | 62 | 39 | 32 | 22 |
| Robbery | 127 | 119 | 103 | 100 | 365 | 210 | 127 | 76 | 62 | 37 | 16 | 2 | 5 |
| Aggravated assault | 768 | 661 | 692 | 681 | 3,115 | 2,310 | 2,120 | 1,869 | 1,722 | 1,101 | 569 | 327 | 306 |
| **Property Crime** | 2,530 | 2,232 | 2,042 | 1,894 | 8,195 | 5,460 | 4,286 | 3,653 | 2,884 | 1,588 | 853 | 389 | 326 |
| Property crime percent distribution[1] | 4.4 | 3.9 | 3.5 | 3.3 | 14.2 | 9.5 | 7.4 | 6.3 | 5.0 | 2.8 | 1.5 | 0.7 | 0.6 |
| Burglary | 895 | 808 | 722 | 647 | 2,675 | 1,588 | 1,148 | 897 | 644 | 325 | 145 | 58 | 40 |
| Larceny-theft | 1,455 | 1,234 | 1,171 | 1,101 | 4,955 | 3,422 | 2,792 | 2,466 | 1,992 | 1,131 | 641 | 303 | 268 |
| Motor vehicle theft | 161 | 167 | 133 | 133 | 485 | 387 | 290 | 256 | 201 | 95 | 44 | 15 | 8 |
| Arson | 19 | 23 | 16 | 13 | 80 | 63 | 56 | 34 | 47 | 37 | 23 | 13 | 10 |
| **Other** | | | | | | | | | | | | | |
| Other assaults | 2,485 | 2,204 | 2,350 | 2,298 | 10,804 | 8,764 | 8,042 | 7,263 | 6,269 | 3,702 | 1,913 | 1,032 | 1,054 |
| Forgery and counterfeiting | 178 | 189 | 174 | 185 | 872 | 671 | 472 | 457 | 311 | 156 | 90 | 31 | 16 |
| Fraud | 604 | 634 | 624 | 624 | 3,837 | 3,435 | 3,156 | 2,544 | 1,876 | 1,336 | 664 | 353 | 257 |
| Embezzlement | 30 | 26 | 31 | 25 | 113 | 103 | 95 | 69 | 75 | 56 | 36 | 10 | 12 |
| Stolen property; buying, receiving, possessing | 199 | 188 | 196 | 160 | 750 | 572 | 425 | 335 | 299 | 187 | 62 | 35 | 21 |
| Vandalism | 543 | 511 | 442 | 422 | 1,571 | 1,037 | 792 | 709 | 611 | 353 | 163 | 105 | 89 |
| Weapons; carrying, possessing, etc. | 293 | 256 | 215 | 268 | 1,116 | 793 | 627 | 563 | 526 | 384 | 235 | 135 | 118 |
| Prostitution and commercialized vice | 3 | 9 | 9 | 3 | 27 | 21 | 17 | 23 | 14 | 18 | 13 | 2 | 4 |
| Sex offenses (except forcible rape and prostitution) | 162 | 152 | 121 | 133 | 535 | 455 | 464 | 387 | 352 | 254 | 158 | 122 | 163 |
| Drug abuse violations | 4,495 | 4,085 | 3,916 | 3,765 | 15,274 | 10,076 | 7,551 | 6,195 | 5,601 | 3,427 | 1,619 | 677 | 343 |
| Gambling | 8 | 10 | 10 | 11 | 38 | 31 | 28 | 28 | 31 | 13 | 16 | 10 | 12 |
| Offenses against the family and children | 279 | 299 | 318 | 381 | 2,137 | 2,127 | 2,011 | 1,578 | 1,157 | 591 | 187 | 78 | 67 |
| Driving under the influence | 6,051 | 6,092 | 5,933 | 5,742 | 24,883 | 18,614 | 16,842 | 16,053 | 16,445 | 11,478 | 6,812 | 3,521 | 2,549 |
| Liquor laws | 892 | 584 | 481 | 449 | 1,547 | 1,080 | 921 | 868 | 856 | 599 | 351 | 186 | 150 |
| Drunkenness | 830 | 715 | 710 | 698 | 2,962 | 2,422 | 2,230 | 2,175 | 2,210 | 1,355 | 700 | 291 | 196 |
| Disorderly conduct | 874 | 817 | 771 | 690 | 2,820 | 2,250 | 1,935 | 1,960 | 1,757 | 1,151 | 599 | 275 | 282 |
| Vagrancy | 9 | 12 | 6 | 12 | 57 | 48 | 30 | 34 | 52 | 32 | 17 | 10 | 2 |
| All other offenses (except traffic) | 9,498 | 9,169 | 9,262 | 8,980 | 41,281 | 30,942 | 25,741 | 21,829 | 18,295 | 11,148 | 5,390 | 2,686 | 2,227 |
| Suspicion | 5 | 8 | 4 | 6 | 28 | 15 | 14 | 7 | 6 | 6 | 2 | 0 | 0 |
| Curfew and loitering law violations | - | - | - | - | - | - | - | - | - | - | - | - | - |
| Runaways | - | - | - | - | - | - | - | - | - | - | - | - | - |

[1] Because of rounding, the percentages may not add to 100.0.

## Table 59. Nonmetropolitan County Arrests of Persons Under 15, 18, 21, and 25 Years of Age, 2009

(Number, percent; 1,976 agencies; 2009 estimated population 21,430,124.)

| Offense charged | Total all ages | Number of persons arrested | | | | Percent of total all ages | | | |
|---|---|---|---|---|---|---|---|---|---|
| | | Under 15 | Under 18 | Under 21 | Under 25 | Under 15 | Under 18 | Under 21 | Under 25 |
| **TOTAL** | 781,970 | 14,454 | 62,025 | 164,792 | 280,902 | 1.8 | 7.9 | 21.1 | 35.9 |
| **Violent Crime** | 24,281 | 525 | 2,056 | 4,973 | 8,562 | 2.2 | 8.5 | 20.5 | 35.3 |
| Murder and nonnegligent manslaughter | 755 | 10 | 48 | 134 | 262 | 1.3 | 6.4 | 17.7 | 34.7 |
| Forcible rape | 1,564 | 72 | 228 | 467 | 677 | 4.6 | 14.6 | 29.9 | 43.3 |
| Robbery | 2,068 | 20 | 235 | 719 | 1,168 | 1.0 | 11.4 | 34.8 | 56.5 |
| Aggravated assault | 19,894 | 423 | 1,545 | 3,653 | 6,455 | 2.1 | 7.8 | 18.4 | 32.4 |
| **Property Crime** | 57,654 | 2,535 | 10,043 | 21,322 | 30,020 | 4.4 | 17.4 | 37.0 | 52.1 |
| Burglary | 18,638 | 821 | 3,534 | 8,046 | 11,118 | 4.4 | 19.0 | 43.2 | 59.7 |
| Larceny-theft | 34,388 | 1,448 | 5,508 | 11,457 | 16,418 | 4.2 | 16.0 | 33.3 | 47.7 |
| Motor vehicle theft | 3,838 | 173 | 774 | 1,463 | 2,057 | 4.5 | 20.2 | 38.1 | 53.6 |
| Arson | 790 | 93 | 227 | 356 | 427 | 11.8 | 28.7 | 45.1 | 54.1 |
| **Other** | | | | | | | | | |
| Other assaults | 73,818 | 2,817 | 8,735 | 15,638 | 24,975 | 3.8 | 11.8 | 21.2 | 33.8 |
| Forgery and counterfeiting | 4,334 | 15 | 77 | 532 | 1,258 | 0.3 | 1.8 | 12.3 | 29.0 |
| Fraud | 21,541 | 50 | 272 | 1,597 | 4,083 | 0.2 | 1.3 | 7.4 | 19.0 |
| Embezzlement | 775 | 0 | 17 | 94 | 206 | 0.0 | 2.2 | 12.1 | 26.6 |
| Stolen property; buying, receiving, possessing | 4,708 | 82 | 509 | 1,279 | 2,022 | 1.7 | 10.8 | 27.2 | 42.9 |
| Vandalism | 13,375 | 1,218 | 3,551 | 6,027 | 7,945 | 9.1 | 26.5 | 45.1 | 59.4 |
| Weapons; carrying, possessing, etc. | 7,092 | 222 | 683 | 1,563 | 2,595 | 3.1 | 9.6 | 22.0 | 36.6 |
| Prostitution and commercialized vice | 183 | 2 | 8 | 20 | 44 | 1.1 | 4.4 | 10.9 | 24.0 |
| Sex offenses (except forcible rape and prostitution) | 5,052 | 410 | 925 | 1,594 | 2,162 | 8.1 | 18.3 | 31.6 | 42.8 |
| Drug abuse violations | 87,691 | 731 | 5,473 | 20,667 | 36,928 | 0.8 | 6.2 | 23.6 | 42.1 |
| Gambling | 313 | 2 | 9 | 67 | 106 | 0.6 | 2.9 | 21.4 | 33.9 |
| Offenses against the family and children | 12,133 | 80 | 288 | 923 | 2,200 | 0.7 | 2.4 | 7.6 | 18.1 |
| Driving under the influence | 154,096 | 18 | 1,550 | 13,081 | 36,899 | * | 1.0 | 8.5 | 23.9 |
| Liquor laws | 32,777 | 612 | 7,170 | 23,813 | 26,219 | 1.9 | 21.9 | 72.7 | 80.0 |
| Drunkenness | 19,883 | 41 | 434 | 2,389 | 5,342 | 0.2 | 2.2 | 12.0 | 26.9 |
| Disorderly conduct | 23,314 | 1,477 | 4,466 | 7,133 | 10,285 | 6.3 | 19.2 | 30.6 | 44.1 |
| Vagrancy | 380 | 10 | 26 | 59 | 98 | 2.6 | 6.8 | 15.5 | 25.8 |
| All other offenses (except traffic) | 234,185 | 2,422 | 11,466 | 37,737 | 74,646 | 1.0 | 4.9 | 16.1 | 31.9 |
| Suspicion | 129 | 5 | 11 | 28 | 51 | 3.9 | 8.5 | 21.7 | 39.5 |
| Curfew and loitering law violations | 502 | 153 | 502 | 502 | 502 | 30.5 | 100.0 | 100.0 | 100.0 |
| Runaways | 3,754 | 1,027 | 3,754 | 3,754 | 3,754 | 27.4 | 100.0 | 100.0 | 100.0 |

* Less than one-tenth of 1 percent.

## Table 60. Nonmetropolitan County Arrests, Distribution by Sex, 2009

(Number, percent; 1,976 agencies; 2009 estimated population 21,430,124.)

| Offense charged | Number of persons arrested | | | Percent male | Percent female | Percent distribution[1] | | |
|---|---|---|---|---|---|---|---|---|
| | Total | Male | Female | | | Total | Male | Female |
| **TOTAL** | 781,970 | 598,163 | 183,807 | 76.5 | 23.5 | 100.0 | 100.0 | 100.0 |
| **Violent Crime** | 24,281 | 20,072 | 4,209 | 82.7 | 17.3 | 3.1 | 3.4 | 2.3 |
| Murder and nonnegligent manslaughter | 755 | 650 | 105 | 86.1 | 13.9 | 0.1 | 0.1 | 0.1 |
| Forcible rape | 1,564 | 1,538 | 26 | 98.3 | 1.7 | 0.2 | 0.3 | * |
| Robbery | 2,068 | 1,827 | 241 | 88.3 | 11.7 | 0.3 | 0.3 | 0.1 |
| Aggravated assault | 19,894 | 16,057 | 3,837 | 80.7 | 19.3 | 2.5 | 2.7 | 2.1 |
| **Property Crime** | 57,654 | 42,988 | 14,666 | 74.6 | 25.4 | 7.4 | 7.2 | 8.0 |
| Burglary | 18,638 | 16,198 | 2,440 | 86.9 | 13.1 | 2.4 | 2.7 | 1.3 |
| Larceny-theft | 34,388 | 22,960 | 11,428 | 66.8 | 33.2 | 4.4 | 3.8 | 6.2 |
| Motor vehicle theft | 3,838 | 3,168 | 670 | 82.5 | 17.5 | 0.5 | 0.5 | 0.4 |
| Arson | 790 | 662 | 128 | 83.8 | 16.2 | 0.1 | 0.1 | 0.1 |
| **Other** | | | | | | | | |
| Other assaults | 73,818 | 55,156 | 18,662 | 74.7 | 25.3 | 9.4 | 9.2 | 10.2 |
| Forgery and counterfeiting | 4,334 | 2,544 | 1,790 | 58.7 | 41.3 | 0.6 | 0.4 | 1.0 |
| Fraud | 21,541 | 11,143 | 10,398 | 51.7 | 48.3 | 2.8 | 1.9 | 5.7 |
| Embezzlement | 775 | 374 | 401 | 48.3 | 51.7 | 0.1 | 0.1 | 0.2 |
| Stolen property; buying, receiving, possessing | 4,708 | 3,912 | 796 | 83.1 | 16.9 | 0.6 | 0.7 | 0.4 |
| Vandalism | 13,375 | 11,032 | 2,343 | 82.5 | 17.5 | 1.7 | 1.8 | 1.3 |
| Weapons; carrying, possessing, etc. | 7,092 | 6,566 | 526 | 92.6 | 7.4 | 0.9 | 1.1 | 0.3 |
| Prostitution and commercialized vice | 183 | 105 | 78 | 57.4 | 42.6 | * | * | * |
| Sex offenses (except forcible rape and prostitution) | 5,052 | 4,732 | 320 | 93.7 | 6.3 | 0.6 | 0.8 | 0.2 |
| Drug abuse violations | 87,691 | 69,204 | 18,487 | 78.9 | 21.1 | 11.2 | 11.6 | 10.1 |
| Gambling | 313 | 264 | 49 | 84.3 | 15.7 | * | * | * |
| Offenses against the family and children | 12,133 | 9,735 | 2,398 | 80.2 | 19.8 | 1.6 | 1.6 | 1.3 |
| Driving under the influence | 154,096 | 122,520 | 31,576 | 79.5 | 20.5 | 19.7 | 20.5 | 17.2 |
| Liquor laws | 32,777 | 23,135 | 9,642 | 70.6 | 29.4 | 4.2 | 3.9 | 5.2 |
| Drunkenness | 19,883 | 15,943 | 3,940 | 80.2 | 19.8 | 2.5 | 2.7 | 2.1 |
| Disorderly conduct | 23,314 | 16,885 | 6,429 | 72.4 | 27.6 | 3.0 | 2.8 | 3.5 |
| Vagrancy | 380 | 301 | 79 | 79.2 | 20.8 | * | 0.1 | * |
| All other offenses (except traffic) | 234,185 | 179,426 | 54,759 | 76.6 | 23.4 | 29.9 | 30.0 | 29.8 |
| Suspicion | 129 | 94 | 35 | 72.9 | 27.1 | * | * | * |
| Curfew and loitering law violations | 502 | 289 | 213 | 57.6 | 42.4 | 0.1 | * | 0.1 |
| Runaways | 3,754 | 1,743 | 2,011 | 46.4 | 53.6 | 0.5 | 0.3 | 1.1 |

[1] Because of rounding, the percentages may not add to 100.0.
* Less than one-tenth of 1 percent.

## Table 61. Nonmetropolitan County Arrests, Distribution by Race, 2009

(Number, percent; 1,976 agencies; 2009 estimated population 21,430,124.)

| Offense charged | Total arrests | | | | | Percent distribution[1] | | | | |
|---|---|---|---|---|---|---|---|---|---|---|
| | Total | White | Black | American Indian or Alaskan Native | Asian or Pacific Islander | Total | White | Black | American Indian or Alaskan Native | Asian or Pacific Islander |
| **TOTAL** | 773,902 | 631,977 | 107,923 | 24,628 | 9,374 | 100.0 | 81.7 | 13.9 | 3.2 | 1.2 |
| **Violent Crime** | 24,107 | 17,659 | 5,104 | 1,104 | 240 | 100.0 | 73.3 | 21.2 | 4.6 | 1.0 |
| Murder and nonnegligent manslaughter | 750 | 508 | 211 | 27 | 4 | 100.0 | 67.7 | 28.1 | 3.6 | 0.5 |
| Forcible rape | 1,552 | 1,275 | 225 | 34 | 18 | 100.0 | 82.2 | 14.5 | 2.2 | 1.2 |
| Robbery | 2,063 | 1,086 | 860 | 83 | 34 | 100.0 | 52.6 | 41.7 | 4.0 | 1.6 |
| Aggravated assault | 19,742 | 14,790 | 3,808 | 960 | 184 | 100.0 | 74.9 | 19.3 | 4.9 | 0.9 |
| **Property Crime** | 57,237 | 46,611 | 7,945 | 1,754 | 927 | 100.0 | 81.4 | 13.9 | 3.1 | 1.6 |
| Burglary | 18,506 | 14,823 | 2,858 | 627 | 198 | 100.0 | 80.1 | 15.4 | 3.4 | 1.1 |
| Larceny-theft | 34,153 | 27,990 | 4,579 | 947 | 637 | 100.0 | 82.0 | 13.4 | 2.8 | 1.9 |
| Motor vehicle theft | 3,793 | 3,124 | 418 | 163 | 88 | 100.0 | 82.4 | 11.0 | 4.3 | 2.3 |
| Arson | 785 | 674 | 90 | 17 | 4 | 100.0 | 85.9 | 11.5 | 2.2 | 0.5 |
| **Other** | | | | | | | | | | |
| Other assaults | 73,382 | 58,575 | 11,242 | 2,660 | 905 | 100.0 | 79.8 | 15.3 | 3.6 | 1.2 |
| Forgery and counterfeiting | 4,289 | 3,486 | 729 | 53 | 21 | 100.0 | 81.3 | 17.0 | 1.2 | 0.5 |
| Fraud | 21,342 | 16,732 | 4,206 | 301 | 103 | 100.0 | 78.4 | 19.7 | 1.4 | 0.5 |
| Embezzlement | 769 | 627 | 119 | 13 | 10 | 100.0 | 81.5 | 15.5 | 1.7 | 1.3 |
| Stolen property; buying, receiving, possessing | 4,685 | 3,637 | 892 | 137 | 19 | 100.0 | 77.6 | 19.0 | 2.9 | 0.4 |
| Vandalism | 13,256 | 11,251 | 1,334 | 527 | 144 | 100.0 | 84.9 | 10.1 | 4.0 | 1.1 |
| Weapons; carrying, possessing, etc. | 7,058 | 5,342 | 1,424 | 234 | 58 | 100.0 | 75.7 | 20.2 | 3.3 | 0.8 |
| Prostitution and commercialized vice | 183 | 132 | 33 | 3 | 15 | 100.0 | 72.1 | 18.0 | 1.6 | 8.2 |
| Sex offenses (except forcible rape and prostitution) | 5,015 | 4,316 | 528 | 112 | 59 | 100.0 | 86.1 | 10.5 | 2.2 | 1.2 |
| Drug abuse violations | 87,140 | 70,728 | 14,181 | 1,493 | 738 | 100.0 | 81.2 | 16.3 | 1.7 | 0.8 |
| Gambling | 312 | 262 | 36 | 3 | 11 | 100.0 | 84.0 | 11.5 | 1.0 | 3.5 |
| Offenses against the family and children | 12,056 | 8,579 | 2,833 | 614 | 30 | 100.0 | 71.2 | 23.5 | 5.1 | 0.2 |
| Driving under the influence | 151,155 | 132,840 | 13,055 | 3,797 | 1,463 | 100.0 | 87.9 | 8.6 | 2.5 | 1.0 |
| Liquor laws | 32,262 | 29,193 | 1,416 | 1,180 | 473 | 100.0 | 90.5 | 4.4 | 3.7 | 1.5 |
| Drunkenness | 19,814 | 17,454 | 1,440 | 870 | 50 | 100.0 | 88.1 | 7.3 | 4.4 | 0.3 |
| Disorderly conduct | 23,157 | 17,897 | 3,925 | 1,115 | 220 | 100.0 | 77.3 | 16.9 | 4.8 | 1.0 |
| Vagrancy | 380 | 236 | 61 | 19 | 64 | 100.0 | 62.1 | 16.1 | 5.0 | 16.8 |
| All other offenses (except traffic) | 231,944 | 183,161 | 37,071 | 8,494 | 3,218 | 100.0 | 79.0 | 16.0 | 3.7 | 1.4 |
| Suspicion | 128 | 86 | 42 | 0 | 0 | 100.0 | 67.2 | 32.8 | 0.0 | 0.0 |
| Curfew and loitering law violations | 499 | 401 | 24 | 20 | 54 | 100.0 | 80.4 | 4.8 | 4.0 | 10.8 |
| Runaways | 3,732 | 2,772 | 283 | 125 | 552 | 100.0 | 74.3 | 7.6 | 3.3 | 14.8 |

[1] Because of rounding, the percentages may not add to 100.0.

## Table 61. Nonmetropolitan County Arrests, Distribution by Race, 2009—*Continued*

(Number, percent; 1,976 agencies; 2009 estimated population 21,430,124.)

| Offense charged | Arrests under 18 | | | | | Percent distribution[1] | | | | |
|---|---|---|---|---|---|---|---|---|---|---|
| | Total | White | Black | American Indian or Alaskan Native | Asian or Pacific Islander | Total | White | Black | American Indian or Alaskan Native | Asian or Pacific Islander |
| **TOTAL** | 61,456 | 48,993 | 8,281 | 2,311 | 1,871 | 100.0 | 79.7 | 13.5 | 3.8 | 3.0 |
| **Violent Crime** | 2,036 | 1,388 | 548 | 72 | 28 | 100.0 | 68.2 | 26.9 | 3.5 | 1.4 |
| Murder and nonnegligent manslaughter | 48 | 31 | 17 | 0 | 0 | 100.0 | 64.6 | 35.4 | 0.0 | 0.0 |
| Forcible rape | 226 | 198 | 24 | 2 | 2 | 100.0 | 87.6 | 10.6 | 0.9 | 0.9 |
| Robbery | 235 | 85 | 138 | 3 | 9 | 100.0 | 36.2 | 58.7 | 1.3 | 3.8 |
| Aggravated assault | 1,527 | 1,074 | 369 | 67 | 17 | 100.0 | 70.3 | 24.2 | 4.4 | 1.1 |
| **Property Crime** | 9,929 | 7,996 | 1,279 | 334 | 320 | 100.0 | 80.5 | 12.9 | 3.4 | 3.2 |
| Burglary | 3,496 | 2,812 | 486 | 149 | 49 | 100.0 | 80.4 | 13.9 | 4.3 | 1.4 |
| Larceny-theft | 5,448 | 4,361 | 695 | 157 | 235 | 100.0 | 80.0 | 12.8 | 2.9 | 4.3 |
| Motor vehicle theft | 759 | 628 | 73 | 24 | 34 | 100.0 | 82.7 | 9.6 | 3.2 | 4.5 |
| Arson | 226 | 195 | 25 | 4 | 2 | 100.0 | 86.3 | 11.1 | 1.8 | 0.9 |
| **Other** | | | | | | | | | | |
| Other assaults | 8,656 | 6,281 | 1,947 | 285 | 143 | 100.0 | 72.6 | 22.5 | 3.3 | 1.7 |
| Forgery and counterfeiting | 77 | 60 | 15 | 1 | 1 | 100.0 | 77.9 | 19.5 | 1.3 | 1.3 |
| Fraud | 267 | 233 | 32 | 2 | 0 | 100.0 | 87.3 | 12.0 | 0.7 | 0.0 |
| Embezzlement | 17 | 16 | 1 | 0 | 0 | 100.0 | 94.1 | 5.9 | 0.0 | 0.0 |
| Stolen property; buying, receiving, possessing | 505 | 396 | 91 | 15 | 3 | 100.0 | 78.4 | 18.0 | 3.0 | 0.6 |
| Vandalism | 3,522 | 3,064 | 274 | 138 | 46 | 100.0 | 87.0 | 7.8 | 3.9 | 1.3 |
| Weapons; carrying, possessing, etc. | 682 | 494 | 157 | 27 | 4 | 100.0 | 72.4 | 23.0 | 4.0 | 0.6 |
| Prostitution and commercialized vice | 8 | 7 | 1 | 0 | 0 | 100.0 | 87.5 | 12.5 | 0.0 | 0.0 |
| Sex offenses (except forcible rape and prostitution) | 916 | 804 | 81 | 20 | 11 | 100.0 | 87.8 | 8.8 | 2.2 | 1.2 |
| Drug abuse violations | 5,435 | 4,629 | 568 | 120 | 118 | 100.0 | 85.2 | 10.5 | 2.2 | 2.2 |
| Gambling | 9 | 6 | 2 | 0 | 1 | 100.0 | 66.7 | 22.2 | 0.0 | 11.1 |
| Offenses against the family and children | 282 | 252 | 29 | 1 | 0 | 100.0 | 89.4 | 10.3 | 0.4 | 0.0 |
| Driving under the influence | 1,522 | 1,405 | 66 | 37 | 14 | 100.0 | 92.3 | 4.3 | 2.4 | 0.9 |
| Liquor laws | 7,084 | 6,553 | 143 | 300 | 88 | 100.0 | 92.5 | 2.0 | 4.2 | 1.2 |
| Drunkenness | 434 | 388 | 9 | 37 | 0 | 100.0 | 89.4 | 2.1 | 8.5 | 0.0 |
| Disorderly conduct | 4,448 | 2,939 | 1,269 | 189 | 51 | 100.0 | 66.1 | 28.5 | 4.2 | 1.1 |
| Vagrancy | 26 | 22 | 3 | 1 | 0 | 100.0 | 84.6 | 11.5 | 3.8 | 0.0 |
| All other offenses (except traffic) | 11,359 | 8,876 | 1,459 | 587 | 437 | 100.0 | 78.1 | 12.8 | 5.2 | 3.8 |
| Suspicion | 11 | 11 | 0 | 0 | 0 | 100.0 | 100.0 | 0.0 | 0.0 | 0.0 |
| Curfew and loitering law violations | 499 | 401 | 24 | 20 | 54 | 100.0 | 80.4 | 4.8 | 4.0 | 10.8 |
| Runaways | 3,732 | 2,772 | 283 | 125 | 552 | 100.0 | 74.3 | 7.6 | 3.3 | 14.8 |

[1] Because of rounding, the percentages may not add to 100.0.

# Table 61. Nonmetropolitan County Arrests, Distribution by Race, 2009—*Continued*

(Number, percent; 1,976 agencies; 2009 estimated population 21,430,124.)

| Offense charged | Arrests 18 and over | | | | | Percent distribution[1] | | | | |
|---|---|---|---|---|---|---|---|---|---|---|
| | Total | White | Black | American Indian or Alaskan Native | Asian or Pacific Islander | Total | White | Black | American Indian or Alaskan Native | Asian or Pacific Islander |
| **TOTAL** | 712,446 | 582,984 | 99,642 | 22,317 | 7,503 | 100.0 | 81.8 | 14.0 | 3.1 | 1.1 |
| **Violent Crime** | 22,071 | 16,271 | 4,556 | 1,032 | 212 | 100.0 | 73.7 | 20.6 | 4.7 | 1.0 |
| Murder and nonnegligent manslaughter | 702 | 477 | 194 | 27 | 4 | 100.0 | 67.9 | 27.6 | 3.8 | 0.6 |
| Forcible rape | 1,326 | 1,077 | 201 | 32 | 16 | 100.0 | 81.2 | 15.2 | 2.4 | 1.2 |
| Robbery | 1,828 | 1,001 | 722 | 80 | 25 | 100.0 | 54.8 | 39.5 | 4.4 | 1.4 |
| Aggravated assault | 18,215 | 13,716 | 3,439 | 893 | 167 | 100.0 | 75.3 | 18.9 | 4.9 | 0.9 |
| **Property Crime** | 47,308 | 38,615 | 6,666 | 1,420 | 607 | 100.0 | 81.6 | 14.1 | 3.0 | 1.3 |
| Burglary | 15,010 | 12,011 | 2,372 | 478 | 149 | 100.0 | 80.0 | 15.8 | 3.2 | 1.0 |
| Larceny-theft | 28,705 | 23,629 | 3,884 | 790 | 402 | 100.0 | 82.3 | 13.5 | 2.8 | 1.4 |
| Motor vehicle theft | 3,034 | 2,496 | 345 | 139 | 54 | 100.0 | 82.3 | 11.4 | 4.6 | 1.8 |
| Arson | 559 | 479 | 65 | 13 | 2 | 100.0 | 85.7 | 11.6 | 2.3 | 0.4 |
| **Other** | | | | | | | | | | |
| Other assaults | 64,726 | 52,294 | 9,295 | 2,375 | 762 | 100.0 | 80.8 | 14.4 | 3.7 | 1.2 |
| Forgery and counterfeiting | 4,212 | 3,426 | 714 | 52 | 20 | 100.0 | 81.3 | 17.0 | 1.2 | 0.5 |
| Fraud | 21,075 | 16,499 | 4,174 | 299 | 103 | 100.0 | 78.3 | 19.8 | 1.4 | 0.5 |
| Embezzlement | 752 | 611 | 118 | 13 | 10 | 100.0 | 81.3 | 15.7 | 1.7 | 1.3 |
| Stolen property; buying, receiving, possessing | 4,180 | 3,241 | 801 | 122 | 16 | 100.0 | 77.5 | 19.2 | 2.9 | 0.4 |
| Vandalism | 9,734 | 8,187 | 1,060 | 389 | 98 | 100.0 | 84.1 | 10.9 | 4.0 | 1.0 |
| Weapons; carrying, possessing, etc. | 6,376 | 4,848 | 1,267 | 207 | 54 | 100.0 | 76.0 | 19.9 | 3.2 | 0.8 |
| Prostitution and commercialized vice | 175 | 125 | 32 | 3 | 15 | 100.0 | 71.4 | 18.3 | 1.7 | 8.6 |
| Sex offenses (except forcible rape and prostitution) | 4,099 | 3,512 | 447 | 92 | 48 | 100.0 | 85.7 | 10.9 | 2.2 | 1.2 |
| Drug abuse violations | 81,705 | 66,099 | 13,613 | 1,373 | 620 | 100.0 | 80.9 | 16.7 | 1.7 | 0.8 |
| Gambling | 303 | 256 | 34 | 3 | 10 | 100.0 | 84.5 | 11.2 | 1.0 | 3.3 |
| Offenses against the family and children | 11,774 | 8,327 | 2,804 | 613 | 30 | 100.0 | 70.7 | 23.8 | 5.2 | 0.3 |
| Driving under the influence | 149,633 | 131,435 | 12,989 | 3,760 | 1,449 | 100.0 | 87.8 | 8.7 | 2.5 | 1.0 |
| Liquor laws | 25,178 | 22,640 | 1,273 | 880 | 385 | 100.0 | 89.9 | 5.1 | 3.5 | 1.5 |
| Drunkenness | 19,380 | 17,066 | 1,431 | 833 | 50 | 100.0 | 88.1 | 7.4 | 4.3 | 0.3 |
| Disorderly conduct | 18,709 | 14,958 | 2,656 | 926 | 169 | 100.0 | 80.0 | 14.2 | 4.9 | 0.9 |
| Vagrancy | 354 | 214 | 58 | 18 | 64 | 100.0 | 60.5 | 16.4 | 5.1 | 18.1 |
| All other offenses (except traffic) | 220,585 | 174,285 | 35,612 | 7,907 | 2,781 | 100.0 | 79.0 | 16.1 | 3.6 | 1.3 |
| Suspicion | 117 | 75 | 42 | 0 | 0 | 100.0 | 64.1 | 35.9 | 0.0 | 0.0 |
| Curfew and loitering law violations | - | - | - | - | - | - | - | - | - | - |
| Runaways | - | - | - | - | - | - | - | - | - | - |

[1] Because of rounding, the percentages may not add to 100.0.

## Table 62. Suburban Area[1] Arrest Trends, 2008–2009

(Number, percent change; 6,008 agencies; 2009 estimated population 94,512,203; 2008 estimated population 93,792,021.)

| Offense charged | Number of persons arrested | | | | | | | | |
|---|---|---|---|---|---|---|---|---|---|
| | Total all ages | | | Under 18 years of age | | | 18 years of age and over | | |
| | 2008 | 2009 | Percent change | 2008 | 2009 | Percent change | 2008 | 2009 | Percent change |
| **TOTAL[2]** | 3,787,825 | 3,700,060 | -2.3 | 560,262 | 513,555 | -8.3 | 3,227,563 | 3,186,505 | -1.3 |
| **Violent Crime** | 136,905 | 135,954 | -0.7 | 21,794 | 20,485 | -6.0 | 115,111 | 115,469 | +0.3 |
| Murder and nonnegligent manslaughter | 2,650 | 2,481 | -6.4 | 214 | 200 | -6.5 | 2,436 | 2,281 | -6.4 |
| Forcible rape | 5,411 | 5,051 | -6.7 | 810 | 812 | +0.2 | 4,601 | 4,239 | -7.9 |
| Robbery | 24,442 | 24,586 | +0.6 | 6,433 | 5,857 | -9.0 | 18,009 | 18,729 | +4.0 |
| Aggravated assault | 104,402 | 103,836 | -0.5 | 14,337 | 13,616 | -5.0 | 90,065 | 90,220 | +0.2 |
| **Property Crime** | 432,312 | 440,560 | +1.9 | 112,651 | 106,158 | -5.8 | 319,661 | 334,402 | +4.6 |
| Burglary | 80,136 | 77,077 | -3.8 | 22,091 | 18,848 | -14.7 | 58,045 | 58,229 | +0.3 |
| Larceny-theft | 325,671 | 340,094 | +4.4 | 82,994 | 80,921 | -2.5 | 242,677 | 259,173 | +6.8 |
| Motor vehicle theft | 22,274 | 19,661 | -11.7 | 5,417 | 4,597 | -15.1 | 16,857 | 15,064 | -10.6 |
| Arson | 4,231 | 3,728 | -11.9 | 2,149 | 1,792 | -16.6 | 2,082 | 1,936 | -7.0 |
| Other assaults | 330,375 | 334,767 | +1.3 | 66,053 | 62,914 | -4.8 | 264,322 | 271,853 | +2.8 |
| Forgery and counterfeiting | 24,528 | 23,391 | -4.6 | 761 | 637 | -16.3 | 23,767 | 22,754 | -4.3 |
| Fraud | 81,199 | 71,488 | -12.0 | 2,110 | 1,804 | -14.5 | 79,089 | 69,684 | -11.9 |
| Embezzlement | 5,483 | 4,714 | -14.0 | 316 | 155 | -50.9 | 5,167 | 4,559 | -11.8 |
| Stolen property; buying, receiving, possessing | 30,666 | 29,036 | -5.3 | 5,543 | 5,065 | -8.6 | 25,123 | 23,971 | -4.6 |
| Vandalism | 75,986 | 71,975 | -5.3 | 30,589 | 25,716 | -15.9 | 45,397 | 46,259 | +1.9 |
| Weapons; carrying, possessing, etc. | 40,954 | 38,451 | -6.1 | 10,021 | 8,697 | -13.2 | 30,933 | 29,754 | -3.8 |
| Prostitution and commercialized vice | 5,431 | 5,038 | -7.2 | 160 | 151 | -5.6 | 5,271 | 4,887 | -7.3 |
| Sex offenses (except forcible rape and prostitution) | 20,745 | 20,045 | -3.4 | 4,134 | 3,851 | -6.8 | 16,611 | 16,194 | -2.5 |
| Drug abuse violations | 430,475 | 426,396 | -0.9 | 51,242 | 49,613 | -3.2 | 379,233 | 376,783 | -0.6 |
| Gambling | 807 | 1,235 | +53.0 | 77 | 109 | +41.6 | 730 | 1,126 | +54.2 |
| Offenses against the family and children | 45,314 | 41,033 | -9.4 | 2,142 | 1,466 | -31.6 | 43,172 | 39,567 | -8.4 |
| Driving under the influence | 476,071 | 469,875 | -1.3 | 5,010 | 4,323 | -13.7 | 471,061 | 465,552 | -1.2 |
| Liquor laws | 176,579 | 168,074 | -4.8 | 42,844 | 38,136 | -11.0 | 133,735 | 129,938 | -2.8 |
| Drunkenness | 140,758 | 134,923 | -4.1 | 4,542 | 4,110 | -9.5 | 136,216 | 130,813 | -4.0 |
| Disorderly conduct | 179,979 | 172,335 | -4.2 | 54,567 | 49,499 | -9.3 | 125,412 | 122,836 | -2.1 |
| Vagrancy | 4,737 | 5,352 | +13.0 | 646 | 502 | -22.3 | 4,091 | 4,850 | +18.6 |
| All other offenses (except traffic) | 1,104,268 | 1,065,473 | -3.5 | 100,807 | 90,219 | -10.5 | 1,003,461 | 975,254 | -2.8 |
| Suspicion | 538 | 934 | +73.6 | 89 | 109 | +22.5 | 449 | 825 | +83.7 |
| Curfew and loitering law violations | 19,626 | 18,229 | -7.1 | 19,626 | 18,229 | -7.1 | - | - | - |
| Runaways | 24,627 | 21,716 | -11.8 | 24,627 | 21,716 | -11.8 | - | - | - |

[1] Suburban areas include law enforcement agencies in cities with less than 50,000 inhabitants and county law enforcement agencies that are within a metropolitan statistical area. Suburban areas exclude all metropolitan agencies associated with a principal city.

[2] Does not include suspicion.

## Table 63. Suburban Area[1] Arrest Trends, by Age and Sex, 2008–2009

(Number, percent change; 6,008 agencies; 2009 estimated population 94,512,203; 2008 estimated population 93,792,021.)

| Offense charged | Male | | | | | | Female | | | | | |
|---|---|---|---|---|---|---|---|---|---|---|---|---|
| | Total | | | Under 18 | | | Total | | | Under 18 | | |
| | 2008 | 2009 | Percent change | 2008 | 2009 | Percent change | 2008 | 2009 | Percent change | 2008 | 2009 | Percent change |
| **TOTAL[2]** | 2,855,567 | 2,764,735 | -3.2 | 397,850 | 361,410 | -9.2 | 932,258 | 935,325 | +0.3 | 162,412 | 152,145 | -6.3 |
| **Violent Crime** | 112,181 | 110,880 | -1.2 | 17,818 | 16,554 | -7.1 | 24,724 | 25,074 | +1.4 | 3,976 | 3,931 | -1.1 |
| Murder and nonnegligent manslaughter | 2,355 | 2,193 | -6.9 | 200 | 182 | -9.0 | 295 | 288 | -2.4 | 14 | 18 | +28.6 |
| Forcible rape | 5,348 | 4,984 | -6.8 | 802 | 797 | -0.6 | 63 | 67 | +6.3 | 8 | 15 | +87.5 |
| Robbery | 21,703 | 21,796 | +0.4 | 5,896 | 5,329 | -9.6 | 2,739 | 2,790 | +1.9 | 537 | 528 | -1.7 |
| Aggravated assault | 82,775 | 81,907 | -1.0 | 10,920 | 10,246 | -6.2 | 21,627 | 21,929 | +1.4 | 3,417 | 3,370 | -1.4 |
| **Property Crime** | 285,906 | 280,284 | -2.0 | 75,041 | 68,574 | -8.6 | 146,406 | 160,276 | +9.5 | 37,610 | 37,584 | -0.1 |
| Burglary | 69,118 | 66,127 | -4.3 | 19,702 | 16,871 | -14.4 | 11,018 | 10,950 | -0.6 | 2,389 | 1,977 | -17.2 |
| Larceny-theft | 194,747 | 194,848 | +0.1 | 48,941 | 46,307 | -5.4 | 130,924 | 145,246 | +10.9 | 34,053 | 34,614 | +1.6 |
| Motor vehicle theft | 18,428 | 16,151 | -12.4 | 4,512 | 3,818 | -15.4 | 3,846 | 3,510 | -8.7 | 905 | 779 | -13.9 |
| Arson | 3,613 | 3,158 | -12.6 | 1,886 | 1,578 | -16.3 | 618 | 570 | -7.8 | 263 | 214 | -18.6 |
| **Other** | | | | | | | | | | | | |
| Other assaults | 244,098 | 246,006 | +0.8 | 44,201 | 41,948 | -5.1 | 86,277 | 88,761 | +2.9 | 21,852 | 20,966 | -4.1 |
| Forgery and counterfeiting | 14,985 | 14,553 | -2.9 | 505 | 466 | -7.7 | 9,543 | 8,838 | -7.4 | 256 | 171 | -33.2 |
| Fraud | 44,356 | 39,896 | -10.1 | 1,370 | 1,194 | -12.8 | 36,843 | 31,592 | -14.3 | 740 | 610 | -17.6 |
| Embezzlement | 2,708 | 2,306 | -14.8 | 191 | 75 | -60.7 | 2,775 | 2,408 | -13.2 | 125 | 80 | -36.0 |
| Stolen property; buying, receiving, possessing | 24,518 | 23,283 | -5.0 | 4,524 | 4,139 | -8.5 | 6,148 | 5,753 | -6.4 | 1,019 | 926 | -9.1 |
| Vandalism | 63,615 | 59,784 | -6.0 | 26,464 | 22,147 | -16.3 | 12,371 | 12,191 | -1.5 | 4,125 | 3,569 | -13.5 |
| Weapons; carrying, possessing, etc. | 37,696 | 35,083 | -6.9 | 8,997 | 7,650 | -15.0 | 3,258 | 3,368 | +3.4 | 1,024 | 1,047 | +2.2 |
| Prostitution and commercialized vice | 1,935 | 1,857 | -4.0 | 58 | 63 | +8.6 | 3,496 | 3,181 | -9.0 | 102 | 88 | -13.7 |
| Sex offenses (except forcible rape and prostitution) | 19,448 | 18,688 | -3.9 | 3,776 | 3,462 | -8.3 | 1,297 | 1,357 | +4.6 | 358 | 389 | +8.7 |
| Drug abuse violations | 346,821 | 342,702 | -1.2 | 42,438 | 41,141 | -3.1 | 83,654 | 83,694 | * | 8,804 | 8,472 | -3.8 |
| Gambling | 680 | 976 | +43.5 | 69 | 104 | +50.7 | 127 | 259 | +103.9 | 8 | 5 | -37.5 |
| Offenses against the family and children | 35,867 | 32,555 | -9.2 | 1,422 | 941 | -33.8 | 9,447 | 8,478 | -10.3 | 720 | 525 | -27.1 |
| Driving under the influence | 371,886 | 362,717 | -2.5 | 3,771 | 3,277 | -13.1 | 104,185 | 107,158 | +2.9 | 1,239 | 1,046 | -15.6 |
| Liquor laws | 125,109 | 117,333 | -6.2 | 26,650 | 23,326 | -12.5 | 51,470 | 50,741 | -1.4 | 16,194 | 14,810 | -8.5 |
| Drunkenness | 115,485 | 110,265 | -4.5 | 3,399 | 3,000 | -11.7 | 25,273 | 24,658 | -2.4 | 1,143 | 1,110 | -2.9 |
| Disorderly conduct | 132,422 | 125,390 | -5.3 | 37,425 | 33,765 | -9.8 | 47,557 | 46,945 | -1.3 | 17,142 | 15,734 | -8.2 |
| Vagrancy | 3,637 | 3,933 | +8.1 | 498 | 364 | -26.9 | 1,100 | 1,419 | +29.0 | 148 | 138 | -6.8 |
| All other offenses (except traffic) | 847,782 | 813,856 | -4.0 | 74,801 | 66,832 | -10.7 | 256,486 | 251,617 | -1.9 | 26,006 | 23,387 | -10.1 |
| Suspicion | 405 | 641 | +58.3 | 68 | 84 | +23.5 | 133 | 293 | +120.3 | 21 | 25 | +19.0 |
| Curfew and loitering law violations | 13,195 | 12,158 | -7.9 | 13,195 | 12,158 | -7.9 | 6,431 | 6,071 | -5.6 | 6,431 | 6,071 | -5.6 |
| Runaways | 11,237 | 10,230 | -9.0 | 11,237 | 10,230 | -9.0 | 13,390 | 11,486 | -14.2 | 13,390 | 11,486 | -14.2 |

[1] Suburban areas include law enforcement agencies in cities with less than 50,000 inhabitants and county law enforcement agencies that are within a metropolitan statistical area. Suburban areas exclude all metropolitan agencies associated with a principal city.

[2] Does not include suspicion.

## Table 64. Suburban Area[1] Arrests, Distribution by Age, 2009

(Number, percent; 6,651 agencies; 2009 estimated population 104,853,682.)

| Offense charged | Total all ages | Ages under 15 | Ages under 18 | Ages 18 and over | Under 10 | 10–12 | 13–14 | 15 | 16 | 17 | 18 | 19 | 20 |
|---|---|---|---|---|---|---|---|---|---|---|---|---|---|
| **TOTAL** | 4,209,800 | 154,137 | 582,161 | 3,627,639 | 3,896 | 32,078 | 118,163 | 110,519 | 144,268 | 173,237 | 216,328 | 222,666 | 202,644 |
| Total percent distribution[2] | 100.0 | 3.7 | 13.8 | 86.2 | 0.1 | 0.8 | 2.8 | 2.6 | 3.4 | 4.1 | 5.1 | 5.3 | 4.8 |
| | | | | | | | | | | | | | |
| **Violent Crime** | 153,068 | 6,182 | 22,914 | 130,154 | 163 | 1,453 | 4,566 | 4,288 | 5,593 | 6,851 | 7,868 | 7,494 | 6,769 |
| Violent crime percent distribution[2] | 100.0 | 4.0 | 15.0 | 85.0 | 0.1 | 0.9 | 3.0 | 2.8 | 3.7 | 4.5 | 5.1 | 4.9 | 4.4 |
| Murder and nonnegligent manslaughter | 2,913 | 25 | 238 | 2,675 | 1 | 5 | 19 | 25 | 80 | 108 | 174 | 176 | 166 |
| Forcible rape | 5,681 | 278 | 880 | 4,801 | 3 | 70 | 205 | 172 | 187 | 243 | 326 | 301 | 274 |
| Robbery | 29,120 | 1,152 | 6,836 | 22,284 | 6 | 138 | 1,008 | 1,316 | 1,886 | 2,482 | 2,909 | 2,466 | 1,957 |
| Aggravated assault | 115,354 | 4,727 | 14,960 | 100,394 | 153 | 1,240 | 3,334 | 2,775 | 3,440 | 4,018 | 4,459 | 4,551 | 4,372 |
| | | | | | | | | | | | | | |
| **Property Crime** | 515,589 | 32,482 | 123,536 | 392,053 | 741 | 6,626 | 25,115 | 23,791 | 31,350 | 35,913 | 37,827 | 32,486 | 25,687 |
| Property crime percent distribution[2] | 100.0 | 6.3 | 24.0 | 76.0 | 0.1 | 1.3 | 4.9 | 4.6 | 6.1 | 7.0 | 7.3 | 6.3 | 5.0 |
| Burglary | 87,132 | 5,634 | 21,476 | 65,656 | 189 | 1,165 | 4,280 | 4,165 | 5,435 | 6,242 | 7,309 | 6,450 | 4,956 |
| Larceny-theft | 403,074 | 24,680 | 95,130 | 307,944 | 443 | 4,995 | 19,242 | 18,218 | 24,257 | 27,975 | 28,842 | 24,659 | 19,614 |
| Motor vehicle theft | 21,268 | 1,002 | 4,975 | 16,293 | 14 | 120 | 868 | 1,090 | 1,382 | 1,501 | 1,480 | 1,211 | 972 |
| Arson | 4,115 | 1,166 | 1,955 | 2,160 | 95 | 346 | 725 | 318 | 276 | 195 | 196 | 166 | 145 |
| | | | | | | | | | | | | | |
| **Other** | | | | | | | | | | | | | |
| Other assaults | 386,216 | 27,294 | 72,219 | 313,997 | 792 | 7,340 | 19,162 | 14,076 | 15,745 | 15,104 | 13,484 | 12,802 | 12,810 |
| Forgery and counterfeiting | 27,663 | 90 | 711 | 26,952 | 2 | 26 | 62 | 90 | 182 | 349 | 895 | 1,193 | 1,285 |
| Fraud | 75,757 | 340 | 2,056 | 73,701 | 13 | 53 | 274 | 295 | 552 | 869 | 1,741 | 2,283 | 2,465 |
| Embezzlement | 5,583 | 13 | 183 | 5,400 | 0 | 6 | 7 | 18 | 38 | 114 | 282 | 373 | 324 |
| Stolen property; buying, receiving, possessing | 33,061 | 1,259 | 5,806 | 27,255 | 22 | 202 | 1,035 | 1,173 | 1,503 | 1,871 | 2,194 | 2,109 | 1,801 |
| Vandalism | 81,553 | 10,876 | 28,524 | 53,029 | 458 | 2,852 | 7,566 | 5,248 | 6,103 | 6,297 | 5,986 | 4,727 | 3,744 |
| Weapons; carrying, possessing, etc. | 43,550 | 3,519 | 9,661 | 33,889 | 213 | 982 | 2,324 | 1,653 | 1,938 | 2,551 | 2,896 | 2,515 | 2,234 |
| Prostitution and commercialized vice | 6,310 | 35 | 168 | 6,142 | 0 | 10 | 25 | 32 | 47 | 54 | 157 | 270 | 274 |
| Sex offenses (except forcible rape and prostitution) | 22,364 | 2,082 | 4,316 | 18,048 | 98 | 546 | 1,438 | 733 | 705 | 796 | 969 | 957 | 825 |
| Drug abuse violations | 481,904 | 8,585 | 55,191 | 426,713 | 61 | 918 | 7,606 | 9,140 | 14,558 | 22,908 | 35,500 | 35,126 | 30,575 |
| Gambling | 1,733 | 20 | 149 | 1,584 | 1 | 0 | 19 | 29 | 46 | 54 | 90 | 111 | 115 |
| Offenses against the family and children | 46,970 | 444 | 1,735 | 45,235 | 7 | 93 | 344 | 352 | 445 | 494 | 699 | 790 | 841 |
| Driving under the influence | 516,126 | 83 | 4,710 | 511,416 | 9 | 7 | 67 | 178 | 1,007 | 3,442 | 10,142 | 14,492 | 16,656 |
| Liquor laws | 186,592 | 3,317 | 41,409 | 145,183 | 37 | 246 | 3,034 | 5,898 | 11,647 | 20,547 | 36,374 | 38,140 | 29,688 |
| Drunkenness | 162,236 | 495 | 4,471 | 157,765 | 18 | 41 | 436 | 674 | 1,155 | 2,147 | 5,151 | 5,816 | 5,494 |
| Disorderly conduct | 199,191 | 20,202 | 56,803 | 142,388 | 279 | 4,586 | 15,337 | 11,777 | 12,819 | 12,005 | 10,288 | 8,403 | 7,569 |
| Vagrancy | 6,500 | 105 | 558 | 5,942 | 1 | 12 | 92 | 122 | 107 | 224 | 391 | 304 | 229 |
| All other offenses (except traffic) | 1,212,515 | 24,513 | 102,562 | 1,109,953 | 811 | 4,318 | 19,384 | 20,069 | 26,045 | 31,935 | 43,349 | 52,233 | 53,221 |
| Suspicion | 954 | 34 | 114 | 840 | 5 | 10 | 19 | 19 | 38 | 23 | 45 | 42 | 38 |
| Curfew and loitering law violations | 20,296 | 5,271 | 20,296 | - | 44 | 775 | 4,452 | 4,806 | 5,801 | 4,418 | - | - | - |
| Runaways | 24,069 | 6,896 | 24,069 | - | 121 | 976 | 5,799 | 6,058 | 6,844 | 4,271 | - | - | - |

[1] Suburban areas include law enforcement agencies in cities with less than 50,000 inhabitants and county law enforcement agencies that are within a metropolitan statistical area. Suburban areas exclude all metropolitan agencies associated with a principal city.

[2] Because of rounding, the percentages may not add to 100.0.

## Table 64. Suburban Area[1] Arrests, Distribution by Age, 2009—*Continued*

(Number, percent; 6,651 agencies; 2009 estimated population 104,853,682.)

| Offense charged | 21 | 22 | 23 | 24 | 25–29 | 30–34 | 35–39 | 40–44 | 45–49 | 50–54 | 55–59 | 60–64 | 65 and over |
|---|---|---|---|---|---|---|---|---|---|---|---|---|---|
| **TOTAL** | 177,724 | 162,527 | 153,621 | 144,912 | 612,131 | 433,634 | 363,219 | 326,031 | 282,973 | 175,853 | 85,028 | 39,077 | 29,271 |
| Total percent distribution[2] | 4.2 | 3.9 | 3.6 | 3.4 | 14.5 | 10.3 | 8.6 | 7.7 | 6.7 | 4.2 | 2.0 | 0.9 | 0.7 |
| | | | | | | | | | | | | | |
| **Violent Crime** | 6,354 | 5,751 | 5,590 | 5,115 | 22,367 | 16,074 | 13,306 | 11,824 | 9,918 | 6,054 | 2,966 | 1,417 | 1,287 |
| Violent crime percent distribution[2] | 4.2 | 3.8 | 3.7 | 3.3 | 14.6 | 10.5 | 8.7 | 7.7 | 6.5 | 4.0 | 1.9 | 0.9 | 0.8 |
| Murder and nonnegligent manslaughter | 160 | 145 | 131 | 102 | 482 | 308 | 245 | 196 | 159 | 89 | 52 | 47 | 43 |
| Forcible rape | 257 | 193 | 190 | 164 | 719 | 608 | 554 | 434 | 320 | 200 | 125 | 79 | 57 |
| Robbery | 1,551 | 1,306 | 1,147 | 968 | 3,604 | 2,049 | 1,492 | 1,247 | 872 | 452 | 173 | 65 | 26 |
| Aggravated assault | 4,386 | 4,107 | 4,122 | 3,881 | 17,562 | 13,109 | 11,015 | 9,947 | 8,567 | 5,313 | 2,616 | 1,226 | 1,161 |
| | | | | | | | | | | | | | |
| **Property Crime** | 21,439 | 17,980 | 16,088 | 14,953 | 61,182 | 42,120 | 35,308 | 31,720 | 26,098 | 15,709 | 7,226 | 3,413 | 2,817 |
| Property crime percent distribution[2] | 4.2 | 3.5 | 3.1 | 2.9 | 11.9 | 8.2 | 6.8 | 6.2 | 5.1 | 3.0 | 1.4 | 0.7 | 0.5 |
| Burglary | 4,137 | 3,356 | 2,901 | 2,613 | 10,829 | 7,018 | 5,360 | 4,637 | 3,309 | 1,750 | 650 | 233 | 148 |
| Larceny-theft | 16,323 | 13,799 | 12,351 | 11,609 | 47,188 | 32,817 | 28,091 | 25,618 | 21,630 | 13,388 | 6,328 | 3,083 | 2,604 |
| Motor vehicle theft | 866 | 726 | 752 | 649 | 2,862 | 2,081 | 1,686 | 1,280 | 976 | 461 | 187 | 67 | 37 |
| Arson | 113 | 99 | 84 | 82 | 303 | 204 | 171 | 185 | 183 | 110 | 61 | 30 | 28 |
| | | | | | | | | | | | | | |
| **Other** | | | | | | | | | | | | | |
| Other assaults | 13,206 | 12,599 | 12,371 | 11,855 | 54,025 | 41,562 | 37,012 | 33,495 | 28,161 | 16,303 | 7,532 | 3,587 | 3,193 |
| Forgery and counterfeiting | 1,184 | 1,170 | 1,182 | 1,133 | 5,226 | 3,950 | 3,216 | 2,638 | 1,934 | 1,113 | 476 | 230 | 127 |
| Fraud | 2,357 | 2,376 | 2,440 | 2,476 | 12,429 | 11,071 | 10,593 | 8,909 | 6,577 | 4,048 | 2,096 | 1,055 | 785 |
| Embezzlement | 297 | 238 | 206 | 198 | 867 | 632 | 594 | 487 | 415 | 252 | 139 | 65 | 31 |
| Stolen property; buying, receiving, possessing | 1,519 | 1,293 | 1,252 | 1,079 | 4,772 | 3,229 | 2,629 | 2,328 | 1,636 | 823 | 351 | 153 | 87 |
| Vandalism | 3,342 | 2,844 | 2,464 | 2,159 | 8,558 | 5,452 | 4,039 | 3,592 | 2,950 | 1,702 | 784 | 362 | 324 |
| Weapons; carrying, possessing, etc. | 2,006 | 1,813 | 1,592 | 1,576 | 6,045 | 3,593 | 2,699 | 2,235 | 1,888 | 1,269 | 762 | 423 | 343 |
| Prostitution and commercialized vice | 261 | 279 | 257 | 219 | 1,017 | 786 | 733 | 705 | 551 | 302 | 176 | 80 | 75 |
| Sex offenses (except forcible rape and prostitution) | 777 | 686 | 566 | 545 | 2,364 | 1,879 | 1,976 | 1,825 | 1,667 | 1,139 | 754 | 498 | 621 |
| Drug abuse violations | 25,491 | 22,754 | 21,077 | 19,160 | 75,896 | 47,603 | 34,878 | 29,429 | 25,103 | 14,877 | 6,040 | 2,207 | 997 |
| Gambling | 30 | 42 | 29 | 22 | 123 | 115 | 153 | 146 | 187 | 137 | 117 | 84 | 83 |
| Offenses against the family and children | 1,127 | 1,138 | 1,292 | 1,437 | 7,613 | 7,836 | 7,538 | 6,263 | 4,669 | 2,486 | 934 | 342 | 230 |
| Driving under the influence | 23,745 | 24,155 | 23,614 | 22,712 | 93,998 | 64,491 | 54,274 | 49,872 | 47,228 | 32,453 | 18,063 | 9,132 | 6,389 |
| Liquor laws | 4,339 | 2,835 | 2,297 | 1,910 | 6,883 | 4,543 | 4,046 | 4,184 | 4,276 | 2,966 | 1,494 | 680 | 528 |
| Drunkenness | 7,754 | 6,685 | 6,233 | 5,870 | 23,936 | 17,383 | 15,810 | 17,390 | 17,772 | 12,473 | 6,073 | 2,489 | 1,436 |
| Disorderly conduct | 8,489 | 7,171 | 6,546 | 5,821 | 22,753 | 15,010 | 12,714 | 12,144 | 11,674 | 7,307 | 3,541 | 1,562 | 1,396 |
| Vagrancy | 255 | 195 | 176 | 169 | 782 | 582 | 641 | 659 | 718 | 449 | 225 | 111 | 56 |
| All other offenses (except traffic) | 53,709 | 50,479 | 48,309 | 46,465 | 201,154 | 145,629 | 120,963 | 106,117 | 89,492 | 53,946 | 25,252 | 11,176 | 8,459 |
| Suspicion | 43 | 44 | 40 | 38 | 141 | 94 | 97 | 69 | 59 | 45 | 27 | 11 | 7 |
| Curfew and loitering law violations | - | - | - | - | - | - | - | - | - | - | - | - | - |
| Runaways | - | - | - | - | - | - | - | - | - | - | - | - | - |

[1] Suburban areas include law enforcement agencies in cities with less than 50,000 inhabitants and county law enforcement agencies that are within a metropolitan statistical area. Suburban areas exclude all metropolitan agencies associated with a principal city.
[2] Because of rounding, the percentages may not add to 100.0.

## Table 65. Suburban Area[1] Arrests of Persons Under 15, 18, 21, and 25 Years of Age, 2009

(Number, percent; 6,651 agencies; 2009 estimated population 104,853,682.)

| Offense charged | Total all ages | Number of persons arrested | | | | Percent of total all ages | | | |
|---|---|---|---|---|---|---|---|---|---|
| | | Under 15 | Under 18 | Under 21 | Under 25 | Under 15 | Under 18 | Under 21 | Under 25 |
| **TOTAL** | 4,209,800 | 154,137 | 582,161 | 1,223,799 | 1,862,583 | 3.7 | 13.8 | 29.1 | 44.2 |
| **Violent Crime** | 153,068 | 6,182 | 22,914 | 45,045 | 67,855 | 4.0 | 15.0 | 29.4 | 44.3 |
| Murder and nonnegligent manslaughter | 2,913 | 25 | 238 | 754 | 1,292 | 0.9 | 8.2 | 25.9 | 44.4 |
| Forcible rape | 5,681 | 278 | 880 | 1,781 | 2,585 | 4.9 | 15.5 | 31.4 | 45.5 |
| Robbery | 29,120 | 1,152 | 6,836 | 14,168 | 19,140 | 4.0 | 23.5 | 48.7 | 65.7 |
| Aggravated assault | 115,354 | 4,727 | 14,960 | 28,342 | 44,838 | 4.1 | 13.0 | 24.6 | 38.9 |
| **Property Crime** | 515,589 | 32,482 | 123,536 | 219,536 | 289,996 | 6.3 | 24.0 | 42.6 | 56.2 |
| Burglary | 87,132 | 5,634 | 21,476 | 40,191 | 53,198 | 6.5 | 24.6 | 46.1 | 61.1 |
| Larceny-theft | 403,074 | 24,680 | 95,130 | 168,245 | 222,327 | 6.1 | 23.6 | 41.7 | 55.2 |
| Motor vehicle theft | 21,268 | 1,002 | 4,975 | 8,638 | 11,631 | 4.7 | 23.4 | 40.6 | 54.7 |
| Arson | 4,115 | 1,166 | 1,955 | 2,462 | 2,840 | 28.3 | 47.5 | 59.8 | 69.0 |
| **Other** | | | | | | | | | |
| Other assaults | 386,216 | 27,294 | 72,219 | 111,315 | 161,346 | 7.1 | 18.7 | 28.8 | 41.8 |
| Forgery and counterfeiting | 27,663 | 90 | 711 | 4,084 | 8,753 | 0.3 | 2.6 | 14.8 | 31.6 |
| Fraud | 75,757 | 340 | 2,056 | 8,545 | 18,194 | 0.4 | 2.7 | 11.3 | 24.0 |
| Embezzlement | 5,583 | 13 | 183 | 1,162 | 2,101 | 0.2 | 3.3 | 20.8 | 37.6 |
| Stolen property; buying, receiving, possessing | 33,061 | 1,259 | 5,806 | 11,910 | 17,053 | 3.8 | 17.6 | 36.0 | 51.6 |
| Vandalism | 81,553 | 10,876 | 28,524 | 42,981 | 53,790 | 13.3 | 35.0 | 52.7 | 66.0 |
| Weapons; carrying, possessing, etc. | 43,550 | 3,519 | 9,661 | 17,306 | 24,293 | 8.1 | 22.2 | 39.7 | 55.8 |
| Prostitution and commercialized vice | 6,310 | 35 | 168 | 869 | 1,885 | 0.6 | 2.7 | 13.8 | 29.9 |
| Sex offenses (except forcible rape and prostitution) | 22,364 | 2,082 | 4,316 | 7,067 | 9,641 | 9.3 | 19.3 | 31.6 | 43.1 |
| Drug abuse violations | 481,904 | 8,585 | 55,191 | 156,392 | 244,874 | 1.8 | 11.5 | 32.5 | 50.8 |
| Gambling | 1,733 | 20 | 149 | 465 | 588 | 1.2 | 8.6 | 26.8 | 33.9 |
| Offenses against the family and children | 46,970 | 444 | 1,735 | 4,065 | 9,059 | 0.9 | 3.7 | 8.7 | 19.3 |
| Driving under the influence | 516,126 | 83 | 4,710 | 46,000 | 140,226 | * | 0.9 | 8.9 | 27.2 |
| Liquor laws | 186,592 | 3,317 | 41,409 | 145,611 | 156,992 | 1.8 | 22.2 | 78.0 | 84.1 |
| Drunkenness | 162,236 | 495 | 4,471 | 20,932 | 47,474 | 0.3 | 2.8 | 12.9 | 29.3 |
| Disorderly conduct | 199,191 | 20,202 | 56,803 | 83,063 | 111,090 | 10.1 | 28.5 | 41.7 | 55.8 |
| Vagrancy | 6,500 | 105 | 558 | 1,482 | 2,277 | 1.6 | 8.6 | 22.8 | 35.0 |
| All other offenses (except traffic) | 1,212,515 | 24,513 | 102,562 | 251,365 | 450,327 | 2.0 | 8.5 | 20.7 | 37.1 |
| Suspicion | 954 | 34 | 114 | 239 | 404 | 3.6 | 11.9 | 25.1 | 42.3 |
| Curfew and loitering law violations | 20,296 | 5,271 | 20,296 | 20,296 | 20,296 | 26.0 | 100.0 | 100.0 | 100.0 |
| Runaways | 24,069 | 6,896 | 24,069 | 24,069 | 24,069 | 28.7 | 100.0 | 100.0 | 100.0 |

[1] Suburban areas include law enforcement agencies in cities with less than 50,000 inhabitants and county law enforcement agencies that are within a metropolitan statistical area. Suburban areas exclude all metropolitan agencies associated with a principal city.

* Less than one-tenth of 1 percent.

## Table 66. Suburban Area[1] Arrests, Distribution by Sex, 2009

(Number, percent; 6,651 agencies; 2009 estimated population 104,853,682.)

| Offense charged | Number of persons arrested | | | Percent male | Percent female | Percent distribution[2] | | |
|---|---|---|---|---|---|---|---|---|
| | Total | Male | Female | | | Total | Male | Female |
| **TOTAL** | 4,209,800 | 3,129,077 | 1,080,723 | 74.3 | 25.7 | 100.0 | 100.0 | 100.0 |
| **Violent Crime** | 153,068 | 124,622 | 28,446 | 81.4 | 18.6 | 3.6 | 4.0 | 2.6 |
| Murder and nonnegligent manslaughter | 2,913 | 2,586 | 327 | 88.8 | 11.2 | 0.1 | 0.1 | * |
| Forcible rape | 5,681 | 5,598 | 83 | 98.5 | 1.5 | 0.1 | 0.2 | * |
| Robbery | 29,120 | 25,738 | 3,382 | 88.4 | 11.6 | 0.7 | 0.8 | 0.3 |
| Aggravated assault | 115,354 | 90,700 | 24,654 | 78.6 | 21.4 | 2.7 | 2.9 | 2.3 |
| **Property Crime** | 515,589 | 324,014 | 191,575 | 62.8 | 37.2 | 12.2 | 10.4 | 17.7 |
| Burglary | 87,132 | 74,627 | 12,505 | 85.6 | 14.4 | 2.1 | 2.4 | 1.2 |
| Larceny-theft | 403,074 | 228,516 | 174,558 | 56.7 | 43.3 | 9.6 | 7.3 | 16.2 |
| Motor vehicle theft | 21,268 | 17,399 | 3,869 | 81.8 | 18.2 | 0.5 | 0.6 | 0.4 |
| Arson | 4,115 | 3,472 | 643 | 84.4 | 15.6 | 0.1 | 0.1 | 0.1 |
| **Other** | | | | | | | | |
| Other assaults | 386,216 | 283,582 | 102,634 | 73.4 | 26.6 | 9.2 | 9.1 | 9.5 |
| Forgery and counterfeiting | 27,663 | 17,139 | 10,524 | 62.0 | 38.0 | 0.7 | 0.5 | 1.0 |
| Fraud | 75,757 | 42,590 | 33,167 | 56.2 | 43.8 | 1.8 | 1.4 | 3.1 |
| Embezzlement | 5,583 | 2,704 | 2,879 | 48.4 | 51.6 | 0.1 | 0.1 | 0.3 |
| Stolen property; buying, receiving, possessing | 33,061 | 26,415 | 6,646 | 79.9 | 20.1 | 0.8 | 0.8 | 0.6 |
| Vandalism | 81,553 | 67,398 | 14,155 | 82.6 | 17.4 | 1.9 | 2.2 | 1.3 |
| Weapons; carrying, possessing, etc. | 43,550 | 39,687 | 3,863 | 91.1 | 8.9 | 1.0 | 1.3 | 0.4 |
| Prostitution and commercialized vice | 6,310 | 2,227 | 4,083 | 35.3 | 64.7 | 0.1 | 0.1 | 0.4 |
| Sex offenses (except forcible rape and prostitution) | 22,364 | 20,745 | 1,619 | 92.8 | 7.2 | 0.5 | 0.7 | 0.1 |
| Drug abuse violations | 481,904 | 386,339 | 95,565 | 80.2 | 19.8 | 11.4 | 12.3 | 8.8 |
| Gambling | 1,733 | 1,219 | 514 | 70.3 | 29.7 | * | * | * |
| Offenses against the family and children | 46,970 | 36,880 | 10,090 | 78.5 | 21.5 | 1.1 | 1.2 | 0.9 |
| Driving under the influence | 516,126 | 395,892 | 120,234 | 76.7 | 23.3 | 12.3 | 12.7 | 11.1 |
| Liquor laws | 186,592 | 130,799 | 55,793 | 70.1 | 29.9 | 4.4 | 4.2 | 5.2 |
| Drunkenness | 162,236 | 133,303 | 28,933 | 82.2 | 17.8 | 3.9 | 4.3 | 2.7 |
| Disorderly conduct | 199,191 | 144,205 | 54,986 | 72.4 | 27.6 | 4.7 | 4.6 | 5.1 |
| Vagrancy | 6,500 | 4,773 | 1,727 | 73.4 | 26.6 | 0.2 | 0.2 | 0.2 |
| All other offenses (except traffic) | 1,212,515 | 919,056 | 293,459 | 75.8 | 24.2 | 28.8 | 29.4 | 27.2 |
| Suspicion | 954 | 659 | 295 | 69.1 | 30.9 | * | * | * |
| Curfew and loitering law violations | 20,296 | 13,602 | 6,694 | 67.0 | 33.0 | 0.5 | 0.4 | 0.6 |
| Runaways | 24,069 | 11,227 | 12,842 | 46.6 | 53.4 | 0.6 | 0.4 | 1.2 |

[1] Suburban areas include law enforcement agencies in cities with less than 50,000 inhabitants and county law enforcement agencies that are within a metropolitan statistical area. Suburban areas exclude all metropolitan agencies associated with a principal city.
[2] Because of rounding, the percentages may not add to 100.0.
* Less than one-tenth of 1 percent.

## Table 67. Suburban Area[1] Arrests, Distribution by Race, 2009

(Number, percent; 6,651 agencies; 2009 estimated population 104,853,682.)

| Offense charged | Total arrests | | | | | Percent distribution[2] | | | | |
|---|---|---|---|---|---|---|---|---|---|---|
| | Total | White | Black | American Indian or Alaskan Native | Asian or Pacific Islander | Total | White | Black | American Indian or Alaskan Native | Asian or Pacific Islander |
| **TOTAL** | 4,190,384 | 3,127,514 | 995,665 | 33,211 | 33,994 | 100.0 | 74.6 | 23.8 | 0.8 | 0.8 |
| **Violent Crime** | 152,661 | 100,222 | 50,167 | 1,113 | 1,159 | 100.0 | 65.7 | 32.9 | 0.7 | 0.8 |
| Murder and nonnegligent manslaughter | 2,903 | 1,683 | 1,184 | 12 | 24 | 100.0 | 58.0 | 40.8 | 0.4 | 0.8 |
| Forcible rape | 5,657 | 4,179 | 1,388 | 34 | 56 | 100.0 | 73.9 | 24.5 | 0.6 | 1.0 |
| Robbery | 29,055 | 13,486 | 15,292 | 126 | 151 | 100.0 | 46.4 | 52.6 | 0.4 | 0.5 |
| Aggravated assault | 115,046 | 80,874 | 32,303 | 941 | 928 | 100.0 | 70.3 | 28.1 | 0.8 | 0.8 |
| **Property Crime** | 513,607 | 362,044 | 142,753 | 3,630 | 5,180 | 100.0 | 70.5 | 27.8 | 0.7 | 1.0 |
| Burglary | 86,876 | 63,701 | 22,258 | 362 | 555 | 100.0 | 73.3 | 25.6 | 0.4 | 0.6 |
| Larceny-theft | 401,449 | 279,936 | 113,980 | 3,071 | 4,462 | 100.0 | 69.7 | 28.4 | 0.8 | 1.1 |
| Motor vehicle theft | 21,183 | 15,097 | 5,785 | 170 | 131 | 100.0 | 71.3 | 27.3 | 0.8 | 0.6 |
| Arson | 4,099 | 3,310 | 730 | 27 | 32 | 100.0 | 80.8 | 17.8 | 0.7 | 0.8 |
| **Other** | | | | | | | | | | |
| Other assaults | 385,008 | 279,089 | 99,886 | 2,960 | 3,073 | 100.0 | 72.5 | 25.9 | 0.8 | 0.8 |
| Forgery and counterfeiting | 27,509 | 18,842 | 8,319 | 84 | 264 | 100.0 | 68.5 | 30.2 | 0.3 | 1.0 |
| Fraud | 75,281 | 51,621 | 22,782 | 319 | 559 | 100.0 | 68.6 | 30.3 | 0.4 | 0.7 |
| Embezzlement | 5,524 | 3,613 | 1,841 | 19 | 51 | 100.0 | 65.4 | 33.3 | 0.3 | 0.9 |
| Stolen property; buying, receiving, possessing | 32,949 | 22,442 | 10,065 | 180 | 262 | 100.0 | 68.1 | 30.5 | 0.5 | 0.8 |
| Vandalism | 81,267 | 64,579 | 15,517 | 561 | 610 | 100.0 | 79.5 | 19.1 | 0.7 | 0.8 |
| Weapons; carrying, possessing, etc. | 43,416 | 28,650 | 14,220 | 234 | 312 | 100.0 | 66.0 | 32.8 | 0.5 | 0.7 |
| Prostitution and commercialized vice | 6,286 | 4,183 | 1,766 | 31 | 306 | 100.0 | 66.5 | 28.1 | 0.5 | 4.9 |
| Sex offenses (except forcible rape and prostitution) | 22,246 | 17,500 | 4,378 | 145 | 223 | 100.0 | 78.7 | 19.7 | 0.7 | 1.0 |
| Drug abuse violations | 480,291 | 355,030 | 119,879 | 2,307 | 3,075 | 100.0 | 73.9 | 25.0 | 0.5 | 0.6 |
| Gambling | 1,726 | 991 | 600 | 15 | 120 | 100.0 | 57.4 | 34.8 | 0.9 | 7.0 |
| Offenses against the family and children | 46,536 | 30,842 | 15,013 | 379 | 302 | 100.0 | 66.3 | 32.3 | 0.8 | 0.6 |
| Driving under the influence | 513,782 | 451,685 | 53,136 | 3,587 | 5,374 | 100.0 | 87.9 | 10.3 | 0.7 | 1.0 |
| Liquor laws | 184,979 | 162,618 | 17,375 | 2,808 | 2,178 | 100.0 | 87.9 | 9.4 | 1.5 | 1.2 |
| Drunkenness | 161,638 | 140,772 | 18,428 | 1,544 | 894 | 100.0 | 87.1 | 11.4 | 1.0 | 0.6 |
| Disorderly conduct | 198,304 | 139,218 | 56,247 | 1,375 | 1,464 | 100.0 | 70.2 | 28.4 | 0.7 | 0.7 |
| Vagrancy | 6,495 | 3,976 | 2,479 | 13 | 27 | 100.0 | 61.2 | 38.2 | 0.2 | 0.4 |
| All other offenses (except traffic) | 1,205,676 | 856,446 | 329,531 | 11,524 | 8,175 | 100.0 | 71.0 | 27.3 | 1.0 | 0.7 |
| Suspicion | 951 | 330 | 616 | 0 | 5 | 100.0 | 34.7 | 64.8 | 0.0 | 0.5 |
| Curfew and loitering law violations | 20,232 | 15,441 | 4,568 | 77 | 146 | 100.0 | 76.3 | 22.6 | 0.4 | 0.7 |
| Runaways | 24,020 | 17,380 | 6,099 | 306 | 235 | 100.0 | 72.4 | 25.4 | 1.3 | 1.0 |

[1] Suburban areas include law enforcement agencies in cities with less than 50,000 inhabitants and county law enforcement agencies that are within a metropolitan statistical area. Suburban areas exclude all metropolitan agencies associated with a principal city.

[2] Because of rounding, the percentages may not add to 100.0.

## Table 67. Suburban Area[1] Arrests, Distribution by Race, 2009—*Continued*

(Number, percent; 6,651 agencies; 2009 estimated population 104,853,682.)

| Offense charged | Arrests under 18 | | | | | Percent distribution[2] | | | | |
|---|---|---|---|---|---|---|---|---|---|---|
| | Total | White | Black | American Indian or Alaskan Native | Asian or Pacific Islander | Total | White | Black | American Indian or Alaskan Native | Asian or Pacific Islander |
| **TOTAL** | 579,999 | 410,716 | 160,231 | 3,671 | 5,381 | 100.0 | 70.8 | 27.6 | 0.6 | 0.9 |
| **Violent Crime** | 22,873 | 11,733 | 10,872 | 109 | 159 | 100.0 | 51.3 | 47.5 | 0.5 | 0.7 |
| Murder and nonnegligent manslaughter | 238 | 111 | 122 | 2 | 3 | 100.0 | 46.6 | 51.3 | 0.8 | 1.3 |
| Forcible rape | 875 | 647 | 213 | 6 | 9 | 100.0 | 73.9 | 24.3 | 0.7 | 1.0 |
| Robbery | 6,828 | 2,144 | 4,632 | 17 | 35 | 100.0 | 31.4 | 67.8 | 0.2 | 0.5 |
| Aggravated assault | 14,932 | 8,831 | 5,905 | 84 | 112 | 100.0 | 59.1 | 39.5 | 0.6 | 0.8 |
| **Property Crime** | 122,974 | 80,174 | 40,549 | 729 | 1,522 | 100.0 | 65.2 | 33.0 | 0.6 | 1.2 |
| Burglary | 21,413 | 14,532 | 6,646 | 88 | 147 | 100.0 | 67.9 | 31.0 | 0.4 | 0.7 |
| Larceny-theft | 94,649 | 60,857 | 31,897 | 579 | 1,316 | 100.0 | 64.3 | 33.7 | 0.6 | 1.4 |
| Motor vehicle theft | 4,961 | 3,196 | 1,674 | 50 | 41 | 100.0 | 64.4 | 33.7 | 1.0 | 0.8 |
| Arson | 1,951 | 1,589 | 332 | 12 | 18 | 100.0 | 81.4 | 17.0 | 0.6 | 0.9 |
| **Other** | | | | | | | | | | |
| Other assaults | 71,993 | 45,632 | 25,487 | 410 | 464 | 100.0 | 63.4 | 35.4 | 0.6 | 0.6 |
| Forgery and counterfeiting | 709 | 505 | 197 | 4 | 3 | 100.0 | 71.2 | 27.8 | 0.6 | 0.4 |
| Fraud | 2,043 | 1,330 | 682 | 11 | 20 | 100.0 | 65.1 | 33.4 | 0.5 | 1.0 |
| Embezzlement | 182 | 111 | 64 | 1 | 6 | 100.0 | 61.0 | 35.2 | 0.5 | 3.3 |
| Stolen property; buying, receiving, possessing | 5,784 | 3,481 | 2,210 | 27 | 66 | 100.0 | 60.2 | 38.2 | 0.5 | 1.1 |
| Vandalism | 28,394 | 22,831 | 5,188 | 156 | 219 | 100.0 | 80.4 | 18.3 | 0.5 | 0.8 |
| Weapons; carrying, possessing, etc. | 9,626 | 6,405 | 3,061 | 61 | 99 | 100.0 | 66.5 | 31.8 | 0.6 | 1.0 |
| Prostitution and commercialized vice | 168 | 97 | 68 | 1 | 2 | 100.0 | 57.7 | 40.5 | 0.6 | 1.2 |
| Sex offenses (except forcible rape and prostitution) | 4,290 | 3,167 | 1,072 | 27 | 24 | 100.0 | 73.8 | 25.0 | 0.6 | 0.6 |
| Drug abuse violations | 55,035 | 44,276 | 9,954 | 316 | 489 | 100.0 | 80.5 | 18.1 | 0.6 | 0.9 |
| Gambling | 149 | 54 | 93 | 0 | 2 | 100.0 | 36.2 | 62.4 | 0.0 | 1.3 |
| Offenses against the family and children | 1,725 | 1,352 | 358 | 9 | 6 | 100.0 | 78.4 | 20.8 | 0.5 | 0.3 |
| Driving under the influence | 4,676 | 4,357 | 238 | 40 | 41 | 100.0 | 93.2 | 5.1 | 0.9 | 0.9 |
| Liquor laws | 41,189 | 37,784 | 2,440 | 442 | 523 | 100.0 | 91.7 | 5.9 | 1.1 | 1.3 |
| Drunkenness | 4,455 | 4,079 | 311 | 43 | 22 | 100.0 | 91.6 | 7.0 | 1.0 | 0.5 |
| Disorderly conduct | 56,652 | 34,781 | 21,189 | 234 | 448 | 100.0 | 61.4 | 37.4 | 0.4 | 0.8 |
| Vagrancy | 558 | 352 | 196 | 2 | 8 | 100.0 | 63.1 | 35.1 | 0.4 | 1.4 |
| All other offenses (except traffic) | 102,158 | 75,366 | 25,250 | 666 | 876 | 100.0 | 73.8 | 24.7 | 0.7 | 0.9 |
| Suspicion | 114 | 28 | 85 | 0 | 1 | 100.0 | 24.6 | 74.6 | 0.0 | 0.9 |
| Curfew and loitering law violations | 20,232 | 15,441 | 4,568 | 77 | 146 | 100.0 | 76.3 | 22.6 | 0.4 | 0.7 |
| Runaways | 24,020 | 17,380 | 6,099 | 306 | 235 | 100.0 | 72.4 | 25.4 | 1.3 | 1.0 |

[1] Suburban areas include law enforcement agencies in cities with less than 50,000 inhabitants and county law enforcement agencies that are within a metropolitan statistical area. Suburban areas exclude all metropolitan agencies associated with a principal city.

[2] Because of rounding, the percentages may not add to 100.0.

## Table 67. Suburban Area[1] Arrests, Distribution by Race, 2009—*Continued*

(Number, percent; 6,651 agencies; 2009 estimated population 104,853,682.)

| Offense charged | Arrests 18 and over | | | | | Percent distribution[2] | | | | |
|---|---|---|---|---|---|---|---|---|---|---|
| | Total | White | Black | American Indian or Alaskan Native | Asian or Pacific Islander | Total | White | Black | American Indian or Alaskan Native | Asian or Pacific Islander |
| **TOTAL** | 3,610,385 | 2,716,798 | 835,434 | 29,540 | 28,613 | 100.0 | 75.2 | 23.1 | 0.8 | 0.8 |
| **Violent Crime** | 129,788 | 88,489 | 39,295 | 1,004 | 1,000 | 100.0 | 68.2 | 30.3 | 0.8 | 0.8 |
| Murder and nonnegligent manslaughter | 2,665 | 1,572 | 1,062 | 10 | 21 | 100.0 | 59.0 | 39.8 | 0.4 | 0.8 |
| Forcible rape | 4,782 | 3,532 | 1,175 | 28 | 47 | 100.0 | 73.9 | 24.6 | 0.6 | 1.0 |
| Robbery | 22,227 | 11,342 | 10,660 | 109 | 116 | 100.0 | 51.0 | 48.0 | 0.5 | 0.5 |
| Aggravated assault | 100,114 | 72,043 | 26,398 | 857 | 816 | 100.0 | 72.0 | 26.4 | 0.9 | 0.8 |
| **Property Crime** | 390,633 | 281,870 | 102,204 | 2,901 | 3,658 | 100.0 | 72.2 | 26.2 | 0.7 | 0.9 |
| Burglary | 65,463 | 49,169 | 15,612 | 274 | 408 | 100.0 | 75.1 | 23.8 | 0.4 | 0.6 |
| Larceny-theft | 306,800 | 219,079 | 82,083 | 2,492 | 3,146 | 100.0 | 71.4 | 26.8 | 0.8 | 1.0 |
| Motor vehicle theft | 16,222 | 11,901 | 4,111 | 120 | 90 | 100.0 | 73.4 | 25.3 | 0.7 | 0.6 |
| Arson | 2,148 | 1,721 | 398 | 15 | 14 | 100.0 | 80.1 | 18.5 | 0.7 | 0.7 |
| **Other** | | | | | | | | | | |
| Other assaults | 313,015 | 233,457 | 74,399 | 2,550 | 2,609 | 100.0 | 74.6 | 23.8 | 0.8 | 0.8 |
| Forgery and counterfeiting | 26,800 | 18,337 | 8,122 | 80 | 261 | 100.0 | 68.4 | 30.3 | 0.3 | 1.0 |
| Fraud | 73,238 | 50,291 | 22,100 | 308 | 539 | 100.0 | 68.7 | 30.2 | 0.4 | 0.7 |
| Embezzlement | 5,342 | 3,502 | 1,777 | 18 | 45 | 100.0 | 65.6 | 33.3 | 0.3 | 0.8 |
| Stolen property; buying, receiving, possessing | 27,165 | 18,961 | 7,855 | 153 | 196 | 100.0 | 69.8 | 28.9 | 0.6 | 0.7 |
| Vandalism | 52,873 | 41,748 | 10,329 | 405 | 391 | 100.0 | 79.0 | 19.5 | 0.8 | 0.7 |
| Weapons; carrying, possessing, etc. | 33,790 | 22,245 | 11,159 | 173 | 213 | 100.0 | 65.8 | 33.0 | 0.5 | 0.6 |
| Prostitution and commercialized vice | 6,118 | 4,086 | 1,698 | 30 | 304 | 100.0 | 66.8 | 27.8 | 0.5 | 5.0 |
| Sex offenses (except forcible rape and prostitution) | 17,956 | 14,333 | 3,306 | 118 | 199 | 100.0 | 79.8 | 18.4 | 0.7 | 1.1 |
| Drug abuse violations | 425,256 | 310,754 | 109,925 | 1,991 | 2,586 | 100.0 | 73.1 | 25.8 | 0.5 | 0.6 |
| Gambling | 1,577 | 937 | 507 | 15 | 118 | 100.0 | 59.4 | 32.1 | 1.0 | 7.5 |
| Offenses against the family and children | 44,811 | 29,490 | 14,655 | 370 | 296 | 100.0 | 65.8 | 32.7 | 0.8 | 0.7 |
| Driving under the influence | 509,106 | 447,328 | 52,898 | 3,547 | 5,333 | 100.0 | 87.9 | 10.4 | 0.7 | 1.0 |
| Liquor laws | 143,790 | 124,834 | 14,935 | 2,366 | 1,655 | 100.0 | 86.8 | 10.4 | 1.6 | 1.2 |
| Drunkenness | 157,183 | 136,693 | 18,117 | 1,501 | 872 | 100.0 | 87.0 | 11.5 | 1.0 | 0.6 |
| Disorderly conduct | 141,652 | 104,437 | 35,058 | 1,141 | 1,016 | 100.0 | 73.7 | 24.7 | 0.8 | 0.7 |
| Vagrancy | 5,937 | 3,624 | 2,283 | 11 | 19 | 100.0 | 61.0 | 38.5 | 0.2 | 0.3 |
| All other offenses (except traffic) | 1,103,518 | 781,080 | 304,281 | 10,858 | 7,299 | 100.0 | 70.8 | 27.6 | 1.0 | 0.7 |
| Suspicion | 837 | 302 | 531 | 0 | 4 | 100.0 | 36.1 | 63.4 | 0.0 | 0.5 |
| Curfew and loitering law violations | - | - | - | - | - | - | - | - | - | - |
| Runaways | - | - | - | - | - | - | - | - | - | - |

[1] Suburban areas include law enforcement agencies in cities with less than 50,000 inhabitants and county law enforcement agencies that are within a metropolitan statistical area. Suburban areas exclude all metropolitan agencies associated with a principal city.

[2] Because of rounding, the percentages may not add to 100.0.

## Table 68. Police Disposition of Juvenile Offenders Taken into Custody, 2009

(Number, percent.)

| Population group | Total[1] | Handled within department and released | Referred to juvenile court jurisdiction | Referred to welfare agency | Referred to other police agency | Referred to criminal or adult court | Number of agencies | 2009 estimated population |
|---|---|---|---|---|---|---|---|---|
| **TOTAL AGENCIES:** | | | | | | | | |
| Number | 543,200 | 121,162 | 365,961 | 2,758 | 5,731 | 47,588 | 5,139 | 116,830,401 |
| Percent[2] | 100.0 | 22.3 | 67.4 | 0.5 | 1.1 | 8.8 | | |
| **Total Cities** | | | | | | | | |
| Number | 461,209 | 109,243 | 308,037 | 2,175 | 5,046 | 36,708 | 4,007 | 85,067,747 |
| Percent[2] | 100.0 | 23.7 | 66.8 | 0.5 | 1.1 | 8.0 | | |
| GROUP I (250,000 and over) | | | | | | | | |
| Number | 118,873 | 37,099 | 78,213 | 11 | 608 | 2,942 | 34 | 22,902,229 |
| Percent[2] | 100.0 | 31.2 | 65.8 | * | 0.5 | 2.5 | | |
| GROUP II (100,000 to 249,999) | | | | | | | | |
| Number | 67,487 | 14,463 | 49,091 | 716 | 965 | 2,252 | 85 | 12,505,038 |
| Percent[2] | 100.0 | 21.4 | 72.7 | 1.1 | 1.4 | 3.3 | | |
| GROUP III (50,000 to 99,999) | | | | | | | | |
| Number | 90,908 | 21,312 | 61,923 | 400 | 1,379 | 5,894 | 236 | 15,961,680 |
| Percent[2] | 100.0 | 23.4 | 68.1 | 0.4 | 1.5 | 6.5 | | |
| GROUP IV (25,000 to 49,999) | | | | | | | | |
| Number | 60,978 | 10,857 | 42,859 | 332 | 657 | 6,273 | 348 | 11,999,775 |
| Percent[2] | 100.0 | 17.8 | 70.3 | 0.5 | 1.1 | 10.3 | | |
| GROUP V (10,000 to 24,999) | | | | | | | | |
| Number | 67,593 | 14,093 | 43,038 | 385 | 655 | 9,422 | 795 | 12,656,463 |
| Percent[2] | 100.0 | 20.8 | 63.7 | 0.6 | 1.0 | 13.9 | | |
| GROUP VI (under 10,000) | | | | | | | | |
| Number | 55,370 | 11,419 | 32,913 | 331 | 782 | 9,925 | 2,509 | 9,042,562 |
| Percent[2] | 100.0 | 20.6 | 59.4 | 0.6 | 1.4 | 17.9 | | |
| **Metropolitan Counties** | | | | | | | | |
| Number | 63,989 | 9,139 | 45,741 | 404 | 569 | 8,136 | 579 | 23,714,860 |
| Percent[2] | 100.0 | 14.3 | 71.5 | 0.6 | 0.9 | 12.7 | | |
| **Nonmetropolitan Counties** | | | | | | | | |
| Number | 18,002 | 2,780 | 12,183 | 179 | 116 | 2,744 | 553 | 8,047,794 |
| Percent[2] | 100.0 | 15.4 | 67.7 | 1.0 | 0.6 | 15.2 | | |
| **SUBURBAN AREAS[3]** | | | | | | | | |
| Number | 228,467 | 46,517 | 148,643 | 1,398 | 2,283 | 29,626 | 3,268 | 58,163,860 |
| Percent[2] | 100.0 | 20.4 | 65.1 | 0.6 | 1.0 | 13.0 | | |

[1] Includes all offenses except traffic and neglect cases.
[2] Because of rounding, the percentages may not add to 100.0.
[3] Suburban areas include law enforcement agencies in cities with less than 50,000 inhabitants and county law enforcement agencies that are within a metropolitan statistical area. Suburban areas exclude all metropolitan agencies associated with a principal city. The agencies associated with suburban areas also appear in other groups within this table.
* Less than one-tenth of 1 percent.

## Table 69. State Arrests, 2009

(Number.)

| State | Total all classes[1] | Violent crime[2] | Property crime[2] | Murder and non-negligent man-slaughter | Forcible rape | Robbery | Aggra-vated assault | Burglary | Larceny-theft | Motor vehicle theft | Arson | Other assaults |
|---|---|---|---|---|---|---|---|---|---|---|---|---|
| **ALABAMA** | | | | | | | | | | | | |
| Under 18 | 11,035 | 620 | 3,735 | 28 | 20 | 336 | 236 | 758 | 2,863 | 94 | 20 | 1,829 |
| Total all ages | 193,586 | 5,759 | 24,104 | 292 | 325 | 1,657 | 3,485 | 4,031 | 19,080 | 868 | 125 | 24,341 |
| **ALASKA** | | | | | | | | | | | | |
| Under 18 | 3,780 | 201 | 1,077 | 0 | 7 | 37 | 157 | 85 | 904 | 57 | 31 | 361 |
| Total all ages | 40,349 | 2,145 | 3,937 | 22 | 77 | 283 | 1,763 | 390 | 3,236 | 269 | 42 | 4,947 |
| **ARIZONA** | | | | | | | | | | | | |
| Under 18 | 50,921 | 1,344 | 10,980 | 13 | 29 | 370 | 932 | 1,378 | 9,025 | 455 | 122 | 4,874 |
| Total all ages | 336,686 | 9,364 | 44,116 | 202 | 226 | 2,214 | 6,722 | 4,547 | 37,430 | 1,911 | 228 | 27,565 |
| **ARKANSAS** | | | | | | | | | | | | |
| Under 18 | 11,745 | 352 | 3,323 | 5 | 32 | 63 | 252 | 572 | 2,675 | 63 | 13 | 1,588 |
| Total all ages | 125,958 | 3,988 | 15,785 | 113 | 240 | 632 | 3,003 | 2,767 | 12,587 | 355 | 76 | 10,525 |
| **CALIFORNIA** | | | | | | | | | | | | |
| Under 18 | 203,345 | 15,146 | 43,399 | 183 | 235 | 6,231 | 8,497 | 13,926 | 25,822 | 3,010 | 641 | 19,004 |
| Total all ages | 1,474,004 | 121,369 | 164,744 | 1,811 | 2,044 | 21,577 | 95,937 | 55,269 | 93,762 | 14,442 | 1,271 | 91,615 |
| **COLORADO[4]** | | | | | | | | | | | | |
| Under 18 | 37,890 | 814 | 7,687 | 17 | 67 | 206 | 524 | 824 | 6,396 | 316 | 151 | 1,997 |
| Total all ages | 213,163 | 6,470 | 25,826 | 166 | 421 | 1,088 | 4,795 | 2,792 | 21,589 | 1,218 | 227 | 14,544 |
| **CONNECTICUT** | | | | | | | | | | | | |
| Under 18 | 18,665 | 1,170 | 4,087 | 7 | 29 | 327 | 807 | 576 | 3,255 | 214 | 42 | 4,009 |
| Total all ages | 138,703 | 6,861 | 19,042 | 118 | 247 | 1,473 | 5,023 | 2,938 | 15,351 | 654 | 99 | 23,501 |
| **DELAWARE** | | | | | | | | | | | | |
| Under 18 | 6,647 | 499 | 1,645 | 4 | 23 | 175 | 297 | 286 | 1,288 | 42 | 29 | 1,451 |
| Total all ages | 42,366 | 2,829 | 7,448 | 31 | 105 | 716 | 1,977 | 1,215 | 6,044 | 130 | 59 | 8,597 |
| **DISTRICT OF COLUMBIA[4,5]** | | | | | | | | | | | | |
| Under 18 | 768 | 67 | 68 | 0 | 0 | 47 | 20 | 0 | 56 | 12 | 0 | 76 |
| Total all ages | 8,416 | 140 | 143 | 0 | 0 | 96 | 44 | 0 | 121 | 22 | 0 | 278 |
| **FLORIDA[4,6]** | | | | | | | | | | | | |
| Under 18 | 105,805 | 7,211 | 32,803 | 69 | 190 | 2,618 | 4,334 | 8,917 | 22,054 | 1,672 | 160 | 14,846 |
| Total all ages | 1,049,817 | 49,859 | 145,011 | 779 | 1,642 | 10,964 | 36,474 | 29,681 | 108,081 | 6,859 | 390 | 91,706 |
| **GEORGIA** | | | | | | | | | | | | |
| Under 18 | 42,572 | 2,167 | 10,907 | 54 | 50 | 658 | 1,405 | 2,377 | 7,796 | 668 | 66 | 5,338 |
| Total all ages | 320,569 | 13,014 | 45,965 | 430 | 339 | 3,119 | 9,126 | 8,189 | 35,352 | 2,180 | 244 | 30,273 |
| **HAWAII** | | | | | | | | | | | | |
| Under 18 | 11,341 | 239 | 1,722 | 0 | 17 | 112 | 110 | 131 | 1,470 | 108 | 13 | 925 |
| Total all ages | 51,974 | 1,394 | 5,326 | 16 | 120 | 406 | 852 | 528 | 4,277 | 488 | 33 | 4,914 |
| **IDAHO** | | | | | | | | | | | | |
| Under 18 | 13,735 | 205 | 2,907 | 2 | 25 | 11 | 167 | 358 | 2,400 | 90 | 59 | 1,109 |
| Total all ages | 73,268 | 1,568 | 7,318 | 16 | 117 | 122 | 1,313 | 1,027 | 6,018 | 193 | 80 | 5,882 |
| **ILLINOIS[7]** | | | | | | | | | | | | |
| Under 18 | 29,961 | 3,016 | 5,651 | 58 | 87 | 1,322 | 1,549 | 1,142 | 3,191 | 1,299 | 19 | 4,615 |
| Total all ages | 157,242 | 8,311 | 22,180 | 380 | 464 | 2,875 | 4,592 | 3,028 | 15,249 | 3,832 | 71 | 22,945 |
| **INDIANA** | | | | | | | | | | | | |
| Under 18 | 35,390 | 1,185 | 8,078 | 14 | 19 | 337 | 815 | 1,255 | 6,358 | 378 | 87 | 4,922 |
| Total all ages | 217,684 | 7,710 | 29,597 | 202 | 210 | 1,804 | 5,494 | 4,217 | 23,753 | 1,443 | 184 | 21,160 |
| **IOWA** | | | | | | | | | | | | |
| Under 18 | 18,341 | 681 | 5,067 | 1 | 27 | 103 | 550 | 659 | 4,195 | 167 | 46 | 2,267 |
| Total all ages | 110,553 | 3,938 | 14,625 | 27 | 90 | 418 | 3,403 | 1,937 | 12,151 | 442 | 95 | 10,170 |
| **KANSAS** | | | | | | | | | | | | |
| Under 18 | 9,585 | 284 | 2,344 | 7 | 23 | 48 | 206 | 247 | 1,991 | 76 | 30 | 1,144 |
| Total all ages | 75,034 | 2,326 | 7,126 | 46 | 150 | 282 | 1,848 | 902 | 5,842 | 316 | 66 | 10,738 |
| **KENTUCKY** | | | | | | | | | | | | |
| Under 18 | 7,946 | 420 | 2,647 | 10 | 16 | 190 | 204 | 498 | 2,042 | 79 | 28 | 1,084 |
| Total all ages | 133,542 | 3,536 | 15,541 | 142 | 196 | 1,055 | 2,143 | 2,714 | 12,364 | 347 | 116 | 8,803 |
| **LOUISIANA** | | | | | | | | | | | | |
| Under 18 | 18,674 | 1,654 | 4,618 | 17 | 39 | 230 | 1,368 | 866 | 3,554 | 160 | 38 | 3,088 |
| Total all ages | 139,698 | 9,894 | 22,359 | 182 | 224 | 1,004 | 8,484 | 3,675 | 17,812 | 728 | 144 | 15,489 |
| **MAINE** | | | | | | | | | | | | |
| Under 18 | 6,899 | 73 | 1,893 | 1 | 19 | 18 | 35 | 321 | 1,466 | 76 | 30 | 895 |
| Total all ages | 56,567 | 712 | 8,173 | 19 | 83 | 194 | 416 | 1,362 | 6,481 | 250 | 80 | 6,878 |
| **MARYLAND** | | | | | | | | | | | | |
| Under 18 | 41,400 | 3,216 | 10,977 | 38 | 55 | 1,756 | 1,367 | 1,846 | 7,915 | 948 | 268 | 6,873 |
| Total all ages | 283,407 | 12,464 | 35,779 | 318 | 442 | 4,185 | 7,519 | 6,595 | 26,228 | 2,467 | 489 | 29,465 |
| **MASSACHUSETTS** | | | | | | | | | | | | |
| Under 18 | 16,079 | 1,771 | 3,390 | 4 | 29 | 484 | 1,254 | 698 | 2,541 | 112 | 39 | 2,497 |
| Total all ages | 148,266 | 13,003 | 20,097 | 76 | 323 | 2,129 | 10,475 | 3,758 | 15,546 | 696 | 97 | 22,234 |
| **MICHIGAN** | | | | | | | | | | | | |
| Under 18 | 35,771 | 2,106 | 10,751 | 23 | 115 | 664 | 1,304 | 1,737 | 8,214 | 690 | 110 | 4,131 |
| Total all ages | 296,005 | 13,330 | 38,817 | 221 | 633 | 2,571 | 9,905 | 6,461 | 29,569 | 2,495 | 292 | 30,626 |

[1] Does not include traffic arrests.

[2] Violent crimes are offenses of murder and nonnegligent manslaughter, forcible rape, robbery, and aggravated assault. Property crimes are offenses of burglary, larceny-theft, motor vehicle theft, and arson.

[4] See Appendix I for details.

[5] Includes arrests reported by the Metro Transit Police. This agency has no population associated with it.

[6] The arrest category *All other offenses* for Florida also includes the arrest counts for offenses against the family and children, drunkenness, disorderly conduct, vagrancy, suspicion, curfew and loitering law violations, and runaways.

[7] Forcible rape figures for Illinois include only those data provided by Rockford. The forcible rape figures for Minnesota include only those provided by the cities of St. Paul and Minneapolis. See Appendix I for details.

## Table 69. State Arrests, 2009—*Continued*

(Number.)

| State | Forgery and counter-feiting | Fraud | Embezzle-ment | Stolen property; buying, receiving, possessing | Vandal-ism | Weapons; carrying, possessing, etc. | Prostitu-tion and commer-cialized vice | Sex offenses (except forcible rape and prosti-tution) | Drug abuse violations | Gamb-ling | Offenses against the family and children | Driving under the influence |
|---|---|---|---|---|---|---|---|---|---|---|---|---|
| **ALABAMA** | | | | | | | | | | | | |
| Under 18 | 29 | 58 | 2 | 135 | 232 | 123 | 0 | 18 | 818 | 21 | 4 | 81 |
| Total all ages | 1,569 | 7,614 | 158 | 1,932 | 2,034 | 1,379 | 296 | 550 | 15,180 | 120 | 860 | 13,924 |
| **ALASKA** | | | | | | | | | | | | |
| Under 18 | 3 | 11 | 10 | 7 | 139 | 39 | 2 | 35 | 314 | 0 | 2 | 66 |
| Total all ages | 116 | 276 | 90 | 37 | 764 | 365 | 217 | 191 | 2,050 | 0 | 315 | 5,428 |
| **ARIZONA** | | | | | | | | | | | | |
| Under 18 | 45 | 75 | 6 | 148 | 3,428 | 393 | 28 | 305 | 5,422 | 0 | 238 | 487 |
| Total all ages | 2,407 | 2,255 | 260 | 1,234 | 12,319 | 3,193 | 1,503 | 1,906 | 35,087 | 3 | 2,998 | 39,260 |
| **ARKANSAS** | | | | | | | | | | | | |
| Under 18 | 15 | 32 | 2 | 104 | 319 | 143 | 0 | 40 | 863 | 4 | 4 | 105 |
| Total all ages | 815 | 2,736 | 38 | 968 | 1,554 | 1,158 | 298 | 176 | 11,213 | 34 | 150 | 10,130 |
| **CALIFORNIA** | | | | | | | | | | | | |
| Under 18 | 200 | 531 | 25 | 2,857 | 13,916 | 7,094 | 429 | 1,958 | 21,882 | 43 | 2 | 1,260 |
| Total all ages | 8,128 | 9,542 | 1,557 | 17,271 | 29,528 | 29,835 | 12,904 | 13,831 | 251,740 | 658 | 272 | 208,831 |
| **COLORADO**[4] | | | | | | | | | | | | |
| Under 18 | 43 | 139 | 10 | 123 | 1,574 | 473 | 13 | 214 | 3,180 | 0 | 76 | 392 |
| Total all ages | 1,004 | 2,482 | 168 | 659 | 5,571 | 1,836 | 651 | 921 | 16,658 | 11 | 2,855 | 27,043 |
| **CONNECTICUT** | | | | | | | | | | | | |
| Under 18 | 17 | 39 | 6 | 77 | 802 | 289 | 0 | 151 | 1,664 | 2 | 76 | 65 |
| Total all ages | 819 | 1,603 | 224 | 423 | 2,719 | 1,487 | 346 | 614 | 17,757 | 73 | 1,530 | 10,178 |
| **DELAWARE** | | | | | | | | | | | | |
| Under 18 | 5 | 106 | 4 | 81 | 333 | 137 | 0 | 53 | 667 | 1 | 4 | 0 |
| Total all ages | 599 | 1,914 | 237 | 422 | 1,183 | 410 | 67 | 173 | 5,752 | 15 | 229 | 230 |
| **DISTRICT OF COLUMBIA**[4,5] | | | | | | | | | | | | |
| Under 18 | 0 | 1 | 0 | 4 | 35 | 13 | 0 | 0 | 20 | 0 | 0 | 1 |
| Total all ages | 2 | 2 | 0 | 12 | 50 | 39 | 0 | 0 | 121 | 2 | 0 | 49 |
| **FLORIDA**[4,6] | | | | | | | | | | | | |
| Under 18 | 85 | 521 | 12 | 253 | 2,292 | 1,462 | 51 | 299 | 11,561 | 64 | | 269 |
| Total all ages | 4,220 | 15,129 | 957 | 3,227 | 8,225 | 6,908 | 5,296 | 3,300 | 146,056 | 356 | | 53,004 |
| **GEORGIA** | | | | | | | | | | | | |
| Under 18 | 98 | 255 | 16 | 472 | 867 | 1,060 | 48 | 568 | 3,444 | 32 | 146 | 184 |
| Total all ages | 4,702 | 7,095 | 362 | 3,406 | 3,760 | 4,475 | 1,702 | 3,700 | 39,395 | 351 | 3,195 | 26,982 |
| **HAWAII** | | | | | | | | | | | | |
| Under 18 | 1 | 7 | 1 | 13 | 341 | 31 | 4 | 80 | 482 | 0 | 1 | 49 |
| Total all ages | 198 | 513 | 62 | 111 | 815 | 237 | 315 | 298 | 2,055 | 19 | 32 | 5,588 |
| **IDAHO** | | | | | | | | | | | | |
| Under 18 | 13 | 35 | 7 | 49 | 537 | 137 | 0 | 83 | 804 | 0 | 14 | 180 |
| Total all ages | 183 | 484 | 88 | 174 | 1,292 | 549 | 5 | 333 | 5,751 | 0 | 785 | 12,226 |
| **ILLINOIS**[7] | | | | | | | | | | | | |
| Under 18 | 10 | 27 | 0 | 18 | 1,515 | 948 | 41 | 72 | 5,664 | 854 | 12 | 23 |
| Total all ages | 319 | 323 | 2 | 54 | 4,641 | 4,172 | 3,473 | 832 | 43,536 | 3,046 | 344 | 4,250 |
| **INDIANA** | | | | | | | | | | | | |
| Under 18 | 20 | 55 | 0 | 1,553 | 992 | 300 | 11 | 230 | 2,326 | 0 | 149 | 156 |
| Total all ages | 1,425 | 1,671 | 6 | 6,608 | 2,319 | 1,913 | 1,185 | 1,427 | 23,203 | 36 | 1,510 | 22,618 |
| **IOWA** | | | | | | | | | | | | |
| Under 18 | 29 | 41 | 12 | 87 | 1,408 | 111 | 2 | 63 | 1,032 | 0 | 5 | 185 |
| Total all ages | 562 | 1,002 | 102 | 220 | 2,945 | 486 | 141 | 210 | 8,376 | 6 | 954 | 13,516 |
| **KANSAS** | | | | | | | | | | | | |
| Under 18 | 17 | 22 | 18 | 38 | 390 | 99 | 0 | 82 | 809 | 0 | 22 | 194 |
| Total all ages | 401 | 1,195 | 148 | 215 | 1,818 | 663 | 239 | 261 | 6,316 | 0 | 211 | 13,223 |
| **KENTUCKY** | | | | | | | | | | | | |
| Under 18 | 24 | 15 | 6 | 204 | 187 | 96 | 1 | 63 | 875 | 3 | 4 | 118 |
| Total all ages | 1,243 | 1,759 | 107 | 1,437 | 951 | 1,056 | 379 | 331 | 18,553 | 28 | 3,021 | 19,733 |
| **LOUISIANA** | | | | | | | | | | | | |
| Under 18 | 5 | 28 | 5 | 237 | 549 | 252 | 10 | 96 | 1,414 | 11 | 100 | 64 |
| Total all ages | 574 | 2,029 | 235 | 1,314 | 2,355 | 1,607 | 288 | 648 | 19,334 | 59 | 1,404 | 8,488 |
| **MAINE** | | | | | | | | | | | | |
| Under 18 | 4 | 27 | 1 | 34 | 471 | 47 | 0 | 33 | 625 | 0 | 4 | 67 |
| Total all ages | 276 | 878 | 37 | 194 | 1,581 | 411 | 27 | 245 | 5,897 | 3 | 104 | 6,861 |
| **MARYLAND** | | | | | | | | | | | | |
| Under 18 | 29 | 59 | 14 | 23 | 1,628 | 1,072 | 23 | 279 | 6,516 | 60 | 40 | 200 |
| Total all ages | 1,239 | 1,989 | 349 | 164 | 3,870 | 3,590 | 1,322 | 1,374 | 51,629 | 314 | 2,223 | 23,180 |
| **MASSACHUSETTS** | | | | | | | | | | | | |
| Under 18 | 13 | 55 | 0 | 246 | 811 | 240 | 5 | 83 | 682 | 0 | 145 | 88 |
| Total all ages | 696 | 1,547 | 139 | 1,457 | 3,393 | 1,514 | 836 | 711 | 12,127 | 21 | 1,853 | 12,369 |
| **MICHIGAN** | | | | | | | | | | | | |
| Under 18 | 29 | 398 | 21 | 393 | 1,091 | 713 | 7 | 215 | 3,579 | 9 | 13 | 523 |
| Total all ages | 893 | 5,912 | 1,010 | 1,729 | 3,684 | 4,270 | 732 | 954 | 34,910 | 154 | 2,921 | 38,941 |

[4] See Appendix I for details.
[5] Includes arrests reported by the Metro Transit Police. This agency has no population associated with it.
[6] The arrest category *All other offenses* for Florida also includes the arrest counts for offenses against the family and children, drunkenness, disorderly conduct, vagrancy, suspicion, curfew and loitering law violations, and runaways.
[7] Forcible rape figures for Illinois include only those data provided by Rockford. The forcible rape figures for Minnesota include only those provided by the cities of St. Paul and Minneapolis. See Appendix I for details.

## Table 69. State Arrests, 2009—*Continued*

(Number.)

| State | Liquor laws | Drunken-ness[3] | Disorderly conduct | Vagrancy | All other offenses (except traffic) | Suspi-cion | Curfew and loitering law violations | Run-aways | Number of agencies | 2008 estimated population |
|---|---|---|---|---|---|---|---|---|---|---|
| **ALABAMA** | | | | | | | | | | |
| Under 18 | 547 | 70 | 1,149 | 8 | 1,345 | 0 | 27 | 184 | 306 | 3,682,108 |
| Total all ages | 4,854 | 8,868 | 4,093 | 274 | 75,466 | 0 | 27 | 184 | | |
| **ALASKA** | | | | | | | | | | |
| Under 18 | 554 | 8 | 57 | 0 | 712 | 0 | 16 | 166 | 33 | 682,496 |
| Total all ages | 2,391 | 367 | 949 | 0 | 15,579 | 3 | 16 | 166 | | |
| **ARIZONA** | | | | | | | | | | |
| Under 18 | 5,468 | 4 | 3,094 | 28 | 5,101 | 0 | 4,768 | 4,685 | 89 | 6,505,613 |
| Total all ages | 30,113 | 6 | 18,713 | 1,919 | 93,012 | 0 | 4,768 | 4,685 | | |
| **ARKANSAS** | | | | | | | | | | |
| Under 18 | 190 | 179 | 1,031 | 0 | 2,432 | 0 | 747 | 272 | 228 | 2,470,159 |
| Total all ages | 1,988 | 8,932 | 3,457 | 653 | 50,341 | 0 | 747 | 272 | | |
| **CALIFORNIA** | | | | | | | | | | |
| Under 18 | 4,456 | 3,772 | 9,161 | 312 | 42,837 | 0 | 11,539 | 3,522 | 692 | 36,772,788 |
| Total all ages | 17,948 | 115,611 | 13,569 | 4,167 | 345,823 | 0 | 11,539 | 3,522 | | |
| **COLORADO**[4] | | | | | | | | | | |
| Under 18 | 3,738 | 35 | 3,064 | 9 | 8,425 | 5 | 1,652 | 4,227 | 204 | 4,524,405 |
| Total all ages | 13,169 | 229 | 10,988 | 166 | 76,023 | 10 | 1,652 | 4,227 | | |
| **CONNECTICUT** | | | | | | | | | | |
| Under 18 | 317 | 0 | 3,087 | 2 | 2,750 | 0 | 52 | 3 | 102 | 3,518,288 |
| Total all ages | 1,507 | 1 | 16,146 | 45 | 33,772 | 0 | 52 | 3 | | |
| **DELAWARE** | | | | | | | | | | |
| Under 18 | 340 | 15 | 541 | 0 | 577 | 0 | 188 | 0 | 54 | 884,338 |
| Total all ages | 2,302 | 674 | 2,048 | 1,258 | 5,791 | 0 | 188 | 0 | | |
| **DISTRICT OF COLUMBIA**[4,5] | | | | | | | | | | |
| Under 18 | 6 | 0 | 97 | 0 | 377 | 0 | 3 | 0 | 1 | |
| Total all ages | 1,713 | 81 | 286 | 167 | 5,328 | 0 | 3 | 0 | | |
| **FLORIDA**[4,6] | | | | | | | | | | |
| Under 18 | 1,440 | | | | 32,636 | | | | 593 | 18,514,171 |
| Total all ages | 37,715 | | | | 478,848 | | | | | |
| **GEORGIA** | | | | | | | | | | |
| Under 18 | 1,005 | 101 | 4,866 | 162 | 7,985 | 80 | 663 | 2,108 | 351 | 6,766,841 |
| Total all ages | 11,456 | 3,385 | 27,605 | 1,818 | 84,454 | 703 | 663 | 2,108 | | |
| **HAWAII** | | | | | | | | | | |
| Under 18 | 208 | 0 | 160 | 0 | 2,720 | 0 | 196 | 4,161 | 3 | 1,150,076 |
| Total all ages | 1,471 | 0 | 782 | 105 | 23,382 | 0 | 196 | 4,161 | | |
| **IDAHO** | | | | | | | | | | |
| Under 18 | 1,800 | 15 | 549 | 0 | 3,320 | 0 | 534 | 1,437 | 103 | 1,519,531 |
| Total all ages | 6,448 | 351 | 2,668 | 7 | 25,185 | 0 | 534 | 1,437 | | |
| **ILLINOIS**[7] | | | | | | | | | | |
| Under 18 | 255 | 0 | 3,188 | 0 | 3,556 | 0 | 489 | 7 | 2 | 3,006,374 |
| Total all ages | 1,288 | 0 | 14,961 | 105 | 21,964 | 0 | 489 | 7 | | |
| **INDIANA** | | | | | | | | | | |
| Under 18 | 2,625 | 384 | 2,349 | 19 | 6,507 | 10 | 755 | 2,764 | 159 | 4,679,770 |
| Total all ages | 12,250 | 16,936 | 7,822 | 54 | 54,613 | 102 | 755 | 2,764 | | |
| **IOWA** | | | | | | | | | | |
| Under 18 | 1,683 | 248 | 2,039 | 0 | 2,443 | 0 | 545 | 393 | 193 | 2,756,917 |
| Total all ages | 8,663 | 10,917 | 6,114 | 22 | 26,646 | 0 | 545 | 393 | | |
| **KANSAS** | | | | | | | | | | |
| Under 18 | 1,170 | 0 | 681 | 0 | 1,010 | 0 | 0 | 1,261 | 188 | 1,813,396 |
| Total all ages | 5,957 | 308 | 3,662 | 0 | 18,966 | 0 | 0 | 1,261 | | |
| **KENTUCKY** | | | | | | | | | | |
| Under 18 | 121 | 239 | 571 | 17 | 1,160 | 0 | 16 | 75 | 235 | 2,295,577 |
| Total all ages | 374 | 17,260 | 4,828 | 482 | 34,029 | 0 | 16 | 75 | | |
| **LOUISIANA** | | | | | | | | | | |
| Under 18 | 219 | 88 | 2,264 | 13 | 3,186 | 3 | 421 | 349 | 118 | 2,410,236 |
| Total all ages | 2,274 | 2,578 | 7,581 | 265 | 40,141 | 12 | 421 | 349 | | |
| **MAINE** | | | | | | | | | | |
| Under 18 | 1,209 | 14 | 208 | 0 | 1,101 | 0 | 90 | 103 | 164 | 1,316,989 |
| Total all ages | 5,528 | 40 | 1,886 | 9 | 16,634 | 0 | 90 | 103 | | |
| **MARYLAND** | | | | | | | | | | |
| Under 18 | 1,220 | 0 | 2,089 | 18 | 6,343 | 52 | 226 | 443 | 149 | 5,674,380 |
| Total all ages | 7,446 | 0 | 7,082 | 135 | 98,707 | 417 | 226 | 443 | | |
| **MASSACHUSETTS** | | | | | | | | | | |
| Under 18 | 922 | 276 | 1,290 | 0 | 3,303 | 3 | 10 | 249 | 328 | 6,130,470 |
| Total all ages | 5,077 | 7,144 | 8,134 | 16 | 35,618 | 21 | 10 | 249 | | |
| **MICHIGAN** | | | | | | | | | | |
| Under 18 | 3,398 | 3 | 1,267 | 0 | 5,177 | 0 | 910 | 1,037 | 568 | 9,569,737 |
| Total all ages | 18,679 | 332 | 9,813 | 291 | 86,060 | 0 | 910 | 1,037 | | |

[3] Drunkenness is not considered a crime in some states; therefore, the figures vary widely from state to state.
[4] See Appendix I for details.
[5] Includes arrests reported by the Metro Transit Police. This agency has no population associated with it.
[6] The arrest category *All other offenses* for Florida also includes the arrest counts for offenses against the family and children, drunkenness, disorderly conduct, vagrancy, suspicion, curfew and loitering law violations, and runaways.
[7] Forcible rape figures for Illinois include only those data provided by Rockford. The forcible rape figures for Minnesota include only those provided by the cities of St. Paul and Minneapolis. See Appendix I for details.

## Table 69. State Arrests, 2009—*Continued*

(Number.)

| State | Total all classes[1] | Violent crime[2] | Property crime[2] | Murder and non-negligent man-slaughter | Forcible rape | Robbery | Aggra-vated assault | Burglary | Larceny-theft | Motor vehicle theft | Arson | Other assaults |
|---|---|---|---|---|---|---|---|---|---|---|---|---|
| **MINNESOTA[7]** | | | | | | | | | | | | |
| Under 18 | 42,324 | 1,000 | 10,128 | 3 | 11 | 359 | 627 | 894 | 8,837 | 284 | 113 | 3,284 |
| Total all ages | 191,480 | 5,419 | 30,539 | 103 | 111 | 1,214 | 3,991 | 3,001 | 26,251 | 1,103 | 184 | 17,220 |
| **MISSISSIPPI** | | | | | | | | | | | | |
| Under 18 | 11,715 | 251 | 2,923 | 4 | 12 | 139 | 96 | 778 | 2,075 | 41 | 29 | 1,643 |
| Total all ages | 123,587 | 2,065 | 13,355 | 109 | 139 | 657 | 1,160 | 2,673 | 10,191 | 385 | 106 | 12,861 |
| **MISSOURI** | | | | | | | | | | | | |
| Under 18 | 43,005 | 1,689 | 11,332 | 49 | 61 | 500 | 1,079 | 1,799 | 8,762 | 656 | 115 | 6,109 |
| Total all ages | 324,277 | 12,169 | 44,812 | 388 | 531 | 2,394 | 8,856 | 6,654 | 35,072 | 2,781 | 305 | 34,915 |
| **MONTANA** | | | | | | | | | | | | |
| Under 18 | 6,948 | 117 | 1,545 | 2 | 5 | 10 | 100 | 68 | 1,363 | 96 | 18 | 593 |
| Total all ages | 31,237 | 893 | 4,485 | 18 | 27 | 52 | 796 | 248 | 3,979 | 227 | 31 | 3,761 |
| **NEBRASKA** | | | | | | | | | | | | |
| Under 18 | 14,591 | 270 | 3,666 | 4 | 20 | 103 | 143 | 300 | 3,197 | 114 | 55 | 1,996 |
| Total all ages | 84,107 | 1,943 | 10,147 | 35 | 158 | 377 | 1,373 | 883 | 8,824 | 348 | 92 | 8,968 |
| **NEVADA** | | | | | | | | | | | | |
| Under 18 | 23,988 | 997 | 4,665 | 13 | 16 | 437 | 531 | 822 | 3,638 | 145 | 60 | 2,747 |
| Total all ages | 172,548 | 7,501 | 18,250 | 149 | 194 | 2,048 | 5,110 | 3,018 | 14,367 | 715 | 150 | 18,590 |
| **NEW HAMPSHIRE** | | | | | | | | | | | | |
| Under 18 | 7,417 | 90 | 1,131 | 0 | 2 | 18 | 70 | 153 | 917 | 36 | 25 | 1,070 |
| Total all ages | 49,351 | 694 | 4,343 | 3 | 45 | 176 | 470 | 550 | 3,624 | 115 | 54 | 6,499 |
| **NEW JERSEY** | | | | | | | | | | | | |
| Under 18 | 48,407 | 2,813 | 8,225 | 28 | 70 | 1,439 | 1,276 | 1,533 | 6,302 | 218 | 172 | 3,765 |
| Total all ages | 387,595 | 13,749 | 34,845 | 229 | 362 | 4,413 | 8,745 | 6,231 | 27,505 | 796 | 313 | 27,102 |
| **NEW MEXICO** | | | | | | | | | | | | |
| Under 18 | 9,666 | 416 | 2,614 | 4 | 18 | 30 | 364 | 279 | 2,184 | 109 | 42 | 1,316 |
| Total all ages | 95,965 | 3,638 | 10,739 | 69 | 105 | 296 | 3,168 | 1,302 | 8,891 | 445 | 101 | 8,606 |
| **NEW YORK[4]** | | | | | | | | | | | | |
| Under 18 | 41,671 | 2,619 | 11,831 | 32 | 63 | 1,168 | 1,356 | 2,002 | 9,215 | 482 | 132 | 4,824 |
| Total all ages | 347,436 | 15,628 | 59,064 | 279 | 522 | 4,323 | 10,504 | 8,158 | 48,308 | 2,186 | 412 | 36,315 |
| **NORTH CAROLINA** | | | | | | | | | | | | |
| Under 18 | 36,830 | 1,913 | 10,337 | 45 | 39 | 730 | 1,099 | 2,858 | 7,159 | 205 | 115 | 5,768 |
| Total all ages | 389,370 | 17,790 | 58,545 | 483 | 474 | 3,729 | 13,104 | 14,315 | 42,756 | 1,191 | 283 | 48,526 |
| **NORTH DAKOTA** | | | | | | | | | | | | |
| Under 18 | 6,170 | 57 | 1,263 | 0 | 16 | 5 | 36 | 108 | 1,060 | 89 | 6 | 428 |
| Total all ages | 27,209 | 465 | 3,125 | 8 | 38 | 41 | 378 | 331 | 2,604 | 175 | 15 | 2,020 |
| **OHIO** | | | | | | | | | | | | |
| Under 18 | 40,191 | 1,263 | 8,708 | 17 | 95 | 747 | 404 | 1,568 | 6,594 | 415 | 131 | 6,677 |
| Total all ages | 266,624 | 7,342 | 39,106 | 232 | 466 | 3,244 | 3,400 | 6,370 | 31,106 | 1,343 | 287 | 36,372 |
| **OKLAHOMA** | | | | | | | | | | | | |
| Under 18 | 20,280 | 652 | 5,566 | 21 | 33 | 172 | 426 | 840 | 4,457 | 154 | 115 | 1,250 |
| Total all ages | 159,508 | 5,953 | 19,557 | 197 | 261 | 852 | 4,643 | 2,975 | 15,850 | 481 | 251 | 9,707 |
| **OREGON** | | | | | | | | | | | | |
| Under 18 | 24,411 | 548 | 6,131 | 5 | 21 | 168 | 354 | 638 | 5,175 | 180 | 138 | 1,794 |
| Total all ages | 132,035 | 4,214 | 24,125 | 72 | 245 | 1,012 | 2,885 | 2,447 | 20,349 | 1,103 | 226 | 14,044 |
| **PENNSYLVANIA** | | | | | | | | | | | | |
| Under 18 | 87,747 | 4,475 | 11,852 | 36 | 201 | 1,685 | 2,553 | 1,811 | 9,135 | 630 | 276 | 7,259 |
| Total all ages | 446,511 | 23,505 | 57,552 | 526 | 1,090 | 6,753 | 15,136 | 9,278 | 44,895 | 2,753 | 626 | 44,291 |
| **RHODE ISLAND** | | | | | | | | | | | | |
| Under 18 | 5,184 | 195 | 1,131 | 0 | 16 | 99 | 80 | 206 | 846 | 39 | 40 | 702 |
| Total all ages | 34,247 | 923 | 3,989 | 12 | 66 | 282 | 563 | 801 | 3,012 | 117 | 59 | 4,404 |
| **SOUTH CAROLINA** | | | | | | | | | | | | |
| Under 18 | 21,129 | 1,098 | 5,345 | 19 | 54 | 293 | 732 | 1,128 | 4,044 | 130 | 43 | 3,284 |
| Total all ages | 198,552 | 9,435 | 25,534 | 234 | 341 | 1,656 | 7,204 | 4,512 | 20,015 | 868 | 139 | 20,497 |
| **SOUTH DAKOTA** | | | | | | | | | | | | |
| Under 18 | 6,091 | 55 | 1,408 | 0 | 8 | 4 | 43 | 82 | 1,272 | 46 | 8 | 497 |
| Total all ages | 28,206 | 466 | 3,636 | 7 | 59 | 42 | 358 | 330 | 3,162 | 134 | 10 | 3,260 |
| **TENNESSEE** | | | | | | | | | | | | |
| Under 18 | 34,792 | 1,598 | 7,548 | 44 | 61 | 507 | 986 | 1,454 | 5,714 | 320 | 60 | 5,667 |
| Total all ages | 305,259 | 13,150 | 41,924 | 321 | 313 | 2,731 | 9,785 | 6,270 | 33,703 | 1,746 | 205 | 31,772 |
| **TEXAS** | | | | | | | | | | | | |
| Under 18 | 170,190 | 4,857 | 33,363 | 84 | 246 | 1,599 | 2,928 | 5,191 | 26,995 | 949 | 228 | 23,056 |
| Total all ages | 1,174,813 | 34,683 | 143,518 | 823 | 1,908 | 8,330 | 23,622 | 20,432 | 117,211 | 5,212 | 663 | 116,411 |
| **UTAH** | | | | | | | | | | | | |
| Under 18 | 26,491 | 358 | 6,678 | 4 | 60 | 74 | 220 | 395 | 6,066 | 150 | 67 | 2,298 |
| Total all ages | 135,850 | 2,227 | 20,677 | 37 | 191 | 515 | 1,484 | 1,471 | 18,657 | 436 | 113 | 11,915 |
| **VERMONT** | | | | | | | | | | | | |
| Under 18 | 1,531 | 43 | 353 | 0 | 8 | 5 | 30 | 78 | 243 | 23 | 9 | 250 |
| Total all ages | 15,630 | 539 | 2,147 | 6 | 61 | 25 | 447 | 351 | 1,676 | 101 | 19 | 1,794 |

[1] Does not include traffic arrests.
[2] Violent crimes are offenses of murder and nonnegligent manslaughter, forcible rape, robbery, and aggravated assault. Property crimes are offenses of burglary, larceny-theft, motor vehicle theft, and arson.
[4] See Appendix I for details.
[7] Forcible rape figures for Illinois include only those data provided by Rockford. The forcible rape figures for Minnesota include only those provided by the cities of St. Paul and Minneapolis. See Appendix I for details.

## Table 69. State Arrests, 2009—*Continued*

(Number.)

| State | Forgery and counter-feiting | Fraud | Embezzle-ment | Stolen property; buying, receiving, possessing | Vandal-ism | Weapons; carrying, possessing, etc. | Prostitu-tion and commer-cialized vice | Sex offenses (except forcible rape and prosti-tution) | Drug abuse violations | Gamb-ling | Offenses against the family and children | Driving under the influence |
|---|---|---|---|---|---|---|---|---|---|---|---|---|
| **MINNESOTA**[7] | | | | | | | | | | | | |
| Under 18 | 62 | 185 | 6 | 511 | 1,680 | 611 | 30 | 255 | 2,730 | 0 | 27 | 383 |
| Total all ages | 1,356 | 3,066 | 51 | 1,862 | 4,342 | 1,858 | 1,087 | 1,444 | 17,040 | 19 | 754 | 26,240 |
| **MISSISSIPPI** | | | | | | | | | | | | |
| Under 18 | 5 | 53 | 5 | 100 | 232 | 240 | 8 | 34 | 772 | 31 | 247 | 110 |
| Total all ages | 847 | 2,042 | 733 | 755 | 1,136 | 1,085 | 225 | 389 | 13,240 | 163 | 3,561 | 12,644 |
| **MISSOURI** | | | | | | | | | | | | |
| Under 18 | 58 | 73 | 16 | 655 | 1,784 | 611 | 3 | 439 | 3,453 | 4 | 104 | 409 |
| Total all ages | 2,229 | 3,367 | 221 | 3,083 | 6,642 | 3,817 | 569 | 2,342 | 35,321 | 101 | 4,515 | 33,020 |
| **MONTANA** | | | | | | | | | | | | |
| Under 18 | 6 | 5 | 3 | 8 | 384 | 13 | 0 | 16 | 304 | 0 | 49 | 65 |
| Total all ages | 58 | 183 | 33 | 21 | 1,006 | 62 | 1 | 57 | 1,539 | 0 | 320 | 4,373 |
| **NEBRASKA** | | | | | | | | | | | | |
| Under 18 | 19 | 88 | 12 | 146 | 1,158 | 132 | 2 | 105 | 1,120 | 0 | 31 | 223 |
| Total all ages | 440 | 1,529 | 103 | 739 | 2,887 | 903 | 180 | 614 | 9,731 | 19 | 1,467 | 13,016 |
| **NEVADA** | | | | | | | | | | | | |
| Under 18 | 30 | 52 | 9 | 264 | 1,539 | 371 | 76 | 101 | 1,834 | 0 | 7 | 116 |
| Total all ages | 1,254 | 1,765 | 505 | 2,006 | 2,928 | 1,950 | 4,561 | 1,555 | 16,976 | 33 | 1,209 | 15,234 |
| **NEW HAMPSHIRE** | | | | | | | | | | | | |
| Under 18 | 6 | 20 | 1 | 110 | 371 | 15 | 0 | 39 | 773 | 0 | 11 | 68 |
| Total all ages | 221 | 774 | 47 | 571 | 1,317 | 108 | 46 | 175 | 4,020 | 3 | 188 | 4,676 |
| **NEW JERSEY** | | | | | | | | | | | | |
| Under 18 | 48 | 124 | 6 | 941 | 2,508 | 1,325 | 16 | 267 | 5,440 | 33 | 125 | 281 |
| Total all ages | 1,766 | 5,039 | 145 | 3,739 | 6,398 | 4,848 | 1,372 | 1,543 | 52,461 | 275 | 14,411 | 27,345 |
| **NEW MEXICO** | | | | | | | | | | | | |
| Under 18 | 6 | 34 | 8 | 58 | 319 | 201 | 2 | 22 | 1,021 | 0 | 56 | 131 |
| Total all ages | 154 | 403 | 141 | 583 | 872 | 601 | 287 | 150 | 6,478 | 0 | 1,262 | 11,674 |
| **NEW YORK**[4] | | | | | | | | | | | | |
| Under 18 | 105 | 309 | 4 | 1,035 | 3,718 | 656 | 15 | 726 | 5,217 | 24 | 117 | 279 |
| Total all ages | 3,473 | 7,114 | 154 | 5,416 | 16,078 | 4,036 | 871 | 4,073 | 60,543 | 237 | 1,315 | 36,093 |
| **NORTH CAROLINA** | | | | | | | | | | | | |
| Under 18 | 51 | 368 | 43 | 540 | 1,685 | 1,256 | 11 | 102 | 2,884 | 3 | 67 | 560 |
| Total all ages | 2,205 | 17,284 | 1,353 | 4,485 | 7,299 | 6,454 | 1,080 | 1,185 | 33,062 | 111 | 6,546 | 50,261 |
| **NORTH DAKOTA** | | | | | | | | | | | | |
| Under 18 | 9 | 11 | 3 | 52 | 285 | 28 | 0 | 28 | 281 | 0 | 89 | 45 |
| Total all ages | 108 | 728 | 32 | 124 | 548 | 132 | 4 | 104 | 1,851 | 1 | 188 | 3,904 |
| **OHIO** | | | | | | | | | | | | |
| Under 18 | 54 | 156 | 7 | 724 | 1,881 | 542 | 10 | 250 | 2,565 | 12 | 595 | 179 |
| Total all ages | 1,497 | 3,274 | 47 | 3,615 | 5,035 | 3,518 | 1,891 | 960 | 30,904 | 131 | 5,165 | 18,993 |
| **OKLAHOMA** | | | | | | | | | | | | |
| Under 18 | 10 | 37 | 38 | 375 | 451 | 278 | 8 | 68 | 1,791 | 0 | 73 | 223 |
| Total all ages | 820 | 2,737 | 552 | 2,405 | 1,443 | 1,966 | 411 | 784 | 20,311 | 10 | 942 | 18,996 |
| **OREGON** | | | | | | | | | | | | |
| Under 18 | 19 | 81 | 1 | 49 | 1,495 | 217 | 26 | 186 | 2,178 | 0 | 13 | 101 |
| Total all ages | 763 | 1,300 | 42 | 386 | 4,474 | 1,456 | 660 | 1,226 | 15,469 | 4 | 602 | 14,477 |
| **PENNSYLVANIA** | | | | | | | | | | | | |
| Under 18 | 65 | 236 | 19 | 523 | 3,840 | 1,233 | 9 | 582 | 5,147 | 7 | 32 | 491 |
| Total all ages | 2,529 | 7,895 | 419 | 2,747 | 11,442 | 4,056 | 1,871 | 2,625 | 52,549 | 162 | 1,072 | 50,177 |
| **RHODE ISLAND** | | | | | | | | | | | | |
| Under 18 | 6 | 19 | 3 | 93 | 351 | 170 | 1 | 17 | 546 | 0 | 106 | 16 |
| Total all ages | 140 | 642 | 128 | 352 | 1,184 | 457 | 97 | 102 | 4,081 | 3 | 172 | 2,601 |
| **SOUTH CAROLINA** | | | | | | | | | | | | |
| Under 18 | 26 | 59 | 19 | 235 | 769 | 538 | 2 | 110 | 2,478 | 1 | 13 | 106 |
| Total all ages | 1,818 | 10,245 | 418 | 2,036 | 3,212 | 2,436 | 642 | 573 | 27,548 | 337 | 1,307 | 16,993 |
| **SOUTH DAKOTA** | | | | | | | | | | | | |
| Under 18 | 2 | 46 | 7 | 32 | 220 | 65 | 1 | 22 | 456 | 0 | 188 | 84 |
| Total all ages | 95 | 688 | 40 | 86 | 610 | 140 | 14 | 77 | 2,868 | 0 | 404 | 5,720 |
| **TENNESSEE** | | | | | | | | | | | | |
| Under 18 | 54 | 165 | 13 | 83 | 1,396 | 663 | 19 | 158 | 3,002 | 100 | 38 | 135 |
| Total all ages | 2,983 | 7,757 | 879 | 863 | 4,362 | 3,244 | 2,531 | 708 | 35,812 | 443 | 2,004 | 24,141 |
| **TEXAS** | | | | | | | | | | | | |
| Under 18 | 218 | 399 | 22 | 177 | 5,433 | 1,413 | 124 | 642 | 16,236 | 70 | 57 | 993 |
| Total all ages | 7,768 | 12,843 | 492 | 901 | 14,122 | 11,365 | 8,604 | 4,139 | 144,329 | 688 | 5,271 | 93,856 |
| **UTAH** | | | | | | | | | | | | |
| Under 18 | 18 | 82 | 3 | 180 | 1,754 | 383 | 24 | 321 | 1,900 | 11 | 76 | 119 |
| Total all ages | 1,062 | 1,171 | 28 | 795 | 4,293 | 1,308 | 550 | 886 | 11,224 | 53 | 2,010 | 7,805 |
| **VERMONT** | | | | | | | | | | | | |
| Under 18 | 4 | 6 | 1 | 24 | 114 | 15 | 1 | 9 | 137 | 0 | 8 | 25 |
| Total all ages | 76 | 316 | 48 | 146 | 469 | 24 | 7 | 41 | 1,433 | 0 | 361 | 3,396 |

[4] See Appendix I for details.

[7] Forcible rape figures for Illinois include only those data provided by Rockford. The forcible rape figures for Minnesota include only those provided by the cities of St. Paul and Minneapolis. See Appendix I for details.

## Table 69. State Arrests, 2009—*Continued*

(Number.)

| State | Liquor laws | Drunkenness[3] | Disorderly conduct | Vagrancy | All other offenses (except traffic) | Suspicion | Curfew and loitering law violations | Runaways | Number of agencies | 2009 estimated population |
|---|---|---|---|---|---|---|---|---|---|---|
| **MINNESOTA[7]** | | | | | | | | | | |
| Under 18 | 5,598 | 0 | 3,581 | 8 | 5,138 | 0 | 3,047 | 4,060 | 320 | 5,094,567 |
| Total all ages | 25,784 | 0 | 13,099 | 432 | 32,761 | 0 | 3,047 | 4,060 | | |
| **MISSISSIPPI** | | | | | | | | | | |
| Under 18 | 225 | 132 | 1,970 | 5 | 2,012 | 3 | 492 | 222 | 94 | 1,630,766 |
| Total all ages | 2,181 | 6,062 | 8,928 | 119 | 40,364 | 118 | 492 | 222 | | |
| **MISSOURI** | | | | | | | | | | |
| Under 18 | 2,460 | 19 | 2,370 | 35 | 6,683 | 0 | 1,832 | 2,867 | 385 | 5,543,053 |
| Total all ages | 12,897 | 249 | 14,097 | 172 | 105,040 | 0 | 1,832 | 2,867 | | |
| **MONTANA** | | | | | | | | | | |
| Under 18 | 1,261 | 0 | 588 | 0 | 934 | 0 | 553 | 504 | 96 | 905,870 |
| Total all ages | 4,581 | 0 | 3,216 | 12 | 5,579 | 0 | 553 | 504 | | |
| **NEBRASKA** | | | | | | | | | | |
| Under 18 | 1,924 | 0 | 790 | 3 | 2,166 | 0 | 292 | 448 | 201 | 1,591,339 |
| Total all ages | 10,741 | 0 | 3,993 | 30 | 15,917 | 0 | 292 | 448 | | |
| **NEVADA** | | | | | | | | | | |
| Under 18 | 2,175 | 43 | 1,228 | 25 | 3,964 | 8 | 2,697 | 1,040 | 33 | 2,546,856 |
| Total all ages | 10,299 | 145 | 3,417 | 2,123 | 58,500 | 10 | 2,697 | 1,040 | | |
| **NEW HAMPSHIRE** | | | | | | | | | | |
| Under 18 | 955 | 263 | 289 | 0 | 1,840 | 0 | 27 | 338 | 151 | 1,160,414 |
| Total all ages | 5,436 | 4,022 | 1,500 | 78 | 14,268 | 0 | 27 | 338 | | |
| **NEW JERSEY** | | | | | | | | | | |
| Under 18 | 2,239 | 0 | 3,653 | 30 | 7,106 | 0 | 5,659 | 3,803 | 508 | 8,522,309 |
| Total all ages | 6,956 | 0 | 21,799 | 1,483 | 152,857 | 0 | 5,659 | 3,803 | | |
| **NEW MEXICO** | | | | | | | | | | |
| Under 18 | 597 | 21 | 561 | 63 | 1,756 | 0 | 15 | 449 | 67 | 1,531,579 |
| Total all ages | 4,488 | 778 | 3,079 | 65 | 41,453 | 50 | 15 | 449 | | |
| **NEW YORK[4]** | | | | | | | | | | |
| Under 18 | 895 | 0 | 2,163 | 48 | 7,086 | 0 | 0 | 0 | 530 | 10,719,319 |
| Total all ages | 5,165 | 0 | 14,615 | 875 | 76,371 | 0 | 0 | 0 | | |
| **NORTH CAROLINA** | | | | | | | | | | |
| Under 18 | 1,187 | 0 | 3,354 | 0 | 5,608 | 0 | 0 | 1,093 | 322 | 6,933,046 |
| Total all ages | 8,567 | 0 | 12,200 | 0 | 111,324 | 0 | 0 | 1,093 | | |
| **NORTH DAKOTA** | | | | | | | | | | |
| Under 18 | 957 | 0 | 752 | 0 | 1,019 | 0 | 328 | 535 | 81 | 611,734 |
| Total all ages | 5,430 | 399 | 1,867 | 4 | 5,312 | 0 | 328 | 535 | | |
| **OHIO** | | | | | | | | | | |
| Under 18 | 1,984 | 67 | 3,171 | 23 | 9,073 | 7 | 1,570 | 673 | 414 | 8,137,156 |
| Total all ages | 12,405 | 4,096 | 21,065 | 55 | 68,869 | 41 | 1,570 | 673 | | |
| **OKLAHOMA** | | | | | | | | | | |
| Under 18 | 345 | 705 | 1,314 | 0 | 2,717 | 0 | 1,877 | 2,502 | 300 | 3,526,827 |
| Total all ages | 2,679 | 22,586 | 3,627 | 3 | 39,640 | 0 | 1,877 | 2,502 | | |
| **OREGON** | | | | | | | | | | |
| Under 18 | 3,434 | 0 | 1,506 | 0 | 3,276 | 0 | 1,785 | 1,571 | 154 | 3,612,440 |
| Total all ages | 16,900 | 0 | 8,818 | 8 | 19,711 | 0 | 1,785 | 1,571 | | |
| **PENNSYLVANIA** | | | | | | | | | | |
| Under 18 | 5,717 | 319 | 15,481 | 176 | 6,409 | 0 | 22,221 | 1,654 | 1,071 | 11,813,884 |
| Total all ages | 23,047 | 23,852 | 59,739 | 1,342 | 51,764 | 0 | 22,221 | 1,654 | | |
| **RHODE ISLAND** | | | | | | | | | | |
| Under 18 | 122 | 0 | 902 | 0 | 756 | 0 | 18 | 30 | 46 | 1,018,309 |
| Total all ages | 894 | 9 | 3,128 | 2 | 10,891 | 0 | 18 | 30 | | |
| **SOUTH CAROLINA** | | | | | | | | | | |
| Under 18 | 784 | 108 | 3,072 | 0 | 2,588 | 0 | 61 | 433 | 432 | 4,397,223 |
| Total all ages | 10,325 | 11,750 | 16,183 | 1,239 | 35,530 | 0 | 61 | 433 | | |
| **SOUTH DAKOTA** | | | | | | | | | | |
| Under 18 | 1,400 | 14 | 298 | 0 | 520 | 0 | 114 | 662 | 105 | 674,759 |
| Total all ages | 5,023 | 96 | 1,843 | 167 | 2,197 | 0 | 114 | 662 | | |
| **TENNESSEE** | | | | | | | | | | |
| Under 18 | 1,118 | 279 | 3,289 | 0 | 5,644 | 0 | 1,992 | 1,831 | 386 | 4,889,352 |
| Total all ages | 7,110 | 19,681 | 9,941 | 71 | 92,060 | 0 | 1,992 | 1,831 | | |
| **TEXAS** | | | | | | | | | | |
| Under 18 | 5,344 | 3,099 | 20,955 | 1,050 | 28,876 | 0 | 11,644 | 12,162 | 996 | 24,280,041 |
| Total all ages | 28,517 | 139,684 | 40,885 | 2,530 | 340,401 | 0 | 11,644 | 12,162 | | |
| **UTAH** | | | | | | | | | | |
| Under 18 | 2,421 | 241 | 1,857 | 72 | 5,727 | 0 | 1,375 | 593 | 121 | 2,747,172 |
| Total all ages | 11,099 | 5,123 | 5,839 | 215 | 45,602 | 0 | 1,375 | 593 | | |
| **VERMONT** | | | | | | | | | | |
| Under 18 | 203 | 1 | 125 | 0 | 210 | 0 | 0 | 2 | 77 | 605,536 |
| Total all ages | 686 | 5 | 830 | 0 | 3,310 | 0 | 0 | 2 | | |

[3] Drunkenness is not considered a crime in some states; therefore, the figures vary widely from state to state.
[4] See Appendix I for details.
[7] Forcible rape figures for Illinois include only those data provided by Rockford. The forcible rape figures for Minnesota include only those provided by the cities of St. Paul and Minneapolis. See Appendix I for details.

## Table 69. State Arrests, 2009—*Continued*

(Number.)

| State | Total all classes[1] | Violent crime[2] | Property crime[2] | Murder and non-negligent man-slaughter | Forcible rape | Robbery | Aggra-vated assault | Burglary | Larceny-theft | Motor vehicle theft | Arson | Other assaults |
|---|---|---|---|---|---|---|---|---|---|---|---|---|
| **VIRGINIA** | | | | | | | | | | | | |
| Under 18 | 33,789 | 783 | 6,602 | 12 | 40 | 300 | 431 | 966 | 5,341 | 186 | 109 | 4,514 |
| Total all ages | 326,202 | 6,638 | 35,284 | 267 | 300 | 1,866 | 4,205 | 4,304 | 29,782 | 919 | 279 | 37,837 |
| **WASHINGTON** | | | | | | | | | | | | |
| Under 18 | 26,080 | 1,210 | 7,662 | 16 | 91 | 452 | 651 | 1,228 | 5,966 | 339 | 129 | 3,801 |
| Total all ages | 200,290 | 7,580 | 32,771 | 138 | 620 | 1,954 | 4,868 | 4,453 | 26,871 | 1,204 | 243 | 26,202 |
| **WEST VIRGINIA** | | | | | | | | | | | | |
| Under 18 | 2,244 | 56 | 625 | 2 | 4 | 18 | 32 | 60 | 532 | 30 | 3 | 325 |
| Total all ages | 47,529 | 1,459 | 6,015 | 42 | 63 | 201 | 1,153 | 791 | 5,016 | 180 | 28 | 5,841 |
| **WISCONSIN** | | | | | | | | | | | | |
| Under 18 | 84,143 | 1,374 | 13,644 | 10 | 142 | 494 | 728 | 1,582 | 11,482 | 494 | 86 | 3,321 |
| Total all ages | 369,962 | 7,521 | 40,465 | 142 | 633 | 1,589 | 5,157 | 4,449 | 34,590 | 1,241 | 185 | 18,164 |
| **WYOMING** | | | | | | | | | | | | |
| Under 18 | 6,071 | 47 | 1,008 | 2 | 9 | 0 | 36 | 71 | 877 | 50 | 10 | 669 |
| Total all ages | 38,737 | 577 | 3,061 | 16 | 43 | 30 | 488 | 286 | 2,645 | 118 | 12 | 3,370 |

[1] Does not include traffic arrests.

[2] Violent crimes are offenses of murder and nonnegligent manslaughter, forcible rape, robbery, and aggravated assault. Property crimes are offenses of burglary, larceny-theft, motor vehicle theft, and arson.

## Table 69. State Arrests, 2009—*Continued*

(Number.)

| State | Forgery and counter-feiting | Fraud | Embezzle-ment | Stolen property; buying, receiving, possessing | Vandal-ism | Weapons; carrying, possessing, etc. | Prostitu-tion and commer-cialized vice | Sex offenses (except forcible rape and prosti-tution) | Drug abuse violations | Gamb-ling | Offenses against the family and children | Driving under the influence |
|---|---|---|---|---|---|---|---|---|---|---|---|---|
| **VIRGINIA** | | | | | | | | | | | | |
| Under 18 | 59 | 123 | 53 | 137 | 1,192 | 392 | 1 | 206 | 2,332 | 2 | 40 | 187 |
| Total all ages | 2,229 | 8,195 | 1,660 | 991 | 4,621 | 3,712 | 848 | 1,063 | 29,780 | 89 | 1,484 | 27,623 |
| **WASHINGTON** | | | | | | | | | | | | |
| Under 18 | 40 | 52 | 1 | 318 | 1,683 | 503 | 57 | 165 | 2,217 | 1 | 14 | 224 |
| Total all ages | 1,459 | 1,007 | 100 | 2,215 | 5,981 | 2,378 | 795 | 988 | 16,561 | 3 | 702 | 16,421 |
| **WEST VIRGINIA** | | | | | | | | | | | | |
| Under 18 | 3 | 6 | 4 | 11 | 88 | 20 | 0 | 11 | 201 | 0 | 2 | 25 |
| Total all ages | 383 | 764 | 109 | 254 | 888 | 305 | 125 | 169 | 6,167 | 12 | 74 | 4,780 |
| **WISCONSIN** | | | | | | | | | | | | |
| Under 18 | 56 | 197 | 10 | 578 | 3,370 | 1,095 | 9 | 948 | 4,061 | 53 | 349 | 541 |
| Total all ages | 1,340 | 5,069 | 225 | 1,664 | 9,481 | 3,964 | 371 | 2,600 | 24,446 | 214 | 2,602 | 38,215 |
| **WYOMING** | | | | | | | | | | | | |
| Under 18 | 3 | 12 | 1 | 13 | 237 | 35 | 0 | 17 | 452 | 3 | 17 | 105 |
| Total all ages | 114 | 225 | 13 | 63 | 765 | 113 | 14 | 164 | 2,807 | 3 | 215 | 6,662 |

## Table 69. State Arrests, 2009—*Continued*

(Number.)

| State | Liquor laws | Drunken- ness[3] | Disorderly conduct | Vagrancy | All other offenses (except traffic) | Suspi- cion | Curfew and loitering law violations | Run- aways | Number of agencies | 2009 estimated population |
|---|---|---|---|---|---|---|---|---|---|---|
| **VIRGINIA** | | | | | | | | | | |
| Under 18 | 2,000 | 267 | 1,249 | 0 | 7,722 | 0 | 2,221 | 3,707 | 380 | 7,481,379 |
| Total all ages | 11,864 | 32,711 | 5,575 | 173 | 107,897 | 0 | 2,221 | 3,707 | | |
| **WASHINGTON** | | | | | | | | | | |
| Under 18 | 2,802 | 5 | 612 | 7 | 3,230 | 0 | 30 | 1,446 | 208 | 4,880,479 |
| Total all ages | 9,738 | 6 | 4,542 | 52 | 69,313 | 0 | 30 | 1,446 | | |
| **WEST VIRGINIA** | | | | | | | | | | |
| Under 18 | 154 | 16 | 69 | 0 | 527 | 0 | 65 | 36 | 201 | 925,274 |
| Total all ages | 1,803 | 3,753 | 1,041 | 11 | 13,475 | 0 | 65 | 36 | | |
| **WISCONSIN** | | | | | | | | | | |
| Under 18 | 7,655 | 0 | 16,112 | 15 | 21,982 | 0 | 5,492 | 3,281 | 359 | 5,389,299 |
| Total all ages | 36,051 | 0 | 58,992 | 3,111 | 106,694 | 0 | 5,492 | 3,281 | | |
| **WYOMING** | | | | | | | | | | |
| Under 18 | 963 | 52 | 188 | 3 | 1,357 | 4 | 479 | 406 | 63 | 539,500 |
| Total all ages | 3,934 | 2,700 | 1,329 | 50 | 11,643 | 30 | 479 | 406 | | |

[3] Drunkenness is not considered a crime in some states; therefore, the figures vary widely from state to state.

## SECTION V:

# LAW ENFORCEMENT PERSONNEL

## LAW ENFORCEMENT PERSONNEL

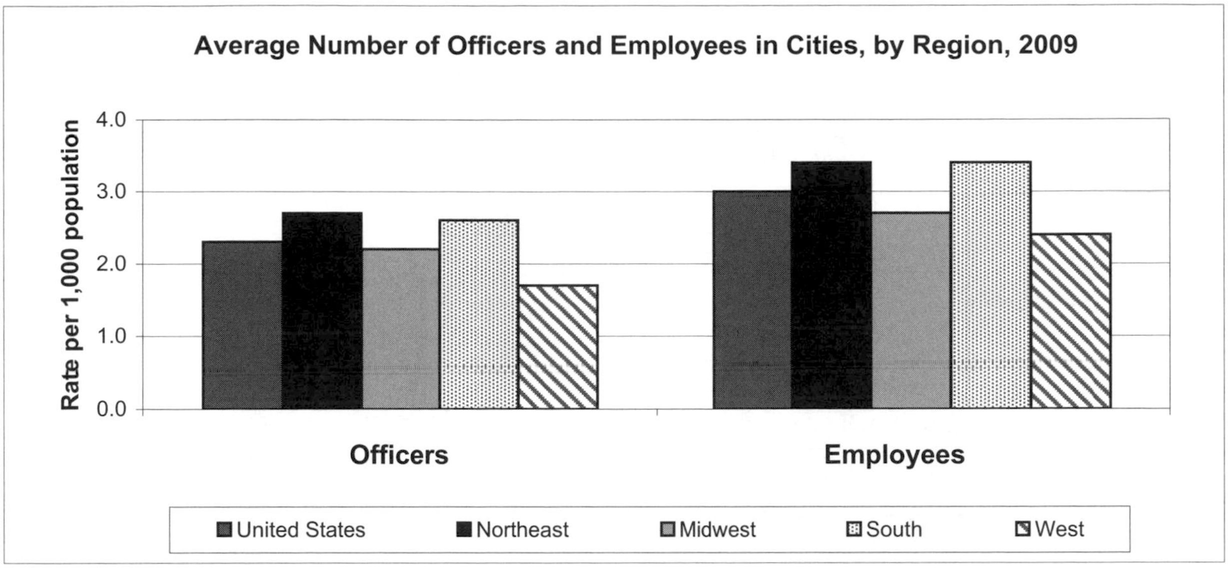


The Uniform Crime Reporting (UCR) Program defines law enforcement officers as individuals who ordinarily carry a firearm and a badge, have full arrest powers, and are paid from governmental funds set aside specifically for sworn law enforcement representatives. Because of law enforcement's varied service requirements and functions, as well as the distinct demographic traits and characteristics of jurisdictions, readers should use caution when drawing comparisons between agencies' staffing levels based upon police employment data from the UCR Program. In addition, the data presented here reflect existing staff levels and should not be interpreted as preferred officer strengths recommended by the FBI. Lastly, it should be noted that the totals given for sworn officers for any particular agency reflect not only the patrol officers on the street but also officers assigned to various other duties such as those in administrative and investigative positions and those assigned to special teams.

Each year, law enforcement agencies across the United States report the total number of sworn law enforcement officers and civilians in their agencies as of October 31 to the UCR Program. Civilian employees include personnel such as clerks, radio dispatchers, meter attendants, stenographers, jailers, correctional officers, and mechanics provided that they are full-time employees of the agency.

This section of *Crime in the United States* presents those data as the number and rate of law enforcement officers and civilian employees throughout the United States. In 2009, 14,614 state, city, university and college, metropolitan and nonmetropolitan county, and other law enforcement agencies employed 706,886 sworn officers and 314,570 civilians, who provided law enforcement services to more than 289 million people nationwide. (Table 74)

The data in this section are broken down by geographic region and division, population group, state, city, university and college, metropolitan and nonmetropolitan county, and other law enforcement agencies. (Information about geographic regions and divisions and population groups can be found in Appendix III.) UCR Program staff compute the rate of sworn officers and law enforcement employees by taking the number of employees (sworn officers only or in combination with civilians), dividing by the population for which the agency provides law enforcement service, and multiplying by 1,000.

- Tables 70 and 71 present the number and rate of law enforcement personnel per 1,000 inhabitants collectively employed by agencies, broken down by geographic region and division by population group.
- Tables 72 and 73 provide a count of law enforcement agencies by population group, based on the employment rate ranges for sworn officer and civilian employees per 1,000 inhabitants.
- Table 74 provides the number and percentage of male and female sworn officers and civilian employees by population group.
- Table 75 lists the percentage of full-time civilian law enforcement employees by population group.
- Table 76 breaks down by state the number of sworn law enforcement officers and civilians employed by state law enforcement agencies.
- Tables 78 to 80 list the number of law enforcement employees for cities, universities and colleges, and metropolitan and nonmetropolitan counties.

- Table 81 supplies employee data for those law enforcement agencies that serve the nation's transit systems, parks and forests, schools and school districts, hospitals, etc.

The demographic traits and characteristics of a jurisdiction affect its requirements for law enforcement service. For instance, a village between two large cities may require more law enforcement than a community of the same size with no urban center nearby. A town with legal gambling may have different law enforcement needs than a town near a military base. A city largely made up of college students may have different law enforcement needs than a city whose residents are mainly retirees.

Similarly, the functions of law enforcement agencies are diverse. Employees of these agencies patrol local streets and major highways, protect citizens in the nation's smallest towns and largest cities, and conduct investigations on offenses at the local and state level. State police in one area may enforce traffic laws on state highways and interstates; in another area, they may be responsible for investigating violent crimes. Sheriff's departments may collect tax monies, serve as the enforcement authority for local and state courts, administer jail facilities, or carry out some combination of these duties. This has an impact on an agency's staffing levels.

Because of the differing service requirements and functions, care should be taken when drawing comparisons between and among the staffing levels of law enforcement agencies. The data in this section are not intended as recommended or preferred officer strength; they should be used merely as guides. Adequate staffing levels can be determined only after careful study of the conditions that affect the service requirements in a particular jurisdiction.

## Rate

The UCR Program computes these rates by taking the number of employees, dividing by the population of the agency's jurisdiction, and multiplying by 1,000. The rate of full-time law enforcement employees (civilian and sworn) per 1,000 inhabitants in the nation for 2009 was 3.5.

Among the nation's four regions, law enforcement agencies in the Northeast and the South had the highest rate of law enforcement employees in 2009, with 3.4 per 1,000 inhabitants. Agencies in the Midwest had 2.7 law enforcement employees per 1,000 inhabitants, followed by the West (2.4). (Table 70)

An examination of the 2009 law enforcement employee data by population group showed that the nation's cities had a collective rate of 3.0 law enforcement employees per 1,000 inhabitants. Cities with fewer than 10,000 inhabitants had the highest rate of law enforcement employees, with 4.5 per 1,000 inhabitants. Cities with 25,000 to 49,999 inhabitants and cities with 50,000 to 99,999 inhabitants had the lowest rate of law enforcement employees (2.3 per 1,000 in population). The nation's largest cities, those with 250,000 or more inhabitants, averaged 3.6 law enforcement employees for every 1,000 inhabitants. (Table 70)

## Sworn Personnel

An analysis of the 2009 data showed that law enforcement agencies in the cities in the Northeast had the highest rate of sworn officers—2.7 per 1,000 inhabitants, followed by the South (2.6), the Midwest (2.2), and the West (1.7). (Table 71)

By population group in 2009, there were 2.3 sworn officers for each 1,000 resident population in the nation's cities collectively. This rate was unchanged from the 2007 and 2008 data. Cities with fewer than 10,000 inhabitants had the highest rate at 3.5 sworn officers per 1,000 inhabitants. The nation's largest cities, those with 250,000 or more inhabitants, averaged 2.8 officers per 1,000 inhabitants. (Table 71)

Males accounted for 88.3 percent of all full-time sworn law enforcement officers in 2009. Cities with populations of 1 million and over employed the highest percentage (18.2) of full-time female officers. Of the city population groups, cities with populations of 10,000 to 24,999 inhabitants employed the highest percentage (92.2) of male officers. In metropolitan counties, 86.5 percent of officers were male, and in nonmetropolitan counties, 92.7 percent of officers were male. (Table 74)

## Civilian Employees

Civilian employees provide a myriad of services to the nation's law enforcement and criminal justice agencies. Among other duties, they dispatch officers, provide administrative and record-keeping support, and query local, state, and national databases.

In 2009, 30.8 percent of all law enforcement employees in the nation were civilians. Female employees accounted for 61.0 percent of all full-time civilian law enforcement employees in 2009. In cities, civilians made up 22.7 percent of law enforcement agencies employees. Civilians made up 41.6 percent of law enforcement employees in metropolitan counties, 41.9 percent of law enforcement employees in nonmetropolitan counties, and 34.5 percent of law enforcement employees in suburban areas. (Table 74)

## Table 70. Full-Time Law Enforcement Employees,[1] by Geographic Region and Division and Population Group, 2009

(Number, rate per 1,000 population.)

| Geographic region/division | Total (11,218 cities; population 195,945,107) | Group I (75 cities, 250,000 and over; population 56,942,042) | Group II (188 cities, 100,000 to 249,999; population 27,843,405) | Group III (439 cities, 50,000 to 99,999; population 29,972,217) | Group IV (815 cities, 25,000 to 49,999; population 27,953,975) | Group V (1,839 cities, 10,000 to 24,999; population 29,047,897) |
|---|---|---|---|---|---|---|
| **TOTAL** | | | | | | |
| Number of employees | 584,672 | 206,064 | 67,620 | 67,603 | 64,238 | 70,228 |
| Average number of employees per 1,000 inhabitants | 3.0 | 3.6 | 2.4 | 2.3 | 2.3 | 2.4 |
| **Northeast** | | | | | | |
| Number of employees | 151,716 | 64,615 | 9,687 | 16,159 | 18,881 | 20,248 |
| Average number of employees per 1,000 inhabitants | 3.4 | 5.7 | 3.4 | 2.6 | 2.3 | 2.2 |
| New England | | | | | | |
| Number of employees | 34,094 | 2,760 | 4,645 | 5,886 | 6,891 | 7,274 |
| Average number of employees per 1,000 inhabitants | 2.7 | 4.4 | 3.2 | 2.3 | 2.2 | 2.2 |
| Middle Atlantic | | | | | | |
| Number of employees | 117,622 | 61,855 | 5,042 | 10,273 | 11,990 | 12,974 |
| Average number of employees per 1,000 inhabitants | 3.7 | 5.7 | 3.7 | 2.7 | 2.4 | 2.2 |
| **Midwest** | | | | | | |
| Number of employees | 121,536 | 36,221 | 9,015 | 14,556 | 16,570 | 19,284 |
| Average number of employees per 1,000 inhabitants | 2.7 | 3.7 | 2.2 | 2.0 | 2.1 | 2.2 |
| East North Central | | | | | | |
| Number of employees | 88,596 | 28,177 | 6,120 | 10,470 | 13,110 | 13,888 |
| Average number of employees per 1,000 inhabitants | 2.7 | 3.9 | 2.3 | 2.1 | 2.1 | 2.2 |
| West North Central | | | | | | |
| Number of employees | 32,940 | 8,044 | 2,895 | 4,086 | 3,460 | 5,396 |
| Average number of employees per 1,000 inhabitants | 2.5 | 3.1 | 2.1 | 1.7 | 2.0 | 2.2 |
| **South** | | | | | | |
| Number of employees | 192,563 | 52,258 | 29,507 | 20,382 | 18,880 | 23,655 |
| Average number of employees per 1,000 inhabitants | 3.4 | 3.2 | 2.8 | 2.7 | 2.8 | 3.1 |
| South Atlantic | | | | | | |
| Number of employees | 90,954 | 22,032 | 15,954 | 10,956 | 9,003 | 10,685 |
| Average number of employees per 1,000 inhabitants | 3.9 | 4.2 | 3.0 | 3.0 | 3.1 | 3.3 |
| East South Central | | | | | | |
| Number of employees | 34,869 | 6,482 | 5,328 | 2,346 | 4,301 | 5,706 |
| Average number of employees per 1,000 inhabitants | 3.5 | 2.9 | 3.3 | 3.1 | 2.9 | 3.1 |
| West South Central | | | | | | |
| Number of employees | 66,740 | 23,744 | 8,225 | 7,080 | 5,576 | 7,264 |
| Average number of employees per 1,000 inhabitants | 2.8 | 2.7 | 2.2 | 2.3 | 2.4 | 2.7 |
| **West** | | | | | | |
| Number of employees | 118,857 | 52,970 | 19,411 | 16,506 | 9,907 | 7,041 |
| Average number of employees per 1,000 inhabitants | 2.4 | 2.7 | 1.9 | 1.8 | 1.9 | 2.2 |
| Mountain | | | | | | |
| Number of employees | 42,897 | 18,788 | 6,466 | 4,751 | 3,737 | 2,625 |
| Average number of employees per 1,000 inhabitants | 2.6 | 2.8 | 2.1 | 2.0 | 2.0 | 2.5 |
| Pacific | | | | | | |
| Number of employees | 75,960 | 34,182 | 12,945 | 11,755 | 6,170 | 4,416 |
| Average number of employees per 1,000 inhabitants | 2.3 | 2.7 | 1.8 | 1.8 | 1.9 | 2.0 |

[1] Full-time law enforcement employees include civilians.

# Table 70. Full-Time Law Enforcement Employees,[1] by Geographic Region and Division and Population Group, 2009—*Continued*

(Number, rate per 1,000 population.)

| Geographic region/division | Group VI (7,862 cities, under 10,000; population 24,185,571) | Total city agencies | 2009 estimated city population | County[2] (3,396 agencies; population 93,472,364) | Total city and county agencies | 2009 estimated total agency population | Suburban Area[3] (7,561 agencies; population 122,719,200) |
|---|---|---|---|---|---|---|---|
| **TOTAL** | | | | | | | |
| Number of employees | 108,919 | 11,218 | 195,945,107 | 436,784 | 14,614 | 289,417,471 | 471,235 |
| Average number of employees per 1,000 inhabitants | 4.5 | | | 4.7 | | | 3.8 |
| **Northeast** | | | | | | | |
| Number of employees | 22,126 | 2,555 | 44,463,787 | | | | |
| Average number of employees per 1,000 inhabitants | 3.4 | 5.7 | 3.4 | 2.6 | 2.3 | 2.2 | 3.4 |
| New England | | | | | | | |
| Number of employees | 6,638 | 767 | 12,718,661 | | | | |
| Average number of employees per 1,000 inhabitants | 3.8 | | | | | | |
| Middle Atlantic | | | | | | | |
| Number of employees | 15,488 | 1,788 | 31,745,126 | | | | |
| Average number of employees per 1,000 inhabitants | 3.3 | | | | | | |
| **Midwest** | | | | | | | |
| Number of employees | 25,890 | 3,329 | 45,346,245 | | | | |
| Average number of employees per 1,000 inhabitants | 3.5 | | | | | | |
| East North Central | | | | | | | |
| Number of employees | 16,831 | 2,105 | 32,243,478 | | | | |
| Average number of employees per 1,000 inhabitants | 3.4 | | | | | | |
| West North Central | | | | | | | |
| Number of employees | 9,059 | 1,224 | 13,102,767 | | | | |
| Average number of employees per 1,000 inhabitants | 3.5 | | | | | | |
| **South** | | | | | | | |
| Number of employees | 47,881 | 3,945 | 56,670,646 | | | | |
| Average number of employees per 1,000 inhabitants | 6.2 | | | | | | |
| South Atlantic | | | | | | | |
| Number of employees | 22,324 | 1,621 | 23,306,717 | | | | |
| Average number of employees per 1,000 inhabitants | 7.6 | | | | | | |
| East South Central | | | | | | | |
| Number of employees | 10,706 | 1,016 | 9,875,872 | | | | |
| Average number of employees per 1,000 inhabitants | 5.4 | | | | | | |
| West South Central | | | | | | | |
| Number of employees | 14,851 | 1,308 | 23,488,057 | | | | |
| Average number of employees per 1,000 inhabitants | 5.4 | | | | | | |
| **West** | | | | | | | |
| Number of employees | 13,022 | 1,389 | 49,464,429 | | | | |
| Average number of employees per 1,000 inhabitants | 5.2 | | | | | | |
| Mountain | | | | | | | |
| Number of employees | 6,530 | 625 | 16,208,175 | | | | |
| Average number of employees per 1,000 inhabitants | 5.1 | | | | | | |
| Pacific | | | | | | | |
| Number of employees | 6,492 | 764 | 33,256,254 | | | | |
| Average number of employees per 1,000 inhabitants | 5.3 | | | | | | |

[1] Full-time law enforcement employees include civilians.
[2] The designation county is a combination of both metropolitan and nonmetropolitan counties.
[3] Suburban areas include law enforcement agencies in cities with less than 50,000 inhabitants and county law enforcement agencies that are within a metropolitan statistical area. Suburban areas exclude all metropolitan agencies associated with a principal city. The agencies associated with suburban areas also appear in other groups within this table.

## Table 71. Full-Time Law Enforcement Officers, by Geographic Region and Division and Population Group, 2009

(Number, rate per 1,000 population.)

| Geographic region/division | Total (11,218 cities; population 195,945,107) | Group I (75 cities, 250,000 and over; population 56,942,042) | Group II (188 cities, 100,000 to 249,999; population 27,843,405) | Group III (439 cities, 50,000 to 99,999; population 29,972,217) | Group IV (815 cities, 25,000 to 49,999; population 27,953,975) | Group V (1,839 cities, 10,000 to 24,999; population 29,047,897) |
|---|---|---|---|---|---|---|
| **TOTAL** | | | | | | |
| Number of officers | 452,037 | 157,079 | 51,236 | 51,954 | 50,701 | 56,342 |
| Average number of officers per 1,000 inhabitants | 2.3 | 2.8 | 1.8 | 1.7 | 1.8 | 1.9 |
| **Northeast** | | | | | | |
| Number of officers | 119,716 | 46,977 | 8,037 | 13,362 | 15,834 | 17,095 |
| Average number of officers per 1,000 inhabitants | 2.7 | 4.1 | 2.9 | 2.1 | 2.0 | 1.8 |
| New England | | | | | | |
| Number of officers | 28,095 | 2,177 | 3,913 | 5,029 | 5,753 | 5,937 |
| Average number of officers per 1,000 inhabitants | 2.2 | 3.5 | 2.7 | 2.0 | 1.9 | 1.8 |
| Middle Atlantic | | | | | | |
| Number of officers | 91,621 | 44,800 | 4,124 | 8,333 | 10,081 | 11,158 |
| Average number of officers per 1,000 inhabitants | 2.9 | 4.1 | 3.0 | 2.2 | 2.0 | 1.9 |
| **Midwest** | | | | | | |
| Number of officers | 100,076 | 31,280 | 7,271 | 11,665 | 13,125 | 15,557 |
| Average number of officers per 1,000 inhabitants | 2.2 | 3.2 | 1.8 | 1.6 | 1.6 | 1.8 |
| East North Central | | | | | | |
| Number of officers | 73,889 | 25,247 | 5,006 | 8,366 | 10,411 | 11,219 |
| Average number of officers per 1,000 inhabitants | 2.3 | 3.5 | 1.9 | 1.7 | 1.7 | 1.8 |
| West North Central | | | | | | |
| Number of officers | 26,187 | 6,033 | 2,265 | 3,299 | 2,714 | 4,338 |
| Average number of officers per 1,000 inhabitants | 2.0 | 2.3 | 1.7 | 1.4 | 1.6 | 1.7 |
| **South** | | | | | | |
| Number of officers | 147,235 | 40,469 | 22,404 | 15,406 | 14,603 | 18,448 |
| Average number of officers per 1,000 inhabitants | 2.6 | 2.5 | 2.1 | 2.1 | 2.2 | 2.4 |
| South Atlantic | | | | | | |
| Number of officers | 69,384 | 16,420 | 12,115 | 8,217 | 7,099 | 8,512 |
| Average number of officers per 1,000 inhabitants | 3.0 | 3.1 | 2.2 | 2.3 | 2.5 | 2.6 |
| East South Central | | | | | | |
| Number of officers | 27,569 | 5,393 | 4,079 | 1,822 | 3,369 | 4,439 |
| Average number of officers per 1,000 inhabitants | 2.8 | 2.4 | 2.5 | 2.4 | 2.2 | 2.4 |
| West South Central | | | | | | |
| Number of officers | 50,282 | 18,656 | 6,210 | 5,367 | 4,135 | 5,497 |
| Average number of officers per 1,000 inhabitants | 2.1 | 2.1 | 1.7 | 1.7 | 1.8 | 2.1 |
| **West** | | | | | | |
| Number of officers | 85,010 | 38,353 | 13,524 | 11,521 | 7,139 | 5,242 |
| Average number of officers per 1,000 inhabitants | 1.7 | 2.0 | 1.3 | 1.3 | 1.4 | 1.6 |
| Mountain | | | | | | |
| Number of officers | 30,029 | 12,819 | 4,542 | 3,345 | 2,725 | 1,947 |
| Average number of officers per 1,000 inhabitants | 1.9 | 1.9 | 1.5 | 1.4 | 1.5 | 1.9 |
| Pacific | | | | | | |
| Number of officers | 54,981 | 25,534 | 8,982 | 8,176 | 4,414 | 3,295 |
| Average number of officers per 1,000 inhabitants | 1.7 | 2.0 | 1.2 | 1.2 | 1.3 | 1.5 |

**Table 71. Full-Time Law Enforcement Officers, by Geographic Region and Division and Population Group, 2009** *(Contd.)*

(Number, rate per 1,000 population.)

| Geographic region/division | Group VI (7,862 cities, under 10,000; population 24,185,571) | Total city agencies | 2009 estimated city population | County[1] (3,396 agencies; population 93,472,364) | Total city and county agencies | 2009 estimated total agency population | Suburban Area[2] (7,561 agencies; population 122,719,200) |
|---|---|---|---|---|---|---|---|
| **TOTAL** | | | | | | | |
| Number of officers | 84,725 | 11,218 | 195,945,107 | 254,849 | 14,614 | 289,417,471 | 308,436 |
| Average number of officers per 1,000 inhabitants | 3.5 | | | 2.7 | | | 2.5 |
| **Northeast** | | | | | | | |
| Number of officers | 18,411 | 2,555 | 44,463,787 | | | | |
| Average number of officers per 1,000 inhabitants | 2.8 | | | | | | |
| New England | | | | | | | |
| Number of officers | 5,286 | 767 | 12,718,661 | | | | |
| Average number of officers per 1,000 inhabitants | 3.0 | | | | | | |
| Middle Atlantic | | | | | | | |
| Number of officers | 13,125 | 1,788 | 31,745,126 | | | | |
| Average number of officers per 1,000 inhabitants | 2.8 | | | | | | |
| **Midwest** | | | | | | | |
| Number of officers | 21,178 | 3,329 | 45,346,245 | | | | |
| Average number of officers per 1,000 inhabitants | 2.8 | | | | | | |
| East North Central | | | | | | | |
| Number of officers | 13,640 | 2,105 | 32,243,478 | | | | |
| Average number of officers per 1,000 inhabitants | 2.8 | | | | | | |
| West North Central | | | | | | | |
| Number of officers | 7,538 | 1,224 | 13,102,767 | | | | |
| Average number of officers per 1,000 inhabitants | 2.9 | | | | | | |
| **South** | | | | | | | |
| Number of officers | 35,905 | 3,945 | 56,670,646 | | | | |
| Average number of officers per 1,000 inhabitants | 4.7 | | | | | | |
| South Atlantic | | | | | | | |
| Number of officers | 17,021 | 1,621 | 23,306,717 | | | | |
| Average number of officers per 1,000 inhabitants | 5.8 | | | | | | |
| East South Central | | | | | | | |
| Number of officers | 8,467 | 1,016 | 9,875,872 | | | | |
| Average number of officers per 1,000 inhabitants | 4.3 | | | | | | |
| West South Central | | | | | | | |
| Number of officers | 10,417 | 1,308 | 23,488,057 | | | | |
| Average number of officers per 1,000 inhabitants | 3.8 | | | | | | |
| **West** | | | | | | | |
| Number of officers | 9,231 | 1,389 | 49,464,429 | | | | |
| Average number of officers per 1,000 inhabitants | 3.7 | | | | | | |
| Mountain | | | | | | | |
| Number of officers | 4,651 | 625 | 16,208,175 | | | | |
| Average number of officers per 1,000 inhabitants | 3.6 | | | | | | |
| Pacific | | | | | | | |
| Number of officers | 4,580 | 764 | 33,256,254 | | | | |
| Average number of officers per 1,000 inhabitants | 3.7 | | | | | | |

[1] The designation county is a combination of both metropolitan and nonmetropolitan counties.

[2] Suburban areas include law enforcement agencies in cities with less than 50,000 inhabitants and county law enforcement agencies that are within a metropolitan statistical area. Suburban areas exclude all metropolitan agencies associated with a principal city. The agencies associated with suburban areas also appear in other groups within this table.

## Table 72. Full-Time Law Enforcement Employees,[1] by Rate Range, 2009

(Number, rate per 1,000 population.)

| Rate range | Total cities[2] (10,127 cities; population 195,945,107) | Group I (75 cities, 250,000 and over; population 56,942,042) | Group II (188 cities, 100,000 to 249,999; population 27,843,405) | Group III (439 cities; 50,000 to 99,999; population 29,972,217) | Group IV (815 cities, 25,000 to 49,999; population 27,953,975) | Group V (1,839 cities, 10,000 to 24,999; population 29,047,897) | Group VI (6,771 cities, under 10,000; population 24,185,571) |
|---|---|---|---|---|---|---|---|
| **Total Cities** | | | | | | | |
| Number | 10,127 | 75 | 188 | 439 | 815 | 1,839 | 6,771 |
| Percent[3] | 100.0 | 100.0 | 100.0 | 100.0 | 100.0 | 100.0 | 100.0 |
| 0.1–0.5 | | | | | | | |
| Number | 113 | 0 | 0 | 0 | 1 | 5 | 107 |
| Percent | 1.1 | 0.0 | 0.0 | 0.0 | 0.1 | 0.3 | 1.6 |
| 0.6–1.0 | | | | | | | |
| Number | 458 | 0 | 0 | 8 | 18 | 44 | 388 |
| Percent | 4.5 | 0.0 | 0.0 | 1.8 | 2.2 | 2.4 | 5.7 |
| 1.1–1.5 | | | | | | | |
| Number | 1,171 | 1 | 24 | 60 | 113 | 205 | 768 |
| Percent | 11.6 | 1.3 | 12.8 | 13.7 | 13.9 | 11.1 | 11.3 |
| 1.6–2.0 | | | | | | | |
| Number | 1,937 | 12 | 54 | 132 | 208 | 422 | 1,109 |
| Percent | 19.1 | 16.0 | 28.7 | 30.1 | 25.5 | 22.9 | 16.4 |
| 2.1–2.5 | | | | | | | |
| Number | 1,968 | 21 | 48 | 123 | 242 | 450 | 1,084 |
| Percent | 19.4 | 28.0 | 25.5 | 28.0 | 29.7 | 24.5 | 16.0 |
| 2.6–3.0 | | | | | | | |
| Number | 1,420 | 14 | 29 | 58 | 118 | 314 | 887 |
| Percent | 14.0 | 18.7 | 15.4 | 13.2 | 14.5 | 17.1 | 13.1 |
| 3.1–3.5 | | | | | | | |
| Number | 920 | 8 | 16 | 29 | 64 | 197 | 606 |
| Percent | 9.1 | 10.7 | 8.5 | 6.6 | 7.9 | 10.7 | 8.9 |
| 3.6–4.0 | | | | | | | |
| Number | 666 | 7 | 7 | 14 | 30 | 102 | 506 |
| Percent | 6.6 | 9.3 | 3.7 | 3.2 | 3.7 | 5.5 | 7.5 |
| 4.1–4.5 | | | | | | | |
| Number | 421 | 5 | 8 | 9 | 10 | 49 | 340 |
| Percent | 4.2 | 6.7 | 4.3 | 2.1 | 1.2 | 2.7 | 5.0 |
| 4.6–5.0 | | | | | | | |
| Number | 252 | 2 | 2 | 1 | 6 | 28 | 213 |
| Percent | 2.5 | 2.7 | 1.1 | 0.2 | 0.7 | 1.5 | 3.1 |
| 5.1 and over | | | | | | | |
| Number | 801 | 5 | 0 | 5 | 5 | 23 | 763 |
| Percent | 7.9 | 6.7 | 0.0 | 1.1 | 0.6 | 1.3 | 11.3 |

[1] Full-time law enforcement employees include civilians.
[2] The number of agencies used to compile these figures differs from other tables that include data about law enforcement employees because agencies with no resident population are excluded from this table. These agencies include those associated with universities and colleges (see Table 79) and other agencies (see Table 81), as well as some state agencies that have concurrent jurisdiction with other local law enforcement.
[3] Because of rounding, the percentages may not add to 100.0.

# Table 73. Full-Time Law Enforcement Officers, by Rate Range, 2009

(Number, rate per 1,000 population.)

| Rate range | Total cities[1] (10,127 cities; population 195,945,107) | Group I (75 cities, 250,000 and over; population 56,942,042) | Group II (188 cities, 100,000 to 249,999; population 27,843,405) | Group III (439 cities, 50,000 to 99,999; population 29,972,217) | Group IV (815 cities, 25,000 to 49,999; population 27,953,975) | Group V (1,839 cities, 10,000 to 24,999; population 29,047,897) | Group VI (6,771 cities, under 10,000; population 24,185,571) |
|---|---|---|---|---|---|---|---|
| **Total Cities** | | | | | | | |
| Number | 10,127 | 75 | 188 | 439 | 815 | 1,839 | 6,771 |
| Percent[2] | 100.0 | 100.0 | 100.0 | 100.0 | 100.0 | 100.0 | 100.0 |
| 0.1–0.5 | | | | | | | |
| Number | 133 | 0 | 0 | 0 | 1 | 7 | 125 |
| Percent | 1.3 | 0.0 | 0.0 | 0.0 | 0.1 | 0.4 | 1.8 |
| 0.6–1.0 | | | | | | | |
| Number | 635 | 2 | 14 | 41 | 54 | 87 | 437 |
| Percent | 6.3 | 2.7 | 7.4 | 9.3 | 6.6 | 4.7 | 6.5 |
| 1.1–1.5 | | | | | | | |
| Number | 1,904 | 11 | 64 | 144 | 236 | 424 | 1,025 |
| Percent | 18.8 | 14.7 | 34.0 | 32.8 | 29.0 | 23.1 | 15.1 |
| 1.6–2.0 | | | | | | | |
| Number | 2,593 | 24 | 56 | 145 | 291 | 644 | 1,433 |
| Percent | 25.6 | 32.0 | 29.8 | 33.0 | 35.7 | 35.0 | 21.2 |
| 2.1–2.5 | | | | | | | |
| Number | 1,840 | 16 | 29 | 70 | 137 | 364 | 1,224 |
| Percent | 18.2 | 21.3 | 15.4 | 15.9 | 16.8 | 19.8 | 18.1 |
| 2.6–3.0 | | | | | | | |
| Number | 1,104 | 9 | 14 | 20 | 72 | 181 | 808 |
| Percent | 10.9 | 12.0 | 7.4 | 4.6 | 8.8 | 9.8 | 11.9 |
| 3.1–3.5 | | | | | | | |
| Number | 657 | 5 | 5 | 11 | 15 | 83 | 538 |
| Percent | 6.5 | 6.7 | 2.7 | 2.5 | 1.8 | 4.5 | 7.9 |
| 3.6–4.0 | | | | | | | |
| Number | 390 | 2 | 6 | 3 | 6 | 32 | 341 |
| Percent | 3.9 | 2.7 | 3.2 | 0.7 | 0.7 | 1.7 | 5.0 |
| 4.1–4.5 | | | | | | | |
| Number | 244 | 2 | 0 | 4 | 1 | 10 | 227 |
| Percent | 2.4 | 2.7 | 0.0 | 0.9 | 0.1 | 0.5 | 3.4 |
| 4.6–5.0 | | | | | | | |
| Number | 159 | 3 | 0 | 1 | 0 | 2 | 153 |
| Percent | 1.6 | 4.0 | 0.0 | 0.2 | 0.0 | 0.1 | 2.3 |
| 5.1 and over | | | | | | | |
| Number | 468 | 1 | 0 | 0 | 2 | 5 | 460 |
| Percent | 4.6 | 1.3 | 0.0 | 0.0 | 0.2 | 0.3 | 6.8 |

[1] The number of agencies used to compile these figures differs from other tables that include data about law enforcement officers because agencies with no resident population are excluded from this table. These agencies include those associated with universities and colleges (see Table 79) and other agencies (see Table 81), as well as some state agencies that have concurrent jurisdiction with other local law enforcement.

[2] Because of rounding, the percentages may not add to 100.0.

## Table 74. Full-Time Law Enforcement Employees, by Population Group, Percent Male and Female, 2009

(Number, percent.)

| Population group | Total law enforcement employees | Percent law enforcement employees | | Total officers | Percent officers | | Total civilians | Percent civilians | | Number of agencies | 2009 estimated population |
|---|---|---|---|---|---|---|---|---|---|---|---|
| | | Male | Female | | Male | Female | | Male | Female | | |
| **TOTAL AGENCIES:** | 1,021,456 | 73.1 | 26.9 | 706,886 | 88.3 | 11.7 | 314,570 | 39.0 | 61.0 | 14,614 | 289,417,471 |
| **Total Cities** | 584,672 | 75.4 | 24.6 | 452,037 | 88.2 | 11.8 | 132,635 | 31.5 | 68.5 | 11,218 | 195,945,107 |
| GROUP I (250,000 and over) | 206,064 | 71.6 | 28.4 | 157,079 | 83.2 | 16.8 | 48,985 | 34.2 | 65.8 | 75 | 56,942,042 |
| 1,000,000 and over (Group I subset) | 111,779 | 70.0 | 30.0 | 83,976 | 81.8 | 18.2 | 27,803 | 34.4 | 65.6 | 10 | 25,873,144 |
| 500,000 to 999,999 (Group I subset) | 56,824 | 74.6 | 25.4 | 44,603 | 84.5 | 15.5 | 12,221 | 38.3 | 61.7 | 25 | 17,183,941 |
| 250,000 to 499,999 (Group I subset) | 37,461 | 71.7 | 28.3 | 28,500 | 85.4 | 14.6 | 8,961 | 27.9 | 72.1 | 40 | 13,884,957 |
| GROUP II (100,000 to 249,999) | 67,620 | 73.0 | 27.0 | 51,236 | 88.1 | 11.9 | 16,384 | 25.9 | 74.1 | 188 | 27,843,405 |
| GROUP III (50,000 to 99,999) | 67,603 | 76.1 | 23.9 | 51,954 | 90.6 | 9.4 | 15,649 | 27.9 | 72.1 | 439 | 29,972,217 |
| GROUP IV (25,000 to 49,999) | 64,238 | 77.8 | 22.2 | 50,701 | 91.4 | 8.6 | 13,537 | 26.7 | 73.3 | 815 | 27,953,975 |
| GROUP V (10,000 to 24,999) | 70,228 | 79.4 | 20.6 | 56,342 | 92.2 | 7.8 | 13,886 | 27.6 | 72.4 | 1,839 | 29,047,897 |
| GROUP VI (under 10,000) | 108,919 | 79.4 | 20.6 | 84,725 | 91.5 | 8.5 | 24,194 | 37.2 | 62.8 | 7,862 | 24,185,571 |
| **Metropolitan Counties** | 303,722 | 69.2 | 30.8 | 177,518 | 86.5 | 13.5 | 126,204 | 45.0 | 55.0 | 1,245 | 65,937,797 |
| **Nonmetropolitan Counties** | 133,062 | 71.9 | 28.1 | 77,331 | 92.7 | 7.3 | 55,731 | 43.0 | 57.0 | 2,151 | 27,534,567 |
| **SUBURBAN AREAS**[1] | 471,235 | 72.7 | 27.3 | 308,436 | 88.6 | 11.4 | 162,799 | 42.6 | 57.4 | 7,561 | 122,719,200 |

[1] Suburban areas include law enforcement agencies in cities with less than 50,000 inhabitants and county law enforcement agencies that are within a metropolitan statistical area. Suburban areas exclude all metropolitan agencies associated with a principal city. The agencies associated with suburban areas also appear in other groups within this table.

## Table 75. Full-Time Civilian Law Enforcement Employees, by Population Group, 2009

(Number, percent.)

| Population group | Percent civilian employees | Number of Agencies | 2009 estimated population |
|---|---|---|---|
| **TOTAL AGENCIES:** | 30.8 | 14,614 | 289,417,471 |
| **Total Cities** | 22.7 | 11,218 | 195,945,107 |
| GROUP I (250,000 and over) | 23.8 | 75 | 56,942,042 |
| 1,000,000 and over (Group I subset) | 24.9 | 10 | 25,873,144 |
| 500,000 to 999,999 (Group I subset) | 21.5 | 25 | 17,183,941 |
| 250,000 to 499,999 (Group I subset) | 23.9 | 40 | 13,884,957 |
| GROUP II (100,000 to 249,999) | 24.2 | 188 | 27,843,405 |
| GROUP III (50,000 to 99,999) | 23.1 | 439 | 29,972,217 |
| GROUP IV (25,000 to 49,999) | 21.1 | 815 | 27,953,975 |
| GROUP V (10,000 to 24,999) | 19.8 | 1,839 | 29,047,897 |
| GROUP VI (under 10,000) | 22.2 | 7,862 | 24,185,571 |
| **Metropolitan Counties** | 41.6 | 1,245 | 65,937,797 |
| **Nonmetropolitan Counties** | 41.9 | 2,151 | 27,534,567 |
| **SUBURBAN AREAS**[1] | 34.5 | 7,561 | 122,719,200 |

[1] Suburban areas include law enforcement agencies in cities with less than 50,000 inhabitants and county law enforcement agencies that are within a metropolitan statistical area. Suburban areas exclude all metropolitan agencies associated with a principal city. The agencies associated with suburban areas also appear in other groups within this table.

## Table 76. Full-Time State Law Enforcement Employees, by State, 2009

(Number.)

| State/agency | Total law enforcement employees | Total officers | | Total civilians | |
|---|---|---|---|---|---|
| | | Male | Female | Male | Female |
| **Alabama** | | | | | |
| Department of Public Safety | 1,438 | 766 | 22 | 174 | 476 |
| Other state agencies | 268 | 211 | 10 | 7 | 40 |
| **Alaska** | | | | | |
| State Troopers | 608 | 352 | 11 | 111 | 134 |
| **Arizona** | | | | | |
| Department of Public Safety | 2,065 | 1,143 | 67 | 341 | 514 |
| Other state agencies | 62 | 29 | 2 | 19 | 12 |
| **Arkansas** | | | | | |
| State Police | 963 | 533 | 26 | 122 | 282 |
| Other state agencies | 34 | 29 | 1 | 0 | 4 |
| **California** | | | | | |
| Highway Patrol | 11,182 | 6,905 | 627 | 1,654 | 1,996 |
| Other state agencies | 1,117 | 846 | 229 | 9 | 33 |
| **Colorado** | | | | | |
| State Patrol | 1,010 | 686 | 50 | 81 | 193 |
| Other state agencies | 277 | 76 | 32 | 44 | 125 |
| **Connecticut** | | | | | |
| State Police | 1,679 | 1,065 | 79 | 227 | 308 |
| Other state agencies | 35 | 25 | 1 | 7 | 2 |
| **Delaware** | | | | | |
| State Police | 893 | 593 | 75 | 98 | 127 |
| Other state agencies | 610 | 267 | 100 | 57 | 186 |
| **Florida** | | | | | |
| Highway Patrol | 2,226 | 1,501 | 181 | 225 | 319 |
| Other state agencies | 1,293 | 914 | 98 | 103 | 178 |
| **Georgia** | | | | | |
| Department of Public Safety | 1,515 | 781 | 23 | 350 | 361 |
| Other state agencies | 1,258 | 413 | 53 | 307 | 485 |
| **Idaho** | | | | | |
| State Police | 468 | 245 | 11 | 67 | 145 |
| **Illinois** | | | | | |
| State Police | 3,413 | 1,854 | 223 | 500 | 836 |
| Other state agencies | 457 | 291 | 23 | 87 | 56 |
| **Indiana** | | | | | |
| State Police | 1,921 | 1,227 | 66 | 263 | 365 |
| Other state agencies | 106 | 81 | 17 | 0 | 8 |
| **Iowa** | | | | | |
| Department of Public Safety | 991 | 613 | 45 | 156 | 177 |
| **Kansas** | | | | | |
| Highway Patrol | 845 | 524 | 18 | 120 | 183 |
| Other state agencies | 542 | 300 | 16 | 90 | 136 |
| **Kentucky** | | | | | |
| State Police | 1,694 | 860 | 26 | 429 | 379 |
| Other state agencies | 544 | 495 | 32 | 7 | 10 |
| **Louisiana** | | | | | |
| State Police | 1,692 | 1,154 | 50 | 126 | 362 |
| Other state agencies | 44 | 35 | 3 | 0 | 6 |
| **Maine** | | | | | |
| State Police | 435 | 295 | 23 | 55 | 62 |
| Other state agencies[1] | 53 | 23 | 1 | 19 | 10 |
| **Maryland** | | | | | |
| State Police | 2,184 | 1,388 | 107 | 352 | 337 |
| Other state agencies | 1,637 | 859 | 136 | 313 | 329 |
| **Massachusetts** | | | | | |
| State Police | 2,774 | 2,074 | 173 | 220 | 307 |
| Other state agencies | 390 | 299 | 49 | 17 | 25 |
| **Michigan** | | | | | |
| State Police | 2,539 | 1,470 | 199 | 357 | 513 |
| **Minnesota** | | | | | |
| State Patrol | 808 | 510 | 56 | 120 | 122 |
| Other state agencies | 52 | 10 | 0 | 32 | 10 |
| **Mississippi** | | | | | |
| Other State Agencies | 63 | 54 | 3 | 0 | 6 |
| **Missouri** | | | | | |
| State Highway Patrol | 2,336 | 1,042 | 45 | 546 | 703 |
| Other state agencies | 570 | 498 | 26 | 6 | 40 |
| **Montana** | | | | | |
| Highway Patrol | 278 | 214 | 9 | 13 | 42 |
| Other state agencies | 24 | 21 | 0 | 0 | 3 |
| **Nebraska** | | | | | |
| State Patrol | 720 | 458 | 27 | 83 | 152 |
| **Nevada** | | | | | |
| Highway Patrol | 911 | 450 | 48 | 126 | 287 |
| Other state agencies | 52 | 22 | 3 | 12 | 15 |

*Note:* Caution should be used when comparing data from one state to that of another. The responsibilities of the various state police, highway patrol, and department of public safety agencies range from full law enforcement duties to only traffic patrol, which can impact both the level of employment for agencies as well as the ratio of sworn officers to civilians employed. Any valid comparison must take these factors and the other identified variables affecting crime into consideration.

[1] The total employee count includes employees from agencies that are not represented in other law enforcement employee tables.

## Table 76. Full-Time State Law Enforcement Employees, by State, 2009 *(Contd.)*

(Number.)

| State/agency | Total law enforcement employees | Total officers | | Total civilians | |
|---|---|---|---|---|---|
| | | Male | Female | Male | Female |
| **New Hampshire** | | | | | |
| State Police | 496 | 309 | 33 | 49 | 105 |
| Other state agencies | 36 | 20 | 3 | 5 | 8 |
| **New Jersey** | | | | | |
| State Police | 4,392 | 2,924 | 116 | 637 | 715 |
| Other state agencies | 577 | 458 | 40 | 51 | 28 |
| Port Authority of New York and New Jersey[2] | 1,019 | 854 | 89 | 19 | 57 |
| **New Mexico** | | | | | |
| State Police | 1,132 | 519 | 23 | 324 | 266 |
| **New York** | | | | | |
| State Police | 5,929 | 4,422 | 405 | 468 | 634 |
| Other state agencies | 284 | 242 | 23 | 5 | 14 |
| **North Carolina** | | | | | |
| Highway Patrol | 2,307 | 1,689 | 48 | 332 | 238 |
| Other state agencies | 668 | 491 | 61 | 52 | 64 |
| **North Dakota** | | | | | |
| Highway Patrol | 183 | 126 | 6 | 20 | 31 |
| **Ohio** | | | | | |
| Highway Patrol | 2,576 | 1,386 | 136 | 523 | 531 |
| Other state agencies | 802 | 465 | 37 | 86 | 214 |
| **Oklahoma** | | | | | |
| Department of Public Safety | 1,521 | 813 | 15 | 292 | 401 |
| Other state agencies | 76 | 31 | 3 | 28 | 14 |
| **Oregon** | | | | | |
| State Police | 767 | 528 | 46 | 77 | 116 |
| Other state agencies | 40 | 29 | 9 | 0 | 2 |
| **Pennsylvania** | | | | | |
| State Police | 6,146 | 4,295 | 215 | 725 | 911 |
| Other state agencies | 167 | 139 | 8 | 12 | 8 |
| **Rhode Island** | | | | | |
| State Police | 308 | 236 | 22 | 32 | 18 |
| Other state agencies | 95 | 73 | 4 | 11 | 7 |
| **South Carolina** | | | | | |
| Highway Patrol | 1,032 | 812 | 24 | 66 | 130 |
| Other state agencies[1] | 1,195 | 715 | 133 | 109 | 238 |
| **South Dakota** | | | | | |
| Highway Patrol | 261 | 159 | 5 | 69 | 28 |
| Other state agencies | 145 | 41 | 3 | 36 | 65 |
| **Tennessee** | | | | | |
| Department of Safety | 1,586 | 775 | 36 | 233 | 542 |
| Other state agencies | 1,034 | 582 | 75 | 115 | 262 |
| **Texas** | | | | | |
| Department of Public Safety | 8,196 | 3,309 | 195 | 1,587 | 3,105 |
| **Utah** | | | | | |
| Highway Patrol | 561 | 408 | 18 | 33 | 102 |
| Other state agencies | 160 | 138 | 12 | 6 | 4 |
| **Vermont** | | | | | |
| State Police | 431 | 287 | 29 | 39 | 76 |
| Other state agencies | 104 | 81 | 2 | 4 | 17 |
| **Virginia** | | | | | |
| State Police | 2,551 | 1,760 | 103 | 209 | 479 |
| Other state agencies | 577 | 328 | 49 | 81 | 119 |
| **Washington** | | | | | |
| State Patrol | 2,254 | 1,011 | 83 | 556 | 604 |
| Other State Agencies | 6 | 4 | 0 | 0 | 2 |
| **West Virginia** | | | | | |
| State Police | 1,044 | 664 | 20 | 129 | 231 |
| Other state agencies | 191 | 158 | 1 | 11 | 21 |
| **Wisconsin** | | | | | |
| State Patrol | 646 | 442 | 54 | 61 | 89 |
| Other state agencies | 514 | 407 | 20 | 59 | 28 |
| **Wyoming** | | | | | |
| Highway Patrol | 366 | 196 | 7 | 49 | 114 |

*Note:* Caution should be used when comparing data from one state to that of another. The responsibilities of the various state police, highway patrol, and department of public safety agencies range from full law enforcement duties to only traffic patrol, which can impact both the level of employment for agencies as well as the ratio of sworn officers to civilians employed. Any valid comparison must take these factors and the other identified variables affecting crime into consideration.

[1] The total employee count includes employees from agencies that are not represented in other law enforcement employee tables.

[2] Data reported are the number of law enforcement employees for the state of New Jersey.

## Table 77. Full-Time Law Enforcement Employees, by State, 2009

(Number.)

| State | Total law enforcement employees | Total officers | | Total civilians | | Number of agencies | 2009 estimated population |
|---|---|---|---|---|---|---|---|
| | | Male | Female | Male | Female | | |
| Alabama | 16,917 | 10,438 | 807 | 2,151 | 3,521 | 349 | 4,587,633 |
| Alaska | 1,977 | 1,156 | 106 | 246 | 469 | 39 | 696,273 |
| Arizona | 22,910 | 11,596 | 1,375 | 4,534 | 5,405 | 106 | 6,482,281 |
| Arkansas | 9,970 | 5,682 | 518 | 1,478 | 2,292 | 281 | 2,888,639 |
| California | 121,879 | 69,749 | 10,572 | 14,550 | 27,008 | 461 | 31,832,381 |
| Colorado | 17,435 | 10,286 | 1,499 | 1,868 | 3,782 | 233 | 5,018,161 |
| Connecticut | 10,556 | 7,830 | 792 | 768 | 1,166 | 104 | 3,518,288 |
| Delaware | 3,127 | 1,986 | 310 | 310 | 521 | 54 | 884,765 |
| District of Columbia | 5,189 | 3,492 | 981 | 292 | 424 | 2 | 599,657 |
| Florida | 72,235 | 37,894 | 6,224 | 10,001 | 18,116 | 365 | 17,648,382 |
| Georgia | 34,809 | 21,107 | 3,921 | 3,413 | 6,368 | 444 | 9,154,201 |
| Hawaii | 3,802 | 2,684 | 306 | 251 | 561 | 4 | 1,295,178 |
| Idaho | 4,215 | 2,511 | 179 | 320 | 1,205 | 108 | 1,543,324 |
| Illinois | 50,833 | 30,663 | 5,574 | 6,940 | 7,656 | 736 | 12,675,815 |
| Indiana | 16,856 | 10,326 | 907 | 2,638 | 2,985 | 242 | 5,995,956 |
| Iowa | 8,057 | 4,842 | 439 | 1,067 | 1,709 | 234 | 2,988,922 |
| Kansas | 10,227 | 6,151 | 610 | 1,388 | 2,078 | 342 | 2,498,126 |
| Kentucky | 10,483 | 7,700 | 548 | 925 | 1,310 | 395 | 4,239,650 |
| Louisiana | 15,453 | 9,215 | 1,925 | 1,605 | 2,708 | 156 | 2,771,692 |
| Maine | 2,859 | 2,117 | 134 | 245 | 363 | 134 | 1,317,341 |
| Maryland | 20,609 | 13,584 | 2,080 | 1,863 | 3,082 | 131 | 5,519,662 |
| Massachusetts | 16,783 | 12,802 | 1,153 | 1,138 | 1,690 | 324 | 6,396,251 |
| Michigan | 25,419 | 16,302 | 2,498 | 2,935 | 3,684 | 630 | 9,845,506 |
| Minnesota | 13,709 | 7,806 | 1,076 | 1,984 | 2,843 | 320 | 5,180,883 |
| Mississippi | 8,764 | 4,924 | 493 | 1,419 | 1,928 | 192 | 2,675,080 |
| Missouri | 20,486 | 13,218 | 1,420 | 2,160 | 3,688 | 555 | 5,874,396 |
| Montana | 2,965 | 1,678 | 102 | 539 | 646 | 110 | 972,240 |
| Nebraska | 4,815 | 3,124 | 394 | 334 | 963 | 162 | 1,750,280 |
| Nevada | 10,115 | 5,410 | 574 | 1,440 | 2,691 | 45 | 2,643,085 |
| New Hampshire | 3,353 | 2,349 | 192 | 246 | 566 | 149 | 1,166,104 |
| New Jersey | 41,609 | 29,437 | 2,653 | 3,510 | 6,009 | 543 | 8,415,289 |
| New Mexico | 6,615 | 4,048 | 427 | 844 | 1,296 | 107 | 1,958,665 |
| New York | 83,941 | 53,588 | 8,572 | 7,711 | 14,070 | 436 | 19,120,958 |
| North Carolina | 32,357 | 19,851 | 2,455 | 4,583 | 5,468 | 499 | 9,260,266 |
| North Dakota | 1,735 | 1,128 | 132 | 176 | 299 | 103 | 646,844 |
| Ohio | 29,797 | 19,818 | 2,292 | 2,720 | 4,967 | 610 | 10,223,161 |
| Oklahoma | 11,984 | 7,250 | 698 | 1,718 | 2,318 | 318 | 3,681,857 |
| Oregon | 10,230 | 5,447 | 588 | 1,821 | 2,374 | 207 | 3,790,072 |
| Pennsylvania | 29,505 | 22,382 | 2,628 | 1,670 | 2,825 | 952 | 9,523,147 |
| Rhode Island | 3,191 | 2,370 | 184 | 290 | 347 | 48 | 1,053,209 |
| South Carolina | 12,881 | 8,449 | 1,112 | 1,130 | 2,190 | 268 | 3,779,301 |
| South Dakota | 2,336 | 1,396 | 88 | 351 | 501 | 143 | 809,838 |
| Tennessee | 25,407 | 14,385 | 1,505 | 4,302 | 5,215 | 454 | 6,293,243 |
| Texas | 89,867 | 48,579 | 6,278 | 15,472 | 19,538 | 1,010 | 24,590,665 |
| Utah | 7,830 | 4,430 | 355 | 1,460 | 1,585 | 133 | 2,783,798 |
| Vermont | 1,419 | 976 | 96 | 108 | 239 | 52 | 303,744 |
| Virginia | 23,395 | 16,168 | 2,155 | 1,313 | 3,759 | 279 | 7,880,881 |
| Washington | 14,862 | 9,612 | 981 | 1,447 | 2,822 | 243 | 6,642,851 |
| West Virginia | 4,460 | 3,362 | 114 | 374 | 610 | 347 | 1,810,824 |
| Wisconsin | 19,156 | 11,326 | 1,794 | 2,399 | 3,637 | 389 | 5,648,330 |
| Wyoming | 2,072 | 1,331 | 115 | 145 | 481 | 66 | 540,376 |

## Table 78. Full-Time Law Enforcement Employees, by State, by City, 2009

(Number.)

| State/city | Population | Total law enforcement employees | Total officers | Total civilians |
|---|---|---|---|---|
| **ALABAMA** | | | | |
| Abbeville | 2,932 | 16 | 8 | 8 |
| Adamsville | 4,704 | 32 | 21 | 11 |
| Addison | 710 | 3 | 3 | 0 |
| Alabaster | 30,002 | 77 | 62 | 15 |
| Albertville | 20,078 | 55 | 34 | 21 |
| Alexander City | 15,057 | 66 | 48 | 18 |
| Aliceville | 2,456 | 10 | 9 | 1 |
| Andalusia | 8,994 | 39 | 29 | 10 |
| Anniston | 23,598 | 128 | 91 | 37 |
| Arab | 8,007 | 38 | 25 | 13 |
| Argo | 1,930 | 6 | 6 | 0 |
| Ashford | 2,087 | 9 | 5 | 4 |
| Ashland | 1,873 | 10 | 6 | 4 |
| Ashville | 2,599 | 5 | 5 | 0 |
| Athens | 24,261 | 57 | 46 | 11 |
| Atmore | 7,396 | 36 | 31 | 5 |
| Attalla | 6,514 | 26 | 21 | 5 |
| Auburn | 57,342 | 111 | 105 | 6 |
| Bay Minette | 8,065 | 34 | 25 | 9 |
| Bayou La Batre | 2,886 | 19 | 14 | 5 |
| Bear Creek | 995 | 1 | 1 | 0 |
| Berry | 1,184 | 3 | 3 | 0 |
| Bessemer | 28,372 | 146 | 110 | 36 |
| Birmingham | 227,373 | 1,127 | 854 | 273 |
| Blountsville | 2,010 | 5 | 5 | 0 |
| Boaz | 8,418 | 32 | 22 | 10 |
| Brantley | 910 | 4 | 4 | 0 |
| Brent | 4,381 | 5 | 5 | 0 |
| Brewton | 5,257 | 34 | 26 | 8 |
| Brighton | 3,234 | 12 | 8 | 4 |
| Brilliant | 717 | 2 | 2 | 0 |
| Brookside | 1,317 | 1 | 1 | 0 |
| Brundidge | 2,262 | 13 | 8 | 5 |
| Butler | 1,687 | 5 | 5 | 0 |
| Calera | 12,159 | 31 | 25 | 6 |
| Camden | 2,225 | 9 | 8 | 1 |
| Carbon Hill | 2,032 | 4 | 4 | 0 |
| Carrollton | 923 | 4 | 4 | 0 |
| Centre | 3,522 | 10 | 9 | 1 |
| Centreville | 2,563 | 6 | 6 | 0 |
| Chatom | 1,161 | 5 | 5 | 0 |
| Cherokee | 1,160 | 4 | 4 | 0 |
| Chickasaw | 5,906 | 20 | 20 | 0 |
| Childersburg | 4,991 | 16 | 12 | 4 |
| Citronelle | 3,744 | 15 | 9 | 6 |
| Clanton | 8,943 | 28 | 26 | 2 |
| Clayhatchee | 492 | 1 | 1 | 0 |
| Clayton | 1,367 | 4 | 4 | 0 |
| Clio | 2,211 | 3 | 3 | 0 |
| Coffeeville | 342 | 1 | 1 | 0 |
| Collinsville | 1,698 | 9 | 4 | 5 |
| Columbiana | 3,873 | 12 | 8 | 4 |
| Coosada | 1,676 | 3 | 3 | 0 |
| Cordova | 2,270 | 7 | 5 | 2 |
| Cottonwood | 1,206 | 3 | 3 | 0 |
| Creola | 2,086 | 13 | 8 | 5 |
| Crossville | 1,515 | 3 | 3 | 0 |
| Cullman | 15,412 | 63 | 45 | 18 |
| Dadeville | 3,231 | 14 | 13 | 1 |
| Daleville | 4,535 | 24 | 18 | 6 |
| Daphne | 19,368 | 84 | 45 | 39 |
| Dauphin Island | 1,610 | 20 | 10 | 10 |
| Decatur | 56,290 | 155 | 130 | 25 |
| Dora | 2,424 | 6 | 3 | 3 |
| Dothan | 67,496 | 226 | 154 | 72 |
| Double Springs | 969 | 6 | 5 | 1 |
| Douglas | 601 | 2 | 2 | 0 |
| Dozier | 396 | 1 | 1 | 0 |
| East Brewton | 2,482 | 7 | 5 | 2 |
| Eclectic | 1,159 | 9 | 5 | 4 |
| Elba | 4,163 | 26 | 17 | 9 |
| Elberta | 1,474 | 5 | 5 | 0 |
| Enterprise | 25,868 | 73 | 54 | 19 |
| Eufaula | 14,564 | 52 | 34 | 18 |
| Eutaw | 2,948 | 10 | 9 | 1 |
| Evergreen | 3,440 | 15 | 13 | 2 |
| Excel | 605 | 1 | 1 | 0 |
| Fairfield | 11,212 | 48 | 37 | 11 |
| Fairhope | 17,723 | 54 | 34 | 20 |
| Falkville | 1,165 | 8 | 6 | 2 |
| Fayette | 4,766 | 13 | 12 | 1 |
| Flomaton | 1,532 | 10 | 5 | 5 |
| Florala | 1,877 | 5 | 5 | 0 |
| Florence | 38,055 | 122 | 96 | 26 |
| Foley | 14,566 | 87 | 59 | 28 |
| Fort Payne | 14,189 | 36 | 33 | 3 |
| Fultondale | 6,953 | 29 | 25 | 4 |
| Gadsden | 36,595 | 129 | 98 | 31 |
| Gardendale | 13,880 | 36 | 28 | 8 |
| Geneva | 4,448 | 16 | 12 | 4 |
| Georgiana | 1,549 | 11 | 8 | 3 |
| Geraldine | 845 | 4 | 3 | 1 |
| Glencoe | 5,399 | 7 | 5 | 2 |
| Gordo | 1,545 | 4 | 4 | 0 |
| Grant | 713 | 6 | 6 | 0 |
| Greensboro | 2,546 | 10 | 10 | 0 |
| Greenville | 6,999 | 33 | 26 | 7 |
| Grove Hill | 1,332 | 5 | 5 | 0 |
| Gulf Shores | 10,947 | 51 | 39 | 12 |
| Guntersville | 8,510 | 46 | 34 | 12 |
| Gurley | 846 | 4 | 4 | 0 |
| Hackleburg | 1,440 | 4 | 4 | 0 |
| Haleyville | 4,024 | 16 | 11 | 5 |
| Hamilton | 6,350 | 12 | 11 | 1 |
| Hammondville | 547 | 2 | 2 | 0 |
| Hanceville | 3,476 | 14 | 10 | 4 |
| Harpersville | 1,728 | 9 | 9 | 0 |
| Hartford | 2,432 | 14 | 9 | 5 |
| Hartselle | 14,070 | 37 | 29 | 8 |
| Hayneville | 1,117 | 4 | 4 | 0 |
| Headland | 4,053 | 14 | 10 | 4 |
| Heflin | 3,583 | 12 | 11 | 1 |
| Helena | 15,192 | 25 | 21 | 4 |
| Henagar | 2,597 | 9 | 5 | 4 |
| Hokes Bluff | 4,485 | 7 | 7 | 0 |
| Hollywood | 921 | 3 | 2 | 1 |
| Homewood | 23,708 | 112 | 78 | 34 |
| Hoover | 71,919 | 215 | 158 | 57 |
| Hueytown | 15,692 | 34 | 34 | 0 |
| Huntsville | 178,601 | 527 | 419 | 108 |
| Irondale | 9,666 | 35 | 28 | 7 |
| Jackson | 5,069 | 26 | 20 | 6 |
| Jacksonville | 10,276 | 31 | 26 | 5 |
| Jasper | 14,129 | 75 | 48 | 27 |
| Jemison | 3,008 | 10 | 10 | 0 |
| Killen | 1,145 | 5 | 5 | 0 |
| Kimberly | 2,887 | 4 | 3 | 1 |
| Kinsey | 1,985 | 3 | 2 | 1 |
| Kinston | 615 | 1 | 1 | 0 |
| Lafayette | 2,858 | 15 | 14 | 1 |
| Lake View | 2,468 | 4 | 3 | 1 |
| Lanett | 7,038 | 30 | 27 | 3 |
| Leeds | 11,398 | 31 | 25 | 6 |
| Leesburg | 823 | 3 | 3 | 0 |
| Leighton | 827 | 3 | 2 | 1 |
| Level Plains | 1,507 | 4 | 4 | 0 |
| Lexington | 843 | 2 | 2 | 0 |
| Lincoln | 5,963 | 17 | 16 | 1 |
| Linden | 2,237 | 7 | 7 | 0 |
| Lineville | 2,371 | 12 | 8 | 4 |
| Littleville | 1,043 | 8 | 5 | 3 |
| Livingston | 2,993 | 13 | 7 | 6 |
| Loxley | 1,830 | 21 | 13 | 8 |
| Luverne | 2,768 | 14 | 10 | 4 |
| Madison | 39,880 | 99 | 71 | 28 |
| Maplesville | 692 | 5 | 5 | 0 |
| Marion | 3,270 | 8 | 6 | 2 |

## Table 78. Full-time Law Enforcement Employees, by State, by City, 2009—*Continued*

(Number.)

| State/city | Population | Total law enforcement employees | Total officers | Total civilians |
|---|---|---|---|---|
| McIntosh | 233 | 10 | 10 | 0 |
| McKenzie | 602 | 1 | 1 | 0 |
| Mentone | 485 | 1 | 1 | 0 |
| Midfield | 5,139 | 11 | 7 | 4 |
| Midland City | 1,904 | 8 | 5 | 3 |
| Millbrook | 17,383 | 35 | 29 | 6 |
| Millport | 999 | 1 | 1 | 0 |
| Millry | 590 | 3 | 3 | 0 |
| Mobile | 246,171 | 716 | 543 | 173 |
| Monroeville | 6,320 | 29 | 23 | 6 |
| Montevallo | 6,469 | 16 | 13 | 3 |
| Montgomery | 202,818 | 649 | 501 | 148 |
| Moody | 14,175 | 20 | 19 | 1 |
| Morris | 1,894 | 9 | 6 | 3 |
| Moulton | 3,267 | 12 | 12 | 0 |
| Moundville | 2,696 | 8 | 7 | 1 |
| Mountain Brook | 21,094 | 65 | 50 | 15 |
| Muscle Shoals | 13,125 | 43 | 34 | 9 |
| Napier Field | 395 | 2 | 2 | 0 |
| New Brockton | 1,233 | 3 | 3 | 0 |
| New Hope | 2,778 | 4 | 4 | 0 |
| New Site | 829 | 1 | 1 | 0 |
| Newton | 1,647 | 4 | 3 | 1 |
| Newville | 542 | 2 | 1 | 1 |
| North Courtland | 798 | 5 | 4 | 1 |
| Northport | 23,498 | 81 | 60 | 21 |
| Notasulga | 838 | 7 | 4 | 3 |
| Oakman | 925 | 2 | 2 | 0 |
| Odenville | 2,291 | 9 | 9 | 0 |
| Ohatchee | 1,247 | 5 | 5 | 0 |
| Oneonta | 7,220 | 20 | 19 | 1 |
| Opelika | 27,087 | 98 | 78 | 20 |
| Opp | 6,555 | 26 | 20 | 6 |
| Orange Beach | 6,563 | 47 | 31 | 16 |
| Owens Crossroads | 1,531 | 4 | 4 | 0 |
| Oxford | 20,808 | 59 | 47 | 12 |
| Ozark | 14,670 | 42 | 37 | 5 |
| Parrish | 1,244 | 10 | 4 | 6 |
| Pelham | 22,172 | 82 | 67 | 15 |
| Pell City | 13,252 | 36 | 33 | 3 |
| Phenix City | 31,438 | 102 | 80 | 22 |
| Phil Campbell | 1,048 | 2 | 2 | 0 |
| Pickensville | 627 | 2 | 1 | 1 |
| Piedmont | 4,952 | 16 | 11 | 5 |
| Pinckard | 623 | 2 | 2 | 0 |
| Pine Hill | 907 | 3 | 3 | 0 |
| Pleasant Grove | 10,281 | 24 | 18 | 6 |
| Powell | 983 | 2 | 2 | 0 |
| Prattville | 33,279 | 92 | 82 | 10 |
| Priceville | 2,981 | 5 | 5 | 0 |
| Prichard | 27,560 | 63 | 39 | 24 |
| Ragland | 2,161 | 4 | 4 | 0 |
| Rainbow City | 9,425 | 32 | 21 | 11 |
| Rainsville | 5,046 | 15 | 11 | 4 |
| Ranburne | 487 | 2 | 2 | 0 |
| Red Bay | 3,288 | 10 | 6 | 4 |
| Reform | 1,771 | 5 | 5 | 0 |
| Riverside | 2,084 | 4 | 4 | 0 |
| Roanoke | 6,701 | 25 | 20 | 5 |
| Robertsdale | 5,111 | 26 | 13 | 13 |
| Rogersville | 1,205 | 6 | 6 | 0 |
| Russellville | 8,913 | 26 | 22 | 4 |
| Samson | 2,025 | 6 | 5 | 1 |
| Saraland | 13,019 | 47 | 36 | 11 |
| Sardis City | 2,206 | 4 | 4 | 0 |
| Scottsboro | 15,015 | 69 | 45 | 24 |
| Section | 758 | 2 | 2 | 0 |
| Selma | 18,679 | 73 | 53 | 20 |
| Sheffield | 9,072 | 36 | 30 | 6 |
| Shorter | 377 | 12 | 5 | 7 |
| Silas | 470 | 2 | 1 | 1 |
| Silverhill | 707 | 2 | 2 | 0 |
| Sipsey | 542 | 1 | 1 | 0 |
| Skyline | 834 | 3 | 1 | 2 |
| Slocomb | 2,046 | 7 | 6 | 1 |
| Snead | 860 | 4 | 4 | 0 |
| Southside | 8,572 | 16 | 10 | 6 |
| Spanish Fort | 5,809 | 22 | 21 | 1 |
| Springville | 3,814 | 15 | 15 | 0 |
| Stevenson | 2,015 | 7 | 4 | 3 |
| St. Florian | 492 | 2 | 2 | 0 |
| Sulligent | 1,949 | 5 | 5 | 0 |
| Sylacauga | 12,844 | 45 | 39 | 6 |
| Sylvania | 1,276 | 3 | 3 | 0 |
| Talladega | 16,902 | 48 | 39 | 9 |
| Tallassee | 5,199 | 26 | 20 | 6 |
| Tarrant | 6,445 | 28 | 23 | 5 |
| Thomasville | 4,460 | 20 | 15 | 5 |
| Thorsby | 2,097 | 5 | 5 | 0 |
| Town Creek | 1,208 | 3 | 3 | 0 |
| Triana | 493 | 2 | 2 | 0 |
| Trinity | 2,003 | 5 | 5 | 0 |
| Troy | 15,278 | 69 | 49 | 20 |
| Trussville | 19,596 | 54 | 44 | 10 |
| Tuscaloosa | 91,688 | 346 | 279 | 67 |
| Tuscumbia | 8,346 | 29 | 21 | 8 |
| Tuskegee | 11,281 | 36 | 25 | 11 |
| Union Springs | 4,682 | 18 | 11 | 7 |
| Uniontown | 1,397 | 8 | 8 | 0 |
| Valley | 10,017 | 36 | 30 | 6 |
| Valley Head | 654 | 3 | 2 | 1 |
| Vance | 1,018 | 3 | 3 | 0 |
| Vernon | 1,867 | 7 | 7 | 0 |
| Vestavia Hills | 30,906 | 70 | 68 | 2 |
| Warrior | 3,100 | 17 | 12 | 5 |
| Weaver | 2,738 | 10 | 7 | 3 |
| Webb | 1,375 | 2 | 2 | 0 |
| Wedowee | 825 | 8 | 8 | 0 |
| West Blocton | 1,433 | 2 | 2 | 0 |
| Wetumpka | 7,964 | 41 | 30 | 11 |
| Winfield | 4,626 | 11 | 10 | 1 |
| Woodstock | 1,029 | 4 | 4 | 0 |
| Woodville | 750 | 1 | 1 | 0 |
| York | 2,481 | 11 | 6 | 5 |
| **ALASKA** | | | | |
| Anchorage | 283,300 | 544 | 383 | 161 |
| Bethel | 6,584 | 20 | 11 | 9 |
| Bristol Bay Borough | 933 | 8 | 3 | 5 |
| Cordova | 2,219 | 12 | 6 | 6 |
| Craig | 1,150 | 11 | 5 | 6 |
| Dillingham | 2,465 | 18 | 6 | 12 |
| Fairbanks | 35,735 | 51 | 48 | 3 |
| Haines | 2,273 | 9 | 5 | 4 |
| Homer | 5,921 | 21 | 14 | 7 |
| Hoonah | 701 | 5 | 3 | 2 |
| Houston | 2,298 | 4 | 2 | 2 |
| Juneau | 31,024 | 80 | 48 | 32 |
| Kenai | 7,836 | 28 | 19 | 9 |
| Ketchikan | 7,215 | 33 | 22 | 11 |
| Kodiak | 6,212 | 33 | 15 | 18 |
| Kotzebue | 3,187 | 16 | 7 | 9 |
| Nome | 3,585 | 15 | 9 | 6 |
| North Pole | 2,299 | 14 | 13 | 1 |
| North Slope Borough | 6,581 | 63 | 38 | 25 |
| Palmer | 8,706 | 31 | 15 | 16 |
| Petersburg | 2,784 | 14 | 8 | 6 |
| Sand Point | 996 | 4 | 3 | 1 |
| Seldovia | 312 | 1 | 1 | 0 |
| Seward | 3,161 | 23 | 9 | 14 |
| Sitka | 8,896 | 30 | 17 | 13 |
| Skagway | 895 | 8 | 4 | 4 |
| Soldotna | 4,461 | 15 | 13 | 2 |
| St. Paul | 405 | 5 | 3 | 2 |
| Togiak | 811 | 3 | 3 | 0 |
| Unalaska | 3,462 | 29 | 13 | 16 |
| Valdez | 3,758 | 19 | 10 | 9 |
| Wasilla | 10,980 | 52 | 24 | 28 |
| Whittier | 157 | 3 | 3 | 0 |
| Wrangell | 1,958 | 16 | 7 | 9 |
| **ARIZONA** | | | | |
| Apache Junction | 32,869 | 85 | 51 | 34 |
| Avondale | 88,773 | 155 | 102 | 53 |

## Table 78. Full-time Law Enforcement Employees, by State, by City, 2009—*Continued*

(Number.)

| State/city | Population | Total law enforcement employees | Total officers | Total civilians |
|---|---|---|---|---|
| Benson | 4,863 | 23 | 14 | 9 |
| Bisbee | 5,965 | 20 | 13 | 7 |
| Buckeye | 56,780 | 89 | 68 | 21 |
| Bullhead City | 41,721 | 126 | 79 | 47 |
| Camp Verde | 11,012 | 34 | 22 | 12 |
| Casa Grande | 43,254 | 109 | 74 | 35 |
| Chandler | 256,091 | 493 | 329 | 164 |
| Chino Valley | 11,453 | 37 | 28 | 9 |
| Clarkdale | 4,374 | 11 | 9 | 2 |
| Clifton | 2,438 | 9 | 5 | 4 |
| Colorado City | 4,934 | 10 | 6 | 4 |
| Coolidge | 10,540 | 43 | 32 | 11 |
| Cottonwood | 11,664 | 48 | 32 | 16 |
| Douglas | 17,622 | 49 | 35 | 14 |
| Eagar | 4,541 | 10 | 8 | 2 |
| El Mirage | 28,196 | 52 | 45 | 7 |
| Eloy | 13,049 | 40 | 28 | 12 |
| Flagstaff | 61,072 | 159 | 110 | 49 |
| Florence | 21,229 | 44 | 30 | 14 |
| Fredonia | 1,135 | 4 | 4 | 0 |
| Gilbert | 231,799 | 340 | 225 | 115 |
| Glendale | 255,080 | 569 | 419 | 150 |
| Globe | 7,167 | 32 | 24 | 8 |
| Goodyear | 67,390 | 130 | 95 | 35 |
| Hayden | 1,234 | 9 | 8 | 1 |
| Holbrook | 5,094 | 22 | 15 | 7 |
| Huachuca City | 1,988 | 9 | 4 | 5 |
| Jerome | 356 | 5 | 5 | 0 |
| Kearny | 3,438 | 9 | 6 | 3 |
| Kingman | 28,700 | 81 | 55 | 26 |
| Lake Havasu City | 58,406 | 117 | 88 | 29 |
| Mammoth | 2,682 | 6 | 3 | 3 |
| Marana | 38,028 | 107 | 78 | 29 |
| Maricopa | 52,200 | 63 | 56 | 7 |
| Mesa | 470,833 | 1,256 | 801 | 455 |
| Miami | 1,762 | 11 | 7 | 4 |
| Nogales | 19,433 | 84 | 65 | 19 |
| Oro Valley | 44,854 | 126 | 100 | 26 |
| Page | 6,940 | 29 | 20 | 9 |
| Paradise Valley | 15,141 | 38 | 29 | 9 |
| Parker | 3,180 | 14 | 12 | 2 |
| Patagonia | 768 | 3 | 3 | 0 |
| Payson | 15,701 | 45 | 29 | 16 |
| Peoria | 164,366 | 287 | 184 | 103 |
| Phoenix | 1,597,397 | 4,360 | 3,279 | 1,081 |
| Pima | 2,173 | 4 | 4 | 0 |
| Pinetop-Lakeside | 4,654 | 23 | 15 | 8 |
| Prescott | 43,748 | 88 | 69 | 19 |
| Prescott Valley | 40,539 | 78 | 62 | 16 |
| Quartzsite | 3,497 | 14 | 13 | 1 |
| Safford | 9,894 | 24 | 20 | 4 |
| Sahuarita | 28,201 | 50 | 43 | 7 |
| San Luis | 26,222 | 48 | 31 | 17 |
| Scottsdale | 239,115 | 682 | 426 | 256 |
| Sedona | 11,759 | 40 | 30 | 10 |
| Show Low | 12,929 | 42 | 29 | 13 |
| Sierra Vista | 43,956 | 97 | 68 | 29 |
| Snowflake-Taylor | 10,084 | 22 | 13 | 9 |
| Somerton | 13,041 | 32 | 23 | 9 |
| South Tucson | 6,071 | 16 | 12 | 4 |
| Springerville | 1,994 | 10 | 7 | 3 |
| St. Johns | 3,613 | 14 | 11 | 3 |
| Superior | 3,346 | 12 | 9 | 3 |
| Surprise | 104,692 | 176 | 126 | 50 |
| Tempe | 177,486 | 546 | 356 | 190 |
| Thatcher | 5,122 | 12 | 11 | 1 |
| Tolleson | 7,498 | 40 | 31 | 9 |
| Tucson | 547,981 | 1,365 | 1,012 | 353 |
| Wellton | 1,916 | 6 | 6 | 0 |
| Wickenburg | 6,707 | 22 | 14 | 8 |
| Willcox | 3,807 | 20 | 11 | 9 |
| Williams | 3,361 | 19 | 12 | 7 |
| Winslow | 9,903 | 39 | 26 | 13 |
| Youngtown | 5,177 | 15 | 14 | 1 |
| Yuma | 91,433 | 236 | 153 | 83 |

| State/city | Population | Total law enforcement employees | Total officers | Total civilians |
|---|---|---|---|---|
| **ARIZONA** | | | | |
| Apache Junction | 32,869 | 85 | 51 | 34 |
| Avondale | 88,773 | 155 | 102 | 53 |
| Benson | 4,863 | 23 | 14 | 9 |
| Bisbee | 5,965 | 20 | 13 | 7 |
| Buckeye | 56,780 | 89 | 68 | 21 |
| Bullhead City | 41,721 | 126 | 79 | 47 |
| Camp Verde | 11,012 | 34 | 22 | 12 |
| Casa Grande | 43,254 | 109 | 74 | 35 |
| Chandler | 256,091 | 493 | 329 | 164 |
| Chino Valley | 11,453 | 37 | 28 | 9 |
| Clarkdale | 4,374 | 11 | 9 | 2 |
| Clifton | 2,438 | 9 | 5 | 4 |
| Colorado City | 4,934 | 10 | 6 | 4 |
| Coolidge | 10,540 | 43 | 32 | 11 |
| Cottonwood | 11,664 | 48 | 32 | 16 |
| Douglas | 17,622 | 49 | 35 | 14 |
| Eagar | 4,541 | 10 | 8 | 2 |
| El Mirage | 28,196 | 52 | 45 | 7 |
| Eloy | 13,049 | 40 | 28 | 12 |
| Flagstaff | 61,072 | 159 | 110 | 49 |
| Florence | 21,229 | 44 | 30 | 14 |
| Fredonia | 1,135 | 4 | 4 | 0 |
| Gilbert | 231,799 | 340 | 225 | 115 |
| Glendale | 255,080 | 569 | 419 | 150 |
| Globe | 7,167 | 32 | 24 | 8 |
| Goodyear | 67,390 | 130 | 95 | 35 |
| Hayden | 1,234 | 9 | 8 | 1 |
| Holbrook | 5,094 | 22 | 15 | 7 |
| Huachuca City | 1,988 | 9 | 4 | 5 |
| Jerome | 356 | 5 | 5 | 0 |
| Kearny | 3,438 | 9 | 6 | 3 |
| Kingman | 28,700 | 81 | 55 | 26 |
| Lake Havasu City | 58,406 | 117 | 88 | 29 |
| Mammoth | 2,682 | 6 | 3 | 3 |
| Marana | 38,028 | 107 | 78 | 29 |
| Maricopa | 52,200 | 63 | 56 | 7 |
| Mesa | 470,833 | 1,256 | 801 | 455 |
| Miami | 1,762 | 11 | 7 | 4 |
| Nogales | 19,433 | 84 | 65 | 19 |
| Oro Valley | 44,854 | 126 | 100 | 26 |
| Page | 6,940 | 29 | 20 | 9 |
| Paradise Valley | 15,141 | 38 | 29 | 9 |
| Parker | 3,180 | 14 | 12 | 2 |
| Patagonia | 768 | 3 | 3 | 0 |
| Payson | 15,701 | 45 | 29 | 16 |
| Peoria | 164,366 | 287 | 184 | 103 |
| Phoenix | 1,597,397 | 4,360 | 3,279 | 1,081 |
| Pima | 2,173 | 4 | 4 | 0 |
| Pinetop-Lakeside | 4,654 | 23 | 15 | 8 |
| Prescott | 43,748 | 88 | 69 | 19 |
| Prescott Valley | 40,539 | 78 | 62 | 16 |
| Quartzsite | 3,497 | 14 | 13 | 1 |
| Safford | 9,894 | 24 | 20 | 4 |
| Sahuarita | 28,201 | 50 | 43 | 7 |
| San Luis | 26,222 | 48 | 31 | 17 |
| Scottsdale | 239,115 | 682 | 426 | 256 |
| Sedona | 11,759 | 40 | 30 | 10 |
| Show Low | 12,929 | 42 | 29 | 13 |
| Sierra Vista | 43,956 | 97 | 68 | 29 |
| Snowflake-Taylor | 10,084 | 22 | 13 | 9 |
| Somerton | 13,041 | 32 | 23 | 9 |
| South Tucson | 6,071 | 16 | 12 | 4 |
| Springerville | 1,994 | 10 | 7 | 3 |
| St. Johns | 3,613 | 14 | 11 | 3 |
| Superior | 3,346 | 12 | 9 | 3 |
| Surprise | 104,692 | 176 | 126 | 50 |
| Tempe | 177,486 | 546 | 356 | 190 |
| Thatcher | 5,122 | 12 | 11 | 1 |
| Tolleson | 7,498 | 40 | 31 | 9 |
| Tucson | 547,981 | 1,365 | 1,012 | 353 |
| Wellton | 1,916 | 6 | 6 | 0 |
| Wickenburg | 6,707 | 22 | 14 | 8 |
| Willcox | 3,807 | 20 | 11 | 9 |
| Williams | 3,361 | 19 | 12 | 7 |

## Table 78. Full-time Law Enforcement Employees, by State, by City, 2009—*Continued*

(Number.)

| State/city | Population | Total law enforcement employees | Total officers | Total civilians |
|---|---|---|---|---|
| Winslow | 9,903 | 39 | 26 | 13 |
| Youngtown | 5,177 | 15 | 14 | 1 |
| Yuma | 91,433 | 236 | 153 | 83 |
| **ARKANSAS** | | | | |
| Alma | 5,219 | 19 | 11 | 8 |
| Altheimer | 1,101 | 1 | 1 | 0 |
| Arkadelphia | 11,158 | 25 | 21 | 4 |
| Arkansas City | 510 | 1 | 1 | 0 |
| Ashdown | 4,405 | 13 | 11 | 2 |
| Ash Flat | 1,106 | 3 | 3 | 0 |
| Atkins | 2,968 | 7 | 6 | 1 |
| Augusta | 2,210 | 8 | 8 | 0 |
| Austin | 2,054 | 3 | 3 | 0 |
| Bald Knob | 3,443 | 9 | 5 | 4 |
| Barling | 4,507 | 10 | 10 | 0 |
| Bay | 2,055 | 4 | 3 | 1 |
| Bearden | 977 | 2 | 2 | 0 |
| Beebe | 7,096 | 20 | 13 | 7 |
| Bella Vista | 27,167 | 29 | 20 | 9 |
| Benton | 30,276 | 67 | 56 | 11 |
| Bentonville | 37,816 | 80 | 54 | 26 |
| Berryville | 5,335 | 13 | 11 | 2 |
| Blytheville | 15,889 | 62 | 43 | 19 |
| Bono | 1,608 | 4 | 4 | 0 |
| Booneville | 4,083 | 12 | 8 | 4 |
| Bradford | 859 | 3 | 3 | 0 |
| Brinkley | 3,142 | 17 | 13 | 4 |
| Bryant | 15,573 | 41 | 31 | 10 |
| Bull Shoals | 2,155 | 3 | 3 | 0 |
| Cabot | 24,766 | 49 | 36 | 13 |
| Caddo Valley | 649 | 5 | 4 | 1 |
| Camden | 11,349 | 39 | 25 | 14 |
| Cammack Village | 776 | 5 | 4 | 1 |
| Caraway | 1,398 | 2 | 2 | 0 |
| Carlisle | 2,420 | 10 | 6 | 4 |
| Cave City | 2,057 | 3 | 3 | 0 |
| Cave Springs | 1,782 | 4 | 4 | 0 |
| Centerton | 9,911 | 11 | 10 | 1 |
| Charleston | 3,035 | 4 | 4 | 0 |
| Cherokee Village | 4,792 | 9 | 8 | 1 |
| Clarendon | 1,637 | 4 | 4 | 0 |
| Clarksville | 8,679 | 22 | 18 | 4 |
| Clinton | 2,482 | 9 | 8 | 1 |
| Conway | 59,343 | 154 | 111 | 43 |
| Corning | 3,270 | 11 | 7 | 4 |
| Cotter | 1,098 | 2 | 2 | 0 |
| Crossett | 5,459 | 24 | 15 | 9 |
| Danville | 2,486 | 6 | 5 | 1 |
| Dardanelle | 4,458 | 14 | 10 | 4 |
| Decatur | 1,990 | 6 | 6 | 0 |
| De Queen | 5,970 | 16 | 13 | 3 |
| Dermott | 3,172 | 13 | 7 | 6 |
| Des Arc | 1,685 | 4 | 4 | 0 |
| De Valls Bluff | 684 | 1 | 1 | 0 |
| De Witt | 3,223 | 12 | 8 | 4 |
| Diaz | 1,143 | 2 | 2 | 0 |
| Dierks | 1,216 | 3 | 3 | 0 |
| Dover | 1,407 | 4 | 4 | 0 |
| Dumas | 4,560 | 25 | 12 | 13 |
| Earle | 2,704 | 8 | 6 | 2 |
| El Dorado | 19,741 | 66 | 49 | 17 |
| Elkins | 2,730 | 6 | 6 | 0 |
| England | 3,023 | 11 | 6 | 5 |
| Etowah | 339 | 1 | 1 | 0 |
| Eudora | 2,292 | 6 | 5 | 1 |
| Eureka Springs | 2,361 | 16 | 10 | 6 |
| Fairfield Bay | 2,500 | 17 | 8 | 9 |
| Farmington | 4,802 | 11 | 10 | 1 |
| Fayetteville | 75,120 | 166 | 119 | 47 |
| Flippin | 1,384 | 6 | 6 | 0 |
| Fordyce | 4,171 | 12 | 8 | 4 |
| Forrest City | 13,123 | 42 | 32 | 10 |
| Fort Smith | 85,175 | 207 | 162 | 45 |
| Gassville | 2,203 | 4 | 4 | 0 |
| Gentry | 3,041 | 10 | 8 | 2 |
| Glenwood | 1,985 | 3 | 3 | 0 |
| Gosnell | 3,541 | 9 | 9 | 0 |
| Gould | 1,127 | 2 | 2 | 0 |
| Gravette | 2,653 | 8 | 7 | 1 |
| Greenbrier | 4,642 | 14 | 10 | 4 |
| Green Forest | 3,081 | 7 | 6 | 1 |
| Greenland | 1,282 | 4 | 4 | 0 |
| Greenwood | 8,814 | 22 | 20 | 2 |
| Greers Ferry | 967 | 4 | 3 | 1 |
| Gurdon | 2,286 | 4 | 3 | 1 |
| Guy | 566 | 1 | 1 | 0 |
| Hamburg | 2,689 | 5 | 4 | 1 |
| Hampton | 1,457 | 4 | 4 | 0 |
| Hardy | 815 | 4 | 3 | 1 |
| Harrisburg | 2,109 | 4 | 4 | 0 |
| Harrison | 13,312 | 40 | 28 | 12 |
| Hazen | 1,441 | 4 | 4 | 0 |
| Heber Springs | 7,279 | 24 | 14 | 10 |
| Helena-West Helena | 11,921 | 55 | 40 | 15 |
| Hermitage | 748 | 3 | 3 | 0 |
| Highfill | 785 | 2 | 2 | 0 |
| Highland | 1,096 | 3 | 3 | 0 |
| Hope | 10,354 | 35 | 24 | 11 |
| Horseshoe Bend | 2,213 | 5 | 5 | 0 |
| Hot Springs | 39,864 | 129 | 100 | 29 |
| Hoxie | 2,630 | 5 | 4 | 1 |
| Huntsville | 2,444 | 8 | 7 | 1 |
| Jacksonville | 31,483 | 83 | 72 | 11 |
| Jonesboro | 64,944 | 156 | 145 | 11 |
| Judsonia | 2,202 | 3 | 2 | 1 |
| Keiser | 801 | 1 | 1 | 0 |
| Kensett | 1,852 | 4 | 4 | 0 |
| Lake City | 2,147 | 4 | 4 | 0 |
| Lakeview | 857 | 2 | 2 | 0 |
| Lake Village | 2,342 | 14 | 8 | 6 |
| Leachville | 1,834 | 4 | 3 | 1 |
| Lepanto | 2,007 | 6 | 4 | 2 |
| Lewisville | 1,134 | 2 | 2 | 0 |
| Lincoln | 2,118 | 5 | 5 | 0 |
| Little Flock | 3,210 | 7 | 7 | 0 |
| Little Rock | 190,205 | 647 | 531 | 116 |
| Lonoke | 4,636 | 16 | 11 | 5 |
| Lowell | 7,397 | 21 | 14 | 7 |
| Luxora | 1,209 | 2 | 2 | 0 |
| Magnolia | 11,011 | 28 | 21 | 7 |
| Malvern | 8,949 | 22 | 19 | 3 |
| Mammoth Spring | 1,108 | 2 | 2 | 0 |
| Mansfield | 1,122 | 4 | 4 | 0 |
| Marianna | 4,319 | 15 | 10 | 5 |
| Marion | 12,641 | 25 | 23 | 2 |
| Marked Tree | 2,615 | 12 | 8 | 4 |
| Marmaduke | 1,175 | 4 | 4 | 0 |
| Marvell | 1,102 | 10 | 7 | 3 |
| Maumelle | 16,958 | 37 | 29 | 8 |
| Mayflower | 2,310 | 5 | 4 | 1 |
| McCrory | 1,520 | 5 | 5 | 0 |
| McGehee | 3,888 | 26 | 9 | 17 |
| McRae | 712 | 2 | 2 | 0 |
| Mena | 5,626 | 14 | 13 | 1 |
| Mineral Springs | 1,271 | 3 | 3 | 0 |
| Monette | 1,234 | 3 | 3 | 0 |
| Monticello | 9,281 | 28 | 22 | 6 |
| Morrilton | 6,584 | 31 | 21 | 10 |
| Mountain Home | 12,767 | 34 | 27 | 7 |
| Mountain View | 3,133 | 9 | 8 | 1 |
| Mulberry | 1,730 | 3 | 3 | 0 |
| Murfreesboro | 1,629 | 3 | 3 | 0 |
| Nashville | 4,806 | 17 | 16 | 1 |
| Newport | 7,364 | 20 | 13 | 7 |
| North Little Rock | 59,320 | 214 | 184 | 30 |
| Ola | 1,242 | 3 | 3 | 0 |
| Osceola | 7,816 | 38 | 24 | 14 |
| Ozark | 3,587 | 12 | 10 | 2 |
| Pangburn | 705 | 1 | 1 | 0 |
| Paragould | 25,113 | 51 | 41 | 10 |
| Paris | 3,602 | 14 | 9 | 5 |
| Pea Ridge | 4,924 | 10 | 10 | 0 |

**Table 78. Full-time Law Enforcement Employees, by State, by City, 2009**—*Continued*

(Number.)

| State/city | Population | Total law enforcement employees | Total officers | Total civilians |
|---|---|---|---|---|
| Perryville | 1,440 | 4 | 4 | 0 |
| Piggott | 3,440 | 9 | 8 | 1 |
| Pine Bluff | 49,915 | 164 | 138 | 26 |
| Plainview | 778 | 1 | 1 | 0 |
| Plummerville | 865 | 3 | 3 | 0 |
| Pocahontas | 6,736 | 14 | 13 | 1 |
| Pottsville | 2,902 | 5 | 5 | 0 |
| Prairie Grove | 3,809 | 9 | 9 | 0 |
| Prescott | 4,439 | 9 | 8 | 1 |
| Quitman | 738 | 4 | 4 | 0 |
| Ravenden | 490 | 1 | 1 | 0 |
| Redfield | 1,171 | 5 | 4 | 1 |
| Rison | 1,282 | 3 | 3 | 0 |
| Rockport | 809 | 6 | 5 | 1 |
| Rogers | 58,992 | 129 | 91 | 38 |
| Rose Bud | 460 | 3 | 2 | 1 |
| Russellville | 28,035 | 62 | 54 | 8 |
| Salem | 1,613 | 3 | 3 | 0 |
| Searcy | 22,647 | 64 | 46 | 18 |
| Sheridan | 4,640 | 28 | 14 | 14 |
| Sherwood | 24,888 | 97 | 72 | 25 |
| Siloam Springs | 15,325 | 56 | 33 | 23 |
| Smackover | 1,868 | 4 | 4 | 0 |
| Springdale | 70,935 | 162 | 116 | 46 |
| Stamps | 1,888 | 3 | 3 | 0 |
| Star City | 2,203 | 6 | 5 | 1 |
| Stuttgart | 8,891 | 24 | 17 | 7 |
| Sulphur Springs | 693 | 2 | 2 | 0 |
| Swifton | 776 | 2 | 1 | 1 |
| Texarkana | 30,348 | 122 | 82 | 40 |
| Trumann | 6,781 | 22 | 14 | 8 |
| Tuckerman | 1,621 | 4 | 3 | 1 |
| Van Buren | 22,964 | 58 | 43 | 15 |
| Vilonia | 3,685 | 6 | 6 | 0 |
| Waldron | 3,574 | 11 | 9 | 2 |
| Walnut Ridge | 4,636 | 9 | 8 | 1 |
| Ward | 4,086 | 6 | 5 | 1 |
| Warren | 6,079 | 19 | 14 | 5 |
| Weiner | 719 | 1 | 1 | 0 |
| West Fork | 2,355 | 7 | 6 | 1 |
| West Memphis | 26,995 | 100 | 82 | 18 |
| White Hall | 5,158 | 16 | 14 | 2 |
| Wynne | 8,419 | 18 | 16 | 2 |
| **CALIFORNIA** | | | | |
| Alameda | 70,372 | 134 | 91 | 43 |
| Albany | 15,950 | 34 | 25 | 9 |
| Alhambra | 85,956 | 128 | 83 | 45 |
| Alturas | 2,778 | 7 | 6 | 1 |
| Anaheim | 335,970 | 609 | 405 | 204 |
| Anderson | 10,718 | 27 | 17 | 10 |
| Antioch | 101,243 | 158 | 114 | 44 |
| Arcadia | 56,596 | 99 | 68 | 31 |
| Arcata | 17,093 | 35 | 25 | 10 |
| Arroyo Grande | 17,323 | 33 | 25 | 8 |
| Arvin | 15,320 | 26 | 18 | 8 |
| Atascadero | 28,675 | 38 | 27 | 11 |
| Atherton | 7,430 | 23 | 18 | 5 |
| Atwater | 26,966 | 44 | 34 | 10 |
| Auburn | 13,306 | 29 | 22 | 7 |
| Azusa | 47,078 | 89 | 60 | 29 |
| Bakersfield | 330,897 | 465 | 339 | 126 |
| Baldwin Park | 77,539 | 105 | 75 | 30 |
| Banning | 29,568 | 48 | 35 | 13 |
| Barstow | 24,822 | 53 | 39 | 14 |
| Bear Valley | 4,618 | 17 | 8 | 9 |
| Beaumont | 36,800 | 77 | 57 | 20 |
| Bell | 36,651 | 44 | 31 | 13 |
| Bell Gardens | 44,756 | 68 | 48 | 20 |
| Belmont | 24,742 | 43 | 30 | 13 |
| Belvedere | 2,052 | 9 | 8 | 1 |
| Benicia | 26,089 | 52 | 36 | 16 |
| Berkeley | 101,190 | 280 | 180 | 100 |
| Beverly Hills | 34,506 | 200 | 133 | 67 |
| Bishop | 3,393 | 19 | 13 | 6 |
| Blythe | 21,841 | 32 | 21 | 11 |
| Brawley | 22,810 | 49 | 34 | 15 |
| Brea | 38,637 | 134 | 99 | 35 |
| Brentwood | 53,494 | 78 | 61 | 17 |
| Brisbane | 3,686 | 19 | 15 | 4 |
| Broadmoor | 4,393 | 11 | 10 | 1 |
| Buena Park | 79,525 | 136 | 90 | 46 |
| Burbank | 103,248 | 257 | 160 | 97 |
| Burlingame | 27,656 | 57 | 39 | 18 |
| Calexico | 39,820 | 71 | 43 | 28 |
| California City | 15,492 | 23 | 16 | 7 |
| Calipatria | 7,623 | 4 | 4 | 0 |
| Calistoga | 5,178 | 15 | 11 | 4 |
| Campbell | 38,584 | 63 | 41 | 22 |
| Capitola | 9,565 | 30 | 24 | 6 |
| Carlsbad | 98,482 | 156 | 109 | 47 |
| Carmel | 3,864 | 21 | 14 | 7 |
| Cathedral City | 53,236 | 94 | 55 | 39 |
| Ceres | 43,669 | 67 | 49 | 18 |
| Chico | 84,724 | 150 | 95 | 55 |
| Chino | 84,626 | 146 | 97 | 49 |
| Chowchilla | 19,817 | 25 | 19 | 6 |
| Chula Vista | 224,841 | 325 | 232 | 93 |
| Citrus Heights | 84,333 | 127 | 87 | 40 |
| City of Angels | 3,804 | 10 | 9 | 1 |
| Claremont | 35,628 | 61 | 39 | 22 |
| Clayton | 11,333 | 12 | 11 | 1 |
| Clearlake | 15,261 | 30 | 22 | 8 |
| Cloverdale | 8,304 | 25 | 17 | 8 |
| Clovis | 95,229 | 138 | 93 | 45 |
| Coalinga | 19,308 | 30 | 20 | 10 |
| Colma | 1,452 | 25 | 18 | 7 |
| Colton | 50,803 | 97 | 62 | 35 |
| Colusa | 5,946 | 10 | 9 | 1 |
| Concord | 121,042 | 200 | 152 | 48 |
| Corcoran | 25,474 | 31 | 21 | 10 |
| Corning | 7,253 | 25 | 15 | 10 |
| Corona | 152,438 | 245 | 174 | 71 |
| Coronado | 22,482 | 61 | 41 | 20 |
| Costa Mesa | 110,150 | 234 | 160 | 74 |
| Cotati | 7,248 | 18 | 12 | 6 |
| Covina | 46,946 | 88 | 56 | 32 |
| Crescent City | 7,889 | 14 | 13 | 1 |
| Culver City | 38,545 | 150 | 108 | 42 |
| Cypress | 47,181 | 73 | 55 | 18 |
| Daly City | 101,284 | 151 | 109 | 42 |
| Davis | 62,994 | 93 | 58 | 35 |
| Delano | 54,801 | 75 | 48 | 27 |
| Del Rey Oaks | 1,516 | 6 | 6 | 0 |
| Desert Hot Springs | 25,577 | 36 | 30 | 6 |
| Dinuba | 20,682 | 48 | 37 | 11 |
| Dixon | 17,562 | 28 | 24 | 4 |
| Dos Palos | 5,015 | 9 | 7 | 2 |
| Downey | 107,598 | 169 | 119 | 50 |
| East Palo Alto | 34,005 | 47 | 36 | 11 |
| El Cajon | 92,466 | 184 | 117 | 67 |
| El Centro | 40,337 | 78 | 55 | 23 |
| El Cerrito | 22,116 | 52 | 41 | 11 |
| Elk Grove | 140,576 | 194 | 127 | 67 |
| El Monte | 122,428 | 174 | 127 | 47 |
| El Segundo | 16,235 | 104 | 70 | 34 |
| Emeryville | 9,929 | 56 | 39 | 17 |
| Escalon | 7,414 | 14 | 10 | 4 |
| Escondido | 137,432 | 209 | 158 | 51 |
| Etna | 768 | 3 | 2 | 1 |
| Eureka | 25,216 | 75 | 47 | 28 |
| Exeter | 10,054 | 17 | 16 | 1 |
| Fairfax | 7,038 | 16 | 11 | 5 |
| Fairfield | 104,478 | 183 | 122 | 61 |
| Farmersville | 10,214 | 18 | 16 | 2 |
| Ferndale | 1,384 | 4 | 4 | 0 |
| Firebaugh | 7,032 | 16 | 12 | 4 |
| Folsom | 69,728 | 108 | 81 | 27 |
| Fontana | 190,303 | 293 | 197 | 96 |
| Fort Bragg | 6,581 | 23 | 17 | 6 |
| Fortuna | 11,424 | 25 | 16 | 9 |
| Foster City | 29,123 | 54 | 39 | 15 |
| Fountain Valley | 55,570 | 80 | 59 | 21 |

**Table 78. Full-time Law Enforcement Employees, by State, by City, 2009—*Continued***

(Number.)

| State/city | Population | Total law enforcement employees | Total officers | Total civilians |
|---|---|---|---|---|
| Fowler | 5,769 | 11 | 10 | 1 |
| Fremont | 202,714 | 275 | 177 | 98 |
| Fresno | 481,370 | 1,217 | 827 | 390 |
| Fullerton | 132,478 | 224 | 156 | 68 |
| Galt | 24,554 | 46 | 33 | 13 |
| Gardena | 58,623 | 115 | 89 | 26 |
| Garden Grove | 165,837 | 240 | 166 | 74 |
| Gilroy | 50,946 | 85 | 55 | 30 |
| Glendale | 197,384 | 371 | 258 | 113 |
| Glendora | 49,400 | 96 | 53 | 43 |
| Gonzales | 8,637 | 15 | 13 | 2 |
| Grass Valley | 12,271 | 34 | 25 | 9 |
| Greenfield | 15,511 | 19 | 15 | 4 |
| Gridley | 6,589 | 21 | 16 | 5 |
| Grover Beach | 13,135 | 29 | 19 | 10 |
| Guadalupe | 6,708 | 12 | 10 | 2 |
| Gustine | 5,133 | 11 | 9 | 2 |
| Half Moon Bay | 12,514 | 17 | 14 | 3 |
| Hanford | 51,102 | 73 | 51 | 22 |
| Hawthorne | 84,314 | 133 | 99 | 34 |
| Hayward | 142,227 | 292 | 185 | 107 |
| Healdsburg | 10,968 | 26 | 17 | 9 |
| Hemet | 72,417 | 93 | 68 | 25 |
| Hercules | 25,120 | 33 | 30 | 3 |
| Hermosa Beach | 19,431 | 61 | 36 | 25 |
| Hillsborough | 10,846 | 35 | 26 | 9 |
| Hollister | 34,883 | 37 | 27 | 10 |
| Holtville | 5,392 | 6 | 5 | 1 |
| Huntington Beach | 192,911 | 358 | 225 | 133 |
| Huntington Park | 60,840 | 111 | 71 | 40 |
| Huron | 7,764 | 17 | 13 | 4 |
| Imperial | 14,565 | 19 | 17 | 2 |
| Indio | 89,459 | 122 | 72 | 50 |
| Inglewood | 112,712 | 270 | 189 | 81 |
| Ione | 7,518 | 7 | 6 | 1 |
| Irvine | 215,673 | 282 | 195 | 87 |
| Irwindale | 1,438 | 37 | 28 | 9 |
| Isleton | 839 | 4 | 4 | 0 |
| Jackson | 4,359 | 12 | 11 | 1 |
| Kensington | 5,387 | 9 | 9 | 0 |
| Kerman | 13,285 | 19 | 16 | 3 |
| King City | 11,683 | 22 | 19 | 3 |
| Kingsburg | 11,276 | 21 | 15 | 6 |
| Laguna Beach | 24,019 | 82 | 47 | 35 |
| La Habra | 59,120 | 103 | 68 | 35 |
| Lakeport | 5,171 | 15 | 13 | 2 |
| Lake Shastina | 2,390 | 5 | 4 | 1 |
| La Mesa | 54,663 | 96 | 66 | 30 |
| La Palma | 15,619 | 32 | 24 | 8 |
| La Verne | 33,842 | 65 | 45 | 20 |
| Lemoore | 24,375 | 38 | 31 | 7 |
| Lincoln | 50,654 | 42 | 32 | 10 |
| Lindsay | 10,587 | 25 | 21 | 4 |
| Livermore | 80,915 | 145 | 90 | 55 |
| Livingston | 13,764 | 28 | 18 | 10 |
| Lodi | 61,748 | 105 | 71 | 34 |
| Lompoc | 41,085 | 71 | 51 | 20 |
| Long Beach | 463,969 | 1,328 | 955 | 373 |
| Los Alamitos | 11,668 | 26 | 22 | 4 |
| Los Altos | 28,380 | 45 | 29 | 16 |
| Los Angeles | 3,848,776 | 13,195 | 9,980 | 3,215 |
| Los Banos | 36,097 | 56 | 39 | 17 |
| Los Gatos | 29,388 | 61 | 42 | 19 |
| Madera | 58,372 | 80 | 59 | 21 |
| Mammoth Lakes | 7,433 | 23 | 20 | 3 |
| Manhattan Beach | 36,907 | 98 | 64 | 34 |
| Manteca | 66,908 | 96 | 66 | 30 |
| Marina | 17,837 | 38 | 29 | 9 |
| Martinez | 35,059 | 53 | 39 | 14 |
| Marysville | 11,638 | 30 | 19 | 11 |
| Maywood | 28,234 | 61 | 39 | 22 |
| Mendota | 10,652 | 10 | 9 | 1 |
| Menlo Park | 30,011 | 73 | 48 | 25 |
| Merced | 78,693 | 136 | 99 | 37 |
| Millbrae | 20,811 | 24 | 19 | 5 |
| Mill Valley | 13,230 | 27 | 22 | 5 |
| Milpitas | 68,047 | 109 | 86 | 23 |
| Modesto | 204,474 | 339 | 245 | 94 |
| Monrovia | 37,723 | 83 | 53 | 30 |
| Montclair | 36,819 | 70 | 47 | 23 |
| Montebello | 61,870 | 126 | 83 | 43 |
| Monterey | 27,554 | 72 | 53 | 19 |
| Monterey Park | 61,353 | 106 | 77 | 29 |
| Moraga | 17,131 | 10 | 9 | 1 |
| Morgan Hill | 38,568 | 54 | 37 | 17 |
| Morro Bay | 10,327 | 20 | 14 | 6 |
| Mountain View | 71,423 | 142 | 94 | 48 |
| Mount Shasta | 3,528 | 13 | 9 | 4 |
| Murrieta | 105,238 | 132 | 90 | 42 |
| Napa | 74,736 | 114 | 71 | 43 |
| National City | 59,230 | 125 | 90 | 35 |
| Nevada City | 2,920 | 10 | 10 | 0 |
| Newark | 41,685 | 77 | 55 | 22 |
| Newman | 10,646 | 16 | 13 | 3 |
| Newport Beach | 79,912 | 228 | 139 | 89 |
| Novato | 53,374 | 77 | 58 | 19 |
| Oakdale | 20,902 | 35 | 26 | 9 |
| Oakland | 404,553 | 1,057 | 793 | 264 |
| Oceanside | 170,579 | 304 | 206 | 98 |
| Ontario | 173,212 | 324 | 220 | 104 |
| Orange | 137,132 | 229 | 159 | 70 |
| Orland | 7,281 | 10 | 8 | 2 |
| Oroville | 14,765 | 34 | 23 | 11 |
| Oxnard | 187,357 | 374 | 233 | 141 |
| Pacifica | 37,668 | 48 | 36 | 12 |
| Pacific Grove | 14,502 | 26 | 19 | 7 |
| Palm Springs | 48,537 | 148 | 92 | 56 |
| Palo Alto | 59,490 | 154 | 86 | 68 |
| Palos Verdes Estates | 13,610 | 35 | 25 | 10 |
| Paradise | 26,471 | 40 | 26 | 14 |
| Parlier | 13,500 | 19 | 16 | 3 |
| Pasadena | 144,063 | 367 | 244 | 123 |
| Paso Robles | 29,204 | 46 | 36 | 10 |
| Petaluma | 54,649 | 94 | 67 | 27 |
| Piedmont | 10,427 | 27 | 19 | 8 |
| Pinole | 18,766 | 47 | 32 | 15 |
| Pismo Beach | 8,573 | 34 | 23 | 11 |
| Pittsburg | 64,989 | 98 | 75 | 23 |
| Placentia | 50,041 | 65 | 49 | 16 |
| Placerville | 10,025 | 26 | 17 | 9 |
| Pleasant Hill | 32,841 | 61 | 43 | 18 |
| Pleasanton | 67,116 | 117 | 83 | 34 |
| Pomona | 153,217 | 289 | 178 | 111 |
| Porterville | 52,555 | 84 | 58 | 26 |
| Port Hueneme | 21,440 | 32 | 24 | 8 |
| Red Bluff | 14,111 | 34 | 22 | 12 |
| Redding | 91,242 | 150 | 112 | 38 |
| Redlands | 70,360 | 140 | 82 | 58 |
| Redondo Beach | 67,268 | 152 | 87 | 65 |
| Redwood City | 73,905 | 134 | 94 | 40 |
| Reedley | 23,744 | 45 | 32 | 13 |
| Rialto | 99,386 | 152 | 111 | 41 |
| Richmond | 102,566 | 275 | 179 | 96 |
| Ridgecrest | 25,719 | 50 | 33 | 17 |
| Rio Dell | 3,184 | 7 | 6 | 1 |
| Rio Vista | 8,256 | 10 | 9 | 1 |
| Ripon | 15,039 | 40 | 27 | 13 |
| Riverside | 299,871 | 537 | 370 | 167 |
| Rocklin | 54,919 | 80 | 52 | 28 |
| Rohnert Park | 40,401 | 88 | 70 | 18 |
| Roseville | 116,846 | 201 | 122 | 79 |
| Ross | 2,272 | 8 | 8 | 0 |
| Sacramento | 470,308 | 1,027 | 700 | 327 |
| Salinas | 143,660 | 222 | 164 | 58 |
| San Anselmo | 11,943 | 26 | 19 | 7 |
| San Bernardino | 199,683 | 468 | 324 | 144 |
| San Bruno | 40,333 | 59 | 45 | 14 |
| San Carlos | 27,187 | 39 | 31 | 8 |
| Sand City | 375 | 11 | 10 | 1 |
| San Diego | 1,314,773 | 2,647 | 1,894 | 753 |
| San Fernando | 23,856 | 54 | 36 | 18 |
| San Francisco | 809,755 | 2,853 | 2,367 | 486 |

**Table 78. Full-time Law Enforcement Employees, by State, by City, 2009**—*Continued*

(Number.)

| State/city | Population | Total law enforcement employees | Total officers | Total civilians |
|---|---|---|---|---|
| San Gabriel | 40,507 | 70 | 56 | 14 |
| Sanger | 26,285 | 38 | 30 | 8 |
| San Jose | 954,009 | 1,749 | 1,371 | 378 |
| San Leandro | 77,676 | 136 | 92 | 44 |
| San Luis Obispo | 43,565 | 86 | 59 | 27 |
| San Marino | 12,792 | 33 | 26 | 7 |
| San Mateo | 92,208 | 150 | 114 | 36 |
| San Pablo | 30,783 | 74 | 54 | 20 |
| San Rafael | 55,544 | 96 | 69 | 27 |
| San Ramon | 49,660 | 75 | 56 | 19 |
| Santa Ana | 339,196 | 646 | 353 | 293 |
| Santa Barbara | 85,715 | 193 | 131 | 62 |
| Santa Clara | 111,106 | 218 | 145 | 73 |
| Santa Cruz | 56,155 | 113 | 91 | 22 |
| Santa Maria | 87,381 | 158 | 111 | 47 |
| Santa Monica | 88,038 | 397 | 203 | 194 |
| Santa Paula | 28,603 | 41 | 32 | 9 |
| Santa Rosa | 156,541 | 242 | 169 | 73 |
| Sausalito | 7,139 | 23 | 18 | 5 |
| Scotts Valley | 11,098 | 27 | 19 | 8 |
| Seal Beach | 24,121 | 55 | 31 | 24 |
| Seaside | 33,875 | 63 | 47 | 16 |
| Sebastopol | 7,487 | 20 | 14 | 6 |
| Selma | 23,181 | 46 | 36 | 10 |
| Shafter | 16,174 | 26 | 18 | 8 |
| Sierra Madre | 10,860 | 22 | 17 | 5 |
| Signal Hill | 11,062 | 47 | 34 | 13 |
| Simi Valley | 121,538 | 176 | 119 | 57 |
| Soledad | 28,748 | 29 | 24 | 5 |
| Sonora | 4,573 | 17 | 13 | 4 |
| South Gate | 96,651 | 125 | 84 | 41 |
| South Lake Tahoe | 23,300 | 62 | 40 | 22 |
| South Pasadena | 24,462 | 50 | 35 | 15 |
| South San Francisco | 62,716 | 107 | 78 | 29 |
| Stallion Springs | 1,661 | 3 | 3 | 0 |
| St. Helena | 5,803 | 16 | 12 | 4 |
| Stockton | 292,212 | 599 | 384 | 215 |
| Suisun City | 27,056 | 38 | 26 | 12 |
| Sunnyvale | 132,144 | 284 | 215 | 69 |
| Susanville | 17,308 | 15 | 13 | 2 |
| Sutter Creek | 2,770 | 8 | 7 | 1 |
| Taft | 9,184 | 24 | 14 | 10 |
| Tehachapi | 11,807 | 15 | 13 | 2 |
| Tiburon | 8,675 | 17 | 13 | 4 |
| Torrance | 141,109 | 331 | 226 | 105 |
| Tracy | 82,019 | 136 | 91 | 45 |
| Trinidad | 309 | 2 | 2 | 0 |
| Truckee | 16,447 | 29 | 25 | 4 |
| Tulare | 58,006 | 101 | 72 | 29 |
| Tulelake | 952 | 4 | 4 | 0 |
| Turlock | 69,859 | 123 | 79 | 44 |
| Tustin | 72,286 | 142 | 91 | 51 |
| Twin Cities | 20,918 | 40 | 31 | 9 |
| Ukiah | 14,896 | 41 | 27 | 14 |
| Union City | 72,666 | 96 | 70 | 26 |
| Upland | 72,461 | 111 | 76 | 35 |
| Vacaville | 92,538 | 167 | 106 | 61 |
| Vallejo | 114,443 | 145 | 111 | 34 |
| Ventura | 103,997 | 172 | 131 | 41 |
| Vernon | 90 | 72 | 53 | 19 |
| Visalia | 124,263 | 189 | 132 | 57 |
| Walnut Creek | 63,356 | 115 | 78 | 37 |
| Watsonville | 50,898 | 87 | 64 | 23 |
| Weed | 3,031 | 16 | 10 | 6 |
| West Covina | 105,846 | 178 | 113 | 65 |
| Westminster | 89,057 | 140 | 96 | 44 |
| Westmorland | 2,207 | 5 | 5 | 0 |
| West Sacramento | 49,646 | 109 | 75 | 34 |
| Wheatland | 3,771 | 8 | 8 | 0 |
| Whittier | 82,096 | 179 | 125 | 54 |
| Williams | 4,900 | 12 | 10 | 2 |
| Willits | 4,960 | 19 | 13 | 6 |
| Willows | 6,272 | 13 | 11 | 2 |
| Winters | 7,074 | 12 | 10 | 2 |
| Woodlake | 7,506 | 15 | 13 | 2 |
| Woodland | 55,138 | 87 | 65 | 22 |
| Yreka | 7,379 | 21 | 15 | 6 |
| Yuba City | 62,495 | 92 | 65 | 27 |
| **COLORADO** | | | | |
| Alamosa | 8,781 | 28 | 24 | 4 |
| Arvada | 107,943 | 236 | 159 | 77 |
| Aspen | 5,897 | 35 | 25 | 10 |
| Ault | 1,444 | 6 | 6 | 0 |
| Aurora | 324,014 | 752 | 627 | 125 |
| Avon | 6,691 | 20 | 18 | 2 |
| Basalt | 3,304 | 12 | 9 | 3 |
| Bayfield | 2,079 | 5 | 5 | 0 |
| Berthoud | 5,477 | 10 | 9 | 1 |
| Black Hawk | 104 | 32 | 22 | 10 |
| Boulder | 100,035 | 255 | 166 | 89 |
| Bow Mar | 808 | 9 | 7 | 2 |
| Breckenridge | 3,493 | 28 | 22 | 6 |
| Brighton | 32,770 | 70 | 53 | 17 |
| Broomfield | 56,991 | 189 | 106 | 83 |
| Brush | 5,356 | 11 | 10 | 1 |
| Buena Vista | 2,127 | 9 | 7 | 2 |
| Burlington | 3,900 | 9 | 8 | 1 |
| Calhan | 865 | 3 | 3 | 0 |
| Campo | 125 | 2 | 2 | 0 |
| Canon City | 15,925 | 48 | 35 | 13 |
| Carbondale | 6,387 | 16 | 13 | 3 |
| Castle Rock | 48,287 | 68 | 50 | 18 |
| Cedaredge | 2,300 | 6 | 4 | 2 |
| Centennial | 99,385 | 148 | 114 | 34 |
| Center | 2,389 | 6 | 5 | 1 |
| Central City | 572 | 4 | 4 | 0 |
| Cherry Hills Village | 6,397 | 27 | 22 | 5 |
| Collbran | 430 | 2 | 2 | 0 |
| Colorado Springs | 401,626 | 945 | 660 | 285 |
| Columbine Valley | 1,341 | 6 | 6 | 0 |
| Commerce City | 45,914 | 114 | 89 | 25 |
| Cortez | 8,680 | 52 | 28 | 24 |
| Craig | 9,250 | 31 | 24 | 7 |
| Crested Butte | 1,665 | 9 | 7 | 2 |
| Cripple Creek | 1,001 | 23 | 12 | 11 |
| Dacono | 4,179 | 11 | 9 | 2 |
| De Beque | 528 | 3 | 3 | 0 |
| Del Norte | 1,576 | 6 | 5 | 1 |
| Delta | 9,162 | 19 | 15 | 4 |
| Denver | 604,680 | 1,757 | 1,510 | 247 |
| Dillon | 809 | 11 | 9 | 2 |
| Durango | 16,644 | 64 | 54 | 10 |
| Eagle | 6,349 | 11 | 9 | 2 |
| Eaton | 4,415 | 9 | 8 | 1 |
| Edgewater | 5,101 | 18 | 15 | 3 |
| Elizabeth | 1,434 | 6 | 5 | 1 |
| Empire | 321 | 1 | 1 | 0 |
| Englewood | 32,750 | 99 | 71 | 28 |
| Erie | 18,195 | 22 | 20 | 2 |
| Estes Park | 6,539 | 28 | 17 | 11 |
| Evans | 20,145 | 33 | 31 | 2 |
| Federal Heights | 11,695 | 34 | 24 | 10 |
| Firestone | 9,408 | 25 | 21 | 4 |
| Florence | 3,618 | 18 | 8 | 10 |
| Fort Collins | 138,487 | 243 | 169 | 74 |
| Fort Lupton | 7,668 | 23 | 18 | 5 |
| Fort Morgan | 10,485 | 34 | 28 | 6 |
| Fountain | 20,205 | 51 | 39 | 12 |
| Fraser/Winter Park | 1,809 | 10 | 9 | 1 |
| Frederick | 9,190 | 19 | 16 | 3 |
| Frisco | 2,727 | 15 | 13 | 2 |
| Fruita | 7,501 | 18 | 16 | 2 |
| Georgetown | 1,020 | 3 | 3 | 0 |
| Glendale | 4,830 | 38 | 24 | 14 |
| Glenwood Springs | 9,198 | 31 | 25 | 6 |
| Golden | 17,334 | 59 | 41 | 18 |
| Granby | 1,658 | 7 | 6 | 1 |
| Grand Junction | 50,195 | 200 | 109 | 91 |
| Greeley | 93,070 | 261 | 145 | 116 |
| Green Mountain Falls | 806 | 2 | 2 | 0 |
| Greenwood Village | 14,552 | 88 | 63 | 25 |
| Gunnison | 5,468 | 27 | 14 | 13 |

## Table 78. Full-time Law Enforcement Employees, by State, by City, 2009—*Continued*

(Number.)

| State/city | Population | Total law enforcement employees | Total officers | Total civilians |
|---|---|---|---|---|
| Hayden | 1,573 | 5 | 4 | 1 |
| Holyoke | 2,220 | 4 | 4 | 0 |
| Hotchkiss | 1,093 | 3 | 3 | 0 |
| Hugo | 728 | 2 | 2 | 0 |
| Idaho Springs | 1,715 | 9 | 7 | 2 |
| Ignacio | 761 | 7 | 7 | 0 |
| Johnstown | 10,116 | 15 | 13 | 2 |
| Kersey | 1,467 | 3 | 3 | 0 |
| Kiowa | 596 | 2 | 2 | 0 |
| Kremmling | 1,523 | 4 | 4 | 0 |
| Lafayette | 25,267 | 46 | 38 | 8 |
| La Junta | 6,992 | 21 | 16 | 5 |
| Lakeside | 19 | 9 | 9 | 0 |
| Lakewood | 140,618 | 419 | 275 | 144 |
| Lamar | 7,860 | 27 | 22 | 5 |
| La Salle | 2,001 | 6 | 6 | 0 |
| Las Animas | 2,305 | 5 | 4 | 1 |
| La Veta | 878 | 3 | 3 | 0 |
| Leadville | 2,736 | 11 | 9 | 2 |
| Limon | 1,719 | 6 | 5 | 1 |
| Littleton | 40,815 | 94 | 68 | 26 |
| Lochbuie | 5,251 | 8 | 7 | 1 |
| Lone Tree | 9,668 | 48 | 43 | 5 |
| Longmont | 87,611 | 202 | 138 | 64 |
| Louisville | 19,147 | 37 | 32 | 5 |
| Loveland | 67,324 | 132 | 91 | 41 |
| Mancos | 1,278 | 3 | 3 | 0 |
| Manitou Springs | 5,182 | 27 | 20 | 7 |
| Manzanola | 467 | 2 | 2 | 0 |
| Meeker | 2,405 | 8 | 6 | 2 |
| Milliken | 6,670 | 10 | 9 | 1 |
| Minturn | 1,198 | 4 | 3 | 1 |
| Monte Vista | 3,950 | 16 | 11 | 5 |
| Montrose | 18,651 | 58 | 39 | 19 |
| Monument | 2,673 | 16 | 13 | 3 |
| Morrison | 413 | 3 | 2 | 1 |
| Mountain View | 515 | 3 | 2 | 1 |
| Mount Crested Butte | 864 | 8 | 7 | 1 |
| Nederland | 1,366 | 5 | 4 | 1 |
| New Castle | 4,065 | 9 | 8 | 1 |
| Northglenn | 33,849 | 79 | 65 | 14 |
| Olathe | 1,758 | 5 | 4 | 1 |
| Ouray | 946 | 5 | 5 | 0 |
| Pagosa Springs | 1,762 | 9 | 8 | 1 |
| Palisade | 2,870 | 8 | 7 | 1 |
| Paonia | 1,645 | 6 | 5 | 1 |
| Parachute | 1,326 | 7 | 6 | 1 |
| Parker | 46,676 | 83 | 58 | 25 |
| Platteville | 2,664 | 8 | 8 | 0 |
| Pueblo | 105,271 | 253 | 200 | 53 |
| Rangely | 2,143 | 10 | 5 | 5 |
| Ridgway | 813 | 3 | 3 | 0 |
| Rifle | 9,504 | 24 | 20 | 4 |
| Rocky Ford | 3,916 | 10 | 9 | 1 |
| Salida | 5,375 | 18 | 15 | 3 |
| Sheridan | 5,398 | 34 | 24 | 10 |
| Silt | 2,791 | 7 | 6 | 1 |
| Silverthorne | 4,074 | 18 | 15 | 3 |
| Simla | 687 | 2 | 2 | 0 |
| Snowmass Village | 1,923 | 13 | 10 | 3 |
| South Fork | 526 | 1 | 1 | 0 |
| Springfield | 1,265 | 4 | 4 | 0 |
| Steamboat Springs | 9,560 | 38 | 24 | 14 |
| Sterling | 12,800 | 25 | 22 | 3 |
| Stratton | 600 | 1 | 1 | 0 |
| Telluride | 2,377 | 12 | 7 | 5 |
| Thornton | 117,415 | 216 | 157 | 59 |
| Trinidad | 9,125 | 34 | 22 | 12 |
| Vail | 4,783 | 58 | 27 | 31 |
| Walsenburg | 3,796 | 15 | 13 | 2 |
| Walsh | 629 | 2 | 2 | 0 |
| Westminster | 107,705 | 252 | 173 | 79 |
| Wheat Ridge | 30,683 | 98 | 71 | 27 |
| Wiggins | 956 | 2 | 2 | 0 |
| Windsor | 19,217 | 23 | 20 | 3 |
| Woodland Park | 6,490 | 29 | 19 | 10 |

| State/city | Population | Total law enforcement employees | Total officers | Total civilians |
|---|---|---|---|---|
| Wray | 2,100 | 7 | 6 | 1 |
| Yuma | 3,261 | 9 | 8 | 1 |
| **CONNECTICUT** | | | | |
| Ansonia | 18,496 | 51 | 44 | 7 |
| Avon | 17,495 | 38 | 30 | 8 |
| Berlin | 20,610 | 52 | 41 | 11 |
| Bethel | 18,476 | 46 | 34 | 12 |
| Bloomfield | 20,856 | 61 | 48 | 13 |
| Branford | 28,999 | 63 | 51 | 12 |
| Bridgeport | 136,049 | 483 | 409 | 74 |
| Bristol | 60,998 | 148 | 122 | 26 |
| Brookfield | 16,766 | 40 | 30 | 10 |
| Canton | 10,253 | 15 | 10 | 5 |
| Cheshire | 29,120 | 59 | 47 | 12 |
| Clinton | 13,602 | 30 | 24 | 6 |
| Coventry | 12,286 | 19 | 14 | 5 |
| Cromwell | 13,676 | 34 | 26 | 8 |
| Danbury | 79,729 | 152 | 147 | 5 |
| Darien | 20,237 | 58 | 51 | 7 |
| Derby | 12,392 | 33 | 31 | 2 |
| East Hampton | 12,887 | 18 | 16 | 2 |
| East Hartford | 48,459 | 161 | 127 | 34 |
| East Haven | 28,633 | 54 | 51 | 3 |
| Easton | 7,344 | 18 | 15 | 3 |
| East Windsor | 10,936 | 31 | 24 | 7 |
| Enfield | 44,857 | 114 | 93 | 21 |
| Fairfield | 57,341 | 111 | 105 | 6 |
| Farmington | 25,278 | 60 | 44 | 16 |
| Glastonbury | 33,411 | 72 | 56 | 16 |
| Granby | 11,315 | 20 | 14 | 6 |
| Greenwich | 62,018 | 178 | 150 | 28 |
| Groton | 9,319 | 39 | 31 | 8 |
| Groton Long Point | 682 | 9 | 8 | 1 |
| Groton Town | 29,105 | 73 | 69 | 4 |
| Guilford | 22,506 | 45 | 37 | 8 |
| Hamden | 57,975 | 133 | 106 | 27 |
| Hartford | 124,049 | 497 | 448 | 49 |
| Madison | 18,900 | 23 | 20 | 3 |
| Manchester | 56,566 | 148 | 115 | 33 |
| Meriden | 59,289 | 129 | 118 | 11 |
| Middlebury | 7,447 | 17 | 11 | 6 |
| Middletown | 48,299 | 114 | 97 | 17 |
| Milford | 56,310 | 121 | 104 | 17 |
| Monroe | 19,366 | 49 | 38 | 11 |
| Naugatuck | 32,033 | 70 | 58 | 12 |
| New Britain | 70,368 | 164 | 152 | 12 |
| New Canaan | 19,965 | 47 | 42 | 5 |
| New Haven | 123,659 | 518 | 423 | 95 |
| Newington | 29,739 | 65 | 52 | 13 |
| New London | 25,859 | 104 | 87 | 17 |
| New Milford | 28,471 | 65 | 49 | 16 |
| Newtown | 26,924 | 53 | 47 | 6 |
| North Branford | 14,426 | 31 | 25 | 6 |
| North Haven | 24,060 | 57 | 48 | 9 |
| Norwalk | 83,198 | 191 | 175 | 16 |
| Norwich | 36,418 | 96 | 80 | 16 |
| Old Saybrook | 10,537 | 26 | 19 | 7 |
| Orange | 13,843 | 52 | 42 | 10 |
| Plainfield | 15,519 | 20 | 16 | 4 |
| Plainville | 17,221 | 42 | 35 | 7 |
| Plymouth | 12,003 | 24 | 24 | 0 |
| Portland | 9,642 | 12 | 11 | 1 |
| Putnam | 9,342 | 18 | 15 | 3 |
| Redding | 8,855 | 21 | 15 | 6 |
| Ridgefield | 24,046 | 45 | 40 | 5 |
| Rocky Hill | 18,948 | 43 | 34 | 9 |
| Seymour | 16,340 | 42 | 40 | 2 |
| Shelton | 40,195 | 63 | 56 | 7 |
| Simsbury | 23,654 | 44 | 35 | 9 |
| Southington | 42,523 | 85 | 66 | 19 |
| South Windsor | 26,139 | 55 | 41 | 14 |
| Stamford | 119,507 | 347 | 284 | 63 |
| Stonington | 18,420 | 47 | 35 | 12 |
| Stratford | 48,726 | 111 | 104 | 7 |
| Suffield | 15,317 | 24 | 19 | 5 |
| Thomaston | 7,792 | 15 | 12 | 3 |

## Table 78. Full-time Law Enforcement Employees, by State, by City, 2009—*Continued*

(Number.)

| State/city | Population | Total law enforcement employees | Total officers | Total civilians |
|---|---|---|---|---|
| Torrington | 35,321 | 97 | 83 | 14 |
| Trumbull | 34,731 | 81 | 72 | 9 |
| Vernon | 30,038 | 65 | 52 | 13 |
| Wallingford | 45,059 | 94 | 68 | 26 |
| Waterbury | 107,007 | 356 | 291 | 65 |
| Waterford | 18,808 | 53 | 46 | 7 |
| Watertown | 22,139 | 45 | 36 | 9 |
| West Hartford | 60,430 | 145 | 126 | 19 |
| West Haven | 52,425 | 135 | 122 | 13 |
| Weston | 10,196 | 15 | 14 | 1 |
| Westport | 26,681 | 84 | 63 | 21 |
| Wethersfield | 25,656 | 58 | 47 | 11 |
| Willimantic | 16,346 | 46 | 41 | 5 |
| Wilton | 17,701 | 46 | 42 | 4 |
| Winchester | 10,721 | 26 | 22 | 4 |
| Windsor | 28,915 | 60 | 48 | 12 |
| Windsor Locks | 12,543 | 31 | 25 | 6 |
| Wolcott | 16,571 | 31 | 23 | 8 |
| Woodbridge | 9,215 | 34 | 26 | 8 |
| **DELAWARE** | | | | |
| Bethany Beach | 971 | 10 | 9 | 1 |
| Blades | 1,166 | 1 | 1 | 0 |
| Bridgeville | 1,645 | 7 | 7 | 0 |
| Camden | 2,621 | 13 | 12 | 1 |
| Cheswold | 479 | 3 | 3 | 0 |
| Clayton | 1,501 | 8 | 7 | 1 |
| Dagsboro | 585 | 2 | 2 | 0 |
| Delaware City | 1,523 | 3 | 3 | 0 |
| Delmar | 1,528 | 13 | 12 | 1 |
| Dewey Beach | 320 | 8 | 8 | 0 |
| Dover | 36,571 | 120 | 91 | 29 |
| Elsmere | 5,676 | 11 | 10 | 1 |
| Felton | 916 | 4 | 4 | 0 |
| Fenwick Island | 369 | 6 | 5 | 1 |
| Frankford | 784 | 1 | 1 | 0 |
| Georgetown | 5,277 | 20 | 18 | 2 |
| Greenwood | 914 | 1 | 1 | 0 |
| Harrington | 3,466 | 10 | 9 | 1 |
| Laurel | 4,009 | 17 | 16 | 1 |
| Lewes | 3,150 | 14 | 13 | 1 |
| Middletown | 13,093 | 30 | 27 | 3 |
| Milford | 8,704 | 40 | 30 | 10 |
| Millsboro | 2,724 | 15 | 14 | 1 |
| Milton | 1,848 | 11 | 9 | 2 |
| Newark | 29,983 | 77 | 61 | 16 |
| New Castle | 4,976 | 18 | 16 | 2 |
| Newport | 1,104 | 7 | 7 | 0 |
| Ocean View | 1,149 | 8 | 7 | 1 |
| Rehoboth Beach | 1,597 | 29 | 18 | 11 |
| Seaford | 7,310 | 38 | 27 | 11 |
| Selbyville | 1,871 | 9 | 8 | 1 |
| Smyrna | 8,981 | 29 | 22 | 7 |
| South Bethany | 530 | 6 | 6 | 0 |
| Wilmington | 72,580 | 405 | 318 | 87 |
| Wyoming | 1,443 | 4 | 4 | 0 |
| **DISTRICT OF COLUMBIA** | | | | |
| Washington | 599,657 | 4,613 | 4,052 | 561 |
| **FLORIDA** | | | | |
| Alachua | 9,669 | 27 | 21 | 6 |
| Altamonte Springs | 39,797 | 123 | 104 | 19 |
| Altha | 521 | 1 | 1 | 0 |
| Apalachicola | 2,197 | 8 | 7 | 1 |
| Apopka | 39,308 | 111 | 82 | 29 |
| Arcadia | 6,788 | 26 | 21 | 5 |
| Astatula | 1,887 | 5 | 5 | 0 |
| Atlantic Beach | 13,124 | 40 | 29 | 11 |
| Atlantis | 2,074 | 18 | 13 | 5 |
| Auburndale | 14,619 | 44 | 35 | 9 |
| Aventura | 29,743 | 117 | 81 | 36 |
| Avon Park | 9,090 | 23 | 20 | 3 |
| Bal Harbour Village | 3,099 | 36 | 28 | 8 |
| Bartow | 17,069 | 63 | 40 | 23 |
| Bay Harbor Islands | 4,912 | 29 | 23 | 6 |
| Belleair | 4,073 | 14 | 13 | 1 |
| Belle Isle | 6,553 | 12 | 11 | 1 |
| Belleview | 4,538 | 17 | 15 | 2 |
| Biscayne Park | 2,930 | 11 | 10 | 1 |
| Blountstown | 2,517 | 9 | 7 | 2 |
| Boca Raton | 85,956 | 282 | 192 | 90 |
| Bonifay | 2,772 | 6 | 5 | 1 |
| Bowling Green | 2,958 | 7 | 7 | 0 |
| Boynton Beach | 69,211 | 243 | 164 | 79 |
| Bradenton | 53,951 | 151 | 120 | 31 |
| Bradenton Beach | 1,560 | 10 | 10 | 0 |
| Brooksville | 8,375 | 27 | 24 | 3 |
| Bunnell | 3,281 | 15 | 13 | 2 |
| Bushnell | 2,301 | 10 | 9 | 1 |
| Cape Coral | 164,344 | 333 | 236 | 97 |
| Carrabelle | 1,222 | 6 | 6 | 0 |
| Casselberry | 24,782 | 69 | 52 | 17 |
| Cedar Key | 999 | 4 | 4 | 0 |
| Center Hill | 1,124 | 3 | 3 | 0 |
| Chattahoochee | 3,746 | 10 | 9 | 1 |
| Chiefland | 2,149 | 14 | 12 | 2 |
| Chipley | 3,800 | 11 | 10 | 1 |
| Clearwater | 105,383 | 353 | 248 | 105 |
| Clermont | 13,484 | 64 | 49 | 15 |
| Clewiston | 7,248 | 29 | 19 | 10 |
| Cocoa | 16,418 | 93 | 68 | 25 |
| Cocoa Beach | 11,860 | 52 | 34 | 18 |
| Coconut Creek | 50,385 | 128 | 89 | 39 |
| Coleman | 775 | 2 | 2 | 0 |
| Coral Gables | 42,784 | 251 | 177 | 74 |
| Coral Springs | 125,656 | 290 | 190 | 100 |
| Cottondale | 879 | 3 | 3 | 0 |
| Crescent City | 1,817 | 8 | 7 | 1 |
| Crestview | 20,023 | 65 | 50 | 15 |
| Cross City | 1,824 | 5 | 5 | 0 |
| Dade City | 7,321 | 34 | 24 | 10 |
| Davenport | 2,646 | 10 | 9 | 1 |
| Davie | 90,147 | 232 | 164 | 68 |
| Daytona Beach | 64,257 | 289 | 237 | 52 |
| Daytona Beach Shores | 5,225 | 35 | 29 | 6 |
| De Funiak Springs | 5,008 | 23 | 18 | 5 |
| Deland | 28,009 | 82 | 63 | 19 |
| Delray Beach | 64,522 | 216 | 146 | 70 |
| Doral | 32,209 | 121 | 89 | 32 |
| Dunnellon | 2,021 | 8 | 6 | 2 |
| Eatonville | 2,354 | 17 | 15 | 2 |
| Edgewater | 21,714 | 30 | 28 | 2 |
| Edgewood | 2,101 | 11 | 10 | 1 |
| El Portal | 2,297 | 7 | 7 | 0 |
| Eustis | 19,500 | 55 | 42 | 13 |
| Fellsmere | 5,054 | 9 | 8 | 1 |
| Fernandina Beach | 11,714 | 46 | 35 | 11 |
| Flagler Beach | 5,963 | 17 | 14 | 3 |
| Florida City | 10,204 | 41 | 31 | 10 |
| Fort Lauderdale | 182,942 | 671 | 489 | 182 |
| Fort Myers | 67,031 | 241 | 173 | 68 |
| Fort Pierce | 41,114 | 143 | 111 | 32 |
| Fort Walton Beach | 18,759 | 61 | 48 | 13 |
| Fruitland Park | 4,413 | 14 | 13 | 1 |
| Gainesville | 115,265 | 358 | 292 | 66 |
| Golden Beach | 870 | 22 | 20 | 2 |
| Graceville | 2,428 | 10 | 8 | 2 |
| Greenacres City | 32,649 | 73 | 52 | 21 |
| Green Cove Springs | 6,693 | 24 | 19 | 5 |
| Greensboro | 598 | 1 | 1 | 0 |
| Gretna | 1,603 | 5 | 5 | 0 |
| Groveland | 8,445 | 29 | 22 | 7 |
| Gulf Breeze | 6,689 | 25 | 17 | 8 |
| Gulfport | 12,286 | 37 | 28 | 9 |
| Gulf Stream | 737 | 11 | 11 | 0 |
| Haines City | 19,610 | 65 | 42 | 23 |
| Hallandale | 38,644 | 131 | 95 | 36 |
| Hampton | 460 | 2 | 2 | 0 |
| Havana | 1,689 | 13 | 9 | 4 |
| Hialeah | 208,874 | 429 | 343 | 86 |
| Hialeah Gardens | 19,667 | 51 | 37 | 14 |
| Highland Beach | 3,988 | 14 | 13 | 1 |
| High Springs | 4,696 | 17 | 13 | 4 |
| Hillsboro Beach | 2,252 | 18 | 15 | 3 |

**Table 78. Full-time Law Enforcement Employees, by State, by City, 2009—*Continued***

(Number.)

| State/city | Population | Total law enforcement employees | Total officers | Total civilians |
|---|---|---|---|---|
| Holly Hill | 13,321 | 31 | 27 | 4 |
| Hollywood | 141,597 | 481 | 316 | 165 |
| Holmes Beach | 5,023 | 21 | 14 | 7 |
| Homestead | 62,037 | 153 | 105 | 48 |
| Howey-in-the-Hills | 1,282 | 7 | 6 | 1 |
| Indialantic | 2,930 | 17 | 11 | 6 |
| Indian Creek Village | 37 | 14 | 10 | 4 |
| Indian Harbour Beach | 8,328 | 26 | 19 | 7 |
| Indian River Shores | 3,387 | 22 | 19 | 3 |
| Indian Shores | 4,235 | 13 | 11 | 2 |
| Inglis | 1,652 | 6 | 5 | 1 |
| Interlachen | 1,508 | 4 | 4 | 0 |
| Jacksonville | 810,064 | 3,241 | 1,746 | 1,495 |
| Jacksonville Beach | 21,750 | 81 | 61 | 20 |
| Jasper | 2,047 | 9 | 8 | 1 |
| Jennings | 844 | 2 | 2 | 0 |
| Juno Beach | 3,338 | 22 | 16 | 6 |
| Jupiter | 51,514 | 136 | 106 | 30 |
| Jupiter Inlet Colony | 387 | 5 | 5 | 0 |
| Jupiter Island | 672 | 21 | 16 | 5 |
| Kenneth City | 4,285 | 15 | 14 | 1 |
| Key Biscayne | 9,655 | 39 | 30 | 9 |
| Key Colony Beach | 757 | 5 | 5 | 0 |
| Key West | 22,049 | 109 | 84 | 25 |
| Kissimmee | 63,986 | 197 | 127 | 70 |
| Lady Lake | 15,282 | 42 | 29 | 13 |
| Lake Alfred | 4,560 | 12 | 7 | 5 |
| Lake City | 12,709 | 47 | 35 | 12 |
| Lake Clarke Shores | 3,313 | 11 | 11 | 0 |
| Lake Hamilton | 1,450 | 7 | 6 | 1 |
| Lake Helen | 2,784 | 8 | 7 | 1 |
| Lakeland | 94,322 | 335 | 221 | 114 |
| Lake Mary | 15,604 | 51 | 34 | 17 |
| Lake Placid | 1,897 | 9 | 7 | 2 |
| Lake Wales | 14,875 | 52 | 46 | 6 |
| Lantana | 10,150 | 37 | 30 | 7 |
| Largo | 72,567 | 183 | 137 | 46 |
| Lauderhill | 67,005 | 143 | 115 | 28 |
| Lawtey | 705 | 1 | 1 | 0 |
| Leesburg | 22,836 | 93 | 70 | 23 |
| Lighthouse Point | 11,107 | 42 | 33 | 9 |
| Live Oak | 7,298 | 21 | 17 | 4 |
| Longboat Key | 7,277 | 22 | 15 | 7 |
| Longwood | 13,453 | 47 | 40 | 7 |
| Lynn Haven | 15,606 | 34 | 25 | 9 |
| Madison | 3,036 | 15 | 14 | 1 |
| Maitland | 14,984 | 45 | 39 | 6 |
| Manalapan | 341 | 15 | 10 | 5 |
| Marco Island | 15,713 | 34 | 32 | 2 |
| Margate | 54,032 | 168 | 109 | 59 |
| Marianna | 6,290 | 25 | 18 | 7 |
| Mascotte | 6,032 | 11 | 10 | 1 |
| Medley | 1,017 | 46 | 36 | 10 |
| Melbourne | 77,854 | 233 | 166 | 67 |
| Melbourne Beach | 3,130 | 9 | 8 | 1 |
| Melbourne Village | 667 | 5 | 5 | 0 |
| Mexico Beach | 1,298 | 8 | 7 | 1 |
| Miami | 419,205 | 1,508 | 1,124 | 384 |
| Miami Beach | 84,260 | 512 | 365 | 147 |
| Miami Gardens | 110,346 | 258 | 197 | 61 |
| Miami Shores | 9,464 | 40 | 32 | 8 |
| Miami Springs | 12,412 | 54 | 41 | 13 |
| Milton | 8,789 | 26 | 18 | 8 |
| Miramar | 108,375 | 253 | 189 | 64 |
| Monticello | 2,541 | 13 | 9 | 4 |
| Mount Dora | 13,226 | 48 | 33 | 15 |
| Mulberry | 3,180 | 13 | 9 | 4 |
| Naples | 21,587 | 107 | 70 | 37 |
| Neptune Beach | 6,731 | 25 | 19 | 6 |
| New Port Richey | 17,766 | 51 | 37 | 14 |
| New Smyrna Beach | 23,656 | 61 | 50 | 11 |
| Niceville | 12,368 | 24 | 19 | 5 |
| North Bay Village | 8,024 | 33 | 25 | 8 |
| North Miami | 55,495 | 160 | 122 | 38 |
| North Miami Beach | 41,324 | 160 | 112 | 48 |
| North Palm Beach | 12,155 | 43 | 31 | 12 |
| North Port | 60,512 | 124 | 97 | 27 |
| Oak Hill | 1,611 | 7 | 7 | 0 |
| Oakland | 1,167 | 8 | 7 | 1 |
| Ocala | 55,847 | 232 | 155 | 77 |
| Ocean Ridge | 1,639 | 19 | 14 | 5 |
| Ocoee | 33,251 | 87 | 75 | 12 |
| Okeechobee | 6,060 | 26 | 20 | 6 |
| Opa Locka | 16,775 | 65 | 45 | 20 |
| Orange City | 10,033 | 26 | 23 | 3 |
| Orange Park | 9,038 | 29 | 22 | 7 |
| Orlando | 235,109 | 960 | 725 | 235 |
| Ormond Beach | 38,153 | 88 | 67 | 21 |
| Oviedo | 33,382 | 78 | 61 | 17 |
| Palatka | 10,902 | 44 | 38 | 6 |
| Palm Bay | 103,475 | 246 | 160 | 86 |
| Palm Beach | 9,519 | 121 | 76 | 45 |
| Palm Beach Gardens | 50,937 | 146 | 114 | 32 |
| Palm Beach Shores | 1,569 | 16 | 10 | 6 |
| Palmetto | 14,453 | 51 | 36 | 15 |
| Palm Springs | 16,514 | 52 | 40 | 12 |
| Panama City | 36,619 | 123 | 86 | 37 |
| Panama City Beach | 15,758 | 66 | 51 | 15 |
| Parker | 4,532 | 10 | 9 | 1 |
| Pembroke Pines | 145,514 | 292 | 229 | 63 |
| Pensacola | 53,570 | 200 | 148 | 52 |
| Perry | 6,780 | 25 | 23 | 2 |
| Pinellas Park | 47,173 | 120 | 99 | 21 |
| Plantation | 83,544 | 274 | 175 | 99 |
| Plant City | 33,048 | 83 | 65 | 18 |
| Ponce Inlet | 3,217 | 17 | 11 | 6 |
| Port Orange | 55,604 | 99 | 83 | 16 |
| Port Richey | 3,458 | 18 | 12 | 6 |
| Port St. Joe | 3,537 | 10 | 9 | 1 |
| Port St. Lucie | 164,069 | 308 | 239 | 69 |
| Punta Gorda | 16,567 | 51 | 35 | 16 |
| Quincy | 6,842 | 32 | 25 | 7 |
| Riviera Beach | 37,247 | 159 | 115 | 44 |
| Rockledge | 25,289 | 67 | 49 | 18 |
| Sanford | 52,118 | 146 | 126 | 20 |
| Sanibel | 5,601 | 30 | 24 | 6 |
| Sarasota | 52,308 | 233 | 176 | 57 |
| Satellite Beach | 11,774 | 31 | 22 | 9 |
| Sea Ranch Lakes | 734 | 10 | 6 | 4 |
| Sebastian | 20,777 | 55 | 37 | 18 |
| Sebring | 10,796 | 39 | 33 | 6 |
| Sewall's Point | 2,010 | 9 | 9 | 0 |
| Shalimar | 699 | 4 | 4 | 0 |
| Sneads | 1,942 | 9 | 5 | 4 |
| South Daytona | 13,662 | 34 | 26 | 8 |
| South Miami | 10,708 | 57 | 49 | 8 |
| South Palm Beach | 1,461 | 9 | 9 | 0 |
| Springfield | 8,792 | 21 | 15 | 6 |
| Starke | 6,011 | 21 | 19 | 2 |
| St. Augustine | 12,476 | 64 | 51 | 13 |
| St. Augustine Beach | 6,400 | 17 | 15 | 2 |
| St. Cloud | 29,604 | 104 | 70 | 34 |
| St. Pete Beach | 9,925 | 34 | 24 | 10 |
| St. Petersburg | 244,933 | 775 | 540 | 235 |
| Stuart | 16,000 | 63 | 45 | 18 |
| Sunny Isles Beach | 16,438 | 58 | 46 | 12 |
| Sunrise | 88,936 | 259 | 173 | 86 |
| Surfside | 4,480 | 37 | 28 | 9 |
| Sweetwater | 12,952 | 25 | 20 | 5 |
| Tallahassee | 174,183 | 477 | 347 | 130 |
| Tampa | 345,233 | 1,242 | 964 | 278 |
| Tarpon Springs | 23,628 | 63 | 48 | 15 |
| Tavares | 14,227 | 39 | 29 | 10 |
| Temple Terrace | 22,713 | 73 | 49 | 24 |
| Tequesta | 5,757 | 23 | 18 | 5 |
| Titusville | 45,197 | 137 | 88 | 49 |
| Treasure Island | 7,454 | 26 | 19 | 7 |
| Trenton | 1,889 | 4 | 3 | 1 |
| Umatilla | 3,107 | 9 | 8 | 1 |
| Valparaiso | 5,991 | 13 | 9 | 4 |
| Venice | 21,236 | 70 | 52 | 18 |
| Vero Beach | 16,908 | 80 | 55 | 25 |

## Table 78. Full-time Law Enforcement Employees, by State, by City, 2009—*Continued*

(Number.)

| State/city | Population | Total law enforcement employees | Total officers | Total civilians |
|---|---|---|---|---|
| Village of Pinecrest | 18,565 | 65 | 49 | 16 |
| Virginia Gardens | 2,150 | 7 | 6 | 1 |
| Waldo | 812 | 8 | 8 | 0 |
| Wauchula | 4,522 | 19 | 15 | 4 |
| Webster | 924 | 3 | 3 | 0 |
| Welaka | 818 | 1 | 1 | 0 |
| West Melbourne | 16,034 | 45 | 35 | 10 |
| West Miami | 5,497 | 21 | 17 | 4 |
| West Palm Beach | 100,763 | 397 | 294 | 103 |
| White Springs | 830 | 3 | 3 | 0 |
| Wildwood | 3,809 | 25 | 18 | 7 |
| Williston | 2,979 | 20 | 12 | 8 |
| Wilton Manors | 12,603 | 39 | 30 | 9 |
| Windermere | 2,582 | 13 | 12 | 1 |
| Winter Garden | 31,554 | 82 | 66 | 16 |
| Winter Haven | 34,103 | 93 | 74 | 19 |
| Winter Park | 27,917 | 111 | 85 | 26 |
| Winter Springs | 32,846 | 84 | 67 | 17 |
| Zephyrhills | 13,377 | 48 | 33 | 15 |
| Zolfo Springs | 1,708 | 1 | 1 | 0 |
| **GEORGIA** | | | | |
| Abbeville | 2,802 | 4 | 3 | 1 |
| Acworth | 20,193 | 52 | 39 | 13 |
| Adairsville | 3,280 | 16 | 14 | 2 |
| Adel | 5,405 | 21 | 19 | 2 |
| Alamo | 2,722 | 4 | 3 | 1 |
| Alapaha | 693 | 1 | 1 | 0 |
| Albany | 75,734 | 197 | 166 | 31 |
| Alpharetta | 50,279 | 139 | 106 | 33 |
| Alto | 915 | 3 | 2 | 1 |
| Americus | 16,467 | 47 | 39 | 8 |
| Aragon | 1,083 | 5 | 4 | 1 |
| Arcade | 1,981 | 3 | 3 | 0 |
| Ashburn | 4,215 | 16 | 15 | 1 |
| Athens-Clarke County | 114,540 | 289 | 230 | 59 |
| Atlanta | 552,901 | 1,881 | 1,506 | 375 |
| Auburn | 7,563 | 24 | 17 | 7 |
| Avondale Estates | 2,854 | 12 | 12 | 0 |
| Bainbridge | 12,380 | 51 | 41 | 10 |
| Ball Ground | 972 | 3 | 3 | 0 |
| Barnesville | 6,001 | 19 | 17 | 2 |
| Baxley | 4,575 | 12 | 11 | 1 |
| Berlin | 618 | 3 | 3 | 0 |
| Blackshear | 3,528 | 15 | 12 | 3 |
| Blythe | 827 | 1 | 1 | 0 |
| Braselton | 5,647 | 13 | 12 | 1 |
| Bremen | 5,842 | 24 | 22 | 2 |
| Brooklet | 1,363 | 4 | 4 | 0 |
| Brunswick | 16,348 | 82 | 73 | 9 |
| Buchanan | 1,054 | 9 | 8 | 1 |
| Buena Vista | 1,639 | 6 | 6 | 0 |
| Butler | 1,808 | 6 | 5 | 1 |
| Byron | 4,515 | 22 | 19 | 3 |
| Cairo | 9,871 | 24 | 21 | 3 |
| Calhoun | 15,295 | 49 | 42 | 7 |
| Camilla | 5,658 | 21 | 18 | 3 |
| Canton | 25,370 | 48 | 43 | 5 |
| Carrollton | 23,679 | 74 | 61 | 13 |
| Cartersville | 19,325 | 63 | 53 | 10 |
| Centerville | 7,502 | 19 | 16 | 3 |
| Chamblee | 11,410 | 43 | 30 | 13 |
| Chatsworth | 4,193 | 17 | 14 | 3 |
| Chickamauga | 2,608 | 5 | 5 | 0 |
| Clarkesville | 1,749 | 8 | 6 | 2 |
| Clarkston | 7,871 | 21 | 18 | 3 |
| Claxton | 2,422 | 9 | 8 | 1 |
| Clayton | 2,203 | 11 | 10 | 1 |
| Cleveland | 2,732 | 13 | 12 | 1 |
| Cochran | 5,302 | 15 | 14 | 1 |
| College Park | 19,936 | 128 | 102 | 26 |
| Colquitt | 1,911 | 9 | 9 | 0 |
| Columbus | 186,224 | 562 | 462 | 100 |
| Commerce | 6,508 | 28 | 22 | 6 |
| Conyers | 13,798 | 69 | 51 | 18 |
| Coolidge | 559 | 4 | 4 | 0 |
| Cordele | 11,507 | 36 | 30 | 6 |
| Covington | 15,385 | 62 | 53 | 9 |
| Cumming | 5,909 | 20 | 14 | 6 |
| Cuthbert | 3,387 | 5 | 5 | 0 |
| Dallas | 11,387 | 22 | 17 | 5 |
| Dalton | 34,299 | 101 | 86 | 15 |
| Danielsville | 452 | 2 | 2 | 0 |
| Dawson | 4,549 | 24 | 18 | 6 |
| Decatur | 19,071 | 56 | 43 | 13 |
| Dillard | 236 | 4 | 3 | 1 |
| Doerun | 844 | 4 | 3 | 1 |
| Donalsonville | 2,684 | 12 | 9 | 3 |
| Doraville | 10,308 | 71 | 45 | 26 |
| Douglas | 11,477 | 44 | 36 | 8 |
| Douglasville | 32,586 | 108 | 89 | 19 |
| Dublin | 17,666 | 60 | 52 | 8 |
| Duluth | 26,495 | 70 | 54 | 16 |
| Dunwoody | 33,294 | 47 | 40 | 7 |
| East Dublin | 2,798 | 8 | 8 | 0 |
| Eastman | 5,697 | 12 | 11 | 1 |
| East Point | 43,753 | 155 | 110 | 45 |
| Eatonton | 6,331 | 22 | 15 | 7 |
| Elberton | 4,524 | 21 | 18 | 3 |
| Ellaville | 1,861 | 4 | 4 | 0 |
| Emerson | 1,473 | 6 | 6 | 0 |
| Eton | 481 | 3 | 3 | 0 |
| Fairburn | 11,750 | 36 | 31 | 5 |
| Fairmount | 813 | 3 | 3 | 0 |
| Fayetteville | 15,625 | 46 | 42 | 4 |
| Folkston | 3,230 | 7 | 6 | 1 |
| Forest Park | 21,760 | 89 | 69 | 20 |
| Forsyth | 5,148 | 22 | 16 | 6 |
| Fort Gaines | 991 | 7 | 7 | 0 |
| Fort Oglethorpe | 10,000 | 31 | 30 | 1 |
| Fort Valley | 8,178 | 30 | 28 | 2 |
| Franklin | 883 | 9 | 7 | 2 |
| Franklin Springs | 803 | 7 | 6 | 1 |
| Gainesville | 36,896 | 114 | 98 | 16 |
| Garden City | 9,329 | 52 | 43 | 9 |
| Glennville | 5,464 | 17 | 12 | 5 |
| Glenwood | 897 | 1 | 1 | 0 |
| Gordon | 2,103 | 11 | 6 | 5 |
| Grantville | 2,885 | 11 | 10 | 1 |
| Gray | 2,240 | 14 | 13 | 1 |
| Greensboro | 3,281 | 21 | 18 | 3 |
| Greenville | 921 | 5 | 4 | 1 |
| Griffin | 23,795 | 106 | 94 | 12 |
| Grovetown | 9,654 | 39 | 22 | 17 |
| Guyton | 2,006 | 4 | 3 | 1 |
| Hahira | 2,579 | 6 | 5 | 1 |
| Hampton | 5,464 | 20 | 18 | 2 |
| Hapeville | 5,964 | 37 | 24 | 13 |
| Harrison | 478 | 3 | 3 | 0 |
| Hartwell | 4,306 | 28 | 23 | 5 |
| Hawkinsville | 4,254 | 10 | 9 | 1 |
| Helen | 903 | 11 | 9 | 2 |
| Helena | 2,466 | 3 | 3 | 0 |
| Hephzibah | 4,610 | 5 | 5 | 0 |
| Hiawassee | 862 | 4 | 4 | 0 |
| Hinesville | 30,130 | 97 | 84 | 13 |
| Hiram | 2,129 | 21 | 15 | 6 |
| Hoboken | 528 | 3 | 2 | 1 |
| Hogansville | 2,929 | 19 | 12 | 7 |
| Holly Springs | 9,753 | 19 | 19 | 0 |
| Homeland | 795 | 2 | 2 | 0 |
| Ideal | 476 | 1 | 1 | 0 |
| Jefferson | 8,531 | 26 | 22 | 4 |
| Jesup | 10,600 | 29 | 25 | 4 |
| Johns Creek | 59,305 | 68 | 59 | 9 |
| Jonesboro | 4,167 | 24 | 20 | 4 |
| Keysville | 246 | 1 | 1 | 0 |
| Kingsland | 14,049 | 47 | 44 | 3 |
| Lafayette | 7,632 | 23 | 21 | 2 |
| LaGrange | 28,634 | 95 | 81 | 14 |
| Lavonia | 2,102 | 15 | 14 | 1 |
| Lawrenceville | 30,046 | 91 | 71 | 20 |
| Leesburg | 2,987 | 12 | 11 | 1 |

## Table 78. Full-time Law Enforcement Employees, by State, by City, 2009—*Continued*

(Number.)

| State/city | Population | Total law enforcement employees | Total officers | Total civilians |
|---|---|---|---|---|
| Lilburn | 11,625 | 42 | 30 | 12 |
| Lincolnton | 1,523 | 4 | 4 | 0 |
| Lithonia | 2,387 | 13 | 11 | 2 |
| Loganville | 11,291 | 30 | 27 | 3 |
| Lookout Mountain | 1,515 | 8 | 7 | 1 |
| Louisville | 2,637 | 7 | 7 | 0 |
| Ludowici | 1,568 | 11 | 7 | 4 |
| Lumber City | 1,175 | 2 | 2 | 0 |
| Lumpkin | 1,205 | 4 | 4 | 0 |
| Luthersville | 825 | 3 | 3 | 0 |
| Lyons | 4,535 | 17 | 16 | 1 |
| Macon | 92,299 | 393 | 295 | 98 |
| Madison | 3,959 | 15 | 13 | 2 |
| Manchester | 3,755 | 19 | 14 | 5 |
| Marietta | 68,037 | 160 | 128 | 32 |
| McCaysville | 977 | 4 | 4 | 0 |
| McDonough | 21,635 | 40 | 36 | 4 |
| McIntyre | 712 | 5 | 5 | 0 |
| Midway | 1,034 | 6 | 5 | 1 |
| Milan | 1,030 | 1 | 1 | 0 |
| Milledgeville | 20,922 | 61 | 39 | 22 |
| Millen | 3,445 | 10 | 10 | 0 |
| Milton | 15,134 | 26 | 23 | 3 |
| Molena | 473 | 1 | 1 | 0 |
| Monroe | 13,607 | 44 | 40 | 4 |
| Montezuma | 3,839 | 13 | 11 | 2 |
| Monticello | 2,632 | 15 | 13 | 2 |
| Morrow | 5,575 | 35 | 30 | 5 |
| Moultrie | 15,515 | 47 | 42 | 5 |
| Mountain City | 737 | 3 | 3 | 0 |
| Nashville | 4,884 | 18 | 15 | 3 |
| Nelson | 964 | 1 | 1 | 0 |
| Newington | 304 | 2 | 2 | 0 |
| Newnan | 32,645 | 84 | 72 | 12 |
| Newton | 794 | 1 | 1 | 0 |
| Nicholls | 2,846 | 5 | 4 | 1 |
| Norcross | 11,031 | 48 | 37 | 11 |
| Oakwood | 4,531 | 14 | 12 | 2 |
| Ocilla | 3,130 | 13 | 12 | 1 |
| Oconee | 290 | 1 | 1 | 0 |
| Omega | 1,389 | 5 | 5 | 0 |
| Oxford | 2,631 | 4 | 4 | 0 |
| Patterson | 687 | 2 | 2 | 0 |
| Pavo | 700 | 4 | 4 | 0 |
| Peachtree City | 35,147 | 67 | 63 | 4 |
| Pearson | 1,966 | 6 | 5 | 1 |
| Pembroke | 2,565 | 8 | 6 | 2 |
| Perry | 13,358 | 43 | 38 | 5 |
| Pine Lake | 714 | 3 | 2 | 1 |
| Pine Mountain | 1,323 | 9 | 8 | 1 |
| Pineview | 516 | 1 | 1 | 0 |
| Plains | 602 | 2 | 2 | 0 |
| Pooler | 16,223 | 33 | 28 | 5 |
| Porterdale | 1,909 | 8 | 7 | 1 |
| Port Wentworth | 4,744 | 24 | 21 | 3 |
| Powder Springs | 15,947 | 35 | 31 | 4 |
| Quitman | 4,616 | 18 | 15 | 3 |
| Ray City | 803 | 2 | 2 | 0 |
| Reidsville | 2,490 | 9 | 8 | 1 |
| Reynolds | 1,060 | 7 | 7 | 0 |
| Richmond Hill | 11,096 | 36 | 29 | 7 |
| Rincon | 8,424 | 16 | 15 | 1 |
| Ringgold | 2,822 | 8 | 8 | 0 |
| Riverdale | 15,619 | 60 | 45 | 15 |
| Roberta | 748 | 4 | 4 | 0 |
| Rochelle | 1,367 | 7 | 5 | 2 |
| Rockmart | 4,622 | 19 | 17 | 2 |
| Rome | 36,091 | 104 | 89 | 15 |
| Rossville | 3,392 | 11 | 10 | 1 |
| Roswell | 88,371 | 206 | 139 | 67 |
| Royston | 2,762 | 26 | 20 | 6 |
| Sale City | 317 | 2 | 1 | 1 |
| Sandersville | 6,224 | 20 | 17 | 3 |
| Sandy Springs | 82,435 | 114 | 102 | 12 |
| Savannah-Chatham Metropolitan | 212,711 | 830 | 599 | 231 |
| Screven | 796 | 2 | 2 | 0 |
| Shiloh | 434 | 2 | 1 | 1 |
| Sky Valley | 217 | 5 | 5 | 0 |
| Smithville | 988 | 6 | 5 | 1 |
| Smyrna | 50,485 | 116 | 87 | 29 |
| Snellville | 20,464 | 56 | 47 | 9 |
| Social Circle | 4,940 | 20 | 16 | 4 |
| Sparta | 1,240 | 12 | 7 | 5 |
| Springfield | 2,158 | 8 | 7 | 1 |
| Statesboro | 27,682 | 75 | 62 | 13 |
| St. Marys | 16,997 | 35 | 32 | 3 |
| Stone Mountain | 7,706 | 19 | 18 | 1 |
| Suwanee | 17,197 | 43 | 35 | 8 |
| Sycamore | 528 | 1 | 1 | 0 |
| Sylvania | 2,494 | 14 | 10 | 4 |
| Sylvester | 5,816 | 25 | 22 | 3 |
| Tallapoosa | 3,151 | 16 | 15 | 1 |
| Tallulah Falls | 161 | 1 | 1 | 0 |
| Temple | 4,801 | 12 | 11 | 1 |
| Thomaston | 9,166 | 26 | 23 | 3 |
| Thomasville | 19,416 | 67 | 59 | 8 |
| Thomson | 6,850 | 14 | 13 | 1 |
| Thunderbolt | 2,627 | 9 | 8 | 1 |
| Tifton | 17,469 | 55 | 46 | 9 |
| Tignall | 611 | 2 | 2 | 0 |
| Toccoa | 9,130 | 32 | 28 | 4 |
| Toomsboro | 616 | 3 | 1 | 2 |
| Tunnel Hill | 1,253 | 3 | 3 | 0 |
| Tybee Island | 3,914 | 27 | 18 | 9 |
| Tyrone | 6,857 | 18 | 17 | 1 |
| Union Point | 1,519 | 8 | 8 | 0 |
| Uvalda | 552 | 1 | 1 | 0 |
| Valdosta | 49,041 | 153 | 133 | 20 |
| Vidalia | 11,449 | 42 | 34 | 8 |
| Villa Rica | 14,456 | 39 | 32 | 7 |
| Warm Springs | 476 | 2 | 1 | 1 |
| Warner Robins | 62,769 | 149 | 112 | 37 |
| Warwick | 398 | 1 | 1 | 0 |
| Washington | 4,037 | 15 | 15 | 0 |
| Watkinsville | 2,983 | 7 | 7 | 0 |
| Waverly Hall | 789 | 5 | 5 | 0 |
| Waycross | 14,712 | 68 | 57 | 11 |
| Waynesboro | 5,881 | 25 | 17 | 8 |
| West Point | 3,356 | 18 | 13 | 5 |
| Winder | 14,549 | 46 | 37 | 9 |
| Woodbury | 1,060 | 12 | 6 | 6 |
| Woodland | 388 | 3 | 2 | 1 |
| Wrens | 2,205 | 10 | 8 | 2 |
| Zebulon | 1,257 | 8 | 6 | 2 |
| **HAWAII** | | | | |
| Honolulu | 907,124 | 2,610 | 2,105 | 505 |
| **IDAHO** | | | | |
| Aberdeen | 1,740 | 6 | 3 | 3 |
| American Falls | 4,067 | 9 | 8 | 1 |
| Bellevue | 2,200 | 5 | 4 | 1 |
| Blackfoot | 11,072 | 29 | 26 | 3 |
| Boise | 206,437 | 358 | 288 | 70 |
| Bonners Ferry | 2,592 | 7 | 7 | 0 |
| Buhl | 4,088 | 10 | 8 | 2 |
| Caldwell | 44,391 | 76 | 60 | 16 |
| Cascade | 989 | 5 | 4 | 1 |
| Chubbuck | 12,087 | 33 | 20 | 13 |
| Coeur d'Alene | 44,406 | 87 | 70 | 17 |
| Cottonwood | 1,053 | 1 | 1 | 0 |
| Emmett | 6,437 | 14 | 13 | 1 |
| Filer | 2,189 | 5 | 5 | 0 |
| Fruitland | 4,836 | 7 | 6 | 1 |
| Garden City | 11,833 | 32 | 24 | 8 |
| Gooding | 3,180 | 7 | 6 | 1 |
| Grangeville | 3,099 | 6 | 6 | 0 |
| Hagerman | 795 | 2 | 2 | 0 |
| Hailey | 8,081 | 17 | 16 | 1 |
| Heyburn | 2,674 | 6 | 5 | 1 |
| Homedale | 2,464 | 5 | 5 | 0 |
| Idaho City | 478 | 1 | 1 | 0 |
| Idaho Falls | 54,702 | 133 | 89 | 44 |
| Jerome | 9,280 | 21 | 18 | 3 |

## Table 78. Full-time Law Enforcement Employees, by State, by City, 2009—*Continued*

(Number.)

| State/city | Population | Total law enforcement employees | Total officers | Total civilians |
|---|---|---|---|---|
| Kamiah | 1,081 | 3 | 3 | 0 |
| Kellogg | 2,208 | 8 | 7 | 1 |
| Ketchum | 3,302 | 12 | 8 | 4 |
| Kimberly | 3,213 | 7 | 6 | 1 |
| Lewiston | 31,864 | 67 | 46 | 21 |
| McCall | 2,656 | 18 | 13 | 5 |
| Meridian | 71,581 | 101 | 78 | 23 |
| Montpelier | 2,313 | 7 | 6 | 1 |
| Moscow | 24,604 | 42 | 34 | 8 |
| Mountain Home | 12,482 | 34 | 28 | 6 |
| Nampa | 83,875 | 173 | 122 | 51 |
| Orofino | 3,024 | 7 | 6 | 1 |
| Osburn | 1,373 | 2 | 2 | 0 |
| Parma | 1,881 | 4 | 4 | 0 |
| Payette | 7,682 | 14 | 12 | 2 |
| Pinehurst | 1,582 | 1 | 1 | 0 |
| Pocatello | 55,272 | 124 | 88 | 36 |
| Ponderay | 702 | 7 | 6 | 1 |
| Post Falls | 27,603 | 62 | 37 | 25 |
| Preston | 5,101 | 7 | 6 | 1 |
| Priest River | 1,930 | 6 | 4 | 2 |
| Rathdrum | 7,086 | 16 | 13 | 3 |
| Rexburg | 30,020 | 36 | 29 | 7 |
| Rigby | 3,438 | 10 | 8 | 2 |
| Rupert | 5,025 | 15 | 13 | 2 |
| Salmon | 2,975 | 9 | 8 | 1 |
| Sandpoint | 8,519 | 26 | 21 | 5 |
| Shelley | 4,304 | 8 | 8 | 0 |
| Soda Springs | 3,040 | 8 | 7 | 1 |
| Spirit Lake | 1,772 | 5 | 4 | 1 |
| St. Anthony | 3,409 | 4 | 4 | 0 |
| St. Maries | 2,642 | 5 | 5 | 0 |
| Sun Valley | 1,470 | 11 | 10 | 1 |
| Twin Falls | 43,095 | 99 | 68 | 31 |
| Weiser | 5,275 | 16 | 13 | 3 |
| Wendell | 2,423 | 6 | 5 | 1 |
| Wilder | 1,474 | 3 | 3 | 0 |
| **ILLINOIS** | | | | |
| Abingdon | 3,234 | 5 | 5 | 0 |
| Addison | 36,968 | 100 | 72 | 28 |
| Albany | 915 | 1 | 1 | 0 |
| Albion | 1,801 | 3 | 3 | 0 |
| Aledo | 3,560 | 8 | 7 | 1 |
| Algonquin | 31,273 | 59 | 49 | 10 |
| Alorton | 2,503 | 4 | 4 | 0 |
| Alsip | 18,583 | 53 | 38 | 15 |
| Altamont | 2,251 | 6 | 6 | 0 |
| Alton | 29,271 | 85 | 63 | 22 |
| Amboy | 2,568 | 4 | 4 | 0 |
| Anna | 5,011 | 8 | 8 | 0 |
| Annawan | 908 | 1 | 1 | 0 |
| Antioch | 14,579 | 41 | 28 | 13 |
| Arcola | 2,776 | 6 | 5 | 1 |
| Arlington Heights | 73,061 | 145 | 112 | 33 |
| Arthur | 2,121 | 5 | 5 | 0 |
| Ashland | 1,317 | 1 | 1 | 0 |
| Athens | 1,786 | 3 | 3 | 0 |
| Atkinson | 950 | 1 | 1 | 0 |
| Atwood | 1,217 | 2 | 2 | 0 |
| Auburn | 4,360 | 10 | 6 | 4 |
| Aurora | 175,135 | 371 | 300 | 71 |
| Aviston | 1,784 | 1 | 1 | 0 |
| Bannockburn | 1,937 | 7 | 7 | 0 |
| Barrington | 10,394 | 27 | 23 | 4 |
| Barrington Hills | 4,402 | 29 | 19 | 10 |
| Bartlett | 42,856 | 71 | 53 | 18 |
| Bartonville | 6,142 | 15 | 10 | 5 |
| Batavia | 27,872 | 51 | 44 | 7 |
| Beardstown | 5,867 | 13 | 9 | 4 |
| Beckemeyer | 1,088 | 1 | 1 | 0 |
| Bedford Park | 529 | 44 | 36 | 8 |
| Beecher | 3,151 | 8 | 7 | 1 |
| Belleville | 40,975 | 98 | 80 | 18 |
| Bellwood | 18,810 | 43 | 40 | 3 |
| Belvidere | 27,128 | 49 | 44 | 5 |
| Benld | 1,455 | 4 | 4 | 0 |
| Bensenville | 20,073 | 43 | 32 | 11 |
| Benton | 6,961 | 11 | 10 | 1 |
| Berkeley | 4,878 | 20 | 16 | 4 |
| Berwyn | 49,489 | 138 | 104 | 34 |
| Bethalto | 9,974 | 21 | 15 | 6 |
| Bloomingdale | 21,855 | 64 | 47 | 17 |
| Bloomington | 73,897 | 155 | 122 | 33 |
| Blue Island | 22,203 | 68 | 38 | 30 |
| Blue Mound | 1,009 | 1 | 1 | 0 |
| Bolingbrook | 72,566 | 154 | 112 | 42 |
| Bourbonnais | 19,479 | 30 | 23 | 7 |
| Braidwood | 6,844 | 11 | 10 | 1 |
| Breese | 4,386 | 8 | 7 | 1 |
| Bridgeport | 2,077 | 2 | 2 | 0 |
| Bridgeview | 14,953 | 43 | 41 | 2 |
| Brighton | 2,397 | 6 | 4 | 2 |
| Broadview | 7,558 | 32 | 25 | 7 |
| Brookfield | 17,971 | 36 | 31 | 5 |
| Buffalo Grove | 42,939 | 85 | 70 | 15 |
| Bull Valley | 855 | 2 | 2 | 0 |
| Burbank | 27,529 | 70 | 53 | 17 |
| Burnham | 3,952 | 12 | 7 | 5 |
| Burr Ridge | 11,471 | 31 | 28 | 3 |
| Byron | 3,951 | 8 | 7 | 1 |
| Cahokia | 14,970 | 44 | 32 | 12 |
| Cairo | 3,052 | 14 | 9 | 5 |
| Calumet City | 36,560 | 118 | 93 | 25 |
| Calumet Park | 7,924 | 29 | 22 | 7 |
| Cambridge | 2,084 | 1 | 1 | 0 |
| Camp Point | 1,188 | 2 | 2 | 0 |
| Campton Hills | 11,100 | 6 | 6 | 0 |
| Canton | 14,463 | 33 | 23 | 10 |
| Carbondale | 26,225 | 77 | 59 | 18 |
| Carlinville | 5,953 | 17 | 12 | 5 |
| Carlyle | 3,375 | 8 | 7 | 1 |
| Carmi | 5,181 | 11 | 9 | 2 |
| Carol Stream | 39,951 | 89 | 64 | 25 |
| Carpentersville | 38,565 | 81 | 67 | 14 |
| Carrier Mills | 1,827 | 2 | 2 | 0 |
| Carrollton | 2,445 | 6 | 6 | 0 |
| Carterville | 5,529 | 7 | 7 | 0 |
| Carthage | 2,481 | 3 | 3 | 0 |
| Casey | 2,911 | 7 | 7 | 0 |
| Caseyville | 4,262 | 15 | 11 | 4 |
| Central City | 1,307 | 4 | 4 | 0 |
| Centralia | 13,484 | 36 | 27 | 9 |
| Centreville | 5,602 | 14 | 11 | 3 |
| Chadwick | 468 | 1 | 1 | 0 |
| Champaign | 80,467 | 153 | 120 | 33 |
| Channahon | 14,933 | 29 | 25 | 4 |
| Charleston | 21,779 | 35 | 33 | 2 |
| Chatham | 10,925 | 21 | 15 | 6 |
| Chenoa | 3,260 | 4 | 4 | 0 |
| Cherry Valley | 2,274 | 16 | 15 | 1 |
| Chester | 7,775 | 11 | 8 | 3 |
| Chicago | 2,848,431 | 13,960 | 13,088 | 872 |
| Chicago Heights | 30,354 | 110 | 81 | 29 |
| Chicago Ridge | 13,286 | 35 | 31 | 4 |
| Chillicothe | 5,893 | 13 | 8 | 5 |
| Christopher | 2,816 | 5 | 5 | 0 |
| Cicero | 79,870 | 176 | 147 | 29 |
| Clarendon Hills | 8,666 | 16 | 15 | 1 |
| Clinton | 7,117 | 15 | 13 | 2 |
| Coal City | 5,836 | 13 | 12 | 1 |
| Coal Valley | 4,045 | 8 | 7 | 1 |
| Cobden | 1,096 | 3 | 3 | 0 |
| Colfax | 1,002 | 1 | 1 | 0 |
| Collinsville | 26,074 | 64 | 45 | 19 |
| Colona | 5,233 | 12 | 11 | 1 |
| Columbia | 9,505 | 19 | 12 | 7 |
| Cordova | 686 | 1 | 1 | 0 |
| Cortland | 4,489 | 4 | 4 | 0 |
| Coulterville | 1,139 | 2 | 2 | 0 |
| Country Club Hills | 16,783 | 64 | 44 | 20 |
| Countryside | 5,766 | 31 | 24 | 7 |
| Crest Hill | 21,405 | 28 | 26 | 2 |

## Table 78. Full-time Law Enforcement Employees, by State, by City, 2009—*Continued*

(Number.)

| State/city | Population | Total law enforcement employees | Total officers | Total civilians |
|---|---|---|---|---|
| Crestwood | 11,028 | 3 | 2 | 1 |
| Crete | 9,189 | 21 | 19 | 2 |
| Creve Coeur | 5,181 | 7 | 6 | 1 |
| Crystal Lake | 42,198 | 78 | 65 | 13 |
| Cuba | 1,324 | 2 | 2 | 0 |
| Danvers | 1,145 | 2 | 2 | 0 |
| Danville | 32,076 | 70 | 60 | 10 |
| Darien | 22,304 | 55 | 39 | 16 |
| Decatur | 75,651 | 195 | 162 | 33 |
| Deer Creek-Goodfield | 1,621 | 1 | 1 | 0 |
| Deerfield | 19,797 | 53 | 39 | 14 |
| Deer Park | 3,373 | 21 | 19 | 2 |
| De Kalb | 46,253 | 74 | 61 | 13 |
| Delavan | 1,747 | 3 | 3 | 0 |
| De Pue | 1,744 | 3 | 3 | 0 |
| De Soto | 1,549 | 4 | 3 | 1 |
| Des Plaines | 57,061 | 124 | 100 | 24 |
| Divernon | 1,121 | 1 | 1 | 0 |
| Dixon | 14,931 | 32 | 28 | 4 |
| Downers Grove | 49,170 | 109 | 79 | 30 |
| Dupo | 4,089 | 6 | 6 | 0 |
| Du Quoin | 6,312 | 15 | 11 | 4 |
| Durand | 1,085 | 1 | 1 | 0 |
| Dwight | 4,255 | 10 | 9 | 1 |
| Earlville | 1,828 | 3 | 3 | 0 |
| East Alton | 6,535 | 16 | 11 | 5 |
| East Dubuque | 1,913 | 6 | 6 | 0 |
| East Dundee | 3,137 | 14 | 13 | 1 |
| East Hazel Crest | 1,528 | 10 | 9 | 1 |
| East Moline | 20,828 | 49 | 39 | 10 |
| East Peoria | 22,769 | 55 | 41 | 14 |
| East St. Louis | 28,479 | 88 | 65 | 23 |
| Edwardsville | 24,803 | 57 | 42 | 15 |
| Effingham | 12,498 | 35 | 22 | 13 |
| Elburn | 5,652 | 9 | 8 | 1 |
| Eldorado | 4,378 | 11 | 7 | 4 |
| Elgin | 107,686 | 233 | 180 | 53 |
| Elizabeth | 646 | 1 | 1 | 0 |
| Elk Grove Village | 33,164 | 106 | 92 | 14 |
| Elmhurst | 46,372 | 91 | 69 | 22 |
| Elmwood | 1,864 | 1 | 1 | 0 |
| Elmwood Park | 23,909 | 41 | 34 | 7 |
| El Paso | 2,814 | 5 | 5 | 0 |
| Elwood | 2,434 | 11 | 10 | 1 |
| Energy | 1,202 | 4 | 4 | 0 |
| Erie | 1,544 | 2 | 2 | 0 |
| Eureka | 5,405 | 6 | 6 | 0 |
| Evanston | 78,101 | 218 | 165 | 53 |
| Evergreen Park | 19,206 | 72 | 60 | 12 |
| Fairbury | 3,762 | 9 | 8 | 1 |
| Fairfield | 5,139 | 17 | 13 | 4 |
| Fairview | 479 | 1 | 1 | 0 |
| Fairview Heights | 16,841 | 50 | 40 | 10 |
| Farmer City | 1,941 | 6 | 4 | 2 |
| Fisher | 1,767 | 2 | 2 | 0 |
| Flora | 4,742 | 16 | 11 | 5 |
| Flossmoor | 9,305 | 24 | 19 | 5 |
| Forest Park | 15,176 | 54 | 38 | 16 |
| Forest View | 712 | 12 | 9 | 3 |
| Fox Lake | 11,314 | 26 | 22 | 4 |
| Fox River Grove | 5,192 | 12 | 12 | 0 |
| Frankfort | 19,060 | 35 | 31 | 4 |
| Franklin Park | 17,810 | 54 | 50 | 4 |
| Freeburg | 4,530 | 10 | 9 | 1 |
| Freeport | 24,424 | 72 | 54 | 18 |
| Fulton | 3,826 | 9 | 8 | 1 |
| Galena | 3,319 | 13 | 10 | 3 |
| Galesburg | 30,910 | 82 | 53 | 29 |
| Galva | 2,632 | 3 | 3 | 0 |
| Geneseo | 6,430 | 17 | 12 | 5 |
| Geneva | 24,862 | 49 | 35 | 14 |
| Genoa | 5,207 | 8 | 7 | 1 |
| Georgetown | 3,421 | 4 | 4 | 0 |
| Germantown | 1,228 | 1 | 1 | 0 |
| Gibson City | 3,277 | 9 | 7 | 2 |
| Gifford | 1,011 | 1 | 1 | 0 |
| Gilberts | 7,298 | 9 | 8 | 1 |
| Gillespie | 3,159 | 10 | 7 | 3 |
| Gilman | 1,706 | 3 | 3 | 0 |
| Girard | 2,158 | 5 | 5 | 0 |
| Glasford | 1,029 | 2 | 2 | 0 |
| Glen Carbon | 12,851 | 28 | 19 | 9 |
| Glencoe | 9,067 | 41 | 32 | 9 |
| Glendale Heights | 31,832 | 79 | 56 | 23 |
| Glen Ellyn | 27,132 | 48 | 40 | 8 |
| Glenview | 46,528 | 84 | 73 | 11 |
| Glenwood | 8,433 | 23 | 22 | 1 |
| Golf | 444 | 4 | 4 | 0 |
| Grafton | 739 | 5 | 5 | 0 |
| Granite City | 30,568 | 70 | 60 | 10 |
| Grant Park | 1,756 | 3 | 3 | 0 |
| Granville | 1,336 | 2 | 2 | 0 |
| Grayslake | 22,099 | 38 | 33 | 5 |
| Grayville | 1,570 | 5 | 3 | 2 |
| Greenfield | 1,062 | 2 | 2 | 0 |
| Greenup | 1,471 | 4 | 4 | 0 |
| Greenville | 7,415 | 13 | 9 | 4 |
| Gurnee | 30,800 | 89 | 61 | 28 |
| Hainesville | 3,940 | 6 | 5 | 1 |
| Hamilton | 2,751 | 4 | 4 | 0 |
| Hampshire | 5,968 | 11 | 11 | 0 |
| Hampton | 1,791 | 4 | 4 | 0 |
| Hanover Park | 36,617 | 80 | 57 | 23 |
| Harrisburg | 9,554 | 15 | 14 | 1 |
| Hartford | 1,470 | 5 | 4 | 1 |
| Harvard | 10,072 | 24 | 18 | 6 |
| Harvey | 27,852 | 93 | 69 | 24 |
| Harwood Heights | 8,031 | 35 | 24 | 11 |
| Havana | 3,302 | 11 | 7 | 4 |
| Hawthorn Woods | 8,312 | 10 | 9 | 1 |
| Hazel Crest | 13,995 | 34 | 28 | 6 |
| Hebron | 1,434 | 4 | 4 | 0 |
| Henry | 2,402 | 3 | 3 | 0 |
| Herrin | 12,439 | 24 | 17 | 7 |
| Herscher | 1,625 | 3 | 3 | 0 |
| Hickory Hills | 13,263 | 37 | 29 | 8 |
| Highland | 9,893 | 28 | 20 | 8 |
| Highland Park | 31,576 | 79 | 58 | 21 |
| Highwood | 5,378 | 14 | 13 | 1 |
| Hillsboro | 6,142 | 8 | 8 | 0 |
| Hillside | 8,367 | 35 | 28 | 7 |
| Hinckley | 2,091 | 3 | 3 | 0 |
| Hinsdale | 18,553 | 35 | 28 | 7 |
| Hodgkins | 2,001 | 23 | 21 | 2 |
| Hoffman Estates | 54,100 | 116 | 101 | 15 |
| Homer | 1,114 | 1 | 1 | 0 |
| Hometown | 4,075 | 5 | 1 | 4 |
| Homewood | 18,361 | 42 | 37 | 5 |
| Hoopeston | 5,621 | 16 | 11 | 5 |
| Hopedale | 924 | 2 | 2 | 0 |
| Huntley | 26,597 | 38 | 32 | 6 |
| Indian Head Park | 3,606 | 11 | 10 | 1 |
| Island Lake | 8,634 | 21 | 15 | 6 |
| Itasca | 8,645 | 32 | 24 | 8 |
| Jacksonville | 19,353 | 50 | 40 | 10 |
| Jerome | 1,282 | 8 | 8 | 0 |
| Jerseyville | 8,415 | 21 | 15 | 6 |
| Johnsburg | 6,894 | 10 | 9 | 1 |
| Joliet | 151,103 | 352 | 269 | 83 |
| Jonesboro | 1,815 | 2 | 2 | 0 |
| Justice | 12,481 | 32 | 25 | 7 |
| Kankakee | 26,615 | 85 | 73 | 12 |
| Kenilworth | 2,387 | 14 | 11 | 3 |
| Kewanee | 12,229 | 32 | 24 | 8 |
| Kildeer | 4,196 | 21 | 19 | 2 |
| Kincaid | 1,451 | 1 | 1 | 0 |
| Kingston | 1,069 | 2 | 2 | 0 |
| Kirkland | 1,772 | 3 | 3 | 0 |
| Knoxville | 2,890 | 5 | 5 | 0 |
| La Grange | 15,206 | 43 | 29 | 14 |
| La Grange Park | 12,311 | 28 | 22 | 6 |
| Lake Bluff | 6,239 | 22 | 16 | 6 |

## Table 78. Full-time Law Enforcement Employees, by State, by City, 2009—*Continued*

(Number.)

| State/city | Population | Total law enforcement employees | Total officers | Total civilians |
|---|---|---|---|---|
| Lake Forest | 21,083 | 59 | 40 | 19 |
| Lake in the Hills | 30,405 | 59 | 42 | 17 |
| Lake Villa | 9,054 | 18 | 17 | 1 |
| Lakewood | 3,875 | 9 | 8 | 1 |
| Lake Zurich | 20,835 | 51 | 34 | 17 |
| La Moille | 740 | 1 | 1 | 0 |
| Lanark | 1,444 | 2 | 1 | 1 |
| Lansing | 26,496 | 74 | 55 | 19 |
| La Salle | 9,480 | 30 | 24 | 6 |
| Lawrenceville | 4,346 | 7 | 7 | 0 |
| Lebanon | 4,595 | 12 | 12 | 0 |
| Leland | 961 | 1 | 1 | 0 |
| Leland Grove | 1,428 | 6 | 5 | 1 |
| Lemont | 16,516 | 37 | 33 | 4 |
| Lenzburg | 525 | 1 | 1 | 0 |
| Le Roy | 3,548 | 6 | 6 | 0 |
| Lewistown | 2,358 | 3 | 3 | 0 |
| Lexington | 1,897 | 2 | 2 | 0 |
| Libertyville | 21,961 | 53 | 38 | 15 |
| Lincoln | 14,454 | 26 | 25 | 1 |
| Lincolnshire | 8,196 | 36 | 25 | 11 |
| Lincolnwood | 11,752 | 41 | 31 | 10 |
| Lindenhurst | 14,923 | 18 | 16 | 2 |
| Lisle | 23,194 | 55 | 43 | 12 |
| Litchfield | 6,613 | 23 | 16 | 7 |
| Lockport | 26,106 | 44 | 37 | 7 |
| Lombard | 42,905 | 86 | 68 | 18 |
| Loves Park | 24,965 | 35 | 31 | 4 |
| Lynwood | 8,582 | 26 | 19 | 7 |
| Lyons | 10,251 | 34 | 27 | 7 |
| Machesney Park | 23,053 | 27 | 26 | 1 |
| Mackinaw | 1,732 | 1 | 1 | 0 |
| Macomb | 19,885 | 34 | 31 | 3 |
| Madison | 4,556 | 16 | 12 | 4 |
| Mahomet | 6,597 | 9 | 8 | 1 |
| Manhattan | 7,793 | 10 | 9 | 1 |
| Manito | 1,620 | 10 | 10 | 0 |
| Manteno | 8,821 | 18 | 17 | 1 |
| Marengo | 7,659 | 22 | 16 | 6 |
| Marion | 17,524 | 40 | 30 | 10 |
| Marissa | 1,965 | 4 | 4 | 0 |
| Maroa | 1,526 | 3 | 3 | 0 |
| Marquette Heights | 2,835 | 4 | 4 | 0 |
| Marseilles | 4,952 | 14 | 9 | 5 |
| Marshall | 3,841 | 10 | 9 | 1 |
| Martinsville | 1,211 | 2 | 2 | 0 |
| Maryville | 7,747 | 18 | 13 | 5 |
| Mascoutah | 6,815 | 14 | 13 | 1 |
| Mason City | 2,345 | 5 | 5 | 0 |
| Matteson | 17,993 | 46 | 36 | 10 |
| Mattoon | 17,064 | 47 | 40 | 7 |
| Maywood | 24,830 | 76 | 59 | 17 |
| McCook | 235 | 23 | 18 | 5 |
| McCullom Lake | 1,107 | 4 | 4 | 0 |
| McHenry | 27,489 | 62 | 47 | 15 |
| McLean | 789 | 1 | 1 | 0 |
| McLeansboro | 2,763 | 5 | 5 | 0 |
| Melrose Park | 21,712 | 81 | 71 | 10 |
| Mendota | 6,965 | 20 | 15 | 5 |
| Meredosia | 958 | 1 | 1 | 0 |
| Metamora | 3,482 | 4 | 4 | 0 |
| Metropolis | 6,537 | 22 | 17 | 5 |
| Midlothian | 13,583 | 29 | 26 | 3 |
| Milan | 5,167 | 19 | 14 | 5 |
| Milledgeville | 922 | 2 | 2 | 0 |
| Millstadt | 3,398 | 8 | 8 | 0 |
| Minier | 1,247 | 2 | 2 | 0 |
| Minonk | 2,153 | 3 | 3 | 0 |
| Minooka | 11,738 | 24 | 21 | 3 |
| Mokena | 19,817 | 36 | 33 | 3 |
| Moline | 42,996 | 105 | 83 | 22 |
| Momence | 3,177 | 9 | 9 | 0 |
| Monee | 5,278 | 15 | 14 | 1 |
| Monmouth | 9,268 | 31 | 19 | 12 |
| Montgomery | 17,071 | 32 | 22 | 10 |
| Monticello | 5,374 | 7 | 6 | 1 |
| Morris | 14,027 | 34 | 25 | 9 |
| Morrison | 4,287 | 7 | 7 | 0 |
| Morton | 16,105 | 29 | 22 | 7 |
| Morton Grove | 22,485 | 60 | 46 | 14 |
| Mount Carmel | 7,343 | 17 | 12 | 5 |
| Mount Carroll | 1,641 | 3 | 3 | 0 |
| Mount Morris | 3,083 | 5 | 4 | 1 |
| Mount Olive | 2,042 | 5 | 3 | 2 |
| Mount Prospect | 53,028 | 113 | 89 | 24 |
| Mount Pulaski | 1,568 | 2 | 2 | 0 |
| Mount Sterling | 1,889 | 8 | 4 | 4 |
| Mount Zion | 5,191 | 12 | 10 | 2 |
| Moweaqua | 1,810 | 1 | 1 | 0 |
| Mundelein | 34,021 | 70 | 52 | 18 |
| Murphysboro | 8,129 | 23 | 16 | 7 |
| Naperville | 144,731 | 292 | 185 | 107 |
| Nashville | 3,014 | 8 | 7 | 1 |
| Nauvoo | 1,165 | 3 | 3 | 0 |
| Neoga | 1,742 | 3 | 3 | 0 |
| New Athens | 2,001 | 4 | 4 | 0 |
| New Baden | 3,276 | 5 | 5 | 0 |
| New Lenox | 24,896 | 41 | 38 | 3 |
| Newton | 2,930 | 7 | 6 | 1 |
| Niles | 28,518 | 75 | 60 | 15 |
| Nokomis | 2,246 | 5 | 4 | 1 |
| Normal | 52,827 | 92 | 78 | 14 |
| North Aurora | 16,470 | 31 | 29 | 2 |
| Northbrook | 33,980 | 94 | 65 | 29 |
| North Chicago | 32,272 | 78 | 57 | 21 |
| Northfield | 5,418 | 28 | 19 | 9 |
| Northlake | 11,417 | 56 | 40 | 16 |
| North Pekin | 1,735 | 3 | 3 | 0 |
| North Riverside | 6,193 | 36 | 28 | 8 |
| Oak Brook | 8,819 | 52 | 42 | 10 |
| Oakbrook Terrace | 2,236 | 24 | 21 | 3 |
| Oak Forest | 27,699 | 54 | 42 | 12 |
| Oak Lawn | 53,028 | 125 | 103 | 22 |
| Oak Park | 53,286 | 145 | 116 | 29 |
| Oakwood | 1,418 | 1 | 1 | 0 |
| Oblong | 1,517 | 1 | 1 | 0 |
| O'Fallon | 28,194 | 58 | 44 | 14 |
| Oglesby | 3,674 | 12 | 9 | 3 |
| Okawville | 1,335 | 3 | 3 | 0 |
| Olney | 8,367 | 18 | 12 | 6 |
| Olympia Fields | 4,735 | 22 | 20 | 2 |
| Oregon | 4,130 | 9 | 8 | 1 |
| Orion | 1,685 | 3 | 3 | 0 |
| Orland Hills | 7,240 | 14 | 13 | 1 |
| Orland Park | 55,990 | 126 | 97 | 29 |
| Oswego | 34,521 | 60 | 50 | 10 |
| Ottawa | 19,509 | 47 | 36 | 11 |
| Palatine | 67,162 | 152 | 112 | 40 |
| Palestine | 1,319 | 2 | 2 | 0 |
| Palmyra | 703 | 5 | 5 | 0 |
| Palos Heights | 12,604 | 30 | 27 | 3 |
| Palos Hills | 16,844 | 36 | 33 | 3 |
| Palos Park | 4,879 | 12 | 11 | 1 |
| Pana | 5,694 | 13 | 9 | 4 |
| Paris | 8,644 | 22 | 17 | 5 |
| Park City | 6,603 | 12 | 10 | 2 |
| Park Forest | 22,482 | 55 | 42 | 13 |
| Park Ridge | 36,835 | 73 | 60 | 13 |
| Pawnee | 2,534 | 10 | 6 | 4 |
| Paxton | 4,514 | 7 | 7 | 0 |
| Pecatonica | 2,232 | 3 | 3 | 0 |
| Pekin | 33,382 | 64 | 55 | 9 |
| Peoria | 114,241 | 277 | 238 | 39 |
| Peoria Heights | 6,190 | 16 | 12 | 4 |
| Peotone | 4,406 | 11 | 10 | 1 |
| Peru | 9,805 | 33 | 26 | 7 |
| Petersburg | 2,179 | 4 | 4 | 0 |
| Pinckneyville | 5,373 | 7 | 6 | 1 |
| Piper City | 731 | 1 | 1 | 0 |
| Pittsfield | 4,435 | 6 | 6 | 0 |
| Plainfield | 40,764 | 78 | 55 | 23 |
| Plano | 12,945 | 20 | 18 | 2 |

**Table 78. Full-time Law Enforcement Employees, by State, by City, 2009**—*Continued*

(Number.)

| State/city | Population | Total law enforcement employees | Total officers | Total civilians |
|---|---|---|---|---|
| Polo | 2,477 | 4 | 4 | 0 |
| Pontiac | 11,182 | 24 | 22 | 2 |
| Pontoon Beach | 6,119 | 21 | 15 | 6 |
| Posen | 4,926 | 17 | 15 | 2 |
| Potomac | 653 | 1 | 1 | 0 |
| Princeton | 7,494 | 17 | 16 | 1 |
| Prophetstown | 1,915 | 3 | 3 | 0 |
| Prospect Heights | 15,940 | 28 | 26 | 2 |
| Quincy | 39,906 | 90 | 76 | 14 |
| Rankin | 581 | 1 | 1 | 0 |
| Rantoul | 12,109 | 38 | 30 | 8 |
| Raymond | 896 | 2 | 2 | 0 |
| Red Bud | 3,656 | 6 | 6 | 0 |
| Richmond | 2,510 | 3 | 3 | 0 |
| Richton Park | 12,873 | 33 | 28 | 5 |
| Ridge Farm | 851 | 1 | 1 | 0 |
| Ridgway | 853 | 3 | 3 | 0 |
| Riverdale | 14,069 | 45 | 37 | 8 |
| River Forest | 11,128 | 30 | 27 | 3 |
| River Grove | 9,921 | 29 | 23 | 6 |
| Riverside | 8,207 | 23 | 18 | 5 |
| Riverwoods | 4,107 | 7 | 7 | 0 |
| Robbins | 6,299 | 11 | 3 | 8 |
| Robinson | 6,323 | 15 | 14 | 1 |
| Rochelle | 9,867 | 28 | 20 | 8 |
| Rochester | 3,277 | 8 | 8 | 0 |
| Rockdale | 2,005 | 5 | 5 | 0 |
| Rock Falls | 9,277 | 26 | 19 | 7 |
| Rockford | 157,943 | 315 | 284 | 31 |
| Rock Island | 37,976 | 110 | 83 | 27 |
| Rockton | 5,520 | 16 | 15 | 1 |
| Rolling Meadows | 23,335 | 63 | 51 | 12 |
| Romeoville | 40,465 | 88 | 68 | 20 |
| Roodhouse | 1,909 | 8 | 4 | 4 |
| Roscoe | 9,135 | 14 | 13 | 1 |
| Roselle | 23,197 | 52 | 36 | 16 |
| Rosemont | 3,898 | 88 | 75 | 13 |
| Rossville | 1,147 | 2 | 2 | 0 |
| Round Lake | 18,836 | 27 | 21 | 6 |
| Round Lake Beach | 28,054 | 51 | 40 | 11 |
| Round Lake Heights | 3,051 | 4 | 4 | 0 |
| Round Lake Park | 6,189 | 14 | 12 | 2 |
| Roxana | 1,546 | 6 | 5 | 1 |
| Royalton | 1,162 | 2 | 2 | 0 |
| Rushville | 3,083 | 4 | 4 | 0 |
| Salem | 7,398 | 19 | 13 | 6 |
| Sandwich | 7,424 | 22 | 16 | 6 |
| Sauget | 236 | 14 | 13 | 1 |
| Sauk Village | 10,236 | 33 | 25 | 8 |
| Savanna | 3,176 | 8 | 8 | 0 |
| Schaumburg | 71,325 | 160 | 116 | 44 |
| Schiller Park | 11,544 | 41 | 33 | 8 |
| Seneca | 2,134 | 8 | 4 | 4 |
| Sesser | 2,121 | 6 | 5 | 1 |
| Shannon | 789 | 1 | 1 | 0 |
| Shawneetown | 1,298 | 4 | 4 | 0 |
| Shelbyville | 4,568 | 8 | 7 | 1 |
| Sheridan | 2,042 | 3 | 3 | 0 |
| Sherman | 3,947 | 6 | 6 | 0 |
| Shiloh | 11,500 | 18 | 17 | 1 |
| Shorewood | 16,707 | 30 | 26 | 4 |
| Silvis | 7,829 | 22 | 15 | 7 |
| Skokie | 66,996 | 144 | 110 | 34 |
| Sleepy Hollow | 3,701 | 8 | 7 | 1 |
| Somonauk | 1,676 | 5 | 5 | 0 |
| South Barrington | 4,545 | 20 | 17 | 3 |
| South Beloit | 5,546 | 16 | 15 | 1 |
| South Chicago Heights | 3,759 | 11 | 7 | 4 |
| South Elgin | 21,729 | 42 | 32 | 10 |
| Southern View | 1,627 | 2 | 2 | 0 |
| South Holland | 20,969 | 49 | 47 | 2 |
| South Jacksonville | 3,226 | 6 | 5 | 1 |
| South Pekin | 1,202 | 2 | 2 | 0 |
| South Roxana | 1,798 | 5 | 5 | 0 |
| Sparta | 4,286 | 15 | 10 | 5 |
| Springfield | 117,973 | 317 | 268 | 49 |
| Spring Grove | 6,009 | 12 | 10 | 2 |
| Spring Valley | 5,451 | 13 | 10 | 3 |
| St. Anne | 1,249 | 2 | 2 | 0 |
| Staunton | 5,139 | 12 | 7 | 5 |
| St. Charles | 33,379 | 64 | 52 | 12 |
| Steger | 10,504 | 24 | 16 | 8 |
| Sterling | 15,051 | 43 | 30 | 13 |
| St. Francisville | 725 | 1 | 1 | 0 |
| Stickney | 5,735 | 22 | 15 | 7 |
| Stockton | 1,782 | 5 | 4 | 1 |
| Stone Park | 4,832 | 22 | 16 | 6 |
| Stonington | 894 | 2 | 2 | 0 |
| Streamwood | 37,175 | 68 | 58 | 10 |
| Streator | 13,736 | 33 | 26 | 7 |
| Sugar Grove | 10,626 | 15 | 14 | 1 |
| Sullivan | 4,385 | 10 | 8 | 2 |
| Summit | 10,179 | 34 | 28 | 6 |
| Sumner | 3,418 | 2 | 2 | 0 |
| Swansea | 13,160 | 28 | 22 | 6 |
| Sycamore | 18,384 | 31 | 28 | 3 |
| Taylorville | 12,193 | 26 | 20 | 6 |
| Thornton | 2,366 | 13 | 12 | 1 |
| Tilton | 2,759 | 3 | 3 | 0 |
| Tinley Park | 60,427 | 104 | 77 | 27 |
| Tolono | 2,850 | 2 | 2 | 0 |
| Toluca | 1,241 | 2 | 2 | 0 |
| Tremont | 2,075 | 3 | 3 | 0 |
| Trenton | 2,666 | 5 | 5 | 0 |
| Troy | 9,993 | 25 | 18 | 7 |
| Tuscola | 4,518 | 8 | 7 | 1 |
| University Park | 8,351 | 19 | 14 | 5 |
| Urbana | 39,838 | 68 | 53 | 15 |
| Valmeyer | 1,252 | 2 | 2 | 0 |
| Vandalia | 6,258 | 18 | 13 | 5 |
| Venice | 2,410 | 6 | 4 | 2 |
| Vernon Hills | 24,965 | 67 | 46 | 21 |
| Vienna | 1,287 | 4 | 4 | 0 |
| Villa Grove | 2,438 | 5 | 4 | 1 |
| Villa Park | 22,185 | 54 | 39 | 15 |
| Virden | 3,351 | 10 | 6 | 4 |
| Virginia | 1,657 | 1 | 1 | 0 |
| Wamac | 1,259 | 3 | 3 | 0 |
| Warren | 1,357 | 4 | 3 | 1 |
| Warrensburg | 1,160 | 2 | 2 | 0 |
| Warrenville | 12,997 | 41 | 33 | 8 |
| Warsaw | 1,584 | 3 | 3 | 0 |
| Washburn | 1,095 | 1 | 1 | 0 |
| Washington | 14,215 | 29 | 22 | 7 |
| Washington Park | 5,518 | 5 | 5 | 0 |
| Waterloo | 10,015 | 17 | 15 | 2 |
| Waterman | 1,563 | 2 | 2 | 0 |
| Watseka | 5,460 | 11 | 10 | 1 |
| Wauconda | 12,549 | 37 | 26 | 11 |
| Waukegan | 91,059 | 199 | 147 | 52 |
| Wayne | 2,421 | 5 | 5 | 0 |
| Wayne City | 1,055 | 1 | 1 | 0 |
| Westchester | 15,593 | 47 | 34 | 13 |
| West Chicago | 26,756 | 64 | 48 | 16 |
| West City | 767 | 9 | 5 | 4 |
| West Dundee | 8,293 | 22 | 20 | 2 |
| Western Springs | 12,705 | 29 | 21 | 8 |
| West Frankfort | 8,185 | 19 | 14 | 5 |
| Westmont | 24,985 | 52 | 39 | 13 |
| West Salem | 930 | 1 | 1 | 0 |
| Westville | 2,983 | 2 | 2 | 0 |
| Wheaton | 54,346 | 85 | 66 | 19 |
| Wheeling | 36,041 | 91 | 65 | 26 |
| White Hall | 2,437 | 8 | 5 | 3 |
| Williamsfield | 568 | 2 | 2 | 0 |
| Williamsville | 1,383 | 3 | 3 | 0 |
| Willowbrook | 8,710 | 29 | 25 | 4 |
| Willow Springs | 5,989 | 25 | 18 | 7 |
| Wilmette | 26,288 | 60 | 44 | 16 |
| Wilmington | 6,234 | 21 | 15 | 6 |
| Winchester | 1,536 | 2 | 2 | 0 |
| Winfield | 10,117 | 21 | 19 | 2 |

## Table 78. Full-time Law Enforcement Employees, by State, by City, 2009—*Continued*

(Number.)

| State/city | Popula-tion | Total law enforce-ment employees | Total officers | Total civilians |
|---|---|---|---|---|
| Winnebago | 3,245 | 5 | 5 | 0 |
| Winnetka | 12,365 | 37 | 28 | 9 |
| Winthrop Harbor | 7,263 | 16 | 11 | 5 |
| Wonder Lake | 3,995 | 3 | 2 | 1 |
| Wood Dale | 13,884 | 51 | 34 | 17 |
| Woodhull | 788 | 1 | 1 | 0 |
| Woodridge | 32,487 | 75 | 50 | 25 |
| Wood River | 10,935 | 25 | 19 | 6 |
| Woodstock | 24,370 | 50 | 38 | 12 |
| Worden | 1,051 | 2 | 2 | 0 |
| Worth | 10,360 | 26 | 24 | 2 |
| Yates City | 661 | 1 | 1 | 0 |
| Yorkville | 18,302 | 35 | 30 | 5 |
| Zeigler | 1,665 | 4 | 4 | 0 |
| **INDIANA** | | | | |
| Albion | 2,337 | 7 | 6 | 1 |
| Alexandria | 5,811 | 17 | 13 | 4 |
| Anderson | 57,020 | 137 | 118 | 19 |
| Angola | 7,936 | 20 | 16 | 4 |
| Attica | 3,271 | 6 | 6 | 0 |
| Auburn | 13,128 | 29 | 23 | 6 |
| Aurora | 4,072 | 13 | 10 | 3 |
| Austin | 4,587 | 6 | 6 | 0 |
| Avon | 12,722 | 23 | 21 | 2 |
| Bargersville | 2,770 | 7 | 6 | 1 |
| Batesville | 6,477 | 17 | 12 | 5 |
| Bedford | 13,458 | 38 | 29 | 9 |
| Beech Grove | 14,257 | 43 | 32 | 11 |
| Berne | 4,389 | 7 | 6 | 1 |
| Bicknell | 3,220 | 9 | 6 | 3 |
| Bloomington | 71,845 | 129 | 92 | 37 |
| Bluffton | 9,293 | 33 | 20 | 13 |
| Boonville | 6,736 | 15 | 14 | 1 |
| Brazil | 8,296 | 14 | 10 | 4 |
| Bremen | 4,660 | 15 | 11 | 4 |
| Brownsburg | 20,651 | 48 | 40 | 8 |
| Brownstown | 2,978 | 5 | 5 | 0 |
| Burns Harbor | 1,148 | 6 | 5 | 1 |
| Carmel | 68,424 | 128 | 107 | 21 |
| Cedar Lake | 11,188 | 22 | 17 | 5 |
| Charlestown | 7,359 | 20 | 15 | 5 |
| Chesterfield | 2,733 | 6 | 6 | 0 |
| Chesterton | 12,968 | 27 | 21 | 6 |
| Clarksville | 21,921 | 46 | 38 | 8 |
| Clinton | 4,766 | 8 | 7 | 1 |
| Columbia City | 8,386 | 20 | 18 | 2 |
| Columbus | 40,087 | 81 | 73 | 8 |
| Connersville | 13,815 | 30 | 29 | 1 |
| Corydon | 2,787 | 7 | 7 | 0 |
| Covington | 2,416 | 6 | 6 | 0 |
| Crawfordsville | 15,036 | 44 | 31 | 13 |
| Crown Point | 24,942 | 53 | 40 | 13 |
| Culver | 1,502 | 4 | 4 | 0 |
| Danville | 8,319 | 21 | 19 | 2 |
| Decatur | 9,576 | 21 | 17 | 4 |
| Delphi | 2,844 | 8 | 7 | 1 |
| Dyer | 16,148 | 33 | 25 | 8 |
| East Chicago | 29,728 | 121 | 108 | 13 |
| Elkhart | 52,661 | 144 | 123 | 21 |
| Elwood | 8,956 | 20 | 15 | 5 |
| Evansville | 115,770 | 307 | 275 | 32 |
| Fairmount | 2,701 | 8 | 5 | 3 |
| Fishers | 73,538 | 97 | 90 | 7 |
| Fort Wayne | 251,584 | 488 | 452 | 36 |
| Fowler | 2,177 | 4 | 4 | 0 |
| Franklin | 23,704 | 56 | 40 | 16 |
| Garrett | 5,664 | 17 | 13 | 4 |
| Gary | 95,219 | 286 | 231 | 55 |
| Georgetown | 3,172 | 3 | 3 | 0 |
| Goshen | 32,952 | 63 | 58 | 5 |
| Greencastle | 10,172 | 18 | 16 | 2 |
| Greendale | 4,372 | 14 | 10 | 4 |
| Greenfield | 19,262 | 41 | 38 | 3 |
| Greenwood | 49,136 | 74 | 53 | 21 |
| Griffith | 16,205 | 39 | 31 | 8 |
| Hagerstown | 1,613 | 4 | 4 | 0 |
| Hammond | 76,085 | 253 | 206 | 47 |
| Hartford City | 6,239 | 15 | 13 | 2 |
| Hebron | 3,707 | 7 | 6 | 1 |
| Highland | 22,544 | 49 | 41 | 8 |
| Hobart | 28,173 | 70 | 55 | 15 |
| Huntingburg | 6,147 | 11 | 10 | 1 |
| Huntington | 16,424 | 44 | 34 | 10 |
| Indianapolis | 813,471 | 1,898 | 1,619 | 279 |
| Jasonville | 2,433 | 5 | 5 | 0 |
| Jasper | 14,224 | 29 | 21 | 8 |
| Jeffersonville | 30,783 | 73 | 64 | 9 |
| Kendallville | 10,472 | 26 | 18 | 8 |
| Knox | 3,844 | 7 | 7 | 0 |
| Kokomo | 45,562 | 130 | 100 | 30 |
| Lafayette | 64,370 | 163 | 128 | 35 |
| Lake Station | 13,172 | 27 | 24 | 3 |
| La Porte | 21,128 | 49 | 41 | 8 |
| Lawrence | 43,737 | 64 | 56 | 8 |
| Lawrenceburg | 4,798 | 25 | 20 | 5 |
| Lebanon | 15,522 | 30 | 29 | 1 |
| Ligonier | 4,551 | 10 | 9 | 1 |
| Linton | 5,683 | 15 | 11 | 4 |
| Logansport | 18,551 | 43 | 39 | 4 |
| Long Beach | 1,546 | 6 | 5 | 1 |
| Loogootee | 2,568 | 5 | 4 | 1 |
| Lowell | 8,504 | 19 | 14 | 5 |
| Lynn | 1,041 | 2 | 2 | 0 |
| Madison | 12,796 | 35 | 27 | 8 |
| Marion | 29,987 | 90 | 72 | 18 |
| Martinsville | 11,812 | 29 | 20 | 9 |
| Merrillville | 33,349 | 65 | 50 | 15 |
| Michigan City | 32,355 | 94 | 85 | 9 |
| Mishawaka | 50,378 | 125 | 102 | 23 |
| Mitchell | 4,564 | 11 | 7 | 4 |
| Monticello | 5,249 | 18 | 12 | 6 |
| Mooresville | 12,037 | 28 | 22 | 6 |
| Mount Vernon | 6,925 | 15 | 14 | 1 |
| Muncie | 64,639 | 105 | 98 | 7 |
| Munster | 22,173 | 47 | 37 | 10 |
| Nappanee | 7,196 | 22 | 15 | 7 |
| New Albany | 37,237 | 66 | 61 | 5 |
| New Castle | 18,236 | 34 | 32 | 2 |
| New Chicago | 1,984 | 5 | 2 | 3 |
| New Haven | 13,729 | 27 | 19 | 8 |
| New Whiteland | 5,961 | 13 | 8 | 5 |
| Noblesville | 43,820 | 83 | 71 | 12 |
| North Liberty | 1,397 | 3 | 3 | 0 |
| North Manchester | 5,784 | 16 | 11 | 5 |
| North Vernon | 6,269 | 21 | 18 | 3 |
| Oakland City | 2,505 | 4 | 4 | 0 |
| Peru | 12,225 | 31 | 29 | 2 |
| Petersburg | 2,435 | 5 | 5 | 0 |
| Plainfield | 28,811 | 47 | 42 | 5 |
| Plymouth | 11,170 | 29 | 24 | 5 |
| Portage | 37,373 | 76 | 61 | 15 |
| Portland | 6,131 | 17 | 13 | 4 |
| Prince's Lakes | 1,624 | 3 | 3 | 0 |
| Princeton | 8,471 | 18 | 16 | 2 |
| Rensselaer | 6,285 | 15 | 10 | 5 |
| Richmond | 36,479 | 83 | 72 | 11 |
| Rochester | 6,459 | 19 | 14 | 5 |
| Rushville | 6,011 | 18 | 13 | 5 |
| Salem | 6,538 | 17 | 12 | 5 |
| Schererville | 29,361 | 59 | 48 | 11 |
| Scottsburg | 5,896 | 13 | 13 | 0 |
| Sellersburg | 6,369 | 20 | 15 | 5 |
| Seymour | 19,342 | 55 | 39 | 16 |
| Shelbyville | 18,568 | 55 | 43 | 12 |
| South Bend | 103,326 | 316 | 249 | 67 |
| South Whitley | 1,852 | 4 | 4 | 0 |
| Speedway | 12,567 | 49 | 34 | 15 |
| St. John | 13,616 | 25 | 19 | 6 |
| Tell City | 7,493 | 20 | 12 | 8 |
| Terre Haute | 60,065 | 142 | 131 | 11 |
| Tipton | 4,968 | 14 | 12 | 2 |
| Union City | 3,294 | 10 | 8 | 2 |

## Table 78. Full-time Law Enforcement Employees, by State, by City, 2009—*Continued*

(Number.)

| State/city | Population | Total law enforcement employees | Total officers | Total civilians |
|---|---|---|---|---|
| Valparaiso | 30,680 | 56 | 50 | 6 |
| Vincennes | 17,902 | 37 | 33 | 4 |
| Wabash | 10,718 | 33 | 27 | 6 |
| Walkerton | 2,164 | 10 | 6 | 4 |
| Warsaw | 13,733 | 39 | 32 | 7 |
| Washington | 11,400 | 23 | 17 | 6 |
| Waterloo | 2,160 | 7 | 6 | 1 |
| Westfield | 21,946 | 42 | 37 | 5 |
| West Lafayette | 31,092 | 67 | 48 | 19 |
| Westville | 5,179 | 3 | 3 | 0 |
| Whitestown | 709 | 10 | 8 | 2 |
| Whiting | 4,712 | 24 | 19 | 5 |
| Winchester | 4,562 | 15 | 11 | 4 |
| Winona Lake | 4,327 | 5 | 5 | 0 |
| Zionsville | 14,065 | 23 | 22 | 1 |
| **IOWA** | | | | |
| Adel | 4,553 | 8 | 7 | 1 |
| Albia | 3,537 | 7 | 6 | 1 |
| Algona | 5,285 | 14 | 10 | 4 |
| Altoona | 14,297 | 26 | 24 | 2 |
| Ames | 57,173 | 72 | 50 | 22 |
| Anamosa | 5,764 | 8 | 7 | 1 |
| Ankeny | 44,339 | 60 | 52 | 8 |
| Atlantic | 6,726 | 14 | 12 | 2 |
| Audubon | 2,082 | 3 | 3 | 0 |
| Belle Plaine | 2,805 | 4 | 4 | 0 |
| Belmond | 2,278 | 5 | 5 | 0 |
| Bettendorf | 32,734 | 59 | 46 | 13 |
| Bloomfield | 2,580 | 5 | 5 | 0 |
| Boone | 12,592 | 16 | 15 | 1 |
| Burlington | 25,172 | 57 | 41 | 16 |
| Camanche | 4,288 | 7 | 7 | 0 |
| Carlisle | 3,708 | 5 | 4 | 1 |
| Carroll | 9,974 | 16 | 15 | 1 |
| Carter Lake | 3,270 | 10 | 9 | 1 |
| Cedar Falls | 38,271 | 43 | 42 | 1 |
| Cedar Rapids | 128,779 | 258 | 202 | 56 |
| Centerville | 5,393 | 15 | 10 | 5 |
| Chariton | 4,401 | 8 | 7 | 1 |
| Charles City | 7,435 | 20 | 14 | 6 |
| Cherokee | 4,629 | 9 | 8 | 1 |
| Clarinda | 5,474 | 15 | 9 | 6 |
| Clarion | 2,692 | 8 | 7 | 1 |
| Clear Lake | 7,781 | 22 | 16 | 6 |
| Clinton | 26,266 | 53 | 45 | 8 |
| Clive | 15,522 | 27 | 24 | 3 |
| Coralville | 18,884 | 35 | 31 | 4 |
| Council Bluffs | 59,669 | 131 | 110 | 21 |
| Cresco | 3,712 | 7 | 7 | 0 |
| Creston | 7,597 | 15 | 11 | 4 |
| Davenport | 101,116 | 210 | 161 | 49 |
| Decorah | 7,877 | 19 | 12 | 7 |
| Denison | 7,167 | 17 | 12 | 5 |
| Des Moines | 196,794 | 480 | 373 | 107 |
| De Witt | 5,286 | 10 | 10 | 0 |
| Dubuque | 57,192 | 105 | 99 | 6 |
| Dyersville | 4,222 | 10 | 6 | 4 |
| Eagle Grove | 3,269 | 7 | 7 | 0 |
| Eldora | 2,703 | 4 | 4 | 0 |
| Eldridge | 4,962 | 6 | 6 | 0 |
| Emmetsburg | 3,586 | 7 | 6 | 1 |
| Estherville | 6,255 | 12 | 12 | 0 |
| Evansdale | 5,121 | 8 | 7 | 1 |
| Fairfield | 9,177 | 19 | 13 | 6 |
| Forest City | 4,066 | 7 | 7 | 0 |
| Fort Dodge | 25,058 | 41 | 38 | 3 |
| Fort Madison | 10,818 | 23 | 18 | 5 |
| Garner | 2,932 | 5 | 5 | 0 |
| Glenwood | 5,675 | 9 | 8 | 1 |
| Grinnell | 9,174 | 17 | 15 | 2 |
| Grundy Center | 2,510 | 5 | 5 | 0 |
| Hampton | 4,126 | 12 | 7 | 5 |
| Harlan | 4,954 | 9 | 8 | 1 |
| Hawarden | 2,396 | 4 | 4 | 0 |
| Hiawatha | 6,708 | 13 | 12 | 1 |
| Humboldt | 4,170 | 6 | 6 | 0 |
| Independence | 6,125 | 10 | 10 | 0 |
| Indianola | 14,500 | 19 | 17 | 2 |
| Iowa City | 68,427 | 95 | 74 | 21 |
| Iowa Falls | 4,940 | 15 | 11 | 4 |
| Jefferson | 4,095 | 7 | 7 | 0 |
| Johnston | 16,725 | 23 | 22 | 1 |
| Keokuk | 10,283 | 33 | 25 | 8 |
| Knoxville | 7,204 | 14 | 12 | 2 |
| Le Claire | 3,007 | 7 | 6 | 1 |
| Le Mars | 9,114 | 15 | 14 | 1 |
| Leon | 1,875 | 2 | 2 | 0 |
| Manchester | 4,834 | 13 | 9 | 4 |
| Maquoketa | 5,882 | 17 | 11 | 6 |
| Marion | 33,590 | 50 | 41 | 9 |
| Marshalltown | 25,833 | 58 | 42 | 16 |
| Mason City | 27,142 | 52 | 47 | 5 |
| Missouri Valley | 2,726 | 4 | 4 | 0 |
| Monticello | 3,652 | 7 | 6 | 1 |
| Mount Pleasant | 8,780 | 16 | 14 | 2 |
| Mount Vernon | 4,196 | 6 | 6 | 0 |
| Muscatine | 22,480 | 44 | 40 | 4 |
| Nevada | 6,688 | 9 | 8 | 1 |
| New Hampton | 3,369 | 7 | 7 | 0 |
| New London | 1,832 | 3 | 3 | 0 |
| Newton | 14,981 | 28 | 23 | 5 |
| North Liberty | 12,569 | 13 | 12 | 1 |
| Norwalk | 9,048 | 15 | 13 | 2 |
| Oelwein | 6,019 | 16 | 11 | 5 |
| Ogden | 1,968 | 3 | 3 | 0 |
| Onawa | 2,710 | 6 | 6 | 0 |
| Orange City | 5,922 | 7 | 7 | 0 |
| Osage | 3,424 | 6 | 5 | 1 |
| Osceola | 4,708 | 11 | 10 | 1 |
| Oskaloosa | 11,077 | 19 | 17 | 2 |
| Ottumwa | 24,276 | 47 | 40 | 7 |
| Pella | 10,238 | 20 | 14 | 6 |
| Perry | 9,809 | 20 | 13 | 7 |
| Pleasant Hill | 8,873 | 18 | 16 | 2 |
| Pleasantville | 1,584 | 2 | 2 | 0 |
| Polk City | 3,314 | 6 | 6 | 0 |
| Prairie City | 1,444 | 3 | 3 | 0 |
| Rock Rapids | 2,423 | 1 | 1 | 0 |
| Rock Valley | 2,967 | 5 | 5 | 0 |
| Sac City | 2,118 | 4 | 4 | 0 |
| Sergeant Bluff | 4,093 | 9 | 8 | 1 |
| Sheldon | 4,740 | 7 | 7 | 0 |
| Shenandoah | 4,884 | 11 | 8 | 3 |
| Sioux Center | 6,638 | 7 | 7 | 0 |
| Sioux City | 82,573 | 152 | 127 | 25 |
| Spencer | 10,949 | 27 | 19 | 8 |
| Spirit Lake | 4,742 | 11 | 10 | 1 |
| St. Ansgar | 1,060 | 1 | 1 | 0 |
| State Center | 1,340 | 1 | 1 | 0 |
| Storm Lake | 9,542 | 23 | 19 | 4 |
| Story City | 3,406 | 5 | 5 | 0 |
| Tama | 2,539 | 5 | 5 | 0 |
| Tipton | 2,997 | 6 | 6 | 0 |
| Urbandale | 39,518 | 51 | 47 | 4 |
| Vinton | 5,078 | 8 | 8 | 0 |
| Washington | 7,276 | 11 | 10 | 1 |
| Waterloo | 66,436 | 134 | 120 | 14 |
| Waukee | 13,558 | 13 | 12 | 1 |
| Waukon | 3,885 | 7 | 7 | 0 |
| Waverly | 9,334 | 16 | 15 | 1 |
| Webster City | 7,672 | 17 | 13 | 4 |
| West Burlington | 3,298 | 12 | 11 | 1 |
| West Des Moines | 56,400 | 81 | 66 | 15 |
| West Liberty | 3,685 | 8 | 7 | 1 |
| West Union | 2,416 | 4 | 4 | 0 |
| Williamsburg | 2,831 | 6 | 6 | 0 |
| Wilton | 2,820 | 4 | 4 | 0 |
| Windsor Heights | 4,616 | 15 | 13 | 2 |
| Winterset | 4,825 | 8 | 8 | 0 |
| **KANSAS** | | | | |
| Abilene | 6,383 | 16 | 14 | 2 |
| Alma | 751 | 1 | 1 | 0 |

## Table 78. Full-time Law Enforcement Employees, by State, by City, 2009—*Continued*

(Number.)

| State/city | Population | Total law enforcement employees | Total officers | Total civilians |
|---|---|---|---|---|
| Altamont | 1,045 | 3 | 3 | 0 |
| Andale | 892 | 2 | 2 | 0 |
| Andover | 10,792 | 29 | 21 | 8 |
| Anthony | 2,196 | 6 | 5 | 1 |
| Argonia | 466 | 1 | 1 | 0 |
| Arkansas City | 10,975 | 35 | 25 | 10 |
| Arma | 1,511 | 5 | 5 | 0 |
| Atchison | 10,378 | 23 | 22 | 1 |
| Attica | 581 | 1 | 1 | 0 |
| Atwood | 1,048 | 2 | 2 | 0 |
| Augusta | 8,715 | 32 | 23 | 9 |
| Baldwin City | 4,416 | 9 | 7 | 2 |
| Basehor | 4,525 | 14 | 12 | 2 |
| Baxter Springs | 4,108 | 13 | 9 | 4 |
| Bel Aire | 6,883 | 13 | 12 | 1 |
| Belle Plaine | 1,509 | 4 | 4 | 0 |
| Belleville | 1,793 | 5 | 5 | 0 |
| Benton | 804 | 2 | 2 | 0 |
| Blue Rapids | 1,011 | 1 | 1 | 0 |
| Bonner Springs | 7,205 | 26 | 24 | 2 |
| Buhler | 1,329 | 3 | 3 | 0 |
| Burden | 525 | 1 | 1 | 0 |
| Burlingame | 952 | 2 | 2 | 0 |
| Burlington | 2,667 | 9 | 7 | 2 |
| Burrton | 892 | 2 | 2 | 0 |
| Caldwell | 1,130 | 3 | 3 | 0 |
| Canton | 786 | 1 | 1 | 0 |
| Carbondale | 1,367 | 2 | 2 | 0 |
| Cawker City | 457 | 1 | 1 | 0 |
| Cedar Vale | 606 | 1 | 1 | 0 |
| Chanute | 8,784 | 22 | 19 | 3 |
| Chapman | 1,343 | 4 | 4 | 0 |
| Chase | 442 | 1 | 1 | 0 |
| Cheney | 2,059 | 4 | 4 | 0 |
| Cherryvale | 2,238 | 5 | 5 | 0 |
| Claflin | 649 | 1 | 1 | 0 |
| Clay Center | 4,430 | 8 | 7 | 1 |
| Clearwater | 2,427 | 6 | 5 | 1 |
| Coffeyville | 10,235 | 32 | 25 | 7 |
| Colby | 4,737 | 17 | 12 | 5 |
| Coldwater | 778 | 1 | 1 | 0 |
| Columbus | 3,163 | 11 | 9 | 2 |
| Colwich | 1,426 | 2 | 2 | 0 |
| Concordia | 5,158 | 15 | 9 | 6 |
| Conway Springs | 1,180 | 2 | 2 | 0 |
| Council Grove | 2,269 | 7 | 6 | 1 |
| Derby | 23,041 | 50 | 38 | 12 |
| Dodge City | 25,738 | 65 | 50 | 15 |
| Eastborough | 803 | 7 | 7 | 0 |
| Edwardsville | 4,494 | 16 | 15 | 1 |
| El Dorado | 12,566 | 26 | 24 | 2 |
| Elkhart | 1,868 | 2 | 2 | 0 |
| Ellinwood | 2,022 | 5 | 5 | 0 |
| Ellis | 1,960 | 5 | 5 | 0 |
| Ellsworth | 2,847 | 7 | 6 | 1 |
| Elwood | 1,118 | 5 | 5 | 0 |
| Emporia | 26,330 | 66 | 43 | 23 |
| Enterprise | 814 | 2 | 1 | 1 |
| Erie | 1,154 | 3 | 2 | 1 |
| Eskridge | 562 | 1 | 1 | 0 |
| Eudora | 6,482 | 10 | 9 | 1 |
| Fairway | 3,831 | 11 | 9 | 2 |
| Florence | 588 | 1 | 1 | 0 |
| Fort Scott | 7,903 | 28 | 19 | 9 |
| Fredonia | 2,372 | 7 | 6 | 1 |
| Frontenac | 3,214 | 9 | 6 | 3 |
| Galena | 3,110 | 12 | 7 | 5 |
| Galva | 816 | 1 | 1 | 0 |
| Garden City | 28,561 | 87 | 57 | 30 |
| Garden Plain | 860 | 2 | 2 | 0 |
| Gardner | 18,650 | 40 | 36 | 4 |
| Garnett | 3,207 | 9 | 9 | 0 |
| Girard | 2,712 | 7 | 6 | 1 |
| Goddard | 4,140 | 11 | 10 | 1 |
| Goodland | 4,332 | 10 | 9 | 1 |
| Grandview Plaza | 1,425 | 6 | 6 | 0 |
| Great Bend | 15,671 | 33 | 29 | 4 |
| Halstead | 1,892 | 8 | 6 | 2 |
| Harper | 1,401 | 3 | 3 | 0 |
| Haven | 1,161 | 3 | 3 | 0 |
| Havensville | 144 | 1 | 1 | 0 |
| Hays | 20,405 | 51 | 32 | 19 |
| Haysville | 10,561 | 33 | 26 | 7 |
| Herington | 2,439 | 8 | 7 | 1 |
| Hesston | 3,758 | 7 | 6 | 1 |
| Hiawatha | 3,143 | 7 | 6 | 1 |
| Highland | 942 | 2 | 2 | 0 |
| Hill City | 1,372 | 4 | 4 | 0 |
| Hillsboro | 2,615 | 5 | 5 | 0 |
| Hoisington | 2,875 | 9 | 7 | 2 |
| Holcomb | 1,992 | 3 | 2 | 1 |
| Horton | 1,782 | 10 | 6 | 4 |
| Howard | 753 | 1 | 1 | 0 |
| Hoxie | 1,102 | 2 | 2 | 0 |
| Hugoton | 3,381 | 7 | 5 | 2 |
| Humboldt | 1,814 | 6 | 6 | 0 |
| Hutchinson | 40,787 | 109 | 69 | 40 |
| Independence | 9,182 | 28 | 20 | 8 |
| Inman | 1,183 | 2 | 2 | 0 |
| Iola | 5,727 | 24 | 16 | 8 |
| Junction City | 20,880 | 65 | 43 | 22 |
| Kechi | 1,793 | 6 | 5 | 1 |
| Kingman | 2,953 | 7 | 7 | 0 |
| Kiowa | 894 | 3 | 3 | 0 |
| La Crosse | 1,228 | 3 | 3 | 0 |
| La Cygne | 1,106 | 2 | 2 | 0 |
| Lake Quivira | 942 | 2 | 2 | 0 |
| Lansing | 10,812 | 19 | 18 | 1 |
| Larned | 3,536 | 14 | 9 | 5 |
| Lawrence | 91,703 | 171 | 137 | 34 |
| Leavenworth | 34,647 | 92 | 66 | 26 |
| Leawood | 31,765 | 81 | 60 | 21 |
| Lebo | 907 | 1 | 1 | 0 |
| Lenexa | 47,601 | 126 | 85 | 41 |
| Liberal | 20,118 | 49 | 38 | 11 |
| Lindsborg | 3,236 | 7 | 6 | 1 |
| Linn Valley | 587 | 2 | 2 | 0 |
| Little River | 516 | 1 | 1 | 0 |
| Louisburg | 4,117 | 8 | 8 | 0 |
| Lyndon | 1,003 | 2 | 2 | 0 |
| Lyons | 3,366 | 7 | 6 | 1 |
| Macksville | 472 | 1 | 1 | 0 |
| Maize | 3,200 | 10 | 9 | 1 |
| Marion | 1,856 | 5 | 5 | 0 |
| Marquette | 582 | 1 | 1 | 0 |
| Marysville | 3,101 | 8 | 7 | 1 |
| McLouth | 828 | 2 | 2 | 0 |
| McPherson | 13,353 | 36 | 30 | 6 |
| Meade | 1,524 | 3 | 3 | 0 |
| Medicine Lodge | 1,890 | 7 | 6 | 1 |
| Merriam | 10,793 | 33 | 28 | 5 |
| Minneapolis | 1,970 | 5 | 5 | 0 |
| Mission | 9,738 | 31 | 29 | 2 |
| Moran | 518 | 1 | 1 | 0 |
| Mound City | 788 | 2 | 2 | 0 |
| Moundridge | 1,633 | 3 | 3 | 0 |
| Mount Hope | 858 | 2 | 2 | 0 |
| Mulberry | 566 | 2 | 2 | 0 |
| Mulvane | 5,947 | 18 | 12 | 6 |
| Neodesha | 2,611 | 8 | 7 | 1 |
| Newton | 18,175 | 35 | 30 | 5 |
| Nickerson | 1,139 | 3 | 3 | 0 |
| North Newton | 1,600 | 2 | 2 | 0 |
| Norton | 2,614 | 6 | 6 | 0 |
| Norwich | 493 | 1 | 1 | 0 |
| Oakley | 1,812 | 11 | 6 | 5 |
| Oberlin | 1,623 | 4 | 4 | 0 |
| Onaga | 672 | 1 | 1 | 0 |
| Osage City | 2,803 | 6 | 6 | 0 |
| Osawatomie | 4,468 | 17 | 12 | 5 |
| Osborne | 1,329 | 3 | 3 | 0 |
| Oswego | 1,973 | 5 | 5 | 0 |

**Table 78. Full-time Law Enforcement Employees, by State, by City, 2009—*Continued***

(Number.)

| State/city | Population | Total law enforcement employees | Total officers | Total civilians |
|---|---|---|---|---|
| Ottawa | 12,950 | 29 | 24 | 5 |
| Overbrook | 925 | 2 | 2 | 0 |
| Overland Park | 173,688 | 304 | 251 | 53 |
| Paola | 5,386 | 21 | 15 | 6 |
| Park City | 7,984 | 21 | 19 | 2 |
| Parsons | 11,020 | 31 | 24 | 7 |
| Peabody | 1,185 | 3 | 3 | 0 |
| Pittsburg | 19,693 | 55 | 38 | 17 |
| Plainville | 1,800 | 5 | 5 | 0 |
| Pleasanton | 1,307 | 2 | 2 | 0 |
| Prairie Village | 21,416 | 57 | 45 | 12 |
| Pratt | 6,380 | 19 | 14 | 5 |
| Protection | 546 | 1 | 1 | 0 |
| Roeland Park | 6,934 | 18 | 16 | 2 |
| Rolla | 406 | 1 | 1 | 0 |
| Rose Hill | 4,103 | 11 | 9 | 2 |
| Rossville | 1,126 | 3 | 3 | 0 |
| Russell | 4,168 | 10 | 8 | 2 |
| Sabetha | 2,471 | 5 | 5 | 0 |
| Salina | 46,561 | 111 | 82 | 29 |
| Scott City | 3,462 | 12 | 7 | 5 |
| Scranton | 676 | 1 | 1 | 0 |
| Sedgwick | 1,680 | 2 | 2 | 0 |
| Seneca | 2,003 | 5 | 5 | 0 |
| Shawnee | 62,508 | 107 | 85 | 22 |
| Silver Lake | 1,382 | 1 | 1 | 0 |
| Smith Center | 1,616 | 3 | 3 | 0 |
| South Hutchinson | 2,548 | 10 | 8 | 2 |
| Spearville | 866 | 1 | 1 | 0 |
| Spring Hill | 5,578 | 15 | 13 | 2 |
| Stafford | 1,015 | 3 | 3 | 0 |
| Sterling | 2,520 | 5 | 5 | 0 |
| St. Francis | 1,261 | 5 | 4 | 1 |
| St. George | 575 | 1 | 1 | 0 |
| St. John | 1,159 | 4 | 4 | 0 |
| St. Marys | 2,284 | 5 | 5 | 0 |
| Stockton | 1,386 | 5 | 5 | 0 |
| Tonganoxie | 4,520 | 10 | 9 | 1 |
| Topeka | 123,449 | 354 | 283 | 71 |
| Udall | 738 | 1 | 1 | 0 |
| Ulysses | 5,515 | 12 | 11 | 1 |
| Valley Center | 6,631 | 16 | 12 | 4 |
| Valley Falls | 1,146 | 2 | 2 | 0 |
| Victoria | 1,204 | 2 | 2 | 0 |
| Wa Keeney | 1,692 | 5 | 5 | 0 |
| Walton | 286 | 1 | 1 | 0 |
| Wamego | 4,317 | 12 | 8 | 4 |
| Waterville | 609 | 1 | 1 | 0 |
| Wathena | 1,291 | 2 | 2 | 0 |
| Wellington | 7,639 | 20 | 17 | 3 |
| Wellsville | 1,751 | 5 | 4 | 1 |
| Westwood | 1,838 | 8 | 7 | 1 |
| Wichita | 367,635 | 825 | 643 | 182 |
| Winfield | 11,421 | 28 | 22 | 6 |
| Yates Center | 1,354 | 3 | 3 | 0 |
| **KENTUCKY** | | | | |
| Adairville | 921 | 1 | 1 | 0 |
| Albany | 2,321 | 8 | 8 | 0 |
| Alexandria | 8,605 | 15 | 13 | 2 |
| Allen | 148 | 2 | 1 | 1 |
| Anchorage | 3,417 | 14 | 10 | 4 |
| Ashland | 21,276 | 52 | 46 | 6 |
| Auburn | 1,506 | 2 | 2 | 0 |
| Audubon Park | 1,676 | 8 | 7 | 1 |
| Augusta | 1,257 | 3 | 3 | 0 |
| Barbourville | 3,614 | 17 | 13 | 4 |
| Bardstown | 11,292 | 23 | 22 | 1 |
| Bardwell | 772 | 1 | 1 | 0 |
| Beattyville | 1,113 | 7 | 5 | 2 |
| Beaver Dam | 3,144 | 9 | 6 | 3 |
| Bellefonte | 844 | 4 | 4 | 0 |
| Bellevue | 5,788 | 11 | 10 | 1 |
| Benham | 524 | 2 | 2 | 0 |
| Benton | 4,370 | 9 | 7 | 2 |
| Berea | 14,825 | 30 | 28 | 2 |
| Bloomfield | 895 | 1 | 1 | 0 |
| Booneville | 147 | 2 | 2 | 0 |
| Bowling Green | 55,754 | 147 | 110 | 37 |
| Bradfordsville | 324 | 1 | 1 | 0 |
| Brandenburg | 2,196 | 5 | 5 | 0 |
| Brooksville | 573 | 1 | 1 | 0 |
| Brownsville | 1,049 | 3 | 3 | 0 |
| Burgin | 884 | 1 | 1 | 0 |
| Burkesville | 1,672 | 9 | 5 | 4 |
| Burnside | 697 | 4 | 4 | 0 |
| Butler | 628 | 1 | 1 | 0 |
| Cadiz | 2,592 | 9 | 8 | 1 |
| Calhoun | 783 | 1 | 1 | 0 |
| Calvert City | 2,769 | 7 | 6 | 1 |
| Campbellsville | 11,072 | 23 | 21 | 2 |
| Caneyville | 664 | 1 | 1 | 0 |
| Carlisle | 2,068 | 9 | 5 | 4 |
| Carrollton | 3,933 | 11 | 10 | 1 |
| Catlettsburg | 1,928 | 8 | 8 | 0 |
| Cave City | 2,014 | 6 | 6 | 0 |
| Central City | 5,678 | 12 | 12 | 0 |
| Clarkson | 843 | 1 | 1 | 0 |
| Clay City | 1,364 | 2 | 2 | 0 |
| Clinton | 1,321 | 3 | 3 | 0 |
| Cloverport | 1,232 | 1 | 1 | 0 |
| Coal Run Village | 625 | 3 | 2 | 1 |
| Cold Spring | 6,072 | 11 | 11 | 0 |
| Columbia | 4,296 | 11 | 10 | 1 |
| Corbin | 8,376 | 30 | 22 | 8 |
| Covington | 43,215 | 138 | 110 | 28 |
| Cumberland | 2,327 | 5 | 5 | 0 |
| Cynthiana | 6,277 | 14 | 13 | 1 |
| Danville | 15,530 | 33 | 31 | 2 |
| Dawson Springs | 2,895 | 7 | 4 | 3 |
| Dayton | 5,400 | 10 | 9 | 1 |
| Dry Ridge | 2,245 | 1 | 1 | 0 |
| Earlington | 1,563 | 1 | 1 | 0 |
| Eddyville | 2,423 | 6 | 6 | 0 |
| Edgewood | 8,858 | 14 | 14 | 0 |
| Edmonton | 1,650 | 7 | 7 | 0 |
| Elizabethtown | 24,321 | 59 | 43 | 16 |
| Elkhorn City | 996 | 4 | 4 | 0 |
| Elkton | 1,981 | 7 | 7 | 0 |
| Elsmere | 7,908 | 11 | 10 | 1 |
| Eminence | 2,213 | 6 | 6 | 0 |
| Erlanger | 21,299 | 55 | 43 | 12 |
| Eubank | 378 | 1 | 1 | 0 |
| Evarts | 1,019 | 4 | 4 | 0 |
| Falmouth | 2,058 | 8 | 7 | 1 |
| Ferguson | 943 | 1 | 1 | 0 |
| Flatwoods | 7,663 | 11 | 10 | 1 |
| Fleming-Neon | 784 | 1 | 1 | 0 |
| Flemingsburg | 2,682 | 7 | 7 | 0 |
| Florence | 28,232 | 64 | 60 | 4 |
| Fort Mitchell | 7,507 | 13 | 13 | 0 |
| Fort Thomas | 15,089 | 24 | 23 | 1 |
| Fort Wright | 5,425 | 13 | 12 | 1 |
| Frankfort | 27,272 | 70 | 65 | 5 |
| Franklin | 7,981 | 21 | 20 | 1 |
| Fulton | 2,406 | 14 | 10 | 4 |
| Gamaliel | 426 | 1 | 1 | 0 |
| Georgetown | 21,962 | 47 | 44 | 3 |
| Glasgow | 14,440 | 48 | 35 | 13 |
| Glencoe | 379 | 1 | 1 | 0 |
| Graymoor-Devondale | 3,215 | 2 | 2 | 0 |
| Grayson | 3,996 | 11 | 11 | 0 |
| Greensburg | 2,416 | 12 | 7 | 5 |
| Greenup | 1,184 | 3 | 3 | 0 |
| Greenville | 4,218 | 9 | 9 | 0 |
| Guthrie | 1,453 | 4 | 4 | 0 |
| Hardinsburg | 2,443 | 4 | 4 | 0 |
| Harlan | 1,843 | 11 | 9 | 2 |
| Harrodsburg | 8,195 | 23 | 15 | 8 |
| Hartford | 2,677 | 6 | 6 | 0 |
| Hawesville | 983 | 1 | 1 | 0 |
| Hazard | 4,789 | 24 | 15 | 9 |
| Henderson | 27,984 | 67 | 53 | 14 |

## Table 78. Full-time Law Enforcement Employees, by State, by City, 2009—*Continued*

(Number.)

| State/city | Population | Total law enforcement employees | Total officers | Total civilians |
|---|---|---|---|---|
| Heritage Creek | 1,831 | 9 | 9 | 0 |
| Hickman | 2,208 | 3 | 3 | 0 |
| Highland Heights Southgate | 8,948 | 20 | 20 | 0 |
| Hillview | 7,630 | 13 | 13 | 0 |
| Hindman | 765 | 2 | 2 | 0 |
| Hodgenville | 2,762 | 5 | 5 | 0 |
| Hopkinsville | 32,294 | 78 | 72 | 6 |
| Horse Cave | 2,334 | 4 | 4 | 0 |
| Hustonville | 350 | 1 | 1 | 0 |
| Hyden | 189 | 3 | 3 | 0 |
| Independence | 22,572 | 32 | 30 | 2 |
| Indian Hills | 3,552 | 8 | 8 | 0 |
| Inez | 431 | 2 | 2 | 0 |
| Irvine | 2,648 | 5 | 5 | 0 |
| Jackson | 2,387 | 12 | 9 | 3 |
| Jamestown | 1,750 | 4 | 4 | 0 |
| Jeffersontown | 26,199 | 60 | 50 | 10 |
| Jenkins | 2,228 | 3 | 3 | 0 |
| Junction City | 2,212 | 3 | 3 | 0 |
| La Center | 1,039 | 1 | 1 | 0 |
| La Grange | 6,354 | 12 | 12 | 0 |
| Lakeside Park-Crestview Hills | 6,470 | 12 | 11 | 1 |
| Lancaster | 4,473 | 13 | 13 | 0 |
| Lawrenceburg | 10,071 | 23 | 15 | 8 |
| Lebanon | 5,993 | 22 | 15 | 7 |
| Lebanon Junction | 2,036 | 5 | 5 | 0 |
| Leitchfield | 6,572 | 14 | 13 | 1 |
| Lewisburg | 913 | 1 | 1 | 0 |
| Lewisport | 1,660 | 2 | 2 | 0 |
| Lexington | 296,406 | 631 | 552 | 79 |
| Liberty | 1,898 | 5 | 5 | 0 |
| London | 8,020 | 35 | 32 | 3 |
| Louisa | 2,096 | 6 | 6 | 0 |
| Louisville Metro | 631,260 | 1,374 | 1,206 | 168 |
| Loyall | 697 | 2 | 2 | 0 |
| Ludlow | 4,856 | 11 | 10 | 1 |
| Lynch | 812 | 2 | 2 | 0 |
| Lynnview | 1,044 | 2 | 2 | 0 |
| Madisonville | 19,083 | 56 | 45 | 11 |
| Manchester | 1,939 | 11 | 11 | 0 |
| Marion | 3,091 | 7 | 6 | 1 |
| Martin | 632 | 4 | 3 | 1 |
| Mayfield | 10,167 | 24 | 24 | 0 |
| Maysville | 9,277 | 32 | 23 | 9 |
| McKee | 856 | 1 | 1 | 0 |
| Meadow Vale | 859 | 1 | 1 | 0 |
| Middlesboro | 9,881 | 28 | 24 | 4 |
| Millersburg | 864 | 1 | 1 | 0 |
| Monticello | 6,182 | 11 | 10 | 1 |
| Morehead | 7,718 | 28 | 18 | 10 |
| Morganfield | 3,274 | 13 | 8 | 5 |
| Morgantown | 2,566 | 6 | 6 | 0 |
| Mortons Gap | 935 | 1 | 1 | 0 |
| Mount Sterling | 7,026 | 23 | 21 | 2 |
| Mount Vernon | 2,612 | 9 | 9 | 0 |
| Mount Washington | 12,414 | 15 | 14 | 1 |
| Muldraugh | 1,214 | 3 | 3 | 0 |
| Munfordville | 1,616 | 4 | 4 | 0 |
| Murray | 16,709 | 38 | 32 | 6 |
| New Castle | 908 | 1 | 1 | 0 |
| New Haven | 886 | 1 | 1 | 0 |
| Newport | 15,632 | 49 | 45 | 4 |
| Nicholasville | 27,162 | 64 | 57 | 7 |
| Nortonville | 1,231 | 1 | 1 | 0 |
| Oak Grove | 9,480 | 23 | 17 | 6 |
| Olive Hill | 1,820 | 6 | 5 | 1 |
| Owensboro | 55,651 | 129 | 99 | 30 |
| Owenton | 1,486 | 4 | 4 | 0 |
| Owingsville | 1,684 | 5 | 5 | 0 |
| Paducah | 25,439 | 84 | 73 | 11 |
| Paintsville | 4,226 | 12 | 11 | 1 |
| Paris | 9,297 | 24 | 22 | 2 |
| Park Hills | 2,762 | 6 | 6 | 0 |
| Pembroke | 963 | 1 | 1 | 0 |
| Perryville | 759 | 1 | 1 | 0 |
| Pewee Valley | 1,625 | 1 | 1 | 0 |
| Pikeville | 6,406 | 29 | 22 | 7 |
| Pineville | 1,979 | 9 | 9 | 0 |
| Pioneer Village | 2,732 | 6 | 6 | 0 |
| Pippa Passes | 447 | 1 | 1 | 0 |
| Powderly | 878 | 1 | 1 | 0 |
| Prestonsburg | 3,861 | 17 | 17 | 0 |
| Princeton | 6,384 | 16 | 15 | 1 |
| Prospect | 5,953 | 10 | 9 | 1 |
| Providence | 3,399 | 7 | 7 | 0 |
| Raceland | 2,630 | 6 | 6 | 0 |
| Radcliff | 22,008 | 51 | 39 | 12 |
| Ravenna | 668 | 1 | 1 | 0 |
| Richmond | 33,546 | 90 | 65 | 25 |
| Russell | 3,584 | 11 | 11 | 0 |
| Russell Springs | 2,345 | 8 | 7 | 1 |
| Russellville | 7,281 | 20 | 19 | 1 |
| Sadieville | 326 | 1 | 1 | 0 |
| Salyersville | 1,566 | 3 | 3 | 0 |
| Science Hill | 674 | 2 | 2 | 0 |
| Scottsville | 4,610 | 20 | 13 | 7 |
| Sebree | 1,501 | 1 | 1 | 0 |
| Shelbyville | 11,422 | 22 | 21 | 1 |
| Shepherdsville | 9,293 | 26 | 24 | 2 |
| Shively | 16,816 | 33 | 28 | 5 |
| Silver Grove | 1,147 | 1 | 1 | 0 |
| Simpsonville | 1,454 | 4 | 4 | 0 |
| Smiths Grove | 781 | 1 | 1 | 0 |
| Somerset | 12,570 | 43 | 39 | 4 |
| South Shore | 1,255 | 1 | 1 | 0 |
| Springfield | 2,894 | 13 | 8 | 5 |
| Stamping Ground | 691 | 1 | 1 | 0 |
| Stanford | 3,396 | 10 | 10 | 0 |
| Stanton | 3,162 | 6 | 6 | 0 |
| St. Matthews | 18,871 | 36 | 30 | 6 |
| Strathmoor Village | 697 | 2 | 2 | 0 |
| Sturgis | 1,912 | 3 | 3 | 0 |
| Taylor Mill | 6,728 | 11 | 10 | 1 |
| Taylorsville | 1,258 | 5 | 5 | 0 |
| Tompkinsville | 2,604 | 12 | 9 | 3 |
| Uniontown | 1,015 | 2 | 2 | 0 |
| Vanceburg | 1,693 | 5 | 5 | 0 |
| Versailles | 7,817 | 41 | 40 | 1 |
| Villa Hills | 7,703 | 9 | 8 | 1 |
| Vine Grove | 4,386 | 8 | 8 | 0 |
| Warsaw | 1,788 | 6 | 6 | 0 |
| Wayland | 290 | 1 | 1 | 0 |
| West Liberty | 3,289 | 14 | 8 | 6 |
| West Point | 961 | 4 | 4 | 0 |
| Wheelwright | 1,028 | 1 | 1 | 0 |
| Whitesburg | 1,466 | 5 | 5 | 0 |
| Wilder | 2,959 | 6 | 6 | 0 |
| Williamsburg | 5,230 | 12 | 12 | 0 |
| Williamstown | 3,565 | 8 | 7 | 1 |
| Wilmore | 6,016 | 10 | 9 | 1 |
| Winchester | 16,583 | 38 | 34 | 4 |
| Wingo | 595 | 1 | 1 | 0 |
| Worthington | 1,677 | 5 | 5 | 0 |
| Wurtland | 1,047 | 1 | 1 | 0 |
| **LOUISIANA** | | | | |
| Abbeville | 12,125 | 41 | 38 | 3 |
| Addis | 3,652 | 15 | 14 | 1 |
| Alexandria | 48,886 | 197 | 162 | 35 |
| Amite | 4,343 | 27 | 27 | 0 |
| Baker | 13,315 | 40 | 38 | 2 |
| Baldwin | 2,601 | 7 | 6 | 1 |
| Bastrop | 11,687 | 37 | 37 | 0 |
| Bernice | 1,626 | 5 | 5 | 0 |
| Berwick | 4,268 | 13 | 12 | 1 |
| Blanchard | 2,655 | 6 | 5 | 1 |
| Bogalusa | 12,531 | 61 | 39 | 22 |
| Bossier City | 63,077 | 242 | 201 | 41 |
| Broussard | 7,973 | 29 | 25 | 4 |
| Brusly | 2,176 | 7 | 6 | 1 |
| Church Point | 4,652 | 19 | 19 | 0 |
| Clarence | 498 | 2 | 2 | 0 |
| Clinton | 1,880 | 8 | 7 | 1 |

**Table 78. Full-time Law Enforcement Employees, by State, by City, 2009**—*Continued*

(Number.)

| State/city | Population | Total law enforcement employees | Total officers | Total civilians |
|---|---|---|---|---|
| Coushatta | 2,067 | 7 | 7 | 0 |
| Covington | 9,218 | 51 | 39 | 12 |
| Crowley | 13,865 | 44 | 38 | 6 |
| Cullen | 1,365 | 4 | 4 | 0 |
| Denham Springs | 10,398 | 41 | 33 | 8 |
| De Ridder | 10,043 | 29 | 23 | 6 |
| Dixie Inn | 343 | 2 | 2 | 0 |
| Erath | 2,173 | 8 | 8 | 0 |
| Eunice | 11,501 | 41 | 31 | 10 |
| Franklin | 7,613 | 26 | 23 | 3 |
| Franklinton | 3,759 | 21 | 16 | 5 |
| French Settlement | 1,070 | 2 | 2 | 0 |
| Glenmora | 1,554 | 8 | 8 | 0 |
| Golden Meadow | 2,102 | 6 | 5 | 1 |
| Gonzales | 9,531 | 44 | 44 | 0 |
| Grambling | 4,479 | 15 | 10 | 5 |
| Gramercy | 3,278 | 5 | 5 | 0 |
| Gretna | 16,299 | 125 | 97 | 28 |
| Harahan | 9,249 | 27 | 20 | 7 |
| Haughton | 3,015 | 9 | 7 | 2 |
| Homer | 3,345 | 12 | 11 | 1 |
| Houma | 32,477 | 99 | 80 | 19 |
| Iowa | 2,616 | 16 | 11 | 5 |
| Jeanerette | 5,871 | 17 | 10 | 7 |
| Jennings | 10,483 | 35 | 25 | 10 |
| Kaplan | 5,035 | 21 | 21 | 0 |
| Kenner | 66,592 | 231 | 163 | 68 |
| Kentwood | 2,283 | 7 | 7 | 0 |
| Kinder | 2,399 | 17 | 16 | 1 |
| Lafayette | 113,868 | 308 | 253 | 55 |
| Lake Arthur | 2,866 | 9 | 9 | 0 |
| Lake Providence | 4,151 | 12 | 10 | 2 |
| Lecompte | 1,312 | 5 | 5 | 0 |
| Leesville | 5,600 | 43 | 28 | 15 |
| Mandeville | 12,645 | 51 | 36 | 15 |
| Mansfield | 5,386 | 19 | 14 | 5 |
| Many | 2,739 | 10 | 10 | 0 |
| McNary | 199 | 1 | 1 | 0 |
| Minden | 12,926 | 35 | 35 | 0 |
| Monroe | 51,020 | 228 | 177 | 51 |
| Moreauville | 930 | 2 | 2 | 0 |
| Natchitoches | 18,264 | 68 | 52 | 16 |
| Olla | 1,348 | 4 | 4 | 0 |
| Opelousas | 23,267 | 78 | 62 | 16 |
| Pearl River | 2,230 | 14 | 10 | 4 |
| Pineville | 14,885 | 63 | 56 | 7 |
| Plaquemine | 6,718 | 32 | 22 | 10 |
| Ponchatoula | 6,449 | 29 | 23 | 6 |
| Port Allen | 4,955 | 18 | 18 | 0 |
| Port Barre | 2,408 | 16 | 11 | 5 |
| Port Vincent | 534 | 2 | 2 | 0 |
| Rayne | 8,608 | 28 | 24 | 4 |
| Ruston | 21,181 | 49 | 42 | 7 |
| Scott | 9,096 | 24 | 23 | 1 |
| Sicily Island | 445 | 5 | 4 | 1 |
| Simmesport | 2,204 | 8 | 8 | 0 |
| Slidell | 27,355 | 132 | 76 | 56 |
| Springhill | 5,082 | 17 | 17 | 0 |
| St. Gabriel | 5,555 | 17 | 10 | 7 |
| Stonewall | 1,937 | 4 | 4 | 0 |
| Sulphur | 19,341 | 64 | 49 | 15 |
| Tallulah | 7,504 | 17 | 12 | 5 |
| Thibodaux | 14,012 | 64 | 56 | 8 |
| Tickfaw | 694 | 7 | 7 | 0 |
| Ville Platte | 8,149 | 27 | 27 | 0 |
| Vinton | 3,247 | 12 | 9 | 3 |
| Walker | 6,427 | 21 | 17 | 4 |
| Washington | 1,050 | 8 | 6 | 2 |
| Westlake | 4,566 | 22 | 22 | 0 |
| West Monroe | 12,863 | 79 | 76 | 3 |
| Westwego | 10,033 | 42 | 41 | 1 |
| Winnfield | 5,031 | 21 | 21 | 0 |
| Woodworth | 1,135 | 7 | 5 | 2 |
| Youngsville | 7,420 | 16 | 15 | 1 |
| **MAINE** | | | | |
| Ashland | 1,441 | 3 | 3 | 0 |
| Auburn | 23,176 | 53 | 48 | 5 |
| Augusta | 18,252 | 56 | 41 | 15 |
| Baileyville | 1,540 | 4 | 4 | 0 |
| Bangor | 31,789 | 96 | 79 | 17 |
| Bar Harbor | 5,163 | 14 | 10 | 4 |
| Bath | 8,847 | 25 | 20 | 5 |
| Belfast | 6,754 | 14 | 13 | 1 |
| Berwick | 7,681 | 12 | 11 | 1 |
| Bethel | 2,687 | 3 | 3 | 0 |
| Biddeford | 21,479 | 66 | 45 | 21 |
| Boothbay Harbor | 2,242 | 7 | 6 | 1 |
| Brewer | 9,041 | 22 | 20 | 2 |
| Bridgton | 5,507 | 12 | 8 | 4 |
| Brownville | 1,292 | 2 | 2 | 0 |
| Brunswick | 21,781 | 50 | 35 | 15 |
| Bucksport | 4,892 | 11 | 7 | 4 |
| Buxton | 8,138 | 14 | 9 | 5 |
| Calais | 3,157 | 11 | 7 | 4 |
| Camden | 5,216 | 14 | 11 | 3 |
| Cape Elizabeth | 8,769 | 14 | 13 | 1 |
| Caribou | 8,070 | 16 | 15 | 1 |
| Carrabassett Valley | 479 | 1 | 1 | 0 |
| Clinton | 3,312 | 3 | 3 | 0 |
| Cumberland | 7,639 | 11 | 10 | 1 |
| Damariscotta | 1,900 | 6 | 5 | 1 |
| Dexter | 3,666 | 6 | 5 | 1 |
| Dixfield | 2,532 | 4 | 4 | 0 |
| Dover-Foxcroft | 4,221 | 5 | 5 | 0 |
| East Millinocket | 3,157 | 4 | 4 | 0 |
| Eastport | 1,525 | 4 | 4 | 0 |
| Eliot | 6,339 | 10 | 9 | 1 |
| Ellsworth | 7,177 | 19 | 16 | 3 |
| Fairfield | 6,718 | 12 | 11 | 1 |
| Falmouth | 10,768 | 23 | 18 | 5 |
| Farmington | 7,561 | 15 | 14 | 1 |
| Fort Fairfield | 3,437 | 4 | 4 | 0 |
| Fort Kent | 4,177 | 8 | 4 | 4 |
| Freeport | 8,239 | 17 | 12 | 5 |
| Fryeburg | 3,363 | 6 | 6 | 0 |
| Gardiner | 6,090 | 14 | 12 | 2 |
| Gorham | 15,725 | 25 | 23 | 2 |
| Gouldsboro | 1,999 | 2 | 2 | 0 |
| Greenville | 1,722 | 3 | 2 | 1 |
| Hallowell | 2,434 | 5 | 5 | 0 |
| Hampden | 6,984 | 12 | 11 | 1 |
| Holden | 3,006 | 3 | 3 | 0 |
| Houlton | 6,109 | 19 | 14 | 5 |
| Jay | 4,749 | 8 | 7 | 1 |
| Kennebunk | 11,551 | 27 | 20 | 7 |
| Kennebunkport | 4,012 | 16 | 11 | 5 |
| Kittery | 10,524 | 27 | 20 | 7 |
| Lewiston | 35,074 | 97 | 82 | 15 |
| Limestone | 2,252 | 3 | 3 | 0 |
| Lincoln | 5,263 | 7 | 6 | 1 |
| Lincolnville | 2,202 | 1 | 1 | 0 |
| Lisbon | 9,343 | 21 | 15 | 6 |
| Livermore Falls | 3,124 | 10 | 6 | 4 |
| Machias | 2,112 | 4 | 4 | 0 |
| Madawaska | 4,315 | 6 | 5 | 1 |
| Madison | 4,575 | 8 | 7 | 1 |
| Mechanic Falls | 3,242 | 5 | 5 | 0 |
| Mexico | 2,856 | 5 | 5 | 0 |
| Milbridge | 1,312 | 2 | 2 | 0 |
| Millinocket | 4,871 | 9 | 9 | 0 |
| Milo | 2,313 | 2 | 2 | 0 |
| Monmouth | 3,862 | 4 | 4 | 0 |
| Mount Desert | 2,169 | 11 | 7 | 4 |
| Newport | 3,114 | 7 | 7 | 0 |
| North Berwick | 4,891 | 9 | 8 | 1 |
| Norway | 4,779 | 8 | 7 | 1 |
| Oakland | 6,209 | 10 | 9 | 1 |
| Ogunquit | 1,266 | 11 | 9 | 2 |
| Old Orchard Beach | 9,451 | 27 | 19 | 8 |
| Old Town | 7,689 | 17 | 15 | 2 |
| Orono | 9,708 | 15 | 14 | 1 |
| Oxford | 3,922 | 6 | 5 | 1 |
| Paris | 4,980 | 8 | 7 | 1 |
| Phippsburg | 2,167 | 1 | 1 | 0 |

## Table 78. Full-time Law Enforcement Employees, by State, by City, 2009—*Continued*

(Number.)

| State/city | Population | Total law enforcement employees | Total officers | Total civilians |
|---|---|---|---|---|
| Pittsfield | 4,217 | 6 | 6 | 0 |
| Portland | 62,382 | 208 | 157 | 51 |
| Presque Isle | 8,996 | 21 | 19 | 2 |
| Rangeley | 1,188 | 2 | 2 | 0 |
| Richmond | 3,429 | 4 | 4 | 0 |
| Rockland | 7,417 | 22 | 19 | 3 |
| Rockport | 3,553 | 6 | 6 | 0 |
| Rumford | 6,293 | 13 | 12 | 1 |
| Sabattus | 4,666 | 6 | 5 | 1 |
| Saco | 18,262 | 47 | 34 | 13 |
| Sanford | 21,183 | 63 | 41 | 22 |
| Scarborough | 19,281 | 50 | 35 | 15 |
| Searsport | 2,577 | 3 | 3 | 0 |
| Skowhegan | 8,664 | 17 | 15 | 2 |
| South Berwick | 7,205 | 12 | 8 | 4 |
| South Portland | 23,852 | 55 | 52 | 3 |
| Southwest Harbor | 1,939 | 5 | 5 | 0 |
| Swan's Island | 300 | 1 | 1 | 0 |
| Thomaston | 3,646 | 5 | 5 | 0 |
| Topsham | 9,909 | 14 | 13 | 1 |
| Van Buren | 2,463 | 3 | 3 | 0 |
| Veazie | 1,908 | 5 | 5 | 0 |
| Waldoboro | 5,015 | 9 | 8 | 1 |
| Washburn | 1,571 | 1 | 1 | 0 |
| Waterville | 16,063 | 41 | 31 | 10 |
| Wells | 9,944 | 30 | 22 | 8 |
| Westbrook | 16,579 | 39 | 37 | 2 |
| Wilton | 4,176 | 9 | 7 | 2 |
| Windham | 16,927 | 33 | 25 | 8 |
| Winslow | 7,856 | 10 | 9 | 1 |
| Winthrop | 6,451 | 15 | 10 | 5 |
| Wiscasset | 3,768 | 4 | 3 | 1 |
| Yarmouth | 8,069 | 18 | 12 | 6 |
| York | 14,195 | 38 | 27 | 11 |
| **MARYLAND** | | | | |
| Aberdeen | 14,003 | 55 | 45 | 10 |
| Annapolis | 36,586 | 162 | 121 | 41 |
| Baltimore | 638,755 | 3,586 | 3,013 | 573 |
| Baltimore City Sheriff | | 171 | 127 | 44 |
| Bel Air | 9,824 | 44 | 30 | 14 |
| Berlin | 4,111 | 18 | 13 | 5 |
| Berwyn Heights | 2,929 | 9 | 8 | 1 |
| Bladensburg | 7,557 | 24 | 18 | 6 |
| Boonsboro | 3,463 | 4 | 4 | 0 |
| Bowie | 52,577 | 52 | 47 | 5 |
| Brunswick | 5,262 | 12 | 10 | 2 |
| Cambridge | 11,840 | 63 | 49 | 14 |
| Capitol Heights | 4,094 | 4 | 4 | 0 |
| Centreville | 3,681 | 10 | 9 | 1 |
| Chestertown | 4,915 | 13 | 12 | 1 |
| Cheverly | 6,365 | 16 | 14 | 2 |
| Chevy Chase Village | 2,116 | 19 | 12 | 7 |
| Colmar Manor | 1,256 | 6 | 4 | 2 |
| Cottage City | 1,120 | 8 | 6 | 2 |
| Crisfield | 2,751 | 15 | 12 | 3 |
| Cumberland | 20,372 | 56 | 53 | 3 |
| Delmar | 3,576 | 13 | 12 | 1 |
| Denton | 4,147 | 14 | 13 | 1 |
| District Heights | 6,026 | 14 | 11 | 3 |
| Easton | 15,030 | 62 | 47 | 15 |
| Edmonston | 1,328 | 9 | 6 | 3 |
| Elkton | 15,202 | 47 | 40 | 7 |
| Fairmount Heights | 1,493 | 3 | 3 | 0 |
| Federalsburg | 2,627 | 9 | 9 | 0 |
| Forest Heights | 2,550 | 4 | 3 | 1 |
| Frederick | 59,936 | 170 | 133 | 37 |
| Frostburg | 7,669 | 19 | 15 | 4 |
| Fruitland | 4,511 | 19 | 17 | 2 |
| Glenarden | 6,304 | 9 | 8 | 1 |
| Greenbelt | 21,087 | 68 | 55 | 13 |
| Greensboro | 2,043 | 3 | 3 | 0 |
| Hagerstown | 40,062 | 117 | 100 | 17 |
| Hampstead | 5,501 | 10 | 9 | 1 |
| Hancock | 1,743 | 4 | 3 | 1 |
| Havre de Grace | 13,289 | 44 | 36 | 8 |
| Hurlock | 2,069 | 10 | 9 | 1 |
| Hyattsville | 15,346 | 54 | 42 | 12 |
| Landover Hills | 1,512 | 5 | 4 | 1 |
| La Plata | 9,170 | 16 | 14 | 2 |
| Laurel | 22,463 | 82 | 64 | 18 |
| Luke | 72 | 1 | 1 | 0 |
| Manchester | 3,567 | 6 | 5 | 1 |
| Morningside | 1,305 | 5 | 4 | 1 |
| Mount Rainier | 8,303 | 20 | 17 | 3 |
| New Carrollton | 12,445 | 16 | 13 | 3 |
| North East | 2,872 | 10 | 9 | 1 |
| Oakland | 1,832 | 5 | 4 | 1 |
| Ocean City | 7,026 | 133 | 106 | 27 |
| Ocean Pines | 11,295 | 19 | 15 | 4 |
| Oxford | 699 | 3 | 3 | 0 |
| Perryville | 3,816 | 13 | 9 | 4 |
| Pocomoke City | 3,854 | 21 | 14 | 7 |
| Port Deposit | 704 | 3 | 3 | 0 |
| Preston | 685 | 2 | 2 | 0 |
| Princess Anne | 3,104 | 15 | 13 | 2 |
| Ridgely | 1,536 | 4 | 4 | 0 |
| Rising Sun | 1,815 | 7 | 6 | 1 |
| Riverdale Park | 6,413 | 27 | 18 | 9 |
| Rock Hall | 1,496 | 5 | 5 | 0 |
| Salisbury | 28,800 | 112 | 76 | 36 |
| Seat Pleasant | 4,822 | 13 | 11 | 2 |
| Smithsburg | 3,002 | 5 | 4 | 1 |
| Snow Hill | 2,305 | 9 | 8 | 1 |
| St. Michaels | 1,054 | 9 | 8 | 1 |
| Sykesville | 4,444 | 9 | 8 | 1 |
| Takoma Park | 17,741 | 53 | 40 | 13 |
| Taneytown | 5,455 | 13 | 12 | 1 |
| Thurmont | 6,082 | 10 | 9 | 1 |
| Trappe | 1,136 | 1 | 1 | 0 |
| University Park | 2,278 | 8 | 8 | 0 |
| Upper Marlboro | 658 | 4 | 4 | 0 |
| Westernport | 1,929 | 4 | 4 | 0 |
| Westminster | 17,787 | 59 | 45 | 14 |
| **MASSACHUSETTS** | | | | |
| Abington | 16,732 | 28 | 26 | 2 |
| Acton | 21,104 | 43 | 35 | 8 |
| Acushnet | 10,606 | 18 | 16 | 2 |
| Adams | 8,232 | 20 | 15 | 5 |
| Amesbury | 16,623 | 37 | 31 | 6 |
| Amherst | 36,845 | 48 | 45 | 3 |
| Andover | 33,853 | 70 | 51 | 19 |
| Aquinnah | 358 | 4 | 4 | 0 |
| Arlington | 41,598 | 69 | 54 | 15 |
| Ashburnham | 6,054 | 14 | 9 | 5 |
| Ashby | 2,999 | 5 | 5 | 0 |
| Ashland | 16,164 | 31 | 26 | 5 |
| Athol | 11,724 | 23 | 18 | 5 |
| Attleboro | 43,772 | 91 | 78 | 13 |
| Auburn | 16,420 | 44 | 36 | 8 |
| Avon | 4,354 | 20 | 15 | 5 |
| Ayer | 7,488 | 22 | 17 | 5 |
| Barnstable | 48,042 | 123 | 107 | 16 |
| Barre | 5,496 | 11 | 7 | 4 |
| Becket | 1,822 | 2 | 2 | 0 |
| Bedford | 13,411 | 37 | 29 | 8 |
| Belchertown | 14,383 | 24 | 19 | 5 |
| Bellingham | 16,235 | 34 | 27 | 7 |
| Belmont | 23,597 | 60 | 46 | 14 |
| Berkley | 6,601 | 6 | 6 | 0 |
| Berlin | 2,760 | 11 | 7 | 4 |
| Bernardston | 2,258 | 3 | 3 | 0 |
| Beverly | 39,919 | 76 | 68 | 8 |
| Billerica | 43,058 | 75 | 64 | 11 |
| Blackstone | 9,126 | 19 | 16 | 3 |
| Bolton | 4,556 | 15 | 10 | 5 |
| Boston | 624,222 | 2,760 | 2,177 | 583 |
| Bourne | 19,133 | 44 | 37 | 7 |
| Boxborough | 5,200 | 11 | 10 | 1 |
| Boxford | 8,187 | 14 | 13 | 1 |
| Boylston | 4,330 | 13 | 10 | 3 |
| Braintree | 35,047 | 80 | 73 | 7 |
| Brewster | 10,054 | 26 | 20 | 6 |

**Table 78. Full-time Law Enforcement Employees, by State, by City, 2009**—*Continued*

(Number.)

| State/city | Population | Total law enforcement employees | Total officers | Total civilians |
|---|---|---|---|---|
| Bridgewater | 25,765 | 27 | 26 | 1 |
| Brockton | 96,471 | 200 | 180 | 20 |
| Brookfield | 3,049 | 5 | 4 | 1 |
| Brookline | 55,400 | 164 | 129 | 35 |
| Buckland | 2,011 | 2 | 2 | 0 |
| Burlington | 25,695 | 72 | 64 | 8 |
| Cambridge | 102,866 | 303 | 272 | 31 |
| Canton | 22,407 | 43 | 42 | 1 |
| Carlisle | 4,973 | 14 | 10 | 4 |
| Carver | 11,691 | 22 | 16 | 6 |
| Charlton | 12,835 | 23 | 20 | 3 |
| Chatham | 6,765 | 27 | 21 | 6 |
| Chelmsford | 34,695 | 63 | 49 | 14 |
| Chelsea | 39,883 | 99 | 93 | 6 |
| Chicopee | 54,589 | 133 | 129 | 4 |
| Chilmark | 986 | 4 | 4 | 0 |
| Clinton | 14,206 | 31 | 26 | 5 |
| Cohasset | 7,286 | 22 | 16 | 6 |
| Concord | 17,804 | 45 | 35 | 10 |
| Dalton | 6,616 | 12 | 11 | 1 |
| Danvers | 27,289 | 58 | 46 | 12 |
| Dartmouth | 34,879 | 79 | 65 | 14 |
| Dedham | 24,605 | 63 | 60 | 3 |
| Deerfield | 4,780 | 9 | 8 | 1 |
| Dennis | 15,475 | 50 | 41 | 9 |
| Dighton | 6,905 | 11 | 10 | 1 |
| Douglas | 8,093 | 20 | 15 | 5 |
| Dover | 5,724 | 18 | 16 | 2 |
| Dracut | 30,048 | 42 | 37 | 5 |
| Dudley | 11,264 | 15 | 11 | 4 |
| Dunstable | 3,399 | 7 | 7 | 0 |
| Duxbury | 14,588 | 33 | 26 | 7 |
| East Bridgewater | 14,108 | 23 | 21 | 2 |
| East Brookfield | 2,080 | 4 | 4 | 0 |
| Eastham | 5,464 | 23 | 14 | 9 |
| Easthampton | 16,401 | 33 | 25 | 8 |
| East Longmeadow | 15,595 | 25 | 24 | 1 |
| Easton | 23,337 | 33 | 32 | 1 |
| Edgartown | 3,968 | 16 | 15 | 1 |
| Egremont | 1,365 | 2 | 2 | 0 |
| Erving | 1,563 | 3 | 3 | 0 |
| Essex | 3,369 | 8 | 7 | 1 |
| Everett | 37,724 | 103 | 94 | 9 |
| Fairhaven | 16,318 | 35 | 28 | 7 |
| Fall River | 91,901 | 258 | 204 | 54 |
| Falmouth | 33,451 | 68 | 62 | 6 |
| Fitchburg | 40,678 | 83 | 76 | 7 |
| Foxborough | 16,562 | 36 | 28 | 8 |
| Framingham | 65,478 | 130 | 119 | 11 |
| Franklin | 32,114 | 56 | 45 | 11 |
| Freetown | 9,103 | 16 | 16 | 0 |
| Georgetown | 8,342 | 13 | 11 | 2 |
| Gill | 1,396 | 2 | 2 | 0 |
| Gloucester | 30,675 | 60 | 56 | 4 |
| Goshen | 980 | 1 | 1 | 0 |
| Grafton | 18,005 | 23 | 18 | 5 |
| Granby | 6,432 | 12 | 10 | 2 |
| Great Barrington | 7,431 | 15 | 14 | 1 |
| Greenfield | 17,840 | 38 | 34 | 4 |
| Groton | 10,936 | 21 | 15 | 6 |
| Groveland | 7,127 | 11 | 8 | 3 |
| Hadley | 4,884 | 15 | 11 | 4 |
| Halifax | 7,788 | 10 | 10 | 0 |
| Hamilton | 8,270 | 13 | 12 | 1 |
| Hampden | 5,401 | 15 | 10 | 5 |
| Hanover | 14,185 | 32 | 28 | 4 |
| Hanson | 10,096 | 25 | 21 | 4 |
| Hardwick | 2,673 | 3 | 3 | 0 |
| Harvard | 6,046 | 13 | 9 | 4 |
| Harwich | 12,436 | 35 | 33 | 2 |
| Haverhill | 60,738 | 100 | 90 | 10 |
| Hingham | 22,919 | 57 | 45 | 12 |
| Hinsdale | 1,966 | 2 | 2 | 0 |
| Holbrook | 10,817 | 21 | 20 | 1 |
| Holden | 16,819 | 27 | 24 | 3 |
| Holland | 2,586 | 1 | 1 | 0 |
| Holliston | 14,160 | 25 | 24 | 1 |
| Holyoke | 40,322 | 137 | 118 | 19 |
| Hopedale | 6,241 | 13 | 12 | 1 |
| Hopkinton | 14,633 | 26 | 21 | 5 |
| Hubbardston | 4,565 | 7 | 6 | 1 |
| Hudson | 20,060 | 37 | 31 | 6 |
| Hull | 11,159 | 30 | 24 | 6 |
| Ipswich | 13,435 | 32 | 25 | 7 |
| Kingston | 12,511 | 31 | 22 | 9 |
| Lakeville | 10,769 | 14 | 12 | 2 |
| Lancaster | 7,183 | 12 | 11 | 1 |
| Lanesboro | 2,910 | 7 | 7 | 0 |
| Lawrence | 70,670 | 173 | 146 | 27 |
| Leicester | 11,124 | 23 | 18 | 5 |
| Lenox | 5,160 | 10 | 10 | 0 |
| Leominster | 41,401 | 88 | 70 | 18 |
| Leverett | 1,772 | 2 | 2 | 0 |
| Lexington | 30,771 | 61 | 47 | 14 |
| Lincoln | 8,103 | 14 | 13 | 1 |
| Littleton | 8,906 | 20 | 14 | 6 |
| Lowell | 111,772 | 293 | 229 | 64 |
| Ludlow | 22,870 | 38 | 33 | 5 |
| Lunenburg | 10,087 | 13 | 13 | 0 |
| Lynn | 91,149 | 191 | 173 | 18 |
| Lynnfield | 11,500 | 22 | 17 | 5 |
| Malden | 56,455 | 113 | 104 | 9 |
| Manchester-by-the-Sea | 5,333 | 19 | 14 | 5 |
| Mansfield | 23,347 | 45 | 34 | 11 |
| Marblehead | 20,240 | 40 | 31 | 9 |
| Marion | 5,271 | 14 | 14 | 0 |
| Marlborough | 38,821 | 78 | 66 | 12 |
| Marshfield | 24,811 | 45 | 42 | 3 |
| Mashpee | 14,481 | 46 | 34 | 12 |
| Maynard | 10,295 | 24 | 21 | 3 |
| Medfield | 12,457 | 19 | 16 | 3 |
| Medford | 56,380 | 110 | 106 | 4 |
| Medway | 12,987 | 24 | 19 | 5 |
| Melrose | 27,134 | 44 | 44 | 0 |
| Mendon | 5,866 | 19 | 13 | 6 |
| Methuen | 44,527 | 98 | 85 | 13 |
| Middleboro | 21,585 | 43 | 39 | 4 |
| Middleton | 9,662 | 14 | 13 | 1 |
| Milford | 27,526 | 54 | 45 | 9 |
| Millbury | 13,652 | 24 | 19 | 5 |
| Millis | 8,055 | 18 | 15 | 3 |
| Millville | 2,878 | 5 | 5 | 0 |
| Milton | 26,719 | 63 | 51 | 12 |
| Monson | 8,974 | 16 | 10 | 6 |
| Montague | 8,407 | 20 | 15 | 5 |
| Monterey | 973 | 1 | 1 | 0 |
| Nahant | 3,548 | 13 | 12 | 1 |
| Nantucket | 11,380 | 41 | 37 | 4 |
| Natick | 32,418 | 64 | 52 | 12 |
| Needham | 28,683 | 56 | 46 | 10 |
| New Bedford | 92,621 | 304 | 261 | 43 |
| New Braintree | 1,144 | 1 | 1 | 0 |
| Newbury | 7,035 | 15 | 13 | 2 |
| Newburyport | 17,343 | 36 | 33 | 3 |
| Newton | 84,427 | 180 | 138 | 42 |
| Norfolk | 10,837 | 19 | 17 | 2 |
| North Adams | 13,927 | 31 | 26 | 5 |
| Northampton | 28,921 | 66 | 61 | 5 |
| North Andover | 28,116 | 53 | 40 | 13 |
| North Attleboro | 28,346 | 57 | 44 | 13 |
| Northborough | 14,792 | 27 | 20 | 7 |
| Northbridge | 14,634 | 22 | 17 | 5 |
| North Brookfield | 4,870 | 5 | 5 | 0 |
| Northfield | 3,022 | 2 | 2 | 0 |
| Norton | 19,610 | 27 | 26 | 1 |
| Norwell | 10,418 | 31 | 22 | 9 |
| Norwood | 28,569 | 71 | 60 | 11 |
| Oakham | 1,950 | 3 | 3 | 0 |
| Orange | 7,915 | 13 | 12 | 1 |
| Orleans | 6,337 | 27 | 21 | 6 |
| Oxford | 13,773 | 25 | 20 | 5 |
| Palmer | 13,086 | 26 | 20 | 6 |

## Table 78. Full-time Law Enforcement Employees, by State, by City, 2009—*Continued*

(Number.)

| State/city | Population | Total law enforcement employees | Total officers | Total civilians |
|---|---|---|---|---|
| Paxton | 4,580 | 11 | 7 | 4 |
| Peabody | 52,483 | 110 | 94 | 16 |
| Pembroke | 18,967 | 30 | 28 | 2 |
| Pepperell | 11,608 | 17 | 16 | 1 |
| Petersham | 1,306 | 2 | 2 | 0 |
| Phillipston | 1,821 | 3 | 2 | 1 |
| Pittsfield | 43,050 | 102 | 85 | 17 |
| Plainville | 8,522 | 19 | 14 | 5 |
| Plymouth | 56,084 | 116 | 100 | 16 |
| Plympton | 2,812 | 7 | 7 | 0 |
| Princeton | 3,536 | 8 | 5 | 3 |
| Provincetown | 3,398 | 25 | 17 | 8 |
| Quincy | 96,580 | 219 | 187 | 32 |
| Randolph | 30,549 | 59 | 59 | 0 |
| Raynham | 14,068 | 34 | 25 | 9 |
| Reading | 23,398 | 51 | 39 | 12 |
| Rehoboth | 11,795 | 27 | 22 | 5 |
| Revere | 58,290 | 95 | 87 | 8 |
| Rochester | 5,346 | 10 | 10 | 0 |
| Rockland | 17,941 | 36 | 29 | 7 |
| Rockport | 7,709 | 17 | 15 | 2 |
| Rowley | 5,953 | 17 | 13 | 4 |
| Rutland | 8,109 | 9 | 8 | 1 |
| Salem | 42,041 | 85 | 81 | 4 |
| Salisbury | 8,715 | 20 | 15 | 5 |
| Sandwich | 20,349 | 34 | 33 | 1 |
| Saugus | 27,663 | 69 | 53 | 16 |
| Scituate | 18,032 | 31 | 27 | 4 |
| Seekonk | 13,781 | 34 | 32 | 2 |
| Sharon | 17,256 | 32 | 28 | 4 |
| Shelburne | 2,056 | 2 | 2 | 0 |
| Sherborn | 4,281 | 14 | 14 | 0 |
| Shirley | 7,853 | 14 | 9 | 5 |
| Shrewsbury | 33,957 | 55 | 42 | 13 |
| Somerset | 18,495 | 40 | 35 | 5 |
| Somerville | 75,112 | 153 | 128 | 25 |
| Southampton | 6,160 | 8 | 8 | 0 |
| Southborough | 9,640 | 19 | 15 | 4 |
| Southbridge | 17,012 | 36 | 33 | 3 |
| South Hadley | 17,267 | 31 | 26 | 5 |
| Southwick | 9,651 | 21 | 16 | 5 |
| Spencer | 12,131 | 21 | 17 | 4 |
| Springfield | 153,533 | 539 | 450 | 89 |
| Sterling | 8,009 | 17 | 13 | 4 |
| Stockbridge | 2,251 | 6 | 6 | 0 |
| Stoughton | 27,355 | 54 | 48 | 6 |
| Stow | 6,473 | 16 | 11 | 5 |
| Sturbridge | 9,335 | 23 | 18 | 5 |
| Sudbury | 17,445 | 32 | 27 | 5 |
| Sunderland | 3,754 | 5 | 5 | 0 |
| Sutton | 9,175 | 20 | 15 | 5 |
| Swampscott | 14,111 | 33 | 32 | 1 |
| Swansea | 16,479 | 37 | 31 | 6 |
| Taunton | 56,446 | 111 | 106 | 5 |
| Templeton | 7,970 | 15 | 10 | 5 |
| Tewksbury | 30,133 | 65 | 51 | 14 |
| Tisbury | 3,841 | 13 | 12 | 1 |
| Topsfield | 6,130 | 14 | 10 | 4 |
| Townsend | 9,534 | 16 | 14 | 2 |
| Truro | 2,149 | 17 | 12 | 5 |
| Tyngsboro | 12,133 | 28 | 22 | 6 |
| Uxbridge | 12,916 | 22 | 17 | 5 |
| Wakefield | 25,057 | 41 | 40 | 1 |
| Walpole | 23,483 | 40 | 36 | 4 |
| Waltham | 61,357 | 176 | 147 | 29 |
| Ware | 10,165 | 17 | 17 | 0 |
| Wareham | 21,432 | 55 | 47 | 8 |
| Warren | 5,146 | 10 | 6 | 4 |
| Watertown | 32,944 | 68 | 64 | 4 |
| Wayland | 13,195 | 30 | 22 | 8 |
| Webster | 16,861 | 35 | 30 | 5 |
| Wellesley | 27,407 | 54 | 40 | 14 |
| Wellfleet | 2,758 | 18 | 13 | 5 |
| Wenham | 4,665 | 10 | 9 | 1 |
| Westborough | 18,647 | 35 | 29 | 6 |
| West Boylston | 8,364 | 18 | 13 | 5 |
| West Bridgewater | 6,739 | 20 | 20 | 0 |
| West Brookfield | 3,856 | 6 | 6 | 0 |
| Westfield | 41,474 | 87 | 75 | 12 |
| Westford | 22,239 | 50 | 40 | 10 |
| Westminster | 7,502 | 18 | 13 | 5 |
| West Newbury | 4,336 | 8 | 7 | 1 |
| Weston | 11,897 | 29 | 25 | 4 |
| Westport | 15,445 | 32 | 28 | 4 |
| West Springfield | 27,981 | 88 | 78 | 10 |
| West Tisbury | 2,668 | 10 | 9 | 1 |
| Westwood | 14,219 | 36 | 28 | 8 |
| Weymouth | 54,031 | 102 | 86 | 16 |
| Whitman | 14,564 | 27 | 26 | 1 |
| Wilbraham | 14,311 | 27 | 26 | 1 |
| Williamstown | 8,157 | 16 | 12 | 4 |
| Wilmington | 22,035 | 49 | 47 | 2 |
| Winchendon | 10,268 | 15 | 14 | 1 |
| Winchester | 21,486 | 46 | 38 | 8 |
| Winthrop | 21,071 | 31 | 29 | 2 |
| Woburn | 37,555 | 80 | 74 | 6 |
| Worcester | 178,474 | 472 | 423 | 49 |
| Wrentham | 11,360 | 17 | 15 | 2 |
| Yarmouth | 24,010 | 58 | 50 | 8 |
| **MICHIGAN** | | | | |
| Adrian | 21,295 | 36 | 33 | 3 |
| Adrian Township | 7,422 | 2 | 2 | 0 |
| Albion | 9,100 | 27 | 24 | 3 |
| Algonac | 4,532 | 9 | 8 | 1 |
| Allegan | 4,826 | 10 | 9 | 1 |
| Allen Park | 25,658 | 54 | 46 | 8 |
| Alma | 9,215 | 14 | 14 | 0 |
| Almont | 2,737 | 7 | 7 | 0 |
| Alpena | 10,378 | 19 | 17 | 2 |
| Ann Arbor | 114,367 | 173 | 124 | 49 |
| Argentine Township | 7,099 | 5 | 4 | 1 |
| Armada | 1,661 | 2 | 2 | 0 |
| Auburn | 2,034 | 1 | 1 | 0 |
| Auburn Hills | 21,021 | 70 | 55 | 15 |
| Augusta | 852 | 6 | 5 | 1 |
| Bad Axe | 3,029 | 8 | 8 | 0 |
| Bancroft | 584 | 1 | 1 | 0 |
| Bangor | 1,828 | 5 | 5 | 0 |
| Baraga | 1,175 | 3 | 3 | 0 |
| Barry Township | 3,537 | 3 | 3 | 0 |
| Bath Township | 11,886 | 12 | 11 | 1 |
| Battle Creek | 61,139 | 133 | 114 | 19 |
| Bay City | 33,572 | 61 | 57 | 4 |
| Beaverton | 1,054 | 1 | 1 | 0 |
| Belding | 5,672 | 8 | 7 | 1 |
| Bellaire | 1,118 | 3 | 3 | 0 |
| Belleville | 3,510 | 9 | 7 | 2 |
| Bellevue | 1,353 | 2 | 2 | 0 |
| Benton Harbor | 10,760 | 30 | 24 | 6 |
| Benton Township | 15,043 | 35 | 25 | 10 |
| Berkley | 14,708 | 33 | 27 | 6 |
| Berrien Springs-Oronoko Township | 9,534 | 10 | 9 | 1 |
| Beverly Hills | 9,805 | 27 | 23 | 4 |
| Big Rapids | 10,194 | 20 | 19 | 1 |
| Birch Run | 1,636 | 6 | 5 | 1 |
| Birmingham | 18,895 | 42 | 33 | 9 |
| Blackman Township | 24,512 | 29 | 28 | 1 |
| Blissfield | 3,164 | 6 | 6 | 0 |
| Bloomfield Hills | 3,755 | 30 | 26 | 4 |
| Bloomfield Township | 40,699 | 96 | 75 | 21 |
| Boyne City | 3,103 | 8 | 7 | 1 |
| Breckenridge | 1,278 | 2 | 2 | 0 |
| Bridgeport Township | 10,727 | 10 | 9 | 1 |
| Bridgman | 2,396 | 4 | 4 | 0 |
| Brighton | 7,256 | 19 | 17 | 2 |
| Bronson | 2,258 | 5 | 5 | 0 |
| Brown City | 1,243 | 2 | 2 | 0 |
| Brownstown Township | 29,045 | 45 | 35 | 10 |
| Buchanan | 4,320 | 10 | 9 | 1 |
| Buena Vista Township | 9,253 | 17 | 15 | 2 |
| Burr Oak | 745 | 1 | 1 | 0 |
| Burton | 29,788 | 45 | 40 | 5 |

**Table 78. Full-time Law Enforcement Employees, by State, by City, 2009—*Continued***

(Number.)

| State/city | Population | Total law enforcement employees | Total officers | Total civilians |
|---|---|---|---|---|
| Cadillac | 10,271 | 17 | 15 | 2 |
| Calumet | 795 | 1 | 1 | 0 |
| Cambridge Township | 5,865 | 3 | 3 | 0 |
| Canton Township | 82,634 | 121 | 86 | 35 |
| Capac | 2,089 | 2 | 2 | 0 |
| Carleton | 2,572 | 4 | 3 | 1 |
| Caro | 3,994 | 7 | 7 | 0 |
| Carrollton Township | 5,904 | 8 | 7 | 1 |
| Carson City | 1,174 | 3 | 3 | 0 |
| Caseville | 829 | 2 | 2 | 0 |
| Cass City | 2,477 | 4 | 4 | 0 |
| Cassopolis | 1,924 | 5 | 5 | 0 |
| Cedar Springs | 3,259 | 7 | 7 | 0 |
| Center Line | 8,093 | 22 | 20 | 2 |
| Central Lake | 962 | 1 | 1 | 0 |
| Charlevoix | 2,622 | 8 | 7 | 1 |
| Charlotte | 8,996 | 19 | 18 | 1 |
| Cheboygan | 4,904 | 8 | 7 | 1 |
| Chelsea | 5,075 | 12 | 8 | 4 |
| Chesterfield Township | 45,432 | 60 | 47 | 13 |
| Chikaming Township | 3,653 | 6 | 5 | 1 |
| Chocolay Township | 6,040 | 5 | 4 | 1 |
| Clare | 3,080 | 9 | 8 | 1 |
| Clarkston | 908 | 2 | 2 | 0 |
| Clawson | 12,097 | 19 | 18 | 1 |
| Clayton Township | 7,750 | 7 | 7 | 0 |
| Clay Township | 9,458 | 16 | 12 | 4 |
| Clinton | 2,400 | 4 | 4 | 0 |
| Clinton Township | 95,956 | 137 | 107 | 30 |
| Clio | 2,490 | 4 | 4 | 0 |
| Coldwater | 10,527 | 19 | 18 | 1 |
| Coleman | 1,221 | 2 | 2 | 0 |
| Coloma Township | 6,503 | 10 | 8 | 2 |
| Colon | 1,160 | 3 | 3 | 0 |
| Columbia Township | 7,552 | 6 | 6 | 0 |
| Concord | 1,069 | 2 | 2 | 0 |
| Constantine | 2,103 | 7 | 6 | 1 |
| Corunna | 3,273 | 3 | 2 | 1 |
| Covert Township | 3,049 | 6 | 6 | 0 |
| Croswell | 2,455 | 6 | 6 | 0 |
| Crystal Falls | 1,574 | 3 | 3 | 0 |
| Davison | 5,093 | 12 | 10 | 2 |
| Davison Township | 18,561 | 20 | 18 | 2 |
| Dearborn | 85,305 | 224 | 193 | 31 |
| Dearborn Heights | 51,308 | 111 | 84 | 27 |
| Decatur | 1,765 | 5 | 5 | 0 |
| Deckerville | 884 | 1 | 1 | 0 |
| Denmark Township | 1,771 | 1 | 1 | 0 |
| Denton Township | 5,375 | 5 | 5 | 0 |
| Detroit | 908,441 | 3,273 | 2,930 | 343 |
| Dewitt | 4,399 | 7 | 6 | 1 |
| Dewitt Township | 13,188 | 16 | 15 | 1 |
| Dowagiac | 5,670 | 15 | 14 | 1 |
| Dryden Township | 4,591 | 4 | 4 | 0 |
| Durand | 3,718 | 5 | 5 | 0 |
| East Grand Rapids | 10,435 | 32 | 29 | 3 |
| East Jordan | 2,206 | 6 | 5 | 1 |
| East Lansing | 45,779 | 88 | 59 | 29 |
| Eastpointe | 32,331 | 59 | 54 | 5 |
| East Tawas | 2,699 | 5 | 4 | 1 |
| Eaton Rapids | 5,236 | 11 | 10 | 1 |
| Ecorse | 9,717 | 24 | 20 | 4 |
| Edmore-Home Township | 2,744 | 1 | 1 | 0 |
| Elk Rapids | 1,669 | 5 | 5 | 0 |
| Elkton | 747 | 2 | 2 | 0 |
| Elsie | 971 | 2 | 2 | 0 |
| Emmett Township | 11,791 | 22 | 19 | 3 |
| Erie Township | 4,654 | 4 | 3 | 1 |
| Escanaba | 12,117 | 44 | 31 | 13 |
| Essexville | 3,465 | 8 | 8 | 0 |
| Evart | 1,659 | 6 | 5 | 1 |
| Fair Haven Township | 1,108 | 1 | 1 | 0 |
| Farmington | 9,778 | 10 | 3 | 7 |
| Farmington Hills | 78,140 | 158 | 116 | 42 |
| Fenton | 11,796 | 19 | 15 | 4 |
| Ferndale | 21,008 | 57 | 48 | 9 |
| Flat Rock | 8,797 | 26 | 23 | 3 |
| Flint | 111,657 | 205 | 186 | 19 |
| Flint Township | 31,391 | 52 | 44 | 8 |
| Flushing | 7,759 | 14 | 13 | 1 |
| Flushing Township | 10,078 | 9 | 8 | 1 |
| Forsyth Township | 4,894 | 7 | 6 | 1 |
| Fowlerville | 3,113 | 7 | 6 | 1 |
| Frankenmuth | 4,631 | 7 | 7 | 0 |
| Frankfort | 1,444 | 3 | 3 | 0 |
| Franklin | 2,912 | 10 | 10 | 0 |
| Fraser | 14,861 | 52 | 39 | 13 |
| Fremont | 4,182 | 9 | 8 | 1 |
| Frost Township | 1,109 | 1 | 1 | 0 |
| Fruitport | 1,075 | 10 | 9 | 1 |
| Gagetown | 364 | 1 | 1 | 0 |
| Galesburg | 1,927 | 3 | 2 | 1 |
| Garden City | 26,398 | 39 | 31 | 8 |
| Gaylord | 3,580 | 13 | 11 | 2 |
| Genesee Township | 22,926 | 25 | 23 | 2 |
| Gerrish Township | 3,075 | 7 | 7 | 0 |
| Gibraltar | 4,893 | 11 | 10 | 1 |
| Gladstone | 5,068 | 10 | 9 | 1 |
| Gladwin | 2,891 | 5 | 5 | 0 |
| Grand Beach | 242 | 4 | 4 | 0 |
| Grand Blanc | 7,479 | 19 | 17 | 2 |
| Grand Blanc Township | 35,451 | 51 | 46 | 5 |
| Grand Haven | 10,548 | 38 | 33 | 5 |
| Grand Ledge | 7,653 | 16 | 15 | 1 |
| Grand Rapids | 192,901 | 395 | 325 | 70 |
| Grandville | 16,763 | 26 | 24 | 2 |
| Grant | 853 | 1 | 1 | 0 |
| Grayling | 1,822 | 5 | 5 | 0 |
| Green Oak Township | 17,836 | 17 | 15 | 2 |
| Greenville | 8,165 | 20 | 16 | 4 |
| Grosse Ile Township | 9,776 | 24 | 17 | 7 |
| Grosse Pointe | 4,926 | 26 | 24 | 2 |
| Grosse Pointe Farms | 8,495 | 47 | 34 | 13 |
| Grosse Pointe Park | 10,802 | 49 | 43 | 6 |
| Grosse Pointe Shores | 2,476 | 21 | 18 | 3 |
| Grosse Pointe Woods | 14,954 | 44 | 38 | 6 |
| Hamburg Township | 21,772 | 13 | 12 | 1 |
| Hampton Township | 9,679 | 12 | 11 | 1 |
| Hamtramck | 20,255 | 43 | 43 | 0 |
| Hancock | 4,141 | 7 | 7 | 0 |
| Harbor Beach | 1,595 | 4 | 4 | 0 |
| Harbor Springs | 1,545 | 6 | 5 | 1 |
| Harper Woods | 12,411 | 40 | 36 | 4 |
| Hart | 1,911 | 4 | 4 | 0 |
| Hartford | 2,451 | 6 | 6 | 0 |
| Hastings | 6,832 | 16 | 14 | 2 |
| Hazel Park | 17,851 | 41 | 36 | 5 |
| Hesperia | 948 | 2 | 2 | 0 |
| Hillsdale | 7,710 | 16 | 14 | 2 |
| Holland | 33,970 | 70 | 60 | 10 |
| Holly | 6,283 | 17 | 13 | 4 |
| Homer | 1,736 | 3 | 3 | 0 |
| Hopkins | 548 | 2 | 2 | 0 |
| Houghton | 6,852 | 8 | 7 | 1 |
| Howard City | 1,574 | 3 | 3 | 0 |
| Howell | 9,733 | 21 | 19 | 2 |
| Hudson | 2,294 | 3 | 3 | 0 |
| Huntington Woods | 5,776 | 18 | 17 | 1 |
| Huron Township | 16,133 | 24 | 19 | 5 |
| Imlay City | 3,667 | 10 | 9 | 1 |
| Inkster | 26,261 | 70 | 61 | 9 |
| Ionia | 12,713 | 18 | 16 | 2 |
| Iron Mountain | 7,722 | 14 | 14 | 0 |
| Iron River | 2,964 | 8 | 7 | 1 |
| Ironwood | 5,277 | 12 | 12 | 0 |
| Ishpeming | 6,459 | 11 | 10 | 1 |
| Ishpeming Township | 3,615 | 1 | 1 | 0 |
| Ithaca | 3,008 | 4 | 4 | 0 |
| Jackson | 33,228 | 81 | 64 | 17 |
| Jonesville | 2,216 | 5 | 5 | 0 |
| Kalamazoo | 71,664 | 295 | 242 | 53 |
| Kalamazoo Township | 22,008 | 40 | 32 | 8 |

## Table 78. Full-time Law Enforcement Employees, by State, by City, 2009—*Continued*

(Number.)

| State/city | Population | Total law enforcement employees | Total officers | Total civilians |
|---|---|---|---|---|
| Kalkaska | 2,164 | 4 | 3 | 1 |
| Keego Harbor | 2,846 | 6 | 5 | 1 |
| Kentwood | 47,646 | 82 | 66 | 16 |
| Kingsford | 5,270 | 19 | 19 | 0 |
| Kingston | 420 | 1 | 1 | 0 |
| Kinross Township | 8,869 | 3 | 3 | 0 |
| L'Anse | 1,860 | 4 | 4 | 0 |
| Laingsburg | 1,251 | 2 | 2 | 0 |
| Lake Angelus | 311 | 5 | 5 | 0 |
| Lake Linden | 1,044 | 1 | 1 | 0 |
| Lake Odessa | 2,209 | 4 | 4 | 0 |
| Lake Orion | 2,712 | 8 | 4 | 4 |
| Lakeview | 1,089 | 2 | 2 | 0 |
| Lansing | 113,392 | 328 | 246 | 82 |
| Lansing Township | 7,832 | 17 | 16 | 1 |
| Lapeer | 9,007 | 24 | 21 | 3 |
| Lapeer Township | 5,012 | 1 | 1 | 0 |
| Lathrup Village | 4,042 | 7 | 7 | 0 |
| Laurium | 1,991 | 4 | 4 | 0 |
| Lawton | 1,794 | 6 | 6 | 0 |
| Leoni Township | 13,505 | 8 | 7 | 1 |
| Leslie | 2,302 | 3 | 3 | 0 |
| Lexington | 1,040 | 3 | 3 | 0 |
| Lincoln Park | 34,832 | 58 | 50 | 8 |
| Lincoln Township | 14,342 | 13 | 11 | 2 |
| Linden | 3,417 | 5 | 5 | 0 |
| Litchfield | 1,385 | 3 | 3 | 0 |
| Livonia | 90,232 | 179 | 148 | 31 |
| Lowell | 4,167 | 8 | 6 | 2 |
| Ludington | 8,319 | 15 | 14 | 1 |
| Luna Pier | 1,524 | 4 | 4 | 0 |
| Mackinac Island | 456 | 7 | 6 | 1 |
| Mackinaw City | 838 | 6 | 6 | 0 |
| Madison Heights | 29,367 | 68 | 55 | 13 |
| Madison Township | 8,155 | 2 | 2 | 0 |
| Mancelona | 1,349 | 2 | 2 | 0 |
| Manistee | 6,058 | 14 | 13 | 1 |
| Manistique | 3,034 | 8 | 8 | 0 |
| Manton | 1,161 | 1 | 1 | 0 |
| Marenisco Township | 1,801 | 1 | 1 | 0 |
| Marine City | 4,349 | 5 | 5 | 0 |
| Marion | 798 | 1 | 1 | 0 |
| Marlette | 1,971 | 3 | 3 | 0 |
| Marquette | 20,943 | 37 | 31 | 6 |
| Marshall | 7,085 | 18 | 14 | 4 |
| Marysville | 9,972 | 16 | 13 | 3 |
| Mason | 8,204 | 14 | 13 | 1 |
| Mattawan | 2,830 | 5 | 5 | 0 |
| Mayville | 981 | 2 | 2 | 0 |
| Melvindale | 9,715 | 24 | 21 | 3 |
| Memphis | 1,108 | 1 | 1 | 0 |
| Mendon | 906 | 2 | 2 | 0 |
| Menominee | 8,239 | 14 | 13 | 1 |
| Meridian Township | 38,414 | 48 | 42 | 6 |
| Metamora Township | 4,625 | 5 | 5 | 0 |
| Michiana | 192 | 3 | 3 | 0 |
| Midland | 40,821 | 50 | 48 | 2 |
| Milan | 5,762 | 12 | 8 | 4 |
| Milford | 16,661 | 26 | 20 | 6 |
| Millington | 1,062 | 1 | 1 | 0 |
| Monroe | 21,301 | 43 | 38 | 5 |
| Montague | 2,282 | 5 | 5 | 0 |
| Montrose Township | 7,659 | 9 | 8 | 1 |
| Morenci | 2,245 | 3 | 3 | 0 |
| Morrice | 871 | 2 | 2 | 0 |
| Mount Morris | 3,166 | 8 | 7 | 1 |
| Mount Morris Township | 22,058 | 34 | 31 | 3 |
| Mount Pleasant | 26,765 | 39 | 32 | 7 |
| Mundy Township | 14,141 | 21 | 18 | 3 |
| Munising | 2,289 | 5 | 5 | 0 |
| Muskegon | 39,327 | 88 | 79 | 9 |
| Muskegon Heights | 11,578 | 19 | 16 | 3 |
| Muskegon Township | 18,354 | 16 | 15 | 1 |
| Napoleon Township | 6,959 | 2 | 2 | 0 |
| Nashville | 1,651 | 2 | 2 | 0 |
| Negaunee | 4,444 | 9 | 8 | 1 |
| Newaygo | 1,621 | 5 | 4 | 1 |
| New Baltimore | 11,869 | 21 | 17 | 4 |
| New Buffalo | 2,449 | 8 | 7 | 1 |
| New Haven | 5,425 | 10 | 9 | 1 |
| Niles | 11,159 | 27 | 19 | 8 |
| North Branch | 972 | 2 | 2 | 0 |
| Northfield Township | 8,505 | 12 | 11 | 1 |
| North Muskegon | 3,902 | 7 | 7 | 0 |
| Northville | 5,947 | 15 | 15 | 0 |
| Northville Township | 25,266 | 46 | 34 | 12 |
| Norton Shores | 23,389 | 29 | 27 | 2 |
| Norway | 2,806 | 4 | 4 | 0 |
| Novi | 54,842 | 96 | 69 | 27 |
| Oak Park | 30,350 | 75 | 64 | 11 |
| Olivet | 1,820 | 2 | 2 | 0 |
| Onaway | 893 | 1 | 1 | 0 |
| Ontwa Township-Edwardsburg | 5,872 | 9 | 8 | 1 |
| Orchard Lake | 2,207 | 9 | 8 | 1 |
| Oscoda Township | 6,764 | 13 | 12 | 1 |
| Otsego | 3,807 | 7 | 6 | 1 |
| Ovid | 1,387 | 3 | 3 | 0 |
| Owosso | 14,885 | 22 | 20 | 2 |
| Oxford | 3,524 | 18 | 9 | 9 |
| Parchment | 1,795 | 3 | 3 | 0 |
| Parma-Sandstone | 6,782 | 2 | 2 | 0 |
| Paw Paw | 3,206 | 9 | 8 | 1 |
| Pentwater | 940 | 3 | 3 | 0 |
| Perry | 2,016 | 6 | 6 | 0 |
| Petoskey | 6,022 | 21 | 18 | 3 |
| Pigeon | 1,052 | 1 | 1 | 0 |
| Pinckney | 2,449 | 5 | 5 | 0 |
| Pinconning | 1,306 | 3 | 3 | 0 |
| Pittsfield Township | 34,699 | 51 | 39 | 12 |
| Plainwell | 3,840 | 9 | 8 | 1 |
| Pleasant Ridge | 2,456 | 6 | 6 | 0 |
| Plymouth | 8,430 | 16 | 15 | 1 |
| Plymouth Township | 25,071 | 42 | 30 | 12 |
| Pontiac | 65,924 | 105 | 76 | 29 |
| Portage | 46,269 | 69 | 53 | 16 |
| Port Austin | 643 | 1 | 1 | 0 |
| Port Huron | 30,718 | 58 | 49 | 9 |
| Portland | 3,672 | 6 | 6 | 0 |
| Potterville | 2,144 | 5 | 4 | 1 |
| Prairieville Township | 3,512 | 3 | 3 | 0 |
| Raisin Township | 7,368 | 5 | 4 | 1 |
| Reading | 1,064 | 3 | 2 | 1 |
| Redford Township | 45,291 | 76 | 63 | 13 |
| Reed City | 2,319 | 4 | 4 | 0 |
| Reese | 1,338 | 2 | 2 | 0 |
| Richfield Township, Genesee County | 8,570 | 10 | 8 | 2 |
| Richfield Township, Roscommon County | 4,072 | 8 | 7 | 1 |
| Richland | 771 | 2 | 2 | 0 |
| Richland Township, Saginaw County | 4,214 | 4 | 4 | 0 |
| Richmond | 5,684 | 12 | 9 | 3 |
| River Rouge | 8,303 | 23 | 20 | 3 |
| Riverview | 11,665 | 29 | 26 | 3 |
| Rochester | 11,057 | 26 | 20 | 6 |
| Rockford | 5,503 | 11 | 10 | 1 |
| Rockwood | 3,127 | 9 | 8 | 1 |
| Rogers City | 3,002 | 7 | 7 | 0 |
| Romeo | 3,739 | 12 | 8 | 4 |
| Romulus | 22,957 | 67 | 54 | 13 |
| Roosevelt Park | 3,756 | 5 | 5 | 0 |
| Rose City | 681 | 1 | 1 | 0 |
| Roseville | 46,642 | 95 | 86 | 9 |
| Royal Oak | 56,800 | 95 | 79 | 16 |
| Saginaw | 54,997 | 113 | 102 | 11 |
| Saginaw Township | 38,436 | 50 | 45 | 5 |
| Saline | 8,977 | 19 | 14 | 5 |
| Sandusky | 2,593 | 4 | 3 | 1 |
| Saugatuck-Douglas | 2,171 | 9 | 8 | 1 |
| Sault Ste. Marie | 14,063 | 68 | 55 | 13 |
| Schoolcraft | 1,504 | 11 | 3 | 8 |
| Scottville | 1,247 | 3 | 3 | 0 |
| Sebewaing | 1,726 | 3 | 3 | 0 |
| Shelby | 1,882 | 3 | 3 | 0 |

**Table 78. Full-time Law Enforcement Employees, by State, by City, 2009**—*Continued*

(Number.)

| State/city | Population | Total law enforcement employees | Total officers | Total civilians |
|---|---|---|---|---|
| Shelby Township | 72,094 | 90 | 70 | 20 |
| Shepherd | 1,338 | 2 | 2 | 0 |
| Somerset Township | 4,703 | 4 | 3 | 1 |
| Southfield | 75,074 | 184 | 147 | 37 |
| Southgate | 27,455 | 50 | 40 | 10 |
| South Haven | 5,151 | 24 | 17 | 7 |
| South Lyon | 11,052 | 18 | 17 | 1 |
| South Rockwood | 1,705 | 4 | 4 | 0 |
| Sparta | 4,041 | 5 | 5 | 0 |
| Spaulding Township | 2,168 | 1 | 1 | 0 |
| Spring Arbor Township | 8,409 | 2 | 2 | 0 |
| Springfield | 5,020 | 14 | 13 | 1 |
| Spring Lake-Ferrysburg | 5,464 | 10 | 9 | 1 |
| Springport Township | 2,192 | 2 | 2 | 0 |
| Standish | 1,972 | 1 | 1 | 0 |
| Stanton | 1,480 | 1 | 1 | 0 |
| St. Charles | 1,999 | 3 | 3 | 0 |
| St. Clair | 5,760 | 9 | 9 | 0 |
| St. Clair Shores | 60,076 | 100 | 84 | 16 |
| Sterling Heights | 127,440 | 226 | 171 | 55 |
| St. Ignace | 2,301 | 7 | 6 | 1 |
| St. Johns | 7,225 | 12 | 10 | 2 |
| St. Joseph | 8,423 | 24 | 18 | 6 |
| St. Joseph Township | 9,580 | 12 | 11 | 1 |
| St. Louis | 7,008 | 6 | 5 | 1 |
| Stockbridge | 1,275 | 2 | 2 | 0 |
| Sturgis | 10,866 | 23 | 18 | 5 |
| Summit Township | 21,642 | 5 | 5 | 0 |
| Sumpter Township | 11,114 | 19 | 14 | 5 |
| Suttons Bay | 576 | 2 | 2 | 0 |
| Swartz Creek | 5,235 | 8 | 7 | 1 |
| Sylvan Lake | 1,629 | 5 | 5 | 0 |
| Taylor | 60,054 | 105 | 89 | 16 |
| Tecumseh | 8,602 | 17 | 15 | 2 |
| Thetford Township | 7,784 | 2 | 2 | 0 |
| Thomas Township | 12,252 | 8 | 7 | 1 |
| Three Oaks | 1,681 | 1 | 1 | 0 |
| Three Rivers | 7,136 | 20 | 16 | 4 |
| Tittabawassee Township | 8,833 | 6 | 5 | 1 |
| Traverse City | 14,385 | 34 | 32 | 2 |
| Trenton | 17,792 | 35 | 34 | 1 |
| Troy | 80,182 | 179 | 128 | 51 |
| Tuscarora Township | 3,014 | 8 | 7 | 1 |
| Ubly | 761 | 2 | 2 | 0 |
| Unadilla Township | 3,443 | 2 | 2 | 0 |
| Union City | 1,705 | 4 | 4 | 0 |
| Utica | 4,961 | 20 | 16 | 4 |
| Vassar | 2,648 | 4 | 4 | 0 |
| Vernon | 784 | 1 | 1 | 0 |
| Vicksburg | 2,181 | 8 | 8 | 0 |
| Walker | 23,918 | 38 | 34 | 4 |
| Walled Lake | 6,895 | 14 | 13 | 1 |
| Warren | 133,485 | 263 | 224 | 39 |
| Waterford Township | 70,403 | 109 | 77 | 32 |
| Waterloo Township | 2,958 | 3 | 3 | 0 |
| Watertown Township | 2,145 | 1 | 1 | 0 |
| Watervliet | 1,726 | 2 | 2 | 0 |
| Wayland | 3,794 | 6 | 5 | 1 |
| Wayne | 16,990 | 46 | 38 | 8 |
| West Bloomfield Township | 63,728 | 104 | 81 | 23 |
| West Branch | 1,803 | 6 | 5 | 1 |
| Westland | 78,149 | 118 | 96 | 22 |
| White Cloud | 1,387 | 2 | 2 | 0 |
| Whitehall | 2,794 | 8 | 8 | 0 |
| White Lake Township | 30,102 | 37 | 27 | 10 |
| White Pigeon | 1,552 | 4 | 4 | 0 |
| Williamston | 3,799 | 11 | 10 | 1 |
| Wixom | 13,431 | 24 | 20 | 4 |
| Wolverine Lake | 4,292 | 6 | 6 | 0 |
| Woodhaven | 12,643 | 33 | 30 | 3 |
| Wyandotte | 24,399 | 48 | 38 | 10 |
| Yale | 1,945 | 4 | 4 | 0 |
| Ypsilanti | 21,369 | 42 | 33 | 9 |
| Zeeland | 5,410 | 10 | 9 | 1 |
| Zilwaukee | 1,636 | 2 | 2 | 0 |

| State/city | Population | Total law enforcement employees | Total officers | Total civilians |
|---|---|---|---|---|
| **MINNESOTA** | | | | |
| Albany | 2,148 | 5 | 5 | 0 |
| Albert Lea | 17,279 | 39 | 28 | 11 |
| Alexandria | 11,409 | 25 | 20 | 5 |
| Annandale | 3,150 | 4 | 4 | 0 |
| Anoka | 17,203 | 34 | 27 | 7 |
| Appleton | 3,011 | 4 | 4 | 0 |
| Apple Valley | 50,480 | 59 | 49 | 10 |
| Aurora | 1,735 | 4 | 4 | 0 |
| Austin | 22,721 | 34 | 31 | 3 |
| Avon | 1,324 | 3 | 3 | 0 |
| Babbitt | 1,578 | 4 | 4 | 0 |
| Baxter | 8,625 | 16 | 15 | 1 |
| Bayport | 3,305 | 5 | 5 | 0 |
| Becker | 4,381 | 6 | 5 | 1 |
| Belgrade | 710 | 1 | 1 | 0 |
| Belle Plaine | 7,067 | 10 | 8 | 2 |
| Bemidji | 13,694 | 33 | 31 | 2 |
| Benson | 3,014 | 8 | 7 | 1 |
| Big Lake | 10,282 | 13 | 11 | 2 |
| Blackduck | 768 | 2 | 2 | 0 |
| Blaine | 56,228 | 71 | 59 | 12 |
| Blooming Prairie | 1,970 | 3 | 3 | 0 |
| Bloomington | 80,864 | 144 | 113 | 31 |
| Blue Earth | 3,209 | 5 | 5 | 0 |
| Brainerd | 13,694 | 33 | 26 | 7 |
| Breckenridge | 3,159 | 6 | 6 | 0 |
| Brooklyn Center | 27,217 | 56 | 44 | 12 |
| Brooklyn Park | 71,740 | 130 | 103 | 27 |
| Brownton | 782 | 2 | 2 | 0 |
| Buffalo | 14,741 | 20 | 17 | 3 |
| Burnsville | 59,015 | 84 | 75 | 9 |
| Caledonia | 2,805 | 5 | 4 | 1 |
| Cambridge | 7,965 | 14 | 13 | 1 |
| Cannon Falls | 4,049 | 10 | 9 | 1 |
| Centennial Lakes | 11,262 | 18 | 16 | 2 |
| Champlin | 23,640 | 29 | 24 | 5 |
| Chaska | 24,939 | 27 | 24 | 3 |
| Chisholm | 4,555 | 12 | 11 | 1 |
| Cloquet | 11,407 | 21 | 19 | 2 |
| Cold Spring | 3,802 | 9 | 8 | 1 |
| Columbia Heights | 18,176 | 31 | 26 | 5 |
| Coon Rapids | 61,844 | 72 | 64 | 8 |
| Corcoran | 5,629 | 8 | 7 | 1 |
| Cottage Grove | 33,969 | 46 | 39 | 7 |
| Crookston | 7,744 | 16 | 14 | 2 |
| Crosby | 2,237 | 9 | 8 | 1 |
| Crystal | 21,600 | 37 | 30 | 7 |
| Dawson | 1,339 | 2 | 2 | 0 |
| Dayton | 4,635 | 6 | 5 | 1 |
| Deephaven-Woodland | 4,235 | 8 | 7 | 1 |
| Detroit Lakes | 8,209 | 17 | 15 | 2 |
| Dilworth | 3,757 | 7 | 6 | 1 |
| Duluth | 84,071 | 175 | 145 | 30 |
| Eagan | 64,014 | 80 | 69 | 11 |
| Eagle Lake | 2,340 | 2 | 2 | 0 |
| East Grand Forks | 7,839 | 23 | 21 | 2 |
| Eden Prairie | 61,893 | 89 | 65 | 24 |
| Edina | 45,414 | 68 | 51 | 17 |
| Elk River | 24,061 | 39 | 31 | 8 |
| Elmore | 648 | 1 | 1 | 0 |
| Ely | 3,447 | 7 | 6 | 1 |
| Eveleth | 3,553 | 11 | 10 | 1 |
| Fairmont | 10,148 | 19 | 17 | 2 |
| Faribault | 22,129 | 41 | 33 | 8 |
| Farmington | 19,945 | 27 | 24 | 3 |
| Fergus Falls | 13,631 | 28 | 23 | 5 |
| Floodwood | 494 | 2 | 2 | 0 |
| Forest Lake | 17,727 | 29 | 26 | 3 |
| Fridley | 25,696 | 44 | 38 | 6 |
| Gilbert | 1,745 | 7 | 7 | 0 |
| Glencoe | 5,560 | 10 | 9 | 1 |
| Glenwood | 2,518 | 4 | 4 | 0 |
| Golden Valley | 20,345 | 40 | 30 | 10 |
| Goodview | 3,577 | 4 | 4 | 0 |

## Table 78. Full-time Law Enforcement Employees, by State, by City, 2009—*Continued*

(Number.)

| State/city | Population | Total law enforcement employees | Total officers | Total civilians |
|---|---|---|---|---|
| Grand Rapids | 8,736 | 23 | 20 | 3 |
| Granite Falls | 2,885 | 5 | 5 | 0 |
| Hallock | 1,003 | 1 | 1 | 0 |
| Hastings | 22,600 | 34 | 29 | 5 |
| Hermantown | 9,518 | 15 | 13 | 2 |
| Hibbing | 16,115 | 33 | 29 | 4 |
| Hokah | 556 | 1 | 1 | 0 |
| Hopkins | 16,915 | 39 | 26 | 13 |
| Houston | 949 | 2 | 2 | 0 |
| Hoyt Lakes | 1,943 | 5 | 5 | 0 |
| Hutchinson | 13,995 | 32 | 21 | 11 |
| International Falls | 5,827 | 12 | 11 | 1 |
| Inver Grove Heights | 33,800 | 40 | 33 | 7 |
| Jackson | 3,285 | 7 | 7 | 0 |
| Janesville | 2,255 | 3 | 3 | 0 |
| Jordan | 5,642 | 10 | 8 | 2 |
| Kasson | 5,697 | 8 | 8 | 0 |
| Kimball | 710 | 4 | 4 | 0 |
| La Crescent | 4,908 | 7 | 6 | 1 |
| Lake City | 5,310 | 11 | 10 | 1 |
| Lake Crystal | 2,619 | 4 | 4 | 0 |
| Lakefield | 1,603 | 3 | 3 | 0 |
| Lakes Area | 8,373 | 14 | 12 | 2 |
| Lakeville | 55,921 | 60 | 52 | 8 |
| Lester Prairie | 1,795 | 3 | 3 | 0 |
| Le Sueur | 4,286 | 8 | 7 | 1 |
| Lewiston | 1,479 | 2 | 2 | 0 |
| Lino Lakes | 20,565 | 29 | 27 | 2 |
| Litchfield | 6,557 | 10 | 9 | 1 |
| Little Falls | 8,105 | 15 | 13 | 2 |
| Long Prairie | 2,785 | 6 | 6 | 0 |
| Madison | 1,542 | 3 | 3 | 0 |
| Mankato | 36,676 | 61 | 50 | 11 |
| Maple Grove | 62,801 | 79 | 65 | 14 |
| Mapleton | 1,656 | 3 | 3 | 0 |
| Maplewood | 36,165 | 58 | 53 | 5 |
| Marshall | 12,634 | 22 | 19 | 3 |
| Medina | 5,209 | 11 | 10 | 1 |
| Melrose | 3,150 | 6 | 5 | 1 |
| Mendota Heights | 11,610 | 18 | 17 | 1 |
| Milaca | 3,052 | 6 | 5 | 1 |
| Minneapolis | 382,618 | 1,113 | 888 | 225 |
| Minnetonka | 49,968 | 75 | 57 | 18 |
| Minnetrista | 8,588 | 16 | 12 | 4 |
| Montevideo | 5,203 | 12 | 11 | 1 |
| Montgomery | 3,323 | 6 | 5 | 1 |
| Moorhead | 36,429 | 63 | 49 | 14 |
| Moose Lake | 2,404 | 4 | 4 | 0 |
| Mora | 3,438 | 7 | 6 | 1 |
| Morris | 4,975 | 10 | 8 | 2 |
| Mound | 9,558 | 14 | 12 | 2 |
| Mounds View | 11,925 | 19 | 17 | 2 |
| Mountain Iron | 2,911 | 5 | 5 | 0 |
| Mountain Lake | 1,912 | 4 | 4 | 0 |
| New Brighton | 21,494 | 32 | 27 | 5 |
| New Hope | 20,381 | 36 | 29 | 7 |
| Newport | 3,459 | 7 | 7 | 0 |
| New Prague | 7,001 | 11 | 9 | 2 |
| New Richland | 1,152 | 2 | 2 | 0 |
| New Ulm | 12,989 | 24 | 21 | 3 |
| North Branch | 10,705 | 14 | 12 | 2 |
| Northfield | 19,919 | 27 | 22 | 5 |
| North Mankato | 12,605 | 13 | 12 | 1 |
| North St. Paul | 11,177 | 20 | 17 | 3 |
| Oakdale | 27,068 | 41 | 31 | 10 |
| Oak Park Heights | 4,802 | 10 | 9 | 1 |
| Olivia | 2,340 | 5 | 4 | 1 |
| Orono | 12,002 | 22 | 19 | 3 |
| Ortonville | 1,956 | 3 | 3 | 0 |
| Osakis | 1,573 | 3 | 3 | 0 |
| Osseo | 2,565 | 6 | 5 | 1 |
| Owatonna | 25,119 | 36 | 33 | 3 |
| Park Rapids | 3,673 | 11 | 10 | 1 |
| Paynesville | 2,260 | 5 | 4 | 1 |
| Plainview | 3,228 | 6 | 6 | 0 |
| Plymouth | 72,121 | 79 | 69 | 10 |
| Princeton | 4,858 | 13 | 11 | 2 |
| Prior Lake | 24,870 | 25 | 22 | 3 |
| Proctor | 2,838 | 8 | 7 | 1 |
| Ramsey | 24,391 | 27 | 23 | 4 |
| Red Wing | 15,643 | 31 | 25 | 6 |
| Redwood Falls | 5,035 | 13 | 11 | 2 |
| Richfield | 32,547 | 55 | 44 | 11 |
| Robbinsdale | 13,452 | 25 | 21 | 4 |
| Rochester | 101,884 | 180 | 125 | 55 |
| Rogers | 8,111 | 16 | 13 | 3 |
| Roseau | 2,759 | 6 | 5 | 1 |
| Rosemount | 22,061 | 25 | 22 | 3 |
| Roseville | 32,719 | 55 | 48 | 7 |
| Sartell | 14,467 | 18 | 17 | 1 |
| Sauk Centre | 3,946 | 7 | 6 | 1 |
| Sauk Rapids | 12,197 | 14 | 13 | 1 |
| Savage | 28,473 | 39 | 32 | 7 |
| Shakopee | 35,231 | 53 | 45 | 8 |
| Silver Bay | 1,817 | 5 | 5 | 0 |
| Silver Lake | 802 | 2 | 2 | 0 |
| Slayton | 1,810 | 4 | 4 | 0 |
| Sleepy Eye | 3,399 | 6 | 6 | 0 |
| South Lake Minnetonka | 12,071 | 16 | 14 | 2 |
| South St. Paul | 19,485 | 28 | 26 | 2 |
| Springfield | 2,141 | 5 | 5 | 0 |
| Spring Grove | 1,232 | 2 | 2 | 0 |
| Spring Lake Park | 6,426 | 13 | 11 | 2 |
| St. Anthony | 8,459 | 26 | 23 | 3 |
| Staples | 3,006 | 6 | 5 | 1 |
| St. Charles | 3,606 | 4 | 4 | 0 |
| St. Cloud | 67,804 | 125 | 98 | 27 |
| St. Francis | 7,568 | 12 | 10 | 2 |
| Stillwater | 18,168 | 24 | 21 | 3 |
| St. James | 4,241 | 8 | 7 | 1 |
| St. Joseph | 6,257 | 8 | 7 | 1 |
| St. Louis Park | 45,613 | 68 | 51 | 17 |
| St. Paul | 280,194 | 823 | 614 | 209 |
| St. Paul Park | 5,256 | 9 | 9 | 0 |
| St. Peter | 11,103 | 18 | 13 | 5 |
| Thief River Falls | 8,482 | 16 | 14 | 2 |
| Tracy | 2,044 | 3 | 3 | 0 |
| Two Harbors | 3,252 | 8 | 7 | 1 |
| Virginia | 8,409 | 21 | 20 | 1 |
| Wabasha | 2,511 | 7 | 6 | 1 |
| Wadena | 3,947 | 9 | 8 | 1 |
| Waite Park | 6,809 | 15 | 12 | 3 |
| Warroad | 1,650 | 7 | 6 | 1 |
| Waseca | 9,416 | 16 | 14 | 2 |
| Wayzata | 3,859 | 12 | 11 | 1 |
| Wells | 2,319 | 4 | 4 | 0 |
| West Hennepin | 5,550 | 10 | 8 | 2 |
| West St. Paul | 18,871 | 34 | 29 | 5 |
| Wheaton | 1,402 | 4 | 3 | 1 |
| White Bear Lake | 24,068 | 35 | 28 | 7 |
| Willmar | 17,698 | 37 | 33 | 4 |
| Windom | 4,165 | 9 | 8 | 1 |
| Winnebago | 1,319 | 3 | 3 | 0 |
| Winona | 26,752 | 41 | 37 | 4 |
| Winsted | 2,455 | 4 | 4 | 0 |
| Woodbury | 57,259 | 75 | 63 | 12 |
| Worthington | 11,013 | 32 | 24 | 8 |
| Wyoming | 3,889 | 9 | 8 | 1 |
| Zumbrota | 3,104 | 4 | 4 | 0 |
| **MISSISSIPPI** | | | | |
| Aberdeen | 6,054 | 21 | 17 | 4 |
| Ackerman | 1,507 | 5 | 5 | 0 |
| Amory | 7,226 | 24 | 17 | 7 |
| Batesville | 7,928 | 47 | 37 | 10 |
| Bay Springs | 2,209 | 7 | 6 | 1 |
| Bay St. Louis | 7,774 | 35 | 31 | 4 |
| Belzoni | 2,407 | 15 | 9 | 6 |
| Biloxi | 45,160 | 182 | 130 | 52 |
| Booneville | 8,763 | 30 | 26 | 4 |
| Brandon | 22,716 | 54 | 39 | 15 |
| Brookhaven | 13,334 | 41 | 35 | 6 |
| Bruce | 1,995 | 7 | 6 | 1 |

## Table 78. Full-time Law Enforcement Employees, by State, by City, 2009—*Continued*

(Number.)

| State/city | Population | Total law enforcement employees | Total officers | Total civilians |
|---|---|---|---|---|
| Byhalia | 1,313 | 13 | 8 | 5 |
| Calhoun City | 1,777 | 5 | 5 | 0 |
| Carthage | 4,836 | 19 | 15 | 4 |
| Charleston | 1,850 | 11 | 10 | 1 |
| Clarksdale | 17,741 | 36 | 28 | 8 |
| Cleveland | 12,057 | 52 | 45 | 7 |
| Clinton | 26,444 | 64 | 45 | 19 |
| Collins | 2,774 | 13 | 9 | 4 |
| Columbia | 6,563 | 30 | 22 | 8 |
| Columbus | 23,577 | 79 | 72 | 7 |
| Como | 1,315 | 3 | 3 | 0 |
| Corinth | 14,274 | 56 | 42 | 14 |
| Crenshaw | 909 | 3 | 3 | 0 |
| Crystal Springs | 5,959 | 20 | 14 | 6 |
| De Kalb | 866 | 6 | 6 | 0 |
| Durant | 2,698 | 10 | 10 | 0 |
| Edwards | 1,286 | 1 | 1 | 0 |
| Eupora | 2,201 | 7 | 6 | 1 |
| Fayette | 1,961 | 10 | 7 | 3 |
| Florence | 3,612 | 22 | 14 | 8 |
| Flowood | 7,182 | 60 | 46 | 14 |
| Fulton | 4,093 | 11 | 11 | 0 |
| Gautier | 16,248 | 53 | 43 | 10 |
| Gloster | 1,021 | 7 | 5 | 2 |
| Greenville | 35,187 | 167 | 92 | 75 |
| Greenwood | 15,842 | 73 | 57 | 16 |
| Grenada | 14,647 | 44 | 41 | 3 |
| Gulfport | 69,926 | 257 | 190 | 67 |
| Hattiesburg | 52,716 | 192 | 121 | 71 |
| Hazlehurst | 4,386 | 18 | 18 | 0 |
| Heidelberg | 809 | 5 | 4 | 1 |
| Hernando | 12,913 | 45 | 35 | 10 |
| Hollandale | 2,915 | 9 | 5 | 4 |
| Holly Springs | 7,997 | 25 | 18 | 7 |
| Horn Lake | 25,238 | 77 | 60 | 17 |
| Houston | 3,857 | 10 | 6 | 4 |
| Iuka | 2,926 | 12 | 9 | 3 |
| Jackson | 172,799 | 749 | 485 | 264 |
| Kosciusko | 7,371 | 19 | 19 | 0 |
| Laurel | 18,741 | 81 | 56 | 25 |
| Leakesville | 1,025 | 5 | 1 | 4 |
| Leland | 4,720 | 21 | 15 | 6 |
| Long Beach | 11,879 | 47 | 34 | 13 |
| Louisville | 6,561 | 27 | 21 | 6 |
| Lucedale | 3,152 | 18 | 14 | 4 |
| Macon | 2,718 | 11 | 9 | 2 |
| Madison | 18,040 | 86 | 63 | 23 |
| Magee | 4,347 | 18 | 14 | 4 |
| Magnolia | 2,090 | 8 | 7 | 1 |
| McComb | 13,726 | 61 | 29 | 32 |
| McLain | 594 | 1 | 1 | 0 |
| Meridian | 38,054 | 109 | 92 | 17 |
| Moorhead | 2,319 | 6 | 5 | 1 |
| Morton | 3,432 | 14 | 14 | 0 |
| Moss Point | 13,757 | 42 | 27 | 15 |
| Natchez | 16,209 | 69 | 43 | 26 |
| New Albany | 8,234 | 27 | 25 | 2 |
| Newton | 3,672 | 17 | 10 | 7 |
| Ocean Springs | 17,140 | 55 | 40 | 15 |
| Okolona | 2,852 | 10 | 10 | 0 |
| Olive Branch | 33,284 | 88 | 70 | 18 |
| Oxford | 17,719 | 67 | 58 | 9 |
| Pascagoula | 23,346 | 98 | 63 | 35 |
| Pass Christian | 3,864 | 23 | 21 | 2 |
| Pearl | 24,592 | 74 | 56 | 18 |
| Pelahatchie | 1,475 | 8 | 6 | 2 |
| Petal | 10,659 | 31 | 23 | 8 |
| Philadelphia | 8,046 | 33 | 26 | 7 |
| Picayune | 11,937 | 52 | 34 | 18 |
| Pickens | 1,188 | 2 | 2 | 0 |
| Poplarville | 3,054 | 13 | 12 | 1 |
| Port Gibson | 1,650 | 9 | 5 | 4 |
| Purvis | 2,706 | 10 | 8 | 2 |
| Quitman | 2,305 | 6 | 6 | 0 |
| Raymond | 1,627 | 7 | 6 | 1 |
| Ridgeland | 21,644 | 94 | 68 | 26 |
| Ripley | 5,664 | 12 | 11 | 1 |
| Rolling Fork | 2,043 | 6 | 5 | 1 |
| Roxie | 556 | 1 | 1 | 0 |
| Ruleville | 2,791 | 13 | 9 | 4 |
| Senatobia | 7,442 | 21 | 16 | 5 |
| Shaw | 2,116 | 8 | 4 | 4 |
| Shelby | 2,568 | 9 | 5 | 4 |
| Southaven | 46,093 | 120 | 100 | 20 |
| Starkville | 24,444 | 59 | 49 | 10 |
| Stonewall | 1,067 | 1 | 1 | 0 |
| Summit | 1,627 | 8 | 6 | 2 |
| Sunflower | 1,149 | 3 | 3 | 0 |
| Tylertown | 1,915 | 7 | 6 | 1 |
| Utica | 903 | 3 | 3 | 0 |
| Vaiden | 886 | 4 | 4 | 0 |
| Verona | 3,400 | 8 | 8 | 0 |
| Vicksburg | 24,827 | 95 | 67 | 28 |
| Water Valley | 3,979 | 11 | 11 | 0 |
| Waveland | 5,091 | 27 | 26 | 1 |
| Waynesboro | 5,635 | 17 | 14 | 3 |
| West Point | 11,203 | 29 | 24 | 5 |
| Wiggins | 5,033 | 18 | 15 | 3 |
| Winona | 4,434 | 12 | 10 | 2 |
| Yazoo City | 11,346 | 41 | 31 | 10 |
| **MISSOURI** | | | | |
| Adrian | 1,912 | 3 | 3 | 0 |
| Advance | 1,212 | 3 | 3 | 0 |
| Alton | 635 | 3 | 3 | 0 |
| Anderson | 2,061 | 4 | 4 | 0 |
| Appleton City | 1,257 | 2 | 2 | 0 |
| Arbyrd | 485 | 1 | 1 | 0 |
| Archie | 1,008 | 3 | 3 | 0 |
| Arnold | 20,676 | 62 | 50 | 12 |
| Ash Grove | 1,540 | 3 | 3 | 0 |
| Ashland | 2,185 | 6 | 6 | 0 |
| Aurora | 7,529 | 21 | 15 | 6 |
| Ava | 3,164 | 11 | 7 | 4 |
| Ballwin | 29,897 | 62 | 50 | 12 |
| Bates City | 268 | 1 | 1 | 0 |
| Battlefield | 4,521 | 6 | 5 | 1 |
| Bella Villa | 631 | 5 | 3 | 2 |
| Belle | 1,386 | 4 | 3 | 1 |
| Bellefontaine Neighbors | 10,152 | 31 | 30 | 1 |
| Bellerive | 252 | 9 | 8 | 1 |
| Bellflower | 385 | 1 | 1 | 0 |
| Bel-Nor | 1,469 | 9 | 8 | 1 |
| Bel-Ridge | 2,879 | 19 | 19 | 0 |
| Belton | 24,908 | 62 | 43 | 19 |
| Berkeley | 9,316 | 55 | 42 | 13 |
| Bernie | 1,789 | 9 | 5 | 4 |
| Bethany | 3,066 | 6 | 6 | 0 |
| Beverly Hills | 553 | 5 | 3 | 2 |
| Billings | 1,120 | 4 | 4 | 0 |
| Birch Tree | 623 | 2 | 2 | 0 |
| Birmingham | 223 | 1 | 1 | 0 |
| Bloomfield | 1,861 | 4 | 4 | 0 |
| Blue Springs | 56,567 | 114 | 83 | 31 |
| Bolivar | 11,240 | 25 | 21 | 4 |
| Bonne Terre | 7,307 | 10 | 10 | 0 |
| Boonville | 8,841 | 28 | 21 | 7 |
| Bourbon | 1,533 | 7 | 6 | 1 |
| Bowling Green | 5,300 | 13 | 9 | 4 |
| Branson | 7,734 | 60 | 44 | 16 |
| Branson West | 520 | 6 | 6 | 0 |
| Breckenridge Hills | 4,444 | 15 | 14 | 1 |
| Brentwood | 7,129 | 31 | 25 | 6 |
| Bridgeton | 14,972 | 64 | 52 | 12 |
| Brookfield | 4,275 | 18 | 11 | 7 |
| Brunswick | 846 | 1 | 1 | 0 |
| Bucklin | 469 | 1 | 1 | 0 |
| Buckner | 2,796 | 8 | 7 | 1 |
| Buffalo | 3,348 | 7 | 6 | 1 |
| Butler | 4,314 | 15 | 10 | 5 |
| Butterfield Village | 422 | 2 | 1 | 1 |
| Byrnes Mill | 2,970 | 6 | 6 | 0 |
| Cabool | 2,138 | 10 | 6 | 4 |

## Table 78. Full-time Law Enforcement Employees, by State, by City, 2009—*Continued*

(Number.)

| State/city | Population | Total law enforcement employees | Total officers | Total civilians |
|---|---|---|---|---|
| California | 4,165 | 7 | 6 | 1 |
| Calverton Park | 1,265 | 6 | 6 | 0 |
| Camdenton | 3,569 | 17 | 13 | 4 |
| Cameron | 9,226 | 25 | 17 | 8 |
| Campbell | 1,832 | 7 | 4 | 3 |
| Canton | 2,459 | 5 | 4 | 1 |
| Cape Girardeau | 37,588 | 89 | 72 | 17 |
| Cardwell | 716 | 2 | 2 | 0 |
| Carl Junction | 7,588 | 17 | 12 | 5 |
| Carrollton | 3,830 | 8 | 8 | 0 |
| Carterville | 1,985 | 6 | 6 | 0 |
| Carthage | 14,054 | 37 | 29 | 8 |
| Caruthersville | 6,082 | 23 | 22 | 1 |
| Cassville | 3,337 | 10 | 10 | 0 |
| Center | 641 | 1 | 1 | 0 |
| Centralia | 3,658 | 11 | 6 | 5 |
| Chaffee | 2,940 | 10 | 6 | 4 |
| Charlack | 1,336 | 9 | 9 | 0 |
| Charleston | 5,160 | 19 | 13 | 6 |
| Chesterfield | 45,977 | 99 | 89 | 10 |
| Chillicothe | 8,678 | 24 | 18 | 6 |
| Clarence | 863 | 1 | 1 | 0 |
| Clarkton | 1,228 | 4 | 4 | 0 |
| Claycomo | 1,316 | 15 | 11 | 4 |
| Clayton | 16,105 | 59 | 52 | 7 |
| Cleveland | 689 | 1 | 1 | 0 |
| Clever | 1,720 | 5 | 5 | 0 |
| Clinton | 9,387 | 22 | 21 | 1 |
| Cole Camp | 1,143 | 3 | 3 | 0 |
| Columbia | 102,588 | 180 | 152 | 28 |
| Cool Valley | 996 | 10 | 9 | 1 |
| Cooter | 411 | 2 | 1 | 1 |
| Cottleville | 3,331 | 12 | 12 | 0 |
| Country Club Hills | 1,269 | 12 | 12 | 0 |
| Country Club Village | 2,447 | 2 | 2 | 0 |
| Crane | 1,372 | 2 | 2 | 0 |
| Crestwood | 11,358 | 35 | 28 | 7 |
| Creve Coeur | 16,881 | 61 | 50 | 11 |
| Crocker | 995 | 1 | 1 | 0 |
| Crystal City | 4,568 | 20 | 15 | 5 |
| Cuba | 3,592 | 12 | 11 | 1 |
| Deepwater | 488 | 1 | 1 | 0 |
| Dellwood | 4,864 | 18 | 17 | 1 |
| Desloge | 5,228 | 10 | 10 | 0 |
| De Soto | 6,479 | 19 | 15 | 4 |
| Des Peres | 8,604 | 48 | 40 | 8 |
| Dexter | 7,674 | 23 | 17 | 6 |
| Diamond | 905 | 2 | 2 | 0 |
| Dixon | 1,530 | 8 | 5 | 3 |
| Doniphan | 1,883 | 12 | 8 | 4 |
| Doolittle | 654 | 2 | 2 | 0 |
| Drexel | 1,097 | 2 | 2 | 0 |
| Duenweg | 1,260 | 3 | 3 | 0 |
| Duquesne | 1,758 | 7 | 7 | 0 |
| East Prairie | 3,053 | 9 | 6 | 3 |
| Edmundson | 775 | 10 | 9 | 1 |
| Eldon | 4,996 | 9 | 8 | 1 |
| El Dorado Springs | 3,672 | 11 | 7 | 4 |
| Ellington | 977 | 2 | 2 | 0 |
| Ellisville | 9,224 | 21 | 20 | 1 |
| Elsberry | 2,707 | 5 | 5 | 0 |
| Eminence | 555 | 1 | 1 | 0 |
| Eureka | 9,505 | 28 | 23 | 5 |
| Everton | 303 | 1 | 1 | 0 |
| Excelsior Springs | 12,132 | 34 | 23 | 11 |
| Fair Grove | 1,443 | 4 | 4 | 0 |
| Fair Play | 459 | 1 | 1 | 0 |
| Farmington | 16,351 | 33 | 25 | 8 |
| Fayette | 2,685 | 6 | 6 | 0 |
| Ferguson | 20,814 | 59 | 50 | 9 |
| Ferrelview | 576 | 1 | 1 | 0 |
| Festus | 11,417 | 40 | 28 | 12 |
| Flordell Hills | 854 | 12 | 12 | 0 |
| Florissant | 50,205 | 112 | 88 | 24 |
| Foley | 215 | 1 | 1 | 0 |
| Fordland | 771 | 2 | 2 | 0 |
| Foristell | 330 | 8 | 7 | 1 |
| Forsyth | 1,725 | 8 | 7 | 1 |
| Fredericktown | 4,177 | 8 | 8 | 0 |
| Freeman | 607 | 1 | 1 | 0 |
| Frontenac | 3,842 | 27 | 21 | 6 |
| Fulton | 12,771 | 34 | 28 | 6 |
| Galena | 500 | 1 | 1 | 0 |
| Gallatin | 1,724 | 2 | 2 | 0 |
| Garden City | 1,669 | 4 | 4 | 0 |
| Gerald | 1,254 | 4 | 4 | 0 |
| Gideon | 945 | 3 | 3 | 0 |
| Gladstone | 28,454 | 59 | 42 | 17 |
| Glasgow | 1,193 | 3 | 3 | 0 |
| Glendale | 5,461 | 15 | 12 | 3 |
| Glen Echo Park | 157 | 5 | 3 | 2 |
| Gower | 1,435 | 3 | 3 | 0 |
| Grain Valley | 11,146 | 23 | 20 | 3 |
| Granby | 2,243 | 4 | 4 | 0 |
| Grandview | 23,939 | 67 | 52 | 15 |
| Greendale | 687 | 9 | 8 | 1 |
| Greenfield | 1,220 | 3 | 3 | 0 |
| Greenwood | 4,728 | 12 | 12 | 0 |
| Hallsville | 956 | 2 | 2 | 0 |
| Hamilton | 1,781 | 4 | 4 | 0 |
| Hannibal | 17,396 | 48 | 38 | 10 |
| Harrisonville | 9,837 | 28 | 20 | 8 |
| Hartville | 604 | 2 | 2 | 0 |
| Hayti | 2,933 | 9 | 8 | 1 |
| Hazelwood | 25,254 | 85 | 70 | 15 |
| Herculaneum | 3,675 | 14 | 13 | 1 |
| Hermann | 2,720 | 11 | 7 | 4 |
| Higginsville | 4,558 | 15 | 9 | 6 |
| Highlandville | 915 | 2 | 2 | 0 |
| Hillsboro | 2,111 | 8 | 8 | 0 |
| Hillsdale | 1,401 | 13 | 11 | 2 |
| Holcomb | 668 | 2 | 2 | 0 |
| Holden | 2,546 | 6 | 5 | 1 |
| Hollister | 4,054 | 15 | 11 | 4 |
| Holt | 477 | 2 | 2 | 0 |
| Holts Summit | 3,833 | 13 | 11 | 2 |
| Houston | 2,043 | 6 | 6 | 0 |
| Howardville | 311 | 1 | 1 | 0 |
| Humansville | 1,025 | 2 | 2 | 0 |
| Huntsville | 1,645 | 3 | 3 | 0 |
| Iberia | 682 | 2 | 2 | 0 |
| Independence | 122,174 | 300 | 204 | 96 |
| Indian Point | 722 | 2 | 2 | 0 |
| Iron Mountain Lake | 700 | 1 | 1 | 0 |
| Ironton | 1,310 | 5 | 4 | 1 |
| Jackson | 13,956 | 30 | 22 | 8 |
| Jasper | 1,073 | 1 | 1 | 0 |
| Jefferson City | 40,829 | 119 | 88 | 31 |
| Jennings | 14,536 | 42 | 39 | 3 |
| Jonesburg | 729 | 1 | 1 | 0 |
| Joplin | 50,257 | 129 | 104 | 25 |
| Kansas City | 484,684 | 2,033 | 1,392 | 641 |
| Kearney | 9,018 | 13 | 12 | 1 |
| Kennett | 10,649 | 25 | 20 | 5 |
| Kimberling City | 2,466 | 8 | 7 | 1 |
| King City | 879 | 1 | 1 | 0 |
| Kirksville | 17,376 | 29 | 26 | 3 |
| Kirkwood | 26,698 | 65 | 55 | 10 |
| Knob Noster | 3,349 | 12 | 6 | 6 |
| Ladue | 8,169 | 32 | 26 | 6 |
| La Grange | 918 | 9 | 8 | 1 |
| Lake Lotawana | 1,963 | 7 | 6 | 1 |
| Lake Ozark | 2,093 | 17 | 11 | 6 |
| Lakeshire | 1,276 | 4 | 4 | 0 |
| Lake St. Louis | 14,686 | 39 | 30 | 9 |
| Lake Tapawingo | 780 | 3 | 3 | 0 |
| Lake Waukomis | 897 | 1 | 1 | 0 |
| Lake Winnebago | 1,168 | 5 | 5 | 0 |
| Lamar | 4,478 | 11 | 10 | 1 |
| La Monte | 1,101 | 2 | 2 | 0 |
| Lanagan | 432 | 1 | 1 | 0 |
| La Plata | 1,470 | 3 | 3 | 0 |

## Table 78. Full-time Law Enforcement Employees, by State, by City, 2009—*Continued*

(Number.)

| State/city | Population | Total law enforcement employees | Total officers | Total civilians |
|---|---|---|---|---|
| Laurie | 740 | 6 | 6 | 0 |
| Lawson | 2,340 | 6 | 5 | 1 |
| Leadington | 420 | 6 | 5 | 1 |
| Lebanon | 14,574 | 35 | 28 | 7 |
| Lee's Summit | 85,792 | 186 | 131 | 55 |
| Lexington | 4,528 | 10 | 9 | 1 |
| Liberal | 773 | 2 | 2 | 0 |
| Liberty | 31,073 | 55 | 40 | 15 |
| Licking | 3,023 | 4 | 4 | 0 |
| Lincoln | 1,087 | 3 | 3 | 0 |
| Linn | 1,434 | 3 | 3 | 0 |
| Linn Creek | 312 | 2 | 2 | 0 |
| Lockwood | 910 | 2 | 2 | 0 |
| Lone Jack | 977 | 6 | 6 | 0 |
| Lowry City | 723 | 1 | 1 | 0 |
| Macon | 5,484 | 15 | 13 | 2 |
| Malden | 4,448 | 16 | 11 | 5 |
| Manchester | 18,504 | 43 | 38 | 5 |
| Mansfield | 1,363 | 4 | 4 | 0 |
| Maplewood | 8,563 | 33 | 31 | 2 |
| Marble Hill | 1,479 | 4 | 4 | 0 |
| Marceline | 2,280 | 9 | 6 | 3 |
| Marionville | 2,183 | 5 | 5 | 0 |
| Marquand | 267 | 1 | 1 | 0 |
| Marshall | 12,055 | 36 | 24 | 12 |
| Marshfield | 7,463 | 10 | 10 | 0 |
| Marthasville | 866 | 1 | 1 | 0 |
| Maryland Heights | 25,815 | 98 | 79 | 19 |
| Maryville | 10,815 | 26 | 21 | 5 |
| Matthews | 526 | 2 | 2 | 0 |
| Maysville | 1,131 | 1 | 1 | 0 |
| Memphis | 1,949 | 4 | 4 | 0 |
| Merriam Woods | 1,486 | 2 | 2 | 0 |
| Mexico | 11,050 | 36 | 34 | 2 |
| Milan | 1,754 | 4 | 4 | 0 |
| Miller | 801 | 3 | 2 | 1 |
| Miner | 1,343 | 14 | 9 | 5 |
| Moberly | 14,282 | 46 | 33 | 13 |
| Moline Acres | 2,502 | 13 | 12 | 1 |
| Monett | 9,082 | 28 | 19 | 9 |
| Monroe City | 2,460 | 7 | 7 | 0 |
| Montgomery City | 2,490 | 6 | 6 | 0 |
| Morehouse | 910 | 2 | 2 | 0 |
| Morley | 796 | 1 | 1 | 0 |
| Moscow Mills | 2,553 | 7 | 7 | 0 |
| Mound City | 1,062 | 3 | 3 | 0 |
| Mountain Grove | 4,694 | 16 | 11 | 5 |
| Mountain View | 2,623 | 10 | 9 | 1 |
| Mount Vernon | 4,666 | 11 | 11 | 0 |
| Napoleon | 195 | 1 | 1 | 0 |
| Naylor | 595 | 1 | 1 | 0 |
| Neosho | 11,398 | 28 | 25 | 3 |
| Newburg | 465 | 1 | 1 | 0 |
| New Franklin | 1,108 | 2 | 2 | 0 |
| New Haven | 2,045 | 6 | 6 | 0 |
| New London | 1,010 | 1 | 1 | 0 |
| New Madrid | 2,980 | 7 | 6 | 1 |
| New Melle | 281 | 3 | 3 | 0 |
| Niangua | 499 | 1 | 1 | 0 |
| Nixa | 19,782 | 32 | 22 | 10 |
| Noel | 1,624 | 4 | 4 | 0 |
| Norborne | 748 | 1 | 1 | 0 |
| Normandy | 4,866 | 21 | 20 | 1 |
| North Kansas City | 5,876 | 55 | 39 | 16 |
| Northmoor | 399 | 2 | 2 | 0 |
| Northwoods | 4,276 | 19 | 17 | 2 |
| Oak Grove | 7,010 | 16 | 15 | 1 |
| Oakland | 1,557 | 65 | 55 | 10 |
| Oakview Village | 397 | 4 | 4 | 0 |
| Odessa | 4,725 | 11 | 10 | 1 |
| O'Fallon | 80,528 | 137 | 110 | 27 |
| Old Monroe | 313 | 1 | 1 | 0 |
| Olivette | 7,449 | 24 | 23 | 1 |
| Oran | 1,247 | 1 | 1 | 0 |
| Orrick | 815 | 1 | 1 | 0 |
| Osage Beach | 4,845 | 40 | 26 | 14 |
| Osceola | 780 | 3 | 3 | 0 |
| Overland | 15,507 | 60 | 46 | 14 |
| Owensville | 2,583 | 6 | 6 | 0 |
| Ozark | 19,259 | 37 | 30 | 7 |
| Pacific | 7,345 | 23 | 17 | 6 |
| Pagedale | 3,379 | 15 | 14 | 1 |
| Palmyra | 3,410 | 10 | 6 | 4 |
| Parkville | 5,417 | 15 | 14 | 1 |
| Parma | 731 | 3 | 2 | 1 |
| Peculiar | 4,928 | 10 | 9 | 1 |
| Perry | 663 | 1 | 1 | 0 |
| Perryville | 8,222 | 29 | 26 | 3 |
| Pevely | 6,098 | 20 | 14 | 6 |
| Piedmont | 1,905 | 7 | 7 | 0 |
| Pierce City | 1,473 | 4 | 4 | 0 |
| Pilot Grove | 746 | 1 | 1 | 0 |
| Pilot Knob | 667 | 1 | 1 | 0 |
| Pine Lawn | 3,964 | 25 | 22 | 3 |
| Pineville | 865 | 5 | 5 | 0 |
| Platte City | 4,920 | 11 | 10 | 1 |
| Platte Woods | 455 | 2 | 2 | 0 |
| Plattsburg | 2,424 | 6 | 6 | 0 |
| Pleasant Hill | 7,374 | 18 | 12 | 6 |
| Pleasant Hope | 604 | 1 | 1 | 0 |
| Pleasant Valley | 3,548 | 14 | 9 | 5 |
| Polo | 603 | 1 | 1 | 0 |
| Poplar Bluff | 17,109 | 53 | 42 | 11 |
| Potosi | 2,702 | 12 | 11 | 1 |
| Purdy | 1,164 | 1 | 1 | 0 |
| Puxico | 1,138 | 2 | 2 | 0 |
| Randolph | 51 | 2 | 2 | 0 |
| Raymore | 18,620 | 37 | 23 | 14 |
| Raytown | 27,966 | 72 | 52 | 20 |
| Reeds Spring | 786 | 1 | 1 | 0 |
| Republic | 14,380 | 36 | 23 | 13 |
| Rich Hill | 1,497 | 2 | 2 | 0 |
| Richland | 1,778 | 6 | 5 | 1 |
| Richmond | 5,865 | 17 | 11 | 6 |
| Richmond Heights | 9,040 | 42 | 41 | 1 |
| Riverside | 2,987 | 35 | 28 | 7 |
| Riverview | 2,895 | 12 | 11 | 1 |
| Rockaway Beach | 597 | 2 | 2 | 0 |
| Rock Hill | 4,561 | 9 | 8 | 1 |
| Rock Port | 1,284 | 3 | 3 | 0 |
| Rogersville | 3,278 | 6 | 6 | 0 |
| Rolla | 18,669 | 57 | 35 | 22 |
| Salem | 4,873 | 19 | 14 | 5 |
| Salisbury | 1,541 | 4 | 3 | 1 |
| Sarcoxie | 1,379 | 3 | 3 | 0 |
| Savannah | 5,107 | 6 | 6 | 0 |
| Scott City | 4,533 | 25 | 21 | 4 |
| Sedalia | 21,065 | 57 | 44 | 13 |
| Senath | 1,579 | 3 | 3 | 0 |
| Seneca | 2,282 | 5 | 5 | 0 |
| Seymour | 2,101 | 6 | 6 | 0 |
| Shrewsbury | 6,192 | 20 | 18 | 2 |
| Sikeston | 17,063 | 80 | 68 | 12 |
| Silex | 249 | 1 | 1 | 0 |
| Slater | 1,881 | 7 | 4 | 3 |
| Smithville | 8,416 | 14 | 14 | 0 |
| Southwest City | 930 | 4 | 4 | 0 |
| Sparta | 1,204 | 3 | 3 | 0 |
| Springfield | 156,659 | 370 | 295 | 75 |
| St. Ann | 12,678 | 53 | 39 | 14 |
| St. Charles | 64,807 | 156 | 112 | 44 |
| St. Clair | 4,475 | 16 | 14 | 2 |
| Steele | 2,076 | 7 | 7 | 0 |
| Steelville | 1,500 | 6 | 6 | 0 |
| Ste. Genevieve | 4,407 | 10 | 9 | 1 |
| Stewartsville | 740 | 3 | 3 | 0 |
| St. James | 4,045 | 7 | 6 | 1 |
| St. John | 6,330 | 25 | 23 | 2 |
| St. Joseph | 76,436 | 162 | 116 | 46 |
| St. Louis | 355,208 | 1,923 | 1,408 | 515 |
| St. Marys | 380 | 1 | 1 | 0 |
| Stover | 1,051 | 3 | 3 | 0 |

**Table 78. Full-time Law Enforcement Employees, by State, by City, 2009**—*Continued*

(Number.)

| State/city | Population | Total law enforcement employees | Total officers | Total civilians |
|---|---|---|---|---|
| St. Peters | 55,967 | 107 | 86 | 21 |
| Strafford | 2,218 | 8 | 7 | 1 |
| St. Robert | 3,525 | 27 | 18 | 9 |
| Sturgeon | 912 | 2 | 2 | 0 |
| Sugar Creek | 3,498 | 22 | 17 | 5 |
| Sullivan | 6,769 | 26 | 18 | 8 |
| Summersville | 555 | 2 | 2 | 0 |
| Sunset Hills | 8,181 | 33 | 26 | 7 |
| Tarkio | 1,793 | 3 | 3 | 0 |
| Thayer | 2,145 | 11 | 7 | 4 |
| Tipton | 3,284 | 3 | 3 | 0 |
| Town and Country | 10,692 | 42 | 34 | 8 |
| Tracy | 209 | 1 | 1 | 0 |
| Trenton | 6,030 | 19 | 12 | 7 |
| Troy | 13,093 | 25 | 22 | 3 |
| Truesdale | 701 | 2 | 2 | 0 |
| Union | 9,932 | 23 | 21 | 2 |
| University City | 36,135 | 86 | 69 | 17 |
| Uplands Park | 435 | 9 | 8 | 1 |
| Urbana | 436 | 1 | 1 | 0 |
| Van Buren | 812 | 3 | 3 | 0 |
| Velda City | 1,485 | 6 | 5 | 1 |
| Velda Village Hills | 1,029 | 5 | 3 | 2 |
| Versailles | 2,732 | 10 | 10 | 0 |
| Viburnum | 778 | 1 | 1 | 0 |
| Vienna | 639 | 1 | 1 | 0 |
| Vinita Park | 1,769 | 12 | 11 | 1 |
| Walnut Grove | 671 | 2 | 2 | 0 |
| Wardell | 395 | 1 | 1 | 0 |
| Warrensburg | 19,351 | 37 | 32 | 5 |
| Warrenton | 7,664 | 24 | 20 | 4 |
| Warsaw | 2,236 | 7 | 7 | 0 |
| Warson Woods | 1,853 | 8 | 7 | 1 |
| Washington | 14,516 | 31 | 28 | 3 |
| Waverly | 785 | 1 | 1 | 0 |
| Waynesville | 4,006 | 10 | 9 | 1 |
| Weatherby Lake | 1,862 | 5 | 5 | 0 |
| Webb City | 11,734 | 27 | 21 | 6 |
| Webster Groves | 22,237 | 46 | 44 | 2 |
| Wellsville | 1,314 | 3 | 3 | 0 |
| Wentzville | 27,090 | 75 | 56 | 19 |
| Weston | 1,666 | 4 | 4 | 0 |
| West Plains | 12,175 | 29 | 24 | 5 |
| Wheaton | 752 | 1 | 1 | 0 |
| Willard | 3,350 | 11 | 10 | 1 |
| Willow Springs | 2,158 | 7 | 6 | 1 |
| Winfield | 1,199 | 4 | 4 | 0 |
| Winona | 1,330 | 4 | 4 | 0 |
| Wood Heights | 749 | 6 | 4 | 2 |
| Woodson Terrace | 3,986 | 20 | 17 | 3 |
| Wright City | 3,168 | 9 | 8 | 1 |
| **MONTANA** | | | | |
| Baker | 1,629 | 3 | 3 | 0 |
| Belgrade | 8,485 | 18 | 15 | 3 |
| Billings | 105,427 | 163 | 143 | 20 |
| Boulder | 1,458 | 3 | 3 | 0 |
| Bozeman | 40,910 | 45 | 35 | 10 |
| Bridger | 723 | 2 | 2 | 0 |
| Brockton | 237 | 1 | 1 | 0 |
| Chinook | 1,263 | 4 | 4 | 0 |
| Colstrip | 2,345 | 12 | 6 | 6 |
| Columbia Falls | 5,441 | 14 | 9 | 5 |
| Columbus | 1,982 | 5 | 4 | 1 |
| Conrad | 2,477 | 5 | 5 | 0 |
| Cut Bank | 3,106 | 7 | 7 | 0 |
| Dillon | 4,186 | 9 | 8 | 1 |
| East Helena | 2,173 | 4 | 4 | 0 |
| Ennis | 1,081 | 1 | 1 | 0 |
| Eureka | 1,013 | 2 | 2 | 0 |
| Fort Benton | 1,445 | 9 | 4 | 5 |
| Glasgow | 2,888 | 11 | 9 | 2 |
| Glendive | 4,555 | 14 | 9 | 5 |
| Great Falls | 59,499 | 118 | 79 | 39 |
| Hamilton | 4,951 | 16 | 15 | 1 |
| Havre | 9,572 | 25 | 19 | 6 |
| Helena | 29,718 | 74 | 53 | 21 |
| Hot Springs | 568 | 2 | 2 | 0 |
| Joliet | 631 | 1 | 1 | 0 |
| Kalispell | 21,986 | 41 | 31 | 10 |
| Laurel | 6,645 | 16 | 12 | 4 |
| Lewistown | 5,915 | 20 | 14 | 6 |
| Libby | 2,925 | 5 | 5 | 0 |
| Livingston | 7,550 | 15 | 14 | 1 |
| Manhattan | 1,649 | 3 | 3 | 0 |
| Miles City | 8,062 | 18 | 17 | 1 |
| Missoula | 69,479 | 122 | 101 | 21 |
| Pinesdale | 831 | 3 | 3 | 0 |
| Plains | 1,257 | 3 | 3 | 0 |
| Polson | 5,356 | 12 | 11 | 1 |
| Poplar | 861 | 3 | 3 | 0 |
| Red Lodge | 2,481 | 7 | 7 | 0 |
| Ronan City | 2,030 | 6 | 6 | 0 |
| Sidney | 4,759 | 11 | 10 | 1 |
| Stevensville | 2,036 | 4 | 3 | 1 |
| Thompson Falls | 1,435 | 3 | 3 | 0 |
| Three Forks | 1,951 | 3 | 3 | 0 |
| Troy | 987 | 3 | 3 | 0 |
| West Yellowstone | 1,554 | 11 | 5 | 6 |
| Whitefish | 8,625 | 22 | 17 | 5 |
| Wolf Point | 2,492 | 9 | 8 | 1 |
| **NEBRASKA** | | | | |
| Albion | 1,582 | 3 | 3 | 0 |
| Alliance | 8,024 | 24 | 17 | 7 |
| Auburn | 3,340 | 6 | 6 | 0 |
| Aurora | 4,195 | 9 | 8 | 1 |
| Bayard | 1,104 | 4 | 4 | 0 |
| Beatrice | 12,793 | 32 | 22 | 10 |
| Bellevue | 50,311 | 115 | 98 | 17 |
| Bennington | 1,011 | 2 | 2 | 0 |
| Blair | 7,820 | 19 | 17 | 2 |
| Bridgeport | 1,433 | 3 | 3 | 0 |
| Broken Bow | 3,119 | 7 | 6 | 1 |
| Central City | 2,810 | 6 | 5 | 1 |
| Chadron | 5,409 | 19 | 14 | 5 |
| Columbus | 21,652 | 51 | 36 | 15 |
| Cozad | 4,222 | 7 | 7 | 0 |
| Crete | 6,258 | 17 | 11 | 6 |
| David City | 2,460 | 4 | 3 | 1 |
| Emerson | 819 | 2 | 2 | 0 |
| Fairbury | 3,698 | 7 | 6 | 1 |
| Falls City | 3,952 | 10 | 6 | 4 |
| Fremont | 25,220 | 51 | 41 | 10 |
| Gering | 7,672 | 18 | 15 | 3 |
| Gordon | 1,474 | 4 | 3 | 1 |
| Gothenburg | 3,695 | 7 | 6 | 1 |
| Grand Island | 46,083 | 86 | 75 | 11 |
| Hastings | 25,476 | 50 | 36 | 14 |
| Holdrege | 5,122 | 16 | 10 | 6 |
| Imperial | 1,740 | 4 | 4 | 0 |
| Kearney | 30,759 | 65 | 52 | 13 |
| Kimball | 2,156 | 7 | 6 | 1 |
| La Vista | 17,293 | 37 | 33 | 4 |
| Lexington | 10,138 | 15 | 13 | 2 |
| Lincoln | 254,438 | 414 | 319 | 95 |
| Lyons | 847 | 2 | 2 | 0 |
| Madison | 2,168 | 4 | 4 | 0 |
| McCook | 7,377 | 20 | 16 | 4 |
| Milford | 2,037 | 5 | 5 | 0 |
| Minden | 2,782 | 5 | 5 | 0 |
| Mitchell | 1,780 | 4 | 4 | 0 |
| Nebraska City | 7,011 | 15 | 14 | 1 |
| Neligh | 1,440 | 3 | 3 | 0 |
| Norfolk | 22,892 | 56 | 38 | 18 |
| North Platte | 24,127 | 67 | 42 | 25 |
| Ogallala | 4,361 | 11 | 10 | 1 |
| Omaha | 443,037 | 913 | 769 | 144 |
| O'Neill | 3,267 | 8 | 7 | 1 |
| Ord | 2,003 | 4 | 4 | 0 |
| Papillion | 24,390 | 43 | 39 | 4 |
| Pierce | 1,626 | 3 | 3 | 0 |
| Plainview | 1,185 | 2 | 2 | 0 |
| Plattsmouth | 6,902 | 17 | 15 | 2 |

## Table 78. Full-time Law Enforcement Employees, by State, by City, 2009—*Continued*

(Number.)

| State/city | Population | Total law enforcement employees | Total officers | Total civilians |
|---|---|---|---|---|
| Ralston | 6,077 | 13 | 11 | 2 |
| Schuyler | 5,136 | 8 | 6 | 2 |
| Scottsbluff | 14,773 | 35 | 30 | 5 |
| Scribner | 952 | 1 | 1 | 0 |
| Seward | 6,883 | 11 | 9 | 2 |
| Sidney | 6,514 | 15 | 13 | 2 |
| St. Paul | 2,197 | 4 | 4 | 0 |
| Superior | 1,767 | 4 | 4 | 0 |
| Tecumseh | 1,563 | 4 | 3 | 1 |
| Tekamah | 1,701 | 3 | 3 | 0 |
| Valentine | 2,568 | 6 | 5 | 1 |
| Valley | 1,937 | 3 | 3 | 0 |
| Wahoo | 3,968 | 6 | 6 | 0 |
| Waterloo | 842 | 2 | 2 | 0 |
| Wayne | 5,268 | 15 | 9 | 6 |
| West Point | 3,322 | 8 | 7 | 1 |
| Wilber | 1,725 | 4 | 4 | 0 |
| Wymore | 1,580 | 3 | 3 | 0 |
| York | 7,847 | 20 | 14 | 6 |
| **NEVADA** | | | | |
| Boulder City | 14,686 | 43 | 31 | 12 |
| Carlin | 2,075 | 6 | 5 | 1 |
| Elko | 17,177 | 43 | 38 | 5 |
| Fallon | 8,589 | 36 | 22 | 14 |
| Henderson | 261,883 | 554 | 360 | 194 |
| Las Vegas Metropolitan Police Department | 1,377,282 | 5,264 | 2,735 | 2,529 |
| Lovelock | 1,840 | 7 | 6 | 1 |
| Mesquite | 17,453 | 57 | 32 | 25 |
| North Las Vegas | 232,631 | 473 | 308 | 165 |
| Reno | 221,010 | 462 | 369 | 93 |
| Sparks | 91,421 | 155 | 108 | 47 |
| West Wendover | 5,025 | 22 | 13 | 9 |
| Winnemucca | 8,202 | 21 | 18 | 3 |
| Yerington | 3,960 | 6 | 5 | 1 |
| **NEW HAMPSHIRE** | | | | |
| Alexandria | 1,561 | 2 | 2 | 0 |
| Alstead | 2,115 | 2 | 2 | 0 |
| Alton | 5,148 | 14 | 12 | 2 |
| Amherst | 11,914 | 19 | 18 | 1 |
| Antrim | 2,640 | 5 | 5 | 0 |
| Ashland | 2,102 | 5 | 5 | 0 |
| Auburn | 5,216 | 9 | 7 | 2 |
| Barnstead | 4,678 | 5 | 5 | 0 |
| Barrington | 8,580 | 11 | 10 | 1 |
| Bartlett | 2,934 | 4 | 3 | 1 |
| Bedford | 21,438 | 49 | 35 | 14 |
| Belmont | 7,181 | 15 | 13 | 2 |
| Bennington | 1,470 | 2 | 2 | 0 |
| Berlin | 9,474 | 30 | 22 | 8 |
| Bethlehem | 2,490 | 6 | 5 | 1 |
| Boscawen | 3,984 | 8 | 7 | 1 |
| Bow | 8,186 | 20 | 14 | 6 |
| Bradford | 1,545 | 2 | 2 | 0 |
| Brentwood | 4,057 | 5 | 5 | 0 |
| Bristol | 3,133 | 11 | 9 | 2 |
| Campton | 3,039 | 6 | 5 | 1 |
| Candia | 4,205 | 8 | 7 | 1 |
| Canterbury | 2,334 | 2 | 2 | 0 |
| Carroll | 750 | 4 | 4 | 0 |
| Center Harbor | 1,118 | 3 | 3 | 0 |
| Charlestown | 4,849 | 8 | 5 | 3 |
| Chester | 4,831 | 5 | 4 | 1 |
| Claremont | 12,940 | 27 | 22 | 5 |
| Colebrook | 2,344 | 5 | 5 | 0 |
| Concord | 42,427 | 94 | 75 | 19 |
| Conway | 9,240 | 31 | 22 | 9 |
| Danville | 4,375 | 6 | 5 | 1 |
| Deerfield | 4,261 | 9 | 8 | 1 |
| Deering | 2,066 | 2 | 2 | 0 |
| Derry | 34,189 | 71 | 58 | 13 |
| Dover | 28,794 | 64 | 44 | 20 |
| Dublin | 1,598 | 4 | 3 | 1 |
| Dunbarton | 2,684 | 3 | 3 | 0 |
| Durham | 13,782 | 21 | 19 | 2 |
| Enfield | 4,872 | 8 | 7 | 1 |
| Epping | 6,341 | 14 | 13 | 1 |
| Epsom | 4,643 | 6 | 5 | 1 |
| Exeter | 14,838 | 33 | 23 | 10 |
| Farmington | 6,821 | 16 | 14 | 2 |
| Fitzwilliam | 2,315 | 3 | 3 | 0 |
| Franconia | 1,059 | 3 | 3 | 0 |
| Franklin | 8,748 | 23 | 16 | 7 |
| Freedom | 1,448 | 3 | 3 | 0 |
| Fremont | 4,204 | 4 | 3 | 1 |
| Gilford | 7,526 | 23 | 17 | 6 |
| Gilmanton | 3,565 | 6 | 5 | 1 |
| Goffstown | 17,634 | 42 | 28 | 14 |
| Gorham | 2,787 | 10 | 7 | 3 |
| Grantham | 2,558 | 5 | 4 | 1 |
| Greenland | 3,444 | 7 | 7 | 0 |
| Hampstead | 9,026 | 7 | 7 | 0 |
| Hampton | 15,412 | 43 | 34 | 9 |
| Hancock | 1,807 | 3 | 3 | 0 |
| Hanover | 11,093 | 35 | 21 | 14 |
| Haverhill | 4,694 | 7 | 6 | 1 |
| Henniker | 5,125 | 10 | 8 | 2 |
| Hillsborough | 5,618 | 19 | 12 | 7 |
| Hinsdale | 4,178 | 7 | 6 | 1 |
| Hooksett | 14,027 | 36 | 26 | 10 |
| Hopkinton | 5,616 | 7 | 7 | 0 |
| Hudson | 24,978 | 61 | 46 | 15 |
| Jaffrey | 5,686 | 12 | 11 | 1 |
| Keene | 22,376 | 58 | 43 | 15 |
| Kingston | 6,250 | 10 | 9 | 1 |
| Laconia | 17,127 | 48 | 38 | 10 |
| Lancaster | 3,246 | 8 | 7 | 1 |
| Lebanon | 12,832 | 48 | 35 | 13 |
| Lee | 4,495 | 8 | 7 | 1 |
| Lincoln | 1,358 | 13 | 8 | 5 |
| Lisbon | 1,668 | 4 | 4 | 0 |
| Litchfield | 8,884 | 12 | 10 | 2 |
| Littleton | 6,221 | 12 | 11 | 1 |
| Londonderry | 25,205 | 84 | 69 | 15 |
| Loudon | 5,168 | 7 | 6 | 1 |
| Madison | 2,339 | 4 | 3 | 1 |
| Manchester | 108,671 | 276 | 213 | 63 |
| Marlborough | 2,077 | 3 | 3 | 0 |
| Meredith | 6,700 | 18 | 14 | 4 |
| Merrimack | 26,594 | 54 | 40 | 14 |
| Middleton | 1,872 | 4 | 4 | 0 |
| Milford | 15,133 | 30 | 25 | 5 |
| Milton | 4,655 | 8 | 7 | 1 |
| Mont Vernon | 2,404 | 3 | 3 | 0 |
| Moultonborough | 5,041 | 15 | 12 | 3 |
| Nashua | 86,554 | 227 | 170 | 57 |
| New Boston | 5,186 | 7 | 6 | 1 |
| Newbury | 2,134 | 4 | 4 | 0 |
| New Durham | 2,590 | 6 | 5 | 1 |
| Newfields | 1,635 | 4 | 4 | 0 |
| New Hampton | 2,280 | 6 | 6 | 0 |
| Newington | 805 | 11 | 10 | 1 |
| New Ipswich | 5,430 | 7 | 6 | 1 |
| New London | 4,509 | 13 | 8 | 5 |
| Newmarket | 9,602 | 20 | 13 | 7 |
| Newport | 6,550 | 19 | 14 | 5 |
| Newton | 4,594 | 8 | 5 | 3 |
| Northfield | 5,187 | 11 | 10 | 1 |
| North Hampton | 4,536 | 13 | 12 | 1 |
| Northumberland | 2,302 | 4 | 4 | 0 |
| Northwood | 4,192 | 8 | 7 | 1 |
| Nottingham | 4,628 | 7 | 6 | 1 |
| Ossipee | 4,733 | 10 | 9 | 1 |
| Pelham | 12,770 | 26 | 19 | 7 |
| Pembroke | 7,379 | 14 | 12 | 2 |
| Peterborough | 6,218 | 13 | 11 | 2 |
| Pittsfield | 4,409 | 9 | 8 | 1 |
| Plaistow | 7,607 | 25 | 17 | 8 |
| Plymouth | 6,444 | 16 | 10 | 6 |
| Portsmouth | 20,401 | 82 | 62 | 20 |
| Raymond | 10,296 | 26 | 17 | 9 |
| Rindge | 6,669 | 9 | 8 | 1 |
| Rochester | 30,889 | 75 | 56 | 19 |

## Table 78. Full-time Law Enforcement Employees, by State, by City, 2009—*Continued*

(Number.)

| State/city | Population | Total law enforcement employees | Total officers | Total civilians |
|---|---|---|---|---|
| Rollinsford | 2,642 | 4 | 4 | 0 |
| Rye | 5,140 | 10 | 9 | 1 |
| Sandown | 5,948 | 7 | 7 | 0 |
| Sandwich | 1,319 | 2 | 2 | 0 |
| Seabrook | 8,551 | 34 | 27 | 7 |
| Somersworth | 12,020 | 31 | 24 | 7 |
| South Hampton | 879 | 1 | 1 | 0 |
| Strafford | 4,115 | 4 | 4 | 0 |
| Stratham | 7,394 | 11 | 10 | 1 |
| Sugar Hill | 618 | 2 | 2 | 0 |
| Sunapee | 3,396 | 5 | 5 | 0 |
| Thornton | 2,166 | 4 | 3 | 1 |
| Tilton | 3,604 | 19 | 17 | 2 |
| Troy | 2,073 | 4 | 4 | 0 |
| Wakefield | 5,485 | 10 | 9 | 1 |
| Walpole | 3,684 | 4 | 3 | 1 |
| Warner | 2,967 | 4 | 3 | 1 |
| Washington | 1,097 | 1 | 1 | 0 |
| Waterville Valley | 271 | 7 | 6 | 1 |
| Weare | 9,242 | 12 | 11 | 1 |
| Webster | 1,902 | 1 | 1 | 0 |
| Wilton | 3,940 | 7 | 6 | 1 |
| Winchester | 4,301 | 8 | 7 | 1 |
| Windham | 13,528 | 24 | 17 | 7 |
| Wolfeboro | 6,578 | 17 | 12 | 5 |
| Woodstock | 1,168 | 5 | 5 | 0 |
| **NEW JERSEY** | | | | |
| Aberdeen Township | 18,493 | 42 | 35 | 7 |
| Absecon | 8,478 | 30 | 24 | 6 |
| Allendale | 6,587 | 19 | 14 | 5 |
| Allenhurst | 697 | 13 | 9 | 4 |
| Allentown | 1,840 | 5 | 4 | 1 |
| Alpine | 2,514 | 13 | 13 | 0 |
| Andover Township | 6,585 | 18 | 12 | 6 |
| Asbury Park | 16,499 | 101 | 89 | 12 |
| Atlantic City | 39,295 | 529 | 375 | 154 |
| Atlantic Highlands | 4,589 | 20 | 15 | 5 |
| Audubon | 8,852 | 22 | 20 | 2 |
| Avalon | 2,087 | 29 | 21 | 8 |
| Avon-by-the-Sea | 2,196 | 11 | 11 | 0 |
| Barnegat Township | 23,196 | 56 | 46 | 10 |
| Barrington | 6,924 | 15 | 14 | 1 |
| Bay Head | 1,268 | 9 | 8 | 1 |
| Bayonne | 56,982 | 239 | 203 | 36 |
| Beach Haven | 1,404 | 13 | 11 | 2 |
| Beachwood | 10,886 | 20 | 18 | 2 |
| Bedminster Township | 8,356 | 18 | 16 | 2 |
| Belleville | 33,610 | 110 | 101 | 9 |
| Bellmawr | 11,168 | 25 | 23 | 2 |
| Belmar | 5,891 | 26 | 20 | 6 |
| Belvidere | 2,622 | 7 | 6 | 1 |
| Bergenfield | 25,542 | 52 | 44 | 8 |
| Berkeley Heights Township | 13,335 | 34 | 26 | 8 |
| Berkeley Township | 43,044 | 95 | 73 | 22 |
| Berlin | 8,142 | 21 | 20 | 1 |
| Berlin Township | 5,429 | 20 | 19 | 1 |
| Bernards Township | 26,681 | 54 | 39 | 15 |
| Bernardsville | 7,799 | 24 | 18 | 6 |
| Beverly | 2,553 | 7 | 7 | 0 |
| Blairstown Township | 5,961 | 8 | 6 | 2 |
| Bloomfield | 43,489 | 138 | 126 | 12 |
| Bloomingdale | 7,436 | 19 | 18 | 1 |
| Bogota | 7,881 | 20 | 15 | 5 |
| Boonton | 8,467 | 24 | 19 | 5 |
| Boonton Township | 4,509 | 13 | 13 | 0 |
| Bordentown | 3,801 | 14 | 12 | 2 |
| Bordentown Township | 10,301 | 29 | 24 | 5 |
| Bound Brook | 10,398 | 27 | 22 | 5 |
| Bradley Beach | 4,849 | 20 | 16 | 4 |
| Branchburg Township | 15,087 | 28 | 26 | 2 |
| Brick Township | 78,666 | 171 | 127 | 44 |
| Bridgeton | 24,980 | 76 | 64 | 12 |
| Bridgewater Township | 44,519 | 94 | 77 | 17 |
| Brielle | 4,879 | 13 | 13 | 0 |
| Brigantine | 12,654 | 46 | 35 | 11 |
| Brooklawn | 2,253 | 7 | 7 | 0 |
| Buena | 3,693 | 16 | 10 | 6 |
| Burlington | 9,360 | 41 | 36 | 5 |
| Burlington Township | 21,413 | 53 | 43 | 10 |
| Butler | 8,188 | 18 | 17 | 1 |
| Byram Township | 8,479 | 17 | 16 | 1 |
| Caldwell | 7,085 | 21 | 20 | 1 |
| Camden | 78,980 | 447 | 361 | 86 |
| Cape May | 3,650 | 30 | 24 | 6 |
| Carlstadt | 6,030 | 31 | 28 | 3 |
| Carney's Point Township | 8,002 | 27 | 22 | 5 |
| Carteret | 23,669 | 73 | 62 | 11 |
| Cedar Grove Township | 12,685 | 34 | 32 | 2 |
| Chatham | 8,187 | 26 | 20 | 6 |
| Chatham Township | 10,167 | 26 | 22 | 4 |
| Cherry Hill Township | 70,953 | 170 | 139 | 31 |
| Chesilhurst | 1,959 | 11 | 10 | 1 |
| Chester | 1,682 | 10 | 9 | 1 |
| Chesterfield Township | 7,609 | 11 | 10 | 1 |
| Chester Township | 7,812 | 16 | 15 | 1 |
| Cinnaminson Township | 15,448 | 33 | 31 | 2 |
| Clark Township | 14,330 | 52 | 41 | 11 |
| Clayton | 7,601 | 21 | 19 | 2 |
| Clementon | 4,876 | 15 | 13 | 2 |
| Cliffside Park | 22,848 | 51 | 42 | 9 |
| Clifton | 78,124 | 173 | 144 | 29 |
| Clinton | 2,534 | 10 | 10 | 0 |
| Clinton Township | 13,913 | 29 | 26 | 3 |
| Closter | 8,689 | 25 | 20 | 5 |
| Collingswood | 13,764 | 38 | 33 | 5 |
| Colts Neck Township | 10,119 | 23 | 22 | 1 |
| Cranbury Township | 4,013 | 19 | 18 | 1 |
| Cranford Township | 21,820 | 67 | 51 | 16 |
| Cresskill | 8,716 | 26 | 21 | 5 |
| Deal | 1,042 | 20 | 16 | 4 |
| Delanco Township | 4,848 | 9 | 8 | 1 |
| Delaware Township | 4,691 | 8 | 7 | 1 |
| Delran Township | 16,936 | 36 | 31 | 5 |
| Demarest | 5,162 | 15 | 15 | 0 |
| Denville Township | 16,558 | 44 | 35 | 9 |
| Deptford Township | 31,090 | 71 | 66 | 5 |
| Dover | 17,827 | 38 | 34 | 4 |
| Dumont | 16,910 | 43 | 36 | 7 |
| Dunellen | 7,011 | 22 | 18 | 4 |
| Eastampton Township | 6,578 | 17 | 16 | 1 |
| East Brunswick Township | 47,323 | 114 | 87 | 27 |
| East Greenwich Township | 8,105 | 21 | 19 | 2 |
| East Hanover Township | 11,395 | 42 | 34 | 8 |
| East Newark | 2,113 | 10 | 7 | 3 |
| East Orange | 64,924 | 339 | 277 | 62 |
| East Rutherford | 10,248 | 45 | 41 | 4 |
| East Windsor Township | 26,965 | 61 | 47 | 14 |
| Eatontown | 14,212 | 47 | 37 | 10 |
| Edgewater | 9,846 | 33 | 32 | 1 |
| Edgewater Park Township | 7,674 | 13 | 12 | 1 |
| Edison Township | 99,356 | 238 | 191 | 47 |
| Egg Harbor City | 4,362 | 15 | 14 | 1 |
| Egg Harbor Township | 41,005 | 126 | 91 | 35 |
| Elizabeth | 124,910 | 545 | 335 | 210 |
| Elk Township | 4,001 | 13 | 12 | 1 |
| Elmer | 1,341 | 2 | 2 | 0 |
| Elmwood Park | 18,602 | 43 | 41 | 2 |
| Emerson | 7,370 | 21 | 18 | 3 |
| Englewood | 29,463 | 111 | 83 | 28 |
| Englewood Cliffs | 5,858 | 25 | 24 | 1 |
| Englishtown | 1,934 | 8 | 8 | 0 |
| Essex Fells | 2,102 | 13 | 13 | 0 |
| Evesham Township | 45,633 | 84 | 76 | 8 |
| Ewing Township | 36,098 | 98 | 81 | 17 |
| Fairfield Township, Essex County | 7,529 | 46 | 40 | 6 |
| Fair Haven | 5,905 | 13 | 13 | 0 |
| Fair Lawn | 30,400 | 77 | 64 | 13 |
| Fairview | 13,571 | 37 | 33 | 4 |
| Fanwood | 7,078 | 19 | 18 | 1 |
| Far Hills | 903 | 7 | 6 | 1 |
| Flemington | 4,285 | 16 | 15 | 1 |
| Florence Township | 11,458 | 32 | 26 | 6 |

**Table 78. Full-time Law Enforcement Employees, by State, by City, 2009**—*Continued*

(Number.)

| State/city | Population | Total law enforcement employees | Total officers | Total civilians |
|---|---|---|---|---|
| Florham Park | 12,605 | 39 | 33 | 6 |
| Fort Lee | 36,342 | 128 | 108 | 20 |
| Franklin | 5,068 | 14 | 14 | 0 |
| Franklin Lakes | 11,757 | 27 | 22 | 5 |
| Franklin Township, Gloucester County | 17,499 | 32 | 29 | 3 |
| Franklin Township, Hunterdon County | 3,254 | 6 | 6 | 0 |
| Franklin Township, Somerset County | 60,364 | 139 | 120 | 19 |
| Freehold | 11,474 | 39 | 31 | 8 |
| Freehold Township | 35,099 | 76 | 70 | 6 |
| Frenchtown | 1,450 | 4 | 3 | 1 |
| Galloway Township | 37,051 | 83 | 69 | 14 |
| Garfield | 28,882 | 71 | 63 | 8 |
| Garwood | 4,438 | 19 | 16 | 3 |
| Gibbsboro | 2,434 | 5 | 5 | 0 |
| Glassboro | 19,829 | 49 | 43 | 6 |
| Glen Ridge | 6,599 | 35 | 28 | 7 |
| Glen Rock | 11,086 | 23 | 21 | 2 |
| Gloucester City | 11,508 | 33 | 30 | 3 |
| Gloucester Township | 64,909 | 132 | 110 | 22 |
| Green Brook Township | 7,034 | 28 | 23 | 5 |
| Greenwich Township, Gloucester County | 4,997 | 20 | 18 | 2 |
| Greenwich Township, Warren County | 5,195 | 12 | 11 | 1 |
| Guttenberg | 10,493 | 27 | 22 | 5 |
| Hackensack | 42,801 | 125 | 103 | 22 |
| Hackettstown | 9,565 | 18 | 17 | 1 |
| Haddonfield | 11,420 | 24 | 22 | 2 |
| Haddon Heights | 7,596 | 16 | 15 | 1 |
| Haddon Township | 14,293 | 28 | 26 | 2 |
| Haledon | 8,546 | 18 | 16 | 2 |
| Hamburg | 3,504 | 8 | 7 | 1 |
| Hamilton Township, Atlantic County | 24,863 | 89 | 68 | 21 |
| Hamilton Township, Mercer County | 90,491 | 209 | 176 | 33 |
| Hammonton | 13,517 | 39 | 32 | 7 |
| Hanover Township | 13,736 | 39 | 32 | 7 |
| Harding Township | 3,332 | 13 | 12 | 1 |
| Hardyston Township | 8,559 | 25 | 19 | 6 |
| Harrington Park | 4,883 | 11 | 11 | 0 |
| Harrison | 15,296 | 61 | 47 | 14 |
| Harrison Township | 12,916 | 18 | 18 | 0 |
| Harvey Cedars | 397 | 9 | 9 | 0 |
| Hasbrouck Heights | 11,383 | 31 | 29 | 2 |
| Haworth | 3,416 | 13 | 12 | 1 |
| Hawthorne | 17,972 | 38 | 33 | 5 |
| Hazlet Township | 20,893 | 48 | 43 | 5 |
| Helmetta | 2,031 | 5 | 5 | 0 |
| High Bridge | 3,662 | 7 | 7 | 0 |
| Highland Park | 14,271 | 34 | 27 | 7 |
| Highlands | 5,292 | 18 | 14 | 4 |
| Hightstown | 5,303 | 19 | 14 | 5 |
| Hillsborough Township | 39,265 | 69 | 55 | 14 |
| Hillsdale | 9,822 | 21 | 20 | 1 |
| Hillside Township | 21,108 | 89 | 74 | 15 |
| Hi-Nella | 995 | 6 | 6 | 0 |
| Hoboken | 40,792 | 168 | 155 | 13 |
| Ho-Ho-Kus | 3,995 | 19 | 16 | 3 |
| Holland Township | 5,226 | 7 | 6 | 1 |
| Holmdel Township | 17,009 | 54 | 44 | 10 |
| Hopatcong | 15,447 | 36 | 26 | 10 |
| Hopewell Township | 17,941 | 38 | 30 | 8 |
| Howell Township | 51,596 | 112 | 95 | 17 |
| Independence Township | 5,705 | 9 | 8 | 1 |
| Interlaken | 874 | 6 | 6 | 0 |
| Irvington | 55,838 | 217 | 187 | 30 |
| Island Heights | 1,884 | 5 | 5 | 0 |
| Jackson Township | 53,734 | 105 | 84 | 21 |
| Jamesburg | 6,401 | 17 | 13 | 4 |
| Jefferson Township | 21,903 | 45 | 38 | 7 |
| Jersey City | 240,858 | 1,059 | 885 | 174 |
| Keansburg | 10,527 | 42 | 34 | 8 |
| Kearny | 36,352 | 126 | 119 | 7 |
| Kenilworth | 7,612 | 31 | 30 | 1 |
| Keyport | 7,464 | 25 | 19 | 6 |
| Kinnelon | 9,606 | 16 | 15 | 1 |
| Lacey Township | 26,491 | 59 | 45 | 14 |
| Lake Como | 1,769 | 11 | 11 | 0 |
| Lakehurst | 2,714 | 12 | 10 | 2 |
| Lakewood Township | 72,206 | 162 | 134 | 28 |
| Lambertville | 3,727 | 13 | 11 | 2 |
| Laurel Springs | 1,896 | 7 | 7 | 0 |
| Lavallette | 2,764 | 17 | 12 | 5 |
| Lawnside | 2,858 | 8 | 6 | 2 |
| Lawrence Township, Mercer County | 31,913 | 81 | 69 | 12 |
| Lebanon Township | 6,208 | 10 | 9 | 1 |
| Leonia | 8,563 | 25 | 19 | 6 |
| Lincoln Park | 10,604 | 30 | 24 | 6 |
| Linden | 39,131 | 162 | 132 | 30 |
| Lindenwold | 17,496 | 45 | 42 | 3 |
| Linwood | 7,220 | 23 | 20 | 3 |
| Little Egg Harbor Township | 21,291 | 65 | 47 | 18 |
| Little Falls Township | 11,625 | 31 | 25 | 6 |
| Little Ferry | 10,442 | 30 | 27 | 3 |
| Little Silver | 6,111 | 21 | 16 | 5 |
| Livingston Township | 27,722 | 87 | 74 | 13 |
| Lodi | 23,754 | 50 | 41 | 9 |
| Logan Township | 6,270 | 21 | 20 | 1 |
| Long Beach Township | 3,571 | 51 | 40 | 11 |
| Long Branch | 32,758 | 119 | 100 | 19 |
| Long Hill Township | 8,593 | 28 | 25 | 3 |
| Longport | 1,092 | 19 | 14 | 5 |
| Lopatcong Township | 8,748 | 14 | 13 | 1 |
| Lower Alloways Creek Township | 1,888 | 19 | 14 | 5 |
| Lower Township | 20,060 | 58 | 43 | 15 |
| Lumberton Township | 12,174 | 27 | 24 | 3 |
| Lyndhurst Township | 19,286 | 60 | 53 | 7 |
| Madison | 16,073 | 39 | 33 | 6 |
| Magnolia | 4,321 | 11 | 11 | 0 |
| Mahwah Township | 24,180 | 59 | 50 | 9 |
| Manalapan Township | 39,615 | 79 | 64 | 15 |
| Manasquan | 6,243 | 24 | 18 | 6 |
| Manchester Township | 41,921 | 83 | 66 | 17 |
| Mansfield Township, Burlington County | 8,373 | 18 | 15 | 3 |
| Mansfield Township, Warren County | 8,123 | 16 | 15 | 1 |
| Mantoloking | 455 | 9 | 8 | 1 |
| Mantua Township | 15,285 | 29 | 27 | 2 |
| Manville | 10,863 | 28 | 22 | 6 |
| Maple Shade Township | 19,165 | 44 | 36 | 8 |
| Maplewood Township | 21,795 | 72 | 60 | 12 |
| Margate City | 8,536 | 44 | 33 | 11 |
| Marlboro Township | 41,009 | 91 | 72 | 19 |
| Matawan | 8,735 | 25 | 23 | 2 |
| Maywood | 9,104 | 27 | 23 | 4 |
| Medford Lakes | 4,097 | 8 | 7 | 1 |
| Medford Township | 22,872 | 64 | 49 | 15 |
| Mendham | 5,048 | 12 | 11 | 1 |
| Mendham Township | 5,513 | 17 | 14 | 3 |
| Merchantville | 3,760 | 16 | 14 | 2 |
| Metuchen | 13,121 | 33 | 28 | 5 |
| Middlesex | 13,634 | 32 | 30 | 2 |
| Middle Township | 16,263 | 61 | 48 | 13 |
| Middletown Township | 66,565 | 135 | 107 | 28 |
| Midland Park | 6,743 | 15 | 14 | 1 |
| Millburn Township | 18,418 | 61 | 51 | 10 |
| Milltown | 6,959 | 19 | 16 | 3 |
| Millville | 29,175 | 94 | 81 | 13 |
| Monmouth Beach | 3,566 | 9 | 9 | 0 |
| Monroe Township, Gloucester County | 33,420 | 74 | 67 | 7 |
| Monroe Township, Middlesex County | 38,264 | 68 | 49 | 19 |
| Montclair | 36,788 | 129 | 108 | 21 |
| Montgomery Township | 23,524 | 35 | 30 | 5 |
| Montvale | 7,625 | 23 | 22 | 1 |
| Montville Township | 21,078 | 47 | 41 | 6 |
| Moonachie | 2,722 | 20 | 17 | 3 |
| Moorestown Township | 19,559 | 42 | 36 | 6 |
| Morris Plains | 6,050 | 20 | 16 | 4 |
| Morristown | 19,351 | 64 | 57 | 7 |
| Morris Township | 21,214 | 55 | 43 | 12 |
| Mountain Lakes | 4,276 | 13 | 13 | 0 |
| Mountainside | 6,545 | 27 | 22 | 5 |
| Mount Arlington | 5,968 | 15 | 14 | 1 |
| Mount Ephraim | 4,381 | 15 | 14 | 1 |
| Mount Holly Township | 10,195 | 24 | 22 | 2 |
| Mount Laurel Township | 39,071 | 78 | 63 | 15 |

## Table 78. Full-time Law Enforcement Employees, by State, by City, 2009—*Continued*

(Number.)

| State/city | Population | Total law enforcement employees | Total officers | Total civilians |
|---|---|---|---|---|
| Mount Olive Township | 25,989 | 64 | 55 | 9 |
| Mullica Township | 6,032 | 15 | 14 | 1 |
| Neptune City | 5,100 | 20 | 16 | 4 |
| Neptune Township | 28,484 | 94 | 75 | 19 |
| Netcong | 3,221 | 11 | 9 | 2 |
| Newark | 279,203 | 1,671 | 1,297 | 374 |
| New Brunswick | 51,474 | 168 | 139 | 29 |
| Newfield | 1,675 | 6 | 6 | 0 |
| New Hanover Township | 9,442 | 3 | 3 | 0 |
| New Milford | 15,898 | 34 | 32 | 2 |
| New Providence | 11,904 | 30 | 24 | 6 |
| Newton | 8,079 | 34 | 25 | 9 |
| North Arlington | 14,648 | 38 | 30 | 8 |
| North Bergen Township | 54,948 | 136 | 117 | 19 |
| North Brunswick Township | 39,904 | 99 | 78 | 21 |
| North Caldwell | 7,016 | 20 | 16 | 4 |
| Northfield | 7,903 | 24 | 23 | 1 |
| North Haledon | 9,021 | 23 | 18 | 5 |
| North Hanover Township | 7,335 | 10 | 9 | 1 |
| North Plainfield | 21,077 | 54 | 47 | 7 |
| Northvale | 4,748 | 15 | 15 | 0 |
| North Wildwood | 4,786 | 38 | 28 | 10 |
| Norwood | 6,256 | 15 | 14 | 1 |
| Nutley Township | 26,033 | 77 | 66 | 11 |
| Oakland | 13,400 | 30 | 25 | 5 |
| Oaklyn | 4,014 | 13 | 12 | 1 |
| Ocean City | 14,686 | 74 | 59 | 15 |
| Ocean Gate | 2,143 | 7 | 6 | 1 |
| Oceanport | 5,723 | 19 | 15 | 4 |
| Ocean Township, Monmouth County | 28,360 | 76 | 63 | 13 |
| Ocean Township, Ocean County | 9,329 | 25 | 20 | 5 |
| Ogdensburg | 2,535 | 6 | 6 | 0 |
| Old Bridge Township | 66,460 | 139 | 104 | 35 |
| Old Tappan | 6,091 | 14 | 13 | 1 |
| Oradell | 7,751 | 22 | 21 | 1 |
| Orange | 30,873 | 125 | 107 | 18 |
| Oxford Township | 2,603 | 4 | 3 | 1 |
| Palisades Park | 19,639 | 39 | 30 | 9 |
| Palmyra | 7,374 | 18 | 16 | 2 |
| Paramus | 26,168 | 118 | 92 | 26 |
| Park Ridge | 8,940 | 18 | 17 | 1 |
| Parsippany-Troy Hills Township | 50,095 | 133 | 107 | 26 |
| Passaic | 66,773 | 224 | 189 | 35 |
| Paterson | 144,943 | 579 | 488 | 91 |
| Paulsboro | 6,066 | 19 | 18 | 1 |
| Peapack and Gladstone | 2,572 | 8 | 7 | 1 |
| Pemberton | 1,583 | 6 | 6 | 0 |
| Pemberton Township | 27,914 | 61 | 56 | 5 |
| Pennington | 2,651 | 6 | 6 | 0 |
| Pennsauken Township | 34,905 | 113 | 89 | 24 |
| Penns Grove | 4,668 | 19 | 14 | 5 |
| Pennsville Township | 13,365 | 25 | 23 | 2 |
| Pequannock Township | 17,003 | 36 | 31 | 5 |
| Perth Amboy | 48,897 | 141 | 115 | 26 |
| Phillipsburg | 14,459 | 38 | 37 | 1 |
| Pine Beach | 2,093 | 6 | 5 | 1 |
| Pine Hill | 11,358 | 23 | 21 | 2 |
| Pine Valley | 25 | 4 | 4 | 0 |
| Piscataway Township | 52,605 | 105 | 87 | 18 |
| Pitman | 9,193 | 16 | 15 | 1 |
| Plainfield | 45,939 | 180 | 148 | 32 |
| Plainsboro Township | 21,243 | 46 | 34 | 12 |
| Pleasantville | 18,838 | 67 | 53 | 14 |
| Plumsted Township | 8,318 | 12 | 11 | 1 |
| Pohatcong Township | 3,321 | 15 | 14 | 1 |
| Point Pleasant | 20,232 | 41 | 33 | 8 |
| Point Pleasant Beach | 5,430 | 30 | 24 | 6 |
| Pompton Lakes | 11,075 | 28 | 24 | 4 |
| Princeton | 13,373 | 37 | 27 | 10 |
| Princeton Township | 17,517 | 40 | 31 | 9 |
| Prospect Park | 5,574 | 15 | 15 | 0 |
| Rahway | 28,869 | 87 | 76 | 11 |
| Ramsey | 14,620 | 35 | 29 | 6 |
| Randolph Township | 25,226 | 47 | 38 | 9 |
| Raritan | 7,413 | 23 | 18 | 5 |
| Raritan Township | 22,637 | 35 | 32 | 3 |
| Readington Township | 16,053 | 25 | 23 | 2 |
| Red Bank | 11,866 | 48 | 42 | 6 |
| Ridgefield | 10,852 | 29 | 27 | 2 |
| Ridgefield Park | 12,316 | 39 | 30 | 9 |
| Ridgewood | 24,080 | 48 | 43 | 5 |
| Ringwood | 12,711 | 26 | 21 | 5 |
| Riverdale | 2,902 | 22 | 18 | 4 |
| River Edge | 10,644 | 25 | 22 | 3 |
| Riverside Township | 7,671 | 16 | 16 | 0 |
| Riverton | 2,613 | 5 | 4 | 1 |
| River Vale Township | 9,634 | 24 | 21 | 3 |
| Robbinsville Township | 12,314 | 34 | 26 | 8 |
| Rochelle Park Township | 6,144 | 24 | 20 | 4 |
| Rockaway | 6,241 | 16 | 15 | 1 |
| Rockaway Township | 25,828 | 68 | 57 | 11 |
| Roseland | 5,358 | 27 | 27 | 0 |
| Roselle | 20,523 | 68 | 56 | 12 |
| Roselle Park | 12,750 | 41 | 34 | 7 |
| Roxbury Township | 23,311 | 60 | 48 | 12 |
| Rumson | 7,276 | 22 | 21 | 1 |
| Runnemede | 8,398 | 20 | 19 | 1 |
| Rutherford | 17,384 | 43 | 40 | 3 |
| Saddle Brook Township | 14,019 | 35 | 32 | 3 |
| Saddle River | 3,858 | 23 | 18 | 5 |
| Salem | 5,641 | 26 | 23 | 3 |
| Sayreville | 42,401 | 104 | 88 | 16 |
| Scotch Plains Township | 22,907 | 52 | 46 | 6 |
| Sea Bright | 1,802 | 11 | 10 | 1 |
| Sea Girt | 2,061 | 14 | 12 | 2 |
| Sea Isle City | 2,915 | 36 | 24 | 12 |
| Seaside Heights | 3,364 | 33 | 25 | 8 |
| Seaside Park | 2,317 | 19 | 15 | 4 |
| Secaucus | 15,312 | 64 | 57 | 7 |
| Ship Bottom | 1,456 | 12 | 11 | 1 |
| Shrewsbury | 3,798 | 21 | 16 | 5 |
| Somerdale | 5,074 | 14 | 13 | 1 |
| Somers Point | 11,316 | 32 | 27 | 5 |
| Somerville | 12,672 | 39 | 32 | 7 |
| South Amboy | 7,761 | 31 | 25 | 6 |
| South Bound Brook | 5,191 | 13 | 12 | 1 |
| South Brunswick Township | 41,448 | 101 | 78 | 23 |
| South Hackensack Township | 2,262 | 19 | 17 | 2 |
| South Harrison Township | 3,223 | 6 | 6 | 0 |
| South Orange | 15,767 | 56 | 51 | 5 |
| South Plainfield | 22,710 | 71 | 56 | 15 |
| South River | 15,715 | 40 | 32 | 8 |
| South Toms River | 3,718 | 13 | 12 | 1 |
| Sparta Township | 19,336 | 49 | 37 | 12 |
| Spotswood | 8,173 | 23 | 19 | 4 |
| Springfield | 14,873 | 47 | 41 | 6 |
| Springfield Township | 3,492 | 9 | 8 | 1 |
| Spring Lake | 3,514 | 18 | 14 | 4 |
| Spring Lake Heights | 5,122 | 13 | 13 | 0 |
| Stafford Township | 26,985 | 84 | 58 | 26 |
| Stanhope | 3,559 | 10 | 9 | 1 |
| Stillwater Township | 4,294 | 3 | 3 | 0 |
| Stone Harbor | 1,000 | 23 | 17 | 6 |
| Stratford | 7,026 | 16 | 15 | 1 |
| Summit | 20,494 | 57 | 48 | 9 |
| Surf City | 1,571 | 10 | 10 | 0 |
| Teaneck Township | 37,985 | 110 | 95 | 15 |
| Tenafly | 14,759 | 44 | 37 | 7 |
| Tewksbury Township | 6,088 | 12 | 11 | 1 |
| Tinton Falls | 20,069 | 42 | 41 | 1 |
| Toms River Township | 96,614 | 207 | 159 | 48 |
| Totowa | 10,705 | 30 | 27 | 3 |
| Trenton | 82,609 | 466 | 372 | 94 |
| Tuckerton | 3,918 | 10 | 10 | 0 |
| Union Beach | 6,615 | 18 | 14 | 4 |
| Union City | 61,665 | 208 | 162 | 46 |
| Union Township | 53,579 | 181 | 130 | 51 |
| Upper Saddle River | 8,537 | 24 | 18 | 6 |
| Ventnor City | 12,111 | 50 | 39 | 11 |
| Vernon Township | 24,870 | 41 | 32 | 9 |
| Verona | 12,384 | 33 | 29 | 4 |
| Vineland | 59,121 | 187 | 157 | 30 |

**Table 78. Full-time Law Enforcement Employees, by State, by City, 2009**—*Continued*

(Number.)

| State/city | Population | Total law enforcement employees | Total officers | Total civilians |
|---|---|---|---|---|
| Voorhees Township | 31,686 | 65 | 52 | 13 |
| Waldwick | 9,511 | 24 | 19 | 5 |
| Wallington | 11,265 | 22 | 21 | 1 |
| Wall Township | 26,265 | 84 | 67 | 17 |
| Wanaque | 12,433 | 27 | 23 | 4 |
| Warren Township | 16,150 | 38 | 30 | 8 |
| Washington Township, Bergen County | 9,615 | 22 | 22 | 0 |
| Washington Township, Gloucester County | 51,757 | 90 | 83 | 7 |
| Washington Township, Morris County | 18,468 | 35 | 31 | 4 |
| Washington Township, Warren County | 6,935 | 26 | 24 | 2 |
| Watchung | 6,720 | 37 | 30 | 7 |
| Waterford Township | 10,674 | 25 | 22 | 3 |
| Wayne Township | 53,891 | 148 | 120 | 28 |
| Weehawken Township | 12,252 | 63 | 57 | 6 |
| Wenonah | 2,360 | 7 | 7 | 0 |
| Westampton Township | 8,799 | 24 | 22 | 2 |
| West Amwell Township | 2,970 | 7 | 6 | 1 |
| West Caldwell Township | 10,358 | 34 | 28 | 6 |
| West Deptford Township | 22,326 | 44 | 40 | 4 |
| Westfield | 29,426 | 68 | 56 | 12 |
| West Long Branch | 8,346 | 26 | 21 | 5 |
| West Milford Township | 27,879 | 52 | 45 | 7 |
| West New York | 46,528 | 122 | 111 | 11 |
| West Orange | 42,357 | 135 | 119 | 16 |
| Westville | 4,464 | 15 | 14 | 1 |
| West Wildwood | 395 | 8 | 8 | 0 |
| West Windsor Township | 27,061 | 60 | 47 | 13 |
| Westwood | 10,666 | 38 | 26 | 12 |
| Wharton | 6,060 | 22 | 21 | 1 |
| Wildwood | 5,242 | 49 | 46 | 3 |
| Wildwood Crest | 3,987 | 27 | 21 | 6 |
| Willingboro Township | 36,977 | 83 | 71 | 12 |
| Winfield Township | 1,435 | 9 | 9 | 0 |
| Winslow Township | 39,975 | 101 | 84 | 17 |
| Woodbridge Township | 98,013 | 250 | 204 | 46 |
| Woodbury | 10,467 | 30 | 27 | 3 |
| Woodbury Heights | 3,059 | 8 | 7 | 1 |
| Woodcliff Lake | 5,962 | 18 | 17 | 1 |
| Woodland Park | 12,014 | 30 | 26 | 4 |
| Wood-Ridge | 7,432 | 24 | 20 | 4 |
| Woodstown | 3,385 | 10 | 9 | 1 |
| Woolwich Township | 12,624 | 22 | 21 | 1 |
| Wyckoff Township | 16,938 | 31 | 23 | 8 |
| **NEW MEXICO** | | | | |
| Alamogordo | 35,823 | 114 | 71 | 43 |
| Albuquerque | 530,636 | 1,473 | 1,087 | 386 |
| Angel Fire | 974 | 6 | 5 | 1 |
| Artesia | 11,015 | 53 | 33 | 20 |
| Aztec | 6,977 | 16 | 13 | 3 |
| Bayard | 2,386 | 6 | 6 | 0 |
| Belen | 7,342 | 25 | 20 | 5 |
| Bernalillo | 9,608 | 24 | 21 | 3 |
| Bloomfield | 7,292 | 26 | 20 | 6 |
| Bosque Farms | 4,073 | 14 | 13 | 1 |
| Capitan | 1,517 | 4 | 4 | 0 |
| Carlsbad | 25,638 | 70 | 50 | 20 |
| Carrizozo | 1,048 | 3 | 2 | 1 |
| Clayton | 2,281 | 15 | 8 | 7 |
| Cloudcroft | 898 | 46 | 33 | 13 |
| Clovis | 32,332 | 88 | 60 | 28 |
| Corrales | 7,848 | 19 | 16 | 3 |
| Cuba | 1,498 | 7 | 6 | 1 |
| Deming | 15,625 | 39 | 34 | 5 |
| Dexter | 1,230 | 5 | 4 | 1 |
| Espanola | 9,690 | 35 | 25 | 10 |
| Estancia | 1,571 | 6 | 5 | 1 |
| Eunice | 2,798 | 14 | 7 | 7 |
| Gallup | 19,916 | 82 | 61 | 21 |
| Grants | 8,877 | 20 | 15 | 5 |
| Hatch | 1,646 | 10 | 8 | 2 |
| Hobbs | 30,710 | 118 | 70 | 48 |
| Hurley | 1,405 | 5 | 4 | 1 |
| Jal | 2,052 | 10 | 5 | 5 |
| Las Cruces | 94,024 | 259 | 176 | 83 |
| Las Vegas | 13,737 | 50 | 33 | 17 |
| Logan | 992 | 4 | 4 | 0 |
| Lordsburg | 2,765 | 12 | 11 | 1 |
| Los Alamos | 18,187 | 71 | 33 | 38 |
| Los Lunas | 14,701 | 58 | 34 | 24 |
| Lovington | 10,040 | 31 | 23 | 8 |
| Magdalena | 981 | 4 | 4 | 0 |
| Mesilla | 2,198 | 6 | 6 | 0 |
| Milan | 2,577 | 9 | 5 | 4 |
| Moriarty | 1,962 | 11 | 10 | 1 |
| Portales | 12,343 | 40 | 23 | 17 |
| Questa | 1,912 | 2 | 1 | 1 |
| Raton | 6,381 | 24 | 16 | 8 |
| Red River | 519 | 5 | 4 | 1 |
| Rio Rancho | 83,417 | 209 | 125 | 84 |
| Roswell | 46,314 | 119 | 83 | 36 |
| Ruidoso | 9,233 | 41 | 26 | 15 |
| Ruidoso Downs | 2,638 | 17 | 9 | 8 |
| Santa Clara | 1,847 | 3 | 3 | 0 |
| Santa Fe | 72,845 | 201 | 155 | 46 |
| Santa Rosa | 2,630 | 15 | 8 | 7 |
| Silver City | 10,310 | 35 | 30 | 5 |
| Socorro | 9,004 | 29 | 20 | 9 |
| Springer | 1,132 | 2 | 2 | 0 |
| Sunland Park | 14,574 | 24 | 21 | 3 |
| Taos | 5,646 | 31 | 23 | 8 |
| Taos Ski Valley | 58 | 3 | 3 | 0 |
| Tatum | 764 | 7 | 3 | 4 |
| Texico | 979 | 2 | 2 | 0 |
| Truth or Consequences | 6,732 | 17 | 15 | 2 |
| Tucumcari | 5,198 | 19 | 16 | 3 |
| Tularosa | 3,018 | 12 | 6 | 6 |
| **NEW YORK** | | | | |
| Addison Town and Village | 2,498 | 2 | 2 | 0 |
| Akron Village | 2,955 | 2 | 2 | 0 |
| Albany | 93,445 | 463 | 327 | 136 |
| Albion Village | 5,505 | 12 | 12 | 0 |
| Alexandria Bay Village | 1,118 | 2 | 2 | 0 |
| Alfred Village | 4,943 | 6 | 6 | 0 |
| Allegany Village | 1,747 | 3 | 2 | 1 |
| Amherst Town | 110,399 | 185 | 152 | 33 |
| Amity Town and Belmont Village | 2,158 | 1 | 1 | 0 |
| Amityville Village | 9,974 | 29 | 27 | 2 |
| Amsterdam | 17,448 | 40 | 38 | 2 |
| Arcade Village | 1,874 | 6 | 6 | 0 |
| Ardsley Village | 4,910 | 20 | 20 | 0 |
| Asharoken Village | 664 | 3 | 3 | 0 |
| Attica Village | 2,393 | 5 | 5 | 0 |
| Auburn | 26,991 | 77 | 69 | 8 |
| Baldwinsville Village | 7,266 | 17 | 14 | 3 |
| Ballston Spa Village | 5,453 | 4 | 4 | 0 |
| Batavia | 15,092 | 32 | 30 | 2 |
| Bath Village | 5,409 | 14 | 12 | 2 |
| Beacon | 14,545 | 37 | 35 | 2 |
| Bedford Town | 18,627 | 43 | 39 | 4 |
| Bethlehem Town | 33,286 | 57 | 40 | 17 |
| Binghamton | 44,455 | 145 | 132 | 13 |
| Blooming Grove Town | 12,352 | 17 | 15 | 2 |
| Bolivar Village | 1,107 | 1 | 1 | 0 |
| Boonville Village | 2,032 | 3 | 3 | 0 |
| Briarcliff Manor Village | 8,018 | 19 | 19 | 0 |
| Brighton Town | 34,275 | 45 | 39 | 6 |
| Brockport Village | 8,370 | 13 | 12 | 1 |
| Bronxville Village | 6,513 | 24 | 22 | 2 |
| Buchanan Village | 2,251 | 6 | 6 | 0 |
| Buffalo | 268,655 | 944 | 796 | 148 |
| Cairo Town | 6,524 | 2 | 2 | 0 |
| Caledonia Village | 2,124 | 2 | 2 | 0 |
| Cambridge Village | 1,808 | 4 | 4 | 0 |
| Camillus Town and Village | 23,316 | 26 | 24 | 2 |
| Canandaigua | 11,145 | 28 | 25 | 3 |
| Canastota Village | 4,295 | 8 | 7 | 1 |
| Canisteo Village | 2,209 | 2 | 2 | 0 |
| Canton Village | 6,090 | 10 | 8 | 2 |
| Carmel Town | 34,492 | 42 | 35 | 7 |
| Carthage Village | 3,748 | 4 | 4 | 0 |
| Catskill Village | 4,193 | 16 | 15 | 1 |
| Cayuga Heights Village | 3,663 | 8 | 6 | 2 |

## Table 78. Full-time Law Enforcement Employees, by State, by City, 2009—*Continued*

(Number.)

| State/city | Population | Total law enforcement employees | Total officers | Total civilians |
|---|---|---|---|---|
| Cazenovia Village | 2,948 | 6 | 6 | 0 |
| Centre Island Village | 445 | 5 | 5 | 0 |
| Chatham Village | 1,674 | 5 | 4 | 1 |
| Cheektowaga Town | 77,772 | 168 | 127 | 41 |
| Chester Town | 10,047 | 13 | 13 | 0 |
| Chester Village | 3,584 | 15 | 14 | 1 |
| Chittenango Village | 4,888 | 5 | 4 | 1 |
| Cicero Town | 28,354 | 15 | 14 | 1 |
| Clarkstown Town | 78,899 | 192 | 169 | 23 |
| Clayton Village | 1,879 | 3 | 3 | 0 |
| Clifton Springs Village | 2,132 | 2 | 2 | 0 |
| Clyde Village | 2,082 | 2 | 1 | 1 |
| Cobleskill Village | 4,601 | 12 | 12 | 0 |
| Coeymans Town | 7,993 | 10 | 6 | 4 |
| Cohoes | 14,973 | 49 | 36 | 13 |
| Colchester Town | 2,030 | 2 | 2 | 0 |
| Colonie Town | 78,003 | 152 | 108 | 44 |
| Cooperstown Village | 1,884 | 8 | 6 | 2 |
| Corning | 10,222 | 27 | 23 | 4 |
| Cornwall Town | 9,815 | 16 | 12 | 4 |
| Cortland | 18,404 | 46 | 43 | 3 |
| Crawford Town | 9,581 | 14 | 12 | 2 |
| Cuba Town | 3,316 | 4 | 4 | 0 |
| Dansville Village | 4,448 | 5 | 5 | 0 |
| Deerpark Town | 8,501 | 6 | 6 | 0 |
| Delhi Village | 2,846 | 4 | 4 | 0 |
| Depew Village | 15,173 | 37 | 31 | 6 |
| Deposit Village | 1,581 | 2 | 2 | 0 |
| Dewitt Town | 21,451 | 42 | 38 | 4 |
| Dobbs Ferry Village | 11,187 | 28 | 26 | 2 |
| Dryden Village | 1,819 | 7 | 6 | 1 |
| Dunkirk | 11,978 | 37 | 36 | 1 |
| East Aurora-Aurora Town | 13,451 | 22 | 17 | 5 |
| Eastchester Town | 18,698 | 51 | 46 | 5 |
| East Fishkill Town | 29,193 | 40 | 32 | 8 |
| East Greenbush Town | 17,066 | 32 | 24 | 8 |
| East Hampton Town | 19,964 | 90 | 64 | 26 |
| East Hampton Village | 1,400 | 31 | 26 | 5 |
| East Rochester Village | 6,229 | 9 | 8 | 1 |
| East Syracuse Village | 2,950 | 11 | 10 | 1 |
| Eden Town | 7,700 | 5 | 4 | 1 |
| Ellenville Village | 3,889 | 11 | 11 | 0 |
| Ellicott Town | 5,219 | 13 | 12 | 1 |
| Ellicottville | 1,910 | 2 | 2 | 0 |
| Elmira | 29,090 | 87 | 76 | 11 |
| Elmira Heights Village | 3,869 | 9 | 9 | 0 |
| Elmira Town | 5,833 | 4 | 4 | 0 |
| Elmsford Village | 4,765 | 18 | 18 | 0 |
| Endicott Village | 12,346 | 38 | 35 | 3 |
| Evans Town | 16,756 | 31 | 24 | 7 |
| Fairport Village | 5,444 | 11 | 10 | 1 |
| Fallsburg Town | 12,385 | 23 | 19 | 4 |
| Floral Park Village | 15,832 | 40 | 33 | 7 |
| Florida Village | 2,831 | 1 | 1 | 0 |
| Fort Plain Village | 2,174 | 3 | 3 | 0 |
| Frankfort Village | 2,343 | 4 | 4 | 0 |
| Franklinville Village | 1,688 | 2 | 2 | 0 |
| Freeport Village | 43,890 | 101 | 84 | 17 |
| Fulton City | 11,151 | 37 | 35 | 2 |
| Garden City Village | 22,342 | 60 | 48 | 12 |
| Gates Town | 28,590 | 35 | 29 | 6 |
| Geddes Town | 10,367 | 17 | 15 | 2 |
| Geneseo Village | 7,715 | 8 | 8 | 0 |
| Geneva | 13,177 | 42 | 37 | 5 |
| Glen Cove | 26,920 | 56 | 52 | 4 |
| Glens Falls | 13,828 | 37 | 31 | 6 |
| Glenville Town | 21,971 | 36 | 22 | 14 |
| Gloversville | 14,948 | 32 | 30 | 2 |
| Goshen Town | 8,491 | 12 | 11 | 1 |
| Goshen Village | 5,573 | 20 | 17 | 3 |
| Gouverneur Village | 3,986 | 9 | 6 | 3 |
| Granville Village | 2,530 | 6 | 6 | 0 |
| Great Neck Estates Village | 2,770 | 15 | 12 | 3 |
| Greece Town | 93,274 | 89 | 82 | 7 |
| Greenburgh Town | 43,643 | 133 | 116 | 17 |
| Greene Village | 1,640 | 1 | 1 | 0 |

| State/city | Population | Total law enforcement employees | Total officers | Total civilians |
|---|---|---|---|---|
| Green Island Village | 2,565 | 1 | 1 | 0 |
| Greenwich Village | 1,819 | 4 | 4 | 0 |
| Greenwood Lake Village | 3,417 | 9 | 7 | 2 |
| Groton Village | 2,394 | 2 | 1 | 1 |
| Guilderland Town | 33,161 | 51 | 34 | 17 |
| Hamburg Town | 44,012 | 78 | 61 | 17 |
| Hamburg Village | 9,327 | 15 | 13 | 2 |
| Hamilton Village | 3,818 | 2 | 2 | 0 |
| Hammondsport Village | 731 | 1 | 1 | 0 |
| Harriman Village | 2,247 | 7 | 7 | 0 |
| Harrison Town | 26,953 | 82 | 72 | 10 |
| Hastings-on-Hudson Village | 7,939 | 20 | 20 | 0 |
| Haverstraw Town | 37,449 | 77 | 71 | 6 |
| Hempstead Village | 53,996 | 135 | 109 | 26 |
| Herkimer Village | 6,915 | 22 | 21 | 1 |
| Highland Falls Village | 3,706 | 13 | 9 | 4 |
| Hoosick Falls Village | 3,252 | 6 | 4 | 2 |
| Hornell | 8,454 | 21 | 20 | 1 |
| Horseheads Village | 6,221 | 14 | 13 | 1 |
| Hudson | 6,864 | 30 | 24 | 6 |
| Hudson Falls Village | 6,615 | 16 | 13 | 3 |
| Hunter Town | 2,690 | 1 | 1 | 0 |
| Huntington Bay Village | 1,515 | 6 | 6 | 0 |
| Hyde Park Town | 20,207 | 15 | 12 | 3 |
| Ilion Village | 7,953 | 20 | 18 | 2 |
| Irondequoit Town | 49,755 | 67 | 55 | 12 |
| Irvington Village | 6,669 | 22 | 21 | 1 |
| Ithaca | 29,862 | 88 | 72 | 16 |
| Jamestown | 29,204 | 69 | 60 | 9 |
| Johnson City Village | 14,646 | 44 | 40 | 4 |
| Johnstown | 8,421 | 26 | 25 | 1 |
| Kenmore Village | 14,856 | 26 | 26 | 0 |
| Kensington Village | 1,203 | 6 | 6 | 0 |
| Kent Town | 14,190 | 25 | 20 | 5 |
| Kings Point Village | 5,430 | 24 | 22 | 2 |
| Kingston | 22,333 | 83 | 80 | 3 |
| Kirkland Town | 8,344 | 5 | 5 | 0 |
| Lackawanna | 17,435 | 55 | 48 | 7 |
| Lake Placid Village | 2,763 | 17 | 14 | 3 |
| Lake Success Village | 2,898 | 26 | 23 | 3 |
| Lakewood-Busti | 7,355 | 10 | 9 | 1 |
| Lancaster Town | 23,502 | 65 | 50 | 15 |
| Larchmont Village | 6,575 | 25 | 25 | 0 |
| Le Roy Village | 4,109 | 10 | 9 | 1 |
| Lewisboro Town | 12,530 | 1 | 1 | 0 |
| Lewiston Town and Village | 16,737 | 9 | 9 | 0 |
| Liberty Village | 3,844 | 19 | 16 | 3 |
| Little Falls | 4,833 | 12 | 11 | 1 |
| Liverpool Village | 2,326 | 6 | 5 | 1 |
| Lloyd Harbor Village | 3,748 | 14 | 13 | 1 |
| Lloyd Town | 10,808 | 13 | 10 | 3 |
| Lockport | 20,461 | 55 | 52 | 3 |
| Long Beach | 35,722 | 90 | 71 | 19 |
| Lowville Village | 3,133 | 6 | 6 | 0 |
| Lyons Village | 3,391 | 14 | 12 | 2 |
| Macedon Town and Village | 8,845 | 5 | 4 | 1 |
| Malone Village | 5,764 | 13 | 13 | 0 |
| Mamaroneck Town | 11,538 | 41 | 40 | 1 |
| Manlius Town | 24,850 | 46 | 38 | 8 |
| Marcellus Village | 1,813 | 1 | 1 | 0 |
| Marlborough Town | 8,301 | 12 | 9 | 3 |
| Massena Village | 10,470 | 26 | 21 | 5 |
| Maybrook Village | 4,110 | 3 | 3 | 0 |
| Mechanicville | 4,839 | 13 | 12 | 1 |
| Medina Village | 6,007 | 12 | 11 | 1 |
| Menands Village | 3,783 | 13 | 10 | 3 |
| Middleport Village | 1,765 | 3 | 3 | 0 |
| Mohawk Village | 2,451 | 4 | 4 | 0 |
| Montgomery Town | 8,736 | 15 | 14 | 1 |
| Monticello Village | 6,487 | 27 | 24 | 3 |
| Moriah Town | 3,432 | 2 | 2 | 0 |
| Mount Kisco Village | 10,434 | 38 | 34 | 4 |
| Mount Morris Village | 2,852 | 5 | 5 | 0 |
| Mount Pleasant Town | 26,437 | 54 | 45 | 9 |
| Mount Vernon | 68,677 | 231 | 199 | 32 |
| Newark Village | 9,033 | 18 | 17 | 1 |

## Table 78. Full-time Law Enforcement Employees, by State, by City, 2009—*Continued*

(Number.)

| State/city | Population | Total law enforcement employees | Total officers | Total civilians |
|---|---|---|---|---|
| Newburgh | 28,071 | 104 | 89 | 15 |
| Newburgh Town | 31,394 | 68 | 56 | 12 |
| New Castle Town | 17,750 | 45 | 41 | 4 |
| New Hartford Town and Village | 19,145 | 32 | 21 | 11 |
| New Paltz Town and Village | 13,854 | 27 | 23 | 4 |
| New Rochelle | 74,320 | 252 | 188 | 64 |
| New Windsor Town | 25,407 | 55 | 44 | 11 |
| New York | 8,400,907 | 50,688 | 35,071 | 15,617 |
| New York Mills Village | 3,303 | 5 | 5 | 0 |
| Niagara Falls | 50,909 | 165 | 145 | 20 |
| Niagara Town | 8,344 | 7 | 6 | 1 |
| Niskayuna Town | 21,920 | 37 | 29 | 8 |
| Nissequogue Village | 1,611 | 3 | 3 | 0 |
| North Castle Town | 12,293 | 39 | 36 | 3 |
| North Greenbush Town | 11,954 | 19 | 17 | 2 |
| Northport Village | 7,683 | 19 | 15 | 4 |
| North Syracuse Village | 6,537 | 14 | 13 | 1 |
| North Tonawanda | 31,012 | 57 | 47 | 10 |
| Norwich | 6,954 | 20 | 19 | 1 |
| Ocean Beach Village | 148 | 4 | 4 | 0 |
| Ogdensburg | 10,993 | 32 | 27 | 5 |
| Ogden Town | 19,377 | 15 | 12 | 3 |
| Old Brookville Village | 2,330 | 49 | 38 | 11 |
| Old Westbury Village | 5,430 | 31 | 26 | 5 |
| Olean | 14,025 | 39 | 33 | 6 |
| Olive Town | 4,647 | 1 | 1 | 0 |
| Oneida | 10,695 | 27 | 24 | 3 |
| Oneonta City | 13,205 | 30 | 26 | 4 |
| Orangetown Town | 36,108 | 101 | 91 | 10 |
| Orchard Park Town | 28,626 | 36 | 32 | 4 |
| Ossining Town | 5,731 | 16 | 16 | 0 |
| Ossining Village | 23,773 | 65 | 57 | 8 |
| Oswego City | 17,271 | 55 | 47 | 8 |
| Owego Village | 3,687 | 9 | 8 | 1 |
| Oxford Village | 1,529 | 1 | 1 | 0 |
| Oyster Bay Cove Village | 2,303 | 10 | 10 | 0 |
| Painted Post Village | 1,772 | 4 | 4 | 0 |
| Peekskill | 24,711 | 76 | 62 | 14 |
| Pelham Manor Village | 5,449 | 28 | 27 | 1 |
| Pelham Village | 6,438 | 31 | 28 | 3 |
| Penn Yan Village | 5,157 | 11 | 10 | 1 |
| Perry Village | 3,638 | 4 | 4 | 0 |
| Piermont Village | 2,562 | 8 | 8 | 0 |
| Plattsburgh City | 19,457 | 52 | 46 | 6 |
| Pleasantville Village | 7,142 | 25 | 23 | 2 |
| Port Chester Village | 28,202 | 65 | 62 | 3 |
| Port Dickinson Village | 1,584 | 5 | 4 | 1 |
| Port Jervis | 9,139 | 33 | 32 | 1 |
| Port Washington | 18,980 | 73 | 65 | 8 |
| Potsdam Village | 9,877 | 18 | 14 | 4 |
| Poughkeepsie | 29,599 | 138 | 104 | 34 |
| Poughkeepsie Town | 43,027 | 98 | 86 | 12 |
| Pound Ridge Town | 4,960 | 3 | 2 | 1 |
| Pulaski Village | 2,270 | 1 | 1 | 0 |
| Quogue Village | 1,172 | 14 | 13 | 1 |
| Ramapo Town | 76,611 | 143 | 119 | 24 |
| Red Hook Village | 1,890 | 2 | 2 | 0 |
| Rensselaer City | 7,906 | 29 | 24 | 5 |
| Riverhead Town | 36,318 | 98 | 83 | 15 |
| Rochester | 205,537 | 934 | 773 | 161 |
| Rockville Centre Village | 24,396 | 59 | 49 | 10 |
| Rome | 33,543 | 80 | 76 | 4 |
| Rosendale Town | 6,232 | 3 | 2 | 1 |
| Rotterdam Town | 30,223 | 62 | 44 | 18 |
| Rouses Point Village | 2,325 | 1 | 1 | 0 |
| Rye | 15,070 | 43 | 38 | 5 |
| Rye Brook Village | 9,672 | 28 | 27 | 1 |
| Sag Harbor Village | 2,439 | 13 | 12 | 1 |
| Sands Point Village | 2,929 | 20 | 20 | 0 |
| Saranac Lake Village | 4,783 | 13 | 13 | 0 |
| Saratoga Springs | 29,125 | 78 | 65 | 13 |
| Saugerties Town | 15,844 | 21 | 16 | 5 |
| Saugerties Village | 3,852 | 11 | 10 | 1 |
| Scarsdale Village | 17,677 | 50 | 45 | 5 |
| Schenectady | 61,087 | 208 | 160 | 48 |
| Schodack Town | 11,533 | 12 | 10 | 2 |
| Scotia Village | 8,043 | 14 | 13 | 1 |
| Seneca Falls Village | 6,604 | 16 | 13 | 3 |
| Shandaken Town | 3,045 | 4 | 4 | 0 |
| Shelter Island Town | 2,569 | 10 | 9 | 1 |
| Sherrill | 3,111 | 3 | 3 | 0 |
| Sidney Village | 3,654 | 8 | 8 | 0 |
| Silver Creek Village | 2,789 | 5 | 5 | 0 |
| Skaneateles Village | 2,531 | 5 | 5 | 0 |
| Sleepy Hollow Village | 10,331 | 24 | 24 | 0 |
| Sodus Village | 1,598 | 1 | 1 | 0 |
| Solvay Village | 6,372 | 14 | 12 | 2 |
| Southampton Town | 53,044 | 138 | 98 | 40 |
| Southampton Village | 4,363 | 42 | 31 | 11 |
| South Glens Falls Village | 3,383 | 6 | 6 | 0 |
| South Nyack Village | 3,361 | 7 | 6 | 1 |
| Southold Town | 20,552 | 72 | 56 | 16 |
| Spring Valley Village | 26,340 | 68 | 60 | 8 |
| St. Johnsville Village | 1,600 | 2 | 2 | 0 |
| Stony Point Town | 15,229 | 28 | 27 | 1 |
| Suffern Village | 11,099 | 31 | 26 | 5 |
| Syracuse | 137,208 | 571 | 505 | 66 |
| Tarrytown Village | 11,019 | 40 | 33 | 7 |
| Ticonderoga Town | 4,941 | 7 | 7 | 0 |
| Tonawanda | 14,683 | 33 | 28 | 5 |
| Tonawanda Town | 56,203 | 158 | 106 | 52 |
| Troy | 47,268 | 140 | 129 | 11 |
| Tuckahoe Village | 6,247 | 28 | 25 | 3 |
| Tuxedo Park Village | 718 | 6 | 3 | 3 |
| Tuxedo Town | 2,990 | 15 | 12 | 3 |
| Ulster Town | 12,674 | 34 | 30 | 4 |
| Utica | 57,831 | 204 | 183 | 21 |
| Vestal Town | 27,332 | 41 | 37 | 4 |
| Walden Village | 7,055 | 17 | 14 | 3 |
| Wallkill Town | 27,760 | 47 | 40 | 7 |
| Walton Village | 2,823 | 7 | 6 | 1 |
| Wappingers Falls Village | 5,748 | 6 | 3 | 3 |
| Warsaw Village | 3,602 | 5 | 5 | 0 |
| Warwick Town | 20,040 | 38 | 31 | 7 |
| Washingtonville Village | 6,167 | 15 | 13 | 2 |
| Waterford Town and Village | 8,534 | 13 | 10 | 3 |
| Waterloo Village | 4,975 | 9 | 8 | 1 |
| Watertown | 27,387 | 69 | 65 | 4 |
| Watervliet | 9,718 | 30 | 26 | 4 |
| Watkins Glen Village | 2,015 | 6 | 6 | 0 |
| Waverly Village | 4,272 | 11 | 10 | 1 |
| Webb Town | 1,933 | 5 | 5 | 0 |
| Webster Town and Village | 42,179 | 37 | 31 | 6 |
| Wellsville Village | 4,868 | 14 | 10 | 4 |
| Westfield Village | 3,349 | 5 | 5 | 0 |
| Westhampton Beach Village | 2,023 | 19 | 16 | 3 |
| West Seneca Town | 43,574 | 78 | 64 | 14 |
| Whitehall Village | 2,557 | 4 | 4 | 0 |
| White Plains | 57,810 | 229 | 215 | 14 |
| Whitesboro Village | 3,742 | 7 | 7 | 0 |
| Whitestown Town | 9,219 | 7 | 7 | 0 |
| Windham Town | 1,911 | 2 | 2 | 0 |
| Wolcott Village | 1,585 | 1 | 1 | 0 |
| Woodbury Town | 10,301 | 27 | 22 | 5 |
| Woodstock Town | 6,139 | 14 | 10 | 4 |
| Yonkers | 202,192 | 695 | 615 | 80 |
| Yorktown Town | 37,955 | 67 | 58 | 9 |
| Yorkville Village | 2,548 | 3 | 3 | 0 |
| **NORTH CAROLINA** | | | | |
| Aberdeen | 5,936 | 28 | 26 | 2 |
| Ahoskie | 4,232 | 22 | 17 | 5 |
| Albemarle | 15,471 | 55 | 49 | 6 |
| Andrews | 1,700 | 6 | 6 | 0 |
| Angier | 4,467 | 13 | 12 | 1 |
| Apex | 34,766 | 69 | 54 | 15 |
| Archdale | 9,358 | 27 | 21 | 6 |
| Asheboro | 24,891 | 84 | 77 | 7 |
| Asheville | 74,923 | 263 | 195 | 68 |
| Atlantic Beach | 1,817 | 22 | 18 | 4 |
| Ayden | 5,041 | 22 | 18 | 4 |
| Badin | 1,328 | 5 | 5 | 0 |
| Bailey | 685 | 3 | 3 | 0 |

## Table 78. Full-time Law Enforcement Employees, by State, by City, 2009—*Continued*

(Number.)

| State/city | Population | Total law enforcement employees | Total officers | Total civilians |
|---|---|---|---|---|
| Bakersville | 349 | 1 | 1 | 0 |
| Bald Head Island | 308 | 21 | 10 | 11 |
| Banner Elk | 905 | 10 | 9 | 1 |
| Beaufort | 4,236 | 18 | 17 | 1 |
| Beech Mountain | 341 | 13 | 9 | 4 |
| Belhaven | 2,043 | 12 | 8 | 4 |
| Belmont | 9,433 | 41 | 31 | 10 |
| Benson | 3,554 | 13 | 12 | 1 |
| Beulaville | 1,147 | 6 | 5 | 1 |
| Biltmore Forest | 1,573 | 14 | 12 | 2 |
| Biscoe | 1,671 | 9 | 8 | 1 |
| Black Creek | 695 | 2 | 2 | 0 |
| Black Mountain | 7,915 | 22 | 18 | 4 |
| Bladenboro | 1,668 | 6 | 6 | 0 |
| Blowing Rock | 1,497 | 15 | 11 | 4 |
| Boiling Spring Lakes | 4,920 | 9 | 8 | 1 |
| Boiling Springs | 3,883 | 8 | 8 | 0 |
| Boone | 13,995 | 44 | 35 | 9 |
| Boonville | 1,117 | 5 | 5 | 0 |
| Brevard | 6,708 | 28 | 22 | 6 |
| Broadway | 1,167 | 4 | 4 | 0 |
| Brookford | 426 | 1 | 1 | 0 |
| Bryson City | 1,370 | 8 | 7 | 1 |
| Bunn | 415 | 2 | 2 | 0 |
| Burgaw | 4,377 | 11 | 10 | 1 |
| Burlington | 51,440 | 153 | 111 | 42 |
| Burnsville | 1,639 | 8 | 8 | 0 |
| Butner | 6,146 | 50 | 43 | 7 |
| Cameron | 304 | 1 | 1 | 0 |
| Candor | 839 | 5 | 5 | 0 |
| Canton | 3,852 | 20 | 14 | 6 |
| Cape Carteret | 1,407 | 7 | 7 | 0 |
| Carolina Beach | 5,955 | 30 | 28 | 2 |
| Carrboro | 18,213 | 41 | 38 | 3 |
| Carthage | 2,039 | 11 | 10 | 1 |
| Cary | 133,757 | 193 | 163 | 30 |
| Caswell Beach | 483 | 4 | 4 | 0 |
| Catawba | 817 | 3 | 3 | 0 |
| Chadbourn | 2,053 | 11 | 10 | 1 |
| Chapel Hill | 53,069 | 130 | 112 | 18 |
| Charlotte-Mecklenburg[1] | 777,708 | 2,141 | 1,635 | 506 |
| Cherryville | 5,651 | 23 | 18 | 5 |
| China Grove | 3,755 | 13 | 13 | 0 |
| Chocowinity | 719 | 3 | 3 | 0 |
| Claremont | 1,153 | 9 | 8 | 1 |
| Clayton | 16,952 | 45 | 41 | 4 |
| Cleveland | 841 | 5 | 5 | 0 |
| Clinton | 8,896 | 32 | 29 | 3 |
| Clyde | 1,319 | 4 | 4 | 0 |
| Coats | 2,166 | 7 | 7 | 0 |
| Columbus | 973 | 5 | 5 | 0 |
| Concord | 67,478 | 180 | 154 | 26 |
| Conover | 7,348 | 22 | 21 | 1 |
| Conway | 658 | 1 | 1 | 0 |
| Cooleemee | 986 | 4 | 4 | 0 |
| Cornelius | 26,027 | 58 | 42 | 16 |
| Cramerton | 3,162 | 11 | 11 | 0 |
| Creedmoor | 3,859 | 17 | 13 | 4 |
| Dallas | 3,813 | 16 | 12 | 4 |
| Davidson | 10,716 | 19 | 18 | 1 |
| Denton | 1,490 | 6 | 6 | 0 |
| Dobson | 1,457 | 5 | 5 | 0 |
| Drexel | 1,877 | 5 | 5 | 0 |
| Duck | 497 | 8 | 7 | 1 |
| Dunn | 10,115 | 49 | 35 | 14 |
| Durham | 227,492 | 608 | 460 | 148 |
| East Bend | 665 | 2 | 2 | 0 |
| East Spencer | 1,795 | 6 | 5 | 1 |
| Eden | 15,426 | 52 | 44 | 8 |
| Edenton | 4,964 | 16 | 14 | 2 |
| Elizabeth City | 20,363 | 66 | 53 | 13 |
| Elizabethtown | 3,702 | 15 | 14 | 1 |
| Elkin | 4,104 | 21 | 17 | 4 |
| Elon | 7,092 | 16 | 15 | 1 |
| Emerald Isle | 3,659 | 19 | 14 | 5 |
| Enfield | 2,337 | 11 | 10 | 1 |
| Erwin | 4,866 | 10 | 9 | 1 |
| Fair Bluff | 1,137 | 1 | 1 | 0 |
| Fairmont | 2,734 | 13 | 10 | 3 |
| Farmville | 4,637 | 21 | 16 | 5 |
| Fayetteville | 173,995 | 504 | 347 | 157 |
| Fletcher | 4,770 | 16 | 15 | 1 |
| Forest City | 7,117 | 34 | 32 | 2 |
| Four Oaks | 2,100 | 5 | 5 | 0 |
| Foxfire Village | 491 | 2 | 2 | 0 |
| Franklin | 3,982 | 19 | 18 | 1 |
| Franklinton | 2,013 | 8 | 7 | 1 |
| Fremont | 1,427 | 5 | 3 | 2 |
| Fuquay-Varina | 18,457 | 34 | 29 | 5 |
| Garner | 28,268 | 66 | 61 | 5 |
| Garysburg | 1,121 | 2 | 2 | 0 |
| Gaston | 872 | 2 | 2 | 0 |
| Gastonia | 73,060 | 205 | 172 | 33 |
| Gibsonville | 4,757 | 15 | 14 | 1 |
| Glen Alpine | 1,081 | 3 | 3 | 0 |
| Goldsboro | 37,421 | 120 | 103 | 17 |
| Graham | 14,684 | 36 | 33 | 3 |
| Granite Falls | 4,606 | 16 | 14 | 2 |
| Granite Quarry | 2,278 | 7 | 7 | 0 |
| Greensboro | 253,191 | 743 | 602 | 141 |
| Greenville | 81,814 | 231 | 182 | 49 |
| Grifton | 2,238 | 6 | 6 | 0 |
| Hamlet | 5,764 | 23 | 19 | 4 |
| Havelock | 21,691 | 35 | 28 | 7 |
| Haw River | 2,023 | 8 | 8 | 0 |
| Henderson | 15,795 | 62 | 52 | 10 |
| Hendersonville | 12,077 | 50 | 38 | 12 |
| Hertford | 2,198 | 8 | 7 | 1 |
| Hickory | 41,718 | 143 | 114 | 29 |
| Highlands | 955 | 12 | 12 | 0 |
| High Point | 103,675 | 260 | 219 | 41 |
| Hillsborough | 5,669 | 31 | 28 | 3 |
| Holden Beach | 857 | 9 | 9 | 0 |
| Holly Ridge | 917 | 9 | 8 | 1 |
| Holly Springs | 22,639 | 47 | 36 | 11 |
| Hope Mills | 13,442 | 41 | 30 | 11 |
| Hot Springs | 637 | 1 | 1 | 0 |
| Hudson | 3,042 | 12 | 11 | 1 |
| Huntersville | 46,695 | 92 | 82 | 10 |
| Indian Beach | 92 | 4 | 4 | 0 |
| Jackson | 638 | 1 | 1 | 0 |
| Jacksonville | 77,508 | 139 | 112 | 27 |
| Jefferson | 1,344 | 3 | 3 | 0 |
| Jonesville | 2,271 | 11 | 10 | 1 |
| Kannapolis | 43,166 | 96 | 75 | 21 |
| Kenansville | 1,186 | 4 | 4 | 0 |
| Kenly | 1,977 | 9 | 8 | 1 |
| Kernersville | 22,822 | 87 | 67 | 20 |
| Kill Devil Hills | 6,726 | 31 | 25 | 6 |
| King | 7,011 | 22 | 19 | 3 |
| Kings Mountain | 11,275 | 35 | 29 | 6 |
| Kinston | 22,203 | 93 | 84 | 9 |
| Kitty Hawk | 3,290 | 17 | 15 | 2 |
| Knightdale | 8,419 | 24 | 23 | 1 |
| Kure Beach | 2,658 | 11 | 10 | 1 |
| Lake Lure | 1,010 | 11 | 10 | 1 |
| Lake Royale | | 6 | 6 | 0 |
| Lake Waccamaw | 1,449 | 5 | 5 | 0 |
| Landis | 3,133 | 9 | 8 | 1 |
| Laurel Park | 2,178 | 7 | 7 | 0 |
| Laurinburg | 15,506 | 42 | 36 | 6 |
| Leland | 5,216 | 33 | 30 | 3 |
| Lenoir | 17,869 | 69 | 54 | 15 |
| Lexington | 20,450 | 75 | 67 | 8 |
| Liberty | 2,739 | 11 | 10 | 1 |
| Lilesville | 420 | 1 | 1 | 0 |
| Lillington | 3,327 | 13 | 12 | 1 |
| Lincolnton | 10,944 | 36 | 31 | 5 |
| Littleton | 641 | 5 | 5 | 0 |
| Locust | 2,649 | 12 | 11 | 1 |
| Long View | 4,967 | 14 | 14 | 0 |
| Louisburg | 3,856 | 14 | 13 | 1 |

## Table 78. Full-time Law Enforcement Employees, by State, by City, 2009—*Continued*

(Number.)

| State/city | Population | Total law enforcement employees | Total officers | Total civilians |
|---|---|---|---|---|
| Lowell | 2,807 | 9 | 9 | 0 |
| Lumberton | 22,111 | 89 | 78 | 11 |
| Madison | 2,255 | 14 | 13 | 1 |
| Maggie Valley | 814 | 9 | 8 | 1 |
| Maiden | 3,523 | 14 | 13 | 1 |
| Manteo | 1,331 | 8 | 7 | 1 |
| Marion | 5,168 | 27 | 22 | 5 |
| Marshall | 831 | 3 | 3 | 0 |
| Mars Hill | 1,773 | 5 | 5 | 0 |
| Marshville | 3,317 | 8 | 8 | 0 |
| Matthews | 27,359 | 69 | 57 | 12 |
| Maxton | 2,699 | 14 | 9 | 5 |
| Mayodan | 2,595 | 16 | 13 | 3 |
| Maysville | 955 | 3 | 3 | 0 |
| McAdenville | 669 | 2 | 2 | 0 |
| Mebane | 11,024 | 27 | 20 | 7 |
| Middlesex | 860 | 4 | 4 | 0 |
| Mint Hill | 20,740 | 30 | 28 | 2 |
| Misenheimer | 683 | 5 | 5 | 0 |
| Mocksville | 4,686 | 23 | 22 | 1 |
| Monroe | 33,178 | 99 | 85 | 14 |
| Montreat | 704 | 5 | 5 | 0 |
| Mooresville | 22,247 | 75 | 58 | 17 |
| Morehead City | 9,715 | 48 | 38 | 10 |
| Morganton | 17,169 | 97 | 63 | 34 |
| Morrisville | 15,207 | 34 | 32 | 2 |
| Mount Airy | 9,487 | 51 | 38 | 13 |
| Mount Gilead | 1,396 | 7 | 7 | 0 |
| Mount Holly | 10,130 | 35 | 29 | 6 |
| Mount Olive | 4,371 | 17 | 16 | 1 |
| Murfreesboro | 2,372 | 14 | 9 | 5 |
| Murphy | 1,558 | 11 | 8 | 3 |
| Nags Head | 3,051 | 21 | 19 | 2 |
| Nashville | 4,551 | 13 | 12 | 1 |
| Navassa | 1,908 | 4 | 4 | 0 |
| New Bern | 29,251 | 133 | 87 | 46 |
| Newland | 650 | 5 | 5 | 0 |
| Newport | 4,419 | 10 | 10 | 0 |
| Newton | 13,449 | 43 | 34 | 9 |
| Newton Grove | 633 | 3 | 3 | 0 |
| Norlina | 1,010 | 6 | 6 | 0 |
| North Topsail Beach | 969 | 12 | 11 | 1 |
| North Wilkesboro | 4,158 | 27 | 23 | 4 |
| Norwood | 2,403 | 7 | 6 | 1 |
| Oakboro | 1,165 | 5 | 5 | 0 |
| Oak Island | 8,375 | 32 | 25 | 7 |
| Ocean Isle Beach | 539 | 13 | 13 | 0 |
| Old Fort | 959 | 5 | 4 | 1 |
| Oxford | 8,667 | 39 | 32 | 7 |
| Pembroke | 2,763 | 19 | 14 | 5 |
| Pikeville | 703 | 3 | 3 | 0 |
| Pilot Mountain | 1,271 | 9 | 8 | 1 |
| Pinebluff | 1,422 | 4 | 4 | 0 |
| Pinehurst | 12,649 | 29 | 25 | 4 |
| Pine Knoll Shores | 1,550 | 9 | 8 | 1 |
| Pine Level | 1,805 | 5 | 5 | 0 |
| Pinetops | 1,251 | 10 | 7 | 3 |
| Pineville | 6,878 | 47 | 36 | 11 |
| Pink Hill | 526 | 2 | 2 | 0 |
| Pittsboro | 2,664 | 13 | 13 | 0 |
| Plymouth | 3,834 | 10 | 10 | 0 |
| Princeton | 1,310 | 4 | 4 | 0 |
| Raeford | 3,534 | 17 | 15 | 2 |
| Raleigh | 406,005 | 858 | 704 | 154 |
| Ramseur | 1,769 | 6 | 6 | 0 |
| Randleman | 3,696 | 14 | 14 | 0 |
| Ranlo | 2,353 | 7 | 7 | 0 |
| Red Springs | 3,530 | 20 | 15 | 5 |
| Reidsville | 14,899 | 58 | 49 | 9 |
| Richlands | 934 | 6 | 6 | 0 |
| Rich Square | 862 | 2 | 2 | 0 |
| River Bend | 3,148 | 5 | 5 | 0 |
| Roanoke Rapids | 16,339 | 41 | 37 | 4 |
| Robbins | 1,228 | 5 | 5 | 0 |
| Robersonville | 1,535 | 7 | 7 | 0 |
| Rockingham | 8,810 | 37 | 32 | 5 |
| Rockwell | 2,017 | 5 | 5 | 0 |
| Rocky Mount | 57,121 | 203 | 150 | 53 |
| Rolesville | 3,220 | 11 | 10 | 1 |
| Rose Hill | 1,418 | 4 | 4 | 0 |
| Rowland | 1,160 | 7 | 6 | 1 |
| Roxboro | 8,663 | 34 | 30 | 4 |
| Rutherfordton | 4,031 | 15 | 15 | 0 |
| Salisbury | 29,008 | 105 | 87 | 18 |
| Saluda | 579 | 3 | 3 | 0 |
| Sanford | 30,020 | 97 | 83 | 14 |
| Scotland Neck | 2,150 | 9 | 8 | 1 |
| Selma | 7,049 | 25 | 23 | 2 |
| Seven Devils | 174 | 5 | 5 | 0 |
| Shallotte | 2,218 | 14 | 13 | 1 |
| Sharpsburg | 2,403 | 9 | 9 | 0 |
| Shelby | 21,515 | 85 | 71 | 14 |
| Siler City | 8,744 | 26 | 21 | 5 |
| Smithfield | 13,199 | 43 | 39 | 4 |
| Southern Pines | 12,865 | 37 | 28 | 9 |
| Southern Shores | 2,631 | 10 | 9 | 1 |
| Southport | 3,165 | 12 | 11 | 1 |
| Sparta | 1,770 | 6 | 6 | 0 |
| Spencer | 3,394 | 13 | 12 | 1 |
| Spindale | 3,863 | 11 | 11 | 0 |
| Spring Hope | 1,291 | 5 | 5 | 0 |
| Spring Lake | 8,112 | 13 | 10 | 3 |
| Spruce Pine | 1,975 | 12 | 12 | 0 |
| Stallings | 9,186 | 23 | 21 | 2 |
| Stanfield | 1,112 | 4 | 4 | 0 |
| Stanley | 3,201 | 12 | 8 | 4 |
| Stantonsburg | 705 | 3 | 3 | 0 |
| Star | 791 | 4 | 4 | 0 |
| Statesville | 26,763 | 96 | 75 | 21 |
| Stoneville | 971 | 4 | 4 | 0 |
| St. Pauls | 2,044 | 17 | 13 | 4 |
| Sugar Mountain | 211 | 5 | 5 | 0 |
| Sunset Beach | 2,663 | 12 | 12 | 0 |
| Surf City | 2,132 | 18 | 17 | 1 |
| Swansboro | 1,988 | 9 | 9 | 0 |
| Sylva | 2,437 | 14 | 13 | 1 |
| Tabor City | 2,764 | 10 | 9 | 1 |
| Tarboro | 10,155 | 35 | 28 | 7 |
| Taylorsville | 1,858 | 11 | 11 | 0 |
| Taylortown | 886 | 2 | 2 | 0 |
| Thomasville | 26,759 | 72 | 65 | 7 |
| Topsail Beach | 594 | 7 | 6 | 1 |
| Trent Woods | 3,960 | 5 | 5 | 0 |
| Troutman | 1,841 | 13 | 13 | 0 |
| Troy | 3,403 | 12 | 11 | 1 |
| Tryon | 1,702 | 10 | 8 | 2 |
| Valdese | 4,542 | 13 | 12 | 1 |
| Vanceboro | 844 | 1 | 1 | 0 |
| Vass | 803 | 3 | 3 | 0 |
| Wadesboro | 5,026 | 30 | 25 | 5 |
| Wagram | 772 | 2 | 2 | 0 |
| Wake Forest | 29,368 | 64 | 54 | 10 |
| Wallace | 3,619 | 16 | 13 | 3 |
| Walnut Cove | 1,611 | 7 | 7 | 0 |
| Walnut Creek | 855 | 2 | 2 | 0 |
| Warrenton | 832 | 6 | 5 | 1 |
| Warsaw | 3,192 | 13 | 11 | 2 |
| Washington | 10,157 | 48 | 38 | 10 |
| Waxhaw | 3,808 | 17 | 16 | 1 |
| Waynesville | 9,915 | 42 | 34 | 8 |
| Weaverville | 3,102 | 14 | 13 | 1 |
| Weldon | 1,656 | 9 | 9 | 0 |
| Wendell | 5,414 | 17 | 15 | 2 |
| West Jefferson | 1,118 | 7 | 7 | 0 |
| Whispering Pines | 2,157 | 8 | 7 | 1 |
| Whitakers | 770 | 2 | 2 | 0 |
| White Lake | 515 | 6 | 6 | 0 |
| Whiteville | 5,242 | 29 | 25 | 4 |
| Wilkesboro | 3,134 | 21 | 19 | 2 |
| Williamston | 5,323 | 21 | 19 | 2 |
| Wilmington | 101,438 | 308 | 255 | 53 |
| Wilson | 48,807 | 136 | 115 | 21 |

## Table 78. Full-time Law Enforcement Employees, by State, by City, 2009—*Continued*

(Number.)

| State/city | Population | Total law enforcement employees | Total officers | Total civilians |
|---|---|---|---|---|
| Wilson's Mills | 1,634 | 3 | 3 | 0 |
| Windsor | 3,093 | 9 | 9 | 0 |
| Wingate | 4,097 | 7 | 7 | 0 |
| Winston-Salem | 230,978 | 672 | 519 | 153 |
| Winterville | 4,812 | 20 | 18 | 2 |
| Woodfin | 5,750 | 16 | 15 | 1 |
| Woodland | 760 | 1 | 1 | 0 |
| Wrightsville Beach | 2,654 | 25 | 23 | 2 |
| Yadkinville | 2,865 | 13 | 12 | 1 |
| Youngsville | 786 | 9 | 8 | 1 |
| Zebulon | 4,809 | 23 | 22 | 1 |
| **NORTH DAKOTA** | | | | |
| Beulah | 2,834 | 6 | 5 | 1 |
| Bismarck | 60,923 | 122 | 94 | 28 |
| Bowman | 1,491 | 3 | 3 | 0 |
| Burlington | 990 | 2 | 2 | 0 |
| Cando | 989 | 2 | 2 | 0 |
| Carrington | 2,052 | 4 | 4 | 0 |
| Cavalier | 1,301 | 4 | 4 | 0 |
| Crosby | 939 | 2 | 2 | 0 |
| Devils Lake | 6,654 | 18 | 16 | 2 |
| Dickinson | 16,043 | 46 | 31 | 15 |
| Elgin | 532 | 1 | 1 | 0 |
| Ellendale | 1,446 | 2 | 2 | 0 |
| Emerado | 473 | 1 | 1 | 0 |
| Fargo | 93,830 | 151 | 133 | 18 |
| Fessenden | 488 | 1 | 1 | 0 |
| Grafton | 3,924 | 11 | 10 | 1 |
| Grand Forks | 51,553 | 98 | 82 | 16 |
| Harvey | 1,583 | 4 | 4 | 0 |
| Hazen | 2,181 | 4 | 4 | 0 |
| Hillsboro | 1,459 | 2 | 2 | 0 |
| Jamestown | 14,535 | 33 | 29 | 4 |
| Lamoure | 788 | 1 | 1 | 0 |
| Larimore | 1,300 | 2 | 2 | 0 |
| Lincoln | 2,875 | 3 | 3 | 0 |
| Linton | 987 | 2 | 2 | 0 |
| Lisbon | 2,170 | 3 | 3 | 0 |
| Mandan | 18,244 | 36 | 27 | 9 |
| Mayville | 1,751 | 3 | 3 | 0 |
| Minot | 35,293 | 84 | 60 | 24 |
| Napoleon | 705 | 1 | 1 | 0 |
| Northwood | 924 | 2 | 2 | 0 |
| Oakes | 1,740 | 4 | 4 | 0 |
| Powers Lake | 238 | 1 | 1 | 0 |
| Rolla | 1,420 | 4 | 4 | 0 |
| Rugby | 2,538 | 4 | 4 | 0 |
| South Heart | 297 | 1 | 1 | 0 |
| Stanley | 1,212 | 3 | 3 | 0 |
| Steele | 639 | 1 | 1 | 0 |
| St. John | 354 | 1 | 1 | 0 |
| Thompson | 954 | 1 | 1 | 0 |
| Valley City | 6,172 | 19 | 13 | 6 |
| Wahpeton | 7,484 | 16 | 14 | 2 |
| Watford City | 1,382 | 5 | 5 | 0 |
| West Fargo | 24,862 | 43 | 33 | 10 |
| Williston | 12,662 | 31 | 23 | 8 |
| Wishek | 853 | 2 | 2 | 0 |
| **OHIO** | | | | |
| Aberdeen | 1,499 | 5 | 4 | 1 |
| Ada | 6,109 | 10 | 7 | 3 |
| Addyston | 991 | 1 | 1 | 0 |
| Akron | 206,497 | 506 | 460 | 46 |
| Alliance | 22,402 | 54 | 41 | 13 |
| Amberley Village | 3,573 | 22 | 18 | 4 |
| Amelia | 3,648 | 7 | 6 | 1 |
| Amherst | 11,718 | 26 | 20 | 6 |
| Arcanum | 1,953 | 3 | 3 | 0 |
| Archbold | 4,450 | 8 | 8 | 0 |
| Arlington Heights | 830 | 3 | 3 | 0 |
| Ashland | 21,916 | 34 | 27 | 7 |
| Ashtabula | 19,557 | 34 | 29 | 5 |
| Ashville | 3,300 | 9 | 9 | 0 |
| Athens | 22,173 | 33 | 26 | 7 |
| Aurora | 14,651 | 35 | 27 | 8 |
| Austintown | 34,821 | 48 | 39 | 9 |
| Avon Lake | 24,723 | 34 | 29 | 5 |
| Bainbridge Township | 11,175 | 27 | 19 | 8 |
| Barberton | 26,436 | 55 | 42 | 13 |
| Barnesville | 4,024 | 8 | 6 | 2 |
| Batavia | 1,757 | 4 | 4 | 0 |
| Bath Township, Summit County | 10,247 | 27 | 20 | 7 |
| Bay Village | 14,454 | 28 | 24 | 4 |
| Bazetta Township | 5,951 | 6 | 6 | 0 |
| Beach City | 1,091 | 2 | 2 | 0 |
| Beachwood | 10,997 | 58 | 44 | 14 |
| Beavercreek | 40,119 | 63 | 46 | 17 |
| Beaver Township | 6,045 | 16 | 12 | 4 |
| Bedford | 12,836 | 42 | 31 | 11 |
| Bedford Heights | 10,393 | 54 | 33 | 21 |
| Bellaire | 4,528 | 10 | 10 | 0 |
| Bellbrook | 7,000 | 17 | 12 | 5 |
| Bellefontaine | 12,622 | 30 | 23 | 7 |
| Bellville | 1,694 | 4 | 4 | 0 |
| Belpre | 6,515 | 11 | 6 | 5 |
| Bentleyville Village | 890 | 3 | 3 | 0 |
| Berea | 17,883 | 39 | 32 | 7 |
| Berlin Heights | 630 | 1 | 1 | 0 |
| Bethesda | 1,350 | 1 | 1 | 0 |
| Beverly | 1,331 | 3 | 3 | 0 |
| Bexley | 12,435 | 34 | 28 | 6 |
| Blanchester | 4,306 | 7 | 7 | 0 |
| Blendon Township | 7,830 | 12 | 11 | 1 |
| Boardman | 38,827 | 61 | 48 | 13 |
| Bolivar | 884 | 1 | 1 | 0 |
| Boston Heights | 1,224 | 16 | 16 | 0 |
| Bowling Green | 29,536 | 58 | 43 | 15 |
| Brady Lake | 495 | 1 | 1 | 0 |
| Bratenahl | 1,255 | 12 | 9 | 3 |
| Brecksville | 12,792 | 35 | 29 | 6 |
| Bridgeport | 2,031 | 5 | 5 | 0 |
| Brimfield Township | 7,903 | 15 | 13 | 2 |
| Broadview Heights | 17,422 | 43 | 30 | 13 |
| Brookfield Township | 9,360 | 10 | 9 | 1 |
| Brooklyn | 10,290 | 42 | 34 | 8 |
| Brooklyn Heights | 1,443 | 17 | 17 | 0 |
| Brook Park | 18,987 | 55 | 44 | 11 |
| Brookville | 5,430 | 12 | 11 | 1 |
| Brunswick | 34,842 | 52 | 39 | 13 |
| Brunswick Hills Township | 7,486 | 10 | 9 | 1 |
| Bryan | 8,286 | 26 | 19 | 7 |
| Buchtel | 598 | 1 | 1 | 0 |
| Buckeye Lake | 3,041 | 3 | 3 | 0 |
| Bucyrus | 12,150 | 25 | 19 | 6 |
| Burton | 1,423 | 3 | 3 | 0 |
| Butler Township | 8,101 | 16 | 15 | 1 |
| Cadiz | 3,281 | 5 | 5 | 0 |
| Caldwell | 2,283 | 1 | 1 | 0 |
| Cambridge | 11,156 | 26 | 22 | 4 |
| Campbell | 8,333 | 13 | 13 | 0 |
| Canal Fulton | 5,016 | 9 | 8 | 1 |
| Canfield | 6,805 | 20 | 15 | 5 |
| Canton | 78,085 | 198 | 159 | 39 |
| Carey | 3,759 | 11 | 7 | 4 |
| Carlisle | 6,156 | 9 | 8 | 1 |
| Carrollton | 3,209 | 7 | 7 | 0 |
| Celina | 10,242 | 22 | 16 | 6 |
| Centerville | 22,891 | 55 | 43 | 12 |
| Chagrin Falls | 3,602 | 18 | 10 | 8 |
| Champion Township | 9,145 | 9 | 8 | 1 |
| Chardon | 5,213 | 17 | 11 | 6 |
| Cheshire | 79 | 1 | 1 | 0 |
| Chester Township | 10,902 | 13 | 13 | 0 |
| Cheviot | 8,322 | 10 | 10 | 0 |
| Chillicothe | 22,312 | 53 | 47 | 6 |
| Cincinnati | 333,568 | 1,340 | 1,113 | 227 |
| Circleville | 13,701 | 32 | 24 | 8 |
| Clayton | 12,858 | 14 | 14 | 0 |
| Clay Township, Ottawa County | 2,722 | 4 | 4 | 0 |
| Clearcreek Township | 12,850 | 15 | 15 | 0 |
| Cleveland | 429,238 | 1,908 | 1,642 | 266 |
| Cleveland Heights | 45,320 | 110 | 104 | 6 |

## Table 78. Full-time Law Enforcement Employees, by State, by City, 2009—*Continued*

(Number.)

| State/city | Population | Total law enforcement employees | Total officers | Total civilians |
|---|---|---|---|---|
| Cleves | 2,678 | 4 | 4 | 0 |
| Clinton Township | 4,019 | 9 | 9 | 0 |
| Clyde | 6,120 | 16 | 12 | 4 |
| Coitsville Township | 1,619 | 2 | 2 | 0 |
| Coldwater | 4,387 | 6 | 6 | 0 |
| Columbiana | 6,018 | 16 | 12 | 4 |
| Columbus | 759,391 | 2,179 | 1,878 | 301 |
| Conneaut | 12,342 | 23 | 18 | 5 |
| Copley Township | 14,060 | 24 | 23 | 1 |
| Covington | 2,623 | 6 | 5 | 1 |
| Crestline | 4,853 | 12 | 8 | 4 |
| Creston | 2,109 | 1 | 1 | 0 |
| Crooksville | 2,438 | 5 | 4 | 1 |
| Cuyahoga Falls | 51,281 | 94 | 86 | 8 |
| Dalton | 1,709 | 2 | 2 | 0 |
| Danville | 1,070 | 2 | 2 | 0 |
| Dayton | 152,965 | 477 | 398 | 79 |
| Deer Park | 5,725 | 15 | 11 | 4 |
| Defiance | 16,006 | 30 | 27 | 3 |
| Delaware | 34,734 | 65 | 50 | 15 |
| Delhi Township | 31,419 | 31 | 29 | 2 |
| Delphos | 6,704 | 17 | 13 | 4 |
| Delta | 2,897 | 8 | 7 | 1 |
| Dennison | 2,866 | 4 | 4 | 0 |
| Deshler | 1,793 | 2 | 2 | 0 |
| Dover | 12,487 | 22 | 21 | 1 |
| Doylestown | 2,907 | 7 | 6 | 1 |
| Dublin | 39,390 | 84 | 63 | 21 |
| Eastlake | 19,443 | 46 | 33 | 13 |
| East Liverpool | 11,880 | 24 | 19 | 5 |
| East Palestine | 4,666 | 7 | 6 | 1 |
| Eaton | 7,983 | 20 | 14 | 6 |
| Edgerton | 1,945 | 3 | 3 | 0 |
| Elida | 1,897 | 2 | 2 | 0 |
| Elmwood Place | 2,461 | 3 | 3 | 0 |
| Elyria | 54,857 | 102 | 85 | 17 |
| Empire | 274 | 1 | 1 | 0 |
| Englewood | 12,734 | 24 | 19 | 5 |
| Enon | 2,532 | 4 | 4 | 0 |
| Euclid | 46,871 | 142 | 98 | 44 |
| Evendale | 2,942 | 22 | 19 | 3 |
| Fairborn | 32,451 | 59 | 42 | 17 |
| Fairfax | 1,847 | 10 | 9 | 1 |
| Fairfield | 42,414 | 80 | 61 | 19 |
| Fairfield Township | 17,487 | 18 | 17 | 1 |
| Fairlawn | 7,000 | 35 | 24 | 11 |
| Fairport Harbor | 3,214 | 8 | 7 | 1 |
| Fairview Park | 15,577 | 28 | 27 | 1 |
| Fayette | 1,281 | 3 | 3 | 0 |
| Fayetteville | 365 | 5 | 4 | 1 |
| Findlay | 36,751 | 85 | 68 | 17 |
| Forest | 1,444 | 2 | 2 | 0 |
| Forest Park | 18,418 | 48 | 40 | 8 |
| Fort Recovery | 1,338 | 2 | 2 | 0 |
| Fort Shawnee | 3,687 | 6 | 5 | 1 |
| Franklin | 13,113 | 31 | 24 | 7 |
| Fredericktown | 2,480 | 4 | 4 | 0 |
| Fremont | 16,556 | 38 | 32 | 6 |
| Gahanna | 34,028 | 73 | 59 | 14 |
| Galion | 10,644 | 21 | 17 | 4 |
| Garfield Heights | 27,424 | 79 | 60 | 19 |
| Gates Mills | 2,254 | 15 | 11 | 4 |
| Geneva | 6,259 | 15 | 11 | 4 |
| Geneva-on-the-Lake | 1,478 | 5 | 5 | 0 |
| Genoa | 2,270 | 4 | 4 | 0 |
| Genoa Township | 16,119 | 28 | 25 | 3 |
| Georgetown | 3,405 | 7 | 7 | 0 |
| Germantown | 5,031 | 12 | 11 | 1 |
| German Township, Clark County | 7,186 | 4 | 4 | 0 |
| German Township, Montgomery County | 3,290 | 6 | 6 | 0 |
| Gibsonburg | 2,430 | 5 | 5 | 0 |
| Girard | 9,982 | 19 | 16 | 3 |
| Glendale | 2,217 | 7 | 7 | 0 |
| Glenwillow | 640 | 4 | 4 | 0 |
| Gnadenhutten | 1,283 | 2 | 2 | 0 |
| Goshen Township, Clermont County | 16,564 | 12 | 11 | 1 |
| Goshen Township, Mahoning County | 3,429 | 7 | 7 | 0 |
| Grandview Heights | 6,265 | 23 | 19 | 4 |
| Granville | 5,414 | 13 | 10 | 3 |
| Greenfield | 5,076 | 8 | 8 | 0 |
| Greenhills | 3,810 | 8 | 7 | 1 |
| Greenville | 12,908 | 31 | 24 | 7 |
| Greenwich | 1,500 | 4 | 4 | 0 |
| Grove City | 34,598 | 78 | 61 | 17 |
| Groveport | 5,409 | 21 | 20 | 1 |
| Hamilton | 62,690 | 147 | 125 | 22 |
| Hamler-Marion Township | 1,392 | 1 | 1 | 0 |
| Hanging Rock | 290 | 3 | 3 | 0 |
| Harrison | 9,628 | 25 | 22 | 3 |
| Hartville | 2,598 | 6 | 6 | 0 |
| Harveysburg | 638 | 1 | 1 | 0 |
| Heath | 8,938 | 25 | 18 | 7 |
| Hebron | 2,161 | 8 | 7 | 1 |
| Hicksville | 3,383 | 8 | 7 | 1 |
| Highland Heights | 8,580 | 29 | 22 | 7 |
| Highland Hills | 1,366 | 7 | 6 | 1 |
| Hilliard | 28,326 | 68 | 52 | 16 |
| Hillsboro | 6,688 | 19 | 15 | 4 |
| Hinckley Township | 8,059 | 11 | 9 | 2 |
| Holland | 1,329 | 9 | 9 | 0 |
| Howland Township | 16,245 | 21 | 20 | 1 |
| Hubbard Township | 5,649 | 8 | 7 | 1 |
| Huber Heights | 37,027 | 67 | 51 | 16 |
| Hudson | 23,098 | 35 | 28 | 7 |
| Huron | 7,285 | 16 | 12 | 4 |
| Indian Hill | 6,047 | 25 | 20 | 5 |
| Ironton | 11,307 | 22 | 17 | 5 |
| Jackson | 6,135 | 22 | 16 | 6 |
| Jackson Center | 1,450 | 2 | 2 | 0 |
| Jackson Township, Mahoning County | 2,257 | 5 | 5 | 0 |
| Jackson Township, Montgomery County | 3,844 | 5 | 5 | 0 |
| Jackson Township, Starke County | 40,989 | 50 | 41 | 9 |
| Jamestown | 1,855 | 4 | 4 | 0 |
| Jefferson | 3,399 | 7 | 6 | 1 |
| Jewett | 765 | 1 | 1 | 0 |
| Johnstown | 4,086 | 15 | 10 | 5 |
| Junction City | 843 | 1 | 1 | 0 |
| Kalida | 1,263 | 1 | 1 | 0 |
| Kent | 27,964 | 56 | 42 | 14 |
| Kenton | 8,021 | 16 | 16 | 0 |
| Kettering | 53,288 | 111 | 80 | 31 |
| Kirtland | 7,439 | 15 | 9 | 6 |
| Kirtland Hills | 812 | 11 | 10 | 1 |
| Lagrange | 2,031 | 6 | 6 | 0 |
| Lake Township | 7,446 | 15 | 14 | 1 |
| Lakewood | 50,098 | 120 | 93 | 27 |
| Lancaster | 37,143 | 83 | 65 | 18 |
| Lawrence Township | 8,483 | 6 | 6 | 0 |
| Lebanon | 20,944 | 36 | 27 | 9 |
| Leipsic | 2,166 | 4 | 4 | 0 |
| Lexington | 4,086 | 13 | 9 | 4 |
| Liberty Township | 11,749 | 24 | 19 | 5 |
| Lima | 37,437 | 97 | 77 | 20 |
| Lisbon | 2,969 | 10 | 6 | 4 |
| Lithopolis | 1,133 | 3 | 3 | 0 |
| Liverpool Township | 4,129 | 4 | 4 | 0 |
| Lockland | 3,450 | 15 | 14 | 1 |
| Logan | 7,489 | 19 | 15 | 4 |
| London | 9,679 | 21 | 17 | 4 |
| Lorain | 70,410 | 116 | 93 | 23 |
| Lordstown | 3,509 | 13 | 9 | 4 |
| Loudonville | 3,083 | 9 | 5 | 4 |
| Louisville | 9,516 | 11 | 8 | 3 |
| Loveland | 11,736 | 19 | 17 | 2 |
| Lowellville | 1,132 | 3 | 3 | 0 |
| Luckey | 988 | 1 | 1 | 0 |
| Lyndhurst | 13,702 | 37 | 28 | 9 |
| Madeira | 8,521 | 13 | 12 | 1 |
| Madison | 3,124 | 5 | 5 | 0 |
| Madison Township, Franklin County | 18,389 | 16 | 14 | 2 |
| Madison Township, Lake County | 17,005 | 20 | 16 | 4 |
| Magnolia | 923 | 2 | 2 | 0 |

**Table 78. Full-time Law Enforcement Employees, by State, by City, 2009—*Continued***

(Number.)

| State/city | Population | Total law enforcement employees | Total officers | Total civilians |
|---|---|---|---|---|
| Maineville | 1,050 | 2 | 2 | 0 |
| Mansfield | 49,349 | 125 | 90 | 35 |
| Maple Heights | 23,411 | 61 | 43 | 18 |
| Marblehead | 829 | 4 | 4 | 0 |
| Mariemont | 3,161 | 10 | 9 | 1 |
| Marietta | 14,272 | 36 | 30 | 6 |
| Marion | 35,683 | 77 | 62 | 15 |
| Marlboro Township | 4,753 | 4 | 3 | 1 |
| Marysville | 18,447 | 37 | 31 | 6 |
| Mason | 30,624 | 50 | 42 | 8 |
| Massillon | 32,736 | 49 | 47 | 2 |
| Matamoras | 902 | 1 | 1 | 0 |
| Maumee | 13,729 | 60 | 45 | 15 |
| Mayfield Heights | 17,568 | 46 | 37 | 9 |
| Mayfield Village | 3,089 | 24 | 16 | 8 |
| McArthur | 2,036 | 4 | 4 | 0 |
| McClure | 708 | 1 | 1 | 0 |
| McConnelsville | 1,551 | 4 | 4 | 0 |
| Mechanicsburg | 1,694 | 3 | 3 | 0 |
| Medina | 26,088 | 49 | 37 | 12 |
| Medina Township | 9,023 | 9 | 8 | 1 |
| Mentor | 51,993 | 116 | 82 | 34 |
| Mentor-on-the-Lake | 8,306 | 15 | 10 | 5 |
| Miamisburg | 19,819 | 44 | 40 | 4 |
| Miami Township, Clermont County | 40,027 | 45 | 42 | 3 |
| Miami Township, Montgomery County | 25,016 | 45 | 38 | 7 |
| Middlefield | 2,392 | 13 | 10 | 3 |
| Middletown | 51,401 | 114 | 79 | 35 |
| Midvale | 587 | 1 | 1 | 0 |
| Milford | 6,334 | 16 | 14 | 2 |
| Millersburg | 3,636 | 10 | 10 | 0 |
| Millersport | 928 | 1 | 1 | 0 |
| Milton Township | 2,827 | 4 | 4 | 0 |
| Minerva | 3,903 | 14 | 9 | 5 |
| Mingo Junction | 3,288 | 10 | 9 | 1 |
| Minster | 2,778 | 7 | 6 | 1 |
| Monroe | 15,319 | 32 | 26 | 6 |
| Monroeville | 1,336 | 4 | 4 | 0 |
| Montgomery | 10,497 | 24 | 21 | 3 |
| Montpelier | 3,983 | 9 | 8 | 1 |
| Montville Township | 6,517 | 11 | 11 | 0 |
| Moraine | 6,421 | 39 | 32 | 7 |
| Moreland Hills | 3,039 | 15 | 14 | 1 |
| Mount Eaton | 239 | 5 | 5 | 0 |
| Mount Gilead | 3,593 | 7 | 7 | 0 |
| Mount Healthy | 6,044 | 11 | 10 | 1 |
| Mount Orab | 2,781 | 8 | 8 | 0 |
| Mount Sterling | 1,827 | 9 | 5 | 4 |
| Mount Vernon | 16,074 | 32 | 29 | 3 |
| Munroe Falls | 5,149 | 8 | 8 | 0 |
| Napoleon | 8,764 | 22 | 16 | 6 |
| Navarre | 1,892 | 5 | 5 | 0 |
| Nelsonville | 5,390 | 8 | 8 | 0 |
| New Albany | 7,546 | 22 | 16 | 6 |
| Newark | 47,338 | 102 | 81 | 21 |
| New Boston | 2,151 | 14 | 10 | 4 |
| New Bremen | 3,087 | 6 | 6 | 0 |
| Newcomerstown | 3,882 | 10 | 6 | 4 |
| New Concord | 2,582 | 4 | 4 | 0 |
| New Franklin | 14,986 | 18 | 13 | 5 |
| New London | 2,586 | 4 | 4 | 0 |
| New Middletown | 1,539 | 3 | 3 | 0 |
| New Philadelphia | 17,342 | 26 | 22 | 4 |
| New Richmond | 2,544 | 3 | 3 | 0 |
| Newton Falls | 4,603 | 11 | 7 | 4 |
| Newtown | 4,148 | 8 | 7 | 1 |
| New Washington | 903 | 2 | 2 | 0 |
| Niles | 19,095 | 41 | 35 | 6 |
| North Baltimore | 3,339 | 11 | 5 | 6 |
| North Canton | 16,929 | 32 | 24 | 8 |
| North College Hill | 9,496 | 15 | 14 | 1 |
| Northfield | 3,635 | 10 | 10 | 0 |
| North Kingsville | 2,555 | 4 | 4 | 0 |
| North Olmsted | 31,025 | 63 | 49 | 14 |
| North Ridgeville | 28,875 | 46 | 38 | 8 |
| North Royalton | 29,402 | 61 | 39 | 22 |
| Northwood | 5,524 | 27 | 21 | 6 |
| Norton | 11,465 | 21 | 14 | 7 |
| Norwalk | 16,652 | 30 | 23 | 7 |
| Norwood | 20,207 | 62 | 54 | 8 |
| Oak Harbor | 2,790 | 6 | 4 | 2 |
| Oak Hill | 1,606 | 2 | 2 | 0 |
| Oakwood, Montgomery County | 8,360 | 38 | 32 | 6 |
| Oakwood, Paulding County | 552 | 1 | 1 | 0 |
| Oakwood Village | 3,725 | 13 | 11 | 2 |
| Oberlin | 8,404 | 23 | 17 | 6 |
| Olmsted Falls | 8,183 | 16 | 10 | 6 |
| Olmsted Township | 10,029 | 18 | 16 | 2 |
| Ontario | 5,193 | 23 | 19 | 4 |
| Orange Village | 3,249 | 15 | 14 | 1 |
| Oregon | 18,872 | 60 | 46 | 14 |
| Orrville | 8,367 | 19 | 14 | 5 |
| Orwell | 1,466 | 5 | 5 | 0 |
| Ottawa | 4,390 | 8 | 8 | 0 |
| Owensville | 850 | 1 | 1 | 0 |
| Oxford | 22,995 | 39 | 28 | 11 |
| Oxford Township | 2,695 | 3 | 3 | 0 |
| Painesville | 18,569 | 43 | 39 | 4 |
| Parma | 77,148 | 149 | 91 | 58 |
| Parma Heights | 19,559 | 37 | 31 | 6 |
| Pataskala | 12,967 | 16 | 15 | 1 |
| Paulding | 3,331 | 5 | 4 | 1 |
| Payne | 1,145 | 1 | 1 | 0 |
| Peebles | 1,838 | 1 | 1 | 0 |
| Peninsula | 699 | 3 | 3 | 0 |
| Pepper Pike | 5,681 | 27 | 20 | 7 |
| Perkins Township | 12,820 | 25 | 19 | 6 |
| Perrysburg | 17,051 | 43 | 32 | 11 |
| Perry Township, Allen County | 3,580 | 1 | 1 | 0 |
| Perry Township, Columbiana County | 4,578 | 5 | 5 | 0 |
| Perry Township, Franklin County | 3,653 | 11 | 10 | 1 |
| Perry Township, Starke County | 28,005 | 29 | 23 | 6 |
| Pickerington | 18,672 | 36 | 26 | 10 |
| Pierce Township | 11,177 | 17 | 17 | 0 |
| Pioneer | 1,374 | 4 | 4 | 0 |
| Piqua | 20,559 | 38 | 32 | 6 |
| Plain City | 3,629 | 8 | 8 | 0 |
| Poland Township | 11,014 | 13 | 11 | 2 |
| Poland Village | 2,640 | 5 | 5 | 0 |
| Port Clinton | 6,108 | 18 | 17 | 1 |
| Portsmouth | 20,235 | 45 | 41 | 4 |
| Powell | 13,869 | 20 | 18 | 2 |
| Powhatan Point | 1,647 | 3 | 3 | 0 |
| Ravenna | 11,335 | 33 | 24 | 9 |
| Reading | 10,446 | 25 | 21 | 4 |
| Reminderville | 2,799 | 8 | 8 | 0 |
| Republic | 573 | 1 | 1 | 0 |
| Reynoldsburg | 33,825 | 68 | 54 | 14 |
| Richfield | 3,598 | 24 | 17 | 7 |
| Richland Township | 9,285 | 2 | 2 | 0 |
| Richmond Heights | 10,093 | 23 | 17 | 6 |
| Richwood | 2,176 | 5 | 5 | 0 |
| Rio Grande | 866 | 1 | 1 | 0 |
| Rittman | 6,260 | 11 | 8 | 3 |
| Riverside | 25,147 | 29 | 28 | 1 |
| Roaming Shores Village | 1,190 | 2 | 2 | 0 |
| Rockford | 1,103 | 2 | 2 | 0 |
| Rocky Ridge | 383 | 1 | 1 | 0 |
| Roseville | 1,893 | 3 | 3 | 0 |
| Ross Township | 8,026 | 2 | 2 | 0 |
| Russell Township | 5,575 | 9 | 8 | 1 |
| Russells Point | 1,509 | 3 | 3 | 0 |
| Russia | 621 | 1 | 1 | 0 |
| Sabina | 2,783 | 5 | 5 | 0 |
| Salem | 11,709 | 22 | 21 | 1 |
| Saline Township | 1,331 | 5 | 5 | 0 |
| Sandusky | 25,461 | 61 | 52 | 9 |
| Sebring | 4,484 | 9 | 6 | 3 |
| Seven Hills | 11,565 | 19 | 18 | 1 |
| Seville | 2,419 | 7 | 7 | 0 |
| Shadyside | 3,508 | 6 | 5 | 1 |
| Shaker Heights | 26,159 | 91 | 67 | 24 |

**Table 78. Full-time Law Enforcement Employees, by State, by City, 2009—*Continued***

(Number.)

| State/city | Population | Total law enforcement employees | Total officers | Total civilians |
|---|---|---|---|---|
| Sharonville | 13,334 | 47 | 37 | 10 |
| Shawnee Township | 8,775 | 17 | 11 | 6 |
| Sheffield Lake | 8,858 | 13 | 10 | 3 |
| Shelby | 9,256 | 19 | 15 | 4 |
| Sidney | 19,899 | 52 | 40 | 12 |
| Smith Township | 4,792 | 5 | 5 | 0 |
| Smithville | 1,294 | 3 | 3 | 0 |
| Solon | 21,870 | 76 | 46 | 30 |
| Somerset | 1,557 | 2 | 2 | 0 |
| South Charleston | 1,766 | 2 | 2 | 0 |
| South Euclid | 20,970 | 53 | 40 | 13 |
| South Russell | 3,902 | 9 | 9 | 0 |
| Spencerville | 2,152 | 4 | 4 | 0 |
| Springboro | 18,209 | 28 | 24 | 4 |
| Springdale | 10,370 | 46 | 38 | 8 |
| Springfield | 61,881 | 149 | 129 | 20 |
| Springfield Township, Hamilton County | 40,051 | 57 | 51 | 6 |
| Springfield Township, Mahoning County | 5,956 | 8 | 8 | 0 |
| Springfield Township, Summit County | 15,263 | 25 | 22 | 3 |
| St. Bernard | 4,596 | 18 | 17 | 1 |
| St. Clairsville | 5,045 | 14 | 10 | 4 |
| St. Clair Township | 7,596 | 12 | 11 | 1 |
| Steubenville | 18,710 | 46 | 40 | 6 |
| St. Henry | 2,421 | 2 | 2 | 0 |
| St. Marys | 8,116 | 20 | 15 | 5 |
| Stow | 34,067 | 51 | 41 | 10 |
| St. Paris | 1,960 | 3 | 3 | 0 |
| Strasburg | 2,719 | 5 | 5 | 0 |
| Streetsboro | 14,749 | 34 | 26 | 8 |
| Strongsville | 42,478 | 97 | 77 | 20 |
| Struthers | 10,629 | 20 | 16 | 4 |
| Sugarcreek | 2,194 | 5 | 5 | 0 |
| Sugarcreek Township | 7,005 | 24 | 17 | 7 |
| Sunbury | 3,465 | 12 | 11 | 1 |
| Swanton | 3,676 | 6 | 5 | 1 |
| Sycamore | 862 | 1 | 1 | 0 |
| Sylvania | 19,203 | 41 | 34 | 7 |
| Sylvania Township | 26,142 | 61 | 45 | 16 |
| Tallmadge | 17,390 | 27 | 24 | 3 |
| Terrace Park | 2,215 | 6 | 6 | 0 |
| Tipp City | 9,255 | 22 | 19 | 3 |
| Toledo | 291,066 | 728 | 604 | 124 |
| Toronto | 5,175 | 10 | 10 | 0 |
| Trenton | 11,122 | 23 | 14 | 9 |
| Trotwood | 25,894 | 39 | 36 | 3 |
| Troy | 21,965 | 47 | 42 | 5 |
| Twinsburg | 17,432 | 45 | 32 | 13 |
| Uhrichsville | 5,501 | 8 | 8 | 0 |
| Union City | 1,637 | 5 | 5 | 0 |
| Uniontown | 2,849 | 10 | 8 | 2 |
| Union Township, Clermont County | 44,511 | 71 | 57 | 14 |
| Union Township, Licking County | 3,877 | 2 | 2 | 0 |
| University Heights | 12,353 | 36 | 30 | 6 |
| Upper Arlington | 31,686 | 63 | 50 | 13 |
| Upper Sandusky | 6,343 | 17 | 13 | 4 |
| Urbana | 11,424 | 22 | 22 | 0 |
| Valley View, Cuyahoga County | 1,994 | 20 | 18 | 2 |
| Valleyview, Franklin County | 566 | 1 | 1 | 0 |
| Van Wert | 10,139 | 29 | 21 | 8 |
| Vermilion | 10,735 | 24 | 19 | 5 |
| Wadsworth | 20,943 | 39 | 30 | 9 |
| Waite Hill | 567 | 6 | 6 | 0 |
| Walbridge | 3,088 | 6 | 5 | 1 |
| Walton Hills | 2,265 | 23 | 15 | 8 |
| Wapakoneta | 9,427 | 17 | 12 | 5 |
| Warren | 43,331 | 78 | 61 | 17 |
| Warrensville Heights | 13,465 | 47 | 34 | 13 |
| Warren Township | 5,968 | 8 | 8 | 0 |
| Washington Court House | 13,659 | 27 | 22 | 5 |
| Waterville Township | 5,793 | 3 | 3 | 0 |
| Wauseon | 7,261 | 18 | 14 | 4 |
| Waynesville | 3,112 | 3 | 2 | 1 |
| Weathersfield | 8,095 | 8 | 8 | 0 |
| Wellington | 4,718 | 8 | 6 | 2 |
| Wellston | 5,923 | 16 | 12 | 4 |
| Wells Township | 2,817 | 4 | 4 | 0 |
| Wellsville | 3,867 | 9 | 9 | 0 |
| West Alexandria | 1,289 | 3 | 3 | 0 |
| West Carrollton | 12,652 | 30 | 24 | 6 |
| West Chester Township | 56,060 | 115 | 88 | 27 |
| Westerville | 36,319 | 87 | 73 | 14 |
| Westfield Center | 1,181 | 1 | 1 | 0 |
| West Jefferson | 4,252 | 14 | 11 | 3 |
| West Lafayette | 2,462 | 5 | 5 | 0 |
| Westlake | 30,413 | 72 | 54 | 18 |
| Whitehall | 18,071 | 59 | 47 | 12 |
| Wickliffe | 12,930 | 40 | 30 | 10 |
| Willard | 6,640 | 20 | 16 | 4 |
| Williamsburg | 2,385 | 6 | 6 | 0 |
| Willoughby | 22,555 | 59 | 44 | 15 |
| Willoughby Hills | 8,535 | 24 | 18 | 6 |
| Willowick | 13,661 | 35 | 25 | 10 |
| Wilmington | 12,680 | 25 | 23 | 2 |
| Winchester | 1,083 | 3 | 3 | 0 |
| Windham | 2,715 | 7 | 4 | 3 |
| Wintersville | 3,873 | 9 | 8 | 1 |
| Woodlawn | 2,628 | 15 | 15 | 0 |
| Woodsfield | 2,406 | 6 | 6 | 0 |
| Woodville | 1,971 | 5 | 5 | 0 |
| Wooster | 26,318 | 41 | 36 | 5 |
| Worthington | 13,230 | 46 | 33 | 13 |
| Wyoming | 8,364 | 20 | 18 | 2 |
| Xenia | 27,718 | 66 | 43 | 23 |
| Yellow Springs | 3,391 | 10 | 8 | 2 |
| Youngstown | 72,008 | 211 | 169 | 42 |
| Zanesville | 25,080 | 93 | 56 | 37 |
| **OKLAHOMA** | | | | |
| Achille | 537 | 5 | 4 | 1 |
| Ada | 16,807 | 43 | 34 | 9 |
| Allen | 998 | 2 | 2 | 0 |
| Altus | 18,664 | 66 | 48 | 18 |
| Alva | 4,805 | 11 | 9 | 2 |
| Anadarko | 6,289 | 21 | 14 | 7 |
| Antlers | 2,478 | 11 | 6 | 5 |
| Apache | 1,528 | 4 | 4 | 0 |
| Ardmore | 24,933 | 52 | 40 | 12 |
| Arkoma | 2,175 | 6 | 3 | 3 |
| Atoka | 3,115 | 16 | 15 | 1 |
| Bartlesville | 36,045 | 80 | 54 | 26 |
| Beaver | 1,352 | 2 | 2 | 0 |
| Beggs | 1,354 | 10 | 4 | 6 |
| Bethany | 19,667 | 39 | 29 | 10 |
| Bixby | 21,681 | 34 | 24 | 10 |
| Blackwell | 7,092 | 22 | 15 | 7 |
| Blanchard | 6,825 | 19 | 13 | 6 |
| Boise City | 1,158 | 2 | 2 | 0 |
| Boley | 1,083 | 1 | 1 | 0 |
| Bristow | 4,395 | 13 | 9 | 4 |
| Broken Arrow | 94,415 | 164 | 122 | 42 |
| Broken Bow | 4,136 | 17 | 13 | 4 |
| Caddo | 994 | 4 | 3 | 1 |
| Calera | 1,841 | 10 | 9 | 1 |
| Calumet | 532 | 3 | 2 | 1 |
| Caney | 214 | 4 | 3 | 1 |
| Carnegie | 1,534 | 8 | 4 | 4 |
| Catoosa | 6,748 | 15 | 14 | 1 |
| Chandler | 2,820 | 11 | 7 | 4 |
| Checotah | 3,468 | 13 | 10 | 3 |
| Chelsea | 2,237 | 8 | 3 | 5 |
| Cherokee | 1,418 | 6 | 2 | 4 |
| Chickasha | 17,195 | 39 | 28 | 11 |
| Choctaw | 11,579 | 13 | 12 | 1 |
| Chouteau | 2,021 | 9 | 8 | 1 |
| Claremore | 17,635 | 54 | 38 | 16 |
| Clayton | 728 | 7 | 3 | 4 |
| Cleveland | 3,123 | 5 | 5 | 0 |
| Clinton | 8,761 | 29 | 19 | 10 |
| Coalgate | 1,861 | 6 | 6 | 0 |
| Colbert | 1,129 | 4 | 3 | 1 |
| Collinsville | 5,150 | 16 | 10 | 6 |
| Comanche | 1,519 | 3 | 3 | 0 |
| Cordell | 2,936 | 10 | 7 | 3 |

**Table 78. Full-time Law Enforcement Employees, by State, by City, 2009—*Continued***

(Number.)

| State/city | Population | Total law enforcement employees | Total officers | Total civilians |
|---|---|---|---|---|
| Coweta | 9,282 | 24 | 18 | 6 |
| Crescent | 1,415 | 4 | 4 | 0 |
| Cushing | 8,818 | 21 | 15 | 6 |
| Davenport | 873 | 2 | 2 | 0 |
| Davis | 2,640 | 11 | 9 | 2 |
| Del City | 22,060 | 41 | 29 | 12 |
| Dewar | 896 | 2 | 2 | 0 |
| Dewey | 3,324 | 12 | 10 | 2 |
| Dibble | 648 | 5 | 4 | 1 |
| Drumright | 2,881 | 6 | 6 | 0 |
| Duncan | 22,630 | 50 | 43 | 7 |
| Durant | 16,726 | 37 | 34 | 3 |
| Edmond | 80,889 | 144 | 114 | 30 |
| Elk City | 11,408 | 37 | 25 | 12 |
| El Reno | 16,583 | 42 | 28 | 14 |
| Enid | 47,448 | 114 | 97 | 17 |
| Eufaula | 2,767 | 16 | 12 | 4 |
| Fairfax | 1,443 | 6 | 3 | 3 |
| Fairview | 2,503 | 8 | 5 | 3 |
| Fletcher | 1,084 | 1 | 1 | 0 |
| Forest Park | 1,190 | 3 | 3 | 0 |
| Fort Gibson | 4,404 | 12 | 8 | 4 |
| Frederick | 3,794 | 13 | 11 | 2 |
| Geary | 1,234 | 10 | 6 | 4 |
| Glenpool | 10,097 | 27 | 18 | 9 |
| Goodwell | 1,182 | 4 | 4 | 0 |
| Grandfield | 925 | 1 | 1 | 0 |
| Grove | 6,476 | 33 | 20 | 13 |
| Guthrie | 11,175 | 29 | 22 | 7 |
| Guymon | 10,721 | 26 | 19 | 7 |
| Haileyville | 905 | 4 | 3 | 1 |
| Harrah | 5,259 | 9 | 9 | 0 |
| Hartshorne | 2,077 | 5 | 5 | 0 |
| Haskell | 1,989 | 7 | 6 | 1 |
| Healdton | 2,782 | 5 | 3 | 2 |
| Heavener | 3,236 | 13 | 8 | 5 |
| Henryetta | 6,016 | 17 | 13 | 4 |
| Hinton | 2,129 | 4 | 4 | 0 |
| Hobart | 3,595 | 15 | 9 | 6 |
| Holdenville | 5,388 | 14 | 9 | 5 |
| Hollis | 1,931 | 10 | 5 | 5 |
| Hominy | 3,613 | 11 | 6 | 5 |
| Hooker | 1,715 | 3 | 3 | 0 |
| Howe | 718 | 3 | 2 | 1 |
| Hugo | 5,371 | 19 | 17 | 2 |
| Hulbert | 539 | 3 | 3 | 0 |
| Hydro | 1,004 | 2 | 2 | 0 |
| Idabel | 6,831 | 25 | 19 | 6 |
| Jay | 3,057 | 12 | 8 | 4 |
| Jenks | 16,438 | 22 | 16 | 6 |
| Jones | 2,723 | 5 | 5 | 0 |
| Kaw City | 367 | 1 | 1 | 0 |
| Kiefer | 1,646 | 5 | 4 | 1 |
| Kingfisher | 4,357 | 12 | 10 | 2 |
| Kingston | 1,599 | 7 | 7 | 0 |
| Kiowa | 706 | 8 | 7 | 1 |
| Krebs | 2,139 | 9 | 7 | 2 |
| Lawton | 89,835 | 223 | 162 | 61 |
| Lexington | 2,117 | 11 | 6 | 5 |
| Lindsay | 2,913 | 14 | 8 | 6 |
| Locust Grove | 1,596 | 10 | 6 | 4 |
| Lone Grove | 5,356 | 9 | 6 | 3 |
| Luther | 1,147 | 4 | 4 | 0 |
| Madlll | 3,808 | 12 | 11 | 1 |
| Mangum | 2,689 | 10 | 5 | 5 |
| Mannford | 2,878 | 10 | 8 | 2 |
| Marietta | 2,540 | 6 | 5 | 1 |
| Marlow | 4,601 | 11 | 10 | 1 |
| Maysville | 1,300 | 4 | 3 | 1 |
| McAlester | 18,459 | 59 | 46 | 13 |
| McLoud | 4,448 | 11 | 6 | 5 |
| Medicine Park | 379 | 3 | 2 | 1 |
| Meeker | 982 | 4 | 4 | 0 |
| Miami | 12,953 | 42 | 30 | 12 |
| Midwest City | 56,631 | 120 | 93 | 27 |
| Minco | 1,817 | 5 | 5 | 0 |
| Moore | 54,059 | 80 | 75 | 5 |
| Mooreland | 1,256 | 2 | 2 | 0 |
| Morris | 1,311 | 3 | 3 | 0 |
| Mountain View | 777 | 3 | 3 | 0 |
| Muldrow | 3,158 | 10 | 6 | 4 |
| Muskogee | 40,197 | 113 | 90 | 23 |
| Mustang | 18,314 | 27 | 20 | 7 |
| Newcastle | 7,474 | 21 | 16 | 5 |
| Newkirk | 2,112 | 7 | 6 | 1 |
| Nichols Hills | 4,031 | 21 | 16 | 5 |
| Nicoma Park | 2,398 | 6 | 6 | 0 |
| Noble | 5,875 | 16 | 11 | 5 |
| Norman | 108,152 | 212 | 159 | 53 |
| Nowata | 3,997 | 9 | 7 | 2 |
| Oilton | 1,125 | 3 | 3 | 0 |
| Okemah | 2,897 | 11 | 7 | 4 |
| Oklahoma City | 556,939 | 1,297 | 1,048 | 249 |
| Okmulgee | 12,595 | 29 | 23 | 6 |
| Oologah | 1,158 | 4 | 4 | 0 |
| Owasso | 28,631 | 50 | 46 | 4 |
| Pauls Valley | 6,106 | 19 | 13 | 6 |
| Pawhuska | 3,403 | 10 | 6 | 4 |
| Pawnee | 2,140 | 5 | 5 | 0 |
| Perkins | 2,412 | 7 | 7 | 0 |
| Perry | 5,041 | 21 | 15 | 6 |
| Piedmont | 5,756 | 13 | 10 | 3 |
| Pocola | 4,518 | 9 | 5 | 4 |
| Ponca City | 24,359 | 82 | 55 | 27 |
| Porum | 736 | 2 | 2 | 0 |
| Poteau | 8,287 | 34 | 26 | 8 |
| Prague | 2,126 | 11 | 6 | 5 |
| Pryor | 9,345 | 31 | 23 | 8 |
| Purcell | 6,194 | 21 | 20 | 1 |
| Ringling | 1,035 | 2 | 2 | 0 |
| Roland | 3,453 | 7 | 5 | 2 |
| Rush Springs | 1,352 | 5 | 4 | 1 |
| Sallisaw | 8,823 | 32 | 24 | 8 |
| Sand Springs | 18,602 | 43 | 30 | 13 |
| Sapulpa | 21,288 | 59 | 47 | 12 |
| Sayre | 4,413 | 14 | 8 | 6 |
| Seminole | 6,797 | 16 | 12 | 4 |
| Shawnee | 30,724 | 74 | 55 | 19 |
| Skiatook | 6,973 | 26 | 19 | 7 |
| Snyder | 1,365 | 3 | 3 | 0 |
| South Coffeyville | 787 | 3 | 3 | 0 |
| Spencer | 4,056 | 9 | 8 | 1 |
| Spiro | 2,334 | 4 | 4 | 0 |
| Stigler | 2,876 | 14 | 9 | 5 |
| Stillwater | 48,690 | 109 | 75 | 34 |
| Stilwell | 3,519 | 18 | 13 | 5 |
| Stonewall | 496 | 2 | 2 | 0 |
| Stratford | 1,491 | 3 | 3 | 0 |
| Stringtown | 424 | 4 | 4 | 0 |
| Stroud | 2,721 | 13 | 8 | 5 |
| Sulphur | 4,844 | 12 | 11 | 1 |
| Tahlequah | 16,865 | 38 | 30 | 8 |
| Talihina | 1,237 | 10 | 6 | 4 |
| Tecumseh | 6,732 | 12 | 11 | 1 |
| The Village | 9,728 | 26 | 22 | 4 |
| Tishomingo | 3,151 | 7 | 6 | 1 |
| Tonkawa | 3,121 | 12 | 7 | 5 |
| Tryon | 448 | 1 | 1 | 0 |
| Tulsa | 384,851 | 911 | 812 | 99 |
| Tushka | 373 | 3 | 3 | 0 |
| Tuttle | 6,265 | 17 | 10 | 7 |
| Valliant | 740 | 6 | 3 | 3 |
| Verdigris | 3,126 | 3 | 3 | 0 |
| Vian | 1,447 | 3 | 3 | 0 |
| Vinita | 6,052 | 21 | 15 | 6 |
| Wagoner | 8,122 | 19 | 13 | 6 |
| Walters | 2,408 | 4 | 4 | 0 |
| Warner | 1,449 | 4 | 4 | 0 |
| Warr Acres | 9,394 | 26 | 20 | 6 |
| Washington | 555 | 2 | 1 | 1 |
| Watonga | 5,818 | 11 | 8 | 3 |
| Waukomis | 1,209 | 2 | 2 | 0 |

**Table 78. Full-time Law Enforcement Employees, by State, by City, 2009—*Continued***

(Number.)

| State/city | Population | Total law enforcement employees | Total officers | Total civilians |
|---|---|---|---|---|
| Waurika | 1,802 | 2 | 2 | 0 |
| Waynoka | 892 | 4 | 4 | 0 |
| Weatherford | 10,224 | 32 | 20 | 12 |
| Weleetka | 917 | 8 | 4 | 4 |
| Westville | 1,643 | 10 | 6 | 4 |
| Wetumka | 1,400 | 5 | 5 | 0 |
| Wewoka | 3,289 | 13 | 9 | 4 |
| Wilburton | 2,885 | 7 | 6 | 1 |
| Wilson | 1,640 | 4 | 4 | 0 |
| Woodward | 12,355 | 40 | 25 | 15 |
| Wright City | 785 | 2 | 2 | 0 |
| Wynnewood | 2,280 | 5 | 4 | 1 |
| Yale | 1,359 | 7 | 4 | 3 |
| Yukon | 23,058 | 55 | 36 | 19 |
| **OREGON** | | | | |
| Albany | 48,933 | 95 | 63 | 32 |
| Amity | 1,466 | 2 | 2 | 0 |
| Ashland | 21,611 | 35 | 28 | 7 |
| Astoria | 9,859 | 26 | 17 | 9 |
| Athena | 1,180 | 2 | 2 | 0 |
| Aumsville | 3,673 | 7 | 6 | 1 |
| Aurora | 1,053 | 9 | 8 | 1 |
| Baker City | 9,367 | 18 | 15 | 3 |
| Bandon | 3,299 | 7 | 6 | 1 |
| Beaverton | 93,221 | 165 | 134 | 31 |
| Bend | 80,550 | 113 | 88 | 25 |
| Black Butte | | 7 | 6 | 1 |
| Boardman | 2,919 | 7 | 6 | 1 |
| Brookings | 6,292 | 20 | 13 | 7 |
| Burns | 2,622 | 5 | 4 | 1 |
| Canby | 15,982 | 30 | 25 | 5 |
| Cannon Beach | 1,741 | 9 | 8 | 1 |
| Carlton | 1,699 | 3 | 3 | 0 |
| Central Point | 16,971 | 28 | 22 | 6 |
| Clatskanie | 1,650 | 6 | 5 | 1 |
| Coburg | 1,080 | 2 | 2 | 0 |
| Columbia City | 2,013 | 1 | 1 | 0 |
| Condon | 659 | 2 | 1 | 1 |
| Coos Bay | 15,703 | 37 | 24 | 13 |
| Coquille | 4,110 | 8 | 7 | 1 |
| Cornelius | 11,676 | 15 | 14 | 1 |
| Corvallis | 51,302 | 80 | 53 | 27 |
| Cottage Grove | 9,200 | 27 | 16 | 11 |
| Dallas | 16,317 | 31 | 20 | 11 |
| Eagle Point | 8,787 | 15 | 13 | 2 |
| Elgin | 1,652 | 4 | 3 | 1 |
| Enterprise | 1,691 | 4 | 4 | 0 |
| Eugene | 151,383 | 324 | 191 | 133 |
| Fairview | 10,080 | 14 | 13 | 1 |
| Florence | 8,867 | 23 | 14 | 9 |
| Forest Grove | 21,333 | 33 | 29 | 4 |
| Gearhart | 1,202 | 3 | 3 | 0 |
| Gervais | 2,453 | 4 | 3 | 1 |
| Gladstone | 12,152 | 17 | 15 | 2 |
| Gold Beach | 1,815 | 5 | 4 | 1 |
| Grants Pass | 33,670 | 69 | 42 | 27 |
| Gresham | 102,463 | 158 | 124 | 34 |
| Hermiston | 15,544 | 35 | 24 | 11 |
| Hillsboro | 96,563 | 170 | 126 | 44 |
| Hines | 1,384 | 3 | 3 | 0 |
| Hood River | 6,967 | 16 | 14 | 2 |
| Hubbard | 2,850 | 5 | 4 | 1 |
| Independence | 9,822 | 16 | 14 | 2 |
| Jacksonville | 2,177 | 6 | 5 | 1 |
| John Day | 1,482 | 9 | 4 | 5 |
| Junction City | 5,657 | 16 | 10 | 6 |
| Keizer | 36,275 | 48 | 40 | 8 |
| King City | 2,989 | 6 | 5 | 1 |
| Klamath Falls | 20,358 | 45 | 39 | 6 |
| La Grande | 12,697 | 33 | 18 | 15 |
| Lake Oswego | 37,100 | 73 | 43 | 30 |
| Lakeview | 2,423 | 5 | 5 | 0 |
| Lebanon | 15,665 | 38 | 26 | 12 |
| Lincoln City | 8,121 | 38 | 26 | 12 |
| Madras | 6,093 | 13 | 11 | 2 |
| Malin | 616 | 2 | 1 | 1 |
| Manzanita | 624 | 3 | 3 | 0 |
| McMinnville | 31,730 | 43 | 33 | 10 |
| Medford | 74,042 | 155 | 103 | 52 |
| Milton-Freewater | 6,415 | 17 | 11 | 6 |
| Milwaukie | 20,732 | 41 | 37 | 4 |
| Molalla | 7,451 | 15 | 12 | 3 |
| Monmouth | 9,836 | 15 | 13 | 2 |
| Mount Angel | 3,511 | 7 | 4 | 3 |
| Myrtle Creek | 3,489 | 9 | 7 | 2 |
| Myrtle Point | 2,442 | 5 | 5 | 0 |
| Newberg-Dundee | 26,669 | 35 | 22 | 13 |
| Newport | 9,993 | 23 | 19 | 4 |
| North Bend | 9,648 | 23 | 16 | 7 |
| North Plains | 1,930 | 2 | 2 | 0 |
| Nyssa | 2,981 | 7 | 7 | 0 |
| Oakridge | 3,195 | 12 | 6 | 6 |
| Ontario | 10,986 | 31 | 24 | 7 |
| Oregon City | 31,976 | 46 | 38 | 8 |
| Pendleton | 16,378 | 24 | 21 | 3 |
| Philomath | 4,558 | 10 | 9 | 1 |
| Phoenix | 4,429 | 11 | 9 | 2 |
| Pilot Rock | 1,512 | 3 | 3 | 0 |
| Portland | 560,908 | 1,242 | 957 | 285 |
| Prairie City | 882 | 1 | 1 | 0 |
| Prineville | 10,293 | 26 | 16 | 10 |
| Rainier | 1,820 | 6 | 5 | 1 |
| Redmond | 25,856 | 52 | 37 | 15 |
| Reedsport | 4,195 | 15 | 10 | 5 |
| Rockaway Beach | 1,378 | 3 | 3 | 0 |
| Rogue River | 1,942 | 5 | 4 | 1 |
| Roseburg | 20,741 | 42 | 37 | 5 |
| Salem | 155,329 | 349 | 206 | 143 |
| Sandy | 9,282 | 15 | 12 | 3 |
| Scappoose | 6,543 | 11 | 10 | 1 |
| Seaside | 6,300 | 29 | 20 | 9 |
| Shady Cove | 2,647 | 6 | 4 | 2 |
| Sherwood | 18,111 | 27 | 23 | 4 |
| Silverton | 9,895 | 16 | 13 | 3 |
| Springfield | 57,653 | 108 | 70 | 38 |
| Stanfield | 1,920 | 4 | 4 | 0 |
| Stayton | 7,375 | 18 | 15 | 3 |
| St. Helens | 12,804 | 20 | 19 | 1 |
| Sunriver | | 12 | 11 | 1 |
| Sutherlin | 7,154 | 17 | 15 | 2 |
| Sweet Home | 9,039 | 22 | 15 | 7 |
| Talent | 6,287 | 8 | 7 | 1 |
| The Dalles | 11,874 | 23 | 21 | 2 |
| Tigard | 49,422 | 94 | 76 | 18 |
| Tillamook | 4,414 | 12 | 8 | 4 |
| Toledo | 3,278 | 16 | 10 | 6 |
| Troutdale | 15,630 | 30 | 25 | 5 |
| Tualatin | 26,903 | 42 | 34 | 8 |
| Turner | 1,784 | 3 | 3 | 0 |
| Umatilla | 6,443 | 10 | 8 | 2 |
| Vernonia | 2,280 | 5 | 5 | 0 |
| Warrenton | 4,489 | 9 | 8 | 1 |
| West Linn | 25,568 | 37 | 31 | 6 |
| Weston | 690 | 2 | 2 | 0 |
| Winston | 5,622 | 8 | 7 | 1 |
| Woodburn | 23,103 | 39 | 32 | 7 |
| Yamhill | 928 | 3 | 3 | 0 |
| **PENNSYLVANIA** | | | | |
| Abington Township | 53,761 | 118 | 91 | 27 |
| Adams Township, Butler County | 9,823 | 4 | 4 | 0 |
| Akron | 4,014 | 5 | 5 | 0 |
| Albion | 1,490 | 2 | 2 | 0 |
| Alburtis | 2,425 | 4 | 4 | 0 |
| Aldan | 4,229 | 6 | 6 | 0 |
| Aleppo Township | 1,271 | 14 | 11 | 3 |
| Aliquippa | 10,525 | 18 | 18 | 0 |
| Allegheny Township, Blair County | 6,845 | 6 | 5 | 1 |
| Allegheny Township, Westmoreland County | 8,199 | 9 | 8 | 1 |
| Allentown | 107,326 | 272 | 203 | 69 |
| Altoona | 45,793 | 82 | 74 | 8 |
| Ambler | 6,171 | 16 | 14 | 2 |
| Ambridge | 6,949 | 9 | 9 | 0 |

## Table 78. Full-time Law Enforcement Employees, by State, by City, 2009—*Continued*

(Number.)

| State/city | Population | Total law enforcement employees | Total officers | Total civilians |
|---|---|---|---|---|
| Amity Township | 12,149 | 13 | 12 | 1 |
| Annville Township | 4,786 | 8 | 5 | 3 |
| Apollo | 1,619 | 1 | 1 | 0 |
| Archbald | 6,519 | 5 | 5 | 0 |
| Arnold | 5,165 | 12 | 11 | 1 |
| Ashland | 3,080 | 3 | 3 | 0 |
| Ashley | 2,642 | 3 | 3 | 0 |
| Aspinwall | 2,678 | 7 | 6 | 1 |
| Aston Township | 16,886 | 18 | 16 | 2 |
| Athens | 3,188 | 6 | 5 | 1 |
| Athens Township | 4,998 | 10 | 9 | 1 |
| Auburn | 795 | 1 | 1 | 0 |
| Austin | 556 | 1 | 1 | 0 |
| Avalon | 4,763 | 6 | 6 | 0 |
| Avoca | 2,637 | 2 | 2 | 0 |
| Avonmore Boro | 754 | 2 | 2 | 0 |
| Baden | 3,978 | 5 | 5 | 0 |
| Baldwin Borough | 18,414 | 24 | 23 | 1 |
| Baldwin Township | 2,016 | 5 | 5 | 0 |
| Bally | 1,098 | 2 | 2 | 0 |
| Bangor | 5,249 | 10 | 9 | 1 |
| Barrett Township | 4,278 | 7 | 7 | 0 |
| Beaver | 4,330 | 10 | 9 | 1 |
| Beaver Falls | 8,967 | 19 | 18 | 1 |
| Beaver Meadows | 944 | 1 | 1 | 0 |
| Bedford | 2,984 | 5 | 5 | 0 |
| Bedminster Township | 6,273 | 7 | 6 | 1 |
| Bell Acres | 1,384 | 4 | 4 | 0 |
| Bellefonte | 6,125 | 12 | 10 | 2 |
| Bellevue | 7,899 | 15 | 12 | 3 |
| Bellwood | 1,854 | 2 | 2 | 0 |
| Ben Avon | 1,730 | 14 | 11 | 3 |
| Ben Avon Heights | 356 | 14 | 11 | 3 |
| Bensalem Township | 58,284 | 206 | 101 | 105 |
| Berks-Lehigh Regional | 30,216 | 31 | 30 | 1 |
| Berlin | 2,059 | 2 | 2 | 0 |
| Bern Township | 7,231 | 13 | 13 | 0 |
| Berwick | 10,160 | 16 | 15 | 1 |
| Bethel Park | 31,354 | 44 | 38 | 6 |
| Bethel Township, Berks County | 4,521 | 2 | 2 | 0 |
| Bethlehem | 72,349 | 177 | 159 | 18 |
| Bethlehem Township | 23,846 | 36 | 34 | 2 |
| Biglerville | 1,151 | 2 | 2 | 0 |
| Birdsboro | 5,178 | 8 | 7 | 1 |
| Birmingham Township | 4,257 | 4 | 4 | 0 |
| Blairsville | 3,346 | 3 | 3 | 0 |
| Blair Township | 4,712 | 5 | 5 | 0 |
| Blakely | 6,718 | 3 | 3 | 0 |
| Blawnox | 1,424 | 4 | 4 | 0 |
| Bloomsburg Town | 12,821 | 21 | 15 | 6 |
| Blossburg | 1,444 | 2 | 2 | 0 |
| Boyertown | 3,917 | 8 | 7 | 1 |
| Brackenridge | 3,195 | 4 | 4 | 0 |
| Braddock Hills | 1,809 | 2 | 2 | 0 |
| Bradford | 8,312 | 22 | 22 | 0 |
| Bradford Township | 4,811 | 5 | 5 | 0 |
| Brecknock Township, Berks County | 4,949 | 6 | 6 | 0 |
| Brentwood | 9,426 | 15 | 15 | 0 |
| Briar Creek Township | 3,102 | 8 | 8 | 0 |
| Bridgeport | 4,347 | 10 | 9 | 1 |
| Bridgeville | 4,828 | 9 | 8 | 1 |
| Bridgewater | 877 | 3 | 3 | 0 |
| Bristol | 9,602 | 18 | 16 | 2 |
| Bristol Township | 53,660 | 91 | 78 | 13 |
| Brockway | 2,044 | 2 | 2 | 0 |
| Brookhaven | 7,876 | 9 | 8 | 1 |
| Brookville | 3,968 | 7 | 6 | 1 |
| Brownsville | 2,613 | 2 | 2 | 0 |
| Bryn Athyn | 1,324 | 5 | 5 | 0 |
| Buckingham Township | 19,847 | 23 | 21 | 2 |
| Buffalo Township | 7,284 | 7 | 7 | 0 |
| Burgettstown | 1,468 | 1 | 1 | 0 |
| Bushkill Township | 8,361 | 12 | 10 | 2 |
| Butler | 13,809 | 24 | 23 | 1 |
| Butler Township, Butler County | 16,514 | 23 | 21 | 2 |
| Butler Township, Luzerne County | 9,589 | 9 | 8 | 1 |
| Butler Township, Schuylkill County | 6,120 | 4 | 4 | 0 |
| Caernarvon Township | 3,601 | 10 | 9 | 1 |
| California | 6,384 | 8 | 7 | 1 |
| Caln Township | 12,217 | 22 | 20 | 2 |
| Cambria Township | 6,164 | 4 | 4 | 0 |
| Cambridge Springs | 2,665 | 3 | 3 | 0 |
| Camp Hill | 7,351 | 6 | 5 | 1 |
| Canonsburg | 8,730 | 17 | 16 | 1 |
| Canton | 1,683 | 3 | 3 | 0 |
| Carbondale | 9,147 | 15 | 15 | 0 |
| Carlisle | 18,406 | 37 | 32 | 5 |
| Carnegie | 7,871 | 13 | 12 | 1 |
| Carrolltown | 950 | 1 | 1 | 0 |
| Carroll Township, Washington County | 5,449 | 2 | 2 | 0 |
| Carroll Township, York County | 5,855 | 11 | 11 | 0 |
| Carroll Valley | 3,558 | 5 | 4 | 1 |
| Castle Shannon | 7,974 | 13 | 12 | 1 |
| Catasauqua | 6,555 | 9 | 8 | 1 |
| Catawissa | 1,533 | 2 | 2 | 0 |
| Cecil Township | 10,600 | 18 | 17 | 1 |
| Center Township | 11,666 | 26 | 26 | 0 |
| Centerville | 3,192 | 3 | 3 | 0 |
| Central Berks Regional | 7,525 | 12 | 11 | 1 |
| Chalfont | 4,191 | 7 | 6 | 1 |
| Chambersburg | 18,352 | 37 | 34 | 3 |
| Charleroi | 5,673 | 8 | 6 | 2 |
| Chartiers Township | 7,455 | 11 | 11 | 0 |
| Cheltenham Township | 35,760 | 98 | 85 | 13 |
| Chester | 36,529 | 109 | 103 | 6 |
| Chester Township | 4,431 | 12 | 11 | 1 |
| Cheswick | 1,725 | 3 | 3 | 0 |
| Chippewa Township | 9,789 | 8 | 7 | 1 |
| Churchill | 3,222 | 10 | 10 | 0 |
| Clarion | 5,170 | 9 | 8 | 1 |
| Clarks Summit | 6,490 | 7 | 6 | 1 |
| Clay Township | 5,965 | 4 | 4 | 0 |
| Clearfield | 6,124 | 7 | 7 | 0 |
| Cleona | 2,118 | 4 | 4 | 0 |
| Clifford Township | 2,459 | 2 | 2 | 0 |
| Clifton Heights | 6,516 | 10 | 9 | 1 |
| Coaldale | 2,104 | 4 | 4 | 0 |
| Coal Township | 10,194 | 13 | 12 | 1 |
| Coatesville | 11,711 | 44 | 36 | 8 |
| Cochranton | 1,057 | 2 | 2 | 0 |
| Colebrookdale District | 6,413 | 11 | 10 | 1 |
| Collegeville | 5,066 | 9 | 8 | 1 |
| Collier Township | 6,582 | 15 | 14 | 1 |
| Collingdale | 8,334 | 9 | 8 | 1 |
| Colonial Regional | 20,125 | 26 | 24 | 2 |
| Columbia | 10,001 | 19 | 16 | 3 |
| Conemaugh Township, Cambria County | 2,441 | 2 | 2 | 0 |
| Conemaugh Township, Somerset County | 7,194 | 7 | 6 | 1 |
| Conewago Township, Adams County | 6,130 | 9 | 8 | 1 |
| Conewango Township | 3,518 | 4 | 4 | 0 |
| Conneaut Lake Regional | 3,488 | 4 | 3 | 1 |
| Connellsville | 8,404 | 17 | 16 | 1 |
| Conshohocken | 8,509 | 21 | 19 | 2 |
| Conyngham | 1,823 | 2 | 2 | 0 |
| Coopersburg | 2,560 | 7 | 7 | 0 |
| Coplay | 3,365 | 4 | 4 | 0 |
| Coraopolis | 5,552 | 12 | 9 | 3 |
| Cornwall | 3,501 | 8 | 7 | 1 |
| Corry | 6,253 | 14 | 12 | 2 |
| Coudersport | 2,346 | 4 | 4 | 0 |
| Covington Township | 2,203 | 3 | 3 | 0 |
| Crafton | 6,473 | 10 | 9 | 1 |
| Cranberry Township | 27,605 | 32 | 28 | 4 |
| Crescent Township | 2,790 | 3 | 3 | 0 |
| Cresson | 1,466 | 10 | 10 | 0 |
| Cresson Township | 4,539 | 3 | 2 | 1 |
| Croyle Township | 2,221 | 1 | 1 | 0 |
| Cumberland Township, Adams County | 6,357 | 6 | 6 | 0 |
| Cumberland Township, Greene County | 6,381 | 4 | 4 | 0 |
| Cumru Township | 17,607 | 27 | 24 | 3 |
| Curwensville | 2,443 | 1 | 1 | 0 |
| Dale | 1,343 | 2 | 2 | 0 |

**Table 78. Full-time Law Enforcement Employees, by State, by City, 2009—*Continued***

(Number.)

| State/city | Population | Total law enforcement employees | Total officers | Total civilians |
|---|---|---|---|---|
| Dallas | 2,467 | 4 | 4 | 0 |
| Dallas Township | 8,908 | 8 | 8 | 0 |
| Dalton | 1,217 | 2 | 2 | 0 |
| Danville | 4,403 | 10 | 9 | 1 |
| Darby | 9,861 | 13 | 12 | 1 |
| Darby Township | 9,509 | 14 | 14 | 0 |
| Decatur Township | 4,736 | 1 | 1 | 0 |
| Delmont | 2,409 | 4 | 4 | 0 |
| Derry | 2,753 | 3 | 3 | 0 |
| Derry Township, Dauphin County | 22,091 | 46 | 38 | 8 |
| Dickson City | 5,872 | 7 | 7 | 0 |
| Donora | 5,221 | 6 | 6 | 0 |
| Dormont | 8,330 | 16 | 15 | 1 |
| Douglass Township, Berks County | 3,503 | 3 | 3 | 0 |
| Douglass Township, Montgomery County | 10,259 | 11 | 10 | 1 |
| Downingtown | 7,974 | 19 | 16 | 3 |
| Doylestown | 8,100 | 21 | 16 | 5 |
| Doylestown Township | 18,705 | 23 | 21 | 2 |
| Dublin Borough | 2,146 | 2 | 2 | 0 |
| Du Bois | 7,598 | 13 | 13 | 0 |
| Duboistown | 1,186 | 1 | 1 | 0 |
| Duncannon | 1,492 | 2 | 2 | 0 |
| Duncansville | 1,159 | 2 | 2 | 0 |
| Dunmore | 13,942 | 22 | 22 | 0 |
| Dunnstable Township | 990 | 1 | 1 | 0 |
| Dupont | 2,563 | 1 | 1 | 0 |
| Duquesne | 6,616 | 14 | 13 | 1 |
| Duryea | 4,305 | 1 | 1 | 0 |
| East Bangor | 1,129 | 1 | 1 | 0 |
| East Berlin | 1,432 | 1 | 1 | 0 |
| East Bethlehem Township | 2,332 | 1 | 1 | 0 |
| East Brandywine Township | 6,792 | 10 | 9 | 1 |
| East Buffalo Township | 5,916 | 8 | 8 | 0 |
| East Cocalico Township | 10,509 | 23 | 21 | 2 |
| East Conemaugh | 1,150 | 2 | 2 | 0 |
| East Coventry Township | 6,853 | 8 | 7 | 1 |
| East Deer Township | 1,318 | 2 | 2 | 0 |
| East Earl Township | 6,669 | 7 | 7 | 0 |
| Eastern Adams Regional | 9,948 | 10 | 9 | 1 |
| Eastern Pike Regional | 5,535 | 10 | 9 | 1 |
| East Fallowfield Township | 7,817 | 7 | 7 | 0 |
| East Franklin Township | 3,950 | 3 | 2 | 1 |
| East Hempfield Township | 23,680 | 36 | 32 | 4 |
| East Lampeter Township | 15,147 | 48 | 40 | 8 |
| East Lansdowne | 2,461 | 5 | 3 | 2 |
| East McKeesport | 2,772 | 2 | 2 | 0 |
| East Norriton Township | 13,627 | 30 | 27 | 3 |
| Easton | 26,065 | 63 | 57 | 6 |
| East Pennsboro Township | 19,992 | 20 | 19 | 1 |
| East Pikeland Township | 6,940 | 8 | 7 | 1 |
| East Pittsburgh | 1,821 | 1 | 1 | 0 |
| Easttown Township | 10,549 | 16 | 15 | 1 |
| East Union Township | 1,423 | 1 | 1 | 0 |
| East Vincent Township | 6,589 | 7 | 7 | 0 |
| East Washington | 1,847 | 1 | 1 | 0 |
| East Whiteland Township | 10,790 | 22 | 20 | 2 |
| Ebensburg | 2,907 | 3 | 3 | 0 |
| Economy | 9,112 | 12 | 11 | 1 |
| Eddystone | 2,330 | 10 | 9 | 1 |
| Edgewood | 2,987 | 12 | 10 | 2 |
| Edgeworth | 1,575 | 6 | 4 | 2 |
| Edinboro | 6,625 | 8 | 8 | 0 |
| Edwardsville | 4,625 | 4 | 4 | 0 |
| Elizabethtown | 12,090 | 18 | 16 | 2 |
| Elizabeth Township | 12,752 | 11 | 10 | 1 |
| Elkland | 1,651 | 2 | 2 | 0 |
| Ellwood City | 7,889 | 11 | 10 | 1 |
| Emlenton Borough | 728 | 2 | 2 | 0 |
| Emmaus | 11,354 | 21 | 19 | 2 |
| Emporium | 2,176 | 2 | 2 | 0 |
| Emsworth | 2,354 | 14 | 11 | 3 |
| Ephrata | 13,059 | 35 | 30 | 5 |
| Erie | 103,837 | 202 | 168 | 34 |
| Etna | 3,523 | 7 | 7 | 0 |
| Evans City | 1,870 | 2 | 2 | 0 |
| Everett | 1,843 | 3 | 3 | 0 |
| Exeter | 5,899 | 4 | 3 | 1 |
| Exeter Township, Berks County | 27,355 | 35 | 32 | 3 |
| Exeter Township, Luzerne County | 2,519 | 1 | 1 | 0 |
| Fairview Township, Luzerne County | 4,301 | 5 | 5 | 0 |
| Fairview Township, York County | 17,114 | 19 | 17 | 2 |
| Fallowfield Township | 4,172 | 2 | 2 | 0 |
| Falls Township, Bucks County | 33,445 | 60 | 53 | 7 |
| Fawn Township | 2,291 | 3 | 3 | 0 |
| Ferguson Township | 16,747 | 23 | 20 | 3 |
| Ferndale | 1,635 | 1 | 1 | 0 |
| Findlay Township | 5,045 | 23 | 16 | 7 |
| Folcroft | 6,806 | 10 | 10 | 0 |
| Ford City | 3,150 | 3 | 3 | 0 |
| Forest City | 1,712 | 2 | 2 | 0 |
| Forest Hills | 6,179 | 11 | 10 | 1 |
| Forks Township | 15,173 | 24 | 23 | 1 |
| Forty Fort | 4,209 | 2 | 2 | 0 |
| Forward Township | 3,458 | 5 | 5 | 0 |
| Foster Township | 4,204 | 4 | 4 | 0 |
| Fountain Hill | 4,571 | 11 | 10 | 1 |
| Fox Chapel | 5,107 | 12 | 12 | 0 |
| Frackville | 4,098 | 5 | 5 | 0 |
| Franconia Township | 12,920 | 17 | 15 | 2 |
| Franklin | 6,608 | 23 | 17 | 6 |
| Franklin Park | 12,264 | 13 | 12 | 1 |
| Franklin Township, Carbon County | 4,906 | 4 | 4 | 0 |
| Frazer Township | 1,196 | 3 | 3 | 0 |
| Freedom Township | 3,171 | 2 | 2 | 0 |
| Freeland | 3,357 | 2 | 2 | 0 |
| Freemansburg | 2,037 | 3 | 3 | 0 |
| Freeport | 1,794 | 2 | 2 | 0 |
| Galeton | 1,196 | 2 | 2 | 0 |
| Gallitzin | 1,855 | 5 | 5 | 0 |
| Geistown | 2,331 | 1 | 1 | 0 |
| Gettysburg | 8,103 | 14 | 10 | 4 |
| Gilberton | 817 | 1 | 1 | 0 |
| Gilpin Township | 2,509 | 1 | 1 | 0 |
| Girard | 2,904 | 4 | 4 | 0 |
| Glassport | 4,503 | 6 | 6 | 0 |
| Glenolden | 7,174 | 11 | 10 | 1 |
| Granville Township | 4,953 | 9 | 7 | 2 |
| Greencastle | 4,092 | 6 | 5 | 1 |
| Greenfield Township, Blair County | 3,709 | 3 | 3 | 0 |
| Greensburg | 15,183 | 38 | 28 | 10 |
| Green Tree | 4,295 | 12 | 11 | 1 |
| Greenville | 6,077 | 10 | 9 | 1 |
| Greenwood Township | 2,059 | 1 | 1 | 0 |
| Grove City | 7,684 | 11 | 10 | 1 |
| Hamburg | 4,222 | 6 | 5 | 1 |
| Hamiltonban Township | 2,777 | 1 | 1 | 0 |
| Hampden Township | 27,352 | 25 | 24 | 1 |
| Hampton Township | 17,183 | 19 | 18 | 1 |
| Hanover | 15,076 | 24 | 22 | 2 |
| Hanover Township, Luzerne County | 10,931 | 16 | 15 | 1 |
| Hanover Township, Washington County | 2,711 | 9 | 3 | 6 |
| Harmar Township | 3,015 | 7 | 7 | 0 |
| Harmony Township | 3,029 | 5 | 5 | 0 |
| Harrisburg | 46,961 | 230 | 179 | 51 |
| Harrison Township | 9,922 | 21 | 18 | 3 |
| Harveys Lake | 2,936 | 4 | 4 | 0 |
| Hastings | 1,285 | 1 | 1 | 0 |
| Hatboro | 7,096 | 17 | 14 | 3 |
| Hatfield Township | 20,037 | 31 | 26 | 5 |
| Haverford Township | 47,827 | 79 | 68 | 11 |
| Hazleton | 21,569 | 41 | 38 | 3 |
| Hegins Township | 3,353 | 2 | 2 | 0 |
| Heidelberg | 1,135 | 3 | 3 | 0 |
| Heidelberg Township, Berks County | 1,768 | 1 | 1 | 0 |
| Heidelberg Township, Lebanon County | 4,192 | 2 | 2 | 0 |
| Hellam Township | 9,149 | 7 | 7 | 0 |
| Hellertown | 5,666 | 11 | 10 | 1 |
| Hemlock Township | 2,273 | 6 | 6 | 0 |
| Hempfield Township, Mercer County | 3,833 | 7 | 6 | 1 |
| Hermitage | 16,340 | 33 | 30 | 3 |
| Highspire | 2,594 | 7 | 6 | 1 |
| Hilltown Township | 13,602 | 20 | 17 | 3 |

## Table 78. Full-time Law Enforcement Employees, by State, by City, 2009—*Continued*

(Number.)

| State/city | Population | Total law enforcement employees | Total officers | Total civilians |
|---|---|---|---|---|
| Hollidaysburg | 5,477 | 10 | 8 | 2 |
| Homer City | 1,697 | 2 | 2 | 0 |
| Homestead | 3,483 | 11 | 10 | 1 |
| Honesdale | 4,702 | 9 | 9 | 0 |
| Honey Brook | 1,609 | 1 | 1 | 0 |
| Hooversville | 701 | 1 | 1 | 0 |
| Hopewell Township | 12,297 | 16 | 15 | 1 |
| Horsham Township | 24,765 | 49 | 40 | 9 |
| Hughesville | 2,028 | 1 | 1 | 0 |
| Hummelstown | 4,432 | 7 | 7 | 0 |
| Huntingdon | 6,742 | 12 | 12 | 0 |
| Independence Township, Beaver County | 2,666 | 3 | 3 | 0 |
| Indiana | 14,727 | 24 | 22 | 2 |
| Indiana Township | 7,059 | 10 | 10 | 0 |
| Industry | 1,775 | 12 | 12 | 0 |
| Ingram | 3,336 | 4 | 4 | 0 |
| Irwin | 4,017 | 3 | 3 | 0 |
| Ivyland | 853 | 2 | 2 | 0 |
| Jackson Township, Butler County | 3,720 | 10 | 8 | 2 |
| Jackson Township, Cambria County | 4,669 | 2 | 2 | 0 |
| Jackson Township, Luzerne County | 4,801 | 4 | 4 | 0 |
| Jamestown | 571 | 1 | 1 | 0 |
| Jeannette | 9,777 | 17 | 14 | 3 |
| Jefferson Hills Borough | 9,660 | 19 | 18 | 1 |
| Jefferson Township, Mercer County | 2,293 | 1 | 1 | 0 |
| Jenkins Township | 4,893 | 2 | 2 | 0 |
| Jenkintown | 4,280 | 13 | 11 | 2 |
| Jermyn | 2,225 | 1 | 1 | 0 |
| Jersey Shore | 4,282 | 8 | 7 | 1 |
| Jessup | 4,534 | 2 | 2 | 0 |
| Jim Thorpe | 4,870 | 7 | 6 | 1 |
| Johnsonburg | 2,645 | 3 | 3 | 0 |
| Johnstown | 22,929 | 47 | 42 | 5 |
| Kane | 3,729 | 5 | 5 | 0 |
| Kennedy Township | 9,656 | 15 | 11 | 4 |
| Kennett Square | 5,269 | 14 | 12 | 2 |
| Kidder Township | 1,477 | 10 | 10 | 0 |
| Kilbuck Township | 652 | 14 | 11 | 3 |
| Kingston | 12,850 | 25 | 19 | 6 |
| Kingston Township | 7,038 | 11 | 11 | 0 |
| Kiskiminetas Township | 4,768 | 1 | 1 | 0 |
| Kittanning | 4,312 | 9 | 8 | 1 |
| Knox | 1,089 | 2 | 2 | 0 |
| Koppel | 766 | 1 | 1 | 0 |
| Kulpmont | 2,740 | 1 | 1 | 0 |
| Kutztown | 5,107 | 12 | 10 | 2 |
| Laflin Borough | 1,485 | 3 | 3 | 0 |
| Lake City | 2,880 | 3 | 3 | 0 |
| Lancaster | 54,441 | 184 | 158 | 26 |
| Lancaster Township, Butler County | 2,578 | 1 | 1 | 0 |
| Lansdale | 15,466 | 26 | 20 | 6 |
| Lansdowne | 10,595 | 19 | 16 | 3 |
| Lansford | 4,122 | 10 | 9 | 1 |
| Larksville | 4,408 | 4 | 4 | 0 |
| Latimore Township | 2,867 | 1 | 1 | 0 |
| Latrobe | 8,281 | 14 | 13 | 1 |
| Laureldale | 3,734 | 5 | 5 | 0 |
| Lawrence Park Township | 3,650 | 8 | 7 | 1 |
| Lawrence Township, Clearfield County | 7,436 | 10 | 9 | 1 |
| Lebanon | 24,061 | 54 | 47 | 7 |
| Leechburg | 2,194 | 3 | 3 | 0 |
| Leetsdale | 1,105 | 4 | 4 | 0 |
| Leet Township | 1,485 | 5 | 5 | 0 |
| Lehighton | 5,417 | 10 | 9 | 1 |
| Lehigh Township, Northampton County | 10,926 | 13 | 12 | 1 |
| Lehman Township | 3,324 | 2 | 2 | 0 |
| Lewisburg | 5,435 | 10 | 8 | 2 |
| Liberty | 2,412 | 1 | 1 | 0 |
| Liberty Township, Adams County | 1,303 | 1 | 1 | 0 |
| Ligonier | 1,589 | 3 | 3 | 0 |
| Limerick Township | 17,276 | 17 | 16 | 1 |
| Lincoln | 1,110 | 1 | 1 | 0 |
| Linesville | 1,084 | 1 | 1 | 0 |
| Lititz | 9,034 | 16 | 13 | 3 |
| Littlestown | 4,134 | 7 | 6 | 1 |
| Lock Haven | 8,477 | 15 | 13 | 2 |

| State/city | Population | Total law enforcement employees | Total officers | Total civilians |
|---|---|---|---|---|
| Locust Township | 2,536 | 3 | 3 | 0 |
| Logan Township | 12,185 | 18 | 16 | 2 |
| Lower Allen Township | 17,471 | 21 | 20 | 1 |
| Lower Burrell | 12,032 | 16 | 16 | 0 |
| Lower Chichester Township | 3,424 | 4 | 4 | 0 |
| Lower Frederick Township | 4,813 | 3 | 3 | 0 |
| Lower Gwynedd Township | 11,433 | 19 | 18 | 1 |
| Lower Heidelberg Township | 5,470 | 9 | 8 | 1 |
| Lower Makefield Township | 32,111 | 42 | 38 | 4 |
| Lower Merion Township | 57,033 | 155 | 136 | 19 |
| Lower Milford Township | 3,915 | 1 | 1 | 0 |
| Lower Moreland Township | 12,807 | 27 | 22 | 5 |
| Lower Paxton Township | 45,534 | 67 | 60 | 7 |
| Lower Pottsgrove Township | 12,266 | 18 | 16 | 2 |
| Lower Providence Township | 26,271 | 38 | 33 | 5 |
| Lower Salford Township | 14,683 | 21 | 19 | 2 |
| Lower Saucon Township | 11,435 | 16 | 14 | 2 |
| Lower Southampton Township | 18,954 | 33 | 30 | 3 |
| Lower Swatara Township | 8,563 | 11 | 10 | 1 |
| Lower Windsor Township | 7,875 | 11 | 10 | 1 |
| Luzerne Township | 6,753 | 1 | 1 | 0 |
| Lykens | 1,839 | 1 | 1 | 0 |
| Macungie | 3,131 | 5 | 5 | 0 |
| Mahanoy City | 4,347 | 4 | 4 | 0 |
| Mahoning Township, Montour County | 4,238 | 7 | 6 | 1 |
| Malvern | 3,102 | 5 | 4 | 1 |
| Manheim | 4,631 | 9 | 8 | 1 |
| Manheim Township | 36,582 | 69 | 54 | 15 |
| Manor | 2,927 | 3 | 3 | 0 |
| Manor Township, Lancaster County | 19,812 | 22 | 20 | 2 |
| Mansfield | 3,152 | 5 | 5 | 0 |
| Marcus Hook | 2,219 | 7 | 6 | 1 |
| Marion Township, Beaver County | 880 | 1 | 1 | 0 |
| Marion Township, Berks County | 1,782 | 3 | 3 | 0 |
| Marlborough Township | 3,283 | 3 | 3 | 0 |
| Marple Township | 23,407 | 35 | 30 | 5 |
| Martinsburg | 2,109 | 2 | 2 | 0 |
| Marysville | 2,439 | 1 | 1 | 0 |
| Masontown | 3,371 | 5 | 5 | 0 |
| Mayfield | 1,698 | 1 | 1 | 0 |
| McAdoo | 2,069 | 2 | 2 | 0 |
| McCandless | 27,119 | 29 | 27 | 2 |
| McDonald Borough | 2,103 | 2 | 2 | 0 |
| McKeesport | 21,932 | 55 | 52 | 3 |
| McKees Rocks | 5,956 | 11 | 10 | 1 |
| McSherrystown | 2,803 | 5 | 5 | 0 |
| Meadville | 13,186 | 25 | 22 | 3 |
| Mechanicsburg | 8,688 | 17 | 16 | 1 |
| Media | 5,381 | 24 | 16 | 8 |
| Mercer | 2,188 | 4 | 4 | 0 |
| Mercersburg | 1,589 | 2 | 2 | 0 |
| Meshoppen | 424 | 1 | 1 | 0 |
| Meyersdale | 2,252 | 3 | 2 | 1 |
| Middleburg | 1,321 | 3 | 2 | 1 |
| Middlesex Township, Butler County | 5,438 | 3 | 3 | 0 |
| Middlesex Township, Cumberland County | 6,920 | 10 | 9 | 1 |
| Middletown | 8,799 | 16 | 15 | 1 |
| Middletown Township | 46,978 | 59 | 52 | 7 |
| Midland | 2,817 | 5 | 4 | 1 |
| Mifflin | 603 | 1 | 1 | 0 |
| Mifflinburg | 3,509 | 10 | 9 | 1 |
| Mifflin County Regional | 26,265 | 27 | 25 | 2 |
| Mifflin Township | 2,249 | 4 | 4 | 0 |
| Milford | 2,904 | 2 | 2 | 0 |
| Millbourne | 901 | 1 | 1 | 0 |
| Millcreek Township, Erie County | 51,758 | 71 | 57 | 14 |
| Millcreek Township, Lebanon County | 3,210 | 3 | 3 | 0 |
| Millersburg | 2,449 | 5 | 4 | 1 |
| Millersville | 7,296 | 13 | 11 | 2 |
| Millvale | 3,618 | 5 | 5 | 0 |
| Millville | 940 | 1 | 1 | 0 |
| Milton | 6,331 | 10 | 9 | 1 |
| Minersville | 4,187 | 5 | 5 | 0 |
| Mohnton | 3,081 | 5 | 5 | 0 |
| Monaca | 5,694 | 9 | 9 | 0 |
| Monessen | 7,958 | 12 | 12 | 0 |

**Table 78. Full-time Law Enforcement Employees, by State, by City, 2009**—*Continued*

(Number.)

| State/city | Population | Total law enforcement employees | Total officers | Total civilians |
|---|---|---|---|---|
| Monongahela | 4,387 | 10 | 8 | 2 |
| Monroeville | 27,462 | 62 | 51 | 11 |
| Montgomery | 5,184 | 3 | 3 | 0 |
| Montgomery Township | 24,360 | 44 | 35 | 9 |
| Montoursville | 4,536 | 6 | 6 | 0 |
| Montrose | 1,518 | 1 | 1 | 0 |
| Moon Township | 22,923 | 36 | 30 | 6 |
| Moore Township | 9,494 | 8 | 7 | 1 |
| Moosic | 5,779 | 10 | 10 | 0 |
| Morris-Cooper Regional | 5,625 | 1 | 1 | 0 |
| Morrisville | 9,547 | 12 | 11 | 1 |
| Morton | 2,625 | 5 | 4 | 1 |
| Moscow | 1,945 | 3 | 3 | 0 |
| Mount Carmel | 5,836 | 9 | 9 | 0 |
| Mount Carmel Township | 2,568 | 6 | 6 | 0 |
| Mount Holly Springs | 1,907 | 2 | 2 | 0 |
| Mount Joy | 7,304 | 14 | 12 | 2 |
| Mount Lebanon | 30,106 | 54 | 44 | 10 |
| Mount Oliver | 3,621 | 10 | 10 | 0 |
| Mount Pleasant | 4,344 | 3 | 3 | 0 |
| Mount Pleasant Township | 3,633 | 2 | 2 | 0 |
| Mount Union | 2,327 | 4 | 4 | 0 |
| Muhlenberg Township | 18,767 | 33 | 30 | 3 |
| Muncy | 2,438 | 3 | 3 | 0 |
| Munhall | 11,090 | 26 | 22 | 4 |
| Murrysville | 19,563 | 26 | 21 | 5 |
| Myerstown | 3,115 | 3 | 3 | 0 |
| Nanticoke | 10,122 | 14 | 13 | 1 |
| Nanty Glo | 2,766 | 2 | 2 | 0 |
| Narberth | 4,019 | 6 | 6 | 0 |
| Nazareth Area | 6,021 | 8 | 7 | 1 |
| Neshannock Township | 9,290 | 8 | 8 | 0 |
| Nether Providence Township | 13,123 | 17 | 16 | 1 |
| Neville Township | 1,114 | 14 | 11 | 3 |
| Newberry Township | 15,577 | 18 | 16 | 2 |
| New Bethlehem | 974 | 42 | 40 | 2 |
| New Brighton | 9,252 | 9 | 9 | 0 |
| New Britain | 2,255 | 6 | 5 | 1 |
| New Britain Township | 10,981 | 14 | 12 | 2 |
| New Castle | 23,994 | 39 | 36 | 3 |
| New Castle Township | 393 | 1 | 1 | 0 |
| New Garden Township | 12,073 | 12 | 11 | 1 |
| New Hanover Township | 9,694 | 11 | 10 | 1 |
| New Holland | 5,158 | 13 | 12 | 1 |
| New Hope | 2,280 | 11 | 9 | 2 |
| New Kensington | 13,561 | 23 | 23 | 0 |
| New Philadelphia | 1,083 | 1 | 1 | 0 |
| Newport | 1,459 | 2 | 2 | 0 |
| Newport Township | 4,735 | 2 | 2 | 0 |
| New Sewickley Township | 7,591 | 7 | 7 | 0 |
| Newton Township | 2,774 | 1 | 1 | 0 |
| Newtown | 2,384 | 5 | 5 | 0 |
| Newtown Township, Bucks County | 19,327 | 32 | 28 | 4 |
| Newtown Township, Delaware County | 11,796 | 18 | 16 | 2 |
| Newville | 1,296 | 2 | 2 | 0 |
| Norristown | 31,909 | 82 | 70 | 12 |
| Northampton | 9,892 | 14 | 12 | 2 |
| Northampton Township | 40,813 | 49 | 43 | 6 |
| North Belle Vernon | 1,933 | 3 | 2 | 1 |
| North Braddock | 5,761 | 3 | 3 | 0 |
| North Catasauqua | 2,837 | 5 | 5 | 0 |
| North Charleroi | 1,304 | 1 | 1 | 0 |
| North Cornwall Township | 6,589 | 10 | 9 | 1 |
| North Coventry Township | 7,747 | 14 | 13 | 1 |
| North East, Erie County | 4,146 | 7 | 6 | 1 |
| Northeastern Regional | 11,264 | 12 | 10 | 2 |
| Northern Berks Regional | 12,590 | 15 | 14 | 1 |
| Northern Cambria Borough | 3,877 | 4 | 4 | 0 |
| Northern Regional | 28,544 | 30 | 28 | 2 |
| Northern York Regional | 66,764 | 50 | 46 | 4 |
| North Fayette Township | 13,147 | 24 | 20 | 4 |
| North Franklin Township | 4,619 | 6 | 6 | 0 |
| North Huntingdon Township | 29,516 | 35 | 28 | 7 |
| North Lebanon Township | 10,987 | 12 | 10 | 2 |
| North Londonderry Township | 7,012 | 9 | 8 | 1 |
| North Middleton Township | 11,066 | 10 | 9 | 1 |
| North Sewickley Township | 5,615 | 1 | 1 | 0 |
| North Strabane Township | 12,647 | 20 | 19 | 1 |
| Northumberland | 3,491 | 5 | 5 | 0 |
| North Versailles Township | 12,112 | 22 | 18 | 4 |
| North Wales | 3,213 | 5 | 4 | 1 |
| Northwest Lancaster County Regional | 18,094 | 16 | 15 | 1 |
| Northwest Lawrence County Regional | 6,627 | 2 | 2 | 0 |
| Norwood | 5,752 | 8 | 7 | 1 |
| Oakmont | 6,373 | 7 | 7 | 0 |
| O'Hara Township | 9,578 | 16 | 15 | 1 |
| Ohio Township | 4,166 | 14 | 11 | 3 |
| Ohioville | 3,599 | 2 | 2 | 0 |
| Oil City | 10,504 | 23 | 18 | 5 |
| Old Forge | 8,497 | 5 | 5 | 0 |
| Old Lycoming Township | 5,248 | 9 | 8 | 1 |
| Oley Township | 3,681 | 5 | 5 | 0 |
| Oliver Township | 2,064 | 1 | 1 | 0 |
| Orangeville Area | 1,637 | 1 | 1 | 0 |
| Orwigsburg | 2,966 | 4 | 4 | 0 |
| Oxford | 4,696 | 12 | 11 | 1 |
| Paint Township | 3,133 | 5 | 4 | 1 |
| Palmerton | 5,205 | 9 | 8 | 1 |
| Palmer Township | 20,742 | 34 | 31 | 3 |
| Palmyra | 6,987 | 10 | 9 | 1 |
| Parkesburg | 3,436 | 11 | 10 | 1 |
| Parkside | 2,166 | 3 | 3 | 0 |
| Patterson Area | 3,539 | 4 | 4 | 0 |
| Patton | 1,830 | 2 | 2 | 0 |
| Patton Township | 13,425 | 19 | 17 | 2 |
| Paxtang | 1,477 | 3 | 3 | 0 |
| Pen Argyl | 3,629 | 4 | 4 | 0 |
| Penbrook | 2,906 | 6 | 6 | 0 |
| Penn Hills | 43,755 | 57 | 53 | 4 |
| Pennridge Regional | 10,633 | 15 | 13 | 2 |
| Penn Township, Butler County | 5,142 | 4 | 3 | 1 |
| Penn Township, Lancaster County | 8,688 | 12 | 11 | 1 |
| Penn Township, Perry County | 3,246 | 6 | 5 | 1 |
| Penn Township, Westmoreland County | 20,193 | 23 | 21 | 2 |
| Penn Township, York County | 15,959 | 25 | 23 | 2 |
| Pequea Township | 4,542 | 9 | 9 | 0 |
| Perkasie | 8,614 | 20 | 18 | 2 |
| Perryopolis | 1,707 | 2 | 2 | 0 |
| Peters Township | 20,540 | 23 | 21 | 2 |
| Philadelphia | 1,547,605 | 7,576 | 6,722 | 854 |
| Phoenixville | 16,569 | 29 | 28 | 1 |
| Pine Creek Township | 3,199 | 1 | 1 | 0 |
| Pine Grove | 2,031 | 2 | 2 | 0 |
| Pitcairn | 3,308 | 4 | 4 | 0 |
| Pittsburgh | 312,232 | 976 | 914 | 62 |
| Pittston | 7,490 | 7 | 7 | 0 |
| Plainfield Township | 6,235 | 13 | 12 | 1 |
| Plains Township | 10,364 | 17 | 16 | 1 |
| Pleasant Hills | 7,684 | 18 | 16 | 2 |
| Plum | 26,118 | 30 | 24 | 6 |
| Plumstead Township | 11,811 | 16 | 14 | 2 |
| Plymouth Township, Montgomery County | 16,350 | 53 | 46 | 7 |
| Pocono Mountain Regional | 35,793 | 50 | 44 | 6 |
| Pocono Township | 11,295 | 19 | 18 | 1 |
| Point Marion | 1,238 | 1 | 1 | 0 |
| Point Township | 3,885 | 5 | 5 | 0 |
| Polk | 991 | 2 | 2 | 0 |
| Portage | 2,555 | 2 | 2 | 0 |
| Port Allegany | 2,173 | 4 | 4 | 0 |
| Port Carbon | 1,733 | 2 | 2 | 0 |
| Porter Township | 1,591 | 3 | 3 | 0 |
| Port Vue | 3,804 | 4 | 4 | 0 |
| Pottstown | 21,226 | 60 | 47 | 13 |
| Pottsville | 14,288 | 28 | 28 | 0 |
| Prospect Park | 6,351 | 9 | 9 | 0 |
| Punxsutawney | 5,910 | 11 | 8 | 3 |
| Pymatuning Township | 3,530 | 5 | 5 | 0 |
| Quakertown | 8,612 | 23 | 15 | 8 |
| Quarryville | 2,163 | 4 | 4 | 0 |
| Raccoon Township | 3,199 | 4 | 4 | 0 |
| Radnor Township | 30,958 | 57 | 47 | 10 |
| Rankin | 2,087 | 1 | 1 | 0 |

## Table 78. Full-time Law Enforcement Employees, by State, by City, 2009—*Continued*

(Number.)

| State/city | Population | Total law enforcement employees | Total officers | Total civilians |
|---|---|---|---|---|
| Reading | 80,418 | 216 | 196 | 20 |
| Redstone Township | 6,006 | 2 | 2 | 0 |
| Reilly Township | 826 | 1 | 1 | 0 |
| Reserve Township | 3,497 | 6 | 6 | 0 |
| Reynoldsville | 2,535 | 2 | 2 | 0 |
| Rice Township | 3,055 | 5 | 5 | 0 |
| Richland Township, Bucks County | 12,914 | 14 | 12 | 2 |
| Richland Township, Cambria County | 12,275 | 21 | 20 | 1 |
| Ridgway | 4,046 | 5 | 4 | 1 |
| Ridley Park | 6,956 | 15 | 10 | 5 |
| Ridley Township | 29,767 | 37 | 32 | 5 |
| Riverside | 1,852 | 3 | 3 | 0 |
| Roaring Brook Township | 1,804 | 2 | 2 | 0 |
| Roaring Spring | 2,235 | 3 | 3 | 0 |
| Robesonia | 2,050 | 1 | 1 | 0 |
| Robeson Township | 7,682 | 7 | 6 | 1 |
| Robinson Township, Allegheny County | 13,534 | 26 | 21 | 5 |
| Robinson Township, Washington County | 2,114 | 3 | 2 | 1 |
| Rochester | 3,626 | 11 | 9 | 2 |
| Rochester Township | 2,846 | 3 | 3 | 0 |
| Rockledge | 2,467 | 5 | 5 | 0 |
| Roseto | 1,642 | 2 | 2 | 0 |
| Rosslyn Farms | 419 | 2 | 2 | 0 |
| Ross Township | 30,340 | 43 | 43 | 0 |
| Rostraver Township | 11,621 | 15 | 14 | 1 |
| Royersford | 4,368 | 8 | 7 | 1 |
| Rush Township | 3,724 | 3 | 3 | 0 |
| Rye Township | 2,548 | 1 | 1 | 0 |
| Sadsbury Township, Chester County | 3,393 | 2 | 2 | 0 |
| Salem Township, Luzerne County | 4,075 | 4 | 4 | 0 |
| Salisbury Township | 14,068 | 18 | 16 | 2 |
| Sandy Lake | 686 | 1 | 1 | 0 |
| Sandy Township | 11,577 | 10 | 9 | 1 |
| Saxonburg | 1,589 | 2 | 2 | 0 |
| Saxton | 758 | 1 | 1 | 0 |
| Sayre | 5,401 | 14 | 14 | 0 |
| Schuylkill Haven | 5,121 | 8 | 8 | 0 |
| Schuylkill Township, Chester County | 7,779 | 13 | 11 | 2 |
| Scottdale | 4,372 | 7 | 7 | 0 |
| Scott Township, Allegheny County | 15,732 | 21 | 20 | 1 |
| Scott Township, Columbia County | 5,062 | 6 | 6 | 0 |
| Scott Township, Lackawanna County | 4,892 | 5 | 5 | 0 |
| Scranton | 71,843 | 170 | 150 | 20 |
| Selinsgrove | 5,341 | 7 | 6 | 1 |
| Seven Springs | 116 | 7 | 6 | 1 |
| Sewickley | 4,045 | 13 | 12 | 1 |
| Sewickley Heights | 912 | 5 | 3 | 2 |
| Shaler Township | 27,750 | 25 | 25 | 0 |
| Shamokin | 7,301 | 13 | 13 | 0 |
| Shamokin Dam | 1,432 | 3 | 3 | 0 |
| Sharon | 14,721 | 28 | 27 | 1 |
| Sharon Hill | 5,291 | 10 | 9 | 1 |
| Sharpsburg | 3,229 | 6 | 6 | 0 |
| Sharpsville | 4,059 | 6 | 5 | 1 |
| Sheffield Township | 2,185 | 1 | 1 | 0 |
| Shenandoah | 5,107 | 7 | 7 | 0 |
| Shenango Township, Lawrence County | 7,614 | 6 | 6 | 0 |
| Shillington | 4,990 | 7 | 7 | 0 |
| Shinglehouse | 1,090 | 1 | 1 | 0 |
| Shippingport | 217 | 2 | 2 | 0 |
| Shiremanstown | 1,458 | 2 | 2 | 0 |
| Shohola Township | 2,469 | 1 | 1 | 0 |
| Silver Lake Township | 1,723 | 3 | 3 | 0 |
| Silver Spring Township | 13,488 | 16 | 15 | 1 |
| Sinking Spring | 3,726 | 7 | 6 | 1 |
| Slatington | 4,401 | 7 | 7 | 0 |
| Slippery Rock | 3,069 | 4 | 4 | 0 |
| Smith Township | 4,467 | 1 | 1 | 0 |
| Solebury Township | 8,889 | 15 | 13 | 2 |
| Somerset | 6,316 | 8 | 7 | 1 |
| Souderton | 6,533 | 6 | 6 | 0 |
| South Abington Township | 9,663 | 12 | 10 | 2 |
| South Annville Township | 3,226 | 2 | 2 | 0 |
| South Beaver Township | 2,827 | 4 | 4 | 0 |
| South Buffalo Township | 2,797 | 2 | 2 | 0 |
| South Centre Township | 1,903 | 10 | 10 | 0 |
| South Coatesville | 1,067 | 2 | 2 | 0 |
| South Connellsville Borough | 2,137 | 2 | 2 | 0 |
| Southern Regional Lancaster County | 3,842 | 9 | 9 | 0 |
| Southern Regional York County | 10,027 | 12 | 11 | 1 |
| South Fayette Township | 13,304 | 18 | 17 | 1 |
| South Fork | 1,017 | 2 | 2 | 0 |
| South Greensburg | 2,210 | 2 | 2 | 0 |
| South Heidelberg Township | 7,409 | 7 | 7 | 0 |
| South Lebanon Township | 8,732 | 8 | 7 | 1 |
| South Londonderry Township | 7,503 | 7 | 6 | 1 |
| South Park Township | 13,823 | 18 | 17 | 1 |
| South Pymatuning Township | 2,779 | 2 | 2 | 0 |
| South Strabane Township | 8,807 | 15 | 14 | 1 |
| South Waverly | 962 | 3 | 3 | 0 |
| Southwestern Regional | 18,230 | 14 | 13 | 1 |
| Southwest Greensburg | 2,181 | 2 | 2 | 0 |
| Southwest Mercer County Regional | 11,096 | 24 | 23 | 1 |
| Southwest Regional | 2,842 | 3 | 2 | 1 |
| South Whitehall Township | 19,853 | 40 | 37 | 3 |
| South Williamsport | 5,976 | 8 | 7 | 1 |
| Spring City | 3,383 | 4 | 3 | 1 |
| Springdale | 3,452 | 3 | 3 | 0 |
| Springettsbury Township | 24,940 | 35 | 32 | 3 |
| Springfield Township, Bucks County | 5,079 | 4 | 4 | 0 |
| Springfield Township, Delaware County | 22,682 | 40 | 34 | 6 |
| Springfield Township, Montgomery County | 18,778 | 30 | 29 | 1 |
| Spring Garden Township | 12,154 | 20 | 17 | 3 |
| Spring Township, Berks County | 26,803 | 32 | 30 | 2 |
| Spring Township, Centre County | 7,083 | 8 | 7 | 1 |
| State College | 53,587 | 77 | 64 | 13 |
| St. Clair Boro | 2,960 | 6 | 6 | 0 |
| Steelton | 5,571 | 9 | 8 | 1 |
| Stewartstown | 2,024 | 6 | 5 | 1 |
| St. Marys City | 13,296 | 16 | 15 | 1 |
| Stoneboro | 1,006 | 1 | 1 | 0 |
| Stonycreek Township | 2,874 | 2 | 2 | 0 |
| Stowe Township | 6,032 | 8 | 7 | 1 |
| Strasburg | 2,774 | 4 | 4 | 0 |
| Stroud Area Regional | 34,763 | 62 | 56 | 6 |
| Sugarcreek | 4,931 | 4 | 4 | 0 |
| Sugar Notch | 949 | 4 | 1 | 3 |
| Summerhill Township | 2,565 | 2 | 2 | 0 |
| Summit Hill | 2,954 | 6 | 4 | 2 |
| Summit Township | 2,234 | 1 | 1 | 0 |
| Sunbury | 9,737 | 13 | 11 | 2 |
| Susquehanna Township, Dauphin County | 23,181 | 42 | 40 | 2 |
| Swarthmore | 6,082 | 9 | 9 | 0 |
| Swatara Township | 22,426 | 52 | 49 | 3 |
| Swissvale | 8,674 | 14 | 12 | 2 |
| Swoyersville | 7,534 | 7 | 7 | 0 |
| Sykesville | 1,163 | 2 | 2 | 0 |
| Tamaqua | 6,521 | 10 | 9 | 1 |
| Tarentum | 4,487 | 8 | 7 | 1 |
| Taylor | 6,118 | 7 | 7 | 0 |
| Throop | 4,057 | 4 | 4 | 0 |
| Tidioute | 710 | 1 | 1 | 0 |
| Tilden Township | 3,825 | 2 | 2 | 0 |
| Tinicum Township, Bucks County | 4,201 | 5 | 5 | 0 |
| Tinicum Township, Delaware County | 4,178 | 17 | 15 | 2 |
| Titusville | 5,735 | 10 | 10 | 0 |
| Towamencin Township | 17,619 | 36 | 24 | 12 |
| Towanda | 2,805 | 6 | 6 | 0 |
| Trafford | 2,987 | 3 | 3 | 0 |
| Trainer | 1,824 | 6 | 6 | 0 |
| Tredyffrin Township | 28,915 | 56 | 47 | 9 |
| Troy | 1,451 | 3 | 3 | 0 |
| Tullytown | 1,948 | 7 | 6 | 1 |
| Tulpehocken Township | 3,570 | 3 | 3 | 0 |
| Tunkhannock | 1,759 | 5 | 5 | 0 |
| Tunkhannock Township, Wyoming County | 4,284 | 2 | 2 | 0 |
| Union City | 3,257 | 3 | 3 | 0 |
| Uniontown | 11,603 | 19 | 19 | 0 |
| Union Township, Lawrence County | 4,992 | 3 | 3 | 0 |
| Upland | 2,852 | 5 | 4 | 1 |
| Upper Allen Township | 18,353 | 21 | 20 | 1 |
| Upper Burrell Township | 2,113 | 2 | 2 | 0 |

# Table 78. Full-time Law Enforcement Employees, by State, by City, 2009—*Continued*

(Number.)

| State/city | Population | Total law enforcement employees | Total officers | Total civilians |
|---|---|---|---|---|
| Upper Chichester Township | 17,621 | 24 | 22 | 2 |
| Upper Darby Township | 78,088 | 145 | 126 | 19 |
| Upper Dublin Township | 25,904 | 49 | 41 | 8 |
| Upper Gwynedd Township | 16,234 | 25 | 22 | 3 |
| Upper Makefield Township | 8,630 | 17 | 16 | 1 |
| Upper Merion Township | 26,410 | 84 | 64 | 20 |
| Upper Moreland Township | 24,093 | 45 | 35 | 10 |
| Upper Nazareth Township | 6,026 | 4 | 3 | 1 |
| Upper Perkiomen | 6,372 | 10 | 9 | 1 |
| Upper Pottsgrove Township | 5,330 | 9 | 8 | 1 |
| Upper Providence Township, Delaware County | 11,131 | 12 | 12 | 0 |
| Upper Providence Township, Montgomery County | 20,048 | 27 | 25 | 2 |
| Upper Saucon Township | 15,182 | 21 | 20 | 1 |
| Upper Southampton Township | 15,192 | 25 | 22 | 3 |
| Upper St. Clair Township | 18,723 | 35 | 28 | 7 |
| Upper Uwchlan Township | 11,728 | 10 | 10 | 0 |
| Upper Yoder Township | 5,455 | 13 | 13 | 0 |
| Uwchlan Township | 18,869 | 24 | 22 | 2 |
| Valley Township | 6,869 | 5 | 5 | 0 |
| Vandergrift | 4,950 | 8 | 8 | 0 |
| Vernon Township | 5,413 | 5 | 4 | 1 |
| Verona | 2,813 | 4 | 3 | 1 |
| Walker Township | 976 | 1 | 1 | 0 |
| Walnutport | 2,202 | 4 | 4 | 0 |
| Warminster Township | 33,914 | 54 | 49 | 5 |
| Warren | 9,316 | 20 | 17 | 3 |
| Warrington Township | 23,417 | 33 | 31 | 2 |
| Warwick Township, Bucks County | 14,980 | 22 | 20 | 2 |
| Warwick Township, Lancaster County | 17,426 | 17 | 15 | 2 |
| Washington, Washington County | 14,709 | 33 | 31 | 2 |
| Washington Township, Fayette County | 4,126 | 3 | 3 | 0 |
| Washington Township, Franklin County | 12,201 | 18 | 16 | 2 |
| Washington Township, Northampton County | 4,932 | 5 | 5 | 0 |
| Washington Township, Westmoreland County | 7,347 | 7 | 7 | 0 |
| Watsontown | 2,086 | 5 | 5 | 0 |
| Waynesboro | 9,985 | 21 | 19 | 2 |
| Waynesburg | 4,144 | 10 | 8 | 2 |
| Weatherly | 2,586 | 3 | 3 | 0 |
| Weissport | 423 | 1 | 1 | 0 |
| Wellsboro | 3,233 | 6 | 6 | 0 |
| Wernersville | 2,478 | 2 | 2 | 0 |
| Wesleyville | 3,267 | 11 | 10 | 1 |
| West Brandywine Township | 7,936 | 5 | 5 | 0 |
| West Caln Township | 8,477 | 2 | 2 | 0 |
| West Chester | 18,366 | 60 | 47 | 13 |
| West Conshohocken | 1,501 | 10 | 9 | 1 |
| West Deer Township | 11,974 | 12 | 11 | 1 |
| West Earl Township | 7,779 | 6 | 6 | 0 |
| West Fallowfield Township | 2,603 | 1 | 1 | 0 |
| Westfield | 1,108 | 2 | 2 | 0 |
| West Goshen Township | 21,262 | 34 | 30 | 4 |
| West Grove Borough | 2,773 | 2 | 2 | 0 |
| West Hazleton | 3,278 | 3 | 2 | 1 |
| West Hempfield Township | 16,179 | 23 | 20 | 3 |
| West Hills Regional | 10,568 | 12 | 11 | 1 |
| West Lampeter Township | 15,819 | 16 | 15 | 1 |
| West Mahanoy Township | 2,970 | 3 | 3 | 0 |
| West Manchester Township | 18,393 | 29 | 26 | 3 |
| West Manheim Township | 7,762 | 9 | 8 | 1 |
| West Mead Township | 5,047 | 2 | 2 | 0 |
| West Mifflin | 20,484 | 42 | 36 | 6 |
| West Newton | 2,824 | 2 | 2 | 0 |
| West Norriton Township | 14,488 | 33 | 28 | 5 |
| West Penn Township | 4,343 | 3 | 3 | 0 |
| West Pikeland Township | 4,089 | 4 | 4 | 0 |
| West Pike Run | 1,829 | 1 | 1 | 0 |
| West Pittston | 4,901 | 4 | 4 | 0 |
| West Pottsgrove Township | 3,755 | 10 | 9 | 1 |
| West Sadsbury Township | 2,510 | 4 | 3 | 1 |
| West Salem Township | 3,324 | 10 | 9 | 1 |
| West Shore Regional | 6,568 | 12 | 10 | 2 |
| Westtown-East Goshen Regional | 31,830 | 34 | 31 | 3 |
| West View | 6,615 | 12 | 8 | 4 |
| West Vincent Township | 5,082 | 6 | 5 | 1 |
| West Whiteland Township | 18,397 | 30 | 28 | 2 |

| State/city | Population | Total law enforcement employees | Total officers | Total civilians |
|---|---|---|---|---|
| West Wyoming | 2,668 | 1 | 1 | 0 |
| Whitehall | 13,293 | 24 | 19 | 5 |
| Whitehall Township | 27,053 | 55 | 48 | 7 |
| Whitemarsh Township | 17,840 | 44 | 36 | 8 |
| White Oak | 7,958 | 12 | 11 | 1 |
| White Township | 1,298 | 5 | 5 | 0 |
| Whitpain Township | 18,829 | 39 | 31 | 8 |
| Wiconisco Township | 1,100 | 1 | 1 | 0 |
| Wilkes-Barre | 40,710 | 95 | 92 | 3 |
| Wilkes-Barre Township | 3,045 | 18 | 16 | 2 |
| Wilkinsburg | 17,351 | 27 | 24 | 3 |
| Wilkins Township | 6,146 | 12 | 12 | 0 |
| Williamsburg | 1,238 | 1 | 1 | 0 |
| Williamsport | 29,329 | 57 | 53 | 4 |
| Willistown Township | 10,838 | 19 | 17 | 2 |
| Wilson | 7,622 | 9 | 8 | 1 |
| Windber | 3,973 | 3 | 2 | 1 |
| Wind Gap | 2,782 | 5 | 5 | 0 |
| Womelsdorf | 2,811 | 1 | 1 | 0 |
| Wrightsville | 2,234 | 3 | 3 | 0 |
| Wright Township | 5,920 | 7 | 7 | 0 |
| Wyoming | 2,972 | 4 | 4 | 0 |
| Wyomissing | 10,396 | 28 | 23 | 5 |
| Yardley | 2,491 | 3 | 3 | 0 |
| Yeadon | 11,325 | 16 | 14 | 2 |
| York | 39,970 | 123 | 108 | 15 |
| York Area Regional | 58,530 | 56 | 51 | 5 |
| Youngsville | 1,649 | 2 | 2 | 0 |
| Zelienople | 3,902 | 10 | 9 | 1 |
| **RHODE ISLAND** | | | | |
| Barrington | 16,353 | 28 | 21 | 7 |
| Bristol | 22,510 | 49 | 38 | 11 |
| Burrillville | 16,590 | 31 | 23 | 8 |
| Central Falls | 18,696 | 51 | 42 | 9 |
| Charlestown | 8,067 | 24 | 19 | 5 |
| Coventry | 34,837 | 74 | 59 | 15 |
| Cranston | 80,223 | 171 | 141 | 30 |
| Cumberland | 34,546 | 56 | 45 | 11 |
| East Greenwich | 13,357 | 40 | 32 | 8 |
| East Providence | 48,557 | 115 | 97 | 18 |
| Foster | 4,537 | 12 | 8 | 4 |
| Glocester | 10,583 | 18 | 13 | 5 |
| Hopkinton | 7,988 | 20 | 15 | 5 |
| Jamestown | 5,467 | 21 | 15 | 6 |
| Johnston | 28,617 | 84 | 69 | 15 |
| Lincoln | 22,156 | 44 | 37 | 7 |
| Little Compton | 3,513 | 14 | 10 | 4 |
| Middletown | 16,009 | 36 | 32 | 4 |
| Narragansett | 16,476 | 53 | 41 | 12 |
| Newport | 23,260 | 100 | 81 | 19 |
| New Shoreham | 1,036 | 9 | 5 | 4 |
| North Kingstown | 26,615 | 61 | 49 | 12 |
| North Providence | 32,794 | 81 | 60 | 21 |
| North Smithfield | 11,640 | 28 | 21 | 7 |
| Pawtucket | 71,787 | 181 | 144 | 37 |
| Portsmouth | 16,913 | 33 | 31 | 2 |
| Providence | 171,664 | 561 | 471 | 90 |
| Richmond | 7,657 | 17 | 13 | 4 |
| Scituate | 10,894 | 23 | 17 | 6 |
| Smithfield | 21,289 | 55 | 41 | 14 |
| South Kingstown | 29,270 | 70 | 52 | 18 |
| Tiverton | 14,944 | 36 | 26 | 10 |
| Warren | 10,990 | 28 | 22 | 6 |
| Warwick | 84,488 | 206 | 161 | 45 |
| Westerly | 23,466 | 60 | 48 | 12 |
| West Greenwich | 6,540 | 17 | 11 | 6 |
| West Warwick | 29,282 | 69 | 57 | 12 |
| Woonsocket | 43,366 | 104 | 89 | 15 |
| **SOUTH CAROLINA** | | | | |
| Abbeville | 5,514 | 24 | 19 | 5 |
| Aiken | 29,829 | 115 | 90 | 25 |
| Allendale | 3,617 | 11 | 10 | 1 |
| Anderson | 27,144 | 133 | 96 | 37 |
| Andrews | 2,968 | 8 | 7 | 1 |
| Aynor | 642 | 8 | 6 | 2 |
| Bamberg | 3,401 | 12 | 10 | 2 |

## Table 78. Full-time Law Enforcement Employees, by State, by City, 2009—*Continued*

(Number.)

| State/city | Population | Total law enforcement employees | Total officers | Total civilians |
|---|---|---|---|---|
| Barnwell | 4,766 | 18 | 16 | 2 |
| Belton | 4,691 | 14 | 13 | 1 |
| Bennettsville | 8,956 | 38 | 34 | 4 |
| Bishopville | 3,880 | 14 | 12 | 2 |
| Bluffton | 12,557 | 38 | 35 | 3 |
| Bonneau | 352 | 7 | 3 | 4 |
| Bowman | 1,143 | 4 | 4 | 0 |
| Burnettown | 2,669 | 2 | 2 | 0 |
| Camden | 7,072 | 30 | 27 | 3 |
| Cayce | 12,700 | 67 | 48 | 19 |
| Central | 4,154 | 9 | 8 | 1 |
| Chapin | 718 | 6 | 6 | 0 |
| Charleston | 113,681 | 537 | 390 | 147 |
| Cheraw | 5,411 | 28 | 22 | 6 |
| Chesterfield | 1,313 | 6 | 5 | 1 |
| Clemson | 13,147 | 34 | 26 | 8 |
| Clinton | 8,865 | 40 | 30 | 10 |
| Clio | 715 | 6 | 4 | 2 |
| Clover | 5,032 | 19 | 15 | 4 |
| Columbia | 127,884 | 383 | 345 | 38 |
| Conway | 16,295 | 65 | 50 | 15 |
| Coward | 679 | 2 | 2 | 0 |
| Darlington | 6,645 | 31 | 28 | 3 |
| Denmark | 2,972 | 10 | 9 | 1 |
| Dillon | 6,350 | 29 | 26 | 3 |
| Duncan | 3,141 | 15 | 14 | 1 |
| Easley | 20,589 | 56 | 45 | 11 |
| Edisto Beach | 726 | 6 | 6 | 0 |
| Elgin | 1,294 | 7 | 6 | 1 |
| Fairfax | 3,154 | 8 | 7 | 1 |
| Florence | 31,642 | 127 | 100 | 27 |
| Folly Beach | 2,445 | 21 | 14 | 7 |
| Forest Acres | 9,859 | 36 | 28 | 8 |
| Fort Lawn | 804 | 3 | 3 | 0 |
| Fort Mill | 10,316 | 38 | 32 | 6 |
| Fountain Inn | 7,944 | 29 | 23 | 6 |
| Goose Creek | 38,770 | 84 | 59 | 25 |
| Greenville | 60,355 | 225 | 183 | 42 |
| Greenwood | 22,551 | 57 | 50 | 7 |
| Greer | 25,463 | 70 | 54 | 16 |
| Hampton | 2,745 | 11 | 11 | 0 |
| Hanahan | 16,460 | 40 | 32 | 8 |
| Hardeeville | 2,918 | 19 | 17 | 2 |
| Hartsville | 7,454 | 36 | 33 | 3 |
| Hemingway | 493 | 6 | 6 | 0 |
| Honea Path | 3,691 | 16 | 16 | 0 |
| Inman | 2,107 | 9 | 9 | 0 |
| Irmo | 11,738 | 25 | 23 | 2 |
| Isle of Palms | 4,690 | 28 | 18 | 10 |
| Jackson | 1,650 | 4 | 4 | 0 |
| Johnsonville | 1,496 | 6 | 5 | 1 |
| Johnston | 2,330 | 8 | 8 | 0 |
| Jonesville | 893 | 2 | 2 | 0 |
| Kingstree | 3,211 | 21 | 19 | 2 |
| Lake City | 6,687 | 27 | 22 | 5 |
| Lake View | 781 | 4 | 2 | 2 |
| Lamar | 988 | 4 | 4 | 0 |
| Lancaster | 10,193 | 47 | 37 | 10 |
| Landrum | 2,630 | 10 | 9 | 1 |
| Lane | 509 | 2 | 2 | 0 |
| Laurens | 9,582 | 34 | 27 | 7 |
| Lexington | 16,628 | 48 | 43 | 5 |
| Liberty | 3,070 | 16 | 10 | 6 |
| Lyman | 2,890 | 9 | 7 | 2 |
| Lynchburg | 549 | 3 | 3 | 0 |
| McBee | 705 | 1 | 1 | 0 |
| McColl | 2,288 | 13 | 6 | 7 |
| McCormick | 2,660 | 6 | 6 | 0 |
| Moncks Corner | 7,160 | 28 | 25 | 3 |
| Mount Pleasant | 67,641 | 173 | 134 | 39 |
| Mullins | 4,683 | 23 | 20 | 3 |
| Myrtle Beach | 31,465 | 272 | 202 | 70 |
| Newberry | 10,952 | 32 | 29 | 3 |
| New Ellenton | 2,224 | 7 | 7 | 0 |
| Ninety Six | 1,920 | 6 | 5 | 1 |
| North | 772 | 3 | 3 | 0 |
| North Augusta | 21,066 | 71 | 52 | 19 |
| North Charleston | 95,982 | 408 | 313 | 95 |
| Orangeburg | 13,278 | 96 | 70 | 26 |
| Pacolet | 2,834 | 5 | 5 | 0 |
| Pageland | 2,512 | 15 | 10 | 5 |
| Pelion | 597 | 3 | 3 | 0 |
| Pickens | 3,024 | 14 | 13 | 1 |
| Pine Ridge | 2,007 | 3 | 2 | 1 |
| Port Royal | 11,282 | 21 | 20 | 1 |
| Prosperity | 1,065 | 4 | 4 | 0 |
| Ridgeland | 2,586 | 16 | 14 | 2 |
| Ridgeville | 2,015 | 1 | 1 | 0 |
| Saluda | 2,894 | 12 | 10 | 2 |
| Santee | 715 | 9 | 8 | 1 |
| Scranton | 1,039 | 2 | 2 | 0 |
| Seneca | 8,074 | 45 | 33 | 12 |
| Simpsonville | 17,433 | 49 | 39 | 10 |
| South Congaree | 2,379 | 8 | 6 | 2 |
| Spartanburg | 39,561 | 145 | 120 | 25 |
| Springdale | 2,946 | 8 | 8 | 0 |
| St. George | 2,127 | 10 | 10 | 0 |
| St. Matthews | 1,931 | 6 | 6 | 0 |
| Sullivans Island | 1,866 | 9 | 8 | 1 |
| Summerton | 1,025 | 7 | 6 | 1 |
| Summerville | 47,507 | 104 | 82 | 22 |
| Sumter | 38,399 | 158 | 117 | 41 |
| Surfside Beach | 4,823 | 29 | 22 | 7 |
| Swansea | 805 | 4 | 3 | 1 |
| Tega Cay | 5,103 | 25 | 19 | 6 |
| Timmonsville | 2,380 | 6 | 6 | 0 |
| Travelers Rest | 4,574 | 21 | 15 | 6 |
| Turbeville | 705 | 5 | 4 | 1 |
| Union | 7,960 | 33 | 31 | 2 |
| Wagener | 876 | 3 | 3 | 0 |
| Walhalla | 3,551 | 16 | 14 | 2 |
| Wellford | 2,479 | 9 | 9 | 0 |
| West Columbia | 13,982 | 68 | 54 | 14 |
| Westminster | 2,654 | 9 | 9 | 0 |
| Williston | 3,178 | 9 | 8 | 1 |
| Winnsboro | 3,562 | 25 | 24 | 1 |
| Woodruff | 4,089 | 13 | 12 | 1 |
| Yemassee | 866 | 7 | 7 | 0 |
| York | 8,083 | 35 | 28 | 7 |
| **SOUTH DAKOTA** | | | | |
| Aberdeen | 24,441 | 50 | 42 | 8 |
| Alcester | 893 | 2 | 2 | 0 |
| Armour | 642 | 1 | 1 | 0 |
| Avon | 511 | 1 | 1 | 0 |
| Belle Fourche | 5,001 | 8 | 7 | 1 |
| Beresford | 2,166 | 8 | 4 | 4 |
| Box Elder | 3,601 | 10 | 9 | 1 |
| Brandon | 9,195 | 12 | 11 | 1 |
| Brookings | 19,986 | 37 | 28 | 9 |
| Burke | 561 | 1 | 1 | 0 |
| Canton | 3,680 | 5 | 5 | 0 |
| Centerville | 837 | 1 | 1 | 0 |
| Chamberlain | 2,255 | 5 | 5 | 0 |
| Colman | 546 | 1 | 1 | 0 |
| Corsica | 563 | 1 | 1 | 0 |
| Deadwood | 1,273 | 14 | 11 | 3 |
| Eagle Butte | 927 | 2 | 2 | 0 |
| Elk Point | 1,965 | 5 | 5 | 0 |
| Estelline | 665 | 1 | 1 | 0 |
| Eureka | 921 | 2 | 2 | 0 |
| Faith | 436 | 2 | 1 | 1 |
| Flandreau | 2,206 | 5 | 3 | 2 |
| Freeman | 1,181 | 2 | 2 | 0 |
| Gettysburg | 1,031 | 2 | 2 | 0 |
| Gregory | 1,161 | 3 | 3 | 0 |
| Groton | 1,414 | 3 | 3 | 0 |
| Highmore | 701 | 1 | 1 | 0 |
| Hot Springs | 4,015 | 8 | 7 | 1 |
| Hoven | 384 | 1 | 1 | 0 |
| Huron | 10,945 | 31 | 25 | 6 |
| Jefferson | 600 | 2 | 2 | 0 |
| Kadoka | 628 | 1 | 1 | 0 |

## Table 78. Full-time Law Enforcement Employees, by State, by City, 2009—*Continued*

(Number.)

| State/city | Population | Total law enforcement employees | Total officers | Total civilians |
|---|---|---|---|---|
| Kimball | 687 | 1 | 1 | 0 |
| Lead | 2,878 | 6 | 5 | 1 |
| Lemmon | 1,164 | 3 | 3 | 0 |
| Lennox | 2,453 | 4 | 4 | 0 |
| Leola | 383 | 1 | 1 | 0 |
| Madison | 6,478 | 11 | 10 | 1 |
| Martin | 986 | 2 | 2 | 0 |
| McIntosh | 204 | 1 | 1 | 0 |
| McLaughlin | 726 | 2 | 1 | 1 |
| Menno | 648 | 1 | 1 | 0 |
| Milbank | 3,159 | 6 | 6 | 0 |
| Miller | 1,321 | 4 | 4 | 0 |
| Mitchell | 14,769 | 30 | 28 | 2 |
| Mobridge | 3,113 | 13 | 7 | 6 |
| North Sioux City | 2,547 | 9 | 7 | 2 |
| Parkston | 1,467 | 3 | 3 | 0 |
| Philip | 716 | 2 | 2 | 0 |
| Pierre | 13,901 | 37 | 24 | 13 |
| Platte | 1,276 | 2 | 2 | 0 |
| Rapid City | 66,170 | 127 | 105 | 22 |
| Rosholt | 427 | 1 | 1 | 0 |
| Scotland | 780 | 1 | 1 | 0 |
| Selby | 638 | 1 | 1 | 0 |
| Sioux Falls | 158,672 | 259 | 219 | 40 |
| Sisseton | 2,437 | 7 | 7 | 0 |
| Spearfish | 10,171 | 29 | 20 | 9 |
| Springfield | 1,479 | 2 | 2 | 0 |
| Sturgis | 5,899 | 19 | 16 | 3 |
| Summerset | 442 | 1 | 1 | 0 |
| Tea | 4,073 | 5 | 5 | 0 |
| Tripp | 623 | 1 | 1 | 0 |
| Tyndall | 1,088 | 2 | 2 | 0 |
| Vermillion | 10,523 | 18 | 17 | 1 |
| Viborg | 768 | 1 | 1 | 0 |
| Wagner | 1,538 | 4 | 4 | 0 |
| Watertown | 20,515 | 51 | 36 | 15 |
| Webster | 1,641 | 5 | 5 | 0 |
| Whitewood | 850 | 3 | 3 | 0 |
| Winner | 2,705 | 8 | 6 | 2 |
| Worthing | 1,047 | 1 | 1 | 0 |
| Yankton | 13,831 | 38 | 26 | 12 |
| **TENNESSEE** | | | | |
| Adamsville | 2,138 | 9 | 6 | 3 |
| Alamo | 2,307 | 4 | 4 | 0 |
| Alcoa | 8,681 | 45 | 37 | 8 |
| Alexandria | 879 | 3 | 3 | 0 |
| Algood | 3,430 | 11 | 11 | 0 |
| Ardmore | 1,172 | 12 | 8 | 4 |
| Ashland City | 4,695 | 15 | 14 | 1 |
| Athens | 14,388 | 31 | 29 | 2 |
| Atoka | 7,900 | 18 | 17 | 1 |
| Baileyton | 491 | 2 | 2 | 0 |
| Bartlett | 47,881 | 138 | 107 | 31 |
| Baxter | 1,422 | 4 | 4 | 0 |
| Bean Station | 3,072 | 7 | 7 | 0 |
| Belle Meade | 3,513 | 20 | 16 | 4 |
| Bells | 2,247 | 4 | 4 | 0 |
| Benton | 1,189 | 8 | 7 | 1 |
| Berry Hill | 822 | 17 | 13 | 4 |
| Bethel Springs | 777 | 1 | 1 | 0 |
| Big Sandy | 508 | 2 | 2 | 0 |
| Blaine | 1,770 | 3 | 1 | 2 |
| Bluff City | 1,664 | 8 | 8 | 0 |
| Bolivar | 5,627 | 27 | 22 | 5 |
| Bradford | 1,063 | 3 | 3 | 0 |
| Brentwood | 37,479 | 71 | 57 | 14 |
| Brighton | 2,736 | 5 | 5 | 0 |
| Bristol | 25,859 | 91 | 68 | 23 |
| Brownsville | 10,267 | 38 | 30 | 8 |
| Bruceton | 1,439 | 4 | 4 | 0 |
| Burns | 1,401 | 1 | 1 | 0 |
| Calhoun | 526 | 3 | 3 | 0 |
| Camden | 3,640 | 17 | 13 | 4 |
| Carthage | 2,234 | 11 | 7 | 4 |
| Caryville | 2,400 | 6 | 6 | 0 |
| Celina | 1,332 | 6 | 3 | 3 |
| Centerville | 3,994 | 21 | 13 | 8 |
| Chapel Hill | 1,363 | 5 | 5 | 0 |
| Charleston | 668 | 3 | 3 | 0 |
| Chattanooga | 172,536 | 511 | 432 | 79 |
| Church Hill | 6,864 | 11 | 10 | 1 |
| Clarksville | 121,661 | 295 | 239 | 56 |
| Cleveland | 40,024 | 99 | 88 | 11 |
| Clifton | 2,694 | 6 | 6 | 0 |
| Clinton | 9,646 | 31 | 24 | 7 |
| Collegedale | 8,106 | 21 | 20 | 1 |
| Collierville | 39,973 | 130 | 95 | 35 |
| Collinwood | 1,011 | 3 | 3 | 0 |
| Columbia | 34,529 | 99 | 88 | 11 |
| Cookeville | 29,609 | 86 | 68 | 18 |
| Coopertown | 3,428 | 6 | 5 | 1 |
| Copperhill | 435 | 1 | 1 | 0 |
| Cornersville | 965 | 3 | 3 | 0 |
| Covington | 9,339 | 36 | 35 | 1 |
| Cowan | 1,710 | 6 | 6 | 0 |
| Cross Plains | 1,671 | 3 | 3 | 0 |
| Crossville | 11,908 | 41 | 38 | 3 |
| Crump | 1,463 | 3 | 3 | 0 |
| Cumberland City | 328 | 3 | 3 | 0 |
| Cumberland Gap | 208 | 1 | 1 | 0 |
| Dandridge | 2,760 | 11 | 10 | 1 |
| Dayton | 6,799 | 19 | 17 | 2 |
| Decatur | 1,485 | 5 | 5 | 0 |
| Decaturville | 819 | 1 | 1 | 0 |
| Decherd | 2,112 | 13 | 12 | 1 |
| Dickson | 14,095 | 52 | 46 | 6 |
| Dover | 1,633 | 6 | 5 | 1 |
| Dresden | 2,816 | 9 | 8 | 1 |
| Dunlap | 5,521 | 14 | 12 | 2 |
| Dyer | 2,415 | 6 | 6 | 0 |
| Dyersburg | 17,088 | 68 | 58 | 10 |
| East Ridge | 19,546 | 42 | 38 | 4 |
| Elizabethton | 13,944 | 43 | 38 | 5 |
| Elkton | 593 | 2 | 2 | 0 |
| Englewood | 1,768 | 5 | 5 | 0 |
| Erin | 1,458 | 6 | 5 | 1 |
| Erwin | 5,798 | 12 | 12 | 0 |
| Estill Springs | 2,263 | 8 | 8 | 0 |
| Ethridge | 555 | 1 | 1 | 0 |
| Etowah | 3,787 | 13 | 9 | 4 |
| Fairview | 8,094 | 19 | 18 | 1 |
| Fayetteville | 7,184 | 27 | 25 | 2 |
| Franklin | 60,074 | 154 | 131 | 23 |
| Friendship | 592 | 1 | 1 | 0 |
| Gainesboro | 841 | 8 | 4 | 4 |
| Gallatin | 30,102 | 87 | 64 | 23 |
| Gallaway | 694 | 4 | 4 | 0 |
| Gates | 846 | 2 | 2 | 0 |
| Gatlinburg | 5,862 | 53 | 43 | 10 |
| Germantown | 41,419 | 108 | 87 | 21 |
| Gibson | 400 | 2 | 2 | 0 |
| Gleason | 1,395 | 5 | 5 | 0 |
| Goodlettsville | 17,481 | 52 | 38 | 14 |
| Gordonsville | 1,319 | 4 | 4 | 0 |
| Grand Junction | 304 | 1 | 1 | 0 |
| Graysville | 1,430 | 5 | 5 | 0 |
| Greenbrier | 6,752 | 13 | 12 | 1 |
| Greeneville | 15,446 | 45 | 43 | 2 |
| Greenfield | 2,022 | 8 | 7 | 1 |
| Halls | 2,178 | 8 | 8 | 0 |
| Harriman | 6,646 | 21 | 20 | 1 |
| Henderson | 6,483 | 15 | 15 | 0 |
| Hendersonville | 48,513 | 114 | 87 | 27 |
| Henning | 1,270 | 4 | 4 | 0 |
| Henry | 549 | 2 | 2 | 0 |
| Hohenwald | 3,803 | 14 | 13 | 1 |
| Hollow Rock | 930 | 1 | 1 | 0 |
| Hornbeak | 414 | 1 | 1 | 0 |
| Humboldt | 9,126 | 30 | 24 | 6 |
| Huntingdon | 4,101 | 15 | 11 | 4 |
| Huntland | 861 | 5 | 5 | 0 |
| Jacksboro | 2,127 | 6 | 6 | 0 |

## Table 78. Full-time Law Enforcement Employees, by State, by City, 2009—*Continued*

(Number.)

| State/city | Population | Total law enforcement employees | Total officers | Total civilians |
|---|---|---|---|---|
| Jackson | 63,530 | 242 | 201 | 41 |
| Jamestown | 1,927 | 11 | 11 | 0 |
| Jasper | 3,113 | 8 | 8 | 0 |
| Jefferson City | 8,188 | 21 | 19 | 2 |
| Jellico | 2,532 | 9 | 8 | 1 |
| Johnson City | 62,689 | 172 | 144 | 28 |
| Jonesborough | 5,351 | 21 | 17 | 4 |
| Kenton | 1,289 | 5 | 5 | 0 |
| Kimball | 1,411 | 9 | 9 | 0 |
| Kingsport | 44,402 | 161 | 105 | 56 |
| Kingston | 5,641 | 13 | 12 | 1 |
| Kingston Springs | 2,972 | 6 | 5 | 1 |
| Knoxville | 185,850 | 485 | 388 | 97 |
| Lafayette | 4,482 | 20 | 14 | 6 |
| La Follette | 8,218 | 33 | 24 | 9 |
| La Grange | 143 | 1 | 1 | 0 |
| Lake City | 1,843 | 10 | 7 | 3 |
| Lakewood | 2,624 | 4 | 4 | 0 |
| La Vergne | 31,620 | 62 | 44 | 18 |
| Lawrenceburg | 10,779 | 40 | 34 | 6 |
| Lebanon | 25,161 | 86 | 71 | 15 |
| Lenoir City | 8,147 | 24 | 23 | 1 |
| Lewisburg | 11,048 | 43 | 32 | 11 |
| Lexington | 7,908 | 31 | 26 | 5 |
| Livingston | 3,574 | 21 | 16 | 5 |
| Lookout Mountain | 1,853 | 22 | 17 | 5 |
| Loretto | 1,710 | 3 | 3 | 0 |
| Loudon | 4,959 | 17 | 16 | 1 |
| Madisonville | 4,800 | 17 | 14 | 3 |
| Manchester | 10,188 | 40 | 34 | 6 |
| Martin | 10,172 | 36 | 28 | 8 |
| Maryville | 27,641 | 59 | 52 | 7 |
| Mason | 1,248 | 4 | 4 | 0 |
| Maynardville | 1,923 | 4 | 4 | 0 |
| McEwen | 1,671 | 5 | 4 | 1 |
| McKenzie | 5,362 | 19 | 15 | 4 |
| McMinnville | 13,318 | 34 | 31 | 3 |
| Medina | 2,342 | 11 | 8 | 3 |
| Memphis | 667,421 | 2,724 | 2,202 | 522 |
| Middleton | 609 | 4 | 4 | 0 |
| Milan | 7,939 | 29 | 23 | 6 |
| Millersville | 6,387 | 17 | 12 | 5 |
| Millington | 10,137 | 50 | 38 | 12 |
| Minor Hill | 450 | 2 | 2 | 0 |
| Monteagle | 1,197 | 13 | 6 | 7 |
| Monterey | 2,943 | 7 | 7 | 0 |
| Morristown | 27,775 | 91 | 84 | 7 |
| Moscow | 558 | 4 | 4 | 0 |
| Mountain City | 2,398 | 8 | 8 | 0 |
| Mount Carmel | 5,538 | 7 | 7 | 0 |
| Mount Juliet | 22,778 | 53 | 42 | 11 |
| Mount Pleasant | 4,438 | 17 | 12 | 5 |
| Munford | 6,851 | 16 | 14 | 2 |
| Murfreesboro | 105,910 | 269 | 218 | 51 |
| Nashville | 610,176 | 1,753 | 1,433 | 320 |
| Newbern | 3,158 | 24 | 13 | 11 |
| New Hope | 1,049 | 1 | 1 | 0 |
| New Johnsonville | 1,959 | 4 | 4 | 0 |
| New Market | 1,330 | 9 | 5 | 4 |
| Newport | 7,539 | 29 | 24 | 5 |
| New Tazewell | 2,883 | 11 | 11 | 0 |
| Niota | 802 | 3 | 3 | 0 |
| Nolensville | 2,713 | 6 | 6 | 0 |
| Norris | 1,481 | 7 | 7 | 0 |
| Oakland | 5,792 | 15 | 13 | 2 |
| Oak Ridge | 27,718 | 76 | 60 | 16 |
| Obion | 1,063 | 4 | 4 | 0 |
| Oliver Springs | 3,329 | 12 | 8 | 4 |
| Oneida | 3,861 | 18 | 13 | 5 |
| Paris | 9,990 | 37 | 26 | 11 |
| Parsons | 2,338 | 6 | 6 | 0 |
| Petersburg | 606 | 2 | 2 | 0 |
| Pigeon Forge | 6,318 | 66 | 54 | 12 |
| Pikeville | 1,907 | 3 | 3 | 0 |
| Piperton | 1,297 | 9 | 9 | 0 |
| Pittman Center | 697 | 2 | 2 | 0 |
| Pleasant View | 4,232 | 5 | 5 | 0 |
| Portland | 11,476 | 37 | 29 | 8 |
| Powells Crossroads | 1,267 | 1 | 1 | 0 |
| Pulaski | 7,835 | 28 | 25 | 3 |
| Puryear | 676 | 2 | 2 | 0 |
| Red Bank | 11,488 | 24 | 22 | 2 |
| Red Boiling Springs | 1,116 | 6 | 5 | 1 |
| Ridgely | 1,496 | 6 | 5 | 1 |
| Ridgetop | 1,758 | 6 | 6 | 0 |
| Ripley | 7,616 | 30 | 24 | 6 |
| Rockwood | 5,553 | 16 | 15 | 1 |
| Rogersville | 4,357 | 18 | 14 | 4 |
| Rossville | 582 | 4 | 4 | 0 |
| Rutherford | 1,253 | 3 | 3 | 0 |
| Rutledge | 1,295 | 4 | 4 | 0 |
| Savannah | 7,354 | 20 | 18 | 2 |
| Scotts Hill | 925 | 1 | 1 | 0 |
| Selmer | 4,716 | 19 | 17 | 2 |
| Sevierville | 17,489 | 66 | 54 | 12 |
| Sewanee | 2,613 | 13 | 9 | 4 |
| Sharon | 908 | 1 | 1 | 0 |
| Shelbyville | 20,078 | 50 | 41 | 9 |
| Signal Mountain | 7,075 | 14 | 13 | 1 |
| Smithville | 4,435 | 12 | 11 | 1 |
| Smyrna | 39,260 | 99 | 73 | 26 |
| Sneedville | 1,308 | 1 | 1 | 0 |
| Soddy-Daisy | 12,624 | 33 | 26 | 7 |
| Somerville | 2,966 | 12 | 10 | 2 |
| South Carthage | 1,363 | 4 | 4 | 0 |
| South Fulton | 2,389 | 7 | 6 | 1 |
| South Pittsburg | 3,125 | 7 | 7 | 0 |
| Sparta | 4,976 | 16 | 15 | 1 |
| Spencer | 1,696 | 3 | 3 | 0 |
| Spring City | 2,021 | 8 | 8 | 0 |
| Springfield | 17,608 | 52 | 39 | 13 |
| Spring Hill | 29,870 | 51 | 39 | 12 |
| St. Joseph | 859 | 3 | 1 | 2 |
| Surgoinsville | 1,830 | 2 | 2 | 0 |
| Sweetwater | 6,758 | 20 | 18 | 2 |
| Tazewell | 2,221 | 6 | 6 | 0 |
| Tellico Plains | 976 | 6 | 5 | 1 |
| Tiptonville | 3,978 | 6 | 6 | 0 |
| Townsend | 275 | 4 | 4 | 0 |
| Tracy City | 1,649 | 5 | 5 | 0 |
| Trenton | 4,499 | 24 | 18 | 6 |
| Trezevant | 878 | 1 | 1 | 0 |
| Trimble | 717 | 1 | 1 | 0 |
| Troy | 1,201 | 4 | 4 | 0 |
| Tullahoma | 18,636 | 41 | 34 | 7 |
| Tusculum | 2,309 | 2 | 2 | 0 |
| Union City | 10,533 | 41 | 34 | 7 |
| Vonore | 1,533 | 10 | 9 | 1 |
| Wartburg | 932 | 4 | 4 | 0 |
| Wartrace | 593 | 1 | 1 | 0 |
| Watertown | 1,425 | 7 | 4 | 3 |
| Waverly | 4,201 | 14 | 13 | 1 |
| Waynesboro | 2,130 | 8 | 8 | 0 |
| Westmoreland | 2,199 | 10 | 6 | 4 |
| White Bluff | 2,556 | 4 | 4 | 0 |
| White House | 10,385 | 29 | 16 | 13 |
| White Pine | 2,159 | 8 | 8 | 0 |
| Whiteville | 4,456 | 7 | 7 | 0 |
| Whitwell | 1,597 | 8 | 5 | 3 |
| Winchester | 7,919 | 26 | 24 | 2 |
| Winfield | 1,002 | 3 | 3 | 0 |
| Woodbury | 2,630 | 9 | 8 | 1 |
| **TEXAS** | | | | |
| Abernathy | 2,721 | 4 | 4 | 0 |
| Abilene | 116,557 | 256 | 181 | 75 |
| Addison | 15,063 | 83 | 60 | 23 |
| Alamo | 16,810 | 37 | 26 | 11 |
| Alamo Heights | 7,378 | 29 | 19 | 10 |
| Alice | 19,886 | 46 | 36 | 10 |
| Allen | 86,901 | 153 | 106 | 47 |
| Alpine | 6,322 | 15 | 9 | 6 |
| Alto | 1,175 | 5 | 5 | 0 |

**Table 78. Full-time Law Enforcement Employees, by State, by City, 2009**—*Continued*

(Number.)

| State/city | Population | Total law enforcement employees | Total officers | Total civilians |
|---|---|---|---|---|
| Alton | 11,945 | 17 | 13 | 4 |
| Alvarado | 4,290 | 24 | 17 | 7 |
| Alvin | 23,013 | 71 | 48 | 23 |
| Amarillo | 188,767 | 364 | 308 | 56 |
| Andrews | 10,209 | 25 | 16 | 9 |
| Angleton | 18,665 | 49 | 37 | 12 |
| Anna | 1,906 | 13 | 11 | 2 |
| Anson | 2,252 | 4 | 4 | 0 |
| Anthony | 4,401 | 16 | 14 | 2 |
| Aransas Pass | 8,885 | 34 | 25 | 9 |
| Arcola | 1,251 | 7 | 6 | 1 |
| Argyle | 3,681 | 8 | 8 | 0 |
| Arlington | 379,104 | 804 | 623 | 181 |
| Arp | 969 | 4 | 4 | 0 |
| Athens | 12,402 | 34 | 26 | 8 |
| Atlanta | 5,444 | 19 | 15 | 4 |
| Austin | 768,970 | 2,146 | 1,564 | 582 |
| Azle | 11,555 | 30 | 24 | 6 |
| Baird | 1,677 | 2 | 2 | 0 |
| Balch Springs | 20,052 | 52 | 35 | 17 |
| Ballinger | 3,672 | 8 | 6 | 2 |
| Bangs | 1,561 | 3 | 3 | 0 |
| Bastrop | 8,792 | 24 | 20 | 4 |
| Bay City | 17,811 | 54 | 35 | 19 |
| Bayou Vista | 1,691 | 5 | 5 | 0 |
| Baytown | 70,764 | 186 | 130 | 56 |
| Beaumont | 110,237 | 292 | 261 | 31 |
| Bedford | 49,375 | 130 | 77 | 53 |
| Bee Cave | 2,996 | 15 | 14 | 1 |
| Beeville | 12,642 | 28 | 23 | 5 |
| Bellaire | 18,492 | 56 | 44 | 12 |
| Bellmead | 9,610 | 28 | 18 | 10 |
| Bellville | 4,486 | 12 | 11 | 1 |
| Belton | 18,130 | 38 | 29 | 9 |
| Benbrook | 23,280 | 49 | 39 | 10 |
| Bertram | 1,444 | 4 | 4 | 0 |
| Beverly Hills | 2,040 | 12 | 8 | 4 |
| Big Sandy | 1,368 | 6 | 6 | 0 |
| Big Spring | 24,181 | 64 | 46 | 18 |
| Bishop | 3,122 | 11 | 6 | 5 |
| Blanco | 1,562 | 5 | 4 | 1 |
| Bloomburg | 359 | 1 | 1 | 0 |
| Blue Mound | 2,362 | 13 | 8 | 5 |
| Boerne | 10,835 | 45 | 29 | 16 |
| Bogata | 1,219 | 4 | 4 | 0 |
| Bonham | 10,735 | 26 | 18 | 8 |
| Borger | 12,516 | 42 | 27 | 15 |
| Bovina | 1,680 | 5 | 4 | 1 |
| Bowie | 5,601 | 19 | 13 | 6 |
| Brady | 5,306 | 15 | 9 | 6 |
| Brazoria | 2,970 | 11 | 7 | 4 |
| Breckenridge | 5,610 | 17 | 12 | 5 |
| Bremond | 853 | 4 | 3 | 1 |
| Brenham | 15,415 | 34 | 30 | 4 |
| Bridge City | 8,587 | 15 | 10 | 5 |
| Bridgeport | 6,231 | 25 | 17 | 8 |
| Brookshire | 4,009 | 17 | 12 | 5 |
| Brookside Village | 1,987 | 5 | 5 | 0 |
| Brownfield | 8,893 | 26 | 19 | 7 |
| Brownsville | 179,491 | 311 | 244 | 67 |
| Brownwood | 19,115 | 58 | 38 | 20 |
| Bruceville-Eddy | 1,544 | 3 | 3 | 0 |
| Bryan | 73,111 | 168 | 123 | 45 |
| Bullard | 1,909 | 7 | 6 | 1 |
| Bulverde | 4,704 | 15 | 14 | 1 |
| Burkburnett | 10,361 | 25 | 19 | 6 |
| Burleson | 36,807 | 75 | 55 | 20 |
| Burnet | 6,105 | 14 | 13 | 1 |
| Cactus | 2,612 | 7 | 5 | 2 |
| Caddo Mills | 1,210 | 3 | 3 | 0 |
| Caldwell | 3,744 | 13 | 12 | 1 |
| Calvert | 1,351 | 4 | 4 | 0 |
| Cameron | 5,750 | 12 | 8 | 4 |
| Canton | 3,703 | 18 | 14 | 4 |
| Canyon | 14,781 | 23 | 20 | 3 |
| Carrollton | 127,432 | 222 | 161 | 61 |
| Carthage | 6,632 | 24 | 16 | 8 |
| Castle Hills | 4,206 | 27 | 21 | 6 |
| Castroville | 3,104 | 11 | 9 | 2 |
| Cedar Hill | 46,480 | 88 | 66 | 22 |
| Cedar Park | 68,464 | 98 | 76 | 22 |
| Celina | 6,017 | 9 | 9 | 0 |
| Center | 5,754 | 27 | 19 | 8 |
| Childress | 6,484 | 9 | 8 | 1 |
| Chillicothe | 676 | 1 | 1 | 0 |
| Cibolo | 17,291 | 21 | 19 | 2 |
| Cisco | 3,711 | 9 | 8 | 1 |
| Clarksville | 3,436 | 13 | 9 | 4 |
| Cleburne | 30,287 | 73 | 54 | 19 |
| Cleveland | 7,979 | 32 | 20 | 12 |
| Clifton | 3,567 | 8 | 7 | 1 |
| Clint | 971 | 1 | 1 | 0 |
| Clute | 10,803 | 39 | 28 | 11 |
| Clyde | 3,833 | 10 | 9 | 1 |
| Cockrell Hill | 4,254 | 20 | 14 | 6 |
| Coffee City | 209 | 3 | 2 | 1 |
| Coleman | 4,648 | 16 | 10 | 6 |
| College Station | 86,072 | 169 | 110 | 59 |
| Colleyville | 25,006 | 46 | 36 | 10 |
| Collinsville | 1,524 | 2 | 2 | 0 |
| Colorado City | 3,851 | 14 | 7 | 7 |
| Columbus | 3,886 | 10 | 9 | 1 |
| Comanche | 4,173 | 9 | 8 | 1 |
| Combes | 2,850 | 5 | 4 | 1 |
| Commerce | 9,427 | 23 | 18 | 5 |
| Conroe | 57,685 | 139 | 102 | 37 |
| Converse | 18,353 | 48 | 34 | 14 |
| Coppell | 39,465 | 80 | 62 | 18 |
| Copperas Cove | 30,793 | 70 | 51 | 19 |
| Corinth | 22,152 | 31 | 28 | 3 |
| Corpus Christi | 287,507 | 646 | 446 | 200 |
| Corrigan | 1,887 | 13 | 7 | 6 |
| Corsicana | 26,678 | 55 | 43 | 12 |
| Cottonwood Shores | 1,221 | 3 | 3 | 0 |
| Crandall | 3,983 | 9 | 9 | 0 |
| Crane | 3,199 | 11 | 7 | 4 |
| Crockett | 6,782 | 19 | 17 | 2 |
| Crowell | 935 | 1 | 1 | 0 |
| Crowley | 13,077 | 36 | 26 | 10 |
| Crystal City | 7,159 | 12 | 8 | 4 |
| Cuero | 6,401 | 14 | 13 | 1 |
| Cuney | 147 | 2 | 1 | 1 |
| Daingerfield | 2,446 | 7 | 6 | 1 |
| Dalhart | 7,008 | 17 | 14 | 3 |
| Dallas | 1,290,266 | 4,141 | 3,577 | 564 |
| Dalworthington Gardens | 2,437 | 20 | 14 | 6 |
| Danbury | 1,692 | 3 | 3 | 0 |
| Dayton | 7,461 | 23 | 17 | 6 |
| Decatur | 6,575 | 27 | 21 | 6 |
| Deer Park | 31,164 | 76 | 53 | 23 |
| De Kalb | 1,804 | 7 | 6 | 1 |
| De Leon | 2,325 | 5 | 5 | 0 |
| Del Rio | 36,996 | 95 | 69 | 26 |
| Denison | 24,142 | 59 | 45 | 14 |
| Denton | 124,308 | 205 | 154 | 51 |
| Denver City | 4,085 | 12 | 7 | 5 |
| DeSoto | 48,798 | 93 | 68 | 25 |
| Devine | 4,589 | 11 | 9 | 2 |
| Diboll | 5,545 | 20 | 14 | 6 |
| Dickinson | 17,975 | 42 | 31 | 11 |
| Dilley | 3,597 | 7 | 6 | 1 |
| Dimmitt | 3,636 | 7 | 6 | 1 |
| Donna | 17,323 | 33 | 24 | 9 |
| Double Oak | 3,426 | 6 | 6 | 0 |
| Driscoll | 800 | 2 | 1 | 1 |
| Dublin | 3,808 | 12 | 8 | 4 |
| Dumas | 13,933 | 31 | 26 | 5 |
| Duncanville | 36,115 | 62 | 52 | 10 |
| Eagle Lake | 3,681 | 9 | 8 | 1 |
| Early | 2,774 | 8 | 7 | 1 |
| Earth | 990 | 1 | 1 | 0 |
| Eastland | 3,888 | 11 | 9 | 2 |

## Table 78. Full-time Law Enforcement Employees, by State, by City, 2009—*Continued*

(Number.)

| State/city | Population | Total law enforcement employees | Total officers | Total civilians |
|---|---|---|---|---|
| East Mountain | 633 | 2 | 2 | 0 |
| Edcouch | 4,771 | 7 | 6 | 1 |
| Eden | 2,362 | 4 | 4 | 0 |
| Edgewood | 1,452 | 2 | 2 | 0 |
| Edinburg | 74,611 | 166 | 117 | 49 |
| Edna | 5,792 | 11 | 9 | 2 |
| El Campo | 10,735 | 38 | 29 | 9 |
| Electra | 2,867 | 14 | 7 | 7 |
| Elgin | 10,524 | 24 | 18 | 6 |
| El Paso | 618,812 | 1,459 | 1,117 | 342 |
| Elsa | 6,744 | 19 | 14 | 5 |
| Euless | 53,339 | 124 | 85 | 39 |
| Everman | 5,767 | 17 | 13 | 4 |
| Fairfield | 3,677 | 15 | 11 | 4 |
| Fair Oaks Ranch | 6,565 | 17 | 16 | 1 |
| Falfurrias | 4,906 | 12 | 11 | 1 |
| Farmers Branch | 26,344 | 122 | 75 | 47 |
| Farmersville | 3,516 | 5 | 5 | 0 |
| Farwell | 1,240 | 2 | 2 | 0 |
| Ferris | 2,611 | 13 | 9 | 4 |
| Flatonia | 1,437 | 4 | 4 | 0 |
| Florence | 1,140 | 10 | 10 | 0 |
| Floresville | 7,859 | 17 | 15 | 2 |
| Flower Mound | 71,605 | 118 | 83 | 35 |
| Floydada | 2,999 | 6 | 6 | 0 |
| Forest Hill | 13,961 | 37 | 25 | 12 |
| Forney | 16,977 | 33 | 22 | 11 |
| Fort Stockton | 7,498 | 29 | 18 | 11 |
| Fort Worth | 723,456 | 1,915 | 1,502 | 413 |
| Frankston | 1,237 | 5 | 4 | 1 |
| Fredericksburg | 11,339 | 34 | 30 | 4 |
| Freeport | 12,471 | 40 | 29 | 11 |
| Freer | 2,906 | 13 | 7 | 6 |
| Friendswood | 34,558 | 74 | 57 | 17 |
| Friona | 3,489 | 10 | 6 | 4 |
| Frisco | 108,244 | 192 | 133 | 59 |
| Gainesville | 16,547 | 51 | 38 | 13 |
| Galena Park | 10,166 | 25 | 19 | 6 |
| Galveston | 57,040 | 194 | 154 | 40 |
| Ganado | 1,833 | 3 | 3 | 0 |
| Garland | 218,872 | 445 | 319 | 126 |
| Gatesville | 15,198 | 23 | 16 | 7 |
| Georgetown | 52,555 | 102 | 72 | 30 |
| Giddings | 5,455 | 16 | 11 | 5 |
| Gilmer | 5,300 | 22 | 18 | 4 |
| Gladewater | 6,298 | 21 | 15 | 6 |
| Glenn Heights | 11,594 | 26 | 18 | 8 |
| Godley | 1,021 | 6 | 6 | 0 |
| Gonzales | 7,305 | 22 | 15 | 7 |
| Gorman | 1,230 | 3 | 3 | 0 |
| Graham | 8,455 | 23 | 21 | 2 |
| Granbury | 8,931 | 39 | 33 | 6 |
| Grand Prairie | 164,766 | 319 | 217 | 102 |
| Grand Saline | 3,187 | 7 | 7 | 0 |
| Granger | 1,371 | 3 | 3 | 0 |
| Granite Shoals | 2,877 | 7 | 7 | 0 |
| Grapeland | 1,373 | 3 | 2 | 1 |
| Grapevine | 51,427 | 131 | 93 | 38 |
| Greenville | 25,865 | 71 | 51 | 20 |
| Gregory | 2,188 | 4 | 4 | 0 |
| Groesbeck | 4,279 | 9 | 8 | 1 |
| Groves | 14,255 | 23 | 21 | 2 |
| Gruver | 1,124 | 1 | 1 | 0 |
| Gun Barrel City | 6,057 | 20 | 15 | 5 |
| Hale Center | 2,102 | 3 | 3 | 0 |
| Hallettsville | 2,480 | 8 | 7 | 1 |
| Hallsville | 3,037 | 7 | 6 | 1 |
| Haltom City | 40,303 | 90 | 70 | 20 |
| Hamlin | 1,870 | 8 | 4 | 4 |
| Harker Heights | 26,468 | 55 | 45 | 10 |
| Harlingen | 65,552 | 168 | 131 | 37 |
| Haskell | 2,577 | 4 | 4 | 0 |
| Hawk Cove | 618 | 2 | 2 | 0 |
| Hawkins | 1,547 | 4 | 4 | 0 |
| Hawley | 569 | 1 | 1 | 0 |
| Hearne | 4,566 | 18 | 12 | 6 |
| Heath | 8,267 | 18 | 17 | 1 |
| Hedwig Village | 2,345 | 22 | 16 | 6 |
| Helotes | 8,176 | 21 | 19 | 2 |
| Hemphill | 1,018 | 4 | 4 | 0 |
| Hempstead | 7,763 | 19 | 16 | 3 |
| Henderson | 11,675 | 39 | 31 | 8 |
| Hereford | 14,495 | 29 | 23 | 6 |
| Hewitt | 13,853 | 31 | 22 | 9 |
| Hickory Creek | 4,032 | 12 | 12 | 0 |
| Hidalgo | 12,590 | 47 | 35 | 12 |
| Highland Park | 9,222 | 70 | 55 | 15 |
| Highland Village | 17,317 | 37 | 29 | 8 |
| Hill Country Village | 1,124 | 11 | 11 | 0 |
| Hillsboro | 9,002 | 34 | 24 | 10 |
| Hitchcock | 7,289 | 18 | 14 | 4 |
| Holliday | 1,809 | 3 | 3 | 0 |
| Hollywood Park | 3,345 | 12 | 11 | 1 |
| Hondo | 9,121 | 22 | 18 | 4 |
| Hooks | 2,953 | 7 | 7 | 0 |
| Horizon City | 14,408 | 20 | 16 | 4 |
| Horseshoe Bay | 2,487 | 18 | 16 | 2 |
| Houston | 2,273,771 | 7,139 | 5,371 | 1,768 |
| Howe | 2,717 | 6 | 6 | 0 |
| Hubbard | 1,770 | 5 | 5 | 0 |
| Hudson | 4,358 | 5 | 5 | 0 |
| Hudson Oaks | 2,123 | 11 | 10 | 1 |
| Humble | 14,934 | 81 | 59 | 22 |
| Huntington | 2,110 | 5 | 4 | 1 |
| Huntsville | 38,875 | 52 | 46 | 6 |
| Hurst | 38,801 | 115 | 71 | 44 |
| Hutchins | 3,129 | 25 | 18 | 7 |
| Hutto | 17,482 | 30 | 26 | 4 |
| Idalou | 2,114 | 4 | 4 | 0 |
| Ingleside | 9,004 | 23 | 16 | 7 |
| Ingram | 1,928 | 6 | 6 | 0 |
| Iowa Park | 6,256 | 17 | 11 | 6 |
| Irving | 202,447 | 485 | 344 | 141 |
| Italy | 2,161 | 6 | 5 | 1 |
| Itasca | 1,717 | 5 | 5 | 0 |
| Jacinto City | 9,883 | 25 | 18 | 7 |
| Jacksboro | 4,488 | 10 | 8 | 2 |
| Jacksonville | 14,424 | 35 | 24 | 11 |
| Jamaica Beach | 1,103 | 5 | 5 | 0 |
| Jarrell | 1,462 | 3 | 3 | 0 |
| Jasper | 7,319 | 31 | 24 | 7 |
| Jefferson | 1,908 | 7 | 6 | 1 |
| Jersey Village | 7,324 | 37 | 28 | 9 |
| Johnson City | 1,606 | 3 | 3 | 0 |
| Jones Creek | 2,100 | 3 | 3 | 0 |
| Jonestown | 2,533 | 16 | 15 | 1 |
| Joshua | 5,967 | 14 | 13 | 1 |
| Jourdanton | 4,382 | 8 | 8 | 0 |
| Junction | 2,546 | 5 | 5 | 0 |
| Karnes City | 3,326 | 7 | 6 | 1 |
| Katy | 14,166 | 60 | 43 | 17 |
| Kaufman | 9,073 | 24 | 18 | 6 |
| Keene | 6,452 | 22 | 11 | 11 |
| Keller | 40,421 | 76 | 47 | 29 |
| Kemah | 2,518 | 17 | 12 | 5 |
| Kemp | 1,355 | 6 | 6 | 0 |
| Kempner | 1,199 | 1 | 1 | 0 |
| Kenedy | 3,288 | 8 | 7 | 1 |
| Kennedale | 7,252 | 26 | 19 | 7 |
| Kerens | 1,824 | 3 | 3 | 0 |
| Kermit | 5,189 | 17 | 10 | 7 |
| Kerrville | 23,091 | 67 | 52 | 15 |
| Kilgore | 12,094 | 44 | 34 | 10 |
| Killeen | 120,670 | 278 | 213 | 65 |
| Kingsville | 24,612 | 63 | 47 | 16 |
| Kirby | 8,599 | 17 | 11 | 6 |
| Kirbyville | 1,931 | 6 | 5 | 1 |
| Kountze | 2,177 | 8 | 7 | 1 |
| Kress | 761 | 1 | 1 | 0 |
| Kyle | 30,846 | 40 | 29 | 11 |
| Lacy-Lakeview | 5,896 | 21 | 13 | 8 |
| La Feria | 7,042 | 17 | 13 | 4 |

**Table 78. Full-time Law Enforcement Employees, by State, by City, 2009—*Continued***

(Number.)

| State/city | Population | Total law enforcement employees | Total officers | Total civilians |
|---|---|---|---|---|
| Lago Vista | 6,506 | 23 | 16 | 7 |
| La Grange | 4,733 | 9 | 9 | 0 |
| Laguna Vista | 4,291 | 7 | 7 | 0 |
| La Joya | 4,983 | 18 | 12 | 6 |
| Lake Dallas | 8,011 | 21 | 13 | 8 |
| Lake Jackson | 27,531 | 60 | 45 | 15 |
| Lakeside | 1,359 | 4 | 4 | 0 |
| Lakeview | 6,477 | 17 | 13 | 4 |
| Lakeway | 11,587 | 37 | 27 | 10 |
| Lake Worth | 4,832 | 37 | 26 | 11 |
| La Marque | 14,297 | 34 | 24 | 10 |
| Lamesa | 8,772 | 23 | 17 | 6 |
| Lampasas | 8,107 | 26 | 18 | 8 |
| Lancaster | 37,061 | 70 | 55 | 15 |
| La Porte | 34,535 | 102 | 72 | 30 |
| Laredo | 226,944 | 507 | 432 | 75 |
| La Vernia | 1,252 | 7 | 6 | 1 |
| La Villa | 1,447 | 6 | 5 | 1 |
| Lavon | 426 | 9 | 8 | 1 |
| League City | 74,801 | 141 | 104 | 37 |
| Leander | 28,646 | 49 | 34 | 15 |
| Leon Valley | 10,390 | 31 | 23 | 8 |
| Levelland | 12,410 | 32 | 22 | 10 |
| Lewisville | 104,601 | 193 | 134 | 59 |
| Lexington | 1,241 | 4 | 3 | 1 |
| Liberty | 8,362 | 29 | 20 | 9 |
| Lindale | 4,910 | 20 | 14 | 6 |
| Linden | 2,116 | 6 | 5 | 1 |
| Little Elm | 30,392 | 38 | 34 | 4 |
| Littlefield | 5,871 | 21 | 13 | 8 |
| Live Oak | 13,677 | 45 | 32 | 13 |
| Livingston | 6,280 | 24 | 17 | 7 |
| Llano | 3,226 | 9 | 8 | 1 |
| Lockhart | 13,891 | 30 | 23 | 7 |
| Lockney | 1,631 | 3 | 3 | 0 |
| Lone Star | 1,584 | 6 | 5 | 1 |
| Longview | 77,663 | 189 | 170 | 19 |
| Lorena | 1,698 | 3 | 2 | 1 |
| Lorenzo | 1,166 | 3 | 3 | 0 |
| Los Fresnos | 5,657 | 21 | 14 | 7 |
| Lott | 670 | 3 | 3 | 0 |
| Lubbock | 222,884 | 466 | 354 | 112 |
| Lufkin | 34,668 | 96 | 74 | 22 |
| Luling | 5,499 | 24 | 15 | 9 |
| Lumberton | 10,530 | 18 | 15 | 3 |
| Lytle | 2,869 | 5 | 5 | 0 |
| Madisonville | 4,396 | 11 | 10 | 1 |
| Magnolia | 1,267 | 14 | 11 | 3 |
| Malakoff | 2,333 | 6 | 6 | 0 |
| Manor | 3,928 | 14 | 12 | 2 |
| Mansfield | 48,710 | 207 | 84 | 123 |
| Manvel | 6,570 | 12 | 9 | 3 |
| Marble Falls | 7,785 | 39 | 27 | 12 |
| Marlin | 5,736 | 20 | 15 | 5 |
| Marshall | 23,791 | 69 | 52 | 17 |
| Mart | 2,433 | 4 | 4 | 0 |
| Martindale | 1,171 | 5 | 5 | 0 |
| Mathis | 5,286 | 16 | 9 | 7 |
| McAllen | 132,598 | 398 | 261 | 137 |
| McGregor | 4,909 | 18 | 11 | 7 |
| McKinney | 132,146 | 202 | 159 | 43 |
| Meadows Place | 6,624 | 15 | 14 | 1 |
| Melissa | 4,859 | 7 | 6 | 1 |
| Memorial Villages | 12,024 | 40 | 34 | 6 |
| Memphis | 2,169 | 3 | 2 | 1 |
| Mercedes | 15,261 | 39 | 32 | 7 |
| Meridian | 1,495 | 2 | 2 | 0 |
| Merkel | 2,612 | 4 | 4 | 0 |
| Mesquite | 132,941 | 307 | 224 | 83 |
| Mexia | 6,545 | 29 | 19 | 10 |
| Midland | 107,933 | 219 | 170 | 49 |
| Midlothian | 17,718 | 31 | 29 | 2 |
| Milford | 754 | 4 | 4 | 0 |
| Mineola | 5,253 | 18 | 12 | 6 |
| Mineral Wells | 16,872 | 36 | 28 | 8 |
| Missouri City | 77,543 | 101 | 76 | 25 |
| Monahans | 6,489 | 17 | 11 | 6 |
| Mont Belvieu | 2,737 | 14 | 9 | 5 |
| Montgomery | 609 | 8 | 8 | 0 |
| Morgans Point Resort | 4,603 | 8 | 7 | 1 |
| Mount Pleasant | 15,111 | 38 | 26 | 12 |
| Muleshoe | 4,234 | 13 | 8 | 5 |
| Munday | 1,178 | 2 | 2 | 0 |
| Murphy | 17,459 | 30 | 21 | 9 |
| Nacogdoches | 32,459 | 73 | 56 | 17 |
| Naples | 1,401 | 3 | 3 | 0 |
| Nash | 2,430 | 9 | 8 | 1 |
| Nassau Bay | 4,026 | 13 | 12 | 1 |
| Navasota | 7,647 | 26 | 20 | 6 |
| Nederland | 15,959 | 36 | 24 | 12 |
| Needville | 3,564 | 5 | 5 | 0 |
| New Boston | 4,642 | 13 | 9 | 4 |
| New Braunfels | 55,584 | 126 | 102 | 24 |
| New Deal | 753 | 1 | 1 | 0 |
| Nixon | 2,188 | 4 | 3 | 1 |
| Nocona | 3,241 | 9 | 5 | 4 |
| Nolanville | 3,015 | 3 | 3 | 0 |
| Northlake | 2,260 | 8 | 8 | 0 |
| North Richland Hills | 66,181 | 153 | 105 | 48 |
| Oak Ridge | 249 | 1 | 1 | 0 |
| Oak Ridge North | 3,446 | 18 | 18 | 0 |
| Odessa | 99,770 | 203 | 154 | 49 |
| O'Donnell | 901 | 1 | 1 | 0 |
| Olney | 3,220 | 9 | 5 | 4 |
| Olton | 2,137 | 5 | 5 | 0 |
| Onalaska | 1,452 | 6 | 6 | 0 |
| Orange | 19,366 | 55 | 42 | 13 |
| Orange Grove | 1,417 | 4 | 4 | 0 |
| Ore City | 1,178 | 6 | 6 | 0 |
| Overton | 2,381 | 9 | 6 | 3 |
| Ovilla | 4,026 | 10 | 9 | 1 |
| Oyster Creek | 1,244 | 9 | 5 | 4 |
| Paducah | 1,234 | 7 | 1 | 6 |
| Palacios | 5,058 | 16 | 11 | 5 |
| Palestine | 18,477 | 47 | 36 | 11 |
| Palmer | 2,316 | 10 | 9 | 1 |
| Palmhurst | 5,002 | 10 | 9 | 1 |
| Palmview | 5,537 | 25 | 17 | 8 |
| Pampa | 17,345 | 26 | 23 | 3 |
| Panhandle | 2,474 | 4 | 4 | 0 |
| Pantego | 2,388 | 16 | 11 | 5 |
| Paris | 26,080 | 83 | 62 | 21 |
| Parker | 3,066 | 7 | 7 | 0 |
| Pasadena | 146,963 | 346 | 270 | 76 |
| Pearland | 88,528 | 159 | 126 | 33 |
| Pearsall | 7,663 | 11 | 10 | 1 |
| Pecos | 7,643 | 41 | 18 | 23 |
| Pelican Bay | 1,626 | 3 | 3 | 0 |
| Penitas | 1,183 | 12 | 7 | 5 |
| Perryton | 8,365 | 16 | 8 | 8 |
| Pflugerville | 42,395 | 97 | 74 | 23 |
| Pharr | 67,628 | 156 | 112 | 44 |
| Pilot Point | 4,513 | 5 | 5 | 0 |
| Pinehurst | 2,151 | 10 | 6 | 4 |
| Pineland | 864 | 2 | 2 | 0 |
| Pittsburg | 4,703 | 12 | 10 | 2 |
| Plainview | 21,227 | 41 | 33 | 8 |
| Plano | 272,747 | 477 | 337 | 140 |
| Pleasanton | 9,844 | 25 | 19 | 6 |
| Point Comfort | 706 | 1 | 1 | 0 |
| Ponder | 1,427 | 1 | 1 | 0 |
| Port Aransas | 3,896 | 22 | 14 | 8 |
| Port Arthur | 55,725 | 153 | 115 | 38 |
| Port Isabel | 5,322 | 25 | 18 | 7 |
| Portland | 16,675 | 31 | 21 | 10 |
| Port Lavaca | 11,375 | 24 | 18 | 6 |
| Port Neches | 12,501 | 21 | 18 | 3 |
| Poteet | 3,677 | 5 | 5 | 0 |
| Poth | 2,418 | 3 | 3 | 0 |
| Pottsboro | 2,162 | 7 | 7 | 0 |
| Premont | 2,791 | 6 | 6 | 0 |
| Presidio | 4,753 | 5 | 4 | 1 |

**Table 78. Full-time Law Enforcement Employees, by State, by City, 2009—*Continued***

(Number.)

| State/city | Population | Total law enforcement employees | Total officers | Total civilians |
|---|---|---|---|---|
| Primera | 4,319 | 6 | 6 | 0 |
| Princeton | 6,519 | 12 | 11 | 1 |
| Progreso | 5,588 | 9 | 9 | 0 |
| Prosper | 8,005 | 15 | 9 | 6 |
| Queen City | 1,541 | 6 | 6 | 0 |
| Quinlan | 1,438 | 4 | 4 | 0 |
| Quitman | 2,254 | 6 | 6 | 0 |
| Ralls | 1,946 | 3 | 3 | 0 |
| Rancho Viejo | 1,854 | 8 | 8 | 0 |
| Ranger | 2,557 | 5 | 5 | 0 |
| Ransom Canyon | 1,125 | 3 | 3 | 0 |
| Raymondville | 9,502 | 22 | 13 | 9 |
| Red Oak | 9,852 | 22 | 20 | 2 |
| Refugio | 2,694 | 7 | 6 | 1 |
| Reno | 3,121 | 5 | 4 | 1 |
| Richardson | 102,675 | 237 | 147 | 90 |
| Richland Hills | 8,090 | 28 | 19 | 9 |
| Richmond | 13,706 | 41 | 30 | 11 |
| Richwood | 3,502 | 10 | 8 | 2 |
| Riesel | 1,016 | 3 | 3 | 0 |
| Rio Grande City | 14,167 | 35 | 26 | 9 |
| Rising Star | 826 | 1 | 1 | 0 |
| River Oaks | 6,961 | 24 | 18 | 6 |
| Roanoke | 4,429 | 31 | 23 | 8 |
| Robinson | 10,642 | 29 | 20 | 9 |
| Robstown | 12,106 | 32 | 25 | 7 |
| Rockdale | 5,983 | 15 | 9 | 6 |
| Rockport | 10,026 | 23 | 21 | 2 |
| Rockwall | 37,856 | 93 | 68 | 25 |
| Rollingwood | 1,438 | 6 | 6 | 0 |
| Roma | 11,441 | 36 | 27 | 9 |
| Roman Forest | 4,219 | 7 | 7 | 0 |
| Ropesville | 508 | 1 | 1 | 0 |
| Roscoe | 1,260 | 1 | 1 | 0 |
| Rosebud | 1,320 | 2 | 2 | 0 |
| Rose City | 502 | 2 | 1 | 1 |
| Rosenberg | 34,838 | 83 | 62 | 21 |
| Round Rock | 110,531 | 200 | 141 | 59 |
| Rowlett | 57,119 | 129 | 75 | 54 |
| Royse City | 10,277 | 16 | 15 | 1 |
| Runaway Bay | 1,463 | 4 | 4 | 0 |
| Rusk | 5,330 | 12 | 11 | 1 |
| Sabinal | 1,625 | 3 | 3 | 0 |
| Sachse | 19,996 | 38 | 27 | 11 |
| Saginaw | 21,388 | 44 | 37 | 7 |
| Salado | 2,071 | 4 | 4 | 0 |
| San Angelo | 92,269 | 191 | 158 | 33 |
| San Antonio | 1,373,936 | 2,809 | 2,259 | 550 |
| San Augustine | 2,333 | 7 | 6 | 1 |
| San Benito | 25,176 | 50 | 42 | 8 |
| San Diego | 4,401 | 7 | 6 | 1 |
| San Felipe | 985 | 4 | 3 | 1 |
| Sanger | 8,209 | 15 | 13 | 2 |
| San Juan | 34,896 | 48 | 38 | 10 |
| San Marcos | 55,187 | 127 | 96 | 31 |
| San Saba | 2,481 | 4 | 4 | 0 |
| Sansom Park Village | 4,198 | 17 | 12 | 5 |
| Santa Anna | 1,010 | 2 | 2 | 0 |
| Santa Fe | 10,578 | 28 | 21 | 7 |
| Santa Rosa | 3,163 | 6 | 6 | 0 |
| Schertz | 31,984 | 63 | 46 | 17 |
| Schulenburg | 2,690 | 7 | 6 | 1 |
| Seabrook | 11,777 | 39 | 33 | 6 |
| Seadrift | 1,442 | 2 | 2 | 0 |
| Seagoville | 12,133 | 29 | 21 | 8 |
| Seagraves | 2,351 | 5 | 4 | 1 |
| Sealy | 6,383 | 18 | 16 | 2 |
| Seguin | 26,705 | 64 | 47 | 17 |
| Selma | 5,626 | 29 | 26 | 3 |
| Seminole | 6,149 | 12 | 11 | 1 |
| Seven Points | 1,328 | 11 | 6 | 5 |
| Seymour | 2,590 | 10 | 7 | 3 |
| Shallowater | 2,312 | 5 | 5 | 0 |
| Shamrock | 1,786 | 7 | 3 | 4 |
| Shavano Park | 3,332 | 17 | 16 | 1 |
| Shenandoah | 2,066 | 26 | 23 | 3 |
| Sherman | 38,414 | 88 | 64 | 24 |
| Silsbee | 6,923 | 24 | 16 | 8 |
| Sinton | 5,321 | 11 | 10 | 1 |
| Slaton | 5,770 | 17 | 13 | 4 |
| Smithville | 4,534 | 17 | 10 | 7 |
| Snyder | 10,376 | 22 | 20 | 2 |
| Socorro | 32,522 | 33 | 24 | 9 |
| Somerville | 1,683 | 6 | 6 | 0 |
| Sonora | 3,054 | 7 | 5 | 2 |
| Sour Lake | 1,744 | 8 | 7 | 1 |
| South Houston | 16,410 | 38 | 30 | 8 |
| Southlake | 27,189 | 61 | 52 | 9 |
| South Padre Island | 2,884 | 38 | 27 | 11 |
| Southside Place | 1,680 | 9 | 5 | 4 |
| Spearman | 2,937 | 4 | 4 | 0 |
| Springtown | 3,274 | 16 | 11 | 5 |
| Spring Valley | 3,910 | 23 | 18 | 5 |
| Spur | 923 | 2 | 2 | 0 |
| Stafford | 19,990 | 64 | 46 | 18 |
| Stamford | 3,060 | 9 | 7 | 2 |
| Stanton | 2,193 | 4 | 4 | 0 |
| Stephenville | 17,151 | 48 | 36 | 12 |
| Stratford | 1,905 | 4 | 4 | 0 |
| Sudan | 973 | 1 | 1 | 0 |
| Sugar Land | 82,696 | 179 | 139 | 40 |
| Sullivan City | 4,485 | 14 | 10 | 4 |
| Sulphur Springs | 15,564 | 40 | 29 | 11 |
| Sunrise Beach Village | 758 | 5 | 5 | 0 |
| Sunset Valley | 903 | 13 | 13 | 0 |
| Surfside Beach | 896 | 6 | 6 | 0 |
| Sweeny | 3,612 | 7 | 7 | 0 |
| Sweetwater | 10,581 | 27 | 24 | 3 |
| Taft | 3,331 | 9 | 8 | 1 |
| Tahoka | 2,479 | 4 | 4 | 0 |
| Tatum | 1,215 | 4 | 3 | 1 |
| Taylor | 16,394 | 37 | 27 | 10 |
| Teague | 4,754 | 9 | 8 | 1 |
| Temple | 60,243 | 155 | 130 | 25 |
| Terrell | 20,300 | 49 | 33 | 16 |
| Terrell Hills | 5,266 | 15 | 14 | 1 |
| Texarkana | 36,812 | 102 | 92 | 10 |
| Texas City | 44,807 | 114 | 89 | 25 |
| The Colony | 44,448 | 75 | 51 | 24 |
| Thorndale | 1,313 | 2 | 2 | 0 |
| Thrall | 939 | 3 | 3 | 0 |
| Three Rivers | 1,655 | 7 | 6 | 1 |
| Tioga | 947 | 2 | 2 | 0 |
| Tolar | 704 | 2 | 1 | 1 |
| Tomball | 10,345 | 51 | 37 | 14 |
| Tom Bean | 1,039 | 4 | 4 | 0 |
| Tool | 2,457 | 11 | 7 | 4 |
| Trinity | 2,725 | 13 | 6 | 7 |
| Trophy Club | 8,276 | 16 | 15 | 1 |
| Troup | 2,138 | 9 | 8 | 1 |
| Troy | 1,428 | 4 | 4 | 0 |
| Tulia | 4,535 | 12 | 7 | 5 |
| Tye | 1,138 | 4 | 4 | 0 |
| Tyler | 99,279 | 238 | 183 | 55 |
| Universal City | 18,821 | 37 | 27 | 10 |
| University Park | 25,026 | 49 | 38 | 11 |
| Uvalde | 16,171 | 51 | 39 | 12 |
| Valley View | 793 | 3 | 3 | 0 |
| Van | 2,603 | 8 | 8 | 0 |
| Van Alstyne | 3,013 | 12 | 8 | 4 |
| Vernon | 10,849 | 33 | 22 | 11 |
| Victoria | 62,788 | 144 | 105 | 39 |
| Vidor | 11,023 | 31 | 23 | 8 |
| Waco | 125,098 | 329 | 246 | 83 |
| Waelder | 997 | 5 | 4 | 1 |
| Wake Village | 5,659 | 8 | 7 | 1 |
| Waller | 2,051 | 7 | 6 | 1 |
| Wallis | 1,343 | 3 | 3 | 0 |
| Watauga | 24,235 | 54 | 36 | 18 |
| Waxahachie | 29,576 | 68 | 52 | 16 |
| Weatherford | 27,667 | 70 | 55 | 15 |
| Webster | 10,868 | 64 | 47 | 17 |

**Table 78. Full-time Law Enforcement Employees, by State, by City, 2009**—*Continued*

(Number.)

| State/city | Population | Total law enforcement employees | Total officers | Total civilians |
|---|---|---|---|---|
| Weimar | 2,021 | 8 | 7 | 1 |
| Wells | 799 | 1 | 1 | 0 |
| Weslaco | 33,998 | 98 | 70 | 28 |
| West | 2,688 | 8 | 8 | 0 |
| West Columbia | 4,175 | 16 | 10 | 6 |
| West Lake Hills | 3,160 | 20 | 14 | 6 |
| West Orange | 3,803 | 11 | 9 | 2 |
| Westover Hills | 730 | 14 | 11 | 3 |
| West Tawakoni | 1,760 | 6 | 6 | 0 |
| West University Place | 15,736 | 29 | 20 | 9 |
| Westworth | 3,141 | 19 | 14 | 5 |
| Wharton | 9,137 | 34 | 24 | 10 |
| Whitehouse | 7,957 | 22 | 15 | 7 |
| White Oak | 6,377 | 19 | 15 | 4 |
| Whitesboro | 4,056 | 13 | 8 | 5 |
| White Settlement | 16,471 | 48 | 34 | 14 |
| Whitney | 2,076 | 9 | 7 | 2 |
| Wichita Falls | 100,884 | 285 | 194 | 91 |
| Willis | 4,325 | 15 | 13 | 2 |
| Willow Park | 4,755 | 18 | 12 | 6 |
| Wills Point | 3,839 | 12 | 10 | 2 |
| Wilmer | 3,594 | 15 | 10 | 5 |
| Windcrest | 5,386 | 26 | 18 | 8 |
| Wink | 907 | 1 | 1 | 0 |
| Winnsboro | 3,969 | 14 | 9 | 5 |
| Winters | 2,535 | 5 | 4 | 1 |
| Wolfe City | 1,640 | 2 | 2 | 0 |
| Wolfforth | 3,619 | 11 | 9 | 2 |
| Woodville | 2,266 | 10 | 9 | 1 |
| Woodway | 8,823 | 35 | 25 | 10 |
| Wortham | 1,090 | 4 | 3 | 1 |
| Wylie | 41,824 | 49 | 44 | 5 |
| Yoakum | 5,443 | 16 | 9 | 7 |
| Yorktown | 2,145 | 4 | 4 | 0 |
| **UTAH** | | | | |
| Alta | 372 | 8 | 4 | 4 |
| American Fork/Cedar Hills | 38,183 | 37 | 32 | 5 |
| Big Water | 403 | 1 | 1 | 0 |
| Blanding | 3,280 | 5 | 5 | 0 |
| Bountiful | 44,591 | 52 | 37 | 15 |
| Brian Head | 127 | 5 | 5 | 0 |
| Brigham City | 18,750 | 30 | 25 | 5 |
| Cedar City | 29,568 | 40 | 34 | 6 |
| Centerville | 15,763 | 20 | 17 | 3 |
| Clearfield | 27,913 | 43 | 30 | 13 |
| Clinton | 20,745 | 18 | 17 | 1 |
| Cottonwood Heights | 35,258 | 39 | 34 | 5 |
| Draper | 44,537 | 40 | 33 | 7 |
| East Carbon | 1,238 | 4 | 4 | 0 |
| Enoch | 5,263 | 6 | 4 | 2 |
| Ephraim | 5,341 | 5 | 5 | 0 |
| Fairview | 1,209 | 1 | 1 | 0 |
| Farmington | 17,788 | 16 | 13 | 3 |
| Garland | 2,060 | 4 | 4 | 0 |
| Grantsville | 9,402 | 12 | 10 | 2 |
| Gunnison | 3,080 | 3 | 3 | 0 |
| Harrisville | 6,367 | 10 | 9 | 1 |
| Heber | 10,068 | 15 | 13 | 2 |
| Helper | 1,852 | 7 | 6 | 1 |
| Hildale | 1,967 | 10 | 5 | 5 |
| Hurricane | 13,961 | 20 | 16 | 4 |
| Ivins | 8,294 | 10 | 7 | 3 |
| Kamas | 1,505 | 2 | 2 | 0 |
| Kanab | 3,786 | 8 | 6 | 2 |
| Kaysville | 26,363 | 22 | 20 | 2 |
| La Verkin | 4,602 | 4 | 4 | 0 |
| Layton | 65,947 | 98 | 71 | 27 |
| Lehi | 51,307 | 43 | 39 | 4 |
| Lindon | 10,666 | 15 | 14 | 1 |
| Logan | 49,105 | 94 | 60 | 34 |
| Lone Peak | 27,542 | 21 | 19 | 2 |
| Mantua | 748 | 1 | 1 | 0 |
| Mapleton | 8,183 | 9 | 8 | 1 |
| Midvale | 28,099 | 56 | 46 | 10 |
| Minersville | 813 | 1 | 1 | 0 |
| Moab | 5,130 | 19 | 14 | 5 |
| Monticello | 2,015 | 5 | 4 | 1 |
| Moroni | 1,326 | 1 | 1 | 0 |
| Mount Pleasant | 2,811 | 4 | 4 | 0 |
| Murray | 46,026 | 99 | 79 | 20 |
| Naples | 1,735 | 7 | 6 | 1 |
| Nephi | 5,459 | 10 | 8 | 2 |
| North Ogden | 17,897 | 20 | 17 | 3 |
| North Park | 12,739 | 10 | 9 | 1 |
| North Salt Lake | 14,026 | 18 | 16 | 2 |
| Ogden | 83,016 | 159 | 130 | 29 |
| Orem | 93,785 | 126 | 90 | 36 |
| Park City | 7,998 | 39 | 30 | 9 |
| Parowan | 2,615 | 3 | 3 | 0 |
| Payson | 17,890 | 18 | 17 | 1 |
| Perry | 4,080 | 6 | 6 | 0 |
| Pleasant Grove | 35,016 | 33 | 25 | 8 |
| Pleasant View | 7,183 | 9 | 8 | 1 |
| Price | 7,957 | 19 | 17 | 2 |
| Provo | 119,472 | 147 | 100 | 47 |
| Richfield | 7,220 | 15 | 13 | 2 |
| Riverdale | 8,135 | 23 | 19 | 4 |
| Roosevelt | 5,088 | 14 | 12 | 2 |
| Roy | 35,761 | 44 | 37 | 7 |
| Salem | 6,635 | 10 | 9 | 1 |
| Salina | 2,403 | 5 | 4 | 1 |
| Salt Lake City | 180,724 | 584 | 427 | 157 |
| Sandy | 97,031 | 145 | 115 | 30 |
| Santaquin/Genola | 9,990 | 10 | 10 | 0 |
| Saratoga Springs | 21,450 | 20 | 17 | 3 |
| Smithfield | 9,770 | 9 | 8 | 1 |
| South Jordan | 54,042 | 58 | 48 | 10 |
| South Ogden | 15,989 | 30 | 25 | 5 |
| South Salt Lake | 21,448 | 77 | 63 | 14 |
| Spanish Fork | 32,882 | 31 | 28 | 3 |
| Springville | 29,395 | 38 | 27 | 11 |
| St. George | 75,391 | 141 | 102 | 39 |
| Stockton | 588 | 1 | 1 | 0 |
| Sunset | 4,892 | 9 | 8 | 1 |
| Syracuse | 24,168 | 21 | 19 | 2 |
| Taylorsville City | 58,472 | 60 | 57 | 3 |
| Tooele | 30,851 | 36 | 32 | 4 |
| Tremonton | 6,891 | 12 | 10 | 2 |
| Vernal | 8,769 | 26 | 23 | 3 |
| Washington | 19,183 | 21 | 17 | 4 |
| Wellington | 1,553 | 4 | 4 | 0 |
| West Bountiful | 5,402 | 11 | 10 | 1 |
| West Jordan | 107,113 | 142 | 103 | 39 |
| West Valley | 124,472 | 232 | 188 | 44 |
| Willard | 1,752 | 2 | 2 | 0 |
| Woods Cross | 8,946 | 14 | 12 | 2 |
| **VERMONT** | | | | |
| Barre | 8,790 | 28 | 19 | 9 |
| Barre Town | 8,049 | 7 | 6 | 1 |
| Bellows Falls | 2,873 | 11 | 7 | 4 |
| Bennington | 15,026 | 32 | 25 | 7 |
| Berlin | 2,818 | 7 | 6 | 1 |
| Brandon | 3,860 | 8 | 7 | 1 |
| Brattleboro | 11,438 | 31 | 25 | 6 |
| Burlington | 38,794 | 127 | 93 | 34 |
| Chester | 2,995 | 5 | 4 | 1 |
| Colchester | 17,274 | 35 | 28 | 7 |
| Dover | 1,434 | 6 | 5 | 1 |
| Essex | 19,759 | 32 | 26 | 6 |
| Hardwick | 3,209 | 6 | 5 | 1 |
| Hartford | 10,730 | 31 | 21 | 10 |
| Lyndonville | 1,214 | 3 | 3 | 0 |
| Manchester | 4,279 | 12 | 8 | 4 |
| Middlebury | 8,281 | 16 | 14 | 2 |
| Milton | 10,853 | 13 | 12 | 1 |
| Montpelier | 7,731 | 25 | 17 | 8 |
| Morristown | 5,606 | 11 | 11 | 0 |
| Newport | 5,163 | 13 | 11 | 2 |
| Northfield | 5,735 | 6 | 5 | 1 |
| Randolph | 5,057 | 5 | 5 | 0 |
| Richmond | 4,167 | 4 | 4 | 0 |
| Rutland | 16,688 | 49 | 38 | 11 |

**Table 78. Full-time Law Enforcement Employees, by State, by City, 2009**—*Continued*

(Number.)

| State/city | Population | Total law enforcement employees | Total officers | Total civilians |
|---|---|---|---|---|
| Shelburne | 7,161 | 19 | 11 | 8 |
| South Burlington | 17,893 | 47 | 39 | 8 |
| Springfield | 8,551 | 21 | 16 | 5 |
| St. Albans | 7,207 | 28 | 17 | 11 |
| Swanton | 6,451 | 6 | 5 | 1 |
| Waterbury | 5,399 | 4 | 4 | 0 |
| Windsor | 3,585 | 8 | 7 | 1 |
| Winhall | 796 | 6 | 5 | 1 |
| Winooski | 6,401 | 20 | 15 | 5 |
| **VIRGINIA** | | | | |
| Abingdon | 8,034 | 27 | 25 | 2 |
| Alexandria | 146,145 | 445 | 316 | 129 |
| Altavista | 3,362 | 12 | 12 | 0 |
| Amherst | 2,216 | 5 | 5 | 0 |
| Appalachia | 1,729 | 6 | 5 | 1 |
| Ashland | 7,152 | 27 | 24 | 3 |
| Bedford | 6,335 | 26 | 23 | 3 |
| Berryville | 3,187 | 10 | 9 | 1 |
| Big Stone Gap | 5,652 | 18 | 16 | 2 |
| Blacksburg | 42,047 | 79 | 62 | 17 |
| Blackstone | 3,568 | 14 | 10 | 4 |
| Bluefield | 5,122 | 23 | 17 | 6 |
| Boykins | 599 | 1 | 1 | 0 |
| Bridgewater | 5,458 | 9 | 9 | 0 |
| Bristol | 17,502 | 76 | 55 | 21 |
| Broadway | 3,335 | 4 | 4 | 0 |
| Brookneal | 1,248 | 3 | 3 | 0 |
| Buena Vista | 6,509 | 17 | 15 | 2 |
| Burkeville | 470 | 1 | 1 | 0 |
| Cape Charles | 1,510 | 5 | 5 | 0 |
| Cedar Bluff | 1,039 | 2 | 2 | 0 |
| Charlottesville | 41,798 | 144 | 116 | 28 |
| Chase City | 2,307 | 10 | 9 | 1 |
| Chatham | 1,543 | 3 | 3 | 0 |
| Chesapeake | 223,261 | 501 | 371 | 130 |
| Chilhowie | 1,737 | 6 | 6 | 0 |
| Chincoteague | 4,293 | 14 | 10 | 4 |
| Christiansburg | 19,775 | 69 | 53 | 16 |
| Clarksville | 1,251 | 8 | 7 | 1 |
| Clifton Forge | 3,895 | 14 | 10 | 4 |
| Clintwood | 1,517 | 4 | 4 | 0 |
| Coeburn | 1,974 | 8 | 7 | 1 |
| Colonial Beach | 3,859 | 16 | 11 | 5 |
| Colonial Heights | 17,932 | 53 | 49 | 4 |
| Covington | 6,124 | 28 | 17 | 11 |
| Crewe | 2,274 | 5 | 5 | 0 |
| Culpeper | 14,562 | 49 | 41 | 8 |
| Damascus | 1,081 | 5 | 5 | 0 |
| Danville | 44,442 | 144 | 135 | 9 |
| Dayton | 1,354 | 9 | 8 | 1 |
| Dublin | 2,180 | 9 | 8 | 1 |
| Dumfries | 4,792 | 15 | 13 | 2 |
| Edinburg | 903 | 2 | 2 | 0 |
| Elkton | 2,625 | 7 | 6 | 1 |
| Emporia | 5,662 | 36 | 26 | 10 |
| Exmore | 1,341 | 7 | 7 | 0 |
| Fairfax City | 24,194 | 83 | 65 | 18 |
| Falls Church | 11,301 | 41 | 32 | 9 |
| Farmville | 7,462 | 25 | 24 | 1 |
| Franklin | 8,980 | 39 | 26 | 13 |
| Fredericksburg | 23,326 | 98 | 72 | 26 |
| Fries | 546 | 1 | 1 | 0 |
| Front Royal | 14,731 | 45 | 35 | 10 |
| Galax | 6,828 | 38 | 24 | 14 |
| Gate City | 2,037 | 5 | 5 | 0 |
| Glade Spring | 1,538 | 2 | 2 | 0 |
| Glasgow | 1,003 | 1 | 1 | 0 |
| Glen Lyn | 164 | 1 | 1 | 0 |
| Gordonsville | 1,720 | 6 | 6 | 0 |
| Gretna | 1,185 | 4 | 4 | 0 |
| Grottoes | 2,192 | 6 | 5 | 1 |
| Grundy | 947 | 4 | 4 | 0 |
| Halifax | 1,280 | 5 | 5 | 0 |
| Hampton | 145,932 | 348 | 277 | 71 |
| Harrisonburg | 44,597 | 103 | 87 | 16 |
| Haymarket | 1,268 | 6 | 5 | 1 |
| Haysi | 308 | 2 | 2 | 0 |
| Herndon | 22,078 | 72 | 56 | 16 |
| Hillsville | 2,630 | 12 | 11 | 1 |
| Honaker | 1,438 | 4 | 3 | 1 |
| Hopewell | 23,324 | 67 | 56 | 11 |
| Hurt | 1,208 | 2 | 2 | 0 |
| Independence | 887 | 2 | 2 | 0 |
| Jonesville | 964 | 3 | 3 | 0 |
| Kenbridge | 1,273 | 5 | 5 | 0 |
| Kilmarnock | 1,287 | 5 | 5 | 0 |
| La Crosse | 586 | 2 | 2 | 0 |
| Lawrenceville | 1,342 | 6 | 6 | 0 |
| Lebanon | 3,186 | 12 | 11 | 1 |
| Leesburg | 41,092 | 96 | 80 | 16 |
| Lexington | 7,049 | 17 | 15 | 2 |
| Louisa | 1,583 | 6 | 6 | 0 |
| Luray | 4,840 | 13 | 11 | 2 |
| Lynchburg | 73,735 | 226 | 169 | 57 |
| Manassas | 35,321 | 122 | 90 | 32 |
| Manassas Park | 11,477 | 47 | 31 | 16 |
| Marion | 5,965 | 21 | 19 | 2 |
| Martinsville | 14,509 | 59 | 53 | 6 |
| Middleburg | 979 | 5 | 5 | 0 |
| Middletown | 1,154 | 2 | 2 | 0 |
| Mount Jackson | 2,014 | 4 | 4 | 0 |
| Narrows | 2,151 | 4 | 4 | 0 |
| New Market | 1,865 | 5 | 5 | 0 |
| Newport News | 180,174 | 554 | 408 | 146 |
| Norfolk | 235,097 | 877 | 755 | 122 |
| Norton | 3,697 | 24 | 17 | 7 |
| Occoquan | 824 | 1 | 1 | 0 |
| Onancock | 1,375 | 4 | 4 | 0 |
| Onley | 468 | 4 | 4 | 0 |
| Orange | 4,688 | 17 | 14 | 3 |
| Parksley | 785 | 3 | 3 | 0 |
| Pearisburg | 2,767 | 8 | 7 | 1 |
| Pembroke | 1,166 | 2 | 2 | 0 |
| Pennington Gap | 1,721 | 6 | 6 | 0 |
| Petersburg | 32,966 | 143 | 96 | 47 |
| Pocahontas | 417 | 1 | 1 | 0 |
| Poquoson | 11,902 | 24 | 22 | 2 |
| Portsmouth | 100,970 | 330 | 241 | 89 |
| Pound | 1,070 | 5 | 5 | 0 |
| Pulaski | 8,932 | 36 | 27 | 9 |
| Purcellville | 5,338 | 15 | 14 | 1 |
| Quantico | 614 | 2 | 2 | 0 |
| Radford | 16,216 | 48 | 34 | 14 |
| Rich Creek | 682 | 1 | 1 | 0 |
| Richlands | 3,983 | 25 | 19 | 6 |
| Richmond | 203,233 | 872 | 724 | 148 |
| Roanoke | 93,110 | 302 | 252 | 50 |
| Rocky Mount | 4,536 | 20 | 18 | 2 |
| Rural Retreat | 1,346 | 1 | 1 | 0 |
| Salem | 25,616 | 95 | 66 | 29 |
| Saltville | 2,207 | 6 | 6 | 0 |
| Shenandoah | 1,856 | 5 | 5 | 0 |
| Smithfield | 7,115 | 26 | 22 | 4 |
| South Boston | 7,822 | 29 | 27 | 2 |
| South Hill | 4,558 | 22 | 20 | 2 |
| Stanley | 1,562 | 3 | 3 | 0 |
| Staunton | 24,072 | 64 | 49 | 15 |
| Stephens City | 1,505 | 4 | 4 | 0 |
| St. Paul | 963 | 4 | 4 | 0 |
| Strasburg | 4,405 | 22 | 20 | 2 |
| Suffolk | 84,929 | 234 | 181 | 53 |
| Tappahannock | 2,202 | 11 | 10 | 1 |
| Tazewell | 4,247 | 16 | 14 | 2 |
| Timberville | 1,714 | 4 | 4 | 0 |
| Victoria | 1,722 | 6 | 5 | 1 |
| Vienna | 14,946 | 51 | 40 | 11 |
| Vinton | 7,879 | 28 | 22 | 6 |
| Virginia Beach | 436,175 | 944 | 780 | 164 |
| Warrenton | 9,235 | 22 | 20 | 2 |
| Warsaw | 1,350 | 3 | 3 | 0 |
| Waverly | 2,142 | 12 | 6 | 6 |
| Waynesboro | 22,313 | 60 | 51 | 9 |

**Table 78. Full-time Law Enforcement Employees, by State, by City, 2009—*Continued***

(Number.)

| State/city | Population | Total law enforcement employees | Total officers | Total civilians |
|---|---|---|---|---|
| Weber City | 1,322 | 5 | 5 | 0 |
| West Point | 3,177 | 9 | 8 | 1 |
| White Stone | 336 | 1 | 1 | 0 |
| Williamsburg | 12,584 | 42 | 37 | 5 |
| Winchester | 26,252 | 101 | 75 | 26 |
| Wise | 3,226 | 13 | 12 | 1 |
| Woodstock | 4,315 | 17 | 16 | 1 |
| Wytheville | 8,336 | 40 | 26 | 14 |
| **WASHINGTON** | | | | |
| Aberdeen | 16,000 | 48 | 36 | 12 |
| Airway Heights | 5,384 | 14 | 13 | 1 |
| Algona | 2,763 | 9 | 8 | 1 |
| Anacortes | 17,063 | 33 | 25 | 8 |
| Arlington | 17,413 | 35 | 29 | 6 |
| Asotin | 1,133 | 4 | 2 | 2 |
| Auburn | 56,934 | 129 | 98 | 31 |
| Bainbridge Island | 22,061 | 26 | 21 | 5 |
| Battle Ground | 17,865 | 33 | 27 | 6 |
| Bellevue | 125,054 | 218 | 175 | 43 |
| Bellingham | 80,243 | 157 | 110 | 47 |
| Black Diamond | 4,007 | 12 | 11 | 1 |
| Blaine | 5,128 | 15 | 12 | 3 |
| Bonney Lake | 17,461 | 35 | 30 | 5 |
| Bothell | 32,517 | 84 | 58 | 26 |
| Bremerton | 35,888 | 78 | 63 | 15 |
| Brewster | 2,076 | 8 | 6 | 2 |
| Brier | 6,340 | 8 | 6 | 2 |
| Buckley | 5,514 | 19 | 9 | 10 |
| Burien | 31,263 | 39 | 38 | 1 |
| Burlington | 8,920 | 31 | 25 | 6 |
| Camas | 18,618 | 30 | 25 | 5 |
| Castle Rock | 2,120 | 6 | 5 | 1 |
| Centralia | 15,811 | 39 | 32 | 7 |
| Chehalis | 7,397 | 22 | 17 | 5 |
| Cheney | 10,572 | 20 | 14 | 6 |
| Chewelah | 2,313 | 7 | 6 | 1 |
| Clarkston | 7,194 | 15 | 14 | 1 |
| Cle Elum | 3,514 | 11 | 9 | 2 |
| Clyde Hill | 2,708 | 9 | 8 | 1 |
| Colfax | 2,744 | 7 | 6 | 1 |
| College Place | 9,106 | 13 | 10 | 3 |
| Colton | 395 | 1 | 1 | 0 |
| Colville | 4,919 | 14 | 12 | 2 |
| Connell | 3,214 | 6 | 6 | 0 |
| Cosmopolis | 1,669 | 4 | 3 | 1 |
| Coulee Dam | 1,051 | 7 | 7 | 0 |
| Coupeville | 1,907 | 4 | 4 | 0 |
| Covington | 18,619 | 15 | 15 | 0 |
| Des Moines | 28,667 | 60 | 45 | 15 |
| Dupont | 7,799 | 11 | 10 | 1 |
| Duvall | 6,150 | 17 | 15 | 2 |
| East Wenatchee | 12,355 | 24 | 21 | 3 |
| Eatonville | 2,512 | 6 | 5 | 1 |
| Edgewood | 9,778 | 10 | 9 | 1 |
| Edmonds | 40,227 | 63 | 54 | 9 |
| Ellensburg | 17,331 | 37 | 27 | 10 |
| Elma | 3,114 | 8 | 7 | 1 |
| Enumclaw | 10,640 | 30 | 17 | 13 |
| Ephrata | 7,399 | 18 | 15 | 3 |
| Everett | 98,431 | 245 | 199 | 46 |
| Everson | 2,210 | 6 | 6 | 0 |
| Federal Way | 84,219 | 163 | 132 | 31 |
| Ferndale | 11,669 | 21 | 19 | 2 |
| Fife | 8,622 | 52 | 28 | 24 |
| Fircrest | 6,251 | 9 | 9 | 0 |
| Forks | 3,276 | 14 | 7 | 7 |
| Gig Harbor | 7,059 | 19 | 17 | 2 |
| Goldendale | 3,733 | 10 | 9 | 1 |
| Grand Coulee | 1,924 | 7 | 7 | 0 |
| Grandview | 9,498 | 24 | 18 | 6 |
| Granger | 3,019 | 5 | 5 | 0 |
| Granite Falls | 3,180 | 8 | 7 | 1 |
| Hoquiam | 8,823 | 19 | 18 | 1 |
| Issaquah | 25,019 | 58 | 31 | 27 |
| Kalama | 2,295 | 5 | 5 | 0 |
| Kelso | 12,226 | 31 | 27 | 4 |
| Kenmore | 20,568 | 15 | 15 | 0 |
| Kennewick | 64,009 | 105 | 87 | 18 |
| Kent | 84,363 | 179 | 127 | 52 |
| Kettle Falls | 1,430 | 5 | 4 | 1 |
| Kirkland | 47,565 | 92 | 66 | 26 |
| Kittitas | 1,246 | 2 | 2 | 0 |
| La Center | 2,660 | 11 | 9 | 2 |
| Lacey | 41,915 | 69 | 55 | 14 |
| Lake Forest Park | 12,394 | 23 | 19 | 4 |
| Lake Stevens | 13,758 | 26 | 21 | 5 |
| Lakewood | 56,824 | 120 | 100 | 20 |
| Langley | 1,085 | 4 | 4 | 0 |
| Liberty Lake | 7,592 | 10 | 9 | 1 |
| Long Beach | 1,361 | 7 | 6 | 1 |
| Longview | 36,778 | 69 | 54 | 15 |
| Lynden | 12,022 | 18 | 14 | 4 |
| Lynnwood | 33,544 | 114 | 80 | 34 |
| Mabton | 2,088 | 1 | 1 | 0 |
| Maple Valley | 20,700 | 12 | 12 | 0 |
| Marysville | 35,110 | 78 | 50 | 28 |
| Mattawa | 3,227 | 4 | 4 | 0 |
| McCleary | 1,616 | 4 | 4 | 0 |
| Medina | 3,634 | 9 | 8 | 1 |
| Mercer Island | 24,411 | 34 | 31 | 3 |
| Mill Creek | 17,270 | 31 | 24 | 7 |
| Milton | 6,901 | 13 | 12 | 1 |
| Monroe | 17,458 | 45 | 34 | 11 |
| Montesano | 3,633 | 10 | 8 | 2 |
| Morton | 1,090 | 4 | 3 | 1 |
| Moses Lake | 19,214 | 40 | 32 | 8 |
| Mossyrock | 505 | 2 | 2 | 0 |
| Mountlake Terrace | 19,853 | 38 | 28 | 10 |
| Mount Vernon | 32,096 | 54 | 42 | 12 |
| Moxee | 2,601 | 4 | 4 | 0 |
| Mukilteo | 21,057 | 32 | 28 | 4 |
| Napavine | 1,618 | 3 | 2 | 1 |
| Newcastle | 10,138 | 7 | 7 | 0 |
| Normandy Park | 6,225 | 15 | 13 | 2 |
| North Bend | 4,618 | 7 | 7 | 0 |
| Oak Harbor | 23,098 | 40 | 27 | 13 |
| Ocean Shores | 5,180 | 13 | 12 | 1 |
| Odessa | 913 | 2 | 2 | 0 |
| Olympia | 45,603 | 91 | 65 | 26 |
| Omak | 4,697 | 15 | 12 | 3 |
| Oroville | 1,653 | 6 | 5 | 1 |
| Orting | 6,511 | 10 | 9 | 1 |
| Othello | 6,662 | 21 | 15 | 6 |
| Pacific | 6,102 | 14 | 12 | 2 |
| Palouse | 926 | 3 | 3 | 0 |
| Pasco | 58,316 | 78 | 67 | 11 |
| Port Angeles | 19,044 | 55 | 33 | 22 |
| Port Orchard | 7,973 | 23 | 21 | 2 |
| Port Townsend | 9,223 | 19 | 15 | 4 |
| Poulsbo | 8,271 | 21 | 17 | 4 |
| Prosser | 5,148 | 19 | 12 | 7 |
| Pullman | 27,141 | 40 | 28 | 12 |
| Puyallup | 36,659 | 79 | 58 | 21 |
| Quincy | 5,977 | 15 | 13 | 2 |
| Raymond | 2,853 | 7 | 6 | 1 |
| Reardan | 596 | 1 | 1 | 0 |
| Redmond | 50,009 | 122 | 82 | 40 |
| Renton | 63,599 | 167 | 123 | 44 |
| Republic | 939 | 3 | 3 | 0 |
| Richland | 47,040 | 65 | 57 | 8 |
| Ridgefield | 4,681 | 8 | 7 | 1 |
| Ritzville | 1,736 | 4 | 4 | 0 |
| Rosalia | 581 | 1 | 1 | 0 |
| Roy | 809 | 3 | 3 | 0 |
| Royal City | 1,981 | 3 | 3 | 0 |
| Ruston | 733 | 3 | 3 | 0 |
| Sammamish | 40,837 | 23 | 23 | 0 |
| SeaTac | 25,886 | 46 | 43 | 3 |
| Seattle | 602,531 | 1,857 | 1,351 | 506 |
| Sedro Woolley | 11,114 | 17 | 13 | 4 |
| Selah | 7,215 | 15 | 14 | 1 |
| Sequim | 5,979 | 21 | 18 | 3 |

**Table 78. Full-time Law Enforcement Employees, by State, by City, 2009**—*Continued*

(Number.)

| State/city | Population | Total law enforcement employees | Total officers | Total civilians |
|---|---|---|---|---|
| Shelton | 9,372 | 23 | 19 | 4 |
| Shoreline | 51,877 | 51 | 49 | 2 |
| Snohomish | 8,794 | 24 | 20 | 4 |
| Snoqualmie | 9,772 | 16 | 13 | 3 |
| Soap Lake | 1,838 | 4 | 4 | 0 |
| South Bend | 1,783 | 4 | 3 | 1 |
| Spokane | 202,932 | 393 | 291 | 102 |
| Spokane Valley | 86,756 | 102 | 101 | 1 |
| Springdale | 276 | 1 | 1 | 0 |
| Stanwood | 6,340 | 13 | 11 | 2 |
| Steilacoom | 6,061 | 13 | 12 | 1 |
| Sumas | 1,265 | 6 | 6 | 0 |
| Sumner | 9,832 | 32 | 19 | 13 |
| Sunnyside | 15,040 | 42 | 23 | 19 |
| Tacoma | 197,557 | 432 | 389 | 43 |
| Tenino | 2,241 | 7 | 6 | 1 |
| Tieton | 1,161 | 2 | 2 | 0 |
| Toledo | 681 | 2 | 2 | 0 |
| Tonasket | 942 | 5 | 4 | 1 |
| Toppenish | 9,185 | 21 | 15 | 6 |
| Tukwila | 17,084 | 81 | 66 | 15 |
| Tumwater | 14,235 | 29 | 24 | 5 |
| Twisp | 896 | 2 | 2 | 0 |
| Union Gap | 5,707 | 20 | 17 | 3 |
| University Place | 30,385 | 23 | 22 | 1 |
| Vader | 614 | 1 | 1 | 0 |
| Vancouver | 165,147 | 228 | 199 | 29 |
| Walla Walla | 30,658 | 75 | 45 | 30 |
| Wapato | 4,537 | 18 | 11 | 7 |
| Warden | 2,585 | 5 | 4 | 1 |
| Washougal | 14,182 | 21 | 19 | 2 |
| Wenatchee | 30,051 | 53 | 42 | 11 |
| Westport | 2,631 | 9 | 7 | 2 |
| West Richland | 11,162 | 18 | 15 | 3 |
| White Salmon | 2,434 | 6 | 6 | 0 |
| Wilbur | 874 | 2 | 2 | 0 |
| Winlock | 1,254 | 2 | 2 | 0 |
| Winthrop | 392 | 3 | 3 | 0 |
| Woodinville | 11,417 | 13 | 13 | 0 |
| Woodland | 4,952 | 12 | 10 | 2 |
| Yakima | 84,167 | 185 | 137 | 48 |
| Yelm | 6,182 | 15 | 13 | 2 |
| Zillah | 2,735 | 8 | 7 | 1 |
| **WEST VIRGINIA** | | | | |
| Alderson | 1,068 | 2 | 2 | 0 |
| Anmoore | 778 | 2 | 2 | 0 |
| Ansted | 1,578 | 2 | 2 | 0 |
| Athens | 1,181 | 1 | 1 | 0 |
| Barboursville | 3,428 | 19 | 17 | 2 |
| Barrackville | 1,289 | 1 | 1 | 0 |
| Bayard | 287 | 1 | 1 | 0 |
| Beckley | 16,777 | 68 | 48 | 20 |
| Belington | 1,798 | 3 | 3 | 0 |
| Belle | 1,148 | 4 | 4 | 0 |
| Benwood | 1,416 | 12 | 6 | 6 |
| Berkeley Springs | 677 | 2 | 2 | 0 |
| Bethlehem | 2,470 | 5 | 4 | 1 |
| Bluefield | 11,056 | 28 | 21 | 7 |
| Bradshaw | 243 | 3 | 3 | 0 |
| Bramwell | 410 | 1 | 1 | 0 |
| Bridgeport | 7,982 | 27 | 25 | 2 |
| Buckhannon | 5,476 | 11 | 10 | 1 |
| Burnsville | 465 | 2 | 1 | 1 |
| Cameron | 1,064 | 4 | 2 | 2 |
| Capon Bridge | 279 | 1 | 1 | 0 |
| Cedar Grove | 796 | 2 | 2 | 0 |
| Ceredo | 1,575 | 9 | 6 | 3 |
| Chapmanville | 1,108 | 5 | 5 | 0 |
| Charleston | 49,976 | 202 | 179 | 23 |
| Charles Town | 5,005 | 18 | 15 | 3 |
| Chesapeake | 1,532 | 2 | 2 | 0 |
| Chester | 2,305 | 7 | 6 | 1 |
| Clarksburg | 16,409 | 45 | 40 | 5 |
| Clendenin | 1,034 | 4 | 4 | 0 |
| Danville | 531 | 3 | 3 | 0 |
| Delbarton | 428 | 3 | 3 | 0 |
| Dunbar | 7,614 | 16 | 13 | 3 |
| East Bank | 883 | 3 | 3 | 0 |
| Eleanor | 1,577 | 2 | 2 | 0 |
| Elkins | 6,972 | 11 | 8 | 3 |
| Fairmont | 18,997 | 41 | 35 | 6 |
| Fairview | 441 | 2 | 2 | 0 |
| Farmington | 387 | 1 | 1 | 0 |
| Fayetteville | 2,652 | 12 | 11 | 1 |
| Follansbee | 2,829 | 7 | 7 | 0 |
| Fort Gay | 793 | 3 | 3 | 0 |
| Gary | 732 | 1 | 1 | 0 |
| Gassaway | 872 | 2 | 2 | 0 |
| Gauley Bridge | 685 | 6 | 4 | 2 |
| Gilbert | 384 | 2 | 2 | 0 |
| Glasgow | 727 | 3 | 3 | 0 |
| Glen Dale | 1,380 | 8 | 5 | 3 |
| Glenville | 1,447 | 4 | 3 | 1 |
| Grafton | 5,297 | 6 | 5 | 1 |
| Grantsville | 530 | 1 | 1 | 0 |
| Grant Town | 635 | 1 | 1 | 0 |
| Granville | 816 | 14 | 13 | 1 |
| Hamlin | 1,100 | 3 | 2 | 1 |
| Harpers Ferry/Bolivar | 1,369 | 5 | 4 | 1 |
| Harrisville | 1,814 | 1 | 1 | 0 |
| Henderson | 307 | 1 | 1 | 0 |
| Hinton | 2,498 | 12 | 10 | 2 |
| Huntington | 48,904 | 105 | 98 | 7 |
| Hurricane | 6,435 | 18 | 16 | 2 |
| Iaeger | 288 | 1 | 1 | 0 |
| Kenova | 3,245 | 11 | 7 | 4 |
| Kermit | 218 | 1 | 1 | 0 |
| Keyser | 5,217 | 17 | 12 | 5 |
| Keystone | 358 | 1 | 1 | 0 |
| Kimball | 330 | 3 | 3 | 0 |
| Kingwood | 2,949 | 3 | 3 | 0 |
| Lewisburg | 3,524 | 13 | 11 | 2 |
| Logan | 1,488 | 11 | 8 | 3 |
| Lumberport | 970 | 2 | 2 | 0 |
| Mabscott | 1,345 | 5 | 4 | 1 |
| Madison | 2,566 | 6 | 5 | 1 |
| Man | 684 | 4 | 4 | 0 |
| Mannington | 2,075 | 4 | 4 | 0 |
| Marlinton | 1,189 | 1 | 1 | 0 |
| Marmet | 1,596 | 5 | 5 | 0 |
| Martinsburg | 17,275 | 57 | 46 | 11 |
| Mason | 1,037 | 5 | 4 | 1 |
| Masontown | 654 | 1 | 1 | 0 |
| Matewan | 477 | 1 | 1 | 0 |
| Matoaka | 304 | 2 | 2 | 0 |
| McMechen | 1,703 | 3 | 3 | 0 |
| Milton | 2,420 | 6 | 5 | 1 |
| Monongah | 908 | 1 | 1 | 0 |
| Montgomery | 1,920 | 6 | 5 | 1 |
| Moorefield | 2,444 | 4 | 4 | 0 |
| Morgantown | 29,989 | 68 | 58 | 10 |
| Moundsville | 9,019 | 22 | 18 | 4 |
| Mount Hope | 1,370 | 5 | 4 | 1 |
| Mullens | 1,565 | 5 | 5 | 0 |
| New Cumberland | 979 | 4 | 3 | 1 |
| New Haven | 1,525 | 4 | 3 | 1 |
| New Martinsville | 5,520 | 14 | 10 | 4 |
| Nitro | 6,770 | 14 | 13 | 1 |
| Northfork | 411 | 3 | 3 | 0 |
| Nutter Fort | 1,628 | 6 | 6 | 0 |
| Oak Hill | 7,172 | 16 | 14 | 2 |
| Oceana | 1,397 | 5 | 4 | 1 |
| Paden City | 2,572 | 5 | 4 | 1 |
| Parkersburg | 31,419 | 73 | 63 | 10 |
| Parsons | 1,367 | 1 | 1 | 0 |
| Paw Paw | 485 | 2 | 1 | 1 |
| Pennsboro | 1,150 | 3 | 1 | 2 |
| Petersburg | 2,814 | 6 | 3 | 3 |
| Philippi | 2,774 | 7 | 7 | 0 |
| Pineville | 649 | 3 | 3 | 0 |

## Table 78. Full-time Law Enforcement Employees, by State, by City, 2009—*Continued*

(Number.)

| State/city | Population | Total law enforcement employees | Total officers | Total civilians |
|---|---|---|---|---|
| Point Pleasant | 4,432 | 10 | 9 | 1 |
| Pratt | 527 | 1 | 1 | 0 |
| Princeton | 6,248 | 23 | 19 | 4 |
| Rainelle | 1,462 | 2 | 2 | 0 |
| Ranson | 4,838 | 14 | 13 | 1 |
| Ravenswood | 3,925 | 11 | 10 | 1 |
| Reedsville | 538 | 4 | 1 | 3 |
| Richwood | 2,292 | 5 | 5 | 0 |
| Ridgeley | 673 | 3 | 3 | 0 |
| Ripley | 3,239 | 10 | 9 | 1 |
| Rivesville | 905 | 1 | 1 | 0 |
| Romney | 1,909 | 4 | 3 | 1 |
| Ronceverte | 1,598 | 5 | 5 | 0 |
| Rowlesburg | 613 | 1 | 1 | 0 |
| Salem | 2,046 | 4 | 3 | 1 |
| Shepherdstown | 1,140 | 7 | 4 | 3 |
| Shinnston | 2,238 | 8 | 8 | 0 |
| Sistersville | 1,395 | 4 | 4 | 0 |
| Smithers | 838 | 5 | 4 | 1 |
| Sophia | 1,227 | 5 | 5 | 0 |
| South Charleston | 12,326 | 45 | 40 | 5 |
| Spencer | 2,136 | 6 | 6 | 0 |
| St. Albans | 10,938 | 25 | 21 | 4 |
| Star City | 1,691 | 6 | 5 | 1 |
| St. Marys | 1,913 | 4 | 4 | 0 |
| Stonewood | 1,843 | 2 | 2 | 0 |
| Summersville | 3,305 | 16 | 15 | 1 |
| Sutton | 980 | 2 | 1 | 1 |
| Sylvester | 530 | 2 | 2 | 0 |
| Terra Alta | 1,509 | 1 | 1 | 0 |
| Triadelphia | 798 | 1 | 1 | 0 |
| Vienna | 10,509 | 23 | 18 | 5 |
| Wardensville | 259 | 2 | 2 | 0 |
| Wayne | 1,117 | 1 | 1 | 0 |
| Webster Springs | 741 | 3 | 3 | 0 |
| Weirton | 18,577 | 41 | 38 | 3 |
| Welch | 2,176 | 11 | 10 | 1 |
| Wellsburg | 2,561 | 7 | 6 | 1 |
| West Logan | 386 | 1 | 1 | 0 |
| Weston | 4,261 | 7 | 5 | 2 |
| Westover | 4,105 | 8 | 8 | 0 |
| West Union | 774 | 1 | 1 | 0 |
| Wheeling | 28,660 | 80 | 78 | 2 |
| White Sulphur Springs | 2,275 | 8 | 7 | 1 |
| Whitesville | 502 | 2 | 1 | 1 |
| Williamson | 3,018 | 9 | 7 | 2 |
| Williamstown | 2,981 | 6 | 5 | 1 |
| Winfield | 2,072 | 2 | 2 | 0 |
| **WISCONSIN** | | | | |
| Adams | 1,734 | 4 | 4 | 0 |
| Albany | 1,108 | 3 | 3 | 0 |
| Algoma | 3,091 | 6 | 6 | 0 |
| Altoona | 6,759 | 13 | 12 | 1 |
| Amery | 2,770 | 8 | 7 | 1 |
| Antigo | 7,849 | 19 | 16 | 3 |
| Appleton | 70,294 | 135 | 109 | 26 |
| Arcadia | 2,312 | 5 | 5 | 0 |
| Ashland | 8,066 | 20 | 19 | 1 |
| Ashwaubenon | 17,197 | 54 | 46 | 8 |
| Athens | 1,029 | 1 | 1 | 0 |
| Avoca | 563 | 1 | 1 | 0 |
| Bangor | 1,405 | 2 | 2 | 0 |
| Baraboo | 11,302 | 32 | 27 | 5 |
| Barron | 3,104 | 6 | 6 | 0 |
| Bayfield | 566 | 3 | 3 | 0 |
| Bayside | 4,203 | 19 | 12 | 7 |
| Beaver Dam | 15,116 | 35 | 30 | 5 |
| Belleville | 2,306 | 5 | 5 | 0 |
| Beloit | 36,197 | 86 | 74 | 12 |
| Beloit Town | 7,555 | 14 | 13 | 1 |
| Berlin | 4,965 | 13 | 12 | 1 |
| Big Bend | 1,334 | 3 | 3 | 0 |
| Black River Falls | 3,382 | 8 | 7 | 1 |
| Blair | 1,243 | 2 | 2 | 0 |
| Bloomer | 3,294 | 8 | 7 | 1 |
| Bloomfield | 5,087 | 7 | 7 | 0 |
| Boscobel | 3,198 | 6 | 6 | 0 |
| Brillion | 2,857 | 8 | 7 | 1 |
| Brodhead | 3,118 | 12 | 8 | 4 |
| Brookfield | 39,049 | 82 | 65 | 17 |
| Brookfield Township | 6,154 | 15 | 14 | 1 |
| Brown Deer | 11,671 | 37 | 31 | 6 |
| Burlington | 11,030 | 26 | 20 | 6 |
| Burlington Town | 6,671 | 10 | 9 | 1 |
| Butler | 1,759 | 9 | 8 | 1 |
| Caledonia | 24,291 | 44 | 34 | 10 |
| Campbellsport | 1,943 | 2 | 2 | 0 |
| Campbell Township | 4,551 | 5 | 5 | 0 |
| Cashton | 1,060 | 2 | 2 | 0 |
| Cedarburg | 11,092 | 29 | 20 | 9 |
| Chenequa | 591 | 8 | 8 | 0 |
| Chetek | 2,135 | 6 | 5 | 1 |
| Chilton | 3,563 | 6 | 6 | 0 |
| Chippewa Falls | 12,897 | 30 | 24 | 6 |
| Cleveland | 1,408 | 3 | 2 | 1 |
| Clinton | 3,298 | 6 | 6 | 0 |
| Clintonville | 4,235 | 15 | 11 | 4 |
| Colby-Abbotsford | 3,540 | 7 | 6 | 1 |
| Columbus | 5,162 | 11 | 10 | 1 |
| Combined Locks | 3,348 | 7 | 5 | 2 |
| Coon Valley | 747 | 1 | 1 | 0 |
| Cornell | 1,377 | 3 | 3 | 0 |
| Cottage Grove | 6,445 | 14 | 13 | 1 |
| Crandon | 1,801 | 4 | 3 | 1 |
| Cross Plains | 3,603 | 5 | 4 | 1 |
| Cuba City | 2,035 | 4 | 3 | 1 |
| Cudahy | 18,856 | 44 | 33 | 11 |
| Cumberland | 2,231 | 5 | 5 | 0 |
| Darien | 1,708 | 5 | 5 | 0 |
| Darlington | 2,191 | 5 | 5 | 0 |
| DeForest | 9,006 | 20 | 17 | 3 |
| Delafield | 6,821 | 17 | 15 | 2 |
| Delavan | 8,555 | 25 | 19 | 6 |
| Delavan Town | 4,521 | 12 | 11 | 1 |
| Denmark | 2,138 | 2 | 2 | 0 |
| De Pere | 25,288 | 37 | 32 | 5 |
| Dodgeville | 5,063 | 11 | 10 | 1 |
| Durand | 1,847 | 3 | 3 | 0 |
| Eagle River | 1,754 | 6 | 6 | 0 |
| Eagle Village | 1,836 | 3 | 3 | 0 |
| East Troy | 4,591 | 8 | 8 | 0 |
| Eau Claire | 65,802 | 130 | 95 | 35 |
| Edgar | 1,339 | 1 | 1 | 0 |
| Edgerton | 5,374 | 11 | 10 | 1 |
| Eleva | 637 | 4 | 4 | 0 |
| Elkhart Lake | 1,186 | 3 | 3 | 0 |
| Elkhorn | 9,480 | 19 | 16 | 3 |
| Elk Mound | 814 | 1 | 1 | 0 |
| Ellsworth | 3,119 | 5 | 5 | 0 |
| Elm Grove | 6,118 | 25 | 17 | 8 |
| Elroy | 1,471 | 2 | 2 | 0 |
| Evansville | 5,061 | 10 | 9 | 1 |
| Everest | 15,718 | 27 | 24 | 3 |
| Fall Creek | 1,280 | 2 | 2 | 0 |
| Fennimore | 2,306 | 5 | 5 | 0 |
| Fitchburg | 23,668 | 56 | 44 | 12 |
| Fond du Lac | 42,001 | 78 | 72 | 6 |
| Fontana | 1,957 | 7 | 6 | 1 |
| Fort Atkinson | 11,923 | 27 | 20 | 7 |
| Fountain City | 993 | 1 | 1 | 0 |
| Fox Lake | 1,461 | 2 | 2 | 0 |
| Fox Point | 6,797 | 18 | 17 | 1 |
| Fox Valley Metro | 17,428 | 28 | 25 | 3 |
| Franklin | 36,217 | 72 | 57 | 15 |
| Frederic | 1,190 | 2 | 2 | 0 |
| Freedom | 5,994 | 2 | 2 | 0 |
| Geneva Town | 4,174 | 7 | 6 | 1 |
| Genoa City | 2,994 | 6 | 5 | 1 |
| Germantown | 19,740 | 42 | 31 | 11 |
| Glendale | 12,956 | 48 | 44 | 4 |
| Grafton | 11,728 | 29 | 22 | 7 |
| Grand Chute | 21,079 | 33 | 29 | 4 |

**Table 78. Full-time Law Enforcement Employees, by State, by City, 2009**—*Continued*

(Number.)

| State/city | Population | Total law enforcement employees | Total officers | Total civilians |
|---|---|---|---|---|
| Grand Rapids | 7,347 | 6 | 4 | 2 |
| Grantsburg | 1,354 | 3 | 3 | 0 |
| Green Bay | 100,836 | 219 | 181 | 38 |
| Greendale | 13,937 | 37 | 29 | 8 |
| Greenfield | 36,148 | 79 | 57 | 22 |
| Green Lake | 1,092 | 4 | 4 | 0 |
| Hales Corners | 7,556 | 20 | 17 | 3 |
| Hartford | 14,207 | 29 | 25 | 4 |
| Hartland | 8,774 | 18 | 16 | 2 |
| Hayward | 2,365 | 9 | 8 | 1 |
| Hazel Green | 1,176 | 2 | 2 | 0 |
| Highland | 795 | 1 | 1 | 0 |
| Hillsboro | 1,350 | 2 | 2 | 0 |
| Hobart-Lawrence | 9,229 | 5 | 4 | 1 |
| Holmen | 8,769 | 10 | 9 | 1 |
| Horicon | 3,466 | 11 | 9 | 2 |
| Hortonville | 2,777 | 5 | 4 | 1 |
| Hudson | 12,623 | 23 | 23 | 0 |
| Hurley | 1,514 | 7 | 6 | 1 |
| Independence | 1,208 | 2 | 2 | 0 |
| Iron Ridge | 975 | 1 | 1 | 0 |
| Jackson | 6,978 | 13 | 12 | 1 |
| Janesville | 62,761 | 112 | 99 | 13 |
| Jefferson | 7,874 | 17 | 14 | 3 |
| Juneau | 2,615 | 5 | 4 | 1 |
| Kaukauna | 15,695 | 26 | 24 | 2 |
| Kenosha | 97,657 | 209 | 199 | 10 |
| Kewaskum | 3,999 | 7 | 7 | 0 |
| Kewaunee | 2,748 | 6 | 6 | 0 |
| Kiel | 3,600 | 8 | 7 | 1 |
| Kohler | 1,951 | 8 | 7 | 1 |
| Kronenwetter | 7,118 | 7 | 6 | 1 |
| La Crosse | 50,791 | 112 | 93 | 19 |
| Ladysmith | 3,279 | 11 | 10 | 1 |
| Lake Delton | 3,311 | 20 | 18 | 2 |
| Lake Geneva | 8,437 | 31 | 22 | 9 |
| Lake Hallie | 4,455 | 7 | 6 | 1 |
| Lake Mills | 5,639 | 10 | 10 | 0 |
| Lancaster | 3,904 | 7 | 7 | 0 |
| Lodi | 3,021 | 6 | 5 | 1 |
| Lomira | 2,344 | 4 | 3 | 1 |
| Luxemburg | 2,271 | 2 | 2 | 0 |
| Madison | 234,461 | 548 | 443 | 105 |
| Manitowoc | 33,056 | 73 | 64 | 9 |
| Maple Bluff | 1,354 | 6 | 6 | 0 |
| Marathon City | 1,527 | 2 | 2 | 0 |
| Marinette | 10,699 | 27 | 23 | 4 |
| Marion | 1,163 | 3 | 3 | 0 |
| Markesan | 1,270 | 3 | 3 | 0 |
| Marshall Village | 3,778 | 8 | 7 | 1 |
| Marshfield | 18,205 | 47 | 39 | 8 |
| Mauston | 4,491 | 9 | 8 | 1 |
| Mayville | 5,107 | 12 | 10 | 2 |
| McFarland | 7,923 | 16 | 14 | 2 |
| Medford | 4,085 | 9 | 8 | 1 |
| Menasha | 16,651 | 38 | 31 | 7 |
| Menomonee Falls | 34,822 | 80 | 58 | 22 |
| Menomonie | 15,652 | 32 | 26 | 6 |
| Mequon | 23,688 | 44 | 36 | 8 |
| Merrill | 9,617 | 25 | 22 | 3 |
| Middleton | 16,284 | 46 | 36 | 10 |
| Milton | 5,629 | 11 | 9 | 2 |
| Milwaukee | 604,673 | 2,403 | 1,921 | 482 |
| Mineral Point | 2,446 | 6 | 6 | 0 |
| Minocqua | 4,749 | 15 | 10 | 5 |
| Mishicot | 1,380 | 1 | 1 | 0 |
| Mondovi | 2,553 | 4 | 4 | 0 |
| Monona | 7,814 | 25 | 20 | 5 |
| Monroe | 10,442 | 32 | 25 | 7 |
| Mosinee | 3,962 | 8 | 7 | 1 |
| Mount Horeb | 6,799 | 11 | 10 | 1 |
| Mount Pleasant | 26,985 | 54 | 41 | 13 |
| Mukwonago | 7,341 | 21 | 14 | 7 |
| Muskego | 23,440 | 46 | 36 | 10 |
| Neenah | 25,105 | 49 | 40 | 9 |
| Neillsville | 2,576 | 7 | 6 | 1 |
| New Berlin | 38,686 | 90 | 71 | 19 |
| New Glarus | 2,065 | 4 | 4 | 0 |
| New Holstein | 3,150 | 8 | 7 | 1 |
| New Lisbon | 2,553 | 4 | 4 | 0 |
| New London | 6,702 | 18 | 16 | 2 |
| New Richmond | 8,486 | 16 | 16 | 0 |
| Niagara | 1,720 | 4 | 4 | 0 |
| North Fond du Lac | 5,271 | 14 | 12 | 2 |
| North Hudson | 3,869 | 6 | 5 | 1 |
| Oak Creek | 34,069 | 79 | 58 | 21 |
| Oconomowoc | 14,359 | 28 | 22 | 6 |
| Oconomowoc Town | 8,251 | 13 | 11 | 2 |
| Oconto | 4,278 | 8 | 8 | 0 |
| Oconto Falls | 2,582 | 5 | 5 | 0 |
| Omro | 3,446 | 7 | 6 | 1 |
| Onalaska | 16,998 | 29 | 26 | 3 |
| Oregon | 9,594 | 17 | 15 | 2 |
| Osceola | 2,754 | 7 | 6 | 1 |
| Oshkosh | 63,700 | 115 | 99 | 16 |
| Osseo | 1,624 | 4 | 4 | 0 |
| Palmyra | 1,745 | 5 | 5 | 0 |
| Park Falls | 2,210 | 8 | 7 | 1 |
| Pepin | 912 | 1 | 1 | 0 |
| Peshtigo | 3,200 | 7 | 6 | 1 |
| Pewaukee | 12,631 | 27 | 25 | 2 |
| Pewaukee Village | 8,874 | 20 | 18 | 2 |
| Phillips | 1,377 | 5 | 5 | 0 |
| Plainfield | 883 | 2 | 2 | 0 |
| Platteville | 10,330 | 26 | 20 | 6 |
| Pleasant Prairie | 20,297 | 30 | 28 | 2 |
| Plover | 11,852 | 22 | 19 | 3 |
| Plymouth | 8,276 | 16 | 16 | 0 |
| Portage | 9,939 | 29 | 22 | 7 |
| Port Washington | 11,247 | 24 | 19 | 5 |
| Poynette | 2,577 | 5 | 4 | 1 |
| Prairie du Chien | 5,820 | 14 | 13 | 1 |
| Prescott | 4,039 | 9 | 8 | 1 |
| Princeton | 1,388 | 5 | 5 | 0 |
| Pulaski | 3,602 | 7 | 6 | 1 |
| Racine | 82,232 | 260 | 199 | 61 |
| Readstown | 385 | 1 | 1 | 0 |
| Reedsburg | 8,758 | 28 | 20 | 8 |
| Rhinelander | 7,602 | 20 | 17 | 3 |
| Rice Lake | 8,247 | 20 | 18 | 2 |
| Richland Center | 5,040 | 13 | 11 | 2 |
| Ripon | 7,392 | 19 | 14 | 5 |
| River Falls | 14,549 | 24 | 22 | 2 |
| River Hills | 1,660 | 12 | 12 | 0 |
| Rome Town | 2,997 | 8 | 7 | 1 |
| Rosendale | 1,033 | 1 | 1 | 0 |
| Rothschild | 5,052 | 12 | 10 | 2 |
| Sauk Prairie | 4,050 | 15 | 13 | 2 |
| Saukville | 4,301 | 11 | 11 | 0 |
| Seymour | 3,490 | 9 | 7 | 2 |
| Shawano | 8,706 | 21 | 19 | 2 |
| Sheboygan | 47,578 | 107 | 81 | 26 |
| Sheboygan Falls | 8,025 | 16 | 14 | 2 |
| Shiocton | 913 | 1 | 1 | 0 |
| Shorewood | 13,173 | 30 | 25 | 5 |
| Shorewood Hills | 1,675 | 7 | 6 | 1 |
| Silver Lake | 2,543 | 5 | 4 | 1 |
| Siren | 998 | 3 | 3 | 0 |
| Slinger | 4,757 | 10 | 9 | 1 |
| Somerset | 2,836 | 6 | 5 | 1 |
| South Milwaukee | 21,122 | 39 | 33 | 6 |
| Sparta | 8,836 | 20 | 18 | 2 |
| Spencer | 1,792 | 3 | 3 | 0 |
| Spooner | 2,653 | 7 | 6 | 1 |
| Spring Green | 1,503 | 4 | 3 | 1 |
| Stanley | 3,567 | 4 | 4 | 0 |
| St. Croix Falls | 2,163 | 5 | 5 | 0 |
| Stevens Point | 25,320 | 57 | 44 | 13 |
| St. Francis | 9,862 | 26 | 21 | 5 |
| Stoughton | 13,013 | 26 | 20 | 6 |
| Strum | 1,022 | 9 | 9 | 0 |
| Sturgeon Bay | 8,721 | 22 | 21 | 1 |

## Table 78. Full-time Law Enforcement Employees, by State, by City, 2009—*Continued*

(Number.)

| State/city | Population | Total law enforcement employees | Total officers | Total civilians |
|---|---|---|---|---|
| Sturtevant | 7,120 | 9 | 9 | 0 |
| Summit | 5,055 | 8 | 8 | 0 |
| Sun Prairie | 29,324 | 72 | 50 | 22 |
| Superior | 26,098 | 63 | 57 | 6 |
| Theresa | 1,249 | 2 | 2 | 0 |
| Thiensville | 3,013 | 8 | 7 | 1 |
| Three Lakes | 2,251 | 4 | 4 | 0 |
| Tomah | 8,692 | 21 | 19 | 2 |
| Tomahawk | 3,684 | 8 | 7 | 1 |
| Town of East Troy | 3,970 | 6 | 6 | 0 |
| Town of Madison | 6,309 | 20 | 18 | 2 |
| Town of Menasha | 16,005 | 32 | 25 | 7 |
| Trempealeau | 1,529 | 2 | 2 | 0 |
| Twin Lakes | 5,809 | 18 | 13 | 5 |
| Two Rivers | 11,716 | 29 | 26 | 3 |
| Valders | 973 | 1 | 1 | 0 |
| Verona | 12,056 | 19 | 17 | 2 |
| Viroqua | 4,437 | 11 | 9 | 2 |
| Walworth | 2,738 | 7 | 6 | 1 |
| Washburn | 2,155 | 5 | 5 | 0 |
| Waterloo | 3,273 | 9 | 8 | 1 |
| Watertown | 23,066 | 52 | 38 | 14 |
| Waukesha | 68,248 | 153 | 116 | 37 |
| Waunakee | 11,569 | 18 | 16 | 2 |
| Waupaca | 5,837 | 15 | 14 | 1 |
| Waupun | 10,441 | 20 | 18 | 2 |
| Wausau | 37,459 | 79 | 70 | 9 |
| Wautoma | 2,122 | 7 | 6 | 1 |
| Wauwatosa | 44,777 | 122 | 94 | 28 |
| West Allis | 59,240 | 156 | 132 | 24 |
| West Bend | 30,070 | 75 | 56 | 19 |
| Westby | 2,188 | 3 | 3 | 0 |
| Westfield | 1,174 | 3 | 3 | 0 |
| West Milwaukee | 4,008 | 22 | 18 | 4 |
| West Salem | 4,829 | 7 | 6 | 1 |
| Whitefish Bay | 13,527 | 28 | 24 | 4 |
| Whitehall | 1,593 | 4 | 4 | 0 |
| Whitewater | 14,380 | 35 | 24 | 11 |
| Williams Bay | 2,734 | 8 | 7 | 1 |
| Winneconne | 2,469 | 6 | 5 | 1 |
| Wisconsin Dells | 2,474 | 18 | 12 | 6 |
| Wisconsin Rapids | 17,020 | 42 | 37 | 5 |
| Woodruff | 1,895 | 6 | 5 | 1 |
| **WYOMING** | | | | |
| Afton | 1,866 | 5 | 5 | 0 |
| Alpine | 845 | 2 | 2 | 0 |
| Baggs | 406 | 2 | 2 | 0 |
| Basin | 1,243 | 4 | 4 | 0 |
| Buffalo | 4,945 | 22 | 14 | 8 |
| Casper | 54,550 | 110 | 94 | 16 |
| Cheyenne | 57,317 | 135 | 103 | 32 |
| Cody | 9,358 | 23 | 20 | 3 |
| Diamondville | 657 | 5 | 3 | 2 |
| Douglas | 6,049 | 23 | 17 | 6 |
| Evanston | 11,823 | 33 | 27 | 6 |
| Evansville | 2,408 | 12 | 10 | 2 |
| Gillette | 27,709 | 84 | 53 | 31 |
| Glenrock | 2,443 | 11 | 5 | 6 |
| Green River | 12,194 | 41 | 31 | 10 |
| Greybull | 1,732 | 7 | 5 | 2 |
| Guernsey | 1,065 | 3 | 3 | 0 |
| Hanna | 866 | 5 | 4 | 1 |
| Jackson | 9,937 | 29 | 20 | 9 |
| Kemmerer | 2,449 | 9 | 8 | 1 |
| La Barge | 470 | 2 | 2 | 0 |
| Lander | 7,304 | 18 | 17 | 1 |
| Laramie | 27,730 | 75 | 49 | 26 |
| Lovell | 2,268 | 10 | 6 | 4 |
| Lusk | 1,485 | 4 | 4 | 0 |
| Mills | 3,177 | 13 | 11 | 2 |
| Moorcroft | 900 | 5 | 4 | 1 |
| Newcastle | 3,406 | 16 | 8 | 8 |
| Pine Bluffs | 1,155 | 9 | 2 | 7 |
| Powell | 5,540 | 24 | 17 | 7 |
| Rawlins | 8,716 | 30 | 20 | 10 |
| Riverton | 10,123 | 38 | 25 | 13 |
| Rock Springs | 20,391 | 69 | 47 | 22 |
| Saratoga | 1,763 | 11 | 6 | 5 |
| Sheridan | 17,350 | 49 | 27 | 22 |
| Sundance | 1,264 | 3 | 3 | 0 |
| Thermopolis | 2,951 | 13 | 7 | 6 |
| Torrington | 5,486 | 21 | 15 | 6 |
| Wheatland | 3,273 | 10 | 9 | 1 |
| Worland | 4,926 | 11 | 11 | 0 |

## Table 79. Full-Time Law Enforcement Employees, by State and University and College, 2009

(Number.)

| State, University/College | Campus | Student enrollment[1] | Total law enforcement employees | Total officers | Total civilians |
|---|---|---|---|---|---|
| **ALABAMA** | | | | | |
| Alabama A&M University | | 5,124 | 20 | 11 | 9 |
| Alabama State University | | 5,695 | 29 | 22 | 7 |
| Auburn University | Montgomery | 5,296 | 21 | 12 | 9 |
| Calhoun Community College[2] | | | 7 | 6 | 1 |
| George C. Wallace State Community College | | 3,956 | 2 | 2 | 0 |
| Jacksonville State University | | 9,481 | 18 | 14 | 4 |
| Troy University | | 28,303 | 15 | 10 | 5 |
| University of Alabama: | Birmingham | 16,149 | 158 | 86 | 72 |
| | Huntsville | 7,431 | 17 | 13 | 4 |
| | Tuscaloosa | 27,014 | 76 | 64 | 12 |
| University of Montevallo | | 3,023 | 17 | 9 | 8 |
| University of North Alabama | | 7,203 | 23 | 14 | 9 |
| University of South Alabama | | 14,064 | 45 | 27 | 18 |
| University of West Alabama | | 4,888 | 9 | 6 | 3 |
| **ALASKA** | | | | | |
| University of Alaska: | Anchorage | 16,649 | 20 | 14 | 6 |
| | Fairbanks | 8,575 | 18 | 11 | 7 |
| **ARIZONA** | | | | | |
| Arizona State University | Main Campus | 67,082 | 132 | 70 | 62 |
| Arizona Western College | | 7,290 | 12 | 7 | 5 |
| Central Arizona College | | 5,865 | 10 | 7 | 3 |
| Northern Arizona University | | 22,502 | 26 | 16 | 10 |
| Pima Community College | | 34,136 | 32 | 25 | 7 |
| University of Arizona | | 38,057 | 104 | 53 | 51 |
| Yavapai College | | 9,033 | 9 | 8 | 1 |
| **ARKANSAS** | | | | | |
| Arkansas State University: | Beebe | 4,459 | 5 | 4 | 1 |
| | Jonesboro | 11,490 | 22 | 18 | 4 |
| Arkansas Tech University | | 7,492 | 11 | 9 | 2 |
| Henderson State University | | 3,652 | 8 | 7 | 1 |
| Northwest Arkansas Community College | | 7,216 | 14 | 8 | 6 |
| Southern Arkansas University | | 3,118 | 6 | 5 | 1 |
| University of Arkansas: | Fayetteville | 19,194 | 39 | 31 | 8 |
| | Little Rock | 11,965 | 41 | 26 | 15 |
| | Medical Sciences | 2,652 | 50 | 39 | 11 |
| | Monticello | 3,302 | 7 | 6 | 1 |
| | Pine Bluff | 3,525 | 21 | 15 | 6 |
| University of Central Arkansas | | 12,974 | 34 | 24 | 10 |
| **CALIFORNIA** | | | | | |
| Allan Hancock College | | 11,552 | 5 | 4 | 1 |
| California State Polytechnic University: | Pomona | 21,190 | 31 | 20 | 11 |
| | San Luis Obispo | 19,471 | 39 | 19 | 20 |
| California State University: | Bakersfield | 7,684 | 15 | 11 | 4 |
| | Channel Islands | 3,783 | 24 | 12 | 12 |
| | Chico | 17,132 | 24 | 16 | 8 |
| | Dominguez Hills | 12,851 | 22 | 16 | 6 |
| | East Bay | 14,167 | 23 | 14 | 9 |
| | Fresno | 22,613 | 30 | 21 | 9 |
| | Fullerton | 36,996 | 27 | 22 | 5 |
| | Long Beach | 37,891 | 53 | 26 | 27 |
| | Los Angeles | 20,743 | 34 | 20 | 14 |
| | Monterey Bay | 4,340 | 17 | 15 | 2 |
| | Northridge | 36,208 | 38 | 23 | 15 |
| | Sacramento | 29,011 | 28 | 22 | 6 |
| | San Bernardino | 17,646 | 25 | 16 | 9 |
| | San Jose[2] | | 51 | 28 | 23 |
| | San Marcos | 9,148 | 37 | 16 | 21 |
| | Stanislaus | 8,601 | 21 | 11 | 10 |
| College of the Sequoias | | 13,449 | 5 | 4 | 1 |
| Contra Costa Community College | | 7,580 | 36 | 24 | 12 |
| Cuesta College | | 11,341 | 5 | 5 | 0 |
| El Camino College | | 27,098 | 32 | 25 | 7 |
| Foothill-De Anza College | | 45,541 | 21 | 11 | 10 |
| Fresno Community College | | 24,783 | 18 | 15 | 3 |
| Humboldt State University | | 7,800 | 21 | 13 | 8 |
| Marin Community College | | 6,047 | 7 | 6 | 1 |
| Pasadena Community College | | 26,713 | 14 | 8 | 6 |
| Reedley Community College | | 14,223 | 3 | 2 | 1 |
| Riverside Community College | | 36,146 | 25 | 17 | 8 |
| San Bernardino Community College | | 14,136 | 17 | 11 | 6 |
| San Diego State University | | 34,889 | 49 | 28 | 21 |
| San Francisco State University | | 30,014 | 48 | 26 | 22 |

[1] The student enrollment figures provided by the United States Department of Education are for the 2008 school year, the most recent available. The enrollment figures include full-time and part-time students.

[2] Student enrollment figures were not available.

**Table 79. Full-Time Law Enforcement Employees, by State and University and College, 2009—*Continued***

(Number.)

| State, University/College | Campus | Student enrollment[1] | Total law enforcement employees | Total officers | Total civilians |
|---|---|---|---|---|---|
| San Jose/Evergreen Community College | | 22,826 | 11 | 5 | 6 |
| Santa Rosa Junior College | | 20,298 | 24 | 12 | 12 |
| Solano Community College | | 11,055 | 6 | 4 | 2 |
| Sonoma State University | | 8,921 | 18 | 11 | 7 |
| University of California: | Berkeley | 35,396 | 111 | 62 | 49 |
| | Davis | 30,568 | 78 | 46 | 32 |
| | Hastings College of Law | 1,306 | 14 | 14 | 0 |
| | Irvine | 26,984 | 40 | 30 | 10 |
| | Los Angeles | 38,220 | 92 | 63 | 29 |
| | Merced | 2,718 | 19 | 10 | 9 |
| | Riverside | 18,079 | 40 | 28 | 12 |
| | San Diego | 27,520 | 66 | 34 | 32 |
| | San Francisco | 2,998 | 123 | 41 | 82 |
| | Santa Barbara | 21,868 | 45 | 30 | 15 |
| | Santa Cruz | 16,615 | 44 | 18 | 26 |
| Ventura County Community College District | | 14,207 | 17 | 16 | 1 |
| West Valley-Mission College | | 22,159 | 12 | 8 | 4 |
| **COLORADO** | | | | | |
| Adams State College | | 2,920 | 6 | 5 | 1 |
| Arapahoe Community College | | 7,204 | 10 | 7 | 3 |
| Auraria Higher Education Center[2] | | | 35 | 23 | 12 |
| Colorado School of Mines | | 4,704 | 8 | 7 | 1 |
| Colorado State University: | Fort Collins | 28,882 | 50 | 38 | 12 |
| | Pueblo | 6,759 | 7 | 5 | 2 |
| Fort Lewis College | | 3,740 | 8 | 6 | 2 |
| Pikes Peak Community College | | 11,873 | 17 | 15 | 2 |
| Red Rocks Community College | | 7,667 | 2 | 2 | 0 |
| University of Colorado: | Boulder | 32,469 | 59 | 40 | 19 |
| | Colorado Springs | 9,373 | 26 | 16 | 10 |
| | Denver | 21,903 | 61 | 27 | 34 |
| University of Northern Colorado | | 12,498 | 18 | 12 | 6 |
| **CONNECTICUT** | | | | | |
| Central Connecticut State University | | 12,233 | 27 | 20 | 7 |
| Eastern Connecticut State University | | 5,427 | 25 | 19 | 6 |
| Southern Connecticut State University | | 11,769 | 32 | 26 | 6 |
| University of Connecticut: | Health Center[2] | | 29 | 12 | 17 |
| | Storrs, Avery Point, and Hartford[2] | | 81 | 63 | 18 |
| Western Connecticut State University | | 6,462 | 25 | 18 | 7 |
| Yale University | | 10,192 | 101 | 86 | 15 |
| **DELAWARE** | | | | | |
| Delaware State University | | 3,534 | 39 | 18 | 21 |
| University of Delaware | | 20,500 | 82 | 48 | 34 |
| **FLORIDA** | | | | | |
| Florida A&M University | | 11,857 | 61 | 35 | 26 |
| Florida Atlantic University | | 26,839 | 53 | 42 | 11 |
| Florida Gulf Coast University | | 10,204 | 19 | 14 | 5 |
| Florida International University | | 38,759 | 61 | 44 | 17 |
| Florida State University: | Panama City[2] | | 6 | 5 | 1 |
| | Tallahassee | 38,682 | 75 | 56 | 19 |
| New College of Florida | | 785 | 18 | 12 | 6 |
| Pensacola Junior College | | 10,665 | 15 | 12 | 3 |
| Santa Fe College | | 14,796 | 23 | 19 | 4 |
| Tallahassee Community College | | 14,005 | 22 | 9 | 13 |
| University of Central Florida | | 50,121 | 90 | 55 | 35 |
| University of Florida | | 51,474 | 129 | 78 | 51 |
| University of North Florida | | 15,280 | 37 | 29 | 8 |
| University of South Florida: | St. Petersburg[2] | | 16 | 11 | 5 |
| | Tampa | 46,189 | 58 | 43 | 15 |
| University of West Florida | | 10,491 | 28 | 20 | 8 |
| **GEORGIA** | | | | | |
| Abraham Baldwin Agricultural College | | 3,600 | 13 | 13 | 0 |
| Albany State University | | 4,176 | 29 | 17 | 12 |
| Berry College | | 1,795 | 17 | 13 | 4 |
| Clark Atlanta University | | 4,068 | 37 | 13 | 24 |
| Columbus State University | | 7,951 | 33 | 21 | 12 |
| Dalton State College | | 4,957 | 15 | 13 | 2 |
| Darton College | | 5,018 | 6 | 6 | 0 |
| Fort Valley State University | | 3,106 | 33 | 15 | 18 |
| Georgia College and State University | | 6,506 | 21 | 17 | 4 |
| Georgia Gwinnett College | | 360 | 8 | 5 | 3 |
| Georgia Institute of Technology | | 19,413 | 86 | 65 | 21 |
| Georgia Military College[2] | | | 4 | 3 | 1 |
| Georgia Perimeter College | | 22,808 | 72 | 32 | 40 |
| Georgia Southern University | | 17,764 | 35 | 29 | 6 |

[1] The student enrollment figures provided by the United States Department of Education are for the 2008 school year, the most recent available. The enrollment figures include full-time and part-time students.

[2] Student enrollment figures were not available.

**Table 79. Full-Time Law Enforcement Employees, by State and University and College, 2009—*Continued***

(Number.)

| State, University/College | Campus | Student enrollment[1] | Total law enforcement employees | Total officers | Total civilians |
|---|---|---|---|---|---|
| Georgia Southwestern State University | | 2,717 | 11 | 10 | 1 |
| Georgia State University | | 28,229 | 112 | 65 | 47 |
| Gordon College | | 3,855 | 10 | 8 | 2 |
| Kennesaw State University | | 21,449 | 53 | 26 | 27 |
| Medical College of Georgia | | 2,443 | 44 | 33 | 11 |
| Mercer University | | 7,622 | 31 | 23 | 8 |
| Middle Georgia College | | 3,434 | 16 | 13 | 3 |
| Morehouse College | | 2,781 | 37 | 14 | 23 |
| North Georgia College and State University | | 5,500 | 22 | 12 | 10 |
| Savannah State University | | 3,453 | 37 | 15 | 22 |
| Southern Polytechnic State University | | 4,818 | 17 | 15 | 2 |
| University of Georgia | | 34,180 | 95 | 74 | 21 |
| University of West Georgia | | 11,252 | 31 | 22 | 9 |
| Valdosta State University | | 11,490 | 30 | 21 | 9 |
| Young Harris College | | 654 | 4 | 4 | 0 |
| **ILLINOIS** | | | | | |
| Black Hawk College | | 6,179 | 9 | 8 | 1 |
| Chicago State University | | 6,820 | 38 | 26 | 12 |
| College of DuPage | | 25,668 | 19 | 14 | 5 |
| College of Lake County | | 16,359 | 21 | 14 | 7 |
| Eastern Illinois University | | 12,040 | 23 | 20 | 3 |
| Governors State University | | 5,636 | 12 | 8 | 4 |
| Illinois State University | | 20,799 | 29 | 23 | 6 |
| John A. Logan College | | 7,608 | 7 | 7 | 0 |
| Joliet Junior College | | 14,088 | 21 | 12 | 9 |
| Moraine Valley Community College | | 17,477 | 17 | 11 | 6 |
| Northeastern Illinois University | | 12,320 | 26 | 21 | 5 |
| Northern Illinois University | | 24,397 | 77 | 59 | 18 |
| Northwestern University: | Chicago[2] | | 14 | 14 | 0 |
| | Evanston[2] | | 73 | 31 | 42 |
| Oakton Community College | | 10,747 | 12 | 11 | 1 |
| Parkland College | | 9,273 | 20 | 14 | 6 |
| Rock Valley College | | 8,072 | 17 | 13 | 4 |
| Southern Illinois University: | Carbondale | 20,673 | 53 | 36 | 17 |
| | Edwardsville | 13,602 | 42 | 33 | 9 |
| | School of Medicine[2] | | 14 | 4 | 10 |
| South Suburban College | | 7,989 | 13 | 9 | 4 |
| Triton College | | 15,547 | 15 | 10 | 5 |
| University of Illinois: | Chicago | 25,835 | 126 | 73 | 53 |
| | Springfield | 4,711 | 22 | 15 | 7 |
| | Urbana | 43,246 | 68 | 53 | 15 |
| Waubonsee College | | 9,307 | 2 | 2 | 0 |
| Western Illinois University | | 13,175 | 31 | 26 | 5 |
| William Rainey Harper College[2] | | | 17 | 11 | 6 |
| **INDIANA** | | | | | |
| Ball State University | | 20,243 | 32 | 25 | 7 |
| Indiana State University | | 10,457 | 33 | 24 | 9 |
| Indiana University: | Bloomington | 40,354 | 53 | 43 | 10 |
| | Gary | 4,794 | 15 | 11 | 4 |
| | Indianapolis[2] | | 44 | 35 | 9 |
| | New Albany | 6,482 | 12 | 9 | 3 |
| Marian University | | 2,143 | 8 | 5 | 3 |
| Purdue University | | 41,433 | 53 | 42 | 11 |
| **IOWA** | | | | | |
| Iowa State University | | 26,856 | 39 | 31 | 8 |
| University of Iowa | | 29,152 | 64 | 38 | 26 |
| University of Northern Iowa | | 12,998 | 25 | 17 | 8 |
| **KANSAS** | | | | | |
| Emporia State University | | 6,404 | 9 | 9 | 0 |
| Fort Hays State University | | 10,107 | 11 | 9 | 2 |
| Kansas City Community College | | 5,820 | 12 | 11 | 1 |
| Kansas State University | | 23,520 | 36 | 20 | 16 |
| Pittsburg State University | | 7,127 | 17 | 13 | 4 |
| University of Kansas: | Main Campus | 29,365 | 47 | 25 | 22 |
| | Medical Center[2] | | 62 | 28 | 34 |
| Washburn University | | 6,545 | 18 | 13 | 5 |
| Wichita State University | | 14,405 | 36 | 24 | 12 |
| **KENTUCKY** | | | | | |
| Eastern Kentucky University | | 16,031 | 29 | 25 | 4 |
| Kentucky State University | | 2,659 | 19 | 12 | 7 |
| Morehead State University | | 8,832 | 26 | 16 | 10 |
| Murray State University | | 10,014 | 22 | 15 | 7 |
| Northern Kentucky University | | 15,082 | 18 | 11 | 7 |
| University of Kentucky | | 26,054 | 115 | 46 | 69 |
| University of Louisville | | 20,834 | 72 | 34 | 38 |
| Western Kentucky University | | 19,742 | 38 | 28 | 10 |

[1] The student enrollment figures provided by the United States Department of Education are for the 2008 school year, the most recent available. The enrollment figures include full-time and part-time students.
[2] Student enrollment figures were not available.

## Table 79. Full-Time Law Enforcement Employees, by State and University and College, 2009—*Continued*

(Number.)

| State, University/College | Campus | Student enrollment[1] | Total law enforcement employees | Total officers | Total civilians |
|---|---|---|---|---|---|
| **LOUISIANA** | | | | | |
| Delgado Community College | | 14,450 | 30 | 23 | 7 |
| Grambling State University | | 5,253 | 24 | 9 | 15 |
| Louisiana State University: | Baton Rouge[2] | | 67 | 64 | 3 |
| | Health Sciences Center, New Orleans | 2,431 | 30 | 30 | 0 |
| | Health Sciences Center, Shreveport | 814 | 65 | 47 | 18 |
| | Shreveport | 4,281 | 9 | 9 | 0 |
| Nicholls State University | | 6,916 | 13 | 11 | 2 |
| Northwestern State University | | 9,111 | 23 | 19 | 4 |
| Southeastern Louisiana University | | 15,215 | 38 | 24 | 14 |
| Southern University and A&M College | Baton Rouge | 7,669 | 30 | 23 | 7 |
| Tulane University | | 10,737 | 57 | 43 | 14 |
| University of Louisiana | Monroe | 8,754 | 27 | 19 | 8 |
| University of New Orleans | | 11,428 | 25 | 25 | 0 |
| **MAINE** | | | | | |
| University of Maine: | Farmington | 2,174 | 6 | 5 | 1 |
| | Orono | 11,818 | 32 | 19 | 13 |
| University of Southern Maine | | 10,009 | 21 | 12 | 9 |
| **MARYLAND** | | | | | |
| Bowie State University | | 5,483 | 27 | 14 | 13 |
| Coppin State University | | 4,051 | 40 | 24 | 16 |
| Frostburg State University | | 5,215 | 18 | 14 | 4 |
| Morgan State University | | 7,005 | 51 | 33 | 18 |
| Salisbury University | | 7,868 | 30 | 18 | 12 |
| St. Mary's College | | 2,068 | 13 | 1 | 12 |
| Towson University | | 21,111 | 62 | 41 | 21 |
| University of Baltimore | | 5,843 | 39 | 13 | 26 |
| University of Maryland: | Baltimore City | 6,156 | 153 | 61 | 92 |
| | Baltimore County | 12,268 | 33 | 25 | 8 |
| | College Park | 37,000 | 126 | 84 | 42 |
| | Eastern Shore | 4,290 | 19 | 16 | 3 |
| **MASSACHUSETTS** | | | | | |
| Amherst College | | 1,697 | 14 | 9 | 5 |
| Assumption College | | 2,876 | 28 | 16 | 12 |
| Bentley College | | 5,693 | 33 | 22 | 11 |
| Boston College | | 14,836 | 66 | 51 | 15 |
| Boston University | | 31,766 | 63 | 51 | 12 |
| Brandeis University | | 5,327 | 23 | 21 | 2 |
| Bridgewater State College | | 10,269 | 38 | 21 | 17 |
| Bristol Community College | | 8,100 | 10 | 6 | 4 |
| Clark University | | 3,330 | 16 | 12 | 4 |
| Dean College | | 1,341 | 13 | 7 | 6 |
| Fitchburg State College | | 6,761 | 19 | 16 | 3 |
| Framingham State College | | 6,086 | 15 | 12 | 3 |
| Harvard University | | 26,496 | 106 | 86 | 20 |
| Lasell College | | 1,488 | 16 | 15 | 1 |
| Massachusetts College of Art | | 2,340 | 23 | 9 | 14 |
| Massachusetts College of Liberal Arts | | 1,942 | 14 | 11 | 3 |
| Massachusetts Institute of Technology | | 10,299 | 56 | 53 | 3 |
| Merrimack College | | 2,143 | 17 | 13 | 4 |
| Mount Holyoke College | | 2,241 | 22 | 16 | 6 |
| Northeastern University | | 25,837 | 80 | 56 | 24 |
| North Shore Community College | | 7,224 | 20 | 19 | 1 |
| Quinsigamond Community College | | 7,227 | 13 | 13 | 0 |
| Salem State College | | 10,157 | 27 | 23 | 4 |
| Smith College | | 3,101 | 16 | 14 | 2 |
| Springfield College | | 4,806 | 38 | 13 | 25 |
| University of Massachusetts: | Amherst | 26,359 | 77 | 61 | 16 |
| | Dartmouth | 9,155 | 39 | 26 | 13 |
| | Harbor Campus, Boston | 14,117 | 33 | 27 | 6 |
| | Medical Center, Worcester | 1,025 | 34 | 23 | 11 |
| Wellesley College | | 2,498 | 19 | 14 | 5 |
| Western New England College | | 3,722 | 24 | 18 | 6 |
| Westfield State College | | 5,548 | 23 | 17 | 6 |
| Worcester Polytechnic Institute | | 4,556 | 22 | 16 | 6 |
| **MICHIGAN** | | | | | |
| Central Michigan University | | 27,225 | 31 | 20 | 11 |
| Delta College | | 10,899 | 11 | 8 | 3 |
| Eastern Michigan University | | 22,032 | 39 | 32 | 7 |
| Ferris State University | | 13,532 | 19 | 13 | 6 |
| Grand Rapids Community College | | 15,403 | 15 | 11 | 4 |
| Grand Valley State University | | 23,892 | 20 | 16 | 4 |
| Lansing Community College | | 19,445 | 16 | 13 | 3 |

[1] The student enrollment figures provided by the United States Department of Education are for the 2008 school year, the most recent available. The enrollment figures include full-time and part-time students.
[2] Student enrollment figures were not available.

## Table 79. Full-Time Law Enforcement Employees, by State and University and College, 2009—*Continued*

(Number.)

| State, University/College | Campus | Student enrollment[1] | Total law enforcement employees | Total officers | Total civilians |
|---|---|---|---|---|---|
| Macomb Community College | | 22,985 | 37 | 30 | 7 |
| Michigan State University | | 46,510 | 101 | 67 | 34 |
| Michigan Technological University | | 7,009 | 14 | 11 | 3 |
| Mott Community College | | 10,813 | 9 | 5 | 4 |
| Northern Michigan University | | 9,347 | 25 | 21 | 4 |
| Oakland Community College | | 24,957 | 30 | 26 | 4 |
| Oakland University | | 18,175 | 27 | 21 | 6 |
| Saginaw Valley State University | | 9,837 | 12 | 10 | 2 |
| University of Michigan: | Ann Arbor | 41,028 | 90 | 52 | 38 |
| | Dearborn | 8,311 | 19 | 7 | 12 |
| | Flint | 7,260 | 24 | 8 | 16 |
| Western Michigan University | | 24,818 | 59 | 28 | 31 |
| **MINNESOTA** | | | | | |
| University of Minnesota: | Duluth | 11,366 | 10 | 9 | 1 |
| | Morris | 1,607 | 5 | 3 | 2 |
| | Twin Cities | 51,140 | 60 | 45 | 15 |
| **MISSISSIPPI** | | | | | |
| Coahoma Community College | | 2,263 | 8 | 7 | 1 |
| Itawamba Community College | | 6,627 | 12 | 11 | 1 |
| Jackson State University | | 8,377 | 65 | 36 | 29 |
| Mississippi State University | | 17,824 | 38 | 30 | 8 |
| Northeast Mississippi Community College | | 3,190 | 7 | 5 | 2 |
| University of Mississippi: | Medical Center | 2,266 | 75 | 57 | 18 |
| | Oxford | 15,289 | 45 | 28 | 17 |
| **MISSOURI** | | | | | |
| Lincoln University | | 3,109 | 22 | 10 | 12 |
| Mineral Area College | | 3,238 | 11 | 6 | 5 |
| Missouri Southern State University | | 5,264 | 10 | 5 | 5 |
| Missouri University of Science and Technology | | 6,367 | 20 | 10 | 10 |
| Missouri Western State University | | 5,508 | 13 | 10 | 3 |
| Northwest Missouri State University | | 6,687 | 12 | 10 | 2 |
| Southeast Missouri State University | | 10,736 | 26 | 19 | 7 |
| St. Louis Community College: | Florissant Valley | 6,514 | 12 | 9 | 3 |
| | Meramec | 10,209 | 12 | 9 | 3 |
| Truman State University | | 5,880 | 11 | 10 | 1 |
| University of Central Missouri | | 11,063 | 21 | 17 | 4 |
| University of Missouri: | Columbia | 30,130 | 54 | 33 | 21 |
| | Kansas City | 14,481 | 44 | 28 | 16 |
| | St. Louis | 15,741 | 25 | 19 | 6 |
| Washington University | | 13,339 | 42 | 25 | 17 |
| **MONTANA** | | | | | |
| Montana State University | | 11,976 | 33 | 17 | 16 |
| University of Montana | | 14,207 | 26 | 13 | 13 |
| **NEBRASKA** | | | | | |
| University of Nebraska: | Kearney | 6,543 | 8 | 7 | 1 |
| | Lincoln | 23,573 | 52 | 30 | 22 |
| **NEVADA** | | | | | |
| Truckee Meadows Community College | | 12,492 | 11 | 6 | 5 |
| University of Nevada: | Las Vegas | 28,600 | 52 | 33 | 19 |
| | Reno | 16,867 | 23 | 17 | 6 |
| **NEW JERSEY** | | | | | |
| Brookdale Community College | | 14,642 | 27 | 14 | 13 |
| Essex County College | | 12,318 | 53 | 13 | 40 |
| Kean University | | 14,203 | 55 | 27 | 28 |
| Middlesex County College | | 12,381 | 16 | 11 | 5 |
| Monmouth University | | 6,442 | 39 | 21 | 18 |
| Montclair State University | | 17,475 | 43 | 32 | 11 |
| New Jersey Institute of Technology | | 8,398 | 71 | 29 | 42 |
| Richard Stockton College of New Jersey | | 7,307 | 30 | 22 | 8 |
| Rowan University | | 10,270 | 62 | 22 | 40 |
| Rutgers University: | Camden | 5,398 | 37 | 18 | 19 |
| | Newark | 11,032 | 57 | 32 | 25 |
| | New Brunswick | 36,041 | 75 | 49 | 26 |
| Stevens Institute of Technology | | 5,595 | 21 | 15 | 6 |
| The College of New Jersey | | 6,949 | 29 | 18 | 11 |
| University of Medicine and Dentistry: | Camden[2] | | 19 | 19 | 0 |
| | Newark | 5,906 | 180 | 90 | 90 |
| | New Brunswick[2] | | 36 | 24 | 12 |
| William Paterson University | | 10,256 | 44 | 28 | 16 |
| **NEW MEXICO** | | | | | |
| Eastern New Mexico University | | 4,294 | 9 | 8 | 1 |
| New Mexico Highlands University | | 3,524 | 12 | 3 | 9 |
| New Mexico State University | | 17,239 | 32 | 20 | 12 |
| University of New Mexico | | 25,754 | 54 | 33 | 21 |
| Western New Mexico University | | 2,822 | 5 | 4 | 1 |

[1] The student enrollment figures provided by the United States Department of Education are for the 2008 school year, the most recent available. The enrollment figures include full-time and part-time students.
[2] Student enrollment figures were not available.

## Table 79. Full-Time Law Enforcement Employees, by State and University and College, 2009—*Continued*

(Number.)

| State, University/College | Campus | Student enrollment[1] | Total law enforcement employees | Total officers | Total civilians |
|---|---|---|---|---|---|
| **NEW YORK** | | | | | |
| Cornell University | | 20,273 | 58 | 46 | 12 |
| Ithaca College | | 6,448 | 23 | 17 | 6 |
| State University of New York: | Albany | 18,204 | 70 | 40 | 30 |
| | Binghamton | 14,882 | 49 | 36 | 13 |
| | Buffalo[2] | | 68 | 62 | 6 |
| | Downstate Medical Center[2] | | 126 | 31 | 95 |
| | Maritime College | 1,630 | 11 | 6 | 5 |
| | Stony Brook[2] | | 154 | 73 | 81 |
| | Upstate Medical Center[2] | | 91 | 13 | 78 |
| State University of New York Agricultural and Technical College: | Alfred | 3,276 | 15 | 10 | 5 |
| | Canton | 2,970 | 9 | 8 | 1 |
| | Cobleskill | 2,615 | 11 | 10 | 1 |
| | Farmingdale[2] | | 27 | 17 | 10 |
| | Morrisville[2] | | 11 | 10 | 1 |
| State University of New York College: | Brockport | 8,275 | 19 | 17 | 2 |
| | Buffalo | 11,234 | 35 | 33 | 2 |
| | Cortland | 7,234 | 24 | 19 | 5 |
| | Environmental Science and Forestry | 2,523 | 12 | 10 | 2 |
| | Fredonia[2] | | 16 | 15 | 1 |
| | Geneseo[2] | | 18 | 13 | 5 |
| | New Paltz | 8,205 | 27 | 23 | 4 |
| | Old Westbury | 3,505 | 20 | 18 | 2 |
| | Oneonta | 5,757 | 27 | 17 | 10 |
| | Optometry | 303 | 17 | 6 | 11 |
| | Oswego | 8,909 | 24 | 20 | 4 |
| | Plattsburgh | 6,358 | 22 | 14 | 8 |
| | Potsdam | 4,325 | 14 | 12 | 2 |
| | Purchase | 4,251 | 28 | 24 | 4 |
| | Utica-Rome[2] | | 14 | 10 | 4 |
| **NORTH CAROLINA** | | | | | |
| Appalachian State University | | 16,610 | 42 | 26 | 16 |
| Beaufort County Community College | | 1,763 | 3 | 3 | 0 |
| Belmont Abbey College | | 1,497 | 9 | 6 | 3 |
| Davidson College | | 1,668 | 9 | 8 | 1 |
| Duke University | | 14,060 | 151 | 51 | 100 |
| East Carolina University | | 27,677 | 71 | 52 | 19 |
| Elizabeth City State University | | 3,104 | 21 | 12 | 9 |
| Elon University | | 5,628 | 15 | 14 | 1 |
| Fayetteville State University | | 6,217 | 31 | 15 | 16 |
| Methodist College | | 2,190 | 10 | 6 | 4 |
| North Carolina Agricultural and Technical State University | | 10,388 | 66 | 25 | 41 |
| North Carolina Central University | | 8,035 | 52 | 26 | 26 |
| North Carolina School of the Arts | | 879 | 18 | 12 | 6 |
| North Carolina State University | Raleigh | 32,872 | 61 | 46 | 15 |
| Queens University | | 2,302 | 8 | 5 | 3 |
| University of North Carolina: | Asheville | 3,629 | 20 | 13 | 7 |
| | Chapel Hill | 28,567 | 98 | 49 | 49 |
| | Greensboro | 19,976 | 50 | 30 | 20 |
| | Pembroke | 6,303 | 17 | 14 | 3 |
| | Wilmington | 12,643 | 46 | 30 | 16 |
| Wake Forest University | | 6,862 | 39 | 22 | 17 |
| Western Carolina University | | 9,050 | 21 | 17 | 4 |
| Winston-Salem State University | | 6,442 | 35 | 16 | 19 |
| **NORTH DAKOTA** | | | | | |
| North Dakota State College of Science | | 2,707 | 3 | 3 | 0 |
| North Dakota State University | | 13,230 | 22 | 14 | 8 |
| University of North Dakota | | 12,748 | 14 | 12 | 2 |
| **OHIO** | | | | | |
| Bowling Green State University | | 17,874 | 27 | 22 | 5 |
| Capital University | | 3,632 | 11 | 8 | 3 |
| Cleveland State University | | 15,139 | 40 | 24 | 16 |
| Columbus State Community College | | 24,482 | 39 | 19 | 20 |
| Hocking College | | 5,636 | 5 | 5 | 0 |
| Kent State University | | 22,944 | 36 | 26 | 10 |
| Lakeland Community College | | 9,017 | 11 | 10 | 1 |
| Marietta College | | 1,606 | 9 | 7 | 2 |
| Miami University | | 17,191 | 33 | 24 | 9 |
| Notre Dame College | | 1,637 | 5 | 4 | 1 |
| Ohio State University: | Columbus | 53,715 | 129 | 51 | 78 |
| | Wooster[2] | | 4 | 4 | 0 |
| Ohio University | | 21,369 | 28 | 22 | 6 |
| Sinclair Community College | | 19,466 | 26 | 22 | 4 |
| University of Akron | | 24,119 | 44 | 38 | 6 |
| University of Cincinnati | | 29,617 | 104 | 59 | 45 |

[1] The student enrollment figures provided by the United States Department of Education are for the 2008 school year, the most recent available. The enrollment figures include full-time and part-time students.

[2] Student enrollment figures were not available.

## Table 79. Full-Time Law Enforcement Employees, by State and University and College, 2009—*Continued*

(Number.)

| State University/College | Campus | Student enrollment[1] | Total law enforcement employees | Total officers | Total civilians |
|---|---|---|---|---|---|
| University of Rio Grande | | 1,967 | 7 | 6 | 1 |
| University of Toledo | | 22,336 | 57 | 36 | 21 |
| Wilberforce University | | 785 | 3 | 3 | 0 |
| Wright State University | | 16,672 | 27 | 19 | 8 |
| Youngstown State University | | 13,704 | 25 | 20 | 5 |
| **OKLAHOMA** | | | | | |
| Cameron University | | 5,449 | 12 | 12 | 0 |
| East Central University | | 4,361 | 5 | 5 | 0 |
| Murray State College | | 2,379 | 1 | 1 | 0 |
| Northeastern Oklahoma A&M College | | 1,807 | 8 | 7 | 1 |
| Northeastern State University: | Broken Arrow[2] | | 4 | 4 | 0 |
| | Tahlequah[2] | | 18 | 14 | 4 |
| Oklahoma State University: | Main Campus | 22,995 | 41 | 31 | 10 |
| | Okmulgee[2] | | 7 | 6 | 1 |
| | Tulsa[2] | | 6 | 4 | 2 |
| Rogers State University | | 3,913 | 4 | 4 | 0 |
| Seminole State College | | 2,031 | 3 | 3 | 0 |
| Southeastern Oklahoma State University | | 3,866 | 8 | 7 | 1 |
| Southwestern Oklahoma State University | | 4,850 | 6 | 5 | 1 |
| Tulsa Community College | | 18,325 | 16 | 10 | 6 |
| University of Central Oklahoma | | 15,724 | 21 | 16 | 5 |
| University of Oklahoma: | Health Sciences Center | 3,926 | 58 | 44 | 14 |
| | Norman | 26,140 | 69 | 39 | 30 |
| **PENNSYLVANIA** | | | | | |
| Bloomsburg University | | 8,855 | 18 | 14 | 4 |
| California University | | 8,519 | 16 | 13 | 3 |
| Cheyney University | | 1,488 | 15 | 14 | 1 |
| Clarion University | | 7,100 | 14 | 10 | 4 |
| Dickinson College | | 2,388 | 20 | 15 | 5 |
| East Stroudsburg University | | 7,234 | 19 | 16 | 3 |
| Edinboro University | | 7,671 | 15 | 14 | 1 |
| Elizabethtown College | | 2,311 | 17 | 11 | 6 |
| Indiana University | | 14,310 | 30 | 22 | 8 |
| Lehigh University | | 6,994 | 28 | 20 | 8 |
| Lock Haven University | | 5,266 | 12 | 10 | 2 |
| Mansfield University | | 3,422 | 13 | 10 | 3 |
| Millersville University | | 8,320 | 18 | 15 | 3 |
| Moravian College | | 2,040 | 13 | 10 | 3 |
| Pennsylvania State University: | Altoona | 4,013 | 11 | 9 | 2 |
| | Beaver | 845 | 6 | 6 | 0 |
| | Behrend | 4,334 | 10 | 6 | 4 |
| | Berks | 2,800 | 9 | 8 | 1 |
| | Harrisburg | 3,936 | 8 | 7 | 1 |
| | Hazelton | 1,228 | 5 | 5 | 0 |
| | McKeesport[2] | | 4 | 3 | 1 |
| | Mont Alto | 1,189 | 5 | 5 | 0 |
| Shippensburg University | | 7,942 | 20 | 17 | 3 |
| Slippery Rock University | | 8,458 | 22 | 16 | 6 |
| University of Pittsburgh: | Bradford | 1,502 | 6 | 5 | 1 |
| | Pittsburgh | 27,562 | 130 | 72 | 58 |
| West Chester University | | 13,619 | 20 | 20 | 0 |
| **RHODE ISLAND** | | | | | |
| Brown University | | 8,318 | 80 | 40 | 40 |
| University of Rhode Island | | 15,904 | 28 | 23 | 5 |
| **SOUTH CAROLINA** | | | | | |
| Benedict College | | 2,883 | 28 | 23 | 5 |
| Bob Jones University | | 4,141 | 4 | 4 | 0 |
| Clemson University | | 18,317 | 36 | 27 | 9 |
| Coastal Carolina University | | 8,154 | 71 | 25 | 46 |
| Columbia College | | 1,445 | 13 | 11 | 2 |
| Francis Marion University | | 4,020 | 12 | 11 | 1 |
| Lander University | | 2,614 | 13 | 11 | 2 |
| Medical University of South Carolina | | 2,528 | 74 | 53 | 21 |
| Midlands Technical College | | 11,234 | 26 | 6 | 20 |
| South Carolina State University | | 4,888 | 30 | 18 | 12 |
| Spartanburg Methodist College | | 750 | 3 | 3 | 0 |
| The Citadel | | 3,328 | 15 | 14 | 1 |
| Trident Technical College | | 12,763 | 24 | 19 | 5 |
| University of South Carolina: | Aiken | 3,232 | 8 | 8 | 0 |
| | Columbia | 27,488 | 83 | 55 | 28 |
| | Upstate | 5,063 | 12 | 11 | 1 |
| Winthrop University | | 6,249 | 22 | 15 | 7 |
| **SOUTH DAKOTA** | | | | | |
| South Dakota State University | | 11,995 | 20 | 15 | 5 |

[1] The student enrollment figures provided by the United States Department of Education are for the 2008 school year, the most recent available. The enrollment figures include full-time and part-time students.

[2] Student enrollment figures were not available.

## Table 79. Full-Time Law Enforcement Employees, by State and University and College, 2009—*Continued*

(Number.)

| State, University/College | Campus | Student enrollment[1] | Total law enforcement employees | Total officers | Total civilians |
|---|---|---|---|---|---|
| **TENNESSEE** | | | | | |
| Austin Peay State University | | 9,401 | 25 | 14 | 11 |
| Christian Brothers University | | 1,869 | 16 | 9 | 7 |
| East Tennessee State University | | 13,646 | 25 | 20 | 5 |
| Middle Tennessee State University | | 23,872 | 35 | 28 | 7 |
| Northeast State Technical Community College | | 5,470 | 5 | 5 | 0 |
| Southwest Tennessee Community College | | 11,427 | 36 | 25 | 11 |
| Tennessee State University | | 8,254 | 40 | 26 | 14 |
| Tennessee Technological University | | 10,793 | 22 | 14 | 8 |
| University of Memphis | | 20,220 | 36 | 31 | 5 |
| University of Tennessee: | Chattanooga | 9,807 | 28 | 18 | 10 |
| | Knoxville | 30,410 | 74 | 47 | 27 |
| | Martin | 7,574 | 16 | 12 | 4 |
| | Memphis[2] | | 57 | 26 | 31 |
| Vanderbilt University | | 12,093 | 122 | 94 | 28 |
| Volunteer State Community College | | 7,241 | 7 | 6 | 1 |
| Walters State Community College | | 5,918 | 9 | 9 | 0 |
| **TEXAS** | | | | | |
| Abilene Christian University | | 4,669 | 14 | 13 | 1 |
| Alvin Community College | | 4,402 | 12 | 10 | 2 |
| Amarillo College | | 10,224 | 15 | 13 | 2 |
| Angelo State University | | 6,155 | 18 | 12 | 6 |
| Austin College | | 1,298 | 9 | 7 | 2 |
| Baylor Health Care System[2] | | | 171 | 57 | 114 |
| Baylor University | Waco | 14,541 | 31 | 24 | 7 |
| Blinn College | | 15,608 | 18 | 16 | 2 |
| Brookhaven College | | 11,173 | 23 | 14 | 9 |
| Central Texas College | | 24,498 | 10 | 9 | 1 |
| College of the Mainland | | 3,561 | 8 | 7 | 1 |
| Eastfield College | | 10,501 | 10 | 9 | 1 |
| El Paso Community College | | 25,818 | 40 | 33 | 7 |
| Grayson County College | | 3,676 | 4 | 3 | 1 |
| Hardin-Simmons University | | 2,387 | 7 | 6 | 1 |
| Lamar University | Beaumont | 13,465 | 29 | 17 | 12 |
| Laredo Community College | | 8,256 | 23 | 21 | 2 |
| McLennan Community College | | 7,884 | 17 | 7 | 10 |
| Midwestern State University | | 6,093 | 10 | 9 | 1 |
| Mountain View College | | 7,126 | 13 | 13 | 0 |
| North Lake College | | 10,174 | 20 | 19 | 1 |
| Paris Junior College | | 4,733 | 3 | 3 | 0 |
| Rice University | | 5,357 | 44 | 26 | 18 |
| Southern Methodist University | | 10,965 | 33 | 26 | 7 |
| South Plains College | | 9,111 | 6 | 6 | 0 |
| Southwestern University | | 1,270 | 7 | 6 | 1 |
| Stephen F. Austin State University | | 12,000 | 40 | 23 | 17 |
| St. Thomas University | | 3,165 | 11 | 2 | 9 |
| Sul Ross State University | | 2,772 | 7 | 5 | 2 |
| Tarleton State University | | 9,633 | 14 | 13 | 1 |
| Texas A&M International University | | 5,856 | 21 | 14 | 7 |
| Texas A&M University: | College Station | 48,039 | 129 | 63 | 66 |
| | Commerce | 8,725 | 25 | 15 | 10 |
| | Corpus Christi | 9,007 | 27 | 16 | 11 |
| | Galveston | 1,612 | 9 | 8 | 1 |
| | Kingsville | 7,133 | 18 | 12 | 6 |
| Texas Christian University | | 8,696 | 40 | 24 | 16 |
| Texas Southern University | | 9,102 | 61 | 35 | 26 |
| Texas State Technical College: | Harlingen | 5,466 | 12 | 8 | 4 |
| | Marshall | 946 | 5 | 5 | 0 |
| | Waco | 5,093 | 18 | 16 | 2 |
| Texas State University | San Marcos | 29,105 | 54 | 33 | 21 |
| Texas Tech University | Lubbock | 28,422 | 86 | 50 | 36 |
| Texas Woman's University | | 12,465 | 37 | 16 | 21 |
| Trinity University | | 2,703 | 25 | 15 | 10 |
| Tyler Junior College | | 9,928 | 15 | 5 | 10 |
| University of Houston: | Central Campus | 36,104 | 124 | 43 | 81 |
| | Clearlake | 7,658 | 23 | 14 | 9 |
| | Downtown Campus | 12,283 | 29 | 15 | 14 |
| University of Mary Hardin-Baylor | | 2,648 | 9 | 8 | 1 |
| University of North Texas: | Denton | 34,830 | 82 | 42 | 40 |
| | Health Science Center | 1,225 | 21 | 11 | 10 |
| University of Texas: | Arlington | 25,084 | 104 | 37 | 67 |
| | Austin | 49,984 | 144 | 62 | 82 |
| | Brownsville | 17,189 | 42 | 18 | 24 |
| | Dallas | 14,913 | 49 | 17 | 32 |
| | El Paso | 20,458 | 51 | 22 | 29 |

[1] The student enrollment figures provided by the United States Department of Education are for the 2008 school year, the most recent available. The enrollment figures include full-time and part-time students.
[2] Student enrollment figures were not available.

**Table 79. Full-Time Law Enforcement Employees, by State and University and College, 2009—*Continued***

(Number.)

| State, University/College | Campus | Student enrollment[1] | Total law enforcement employees | Total officers | Total civilians |
|---|---|---|---|---|---|
| | Health Science Center, San Antonio | 3,093 | 121 | 32 | 89 |
| | Health Science Center, Tyler[2] | | 22 | 6 | 16 |
| | Houston[2] | | 316 | 87 | 229 |
| | Medical Branch | 2,338 | 81 | 48 | 33 |
| | Pan American | 17,534 | 38 | 15 | 23 |
| | Permian Basin | 3,496 | 17 | 8 | 9 |
| | San Antonio | 28,413 | 112 | 44 | 68 |
| | Southwestern Medical School | 2,461 | 133 | 38 | 95 |
| | Tyler | 6,117 | 19 | 10 | 9 |
| Western Texas College | | 2,090 | 1 | 1 | 0 |
| West Texas A&M University | | 7,535 | 14 | 10 | 4 |
| **UTAH** | | | | | |
| Brigham Young University | | 34,244 | 40 | 28 | 12 |
| College of Eastern Utah | | 1,438 | 1 | 1 | 0 |
| Southern Utah University | | 7,516 | 5 | 4 | 1 |
| University of Utah | | 28,211 | 92 | 29 | 63 |
| Utah State University | | 15,099 | 16 | 11 | 5 |
| Utah Valley University | | 26,696 | 10 | 9 | 1 |
| Weber State University | | 21,388 | 10 | 9 | 1 |
| **VERMONT** | | | | | |
| University of Vermont | | 12,800 | 33 | 22 | 11 |
| **VIRGINIA** | | | | | |
| Christopher Newport University | | 4,904 | 23 | 17 | 6 |
| College of William and Mary | | 7,892 | 23 | 18 | 5 |
| Emory and Henry College | | 1,015 | 4 | 2 | 2 |
| Ferrum College | | 1,397 | 6 | 6 | 0 |
| George Mason University | | 30,613 | 69 | 53 | 16 |
| Hampton University | | 5,427 | 33 | 21 | 12 |
| James Madison University | | 18,454 | 36 | 28 | 8 |
| J. Sargeant Reynolds Community College | | 13,079 | 28 | 11 | 17 |
| Longwood University | | 4,727 | 21 | 15 | 6 |
| Norfolk State University | | 6,325 | 37 | 23 | 14 |
| Northern Virginia Community College | | 42,663 | 46 | 45 | 1 |
| Old Dominion University | | 23,086 | 57 | 47 | 10 |
| Radford University | | 9,157 | 25 | 20 | 5 |
| Richard Bland College | | 1,634 | 7 | 7 | 0 |
| Thomas Nelson Community College | | 10,557 | 16 | 12 | 4 |
| University of Mary Washington | | 5,084 | 22 | 15 | 7 |
| University of Richmond | | 4,249 | 32 | 19 | 13 |
| University of Virginia | | 24,541 | 121 | 56 | 65 |
| University of Virginia's College at Wise | | 1,964 | 10 | 9 | 1 |
| Virginia Commonwealth University | | 32,044 | 201 | 81 | 120 |
| Virginia Military Institute | | 1,428 | 8 | 8 | 0 |
| Virginia Polytechnic Institute and State University | | 30,739 | 72 | 47 | 25 |
| Virginia State University | | 5,042 | 35 | 19 | 16 |
| Virginia Western Community College | | 8,532 | 8 | 8 | 0 |
| **WASHINGTON** | | | | | |
| Central Washington University | | 10,662 | 14 | 13 | 1 |
| Eastern Washington University | | 10,809 | 13 | 12 | 1 |
| Evergreen State College | | 4,696 | 16 | 10 | 6 |
| University of Washington | | 39,675 | 75 | 47 | 28 |
| Washington State University: | Pullman | 25,352 | 24 | 17 | 7 |
| | Vancouver[2] | | 4 | 3 | 1 |
| Western Washington University | | 14,620 | 21 | 15 | 6 |
| **WEST VIRGINIA** | | | | | |
| Bluefield State College | | 1,868 | 2 | 2 | 0 |
| Concord University | | 2,812 | 9 | 6 | 3 |
| Fairmont State University | | 4,547 | 5 | 3 | 2 |
| Glenville State College | | 1,443 | 5 | 2 | 3 |
| Marshall University | | 13,573 | 24 | 22 | 2 |
| Potomac State College | | 1,582 | 6 | 5 | 1 |
| Shepherd University | | 4,185 | 10 | 9 | 1 |
| West Liberty State College | | 2,513 | 5 | 5 | 0 |
| West Virginia State University | | 3,003 | 11 | 9 | 2 |
| West Virginia Tech | | 1,224 | 6 | 6 | 0 |
| West Virginia University | | 28,840 | 54 | 52 | 2 |
| **WISCONSIN** | | | | | |
| University of Wisconsin: | Eau Claire | 11,140 | 11 | 10 | 1 |
| | Green Bay | 6,286 | 11 | 5 | 6 |
| | La Crosse | 9,880 | 10 | 8 | 2 |
| | Madison | 41,620 | 110 | 62 | 48 |
| | Milwaukee | 29,215 | 46 | 34 | 12 |
| | Oshkosh | 12,753 | 12 | 10 | 2 |

[1] The student enrollment figures provided by the United States Department of Education are for the 2008 school year, the most recent available. The enrollment figures include full-time and part-time students.

[2] Student enrollment figures were not available.

## Table 79. Full-Time Law Enforcement Employees, by State and University and College, 2009—*Continued*

(Number.)

| State, University/College | Campus | Student enrollment[1] | Total law enforcement employees | Total officers | Total civilians |
|---|---|---|---|---|---|
| | Parkside | 5,167 | 13 | 8 | 5 |
| | Platteville | 7,512 | 8 | 7 | 1 |
| | Stevens Point | 9,163 | 8 | 4 | 4 |
| | Stout | 8,839 | 9 | 8 | 1 |
| | Superior | 2,689 | 63 | 57 | 6 |
| | Whitewater | 10,962 | 13 | 12 | 1 |
| **WYOMING** | | | | | |
| Sheridan College | | 4,130 | 2 | 2 | 0 |
| University of Wyoming | | 12,067 | 25 | 14 | 11 |
| George Mason University | | 30,613 | 69 | 53 | 16 |
| Hampton University | | 5,427 | 33 | 21 | 12 |
| James Madison University | | 18,454 | 36 | 28 | 8 |
| J. Sargeant Reynolds Community College | | 13,079 | 28 | 11 | 17 |
| Longwood University | | 4,727 | 21 | 15 | 6 |
| Norfolk State University | | 6,325 | 37 | 23 | 14 |
| Northern Virginia Community College | | 42,663 | 46 | 45 | 1 |
| Old Dominion University | | 23,086 | 57 | 47 | 10 |
| Radford University | | 9,157 | 25 | 20 | 5 |
| Richard Bland College | | 1,634 | 7 | 7 | 0 |
| Thomas Nelson Community College | | 10,557 | 16 | 12 | 4 |
| University of Mary Washington | | 5,084 | 22 | 15 | 7 |
| University of Richmond | | 4,249 | 32 | 19 | 13 |
| University of Virginia | | 24,541 | 121 | 56 | 65 |
| University of Virginia's College at Wise | | 1,964 | 10 | 9 | 1 |
| Virginia Commonwealth University | | 32,044 | 201 | 81 | 120 |
| Virginia Military Institute | | 1,428 | 8 | 8 | 0 |
| Virginia Polytechnic Institute and State University | | 30,739 | 72 | 47 | 25 |
| Virginia State University | | 5,042 | 35 | 19 | 16 |
| Virginia Western Community College | | 8,532 | 8 | 8 | 0 |
| **WASHINGTON** | | | | | |
| Central Washington University | | 10,662 | 14 | 13 | 1 |
| Eastern Washington University | | 10,809 | 13 | 12 | 1 |
| Evergreen State College | | 4,696 | 16 | 10 | 6 |
| University of Washington | | 39,675 | 75 | 47 | 28 |
| Washington State University: | | | | | |
| Pullman | | 25,352 | 24 | 17 | 7 |
| Vancouver[2] | | | 4 | 3 | 1 |
| Western Washington University | | 14,620 | 21 | 15 | 6 |
| **WEST VIRGINIA** | | | | | |
| Bluefield State College | | 1,868 | 2 | 2 | 0 |
| Concord University | | 2,812 | 9 | 6 | 3 |
| Fairmont State University | | 4,547 | 5 | 3 | 2 |
| Glenville State College | | 1,443 | 5 | 2 | 3 |
| Marshall University | | 13,573 | 24 | 22 | 2 |
| Potomac State College | | 1,582 | 6 | 5 | 1 |
| Shepherd University | | 4,185 | 10 | 9 | 1 |
| West Liberty State College | | 2,513 | 5 | 5 | 0 |
| West Virginia State University | | 3,003 | 11 | 9 | 2 |
| West Virginia Tech | | 1,224 | 6 | 6 | 0 |
| West Virginia University | | 28,840 | 54 | 52 | 2 |
| **WISCONSIN** | | | | | |
| University of Wisconsin: | | | | | |
| Eau Claire | | 11,140 | 11 | 10 | 1 |
| Green Bay | | 6,286 | 11 | 5 | 6 |
| La Crosse | | 9,880 | 10 | 8 | 2 |
| Madison | | 41,620 | 110 | 62 | 48 |
| Milwaukee | | 29,215 | 46 | 34 | 12 |
| Oshkosh | | 12,753 | 12 | 10 | 2 |
| Parkside | | 5,167 | 13 | 8 | 5 |
| Platteville | | 7,512 | 8 | 7 | 1 |
| Stevens Point | | 9,163 | 8 | 4 | 4 |
| Stout | | 8,839 | 9 | 8 | 1 |
| Superior | | 2,689 | 63 | 57 | 6 |
| Whitewater | | 10,962 | 13 | 12 | 1 |
| **WYOMING** | | | | | |
| Sheridan College | | 4,130 | 2 | 2 | 0 |
| University of Wyoming | | 12,067 | 25 | 14 | 11 |

[1] The student enrollment figures provided by the United States Department of Education are for the 2008 school year, the most recent available. The enrollment figures include full-time and part-time students.

[2] Student enrollment figures were not available.

## Table 80. Full-Time Law Enforcement Employees, by State and Metropolitan and Nonmetropolitan Counties, 2009

(Number.)

| State/County | Total law enforce-ment employees | Total officers | Total civilians |
|---|---|---|---|
| **ALABAMA–Metropolitan Counties** | | | |
| Autauga | 58 | 23 | 35 |
| Bibb | 12 | 11 | 1 |
| Blount | 47 | 43 | 4 |
| Calhoun | 52 | 47 | 5 |
| Chilton | 58 | 33 | 25 |
| Colbert | 55 | 31 | 24 |
| Elmore | 84 | 37 | 47 |
| Etowah | 166 | 62 | 104 |
| Geneva | 27 | 12 | 15 |
| Greene | 33 | 13 | 20 |
| Hale | 11 | 8 | 3 |
| Henry | 25 | 12 | 13 |
| Houston | 89 | 58 | 31 |
| Jefferson | 681 | 518 | 163 |
| Lawrence | 45 | 25 | 20 |
| Lee | 156 | 67 | 89 |
| Limestone | 104 | 42 | 62 |
| Lowndes | 41 | 15 | 26 |
| Madison | 305 | 110 | 195 |
| Mobile | 483 | 171 | 312 |
| Montgomery | 171 | 127 | 44 |
| Morgan | 184 | 56 | 128 |
| Russell | 89 | 32 | 57 |
| Shelby | 206 | 120 | 86 |
| St. Clair | 46 | 40 | 6 |
| Tuscaloosa | 207 | 99 | 108 |
| Walker | 80 | 34 | 46 |
| **ALABAMA-Nonmetropolitan Counties** | | | |
| Baldwin | 266 | 93 | 173 |
| Bullock | 13 | 6 | 7 |
| Butler | 22 | 10 | 12 |
| Chambers | 50 | 22 | 28 |
| Cherokee | 40 | 20 | 20 |
| Choctaw | 13 | 6 | 7 |
| Clarke | 37 | 14 | 23 |
| Clay | 26 | 10 | 16 |
| Cleburne | 26 | 11 | 15 |
| Coffee | 43 | 19 | 24 |
| Conecuh | 36 | 12 | 24 |
| Coosa | 24 | 9 | 15 |
| Covington | 25 | 23 | 2 |
| Crenshaw | 11 | 9 | 2 |
| Cullman | 135 | 80 | 55 |
| Dale | 37 | 24 | 13 |
| Dallas | 50 | 26 | 24 |
| De Kalb | 103 | 35 | 68 |
| Escambia | 80 | 22 | 58 |
| Fayette | 16 | 10 | 6 |
| Franklin | 16 | 13 | 3 |
| Jackson | 84 | 32 | 52 |
| Lamar | 20 | 8 | 12 |
| Macon | 38 | 19 | 19 |
| Marengo | 27 | 11 | 16 |
| Marshall | 80 | 36 | 44 |
| Monroe | 54 | 19 | 35 |
| Perry | 18 | 8 | 10 |
| Pickens | 29 | 7 | 22 |
| Pike | 29 | 16 | 13 |
| Randolph | 14 | 14 | 0 |
| Sumter | 25 | 7 | 18 |
| Talladega | 100 | 38 | 62 |
| Tallapoosa | 55 | 25 | 30 |
| Washington | 10 | 6 | 4 |
| Wilcox | 23 | 8 | 15 |
| Winston | 23 | 10 | 13 |
| **ARIZONA-Metropolitan Counties** | | | |
| Maricopa | 3,396 | 746 | 2,650 |
| Mohave | 241 | 90 | 151 |
| Pima | 1,428 | 525 | 903 |
| Pinal | 540 | 170 | 370 |
| Yavapai | 372 | 125 | 247 |
| Yuma | 332 | 80 | 252 |
| **ARIZONA-Nonmetropolitan Counties** | | | |
| Cochise | 198 | 85 | 113 |
| Gila | 147 | 52 | 95 |
| Graham | 72 | 23 | 49 |
| Greenlee | 41 | 17 | 24 |
| La Paz | 96 | 35 | 61 |
| Navajo | 132 | 53 | 79 |
| Santa Cruz | 88 | 43 | 45 |
| **ARKANSAS-Metropolitan Counties** | | | |
| Benton | 205 | 129 | 76 |
| Cleveland | 12 | 8 | 4 |
| Craighead | 92 | 30 | 62 |
| Crawford | 60 | 27 | 33 |
| Crittenden | 147 | 34 | 113 |
| Faulkner | 160 | 45 | 115 |
| Franklin | 20 | 9 | 11 |
| Garland | 120 | 41 | 79 |
| Grant | 17 | 14 | 3 |
| Jefferson | 156 | 49 | 107 |
| Lincoln | 22 | 9 | 13 |
| Lonoke | 42 | 25 | 17 |
| Madison | 18 | 10 | 8 |
| Miller | 71 | 25 | 46 |
| Perry | 18 | 10 | 8 |
| Poinsett | 41 | 12 | 29 |
| Pulaski | 478 | 121 | 357 |
| Saline | 84 | 40 | 44 |
| Sebastian | 135 | 42 | 93 |
| Washington | 286 | 151 | 135 |
| **ARKANSAS-Nonmetropolitan Counties** | | | |
| Arkansas | 48 | 10 | 38 |
| Ashley | 44 | 19 | 25 |
| Baxter | 50 | 32 | 18 |
| Boone | 57 | 23 | 34 |
| Bradley | 6 | 4 | 2 |
| Calhoun | 19 | 8 | 11 |
| Carroll | 20 | 17 | 3 |
| Chicot | 6 | 5 | 1 |
| Clark | 30 | 15 | 15 |
| Clay | 21 | 9 | 12 |
| Cleburne | 37 | 22 | 15 |
| Columbia | 34 | 17 | 17 |
| Conway | 33 | 15 | 18 |
| Cross | 35 | 16 | 19 |
| Dallas | 27 | 6 | 21 |
| Desha | 8 | 7 | 1 |
| Drew | 24 | 10 | 14 |
| Fulton | 14 | 7 | 7 |
| Greene | 49 | 12 | 37 |
| Hempstead | 49 | 19 | 30 |
| Hot Spring | 25 | 23 | 2 |
| Howard | 22 | 11 | 11 |
| Independence | 75 | 47 | 28 |
| Izard | 24 | 12 | 12 |
| Jackson | 21 | 12 | 9 |
| Johnson | 34 | 12 | 22 |
| Lafayette | 20 | 15 | 5 |
| Lawrence | 23 | 13 | 10 |
| Lee | 7 | 5 | 2 |
| Little River | 19 | 8 | 11 |
| Logan | 26 | 13 | 13 |
| Marion | 13 | 11 | 2 |
| Mississippi | 86 | 33 | 53 |
| Monroe | 12 | 5 | 7 |
| Montgomery | 16 | 8 | 8 |
| Nevada | 16 | 6 | 10 |
| Newton | 11 | 7 | 4 |
| Ouachita | 32 | 16 | 16 |
| Phillips | 18 | 15 | 3 |
| Pike | 17 | 8 | 9 |
| Polk | 24 | 11 | 13 |
| Pope | 85 | 32 | 53 |
| Prairie | 17 | 7 | 10 |
| Randolph | 20 | 10 | 10 |
| Scott | 13 | 8 | 5 |
| Searcy | 17 | 6 | 11 |
| Sevier | 28 | 12 | 16 |
| Sharp | 19 | 10 | 9 |
| St. Francis | 43 | 20 | 23 |

## Table 80. Full-Time Law Enforcement Employees, by State and Metropolitan and Nonmetropolitan Counties, 2009—*Continued*

(Number.)

| State/County | Total law enforcement employees | Total officers | Total civilians |
|---|---|---|---|
| Stone | 18 | 8 | 10 |
| Union | 60 | 27 | 33 |
| Van Buren | 34 | 15 | 19 |
| White | 96 | 52 | 44 |
| Woodruff | 13 | 6 | 7 |
| Yell | 27 | 14 | 13 |
| **CALIFORNIA-Metropolitan Counties** | | | |
| Alameda | 1,659 | 999 | 660 |
| Butte | 256 | 101 | 155 |
| Contra Costa | 956 | 640 | 316 |
| El Dorado | 379 | 184 | 195 |
| Fresno | 1,044 | 831 | 213 |
| Imperial | 270 | 182 | 88 |
| Kern | 1,140 | 856 | 284 |
| Kings | 221 | 80 | 141 |
| Los Angeles | 16,589 | 9,567 | 7,022 |
| Madera | 110 | 74 | 36 |
| Marin | 312 | 202 | 110 |
| Merced | 252 | 198 | 54 |
| Monterey | 431 | 311 | 120 |
| Napa | 127 | 96 | 31 |
| Orange | 3,604 | 1,807 | 1,797 |
| Placer | 433 | 233 | 200 |
| Riverside | 3,857 | 2,049 | 1,808 |
| Sacramento | 1,973 | 1,229 | 744 |
| San Benito | 64 | 55 | 9 |
| San Bernardino | 3,389 | 1,790 | 1,599 |
| San Diego | 3,757 | 2,261 | 1,496 |
| San Francisco | 1,102 | 925 | 177 |
| San Joaquin | 782 | 320 | 462 |
| San Luis Obispo | 372 | 153 | 219 |
| San Mateo | 585 | 304 | 281 |
| Santa Barbara | 634 | 457 | 177 |
| Santa Clara | 672 | 504 | 168 |
| Santa Cruz | 337 | 145 | 192 |
| Shasta | 219 | 142 | 77 |
| Solano | 450 | 112 | 338 |
| Sonoma | 698 | 490 | 208 |
| Stanislaus | 621 | 445 | 176 |
| Sutter | 133 | 107 | 26 |
| Tulare | 669 | 485 | 184 |
| Ventura | 1,193 | 731 | 462 |
| Yolo | 248 | 84 | 164 |
| Yuba | 177 | 137 | 40 |
| **CALIFORNIA-Nonmetropolitan Counties** | | | |
| Alpine | 14 | 11 | 3 |
| Amador | 91 | 48 | 43 |
| Calaveras | 106 | 58 | 48 |
| Colusa | 64 | 32 | 32 |
| Del Norte | 63 | 30 | 33 |
| Glenn | 61 | 25 | 36 |
| Humboldt | 231 | 181 | 50 |
| Inyo | 57 | 38 | 19 |
| Lake | 158 | 59 | 99 |
| Lassen | 95 | 73 | 22 |
| Mariposa | 70 | 56 | 14 |
| Mendocino | 168 | 128 | 40 |
| Modoc | 25 | 22 | 3 |
| Mono | 49 | 26 | 23 |
| Nevada | 187 | 72 | 115 |
| Plumas | 65 | 33 | 32 |
| Sierra | 14 | 10 | 4 |
| Siskiyou | 107 | 82 | 25 |
| Tehama | 114 | 79 | 35 |
| Trinity | 32 | 16 | 16 |
| Tuolumne | 126 | 63 | 63 |
| **COLORADO-Metropolitan Counties** | | | |
| Adams | 517 | 365 | 152 |
| Arapahoe | 515 | 335 | 180 |
| Boulder | 372 | 216 | 156 |
| Clear Creek | 70 | 26 | 44 |
| Douglas | 429 | 286 | 143 |
| Elbert | 35 | 28 | 7 |
| El Paso | 597 | 413 | 184 |
| Gilpin | 42 | 28 | 14 |
| Jefferson | 813 | 564 | 249 |
| Larimer | 400 | 148 | 252 |
| Mesa | 235 | 122 | 113 |
| Park | 60 | 27 | 33 |
| Pueblo | 312 | 153 | 159 |
| Teller | 85 | 58 | 27 |
| Weld | 337 | 129 | 208 |
| **COLORADO-Nonmetropolitan Counties** | | | |
| Alamosa | 41 | 23 | 18 |
| Archuleta | 37 | 14 | 23 |
| Baca | 10 | 4 | 6 |
| Bent | 15 | 7 | 8 |
| Chaffee | 53 | 22 | 31 |
| Cheyenne | 10 | 6 | 4 |
| Conejos | 18 | 6 | 12 |
| Costilla | 12 | 6 | 6 |
| Crowley | 12 | 7 | 5 |
| Custer | 22 | 11 | 11 |
| Delta | 62 | 29 | 33 |
| Dolores | 7 | 5 | 2 |
| Eagle | 103 | 54 | 49 |
| Fremont | 81 | 32 | 49 |
| Garfield | 131 | 44 | 87 |
| Grand | 50 | 23 | 27 |
| Gunnison | 30 | 13 | 17 |
| Hinsdale | 5 | 4 | 1 |
| Huerfano | 24 | 11 | 13 |
| Jackson | 7 | 4 | 3 |
| Kiowa | 4 | 3 | 1 |
| Kit Carson | 23 | 7 | 16 |
| Lake | 19 | 9 | 10 |
| La Plata | 128 | 97 | 31 |
| Las Animas | 40 | 14 | 26 |
| Lincoln | 19 | 8 | 11 |
| Logan | 51 | 23 | 28 |
| Mineral | 4 | 3 | 1 |
| Moffat | 43 | 16 | 27 |
| Montezuma | 67 | 24 | 43 |
| Montrose | 109 | 56 | 53 |
| Morgan | 53 | 48 | 5 |
| Otero | 21 | 9 | 12 |
| Ouray | 8 | 8 | 0 |
| Phillips | 5 | 4 | 1 |
| Pitkin | 40 | 23 | 17 |
| Prowers | 31 | 9 | 22 |
| Rio Blanco | 30 | 15 | 15 |
| Rio Grande | 32 | 10 | 22 |
| Routt | 47 | 22 | 25 |
| Saguache | 18 | 8 | 10 |
| San Juan | 4 | 3 | 1 |
| San Miguel | 37 | 33 | 4 |
| Sedgwick | 11 | 6 | 5 |
| Summit | 70 | 54 | 16 |
| Washington | 42 | 14 | 28 |
| Yuma | 20 | 18 | 2 |
| **DELAWARE-Metropolitan Counties** | | | |
| New Castle County Police Department | 468 | 360 | 108 |
| **FLORIDA-Metropolitan Counties** | | | |
| Alachua | 818 | 294 | 524 |
| Baker | 150 | 105 | 45 |
| Bay | 287 | 218 | 69 |
| Brevard | 1,168 | 496 | 672 |
| Broward | 3,246 | 1,584 | 1,662 |
| Charlotte | 399 | 282 | 117 |
| Clay | 557 | 265 | 292 |
| Collier | 972 | 609 | 363 |
| Escambia | 1,080 | 394 | 686 |
| Flagler | 175 | 121 | 54 |
| Gadsden | 61 | 45 | 16 |
| Gilchrist | 38 | 24 | 14 |
| Hernando | 378 | 233 | 145 |
| Hillsborough | 3,346 | 1,172 | 2,174 |
| Indian River | 482 | 328 | 154 |
| Jefferson | 50 | 21 | 29 |
| Lake | 420 | 276 | 144 |
| Lee | 952 | 566 | 386 |
| Leon | 354 | 241 | 113 |

**Table 80. Full-Time Law Enforcement Employees, by State and Metropolitan and Nonmetropolitan Counties, 2009**—*Continued*

(Number.)

| State/County | Total law enforcement employees | Total officers | Total civilians |
|---|---|---|---|
| Manatee | 843 | 468 | 375 |
| Marion | 850 | 350 | 500 |
| Martin | 522 | 256 | 266 |
| Miami-Dade | 4,494 | 3,074 | 1,420 |
| Nassau | 221 | 147 | 74 |
| Okaloosa | 350 | 257 | 93 |
| Orange | 2,115 | 1,442 | 673 |
| Osceola | 588 | 377 | 211 |
| Palm Beach | 3,385 | 1,549 | 1,836 |
| Pasco | 1,141 | 493 | 648 |
| Pinellas | 1,320 | 818 | 502 |
| Polk | 1,560 | 637 | 923 |
| Santa Rosa | 264 | 186 | 78 |
| Sarasota | 920 | 400 | 520 |
| Seminole | 1,083 | 390 | 693 |
| St. Johns | 563 | 266 | 297 |
| St. Lucie | 628 | 260 | 368 |
| Volusia | 712 | 426 | 286 |
| Wakulla | 90 | 56 | 34 |
| **FLORIDA-Nonmetropolitan Counties** | | | |
| Bradford | 87 | 21 | 66 |
| Calhoun | 28 | 15 | 13 |
| Citrus | 368 | 221 | 147 |
| Columbia | 174 | 94 | 80 |
| DeSoto | 83 | 54 | 29 |
| Dixie | 72 | 26 | 46 |
| Franklin | 73 | 37 | 36 |
| Glades | 157 | 106 | 51 |
| Gulf | 41 | 28 | 13 |
| Hamilton | 57 | 17 | 40 |
| Hardee | 94 | 43 | 51 |
| Hendry | 135 | 61 | 74 |
| Highlands | 322 | 130 | 192 |
| Holmes | 46 | 18 | 28 |
| Jackson | 78 | 59 | 19 |
| Lafayette | 26 | 11 | 15 |
| Levy | 149 | 68 | 81 |
| Liberty | 25 | 15 | 10 |
| Madison | 69 | 30 | 39 |
| Monroe | 494 | 199 | 295 |
| Okeechobee | 128 | 85 | 43 |
| Putnam | 243 | 118 | 125 |
| Sumter | 185 | 114 | 71 |
| Suwannee | 103 | 57 | 46 |
| Taylor | 48 | 36 | 12 |
| Union | 18 | 11 | 7 |
| Walton | 233 | 165 | 68 |
| Washington | 82 | 57 | 25 |
| **GEORGIA-Metropolitan Counties** | | | |
| Augusta-Richmond | 718 | 645 | 73 |
| Baker | 6 | 5 | 1 |
| Barrow | 185 | 124 | 61 |
| Bibb | 328 | 279 | 49 |
| Brantley | 47 | 20 | 27 |
| Brooks | 42 | 20 | 22 |
| Bryan | 46 | 41 | 5 |
| Butts | 77 | 37 | 40 |
| Carroll | 181 | 99 | 82 |
| Catoosa | 137 | 71 | 66 |
| Chatham | 452 | 359 | 93 |
| Cherokee | 391 | 338 | 53 |
| Clarke | 161 | 137 | 24 |
| Clayton | 314 | 250 | 64 |
| Clayton County Police Department | 388 | 329 | 59 |
| Cobb County Police Department | 739 | 601 | 138 |
| Columbia | 271 | 217 | 54 |
| Coweta | 210 | 139 | 71 |
| Crawford | 31 | 14 | 17 |
| Dade | 27 | 24 | 3 |
| Dawson | 114 | 60 | 54 |
| DeKalb | 1,518 | 705 | 813 |
| DeKalb County Police Department | 1,423 | 1,055 | 368 |
| Dougherty | 249 | 233 | 16 |
| Dougherty County Police Department | 42 | 35 | 7 |
| Douglas | 314 | 281 | 33 |
| Echols | 9 | 8 | 1 |
| Effingham | 104 | 67 | 37 |
| Fayette | 226 | 143 | 83 |
| Floyd County Police Department | 79 | 74 | 5 |
| Forsyth | 373 | 287 | 86 |
| Fulton | 1,146 | 851 | 295 |
| Fulton County Police Department | 188 | 134 | 54 |
| Glynn | 42 | 32 | 10 |
| Glynn County Police Department | 127 | 114 | 13 |
| Gwinnett County Police Department | 947 | 677 | 270 |
| Hall | 491 | 294 | 197 |
| Harris | 63 | 61 | 2 |
| Heard | 38 | 21 | 17 |
| Henry | 261 | 135 | 126 |
| Henry County Police Department | 273 | 234 | 39 |
| Houston | 311 | 112 | 199 |
| Jasper | 38 | 22 | 16 |
| Jones | 70 | 40 | 30 |
| Lamar | 55 | 33 | 22 |
| Lanier | 17 | 13 | 4 |
| Lee | 82 | 44 | 38 |
| Lowndes | 225 | 151 | 74 |
| Madison | 60 | 38 | 22 |
| Marion | 13 | 6 | 7 |
| McDuffie | 41 | 36 | 5 |
| McIntosh | 76 | 44 | 32 |
| Meriwether | 48 | 30 | 18 |
| Monroe | 90 | 49 | 41 |
| Murray | 66 | 37 | 29 |
| Newton | 255 | 154 | 101 |
| Oconee | 85 | 49 | 36 |
| Oglethorpe | 48 | 20 | 28 |
| Paulding | 280 | 246 | 34 |
| Pickens | 96 | 76 | 20 |
| Rockdale | 267 | 249 | 18 |
| Spalding | 179 | 151 | 28 |
| Terrell | 31 | 13 | 18 |
| Twiggs | 42 | 23 | 19 |
| Walker | 116 | 78 | 38 |
| Walton | 140 | 119 | 21 |
| Whitfield | 192 | 163 | 29 |
| Worth | 34 | 23 | 11 |
| **GEORGIA-Nonmetropolitan Counties** | | | |
| Baldwin | 107 | 61 | 46 |
| Ben Hill | 58 | 54 | 4 |
| Berrien | 43 | 22 | 21 |
| Bleckley | 41 | 12 | 29 |
| Calhoun | 16 | 7 | 9 |
| Camden | 56 | 50 | 6 |
| Charlton | 28 | 18 | 10 |
| Chattooga | 49 | 28 | 21 |
| Clinch | 20 | 10 | 10 |
| Coffee | 104 | 55 | 49 |
| Colquitt | 96 | 89 | 7 |
| Cook | 41 | 19 | 22 |
| Crisp | 56 | 51 | 5 |
| Decatur | 46 | 39 | 7 |
| Dodge | 34 | 20 | 14 |
| Dooly | 72 | 28 | 44 |
| Early | 53 | 24 | 29 |
| Elbert | 69 | 35 | 34 |
| Emanuel | 36 | 19 | 17 |
| Fannin | 40 | 25 | 15 |
| Gilmer | 105 | 58 | 47 |
| Gordon | 119 | 69 | 50 |
| Greene | 53 | 34 | 19 |
| Habersham | 35 | 33 | 2 |
| Hart | 38 | 22 | 16 |
| Jackson | 144 | 96 | 48 |
| Jefferson | 26 | 23 | 3 |
| Laurens | 104 | 61 | 43 |
| Lumpkin | 62 | 55 | 7 |
| Macon | 21 | 10 | 11 |
| Miller | 20 | 10 | 10 |
| Mitchell | 54 | 26 | 28 |
| Peach | 58 | 51 | 7 |
| Pierce | 29 | 27 | 2 |

## Table 80. Full-Time Law Enforcement Employees, by State and Metropolitan and Nonmetropolitan Counties, 2009—*Continued*

(Number.)

| State/County | Total law enforcement employees | Total officers | Total civilians |
|---|---|---|---|
| Polk | 77 | 70 | 7 |
| Polk County Police Department | 40 | 37 | 3 |
| Pulaski | 27 | 15 | 12 |
| Putnam | 66 | 37 | 29 |
| Rabun | 53 | 51 | 2 |
| Schley | 8 | 4 | 4 |
| Seminole | 21 | 11 | 10 |
| Stephens | 70 | 34 | 36 |
| Stewart | 11 | 5 | 6 |
| Sumter | 105 | 48 | 57 |
| Taliaferro | 15 | 9 | 6 |
| Tattnall | 43 | 18 | 25 |
| Taylor | 21 | 21 | 0 |
| Telfair | 11 | 10 | 1 |
| Thomas | 80 | 76 | 4 |
| Tift | 113 | 56 | 57 |
| Toombs | 53 | 25 | 28 |
| Towns | 23 | 21 | 2 |
| Treutlen | 14 | 9 | 5 |
| Troup | 138 | 78 | 60 |
| Union | 35 | 32 | 3 |
| Upson | 68 | 34 | 34 |
| Ware | 123 | 43 | 80 |
| Warren | 6 | 6 | 0 |
| Washington | 35 | 18 | 17 |
| Wayne | 30 | 30 | 0 |
| Webster | 6 | 5 | 1 |
| Wheeler | 9 | 4 | 5 |
| White | 64 | 42 | 22 |
| Wilcox | 13 | 8 | 5 |
| Wilkes | 31 | 13 | 18 |
| Wilkinson | 27 | 16 | 11 |
| **HAWAII-Nonmetropolitan Counties** | | | |
| Hawaii Police Department | 561 | 426 | 135 |
| Kauai Police Department | 177 | 130 | 47 |
| Maui Police Department | 454 | 329 | 125 |
| **IDAHO-Metropolitan Counties** | | | |
| Ada | 392 | 136 | 256 |
| Bannock | 66 | 40 | 26 |
| Boise | 14 | 11 | 3 |
| Bonneville | 98 | 64 | 34 |
| Canyon | 193 | 79 | 114 |
| Franklin | 15 | 12 | 3 |
| Gem | 25 | 13 | 12 |
| Jefferson | 33 | 19 | 14 |
| Kootenai | 161 | 81 | 80 |
| Nez Perce | 41 | 23 | 18 |
| Owyhee | 20 | 11 | 9 |
| Power | 17 | 9 | 8 |
| **IDAHO-Nonmetropolitan Counties** | | | |
| Adams | 18 | 11 | 7 |
| Bear Lake | 13 | 6 | 7 |
| Benewah | 18 | 9 | 9 |
| Bingham | 52 | 33 | 19 |
| Blaine | 24 | 19 | 5 |
| Bonner | 55 | 38 | 17 |
| Boundary | 21 | 11 | 10 |
| Butte | 13 | 7 | 6 |
| Camas | 6 | 4 | 2 |
| Caribou | 15 | 9 | 6 |
| Cassia | 52 | 33 | 19 |
| Clark | 7 | 3 | 4 |
| Clearwater | 22 | 14 | 8 |
| Custer | 14 | 8 | 6 |
| Elmore | 41 | 21 | 20 |
| Fremont | 25 | 16 | 9 |
| Gooding | 18 | 12 | 6 |
| Idaho | 30 | 20 | 10 |
| Jerome | 21 | 15 | 6 |
| Latah | 33 | 23 | 10 |
| Lemhi | 7 | 6 | 1 |
| Lewis | 12 | 6 | 6 |
| Lincoln | 6 | 5 | 1 |
| Madison | 34 | 23 | 11 |
| Minidoka | 26 | 17 | 9 |
| Oneida | 14 | 8 | 6 |

| State/County | Total law enforcement employees | Total officers | Total civilians |
|---|---|---|---|
| Payette | 32 | 17 | 15 |
| Shoshone | 28 | 17 | 11 |
| Teton | 21 | 10 | 11 |
| Twin Falls | 66 | 43 | 23 |
| Valley | 30 | 15 | 15 |
| Washington | 16 | 11 | 5 |
| **ILLINOIS-Metropolitan Counties** | | | |
| Alexander | 7 | 5 | 2 |
| Bond | 19 | 11 | 8 |
| Boone | 99 | 37 | 62 |
| Calhoun | 11 | 5 | 6 |
| Champaign | 77 | 56 | 21 |
| Clinton | 34 | 16 | 18 |
| Cook | 6,731 | 2,227 | 4,504 |
| De Kalb | 99 | 44 | 55 |
| Du Page | 537 | 385 | 152 |
| Ford | 25 | 8 | 17 |
| Grundy | 65 | 31 | 34 |
| Henry | 66 | 23 | 43 |
| Jersey | 30 | 14 | 16 |
| Kane | 119 | 91 | 28 |
| Kankakee | 207 | 62 | 145 |
| Kendall | 66 | 57 | 9 |
| Lake | 503 | 190 | 313 |
| Macon | 138 | 64 | 74 |
| Macoupin | 47 | 34 | 13 |
| Madison | 165 | 80 | 85 |
| Marshall | 18 | 8 | 10 |
| McHenry | 387 | 108 | 279 |
| McLean | 139 | 56 | 83 |
| Menard | 20 | 8 | 12 |
| Mercer | 27 | 12 | 15 |
| Monroe | 31 | 16 | 15 |
| Peoria | 200 | 73 | 127 |
| Piatt | 33 | 11 | 22 |
| Rock Island | 159 | 65 | 94 |
| Sangamon | 218 | 72 | 146 |
| Stark | 13 | 5 | 8 |
| St. Clair | 165 | 150 | 15 |
| Tazewell | 108 | 41 | 67 |
| Vermilion | 83 | 36 | 47 |
| Will | 580 | 249 | 331 |
| Winnebago | 382 | 112 | 270 |
| Woodford | 42 | 39 | 3 |
| **ILLINOIS-Nonmetropolitan Counties** | | | |
| Adams | 58 | 58 | 0 |
| Brown | 7 | 6 | 1 |
| Bureau | 39 | 20 | 19 |
| Carroll | 25 | 9 | 16 |
| Cass | 8 | 7 | 1 |
| Christian | 35 | 17 | 18 |
| Clark | 11 | 10 | 1 |
| Clay | 17 | 11 | 6 |
| Coles | 48 | 24 | 24 |
| Crawford | 21 | 14 | 7 |
| Cumberland | 15 | 6 | 9 |
| De Witt | 37 | 16 | 21 |
| Douglas | 31 | 14 | 17 |
| Edgar | 19 | 8 | 11 |
| Edwards | 9 | 4 | 5 |
| Effingham | 43 | 20 | 23 |
| Fayette | 32 | 11 | 21 |
| Franklin | 46 | 17 | 29 |
| Fulton | 53 | 21 | 32 |
| Gallatin | 3 | 3 | 0 |
| Greene | 14 | 6 | 8 |
| Hamilton | 8 | 4 | 4 |
| Hancock | 21 | 9 | 12 |
| Hardin | 6 | 3 | 3 |
| Henderson | 13 | 8 | 5 |
| Iroquois | 28 | 17 | 11 |
| Jackson | 77 | 27 | 50 |
| Jasper | 18 | 9 | 9 |
| Jefferson | 66 | 19 | 47 |
| Jo Daviess | 36 | 18 | 18 |
| Johnson | 14 | 8 | 6 |

**Table 80. Full-Time Law Enforcement Employees, by State and Metropolitan and Nonmetropolitan Counties, 2009**—*Continued*

(Number.)

| State/County | Total law enforcement employees | Total officers | Total civilians |
|---|---|---|---|
| Knox | 61 | 22 | 39 |
| La Salle | 107 | 37 | 70 |
| Lawrence | 17 | 7 | 10 |
| Lee | 40 | 22 | 18 |
| Livingston | 56 | 30 | 26 |
| Logan | 30 | 20 | 10 |
| Marion | 35 | 14 | 21 |
| Mason | 22 | 9 | 13 |
| Massac | 30 | 12 | 18 |
| McDonough | 25 | 13 | 12 |
| Montgomery | 30 | 15 | 15 |
| Morgan | 41 | 15 | 26 |
| Moultrie | 23 | 10 | 13 |
| Ogle | 73 | 30 | 43 |
| Perry | 29 | 26 | 3 |
| Pike | 29 | 13 | 16 |
| Pope | 3 | 3 | 0 |
| Pulaski | 17 | 10 | 7 |
| Putnam | 12 | 7 | 5 |
| Randolph | 31 | 15 | 16 |
| Richland | 23 | 8 | 15 |
| Saline | 12 | 12 | 0 |
| Schuyler | 10 | 4 | 6 |
| Scott | 6 | 2 | 4 |
| Shelby | 25 | 12 | 13 |
| Stephenson | 71 | 28 | 43 |
| Union | 16 | 16 | 0 |
| Wabash | 8 | 4 | 4 |
| Warren | 21 | 11 | 10 |
| Washington | 21 | 9 | 12 |
| Wayne | 22 | 12 | 10 |
| White | 13 | 6 | 7 |
| Whiteside | 52 | 24 | 28 |
| Williamson | 70 | 38 | 32 |
| **INDIANA-Metropolitan Counties** | | | |
| Allen | 348 | 124 | 224 |
| Bartholomew | 88 | 38 | 50 |
| Benton | 19 | 6 | 13 |
| Boone | 62 | 26 | 36 |
| Brown | 38 | 13 | 25 |
| Carroll | 23 | 10 | 13 |
| Clay | 40 | 13 | 27 |
| Delaware | 109 | 48 | 61 |
| Elkhart | 213 | 71 | 142 |
| Floyd | 96 | 31 | 65 |
| Gibson | 40 | 16 | 24 |
| Greene | 41 | 15 | 26 |
| Hamilton | 246 | 65 | 181 |
| Harrison | 61 | 22 | 39 |
| Howard | 119 | 35 | 84 |
| Jasper | 52 | 21 | 31 |
| Johnson | 141 | 111 | 30 |
| Lake | 481 | 331 | 150 |
| La Porte | 165 | 59 | 106 |
| Madison | 140 | 50 | 90 |
| Monroe | 108 | 32 | 76 |
| Morgan | 77 | 26 | 51 |
| Newton | 44 | 18 | 26 |
| Ohio | 9 | 9 | 0 |
| Porter | 150 | 65 | 85 |
| Posey | 14 | 13 | 1 |
| Putnam | 36 | 18 | 18 |
| Shelby | 85 | 29 | 56 |
| St. Joseph | 262 | 109 | 153 |
| Sullivan | 34 | 10 | 24 |
| Tippecanoe | 150 | 47 | 103 |
| Tipton | 27 | 11 | 16 |
| Vanderburgh | 261 | 104 | 157 |
| Vermillion | 24 | 9 | 15 |
| Vigo | 114 | 37 | 77 |
| Warrick | 82 | 38 | 44 |
| Washington | 35 | 12 | 23 |
| Wells | 42 | 15 | 27 |
| Whitley | 46 | 15 | 31 |
| **INDIANA-Nonmetropolitan Counties** | | | |
| Adams | 42 | 16 | 26 |
| Blackford | 30 | 9 | 21 |
| Cass | 55 | 18 | 37 |
| Clinton | 76 | 22 | 54 |
| Crawford | 16 | 8 | 8 |
| Daviess | 64 | 19 | 45 |
| Decatur | 37 | 12 | 25 |
| Fayette | 33 | 11 | 22 |
| Fulton | 23 | 10 | 13 |
| Grant | 114 | 46 | 68 |
| Henry | 59 | 29 | 30 |
| Huntington | 40 | 14 | 26 |
| Jackson | 55 | 15 | 40 |
| Jay | 36 | 11 | 25 |
| Jefferson | 35 | 14 | 21 |
| Jennings | 42 | 14 | 28 |
| Knox | 36 | 12 | 24 |
| Kosciusko | 77 | 36 | 41 |
| LaGrange | 67 | 18 | 49 |
| Marshall | 58 | 21 | 37 |
| Martin | 19 | 9 | 10 |
| Miami | 47 | 34 | 13 |
| Montgomery | 66 | 18 | 48 |
| Noble | 72 | 20 | 52 |
| Orange | 30 | 9 | 21 |
| Parke | 37 | 11 | 26 |
| Perry | 17 | 7 | 10 |
| Pike | 27 | 8 | 19 |
| Pulaski | 43 | 14 | 29 |
| Randolph | 41 | 15 | 26 |
| Ripley | 29 | 11 | 18 |
| Rush | 26 | 11 | 15 |
| Spencer | 15 | 14 | 1 |
| Starke | 25 | 13 | 12 |
| Steuben | 58 | 21 | 37 |
| Wabash | 38 | 15 | 23 |
| Wayne | 104 | 64 | 40 |
| White | 31 | 13 | 18 |
| **IOWA-Metropolitan Counties** | | | |
| Benton | 24 | 12 | 12 |
| Black Hawk | 135 | 102 | 33 |
| Bremer | 29 | 11 | 18 |
| Dallas | 45 | 21 | 24 |
| Dubuque | 83 | 71 | 12 |
| Grundy | 16 | 12 | 4 |
| Guthrie | 11 | 5 | 6 |
| Harrison | 19 | 9 | 10 |
| Johnson | 96 | 64 | 32 |
| Jones | 23 | 10 | 13 |
| Linn | 167 | 107 | 60 |
| Madison | 15 | 7 | 8 |
| Mills | 20 | 11 | 9 |
| Polk | 450 | 136 | 314 |
| Pottawattamie | 162 | 49 | 113 |
| Scott | 164 | 44 | 120 |
| Story | 80 | 30 | 50 |
| Warren | 34 | 23 | 11 |
| Washington | 36 | 18 | 18 |
| Woodbury | 114 | 104 | 10 |
| **IOWA-Nonmetropolitan Counties** | | | |
| Adair | 11 | 5 | 6 |
| Adams | 11 | 6 | 5 |
| Allamakee | 14 | 8 | 6 |
| Appanoose | 15 | 8 | 7 |
| Audubon | 8 | 5 | 3 |
| Boone | 27 | 11 | 16 |
| Buchanan | 19 | 13 | 6 |
| Buena Vista | 27 | 9 | 18 |
| Butler | 20 | 11 | 9 |
| Calhoun | 11 | 6 | 5 |
| Carroll | 10 | 9 | 1 |
| Cass | 11 | 8 | 3 |
| Cedar | 39 | 11 | 28 |
| Cerro Gordo | 73 | 20 | 53 |
| Cherokee | 17 | 6 | 11 |
| Chickasaw | 13 | 8 | 5 |
| Clarke | 26 | 6 | 20 |
| Clay | 18 | 10 | 8 |
| Clayton | 27 | 12 | 15 |

**Table 80. Full-Time Law Enforcement Employees, by State and Metropolitan and Nonmetropolitan Counties, 2009**—*Continued*

(Number.)

| State/County | Total law enforcement employees | Total officers | Total civilians |
|---|---|---|---|
| Clinton | 42 | 24 | 18 |
| Crawford | 12 | 10 | 2 |
| Davis | 12 | 5 | 7 |
| Decatur | 11 | 6 | 5 |
| Delaware | 15 | 11 | 4 |
| Des Moines | 49 | 21 | 28 |
| Dickinson | 20 | 9 | 11 |
| Emmet | 15 | 7 | 8 |
| Fayette | 35 | 11 | 24 |
| Floyd | 18 | 11 | 7 |
| Franklin | 11 | 8 | 3 |
| Fremont | 19 | 8 | 11 |
| Greene | 15 | 7 | 8 |
| Hamilton | 31 | 10 | 21 |
| Hancock | 10 | 8 | 2 |
| Hardin | 29 | 10 | 19 |
| Henry | 29 | 12 | 17 |
| Howard | 14 | 7 | 7 |
| Humboldt | 9 | 9 | 0 |
| Ida | 17 | 9 | 8 |
| Iowa | 25 | 11 | 14 |
| Jackson | 16 | 9 | 7 |
| Jasper | 46 | 14 | 32 |
| Jefferson | 30 | 10 | 20 |
| Keokuk | 8 | 5 | 3 |
| Kossuth | 24 | 9 | 15 |
| Lee | 30 | 15 | 15 |
| Louisa | 26 | 10 | 16 |
| Lucas | 13 | 5 | 8 |
| Lyon | 25 | 11 | 14 |
| Mahaska | 24 | 9 | 15 |
| Marion | 33 | 12 | 21 |
| Marshall | 52 | 18 | 34 |
| Mitchell | 16 | 6 | 10 |
| Monroe | 11 | 4 | 7 |
| Muscatine | 26 | 22 | 4 |
| O'Brien | 28 | 9 | 19 |
| Osceola | 13 | 9 | 4 |
| Page | 14 | 8 | 6 |
| Palo Alto | 16 | 8 | 8 |
| Plymouth | 29 | 10 | 19 |
| Pocahontas | 17 | 8 | 9 |
| Poweshiek | 23 | 11 | 12 |
| Ringgold | 11 | 7 | 4 |
| Sac | 19 | 8 | 11 |
| Shelby | 14 | 8 | 6 |
| Sioux | 38 | 14 | 24 |
| Tama | 23 | 13 | 10 |
| Taylor | 10 | 10 | 0 |
| Union | 11 | 5 | 6 |
| Van Buren | 11 | 5 | 6 |
| Wapello | 38 | 10 | 28 |
| Wayne | 16 | 6 | 10 |
| Webster | 35 | 17 | 18 |
| Winnebago | 8 | 5 | 3 |
| Winneshiek | 23 | 10 | 13 |
| Worth | 20 | 8 | 12 |
| Wright | 20 | 8 | 12 |
| **KANSAS-Metropolitan Counties** | | | |
| Butler | 55 | 51 | 4 |
| Doniphan | 10 | 4 | 6 |
| Douglas | 135 | 79 | 56 |
| Franklin | 53 | 25 | 28 |
| Geary | 84 | 29 | 55 |
| Harvey | 37 | 15 | 22 |
| Jackson | 24 | 13 | 11 |
| Jefferson | 40 | 22 | 18 |
| Johnson | 607 | 481 | 126 |
| Leavenworth | 96 | 58 | 38 |
| Linn | 22 | 11 | 11 |
| Miami | 42 | 27 | 15 |
| Osage | 41 | 23 | 18 |
| Pottawatomie | 45 | 27 | 18 |
| Riley County Police Department | 183 | 104 | 79 |
| Sedgwick | 522 | 172 | 350 |
| Shawnee | 208 | 115 | 93 |

| State/County | Total law enforcement employees | Total officers | Total civilians |
|---|---|---|---|
| Wabaunsee | 20 | 8 | 12 |
| Wyandotte | 157 | 66 | 91 |
| **KANSAS-Nonmetropolitan Counties** | | | |
| Allen | 26 | 10 | 16 |
| Anderson | 29 | 11 | 18 |
| Atchison | 36 | 23 | 13 |
| Barber | 9 | 4 | 5 |
| Barton | 39 | 19 | 20 |
| Bourbon | 9 | 7 | 2 |
| Brown | 19 | 8 | 11 |
| Chase | 9 | 5 | 4 |
| Cherokee | 26 | 16 | 10 |
| Cheyenne | 4 | 4 | 0 |
| Clark | 10 | 5 | 5 |
| Clay | 18 | 7 | 11 |
| Cloud | 9 | 9 | 0 |
| Coffey | 31 | 12 | 19 |
| Comanche | 4 | 4 | 0 |
| Cowley | 47 | 23 | 24 |
| Crawford | 70 | 34 | 36 |
| Decatur | 3 | 3 | 0 |
| Dickinson | 26 | 14 | 12 |
| Edwards | 10 | 6 | 4 |
| Elk | 10 | 4 | 6 |
| Ellis | 30 | 18 | 12 |
| Ellsworth | 16 | 8 | 8 |
| Finney | 96 | 36 | 60 |
| Ford | 59 | 26 | 33 |
| Gove | 5 | 4 | 1 |
| Graham | 7 | 3 | 4 |
| Grant | 16 | 7 | 9 |
| Gray | 16 | 10 | 6 |
| Greeley | 7 | 3 | 4 |
| Greenwood | 24 | 14 | 10 |
| Hamilton | 9 | 5 | 4 |
| Harper | 10 | 5 | 5 |
| Haskell | 16 | 11 | 5 |
| Hodgeman | 8 | 4 | 4 |
| Jewell | 8 | 4 | 4 |
| Kearny | 19 | 11 | 8 |
| Kingman | 17 | 7 | 10 |
| Kiowa | 15 | 8 | 7 |
| Labette | 37 | 18 | 19 |
| Lane | 9 | 5 | 4 |
| Lincoln | 13 | 8 | 5 |
| Logan | 4 | 3 | 1 |
| Lyon | 80 | 27 | 53 |
| Marion | 7 | 6 | 1 |
| Marshall | 17 | 7 | 10 |
| McPherson | 34 | 16 | 18 |
| Meade | 17 | 5 | 12 |
| Mitchell | 14 | 8 | 6 |
| Montgomery | 35 | 23 | 12 |
| Morris | 12 | 7 | 5 |
| Morton | 11 | 6 | 5 |
| Nemaha | 18 | 8 | 10 |
| Neosho | 15 | 14 | 1 |
| Ness | 14 | 6 | 8 |
| Norton | 10 | 5 | 5 |
| Osborne | 14 | 8 | 6 |
| Ottawa | 16 | 5 | 11 |
| Pawnee | 13 | 7 | 6 |
| Phillips | 15 | 9 | 6 |
| Pratt | 9 | 8 | 1 |
| Rawlins | 4 | 3 | 1 |
| Reno | 86 | 47 | 39 |
| Republic | 12 | 6 | 6 |
| Rice | 7 | 5 | 2 |
| Rooks | 10 | 5 | 5 |
| Rush | 9 | 4 | 5 |
| Russell | 18 | 11 | 7 |
| Saline | 104 | 47 | 57 |
| Scott | 9 | 4 | 5 |
| Seward | 50 | 16 | 34 |
| Sheridan | 8 | 3 | 5 |
| Sherman | 13 | 6 | 7 |

**Table 80. Full-Time Law Enforcement Employees, by State and Metropolitan and Nonmetropolitan Counties, 2009**—*Continued*

(Number.)

| State/County | Total law enforcement employees | Total officers | Total civilians |
|---|---|---|---|
| Smith | 5 | 5 | 0 |
| Stafford | 9 | 4 | 5 |
| Stanton | 13 | 5 | 8 |
| Stevens | 23 | 9 | 14 |
| Trego | 4 | 3 | 1 |
| Wallace | 2 | 2 | 0 |
| Washington | 5 | 5 | 0 |
| Wichita | 9 | 4 | 5 |
| Wilson | 31 | 12 | 19 |
| Woodson | 12 | 8 | 4 |
| **KENTUCKY-Metropolitan Counties** | | | |
| Boone | 143 | 134 | 9 |
| Boyd | 32 | 25 | 7 |
| Bracken | 4 | 3 | 1 |
| Bullitt | 45 | 40 | 5 |
| Campbell | 12 | 9 | 3 |
| Campbell County Police Department | 32 | 31 | 1 |
| Christian | 31 | 27 | 4 |
| Clark | 16 | 12 | 4 |
| Daviess | 52 | 39 | 13 |
| Edmonson | 12 | 6 | 6 |
| Fayette | 85 | 52 | 33 |
| Gallatin | 9 | 7 | 2 |
| Gallatin County Police Department | 1 | 1 | 0 |
| Grant | 15 | 13 | 2 |
| Greenup | 15 | 14 | 1 |
| Hancock | 7 | 6 | 1 |
| Hardin | 40 | 31 | 9 |
| Henderson | 24 | 20 | 4 |
| Henry | 8 | 6 | 2 |
| Jefferson | 278 | 228 | 50 |
| Jessamine | 33 | 24 | 9 |
| Kenton | 33 | 27 | 6 |
| Kenton County Police Department | 52 | 32 | 20 |
| Larue | 5 | 4 | 1 |
| McLean | 10 | 8 | 2 |
| Meade | 14 | 11 | 3 |
| Nelson | 30 | 22 | 8 |
| Oldham | 18 | 16 | 2 |
| Oldham County Police Department | 30 | 28 | 2 |
| Pendleton | 7 | 6 | 1 |
| Scott | 34 | 32 | 2 |
| Shelby | 24 | 24 | 0 |
| Spencer | 7 | 6 | 1 |
| Trigg | 8 | 7 | 1 |
| Trimble | 4 | 3 | 1 |
| Warren | 74 | 36 | 38 |
| Webster | 8 | 6 | 2 |
| Woodford | 9 | 8 | 1 |
| **KENTUCKY-Nonmetropolitan Counties** | | | |
| Adair | 8 | 6 | 2 |
| Allen | 17 | 15 | 2 |
| Anderson | 17 | 16 | 1 |
| Ballard | 13 | 13 | 0 |
| Barren | 22 | 18 | 4 |
| Bath | 1 | 1 | 0 |
| Bell | 25 | 10 | 15 |
| Boyle | 8 | 8 | 0 |
| Breathitt | 2 | 2 | 0 |
| Breckinridge | 9 | 7 | 2 |
| Butler | 6 | 6 | 0 |
| Caldwell | 10 | 8 | 2 |
| Calloway | 27 | 14 | 13 |
| Carlisle | 3 | 2 | 1 |
| Carroll | 5 | 4 | 1 |
| Carter | 11 | 9 | 2 |
| Casey | 8 | 7 | 1 |
| Clay | 17 | 14 | 3 |
| Clinton | 4 | 3 | 1 |
| Crittenden | 4 | 3 | 1 |
| Cumberland | 6 | 4 | 2 |
| Elliott | 3 | 2 | 1 |
| Estill | 7 | 5 | 2 |
| Fleming | 9 | 9 | 0 |
| Franklin | 19 | 18 | 1 |
| Fulton | 4 | 3 | 1 |
| Garrard | 10 | 7 | 3 |
| Graves | 14 | 11 | 3 |
| Grayson | 10 | 7 | 3 |
| Harlan | 27 | 23 | 4 |
| Harrison | 10 | 10 | 0 |
| Hart | 9 | 7 | 2 |
| Hickman | 3 | 3 | 0 |
| Hopkins | 26 | 18 | 8 |
| Jackson | 4 | 3 | 1 |
| Johnson | 15 | 11 | 4 |
| Knott | 7 | 5 | 2 |
| Knox | 13 | 7 | 6 |
| Laurel | 34 | 21 | 13 |
| Lawrence | 6 | 4 | 2 |
| Lee | 1 | 1 | 0 |
| Leslie | 7 | 6 | 1 |
| Letcher | 15 | 12 | 3 |
| Lewis | 7 | 5 | 2 |
| Lincoln | 12 | 10 | 2 |
| Livingston | 7 | 7 | 0 |
| Logan | 23 | 23 | 0 |
| Lyon | 5 | 5 | 0 |
| Madison | 40 | 24 | 16 |
| Magoffin | 5 | 4 | 1 |
| Marion | 8 | 6 | 2 |
| Marshall | 24 | 21 | 3 |
| Martin | 6 | 4 | 2 |
| Mason | 13 | 11 | 2 |
| McCracken | 44 | 39 | 5 |
| McCreary | 7 | 6 | 1 |
| Menifee | 7 | 5 | 2 |
| Mercer | 11 | 10 | 1 |
| Metcalfe | 5 | 3 | 2 |
| Monroe | 7 | 4 | 3 |
| Montgomery | 14 | 13 | 1 |
| Morgan | 5 | 3 | 2 |
| Muhlenberg | 13 | 12 | 1 |
| Nicholas | 3 | 2 | 1 |
| Ohio | 21 | 18 | 3 |
| Owen | 7 | 5 | 2 |
| Owsley | 3 | 3 | 0 |
| Perry | 14 | 11 | 3 |
| Pike | 31 | 14 | 17 |
| Powell | 11 | 5 | 6 |
| Pulaski | 38 | 30 | 8 |
| Robertson | 1 | 1 | 0 |
| Rockcastle | 5 | 4 | 1 |
| Rowan | 12 | 9 | 3 |
| Russell | 11 | 10 | 1 |
| Simpson | 15 | 12 | 3 |
| Taylor | 13 | 11 | 2 |
| Union | 9 | 7 | 2 |
| Washington | 5 | 4 | 1 |
| Wayne | 12 | 9 | 3 |
| Whitley | 15 | 12 | 3 |
| Wolfe | 3 | 2 | 1 |
| **LOUISIANA-Metropolitan Counties** | | | |
| Ascension | 275 | 241 | 34 |
| Bossier | 384 | 334 | 50 |
| Caddo | 648 | 440 | 208 |
| Calcasieu | 834 | 424 | 410 |
| Cameron | 72 | 58 | 14 |
| De Soto | 105 | 92 | 13 |
| East Baton Rouge | 818 | 675 | 143 |
| East Feliciana | 62 | 62 | 0 |
| Grant | 72 | 32 | 40 |
| Lafayette | 618 | 289 | 329 |
| Livingston | 240 | 240 | 0 |
| Ouachita | 407 | 407 | 0 |
| Plaquemines | 212 | 211 | 1 |
| St. Charles | 393 | 273 | 120 |
| St. Helena | 54 | 36 | 18 |
| St. John the Baptist | 258 | 224 | 34 |
| St. Martin | 247 | 119 | 128 |
| St. Tammany | 675 | 400 | 275 |
| Terrebonne | 334 | 258 | 76 |

## Table 80. Full-Time Law Enforcement Employees, by State and Metropolitan and Nonmetropolitan Counties, 2009—*Continued*

(Number.)

| State/County | Total law enforcement employees | Total officers | Total civilians |
|---|---|---|---|
| Union | 49 | 32 | 17 |
| West Baton Rouge | 192 | 149 | 43 |
| West Feliciana | 73 | 46 | 27 |
| **LOUISIANA-Nonmetropolitan Counties** | | | |
| Acadia | 113 | 61 | 52 |
| Allen | 81 | 81 | 0 |
| Assumption | 81 | 35 | 46 |
| Beauregard | 72 | 53 | 19 |
| Bienville | 51 | 32 | 19 |
| Caldwell | 29 | 29 | 0 |
| Catahoula | 117 | 15 | 102 |
| Claiborne | 96 | 36 | 60 |
| Evangeline | 57 | 19 | 38 |
| Iberia | 316 | 227 | 89 |
| Jackson | 176 | 176 | 0 |
| Jefferson Davis | 61 | 47 | 14 |
| La Salle | 45 | 45 | 0 |
| Lincoln | 63 | 46 | 17 |
| Morehouse | 158 | 38 | 120 |
| Natchitoches | 81 | 62 | 19 |
| Red River | 37 | 18 | 19 |
| Sabine | 70 | 70 | 0 |
| St. Mary | 196 | 160 | 36 |
| Tangipahoa | 259 | 111 | 148 |
| Tensas | 30 | 17 | 13 |
| Vermilion | 138 | 64 | 74 |
| Vernon | 162 | 124 | 38 |
| Washington | 106 | 49 | 57 |
| Webster | 138 | 33 | 105 |
| West Carroll | 19 | 19 | 0 |
| Winn | 27 | 14 | 13 |
| **MAINE-Metropolitan Counties** | | | |
| Androscoggin | 25 | 16 | 9 |
| Cumberland | 72 | 54 | 18 |
| Penobscot | 28 | 24 | 4 |
| Sagadahoc | 23 | 20 | 3 |
| York | 24 | 20 | 4 |
| **MAINE-Nonmetropolitan Counties** | | | |
| Aroostook | 16 | 14 | 2 |
| Franklin | 26 | 15 | 11 |
| Hancock | 18 | 15 | 3 |
| Kennebec | 20 | 17 | 3 |
| Knox | 19 | 18 | 1 |
| Lincoln | 26 | 24 | 2 |
| Oxford | 19 | 18 | 1 |
| Piscataquis | 19 | 8 | 11 |
| Somerset | 17 | 15 | 2 |
| Waldo | 19 | 17 | 2 |
| Washington | 16 | 15 | 1 |
| **MARYLAND-Metropolitan Counties** | | | |
| Allegany | 12 | 10 | 2 |
| Allegany County Bureau of Police | 16 | 16 | 0 |
| Anne Arundel | 99 | 71 | 28 |
| Anne Arundel County Police Department | 865 | 641 | 224 |
| Baltimore County | 95 | 79 | 16 |
| Baltimore County Police Department | 2,251 | 1,902 | 349 |
| Calvert | 133 | 113 | 20 |
| Carroll | 99 | 71 | 28 |
| Cecil | 93 | 81 | 12 |
| Charles | 441 | 288 | 153 |
| Frederick | 237 | 173 | 64 |
| Harford | 369 | 286 | 83 |
| Howard | 67 | 46 | 21 |
| Howard County Police Department | 595 | 432 | 163 |
| Montgomery | 164 | 141 | 23 |
| Montgomery County Police Department | 1,578 | 1,164 | 414 |
| Prince George's | 320 | 234 | 86 |
| Prince George's County Police Department | 1,818 | 1,564 | 254 |
| Queen Anne's | 54 | 50 | 4 |
| Somerset | 26 | 22 | 4 |
| Washington | 237 | 95 | 142 |
| Wicomico | 108 | 86 | 22 |
| **MARYLAND-Nonmetropolitan Counties** | | | |
| Caroline | 32 | 29 | 3 |
| Dorchester | 44 | 38 | 6 |
| Garrett | 54 | 29 | 25 |
| Kent | 28 | 23 | 5 |
| St. Mary's | 241 | 131 | 110 |
| Talbot | 31 | 28 | 3 |
| Worcester | 49 | 42 | 7 |
| **MICHIGAN-Metropolitan Counties** | | | |
| Barry | 57 | 30 | 27 |
| Bay | 81 | 36 | 45 |
| Berrien | 161 | 70 | 91 |
| Calhoun | 176 | 75 | 101 |
| Cass | 70 | 33 | 37 |
| Clinton | 59 | 25 | 34 |
| Eaton | 138 | 70 | 68 |
| Genesee | 253 | 144 | 109 |
| Ingham | 186 | 109 | 77 |
| Ionia | 54 | 22 | 32 |
| Jackson | 132 | 52 | 80 |
| Kalamazoo | 203 | 168 | 35 |
| Kent | 541 | 201 | 340 |
| Lapeer | 80 | 46 | 34 |
| Livingston | 115 | 66 | 49 |
| Macomb | 496 | 245 | 251 |
| Monroe | 189 | 93 | 96 |
| Muskegon | 125 | 48 | 77 |
| Newaygo | 60 | 26 | 34 |
| Oakland | 1,005 | 829 | 176 |
| Ottawa | 223 | 128 | 95 |
| Saginaw | 125 | 58 | 67 |
| St. Clair | 172 | 65 | 107 |
| Van Buren | 87 | 44 | 43 |
| Washtenaw | 285 | 129 | 156 |
| Wayne | 1,028 | 899 | 129 |
| **MICHIGAN-Nonmetropolitan Counties** | | | |
| Alcona | 25 | 14 | 11 |
| Alger | 13 | 11 | 2 |
| Allegan | 108 | 61 | 47 |
| Alpena | 26 | 13 | 13 |
| Antrim | 48 | 20 | 28 |
| Arenac | 20 | 11 | 9 |
| Baraga | 13 | 6 | 7 |
| Benzie | 41 | 13 | 28 |
| Branch | 49 | 25 | 24 |
| Charlevoix | 34 | 18 | 16 |
| Cheboygan | 35 | 17 | 18 |
| Chippewa | 14 | 13 | 1 |
| Clare | 26 | 23 | 3 |
| Crawford | 28 | 16 | 12 |
| Delta | 30 | 16 | 14 |
| Dickinson | 33 | 13 | 20 |
| Emmet | 46 | 24 | 22 |
| Gladwin | 40 | 16 | 24 |
| Gogebic | 22 | 15 | 7 |
| Grand Traverse | 132 | 67 | 65 |
| Gratiot | 35 | 19 | 16 |
| Hillsdale | 44 | 28 | 16 |
| Houghton | 20 | 20 | 0 |
| Huron | 36 | 20 | 16 |
| Iosco | 21 | 4 | 17 |
| Iron | 17 | 8 | 9 |
| Isabella | 48 | 23 | 25 |
| Kalkaska | 35 | 18 | 17 |
| Keweenaw | 7 | 6 | 1 |
| Lake | 70 | 16 | 54 |
| Leelanau | 19 | 18 | 1 |
| Lenawee | 105 | 42 | 63 |
| Luce | 5 | 4 | 1 |
| Mackinac | 23 | 10 | 13 |
| Manistee | 30 | 14 | 16 |
| Marquette | 52 | 22 | 30 |
| Mason | 40 | 20 | 20 |
| Mecosta | 48 | 23 | 25 |
| Menominee | 14 | 13 | 1 |
| Midland | 55 | 33 | 22 |
| Missaukee | 27 | 12 | 15 |
| Montcalm | 61 | 29 | 32 |
| Montmorency | 26 | 12 | 14 |
| Oceana | 35 | 20 | 15 |

**Table 80. Full-Time Law Enforcement Employees, by State and Metropolitan and Nonmetropolitan Counties, 2009**—*Continued*

(Number.)

| State/County | Total law enforcement employees | Total officers | Total civilians |
|---|---|---|---|
| Ogemaw | 27 | 16 | 11 |
| Ontonagon | 12 | 9 | 3 |
| Osceola | 36 | 18 | 18 |
| Oscoda | 17 | 11 | 6 |
| Otsego | 23 | 10 | 13 |
| Presque Isle | 14 | 14 | 0 |
| Roscommon | 39 | 24 | 15 |
| Sanilac | 55 | 25 | 30 |
| Schoolcraft | 11 | 3 | 8 |
| Shiawassee | 69 | 34 | 35 |
| St. Joseph | 47 | 22 | 25 |
| Tuscola | 49 | 24 | 25 |
| Wexford | 50 | 24 | 26 |
| **MINNESOTA-Metropolitan Counties** | | | |
| Anoka | 247 | 128 | 119 |
| Benton | 74 | 27 | 47 |
| Blue Earth | 81 | 25 | 56 |
| Carlton | 46 | 19 | 27 |
| Carver | 157 | 86 | 71 |
| Chisago | 80 | 39 | 41 |
| Clay | 65 | 32 | 33 |
| Dakota | 155 | 72 | 83 |
| Dodge | 32 | 22 | 10 |
| Hennepin | 788 | 330 | 458 |
| Houston | 25 | 13 | 12 |
| Isanti | 55 | 19 | 36 |
| Nicollet | 38 | 12 | 26 |
| Olmsted | 156 | 60 | 96 |
| Polk | 29 | 23 | 6 |
| Ramsey | 392 | 228 | 164 |
| Scott | 130 | 40 | 90 |
| Sherburne | 263 | 75 | 188 |
| Stearns | 173 | 60 | 113 |
| St. Louis | 230 | 94 | 136 |
| Wabasha | 35 | 19 | 16 |
| Washington | 225 | 90 | 135 |
| Wright | 214 | 137 | 77 |
| **MINNESOTA-Nonmetropolitan Counties** | | | |
| Aitkin | 48 | 19 | 29 |
| Becker | 56 | 21 | 35 |
| Beltrami | 76 | 31 | 45 |
| Big Stone | 8 | 5 | 3 |
| Brown | 36 | 10 | 26 |
| Cass | 57 | 36 | 21 |
| Chippewa | 18 | 8 | 10 |
| Clearwater | 20 | 9 | 11 |
| Cook | 18 | 12 | 6 |
| Cottonwood | 19 | 8 | 11 |
| Crow Wing | 121 | 38 | 83 |
| Douglas | 75 | 26 | 49 |
| Faribault | 27 | 9 | 18 |
| Fillmore | 31 | 19 | 12 |
| Freeborn | 67 | 23 | 44 |
| Goodhue | 104 | 38 | 66 |
| Grant | 11 | 6 | 5 |
| Hubbard | 42 | 14 | 28 |
| Itasca | 67 | 60 | 7 |
| Jackson | 19 | 8 | 11 |
| Kanabec | 33 | 14 | 19 |
| Kandiyohi | 109 | 34 | 75 |
| Kittson | 10 | 5 | 5 |
| Koochiching | 18 | 10 | 8 |
| Lac Qui Parle | 6 | 6 | 0 |
| Lake | 27 | 16 | 11 |
| Lake of the Woods | 9 | 5 | 4 |
| Le Sueur | 34 | 18 | 16 |
| Lincoln | 10 | 4 | 6 |
| Lyon | 47 | 13 | 34 |
| Mahnomen | 18 | 11 | 7 |
| Marshall | 18 | 12 | 6 |
| Martin | 29 | 11 | 18 |
| McLeod | 60 | 24 | 36 |
| Meeker | 44 | 20 | 24 |
| Mille Lacs | 65 | 26 | 39 |
| Morrison | 58 | 19 | 39 |
| Mower | 51 | 22 | 29 |
| Murray | 13 | 9 | 4 |

| State/County | Total law enforcement employees | Total officers | Total civilians |
|---|---|---|---|
| Nobles | 34 | 12 | 22 |
| Norman | 8 | 5 | 3 |
| Otter Tail | 79 | 32 | 47 |
| Pennington | 29 | 8 | 21 |
| Pine | 77 | 28 | 49 |
| Pipestone | 22 | 12 | 10 |
| Pope | 15 | 7 | 8 |
| Red Lake | 10 | 6 | 4 |
| Redwood | 24 | 12 | 12 |
| Renville | 26 | 11 | 15 |
| Rice | 46 | 25 | 21 |
| Rock | 15 | 10 | 5 |
| Roseau | 22 | 12 | 10 |
| Sibley | 23 | 11 | 12 |
| Steele | 24 | 18 | 6 |
| Stevens | 13 | 6 | 7 |
| Swift | 15 | 9 | 6 |
| Todd | 33 | 14 | 19 |
| Traverse | 13 | 6 | 7 |
| Wadena | 19 | 8 | 11 |
| Waseca | 27 | 12 | 15 |
| Watonwan | 21 | 9 | 12 |
| Wilkin | 17 | 6 | 11 |
| Winona | 57 | 19 | 38 |
| Yellow Medicine | 20 | 8 | 12 |
| **MISSISSIPPI-Metropolitan Counties** | | | |
| Copiah | 42 | 23 | 19 |
| DeSoto | 240 | 115 | 125 |
| Forrest | 118 | 83 | 35 |
| George | 20 | 16 | 4 |
| Hancock | 56 | 50 | 6 |
| Harrison | 365 | 104 | 261 |
| Hinds | 502 | 114 | 388 |
| Lamar | 73 | 38 | 35 |
| Madison | 116 | 54 | 62 |
| Marshall | 54 | 26 | 28 |
| Perry | 14 | 6 | 8 |
| Rankin | 186 | 80 | 106 |
| Simpson | 39 | 17 | 22 |
| Stone | 22 | 20 | 2 |
| Tate | 31 | 23 | 8 |
| Tunica | 150 | 70 | 80 |
| **MISSISSIPPI-Nonmetropolitan Counties** | | | |
| Adams | 64 | 38 | 26 |
| Amite | 13 | 6 | 7 |
| Attala | 13 | 8 | 5 |
| Benton | 15 | 5 | 10 |
| Bolivar | 113 | 18 | 95 |
| Calhoun | 6 | 5 | 1 |
| Carroll | 10 | 9 | 1 |
| Chickasaw | 15 | 14 | 1 |
| Choctaw | 12 | 6 | 6 |
| Claiborne | 24 | 11 | 13 |
| Clay | 31 | 10 | 21 |
| Coahoma | 25 | 22 | 3 |
| Covington | 14 | 10 | 4 |
| Franklin | 6 | 3 | 3 |
| Greene | 16 | 8 | 8 |
| Grenada | 14 | 12 | 2 |
| Holmes | 11 | 11 | 0 |
| Humphreys | 15 | 7 | 8 |
| Itawamba | 11 | 10 | 1 |
| Jefferson Davis | 9 | 9 | 0 |
| Jones | 37 | 32 | 5 |
| Kemper | 12 | 6 | 6 |
| Lafayette | 33 | 30 | 3 |
| Lauderdale | 121 | 55 | 66 |
| Lawrence | 24 | 12 | 12 |
| Leake | 16 | 14 | 2 |
| Lee | 126 | 45 | 81 |
| Leflore | 33 | 22 | 11 |
| Lincoln | 43 | 20 | 23 |
| Lowndes | 109 | 42 | 67 |
| Marion | 20 | 14 | 6 |
| Monroe | 55 | 23 | 32 |
| Montgomery | 9 | 7 | 2 |
| Neshoba | 17 | 17 | 0 |

**Table 80. Full-Time Law Enforcement Employees, by State and Metropolitan and Nonmetropolitan Counties, 2009**—*Continued*

(Number.)

| State/County | Total law enforcement employees | Total officers | Total civilians |
|---|---|---|---|
| Newton | 19 | 10 | 9 |
| Noxubee | 11 | 5 | 6 |
| Oktibbeha | 29 | 26 | 3 |
| Panola | 73 | 28 | 45 |
| Pearl River | 99 | 41 | 58 |
| Pike | 56 | 29 | 27 |
| Pontotoc | 34 | 18 | 16 |
| Prentiss | 32 | 13 | 19 |
| Sharkey | 11 | 6 | 5 |
| Smith | 15 | 10 | 5 |
| Sunflower | 13 | 12 | 1 |
| Tallahatchie | 27 | 12 | 15 |
| Tippah | 13 | 9 | 4 |
| Tishomingo | 26 | 12 | 14 |
| Union | 34 | 17 | 17 |
| Walthall | 18 | 10 | 8 |
| Warren | 58 | 40 | 18 |
| Washington | 64 | 37 | 27 |
| Wayne | 22 | 10 | 12 |
| Webster | 7 | 5 | 2 |
| Winston | 11 | 10 | 1 |
| Yazoo | 17 | 15 | 2 |
| **MISSOURI-Metropolitan Counties** | | | |
| Andrew | 14 | 10 | 4 |
| Bates | 34 | 12 | 22 |
| Bollinger | 11 | 8 | 3 |
| Boone | 73 | 60 | 13 |
| Buchanan | 104 | 71 | 33 |
| Caldwell | 45 | 8 | 37 |
| Callaway | 25 | 23 | 2 |
| Cape Girardeau | 70 | 46 | 24 |
| Cass | 93 | 73 | 20 |
| Christian | 68 | 42 | 26 |
| Clay | 182 | 113 | 69 |
| Clinton | 24 | 17 | 7 |
| Cole | 62 | 46 | 16 |
| Dallas | 15 | 12 | 3 |
| De Kalb | 11 | 5 | 6 |
| Franklin | 135 | 114 | 21 |
| Greene | 306 | 171 | 135 |
| Howard | 7 | 6 | 1 |
| Jackson | 120 | 89 | 31 |
| Jasper | 141 | 127 | 14 |
| Jefferson | 213 | 144 | 69 |
| Lafayette | 37 | 33 | 4 |
| Lincoln | 93 | 55 | 38 |
| McDonald | 30 | 28 | 2 |
| Moniteau | 8 | 4 | 4 |
| Newton | 51 | 40 | 11 |
| Osage | 11 | 10 | 1 |
| Platte | 107 | 72 | 35 |
| Polk | 36 | 22 | 14 |
| Ray | 35 | 14 | 21 |
| St. Charles | 224 | 154 | 70 |
| St. Louis County Police Department | 1,012 | 784 | 228 |
| Warren | 60 | 35 | 25 |
| Washington | 33 | 20 | 13 |
| Webster | 28 | 17 | 11 |
| **MISSOURI-Nonmetropolitan Counties** | | | |
| Adair | 29 | 12 | 17 |
| Atchison | 10 | 5 | 5 |
| Audrain | 36 | 18 | 18 |
| Barry | 35 | 21 | 14 |
| Barton | 17 | 7 | 10 |
| Benton | 22 | 15 | 7 |
| Butler | 42 | 25 | 17 |
| Camden | 61 | 55 | 6 |
| Carroll | 10 | 8 | 2 |
| Carter | 10 | 4 | 6 |
| Cedar | 16 | 13 | 3 |
| Clark | 13 | 7 | 6 |
| Cooper | 9 | 8 | 1 |
| Crawford | 38 | 28 | 10 |
| Daviess | 6 | 5 | 1 |
| Dent | 19 | 13 | 6 |
| Douglas | 9 | 6 | 3 |
| Dunklin | 11 | 9 | 2 |
| Gasconade | 13 | 12 | 1 |
| Gentry | 8 | 8 | 0 |
| Grundy | 14 | 4 | 10 |
| Harrison | 14 | 5 | 9 |
| Henry | 29 | 21 | 8 |
| Hickory | 13 | 8 | 5 |
| Holt | 9 | 5 | 4 |
| Howell | 34 | 23 | 11 |
| Iron | 15 | 10 | 5 |
| Johnson | 40 | 33 | 7 |
| Knox | 5 | 3 | 2 |
| Laclede | 23 | 22 | 1 |
| Lawrence | 38 | 28 | 10 |
| Lewis | 10 | 4 | 6 |
| Linn | 5 | 4 | 1 |
| Livingston | 21 | 9 | 12 |
| Macon | 14 | 11 | 3 |
| Madison | 10 | 8 | 2 |
| Maries | 12 | 7 | 5 |
| Marion | 38 | 16 | 22 |
| Mercer | 8 | 3 | 5 |
| Mississippi | 43 | 10 | 33 |
| Monroe | 9 | 8 | 1 |
| Montgomery | 16 | 14 | 2 |
| Morgan | 44 | 24 | 20 |
| New Madrid | 26 | 12 | 14 |
| Nodaway | 10 | 10 | 0 |
| Oregon | 10 | 6 | 4 |
| Ozark | 16 | 8 | 8 |
| Pemiscot | 50 | 22 | 28 |
| Perry | 30 | 20 | 10 |
| Pettis | 50 | 26 | 24 |
| Phelps | 62 | 30 | 32 |
| Pike | 31 | 11 | 20 |
| Pulaski | 31 | 23 | 8 |
| Putnam | 4 | 3 | 1 |
| Ralls | 8 | 7 | 1 |
| Randolph | 37 | 18 | 19 |
| Reynolds | 9 | 8 | 1 |
| Ripley | 10 | 7 | 3 |
| Saline | 32 | 19 | 13 |
| Scott | 41 | 22 | 19 |
| Shannon | 9 | 5 | 4 |
| Shelby | 10 | 5 | 5 |
| St. Clair | 66 | 20 | 46 |
| Ste. Genevieve | 47 | 35 | 12 |
| St. Francois | 69 | 57 | 12 |
| Stoddard | 23 | 12 | 11 |
| Stone | 61 | 49 | 12 |
| Sullivan | 5 | 4 | 1 |
| Taney | 61 | 45 | 16 |
| Texas | 23 | 7 | 16 |
| Vernon | 27 | 11 | 16 |
| Worth | 4 | 3 | 1 |
| Wright | 14 | 6 | 8 |
| **MONTANA-Metropolitan Counties** | | | |
| Carbon | 13 | 8 | 5 |
| Cascade | 130 | 33 | 97 |
| Missoula | 172 | 50 | 122 |
| Yellowstone | 160 | 51 | 109 |
| **MONTANA-Nonmetropolitan Counties** | | | |
| Beaverhead | 18 | 7 | 11 |
| Big Horn | 29 | 12 | 17 |
| Blaine | 14 | 9 | 5 |
| Broadwater | 22 | 9 | 13 |
| Carter | 3 | 3 | 0 |
| Chouteau | 19 | 9 | 10 |
| Custer | 15 | 6 | 9 |
| Daniels | 3 | 3 | 0 |
| Dawson | 16 | 6 | 10 |
| Deer Lodge | 36 | 20 | 16 |
| Fallon | 3 | 3 | 0 |
| Fergus | 21 | 9 | 12 |
| Flathead | 117 | 50 | 67 |
| Gallatin | 89 | 51 | 38 |

**Table 80. Full-Time Law Enforcement Employees, by State and Metropolitan and Nonmetropolitan Counties, 2009**—*Continued*

(Number.)

| State/County | Total law enforcement employees | Total officers | Total civilians |
|---|---|---|---|
| Garfield | 2 | 2 | 0 |
| Glacier | 21 | 14 | 7 |
| Granite | 9 | 5 | 4 |
| Hill | 28 | 12 | 16 |
| Jefferson | 22 | 13 | 9 |
| Judith Basin | 5 | 4 | 1 |
| Lake | 58 | 25 | 33 |
| Lewis and Clark | 71 | 41 | 30 |
| Liberty | 9 | 5 | 4 |
| Lincoln | 37 | 20 | 17 |
| Madison | 14 | 8 | 6 |
| McCone | 4 | 4 | 0 |
| Meagher | 11 | 4 | 7 |
| Mineral | 17 | 6 | 11 |
| Musselshell | 9 | 9 | 0 |
| Park | 23 | 15 | 8 |
| Petroleum | 2 | 2 | 0 |
| Phillips | 11 | 7 | 4 |
| Pondera | 10 | 9 | 1 |
| Powder River | 11 | 3 | 8 |
| Powell | 17 | 10 | 7 |
| Prairie | 3 | 3 | 0 |
| Ravalli | 63 | 29 | 34 |
| Richland | 17 | 8 | 9 |
| Roosevelt | 32 | 10 | 22 |
| Rosebud | 25 | 14 | 11 |
| Sanders | 17 | 7 | 10 |
| Sheridan | 10 | 6 | 4 |
| Silver Bow | 94 | 46 | 48 |
| Stillwater | 12 | 7 | 5 |
| Sweet Grass | 12 | 6 | 6 |
| Teton | 12 | 9 | 3 |
| Toole | 20 | 12 | 8 |
| Treasure | 2 | 2 | 0 |
| Valley | 16 | 7 | 9 |
| Wheatland | 10 | 5 | 5 |
| **NEBRASKA-Metropolitan Counties** | | | |
| Cass | 72 | 51 | 21 |
| Dakota | 15 | 14 | 1 |
| Dixon | 14 | 7 | 7 |
| Douglas | 205 | 132 | 73 |
| Lancaster | 99 | 82 | 17 |
| Sarpy | 198 | 132 | 66 |
| Saunders | 18 | 11 | 7 |
| **NEBRASKA-Nonmetropolitan Counties** | | | |
| Adams | 18 | 16 | 2 |
| Antelope | 12 | 6 | 6 |
| Arthur | 1 | 1 | 0 |
| Banner | 1 | 1 | 0 |
| Boone | 13 | 5 | 8 |
| Box Butte | 17 | 5 | 12 |
| Boyd | 3 | 3 | 0 |
| Brown | 8 | 4 | 4 |
| Buffalo | 44 | 25 | 19 |
| Burt | 9 | 5 | 4 |
| Butler | 8 | 7 | 1 |
| Cedar | 8 | 4 | 4 |
| Chase | 8 | 4 | 4 |
| Cherry | 12 | 5 | 7 |
| Cheyenne | 9 | 7 | 2 |
| Clay | 11 | 7 | 4 |
| Colfax | 9 | 7 | 2 |
| Cuming | 6 | 5 | 1 |
| Custer | 7 | 6 | 1 |
| Dawes | 8 | 3 | 5 |
| Dawson | 46 | 27 | 19 |
| Deuel | 5 | 4 | 1 |
| Dodge | 25 | 18 | 7 |
| Dundy | 8 | 4 | 4 |
| Fillmore | 12 | 7 | 5 |
| Franklin | 7 | 3 | 4 |
| Frontier | 9 | 5 | 4 |
| Furnas | 15 | 9 | 6 |
| Gage | 15 | 12 | 3 |
| Garden | 8 | 3 | 5 |
| Garfield | 2 | 2 | 0 |
| Gosper | 5 | 4 | 1 |
| Grant | 3 | 2 | 1 |
| Hall | 36 | 28 | 8 |
| Hamilton | 16 | 8 | 8 |
| Harlan | 8 | 4 | 4 |
| Hayes | 2 | 2 | 0 |
| Hitchcock | 6 | 3 | 3 |
| Holt | 6 | 5 | 1 |
| Hooker | 2 | 2 | 0 |
| Howard | 11 | 5 | 6 |
| Jefferson | 14 | 7 | 7 |
| Johnson | 10 | 5 | 5 |
| Kearney | 12 | 7 | 5 |
| Keith | 15 | 8 | 7 |
| Keya Paha | 2 | 2 | 0 |
| Kimball | 9 | 4 | 5 |
| Knox | 11 | 5 | 6 |
| Lincoln | 29 | 23 | 6 |
| Logan | 2 | 2 | 0 |
| Loup | 1 | 1 | 0 |
| Madison | 45 | 25 | 20 |
| McPherson | 1 | 1 | 0 |
| Merrick | 11 | 6 | 5 |
| Morrill | 9 | 4 | 5 |
| Nance | 11 | 7 | 4 |
| Nemaha | 5 | 5 | 0 |
| Nuckolls | 7 | 4 | 3 |
| Otoe | 27 | 16 | 11 |
| Pawnee | 4 | 3 | 1 |
| Perkins | 9 | 5 | 4 |
| Phelps | 9 | 6 | 3 |
| Pierce | 8 | 3 | 5 |
| Platte | 63 | 18 | 45 |
| Polk | 12 | 7 | 5 |
| Red Willow | 8 | 6 | 2 |
| Richardson | 11 | 6 | 5 |
| Rock | 8 | 3 | 5 |
| Saline | 9 | 9 | 0 |
| Scotts Bluff | 24 | 16 | 8 |
| Sheridan | 7 | 6 | 1 |
| Sherman | 6 | 5 | 1 |
| Sioux | 1 | 1 | 0 |
| Stanton | 8 | 7 | 1 |
| Thayer | 11 | 7 | 4 |
| Thomas | 1 | 1 | 0 |
| Valley | 7 | 3 | 4 |
| Wayne | 6 | 5 | 1 |
| Webster | 11 | 6 | 5 |
| Wheeler | 2 | 2 | 0 |
| York | 23 | 9 | 14 |
| **NEVADA-Metropolitan Counties** | | | |
| Carson City | 142 | 98 | 44 |
| Storey | 27 | 25 | 2 |
| Washoe | 716 | 429 | 287 |
| **NEVADA-Nonmetropolitan Counties** | | | |
| Churchill | 57 | 49 | 8 |
| Douglas | 112 | 99 | 13 |
| Elko | 68 | 51 | 17 |
| Esmeralda | 16 | 12 | 4 |
| Eureka | 21 | 14 | 7 |
| Humboldt | 48 | 35 | 13 |
| Lander | 32 | 21 | 11 |
| Lincoln | 32 | 27 | 5 |
| Lyon | 110 | 77 | 33 |
| Mineral | 25 | 19 | 6 |
| Nye | 153 | 109 | 44 |
| Pershing | 20 | 12 | 8 |
| White Pine | 30 | 25 | 5 |
| **NEW HAMPSHIRE-Metropolitan Counties** | | | |
| Rockingham | 47 | 24 | 23 |
| **NEW HAMPSHIRE-Nonmetropolitan Counties** | | | |
| Carroll | 24 | 13 | 11 |
| Cheshire | 21 | 10 | 11 |
| Merrimack | 34 | 15 | 19 |
| **NEW JERSEY-Metropolitan Counties** | | | |
| Atlantic | 135 | 107 | 28 |
| Bergen | 547 | 452 | 95 |
| Bergen County Police Department | 165 | 92 | 73 |

**Table 80. Full-Time Law Enforcement Employees, by State and Metropolitan and Nonmetropolitan Counties, 2009**—*Continued*

(Number.)

| State/County | Total law enforcement employees | Total officers | Total civilians |
|---|---|---|---|
| Burlington | 88 | 68 | 20 |
| Camden | 192 | 165 | 27 |
| Cape May | 152 | 133 | 19 |
| Cumberland | 64 | 56 | 8 |
| Essex | 485 | 415 | 70 |
| Gloucester | 108 | 92 | 16 |
| Hudson | 328 | 225 | 103 |
| Hunterdon | 27 | 23 | 4 |
| Mercer | 158 | 128 | 30 |
| Middlesex | 218 | 178 | 40 |
| Monmouth | 563 | 403 | 160 |
| Morris | 328 | 253 | 75 |
| Ocean | 251 | 140 | 111 |
| Passaic | 700 | 547 | 153 |
| Salem | 188 | 162 | 26 |
| Somerset | 222 | 179 | 43 |
| Sussex | 157 | 128 | 29 |
| Union | 208 | 164 | 44 |
| Warren | 23 | 19 | 4 |
| **NEW MEXICO-Metropolitan Counties** | | | |
| Bernalillo | 342 | 272 | 70 |
| Dona Ana | 220 | 131 | 89 |
| Sandoval | 56 | 48 | 8 |
| San Juan | 122 | 97 | 25 |
| Santa Fe | 104 | 79 | 25 |
| Torrance | 18 | 15 | 3 |
| Valencia | 54 | 39 | 15 |
| **NEW MEXICO-Nonmetropolitan Counties** | | | |
| Catron | 12 | 7 | 5 |
| Chaves | 49 | 39 | 10 |
| Cibola | 19 | 13 | 6 |
| Colfax | 13 | 11 | 2 |
| Curry | 26 | 17 | 9 |
| De Baca | 4 | 4 | 0 |
| Eddy | 55 | 46 | 9 |
| Grant | 39 | 36 | 3 |
| Harding | 2 | 2 | 0 |
| Hidalgo | 21 | 13 | 8 |
| Lea | 62 | 43 | 19 |
| Lincoln | 27 | 18 | 9 |
| Luna | 35 | 32 | 3 |
| McKinley | 51 | 40 | 11 |
| Mora | 7 | 5 | 2 |
| Otero | 53 | 35 | 18 |
| Quay | 8 | 8 | 0 |
| Rio Arriba | 29 | 22 | 7 |
| Roosevelt | 17 | 14 | 3 |
| San Miguel | 11 | 9 | 2 |
| Sierra | 16 | 14 | 2 |
| Socorro | 13 | 11 | 2 |
| Taos | 25 | 18 | 7 |
| Union | 5 | 4 | 1 |
| **NEW YORK-Metropolitan Counties** | | | |
| Albany | 172 | 126 | 46 |
| Broome | 71 | 54 | 17 |
| Chemung | 52 | 43 | 9 |
| Dutchess | 140 | 107 | 33 |
| Erie | 191 | 147 | 44 |
| Herkimer | 11 | 6 | 5 |
| Livingston | 72 | 48 | 24 |
| Madison | 41 | 32 | 9 |
| Monroe | 333 | 277 | 56 |
| Nassau | 3,312 | 2,580 | 732 |
| Niagara | 145 | 112 | 33 |
| Oneida | 113 | 88 | 25 |
| Onondaga | 304 | 262 | 42 |
| Ontario | 102 | 68 | 34 |
| Orange | 113 | 101 | 12 |
| Orleans | 29 | 26 | 3 |
| Oswego | 72 | 57 | 15 |
| Putnam | 98 | 80 | 18 |
| Rensselaer | 39 | 33 | 6 |
| Rockland | 120 | 87 | 33 |
| Saratoga | 148 | 112 | 36 |
| Schenectady | 20 | 14 | 6 |
| Schoharie | 29 | 15 | 14 |
| Suffolk | 403 | 268 | 135 |
| Suffolk County Police Department | 3,123 | 2,537 | 586 |
| Tioga | 51 | 34 | 17 |
| Tompkins | 44 | 40 | 4 |
| Warren | 106 | 70 | 36 |
| Washington | 37 | 31 | 6 |
| Wayne | 58 | 50 | 8 |
| Westchester Public Safety | 339 | 264 | 75 |
| **NEW YORK-Nonmetropolitan Counties** | | | |
| Allegany | 50 | 35 | 15 |
| Cayuga | 43 | 37 | 6 |
| Chautauqua | 116 | 72 | 44 |
| Chenango | 41 | 24 | 17 |
| Clinton | 23 | 23 | 0 |
| Columbia | 57 | 47 | 10 |
| Cortland | 54 | 32 | 22 |
| Delaware | 24 | 13 | 11 |
| Essex | 20 | 18 | 2 |
| Franklin | 7 | 3 | 4 |
| Fulton | 44 | 27 | 17 |
| Genesee | 76 | 49 | 27 |
| Greene | 33 | 29 | 4 |
| Hamilton | 5 | 4 | 1 |
| Jefferson | 54 | 45 | 9 |
| Lewis | 31 | 19 | 12 |
| Montgomery | 47 | 25 | 22 |
| Otsego | 20 | 17 | 3 |
| Schuyler | 19 | 17 | 2 |
| Seneca | 39 | 28 | 11 |
| Steuben | 54 | 42 | 12 |
| St. Lawrence | 34 | 33 | 1 |
| Sullivan | 47 | 46 | 1 |
| Wyoming | 42 | 30 | 12 |
| Yates | 44 | 27 | 17 |
| **NORTH CAROLINA-Metropolitan Counties** | | | |
| Alamance | 276 | 126 | 150 |
| Alexander | 46 | 27 | 19 |
| Anson | 44 | 29 | 15 |
| Brunswick | 199 | 125 | 74 |
| Buncombe | 367 | 225 | 142 |
| Burke | 116 | 87 | 29 |
| Cabarrus | 224 | 185 | 39 |
| Caldwell | 117 | 67 | 50 |
| Catawba | 177 | 126 | 51 |
| Chatham | 97 | 75 | 22 |
| Cumberland | 534 | 297 | 237 |
| Currituck | 99 | 64 | 35 |
| Davie | 77 | 47 | 30 |
| Durham | 426 | 160 | 266 |
| Edgecombe | 127 | 51 | 76 |
| Forsyth | 507 | 207 | 300 |
| Franklin | 99 | 60 | 39 |
| Gaston | 212 | 122 | 90 |
| Gaston County Police Department | 226 | 136 | 90 |
| Greene | 40 | 24 | 16 |
| Guilford | 558 | 252 | 306 |
| Haywood | 92 | 51 | 41 |
| Henderson | 187 | 134 | 53 |
| Hoke | 59 | 53 | 6 |
| Johnston | 172 | 95 | 77 |
| Madison | 29 | 17 | 12 |
| Mecklenburg[1] | 1,275 | 294 | 981 |
| Nash | 134 | 76 | 58 |
| New Hanover | 386 | 287 | 99 |
| Orange | 141 | 107 | 34 |
| Pender | 97 | 57 | 40 |
| Person | 82 | 42 | 40 |
| Pitt | 316 | 132 | 184 |
| Randolph | 222 | 160 | 62 |
| Rockingham | 134 | 93 | 41 |
| Stokes | 64 | 43 | 21 |
| Union | 242 | 175 | 67 |
| Wake | 808 | 350 | 458 |
| Wayne | 148 | 83 | 65 |
| Yadkin | 64 | 36 | 28 |
| **NORTH CAROLINA-Nonmetropolitan Counties** | | | |
| Alleghany | 19 | 12 | 7 |
| Avery | 34 | 26 | 8 |

[1] The employee data presented in this table for Mecklenburg represent only Mecklenburg County Sheriff's Office and exclude Charlotte-Mecklenburg Police Department.

**Table 80. Full-Time Law Enforcement Employees, by State and Metropolitan and Nonmetropolitan Counties, 2009**—*Continued*

(Number.)

| State/County | Total law enforcement employees | Total officers | Total civilians |
|---|---|---|---|
| Beaufort | 77 | 46 | 31 |
| Bertie | 31 | 22 | 9 |
| Bladen | 84 | 56 | 28 |
| Camden | 18 | 17 | 1 |
| Carteret | 91 | 47 | 44 |
| Caswell | 47 | 35 | 12 |
| Cherokee | 63 | 28 | 35 |
| Chowan | 37 | 17 | 20 |
| Clay | 41 | 15 | 26 |
| Cleveland | 126 | 84 | 42 |
| Columbus | 111 | 65 | 46 |
| Craven | 122 | 69 | 53 |
| Dare | 123 | 63 | 60 |
| Davidson | 191 | 125 | 66 |
| Duplin | 90 | 59 | 31 |
| Gates | 13 | 12 | 1 |
| Graham | 20 | 13 | 7 |
| Granville | 84 | 45 | 39 |
| Halifax | 84 | 58 | 26 |
| Harnett | 187 | 107 | 80 |
| Hertford | 60 | 21 | 39 |
| Hyde | 19 | 14 | 5 |
| Iredell | 206 | 150 | 56 |
| Jackson | 72 | 47 | 25 |
| Jones | 22 | 13 | 9 |
| Lee | 77 | 47 | 30 |
| Lenoir | 101 | 64 | 37 |
| Lincoln | 151 | 104 | 47 |
| Macon | 64 | 46 | 18 |
| Martin | 36 | 34 | 2 |
| McDowell | 62 | 41 | 21 |
| Mitchell | 16 | 14 | 2 |
| Montgomery | 62 | 31 | 31 |
| Moore | 114 | 74 | 40 |
| Northampton | 51 | 26 | 25 |
| Pamlico | 36 | 14 | 22 |
| Pasquotank | 46 | 40 | 6 |
| Perquimans | 16 | 13 | 3 |
| Polk | 35 | 22 | 13 |
| Richmond | 74 | 49 | 25 |
| Robeson | 242 | 128 | 114 |
| Rowan | 186 | 131 | 55 |
| Rutherford | 127 | 76 | 51 |
| Sampson | 130 | 82 | 48 |
| Scotland | 68 | 41 | 27 |
| Stanly | 91 | 49 | 42 |
| Surry | 103 | 67 | 36 |
| Swain | 34 | 14 | 20 |
| Transylvania | 79 | 57 | 22 |
| Tyrrell | 16 | 10 | 6 |
| Vance | 93 | 45 | 48 |
| Warren | 60 | 32 | 28 |
| Washington | 42 | 22 | 20 |
| Watauga | 81 | 44 | 37 |
| Wilkes | 117 | 70 | 47 |
| Wilson | 137 | 88 | 49 |
| Yancey | 30 | 14 | 16 |
| **NORTH DAKOTA-Metropolitan Counties** | | | |
| Burleigh | 81 | 44 | 37 |
| Cass | 136 | 70 | 66 |
| Grand Forks | 34 | 27 | 7 |
| Morton | 35 | 21 | 14 |
| **NORTH DAKOTA-Nonmetropolitan Counties** | | | |
| Adams | 3 | 3 | 0 |
| Barnes | 17 | 6 | 11 |
| Benson | 4 | 4 | 0 |
| Billings | 4 | 4 | 0 |
| Bottineau | 14 | 10 | 4 |
| Bowman | 3 | 3 | 0 |
| Burke | 4 | 4 | 0 |
| Cavalier | 11 | 5 | 6 |
| Dickey | 5 | 4 | 1 |
| Divide | 4 | 4 | 0 |
| Dunn | 5 | 4 | 1 |
| Eddy | 5 | 4 | 1 |
| Emmons | 4 | 3 | 1 |
| Foster | 4 | 3 | 1 |
| Golden Valley | 5 | 4 | 1 |
| Grant | 3 | 3 | 0 |
| Griggs | 3 | 2 | 1 |
| Hettinger | 3 | 3 | 0 |
| Kidder | 4 | 3 | 1 |
| Lamoure | 5 | 4 | 1 |
| Logan | 2 | 2 | 0 |
| McHenry | 7 | 7 | 0 |
| McIntosh | 3 | 3 | 0 |
| McKenzie | 15 | 15 | 0 |
| McLean | 32 | 20 | 12 |
| Mercer | 22 | 14 | 8 |
| Mountrail | 12 | 7 | 5 |
| Nelson | 4 | 3 | 1 |
| Oliver | 4 | 3 | 1 |
| Pembina | 13 | 7 | 6 |
| Pierce | 7 | 3 | 4 |
| Ramsey | 7 | 6 | 1 |
| Ransom | 6 | 4 | 2 |
| Renville | 5 | 5 | 0 |
| Richland | 25 | 13 | 12 |
| Rolette | 15 | 7 | 8 |
| Sargent | 5 | 4 | 1 |
| Sheridan | 3 | 3 | 0 |
| Sioux | 1 | 1 | 0 |
| Slope | 1 | 1 | 0 |
| Stark | 15 | 12 | 3 |
| Steele | 3 | 3 | 0 |
| Stutsman | 10 | 8 | 2 |
| Towner | 3 | 2 | 1 |
| Traill | 11 | 6 | 5 |
| Walsh | 17 | 10 | 7 |
| Ward | 46 | 21 | 25 |
| Wells | 3 | 3 | 0 |
| Williams | 30 | 18 | 12 |
| **OHIO-Metropolitan Counties** | | | |
| Brown | 41 | 25 | 16 |
| Butler | 366 | 226 | 140 |
| Carroll | 25 | 18 | 7 |
| Clark | 159 | 131 | 28 |
| Delaware | 194 | 90 | 104 |
| Erie | 74 | 35 | 39 |
| Fairfield | 129 | 104 | 25 |
| Fulton | 31 | 20 | 11 |
| Geauga | 117 | 48 | 69 |
| Greene | 142 | 93 | 49 |
| Lake | 200 | 57 | 143 |
| Lawrence | 43 | 31 | 12 |
| Licking | 185 | 130 | 55 |
| Lucas | 504 | 296 | 208 |
| Madison | 36 | 33 | 3 |
| Mahoning | 300 | 283 | 17 |
| Medina | 84 | 60 | 24 |
| Miami | 115 | 48 | 67 |
| Montgomery | 449 | 206 | 243 |
| Morrow | 43 | 18 | 25 |
| Ottawa | 63 | 22 | 41 |
| Pickaway | 91 | 39 | 52 |
| Portage | 130 | 54 | 76 |
| Preble | 44 | 11 | 33 |
| Richland | 123 | 39 | 84 |
| Stark | 225 | 131 | 94 |
| Trumbull | 129 | 42 | 87 |
| Warren | 186 | 99 | 87 |
| Washington | 81 | 40 | 41 |
| Wood | 121 | 115 | 6 |
| **OHIO-Nonmetropolitan Counties** | | | |
| Ashland | 66 | 39 | 27 |
| Athens | 29 | 24 | 5 |
| Auglaize | 56 | 22 | 34 |
| Champaign | 24 | 22 | 2 |
| Clinton | 66 | 35 | 31 |
| Columbiana | 30 | 20 | 10 |
| Crawford | 61 | 17 | 44 |
| Darke | 64 | 39 | 25 |
| Defiance | 36 | 20 | 16 |
| Fayette | 36 | 23 | 13 |

## Table 80. Full-Time Law Enforcement Employees, by State and Metropolitan and Nonmetropolitan Counties, 2009—*Continued*

(Number.)

| State/County | Total law enforcement employees | Total officers | Total civilians |
|---|---|---|---|
| Gallia | 32 | 21 | 11 |
| Guernsey | 40 | 19 | 21 |
| Hancock | 79 | 30 | 49 |
| Harrison | 22 | 16 | 6 |
| Henry | 23 | 23 | 0 |
| Highland | 48 | 31 | 17 |
| Hocking | 24 | 20 | 4 |
| Holmes | 48 | 28 | 20 |
| Jackson | 19 | 14 | 5 |
| Logan | 69 | 31 | 38 |
| Mercer | 46 | 29 | 17 |
| Monroe | 20 | 16 | 4 |
| Morgan | 13 | 9 | 4 |
| Muskingum | 117 | 77 | 40 |
| Paulding | 20 | 13 | 7 |
| Perry | 17 | 12 | 5 |
| Putnam | 54 | 32 | 22 |
| Ross | 70 | 44 | 26 |
| Sandusky | 54 | 30 | 24 |
| Scioto | 74 | 43 | 31 |
| Seneca | 82 | 33 | 49 |
| Shelby | 58 | 35 | 23 |
| Tuscarawas | 98 | 27 | 71 |
| Van Wert | 24 | 18 | 6 |
| Vinton | 16 | 11 | 5 |
| Williams | 21 | 17 | 4 |
| Wyandot | 24 | 13 | 11 |
| **OKLAHOMA-Metropolitan Counties** | | | |
| Canadian | 59 | 31 | 28 |
| Cleveland | 112 | 49 | 63 |
| Comanche | 40 | 29 | 11 |
| Creek | 72 | 36 | 36 |
| Grady | 25 | 18 | 7 |
| Le Flore | 19 | 13 | 6 |
| Lincoln | 35 | 13 | 22 |
| Logan | 49 | 15 | 34 |
| McClain | 25 | 14 | 11 |
| Oklahoma | 779 | 203 | 576 |
| Okmulgee | 15 | 14 | 1 |
| Osage | 79 | 41 | 38 |
| Pawnee | 18 | 10 | 8 |
| Rogers | 34 | 29 | 5 |
| Sequoyah | 41 | 14 | 27 |
| Tulsa | 570 | 530 | 40 |
| Wagoner | 49 | 21 | 28 |
| **OKLAHOMA-Nonmetropolitan Counties** | | | |
| Adair | 35 | 10 | 25 |
| Alfalfa | 9 | 4 | 5 |
| Atoka | 23 | 7 | 16 |
| Beaver | 13 | 7 | 6 |
| Beckham | 33 | 11 | 22 |
| Blaine | 15 | 8 | 7 |
| Bryan | 43 | 16 | 27 |
| Caddo | 31 | 16 | 15 |
| Carter | 59 | 18 | 41 |
| Cherokee | 26 | 20 | 6 |
| Choctaw | 17 | 6 | 11 |
| Cimarron | 5 | 2 | 3 |
| Coal | 12 | 9 | 3 |
| Cotton | 13 | 7 | 6 |
| Craig | 27 | 11 | 16 |
| Custer | 32 | 12 | 20 |
| Delaware | 45 | 18 | 27 |
| Dewey | 11 | 4 | 7 |
| Ellis | 15 | 5 | 10 |
| Garfield | 65 | 23 | 42 |
| Garvin | 31 | 17 | 14 |
| Grant | 11 | 5 | 6 |
| Greer | 7 | 3 | 4 |
| Harmon | 3 | 3 | 0 |
| Harper | 7 | 4 | 3 |
| Haskell | 27 | 5 | 22 |
| Hughes | 12 | 6 | 6 |
| Jackson | 38 | 13 | 25 |
| Jefferson | 12 | 6 | 6 |
| Johnston | 27 | 8 | 19 |
| Kay | 40 | 12 | 28 |
| Kingfisher | 14 | 7 | 7 |
| Kiowa | 11 | 6 | 5 |
| Latimer | 5 | 5 | 0 |
| Love | 21 | 6 | 15 |
| Major | 12 | 5 | 7 |
| Marshall | 27 | 6 | 21 |
| Mayes | 48 | 19 | 29 |
| McCurtain | 22 | 18 | 4 |
| McIntosh | 21 | 15 | 6 |
| Murray | 12 | 6 | 6 |
| Muskogee | 43 | 36 | 7 |
| Noble | 18 | 5 | 13 |
| Nowata | 19 | 10 | 9 |
| Okfuskee | 16 | 9 | 7 |
| Ottawa | 46 | 18 | 28 |
| Payne | 70 | 30 | 40 |
| Pittsburg | 62 | 17 | 45 |
| Pontotoc | 34 | 11 | 23 |
| Pottawatomie | 27 | 23 | 4 |
| Pushmataha | 13 | 6 | 7 |
| Roger Mills | 13 | 8 | 5 |
| Seminole | 27 | 16 | 11 |
| Stephens | 43 | 15 | 28 |
| Texas | 38 | 11 | 27 |
| Tillman | 15 | 6 | 9 |
| Washington | 40 | 17 | 23 |
| Washita | 17 | 7 | 10 |
| Woods | 10 | 5 | 5 |
| Woodward | 19 | 9 | 10 |
| **OREGON-Metropolitan Counties** | | | |
| Benton | 75 | 62 | 13 |
| Clackamas | 448 | 222 | 226 |
| Columbia | 34 | 10 | 24 |
| Deschutes | 210 | 82 | 128 |
| Jackson | 163 | 117 | 46 |
| Lane | 371 | 69 | 302 |
| Marion | 327 | 87 | 240 |
| Multnomah | 795 | 95 | 700 |
| Polk | 64 | 47 | 17 |
| Washington | 519 | 231 | 288 |
| Yamhill | 96 | 45 | 51 |
| **OREGON-Nonmetropolitan Counties** | | | |
| Baker | 26 | 12 | 14 |
| Clatsop | 54 | 26 | 28 |
| Coos | 85 | 23 | 62 |
| Crook | 28 | 15 | 13 |
| Curry | 36 | 14 | 22 |
| Douglas | 144 | 112 | 32 |
| Gilliam | 6 | 5 | 1 |
| Grant | 16 | 4 | 12 |
| Harney | 20 | 5 | 15 |
| Hood River | 35 | 18 | 17 |
| Jefferson | 49 | 13 | 36 |
| Josephine | 93 | 34 | 59 |
| Klamath | 88 | 37 | 51 |
| Lake | 19 | 7 | 12 |
| Lincoln | 87 | 27 | 60 |
| Linn | 188 | 81 | 107 |
| Malheur | 51 | 20 | 31 |
| Morrow | 18 | 18 | 0 |
| Sherman | 8 | 6 | 2 |
| Tillamook | 60 | 56 | 4 |
| Umatilla | 74 | 49 | 25 |
| Union | 11 | 9 | 2 |
| Wallowa | 12 | 6 | 6 |
| Wasco | 29 | 14 | 15 |
| Wheeler | 14 | 3 | 11 |
| **PENNSYLVANIA-Metropolitan Counties** | | | |
| Allegheny County Police Department | 261 | 203 | 58 |
| Beaver | 31 | 25 | 6 |
| Cumberland | 34 | 28 | 6 |
| Erie | 42 | 35 | 7 |
| Luzerne | 10 | 10 | 0 |
| Lycoming | 16 | 11 | 5 |
| Mercer | 16 | 13 | 3 |

**Table 80. Full-Time Law Enforcement Employees, by State and Metropolitan and Nonmetropolitan Counties, 2009**—*Continued*

(Number.)

| State/County | Total law enforcement employees | Total officers | Total civilians |
|---|---|---|---|
| Montgomery | 124 | 104 | 20 |
| Northampton | 56 | 52 | 4 |
| Pike | 21 | 17 | 4 |
| Washington | 32 | 28 | 4 |
| York | 114 | 104 | 10 |
| **PENNSYLVANIA-Nonmetropolitan Counties** | | | |
| Bradford | 11 | 9 | 2 |
| Clarion | 10 | 7 | 3 |
| Elk | 6 | 5 | 1 |
| Franklin | 19 | 15 | 4 |
| Greene | 7 | 6 | 1 |
| Jefferson | 4 | 3 | 1 |
| Snyder | 4 | 4 | 0 |
| Tioga | 7 | 5 | 2 |
| **SOUTH CAROLINA-Metropolitan Counties** | | | |
| Aiken | 234 | 128 | 106 |
| Anderson | 272 | 188 | 84 |
| Berkeley | 200 | 131 | 69 |
| Charleston | 712 | 251 | 461 |
| Darlington | 74 | 66 | 8 |
| Dorchester | 162 | 122 | 40 |
| Edgefield | 62 | 32 | 30 |
| Fairfield | 49 | 43 | 6 |
| Greenville | 500 | 403 | 97 |
| Horry | 294 | 222 | 72 |
| Kershaw | 73 | 61 | 12 |
| Laurens | 72 | 65 | 7 |
| Lexington | 397 | 254 | 143 |
| Pickens | 141 | 98 | 43 |
| Richland | 547 | 446 | 101 |
| Saluda | 54 | 21 | 33 |
| Spartanburg | 328 | 299 | 29 |
| Sumter | 127 | 117 | 10 |
| **SOUTH CAROLINA-Nonmetropolitan Counties** | | | |
| Abbeville | 55 | 29 | 26 |
| Allendale | 15 | 13 | 2 |
| Bamberg | 15 | 12 | 3 |
| Barnwell | 44 | 25 | 19 |
| Beaufort | 255 | 228 | 27 |
| Cherokee | 91 | 45 | 46 |
| Chester | 101 | 48 | 53 |
| Clarendon | 49 | 45 | 4 |
| Colleton | 72 | 62 | 10 |
| Dillon | 35 | 32 | 3 |
| Georgetown | 158 | 81 | 77 |
| Greenwood | 118 | 73 | 45 |
| Hampton | 32 | 29 | 3 |
| Jasper | 34 | 29 | 5 |
| Lancaster | 145 | 96 | 49 |
| Marion | 38 | 34 | 4 |
| Marlboro | 53 | 25 | 28 |
| McCormick | 35 | 13 | 22 |
| Newberry | 97 | 48 | 49 |
| Orangeburg | 125 | 93 | 32 |
| Union | 66 | 29 | 37 |
| **SOUTH DAKOTA-Metropolitan Counties** | | | |
| Lincoln | 17 | 15 | 2 |
| McCook | 7 | 6 | 1 |
| Meade | 52 | 17 | 35 |
| Minnehaha | 206 | 75 | 131 |
| Pennington | 100 | 65 | 35 |
| Turner | 10 | 8 | 2 |
| Union | 24 | 7 | 17 |
| **SOUTH DAKOTA-Nonmetropolitan Counties** | | | |
| Aurora | 4 | 3 | 1 |
| Beadle | 26 | 7 | 19 |
| Bennett | 4 | 3 | 1 |
| Bon Homme | 7 | 3 | 4 |
| Brookings | 19 | 11 | 8 |
| Brown | 49 | 15 | 34 |
| Brule | 9 | 4 | 5 |
| Buffalo | 1 | 1 | 0 |
| Butte | 12 | 4 | 8 |
| Campbell | 2 | 2 | 0 |
| Charles Mix | 12 | 5 | 7 |
| Clark | 4 | 4 | 0 |
| Clay | 10 | 7 | 3 |
| Codington | 24 | 8 | 16 |
| Corson | 3 | 2 | 1 |
| Custer | 14 | 12 | 2 |
| Davison | 8 | 6 | 2 |
| Day | 7 | 4 | 3 |
| Deuel | 8 | 4 | 4 |
| Dewey | 4 | 3 | 1 |
| Douglas | 2 | 2 | 0 |
| Edmunds | 7 | 4 | 3 |
| Fall River | 15 | 5 | 10 |
| Faulk | 9 | 3 | 6 |
| Grant | 8 | 3 | 5 |
| Gregory | 4 | 3 | 1 |
| Haakon | 2 | 2 | 0 |
| Hamlin | 4 | 4 | 0 |
| Hand | 3 | 2 | 1 |
| Hanson | 2 | 2 | 0 |
| Harding | 3 | 2 | 1 |
| Hughes | 8 | 6 | 2 |
| Hutchinson | 3 | 3 | 0 |
| Jackson | 2 | 2 | 0 |
| Jerauld | 4 | 3 | 1 |
| Jones | 2 | 2 | 0 |
| Kingsbury | 5 | 4 | 1 |
| Lake | 10 | 5 | 5 |
| Lawrence | 44 | 14 | 30 |
| Lyman | 5 | 4 | 1 |
| Marshall | 11 | 6 | 5 |
| McPherson | 1 | 1 | 0 |
| Mellette | 4 | 4 | 0 |
| Miner | 4 | 3 | 1 |
| Moody | 8 | 4 | 4 |
| Perkins | 4 | 3 | 1 |
| Potter | 3 | 2 | 1 |
| Roberts | 30 | 4 | 26 |
| Sanborn | 3 | 2 | 1 |
| Shannon | 1 | 1 | 0 |
| Spink | 13 | 8 | 5 |
| Stanley | 6 | 5 | 1 |
| Sully | 3 | 3 | 0 |
| Todd | 1 | 1 | 0 |
| Tripp | 7 | 6 | 1 |
| Walworth | 10 | 3 | 7 |
| Yankton | 12 | 10 | 2 |
| Ziebach | 2 | 2 | 0 |
| **TENNESSEE-Metropolitan Counties** | | | |
| Anderson | 148 | 64 | 84 |
| Blount | 175 | 140 | 35 |
| Bradley | 200 | 103 | 97 |
| Cannon | 35 | 12 | 23 |
| Carter | 88 | 46 | 42 |
| Cheatham | 65 | 31 | 34 |
| Chester | 33 | 12 | 21 |
| Dickson | 125 | 57 | 68 |
| Fayette | 85 | 38 | 47 |
| Grainger | 41 | 18 | 23 |
| Hamblen | 68 | 32 | 36 |
| Hamilton | 385 | 156 | 229 |
| Hartsville-Trousdale | 40 | 17 | 23 |
| Hawkins | 58 | 39 | 19 |
| Hickman | 44 | 27 | 17 |
| Jefferson | 83 | 42 | 41 |
| Knox | 1,008 | 386 | 622 |
| Loudon | 63 | 39 | 24 |
| Macon | 59 | 27 | 32 |
| Madison | 228 | 72 | 156 |
| Marion | 43 | 19 | 24 |
| Montgomery | 316 | 80 | 236 |
| Polk | 49 | 18 | 31 |
| Robertson | 155 | 50 | 105 |
| Rutherford | 404 | 192 | 212 |
| Sequatchie | 40 | 17 | 23 |
| Shelby | 1,894 | 520 | 1,374 |
| Smith | 29 | 20 | 9 |
| Stewart | 41 | 18 | 23 |

**Table 80. Full-Time Law Enforcement Employees, by State and Metropolitan and Nonmetropolitan Counties, 2009**—*Continued*

(Number.)

| State/County | Total law enforcement employees | Total officers | Total civilians |
|---|---|---|---|
| Sullivan | 251 | 100 | 151 |
| Sumner | 241 | 69 | 172 |
| Tipton | 80 | 43 | 37 |
| Unicoi | 39 | 22 | 17 |
| Union | 37 | 22 | 15 |
| Washington | 197 | 80 | 117 |
| Williamson | 208 | 110 | 98 |
| Wilson | 222 | 88 | 134 |
| **TENNESSEE-Nonmetropolitan Counties** | | | |
| Bedford | 106 | 36 | 70 |
| Benton | 46 | 21 | 25 |
| Bledsoe | 21 | 8 | 13 |
| Campbell | 76 | 50 | 26 |
| Carroll | 47 | 24 | 23 |
| Claiborne | 85 | 29 | 56 |
| Clay | 18 | 10 | 8 |
| Cocke | 60 | 30 | 30 |
| Coffee | 69 | 39 | 30 |
| Crockett | 33 | 14 | 19 |
| Cumberland | 88 | 45 | 43 |
| Decatur | 33 | 14 | 19 |
| DeKalb | 37 | 16 | 21 |
| Dyer | 69 | 28 | 41 |
| Fentress | 26 | 15 | 11 |
| Franklin | 62 | 34 | 28 |
| Gibson | 73 | 32 | 41 |
| Giles | 62 | 29 | 33 |
| Greene | 153 | 59 | 94 |
| Grundy | 23 | 14 | 9 |
| Hancock | 32 | 14 | 18 |
| Hardeman | 39 | 19 | 20 |
| Hardin | 50 | 19 | 31 |
| Haywood | 45 | 18 | 27 |
| Henderson | 35 | 24 | 11 |
| Henry | 68 | 34 | 34 |
| Houston | 23 | 11 | 12 |
| Humphreys | 34 | 18 | 16 |
| Jackson | 44 | 11 | 33 |
| Johnson | 38 | 15 | 23 |
| Lake | 18 | 8 | 10 |
| Lauderdale | 59 | 20 | 39 |
| Lawrence | 81 | 43 | 38 |
| Lewis | 29 | 14 | 15 |
| Lincoln | 61 | 26 | 35 |
| Marshall | 50 | 23 | 27 |
| Maury | 144 | 82 | 62 |
| McMinn | 68 | 32 | 36 |
| McNairy | 35 | 14 | 21 |
| Meigs | 28 | 12 | 16 |
| Monroe | 64 | 35 | 29 |
| Moore | 26 | 13 | 13 |
| Morgan | 40 | 15 | 25 |
| Obion | 60 | 22 | 38 |
| Overton | 56 | 23 | 33 |
| Perry | 34 | 13 | 21 |
| Pickett | 17 | 11 | 6 |
| Putnam | 123 | 57 | 66 |
| Rhea | 54 | 54 | 0 |
| Roane | 73 | 39 | 34 |
| Scott | 56 | 30 | 26 |
| Sevier | 116 | 93 | 23 |
| Van Buren | 18 | 18 | 0 |
| Warren | 79 | 39 | 40 |
| Wayne | 32 | 16 | 16 |
| Weakley | 42 | 21 | 21 |
| White | 64 | 31 | 33 |
| **TEXAS-Metropolitan Counties** | | | |
| Aransas | 71 | 26 | 45 |
| Archer | 12 | 8 | 4 |
| Armstrong | 6 | 2 | 4 |
| Atascosa | 74 | 31 | 43 |
| Austin | 60 | 37 | 23 |
| Bandera | 60 | 28 | 32 |
| Bastrop | 205 | 70 | 135 |
| Bell | 260 | 85 | 175 |
| Bexar | 1,790 | 537 | 1,253 |
| Bowie | 45 | 40 | 5 |
| Brazoria | 341 | 162 | 179 |
| Brazos | 231 | 96 | 135 |
| Burleson | 33 | 13 | 20 |
| Caldwell | 104 | 25 | 79 |
| Calhoun | 67 | 25 | 42 |
| Callahan | 13 | 5 | 8 |
| Cameron | 384 | 108 | 276 |
| Carson | 13 | 5 | 8 |
| Chambers | 80 | 38 | 42 |
| Clay | 19 | 10 | 9 |
| Collin | 482 | 149 | 333 |
| Comal | 245 | 118 | 127 |
| Coryell | 66 | 27 | 39 |
| Crosby | 19 | 5 | 14 |
| Dallas | 2,128 | 446 | 1,682 |
| Delta | 20 | 10 | 10 |
| Denton | 568 | 219 | 349 |
| Ector | 210 | 96 | 114 |
| Ellis | 216 | 76 | 140 |
| El Paso | 1,044 | 242 | 802 |
| Fort Bend | 741 | 491 | 250 |
| Galveston | 410 | 232 | 178 |
| Goliad | 26 | 13 | 13 |
| Grayson | 135 | 59 | 76 |
| Gregg | 248 | 96 | 152 |
| Guadalupe | 213 | 82 | 131 |
| Hardin | 69 | 32 | 37 |
| Harris | 4,038 | 2,370 | 1,668 |
| Hays | 281 | 130 | 151 |
| Hidalgo | 728 | 260 | 468 |
| Hunt | 126 | 50 | 76 |
| Irion | 9 | 4 | 5 |
| Jefferson | 399 | 112 | 287 |
| Johnson | 128 | 81 | 47 |
| Jones | 24 | 9 | 15 |
| Kaufman | 262 | 87 | 175 |
| Kendall | 70 | 50 | 20 |
| Lampasas | 34 | 18 | 16 |
| Liberty | 65 | 46 | 19 |
| Lubbock | 387 | 139 | 248 |
| McLennan | 307 | 110 | 197 |
| Medina | 65 | 24 | 41 |
| Midland | 181 | 74 | 107 |
| Montgomery | 613 | 346 | 267 |
| Nueces | 309 | 89 | 220 |
| Orange | 140 | 64 | 76 |
| Parker | 117 | 85 | 32 |
| Potter | 196 | 91 | 105 |
| Randall | 161 | 79 | 82 |
| Robertson | 33 | 13 | 20 |
| Rockwall | 115 | 37 | 78 |
| Rusk | 73 | 42 | 31 |
| San Jacinto | 60 | 28 | 32 |
| San Patricio | 108 | 47 | 61 |
| Smith | 321 | 162 | 159 |
| Tarrant | 1,375 | 1,240 | 135 |
| Taylor | 197 | 83 | 114 |
| Tom Green | 190 | 74 | 116 |
| Travis | 1,497 | 695 | 802 |
| Upshur | 78 | 48 | 30 |
| Victoria | 187 | 102 | 85 |
| Waller | 69 | 38 | 31 |
| Webb | 294 | 166 | 128 |
| Wichita | 187 | 39 | 148 |
| Williamson | 483 | 212 | 271 |
| Wilson | 70 | 26 | 44 |
| Wise | 132 | 54 | 78 |
| **TEXAS-Nonmetropolitan Counties** | | | |
| Anderson | 83 | 36 | 47 |
| Andrews | 32 | 12 | 20 |
| Angelina | 116 | 56 | 60 |
| Bailey | 24 | 5 | 19 |
| Baylor | 8 | 3 | 5 |

**Table 80. Full-Time Law Enforcement Employees, by State and Metropolitan and Nonmetropolitan Counties, 2009***—Continued*

(Number.)

| State/County | Total law enforcement employees | Total officers | Total civilians |
|---|---|---|---|
| Bee | 46 | 19 | 27 |
| Blanco | 18 | 10 | 8 |
| Borden | 3 | 2 | 1 |
| Bosque | 35 | 16 | 19 |
| Brewster | 29 | 15 | 14 |
| Briscoe | 2 | 1 | 1 |
| Brooks | 34 | 13 | 21 |
| Brown | 66 | 26 | 40 |
| Burnet | 58 | 43 | 15 |
| Camp | 18 | 7 | 11 |
| Cass | 45 | 19 | 26 |
| Castro | 18 | 7 | 11 |
| Cherokee | 74 | 32 | 42 |
| Childress | 22 | 4 | 18 |
| Cochran | 14 | 8 | 6 |
| Coke | 6 | 5 | 1 |
| Coleman | 12 | 6 | 6 |
| Collingsworth | 9 | 5 | 4 |
| Colorado | 45 | 18 | 27 |
| Comanche | 28 | 10 | 18 |
| Concho | 9 | 5 | 4 |
| Cooke | 74 | 22 | 52 |
| Cottle | 2 | 2 | 0 |
| Crane | 11 | 6 | 5 |
| Crockett | 14 | 8 | 6 |
| Culberson | 11 | 5 | 6 |
| Dallam | 25 | 5 | 20 |
| Dawson | 19 | 7 | 12 |
| Deaf Smith | 30 | 10 | 20 |
| Dewitt | 41 | 11 | 30 |
| Dickens | 6 | 2 | 4 |
| Dimmit | 39 | 14 | 25 |
| Donley | 10 | 6 | 4 |
| Eastland | 26 | 9 | 17 |
| Edwards | 10 | 4 | 6 |
| Erath | 55 | 23 | 32 |
| Falls | 8 | 3 | 5 |
| Fayette | 43 | 21 | 22 |
| Fisher | 8 | 5 | 3 |
| Floyd | 7 | 3 | 4 |
| Foard | 3 | 2 | 1 |
| Franklin | 19 | 9 | 10 |
| Freestone | 40 | 16 | 24 |
| Frio | 21 | 11 | 10 |
| Gaines | 26 | 12 | 14 |
| Garza | 31 | 9 | 22 |
| Gillespie | 39 | 24 | 15 |
| Glasscock | 4 | 3 | 1 |
| Gonzales | 47 | 15 | 32 |
| Gray | 39 | 14 | 25 |
| Grimes | 52 | 25 | 27 |
| Hale | 70 | 23 | 47 |
| Hall | 9 | 3 | 6 |
| Hamilton | 23 | 13 | 10 |
| Hansford | 9 | 4 | 5 |
| Hardeman | 13 | 7 | 6 |
| Harrison | 92 | 44 | 48 |
| Hartley | 5 | 5 | 0 |
| Haskell | 6 | 3 | 3 |
| Hemphill | 17 | 10 | 7 |
| Henderson | 158 | 77 | 81 |
| Hill | 74 | 30 | 44 |
| Hockley | 25 | 15 | 10 |
| Hood | 128 | 45 | 83 |
| Hopkins | 52 | 25 | 27 |
| Houston | 38 | 18 | 20 |
| Howard | 42 | 14 | 28 |
| Hudspeth | 38 | 17 | 21 |
| Hutchinson | 35 | 12 | 23 |
| Jack | 37 | 11 | 26 |
| Jackson | 33 | 15 | 18 |
| Jasper | 47 | 18 | 29 |
| Jeff Davis | 3 | 3 | 0 |
| Jim Hogg | 33 | 20 | 13 |
| Jim Wells | 65 | 27 | 38 |
| Karnes | 18 | 9 | 9 |
| Kenedy | 18 | 11 | 7 |
| Kent | 10 | 3 | 7 |
| Kerr | 96 | 45 | 51 |
| Kimble | 14 | 9 | 5 |
| King | 2 | 2 | 0 |
| Kinney | 14 | 6 | 8 |
| Kleberg | 70 | 22 | 48 |
| Knox | 9 | 3 | 6 |
| Lamar | 78 | 27 | 51 |
| Lamb | 31 | 14 | 17 |
| La Salle | 30 | 14 | 16 |
| Lavaca | 29 | 12 | 17 |
| Lee | 34 | 12 | 22 |
| Leon | 40 | 24 | 16 |
| Limestone | 58 | 21 | 37 |
| Lipscomb | 13 | 7 | 6 |
| Live Oak | 40 | 12 | 28 |
| Llano | 50 | 24 | 26 |
| Loving | 4 | 3 | 1 |
| Lynn | 21 | 7 | 14 |
| Madison | 22 | 9 | 13 |
| Marion | 15 | 14 | 1 |
| Martin | 8 | 4 | 4 |
| Mason | 8 | 4 | 4 |
| Matagorda | 70 | 35 | 35 |
| McCulloch | 13 | 6 | 7 |
| McMullen | 5 | 4 | 1 |
| Menard | 9 | 5 | 4 |
| Milam | 50 | 16 | 34 |
| Mills | 9 | 6 | 3 |
| Mitchell | 11 | 5 | 6 |
| Montague | 32 | 12 | 20 |
| Moore | 48 | 17 | 31 |
| Morris | 22 | 9 | 13 |
| Motley | 2 | 2 | 0 |
| Nacogdoches | 103 | 49 | 54 |
| Navarro | 124 | 59 | 65 |
| Newton | 23 | 12 | 11 |
| Nolan | 30 | 11 | 19 |
| Ochiltree | 19 | 8 | 11 |
| Oldham | 11 | 6 | 5 |
| Palo Pinto | 55 | 23 | 32 |
| Panola | 57 | 21 | 36 |
| Parmer | 19 | 6 | 13 |
| Pecos | 31 | 17 | 14 |
| Polk | 96 | 51 | 45 |
| Presidio | 11 | 5 | 6 |
| Rains | 22 | 11 | 11 |
| Reagan | 20 | 8 | 12 |
| Real | 8 | 3 | 5 |
| Red River | 29 | 13 | 16 |
| Reeves | 465 | 20 | 445 |
| Refugio | 43 | 15 | 28 |
| Roberts | 6 | 5 | 1 |
| Runnels | 25 | 7 | 18 |
| Sabine | 17 | 7 | 10 |
| San Augustine | 16 | 6 | 10 |
| San Saba | 10 | 5 | 5 |
| Schleicher | 11 | 5 | 6 |
| Scurry | 25 | 11 | 14 |
| Shackelford | 15 | 5 | 10 |
| Shelby | 30 | 15 | 15 |
| Sherman | 10 | 5 | 5 |
| Somervell | 41 | 20 | 21 |
| Starr | 95 | 42 | 53 |
| Stephens | 15 | 7 | 8 |
| Sterling | 4 | 4 | 0 |
| Stonewall | 7 | 2 | 5 |
| Sutton | 13 | 4 | 9 |
| Swisher | 10 | 4 | 6 |
| Terrell | 14 | 7 | 7 |
| Terry | 41 | 10 | 31 |
| Throckmorton | 6 | 2 | 4 |
| Titus | 61 | 23 | 38 |
| Trinity | 17 | 11 | 6 |
| Tyler | 31 | 16 | 15 |

**Table 80. Full-Time Law Enforcement Employees, by State and Metropolitan and Nonmetropolitan Counties, 2009**—*Continued*

(Number.)

| State/County | Total law enforcement employees | Total officers | Total civilians |
|---|---|---|---|
| Upton | 24 | 11 | 13 |
| Uvalde | 37 | 17 | 20 |
| Val Verde | 52 | 35 | 17 |
| Van Zandt | 68 | 27 | 41 |
| Walker | 68 | 33 | 35 |
| Ward | 30 | 14 | 16 |
| Washington | 58 | 32 | 26 |
| Wharton | 70 | 46 | 24 |
| Wheeler | 11 | 6 | 5 |
| Wilbarger | 18 | 7 | 11 |
| Willacy | 41 | 14 | 27 |
| Winkler | 28 | 10 | 18 |
| Wood | 64 | 26 | 38 |
| Yoakum | 21 | 8 | 13 |
| Young | 35 | 13 | 22 |
| Zapata | 114 | 48 | 66 |
| Zavala | 30 | 11 | 19 |
| **UTAH-Metropolitan Counties** | | | |
| Cache | 145 | 112 | 33 |
| Davis | 353 | 95 | 258 |
| Juab | 22 | 9 | 13 |
| Morgan | 13 | 11 | 2 |
| Salt Lake | 1,263 | 324 | 939 |
| Summit | 104 | 53 | 51 |
| Tooele | 92 | 36 | 56 |
| Utah | 363 | 146 | 217 |
| Washington | 152 | 43 | 109 |
| Weber | 91 | 89 | 2 |
| **UTAH-Nonmetropolitan Counties** | | | |
| Beaver | 78 | 22 | 56 |
| Box Elder | 88 | 74 | 14 |
| Carbon | 45 | 20 | 25 |
| Daggett | 6 | 5 | 1 |
| Duchesne | 52 | 16 | 36 |
| Emery | 43 | 25 | 18 |
| Garfield | 27 | 6 | 21 |
| Grand | 34 | 19 | 15 |
| Iron | 77 | 39 | 38 |
| Kane | 26 | 18 | 8 |
| Millard | 50 | 25 | 25 |
| Piute | 3 | 3 | 0 |
| Rich | 10 | 5 | 5 |
| San Juan | 37 | 16 | 21 |
| Sanpete | 54 | 37 | 17 |
| Sevier | 67 | 35 | 32 |
| Uintah | 63 | 52 | 11 |
| Wasatch | 42 | 19 | 23 |
| Wayne | 6 | 6 | 0 |
| **VERMONT-Metropolitan Counties** | | | |
| Chittenden | 20 | 16 | 4 |
| Franklin | 19 | 15 | 4 |
| **VERMONT-Nonmetropolitan Counties** | | | |
| Addison | 10 | 7 | 3 |
| Bennington | 14 | 11 | 3 |
| Caledonia | 5 | 4 | 1 |
| Essex | 2 | 1 | 1 |
| Lamoille | 23 | 11 | 12 |
| Orange | 4 | 4 | 0 |
| Orleans | 10 | 8 | 2 |
| Rutland | 20 | 17 | 3 |
| Washington | 13 | 11 | 2 |
| Windham | 15 | 11 | 4 |
| Windsor | 14 | 11 | 3 |
| **VIRGINIA-Metropolitan Counties** | | | |
| Albemarle County Police Department | 146 | 118 | 28 |
| Amelia | 22 | 14 | 8 |
| Amherst | 68 | 63 | 5 |
| Appomattox | 33 | 30 | 3 |
| Arlington County Police Department | 436 | 355 | 81 |
| Bedford | 86 | 84 | 2 |
| Botetourt | 117 | 95 | 22 |
| Campbell | 65 | 57 | 8 |
| Caroline | 68 | 48 | 20 |
| Charles City | 17 | 10 | 7 |
| Chesterfield County Police Department | 580 | 478 | 102 |
| Clarke | 29 | 17 | 12 |
| Craig | 13 | 8 | 5 |
| Cumberland | 22 | 15 | 7 |
| Dinwiddie | 43 | 39 | 4 |
| Fairfax County Police Department | 1,786 | 1,422 | 364 |
| Fauquier | 124 | 108 | 16 |
| Fluvanna | 37 | 27 | 10 |
| Franklin | 92 | 72 | 20 |
| Frederick | 118 | 104 | 14 |
| Giles | 35 | 25 | 10 |
| Gloucester | 94 | 78 | 16 |
| Goochland | 41 | 32 | 9 |
| Greene | 33 | 25 | 8 |
| Hanover | 228 | 210 | 18 |
| Henrico County Police Department | 766 | 585 | 181 |
| Isle of Wight | 49 | 42 | 7 |
| James City County Police Department | 98 | 93 | 5 |
| King and Queen | 20 | 12 | 8 |
| King William | 33 | 21 | 12 |
| Loudoun | 580 | 478 | 102 |
| Louisa | 56 | 48 | 8 |
| Mathews | 19 | 12 | 7 |
| Montgomery | 119 | 104 | 15 |
| Nelson | 17 | 16 | 1 |
| New Kent | 39 | 28 | 11 |
| Pittsylvania | 132 | 114 | 18 |
| Powhatan | 57 | 41 | 16 |
| Prince George County Police Department | 76 | 57 | 19 |
| Prince William County Police Department | 680 | 548 | 132 |
| Pulaski | 51 | 41 | 10 |
| Roanoke County Police Department | 140 | 128 | 12 |
| Rockingham | 66 | 51 | 15 |
| Scott | 35 | 26 | 9 |
| Spotsylvania | 205 | 156 | 49 |
| Stafford | 219 | 156 | 63 |
| Surry | 22 | 13 | 9 |
| Sussex | 44 | 39 | 5 |
| Warren | 92 | 46 | 46 |
| Washington | 69 | 52 | 17 |
| York | 111 | 104 | 7 |
| **VIRGINIA-Nonmetropolitan Counties** | | | |
| Accomack | 67 | 56 | 11 |
| Alleghany | 57 | 41 | 16 |
| Augusta | 75 | 64 | 11 |
| Bath | 17 | 11 | 6 |
| Bland | 17 | 11 | 6 |
| Brunswick | 52 | 39 | 13 |
| Buchanan | 43 | 31 | 12 |
| Buckingham | 24 | 17 | 7 |
| Carroll | 36 | 30 | 6 |
| Charlotte | 35 | 32 | 3 |
| Culpeper | 92 | 77 | 15 |
| Dickenson | 31 | 24 | 7 |
| Essex | 20 | 20 | 0 |
| Floyd | 26 | 19 | 7 |
| Grayson | 28 | 22 | 6 |
| Greensville | 33 | 22 | 11 |
| Halifax | 42 | 34 | 8 |
| Henry | 124 | 111 | 13 |
| Highland | 12 | 7 | 5 |
| King George | 44 | 30 | 14 |
| Lancaster | 36 | 30 | 6 |
| Lee | 37 | 37 | 0 |
| Lunenburg | 20 | 14 | 6 |
| Madison | 32 | 19 | 13 |
| Mecklenburg | 53 | 50 | 3 |
| Middlesex | 23 | 17 | 6 |
| Northampton | 83 | 65 | 18 |
| Northumberland | 28 | 17 | 11 |
| Nottoway | 25 | 14 | 11 |
| Orange | 47 | 37 | 10 |
| Page | 65 | 55 | 10 |
| Patrick | 50 | 36 | 14 |
| Prince Edward | 29 | 29 | 0 |
| Rappahannock | 24 | 24 | 0 |

## Table 80. Full-Time Law Enforcement Employees, by State and Metropolitan and Nonmetropolitan Counties, 2009—*Continued*

(Number.)

| State/County | Total law enforcement employees | Total officers | Total civilians |
|---|---|---|---|
| Richmond | 20 | 12 | 8 |
| Rockbridge | 38 | 29 | 9 |
| Russell | 51 | 34 | 17 |
| Shenandoah | 76 | 68 | 8 |
| Smyth | 47 | 47 | 0 |
| Southampton | 41 | 30 | 11 |
| Tazewell | 48 | 40 | 8 |
| Westmoreland | 31 | 21 | 10 |
| Wise | 60 | 46 | 14 |
| Wythe | 47 | 40 | 7 |
| **WASHINGTON-Metropolitan Counties** | | | |
| Asotin | 15 | 13 | 2 |
| Benton | 67 | 56 | 11 |
| Chelan | 63 | 52 | 11 |
| Clark | 241 | 144 | 97 |
| Cowlitz | 49 | 40 | 9 |
| Douglas | 33 | 26 | 7 |
| Franklin | 29 | 27 | 2 |
| King | 779 | 463 | 316 |
| Kitsap | 151 | 120 | 31 |
| Pierce | 380 | 318 | 62 |
| Skagit | 109 | 56 | 53 |
| Skamania | 27 | 23 | 4 |
| Snohomish | 357 | 281 | 76 |
| Spokane | 197 | 141 | 56 |
| Thurston | 108 | 87 | 21 |
| Whatcom | 101 | 84 | 17 |
| Yakima | 100 | 64 | 36 |
| **WASHINGTON-Nonmetropolitan Counties** | | | |
| Adams | 28 | 17 | 11 |
| Clallam | 45 | 35 | 10 |
| Columbia | 14 | 9 | 5 |
| Ferry | 22 | 7 | 15 |
| Garfield | 16 | 8 | 8 |
| Grant | 63 | 48 | 15 |
| Grays Harbor | 79 | 41 | 38 |
| Island | 67 | 40 | 27 |
| Jefferson | 44 | 22 | 22 |
| Kittitas | 68 | 36 | 32 |
| Klickitat | 49 | 19 | 30 |
| Lewis | 60 | 42 | 18 |
| Lincoln | 27 | 16 | 11 |
| Mason | 64 | 48 | 16 |
| Okanogan | 34 | 29 | 5 |
| Pacific | 24 | 20 | 4 |
| Pend Oreille | 22 | 18 | 4 |
| San Juan | 31 | 20 | 11 |
| Stevens | 32 | 27 | 5 |
| Wahkiakum | 16 | 7 | 9 |
| Walla Walla | 33 | 27 | 6 |
| Whitman | 21 | 19 | 2 |
| **WEST VIRGINIA-Metropolitan Counties** | | | |
| Berkeley | 78 | 54 | 24 |
| Boone | 26 | 23 | 3 |
| Brooke | 28 | 17 | 11 |
| Cabell | 53 | 41 | 12 |
| Clay | 11 | 6 | 5 |
| Hampshire | 18 | 16 | 2 |
| Hancock | 37 | 26 | 11 |
| Jefferson | 33 | 25 | 8 |
| Kanawha | 131 | 100 | 31 |
| Lincoln | 8 | 8 | 0 |
| Marshall | 27 | 24 | 3 |
| Mineral | 14 | 12 | 2 |
| Monongalia | 57 | 35 | 22 |
| Morgan | 12 | 11 | 1 |
| Ohio | 30 | 28 | 2 |
| Pleasants | 7 | 6 | 1 |
| Preston | 24 | 16 | 8 |
| Putnum | 49 | 38 | 11 |
| Wayne | 27 | 22 | 5 |
| Wirt | 2 | 2 | 0 |
| Wood | 72 | 38 | 34 |
| **WEST VIRGINIA-Nonmetropolitan Counties** | | | |
| Barbour | 10 | 6 | 4 |
| Braxton | 11 | 10 | 1 |

| State/County | Total law enforcement employees | Total officers | Total civilians |
|---|---|---|---|
| Calhoun | 7 | 4 | 3 |
| Doddridge | 9 | 6 | 3 |
| Fayette | 37 | 32 | 5 |
| Gilmer | 8 | 5 | 3 |
| Grant | 11 | 8 | 3 |
| Greenbrier | 34 | 29 | 5 |
| Hardy | 8 | 7 | 1 |
| Harrison | 45 | 43 | 2 |
| Jackson | 28 | 15 | 13 |
| Lewis | 16 | 13 | 3 |
| Logan | 40 | 20 | 20 |
| Marion | 41 | 31 | 10 |
| Mason | 24 | 18 | 6 |
| McDowell | 17 | 15 | 2 |
| Mercer | 31 | 27 | 4 |
| Mingo | 22 | 19 | 3 |
| Monroe | 7 | 7 | 0 |
| Nicholas | 27 | 23 | 4 |
| Pendleton | 4 | 4 | 0 |
| Pocahontas | 13 | 8 | 5 |
| Raleigh | 62 | 45 | 17 |
| Randolph | 9 | 9 | 0 |
| Ritchie | 10 | 8 | 2 |
| Roane | 7 | 6 | 1 |
| Summers | 9 | 6 | 3 |
| Taylor | 15 | 7 | 8 |
| Tucker | 4 | 4 | 0 |
| Tyler | 7 | 6 | 1 |
| Upshur | 13 | 11 | 2 |
| Webster | 9 | 6 | 3 |
| Wetzel | 15 | 10 | 5 |
| Wyoming | 24 | 19 | 5 |
| **WISCONSIN-Metropolitan Counties** | | | |
| Brown | 315 | 149 | 166 |
| Calumet | 48 | 22 | 26 |
| Chippewa | 69 | 55 | 14 |
| Columbia | 97 | 40 | 57 |
| Dane | 554 | 452 | 102 |
| Douglas | 94 | 37 | 57 |
| Eau Claire | 90 | 42 | 48 |
| Fond du Lac | 120 | 57 | 63 |
| Iowa | 21 | 19 | 2 |
| Kenosha | 323 | 107 | 216 |
| Kewaunee | 37 | 35 | 2 |
| La Crosse | 108 | 41 | 67 |
| Marathon | 176 | 67 | 109 |
| Milwaukee | 1,433 | 449 | 984 |
| Oconto | 57 | 26 | 31 |
| Outagamie | 200 | 76 | 124 |
| Ozaukee | 102 | 79 | 23 |
| Pierce | 48 | 44 | 4 |
| Racine | 236 | 141 | 95 |
| Rock | 199 | 93 | 106 |
| Sheboygan | 177 | 77 | 100 |
| St. Croix | 85 | 77 | 8 |
| Washington | 173 | 71 | 102 |
| Waukesha | 324 | 147 | 177 |
| Winnebago | 190 | 129 | 61 |
| **WISCONSIN-Nonmetropolitan Counties** | | | |
| Adams | 61 | 29 | 32 |
| Ashland | 35 | 18 | 17 |
| Barron | 71 | 35 | 36 |
| Bayfield | 41 | 19 | 22 |
| Buffalo | 22 | 11 | 11 |
| Burnett | 33 | 17 | 16 |
| Clark | 50 | 46 | 4 |
| Crawford | 31 | 30 | 1 |
| Dodge | 173 | 75 | 98 |
| Door | 66 | 51 | 15 |
| Dunn | 56 | 25 | 31 |
| Florence | 12 | 12 | 0 |
| Forest | 38 | 18 | 20 |
| Grant | 47 | 26 | 21 |
| Green | 53 | 36 | 17 |
| Green Lake | 31 | 17 | 14 |
| Iron | 19 | 10 | 9 |

**Table 80. Full-Time Law Enforcement Employees, by State and Metropolitan and Nonmetropolitan Counties, 2009**—*Continued*

(Number.)

| State/County | Total law enforcement employees | Total officers | Total civilians |
|---|---|---|---|
| Jackson | 44 | 20 | 24 |
| Jefferson | 123 | 97 | 26 |
| Juneau | 57 | 43 | 14 |
| Lafayette | 27 | 15 | 12 |
| Langlade | 35 | 16 | 19 |
| Lincoln | 61 | 28 | 33 |
| Manitowoc | 96 | 58 | 38 |
| Marinette | 58 | 29 | 29 |
| Marquette | 37 | 18 | 19 |
| Menominee | 12 | 11 | 1 |
| Monroe | 55 | 23 | 32 |
| Oneida | 87 | 38 | 49 |
| Pepin | 18 | 7 | 11 |
| Polk | 75 | 29 | 46 |
| Portage | 91 | 46 | 45 |
| Price | 31 | 19 | 12 |
| Richland | 30 | 17 | 13 |
| Rusk | 30 | 16 | 14 |
| Sauk | 166 | 127 | 39 |
| Sawyer | 41 | 28 | 13 |
| Shawano | 110 | 39 | 71 |
| Taylor | 41 | 19 | 22 |
| Trempealeau | 52 | 25 | 27 |
| Vernon | 44 | 26 | 18 |
| Vilas | 71 | 35 | 36 |
| Walworth | 208 | 82 | 126 |
| Washburn | 32 | 15 | 17 |
| Waupaca | 97 | 36 | 61 |
| Waushara | 64 | 24 | 40 |
| Wood | 74 | 43 | 31 |
| **WYOMING-Metropolitan Counties** | | | |
| Laramie | 66 | 50 | 16 |
| Natrona | 59 | 47 | 12 |
| **WYOMING-Nonmetropolitan Counties** | | | |
| Albany | 22 | 21 | 1 |
| Big Horn | 13 | 11 | 2 |
| Campbell | 60 | 45 | 15 |
| Carbon | 29 | 17 | 12 |
| Converse | 21 | 12 | 9 |
| Crook | 21 | 9 | 12 |
| Fremont | 40 | 36 | 4 |
| Goshen | 13 | 11 | 2 |
| Hot Springs | 10 | 8 | 2 |
| Johnson | 13 | 12 | 1 |
| Lincoln | 48 | 35 | 13 |
| Niobrara | 17 | 5 | 12 |
| Park | 30 | 20 | 10 |
| Platte | 11 | 9 | 2 |
| Sheridan | 28 | 21 | 7 |
| Sublette | 40 | 35 | 5 |
| Sweetwater | 51 | 43 | 8 |
| Teton | 37 | 21 | 16 |
| Uinta | 36 | 22 | 14 |
| Washakie | 10 | 9 | 1 |
| Weston | 8 | 8 | 0 |

## Table 81. Full-Time Law Enforcement Employees, by State and Agency, 2009

(Number.)

| State, agency, unit/office | Total law enforcement employees | Total officers | Total civilians |
|---|---|---|---|
| **ALABAMA—State Agencies** | | | |
| Alabama Alcoholic Beverage Control Board | 149 | 126 | 23 |
| Alabama Conservation Department Marine Police | 74 | 60 | 14 |
| Alabama Department of Mental Health | 5 | 4 | 1 |
| Alabama Public Service Commission Enforcement Division | 9 | 8 | 1 |
| State Capitol Police | 31 | 23 | 8 |
| **ALABAMA—Tribal Agencies** | | | |
| Poarch Creek Tribal | 42 | 40 | 2 |
| **ALABAMA—Other Agencies** | | | |
| 24th Judicial Circuit Drug and Violent Crime Task Force | 5 | 4 | 1 |
| Huntsville International Airport | 20 | 19 | 1 |
| Marshall County Drug Enforcement Unit | 7 | 5 | 2 |
| **ALASKA—Other Agencies** | | | |
| Anchorage International Airport | 61 | 59 | 2 |
| Fairbanks International Airport | 32 | 25 | 7 |
| **ARIZONA—State Agencies** | | | |
| Arizona State Capitol | 62 | 31 | 31 |
| **ARIZONA—Tribal Agencies** | | | |
| Fort McDowell Tribal | 28 | 22 | 6 |
| Fort Mojave Tribal | 50 | 21 | 29 |
| Hualapai Tribal | 14 | 13 | 1 |
| Quechan Tribal | 12 | 8 | 4 |
| Yavapai Apache Tribal | 19 | 16 | 3 |
| Yavapai-Prescott Tribal | 11 | 8 | 3 |
| **ARIZONA—Other Agencies** | | | |
| Tucson Airport Authority | 47 | 21 | 26 |
| **ARKANSAS—State Agencies** | | | |
| Camp Robinson | 12 | 11 | 1 |
| State Capitol Police | 22 | 19 | 3 |
| **CALIFORNIA—State Agencies** | | | |
| Atascadero State Hospital | 133 | 118 | 15 |
| California State Fair | 8 | 3 | 5 |
| Coalinga State Hospital | 229 | 217 | 12 |
| Department of Parks and Recreation | | | |
| Capital | 606 | 606 | 0 |
| Napa State Hospital | 94 | 91 | 3 |
| Patton State Hospital | 47 | 40 | 7 |
| **CALIFORNIA—Other Agencies** | | | |
| East Bay Regional Parks | | | |
| Alameda County | 80 | 57 | 23 |
| Fontana Unified School District | 75 | 14 | 61 |
| Monterey Peninsula Airport | 6 | 6 | 0 |
| Port of San Diego Harbor | 162 | 136 | 26 |
| San Bernardino Unified School District | 82 | 25 | 57 |
| San Francisco Bay Area Rapid Transit | | | |
| Contra Costa County | 260 | 184 | 76 |
| Stockton Unified School District | 26 | 19 | 7 |
| Twin Rivers Unified School District | 27 | 21 | 6 |
| **COLORADO—State Agencies** | | | |
| Colorado Bureau of Investigation | 200 | 90 | 110 |
| Colorado Mental Health Institute | 77 | 18 | 59 |
| **COLORADO—Tribal Agencies** | | | |
| Southern Ute Tribal | 41 | 21 | 20 |
| **COLORADO—Other Agencies** | | | |
| 22nd Judicial District Drug Task Force | 2 | 1 | 1 |
| Southwest Drug Task Force | 7 | 6 | 1 |
| Two Rivers Drug Enforcement Team | 8 | 7 | 1 |
| **CONNECTICUT—State Agencies** | | | |
| State Capitol Police | 35 | 26 | 9 |
| **CONNECTICUT—Tribal Agencies** | | | |
| Mashantucket Pequot Tribal | 14 | 12 | 2 |
| Mohegan Tribal | 25 | 17 | 8 |
| **CONNECTICUT—Other Agencies** | | | |
| Metropolitan Transportation Authority | 768 | 695 | 73 |
| **DELAWARE—State Agencies** | | | |
| Attorney General: | | | |
| Kent County | 56 | 29 | 27 |
| New Castle County | 243 | 140 | 103 |
| Sussex County | 50 | 22 | 28 |
| Division of Alcohol and Tobacco Enforcement | 15 | 12 | 3 |
| Environmental Control | 14 | 12 | 2 |
| Fish and Wildlife | 29 | 24 | 5 |
| Park Rangers | 19 | 19 | 0 |
| River and Bay Authority | 65 | 48 | 17 |
| State Capitol Police | 65 | 41 | 24 |
| State Fire Marshal | 54 | 20 | 34 |

## Table 81. Full-Time Law Enforcement Employees, by State and Agency, 2009—*Continued*

(Number.)

| State, agency, unit/office | Total law enforcement employees | Total officers | Total civilians |
|---|---|---|---|
| **DELAWARE—Other Agencies** | | | |
| Amtrak Police | 12 | 12 | 0 |
| Drug Enforcement Administration | | | |
| Wilmington Resident Office | 8 | 5 | 3 |
| Wilmington Fire Department | 17 | 12 | 5 |
| **DISTRICT OF COLUMBIA—Other Agencies** | | | |
| Metro Transit Police | 576 | 421 | 155 |
| **FLORIDA—State Agencies** | | | |
| Capitol Police | 79 | 60 | 19 |
| Department of Environmental Protection, | | | |
| Division of Law Enforcement | | | |
| Leon County | 170 | 126 | 44 |
| Florida Game Commission | | | |
| Leon County | 870 | 692 | 178 |
| State Treasurer's Office | | | |
| Division of Insurance Fraud | 174 | 134 | 40 |
| **FLORIDA—Tribal Agencies** | | | |
| Miccosukee Tribal | 49 | 37 | 12 |
| Seminole Tribal | 219 | 148 | 71 |
| **FLORIDA—Other Agencies** | | | |
| Duval County Schools | 28 | 18 | 10 |
| Florida School for the Deaf and Blind | 18 | 10 | 8 |
| Jacksonville Airport Authority | 30 | 27 | 3 |
| Lee County Port Authority | 63 | 39 | 24 |
| Melbourne International Airport | 12 | 11 | 1 |
| Miami-Dade County Public Schools | 180 | 156 | 24 |
| Palm Beach County School District | 233 | 151 | 82 |
| Sarasota-Bradenton International Airport | 12 | 11 | 1 |
| Tampa International Airport | 129 | 59 | 70 |
| Volusia County Beach Management | 65 | 61 | 4 |
| **GEORGIA—State Agencies** | | | |
| Atlanta State Farmers Market | 15 | 14 | 1 |
| Department of Natural Resources | | | |
| Social Circle | 214 | 195 | 19 |
| Georgia Bureau of Investigation | | | |
| Headquarters | 854 | 151 | 703 |
| Georgia Department of Transportation | | | |
| Office of Investigations | 3 | 3 | 0 |
| Georgia World Congress | 54 | 24 | 30 |
| Ports Authority | | | |
| Savannah | 118 | 79 | 39 |
| **GEORGIA—Other Agencies** | | | |
| Atlanta Public Schools | 23 | 8 | 15 |
| Augusta Board of Education | 39 | 32 | 7 |
| Bibb County Board of Education | 30 | 25 | 5 |
| Chatham County Board of Education | 45 | 37 | 8 |
| Cherokee County Board of Education | 16 | 14 | 2 |
| Cobb County Board of Education | 42 | 39 | 3 |
| DeKalb County School System | 88 | 84 | 4 |
| Fulton County Marshal | 72 | 61 | 11 |
| Fulton County School System | 64 | 62 | 2 |
| Gwinnett County Public Schools | 26 | 22 | 4 |
| Habersham County Public Schools | 2 | 2 | 0 |
| Hartsfield-Jackson Atlanta International Airport | 145 | 126 | 19 |
| Macon County Schools | 4 | 4 | 0 |
| Metropolitan Atlanta Rapid Transit Authority | 351 | 305 | 46 |
| Muscogee City Marshal | 20 | 18 | 2 |
| Richmond County Marshal | 51 | 45 | 6 |
| Stone Mountain Park | 26 | 22 | 4 |
| Troup County Marshal | 8 | 7 | 1 |
| Twiggs County Board of Education | 1 | 1 | 0 |
| **IDAHO—Tribal Agencies** | | | |
| Coeur d'Alene Tribal | 17 | 15 | 2 |
| **ILLINOIS—State Agencies** | | | |
| Illinois Commerce Commission | 20 | 12 | 8 |
| Illinois Department of Natural Resources | 161 | 145 | 16 |
| Secretary of State Police | 256 | 139 | 117 |
| State Fire Marshal | 20 | 18 | 2 |
| **ILLINOIS—Other Agencies** | | | |
| Burlington Northern Santa Fe Railroad | 22 | 19 | 3 |
| Capitol Airport Authority | 6 | 6 | 0 |
| Chicago Fire Department | | | |
| Arson Investigations | 11 | 3 | 8 |
| Cook County Forest Preserve | 112 | 105 | 7 |
| Crystal Lake Park District | 3 | 3 | 0 |
| CSX Transportation | 18 | 18 | 0 |

**Table 81. Full-Time Law Enforcement Employees, by State and Agency, 2009—*Continued***

(Number.)

| State, agency, unit/office | Total law enforcement employees | Total officers | Total civilians |
|---|---|---|---|
| Decatur Park District | 5 | 5 | 0 |
| Du Page County Forest Preserve | 29 | 25 | 4 |
| Indian Harbor Belt Railroad | 13 | 12 | 1 |
| John H. Stroger Hospital | 56 | 51 | 5 |
| Kane County Forest Preserve | 6 | 6 | 0 |
| Lake County Forest Preserve | 20 | 17 | 3 |
| Norfolk Southern Railway | 45 | 44 | 1 |
| Pekin Park District | 1 | 1 | 0 |
| Rockford Park District | 19 | 18 | 1 |
| Springfield Park District | 7 | 7 | 0 |
| Will County Forest Preserve | 13 | 11 | 2 |
| **INDIANA—State Agencies** | | | |
| Indiana State Excise Police | 97 | 90 | 7 |
| Northern Indiana Commuter Transportation District | 9 | 8 | 1 |
| **INDIANA—Other Agencies** | | | |
| Indianapolis International Airport | 102 | 48 | 54 |
| St. Joseph County Airport Authority | 17 | 17 | 0 |
| **KANSAS—State Agencies** | | | |
| Kansas Alcoholic Beverage Control | 21 | 21 | 0 |
| Kansas Bureau of Investigation | 256 | 82 | 174 |
| Kansas Department of Wildlife and Parks | 178 | 176 | 2 |
| Kansas Lottery Security Division | 9 | 5 | 4 |
| Kansas Racing Commission Security Division | 35 | 14 | 21 |
| Securities Office Investigation Section | 30 | 7 | 23 |
| State Fire Marshal | 13 | 11 | 2 |
| **KANSAS—Tribal Agencies** | | | |
| Iowa Tribal | 8 | 8 | 0 |
| Kickapoo Tribal | 8 | 4 | 4 |
| Sac and Fox Tribal | 7 | 6 | 1 |
| **KANSAS—Other Agencies** | | | |
| Blue Valley School District | 6 | 6 | 0 |
| Johnson County Park | 20 | 19 | 1 |
| Metropolitan Topeka Airport Authority | 23 | 19 | 4 |
| Shawnee Mission Public Schools | 8 | 8 | 0 |
| Topeka Fire Department Arson Investigation | 3 | 3 | 0 |
| Unified School District: | | | |
| Auburn-Washburn | 1 | 1 | 0 |
| Bluestem | 1 | 1 | 0 |
| Goddard | 6 | 4 | 2 |
| Maize | 4 | 4 | 0 |
| Seaman | 4 | 4 | 0 |
| Topeka | 9 | 9 | 0 |
| **KENTUCKY—State Agencies** | | | |
| Alcohol Beverage Control | 31 | 28 | 3 |
| Fish and Wildlife Enforcement | 150 | 142 | 8 |
| Forestry Enforcement | 138 | 136 | 2 |
| Kentucky Horse Park | 10 | 9 | 1 |
| Motor Vehicle Enforcement | 142 | 142 | 0 |
| Park Security | 52 | 52 | 0 |
| Unlawful Narcotics Investigation Treatment and Education | 21 | 18 | 3 |
| **KENTUCKY—Other Agencies** | | | |
| Adair County Constable District 6 | 1 | 1 | 0 |
| Barren County Drug Task Force | 2 | 1 | 1 |
| Buffalo Trace-Gateway Narcotics Task Force | 4 | 4 | 0 |
| Central Kentucky Area Drug Task Force | 2 | 1 | 1 |
| Cincinnati-Northern Kentucky International Airport | 64 | 49 | 15 |
| Clark County School System | 2 | 2 | 0 |
| Daniel Boone National Forest | 18 | 18 | 0 |
| Fayette County Schools | 25 | 21 | 4 |
| FIVCO Area Drug Task Force | 7 | 6 | 1 |
| Floyd County Constable District 1 | 1 | 1 | 0 |
| Graves County Schools | 1 | 1 | 0 |
| Greater Hardin County Narcotics Task Force | 7 | 6 | 1 |
| Jefferson County Board of Education | 27 | 21 | 6 |
| Kentucky Dam | 21 | 21 | 0 |
| Lake Cumberland Area Drug Enforcement Task Force | 8 | 7 | 1 |
| Lexington Bluegrass Airport | 28 | 20 | 8 |
| Louisville Regional Airport Authority | 49 | 40 | 9 |
| McCracken County Public Schools | 4 | 4 | 0 |
| Montgomery County School District | 2 | 2 | 0 |

## Table 81. Full-Time Law Enforcement Employees, by State and Agency, 2009—*Continued*

(Number.)

| State, agency, unit/office | Total law enforcement employees | Total officers | Total civilians |
|---|---|---|---|
| Nicholas County Schools | 1 | 1 | 0 |
| Northern Kentucky Narcotics Enforcement Unit | 3 | 2 | 1 |
| Ohio County School System | 2 | 2 | 0 |
| Owen County Constable District 3 | 1 | 1 | 0 |
| Pennyrile Narcotics Task Force | 19 | 16 | 3 |
| South Central Kentucky Drug Task Force | 5 | 5 | 0 |
| Tennessee Valley Authority | 11 | 10 | 1 |
| United States Marshals Service Lexington | 28 | 23 | 5 |
| Warren County Constable District 4 | 2 | 2 | 0 |
| Warren County Drug Task Force | 1 | 1 | 0 |
| **LOUISIANA—State Agencies** | | | |
| Department of Public Safety State Capitol Detail | 44 | 38 | 6 |
| **LOUISIANA—Tribal Agencies** | | | |
| Chitimacha Tribal | 14 | 9 | 5 |
| **MAINE—Tribal Agencies** | | | |
| Passamaquoddy Indian Township | 11 | 6 | 5 |
| **MARYLAND—State Agencies** | | | |
| Comptroller of the Treasury Field Enforcement Division | 52 | 23 | 29 |
| Department of Public Safety and Correctional Services Internal Investigations Unit | 24 | 19 | 5 |
| General Services: | | | |
| Annapolis, Anne Arundel County | 65 | 30 | 35 |
| Baltimore City | 105 | 35 | 70 |
| Natural Resources Police | 535 | 267 | 268 |
| Springfield Hospital | 17 | 5 | 12 |
| State Fire Marshal | 75 | 43 | 32 |
| Transit Administration | 159 | 142 | 17 |
| Transportation Authority | 605 | 431 | 174 |
| **MARYLAND—Other Agencies** | | | |
| Maryland-National Capital Park Police: | | | |
| Montgomery County | 109 | 84 | 25 |
| Prince George's County | 136 | 105 | 31 |
| **MASSACHUSETTS-State Agencies** | | | |
| Division of Law Enforcement Environmental Police | 118 | 85 | 33 |
| **MASSACHUSETTS-Other Agencies** | | | |
| Beth Israel Deaconess Medical Center | 54 | 13 | 41 |
| **MICHIGAN—Tribal Agencies** | | | |
| Bay Mills Tribal | 18 | 14 | 4 |
| Hannahville Tribal | 12 | 11 | 1 |
| Keweenaw Bay Tribal | 14 | 13 | 1 |
| Lac Vieux Desert Tribal | 7 | 7 | 0 |
| Little River Band of Ottawa Tribal | 17 | 16 | 1 |
| Little Traverse Bay Tribal | 16 | 11 | 5 |
| **MICHIGAN—Other Agencies** | | | |
| Bishop International Airport | 8 | 7 | 1 |
| Capitol Region Airport Authority | 21 | 13 | 8 |
| Gerald R. Ford International Airport | 19 | 17 | 2 |
| Huron-Clinton Metropolitan Authority: | | | |
| Hudson Mills Metropark | 5 | 5 | 0 |
| Kensington Metropark | 8 | 8 | 0 |
| Lower Huron Metropark | 10 | 10 | 0 |
| Stony Creek Metropark | 9 | 9 | 0 |
| Wayne County Airport | 112 | 102 | 10 |
| **MINNESOTA—State Agencies** | | | |
| Capitol Security St. Paul | 52 | 10 | 42 |
| **MINNESOTA—Tribal Agencies** | | | |
| Mille Lacs Tribal | 22 | 19 | 3 |
| Nett Lake Tribal | 6 | 5 | 1 |
| **MINNESOTA—Other Agencies** | | | |
| Minneapolis-St. Paul International Airport | 116 | 81 | 35 |
| Three Rivers Park District | 46 | 28 | 18 |
| **MISSISSIPPI—State Agencies** | | | |
| State Capitol Police | 63 | 57 | 6 |
| **MISSOURI—State Agencies** | | | |
| Capitol Police | 36 | 30 | 6 |
| Department of Conservation | 207 | 198 | 9 |
| Division of Alcohol and Tobacco Control | 32 | 29 | 3 |
| Gaming Commission Enforcement Division | 110 | 108 | 2 |

**Table 81. Full-Time Law Enforcement Employees, by State and Agency, 2009—*Continued***

(Number.)

| State, agency, unit/office | Total law enforcement employees | Total officers | Total civilians |
|---|---|---|---|
| State Fire Marshal | 23 | 21 | 2 |
| State Park Rangers | 45 | 44 | 1 |
| State Water Patrol | 117 | 94 | 23 |
| **MISSOURI—Other Agencies** | | | |
| Bootheel Drug Task Force | 7 | 7 | 0 |
| Clay County Drug Task Force | 3 | 3 | 0 |
| Clay County Park Authority | 8 | 8 | 0 |
| Jackson County Drug Task Force | 21 | 19 | 2 |
| Jackson County Park Rangers | 21 | 19 | 2 |
| Lambert-St. Louis International Airport | 102 | 87 | 15 |
| Springfield-Branson Airport | 10 | 10 | 0 |
| St. Charles County Park Rangers | 12 | 12 | 0 |
| St. Peters Ranger Division | 6 | 6 | 0 |
| **MONTANA—State Agencies** | | | |
| Gambling Investigations Bureau | 24 | 21 | 3 |
| **MONTANA—Tribal Agencies** | | | |
| Crow Tribal | 24 | 15 | 9 |
| Flathead Tribal | 20 | 19 | 1 |
| Fort Belknap Tribal | 9 | 8 | 1 |
| Northern Cheyenne Tribal | 27 | 11 | 16 |
| **NEBRASKA—Tribal Agencies** | | | |
| Winnebago Tribal | 18 | 10 | 8 |
| **NEVADA—State Agencies** | | | |
| Taxicab Authority | 52 | 25 | 27 |
| **NEVADA—Tribal Agencies** | | | |
| Ely Shoshone Tribal | 2 | 2 | 0 |
| Moapa Tribal | 6 | 3 | 3 |
| Pyramid Lake Tribal | 17 | 14 | 3 |
| Walker River Tribal | 5 | 5 | 0 |
| Washoe Tribal | 14 | 12 | 2 |
| Western Nevada Tribal | 6 | 5 | 1 |
| Yerington Paiute Tribal | 3 | 3 | 0 |
| Yomba Shoshone Tribal | 2 | 2 | 0 |
| **NEVADA—Other Agencies** | | | |
| Clark County School District | 210 | 168 | 42 |
| Washoe County School District | 43 | 39 | 4 |
| **NEW HAMPSHIRE—State Agencies** | | | |
| Liquor Commission | 36 | 23 | 13 |
| **NEW JERSEY—State Agencies** | | | |
| Department of Human Services | 130 | 123 | 7 |
| Division of Fish and Wildlife | 54 | 51 | 3 |
| New Jersey Transit Police | 282 | 217 | 65 |
| Palisades Interstate Parkway | 26 | 25 | 1 |
| State Park Police | 85 | 82 | 3 |
| **NEW JERSEY—Other Agencies** | | | |
| Park Police: | | | |
| Camden County | 21 | 20 | 1 |
| Morris County | 32 | 31 | 1 |
| Union County | 81 | 73 | 8 |
| Prosecutor: | | | |
| Atlantic County | 175 | 78 | 97 |
| Bergen County | 254 | 110 | 144 |
| Burlington County | 149 | 85 | 64 |
| Camden County | 232 | 157 | 75 |
| Cape May County | 77 | 36 | 41 |
| Cumberland County | 111 | 41 | 70 |
| Essex County | 319 | 195 | 124 |
| Gloucester County | 95 | 34 | 61 |
| Hudson County | 221 | 97 | 124 |
| Hunterdon County | 60 | 26 | 34 |
| Mercer County | 164 | 50 | 114 |
| Middlesex County | 204 | 76 | 128 |
| Monmouth County | 283 | 81 | 202 |
| Morris County | 148 | 67 | 81 |
| Ocean County | 170 | 80 | 90 |
| Passaic County | 186 | 82 | 104 |
| Salem County | 54 | 20 | 34 |
| Somerset County | 117 | 51 | 66 |
| Sussex County | 53 | 33 | 20 |
| Union County | 253 | 77 | 176 |
| Warren County | 60 | 21 | 39 |
| **NEW MEXICO—Tribal Agencies** | | | |
| Acoma Tribal | 20 | 12 | 8 |
| Jemez Tribal | 7 | 6 | 1 |
| Northern Pueblos Tribal | 10 | 8 | 2 |
| Ramah Navajo Tribal | 17 | 10 | 7 |
| Santa Ana Tribal | 20 | 14 | 6 |
| Santa Clara Tribal | 16 | 9 | 7 |

**Table 81. Full-Time Law Enforcement Employees, by State and Agency, 2009—*Continued***

(Number.)

| State, agency, unit/office | Total law enforcement employees | Total officers | Total civilians |
|---|---|---|---|
| Taos Pueblo Tribal | 10 | 5 | 5 |
| Zuni Tribal | 31 | 20 | 11 |
| **NEW YORK—State Agencies** | | | |
| StatePark: | | | |
| Allegany Region | 15 | 12 | 3 |
| Central Region | 16 | 13 | 3 |
| Finger Lakes Region | 18 | 16 | 2 |
| Genesee Region | 15 | 14 | 1 |
| Long Island Region | 70 | 68 | 2 |
| New York City Region | 27 | 23 | 4 |
| Niagara Region | 31 | 30 | 1 |
| Palisades Region | 45 | 44 | 1 |
| Saratoga/Capital Region | 18 | 18 | 0 |
| Taconic Region | 14 | 13 | 1 |
| Thousand Island Region | 15 | 14 | 1 |
| **NEW YORK—Tribal Agencies** | | | |
| Oneida Indian Nation | 37 | 31 | 6 |
| St. Regis Tribal | 26 | 20 | 6 |
| **NEW YORK—Other Agencies** | | | |
| New York City Metropolitan Transportation Authority | 768 | 695 | 73 |
| Suffolk County Parks | 47 | 45 | 2 |
| **NORTH CAROLINA—State Agencies** | | | |
| Caswell Center Hospital | 4 | 4 | 0 |
| Department of Human Resources | 9 | 9 | 0 |
| Department of Wildlife | 227 | 206 | 21 |
| Division of Alcohol Law Enforcement | 124 | 111 | 13 |
| North Carolina Arboretum | 2 | 2 | 0 |
| State Capitol Police | 81 | 54 | 27 |
| State Fairgrounds | 6 | 1 | 5 |
| State Park Rangers: | | | |
| Carolina Beach | 6 | 4 | 2 |
| Cliffs of the Neuse | 7 | 5 | 2 |
| Crowders Mountain | 6 | 5 | 1 |
| Dismal Swamp | 4 | 3 | 1 |
| Elk Knob | 5 | 3 | 2 |
| Eno River | 5 | 5 | 0 |
| Falls Lake Recreation Area | 19 | 18 | 1 |
| Fort Fisher | 4 | 3 | 1 |
| Fort Macon | 4 | 4 | 0 |
| Goose Creek | 6 | 4 | 2 |
| Gorges | 3 | 3 | 0 |
| Hammocks Beach | 4 | 4 | 0 |
| Hanging Rock | 11 | 6 | 5 |
| Jockey's Ridge | 4 | 4 | 0 |
| Jones Lake | 6 | 5 | 1 |
| Jordan Lake State Recreation Area | 17 | 15 | 2 |
| Kerr Lake | 12 | 10 | 2 |
| Lake James | 5 | 3 | 2 |
| Lake Norman | 5 | 4 | 1 |
| Lake Waccamaw | 4 | 4 | 0 |
| Lumber River | 7 | 5 | 2 |
| Medoc Mountain | 4 | 1 | 3 |
| Merchants Millpond | 7 | 4 | 3 |
| Morrow Mountain | 9 | 4 | 5 |
| Mount Mitchell | 4 | 3 | 1 |
| New River-Mount Jefferson | 7 | 7 | 0 |
| Pettigrew | 4 | 3 | 1 |
| Raven Rock | 4 | 3 | 1 |
| Singletary Lake | 4 | 1 | 3 |
| South Mountains | 10 | 7 | 3 |
| Stone Mountain | 9 | 7 | 2 |
| Weymouth Woods/Sandhills Nature Preserve | 2 | 2 | 0 |
| William B. Umstead | 7 | 6 | 1 |
| **NORTH CAROLINA—Tribal Agencies** | | | |
| Cherokee Tribal | 54 | 48 | 6 |
| **NORTH CAROLINA—Other Agencies** | | | |
| Asheville Regional Airport | 19 | 14 | 5 |
| Durham County Alcohol Beverage Control Law Enforcement Office | 2 | 2 | 0 |
| Nash County Alcohol Beverage Control Enforcement | 2 | 2 | 0 |
| Piedmont Triad International Airport | 20 | 17 | 3 |
| Raleigh-Durham International Airport | 30 | 28 | 2 |
| Triad Alcohol Beverage Control Law Enforcement | 6 | 5 | 1 |
| WakeMed Campus Police | 74 | 44 | 30 |
| Wilmington International Airport | 13 | 9 | 4 |
| **OHIO—State Agencies** | | | |
| Bureau of Criminal Identification and Investigation | 305 | 89 | 216 |
| Ohio Department of Natural Resources | 497 | 413 | 84 |

**Table 81. Full-Time Law Enforcement Employees, by State and Agency, 2009**—*Continued*

(Number.)

| State, agency, unit/office | Total law enforcement employees | Total officers | Total civilians |
|---|---|---|---|
| **OHIO—Other Agencies** | | | |
| Cedar Point | 11 | 11 | 0 |
| Cleveland Metropolitan Park District | 79 | 69 | 10 |
| Columbus and Franklin County Metropolitan Park District | 42 | 40 | 2 |
| Erie MetroParks | 4 | 4 | 0 |
| Greater Cleveland Regional Transit Authority | 111 | 100 | 11 |
| Hamilton County Park District | 37 | 34 | 3 |
| Johnny Appleseed Metropolitan Park District | 8 | 8 | 0 |
| Lake Metroparks | 15 | 13 | 2 |
| Lima Park Services | | | |
| Ranger Division | 4 | 4 | 0 |
| Lorain County Metropolitan Park District | 13 | 13 | 0 |
| Port Columbus International Airport | 58 | 39 | 19 |
| Robinson Memorial Hospital | 7 | 7 | 0 |
| Sandusky County Park District | 4 | 4 | 0 |
| Toledo-Lucas County Port Authority | 9 | 9 | 0 |
| Toledo Metropolitan Park District | 22 | 22 | 0 |
| Wood County Park District | 6 | 6 | 0 |
| **OKLAHOMA—State Agencies** | | | |
| Capitol Park Police | 66 | 25 | 41 |
| Grand River Dam Authority | | | |
| Lake Patrol | 10 | 9 | 1 |
| **OKLAHOMA—Tribal Agencies** | | | |
| Absentee Shawnee Tribal | 10 | 7 | 3 |
| Choctaw Tribal | 31 | 30 | 1 |
| Comanche Tribal | 22 | 17 | 5 |
| Eastern Shawnee Tribal | 10 | 9 | 1 |
| **OKLAHOMA—Other Agencies** | | | |
| Guymon Public Schools | 2 | 2 | 0 |
| Jenks Public Schools | 8 | 7 | 1 |
| Madill Public Schools | 1 | 1 | 0 |
| McAlester Public Schools | 3 | 3 | 0 |
| Norman Public Schools | 4 | 4 | 0 |
| Putnam City Campus | 12 | 8 | 4 |
| **OREGON—State Agencies** | | | |
| Liquor Commission: | | | |
| Clatsop County | 1 | 1 | 0 |
| Columbia County | 1 | 1 | 0 |
| Coos County | 1 | 1 | 0 |
| Curry County | 1 | 1 | 0 |
| Douglas County | 1 | 1 | 0 |
| Hood River | 1 | 1 | 0 |
| Jackson County | 6 | 6 | 0 |
| Klamath County | 1 | 1 | 0 |
| Lane County | 7 | 6 | 1 |
| Malheur County | 1 | 1 | 0 |
| Marion County | 7 | 6 | 1 |
| Multnomah County | 7 | 7 | 0 |
| Umatilla County | 2 | 2 | 0 |
| Washington County | 2 | 2 | 0 |
| Yamhill County | 1 | 1 | 0 |
| **OREGON—Tribal Agencies** | | | |
| Burns Paiute Tribal | 5 | 4 | 1 |
| Coquille Tribal | 4 | 4 | 0 |
| Umatilla Tribal | 21 | 16 | 5 |
| **OREGON—Other Agencies** | | | |
| Port of Portland | 69 | 52 | 17 |
| **PENNSYLVANIA—State Agencies** | | | |
| Department of Environmental Resources | 11 | 5 | 6 |
| State Capitol Police | 141 | 132 | 9 |
| State Park Police: | | | |
| Pine Grove Furnace | 7 | 2 | 5 |
| Presque Isle | 5 | 5 | 0 |
| Pymatuning | 3 | 3 | 0 |
| **PENNSYLVANIA—Other Agencies** | | | |
| Allegheny County Port Authority | 57 | 40 | 17 |
| County Detective: | | | |
| Berks County | 30 | 28 | 2 |
| Bucks County | 20 | 16 | 4 |
| Butler County | 4 | 4 | 0 |
| Chester County | 23 | 20 | 3 |
| Dauphin County | 15 | 12 | 3 |
| Lackawanna County | 13 | 13 | 0 |
| Lebanon County | 9 | 6 | 3 |
| Lehigh County | 18 | 16 | 2 |
| Pike County | 3 | 3 | 0 |
| Schuylkill County | 7 | 7 | 0 |

**Table 81. Full-Time Law Enforcement Employees, by State and Agency, 2009—*Continued***

(Number.)

| State, agency, unit/office | Total law enforcement employees | Total officers | Total civilians |
|---|---|---|---|
| Westmoreland County | 57 | 15 | 42 |
| York County | 11 | 10 | 1 |
| Delaware County Park | 56 | 55 | 1 |
| Easton Area School District | 7 | 6 | 1 |
| Fort Indiantown Gap | 28 | 8 | 20 |
| Harrisburg International Airport | 16 | 9 | 7 |
| Tyrone Area School District | 1 | 1 | 0 |
| Washington County Alternative Education | 1 | 1 | 0 |
| Westmoreland County Park | 21 | 21 | 0 |
| Wilkes-Barre Area School District | 5 | 5 | 0 |
| **RHODE ISLAND—State Agencies** | | | |
| Department of Environmental Management | 42 | 33 | 9 |
| Rhode Island State Airport | 53 | 44 | 9 |
| **SOUTH CAROLINA—State Agencies** | | | |
| Bureau of Protective Services | 73 | 68 | 5 |
| Employment Security Commission | 4 | 4 | 0 |
| Forestry Commission: | | | |
| Aiken County | 1 | 1 | 0 |
| Anderson County | 1 | 1 | 0 |
| Barnwell County | 1 | 1 | 0 |
| Beaufort County | 1 | 1 | 0 |
| Berkeley County | 1 | 1 | 0 |
| Charleston County | 1 | 1 | 0 |
| Chesterfield County | 4 | 4 | 0 |
| Colleton County | 1 | 1 | 0 |
| Darlington County | 2 | 2 | 0 |
| Fairfield County | 1 | 1 | 0 |
| Florence County | 1 | 1 | 0 |
| Georgetown County | 1 | 1 | 0 |
| Greenville County | 1 | 1 | 0 |
| Hampton County | 1 | 1 | 0 |
| Horry County | 1 | 1 | 0 |
| Kershaw County | 3 | 3 | 0 |
| Lancaster County | 1 | 1 | 0 |
| Lee County | 1 | 1 | 0 |
| Lexington County | 2 | 2 | 0 |
| Oconee County | 1 | 1 | 0 |
| Orangeburg County | 1 | 1 | 0 |
| Pickens County | 1 | 1 | 0 |
| Richland County | 2 | 2 | 0 |
| Sumter County | 5 | 5 | 0 |
| Williamsburg County | 2 | 2 | 0 |
| York County | 1 | 1 | 0 |
| State Museum | 3 | 2 | 1 |
| State Transport Police: | | | |
| Abbeville County | 13 | 13 | 0 |
| Aiken County | 45 | 27 | 18 |
| Allendale County | 9 | 9 | 0 |
| Anderson County | 20 | 17 | 3 |
| Berkeley County | 20 | 17 | 3 |
| Cherokee County | 10 | 10 | 0 |
| Darlington County | 11 | 11 | 0 |
| United States Department of Energy | | | |
| Savannah River Plant | 61 | 54 | 7 |
| **SOUTH CAROLINA—Other Agencies** | | | |
| Charleston County Aviation Authority | 39 | 28 | 11 |
| Greenville-Spartanburg International Airport | 21 | 16 | 5 |
| Whitten Center | 1 | 1 | 0 |
| **SOUTH DAKOTA—State Agencies** | | | |
| Division of Criminal Investigation | 145 | 44 | 101 |
| **SOUTH DAKOTA—Tribal Agencies** | | | |
| Rosebud Tribal | 32 | 23 | 9 |
| Sisseton-Wahpeton Tribal | 20 | 11 | 9 |
| **TENNESSEE—State Agencies** | | | |
| Alcoholic Beverage Commission | 50 | 30 | 20 |
| Department of Correction | | | |
| Internal Affairs | 12 | 8 | 4 |
| State Fire Marshal | 30 | 26 | 4 |
| State Park Rangers: | | | |
| Bicentennial Capitol Mall | 6 | 6 | 0 |
| Big Hill Pond | 3 | 3 | 0 |
| Big Ridge | 4 | 4 | 0 |
| Bledsoe Creek | 2 | 2 | 0 |
| Booker T. Washington | 4 | 4 | 0 |
| Burgess Falls Natural Area | 2 | 2 | 0 |
| Cedars of Lebanon | 4 | 4 | 0 |
| Chickasaw | 5 | 5 | 0 |

## Table 81. Full-Time Law Enforcement Employees, by State and Agency, 2009—*Continued*

(Number.)

| State, agency, unit/office | Total law enforcement employees | Total officers | Total civilians |
|---|---|---|---|
| Cove Lake | 4 | 4 | 0 |
| Cumberland Mountain | 3 | 3 | 0 |
| Cumberland Trail | 5 | 5 | 0 |
| David Crockett | 4 | 4 | 0 |
| Davy Crockett Birthplace | 3 | 3 | 0 |
| Dunbar Cave Natural Area | 3 | 3 | 0 |
| Edgar Evins | 4 | 4 | 0 |
| Fall Creek Falls | 8 | 8 | 0 |
| Fort Loudon State Historic Park | 4 | 4 | 0 |
| Fort Pillow State Historic Park | 3 | 3 | 0 |
| Frozen Head Natural Area | 3 | 3 | 0 |
| Harpeth Scenic Rivers | 3 | 3 | 0 |
| Harrison Bay | 5 | 5 | 0 |
| Henry Horton | 4 | 4 | 0 |
| Hiwassee/Ocoee State Scenic Rivers | 6 | 6 | 0 |
| Indian Mountain | 2 | 2 | 0 |
| Johnsonville State Historic Park | 1 | 1 | 0 |
| Long Hunter | 4 | 4 | 0 |
| Meeman-Shelby Forest | 5 | 5 | 0 |
| Montgomery Bell | 7 | 7 | 0 |
| Mousetail Landing | 3 | 3 | 0 |
| Natchez Trace | 4 | 4 | 0 |
| Nathan Bedford Forrest | 2 | 2 | 0 |
| Norris Dam | 4 | 4 | 0 |
| Old Stone Fort State Archaeological Park | 3 | 3 | 0 |
| Panther Creek | 3 | 3 | 0 |
| Paris Landing | 5 | 5 | 0 |
| Pickett | 5 | 5 | 0 |
| Pickwick Landing | 5 | 5 | 0 |
| Pinson Mounds State Archaeological Park | 2 | 2 | 0 |
| Radnor Lake Natural Area | 5 | 5 | 0 |
| Red Clay State Historic Park | 2 | 2 | 0 |
| Reelfoot Lake | 4 | 4 | 0 |
| Roan Mountain | 3 | 3 | 0 |
| Rock Island | 4 | 4 | 0 |
| Sgt. Alvin C. York | 1 | 1 | 0 |
| South Cumberland Recreation Area | 6 | 6 | 0 |
| Standing Stone | 4 | 4 | 0 |
| Sycamore Shoals State Historic Park | 2 | 2 | 0 |
| Tim's Ford | 5 | 5 | 0 |
| T.O. Fuller | 3 | 3 | 0 |
| Warrior's Path | 5 | 5 | 0 |
| TennCare Office of Inspector General | 48 | 16 | 32 |
| Tennessee Bureau of Investigation | 465 | 178 | 287 |
| Tennessee Department of Revenue | | | |
| Special Investigations Unit | 52 | 29 | 23 |
| Wildlife Resources Agency: | | | |
| Region 1 | 41 | 41 | 0 |
| Region 2 | 56 | 49 | 7 |
| Region 3 | 43 | 43 | 0 |
| Region 4 | 46 | 46 | 0 |
| **TENNESSEE—Other Agencies** | | | |
| Chattanooga Housing Authority | 6 | 5 | 1 |
| Chattanooga Metropolitan Airport | 10 | 10 | 0 |
| Dickson Parks and Recreation | 11 | 3 | 8 |
| Drug Task Force: | | | |
| 1st Judicial District | 6 | 5 | 1 |
| 3rd Judicial District | 5 | 4 | 1 |
| 4th Judicial District | 3 | 2 | 1 |
| 5th Judicial District | 9 | 8 | 1 |
| 8th Judicial District | 4 | 3 | 1 |
| 9th Judicial District | 2 | 2 | 0 |
| 10th Judicial District | 16 | 15 | 1 |
| 12th Judicial District | 2 | 2 | 0 |
| 13th Judicial District | 5 | 4 | 1 |
| 14th Judicial District | 2 | 2 | 0 |
| 15th Judicial District | 5 | 4 | 1 |
| 17th Judicial District | 7 | 6 | 1 |
| 18th Judicial District | 6 | 6 | 0 |
| 19th Judicial District | 10 | 9 | 1 |
| 21st Judicial District | 13 | 10 | 3 |
| 22nd Judicial District | 3 | 3 | 0 |
| 23rd Judicial District | 10 | 7 | 3 |
| 24th Judicial District | 4 | 3 | 1 |
| 25th Judicial District | 3 | 2 | 1 |
| 27th Judicial District | 2 | 1 | 1 |
| 31st Judicial District | 3 | 1 | 2 |

**Table 81. Full-Time Law Enforcement Employees, by State and Agency, 2009**—*Continued*

(Number.)

| State, agency, unit/office | Total law enforcement employees | Total officers | Total civilians |
|---|---|---|---|
| Knoxville Metropolitan Airport | 45 | 27 | 18 |
| Memphis International Airport | 63 | 50 | 13 |
| Metropolitan Board of Parks and Recreation | | | |
| Nashville-Davidson | 24 | 23 | 1 |
| Nashville International Airport | 78 | 62 | 16 |
| Smyrna/Rutherford County Airport Authority | 7 | 4 | 3 |
| Tri-Cities Regional Airport | 15 | 14 | 1 |
| West Tennessee Violent Crime Task Force | 7 | 6 | 1 |
| **TEXAS—Tribal Agencies** | | | |
| Ysleta Del Sur Pueblo Tribal | 6 | 5 | 1 |
| **TEXAS—Other Agencies** | | | |
| Amarillo International Airport | 12 | 12 | 0 |
| Dallas-Fort Worth International Airport | 396 | 260 | 136 |
| Hospital District: | | | |
| Dallas County | 78 | 51 | 27 |
| Tarrant County | 65 | 44 | 21 |
| Houston Metropolitan Transit Authority | 250 | 183 | 67 |
| Independent School District: | | | |
| Aldine | 50 | 44 | 6 |
| Alvin | 23 | 18 | 5 |
| Angleton | 5 | 4 | 1 |
| Athens | 3 | 2 | 1 |
| Austin | 104 | 70 | 34 |
| Barbers Hill | 3 | 2 | 1 |
| Bay City | 7 | 6 | 1 |
| Brownsville | 136 | 32 | 104 |
| Cedar Hill | 23 | 5 | 18 |
| Conroe | 63 | 46 | 17 |
| Corpus Christi | 56 | 31 | 25 |
| East Central | 9 | 8 | 1 |
| Ector County | 30 | 28 | 2 |
| El Paso | 52 | 42 | 10 |
| Fort Bend | 52 | 44 | 8 |
| Humble | 32 | 24 | 8 |
| Judson | 22 | 20 | 2 |
| Katy | 43 | 34 | 9 |
| Kaufman | 5 | 4 | 1 |
| Killeen | 13 | 13 | 0 |
| Klein | 48 | 30 | 18 |
| Laredo | 91 | 26 | 65 |
| Mexia | 4 | 4 | 0 |
| Midland | 16 | 10 | 6 |
| Pasadena | 39 | 32 | 7 |
| Pflugerville | 17 | 16 | 1 |
| Raymondville | 4 | 4 | 0 |
| Rio Grande City | 58 | 12 | 46 |
| Spring | 43 | 41 | 2 |
| Spring Branch | 38 | 32 | 6 |
| Taft | 1 | 1 | 0 |
| United | 162 | 51 | 111 |
| Weslaco | 4 | 4 | 0 |
| **UTAH—State Agencies** | | | |
| Parks and Recreation | 77 | 76 | 1 |
| Wildlife Resources | 83 | 74 | 9 |
| **UTAH—Other Agencies** | | | |
| Granite School District | 40 | 16 | 24 |
| Utah County Attorney | | | |
| Investigations Division | 7 | 5 | 2 |
| Utah Transit Authority | 50 | 38 | 12 |
| **VERMONT—State Agencies** | | | |
| Department of Liquor Control | | | |
| Division of Enforcement and Licensing | 21 | 16 | 5 |
| Department of Motor Vehicles | 43 | 29 | 14 |
| Fish and Wildlife Department | | | |
| Law Enforcement Division | 40 | 38 | 2 |
| **VIRGINIA—State Agencies** | | | |
| Alcoholic Beverage Control Commission | 138 | 111 | 27 |
| Department of Conservation and Recreation | 251 | 107 | 144 |
| Department of Motor Vehicles | 86 | 72 | 14 |
| Southside Virginia Training Center | 18 | 16 | 2 |
| Virginia State Capitol | 84 | 71 | 13 |
| **VIRGINIA—Other Agencies** | | | |
| Norfolk Airport Authority | 44 | 37 | 7 |
| Port Authority | | | |
| Norfolk | 88 | 81 | 7 |
| Reagan National Airport | 265 | 191 | 74 |
| Richmond International Airport | 34 | 26 | 8 |

## Table 81. Full-Time Law Enforcement Employees, by State and Agency, 2009—*Continued*

(Number.)

| State, agency, unit/office | Total law enforcement employees | Total officers | Total civilians |
|---|---|---|---|
| **WASHINGTON—State Agencies** | | | |
| State Insurance Commissioner Special Investigations Unit | 6 | 4 | 2 |
| **WASHINGTON—Tribal Agencies** | | | |
| Colville Tribal | 41 | 27 | 14 |
| Kalispel Tribal | 15 | 13 | 2 |
| Lummi Tribal | 16 | 14 | 2 |
| Nisqually Tribal | 17 | 13 | 4 |
| Nooksack Tribal | 6 | 5 | 1 |
| Skokomish Tribal | 5 | 4 | 1 |
| Spokane Tribal | 23 | 16 | 7 |
| Swinomish Tribal | 13 | 11 | 2 |
| **WASHINGTON—Other Agencies** | | | |
| Port of Seattle | 121 | 94 | 27 |
| **WEST VIRGINIA—State Agencies** | | | |
| Capitol Protective Services | 35 | 19 | 16 |
| Division of Natural Resources: | | | |
| Berkeley County | 2 | 2 | 0 |
| Boone County | 1 | 1 | 0 |
| Braxton County | 2 | 2 | 0 |
| Brooke County | 1 | 1 | 0 |
| Cabell County | 3 | 3 | 0 |
| Clay County | 2 | 2 | 0 |
| Doddridge County | 1 | 1 | 0 |
| Fayette County | 4 | 4 | 0 |
| Gilmer County | 2 | 2 | 0 |
| Grant County | 2 | 2 | 0 |
| Greenbrier County | 2 | 2 | 0 |
| Hampshire County | 5 | 4 | 1 |
| Hancock County | 1 | 1 | 0 |
| Hardy County | 3 | 3 | 0 |
| Harrison County | 3 | 3 | 0 |
| Jackson County | 2 | 2 | 0 |
| Jefferson County | 1 | 1 | 0 |
| Kanawha County | 3 | 3 | 0 |
| Lewis County | 1 | 1 | 0 |
| Lincoln County | 2 | 2 | 0 |
| Logan County | 2 | 2 | 0 |
| Marion County | 6 | 5 | 1 |
| Marshall County | 1 | 1 | 0 |
| Mason County | 1 | 1 | 0 |
| McDowell County | 1 | 1 | 0 |
| Mercer County | 4 | 4 | 0 |
| Mineral County | 2 | 2 | 0 |
| Mingo County | 1 | 1 | 0 |
| Monongalia County | 2 | 2 | 0 |
| Monroe County | 1 | 1 | 0 |
| Morgan County | 1 | 1 | 0 |
| Nicholas County | 3 | 3 | 0 |
| Pendleton County | 2 | 2 | 0 |
| Pleasants County | 2 | 1 | 1 |
| Pocahontas County | 3 | 3 | 0 |
| Preston County | 2 | 2 | 0 |
| Putnam County | 5 | 4 | 1 |
| Raleigh County | 3 | 3 | 0 |
| Randolph County | 3 | 2 | 1 |
| Ritchie County | 1 | 1 | 0 |
| Roane County | 1 | 1 | 0 |
| Summers County | 6 | 5 | 1 |
| Taylor County | 1 | 1 | 0 |
| Tucker County | 2 | 2 | 0 |
| Tyler County | 1 | 1 | 0 |
| Upshur County | 3 | 3 | 0 |
| Wayne County | 2 | 2 | 0 |
| Webster County | 3 | 3 | 0 |
| Wetzel County | 1 | 1 | 0 |
| Wirt County | 2 | 2 | 0 |
| Wood County | 2 | 2 | 0 |
| Wyoming County | 1 | 1 | 0 |
| State Fire Marshal Kanawha County | 42 | 32 | 10 |
| **WEST VIRGINIA—Other Agencies** | | | |
| Eastern Panhandle Drug and Violent Crime Task Force | 3 | 3 | 0 |
| Huntington Drug and Violent Crime Task Force | 5 | 4 | 1 |
| Kanawha County Parks and Recreation | 3 | 3 | 0 |
| Metropolitan Drug Enforcement Network Team | 16 | 15 | 1 |
| Potomac Highlands Drug and Violent Crime Task Force | 4 | 4 | 0 |

## Table 81. Full-Time Law Enforcement Employees, by State and Agency, 2009—*Continued*

(Number.)

| State, agency, unit/office | Total law enforcement employees | Total officers | Total civilians |
|---|---|---|---|
| **WISCONSIN—State Agencies** | | | |
| Capitol Police | 49 | 39 | 10 |
| Department of Natural Resources | 465 | 427 | 38 |
| **WISCONSIN—Tribal Agencies** | | | |
| Lac du Flambeau Tribal | 9 | 7 | 2 |
| Menominee Tribal | 30 | 23 | 7 |
| Oneida Tribal | 27 | 20 | 7 |
| Stockbridge Munsee Tribal | 5 | 5 | 0 |
| **PUERTO RICO AND OTHER OUTLYING AREAS** | | | |
| Guam | 374 | 310 | 64 |
| Puerto Rico | 17,947 | 16,445 | 1,502 |
| **FEDERAL AGENCIES** | | | |
| United States Park Police | 736 | 624 | 112 |
| National Institutes of Health | 123 | 97 | 26 |

# SECTION VI:
# HATE CRIMES

## HATE CRIMES

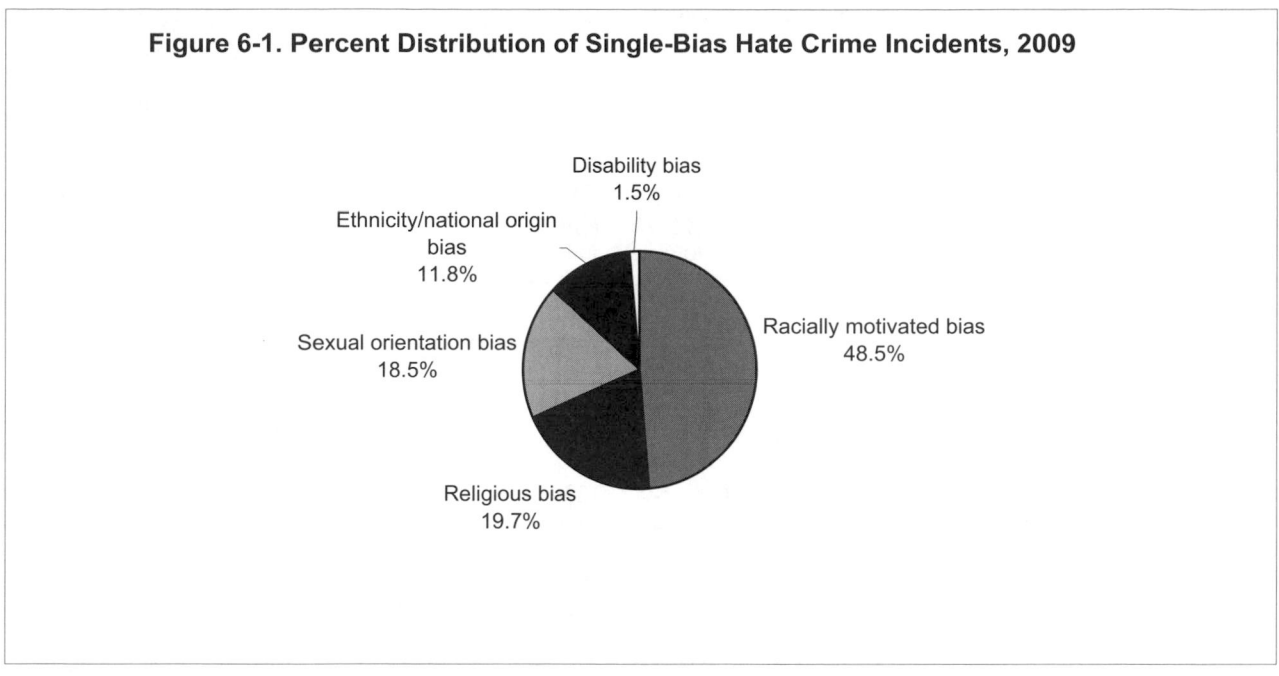

**Figure 6-1. Percent Distribution of Single-Bias Hate Crime Incidents, 2009**

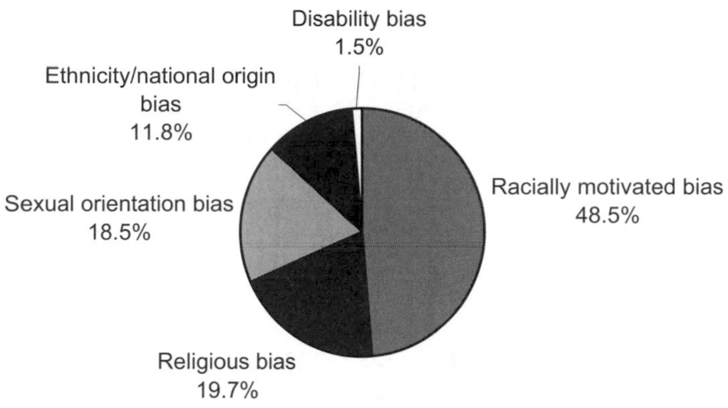


The Federal Bureau of Investigation (FBI) began the procedures for implementing, collecting, and managing hate crime data after Congress passed the Hate Crime Statistics Act in 1990 which required the collection of data "about crimes that manifest evidence of prejudice based on race, religion, sexual orientation, or ethnicity." In 1994, the Hate Crime Statistics Act was amended to include bias against persons with disabilities. The Church Arson Prevention Act, which was signed into law in July 1996, removed the sunset clause from the original statute and mandated that the collection of hate crime data become a permanent part of the UCR Program. In 2009, Congress further amended the Hate Crime Statistics Act by passing the Matthew Shepard and James Byrd, Jr. Hate Crime Prevention Act. The amendment includes the collection of data for crimes motivated by bias against a particular gender and gender identity, as well as for crimes committed by, and crimes directed against, juveniles. The FBI is currently making plans to implement changes to collect these data. (See http://www2.fbi.gov/ucr/hc2009/hatecrimestatistics.html for referenced legislation, as amended.)

### Definition

Hate crimes include any crime motivated by bias against race, religion, sexual orientation, ethnicity/national origin, and/or disability. Because motivation is subjective, it is sometimes difficult to know with certainty whether a crime resulted from the offender's bias. Moreover, the presence of bias alone does not necessarily mean that a crime can be considered a hate crime. Only when law enforcement investigation reveals sufficient evidence to lead a reasonable and prudent person to conclude that the offender's actions were motivated, in whole or in part, by his or her bias, should an incident be reported as a hate crime.

### Data Collection

The UCR (Uniform Crime Reporting) Program collects data about both single-bias and multiple-bias hate crimes. A single-bias incident is defined as an incident in which one or more offense types are motivated by the same bias. A multiple-bias incident is defined as an incident in which more than one offense type occurs and at least two offense types are motivated by different biases.

#### *Crimes against persons, property, or society*

The UCR Program's data collection guidelines stipulate that a hate crime may involve multiple offenses, victims, and offenders within one incident; therefore, the Hate Crime Statistics Program is incident-based. According to UCR counting guidelines:

- One offense is counted for each victim in *crimes against persons*.
- One offense is counted for each offense type in *crimes against property*.
- One offense is counted for each offense type in *crimes against society*.

### *Victims*

In the UCR Program, the victim of a hate crime may be an individual, a business, an institution, or society as a whole.

### *Offenders*

According to the UCR Program, the term *known offender* does not imply that the suspect's identity is known; rather, the term indicates that some aspect of the suspect was identified, thus distinguishing the suspect from an unknown offender. Law enforcement agencies specify the number of offenders and, when possible, the race of the offender or offenders as a group.

### *Race/ethnicity*

The UCR Program uses the following five racial designations in its Hate Crime Statistics Program: White; Black; American Indian/Alaskan Native; Asian/Pacific Islander; and Multiple Races, Group. In addition, the UCR Program uses the ethnic designations of Hispanic and Other Ethnicity/National Origin.

Agencies that participated in the Hate Crime program in 2009 represented nearly 279 million inhabitants, or 90.9 percent of the Nation's population, and their jurisdictions covered 49 states and the District of Columbia. The law enforcement agencies that voluntarily participate in the Hate Crime program collect details about an offender's bias motivation associated with 11 offense types already being reported to the UCR Program: murder and nonnegligent manslaughter, forcible rape, aggravated assault, simple assault, and intimidation (crimes against persons); and robbery, burglary, larceny-theft, motor vehicle theft, arson, and destruction/damage/vandalism (crimes against property). The law enforcement agencies that participate in the UCR Program via the National Incident-Based Reporting System (NIBRS) collect data about additional offenses for *crimes against persons* and *crimes against property*. These data appear in the category of other. These agencies also collect hate crime data for the category called *crimes against society*, which includes drug or narcotic offenses, gambling offenses, prostitution offenses, and weapon law violations.

## National Volume and Percent Distribution

In 2009, 2,025 law enforcement agencies reported 6,604 hate crime incidents involving 7,789 offenses. Of these, 7,775 were single-bias offenses. An analysis of the single-bias incidents revealed 49.1 percent were racially motivated, 17.7 percent were motivated by religious bias, 18.5 percent resulted from sexual-orientation bias, 13.5 percent were based on an ethnicity/national origin bias and 1.2 percent were prompted by a disability bias. (Table 82)

The majority of the hate crime offenses that were racially motivated resulted from an anti-Black bias (71.4 percent) followed by an anti-White basis (17.1 percent). Bias against people of more than one race accounted for 5.5 percent of offenses while an anti-Asian/Pacific Islander bias accounted for 3.9 percent of racially motivated offenses. (Table 82)

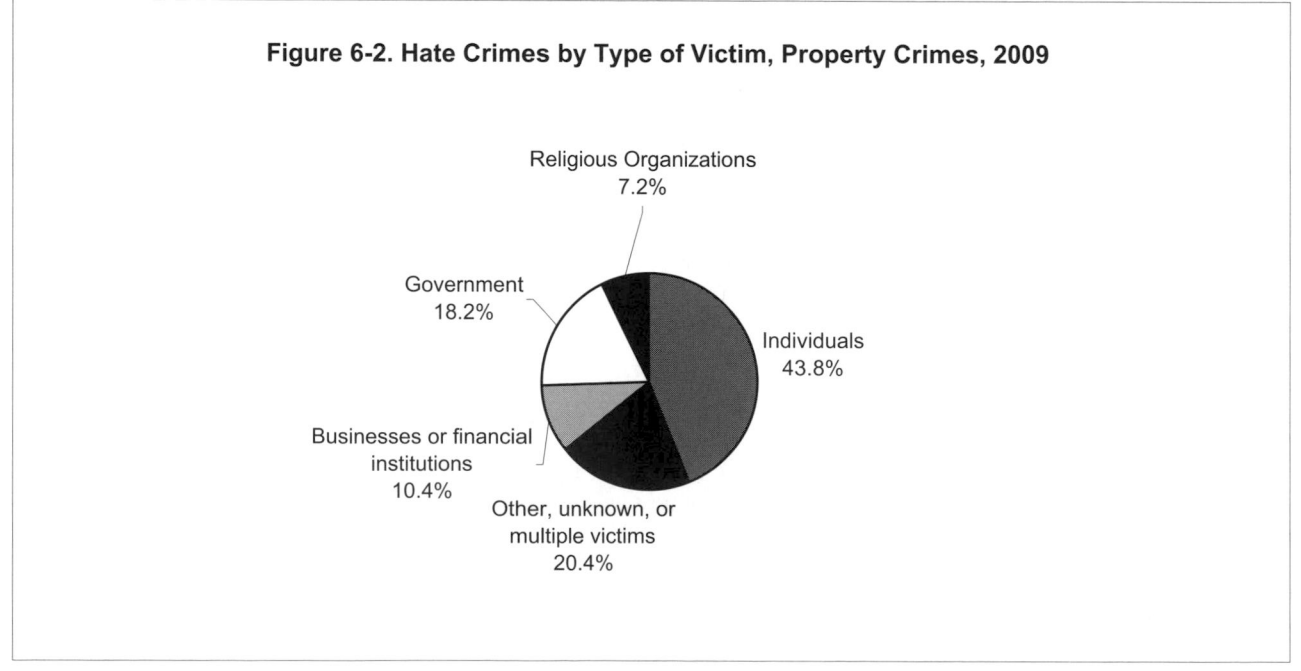

**Figure 6-2. Hate Crimes by Type of Victim, Property Crimes, 2009**

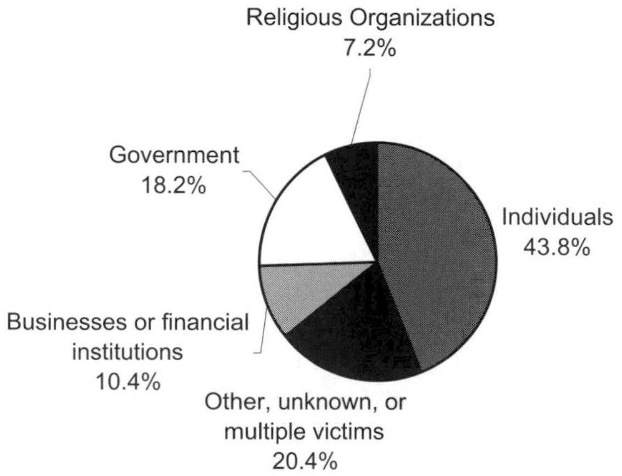

Hate crimes motivated by religious bias accounted for 1,376 offenses reported by law enforcement. A breakdown of these offenses revealed 70.1 percent were motivated by an anti-Jewish bias, 9.3 percent by an anti-Islamic bias, 4.4 percent were anti-multiple religions or groups, 4.0 percent an anti-Catholic bias, 2.9 percent were anti-Protestant, 0.7 percent were anti-Atheism and the remainder of offenses were based on a bias against other religions. (Table 82)

More hate crimes were motivated by sexual orientation than were motivated by religion in 2009. Of the 1,463 offenses based on sexual orientation, 55.6 percent were classified as having an anti-male homosexual bias, 22.6 percent had an anti-homosexual bias, 15.0 percent had an anti-female homosexual basis, 1.7 percent had an anti-bisexual bias, and 1.5 percent had an anti-heterosexual bias. (Table 82)

The vast majority of 1,050 offenses that were committed on the perceived ethnicity or national origin of the victim had an anti-Hispanic basis (62.3 percent). The remaining 37.7 percent were based on a bias against another ethnicity or national origin. (Table 82)

Other hate crimes offenses were committed based on disability. The majority (74.2 percent) were classified as anti-mental disability, with the rest being classified as anti-physical disability. (Table 82)

## Crimes Against Persons

Law enforcement agencies reported 4,793 hate crimes against persons in 2009. Nearly half of them (45.0 percent) involved intimidation, 35.3 percent involved simple assault, and 19.1 percent involved aggravated assault. In addition, there were 8 murders and 9 forcible rapes. (Table 83)

## Crimes Against Property

In 2009, there were 2,970 hate crimes against property. Approximately 83.0 percent of offenses involved destruction/damage or vandalism. The remaining 17.0 percent of crimes against property consisted of robbery, burglary, larceny-theft, motor vehicle theft, arson, and other crimes. (Table 83)

## Table 82. Incidents, Offenses, Victims, and Known Offenders, by Bias Motivation, 2009

(Number.)

| Bias motivation | Incidents | Offenses | Victims[1] | Known offenders[2] |
|---|---|---|---|---|
| **TOTAL** | 6,604 | 7,789 | 8,336 | 6,225 |
| **Single-Bias Incidents** | 6,598 | 7,775 | 8,322 | 6,219 |
| **Race:** | 3,199 | 3,816 | 4,057 | 3,241 |
| Anti-White | 545 | 652 | 668 | 753 |
| Anti-Black | 2,284 | 2,724 | 2,902 | 2,160 |
| Anti-American Indian/Alaskan Native | 65 | 84 | 87 | 88 |
| Anti-Asian/Pacific Islander | 126 | 147 | 149 | 108 |
| Anti-Multiple Races, Group | 179 | 209 | 251 | 132 |
| **Religion:** | 1,303 | 1,376 | 1,575 | 586 |
| Anti-Jewish | 931 | 964 | 1,132 | 353 |
| Anti-Catholic | 51 | 55 | 59 | 25 |
| Anti-Protestant | 38 | 40 | 42 | 17 |
| Anti-Islamic | 107 | 128 | 132 | 95 |
| Anti-Other Religion | 109 | 119 | 131 | 51 |
| Anti-Multiple Religions, Group | 57 | 60 | 68 | 38 |
| Anti-Atheism/Agnosticism/etc. | 10 | 10 | 11 | 7 |
| **Sexual Orientation:** | 1,223 | 1,436 | 1,482 | 1,394 |
| Anti-Male Homosexual | 682 | 798 | 817 | 817 |
| Anti-Female Homosexual | 185 | 216 | 227 | 197 |
| Anti-Homosexual | 312 | 376 | 391 | 349 |
| Anti-Heterosexual | 21 | 21 | 21 | 14 |
| Anti-Bisexual | 23 | 25 | 26 | 17 |
| **Ethnicity/National Origin:** | 777 | 1,050 | 1,109 | 934 |
| Anti-Hispanic | 483 | 654 | 692 | 649 |
| Anti-Other Ethnicity/National Origin | 294 | 396 | 417 | 285 |
| **Disability:** | 96 | 97 | 99 | 64 |
| Anti-Physical | 25 | 25 | 25 | 25 |
| Anti-Mental | 71 | 72 | 74 | 39 |
| **Multiple-Bias Incidents[3]** | 6 | 14 | 14 | 6 |

[1]The term *victim* may refer to a person, business, institution, or society as a whole.
[2]The term *known offender* does not imply that the identity of the suspect is known, but only that an attribute of the suspect has been identified, which distinguishes him/her from an unknown offender.
[3]In a *multiple-bias incident,* two conditions must be met: (a) more than one offense type must occur in the incident and (b) at least two offense types must be motivated by different biases.

## Table 83. Incidents, Offenses, Victims, and Known Offenders, by Offense Type, 2009

(Number.)

| Offense type | Incidents[1] | Offenses | Victims[2] | Known offenders[3] |
|---|---|---|---|---|
| **TOTAL** | 6,604 | 7,789 | 8,336 | 6,225 |
| **Crimes against persons:** | 3,875 | 4,793 | 4,793 | 5,136 |
| Murder and nonnegligent manslaughter | 8 | 8 | 8 | 47 |
| Forcible rape | 9 | 9 | 9 | 16 |
| Aggravated assault | 699 | 914 | 914 | 1,208 |
| Simple assault | 1,446 | 1,691 | 1,691 | 2,072 |
| Intimidation | 1,700 | 2,158 | 2,158 | 1,778 |
| Other[4] | 13 | 13 | 13 | 15 |
| **Crimes against property:** | 2,970 | 2,970 | 3,517 | 1,453 |
| Robbery | 124 | 124 | 142 | 293 |
| Burglary | 137 | 137 | 157 | 78 |
| Larceny-theft | 163 | 163 | 174 | 126 |
| Motor vehicle theft | 11 | 11 | 11 | 7 |
| Arson | 41 | 41 | 61 | 22 |
| Destruction/damage/vandalism | 2,465 | 2,465 | 2,943 | 898 |
| Other[4] | 29 | 29 | 29 | 29 |
| **Crimes against society[4]** | 26 | 26 | 26 | 34 |

[1]The actual number of incidents is 6,604. However, the column figures will not add to the total because incidents may include more than one offense type, and these are counted in each appropriate offense type category.
[2]The term *victim* may refer to a person, business, institution, or society as a whole.
[3]The term known offender does not imply that the identity of the suspect is known, but only that an attribute of the suspect has been identified, which distinguishes him/her from an unknown offender. The actual number of known offenders is 6,225. However, the column figures will not add to the total because some offenders are responsible for more than one offense type, and they are, therefore, counted more than once in this table.
[4]Includes additional offenses collected in the NIBRS.

## Table 84. Known Offender's Race, by Offense Type, 2009

(Number.)

| Offense type | Total offenses | Known offender's race | | | | | | Unknown offender |
|---|---|---|---|---|---|---|---|---|
| | | White | Black | American Indian/ Alaskan Native | Asian/Pacific Islander | Multiple races, group | Unknown race | |
| **TOTAL** | 7,789 | 3,398 | 837 | 60 | 47 | 228 | 571 | 2,648 |
| **Crimes against persons:** | 4,793 | 2,868 | 710 | 55 | 36 | 194 | 314 | 616 |
| Murder and nonnegligent manslaughter | 8 | 6 | 2 | 0 | 0 | 0 | 0 | 0 |
| Forcible rape | 9 | 6 | 1 | 0 | 0 | 1 | 0 | 1 |
| Aggravated assault | 914 | 577 | 192 | 16 | 6 | 47 | 38 | 38 |
| Simple assault | 1,691 | 983 | 309 | 29 | 10 | 98 | 90 | 172 |
| Intimidation | 2,158 | 1,287 | 205 | 10 | 19 | 48 | 184 | 405 |
| Other[1] | 13 | 9 | 1 | 0 | 1 | 0 | 2 | 0 |
| **Crimes against property:** | 2,970 | 509 | 124 | 5 | 11 | 34 | 255 | 2,032 |
| Robbery | 124 | 44 | 46 | 1 | 2 | 15 | 4 | 12 |
| Burglary | 137 | 29 | 5 | 0 | 0 | 1 | 17 | 85 |
| Larceny-theft | 163 | 56 | 14 | 1 | 1 | 1 | 25 | 65 |
| Motor vehicle theft | 11 | 0 | 0 | 0 | 0 | 0 | 7 | 4 |
| Arson | 41 | 11 | 2 | 0 | 0 | 1 | 2 | 25 |
| Destruction/damage/vandalism | 2,465 | 353 | 54 | 2 | 7 | 15 | 197 | 1,837 |
| Other[1] | 29 | 16 | 3 | 1 | 1 | 1 | 3 | 4 |
| **Crimes against society[1]** | 26 | 21 | 3 | 0 | 0 | 0 | 2 | 0 |

[1]Includes additional offenses collected in the NIBRS.

## Table 85. Number of Offenses and Offense Type, by Bias Motivation, 2009

(Number.)

| Bias motivation | Total offenses | Crimes against persons | | | | | Other[1] |
|---|---|---|---|---|---|---|---|
| | | Murder and nonnegligent manslaughter | Forcible rape | Aggravated assault | Simple assault | Intimidation | |
| **TOTAL** | 7789 | 8 | 9 | 914 | 1691 | 2158 | 13 |
| **Single-Bias Incidents** | 7775 | 8 | 9 | 913 | 1689 | 2153 | 13 |
| **Race:** | 3816 | 6 | 4 | 460 | 804 | 1194 | 8 |
| Anti-White | 652 | 3 | 2 | 113 | 191 | 158 | 5 |
| Anti-Black | 2724 | 2 | 2 | 312 | 507 | 935 | 1 |
| Anti-American Indian/Alaskan Native | 84 | 1 | 0 | 13 | 31 | 12 | 2 |
| Anti-Asian/Pacific Islander | 147 | 0 | 0 | 15 | 44 | 40 | 0 |
| Anti-Multiple Races, Group | 209 | 0 | 0 | 7 | 31 | 49 | 0 |
| **Religion:** | 1376 | 0 | 0 | 29 | 129 | 260 | 0 |
| Anti-Jewish | 964 | 0 | 0 | 9 | 82 | 172 | 0 |
| Anti-Catholic | 55 | 0 | 0 | 1 | 4 | 6 | 0 |
| Anti-Protestant | 40 | 0 | 0 | 0 | 0 | 10 | 0 |
| Anti-Islamic | 128 | 0 | 0 | 11 | 34 | 44 | 0 |
| Anti-Other Religion | 119 | 0 | 0 | 4 | 3 | 20 | 0 |
| Anti-Multiple Religions, Group | 60 | 0 | 0 | 4 | 5 | 7 | 0 |
| Anti-Atheism/Agnosticism/etc. | 10 | 0 | 0 | 0 | 1 | 1 | 0 |
| **Sexual Orientation:** | 1436 | 1 | 4 | 227 | 493 | 325 | 2 |
| Anti-Male Homosexual | 798 | 0 | 0 | 137 | 291 | 170 | 1 |
| Anti-Female Homosexual | 216 | 0 | 4 | 36 | 73 | 47 | 1 |
| Anti-Homosexual | 376 | 1 | 0 | 51 | 118 | 100 | 0 |
| Anti-Heterosexual | 21 | 0 | 0 | 3 | 5 | 3 | 0 |
| Anti-Bisexual | 25 | 0 | 0 | 0 | 6 | 5 | 0 |
| **Ethnicity/National Origin:** | 1050 | 1 | 1 | 192 | 242 | 357 | 1 |
| Anti-Hispanic | 654 | 1 | 1 | 143 | 158 | 205 | 1 |
| Anti-Other Ethnicity/National Origin | 396 | 0 | 0 | 49 | 84 | 152 | 0 |
| **Disability:** | 97 | 0 | 0 | 5 | 21 | 17 | 2 |
| Anti-Physical | 25 | 0 | 0 | 3 | 4 | 9 | 0 |
| Anti-Mental | 72 | 0 | 0 | 2 | 17 | 8 | 2 |
| **Multiple-Bias Incidents**[2] | 14 | 0 | 0 | 1 | 2 | 5 | 0 |

| Bias motivation | Crimes against property | | | | | | | Crimes against society[1] |
|---|---|---|---|---|---|---|---|---|
| | Robbery | Burglary | Larceny-theft | Motor vehicle theft | Arson | Destruction/ damage/ vandalism | Other[1] | |
| **TOTAL** | 124 | 137 | 163 | 11 | 41 | 2465 | 29 | 26 |
| **Single-Bias Incidents** | 124 | 135 | 163 | 11 | 41 | 2461 | 29 | 26 |
| **Race:** | 57 | 76 | 79 | 5 | 12 | 1079 | 17 | 15 |
| Anti-White | 31 | 20 | 47 | 1 | 2 | 60 | 13 | 6 |
| Anti-Black | 23 | 49 | 19 | 3 | 8 | 856 | 1 | 6 |
| Anti-American Indian/Alaskan Native | 3 | 2 | 9 | 0 | 0 | 8 | 2 | 1 |
| Anti-Asian/Pacific Islander | 0 | 0 | 2 | 0 | 0 | 45 | 1 | 0 |
| Anti-Multiple Races, Group | 0 | 5 | 2 | 1 | 2 | 110 | 0 | 2 |
| **Religion:** | 1 | 23 | 30 | 1 | 14 | 882 | 5 | 2 |
| Anti-Jewish | 1 | 13 | 6 | 1 | 8 | 671 | 0 | 1 |
| Anti-Catholic | 0 | 0 | 12 | 0 | 1 | 29 | 2 | 0 |
| Anti-Protestant | 0 | 1 | 1 | 0 | 1 | 26 | 1 | 0 |
| Anti-Islamic | 0 | 0 | 4 | 0 | 1 | 33 | 0 | 1 |
| Anti-Other Religion | 0 | 3 | 1 | 0 | 3 | 84 | 1 | 0 |
| Anti-Multiple Religions, Group | 0 | 4 | 4 | 0 | 0 | 35 | 1 | 0 |
| Anti-Atheism/Agnosticism/etc. | 0 | 2 | 2 | 0 | 0 | 4 | 0 | 0 |
| **Sexual Orientation:** | 44 | 16 | 16 | 1 | 8 | 295 | 1 | 3 |
| Anti-Male Homosexual | 30 | 7 | 6 | 1 | 2 | 152 | 0 | 1 |
| Anti-Female Homosexual | 2 | 4 | 3 | 0 | 2 | 43 | 0 | 1 |
| Anti-Homosexual | 11 | 2 | 4 | 0 | 3 | 85 | 1 | 0 |
| Anti-Heterosexual | 0 | 1 | 0 | 0 | 1 | 8 | 0 | 0 |
| Anti-Bisexual | 1 | 2 | 3 | 0 | 0 | 7 | 0 | 1 |
| **Ethnicity/National Origin:** | 22 | 13 | 18 | 4 | 7 | 184 | 4 | 4 |
| Anti-Hispanic | 20 | 11 | 10 | 1 | 3 | 95 | 2 | 3 |
| Anti-Other Ethnicity/National Origin | 2 | 2 | 8 | 3 | 4 | 89 | 2 | 1 |
| **Disability:** | 0 | 7 | 20 | 0 | 0 | 21 | 2 | 2 |
| Anti-Physical | 0 | 0 | 4 | 0 | 0 | 4 | 0 | 1 |
| Anti-Mental | 0 | 7 | 16 | 0 | 0 | 17 | 2 | 1 |
| **Multiple-Bias Incidents**[2] | 0 | 2 | 0 | 0 | 0 | 4 | 0 | 0 |

[1]Includes additional offenses collected in the NIBRS.

[2]In a *multiple-bias incident*, two conditions must be met: (a) more than one offense type must occur in the incident and (b) at least two offense types must be motivated by different biases.

## Table 86. Known Offender's Race, by Bias Motivation, 2009

(Number.)

| Bias motivation | Total offenses | Known offender's race | | | | | | Unknown offender |
|---|---|---|---|---|---|---|---|---|
| | | White | Black | American Indian/ Alaskan Native | Asian/Pacific Islander | Multipleraces, group | Unknown race | |
| **TOTAL** | 7,789 | 3,398 | 837 | 60 | 47 | 228 | 571 | 2,648 |
| **Single-Bias Incidents** | 7,775 | 3,390 | 837 | 60 | 47 | 226 | 569 | 2,646 |
| **Race:** | 3,816 | 1,844 | 392 | 34 | 16 | 103 | 274 | 1,153 |
| Anti-White | 652 | 147 | 304 | 16 | 2 | 22 | 50 | 111 |
| Anti-Black | 2,724 | 1,503 | 63 | 6 | 10 | 62 | 192 | 888 |
| Anti-American Indian/Alaskan Native | 84 | 53 | 5 | 6 | 3 | 5 | 2 | 10 |
| Anti-Asian/Pacific Islander | 147 | 72 | 11 | 2 | 1 | 4 | 9 | 48 |
| Anti-Multiple Races, Group | 209 | 69 | 9 | 4 | 0 | 10 | 21 | 96 |
| **Religion:** | 1,376 | 281 | 54 | 1 | 12 | 18 | 120 | 890 |
| Anti-Jewish | 964 | 165 | 29 | 1 | 9 | 8 | 76 | 676 |
| Anti-Catholic | 55 | 15 | 2 | 0 | 2 | 0 | 5 | 31 |
| Anti-Protestant | 40 | 5 | 0 | 0 | 1 | 0 | 12 | 22 |
| Anti-Islamic | 128 | 49 | 18 | 0 | 0 | 4 | 10 | 47 |
| Anti-Other Religion | 119 | 29 | 3 | 0 | 0 | 1 | 9 | 77 |
| Anti-Multiple Religions, Group | 60 | 12 | 2 | 0 | 0 | 5 | 7 | 34 |
| Anti-Atheism/Agnosticism/etc. | 10 | 6 | 0 | 0 | 0 | 0 | 1 | 3 |
| **Sexual Orientation:** | 1,436 | 663 | 268 | 9 | 9 | 63 | 100 | 324 |
| Anti-Male Homosexual | 798 | 375 | 162 | 7 | 4 | 37 | 55 | 158 |
| Anti-Female Homosexual | 216 | 94 | 41 | 1 | 2 | 14 | 16 | 48 |
| Anti-Homosexual | 376 | 172 | 61 | 1 | 3 | 12 | 24 | 103 |
| Anti-Heterosexual | 21 | 10 | 2 | 0 | 0 | 0 | 2 | 7 |
| Anti-Bisexual | 25 | 12 | 2 | 0 | 0 | 0 | 3 | 8 |
| **Ethnicity/National Origin:** | 1,050 | 562 | 114 | 16 | 9 | 39 | 75 | 235 |
| Anti-Hispanic | 654 | 364 | 79 | 13 | 7 | 25 | 41 | 125 |
| Anti-Other Ethnicity/National Origin | 396 | 198 | 35 | 3 | 2 | 14 | 34 | 110 |
| **Disability:** | 97 | 40 | 9 | 0 | 1 | 3 | 0 | 44 |
| Anti-Physical | 25 | 14 | 2 | 0 | 0 | 2 | 0 | 7 |
| Anti-Mental | 72 | 26 | 7 | 0 | 1 | 1 | 0 | 37 |
| **Multiple-Bias Incidents[1]** | 14 | 8 | 0 | 0 | 0 | 2 | 2 | 2 |

[1]In a *multiple-bias incident,* two conditions must be met: (a) more than one offense type must occur in the incident and (b) at least two offense types must be motivated by different biases.

## Table 87. Victim Type, by Offense Type, 2009

(Number.)

| Offense type | Total offenses | Victim type | | | | | Other/ unknown/ multiple |
|---|---|---|---|---|---|---|---|
| | | Individual | Business/ financial institution | Government | Religious organization | Society/ public[1] | |
| **TOTAL** | 7789 | 6234 | 343 | 291 | 237 | 26 | 658 |
| **Crimes against persons[2]** | 4793 | 4793 | - | - | - | - | - |
| **Crimes against property:** | 2970 | 1441 | 343 | 291 | 237 | 0 | 658 |
| Robbery | 124 | 107 | 1 | 0 | 0 | 0 | 16 |
| Burglary | 137 | 104 | 9 | 4 | 10 | 0 | 10 |
| Larceny-theft | 163 | 115 | 36 | 1 | 3 | 0 | 8 |
| Motor vehicle theft | 11 | 9 | 0 | 0 | 0 | 0 | 2 |
| Arson | 41 | 25 | 7 | 0 | 8 | 0 | 1 |
| Destruction/damage/vandalism | 2465 | 1058 | 286 | 284 | 216 | 0 | 621 |
| Other[2] | 29 | 23 | 4 | 2 | 0 | 0 | 0 |
| **Crimes against society[2]** | 26 | - | - | - | - | 26 | - |

[1]The victim type *society/public* is collected only in the NIBRS.
[2]Includes additional offenses collected in the NIBRS.

## Table 88. Number of Victims and Offense Type, by Bias Motivation, 2009

(Number.)

| Bias motivation | Total offenses | Crimes against persons | | | | | |
|---|---|---|---|---|---|---|---|
| | | Murder and nonnegligent manslaughter | Forcible rape | Aggravated assault | Simple assault | Intimidation | Other[1] |
| **TOTAL** 8336 | 8 | 9 | 914 | 1691 | 2158 | 13 | |
| **Single-Bias Incidents** 8322 | 8 | 9 | 913 | 1689 | 2153 | 13 | |
| **Race:** 4057 | 6 | 4 | 460 | 804 | 1194 | 8 | |
| Anti-White 668 | 3 | 2 | 113 | 191 | 158 | 5 | |
| Anti-Black 2902 | 2 | 2 | 312 | 507 | 935 | 1 | |
| Anti-American Indian/Alaskan Native 87 | 1 | 0 | 13 | 31 | 12 | 2 | |
| Anti-Asian/Pacific Islander 149 | 0 | 0 | 15 | 44 | 40 | 0 | |
| Anti-Multiple Races, Group 251 | 0 | 0 | 7 | 31 | 49 | 0 | |
| **Religion:** 1575 | 0 | 0 | 29 | 129 | 260 | 0 | |
| Anti-Jewish 1132 | 0 | 0 | 9 | 82 | 172 | 0 | |
| Anti-Catholic 59 | 0 | 0 | 1 | 4 | 6 | 0 | |
| Anti-Protestant 42 | 0 | 0 | 0 | 0 | 10 | 0 | |
| Anti-Islamic 132 | 0 | 0 | 11 | 34 | 44 | 0 | |
| Anti-Other Religion 131 | 0 | 0 | 4 | 3 | 20 | 0 | |
| Anti-Multiple Religions, Group 68 | 0 | 0 | 4 | 5 | 7 | 0 | |
| Anti-Atheism/Agnosticism/etc. 11 | 0 | 0 | 0 | 1 | 1 | 0 | |
| **Sexual Orientation:** 1482 | 1 | 4 | 227 | 493 | 325 | 2 | |
| Anti-Male Homosexual 817 | 0 | 0 | 137 | 291 | 170 | 1 | |
| Anti-Female Homosexual 227 | 0 | 4 | 36 | 73 | 47 | 1 | |
| Anti-Homosexual 391 | 1 | 0 | 51 | 118 | 100 | 0 | |
| Anti-Heterosexual 21 | 0 | 0 | 3 | 5 | 3 | 0 | |
| Anti-Bisexual 26 | 0 | 0 | 0 | 6 | 5 | 0 | |
| **Ethnicity/National Origin:** 1109 | 1 | 1 | 192 | 242 | 357 | 1 | |
| Anti-Hispanic 692 | 1 | 1 | 143 | 158 | 205 | 1 | |
| Anti-Other Ethnicity/National Origin 417 | 0 | 0 | 49 | 84 | 152 | 0 | |
| **Disability:** 99 | 0 | 0 | 5 | 21 | 17 | 2 | |
| Anti-Physical 25 | 0 | 0 | 3 | 4 | 9 | 0 | |
| Anti-Mental 74 | 0 | 0 | 2 | 17 | 8 | 2 | |
| **Multiple-Bias Incidents[2]** 14 | 0 | 0 | 1 | 2 | 5 | 0 | |

| Bias motivation | Crimes against property | | | | | | | Crimes against society[1] |
|---|---|---|---|---|---|---|---|---|
| | Robbery | Burglary | Larceny-theft | Motor vehicle theft | Arson | Destruction/ damage/ vandalism | Other[1] | |
| **TOTAL** | 142 | 157 | 174 | 11 | 61 | 2943 | 29 | 26 |
| **Single-Bias Incidents** | 142 | 155 | 174 | 11 | 61 | 2939 | 29 | 26 |
| **Race:** | 63 | 84 | 81 | 5 | 20 | 1296 | 17 | 15 |
| Anti-White | 34 | 22 | 48 | 1 | 2 | 70 | 13 | 6 |
| Anti-Black | 25 | 54 | 19 | 3 | 16 | 1019 | 1 | 6 |
| Anti-American Indian/Alaskan Native | 4 | 2 | 10 | 0 | 0 | 9 | 2 | 1 |
| Anti-Asian/Pacific Islander | 0 | 0 | 2 | 0 | 0 | 47 | 1 | 0 |
| Anti-Multiple Races, Group | 0 | 6 | 2 | 1 | 2 | 151 | 0 | 2 |
| **Religion:** | 1 | 25 | 33 | 1 | 21 | 1069 | 5 | 2 |
| Anti-Jewish | 1 | 14 | 7 | 1 | 13 | 832 | 0 | 1 |
| Anti-Catholic | 0 | 0 | 13 | 0 | 2 | 31 | 2 | 0 |
| Anti-Protestant | 0 | 1 | 1 | 0 | 1 | 28 | 1 | 0 |
| Anti-Islamic | 0 | 0 | 4 | 0 | 1 | 37 | 0 | 1 |
| Anti-Other Religion | 0 | 3 | 1 | 0 | 4 | 95 | 1 | 0 |
| Anti-Multiple Religions, Group | 0 | 5 | 4 | 0 | 0 | 42 | 1 | 0 |
| Anti-Atheism/Agnosticism/etc. | 0 | 2 | 3 | 0 | 0 | 4 | 0 | 0 |
| **Sexual Orientation:** | 49 | 18 | 18 | 1 | 9 | 331 | 1 | 3 |
| Anti-Male Homosexual | 33 | 8 | 6 | 1 | 2 | 167 | 0 | 1 |
| Anti-Female Homosexual | 2 | 5 | 3 | 0 | 3 | 52 | 0 | 1 |
| Anti-Homosexual | 13 | 2 | 5 | 0 | 3 | 97 | 1 | 0 |
| Anti-Heterosexual | 0 | 1 | 0 | 0 | 1 | 8 | 0 | 0 |
| Anti-Bisexual | 1 | 2 | 4 | 0 | 0 | 7 | 0 | 1 |
| **Ethnicity/National Origin:** | 29 | 19 | 22 | 4 | 11 | 222 | 4 | 4 |
| Anti-Hispanic | 27 | 17 | 12 | 1 | 3 | 118 | 2 | 3 |
| Anti-Other Ethnicity/National Origin | 2 | 2 | 10 | 3 | 8 | 104 | 2 | 1 |
| **Disability:** | 0 | 9 | 20 | 0 | 0 | 21 | 2 | 2 |
| Anti-Physical | 0 | 0 | 4 | 0 | 0 | 4 | 0 | 1 |
| Anti-Mental | 0 | 9 | 16 | 0 | 0 | 17 | 2 | 1 |
| **Multiple-Bias Incidents[2]** | 0 | 2 | 0 | 0 | 0 | 4 | 0 | 0 |

[1]Includes additional offenses collected in the NIBRS.

[2]In a *multiple-bias incident,* two conditions must be met: (a) more than one offense type must occur in the incident and (b) at least two offense types must be motivated by different biases.

## Table 89. Number of Incidents and Victim Type, by Bias Motivation, 2009

(Number.)

| Offense type | Total offenses | Victim type | | | | | |
|---|---|---|---|---|---|---|---|
| | | Individual | Business/ financial institution | Government | Religious organization | Society/ public[1] | Other/ unknown/ multiple |
| **TOTAL** | 6604 | 5070 | 327 | 283 | 229 | 18 | 677 |
| **Single-Bias Incidents** | 6598 | 5065 | 326 | 283 | 229 | 18 | 677 |
| Race | 3199 | 2574 | 160 | 174 | 30 | 10 | 251 |
| Religion | 1303 | 608 | 110 | 76 | 190 | 1 | 318 |
| Sexual Orientation | 1223 | 1104 | 26 | 19 | 7 | 2 | 65 |
| Ethnicity/National Origin | 777 | 689 | 28 | 12 | 2 | 3 | 43 |
| Disability | 96 | 90 | 2 | 2 | 0 | 2 | 0 |
| **Multiple-Bias Incidents[2]** | 6 | 5 | 1 | 0 | 0 | 0 | 0 |

[1]The victim type *society/public* is collected only in the NIBRS.
[2]In a *multiple-bias incident,* two conditions must be met: (a) more than one offense type must occur in the incident and (b) at least two offense types must be motivated by different biases.

## Table 90. Known Offender's[1] Race, 2009

(Number.)

| Race | Number |
|---|---|
| **TOTAL** | **6,225** |
| White | 3,885 |
| Black | 1,150 |
| American Indian/Alaskan Native | 60 |
| Asian/Pacific Islander | 45 |
| Multiple Races, Group[2] | 453 |
| Unknown Race | 632 |

[1]The term *known offender* does not imply that the identity of the suspect is known, but only that an attribute of the suspect has been identified, which distinguishes him/her from an unknown offender.
[2]The term *multiple races, group* is used to describe a group of offenders of varying races.

## Table 91. Number of Incidents and Bias Motivation, by Location, 2009

(Number.)

| Location | Total incidents | Bias motivation | | | | | Multiple-bias incidents[1] |
|---|---|---|---|---|---|---|---|
| | | Race | Religion | Sexual orientation | Ethnicity/ national origin | Disability | |
| **TOTAL** | 6604 | 3199 | 1303 | 1223 | 777 | 96 | 6 |
| Air/bus/train terminal | 55 | 29 | 9 | 13 | 2 | 2 | 0 |
| Bank/savings and loan | 8 | 3 | 1 | 2 | 1 | 1 | 0 |
| Bar/nightclub | 133 | 59 | 2 | 62 | 10 | 0 | 0 |
| Church/synagogue/temple | 283 | 41 | 229 | 9 | 2 | 2 | 0 |
| Commercial office building | 123 | 55 | 38 | 16 | 11 | 3 | 0 |
| Construction site | 13 | 6 | 3 | 1 | 3 | 0 | 0 |
| Convenience store | 64 | 32 | 9 | 5 | 18 | 0 | 0 |
| Department/discount store | 59 | 37 | 10 | 8 | 4 | 0 | 0 |
| Drug store/Dr.'s office/hospital | 50 | 27 | 16 | 2 | 5 | 0 | 0 |
| Field/woods | 95 | 59 | 10 | 11 | 12 | 3 | 0 |
| Government/public building | 108 | 60 | 23 | 12 | 12 | 1 | 0 |
| Grocery/supermarket | 44 | 24 | 6 | 2 | 11 | 1 | 0 |
| Highway/road/alley/street | 1135 | 602 | 92 | 261 | 169 | 11 | 0 |
| Hotel/motel/etc. | 35 | 21 | 2 | 6 | 6 | 0 | 0 |
| Jail/prison | 48 | 28 | 5 | 10 | 4 | 1 | 0 |
| Lake/waterway | 12 | 5 | 0 | 4 | 3 | 0 | 0 |
| Liquor store | 12 | 6 | 1 | 1 | 4 | 0 | 0 |
| Parking lot/garage | 403 | 212 | 36 | 84 | 64 | 7 | 0 |
| Rental storage facility | 7 | 5 | 1 | 0 | 1 | 0 | 0 |
| Residence/home | 2070 | 1064 | 324 | 381 | 253 | 46 | 2 |
| Restaurant | 107 | 53 | 10 | 27 | 16 | 0 | 1 |
| School/college | 754 | 396 | 168 | 123 | 64 | 2 | 1 |
| Service/gas station | 42 | 17 | 2 | 7 | 15 | 1 | 0 |
| Specialty store (TV, fur, etc.) | 64 | 31 | 19 | 8 | 6 | 0 | 0 |
| Other/unknown | 877 | 327 | 287 | 168 | 80 | 15 | 0 |
| Multiple locations | 3 | 0 | 0 | 0 | 1 | 0 | 2 |

[1]In a *multiple-bias incident,* two conditions must be met: (a) more than one offense type must occur in the incident and (b) at least two offense types must be motivated by different biases.

## Table 92. Offense Type, by Participating State, 2009

(Number.)

| Participating state | Total offenses | Crimes against persons | | | | | |
|---|---|---|---|---|---|---|---|
| | | Murder and nonnegligent manslaughter | Forcible rape | Aggravated assault | Simple assault | Intimidation | Other[1] |
| **TOTAL** | 7789 | 8 | 9 | 914 | 1691 | 2158 | 13 |
| Alabama | 10 | 0 | 0 | 0 | 0 | 5 | 0 |
| Alaska | 12 | 0 | 0 | 5 | 4 | 1 | 0 |
| Arizona | 274 | 0 | 0 | 39 | 60 | 76 | 0 |
| Arkansas | 85 | 0 | 1 | 5 | 24 | 14 | 0 |
| California | 1285 | 2 | 4 | 200 | 231 | 363 | 0 |
| Colorado | 269 | 1 | 1 | 52 | 65 | 75 | 2 |
| Connecticut | 222 | 0 | 0 | 19 | 21 | 68 | 1 |
| Delaware | 44 | 0 | 0 | 1 | 8 | 12 | 0 |
| District of Columbia | 41 | 0 | 0 | 11 | 13 | 9 | 0 |
| Florida | 147 | 0 | 0 | 34 | 31 | 37 | 0 |
| Georgia | 12 | 0 | 0 | 0 | 2 | 1 | 0 |
| Idaho | 42 | 0 | 0 | 8 | 10 | 12 | 0 |
| Illinois | 178 | 0 | 0 | 22 | 46 | 54 | 0 |
| Indiana | 68 | 0 | 0 | 2 | 22 | 23 | 0 |
| Iowa | 19 | 0 | 0 | 2 | 7 | 4 | 0 |
| Kansas | 143 | 0 | 0 | 18 | 29 | 44 | 0 |
| Kentucky | 176 | 2 | 0 | 10 | 37 | 53 | 1 |
| Louisiana | 21 | 0 | 0 | 8 | 8 | 0 | 0 |
| Maine | 56 | 0 | 0 | 4 | 19 | 22 | 0 |
| Maryland | 107 | 0 | 0 | 7 | 13 | 2 | 0 |
| Massachusetts | 382 | 0 | 0 | 36 | 69 | 142 | 3 |
| Michigan | 409 | 0 | 0 | 85 | 106 | 158 | 0 |
| Minnesota | 189 | 0 | 0 | 39 | 84 | 30 | 0 |
| Mississippi | 2 | 0 | 0 | 0 | 0 | 0 | 0 |
| Missouri | 167 | 0 | 1 | 32 | 43 | 50 | 0 |
| Montana | 31 | 1 | 0 | 2 | 8 | 4 | 2 |
| Nebraska | 82 | 0 | 0 | 5 | 29 | 11 | 0 |
| Nevada | 64 | 0 | 0 | 23 | 12 | 15 | 0 |
| New Hampshire | 27 | 0 | 0 | 0 | 10 | 9 | 0 |
| New Jersey | 549 | 0 | 0 | 8 | 27 | 267 | 0 |
| New Mexico | 18 | 0 | 0 | 6 | 5 | 0 | 0 |
| New York | 648 | 0 | 0 | 33 | 239 | 37 | 0 |
| North Carolina | 125 | 0 | 0 | 13 | 25 | 44 | 0 |
| North Dakota | 14 | 1 | 0 | 2 | 4 | 2 | 1 |
| Ohio | 342 | 0 | 0 | 7 | 58 | 119 | 0 |
| Oklahoma | 68 | 1 | 0 | 10 | 17 | 18 | 0 |
| Oregon | 167 | 0 | 0 | 19 | 25 | 66 | 0 |
| Pennsylvania | 53 | 0 | 0 | 7 | 9 | 24 | 0 |
| Rhode Island | 38 | 0 | 0 | 3 | 10 | 1 | 0 |
| South Carolina | 146 | 0 | 1 | 29 | 24 | 26 | 2 |
| South Dakota | 58 | 0 | 0 | 1 | 33 | 3 | 0 |
| Tennessee | 185 | 0 | 0 | 23 | 35 | 43 | 1 |
| Texas | 185 | 0 | 0 | 36 | 50 | 31 | 0 |
| Utah | 54 | 0 | 0 | 4 | 14 | 10 | 0 |
| Vermont | 28 | 0 | 0 | 2 | 8 | 1 | 0 |
| Virginia | 170 | 0 | 0 | 11 | 33 | 26 | 0 |
| Washington | 272 | 0 | 1 | 20 | 44 | 118 | 0 |
| West Virginia | 27 | 0 | 0 | 3 | 4 | 5 | 0 |
| Wisconsin | 61 | 0 | 0 | 7 | 14 | 10 | 0 |
| Wyoming | 17 | 0 | 0 | 1 | 2 | 13 | 0 |

[1]Includes additional offenses collected in the NIBRS.

## Table 92. Offense Type, by Participating State, 2009—*Continued*

(Number.)

| Participating state | Crimes against property | | | | | | | Crimes against society[1] |
|---|---|---|---|---|---|---|---|---|
| | Robbery | Burglary | Larceny-theft | Motor vehicle theft | Arson | Destruction/ damage/ vandalism | Other[1] | |
| **TOTAL** | 124 | 137 | 163 | 11 | 41 | 2465 | 29 | 26 |
| Alabama | 0 | 0 | 0 | 0 | 1 | 4 | 0 | 0 |
| Alaska | 2 | 0 | 0 | 0 | 0 | 0 | 0 | 0 |
| Arizona | 2 | 6 | 0 | 1 | 1 | 89 | 0 | 0 |
| Arkansas | 3 | 5 | 7 | 0 | 2 | 19 | 1 | 4 |
| California | 33 | 18 | 6 | 1 | 12 | 415 | 0 | 0 |
| Colorado | 16 | 4 | 9 | 1 | 0 | 42 | 1 | 0 |
| Connecticut | 0 | 0 | 1 | 0 | 0 | 111 | 0 | 1 |
| Delaware | 2 | 2 | 0 | 0 | 0 | 19 | 0 | 0 |
| District of Columbia | 3 | 0 | 0 | 0 | 1 | 4 | 0 | 0 |
| Florida | 3 | 3 | 0 | 1 | 0 | 38 | 0 | 0 |
| Georgia | 0 | 1 | 0 | 0 | 0 | 8 | 0 | 0 |
| Idaho | 0 | 0 | 2 | 0 | 0 | 10 | 0 | 0 |
| Illinois | 1 | 1 | 1 | 0 | 2 | 51 | 0 | 0 |
| Indiana | 1 | 0 | 0 | 0 | 0 | 20 | 0 | 0 |
| Iowa | 0 | 0 | 0 | 0 | 0 | 6 | 0 | 0 |
| Kansas | 0 | 3 | 5 | 0 | 0 | 43 | 0 | 1 |
| Kentucky | 5 | 13 | 7 | 1 | 3 | 42 | 2 | 0 |
| Louisiana | 1 | 1 | 1 | 0 | 0 | 2 | 0 | 0 |
| Maine | 0 | 1 | 0 | 0 | 0 | 10 | 0 | 0 |
| Maryland | 0 | 1 | 0 | 0 | 2 | 82 | 0 | 0 |
| Massachusetts | 2 | 8 | 8 | 0 | 1 | 111 | 2 | 0 |
| Michigan | 3 | 6 | 13 | 0 | 0 | 29 | 1 | 8 |
| Minnesota | 2 | 1 | 1 | 0 | 2 | 30 | 0 | 0 |
| Mississippi | 0 | 0 | 1 | 0 | 0 | 1 | 0 | 0 |
| Missouri | 3 | 2 | 0 | 0 | 0 | 36 | 0 | 0 |
| Montana | 0 | 1 | 5 | 0 | 0 | 6 | 2 | 0 |
| Nebraska | 1 | 1 | 1 | 0 | 0 | 34 | 0 | 0 |
| Nevada | 2 | 0 | 0 | 0 | 0 | 12 | 0 | 0 |
| New Hampshire | 0 | 0 | 0 | 0 | 0 | 8 | 0 | 0 |
| New Jersey | 2 | 2 | 0 | 0 | 2 | 241 | 0 | 0 |
| New Mexico | 0 | 0 | 0 | 0 | 0 | 7 | 0 | 0 |
| New York | 15 | 7 | 8 | 0 | 4 | 305 | 0 | 0 |
| North Carolina | 1 | 2 | 2 | 0 | 0 | 38 | 0 | 0 |
| North Dakota | 0 | 1 | 2 | 0 | 0 | 1 | 0 | 0 |
| Ohio | 5 | 14 | 29 | 2 | 2 | 98 | 5 | 3 |
| Oklahoma | 1 | 0 | 0 | 0 | 0 | 21 | 0 | 0 |
| Oregon | 2 | 0 | 4 | 1 | 0 | 49 | 0 | 1 |
| Pennsylvania | 0 | 0 | 0 | 0 | 3 | 10 | 0 | 0 |
| Rhode Island | 0 | 1 | 0 | 0 | 1 | 21 | 0 | 1 |
| South Carolina | 3 | 7 | 15 | 2 | 0 | 32 | 4 | 1 |
| South Dakota | 0 | 1 | 3 | 0 | 0 | 15 | 2 | 0 |
| Tennessee | 3 | 4 | 14 | 1 | 0 | 57 | 4 | 0 |
| Texas | 3 | 2 | 0 | 0 | 2 | 61 | 0 | 0 |
| Utah | 0 | 0 | 6 | 0 | 0 | 17 | 2 | 1 |
| Vermont | 1 | 1 | 3 | 0 | 0 | 11 | 1 | 0 |
| Virginia | 0 | 8 | 2 | 0 | 0 | 90 | 0 | 0 |
| Washington | 1 | 2 | 0 | 0 | 0 | 86 | 0 | 0 |
| West Virginia | 0 | 3 | 3 | 0 | 0 | 5 | 1 | 3 |
| Wisconsin | 2 | 4 | 4 | 0 | 0 | 17 | 1 | 2 |
| Wyoming | 0 | 0 | 0 | 0 | 0 | 1 | 0 | 0 |

[1]Includes additional offenses collected in the NIBRS.

## Table 93. Agency Hate Crime Reporting, by State, 2009

| Participating state | Number of participating agencies | Population covered | Agencies submitting incident reports | Total number of incidents reported |
|---|---|---|---|---|
| **TOTAL** | 14,422 | 278,948,317 | 2,034 | 6,604 |
| Alabama | 218 | 3,211,336 | 6 | 9 |
| Alaska | 2 | 289,884 | 2 | 9 |
| Arizona | 93 | 6,506,963 | 25 | 219 |
| Arkansas | 256 | 2,717,288 | 41 | 74 |
| California | 734 | 36,961,664 | 254 | 1,015 |
| Colorado | 218 | 4,952,740 | 55 | 208 |
| Connecticut | 102 | 3,518,288 | 48 | 198 |
| Delaware | 55 | 885,122 | 9 | 37 |
| District of Columbia | 2 | 599,657 | 2 | 36 |
| Florida | 487 | 18,445,281 | 64 | 130 |
| Georgia | 487 | 7,791,562 | 5 | 11 |
| Idaho | 107 | 1,543,741 | 10 | 35 |
| Illinois | 359 | 8,493,832 | 53 | 129 |
| Indiana | 139 | 3,735,359 | 17 | 55 |
| Iowa | 228 | 2,979,710 | 12 | 18 |
| Kansas | 352 | 2,195,030 | 62 | 122 |
| Kentucky | 347 | 3,213,237 | 84 | 150 |
| Louisiana | 95 | 2,613,140 | 9 | 13 |
| Maine | 149 | 1,318,301 | 24 | 50 |
| Maryland | 156 | 5,699,478 | 18 | 102 |
| Massachusetts | 309 | 6,375,433 | 86 | 322 |
| Michigan | 604 | 9,837,274 | 141 | 314 |
| Minnesota | 87 | 2,563,655 | 31 | 153 |
| Mississippi | 61 | 827,707 | 2 | 2 |
| Missouri | 621 | 5,978,668 | 36 | 124 |
| Montana | 100 | 968,253 | 14 | 28 |
| Nebraska | 190 | 1,521,548 | 7 | 78 |
| Nevada | 31 | 2,279,796 | 5 | 48 |
| New Hampshire | 151 | 1,160,414 | 18 | 24 |
| New Jersey | 510 | 8,695,567 | 175 | 549 |
| New Mexico | 49 | 1,136,341 | 4 | 15 |
| New York | 515 | 18,703,702 | 80 | 626 |
| North Carolina | 516 | 9,378,135 | 42 | 103 |
| North Dakota | 87 | 614,661 | 9 | 14 |
| Ohio | 588 | 9,477,815 | 105 | 297 |
| Oklahoma | 314 | 3,682,123 | 27 | 59 |
| Oregon | 73 | 2,384,990 | 32 | 130 |
| Pennsylvania | 1,299 | 12,538,883 | 22 | 46 |
| Rhode Island | 48 | 1,053,209 | 13 | 36 |
| South Carolina | 475 | 4,554,167 | 50 | 124 |
| South Dakota | 113 | 724,778 | 11 | 42 |
| Tennessee | 462 | 6,296,254 | 60 | 169 |
| Texas | 1,020 | 24,770,372 | 64 | 165 |
| Utah | 123 | 2,747,172 | 24 | 48 |
| Vermont | 82 | 607,236 | 15 | 24 |
| Virginia | 413 | 7,882,590 | 67 | 150 |
| Washington | 250 | 6,651,663 | 52 | 208 |
| West Virginia | 291 | 1,674,227 | 17 | 24 |
| Wisconsin | 391 | 5,650,571 | 21 | 54 |
| Wyoming | 63 | 539,500 | 4 | 8 |

## Table 94. Hate Crime Incidents per Bias Motivation and Quarter, by State and Agency, 2009

| State | Agency type/Agency name | Number of incidents per bias motivation | | | | | Number of incidents per quarter[1] | | | | Popu-lation[2] |
|---|---|---|---|---|---|---|---|---|---|---|---|
| | | Race | Religion | Sexual orient-ation | Ethnicity | Disability | 1st quarter | 2nd quarter | 3rd quarter | 4th quarter | |
| **ALABAMA** | **Total** | 6 | 1 | 2 | 0 | 0 | | | | | |
| | **Cities** | 6 | 1 | 2 | 0 | 0 | | | | | |
| | Alabaster | 1 | 0 | 0 | 0 | 0 | 0 | 0 | 1 | 0 | 30,002 |
| | Hoover | 3 | 0 | 1 | 0 | 0 | 1 | 1 | 2 | 0 | 71,919 |
| | Jasper | 1 | 0 | 0 | 0 | 0 | 0 | 1 | 0 | 0 | 14,129 |
| | Leesburg | 0 | 0 | 1 | 0 | 0 | | 1 | | | 823 |
| | Mobile | 0 | 1 | 0 | 0 | 0 | 1 | | 0 | 0 | 246,171 |
| | Ozark | 1 | 0 | 0 | 0 | 0 | 0 | 1 | 0 | 0 | 14,670 |
| **ALASKA** | **Total** | 7 | 0 | 2 | 0 | 0 | | | | | |
| | **Cities** | 7 | 0 | 2 | 0 | 0 | | | | | |
| | Anchorage | 6 | 0 | 1 | 0 | 0 | 1 | 1 | 3 | 2 | 283,300 |
| | Bethel | 1 | 0 | 1 | 0 | 0 | 0 | 1 | 0 | 1 | 6,584 |
| **ARIZONA** | **Total** | 85 | 50 | 41 | 42 | 1 | | | | | |
| | **Cities** | 69 | 47 | 38 | 37 | 0 | | | | | |
| | Avondale | 2 | 0 | 0 | 2 | 0 | 3 | 0 | 1 | 0 | 88,773 |
| | Buckeye | 0 | 0 | 0 | 1 | 0 | 0 | 0 | 0 | 1 | 56,780 |
| | Bullhead City | 0 | 0 | 0 | 1 | 0 | 0 | 1 | 0 | 0 | 41,721 |
| | Chandler | 0 | 2 | 0 | 0 | 0 | 1 | 1 | 0 | 0 | 256,091 |
| | Coolidge | 1 | 0 | 0 | 0 | 0 | 0 | 0 | 1 | 0 | 10,540 |
| | Glendale | 5 | 2 | 2 | 2 | 0 | 2 | 4 | 4 | 1 | 255,080 |
| | Jerome | 0 | 0 | 1 | 0 | 0 | 1 | 0 | 0 | 0 | 356 |
| | Lake Havasu City | 1 | 0 | 0 | 0 | 0 | 0 | 0 | 0 | 1 | 58,406 |
| | Mesa | 4 | 1 | 2 | 1 | 0 | 1 | 5 | 1 | 1 | 470,833 |
| | Peoria | 1 | 0 | 0 | 0 | 0 | 0 | 0 | 1 | 0 | 164,366 |
| | Phoenix | 36 | 29 | 24 | 26 | 0 | 28 | 27 | 39 | 21 | 1,597,397 |
| | Prescott Valley | 1 | 0 | 0 | 0 | 0 | 1 | 0 | 0 | 0 | 40,539 |
| | Scottsdale | 9 | 4 | 2 | 2 | 0 | 4 | 2 | 4 | 7 | 239,115 |
| | Show Low | 0 | 1 | 1 | 0 | 0 | 0 | 2 | 0 | 0 | 12,929 |
| | Sierra Vista | 1 | 0 | 0 | 1 | 0 | 1 | 1 | 0 | 0 | 43,956 |
| | Tempe | 5 | 2 | 4 | 1 | 0 | 5 | 5 | 1 | 1 | 177,486 |
| | Tucson | 3 | 6 | 2 | 0 | 0 | 2 | 1 | 4 | 4 | 547,981 |
| | **Universities and Colleges** | 6 | 1 | 0 | 1 | 1 | | | | | |
| | Arizona State University, Main Campus | 1 | 1 | 0 | 0 | 0 | 0 | 0 | 1 | 1 | 67,082 |
| | Northern Arizona University | 0 | 0 | 0 | 0 | 1 | 0 | 1 | 0 | 0 | 22,502 |
| | Pima Community College | 2 | 0 | 0 | 0 | 0 | 0 | 0 | 0 | 2 | 34,136 |
| | University of Arizona | 3 | 0 | 0 | 1 | 0 | 0 | 2 | 1 | 1 | 38,057 |
| | **Metropolitan Counties** | 10 | 2 | 3 | 4 | 0 | | | | | |
| | Maricopa | 4 | 1 | 0 | 3 | 0 | 0 | 4 | 3 | 1 | |
| | Pima | 1 | 1 | 2 | 0 | 0 | 1 | 1 | 0 | 2 | |
| | Pinal | 4 | 0 | 0 | 1 | 0 | 0 | 2 | 0 | 3 | |
| | Yavapai | 1 | 0 | 1 | 0 | 0 | 1 | | | 1 | |
| **ARKANSAS** | **Total** | 45 | 5 | 16 | 7 | 1 | | | | | |
| | **Cities** | 36 | 4 | 12 | 7 | 0 | | | | | |
| | Arkadelphia | 0 | 1 | 0 | 0 | 0 | 0 | 0 | 1 | 0 | 11,158 |
| | Barling | 0 | 0 | 0 | 1 | 0 | 1 | 0 | 0 | 0 | 4,507 |
| | Beebe | 1 | 0 | 0 | 0 | 0 | 1 | 0 | 0 | 0 | 7,096 |
| | Berryville | 1 | 0 | 0 | 0 | 0 | 0 | 0 | 0 | 1 | 5,335 |
| | Bryant | 1 | 0 | 1 | 0 | 0 | 1 | 1 | 0 | 0 | 15,573 |
| | Cabot | 1 | 0 | 0 | 0 | 0 | 0 | 0 | 0 | 1 | 24,766 |
| | Cammack Village | 1 | 0 | 0 | 0 | 0 | 0 | 1 | 0 | 0 | 776 |
| | Conway | 2 | 0 | 0 | 1 | 0 | 1 | 2 | 0 | 0 | 59,343 |
| | Farmington | 1 | 0 | 0 | 0 | 0 | 1 | 0 | 0 | 0 | 4,802 |
| | Fayetteville | 0 | 0 | 1 | 0 | 0 | 1 | 0 | 0 | 0 | 75,120 |
| | Fort Smith | 1 | 0 | 0 | 0 | 0 | 0 | 0 | 0 | 1 | 85,175 |
| | Greers Ferry | 0 | 0 | 1 | 0 | 0 | 0 | 0 | 0 | 1 | 967 |
| | Harrison | 1 | 0 | 0 | 0 | 0 | 0 | 0 | 0 | 1 | 13,312 |
| | Hot Springs | 0 | 1 | 0 | 0 | 0 | 1 | 0 | 0 | 0 | 39,864 |
| | Jacksonville | 1 | 0 | 0 | 0 | 0 | 0 | 0 | 1 | 0 | 31,483 |
| | Jonesboro | 2 | 1 | 0 | 0 | 0 | 0 | 1 | 0 | 2 | 64,944 |
| | Judsonia | 2 | 0 | 0 | 0 | 0 | 0 | 1 | 0 | 1 | 2,202 |
| | Magnolia | 0 | 0 | 1 | 0 | 0 | 0 | 1 | 0 | 0 | 11,011 |
| | Mayflower | 2 | 0 | 0 | 0 | 0 | 0 | 0 | 1 | 1 | 2,310 |
| | McGehee | 1 | 0 | 0 | 0 | 0 | 0 | 1 | 0 | 0 | 3,888 |
| | Mena | 0 | 0 | 0 | 1 | 0 | 0 | 0 | 1 | 0 | 5,626 |
| | North Little Rock | 3 | 0 | 0 | 1 | 0 | 0 | 1 | 2 | 1 | 59,320 |
| | Paragould | 0 | 0 | 2 | 0 | 0 | 0 | 1 | 1 | 0 | 25,113 |

[1]Agencies published in this table indicated that at least one hate crime incident occurred in their respective jurisdictions during the quarter(s) for which they submitted a report to the Hate Crime Statistics Program. Blanks indicate quarters for which agencies did not submit reports.

[2]Population figures are published only for the cities. The figures listed for the universities and colleges are student enrollment and were provided by the United States Department of Education for the 2008 school year, the most recent available. The enrollment figures include full-time and part-time students.

## Table 94. Hate Crime Incidents per Bias Motivation and Quarter by State and Agency, 2009—*Continued*

| State | Agency type/Agency name | Number of incidents per bias motivation | | | | | Number of incidents per quarter[1] | | | | Population[2] |
|---|---|---|---|---|---|---|---|---|---|---|---|
| | | Race | Religion | Sexual orientation | Ethnicity | Disability | 1st quarter | 2nd quarter | 3rd quarter | 4th quarter | |
| | Pea Ridge | 1 | 0 | 0 | 0 | 0 | 0 | 0 | 1 | 0 | 4,924 |
| | Pine Bluff | 4 | 0 | 2 | 0 | 0 | 2 | 1 | 1 | 2 | 49,915 |
| | Russellville | 0 | 0 | 1 | 0 | 0 | 1 | 0 | 0 | 0 | 28,035 |
| | Searcy | 1 | 0 | 0 | 1 | 0 | 0 | 1 | 1 | 0 | 22,647 |
| | Sherwood | 6 | 0 | 2 | 0 | 0 | 1 | 3 | 2 | 2 | 24,888 |
| | Springdale | 0 | 1 | 0 | 0 | 0 | 0 | 0 | 1 | 0 | 70,935 |
| | Texarkana | 0 | 0 | 1 | 2 | 0 | 2 | 1 | 0 | 0 | 30,348 |
| | West Memphis | 1 | 0 | 0 | 0 | 0 | 0 | 0 | 1 | 0 | 26,995 |
| | Wynne | 2 | 0 | 0 | 0 | 0 | 0 | 0 | 2 | 0 | 8,419 |
| | **Metropolitan Counties** | 6 | 0 | 1 | 0 | 1 | | | | | |
| | Craighead | 0 | 0 | 1 | 0 | 0 | 0 | 1 | 0 | 0 | |
| | Faulkner | 1 | 0 | 0 | 0 | 0 | 0 | 0 | 1 | 0 | |
| | Pulaski | 4 | 0 | 0 | 0 | 1 | 3 | 0 | 1 | 1 | |
| | Washington | 1 | 0 | 0 | 0 | 0 | 1 | 0 | 0 | 0 | |
| | **Nonmetropolitan Counties** | 3 | 1 | 3 | 0 | 0 | | | | | |
| | Arkansas | 2 | 0 | 0 | 0 | 0 | 2 | 0 | 0 | 0 | |
| | Conway | 0 | 0 | 1 | 0 | 0 | 0 | 1 | 0 | 0 | |
| | Fulton | 0 | 0 | 1 | 0 | 0 | 1 | 0 | 0 | 0 | |
| | Polk | 0 | 1 | 0 | 0 | 0 | 0 | 0 | 1 | 0 | |
| | Yell | 1 | 0 | 1 | 0 | 0 | 1 | 1 | 0 | 0 | |
| **CALIFORNIA**.............. | **Total** | 453 | 194 | 222 | 142 | 4 | | | | | |
| | **Cities** | 374 | 172 | 187 | 122 | 4 | | | | | |
| | Agoura Hills | 1 | 2 | 0 | 0 | 0 | 1 | 1 | 0 | 1 | 22,469 |
| | Albany | 0 | 1 | 1 | 0 | 0 | 1 | 0 | 0 | 1 | 15,950 |
| | Alhambra | 4 | 0 | 1 | 0 | 0 | 0 | 2 | 2 | 1 | 85,956 |
| | Anaheim | 0 | 0 | 1 | 0 | 0 | 0 | 0 | 1 | 0 | 335,970 |
| | Antioch | 1 | 0 | 1 | 0 | 0 | 2 | 0 | 0 | 0 | 101,243 |
| | Arcata | 0 | 0 | 1 | 0 | 0 | 0 | 0 | 0 | 1 | 17,093 |
| | Atherton | 0 | 1 | 0 | 1 | 0 | 0 | 2 | 0 | 0 | 7,430 |
| | Avalon | 0 | 0 | 1 | 0 | 0 | 1 | 0 | 0 | 0 | 3,098 |
| | Azusa | 2 | 0 | 0 | 0 | 0 | 0 | 0 | 2 | 0 | 47,078 |
| | Bakersfield | 1 | 0 | 0 | 1 | 0 | 0 | 1 | 1 | 0 | 330,897 |
| | Bellflower | 1 | 1 | 0 | 0 | 0 | 1 | 0 | 1 | 0 | 73,038 |
| | Belmont | 1 | 0 | 1 | 0 | 0 | 0 | 0 | 1 | 1 | 24,742 |
| | Benicia | 1 | 0 | 0 | 0 | 0 | 0 | 1 | 0 | 0 | 26,089 |
| | Berkeley | 0 | 0 | 0 | 1 | 0 | 0 | 0 | 0 | 1 | 101,190 |
| | Beverly Hills | 2 | 0 | 0 | 0 | 0 | 0 | 0 | 0 | 2 | 34,506 |
| | Blythe | 0 | 1 | 0 | 0 | 0 | 0 | 0 | 0 | 1 | 21,841 |
| | Brawley | 0 | 0 | 1 | 0 | 0 | 0 | 0 | 1 | 0 | 22,810 |
| | Brentwood | 1 | 0 | 0 | 0 | 0 | 0 | 0 | 1 | 0 | 53,494 |
| | Burbank | 1 | 0 | 0 | 1 | 0 | 1 | 1 | 0 | 0 | 103,248 |
| | Camarillo | 0 | 1 | 0 | 0 | 0 | 1 | 0 | 0 | 0 | 64,011 |
| | Campbell | 1 | 2 | 1 | 0 | 0 | 1 | 1 | 1 | 1 | 38,584 |
| | Carpinteria | 0 | 0 | 0 | 1 | 0 | 1 | 0 | 0 | 0 | 13,595 |
| | Carson | 0 | 0 | 0 | 2 | 0 | 0 | 0 | 2 | 0 | 92,635 |
| | Cathedral City | 0 | 1 | 0 | 0 | 0 | 1 | 0 | 0 | 0 | 53,236 |
| | Cerritos | 1 | 0 | 0 | 0 | 0 | 0 | 0 | 1 | 0 | 51,299 |
| | Chico | 1 | 0 | 0 | 0 | 0 | 1 | 0 | 0 | 0 | 84,724 |
| | Chowchilla | 0 | 0 | 0 | 1 | 0 | 0 | 0 | 0 | 1 | 19,817 |
| | Chula Vista | 1 | 2 | 0 | 2 | 0 | 2 | 1 | 1 | 1 | 224,841 |
| | Citrus Heights | 1 | 0 | 0 | 1 | 0 | 0 | 1 | 0 | 1 | 84,333 |
| | City of Angels | 1 | 1 | 0 | 1 | 0 | 2 | 0 | 0 | 1 | 3,804 |
| | Clearlake | 1 | 0 | 0 | 0 | 0 | 0 | 1 | 0 | 0 | 15,261 |
| | Commerce | 0 | 0 | 0 | 1 | 0 | 0 | 0 | 1 | 0 | 13,529 |
| | Compton | 2 | 0 | 0 | 0 | 0 | 0 | 0 | 0 | 2 | 93,872 |
| | Concord | 2 | 0 | 2 | 0 | 0 | 2 | 2 | 0 | 0 | 121,042 |
| | Corona | 1 | 1 | 2 | 1 | 0 | 0 | 2 | 2 | 1 | 152,438 |
| | Coronado | 0 | 1 | 0 | 0 | 0 | 0 | 1 | 0 | 0 | 22,482 |
| | Costa Mesa | 0 | 0 | 1 | 1 | 0 | 1 | 0 | 0 | 1 | 110,150 |
| | Covina | 0 | 1 | 1 | 0 | 0 | 0 | 1 | 1 | 0 | 46,946 |
| | Cudahy | 0 | 0 | 0 | 1 | 0 | 0 | 0 | 0 | 1 | 24,337 |
| | Culver City | 0 | 1 | 0 | 0 | 0 | 0 | 1 | 0 | 0 | 38,545 |
| | Cupertino | 0 | 2 | 0 | 0 | 0 | 1 | 0 | 1 | 0 | 53,760 |

[1]Agencies published in this table indicated that at least one hate crime incident occurred in their respective jurisdictions during the quarter(s) for which they submitted a report to the Hate Crime Statistics Program. Blanks indicate quarters for which agencies did not submit reports.

[2]Population figures are published only for the cities. The figures listed for the universities and colleges are student enrollment and were provided by the United States Department of Education for the 2008 school year, the most recent available. The enrollment figures include full-time and part-time students.

## Table 94. Hate Crime Incidents per Bias Motivation and Quarter, by State and Agency, 2009—*Continued*

| State | Agency type/Agency name | Number of incidents per bias motivation | | | | | Number of incidents per quarter[1] | | | | Population[2] |
|---|---|---|---|---|---|---|---|---|---|---|---|
| | | Race | Religion | Sexual orientation | Ethnicity | Disability | 1st quarter | 2nd quarter | 3rd quarter | 4th quarter | |
| | Cypress | 1 | 2 | 0 | 0 | 0 | 0 | 2 | 0 | 1 | 47,181 |
| | Daly City | 2 | 0 | 0 | 0 | 0 | 1 | 0 | | 1 | 101,284 |
| | Dana Point | 2 | 0 | 0 | 0 | 0 | 1 | 1 | 0 | 0 | 35,756 |
| | Davis | 0 | 0 | 1 | 1 | 1 | 0 | 2 | 1 | 0 | 62,994 |
| | Delano | 1 | 0 | 0 | 0 | 0 | 0 | 0 | 1 | 0 | 54,801 |
| | Del Mar | 1 | 0 | 0 | 0 | 0 | 0 | 1 | 0 | 0 | 4,453 |
| | Downey | 2 | 2 | 0 | 0 | 0 | 0 | 3 | 0 | 1 | 107,598 |
| | Duarte | 2 | 0 | 0 | 0 | 0 | 0 | 1 | 0 | 1 | 21,873 |
| | Dublin | 2 | 0 | 0 | 0 | 0 | 0 | 1 | 0 | 1 | 46,157 |
| | El Cerrito | 0 | 0 | 0 | 1 | 0 | 0 | 1 | 0 | 0 | 22,116 |
| | Elk Grove | 0 | 2 | 0 | 1 | 0 | 0 | 1 | 2 | 0 | 140,576 |
| | El Monte | 4 | 0 | 0 | 0 | 0 | 2 | 2 | 0 | 0 | 122,428 |
| | Escalon | 0 | 1 | 0 | 0 | 0 | 1 | 0 | 0 | 0 | 7,414 |
| | Escondido | 2 | 1 | 0 | 1 | 0 | 2 | 1 | 1 | 0 | 137,432 |
| | Eureka | 4 | 0 | 1 | 0 | 0 | 1 | 2 | 2 | 0 | 25,216 |
| | Fairfield | 1 | 0 | 0 | 0 | 0 | 0 | 1 | 0 | 0 | 104,478 |
| | Farmersville | 0 | 0 | 0 | 1 | 0 | 1 | 0 | 0 | 0 | 10,214 |
| | Fontana | 0 | 0 | 1 | 0 | 0 | 0 | 0 | 0 | 1 | 190,303 |
| | Fountain Valley | 1 | 1 | 1 | 0 | 0 | 0 | 1 | 2 | 0 | 55,570 |
| | Fresno | 1 | 0 | 4 | 1 | 0 | 2 | 2 | 2 | 0 | 481,370 |
| | Fullerton | 6 | 0 | 0 | 1 | 0 | 6 | 0 | 1 | 0 | 132,478 |
| | Galt | 1 | 0 | 1 | 0 | 0 | 1 | 0 | 0 | 1 | 24,554 |
| | Gardena | 0 | 0 | 0 | 1 | 0 | 0 | 1 | 0 | 0 | 58,623 |
| | Garden Grove | 4 | 1 | 0 | 1 | 0 | 1 | 3 | 1 | 1 | 165,837 |
| | Gilroy | 1 | 0 | 0 | 0 | 0 | 0 | 1 | 0 | 0 | 50,946 |
| | Glendale | 0 | 0 | 1 | 1 | 0 | 0 | 2 | 0 | 0 | 197,384 |
| | Gridley | 1 | 0 | 0 | 0 | 0 | 1 | 0 | 0 | 0 | 6,589 |
| | Hawaiian Gardens | 3 | 0 | 0 | 0 | 0 | 2 | 0 | 1 | 0 | 15,276 |
| | Hawthorne | 1 | 0 | 0 | 1 | 0 | 2 | 0 | 0 | 0 | 84,314 |
| | Healdsburg | 0 | 0 | 0 | 1 | 0 | 0 | 1 | 0 | 0 | 10,968 |
| | Hemet | 2 | 0 | 0 | 0 | 0 | 0 | 1 | 1 | 0 | 72,417 |
| | Hermosa Beach | 0 | 0 | 1 | 0 | 0 | 0 | 0 | 0 | 1 | 19,431 |
| | Hesperia | 0 | 0 | 2 | 0 | 0 | 1 | 0 | 1 | 0 | 88,904 |
| | Hollister | 1 | 1 | 0 | 0 | 0 | 1 | 1 | 0 | 0 | 34,883 |
| | Huntington Beach | 2 | 0 | 0 | 2 | 0 | 1 | 2 | 1 | 0 | 192,911 |
| | Huntington Park | 1 | 0 | 0 | 0 | 0 | 0 | 1 | 0 | 0 | 60,840 |
| | Inglewood | 2 | 0 | 1 | 0 | 0 | 1 | 0 | 0 | 2 | 112,712 |
| | Ione | 0 | 0 | 1 | 0 | 0 | 1 | 0 | 0 | 0 | 7,518 |
| | Irvine | 2 | 0 | 0 | 1 | 0 | 1 | 0 | 2 | 0 | 215,673 |
| | Laguna Beach | 1 | 0 | 1 | 0 | 0 | 2 | 0 | 0 | 0 | 24,019 |
| | La Habra | 1 | 1 | 0 | 0 | 0 | 0 | 1 | 1 | 0 | 59,120 |
| | Lake Elsinore | 1 | 0 | 0 | 0 | 0 | 1 | 0 | 0 | 0 | 54,235 |
| | Lake Forest | 1 | 0 | 0 | 0 | 0 | 0 | 0 | 1 | 0 | 75,509 |
| | Lakewood | 2 | 0 | 1 | 0 | 0 | 0 | 1 | 1 | 1 | 78,334 |
| | La Mesa | 0 | 1 | 0 | 0 | 0 | 0 | 0 | 0 | 1 | 54,663 |
| | Lancaster | 6 | 0 | 2 | 2 | 0 | 1 | 3 | 4 | 2 | 148,742 |
| | La Quinta | 3 | 0 | 0 | 0 | 0 | 0 | 0 | 1 | 2 | 46,805 |
| | La Verne | 1 | 0 | 1 | 0 | 0 | 0 | 1 | 1 | 0 | 33,842 |
| | Lawndale | 1 | 0 | 0 | 0 | 0 | 0 | 0 | 0 | 1 | 31,301 |
| | Lemon Grove | 2 | 0 | 1 | 1 | 0 | 0 | 1 | 2 | 1 | 23,997 |
| | Livermore | 0 | 0 | 1 | 0 | 0 | 0 | 1 | 0 | 0 | 80,915 |
| | Lodi | 3 | 0 | 0 | 0 | 0 | 1 | 1 | 0 | 1 | 61,748 |
| | Lompoc | 0 | 0 | 0 | 1 | 0 | 0 | 0 | 1 | 0 | 41,085 |
| | Long Beach | 0 | 2 | 7 | 0 | 0 | 3 | 2 | 2 | 2 | 463,969 |
| | Los Alamitos | 1 | 0 | 0 | 0 | 0 | 0 | 1 | 0 | 0 | 11,668 |
| | Los Angeles | 74 | 57 | 36 | 23 | 0 | 44 | 76 | 53 | 17 | 3,848,776 |
| | Los Gatos | 0 | 0 | 0 | 1 | 0 | 0 | 0 | 1 | 0 | 29,388 |
| | Malibu | 0 | 1 | 0 | 0 | 0 | 1 | 0 | 0 | 0 | 13,058 |
| | Mammoth Lakes | 0 | 0 | 0 | 1 | 0 | 0 | 1 | 0 | 0 | 7,433 |
| | Manhattan Beach | 1 | 0 | 0 | 0 | 0 | 1 | | 0 | 0 | 36,907 |
| | Marina | 1 | 0 | 0 | 0 | 0 | 0 | 0 | 0 | 1 | 17,837 |
| | Marysville | 0 | 0 | 0 | 1 | 0 | 0 | 1 | 0 | 0 | 11,638 |
| | Millbrae | 1 | 0 | 0 | 0 | 0 | 0 | 0 | 1 | 0 | 20,811 |
| | Milpitas | 0 | 0 | 1 | 0 | 0 | 0 | 0 | 0 | 1 | 68,047 |
| | Mission Viejo | 0 | 1 | 0 | 1 | 0 | 0 | 0 | 1 | 1 | 94,552 |
| | Modesto | 0 | 1 | 0 | 0 | 0 | 1 | 0 | 0 | 0 | 204,474 |
| | Monrovia | 0 | 1 | 1 | 0 | 0 | 1 | 0 | 0 | 1 | 37,723 |
| | Monterey Park | 0 | 1 | 0 | 0 | 0 | 1 | 0 | 0 | 0 | 61,353 |
| | Moorpark | 0 | 0 | 0 | 1 | 0 | 0 | 1 | 0 | 0 | 36,919 |
| | Moraga | 1 | 0 | 0 | 0 | 0 | 0 | 0 | 1 | 0 | 17,131 |
| | Moreno Valley | 4 | 0 | 0 | 1 | 0 | 2 | 2 | 0 | 1 | 197,114 |
| | Morro Bay | 1 | 0 | 0 | 0 | 0 | 0 | 1 | 0 | 0 | 10,327 |

[1]Agencies published in this table indicated that at least one hate crime incident occurred in their respective jurisdictions during the quarter(s) for which they submitted a report to the Hate Crime Statistics Program. Blanks indicate quarters for which agencies did not submit reports.

[2]Population figures are published only for the cities. The figures listed for the universities and colleges are student enrollment and were provided by the United States Department of Education for the 2008 school year, the most recent available. The enrollment figures include full-time and part-time students.

## Table 94. Hate Crime Incidents per Bias Motivation and Quarter, by State and Agency, 2009—*Continued*

| State | Agency type/Agency name | Number of incidents per bias motivation | | | | | Number of incidents per quarter[1] | | | | Population[2] |
|---|---|---|---|---|---|---|---|---|---|---|---|
| | | Race | Religion | Sexual orientation | Ethnicity | Disability | 1st quarter | 2nd quarter | 3rd quarter | 4th quarter | |
| | Mountain View | 1 | 0 | 0 | 1 | 0 | 1 | 0 | 1 | 0 | 71,423 |
| | Mount Shasta | 1 | 0 | 0 | 0 | 0 | 0 | 0 | 0 | 1 | 3,528 |
| | Newark | 0 | 0 | 0 | 1 | 0 | 0 | 0 | 0 | 1 | 41,685 |
| | Newport Beach | 2 | 0 | 1 | 2 | 0 | 1 | 1 | 3 | 0 | 79,912 |
| | Norwalk | 0 | 0 | 1 | 1 | 0 | 0 | 1 | 1 | 0 | 102,807 |
| | Novato | 1 | 0 | 0 | 0 | 0 | 1 | 0 | 0 | 0 | 53,374 |
| | Oakland | 4 | 1 | 10 | 3 | 0 | 5 | 4 | 5 | 4 | 404,553 |
| | Oceanside | 4 | 1 | 1 | 1 | 0 | 2 | 0 | 4 | 1 | 170,579 |
| | Ontario | 2 | 0 | 0 | 0 | 0 | 1 | 0 | 1 | 0 | 173,212 |
| | Orange | 3 | 1 | 0 | 0 | 0 | 1 | 3 | 0 | 0 | 137,132 |
| | Orinda | 2 | 0 | 0 | 0 | 0 | 0 | 0 | 1 | 1 | 18,536 |
| | Oroville | 1 | 0 | 0 | 0 | 0 | 0 | 1 | 0 | 0 | 14,765 |
| | Oxnard | 1 | 0 | 2 | 0 | 1 | 3 | 0 | 0 | 1 | 187,357 |
| | Pacifica | 0 | 0 | 1 | 0 | 0 | 1 | 0 | 0 | 0 | 37,668 |
| | Pacific Grove | 1 | 0 | 0 | 0 | 0 | 0 | 1 | 0 | 0 | 14,502 |
| | Palmdale | 6 | 1 | 1 | 1 | 1 | 2 | 3 | 4 | 1 | 146,377 |
| | Palm Springs | 0 | 1 | 3 | 0 | 0 | 0 | 1 | 2 | 1 | 48,537 |
| | Palo Alto | 1 | 1 | 1 | 1 | 0 | 3 | 0 | 0 | 1 | 59,490 |
| | Palos Verdes Estates | 1 | 0 | 0 | 0 | 0 | 0 | 0 | 0 | 1 | 13,610 |
| | Paramount | 1 | 0 | 0 | 1 | 0 | 2 | 0 | 0 | 0 | 55,220 |
| | Pasadena | 2 | 1 | 1 | 1 | 0 | 1 | 1 | 2 | 1 | 144,063 |
| | Pico Rivera | 1 | 0 | 0 | 0 | 0 | 0 | 1 | 0 | 0 | 63,098 |
| | Placentia | 1 | 0 | 0 | 0 | 0 | 0 | 0 | 1 | 0 | 50,041 |
| | Placerville | 2 | 2 | 0 | 0 | 0 | 1 | 1 | 0 | 2 | 10,025 |
| | Pleasant Hill | 3 | 0 | 0 | 0 | 0 | 0 | 0 | 1 | 2 | 32,841 |
| | Pomona | 4 | 0 | 0 | 0 | 0 | 1 | 2 | 0 | 1 | 153,217 |
| | Porterville | 0 | 0 | 0 | 1 | 0 | 0 | 0 | 1 | 0 | 52,555 |
| | Poway | 2 | 1 | 0 | 0 | 0 | 0 | 2 | 1 | 0 | 48,931 |
| | Rancho Palos Verdes | 2 | 0 | 0 | 0 | 0 | 1 | 1 | 0 | 0 | 41,093 |
| | Redding | 10 | 0 | 1 | 2 | 0 | 4 | 1 | 6 | 2 | 91,242 |
| | Redlands | 0 | 0 | 1 | 0 | 0 | 0 | 0 | 0 | 1 | 70,360 |
| | Redondo Beach | 3 | 0 | 0 | 2 | 0 | 1 | 2 | 1 | 1 | 67,268 |
| | Redwood City[3] | 4 | 0 | 0 | 1 | 0 | 2 | 2 | 1 | 0 | 73,905 |
| | Richmond | 3 | 1 | 0 | 0 | 0 | 1 | 0 | 2 | 1 | 102,566 |
| | Rio Vista | 0 | 0 | 0 | 1 | 0 | 1 | 0 | 0 | 0 | 8,256 |
| | Riverside | 2 | 4 | 2 | 2 | 0 | 4 | 1 | 4 | 1 | 299,871 |
| | Roseville | 1 | 0 | 0 | 2 | 0 | 1 | 2 | 0 | 0 | 116,846 |
| | Sacramento | 2 | 1 | 5 | 1 | 0 | 4 | 2 | 2 | 1 | 470,308 |
| | Salinas | 2 | 1 | 0 | 0 | 0 | 0 | 2 | 1 | 0 | 143,660 |
| | San Bernardino | 3 | 0 | 0 | 1 | 0 | 2 | 0 | 1 | 1 | 199,683 |
| | San Diego | 12 | 7 | 15 | 8 | 1 | 14 | 14 | 12 | 3 | 1,314,773 |
| | San Fernando | 0 | 1 | 0 | 0 | 0 | 0 | 0 | 1 | 0 | 23,856 |
| | San Francisco | 4 | 10 | 6 | 3 | 0 | 9 | 7 | 3 | 4 | 809,755 |
| | San Jacinto | 1 | 0 | 0 | 0 | 0 | 0 | 0 | 1 | 0 | 39,848 |
| | San Jose | 23 | 7 | 9 | 1 | 0 | 14 | 15 | 8 | 3 | 954,009 |
| | San Juan Capistrano | 1 | 0 | 0 | 0 | 0 | 0 | 0 | 0 | 1 | 34,896 |
| | San Leandro | 0 | 0 | 1 | 0 | 0 | 0 | 0 | 1 | 0 | 77,676 |
| | San Luis Obispo | 2 | 0 | 5 | 0 | 0 | 1 | 4 | 1 | 1 | 43,565 |
| | San Marcos | 1 | 0 | 1 | 0 | 0 | 1 | 0 | 1 | 0 | 82,258 |
| | San Mateo | 1 | 0 | 0 | 2 | 0 | 1 | 2 | 0 | 0 | 92,208 |
| | San Rafael | 5 | 0 | 2 | 0 | 0 | 0 | 4 | 3 | 0 | 55,544 |
| | Santa Ana | 1 | 0 | 2 | 0 | 0 | 0 | 1 | 2 | 0 | 339,196 |
| | Santa Barbara | 3 | 1 | 1 | 0 | 0 | 2 | 2 | 1 | 0 | 85,715 |
| | Santa Clara | 0 | 0 | 1 | 0 | 0 | 0 | 0 | 1 | 0 | 111,106 |
| | Santa Clarita | 5 | 1 | 3 | 3 | 0 | 4 | 3 | 4 | 1 | 171,112 |
| | Santa Cruz | 1 | 3 | 4 | 0 | 0 | 2 | 2 | 4 | 0 | 56,155 |
| | Santa Maria | 1 | 0 | 0 | 0 | 0 | 0 | 0 | 0 | 1 | 87,381 |
| | Santa Monica | 1 | 0 | 1 | 1 | 0 | 0 | 1 | 1 | 1 | 88,038 |
| | Santa Paula | 0 | 0 | 2 | 1 | 0 | 3 | 0 | 0 | 0 | 28,603 |
| | Santa Rosa | 1 | 0 | 0 | 0 | 0 | 0 | 0 | 1 | 0 | 156,541 |
| | Santee | 4 | 0 | 0 | 1 | 0 | 1 | 0 | 2 | 2 | 53,957 |
| | Saratoga | 0 | 1 | 0 | 0 | 0 | 0 | 1 | 0 | 0 | 30,486 |
| | Scotts Valley | 0 | 1 | 0 | 0 | 0 | 1 | 0 | 0 | 0 | 11,098 |
| | Soledad | 0 | 0 | 0 | 1 | 0 | 0 | 0 | 0 | 1 | 28,748 |
| | Sonora | 1 | 0 | 0 | 0 | 0 | 0 | 1 | 0 | 0 | 4,573 |
| | South El Monte | 1 | 0 | 0 | 0 | 0 | 0 | 0 | 0 | 1 | 21,422 |
| | South Gate | 2 | 0 | 0 | 0 | 0 | 0 | 1 | 0 | 1 | 96,651 |
| | Stockton | 2 | 1 | 0 | 0 | 0 | 1 | 2 | 0 | 0 | 292,212 |
| | Sunnyvale | 1 | 1 | 0 | 0 | 0 | 0 | 0 | 1 | 1 | 132,144 |
| | Tehachapi | 0 | 0 | 0 | 1 | 0 | 0 | 0 | 1 | 0 | 11,807 |
| | Temecula | 1 | 0 | 0 | 0 | 0 | 1 | 0 | 0 | 0 | 100,922 |
| | Temple City | 0 | 0 | 0 | 1 | 0 | 0 | 0 | 1 | 0 | 38,909 |

[1]Agencies published in this table indicated that at least one hate crime incident occurred in their respective jurisdictions during the quarter(s) for which they submitted a report to the Hate Crime Statistics Program. Blanks indicate quarters for which agencies did not submit reports.

[2]Population figures are published only for the cities. The figures listed for the universities and colleges are student enrollment and were provided by the United States Department of Education for the 2008 school year, the most recent available. The enrollment figures include full-time and part-time students.

[3]Includes one incident reported with more than one bias motivation.

## Table 94. Hate Crime Incidents per Bias Motivation and Quarter, by State and Agency, 2009—*Continued*

| State | Agency type/Agency name | Number of incidents per bias motivation | | | | | Number of incidents per quarter[1] | | | | Population[2] |
|---|---|---|---|---|---|---|---|---|---|---|---|
| | | Race | Religion | Sexual orientation | Ethnicity | Disability | 1st quarter | 2nd quarter | 3rd quarter | 4th quarter | |
| | Thousand Oaks | 2 | 6 | 2 | 1 | 0 | 3 | 5 | 3 | 0 | 123,735 |
| | Torrance | 4 | 3 | 0 | 1 | 0 | 3 | 2 | 2 | 1 | 141,109 |
| | Tracy | 1 | 0 | 0 | 0 | 0 | 0 | 0 | 1 | 0 | 82,019 |
| | Tulare | 1 | 0 | 0 | 0 | 0 | 0 | 1 | 0 | 0 | 58,006 |
| | Turlock | 2 | 0 | 1 | 2 | 0 | 1 | 1 | 2 | 1 | 69,859 |
| | Tustin | 0 | 1 | 0 | 0 | 0 | 0 | 0 | 1 | 0 | 72,286 |
| | Twin Cities | 0 | 0 | 1 | 0 | 0 | 0 | 0 | 1 | 0 | 20,918 |
| | Union City | 2 | 0 | 1 | 0 | 0 | 2 | 0 | 0 | 1 | 72,666 |
| | Upland | 0 | 0 | 0 | 1 | 0 | 0 | 0 | 1 | 0 | 72,461 |
| | Vacaville | 3 | 0 | 0 | 2 | 0 | 1 | 2 | 2 | 0 | 92,538 |
| | Vallejo | 2 | 0 | 1 | 1 | 0 | 3 | 0 | 1 | 0 | 114,443 |
| | Ventura | 0 | 0 | 1 | 0 | 0 | 0 | 1 | 0 | 0 | 103,997 |
| | Visalia | 2 | 1 | 3 | 0 | 0 | 2 | 2 | 1 | 1 | 124,263 |
| | Vista | 2 | 0 | 1 | 0 | 0 | 0 | 0 | 2 | 1 | 91,252 |
| | Walnut Creek | 5 | 0 | 0 | 0 | 0 | 0 | 1 | 3 | 1 | 63,356 |
| | Watsonville | 0 | 0 | 2 | 0 | 0 | 0 | 0 | 2 | 0 | 50,898 |
| | West Covina | 2 | 1 | 1 | 0 | 0 | 0 | 2 | 1 | 1 | 105,846 |
| | West Hollywood | 0 | 3 | 6 | 0 | 0 | 3 | 2 | 2 | 2 | 36,020 |
| | Westminster | 2 | 4 | 0 | 0 | 0 | 1 | 1 | 2 | 2 | 89,057 |
| | West Sacramento | 0 | 1 | 0 | 1 | 0 | 1 | 0 | 0 | 1 | 49,646 |
| | Whittier | 1 | 3 | 1 | 0 | 0 | 0 | 0 | 4 | 1 | 82,096 |
| | Wildomar | 0 | 1 | 0 | 0 | 0 | 1 | 0 | 0 | 0 | 31,496 |
| | Woodlake | 1 | 0 | 0 | 0 | 0 | 1 | 0 | 0 | 0 | 7,506 |
| | Yuba City | 1 | 0 | 0 | 0 | 0 | 0 | 1 | 0 | 0 | 62,495 |
| | Yucaipa | 0 | 1 | 0 | 0 | 0 | 1 | 0 | 0 | 0 | 50,782 |
| | **Universities and Colleges** | 10 | 8 | 8 | 2 | 0 | | | | | |
| | California State University: | | | | | | | | | | |
| | Dominguez Hills | 1 | 0 | 0 | 0 | 0 | 0 | 0 | 0 | 1 | 12,851 |
| | Fullerton | 0 | 0 | 1 | 0 | 0 | 1 | 0 | 0 | 0 | 36,996 |
| | Monterey Bay | 1 | 0 | 1 | 0 | 0 | 2 | 0 | 0 | 0 | 4,340 |
| | Northridge | 1 | 0 | 0 | 0 | 0 | 0 | 0 | 1 | 0 | 36,208 |
| | San Jose[4] | 2 | 1 | 1 | 0 | 0 | 1 | 1 | 2 | 0 | |
| | Contra Costa Community College | 1 | 0 | 0 | 0 | 0 | 1 | 0 | 0 | 0 | 7,580 |
| | San Diego State University | 0 | 0 | 0 | 1 | 0 | 0 | 0 | 0 | 1 | 34,889 |
| | University of California: | | | | | | | | | | |
| | Berkeley | 1 | 1 | 1 | 0 | 0 | 2 | 0 | 0 | 1 | 35,396 |
| | Davis | 1 | 1 | 0 | 0 | 0 | 1 | 1 | 0 | 0 | 30,568 |
| | Los Angeles | 0 | 0 | 1 | 0 | 0 | 0 | 1 | 0 | 0 | 38,220 |
| | Riverside | 1 | 1 | 0 | 1 | 0 | 2 | 0 | 0 | 1 | 18,079 |
| | San Diego | 0 | 2 | 2 | 0 | 0 | 1 | 1 | 2 | 0 | 27,520 |
| | Santa Cruz | 1 | 2 | 1 | 0 | 0 | 0 | 3 | 0 | 1 | 16,615 |
| | **Metropolitan Counties** | 60 | 14 | 23 | 17 | 0 | | | | | |
| | Contra Costa | 0 | 0 | 1 | 0 | 0 | 0 | | 1 | 0 | |
| | El Dorado | 1 | 0 | 1 | 0 | 0 | 0 | 0 | 1 | 1 | |
| | Kern | 7 | 0 | 1 | 7 | 0 | 4 | 6 | 4 | 1 | |
| | Los Angeles | 14 | 5 | 10 | 4 | 0 | 13 | 7 | 4 | 9 | |
| | Madera | 1 | 0 | 0 | 0 | 0 | 1 | 0 | 0 | 0 | |
| | Orange | 1 | 1 | 1 | 1 | 0 | 0 | 2 | 2 | 0 | |
| | Placer | 1 | 0 | 1 | 0 | 0 | 0 | 0 | 2 | 0 | |
| | Riverside | 11 | 2 | 1 | 1 | 0 | 3 | 5 | 5 | 2 | |
| | Sacramento | 6 | 1 | 1 | 2 | 0 | 2 | 3 | 2 | 3 | |
| | San Bernardino | 4 | 0 | 0 | 0 | 0 | 0 | 0 | 4 | 0 | |
| | San Diego | 7 | 1 | 4 | 0 | 0 | 0 | 5 | 4 | 3 | |
| | San Luis Obispo | 1 | 0 | 0 | 0 | 0 | 0 | 0 | 1 | 0 | |
| | Santa Barbara | 1 | 2 | 0 | 0 | 0 | 1 | 0 | 1 | 1 | |
| | Santa Clara | 1 | 0 | 0 | 0 | 0 | 0 | 0 | 1 | 0 | |
| | Santa Cruz | 0 | 0 | 0 | 1 | 0 | 1 | 0 | 0 | 0 | |
| | Shasta | 1 | 0 | 0 | 0 | 0 | 1 | 0 | 0 | 0 | |
| | Solano | 1 | 0 | 0 | 0 | 0 | 0 | 1 | 0 | 0 | |
| | Stanislaus | 0 | 0 | 1 | 0 | 0 | 1 | 0 | 0 | 0 | |
| | Sutter | 0 | 1 | 0 | 0 | 0 | 0 | 0 | 0 | 1 | |
| | Ventura | 2 | 1 | 0 | 1 | 0 | 1 | 2 | 1 | 0 | |
| | Yuba | 0 | 0 | 1 | 0 | 0 | 0 | 0 | 1 | 0 | |
| | **Nonmetropolitan Counties** | 5 | 0 | 2 | 0 | 0 | | | | | |
| | Amador | 2 | 0 | 1 | 0 | 0 | 1 | 1 | 1 | 0 | |
| | Humboldt | 1 | 0 | 1 | 0 | 0 | 0 | 1 | 0 | 1 | |
| | Lake | 1 | 0 | 0 | 0 | 0 | 0 | 0 | 1 | 0 | |
| | Mendocino | 1 | 0 | 0 | 0 | 0 | 0 | 0 | 0 | 1 | |

[1]Agencies published in this table indicated that at least one hate crime incident occurred in their respective jurisdictions during the quarter(s) for which they submitted a report to the Hate Crime Statistics Program. Blanks indicate quarters for which agencies did not submit reports.
[2]Population figures are published only for the cities. The figures listed for the universities and colleges are student enrollment and were provided by the United States Department of Education for the 2008 school year, the most recent available. The enrollment figures include full-time and part-time students.
[4]Student enrollment figures were not available.

## Table 94. Hate Crime Incidents per Bias Motivation and Quarter, by State and Agency, 2009—*Continued*

| State | Agency type/Agency name | Number of incidents per bias motivation | | | | | Number of incidents per quarter[1] | | | | Population[2] |
|---|---|---|---|---|---|---|---|---|---|---|---|
| | | Race | Religion | Sexual orientation | Ethnicity | Disability | 1st quarter | 2nd quarter | 3rd quarter | 4th quarter | |
| | **Other Agencies** | 4 | 0 | 2 | 1 | 0 | | | | | |
| | Department of Parks and Recreation: | | | | | | | | | | |
| | Gold Fields District | 1 | 0 | 0 | 0 | 0 | 0 | 0 | 1 | 0 | |
| | San Luis Obispo Coast | 1 | 0 | 0 | 0 | 0 | 0 | 1 | 0 | 0 | |
| | Los Angeles Transportation Services Bureau | 1 | 0 | 1 | 0 | 0 | 1 | 0 | 0 | 1 | |
| | Port of San Diego Harbor | 0 | 0 | 0 | 1 | 0 | 0 | 0 | 1 | 0 | |
| | San Francisco Bay Area Rapid Transit: | | | | | | | | | | |
| | Contra Costa County | 1 | 0 | 0 | 0 | 0 | 0 | 1 | 0 | 0 | |
| | San Francisco County | 0 | 0 | 1 | 0 | 0 | 0 | 0 | 1 | 0 | |
| COLORADO | **Total** | 110 | 16 | 28 | 51 | 3 | | | | | |
| | **Cities** | 94 | 13 | 19 | 39 | 3 | | | | | |
| | Arvada | 0 | 1 | 1 | 0 | 0 | 2 | 0 | 0 | 0 | 107,943 |
| | Aspen | 1 | 0 | 0 | 0 | 0 | 0 | 1 | 0 | 0 | 5,897 |
| | Aurora | 3 | 2 | 0 | 1 | 0 | 1 | 3 | 2 | 0 | 324,014 |
| | Basalt | 0 | 0 | 0 | 1 | 0 | 1 | 0 | 0 | 0 | 3,304 |
| | Berthoud | 0 | 0 | 1 | 0 | 0 | 1 | 0 | 0 | 0 | 5,477 |
| | Boulder | 3 | 1 | 0 | 1 | 0 | 0 | 3 | 1 | 1 | 100,035 |
| | Broomfield | 0 | 1 | 0 | 0 | 0 | 0 | 1 | 0 | 0 | 56,991 |
| | Canon City | 2 | 0 | 0 | 1 | 0 | 2 | 1 | 0 | 0 | 15,925 |
| | Castle Rock | 1 | 0 | 0 | 0 | 0 | 1 | 0 | 0 | 0 | 48,287 |
| | Centennial | 1 | 1 | 0 | 1 | 0 | 0 | 1 | 2 | 0 | 99,385 |
| | Colorado Springs | 16 | 0 | 4 | 3 | 0 | 3 | 7 | 9 | 4 | 401,626 |
| | Commerce City | 0 | 0 | 1 | 0 | 0 | 1 | 0 | 0 | 0 | 45,914 |
| | Craig | 1 | 0 | 0 | 1 | 0 | 0 | 0 | 1 | 1 | 9,250 |
| | Denver | 36 | 5 | 9 | 9 | 2 | 17 | 11 | 24 | 9 | 604,680 |
| | Eaton | 0 | 0 | 0 | 1 | 0 | 1 | 0 | 0 | 0 | 4,415 |
| | Englewood | 1 | 0 | 0 | 0 | 0 | 0 | 0 | 1 | 0 | 32,750 |
| | Estes Park | 2 | 0 | 0 | 0 | 0 | 0 | 0 | 1 | 1 | 6,539 |
| | Fort Collins | 2 | 0 | 0 | 6 | 0 | 1 | 3 | 3 | 1 | 138,487 |
| | Fort Morgan | 2 | 0 | 0 | 0 | 0 | 0 | 1 | 1 | 0 | 10,485 |
| | Fountain | 1 | 0 | 0 | 1 | 0 | 0 | 1 | 1 | 0 | 20,205 |
| | Fruita | 0 | 0 | 0 | 1 | 0 | 0 | 0 | 0 | 1 | 7,501 |
| | Glenwood Springs | 0 | 0 | 0 | 1 | 0 | 0 | 0 | 1 | 0 | 9,198 |
| | Grand Junction | 1 | 0 | 0 | 0 | 0 | 0 | 1 | 0 | 0 | 50,195 |
| | Greeley | 1 | 0 | 0 | 2 | 0 | 1 | 0 | 1 | 1 | 93,070 |
| | Gunnison | 1 | 0 | 0 | 0 | 0 | 0 | 1 | 0 | 0 | 5,468 |
| | Lafayette | 1 | 0 | 0 | 0 | 0 | 0 | 0 | 0 | 1 | 25,267 |
| | Lakewood | 0 | 0 | 1 | 0 | 0 | 1 | 0 | 0 | 0 | 140,618 |
| | Leadville | 1 | 0 | 0 | 0 | 0 | 0 | 1 | 0 | 0 | 2,736 |
| | Littleton | 0 | 0 | 0 | 1 | 0 | 0 | 0 | 0 | 1 | 40,815 |
| | Lone Tree | 2 | 0 | 0 | 1 | 0 | 1 | 2 | 0 | 0 | 9,668 |
| | Longmont[3] | 3 | 1 | 1 | 3 | 0 | 1 | 3 | 2 | 2 | 87,611 |
| | Louisville | 1 | 0 | 1 | 0 | 0 | 1 | 1 | 0 | 0 | 19,147 |
| | Loveland | 2 | 0 | 0 | 2 | 0 | 0 | 1 | 1 | 2 | 67,324 |
| | Montrose | 1 | 0 | 0 | 0 | 0 | 0 | 0 | 1 | 0 | 18,651 |
| | Mount Crested Butte | 0 | 0 | 0 | 1 | 0 | 0 | 0 | 1 | 0 | 864 |
| | Northglenn | 2 | 0 | 0 | 0 | 0 | 2 | 0 | 0 | 0 | 33,849 |
| | Pueblo | 2 | 1 | 0 | 0 | 1 | 0 | 1 | 2 | 1 | 105,271 |
| | Steamboat Springs | 1 | 0 | 0 | 1 | 0 | 0 | 0 | 2 | 0 | 9,560 |
| | Trinidad | 2 | 0 | 0 | 0 | 0 | 0 | 0 | 0 | 2 | 9,125 |
| | Westminster | 1 | 0 | 0 | 0 | 0 | 0 | 1 | 0 | 0 | 107,705 |
| | **Universities and Colleges** | 1 | 1 | 0 | 1 | 0 | | | | | |
| | Colorado State University, Fort Collins | 0 | 1 | 0 | 1 | 0 | 0 | 2 | 0 | 0 | 28,882 |
| | University of Colorado, Boulder | 1 | 0 | 0 | 0 | 0 | 0 | 0 | 0 | 1 | 32,469 |
| | **Metropolitan Counties** | | 11 | 2 | 8 | 10 | 0 | | | | |
| | Adams | 3 | 0 | 1 | 0 | 0 | 1 | 1 | 1 | 1 | |
| | Arapahoe | 1 | 0 | 3 | 1 | 0 | 1 | 2 | 1 | 1 | |
| | Douglas | 2 | 0 | 2 | 3 | 0 | 0 | 2 | 4 | 1 | |
| | Jefferson | 0 | 0 | 1 | 0 | 0 | 0 | 1 | 0 | 0 | |
| | Larimer | 3 | 1 | 1 | 3 | 0 | 0 | 3 | 3 | 2 | |
| | Mesa | 0 | 0 | 0 | 2 | 0 | 1 | 0 | 1 | 0 | |
| | Park | 1 | 0 | 0 | 0 | 0 | 0 | 1 | 0 | 0 | |
| | Weld | 1 | 1 | 0 | 1 | 0 | 1 | 1 | 1 | 0 | |
| | **Nonmetropolitan Counties** | | 4 | 0 | 1 | 1 | 0 | | | | |
| | Bent | 1 | 0 | 0 | 0 | 0 | 0 | 1 | 0 | 0 | |
| | Chaffee | 0 | 0 | 1 | 0 | 0 | 0 | 1 | 0 | 0 | |
| | Custer | 1 | 0 | 0 | 0 | 0 | 0 | 0 | 1 | 0 | |
| | Montrose | 0 | 0 | 0 | 1 | 0 | 0 | 0 | 1 | 0 | |
| | Summit | 2 | 0 | 0 | 0 | 0 | 1 | 0 | 0 | 1 | |

[1]Agencies published in this table indicated that at least one hate crime incident occurred in their respective jurisdictions during the quarter(s) for which they submitted a report to the Hate Crime Statistics Program. Blanks indicate quarters for which agencies did not submit reports.

[2]Population figures are published only for the cities. The figures listed for the universities and colleges are student enrollment and were provided by the United States Department of Education for the 2008 school year, the most recent available. The enrollment figures include full-time and part-time students.

[3]Includes one incident reported with more than one bias motivation.

## Table 94. Hate Crime Incidents per Bias Motivation and Quarter, by State and Agency, 2009—*Continued*

| State | Agency type/Agency name | Number of incidents per bias motivation | | | | | Number of incidents per quarter[1] | | | | Population[2] |
|---|---|---|---|---|---|---|---|---|---|---|---|
| | | Race | Religion | Sexual orientation | Ethnicity | Disability | 1st quarter | 2nd quarter | 3rd quarter | 4th quarter | |
| CONNECTICUT.......... | **Total** | 104 | 43 | 28 | 22 | 2 | | | | | |
| | **Cities** | | 96 | 39 | 26 | 18 | 2 | | | | |
| | Bridgeport | 1 | 2 | 0 | 3 | 0 | 0 | 5 | 0 | 1 | 136,049 |
| | Bristol | 2 | 1 | 1 | 0 | 0 | 1 | 2 | 1 | 0 | 60,998 |
| | Canton | 1 | 0 | 0 | 0 | 0 | 0 | 0 | 1 | 0 | 10,253 |
| | Cheshire | 4 | 0 | 1 | 0 | 0 | 0 | 0 | 1 | 4 | 29,120 |
| | Clinton | 0 | 0 | 1 | 0 | 0 | 0 | 0 | 0 | 1 | 13,602 |
| | Coventry | 11 | 3 | 0 | 1 | 0 | 0 | 13 | 2 | 0 | 12,286 |
| | Danbury | 1 | 0 | 0 | 1 | 0 | 0 | 1 | 0 | 1 | 79,729 |
| | Derby | 0 | 1 | 0 | 0 | 0 | 0 | 1 | 0 | 0 | 12,392 |
| | Easton | 0 | 1 | 0 | 0 | 0 | 1 | 0 | 0 | 0 | 7,344 |
| | Enfield | 2 | 0 | 0 | 0 | 0 | 1 | 0 | 1 | 0 | 44,857 |
| | Farmington | 2 | 0 | 1 | 0 | 0 | 0 | 1 | 0 | 2 | 25,278 |
| | Glastonbury | 0 | 0 | 1 | 0 | 0 | 0 | 0 | 0 | 1 | 33,411 |
| | Greenwich | 0 | 2 | 0 | 0 | 0 | 1 | 0 | 1 | 0 | 62,018 |
| | Groton Town | 2 | 0 | 0 | 1 | 0 | 0 | 0 | 2 | 1 | 29,105 |
| | Guilford | 0 | 0 | 1 | 0 | 0 | 0 | 1 | 0 | 0 | 22,506 |
| | Hartford | 0 | 1 | 4 | 0 | 0 | 0 | 2 | 0 | 3 | 124,049 |
| | Madison | 1 | 0 | 0 | 0 | 0 | 0 | 0 | 0 | 1 | 18,900 |
| | Manchester | 22 | 4 | 3 | 5 | 1 | 3 | 17 | 9 | 6 | 56,566 |
| | Meriden | 3 | 1 | 0 | 0 | 0 | 1 | 1 | 1 | 1 | 59,289 |
| | Middlebury | 1 | 0 | 0 | 0 | 0 | 0 | 0 | 1 | 0 | 7,447 |
| | Middletown | 2 | 0 | 0 | 0 | 0 | 0 | 1 | 1 | 0 | 48,299 |
| | Milford | 3 | 2 | 0 | 0 | 0 | 1 | 3 | 1 | 0 | 56,310 |
| | Naugatuck | 2 | 2 | 0 | 0 | 0 | 1 | 2 | 0 | 1 | 32,033 |
| | New Britain | 2 | 1 | 0 | 0 | 0 | 0 | 1 | 2 | 0 | 70,368 |
| | New Haven | 10 | 1 | 5 | 0 | 0 | 3 | 8 | 3 | 2 | 123,659 |
| | Newington | 0 | 0 | 0 | 1 | 0 | 0 | 1 | 0 | 0 | 29,739 |
| | New London | 0 | 2 | 0 | 0 | 0 | 0 | 0 | 1 | 1 | 25,859 |
| | Newtown | 1 | 1 | 0 | 1 | 0 | 2 | 0 | 1 | 0 | 26,924 |
| | Norwalk | 3 | 0 | 1 | 1 | 0 | 1 | 1 | 2 | 1 | 83,198 |
| | Norwich | 0 | 0 | 1 | 1 | 0 | 1 | 1 | 0 | 0 | 36,418 |
| | Shelton | 1 | 0 | 1 | 0 | 0 | 0 | 0 | 0 | 2 | 40,195 |
| | Simsbury | 1 | 1 | 0 | 0 | 0 | 1 | 0 | 1 | 0 | 23,654 |
| | Southington | 0 | 1 | 1 | 0 | 0 | 0 | 1 | 0 | 1 | 42,523 |
| | Stratford | 3 | 0 | 1 | 0 | 0 | 1 | 0 | 2 | 1 | 48,726 |
| | Torrington | 3 | 1 | 0 | 0 | 0 | 1 | 0 | 3 | 0 | 35,321 |
| | Wallingford | 2 | 3 | 0 | 0 | 0 | 0 | 0 | 0 | 5 | 45,059 |
| | Waterford | 0 | 1 | 0 | 0 | 1 | 0 | 1 | 0 | 1 | 18,808 |
| | Watertown | 1 | 0 | 0 | 0 | 0 | 0 | 0 | 0 | 1 | 22,139 |
| | West Hartford[3] | 0 | 1 | 2 | 1 | 0 | 2 | 1 | 0 | 0 | 60,430 |
| | West Haven | 3 | 3 | 0 | 1 | 0 | 1 | 4 | 1 | 1 | 52,425 |
| | Westport | 4 | 2 | 0 | 0 | 0 | 1 | 4 | 1 | 0 | 26,681 |
| | Willimantic | 0 | 0 | 0 | 1 | 0 | 1 | 0 | 0 | 0 | 16,346 |
| | Winchester | 2 | 0 | 0 | 0 | 0 | 0 | 2 | 0 | 0 | 10,721 |
| | Windsor Locks | 0 | 1 | 1 | 0 | 0 | 0 | 0 | 0 | 2 | 12,543 |
| | **Universities and Colleges** | | 3 | 1 | 0 | 0 | 0 | | | | |
| | Eastern Connecticut State University | 3 | 0 | 0 | 0 | 0 | 0 | 1 | 0 | 2 | 5,427 |
| | University of Connecticut, Storrs, Avery Point, and Hartford[4] | 0 | 1 | 0 | 0 | 0 | 0 | 0 | 0 | 1 | |
| | **State Police Agencies** | | 4 | 3 | 2 | 4 | 0 | | | | |
| | Connecticut State Police | 4 | 3 | 2 | 4 | 0 | 2 | 5 | 1 | 5 | |
| | **Other Agencies** | | 1 | 0 | 0 | 0 | 0 | | | | |
| | Metropolitan Transportation Authority | 1 | 0 | 0 | 0 | 0 | 0 | 0 | 1 | 0 | |
| DELAWARE................ | **Total** | 20 | 10 | 3 | 4 | 0 | | | | | |
| | **Cities** | | 2 | 4 | 1 | 2 | 0 | | | | |
| | Georgetown | 0 | 0 | 0 | 1 | 0 | 0 | 1 | 0 | 0 | 5,277 |
| | Newark | 1 | 4 | 0 | 0 | 0 | 0 | 0 | 0 | 5 | 29,983 |
| | Selbyville | 0 | 0 | 0 | 1 | 0 | 0 | 0 | 1 | 0 | 1,871 |
| | Wilmington | 1 | 0 | 1 | 0 | 0 | 0 | 1 | 1 | 0 | 72,580 |
| | **Universities and Colleges** | | 1 | 5 | 0 | 1 | 0 | | | | |
| | University of Delaware | 1 | 5 | 0 | 1 | 0 | 4 | 1 | 1 | 1 | 20,500 |
| | **Metropolitan Counties** | | 4 | 0 | 1 | 1 | 0 | | | | |
| | New Castle County Police Department | 4 | 0 | 1 | 1 | 0 | 1 | 2 | 3 | 0 | |
| | **State Police Agencies** | | 13 | 1 | 1 | 0 | 0 | | | | |
| | State Police: | | | | | | | | | | |
| | Kent County | 5 | 1 | 0 | 0 | 0 | 2 | 1 | 3 | 0 | |
| | New Castle County | 5 | 0 | 1 | 0 | 0 | 1 | 2 | 2 | 1 | |
| | Sussex County | 3 | 0 | 0 | 0 | 0 | 1 | 1 | 1 | 0 | |

[1]Agencies published in this table indicated that at least one hate crime incident occurred in their respective jurisdictions during the quarter(s) for which they submitted a report to the Hate Crime Statistics Program. Blanks indicate quarters for which agencies did not submit reports.

[2]Population figures are published only for the cities. The figures listed for the universities and colleges are student enrollment and were provided by the United States Department of Education for the 2008 school year, the most recent available. The enrollment figures include full-time and part-time students.

[3]Includes one incident reported with more than one bias motivation.

[4]Student enrollment figures were not available.

## Table 94. Hate Crime Incidents per Bias Motivation and Quarter, by State and Agency, 2009—*Continued*

| State | Agency type/Agency name | Number of incidents per bias motivation | | | | | Number of incidents per quarter[1] | | | | Population[2] |
|---|---|---|---|---|---|---|---|---|---|---|---|
| | | Race | Religion | Sexual orientation | Ethnicity | Disability | 1st quarter | 2nd quarter | 3rd quarter | 4th quarter | |
| DISTRICT OF COLUMBIA | Total | 3 | 0 | 31 | 2 | 0 | | | | | |
| | Cities | | 2 | 0 | 30 | 2 | 0 | | | | |
| | Washington | 2 | 0 | 30 | 2 | 0 | 6 | 12 | 12 | 4 | 599,657 |
| | Other Agencies | | 1 | 0 | 1 | 0 | 0 | | | | |
| | Metro Transit Police | 1 | 0 | 1 | 0 | 0 | 0 | 2 | 0 | 0 | |
| FLORIDA | Total | 68 | 21 | 28 | 13 | 0 | | | | | |
| | Cities | | 47 | 11 | 23 | 8 | 0 | | | | |
| | Arcadia | 1 | 0 | 0 | 0 | 0 | 0 | 0 | 1 | 0 | 6,788 |
| | Atlantic Beach | 1 | 0 | 0 | 0 | 0 | 0 | 0 | 1 | 0 | 13,124 |
| | Aventura | 0 | 1 | 0 | 0 | 0 | 0 | 0 | 1 | 0 | 29,743 |
| | Boca Raton | 1 | 0 | 0 | 0 | 0 | 0 | 1 | 0 | 0 | 85,956 |
| | Chattahoochee | 1 | 0 | 0 | 0 | 0 | 1 | 0 | 0 | 0 | 3,746 |
| | Coconut Creek | 1 | 1 | 0 | 0 | 0 | 0 | 2 | 0 | 0 | 50,385 |
| | Coral Gables | 3 | 0 | 0 | 0 | 0 | 1 | 1 | 0 | 1 | 42,784 |
| | Coral Springs | 0 | 1 | 0 | 0 | 0 | 0 | 0 | 0 | 1 | 125,656 |
| | Dania | 1 | 0 | 1 | 0 | 0 | 0 | 1 | 1 | 0 | 28,065 |
| | Davie | 0 | 1 | 0 | 0 | 0 | 0 | 0 | 1 | 0 | 90,147 |
| | Daytona Beach Shores | 0 | 0 | 1 | 0 | 0 | 0 | 1 | 0 | 0 | 5,225 |
| | Deerfield Beach | 1 | 0 | 1 | 0 | 0 | 2 | 0 | 0 | 0 | 74,509 |
| | Edgewater | 1 | 0 | 0 | 0 | 0 | 0 | 0 | 1 | 0 | 21,714 |
| | Gainesville | 5 | 1 | 4 | 2 | 0 | 0 | 3 | 5 | 4 | 115,265 |
| | Graceville | 1 | 0 | 0 | 0 | 0 | 0 | 1 | 0 | 0 | 2,428 |
| | Homestead | 0 | 0 | 0 | 1 | 0 | 0 | 0 | 0 | 1 | 62,037 |
| | Jacksonville | 2 | 0 | 0 | 0 | 0 | 0 | 1 | 1 | 0 | 810,064 |
| | Jasper | 1 | 0 | 0 | 0 | 0 | 0 | 1 | 0 | 0 | 2,047 |
| | Jupiter | 0 | 0 | 1 | 0 | 0 | 0 | 1 | 0 | 0 | 51,514 |
| | Key West | 0 | 0 | 1 | 1 | 0 | 0 | 0 | 1 | 1 | 22,049 |
| | Largo | 0 | 0 | 0 | 1 | 0 | 0 | 1 | 0 | 0 | 72,567 |
| | Longboat Key | 0 | 1 | 0 | 0 | 0 | 0 | 0 | 1 | 0 | 7,277 |
| | Miami Beach | 0 | 1 | 4 | 0 | 0 | 1 | 2 | 0 | 2 | 84,260 |
| | Miami Gardens | 1 | 0 | 1 | 0 | 0 | 2 | 0 | 0 | 0 | 110,346 |
| | Miramar | 0 | 0 | 2 | 0 | 0 | 0 | 1 | 0 | 1 | 108,375 |
| | New Port Richey | 0 | 0 | 0 | 1 | 0 | 0 | 0 | 1 | 0 | 17,766 |
| | North Miami | 1 | 1 | 0 | 0 | 0 | 0 | 1 | 0 | 1 | 55,495 |
| | North Port | 4 | 0 | 0 | 1 | 0 | 2 | 1 | 1 | 1 | 60,512 |
| | Ocala | 0 | 0 | 1 | 0 | 0 | 0 | 0 | 1 | 0 | 55,847 |
| | Ocoee | 1 | 0 | 0 | 0 | 0 | 0 | 0 | 0 | 1 | 33,251 |
| | Orlando | 1 | 0 | 0 | 0 | 0 | 0 | 0 | 0 | 1 | 235,109 |
| | Palm Bay | 2 | 0 | 1 | 0 | 0 | 0 | 0 | 1 | 2 | 103,475 |
| | Palm Beach Gardens | 2 | 2 | 0 | 0 | 0 | 0 | 0 | 0 | 4 | 50,937 |
| | Panama City | 2 | 0 | 1 | 0 | 0 | 0 | 1 | 0 | 2 | 36,619 |
| | Pensacola | 2 | 0 | 0 | 0 | 0 | 0 | 1 | 1 | 0 | 53,570 |
| | Pompano Beach | 0 | 0 | 1 | 0 | 0 | 0 | 0 | 0 | 1 | 101,840 |
| | Port Orange | 1 | 0 | 0 | 0 | 0 | 0 | 1 | 0 | 0 | 55,604 |
| | St. Petersburg | 1 | 0 | 0 | 0 | 0 | 1 | 0 | 0 | 0 | 244,933 |
| | Sunrise | 0 | 1 | 0 | 0 | 0 | 0 | 0 | 0 | 1 | 88,936 |
| | Tampa | 3 | 0 | 2 | 0 | 0 | 3 | 1 | 1 | 0 | 345,233 |
| | Titusville | 2 | 0 | 0 | 0 | 0 | 0 | 1 | 0 | 1 | 45,197 |
| | Wellington | 1 | 0 | 0 | 0 | 0 | 0 | 1 | 0 | 0 | 56,588 |
| | Wilton Manors | 3 | 0 | 1 | 0 | 0 | 0 | 0 | 0 | 4 | 12,603 |
| | Winter Haven | 0 | 0 | 0 | 1 | 0 | 0 | 1 | 0 | 0 | 34,103 |
| | Universities and Colleges | | 1 | 1 | 0 | 1 | 0 | | | | |
| | University of Central Florida | 0 | 0 | 0 | 1 | 0 | 0 | 1 | 0 | 0 | 50,121 |
| | University of Florida | 0 | 1 | 0 | 0 | 0 | 0 | 1 | 0 | 0 | 51,474 |
| | University of West Florida | 1 | 0 | 0 | 0 | 0 | 0 | 0 | 1 | 0 | 10,491 |
| | Metropolitan Counties | | 18 | 9 | 5 | 4 | 0 | | | | |
| | Alachua | 3 | 1 | 1 | 0 | 0 | 0 | 1 | 3 | 1 | |
| | Broward | 2 | 0 | 0 | 0 | 0 | 1 | 0 | 1 | 0 | |
| | Clay | 1 | 1 | 0 | 0 | 0 | 0 | 1 | 1 | 0 | |
| | Collier | 0 | 2 | 0 | 1 | 0 | 1 | 1 | 1 | 0 | |
| | Escambia | 1 | 0 | 1 | 1 | 0 | 2 | 0 | 1 | 0 | |
| | Hillsborough | 2 | 0 | 1 | 0 | 0 | 0 | 2 | 1 | 0 | |
| | Manatee | 1 | 0 | 0 | 0 | 0 | 0 | 1 | 0 | 0 | |
| | Martin | 0 | 1 | 0 | 0 | 0 | 0 | 1 | 0 | 0 | |
| | Okaloosa | 1 | 1 | 0 | 0 | 0 | 1 | 0 | 0 | 1 | |
| | Orange | 2 | 1 | 1 | 1 | 0 | 1 | 1 | 2 | 1 | |
| | Osceola | 0 | 1 | 0 | 0 | 0 | 0 | 0 | 0 | 1 | |
| | Palm Beach | 1 | 1 | 0 | 0 | 0 | 0 | 0 | 0 | 2 | |
| | Pasco | 0 | 0 | 0 | 1 | 0 | 0 | 1 | 0 | 0 | |
| | Santa Rosa | 2 | 0 | 1 | 0 | 0 | 1 | 1 | 0 | 1 | |
| | Wakulla | 2 | 0 | 0 | 0 | 0 | 0 | 0 | 1 | 1 | |

[1]Agencies published in this table indicated that at least one hate crime incident occurred in their respective jurisdictions during the quarter(s) for which they submitted a report to the Hate Crime Statistics Program. Blanks indicate quarters for which agencies did not submit reports.

[2]Population figures are published only for the cities. The figures listed for the universities and colleges are student enrollment and were provided by the United States Department of Education for the 2008 school year, the most recent available. The enrollment figures include full-time and part-time students.

## Table 94. Hate Crime Incidents per Bias Motivation and Quarter, by State and Agency, 2009—*Continued*

| State | Agency type/Agency name | Number of incidents per bias motivation | | | | | Number of incidents per quarter[1] | | | | Population[2] |
|---|---|---|---|---|---|---|---|---|---|---|---|
| | | Race | Religion | Sexual orientation | Ethnicity | Disability | 1st quarter | 2nd quarter | 3rd quarter | 4th quarter | |
| | **Tribal Agencies** | 1 | 0 | 0 | 0 | 0 | | | | | |
| | Seminole Tribal | 1 | 0 | 0 | 0 | 0 | 0 | 0 | 1 | 0 | |
| | **Other Agencies** | 1 | 0 | 0 | 0 | 0 | | | | | |
| | Fort Lauderdale Airport | 1 | 0 | 0 | 0 | 0 | 0 | 1 | 0 | 0 | |
| **GEORGIA** | **Total** | 6 | 1 | 4 | 0 | 0 | | | | | |
| | **Cities** | 3 | 0 | 0 | 0 | 0 | | | | | |
| | Atlanta | 1 | 0 | 0 | 0 | 0 | 0 | 0 | 1 | 0 | 552,901 |
| | Helen | 1 | 0 | 0 | 0 | 0 | 1 | 0 | 0 | 0 | 903 |
| | Morrow | 1 | 0 | 0 | 0 | 0 | 0 | 0 | 1 | 0 | 5,575 |
| | **Universities and Colleges** | 3 | 1 | 4 | 0 | 0 | | | | | |
| | University of Georgia | 2 | 0 | 4 | 0 | 0 | 1 | 0 | 3 | 2 | 34,180 |
| | University of West Georgia | 1 | 1 | 0 | 0 | 0 | 0 | 0 | 2 | 0 | 11,252 |
| **IDAHO** | **Total** | 15 | 6 | 5 | 9 | 0 | | | | | |
| | **Cities** | 15 | 6 | 5 | 9 | 0 | | | | | |
| | Bellevue | 0 | 0 | 1 | 0 | 0 | 0 | 0 | 1 | 0 | 2,200 |
| | Boise | 3 | 3 | 1 | 0 | 0 | 0 | 3 | 3 | 1 | 206,437 |
| | Caldwell | 0 | 0 | 2 | 0 | 0 | 1 | 1 | 0 | 0 | 44,391 |
| | Coeur d'Alene | 4 | 1 | 0 | 3 | 0 | 2 | 0 | 2 | 4 | 44,406 |
| | Hailey | 1 | 1 | 0 | 0 | 0 | 0 | 1 | 1 | 0 | 8,081 |
| | Jerome | 1 | 0 | 0 | 1 | 0 | 0 | 0 | 1 | 1 | 9,280 |
| | Moscow | 1 | 0 | 0 | 0 | 0 | 0 | 1 | 0 | 0 | 24,604 |
| | Nampa | 4 | 1 | 0 | 5 | 0 | 1 | 5 | 0 | 4 | 83,875 |
| | Pocatello | 1 | 0 | 0 | 0 | 0 | 0 | 0 | 1 | 0 | 55,272 |
| | Twin Falls | 0 | 0 | 1 | 0 | 0 | 0 | 0 | 1 | 0 | 43,095 |
| **ILLINOIS** | **Total** | 76 | 20 | 22 | 11 | 0 | | | | | |
| | **Cities** | 66 | 19 | 15 | 11 | 0 | | | | | |
| | Aurora | 2 | 0 | 0 | 1 | 0 | 0 | 0 | 2 | 1 | 175,135 |
| | Batavia | 1 | 0 | 0 | 0 | 0 | 0 | 1 | 0 | 0 | 27,872 |
| | Beardstown | 1 | 0 | 0 | 1 | 0 | 1 | 1 | 0 | 0 | 5,867 |
| | Bloomington | 1 | 0 | 1 | 0 | 0 | 0 | 1 | 1 | 0 | 73,897 |
| | Bolingbrook | 0 | 1 | 0 | 0 | 0 | 0 | 0 | 0 | 1 | 72,566 |
| | Buffalo Grove | 0 | 1 | 0 | 0 | 0 | 1 | 0 | 0 | 0 | 42,939 |
| | Burbank | 1 | 0 | 0 | 0 | 0 | 0 | 1 | 0 | 0 | 27,529 |
| | Carol Stream | 0 | 1 | 0 | 0 | 0 | 0 | 0 | 1 | 0 | 39,951 |
| | Chicago | 9 | 6 | 8 | 4 | 0 | 8 | 8 | 8 | 3 | 2,848,431 |
| | Decatur | 2 | 0 | 0 | 0 | 0 | 0 | 0 | 0 | 2 | 75,651 |
| | Des Plaines | 1 | 0 | 0 | 0 | 0 | 0 | 0 | 0 | 1 | 57,061 |
| | Downers Grove | 2 | 1 | 0 | 0 | 0 | 1 | 0 | 2 | 0 | 49,170 |
| | Elgin | 1 | 0 | 1 | 0 | 0 | | | 1 | 1 | 107,686 |
| | Evanston | 4 | 2 | 0 | 0 | 0 | 2 | 3 | | 1 | 78,101 |
| | Genoa | 0 | 1 | 0 | 0 | 0 | 0 | 0 | 1 | 0 | 5,207 |
| | Highwood | 0 | 0 | 0 | 1 | 0 | 0 | 1 | 0 | 0 | 5,378 |
| | Jacksonville | 1 | 0 | 0 | 0 | 0 | 0 | 0 | 1 | 0 | 19,353 |
| | Joliet | 1 | 0 | 1 | 0 | 0 | 0 | 2 | 0 | 0 | 151,103 |
| | Kildeer | 0 | 1 | 0 | 0 | 0 | 0 | 0 | 0 | 1 | 4,196 |
| | Lincolnwood | 0 | 1 | 0 | 0 | 0 | 1 | | | | 11,752 |
| | Lindenhurst | 0 | 0 | 0 | 1 | 0 | | | | 1 | 14,923 |
| | Litchfield | 1 | 0 | 0 | 0 | 0 | 0 | 1 | 0 | 0 | 6,613 |
| | Lyons | 2 | 0 | 0 | 0 | 0 | 1 | 1 | 0 | 0 | 10,251 |
| | Mascoutah | 1 | 0 | 0 | 0 | 0 | 0 | 0 | 1 | 0 | 6,815 |
| | Monmouth | 1 | 0 | 0 | 0 | 0 | 0 | 1 | 0 | 0 | 9,268 |
| | Mount Carroll | 1 | 0 | 0 | 0 | 0 | 1 | 0 | 0 | 0 | 1,641 |
| | Mount Sterling | 1 | 0 | 0 | 0 | 0 | 0 | 0 | 1 | 0 | 1,889 |
| | Naperville | 1 | 0 | 0 | 0 | 0 | 1 | 0 | 0 | 0 | 144,731 |
| | New Lenox | 1 | 0 | 0 | 1 | 0 | 2 | | | | 24,896 |
| | Normal | 2 | 0 | 0 | 0 | 0 | 0 | 0 | 0 | 2 | 52,827 |
| | Northfield | 0 | 1 | 0 | 0 | 0 | | 1 | | | 5,418 |
| | Park Ridge | 1 | 0 | 0 | 0 | 0 | 0 | 0 | 0 | 1 | 36,835 |
| | Pekin | 3 | 0 | 0 | 0 | 0 | 1 | 1 | 1 | | 33,382 |
| | Peoria | 2 | 0 | 0 | 0 | 0 | 0 | 0 | 2 | 0 | 114,241 |
| | Plainfield | 1 | 0 | 0 | 0 | 0 | 0 | 0 | 0 | 1 | 40,764 |
| | Rantoul | 1 | 0 | 0 | 0 | 0 | 1 | 0 | 0 | 0 | 12,109 |
| | Robinson | 1 | 0 | 0 | 0 | 0 | 1 | 0 | 0 | 0 | 6,323 |
| | Rockford | 8 | 1 | 2 | 0 | 0 | 3 | 5 | 2 | 1 | 157,943 |
| | Schaumburg | 1 | 0 | 0 | 0 | 0 | | 1 | | | 71,325 |
| | Shiloh | 1 | 0 | 0 | 0 | 0 | 1 | 0 | 0 | 0 | 11,500 |
| | Skokie | 0 | 1 | 0 | 1 | 0 | 0 | 2 | 0 | | 66,996 |
| | Springfield | 7 | 1 | 2 | 1 | 0 | 1 | 5 | 4 | 1 | 117,973 |
| | Tinley Park | 1 | 0 | 0 | 0 | 0 | | | 1 | 0 | 60,427 |
| | Wood River | 1 | 0 | 0 | 0 | 0 | 0 | 0 | 0 | 1 | 10,935 |

[1]Agencies published in this table indicated that at least one hate crime incident occurred in their respective jurisdictions during the quarter(s) for which they submitted a report to the Hate Crime Statistics Program. Blanks indicate quarters for which agencies did not submit reports.

[2]Population figures are published only for the cities. The figures listed for the universities and colleges are student enrollment and were provided by the United States Department of Education for the 2008 school year, the most recent available. The enrollment figures include full-time and part-time students.

## Table 94. Hate Crime Incidents per Bias Motivation and Quarter, by State and Agency, 2009—*Continued*

| State | Agency type/Agency name | Number of incidents per bias motivation | | | | | Number of incidents per quarter[1] | | | | Population[2] |
|---|---|---|---|---|---|---|---|---|---|---|---|
| | | Race | Religion | Sexual orientation | Ethnicity | Disability | 1st quarter | 2nd quarter | 3rd quarter | 4th quarter | |
| | **Universities and Colleges** | 4 | 1 | 5 | 0 | 0 | | | | | |
| | College of DuPage | 1 | 1 | 0 | 0 | 0 | 2 | | | | 25,668 |
| | Northern Illinois University | 3 | 0 | 0 | 0 | 0 | 1 | | | 2 | 24,397 |
| | Southern Illinois University, Edwardsville | 0 | 0 | 1 | 0 | 0 | 0 | 1 | 0 | 0 | 13,602 |
| | University of Illinois, Springfield | 0 | 0 | 1 | 0 | 0 | 0 | 0 | 0 | 1 | 4,711 |
| | Western Illinois University | 0 | 0 | 3 | 0 | 0 | 2 | 0 | 0 | 1 | 13,175 |
| | **Metropolitan Counties** | 5 | 0 | 2 | 0 | 0 | | | | | |
| | Du Page | 1 | 0 | 1 | 0 | 0 | 1 | 0 | 1 | 0 | |
| | Peoria | 2 | 0 | 0 | 0 | 0 | 1 | | | 1 | |
| | Sangamon | 2 | 0 | 1 | 0 | 0 | 1 | 0 | 1 | 1 | |
| | **Nonmetropolitan Counties** | 1 | 0 | 0 | 0 | 0 | | | | | |
| | Knox | 1 | 0 | 0 | 0 | 0 | 0 | 1 | 0 | 0 | |
| INDIANA | **Total** | 34 | 8 | 12 | 1 | 0 | | | | | |
| | **Cities** | 24 | 6 | 9 | 1 | 0 | | | | | |
| | Bloomington | 14 | 3 | 8 | 0 | 0 | 8 | 5 | 8 | 4 | 71,845 |
| | Clarksville | 1 | 0 | 0 | 0 | 0 | 0 | 0 | 0 | 1 | 21,921 |
| | Fishers | 0 | 0 | 0 | 1 | 0 | 1 | 0 | 0 | 0 | 73,538 |
| | Fort Wayne | 2 | 1 | 0 | 0 | 0 | 1 | 0 | 1 | 1 | 251,584 |
| | Goshen | 0 | 0 | 1 | 0 | 0 | 1 | 0 | 0 | 0 | 32,952 |
| | Greenwood | 1 | 0 | 0 | 0 | 0 | 0 | 1 | 0 | 0 | 49,136 |
| | La Porte | 1 | 0 | 0 | 0 | 0 | 0 | 0 | 0 | 1 | 21,128 |
| | Mishawaka | 3 | 0 | 0 | 0 | 0 | | 2 | 1 | | 50,378 |
| | Munster | 0 | 2 | 0 | 0 | 0 | 0 | 1 | 0 | 1 | 22,173 |
| | Plainfield | 1 | 0 | 0 | 0 | 0 | 1 | 0 | 0 | 0 | 28,811 |
| | Walkerton | 1 | 0 | 0 | 0 | 0 | 0 | 1 | 0 | 0 | 2,164 |
| | **Universities and Colleges** | 5 | 2 | 3 | 0 | 0 | | | | | |
| | Indiana State University | 0 | 0 | 2 | 0 | 0 | 0 | 0 | 2 | 0 | 10,457 |
| | Indiana University, Indianapolis[4] | 4 | 1 | 0 | 0 | 0 | 4 | 0 | 0 | 1 | |
| | Purdue University | 1 | 1 | 1 | 0 | 0 | 0 | 1 | 0 | 2 | 41,433 |
| | **Metropolitan Counties** | 3 | 0 | 0 | 0 | 0 | | | | | |
| | Elkhart | 1 | 0 | 0 | 0 | 0 | 0 | 1 | | 0 | |
| | Porter | 2 | 0 | 0 | 0 | 0 | 0 | 2 | 0 | 0 | |
| | **State Police Agencies** | 2 | 0 | 0 | 0 | 0 | | | | | |
| | Indiana State Police | 2 | 0 | 0 | 0 | 0 | 1 | | | 1 | |
| IOWA | **Total** | 10 | 1 | 4 | 3 | 0 | | | | | |
| | **Cities** | 8 | 0 | 4 | 3 | 0 | | | | | |
| | Ames | 1 | 0 | 0 | 0 | 0 | 0 | 1 | 0 | 0 | 57,173 |
| | Bettendorf | 0 | 0 | 0 | 1 | 0 | 0 | 1 | 0 | 0 | 32,734 |
| | Clarion | 1 | 0 | 0 | 0 | 0 | 1 | 0 | 0 | 0 | 2,692 |
| | Davenport | 3 | 0 | 2 | 0 | 0 | 0 | 1 | 3 | 1 | 101,116 |
| | Des Moines | 0 | 0 | 1 | 0 | 0 | 0 | 0 | 1 | 0 | 196,794 |
| | Grinnell | 0 | 0 | 1 | 0 | 0 | 0 | 0 | 0 | 1 | 9,174 |
| | Iowa City | 1 | 0 | 0 | 0 | 0 | 0 | 1 | 0 | 0 | 68,427 |
| | Perry | 1 | 0 | 0 | 1 | 0 | 0 | 1 | 1 | 0 | 9,809 |
| | Urbandale | 1 | 0 | 0 | 0 | 0 | 0 | 1 | 0 | 0 | 39,518 |
| | Vinton | 0 | 0 | 0 | 1 | 0 | 0 | 0 | 0 | 1 | 5,078 |
| | **Metropolitan Counties** | 1 | 1 | 0 | 0 | 0 | | | | | |
| | Linn | 1 | 1 | 0 | 0 | 0 | 1 | 1 | 0 | 0 | |
| | **Nonmetropolitan Counties** | 1 | 0 | 0 | 0 | 0 | | | | | |
| | Marshall | 1 | 0 | 0 | 0 | 0 | 0 | 0 | 0 | 1 | |
| KANSAS | **Total** | 63 | 18 | 20 | 20 | 1 | | | | | |
| | **Cities** | 50 | 14 | 15 | 14 | 1 | | | | | |
| | Abilene | 0 | 0 | 0 | 1 | 0 | 1 | 0 | 0 | 0 | 6,383 |
| | Arma | 0 | 0 | 1 | 0 | 0 | 0 | 0 | 1 | 0 | 1,511 |
| | Atchison | 1 | 0 | 0 | 0 | 0 | 0 | 0 | 0 | 1 | 10,378 |
| | Augusta | 1 | 0 | 0 | 0 | 0 | 1 | 0 | 0 | 0 | 8,715 |
| | Bonner Springs | 0 | 0 | 0 | 1 | 0 | 1 | 0 | 0 | 0 | 7,205 |
| | Chanute | 0 | 0 | 2 | 0 | 0 | 1 | 1 | 0 | 0 | 8,784 |
| | Colby | 0 | 1 | 0 | 0 | 0 | 0 | 1 | 0 | 0 | 4,737 |
| | El Dorado | 1 | 0 | 0 | 0 | 0 | 0 | 0 | 1 | 0 | 12,566 |
| | Fort Scott | 3 | 0 | 0 | 0 | 0 | 2 | 1 | 0 | 0 | 7,903 |
| | Garden City | 0 | 0 | 0 | 1 | 0 | 0 | 1 | 0 | 0 | 28,561 |
| | Goodland | 0 | 0 | 1 | 0 | 0 | 0 | 1 | 0 | 0 | 4,332 |
| | Great Bend | 0 | 0 | 0 | 1 | 0 | 1 | 0 | 0 | 0 | 15,671 |
| | Hesston | 1 | 0 | 0 | 0 | 0 | 0 | 1 | 0 | 0 | 3,758 |
| | Hoisington | 0 | 0 | 0 | 1 | 0 | 1 | 0 | 0 | 0 | 2,875 |
| | Hutchinson | 3 | 5 | 0 | 1 | 0 | 2 | 0 | 7 | 0 | 40,787 |

[1]Agencies published in this table indicated that at least one hate crime incident occurred in their respective jurisdictions during the quarter(s) for which they submitted a report to the Hate Crime Statistics Program. Blanks indicate quarters for which agencies did not submit reports.

[2]Population figures are published only for the cities. The figures listed for the universities and colleges are student enrollment and were provided by the United States Department of Education for the 2008 school year, the most recent available. The enrollment figures include full-time and part-time students.

[4]Student enrollment figures were not available.

## Table 94. Hate Crime Incidents per Bias Motivation and Quarter, by State and Agency, 2009—*Continued*

| State | Agency type/Agency name | Number of incidents per bias motivation | | | | | Number of incidents per quarter[1] | | | | Population[2] |
|---|---|---|---|---|---|---|---|---|---|---|---|
| | | Race | Religion | Sexual orientation | Ethnicity | Disability | 1st quarter | 2nd quarter | 3rd quarter | 4th quarter | |
| | Independence | 0 | 0 | 0 | 1 | 0 | 0 | 0 | 0 | 1 | 9,182 |
| | Iola | 1 | 0 | 1 | 0 | 0 | 0 | 0 | 2 | 0 | 5,727 |
| | Junction City | 3 | 1 | 0 | 0 | 0 | 0 | 3 | 1 | 0 | 20,880 |
| | Lansing | 3 | 0 | 0 | 0 | 0 | 1 | 0 | 2 | 0 | 10,812 |
| | Larned | 1 | 0 | 0 | 0 | 0 | 0 | 0 | 1 | 0 | 3,536 |
| | Lawrence | 1 | 1 | 0 | 0 | 0 | 1 | 0 | 0 | 1 | 91,703 |
| | Leavenworth | 1 | 0 | 0 | 0 | 0 | 0 | 0 | 1 | 0 | 34,647 |
| | Leawood | 1 | 0 | 0 | 0 | 1 | 0 | 1 | 1 | 0 | 31,765 |
| | Lenexa | 2 | 0 | 0 | 0 | 0 | 1 | 0 | 1 | 0 | 47,601 |
| | Maize | 1 | 0 | 0 | 0 | 0 | 0 | 0 | 1 | 0 | 3,200 |
| | Newton | 1 | 1 | 0 | 0 | 0 | 0 | 0 | 1 | 1 | 18,175 |
| | Osawatomie | 0 | 0 | 1 | 0 | 0 | 0 | 0 | 1 | 0 | 4,468 |
| | Oswego | 0 | 0 | 1 | 0 | 0 | 0 | 0 | 1 | 0 | 1,973 |
| | Ottawa | 0 | 1 | 0 | 0 | 0 | 0 | 1 | 0 | 0 | 12,950 |
| | Parsons | 1 | 0 | 1 | 0 | 0 | 1 | 1 | 0 | 0 | 11,020 |
| | Pittsburg | 0 | 0 | 1 | 0 | 0 | 1 | 0 | 0 | 0 | 19,693 |
| | Pratt | 0 | 0 | 0 | 1 | 0 | 0 | 1 | 0 | 0 | 6,380 |
| | Salina | 1 | 0 | 1 | 2 | 0 | 1 | 2 | 1 | 0 | 46,561 |
| | Shawnee | 1 | 0 | 0 | 0 | 0 | 0 | 0 | 0 | 1 | 62,508 |
| | Valley Center | 1 | 2 | 0 | 1 | 0 | 2 | 1 | 1 | 0 | 6,631 |
| | Wamego | 1 | 0 | 0 | 0 | 0 | 1 | 0 | 0 | 0 | 4,317 |
| | Wellington | 2 | 0 | 0 | 0 | 0 | 1 | 0 | 1 | 0 | 7,639 |
| | Wichita | 18 | 2 | 5 | 3 | 0 | 4 | 11 | 10 | 3 | 367,635 |
| | **Universities and Colleges** | 2 | 1 | 1 | 0 | 0 | | | | | |
| | Kansas City Community College | 1 | 0 | 0 | 0 | 0 | 1 | 0 | 0 | 0 | 5,820 |
| | Kansas State University | 0 | 1 | 0 | 0 | 0 | 0 | 0 | 1 | 0 | 23,520 |
| | University of Kansas, Medical Center[4] | | 0 | 0 | 1 | 0 | 0 | 0 | 0 | 1 | 0 |
| | Washburn University | 1 | 0 | 0 | 0 | 0 | 1 | 0 | 0 | 0 | 6,545 |
| | **Metropolitan Counties** | 6 | 1 | 2 | 4 | 0 | | | | | |
| | Doniphan | 0 | 1 | 0 | 0 | 0 | 1 | 0 | 0 | 0 | |
| | Franklin | 1 | 0 | 0 | 0 | 0 | 0 | 0 | 0 | 1 | |
| | Jackson | 1 | 0 | 0 | 1 | 0 | 1 | 0 | 0 | 1 | |
| | Johnson | 0 | 0 | 0 | 1 | 0 | 0 | 1 | 0 | 0 | |
| | Pottawatomie | 1 | 0 | 1 | 0 | 0 | 0 | 2 | 0 | 0 | |
| | Riley County | | | | | | | | | | |
| | Police Department | 0 | 0 | 0 | 1 | 0 | 0 | 0 | 0 | 1 | |
| | Sedgwick | 1 | 0 | 1 | 0 | 0 | 1 | 0 | 1 | 0 | |
| | Shawnee | 1 | 0 | 0 | 1 | 0 | 0 | 1 | 1 | 0 | |
| | Sumner | 1 | 0 | 0 | 0 | 0 | 0 | 1 | 0 | 0 | |
| | **Nonmetropolitan Counties** | 4 | 2 | 1 | 1 | 0 | | | | | |
| | Chautauqua | 1 | 0 | 0 | 0 | 0 | 1 | 0 | 0 | 0 | |
| | Dickinson | 1 | 0 | 0 | 0 | 0 | 1 | 0 | 0 | 0 | |
| | Kearny | 1 | 0 | 0 | 0 | 0 | 0 | 1 | 0 | | |
| | Labette | 0 | 1 | 0 | 0 | 0 | 0 | 0 | 1 | 0 | |
| | Lincoln | 0 | 1 | 0 | 0 | 0 | 1 | 0 | 0 | 0 | |
| | Reno | 0 | 0 | 1 | 0 | 0 | 1 | 0 | 0 | 0 | |
| | Seward | 1 | 0 | 0 | 0 | 0 | 0 | 1 | 0 | 0 | |
| | Wichita | 0 | 0 | 0 | 1 | 0 | 0 | 0 | 0 | 1 | |
| | **Other Agencies** | 1 | 0 | 1 | 1 | 0 | | | | | |
| | Kansas Department of Wildlife and Parks | 1 | 0 | 0 | 0 | 0 | 0 | 0 | 1 | 0 | |
| | Unified School District: | | | | | | | | | | |
| | Goddard | 0 | 0 | 0 | 1 | 0 | 0 | 1 | 0 | 0 | |
| | Maize | 0 | 0 | 1 | 0 | 0 | 0 | 1 | 0 | 0 | |
| **KENTUCKY** | **Total** | 95 | 11 | 24 | 18 | 2 | | | | | |
| | **Cities** | 59 | 5 | 12 | 12 | 2 | | | | | |
| | Audubon Park | 1 | 0 | 0 | 0 | 0 | 0 | 0 | 1 | 0 | 1,676 |
| | Barbourville | 0 | 0 | 1 | 0 | 0 | 0 | 0 | 0 | 1 | 3,614 |
| | Bardstown | 2 | 0 | 0 | 0 | 0 | 1 | 1 | 0 | 0 | 11,292 |
| | Bellevue | 1 | 0 | 1 | 0 | 0 | 0 | 1 | 1 | 0 | 5,788 |
| | Berea | 0 | 1 | 0 | 0 | 0 | 0 | 0 | 1 | 0 | 14,825 |
| | Bowling Green | 5 | 0 | 0 | 0 | 0 | 0 | 3 | 1 | 1 | 55,754 |
| | Campbellsville | 1 | 0 | 0 | 0 | 0 | 0 | 0 | 0 | 1 | 11,072 |
| | Covington | 4 | 1 | 1 | 3 | 0 | 3 | 1 | 2 | 3 | 43,215 |
| | Cynthiana | 1 | 0 | 0 | 0 | 0 | 1 | 0 | 0 | 0 | 6,277 |
| | Danville | 1 | 0 | 0 | 0 | 0 | 1 | 0 | 0 | 0 | 15,530 |
| | Dayton | 0 | 1 | 1 | 0 | 0 | 0 | 1 | 1 | 0 | 5,400 |
| | Elizabethtown | 2 | 1 | 1 | 0 | 0 | 2 | 1 | 0 | 1 | 24,321 |
| | Elkton | 0 | 0 | 0 | 1 | 0 | 0 | 0 | 1 | 0 | 1,981 |
| | Elsmere | 1 | 0 | 0 | 0 | 0 | 0 | 0 | 0 | 1 | 7,908 |
| | Erlanger | 2 | 0 | 0 | 0 | 0 | 0 | 0 | 0 | 2 | 21,299 |

[1]Agencies published in this table indicated that at least one hate crime incident occurred in their respective jurisdictions during the quarter(s) for which they submitted a report to the Hate Crime Statistics Program. Blanks indicate quarters for which agencies did not submit reports.
[2]Population figures are published only for the cities. The figures listed for the universities and colleges are student enrollment and were provided by the United States Department of Education for the 2008 school year, the most recent available. The enrollment figures include full-time and part-time students.
[4]Student enrollment figures were not available.

## Table 94. Hate Crime Incidents per Bias Motivation and Quarter, by State and Agency, 2009—*Continued*

| State | Agency type/Agency name | Number of incidents per bias motivation | | | | | Number of incidents per quarter[1] | | | | Population[2] |
|---|---|---|---|---|---|---|---|---|---|---|---|
| | | Race | Religion | Sexual orientation | Ethnicity | Disability | 1st quarter | 2nd quarter | 3rd quarter | 4th quarter | |
| | Falmouth | 1 | 0 | 0 | 0 | 0 | 1 | 0 | 0 | 0 | 2,058 |
| | Florence | 0 | 0 | 1 | 2 | 0 | 0 | 0 | 1 | 2 | 28,232 |
| | Fulton | 1 | 0 | 0 | 0 | 0 | 0 | 1 | 0 | 0 | 2,406 |
| | Glasgow | 1 | 0 | 0 | 0 | 0 | 1 | 0 | 0 | 0 | 14,440 |
| | Hardinsburg | 1 | 0 | 0 | 0 | 0 | 0 | 1 | 0 | 0 | 2,443 |
| | Harrodsburg | 1 | 0 | 0 | 0 | 0 | 0 | 1 | 0 | 0 | 8,195 |
| | Hopkinsville | 4 | 0 | 1 | 1 | 0 | 1 | 2 | 1 | 2 | 32,294 |
| | Independence | 1 | 0 | 0 | 0 | 0 | 0 | 0 | 1 | 0 | 22,572 |
| | Irvine | 0 | 0 | 0 | 1 | 0 | 1 | 0 | 0 | 0 | 2,648 |
| | Jeffersontown | 1 | 0 | 0 | 0 | 0 | 0 | 1 | 0 | 0 | 26,199 |
| | Lakeside Park-Crestview Hills | 0 | 1 | 0 | 0 | 0 | 0 | 0 | 0 | 1 | 6,470 |
| | Leitchfield | 1 | 0 | 0 | 0 | 0 | 1 | 0 | 0 | 0 | 6,572 |
| | Ludlow | 2 | 0 | 1 | 0 | 0 | 2 | 0 | 1 | 0 | 4,856 |
| | Mayfield | 0 | 0 | 0 | 2 | 0 | 0 | 2 | 0 | 0 | 10,167 |
| | Maysville | 1 | 0 | 0 | 0 | 0 | 0 | 0 | 1 | 0 | 9,277 |
| | Meadow Vale | 0 | 0 | 1 | 0 | 0 | 0 | 0 | 0 | 1 | 859 |
| | Monticello | 1 | 0 | 0 | 0 | 0 | 1 | 0 | 0 | 0 | 6,182 |
| | Mount Washington | 2 | 0 | 0 | 0 | 0 | 0 | 2 | 0 | 0 | 12,414 |
| | Nicholasville | 1 | 0 | 0 | 0 | 0 | 0 | 1 | 0 | 0 | 27,162 |
| | Oak Grove | 2 | 0 | 0 | 0 | 0 | 0 | 0 | 1 | 1 | 9,480 |
| | Paducah | 3 | 0 | 1 | 0 | 0 | 3 | 0 | 1 | 0 | 25,439 |
| | Pikeville | 1 | 0 | 0 | 0 | 0 | 1 | 0 | 0 | 0 | 6,406 |
| | Princeton | 0 | 0 | 0 | 0 | 1 | 0 | 0 | 1 | 0 | 6,384 |
| | Richmond | 1 | 0 | 0 | 0 | 0 | 1 | 0 | 0 | 0 | 33,546 |
| | Shelbyville | 3 | 0 | 2 | 2 | 0 | 2 | 1 | 2 | 2 | 11,422 |
| | Shively | 4 | 0 | 0 | 0 | 0 | 1 | 2 | 1 | 0 | 16,816 |
| | St. Matthews | 1 | 0 | 0 | 0 | 0 | 0 | 1 | 0 | 0 | 18,871 |
| | Versailles | 1 | 0 | 0 | 0 | 0 | 0 | 0 | 0 | 1 | 7,817 |
| | Vine Grove | 1 | 0 | 0 | 0 | 0 | 0 | 0 | 1 | 0 | 4,386 |
| | West Point[3] | 1 | 0 | 0 | 0 | 0 | 0 | 0 | 0 | 1 | 961 |
| | Whitesburg | 1 | 0 | 0 | 0 | 0 | 0 | 0 | 1 | 0 | 1,466 |
| | Wilmore | 0 | 0 | 0 | 0 | 1 | 0 | 0 | 0 | 1 | 6,016 |
| | **Universities and Colleges** | | 4 | 1 | 4 | 0 | 0 | | | | |
| | Eastern Kentucky University | 0 | 1 | 2 | 0 | 0 | 1 | 1 | 0 | 1 | 16,031 |
| | Murray State University | 1 | 0 | 0 | 0 | 0 | 0 | 0 | 1 | 0 | 10,014 |
| | Northern Kentucky University | 1 | 0 | 0 | 0 | 0 | 1 | 0 | 0 | 0 | 15,082 |
| | University of Kentucky | 1 | 0 | 1 | 0 | 0 | 0 | 0 | 1 | 1 | 26,054 |
| | University of Louisville | 1 | 0 | 1 | 0 | 0 | 1 | 0 | 0 | 1 | 20,834 |
| | **Metropolitan Counties** | | 10 | 0 | 3 | 1 | 0 | | | | |
| | Boone | 2 | 0 | 2 | 0 | 0 | 0 | 0 | 0 | 4 | |
| | Bullitt | 2 | 0 | 0 | 0 | 0 | 1 | 0 | 0 | 1 | |
| | Clark | 0 | 0 | 0 | 1 | 0 | 1 | 0 | 0 | 0 | |
| | Kenton County Police Department | 1 | 0 | 1 | 0 | 0 | 1 | 1 | 0 | 0 | |
| | Oldham County Police Department | 1 | 0 | 0 | 0 | 0 | 0 | 0 | 0 | 1 | |
| | Shelby | 2 | 0 | 0 | 0 | 0 | 0 | 0 | 2 | 0 | |
| | Warren | 2 | 0 | 0 | 0 | 0 | 0 | 1 | 1 | 0 | |
| | **Nonmetropolitan Counties** | | 10 | 4 | 3 | 5 | 0 | | | | |
| | Allen | 0 | 1 | 2 | 1 | 0 | 1 | 1 | 1 | 1 | |
| | Ballard | 1 | 0 | 0 | 1 | 0 | 1 | 1 | 0 | 0 | |
| | Fleming | 1 | 0 | 0 | 0 | 0 | 0 | 0 | 0 | 1 | |
| | Franklin | 0 | 0 | 0 | 1 | 0 | 0 | 1 | 0 | 0 | |
| | Graves | 0 | 0 | 1 | 0 | 0 | 0 | 0 | 1 | 0 | |
| | Harrison | 0 | 0 | 0 | 1 | 0 | 0 | 0 | 1 | 0 | |
| | Laurel | 1 | 0 | 0 | 0 | 0 | 1 | 0 | 0 | 0 | |
| | Madison | 1 | 0 | 0 | 0 | 0 | 0 | 0 | 0 | 1 | |
| | Marshall | 0 | 1 | 0 | 0 | 0 | 0 | 0 | 1 | 0 | |
| | McCracken | 4 | 1 | 0 | 1 | 0 | 0 | 3 | 2 | 1 | |
| | Ohio | 1 | 0 | 0 | 0 | 0 | 0 | 1 | 0 | 0 | |
| | Rowan | 0 | 1 | 0 | 0 | 0 | 0 | 0 | 0 | 1 | |
| | Union | 1 | 0 | 0 | 0 | 0 | 1 | 0 | 0 | 0 | |
| | **State Police Agencies** | | 4 | 1 | 1 | 0 | 0 | | | | |
| | State Police: | | | | | | | | | | |
| | Campbellsburg | 1 | 0 | 0 | 0 | 0 | 1 | 0 | 0 | 0 | |
| | Columbia | 1 | 0 | 0 | 0 | 0 | 0 | 0 | 1 | 0 | |
| | Harlan | 0 | 0 | 1 | 0 | 0 | 0 | 0 | 0 | 1 | |
| | London | 1 | 0 | 0 | 0 | 0 | 0 | 0 | 0 | 1 | |
| | Madisonville | 0 | 1 | 0 | 0 | 0 | 0 | 0 | 1 | 0 | |
| | Pikeville | 1 | 0 | 0 | 0 | 0 | 0 | 1 | 0 | 0 | |

[1]Agencies published in this table indicated that at least one hate crime incident occurred in their respective jurisdictions during the quarter(s) for which they submitted a report to the Hate Crime Statistics Program. Blanks indicate quarters for which agencies did not submit reports.

[2]Population figures are published only for the cities. The figures listed for the universities and colleges are student enrollment and were provided by the United States Department of Education for the 2008 school year, the most recent available. The enrollment figures include full-time and part-time students.

[3]Includes one incident reported with more than one bias motivation.

## Table 94. Hate Crime Incidents per Bias Motivation and Quarter, by State and Agency, 2009—*Continued*

| State | Agency type/Agency name | Number of incidents per bias motivation | | | | | Number of incidents per quarter[1] | | | | Population[2] |
|---|---|---|---|---|---|---|---|---|---|---|---|
| | | Race | Religion | Sexual orientation | Ethnicity | Disability | 1st quarter | 2nd quarter | 3rd quarter | 4th quarter | |
| | **Other Agencies** | | 8 | 0 | 1 | 0 | 0 | | | | |
| | Cincinnati-Northern Kentucky International Airport | 1 | 0 | 0 | 0 | 0 | 0 | 0 | 1 | 0 | |
| | Clark County School System | 1 | 0 | 0 | 0 | 0 | 1 | 0 | 0 | 0 | |
| | Fayette County Schools | 2 | 0 | 1 | 0 | 0 | 1 | 1 | 1 | 0 | |
| | Jefferson County Board of Education | 1 | 0 | 0 | 0 | 0 | 0 | 0 | 0 | 1 | |
| | Ohio County School System | 2 | 0 | 0 | 0 | 0 | 0 | 0 | 2 | 0 | |
| | Park Security | 1 | 0 | 0 | 0 | 0 | 0 | 1 | 0 | 0 | |
| **LOUISIANA** | **Total** | 9 | 0 | 3 | 1 | 0 | | | | | |
| | **Cities** | 1 | 0 | 1 | 0 | 0 | | | | | |
| | Farmerville | 1 | 0 | 0 | 0 | 0 | 1 | 0 | | 0 | 3,615 |
| | Houma | 0 | 0 | 1 | 0 | 0 | 0 | 1 | | | 32,477 |
| | **Universities and Colleges** | 1 | 0 | 0 | 0 | 0 | | | | | |
| | University of New Orleans | 1 | 0 | 0 | 0 | 0 | | | | 1 | 11,428 |
| | **Metropolitan Counties** | 5 | 0 | 1 | 1 | 0 | | | | | |
| | Bossier | 1 | 0 | 0 | 0 | 0 | 0 | 1 | 0 | 0 | |
| | Jefferson | 3 | 0 | 1 | 0 | 0 | 1 | 0 | 2 | 1 | |
| | Lafayette | 0 | 0 | 0 | 1 | 0 | 0 | 1 | | 0 | |
| | Livingston | 1 | 0 | 0 | 0 | 0 | | | | 1 | |
| | **Nonmetropolitan Counties** | 2 | 0 | 1 | 0 | 0 | | | | | |
| | East Carroll | 1 | 0 | 1 | 0 | 0 | 0 | 1 | 1 | 0 | |
| | St. James | 1 | 0 | 0 | 0 | 0 | 0 | 0 | 1 | 0 | |
| **MAINE** | **Total** | 28 | 6 | 14 | 2 | 0 | | | | | |
| | **Cities** | 22 | 5 | 13 | 1 | 0 | | | | | |
| | Auburn | 1 | 0 | 0 | 0 | 0 | 0 | 1 | 0 | 0 | 23,176 |
| | Augusta | 5 | 0 | 2 | 0 | 0 | 1 | 0 | 1 | 5 | 18,252 |
| | Biddeford | 0 | 0 | 1 | 0 | 0 | 0 | 0 | 1 | 0 | 21,479 |
| | Ellsworth | 1 | 0 | 0 | 0 | 0 | 0 | 0 | 0 | 1 | 7,177 |
| | Gorham | 1 | 0 | 0 | 1 | 0 | 1 | 1 | 0 | 0 | 15,725 |
| | Kennebunk | 1 | 0 | 0 | 0 | 0 | 0 | 0 | 0 | 1 | 11,551 |
| | Lewiston | 2 | 0 | 0 | 0 | 0 | 0 | 0 | 1 | 1 | 35,074 |
| | Old Orchard Beach | 0 | 1 | 1 | 0 | 0 | 0 | 0 | 1 | 1 | 9,451 |
| | Orono | 0 | 1 | 1 | 0 | 0 | 2 | 0 | 0 | 0 | 9,708 |
| | Portland | 4 | 1 | 3 | 0 | 0 | 4 | 2 | 1 | 1 | 62,382 |
| | Rumford | 1 | 0 | 0 | 0 | 0 | 0 | 0 | 0 | 1 | 6,293 |
| | Saco | 0 | 1 | 1 | 0 | 0 | 0 | 0 | 0 | 2 | 18,262 |
| | Sanford | 3 | 0 | 1 | 0 | 0 | 0 | 1 | 2 | 1 | 21,183 |
| | South Portland | 2 | 1 | 3 | 0 | 0 | 4 | 1 | 0 | 1 | 23,852 |
| | Topsham | 1 | 0 | 0 | 0 | 0 | 0 | 1 | 0 | 0 | 9,909 |
| | **Universities and Colleges** | | 1 | 0 | 0 | 0 | 0 | | | | |
| | University of Southern Maine | 1 | 0 | 0 | 0 | 0 | 0 | 0 | 0 | 1 | 10,009 |
| | **Metropolitan Counties** | | 2 | 1 | 0 | 0 | 0 | | | | |
| | Cumberland | 0 | 1 | 0 | 0 | 0 | 0 | 0 | 0 | 1 | |
| | Sagadahoc | 1 | 0 | 0 | 0 | 0 | 0 | 0 | 0 | 1 | |
| | York | 1 | 0 | 0 | 0 | 0 | 0 | 1 | 0 | 0 | |
| | **Nonmetropolitan Counties** | | 1 | 0 | 0 | 1 | 0 | | | | |
| | Aroostook | 1 | 0 | 0 | 0 | 0 | 0 | 0 | 1 | 0 | |
| | Washington | 0 | 0 | 0 | 1 | 0 | 0 | 0 | 0 | 1 | |
| | **State Police Agencies** | | 2 | 0 | 1 | 0 | 0 | | | | |
| | State Police: Kennebec County | 0 | 0 | 1 | 0 | 0 | 0 | 0 | 0 | 1 | |
| | Somerset County | 1 | 0 | 0 | 0 | 0 | 0 | 1 | 0 | 0 | |
| | York County | 1 | 0 | 0 | 0 | 0 | 0 | 0 | 1 | 0 | |
| **MARYLAND** | **Total** | 62 | 26 | 9 | 5 | 0 | | | | | |
| | **Cities** | 6 | 3 | 1 | 0 | 0 | | | | | |
| | Aberdeen | 1 | 0 | 0 | 0 | 0 | 0 | 0 | 1 | 0 | 14,003 |
| | Annapolis | 0 | 2 | 0 | 0 | 0 | 0 | 0 | 2 | 0 | 36,586 |
| | Baltimore | 5 | 1 | 1 | 0 | 0 | 3 | 1 | 1 | 2 | 638,755 |
| | **Universities and Colleges** | | 2 | 3 | 5 | 0 | 0 | | | | |
| | Towson University | 2 | 2 | 5 | 0 | 0 | 0 | 0 | 0 | 9 | 21,111 |
| | University of Maryland, College Park | 0 | 1 | 0 | 0 | 0 | 0 | 0 | 1 | 0 | 37,000 |
| | **Metropolitan Counties** | | 48 | 20 | 3 | 5 | 0 | | | | |
| | Anne Arundel County Police Department | 1 | 0 | 0 | 0 | 0 | 0 | 1 | 0 | 0 | |
| | Baltimore County Police Department | 30 | 8 | 2 | 1 | 0 | 9 | 8 | 14 | 10 | |

[1]Agencies published in this table indicated that at least one hate crime incident occurred in their respective jurisdictions during the quarter(s) for which they submitted a report to the Hate Crime Statistics Program. Blanks indicate quarters for which agencies did not submit reports.
[2]Population figures are published only for the cities. The figures listed for the universities and colleges are student enrollment and were provided by the United States Department of Education for the 2008 school year, the most recent available. The enrollment figures include full-time and part-time students.

## Table 94. Hate Crime Incidents per Bias Motivation and Quarter, by State and Agency, 2009—*Continued*

| State | Agency type/Agency name | Number of incidents per bias motivation | | | | | Number of incidents per quarter[1] | | | | Population[2] |
|---|---|---|---|---|---|---|---|---|---|---|---|
| | | Race | Religion | Sexual orientation | Ethnicity | Disability | 1st quarter | 2nd quarter | 3rd quarter | 4th quarter | |
| | Charles | 5 | 1 | 0 | 0 | 0 | 6 | 0 | 0 | 0 | |
| | Frederick | 1 | 0 | 0 | 0 | 0 | 0 | 0 | 0 | 1 | |
| | Harford | 1 | 0 | 0 | 0 | 0 | 0 | 1 | 0 | 0 | |
| | Howard County Police Department | 2 | 0 | 0 | 0 | 0 | 0 | 0 | 1 | 1 | |
| | Montgomery County Police Department | 3 | 9 | 1 | 3 | 0 | 4 | 2 | 6 | 4 | |
| | Prince George's County Police Department | 5 | 2 | 0 | 0 | 0 | 2 | 2 | 3 | 0 | |
| | Wicomico | 0 | 0 | 0 | 1 | 0 | 0 | 0 | 0 | 1 | |
| | **State Police Agencies** | | 6 | 0 | 0 | 0 | 0 | | | | |
| | State Police: | | | | | | | | | | |
| | Allegany County | 1 | 0 | 0 | 0 | 0 | 1 | 0 | 0 | 0 | |
| | Carroll County | 2 | 0 | 0 | 0 | 0 | 0 | 0 | 0 | 2 | |
| | Cecil County | 2 | 0 | 0 | 0 | 0 | 0 | 1 | 0 | 1 | |
| | Worcester County | 1 | 0 | 0 | 0 | 0 | 0 | 0 | 0 | 1 | |
| **MASSACHUSETTS....** | **Total** | 158 | 59 | 66 | 36 | 3 | | | | | |
| | **Cities** | 150 | 58 | 57 | 36 | 3 | | | | | |
| | Acton | 1 | 2 | 0 | 0 | 0 | 0 | 0 | 1 | 2 | 21,104 |
| | Amesbury | 1 | 0 | 0 | 0 | 0 | 0 | 0 | 0 | 1 | 16,623 |
| | Amherst | 0 | 0 | 0 | 1 | 0 | 1 | 0 | 0 | 0 | 36,845 |
| | Andover | 1 | 0 | 0 | 0 | 0 | 0 | 0 | 0 | 1 | 33,853 |
| | Arlington | 1 | 0 | 0 | 1 | 0 | 0 | 0 | 2 | 0 | 41,598 |
| | Barnstable | 4 | 3 | 3 | 0 | 0 | 1 | 0 | 4 | 5 | 48,042 |
| | Belmont | 1 | 0 | 0 | 0 | 0 | 0 | 0 | 0 | 1 | 23,597 |
| | Bernardston | 1 | 0 | 0 | 0 | 0 | 0 | 0 | 0 | 1 | 2,258 |
| | Beverly | 1 | 0 | 0 | 0 | 0 | 0 | 0 | 1 | 0 | 39,919 |
| | Boston | 66 | 22 | 32 | 14 | 0 | 35 | 40 | 29 | 30 | 624,222 |
| | Braintree | 0 | 1 | 0 | 0 | 0 | 0 | 1 | 0 | 0 | 35,047 |
| | Burlington | 1 | 0 | 0 | 0 | 0 | 0 | 0 | 0 | 1 | 25,695 |
| | Cambridge | 8 | 2 | 2 | 4 | 1 | 3 | 3 | 8 | 3 | 102,866 |
| | Chelsea | 1 | 0 | 1 | 0 | 0 | 1 | 1 | 0 | 0 | 39,883 |
| | Cohasset | 1 | 0 | 0 | 0 | 0 | 0 | 0 | 0 | 1 | 7,286 |
| | Douglas | 1 | 0 | 0 | 0 | 0 | 1 | 0 | 0 | 0 | 8,093 |
| | Duxbury | 1 | 0 | 0 | 0 | 0 | 0 | 0 | 0 | 1 | 14,588 |
| | East Longmeadow | 2 | 0 | 0 | 0 | 0 | 0 | 0 | 1 | 1 | 15,595 |
| | Erving | 1 | 0 | 0 | 0 | 0 | 0 | 0 | 1 | 0 | 1,563 |
| | Everett | 1 | 0 | 0 | 1 | 0 | 0 | 1 | 1 | 0 | 37,724 |
| | Framingham | 0 | 0 | 0 | 1 | 0 | 0 | 0 | | 1 | 65,478 |
| | Hardwick | 0 | 1 | 0 | 0 | 0 | 0 | 0 | 1 | 0 | 2,673 |
| | Haverhill | 3 | 0 | 0 | 2 | 0 | 3 | 1 | 0 | 1 | 60,738 |
| | Holbrook | 0 | 0 | 3 | 0 | 0 | | 1 | 2 | | 10,817 |
| | Holyoke | 0 | 1 | 0 | 0 | 0 | 1 | 0 | 0 | 0 | 40,322 |
| | Ipswich | 0 | 0 | 1 | 0 | 0 | 0 | 1 | 0 | 0 | 13,435 |
| | Lakeville | 1 | 0 | 1 | 0 | 0 | 0 | 0 | 1 | 1 | 10,769 |
| | Lawrence | 1 | 0 | 0 | 0 | 0 | | | | 1 | 70,670 |
| | Lenox | 1 | 1 | 0 | 0 | 0 | 0 | 2 | 0 | 0 | 5,160 |
| | Lowell | 0 | 1 | 1 | 0 | 0 | 0 | 2 | 0 | 0 | 111,772 |
| | Lynn | 0 | 0 | 0 | 1 | 0 | 0 | 0 | 1 | 0 | 91,149 |
| | Malden | 1 | 0 | 0 | 0 | 0 | 0 | 1 | 0 | 0 | 56,455 |
| | Marion | 0 | 0 | 1 | 0 | 0 | 0 | 1 | 0 | 0 | 5,271 |
| | Medford | 0 | 1 | 0 | 0 | 0 | | 1 | | | 56,380 |
| | Milton | 1 | 0 | 0 | 0 | 0 | | | 1 | | 26,719 |
| | Monson | 0 | 0 | 1 | 0 | 0 | 1 | 0 | 0 | 0 | 8,974 |
| | Nantucket | 0 | 0 | 1 | 0 | 0 | 1 | 0 | 0 | 0 | 11,380 |
| | Natick | 0 | 1 | 0 | 0 | 0 | 0 | 1 | 0 | 0 | 32,418 |
| | Needham | 2 | 0 | 0 | 0 | 0 | 0 | 0 | 1 | 1 | 28,683 |
| | New Bedford | 0 | 0 | 2 | 1 | 0 | 2 | 1 | 0 | 0 | 92,621 |
| | Newbury | 0 | 1 | 0 | 0 | 0 | 1 | 0 | 0 | 0 | 7,035 |
| | Newburyport | 0 | 0 | 0 | 1 | 0 | 0 | 1 | 0 | 0 | 17,343 |
| | Newton | 0 | 1 | 0 | 0 | 0 | 0 | 0 | 1 | 0 | 84,427 |
| | Norfolk | 0 | 1 | 0 | 0 | 0 | 0 | 0 | 1 | 0 | 10,837 |
| | Northampton | 2 | 1 | 1 | 0 | 0 | 1 | 2 | 1 | 0 | 28,921 |
| | North Attleboro | 0 | 0 | 0 | 1 | 0 | 0 | 0 | 0 | 1 | 28,346 |
| | Northborough | 1 | 0 | 0 | 0 | 0 | 0 | 0 | 1 | 0 | 14,792 |
| | North Reading | 1 | 2 | 0 | 0 | 0 | 0 | 2 | 0 | 1 | 14,249 |
| | Norton | 7 | 0 | 0 | 0 | 0 | 0 | 0 | 7 | 0 | 19,610 |
| | Oxford | 2 | 0 | 0 | 0 | 0 | 0 | 1 | 1 | 0 | 13,773 |
| | Pittsfield | 0 | 1 | 0 | 0 | 0 | 1 | 0 | 0 | 0 | 43,050 |
| | Plainville | 2 | 0 | 0 | 0 | 0 | 1 | 1 | 0 | 0 | 8,522 |
| | Plymouth | 6 | 2 | 1 | 1 | 0 | 1 | 3 | 0 | 6 | 56,084 |

[1]Agencies published in this table indicated that at least one hate crime incident occurred in their respective jurisdictions during the quarter(s) for which they submitted a report to the Hate Crime Statistics Program. Blanks indicate quarters for which agencies did not submit reports.

[2]Population figures are published only for the cities. The figures listed for the universities and colleges are student enrollment and were provided by the United States Department of Education for the 2008 school year, the most recent available. The enrollment figures include full-time and part-time students.

# Table 94. Hate Crime Incidents per Bias Motivation and Quarter, by State and Agency, 2009—*Continued*

| State | Agency type/Agency name | Number of incidents per bias motivation | | | | | Number of incidents per quarter[1] | | | | Population[2] |
|---|---|---|---|---|---|---|---|---|---|---|---|
| | | Race | Religion | Sexual orientation | Ethnicity | Disability | 1st quarter | 2nd quarter | 3rd quarter | 4th quarter | |
| | Provincetown | 0 | 0 | 1 | 0 | 0 | 0 | 1 | 0 | 0 | 3,398 |
| | Quincy | 3 | 0 | 0 | 1 | 0 | 2 | 1 | 1 | 0 | 96,580 |
| | Randolph | 2 | 0 | 0 | 0 | 0 | 0 | 0 | 1 | 1 | 30,549 |
| | Revere | 8 | 2 | 1 | 1 | 2 | 6 | 7 | 0 | 1 | 58,290 |
| | Sharon | 1 | 0 | 0 | 0 | 0 | 0 | 1 | 0 | 0 | 17,256 |
| | Somerville | 0 | 1 | 0 | 0 | 0 | 0 | 0 | 1 | 0 | 75,112 |
| | Southbridge | 2 | 0 | 0 | 1 | 0 | 0 | 1 | 2 | 0 | 17,012 |
| | South Hadley | 1 | 0 | 1 | 0 | 0 | 1 | 1 | 0 | 0 | 17,267 |
| | Southwick | 1 | 0 | 0 | 0 | 0 | 0 | 0 | 1 | 0 | 9,651 |
| | Springfield | 1 | 1 | 0 | 3 | 0 | 1 | 3 | 1 | 0 | 153,533 |
| | Stoughton | 0 | 1 | 0 | 0 | 0 | 0 | 1 | 0 | 0 | 27,355 |
| | Sturbridge | 1 | 0 | 0 | 0 | 0 | 0 | 0 | 1 | 0 | 9,335 |
| | Tewksbury | 0 | 1 | 0 | 0 | 0 | 0 | 1 | 0 | 0 | 30,133 |
| | Upton | 1 | 0 | 0 | 0 | 0 | 0 | 1 | 0 | 0 | 6,678 |
| | Waltham | 0 | 0 | 1 | 0 | 0 | 0 | 1 | 0 | 0 | 61,357 |
| | Watertown | 0 | 0 | 1 | 0 | 0 | 0 | 0 | 1 | 0 | 32,944 |
| | Wellesley | 1 | 0 | 0 | 0 | 0 | 0 | 0 | 0 | 1 | 27,407 |
| | West Boylston | 0 | 1 | 0 | 0 | 0 | 0 | 1 | 0 | 0 | 8,364 |
| | Westport | 1 | 0 | 0 | 0 | 0 | 0 | 0 | 0 | 1 | 15,445 |
| | Westwood | 1 | 0 | 0 | 0 | 0 | 0 | 0 | 0 | 1 | 14,219 |
| | Wilbraham | 0 | 0 | 0 | 1 | 0 | 0 | 0 | 0 | 1 | 14,311 |
| | Winthrop | 0 | 0 | 1 | 0 | 0 | 1 | 0 | 0 | 0 | 21,071 |
| | Worcester | 1 | 6 | 0 | 0 | 0 | 0 | 0 | 2 | 5 | 178,474 |
| | **Universities and Colleges** | | 8 | 1 | 9 | 0 | 0 | | | | |
| | Amherst College | 0 | 0 | 1 | 0 | 0 | | | | 1 | 1,697 |
| | Bentley College | 0 | 0 | 1 | 0 | 0 | | | | 1 | 5,693 |
| | Bridgewater State College | 1 | 0 | 0 | 0 | 0 | 0 | 1 | 0 | 0 | 10,269 |
| | Dean College | 1 | 0 | 1 | 0 | 0 | | | | 2 | 1,341 |
| | Framingham State College | 0 | 0 | 3 | 0 | 0 | | | 3 | | 6,086 |
| | Harvard University | 1 | 0 | 0 | 0 | 0 | | | 1 | | 26,496 |
| | Northeastern University | 2 | 1 | 2 | 0 | 0 | | | 3 | 2 | 25,837 |
| | Smith College | 0 | 0 | 1 | 0 | 0 | 0 | 0 | 0 | 1 | 3,101 |
| | University of Massachusetts: | | | | | | | | | | |
| | Amherst | 2 | 0 | 0 | 0 | 0 | 1 | 0 | 1 | 0 | 26,359 |
| | Harbor Campus, Boston | 1 | 0 | 0 | 0 | 0 | 0 | 0 | 1 | 0 | 14,117 |
| MICHIGAN | **Total** | | 194 | 26 | 62 | 25 | 7 | | | | |
| | **Cities** | | 161 | 22 | 54 | 21 | 6 | | | | |
| | Adrian | 2 | 0 | 0 | 0 | 0 | 1 | 0 | 1 | 0 | 21,295 |
| | Adrian Township | 0 | 0 | 0 | 1 | 0 | 0 | 0 | 0 | 1 | 7,422 |
| | Allegan | 1 | 0 | 0 | 0 | 0 | 0 | 0 | 1 | 0 | 4,826 |
| | Ann Arbor | 4 | 2 | 1 | 3 | 0 | 3 | 4 | 1 | 2 | 114,367 |
| | Auburn Hills | 1 | 0 | 0 | 1 | 0 | 0 | 0 | 1 | 1 | 21,021 |
| | Bay City | 2 | 0 | 0 | 0 | 0 | 0 | 1 | 1 | 0 | 33,572 |
| | Bellaire | 0 | 0 | 0 | 0 | 1 | 0 | 0 | 1 | 0 | 1,118 |
| | Benton Township | 0 | 0 | 1 | 0 | 0 | 0 | 0 | 0 | 1 | 15,043 |
| | Berrien Springs-Oronoko Township | 2 | 0 | 0 | 0 | 0 | 1 | 1 | 0 | 0 | 9,534 |
| | Beverly Hills | 1 | 0 | 0 | 0 | 0 | 0 | 1 | 0 | 0 | 9,805 |
| | Blackman Township | 1 | 0 | 0 | 0 | 0 | 1 | 0 | 0 | 0 | 24,512 |
| | Bloomfield Township | 0 | 0 | 1 | 0 | 0 | 0 | 1 | 0 | 0 | 40,699 |
| | Bridgeport Township | 1 | 0 | 0 | 0 | 0 | 0 | 1 | 0 | 0 | 10,727 |
| | Cadillac | 2 | 0 | 1 | 0 | 0 | 1 | 1 | 0 | 1 | 10,271 |
| | Canton Township | 2 | 0 | 0 | 0 | 0 | 0 | 1 | 0 | 1 | 82,634 |
| | Carrollton Township | 1 | 0 | 0 | 0 | 0 | 0 | 0 | 0 | 1 | 5,904 |
| | Cedar Springs | 1 | 0 | 0 | 0 | 0 | 0 | 0 | 0 | 1 | 3,259 |
| | Chesterfield Township | 1 | 1 | 0 | 0 | 0 | 0 | 1 | 1 | 0 | 45,432 |
| | Clinton Township | 2 | 0 | 0 | 0 | 0 | 0 | 1 | 0 | 1 | 95,956 |
| | Coldwater | 1 | 0 | 0 | 0 | 0 | 1 | 0 | 0 | 0 | 10,527 |
| | Covert Township | 1 | 0 | 0 | 0 | 0 | 0 | 0 | 0 | 1 | 3,049 |
| | Croswell | 0 | 0 | 0 | 0 | 2 | 1 | 1 | 0 | 0 | 2,455 |
| | Davison Township | 0 | 1 | 0 | 1 | 0 | 0 | 0 | 2 | 0 | 18,561 |
| | Dearborn | 3 | 1 | 0 | 0 | 0 | 1 | 0 | 3 | 0 | 85,305 |
| | Dearborn Heights | 1 | 0 | 0 | 0 | 0 | 0 | 1 | 0 | 0 | 51,308 |
| | Decatur | 0 | 1 | 0 | 0 | 0 | 0 | 1 | 0 | 0 | 1,765 |
| | Detroit | 9 | 1 | 11 | 1 | 1 | 4 | 6 | 8 | 5 | 908,441 |
| | Dowagiac | 1 | 0 | 0 | 0 | 0 | 0 | 0 | 0 | 1 | 5,670 |
| | East Lansing | 1 | 0 | 1 | 0 | 0 | 1 | 0 | 0 | 1 | 45,779 |
| | Eastpointe | 5 | 0 | 1 | 0 | 0 | 1 | 1 | 3 | 1 | 32,331 |
| | Escanaba | 1 | 0 | 0 | 0 | 0 | 1 | 0 | 0 | 0 | 12,117 |

[1]Agencies published in this table indicated that at least one hate crime incident occurred in their respective jurisdictions during the quarter(s) for which they submitted a report to the Hate Crime Statistics Program. Blanks indicate quarters for which agencies did not submit reports.

[2]Population figures are published only for the cities. The figures listed for the universities and colleges are student enrollment and were provided by the United States Department of Education for the 2008 school year, the most recent available. The enrollment figures include full-time and part-time students.

## Table 94. Hate Crime Incidents per Bias Motivation and Quarter, by State and Agency, 2009—*Continued*

| State | Agency type/Agency name | Number of incidents per bias motivation | | | | | Number of incidents per quarter[1] | | | | Population[2] |
|---|---|---|---|---|---|---|---|---|---|---|---|
| | | Race | Religion | Sexual orientation | Ethnicity | Disability | 1st quarter | 2nd quarter | 3rd quarter | 4th quarter | |
| | Evart | 1 | 0 | 0 | 0 | 0 | 0 | 1 | 0 | 0 | 1,659 |
| | Farmington | 1 | 0 | 0 | 0 | 0 | 0 | 0 | 1 | 0 | 9,778 |
| | Farmington Hills | 0 | 0 | 0 | 1 | 0 | 0 | 1 | 0 | 0 | 78,140 |
| | Fenton | 1 | 0 | 0 | 0 | 0 | 1 | 0 | 0 | 0 | 11,796 |
| | Ferndale | 0 | 1 | 0 | 0 | 0 | 1 | 0 | 0 | 0 | 21,008 |
| | Flint | 4 | 0 | 5 | 0 | 0 | 2 | 3 | 2 | 2 | 111,657 |
| | Forsyth Township | 0 | 0 | 1 | 0 | 0 | 0 | 0 | 1 | 0 | 4,894 |
| | Frankfort | 0 | 1 | 0 | 0 | 0 | 0 | 1 | 0 | 0 | 1,444 |
| | Fruitport | 0 | 0 | 0 | 0 | 1 | 0 | 0 | 0 | 1 | 1,075 |
| | Garden City | 1 | 0 | 0 | 0 | 0 | 0 | 0 | 0 | 1 | 26,398 |
| | Genesee Township | 3 | 0 | 0 | 0 | 0 | 1 | 1 | 0 | 1 | 22,926 |
| | Gibraltar | 2 | 0 | 0 | 0 | 0 | 0 | 1 | 1 | 0 | 4,893 |
| | Grand Blanc | 1 | 0 | 0 | 0 | 0 | 0 | 0 | 1 | 0 | 7,479 |
| | Grand Ledge | 1 | 0 | 0 | 0 | 0 | 0 | 1 | 0 | 0 | 7,653 |
| | Grand Rapids | 3 | 1 | 3 | 1 | 0 | 4 | 3 | 0 | 1 | 192,901 |
| | Grandville | 0 | 0 | 0 | 1 | 0 | 0 | 0 | 1 | 0 | 16,763 |
| | Greenville | 5 | 0 | 0 | 0 | 0 | 2 | 1 | 2 | 0 | 8,165 |
| | Grosse Pointe Farms | 0 | 0 | 0 | 1 | 0 | 1 | 0 | 0 | 0 | 8,495 |
| | Hampton Township | 1 | 0 | 0 | 0 | 0 | 1 | 0 | 0 | 0 | 9,679 |
| | Hamtramck | 2 | 1 | 0 | 0 | 0 | 1 | 0 | 2 | 0 | 20,255 |
| | Hazel Park | 1 | 0 | 0 | 0 | 0 | 0 | 1 | 0 | 0 | 17,851 |
| | Holland | 2 | 0 | 1 | 2 | 0 | 1 | 2 | 2 | 0 | 33,970 |
| | Inkster | 1 | 0 | 0 | 0 | 0 | 0 | 0 | 0 | 1 | 26,261 |
| | Lansing | 3 | 0 | 0 | 0 | 0 | 0 | 1 | 2 | 0 | 113,392 |
| | Lawton | 1 | 0 | 1 | 0 | 0 | 0 | 1 | 0 | 1 | 1,794 |
| | Livonia | 3 | 0 | 2 | 0 | 0 | 1 | 0 | 4 | 0 | 90,232 |
| | Madison Heights | 1 | 0 | 0 | 0 | 0 | 0 | 1 | 0 | 0 | 29,367 |
| | Manistique | 0 | 0 | 1 | 0 | 0 | 0 | 0 | 0 | 1 | 3,034 |
| | Melvindale | 0 | 0 | 1 | 0 | 0 | 1 | 0 | 0 | 0 | 9,715 |
| | Meridian Township | 4 | 0 | 1 | 0 | 0 | 0 | 2 | 2 | 1 | 38,414 |
| | Monroe | 1 | 0 | 0 | 0 | 0 | 0 | 0 | 1 | 0 | 21,301 |
| | Mount Morris | 2 | 0 | 0 | 0 | 0 | 0 | 0 | 0 | 2 | 3,166 |
| | Mount Pleasant | 0 | 0 | 2 | 0 | 0 | 0 | 1 | 0 | 1 | 26,765 |
| | Mundy Township | 1 | 0 | 0 | 0 | 0 | 1 | 0 | 0 | 0 | 14,141 |
| | Muskegon Township | 0 | 0 | 0 | 1 | 0 | 0 | 1 | 0 | 0 | 18,354 |
| | New Baltimore | 1 | 0 | 0 | 0 | 0 | 0 | 0 | 1 | 0 | 11,869 |
| | New Buffalo | 1 | 0 | 0 | 0 | 0 | 1 | 0 | 0 | 0 | 2,449 |
| | Niles | 1 | 1 | 0 | 0 | 0 | 1 | 0 | 0 | 1 | 11,159 |
| | Northfield Township | 0 | 0 | 1 | 0 | 0 | 0 | 0 | 1 | 0 | 8,505 |
| | Northville Township | 0 | 1 | 0 | 0 | 0 | 1 | 0 | 0 | 0 | 25,266 |
| | Oak Park | 0 | 1 | 1 | 0 | 0 | 0 | 0 | 2 | 0 | 30,350 |
| | Owosso | 1 | 0 | 0 | 0 | 0 | 0 | 0 | 0 | 1 | 14,885 |
| | Paw Paw | 1 | 0 | 0 | 0 | 0 | 0 | 0 | 0 | 1 | 3,206 |
| | Plymouth | 1 | 0 | 0 | 0 | 0 | 0 | 1 | 0 | 0 | 8,430 |
| | Plymouth Township | 1 | 0 | 0 | 0 | 0 | 0 | 0 | 0 | 1 | 25,071 |
| | Pontiac | 1 | 0 | 1 | 0 | 0 | 0 | 1 | 0 | 1 | 65,924 |
| | Portage | 0 | 0 | 1 | 0 | 0 | 0 | 0 | 1 | 0 | 46,269 |
| | Port Huron | 2 | 0 | 0 | 0 | 0 | 0 | 1 | 1 | 0 | 30,718 |
| | Redford Township | 0 | 0 | 1 | 0 | 0 | 0 | 1 | 0 | 0 | 45,291 |
| | Reed City | 1 | 0 | 0 | 0 | 0 | 0 | 0 | 0 | 1 | 2,319 |
| | Rochester | 2 | 1 | 0 | 0 | 0 | 0 | 2 | 0 | 1 | 11,057 |
| | Rockwood | 1 | 0 | 0 | 0 | 0 | 0 | 0 | 1 | 0 | 3,127 |
| | Roseville | 4 | 0 | 0 | 0 | 0 | 1 | 1 | 1 | 1 | 46,642 |
| | Royal Oak | 2 | 0 | 3 | 0 | 0 | 1 | 1 | 3 | 0 | 56,800 |
| | Saginaw | 3 | 0 | 0 | 0 | 0 | 0 | 1 | 1 | 1 | 54,997 |
| | Saginaw Township | 3 | 0 | 0 | 1 | 0 | 1 | 0 | 3 | 0 | 38,436 |
| | Saline | 1 | 0 | 0 | 0 | 0 | 0 | 0 | 1 | 0 | 8,977 |
| | Sandusky | 0 | 0 | 0 | 1 | 0 | 0 | 1 | 0 | 0 | 2,593 |
| | Scottville | 0 | 0 | 1 | 0 | 0 | 1 | 0 | 0 | 0 | 1,247 |
| | Shelby Township | 5 | 0 | 0 | 1 | 0 | 3 | 0 | 3 | 0 | 72,094 |
| | Southfield | 1 | 0 | 0 | 0 | 0 | 1 | 0 | 0 | 0 | 75,074 |
| | Sparta | 1 | 0 | 0 | 0 | 0 | 0 | 0 | 1 | 0 | 4,041 |
| | Stephenson | 0 | 0 | 0 | 1 | 0 | 1 | 0 | | 0 | 796 |
| | Sterling Heights | 1 | 0 | 0 | 2 | 0 | 0 | 2 | 1 | 0 | 127,440 |
| | St. Joseph | 0 | 1 | 2 | 0 | 0 | 0 | 1 | 2 | 0 | 8,423 |
| | Stockbridge | 1 | 0 | 0 | 0 | 0 | 0 | 0 | 1 | 0 | 1,275 |
| | Summit Township | 1 | 0 | 0 | 0 | 0 | 0 | 0 | 1 | 0 | 21,642 |
| | Taylor | 2 | 0 | 0 | 0 | 0 | 0 | 1 | 1 | 0 | 60,054 |
| | Tecumseh | 1 | 1 | 0 | 0 | 0 | 2 | 0 | 0 | 0 | 8,602 |
| | Traverse City | 0 | 0 | 2 | 0 | 0 | 0 | 1 | 1 | 0 | 14,385 |
| | Trenton | 0 | 1 | 0 | 0 | 0 | 0 | 0 | 1 | 0 | 17,792 |
| | Troy | 3 | 0 | 1 | 0 | 0 | 1 | 1 | 0 | 2 | 80,182 |
| | Utica | 1 | 0 | 0 | 0 | 0 | 1 | 0 | 0 | 0 | 4,961 |

[1]Agencies published in this table indicated that at least one hate crime incident occurred in their respective jurisdictions during the quarter(s) for which they submitted a report to the Hate Crime Statistics Program. Blanks indicate quarters for which agencies did not submit reports.

[2]Population figures are published only for the cities. The figures listed for the universities and colleges are student enrollment and were provided by the United States Department of Education for the 2008 school year, the most recent available. The enrollment figures include full-time and part-time students.

## Table 94. Hate Crime Incidents per Bias Motivation and Quarter, by State and Agency, 2009—*Continued*

| State | Agency type/Agency name | Number of incidents per bias motivation | | | | | Number of incidents per quarter[1] | | | | Population[2] |
|---|---|---|---|---|---|---|---|---|---|---|---|
| | | Race | Religion | Sexual orientation | Ethnicity | Disability | 1st quarter | 2nd quarter | 3rd quarter | 4th quarter | |
| | Van Buren Township | 1 | 0 | 0 | 0 | 0 | 0 | 1 | 0 | 0 | 26,513 |
| | Warren | 8 | 2 | 2 | 0 | 0 | 2 | 6 | 3 | 1 | 133,485 |
| | Waterford Township | 6 | 0 | 0 | 1 | 1 | 3 | 0 | 5 | 0 | 70,403 |
| | Wayne | 0 | 1 | 0 | 0 | 0 | 0 | 0 | 1 | 0 | 16,990 |
| | West Bloomfield Township | 1 | 0 | 0 | 0 | 0 | 0 | 0 | 0 | 1 | 63,728 |
| | Westland | 1 | 0 | 0 | 0 | 0 | 0 | 0 | 1 | 0 | 78,149 |
| | White Lake Township | 1 | 0 | 0 | 0 | 0 | 1 | 0 | 0 | 0 | 30,102 |
| | Wyandotte | 1 | 0 | 0 | 0 | 0 | 0 | 1 | 0 | 0 | 24,399 |
| | Wyoming | 3 | 0 | 2 | 0 | 0 | 0 | 3 | 2 | 0 | 70,565 |
| | Ypsilanti | 2 | 0 | 1 | 0 | 0 | 1 | 1 | 0 | 1 | 21,369 |
| | Zeeland | 0 | 1 | 0 | 0 | 0 | 1 | 0 | 0 | 0 | 5,410 |
| | **Universities and Colleges** | | 3 | 0 | 1 | 0 | 0 | | | | |
| | Central Michigan University | 0 | 0 | 1 | 0 | 0 | 0 | 0 | 0 | 1 | 27,225 |
| | Michigan State University | 2 | 0 | 0 | 0 | 0 | 0 | 0 | 0 | 2 | 46,510 |
| | University of Michigan, Ann Arbor | 1 | 0 | 0 | 0 | 0 | 0 | 1 | 0 | 0 | 41,028 |
| | **Metropolitan Counties** | | 25 | 4 | 6 | 2 | 0 | | | | |
| | Bay | 2 | 0 | 0 | 0 | 0 | 0 | 0 | 0 | 2 | |
| | Berrien | 1 | 0 | 0 | 0 | 0 | 0 | 0 | 1 | 0 | |
| | Calhoun | 1 | 0 | 1 | 0 | 0 | 2 | 0 | 0 | 0 | |
| | Cass | 1 | 0 | 0 | 0 | 0 | 0 | 0 | 0 | 1 | |
| | Genesee | 0 | 2 | 0 | 0 | 0 | 0 | 2 | 0 | 0 | |
| | Ingham | 1 | 0 | 0 | 0 | 0 | 1 | 0 | 0 | 0 | |
| | Kalamazoo | 1 | 0 | 0 | 0 | 0 | 0 | 1 | 0 | 0 | |
| | Kent | 1 | 0 | 0 | 0 | 0 | 0 | 1 | 0 | 0 | |
| | Macomb | 2 | 1 | 2 | 0 | 0 | 1 | 1 | 2 | 1 | |
| | Monroe | 1 | 0 | 1 | 0 | 0 | 0 | 0 | 2 | 0 | |
| | Oakland | 4 | 0 | 1 | 1 | 0 | 0 | 2 | 2 | 2 | |
| | Ottawa | 1 | 0 | 0 | 0 | 0 | 0 | 0 | 0 | 1 | |
| | Saginaw | 1 | 1 | 0 | 1 | 0 | 0 | 2 | 0 | 1 | |
| | St. Clair | 7 | 0 | 0 | 0 | 0 | 2 | 1 | 1 | 3 | |
| | Washtenaw | 1 | 0 | 1 | 0 | 0 | 2 | 0 | 0 | 0 | |
| | **Nonmetropolitan Counties** | | 4 | 0 | 1 | 1 | 0 | | | | |
| | Branch | 1 | 0 | 0 | 0 | 0 | 0 | 0 | 0 | 1 | |
| | Crawford | 2 | 0 | 0 | 0 | 0 | 0 | 0 | 2 | 0 | |
| | Ogemaw | 0 | 0 | 0 | 1 | 0 | 1 | 0 | 0 | 0 | |
| | St. Joseph | 1 | 0 | 0 | 0 | 0 | 0 | 0 | 1 | 0 | |
| | Tuscola | 0 | 0 | 1 | 0 | 0 | 1 | 0 | 0 | 0 | |
| | **State Police Agencies** | | 1 | 0 | 0 | 1 | 1 | | | | |
| | State Police: | | | | | | | | | | |
| | Clare County | 1 | 0 | 0 | 0 | 0 | 0 | 0 | 0 | 1 | |
| | Grand Traverse County | 0 | 0 | 0 | 1 | 0 | 1 | 0 | 0 | 0 | |
| | Monroe County | 0 | 0 | 0 | 0 | 1 | 0 | 0 | 1 | 0 | |
| **MINNESOTA** | **Total** | | 86 | 15 | 28 | 22 | 2 | | | | |
| | **Cities** | | 81 | 15 | 26 | 21 | 2 | | | | |
| | Blaine | 2 | 0 | 0 | 1 | 0 | 0 | 2 | 1 | | 56,228 |
| | Brooklyn Park | 6 | 0 | 2 | 1 | 0 | 3 | 1 | 5 | | 71,740 |
| | Columbia Heights | 1 | 0 | 0 | 0 | 0 | | | 1 | | 18,176 |
| | Coon Rapids | 0 | 1 | 0 | 0 | 0 | | | 1 | | 61,844 |
| | Cottage Grove | 1 | 0 | 0 | 0 | 0 | 1 | 0 | 0 | 0 | 33,969 |
| | Duluth | 0 | 0 | 1 | 0 | 0 | 1 | | | | 84,071 |
| | Eagan | 1 | 0 | 0 | 0 | 0 | | | 1 | | 64,014 |
| | Eden Prairie | 2 | 0 | 0 | 0 | 0 | 1 | | 1 | | 61,893 |
| | Elk River | 3 | 0 | 0 | 0 | 0 | 1 | | 1 | 1 | 24,061 |
| | Forest Lake | 0 | 0 | 0 | 1 | 0 | 1 | | | | 17,727 |
| | Hibbing | 1 | 0 | 0 | 0 | 0 | | | 1 | | 16,115 |
| | Mankato | 5 | 1 | 0 | 5 | 0 | 1 | 3 | 4 | 3 | 36,676 |
| | Maple Grove | 1 | 0 | 0 | 0 | 0 | 1 | 0 | 0 | | 62,801 |
| | Marshall | 2 | 0 | 1 | 0 | 0 | | 2 | 1 | | 12,634 |
| | Minneapolis | 25 | 5 | 18 | 9 | 2 | 12 | 16 | 16 | 15 | 382,618 |
| | New Brighton | 0 | 0 | 0 | 1 | 0 | 0 | 0 | 1 | 0 | 21,494 |
| | New Hope | 1 | 1 | 0 | 0 | 0 | 0 | 0 | 2 | 0 | 20,381 |
| | Oakdale | 1 | 0 | 1 | 0 | 0 | 0 | 1 | 1 | | 27,068 |
| | Plymouth | 3 | 1 | 0 | 2 | 0 | 1 | 2 | 2 | 1 | 72,121 |
| | Rochester | 6 | 1 | 1 | 1 | 0 | 3 | | 2 | 4 | 101,884 |
| | Savage | 1 | 0 | 0 | 0 | 0 | 0 | 1 | 0 | 0 | 28,473 |
| | South St. Paul | 1 | 0 | 0 | 0 | 0 | | | | 1 | 19,485 |
| | St. Louis Park | 0 | 4 | 0 | 0 | 0 | | 3 | 1 | | 45,613 |
| | St. Paul | 17 | 1 | 2 | 0 | 0 | 8 | 5 | 5 | 2 | 280,194 |
| | Winona | 1 | 0 | 0 | 0 | 0 | 0 | 0 | 1 | 0 | 26,752 |

[1]Agencies published in this table indicated that at least one hate crime incident occurred in their respective jurisdictions during the quarter(s) for which they submitted a report to the Hate Crime Statistics Program. Blanks indicate quarters for which agencies did not submit reports.

[2]Population figures are published only for the cities. The figures listed for the universities and colleges are student enrollment and were provided by the United States Department of Education for the 2008 school year, the most recent available. The enrollment figures include full-time and part-time students.

# Table 94. Hate Crime Incidents per Bias Motivation and Quarter, by State and Agency, 2009—*Continued*

| State | Agency type/Agency name | Number of incidents per bias motivation | | | | | Number of incidents per quarter[1] | | | | Population[2] |
|---|---|---|---|---|---|---|---|---|---|---|---|
| | | Race | Religion | Sexual orientation | Ethnicity | Disability | 1st quarter | 2nd quarter | 3rd quarter | 4th quarter | |
| | **Universities and Colleges** | | 1 | 0 | 1 | 0 | 0 | | | | |
| | University of Minnesota, Twin Cities | 1 | 0 | 1 | 0 | 0 | 1 | 1 | 0 | 0 | 51,140 |
| | **Metropolitan Counties** | | 0 | 0 | 1 | 1 | 0 | | | | |
| | Blue Earth | 0 | 0 | 0 | 1 | 0 | | | | 1 | |
| | Carver | 0 | 0 | 1 | 0 | 0 | | | | 1 | |
| | **Nonmetropolitan Counties** | | 4 | 0 | 0 | 0 | 0 | | | | |
| | Beltrami | 2 | 0 | 0 | 0 | 0 | 1 | 1 | 0 | 0 | |
| | Kanabec | 1 | 0 | 0 | 0 | 0 | | | 1 | | |
| | Mille Lacs | 1 | 0 | 0 | 0 | 0 | | | 1 | | |
| MISSISSIPPI | **Total** | | 1 | 0 | 0 | 1 | 0 | | | | |
| | **Cities** | | 0 | 0 | 0 | 1 | 0 | | | | |
| | Gulfport | 0 | 0 | 0 | 1 | 0 | 0 | 0 | 0 | 1 | 69,926 |
| | **Nonmetropolitan Counties** | | 1 | 0 | 0 | 0 | 0 | | | | |
| | Adams | 1 | 0 | 0 | 0 | 0 | 0 | 0 | 0 | 1 | |
| MISSOURI | **Total** | | 81 | 17 | 21 | 5 | 0 | | | | |
| | **Cities** | | 69 | 17 | 20 | 5 | 0 | | | | |
| | Buffalo | 0 | 1 | 0 | 0 | 0 | 1 | 0 | 0 | 0 | 3,348 |
| | Cape Girardeau | 0 | 0 | 1 | 0 | 0 | 0 | 0 | 0 | 1 | 37,588 |
| | Chesterfield | 1 | 0 | 0 | 0 | 0 | 1 | 0 | 0 | 0 | 45,977 |
| | Clarkton | 1 | 0 | 0 | 0 | 0 | 0 | | 1 | 0 | 1,228 |
| | Clayton | 4 | 0 | 0 | 0 | 0 | 4 | 0 | 0 | 0 | 16,105 |
| | Columbia | 2 | 1 | 1 | 0 | 0 | 0 | 0 | 0 | 4 | 102,588 |
| | Grandview | 1 | 0 | 0 | 0 | 0 | 0 | 0 | 1 | 0 | 23,939 |
| | Herculaneum | 1 | 0 | 0 | 0 | 0 | 0 | 0 | 0 | 1 | 3,675 |
| | Independence | 10 | 4 | 2 | 0 | 0 | 2 | 3 | 1 | 10 | 122,174 |
| | Kansas City | 28 | 5 | 10 | 1 | 0 | 5 | 9 | 16 | 14 | 484,684 |
| | Lee's Summit | 1 | 0 | 0 | 0 | 0 | 0 | 0 | 0 | 1 | 85,792 |
| | Maplewood | 1 | 0 | 0 | 0 | 0 | 0 | 0 | 1 | 0 | 8,563 |
| | Maryland Heights | 0 | 1 | 0 | 0 | 0 | 0 | 0 | 0 | 1 | 25,815 |
| | Maryville | 0 | 0 | 0 | 1 | 0 | 1 | 0 | 0 | 0 | 10,815 |
| | O'Fallon | 1 | 0 | 0 | 1 | 0 | 0 | 0 | 2 | 0 | 80,528 |
| | Oran | 1 | 0 | 0 | 0 | 0 | 1 | | | 0 | 1,247 |
| | Raytown | 3 | 0 | 1 | 0 | 0 | 0 | 1 | 3 | 0 | 27,966 |
| | Rolla | 1 | 0 | 0 | 1 | 0 | 0 | 1 | 1 | 0 | 18,669 |
| | Smithville | 1 | 0 | 0 | 0 | 0 | 1 | 0 | 0 | 0 | 8,416 |
| | Springfield | 6 | 3 | 3 | 0 | 0 | 3 | 2 | 1 | 6 | 156,659 |
| | Steelville | 1 | 0 | 0 | 0 | 0 | 0 | 0 | 1 | 0 | 1,500 |
| | St. Louis | 4 | 1 | 1 | 0 | 0 | 1 | 1 | 2 | 2 | 355,208 |
| | St. Peters | 0 | 1 | 1 | 0 | 0 | 0 | 1 | 0 | 0 | 55,967 |
| | Summersville | 1 | 0 | 0 | 0 | 0 | 1 | 0 | 0 | 0 | 555 |
| | Warrensburg | 0 | 0 | 1 | 0 | 0 | 0 | 0 | 0 | 1 | 19,351 |
| | Willard | 0 | 0 | 0 | 1 | 0 | 0 | 0 | 1 | 0 | 3,350 |
| | **Universities and Colleges** | | 2 | 0 | 1 | 0 | 0 | | | | |
| | Missouri Southern State University | 1 | 0 | 0 | 0 | 0 | 0 | 0 | 1 | 0 | 5,264 |
| | Northwest Missouri State University | 0 | 0 | 1 | 0 | 0 | 1 | 0 | 0 | 0 | 6,687 |
| | University of Missouri, Columbia | 1 | 0 | 0 | 0 | 0 | 0 | 1 | 0 | 0 | 30,130 |
| | **Metropolitan Counties** | | 8 | 0 | 0 | 0 | 0 | | | | |
| | Greene | 2 | 0 | 0 | 0 | 0 | 1 | 1 | 0 | 0 | |
| | Jefferson | 1 | 0 | 0 | 0 | 0 | 1 | 0 | 0 | 0 | |
| | St. Charles | 1 | 0 | 0 | 0 | 0 | 0 | 0 | 0 | 1 | |
| | St. Louis County Police Department | 3 | 0 | 0 | 0 | 0 | 0 | 0 | 1 | 2 | |
| | Warren | 1 | 0 | 0 | 0 | 0 | | 0 | 0 | 1 | |
| | **Nonmetropolitan Counties** | | 2 | 0 | 0 | 0 | 0 | | | | |
| | Audrain | 1 | 0 | 0 | 0 | 0 | 0 | 1 | 0 | 0 | |
| | Shannon | 1 | 0 | 0 | 0 | 0 | 1 | 0 | | 0 | |
| MONTANA | **Total** | | 8 | 6 | 10 | 4 | 0 | | | | |
| | **Cities** | | 4 | 2 | 4 | 2 | 0 | | | | |
| | Belgrade | 0 | 0 | 0 | 1 | 0 | 0 | 0 | 0 | 1 | 8,485 |
| | Billings | 1 | 1 | 0 | 0 | 0 | 1 | 0 | 1 | 0 | 105,427 |
| | Bozeman | 0 | 0 | 0 | 1 | 0 | 0 | 0 | 1 | 0 | 40,910 |
| | Conrad | 0 | 0 | 1 | 0 | 0 | 0 | 0 | 0 | 1 | 2,477 |
| | Eureka | 0 | 0 | 1 | 0 | 0 | 0 | 0 | 0 | 1 | 1,013 |
| | Helena | 0 | 1 | 0 | 0 | 0 | 0 | 1 | 0 | 0 | 29,718 |
| | Missoula | 2 | 0 | 2 | 0 | 0 | 0 | 3 | 1 | 0 | 69,479 |
| | Whitefish | 1 | 0 | 0 | 0 | 0 | 1 | 0 | 0 | 0 | 8,625 |
| | **Metropolitan Counties** | | 0 | 1 | 4 | 1 | 0 | | | | |
| | Missoula | 0 | 1 | 4 | 1 | 0 | 1 | 3 | 1 | 1 | |

[1]Agencies published in this table indicated that at least one hate crime incident occurred in their respective jurisdictions during the quarter(s) for which they submitted a report to the Hate Crime Statistics Program. Blanks indicate quarters for which agencies did not submit reports.

[2]Population figures are published only for the cities. The figures listed for the universities and colleges are student enrollment and were provided by the United States Department of Education for the 2008 school year, the most recent available. The enrollment figures include full-time and part-time students.

# Table 94. Hate Crime Incidents per Bias Motivation and Quarter, by State and Agency, 2009—*Continued*

| State | Agency type/Agency name | Number of incidents per bias motivation | | | | | Number of incidents per quarter[1] | | | | Population[2] |
|---|---|---|---|---|---|---|---|---|---|---|---|
| | | Race | Religion | Sexual orientation | Ethnicity | Disability | 1st quarter | 2nd quarter | 3rd quarter | 4th quarter | |
| | **Nonmetropolitan Counties** | | 4 | 3 | 2 | 1 | 0 | | | | |
| | Flathead | 3 | 0 | 0 | 0 | 0 | 1 | 1 | 1 | 0 | |
| | Lewis and Clark | 0 | 0 | 1 | 0 | 0 | 1 | 0 | 0 | 0 | |
| | Park | 0 | 0 | 1 | 0 | 0 | 0 | 1 | 0 | 0 | |
| | Ravalli | 1 | 1 | 0 | 1 | 0 | 0 | 1 | 1 | 1 | |
| | Silver Bow | 0 | 2 | 0 | 0 | 0 | 0 | 1 | 0 | 1 | |
| **NEBRASKA** | **Total** | | 47 | 10 | 10 | 8 | 3 | | | | |
| | **Cities** | | 46 | 10 | 10 | 8 | 3 | | | | |
| | Hastings | 0 | 0 | 0 | 0 | 1 | 1 | 0 | 0 | 0 | 25,476 |
| | Kearney | 0 | 1 | 1 | 0 | 0 | 2 | 0 | 0 | 0 | 30,759 |
| | Lincoln | 43 | 6 | 8 | 8 | 2 | 28 | 12 | 13 | 14 | 254,438 |
| | Omaha | 2 | 3 | 0 | 0 | 0 | 0 | 3 | 1 | 1 | 443,037 |
| | Papillion | 1 | 0 | 0 | 0 | 0 | 0 | 1 | 0 | 0 | 24,390 |
| | Ralston | 0 | 0 | 1 | 0 | 0 | 0 | 0 | 0 | 1 | 6,077 |
| | **Nonmetropolitan Counties** | | 1 | 0 | 0 | 0 | 0 | | | | |
| | Saline | 1 | 0 | 0 | 0 | 0 | 0 | 0 | 1 | 0 | |
| **NEVADA** | **Total** | | 20 | 4 | 16 | 8 | 0 | | | | |
| | **Cities** | | 20 | 4 | 16 | 6 | 0 | | | | |
| | Las Vegas Metropolitan Police Department | 15 | 4 | 13 | 3 | 0 | 4 | 10 | 7 | 14 | 1,377,282 |
| | North Las Vegas | 2 | 0 | 1 | 3 | 0 | 0 | 1 | 2 | 3 | 232,631 |
| | Reno | 3 | 0 | 2 | 0 | 0 | 2 | 2 | 1 | 0 | 221,010 |
| | **Universities and Colleges** | | 0 | 0 | 0 | 1 | 0 | | | | |
| | University of Nevada, Las Vegas | 0 | 0 | 0 | 1 | 0 | 0 | 0 | 1 | 0 | 28,600 |
| | **Nonmetropolitan Counties** | | 0 | 0 | 0 | 1 | 0 | | | | |
| | Lyon | 0 | 0 | 0 | 1 | 0 | 0 | 0 | 1 | 0 | |
| **NEW HAMPSHIRE** | **Total** | | 14 | 3 | 5 | 2 | 0 | | | | |
| | **Cities** | | 14 | 3 | 5 | 2 | 0 | | | | |
| | Bedford | 1 | 0 | 0 | 0 | 0 | 0 | 0 | 0 | 1 | 21,438 |
| | Bow | 1 | 0 | 0 | 0 | 0 | 0 | 0 | 1 | 0 | 8,186 |
| | Concord | 0 | 0 | 1 | 0 | 0 | 1 | 0 | 0 | 0 | 42,427 |
| | Greenland | 1 | 0 | 0 | 0 | 0 | 0 | 1 | 0 | 0 | 3,444 |
| | Hancock | 1 | 0 | 1 | 0 | 0 | 0 | 0 | 2 | 0 | 1,807 |
| | Hanover | 1 | 0 | 0 | 0 | 0 | 0 | 0 | 0 | 1 | 11,093 |
| | Hudson | 0 | 0 | 0 | 1 | 0 | 0 | 0 | 0 | 1 | 24,978 |
| | Laconia | 2 | 0 | 0 | 0 | 0 | 0 | 0 | 2 | 0 | 17,127 |
| | Lebanon | 1 | 0 | 0 | 0 | 0 | 0 | 0 | 0 | 1 | 12,832 |
| | Manchester | 2 | 0 | 0 | 1 | 0 | 2 | 1 | 0 | 0 | 108,671 |
| | Meredith | 0 | 1 | 0 | 0 | 0 | 0 | 1 | 0 | 0 | 6,700 |
| | Merrimack | 1 | 0 | 0 | 0 | 0 | 0 | 1 | 0 | 0 | 26,594 |
| | Northumberland | 1 | 1 | 1 | 0 | 0 | 0 | 0 | 0 | 3 | 2,302 |
| | Pembroke | 1 | 0 | 0 | 0 | 0 | 1 | 0 | 0 | 0 | 7,379 |
| | Plymouth | 0 | 0 | 1 | 0 | 0 | 0 | 0 | 0 | 1 | 6,444 |
| | Rochester | 0 | 1 | 0 | 0 | 0 | 0 | 0 | 1 | 0 | 30,889 |
| | Seabrook | 0 | 0 | 1 | 0 | 0 | 0 | 1 | 0 | 0 | 8,551 |
| | Wilton | 1 | 0 | 0 | 0 | 0 | 0 | 0 | 0 | 1 | 3,940 |
| **NEW JERSEY** | **Total** | | 221 | 210 | 66 | 50 | 2 | | | | |
| | **Cities** | | 220 | 210 | 66 | 50 | 2 | | | | |
| | Aberdeen Township | 2 | 3 | 3 | 0 | 0 | 1 | 3 | 0 | 4 | 18,493 |
| | Asbury Park | 0 | 0 | 2 | 0 | 0 | 1 | 0 | 1 | 0 | 16,499 |
| | Atlantic City | 3 | 0 | 1 | 0 | 0 | 0 | 1 | 1 | 2 | 39,295 |
| | Bayonne | 0 | 1 | 1 | 0 | 0 | 0 | 0 | 2 | 0 | 56,982 |
| | Bernards Township | 0 | 2 | 0 | 0 | 0 | 1 | 0 | 1 | 0 | 26,681 |
| | Boonton Township | 0 | 2 | 1 | 0 | 0 | 1 | 0 | 0 | 2 | 4,509 |
| | Bound Brook | 0 | 1 | 0 | 0 | 0 | 0 | 1 | 0 | 0 | 10,398 |
| | Branchburg Township | 1 | 0 | 0 | 1 | 0 | 0 | 1 | 1 | 0 | 15,087 |
| | Brick Township | 0 | 0 | 0 | 1 | 0 | 0 | 0 | 0 | 1 | 78,666 |
| | Bridgewater Township | 1 | 1 | 0 | 0 | 0 | 0 | 1 | 0 | 1 | 44,519 |
| | Brooklawn | 1 | 0 | 0 | 0 | 0 | 0 | 1 | 0 | 0 | 2,253 |
| | Camden | 1 | 0 | 0 | 0 | 0 | 1 | 0 | 0 | 0 | 78,980 |
| | Carney's Point Township | 4 | 0 | 0 | 0 | 0 | 0 | 0 | 1 | 3 | 8,002 |
| | Carteret | 0 | 1 | 0 | 0 | 0 | 1 | 0 | 0 | 0 | 23,669 |
| | Cinnaminson Township | 0 | 0 | 0 | 1 | 0 | 0 | 1 | 0 | 0 | 15,448 |
| | Cliffside Park | 0 | 1 | 0 | 2 | 0 | 0 | 0 | 0 | 3 | 22,848 |
| | Clifton | 1 | 0 | 1 | 0 | 0 | 1 | 0 | 1 | 0 | 78,124 |
| | Cranford Township | 0 | 2 | 0 | 0 | 0 | 0 | 0 | 1 | 1 | 21,820 |
| | Cresskill | 0 | 1 | 0 | 0 | 0 | 0 | 1 | 0 | 0 | 8,716 |
| | Delanco Township | 2 | 0 | 0 | 0 | 0 | 1 | 0 | 0 | 1 | 4,848 |
| | Denville Township | 0 | 0 | 0 | 1 | 0 | 0 | 1 | 0 | 0 | 16,558 |
| | East Brunswick Township | 1 | 12 | 1 | 0 | 0 | 8 | 1 | 1 | 4 | 47,323 |
| | East Hanover Township | 0 | 1 | 0 | 0 | 0 | 0 | 1 | 0 | 0 | 11,395 |

[1]Agencies published in this table indicated that at least one hate crime incident occurred in their respective jurisdictions during the quarter(s) for which they submitted a report to the Hate Crime Statistics Program. Blanks indicate quarters for which agencies did not submit reports.
[2]Population figures are published only for the cities. The figures listed for the universities and colleges are student enrollment and were provided by the United States Department of Education for the 2008 school year, the most recent available. The enrollment figures include full-time and part-time students.

## Table 94. Hate Crime Incidents per Bias Motivation and Quarter, by State and Agency, 2009—*Continued*

| State | Agency type/Agency name | Number of incidents per bias motivation | | | | | Number of incidents per quarter[1] | | | | Population[2] |
|---|---|---|---|---|---|---|---|---|---|---|---|
| | | Race | Religion | Sexual orientation | Ethnicity | Disability | 1st quarter | 2nd quarter | 3rd quarter | 4th quarter | |
| | East Windsor Township | 0 | 0 | 0 | 1 | 0 | | 0 | 1 | 0 | 26,965 |
| | Eatontown | 1 | 0 | 0 | 0 | 0 | 0 | 0 | 1 | 0 | 14,212 |
| | Edgewater Park Township | 1 | 0 | 0 | 1 | 0 | 0 | 2 | 0 | 0 | 7,674 |
| | Edison Township | 1 | 1 | 0 | 0 | 0 | 0 | 0 | 1 | 1 | 99,356 |
| | Egg Harbor Township | 2 | 1 | 0 | 0 | 0 | 0 | 0 | 0 | 3 | 41,005 |
| | Elizabeth | 0 | 1 | 0 | 0 | 0 | 0 | 0 | 1 | 0 | 124,910 |
| | Evesham Township | 1 | 0 | 1 | 0 | 0 | 1 | 0 | 0 | 1 | 45,633 |
| | Ewing Township | 2 | 1 | 2 | 0 | 0 | 0 | 1 | 3 | 1 | 36,098 |
| | Fair Lawn | 1 | 5 | 0 | 0 | 0 | 0 | 0 | 2 | 4 | 30,400 |
| | Fanwood | 1 | 0 | 0 | 0 | 0 | 1 | 0 | 0 | 0 | 7,078 |
| | Florham Park | 0 | 2 | 0 | 0 | 0 | 1 | 0 | 0 | 1 | 12,605 |
| | Freehold | 6 | 1 | 2 | 1 | 0 | 3 | 1 | 5 | 1 | 11,474 |
| | Freehold Township | 3 | 5 | 2 | 0 | 0 | 4 | 4 | 2 | 0 | 35,099 |
| | Frenchtown | 1 | 0 | 0 | 0 | 0 | 0 | 0 | 0 | 1 | 1,450 |
| | Galloway Township | 0 | 2 | 2 | 0 | 0 | 1 | 0 | 1 | 2 | 37,051 |
| | Gibbsboro | 1 | 0 | 0 | 0 | 0 | 0 | 0 | 0 | 1 | 2,434 |
| | Glassboro | 4 | 4 | 0 | 1 | 0 | 2 | 2 | 0 | 5 | 19,829 |
| | Glen Rock | 0 | 1 | 0 | 0 | 0 | 1 | 0 | 0 | 0 | 11,086 |
| | Gloucester Township | 1 | 1 | 0 | 0 | 0 | 0 | 0 | 2 | 0 | 64,909 |
| | Greenwich Township, Warren County | 0 | 1 | 0 | 0 | 0 | 0 | 1 | 0 | 0 | 5,195 |
| | Guttenberg | 0 | 1 | 0 | 0 | 0 | 0 | 0 | 1 | 0 | 10,493 |
| | Hackettstown | 2 | 0 | 0 | 1 | 0 | 3 | 0 | 0 | 0 | 9,565 |
| | Haddonfield | 0 | 0 | 1 | 0 | 0 | 0 | 0 | 0 | 1 | 11,420 |
| | Haddon Heights | 2 | 0 | 0 | 0 | 0 | 1 | 0 | 1 | 0 | 7,596 |
| | Hamilton Township, Mercer County | 1 | 4 | 0 | 0 | 0 | 1 | 1 | 2 | 1 | 90,491 |
| | Harding Township | 1 | 0 | 0 | 0 | 0 | 0 | 0 | 1 | 0 | 3,332 |
| | Hardyston Township | 1 | 0 | 0 | 0 | 0 | 1 | 0 | 0 | 0 | 8,559 |
| | Harrison Township | 0 | 2 | 0 | 0 | 0 | 0 | 0 | 1 | 1 | 12,916 |
| | Hawthorne | 0 | 0 | 1 | 0 | 0 | 1 | 0 | 0 | 0 | 17,972 |
| | Hazlet Township | 0 | 0 | 1 | 0 | 0 | 0 | 1 | 0 | 0 | 20,893 |
| | Highland Park | 0 | 1 | 0 | 0 | 0 | 0 | 0 | 1 | 0 | 14,271 |
| | Hillsborough Township | 1 | 1 | 0 | 0 | 0 | 1 | 0 | 1 | 0 | 39,265 |
| | Hillside Township | 0 | 1 | 0 | 0 | 0 | 0 | 0 | 1 | 0 | 21,108 |
| | Hoboken | 2 | 2 | 1 | 2 | 1 | 2 | 3 | 2 | 1 | 40,792 |
| | Holmdel Township | 0 | 1 | 0 | 0 | 0 | 1 | | 0 | 0 | 17,009 |
| | Howell Township | 2 | 1 | 4 | 2 | 0 | 3 | 6 | 0 | 0 | 51,596 |
| | Jackson Township | 2 | 3 | 0 | 0 | 0 | 2 | 3 | 0 | 0 | 53,734 |
| | Jersey City | 6 | 1 | 1 | 0 | 0 | 0 | 2 | 0 | 6 | 240,858 |
| | Keansburg | 28 | 4 | 9 | 4 | 0 | 16 | 10 | 7 | 12 | 10,527 |
| | Lacey Township | 1 | 0 | 0 | 0 | 0 | 1 | 0 | 0 | 0 | 26,491 |
| | Lakehurst | 1 | 0 | 0 | 0 | 0 | 0 | 1 | 0 | 0 | 2,714 |
| | Lakewood Township | 5 | 15 | 0 | 1 | 0 | 6 | 9 | 5 | 1 | 72,206 |
| | Lawrence Township, Mercer County | 0 | 0 | 0 | 2 | 0 | 1 | 0 | 1 | 0 | 31,913 |
| | Lincoln Park | 1 | 0 | 0 | 0 | 0 | 0 | 0 | 1 | 0 | 10,604 |
| | Linden | 2 | 0 | 0 | 0 | 0 | 1 | 1 | 0 | 0 | 39,131 |
| | Lindenwold | 0 | 1 | 0 | 0 | 0 | 0 | 1 | 0 | 0 | 17,496 |
| | Little Egg Harbor Township | 2 | 2 | 0 | 1 | 0 | 1 | 4 | 0 | 0 | 21,291 |
| | Little Falls Township | 1 | 1 | 5 | 0 | 0 | 3 | 1 | 0 | 3 | 11,625 |
| | Little Ferry | 1 | 0 | 0 | 0 | 0 | 0 | 1 | 0 | 0 | 10,442 |
| | Little Silver | 0 | 0 | 1 | 0 | 0 | 0 | 1 | 0 | 0 | 6,111 |
| | Livingston Township | 1 | 1 | 0 | 0 | 0 | 1 | 0 | 0 | 1 | 27,722 |
| | Lodi | 1 | 0 | 1 | 1 | 0 | 2 | 1 | 0 | 0 | 23,754 |
| | Long Branch | 0 | 1 | 0 | 0 | 0 | 0 | 0 | 1 | 0 | 32,758 |
| | Lower Township | 2 | 0 | 0 | 0 | 0 | 0 | 0 | 1 | 1 | 20,060 |
| | Lumberton Township | 7 | 0 | 0 | 0 | 0 | 0 | 6 | 0 | 1 | 12,174 |
| | Madison | 4 | 1 | 1 | 0 | 0 | 0 | 3 | 0 | 3 | 16,073 |
| | Manalapan Township | 3 | 3 | 0 | 0 | 0 | 0 | 1 | 4 | 1 | 39,615 |
| | Manasquan | 1 | 0 | 0 | 0 | 0 | 0 | 1 | 0 | 0 | 6,243 |
| | Manchester Township | 2 | 3 | 0 | 0 | 0 | 1 | 2 | 1 | 1 | 41,921 |
| | Mansfield Township, Burlington County | 1 | 0 | 0 | 0 | 0 | 1 | 0 | 0 | 0 | 8,373 |
| | Mansfield Township, Warren County | 0 | 0 | 0 | 1 | 0 | 1 | 0 | 0 | 0 | 8,123 |
| | Maple Shade Township | 1 | 0 | 0 | 0 | 0 | 0 | 0 | 1 | 0 | 19,165 |
| | Margate City | 1 | 0 | 0 | 0 | 0 | 0 | 0 | 1 | 0 | 8,536 |
| | Marlboro Township | 1 | 5 | 1 | 0 | 0 | 1 | 0 | 2 | 4 | 41,009 |
| | Matawan | 0 | 0 | 0 | 1 | 0 | 0 | 0 | 0 | 1 | 8,735 |
| | Medford Township | 0 | 1 | 0 | 0 | 0 | 0 | 0 | 1 | 0 | 22,872 |

[1]Agencies published in this table indicated that at least one hate crime incident occurred in their respective jurisdictions during the quarter(s) for which they submitted a report to the Hate Crime Statistics Program. Blanks indicate quarters for which agencies did not submit reports.

[2]Population figures are published only for the cities. The figures listed for the universities and colleges are student enrollment and were provided by the United States Department of Education for the 2008 school year, the most recent available. The enrollment figures include full-time and part-time students.

## Table 94. Hate Crime Incidents per Bias Motivation and Quarter, by State and Agency, 2009—*Continued*

| State | Agency type/Agency name | Number of incidents per bias motivation | | | | | Number of incidents per quarter[1] | | | | Popu-lation[2] |
|---|---|---|---|---|---|---|---|---|---|---|---|
| | | Race | Religion | Sexual orient-ation | Ethnicity | Disability | 1st quarter | 2nd quarter | 3rd quarter | 4th quarter | |
| | Mendham Township | 0 | 0 | 0 | 1 | 0 | 0 | 0 | 0 | 1 | 5,513 |
| | Metuchen | 2 | 1 | 0 | 0 | 0 | 0 | 1 | 1 | 1 | 13,121 |
| | Middle Township | 0 | 1 | 0 | 1 | 0 | 1 | 0 | 0 | 1 | 16,263 |
| | Middletown Township | 5 | 4 | 2 | 0 | 0 | 4 | 2 | 1 | 4 | 66,565 |
| | Millburn Township | 1 | 3 | 0 | 0 | 0 | 1 | 1 | 1 | 1 | 18,418 |
| | Milltown | 1 | 0 | 0 | 0 | 0 | 1 | 0 | 0 | 0 | 6,959 |
| | Millville | 1 | 1 | 2 | 0 | 0 | 1 | 0 | 2 | 1 | 29,175 |
| | Monroe Township, Middlesex County | 0 | 1 | 0 | 0 | 0 | 1 | 0 | 0 | 0 | 38,264 |
| | Montgomery Township | 3 | 2 | 0 | 1 | 0 | 3 | 1 | 0 | 2 | 23,524 |
| | Montville Township | 1 | 1 | 0 | 0 | 0 | 0 | 0 | 2 | 0 | 21,078 |
| | Moorestown Township | 1 | 0 | 0 | 0 | 0 | 0 | 0 | 0 | 1 | 19,559 |
| | Morris Township | 2 | 0 | 0 | 1 | 0 | 1 | 0 | 1 | 1 | 21,214 |
| | Mount Laurel Township | 2 | 0 | 0 | 0 | 0 | 1 | 0 | 1 | 0 | 39,071 |
| | Mount Olive Township | 1 | 2 | 1 | 1 | 0 | 2 | 1 | 0 | 2 | 25,989 |
| | Neptune Township | 10 | 0 | 2 | 3 | 0 | 2 | 8 | 3 | 2 | 28,484 |
| | Newark | 0 | 1 | 0 | 1 | 0 | | 0 | 0 | 2 | 279,203 |
| | New Brunswick | 3 | 5 | 0 | 0 | 0 | 3 | 2 | 2 | 1 | 51,474 |
| | North Bergen Township | 0 | 0 | 1 | 0 | 0 | 0 | 0 | 0 | 1 | 54,948 |
| | North Brunswick Township | 4 | 1 | 0 | 0 | 0 | 1 | 1 | 0 | 3 | 39,904 |
| | North Hanover Township | 1 | 1 | 0 | 0 | 0 | 0 | 0 | 1 | 1 | 7,335 |
| | North Plainfield | 0 | 1 | 0 | 0 | 0 | 0 | 1 | 0 | 0 | 21,077 |
| | Oakland | 2 | 0 | 0 | 0 | 0 | 1 | 1 | 0 | 0 | 13,400 |
| | Old Bridge Township | 1 | 1 | 0 | 0 | 0 | 0 | 1 | 1 | 0 | 66,460 |
| | Oradell | 0 | 1 | 0 | 0 | 0 | 1 | 0 | 0 | 0 | 7,751 |
| | Palmyra | 1 | 3 | 0 | 0 | 0 | 1 | 3 | 0 | 0 | 7,374 |
| | Paramus | 6 | 1 | 1 | 0 | 0 | 1 | 2 | 1 | 4 | 26,168 |
| | Park Ridge | 0 | 2 | 0 | 1 | 0 | 1 | 0 | 1 | 1 | 8,940 |
| | Parsippany-Troy Hills Township | 1 | 6 | 0 | 0 | 0 | 1 | 2 | 4 | 0 | 50,095 |
| | Passaic | 1 | 2 | 2 | 0 | 0 | 2 | 0 | 1 | 2 | 66,773 |
| | Paulsboro | 1 | 0 | 1 | 0 | 0 | 1 | 0 | 1 | 0 | 6,066 |
| | Pequannock Township | 0 | 4 | 0 | 0 | 0 | 0 | 0 | 4 | 0 | 17,003 |
| | Phillipsburg | 1 | 0 | 0 | 0 | 0 | 1 | 0 | 0 | 0 | 14,459 |
| | Piscataway Township | 1 | 0 | 0 | 2 | 0 | 0 | 2 | 0 | 1 | 52,605 |
| | Plainsboro Township | 0 | 1 | 0 | 0 | 0 | 0 | 1 | 0 | 0 | 21,243 |
| | Plumsted Township | 0 | 2 | 0 | 0 | 0 | 0 | 0 | 0 | 2 | 8,318 |
| | Point Pleasant | 0 | 0 | 0 | 0 | 1 | 1 | 0 | 0 | 0 | 20,232 |
| | Princeton | 0 | 2 | 0 | 0 | 0 | 0 | 0 | 1 | 1 | 13,373 |
| | Ramsey | 0 | 1 | 0 | 0 | 0 | 0 | 1 | 0 | 0 | 14,620 |
| | Randolph Township | 0 | 2 | 0 | 0 | 0 | 0 | 1 | 1 | 0 | 25,226 |
| | Raritan | 1 | 0 | 0 | 0 | 0 | 0 | 1 | 0 | 0 | 7,413 |
| | Raritan Township | 1 | 0 | 0 | 0 | 0 | 1 | 0 | 0 | 0 | 22,637 |
| | Red Bank | 0 | 1 | 0 | 0 | 0 | 0 | 0 | 0 | 1 | 11,866 |
| | Ridgewood | 0 | 1 | 0 | 1 | 0 | 0 | 0 | 0 | 2 | 24,080 |
| | Ringwood | 0 | 1 | 0 | 0 | 0 | 0 | 0 | 0 | 1 | 12,711 |
| | River Edge | 0 | 1 | 0 | 0 | 0 | 0 | 1 | 0 | 0 | 10,644 |
| | Riverside Township | 1 | 0 | 0 | 0 | 0 | 0 | 0 | 1 | 0 | 7,671 |
| | River Vale Township | 0 | 2 | 0 | 1 | 0 | 0 | 0 | 1 | 2 | 9,634 |
| | Rockaway Township | 1 | 1 | 0 | 0 | 0 | 1 | 0 | 0 | 1 | 25,828 |
| | Roseland | 0 | 1 | 0 | 0 | 0 | 0 | 0 | 1 | 0 | 5,358 |
| | Runnemede | 1 | 0 | 0 | 0 | 0 | 0 | 1 | 0 | 0 | 8,398 |
| | Sayreville | 0 | 0 | 1 | 1 | 0 | 1 | 0 | 0 | 1 | 42,401 |
| | Scotch Plains Township | 0 | 2 | 0 | 0 | 0 | 0 | 1 | 0 | 1 | 22,907 |
| | Sea Bright | 1 | 0 | 0 | 0 | 0 | 0 | 1 | 0 | 0 | 1,802 |
| | Sea Girt | 0 | 1 | 0 | 0 | 0 | 0 | 1 | 0 | 0 | 2,061 |
| | Sea Isle City | 1 | 1 | 0 | 0 | 0 | 0 | 0 | 2 | 0 | 2,915 |
| | Secaucus | 1 | 0 | 0 | 0 | 0 | 1 | 0 | 0 | 0 | 15,312 |
| | Somerville | 1 | 3 | 0 | 0 | 0 | 0 | 1 | 0 | 3 | 12,672 |
| | South Brunswick Township | 4 | 6 | 3 | 2 | 0 | 6 | 0 | 5 | 4 | 41,448 |
| | South Orange | 0 | 1 | 0 | 0 | 0 | 1 | 0 | 0 | 0 | 15,767 |
| | South Plainfield | 0 | 0 | 1 | 0 | 0 | 0 | 0 | 0 | 1 | 22,710 |
| | South Toms River | 1 | 0 | 0 | 0 | 0 | 0 | 0 | 0 | 1 | 3,718 |
| | Spotswood | 1 | 0 | 1 | 0 | 0 | 1 | 1 | 0 | 0 | 8,173 |
| | Stafford Township | 1 | 3 | 0 | 0 | 0 | 3 | 0 | 0 | 1 | 26,985 |
| | Teaneck Township | 1 | 8 | 0 | 2 | 0 | 0 | 4 | 3 | 4 | 37,985 |
| | Tinton Falls | 0 | 3 | 0 | 1 | 0 | 0 | 0 | 2 | 2 | 20,069 |
| | Tuckerton | 0 | 0 | 1 | 0 | 0 | 0 | 0 | 1 | 0 | 3,918 |
| | Union City | 0 | 1 | 0 | 0 | 0 | 0 | 1 | 0 | 0 | 61,665 |
| | Union Township | 1 | 0 | 0 | 0 | 0 | 0 | 0 | 1 | 0 | 53,579 |

[1]Agencies published in this table indicated that at least one hate crime incident occurred in their respective jurisdictions during the quarter(s) for which they submitted a report to the Hate Crime Statistics Program. Blanks indicate quarters for which agencies did not submit reports.

[2]Population figures are published only for the cities. The figures listed for the universities and colleges are student enrollment and were provided by the United States Department of Education for the 2008 school year, the most recent available. The enrollment figures include full-time and part-time students.

[3]Includes one incident reported with more than one bias motivation.

[4]Student enrollment figures were not available.

## Table 94. Hate Crime Incidents per Bias Motivation and Quarter, by State and Agency, 2009—*Continued*

| State | Agency type/Agency name | Number of incidents per bias motivation | | | | | Number of incidents per quarter[1] | | | | Popu-lation[2] |
|---|---|---|---|---|---|---|---|---|---|---|---|
| | | Race | Religion | Sexual orient-ation | Ethnicity | Disability | 1st quarter | 2nd quarter | 3rd quarter | 4th quarter | |
| | Voorhees Township | 1 | 1 | 0 | 0 | 0 | 0 | 0 | 0 | 2 | 31,686 |
| | Waldwick | 1 | 0 | 0 | 0 | 0 | 1 | 0 | 0 | 0 | 9,511 |
| | Warren Township | 2 | 0 | 0 | 0 | 0 | 0 | 0 | 2 | 0 | 16,150 |
| | Washington Township, Gloucester County | 0 | 1 | 0 | 1 | 0 | 1 | 0 | 1 | 0 | 51,757 |
| | West Deptford Township | 0 | 0 | 0 | 1 | 0 | 0 | 0 | 0 | 1 | 22,326 |
| | West Long Branch | 1 | 1 | 0 | 0 | 0 | 1 | 0 | 1 | 0 | 8,346 |
| | West New York | 0 | 1 | 0 | 0 | 0 | 0 | 1 | 0 | 0 | 46,528 |
| | West Orange | 0 | 1 | 0 | 0 | 0 | 0 | 1 | 0 | 0 | 42,357 |
| | West Windsor Township | 1 | 0 | 0 | 0 | 0 | 1 | 0 | 0 | 0 | 27,061 |
| | Wharton | 0 | 0 | 0 | 1 | 0 | 0 | 1 | 0 | 0 | 6,060 |
| | Wildwood | 1 | 0 | 0 | 0 | 0 | 1 | 0 | 0 | 0 | 5,242 |
| | Winfield Township | 1 | 0 | 0 | 0 | 0 | 0 | 1 | 0 | 0 | 1,435 |
| | Winslow Township | 3 | 1 | 0 | 0 | 0 | 0 | 2 | 0 | 2 | 39,975 |
| | Woodbridge Township | 5 | 3 | 0 | 1 | 0 | 0 | 1 | 4 | 4 | 98,013 |
| | Woodbury | 2 | 0 | 1 | 0 | 0 | 0 | 0 | 1 | 2 | 10,467 |
| | Woodcliff Lake | 0 | 1 | 0 | 0 | 0 | 0 | 0 | 0 | 1 | 5,962 |
| | Woodland Park | 1 | 0 | 0 | 0 | 0 | 0 | 0 | 1 | 0 | 12,014 |
| | **State Police Agencies** | 1 | 0 | 0 | 0 | 0 | | | | | |
| | State Police, Sussex County | 1 | 0 | 0 | 0 | 0 | 0 | 0 | 1 | 0 | |
| **NEW MEXICO** | **Total** | 6 | 1 | 5 | 3 | 0 | | | | | |
| | **Cities** | 6 | 0 | 5 | 3 | 0 | | | | | |
| | Albuquerque | 3 | 0 | 5 | 1 | 0 | 3 | 3 | 2 | 1 | 530,636 |
| | Farmington | 2 | 0 | 0 | 2 | 0 | | 2 | 1 | 1 | 43,131 |
| | Gallup | 1 | 0 | 0 | 0 | 0 | 0 | 1 | 0 | 0 | 19,916 |
| | **Metropolitan Counties** | 0 | 1 | 0 | 0 | 0 | | | | | |
| | Valencia | 0 | 1 | 0 | 0 | 0 | 0 | 0 | 0 | 1 | |
| **NEW YORK** | **Total** | 160 | 283 | 114 | 67 | 2 | | | | | |
| | **Cities** | 106 | 172 | 86 | 42 | 1 | | | | | |
| | Albany | 2 | 0 | 1 | 0 | 0 | 1 | 1 | 1 | 0 | 93,445 |
| | Amherst Town | 2 | 2 | 0 | 0 | 0 | 0 | 2 | 2 | 0 | 110,399 |
| | Auburn | 4 | 0 | 0 | 0 | 0 | 1 | 1 | 0 | 2 | 26,991 |
| | Bethlehem Town | 1 | 0 | 0 | 0 | 0 | 0 | 1 | 0 | 0 | 33,286 |
| | Binghamton | 0 | 2 | 1 | 0 | 0 | 0 | 1 | 1 | 1 | 44,455 |
| | Blooming Grove Town | 1 | 0 | 0 | 0 | 0 | 0 | 0 | 0 | 1 | 12,352 |
| | Brighton Town | 1 | 0 | 0 | 0 | 0 | 0 | 0 | 1 | 0 | 34,275 |
| | Buffalo | 19 | 0 | 6 | 6 | 0 | 6 | 9 | 12 | 4 | 268,655 |
| | Catskill Village | 0 | 1 | 1 | 0 | 0 | | 1 | 1 | | 4,193 |
| | Cheektowaga Town | 1 | 0 | 2 | 0 | 0 | | 1 | 1 | 1 | 77,772 |
| | Clarkstown Town | 1 | 4 | 1 | 0 | 0 | 2 | 1 | 2 | 1 | 78,899 |
| | Colonie Town | 1 | 0 | 0 | 0 | 0 | 0 | 0 | 1 | 0 | 78,003 |
| | Dobbs Ferry Village | 0 | 1 | 0 | 0 | 0 | 0 | 0 | 0 | 1 | 11,187 |
| | East Greenbush Town | 0 | 0 | 1 | 0 | 0 | 0 | 0 | 1 | 0 | 17,066 |
| | East Rochester Village | 1 | 0 | 0 | 0 | 1 | 0 | 1 | | 1 | 6,229 |
| | Freeport Village | 0 | 0 | 1 | 0 | 0 | 1 | 0 | 0 | 0 | 43,890 |
| | Goshen Village | 0 | 1 | 0 | 0 | 0 | 0 | 0 | 0 | 1 | 5,573 |
| | Greece Town | 1 | 0 | 0 | 0 | 0 | 0 | 0 | 1 | 0 | 93,274 |
| | Hastings-on-Hudson Village | 0 | 2 | 0 | 0 | 0 | 0 | 0 | 0 | 2 | 7,939 |
| | Hudson Falls Village | 1 | 0 | 0 | 1 | 0 | 1 | 1 | 0 | 0 | 6,615 |
| | Ithaca | 6 | 0 | 2 | 1 | 0 | 3 | 0 | 4 | 2 | 29,862 |
| | New Rochelle | 3 | 1 | 0 | 0 | 0 | 0 | 0 | 3 | 1 | 74,320 |
| | New York | 45 | 139 | 61 | 26 | 0 | 42 | 71 | 63 | 95 | 8,400,907 |
| | Niagara Falls | 0 | 0 | 0 | 1 | 0 | 0 | 0 | 1 | 0 | 50,909 |
| | Niskayuna Town | 0 | 2 | 0 | 0 | 0 | 1 | 0 | 1 | 0 | 21,920 |
| | North Tonawanda | 1 | 0 | 0 | 0 | 0 | 0 | 0 | 0 | 1 | 31,012 |
| | Orangetown Town | 0 | 1 | 0 | 0 | 0 | | | 1 | 0 | 36,108 |
| | Plattsburgh City | 0 | 1 | 0 | 0 | 0 | 0 | 0 | 1 | 0 | 19,457 |
| | Poughkeepsie | 2 | 0 | 0 | 1 | 0 | 2 | 0 | 0 | 1 | 29,599 |
| | Ramapo Town | 0 | 0 | 0 | 2 | 0 | 1 | | 1 | | 76,611 |
| | Rhinebeck Village | 0 | 2 | 0 | 0 | 0 | 0 | 2 | 0 | 0 | 3,046 |
| | Rochester | 0 | 1 | 5 | 0 | 0 | 4 | 1 | 1 | 0 | 205,537 |
| | Rockville Centre Village | 0 | 3 | 0 | 0 | 0 | 0 | 0 | 0 | 3 | 24,396 |
| | Saratoga Springs | 2 | 1 | 0 | 1 | 0 | 0 | 1 | 3 | 0 | 29,125 |
| | Saugerties Town | 1 | 0 | 0 | 0 | 0 | 0 | 0 | 1 | 0 | 15,844 |
| | Scarsdale Village | 0 | 1 | 0 | 0 | 0 | 0 | 0 | 0 | 1 | 17,677 |
| | Schenectady | 3 | 0 | 0 | 0 | 0 | 1 | 1 | 0 | 1 | 61,087 |
| | South Nyack Village | 1 | 0 | 1 | 0 | 0 | 0 | 0 | 2 | 0 | 3,361 |
| | Southold Town | 0 | 1 | 0 | 0 | 0 | 0 | 0 | 0 | 1 | 20,552 |
| | Spring Valley Village | 0 | 0 | 1 | 1 | 0 | 0 | 0 | 0 | 2 | 26,340 |
| | Tarrytown Village | 0 | 1 | 0 | 0 | 0 | 1 | 0 | 0 | 0 | 11,019 |
| | Tonawanda | 2 | 0 | 0 | 0 | 0 | 0 | 1 | 1 | 0 | 14,683 |

[1]Agencies published in this table indicated that at least one hate crime incident occurred in their respective jurisdictions during the quarter(s) for which they submitted a report to the Hate Crime Statistics Program. Blanks indicate quarters for which agencies did not submit reports.

[2]Population figures are published only for the cities. The figures listed for the universities and colleges are student enrollment and were provided by the United States Department of Education for the 2008 school year, the most recent available. The enrollment figures include full-time and part-time students.

## Table 94. Hate Crime Incidents per Bias Motivation and Quarter, by State and Agency, 2009—*Continued*

| State | Agency type/Agency name | Number of incidents per bias motivation | | | | | Number of incidents per quarter[1] | | | | Population[2] |
|---|---|---|---|---|---|---|---|---|---|---|---|
| | | Race | Religion | Sexual orientation | Ethnicity | Disability | 1st quarter | 2nd quarter | 3rd quarter | 4th quarter | |
| | Utica | 0 | 0 | 1 | 0 | 0 | 0 | 1 | 0 | 0 | 57,831 |
| | Vestal Town | 1 | 0 | 0 | 2 | 0 | 0 | 0 | 0 | 3 | 27,332 |
| | Yonkers | 3 | 5 | 1 | 0 | 0 | 2 | 2 | 4 | 1 | 202,192 |
| | **Universities and Colleges** | 11 | 7 | 11 | 3 | 0 | | | | | |
| | Cornell University | 1 | 0 | 0 | 0 | 0 | 1 | 0 | 0 | 0 | 20,273 |
| | State University of New York: | | | | | | | | | | |
| | Albany | 1 | 0 | 1 | 0 | 0 | 0 | 1 | 1 | 0 | 18,204 |
| | Buffalo[4] | 0 | 1 | 0 | 0 | 0 | 0 | 1 | 0 | 0 | |
| | Maritime College | 1 | 0 | 1 | 0 | 0 | 0 | 0 | 1 | 1 | 1,630 |
| | Stony Brook[4] | 1 | 0 | 0 | 0 | 0 | 1 | | | | |
| | State University of New York Agricultural and Technical College, Alfred | 1 | 0 | 0 | 0 | 0 | 0 | 1 | 0 | 0 | 3,276 |
| | State University of New York College: | | | | | | | | | | |
| | Buffalo | 0 | 0 | 0 | 1 | 0 | 0 | 0 | 0 | 1 | 11,234 |
| | Cortland | 0 | 1 | 0 | 1 | 0 | 0 | 1 | 1 | 0 | 7,234 |
| | New Paltz | 0 | 2 | 0 | 0 | 0 | 1 | 0 | 1 | 0 | 8,205 |
| | Oneonta | 1 | 0 | 2 | 0 | 0 | 1 | 0 | 1 | 1 | 5,757 |
| | Oswego | 2 | 3 | 2 | 0 | 0 | 1 | 2 | 0 | 4 | 8,909 |
| | Plattsburgh | 2 | 0 | 4 | 1 | 0 | 4 | 2 | 1 | 0 | 6,358 |
| | Potsdam | 1 | 0 | 1 | 0 | 0 | 0 | 0 | 1 | 1 | 4,325 |
| | **Metropolitan Counties** | 32 | 92 | 15 | 21 | 1 | | | | | |
| | Broome | 1 | 1 | 0 | 0 | 0 | 0 | 0 | 2 | | |
| | Chemung | 1 | 0 | 0 | 0 | 0 | 0 | 1 | 0 | 0 | |
| | Dutchess | 0 | 2 | 1 | 0 | 0 | 1 | 2 | 0 | 0 | |
| | Erie | 2 | 0 | 0 | 0 | 0 | 0 | 1 | 0 | 1 | |
| | Monroe | 2 | 1 | 0 | 0 | 0 | 1 | 1 | 0 | 1 | |
| | Nassau | 15 | 50 | 4 | 5 | 0 | 9 | 17 | 26 | 22 | |
| | Niagara | 0 | 0 | 1 | 0 | 0 | 0 | 0 | 1 | 0 | |
| | Oneida | 0 | 0 | 1 | 0 | 0 | 0 | 0 | 0 | 1 | |
| | Rockland | 0 | 1 | 0 | 0 | 0 | | | | 1 | |
| | Suffolk County Police Department | 11 | 37 | 8 | 16 | 1 | 18 | 13 | 18 | 24 | |
| | **Nonmetropolitan Counties** | 0 | 2 | 0 | 1 | 0 | | | | | |
| | Cattaraugus | 0 | 0 | 0 | 1 | 0 | 1 | 0 | 0 | 0 | |
| | Cayuga | 0 | 1 | 0 | 0 | 0 | 0 | 1 | 0 | | |
| | Sullivan | 0 | 1 | 0 | 0 | 0 | 0 | 1 | 0 | 0 | |
| | **State Police Agencies** | 5 | 1 | 2 | 0 | 0 | | | | | |
| | State Police: | | | | | | | | | | |
| | Albany County | 0 | 0 | 2 | 0 | 0 | 1 | 1 | 0 | 0 | |
| | Broome County | 1 | 0 | 0 | 0 | 0 | 0 | 0 | 1 | 0 | |
| | Columbia County | 1 | 0 | 0 | 0 | 0 | 0 | 0 | 1 | 0 | |
| | Madison County | 0 | 1 | 0 | 0 | 0 | 1 | 0 | 0 | 0 | |
| | Montgomery County | 1 | 0 | 0 | 0 | 0 | 0 | 1 | 0 | 0 | |
| | Niagara County | 1 | 0 | 0 | 0 | 0 | 0 | 0 | 1 | 0 | |
| | Otsego County | 1 | 0 | 0 | 0 | 0 | 0 | 1 | 0 | 0 | |
| | **Other Agencies** | 6 | 9 | 0 | 0 | 0 | | | | | |
| | Broome County Special Investigations Task Force | 1 | 0 | 0 | 0 | 0 | 0 | 0 | 1 | 0 | |
| | New York City Metropolitan Transportation Authority | 5 | 9 | 0 | 0 | 0 | 4 | 1 | 4 | 5 | |
| **NORTH CAROLINA** | **Total** | 67 | 9 | 15 | 12 | 0 | | | | | |
| | **Cities** | 42 | 8 | 14 | 7 | 0 | | | | | |
| | Albemarle | 3 | 1 | 0 | 0 | 0 | 0 | 2 | 1 | 1 | 15,471 |
| | Asheville | 2 | 1 | 2 | 1 | 0 | 3 | 1 | 0 | 2 | 74,923 |
| | Carrboro | 1 | 0 | 3 | 1 | 0 | 0 | 1 | 3 | 1 | 18,213 |
| | Cary | 1 | 0 | 0 | 0 | 0 | 0 | 0 | 1 | 0 | 133,757 |
| | Chapel Hill | 0 | 2 | 0 | 1 | 0 | 2 | 0 | 0 | 1 | 53,069 |
| | Charlotte-Mecklenburg | 7 | 1 | 0 | 0 | 0 | 0 | 4 | 1 | 3 | 777,708 |
| | Cherryville | 1 | 0 | 0 | 0 | 0 | 0 | 0 | 1 | 0 | 5,651 |
| | Eden | 1 | 0 | 0 | 0 | 0 | 0 | 0 | 0 | 1 | 15,426 |
| | Elizabeth City | 2 | 0 | 0 | 0 | 0 | 1 | 0 | 0 | 1 | 20,363 |
| | Fayetteville | 2 | 0 | 0 | 0 | 0 | 1 | 0 | 1 | 0 | 173,995 |
| | Gastonia | 1 | 0 | 0 | 0 | 0 | 0 | 0 | 1 | 0 | 73,060 |

[1]Agencies published in this table indicated that at least one hate crime incident occurred in their respective jurisdictions during the quarter(s) for which they submitted a report to the Hate Crime Statistics Program. Blanks indicate quarters for which agencies did not submit reports.
[2]Population figures are published only for the cities. The figures listed for the universities and colleges are student enrollment and were provided by the United States Department of Education for the 2008 school year, the most recent available. The enrollment figures include full-time and part-time students.
[4]Student enrollment figures were not available.

**Table 94. Hate Crime Incidents per Bias Motivation and Quarter, by State and Agency, 2009—*Continued***

| State | Agency type/Agency name | Number of incidents per bias motivation | | | | | Number of incidents per quarter[1] | | | | Popu- lation[2] |
|---|---|---|---|---|---|---|---|---|---|---|---|
| | | Race | Religion | Sexual orient- ation | Ethnicity | Disability | 1st quarter | 2nd quarter | 3rd quarter | 4th quarter | |
| | Goldsboro | 1 | 0 | 0 | 0 | 0 | 1 | 0 | 0 | 0 | 37,421 |
| | Greensboro | 1 | 1 | 3 | 1 | 0 | 0 | 1 | 3 | 2 | 253,191 |
| | Hamlet | 1 | 0 | 0 | 0 | 0 | 0 | 0 | 0 | 1 | 5,764 |
| | Hickory | 1 | 0 | 1 | 0 | 0 | 0 | 0 | 0 | 2 | 41,718 |
| | High Point | 2 | 0 | 0 | 1 | 0 | 0 | 3 | 0 | 0 | 103,675 |
| | Kernersville | 0 | 0 | 0 | 1 | 0 | 0 | 1 | 0 | 0 | 22,822 |
| | Maiden | 1 | 0 | 0 | 0 | 0 | 0 | 0 | 0 | 1 | 3,523 |
| | Mint Hill | 0 | 1 | 1 | 0 | 0 | 1 | 0 | 1 | 0 | 20,740 |
| | Morganton | 1 | 0 | 0 | 1 | 0 | 0 | 1 | 0 | 1 | 17,169 |
| | Mount Airy | 1 | 0 | 0 | 0 | 0 | 0 | 1 | 0 | 0 | 9,487 |
| | Reidsville | 0 | 0 | 1 | 0 | 0 | 0 | 0 | 0 | 1 | 14,899 |
| | Roxboro | 1 | 0 | 0 | 0 | 0 | 0 | 0 | 0 | 1 | 8,663 |
| | Salisbury | 5 | 0 | 1 | 0 | 0 | 1 | 1 | 2 | 2 | 29,008 |
| | Smithfield | 2 | 0 | 0 | 0 | 0 | 2 | 0 | 0 | 0 | 13,199 |
| | Southern Pines | 1 | 1 | 1 | 0 | 0 | 1 | 0 | 2 | 0 | 12,865 |
| | Stallings | 1 | 0 | 1 | 0 | 0 | 0 | 0 | 1 | 1 | 9,186 |
| | Wendell | 2 | 0 | 0 | 0 | 0 | 0 | 1 | 0 | 1 | 5,414 |
| | **Metropolitan Counties** | | 19 | 1 | 1 | 5 | 0 | | | | |
| | Buncombe | 5 | 1 | 1 | 2 | 0 | 4 | 0 | 3 | 2 | |
| | Caldwell | 1 | 0 | 0 | 0 | 0 | 1 | 0 | 0 | 0 | |
| | Chatham | 1 | 0 | 0 | 0 | 0 | 1 | 0 | 0 | 0 | |
| | Currituck | 4 | 0 | 0 | 0 | 0 | 0 | 2 | 1 | 1 | |
| | Forsyth | 0 | 0 | 0 | 1 | 0 | 0 | 0 | 0 | 1 | |
| | Guilford | 1 | 0 | 0 | 0 | 0 | 0 | 0 | 1 | 0 | |
| | Person | 1 | 0 | 0 | 0 | 0 | 0 | 1 | 0 | 0 | |
| | Pitt | 5 | 0 | 0 | 2 | 0 | 2 | 2 | 0 | 3 | |
| | Rockingham | 1 | 0 | 0 | 0 | 0 | 1 | 0 | 0 | 0 | |
| | **Nonmetropolitan Counties** | | 6 | 0 | 0 | 0 | 0 | | | | |
| | Cherokee | 1 | 0 | 0 | 0 | 0 | 0 | 0 | 1 | 0 | |
| | Iredell | 2 | 0 | 0 | 0 | 0 | 0 | 0 | 0 | 2 | |
| | Pasquotank | 1 | 0 | 0 | 0 | 0 | 0 | 0 | 0 | 1 | |
| | Rutherford | 1 | 0 | 0 | 0 | 0 | 0 | 0 | 1 | 0 | |
| | Transylvania | 1 | 0 | 0 | 0 | 0 | 1 | 0 | 0 | 0 | |
| **NORTH DAKOTA** | **Total** | 10 | 1 | 2 | 1 | 0 | | | | | |
| | **Cities** | 8 | 1 | 1 | 1 | 0 | | | | | |
| | Bismarck | 1 | 0 | 0 | 0 | 0 | 0 | 1 | 0 | 0 | 60,923 |
| | Dickinson | 1 | 0 | 0 | 0 | 0 | 0 | 0 | 1 | 0 | 16,043 |
| | Fargo | 0 | 0 | 1 | 0 | 0 | 1 | 0 | 0 | 0 | 93,830 |
| | Grand Forks | 2 | 0 | 0 | 0 | 0 | 0 | 0 | 2 | 0 | 51,553 |
| | Larimore | 0 | 0 | 0 | 1 | 0 | 0 | 0 | 1 | 0 | 1,300 |
| | Mandan | 4 | 1 | 0 | 0 | 0 | 2 | 1 | 0 | 2 | 18,244 |
| | **Metropolitan Counties** | 1 | 0 | 1 | 0 | 0 | | | | | |
| | Burleigh | 0 | 0 | 1 | 0 | 0 | 0 | 0 | 1 | 0 | |
| | Morton | 1 | 0 | 0 | 0 | 0 | 0 | 0 | 1 | 0 | |
| | **Nonmetropolitan Counties** | 1 | 0 | 0 | 0 | 0 | | | | | |
| | Ward | 1 | 0 | 0 | 0 | 0 | 0 | 0 | 1 | 0 | |
| **OHIO** | **Total** | 142 | 24 | 47 | 31 | 53 | | | | | |
| | **Cities** | 116 | 20 | 31 | 28 | 11 | | | | | |
| | Akron | 8 | 0 | 1 | 2 | 0 | 0 | 4 | 3 | 4 | 206,497 |
| | Amherst | 0 | 1 | 0 | 0 | 0 | 0 | 0 | 0 | 1 | 11,718 |
| | Ashland | 0 | 0 | 0 | 1 | 0 | 1 | 0 | 0 | 0 | 21,916 |
| | Athens | 1 | 0 | 0 | 0 | 0 | 0 | 1 | 0 | 0 | 22,173 |
| | Bath Township, Summit County | 1 | 0 | 0 | 0 | 1 | 1 | 0 | 1 | 0 | 10,247 |
| | Beavercreek | 1 | 0 | 0 | 0 | 0 | 0 | 0 | 1 | 0 | 40,119 |
| | Beaver Township | 2 | 0 | 0 | 0 | 0 | 0 | 1 | 1 | 0 | 6,045 |
| | Berea | 1 | 0 | 0 | 0 | 0 | 1 | 0 | 0 | 0 | 17,883 |
| | Blue Ash | 0 | 1 | 0 | 0 | 0 | 0 | 1 | 0 | 0 | 12,812 |
| | Boardman | 0 | 0 | 0 | 1 | 0 | 0 | 0 | 0 | 1 | 38,827 |
| | Celina | 1 | 0 | 0 | 0 | 0 | 0 | 1 | 0 | 0 | 10,242 |
| | Chillicothe | 9 | 0 | 0 | 0 | 0 | 5 | 1 | 3 | 0 | 22,312 |
| | Cincinnati | 1 | 0 | 2 | 1 | 0 | 1 | 1 | 2 | 0 | 333,568 |
| | Clearcreek Township | 1 | 0 | 0 | 0 | 0 | 0 | 1 | 0 | 0 | 12,850 |
| | Cleveland | 2 | 0 | 1 | 2 | 0 | 1 | 0 | 3 | 1 | 429,238 |
| | Columbus | 14 | 2 | 13 | 8 | 0 | 7 | 14 | 8 | 8 | 759,391 |
| | Dayton | 5 | 1 | 0 | 0 | 0 | 1 | 2 | 1 | 2 | 152,965 |
| | Defiance | 0 | 0 | 0 | 1 | 0 | 1 | 0 | 0 | 0 | 16,006 |
| | Englewood | 1 | 0 | 0 | 0 | 0 | 0 | 0 | 1 | 0 | 12,734 |
| | Fairfield Township | 2 | 0 | 0 | 0 | 0 | 0 | 0 | 0 | 2 | 17,487 |
| | Findlay | 2 | 0 | 1 | 0 | 0 | 0 | 2 | 1 | 0 | 36,751 |
| | Fort Shawnee | 0 | 0 | 1 | 0 | 0 | 1 | 0 | 0 | 0 | 3,687 |
| | Franklin | 4 | 0 | 0 | 0 | 0 | 0 | 1 | 0 | 3 | 13,113 |

[1]Agencies published in this table indicated that at least one hate crime incident occurred in their respective jurisdictions during the quarter(s) for which they submitted a report to the Hate Crime Statistics Program. Blanks indicate quarters for which agencies did not submit reports.

[2]Population figures are published only for the cities. The figures listed for the universities and colleges are student enrollment and were provided by the United States Department of Education for the 2008 school year, the most recent available. The enrollment figures include full-time and part-time students.

# Table 94. Hate Crime Incidents per Bias Motivation and Quarter, by State and Agency, 2009—*Continued*

| State | Agency type/Agency name | Number of incidents per bias motivation | | | | | Number of incidents per quarter[1] | | | | Population[2] |
|---|---|---|---|---|---|---|---|---|---|---|---|
| | | Race | Religion | Sexual orientation | Ethnicity | Disability | 1st quarter | 2nd quarter | 3rd quarter | 4th quarter | |
| | Fremont | 2 | 0 | 0 | 0 | 0 | 0 | 1 | 1 | | 16,556 |
| | Gahanna | 5 | 0 | 0 | 0 | 0 | 2 | 2 | 1 | 0 | 34,028 |
| | Galion | 1 | 0 | 0 | 0 | 0 | 0 | 0 | 0 | 1 | 10,644 |
| | Genoa Township | 0 | 1 | 0 | 0 | 0 | 0 | 1 | 0 | 0 | 16,119 |
| | Germantown | 1 | 0 | 0 | 0 | 0 | 0 | 0 | 0 | 1 | 5,031 |
| | Hamilton | 0 | 1 | 0 | 0 | 0 | 1 | 0 | 0 | 0 | 62,690 |
| | Harrison | 1 | 0 | 0 | 0 | 0 | 0 | 1 | 0 | 0 | 9,628 |
| | Heath | 0 | 0 | 1 | 1 | 0 | 0 | 0 | 2 | 0 | 8,938 |
| | Hilliard | 0 | 1 | 0 | 0 | 0 | 0 | 0 | 1 | 0 | 28,326 |
| | Holland | 0 | 0 | 0 | 1 | 0 | 0 | 0 | 1 | 0 | 1,329 |
| | Howland Township | 1 | 0 | 0 | 0 | 0 | 0 | 0 | 0 | 1 | 16,245 |
| | Huber Heights | 4 | 0 | 1 | 0 | 0 | 1 | 1 | 2 | 1 | 37,027 |
| | Jackson | 1 | 0 | 0 | 0 | 0 | 1 | 0 | 0 | 0 | 6,135 |
| | Jackson Township, Stark County | 1 | 0 | 1 | 0 | 0 | 0 | 1 | 0 | 1 | 40,989 |
| | Lancaster | 0 | 0 | 0 | 1 | 0 | 0 | 0 | 1 | 0 | 37,143 |
| | Lorain | 1 | 0 | 0 | 1 | 0 | 0 | 1 | 0 | 1 | 70,410 |
| | Madison Township, Lake County | 2 | 1 | 0 | 0 | 0 | 2 | 0 | 0 | 1 | 17,005 |
| | Mansfield | 2 | 1 | 1 | 0 | 0 | 0 | 0 | 0 | 4 | 49,349 |
| | Marysville | 2 | 0 | 0 | 0 | 0 | 0 | 1 | 0 | 1 | 18,447 |
| | Maumee | 1 | 0 | 0 | 0 | 0 | 0 | 0 | 0 | 1 | 13,729 |
| | Miami Township, Clermont County | 1 | 0 | 0 | 0 | 0 | 1 | 0 | 0 | 0 | 40,027 |
| | Miami Township, Montgomery County | 2 | 0 | 1 | 0 | 1 | 0 | 0 | 1 | 3 | 25,016 |
| | Moraine | 2 | 0 | 0 | 1 | 0 | 0 | 0 | 2 | 1 | 6,421 |
| | Mount Healthy | 2 | 0 | 0 | 0 | 0 | 2 | 0 | 0 | 0 | 6,044 |
| | Napoleon | 1 | 0 | 0 | 0 | 0 | 0 | 0 | 1 | 0 | 8,764 |
| | Niles | 1 | 1 | 1 | 0 | 0 | 1 | 0 | 2 | 0 | 19,095 |
| | North Canton | 1 | 0 | 0 | 0 | 0 | 0 | 0 | 0 | 1 | 16,929 |
| | Norton | 1 | 0 | 0 | 0 | 1 | 0 | 1 | 1 | 0 | 11,465 |
| | Norwood | 0 | 1 | 0 | 0 | 0 | 1 | 0 | 0 | 0 | 20,207 |
| | Parma | 1 | 1 | 0 | 0 | 0 | 1 | 1 | 0 | 0 | 77,148 |
| | Perkins Township | 1 | 0 | 0 | 0 | 0 | 0 | 0 | 1 | 0 | 12,820 |
| | Pickerington | 1 | 0 | 0 | 0 | 0 | 0 | 0 | 0 | 1 | 18,672 |
| | Piqua | 0 | 0 | 1 | 0 | 0 | 0 | 1 | 0 | 0 | 20,559 |
| | Portsmouth | 2 | 0 | 0 | 4 | 8 | 3 | 5 | 3 | 3 | 20,235 |
| | Reynoldsburg | 2 | 1 | 0 | 0 | 0 | 2 | 0 | 1 | 0 | 33,825 |
| | Shadyside | 0 | 0 | 1 | 0 | 0 | | | 0 | 1 | 3,508 |
| | Shaker Heights | 0 | 1 | 0 | 0 | 0 | 0 | 1 | 0 | 0 | 26,159 |
| | Sidney | 1 | 0 | 0 | 0 | 0 | 1 | 0 | 0 | 0 | 19,899 |
| | Solon | 1 | 0 | 0 | 0 | 0 | 0 | 0 | 1 | 0 | 21,870 |
| | South Euclid | 2 | 0 | 0 | 1 | 0 | 1 | 0 | 0 | 2 | 20,970 |
| | Springdale | 1 | 0 | 0 | 0 | 0 | 1 | 0 | 0 | 0 | 10,370 |
| | Springfield | 0 | 0 | 0 | 1 | 0 | 0 | 0 | 1 | 0 | 61,881 |
| | Stow | 3 | 0 | 0 | 0 | 0 | 2 | 0 | 0 | 1 | 34,067 |
| | Streetsboro | 1 | 0 | 0 | 0 | 0 | 1 | 0 | 0 | 0 | 14,749 |
| | Trotwood | 1 | 0 | 0 | 0 | 0 | 1 | 0 | 0 | 0 | 25,894 |
| | Upper Arlington | 1 | 0 | 1 | 0 | 0 | 1 | 0 | 0 | 1 | 31,686 |
| | Van Wert | 0 | 1 | 0 | 0 | 0 | 1 | 0 | 0 | 0 | 10,139 |
| | Vienna Township | 0 | 0 | 1 | 0 | 0 | 0 | 0 | 1 | 0 | 3,820 |
| | Warren | 0 | 0 | 1 | 0 | 0 | 0 | 0 | 0 | 1 | 43,331 |
| | West Chester Township | 0 | 0 | 0 | 1 | 0 | 0 | 0 | 0 | 1 | 56,060 |
| | Westerville | 1 | 1 | 0 | 0 | 0 | 0 | 1 | 0 | 1 | 36,319 |
| | Willoughby | 1 | 0 | 0 | 0 | 0 | 1 | 0 | 0 | 0 | 22,555 |
| | Wilmington | 1 | 2 | 1 | 0 | 0 | 2 | 0 | 0 | 2 | 12,680 |
| | Worthington | 1 | 0 | 0 | 0 | 0 | 0 | 0 | 0 | 1 | 13,230 |
| | Youngstown | 1 | 1 | 0 | 0 | 0 | 0 | 2 | 0 | 0 | 72,008 |
| | Zanesville | 1 | 0 | 0 | 0 | 0 | 0 | 0 | 0 | 1 | 25,080 |
| | **Universities and Colleges** | | 3 | 1 | 4 | 0 | 0 | | | | |
| | Capital University | 0 | 0 | 1 | 0 | 0 | 0 | 0 | 0 | 1 | 3,632 |
| | Ohio State University: Columbus | 1 | 0 | 2 | 0 | 0 | 0 | 1 | 1 | 1 | 53,715 |
| | Wooster[4] | 0 | 0 | 1 | 0 | 0 | 0 | 0 | 0 | 1 | |
| | Wright State University | 2 | 1 | 0 | 0 | 0 | 0 | 1 | 1 | 1 | 16,672 |
| | **Metropolitan Counties** | | 17 | 2 | 8 | 3 | 2 | | | | |
| | Butler | 0 | 0 | 5 | 0 | 1 | 1 | 3 | 1 | 1 | |
| | Clermont | 1 | 0 | 0 | 0 | 0 | 1 | 0 | 0 | 0 | |
| | Delaware | 0 | 0 | 0 | 1 | 0 | 1 | 0 | 0 | 0 | |
| | Franklin | 4 | 0 | 0 | 2 | 0 | 1 | 3 | 1 | 1 | |
| | Geauga | 1 | 0 | 0 | 0 | 0 | 0 | 1 | 0 | 0 | |
| | Jefferson | 1 | 0 | 0 | 0 | 0 | 1 | 0 | 0 | 0 | |
| | Lawrence | 2 | 0 | 0 | 0 | 0 | 0 | 1 | 1 | 0 | |

[1]Agencies published in this table indicated that at least one hate crime incident occurred in their respective jurisdictions during the quarter(s) for which they submitted a report to the Hate Crime Statistics Program. Blanks indicate quarters for which agencies did not submit reports.
[2]Population figures are published only for the cities. The figures listed for the universities and colleges are student enrollment and were provided by the United States Department of Education for the 2008 school year, the most recent available. The enrollment figures include full-time and part-time students.
[4]Student enrollment figures were not available.

## Table 94. Hate Crime Incidents per Bias Motivation and Quarter, by State and Agency, 2009—*Continued*

| State | Agency type/Agency name | Number of incidents per bias motivation | | | | | Number of incidents per quarter[1] | | | | Popu-lation[2] |
|---|---|---|---|---|---|---|---|---|---|---|---|
| | | Race | Religion | Sexual orient-ation | Ethnicity | Disability | 1st quarter | 2nd quarter | 3rd quarter | 4th quarter | |
| | Lucas | 3 | 0 | 3 | 0 | 0 | 4 | 0 | 1 | 1 | |
| | Madison | 1 | 0 | 0 | 0 | 0 | | 0 | 0 | 1 | |
| | Montgomery | 3 | 2 | 0 | 0 | 0 | 0 | 0 | 3 | 2 | |
| | Stark | 0 | 0 | 0 | 0 | 1 | 0 | 1 | 0 | 0 | |
| | Summit | 1 | 0 | 0 | 0 | 0 | 0 | 1 | 0 | 0 | |
| | **Nonmetropolitan Counties** | | 4 | 1 | 3 | 0 | 40 | | | | |
| | Champaign | 1 | 0 | 0 | 0 | 0 | 0 | 0 | 0 | 1 | |
| | Coshocton | 0 | 1 | 2 | 0 | 0 | 1 | 2 | 0 | 0 | |
| | Gallia | 1 | 0 | 0 | 0 | 0 | 0 | 0 | 1 | 0 | |
| | Hancock | 1 | 0 | 0 | 0 | 0 | 0 | 0 | 1 | 0 | |
| | Holmes | 0 | 0 | 0 | 0 | 1 | 0 | 0 | 1 | 0 | |
| | Mercer | 0 | 0 | 1 | 0 | 0 | 0 | 1 | 0 | 0 | |
| | Ross | 1 | 0 | 0 | 0 | 0 | 0 | 0 | 1 | 0 | |
| | Seneca | 0 | 0 | 0 | 0 | 39 | 10 | 9 | 10 | 10 | |
| | **Other Agencies** | | 2 | 0 | 1 | 0 | 0 | | | | |
| | Cleveland Metropolitan Park District | 1 | 0 | 1 | 0 | 0 | 0 | 2 | 0 | 0 | |
| | Mill Creek Metropolitan Park District | 1 | 0 | 0 | 0 | 0 | 0 | 1 | | | |
| **OKLAHOMA** | **Total** | | 33 | 6 | 14 | 6 | 0 | | | | |
| | **Cities** | | 23 | 6 | 12 | 6 | 0 | | | | |
| | Ada | 1 | 0 | 0 | 0 | 0 | 0 | 0 | 0 | 1 | 16,807 |
| | Altus | 0 | 0 | 1 | 0 | 0 | 0 | 1 | 0 | 0 | 18,664 |
| | Bixby | 1 | 0 | 0 | 0 | 0 | 0 | 0 | 0 | 1 | 21,681 |
| | Broken Arrow | 0 | 0 | 0 | 2 | 0 | 0 | 1 | 0 | 1 | 94,415 |
| | Chickasha | 3 | 1 | 1 | 0 | 0 | 0 | 0 | 4 | 1 | 17,195 |
| | Collinsville | 0 | 0 | 1 | 0 | 0 | 0 | 1 | 0 | 0 | 5,150 |
| | Cushing | 1 | 0 | 0 | 0 | 0 | 0 | 0 | 1 | 0 | 8,818 |
| | Edmond | 0 | 0 | 1 | 0 | 0 | 0 | 0 | 0 | 1 | 80,889 |
| | Lawton | 3 | 0 | 0 | 0 | 0 | 3 | 0 | 0 | 0 | 89,835 |
| | Miami | 2 | 0 | 0 | 0 | 0 | 0 | 1 | 0 | 1 | 12,953 |
| | Muskogee | 0 | 1 | 0 | 0 | 0 | 1 | 0 | 0 | 0 | 40,197 |
| | Norman | 1 | 1 | 0 | 0 | 0 | 1 | 0 | 1 | 0 | 108,152 |
| | Oklahoma City | 9 | 2 | 6 | 3 | 0 | 2 | 5 | 11 | 2 | 556,939 |
| | Owasso | 0 | 0 | 1 | 0 | 0 | 0 | 0 | 1 | 0 | 28,631 |
| | Ponca City | 1 | 0 | 0 | 0 | 0 | 1 | 0 | 0 | 0 | 24,359 |
| | Sallisaw | 0 | 0 | 1 | 0 | 0 | 0 | 0 | 1 | 0 | 8,823 |
| | Sand Springs | 1 | 0 | 0 | 0 | 0 | 0 | 0 | 1 | 0 | 18,602 |
| | Stillwater | 0 | 1 | 0 | 0 | 0 | 0 | 0 | 1 | 0 | 48,690 |
| | Tulsa | 0 | 0 | 0 | 1 | 0 | 1 | 0 | 0 | 0 | 384,851 |
| | **Universities and Colleges** | | 4 | 0 | 0 | 0 | 0 | | | | |
| | University of Central Oklahoma | 1 | 0 | 0 | 0 | 0 | 1 | 0 | 0 | 0 | 15,724 |
| | University of Oklahoma, Health Sciences Center | 3 | 0 | 0 | 0 | 0 | 1 | 1 | 0 | 1 | 3,926 |
| | **Metropolitan Counties** | | 6 | 0 | 0 | 0 | 0 | | | | |
| | Cleveland | 2 | 0 | 0 | 0 | 0 | 0 | 0 | 2 | 0 | |
| | Creek | 1 | 0 | 0 | 0 | 0 | 0 | 0 | 1 | 0 | |
| | Logan | 2 | 0 | 0 | 0 | 0 | 0 | 2 | 0 | 0 | |
| | Tulsa | 1 | 0 | 0 | 0 | 0 | 0 | 0 | 1 | 0 | |
| | **Nonmetropolitan Counties** | | 0 | 0 | 2 | 0 | 0 | | | | |
| | Latimer | 0 | 0 | 1 | 0 | 0 | 0 | 0 | 1 | 0 | |
| | Pittsburg | 0 | 0 | 1 | 0 | 0 | 0 | 1 | 0 | 0 | |
| **OREGON**...................... | **Total** | 64 | 18 | 24 | 22 | 2 | | | | | |
| | **Cities** | 54 | 17 | 23 | 20 | 2 | | | | | |
| | Beaverton | 3 | 2 | 1 | 4 | 0 | 1 | 3 | 3 | 3 | 93,221 |
| | Bend | 1 | 0 | 0 | 0 | 0 | 0 | 0 | 1 | 0 | 80,550 |
| | Boardman | 0 | 1 | 0 | 0 | 0 | 0 | 0 | 1 | 0 | 2,919 |
| | Coos Bay | 2 | 0 | 0 | 0 | 0 | | 2 | | | 15,703 |
| | Corvallis | 2 | 0 | 1 | 2 | 1 | 1 | 1 | 4 | 0 | 51,302 |
| | Eugene | 6 | 2 | 1 | 1 | 0 | 2 | 2 | 1 | 5 | 151,383 |
| | Hermiston | 0 | 0 | 0 | 1 | 0 | | | 1 | | 15,544 |
| | La Grande | 0 | 0 | 0 | 1 | 0 | 0 | 0 | 0 | 1 | 12,697 |
| | Lebanon | 1 | 1 | 0 | 0 | 0 | 0 | 1 | 1 | 0 | 15,665 |
| | McMinnville | 0 | 0 | 0 | 1 | 0 | 0 | 0 | 1 | 0 | 31,730 |
| | Medford | 0 | 0 | 1 | 1 | 0 | 1 | 0 | 0 | 1 | 74,042 |
| | Milton-Freewater | 0 | 0 | 1 | 0 | 0 | | | | 1 | 6,415 |
| | Newport | 1 | 1 | 0 | 1 | 0 | 1 | 2 | 0 | 0 | 9,993 |
| | Pendleton | 1 | 0 | 0 | 0 | 0 | 0 | 0 | 1 | 0 | 16,378 |
| | Portland | 12 | 5 | 15 | 2 | 1 | 8 | 2 | 9 | 16 | 560,908 |
| | Reedsport | 1 | 0 | 0 | 1 | 0 | 2 | 0 | 0 | 0 | 4,195 |
| | Roseburg | 1 | 0 | 0 | 0 | 0 | 0 | 1 | 0 | 0 | 20,741 |
| | Salem | 5 | 3 | 1 | 2 | 0 | 1 | 5 | 4 | 1 | 155,329 |

[1]Agencies published in this table indicated that at least one hate crime incident occurred in their respective jurisdictions during the quarter(s) for which they submitted a report to the Hate Crime Statistics Program. Blanks indicate quarters for which agencies did not submit reports.

[2]Population figures are published only for the cities. The figures listed for the universities and colleges are student enrollment and were provided by the United States Department of Education for the 2008 school year, the most recent available. The enrollment figures include full-time and part-time students.

**Table 94. Hate Crime Incidents per Bias Motivation and Quarter, by State and Agency, 2009—*Continued***

| State | Agency type/Agency name | Number of incidents per bias motivation | | | | | Number of incidents per quarter[1] | | | | Popu- lation[2] |
|---|---|---|---|---|---|---|---|---|---|---|---|
| | | Race | Religion | Sexual orient- ation | Ethnicity | Disability | 1st quarter | 2nd quarter | 3rd quarter | 4th quarter | |
| | Seaside | 0 | 0 | 1 | 0 | 0 | 1 | | | | 6,300 |
| | Silverton | 0 | 0 | 0 | 1 | 0 | 0 | 1 | 0 | 0 | 9,895 |
| | Springfield | 4 | 0 | 0 | 0 | 0 | 0 | 4 | 0 | 0 | 57,653 |
| | Tigard | 11 | 0 | 0 | 1 | 0 | 4 | 4 | 4 | | 49,422 |
| | Troutdale | 2 | 2 | 0 | 1 | 0 | 5 | | | | 15,630 |
| | Winston | 1 | 0 | 0 | 0 | 0 | 0 | 0 | 1 | 0 | 5,622 |
| | Woodburn | 0 | 0 | 1 | 0 | 0 | 1 | 0 | 0 | 0 | 23,103 |
| | **Metropolitan Counties** | | 4 | 1 | 0 | 1 | 0 | | | | |
| | Benton | 1 | 0 | 0 | 0 | 0 | 0 | 1 | 0 | 0 | |
| | Clackamas | 0 | 1 | 0 | 1 | 0 | 1 | 1 | | | |
| | Lane | 3 | 0 | 0 | 0 | 0 | 1 | | 2 | | |
| | **Nonmetropolitan Counties** | | 6 | 0 | 1 | 1 | 0 | | | | |
| | Douglas | 4 | 0 | 1 | 0 | 0 | 1 | 1 | 3 | 0 | |
| | Lincoln | 1 | 0 | 0 | 0 | 0 | 0 | 1 | 0 | 0 | |
| | Tillamook | 0 | 0 | 0 | 1 | 0 | 1 | 0 | 0 | 0 | |
| | Umatilla | 1 | 0 | 0 | 0 | 0 | 0 | 1 | 0 | 0 | |
| **PENNSYLVANIA** ....... | **Total** | 27 | 10 | 5 | 4 | 0 | | | | | |
| | **Cities** | 22 | 10 | 3 | 4 | 0 | | | | | |
| | Abington Township | 3 | 0 | 0 | 0 | 0 | 3 | 0 | 0 | 0 | 53,761 |
| | Bedford | 1 | 0 | 0 | 0 | 0 | 0 | 0 | 0 | 1 | 2,984 |
| | Bensalem Township | 0 | 1 | 0 | 0 | 0 | 1 | 0 | 0 | 0 | 58,284 |
| | Ferguson Township | 1 | 0 | 0 | 0 | 0 | 0 | 0 | 1 | 0 | 16,747 |
| | Harrisburg | 3 | 1 | 1 | 2 | 0 | 2 | 2 | 0 | 3 | 46,961 |
| | Johnstown | 1 | 0 | 0 | 0 | 0 | 0 | 1 | 0 | 0 | 22,929 |
| | Lancaster | 3 | 0 | 0 | 1 | 0 | 0 | 2 | 1 | 1 | 54,441 |
| | Mechanicsburg | 0 | 1 | 0 | 0 | 0 | 1 | 0 | 0 | 0 | 8,688 |
| | Northern York Regional | 2 | 0 | 0 | 0 | 0 | 0 | 1 | 1 | 0 | 66,764 |
| | Patton Township | 1 | 0 | 0 | 0 | 0 | 0 | 0 | 1 | 0 | 13,425 |
| | Philadelphia | 2 | 4 | 0 | 0 | 0 | 4 | 2 | | 0 | 1,547,605 |
| | Pittsburgh | 2 | 2 | 2 | 1 | 0 | 1 | 3 | 3 | 0 | 312,232 |
| | Reading | 0 | 1 | 0 | 0 | 0 | 0 | 0 | 1 | 0 | 80,418 |
| | Springdale | 1 | 0 | 0 | 0 | 0 | 0 | 1 | 0 | 0 | 3,452 |
| | Springfield Township, Montgomery County | 1 | 0 | 0 | 0 | 0 | 0 | 0 | 1 | 0 | 18,778 |
| | West Pottsgrove Township | 1 | 0 | 0 | 0 | 0 | 0 | 0 | 1 | 0 | 3,755 |
| | **Universities and Colleges** | | 3 | 0 | 0 | 0 | 0 | | | | |
| | Pennsylvania State University, University Park | 1 | 0 | 0 | 0 | 0 | 0 | 0 | 0 | 1 | 44,406 |
| | West Chester University | 2 | 0 | 0 | 0 | 0 | 1 | 1 | 0 | 0 | 13,619 |
| | **State Police Agencies** | | 2 | 0 | 2 | 0 | 0 | | | | |
| | State Police: | | | | | | | | | | |
| | Bucks County | 0 | 0 | 1 | 0 | 0 | 1 | 0 | 0 | 0 | |
| | Chester County | 0 | 0 | 1 | 0 | 0 | 1 | 0 | 0 | | |
| | Washington County | 1 | 0 | 0 | 0 | 0 | 0 | 0 | 1 | 0 | |
| | Westmoreland County | 1 | 0 | 0 | 0 | 0 | 1 | 0 | 0 | 0 | |
| **RHODE ISLAND**........ | **Total** | 10 | 11 | 12 | 3 | 0 | | | | | |
| | **Cities** | 7 | 11 | 11 | 3 | 0 | | | | | |
| | Cranston | 0 | 0 | 2 | 0 | 0 | 0 | 0 | 0 | 2 | 80,223 |
| | East Providence | 1 | 0 | 0 | 0 | 0 | 0 | 0 | 1 | 0 | 48,557 |
| | Johnston | 2 | 0 | 0 | 0 | 0 | 2 | 0 | 0 | 0 | 28,617 |
| | Little Compton | 1 | 0 | 0 | 1 | 0 | 0 | 0 | 0 | 2 | 3,513 |
| | Newport | 0 | 0 | 1 | 0 | 0 | 0 | 0 | 1 | 0 | 23,260 |
| | North Smithfield | 0 | 1 | 0 | 0 | 0 | 0 | 0 | 0 | 1 | 11,640 |
| | Pawtucket | 2 | 2 | 0 | 0 | 0 | 0 | 3 | 1 | 0 | 71,787 |
| | Providence | 1 | 4 | 6 | 1 | 0 | 4 | 3 | 2 | 3 | 171,664 |
| | Smithfield | 0 | 1 | 0 | 0 | 0 | 0 | 0 | 0 | 1 | 21,289 |
| | South Kingstown | 0 | 0 | 1 | 0 | 0 | 1 | 0 | 0 | 0 | 29,270 |
| | Warwick | 0 | 2 | 1 | 0 | 0 | 2 | 1 | 0 | 0 | 84,488 |
| | West Warwick | 0 | 1 | 0 | 1 | 0 | 0 | 0 | 1 | 1 | 29,282 |
| | **Universities and Colleges** | | 3 | 0 | 1 | 0 | 0 | | | | |
| | University of Rhode Island | 3 | 0 | 1 | 0 | 0 | 0 | 1 | 0 | 3 | 15,904 |
| **SOUTH CAROLINA**.. | **Total** | 63 | 25 | 18 | 13 | 5 | | | | | |
| | **Cities** | 36 | 4 | 12 | 4 | 1 | | | | | |
| | Allendale | 0 | 0 | 1 | 0 | 0 | 1 | 0 | 0 | 0 | 3,617 |
| | Beaufort | 4 | 0 | 0 | 0 | 0 | 0 | 1 | 3 | 0 | 11,663 |
| | Calhoun Falls | 1 | 0 | 0 | 0 | 0 | 0 | 0 | 1 | 0 | 2,170 |
| | Cayce | 1 | 1 | 1 | 0 | 0 | 1 | 0 | 1 | 1 | 12,700 |
| | Clinton | 1 | 0 | 0 | 0 | 0 | 1 | 0 | 0 | 0 | 8,865 |
| | Clover | 0 | 0 | 1 | 0 | 0 | 1 | 0 | 0 | 0 | 5,032 |

[1]Agencies published in this table indicated that at least one hate crime incident occurred in their respective jurisdictions during the quarter(s) for which they submitted a report to the Hate Crime Statistics Program. Blanks indicate quarters for which agencies did not submit reports.

[2]Population figures are published only for the cities. The figures listed for the universities and colleges are student enrollment and were provided by the United States Department of Education for the 2008 school year, the most recent available. The enrollment figures include full-time and part-time students.

## Table 94. Hate Crime Incidents per Bias Motivation and Quarter, by State and Agency, 2009—*Continued*

| State | Agency type/Agency name | Number of incidents per bias motivation | | | | | Number of incidents per quarter[1] | | | | Popu-lation[2] |
|---|---|---|---|---|---|---|---|---|---|---|---|
| | | Race | Religion | Sexual orient-ation | Ethnicity | Disability | 1st quarter | 2nd quarter | 3rd quarter | 4th quarter | |
| | Columbia | 5 | 1 | 3 | 0 | 0 | 1 | 1 | 4 | 3 | 127,884 |
| | Cowpens | 1 | 0 | 0 | 0 | 0 | 0 | 0 | 0 | 1 | 2,428 |
| | Forest Acres | 1 | 0 | 0 | 0 | 0 | 0 | 1 | 0 | 0 | 9,859 |
| | Fort Mill | 0 | 0 | 0 | 1 | 0 | 0 | 0 | 0 | 1 | 10,316 |
| | Goose Creek | 0 | 1 | 1 | 1 | 0 | 2 | 0 | 1 | 0 | 38,770 |
| | Hampton | 1 | 0 | 0 | 0 | 0 | 1 | 0 | 0 | 0 | 2,745 |
| | Hartsville | 4 | 0 | 0 | 0 | 0 | 4 | 0 | 0 | 0 | 7,454 |
| | Holly Hill | 1 | 0 | 0 | 0 | 0 | 0 | 0 | 0 | 1 | 1,337 |
| | Lamar | 1 | 0 | 0 | 0 | 1 | 1 | 0 | 1 | 0 | 988 |
| | Latta | 0 | 0 | 1 | 0 | 0 | 1 | 0 | 0 | 0 | 1,485 |
| | Laurens | 1 | 0 | 0 | 0 | 0 | 0 | 0 | 0 | 1 | 9,582 |
| | Lexington | 2 | 0 | 0 | 1 | 0 | 0 | 2 | 0 | 1 | 16,628 |
| | Mauldin | 3 | 1 | 0 | 0 | 0 | 1 | 2 | 1 | 0 | 22,602 |
| | Mount Pleasant | 0 | 0 | 1 | 0 | 0 | 0 | 1 | 0 | 0 | 67,641 |
| | New Ellenton | 2 | 0 | 0 | 0 | 0 | 2 | 0 | 0 | 0 | 2,224 |
| | North Charleston | 0 | 0 | 0 | 1 | 0 | 0 | 1 | 0 | 0 | 95,982 |
| | Pacolet | 1 | 0 | 0 | 0 | 0 | 0 | 0 | 1 | 0 | 2,834 |
| | Pageland[3] | 0 | 0 | 1 | 0 | 0 | 0 | 1 | 0 | 0 | 2,512 |
| | Rock Hill | 3 | 0 | 0 | 0 | 0 | 1 | 0 | 1 | 1 | 69,506 |
| | Spartanburg | 1 | 0 | 1 | 0 | 0 | 0 | 0 | 2 | 0 | 39,561 |
| | Springdale | 1 | 0 | 0 | 0 | 0 | 1 | 0 | 0 | 0 | 2,946 |
| | Wellford | 0 | 0 | 1 | 0 | 0 | 0 | 1 | 0 | 0 | 2,479 |
| | York | 1 | 0 | 0 | 0 | 0 | 0 | 1 | 0 | 0 | 8,083 |
| | **Universities and Colleges** | | 1 | 0 | 1 | 0 | 1 | | | | |
| | Coastal Carolina University | 1 | 0 | 1 | 0 | 1 | 0 | 1 | 0 | 2 | 8,154 |
| | **Metropolitan Counties** | | 9 | 5 | 2 | 3 | 1 | | | | |
| | Aiken | 1 | 0 | 0 | 0 | 0 | 1 | 0 | 0 | 0 | |
| | Anderson | 0 | 1 | 0 | 0 | 0 | 1 | 0 | 0 | 0 | |
| | Berkeley | 4 | 0 | 0 | 0 | 0 | 1 | 0 | 1 | 2 | |
| | Greenville | 2 | 4 | 1 | 0 | 0 | 0 | 1 | 3 | 3 | |
| | Horry County Police Department | 1 | 0 | 0 | 0 | 0 | 0 | 0 | 1 | 0 | |
| | Laurens | 1 | 0 | 0 | 0 | 1 | 1 | 0 | 1 | 0 | |
| | Pickens | 0 | 0 | 1 | 1 | 0 | 0 | 0 | 0 | 2 | |
| | Richland | 0 | 0 | 0 | 2 | 0 | 1 | 1 | 0 | 0 | |
| | **Nonmetropolitan Counties** | | 17 | 16 | 3 | 4 | 2 | | | | |
| | Abbeville | 0 | 4 | 0 | 0 | 0 | 2 | 1 | 0 | 1 | |
| | Chester | 0 | 11 | 0 | 1 | 0 | 8 | 4 | 0 | 0 | |
| | Chesterfield | 0 | 0 | 0 | 0 | 1 | 0 | 1 | 0 | 0 | |
| | Clarendon | 0 | 0 | 0 | 1 | 0 | 0 | 0 | 1 | 0 | |
| | Colleton | 3 | 1 | 1 | 0 | 0 | 2 | 0 | 1 | 2 | |
| | Dillon | 1 | 0 | 1 | 1 | 0 | 1 | 1 | 0 | 1 | |
| | Georgetown | 1 | 0 | 0 | 0 | 0 | 0 | 0 | 1 | 0 | |
| | Greenwood | 1 | 0 | 0 | 0 | 0 | 0 | 1 | 0 | 0 | |
| | Hampton | 11 | 0 | 0 | 0 | 0 | 3 | 2 | 2 | 4 | |
| | Jasper | 0 | 0 | 0 | 1 | 0 | 0 | 0 | 1 | 0 | |
| | Lee | 0 | 0 | 1 | 0 | 1 | 0 | 1 | 1 | 0 | |
| | **Other Agencies** | | 0 | 0 | 0 | 2 | 0 | | | | |
| | Charleston County Aviation Authority | 0 | 0 | 0 | 2 | 0 | 0 | 0 | 2 | 0 | |
| SOUTH DAKOTA | **Total** | 26 | 5 | 4 | 7 | 0 | | | | | |
| | **Cities** | 22 | 5 | 3 | 7 | 0 | | | | | |
| | Miller | 1 | 0 | 0 | 0 | 0 | 1 | 0 | 0 | 0 | 1,321 |
| | Pierre | 0 | 2 | 0 | 0 | 0 | 0 | 1 | 1 | 0 | 13,901 |
| | Rapid City | 4 | 0 | 0 | 0 | 0 | 3 | 1 | 0 | 0 | 66,170 |
| | Sioux Falls | 11 | 3 | 3 | 5 | 0 | 6 | 6 | 4 | 6 | 158,672 |
| | Spearfish | 1 | 0 | 0 | 0 | 0 | 0 | 0 | 0 | 1 | 10,171 |
| | Tea | 2 | 0 | 0 | 0 | 0 | 1 | 1 | 0 | 0 | 4,073 |
| | Watertown | 2 | 0 | 0 | 2 | 0 | 0 | 1 | 2 | 1 | 20,515 |
| | Yankton | 1 | 0 | 0 | 0 | 0 | 1 | 0 | 0 | 0 | 13,831 |
| | **Metropolitan Counties** | | 3 | 0 | 0 | 0 | 0 | | | | |
| | Minnehaha | 3 | 0 | 0 | 0 | 0 | 0 | 1 | 2 | 0 | |
| | **Nonmetropolitan Counties** | | 1 | 0 | 1 | 0 | 0 | | | | |
| | Custer | 1 | 0 | 0 | 0 | 0 | 0 | 1 | 0 | 0 | |
| | Miner | 0 | 0 | 1 | 0 | 0 | 1 | 0 | 0 | 0 | |
| TENNESSEE | **Total** | 91 | 18 | 44 | 15 | 1 | | | | | |
| | **Cities** | 48 | 7 | 36 | 8 | 1 | | | | | |
| | Bartlett | 0 | 0 | 0 | 1 | 0 | 0 | 0 | 0 | 1 | 47,881 |
| | Bradford | 1 | 0 | 0 | 0 | 0 | 0 | 0 | 0 | 1 | 1,063 |
| | Chattanooga | 1 | 0 | 0 | 0 | 1 | 0 | 1 | 1 | 0 | 172,536 |
| | Clarksville | 1 | 0 | 2 | 0 | 0 | 1 | 1 | 0 | 1 | 121,661 |

[1]Agencies published in this table indicated that at least one hate crime incident occurred in their respective jurisdictions during the quarter(s) for which they submitted a report to the Hate Crime Statistics Program. Blanks indicate quarters for which agencies did not submit reports.

[2]Population figures are published only for the cities. The figures listed for the universities and colleges are student enrollment and were provided by the United States Department of Education for the 2008 school year, the most recent available. The enrollment figures include full-time and part-time students.

[3]Includes one incident reported with more than one bias motivation.

## Table 94. Hate Crime Incidents per Bias Motivation and Quarter, by State and Agency, 2009—*Continued*

| State | Agency type/Agency name | Number of incidents per bias motivation | | | | | Number of incidents per quarter[1] | | | | Population[2] |
|---|---|---|---|---|---|---|---|---|---|---|---|
| | | Race | Religion | Sexual orientation | Ethnicity | Disability | 1st quarter | 2nd quarter | 3rd quarter | 4th quarter | |
| | Cleveland | 6 | 0 | 1 | 0 | 0 | 2 | 3 | 1 | 1 | 40,024 |
| | Crossville | 0 | 0 | 1 | 0 | 0 | 1 | 0 | 0 | 0 | 11,908 |
| | Dickson | 1 | 0 | 0 | 0 | 0 | 0 | 1 | 0 | 0 | 14,095 |
| | Dunlap | 0 | 0 | 0 | 1 | 0 | 1 | 0 | 0 | 0 | 5,521 |
| | Elizabethton | 2 | 1 | 3 | 0 | 0 | 3 | 1 | 1 | 1 | 13,944 |
| | Franklin | 0 | 1 | 0 | 0 | 0 | 0 | 0 | 1 | 0 | 60,074 |
| | Greenbrier | 1 | 0 | 0 | 0 | 0 | 1 | 0 | 0 | 0 | 6,752 |
| | Hendersonville | 1 | 0 | 1 | 0 | 0 | 0 | 1 | 1 | 0 | 48,513 |
| | Humboldt | 1 | 0 | 1 | 0 | 0 | 0 | 2 | 0 | 0 | 9,126 |
| | Johnson City | 0 | 0 | 1 | 1 | 0 | 0 | 0 | 1 | 1 | 62,689 |
| | Kingsport | 1 | 0 | 1 | 0 | 0 | 0 | 0 | 1 | 1 | 44,402 |
| | Knoxville | 3 | 1 | 0 | 0 | 0 | 2 | 0 | 2 | 0 | 185,850 |
| | Lebanon | 2 | 0 | 0 | 0 | 0 | 0 | 0 | 2 | 0 | 25,161 |
| | Lexington | 5 | 0 | 0 | 0 | 0 | 0 | 2 | 0 | 3 | 7,908 |
| | Livingston | 1 | 0 | 0 | 0 | 0 | 0 | 0 | 1 | 0 | 3,574 |
| | Memphis | 11 | 3 | 18 | 3 | 0 | 12 | 7 | 10 | 6 | 667,421 |
| | Murfreesboro | 1 | 0 | 0 | 0 | 0 | 0 | 1 | 0 | 0 | 105,910 |
| | Nashville | 1 | 0 | 4 | 1 | 0 | 4 | 2 | 0 | 0 | 610,176 |
| | Newport | 1 | 0 | 0 | 0 | 0 | 0 | 0 | 1 | 0 | 7,539 |
| | Savannah | 1 | 0 | 0 | 0 | 0 | 0 | 1 | 0 | 0 | 7,354 |
| | Sevierville | 1 | 0 | 0 | 0 | 0 | 0 | 1 | 0 | 0 | 17,489 |
| | Sewanee | 0 | 1 | 0 | 1 | 0 | 0 | 1 | 0 | 1 | 2,613 |
| | Smyrna | 1 | 0 | 0 | 0 | 0 | 1 | 0 | 0 | 0 | 39,260 |
| | Spring Hill | 2 | 0 | 0 | 0 | 0 | 1 | 1 | 0 | 0 | 29,870 |
| | Tracy City | 0 | 0 | 3 | 0 | 0 | 0 | 0 | 2 | 1 | 1,649 |
| | Union City | 1 | 0 | 0 | 0 | 0 | 0 | 1 | 0 | 0 | 10,533 |
| | Wartrace | 1 | 0 | 0 | 0 | 0 | 0 | 1 | 0 | 0 | 593 |
| | **Universities and Colleges** | | 7 | 1 | 1 | 0 | 0 | | | | |
| | Tennessee Technological University | 1 | 0 | 0 | 0 | 0 | 0 | 1 | 0 | 0 | 10,793 |
| | University of Memphis | 0 | 1 | 0 | 0 | 0 | 0 | 0 | 0 | 1 | 20,220 |
| | University of Tennessee: | | | | | | | | | | |
| | Chattanooga | 1 | 0 | 0 | 0 | 0 | 0 | 0 | 0 | 1 | 9,807 |
| | Knoxville | 4 | 0 | 1 | 0 | 0 | 2 | 0 | 2 | 1 | 30,410 |
| | Walters State Community College | 1 | 0 | 0 | 0 | 0 | 0 | 0 | 1 | 0 | 5,918 |
| | **Metropolitan Counties** | | 23 | 8 | 4 | 3 | 0 | | | | |
| | Anderson | 1 | 1 | 0 | 0 | 0 | 1 | 0 | 0 | 1 | |
| | Bradley | 0 | 4 | 0 | 0 | 0 | 2 | 2 | 0 | 0 | |
| | Cheatham | 0 | 1 | 0 | 0 | 0 | 1 | 0 | 0 | 0 | |
| | Dickson | 0 | 0 | 0 | 1 | 0 | 0 | 1 | 0 | 0 | |
| | Hamilton | 2 | 0 | 0 | 0 | 0 | 0 | 1 | 0 | 1 | |
| | Knox | 1 | 0 | 1 | 1 | 0 | 0 | 1 | 2 | 0 | |
| | Loudon | 2 | 0 | 0 | 0 | 0 | 0 | 0 | 0 | 2 | |
| | Montgomery | 1 | 0 | 0 | 0 | 0 | 1 | 0 | 0 | 0 | |
| | Rutherford | 1 | 0 | 0 | 0 | 0 | 0 | 0 | 0 | 1 | |
| | Shelby | 12 | 2 | 0 | 1 | 0 | 3 | 1 | 3 | 8 | |
| | Sullivan | 0 | 0 | 3 | 0 | 0 | 0 | 0 | 1 | 2 | |
| | Tipton | 1 | 0 | 0 | 0 | 0 | 0 | 1 | 0 | 0 | |
| | Washington | 2 | 0 | 0 | 0 | 0 | 0 | 0 | 2 | 0 | |
| | **Nonmetropolitan Counties** | | 12 | 2 | 3 | 2 | 0 | | | | |
| | Fentress | 0 | 1 | 0 | 0 | 0 | 1 | 0 | 0 | 0 | |
| | Grundy | 1 | 0 | 0 | 0 | 0 | 0 | 1 | 0 | 0 | |
| | Hardin | 0 | 0 | 2 | 0 | 0 | 0 | 0 | 2 | 0 | |
| | Lawrence | 2 | 0 | 0 | 0 | 0 | 1 | 0 | 0 | 1 | |
| | Marshall | 0 | 0 | 1 | 1 | 0 | 0 | 1 | 0 | 1 | |
| | Monroe | 1 | 0 | 0 | 0 | 0 | 0 | 1 | 0 | 0 | |
| | Scott | 0 | 0 | 0 | 1 | 0 | 0 | 1 | 0 | 0 | |
| | Van Buren | 8 | 0 | 0 | 0 | 0 | 1 | 2 | 5 | 0 | |
| | Weakley | 0 | 1 | 0 | 0 | 0 | 0 | 0 | 0 | 1 | |
| | **State Police Agencies** | | 0 | 0 | 0 | 2 | 0 | | | | |
| | Department of Safety | 0 | 0 | 0 | 2 | 0 | 1 | 0 | 1 | 0 | |
| | **Other Agencies** | | 1 | 0 | 0 | 0 | 0 | | | | |
| | Tennessee Bureau of Investigation | 1 | 0 | 0 | 0 | 0 | 0 | 0 | 1 | 0 | |
| **TEXAS** | **Total** | 84 | 18 | 36 | 27 | 0 | | | | | |
| | **Cities** | 74 | 16 | 29 | 27 | 0 | | | | | |
| | Allen | 1 | 0 | 0 | 0 | 0 | 1 | 0 | 0 | 0 | 86,901 |
| | Alvin | 0 | 0 | 0 | 1 | 0 | 0 | 0 | 0 | 1 | 23,013 |
| | Argyle | 0 | 0 | 0 | 1 | 0 | 0 | 0 | 1 | 0 | 3,681 |
| | Austin | 3 | 1 | 4 | 3 | 0 | 2 | 2 | 3 | 4 | 768,970 |
| | Beaumont | 5 | 0 | 0 | 0 | 0 | 3 | 0 | 2 | 0 | 110,237 |

[1]Agencies published in this table indicated that at least one hate crime incident occurred in their respective jurisdictions during the quarter(s) for which they submitted a report to the Hate Crime Statistics Program. Blanks indicate quarters for which agencies did not submit reports.

[2]Population figures are published only for the cities. The figures listed for the universities and colleges are student enrollment and were provided by the United States Department of Education for the 2008 school year, the most recent available. The enrollment figures include full-time and part-time students.

## Table 94. Hate Crime Incidents per Bias Motivation and Quarter, by State and Agency, 2009—*Continued*

| State | Agency type/Agency name | Number of incidents per bias motivation | | | | | Number of incidents per quarter[1] | | | | Popu-lation[2] |
|---|---|---|---|---|---|---|---|---|---|---|---|
| | | Race | Religion | Sexual orient-ation | Ethnicity | Disability | 1st quarter | 2nd quarter | 3rd quarter | 4th quarter | |
| | Bedford | 3 | 0 | 0 | 0 | 0 | 0 | 0 | 3 | 0 | 49,375 |
| | Bellmead | 0 | 0 | 0 | 1 | 0 | 0 | 1 | 0 | 0 | 9,610 |
| | Brownwood | 0 | 0 | 1 | 0 | 0 | 0 | 1 | 0 | 0 | 19,115 |
| | Burleson | 1 | 0 | 0 | 0 | 0 | 0 | 0 | 1 | 0 | 36,807 |
| | Carrollton | 1 | 0 | 1 | 0 | 0 | 2 | 0 | 0 | 0 | 127,432 |
| | Cleburne | 0 | 0 | 1 | 0 | 0 | 1 | 0 | 0 | 0 | 30,287 |
| | Corpus Christi | 2 | 1 | 1 | 0 | 0 | 1 | 1 | 2 | 0 | 287,507 |
| | Dallas | 3 | 2 | 3 | 3 | 0 | 3 | 2 | 3 | 3 | 1,290,266 |
| | Del Rio | 1 | 0 | 0 | 0 | 0 | 1 | 0 | 0 | 0 | 36,996 |
| | Denison | 1 | 0 | 0 | 1 | 0 | 0 | 0 | 0 | 2 | 24,142 |
| | Denton | 1 | 0 | 1 | 0 | 0 | 0 | 1 | 0 | 1 | 124,308 |
| | Eastland | 2 | 0 | 0 | 0 | 0 | 0 | 0 | 0 | 2 | 3,888 |
| | El Paso | 0 | 1 | 2 | 0 | 0 | 2 | 0 | 0 | 1 | 618,812 |
| | Fort Worth | 3 | 2 | 0 | 1 | 0 | 2 | 3 | 1 | 0 | 723,456 |
| | Frisco | 1 | 0 | 0 | 0 | 0 | 0 | 1 | 0 | 0 | 108,244 |
| | Galveston | 0 | 0 | 3 | 2 | 0 | 2 | 0 | 2 | 1 | 57,040 |
| | Garland | 2 | 0 | 0 | 0 | 0 | 2 | 0 | 0 | 0 | 218,872 |
| | Greenville | 1 | 0 | 0 | 0 | 0 | 0 | 0 | 0 | 1 | 25,865 |
| | Harlingen | 0 | 0 | 0 | 1 | 0 | 0 | 0 | 1 | 0 | 65,552 |
| | Highland Village | 1 | 0 | 0 | 0 | 0 | 0 | 0 | 0 | 1 | 17,317 |
| | Houston | 4 | 1 | 5 | 4 | 0 | 4 | 3 | 5 | 2 | 2,273,771 |
| | Kilgore | 1 | 0 | 0 | 0 | 0 | 1 | 0 | 0 | 0 | 12,094 |
| | Killeen | 4 | 1 | 0 | 1 | 0 | 2 | 0 | 2 | 2 | 120,670 |
| | Lake Dallas | 0 | 0 | 0 | 1 | 0 | 0 | 1 | 0 | 0 | 8,011 |
| | Lake Jackson | 1 | 0 | 0 | 0 | 0 | 0 | 1 | 0 | 0 | 27,531 |
| | La Porte | 1 | 0 | 0 | 0 | 0 | 0 | 1 | 0 | 0 | 34,535 |
| | Leander | 1 | 0 | 0 | 0 | 0 | 0 | 0 | 1 | 0 | 28,646 |
| | Longview | 1 | 0 | 0 | 0 | 0 | 1 | 0 | 0 | 0 | 77,663 |
| | Mansfield | 1 | 0 | 0 | 0 | 0 | 0 | 0 | 1 | 0 | 48,710 |
| | McKinney | 1 | 1 | 1 | 0 | 0 | 0 | 1 | 1 | 1 | 132,146 |
| | Midland | 2 | 0 | 0 | 0 | 0 | 0 | 0 | 2 | 0 | 107,933 |
| | Mineral Wells | 1 | 0 | 0 | 0 | 0 | 0 | 0 | 0 | 1 | 16,872 |
| | Missouri City | 1 | 1 | 0 | 0 | 0 | 0 | 1 | 1 | 0 | 77,543 |
| | New Braunfels | 0 | 0 | 0 | 1 | 0 | 1 | 0 | 0 | 0 | 55,584 |
| | North Richland Hills | 3 | 1 | 0 | 0 | 0 | 2 | 1 | 1 | 0 | 66,181 |
| | Odessa | 0 | 0 | 0 | 1 | 0 | 0 | 1 | 0 | 0 | 99,770 |
| | Overton | 1 | 0 | 0 | 0 | 0 | 0 | 0 | 0 | 1 | 2,381 |
| | Paris | 1 | 0 | 0 | 0 | 0 | 0 | 0 | 0 | 1 | 26,080 |
| | Pasadena | 0 | 0 | 1 | 1 | 0 | 1 | 0 | 0 | 1 | 146,963 |
| | Pearland | 0 | 0 | 1 | 0 | 0 | 0 | 0 | 1 | 0 | 88,528 |
| | Plano | 2 | 1 | 0 | 0 | 0 | 0 | 0 | 1 | 2 | 272,747 |
| | Richland Hills | 1 | 0 | 1 | 0 | 0 | 0 | 1 | 0 | 1 | 8,090 |
| | Rockwall | 2 | 0 | 0 | 0 | 0 | 1 | 1 | 0 | 0 | 37,856 |
| | Round Rock | 4 | 2 | 0 | 1 | 0 | 0 | 5 | 2 | 0 | 110,531 |
| | San Antonio | 3 | 1 | 3 | 2 | 0 | 2 | 2 | 4 | 1 | 1,373,936 |
| | Sweetwater | 1 | 0 | 0 | 0 | 0 | 1 | 0 | 0 | 0 | 10,581 |
| | Texas City | 1 | 0 | 0 | 0 | 0 | 1 | 0 | 0 | 0 | 44,807 |
| | Trophy Club | 1 | 0 | 0 | 0 | 0 | 0 | 0 | 1 | 0 | 8,276 |
| | Vidor | 1 | 0 | 0 | 0 | 0 | 1 | 0 | 0 | 0 | 11,023 |
| | Weatherford | 1 | 0 | 0 | 0 | 0 | 0 | 1 | 0 | 0 | 27,667 |
| | Wichita Falls | 1 | 0 | 0 | 1 | 0 | 0 | 0 | 1 | 1 | 100,884 |
| | **Universities and Colleges** | | 2 | 0 | 1 | 0 | 0 | | | | |
| | Grayson County College | 0 | 0 | 1 | 0 | 0 | 0 | 0 | 1 | 0 | 3,676 |
| | Richland College | 1 | 0 | 0 | 0 | 0 | 0 | 0 | 1 | 0 | 15,917 |
| | University of Texas, Austin | 1 | 0 | 0 | 0 | 0 | 1 | 0 | 0 | 0 | 49,984 |
| | **Metropolitan Counties** | | 6 | 2 | 5 | 0 | 0 | | | | |
| | Harris | 6 | 2 | 3 | 0 | 0 | 3 | 2 | 5 | 1 | |
| | Lubbock | 0 | 0 | 2 | 0 | 0 | 0 | 1 | 0 | 1 | |
| | **Nonmetropolitan Counties** | | 2 | 0 | 1 | 0 | 0 | | | | |
| | Anderson | 1 | 0 | 0 | 0 | 0 | 0 | 0 | 1 | 0 | |
| | Cherokee | 0 | 0 | 1 | 0 | 0 | 0 | 1 | 0 | 0 | |
| | Colorado | 1 | 0 | 0 | 0 | 0 | 0 | 1 | 0 | 0 | |
| **UTAH** ........................... | **Total** | 13 | 15 | 8 | 12 | 0 | | | | | |
| | **Cities** | | 8 | 12 | 7 | 10 | 0 | | | | |
| | Draper | 0 | 1 | 2 | 3 | 0 | 2 | 2 | 0 | 2 | 44,537 |
| | Farmington | 0 | 1 | 0 | 0 | 0 | 0 | 0 | 1 | 0 | 17,788 |
| | Midvale | 1 | 0 | 0 | 0 | 0 | 0 | 1 | 0 | 0 | 28,099 |
| | Orem | 1 | 0 | 0 | 0 | 0 | 0 | 0 | 0 | 1 | 93,785 |
| | Provo | 1 | 0 | 0 | 0 | 0 | 0 | 0 | 1 | 0 | 119,472 |
| | Salt Lake City | 0 | 2 | 0 | 0 | 0 | 0 | 0 | 1 | 1 | 180,724 |
| | Sandy | 0 | 1 | 0 | 1 | 0 | 0 | 0 | 1 | 1 | 97,031 |

[1]Agencies published in this table indicated that at least one hate crime incident occurred in their respective jurisdictions during the quarter(s) for which they submitted a report to the Hate Crime Statistics Program. Blanks indicate quarters for which agencies did not submit reports.

[2]Population figures are published only for the cities. The figures listed for the universities and colleges are student enrollment and were provided by the United States Department of Education for the 2008 school year, the most recent available. The enrollment figures include full-time and part-time students.

# Table 94. Hate Crime Incidents per Bias Motivation and Quarter, by State and Agency, 2009—*Continued*

| State | Agency type/Agency name | Number of incidents per bias motivation | | | | | Number of incidents per quarter[1] | | | | Popu-lation[2] |
|---|---|---|---|---|---|---|---|---|---|---|---|
| | | Race | Religion | Sexual orient-ation | Ethnicity | Disability | 1st quarter | 2nd quarter | 3rd quarter | 4th quarter | |
| | Saratoga Springs | 1 | 0 | 0 | 0 | 0 | 0 | 0 | 1 | 0 | 21,450 |
| | South Jordan | 3 | 3 | 0 | 0 | 0 | 1 | 0 | 0 | 5 | 54,042 |
| | South Salt Lake | 0 | 0 | 0 | 1 | 0 | 0 | 0 | 0 | 1 | 21,448 |
| | Springville | 0 | 0 | 0 | 1 | 0 | 1 | 0 | 0 | 0 | 29,395 |
| | St. George | 0 | 1 | 0 | 1 | 0 | 0 | 1 | 1 | 0 | 75,391 |
| | Tooele | 0 | 0 | 3 | 0 | 0 | 1 | 0 | 1 | 1 | 30,851 |
| | West Bountiful | 0 | 1 | 0 | 0 | 0 | 1 | 0 | 0 | 0 | 5,402 |
| | West Jordan | 0 | 1 | 0 | 0 | 0 | 1 | 0 | 0 | 0 | 107,113 |
| | West Valley | 1 | 0 | 2 | 3 | 0 | 2 | 0 | 1 | 3 | 124,472 |
| | Woods Cross | 0 | 1 | 0 | 0 | 0 | 1 | 0 | 0 | 0 | 8,946 |
| | **Metropolitan Counties** | | 2 | 2 | 1 | 2 | 0 | | | | |
| | Davis | 0 | 0 | 0 | 1 | 0 | 1 | 0 | 0 | 0 | |
| | Salt Lake | 0 | 2 | 1 | 0 | 0 | 1 | 0 | 0 | 2 | |
| | Tooele | 1 | 0 | 0 | 1 | 0 | 2 | 0 | 0 | 0 | |
| | Washington | 1 | 0 | 0 | 0 | 0 | 0 | 0 | 0 | 1 | |
| | **Nonmetropolitan Counties** | | 1 | 0 | 0 | 0 | 0 | | | | |
| | Uintah | 1 | 0 | 0 | 0 | 0 | 0 | 0 | 0 | 1 | |
| | **Other Agencies** | | 2 | 1 | 0 | 0 | 0 | | | | |
| | Granite School District | 1 | 0 | 0 | 0 | 0 | 0 | 1 | 0 | 0 | |
| | Utah Transit Authority | 1 | 1 | 0 | 0 | 0 | 0 | 1 | 1 | 0 | |
| **VERMONT** | **Total** | | 8 | 8 | 7 | 0 | 1 | | | | |
| | **Cities** | | 5 | 6 | 7 | 0 | 1 | | | | |
| | Burlington | 2 | 1 | 3 | 0 | 0 | 0 | 2 | 4 | 0 | 38,794 |
| | Colchester | 0 | 1 | 1 | 0 | 0 | 1 | 1 | 0 | 0 | 17,274 |
| | Essex | 1 | 0 | 0 | 0 | 0 | 1 | 0 | 0 | 0 | 19,759 |
| | Hinesburg | 0 | 1 | 0 | 0 | 0 | 0 | 1 | 0 | 0 | 4,660 |
| | Ludlow | 0 | 1 | 0 | 0 | 0 | 1 | 0 | 0 | 0 | 2,659 |
| | Lyndonville | 0 | 0 | 0 | 0 | 1 | 1 | 0 | 0 | 0 | 1,214 |
| | Manchester | 0 | 1 | 0 | 0 | 0 | 1 | 0 | 0 | 0 | 4,279 |
| | Shelburne | 0 | 1 | 0 | 0 | 0 | 0 | 1 | 0 | 0 | 7,161 |
| | South Burlington | 0 | 0 | 3 | 0 | 0 | 2 | 0 | 1 | 0 | 17,893 |
| | Woodstock | 2 | 0 | 0 | 0 | 0 | 0 | 0 | 2 | 0 | 3,122 |
| | **Universities and Colleges** | | 0 | 1 | 0 | 0 | 0 | | | | |
| | University of Vermont | 0 | 1 | 0 | 0 | 0 | 0 | 1 | 0 | 0 | 12,800 |
| | **Nonmetropolitan Counties** | | 1 | 0 | 0 | 0 | 0 | | | | |
| | Caledonia | 1 | 0 | 0 | 0 | 0 | 0 | 0 | 1 | 0 | |
| | **State Police Agencies** | | 2 | 1 | 0 | 0 | 0 | | | | |
| | State Police: | | | | | | | | | | |
| | Middlesex | 0 | 1 | 0 | 0 | 0 | 0 | 0 | 0 | 1 | |
| | Shaftsbury | 1 | 0 | 0 | 0 | 0 | 1 | 0 | 0 | 0 | |
| | St. Albans | 1 | 0 | 0 | 0 | 0 | 0 | 0 | 1 | 0 | |
| **VIRGINIA** | **Total** | | 97 | 27 | 18 | 8 | 0 | | | | |
| | **Cities** | | 54 | 16 | 12 | 8 | 0 | | | | |
| | Alexandria | 3 | 1 | 0 | 0 | 0 | 1 | 0 | 2 | 1 | 146,145 |
| | Bedford | 1 | 0 | 0 | 0 | 0 | 1 | 0 | 0 | 0 | 6,335 |
| | Bluefield | 0 | 0 | 1 | 0 | 0 | 0 | 0 | 0 | 1 | 5,122 |
| | Charlottesville | 3 | 0 | 0 | 0 | 0 | 2 | 0 | 1 | 0 | 41,798 |
| | Chesapeake | 2 | 0 | 2 | 0 | 0 | 1 | 0 | 0 | 3 | 223,261 |
| | Christiansburg | 1 | 0 | 0 | 0 | 0 | 0 | 0 | 1 | 0 | 19,775 |
| | Colonial Beach | 1 | 0 | 0 | 0 | 0 | 0 | 0 | 1 | 0 | 3,859 |
| | Colonial Heights | 1 | 0 | 0 | 0 | 0 | 0 | 1 | 0 | 0 | 17,932 |
| | Covington | 1 | 0 | 0 | 0 | 0 | 1 | 0 | 0 | 0 | 6,124 |
| | Culpeper | 0 | 0 | 0 | 1 | 0 | 0 | 0 | 0 | 1 | 14,562 |
| | Danville | 2 | 0 | 0 | 0 | 0 | 1 | 0 | 0 | 1 | 44,442 |
| | Fairfax City | 2 | 1 | 0 | 1 | 0 | 1 | 1 | 1 | 1 | 24,194 |
| | Falls Church | 1 | 0 | 0 | 0 | 0 | 0 | 0 | 1 | 0 | 11,301 |
| | Fredericksburg | 0 | 0 | 0 | 1 | 0 | 0 | 1 | 0 | 0 | 23,326 |
| | Front Royal | 0 | 0 | 1 | 0 | 0 | 0 | 1 | 0 | 0 | 14,731 |
| | Galax | 0 | 0 | 0 | 1 | 0 | 1 | 0 | 0 | 0 | 6,828 |
| | Hampton | 1 | 0 | 0 | 0 | 0 | 0 | 0 | 1 | 0 | 145,932 |
| | Harrisonburg | 1 | 1 | 0 | 0 | 0 | 0 | 1 | 1 | 0 | 44,597 |
| | Leesburg | 1 | 1 | 0 | 1 | 0 | 1 | 0 | 1 | 1 | 41,092 |
| | Lynchburg | 2 | 0 | 1 | 0 | 0 | 2 | 1 | 0 | 0 | 73,735 |
| | Manassas | 0 | 0 | 1 | 0 | 0 | 0 | 0 | 1 | 0 | 35,321 |
| | Manassas Park | 0 | 1 | 0 | 0 | 0 | 1 | 0 | 0 | 0 | 11,477 |
| | Marion | 1 | 0 | 0 | 0 | 0 | 0 | 0 | 0 | 1 | 5,965 |
| | Newport News | 2 | 1 | 0 | 1 | 0 | 0 | 0 | 3 | 1 | 180,174 |
| | Norfolk | 2 | 3 | 3 | 0 | 0 | 0 | 5 | 1 | 2 | 235,097 |
| | Pearisburg | 1 | 0 | 0 | 0 | 0 | 1 | 0 | 0 | 0 | 2,767 |
| | Portsmouth | 5 | 0 | 0 | 0 | 0 | 0 | 4 | 0 | 1 | 100,970 |
| | Purcellville | 2 | 0 | 0 | 0 | 0 | 0 | 1 | 1 | 0 | 5,338 |
| | Richmond | 6 | 3 | 1 | 0 | 0 | 0 | 2 | 3 | 5 | 203,233 |
| | Roanoke | 1 | 0 | 0 | 0 | 0 | 0 | 1 | 0 | 0 | 93,110 |

[1]Agencies published in this table indicated that at least one hate crime incident occurred in their respective jurisdictions during the quarter(s) for which they submitted a report to the Hate Crime Statistics Program. Blanks indicate quarters for which agencies did not submit reports.

[2]Population figures are published only for the cities. The figures listed for the universities and colleges are student enrollment and were provided by the United States Department of Education for the 2008 school year, the most recent available. The enrollment figures include full-time and part-time students.

## Table 94. Hate Crime Incidents per Bias Motivation and Quarter, by State and Agency, 2009—*Continued*

| State | Agency type/Agency name | Number of incidents per bias motivation | | | | | Number of incidents per quarter[1] | | | | Population[2] |
|---|---|---|---|---|---|---|---|---|---|---|---|
| | | Race | Religion | Sexual orientation | Ethnicity | Disability | 1st quarter | 2nd quarter | 3rd quarter | 4th quarter | |
| | Salem | 0 | 1 | 0 | 0 | 0 | 0 | 0 | 1 | 0 | 25,616 |
| | Suffolk | 3 | 1 | 0 | 1 | 0 | 0 | 2 | 2 | 1 | 84,929 |
| | Virginia Beach | 7 | 2 | 2 | 1 | 0 | 2 | 2 | 2 | 6 | 436,175 |
| | Waynesboro | 1 | 0 | 0 | 0 | 0 | 0 | 0 | 1 | 0 | 22,313 |
| | **Universities and Colleges** | | 9 | 4 | 2 | 0 | 0 | | | | |
| | College of William and Mary | 1 | 0 | 0 | 0 | 0 | 0 | 0 | 0 | 1 | 7,892 |
| | George Mason University | 0 | 0 | 1 | 0 | 0 | 0 | 0 | 0 | 1 | 30,613 |
| | Hampton University | 1 | 0 | 0 | 0 | 0 | 0 | 0 | 0 | 1 | 5,427 |
| | Northern Virginia Community College | 2 | 0 | 0 | 0 | 0 | 0 | 0 | 1 | 1 | 42,663 |
| | Old Dominion University | 0 | 1 | 0 | 0 | 0 | 1 | 0 | 0 | 0 | 23,086 |
| | Radford University | 3 | 1 | 0 | 0 | 0 | 0 | 0 | 0 | 4 | 9,157 |
| | University of Virginia | 0 | 1 | 1 | 0 | 0 | 0 | 2 | 0 | 0 | 24,541 |
| | Virginia Polytechnic Institute and State University | 2 | 1 | 0 | 0 | 0 | 0 | 0 | 2 | 1 | 30,739 |
| | **Metropolitan Counties** | | 32 | 7 | 4 | 0 | 0 | | | | |
| | Albemarle County Police Department | 1 | 1 | 0 | 0 | 0 | 0 | 1 | 1 | 0 | |
| | Amelia | 1 | 0 | 0 | 0 | 0 | 0 | 1 | 0 | 0 | |
| | Amherst | 1 | 0 | 0 | 0 | 0 | 0 | 0 | 1 | 0 | |
| | Arlington County Police Department | 0 | 2 | 0 | 0 | 0 | 0 | 0 | 1 | 1 | |
| | Bedford | 1 | 0 | 0 | 0 | 0 | 0 | 0 | 0 | 1 | |
| | Botetourt | 1 | 0 | 0 | 0 | 0 | 0 | 1 | 0 | 0 | |
| | Chesterfield County Police Department | 3 | 1 | 1 | 0 | 0 | 2 | 2 | 1 | 0 | |
| | Clarke | 1 | 0 | 0 | 0 | 0 | 0 | 0 | 1 | 0 | |
| | Cumberland | 1 | 0 | 0 | 0 | 0 | 1 | 0 | 0 | 0 | |
| | Dinwiddie | 1 | 0 | 1 | 0 | 0 | 0 | 0 | 0 | 2 | |
| | Fairfax County Police Department | 2 | 0 | 0 | 0 | 0 | 0 | 0 | 0 | 2 | |
| | Greene | 0 | 1 | 0 | 0 | 0 | 1 | 0 | 0 | 0 | |
| | Henrico County Police Department | 6 | 1 | 0 | 0 | 0 | 3 | 2 | 1 | 1 | |
| | James City County Police Department | 2 | 0 | 0 | 0 | 0 | 0 | 0 | 1 | 1 | |
| | King and Queen | 1 | 0 | 0 | 0 | 0 | 1 | 0 | 0 | 0 | |
| | Loudoun | 3 | 0 | 1 | 0 | 0 | 0 | 2 | 2 | 0 | |
| | New Kent | 0 | 1 | 0 | 0 | 0 | 0 | 0 | 0 | 1 | |
| | Prince William County Police Department | 1 | 0 | 0 | 0 | 0 | 0 | 0 | 0 | 1 | |
| | Roanoke County Police Department | 1 | 0 | 0 | 0 | 0 | 0 | 1 | 0 | 0 | |
| | Spotsylvania | 1 | 0 | 0 | 0 | 0 | 0 | 1 | 0 | 0 | |
| | Stafford | 1 | 0 | 0 | 0 | 0 | 0 | 1 | 0 | 0 | |
| | Warren | 2 | 0 | 0 | 0 | 0 | 1 | 0 | 0 | 1 | |
| | York | 1 | 0 | 1 | 0 | 0 | 0 | 1 | 1 | 0 | |
| | **Nonmetropolitan Counties** | | 2 | 0 | 0 | 0 | 0 | | | | |
| | Augusta | 1 | 0 | 0 | 0 | 0 | 1 | 0 | 0 | 0 | |
| | Charlotte | 1 | 0 | 0 | 0 | 0 | 0 | 1 | 0 | 0 | |
| **WASHINGTON** .......... | **Total** | | 120 | 27 | 36 | 25 | 0 | | | | |
| | **Cities** | | 76 | 20 | 24 | 18 | 0 | | | | |
| | Auburn | 2 | 0 | 0 | 1 | 0 | 0 | 0 | 1 | 2 | 56,934 |
| | Bellevue | 1 | 1 | 1 | 1 | 0 | 1 | 1 | 1 | 1 | 125,054 |
| | Bellingham | 0 | 0 | 1 | 1 | 0 | 1 | 0 | 0 | 1 | 80,243 |
| | Burien | 1 | 0 | 0 | 0 | 0 | 0 | 1 | 0 | 0 | 31,263 |
| | Burlington | 1 | 0 | 0 | 0 | 0 | 0 | 1 | | 0 | 8,920 |
| | Camas | 1 | 0 | 0 | 0 | 0 | 0 | 1 | 0 | 0 | 18,618 |
| | Cheney | 1 | 0 | 1 | 0 | 0 | 0 | 1 | 0 | 1 | 10,572 |
| | Edmonds | 2 | 1 | 0 | 0 | 0 | 0 | 2 | 1 | 0 | 40,227 |
| | Everett | 1 | 0 | 1 | 0 | 0 | 0 | 1 | 1 | 0 | 98,431 |
| | Federal Way | 3 | 1 | 0 | 0 | 0 | 1 | 0 | 3 | 0 | 84,219 |
| | Kelso | 1 | 0 | 0 | 0 | 0 | 1 | 0 | 0 | 0 | 12,226 |
| | Kennewick | 1 | 0 | 0 | 3 | 0 | 1 | 0 | 2 | 1 | 64,009 |
| | Lakewood | 0 | 0 | 0 | 1 | 0 | 0 | 1 | 0 | 0 | 56,824 |
| | Lynden | 1 | 1 | 0 | 0 | 0 | 0 | 1 | 1 | 0 | 12,022 |
| | Maple Valley | 1 | 0 | 0 | 0 | 0 | 0 | 0 | 1 | 0 | 20,700 |
| | Mill Creek | 0 | 0 | 1 | 0 | 0 | 0 | 0 | 0 | 1 | 17,270 |
| | Monroe | 0 | 0 | 0 | 1 | 0 | 0 | 0 | 0 | 1 | 17,458 |
| | Moses Lake | 1 | 0 | 0 | 0 | 0 | 1 | 0 | 0 | 0 | 19,214 |

[1]Agencies published in this table indicated that at least one hate crime incident occurred in their respective jurisdictions during the quarter(s) for which they submitted a report to the Hate Crime Statistics Program. Blanks indicate quarters for which agencies did not submit reports.

[2]Population figures are published only for the cities. The figures listed for the universities and colleges are student enrollment and were provided by the United States Department of Education for the 2008 school year, the most recent available. The enrollment figures include full-time and part-time students.

## Table 94. Hate Crime Incidents per Bias Motivation and Quarter, by State and Agency, 2009—*Continued*

| State | Agency type/Agency name | Number of incidents per bias motivation | | | | | Number of incidents per quarter[1] | | | | Popu-lation[2] |
|---|---|---|---|---|---|---|---|---|---|---|---|
| | | Race | Religion | Sexual orient-ation | Ethnicity | Disability | 1st quarter | 2nd quarter | 3rd quarter | 4th quarter | |
| | Mossyrock | 1 | 0 | 0 | 0 | 0 | 0 | 1 | 0 | 0 | 505 |
| | Mountlake Terrace | 0 | 2 | 0 | 0 | 0 | 0 | | 0 | 2 | 19,853 |
| | Mount Vernon | 1 | 0 | 0 | 0 | 0 | 1 | 0 | 0 | 0 | 32,096 |
| | Olympia | 0 | 0 | 2 | 0 | 0 | 0 | 0 | 1 | 1 | 45,603 |
| | Pasco | 1 | 0 | 0 | 0 | 0 | 0 | 0 | 1 | 0 | 58,316 |
| | Pullman | 1 | 0 | 0 | 0 | 0 | 0 | 0 | 1 | 0 | 27,141 |
| | Redmond | 0 | 2 | 0 | 0 | 0 | 1 | 0 | 1 | 0 | 50,009 |
| | Richland | 1 | 0 | 0 | 1 | 0 | 1 | 0 | 1 | 0 | 47,040 |
| | SeaTac | 1 | 0 | 0 | 0 | 0 | 0 | 1 | 0 | 0 | 25,886 |
| | Seattle | 3 | 2 | 9 | 0 | 0 | 4 | 4 | 3 | 3 | 602,531 |
| | Sequim | 1 | 0 | 0 | 0 | 0 | 0 | 1 | 0 | 0 | 5,979 |
| | Shelton | 2 | 0 | 0 | 1 | 0 | 0 | 1 | 1 | 1 | 9,372 |
| | Shoreline | 0 | 0 | 0 | 1 | 0 | 1 | 0 | 0 | 0 | 51,877 |
| | Snoqualmie | 2 | 3 | 0 | 0 | 0 | 0 | 5 | 0 | 0 | 9,772 |
| | Spokane | 18 | 3 | 6 | 1 | 0 | 5 | 7 | 11 | 5 | 202,932 |
| | Spokane Valley | 1 | 0 | 0 | 0 | 0 | 1 | 0 | 0 | 0 | 86,756 |
| | Tacoma | 9 | 1 | 0 | 1 | 0 | 5 | 1 | 3 | 2 | 197,557 |
| | Tukwila | 1 | 0 | 0 | 0 | 0 | 0 | 1 | | 0 | 17,084 |
| | Vancouver | 12 | 1 | 2 | 4 | 0 | 6 | 8 | 4 | 1 | 165,147 |
| | Walla Walla | 3 | 1 | 0 | 0 | 0 | 2 | 2 | 0 | 0 | 30,658 |
| | Yakima | 0 | 1 | 0 | 1 | 0 | 1 | 1 | | | 84,167 |
| | **Universities and Colleges** | | 1 | 1 | 2 | 0 | 0 | | | | |
| | Eastern Washington University | 0 | 0 | 1 | 0 | 0 | 0 | 1 | 0 | 0 | 10,809 |
| | Evergreen State College | 1 | 1 | 0 | 0 | 0 | 0 | 1 | 1 | 0 | 4,696 |
| | Washington State University, Pullman | 0 | 0 | 1 | 0 | 0 | 1 | 0 | 0 | 0 | 25,352 |
| | **Metropolitan Counties** | | 42 | 6 | 7 | 7 | 0 | | | | |
| | Clark | 15 | 2 | 1 | 1 | 0 | 5 | 8 | 4 | 2 | |
| | King | 6 | 0 | 2 | 4 | 0 | 1 | 3 | 3 | 5 | |
| | Kitsap | 2 | 1 | 1 | 0 | 0 | 2 | 1 | 1 | 0 | |
| | Pierce | 7 | 0 | 3 | 1 | 0 | 2 | 2 | 4 | 3 | |
| | Snohomish | 5 | 0 | 0 | 0 | 0 | 0 | 2 | 3 | | |
| | Spokane | 2 | 1 | 0 | 0 | 0 | 2 | 0 | 1 | 0 | |
| | Thurston | 5 | 2 | 0 | 1 | 0 | 2 | 1 | 2 | 3 | |
| | **Nonmetropolitan Counties** | | 1 | 0 | 3 | 0 | 0 | | | | |
| | Garfield | 1 | 0 | 0 | 0 | 0 | 0 | 1 | 0 | 0 | |
| | Grays Harbor | 0 | 0 | 2 | 0 | 0 | 1 | 1 | 0 | 0 | |
| | Walla Walla | 0 | 0 | 1 | 0 | 0 | 0 | 0 | 0 | 1 | |
| WEST VIRGINIA........ | **Total** | | 18 | 1 | 3 | 1 | 1 | | | | |
| | **Cities** | | 11 | 1 | 3 | 0 | 1 | | | | |
| | Buckhannon | 1 | 0 | 0 | 0 | 0 | 0 | 0 | 0 | 1 | 5,476 |
| | Clarksburg | 1 | 1 | 0 | 0 | 0 | 1 | 0 | 0 | 1 | 16,409 |
| | Fairmont | 1 | 0 | 0 | 0 | 0 | 1 | 0 | 0 | 0 | 18,997 |
| | Huntington | 2 | 0 | 0 | 0 | 0 | 0 | 0 | 2 | 0 | 48,904 |
| | Martinsburg | 0 | 0 | 1 | 0 | 0 | 0 | 0 | 0 | 1 | 17,275 |
| | Morgantown | 1 | 0 | 0 | 0 | 0 | 1 | 0 | 0 | 0 | 29,989 |
| | Moundsville | 2 | 0 | 0 | 0 | 0 | 0 | 0 | 0 | 2 | 9,019 |
| | South Charleston | 0 | 0 | 1 | 0 | 0 | 0 | 0 | 0 | 1 | 12,326 |
| | Weirton | 3 | 0 | 0 | 0 | 1 | 2 | 0 | 2 | 0 | 18,577 |
| | Wheeling | 0 | 0 | 1 | 0 | 0 | 0 | 1 | 0 | 0 | 28,660 |
| | **Universities and Colleges** | | 2 | 0 | 0 | 0 | 0 | | | | |
| | Marshall University | 2 | 0 | 0 | 0 | 0 | 1 | 0 | 1 | 0 | 13,573 |
| | **Metropolitan Counties** | | 3 | 0 | 0 | 1 | 0 | | | | |
| | Berkeley | 1 | 0 | 0 | 0 | 0 | 0 | 1 | 0 | 0 | |
| | Jefferson | 1 | 0 | 0 | 0 | 0 | 0 | 1 | 0 | 0 | |
| | Kanawha | 1 | 0 | 0 | 0 | 0 | 0 | 0 | 1 | 0 | |
| | Monongalia | 0 | 0 | 0 | 1 | 0 | 0 | 0 | 1 | 0 | |
| | **Nonmetropolitan Counties** | | 2 | 0 | 0 | 0 | 0 | | | | |
| | Summers | 1 | 0 | 0 | 0 | 0 | 0 | 0 | 0 | 1 | |
| | Upshur | 1 | 0 | 0 | 0 | 0 | 0 | 1 | 0 | 0 | |
| WISCONSIN................. | **Total** | | 29 | 9 | 11 | 5 | 0 | | | | |
| | **Cities** | | 25 | 7 | 7 | 4 | 0 | | | | |
| | Appleton | 4 | 0 | 0 | 1 | 0 | 0 | 1 | 2 | 2 | 70,294 |
| | Everest | 1 | 0 | 1 | 0 | 0 | 1 | 0 | 0 | 1 | 15,718 |
| | Fond du Lac | 0 | 2 | 0 | 0 | 0 | 2 | 0 | 0 | 0 | 42,001 |
| | Hudson | 1 | 0 | 0 | 0 | 0 | 0 | 0 | 0 | 1 | 12,623 |
| | Janesville | 1 | 0 | 0 | 0 | 0 | 0 | 0 | 1 | 0 | 62,761 |
| | Kewaunee | 0 | 1 | 0 | 0 | 0 | 0 | 1 | 0 | 0 | 2,748 |
| | Luxemburg | 0 | 1 | 0 | 0 | 0 | 0 | 0 | 1 | 0 | 2,271 |
| | Madison | 2 | 0 | 0 | 0 | 0 | 1 | 1 | 0 | 0 | 234,461 |
| | Manitowoc | 2 | 0 | 1 | 0 | 0 | 1 | 0 | 2 | 0 | 33,056 |

[1]Agencies published in this table indicated that at least one hate crime incident occurred in their respective jurisdictions during the quarter(s) for which they submitted a report to the Hate Crime Statistics Program. Blanks indicate quarters for which agencies did not submit reports.

[2]Population figures are published only for the cities. The figures listed for the universities and colleges are student enrollment and were provided by the United States Department of Education for the 2008 school year, the most recent available. The enrollment figures include full-time and part-time students.

## Table 94. Hate Crime Incidents per Bias Motivation and Quarter, by State and Agency, 2009—*Continued*

| State | Agency type/Agency name | Number of incidents per bias motivation | | | | | Number of incidents per quarter[1] | | | | Population[2] |
|---|---|---|---|---|---|---|---|---|---|---|---|
| | | Race | Religion | Sexual orientation | Ethnicity | Disability | 1st quarter | 2nd quarter | 3rd quarter | 4th quarter | |
| | Merrill | 1 | 0 | 0 | 0 | 0 | 0 | 1 | 0 | 0 | 9,617 |
| | Milwaukee | 10 | 2 | 2 | 2 | 0 | 3 | 5 | 5 | 3 | 604,673 |
| | Rhinelander | 0 | 0 | 3 | 0 | 0 | 0 | 1 | 0 | 2 | 7,602 |
| | River Falls | 1 | 1 | 0 | 1 | 0 | 0 | 1 | 1 | 1 | 14,549 |
| | Shiocton | 1 | 0 | 0 | 0 | 0 | 0 | 0 | 1 | 0 | 913 |
| | Watertown | 1 | 0 | 0 | 0 | 0 | 0 | 1 | 0 | 0 | 23,066 |
| | **Universities and Colleges** | | 0 | 0 | 1 | 0 | 0 | | | | |
| | University of Wisconsin, Whitewater | 0 | 0 | 1 | 0 | 0 | 0 | 0 | 0 | 1 | 10,962 |
| | **Metropolitan Counties** | | 4 | 1 | 3 | 1 | 0 | | | | |
| | Dane | 2 | 1 | 3 | 0 | 0 | 0 | 3 | 3 | 0 | |
| | La Crosse | 1 | 0 | 0 | 0 | 0 | 1 | 0 | 0 | 0 | |
| | Outagamie | 0 | 0 | 0 | 1 | 0 | 0 | 1 | 0 | 0 | |
| | Racine | 1 | 0 | 0 | 0 | 0 | 0 | 1 | 0 | 0 | |
| | **Nonmetropolitan Counties** | | 0 | 1 | 0 | 0 | 0 | | | | |
| | Clark | 0 | 1 | 0 | 0 | 0 | 0 | 0 | 0 | 1 | |
| **WYOMING** | **Total** | | 5 | 0 | 0 | 3 | 0 | | | | |
| | **Cities** | | 5 | 0 | 0 | 3 | 0 | | | | |
| | Gillette | 4 | 0 | 0 | 1 | 0 | 2 | 1 | 2 | 0 | 27,709 |
| | Green River | 0 | 0 | 0 | 1 | 0 | 1 | 0 | 0 | 0 | 12,194 |
| | Jackson | 0 | 0 | 0 | 1 | 0 | 0 | 0 | 0 | 1 | 9,937 |
| | Riverton | 1 | 0 | 0 | 0 | 0 | 0 | 0 | 1 | 0 | 10,123 |

[1]Agencies published in this table indicated that at least one hate crime incident occurred in their respective jurisdictions during the quarter(s) for which they submitted a report to the Hate Crime Statistics Program. Blanks indicate quarters for which agencies did not submit reports.

[2]Population figures are published only for the cities. The figures listed for the universities and colleges are student enrollment and were provided by the United States Department of Education for the 2008 school year, the most recent available. The enrollment figures include full-time and part-time students.

# Table 95. Hate Crime Zero Data Submitted per Quarter by State and Agency, 2009

(Number.)

| State | Agency type | Agency name | Zero data per quarter[1] | | | | Population[2] |
|---|---|---|---|---|---|---|---|
| | | | 1st quarter | 2nd quarter | 3rd quarter | 4th quarter | |
| **ALABAMA** | **Cities** | Abbeville | 0 | 0 | 0 | 0 | 2,932 |
| | | Adamsville | 0 | 0 | 0 | 0 | 4,704 |
| | | Addison | 0 | 0 | 0 | 0 | 710 |
| | | Alexander City | 0 | 0 | 0 | 0 | 15,057 |
| | | Anniston | 0 | 0 | 0 | 0 | 23,598 |
| | | Arab | 0 | 0 | 0 | 0 | 8,007 |
| | | Ardmore | 0 | 0 | 0 | 0 | 1,275 |
| | | Ashford | 0 | | 0 | 0 | 2,087 |
| | | Ashland | 0 | 0 | 0 | 0 | 1,873 |
| | | Ashville | 0 | 0 | 0 | 0 | 2,599 |
| | | Atmore | 0 | 0 | 0 | 0 | 7,396 |
| | | Attalla | 0 | 0 | 0 | 0 | 6,514 |
| | | Auburn | 0 | 0 | 0 | 0 | 57,342 |
| | | Bay Minette | 0 | 0 | 0 | 0 | 8,065 |
| | | Berry | 0 | 0 | 0 | 0 | 1,184 |
| | | Bessemer | 0 | 0 | 0 | 0 | 28,372 |
| | | Boaz | 0 | 0 | 0 | 0 | 8,418 |
| | | Brewton | 0 | 0 | 0 | 0 | 5,257 |
| | | Brilliant | 0 | 0 | 0 | 0 | 717 |
| | | Brundidge | 0 | 0 | 0 | 0 | 2,262 |
| | | Butler | 0 | 0 | 0 | 0 | 1,687 |
| | | Calera | 0 | 0 | 0 | 0 | 12,159 |
| | | Centre | | | | 0 | 3,522 |
| | | Chatom | 0 | 0 | 0 | 0 | 1,161 |
| | | Chickasaw | 0 | 0 | 0 | 0 | 5,906 |
| | | Childersburg | 0 | 0 | 0 | 0 | 4,991 |
| | | Clanton | 0 | 0 | 0 | | 8,943 |
| | | Clayhatchee | 0 | 0 | 0 | 0 | 492 |
| | | Clio | 0 | 0 | 0 | 0 | 2,211 |
| | | Coffeeville | 0 | | | | 342 |
| | | Columbiana | 0 | 0 | 0 | 0 | 3,873 |
| | | Coosada | 0 | 0 | 0 | 0 | 1,676 |
| | | Courtland | 0 | 0 | 0 | 0 | 763 |
| | | Creola | 0 | 0 | 0 | 0 | 2,086 |
| | | Crossville | 0 | 0 | 0 | 0 | 1,515 |
| | | Cullman | 0 | 0 | 0 | 0 | 15,412 |
| | | Dadeville | 0 | 0 | 0 | 0 | 3,231 |
| | | Daleville | 0 | 0 | 0 | 0 | 4,535 |
| | | Daphne | 0 | 0 | 0 | 0 | 19,368 |
| | | Dauphin Island | 0 | 0 | 0 | 0 | 1,610 |
| | | Demopolis | 0 | 0 | 0 | 0 | 7,297 |
| | | Dora | 0 | 0 | 0 | 0 | 2,424 |
| | | Dothan | 0 | 0 | 0 | 0 | 67,496 |
| | | Douglas | 0 | 0 | 0 | 0 | 601 |
| | | Dozier | 0 | 0 | 0 | 0 | 396 |
| | | Elberta | 0 | 0 | 0 | 0 | 1,474 |
| | | Enterprise | 0 | 0 | 0 | 0 | 25,868 |
| | | Eutaw | 0 | 0 | 0 | 0 | 2,948 |
| | | Fairfield | 0 | 0 | 0 | 0 | 11,212 |
| | | Fairhope | 0 | 0 | 0 | 0 | 17,723 |
| | | Falkville | 0 | 0 | 0 | 0 | 1,165 |
| | | Fayette | 0 | 0 | 0 | 0 | 4,766 |
| | | Flomaton | 0 | 0 | 0 | 0 | 1,532 |
| | | Florence | 0 | 0 | 0 | 0 | 38,055 |
| | | Foley | 0 | 0 | 0 | 0 | 14,566 |
| | | Fort Payne | 0 | 0 | 0 | 0 | 14,189 |
| | | Gadsden | 0 | 0 | 0 | 0 | 36,595 |
| | | Gantt | 0 | | | | 237 |
| | | Geneva | 0 | 0 | 0 | 0 | 4,448 |
| | | Georgiana | 0 | 0 | 0 | 0 | 1,549 |
| | | Geraldine | 0 | 0 | 0 | 0 | 845 |
| | | Glencoe | 0 | 0 | 0 | 0 | 5,399 |
| | | Grove Hill | 0 | | | | 1,332 |
| | | Gulf Shores | 0 | 0 | 0 | 0 | 10,947 |
| | | Guntersville | 0 | 0 | 0 | 0 | 8,510 |
| | | Hackleburg | 0 | 0 | | | 1,440 |
| | | Hamilton | 0 | 0 | 0 | 0 | 6,350 |
| | | Hammondville | 0 | 0 | 0 | 0 | 547 |
| | | Hartford | 0 | 0 | | | 2,432 |
| | | Helena | 0 | 0 | | 0 | 15,192 |
| | | Henagar | 0 | 0 | 0 | 0 | 2,597 |
| | | Highland Lake | 0 | 0 | 0 | 0 | 511 |
| | | Hillsboro | 0 | 0 | 0 | | 589 |
| | | Hollywood | 0 | 0 | 0 | 0 | 921 |
| | | Huntsville | 0 | 0 | 0 | 0 | 178,601 |
| | | Irondale | 0 | 0 | 0 | 0 | 9,666 |
| | | Jackson | 0 | 0 | 0 | 0 | 5,069 |
| | | Killen | 0 | 0 | 0 | 0 | 1,145 |
| | | Kimberly | 0 | 0 | 0 | 0 | 2,887 |
| | | Lafayette | 0 | 0 | 0 | 0 | 2,858 |
| | | Lake View | 0 | 0 | 0 | 0 | 2,468 |
| | | Lanett | 0 | | | | 7,038 |
| | | Leeds | 0 | 0 | 0 | 0 | 11,398 |
| | | Leighton | 0 | 0 | 0 | 0 | 827 |
| | | Level Plains | 0 | 0 | 0 | 0 | 1,507 |
| | | Lincoln | | | | 0 | 5,963 |
| | | Linden | 0 | 0 | 0 | 0 | 2,237 |
| | | Lineville | 0 | 0 | 0 | 0 | 2,371 |
| | | Livingston | 0 | 0 | 0 | 0 | 2,993 |
| | | Lockhart | 0 | 0 | 0 | 0 | 538 |
| | | Loxley | 0 | 0 | 0 | 0 | 1,830 |
| | | Madison | 0 | 0 | 0 | 0 | 39,880 |
| | | Marion | 0 | 0 | 0 | 0 | 3,270 |
| | | Mentone | 0 | 0 | 0 | | 485 |
| | | Midfield | 0 | 0 | 0 | 0 | 5,139 |
| | | Midland City | 0 | 0 | 0 | 0 | 1,904 |
| | | Millbrook | 0 | 0 | 0 | 0 | 17,383 |
| | | Montevallo | 0 | 0 | 0 | 0 | 6,469 |
| | | Moody | | | | 0 | 14,175 |
| | | Morris | 0 | 0 | 0 | 0 | 1,894 |
| | | Mountain Brook | 0 | 0 | 0 | 0 | 21,094 |
| | | Muscle Shoals | 0 | 0 | 0 | 0 | 13,125 |
| | | Myrtlewood | 0 | 0 | 0 | 0 | 129 |
| | | Napier Field | 0 | 0 | 0 | | 395 |
| | | New Hope | 0 | 0 | 0 | 0 | 2,778 |
| | | New Site | 0 | 0 | 0 | 0 | 829 |
| | | Newton | 0 | 0 | 0 | 0 | 1,647 |
| | | Newville | 0 | 0 | 0 | 0 | 542 |
| | | Northport | 0 | 0 | 0 | 0 | 23,498 |
| | | Odenville | | | 0 | 0 | 2,291 |
| | | Ohatchee | 0 | 0 | 0 | 0 | 1,247 |
| | | Oneonta | 0 | 0 | 0 | 0 | 7,220 |
| | | Opelika | 0 | 0 | 0 | 0 | 27,087 |
| | | Opp | 0 | 0 | 0 | 0 | 6,555 |
| | | Oxford | 0 | 0 | 0 | 0 | 20,808 |
| | | Pelham | 0 | 0 | 0 | 0 | 22,172 |
| | | Phenix City | 0 | 0 | | | 31,438 |
| | | Phil Campbell | 0 | 0 | 0 | 0 | 1,048 |
| | | Pickensville | 0 | 0 | 0 | 0 | 627 |
| | | Piedmont | 0 | 0 | 0 | 0 | 4,952 |
| | | Pine Hill | 0 | 0 | 0 | 0 | 907 |
| | | Prichard | 0 | 0 | 0 | 0 | 27,560 |
| | | Rainbow City | 0 | 0 | 0 | 0 | 9,425 |
| | | Rainsville | 0 | 0 | 0 | 0 | 5,046 |
| | | Red Bay | 0 | 0 | | 0 | 3,288 |
| | | Red Level | 0 | 0 | 0 | 0 | 547 |
| | | Reform | 0 | 0 | 0 | 0 | 1,771 |
| | | Roanoke | 0 | 0 | 0 | 0 | 6,701 |
| | | Robertsdale | 0 | 0 | 0 | 0 | 5,111 |
| | | Russellville | 0 | 0 | 0 | 0 | 8,913 |
| | | Samson | 0 | 0 | 0 | 0 | 2,025 |
| | | Saraland | 0 | 0 | 0 | 0 | 13,019 |
| | | Sardis City | 0 | 0 | 0 | 0 | 2,206 |
| | | Scottsboro | 0 | | | | 15,015 |
| | | Section | 0 | 0 | 0 | 0 | 758 |
| | | Selma | 0 | 0 | 0 | 0 | 18,679 |
| | | Sheffield | 0 | 0 | | | 9,072 |
| | | Silas | 0 | 0 | 0 | 0 | 470 |
| | | Sipsey | 0 | 0 | 0 | 0 | 542 |
| | | Slocomb | 0 | 0 | 0 | 0 | 2,046 |
| | | Snead | 0 | 0 | 0 | 0 | 860 |
| | | Springville | 0 | 0 | 0 | 0 | 3,814 |
| | | Stevenson | 0 | 0 | 0 | 0 | 2,015 |
| | | Sulligent | 0 | 0 | 0 | 0 | 1,949 |
| | | Summerdale | 0 | 0 | 0 | 0 | 756 |

[1]Agencies published in this table indicated that no hate crimes occurred in their jurisdictions during the quarter(s) for which they submitted reports to the Hate Crime program. Blanks indicate quarters for which agencies did not submit reports.

[2]Population figures are published only for the cities. The figures listed for the universities and colleges are student enrollment and were provided by the United States Department of Education for the 2008 school year, the most recent available. The enrollment figures include full-time and part-time students.

## Table 95. Hate Crime Zero Data Submitted per Quarter, by State and Agency, 2009—*Continued*

(Number.)

| State | Agency type | Agency name | Zero data per quarter[1] 1st quarter | 2nd quarter | 3rd quarter | 4th quarter | Population[2] |
|---|---|---|---|---|---|---|---|
| ALABAMA | | Sylacauga | 0 | 0 | 0 | 0 | 12,844 |
| | | Talladega | 0 | 0 | 0 | 0 | 16,902 |
| | | Tarrant | 0 | 0 | 0 | 0 | 6,445 |
| | | Taylor | 0 | 0 | 0 | 0 | 2,004 |
| | | Town Creek | 0 | 0 | 0 | 0 | 1,208 |
| | | Triana | 0 | 0 | 0 | 0 | 493 |
| | | Trinity | 0 | 0 | 0 | 0 | 2,003 |
| | | Troy | 0 | 0 | 0 | 0 | 15,278 |
| | | Trussville | 0 | 0 | 0 | 0 | 19,596 |
| | | Tuscaloosa | 0 | 0 | 0 | 0 | 91,688 |
| | | Uniontown | 0 | 0 | 0 | 0 | 1,397 |
| | | Valley Head | 0 | 0 | 0 | 0 | 654 |
| | | Vance | 0 | 0 | 0 | 0 | 1,018 |
| | | Vernon | 0 | 0 | 0 | 0 | 1,867 |
| | | Vestavia Hills | 0 | 0 | 0 | 0 | 30,906 |
| | | Weaver | 0 | 0 | 0 | 0 | 2,738 |
| | | Wetumpka | 0 | 0 | 0 | 0 | 7,964 |
| | | Winfield | 0 | 0 | 0 | 0 | 4,626 |
| | Universities and Colleges | Calhoun Community College[3] | 0 | 0 | 0 | 0 | |
| | | Jacksonville State University | 0 | 0 | 0 | 0 | 9,481 |
| | | Troy University | 0 | 0 | 0 | 0 | 28,303 |
| | | University of Alabama: | | | | | |
| | | Birmingham | 0 | 0 | 0 | 0 | 16,149 |
| | | Huntsville | 0 | 0 | 0 | 0 | 7,431 |
| | | University of Montevallo | 0 | 0 | 0 | 0 | 3,023 |
| | | University of South Alabama | 0 | 0 | 0 | 0 | 14,064 |
| | | University of West Alabama | 0 | 0 | 0 | 0 | 4,888 |
| | Metropolitan Counties | Autauga | 0 | 0 | 0 | 0 | |
| | | Bibb | 0 | 0 | 0 | 0 | |
| | | Blount | 0 | 0 | 0 | 0 | |
| | | Colbert | 0 | 0 | 0 | 0 | |
| | | Elmore | 0 | 0 | | | |
| | | Greene | 0 | | | | |
| | | Hale | 0 | 0 | 0 | 0 | |
| | | Henry | 0 | 0 | 0 | 0 | |
| | | Houston | 0 | 0 | 0 | 0 | |
| | | Jefferson | | | | 0 | |
| | | Lee | 0 | | | 0 | |
| | | Lowndes | 0 | 0 | 0 | 0 | |
| | | Madison | 0 | 0 | 0 | 0 | |
| | | Mobile | 0 | 0 | 0 | 0 | |
| | | Morgan | | | | 0 | |
| | | Russell | 0 | 0 | 0 | 0 | |
| | | Shelby | 0 | 0 | 0 | 0 | |
| | | Tuscaloosa | 0 | 0 | 0 | 0 | |
| | | Walker | 0 | 0 | 0 | 0 | |
| | Nonmetropolitan Counties | Baldwin | 0 | | | | |
| | | Choctaw | 0 | 0 | 0 | 0 | |
| | | Cleburne | 0 | 0 | 0 | 0 | |
| | | Coffee | 0 | 0 | 0 | 0 | |
| | | Coosa | 0 | 0 | 0 | 0 | |
| | | Covington | 0 | 0 | 0 | 0 | |
| | | Crenshaw | 0 | 0 | 0 | 0 | |
| | | Cullman | 0 | 0 | 0 | 0 | |
| | | Dale | 0 | 0 | 0 | 0 | |
| | | Dallas | 0 | 0 | 0 | 0 | |
| | | De Kalb | 0 | 0 | 0 | 0 | |
| | | Escambia | 0 | 0 | 0 | 0 | |
| | | Lamar | 0 | 0 | 0 | 0 | |
| | | Macon | 0 | 0 | 0 | 0 | |
| | | Marengo | 0 | 0 | 0 | 0 | |
| | | Marshall | 0 | 0 | 0 | 0 | |
| | | Perry | 0 | 0 | 0 | 0 | |
| | | Pike | 0 | 0 | 0 | 0 | |
| | | Randolph | 0 | 0 | | | |
| | | Talladega | 0 | 0 | 0 | 0 | |
| | | Tallapoosa | 0 | 0 | 0 | 0 | |
| | Other Agencies | 24th Judicial Circuit Drug and Violent Crime Task Force | 0 | 0 | | | |
| ARIZONA | Cities | Apache Junction | 0 | 0 | 0 | 0 | 32,869 |
| | | Benson | 0 | 0 | 0 | 0 | 4,863 |
| | | Bisbee | 0 | 0 | | 0 | 5,965 |
| | | Camp Verde | 0 | 0 | 0 | 0 | 11,012 |
| | | Chino Valley | 0 | 0 | 0 | 0 | 11,453 |
| | | Clarkdale | 0 | 0 | 0 | 0 | 4,374 |
| | | Clifton | 0 | 0 | 0 | 0 | 2,438 |
| | | Colorado City | 0 | 0 | 0 | 0 | 4,934 |
| | | Cottonwood | 0 | 0 | 0 | 0 | 11,664 |
| | | Douglas | 0 | 0 | 0 | 0 | 17,622 |
| | | Eagar | 0 | 0 | 0 | 0 | 4,541 |
| | | El Mirage | 0 | 0 | 0 | 0 | 28,196 |
| | | Eloy | 0 | 0 | 0 | 0 | 13,049 |
| | | Flagstaff | 0 | 0 | 0 | 0 | 61,072 |
| | | Florence | 0 | 0 | 0 | 0 | 21,229 |
| | | Fredonia | 0 | 0 | 0 | 0 | 1,135 |
| | | Gilbert | 0 | 0 | 0 | 0 | 231,799 |
| | | Globe | 0 | 0 | 0 | | 7,167 |
| | | Goodyear | 0 | 0 | 0 | 0 | 67,390 |
| | | Holbrook | 0 | 0 | 0 | 0 | 5,094 |
| | | Huachuca City | 0 | 0 | 0 | 0 | 1,988 |
| | | Kingman | 0 | 0 | 0 | 0 | 28,700 |
| | | Mammoth | 0 | 0 | 0 | 0 | 2,682 |
| | | Marana | 0 | 0 | 0 | 0 | 38,028 |
| | | Maricopa | 0 | 0 | 0 | 0 | 52,200 |
| | | Miami | 0 | 0 | 0 | 0 | 1,762 |
| | | Nogales | 0 | 0 | | 0 | 19,433 |
| | | Oro Valley | 0 | 0 | | | 44,854 |
| | | Paradise Valley | 0 | 0 | 0 | 0 | 15,141 |
| | | Parker | 0 | 0 | 0 | 0 | 3,180 |
| | | Payson | 0 | 0 | 0 | 0 | 15,701 |
| | | Pima | 0 | 0 | | 0 | 2,173 |
| | | Pinetop-Lakeside | 0 | 0 | 0 | 0 | 4,654 |
| | | Prescott | 0 | 0 | 0 | 0 | 43,748 |
| | | Quartzsite | 0 | 0 | 0 | 0 | 3,497 |
| | | Safford | 0 | | 0 | 0 | 9,894 |
| | | Sahuarita | 0 | 0 | 0 | 0 | 28,201 |
| | | Sedona | 0 | 0 | 0 | 0 | 11,759 |
| | | Snowflake-Taylor | 0 | 0 | 0 | 0 | 10,084 |
| | | Somerton | 0 | 0 | 0 | 0 | 13,041 |
| | | South Tucson | 0 | 0 | 0 | 0 | 6,071 |
| | | Springerville | | 0 | 0 | 0 | 1,994 |
| | | Surprise | 0 | 0 | 0 | 0 | 104,692 |
| | | Thatcher | 0 | 0 | 0 | 0 | 5,122 |
| | | Tolleson | 0 | 0 | 0 | | 7,498 |
| | | Tombstone | 0 | | | 0 | 1,573 |
| | | Wellton | 0 | 0 | 0 | 0 | 1,916 |
| | | Wickenburg | 0 | 0 | 0 | 0 | 6,707 |
| | | Willcox | 0 | 0 | 0 | 0 | 3,807 |
| | | Williams | 0 | 0 | 0 | 0 | 3,361 |
| | | Winslow | 0 | 0 | 0 | 0 | 9,903 |
| | | Youngtown | 0 | 0 | 0 | 0 | 5,177 |
| | | Yuma | 0 | 0 | 0 | 0 | 91,433 |
| | Universities and Colleges | Central Arizona College | 0 | 0 | 0 | 0 | 5,865 |
| | | Yavapai College | 0 | 0 | 0 | 0 | 9,033 |

[1]Agencies published in this table indicated that no hate crimes occurred in their jurisdictions during the quarter(s) for which they submitted reports to the Hate Crime Statistics Program. Blanks indicate quarters for which agencies did not submit reports.

[2]Population figures are published only for the cities. The figures listed for the universities and colleges are student enrollment and were provided by the United States Department of Education for the 2008 school year, the most recent available. The enrollment figures include full-time and part-time students.

[3]Student enrollment figures were not available.

## Table 95. Hate Crime Zero Data Submitted per Quarter, by State and Agency, 2009—*Continued*

(Number.)

| State | Agency type | Agency name | Zero data per quarter[1] | | | | Population[2] |
|---|---|---|---|---|---|---|---|
| | | | 1st quarter | 2nd quarter | 3rd quarter | 4th quarter | |
| **ARIZONA** | **Metropolitan Counties** | Coconino | 0 | 0 | 0 | 0 | |
| | | Mohave | 0 | 0 | 0 | 0 | |
| | | Yuma | 0 | 0 | 0 | 0 | |
| | **Nonmetropolitan Counties** | Apache | 0 | 0 | 0 | 0 | |
| | | Cochise | 0 | 0 | 0 | 0 | |
| | | Gila | 0 | 0 | 0 | 0 | |
| | | Graham | 0 | 0 | 0 | 0 | |
| | | Greenlee | 0 | 0 | 0 | 0 | |
| | | La Paz | 0 | 0 | 0 | 0 | |
| | | Navajo | 0 | 0 | 0 | 0 | |
| | | Santa Cruz | 0 | 0 | 0 | 0 | |
| | **State Police Agencies** | Arizona Department of Public Safety | 0 | 0 | 0 | 0 | |
| | **Other Agencies** | Tucson Airport Authority | 0 | 0 | 0 | 0 | |
| **ARKANSAS** .. | **Cities** | Alma | 0 | 0 | 0 | 0 | 5,219 |
| | | Arkansas City | 0 | 0 | 0 | 0 | 510 |
| | | Ashdown | 0 | 0 | 0 | 0 | 4,405 |
| | | Ash Flat | 0 | 0 | 0 | 0 | 1,106 |
| | | Atkins | 0 | 0 | 0 | 0 | 2,968 |
| | | Augusta | 0 | 0 | 0 | 0 | 2,210 |
| | | Austin | 0 | 0 | 0 | 0 | 2,054 |
| | | Bald Knob | 0 | 0 | 0 | 0 | 3,443 |
| | | Bay | 0 | 0 | 0 | 0 | 2,055 |
| | | Bearden | 0 | 0 | 0 | 0 | 977 |
| | | Bella Vista | 0 | 0 | 0 | 0 | 27,167 |
| | | Benton | 0 | 0 | 0 | 0 | 30,276 |
| | | Bentonville | 0 | 0 | 0 | 0 | 37,816 |
| | | Blytheville | 0 | 0 | 0 | 0 | 15,889 |
| | | Bono | 0 | 0 | 0 | 0 | 1,608 |
| | | Booneville | 0 | 0 | 0 | 0 | 4,083 |
| | | Bradford | 0 | 0 | 0 | 0 | 859 |
| | | Brinkley | 0 | 0 | 0 | 0 | 3,142 |
| | | Bull Shoals | 0 | 0 | 0 | 0 | 2,155 |
| | | Caddo Valley | 0 | 0 | 0 | 0 | 649 |
| | | Camden | 0 | 0 | 0 | 0 | 11,349 |
| | | Carlisle | 0 | 0 | 0 | 0 | 2,420 |
| | | Cave City | 0 | 0 | 0 | 0 | 2,057 |
| | | Cave Springs | 0 | 0 | 0 | 0 | 1,782 |
| | | Centerton | 0 | 0 | 0 | 0 | 9,911 |
| | | Charleston | 0 | 0 | 0 | 0 | 3,035 |
| | | Cherokee Village | 0 | 0 | 0 | 0 | 4,792 |
| | | Clarendon | 0 | | 0 | 0 | 1,637 |
| | | Clarksville | 0 | 0 | 0 | 0 | 8,679 |
| | | Clinton | 0 | 0 | 0 | 0 | 2,482 |
| | | Corning | 0 | 0 | 0 | 0 | 3,270 |
| | | Cotter | 0 | 0 | 0 | 0 | 1,098 |
| | | Crossett | 0 | 0 | 0 | 0 | 5,459 |
| | | Danville | 0 | 0 | 0 | 0 | 2,486 |
| | | Dardanelle | 0 | 0 | 0 | 0 | 4,458 |
| | | Decatur | 0 | 0 | 0 | 0 | 1,990 |
| | | De Queen | 0 | 0 | 0 | 0 | 5,970 |
| | | Dermott | 0 | | 0 | | 3,172 |
| | | Des Arc | 0 | 0 | 0 | 0 | 1,685 |
| | | De Witt | 0 | 0 | 0 | 0 | 3,223 |
| | | Diamond City | 0 | 0 | 0 | 0 | 811 |
| | | Diaz | 0 | 0 | 0 | 0 | 1,143 |
| | | Dierks | 0 | 0 | 0 | 0 | 1,216 |
| | | Dover | 0 | 0 | 0 | 0 | 1,407 |
| | | Dumas | 0 | 0 | 0 | 0 | 4,560 |
| | | Earle | 0 | 0 | 0 | 0 | 2,704 |
| | | El Dorado | 0 | 0 | 0 | 0 | 19,741 |
| | | Elkins | 0 | 0 | 0 | 0 | 2,730 |
| | | Etowah | 0 | 0 | 0 | 0 | 339 |
| | | Eudora | 0 | 0 | 0 | 0 | 2,292 |
| | | Eureka Springs | 0 | 0 | 0 | 0 | 2,361 |
| | | Fairfield Bay | 0 | 0 | 0 | 0 | 2,500 |
| | | Flippin | 0 | 0 | 0 | 0 | 1,384 |
| | | Fordyce | 0 | 0 | 0 | 0 | 4,171 |
| | | Forrest City | 0 | 0 | 0 | 0 | 13,123 |
| | | Gassville | 0 | 0 | 0 | 0 | 2,203 |
| | | Gentry | 0 | 0 | 0 | 0 | 3,041 |
| | | Glenwood | 0 | 0 | 0 | 0 | 1,985 |
| | | Gosnell | 0 | 0 | 0 | 0 | 3,541 |
| | | Gravette | 0 | 0 | 0 | 0 | 2,653 |
| | | Greenbrier | 0 | 0 | 0 | 0 | 4,642 |
| | | Green Forest | 0 | 0 | 0 | 0 | 3,081 |
| | | Greenland | 0 | 0 | 0 | 0 | 1,282 |
| | | Greenwood | 0 | 0 | 0 | 0 | 8,814 |
| | | Gurdon | 0 | 0 | 0 | 0 | 2,286 |
| | | Guy | 0 | 0 | 0 | 0 | 566 |
| | | Hamburg | 0 | 0 | 0 | 0 | 2,689 |
| | | Hampton | 0 | 0 | 0 | 0 | 1,457 |
| | | Hardy | 0 | | 0 | 0 | 815 |
| | | Harrisburg | 0 | 0 | 0 | 0 | 2,109 |
| | | Hazen | 0 | 0 | 0 | 0 | 1,441 |
| | | Heber Springs | 0 | 0 | 0 | 0 | 7,279 |
| | | Helena-West Helena | 0 | 0 | 0 | 0 | 11,921 |
| | | Highfill | 0 | 0 | 0 | 0 | 785 |
| | | Highland | 0 | 0 | 0 | 0 | 1,096 |
| | | Hope | 0 | 0 | 0 | 0 | 10,354 |
| | | Horseshoe Bend | 0 | 0 | 0 | 0 | 2,213 |
| | | Hoxie | 0 | 0 | 0 | 0 | 2,630 |
| | | Keiser | 0 | 0 | | 0 | 801 |
| | | Kensett | 0 | 0 | 0 | 0 | 1,852 |
| | | Lake City | 0 | 0 | 0 | 0 | 2,147 |
| | | Lakeview | 0 | 0 | 0 | 0 | 857 |
| | | Lake Village | 0 | 0 | 0 | 0 | 2,342 |
| | | Leachville | 0 | 0 | 0 | 0 | 1,834 |
| | | Lepanto | 0 | 0 | 0 | 0 | 2,007 |
| | | Lewisville | 0 | 0 | 0 | 0 | 1,134 |
| | | Lincoln | 0 | 0 | 0 | 0 | 2,118 |
| | | Little Flock | 0 | 0 | 0 | 0 | 3,210 |
| | | Little Rock | 0 | 0 | 0 | 0 | 190,205 |
| | | Lonoke | 0 | 0 | 0 | 0 | 4,636 |
| | | Lowell | 0 | 0 | 0 | 0 | 7,397 |
| | | Luxora | 0 | 0 | 0 | 0 | 1,209 |
| | | Marianna | 0 | 0 | 0 | 0 | 4,319 |
| | | Marion | 0 | 0 | 0 | 0 | 12,641 |
| | | Marked Tree | 0 | 0 | 0 | 0 | 2,615 |
| | | Marmaduke | 0 | 0 | 0 | 0 | 1,175 |
| | | Marvell | 0 | 0 | 0 | 0 | 1,102 |
| | | Maumelle | 0 | 0 | 0 | 0 | 16,958 |
| | | McCrory | 0 | 0 | 0 | 0 | 1,520 |
| | | McRae | 0 | 0 | 0 | 0 | 712 |
| | | Mineral Springs | | 0 | 0 | 0 | 1,271 |
| | | Monette | 0 | 0 | 0 | 0 | 1,234 |
| | | Monticello | 0 | 0 | 0 | 0 | 9,281 |
| | | Morrilton | 0 | 0 | 0 | 0 | 6,584 |
| | | Mountain Home | 0 | 0 | 0 | 0 | 12,767 |
| | | Mountain View | 0 | 0 | 0 | 0 | 3,133 |
| | | Mulberry | 0 | 0 | 0 | 0 | 1,730 |
| | | Murfreesboro | 0 | 0 | 0 | 0 | 1,629 |
| | | Nashville | 0 | 0 | 0 | 0 | 4,806 |
| | | Newport | 0 | 0 | 0 | 0 | 7,364 |
| | | Ola | 0 | 0 | 0 | 0 | 1,242 |
| | | Osceola | 0 | 0 | 0 | 0 | 7,816 |
| | | Ozark | 0 | 0 | 0 | 0 | 3,587 |
| | | Pangburn | 0 | 0 | | | 705 |
| | | Paris | 0 | 0 | 0 | 0 | 3,602 |
| | | Perryville | 0 | 0 | 0 | 0 | 1,440 |
| | | Piggott | 0 | 0 | 0 | 0 | 3,440 |
| | | Plainview | 0 | 0 | 0 | 0 | 778 |
| | | Plummerville | 0 | 0 | 0 | 0 | 865 |
| | | Pocahontas | 0 | 0 | 0 | 0 | 6,736 |
| | | Pottsville | 0 | 0 | 0 | 0 | 2,902 |
| | | Prairie Grove | 0 | 0 | 0 | 0 | 3,809 |
| | | Prescott | 0 | 0 | 0 | 0 | 4,439 |

[1]Agencies published in this table indicated that no hate crimes occurred in their jurisdictions during the quarter(s) for which they submitted reports to the Hate Crime Statistics Program. Blanks indicate quarters for which agencies did not submit reports.
[2]Population figures are published only for the cities. The figures listed for the universities and colleges are student enrollment and were provided by the United States Department of Education for the 2008 school year, the most recent available. The enrollment figures include full-time and part-time students.

# Table 95. Hate Crime Zero Data Submitted per Quarter, by State and Agency, 2009—*Continued*

(Number.)

| State | Agency type | Agency name | Zero data per quarter[1] 1st quarter | 2nd quarter | 3rd quarter | 4th quarter | Population[2] |
|---|---|---|---|---|---|---|---|
| ARKANSAS | | Quitman | 0 | 0 | 0 | 0 | 738 |
| | | Ravenden | 0 | | 0 | | 490 |
| | | Redfield | 0 | 0 | 0 | 0 | 1,171 |
| | | Rison | 0 | 0 | 0 | 0 | 1,282 |
| | | Rogers | 0 | 0 | 0 | 0 | 58,992 |
| | | Rose Bud | 0 | 0 | 0 | 0 | 460 |
| | | Salem | 0 | 0 | 0 | 0 | 1,613 |
| | | Sheridan | 0 | 0 | 0 | 0 | 4,640 |
| | | Siloam Springs | 0 | 0 | 0 | 0 | 15,325 |
| | | Stamps | 0 | 0 | 0 | 0 | 1,888 |
| | | Star City | 0 | 0 | 0 | 0 | 2,203 |
| | | Stuttgart | 0 | 0 | 0 | 0 | 8,891 |
| | | Trumann | 0 | 0 | 0 | 0 | 6,781 |
| | | Tuckerman | 0 | 0 | | 0 | 1,621 |
| | | Van Buren | 0 | 0 | 0 | 0 | 22,964 |
| | | Vilonia | 0 | 0 | 0 | 0 | 3,685 |
| | | Waldron | 0 | 0 | 0 | 0 | 3,574 |
| | | Walnut Ridge | 0 | 0 | 0 | 0 | 4,636 |
| | | Ward | 0 | 0 | 0 | 0 | 4,086 |
| | | Warren | 0 | 0 | 0 | 0 | 6,079 |
| | | Weiner | 0 | 0 | 0 | 0 | 719 |
| | | West Fork | 0 | 0 | 0 | 0 | 2,355 |
| | | White Hall | 0 | 0 | 0 | 0 | 5,158 |
| | Universities and Colleges | Arkansas State University, Jonesboro | 0 | 0 | 0 | 0 | 11,490 |
| | | Arkansas Tech University | 0 | 0 | 0 | 0 | 7,492 |
| | | Henderson State University | 0 | 0 | 0 | 0 | 3,652 |
| | | University of Arkansas: | | | | | |
| | | Fayetteville | 0 | 0 | 0 | 0 | 19,194 |
| | | Little Rock | 0 | 0 | 0 | 0 | 11,965 |
| | | Medical Sciences | 0 | 0 | 0 | 0 | 2,652 |
| | | Monticello | 0 | 0 | 0 | 0 | 3,302 |
| | | Pine Bluff | 0 | 0 | 0 | 0 | 3,525 |
| | | University of Central Arkansas | 0 | 0 | 0 | 0 | 12,974 |
| | Metropolitan Counties | Benton | 0 | 0 | 0 | 0 | |
| | | Cleveland | 0 | 0 | 0 | 0 | |
| | | Crittenden | 0 | 0 | 0 | 0 | |
| | | Franklin | 0 | 0 | 0 | 0 | |
| | | Garland | 0 | 0 | 0 | 0 | |
| | | Grant | 0 | 0 | 0 | 0 | |
| | | Jefferson | 0 | 0 | 0 | 0 | |
| | | Lincoln | 0 | 0 | 0 | 0 | |
| | | Lonoke | 0 | 0 | 0 | 0 | |
| | | Madison | 0 | 0 | 0 | 0 | |
| | | Perry | 0 | 0 | 0 | 0 | |
| | | Poinsett | 0 | 0 | 0 | 0 | |
| | | Sebastian | 0 | 0 | 0 | 0 | |
| | Nonmetropolitan Counties | Ashley | 0 | 0 | 0 | 0 | |
| | | Baxter | 0 | 0 | 0 | 0 | |
| | | Boone | 0 | 0 | 0 | 0 | |
| | | Bradley | 0 | 0 | 0 | 0 | |
| | | Calhoun | 0 | 0 | 0 | 0 | |
| | | Carroll | 0 | 0 | 0 | 0 | |
| | | Chicot | 0 | 0 | 0 | 0 | |
| | | Clark | 0 | 0 | 0 | 0 | |
| | | Clay | 0 | 0 | 0 | 0 | |
| | | Cleburne | 0 | 0 | 0 | 0 | |
| | | Columbia | 0 | 0 | 0 | 0 | |
| | | Cross | 0 | 0 | 0 | 0 | |
| | | Dallas | 0 | 0 | 0 | 0 | |
| | | Drew | 0 | 0 | 0 | 0 | |
| | | Greene | 0 | 0 | 0 | 0 | |
| | | Hempstead | 0 | 0 | 0 | 0 | |
| | | Howard | 0 | 0 | 0 | 0 | |
| | | Independence | 0 | 0 | 0 | 0 | |
| | | Izard | 0 | 0 | 0 | 0 | |
| | | Jackson | 0 | 0 | 0 | 0 | |
| | | Johnson | 0 | 0 | 0 | 0 | |
| | | Lafayette | 0 | 0 | 0 | 0 | |
| | | Lawrence | 0 | 0 | 0 | 0 | |
| | | Lee | 0 | 0 | 0 | 0 | |
| | | Little River | 0 | 0 | 0 | 0 | |
| | | Logan | 0 | 0 | 0 | 0 | |
| | | Marion | 0 | 0 | 0 | 0 | |
| | | Mississippi | 0 | 0 | 0 | 0 | |
| | | Monroe | 0 | 0 | 0 | 0 | |
| | | Montgomery | 0 | 0 | 0 | 0 | |
| | | Nevada | 0 | 0 | 0 | 0 | |
| | | Newton | 0 | 0 | 0 | 0 | |
| | | Ouachita | 0 | 0 | 0 | 0 | |
| | | Pike | 0 | 0 | 0 | 0 | |
| | | Pope | 0 | 0 | 0 | 0 | |
| | | Prairie | 0 | 0 | 0 | 0 | |
| | | Randolph | 0 | 0 | 0 | 0 | |
| | | Scott | 0 | 0 | 0 | 0 | |
| | | Searcy | 0 | 0 | 0 | 0 | |
| | | Sevier | 0 | 0 | 0 | 0 | |
| | | St. Francis | 0 | 0 | 0 | 0 | |
| | | Stone | 0 | 0 | 0 | 0 | |
| | | Union | 0 | 0 | 0 | 0 | |
| | | Van Buren | 0 | 0 | 0 | 0 | |
| | | White | 0 | 0 | 0 | 0 | |
| | Other Agencies | Camp Robinson | 0 | | | 0 | |
| | | State Capitol Police | 0 | 0 | 0 | 0 | |
| CALIFORNIA | Cities | Adelanto | 0 | 0 | 0 | 0 | 30,045 |
| | | Alameda | 0 | 0 | 0 | 0 | 70,372 |
| | | Aliso Viejo | 0 | 0 | 0 | 0 | 41,740 |
| | | Alturas | 0 | 0 | 0 | 0 | 2,778 |
| | | American Canyon | 0 | 0 | 0 | 0 | 17,259 |
| | | Anderson | 0 | 0 | 0 | 0 | 10,718 |
| | | Apple Valley | 0 | 0 | 0 | 0 | 72,200 |
| | | Arcadia | 0 | 0 | 0 | 0 | 56,596 |
| | | Arroyo Grande | 0 | 0 | 0 | 0 | 17,323 |
| | | Artesia | 0 | 0 | 0 | 0 | 16,226 |
| | | Arvin | 0 | 0 | 0 | 0 | 15,320 |
| | | Atascadero | 0 | 0 | 0 | 0 | 28,675 |
| | | Atwater | 0 | 0 | 0 | 0 | 26,966 |
| | | Auburn | 0 | 0 | 0 | 0 | 13,306 |
| | | Avenal | 0 | 0 | 0 | 0 | 17,451 |
| | | Baldwin Park | 0 | 0 | 0 | 0 | 77,539 |
| | | Banning | 0 | 0 | 0 | 0 | 29,568 |
| | | Barstow | 0 | 0 | 0 | 0 | 24,822 |
| | | Bear Valley | 0 | 0 | 0 | 0 | 4,618 |
| | | Beaumont | 0 | 0 | 0 | 0 | 36,800 |
| | | Bell | 0 | 0 | 0 | 0 | 36,651 |
| | | Bell Gardens | 0 | 0 | 0 | 0 | 44,756 |
| | | Belvedere | 0 | 0 | 0 | 0 | 2,052 |
| | | Big Bear Lake | 0 | 0 | 0 | 0 | 6,210 |
| | | Biggs | 0 | 0 | 0 | 0 | 1,823 |
| | | Bishop | 0 | 0 | 0 | 0 | 3,393 |
| | | Bradbury | 0 | 0 | 0 | 0 | 1,088 |
| | | Brea | 0 | 0 | 0 | 0 | 38,637 |
| | | Brisbane | 0 | 0 | 0 | 0 | 3,686 |
| | | Broadmoor | 0 | 0 | 0 | 0 | 4,393 |
| | | Buellton | 0 | 0 | 0 | 0 | 4,346 |
| | | Buena Park | 0 | 0 | 0 | 0 | 79,525 |
| | | Burlingame | 0 | 0 | 0 | 0 | 27,656 |
| | | Calabasas | 0 | 0 | 0 | 0 | 22,359 |
| | | Calexico | 0 | 0 | 0 | 0 | 39,820 |
| | | California City | 0 | 0 | 0 | 0 | 15,492 |
| | | Calimesa | 0 | 0 | 0 | 0 | 7,497 |
| | | Calipatria | 0 | 0 | 0 | 0 | 7,623 |
| | | Calistoga | 0 | 0 | 0 | 0 | 5,178 |

[1]Agencies published in this table indicated that no hate crimes occurred in their jurisdictions during the quarter(s) for which they submitted reports to the Hate Crime Statistics Program. Blanks indicate quarters for which agencies did not submit reports.
[2]Population figures are published only for the cities. The figures listed for the universities and colleges are student enrollment and were provided by the United States Department of Education for the 2008 school year, the most recent available. The enrollment figures include full-time and part-time students.
[3]Student enrollment figures were not available.

## Table 95. Hate Crime Zero Data Submitted per Quarter, by State and Agency, 2009—*Continued*

(Number.)

| State | Agency type | Agency name | Zero data per quarter[1] | | | | Population[2] |
|---|---|---|---|---|---|---|---|
| | | | 1st quarter | 2nd quarter | 3rd quarter | 4th quarter | |
| CALIFORNIA | | Canyon Lake | 0 | 0 | 0 | 0 | 11,387 |
| | | Capitola | 0 | 0 | 0 | 0 | 9,565 |
| | | Carlsbad | 0 | 0 | 0 | 0 | 98,482 |
| | | Carmel | 0 | 0 | 0 | 0 | 3,864 |
| | | Ceres | 0 | 0 | 0 | 0 | 43,669 |
| | | Chino | 0 | 0 | 0 | 0 | 84,626 |
| | | Chino Hills | 0 | 0 | 0 | 0 | 74,650 |
| | | Claremont | 0 | 0 | 0 | 0 | 35,628 |
| | | Clayton | 0 | 0 | 0 | 0 | 11,333 |
| | | Cloverdale | 0 | 0 | 0 | 0 | 8,304 |
| | | Clovis | 0 | 0 | 0 | 0 | 95,229 |
| | | Coachella | 0 | 0 | 0 | 0 | 41,863 |
| | | Coalinga | 0 | 0 | 0 | 0 | 19,308 |
| | | Colma | 0 | 0 | 0 | 0 | 1,452 |
| | | Colton | 0 | 0 | 0 | 0 | 50,803 |
| | | Colusa | 0 | 0 | 0 | 0 | 5,946 |
| | | Corcoran | 0 | 0 | 0 | 0 | 25,474 |
| | | Corning | 0 | 0 | 0 | 0 | 7,253 |
| | | Cotati | 0 | 0 | 0 | 0 | 7,248 |
| | | Crescent City | 0 | 0 | 0 | 0 | 7,889 |
| | | Danville | 0 | 0 | 0 | 0 | 41,118 |
| | | Del Rey Oaks | 0 | 0 | 0 | 0 | 1,516 |
| | | Desert Hot Springs | 0 | 0 | 0 | 0 | 25,577 |
| | | Diamond Bar | 0 | 0 | 0 | 0 | 57,330 |
| | | Dinuba | 0 | 0 | 0 | 0 | 20,682 |
| | | Dixon | 0 | 0 | 0 | 0 | 17,562 |
| | | Dorris | 0 | 0 | 0 | 0 | 825 |
| | | Dos Palos | 0 | 0 | 0 | 0 | 5,015 |
| | | Dunsmuir | 0 | 0 | 0 | 0 | 1,788 |
| | | East Palo Alto | 0 | 0 | 0 | 0 | 34,005 |
| | | El Cajon | 0 | 0 | 0 | 0 | 92,466 |
| | | El Centro | 0 | 0 | 0 | 0 | 40,337 |
| | | El Segundo | 0 | 0 | 0 | 0 | 16,235 |
| | | Emeryville | 0 | 0 | 0 | 0 | 9,929 |
| | | Encinitas | 0 | 0 | 0 | 0 | 60,625 |
| | | Etna | 0 | 0 | 0 | 0 | 768 |
| | | Exeter | 0 | 0 | 0 | 0 | 10,054 |
| | | Fairfax | 0 | 0 | 0 | 0 | 7,038 |
| | | Ferndale | 0 | 0 | 0 | 0 | 1,384 |
| | | Fillmore | 0 | 0 | 0 | 0 | 15,206 |
| | | Firebaugh | 0 | 0 | 0 | 0 | 7,032 |
| | | Folsom | 0 | 0 | 0 | 0 | 69,728 |
| | | Fort Bragg | 0 | 0 | 0 | 0 | 6,581 |
| | | Fort Jones | 0 | 0 | 0 | 0 | 646 |
| | | Fortuna | 0 | 0 | 0 | 0 | 11,424 |
| | | Foster City | 0 | 0 | 0 | 0 | 29,123 |
| | | Fowler | 0 | 0 | 0 | 0 | 5,769 |
| | | Fremont | | 0 | | 0 | 202,714 |
| | | Glendora | 0 | 0 | 0 | 0 | 49,400 |
| | | Goleta | 0 | 0 | 0 | 0 | 29,471 |
| | | Gonzales | 0 | 0 | 0 | 0 | 8,637 |
| | | Grand Terrace | 0 | 0 | 0 | 0 | 12,266 |
| | | Grass Valley | 0 | 0 | 0 | 0 | 12,271 |
| | | Greenfield | 0 | 0 | 0 | 0 | 15,511 |
| | | Grover Beach | 0 | 0 | 0 | 0 | 13,135 |
| | | Guadalupe | 0 | 0 | 0 | 0 | 6,708 |
| | | Gustine | 0 | 0 | 0 | 0 | 5,133 |
| | | Half Moon Bay | 0 | 0 | 0 | 0 | 12,514 |
| | | Hanford | 0 | 0 | 0 | 0 | 51,102 |
| | | Hayward | 0 | 0 | 0 | 0 | 142,227 |
| | | Hercules | 0 | 0 | 0 | 0 | 25,120 |
| | | Hidden Hills | 0 | 0 | 0 | 0 | 2,037 |
| | | Highland | 0 | 0 | 0 | 0 | 51,847 |
| | | Hillsborough | 0 | 0 | 0 | 0 | 10,846 |
| | | Holtville | 0 | 0 | 0 | 0 | 5,392 |
| | | Hughson | 0 | 0 | 0 | 0 | 6,647 |
| | | Huron | 0 | 0 | 0 | 0 | 7,764 |
| | | Imperial | 0 | 0 | 0 | 0 | 14,565 |
| | | Imperial Beach | 0 | 0 | 0 | 0 | 26,490 |
| | | Indian Wells | 0 | 0 | 0 | 0 | 5,323 |
| | | Indio | 0 | 0 | 0 | 0 | 89,459 |
| | | Industry | 0 | 0 | 0 | 0 | 930 |
| | | Irwindale | 0 | 0 | 0 | 0 | 1,438 |
| | | Isleton | 0 | 0 | 0 | 0 | 839 |
| | | Jackson | 0 | 0 | 0 | 0 | 4,359 |
| | | Kensington | 0 | 0 | 0 | 0 | 5,387 |
| | | Kerman | 0 | 0 | 0 | 0 | 13,285 |
| | | King City | 0 | 0 | 0 | 0 | 11,683 |
| | | Kingsburg | 0 | 0 | 0 | 0 | 11,276 |
| | | La Canada Flintridge | 0 | 0 | 0 | 0 | 20,706 |
| | | Lafayette | 0 | 0 | 0 | 0 | 25,128 |
| | | Laguna Hills | 0 | 0 | 0 | 0 | 31,816 |
| | | Laguna Niguel | 0 | 0 | 0 | 0 | 64,649 |
| | | Laguna Woods | 0 | 0 | 0 | 0 | 18,246 |
| | | La Habra Heights | 0 | 0 | 0 | 0 | 5,911 |
| | | Lakeport | 0 | 0 | 0 | 0 | 5,171 |
| | | Lake Shastina | 0 | 0 | 0 | 0 | 2,390 |
| | | La Mirada | 0 | 0 | 0 | 0 | 50,139 |
| | | La Palma | 0 | 0 | 0 | 0 | 15,619 |
| | | La Puente | 0 | 0 | 0 | 0 | 40,589 |
| | | Lemoore | 0 | 0 | 0 | 0 | 24,375 |
| | | Lincoln | 0 | 0 | 0 | 0 | 50,654 |
| | | Lindsay | 0 | 0 | 0 | 0 | 10,587 |
| | | Livingston | 0 | 0 | 0 | 0 | 13,764 |
| | | Loma Linda | 0 | 0 | 0 | 0 | 21,878 |
| | | Lomita | 0 | 0 | 0 | 0 | 20,164 |
| | | Los Altos | 0 | 0 | 0 | 0 | 28,380 |
| | | Los Altos Hills | 0 | 0 | 0 | 0 | 8,632 |
| | | Los Banos | 0 | 0 | 0 | 0 | 36,097 |
| | | Lynwood | 0 | 0 | 0 | 0 | 70,032 |
| | | Madera | 0 | 0 | 0 | 0 | 58,372 |
| | | Manteca | 0 | 0 | 0 | 0 | 66,908 |
| | | Martinez | 0 | 0 | 0 | 0 | 35,059 |
| | | Maywood | 0 | 0 | 0 | 0 | 28,234 |
| | | Mendota | | | | 0 | 10,652 |
| | | Menifee | 0 | 0 | 0 | 0 | 68,083 |
| | | Menlo Park | 0 | 0 | 0 | 0 | 30,011 |
| | | Merced | 0 | 0 | 0 | 0 | 78,693 |
| | | Mill Valley | 0 | 0 | 0 | 0 | 13,230 |
| | | Montague | 0 | 0 | 0 | 0 | 1,454 |
| | | Montclair | 0 | 0 | 0 | 0 | 36,819 |
| | | Montebello | 0 | 0 | 0 | 0 | 61,870 |
| | | Monterey | 0 | 0 | 0 | 0 | 27,554 |
| | | Monte Sereno | 0 | 0 | 0 | 0 | 3,615 |
| | | Morgan Hill | 0 | 0 | 0 | 0 | 38,568 |
| | | Murrieta | 0 | 0 | 0 | 0 | 105,238 |
| | | Napa | 0 | 0 | 0 | 0 | 74,736 |
| | | National City | 0 | 0 | 0 | 0 | 59,230 |
| | | Needles | 0 | 0 | 0 | 0 | 5,289 |
| | | Nevada City | 0 | 0 | 0 | 0 | 2,920 |
| | | Newman | 0 | 0 | 0 | 0 | 10,646 |
| | | Norco | 0 | 0 | 0 | 0 | 26,933 |
| | | Oakdale | 0 | 0 | 0 | 0 | 20,902 |
| | | Oakley | 0 | 0 | 0 | 0 | 32,818 |
| | | Ojai | 0 | 0 | 0 | 0 | 7,765 |
| | | Orland | 0 | 0 | 0 | 0 | 7,281 |
| | | Palm Desert | 0 | 0 | 0 | 0 | 51,630 |
| | | Paradise | 0 | 0 | 0 | 0 | 26,471 |
| | | Parlier | 0 | 0 | 0 | 0 | 13,500 |
| | | Paso Robles | 0 | 0 | 0 | 0 | 29,204 |
| | | Patterson | 0 | 0 | 0 | 0 | 20,085 |
| | | Perris | 0 | 0 | 0 | 0 | 58,362 |
| | | Petaluma | 0 | 0 | 0 | 0 | 54,649 |
| | | Piedmont | 0 | 0 | 0 | 0 | 10,427 |
| | | Pinole | 0 | 0 | 0 | 0 | 18,766 |
| | | Pismo Beach | 0 | 0 | 0 | 0 | 8,573 |
| | | Pittsburg | 0 | 0 | 0 | 0 | 64,989 |
| | | Pleasanton | 0 | 0 | 0 | 0 | 67,116 |
| | | Port Hueneme | 0 | 0 | 0 | 0 | 21,440 |
| | | Rancho Cordova | 0 | 0 | 0 | 0 | 63,303 |
| | | Rancho Cucamonga | 0 | 0 | 0 | 0 | 176,676 |
| | | Rancho Mirage | 0 | 0 | 0 | 0 | 17,137 |
| | | Rancho Santa Margarita | 0 | 0 | 0 | 0 | 49,854 |

[1]Agencies published in this table indicated that no hate crimes occurred in their jurisdictions during the quarter(s) for which they submitted reports to the Hate Crime program. Blanks indicate quarters for which agencies did not submit reports.

[2]Population figures are published only for the cities. The figures listed for the universities and colleges are student enrollment and were provided by the United States Department of Education for the 2006 school year, the most recent available. The enrollment figures include full-time and part-time students.

# Table 95. Hate Crime Zero Data Submitted per Quarter, by State and Agency, 2009—*Continued*

(Number.)

| State | Agency type | Agency name | Zero data per quarter[1] | | | | Population[2] |
|---|---|---|---|---|---|---|---|
| | | | 1st quarter | 2nd quarter | 3rd quarter | 4th quarter | |
| **CALIFORNIA** | | Red Bluff | 0 | 0 | 0 | 0 | 14,111 |
| | | Reedley | 0 | 0 | 0 | 0 | 23,744 |
| | | Rialto | 0 | 0 | 0 | 0 | 99,386 |
| | | Ridgecrest | 0 | 0 | 0 | 0 | 25,719 |
| | | Rio Dell | 0 | 0 | 0 | 0 | 3,184 |
| | | Ripon | 0 | 0 | 0 | 0 | 15,039 |
| | | Riverbank | 0 | 0 | 0 | 0 | 21,226 |
| | | Rocklin | 0 | 0 | 0 | 0 | 54,919 |
| | | Rohnert Park | 0 | 0 | 0 | 0 | 40,401 |
| | | Rolling Hills | 0 | 0 | 0 | 0 | 1,912 |
| | | Rolling Hills Estates | 0 | 0 | 0 | 0 | 7,879 |
| | | Rosemead | 0 | 0 | 0 | 0 | 54,501 |
| | | Ross | 0 | 0 | 0 | 0 | 2,272 |
| | | San Anselmo | 0 | 0 | 0 | 0 | 11,943 |
| | | San Bruno | 0 | 0 | 0 | 0 | 40,333 |
| | | San Carlos | 0 | 0 | 0 | 0 | 27,187 |
| | | San Clemente | 0 | 0 | 0 | 0 | 62,821 |
| | | Sand City | 0 | 0 | 0 | 0 | 375 |
| | | San Dimas | 0 | 0 | 0 | 0 | 35,043 |
| | | San Gabriel | 0 | 0 | 0 | 0 | 40,507 |
| | | Sanger | 0 | 0 | 0 | 0 | 26,285 |
| | | San Marino | 0 | 0 | 0 | 0 | 12,792 |
| | | San Pablo | 0 | 0 | 0 | 0 | 30,783 |
| | | San Ramon | 0 | 0 | 0 | 0 | 49,660 |
| | | Santa Fe Springs | 0 | 0 | 0 | 0 | 17,239 |
| | | Sausalito | 0 | 0 | 0 | 0 | 7,139 |
| | | Seal Beach | 0 | 0 | 0 | 0 | 24,121 |
| | | Seaside | 0 | 0 | 0 | 0 | 33,875 |
| | | Sebastopol | 0 | 0 | 0 | 0 | 7,487 |
| | | Selma | 0 | 0 | 0 | 0 | 23,181 |
| | | Shafter | 0 | 0 | 0 | 0 | 16,174 |
| | | Sierra Madre | 0 | 0 | 0 | 0 | 10,860 |
| | | Signal Hill | 0 | 0 | 0 | 0 | 11,062 |
| | | Simi Valley | 0 | 0 | 0 | 0 | 121,538 |
| | | Solana Beach | 0 | 0 | 0 | 0 | 12,807 |
| | | Solvang | 0 | 0 | 0 | 0 | 5,127 |
| | | Sonoma | 0 | 0 | 0 | 0 | 9,955 |
| | | South Lake Tahoe | 0 | 0 | 0 | 0 | 23,300 |
| | | South Pasadena | 0 | 0 | 0 | 0 | 24,462 |
| | | South San Francisco | 0 | 0 | 0 | 0 | 62,716 |
| | | Stallion Springs | 0 | 0 | 0 | 0 | 1,661 |
| | | Stanton | 0 | 0 | 0 | 0 | 37,583 |
| | | St. Helena | 0 | 0 | 0 | 0 | 5,803 |
| | | Suisun City | 0 | 0 | 0 | 0 | 27,056 |
| | | Susanville | 0 | 0 | 0 | 0 | 17,308 |
| | | Sutter Creek | 0 | 0 | 0 | 0 | 2,770 |
| | | Taft | 0 | 0 | 0 | 0 | 9,184 |
| | | Tiburon | 0 | 0 | 0 | 0 | 8,675 |
| | | Trinidad | 0 | 0 | 0 | 0 | 309 |
| | | Truckee | 0 | 0 | 0 | 0 | 16,447 |
| | | Tulelake | 0 | 0 | 0 | 0 | 952 |
| | | Twentynine Palms | 0 | 0 | 0 | 0 | 34,083 |
| | | Ukiah | 0 | 0 | 0 | 0 | 14,896 |
| | | Vernon | 0 | 0 | 0 | 0 | 90 |
| | | Victorville | 0 | 0 | 0 | 0 | 117,150 |
| | | Villa Park | 0 | 0 | 0 | 0 | 5,968 |
| | | Walnut | 0 | 0 | 0 | 0 | 30,819 |
| | | Waterford | 0 | 0 | 0 | 0 | 9,124 |
| | | Weed | 0 | 0 | 0 | 0 | 3,031 |
| | | Westlake Village | 0 | 0 | 0 | 0 | 8,479 |
| | | Westmorland | 0 | 0 | 0 | 0 | 2,207 |
| | | Wheatland | 0 | 0 | 0 | 0 | 3,771 |
| | | Williams | 0 | 0 | 0 | 0 | 4,900 |
| | | Willits | 0 | 0 | 0 | 0 | 4,960 |
| | | Willows | 0 | 0 | 0 | 0 | 6,272 |
| | | Windsor | 0 | 0 | 0 | 0 | 25,634 |
| | | Winters | 0 | 0 | 0 | 0 | 7,074 |
| | | Woodland | 0 | 0 | 0 | 0 | 55,138 |
| | | Yorba Linda | 0 | 0 | 0 | 0 | 66,498 |

| State | Agency type | Agency name | Zero data per quarter[1] | | | | Population[2] |
|---|---|---|---|---|---|---|---|
| | | | 1st quarter | 2nd quarter | 3rd quarter | 4th quarter | |
| | | Yountville | 0 | 0 | 0 | 0 | 3,265 |
| | | Yreka | 0 | 0 | 0 | 0 | 7,379 |
| | | Yucca Valley | 0 | 0 | 0 | 0 | 20,798 |
| | **Universities and Colleges** | Allan Hancock College | 0 | 0 | 0 | 0 | 11,552 |
| | | California State Polytechnic University: Pomona | 0 | 0 | 0 | 0 | 21,190 |
| | | San Luis Obispo | 0 | 0 | 0 | 0 | 19,471 |
| | | California State University: Bakersfield | 0 | 0 | 0 | 0 | 7,684 |
| | | Channel Islands | 0 | 0 | 0 | 0 | 3,783 |
| | | Chico | 0 | 0 | 0 | 0 | 17,132 |
| | | East Bay | 0 | 0 | 0 | 0 | 14,167 |
| | | Fresno | 0 | 0 | 0 | 0 | 22,613 |
| | | Long Beach | 0 | 0 | 0 | 0 | 37,891 |
| | | Los Angeles | 0 | 0 | 0 | 0 | 20,743 |
| | | Sacramento | 0 | 0 | 0 | 0 | 29,011 |
| | | San Bernardino | 0 | 0 | 0 | 0 | 17,646 |
| | | San Marcos | 0 | 0 | 0 | 0 | 9,148 |
| | | Stanislaus | 0 | 0 | 0 | 0 | 8,601 |
| | | College of the Sequoias | 0 | 0 | 0 | 0 | 13,449 |
| | | Cuesta College | 0 | 0 | 0 | 0 | 11,341 |
| | | El Camino College | 0 | 0 | 0 | 0 | 27,098 |
| | | Foothill-De Anza College | 0 | 0 | 0 | 0 | 45,541 |
| | | Fresno Community College | 0 | 0 | 0 | | 24,783 |
| | | Humboldt State University | 0 | 0 | 0 | 0 | 7,800 |
| | | Marin Community College | 0 | 0 | 0 | 0 | 6,047 |
| | | Pasadena Community College | 0 | 0 | 0 | 0 | 26,713 |
| | | Reedley Community College | 0 | 0 | 0 | 0 | 14,223 |
| | | Riverside Community College | 0 | 0 | 0 | 0 | 36,146 |
| | | San Bernardino Community College | 0 | 0 | 0 | 0 | 14,136 |
| | | San Francisco State University | 0 | 0 | 0 | 0 | 30,014 |
| | | San Jose/ Evergreen Community College | 0 | 0 | 0 | 0 | 22,826 |
| | | Santa Rosa Junior College | 0 | 0 | 0 | 0 | 20,298 |
| | | Solano Community College | 0 | 0 | 0 | 0 | 11,055 |
| | | Sonoma State University | 0 | 0 | 0 | 0 | 8,921 |
| | | University of California: Hastings College of Law | 0 | 0 | 0 | 0 | 1,306 |
| | | Irvine | 0 | 0 | 0 | 0 | 26,984 |
| | | Medical Center, Sacramento[3] | 0 | 0 | 0 | 0 | |

[1]Agencies published in this table indicated that no hate crimes occurred in their jurisdictions during the quarter(s) for which they submitted reports to the Hate Crime Statistics Program. Blanks indicate quarters for which agencies did not submit reports.

[2]Population figures are published only for the cities. The figures listed for the universities and colleges are student enrollment and were provided by the United States Department of Education for the 2008 school year, the most recent available. The enrollment figures include full-time and part-time students.

[3]Student enrollment figures were not available.

# Table 95. Hate Crime Zero Data Submitted per Quarter, by State and Agency, 2009—*Continued*

(Number.)

| State | Agency type | Agency name | Zero data per quarter[1] | | | | Population[2] |
|---|---|---|---|---|---|---|---|
| | | | 1st quarter | 2nd quarter | 3rd quarter | 4th quarter | |
| **CALIFORNIA** | | Merced | 0 | 0 | 0 | 0 | 2,718 |
| | | San Francisco | 0 | 0 | 0 | 0 | 2,998 |
| | | Santa Barbara | 0 | 0 | 0 | 0 | 21,868 |
| | | Ventura County Community College District | 0 | 0 | 0 | 0 | 14,207 |
| | | West Valley-Mission College | | | 0 | 0 | 22,159 |
| | **Metropolitan Counties** | Alameda | 0 | 0 | 0 | 0 | |
| | | Butte | 0 | 0 | 0 | 0 | |
| | | Fresno | 0 | 0 | 0 | 0 | |
| | | Imperial | 0 | 0 | 0 | 0 | |
| | | Kings | 0 | 0 | 0 | 0 | |
| | | Marin | 0 | 0 | 0 | 0 | |
| | | Merced | 0 | 0 | 0 | 0 | |
| | | Monterey | 0 | 0 | 0 | 0 | |
| | | Napa | 0 | 0 | 0 | 0 | |
| | | San Benito | 0 | 0 | 0 | 0 | |
| | | San Joaquin | 0 | 0 | 0 | 0 | |
| | | San Mateo | 0 | 0 | 0 | 0 | |
| | | Sonoma | 0 | 0 | 0 | 0 | |
| | | Tulare | 0 | 0 | 0 | 0 | |
| | | Yolo | 0 | 0 | 0 | 0 | |
| | **Nonmetropolitan Counties** | Alpine | 0 | 0 | 0 | 0 | |
| | | Calaveras | 0 | 0 | 0 | 0 | |
| | | Colusa | 0 | 0 | 0 | 0 | |
| | | Del Norte | 0 | 0 | 0 | 0 | |
| | | Glenn | 0 | 0 | 0 | 0 | |
| | | Inyo | 0 | 0 | 0 | 0 | |
| | | Lassen | 0 | 0 | 0 | 0 | |
| | | Mariposa | 0 | 0 | 0 | 0 | |
| | | Modoc | 0 | 0 | 0 | 0 | |
| | | Mono | 0 | 0 | 0 | 0 | |
| | | Nevada | 0 | 0 | 0 | 0 | |
| | | Plumas | 0 | 0 | 0 | 0 | |
| | | Sierra | 0 | 0 | 0 | 0 | |
| | | Siskiyou | 0 | 0 | 0 | 0 | |
| | | Tehama | 0 | 0 | 0 | 0 | |
| | | Trinity | 0 | 0 | 0 | 0 | |
| | | Tuolumne | 0 | 0 | 0 | 0 | |
| | **State Police Agencies** | Highway Patrol: | | | | | |
| | | Alameda County | 0 | 0 | 0 | 0 | |
| | | Alpine County | 0 | 0 | 0 | 0 | |
| | | Amador County | 0 | 0 | 0 | 0 | |
| | | Butte County | 0 | 0 | 0 | 0 | |
| | | Calaveras County | 0 | 0 | 0 | 0 | |
| | | Colusa County | 0 | 0 | 0 | 0 | |
| | | Contra Costa County | 0 | 0 | 0 | 0 | |
| | | Del Norte County | 0 | 0 | 0 | 0 | |
| | | El Dorado County | 0 | 0 | 0 | 0 | |
| | | Fresno County | 0 | 0 | 0 | 0 | |
| | | Glenn County | 0 | 0 | 0 | 0 | |
| | | Humboldt County | 0 | 0 | 0 | 0 | |
| | | Imperial County | 0 | 0 | 0 | 0 | |
| | | Inyo County | 0 | 0 | 0 | 0 | |
| | | Kern County | 0 | 0 | 0 | 0 | |
| | | Kings County | 0 | 0 | 0 | 0 | |
| | | Lake County | 0 | 0 | 0 | 0 | |
| | | Lassen County | 0 | 0 | 0 | 0 | |
| | | Los Angeles County | 0 | 0 | 0 | 0 | |
| | | Madera County | 0 | 0 | 0 | 0 | |
| | | Marin County | 0 | 0 | 0 | 0 | |
| | | Mariposa County | 0 | 0 | 0 | 0 | |
| | | Mendocino County | 0 | 0 | 0 | 0 | |
| | | Merced County | 0 | 0 | 0 | 0 | |
| | | Modoc County | 0 | 0 | 0 | 0 | |
| | | Mono County | 0 | 0 | 0 | 0 | |
| | | Monterey County | 0 | 0 | 0 | 0 | |
| | | Napa County | 0 | 0 | 0 | 0 | |
| | | Nevada County | 0 | 0 | 0 | 0 | |
| | | Orange County | 0 | 0 | 0 | 0 | |
| | | Placer County | 0 | 0 | 0 | 0 | |
| | | Plumas County | 0 | 0 | 0 | 0 | |
| | | Riverside County | 0 | 0 | 0 | 0 | |
| | | Sacramento County | 0 | 0 | 0 | 0 | |
| | | San Benito County | 0 | 0 | 0 | 0 | |
| | | San Bernardino County | 0 | 0 | 0 | 0 | |
| | | San Diego County | 0 | 0 | 0 | 0 | |
| | | San Francisco County | 0 | 0 | 0 | 0 | |
| | | San Joaquin County | 0 | 0 | 0 | 0 | |
| | | San Luis Obispo County | 0 | 0 | 0 | 0 | |
| | | San Mateo County | 0 | 0 | 0 | 0 | |
| | | Santa Barbara County | 0 | 0 | 0 | 0 | |
| | | Santa Clara County | 0 | 0 | 0 | 0 | |
| | | Santa Cruz County | 0 | 0 | 0 | 0 | |
| | | Shasta County | 0 | 0 | 0 | 0 | |
| | | Sierra County | 0 | 0 | 0 | 0 | |
| | | Siskiyou County | 0 | 0 | 0 | 0 | |
| | | Solano County | 0 | 0 | 0 | 0 | |
| | | Sonoma County | 0 | 0 | 0 | 0 | |
| | | Stanislaus County | 0 | 0 | 0 | 0 | |
| | | Sutter County | 0 | 0 | 0 | 0 | |
| | | Tehama County | 0 | 0 | 0 | 0 | |
| | | Trinity County | 0 | 0 | 0 | 0 | |
| | | Tulare County | 0 | 0 | 0 | 0 | |
| | | Tuolumne County | 0 | 0 | 0 | 0 | |
| | | Ventura County | 0 | 0 | 0 | 0 | |
| | | Yolo County | 0 | 0 | 0 | 0 | |
| | | Yuba County | 0 | 0 | 0 | 0 | |
| | **Other Agencies** | Agnews Developmental Center | 0 | 0 | | | |
| | | Atascadero State Hospital | 0 | 0 | 0 | 0 | |
| | | California State Fair | 0 | 0 | 0 | 0 | |
| | | Coalinga State Hospital | 0 | 0 | 0 | 0 | |
| | | Department of Parks and Recreation: | | | | | |
| | | Angeles | 0 | 0 | 0 | 0 | |
| | | Bay Area | 0 | 0 | 0 | 0 | |

[1]Agencies published in this table indicated that no hate crimes occurred in their jurisdictions during the quarter(s) for which they submitted reports to the Hate Crime Statistics Program. Blanks indicate quarters for which agencies did not submit reports.

[2]Population figures are published only for the cities. The figures listed for the universities and colleges are student enrollment and were provided by the United States Department of Education for the 2008 school year, the most recent available. The enrollment figures include full-time and part-time students.

# Table 95. Hate Crime Zero Data Submitted per Quarter, by State and Agency, 2009—*Continued*

(Number.)

| State | Agency type | Agency name | Zero data per quarter[1] 1st quarter | 2nd quarter | 3rd quarter | 4th quarter | Population[2] |
|---|---|---|---|---|---|---|---|
| **CALIFORNIA** | | Calaveras County | 0 | 0 | 0 | 0 | |
| | | Capital | 0 | 0 | 0 | 0 | |
| | | Channel Coast | 0 | 0 | 0 | 0 | |
| | | Colorado | 0 | 0 | 0 | 0 | |
| | | Four Rivers District | 0 | 0 | 0 | 0 | |
| | | Hollister Hills | 0 | 0 | 0 | 0 | |
| | | Hungry Valley | 0 | 0 | 0 | 0 | |
| | | Inland Empire | 0 | 0 | 0 | 0 | |
| | | Marin County | 0 | 0 | 0 | 0 | |
| | | Mendocino Headquarters | 0 | 0 | 0 | 0 | |
| | | Monterey County | 0 | 0 | 0 | 0 | |
| | | North Coast Redwoods | 0 | 0 | 0 | 0 | |
| | | Northern Buttes | 0 | 0 | 0 | 0 | |
| | | Oceano Dunes | 0 | 0 | 0 | 0 | |
| | | Ocotillo Wells | 0 | 0 | 0 | 0 | |
| | | Orange Coast | 0 | 0 | 0 | 0 | |
| | | Russian River | 0 | 0 | 0 | 0 | |
| | | San Diego Coast | 0 | 0 | 0 | 0 | |
| | | San Joaquin | 0 | 0 | 0 | 0 | |
| | | Santa Cruz Mountains | 0 | 0 | 0 | 0 | |
| | | Sierra | 0 | 0 | 0 | 0 | |
| | | Silverado | 0 | 0 | 0 | 0 | |
| | | Twin Cities | 0 | 0 | 0 | 0 | |
| | | East Bay Municipal Utility | 0 | 0 | 0 | 0 | |
| | | East Bay Regional Parks: | | | | | |
| | | Alameda County | 0 | 0 | 0 | 0 | |
| | | Contra Costa County | 0 | 0 | 0 | 0 | |
| | | Fairview Developmental Center | 0 | 0 | 0 | 0 | |
| | | Fontana Unified School District | 0 | 0 | 0 | 0 | |
| | | Lanterman State Hospital | 0 | 0 | 0 | 0 | |
| | | Los Angeles County Metropolitan Transportation Authority | 0 | 0 | 0 | 0 | |
| | | Monterey Peninsula Airport | 0 | 0 | 0 | 0 | |
| | | Napa State Hospital | 0 | 0 | 0 | 0 | |
| | | Patton State Hospital | 0 | 0 | 0 | 0 | |
| | | Porterville Developmental Center | 0 | 0 | 0 | 0 | |
| | | San Bernardino Unified School District | 0 | 0 | 0 | 0 | |
| | | San Francisco Bay Area Rapid Transit: | | | | | |
| | | Alameda County | 0 | 0 | 0 | 0 | |
| | | San Mateo County | 0 | 0 | 0 | 0 | |
| | | Santa Clara Transit District | 0 | 0 | 0 | 0 | |
| | | Sonoma Developmental Center | 0 | 0 | 0 | 0 | |
| | | Stockton Unified School District | 0 | 0 | 0 | 0 | |
| | | Twin Rivers Unified School District | 0 | 0 | 0 | 0 | |
| | | Union Pacific Railroad: | | | | | |
| | | Alameda County | 0 | 0 | 0 | 0 | |
| | | Amador County | 0 | 0 | 0 | 0 | |
| | | Butte County | 0 | 0 | 0 | 0 | |
| | | Calaveras County | 0 | 0 | 0 | 0 | |
| | | Colusa County | 0 | 0 | 0 | 0 | |
| | | Contra Costa County | 0 | 0 | 0 | 0 | |
| | | El Dorado County | 0 | 0 | 0 | 0 | |
| | | Fresno County | 0 | 0 | 0 | 0 | |
| | | Glenn County | 0 | 0 | 0 | 0 | |
| | | Humboldt County | 0 | 0 | 0 | 0 | |
| | | Imperial County | 0 | 0 | 0 | 0 | |
| | | Inyo County | 0 | 0 | 0 | 0 | |
| | | Kern County | 0 | 0 | 0 | 0 | |
| | | Kings County | 0 | 0 | 0 | 0 | |
| | | Lassen County | 0 | 0 | 0 | 0 | |
| | | Los Angeles County | 0 | 0 | 0 | 0 | |
| | | Madera County | 0 | 0 | 0 | 0 | |
| | | Marin County | 0 | 0 | 0 | 0 | |
| | | Mendocino County | 0 | 0 | 0 | 0 | |
| | | Merced County | 0 | 0 | 0 | 0 | |
| | | Modoc County | 0 | 0 | 0 | 0 | |
| | | Monterey County | 0 | 0 | 0 | 0 | |
| | | Napa County | 0 | 0 | 0 | 0 | |
| | | Nevada County | 0 | 0 | 0 | 0 | |
| | | Orange County | 0 | 0 | 0 | 0 | |
| | | Placer County | 0 | 0 | 0 | 0 | |
| | | Plumas County | 0 | 0 | 0 | 0 | |
| | | Riverside County | 0 | 0 | 0 | 0 | |
| | | Sacramento County | 0 | 0 | 0 | 0 | |
| | | San Benito County | 0 | 0 | 0 | 0 | |
| | | San Bernardino County | 0 | 0 | 0 | 0 | |
| | | San Francisco County | 0 | 0 | 0 | 0 | |
| | | San Joaquin County | 0 | 0 | 0 | 0 | |
| | | San Luis Obispo County | 0 | 0 | 0 | 0 | |
| | | San Mateo County | 0 | 0 | 0 | 0 | |
| | | Santa Barbara County | 0 | 0 | 0 | 0 | |
| | | Santa Clara County | 0 | 0 | 0 | 0 | |
| | | Santa Cruz County | 0 | 0 | 0 | 0 | |
| | | Shasta County | 0 | 0 | 0 | 0 | |
| | | Sierra County | 0 | 0 | 0 | 0 | |
| | | Siskiyou County | 0 | 0 | 0 | 0 | |

[1]Agencies published in this table indicated that no hate crimes occurred in their jurisdictions during the quarter(s) for which they submitted reports to the Hate Crime program. Blanks indicate quarters for which agencies did not submit reports.

[2]Population figures are published only for the cities. The figures listed for the universities and colleges are student enrollment and were provided by the United States Department of Education for the 2006 school year, the most recent available. The enrollment figures include full-time and part-time students.

# Table 95. Hate Crime Zero Data Submitted per Quarter, by State and Agency, 2009—*Continued*

(Number.)

| State | Agency type | Agency name | Zero data per quarter[1] | | | | Population[2] |
|---|---|---|---|---|---|---|---|
| | | | 1st quarter | 2nd quarter | 3rd quarter | 4th quarter | |
| **CALIFORNIA** | | Solano County | 0 | 0 | 0 | 0 | |
| | | Sonoma County | 0 | 0 | 0 | 0 | |
| | | Stanislaus County | 0 | 0 | 0 | 0 | |
| | | Sutter County | 0 | 0 | 0 | 0 | |
| | | Tehama County | 0 | 0 | 0 | 0 | |
| | | Trinity County | 0 | 0 | 0 | 0 | |
| | | Tulare County | 0 | 0 | 0 | 0 | |
| | | Ventura County | 0 | 0 | 0 | 0 | |
| | | Yolo County | 0 | 0 | 0 | 0 | |
| | | Yuba County | 0 | 0 | 0 | 0 | |
| **COLORADO** | **Cities** | Alamosa | 0 | 0 | 0 | 0 | 8,781 |
| | | Ault | 0 | 0 | 0 | 0 | 1,444 |
| | | Avon | 0 | 0 | 0 | 0 | 6,691 |
| | | Bayfield | 0 | 0 | 0 | 0 | 2,079 |
| | | Black Hawk | 0 | 0 | 0 | 0 | 104 |
| | | Bow Mar | 0 | 0 | 0 | 0 | 808 |
| | | Breckenridge | 0 | 0 | 0 | 0 | 3,493 |
| | | Brighton | 0 | 0 | 0 | 0 | 32,770 |
| | | Brush | 0 | 0 | 0 | 0 | 5,356 |
| | | Buena Vista | 0 | 0 | 0 | 0 | 2,127 |
| | | Burlington | 0 | 0 | 0 | 0 | 3,900 |
| | | Campo | 0 | 0 | 0 | 0 | 125 |
| | | Cedaredge | 0 | 0 | 0 | 0 | 2,300 |
| | | Center | 0 | 0 | 0 | 0 | 2,389 |
| | | Central City | 0 | 0 | 0 | 0 | 572 |
| | | Cherry Hills Village | 0 | 0 | 0 | 0 | 6,397 |
| | | Columbine Valley | 0 | 0 | 0 | 0 | 1,341 |
| | | Cortez | 0 | 0 | 0 | 0 | 8,680 |
| | | Crested Butte | 0 | 0 | 0 | 0 | 1,665 |
| | | Cripple Creek | 0 | 0 | 0 | 0 | 1,001 |
| | | Dacono | 0 | 0 | 0 | 0 | 4,179 |
| | | De Beque | 0 | 0 | 0 | 0 | 528 |
| | | Delta | 0 | 0 | 0 | 0 | 9,162 |
| | | Dillon | 0 | 0 | 0 | 0 | 809 |
| | | Durango | 0 | 0 | 0 | 0 | 16,644 |
| | | Eagle | 0 | 0 | 0 | 0 | 6,349 |
| | | Edgewater | 0 | 0 | 0 | 0 | 5,101 |
| | | Elizabeth | 0 | 0 | 0 | 0 | 1,434 |
| | | Empire | 0 | | | | 321 |
| | | Erie | 0 | 0 | 0 | 0 | 18,195 |
| | | Evans | 0 | 0 | 0 | 0 | 20,145 |
| | | Federal Heights | 0 | 0 | 0 | 0 | 11,695 |
| | | Firestone | 0 | 0 | 0 | 0 | 9,408 |
| | | Florence | 0 | 0 | 0 | 0 | 3,618 |
| | | Fort Lupton | 0 | 0 | 0 | 0 | 7,668 |
| | | Fowler | 0 | 0 | 0 | 0 | 1,082 |
| | | Fraser/Winter Park | 0 | 0 | 0 | 0 | 1,809 |
| | | Frederick | 0 | 0 | 0 | 0 | 9,190 |
| | | Frisco | 0 | 0 | 0 | 0 | 2,727 |
| | | Glendale | 0 | 0 | 0 | 0 | 4,830 |
| | | Golden | 0 | 0 | 0 | 0 | 17,334 |
| | | Granby | 0 | 0 | 0 | 0 | 1,658 |
| | | Green Mountain Falls | 0 | 0 | 0 | 0 | 806 |
| | | Greenwood Village | 0 | 0 | 0 | 0 | 14,552 |
| | | Haxtun | 0 | 0 | 0 | 0 | 963 |
| | | Hayden | 0 | 0 | 0 | 0 | 1,573 |
| | | Holyoke | 0 | 0 | 0 | 0 | 2,220 |
| | | Hotchkiss | 0 | 0 | 0 | 0 | 1,093 |
| | | Idaho Springs | 0 | 0 | 0 | 0 | 1,715 |
| | | Ignacio | 0 | 0 | 0 | 0 | 761 |
| | | Johnstown | 0 | 0 | 0 | 0 | 10,116 |
| | | Kersey | 0 | 0 | 0 | 0 | 1,467 |
| | | Kiowa | 0 | 0 | 0 | 0 | 596 |
| | | Kremmling | 0 | 0 | 0 | 0 | 1,523 |
| | | La Junta | 0 | 0 | 0 | 0 | 6,992 |
| | | Lakeside | 0 | 0 | 0 | 0 | 19 |
| | | Lamar | 0 | | | 0 | 7,860 |
| | | La Salle | 0 | 0 | 0 | 0 | 2,001 |
| | | Las Animas | 0 | 0 | 0 | 0 | 2,305 |
| | | La Veta | 0 | 0 | 0 | 0 | 878 |
| | | Limon | 0 | 0 | 0 | 0 | 1,719 |
| | | Mancos | 0 | 0 | 0 | 0 | 1,278 |
| | | Manitou Springs | 0 | 0 | 0 | 0 | 5,182 |
| | | Meeker | 0 | 0 | 0 | 0 | 2,405 |
| | | Milliken | 0 | 0 | 0 | 0 | 6,670 |
| | | Minturn | 0 | 0 | 0 | 0 | 1,198 |
| | | Monte Vista | 0 | 0 | 0 | 0 | 3,950 |
| | | Monument | 0 | 0 | 0 | 0 | 2,673 |
| | | Morrison | 0 | 0 | 0 | 0 | 413 |
| | | Mountain View | 0 | 0 | 0 | 0 | 515 |
| | | Nederland | 0 | 0 | 0 | 0 | 1,366 |
| | | New Castle | 0 | 0 | 0 | 0 | 4,065 |
| | | Olathe | 0 | 0 | 0 | 0 | 1,758 |
| | | Ouray | 0 | 0 | 0 | 0 | 946 |
| | | Pagosa Springs | 0 | 0 | 0 | 0 | 1,762 |
| | | Palisade | | | 0 | 0 | 2,870 |
| | | Palmer Lake | 0 | 0 | 0 | | 2,343 |
| | | Paonia | 0 | 0 | 0 | 0 | 1,645 |
| | | Parachute | 0 | 0 | 0 | 0 | 1,326 |
| | | Parker | 0 | 0 | 0 | 0 | 46,676 |
| | | Rangely | 0 | 0 | 0 | 0 | 2,143 |
| | | Rocky Ford | 0 | 0 | 0 | 0 | 3,916 |
| | | Salida | 0 | 0 | 0 | 0 | 5,375 |
| | | Sheridan | 0 | 0 | 0 | 0 | 5,398 |
| | | Silt | 0 | 0 | 0 | 0 | 2,791 |
| | | Silverthorne | 0 | 0 | 0 | 0 | 4,074 |
| | | Snowmass Village | 0 | 0 | 0 | 0 | 1,923 |
| | | Springfield | 0 | 0 | 0 | 0 | 1,265 |
| | | Sterling | 0 | 0 | 0 | 0 | 12,800 |
| | | Telluride | 0 | 0 | 0 | 0 | 2,377 |
| | | Thornton | 0 | 0 | 0 | 0 | 117,415 |
| | | Vail | 0 | 0 | 0 | 0 | 4,783 |
| | | Victor | 0 | 0 | 0 | 0 | 402 |
| | | Walsh | 0 | 0 | 0 | 0 | 629 |
| | | Wheat Ridge | 0 | 0 | 0 | 0 | 30,683 |
| | | Wiggins | 0 | 0 | 0 | 0 | 956 |
| | | Windsor | 0 | 0 | 0 | 0 | 19,217 |
| | | Woodland Park | 0 | 0 | 0 | 0 | 6,490 |
| | | Wray | 0 | 0 | 0 | 0 | 2,100 |
| | | Yuma | 0 | 0 | 0 | 0 | 3,261 |
| | **Universities and Colleges** | Adams State College | 0 | 0 | 0 | 0 | 2,920 |
| | | Arapahoe Community College | 0 | 0 | 0 | 0 | 7,204 |
| | | Auraria Higher Education Center[3] | 0 | 0 | 0 | 0 | |
| | | Colorado School of Mines | 0 | 0 | 0 | 0 | 4,704 |
| | | Colorado State University, Pueblo | 0 | 0 | 0 | 0 | 6,759 |
| | | Fort Lewis College | 0 | 0 | 0 | 0 | 3,740 |
| | | Pikes Peak Community College | 0 | 0 | 0 | 0 | 11,873 |
| | | Red Rocks Community College | 0 | 0 | 0 | 0 | 7,667 |
| | | University of Colorado: | | | | | |
| | | Colorado Springs | 0 | 0 | 0 | 0 | 9,373 |
| | | Denver | 0 | 0 | 0 | 0 | 21,903 |
| | | Health Sciences Center[3] | 0 | 0 | 0 | 0 | |

[1]Agencies published in this table indicated that no hate crimes occurred in their jurisdictions during the quarter(s) for which they submitted reports to the Hate Crime Statistics Program. Blanks indicate quarters for which agencies did not submit reports.
[2]Population figures are published only for the cities. The figures listed for the universities and colleges are student enrollment and were provided by the United States Department of Education for the 2008 school year, the most recent available. The enrollment figures include full-time and part-time students.
[3]Student enrollment figures were not available.

## Table 95. Hate Crime Zero Data Submitted per Quarter, by State and Agency, 2009—*Continued*

(Number.)

| State | Agency type | Agency name | Zero data per quarter[1] 1st quarter | 2nd quarter | 3rd quarter | 4th quarter | Population[2] |
|---|---|---|---|---|---|---|---|
| COLORADO | | University of Northern Colorado | 0 | 0 | 0 | 0 | 12,498 |
| | Metropolitan Counties | Boulder | 0 | 0 | 0 | 0 | |
| | | Clear Creek | 0 | 0 | 0 | 0 | |
| | | Elbert | 0 | 0 | 0 | 0 | |
| | | El Paso | 0 | 0 | 0 | 0 | |
| | | Gilpin | 0 | 0 | 0 | 0 | |
| | | Pueblo | 0 | 0 | 0 | 0 | |
| | | Teller | 0 | 0 | 0 | 0 | |
| | Nonmetropolitan Counties | Alamosa | 0 | 0 | 0 | 0 | |
| | | Archuleta | 0 | 0 | 0 | 0 | |
| | | Baca | 0 | 0 | 0 | 0 | |
| | | Cheyenne | 0 | 0 | 0 | 0 | |
| | | Crowley | 0 | 0 | 0 | 0 | |
| | | Delta | 0 | 0 | 0 | 0 | |
| | | Dolores | 0 | 0 | 0 | 0 | |
| | | Eagle | 0 | 0 | 0 | 0 | |
| | | Fremont | 0 | 0 | 0 | 0 | |
| | | Grand | 0 | 0 | 0 | 0 | |
| | | Gunnison | 0 | 0 | 0 | 0 | |
| | | Hinsdale | 0 | 0 | 0 | 0 | |
| | | Huerfano | 0 | 0 | 0 | 0 | |
| | | Jackson | 0 | 0 | 0 | 0 | |
| | | Kiowa | 0 | 0 | 0 | 0 | |
| | | Kit Carson | 0 | 0 | 0 | 0 | |
| | | Lake | 0 | 0 | 0 | 0 | |
| | | La Plata | 0 | 0 | 0 | 0 | |
| | | Las Animas | | | 0 | 0 | |
| | | Lincoln | 0 | 0 | 0 | 0 | |
| | | Logan | 0 | 0 | 0 | 0 | |
| | | Mineral | 0 | 0 | 0 | 0 | |
| | | Moffat | 0 | 0 | 0 | 0 | |
| | | Montezuma | 0 | 0 | 0 | 0 | |
| | | Morgan | 0 | 0 | 0 | 0 | |
| | | Otero | 0 | 0 | 0 | 0 | |
| | | Ouray | 0 | 0 | 0 | 0 | |
| | | Phillips | 0 | 0 | 0 | 0 | |
| | | Pitkin | 0 | 0 | 0 | 0 | |
| | | Prowers | 0 | 0 | 0 | 0 | |
| | | Rio Blanco | 0 | 0 | 0 | 0 | |
| | | Rio Grande | 0 | 0 | 0 | 0 | |
| | | Routt | 0 | 0 | 0 | 0 | |
| | | Saguache | 0 | 0 | 0 | 0 | |
| | | San Juan | 0 | 0 | 0 | 0 | |
| | | San Miguel | 0 | 0 | 0 | 0 | |
| | | Sedgwick | 0 | 0 | 0 | 0 | |
| | | Washington | 0 | 0 | 0 | 0 | |
| | | Yuma | 0 | 0 | 0 | 0 | |
| | State Police Agencies | State Patrol | 0 | 0 | 0 | 0 | |
| | Other Agencies | 22nd Judicial District Drug Task Force | 0 | 0 | 0 | 0 | |
| | | Colorado Bureau of Investigation | 0 | 0 | 0 | 0 | |
| | | Colorado Mental Health Institute | 0 | 0 | 0 | 0 | |
| | | Delta Montrose Drug Task Force | 0 | 0 | 0 | 0 | |
| CONNECTICUT | Cities | Ansonia | 0 | 0 | 0 | 0 | 18,496 |
| | | Avon | 0 | 0 | 0 | 0 | 17,495 |
| | | Berlin | 0 | 0 | 0 | 0 | 20,610 |
| | | Bethel | 0 | 0 | 0 | 0 | 18,476 |
| | | Bloomfield | 0 | 0 | 0 | 0 | 20,856 |
| | | Branford | 0 | 0 | 0 | 0 | 28,999 |
| | | Brookfield | 0 | 0 | 0 | 0 | 16,766 |
| | | Cromwell | 0 | 0 | 0 | 0 | 13,676 |
| | | Darien | 0 | 0 | 0 | 0 | 20,237 |
| | | East Hampton | 0 | 0 | 0 | 0 | 12,887 |
| | | East Hartford | 0 | 0 | 0 | 0 | 48,459 |
| | | East Haven | 0 | 0 | 0 | 0 | 28,633 |
| | | East Windsor | 0 | 0 | 0 | 0 | 10,936 |
| | | Fairfield | 0 | 0 | 0 | 0 | 57,341 |
| | | Granby | 0 | 0 | 0 | 0 | 11,315 |
| | | Groton | 0 | 0 | 0 | 0 | 9,319 |
| | | Groton Long Point | 0 | 0 | 0 | 0 | 682 |
| | | Hamden | 0 | 0 | 0 | 0 | 57,975 |
| | | Monroe | 0 | 0 | 0 | 0 | 19,366 |
| | | New Canaan | 0 | 0 | 0 | 0 | 19,965 |
| | | New Milford | 0 | 0 | 0 | 0 | 28,471 |
| | | North Branford | 0 | 0 | 0 | 0 | 14,426 |
| | | North Haven | 0 | 0 | 0 | 0 | 24,060 |
| | | Old Saybrook | 0 | 0 | 0 | 0 | 10,537 |
| | | Orange | 0 | 0 | 0 | 0 | 13,843 |
| | | Plainfield | 0 | 0 | 0 | 0 | 15,519 |
| | | Plainville | 0 | 0 | 0 | 0 | 17,221 |
| | | Plymouth | 0 | 0 | 0 | 0 | 12,003 |
| | | Portland | 0 | 0 | 0 | 0 | 9,642 |
| | | Putnam | 0 | 0 | 0 | 0 | 9,342 |
| | | Redding | 0 | 0 | 0 | 0 | 8,855 |
| | | Ridgefield | 0 | 0 | 0 | 0 | 24,046 |
| | | Rocky Hill | 0 | 0 | 0 | 0 | 18,948 |
| | | Seymour | 0 | 0 | 0 | 0 | 16,340 |
| | | South Windsor | 0 | 0 | 0 | 0 | 26,139 |
| | | Stamford | 0 | 0 | 0 | 0 | 119,507 |
| | | Stonington | 0 | 0 | 0 | 0 | 18,420 |
| | | Suffield | 0 | 0 | 0 | 0 | 15,317 |
| | | Thomaston | 0 | 0 | 0 | 0 | 7,792 |
| | | Trumbull | 0 | 0 | 0 | 0 | 34,731 |
| | | Vernon | 0 | 0 | 0 | 0 | 30,038 |
| | | Waterbury | 0 | 0 | 0 | 0 | 107,007 |
| | | Weston | 0 | 0 | 0 | 0 | 10,196 |
| | | Wethersfield | 0 | 0 | 0 | 0 | 25,656 |
| | | Wilton | 0 | 0 | 0 | 0 | 17,701 |
| | | Windsor | 0 | 0 | 0 | 0 | 28,915 |
| | | Wolcott | 0 | 0 | 0 | 0 | 16,571 |
| | | Woodbridge | 0 | 0 | 0 | 0 | 9,215 |
| | Universities and Colleges | Central Connecticut State University | 0 | 0 | 0 | 0 | 12,233 |
| | | Southern Connecticut State University | 0 | 0 | 0 | 0 | 11,769 |
| | | University of Connecticut, Health Center[3] | 0 | 0 | 0 | 0 | |
| | | Western Connecticut State University | 0 | 0 | 0 | 0 | 6,462 |
| | | Yale University | 0 | 0 | 0 | 0 | 10,192 |
| | Other Agencies | State Capitol Police | 0 | 0 | 0 | 0 | |
| DELAWARE | Cities | Bethany Beach | 0 | 0 | 0 | 0 | 971 |
| | | Blades | 0 | 0 | 0 | 0 | 1,166 |
| | | Bridgeville | 0 | 0 | 0 | 0 | 1,645 |
| | | Camden | 0 | 0 | 0 | 0 | 2,621 |
| | | Cheswold | 0 | 0 | 0 | 0 | 479 |
| | | Clayton | 0 | 0 | 0 | 0 | 1,501 |
| | | Dagsboro | 0 | 0 | 0 | 0 | 585 |
| | | Delaware City | 0 | 0 | 0 | 0 | 1,523 |
| | | Delmar | 0 | 0 | 0 | 0 | 1,528 |
| | | Dewey Beach | 0 | 0 | 0 | 0 | 320 |
| | | Dover | 0 | 0 | 0 | 0 | 36,571 |
| | | Ellendale | 0 | 0 | 0 | 0 | 357 |
| | | Elsmere | 0 | 0 | 0 | 0 | 5,676 |

[1]Agencies published in this table indicated that no hate crimes occurred in their jurisdictions during the quarter(s) for which they submitted reports to the Hate Crime Statistics Program. Blanks indicate quarters for which agencies did not submit reports.
[2]Population figures are published only for the cities. The figures listed for the universities and colleges are student enrollment and were provided by the United States Department of Education for the 2008 school year, the most recent available. The enrollment figures include full-time and part-time students.
[3]Student enrollment figures were not available.

## Table 95. Hate Crime Zero Data Submitted per Quarter, by State and Agency, 2009—*Continued*

(Number.)

| State | Agency type | Agency name | Zero data per quarter[1] | | | | Population[2] |
|---|---|---|---|---|---|---|---|
| | | | 1st quarter | 2nd quarter | 3rd quarter | 4th quarter | |
| **DELAWARE** | Felton | 0 | 0 | 0 | 0 | 916 | |
| | | Fenwick Island | 0 | 0 | 0 | 0 | 369 |
| | | Frankford | | | 0 | | 784 |
| | | Greenwood | 0 | 0 | 0 | 0 | 914 |
| | | Harrington | 0 | 0 | 0 | 0 | 3,466 |
| | | Laurel | 0 | 0 | 0 | 0 | 4,009 |
| | | Lewes | 0 | 0 | 0 | 0 | 3,150 |
| | | Middletown | 0 | 0 | 0 | 0 | 13,093 |
| | | Milford | 0 | 0 | 0 | 0 | 8,704 |
| | | Millsboro | 0 | 0 | 0 | 0 | 2,724 |
| | | Milton | 0 | 0 | 0 | 0 | 1,848 |
| | | New Castle | 0 | 0 | 0 | 0 | 4,976 |
| | | Newport | 0 | 0 | 0 | 0 | 1,104 |
| | | Ocean View | 0 | 0 | 0 | 0 | 1,149 |
| | | Rehoboth Beach | 0 | 0 | 0 | 0 | 1,597 |
| | | Seaford | 0 | 0 | 0 | 0 | 7,310 |
| | | Smyrna | 0 | 0 | 0 | 0 | 8,981 |
| | | South Bethany | 0 | 0 | 0 | 0 | 530 |
| | | Wyoming | 0 | 0 | 0 | 0 | 1,443 |
| | **Universities and Colleges** | Delaware State University | 0 | 0 | 0 | 0 | 3,534 |
| | **Other Agencies** | Amtrak Police | 0 | 0 | 0 | 0 | |
| | | Attorney General: | | | | | |
| | | Kent County | 0 | 0 | 0 | 0 | |
| | | New Castle County | 0 | 0 | 0 | 0 | |
| | | Sussex County | 0 | 0 | 0 | 0 | |
| | | Division of Alcohol and Tobacco Enforcement | 0 | 0 | 0 | 0 | |
| | | Drug Enforcement Administration, Wilmington Resident Office | 0 | 0 | 0 | 0 | |
| | | Environmental Control | 0 | 0 | 0 | 0 | |
| | | Fish and Wildlife | 0 | 0 | 0 | 0 | |
| | | Park Rangers | 0 | 0 | 0 | 0 | |
| | | River and Bay Authority | 0 | 0 | 0 | 0 | |
| | | State Capitol Police | 0 | 0 | 0 | 0 | |
| | | State Fire Marshal | 0 | 0 | 0 | 0 | |
| | | Wilmington Fire Department | 0 | 0 | 0 | 0 | |
| **FLORIDA** ...... | **Cities** | Alachua | 0 | 0 | 0 | 0 | 9,669 |
| | | Altamonte Springs | 0 | 0 | 0 | 0 | 39,797 |
| | | Altha | 0 | 0 | 0 | 0 | 521 |
| | | Apalachicola | 0 | 0 | 0 | 0 | 2,197 |
| | | Apopka | 0 | 0 | 0 | 0 | 39,308 |
| | | Astatula | 0 | 0 | 0 | 0 | 1,887 |
| | | Atlantis | 0 | 0 | 0 | 0 | 2,074 |
| | | Auburndale | 0 | 0 | 0 | 0 | 14,619 |
| | | Avon Park | 0 | 0 | 0 | 0 | 9,090 |
| | | Bal Harbour Village | 0 | 0 | 0 | 0 | 3,099 |
| | | Bartow | 0 | 0 | 0 | 0 | 17,069 |
| | | Bay Harbor Islands | 0 | 0 | 0 | 0 | 4,912 |
| | | Belleair | 0 | 0 | 0 | 0 | 4,073 |
| | | Belleair Beach | 0 | 0 | 0 | 0 | 1,581 |
| | | Belleair Bluffs | 0 | 0 | 0 | 0 | 2,155 |
| | | Belle Glade | 0 | 0 | 0 | 0 | 16,642 |
| | | Belleview | 0 | 0 | 0 | 0 | 4,538 |
| | | Biscayne Park | 0 | 0 | 0 | 0 | 2,930 |
| | | Blountstown | 0 | 0 | 0 | 0 | 2,517 |
| | | Bonifay | 0 | 0 | 0 | 0 | 2,772 |
| | | Bowling Green | 0 | 0 | 0 | 0 | 2,958 |
| | | Boynton Beach | 0 | 0 | 0 | 0 | 69,211 |
| | | Bradenton | 0 | 0 | 0 | 0 | 53,951 |
| | | Bradenton Beach | 0 | 0 | 0 | 0 | 1,560 |
| | | Brooksville | 0 | 0 | 0 | 0 | 8,375 |
| | | Bunnell | 0 | 0 | 0 | 0 | 3,281 |
| | | Bushnell | 0 | 0 | 0 | 0 | 2,301 |
| | | Cape Coral | 0 | 0 | 0 | 0 | 164,344 |
| | | Carrabelle | 0 | 0 | 0 | 0 | 1,222 |
| | | Casselberry | 0 | 0 | 0 | 0 | 24,782 |
| | | Cedar Key | 0 | 0 | 0 | 0 | 999 |
| | | Center Hill | 0 | 0 | 0 | 0 | 1,124 |
| | | Chiefland | 0 | 0 | 0 | 0 | 2,149 |
| | | Chipley | 0 | 0 | 0 | 0 | 3,800 |
| | | Clearwater | 0 | 0 | 0 | 0 | 105,383 |
| | | Clermont | 0 | 0 | 0 | 0 | 13,484 |
| | | Clewiston | 0 | 0 | 0 | 0 | 7,248 |
| | | Cocoa | 0 | 0 | 0 | 0 | 16,418 |
| | | Cocoa Beach | 0 | 0 | 0 | 0 | 11,860 |
| | | Coleman | 0 | 0 | 0 | 0 | 775 |
| | | Cooper City | 0 | 0 | 0 | 0 | 29,392 |
| | | Cottondale | 0 | 0 | 0 | 0 | 879 |
| | | Crescent City | 0 | 0 | 0 | 0 | 1,817 |
| | | Crestview | 0 | 0 | 0 | 0 | 20,023 |
| | | Cross City | 0 | 0 | 0 | 0 | 1,824 |
| | | Crystal River | 0 | 0 | 0 | 0 | 3,559 |
| | | Dade City | 0 | 0 | 0 | 0 | 7,321 |
| | | Davenport | 0 | 0 | 0 | 0 | 2,646 |
| | | Daytona Beach | 0 | 0 | 0 | 0 | 64,257 |
| | | De Funiak Springs | 0 | 0 | 0 | 0 | 5,008 |
| | | Deland | 0 | 0 | 0 | 0 | 28,009 |
| | | Delray Beach | 0 | 0 | 0 | 0 | 64,522 |
| | | Doral | 0 | 0 | 0 | 0 | 32,209 |
| | | Dundee | 0 | 0 | 0 | 0 | 3,309 |
| | | Dunedin | 0 | 0 | 0 | 0 | 35,963 |
| | | Dunnellon | 0 | 0 | 0 | 0 | 2,021 |
| | | Eatonville | 0 | 0 | 0 | 0 | 2,354 |
| | | Edgewood | 0 | 0 | 0 | 0 | 2,101 |
| | | El Portal | 0 | 0 | 0 | 0 | 2,297 |
| | | Eustis | 0 | 0 | 0 | 0 | 19,500 |
| | | Fellsmere | 0 | 0 | 0 | 0 | 5,054 |
| | | Fernandina Beach | 0 | 0 | 0 | 0 | 11,714 |
| | | Flagler Beach | 0 | 0 | 0 | 0 | 5,963 |
| | | Florida City | 0 | 0 | 0 | 0 | 10,204 |
| | | Fort Lauderdale | 0 | 0 | 0 | 0 | 182,942 |
| | | Fort Myers | 0 | 0 | 0 | 0 | 67,031 |
| | | Fort Pierce | 0 | 0 | 0 | 0 | 41,114 |
| | | Fort Walton Beach | 0 | 0 | 0 | 0 | 18,759 |
| | | Fruitland Park | 0 | 0 | 0 | 0 | 4,413 |
| | | Golden Beach | 0 | 0 | 0 | 0 | 870 |
| | | Greenacres City | 0 | 0 | 0 | 0 | 32,649 |
| | | Green Cove Springs | 0 | 0 | 0 | 0 | 6,693 |
| | | Greensboro | 0 | 0 | 0 | 0 | 598 |
| | | Gretna | 0 | 0 | 0 | 0 | 1,603 |
| | | Groveland | 0 | 0 | 0 | 0 | 8,445 |
| | | Gulf Breeze | 0 | 0 | 0 | 0 | 6,689 |
| | | Gulfport | 0 | 0 | 0 | 0 | 12,286 |
| | | Gulf Stream | 0 | 0 | 0 | 0 | 737 |
| | | Haines City | 0 | 0 | 0 | 0 | 19,610 |
| | | Hallandale | 0 | 0 | 0 | 0 | 38,644 |
| | | Hampton | 0 | 0 | 0 | 0 | 460 |
| | | Havana | 0 | 0 | 0 | 0 | 1,689 |
| | | Hialeah | 0 | 0 | 0 | 0 | 208,874 |
| | | Hialeah Gardens | 0 | 0 | 0 | 0 | 19,667 |
| | | Highland Beach | 0 | 0 | 0 | 0 | 3,988 |

[1]Agencies published in this table indicated that no hate crimes occurred in their jurisdictions during the quarter(s) for which they submitted reports to the Hate Crime program. Blanks indicate quarters for which agencies did not submit reports.

[2]Population figures are published only for the cities. The figures listed for the universities and colleges are student enrollment and were provided by the United States Department of Education for the 2008 school year, the most recent available. The enrollment figures include full-time and part-time students.

[3]Student enrollment figures were not available.

## Table 95. Hate Crime Zero Data Submitted per Quarter, by State and Agency, 2009—*Continued*

(Number.)

| State | Agency type | Agency name | Zero data per quarter[1] | | | | Population[2] |
|---|---|---|---|---|---|---|---|
| | | | 1st quarter | 2nd quarter | 3rd quarter | 4th quarter | |
| **FLORIDA** | | High Springs | 0 | 0 | 0 | 0 | 4,696 |
| | | Hillsboro Beach | 0 | 0 | 0 | 0 | 2,252 |
| | | Holly Hill | 0 | 0 | 0 | 0 | 13,321 |
| | | Hollywood | 0 | 0 | 0 | 0 | 141,597 |
| | | Holmes Beach | 0 | 0 | 0 | 0 | 5,023 |
| | | Howey-in-the-Hills | 0 | 0 | 0 | 0 | 1,282 |
| | | Indialantic | 0 | 0 | 0 | 0 | 2,930 |
| | | Indian Creek Village | 0 | 0 | 0 | 0 | 37 |
| | | Indian Harbour Beach | 0 | 0 | 0 | 0 | 8,328 |
| | | Indian River Shores | 0 | 0 | 0 | 0 | 3,387 |
| | | Indian Rocks Beach | 0 | 0 | 0 | 0 | 5,143 |
| | | Indian Shores | 0 | 0 | 0 | 0 | 4,235 |
| | | Inglis | 0 | 0 | 0 | 0 | 1,652 |
| | | Interlachen | 0 | 0 | 0 | 0 | 1,508 |
| | | Jacksonville Beach | 0 | 0 | 0 | 0 | 21,750 |
| | | Jennings | 0 | 0 | 0 | 0 | 844 |
| | | Juno Beach | 0 | 0 | 0 | 0 | 3,338 |
| | | Jupiter Inlet Colony | 0 | 0 | 0 | 0 | 387 |
| | | Jupiter Island | 0 | 0 | 0 | 0 | 672 |
| | | Kenneth City | 0 | 0 | 0 | 0 | 4,285 |
| | | Key Biscayne | 0 | 0 | 0 | 0 | 9,655 |
| | | Key Colony Beach | 0 | 0 | 0 | 0 | 757 |
| | | Kissimmee | 0 | 0 | 0 | 0 | 63,986 |
| | | Lady Lake | 0 | 0 | 0 | 0 | 15,282 |
| | | Lake Alfred | 0 | 0 | 0 | 0 | 4,560 |
| | | Lake City | 0 | 0 | 0 | 0 | 12,709 |
| | | Lake Clarke Shores | 0 | 0 | 0 | 0 | 3,313 |
| | | Lake Hamilton | 0 | 0 | 0 | 0 | 1,450 |
| | | Lake Helen | 0 | 0 | 0 | 0 | 2,784 |
| | | Lakeland | 0 | 0 | 0 | 0 | 94,322 |
| | | Lake Mary | 0 | 0 | 0 | 0 | 15,604 |
| | | Lake Park | 0 | 0 | 0 | 0 | 8,664 |
| | | Lake Placid | 0 | 0 | 0 | 0 | 1,897 |
| | | Lake Wales | 0 | 0 | 0 | 0 | 14,875 |
| | | Lake Worth | 0 | 0 | 0 | 0 | 35,500 |
| | | Lantana | 0 | 0 | 0 | 0 | 10,150 |
| | | Lauderdale-by-the-Sea | 0 | 0 | 0 | 0 | 5,825 |
| | | Lauderdale Lakes | 0 | 0 | 0 | 0 | 32,087 |
| | | Lauderhill | 0 | 0 | 0 | 0 | 67,005 |
| | | Lawtey | 0 | 0 | 0 | 0 | 705 |
| | | Leesburg | 0 | 0 | 0 | 0 | 22,836 |
| | | Lighthouse Point | 0 | 0 | 0 | 0 | 11,107 |
| | | Live Oak | 0 | 0 | 0 | 0 | 7,298 |
| | | Longwood | 0 | 0 | 0 | 0 | 13,453 |
| | | Lynn Haven | 0 | 0 | 0 | 0 | 15,606 |
| | | Madeira Beach | 0 | 0 | 0 | 0 | 4,320 |
| | | Madison | 0 | 0 | 0 | 0 | 3,036 |
| | | Maitland | 0 | 0 | 0 | 0 | 14,984 |
| | | Manalapan | 0 | 0 | 0 | 0 | 341 |
| | | Mangonia Park | 0 | 0 | 0 | 0 | 1,224 |
| | | Marco Island | 0 | 0 | 0 | 0 | 15,713 |
| | | Margate | 0 | 0 | 0 | 0 | 54,032 |
| | | Marianna | 0 | 0 | 0 | 0 | 6,290 |
| | | Mascotte | 0 | 0 | 0 | 0 | 6,032 |
| | | Medley | 0 | 0 | 0 | 0 | 1,017 |
| | | Melbourne | 0 | 0 | 0 | 0 | 77,854 |
| | | Melbourne Beach | 0 | 0 | 0 | 0 | 3,130 |
| | | Melbourne Village | 0 | 0 | 0 | 0 | 667 |
| | | Mexico Beach | 0 | 0 | 0 | 0 | 1,298 |
| | | Miami | 0 | 0 | 0 | 0 | 419,205 |
| | | Miami Shores | 0 | 0 | 0 | 0 | 9,464 |
| | | Miami Springs | 0 | 0 | 0 | 0 | 12,412 |
| | | Milton | 0 | 0 | 0 | 0 | 8,789 |
| | | Minneola | 0 | 0 | 0 | 0 | 9,509 |
| | | Monticello | 0 | 0 | 0 | 0 | 2,541 |
| | | Mount Dora | 0 | 0 | 0 | 0 | 13,226 |
| | | Mulberry | 0 | 0 | 0 | 0 | 3,180 |
| | | Naples | 0 | 0 | 0 | 0 | 21,587 |
| | | Neptune Beach | 0 | 0 | 0 | 0 | 6,731 |
| | | New Smyrna Beach | 0 | 0 | 0 | 0 | 23,656 |
| | | Niceville | 0 | 0 | 0 | 0 | 12,368 |
| | | North Bay Village | 0 | 0 | 0 | 0 | 8,024 |
| | | North Lauderdale | 0 | 0 | 0 | 0 | 41,730 |
| | | North Miami Beach | 0 | 0 | 0 | 0 | 41,324 |
| | | North Palm Beach | 0 | 0 | 0 | 0 | 12,155 |
| | | North Redington Beach | 0 | 0 | 0 | 0 | 1,475 |
| | | Oak Hill | 0 | 0 | 0 | 0 | 1,611 |
| | | Oakland | 0 | 0 | 0 | 0 | 1,167 |
| | | Oakland Park | 0 | 0 | 0 | 0 | 42,250 |
| | | Ocean Ridge | 0 | 0 | 0 | 0 | 1,639 |
| | | Okeechobee | 0 | 0 | 0 | 0 | 6,060 |
| | | Oldsmar | 0 | 0 | 0 | 0 | 13,538 |
| | | Opa Locka | 0 | 0 | 0 | 0 | 16,775 |
| | | Orange City | 0 | 0 | 0 | 0 | 10,033 |
| | | Orange Park | 0 | 0 | 0 | 0 | 9,038 |
| | | Ormond Beach | 0 | 0 | 0 | 0 | 38,153 |
| | | Oviedo | 0 | 0 | 0 | 0 | 33,382 |
| | | Pahokee | 0 | 0 | 0 | 0 | 6,650 |
| | | Palatka | 0 | 0 | 0 | 0 | 10,902 |
| | | Palm Beach | 0 | 0 | 0 | 0 | 9,519 |
| | | Palm Beach Shores | 0 | 0 | 0 | 0 | 1,569 |
| | | Palmetto | 0 | 0 | 0 | 0 | 14,453 |
| | | Palmetto Bay | 0 | 0 | 0 | 0 | 22,543 |
| | | Palm Springs | 0 | 0 | 0 | 0 | 16,514 |
| | | Panama City Beach | 0 | 0 | 0 | 0 | 15,758 |
| | | Parker | 0 | 0 | 0 | 0 | 4,532 |
| | | Parkland | 0 | 0 | 0 | 0 | 23,993 |
| | | Pembroke Park | 0 | 0 | 0 | 0 | 4,739 |
| | | Pembroke Pines | 0 | 0 | 0 | 0 | 145,514 |
| | | Perry | 0 | 0 | 0 | 0 | 6,780 |
| | | Pinellas Park | 0 | 0 | 0 | 0 | 47,173 |
| | | Plantation | 0 | 0 | 0 | 0 | 83,544 |
| | | Plant City | 0 | 0 | 0 | 0 | 33,048 |
| | | Ponce Inlet | 0 | 0 | 0 | 0 | 3,217 |
| | | Port Richey | 0 | 0 | 0 | 0 | 3,458 |
| | | Port St. Joe | 0 | 0 | 0 | 0 | 3,537 |
| | | Port St. Lucie | 0 | 0 | 0 | 0 | 164,069 |
| | | Punta Gorda | 0 | 0 | 0 | 0 | 16,567 |
| | | Quincy | 0 | 0 | 0 | 0 | 6,842 |
| | | Redington Beaches | 0 | 0 | 0 | 0 | 1,476 |
| | | Riviera Beach | 0 | 0 | 0 | 0 | 37,247 |
| | | Rockledge | 0 | 0 | 0 | 0 | 25,289 |
| | | Royal Palm Beach | 0 | 0 | 0 | 0 | 31,468 |
| | | Safety Harbor | 0 | 0 | 0 | 0 | 17,060 |
| | | Sanford | 0 | 0 | 0 | 0 | 52,118 |
| | | Sanibel | 0 | 0 | 0 | 0 | 5,601 |
| | | Sarasota | 0 | 0 | 0 | 0 | 52,308 |
| | | Satellite Beach | 0 | 0 | 0 | 0 | 11,774 |
| | | Sea Ranch Lakes | 0 | 0 | 0 | 0 | 734 |
| | | Sebastian | 0 | 0 | 0 | 0 | 20,777 |
| | | Sebring | 0 | 0 | 0 | 0 | 10,796 |
| | | Seminole | 0 | 0 | 0 | 0 | 19,047 |
| | | Sewall's Point | 0 | 0 | 0 | 0 | 2,010 |
| | | Shalimar | 0 | 0 | 0 | 0 | 699 |

[1]Agencies published in this table indicated that no hate crimes occurred in their jurisdictions during the quarter(s) for which they submitted reports to the Hate Crime Statistics Program. Blanks indicate quarters for which agencies did not submit reports.

[2]Population figures are published only for the cities. The figures listed for the universities and colleges are student enrollment and were provided by the United States Department of Education for the 2008 school year, the most recent available. The enrollment figures include full-time and part-time students.

## Table 95. Hate Crime Zero Data Submitted per Quarter, by State and Agency, 2009—*Continued*

(Number.)

| State | Agency type | Agency name | Zero data per quarter[1] | | | | Population[2] |
|---|---|---|---|---|---|---|---|
| | | | 1st quarter | 2nd quarter | 3rd quarter | 4th quarter | |
| **FLORIDA** | | Sneads | 0 | 0 | 0 | 0 | 1,942 |
| | | South Bay | 0 | 0 | 0 | 0 | 4,584 |
| | | South Daytona | 0 | 0 | 0 | 0 | 13,662 |
| | | South Miami | 0 | 0 | 0 | 0 | 10,708 |
| | | South Palm Beach | 0 | 0 | 0 | 0 | 1,461 |
| | | South Pasadena | 0 | 0 | 0 | 0 | 5,523 |
| | | Southwest Ranches | 0 | 0 | 0 | 0 | 7,222 |
| | | Springfield | 0 | 0 | 0 | 0 | 8,792 |
| | | Starke | 0 | 0 | 0 | 0 | 6,011 |
| | | St. Augustine | 0 | 0 | 0 | 0 | 12,476 |
| | | St. Augustine Beach | 0 | 0 | 0 | 0 | 6,400 |
| | | St. Cloud | 0 | 0 | 0 | 0 | 29,604 |
| | | St. Pete Beach | 0 | 0 | 0 | 0 | 9,925 |
| | | Stuart | 0 | 0 | 0 | 0 | 16,000 |
| | | Sunny Isles Beach | 0 | 0 | 0 | 0 | 16,438 |
| | | Surfside | 0 | 0 | 0 | 0 | 4,480 |
| | | Sweetwater | 0 | 0 | 0 | 0 | 12,952 |
| | | Tallahassee | 0 | 0 | 0 | 0 | 174,183 |
| | | Tamarac | 0 | 0 | 0 | 0 | 59,280 |
| | | Tarpon Springs | 0 | 0 | 0 | 0 | 23,628 |
| | | Tavares | 0 | 0 | 0 | 0 | 14,227 |
| | | Temple Terrace | 0 | 0 | 0 | 0 | 22,713 |
| | | Tequesta | 0 | 0 | 0 | 0 | 5,757 |
| | | Treasure Island | 0 | 0 | 0 | 0 | 7,454 |
| | | Trenton | 0 | 0 | 0 | 0 | 1,889 |
| | | Umatilla | 0 | 0 | 0 | 0 | 3,107 |
| | | Valparaiso | 0 | 0 | 0 | 0 | 5,991 |
| | | Venice | 0 | 0 | 0 | 0 | 21,236 |
| | | Vero Beach | 0 | 0 | 0 | 0 | 16,908 |
| | | Virginia Gardens | 0 | 0 | 0 | 0 | 2,150 |
| | | Waldo | 0 | 0 | 0 | 0 | 812 |
| | | Wauchula | 0 | 0 | 0 | 0 | 4,522 |
| | | Webster | 0 | 0 | 0 | 0 | 924 |
| | | Welaka | 0 | 0 | 0 | 0 | 818 |
| | | West Melbourne | 0 | 0 | 0 | 0 | 16,034 |
| | | West Miami | 0 | 0 | 0 | 0 | 5,497 |
| | | Weston | 0 | 0 | 0 | 0 | 63,564 |
| | | West Palm Beach | 0 | 0 | 0 | 0 | 100,763 |
| | | White Springs | 0 | 0 | 0 | 0 | 830 |
| | | Wildwood | 0 | 0 | 0 | 0 | 3,809 |
| | | Williston | 0 | 0 | 0 | 0 | 2,979 |
| | | Windermere | 0 | 0 | 0 | 0 | 2,582 |
| | | Winter Garden | 0 | 0 | 0 | 0 | 31,554 |
| | | Winter Park | 0 | 0 | 0 | 0 | 27,917 |
| | | Winter Springs | 0 | 0 | 0 | 0 | 32,846 |
| | | Zephyrhills | 0 | 0 | 0 | 0 | 13,377 |
| | | Zolfo Springs | 0 | 0 | 0 | 0 | 1,708 |
| | **Universities and Colleges** | Florida A&M University | 0 | 0 | 0 | 0 | 11,857 |
| | | Florida Atlantic University | 0 | 0 | 0 | 0 | 26,839 |
| | | Florida Gulf Coast University | 0 | 0 | 0 | 0 | 10,204 |
| | | Florida International University | 0 | 0 | 0 | 0 | 38,759 |
| | | Florida State University: | | | | | |
| | | Panama City[3] | 0 | 0 | 0 | 0 | |
| | | Tallahassee | 0 | 0 | 0 | 0 | 38,682 |
| | | New College of Florida | 0 | 0 | 0 | 0 | 785 |
| | | Pensacola Junior College | 0 | 0 | 0 | 0 | 10,665 |
| | | Santa Fe College | 0 | 0 | 0 | 0 | 14,796 |
| | | Tallahassee Community College | 0 | 0 | 0 | 0 | 14,005 |
| | | University of North Florida | 0 | 0 | 0 | 0 | 15,280 |
| | | University of South Florida: | | | | | |
| | | St. Petersburg[3] | 0 | 0 | 0 | 0 | |
| | | Tampa | 0 | 0 | 0 | 0 | 46,189 |
| | **Metropolitan Counties** | Baker | 0 | 0 | 0 | 0 | |
| | | Bay | 0 | 0 | 0 | 0 | |
| | | Brevard | 0 | 0 | 0 | 0 | |
| | | Charlotte | 0 | 0 | 0 | 0 | |
| | | Flagler | 0 | 0 | 0 | 0 | |
| | | Gadsden | 0 | 0 | 0 | 0 | |
| | | Gilchrist | 0 | 0 | 0 | 0 | |
| | | Hernando | 0 | 0 | 0 | 0 | |
| | | Indian River | 0 | 0 | 0 | 0 | |
| | | Jefferson | 0 | 0 | 0 | 0 | |
| | | Lake | 0 | 0 | 0 | 0 | |
| | | Lee | 0 | 0 | 0 | 0 | |
| | | Leon | 0 | 0 | 0 | 0 | |
| | | Marion | 0 | 0 | 0 | 0 | |
| | | Miami-Dade | 0 | 0 | 0 | 0 | |
| | | Nassau | 0 | 0 | 0 | 0 | |
| | | Pinellas | 0 | 0 | 0 | 0 | |
| | | Polk | 0 | 0 | 0 | 0 | |
| | | Sarasota | 0 | 0 | 0 | 0 | |
| | | Seminole | 0 | 0 | 0 | 0 | |
| | | St. Johns | 0 | 0 | 0 | 0 | |
| | | St. Lucie | 0 | 0 | 0 | 0 | |
| | | Volusia | 0 | 0 | 0 | 0 | |
| | **Nonmetropolitan Counties** | Bradford | 0 | 0 | 0 | 0 | |
| | | Calhoun | 0 | 0 | 0 | 0 | |
| | | Citrus | 0 | 0 | 0 | 0 | |
| | | Columbia | 0 | 0 | 0 | 0 | |
| | | DeSoto | 0 | 0 | 0 | 0 | |
| | | Dixie | 0 | 0 | 0 | 0 | |
| | | Franklin | 0 | 0 | 0 | 0 | |
| | | Glades | 0 | 0 | 0 | 0 | |
| | | Gulf | 0 | 0 | 0 | 0 | |
| | | Hamilton | 0 | 0 | 0 | 0 | |
| | | Hardee | 0 | 0 | 0 | 0 | |
| | | Hendry | 0 | 0 | 0 | 0 | |
| | | Highlands | 0 | 0 | 0 | 0 | |
| | | Holmes | 0 | 0 | 0 | 0 | |
| | | Jackson | 0 | 0 | 0 | 0 | |
| | | Lafayette | 0 | 0 | 0 | 0 | |
| | | Levy | 0 | 0 | 0 | 0 | |
| | | Liberty | 0 | 0 | 0 | 0 | |
| | | Madison | 0 | 0 | 0 | 0 | |
| | | Monroe | 0 | 0 | 0 | 0 | |
| | | Okeechobee | 0 | 0 | 0 | 0 | |
| | | Putnam | 0 | 0 | 0 | 0 | |
| | | Sumter | 0 | 0 | 0 | 0 | |
| | | Suwannee | 0 | 0 | 0 | 0 | |
| | | Taylor | 0 | 0 | 0 | 0 | |
| | | Union | 0 | 0 | 0 | 0 | |
| | | Walton | 0 | 0 | 0 | 0 | |
| | | Washington | 0 | 0 | 0 | 0 | |
| | **State Police Agencies** | Highway Patrol: | | | | | |
| | | Alachua County | 0 | 0 | 0 | 0 | |
| | | Baker County | 0 | 0 | 0 | 0 | |
| | | Bay County | 0 | 0 | 0 | 0 | |
| | | Bradford County | 0 | 0 | 0 | 0 | |
| | | Brevard County | 0 | 0 | 0 | 0 | |

[1]Agencies published in this table indicated that no hate crimes occurred in their jurisdictions during the quarter(s) for which they submitted reports to the Hate Crime Statistics Program. Blanks indicate quarters for which agencies did not submit reports.
[2]Population figures are published only for the cities. The figures listed for the universities and colleges are student enrollment and were provided by the United States Department of Education for the 2008 school year, the most recent available. The enrollment figures include full-time and part-time students.
[3]Student enrollment figures were not available.

## Table 95. Hate Crime Zero Data Submitted per Quarter, by State and Agency, 2009—*Continued*

(Number.)

| State | Agency type | Agency name | Zero data per quarter[1] | | | | Population[2] |
|---|---|---|---|---|---|---|---|
| | | | 1st quarter | 2nd quarter | 3rd quarter | 4th quarter | |
| **FLORIDA** | | Broward County | 0 | 0 | 0 | 0 | |
| | | Calhoun County | 0 | 0 | 0 | 0 | |
| | | Charlotte County | 0 | 0 | 0 | 0 | |
| | | Citrus County | 0 | 0 | 0 | 0 | |
| | | Clay County | 0 | 0 | 0 | 0 | |
| | | Collier County | 0 | 0 | 0 | 0 | |
| | | Columbia County | 0 | 0 | 0 | 0 | |
| | | DeSoto County | 0 | 0 | 0 | 0 | |
| | | Dixie County | 0 | 0 | 0 | 0 | |
| | | Duval County | 0 | 0 | 0 | 0 | |
| | | Escambia County | 0 | 0 | 0 | 0 | |
| | | Flagler County | 0 | 0 | 0 | 0 | |
| | | Franklin County | 0 | 0 | 0 | 0 | |
| | | Gadsden County | 0 | 0 | 0 | 0 | |
| | | Gilchrist County | 0 | 0 | 0 | 0 | |
| | | Glades County | 0 | 0 | 0 | 0 | |
| | | Gulf County | 0 | 0 | 0 | 0 | |
| | | Hamilton County | 0 | 0 | 0 | 0 | |
| | | Hardee County | 0 | 0 | 0 | 0 | |
| | | Hendry County | 0 | 0 | 0 | 0 | |
| | | Hernando County | 0 | 0 | 0 | 0 | |
| | | Highlands County | 0 | 0 | 0 | 0 | |
| | | Hillsborough County | 0 | 0 | 0 | 0 | |
| | | Holmes County | 0 | 0 | 0 | 0 | |
| | | Indian River County | 0 | 0 | 0 | 0 | |
| | | Jackson County | 0 | 0 | 0 | 0 | |
| | | Jefferson County | 0 | 0 | 0 | 0 | |
| | | Lafayette County | 0 | 0 | 0 | 0 | |
| | | Lake County | 0 | 0 | 0 | 0 | |
| | | Lee County | 0 | 0 | 0 | 0 | |
| | | Leon County | 0 | 0 | 0 | 0 | |
| | | Levy County | 0 | 0 | 0 | 0 | |
| | | Liberty County | 0 | 0 | 0 | 0 | |
| | | Madison County | 0 | 0 | 0 | 0 | |
| | | Manatee County | 0 | 0 | 0 | 0 | |
| | | Marion County | 0 | 0 | 0 | 0 | |
| | | Martin County | 0 | 0 | 0 | 0 | |
| | | Miami-Dade County | 0 | 0 | 0 | 0 | |
| | | Monroe County | 0 | 0 | 0 | 0 | |
| | | Nassau County | 0 | 0 | 0 | 0 | |
| | | Okaloosa County | 0 | 0 | 0 | 0 | |
| | | Okeechobee County | 0 | 0 | 0 | 0 | |
| | | Orange County | 0 | 0 | 0 | 0 | |
| | | Osceola County | 0 | 0 | 0 | 0 | |
| | | Palm Beach County | 0 | 0 | 0 | 0 | |
| | | Pasco County | 0 | 0 | 0 | 0 | |
| | | Pinellas County | 0 | 0 | 0 | 0 | |
| | | Polk County | 0 | 0 | 0 | 0 | |
| | | Putnam County | 0 | 0 | 0 | 0 | |
| | | Santa Rosa County | 0 | 0 | 0 | 0 | |
| | | Sarasota County | 0 | 0 | 0 | 0 | |
| | | Seminole County | 0 | 0 | 0 | 0 | |
| | | St. Johns County | 0 | 0 | 0 | 0 | |
| | | St. Lucie County | 0 | 0 | 0 | 0 | |
| | | Sumter County | 0 | 0 | 0 | 0 | |
| | | Suwannee County | 0 | 0 | 0 | 0 | |
| | | Taylor County | 0 | 0 | 0 | 0 | |
| | | Union County | 0 | 0 | 0 | 0 | |
| | | Volusia County | 0 | 0 | 0 | 0 | |
| | | Wakulla County | 0 | 0 | 0 | 0 | |
| | | Walton County | 0 | 0 | 0 | 0 | |
| | | Washington County | 0 | 0 | 0 | 0 | |
| | **Tribal Agencies** | Miccosukee Tribal | 0 | 0 | 0 | 0 | |
| | **Other Agencies** | Capitol Police | 0 | 0 | 0 | 0 | |
| | | Department of Environmental Protection, Division of Law Enforcement: | | | | | |
| | | Bay County | 0 | 0 | 0 | 0 | |
| | | Brevard County | 0 | 0 | 0 | 0 | |
| | | Citrus County | 0 | 0 | 0 | 0 | |
| | | Duval County | 0 | 0 | 0 | 0 | |
| | | Escambia County | 0 | 0 | 0 | 0 | |
| | | Franklin County | 0 | 0 | 0 | 0 | |
| | | Hillsborough County | 0 | 0 | 0 | 0 | |
| | | Lee County | 0 | 0 | 0 | 0 | |
| | | Leon County | 0 | 0 | 0 | 0 | |
| | | Miami-Dade County | 0 | 0 | 0 | 0 | |
| | | Monroe County | 0 | 0 | 0 | 0 | |
| | | Palm Beach County | 0 | 0 | 0 | 0 | |
| | | Pinellas County | 0 | 0 | 0 | 0 | |
| | | Department of Law Enforcement: | | | | | |
| | | Duval County, Jacksonville | 0 | 0 | 0 | 0 | |
| | | Escambia County, Pensacola | 0 | 0 | 0 | 0 | |
| | | Hillsborough County, Tampa | 0 | 0 | 0 | 0 | |
| | | Lee County, Fort Myers | 0 | 0 | 0 | 0 | |
| | | Leon County, Tallahassee | 0 | 0 | 0 | 0 | |
| | | Miami-Dade County, Miami | 0 | 0 | 0 | 0 | |
| | | Orange County, Orlando | 0 | 0 | 0 | 0 | |
| | | Duval County Schools | 0 | 0 | 0 | 0 | |
| | | Florida Game Commission, Leon County | 0 | 0 | 0 | 0 | |
| | | Florida School for the Deaf and Blind | 0 | 0 | 0 | 0 | |
| | | Jacksonville Airport Authority | 0 | 0 | 0 | 0 | |
| | | Lee County Port Authority | 0 | 0 | 0 | 0 | |
| | | Melbourne International Airport | 0 | 0 | 0 | 0 | |

[1]Agencies published in this table indicated that no hate crimes occurred in their jurisdictions during the quarter(s) for which they submitted reports to the Hate Crime program. Blanks indicate quarters for which agencies did not submit reports.

[2]Population figures are published only for the cities. The figures listed for the universities and colleges are student enrollment and were provided by the United States Department of Education for the 2006 school year, the most recent available. The enrollment figures include full-time and part-time students.

# Table 95. Hate Crime Zero Data Submitted per Quarter, by State and Agency, 2009—*Continued*

(Number.)

| State | Agency type | Agency name | Zero data per quarter[1] | | | | Population[2] |
|---|---|---|---|---|---|---|---|
| | | | 1st quarter | 2nd quarter | 3rd quarter | 4th quarter | |
| **FLORIDA** | | Miami-Dade County Public Schools | 0 | 0 | 0 | 0 | |
| | | Palm Beach County School District | 0 | 0 | 0 | 0 | |
| | | Port Everglades | 0 | 0 | 0 | 0 | |
| | | Sarasota-Bradenton International Airport | 0 | 0 | 0 | 0 | |
| | | State Fire Marshal | 0 | 0 | 0 | 0 | |
| | | St. Petersburg-Clearwater International Airport | 0 | 0 | 0 | 0 | |
| | | Tampa International Airport | 0 | 0 | 0 | 0 | |
| | | Volusia County Beach Management | 0 | 0 | 0 | 0 | |
| **GEORGIA** | **Cities** | Abbeville | 0 | 0 | 0 | 0 | 2,802 |
| | | Adairsville | 0 | 0 | 0 | 0 | 3,280 |
| | | Adel | 0 | 0 | 0 | 0 | 5,405 |
| | | Adrian | 0 | 0 | 0 | | 565 |
| | | Alamo | 0 | 0 | 0 | 0 | 2,722 |
| | | Albany | 0 | 0 | 0 | 0 | 75,734 |
| | | Alma | 0 | 0 | 0 | | 3,518 |
| | | Alpharetta | 0 | | 0 | 0 | 50,279 |
| | | Alto | 0 | 0 | 0 | 0 | 915 |
| | | Americus | 0 | 0 | 0 | 0 | 16,467 |
| | | Aragon | 0 | 0 | 0 | 0 | 1,083 |
| | | Arcade | 0 | 0 | 0 | 0 | 1,981 |
| | | Arlington | 0 | 0 | 0 | 0 | 1,491 |
| | | Attapulgus | 0 | 0 | | | 468 |
| | | Auburn | 0 | 0 | 0 | 0 | 7,563 |
| | | Avondale Estates | 0 | 0 | 0 | 0 | 2,854 |
| | | Baldwin | 0 | 0 | 0 | 0 | 3,028 |
| | | Ball Ground | 0 | 0 | 0 | 0 | 972 |
| | | Barnesville | 0 | 0 | 0 | 0 | 6,001 |
| | | Bartow | 0 | | | | 278 |
| | | Baxley | 0 | 0 | 0 | 0 | 4,575 |
| | | Berlin | 0 | 0 | 0 | 0 | 618 |
| | | Blackshear | 0 | 0 | 0 | 0 | 3,528 |
| | | Blairsville | 0 | 0 | 0 | 0 | 727 |
| | | Blakely | 0 | | | | 5,212 |
| | | Bloomingdale | 0 | 0 | 0 | 0 | 2,627 |
| | | Blythe | 0 | 0 | 0 | 0 | 827 |
| | | Bowdon | 0 | 0 | 0 | 0 | 2,066 |
| | | Braselton | 0 | 0 | 0 | 0 | 5,647 |
| | | Brooklet | 0 | 0 | 0 | 0 | 1,363 |
| | | Brunswick | 0 | 0 | 0 | 0 | 16,348 |
| | | Buchanan | 0 | 0 | 0 | 0 | 1,054 |
| | | Buena Vista | 0 | 0 | 0 | 0 | 1,639 |
| | | Butler | 0 | 0 | 0 | 0 | 1,808 |
| | | Byron | 0 | 0 | | | 4,515 |
| | | Cairo | 0 | 0 | 0 | 0 | 9,871 |
| | | Calhoun | 0 | 0 | 0 | 0 | 15,295 |
| | | Camilla | 0 | 0 | 0 | 0 | 5,658 |
| | | Canton | 0 | 0 | 0 | 0 | 25,370 |
| | | Carrollton | 0 | 0 | 0 | 0 | 23,679 |
| | | Cartersville | 0 | 0 | 0 | 0 | 19,325 |
| | | Cave Spring | 0 | 0 | 0 | 0 | 1,056 |
| | | Cedartown | 0 | 0 | 0 | 0 | 10,177 |
| | | Centerville | 0 | 0 | 0 | 0 | 7,502 |
| | | Chatsworth | 0 | 0 | 0 | 0 | 4,193 |
| | | Chickamauga | 0 | 0 | 0 | 0 | 2,608 |
| | | Clarkesville | 0 | 0 | 0 | | 1,749 |
| | | Clarkston | 0 | 0 | 0 | 0 | 7,871 |
| | | Claxton | 0 | 0 | 0 | 0 | 2,422 |
| | | Cleveland | 0 | 0 | 0 | 0 | 2,732 |
| | | Climax | 0 | 0 | 0 | 0 | 290 |
| | | Cochran | 0 | 0 | | 0 | 5,302 |
| | | College Park | 0 | 0 | 0 | 0 | 19,936 |
| | | Colquitt | 0 | 0 | 0 | 0 | 1,911 |
| | | Columbus | 0 | | | | 186,224 |
| | | Conyers | 0 | 0 | 0 | 0 | 13,798 |
| | | Coolidge | 0 | 0 | 0 | 0 | 559 |
| | | Cordele | 0 | 0 | 0 | 0 | 11,507 |
| | | Cornelia | 0 | 0 | 0 | 0 | 3,882 |
| | | Covington | 0 | 0 | 0 | 0 | 15,385 |
| | | Cumming | 0 | 0 | 0 | | 5,909 |
| | | Cuthbert | 0 | 0 | 0 | 0 | 3,387 |
| | | Dallas | 0 | 0 | 0 | 0 | 11,387 |
| | | Dalton | 0 | 0 | | | 34,299 |
| | | Danielsville | 0 | 0 | 0 | 0 | 452 |
| | | Darien | 0 | 0 | | | 1,770 |
| | | Davisboro | 0 | 0 | 0 | 0 | 1,879 |
| | | Dawson | 0 | 0 | 0 | | 4,549 |
| | | Decatur | 0 | 0 | 0 | 0 | 19,071 |
| | | Dillard | 0 | 0 | 0 | 0 | 236 |
| | | Doerun | 0 | 0 | 0 | 0 | 844 |
| | | Donalsonville | 0 | 0 | 0 | 0 | 2,684 |
| | | Doraville | 0 | 0 | 0 | | 10,308 |
| | | Douglas | 0 | 0 | 0 | 0 | 11,477 |
| | | Douglasville | 0 | 0 | 0 | 0 | 32,586 |
| | | Dublin | 0 | 0 | 0 | 0 | 17,666 |
| | | Duluth | 0 | 0 | 0 | 0 | 26,495 |
| | | Dunwoody | | 0 | 0 | 0 | 33,294 |
| | | East Dublin | 0 | 0 | 0 | 0 | 2,798 |
| | | Eastman | 0 | 0 | 0 | 0 | 5,697 |
| | | East Point | 0 | | 0 | 0 | 43,753 |
| | | Edison | 0 | 0 | 0 | 0 | 1,241 |
| | | Elberton | 0 | 0 | 0 | 0 | 4,524 |
| | | Ellaville | 0 | 0 | 0 | 0 | 1,861 |
| | | Ellijay | 0 | 0 | 0 | 0 | 1,587 |
| | | Emerson | 0 | 0 | 0 | 0 | 1,473 |
| | | Ephesus | 0 | 0 | 0 | 0 | 386 |
| | | Eton | 0 | 0 | 0 | 0 | 481 |
| | | Euharlee | 0 | 0 | | | 4,324 |
| | | Fairburn | 0 | 0 | 0 | 0 | 11,750 |
| | | Fairmount | 0 | 0 | 0 | 0 | 813 |
| | | Flowery Branch | 0 | 0 | 0 | 0 | 4,318 |
| | | Folkston | 0 | 0 | 0 | 0 | 3,230 |
| | | Forest Park | 0 | 0 | 0 | | 21,760 |
| | | Forsyth | 0 | 0 | 0 | 0 | 5,148 |
| | | Fort Gaines | 0 | 0 | 0 | 0 | 991 |
| | | Fort Oglethorpe | 0 | 0 | 0 | 0 | 10,000 |
| | | Franklin | 0 | 0 | 0 | 0 | 883 |
| | | Franklin Springs | 0 | 0 | 0 | 0 | 803 |
| | | Gainesville | 0 | 0 | 0 | 0 | 36,896 |
| | | Garden City | 0 | 0 | 0 | 0 | 9,329 |
| | | Glennville | 0 | 0 | 0 | 0 | 5,464 |
| | | Glenwood | 0 | 0 | 0 | 0 | 897 |
| | | Gordon | 0 | 0 | 0 | 0 | 2,103 |
| | | Grantville | 0 | 0 | 0 | 0 | 2,885 |
| | | Gray | 0 | 0 | 0 | 0 | 2,240 |
| | | Greensboro | 0 | 0 | 0 | 0 | 3,281 |
| | | Greenville | 0 | 0 | 0 | 0 | 921 |
| | | Griffin | 0 | 0 | 0 | 0 | 23,795 |
| | | Grovetown | 0 | 0 | 0 | 0 | 9,654 |
| | | Guyton | 0 | 0 | 0 | 0 | 2,006 |
| | | Hahira | 0 | 0 | 0 | 0 | 2,579 |
| | | Hampton | 0 | 0 | 0 | 0 | 5,464 |
| | | Hapeville | 0 | 0 | 0 | 0 | 5,964 |
| | | Harlem | 0 | 0 | 0 | 0 | 2,071 |
| | | Harrison | 0 | 0 | 0 | 0 | 478 |
| | | Hartwell | 0 | 0 | 0 | 0 | 4,306 |
| | | Hazlehurst | 0 | 0 | 0 | 0 | 3,898 |
| | | Helena | 0 | 0 | 0 | | 2,466 |
| | | Hephzibah | 0 | 0 | 0 | 0 | 4,610 |
| | | Hiawassee | 0 | 0 | 0 | 0 | 862 |
| | | Hinesville | | | 0 | | 30,130 |
| | | Hiram | 0 | 0 | 0 | 0 | 2,129 |
| | | Hoboken | | 0 | 0 | 0 | 528 |
| | | Hogansville | 0 | 0 | 0 | 0 | 2,929 |

[1] Agencies published in this table indicated that no hate crimes occurred in their jurisdictions during the quarter(s) for which they submitted reports to the Hate Crime Statistics Program. Blanks indicate quarters for which agencies did not submit reports.
[2] Population figures are published only for the cities. The figures listed for the universities and colleges are student enrollment and were provided by the United States Department of Education for the 2008 school year, the most recent available. The enrollment figures include full-time and part-time students.

## Table 95. Hate Crime Zero Data Submitted per Quarter, by State and Agency, 2009—*Continued*

(Number.)

| State | Agency type | Agency name | Zero data per quarter[1] | | | | Population[2] |
|---|---|---|---|---|---|---|---|
| | | | 1st quarter | 2nd quarter | 3rd quarter | 4th quarter | |
| GEORGIA | | Holly Springs | 0 | 0 | 0 | 0 | 9,753 |
| | | Homeland | 0 | 0 | 0 | 0 | 795 |
| | | Hoschton | 0 | 0 | 0 | 0 | 1,682 |
| | | Irwinton | 0 | 0 | 0 | 0 | 583 |
| | | Ivey | 0 | 0 | 0 | 0 | 1,064 |
| | | Jackson | 0 | 0 | 0 | 0 | 4,556 |
| | | Jefferson | 0 | 0 | 0 | 0 | 8,531 |
| | | Jesup | 0 | 0 | 0 | 0 | 10,600 |
| | | Johns Creek | 0 | 0 | 0 | 0 | 59,305 |
| | | Jonesboro | 0 | 0 | 0 | 0 | 4,167 |
| | | Kennesaw | 0 | 0 | 0 | 0 | 33,060 |
| | | Keysville | 0 | 0 | 0 | 0 | 246 |
| | | Kingsland | 0 | 0 | 0 | 0 | 14,049 |
| | | Lafayette | 0 | 0 | | | 7,632 |
| | | LaGrange | 0 | 0 | 0 | 0 | 28,634 |
| | | Lake Park | 0 | 0 | | | 616 |
| | | Lavonia | 0 | 0 | 0 | 0 | 2,102 |
| | | Lawrenceville | 0 | 0 | 0 | 0 | 30,046 |
| | | Leary | 0 | 0 | 0 | 0 | 619 |
| | | Leesburg | 0 | 0 | 0 | 0 | 2,987 |
| | | Lilburn | 0 | 0 | 0 | 0 | 11,625 |
| | | Lincolnton | 0 | 0 | 0 | 0 | 1,523 |
| | | Lithonia | 0 | 0 | 0 | | 2,387 |
| | | Locust Grove | 0 | 0 | 0 | 0 | 5,151 |
| | | Loganville | 0 | 0 | 0 | 0 | 11,291 |
| | | Lookout Mountain | 0 | 0 | 0 | | 1,515 |
| | | Louisville | 0 | | | | 2,637 |
| | | Ludowici | 0 | 0 | 0 | 0 | 1,568 |
| | | Lumber City | 0 | 0 | 0 | 0 | 1,175 |
| | | Lumpkin | 0 | 0 | 0 | 0 | 1,205 |
| | | Macon | | 0 | 0 | | 92,299 |
| | | Madison | 0 | 0 | 0 | 0 | 3,959 |
| | | Manchester | 0 | 0 | 0 | 0 | 3,755 |
| | | Marietta | 0 | 0 | 0 | 0 | 68,037 |
| | | Maysville | 0 | 0 | | | 1,711 |
| | | McCaysville | 0 | 0 | 0 | 0 | 977 |
| | | McDonough | 0 | 0 | 0 | 0 | 21,635 |
| | | McIntyre | 0 | 0 | 0 | 0 | 712 |
| | | Metter | | | 0 | | 4,401 |
| | | Midway | 0 | 0 | 0 | 0 | 1,034 |
| | | Milledgeville | 0 | 0 | 0 | 0 | 20,922 |
| | | Millen | 0 | 0 | 0 | 0 | 3,445 |
| | | Milton | 0 | 0 | 0 | 0 | 15,134 |
| | | Molena | 0 | 0 | 0 | 0 | 473 |
| | | Monroe | 0 | 0 | 0 | 0 | 13,607 |
| | | Montezuma | 0 | 0 | 0 | 0 | 3,839 |
| | | Monticello | 0 | 0 | 0 | 0 | 2,632 |
| | | Moultrie | 0 | 0 | 0 | 0 | 15,515 |
| | | Mountain City | 0 | 0 | 0 | 0 | 737 |
| | | Mount Airy | 0 | 0 | 0 | 0 | 1,209 |
| | | Mount Zion | | | | 0 | 1,612 |
| | | Nahunta | 0 | 0 | 0 | | 991 |
| | | Nashville | 0 | 0 | 0 | 0 | 4,884 |
| | | Newnan | 0 | 0 | 0 | 0 | 32,645 |
| | | Newton | 0 | 0 | 0 | 0 | 794 |
| | | Nicholls | 0 | 0 | 0 | 0 | 2,846 |
| | | Norcross | 0 | 0 | 0 | 0 | 11,031 |
| | | Oakwood | 0 | 0 | 0 | 0 | 4,531 |
| | | Ocilla | 0 | 0 | 0 | 0 | 3,130 |
| | | Oglethorpe | 0 | 0 | | | 1,104 |
| | | Omega | 0 | 0 | 0 | 0 | 1,389 |
| | | Oxford | 0 | 0 | 0 | 0 | 2,631 |
| | | Palmetto | 0 | 0 | 0 | 0 | 5,242 |
| | | Patterson | 0 | 0 | 0 | 0 | 687 |
| | | Pavo | 0 | 0 | 0 | | 700 |
| | | Peachtree City | 0 | 0 | 0 | 0 | 35,147 |
| | | Pearson | 0 | 0 | 0 | 0 | 1,966 |
| | | Pelham | 0 | 0 | 0 | 0 | 3,856 |
| | | Pembroke | 0 | 0 | 0 | 0 | 2,565 |
| | | Pendergrass | 0 | 0 | | | 654 |
| | | Pine Lake | 0 | 0 | 0 | | 714 |
| | | Pine Mountain | 0 | 0 | 0 | 0 | 1,323 |
| | | Pineview | 0 | 0 | 0 | 0 | 516 |
| | | Plains | 0 | 0 | 0 | 0 | 602 |
| | | Pooler | 0 | 0 | 0 | 0 | 16,223 |
| | | Portal | 0 | 0 | 0 | 0 | 609 |
| | | Porterdale | 0 | 0 | 0 | 0 | 1,909 |
| | | Port Wentworth | 0 | 0 | 0 | 0 | 4,744 |
| | | Poulan | 0 | 0 | 0 | | 878 |
| | | Powder Springs | 0 | 0 | 0 | 0 | 15,947 |
| | | Quitman | 0 | 0 | 0 | 0 | 4,616 |
| | | Ray City | 0 | 0 | 0 | 0 | 803 |
| | | Register | 0 | | | | 166 |
| | | Reidsville | 0 | | | | 2,490 |
| | | Resaca | 0 | 0 | 0 | 0 | 785 |
| | | Reynolds | 0 | 0 | | 0 | 1,060 |
| | | Richmond Hill | 0 | 0 | 0 | 0 | 11,096 |
| | | Rincon | 0 | | 0 | 0 | 8,424 |
| | | Ringgold | 0 | 0 | 0 | 0 | 2,822 |
| | | Riverdale | 0 | 0 | 0 | 0 | 15,619 |
| | | Roberta | 0 | 0 | 0 | 0 | 748 |
| | | Rockmart | 0 | 0 | 0 | 0 | 4,622 |
| | | Rome | 0 | 0 | 0 | 0 | 36,091 |
| | | Roswell | 0 | 0 | 0 | 0 | 88,371 |
| | | Royston | 0 | 0 | 0 | 0 | 2,762 |
| | | Sandy Springs | 0 | 0 | | 0 | 82,435 |
| | | Savannah-Chatham Metropolitan | 0 | 0 | 0 | 0 | 212,711 |
| | | Screven | 0 | 0 | 0 | 0 | 796 |
| | | Senoia | 0 | 0 | 0 | 0 | 3,793 |
| | | Shiloh | 0 | 0 | 0 | 0 | 434 |
| | | Sky Valley | 0 | 0 | 0 | 0 | 217 |
| | | Smyrna | 0 | 0 | 0 | 0 | 50,485 |
| | | Snellville | 0 | 0 | 0 | 0 | 20,464 |
| | | Social Circle | 0 | 0 | 0 | 0 | 4,940 |
| | | Sparta | 0 | 0 | 0 | 0 | 1,240 |
| | | Springfield | 0 | 0 | 0 | 0 | 2,158 |
| | | Statesboro | 0 | 0 | 0 | 0 | 27,682 |
| | | St. Marys | 0 | 0 | 0 | 0 | 16,997 |
| | | Stone Mountain | 0 | 0 | 0 | 0 | 7,706 |
| | | Suwanee | 0 | 0 | 0 | 0 | 17,197 |
| | | Sycamore | 0 | 0 | 0 | 0 | 528 |
| | | Sylvania | 0 | 0 | 0 | 0 | 2,494 |
| | | Sylvester | 0 | 0 | 0 | 0 | 5,816 |
| | | Talbotton | 0 | 0 | 0 | 0 | 964 |
| | | Tallapoosa | 0 | 0 | 0 | 0 | 3,151 |
| | | Tallulah Falls | 0 | 0 | 0 | 0 | 161 |
| | | Temple | 0 | 0 | 0 | 0 | 4,801 |
| | | Thomaston | 0 | 0 | 0 | 0 | 9,166 |
| | | Thomasville | 0 | 0 | 0 | 0 | 19,416 |
| | | Thomson | 0 | 0 | 0 | 0 | 6,850 |
| | | Thunderbolt | 0 | 0 | 0 | 0 | 2,627 |
| | | Tifton | 0 | 0 | 0 | 0 | 17,469 |
| | | Tignall | 0 | 0 | 0 | 0 | 611 |
| | | Toccoa | 0 | 0 | 0 | 0 | 9,130 |
| | | Trenton | 0 | 0 | 0 | 0 | 2,425 |
| | | Trion | 0 | 0 | 0 | | 2,066 |
| | | Tybee Island | 0 | 0 | 0 | 0 | 3,914 |
| | | Tyrone | 0 | | 0 | 0 | 6,857 |
| | | Union Point | 0 | 0 | 0 | 0 | 1,519 |
| | | Valdosta | 0 | 0 | 0 | 0 | 49,041 |
| | | Vidalia | 0 | 0 | | 0 | 11,449 |
| | | Vienna | 0 | 0 | | | 2,839 |
| | | Wadley | 0 | 0 | | | 1,925 |
| | | Warm Springs | 0 | 0 | 0 | | 476 |
| | | Warner Robins | 0 | 0 | 0 | 0 | 62,769 |
| | | Warrenton | 0 | 0 | | | 1,907 |
| | | Warwick | | | | 0 | 398 |
| | | Washington | 0 | 0 | 0 | 0 | 4,037 |
| | | Watkinsville | 0 | 0 | 0 | 0 | 2,983 |
| | | Waverly Hall | 0 | 0 | 0 | 0 | 789 |
| | | Waycross | 0 | 0 | 0 | 0 | 14,712 |
| | | Waynesboro | 0 | 0 | 0 | 0 | 5,881 |
| | | West Point | 0 | 0 | 0 | 0 | 3,356 |
| | | Whitesburg | 0 | 0 | 0 | | 592 |
| | | Willacoochee | 0 | 0 | 0 | 0 | 1,539 |
| | | Winder | 0 | 0 | 0 | 0 | 14,549 |
| | | Winterville | 0 | | | | 1,201 |

[1]Agencies published in this table indicated that no hate crimes occurred in their jurisdictions during the quarter(s) for which they submitted reports to the Hate Crime Statistics Program. Blanks indicate quarters for which agencies did not submit reports.

[2]Population figures are published only for the cities. The figures listed for the universities and colleges are student enrollment and were provided by the United States Department of Education for the 2008 school year, the most recent available. The enrollment figures include full-time and part-time students.

## Table 95. Hate Crime Zero Data Submitted per Quarter, by State and Agency, 2009—*Continued*

(Number.)

| State | Agency type | Agency name | Zero data per quarter[1] | | | | Population[2] |
|---|---|---|---|---|---|---|---|
| | | | 1st quarter | 2nd quarter | 3rd quarter | 4th quarter | |
| GEORGIA | | Woodbury | 0 | 0 | 0 | | 1,060 |
| | | Woodland | 0 | | | | 388 |
| | | Wrens | 0 | 0 | 0 | 0 | 2,205 |
| | | Zebulon | 0 | 0 | 0 | | 1,257 |
| | Universities and Colleges | Abraham Baldwin Agricultural College | 0 | 0 | 0 | 0 | 3,600 |
| | | Agnes Scott College | 0 | 0 | | | 832 |
| | | Albany State University | 0 | 0 | 0 | 0 | 4,176 |
| | | Armstrong Atlantic State University | 0 | 0 | 0 | 0 | 7,067 |
| | | Atlanta Metropolitan College | 0 | 0 | 0 | | 2,241 |
| | | Augusta State University | 0 | 0 | 0 | 0 | 6,689 |
| | | Berry College | 0 | 0 | 0 | 0 | 1,795 |
| | | Clark Atlanta University | 0 | 0 | 0 | 0 | 4,068 |
| | | Clayton College and State University | 0 | | | 0 | 6,074 |
| | | Coastal Georgia Community College | 0 | 0 | 0 | 0 | 2,932 |
| | | Columbus State University | 0 | 0 | 0 | | 7,951 |
| | | Dalton State College | 0 | 0 | 0 | 0 | 4,957 |
| | | Darton College | 0 | 0 | 0 | 0 | 5,018 |
| | | Emory University | 0 | 0 | 0 | 0 | 12,755 |
| | | Fort Valley State University | 0 | 0 | | 0 | 3,106 |
| | | Georgia College and State University | 0 | 0 | 0 | 0 | 6,506 |
| | | Georgia Gwinnett College | 0 | | | | 360 |
| | | Georgia Institute of Technology | 0 | 0 | 0 | 0 | 19,413 |
| | | Georgia Military College | 0 | 0 | 0 | 0 | 1,345 |
| | | Georgia Perimeter College | 0 | 0 | 0 | 0 | 22,808 |
| | | Georgia Southern University | 0 | 0 | 0 | 0 | 17,764 |
| | | Georgia Southwestern State University | 0 | 0 | 0 | 0 | 2,717 |
| | | Georgia State University | 0 | 0 | 0 | 0 | 28,229 |
| | | Gordon College | 0 | 0 | 0 | 0 | 3,855 |
| | | Kennesaw State University | 0 | 0 | 0 | 0 | 21,449 |
| | | Medical College of Georgia | 0 | 0 | 0 | 0 | 2,443 |
| | | Mercer University | 0 | 0 | 0 | 0 | 7,622 |
| | | Middle Georgia College | 0 | 0 | 0 | 0 | 3,434 |
| | | Morehouse College | 0 | 0 | 0 | 0 | 2,781 |
| | | Morris-Brown College[3] | 0 | 0 | 0 | 0 | |
| | | North Georgia College and State University | 0 | 0 | 0 | 0 | 5,500 |
| | | Piedmont College | 0 | 0 | 0 | 0 | 2,783 |
| | | Savannah State University | 0 | 0 | 0 | 0 | 3,453 |
| | | Southern Polytechnic State University | 0 | 0 | 0 | 0 | 4,818 |
| | | South Georgia College | 0 | 0 | 0 | 0 | 1,880 |
| | | Valdosta State University | 0 | 0 | 0 | 0 | 11,490 |
| | | Wesleyan College | 0 | 0 | 0 | 0 | 739 |
| | | Young Harris College | 0 | 0 | 0 | 0 | 654 |
| | Metropolitan Counties | Augusta-Richmond | 0 | 0 | 0 | 0 | |
| | | Baker | 0 | | | | |
| | | Bartow | 0 | 0 | 0 | 0 | |
| | | Bibb | 0 | | | | |
| | | Brantley | 0 | 0 | 0 | 0 | |
| | | Brooks | 0 | 0 | 0 | 0 | |
| | | Bryan | 0 | 0 | 0 | 0 | |
| | | Burke | 0 | 0 | | | |
| | | Butts | 0 | 0 | 0 | 0 | |
| | | Carroll | 0 | 0 | 0 | | |
| | | Catoosa | 0 | 0 | 0 | 0 | |
| | | Chatham | 0 | 0 | 0 | 0 | |
| | | Cherokee | 0 | 0 | 0 | 0 | |
| | | Clarke | 0 | 0 | 0 | 0 | |
| | | Clayton | 0 | | 0 | 0 | |
| | | Clayton County Police Department | 0 | 0 | 0 | 0 | |
| | | Cobb | 0 | 0 | 0 | 0 | |
| | | Columbia | 0 | 0 | 0 | 0 | |
| | | Coweta | 0 | 0 | 0 | 0 | |
| | | Dawson | 0 | 0 | 0 | 0 | |
| | | DeKalb | 0 | 0 | 0 | 0 | |
| | | DeKalb County Police Department | 0 | 0 | | | |
| | | Dougherty County Police Department | 0 | 0 | 0 | | |
| | | Douglas | 0 | 0 | 0 | 0 | |
| | | Echols | 0 | 0 | 0 | 0 | |
| | | Fayette | 0 | 0 | 0 | 0 | |
| | | Forsyth | 0 | 0 | | | |
| | | Fulton | 0 | 0 | 0 | 0 | |
| | | Fulton County Police Department | 0 | | | | |
| | | Glynn | 0 | 0 | 0 | 0 | |
| | | Glynn County Police Department | 0 | 0 | 0 | 0 | |
| | | Hall | 0 | 0 | 0 | | |
| | | Harris | 0 | 0 | 0 | 0 | |
| | | Heard | 0 | 0 | 0 | 0 | |
| | | Henry | 0 | 0 | 0 | 0 | |
| | | Henry County Police Department | 0 | 0 | 0 | 0 | |
| | | Houston | 0 | 0 | 0 | | |

[1]Agencies published in this table indicated that no hate crimes occurred in their jurisdictions during the quarter(s) for which they submitted reports to the Hate Crime Statistics Program. Blanks indicate quarters for which agencies did not submit reports.

[2]Population figures are published only for the cities. The figures listed for the universities and colleges are student enrollment and were provided by the United States Department of Education for the 2008 school year, the most recent available. The enrollment figures include full-time and part-time students.

[3]Student enrollment figures were not available.

## Table 95. Hate Crime Zero Data Submitted per Quarter, by State and Agency, 2009—*Continued*

(Number.)

| State | Agency type | Agency name | Zero data per quarter[1] 1st quarter | 2nd quarter | 3rd quarter | 4th quarter | Population[2] |
|---|---|---|---|---|---|---|---|
| **GEORGIA** | | Jasper | 0 | 0 | 0 | 0 | |
| | | Jones | 0 | 0 | 0 | 0 | |
| | | Lamar | 0 | 0 | 0 | | |
| | | Lanier | 0 | 0 | 0 | 0 | |
| | | Lee | 0 | 0 | 0 | 0 | |
| | | Long | 0 | 0 | | | |
| | | Lowndes | 0 | 0 | | | |
| | | Marion | 0 | 0 | 0 | | |
| | | McDuffie | 0 | 0 | 0 | 0 | |
| | | McIntosh | 0 | | | | |
| | | Meriwether | 0 | 0 | 0 | 0 | |
| | | Monroe | 0 | 0 | 0 | 0 | |
| | | Murray | 0 | 0 | 0 | 0 | |
| | | Newton | 0 | 0 | 0 | 0 | |
| | | Oconee | 0 | | | | |
| | | Oglethorpe | 0 | 0 | 0 | 0 | |
| | | Paulding | 0 | 0 | 0 | 0 | |
| | | Pickens | 0 | 0 | 0 | 0 | |
| | | Pike | 0 | 0 | 0 | 0 | |
| | | Rockdale | 0 | 0 | 0 | 0 | |
| | | Spalding | 0 | 0 | 0 | 0 | |
| | | Terrell | 0 | 0 | 0 | 0 | |
| | | Twiggs | 0 | 0 | 0 | 0 | |
| | | Walker | 0 | 0 | 0 | 0 | |
| | | Walton | 0 | | | | |
| | | Whitfield | 0 | 0 | 0 | | |
| | | Worth | 0 | 0 | 0 | 0 | |
| | **Nonmetropolitan Counties** | Appling | 0 | | | | |
| | | Baldwin | 0 | 0 | 0 | 0 | |
| | | Banks | 0 | 0 | 0 | | |
| | | Ben Hill | 0 | 0 | 0 | 0 | |
| | | Berrien | 0 | 0 | 0 | 0 | |
| | | Bleckley | 0 | 0 | 0 | 0 | |
| | | Bulloch | 0 | 0 | 0 | 0 | |
| | | Calhoun | 0 | 0 | 0 | 0 | |
| | | Camden | 0 | 0 | 0 | 0 | |
| | | Candler | 0 | 0 | 0 | 0 | |
| | | Charlton | 0 | 0 | 0 | 0 | |
| | | Chattooga | 0 | | | | |
| | | Clay | 0 | 0 | 0 | 0 | |
| | | Clinch | 0 | 0 | 0 | 0 | |
| | | Coffee | 0 | 0 | | 0 | |
| | | Cook | 0 | 0 | 0 | 0 | |
| | | Crisp | 0 | 0 | 0 | 0 | |
| | | Dooly | 0 | 0 | 0 | 0 | |
| | | Early | 0 | 0 | 0 | 0 | |
| | | Elbert | 0 | 0 | 0 | 0 | |
| | | Emanuel | 0 | 0 | 0 | 0 | |
| | | Evans | 0 | 0 | | | |
| | | Fannin | 0 | 0 | 0 | 0 | |
| | | Franklin | | | 0 | | |
| | | Gilmer | 0 | | 0 | 0 | |
| | | Glascock | 0 | 0 | | | |
| | | Gordon | 0 | 0 | 0 | 0 | |
| | | Grady | 0 | | | | |
| | | Greene | 0 | 0 | 0 | 0 | |
| | | Habersham | 0 | 0 | 0 | 0 | |
| | | Hancock | 0 | | | | |
| | | Hancock County Police Department | 0 | | | | |
| | | Irwin | 0 | 0 | 0 | 0 | |
| | | Jackson | 0 | 0 | 0 | 0 | |
| | | Jeff Davis | 0 | 0 | 0 | 0 | |
| | | Jefferson | 0 | 0 | 0 | 0 | |
| | | Laurens | 0 | 0 | 0 | 0 | |
| | | Lincoln | 0 | | | | |
| | | Lumpkin | 0 | 0 | 0 | | |
| | | Macon | 0 | 0 | | | |
| | | Miller | 0 | | | | |
| | | Mitchell | 0 | 0 | 0 | 0 | |
| | | Peach | 0 | 0 | 0 | 0 | |
| | | Pierce | 0 | 0 | 0 | 0 | |
| | | Polk | 0 | 0 | 0 | 0 | |
| | | Polk County Police Department | 0 | 0 | 0 | 0 | |
| | | Pulaski | 0 | 0 | 0 | 0 | |
| | | Quitman | 0 | 0 | | | |
| | | Rabun | 0 | 0 | 0 | 0 | |
| | | Randolph | 0 | 0 | | | |
| | | Schley | 0 | 0 | 0 | 0 | |
| | | Seminole | 0 | 0 | 0 | 0 | |
| | | Stephens | 0 | 0 | 0 | 0 | |
| | | Stewart | 0 | 0 | 0 | 0 | |
| | | Sumter | 0 | 0 | | | |
| | | Talbot | 0 | 0 | 0 | 0 | |
| | | Taliaferro | 0 | | | | |
| | | Tattnall | 0 | 0 | 0 | | |
| | | Taylor | 0 | 0 | 0 | 0 | |
| | | Telfair | 0 | 0 | 0 | 0 | |
| | | Thomas | 0 | 0 | 0 | 0 | |
| | | Tift | 0 | 0 | 0 | 0 | |
| | | Toombs | 0 | 0 | 0 | 0 | |
| | | Treutlen | 0 | 0 | 0 | 0 | |
| | | Troup | 0 | 0 | 0 | | |
| | | Turner | 0 | 0 | 0 | 0 | |
| | | Union | | | | 0 | |
| | | Upson | 0 | 0 | 0 | 0 | |
| | | Ware | 0 | 0 | 0 | 0 | |
| | | Warren | 0 | | | | |
| | | Washington | 0 | 0 | 0 | | |
| | | Wheeler | 0 | 0 | 0 | 0 | |
| | | White | 0 | 0 | 0 | 0 | |
| | | Wilcox | 0 | 0 | 0 | 0 | |
| | | Wilkes | 0 | 0 | 0 | 0 | |
| | | Wilkinson | 0 | 0 | 0 | 0 | |
| | **State Police Agencies** | Georgia Department of Public Safety | 0 | 0 | 0 | 0 | |
| | **Other Agencies** | Atlanta Public Schools | 0 | 0 | 0 | 0 | |
| | | Atlanta State Farmers Market | 0 | 0 | 0 | 0 | |
| | | Augusta Board of Education | 0 | 0 | 0 | 0 | |
| | | Bibb County Board of Education | 0 | 0 | 0 | 0 | |
| | | Chatham County Board of Education | 0 | 0 | 0 | 0 | |
| | | Cherokee County Board of Education | 0 | 0 | | | |
| | | Cherokee County Marshal | 0 | 0 | 0 | 0 | |
| | | Cobb County Board of Education | 0 | 0 | 0 | 0 | |
| | | Decatur County Schools | 0 | 0 | 0 | 0 | |
| | | DeKalb County School System | 0 | 0 | 0 | 0 | |
| | | Department of Natural Resources, Social Circle | 0 | 0 | 0 | 0 | |
| | | Fayette County Marshal | 0 | 0 | 0 | 0 | |
| | | Forsyth County Fire Investigation Unit | 0 | 0 | 0 | 0 | |

[1]Agencies published in this table indicated that no hate crimes occurred in their jurisdictions during the quarter(s) for which they submitted reports to the Hate Crime Statistics Program. Blanks indicate quarters for which agencies did not submit reports.

[2]Population figures are published only for the cities. The figures listed for the universities and colleges are student enrollment and were provided by the United States Department of Education for the 2008 school year, the most recent available. The enrollment figures include full-time and part-time students.

## Table 95. Hate Crime Zero Data Submitted per Quarter, by State and Agency, 2009—*Continued*

(Number.)

| State | Agency type | Agency name | Zero data per quarter[1] 1st quarter | 2nd quarter | 3rd quarter | 4th quarter | Population[2] |
|---|---|---|---|---|---|---|---|
| GEORGIA | | Fulton County School System | 0 | 0 | 0 | 0 | |
| | | Georgia Department of Transportation, Office of Investigations | 0 | 0 | 0 | 0 | |
| | | Georgia World Congress | 0 | 0 | | | |
| | | Gwinnett County Public Schools | 0 | 0 | 0 | 0 | |
| | | Habersham County Public Schools | 0 | 0 | 0 | 0 | |
| | | Hartsfield-Jackson Atlanta International Airport | 0 | 0 | 0 | 0 | |
| | | Metropolitan Atlanta Rapid Transit Authority | 0 | 0 | 0 | 0 | |
| | | Muscogee City Marshal | 0 | 0 | 0 | 0 | |
| | | Pickens County Board of Education | 0 | 0 | | | |
| | | Ports Authority, Savannah | 0 | 0 | 0 | 0 | |
| | | Richmond County Marshal | | | 0 | 0 | |
| | | State Board of Workers Compensation, Fraud Investigation Division | 0 | 0 | 0 | 0 | |
| | | Stone Mountain Park | 0 | 0 | 0 | 0 | |
| | | Washington County Board of Education | 0 | 0 | 0 | 0 | |
| IDAHO | Cities | Aberdeen | 0 | 0 | 0 | 0 | 1,740 |
| | | American Falls | 0 | 0 | 0 | 0 | 4,067 |
| | | Blackfoot | 0 | 0 | 0 | 0 | 11,072 |
| | | Bonners Ferry | 0 | 0 | 0 | 0 | 2,592 |
| | | Buhl | 0 | 0 | 0 | 0 | 4,088 |
| | | Cascade | 0 | 0 | 0 | 0 | 989 |
| | | Challis | 0 | 0 | 0 | 0 | 895 |
| | | Chubbuck | 0 | 0 | 0 | 0 | 12,087 |
| | | Cottonwood | 0 | 0 | 0 | 0 | 1,053 |
| | | Emmett | 0 | 0 | 0 | 0 | 6,437 |
| | | Filer | 0 | 0 | 0 | 0 | 2,189 |
| | | Fruitland | 0 | 0 | 0 | 0 | 4,836 |
| | | Garden City | 0 | 0 | 0 | 0 | 11,833 |
| | | Gooding | 0 | 0 | 0 | 0 | 3,180 |
| | | Grangeville | 0 | 0 | 0 | 0 | 3,099 |
| | | Hagerman | 0 | 0 | 0 | 0 | 795 |
| | | Heyburn | 0 | 0 | 0 | 0 | 2,674 |
| | | Homedale | 0 | 0 | 0 | 0 | 2,464 |
| | | Idaho Falls | 0 | 0 | 0 | 0 | 54,702 |
| | | Kamiah | 0 | 0 | 0 | 0 | 1,081 |
| | | Kellogg | 0 | 0 | 0 | 0 | 2,208 |
| | | Ketchum | 0 | 0 | 0 | 0 | 3,302 |
| | | Kimberly | 0 | 0 | 0 | 0 | 3,213 |
| | | Lewiston | 0 | 0 | 0 | 0 | 31,864 |
| | | McCall | 0 | 0 | 0 | 0 | 2,656 |
| | | Meridian | 0 | 0 | 0 | 0 | 71,581 |
| | | Montpelier | 0 | 0 | 0 | 0 | 2,313 |
| | | Mountain Home | 0 | 0 | 0 | 0 | 12,482 |
| | | Orofino | 0 | 0 | 0 | 0 | 3,024 |
| | | Osburn | 0 | 0 | 0 | 0 | 1,373 |
| | | Parma | 0 | 0 | 0 | 0 | 1,881 |
| | | Payette | 0 | 0 | 0 | 0 | 7,682 |
| | | Pinehurst | 0 | 0 | 0 | 0 | 1,582 |
| | | Ponderay | 0 | 0 | 0 | 0 | 702 |
| | | Post Falls | 0 | 0 | 0 | 0 | 27,603 |
| | | Preston | 0 | 0 | 0 | 0 | 5,101 |
| | | Priest River | 0 | 0 | 0 | 0 | 1,930 |
| | | Rathdrum | 0 | 0 | 0 | 0 | 7,086 |
| | | Rexburg | 0 | 0 | 0 | 0 | 30,020 |
| | | Rigby | 0 | 0 | 0 | 0 | 3,438 |
| | | Rupert | 0 | 0 | 0 | 0 | 5,025 |
| | | Salmon | 0 | 0 | 0 | 0 | 2,975 |
| | | Sandpoint | 0 | 0 | 0 | 0 | 8,519 |
| | | Shelley | 0 | 0 | 0 | 0 | 4,304 |
| | | Soda Springs | 0 | 0 | 0 | 0 | 3,040 |
| | | Spirit Lake | 0 | 0 | 0 | 0 | 1,772 |
| | | St. Anthony | 0 | 0 | 0 | 0 | 3,409 |
| | | St. Maries | 0 | 0 | 0 | 0 | 2,642 |
| | | Sun Valley | 0 | 0 | 0 | 0 | 1,470 |
| | | Weiser | 0 | 0 | 0 | 0 | 5,275 |
| | | Wendell | 0 | 0 | 0 | 0 | 2,423 |
| | | Wilder | 0 | 0 | 0 | 0 | 1,474 |
| | Metropolitan Counties | Ada | 0 | 0 | 0 | 0 | |
| | | Bannock | 0 | 0 | 0 | 0 | |
| | | Boise | 0 | | | | |
| | | Bonneville | 0 | 0 | 0 | 0 | |
| | | Canyon | 0 | 0 | 0 | 0 | |
| | | Franklin | 0 | 0 | 0 | 0 | |
| | | Gem | 0 | 0 | 0 | 0 | |
| | | Jefferson | 0 | 0 | 0 | 0 | |
| | | Kootenai | 0 | 0 | 0 | 0 | |
| | | Nez Perce | 0 | 0 | 0 | 0 | |
| | | Owyhee | 0 | 0 | 0 | 0 | |
| | | Power | 0 | 0 | 0 | 0 | |
| | Nonmetropolitan Counties | Adams | 0 | 0 | 0 | 0 | |
| | | Bear Lake | 0 | 0 | 0 | 0 | |
| | | Benewah | 0 | 0 | 0 | 0 | |
| | | Bingham | 0 | 0 | 0 | 0 | |
| | | Blaine | 0 | 0 | 0 | 0 | |
| | | Bonner | 0 | 0 | 0 | 0 | |
| | | Boundary | 0 | 0 | 0 | 0 | |
| | | Butte | 0 | 0 | 0 | 0 | |
| | | Camas | 0 | 0 | 0 | 0 | |
| | | Caribou | 0 | 0 | 0 | 0 | |
| | | Cassia | 0 | 0 | 0 | 0 | |
| | | Clark | 0 | 0 | 0 | 0 | |
| | | Clearwater | 0 | 0 | 0 | 0 | |
| | | Custer | 0 | 0 | 0 | 0 | |
| | | Elmore | 0 | 0 | 0 | 0 | |
| | | Fremont | 0 | 0 | 0 | 0 | |
| | | Gooding | 0 | 0 | 0 | 0 | |
| | | Idaho | 0 | 0 | 0 | 0 | |
| | | Jerome | 0 | 0 | 0 | 0 | |
| | | Latah | 0 | 0 | 0 | 0 | |
| | | Lemhi | 0 | 0 | 0 | 0 | |
| | | Lewis | 0 | 0 | 0 | 0 | |
| | | Lincoln | 0 | 0 | 0 | 0 | |
| | | Madison | 0 | 0 | 0 | 0 | |
| | | Minidoka | 0 | 0 | 0 | 0 | |
| | | Oneida | 0 | 0 | 0 | 0 | |
| | | Payette | 0 | 0 | 0 | 0 | |
| | | Shoshone | 0 | 0 | 0 | 0 | |
| | | Teton | 0 | 0 | 0 | 0 | |
| | | Twin Falls | 0 | 0 | 0 | 0 | |
| | | Valley | 0 | 0 | 0 | 0 | |
| | | Washington | 0 | 0 | 0 | 0 | |
| | State Police Agencies | Idaho State Police | 0 | 0 | 0 | 0 | |
| ILLINOIS | Cities | Albers | 0 | 0 | 0 | 0 | 1,110 |
| | | Aledo | 0 | | | | 3,560 |

[1]Agencies published in this table indicated that no hate crimes occurred in their jurisdictions during the quarter(s) for which they submitted reports to the Hate Crime Statistics Program. Blanks indicate quarters for which agencies did not submit reports.

[2]Population figures are published only for the cities. The figures listed for the universities and colleges are student enrollment and were provided by the United States Department of Education for the 2008 school year, the most recent available. The enrollment figures include full-time and part-time students.

## Table 95. Hate Crime Zero Data Submitted per Quarter, by State and Agency, 2009—*Continued*

(Number.)

| State | Agency type | Agency name | Zero data per quarter[1] | | | | Population[2] |
|---|---|---|---|---|---|---|---|
| | | | 1st quarter | 2nd quarter | 3rd quarter | 4th quarter | |
| **ILLINOIS** | | Alorton | 0 | 0 | 0 | 0 | 2,503 |
| | | Alton | 0 | 0 | 0 | 0 | 29,271 |
| | | Antioch | 0 | 0 | 0 | 0 | 14,579 |
| | | Arcola | 0 | 0 | 0 | 0 | 2,776 |
| | | Arlington Heights | 0 | 0 | 0 | 0 | 73,061 |
| | | Arthur | 0 | 0 | 0 | 0 | 2,121 |
| | | Atkinson | 0 | 0 | 0 | | 950 |
| | | Bartlett | 0 | 0 | 0 | 0 | 42,856 |
| | | Bartonville | 0 | 0 | 0 | 0 | 6,142 |
| | | Beckemeyer | 0 | 0 | | | 1,088 |
| | | Beecher | 0 | 0 | 0 | 0 | 3,151 |
| | | Belgium | 0 | 0 | 0 | 0 | 460 |
| | | Belvidere | | | | 0 | 27,128 |
| | | Bensenville | 0 | | | | 20,073 |
| | | Benton | 0 | 0 | 0 | 0 | 6,961 |
| | | Berkeley | 0 | 0 | 0 | 0 | 4,878 |
| | | Berwyn | 0 | 0 | 0 | 0 | 49,489 |
| | | Bethalto | 0 | | | | 9,974 |
| | | Bloomingdale | 0 | 0 | 0 | 0 | 21,855 |
| | | Blue Mound | 0 | 0 | | | 1,009 |
| | | Bridgeport | 0 | | | | 2,077 |
| | | Bridgeview | 0 | 0 | 0 | 0 | 14,953 |
| | | Broadview | 0 | 0 | 0 | 0 | 7,558 |
| | | Bunker Hill | 0 | 0 | 0 | 0 | 1,735 |
| | | Byron | 0 | 0 | 0 | 0 | 3,951 |
| | | Cahokia | 0 | 0 | 0 | 0 | 14,970 |
| | | Calumet Park | 0 | 0 | 0 | 0 | 7,924 |
| | | Cambridge | 0 | 0 | 0 | 0 | 2,084 |
| | | Canton | 0 | 0 | 0 | 0 | 14,463 |
| | | Carlyle | 0 | 0 | 0 | 0 | 3,375 |
| | | Carrier Mills | | 0 | | 0 | 1,827 |
| | | Cary | | 0 | 0 | 0 | 20,066 |
| | | Catlin | 0 | 0 | 0 | 0 | 2,111 |
| | | Champaign | 0 | 0 | 0 | 0 | 80,467 |
| | | Charleston | 0 | 0 | 0 | 0 | 21,779 |
| | | Chatham | 0 | 0 | 0 | 0 | 10,925 |
| | | Chester | 0 | 0 | 0 | 0 | 7,775 |
| | | Chicago Heights | 0 | 0 | 0 | 0 | 30,354 |
| | | Clarendon Hills | 0 | 0 | 0 | 0 | 8,666 |
| | | Clinton | 0 | 0 | 0 | 0 | 7,117 |
| | | Coal Valley | 0 | 0 | 0 | 0 | 4,045 |
| | | Cobden | 0 | 0 | 0 | 0 | 1,096 |
| | | Colfax | 0 | | | | 1,002 |
| | | Columbia | 0 | 0 | 0 | 0 | 9,505 |
| | | Cordova | 0 | 0 | | | 686 |
| | | Country Club Hills | 0 | 0 | 0 | 0 | 16,783 |
| | | Countryside | 0 | 0 | | | 5,766 |
| | | Danvers | 0 | 0 | 0 | 0 | 1,145 |
| | | Danville | 0 | 0 | 0 | 0 | 32,076 |
| | | Darien | 0 | 0 | 0 | 0 | 22,304 |
| | | Deerfield | 0 | 0 | 0 | 0 | 19,797 |
| | | Deer Park | 0 | 0 | 0 | 0 | 3,373 |
| | | Delavan | 0 | 0 | 0 | 0 | 1,747 |
| | | De Soto | 0 | 0 | 0 | 0 | 1,549 |
| | | Dixon | 0 | 0 | 0 | 0 | 14,931 |
| | | Dunfermline | 0 | | | | 306 |
| | | Dupo | 0 | 0 | 0 | 0 | 4,089 |
| | | Durand | 0 | 0 | | | 1,085 |
| | | Dwight | 0 | 0 | 0 | 0 | 4,255 |
| | | East Dubuque | 0 | 0 | 0 | 0 | 1,913 |
| | | East Moline | 0 | 0 | 0 | 0 | 20,828 |
| | | East Peoria | 0 | 0 | 0 | 0 | 22,769 |
| | | Effingham | 0 | 0 | 0 | 0 | 12,498 |
| | | Elizabeth | 0 | 0 | 0 | 0 | 646 |
| | | Elk Grove Village | 0 | 0 | 0 | 0 | 33,164 |
| | | Essex | 0 | 0 | 0 | 0 | 723 |
| | | Eureka | 0 | 0 | 0 | 0 | 5,405 |
| | | Evergreen Park | 0 | 0 | 0 | 0 | 19,206 |
| | | Fairfield | 0 | | | | 5,139 |
| | | Fairmont City | 0 | 0 | 0 | 0 | 2,224 |
| | | Fairmount | 0 | 0 | 0 | 0 | 624 |
| | | Fairview Heights | | | 0 | 0 | 16,841 |
| | | Fithian | 0 | 0 | 0 | 0 | 550 |
| | | Fox Lake | 0 | 0 | 0 | 0 | 11,314 |
| | | Freeburg | | | | 0 | 4,530 |
| | | Fulton | 0 | 0 | 0 | 0 | 3,826 |
| | | Galena | 0 | 0 | 0 | 0 | 3,319 |
| | | Galesburg | 0 | 0 | 0 | 0 | 30,910 |
| | | Geneseo | 0 | 0 | 0 | 0 | 6,430 |
| | | Georgetown | 0 | 0 | 0 | 0 | 3,421 |
| | | Germantown | 0 | 0 | 0 | 0 | 1,228 |
| | | Gibson City | 0 | 0 | 0 | 0 | 3,277 |
| | | Gifford | 0 | 0 | 0 | 0 | 1,011 |
| | | Gillespie | 0 | 0 | 0 | 0 | 3,159 |
| | | Gilman | 0 | 0 | 0 | 0 | 1,706 |
| | | Glencoe | 0 | 0 | 0 | 0 | 9,067 |
| | | Glen Ellyn | 0 | 0 | 0 | 0 | 27,132 |
| | | Glenview | 0 | 0 | 0 | 0 | 46,528 |
| | | Glenwood | 0 | 0 | 0 | | 8,433 |
| | | Grafton | 0 | 0 | | | 739 |
| | | Grand Ridge | 0 | 0 | 0 | 0 | 517 |
| | | Grant Park | 0 | 0 | 0 | 0 | 1,756 |
| | | Green Valley | 0 | 0 | 0 | | 691 |
| | | Hainesville | 0 | 0 | 0 | 0 | 3,940 |
| | | Hanover | 0 | 0 | 0 | 0 | 786 |
| | | Hanover Park | 0 | 0 | 0 | 0 | 36,617 |
| | | Harrisburg | | 0 | 0 | | 9,554 |
| | | Hawthorn Woods | 0 | 0 | 0 | 0 | 8,312 |
| | | Henning | 0 | 0 | 0 | 0 | 228 |
| | | Hickory Hills | 0 | 0 | 0 | 0 | 13,263 |
| | | Highland | | 0 | | | 9,893 |
| | | Hillsboro | 0 | 0 | 0 | 0 | 6,142 |
| | | Hinsdale | 0 | | | | 18,553 |
| | | Holiday Hills | 0 | 0 | 0 | 0 | 770 |
| | | Homer Glen | 0 | 0 | 0 | 0 | 26,554 |
| | | Homewood | 0 | 0 | 0 | 0 | 18,361 |
| | | Indianola | 0 | 0 | 0 | 0 | 220 |
| | | Inverness | | 0 | 0 | 0 | 7,752 |
| | | Itasca | 0 | 0 | 0 | 0 | 8,645 |
| | | Jerome | 0 | 0 | 0 | 0 | 1,282 |
| | | Johnston City | 0 | 0 | 0 | 0 | 3,469 |
| | | Kenilworth | 0 | 0 | 0 | 0 | 2,387 |
| | | Kingston | 0 | 0 | 0 | 0 | 1,069 |
| | | Kirkland | 0 | 0 | 0 | | 1,772 |
| | | La Grange Park | 0 | 0 | 0 | 0 | 12,311 |
| | | Lake Bluff | 0 | | | | 6,239 |
| | | Lake Forest | 0 | 0 | 0 | 0 | 21,083 |
| | | Lakewood | 0 | 0 | 0 | 0 | 3,875 |
| | | Lansing | 0 | 0 | 0 | 0 | 26,496 |
| | | La Salle | 0 | 0 | 0 | 0 | 9,480 |
| | | Lawrenceville | 0 | 0 | 0 | 0 | 4,346 |
| | | Leland Grove | 0 | 0 | 0 | 0 | 1,428 |
| | | Lenzburg | 0 | 0 | 0 | 0 | 525 |
| | | Lincoln | 0 | 0 | 0 | 0 | 14,454 |
| | | Lisle | | 0 | 0 | | 23,194 |
| | | Loami | 0 | 0 | 0 | 0 | 779 |
| | | Lockport | 0 | 0 | 0 | 0 | 26,106 |
| | | Loves Park | | | | 0 | 24,965 |
| | | Macomb | | | | 0 | 19,885 |
| | | Madison | 0 | 0 | 0 | 0 | 4,556 |
| | | Mahomet | | | | 0 | 6,597 |
| | | Maple Park | | | | 0 | 1,365 |
| | | Marengo | 0 | 0 | 0 | 0 | 7,659 |
| | | Marion | 0 | 0 | 0 | 0 | 17,524 |
| | | Marissa | 0 | 0 | 0 | 0 | 1,965 |
| | | Maryville | 0 | 0 | | 0 | 7,747 |
| | | Matteson | 0 | 0 | 0 | 0 | 17,993 |
| | | Mattoon | 0 | 0 | 0 | 0 | 17,064 |
| | | McLean | | 0 | 0 | 0 | 789 |
| | | McLeansboro | 0 | 0 | 0 | 0 | 2,763 |
| | | Melrose Park | 0 | 0 | 0 | 0 | 21,712 |

[1]Agencies published in this table indicated that no hate crimes occurred in their jurisdictions during the quarter(s) for which they submitted reports to the Hate Crime Statistics Program. Blanks indicate quarters for which agencies did not submit reports.

[2]Population figures are published only for the cities. The figures listed for the universities and colleges are student enrollment and were provided by the United States Department of Education for the 2008 school year, the most recent available. The enrollment figures include full-time and part-time students.

## Table 95. Hate Crime Zero Data Submitted per Quarter, by State and Agency, 2009—*Continued*

(Number.)

| State | Agency type | Agency name | Zero data per quarter[1] 1st quarter | 2nd quarter | 3rd quarter | 4th quarter | Population[2] |
|---|---|---|---|---|---|---|---|
| ILLINOIS | | Merrionette Park | 0 | 0 | 0 | 0 | 1,980 |
| | | Milan | | 0 | 0 | 0 | 5,167 |
| | | Millstadt | | | | 0 | 3,398 |
| | | Minier | 0 | | | 0 | 1,247 |
| | | Minooka | 0 | 0 | 0 | 0 | 11,738 |
| | | Mokena | 0 | 0 | 0 | 0 | 19,817 |
| | | Moline | 0 | 0 | 0 | 0 | 42,996 |
| | | Momence | | 0 | 0 | 0 | 3,177 |
| | | Monee | 0 | 0 | 0 | 0 | 5,278 |
| | | Monticello | 0 | 0 | 0 | 0 | 5,374 |
| | | Morris | 0 | 0 | 0 | 0 | 14,027 |
| | | Morrison | 0 | 0 | 0 | 0 | 4,287 |
| | | Mount Carmel | 0 | | | | 7,343 |
| | | Mount Morris | 0 | 0 | 0 | 0 | 3,083 |
| | | Mount Prospect | 0 | 0 | 0 | 0 | 53,028 |
| | | Mount Zion | 0 | 0 | 0 | 0 | 5,191 |
| | | Mundelein | 0 | 0 | 0 | 0 | 34,021 |
| | | Nauvoo | 0 | 0 | 0 | 0 | 1,165 |
| | | Neoga | 0 | 0 | 0 | 0 | 1,742 |
| | | New Athens | 0 | 0 | 0 | | 2,001 |
| | | New Baden | 0 | 0 | 0 | 0 | 3,276 |
| | | Nokomis | 0 | 0 | 0 | 0 | 2,246 |
| | | Norridge | 0 | 0 | 0 | 0 | 13,888 |
| | | North Aurora | 0 | 0 | 0 | 0 | 16,470 |
| | | Northbrook | 0 | 0 | 0 | | 33,980 |
| | | Northlake | 0 | 0 | 0 | 0 | 11,417 |
| | | Norwood | 0 | 0 | 0 | | 454 |
| | | Oak Brook | 0 | 0 | 0 | 0 | 8,819 |
| | | Oak Park | 0 | 0 | 0 | 0 | 53,286 |
| | | Oakwood | 0 | 0 | 0 | 0 | 1,418 |
| | | Oglesby | 0 | 0 | 0 | | 3,674 |
| | | Olney | 0 | 0 | 0 | 0 | 8,367 |
| | | Oswego | 0 | 0 | 0 | 0 | 34,521 |
| | | Palatine | 0 | 0 | 0 | 0 | 67,162 |
| | | Palestine | 0 | 0 | 0 | 0 | 1,319 |
| | | Palos Park | 0 | 0 | 0 | 0 | 4,879 |
| | | Pana | 0 | 0 | 0 | 0 | 5,694 |
| | | Paris | 0 | 0 | 0 | 0 | 8,644 |
| | | Park City | 0 | 0 | 0 | 0 | 6,603 |
| | | Pawnee | 0 | 0 | 0 | 0 | 2,534 |
| | | Pecatonica | 0 | 0 | | | 2,232 |
| | | Peotone | 0 | 0 | 0 | 0 | 4,406 |
| | | Plano | 0 | 0 | 0 | 0 | 12,945 |
| | | Polo | 0 | 0 | 0 | 0 | 2,477 |
| | | Pontiac | 0 | 0 | 0 | 0 | 11,182 |
| | | Posen | 0 | 0 | 0 | 0 | 4,926 |
| | | Potomac | 0 | 0 | 0 | 0 | 653 |
| | | Rankin | 0 | 0 | 0 | 0 | 581 |
| | | Raymond | 0 | 0 | 0 | 0 | 896 |
| | | Richmond | 0 | 0 | 0 | 0 | 2,510 |
| | | Richton Park | 0 | 0 | 0 | | 12,873 |
| | | Ridge Farm | 0 | 0 | 0 | 0 | 851 |
| | | Riverwoods | 0 | 0 | 0 | 0 | 4,107 |
| | | Robbins | 0 | | | | 6,299 |
| | | Rochelle | 0 | 0 | 0 | 0 | 9,867 |
| | | Rochester | 0 | 0 | 0 | 0 | 3,277 |
| | | Rock Island | 0 | 0 | 0 | 0 | 37,976 |
| | | Rockton | 0 | 0 | 0 | 0 | 5,520 |
| | | Roscoe | 0 | 0 | 0 | 0 | 9,135 |
| | | Roselle | 0 | 0 | 0 | 0 | 23,197 |
| | | Round Lake | 0 | 0 | 0 | 0 | 18,836 |
| | | Ruma | 0 | 0 | 0 | 0 | 285 |
| | | Rushville | 0 | 0 | 0 | 0 | 3,083 |
| | | Sauk Village | | 0 | 0 | 0 | 10,236 |
| | | Schiller Park | 0 | 0 | 0 | 0 | 11,544 |
| | | Seneca | 0 | 0 | 0 | 0 | 2,134 |
| | | Sesser | 0 | 0 | 0 | 0 | 2,121 |
| | | Shawneetown | 0 | | | | 1,298 |
| | | Sherman | 0 | 0 | 0 | 0 | 3,947 |
| | | Shorewood | 0 | 0 | 0 | 0 | 16,707 |
| | | Sidell | 0 | 0 | 0 | 0 | 589 |
| | | Silvis | 0 | 0 | 0 | 0 | 7,829 |
| | | Somonauk | 0 | 0 | 0 | 0 | 1,676 |
| | | South Beloit | 0 | 0 | 0 | 0 | 5,546 |
| | | South Elgin | | | 0 | | 21,729 |
| | | South Holland | 0 | 0 | 0 | 0 | 20,969 |
| | | South Jacksonville | 0 | 0 | 0 | 0 | 3,226 |
| | | Stanford | 0 | 0 | 0 | 0 | 672 |
| | | St. Charles | 0 | 0 | 0 | 0 | 33,379 |
| | | Sterling | 0 | 0 | 0 | 0 | 15,051 |
| | | Stickney | 0 | 0 | 0 | 0 | 5,735 |
| | | Stone Park | 0 | 0 | 0 | 0 | 4,832 |
| | | Streator | 0 | 0 | 0 | 0 | 13,736 |
| | | Sycamore | 0 | 0 | 0 | 0 | 18,384 |
| | | Thomasboro | 0 | 0 | 0 | | 1,206 |
| | | Thornton | 0 | 0 | 0 | 0 | 2,366 |
| | | Tilton | 0 | 0 | 0 | 0 | 2,759 |
| | | Toluca | | 0 | 0 | 0 | 1,241 |
| | | Trenton | 0 | 0 | 0 | 0 | 2,666 |
| | | Troy | 0 | 0 | 0 | | 9,993 |
| | | Urbana | 0 | 0 | 0 | 0 | 39,838 |
| | | Vandalia | 0 | 0 | 0 | 0 | 6,258 |
| | | Vermont | 0 | 0 | | | 747 |
| | | Vernon Hills | 0 | 0 | 0 | 0 | 24,965 |
| | | Villa Park | 0 | 0 | 0 | 0 | 22,185 |
| | | Wayne | | 0 | 0 | 0 | 2,421 |
| | | Wayne City | 0 | 0 | 0 | 0 | 1,055 |
| | | Western Springs | 0 | 0 | 0 | 0 | 12,705 |
| | | Westmont | 0 | 0 | 0 | 0 | 24,985 |
| | | West Salem | 0 | 0 | 0 | 0 | 930 |
| | | Westville | 0 | 0 | 0 | 0 | 2,983 |
| | | Wheeling | 0 | 0 | 0 | 0 | 36,041 |
| | | White Hall | 0 | 0 | 0 | 0 | 2,437 |
| | | Williamsfield | 0 | 0 | | | 568 |
| | | Willowbrook | 0 | 0 | 0 | 0 | 8,710 |
| | | Winnetka | 0 | 0 | 0 | 0 | 12,365 |
| | | Winthrop Harbor | 0 | 0 | 0 | 0 | 7,263 |
| | | Wonder Lake | 0 | 0 | 0 | 0 | 3,995 |
| | | Wood Dale | 0 | 0 | 0 | 0 | 13,884 |
| | | Woodstock | 0 | 0 | 0 | 0 | 24,370 |
| | | Worth | 0 | 0 | 0 | 0 | 10,360 |
| | | Zion | 0 | 0 | 0 | 0 | 25,414 |
| | **Universities and Colleges** | Illinois State University | 0 | 0 | 0 | 0 | 20,799 |
| | | Joliet Junior College | 0 | 0 | | | 14,088 |
| | | Moraine Valley Community College | 0 | 0 | 0 | 0 | 17,477 |
| | | Parkland College | 0 | 0 | 0 | 0 | 9,273 |
| | | Southern Illinois University: Carbondale | 0 | 0 | 0 | 0 | 20,673 |
| | | School of Medicine[3] | 0 | 0 | | | |
| | | Triton College | 0 | 0 | 0 | 0 | 15,547 |
| | **Metropolitan Counties** | Boone | 0 | 0 | 0 | 0 | |
| | | Champaign | | | 0 | 0 | |
| | | De Kalb | 0 | 0 | 0 | 0 | |
| | | Grundy | 0 | 0 | 0 | 0 | |
| | | Henry | 0 | 0 | 0 | 0 | |
| | | Macon | 0 | 0 | 0 | 0 | |
| | | Macoupin | 0 | 0 | 0 | 0 | |
| | | Marshall | 0 | 0 | 0 | 0 | |
| | | McLean | 0 | 0 | 0 | 0 | |
| | | Piatt | 0 | 0 | 0 | 0 | |
| | | Rock Island | 0 | 0 | 0 | 0 | |
| | | Stark | 0 | 0 | 0 | 0 | |
| | | St. Clair | 0 | 0 | 0 | 0 | |
| | | Vermilion | 0 | 0 | 0 | 0 | |
| | | Will | 0 | 0 | 0 | 0 | |

[1]Agencies published in this table indicated that no hate crimes occurred in their jurisdictions during the quarter(s) for which they submitted reports to the Hate Crime program. Blanks indicate quarters for which agencies did not submit reports.
[2]Population figures are published only for the cities. The figures listed for the universities and colleges are student enrollment and were provided by the United States Department of Education for the 2008 school year, the most recent available. The enrollment figures include full-time and part-time students.
[3]Student enrollment figures were not available.

## Table 95. Hate Crime Zero Data Submitted per Quarter, by State and Agency, 2009—*Continued*

(Number.)

| State | Agency type | Agency name | Zero data per quarter[1] | | | | Population[2] |
|---|---|---|---|---|---|---|---|
| | | | 1st quarter | 2nd quarter | 3rd quarter | 4th quarter | |
| **ILLINOIS** | **Nonmetropolitan Counties** | Carroll | 0 | 0 | 0 | 0 | |
| | | Cass | 0 | 0 | 0 | 0 | |
| | | Clay | | | | 0 | |
| | | Douglas | 0 | | 0 | 0 | |
| | | Effingham | 0 | 0 | 0 | 0 | |
| | | Franklin | 0 | 0 | 0 | 0 | |
| | | Fulton | 0 | | | | |
| | | Greene | 0 | 0 | 0 | 0 | |
| | | Hancock | 0 | 0 | 0 | | |
| | | Iroquois | 0 | 0 | 0 | 0 | |
| | | Jasper | 0 | 0 | 0 | 0 | |
| | | Lawrence | 0 | 0 | 0 | 0 | |
| | | Livingston | 0 | 0 | 0 | 0 | |
| | | Logan | | 0 | 0 | 0 | |
| | | Massac | 0 | 0 | 0 | 0 | |
| | | Moultrie | 0 | 0 | 0 | 0 | |
| | | Perry | 0 | 0 | 0 | 0 | |
| | | Pope | 0 | 0 | 0 | 0 | |
| | | Randolph | 0 | | 0 | | |
| | | Richland | 0 | 0 | 0 | 0 | |
| | | Saline | 0 | 0 | 0 | 0 | |
| | | Schuyler | 0 | 0 | 0 | 0 | |
| | | Union | 0 | 0 | 0 | 0 | |
| | | Wabash | 0 | 0 | 0 | 0 | |
| | **Other Agencies** | Cook County Forest Preserve | 0 | 0 | 0 | 0 | |
| | | Illinois Commerce Commission | 0 | 0 | 0 | 0 | |
| | | Lake County Forest Preserve | 0 | 0 | 0 | 0 | |
| | | Secretary of State Police | 0 | 0 | 0 | 0 | |
| | | Springfield Park District | 0 | 0 | 0 | | |
| **INDIANA** | **Cities** | Albion | | | 0 | 0 | 2,337 |
| | | Alexandria | 0 | 0 | 0 | 0 | 5,811 |
| | | Anderson | 0 | 0 | | | 57,020 |
| | | Bargersville | 0 | 0 | 0 | 0 | 2,770 |
| | | Batesville | 0 | 0 | 0 | 0 | 6,477 |
| | | Beech Grove | 0 | 0 | 0 | 0 | 14,257 |
| | | Berne | | | 0 | | 4,389 |
| | | Boonville | 0 | 0 | 0 | 0 | 6,736 |
| | | Brazil | 0 | | | | 8,296 |
| | | Bremen | 0 | 0 | 0 | 0 | 4,660 |
| | | Brownsburg | | 0 | | 0 | 20,651 |
| | | Brownstown | 0 | 0 | 0 | | 2,978 |
| | | Burns Harbor | 0 | 0 | 0 | 0 | 1,148 |
| | | Carmel | 0 | 0 | 0 | 0 | 68,424 |
| | | Charlestown | 0 | | 0 | 0 | 7,359 |
| | | Chesterfield | | | | 0 | 2,733 |
| | | Clarks Hill | | | | 0 | 689 |
| | | Columbia City | 0 | 0 | 0 | 0 | 8,386 |
| | | Columbus | 0 | 0 | | 0 | 40,087 |
| | | Corydon | 0 | 0 | 0 | 0 | 2,787 |
| | | Crawfordsville | 0 | 0 | 0 | 0 | 15,036 |
| | | Danville | 0 | | 0 | 0 | 8,319 |
| | | Decatur | 0 | 0 | 0 | 0 | 9,576 |
| | | Delphi | 0 | 0 | 0 | | 2,844 |
| | | Dyer | | 0 | | 0 | 16,148 |
| | | East Chicago | 0 | 0 | 0 | 0 | 29,728 |
| | | Edinburgh | 0 | 0 | 0 | | 4,696 |
| | | Ellettsville | 0 | 0 | 0 | 0 | 6,107 |
| | | Elwood | 0 | 0 | | 0 | 8,956 |
| | | Fairmount | 0 | 0 | 0 | 0 | 2,701 |
| | | Fowler | 0 | 0 | 0 | 0 | 2,177 |
| | | Franklin | 0 | | 0 | 0 | 23,704 |
| | | Gas City | | 0 | | 0 | 5,658 |
| | | Georgetown | 0 | 0 | | | 3,172 |
| | | Hagerstown | 0 | 0 | 0 | | 1,613 |
| | | Hammond | 0 | 0 | 0 | 0 | 76,085 |
| | | Hartford City | 0 | 0 | 0 | 0 | 6,239 |
| | | Hebron | 0 | 0 | 0 | 0 | 3,707 |
| | | Highland | 0 | 0 | 0 | 0 | 22,544 |
| | | Hobart | 0 | 0 | 0 | 0 | 28,173 |
| | | Huntingburg | 0 | 0 | 0 | | 6,147 |
| | | Huntington | 0 | 0 | 0 | 0 | 16,424 |
| | | Indianapolis | 0 | | | | 813,471 |
| | | Jasper | 0 | 0 | 0 | 0 | 14,224 |
| | | Knox | 0 | 0 | 0 | | 3,844 |
| | | Kokomo | 0 | 0 | 0 | 0 | 45,562 |
| | | Lafayette | 0 | | | | 64,370 |
| | | Lebanon | | 0 | | | 15,522 |
| | | Ligonier | 0 | 0 | 0 | 0 | 4,551 |
| | | Logansport | | | | 0 | 18,551 |
| | | Loogootee | 0 | 0 | 0 | 0 | 2,568 |
| | | Lowell | 0 | 0 | | | 8,504 |
| | | Merrillville | 0 | 0 | 0 | 0 | 33,349 |
| | | Monticello | 0 | 0 | 0 | 0 | 5,249 |
| | | Mooresville | 0 | 0 | 0 | 0 | 12,037 |
| | | Nappanee | 0 | 0 | 0 | 0 | 7,196 |
| | | New Albany | 0 | 0 | 0 | | 37,237 |
| | | New Castle | 0 | 0 | 0 | 0 | 18,236 |
| | | New Whiteland | | 0 | 0 | | 5,961 |
| | | Noblesville | 0 | 0 | | | 43,820 |
| | | North Liberty | 0 | 0 | 0 | 0 | 1,397 |
| | | North Vernon | | 0 | 0 | 0 | 6,269 |
| | | Oakland City | 0 | | | | 2,505 |
| | | Peru | | | 0 | | 12,225 |
| | | Plymouth | 0 | 0 | 0 | 0 | 11,170 |
| | | Portland | 0 | 0 | 0 | 0 | 6,131 |
| | | Richmond | 0 | 0 | 0 | 0 | 36,479 |
| | | Rushville | 0 | | 0 | | 6,011 |
| | | Salem | 0 | 0 | 0 | 0 | 6,538 |
| | | Schererville | 0 | 0 | 0 | 0 | 29,361 |
| | | Scottsburg | 0 | 0 | 0 | 0 | 5,896 |
| | | Seymour | 0 | | | 0 | 19,342 |
| | | Tell City | 0 | 0 | 0 | 0 | 7,493 |
| | | Terre Haute | | 0 | 0 | 0 | 60,065 |
| | | Vincennes | 0 | 0 | 0 | 0 | 17,902 |
| | | Wabash | 0 | 0 | 0 | 0 | 10,718 |
| | | Warsaw | 0 | 0 | 0 | 0 | 13,733 |
| | | Washington | | 0 | | | 11,400 |
| | | West Lafayette | 0 | 0 | 0 | 0 | 31,092 |
| | | Westville | 0 | 0 | 0 | 0 | 5,179 |
| | | Winchester | 0 | 0 | 0 | 0 | 4,562 |
| | | Winona Lake | 0 | 0 | 0 | 0 | 4,327 |
| | **Universities and Colleges** | Ball State University | 0 | 0 | 0 | 0 | 20,243 |
| | | Indiana University: Bloomington | | | | 0 | 40,354 |
| | | Gary | 0 | 0 | 0 | | 4,794 |
| | | Marian University | 0 | | | | 2,143 |
| | **Metropolitan Counties** | Bartholomew | 0 | 0 | 0 | 0 | |
| | | Brown | 0 | 0 | 0 | 0 | |
| | | Delaware | | 0 | | | |
| | | Floyd | 0 | 0 | 0 | 0 | |
| | | Greene | 0 | 0 | 0 | 0 | |
| | | Jasper | | 0 | | | |
| | | Monroe | 0 | 0 | 0 | 0 | |
| | | Newton | 0 | 0 | 0 | 0 | |
| | | Putnam | 0 | 0 | 0 | 0 | |
| | | Shelby | 0 | 0 | 0 | 0 | |
| | | St. Joseph | 0 | 0 | 0 | 0 | |
| | | Tippecanoe | 0 | | | 0 | |
| | | Vermillion | 0 | 0 | 0 | 0 | |
| | | Warrick | 0 | 0 | 0 | 0 | |
| | | Wells | 0 | 0 | 0 | 0 | |

[1]Agencies published in this table indicated that no hate crimes occurred in their jurisdictions during the quarter(s) for which they submitted reports to the Hate Crime Statistics Program. Blanks indicate quarters for which agencies did not submit reports.

[2]Population figures are published only for the cities. The figures listed for the universities and colleges are student enrollment and were provided by the United States Department of Education for the 2008 school year, the most recent available. The enrollment figures include full-time and part-time students.

## Table 95. Hate Crime Zero Data Submitted per Quarter, by State and Agency, 2009—*Continued*

(Number.)

| State | Agency type | Agency name | Zero data per quarter[1] | | | | Population[2] |
|---|---|---|---|---|---|---|---|
| | | | 1st quarter | 2nd quarter | 3rd quarter | 4th quarter | |
| **INDIANA** | **Nonmetropolitan Counties** | Blackford | 0 | 0 | 0 | 0 | |
| | | Cass | 0 | 0 | 0 | 0 | |
| | | Clinton | | | | 0 | |
| | | Crawford | 0 | 0 | 0 | 0 | |
| | | Daviess | 0 | 0 | 0 | 0 | |
| | | Fulton | 0 | 0 | 0 | 0 | |
| | | Grant | 0 | 0 | 0 | 0 | |
| | | Henry | 0 | 0 | | 0 | |
| | | Huntington | 0 | 0 | 0 | 0 | |
| | | Jay | 0 | | | 0 | |
| | | Knox | 0 | 0 | 0 | 0 | |
| | | Martin | 0 | 0 | | | |
| | | Noble | 0 | 0 | 0 | 0 | |
| | | Orange | 0 | 0 | | | |
| | | Perry | 0 | 0 | 0 | 0 | |
| | | Randolph | 0 | 0 | 0 | 0 | |
| | | Starke | 0 | 0 | 0 | 0 | |
| | | Steuben | | | 0 | 0 | |
| | **Other Agencies** | Indiana State Excise Police | 0 | 0 | 0 | 0 | |
| | | Northern Indiana Commuter Transportation District | 0 | | 0 | 0 | |
| | | St. Joseph County Airport Authority | 0 | 0 | 0 | 0 | |
| **IOWA** | **Cities** | Adel | 0 | 0 | 0 | 0 | 4,553 |
| | | Albia | 0 | 0 | 0 | 0 | 3,537 |
| | | Algona | 0 | 0 | 0 | 0 | 5,285 |
| | | Altoona | 0 | 0 | 0 | 0 | 14,297 |
| | | Anamosa | 0 | 0 | 0 | 0 | 5,764 |
| | | Ankeny | 0 | 0 | 0 | 0 | 44,339 |
| | | Atlantic | 0 | 0 | 0 | 0 | 6,726 |
| | | Audubon | 0 | 0 | 0 | 0 | 2,082 |
| | | Belmond | 0 | 0 | 0 | 0 | 2,278 |
| | | Bloomfield | 0 | 0 | 0 | 0 | 2,580 |
| | | Boone | 0 | 0 | 0 | 0 | 12,592 |
| | | Burlington | 0 | 0 | 0 | 0 | 25,172 |
| | | Camanche | 0 | 0 | 0 | 0 | 4,288 |
| | | Carlisle | 0 | 0 | 0 | 0 | 3,708 |
| | | Carroll | 0 | 0 | 0 | 0 | 9,974 |
| | | Carter Lake | 0 | | 0 | | 3,270 |
| | | Cedar Falls | 0 | 0 | 0 | 0 | 38,271 |
| | | Cedar Rapids | 0 | 0 | 0 | 0 | 128,779 |
| | | Centerville | 0 | 0 | 0 | 0 | 5,393 |
| | | Chariton | 0 | 0 | 0 | 0 | 4,401 |
| | | Charles City | 0 | 0 | 0 | 0 | 7,435 |
| | | Cherokee | 0 | 0 | 0 | 0 | 4,629 |
| | | Clarinda | 0 | 0 | 0 | 0 | 5,474 |
| | | Clear Lake | 0 | 0 | 0 | 0 | 7,781 |
| | | Clinton | 0 | 0 | 0 | 0 | 26,266 |
| | | Clive | 0 | 0 | 0 | 0 | 15,522 |
| | | Coralville | 0 | 0 | 0 | 0 | 18,884 |
| | | Council Bluffs | 0 | 0 | 0 | 0 | 59,669 |
| | | Cresco | 0 | 0 | 0 | 0 | 3,712 |
| | | Creston | 0 | 0 | 0 | 0 | 7,597 |
| | | Decorah | 0 | 0 | 0 | 0 | 7,877 |
| | | Denison | 0 | 0 | 0 | 0 | 7,167 |
| | | De Witt | 0 | 0 | 0 | 0 | 5,286 |
| | | Dubuque | 0 | 0 | 0 | 0 | 57,192 |
| | | Dyersville | 0 | 0 | 0 | 0 | 4,222 |
| | | Eagle Grove | 0 | 0 | 0 | 0 | 3,269 |
| | | Eldora | 0 | 0 | 0 | 0 | 2,703 |
| | | Eldridge | 0 | 0 | 0 | 0 | 4,962 |
| | | Emmetsburg | 0 | 0 | 0 | 0 | 3,586 |
| | | Estherville | 0 | 0 | 0 | 0 | 6,255 |
| | | Evansdale | 0 | 0 | 0 | 0 | 5,121 |
| | | Fairfield | 0 | 0 | 0 | 0 | 9,177 |
| | | Forest City | 0 | 0 | 0 | 0 | 4,066 |
| | | Fort Dodge | 0 | 0 | 0 | 0 | 25,058 |
| | | Fort Madison | 0 | 0 | 0 | 0 | 10,818 |
| | | Garner | 0 | 0 | 0 | 0 | 2,932 |
| | | Glenwood | 0 | 0 | 0 | 0 | 5,675 |
| | | Grundy Center | 0 | 0 | 0 | 0 | 2,510 |
| | | Hampton | 0 | 0 | 0 | 0 | 4,126 |
| | | Harlan | | 0 | 0 | | 4,954 |
| | | Hawarden | 0 | 0 | 0 | 0 | 2,396 |
| | | Humboldt | 0 | 0 | 0 | 0 | 4,170 |
| | | Independence | 0 | 0 | 0 | 0 | 6,125 |
| | | Indianola | 0 | 0 | 0 | 0 | 14,500 |
| | | Iowa Falls | 0 | 0 | 0 | 0 | 4,940 |
| | | Jefferson | 0 | 0 | 0 | 0 | 4,095 |
| | | Johnston | 0 | 0 | 0 | 0 | 16,725 |
| | | Keokuk | 0 | 0 | 0 | 0 | 10,283 |
| | | Knoxville | | | 0 | | 7,204 |
| | | Le Claire | | | 0 | 0 | 3,007 |
| | | Le Mars | 0 | 0 | 0 | 0 | 9,114 |
| | | Lisbon | 0 | 0 | 0 | | 2,043 |
| | | Manchester | 0 | 0 | 0 | 0 | 4,834 |
| | | Maquoketa | 0 | 0 | 0 | 0 | 5,882 |
| | | Marion | 0 | 0 | 0 | 0 | 33,590 |
| | | Marshalltown | 0 | 0 | 0 | 0 | 25,833 |
| | | Mason City | 0 | 0 | 0 | 0 | 27,142 |
| | | Missouri Valley | | | 0 | | 2,726 |
| | | Monticello | 0 | 0 | 0 | 0 | 3,652 |
| | | Mount Pleasant | 0 | 0 | 0 | 0 | 8,780 |
| | | Mount Vernon | 0 | 0 | 0 | 0 | 4,196 |
| | | Muscatine | 0 | 0 | 0 | 0 | 22,480 |
| | | Nevada | 0 | 0 | 0 | | 6,688 |
| | | Newton | 0 | 0 | 0 | 0 | 14,981 |
| | | North Liberty | 0 | 0 | 0 | 0 | 12,569 |
| | | Norwalk | 0 | 0 | 0 | 0 | 9,048 |
| | | Oelwein | 0 | 0 | 0 | 0 | 6,019 |
| | | Ogden | 0 | 0 | 0 | 0 | 1,968 |
| | | Orange City | 0 | 0 | 0 | 0 | 5,922 |
| | | Osage | 0 | 0 | 0 | 0 | 3,424 |
| | | Osceola | 0 | 0 | 0 | 0 | 4,708 |
| | | Oskaloosa | 0 | 0 | 0 | 0 | 11,077 |
| | | Ottumwa | 0 | 0 | 0 | 0 | 24,276 |
| | | Pella | 0 | 0 | 0 | 0 | 10,238 |
| | | Pleasant Hill | 0 | 0 | 0 | 0 | 8,873 |
| | | Pleasantville | | | 0 | 0 | 1,584 |
| | | Polk City | 0 | 0 | 0 | 0 | 3,314 |
| | | Prairie City | 0 | 0 | 0 | 0 | 1,444 |
| | | Red Oak | 0 | 0 | 0 | 0 | 5,627 |
| | | Rock Valley | 0 | | 0 | 0 | 2,967 |
| | | Sac City | 0 | 0 | 0 | 0 | 2,118 |
| | | Sergeant Bluff | 0 | 0 | 0 | 0 | 4,093 |
| | | Sheldon | 0 | 0 | 0 | 0 | 4,740 |
| | | Shenandoah | 0 | 0 | 0 | 0 | 4,884 |
| | | Sioux Center | | | 0 | 0 | 6,638 |
| | | Sioux City | 0 | 0 | 0 | 0 | 82,573 |
| | | Spencer | 0 | 0 | 0 | 0 | 10,949 |
| | | Spirit Lake | 0 | 0 | 0 | 0 | 4,742 |
| | | St. Ansgar | 0 | 0 | 0 | 0 | 1,060 |
| | | State Center | 0 | 0 | 0 | 0 | 1,340 |
| | | Storm Lake | 0 | 0 | 0 | 0 | 9,542 |
| | | Story City | 0 | 0 | 0 | 0 | 3,406 |
| | | Tipton | 0 | 0 | 0 | 0 | 2,997 |
| | | Washington | 0 | 0 | 0 | 0 | 7,276 |
| | | Waterloo | 0 | 0 | 0 | 0 | 66,436 |
| | | Waukee | 0 | 0 | 0 | 0 | 13,558 |
| | | Waverly | 0 | 0 | 0 | 0 | 9,334 |
| | | Webster City | 0 | 0 | 0 | 0 | 7,672 |
| | | West Burlington | 0 | 0 | 0 | 0 | 3,298 |
| | | West Des Moines | 0 | 0 | 0 | 0 | 56,400 |
| | | West Liberty | 0 | 0 | 0 | 0 | 3,685 |
| | | West Union | 0 | 0 | 0 | 0 | 2,416 |
| | | Williamsburg | 0 | 0 | 0 | 0 | 2,831 |
| | | Wilton | 0 | 0 | 0 | 0 | 2,820 |
| | | Windsor Heights | 0 | 0 | 0 | 0 | 4,616 |
| | | Winterset | 0 | 0 | 0 | 0 | 4,825 |

[1]Agencies published in this table indicated that no hate crimes occurred in their jurisdictions during the quarter(s) for which they submitted reports to the Hate Crime Statistics Program. Blanks indicate quarters for which agencies did not submit reports.

[2]Population figures are published only for the cities. The figures listed for the universities and colleges are student enrollment and were provided by the United States Department of Education for the 2008 school year, the most recent available. The enrollment figures include full-time and part-time students.

# Table 95. Hate Crime Zero Data Submitted per Quarter, by State and Agency, 2009—*Continued*

(Number.)

| State | Agency type | Agency name | Zero data per quarter[1] 1st quarter | 2nd quarter | 3rd quarter | 4th quarter | Population[2] |
|---|---|---|---|---|---|---|---|
| IOWA | Universities and Colleges | Iowa State University | 0 | 0 | 0 | 0 | 26,856 |
| | | University of Iowa | 0 | 0 | 0 | 0 | 29,152 |
| | | University of Northern Iowa | 0 | 0 | 0 | 0 | 12,998 |
| | Metropolitan Counties | Benton | 0 | 0 | 0 | 0 | |
| | | Black Hawk | 0 | 0 | 0 | 0 | |
| | | Bremer | 0 | 0 | 0 | 0 | |
| | | Dallas | 0 | 0 | 0 | 0 | |
| | | Dubuque | 0 | 0 | 0 | 0 | |
| | | Grundy | 0 | 0 | 0 | 0 | |
| | | Guthrie | 0 | 0 | 0 | 0 | |
| | | Harrison | 0 | 0 | 0 | 0 | |
| | | Johnson | 0 | 0 | 0 | 0 | |
| | | Jones | 0 | 0 | 0 | 0 | |
| | | Madison | 0 | 0 | 0 | 0 | |
| | | Mills | 0 | 0 | 0 | 0 | |
| | | Polk | 0 | 0 | 0 | 0 | |
| | | Pottawattamie | 0 | 0 | 0 | 0 | |
| | | Scott | 0 | 0 | 0 | 0 | |
| | | Story | 0 | 0 | 0 | 0 | |
| | | Warren | 0 | 0 | 0 | 0 | |
| | | Washington | 0 | 0 | 0 | 0 | |
| | | Woodbury | 0 | 0 | 0 | 0 | |
| | Nonmetropolitan Counties | Adair | 0 | 0 | 0 | 0 | |
| | | Adams | 0 | 0 | 0 | 0 | |
| | | Allamakee | 0 | | | 0 | |
| | | Appanoose | 0 | 0 | 0 | 0 | |
| | | Audubon | 0 | 0 | 0 | 0 | |
| | | Boone | 0 | 0 | 0 | 0 | |
| | | Buchanan | 0 | 0 | 0 | 0 | |
| | | Buena Vista | 0 | 0 | 0 | 0 | |
| | | Butler | 0 | 0 | 0 | 0 | |
| | | Calhoun | 0 | 0 | 0 | 0 | |
| | | Carroll | 0 | 0 | 0 | 0 | |
| | | Cass | 0 | 0 | 0 | 0 | |
| | | Cedar | 0 | 0 | 0 | 0 | |
| | | Cerro Gordo | 0 | 0 | 0 | 0 | |
| | | Cherokee | 0 | 0 | 0 | 0 | |
| | | Chickasaw | 0 | 0 | 0 | 0 | |
| | | Clarke | 0 | 0 | 0 | 0 | |
| | | Clay | 0 | 0 | 0 | 0 | |
| | | Clayton | 0 | 0 | 0 | 0 | |
| | | Clinton | 0 | 0 | 0 | 0 | |
| | | Crawford | 0 | 0 | 0 | 0 | |
| | | Davis | 0 | 0 | 0 | 0 | |
| | | Decatur | 0 | 0 | 0 | | |
| | | Delaware | 0 | 0 | 0 | 0 | |
| | | Des Moines | 0 | 0 | 0 | 0 | |
| | | Dickinson | 0 | 0 | 0 | 0 | |
| | | Emmet | 0 | 0 | 0 | 0 | |
| | | Fayette | 0 | 0 | 0 | 0 | |
| | | Floyd | 0 | 0 | 0 | 0 | |
| | | Franklin | 0 | 0 | 0 | 0 | |
| | | Fremont | 0 | 0 | 0 | 0 | |
| | | Greene | 0 | | 0 | 0 | |
| | | Hamilton | 0 | 0 | 0 | 0 | |
| | | Hancock | 0 | 0 | 0 | 0 | |
| | | Hardin | 0 | 0 | 0 | 0 | |
| | | Henry | 0 | 0 | 0 | 0 | |
| | | Howard | 0 | 0 | 0 | 0 | |
| | | Humboldt | 0 | 0 | 0 | 0 | |
| | | Ida | 0 | 0 | 0 | 0 | |
| | | Iowa | 0 | 0 | 0 | 0 | |
| | | Jackson | 0 | 0 | | 0 | |
| | | Jasper | 0 | 0 | 0 | 0 | |
| | | Jefferson | 0 | 0 | 0 | 0 | |
| | | Keokuk | 0 | 0 | 0 | 0 | |
| | | Kossuth | 0 | 0 | 0 | 0 | |
| | | Lee | 0 | 0 | 0 | 0 | |
| | | Louisa | 0 | 0 | 0 | 0 | |
| | | Lucas | 0 | 0 | 0 | 0 | |
| | | Lyon | 0 | 0 | 0 | 0 | |
| | | Mahaska | 0 | 0 | 0 | 0 | |
| | | Marion | 0 | 0 | 0 | 0 | |
| | | Mitchell | 0 | 0 | 0 | 0 | |
| | | Monona | | 0 | 0 | 0 | |
| | | Monroe | 0 | 0 | 0 | 0 | |
| | | Montgomery | | | | 0 | |
| | | Muscatine | 0 | 0 | 0 | 0 | |
| | | O'Brien | 0 | 0 | 0 | 0 | |
| | | Osceola | 0 | 0 | 0 | 0 | |
| | | Page | 0 | 0 | 0 | 0 | |
| | | Palo Alto | 0 | 0 | 0 | 0 | |
| | | Plymouth | 0 | 0 | 0 | 0 | |
| | | Pocahontas | 0 | 0 | 0 | 0 | |
| | | Poweshiek | 0 | 0 | 0 | 0 | |
| | | Ringgold | | 0 | | | |
| | | Sac | 0 | 0 | 0 | 0 | |
| | | Shelby | 0 | 0 | 0 | 0 | |
| | | Sioux | 0 | 0 | 0 | 0 | |
| | | Tama | 0 | 0 | 0 | 0 | |
| | | Taylor | 0 | 0 | 0 | 0 | |
| | | Union | 0 | 0 | 0 | 0 | |
| | | Van Buren | 0 | 0 | 0 | 0 | |
| | | Wapello | 0 | 0 | 0 | 0 | |
| | | Wayne | 0 | 0 | 0 | 0 | |
| | | Webster | 0 | 0 | 0 | 0 | |
| | | Winnebago | 0 | 0 | 0 | 0 | |
| | | Winneshiek | 0 | 0 | 0 | 0 | |
| | | Worth | 0 | 0 | 0 | 0 | |
| | | Wright | 0 | 0 | 0 | 0 | |
| KANSAS | Cities | Altamont | 0 | 0 | 0 | | 1,045 |
| | | Americus | 0 | | | 0 | 914 |
| | | Andale | 0 | 0 | | | 892 |
| | | Andover | 0 | 0 | 0 | 0 | 10,792 |
| | | Anthony | 0 | 0 | 0 | 0 | 2,196 |
| | | Arcadia | | 0 | 0 | 0 | 385 |
| | | Argonia | 0 | 0 | 0 | 0 | 466 |
| | | Arkansas City | 0 | 0 | 0 | 0 | 10,975 |
| | | Attica | | | 0 | | 581 |
| | | Atwood | 0 | 0 | 0 | 0 | 1,048 |
| | | Auburn | 0 | 0 | 0 | 0 | 1,155 |
| | | Baldwin City | 0 | 0 | 0 | 0 | 4,416 |
| | | Basehor | 0 | 0 | 0 | 0 | 4,525 |
| | | Baxter Springs | 0 | 0 | 0 | 0 | 4,108 |
| | | Bel Aire | 0 | 0 | 0 | 0 | 6,883 |
| | | Belle Plaine | 0 | | | | 1,509 |
| | | Belleville | | 0 | 0 | 0 | 1,793 |
| | | Beloit | 0 | 0 | 0 | 0 | 3,602 |
| | | Bentley | | | 0 | | 539 |
| | | Benton | 0 | 0 | 0 | 0 | 804 |
| | | Blue Rapids | 0 | 0 | 0 | 0 | 1,011 |
| | | Bucklin | 0 | 0 | 0 | 0 | 727 |
| | | Buhler | 0 | 0 | 0 | 0 | 1,329 |
| | | Burden | 0 | 0 | 0 | 0 | 525 |
| | | Burlingame | 0 | 0 | 0 | | 952 |
| | | Burlington | 0 | 0 | 0 | 0 | 2,667 |
| | | Burns | 0 | 0 | 0 | 0 | 259 |
| | | Burrton | 0 | | | | 892 |
| | | Bushton | 0 | 0 | 0 | 0 | 282 |
| | | Caldwell | 0 | 0 | 0 | 0 | 1,130 |
| | | Caney | 0 | 0 | 0 | | 1,964 |
| | | Canton | 0 | 0 | 0 | 0 | 786 |
| | | Cawker City | 0 | 0 | 0 | 0 | 457 |
| | | Cedar Vale | 0 | 0 | 0 | 0 | 606 |
| | | Chapman | 0 | 0 | 0 | 0 | 1,343 |
| | | Chase | 0 | 0 | 0 | 0 | 442 |
| | | Cheney | | 0 | 0 | 0 | 2,059 |
| | | Cherokee | 0 | 0 | 0 | | 714 |
| | | Cherryvale | 0 | 0 | 0 | 0 | 2,238 |
| | | Chetopa | 0 | 0 | 0 | 0 | 1,228 |

[1]Agencies published in this table indicated that no hate crimes occurred in their jurisdictions during the quarter(s) for which they submitted reports to the Hate Crime Statistics Program. Blanks indicate quarters for which agencies did not submit reports.

[2]Population figures are published only for the cities. The figures listed for the universities and colleges are student enrollment and were provided by the United States Department of Education for the 2008 school year, the most recent available. The enrollment figures include full-time and part-time students.

## Table 95. Hate Crime Zero Data Submitted per Quarter, by State and Agency, 2009—*Continued*

(Number.)

| State | Agency type | Agency name | Zero data per quarter[1] 1st quarter | 2nd quarter | 3rd quarter | 4th quarter | Population[2] |
|---|---|---|---|---|---|---|---|
| KANSAS | | Claflin | 0 | 0 | 0 | 0 | 649 |
| | | Clay Center | 0 | 0 | 0 | 0 | 4,430 |
| | | Clearwater | 0 | 0 | 0 | 0 | 2,427 |
| | | Coffeyville | 0 | 0 | 0 | 0 | 10,235 |
| | | Coldwater | | 0 | | 0 | 778 |
| | | Columbus | 0 | 0 | 0 | 0 | 3,163 |
| | | Colwich | 0 | 0 | 0 | 0 | 1,426 |
| | | Concordia | 0 | 0 | 0 | 0 | 5,158 |
| | | Council Grove | 0 | 0 | 0 | 0 | 2,269 |
| | | Derby | 0 | 0 | 0 | 0 | 23,041 |
| | | Dodge City | 0 | 0 | 0 | 0 | 25,738 |
| | | Eastborough | 0 | 0 | 0 | 0 | 803 |
| | | Edwardsville | 0 | 0 | 0 | 0 | 4,494 |
| | | Elkhart | 0 | 0 | 0 | 0 | 1,868 |
| | | Ellinwood | 0 | 0 | 0 | 0 | 2,022 |
| | | Ellis | 0 | 0 | 0 | 0 | 1,960 |
| | | Ellsworth | 0 | 0 | 0 | 0 | 2,847 |
| | | Elwood | 0 | 0 | 0 | 0 | 1,118 |
| | | Emporia | 0 | 0 | 0 | 0 | 26,330 |
| | | Enterprise | 0 | 0 | | | 814 |
| | | Erie | 0 | 0 | 0 | 0 | 1,154 |
| | | Eskridge | 0 | 0 | 0 | 0 | 562 |
| | | Eudora | 0 | 0 | 0 | 0 | 6,482 |
| | | Fairway | 0 | 0 | 0 | 0 | 3,831 |
| | | Florence | 0 | | | | 588 |
| | | Frankfort | | | 0 | | 768 |
| | | Fredonia | 0 | 0 | 0 | 0 | 2,372 |
| | | Frontenac | 0 | 0 | 0 | 0 | 3,214 |
| | | Galena | 0 | 0 | 0 | 0 | 3,110 |
| | | Garden Plain | 0 | 0 | | | 860 |
| | | Gardner | 0 | 0 | 0 | 0 | 18,650 |
| | | Garnett | 0 | 0 | 0 | 0 | 3,207 |
| | | Girard | 0 | 0 | 0 | 0 | 2,712 |
| | | Goddard | 0 | 0 | 0 | 0 | 4,140 |
| | | Grandview Plaza | 0 | 0 | 0 | 0 | 1,425 |
| | | Halstead | 0 | 0 | 0 | 0 | 1,892 |
| | | Harper | 0 | 0 | 0 | 0 | 1,401 |
| | | Haven | 0 | 0 | 0 | 0 | 1,161 |
| | | Havensville | 0 | | 0 | 0 | 144 |
| | | Hays | 0 | 0 | 0 | 0 | 20,405 |
| | | Haysville | 0 | 0 | 0 | 0 | 10,561 |
| | | Herington | 0 | 0 | 0 | 0 | 2,439 |
| | | Hiawatha | 0 | 0 | 0 | 0 | 3,143 |
| | | Highland | | 0 | 0 | 0 | 942 |
| | | Hill City | 0 | 0 | 0 | 0 | 1,372 |
| | | Hillsboro | 0 | 0 | 0 | 0 | 2,615 |
| | | Holcomb | 0 | 0 | 0 | 0 | 1,992 |
| | | Holton | 0 | 0 | 0 | 0 | 3,248 |
| | | Howard | 0 | 0 | | | 753 |
| | | Hoxie | 0 | 0 | 0 | 0 | 1,102 |
| | | Hugoton | 0 | 0 | 0 | | 3,381 |
| | | Inman | 0 | 0 | 0 | 0 | 1,183 |
| | | Kechi | 0 | 0 | 0 | 0 | 1,793 |
| | | Kingman | 0 | 0 | 0 | | 2,953 |
| | | Kiowa | 0 | 0 | 0 | 0 | 894 |
| | | La Crosse | 0 | 0 | 0 | 0 | 1,228 |
| | | La Cygne | 0 | 0 | 0 | 0 | 1,106 |
| | | Lake Quivira | 0 | 0 | 0 | 0 | 942 |
| | | Lebo | 0 | 0 | 0 | 0 | 907 |
| | | Le Roy | 0 | 0 | | | 544 |
| | | Liberal | 0 | 0 | 0 | 0 | 20,118 |
| | | Lindsborg | 0 | 0 | 0 | 0 | 3,236 |
| | | Linn Valley | 0 | 0 | 0 | 0 | 587 |
| | | Little River | 0 | 0 | 0 | | 516 |
| | | Louisburg | 0 | 0 | 0 | 0 | 4,117 |
| | | Lyndon | 0 | 0 | 0 | 0 | 1,003 |
| | | Lyons | 0 | 0 | 0 | 0 | 3,366 |
| | | Macksville | 0 | 0 | 0 | 0 | 472 |
| | | Maple Hill | 0 | 0 | 0 | 0 | 514 |
| | | Marion | 0 | 0 | 0 | 0 | 1,856 |
| | | Marquette | 0 | 0 | 0 | 0 | 582 |
| | | Marysville | 0 | 0 | 0 | 0 | 3,101 |
| | | Mayetta | 0 | 0 | 0 | 0 | 356 |
| | | McLouth | 0 | 0 | 0 | 0 | 828 |
| | | McPherson | 0 | 0 | 0 | 0 | 13,353 |
| | | Meade | 0 | 0 | 0 | 0 | 1,524 |
| | | Meriden | 0 | 0 | 0 | 0 | 755 |
| | | Minneapolis | 0 | 0 | 0 | 0 | 1,970 |
| | | Mission Hills | | | 0 | 0 | 3,565 |
| | | Moran | 0 | 0 | 0 | 0 | 518 |
| | | Mound City | 0 | 0 | 0 | 0 | 788 |
| | | Moundridge | 0 | 0 | 0 | 0 | 1,633 |
| | | Mount Hope | 0 | 0 | | | 858 |
| | | Mulberry | 0 | 0 | 0 | 0 | 566 |
| | | Mulvane | 0 | 0 | 0 | 0 | 5,947 |
| | | Neodesha | 0 | 0 | 0 | 0 | 2,611 |
| | | Nickerson | 0 | 0 | 0 | 0 | 1,139 |
| | | North Newton | 0 | 0 | 0 | 0 | 1,600 |
| | | Norton | 0 | 0 | 0 | 0 | 2,614 |
| | | Nortonville | 0 | 0 | 0 | 0 | 580 |
| | | Norwich | 0 | 0 | 0 | | 493 |
| | | Oakley | 0 | 0 | 0 | 0 | 1,812 |
| | | Oberlin | 0 | 0 | 0 | 0 | 1,623 |
| | | Onaga | 0 | 0 | 0 | 0 | 672 |
| | | Osage City | 0 | 0 | 0 | 0 | 2,803 |
| | | Oskaloosa | 0 | 0 | 0 | 0 | 1,146 |
| | | Overbrook | 0 | 0 | 0 | | 925 |
| | | Oxford | 0 | | | | 1,057 |
| | | Paola | 0 | 0 | 0 | 0 | 5,386 |
| | | Park City | 0 | 0 | 0 | 0 | 7,984 |
| | | Peabody | 0 | 0 | 0 | 0 | 1,185 |
| | | Perry | 0 | 0 | 0 | 0 | 839 |
| | | Plainville | 0 | 0 | 0 | 0 | 1,800 |
| | | Pleasanton | 0 | 0 | 0 | 0 | 1,307 |
| | | Prairie Village | 0 | 0 | 0 | 0 | 21,416 |
| | | Roeland Park | | 0 | | | 6,934 |
| | | Rolla | 0 | 0 | 0 | 0 | 406 |
| | | Rose Hill | 0 | 0 | 0 | 0 | 4,103 |
| | | Rossville | 0 | 0 | 0 | 0 | 1,126 |
| | | Russell | 0 | 0 | 0 | 0 | 4,168 |
| | | Sabetha | 0 | 0 | 0 | 0 | 2,471 |
| | | Scott City | 0 | 0 | 0 | 0 | 3,462 |
| | | Scranton | 0 | 0 | 0 | 0 | 676 |
| | | Sedan | | 0 | 0 | | 1,151 |
| | | Sedgwick | 0 | 0 | 0 | 0 | 1,680 |
| | | Seneca | 0 | 0 | 0 | 0 | 2,003 |
| | | South Hutchinson | 0 | 0 | 0 | 0 | 2,548 |
| | | Spring Hill | 0 | 0 | 0 | 0 | 5,578 |
| | | Stafford | 0 | 0 | 0 | 0 | 1,015 |
| | | Sterling | 0 | 0 | 0 | 0 | 2,520 |
| | | St. Francis | 0 | 0 | 0 | 0 | 1,261 |
| | | St. George | 0 | 0 | 0 | 0 | 575 |
| | | St. John | 0 | 0 | 0 | | 1,159 |
| | | St. Marys | 0 | 0 | 0 | 0 | 2,284 |
| | | Stockton | 0 | 0 | 0 | 0 | 1,386 |
| | | Tonganoxie | 0 | 0 | 0 | 0 | 4,520 |
| | | Towanda | 0 | 0 | | | 1,362 |
| | | Troy | | 0 | | | 1,010 |
| | | Udall | 0 | 0 | 0 | 0 | 738 |
| | | Ulysses | 0 | 0 | 0 | 0 | 5,515 |
| | | Valley Falls | 0 | 0 | 0 | 0 | 1,146 |
| | | Victoria | 0 | 0 | 0 | 0 | 1,204 |
| | | Wa Keeney | 0 | 0 | 0 | 0 | 1,692 |
| | | Wakefield | 0 | 0 | 0 | 0 | 874 |
| | | Walton | 0 | | 0 | 0 | 286 |
| | | Wathena | 0 | 0 | 0 | 0 | 1,291 |
| | | Waterville | 0 | 0 | 0 | 0 | 609 |
| | | Waverly | | | | 0 | 543 |
| | | Weir | 0 | 0 | 0 | 0 | 698 |
| | | Wellsville | 0 | 0 | 0 | 0 | 1,751 |
| | | Westwood | 0 | 0 | 0 | 0 | 1,838 |
| | | Wilson | 0 | 0 | 0 | 0 | 754 |
| | | Winchester | 0 | 0 | 0 | 0 | 567 |
| | | Winfield | 0 | | | | 11,421 |
| | | Yates Center | 0 | 0 | 0 | 0 | 1,354 |

[1]Agencies published in this table indicated that no hate crimes occurred in their jurisdictions during the quarter(s) for which they submitted reports to the Hate Crime Statistics Program. Blanks indicate quarters for which agencies did not submit reports.

[2]Population figures are published only for the cities. The figures listed for the universities and colleges are student enrollment and were provided by the United States Department of Education for the 2008 school year, the most recent available. The enrollment figures include full-time and part-time students.

# Table 95. Hate Crime Zero Data Submitted per Quarter, by State and Agency, 2009—*Continued*

(Number.)

| State | Agency type | Agency name | Zero data per quarter[1] | | | | Population[2] |
|---|---|---|---|---|---|---|---|
| | | | 1st quarter | 2nd quarter | 3rd quarter | 4th quarter | |
| **KANSAS** | **Universities and Colleges** | Emporia State University | 0 | 0 | 0 | 0 | 6,404 |
| | | Fort Hays State University | 0 | 0 | 0 | 0 | 10,107 |
| | | Pittsburg State University | 0 | 0 | 0 | 0 | 7,127 |
| | | University of Kansas, Main Campus | 0 | 0 | 0 | 0 | 29,365 |
| | | Wichita State University | 0 | 0 | 0 | 0 | 14,405 |
| | **Metropolitan Counties** | Butler | 0 | 0 | 0 | 0 | |
| | | Douglas | 0 | 0 | 0 | 0 | |
| | | Geary | 0 | 0 | 0 | 0 | |
| | | Harvey | 0 | 0 | 0 | 0 | |
| | | Jefferson | 0 | 0 | 0 | 0 | |
| | | Leavenworth | 0 | 0 | 0 | 0 | |
| | | Linn | 0 | 0 | 0 | 0 | |
| | | Miami | 0 | 0 | 0 | 0 | |
| | | Osage | 0 | 0 | 0 | 0 | |
| | | Wabaunsee | 0 | 0 | 0 | 0 | |
| | | Wyandotte | 0 | 0 | 0 | 0 | |
| | **Nonmetropolitan Counties** | Allen | 0 | 0 | 0 | 0 | |
| | | Anderson | 0 | 0 | 0 | 0 | |
| | | Atchison | 0 | 0 | 0 | 0 | |
| | | Barber | 0 | 0 | 0 | 0 | |
| | | Barton | 0 | 0 | 0 | 0 | |
| | | Bourbon | 0 | 0 | 0 | 0 | |
| | | Brown | 0 | 0 | 0 | 0 | |
| | | Chase | 0 | 0 | 0 | 0 | |
| | | Cherokee | 0 | 0 | 0 | 0 | |
| | | Cheyenne | 0 | 0 | 0 | 0 | |
| | | Clark | 0 | 0 | 0 | 0 | |
| | | Clay | 0 | 0 | 0 | 0 | |
| | | Cloud | 0 | 0 | 0 | 0 | |
| | | Coffey | 0 | 0 | 0 | 0 | |
| | | Cowley | 0 | 0 | 0 | 0 | |
| | | Crawford | 0 | 0 | 0 | 0 | |
| | | Edwards | 0 | 0 | 0 | 0 | |
| | | Elk | 0 | 0 | 0 | 0 | |
| | | Ellis | 0 | 0 | 0 | 0 | |
| | | Ellsworth | 0 | 0 | 0 | 0 | |
| | | Finney | 0 | 0 | 0 | 0 | |
| | | Ford | 0 | 0 | 0 | 0 | |
| | | Gove | 0 | 0 | 0 | 0 | |
| | | Graham | 0 | 0 | 0 | 0 | |
| | | Grant | 0 | 0 | 0 | 0 | |
| | | Gray | 0 | 0 | 0 | 0 | |
| | | Greeley | 0 | 0 | 0 | 0 | |
| | | Greenwood | 0 | 0 | 0 | 0 | |
| | | Harper | 0 | 0 | 0 | 0 | |
| | | Hodgeman | 0 | 0 | 0 | 0 | |
| | | Kingman | 0 | 0 | 0 | | |
| | | Kiowa | 0 | 0 | 0 | 0 | |
| | | Lane | 0 | 0 | 0 | 0 | |
| | | Logan | 0 | 0 | 0 | 0 | |
| | | Lyon | 0 | 0 | 0 | 0 | |
| | | Marion | 0 | 0 | 0 | 0 | |
| | | Marshall | 0 | 0 | 0 | 0 | |
| | | McPherson | 0 | 0 | 0 | 0 | |
| | | Mitchell | 0 | 0 | 0 | 0 | |
| | | Montgomery | 0 | 0 | 0 | 0 | |
| | | Morris | 0 | 0 | 0 | 0 | |
| | | Morton | 0 | 0 | 0 | 0 | |
| | | Nemaha | 0 | 0 | 0 | 0 | |
| | | Neosho | 0 | 0 | 0 | 0 | |
| | | Ness | 0 | 0 | 0 | 0 | |
| | | Norton | 0 | 0 | 0 | 0 | |
| | | Osborne | 0 | 0 | 0 | 0 | |
| | | Ottawa | 0 | 0 | 0 | 0 | |
| | | Pawnee | 0 | 0 | 0 | 0 | |
| | | Phillips | 0 | 0 | 0 | 0 | |
| | | Pratt | 0 | 0 | 0 | 0 | |
| | | Rawlins | 0 | 0 | 0 | 0 | |
| | | Republic | 0 | 0 | 0 | 0 | |
| | | Rice | 0 | 0 | 0 | 0 | |
| | | Rooks | 0 | 0 | 0 | 0 | |
| | | Rush | 0 | 0 | 0 | 0 | |
| | | Russell | 0 | 0 | 0 | 0 | |
| | | Saline | 0 | 0 | 0 | 0 | |
| | | Scott | 0 | 0 | 0 | 0 | |
| | | Sheridan | 0 | 0 | 0 | 0 | |
| | | Sherman | 0 | 0 | 0 | 0 | |
| | | Smith | 0 | 0 | 0 | 0 | |
| | | Stafford | 0 | 0 | 0 | 0 | |
| | | Stanton | 0 | 0 | 0 | 0 | |
| | | Thomas | 0 | 0 | 0 | 0 | |
| | | Trego | 0 | 0 | 0 | 0 | |
| | | Wallace | 0 | 0 | 0 | 0 | |
| | | Washington | 0 | 0 | 0 | 0 | |
| | | Wilson | 0 | 0 | 0 | 0 | |
| | | Woodson | 0 | 0 | 0 | 0 | |
| | **State Police Agencies** | Kansas Highway Patrol | 0 | 0 | 0 | 0 | |
| | **Tribal Agencies** | Iowa Tribal | 0 | 0 | | | |
| | | Kickapoo Tribal | 0 | 0 | | 0 | |
| | | Potawatomi Tribal | 0 | 0 | 0 | 0 | |
| | **Other Agencies** | Blue Valley School District | 0 | 0 | 0 | 0 | |
| | | Franklin County Drug Enforcement | 0 | 0 | 0 | 0 | |
| | | Kansas Alcoholic Beverage Control | 0 | | 0 | 0 | |
| | | Kansas Bureau of Investigation | 0 | 0 | 0 | 0 | |
| | | Kansas Lottery Security Division | 0 | 0 | 0 | 0 | |
| | | Kansas Racing Commission, Security Division | 0 | 0 | 0 | 0 | |
| | | Metropolitan Topeka Airport Authority | 0 | 0 | 0 | 0 | |
| | | Shawnee Mission Public Schools | 0 | 0 | 0 | 0 | |
| | | State Fire Marshal | 0 | 0 | 0 | 0 | |
| | | Topeka Fire Department, Arson Investigation | 0 | 0 | 0 | 0 | |
| | | Unified School District: | | | | | |
| | | Auburn-Washburn | 0 | | | | |
| | | Liberal | 0 | 0 | | | |
| | | Seaman | 0 | 0 | 0 | 0 | |
| | | Topeka | 0 | 0 | | | |
| | | Wyandotte County Parks and Recreation | 0 | 0 | 0 | 0 | |
| **KENTUCKY** .. | **Cities** | Albany | 0 | 0 | 0 | 0 | 2,321 |
| | | Alexandria | 0 | 0 | 0 | 0 | 8,605 |

[1]Agencies published in this table indicated that no hate crimes occurred in their jurisdictions during the quarter(s) for which they submitted reports to the Hate Crime program. Blanks indicate quarters for which agencies did not submit reports.

[2]Population figures are published only for the cities. The figures listed for the universities and colleges are student enrollment and were provided by the United States Department of Education for the 2006 school year, the most recent available. The enrollment figures include full-time and part-time students.

## Table 95. Hate Crime Zero Data Submitted per Quarter, by State and Agency, 2009—*Continued*

(Number.)

| State | Agency type | Agency name | Zero data per quarter[1] 1st quarter | 2nd quarter | 3rd quarter | 4th quarter | Population[2] |
|---|---|---|---|---|---|---|---|
| KENTUCKY | | Anchorage | 0 | 0 | 0 | 0 | 3,417 |
| | | Ashland | 0 | 0 | 0 | 0 | 21,276 |
| | | Auburn | 0 | 0 | | 0 | 1,506 |
| | | Bardwell | 0 | 0 | 0 | 0 | 772 |
| | | Beattyville | 0 | 0 | 0 | 0 | 1,113 |
| | | Beaver Dam | 0 | 0 | 0 | 0 | 3,144 |
| | | Bellefonte | | 0 | | | 844 |
| | | Benham | 0 | 0 | 0 | 0 | 524 |
| | | Benton | 0 | 0 | 0 | 0 | 4,370 |
| | | Brandenburg | 0 | 0 | 0 | 0 | 2,196 |
| | | Brownsville | 0 | 0 | 0 | 0 | 1,049 |
| | | Burnside | 0 | 0 | 0 | 0 | 697 |
| | | Cadiz | 0 | 0 | 0 | 0 | 2,592 |
| | | Calhoun | 0 | 0 | 0 | 0 | 783 |
| | | Calvert City | 0 | 0 | 0 | 0 | 2,769 |
| | | Carrollton | 0 | 0 | 0 | 0 | 3,933 |
| | | Catlettsburg | 0 | 0 | 0 | 0 | 1,928 |
| | | Cave City | 0 | 0 | 0 | 0 | 2,014 |
| | | Central City | 0 | 0 | 0 | 0 | 5,678 |
| | | Clarkson | 0 | 0 | 0 | 0 | 843 |
| | | Clay City | 0 | 0 | 0 | 0 | 1,364 |
| | | Clinton | 0 | 0 | 0 | 0 | 1,321 |
| | | Cloverport | 0 | 0 | 0 | 0 | 1,232 |
| | | Coal Run Village | 0 | 0 | 0 | 0 | 625 |
| | | Cold Spring | 0 | 0 | 0 | 0 | 6,072 |
| | | Columbia | 0 | 0 | 0 | 0 | 4,296 |
| | | Corbin | 0 | 0 | 0 | 0 | 8,376 |
| | | Cumberland | 0 | 0 | 0 | 0 | 2,327 |
| | | Dawson Springs | 0 | 0 | 0 | 0 | 2,895 |
| | | Dry Ridge | 0 | 0 | 0 | 0 | 2,245 |
| | | Earlington | 0 | 0 | 0 | 0 | 1,563 |
| | | Eddyville | 0 | 0 | 0 | 0 | 2,423 |
| | | Edgewood | 0 | 0 | 0 | 0 | 8,858 |
| | | Edmonton | 0 | 0 | 0 | 0 | 1,650 |
| | | Eminence | 0 | 0 | 0 | 0 | 2,213 |
| | | Evarts | 0 | 0 | 0 | 0 | 1,019 |
| | | Ferguson | | | | 0 | 943 |
| | | Flatwoods | 0 | 0 | 0 | 0 | 7,663 |
| | | Flemingsburg | 0 | 0 | 0 | 0 | 2,682 |
| | | Fort Mitchell | 0 | 0 | 0 | 0 | 7,507 |
| | | Fort Thomas | 0 | 0 | 0 | 0 | 15,089 |
| | | Fort Wright | 0 | 0 | 0 | 0 | 5,425 |
| | | Frankfort | | 0 | 0 | 0 | 27,272 |
| | | Franklin | 0 | 0 | 0 | 0 | 7,981 |
| | | Gamaliel | 0 | 0 | 0 | 0 | 426 |
| | | Georgetown | 0 | 0 | 0 | 0 | 21,962 |
| | | Graymoor-Devondale | 0 | 0 | 0 | 0 | 3,215 |
| | | Grayson | 0 | 0 | 0 | 0 | 3,996 |
| | | Greensburg | 0 | 0 | 0 | 0 | 2,416 |
| | | Greenup | 0 | 0 | 0 | 0 | 1,184 |
| | | Greenville | 0 | 0 | 0 | 0 | 4,218 |
| | | Guthrie | 0 | 0 | 0 | 0 | 1,453 |
| | | Harlan | 0 | 0 | 0 | 0 | 1,843 |
| | | Hartford | 0 | 0 | 0 | 0 | 2,677 |
| | | Hazard | 0 | 0 | 0 | 0 | 4,789 |
| | | Henderson | 0 | 0 | 0 | 0 | 27,984 |
| | | Heritage Creek | 0 | 0 | 0 | 0 | 1,831 |
| | | Highland Heights Southgate | 0 | 0 | 0 | 0 | 8,948 |
| | | Hillview | 0 | 0 | 0 | 0 | 7,630 |
| | | Hodgenville | 0 | 0 | 0 | 0 | 2,762 |
| | | Horse Cave | 0 | 0 | 0 | 0 | 2,334 |
| | | Indian Hills | 0 | 0 | 0 | 0 | 3,552 |
| | | Inez | 0 | 0 | 0 | 0 | 431 |
| | | Irvington | 0 | 0 | 0 | 0 | 1,417 |
| | | Jackson | 0 | 0 | 0 | 0 | 2,387 |
| | | Jamestown | 0 | 0 | 0 | 0 | 1,750 |
| | | Jenkins | 0 | 0 | 0 | 0 | 2,228 |
| | | Junction City | 0 | 0 | 0 | 0 | 2,212 |
| | | La Grange | 0 | 0 | 0 | 0 | 6,354 |
| | | Lancaster | 0 | 0 | 0 | 0 | 4,473 |
| | | Lawrenceburg | 0 | 0 | 0 | 0 | 10,071 |
| | | Lebanon | 0 | 0 | 0 | 0 | 5,993 |
| | | Lewisburg | 0 | 0 | 0 | 0 | 913 |
| | | Liberty | 0 | 0 | 0 | 0 | 1,898 |
| | | London | 0 | 0 | 0 | 0 | 8,020 |
| | | Louisa | 0 | 0 | 0 | 0 | 2,096 |
| | | Loyall | 0 | 0 | 0 | 0 | 697 |
| | | Lynch | 0 | 0 | 0 | 0 | 812 |
| | | Lynnview | 0 | 0 | 0 | 0 | 1,044 |
| | | Madisonville | 0 | 0 | 0 | 0 | 19,083 |
| | | Manchester | 0 | 0 | 0 | 0 | 1,939 |
| | | Marion | 0 | 0 | 0 | 0 | 3,091 |
| | | Middlesboro | 0 | 0 | 0 | 0 | 9,881 |
| | | Morehead | 0 | 0 | 0 | 0 | 7,718 |
| | | Morganfield | 0 | 0 | 0 | 0 | 3,274 |
| | | Morgantown | 0 | 0 | 0 | 0 | 2,566 |
| | | Mortons Gap | 0 | 0 | 0 | 0 | 935 |
| | | Mount Sterling | 0 | 0 | 0 | 0 | 7,026 |
| | | Mount Vernon | 0 | 0 | 0 | 0 | 2,612 |
| | | Muldraugh | | 0 | | | 1,214 |
| | | Munfordville | 0 | 0 | 0 | 0 | 1,616 |
| | | Murray | 0 | 0 | 0 | 0 | 16,709 |
| | | New Castle | 0 | 0 | 0 | 0 | 908 |
| | | Newport | 0 | 0 | 0 | 0 | 15,632 |
| | | Nortonville | 0 | 0 | 0 | 0 | 1,231 |
| | | Olive Hill | 0 | 0 | 0 | 0 | 1,820 |
| | | Owensboro | 0 | 0 | 0 | 0 | 55,651 |
| | | Owenton | 0 | 0 | 0 | 0 | 1,486 |
| | | Owingsville | 0 | 0 | 0 | 0 | 1,684 |
| | | Paintsville | 0 | 0 | 0 | 0 | 4,226 |
| | | Paris | 0 | 0 | 0 | 0 | 9,297 |
| | | Park Hills | 0 | 0 | 0 | 0 | 2,762 |
| | | Pewee Valley | 0 | 0 | 0 | 0 | 1,625 |
| | | Pineville | 0 | 0 | 0 | 0 | 1,979 |
| | | Pioneer Village | 0 | 0 | 0 | 0 | 2,732 |
| | | Prestonsburg | 0 | 0 | 0 | 0 | 3,861 |
| | | Providence | 0 | 0 | 0 | 0 | 3,399 |
| | | Raceland | 0 | 0 | 0 | 0 | 2,630 |
| | | Radcliff | 0 | | | | 22,008 |
| | | Russell | 0 | 0 | 0 | 0 | 3,584 |
| | | Russell Springs | 0 | 0 | 0 | 0 | 2,345 |
| | | Russellville | 0 | 0 | 0 | 0 | 7,281 |
| | | Sadieville | 0 | 0 | 0 | 0 | 326 |
| | | Salyersville | 0 | 0 | 0 | 0 | 1,566 |
| | | Science Hill | 0 | 0 | 0 | 0 | 674 |
| | | Scottsville | 0 | 0 | 0 | 0 | 4,610 |
| | | Silver Grove | 0 | 0 | 0 | 0 | 1,147 |
| | | Simpsonville | 0 | 0 | 0 | 0 | 1,454 |
| | | Somerset | 0 | 0 | 0 | 0 | 12,570 |
| | | Springfield | 0 | 0 | 0 | 0 | 2,894 |
| | | Stamping Ground | 0 | 0 | 0 | 0 | 691 |
| | | Stanford | 0 | 0 | 0 | 0 | 3,396 |
| | | Stanton | 0 | 0 | 0 | 0 | 3,162 |
| | | Strathmoor Village | 0 | 0 | 0 | 0 | 697 |
| | | Sturgis | 0 | 0 | 0 | 0 | 1,912 |
| | | Taylor Mill | 0 | 0 | 0 | 0 | 6,728 |
| | | Taylorsville | 0 | 0 | 0 | 0 | 1,258 |
| | | Tompkinsville | 0 | 0 | 0 | 0 | 2,604 |
| | | Trenton | 0 | 0 | 0 | 0 | 428 |
| | | Uniontown | 0 | 0 | 0 | 0 | 1,015 |
| | | Vanceburg | 0 | 0 | 0 | 0 | 1,693 |
| | | Villa Hills | 0 | 0 | 0 | 0 | 7,703 |
| | | Warsaw | 0 | 0 | 0 | 0 | 1,788 |
| | | West Liberty | 0 | 0 | 0 | 0 | 3,289 |
| | | Wilder | 0 | 0 | 0 | 0 | 2,959 |
| | | Williamsburg | 0 | 0 | 0 | 0 | 5,230 |
| | | Williamstown | 0 | 0 | 0 | 0 | 3,565 |
| | | Winchester | 0 | 0 | 0 | 0 | 16,583 |
| | | Worthington | 0 | 0 | 0 | 0 | 1,677 |
| | **Universities and Colleges** | Kentucky State University | 0 | 0 | 0 | 0 | 2,659 |

[1]Agencies published in this table indicated that no hate crimes occurred in their jurisdictions during the quarter(s) for which they submitted reports to the Hate Crime Statistics Program. Blanks indicate quarters for which agencies did not submit reports.

[2]Population figures are published only for the cities. The figures listed for the universities and colleges are student enrollment and were provided by the United States Department of Education for the 2008 school year, the most recent available. The enrollment figures include full-time and part-time students.

# Table 95. Hate Crime Zero Data Submitted per Quarter, by State and Agency, 2009—*Continued*

(Number.)

| State | Agency type | Agency name | Zero data per quarter[1] 1st quarter | 2nd quarter | 3rd quarter | 4th quarter | Population[2] |
|---|---|---|---|---|---|---|---|
| KENTUCKY | | Morehead State University | 0 | 0 | 0 | 0 | 8,832 |
| | | Western Kentucky University | 0 | 0 | 0 | 0 | 19,742 |
| | Metropolitan Counties | Bourbon | 0 | 0 | 0 | 0 | |
| | | Boyd | 0 | 0 | 0 | 0 | |
| | | Bracken | 0 | 0 | 0 | 0 | |
| | | Campbell County Police Department | 0 | 0 | 0 | 0 | |
| | | Christian | 0 | 0 | 0 | 0 | |
| | | Daviess | 0 | 0 | 0 | 0 | |
| | | Edmonson | 0 | 0 | 0 | 0 | |
| | | Gallatin | 0 | 0 | 0 | 0 | |
| | | Grant | 0 | 0 | 0 | 0 | |
| | | Greenup | 0 | 0 | 0 | 0 | |
| | | Hancock | | | | 0 | |
| | | Hardin | 0 | 0 | 0 | 0 | |
| | | Henderson | 0 | 0 | 0 | 0 | |
| | | Henry | 0 | 0 | 0 | 0 | |
| | | Jessamine | 0 | 0 | 0 | 0 | |
| | | Kenton | 0 | 0 | 0 | 0 | |
| | | Larue | 0 | 0 | 0 | 0 | |
| | | McLean | 0 | 0 | 0 | 0 | |
| | | Meade | 0 | 0 | 0 | 0 | |
| | | Nelson | 0 | 0 | 0 | 0 | |
| | | Oldham | 0 | 0 | 0 | 0 | |
| | | Pendleton | 0 | 0 | 0 | 0 | |
| | | Scott | 0 | 0 | 0 | 0 | |
| | | Spencer | 0 | 0 | 0 | 0 | |
| | | Trigg | 0 | 0 | 0 | 0 | |
| | | Trimble | 0 | 0 | 0 | 0 | |
| | | Webster | 0 | 0 | 0 | 0 | |
| | | Woodford | 0 | 0 | 0 | 0 | |
| | Nonmetropolitan Counties | Adair | 0 | 0 | 0 | 0 | |
| | | Anderson | 0 | 0 | 0 | 0 | |
| | | Barren | 0 | 0 | 0 | 0 | |
| | | Bell | 0 | 0 | 0 | 0 | |
| | | Boyle | 0 | 0 | 0 | 0 | |
| | | Breckinridge | 0 | 0 | 0 | 0 | |
| | | Butler | 0 | 0 | 0 | 0 | |
| | | Caldwell | 0 | 0 | 0 | 0 | |
| | | Calloway | 0 | 0 | 0 | 0 | |
| | | Carlisle | 0 | 0 | 0 | 0 | |
| | | Carter | 0 | 0 | 0 | 0 | |
| | | Casey | 0 | 0 | 0 | 0 | |
| | | Clay | 0 | 0 | 0 | 0 | |
| | | Crittenden | 0 | 0 | 0 | 0 | |
| | | Cumberland | 0 | 0 | 0 | 0 | |
| | | Estill | 0 | 0 | 0 | 0 | |
| | | Floyd | 0 | 0 | 0 | 0 | |
| | | Fulton | 0 | 0 | 0 | 0 | |
| | | Garrard | 0 | 0 | 0 | 0 | |
| | | Grayson | 0 | 0 | 0 | 0 | |
| | | Green | 0 | 0 | 0 | 0 | |
| | | Harlan | 0 | 0 | 0 | 0 | |
| | | Hart | 0 | 0 | 0 | 0 | |
| | | Hopkins | 0 | 0 | 0 | 0 | |
| | | Jackson | 0 | 0 | 0 | 0 | |
| | | Johnson | | | | 0 | |
| | | Knott | 0 | 0 | 0 | 0 | |
| | | Knox | 0 | 0 | 0 | 0 | |
| | | Lawrence | 0 | 0 | 0 | 0 | |
| | | Lee | 0 | 0 | 0 | 0 | |
| | | Letcher | 0 | 0 | 0 | 0 | |
| | | Lewis | 0 | 0 | 0 | 0 | |
| | | Lincoln | 0 | 0 | 0 | 0 | |
| | | Livingston | 0 | 0 | 0 | 0 | |
| | | Logan | 0 | 0 | 0 | 0 | |
| | | Lyon | 0 | 0 | 0 | 0 | |
| | | Magoffin | 0 | 0 | 0 | 0 | |
| | | Marion | 0 | 0 | 0 | 0 | |
| | | Martin | 0 | 0 | 0 | 0 | |
| | | Mason | 0 | 0 | 0 | 0 | |
| | | McCreary | 0 | 0 | 0 | 0 | |
| | | Menifee | 0 | 0 | 0 | 0 | |
| | | Mercer | 0 | 0 | 0 | 0 | |
| | | Metcalfe | 0 | 0 | 0 | 0 | |
| | | Montgomery | 0 | 0 | 0 | 0 | |
| | | Muhlenberg | 0 | 0 | 0 | 0 | |
| | | Nicholas | 0 | 0 | 0 | 0 | |
| | | Owen | 0 | 0 | 0 | 0 | |
| | | Perry | 0 | 0 | 0 | 0 | |
| | | Pike | 0 | 0 | 0 | 0 | |
| | | Powell | 0 | 0 | 0 | 0 | |
| | | Pulaski | 0 | 0 | 0 | 0 | |
| | | Rockcastle | 0 | 0 | 0 | 0 | |
| | | Russell | 0 | 0 | 0 | 0 | |
| | | Simpson | 0 | 0 | 0 | 0 | |
| | | Taylor | 0 | 0 | 0 | 0 | |
| | | Todd | 0 | 0 | 0 | 0 | |
| | | Washington | 0 | 0 | 0 | 0 | |
| | | Wayne | 0 | 0 | 0 | 0 | |
| | | Wolfe | 0 | 0 | 0 | 0 | |
| | State Police Agencies | State Police: Ashland | 0 | 0 | 0 | 0 | |
| | | Bowling Green | 0 | 0 | 0 | 0 | |
| | | Cannabis Suppression Section | 0 | 0 | 0 | 0 | |
| | | Dry Ridge | 0 | 0 | 0 | 0 | |
| | | East Drug Enforcement Branch | 0 | 0 | 0 | 0 | |
| | | Electronic Crimes | 0 | 0 | 0 | 0 | |
| | | Elizabethtown | 0 | 0 | 0 | 0 | |
| | | Frankfort | 0 | 0 | 0 | 0 | |
| | | Hazard | 0 | 0 | 0 | 0 | |
| | | Henderson | 0 | 0 | 0 | 0 | |
| | | Mayfield | 0 | 0 | 0 | 0 | |
| | | Morehead | 0 | 0 | 0 | 0 | |
| | | Richmond | 0 | 0 | 0 | 0 | |
| | | Special Investigations | 0 | 0 | 0 | 0 | |
| | | West Drug Enforcement Branch | 0 | 0 | 0 | 0 | |
| | Other Agencies | Barren County Drug Task Force | 0 | 0 | 0 | 0 | |
| | | Buffalo Trace-Gateway Narcotics Task Force | 0 | 0 | 0 | 0 | |
| | | Central Kentucky Area Drug Task Force | 0 | 0 | 0 | 0 | |
| | | FIVCO Area Drug Task Force | 0 | 0 | 0 | 0 | |
| | | Graves County Schools | 0 | 0 | 0 | 0 | |
| | | Greater Hardin County Narcotics Task Force | 0 | 0 | 0 | 0 | |
| | | Kentucky Fairgrounds Security | 0 | 0 | 0 | 0 | |
| | | Kentucky Horse Park | 0 | 0 | 0 | 0 | |

[1]Agencies published in this table indicated that no hate crimes occurred in their jurisdictions during the quarter(s) for which they submitted reports to the Hate Crime Statistics Program. Blanks indicate quarters for which agencies did not submit reports.

[2]Population figures are published only for the cities. The figures listed for the universities and colleges are student enrollment and were provided by the United States Department of Education for the 2008 school year, the most recent available. The enrollment figures include full-time and part-time students.

# Table 95. Hate Crime Zero Data Submitted per Quarter, by State and Agency, 2009—*Continued*

(Number.)

| State | Agency type | Agency name | Zero data per quarter[1] | | | | Population[2] |
|---|---|---|---|---|---|---|---|
| | | | 1st quarter | 2nd quarter | 3rd quarter | 4th quarter | |
| **KENTUCKY** | | Lake Cumberland Area Drug Enforcement Task Force | 0 | 0 | 0 | 0 | |
| | | Louisville Regional Airport Authority | 0 | 0 | 0 | 0 | |
| | | Montgomery County School District | 0 | 0 | 0 | 0 | |
| | | Motor Vehicle Enforcement | 0 | 0 | 0 | 0 | |
| | | Northern Kentucky Narcotics Enforcement Unit | | | | 0 | |
| | | Pennyrile Narcotics Task Force | 0 | 0 | 0 | 0 | |
| | | South Central Kentucky Drug Task Force | 0 | 0 | 0 | 0 | |
| | | Unlawful Narcotics Investigation, Treatment and Education | 0 | 0 | 0 | 0 | |
| **LOUISIANA** | **Cities** | Addis | | 0 | 0 | 0 | 3,652 |
| | | Alexandria | | 0 | 0 | 0 | 48,886 |
| | | Amite | 0 | 0 | 0 | | 4,343 |
| | | Baker | 0 | 0 | 0 | 0 | 13,315 |
| | | Baldwin | 0 | | | | 2,601 |
| | | Basile | 0 | 0 | 0 | 0 | 2,372 |
| | | Bastrop | 0 | | 0 | | 11,687 |
| | | Bernice | 0 | 0 | 0 | 0 | 1,626 |
| | | Bossier City | 0 | 0 | 0 | 0 | 63,077 |
| | | Brusly | 0 | 0 | 0 | 0 | 2,176 |
| | | Clinton | 0 | 0 | 0 | 0 | 1,880 |
| | | Coushatta | 0 | 0 | 0 | 0 | 2,067 |
| | | Covington | 0 | 0 | 0 | | 9,218 |
| | | Denham Springs | 0 | 0 | 0 | 0 | 10,398 |
| | | De Quincy | 0 | 0 | 0 | 0 | 3,206 |
| | | Ferriday | 0 | | | | 3,556 |
| | | French Settlement | 0 | | 0 | 0 | 1,070 |
| | | Gonzales | 0 | 0 | | | 9,531 |
| | | Harahan | | 0 | 0 | | 9,249 |
| | | Jeanerette | 0 | 0 | 0 | 0 | 5,871 |
| | | Jennings | 0 | 0 | 0 | 0 | 10,483 |
| | | Kenner | 0 | 0 | 0 | 0 | 66,592 |
| | | Kinder | 0 | 0 | 0 | 0 | 2,399 |
| | | Krotz Springs | 0 | | | | 1,277 |
| | | Lake Arthur | 0 | 0 | 0 | 0 | 2,866 |
| | | Lake Charles | 0 | 0 | 0 | 0 | 70,975 |
| | | Mamou | 0 | 0 | 0 | 0 | 3,399 |
| | | Mandeville | 0 | 0 | | 0 | 12,645 |
| | | Morgan City | 0 | 0 | 0 | | 11,497 |
| | | New Orleans | 0 | 0 | 0 | 0 | 336,425 |
| | | Olla | 0 | 0 | 0 | 0 | 1,348 |
| | | Pearl River | 0 | | | 0 | 2,230 |
| | | Plaquemine | 0 | 0 | 0 | 0 | 6,718 |
| | | Port Allen | 0 | 0 | 0 | 0 | 4,955 |
| | | Ruston | 0 | | 0 | 0 | 21,181 |
| | | Shreveport | 0 | | 0 | 0 | 199,629 |
| | | Sorrento | 0 | | | | 1,452 |
| | | Springhill | 0 | | | | 5,082 |
| | | Sterlington | 0 | 0 | 0 | 0 | 1,415 |
| | | Tallulah | 0 | 0 | 0 | 0 | 7,504 |
| | | Thibodaux | 0 | 0 | | 0 | 14,012 |
| | | Tickfaw | | 0 | | | 694 |
| | | Vinton | 0 | 0 | 0 | 0 | 3,247 |
| | | Westlake | 0 | 0 | 0 | 0 | 4,566 |
| | | West Monroe | 0 | 0 | 0 | 0 | 12,863 |
| | | Westwego | 0 | 0 | 0 | 0 | 10,033 |
| | **Universities and Colleges** | Delgado Community College | 0 | | 0 | | 14,450 |
| | | Louisiana State University: | | | | | |
| | | Baton Rouge[3] | 0 | 0 | 0 | 0 | |
| | | Eunice | 0 | 0 | 0 | | 3,031 |
| | | Shreveport | 0 | 0 | | | 4,281 |
| | | Louisiana Tech University | 0 | | | | 10,917 |
| | | McNeese State University | 0 | 0 | 0 | 0 | 8,283 |
| | | Nicholls State University | 0 | 0 | 0 | 0 | 6,916 |
| | | Northwestern State University | 0 | 0 | 0 | 0 | 9,111 |
| | | Southeastern Louisiana University | 0 | 0 | 0 | 0 | 15,215 |
| | | Southern University and A&M College, New Orleans | 0 | 0 | 0 | 0 | 3,104 |
| | | Tulane University | 0 | 0 | 0 | 0 | 10,737 |
| | | University of Louisiana, Monroe | 0 | 0 | 0 | 0 | 8,754 |
| | **Metropolitan Counties** | Ascension | 0 | 0 | 0 | 0 | |
| | | Caddo | 0 | 0 | 0 | 0 | |
| | | Cameron | 0 | 0 | 0 | 0 | |
| | | De Soto | 0 | 0 | 0 | 0 | |
| | | Grant | 0 | 0 | | | |
| | | Ouachita | 0 | | | | |
| | | Plaquemines | 0 | 0 | 0 | 0 | |
| | | Pointe Coupee | 0 | 0 | | | |
| | | Rapides | 0 | 0 | 0 | 0 | |
| | | St. Bernard | 0 | 0 | | 0 | |
| | | St. Charles | 0 | 0 | 0 | 0 | |
| | | St. Helena | 0 | 0 | | | |
| | | St. Martin | 0 | | | | |
| | | St. Tammany | 0 | 0 | 0 | 0 | |
| | | West Baton Rouge | 0 | 0 | 0 | 0 | |
| | | West Feliciana | 0 | 0 | 0 | 0 | |
| | **Nonmetropolitan Counties** | Acadia | | | 0 | | |
| | | Evangeline | 0 | 0 | 0 | 0 | |
| | | Franklin | 0 | 0 | 0 | 0 | |
| | | Jackson | 0 | | | | |
| | | Jefferson Davis | 0 | 0 | 0 | 0 | |
| | | Madison | 0 | 0 | 0 | 0 | |
| | | Morehouse | 0 | 0 | 0 | 0 | |
| | | Sabine | 0 | 0 | 0 | 0 | |
| | | St. Landry | 0 | 0 | 0 | 0 | |
| | | Tensas | 0 | 0 | 0 | 0 | |
| | | Vernon | 0 | 0 | 0 | | |
| | | Webster | 0 | 0 | 0 | | |
| **MAINE** | **Cities** | Ashland | 0 | 0 | 0 | 0 | 1,441 |
| | | Baileyville | 0 | 0 | 0 | 0 | 1,540 |
| | | Bangor | 0 | 0 | 0 | 0 | 31,789 |
| | | Bar Harbor | 0 | 0 | 0 | 0 | 5,163 |
| | | Bath | 0 | 0 | 0 | 0 | 8,847 |
| | | Belfast | 0 | 0 | 0 | 0 | 6,754 |

[1]Agencies published in this table indicated that no hate crimes occurred in their jurisdictions during the quarter(s) for which they submitted reports to the Hate Crime Statistics Program. Blanks indicate quarters for which agencies did not submit reports.

[2]Population figures are published only for the cities. The figures listed for the universities and colleges are student enrollment and were provided by the United States Department of Education for the 2008 school year, the most recent available. The enrollment figures include full-time and part-time students.

[3]Student enrollment figures were not available.

# Table 95. Hate Crime Zero Data Submitted per Quarter, by State and Agency, 2009—*Continued*

(Number.)

| State | Agency type | Agency name | Zero data per quarter[1] | | | | Population[2] |
|---|---|---|---|---|---|---|---|
| | | | 1st quarter | 2nd quarter | 3rd quarter | 4th quarter | |
| **MAINE** | | Berwick | 0 | 0 | 0 | 0 | 7,681 |
| | | Bethel | 0 | 0 | 0 | 0 | 2,687 |
| | | Boothbay Harbor | 0 | 0 | 0 | 0 | 2,242 |
| | | Brewer | 0 | 0 | 0 | 0 | 9,041 |
| | | Bridgton | 0 | 0 | 0 | 0 | 5,507 |
| | | Brownville | 0 | 0 | 0 | 0 | 1,292 |
| | | Brunswick | 0 | 0 | 0 | 0 | 21,781 |
| | | Bucksport | 0 | 0 | 0 | 0 | 4,892 |
| | | Buxton | 0 | 0 | 0 | 0 | 8,138 |
| | | Calais | 0 | 0 | 0 | 0 | 3,157 |
| | | Camden | 0 | 0 | 0 | 0 | 5,216 |
| | | Cape Elizabeth | 0 | 0 | 0 | 0 | 8,769 |
| | | Caribou | 0 | 0 | 0 | 0 | 8,070 |
| | | Carrabassett Valley | 0 | 0 | 0 | 0 | 479 |
| | | Clinton | 0 | 0 | 0 | 0 | 3,312 |
| | | Cumberland | 0 | 0 | 0 | 0 | 7,639 |
| | | Damariscotta | 0 | 0 | 0 | 0 | 1,900 |
| | | Dexter | 0 | 0 | 0 | 0 | 3,666 |
| | | Dixfield | 0 | 0 | 0 | 0 | 2,532 |
| | | Dover-Foxcroft | 0 | 0 | 0 | 0 | 4,221 |
| | | East Millinocket | 0 | 0 | 0 | 0 | 3,157 |
| | | Eastport | 0 | 0 | 0 | 0 | 1,525 |
| | | Eliot | 0 | 0 | 0 | 0 | 6,339 |
| | | Fairfield | 0 | 0 | 0 | 0 | 6,718 |
| | | Falmouth | 0 | 0 | 0 | 0 | 10,768 |
| | | Farmington | 0 | 0 | 0 | 0 | 7,561 |
| | | Fort Fairfield | 0 | 0 | 0 | 0 | 3,437 |
| | | Fort Kent | 0 | 0 | 0 | 0 | 4,177 |
| | | Freeport | 0 | 0 | 0 | 0 | 8,239 |
| | | Fryeburg | 0 | 0 | 0 | 0 | 3,363 |
| | | Gardiner | 0 | 0 | 0 | 0 | 6,090 |
| | | Gouldsboro | 0 | 0 | 0 | 0 | 1,999 |
| | | Greenville | 0 | 0 | 0 | 0 | 1,722 |
| | | Hallowell | 0 | 0 | 0 | 0 | 2,434 |
| | | Hampden | 0 | 0 | 0 | 0 | 6,984 |
| | | Holden | 0 | 0 | 0 | 0 | 3,006 |
| | | Houlton | 0 | 0 | 0 | 0 | 6,109 |
| | | Jay | 0 | 0 | 0 | 0 | 4,749 |
| | | Kennebunkport | 0 | 0 | 0 | 0 | 4,012 |
| | | Kittery | 0 | 0 | 0 | 0 | 10,524 |
| | | Limestone | 0 | 0 | 0 | 0 | 2,252 |
| | | Lincoln | 0 | 0 | 0 | 0 | 5,263 |
| | | Lincolnville | 0 | 0 | 0 | 0 | 2,202 |
| | | Lisbon | 0 | 0 | 0 | 0 | 9,343 |
| | | Livermore Falls | 0 | 0 | 0 | 0 | 3,124 |
| | | Machias | 0 | 0 | 0 | 0 | 2,112 |
| | | Madawaska | 0 | 0 | 0 | 0 | 4,315 |
| | | Madison | 0 | 0 | 0 | 0 | 4,575 |
| | | Mechanic Falls | | 0 | 0 | 0 | 3,242 |
| | | Mexico | 0 | 0 | 0 | 0 | 2,856 |
| | | Milbridge | 0 | 0 | 0 | 0 | 1,312 |
| | | Millinocket | 0 | 0 | 0 | 0 | 4,871 |
| | | Milo | 0 | 0 | 0 | 0 | 2,313 |
| | | Monmouth | 0 | 0 | 0 | 0 | 3,862 |
| | | Mount Desert | 0 | 0 | 0 | 0 | 2,169 |
| | | Newport | 0 | 0 | 0 | 0 | 3,114 |
| | | North Berwick | 0 | 0 | 0 | 0 | 4,891 |
| | | Norway | 0 | 0 | 0 | 0 | 4,779 |
| | | Oakland | 0 | 0 | 0 | 0 | 6,209 |
| | | Ogunquit | 0 | 0 | 0 | 0 | 1,266 |
| | | Old Town | 0 | 0 | 0 | 0 | 7,689 |
| | | Oxford | 0 | 0 | 0 | 0 | 3,922 |
| | | Paris | 0 | 0 | 0 | 0 | 4,980 |
| | | Phippsburg | 0 | 0 | 0 | 0 | 2,167 |
| | | Pittsfield | 0 | 0 | 0 | 0 | 4,217 |
| | | Presque Isle | 0 | 0 | 0 | 0 | 8,996 |
| | | Rangeley | 0 | 0 | 0 | 0 | 1,188 |
| | | Richmond | 0 | 0 | 0 | 0 | 3,429 |
| | | Rockland | 0 | 0 | 0 | 0 | 7,417 |
| | | Rockport | 0 | 0 | 0 | 0 | 3,553 |
| | | Sabattus | 0 | 0 | 0 | 0 | 4,666 |
| | | Scarborough | 0 | 0 | 0 | 0 | 19,281 |
| | | Searsport | 0 | 0 | 0 | 0 | 2,577 |
| | | Skowhegan | 0 | 0 | 0 | 0 | 8,664 |
| | | South Berwick | 0 | 0 | 0 | 0 | 7,205 |
| | | Southwest Harbor | 0 | 0 | 0 | 0 | 1,939 |
| | | Swan's Island | 0 | 0 | 0 | 0 | 300 |
| | | Thomaston | 0 | 0 | 0 | 0 | 3,646 |
| | | Van Buren | 0 | 0 | 0 | 0 | 2,463 |
| | | Veazie | 0 | 0 | 0 | 0 | 1,908 |
| | | Waldoboro | 0 | 0 | 0 | 0 | 5,015 |
| | | Washburn | 0 | 0 | 0 | 0 | 1,571 |
| | | Waterville | 0 | 0 | 0 | 0 | 16,063 |
| | | Wells | 0 | 0 | 0 | 0 | 9,944 |
| | | Westbrook | 0 | 0 | 0 | 0 | 16,579 |
| | | Wilton | 0 | 0 | 0 | 0 | 4,176 |
| | | Windham | 0 | 0 | 0 | 0 | 16,927 |
| | | Winslow | 0 | 0 | 0 | 0 | 7,856 |
| | | Winter Harbor | 0 | 0 | 0 | 0 | 960 |
| | | Winthrop | 0 | 0 | 0 | 0 | 6,451 |
| | | Wiscasset | 0 | 0 | 0 | 0 | 3,768 |
| | | Yarmouth | 0 | 0 | 0 | 0 | 8,069 |
| | | York | 0 | 0 | 0 | 0 | 14,195 |
| | **Universities and Colleges** | University of Maine: | | | | | |
| | | Farmington | 0 | 0 | 0 | 0 | 2,174 |
| | | Orono | 0 | 0 | 0 | 0 | 11,818 |
| | **Metropolitan Counties** | Androscoggin | 0 | 0 | 0 | 0 | |
| | | Penobscot | 0 | 0 | 0 | 0 | |
| | **Nonmetropolitan Counties** | Franklin | 0 | 0 | 0 | 0 | |
| | | Hancock | 0 | 0 | 0 | 0 | |
| | | Kennebec | 0 | 0 | 0 | 0 | |
| | | Knox | 0 | 0 | 0 | 0 | |
| | | Lincoln | 0 | 0 | 0 | 0 | |
| | | Oxford | 0 | 0 | 0 | 0 | |
| | | Piscataquis | 0 | 0 | 0 | 0 | |
| | | Somerset | 0 | 0 | 0 | 0 | |
| | | Waldo | 0 | 0 | 0 | 0 | |
| | **State Police Agencies** | State Police: | | | | | |
| | | Androscoggin County | 0 | 0 | 0 | 0 | |
| | | Aroostook County | 0 | 0 | 0 | 0 | |
| | | Cumberland County | 0 | 0 | 0 | 0 | |
| | | Franklin County | 0 | 0 | 0 | 0 | |
| | | Hancock County | 0 | 0 | 0 | 0 | |
| | | Knox County | 0 | 0 | 0 | 0 | |
| | | Lincoln County | 0 | 0 | 0 | 0 | |
| | | Oxford County | 0 | 0 | 0 | 0 | |
| | | Penobscot County | 0 | 0 | 0 | 0 | |
| | | Piscataquis County | 0 | 0 | 0 | 0 | |
| | | Sagadahoc County | 0 | 0 | 0 | 0 | |
| | | Waldo County | 0 | 0 | 0 | 0 | |
| | | Washington County | 0 | 0 | 0 | 0 | |
| **MARYLAND** | **Cities** | Baltimore City Sheriff | 0 | 0 | 0 | 0 | |
| | | Bel Air | 0 | 0 | 0 | 0 | 9,824 |
| | | Berlin | 0 | 0 | 0 | 0 | 4,111 |
| | | Berwyn Heights | 0 | 0 | 0 | 0 | 2,929 |
| | | Bladensburg | 0 | 0 | 0 | 0 | 7,557 |
| | | Boonsboro | 0 | 0 | 0 | 0 | 3,463 |
| | | Bowie | 0 | 0 | 0 | 0 | 52,577 |

[1]Agencies published in this table indicated that no hate crimes occurred in their jurisdictions during the quarter(s) for which they submitted reports to the Hate Crime Statistics Program. Blanks indicate quarters for which agencies did not submit reports.

[2]Population figures are published only for the cities. The figures listed for the universities and colleges are student enrollment and were provided by the United States Department of Education for the 2008 school year, the most recent available. The enrollment figures include full-time and part-time students.

## Table 95. Hate Crime Zero Data Submitted per Quarter, by State and Agency, 2009—*Continued*

(Number.)

| State | Agency type | Agency name | Zero data per quarter[1] 1st quarter | 2nd quarter | 3rd quarter | 4th quarter | Population[2] |
|---|---|---|---|---|---|---|---|
| MARYLAND | | Brunswick | 0 | 0 | 0 | 0 | 5,262 |
| | | Cambridge | 0 | 0 | 0 | 0 | 11,840 |
| | | Capitol Heights | 0 | 0 | 0 | 0 | 4,094 |
| | | Centreville | 0 | 0 | 0 | 0 | 3,681 |
| | | Chestertown | 0 | 0 | 0 | 0 | 4,915 |
| | | Cheverly | 0 | 0 | 0 | 0 | 6,365 |
| | | Chevy Chase Village | 0 | 0 | 0 | 0 | 2,116 |
| | | Colmar Manor | 0 | 0 | | 0 | 1,256 |
| | | Cottage City | 0 | 0 | 0 | 0 | 1,120 |
| | | Crisfield | 0 | 0 | 0 | 0 | 2,751 |
| | | Cumberland | 0 | 0 | 0 | 0 | 20,372 |
| | | Delmar | 0 | 0 | 0 | 0 | 3,576 |
| | | Denton | 0 | 0 | 0 | 0 | 4,147 |
| | | District Heights | 0 | 0 | 0 | 0 | 6,026 |
| | | Easton | 0 | 0 | 0 | 0 | 15,030 |
| | | Edmonston | 0 | 0 | 0 | 0 | 1,328 |
| | | Elkton | 0 | 0 | 0 | 0 | 15,202 |
| | | Fairmount Heights | 0 | 0 | 0 | 0 | 1,493 |
| | | Federalsburg | 0 | 0 | 0 | 0 | 2,627 |
| | | Forest Heights | 0 | 0 | 0 | 0 | 2,550 |
| | | Frederick | 0 | 0 | 0 | 0 | 59,936 |
| | | Frostburg | 0 | 0 | 0 | 0 | 7,669 |
| | | Fruitland | 0 | 0 | 0 | 0 | 4,511 |
| | | Glenarden | 0 | 0 | 0 | 0 | 6,304 |
| | | Greenbelt | 0 | 0 | 0 | 0 | 21,087 |
| | | Greensboro | 0 | 0 | 0 | 0 | 2,043 |
| | | Hagerstown | 0 | 0 | 0 | 0 | 40,062 |
| | | Hampstead | 0 | 0 | 0 | 0 | 5,501 |
| | | Hancock | 0 | 0 | 0 | 0 | 1,743 |
| | | Havre de Grace | 0 | 0 | 0 | 0 | 13,289 |
| | | Hurlock | 0 | 0 | 0 | 0 | 2,069 |
| | | Hyattsville | 0 | 0 | 0 | 0 | 15,346 |
| | | Landover Hills | 0 | 0 | 0 | 0 | 1,512 |
| | | La Plata | 0 | 0 | 0 | 0 | 9,170 |
| | | Laurel | 0 | 0 | 0 | 0 | 22,463 |
| | | Lonaconing | 0 | 0 | 0 | 0 | 1,117 |
| | | Luke | 0 | 0 | 0 | 0 | 72 |
| | | Manchester | 0 | 0 | 0 | 0 | 3,567 |
| | | Morningside | 0 | 0 | 0 | 0 | 1,305 |
| | | Mount Rainier | 0 | 0 | 0 | 0 | 8,303 |
| | | New Carrollton | 0 | 0 | 0 | 0 | 12,445 |
| | | North East | 0 | 0 | 0 | 0 | 2,872 |
| | | Oakland | 0 | 0 | 0 | 0 | 1,832 |
| | | Ocean City | 0 | 0 | 0 | 0 | 7,026 |
| | | Ocean Pines | 0 | 0 | 0 | 0 | 11,295 |
| | | Oxford | 0 | 0 | 0 | 0 | 699 |
| | | Perryville | 0 | 0 | 0 | 0 | 3,816 |
| | | Pocomoke City | 0 | 0 | 0 | 0 | 3,854 |
| | | Port Deposit | 0 | 0 | 0 | 0 | 704 |
| | | Preston | 0 | 0 | 0 | 0 | 685 |
| | | Princess Anne | 0 | 0 | 0 | 0 | 3,104 |
| | | Ridgely | 0 | 0 | 0 | 0 | 1,536 |
| | | Rising Sun | 0 | 0 | 0 | 0 | 1,815 |
| | | Riverdale Park | 0 | 0 | 0 | 0 | 6,413 |
| | | Rock Hall | 0 | 0 | 0 | 0 | 1,496 |
| | | Salisbury | 0 | 0 | 0 | 0 | 28,800 |
| | | Seat Pleasant | 0 | 0 | 0 | 0 | 4,822 |
| | | Smithsburg | 0 | 0 | 0 | 0 | 3,002 |
| | | Snow Hill | 0 | 0 | 0 | 0 | 2,305 |
| | | St. Michaels | 0 | 0 | 0 | 0 | 1,054 |
| | | Sykesville | 0 | 0 | 0 | 0 | 4,444 |
| | | Takoma Park | 0 | 0 | 0 | 0 | 17,741 |
| | | Taneytown | 0 | 0 | 0 | 0 | 5,455 |
| | | Thurmont | 0 | 0 | 0 | 0 | 6,082 |
| | | Trappe | 0 | 0 | 0 | 0 | 1,136 |
| | | University Park | 0 | 0 | 0 | 0 | 2,278 |
| | | Upper Marlboro | 0 | 0 | 0 | 0 | 658 |
| | | Westernport | 0 | 0 | 0 | 0 | 1,929 |
| | | Westminster | 0 | 0 | 0 | 0 | 17,787 |
| | **Universities and Colleges** | Bowie State University | 0 | 0 | 0 | 0 | 5,483 |
| | | Coppin State University | 0 | 0 | 0 | 0 | 4,051 |
| | | Frostburg State University | 0 | 0 | 0 | 0 | 5,215 |
| | | Morgan State University | 0 | 0 | 0 | 0 | 7,005 |
| | | Salisbury University | 0 | 0 | 0 | 0 | 7,868 |
| | | St. Mary's College | 0 | 0 | 0 | 0 | 2,068 |
| | | University of Baltimore | 0 | 0 | 0 | 0 | 5,843 |
| | | University of Maryland: Baltimore City | 0 | 0 | 0 | 0 | 6,156 |
| | | Baltimore County | 0 | 0 | 0 | 0 | 12,268 |
| | | Eastern Shore | 0 | 0 | 0 | 0 | 4,290 |
| | **Metropolitan Counties** | Allegany | 0 | 0 | 0 | 0 | |
| | | Allegany County Bureau of Police | 0 | 0 | | 0 | |
| | | Anne Arundel | 0 | 0 | 0 | 0 | |
| | | Baltimore County | 0 | 0 | 0 | 0 | |
| | | Calvert | 0 | 0 | 0 | 0 | |
| | | Carroll | 0 | 0 | 0 | 0 | |
| | | Cecil | 0 | 0 | 0 | 0 | |
| | | Howard | 0 | 0 | 0 | 0 | |
| | | Montgomery | 0 | 0 | 0 | 0 | |
| | | Prince George's | 0 | 0 | 0 | 0 | |
| | | Queen Anne's | 0 | 0 | 0 | 0 | |
| | | Somerset | 0 | 0 | 0 | 0 | |
| | | Washington | 0 | 0 | 0 | 0 | |
| | **Nonmetropolitan Counties** | Caroline | 0 | 0 | 0 | 0 | |
| | | Dorchester | 0 | 0 | 0 | 0 | |
| | | Garrett | 0 | 0 | 0 | 0 | |
| | | Kent | 0 | 0 | 0 | 0 | |
| | | St. Mary's | 0 | 0 | 0 | 0 | |
| | | Talbot | 0 | 0 | 0 | 0 | |
| | | Worcester | 0 | 0 | 0 | 0 | |
| | **State Police Agencies** | Maryland State Police Statewide | 0 | 0 | 0 | 0 | |
| | | State Police: Anne Arundel County | 0 | 0 | 0 | 0 | |
| | | Baltimore City | 0 | 0 | 0 | 0 | |
| | | Baltimore County | 0 | 0 | 0 | 0 | |
| | | Calvert County | 0 | 0 | 0 | 0 | |
| | | Caroline County | 0 | 0 | 0 | 0 | |
| | | Charles County | 0 | 0 | 0 | 0 | |
| | | Dorchester County | 0 | 0 | 0 | 0 | |
| | | Frederick County | 0 | 0 | 0 | 0 | |
| | | Garrett County | 0 | 0 | 0 | 0 | |
| | | Harford County | 0 | 0 | 0 | 0 | |
| | | Howard County | 0 | 0 | 0 | 0 | |
| | | Kent County | 0 | 0 | 0 | 0 | |
| | | Montgomery County | 0 | 0 | 0 | 0 | |
| | | Prince George's County | 0 | 0 | 0 | 0 | |
| | | Queen Anne's County | 0 | 0 | 0 | 0 | |

[1]Agencies published in this table indicated that no hate crimes occurred in their jurisdictions during the quarter(s) for which they submitted reports to the Hate Crime Statistics Program. Blanks indicate quarters for which agencies did not submit reports.

[2]Population figures are published only for the cities. The figures listed for the universities and colleges are student enrollment and were provided by the United States Department of Education for the 2008 school year, the most recent available. The enrollment figures include full-time and part-time students.

# Table 95. Hate Crime Zero Data Submitted per Quarter, by State and Agency, 2009—*Continued*

(Number.)

| State | Agency type | Agency name | Zero data per quarter[1] 1st quarter | 2nd quarter | 3rd quarter | 4th quarter | Population[2] |
|---|---|---|---|---|---|---|---|
| | | Somerset County | 0 | 0 | 0 | 0 | |
| | | St. Mary's County | 0 | 0 | 0 | 0 | |
| | | Talbot County | 0 | 0 | 0 | 0 | |
| | | Washington County | 0 | 0 | 0 | 0 | |
| | | Wicomico County | 0 | 0 | 0 | 0 | |
| | Other Agencies | Comptroller of the Treasury, Field Enforcement Division | 0 | 0 | 0 | 0 | |
| | | Department of Public Safety and Correctional Services, Internal Investigations Unit | 0 | 0 | 0 | 0 | |
| | | General Services: Annapolis, Anne Arundel County | 0 | 0 | 0 | 0 | |
| | | Baltimore City | 0 | 0 | 0 | 0 | |
| | | Maryland-National Capital Park Police: Montgomery County | 0 | 0 | 0 | 0 | |
| | | Prince George's County | 0 | 0 | 0 | 0 | |
| | | Natural Resources Police | 0 | 0 | 0 | 0 | |
| | | Springfield Hospital | 0 | 0 | 0 | 0 | |
| | | State Fire Marshal | 0 | 0 | 0 | 0 | |
| | | Transit Administration | 0 | 0 | 0 | 0 | |
| | | Transportation Authority | 0 | 0 | 0 | 0 | |
| MASSACHUSETTS | Cities | Abington | 0 | 0 | 0 | 0 | 16,732 |
| | | Acushnet | 0 | 0 | 0 | 0 | 10,606 |
| | | Adams | 0 | 0 | 0 | 0 | 8,232 |
| | | Agawam | 0 | 0 | 0 | 0 | 28,781 |
| | | Aquinnah | 0 | 0 | 0 | 0 | 358 |
| | | Ashburnham | 0 | 0 | 0 | 0 | 6,054 |
| | | Ashby | 0 | 0 | 0 | 0 | 2,999 |
| | | Ashland | 0 | 0 | 0 | 0 | 16,164 |
| | | Athol | 0 | 0 | 0 | 0 | 11,724 |
| | | Attleboro | 0 | 0 | 0 | 0 | 43,772 |
| | | Auburn | 0 | 0 | 0 | 0 | 16,420 |
| | | Ayer | 0 | 0 | 0 | 0 | 7,488 |
| | | Barre | 0 | 0 | 0 | 0 | 5,496 |
| | | Bedford | 0 | 0 | 0 | 0 | 13,411 |
| | | Belchertown | 0 | 0 | 0 | 0 | 14,383 |
| | | Bellingham | 0 | 0 | 0 | 0 | 16,235 |
| | | Berkley | 0 | 0 | 0 | 0 | 6,601 |
| | | Berlin | 0 | 0 | 0 | 0 | 2,760 |
| | | Billerica | 0 | 0 | 0 | 0 | 43,058 |
| | | Blackstone | 0 | 0 | 0 | 0 | 9,126 |
| | | Bolton | 0 | 0 | 0 | 0 | 4,556 |
| | | Bourne | 0 | 0 | 0 | 0 | 19,133 |
| | | Boxborough | 0 | 0 | 0 | | 5,200 |
| | | Boxford | 0 | 0 | 0 | 0 | 8,187 |
| | | Boylston | 0 | 0 | 0 | 0 | 4,330 |
| | | Brewster | 0 | 0 | 0 | 0 | 10,054 |
| | | Bridgewater | 0 | 0 | 0 | 0 | 25,765 |
| | | Brimfield | 0 | 0 | 0 | 0 | 3,796 |
| | | Brockton | 0 | 0 | 0 | 0 | 96,471 |
| | | Brookline | 0 | 0 | 0 | 0 | 55,400 |
| | | Canton | 0 | 0 | 0 | 0 | 22,407 |
| | | Carlisle | 0 | 0 | 0 | | 4,973 |
| | | Carver | 0 | 0 | 0 | 0 | 11,691 |
| | | Charlemont | 0 | 0 | 0 | 0 | 1,383 |
| | | Charlton | 0 | 0 | 0 | 0 | 12,835 |
| | | Chatham | 0 | 0 | 0 | 0 | 6,765 |
| | | Chelmsford | 0 | 0 | 0 | 0 | 34,695 |
| | | Chesterfield | | 0 | 0 | 0 | 1,308 |
| | | Chicopee | 0 | 0 | 0 | 0 | 54,589 |
| | | Chilmark | 0 | 0 | 0 | 0 | 986 |
| | | Clinton | 0 | 0 | 0 | 0 | 14,206 |
| | | Concord | 0 | 0 | 0 | 0 | 17,804 |
| | | Dalton | 0 | 0 | 0 | 0 | 6,616 |
| | | Danvers | 0 | 0 | 0 | 0 | 27,289 |
| | | Dartmouth | 0 | 0 | 0 | 0 | 34,879 |
| | | Dedham | 0 | 0 | 0 | 0 | 24,605 |
| | | Deerfield | 0 | 0 | 0 | 0 | 4,780 |
| | | Dennis | 0 | 0 | 0 | 0 | 15,475 |
| | | Dover | 0 | 0 | 0 | 0 | 5,724 |
| | | Dracut | 0 | 0 | 0 | 0 | 30,048 |
| | | Dudley | 0 | 0 | 0 | 0 | 11,264 |
| | | East Bridgewater | 0 | 0 | 0 | 0 | 14,108 |
| | | East Brookfield | 0 | 0 | 0 | 0 | 2,080 |
| | | Eastham | 0 | 0 | 0 | 0 | 5,464 |
| | | Easthampton | 0 | 0 | 0 | 0 | 16,401 |
| | | Easton | 0 | 0 | 0 | 0 | 23,337 |
| | | Edgartown | 0 | 0 | 0 | 0 | 3,968 |
| | | Fairhaven | 0 | 0 | 0 | 0 | 16,318 |
| | | Fall River | 0 | 0 | 0 | 0 | 91,901 |
| | | Falmouth | 0 | 0 | 0 | 0 | 33,451 |
| | | Fitchburg | 0 | 0 | 0 | 0 | 40,678 |
| | | Franklin | 0 | 0 | 0 | 0 | 32,114 |
| | | Freetown | 0 | 0 | 0 | 0 | 9,103 |
| | | Gardner | 0 | 0 | 0 | 0 | 20,741 |
| | | Georgetown | 0 | 0 | 0 | 0 | 8,342 |
| | | Gill | 0 | 0 | 0 | 0 | 1,396 |
| | | Gloucester | 0 | 0 | 0 | 0 | 30,675 |
| | | Goshen | 0 | 0 | 0 | 0 | 980 |
| | | Grafton | 0 | 0 | 0 | 0 | 18,005 |
| | | Granby | 0 | 0 | 0 | 0 | 6,432 |
| | | Great Barrington | 0 | 0 | 0 | 0 | 7,431 |
| | | Greenfield | 0 | 0 | 0 | 0 | 17,840 |
| | | Groton | 0 | 0 | 0 | 0 | 10,936 |
| | | Groveland | 0 | 0 | 0 | 0 | 7,127 |
| | | Hadley | 0 | 0 | 0 | 0 | 4,884 |
| | | Halifax | 0 | 0 | 0 | 0 | 7,788 |
| | | Hamilton | 0 | 0 | 0 | 0 | 8,270 |
| | | Hampden | 0 | 0 | 0 | 0 | 5,401 |
| | | Hanover | 0 | 0 | 0 | 0 | 14,185 |
| | | Hanson | 0 | 0 | 0 | 0 | 10,096 |
| | | Harvard | 0 | 0 | 0 | 0 | 6,046 |
| | | Harwich | 0 | 0 | 0 | 0 | 12,436 |
| | | Hingham | 0 | 0 | 0 | 0 | 22,919 |
| | | Holden | 0 | 0 | 0 | 0 | 16,819 |
| | | Holliston | 0 | 0 | 0 | 0 | 14,160 |
| | | Hopedale | 0 | 0 | 0 | 0 | 6,241 |
| | | Hopkinton | 0 | 0 | 0 | 0 | 14,633 |
| | | Hubbardston | 0 | 0 | 0 | 0 | 4,565 |
| | | Hudson | 0 | 0 | 0 | 0 | 20,060 |
| | | Hull | 0 | 0 | 0 | 0 | 11,159 |
| | | Kingston | 0 | 0 | 0 | 0 | 12,511 |
| | | Lancaster | 0 | 0 | 0 | 0 | 7,183 |
| | | Lanesboro | 0 | 0 | 0 | 0 | 2,910 |
| | | Lee | 0 | 0 | 0 | 0 | 5,843 |
| | | Leicester | 0 | 0 | 0 | 0 | 11,124 |
| | | Leominster | 0 | 0 | 0 | 0 | 41,401 |
| | | Leverett | 0 | 0 | | | 1,772 |
| | | Lexington | 0 | 0 | 0 | 0 | 30,771 |

[1]Agencies published in this table indicated that no hate crimes occurred in their jurisdictions during the quarter(s) for which they submitted reports to the Hate Crime Statistics Program. Blanks indicate quarters for which agencies did not submit reports.

[2]Population figures are published only for the cities. The figures listed for the universities and colleges are student enrollment and were provided by the United States Department of Education for the 2008 school year, the most recent available. The enrollment figures include full-time and part-time students.

## Table 95. Hate Crime Zero Data Submitted per Quarter, by State and Agency, 2009—*Continued*

(Number.)

| State | Agency type | Agency name | Zero data per quarter[1] | | | | Population[2] |
|---|---|---|---|---|---|---|---|
| | | | 1st quarter | 2nd quarter | 3rd quarter | 4th quarter | |
| **MASSACHUSETTS** | | Lincoln | 0 | 0 | 0 | 0 | 8,103 |
| | | Littleton | 0 | 0 | 0 | 0 | 8,906 |
| | | Longmeadow | 0 | 0 | 0 | 0 | 15,506 |
| | | Ludlow | 0 | 0 | 0 | 0 | 22,870 |
| | | Lunenburg | 0 | 0 | 0 | 0 | 10,087 |
| | | Lynnfield | 0 | 0 | 0 | 0 | 11,500 |
| | | Manchester-by-the-Sea | 0 | 0 | 0 | 0 | 5,333 |
| | | Mansfield | 0 | 0 | 0 | 0 | 23,347 |
| | | Marblehead | 0 | 0 | 0 | 0 | 20,240 |
| | | Marlborough | 0 | 0 | 0 | 0 | 38,821 |
| | | Marshfield | 0 | 0 | 0 | 0 | 24,811 |
| | | Mashpee | 0 | 0 | 0 | 0 | 14,481 |
| | | Mattapoisett | 0 | 0 | 0 | 0 | 6,523 |
| | | Maynard | 0 | 0 | 0 | 0 | 10,295 |
| | | Medfield | 0 | 0 | 0 | 0 | 12,457 |
| | | Medway | 0 | 0 | 0 | 0 | 12,987 |
| | | Melrose | 0 | 0 | 0 | 0 | 27,134 |
| | | Mendon | 0 | 0 | 0 | 0 | 5,866 |
| | | Merrimac | 0 | 0 | 0 | 0 | 6,538 |
| | | Methuen | 0 | 0 | 0 | 0 | 44,527 |
| | | Middleboro | 0 | 0 | 0 | 0 | 21,585 |
| | | Middleton | 0 | 0 | 0 | 0 | 9,662 |
| | | Milford | 0 | 0 | 0 | 0 | 27,526 |
| | | Millbury | 0 | 0 | 0 | 0 | 13,652 |
| | | Millis | 0 | | | | 8,055 |
| | | Millville | 0 | 0 | 0 | 0 | 2,878 |
| | | Montague | 0 | 0 | 0 | 0 | 8,407 |
| | | Monterey | 0 | 0 | 0 | 0 | 973 |
| | | Nahant | 0 | 0 | 0 | 0 | 3,548 |
| | | New Salem | 0 | 0 | 0 | 0 | 1,009 |
| | | North Adams | 0 | 0 | 0 | 0 | 13,927 |
| | | North Andover | 0 | 0 | 0 | 0 | 28,116 |
| | | Northbridge | 0 | 0 | 0 | 0 | 14,634 |
| | | North Brookfield | 0 | 0 | 0 | 0 | 4,870 |
| | | Norwell | 0 | 0 | 0 | 0 | 10,418 |
| | | Norwood | 0 | 0 | 0 | 0 | 28,569 |
| | | Oak Bluffs | 0 | | | | 3,762 |
| | | Orange | 0 | 0 | 0 | 0 | 7,915 |
| | | Orleans | 0 | 0 | 0 | 0 | 6,337 |
| | | Palmer | 0 | 0 | 0 | 0 | 13,086 |
| | | Paxton | 0 | 0 | 0 | 0 | 4,580 |
| | | Peabody | 0 | 0 | 0 | 0 | 52,483 |
| | | Pembroke | 0 | 0 | 0 | 0 | 18,967 |
| | | Pepperell | 0 | 0 | 0 | 0 | 11,608 |
| | | Plympton | 0 | 0 | 0 | 0 | 2,812 |
| | | Princeton | 0 | 0 | 0 | 0 | 3,536 |
| | | Raynham | 0 | 0 | 0 | 0 | 14,068 |
| | | Reading | 0 | 0 | 0 | 0 | 23,398 |
| | | Rehoboth | 0 | 0 | 0 | 0 | 11,795 |
| | | Rochester | 0 | 0 | 0 | 0 | 5,346 |
| | | Rockport | 0 | 0 | 0 | 0 | 7,709 |
| | | Rowley | 0 | 0 | 0 | | 5,953 |
| | | Royalston | 0 | 0 | 0 | 0 | 1,406 |
| | | Rutland | 0 | 0 | 0 | 0 | 8,109 |
| | | Salisbury | 0 | 0 | 0 | 0 | 8,715 |
| | | Sandwich | 0 | 0 | 0 | 0 | 20,349 |
| | | Saugus | 0 | 0 | 0 | 0 | 27,663 |
| | | Scituate | 0 | 0 | 0 | 0 | 18,032 |
| | | Seekonk | 0 | 0 | 0 | 0 | 13,781 |
| | | Shelburne | 0 | 0 | 0 | 0 | 2,056 |
| | | Sherborn | 0 | 0 | 0 | 0 | 4,281 |
| | | Shirley | 0 | 0 | 0 | 0 | 7,853 |
| | | Shrewsbury | 0 | 0 | 0 | 0 | 33,957 |
| | | Somerset | 0 | 0 | 0 | 0 | 18,495 |
| | | Southampton | 0 | 0 | 0 | 0 | 6,160 |
| | | Southborough | 0 | 0 | 0 | 0 | 9,640 |
| | | Spencer | 0 | 0 | 0 | 0 | 12,131 |
| | | Sterling | 0 | 0 | 0 | 0 | 8,009 |
| | | Stockbridge | 0 | 0 | 0 | 0 | 2,251 |
| | | Stoneham | 0 | 0 | 0 | 0 | 21,737 |
| | | Stow | 0 | 0 | 0 | 0 | 6,473 |
| | | Sudbury | 0 | 0 | 0 | 0 | 17,445 |
| | | Sunderland | 0 | 0 | | | 3,754 |
| | | Sutton | 0 | 0 | 0 | 0 | 9,175 |
| | | Swampscott | 0 | 0 | 0 | 0 | 14,111 |
| | | Swansea | 0 | 0 | 0 | 0 | 16,479 |
| | | Taunton | 0 | 0 | 0 | 0 | 56,446 |
| | | Templeton | 0 | 0 | 0 | 0 | 7,970 |
| | | Tisbury | 0 | 0 | 0 | 0 | 3,841 |
| | | Topsfield | 0 | 0 | 0 | 0 | 6,130 |
| | | Townsend | 0 | 0 | 0 | 0 | 9,534 |
| | | Truro | 0 | 0 | 0 | 0 | 2,149 |
| | | Tyngsboro | 0 | 0 | 0 | 0 | 12,133 |
| | | Uxbridge | 0 | 0 | 0 | 0 | 12,916 |
| | | Wakefield | 0 | 0 | 0 | 0 | 25,057 |
| | | Wales | 0 | 0 | 0 | 0 | 1,885 |
| | | Walpole | 0 | 0 | 0 | 0 | 23,483 |
| | | Ware | 0 | 0 | 0 | 0 | 10,165 |
| | | Warren | 0 | 0 | 0 | 0 | 5,146 |
| | | Wayland | 0 | 0 | 0 | 0 | 13,195 |
| | | Webster | 0 | 0 | 0 | 0 | 16,861 |
| | | Wellfleet | 0 | 0 | 0 | 0 | 2,758 |
| | | Wenham | 0 | 0 | 0 | 0 | 4,665 |
| | | Westborough | 0 | 0 | 0 | 0 | 18,647 |
| | | West Bridgewater | 0 | 0 | 0 | | 6,739 |
| | | West Brookfield | 0 | 0 | 0 | 0 | 3,856 |
| | | Westfield | 0 | 0 | 0 | 0 | 41,474 |
| | | Westford | 0 | 0 | 0 | 0 | 22,239 |
| | | Westminster | 0 | 0 | 0 | 0 | 7,502 |
| | | West Newbury | 0 | 0 | 0 | 0 | 4,336 |
| | | Weston | 0 | 0 | 0 | 0 | 11,897 |
| | | West Tisbury | 0 | 0 | 0 | 0 | 2,668 |
| | | Weymouth | 0 | 0 | 0 | 0 | 54,031 |
| | | Whately | 0 | 0 | 0 | 0 | 1,571 |
| | | Whitman | 0 | 0 | 0 | 0 | 14,564 |
| | | Williamsburg | 0 | 0 | 0 | 0 | 2,492 |
| | | Williamstown | 0 | 0 | 0 | 0 | 8,157 |
| | | Wilmington | 0 | 0 | 0 | 0 | 22,035 |
| | | Winchendon | 0 | 0 | 0 | 0 | 10,268 |
| | | Winchester | 0 | 0 | 0 | 0 | 21,486 |
| | | Woburn | 0 | 0 | 0 | 0 | 37,555 |
| | | Wrentham | 0 | 0 | 0 | 0 | 11,360 |
| | | Yarmouth | 0 | 0 | 0 | 0 | 24,010 |
| | **Universities and Colleges** | Assumption College | 0 | 0 | 0 | 0 | 2,876 |
| | | Boston University | 0 | 0 | 0 | 0 | 31,766 |
| | | Holyoke Community College | | | | 0 | 6,592 |
| | | Massachusetts College of Liberal Arts | 0 | 0 | 0 | 0 | 1,942 |
| | | Massachusetts Institute of Technology | 0 | 0 | 0 | 0 | 10,299 |
| | | Mount Holyoke College | 0 | 0 | 0 | 0 | 2,241 |
| | | Salem State College | | | 0 | | 10,157 |
| | | Springfield College | | | 0 | | 4,806 |
| | | Westfield State College | 0 | 0 | 0 | 0 | 5,548 |
| | | Worcester Polytechnic Institute | | 0 | 0 | 0 | 4,556 |
| | **Other Agencies** | Beth Israel Deaconess Medical Center | 0 | 0 | 0 | 0 | |

[1]Agencies published in this table indicated that no hate crimes occurred in their jurisdictions during the quarter(s) for which they submitted reports to the Hate Crime Statistics Program. Blanks indicate quarters for which agencies did not submit reports.

[2]Population figures are published only for the cities. The figures listed for the universities and colleges are student enrollment and were provided by the United States Department of Education for the 2008 school year, the most recent available. The enrollment figures include full-time and part-time students.

## Table 95. Hate Crime Zero Data Submitted per Quarter, by State and Agency, 2009—*Continued*

(Number.)

| State | Agency type | Agency name | Zero data per quarter[1] 1st quarter | 2nd quarter | 3rd quarter | 4th quarter | Population[2] |
|---|---|---|---|---|---|---|---|
| MASSACHUSETTS | | Division of Law Enforcement, Environmental Police | 0 | 0 | 0 | 0 | |
| MICHIGAN... | Cities | Albion | 0 | 0 | 0 | 0 | 9,100 |
| | | Algonac | 0 | 0 | 0 | 0 | 4,532 |
| | | Allen Park | 0 | 0 | 0 | 0 | 25,658 |
| | | Alma | 0 | 0 | 0 | 0 | 9,215 |
| | | Almont | 0 | 0 | 0 | 0 | 2,737 |
| | | Alpena | 0 | 0 | 0 | 0 | 10,378 |
| | | Argentine Township | 0 | 0 | 0 | 0 | 7,099 |
| | | Armada | 0 | 0 | 0 | 0 | 1,661 |
| | | Auburn | 0 | 0 | 0 | 0 | 2,034 |
| | | Bad Axe | 0 | 0 | 0 | 0 | 3,029 |
| | | Bangor | 0 | 0 | 0 | 0 | 1,828 |
| | | Barryton | 0 | 0 | | | 369 |
| | | Barry Township | 0 | 0 | 0 | 0 | 3,537 |
| | | Bath Township | 0 | 0 | 0 | 0 | 11,886 |
| | | Battle Creek | 0 | 0 | 0 | 0 | 61,139 |
| | | Beaverton | 0 | 0 | 0 | 0 | 1,054 |
| | | Belding | 0 | 0 | 0 | 0 | 5,672 |
| | | Belleville | 0 | 0 | 0 | 0 | 3,510 |
| | | Benton Harbor | 0 | 0 | 0 | 0 | 10,760 |
| | | Berkley | 0 | 0 | 0 | 0 | 14,708 |
| | | Big Rapids | 0 | 0 | 0 | 0 | 10,194 |
| | | Birch Run | 0 | 0 | 0 | 0 | 1,636 |
| | | Birmingham | 0 | 0 | 0 | 0 | 18,895 |
| | | Blissfield | 0 | 0 | 0 | 0 | 3,164 |
| | | Bloomfield Hills | 0 | 0 | 0 | 0 | 3,755 |
| | | Bloomingdale | 0 | | | | 490 |
| | | Boyne City | 0 | 0 | 0 | 0 | 3,103 |
| | | Breckenridge | 0 | 0 | 0 | 0 | 1,278 |
| | | Bridgman | 0 | 0 | 0 | 0 | 2,396 |
| | | Brighton | 0 | 0 | 0 | 0 | 7,256 |
| | | Bronson | 0 | 0 | 0 | 0 | 2,258 |
| | | Brown City | 0 | 0 | 0 | 0 | 1,243 |
| | | Brownstown Township | 0 | 0 | 0 | 0 | 29,045 |
| | | Buchanan | 0 | 0 | 0 | 0 | 4,320 |
| | | Buena Vista Township | 0 | 0 | 0 | 0 | 9,253 |
| | | Burr Oak | 0 | 0 | 0 | 0 | 745 |
| | | Burton | 0 | 0 | 0 | 0 | 29,788 |
| | | Calumet | 0 | 0 | 0 | 0 | 795 |
| | | Cambridge Township | 0 | 0 | 0 | 0 | 5,865 |
| | | Capac | 0 | 0 | 0 | 0 | 2,089 |
| | | Carleton | 0 | 0 | 0 | 0 | 2,572 |
| | | Caro | 0 | 0 | 0 | 0 | 3,994 |
| | | Caseville | 0 | 0 | 0 | 0 | 829 |
| | | Cassopolis | 0 | 0 | 0 | 0 | 1,924 |
| | | Center Line | 0 | 0 | 0 | 0 | 8,093 |
| | | Central Lake | 0 | 0 | 0 | 0 | 962 |
| | | Charlevoix | 0 | 0 | 0 | 0 | 2,622 |
| | | Charlotte | 0 | 0 | 0 | 0 | 8,996 |
| | | Cheboygan | 0 | 0 | 0 | 0 | 4,904 |
| | | Chelsea | 0 | 0 | 0 | 0 | 5,075 |
| | | Chesaning | 0 | 0 | 0 | 0 | 2,324 |
| | | Chikaming Township | 0 | 0 | 0 | 0 | 3,653 |
| | | Chocolay Township | 0 | 0 | 0 | 0 | 6,040 |
| | | Clare | 0 | 0 | 0 | 0 | 3,080 |
| | | Clarkston | 0 | 0 | 0 | 0 | 908 |
| | | Clawson | 0 | 0 | 0 | 0 | 12,097 |
| | | Clayton Township | 0 | 0 | 0 | 0 | 7,750 |
| | | Clay Township | 0 | 0 | 0 | 0 | 9,458 |
| | | Clinton | 0 | 0 | 0 | 0 | 2,400 |
| | | Clio | 0 | 0 | 0 | 0 | 2,490 |
| | | Coleman | 0 | 0 | 0 | 0 | 1,221 |
| | | Coloma Township | 0 | 0 | 0 | 0 | 6,503 |
| | | Colon | 0 | 0 | 0 | 0 | 1,160 |
| | | Columbia Township | 0 | 0 | 0 | 0 | 7,552 |
| | | Concord | 0 | 0 | 0 | 0 | 1,069 |
| | | Corunna | 0 | 0 | 0 | 0 | 3,273 |
| | | Crystal Falls | 0 | 0 | 0 | 0 | 1,574 |
| | | Davison | 0 | 0 | 0 | 0 | 5,093 |
| | | Denmark Township | | | 0 | | 1,771 |
| | | Denton Township | 0 | 0 | 0 | 0 | 5,375 |
| | | Dewitt | 0 | 0 | 0 | 0 | 4,399 |
| | | Dewitt Township | 0 | 0 | 0 | 0 | 13,188 |
| | | Dryden Township | 0 | 0 | 0 | 0 | 4,591 |
| | | Durand | 0 | 0 | 0 | 0 | 3,718 |
| | | East Grand Rapids | 0 | 0 | 0 | 0 | 10,435 |
| | | East Jordan | 0 | 0 | 0 | 0 | 2,206 |
| | | East Tawas | 0 | 0 | 0 | 0 | 2,699 |
| | | Eaton Rapids | 0 | 0 | 0 | 0 | 5,236 |
| | | Eau Claire | 0 | 0 | 0 | 0 | 620 |
| | | Elk Rapids | 0 | 0 | 0 | 0 | 1,669 |
| | | Elkton | 0 | 0 | 0 | 0 | 747 |
| | | Elsie | 0 | 0 | 0 | 0 | 971 |
| | | Emmett Township | 0 | 0 | 0 | 0 | 11,791 |
| | | Erie Township | 0 | 0 | 0 | 0 | 4,654 |
| | | Essexville | 0 | 0 | 0 | 0 | 3,465 |
| | | Fairgrove | | 0 | 0 | 0 | 587 |
| | | Fair Haven Township | | 0 | 0 | 0 | 1,108 |
| | | Flat Rock | 0 | 0 | 0 | 0 | 8,797 |
| | | Flint Township | 0 | 0 | 0 | 0 | 31,391 |
| | | Flushing | 0 | 0 | 0 | 0 | 7,759 |
| | | Flushing Township | 0 | 0 | 0 | 0 | 10,078 |
| | | Fowlerville | 0 | 0 | 0 | 0 | 3,113 |
| | | Frankenmuth | 0 | 0 | 0 | 0 | 4,631 |
| | | Franklin | 0 | 0 | 0 | 0 | 2,912 |
| | | Fraser | 0 | 0 | 0 | 0 | 14,861 |
| | | Fremont | 0 | 0 | 0 | 0 | 4,182 |
| | | Frost Township | 0 | 0 | 0 | 0 | 1,109 |
| | | Gagetown | 0 | 0 | 0 | 0 | 364 |
| | | Gaylord | 0 | 0 | 0 | 0 | 3,580 |
| | | Gerrish Township | 0 | 0 | 0 | 0 | 3,075 |
| | | Gladstone | 0 | 0 | 0 | 0 | 5,068 |
| | | Gladwin | 0 | 0 | 0 | 0 | 2,891 |
| | | Grand Beach | 0 | 0 | 0 | | 242 |
| | | Grand Blanc Township | 0 | 0 | 0 | 0 | 35,451 |
| | | Grand Haven | 0 | 0 | 0 | 0 | 10,548 |
| | | Grant | 0 | 0 | 0 | 0 | 853 |
| | | Grayling | 0 | 0 | 0 | 0 | 1,822 |
| | | Green Oak Township | 0 | 0 | 0 | 0 | 17,836 |
| | | Grosse Ile Township | 0 | 0 | 0 | 0 | 9,776 |
| | | Grosse Pointe | 0 | 0 | 0 | 0 | 4,926 |
| | | Grosse Pointe Park | 0 | 0 | 0 | 0 | 10,802 |
| | | Grosse Pointe Shores | 0 | 0 | 0 | 0 | 2,476 |
| | | Grosse Pointe Woods | 0 | 0 | 0 | 0 | 14,954 |
| | | Hamburg Township | 0 | 0 | 0 | 0 | 21,772 |
| | | Hancock | 0 | 0 | 0 | 0 | 4,141 |
| | | Harbor Beach | 0 | 0 | 0 | 0 | 1,595 |
| | | Harbor Springs | 0 | 0 | 0 | 0 | 1,545 |
| | | Harper Woods | 0 | 0 | 0 | 0 | 12,411 |

[1]Agencies published in this table indicated that no hate crimes occurred in their jurisdictions during the quarter(s) for which they submitted reports to the Hate Crime Statistics Program. Blanks indicate quarters for which agencies did not submit reports.

[2]Population figures are published only for the cities. The figures listed for the universities and colleges are student enrollment and were provided by the United States Department of Education for the 2008 school year, the most recent available. The enrollment figures include full-time and part-time students.

# Table 95. Hate Crime Zero Data Submitted per Quarter, by State and Agency, 2009—*Continued*

(Number.)

| State | Agency type | Agency name | Zero data per quarter[1] 1st quarter | 2nd quarter | 3rd quarter | 4th quarter | Population[2] |
|---|---|---|---|---|---|---|---|
| MICHIGAN | | Hart | 0 | 0 | 0 | 0 | 1,911 |
| | | Hartford | 0 | 0 | 0 | 0 | 2,451 |
| | | Hastings | 0 | 0 | 0 | 0 | 6,832 |
| | | Hillsdale | 0 | 0 | 0 | 0 | 7,710 |
| | | Holly | 0 | 0 | 0 | 0 | 6,283 |
| | | Homer | 0 | 0 | 0 | 0 | 1,736 |
| | | Houghton | 0 | 0 | 0 | 0 | 6,852 |
| | | Howell | 0 | 0 | 0 | 0 | 9,733 |
| | | Hudson | 0 | 0 | 0 | 0 | 2,294 |
| | | Huntington Woods | 0 | 0 | 0 | 0 | 5,776 |
| | | Huron Township | 0 | 0 | 0 | 0 | 16,133 |
| | | Imlay City | 0 | 0 | 0 | 0 | 3,667 |
| | | Ionia | 0 | 0 | 0 | 0 | 12,713 |
| | | Iron Mountain | 0 | | | | 7,722 |
| | | Iron River | 0 | 0 | 0 | 0 | 2,964 |
| | | Ishpeming | 0 | 0 | 0 | 0 | 6,459 |
| | | Ishpeming Township | 0 | 0 | 0 | 0 | 3,615 |
| | | Ithaca | 0 | 0 | 0 | 0 | 3,008 |
| | | Jackson | 0 | 0 | 0 | 0 | 33,228 |
| | | Jonesville | 0 | 0 | 0 | 0 | 2,216 |
| | | Kalamazoo | 0 | 0 | 0 | 0 | 71,664 |
| | | Kalamazoo Township | 0 | 0 | 0 | 0 | 22,008 |
| | | Kalkaska | 0 | 0 | 0 | 0 | 2,164 |
| | | Keego Harbor | 0 | 0 | 0 | 0 | 2,846 |
| | | Kentwood | 0 | 0 | 0 | 0 | 47,646 |
| | | Kingsford | 0 | 0 | 0 | 0 | 5,270 |
| | | Kingston | 0 | | 0 | 0 | 420 |
| | | Kinross Township | 0 | 0 | 0 | 0 | 8,869 |
| | | Laingsburg | 0 | 0 | 0 | 0 | 1,251 |
| | | Lake Angelus | 0 | 0 | 0 | 0 | 311 |
| | | Lake Linden | 0 | 0 | 0 | 0 | 1,044 |
| | | Lake Odessa | 0 | 0 | 0 | 0 | 2,209 |
| | | Lake Orion | 0 | 0 | 0 | 0 | 2,712 |
| | | Lakeview | 0 | 0 | 0 | 0 | 1,089 |
| | | L'Anse | 0 | 0 | 0 | 0 | 1,860 |
| | | Lapeer | 0 | 0 | 0 | 0 | 9,007 |
| | | Lapeer Township | 0 | 0 | 0 | 0 | 5,012 |
| | | Lathrup Village | 0 | 0 | 0 | 0 | 4,042 |
| | | Laurium | 0 | 0 | 0 | 0 | 1,991 |
| | | Lennon | 0 | 0 | 0 | 0 | 488 |
| | | Leoni Township | 0 | 0 | 0 | 0 | 13,505 |
| | | Leslie | 0 | 0 | 0 | 0 | 2,302 |
| | | Lexington | 0 | 0 | 0 | 0 | 1,040 |
| | | Lincoln Park | 0 | 0 | 0 | 0 | 34,832 |
| | | Lincoln Township | 0 | 0 | 0 | 0 | 14,342 |
| | | Linden | 0 | 0 | 0 | 0 | 3,417 |
| | | Litchfield | 0 | 0 | 0 | 0 | 1,385 |
| | | Lowell | 0 | 0 | 0 | 0 | 4,167 |
| | | Ludington | 0 | 0 | 0 | 0 | 8,319 |
| | | Luna Pier | 0 | 0 | 0 | 0 | 1,524 |
| | | Mackinac Island | 0 | 0 | 0 | 0 | 456 |
| | | Mackinaw City | 0 | 0 | 0 | 0 | 838 |
| | | Madison Township | 0 | 0 | 0 | 0 | 8,155 |
| | | Mancelona | 0 | 0 | 0 | 0 | 1,349 |
| | | Manistee | 0 | 0 | 0 | 0 | 6,058 |
| | | Manton | 0 | 0 | 0 | 0 | 1,161 |
| | | Marine City | 0 | 0 | 0 | 0 | 4,349 |
| | | Marion | 0 | 0 | 0 | 0 | 798 |
| | | Marlette | 0 | 0 | 0 | 0 | 1,971 |
| | | Marquette | 0 | 0 | 0 | 0 | 20,943 |
| | | Marshall | 0 | 0 | 0 | 0 | 7,085 |
| | | Marysville | 0 | 0 | 0 | 0 | 9,972 |
| | | Mason | 0 | 0 | 0 | 0 | 8,204 |
| | | Mattawan | 0 | 0 | 0 | 0 | 2,830 |
| | | Mayville | 0 | 0 | 0 | 0 | 981 |
| | | Memphis | 0 | 0 | 0 | 0 | 1,108 |
| | | Mendon | 0 | 0 | 0 | 0 | 906 |
| | | Metamora Township | 0 | 0 | 0 | 0 | 4,625 |
| | | Michiana | 0 | 0 | 0 | 0 | 192 |
| | | Midland | 0 | 0 | 0 | 0 | 40,821 |
| | | Milan | 0 | 0 | 0 | 0 | 5,762 |
| | | Milford | 0 | 0 | 0 | 0 | 16,661 |
| | | Montague | 0 | 0 | 0 | 0 | 2,282 |
| | | Montrose Township | 0 | 0 | 0 | 0 | 7,659 |
| | | Morenci | 0 | 0 | 0 | 0 | 2,245 |
| | | Morrice | 0 | 0 | 0 | 0 | 871 |
| | | Mount Morris Township | 0 | 0 | 0 | 0 | 22,058 |
| | | Munising | 0 | 0 | 0 | 0 | 2,289 |
| | | Muskegon | 0 | 0 | 0 | 0 | 39,327 |
| | | Muskegon Heights | 0 | 0 | 0 | 0 | 11,578 |
| | | Napoleon Township | 0 | 0 | 0 | 0 | 6,959 |
| | | Nashville | 0 | 0 | 0 | 0 | 1,651 |
| | | Negaunee | 0 | 0 | 0 | 0 | 4,444 |
| | | Newaygo | 0 | 0 | 0 | 0 | 1,621 |
| | | New Haven | 0 | 0 | 0 | 0 | 5,425 |
| | | New Lothrop | 0 | 0 | 0 | 0 | 575 |
| | | North Branch | 0 | 0 | 0 | 0 | 972 |
| | | North Muskegon | 0 | 0 | 0 | 0 | 3,902 |
| | | Northville | 0 | 0 | 0 | 0 | 5,947 |
| | | Norton Shores | 0 | 0 | 0 | 0 | 23,389 |
| | | Novi | 0 | 0 | 0 | 0 | 54,842 |
| | | Onaway | 0 | 0 | 0 | 0 | 893 |
| | | Ontwa Township-Edwardsburg | 0 | 0 | 0 | 0 | 5,872 |
| | | Orchard Lake | 0 | 0 | 0 | 0 | 2,207 |
| | | Oscoda Township | 0 | 0 | 0 | 0 | 6,764 |
| | | Otsego | 0 | 0 | 0 | 0 | 3,807 |
| | | Ovid | 0 | 0 | 0 | 0 | 1,387 |
| | | Owendale | 0 | 0 | 0 | 0 | 262 |
| | | Oxford | 0 | 0 | 0 | 0 | 3,524 |
| | | Parchment | 0 | 0 | 0 | 0 | 1,795 |
| | | Parma-Sandstone | 0 | 0 | 0 | 0 | 6,782 |
| | | Peck | 0 | 0 | 0 | 0 | 558 |
| | | Pentwater | 0 | 0 | 0 | 0 | 940 |
| | | Perry | 0 | 0 | 0 | 0 | 2,016 |
| | | Petoskey | 0 | 0 | 0 | 0 | 6,022 |
| | | Pinckney | 0 | 0 | 0 | 0 | 2,449 |
| | | Pinconning | 0 | 0 | 0 | 0 | 1,306 |
| | | Pittsfield Township | 0 | 0 | 0 | 0 | 34,699 |
| | | Plainwell | 0 | 0 | 0 | 0 | 3,840 |
| | | Pleasant Ridge | 0 | 0 | 0 | 0 | 2,456 |
| | | Port Austin | 0 | 0 | 0 | 0 | 643 |
| | | Portland | 0 | 0 | 0 | 0 | 3,672 |
| | | Potterville | 0 | 0 | 0 | 0 | 2,144 |
| | | Prairieville Township | 0 | 0 | 0 | 0 | 3,512 |
| | | Raisin Township | 0 | 0 | 0 | 0 | 7,368 |
| | | Reading | 0 | 0 | 0 | 0 | 1,064 |
| | | Reese | | | 0 | 0 | 1,338 |
| | | Richfield Township, Genesee County | 0 | 0 | 0 | 0 | 8,570 |
| | | Richfield Township, Roscommon County | 0 | 0 | 0 | 0 | 4,072 |
| | | Richland | 0 | 0 | 0 | 0 | 771 |

[1]Agencies published in this table indicated that no hate crimes occurred in their jurisdictions during the quarter(s) for which they submitted reports to the Hate Crime Statistics Program. Blanks indicate quarters for which agencies did not submit reports.

[2]Population figures are published only for the cities. The figures listed for the universities and colleges are student enrollment and were provided by the United States Department of Education for the 2008 school year, the most recent available. The enrollment figures include full-time and part-time students.

## Table 95. Hate Crime Zero Data Submitted per Quarter, by State and Agency, 2009—*Continued*

(Number.)

| State | Agency type | Agency name | Zero data per quarter[1] 1st quarter | 2nd quarter | 3rd quarter | 4th quarter | Population[2] |
|---|---|---|---|---|---|---|---|
| **MICHIGAN** | | Richland Township, Saginaw County | 0 | 0 | 0 | 0 | 4,214 |
| | | Richmond | 0 | 0 | 0 | 0 | 5,684 |
| | | Riverview | 0 | 0 | 0 | 0 | 11,665 |
| | | Rockford | 0 | 0 | 0 | 0 | 5,503 |
| | | Rogers City | 0 | 0 | 0 | 0 | 3,002 |
| | | Romeo | 0 | 0 | 0 | 0 | 3,739 |
| | | Romulus | 0 | 0 | 0 | 0 | 22,957 |
| | | Roosevelt Park | 0 | 0 | 0 | 0 | 3,756 |
| | | Rothbury | 0 | 0 | 0 | 0 | 435 |
| | | Sand Lake | 0 | 0 | 0 | 0 | 517 |
| | | Saugatuck-Douglas | 0 | 0 | 0 | 0 | 2,171 |
| | | Sault Ste. Marie | 0 | 0 | 0 | 0 | 14,063 |
| | | Schoolcraft | 0 | 0 | 0 | 0 | 1,504 |
| | | Somerset Township | 0 | 0 | 0 | 0 | 4,703 |
| | | Southgate | 0 | 0 | 0 | 0 | 27,455 |
| | | South Haven | 0 | 0 | 0 | 0 | 5,151 |
| | | South Lyon | 0 | 0 | 0 | 0 | 11,052 |
| | | South Rockwood | 0 | 0 | 0 | 0 | 1,705 |
| | | Spaulding Township | 0 | 0 | 0 | 0 | 2,168 |
| | | Spring Arbor Township | 0 | 0 | 0 | 0 | 8,409 |
| | | Springfield | 0 | 0 | 0 | 0 | 5,020 |
| | | Spring Lake-Ferrysburg | 0 | 0 | 0 | 0 | 5,464 |
| | | Standish | 0 | 0 | 0 | 0 | 1,972 |
| | | St. Charles | 0 | 0 | 0 | 0 | 1,999 |
| | | St. Clair | 0 | 0 | 0 | 0 | 5,760 |
| | | St. Clair Shores | 0 | 0 | 0 | 0 | 60,076 |
| | | St. Ignace | 0 | 0 | 0 | 0 | 2,301 |
| | | St. Johns | 0 | 0 | 0 | 0 | 7,225 |
| | | St. Joseph Township | 0 | 0 | 0 | 0 | 9,580 |
| | | St. Louis | 0 | 0 | 0 | 0 | 7,008 |
| | | Sturgis | 0 | 0 | 0 | 0 | 10,866 |
| | | Sumpter Township | 0 | 0 | 0 | 0 | 11,114 |
| | | Suttons Bay | 0 | 0 | 0 | 0 | 576 |
| | | Swartz Creek | 0 | 0 | 0 | 0 | 5,235 |
| | | Sylvan Lake | 0 | 0 | 0 | 0 | 1,629 |
| | | Thetford Township | 0 | 0 | 0 | 0 | 7,784 |
| | | Thomas Township | 0 | 0 | 0 | 0 | 12,252 |
| | | Three Rivers | 0 | 0 | 0 | 0 | 7,136 |
| | | Tittabawassee Township | 0 | 0 | 0 | 0 | 8,833 |
| | | Tuscarora Township | 0 | 0 | 0 | 0 | 3,014 |
| | | Ubly | 0 | 0 | 0 | 0 | 761 |
| | | Unadilla Township | 0 | 0 | 0 | 0 | 3,443 |
| | | Union City | 0 | 0 | 0 | 0 | 1,705 |
| | | Unionville | 0 | 0 | 0 | 0 | 563 |
| | | Vassar | 0 | 0 | 0 | 0 | 2,648 |
| | | Vernon | 0 | 0 | 0 | 0 | 784 |
| | | Vicksburg | 0 | 0 | 0 | 0 | 2,181 |
| | | Walker | 0 | 0 | 0 | 0 | 23,918 |
| | | Walled Lake | 0 | 0 | 0 | 0 | 6,895 |
| | | Waterloo Township | 0 | 0 | 0 | 0 | 2,958 |
| | | Watertown Township | | | 0 | | 2,145 |
| | | Watervliet | 0 | 0 | 0 | 0 | 1,726 |
| | | Wayland | 0 | 0 | 0 | 0 | 3,794 |
| | | West Branch | 0 | 0 | 0 | 0 | 1,803 |
| | | White Cloud | 0 | 0 | 0 | 0 | 1,387 |
| | | Whitehall | 0 | 0 | 0 | 0 | 2,794 |
| | | White Pigeon | 0 | 0 | 0 | 0 | 1,552 |

| State | Agency type | Agency name | Zero data per quarter[1] 1st quarter | 2nd quarter | 3rd quarter | 4th quarter | Population[2] |
|---|---|---|---|---|---|---|---|
| | | Williamston | 0 | 0 | 0 | 0 | 3,799 |
| | | Wixom | 0 | 0 | 0 | 0 | 13,431 |
| | | Wolverine Lake | 0 | 0 | 0 | 0 | 4,292 |
| | | Woodhaven | 0 | 0 | 0 | 0 | 12,643 |
| | | Zilwaukee | 0 | 0 | 0 | 0 | 1,636 |
| | **Universities and Colleges** | Delta College | 0 | 0 | 0 | 0 | 10,899 |
| | | Eastern Michigan University | 0 | 0 | 0 | 0 | 22,032 |
| | | Ferris State University | 0 | 0 | 0 | 0 | 13,532 |
| | | Grand Rapids Community College | 0 | 0 | 0 | 0 | 15,403 |
| | | Grand Valley State University | 0 | 0 | 0 | 0 | 23,892 |
| | | Lansing Community College | 0 | 0 | 0 | 0 | 19,445 |
| | | Macomb Community College | 0 | 0 | 0 | 0 | 22,985 |
| | | Michigan Technological University | 0 | 0 | 0 | 0 | 7,009 |
| | | Mott Community College | 0 | 0 | 0 | 0 | 10,813 |
| | | Northern Michigan University | 0 | 0 | 0 | 0 | 9,347 |
| | | Oakland Community College | 0 | 0 | 0 | 0 | 24,957 |
| | | Oakland University | 0 | 0 | 0 | 0 | 18,175 |
| | | Saginaw Valley State University | 0 | 0 | 0 | 0 | 9,837 |
| | | University of Michigan, Flint | 0 | 0 | 0 | 0 | 7,260 |
| | **Metropolitan Counties** | Barry | 0 | 0 | 0 | 0 | |
| | | Clinton | 0 | 0 | 0 | 0 | |
| | | Eaton | 0 | 0 | 0 | 0 | |
| | | Ionia | 0 | 0 | 0 | 0 | |
| | | Jackson | 0 | 0 | 0 | 0 | |
| | | Lapeer | 0 | 0 | 0 | 0 | |
| | | Livingston | 0 | 0 | 0 | 0 | |
| | | Muskegon | 0 | 0 | 0 | 0 | |
| | | Newaygo | 0 | 0 | 0 | 0 | |
| | | Van Buren | 0 | 0 | 0 | 0 | |
| | | Wayne | 0 | 0 | 0 | 0 | |
| | **Nonmetropolitan Counties** | Alcona | 0 | 0 | 0 | 0 | |
| | | Alger | | 0 | 0 | 0 | |
| | | Allegan | 0 | 0 | 0 | 0 | |
| | | Alpena | 0 | 0 | 0 | 0 | |
| | | Antrim | 0 | 0 | 0 | 0 | |
| | | Arenac | 0 | 0 | 0 | 0 | |
| | | Baraga | 0 | 0 | | | |
| | | Benzie | 0 | 0 | 0 | 0 | |
| | | Charlevoix | 0 | 0 | 0 | 0 | |
| | | Cheboygan | 0 | 0 | 0 | 0 | |
| | | Chippewa | 0 | 0 | 0 | 0 | |
| | | Delta | 0 | 0 | 0 | 0 | |
| | | Dickinson | 0 | 0 | | | |
| | | Emmet | 0 | 0 | 0 | 0 | |
| | | Gladwin | 0 | 0 | 0 | 0 | |

[1]Agencies published in this table indicated that no hate crimes occurred in their jurisdictions during the quarter(s) for which they submitted reports to the Hate Crime Statistics Program. Blanks indicate quarters for which agencies did not submit reports.

[2]Population figures are published only for the cities. The figures listed for the universities and colleges are student enrollment and were provided by the United States Department of Education for the 2008 school year, the most recent available. The enrollment figures include full-time and part-time students.

## Table 95. Hate Crime Zero Data Submitted per Quarter, by State and Agency, 2009—*Continued*

(Number.)

| State | Agency type | Agency name | Zero data per quarter[1] | | | | Population[2] |
|---|---|---|---|---|---|---|---|
| | | | 1st quarter | 2nd quarter | 3rd quarter | 4th quarter | |
| MICHIGAN | | Grand Traverse | 0 | 0 | 0 | 0 | |
| | | Gratiot | 0 | 0 | 0 | 0 | |
| | | Hillsdale | 0 | 0 | 0 | 0 | |
| | | Houghton | 0 | 0 | 0 | 0 | |
| | | Huron | 0 | 0 | 0 | 0 | |
| | | Iosco | 0 | 0 | 0 | 0 | |
| | | Iron | 0 | 0 | 0 | 0 | |
| | | Isabella | 0 | 0 | 0 | 0 | |
| | | Kalkaska | 0 | 0 | 0 | 0 | |
| | | Keweenaw | 0 | 0 | 0 | 0 | |
| | | Lake | 0 | 0 | 0 | 0 | |
| | | Leelanau | 0 | 0 | 0 | 0 | |
| | | Lenawee | 0 | 0 | 0 | 0 | |
| | | Luce | 0 | 0 | 0 | 0 | |
| | | Mackinac | 0 | 0 | 0 | 0 | |
| | | Manistee | 0 | 0 | 0 | 0 | |
| | | Marquette | 0 | 0 | 0 | 0 | |
| | | Mason | 0 | 0 | 0 | 0 | |
| | | Mecosta | 0 | 0 | 0 | 0 | |
| | | Menominee | 0 | 0 | 0 | 0 | |
| | | Midland | 0 | 0 | 0 | 0 | |
| | | Missaukee | 0 | 0 | 0 | 0 | |
| | | Montcalm | 0 | 0 | 0 | 0 | |
| | | Montmorency | 0 | 0 | 0 | 0 | |
| | | Oceana | 0 | 0 | 0 | 0 | |
| | | Ontonagon | 0 | 0 | 0 | 0 | |
| | | Osceola | 0 | 0 | 0 | 0 | |
| | | Oscoda | 0 | 0 | 0 | 0 | |
| | | Otsego | 0 | 0 | 0 | 0 | |
| | | Presque Isle | | | | 0 | |
| | | Roscommon | 0 | 0 | 0 | 0 | |
| | | Sanilac | 0 | 0 | 0 | 0 | |
| | | Schoolcraft | 0 | 0 | 0 | 0 | |
| | | Shiawassee | 0 | 0 | 0 | 0 | |
| | | Wexford | 0 | 0 | 0 | 0 | |
| | State Police Agencies | State Police: | | | | | |
| | | Alcona County | 0 | 0 | 0 | 0 | |
| | | Alger County | 0 | 0 | 0 | 0 | |
| | | Allegan County | 0 | 0 | 0 | 0 | |
| | | Alpena County | 0 | 0 | 0 | 0 | |
| | | Antrim County | 0 | 0 | 0 | 0 | |
| | | Arenac County | 0 | 0 | 0 | 0 | |
| | | Baraga County | 0 | 0 | 0 | 0 | |
| | | Barry County | 0 | 0 | 0 | 0 | |
| | | Bay County | 0 | 0 | 0 | 0 | |
| | | Benzie County | 0 | 0 | 0 | 0 | |
| | | Berrien County | 0 | 0 | 0 | 0 | |
| | | Branch County | 0 | 0 | 0 | 0 | |
| | | Calhoun County | 0 | 0 | 0 | 0 | |
| | | Cass County | 0 | 0 | 0 | 0 | |
| | | Charlevoix County | 0 | 0 | 0 | 0 | |
| | | Cheboygan County | 0 | 0 | 0 | 0 | |
| | | Chippewa County | 0 | 0 | 0 | 0 | |
| | | Clinton County | 0 | 0 | 0 | 0 | |
| | | Crawford County | 0 | 0 | 0 | 0 | |
| | | Delta County | 0 | 0 | 0 | 0 | |
| | | Dickinson County | 0 | 0 | 0 | 0 | |
| | | Eaton County | 0 | 0 | 0 | 0 | |
| | | Emmet County | 0 | 0 | 0 | 0 | |
| | | Genesee County | 0 | 0 | 0 | 0 | |
| | | Gladwin County | 0 | 0 | 0 | 0 | |
| | | Gogebic County | 0 | 0 | 0 | 0 | |
| | | Gratiot County | 0 | 0 | 0 | 0 | |
| | | Hillsdale County | 0 | 0 | 0 | 0 | |
| | | Houghton County | 0 | 0 | 0 | 0 | |
| | | Huron County | 0 | 0 | 0 | 0 | |
| | | Ingham County | 0 | 0 | 0 | 0 | |
| | | Ionia County | 0 | 0 | 0 | 0 | |
| | | Iosco County | 0 | 0 | 0 | 0 | |
| | | Iron County | 0 | 0 | 0 | 0 | |
| | | Isabella County | 0 | 0 | 0 | 0 | |
| | | Jackson County | 0 | 0 | 0 | 0 | |
| | | Kalamazoo County | 0 | 0 | 0 | 0 | |
| | | Kalkaska County | 0 | 0 | 0 | 0 | |
| | | Kent County | 0 | 0 | 0 | 0 | |
| | | Keweenaw County | 0 | 0 | 0 | 0 | |
| | | Lake County | 0 | 0 | 0 | 0 | |
| | | Lapeer County | 0 | 0 | 0 | 0 | |
| | | Leelanau County | 0 | 0 | 0 | 0 | |
| | | Lenawee County | 0 | 0 | 0 | 0 | |
| | | Livingston County | 0 | 0 | 0 | 0 | |
| | | Luce County | 0 | 0 | 0 | 0 | |
| | | Mackinac County | 0 | 0 | 0 | 0 | |
| | | Macomb County | 0 | 0 | 0 | 0 | |
| | | Manistee County | 0 | 0 | 0 | 0 | |
| | | Marquette County | 0 | 0 | 0 | 0 | |
| | | Mason County | 0 | 0 | 0 | 0 | |
| | | Mecosta County | 0 | 0 | 0 | 0 | |
| | | Menominee County | 0 | 0 | 0 | 0 | |
| | | Midland County | 0 | 0 | 0 | 0 | |
| | | Missaukee County | 0 | 0 | 0 | 0 | |
| | | Montcalm County | 0 | 0 | 0 | 0 | |
| | | Montmorency County | 0 | 0 | 0 | 0 | |
| | | Muskegon County | 0 | 0 | 0 | 0 | |
| | | Newaygo County | 0 | 0 | 0 | 0 | |
| | | Oakland County | 0 | 0 | 0 | 0 | |
| | | Oceana County | 0 | 0 | 0 | 0 | |
| | | Ogemaw County | 0 | 0 | 0 | 0 | |
| | | Ontonagon County | 0 | 0 | 0 | 0 | |
| | | Osceola County | 0 | 0 | 0 | 0 | |
| | | Oscoda County | 0 | 0 | 0 | 0 | |
| | | Otsego County | 0 | 0 | 0 | 0 | |
| | | Ottawa County | 0 | 0 | 0 | 0 | |
| | | Presque Isle County | 0 | 0 | 0 | 0 | |
| | | Roscommon County | 0 | 0 | 0 | 0 | |
| | | Saginaw County | 0 | 0 | 0 | 0 | |
| | | Sanilac County | 0 | 0 | 0 | 0 | |
| | | Schoolcraft County | 0 | 0 | 0 | 0 | |
| | | Shiawassee County | 0 | 0 | 0 | 0 | |
| | | St. Clair County | 0 | 0 | 0 | 0 | |
| | | St. Joseph County | 0 | 0 | 0 | 0 | |
| | | Tuscola County | 0 | 0 | 0 | 0 | |

[1] Agencies published in this table indicated that no hate crimes occurred in their jurisdictions during the quarter(s) for which they submitted reports to the Hate Crime Statistics Program. Blanks indicate quarters for which agencies did not submit reports.
[2] Population figures are published only for the cities. The figures listed for the universities and colleges are student enrollment and were provided by the United States Department of Education for the 2008 school year, the most recent available. The enrollment figures include full-time and part-time students.

## Table 95. Hate Crime Zero Data Submitted per Quarter, by State and Agency, 2009—*Continued*

(Number.)

| State | Agency type | Agency name | Zero data per quarter[1] | | | | Population[2] |
|---|---|---|---|---|---|---|---|
| | | | 1st quarter | 2nd quarter | 3rd quarter | 4th quarter | |
| MICHIGAN | | Van Buren County | 0 | 0 | 0 | 0 | |
| | | Washtenaw County | 0 | 0 | 0 | 0 | |
| | | Wayne County | 0 | 0 | 0 | 0 | |
| | | Wexford County | 0 | 0 | 0 | 0 | |
| | Other Agencies | Bishop International Airport | 0 | 0 | 0 | 0 | |
| | | Capitol Region Airport Authority | 0 | 0 | 0 | 0 | |
| | | Gerald R. Ford International Airport | 0 | 0 | 0 | 0 | |
| | | Huron-Clinton Metropolitan Authority: Hudson Mills Metropark | 0 | 0 | 0 | 0 | |
| | | Kensington Metropark | 0 | 0 | 0 | 0 | |
| | | Lower Huron Metropark | 0 | 0 | 0 | 0 | |
| | | Stony Creek Metropark | 0 | 0 | 0 | 0 | |
| | | Wayne County Airport | 0 | 0 | 0 | 0 | |
| MINNESOTA.. | Cities | Alexandria | | 0 | 0 | | 11,409 |
| | | Arden Hills | | | | 0 | 9,604 |
| | | Bemidji | 0 | 0 | 0 | 0 | 13,694 |
| | | Benson | 0 | 0 | 0 | 0 | 3,014 |
| | | Cambridge | 0 | | | | 7,965 |
| | | Cannon Falls | | 0 | 0 | 0 | 4,049 |
| | | Champlin | 0 | 0 | 0 | 0 | 23,640 |
| | | Crystal | 0 | 0 | | 0 | 21,600 |
| | | Dilworth | 0 | 0 | 0 | 0 | 3,757 |
| | | Elmore | | 0 | | | 648 |
| | | Eveleth | 0 | 0 | 0 | 0 | 3,553 |
| | | Farmington | 0 | 0 | | | 19,945 |
| | | Fergus Falls | 0 | | 0 | | 13,631 |
| | | Goodview | 0 | 0 | 0 | 0 | 3,577 |
| | | Hastings | 0 | 0 | 0 | 0 | 22,600 |
| | | Inver Grove Heights | 0 | 0 | 0 | 0 | 33,800 |
| | | Lakeville | | 0 | 0 | 0 | 55,921 |
| | | Little Canada | | | | 0 | 9,544 |
| | | Mendota Heights | 0 | 0 | 0 | | 11,610 |
| | | Montgomery | | 0 | 0 | 0 | 3,323 |
| | | North Oaks | | | | 0 | 4,785 |
| | | Oak Park Heights | 0 | 0 | 0 | 0 | 4,802 |
| | | Osakis | 0 | 0 | 0 | | 1,573 |
| | | Princeton | 0 | 0 | 0 | 0 | 4,858 |
| | | Ramsey | 0 | | | | 24,391 |
| | | Sauk Centre | 0 | 0 | 0 | 0 | 3,946 |
| | | Shoreview | | | | 0 | 25,008 |
| | | South Lake Minnetonka | 0 | 0 | 0 | 0 | 12,071 |
| | | Spring Lake Park | 0 | | | 0 | 6,426 |
| | | Tracy | | | 0 | 0 | 2,044 |
| | | Vadnais Heights | | | | 0 | 12,446 |
| | | Virginia | 0 | | | | 8,409 |
| | | Waite Park | 0 | 0 | 0 | 0 | 6,809 |
| | | West St. Paul | 0 | 0 | | | 18,871 |
| | | White Bear Township | | | | 0 | 11,494 |
| | | Willmar | 0 | 0 | 0 | 0 | 17,698 |
| | | Winnebago | | 0 | | | 1,319 |
| | Universities and Colleges | University of Minnesota, Duluth | 0 | 0 | 0 | 0 | 11,366 |
| | Metropolitan Counties | Carlton | 0 | 0 | 0 | 0 | |
| | | Chisago | 0 | 0 | 0 | 0 | |
| | | Clay | 0 | 0 | 0 | 0 | |
| | | Polk | | 0 | 0 | | |
| | | Ramsey | | | | 0 | |
| | | Washington | 0 | 0 | 0 | | |
| | Nonmetropolitan Counties | Big Stone | | | | 0 | |
| | | Cass | 0 | 0 | 0 | 0 | |
| | | Crow Wing | 0 | | 0 | | |
| | | Douglas | 0 | 0 | 0 | 0 | |
| | | Faribault | | 0 | | | |
| | | Grant | 0 | 0 | | | |
| | | Itasca | 0 | | 0 | 0 | |
| | | Kittson | 0 | 0 | 0 | 0 | |
| | | Pope | 0 | 0 | 0 | 0 | |
| | | Redwood | | 0 | 0 | 0 | |
| | | Rock | 0 | 0 | | 0 | |
| | | Wadena | 0 | 0 | 0 | 0 | |
| MISSISSIPPI .. | Cities | Aberdeen | 0 | 0 | 0 | 0 | 6,054 |
| | | Ackerman | 0 | 0 | 0 | 0 | 1,507 |
| | | Amory | 0 | 0 | 0 | 0 | 7,226 |
| | | Batesville | 0 | 0 | 0 | 0 | 7,928 |
| | | Belzoni | 0 | 0 | 0 | 0 | 2,407 |
| | | Byhalia | 0 | 0 | 0 | 0 | 1,313 |
| | | Columbia | 0 | 0 | 0 | 0 | 6,563 |
| | | Columbus | 0 | 0 | 0 | 0 | 23,577 |
| | | De Kalb | 0 | 0 | 0 | 0 | 866 |
| | | Eupora | 0 | 0 | | 0 | 2,201 |
| | | Florence | 0 | 0 | | | 3,612 |
| | | Fulton | 0 | 0 | 0 | 0 | 4,093 |
| | | Gautier | | | 0 | 0 | 16,248 |
| | | Greenville | 0 | 0 | 0 | 0 | 35,187 |
| | | Hattiesburg | 0 | 0 | | | 52,716 |
| | | Heidelberg | 0 | 0 | 0 | 0 | 809 |
| | | Hernando | | 0 | | | 12,913 |
| | | Hollandale | 0 | 0 | | | 2,915 |
| | | Horn Lake | 0 | 0 | 0 | 0 | 25,238 |
| | | Iuka | 0 | 0 | 0 | 0 | 2,926 |
| | | Magnolia | 0 | 0 | 0 | 0 | 2,090 |
| | | McComb | 0 | 0 | 0 | 0 | 13,726 |
| | | New Albany | 0 | 0 | 0 | 0 | 8,234 |
| | | Newton | 0 | 0 | | | 3,672 |
| | | Olive Branch | 0 | 0 | 0 | 0 | 33,284 |
| | | Pascagoula | 0 | 0 | 0 | 0 | 23,346 |
| | | Petal | 0 | 0 | 0 | | 10,659 |
| | | Picayune | 0 | 0 | 0 | 0 | 11,937 |
| | | Poplarville | 0 | 0 | 0 | 0 | 3,054 |
| | | Raymond | 0 | 0 | | | 1,627 |
| | | Shaw | 0 | 0 | | 0 | 2,116 |
| | | Shelby | 0 | 0 | 0 | 0 | 2,568 |
| | | Starkville | | | 0 | 0 | 24,444 |
| | | Tupelo | | 0 | 0 | 0 | 36,453 |
| | | Waveland | 0 | 0 | 0 | 0 | 5,091 |
| | | Waynesboro | 0 | 0 | 0 | | 5,635 |
| | | West Point | 0 | 0 | 0 | 0 | 11,203 |
| | | Winona | 0 | 0 | | 0 | 4,434 |
| | Universities and Colleges | Coahoma Community College | 0 | 0 | 0 | 0 | 2,263 |
| | | Mississippi State University | | | | 0 | 17,824 |
| | | University of Mississippi, Oxford | 0 | | | 0 | 15,289 |

[1]Agencies published in this table indicated that no hate crimes occurred in their jurisdictions during the quarter(s) for which they submitted reports to the Hate Crime Statistics Program. Blanks indicate quarters for which agencies did not submit reports.

[2]Population figures are published only for the cities. The figures listed for the universities and colleges are student enrollment and were provided by the United States Department of Education for the 2008 school year, the most recent available. The enrollment figures include full-time and part-time students.

# Table 95. Hate Crime Zero Data Submitted per Quarter, by State and Agency, 2009—*Continued*

(Number.)

| State | Agency type | Agency name | Zero data per quarter[1] 1st quarter | 2nd quarter | 3rd quarter | 4th quarter | Population[2] |
|---|---|---|---|---|---|---|---|
| MISSISSIPPI | Metropolitan Counties | Forrest | | | 0 | | |
| | Nonmetropolitan Counties | Attala | | 0 | 0 | | |
| | | Chickasaw | 0 | 0 | 0 | 0 | |
| | | Greene | 0 | 0 | 0 | 0 | |
| | | Grenada | 0 | 0 | 0 | 0 | |
| | | Leflore | | | | 0 | |
| | | Lincoln | 0 | 0 | 0 | 0 | |
| | | Lowndes | 0 | 0 | 0 | 0 | |
| | | Oktibbeha | 0 | 0 | 0 | 0 | |
| | | Panola | 0 | 0 | 0 | 0 | |
| | | Pontotoc | | 0 | | | |
| | | Prentiss | | | 0 | 0 | |
| | | Sunflower | 0 | 0 | 0 | 0 | |
| | | Tippah | 0 | 0 | 0 | 0 | |
| | | Union | 0 | 0 | 0 | 0 | |
| | | Warren | 0 | 0 | 0 | 0 | |
| | | Washington | | | 0 | 0 | |
| | | Winston | 0 | 0 | 0 | | |
| MISSOURI..... | Cities | Adrian | | | 0 | 0 | 1,912 |
| | | Advance | 0 | 0 | 0 | 0 | 1,212 |
| | | Alton | | | | 0 | 635 |
| | | Anderson | 0 | 0 | 0 | 0 | 2,061 |
| | | Appleton City | 0 | 0 | 0 | 0 | 1,257 |
| | | Arbyrd | 0 | 0 | 0 | 0 | 485 |
| | | Archie | 0 | 0 | 0 | 0 | 1,008 |
| | | Arnold | 0 | 0 | 0 | 0 | 20,676 |
| | | Ash Grove | 0 | 0 | 0 | 0 | 1,540 |
| | | Ashland | 0 | 0 | 0 | 0 | 2,185 |
| | | Aurora | 0 | 0 | 0 | 0 | 7,529 |
| | | Auxvasse | 0 | 0 | 0 | 0 | 999 |
| | | Ava | 0 | 0 | 0 | 0 | 3,164 |
| | | Ballwin | 0 | 0 | 0 | 0 | 29,897 |
| | | Bates City | 0 | 0 | | 0 | 268 |
| | | Battlefield | 0 | | 0 | 0 | 4,521 |
| | | Bella Villa | 0 | 0 | 0 | 0 | 631 |
| | | Belle | 0 | 0 | 0 | 0 | 1,386 |
| | | Bellefontaine Neighbors | | 0 | 0 | 0 | 10,152 |
| | | Bellerive | 0 | 0 | 0 | 0 | 252 |
| | | Bellflower | | 0 | 0 | 0 | 385 |
| | | Bel-Nor | 0 | 0 | 0 | 0 | 1,469 |
| | | Bel-Ridge | 0 | 0 | 0 | 0 | 2,879 |
| | | Belton | 0 | 0 | 0 | 0 | 24,908 |
| | | Berkeley | 0 | | | 0 | 9,316 |
| | | Bernie | 0 | 0 | 0 | 0 | 1,789 |
| | | Bethany | 0 | 0 | 0 | 0 | 3,066 |
| | | Beverly Hills | 0 | 0 | 0 | 0 | 553 |
| | | Billings | 0 | 0 | 0 | 0 | 1,120 |
| | | Birch Tree | 0 | 0 | 0 | 0 | 623 |
| | | Birmingham | 0 | 0 | 0 | 0 | 223 |
| | | Bismarck | 0 | | 0 | | 1,545 |
| | | Blackburn | | | | 0 | 268 |
| | | Bloomfield | 0 | 0 | 0 | 0 | 1,861 |
| | | Blue Springs | 0 | 0 | 0 | 0 | 56,567 |
| | | Bolivar | 0 | 0 | 0 | 0 | 11,240 |
| | | Bonne Terre | 0 | 0 | 0 | 0 | 7,307 |
| | | Boonville | 0 | 0 | 0 | 0 | 8,841 |
| | | Bourbon | 0 | 0 | 0 | 0 | 1,533 |
| | | Bowling Green | 0 | 0 | 0 | 0 | 5,300 |
| | | Branson | 0 | 0 | 0 | 0 | 7,734 |
| | | Branson West | 0 | 0 | 0 | 0 | 520 |
| | | Braymer | 0 | 0 | 0 | 0 | 948 |
| | | Breckenridge Hills | 0 | 0 | 0 | 0 | 4,444 |
| | | Brentwood | 0 | 0 | 0 | 0 | 7,129 |
| | | Bridgeton | 0 | 0 | 0 | 0 | 14,972 |
| | | Brookfield | 0 | 0 | 0 | 0 | 4,275 |
| | | Brunswick | | | 0 | 0 | 846 |
| | | Bucklin | 0 | 0 | | 0 | 469 |
| | | Buckner | 0 | 0 | 0 | 0 | 2,796 |
| | | Butler | 0 | 0 | 0 | 0 | 4,314 |
| | | Butterfield Village | 0 | 0 | 0 | 0 | 422 |
| | | Byrnes Mill | | | | 0 | 2,970 |
| | | Cabool | 0 | 0 | 0 | 0 | 2,138 |
| | | California | 0 | 0 | 0 | 0 | 4,165 |
| | | Calverton Park | 0 | 0 | 0 | 0 | 1,265 |
| | | Camden Point | 0 | | 0 | 0 | 545 |
| | | Camdenton | 0 | 0 | 0 | 0 | 3,569 |
| | | Cameron | 0 | | 0 | 0 | 9,226 |
| | | Campbell | 0 | 0 | 0 | 0 | 1,832 |
| | | Canton | 0 | 0 | 0 | 0 | 2,459 |
| | | Cardwell | 0 | 0 | 0 | 0 | 716 |
| | | Carl Junction | 0 | 0 | 0 | 0 | 7,588 |
| | | Carrollton | | | | 0 | 3,830 |
| | | Carterville | | 0 | 0 | 0 | 1,985 |
| | | Carthage | 0 | 0 | 0 | 0 | 14,054 |
| | | Caruthersville | 0 | 0 | 0 | 0 | 6,082 |
| | | Cassville | 0 | 0 | 0 | 0 | 3,337 |
| | | Center | 0 | 0 | 0 | 0 | 641 |
| | | Centralia | 0 | 0 | 0 | 0 | 3,658 |
| | | Chaffee | 0 | 0 | 0 | 0 | 2,940 |
| | | Charlack | 0 | 0 | 0 | 0 | 1,336 |
| | | Charleston | 0 | | | 0 | 5,160 |
| | | Chillicothe | | | | 0 | 8,678 |
| | | Clarence | | | 0 | 0 | 863 |
| | | Claycomo | 0 | 0 | 0 | 0 | 1,316 |
| | | Cleveland | 0 | 0 | 0 | 0 | 689 |
| | | Clever | 0 | 0 | 0 | 0 | 1,720 |
| | | Clinton | 0 | 0 | 0 | 0 | 9,387 |
| | | Concordia | 0 | 0 | 0 | 0 | 2,386 |
| | | Conway | 0 | 0 | 0 | 0 | 784 |
| | | Cool Valley | 0 | 0 | 0 | 0 | 996 |
| | | Cooter | 0 | 0 | 0 | 0 | 411 |
| | | Corder | | | | 0 | 412 |
| | | Cottleville | 0 | 0 | 0 | 0 | 3,331 |
| | | Country Club Hills | 0 | 0 | 0 | 0 | 1,269 |
| | | Country Club Village | 0 | 0 | 0 | 0 | 2,447 |
| | | Crane | 0 | 0 | 0 | 0 | 1,372 |
| | | Creighton | 0 | 0 | 0 | 0 | 348 |
| | | Crestwood | 0 | 0 | 0 | 0 | 11,358 |
| | | Creve Coeur | 0 | 0 | 0 | 0 | 16,881 |
| | | Crocker | 0 | 0 | 0 | 0 | 995 |
| | | Crystal City | 0 | 0 | 0 | 0 | 4,568 |
| | | Cuba | 0 | 0 | 0 | 0 | 3,592 |
| | | Deepwater | 0 | 0 | 0 | 0 | 488 |
| | | Dellwood | 0 | 0 | 0 | 0 | 4,864 |
| | | Delta | 0 | 0 | 0 | 0 | 543 |
| | | Desloge | 0 | 0 | 0 | 0 | 5,228 |
| | | De Soto | 0 | 0 | 0 | 0 | 6,479 |
| | | Des Peres | | 0 | | 0 | 8,604 |
| | | Dexter | 0 | 0 | 0 | 0 | 7,674 |
| | | Diamond | 0 | 0 | 0 | 0 | 905 |
| | | Dixon | 0 | 0 | 0 | 0 | 1,530 |
| | | Doniphan | 0 | 0 | 0 | 0 | 1,883 |
| | | Doolittle | 0 | 0 | 0 | 0 | 654 |
| | | Drexel | 0 | 0 | 0 | 0 | 1,097 |
| | | Duenweg | 0 | 0 | 0 | 0 | 1,260 |
| | | Duquesne | 0 | 0 | 0 | 0 | 1,758 |
| | | East Prairie | 0 | 0 | 0 | 0 | 3,053 |
| | | Edgerton | 0 | 0 | 0 | 0 | 556 |
| | | Edina | 0 | 0 | 0 | 0 | 1,111 |
| | | Edmundson | 0 | 0 | 0 | 0 | 775 |
| | | Eldon | 0 | 0 | 0 | 0 | 4,996 |
| | | El Dorado Springs | 0 | 0 | 0 | 0 | 3,672 |
| | | Ellington | 0 | 0 | 0 | 0 | 977 |
| | | Ellisville | 0 | 0 | 0 | 0 | 9,224 |
| | | Elsberry | 0 | 0 | 0 | 0 | 2,707 |
| | | Eminence | 0 | 0 | | 0 | 555 |
| | | Emma | | | | 0 | 232 |
| | | Eureka | 0 | 0 | 0 | 0 | 9,505 |
| | | Everton | 0 | | 0 | 0 | 303 |

[1]Agencies published in this table indicated that no hate crimes occurred in their jurisdictions during the quarter(s) for which they submitted reports to the Hate Crime Statistics Program. Blanks indicate quarters for which agencies did not submit reports.

[2]Population figures are published only for the cities. The figures listed for the universities and colleges are student enrollment and were provided by the United States Department of Education for the 2008 school year, the most recent available. The enrollment figures include full-time and part-time students.

## Table 95. Hate Crime Zero Data Submitted per Quarter, by State and Agency, 2009—*Continued*

(Number.)

| State | Agency type | Agency name | Zero data per quarter[1] | | | | Population[2] |
|---|---|---|---|---|---|---|---|
| | | | 1st quarter | 2nd quarter | 3rd quarter | 4th quarter | |
| MISSOURI | | Excelsior Springs | 0 | 0 | 0 | 0 | 12,132 |
| | | Exeter | 0 | 0 | 0 | 0 | 753 |
| | | Fair Grove | 0 | 0 | 0 | 0 | 1,443 |
| | | Fair Play | 0 | 0 | 0 | 0 | 459 |
| | | Farber | 0 | 0 | 0 | 0 | 392 |
| | | Farmington | 0 | 0 | 0 | 0 | 16,351 |
| | | Fayette | 0 | 0 | | 0 | 2,685 |
| | | Ferguson | 0 | 0 | 0 | 0 | 20,814 |
| | | Ferrelview | 0 | 0 | 0 | 0 | 576 |
| | | Festus | 0 | 0 | 0 | 0 | 11,417 |
| | | Fleming | 0 | 0 | 0 | 0 | 116 |
| | | Flordell Hills | 0 | 0 | 0 | 0 | 854 |
| | | Florissant | 0 | 0 | 0 | 0 | 50,205 |
| | | Foley | 0 | 0 | 0 | 0 | 215 |
| | | Fordland | 0 | 0 | 0 | 0 | 771 |
| | | Foristell | 0 | 0 | 0 | 0 | 330 |
| | | Forsyth | 0 | 0 | 0 | 0 | 1,725 |
| | | Fredericktown | 0 | 0 | 0 | 0 | 4,177 |
| | | Freeman | 0 | 0 | 0 | 0 | 607 |
| | | Frontenac | 0 | 0 | 0 | 0 | 3,842 |
| | | Fulton | 0 | 0 | 0 | 0 | 12,771 |
| | | Galena | 0 | 0 | 0 | 0 | 500 |
| | | Gallatin | 0 | 0 | 0 | 0 | 1,724 |
| | | Garden City | 0 | 0 | 0 | 0 | 1,669 |
| | | Gerald | 0 | | 0 | 0 | 1,254 |
| | | Gideon | 0 | 0 | | | 945 |
| | | Gladstone | 0 | 0 | 0 | 0 | 28,454 |
| | | Glasgow | 0 | 0 | 0 | 0 | 1,193 |
| | | Glendale | 0 | 0 | 0 | 0 | 5,461 |
| | | Glen Echo Park | 0 | 0 | 0 | 0 | 157 |
| | | Goodman | 0 | 0 | 0 | 0 | 1,262 |
| | | Gower | 0 | 0 | 0 | 0 | 1,435 |
| | | Grain Valley | | | | 0 | 11,146 |
| | | Granby | 0 | 0 | 0 | 0 | 2,243 |
| | | Grandin | 0 | 0 | | 0 | 235 |
| | | Greendale | 0 | 0 | 0 | 0 | 687 |
| | | Greenfield | 0 | 0 | 0 | 0 | 1,220 |
| | | Greenville | 0 | 0 | 0 | 0 | 430 |
| | | Greenwood | 0 | 0 | 0 | 0 | 4,728 |
| | | Hallsville | 0 | 0 | 0 | 0 | 956 |
| | | Hamilton | 0 | 0 | 0 | 0 | 1,781 |
| | | Hannibal | 0 | 0 | 0 | 0 | 17,396 |
| | | Hardin | 0 | 0 | 0 | 0 | 550 |
| | | Harrisonville | 0 | | 0 | 0 | 9,837 |
| | | Hartville | 0 | 0 | 0 | 0 | 604 |
| | | Hawk Point | 0 | 0 | | 0 | 590 |
| | | Hayti | 0 | 0 | 0 | 0 | 2,933 |
| | | Hayti Heights | 0 | 0 | 0 | 0 | 741 |
| | | Hazelwood | 0 | 0 | | 0 | 25,254 |
| | | Henrietta | 0 | 0 | 0 | 0 | 429 |
| | | Hermann | 0 | 0 | 0 | 0 | 2,720 |
| | | Higbee | | | 0 | | 659 |
| | | Higginsville | 0 | 0 | 0 | 0 | 4,558 |
| | | High Hill | 0 | 0 | 0 | 0 | 210 |
| | | Highlandville | 0 | 0 | 0 | 0 | 915 |
| | | Hillsboro | 0 | 0 | 0 | 0 | 2,111 |
| | | Hillsdale | 0 | 0 | 0 | 0 | 1,401 |
| | | Holcomb | 0 | 0 | 0 | 0 | 668 |
| | | Holden | 0 | 0 | 0 | 0 | 2,546 |
| | | Hollister | 0 | 0 | | 0 | 4,054 |
| | | Holt | 0 | 0 | | 0 | 477 |
| | | Holts Summit | 0 | 0 | 0 | 0 | 3,833 |
| | | Hornersville | 0 | 0 | 0 | 0 | 653 |
| | | Houston | 0 | 0 | 0 | 0 | 2,043 |
| | | Howardville | | | | 0 | 311 |
| | | Humansville | 0 | 0 | 0 | 0 | 1,025 |
| | | Huntsville | 0 | 0 | | 0 | 1,645 |
| | | Hurley | 0 | 0 | 0 | 0 | 150 |
| | | Iberia | 0 | 0 | 0 | 0 | 682 |
| | | Indian Point | 0 | 0 | 0 | 0 | 722 |
| | | Iron Mountain Lake | 0 | 0 | | 0 | 700 |
| | | Ironton | 0 | 0 | 0 | 0 | 1,310 |
| | | Jackson | 0 | 0 | 0 | 0 | 13,956 |
| | | Jasper | 0 | 0 | 0 | 0 | 1,073 |
| | | Jefferson City | 0 | 0 | 0 | 0 | 40,829 |
| | | Jennings | 0 | 0 | 0 | 0 | 14,536 |
| | | Jonesburg | 0 | 0 | 0 | 0 | 729 |
| | | Joplin | 0 | 0 | 0 | | 50,257 |
| | | Kahoka | 0 | 0 | 0 | | 2,177 |
| | | Kearney | 0 | 0 | 0 | 0 | 9,018 |
| | | Kennett | 0 | 0 | 0 | 0 | 10,649 |
| | | Kimberling City | 0 | 0 | 0 | 0 | 2,466 |
| | | Kimmswick | 0 | 0 | 0 | 0 | 111 |
| | | King City | | 0 | 0 | 0 | 879 |
| | | Kinloch | | | | 0 | 423 |
| | | Kirksville | 0 | 0 | 0 | 0 | 17,376 |
| | | Kirkwood | 0 | 0 | 0 | 0 | 26,698 |
| | | Knob Noster | 0 | 0 | 0 | 0 | 3,349 |
| | | Ladue | 0 | 0 | 0 | 0 | 8,169 |
| | | La Grange | 0 | 0 | 0 | 0 | 918 |
| | | Lake Lafayette | 0 | 0 | | 0 | 369 |
| | | Lake Lotawana | 0 | 0 | 0 | 0 | 1,963 |
| | | Lake Ozark | 0 | 0 | 0 | 0 | 2,093 |
| | | Lakeshire | 0 | 0 | 0 | 0 | 1,276 |
| | | Lake St. Louis | 0 | 0 | 0 | 0 | 14,686 |
| | | Lake Tapawingo | 0 | 0 | 0 | 0 | 780 |
| | | Lake Waukomis | 0 | 0 | 0 | 0 | 897 |
| | | Lake Winnebago | 0 | 0 | 0 | 0 | 1,168 |
| | | Lamar | 0 | 0 | 0 | 0 | 4,478 |
| | | La Monte | 0 | 0 | 0 | 0 | 1,101 |
| | | Lanagan | 0 | 0 | 0 | 0 | 432 |
| | | La Plata | 0 | 0 | 0 | 0 | 1,470 |
| | | Lathrop | 0 | | 0 | | 2,357 |
| | | Laurie | 0 | | 0 | 0 | 740 |
| | | Lawson | 0 | 0 | 0 | 0 | 2,340 |
| | | Leadington | 0 | 0 | 0 | 0 | 420 |
| | | Leadwood | 0 | 0 | | | 1,159 |
| | | Lebanon | 0 | 0 | 0 | 0 | 14,574 |
| | | Leeton | 0 | 0 | 0 | 0 | 626 |
| | | Lexington | 0 | 0 | 0 | 0 | 4,528 |
| | | Liberal | 0 | 0 | 0 | 0 | 773 |
| | | Liberty | 0 | 0 | 0 | 0 | 31,073 |
| | | Licking | 0 | 0 | 0 | 0 | 3,023 |
| | | Lincoln | 0 | 0 | 0 | 0 | 1,087 |
| | | Linn | | | 0 | 0 | 1,434 |
| | | Linn Creek | 0 | 0 | 0 | 0 | 312 |
| | | Lockwood | 0 | 0 | 0 | 0 | 910 |
| | | Lone Jack | 0 | 0 | 0 | 0 | 977 |
| | | Louisiana | 0 | | 0 | | 3,759 |
| | | Lowry City | 0 | 0 | 0 | 0 | 723 |
| | | Macon | 0 | 0 | 0 | 0 | 5,484 |
| | | Malden | 0 | 0 | 0 | 0 | 4,448 |
| | | Manchester | 0 | 0 | | 0 | 18,504 |
| | | Mansfield | 0 | 0 | 0 | 0 | 1,363 |
| | | Marble Hill | 0 | 0 | 0 | 0 | 1,479 |
| | | Marceline | 0 | | | 0 | 2,280 |
| | | Marionville | 0 | 0 | 0 | 0 | 2,183 |
| | | Marquand | 0 | 0 | 0 | 0 | 267 |
| | | Marshall | 0 | 0 | 0 | 0 | 12,055 |
| | | Marshfield | 0 | 0 | 0 | 0 | 7,463 |
| | | Marthasville | 0 | 0 | 0 | 0 | 866 |
| | | Martinsburg | 0 | 0 | 0 | 0 | 327 |
| | | Matthews | 0 | 0 | 0 | 0 | 526 |
| | | Maysville | 0 | 0 | 0 | 0 | 1,131 |
| | | Mayview | 0 | 0 | | 0 | 285 |
| | | Memphis | 0 | 0 | 0 | 0 | 1,949 |
| | | Merriam Woods | | | | 0 | 1,486 |
| | | Mexico | 0 | 0 | 0 | 0 | 11,050 |
| | | Milan | 0 | 0 | 0 | 0 | 1,754 |
| | | Miller | 0 | 0 | 0 | 0 | 801 |
| | | Miner | 0 | 0 | 0 | 0 | 1,343 |
| | | Moberly | 0 | 0 | 0 | 0 | 14,282 |
| | | Moline Acres | 0 | 0 | 0 | 0 | 2,502 |

[1]Agencies published in this table indicated that no hate crimes occurred in their jurisdictions during the quarter(s) for which they submitted reports to the Hate Crime Statistics Program. Blanks indicate quarters for which agencies did not submit reports.

[2]Population figures are published only for the cities. The figures listed for the universities and colleges are student enrollment and were provided by the United States Department of Education for the 2008 school year, the most recent available. The enrollment figures include full-time and part-time students.

## Table 95. Hate Crime Zero Data Submitted per Quarter, by State and Agency, 2009—*Continued*

(Number.)

| State | Agency type | Agency name | Zero data per quarter[1] | | | | Population[2] |
|---|---|---|---|---|---|---|---|
| | | | 1st quarter | 2nd quarter | 3rd quarter | 4th quarter | |
| **MISSOURI** | | Monett | 0 | 0 | 0 | 0 | 9,082 |
| | | Monroe City | 0 | 0 | 0 | 0 | 2,460 |
| | | Montgomery City | 0 | 0 | 0 | 0 | 2,490 |
| | | Montrose | 0 | 0 | 0 | | 419 |
| | | Morehouse | 0 | 0 | 0 | 0 | 910 |
| | | Morley | 0 | 0 | 0 | 0 | 796 |
| | | Mosby | 0 | 0 | | 0 | 250 |
| | | Moscow Mills | 0 | 0 | 0 | 0 | 2,553 |
| | | Mound City | 0 | 0 | 0 | 0 | 1,062 |
| | | Mountain Grove | | | | 0 | 4,694 |
| | | Mountain View | 0 | 0 | 0 | 0 | 2,623 |
| | | Mount Vernon | 0 | | 0 | 0 | 4,666 |
| | | Napoleon | 0 | 0 | | 0 | 195 |
| | | Naylor | 0 | 0 | 0 | 0 | 595 |
| | | Neosho | 0 | 0 | 0 | 0 | 11,398 |
| | | Nevada | 0 | 0 | 0 | 0 | 8,299 |
| | | New Bloomfield | 0 | 0 | 0 | 0 | 750 |
| | | Newburg | 0 | 0 | 0 | 0 | 465 |
| | | New Florence | 0 | 0 | 0 | 0 | 750 |
| | | New Franklin | | | | 0 | 1,108 |
| | | New Haven | 0 | 0 | 0 | 0 | 2,045 |
| | | New London | 0 | 0 | 0 | 0 | 1,010 |
| | | New Madrid | 0 | 0 | 0 | 0 | 2,980 |
| | | New Melle | 0 | 0 | 0 | 0 | 281 |
| | | Niangua | 0 | 0 | | 0 | 499 |
| | | Nixa | 0 | 0 | 0 | 0 | 19,782 |
| | | Noel | 0 | 0 | 0 | 0 | 1,624 |
| | | Norborne | 0 | | | 0 | 748 |
| | | Normandy | 0 | 0 | 0 | 0 | 4,866 |
| | | North Kansas City | 0 | 0 | 0 | 0 | 5,876 |
| | | Northmoor | 0 | 0 | 0 | 0 | 399 |
| | | Northwoods | 0 | 0 | 0 | 0 | 4,276 |
| | | Norwood | 0 | 0 | 0 | 0 | 581 |
| | | Oak Grove | | | | 0 | 7,010 |
| | | Oakland | 0 | 0 | 0 | 0 | 1,557 |
| | | Oakview Village | 0 | 0 | 0 | 0 | 397 |
| | | Odessa | 0 | 0 | 0 | 0 | 4,725 |
| | | Old Monroe | | | | 0 | 313 |
| | | Olivette | 0 | 0 | 0 | 0 | 7,449 |
| | | Oregon | 0 | 0 | | | 866 |
| | | Orrick | 0 | 0 | 0 | 0 | 815 |
| | | Osage Beach | 0 | 0 | 0 | 0 | 4,845 |
| | | Osceola | 0 | 0 | 0 | 0 | 780 |
| | | Overland | 0 | 0 | 0 | 0 | 15,507 |
| | | Owensville | 0 | 0 | | 0 | 2,583 |
| | | Ozark | 0 | 0 | 0 | 0 | 19,259 |
| | | Pacific | 0 | 0 | 0 | 0 | 7,345 |
| | | Pagedale | 0 | 0 | 0 | 0 | 3,379 |
| | | Palmyra | 0 | 0 | 0 | 0 | 3,410 |
| | | Park Hills | 0 | | | | 8,966 |
| | | Parkville | 0 | 0 | 0 | 0 | 5,417 |
| | | Parma | 0 | 0 | 0 | 0 | 731 |
| | | Pasadena Park | 0 | 0 | 0 | 0 | 454 |
| | | Peculiar | 0 | 0 | 0 | 0 | 4,928 |
| | | Perry | 0 | 0 | 0 | 0 | 663 |
| | | Perryville | 0 | 0 | 0 | 0 | 8,222 |
| | | Pevely | 0 | 0 | 0 | 0 | 6,098 |
| | | Piedmont | 0 | 0 | | 0 | 1,905 |
| | | Pierce City | 0 | 0 | 0 | 0 | 1,473 |
| | | Pilot Grove | 0 | 0 | 0 | 0 | 746 |
| | | Pilot Knob | | | | 0 | 667 |
| | | Pine Lawn | 0 | 0 | 0 | 0 | 3,964 |
| | | Pineville | 0 | | | 0 | 865 |
| | | Platte City | 0 | 0 | 0 | 0 | 4,920 |
| | | Platte Woods | 0 | 0 | | | 455 |
| | | Plattsburg | 0 | 0 | | 0 | 2,424 |
| | | Pleasant Hill | 0 | 0 | 0 | 0 | 7,374 |
| | | Pleasant Hope | 0 | 0 | 0 | 0 | 604 |
| | | Pleasant Valley | 0 | 0 | | 0 | 3,548 |
| | | Polo | | | | 0 | 603 |
| | | Poplar Bluff | 0 | 0 | | 0 | 17,109 |
| | | Portageville | 0 | 0 | | 0 | 2,875 |
| | | Potosi | | 0 | 0 | 0 | 2,702 |
| | | Purdy | 0 | 0 | 0 | 0 | 1,164 |
| | | Puxico | | | 0 | 0 | 1,138 |
| | | Queen City | 0 | 0 | 0 | 0 | 608 |
| | | Qulin | 0 | 0 | 0 | 0 | 480 |
| | | Randolph | 0 | 0 | 0 | 0 | 51 |
| | | Raymore | 0 | 0 | 0 | 0 | 18,620 |
| | | Reeds Spring | 0 | 0 | 0 | 0 | 786 |
| | | Republic | 0 | 0 | 0 | 0 | 14,380 |
| | | Rich Hill | 0 | 0 | 0 | 0 | 1,497 |
| | | Richland | 0 | 0 | 0 | 0 | 1,778 |
| | | Richmond | 0 | 0 | 0 | 0 | 5,865 |
| | | Richmond Heights | 0 | 0 | 0 | 0 | 9,040 |
| | | Riverside | 0 | 0 | 0 | | 2,987 |
| | | Riverview | | 0 | 0 | 0 | 2,895 |
| | | Rockaway Beach | 0 | 0 | 0 | 0 | 597 |
| | | Rock Hill | 0 | | 0 | 0 | 4,561 |
| | | Rock Port | 0 | 0 | 0 | 0 | 1,284 |
| | | Rogersville | 0 | 0 | 0 | 0 | 3,278 |
| | | Rosebud | 0 | | 0 | 0 | 384 |
| | | Salem | 0 | 0 | 0 | 0 | 4,873 |
| | | Salisbury | 0 | 0 | 0 | 0 | 1,541 |
| | | Sarcoxie | 0 | | | 0 | 1,379 |
| | | Savannah | 0 | 0 | 0 | 0 | 5,107 |
| | | Scott City | 0 | 0 | 0 | 0 | 4,533 |
| | | Sedalia | 0 | 0 | 0 | 0 | 21,065 |
| | | Seligman | 0 | 0 | 0 | 0 | 950 |
| | | Senath | 0 | | | 0 | 1,579 |
| | | Seneca | 0 | 0 | 0 | 0 | 2,282 |
| | | Seymour | 0 | 0 | 0 | 0 | 2,101 |
| | | Shelbina | | 0 | 0 | 0 | 1,778 |
| | | Shrewsbury | 0 | 0 | 0 | 0 | 6,192 |
| | | Sikeston | 0 | 0 | 0 | 0 | 17,063 |
| | | Silex | 0 | | 0 | | 249 |
| | | Slater | 0 | 0 | 0 | 0 | 1,881 |
| | | Southwest City | 0 | 0 | 0 | 0 | 930 |
| | | Sparta | 0 | 0 | 0 | 0 | 1,204 |
| | | St. Ann | 0 | 0 | 0 | 0 | 12,678 |
| | | St. Charles | 0 | 0 | 0 | 0 | 64,807 |
| | | St. Clair | 0 | 0 | 0 | 0 | 4,475 |
| | | Steele | 0 | 0 | 0 | 0 | 2,076 |
| | | Ste. Genevieve | 0 | 0 | 0 | 0 | 4,407 |
| | | Stewartsville | 0 | 0 | | 0 | 740 |
| | | St. James | 0 | 0 | 0 | 0 | 4,045 |
| | | St. John | 0 | 0 | 0 | 0 | 6,330 |
| | | St. Joseph | 0 | 0 | 0 | 0 | 76,436 |
| | | St. Marys | 0 | 0 | 0 | 0 | 380 |
| | | Stover | 0 | 0 | 0 | 0 | 1,051 |
| | | Strafford | 0 | 0 | 0 | 0 | 2,218 |
| | | Strasburg | 0 | 0 | 0 | 0 | 136 |
| | | St. Robert | 0 | 0 | 0 | 0 | 3,525 |
| | | Sugar Creek | 0 | 0 | 0 | 0 | 3,498 |
| | | Sullivan | 0 | 0 | 0 | 0 | 6,769 |
| | | Sunset Hills | 0 | 0 | 0 | 0 | 8,181 |
| | | Sweet Springs | 0 | | 0 | 0 | 1,505 |
| | | Tarkio | 0 | 0 | 0 | 0 | 1,793 |
| | | Thayer | 0 | 0 | 0 | 0 | 2,145 |
| | | Theodosia | 0 | 0 | 0 | 0 | 250 |
| | | Tipton | 0 | 0 | 0 | 0 | 3,284 |
| | | Town and Country | 0 | 0 | 0 | 0 | 10,692 |
| | | Tracy | 0 | 0 | 0 | 0 | 209 |
| | | Trenton | 0 | 0 | 0 | 0 | 6,030 |
| | | Trimble | | 0 | | 0 | 478 |
| | | Troy | 0 | 0 | 0 | 0 | 13,093 |
| | | Truesdale | 0 | 0 | 0 | 0 | 701 |
| | | Union | 0 | 0 | 0 | 0 | 9,932 |
| | | Unionville | | | 0 | | 1,846 |
| | | University City | 0 | 0 | 0 | 0 | 36,135 |
| | | Uplands Park | 0 | 0 | 0 | 0 | 435 |
| | | Urbana | 0 | 0 | 0 | 0 | 436 |

[1]Agencies published in this table indicated that no hate crimes occurred in their jurisdictions during the quarter(s) for which they submitted reports to the Hate Crime Statistics Program. Blanks indicate quarters for which agencies did not submit reports.

[2]Population figures are published only for the cities. The figures listed for the universities and colleges are student enrollment and were provided by the United States Department of Education for the 2008 school year, the most recent available. The enrollment figures include full-time and part-time students.

## Table 95. Hate Crime Zero Data Submitted per Quarter, by State and Agency, 2009—*Continued*

(Number.)

| State | Agency type | Agency name | Zero data per quarter[1] 1st quarter | 2nd quarter | 3rd quarter | 4th quarter | Population[2] |
|---|---|---|---|---|---|---|---|
| **MISSOURI** | | Van Buren | 0 | 0 | 0 | 0 | 812 |
| | | Vandalia | 0 | 0 | 0 | | 4,404 |
| | | Velda City | 0 | 0 | 0 | 0 | 1,485 |
| | | Velda Village Hills | 0 | | 0 | 0 | 1,029 |
| | | Verona | 0 | 0 | 0 | 0 | 725 |
| | | Versailles | 0 | 0 | 0 | 0 | 2,732 |
| | | Viburnum | 0 | 0 | 0 | 0 | 778 |
| | | Vienna | 0 | 0 | | 0 | 639 |
| | | Vinita Park | 0 | 0 | 0 | 0 | 1,769 |
| | | Walnut Grove | 0 | 0 | 0 | 0 | 671 |
| | | Wardell | 0 | | 0 | 0 | 395 |
| | | Warrenton | 0 | 0 | 0 | 0 | 7,664 |
| | | Warsaw | 0 | 0 | 0 | 0 | 2,236 |
| | | Warson Woods | 0 | 0 | 0 | 0 | 1,853 |
| | | Washburn | 0 | 0 | 0 | 0 | 485 |
| | | Washington | 0 | 0 | 0 | 0 | 14,516 |
| | | Waverly | | | 0 | 0 | 785 |
| | | Waynesville | 0 | 0 | 0 | 0 | 4,006 |
| | | Weatherby Lake | 0 | 0 | 0 | 0 | 1,862 |
| | | Webb City | 0 | 0 | 0 | 0 | 11,734 |
| | | Webster Groves | 0 | 0 | 0 | 0 | 22,237 |
| | | Wellington | | | | 0 | 760 |
| | | Wellston | 0 | 0 | | | 2,295 |
| | | Wellsville | 0 | 0 | 0 | 0 | 1,314 |
| | | Wentzville | 0 | 0 | 0 | 0 | 27,090 |
| | | Weston | 0 | 0 | 0 | 0 | 1,666 |
| | | West Plains | 0 | 0 | 0 | 0 | 12,175 |
| | | Wheaton | 0 | 0 | | 0 | 752 |
| | | Willow Springs | 0 | 0 | 0 | 0 | 2,158 |
| | | Winfield | 0 | 0 | 0 | 0 | 1,199 |
| | | Winona | 0 | 0 | 0 | 0 | 1,330 |
| | | Wood Heights | | 0 | 0 | 0 | 749 |
| | | Woodson Terrace | | 0 | 0 | 0 | 3,986 |
| | | Wright City | 0 | 0 | 0 | 0 | 3,168 |
| | **Universities and Colleges** | Lincoln University | 0 | | 0 | 0 | 3,109 |
| | | Mineral Area College | 0 | | 0 | 0 | 3,238 |
| | | Missouri University of Science and Technology | 0 | 0 | | 0 | 6,367 |
| | | Missouri Western State University | 0 | 0 | 0 | 0 | 5,508 |
| | | Southeast Missouri State University | 0 | 0 | 0 | 0 | 10,736 |
| | | St. Louis Community College: Florissant Valley | 0 | 0 | 0 | 0 | 6,514 |
| | | Meramec | 0 | 0 | 0 | 0 | 10,209 |
| | | Three Rivers Community College | | | | 0 | 3,114 |
| | | Truman State University | 0 | 0 | 0 | 0 | 5,880 |
| | | University of Central Missouri | 0 | 0 | 0 | 0 | 11,063 |
| | | University of Missouri: Kansas City | 0 | 0 | 0 | 0 | 14,481 |
| | | St. Louis | 0 | 0 | 0 | 0 | 15,741 |
| | | Washington University | 0 | 0 | 0 | 0 | 13,339 |

| State | Agency type | Agency name | Zero data per quarter[1] 1st quarter | 2nd quarter | 3rd quarter | 4th quarter | Population[2] |
|---|---|---|---|---|---|---|---|
| | **Metropolitan Counties** | Andrew | 0 | 0 | 0 | 0 | |
| | | Bates | 0 | 0 | | 0 | |
| | | Bollinger | 0 | 0 | 0 | 0 | |
| | | Boone | 0 | 0 | 0 | 0 | |
| | | Buchanan | 0 | 0 | 0 | 0 | |
| | | Caldwell | 0 | 0 | 0 | 0 | |
| | | Callaway | 0 | 0 | 0 | 0 | |
| | | Cape Girardeau | 0 | 0 | 0 | 0 | |
| | | Cass | 0 | 0 | 0 | 0 | |
| | | Christian | 0 | 0 | 0 | 0 | |
| | | Clay | 0 | 0 | 0 | 0 | |
| | | Clinton | 0 | 0 | 0 | 0 | |
| | | Cole | 0 | 0 | 0 | 0 | |
| | | Dallas | 0 | 0 | 0 | 0 | |
| | | De Kalb | 0 | 0 | 0 | 0 | |
| | | Franklin | 0 | 0 | 0 | 0 | |
| | | Howard | 0 | 0 | 0 | 0 | |
| | | Jackson | 0 | 0 | 0 | 0 | |
| | | Jasper | 0 | 0 | 0 | 0 | |
| | | Lafayette | 0 | 0 | 0 | 0 | |
| | | Lincoln | 0 | 0 | 0 | 0 | |
| | | McDonald | 0 | 0 | 0 | 0 | |
| | | Moniteau | 0 | 0 | 0 | 0 | |
| | | Newton | 0 | 0 | 0 | 0 | |
| | | Osage | 0 | 0 | 0 | 0 | |
| | | Platte | 0 | 0 | 0 | 0 | |
| | | Polk | 0 | 0 | 0 | 0 | |
| | | Ray | 0 | 0 | 0 | 0 | |
| | | Washington | 0 | 0 | | 0 | |
| | | Webster | 0 | 0 | 0 | 0 | |
| | **Nonmetropolitan Counties** | Adair | 0 | 0 | 0 | 0 | |
| | | Atchison | 0 | 0 | 0 | 0 | |
| | | Barry | 0 | 0 | 0 | 0 | |
| | | Barton | | 0 | 0 | 0 | |
| | | Benton | 0 | 0 | 0 | 0 | |
| | | Butler | 0 | 0 | 0 | 0 | |
| | | Camden | 0 | 0 | 0 | 0 | |
| | | Carroll | 0 | 0 | 0 | 0 | |
| | | Carter | 0 | 0 | 0 | 0 | |
| | | Cedar | 0 | 0 | 0 | 0 | |
| | | Clark | 0 | 0 | | 0 | |
| | | Cooper | 0 | 0 | 0 | 0 | |
| | | Crawford | 0 | 0 | 0 | 0 | |
| | | Dade | 0 | 0 | | | |
| | | Daviess | 0 | 0 | 0 | 0 | |
| | | Dent | 0 | 0 | 0 | 0 | |
| | | Douglas | 0 | 0 | 0 | 0 | |
| | | Dunklin | 0 | 0 | 0 | 0 | |
| | | Gasconade | 0 | 0 | 0 | 0 | |
| | | Gentry | 0 | | 0 | 0 | |
| | | Grundy | 0 | 0 | 0 | 0 | |
| | | Harrison | 0 | 0 | 0 | 0 | |
| | | Henry | 0 | 0 | 0 | 0 | |
| | | Hickory | 0 | 0 | 0 | 0 | |
| | | Holt | 0 | 0 | 0 | 0 | |
| | | Howell | 0 | | 0 | 0 | |
| | | Iron | 0 | 0 | | 0 | |
| | | Johnson | 0 | 0 | 0 | 0 | |
| | | Knox | 0 | 0 | 0 | 0 | |
| | | Laclede | 0 | 0 | 0 | 0 | |
| | | Lawrence | 0 | 0 | 0 | 0 | |
| | | Lewis | 0 | 0 | 0 | 0 | |
| | | Linn | 0 | 0 | 0 | 0 | |
| | | Livingston | 0 | 0 | 0 | 0 | |
| | | Macon | 0 | 0 | 0 | 0 | |
| | | Madison | 0 | 0 | 0 | 0 | |
| | | Maries | 0 | 0 | 0 | 0 | |
| | | Marion | 0 | 0 | 0 | 0 | |
| | | Mercer | 0 | 0 | 0 | 0 | |
| | | Miller | | | 0 | | |

[1]Agencies published in this table indicated that no hate crimes occurred in their jurisdictions during the quarter(s) for which they submitted reports to the Hate Crime Statistics Program. Blanks indicate quarters for which agencies did not submit reports.

[2]Population figures are published only for the cities. The figures listed for the universities and colleges are student enrollment and were provided by the United States Department of Education for the 2008 school year, the most recent available. The enrollment figures include full-time and part-time students.

## Table 95. Hate Crime Zero Data Submitted per Quarter, by State and Agency, 2009—*Continued*

(Number.)

| State | Agency type | Agency name | Zero data per quarter[1] | | | | Population[2] |
|---|---|---|---|---|---|---|---|
| | | | 1st quarter | 2nd quarter | 3rd quarter | 4th quarter | |
| **MISSOURI** | | Mississippi | 0 | 0 | 0 | 0 | |
| | | Monroe | 0 | 0 | 0 | 0 | |
| | | Montgomery | 0 | 0 | 0 | 0 | |
| | | Morgan | 0 | 0 | 0 | 0 | |
| | | New Madrid | 0 | 0 | 0 | 0 | |
| | | Nodaway | 0 | 0 | 0 | 0 | |
| | | Oregon | 0 | | 0 | 0 | |
| | | Ozark | 0 | 0 | 0 | 0 | |
| | | Pemiscot | 0 | 0 | 0 | 0 | |
| | | Perry | 0 | 0 | 0 | 0 | |
| | | Pettis | 0 | 0 | 0 | 0 | |
| | | Phelps | 0 | 0 | 0 | 0 | |
| | | Pike | 0 | 0 | 0 | 0 | |
| | | Pulaski | 0 | 0 | 0 | 0 | |
| | | Putnam | 0 | | | | |
| | | Ralls | 0 | 0 | 0 | 0 | |
| | | Randolph | 0 | 0 | 0 | 0 | |
| | | Reynolds | 0 | | 0 | 0 | |
| | | Ripley | 0 | 0 | 0 | 0 | |
| | | Saline | 0 | 0 | 0 | 0 | |
| | | Schuyler | 0 | | | | |
| | | Scotland | | | 0 | | |
| | | Scott | 0 | 0 | 0 | 0 | |
| | | Shelby | 0 | 0 | 0 | 0 | |
| | | St. Clair | 0 | 0 | 0 | 0 | |
| | | Ste. Genevieve | 0 | 0 | 0 | 0 | |
| | | St. Francois | 0 | | 0 | 0 | |
| | | Stoddard | 0 | 0 | 0 | 0 | |
| | | Stone | 0 | 0 | 0 | 0 | |
| | | Sullivan | 0 | 0 | 0 | 0 | |
| | | Taney | 0 | 0 | 0 | 0 | |
| | | Texas | 0 | 0 | 0 | 0 | |
| | | Vernon | | 0 | 0 | 0 | |
| | | Wayne | 0 | | | | |
| | | Worth | 0 | 0 | 0 | 0 | |
| | | Wright | 0 | | | 0 | |
| | **State Police Agencies** | State Highway Patrol: | | | | | |
| | | Jefferson City | 0 | 0 | 0 | 0 | |
| | | Kirkwood | 0 | 0 | 0 | 0 | |
| | | Lee's Summit | 0 | 0 | 0 | 0 | |
| | | Macon | 0 | 0 | | 0 | |
| | | Poplar Bluff | 0 | 0 | 0 | 0 | |
| | | Rolla | 0 | 0 | 0 | 0 | |
| | | Springfield | 0 | 0 | 0 | 0 | |
| | | St. Joseph | 0 | 0 | 0 | 0 | |
| | | Willow Springs | 0 | 0 | 0 | 0 | |
| | **Other Agencies** | Bootheel Drug Task Force | 0 | 0 | | | |
| | | Capitol Police | 0 | 0 | | 0 | |
| | | Clay County Drug Task Force | 0 | 0 | | | |
| | | Clay County Park Authority | 0 | 0 | 0 | 0 | |
| | | Department of Conservation | 0 | 0 | | | |
| | | Division of Alcohol and Tobacco Control | 0 | 0 | | | |
| | | Gaming Commission, Enforcement Division | 0 | 0 | 0 | 0 | |
| | | Jackson County Drug Task Force | 0 | 0 | | | |
| | | Jackson County Park Rangers | 0 | 0 | 0 | 0 | |

| State | Agency type | Agency name | Zero data per quarter[1] | | | | Population[2] |
|---|---|---|---|---|---|---|---|
| | | | 1st quarter | 2nd quarter | 3rd quarter | 4th quarter | |
| | | Lambert-St. Louis International Airport | 0 | 0 | 0 | 0 | |
| | | Platte County Multi-Jurisdictional Enforcement Group | 0 | 0 | | | |
| | | Springfield-Branson Airport | 0 | 0 | 0 | 0 | |
| | | State Fire Marshal | 0 | 0 | 0 | 0 | |
| | | State Park Rangers | 0 | 0 | 0 | 0 | |
| | | State Water Patrol | 0 | 0 | 0 | 0 | |
| | | St. Charles County Park Rangers | 0 | 0 | 0 | 0 | |
| | | St. Peters Ranger Division | 0 | 0 | 0 | 0 | |
| **MONTANA....** | **Cities** | Baker | 0 | 0 | 0 | 0 | 1,629 |
| | | Boulder | 0 | 0 | 0 | 0 | 1,458 |
| | | Bridger | 0 | 0 | 0 | 0 | 723 |
| | | Colstrip | 0 | 0 | 0 | 0 | 2,345 |
| | | Columbia Falls | 0 | 0 | 0 | 0 | 5,441 |
| | | Columbus | 0 | 0 | 0 | 0 | 1,982 |
| | | Cut Bank | 0 | 0 | 0 | 0 | 3,106 |
| | | Dillon | 0 | 0 | 0 | 0 | 4,186 |
| | | East Helena | 0 | 0 | 0 | 0 | 2,173 |
| | | Ennis | 0 | 0 | 0 | 0 | 1,081 |
| | | Fort Benton | 0 | 0 | 0 | 0 | 1,445 |
| | | Glasgow | 0 | 0 | 0 | 0 | 2,888 |
| | | Glendive | 0 | 0 | 0 | 0 | 4,555 |
| | | Great Falls | 0 | 0 | 0 | 0 | 59,499 |
| | | Hamilton | 0 | 0 | 0 | 0 | 4,951 |
| | | Havre | 0 | 0 | 0 | 0 | 9,572 |
| | | Hot Springs | 0 | 0 | 0 | 0 | 568 |
| | | Joliet | 0 | 0 | 0 | 0 | 631 |
| | | Kalispell | 0 | 0 | 0 | 0 | 21,986 |
| | | Laurel | 0 | 0 | 0 | 0 | 6,645 |
| | | Lewistown | 0 | 0 | 0 | 0 | 5,915 |
| | | Libby | 0 | 0 | 0 | 0 | 2,925 |
| | | Livingston | 0 | 0 | 0 | 0 | 7,550 |
| | | Manhattan | 0 | 0 | 0 | 0 | 1,649 |
| | | Miles City | 0 | 0 | 0 | 0 | 8,062 |
| | | Plains | 0 | 0 | 0 | 0 | 1,257 |
| | | Polson | 0 | 0 | 0 | 0 | 5,356 |
| | | Poplar | 0 | 0 | 0 | 0 | 861 |
| | | Red Lodge | 0 | 0 | 0 | 0 | 2,481 |
| | | Ronan City | 0 | 0 | 0 | 0 | 2,030 |
| | | Sidney | 0 | 0 | 0 | 0 | 4,759 |
| | | Stevensville | 0 | 0 | 0 | 0 | 2,036 |
| | | St. Ignatius | 0 | 0 | 0 | 0 | 816 |
| | | Thompson Falls | 0 | 0 | 0 | 0 | 1,435 |
| | | Three Forks | 0 | 0 | 0 | 0 | 1,951 |
| | | Troy | 0 | 0 | 0 | 0 | 987 |
| | | West Yellowstone | 0 | 0 | 0 | 0 | 1,554 |
| | | Wolf Point | 0 | 0 | 0 | 0 | 2,492 |
| | **Universities and Colleges** | Montana State University | 0 | 0 | 0 | 0 | 11,976 |
| | | University of Montana | 0 | 0 | 0 | 0 | 14,207 |
| | **Metropolitan Counties** | Carbon | 0 | 0 | 0 | 0 | |
| | | Cascade | 0 | 0 | 0 | 0 | |
| | | Yellowstone | 0 | 0 | 0 | 0 | |

[1]Agencies published in this table indicated that no hate crimes occurred in their jurisdictions during the quarter(s) for which they submitted reports to the Hate Crime Statistics Program. Blanks indicate quarters for which agencies did not submit reports.

[2]Population figures are published only for the cities. The figures listed for the universities and colleges are student enrollment and were provided by the United States Department of Education for the 2008 school year, the most recent available. The enrollment figures include full-time and part-time students.

## Table 95. Hate Crime Zero Data Submitted per Quarter, by State and Agency, 2009—*Continued*

(Number.)

| State | Agency type | Agency name | Zero data per quarter[1] | | | | Population[2] |
|---|---|---|---|---|---|---|---|
| | | | 1st quarter | 2nd quarter | 3rd quarter | 4th quarter | |
| **MONTANA** | **Nonmetropolitan Counties** | Beaverhead | 0 | 0 | 0 | 0 | |
| | | Big Horn | 0 | 0 | 0 | 0 | |
| | | Blaine | 0 | 0 | 0 | 0 | |
| | | Broadwater | 0 | 0 | 0 | 0 | |
| | | Carter | 0 | 0 | 0 | 0 | |
| | | Chouteau | 0 | 0 | 0 | 0 | |
| | | Custer | 0 | 0 | 0 | 0 | |
| | | Daniels | 0 | 0 | 0 | 0 | |
| | | Dawson | 0 | 0 | 0 | 0 | |
| | | Deer Lodge | 0 | 0 | 0 | 0 | |
| | | Fallon | 0 | 0 | 0 | 0 | |
| | | Fergus | 0 | 0 | 0 | 0 | |
| | | Gallatin | 0 | 0 | 0 | 0 | |
| | | Garfield | 0 | 0 | 0 | 0 | |
| | | Glacier | 0 | 0 | 0 | 0 | |
| | | Golden Valley | 0 | | | | |
| | | Granite | 0 | 0 | 0 | 0 | |
| | | Hill | 0 | 0 | 0 | 0 | |
| | | Jefferson | 0 | 0 | 0 | 0 | |
| | | Judith Basin | 0 | 0 | 0 | 0 | |
| | | Lake | 0 | 0 | 0 | 0 | |
| | | Lincoln | 0 | 0 | 0 | 0 | |
| | | Madison | 0 | 0 | 0 | 0 | |
| | | McCone | 0 | 0 | 0 | 0 | |
| | | Meagher | 0 | 0 | 0 | 0 | |
| | | Mineral | 0 | 0 | 0 | 0 | |
| | | Musselshell | 0 | 0 | 0 | 0 | |
| | | Phillips | 0 | 0 | 0 | 0 | |
| | | Pondera | 0 | 0 | 0 | 0 | |
| | | Powell | 0 | 0 | 0 | 0 | |
| | | Prairie | 0 | 0 | 0 | 0 | |
| | | Richland | 0 | 0 | 0 | 0 | |
| | | Roosevelt | 0 | 0 | 0 | 0 | |
| | | Rosebud | 0 | 0 | 0 | 0 | |
| | | Sanders | 0 | 0 | 0 | 0 | |
| | | Sheridan | 0 | 0 | 0 | 0 | |
| | | Stillwater | 0 | 0 | 0 | 0 | |
| | | Sweet Grass | 0 | 0 | 0 | 0 | |
| | | Teton | 0 | 0 | 0 | 0 | |
| | | Toole | 0 | 0 | 0 | 0 | |
| | | Valley | 0 | 0 | 0 | 0 | |
| | | Wheatland | | 0 | | | |
| | | Wibaux | 0 | 0 | 0 | 0 | |
| **NEBRASKA** .. | **Cities** | Alliance | 0 | 0 | 0 | 0 | 8,024 |
| | | Auburn | | | 0 | 0 | 3,340 |
| | | Aurora | 0 | 0 | 0 | 0 | 4,195 |
| | | Beatrice | 0 | 0 | 0 | 0 | 12,793 |
| | | Bellevue | 0 | 0 | 0 | 0 | 50,311 |
| | | Blair | 0 | 0 | 0 | 0 | 7,820 |
| | | Broken Bow | 0 | 0 | 0 | 0 | 3,119 |
| | | Central City | 0 | 0 | 0 | 0 | 2,810 |
| | | Chadron | 0 | 0 | 0 | 0 | 5,409 |
| | | Columbus | 0 | 0 | 0 | 0 | 21,652 |
| | | Cozad | 0 | 0 | 0 | 0 | 4,222 |
| | | Crete | 0 | 0 | 0 | 0 | 6,258 |
| | | Emerson | 0 | 0 | 0 | 0 | 819 |
| | | Fremont | 0 | 0 | 0 | 0 | 25,220 |
| | | Gering | 0 | 0 | 0 | 0 | 7,672 |
| | | Gordon | 0 | 0 | 0 | 0 | 1,474 |
| | | Gothenburg | 0 | 0 | 0 | 0 | 3,695 |
| | | Grand Island | 0 | 0 | 0 | 0 | 46,083 |
| | | Holdrege | 0 | 0 | 0 | 0 | 5,122 |
| | | La Vista | 0 | 0 | 0 | 0 | 17,293 |
| | | Lexington | 0 | 0 | 0 | 0 | 10,138 |
| | | Lyons | 0 | 0 | 0 | 0 | 847 |
| | | Madison | 0 | 0 | 0 | 0 | 2,168 |
| | | McCook | 0 | 0 | 0 | 0 | 7,377 |
| | | Minden | 0 | 0 | 0 | 0 | 2,782 |
| | | Nebraska City | 0 | 0 | 0 | 0 | 7,011 |
| | | Norfolk | 0 | 0 | 0 | 0 | 22,892 |
| | | North Platte | 0 | 0 | 0 | 0 | 24,127 |
| | | Ogallala | 0 | 0 | 0 | 0 | 4,361 |
| | | Plattsmouth | | | | 0 | 6,902 |

| State | Agency type | Agency name | Zero data per quarter[1] | | | | Population[2] |
|---|---|---|---|---|---|---|---|
| | | | 1st quarter | 2nd quarter | 3rd quarter | 4th quarter | |
| | | Scottsbluff | 0 | 0 | 0 | 0 | 14,773 |
| | | Scribner | 0 | 0 | 0 | 0 | 952 |
| | | Seward | 0 | 0 | 0 | 0 | 6,883 |
| | | Sidney | 0 | 0 | 0 | 0 | 6,514 |
| | | St. Paul | 0 | 0 | 0 | 0 | 2,197 |
| | | Tecumseh | 0 | 0 | 0 | 0 | 1,563 |
| | | Valentine | 0 | 0 | 0 | 0 | 2,568 |
| | | Wahoo | 0 | 0 | 0 | 0 | 3,968 |
| | | West Point | 0 | 0 | 0 | 0 | 3,322 |
| | | Wilber | 0 | 0 | 0 | 0 | 1,725 |
| | | Wymore | 0 | 0 | 0 | 0 | 1,580 |
| | | York | 0 | 0 | 0 | 0 | 7,847 |
| | **Universities and Colleges** | University of Nebraska, Kearney | 0 | 0 | 0 | 0 | 6,543 |
| | **Metropolitan Counties** | Cass | 0 | 0 | 0 | 0 | |
| | | Dixon | 0 | 0 | 0 | 0 | |
| | | Lancaster | 0 | 0 | 0 | 0 | |
| | | Sarpy | 0 | 0 | 0 | 0 | |
| | | Seward | 0 | 0 | | | |
| | | Washington | 0 | 0 | 0 | | |
| | **Nonmetropolitan Counties** | Adams | 0 | 0 | 0 | 0 | |
| | | Arthur | 0 | 0 | 0 | 0 | |
| | | Buffalo | 0 | 0 | 0 | 0 | |
| | | Cedar | 0 | 0 | | | |
| | | Cuming | 0 | 0 | | | |
| | | Custer | 0 | 0 | 0 | 0 | |
| | | Dawson | 0 | 0 | 0 | 0 | |
| | | Deuel | 0 | 0 | 0 | 0 | |
| | | Dodge | 0 | 0 | 0 | 0 | |
| | | Furnas | 0 | | | | |
| | | Gage | 0 | 0 | 0 | 0 | |
| | | Gosper | 0 | 0 | 0 | 0 | |
| | | Hall | 0 | 0 | 0 | 0 | |
| | | Hamilton | 0 | 0 | 0 | 0 | |
| | | Harlan | 0 | 0 | 0 | 0 | |
| | | Hooker | 0 | 0 | 0 | 0 | |
| | | Jefferson | 0 | 0 | 0 | 0 | |
| | | Kearney | 0 | 0 | 0 | 0 | |
| | | Keith | 0 | 0 | 0 | 0 | |
| | | Kimball | | 0 | 0 | 0 | |
| | | Lincoln | | | 0 | 0 | |
| | | Madison | 0 | 0 | 0 | 0 | |
| | | Morrill | 0 | 0 | 0 | 0 | |
| | | Nance | 0 | 0 | 0 | 0 | |
| | | Nemaha | 0 | 0 | 0 | 0 | |
| | | Otoe | 0 | | | | |
| | | Pawnee | 0 | 0 | 0 | 0 | |
| | | Perkins | 0 | 0 | 0 | 0 | |
| | | Phelps | 0 | 0 | 0 | 0 | |
| | | Platte | 0 | 0 | 0 | 0 | |
| | | Polk | 0 | 0 | 0 | 0 | |
| | | Red Willow | 0 | 0 | 0 | 0 | |
| | | Rock | 0 | 0 | 0 | 0 | |
| | | Scotts Bluff | 0 | 0 | 0 | 0 | |
| | | Sherman | 0 | 0 | 0 | 0 | |
| | | Stanton | 0 | 0 | 0 | 0 | |
| | | Thayer | 0 | 0 | 0 | 0 | |
| | | Wayne | 0 | 0 | 0 | 0 | |
| | | Wheeler | 0 | 0 | 0 | 0 | |
| | | York | 0 | 0 | 0 | 0 | |
| | **State Police Agencies** | Nebraska State Patrol | 0 | 0 | 0 | 0 | |
| | | State Patrol: | | | | | |
| | | Adams County | 0 | 0 | 0 | 0 | |
| | | Antelope County | 0 | 0 | 0 | 0 | |
| | | Arthur County | 0 | 0 | 0 | 0 | |
| | | Banner County | 0 | 0 | 0 | 0 | |

[1] Agencies published in this table indicated that no hate crimes occurred in their jurisdictions during the quarter(s) for which they submitted reports to the Hate Crime Statistics Program. Blanks indicate quarters for which agencies did not submit reports.

[2] Population figures are published only for the cities. The figures listed for the universities and colleges are student enrollment and were provided by the United States Department of Education for the 2008 school year, the most recent available. The enrollment figures include full-time and part-time students.

## Table 95. Hate Crime Zero Data Submitted per Quarter, by State and Agency, 2009—*Continued*

(Number.)

| State | Agency type | Agency name | Zero data per quarter[1] | | | | Population[2] |
|---|---|---|---|---|---|---|---|
| | | | 1st quarter | 2nd quarter | 3rd quarter | 4th quarter | |
| NEBRASKA | | Blaine County | 0 | 0 | 0 | 0 | |
| | | Boone County | 0 | 0 | 0 | 0 | |
| | | Box Butte County | 0 | 0 | 0 | 0 | |
| | | Boyd County | 0 | 0 | 0 | 0 | |
| | | Brown County | 0 | 0 | 0 | 0 | |
| | | Buffalo County | 0 | 0 | 0 | 0 | |
| | | Burt County | 0 | 0 | 0 | 0 | |
| | | Butler County | 0 | 0 | 0 | 0 | |
| | | Cass County | 0 | 0 | 0 | 0 | |
| | | Cedar County | 0 | 0 | 0 | 0 | |
| | | Chase County | 0 | 0 | 0 | 0 | |
| | | Cherry County | 0 | 0 | 0 | 0 | |
| | | Cheyenne County | 0 | 0 | 0 | 0 | |
| | | Clay County | 0 | 0 | 0 | 0 | |
| | | Colfax County | 0 | 0 | 0 | 0 | |
| | | Cuming County | 0 | 0 | 0 | 0 | |
| | | Custer County | 0 | 0 | 0 | 0 | |
| | | Dakota County | 0 | 0 | 0 | 0 | |
| | | Dawes County | 0 | 0 | 0 | 0 | |
| | | Dawson County | 0 | 0 | 0 | 0 | |
| | | Deuel County | 0 | 0 | 0 | 0 | |
| | | Dixon County | 0 | 0 | 0 | 0 | |
| | | Dodge County | 0 | 0 | 0 | 0 | |
| | | Douglas County | 0 | 0 | 0 | 0 | |
| | | Dundy County | 0 | 0 | 0 | 0 | |
| | | Fillmore County | 0 | 0 | 0 | 0 | |
| | | Franklin County | 0 | 0 | 0 | 0 | |
| | | Frontier County | 0 | 0 | 0 | 0 | |
| | | Furnas County | 0 | 0 | 0 | 0 | |
| | | Gage County | 0 | 0 | 0 | 0 | |
| | | Garden County | 0 | 0 | 0 | 0 | |
| | | Garfield County | 0 | 0 | 0 | 0 | |
| | | Gosper County | 0 | 0 | 0 | 0 | |
| | | Grant County | 0 | 0 | 0 | 0 | |
| | | Greeley County | 0 | 0 | 0 | 0 | |
| | | Hall County | 0 | 0 | 0 | 0 | |
| | | Hamilton County | 0 | 0 | 0 | 0 | |
| | | Harlan County | 0 | 0 | 0 | 0 | |
| | | Hayes County | 0 | 0 | 0 | 0 | |
| | | Hitchcock County | 0 | 0 | 0 | 0 | |
| | | Holt County | 0 | 0 | 0 | 0 | |
| | | Hooker County | 0 | 0 | 0 | 0 | |
| | | Howard County | 0 | 0 | 0 | 0 | |
| | | Jefferson County | 0 | 0 | 0 | 0 | |
| | | Johnson County | 0 | 0 | 0 | 0 | |
| | | Kearney County | 0 | 0 | 0 | 0 | |
| | | Keith County | 0 | 0 | 0 | 0 | |
| | | Keya Paha County | 0 | 0 | 0 | 0 | |
| | | Kimball County | 0 | 0 | 0 | 0 | |
| | | Knox County | 0 | 0 | 0 | 0 | |
| | | Lancaster County | 0 | 0 | 0 | 0 | |
| | | Lincoln County | 0 | 0 | 0 | 0 | |
| | | Logan County | 0 | 0 | 0 | 0 | |
| | | Loup County | 0 | 0 | 0 | 0 | |
| | | Madison County | 0 | 0 | 0 | 0 | |
| | | McPherson County | 0 | 0 | 0 | 0 | |
| | | Merrick County | 0 | 0 | 0 | 0 | |
| | | Morrill County | 0 | 0 | 0 | 0 | |
| | | Nance County | 0 | 0 | 0 | 0 | |
| | | Nemaha County | 0 | 0 | 0 | 0 | |
| | | Nuckolls County | 0 | 0 | 0 | 0 | |
| | | Otoe County | 0 | 0 | 0 | 0 | |
| | | Pawnee County | 0 | 0 | 0 | 0 | |
| | | Perkins County | 0 | 0 | 0 | 0 | |
| | | Phelps County | 0 | 0 | 0 | 0 | |
| | | Pierce County | 0 | 0 | 0 | 0 | |
| | | Platte County | 0 | 0 | 0 | 0 | |
| | | Polk County | 0 | 0 | 0 | 0 | |
| | | Red Willow County | 0 | 0 | 0 | 0 | |
| | | Richardson County | 0 | 0 | 0 | 0 | |
| | | Rock County | 0 | 0 | 0 | 0 | |
| | | Saline County | 0 | 0 | 0 | 0 | |
| | | Sarpy County | 0 | 0 | 0 | 0 | |
| | | Saunders County | 0 | 0 | 0 | 0 | |
| | | Scotts Bluff County | 0 | 0 | 0 | 0 | |
| | | Seward County | 0 | 0 | 0 | 0 | |
| | | Sheridan County | 0 | 0 | 0 | 0 | |
| | | Sherman County | 0 | 0 | 0 | 0 | |
| | | Sioux County | 0 | 0 | 0 | 0 | |
| | | Stanton County | 0 | 0 | 0 | 0 | |
| | | Thayer County | 0 | 0 | 0 | 0 | |
| | | Thomas County | 0 | 0 | 0 | 0 | |
| | | Thurston County | 0 | 0 | 0 | 0 | |
| | | Valley County | 0 | 0 | 0 | 0 | |
| | | Washington County | 0 | 0 | 0 | 0 | |
| | | Wayne County | 0 | 0 | 0 | 0 | |
| | | Webster County | 0 | 0 | 0 | 0 | |
| | | Wheeler County | 0 | 0 | 0 | 0 | |
| | | York County | 0 | 0 | 0 | 0 | |
| NEVADA | Cities | Boulder City | 0 | 0 | 0 | 0 | 14,686 |
| | | Carlin | 0 | 0 | 0 | 0 | 2,075 |
| | | Elko | 0 | 0 | 0 | 0 | 17,177 |
| | | Fallon | 0 | 0 | 0 | 0 | 8,589 |
| | | Lovelock | 0 | 0 | 0 | 0 | 1,840 |
| | | Mesquite | 0 | 0 | 0 | 0 | 17,453 |
| | | Sparks | 0 | 0 | 0 | 0 | 91,421 |
| | | West Wendover | 0 | 0 | 0 | 0 | 5,025 |
| | | Winnemucca | 0 | 0 | 0 | 0 | 8,202 |
| | | Yerington | 0 | 0 | 0 | 0 | 3,960 |
| | Universities and Colleges | Truckee Meadows Community College | 0 | 0 | 0 | 0 | 12,492 |
| | Metropolitan Counties | Carson City | 0 | 0 | 0 | 0 | |
| | | Storey | 0 | 0 | 0 | 0 | |
| | Nonmetropolitan Counties | Churchill | 0 | 0 | 0 | 0 | |
| | | Douglas | 0 | 0 | 0 | 0 | |
| | | Elko | 0 | 0 | 0 | 0 | |
| | | Esmeralda | 0 | 0 | 0 | 0 | |
| | | Eureka | 0 | 0 | 0 | 0 | |
| | | Humboldt | 0 | 0 | 0 | 0 | |
| | | Lander | 0 | | | | |
| | | Lincoln | 0 | 0 | 0 | 0 | |
| | | Mineral | 0 | 0 | 0 | 0 | |
| | | Nye | 0 | 0 | 0 | 0 | |
| | | Pershing | 0 | 0 | 0 | 0 | |
| | | White Pine | 0 | 0 | 0 | 0 | |
| | Other Agencies | Washoe County School District | 0 | | | | |
| NEW HAMPSHIRE | Cities | Alexandria | 0 | 0 | 0 | 0 | 1,561 |
| | | Alstead | 0 | 0 | 0 | 0 | 2,115 |
| | | Alton | 0 | 0 | 0 | 0 | 5,148 |

[1]Agencies published in this table indicated that no hate crimes occurred in their jurisdictions during the quarter(s) for which they submitted reports to the Hate Crime Statistics Program. Blanks indicate quarters for which agencies did not submit reports.
[2]Population figures are published only for the cities. The figures listed for the universities and colleges are student enrollment and were provided by the United States Department of Education for the 2008 school year, the most recent available. The enrollment figures include full-time and part-time students.

## Table 95. Hate Crime Zero Data Submitted per Quarter, by State and Agency, 2009—*Continued*

(Number.)

| State | Agency type | Agency name | Zero data per quarter[1] | | | | Population[2] |
|---|---|---|---|---|---|---|---|
| | | | 1st quarter | 2nd quarter | 3rd quarter | 4th quarter | |
| NEW HAMPSHIRE | | Amherst | 0 | 0 | 0 | 0 | 11,914 |
| | | Antrim | 0 | 0 | 0 | 0 | 2,640 |
| | | Ashland | 0 | 0 | 0 | 0 | 2,102 |
| | | Auburn | 0 | 0 | 0 | 0 | 5,216 |
| | | Barnstead | 0 | 0 | 0 | 0 | 4,678 |
| | | Barrington | 0 | 0 | 0 | 0 | 8,580 |
| | | Bartlett | 0 | 0 | 0 | 0 | 2,934 |
| | | Belmont | 0 | 0 | 0 | 0 | 7,181 |
| | | Bennington | 0 | 0 | 0 | 0 | 1,470 |
| | | Berlin | 0 | 0 | 0 | 0 | 9,474 |
| | | Bethlehem | 0 | 0 | 0 | 0 | 2,490 |
| | | Boscawen | 0 | 0 | 0 | 0 | 3,984 |
| | | Bradford | 0 | 0 | 0 | 0 | 1,545 |
| | | Brentwood | 0 | 0 | 0 | 0 | 4,057 |
| | | Bristol | 0 | 0 | 0 | 0 | 3,133 |
| | | Campton | 0 | 0 | 0 | 0 | 3,039 |
| | | Candia | 0 | 0 | 0 | 0 | 4,205 |
| | | Canterbury | 0 | 0 | 0 | 0 | 2,334 |
| | | Carroll | 0 | 0 | 0 | 0 | 750 |
| | | Center Harbor | 0 | 0 | 0 | 0 | 1,118 |
| | | Charlestown | 0 | 0 | 0 | 0 | 4,849 |
| | | Chester | 0 | 0 | 0 | 0 | 4,831 |
| | | Claremont | 0 | 0 | 0 | 0 | 12,940 |
| | | Colebrook | 0 | 0 | 0 | 0 | 2,344 |
| | | Conway | 0 | 0 | 0 | 0 | 9,240 |
| | | Dalton | 0 | 0 | 0 | 0 | 880 |
| | | Danville | 0 | 0 | 0 | 0 | 4,375 |
| | | Deerfield | 0 | 0 | 0 | 0 | 4,261 |
| | | Deering | 0 | 0 | 0 | 0 | 2,066 |
| | | Derry | 0 | 0 | 0 | 0 | 34,189 |
| | | Dover | 0 | 0 | 0 | 0 | 28,794 |
| | | Dublin | 0 | 0 | 0 | 0 | 1,598 |
| | | Dunbarton | 0 | 0 | 0 | 0 | 2,684 |
| | | Durham | 0 | 0 | 0 | 0 | 13,782 |
| | | Enfield | 0 | 0 | 0 | 0 | 4,872 |
| | | Epping | 0 | 0 | 0 | 0 | 6,341 |
| | | Epsom | 0 | 0 | 0 | 0 | 4,643 |
| | | Exeter | 0 | 0 | 0 | 0 | 14,838 |
| | | Farmington | 0 | 0 | 0 | 0 | 6,821 |
| | | Fitzwilliam | 0 | 0 | 0 | 0 | 2,315 |
| | | Franconia | 0 | 0 | 0 | 0 | 1,059 |
| | | Freedom | 0 | 0 | 0 | 0 | 1,448 |
| | | Fremont | 0 | 0 | 0 | 0 | 4,204 |
| | | Gilford | 0 | 0 | 0 | 0 | 7,526 |
| | | Gilmanton | 0 | 0 | 0 | 0 | 3,565 |
| | | Goffstown | 0 | 0 | 0 | 0 | 17,634 |
| | | Gorham | 0 | 0 | 0 | 0 | 2,787 |
| | | Grantham | 0 | 0 | 0 | 0 | 2,558 |
| | | Hampstead | 0 | 0 | 0 | 0 | 9,026 |
| | | Hampton | 0 | 0 | 0 | 0 | 15,412 |
| | | Haverhill | 0 | 0 | 0 | 0 | 4,694 |
| | | Henniker | 0 | 0 | 0 | 0 | 5,125 |
| | | Hill | 0 | 0 | 0 | 0 | 1,124 |
| | | Hillsborough | 0 | 0 | 0 | 0 | 5,618 |
| | | Hinsdale | 0 | 0 | 0 | 0 | 4,178 |
| | | Hooksett | 0 | 0 | 0 | 0 | 14,027 |
| | | Hopkinton | 0 | 0 | 0 | 0 | 5,616 |
| | | Jaffrey | 0 | 0 | 0 | 0 | 5,686 |
| | | Keene | 0 | 0 | 0 | 0 | 22,376 |
| | | Kingston | 0 | 0 | 0 | 0 | 6,250 |
| | | Lancaster | 0 | 0 | 0 | 0 | 3,246 |
| | | Lee | 0 | 0 | 0 | 0 | 4,495 |
| | | Lincoln | 0 | 0 | 0 | 0 | 1,358 |
| | | Lisbon | 0 | 0 | 0 | 0 | 1,668 |
| | | Litchfield | 0 | 0 | 0 | 0 | 8,884 |
| | | Littleton | 0 | 0 | 0 | 0 | 6,221 |
| | | Londonderry | 0 | 0 | 0 | 0 | 25,205 |
| | | Loudon | 0 | 0 | 0 | 0 | 5,168 |
| | | Madison | 0 | 0 | 0 | 0 | 2,339 |
| | | Marlborough | 0 | 0 | 0 | 0 | 2,077 |
| | | Middleton | 0 | 0 | 0 | 0 | 1,872 |
| | | Milford | 0 | 0 | 0 | 0 | 15,133 |
| | | Milton | 0 | 0 | 0 | 0 | 4,655 |
| | | Mont Vernon | 0 | 0 | 0 | 0 | 2,404 |
| | | Moultonborough | 0 | 0 | 0 | 0 | 5,041 |
| | | Nashua | 0 | 0 | 0 | 0 | 86,554 |
| | | New Boston | 0 | 0 | 0 | 0 | 5,186 |
| | | Newbury | 0 | 0 | 0 | 0 | 2,134 |
| | | New Durham | 0 | 0 | 0 | 0 | 2,590 |
| | | Newfields | 0 | 0 | 0 | 0 | 1,635 |
| | | New Hampton | 0 | 0 | 0 | 0 | 2,280 |
| | | Newington | 0 | 0 | 0 | 0 | 805 |
| | | New Ipswich | 0 | 0 | 0 | 0 | 5,430 |
| | | New London | 0 | 0 | 0 | 0 | 4,509 |
| | | Newmarket | 0 | 0 | 0 | 0 | 9,602 |
| | | Newport | 0 | 0 | 0 | 0 | 6,550 |
| | | Newton | 0 | 0 | 0 | 0 | 4,594 |
| | | Northfield | 0 | 0 | 0 | 0 | 5,187 |
| | | North Hampton | 0 | 0 | 0 | 0 | 4,536 |
| | | Northwood | 0 | 0 | 0 | 0 | 4,192 |
| | | Nottingham | 0 | 0 | 0 | 0 | 4,628 |
| | | Orford | 0 | 0 | 0 | 0 | 1,054 |
| | | Ossipee | 0 | 0 | 0 | 0 | 4,733 |
| | | Pelham | 0 | 0 | 0 | 0 | 12,770 |
| | | Peterborough | 0 | 0 | 0 | 0 | 6,218 |
| | | Pittsfield | 0 | 0 | 0 | 0 | 4,409 |
| | | Plaistow | 0 | 0 | 0 | 0 | 7,607 |
| | | Portsmouth | 0 | 0 | 0 | 0 | 20,401 |
| | | Raymond | 0 | 0 | 0 | 0 | 10,296 |
| | | Rindge | 0 | 0 | 0 | 0 | 6,669 |
| | | Rollinsford | 0 | 0 | 0 | 0 | 2,642 |
| | | Rye | 0 | 0 | 0 | 0 | 5,140 |
| | | Sandown | 0 | 0 | 0 | 0 | 5,948 |
| | | Sandwich | 0 | 0 | 0 | 0 | 1,319 |
| | | Somersworth | 0 | 0 | 0 | 0 | 12,020 |
| | | South Hampton | 0 | 0 | 0 | 0 | 879 |
| | | Strafford | 0 | 0 | 0 | 0 | 4,115 |
| | | Stratham | 0 | 0 | 0 | 0 | 7,394 |
| | | Sugar Hill | 0 | 0 | 0 | 0 | 618 |
| | | Sunapee | 0 | 0 | 0 | 0 | 3,396 |
| | | Thornton | 0 | 0 | 0 | 0 | 2,166 |
| | | Tilton | 0 | 0 | 0 | 0 | 3,604 |
| | | Troy | 0 | 0 | 0 | 0 | 2,073 |
| | | Wakefield | 0 | 0 | 0 | 0 | 5,485 |
| | | Walpole | 0 | 0 | 0 | 0 | 3,684 |
| | | Warner | 0 | 0 | 0 | 0 | 2,967 |
| | | Washington | 0 | 0 | 0 | 0 | 1,097 |
| | | Waterville Valley | 0 | 0 | 0 | 0 | 271 |
| | | Weare | 0 | 0 | 0 | 0 | 9,242 |
| | | Webster | 0 | 0 | 0 | 0 | 1,902 |
| | | Winchester | 0 | 0 | 0 | 0 | 4,301 |
| | | Windham | 0 | 0 | 0 | 0 | 13,528 |
| | | Wolfeboro | 0 | 0 | 0 | 0 | 6,578 |
| | | Woodstock | 0 | 0 | 0 | 0 | 1,168 |
| | Universities and Colleges | University of New Hampshire | 0 | 0 | 0 | 0 | 14,898 |
| | Metropolitan Counties | Rockingham | 0 | 0 | 0 | 0 | |
| | Nonmetropolitan Counties | Carroll | 0 | 0 | 0 | 0 | |
| | | Cheshire | 0 | 0 | 0 | 0 | |
| | | Merrimack | 0 | 0 | 0 | 0 | |
| | Other Agencies | Liquor Commission | 0 | 0 | 0 | 0 | |
| NEW JERSEY.......... | Cities | Absecon | 0 | 0 | 0 | 0 | 8,478 |
| | | Allendale | | 0 | 0 | 0 | 6,587 |
| | | Allenhurst | 0 | 0 | 0 | 0 | 697 |
| | | Allentown | 0 | 0 | 0 | 0 | 1,840 |
| | | Alpha | 0 | 0 | 0 | 0 | 2,376 |
| | | Alpine | 0 | 0 | 0 | 0 | 2,514 |
| | | Andover Township | | 0 | 0 | 0 | 6,585 |

[1]Agencies published in this table indicated that no hate crimes occurred in their jurisdictions during the quarter(s) for which they submitted reports to the Hate Crime Statistics Program. Blanks indicate quarters for which agencies did not submit reports.

[2]Population figures are published only for the cities. The figures listed for the universities and colleges are student enrollment and were provided by the United States Department of Education for the 2008 school year, the most recent available. The enrollment figures include full-time and part-time students.

## Table 95. Hate Crime Zero Data Submitted per Quarter, by State and Agency, 2009—*Continued*

(Number.)

| State | Agency type | Agency name | Zero data per quarter[1] | | | | Population[2] |
|---|---|---|---|---|---|---|---|
| | | | 1st quarter | 2nd quarter | 3rd quarter | 4th quarter | |
| NEW JERSEY | | Atlantic Highlands | 0 | 0 | 0 | 0 | 4,589 |
| | | Audubon | | 0 | 0 | 0 | 8,852 |
| | | Audubon Park | 0 | 0 | 0 | 0 | 1,053 |
| | | Avalon | 0 | 0 | 0 | 0 | 2,087 |
| | | Avon-by-the-Sea | 0 | 0 | 0 | 0 | 2,196 |
| | | Barnegat Light | | 0 | 0 | 0 | 846 |
| | | Barnegat Township | 0 | 0 | 0 | 0 | 23,196 |
| | | Barrington | 0 | 0 | 0 | 0 | 6,924 |
| | | Bay Head | 0 | 0 | 0 | 0 | 1,268 |
| | | Beach Haven | 0 | 0 | 0 | 0 | 1,404 |
| | | Beachwood | 0 | 0 | 0 | 0 | 10,886 |
| | | Bedminster Township | | 0 | 0 | 0 | 8,356 |
| | | Belleville | | 0 | 0 | 0 | 33,610 |
| | | Bellmawr | 0 | 0 | 0 | 0 | 11,168 |
| | | Belmar | 0 | 0 | 0 | 0 | 5,891 |
| | | Belvidere | 0 | 0 | 0 | 0 | 2,622 |
| | | Bergenfield | 0 | 0 | 0 | 0 | 25,542 |
| | | Berkeley Heights Township | | 0 | 0 | 0 | 13,335 |
| | | Berkeley Township | 0 | 0 | 0 | 0 | 43,044 |
| | | Berlin | 0 | 0 | 0 | 0 | 8,142 |
| | | Berlin Township | 0 | 0 | 0 | 0 | 5,429 |
| | | Bernardsville | 0 | 0 | 0 | 0 | 7,799 |
| | | Beverly | 0 | 0 | 0 | 0 | 2,553 |
| | | Blairstown Township | 0 | 0 | 0 | 0 | 5,961 |
| | | Bloomfield | 0 | 0 | 0 | 0 | 43,489 |
| | | Bloomingdale | | 0 | 0 | 0 | 7,436 |
| | | Bogota | 0 | 0 | 0 | 0 | 7,881 |
| | | Boonton | | 0 | 0 | 0 | 8,467 |
| | | Bordentown | 0 | 0 | 0 | 0 | 3,801 |
| | | Bordentown Township | | 0 | 0 | 0 | 10,301 |
| | | Bradley Beach | 0 | 0 | 0 | 0 | 4,849 |
| | | Bridgeton | | 0 | 0 | 0 | 24,980 |
| | | Brielle | 0 | 0 | 0 | 0 | 4,879 |
| | | Brigantine | 0 | 0 | 0 | 0 | 12,654 |
| | | Buena | 0 | 0 | 0 | 0 | 3,693 |
| | | Burlington | 0 | 0 | 0 | 0 | 9,360 |
| | | Burlington Township | 0 | 0 | 0 | 0 | 21,413 |
| | | Butler | 0 | 0 | 0 | 0 | 8,188 |
| | | Byram Township | 0 | 0 | 0 | 0 | 8,479 |
| | | Caldwell | 0 | 0 | 0 | 0 | 7,085 |
| | | Cape May | 0 | 0 | 0 | 0 | 3,650 |
| | | Cape May Point | 0 | 0 | 0 | 0 | 221 |
| | | Carlstadt | 0 | 0 | 0 | 0 | 6,030 |
| | | Cedar Grove Township | 0 | 0 | 0 | 0 | 12,685 |
| | | Chatham | 0 | 0 | 0 | 0 | 8,187 |
| | | Chatham Township | 0 | 0 | 0 | 0 | 10,167 |
| | | Cherry Hill Township | 0 | 0 | 0 | 0 | 70,953 |
| | | Chesilhurst | 0 | 0 | 0 | 0 | 1,959 |
| | | Chester | 0 | 0 | 0 | 0 | 1,682 |
| | | Chesterfield Township | 0 | 0 | 0 | 0 | 7,609 |
| | | Chester Township | 0 | 0 | 0 | 0 | 7,812 |
| | | Clark Township | 0 | 0 | 0 | 0 | 14,330 |
| | | Clayton | 0 | 0 | 0 | 0 | 7,601 |
| | | Clementon | 0 | 0 | 0 | 0 | 4,876 |
| | | Clinton | 0 | 0 | 0 | 0 | 2,534 |
| | | Clinton Township | 0 | 0 | 0 | 0 | 13,913 |
| | | Closter | 0 | 0 | 0 | 0 | 8,689 |
| | | Collingswood | 0 | 0 | 0 | 0 | 13,764 |
| | | Colts Neck Township | 0 | 0 | 0 | 0 | 10,119 |
| | | Cranbury Township | 0 | 0 | 0 | 0 | 4,013 |
| | | Deal | 0 | 0 | 0 | 0 | 1,042 |
| | | Delaware Township | 0 | 0 | 0 | 0 | 4,691 |
| | | Delran Township | 0 | 0 | 0 | 0 | 16,936 |
| | | Demarest | 0 | 0 | 0 | 0 | 5,162 |
| | | Deptford Township | 0 | 0 | 0 | 0 | 31,090 |
| | | Dover | 0 | 0 | 0 | 0 | 17,827 |
| | | Dumont | 0 | 0 | 0 | 0 | 16,910 |
| | | Dunellen | 0 | 0 | 0 | 0 | 7,011 |
| | | Eastampton Township | 0 | 0 | 0 | 0 | 6,578 |
| | | East Greenwich Township | 0 | 0 | 0 | 0 | 8,105 |
| | | East Newark | 0 | 0 | 0 | 0 | 2,113 |
| | | East Orange | 0 | 0 | 0 | 0 | 64,924 |
| | | East Rutherford | 0 | 0 | 0 | 0 | 10,248 |
| | | Edgewater | 0 | 0 | 0 | 0 | 9,846 |
| | | Egg Harbor City | 0 | 0 | 0 | 0 | 4,362 |
| | | Elk Township | 0 | 0 | 0 | 0 | 4,001 |
| | | Elmer | 0 | 0 | 0 | 0 | 1,341 |
| | | Elmwood Park | 0 | 0 | 0 | 0 | 18,602 |
| | | Elsinboro Township | 0 | 0 | 0 | 0 | 1,046 |
| | | Emerson | 0 | 0 | 0 | 0 | 7,370 |
| | | Englewood | 0 | 0 | 0 | 0 | 29,463 |
| | | Englewood Cliffs | 0 | 0 | 0 | 0 | 5,858 |
| | | Englishtown | 0 | 0 | 0 | 0 | 1,934 |
| | | Essex Fells | 0 | 0 | 0 | 0 | 2,102 |
| | | Fairfield Township, Essex County | 0 | 0 | 0 | 0 | 7,529 |
| | | Fair Haven | 0 | 0 | 0 | 0 | 5,905 |
| | | Fairview | 0 | 0 | 0 | 0 | 13,571 |
| | | Far Hills | 0 | 0 | 0 | 0 | 903 |
| | | Flemington | 0 | 0 | 0 | 0 | 4,285 |
| | | Florence Township | 0 | 0 | 0 | 0 | 11,458 |
| | | Fort Lee | 0 | 0 | 0 | 0 | 36,342 |
| | | Franklin | 0 | 0 | 0 | 0 | 5,068 |
| | | Franklin Lakes | 0 | 0 | 0 | 0 | 11,757 |
| | | Franklin Township, Gloucester County | 0 | 0 | 0 | 0 | 17,499 |
| | | Franklin Township, Hunterdon County | 0 | 0 | 0 | 0 | 3,254 |
| | | Franklin Township, Somerset County | 0 | 0 | 0 | 0 | 60,364 |
| | | Garfield | 0 | 0 | 0 | 0 | 28,882 |
| | | Garwood | 0 | 0 | 0 | 0 | 4,438 |
| | | Glen Ridge | 0 | 0 | 0 | 0 | 6,599 |
| | | Gloucester City | 0 | 0 | 0 | 0 | 11,508 |
| | | Green Brook Township | 0 | 0 | 0 | 0 | 7,034 |
| | | Greenwich Township, Gloucester County | 0 | 0 | 0 | 0 | 4,997 |
| | | Hackensack | 0 | 0 | 0 | 0 | 42,801 |

[1]Agencies published in this table indicated that no hate crimes occurred in their jurisdictions during the quarter(s) for which they submitted reports to the Hate Crime Statistics Program. Blanks indicate quarters for which agencies did not submit reports.

[2]Population figures are published only for the cities. The figures listed for the universities and colleges are student enrollment and were provided by the United States Department of Education for the 2008 school year, the most recent available. The enrollment figures include full-time and part-time students.

## Table 95. Hate Crime Zero Data Submitted per Quarter, by State and Agency, 2009—*Continued*

(Number.)

| State | Agency type | Agency name | Zero data per quarter[1] 1st quarter | 2nd quarter | 3rd quarter | 4th quarter | Population[2] |
|---|---|---|---|---|---|---|---|
| NEW JERSEY | | Haddon Township | 0 | 0 | 0 | 0 | 14,293 |
| | | Haledon | 0 | 0 | 0 | 0 | 8,546 |
| | | Hamburg | | 0 | 0 | 0 | 3,504 |
| | | Hamilton Township, Atlantic County | 0 | 0 | 0 | 0 | 24,863 |
| | | Hammonton | 0 | 0 | 0 | 0 | 13,517 |
| | | Hanover Township | 0 | 0 | | 0 | 13,736 |
| | | Harrington Park | 0 | 0 | 0 | 0 | 4,883 |
| | | Harrison | 0 | 0 | 0 | 0 | 15,296 |
| | | Harvey Cedars | 0 | 0 | 0 | 0 | 397 |
| | | Hasbrouck Heights | 0 | 0 | 0 | 0 | 11,383 |
| | | Haworth | 0 | 0 | 0 | 0 | 3,416 |
| | | Helmetta | 0 | 0 | 0 | 0 | 2,031 |
| | | High Bridge | 0 | 0 | 0 | 0 | 3,662 |
| | | Highlands | 0 | 0 | 0 | 0 | 5,292 |
| | | Hightstown | 0 | 0 | 0 | 0 | 5,303 |
| | | Hillsdale | 0 | 0 | 0 | 0 | 9,822 |
| | | Hi-Nella | 0 | 0 | 0 | 0 | 995 |
| | | Ho-Ho-Kus | 0 | 0 | 0 | 0 | 3,995 |
| | | Holland Township | 0 | 0 | 0 | 0 | 5,226 |
| | | Hopatcong | 0 | 0 | 0 | 0 | 15,447 |
| | | Hopewell | 0 | 0 | 0 | 0 | 1,983 |
| | | Hopewell Township | 0 | 0 | 0 | 0 | 17,941 |
| | | Independence Township | 0 | 0 | 0 | 0 | 5,705 |
| | | Interlaken | 0 | 0 | 0 | 0 | 874 |
| | | Irvington | 0 | 0 | 0 | 0 | 55,838 |
| | | Island Heights | 0 | 0 | 0 | 0 | 1,884 |
| | | Jamesburg | 0 | 0 | 0 | 0 | 6,401 |
| | | Jefferson Township | 0 | 0 | 0 | 0 | 21,903 |
| | | Kearny | 0 | 0 | 0 | 0 | 36,352 |
| | | Kenilworth | 0 | 0 | 0 | 0 | 7,612 |
| | | Keyport | 0 | 0 | 0 | 0 | 7,464 |
| | | Kinnelon | 0 | 0 | 0 | 0 | 9,606 |
| | | Lake Como | 0 | 0 | 0 | 0 | 1,769 |
| | | Lambertville | 0 | 0 | 0 | 0 | 3,727 |
| | | Laurel Springs | 0 | 0 | 0 | 0 | 1,896 |
| | | Lavallette | 0 | 0 | 0 | 0 | 2,764 |
| | | Lawnside | 0 | 0 | 0 | 0 | 2,858 |
| | | Lebanon Township | 0 | 0 | 0 | 0 | 6,208 |
| | | Leonia | 0 | 0 | 0 | 0 | 8,563 |
| | | Linwood | 0 | 0 | 0 | 0 | 7,220 |
| | | Loch Arbour | 0 | 0 | 0 | 0 | 273 |
| | | Logan Township | 0 | 0 | 0 | 0 | 6,270 |
| | | Long Beach Township | 0 | 0 | 0 | 0 | 3,571 |
| | | Long Hill Township | 0 | 0 | 0 | 0 | 8,593 |
| | | Longport | 0 | 0 | 0 | 0 | 1,092 |
| | | Lopatcong Township | 0 | 0 | 0 | 0 | 8,748 |
| | | Lower Alloways Creek Township | 0 | 0 | 0 | 0 | 1,888 |
| | | Lyndhurst Township | 0 | 0 | 0 | 0 | 19,286 |
| | | Magnolia | 0 | 0 | 0 | 0 | 4,321 |
| | | Mahwah Township | 0 | 0 | 0 | 0 | 24,180 |
| | | Mantoloking | 0 | 0 | 0 | 0 | 455 |
| | | Mantua Township | 0 | 0 | 0 | 0 | 15,285 |
| | | Manville | 0 | 0 | 0 | 0 | 10,863 |
| | | Maplewood Township | 0 | 0 | 0 | 0 | 21,795 |
| | | Maywood | 0 | 0 | 0 | 0 | 9,104 |
| | | Medford Lakes | 0 | 0 | 0 | 0 | 4,097 |
| | | Mendham | 0 | 0 | 0 | 0 | 5,048 |
| | | Merchantville | 0 | 0 | 0 | 0 | 3,760 |
| | | Middlesex | 0 | 0 | 0 | 0 | 13,634 |
| | | Midland Park | 0 | 0 | 0 | 0 | 6,743 |
| | | Mine Hill Township | 0 | 0 | 0 | 0 | 3,577 |
| | | Monmouth Beach | 0 | 0 | 0 | 0 | 3,566 |
| | | Monroe Township, Gloucester County | 0 | 0 | 0 | 0 | 33,420 |
| | | Montclair | 0 | 0 | | 0 | 36,788 |
| | | Montvale | 0 | 0 | 0 | 0 | 7,625 |
| | | Moonachie | 0 | 0 | 0 | 0 | 2,722 |
| | | Morris Plains | 0 | 0 | 0 | 0 | 6,050 |
| | | Morristown | 0 | 0 | 0 | 0 | 19,351 |
| | | Mountain Lakes | 0 | 0 | 0 | 0 | 4,276 |
| | | Mountainside | 0 | 0 | 0 | 0 | 6,545 |
| | | Mount Arlington | 0 | 0 | 0 | 0 | 5,968 |
| | | Mount Ephraim | 0 | 0 | 0 | 0 | 4,381 |
| | | Mount Holly Township | 0 | 0 | 0 | 0 | 10,195 |
| | | Mullica Township | 0 | 0 | 0 | 0 | 6,032 |
| | | National Park | 0 | 0 | 0 | 0 | 3,230 |
| | | Neptune City | 0 | 0 | 0 | 0 | 5,100 |
| | | Netcong | 0 | 0 | 0 | 0 | 3,221 |
| | | Newfield | 0 | 0 | 0 | 0 | 1,675 |
| | | New Hanover Township | 0 | 0 | 0 | 0 | 9,442 |
| | | New Milford | 0 | 0 | 0 | 0 | 15,898 |
| | | New Providence | 0 | 0 | 0 | 0 | 11,904 |
| | | Newton | 0 | 0 | 0 | 0 | 8,079 |
| | | North Arlington | 0 | 0 | 0 | 0 | 14,648 |
| | | North Caldwell | 0 | 0 | 0 | 0 | 7,016 |
| | | Northfield | 0 | 0 | 0 | 0 | 7,903 |
| | | North Haledon | 0 | 0 | 0 | 0 | 9,021 |
| | | Northvale | 0 | 0 | 0 | 0 | 4,748 |
| | | North Wildwood | 0 | 0 | 0 | 0 | 4,786 |
| | | Norwood | 0 | 0 | 0 | 0 | 6,256 |
| | | Nutley Township | 0 | 0 | 0 | 0 | 26,033 |
| | | Oaklyn | 0 | 0 | 0 | 0 | 4,014 |
| | | Ocean City | 0 | 0 | 0 | 0 | 14,686 |
| | | Ocean Gate | 0 | 0 | 0 | 0 | 2,143 |
| | | Oceanport | 0 | 0 | 0 | 0 | 5,723 |
| | | Ocean Township, Monmouth County | 0 | 0 | 0 | 0 | 28,360 |
| | | Ocean Township, Ocean County | 0 | 0 | 0 | 0 | 9,329 |
| | | Ogdensburg | 0 | 0 | 0 | 0 | 2,535 |
| | | Old Tappan | 0 | 0 | 0 | 0 | 6,091 |
| | | Orange | 0 | 0 | 0 | 0 | 30,873 |
| | | Oxford Township | 0 | 0 | 0 | 0 | 2,603 |
| | | Palisades Park | 0 | 0 | 0 | 0 | 19,639 |
| | | Paterson | 0 | 0 | 0 | 0 | 144,943 |
| | | Peapack and Gladstone | 0 | 0 | 0 | 0 | 2,572 |
| | | Pemberton | 0 | 0 | 0 | 0 | 1,583 |

[1]Agencies published in this table indicated that no hate crimes occurred in their jurisdictions during the quarter(s) for which they submitted reports to the Hate Crime Statistics Program. Blanks indicate quarters for which agencies did not submit reports.

[2]Population figures are published only for the cities. The figures listed for the universities and colleges are student enrollment and were provided by the United States Department of Education for the 2008 school year, the most recent available. The enrollment figures include full-time and part-time students.

## Table 95. Hate Crime Zero Data Submitted per Quarter, by State and Agency, 2009—*Continued*

(Number.)

| State | Agency type | Agency name | Zero data per quarter[1] 1st quarter | 2nd quarter | 3rd quarter | 4th quarter | Population[2] |
|---|---|---|---|---|---|---|---|
| NEW JERSEY | | Pemberton Township | 0 | 0 | 0 | 0 | 27,914 |
| | | Pennington | 0 | 0 | 0 | 0 | 2,651 |
| | | Pennsauken Township | 0 | 0 | 0 | 0 | 34,905 |
| | | Penns Grove | 0 | 0 | 0 | 0 | 4,668 |
| | | Pennsville Township | 0 | 0 | 0 | 0 | 13,365 |
| | | Perth Amboy | 0 | 0 | 0 | 0 | 48,897 |
| | | Pine Beach | 0 | 0 | 0 | 0 | 2,093 |
| | | Pine Hill | 0 | 0 | 0 | 0 | 11,358 |
| | | Pine Valley | 0 | 0 | 0 | 0 | 25 |
| | | Pitman | 0 | 0 | 0 | 0 | 9,193 |
| | | Plainfield | 0 | 0 | 0 | 0 | 45,939 |
| | | Pleasantville | 0 | 0 | 0 | 0 | 18,838 |
| | | Pohatcong Township | 0 | 0 | 0 | 0 | 3,321 |
| | | Point Pleasant Beach | 0 | 0 | 0 | 0 | 5,430 |
| | | Pompton Lakes | 0 | 0 | 0 | 0 | 11,075 |
| | | Princeton Township | 0 | 0 | 0 | 0 | 17,517 |
| | | Prospect Park | 0 | 0 | 0 | 0 | 5,574 |
| | | Rahway | 0 | 0 | 0 | 0 | 28,869 |
| | | Readington Township | 0 | 0 | 0 | 0 | 16,053 |
| | | Ridgefield | 0 | 0 | 0 | 0 | 10,852 |
| | | Ridgefield Park | 0 | 0 | 0 | 0 | 12,316 |
| | | Riverdale | 0 | 0 | 0 | 0 | 2,902 |
| | | Riverton | 0 | 0 | 0 | 0 | 2,613 |
| | | Robbinsville Township | 0 | 0 | 0 | 0 | 12,314 |
| | | Rochelle Park Township | 0 | 0 | 0 | 0 | 6,144 |
| | | Rockaway | 0 | 0 | 0 | 0 | 6,241 |
| | | Rockleigh | 0 | 0 | 0 | 0 | 388 |
| | | Roselle | 0 | 0 | 0 | 0 | 20,523 |
| | | Roselle Park | 0 | 0 | 0 | 0 | 12,750 |
| | | Roxbury Township | 0 | 0 | 0 | 0 | 23,311 |
| | | Rumson | 0 | 0 | 0 | 0 | 7,276 |
| | | Rutherford | 0 | 0 | 0 | 0 | 17,384 |
| | | Saddle Brook Township | 0 | 0 | 0 | 0 | 14,019 |
| | | Saddle River | 0 | 0 | 0 | 0 | 3,858 |
| | | Salem | 0 | 0 | 0 | 0 | 5,641 |
| | | Seaside Heights | 0 | 0 | 0 | 0 | 3,364 |
| | | Seaside Park | 0 | 0 | 0 | 0 | 2,317 |
| | | Ship Bottom | 0 | 0 | 0 | 0 | 1,456 |
| | | Shrewsbury | 0 | 0 | 0 | 0 | 3,798 |
| | | Somerdale | 0 | 0 | 0 | 0 | 5,074 |
| | | Somers Point | 0 | 0 | 0 | 0 | 11,316 |
| | | South Amboy | 0 | 0 | 0 | 0 | 7,761 |
| | | South Bound Brook | 0 | 0 | 0 | 0 | 5,191 |
| | | South Hackensack Township | 0 | 0 | 0 | 0 | 2,262 |
| | | South Harrison Township | 0 | 0 | 0 | 0 | 3,223 |
| | | South River | 0 | 0 | 0 | 0 | 15,715 |
| | | Sparta Township | 0 | 0 | 0 | 0 | 19,336 |
| | | Springfield | 0 | 0 | 0 | 0 | 14,873 |
| | | Springfield Township | 0 | 0 | 0 | 0 | 3,492 |
| | | Spring Lake | 0 | 0 | 0 | 0 | 3,514 |
| | | Spring Lake Heights | 0 | 0 | 0 | 0 | 5,122 |
| | | Stanhope | 0 | 0 | 0 | 0 | 3,559 |
| | | Stillwater Township | 0 | 0 | 0 | 0 | 4,294 |
| | | Stone Harbor | 0 | 0 | 0 | 0 | 1,000 |
| | | Stratford | 0 | 0 | 0 | 0 | 7,026 |
| | | Summit | 0 | 0 | 0 | 0 | 20,494 |
| | | Surf City | 0 | 0 | 0 | 0 | 1,571 |
| | | Tavistock | 0 | 0 | 0 | 0 | 31 |
| | | Tenafly | 0 | 0 | 0 | 0 | 14,759 |
| | | Teterboro | 0 | 0 | 0 | 0 | 17 |
| | | Tewksbury Township | 0 | 0 | 0 | 0 | 6,088 |
| | | Toms River Township | 0 | 0 | 0 | 0 | 96,614 |
| | | Totowa | 0 | 0 | 0 | 0 | 10,705 |
| | | Trenton | 0 | 0 | | 0 | 82,609 |
| | | Union Beach | 0 | 0 | 0 | 0 | 6,615 |
| | | Upper Saddle River | 0 | 0 | 0 | 0 | 8,537 |
| | | Ventnor City | 0 | 0 | 0 | 0 | 12,111 |
| | | Vernon Township | 0 | 0 | 0 | 0 | 24,870 |
| | | Verona | 0 | 0 | 0 | 0 | 12,384 |
| | | Vineland | 0 | 0 | 0 | 0 | 59,121 |
| | | Wallington | 0 | 0 | 0 | 0 | 11,265 |
| | | Wall Township | 0 | 0 | 0 | 0 | 26,265 |
| | | Wanaque | 0 | 0 | 0 | 0 | 12,433 |
| | | Washington Township, Bergen County | 0 | 0 | 0 | 0 | 9,615 |
| | | Washington Township, Morris County | 0 | 0 | 0 | 0 | 18,468 |
| | | Washington Township, Warren County | 0 | 0 | 0 | 0 | 6,935 |
| | | Watchung | 0 | 0 | 0 | 0 | 6,720 |
| | | Waterford Township | 0 | 0 | 0 | 0 | 10,674 |
| | | Wayne Township | 0 | 0 | 0 | 0 | 53,891 |
| | | Weehawken Township | 0 | 0 | 0 | 0 | 12,252 |
| | | Wenonah | 0 | 0 | 0 | 0 | 2,360 |
| | | Westampton Township | 0 | 0 | 0 | 0 | 8,799 |
| | | West Amwell Township | 0 | 0 | 0 | 0 | 2,970 |
| | | West Caldwell Township | 0 | 0 | 0 | 0 | 10,358 |
| | | West Cape May | 0 | 0 | 0 | 0 | 968 |
| | | Westfield | 0 | 0 | 0 | 0 | 29,426 |
| | | West Milford Township | 0 | 0 | 0 | 0 | 27,879 |
| | | Westville | 0 | 0 | 0 | 0 | 4,464 |
| | | West Wildwood | 0 | 0 | 0 | 0 | 395 |
| | | Westwood | 0 | 0 | 0 | 0 | 10,666 |
| | | Wildwood Crest | 0 | 0 | 0 | 0 | 3,987 |
| | | Willingboro Township | 0 | 0 | 0 | 0 | 36,977 |
| | | Woodbine | 0 | 0 | 0 | 0 | 2,437 |
| | | Woodbury Heights | 0 | 0 | 0 | 0 | 3,059 |
| | | Woodlynne | 0 | 0 | 0 | 0 | 2,676 |
| | | Wood-Ridge | 0 | 0 | 0 | 0 | 7,432 |
| | | Woodstown | 0 | 0 | 0 | 0 | 3,385 |
| | | Woolwich Township | 0 | 0 | 0 | 0 | 12,624 |
| | | Wyckoff Township | 0 | 0 | 0 | 0 | 16,938 |
| | **State Police Agencies** | State Police: Atlantic County | 0 | 0 | 0 | 0 | |
| | | Bergen County | 0 | 0 | 0 | 0 | |
| | | Burlington County | 0 | 0 | 0 | 0 | |
| | | Camden County | 0 | 0 | 0 | 0 | |
| | | Cape May County | 0 | 0 | 0 | 0 | |

[1]Agencies published in this table indicated that no hate crimes occurred in their jurisdictions during the quarter(s) for which they submitted reports to the Hate Crime Statistics Program. Blanks indicate quarters for which agencies did not submit reports.

[2]Population figures are published only for the cities. The figures listed for the universities and colleges are student enrollment and were provided by the United States Department of Education for the 2008 school year, the most recent available. The enrollment figures include full-time and part-time students.

## Table 95. Hate Crime Zero Data Submitted per Quarter, by State and Agency, 2009—*Continued*

(Number.)

| State | Agency type | Agency name | Zero data per quarter[1] | | | | Population[2] |
|---|---|---|---|---|---|---|---|
| | | | 1st quarter | 2nd quarter | 3rd quarter | 4th quarter | |
| **NEW JERSEY** | | Cumberland County | 0 | 0 | 0 | 0 | |
| | | Essex County | 0 | 0 | 0 | 0 | |
| | | Gloucester County | 0 | 0 | 0 | 0 | |
| | | Hudson County | 0 | 0 | 0 | 0 | |
| | | Hunterdon County | 0 | 0 | 0 | 0 | |
| | | Mercer County | 0 | 0 | 0 | 0 | |
| | | Middlesex County | 0 | 0 | 0 | 0 | |
| | | Monmouth County | 0 | 0 | 0 | 0 | |
| | | Morris County | 0 | 0 | 0 | 0 | |
| | | Ocean County | 0 | 0 | 0 | 0 | |
| | | Passaic County | 0 | 0 | 0 | 0 | |
| | | Salem County | 0 | 0 | 0 | 0 | |
| | | Somerset County | 0 | 0 | 0 | 0 | |
| | | Union County | 0 | 0 | 0 | 0 | |
| | | Warren County | 0 | 0 | 0 | 0 | |
| | **Other Agencies** | Human Services, Woodland Township | 0 | 0 | 0 | 0 | |
| | | Hunterdon Developmental Center | 0 | 0 | 0 | 0 | |
| **NEW MEXICO** ........ | **Cities** | Alamogordo | 0 | 0 | 0 | 0 | 35,823 |
| | | Angel Fire | 0 | 0 | | 0 | 974 |
| | | Aztec | 0 | | 0 | | 6,977 |
| | | Bayard | 0 | 0 | 0 | 0 | 2,386 |
| | | Belen | 0 | 0 | 0 | 0 | 7,342 |
| | | Bloomfield | 0 | 0 | 0 | 0 | 7,292 |
| | | Bosque Farms | 0 | 0 | 0 | 0 | 4,073 |
| | | Carrizozo | 0 | 0 | 0 | 0 | 1,048 |
| | | Corrales | 0 | 0 | 0 | 0 | 7,848 |
| | | Deming | 0 | | | | 15,625 |
| | | Espanola | 0 | | 0 | 0 | 9,690 |
| | | Estancia | 0 | | 0 | | 1,571 |
| | | Grants | | 0 | 0 | | 8,877 |
| | | Hatch | 0 | 0 | | | 1,646 |
| | | Hobbs | | 0 | 0 | 0 | 30,710 |
| | | Jal | 0 | 0 | 0 | 0 | 2,052 |
| | | Logan | | 0 | 0 | | 992 |
| | | Lordsburg | 0 | 0 | 0 | 0 | 2,765 |
| | | Los Alamos | 0 | 0 | | | 18,187 |
| | | Lovington | 0 | 0 | 0 | 0 | 10,040 |
| | | Melrose | | 0 | | | 672 |
| | | Portales | 0 | 0 | | | 12,343 |
| | | Raton | 0 | 0 | 0 | 0 | 6,381 |
| | | Red River | 0 | 0 | 0 | 0 | 519 |
| | | Roswell | | 0 | 0 | | 46,314 |
| | | Santa Clara | 0 | 0 | 0 | 0 | 1,847 |
| | | Socorro | 0 | 0 | 0 | | 9,004 |
| | | Tatum | | 0 | | 0 | 764 |
| | | Texico | 0 | 0 | 0 | 0 | 979 |
| | | Tucumcari | | 0 | | | 5,198 |
| | **Universities and Colleges** | Eastern New Mexico University | 0 | 0 | | 0 | 4,294 |
| | | University of New Mexico | 0 | 0 | 0 | 0 | 25,754 |
| | **Metropolitan Counties** | Bernalillo | 0 | 0 | 0 | 0 | |
| | **Nonmetropolitan Counties** | Chaves | 0 | | 0 | 0 | |
| | | Colfax | 0 | | 0 | 0 | |
| | | Curry | 0 | 0 | | | |
| | | Hidalgo | 0 | 0 | | | |
| | | Lea | 0 | 0 | 0 | 0 | |
| | | Luna | | 0 | | 0 | |
| | | McKinley | 0 | 0 | | | |
| | | Mora | 0 | | 0 | | |
| | | Quay | 0 | 0 | 0 | 0 | |
| | | Sierra | 0 | | 0 | 0 | |
| | **Tribal Agencies** | Acoma Tribal | 0 | 0 | 0 | 0 | |
| | | Taos Pueblo Tribal | | | | 0 | |
| **NEW YORK**... | **Cities** | Adams Village | 0 | 0 | 0 | 0 | 1,665 |
| | | Addison Town and Village | 0 | 0 | 0 | 0 | 2,498 |
| | | Afton Village | | | | 0 | 808 |
| | | Akron Village | 0 | 0 | 0 | 0 | 2,955 |
| | | Albion Village | 0 | 0 | | 0 | 5,505 |
| | | Alexandria Bay Village | 0 | 0 | 0 | 0 | 1,118 |
| | | Allegany Village | 0 | 0 | 0 | 0 | 1,747 |
| | | Altamont Village | 0 | 0 | 0 | 0 | 1,695 |
| | | Amity Town and Belmont Village | 0 | 0 | 0 | 0 | 2,158 |
| | | Amityville Village | 0 | 0 | 0 | 0 | 9,974 |
| | | Amsterdam | 0 | 0 | 0 | 0 | 17,448 |
| | | Arcade Village | 0 | 0 | 0 | 0 | 1,874 |
| | | Ardsley Village | 0 | 0 | 0 | 0 | 4,910 |
| | | Asharoken Village | 0 | 0 | 0 | 0 | 664 |
| | | Attica Village | 0 | 0 | 0 | 0 | 2,393 |
| | | Baldwinsville Village | 0 | 0 | 0 | 0 | 7,266 |
| | | Ballston Spa Village | 0 | 0 | 0 | 0 | 5,453 |
| | | Batavia | 0 | 0 | 0 | 0 | 15,092 |
| | | Bath Village | 0 | 0 | 0 | 0 | 5,409 |
| | | Beacon | 0 | 0 | 0 | 0 | 14,545 |
| | | Bolivar Village | 0 | 0 | 0 | 0 | 1,107 |
| | | Bolton Town | 0 | 0 | 0 | 0 | 2,158 |
| | | Boonville Village | 0 | 0 | 0 | 0 | 2,032 |
| | | Brant Town | 0 | 0 | 0 | 0 | 1,814 |
| | | Brewster | 0 | 0 | 0 | 0 | 2,106 |
| | | Briarcliff Manor Village | 0 | 0 | 0 | | 8,018 |
| | | Brockport Village | 0 | 0 | 0 | 0 | 8,370 |
| | | Bronxville Village | 0 | 0 | 0 | 0 | 6,513 |
| | | Brownville Village | 0 | 0 | 0 | 0 | 1,055 |
| | | Cairo Town | 0 | 0 | 0 | 0 | 6,524 |
| | | Caledonia Village | 0 | 0 | 0 | 0 | 2,124 |
| | | Cambridge Village | | | | 0 | 1,808 |
| | | Camden Village | 0 | 0 | 0 | 0 | 2,244 |
| | | Camillus Town and Village | 0 | 0 | 0 | 0 | 23,316 |
| | | Canisteo Village | 0 | 0 | 0 | 0 | 2,209 |
| | | Canton Village | 0 | 0 | 0 | 0 | 6,090 |
| | | Cape Vincent Village | 0 | 0 | 0 | 0 | 785 |
| | | Carmel Town | 0 | 0 | 0 | 0 | 34,492 |
| | | Carroll Town | 0 | 0 | 0 | 0 | 3,442 |
| | | Carthage Village | 0 | 0 | 0 | 0 | 3,748 |
| | | Cattaraugus Village | 0 | 0 | 0 | 0 | 975 |

[1]Agencies published in this table indicated that no hate crimes occurred in their jurisdictions during the quarter(s) for which they submitted reports to the Hate Crime Statistics Program. Blanks indicate quarters for which agencies did not submit reports.

[2]Population figures are published only for the cities. The figures listed for the universities and colleges are student enrollment and were provided by the United States Department of Education for the 2008 school year, the most recent available. The enrollment figures include full-time and part-time students.

# Table 95. Hate Crime Zero Data Submitted per Quarter, by State and Agency, 2009—*Continued*

(Number.)

| State | Agency type | Agency name | Zero data per quarter[1] | | | | Popu-lation[2] |
|---|---|---|---|---|---|---|---|
| | | | 1st quarter | 2nd quarter | 3rd quarter | 4th quarter | |
| NEW YORK | | Cayuga Heights Village | 0 | 0 | 0 | 0 | 3,663 |
| | | Cazenovia Village | 0 | 0 | 0 | 0 | 2,948 |
| | | Central Square Village | 0 | 0 | 0 | 0 | 1,725 |
| | | Centre Island Village | 0 | 0 | 0 | 0 | 445 |
| | | Chatham Village | 0 | 0 | 0 | 0 | 1,674 |
| | | Chester Town | 0 | 0 | 0 | 0 | 10,047 |
| | | Chester Village | 0 | 0 | 0 | 0 | 3,584 |
| | | Chittenango Village | 0 | 0 | 0 | 0 | 4,888 |
| | | Cicero Town | 0 | 0 | 0 | 0 | 28,354 |
| | | Clayton Village | 0 | 0 | 0 | 0 | 1,879 |
| | | Clifton Springs Village | 0 | 0 | 0 | 0 | 2,132 |
| | | Clyde Village | 0 | 0 | 0 | | 2,082 |
| | | Cobleskill Village | 0 | 0 | 0 | 0 | 4,601 |
| | | Coeymans Town | 0 | 0 | 0 | 0 | 7,993 |
| | | Cohoes | 0 | 0 | 0 | 0 | 14,973 |
| | | Colchester Town | 0 | 0 | 0 | 0 | 2,030 |
| | | Cooperstown Village | 0 | 0 | 0 | 0 | 1,884 |
| | | Copake Town | 0 | 0 | 0 | 0 | 3,254 |
| | | Corning | 0 | 0 | 0 | 0 | 10,222 |
| | | Cornwall Town | 0 | 0 | 0 | 0 | 9,815 |
| | | Cortland | 0 | 0 | 0 | 0 | 18,404 |
| | | Coxsackie Village | | | | 0 | 2,745 |
| | | Crawford Town | 0 | 0 | 0 | 0 | 9,581 |
| | | Cuba Town | 0 | 0 | 0 | 0 | 3,316 |
| | | Dansville Village | 0 | 0 | | | 4,448 |
| | | Deerpark Town | 0 | 0 | 0 | 0 | 8,501 |
| | | Delhi Village | 0 | 0 | 0 | 0 | 2,846 |
| | | Depew Village | 0 | 0 | 0 | 0 | 15,173 |
| | | Deposit Village | 0 | 0 | 0 | 0 | 1,581 |
| | | Dewitt Town | 0 | 0 | 0 | 0 | 21,451 |
| | | Dexter Village | 0 | 0 | 0 | 0 | 1,179 |
| | | Dryden Village | 0 | | 0 | 0 | 1,819 |
| | | Dunkirk | 0 | 0 | 0 | 0 | 11,978 |
| | | Durham Town | 0 | | | | 2,685 |
| | | East Aurora-Aurora Town | 0 | 0 | 0 | 0 | 13,451 |
| | | Eastchester Town | 0 | 0 | 0 | 0 | 18,698 |
| | | East Fishkill Town | 0 | 0 | 0 | 0 | 29,193 |
| | | East Hampton Town | 0 | 0 | 0 | 0 | 19,964 |
| | | East Hampton Village | 0 | 0 | 0 | 0 | 1,400 |
| | | East Syracuse Village | 0 | 0 | 0 | 0 | 2,950 |
| | | Eden Town | 0 | 0 | 0 | 0 | 7,700 |
| | | Ellenville Village | 0 | 0 | 0 | 0 | 3,889 |
| | | Ellicott Town | 0 | 0 | 0 | 0 | 5,219 |
| | | Ellicottville | 0 | 0 | 0 | 0 | 1,910 |
| | | Elmira | 0 | 0 | 0 | 0 | 29,090 |
| | | Elmira Heights Village | 0 | 0 | 0 | 0 | 3,869 |
| | | Elmira Town | 0 | 0 | 0 | 0 | 5,833 |
| | | Elmsford Village | 0 | 0 | 0 | 0 | 4,765 |
| | | Endicott Village | 0 | 0 | 0 | 0 | 12,346 |
| | | Evans Town | 0 | 0 | 0 | 0 | 16,756 |
| | | Fairport Village | 0 | 0 | 0 | 0 | 5,444 |
| | | Fishkill Town | 0 | 0 | | | 19,503 |
| | | Fishkill Village | 0 | 0 | 0 | 0 | 1,687 |
| | | Floral Park Village | 0 | 0 | 0 | 0 | 15,832 |
| | | Fort Edward Village | 0 | 0 | 0 | | 3,013 |
| | | Fort Plain Village | 0 | 0 | 0 | | 2,174 |
| | | Frankfort Village | 0 | 0 | 0 | 0 | 2,343 |
| | | Franklinville Village | 0 | 0 | 0 | 0 | 1,688 |
| | | Friendship Town | 0 | 0 | 0 | 0 | 1,833 |
| | | Fulton City | 0 | 0 | 0 | 0 | 11,151 |
| | | Garden City Village | | | 0 | 0 | 22,342 |
| | | Gates Town | 0 | 0 | 0 | 0 | 28,590 |
| | | Geddes Town | 0 | 0 | 0 | 0 | 10,367 |
| | | Geneseo Village | 0 | 0 | 0 | 0 | 7,715 |
| | | Geneva | | | | 0 | 13,177 |
| | | Germantown Town | 0 | 0 | 0 | 0 | 1,964 |
| | | Glen Cove | | 0 | 0 | 0 | 26,920 |
| | | Glen Park Village | 0 | 0 | 0 | 0 | 500 |
| | | Glens Falls | 0 | 0 | | | 13,828 |
| | | Glenville Town | 0 | 0 | 0 | 0 | 21,971 |
| | | Gloversville | 0 | 0 | 0 | 0 | 14,948 |
| | | Goshen Town | 0 | 0 | 0 | 0 | 8,491 |
| | | Granville Village | 0 | 0 | 0 | 0 | 2,530 |
| | | Great Neck Estates Village | 0 | 0 | 0 | 0 | 2,770 |
| | | Greene Village | 0 | 0 | 0 | 0 | 1,640 |
| | | Green Island Village | 0 | 0 | 0 | 0 | 2,565 |
| | | Greenwich Village | | 0 | 0 | 0 | 1,819 |
| | | Greenwood Lake Village | 0 | | | 0 | 3,417 |
| | | Groton Village | 0 | 0 | 0 | 0 | 2,394 |
| | | Guilderland Town | 0 | 0 | 0 | 0 | 33,161 |
| | | Hamburg Town | 0 | 0 | 0 | 0 | 44,012 |
| | | Hamburg Village | 0 | 0 | 0 | 0 | 9,327 |
| | | Hamilton Village | 0 | 0 | 0 | 0 | 3,818 |
| | | Hammondsport Village | | | | 0 | 731 |
| | | Hancock Village | 0 | 0 | 0 | 0 | 1,078 |
| | | Haverstraw Town | 0 | 0 | 0 | 0 | 37,449 |
| | | Hempstead Village | 0 | 0 | 0 | 0 | 53,996 |
| | | Herkimer Village | 0 | | 0 | 0 | 6,915 |
| | | Highland Falls Village | | | | 0 | 3,706 |
| | | Homer Village | 0 | 0 | 0 | 0 | 3,232 |
| | | Hoosick Falls Village | 0 | 0 | 0 | | 3,252 |
| | | Hornell | 0 | 0 | 0 | 0 | 8,454 |
| | | Horseheads Village | 0 | 0 | 0 | 0 | 6,221 |
| | | Hunter Town | 0 | 0 | | 0 | 2,690 |
| | | Huntington Bay Village | 0 | 0 | 0 | 0 | 1,515 |
| | | Hyde Park Town | 0 | 0 | 0 | 0 | 20,207 |
| | | Independence Town | 0 | 0 | 0 | 0 | 1,034 |
| | | Inlet Town | 0 | 0 | 0 | 0 | 376 |

[1]Agencies published in this table indicated that no hate crimes occurred in their jurisdictions during the quarter(s) for which they submitted reports to the Hate Crime Statistics Program. Blanks indicate quarters for which agencies did not submit reports.

[2]Population figures are published only for the cities. The figures listed for the universities and colleges are student enrollment and were provided by the United States Department of Education for the 2008 school year, the most recent available. The enrollment figures include full-time and part-time students.

## Table 95. Hate Crime Zero Data Submitted per Quarter, by State and Agency, 2009—*Continued*

(Number.)

| State | Agency type | Agency name | Zero data per quarter[1] 1st quarter | 2nd quarter | 3rd quarter | 4th quarter | Population[2] |
|---|---|---|---|---|---|---|---|
| NEW YORK | | Irondequoit Town | 0 | 0 | 0 | 0 | 49,755 |
| | | Irvington Village | 0 | 0 | 0 | 0 | 6,669 |
| | | Jamestown | 0 | 0 | 0 | 0 | 29,204 |
| | | Johnson City Village | 0 | 0 | 0 | 0 | 14,646 |
| | | Johnstown | 0 | 0 | 0 | 0 | 8,421 |
| | | Jordan Village | 0 | 0 | 0 | 0 | 1,306 |
| | | Kenmore Village | 0 | 0 | 0 | 0 | 14,856 |
| | | Kensington Village | 0 | 0 | 0 | 0 | 1,203 |
| | | Kent Town | 0 | 0 | 0 | 0 | 14,190 |
| | | Kings Point Village | 0 | 0 | 0 | 0 | 5,430 |
| | | Kingston | 0 | 0 | 0 | 0 | 22,333 |
| | | Lackawanna | 0 | 0 | 0 | 0 | 17,435 |
| | | Lake Placid Village | 0 | 0 | 0 | 0 | 2,763 |
| | | Lake Success Village | 0 | 0 | 0 | 0 | 2,898 |
| | | Lakewood-Busti | 0 | 0 | 0 | | 7,355 |
| | | Lancaster Town | 0 | 0 | 0 | 0 | 23,502 |
| | | Le Roy Village | 0 | 0 | 0 | 0 | 4,109 |
| | | Liberty Village | 0 | 0 | 0 | 0 | 3,844 |
| | | Little Falls | 0 | 0 | 0 | 0 | 4,833 |
| | | Lloyd Harbor Village | 0 | 0 | 0 | 0 | 3,748 |
| | | Lloyd Town | | 0 | 0 | 0 | 10,808 |
| | | Lockport | 0 | 0 | 0 | 0 | 20,461 |
| | | Long Beach | 0 | 0 | 0 | 0 | 35,722 |
| | | Lowville Village | | | | 0 | 3,133 |
| | | Macedon Town and Village | 0 | 0 | 0 | 0 | 8,845 |
| | | Malone Village | 0 | 0 | 0 | 0 | 5,764 |
| | | Malverne Village | 0 | 0 | 0 | 0 | 8,873 |
| | | Mamaroneck Town | 0 | 0 | 0 | 0 | 11,538 |
| | | Manchester Village | 0 | 0 | 0 | 0 | 1,410 |
| | | Manlius Town | 0 | 0 | 0 | 0 | 24,850 |
| | | Marlborough Town | 0 | 0 | 0 | 0 | 8,301 |
| | | Maybrook Village | 0 | 0 | 0 | 0 | 4,110 |
| | | McGraw Village | 0 | 0 | 0 | 0 | 949 |
| | | Medina Village | 0 | 0 | 0 | 0 | 6,007 |
| | | Menands Village | 0 | 0 | 0 | 0 | 3,783 |
| | | Middleport Village | 0 | 0 | 0 | 0 | 1,765 |
| | | Middletown | 0 | 0 | 0 | 0 | 25,921 |
| | | Millbrook Village | | | 0 | | 1,517 |
| | | Monroe Village | 0 | 0 | 0 | 0 | 8,207 |
| | | Montgomery Village | | 0 | | | 4,878 |
| | | Monticello Village | 0 | 0 | 0 | 0 | 6,487 |
| | | Moravia Village | 0 | 0 | 0 | 0 | 1,286 |
| | | Moriah Town | 0 | 0 | 0 | 0 | 3,432 |
| | | Mount Hope Town | 0 | 0 | 0 | 0 | 7,568 |
| | | Mount Kisco Village | 0 | 0 | 0 | 0 | 10,434 |
| | | Mount Pleasant Town | 0 | 0 | 0 | 0 | 26,437 |
| | | New Berlin Town | 0 | 0 | 0 | 0 | 1,698 |
| | | Newburgh | 0 | 0 | 0 | 0 | 28,071 |
| | | Newburgh Town | 0 | 0 | 0 | 0 | 31,394 |
| | | New Castle Town | | 0 | 0 | 0 | 17,750 |
| | | New Hartford Town and Village | 0 | 0 | 0 | 0 | 19,145 |
| | | New Paltz Town and Village | 0 | 0 | 0 | 0 | 13,854 |
| | | New Windsor Town | 0 | 0 | 0 | 0 | 25,407 |
| | | New York Mills Village | 0 | 0 | 0 | 0 | 3,303 |
| | | Niagara Town | 0 | 0 | 0 | 0 | 8,344 |
| | | Nissequogue Village | 0 | 0 | 0 | 0 | 1,611 |
| | | Norfolk Town | | | | 0 | 4,518 |
| | | Northport Village | 0 | 0 | 0 | 0 | 7,683 |
| | | North Syracuse Village | 0 | 0 | 0 | 0 | 6,537 |
| | | Northville Village | 0 | 0 | 0 | 0 | 1,155 |
| | | Norwich | 0 | 0 | 0 | 0 | 6,954 |
| | | Nunda Town and Village | 0 | 0 | 0 | 0 | 2,941 |
| | | Ocean Beach Village | 0 | 0 | 0 | 0 | 148 |
| | | Ogdensburg | 0 | 0 | 0 | 0 | 10,993 |
| | | Ogden Town | 0 | 0 | 0 | 0 | 19,377 |
| | | Old Brookville Village | 0 | 0 | 0 | 0 | 2,330 |
| | | Old Westbury Village | 0 | 0 | 0 | 0 | 5,430 |
| | | Olean | 0 | 0 | 0 | 0 | 14,025 |
| | | Oneida | 0 | 0 | 0 | | 10,695 |
| | | Oneonta City | 0 | 0 | 0 | 0 | 13,205 |
| | | Orchard Park Town | 0 | 0 | 0 | 0 | 28,626 |
| | | Oriskany Village | 0 | 0 | 0 | 0 | 1,398 |
| | | Ossining Town | | | | 0 | 5,731 |
| | | Ossining Village | 0 | 0 | 0 | 0 | 23,773 |
| | | Oswego City | 0 | 0 | 0 | 0 | 17,271 |
| | | Owego Village | 0 | 0 | 0 | 0 | 3,687 |
| | | Oxford Village | 0 | 0 | 0 | 0 | 1,529 |
| | | Oyster Bay Cove Village | 0 | 0 | 0 | 0 | 2,303 |
| | | Painted Post Village | 0 | 0 | 0 | 0 | 1,772 |
| | | Pelham Manor Village | 0 | 0 | 0 | | 5,449 |
| | | Pelham Village | | | 0 | 0 | 6,438 |
| | | Penn Yan Village | 0 | 0 | 0 | 0 | 5,157 |
| | | Perry Village | 0 | 0 | 0 | 0 | 3,638 |
| | | Phelps Village | 0 | 0 | 0 | 0 | 1,896 |
| | | Philmont Village | 0 | 0 | 0 | 0 | 1,354 |
| | | Phoenix Village | 0 | 0 | 0 | 0 | 2,126 |
| | | Piermont Village | 0 | 0 | 0 | 0 | 2,562 |
| | | Pine Plains Town | 0 | 0 | 0 | 0 | 2,704 |
| | | Plattekill Town | 0 | 0 | 0 | 0 | 10,897 |
| | | Pleasantville Village | 0 | 0 | 0 | 0 | 7,142 |
| | | Port Byron Village | 0 | 0 | 0 | 0 | 1,226 |
| | | Port Chester Village | 0 | 0 | 0 | 0 | 28,202 |
| | | Port Dickinson Village | 0 | 0 | 0 | 0 | 1,584 |
| | | Port Jervis | 0 | 0 | 0 | 0 | 9,139 |

[1]Agencies published in this table indicated that no hate crimes occurred in their jurisdictions during the quarter(s) for which they submitted reports to the Hate Crime Statistics Program. Blanks indicate quarters for which agencies did not submit reports.

[2]Population figures are published only for the cities. The figures listed for the universities and colleges are student enrollment and were provided by the United States Department of Education for the 2008 school year, the most recent available. The enrollment figures include full-time and part-time students.

## Table 95. Hate Crime Zero Data Submitted per Quarter, by State and Agency, 2009—*Continued*

(Number.)

| State | Agency type | Agency name | Zero data per quarter[1] 1st quarter | 2nd quarter | 3rd quarter | 4th quarter | Population[2] |
|---|---|---|---|---|---|---|---|
| NEW YORK | | Portville Village | 0 | 0 | 0 | 0 | 943 |
| | | Port Washington | 0 | 0 | 0 | | 18,980 |
| | | Potsdam Village | 0 | 0 | 0 | 0 | 9,877 |
| | | Poughkeepsie Town | 0 | 0 | 0 | 0 | 43,027 |
| | | Pound Ridge Town | | | 0 | 0 | 4,960 |
| | | Pulaski Village | 0 | 0 | 0 | 0 | 2,270 |
| | | Quogue Village | 0 | | | 0 | 1,172 |
| | | Red Hook Village | 0 | 0 | 0 | 0 | 1,890 |
| | | Rensselaer City | 0 | 0 | 0 | 0 | 7,906 |
| | | Riverhead Town | 0 | 0 | 0 | 0 | 36,318 |
| | | Rome | 0 | 0 | 0 | 0 | 33,543 |
| | | Rosendale Town | 0 | 0 | 0 | 0 | 6,232 |
| | | Rotterdam Town | 0 | 0 | 0 | 0 | 30,223 |
| | | Rouses Point Village | 0 | 0 | 0 | 0 | 2,325 |
| | | Rushford Town | 0 | | | | 1,234 |
| | | Rye | | 0 | 0 | 0 | 15,070 |
| | | Rye Brook Village | 0 | 0 | 0 | 0 | 9,672 |
| | | Sackets Harbor Village | | | | 0 | 1,429 |
| | | Sag Harbor Village | 0 | 0 | 0 | 0 | 2,439 |
| | | Sands Point Village | 0 | 0 | 0 | 0 | 2,929 |
| | | Saugerties Village | 0 | 0 | 0 | 0 | 3,852 |
| | | Schodack Town | 0 | 0 | 0 | 0 | 11,533 |
| | | Schoharie Village | 0 | 0 | 0 | 0 | 999 |
| | | Scotia Village | 0 | 0 | 0 | 0 | 8,043 |
| | | Seneca Falls Village | 0 | 0 | 0 | 0 | 6,604 |
| | | Shandaken Town | 0 | 0 | 0 | 0 | 3,045 |
| | | Shawangunk Town | | | | 0 | 12,786 |
| | | Shelter Island Town | 0 | 0 | 0 | 0 | 2,569 |
| | | Sherburne Village | 0 | 0 | 0 | 0 | 1,408 |
| | | Sherrill | 0 | 0 | 0 | 0 | 3,111 |
| | | Shortsville Village | 0 | 0 | 0 | 0 | 1,313 |
| | | Sidney Village | 0 | 0 | 0 | 0 | 3,654 |
| | | Silver Creek Village | 0 | 0 | 0 | 0 | 2,789 |
| | | Skaneateles Village | 0 | 0 | 0 | 0 | 2,531 |
| | | Sleepy Hollow Village | 0 | 0 | 0 | 0 | 10,331 |
| | | Sodus Point Village | 0 | | | | 1,102 |
| | | Solvay Village | 0 | 0 | 0 | 0 | 6,372 |
| | | Southampton Town | 0 | 0 | 0 | 0 | 53,044 |
| | | Southampton Village | 0 | 0 | 0 | 0 | 4,363 |
| | | South Glens Falls Village | 0 | 0 | 0 | 0 | 3,383 |
| | | Stockport Town | 0 | 0 | 0 | 0 | 2,797 |
| | | Suffern Village | 0 | 0 | 0 | 0 | 11,099 |
| | | Syracuse | 0 | 0 | 0 | 0 | 137,208 |
| | | Tonawanda Town | 0 | 0 | 0 | 0 | 56,203 |
| | | Troy | 0 | 0 | 0 | 0 | 47,268 |
| | | Trumansburg Village | 0 | 0 | 0 | 0 | 1,593 |
| | | Tuckahoe Village | 0 | 0 | 0 | 0 | 6,247 |
| | | Tuxedo Park Village | 0 | 0 | 0 | 0 | 718 |
| | | Tuxedo Town | 0 | 0 | 0 | 0 | 2,990 |
| | | Ulster Town | 0 | 0 | 0 | 0 | 12,674 |
| | | Vernon Village | 0 | 0 | 0 | 0 | 1,145 |
| | | Wallkill Town | 0 | 0 | 0 | 0 | 27,760 |
| | | Walton Village | 0 | 0 | 0 | 0 | 2,823 |
| | | Wappingers Falls Village | 0 | 0 | 0 | 0 | 5,748 |
| | | Warsaw Village | 0 | 0 | 0 | 0 | 3,602 |
| | | Warwick Town | 0 | 0 | 0 | 0 | 20,040 |
| | | Washingtonville Village | 0 | 0 | 0 | 0 | 6,167 |
| | | Waterford Town and Village | 0 | 0 | 0 | 0 | 8,534 |
| | | Waterloo Village | 0 | 0 | 0 | 0 | 4,975 |
| | | Watertown | 0 | 0 | 0 | 0 | 27,387 |
| | | Watkins Glen Village | 0 | 0 | 0 | 0 | 2,015 |
| | | Webster Town and Village | 0 | 0 | 0 | 0 | 42,179 |
| | | Weedsport Village | 0 | 0 | 0 | 0 | 1,904 |
| | | Wellsville Village | 0 | 0 | 0 | 0 | 4,868 |
| | | West Carthage Village | 0 | 0 | 0 | 0 | 2,175 |
| | | Westfield Village | 0 | 0 | 0 | | 3,349 |
| | | Westhampton Beach Village | 0 | 0 | 0 | 0 | 2,023 |
| | | West Seneca Town | 0 | 0 | 0 | 0 | 43,574 |
| | | Whitehall Village | 0 | 0 | 0 | 0 | 2,557 |
| | | Whitesboro Village | 0 | 0 | 0 | 0 | 3,742 |
| | | Whitestown Town | 0 | 0 | 0 | 0 | 9,219 |
| | | Windham Town | 0 | 0 | 0 | 0 | 1,911 |
| | | Wolcott Village | 0 | 0 | 0 | 0 | 1,585 |
| | | Woodbury Town | 0 | 0 | 0 | 0 | 10,301 |
| | | Woodridge Village | 0 | 0 | 0 | | 1,084 |
| | | Yorktown Town | 0 | 0 | 0 | | 37,955 |
| | | Yorkville Village | 0 | 0 | 0 | 0 | 2,548 |
| | Universities and Colleges | Ithaca College | 0 | 0 | 0 | 0 | 6,448 |
| | | Rensselaer Polytechnic Institute | 0 | 0 | 0 | 0 | 6,777 |
| | | State University of New York, Upstate Medical Center[3] | 0 | 0 | 0 | 0 | |
| | | State University of New York Agricultural and Technical College: Canton | 0 | 0 | 0 | 0 | 2,970 |
| | | Farmingdale[3] | 0 | 0 | 0 | 0 | |
| | | State University of New York College: Brockport | 0 | 0 | 0 | 0 | 8,275 |

[1]Agencies published in this table indicated that no hate crimes occurred in their jurisdictions during the quarter(s) for which they submitted reports to the Hate Crime program. Blanks indicate quarters for which agencies did not submit reports.

[2]Population figures are published only for the cities. The figures listed for the universities and colleges are student enrollment and were provided by the United States Department of Education for the 2008 school year, the most recent available. The enrollment figures include full-time and part-time students.

[3]Student enrollment figures were not available.

## Table 95. Hate Crime Zero Data Submitted per Quarter, by State and Agency, 2009—*Continued*

(Number.)

| State | Agency type | Agency name | Zero data per quarter[1] | | | | Population[2] |
|---|---|---|---|---|---|---|---|
| | | | 1st quarter | 2nd quarter | 3rd quarter | 4th quarter | |
| **NEW YORK** | | Environmental Science and Forestry | 0 | 0 | 0 | 0 | 2,523 |
| | | Fredonia[3] | 0 | 0 | 0 | 0 | |
| | | Geneseo[3] | 0 | 0 | 0 | 0 | |
| | | Old Westbury | 0 | 0 | 0 | 0 | 3,505 |
| | | Optometry | 0 | 0 | 0 | 0 | 303 |
| | | Purchase | 0 | 0 | 0 | 0 | 4,251 |
| | | Utica-Rome[3] | 0 | 0 | 0 | 0 | |
| | **Metropolitan Counties** | Albany | 0 | 0 | 0 | 0 | |
| | | Herkimer | 0 | 0 | 0 | 0 | |
| | | Livingston | 0 | 0 | 0 | 0 | |
| | | Madison | 0 | 0 | 0 | 0 | |
| | | Onondaga | 0 | 0 | 0 | 0 | |
| | | Ontario | 0 | 0 | 0 | 0 | |
| | | Orange | 0 | 0 | 0 | 0 | |
| | | Orleans | 0 | 0 | 0 | 0 | |
| | | Oswego | 0 | 0 | 0 | 0 | |
| | | Putnam | 0 | 0 | 0 | 0 | |
| | | Rensselaer | | | 0 | 0 | |
| | | Saratoga | 0 | 0 | 0 | 0 | |
| | | Schenectady | 0 | 0 | 0 | 0 | |
| | | Schoharie | 0 | 0 | 0 | 0 | |
| | | Suffolk | 0 | 0 | 0 | 0 | |
| | | Tioga | 0 | 0 | 0 | 0 | |
| | | Tompkins | 0 | 0 | 0 | 0 | |
| | | Ulster | 0 | | 0 | 0 | |
| | | Warren | 0 | 0 | 0 | 0 | |
| | | Westchester Public Safety | 0 | 0 | 0 | 0 | |
| | **Nonmetropolitan Counties** | Chautauqua | 0 | 0 | 0 | 0 | |
| | | Chenango | 0 | 0 | 0 | | |
| | | Cortland | 0 | 0 | 0 | 0 | |
| | | Delaware | 0 | 0 | 0 | 0 | |
| | | Essex | | | | 0 | |
| | | Franklin | 0 | 0 | 0 | 0 | |
| | | Fulton | 0 | 0 | 0 | 0 | |
| | | Genesee | 0 | 0 | 0 | 0 | |
| | | Greene | 0 | 0 | 0 | 0 | |
| | | Hamilton | 0 | 0 | 0 | 0 | |
| | | Jefferson | 0 | 0 | 0 | 0 | |
| | | Lewis | 0 | 0 | 0 | 0 | |
| | | Montgomery | 0 | 0 | 0 | 0 | |
| | | Otsego | 0 | 0 | 0 | 0 | |
| | | Schuyler | 0 | 0 | 0 | 0 | |
| | | Seneca | 0 | 0 | 0 | 0 | |
| | | Steuben | 0 | 0 | 0 | 0 | |
| | | St. Lawrence | 0 | 0 | 0 | 0 | |
| | | Wyoming | 0 | 0 | 0 | 0 | |
| | | Yates | 0 | 0 | 0 | 0 | |
| | **State Police Agencies:** | State Police: Allegany County | 0 | 0 | 0 | 0 | |
| | | Cattaraugus County | 0 | 0 | 0 | 0 | |
| | | Cayuga County | 0 | 0 | 0 | 0 | |
| | | Chautauqua County | 0 | 0 | 0 | 0 | |
| | | Chemung County | 0 | 0 | 0 | 0 | |
| | | Chenango County | 0 | 0 | 0 | 0 | |
| | | Clinton County | 0 | 0 | 0 | 0 | |
| | | Cortland County | 0 | 0 | 0 | 0 | |
| | | Delaware County | 0 | 0 | 0 | 0 | |
| | | Dutchess County | 0 | 0 | 0 | 0 | |
| | | Erie County | 0 | 0 | 0 | 0 | |
| | | Essex County | 0 | 0 | 0 | 0 | |
| | | Franklin County | 0 | 0 | 0 | 0 | |
| | | Fulton County | 0 | 0 | 0 | 0 | |
| | | Genesee County | 0 | 0 | 0 | 0 | |
| | | Greene County | 0 | 0 | 0 | 0 | |
| | | Hamilton County | 0 | 0 | 0 | 0 | |
| | | Herkimer County | 0 | 0 | 0 | 0 | |
| | | Jefferson County | 0 | 0 | 0 | 0 | |
| | | Lewis County | 0 | 0 | 0 | 0 | |
| | | Livingston County | 0 | 0 | 0 | 0 | |
| | | Monroe County | 0 | 0 | 0 | 0 | |
| | | Nassau County | 0 | 0 | 0 | 0 | |
| | | New York County | 0 | 0 | 0 | 0 | |
| | | Oneida County | 0 | 0 | 0 | 0 | |
| | | Onondaga County | 0 | 0 | 0 | 0 | |
| | | Ontario County | 0 | 0 | 0 | 0 | |
| | | Orange County | 0 | 0 | 0 | 0 | |
| | | Orleans County | 0 | 0 | 0 | 0 | |
| | | Oswego County | 0 | 0 | 0 | 0 | |
| | | Putnam County | 0 | 0 | 0 | 0 | |
| | | Rensselaer County | 0 | 0 | 0 | 0 | |
| | | Rockland County | 0 | 0 | 0 | 0 | |
| | | Saratoga County | 0 | 0 | 0 | 0 | |
| | | Schenectady County | 0 | 0 | 0 | 0 | |
| | | Schoharie County | 0 | 0 | 0 | 0 | |
| | | Schuyler County | 0 | 0 | 0 | 0 | |
| | | Seneca County | 0 | 0 | 0 | 0 | |
| | | Steuben County | 0 | 0 | 0 | 0 | |
| | | St. Lawrence County | 0 | 0 | 0 | 0 | |
| | | Suffolk County | 0 | 0 | 0 | 0 | |
| | | Sullivan County | 0 | 0 | 0 | 0 | |
| | | Tioga County | 0 | 0 | 0 | 0 | |
| | | Tompkins County | 0 | 0 | 0 | 0 | |
| | | Ulster County | 0 | 0 | 0 | 0 | |
| | | Warren County | 0 | 0 | 0 | 0 | |
| | | Washington County | 0 | 0 | 0 | 0 | |
| | | Wayne County | 0 | 0 | 0 | 0 | |
| | | Westchester County | 0 | 0 | 0 | 0 | |
| | | Wyoming County | 0 | 0 | 0 | 0 | |
| | | Yates County | 0 | 0 | 0 | 0 | |
| | **Other Agencies** | Board of Water: Delaware County | 0 | 0 | 0 | 0 | |
| | | Sullivan County | 0 | 0 | 0 | 0 | |
| | | Ulster County | 0 | 0 | 0 | 0 | |
| | | Westchester County | 0 | 0 | 0 | 0 | |
| | | Onondaga County Parks | 0 | 0 | 0 | 0 | |
| | | Port Authority: Kings County | 0 | 0 | 0 | | |
| | | New York County | 0 | 0 | | | |
| | | Queens County | 0 | 0 | | | |
| | | Richmond County | | 0 | | | |

[1]Agencies published in this table indicated that no hate crimes occurred in their jurisdictions during the quarter(s) for which they submitted reports to the Hate Crime Statistics Program. Blanks indicate quarters for which agencies did not submit reports.

[2]Population figures are published only for the cities. The figures listed for the universities and colleges are student enrollment and were provided by the United States Department of Education for the 2008 school year, the most recent available. The enrollment figures include full-time and part-time students.

[3]Student enrollment figures were not available.

## Table 95. Hate Crime Zero Data Submitted per Quarter, by State and Agency, 2009—*Continued*

(Number.)

| State | Agency type | Agency name | Zero data per quarter[1] | | | | Population[2] |
|---|---|---|---|---|---|---|---|
| | | | 1st quarter | 2nd quarter | 3rd quarter | 4th quarter | |
| NEW YORK | | State Park: | | | | | |
| | | Allegany Region | 0 | 0 | 0 | 0 | |
| | | Central Region | 0 | 0 | 0 | 0 | |
| | | Finger Lakes Region | 0 | 0 | 0 | 0 | |
| | | Genesee Region | 0 | 0 | 0 | 0 | |
| | | Long Island Region | 0 | 0 | 0 | 0 | |
| | | New York City Region | 0 | 0 | 0 | 0 | |
| | | Niagara Region | 0 | 0 | 0 | 0 | |
| | | Palisades Region | 0 | 0 | 0 | 0 | |
| | | Saratoga/ Capital Region | 0 | 0 | 0 | 0 | |
| | | Taconic Region | 0 | 0 | 0 | 0 | |
| | | Thousand Island Region | 0 | 0 | 0 | 0 | |
| | | Suffolk County Parks | 0 | 0 | 0 | 0 | |
| NORTH CAROLINA... | Cities | Aberdeen | 0 | 0 | 0 | 0 | 5,936 |
| | | Ahoskie | 0 | 0 | 0 | 0 | 4,232 |
| | | Andrews | 0 | 0 | 0 | 0 | 1,700 |
| | | Angier | 0 | 0 | 0 | 0 | 4,467 |
| | | Apex | 0 | 0 | 0 | 0 | 34,766 |
| | | Archdale | 0 | 0 | 0 | 0 | 9,358 |
| | | Asheboro | 0 | 0 | 0 | 0 | 24,891 |
| | | Atlantic Beach | 0 | 0 | 0 | 0 | 1,817 |
| | | Aulander | 0 | 0 | 0 | 0 | 835 |
| | | Aurora | 0 | 0 | 0 | 0 | 596 |
| | | Ayden | 0 | 0 | 0 | 0 | 5,041 |
| | | Badin | 0 | 0 | 0 | 0 | 1,328 |
| | | Bailey | 0 | 0 | 0 | 0 | 685 |
| | | Bakersville | 0 | 0 | 0 | 0 | 349 |
| | | Bald Head Island | 0 | 0 | 0 | 0 | 308 |
| | | Banner Elk | 0 | 0 | 0 | 0 | 905 |
| | | Beaufort | 0 | 0 | 0 | 0 | 4,236 |
| | | Beech Mountain | 0 | 0 | 0 | 0 | 341 |
| | | Belhaven | 0 | 0 | 0 | 0 | 2,043 |
| | | Belmont | 0 | 0 | 0 | 0 | 9,433 |
| | | Benson | 0 | 0 | 0 | 0 | 3,554 |
| | | Bethel | 0 | 0 | 0 | 0 | 1,741 |
| | | Beulaville | 0 | 0 | 0 | 0 | 1,147 |
| | | Biltmore Forest | 0 | 0 | 0 | 0 | 1,573 |
| | | Biscoe | 0 | 0 | 0 | 0 | 1,671 |
| | | Black Creek | 0 | 0 | 0 | 0 | 695 |
| | | Black Mountain | 0 | 0 | 0 | 0 | 7,915 |
| | | Bladenboro | 0 | 0 | 0 | 0 | 1,668 |
| | | Blowing Rock | 0 | 0 | 0 | 0 | 1,497 |
| | | Boiling Spring Lakes | 0 | 0 | 0 | 0 | 4,920 |
| | | Boiling Springs | 0 | 0 | 0 | 0 | 3,883 |
| | | Boone | 0 | 0 | 0 | 0 | 13,995 |
| | | Boonville | 0 | 0 | 0 | 0 | 1,117 |
| | | Brevard | 0 | 0 | 0 | 0 | 6,708 |
| | | Broadway | 0 | 0 | 0 | 0 | 1,167 |
| | | Brookford | 0 | 0 | 0 | 0 | 426 |
| | | Bryson City | 0 | 0 | 0 | 0 | 1,370 |
| | | Bunn | 0 | 0 | 0 | 0 | 415 |
| | | Burgaw | 0 | 0 | 0 | 0 | 4,377 |
| | | Burlington | 0 | 0 | 0 | 0 | 51,440 |
| | | Burnsville | 0 | 0 | 0 | 0 | 1,639 |
| | | Butner | 0 | 0 | 0 | 0 | 6,146 |
| | | Cameron | 0 | 0 | 0 | 0 | 304 |
| | | Candor | 0 | 0 | 0 | 0 | 839 |
| | | Canton | 0 | 0 | 0 | 0 | 3,852 |
| | | Cape Carteret | 0 | 0 | 0 | 0 | 1,407 |
| | | Carolina Beach | 0 | 0 | 0 | 0 | 5,955 |
| | | Carthage | 0 | 0 | 0 | 0 | 2,039 |
| | | Caswell Beach | 0 | 0 | 0 | 0 | 483 |
| | | Catawba | 0 | 0 | 0 | 0 | 817 |
| | | Chadbourn | 0 | 0 | 0 | 0 | 2,053 |
| | | China Grove | 0 | 0 | 0 | 0 | 3,755 |
| | | Chocowinity | 0 | 0 | 0 | 0 | 719 |
| | | Claremont | 0 | 0 | 0 | 0 | 1,153 |
| | | Clayton | 0 | 0 | 0 | 0 | 16,952 |
| | | Cleveland | 0 | 0 | 0 | 0 | 841 |
| | | Clinton | 0 | 0 | 0 | 0 | 8,896 |
| | | Clyde | 0 | 0 | 0 | 0 | 1,319 |
| | | Coats | 0 | 0 | 0 | 0 | 2,166 |
| | | Columbus | 0 | 0 | 0 | 0 | 973 |
| | | Concord | 0 | 0 | 0 | 0 | 67,478 |
| | | Conover | 0 | 0 | 0 | 0 | 7,348 |
| | | Conway | 0 | 0 | 0 | 0 | 658 |
| | | Cooleemee | 0 | 0 | 0 | 0 | 986 |
| | | Cornelius | 0 | 0 | 0 | 0 | 26,027 |
| | | Cramerton | 0 | 0 | 0 | 0 | 3,162 |
| | | Creedmoor | 0 | 0 | 0 | 0 | 3,859 |
| | | Dallas | 0 | 0 | 0 | 0 | 3,813 |
| | | Davidson | 0 | 0 | 0 | 0 | 10,716 |
| | | Denton | 0 | 0 | 0 | 0 | 1,490 |
| | | Dobson | 0 | 0 | 0 | 0 | 1,457 |
| | | Drexel | 0 | 0 | 0 | 0 | 1,877 |
| | | Duck | 0 | 0 | 0 | 0 | 497 |
| | | Dunn | 0 | 0 | 0 | 0 | 10,115 |
| | | Durham | 0 | 0 | 0 | 0 | 227,492 |
| | | East Bend | 0 | 0 | 0 | 0 | 665 |
| | | East Spencer | 0 | 0 | 0 | 0 | 1,795 |
| | | Edenton | 0 | 0 | 0 | 0 | 4,964 |
| | | Elizabethtown | 0 | 0 | 0 | 0 | 3,702 |
| | | Elkin | 0 | 0 | 0 | 0 | 4,104 |
| | | Elon | 0 | 0 | 0 | 0 | 7,092 |
| | | Emerald Isle | 0 | 0 | 0 | 0 | 3,659 |
| | | Enfield | 0 | 0 | 0 | 0 | 2,337 |
| | | Erwin | 0 | 0 | 0 | 0 | 4,866 |
| | | Fair Bluff | 0 | 0 | 0 | 0 | 1,137 |
| | | Fairmont | 0 | 0 | 0 | 0 | 2,734 |
| | | Farmville | 0 | 0 | 0 | 0 | 4,637 |
| | | Fletcher | 0 | 0 | 0 | 0 | 4,770 |
| | | Forest City | 0 | 0 | 0 | 0 | 7,117 |
| | | Four Oaks | 0 | 0 | 0 | 0 | 2,100 |
| | | Foxfire Village | 0 | 0 | 0 | 0 | 491 |
| | | Franklin | 0 | 0 | 0 | 0 | 3,982 |
| | | Franklinton | 0 | 0 | 0 | 0 | 2,013 |
| | | Fremont | 0 | 0 | 0 | 0 | 1,427 |
| | | Fuquay-Varina | 0 | 0 | 0 | 0 | 18,457 |
| | | Garner | 0 | 0 | 0 | 0 | 28,268 |
| | | Garysburg | 0 | 0 | 0 | 0 | 1,121 |
| | | Gaston | 0 | 0 | 0 | 0 | 872 |
| | | Gibsonville | 0 | 0 | 0 | 0 | 4,757 |
| | | Glen Alpine | 0 | 0 | 0 | 0 | 1,081 |
| | | Graham | 0 | 0 | 0 | 0 | 14,684 |
| | | Granite Falls | 0 | 0 | 0 | 0 | 4,606 |
| | | Granite Quarry | 0 | 0 | 0 | 0 | 2,278 |
| | | Greenville | 0 | 0 | 0 | 0 | 81,814 |
| | | Grifton | 0 | 0 | 0 | 0 | 2,238 |
| | | Havelock | 0 | 0 | 0 | 0 | 21,691 |
| | | Haw River | 0 | 0 | 0 | 0 | 2,023 |
| | | Henderson | 0 | 0 | 0 | 0 | 15,795 |
| | | Hendersonville | 0 | 0 | 0 | 0 | 12,077 |
| | | Hertford | 0 | 0 | 0 | 0 | 2,198 |
| | | Highlands | 0 | 0 | 0 | 0 | 955 |
| | | Hillsborough | 0 | 0 | 0 | 0 | 5,669 |
| | | Hobgood | 0 | 0 | 0 | 0 | 375 |
| | | Holden Beach | 0 | 0 | 0 | 0 | 857 |
| | | Holly Ridge | 0 | 0 | 0 | 0 | 917 |
| | | Holly Springs | 0 | 0 | 0 | 0 | 22,639 |
| | | Hope Mills | 0 | 0 | 0 | 0 | 13,442 |
| | | Hot Springs | 0 | 0 | 0 | 0 | 637 |
| | | Hudson | 0 | 0 | 0 | 0 | 3,042 |
| | | Huntersville | 0 | 0 | 0 | 0 | 46,695 |
| | | Indian Beach | 0 | 0 | 0 | 0 | 92 |
| | | Jackson | 0 | 0 | 0 | 0 | 638 |
| | | Jacksonville | 0 | 0 | 0 | 0 | 77,508 |

[1]Agencies published in this table indicated that no hate crimes occurred in their jurisdictions during the quarter(s) for which they submitted reports to the Hate Crime Statistics Program. Blanks indicate quarters for which agencies did not submit reports.

[2]Population figures are published only for the cities. The figures listed for the universities and colleges are student enrollment and were provided by the United States Department of Education for the 2008 school year, the most recent available. The enrollment figures include full-time and part-time students.

## Table 95. Hate Crime Zero Data Submitted per Quarter, by State and Agency, 2009—*Continued*

(Number.)

| State | Agency type | Agency name | Zero data per quarter[1] | | | | Population[2] |
|---|---|---|---|---|---|---|---|
| | | | 1st quarter | 2nd quarter | 3rd quarter | 4th quarter | |
| NORTH CAROLINA | | Jefferson | 0 | 0 | 0 | 0 | 1,344 |
| | | Jonesville | 0 | 0 | 0 | 0 | 2,271 |
| | | Kannapolis | 0 | 0 | 0 | 0 | 43,166 |
| | | Kenansville | 0 | 0 | 0 | 0 | 1,186 |
| | | Kenly | 0 | 0 | 0 | 0 | 1,977 |
| | | Kill Devil Hills | 0 | 0 | 0 | 0 | 6,726 |
| | | King | 0 | 0 | 0 | 0 | 7,011 |
| | | Kings Mountain | 0 | 0 | 0 | 0 | 11,275 |
| | | Kingstown | 0 | 0 | 0 | 0 | 847 |
| | | Kinston | 0 | 0 | 0 | 0 | 22,203 |
| | | Kitty Hawk | 0 | 0 | 0 | 0 | 3,290 |
| | | Knightdale | 0 | 0 | 0 | 0 | 8,419 |
| | | Kure Beach | 0 | 0 | 0 | 0 | 2,658 |
| | | Lake Lure | 0 | 0 | 0 | 0 | 1,010 |
| | | Lake Royale | 0 | 0 | 0 | 0 | |
| | | Lake Waccamaw | 0 | 0 | 0 | 0 | 1,449 |
| | | Landis | 0 | 0 | 0 | 0 | 3,133 |
| | | Laurel Park | 0 | 0 | 0 | 0 | 2,178 |
| | | Laurinburg | 0 | 0 | 0 | 0 | 15,506 |
| | | Leland | 0 | 0 | 0 | 0 | 5,216 |
| | | Lenoir | 0 | 0 | 0 | 0 | 17,869 |
| | | Lexington | 0 | 0 | 0 | 0 | 20,450 |
| | | Liberty | 0 | 0 | 0 | 0 | 2,739 |
| | | Lilesville | 0 | 0 | 0 | 0 | 420 |
| | | Lillington | 0 | 0 | 0 | 0 | 3,327 |
| | | Lincolnton | 0 | 0 | 0 | 0 | 10,944 |
| | | Littleton | 0 | 0 | 0 | 0 | 641 |
| | | Locust | 0 | 0 | 0 | 0 | 2,649 |
| | | Long View | 0 | 0 | 0 | 0 | 4,967 |
| | | Louisburg | 0 | 0 | 0 | 0 | 3,856 |
| | | Lowell | 0 | 0 | 0 | 0 | 2,807 |
| | | Lumberton | 0 | 0 | 0 | 0 | 22,111 |
| | | Madison | 0 | 0 | 0 | 0 | 2,255 |
| | | Maggie Valley | 0 | 0 | 0 | 0 | 814 |
| | | Magnolia | 0 | 0 | 0 | 0 | 995 |
| | | Manteo | 0 | 0 | 0 | 0 | 1,331 |
| | | Marion | 0 | 0 | 0 | 0 | 5,168 |
| | | Marshall | 0 | 0 | 0 | 0 | 831 |
| | | Mars Hill | 0 | 0 | 0 | 0 | 1,773 |
| | | Marshville | 0 | 0 | 0 | 0 | 3,317 |
| | | Matthews | 0 | 0 | 0 | 0 | 27,359 |
| | | Maxton | 0 | 0 | 0 | 0 | 2,699 |
| | | Mayodan | 0 | 0 | 0 | 0 | 2,595 |
| | | Maysville | 0 | 0 | 0 | 0 | 955 |
| | | McAdenville | 0 | 0 | 0 | 0 | 669 |
| | | Mebane | 0 | 0 | 0 | 0 | 11,024 |
| | | Middlesex | 0 | 0 | 0 | 0 | 860 |
| | | Misenheimer | 0 | 0 | 0 | 0 | 683 |
| | | Mocksville | 0 | 0 | 0 | 0 | 4,686 |
| | | Monroe | 0 | 0 | 0 | 0 | 33,178 |
| | | Montreat | 0 | 0 | 0 | 0 | 704 |
| | | Mooresville | 0 | 0 | 0 | 0 | 22,247 |
| | | Morehead City | 0 | 0 | 0 | 0 | 9,715 |
| | | Morrisville | 0 | 0 | 0 | 0 | 15,207 |
| | | Morven | 0 | 0 | 0 | 0 | 537 |
| | | Mount Gilead | 0 | 0 | 0 | 0 | 1,396 |
| | | Mount Holly | 0 | 0 | 0 | 0 | 10,130 |
| | | Mount Olive | 0 | 0 | 0 | 0 | 4,371 |
| | | Murfreesboro | 0 | 0 | 0 | 0 | 2,372 |
| | | Murphy | 0 | 0 | 0 | 0 | 1,558 |
| | | Nags Head | 0 | 0 | 0 | 0 | 3,051 |
| | | Nashville | 0 | 0 | 0 | 0 | 4,551 |
| | | Navassa | 0 | 0 | 0 | 0 | 1,908 |
| | | New Bern | 0 | 0 | 0 | 0 | 29,251 |
| | | Newland | 0 | 0 | 0 | 0 | 650 |
| | | Newport | 0 | 0 | 0 | 0 | 4,419 |
| | | Newton | 0 | 0 | 0 | 0 | 13,449 |
| | | Newton Grove | 0 | 0 | 0 | 0 | 633 |
| | | Norlina | 0 | 0 | 0 | 0 | 1,010 |
| | | North Topsail Beach | 0 | 0 | 0 | 0 | 969 |
| | | Northwest | 0 | 0 | 0 | 0 | 980 |
| | | North Wilkesboro | 0 | 0 | 0 | 0 | 4,158 |
| | | Norwood | 0 | 0 | 0 | 0 | 2,403 |
| | | Oakboro | 0 | 0 | 0 | 0 | 1,165 |
| | | Oak Island | 0 | 0 | 0 | 0 | 8,375 |
| | | Ocean Isle Beach | 0 | 0 | 0 | 0 | 539 |
| | | Old Fort | 0 | 0 | 0 | 0 | 959 |
| | | Oxford | 0 | 0 | 0 | 0 | 8,667 |
| | | Parkton | 0 | 0 | 0 | 0 | 434 |
| | | Pembroke | 0 | 0 | 0 | 0 | 2,763 |
| | | Pikeville | 0 | 0 | 0 | 0 | 703 |
| | | Pilot Mountain | 0 | 0 | 0 | 0 | 1,271 |
| | | Pinebluff | 0 | 0 | 0 | 0 | 1,422 |
| | | Pinehurst | 0 | 0 | 0 | 0 | 12,649 |
| | | Pine Knoll Shores | 0 | 0 | 0 | 0 | 1,550 |
| | | Pine Level | 0 | 0 | 0 | 0 | 1,805 |
| | | Pinetops | 0 | 0 | 0 | 0 | 1,251 |
| | | Pineville | 0 | 0 | 0 | 0 | 6,878 |
| | | Pink Hill | 0 | 0 | 0 | 0 | 526 |
| | | Pittsboro | 0 | 0 | 0 | 0 | 2,664 |
| | | Plymouth | 0 | 0 | 0 | 0 | 3,834 |
| | | Princeton | 0 | 0 | 0 | 0 | 1,310 |
| | | Raeford | 0 | 0 | 0 | 0 | 3,534 |
| | | Raleigh | 0 | 0 | 0 | 0 | 406,005 |
| | | Ramseur | 0 | 0 | 0 | 0 | 1,769 |
| | | Randleman | 0 | 0 | 0 | 0 | 3,696 |
| | | Ranlo | 0 | 0 | 0 | 0 | 2,353 |
| | | Red Springs | 0 | 0 | 0 | 0 | 3,530 |
| | | Richlands | 0 | 0 | 0 | 0 | 934 |
| | | Rich Square | 0 | 0 | 0 | 0 | 862 |
| | | River Bend | 0 | 0 | 0 | 0 | 3,148 |
| | | Roanoke Rapids | 0 | 0 | 0 | 0 | 16,339 |
| | | Robbins | 0 | 0 | 0 | 0 | 1,228 |
| | | Robersonville | 0 | 0 | 0 | 0 | 1,535 |
| | | Rockingham | 0 | 0 | 0 | 0 | 8,810 |
| | | Rockwell | 0 | 0 | 0 | 0 | 2,017 |
| | | Rocky Mount | 0 | 0 | 0 | 0 | 57,121 |
| | | Rolesville | 0 | 0 | 0 | 0 | 3,220 |
| | | Rose Hill | 0 | 0 | 0 | 0 | 1,418 |
| | | Rowland | 0 | 0 | 0 | 0 | 1,160 |
| | | Rutherfordton | 0 | 0 | 0 | 0 | 4,031 |
| | | Salemburg | 0 | 0 | 0 | 0 | 487 |
| | | Saluda | 0 | 0 | 0 | 0 | 579 |
| | | Sanford | 0 | 0 | 0 | 0 | 30,020 |
| | | Scotland Neck | 0 | 0 | 0 | 0 | 2,150 |
| | | Seagrove | 0 | 0 | 0 | 0 | 260 |
| | | Selma | 0 | 0 | 0 | 0 | 7,049 |
| | | Seven Devils | 0 | 0 | 0 | 0 | 174 |
| | | Shallotte | 0 | 0 | 0 | 0 | 2,218 |
| | | Sharpsburg | 0 | 0 | 0 | 0 | 2,403 |
| | | Shelby | 0 | 0 | 0 | 0 | 21,515 |
| | | Siler City | 0 | 0 | 0 | 0 | 8,744 |
| | | Southern Shores | 0 | 0 | 0 | 0 | 2,631 |
| | | Southport | 0 | 0 | 0 | 0 | 3,165 |
| | | Sparta | 0 | 0 | 0 | 0 | 1,770 |
| | | Spencer | 0 | 0 | 0 | 0 | 3,394 |
| | | Spindale | 0 | 0 | 0 | 0 | 3,863 |
| | | Spring Hope | 0 | 0 | 0 | 0 | 1,291 |
| | | Spring Lake | 0 | 0 | 0 | 0 | 8,112 |
| | | Spruce Pine | 0 | 0 | 0 | 0 | 1,975 |
| | | Stanfield | 0 | 0 | 0 | 0 | 1,112 |
| | | Stanley | 0 | 0 | 0 | 0 | 3,201 |
| | | Stantonsburg | 0 | 0 | 0 | 0 | 705 |
| | | Star | 0 | 0 | 0 | 0 | 791 |
| | | Statesville | 0 | 0 | 0 | 0 | 26,763 |
| | | Stoneville | 0 | 0 | 0 | 0 | 971 |
| | | St. Pauls | 0 | 0 | 0 | 0 | 2,044 |
| | | Sugar Mountain | 0 | 0 | 0 | 0 | 211 |
| | | Sunset Beach | 0 | 0 | 0 | 0 | 2,663 |
| | | Surf City | 0 | 0 | 0 | 0 | 2,132 |
| | | Swansboro | 0 | 0 | 0 | 0 | 1,988 |

[1]Agencies published in this table indicated that no hate crimes occurred in their jurisdictions during the quarter(s) for which they submitted reports to the Hate Crime Statistics Program. Blanks indicate quarters for which agencies did not submit reports.

[2]Population figures are published only for the cities. The figures listed for the universities and colleges are student enrollment and were provided by the United States Department of Education for the 2008 school year, the most recent available. The enrollment figures include full-time and part-time students.

## Table 95. Hate Crime Zero Data Submitted per Quarter, by State and Agency, 2009—*Continued*

(Number.)

| State | Agency type | Agency name | Zero data per quarter[1] 1st quarter | 2nd quarter | 3rd quarter | 4th quarter | Population[2] |
|---|---|---|---|---|---|---|---|
| NORTH CAROLINA | | Sylva | 0 | 0 | 0 | 0 | 2,437 |
| | | Tabor City | 0 | 0 | 0 | 0 | 2,764 |
| | | Tarboro | 0 | 0 | 0 | 0 | 10,155 |
| | | Taylorsville | 0 | 0 | 0 | 0 | 1,858 |
| | | Taylortown | 0 | 0 | 0 | 0 | 886 |
| | | Thomasville | 0 | 0 | 0 | 0 | 26,759 |
| | | Topsail Beach | 0 | 0 | 0 | 0 | 594 |
| | | Trent Woods | 0 | 0 | 0 | 0 | 3,960 |
| | | Troutman | 0 | 0 | 0 | 0 | 1,841 |
| | | Troy | 0 | 0 | 0 | 0 | 3,403 |
| | | Tryon | 0 | 0 | 0 | 0 | 1,702 |
| | | Valdese | 0 | 0 | 0 | 0 | 4,542 |
| | | Vanceboro | 0 | 0 | 0 | 0 | 844 |
| | | Vass | 0 | 0 | 0 | 0 | 803 |
| | | Wadesboro | 0 | 0 | 0 | 0 | 5,026 |
| | | Wagram | 0 | 0 | 0 | 0 | 772 |
| | | Wake Forest | 0 | 0 | 0 | 0 | 29,368 |
| | | Wallace | 0 | 0 | 0 | 0 | 3,619 |
| | | Walnut Cove | 0 | 0 | 0 | 0 | 1,611 |
| | | Walnut Creek | 0 | 0 | 0 | 0 | 855 |
| | | Warrenton | 0 | 0 | 0 | 0 | 832 |
| | | Warsaw | 0 | 0 | 0 | 0 | 3,192 |
| | | Washington | 0 | 0 | 0 | 0 | 10,157 |
| | | Waxhaw | 0 | 0 | 0 | 0 | 3,808 |
| | | Waynesville | 0 | 0 | 0 | 0 | 9,915 |
| | | Weaverville | 0 | 0 | 0 | 0 | 3,102 |
| | | Weldon | 0 | 0 | 0 | 0 | 1,656 |
| | | West Jefferson | 0 | 0 | 0 | 0 | 1,118 |
| | | Whispering Pines | 0 | 0 | 0 | 0 | 2,157 |
| | | Whitakers | 0 | 0 | 0 | 0 | 770 |
| | | White Lake | 0 | 0 | 0 | 0 | 515 |
| | | Whiteville | 0 | 0 | 0 | 0 | 5,242 |
| | | Wilkesboro | 0 | 0 | 0 | 0 | 3,134 |
| | | Williamston | 0 | 0 | 0 | 0 | 5,323 |
| | | Wilmington | 0 | 0 | 0 | 0 | 101,438 |
| | | Wilson | 0 | 0 | 0 | 0 | 48,807 |
| | | Wilson's Mills | 0 | 0 | 0 | 0 | 1,634 |
| | | Windsor | 0 | 0 | 0 | 0 | 3,093 |
| | | Wingate | 0 | 0 | 0 | 0 | 4,097 |
| | | Winston-Salem | 0 | 0 | 0 | 0 | 230,978 |
| | | Winterville | 0 | 0 | 0 | 0 | 4,812 |
| | | Winton | 0 | 0 | 0 | 0 | 889 |
| | | Woodfin | 0 | 0 | 0 | 0 | 5,750 |
| | | Woodland | 0 | 0 | 0 | 0 | 760 |
| | | Wrightsville Beach | 0 | 0 | 0 | 0 | 2,654 |
| | | Yadkinville | 0 | 0 | 0 | 0 | 2,865 |
| | | Youngsville | 0 | 0 | 0 | 0 | 786 |
| | | Zebulon | 0 | 0 | 0 | 0 | 4,809 |
| | Universities and Colleges | Appalachian State University | 0 | 0 | 0 | 0 | 16,610 |
| | | Beaufort County Community College | 0 | 0 | 0 | 0 | 1,763 |
| | | Belmont Abbey College | 0 | 0 | 0 | 0 | 1,497 |
| | | Davidson College | 0 | 0 | 0 | 0 | 1,668 |
| | | Duke University | 0 | 0 | 0 | 0 | 14,060 |
| | | East Carolina University | 0 | 0 | 0 | 0 | 27,677 |
| | | Elizabeth City State University | 0 | 0 | 0 | 0 | 3,104 |
| | | Elon University | 0 | 0 | 0 | 0 | 5,628 |
| | | Fayetteville State University | 0 | 0 | 0 | 0 | 6,217 |
| | | Methodist College | 0 | 0 | 0 | 0 | 2,190 |
| | | North Carolina Agricultural and Technical State University | 0 | 0 | 0 | 0 | 10,388 |
| | | North Carolina Central University | 0 | 0 | 0 | 0 | 8,035 |
| | | North Carolina School of the Arts | 0 | 0 | 0 | 0 | 879 |
| | | North Carolina State University, Raleigh | 0 | 0 | 0 | 0 | 32,872 |
| | | Queens University | 0 | 0 | 0 | 0 | 2,302 |
| | | Saint Augustine's College | 0 | 0 | 0 | 0 | 1,451 |
| | | University of North Carolina: | | | | | |
| | | Asheville | 0 | 0 | 0 | 0 | 3,629 |
| | | Chapel Hill | 0 | 0 | 0 | 0 | 28,567 |
| | | Charlotte | 0 | 0 | 0 | 0 | 23,300 |
| | | Greensboro | 0 | 0 | 0 | 0 | 19,976 |
| | | Pembroke | 0 | 0 | 0 | 0 | 6,303 |
| | | Wilmington | 0 | 0 | 0 | 0 | 12,643 |
| | | Wake Forest University | 0 | 0 | 0 | 0 | 6,862 |
| | | Western Carolina University | 0 | 0 | 0 | 0 | 9,050 |
| | | Winston-Salem State University | 0 | 0 | 0 | 0 | 6,442 |
| | Metropolitan Counties | Alamance | 0 | 0 | 0 | 0 | |
| | | Alexander | 0 | 0 | 0 | 0 | |
| | | Anson | 0 | 0 | 0 | 0 | |
| | | Brunswick | 0 | 0 | 0 | 0 | |
| | | Burke | 0 | 0 | 0 | 0 | |
| | | Cabarrus | 0 | 0 | 0 | 0 | |
| | | Catawba | 0 | 0 | 0 | 0 | |
| | | Cumberland | 0 | 0 | 0 | 0 | |
| | | Davie | 0 | 0 | 0 | 0 | |
| | | Durham | 0 | 0 | 0 | 0 | |
| | | Edgecombe | 0 | 0 | 0 | 0 | |
| | | Franklin | 0 | 0 | 0 | 0 | |
| | | Gaston | 0 | 0 | 0 | 0 | |
| | | Gaston County Police Department | 0 | 0 | 0 | 0 | |
| | | Greene | 0 | 0 | 0 | 0 | |
| | | Haywood | 0 | 0 | 0 | 0 | |
| | | Henderson | 0 | 0 | 0 | 0 | |
| | | Hoke | 0 | 0 | 0 | 0 | |
| | | Johnston | 0 | 0 | 0 | 0 | |
| | | Madison | 0 | 0 | 0 | 0 | |
| | | Nash | 0 | 0 | 0 | 0 | |
| | | New Hanover | 0 | 0 | 0 | 0 | |
| | | Onslow | 0 | 0 | 0 | 0 | |
| | | Orange | 0 | 0 | 0 | 0 | |
| | | Pender | 0 | 0 | 0 | 0 | |
| | | Randolph | 0 | 0 | 0 | 0 | |
| | | Stokes | 0 | 0 | 0 | 0 | |
| | | Union | 0 | 0 | 0 | 0 | |
| | | Wake | 0 | 0 | 0 | 0 | |
| | | Wayne | 0 | 0 | 0 | 0 | |
| | | Yadkin | 0 | 0 | 0 | 0 | |
| | Nonmetropolitan Counties | Alleghany | 0 | 0 | 0 | 0 | |
| | | Ashe | 0 | 0 | 0 | 0 | |
| | | Avery | 0 | 0 | 0 | 0 | |

[1]Agencies published in this table indicated that no hate crimes occurred in their jurisdictions during the quarter(s) for which they submitted reports to the Hate Crime Statistics Program. Blanks indicate quarters for which agencies did not submit reports.

[2]Population figures are published only for the cities. The figures listed for the universities and colleges are student enrollment and were provided by the United States Department of Education for the 2008 school year, the most recent available. The enrollment figures include full-time and part-time students.

## Table 95. Hate Crime Zero Data Submitted per Quarter, by State and Agency, 2009—*Continued*

(Number.)

| State | Agency type | Agency name | Zero data per quarter[1] 1st quarter | 2nd quarter | 3rd quarter | 4th quarter | Population[2] |
|---|---|---|---|---|---|---|---|
| NORTH CAROLINA | | Beaufort | 0 | 0 | 0 | 0 | |
| | | Bertie | 0 | 0 | 0 | 0 | |
| | | Bladen | 0 | 0 | 0 | 0 | |
| | | Camden | 0 | 0 | 0 | 0 | |
| | | Carteret | 0 | 0 | 0 | 0 | |
| | | Caswell | 0 | 0 | 0 | 0 | |
| | | Chowan | 0 | 0 | 0 | 0 | |
| | | Clay | 0 | 0 | 0 | 0 | |
| | | Cleveland | 0 | 0 | 0 | 0 | |
| | | Columbus | 0 | 0 | 0 | 0 | |
| | | Craven | 0 | 0 | 0 | 0 | |
| | | Dare | 0 | 0 | 0 | 0 | |
| | | Davidson | 0 | 0 | 0 | 0 | |
| | | Duplin | 0 | 0 | 0 | 0 | |
| | | Gates | 0 | 0 | 0 | 0 | |
| | | Graham | 0 | 0 | 0 | 0 | |
| | | Granville | 0 | 0 | 0 | 0 | |
| | | Halifax | 0 | 0 | 0 | 0 | |
| | | Harnett | 0 | 0 | 0 | 0 | |
| | | Hertford | 0 | 0 | 0 | 0 | |
| | | Hyde | 0 | 0 | 0 | 0 | |
| | | Jackson | 0 | 0 | 0 | 0 | |
| | | Jones | 0 | 0 | 0 | 0 | |
| | | Lee | 0 | 0 | 0 | 0 | |
| | | Lenoir | 0 | 0 | 0 | 0 | |
| | | Lincoln | 0 | 0 | 0 | 0 | |
| | | Macon | 0 | 0 | 0 | 0 | |
| | | Martin | 0 | 0 | 0 | 0 | |
| | | McDowell | 0 | 0 | 0 | 0 | |
| | | Mitchell | 0 | 0 | 0 | 0 | |
| | | Montgomery | 0 | 0 | 0 | 0 | |
| | | Moore | 0 | 0 | 0 | 0 | |
| | | Northampton | 0 | 0 | 0 | 0 | |
| | | Pamlico | 0 | 0 | 0 | 0 | |
| | | Perquimans | 0 | 0 | 0 | 0 | |
| | | Polk | 0 | 0 | 0 | 0 | |
| | | Richmond | 0 | 0 | 0 | 0 | |
| | | Robeson | 0 | 0 | 0 | 0 | |
| | | Rowan | 0 | 0 | 0 | 0 | |
| | | Sampson | 0 | 0 | 0 | 0 | |
| | | Scotland | 0 | 0 | 0 | 0 | |
| | | Stanly | 0 | 0 | 0 | 0 | |
| | | Surry | 0 | 0 | 0 | 0 | |
| | | Swain | 0 | 0 | 0 | 0 | |
| | | Tyrrell | 0 | 0 | 0 | 0 | |
| | | Vance | 0 | 0 | 0 | 0 | |
| | | Warren | 0 | 0 | 0 | 0 | |
| | | Washington | 0 | 0 | 0 | 0 | |
| | | Watauga | 0 | 0 | 0 | 0 | |
| | | Wilkes | 0 | 0 | 0 | 0 | |
| | | Wilson | 0 | 0 | 0 | 0 | |
| | | Yancey | 0 | 0 | 0 | 0 | |
| | State Police Agencies | North Carolina Highway Patrol | 0 | 0 | 0 | 0 | |
| | Tribal Agencies | Cherokee Tribal | 0 | 0 | 0 | 0 | |
| | Other Agencies | Asheville Regional Airport | 0 | 0 | 0 | 0 | |
| | | Caswell Center Hospital | 0 | 0 | 0 | 0 | |
| | | Department of Human Resources | 0 | 0 | 0 | 0 | |
| | | Department of Wildlife | 0 | 0 | 0 | 0 | |
| | | Division of Alcohol Law Enforcement | 0 | 0 | 0 | 0 | |
| | | Durham County Alcohol Beverage Control Law Enforcement Office | 0 | 0 | 0 | 0 | |
| | | Nash County Alcohol Beverage Control Enforcement | 0 | 0 | 0 | 0 | |
| | | North Carolina Arboretum | 0 | 0 | 0 | 0 | |
| | | Piedmont Triad International Airport | 0 | 0 | 0 | 0 | |
| | | Raleigh-Durham International Airport | 0 | 0 | 0 | 0 | |
| | | State Capitol Police | 0 | 0 | 0 | 0 | |
| | | State Fairgrounds | 0 | 0 | 0 | 0 | |
| | | State Park Rangers: Carolina Beach | 0 | 0 | 0 | 0 | |
| | | Cliffs of the Neuse | 0 | 0 | 0 | 0 | |
| | | Crowders Mountain | 0 | 0 | 0 | 0 | |
| | | Dismal Swamp | 0 | 0 | 0 | 0 | |
| | | Elk Knob | 0 | 0 | 0 | 0 | |
| | | Eno River | 0 | 0 | 0 | 0 | |
| | | Falls Lake Recreation Area | 0 | 0 | 0 | 0 | |
| | | Fort Fisher | 0 | 0 | 0 | 0 | |
| | | Fort Macon | 0 | 0 | 0 | 0 | |
| | | Goose Creek | 0 | 0 | 0 | 0 | |
| | | Gorges | 0 | 0 | 0 | 0 | |
| | | Hammocks Beach | 0 | 0 | 0 | 0 | |
| | | Hanging Rock | 0 | 0 | 0 | 0 | |
| | | Jockey's Ridge | 0 | 0 | 0 | 0 | |
| | | Jones Lake | 0 | 0 | 0 | 0 | |
| | | Jordan Lake State Recreation Area | 0 | 0 | 0 | 0 | |
| | | Kerr Lake | 0 | 0 | 0 | 0 | |
| | | Lake James | 0 | 0 | 0 | 0 | |
| | | Lake Norman | 0 | 0 | 0 | 0 | |
| | | Lake Waccamaw | 0 | 0 | 0 | 0 | |
| | | Lumber River | 0 | 0 | 0 | 0 | |
| | | Medoc Mountain | 0 | 0 | 0 | 0 | |
| | | Merchants Millpond | 0 | 0 | 0 | 0 | |
| | | Morrow Mountain | 0 | 0 | 0 | 0 | |
| | | Mount Mitchell | 0 | 0 | 0 | 0 | |
| | | New River/Mount Jefferson | 0 | 0 | 0 | 0 | |
| | | Pettigrew | 0 | 0 | 0 | 0 | |
| | | Pilot Mountain | 0 | 0 | 0 | 0 | |
| | | Raven Rock | 0 | 0 | 0 | 0 | |
| | | Singletary Lake | 0 | 0 | 0 | 0 | |
| | | South Mountains | 0 | 0 | 0 | 0 | |
| | | Stone Mountain | 0 | 0 | 0 | 0 | |

[1]Agencies published in this table indicated that no hate crimes occurred in their jurisdictions during the quarter(s) for which they submitted reports to the Hate Crime Statistics Program. Blanks indicate quarters for which agencies did not submit reports.

[2]Population figures are published only for the cities. The figures listed for the universities and colleges are student enrollment and were provided by the United States Department of Education for the 2008 school year, the most recent available. The enrollment figures include full-time and part-time students.

## Table 95. Hate Crime Zero Data Submitted per Quarter, by State and Agency, 2009—*Continued*

(Number.)

| State | Agency type | Agency name | Zero data per quarter[1] 1st quarter | 2nd quarter | 3rd quarter | 4th quarter | Population[2] |
|---|---|---|---|---|---|---|---|
| NORTH CAROLINA | | Weymouth Woods/ Sandhills Nature Preserve | 0 | 0 | 0 | 0 | |
| | | William B. Umstead | 0 | 0 | 0 | 0 | |
| | | Triad Alcohol Beverage Control Law Enforcement | 0 | 0 | 0 | 0 | |
| | | WakeMed Campus Police | 0 | 0 | 0 | 0 | |
| | | Wilmington International Airport | 0 | 0 | 0 | 0 | |
| NORTH DAKOTA | Cities | Beulah | 0 | 0 | 0 | 0 | 2,834 |
| | | Burlington | | 0 | 0 | 0 | 990 |
| | | Cando | 0 | 0 | 0 | 0 | 989 |
| | | Carrington | 0 | 0 | 0 | 0 | 2,052 |
| | | Cavalier | 0 | 0 | 0 | 0 | 1,301 |
| | | Elgin | 0 | 0 | 0 | 0 | 532 |
| | | Ellendale | 0 | 0 | 0 | 0 | 1,446 |
| | | Emerado | 0 | 0 | 0 | 0 | 473 |
| | | Fessenden | 0 | 0 | 0 | 0 | 488 |
| | | Grafton | 0 | 0 | 0 | 0 | 3,924 |
| | | Harvey | 0 | 0 | 0 | 0 | 1,583 |
| | | Hillsboro | 0 | 0 | 0 | 0 | 1,459 |
| | | Jamestown | 0 | 0 | 0 | 0 | 14,535 |
| | | Lincoln | 0 | 0 | 0 | 0 | 2,875 |
| | | Lisbon | 0 | 0 | 0 | 0 | 2,170 |
| | | Mayville | 0 | 0 | 0 | 0 | 1,751 |
| | | Minot | 0 | 0 | 0 | 0 | 35,293 |
| | | Napoleon | | | | 0 | 705 |
| | | Northwood | 0 | 0 | 0 | 0 | 924 |
| | | Oakes | 0 | 0 | 0 | 0 | 1,740 |
| | | Powers Lake | | | | 0 | 238 |
| | | Rolla | 0 | 0 | 0 | 0 | 1,420 |
| | | Rugby | 0 | 0 | 0 | 0 | 2,538 |
| | | Stanley | 0 | | 0 | | 1,212 |
| | | Steele | 0 | 0 | 0 | 0 | 639 |
| | | St. John | 0 | 0 | 0 | 0 | 354 |
| | | Thompson | 0 | 0 | 0 | 0 | 954 |
| | | Valley City | 0 | 0 | 0 | 0 | 6,172 |
| | | Wahpeton | 0 | 0 | 0 | 0 | 7,484 |
| | | Watford City | 0 | 0 | 0 | 0 | 1,382 |
| | | West Fargo | 0 | 0 | 0 | 0 | 24,862 |
| | | Williston | 0 | 0 | 0 | 0 | 12,662 |
| | Universities and Colleges | North Dakota State College of Science | 0 | 0 | 0 | 0 | 2,707 |
| | | North Dakota State University | 0 | 0 | 0 | 0 | 13,230 |
| | | University of North Dakota | 0 | 0 | 0 | 0 | 12,748 |
| | Metropolitan Counties | Cass | 0 | 0 | 0 | 0 | |
| | | Grand Forks | 0 | 0 | 0 | 0 | |
| | Nonmetropolitan Counties | Adams | 0 | 0 | 0 | 0 | |
| | | Barnes | 0 | 0 | 0 | 0 | |
| | | Benson | | | | 0 | |
| | | Billings | | | | 0 | |
| | | Bottineau | 0 | 0 | 0 | 0 | |
| | | Bowman | | 0 | 0 | 0 | |
| | | Burke | 0 | 0 | 0 | 0 | |
| | | Cavalier | 0 | 0 | 0 | 0 | |
| | | Dickey | 0 | 0 | 0 | 0 | |
| | | Eddy | 0 | 0 | 0 | 0 | |
| | | Emmons | 0 | 0 | 0 | 0 | |
| | | Grant | 0 | 0 | 0 | 0 | |
| | | Griggs | 0 | 0 | 0 | 0 | |
| | | Hettinger | 0 | 0 | 0 | 0 | |
| | | Kidder | 0 | 0 | 0 | 0 | |
| | | Lamoure | 0 | 0 | 0 | 0 | |
| | | Logan | 0 | 0 | 0 | 0 | |
| | | McHenry | 0 | 0 | 0 | 0 | |
| | | McIntosh | 0 | 0 | 0 | 0 | |
| | | McKenzie | 0 | 0 | 0 | 0 | |
| | | McLean | 0 | 0 | 0 | 0 | |
| | | Mercer | 0 | 0 | 0 | 0 | |
| | | Mountrail | 0 | 0 | 0 | 0 | |
| | | Nelson | 0 | 0 | 0 | 0 | |
| | | Oliver | 0 | 0 | 0 | 0 | |
| | | Pembina | 0 | 0 | 0 | 0 | |
| | | Pierce | 0 | 0 | 0 | 0 | |
| | | Ransom | 0 | 0 | 0 | 0 | |
| | | Renville | 0 | 0 | 0 | 0 | |
| | | Richland | 0 | 0 | 0 | 0 | |
| | | Rolette | 0 | 0 | 0 | 0 | |
| | | Sargent | 0 | 0 | 0 | 0 | |
| | | Sheridan | 0 | 0 | 0 | 0 | |
| | | Slope | 0 | 0 | 0 | 0 | |
| | | Stark | 0 | 0 | 0 | 0 | |
| | | Stutsman | 0 | 0 | 0 | 0 | |
| | | Towner | 0 | 0 | 0 | 0 | |
| | | Traill | 0 | 0 | 0 | 0 | |
| | | Walsh | 0 | 0 | 0 | 0 | |
| | | Wells | 0 | 0 | 0 | 0 | |
| | | Williams | 0 | 0 | 0 | 0 | |
| OHIO | Cities | Aberdeen | 0 | 0 | 0 | 0 | 1,499 |
| | | Ada | 0 | 0 | 0 | 0 | 6,109 |
| | | Addyston | 0 | | | 0 | 991 |
| | | Albany | | | 0 | 0 | 835 |
| | | Amberley Village | 0 | 0 | 0 | 0 | 3,573 |
| | | Amelia | 0 | 0 | 0 | 0 | 3,648 |
| | | American Township | 0 | 0 | 0 | 0 | 12,595 |
| | | Arcanum | 0 | 0 | 0 | 0 | 1,953 |
| | | Archbold | 0 | 0 | 0 | 0 | 4,450 |
| | | Arlington Heights | 0 | 0 | 0 | 0 | 830 |
| | | Ashville | 0 | 0 | 0 | 0 | 3,300 |
| | | Aurora | | 0 | 0 | 0 | 14,651 |
| | | Austintown | 0 | 0 | 0 | 0 | 34,821 |
| | | Bainbridge Township | 0 | 0 | 0 | 0 | 11,175 |
| | | Baltimore | 0 | 0 | 0 | 0 | 2,912 |
| | | Barnesville | 0 | 0 | 0 | 0 | 4,024 |
| | | Batavia | 0 | 0 | 0 | 0 | 1,757 |
| | | Bay View | 0 | 0 | 0 | 0 | 633 |
| | | Bay Village | 0 | 0 | 0 | 0 | 14,454 |
| | | Bazetta Township | 0 | | | | 5,951 |
| | | Beach City | | | 0 | | 1,091 |
| | | Beachwood | 0 | 0 | 0 | 0 | 10,997 |
| | | Bellaire | 0 | 0 | 0 | 0 | 4,528 |
| | | Bellbrook | 0 | 0 | 0 | 0 | 7,000 |
| | | Bellville | 0 | 0 | 0 | 0 | 1,694 |
| | | Berlin Heights | | | 0 | | 630 |
| | | Bethel | 0 | 0 | 0 | 0 | 2,645 |
| | | Bethesda | 0 | 0 | 0 | 0 | 1,350 |
| | | Beverly | 0 | 0 | 0 | | 1,331 |
| | | Bexley | 0 | 0 | 0 | 0 | 12,435 |
| | | Blanchester | 0 | 0 | 0 | 0 | 4,306 |
| | | Blendon Township | 0 | 0 | 0 | 0 | 7,830 |
| | | Bloomville | 0 | 0 | | 0 | 977 |
| | | Boston Heights | | 0 | 0 | | 1,224 |
| | | Bowling Green | 0 | 0 | 0 | 0 | 29,536 |
| | | Bratenahl | 0 | | 0 | 0 | 1,255 |
| | | Brecksville | 0 | 0 | 0 | 0 | 12,792 |
| | | Bridgeport | 0 | 0 | 0 | 0 | 2,031 |

[1]Agencies published in this table indicated that no hate crimes occurred in their jurisdictions during the quarter(s) for which they submitted reports to the Hate Crime Statistics Program. Blanks indicate quarters for which agencies did not submit reports.

[2]Population figures are published only for the cities. The figures listed for the universities and colleges are student enrollment and were provided by the United States Department of Education for the 2008 school year, the most recent available. The enrollment figures include full-time and part-time students.

# Table 95. Hate Crime Zero Data Submitted per Quarter, by State and Agency, 2009—*Continued*

(Number.)

| State | Agency type | Agency name | Zero data per quarter[1] | | | | Population[2] |
|---|---|---|---|---|---|---|---|
| | | | 1st quarter | 2nd quarter | 3rd quarter | 4th quarter | |
| OHIO | | Broadview Heights | 0 | 0 | 0 | 0 | 17,422 |
| | | Brooklyn Heights | 0 | 0 | 0 | 0 | 1,443 |
| | | Brook Park | 0 | 0 | 0 | 0 | 18,987 |
| | | Brunswick Hills Township | 0 | 0 | 0 | 0 | 7,486 |
| | | Bryan | 0 | 0 | 0 | 0 | 8,286 |
| | | Buckeye Lake | 0 | 0 | 0 | 0 | 3,041 |
| | | Butler | 0 | 0 | | | 876 |
| | | Cadiz | 0 | 0 | 0 | 0 | 3,281 |
| | | Cairo | 0 | 0 | | | 506 |
| | | Cambridge | 0 | | 0 | 0 | 11,156 |
| | | Camden | 0 | 0 | 0 | 0 | 2,169 |
| | | Campbell | 0 | 0 | 0 | 0 | 8,333 |
| | | Canal Fulton | 0 | 0 | 0 | 0 | 5,016 |
| | | Canfield | 0 | 0 | 0 | 0 | 6,805 |
| | | Cardington | 0 | 0 | 0 | 0 | 2,008 |
| | | Carey | 0 | 0 | 0 | 0 | 3,759 |
| | | Carroll | 0 | 0 | 0 | 0 | 465 |
| | | Centerville | 0 | 0 | 0 | 0 | 22,891 |
| | | Chagrin Falls | | 0 | | | 3,602 |
| | | Champion Township | 0 | 0 | 0 | 0 | 9,145 |
| | | Cheviot | 0 | 0 | 0 | 0 | 8,322 |
| | | Circleville | 0 | 0 | 0 | 0 | 13,701 |
| | | Clay Center | 0 | | | | 303 |
| | | Clayton | 0 | | | | 12,858 |
| | | Clay Township, Ottawa County | 0 | 0 | 0 | 0 | 2,722 |
| | | Cleves | 0 | 0 | 0 | 0 | 2,678 |
| | | Clinton Township | 0 | 0 | 0 | 0 | 4,019 |
| | | Clyde | 0 | 0 | 0 | | 6,120 |
| | | Coal Grove | | | 0 | | 2,070 |
| | | Coitsville Township | 0 | 0 | 0 | 0 | 1,619 |
| | | Coldwater | 0 | 0 | 0 | 0 | 4,387 |
| | | Commercial Point | | 0 | 0 | 0 | 835 |
| | | Cortland | 0 | 0 | 0 | 0 | 6,319 |
| | | Covington | 0 | 0 | 0 | 0 | 2,623 |
| | | Craig Beach | 0 | 0 | 0 | | 1,149 |
| | | Creston | 0 | 0 | 0 | 0 | 2,109 |
| | | Cridersville | 0 | 0 | 0 | 0 | 1,696 |
| | | Crooksville | 0 | 0 | 0 | 0 | 2,438 |
| | | Cross Creek Township | 0 | 0 | 0 | 0 | 5,469 |
| | | Danville | 0 | 0 | 0 | 0 | 1,070 |
| | | Deer Park | 0 | 0 | 0 | 0 | 5,725 |
| | | De Graff | 0 | 0 | 0 | 0 | 1,141 |
| | | Delaware | 0 | 0 | 0 | 0 | 34,734 |
| | | Delhi Township | 0 | 0 | 0 | 0 | 31,419 |
| | | Delphos | 0 | | | | 6,704 |
| | | Delta | 0 | 0 | 0 | 0 | 2,897 |
| | | Dennison | 0 | 0 | 0 | 0 | 2,866 |
| | | Dillonvale | | | | 0 | 715 |
| | | Dover | 0 | 0 | 0 | 0 | 12,487 |
| | | Dresden | | | | 0 | 1,414 |
| | | Eastlake | | 0 | 0 | 0 | 19,443 |
| | | Eaton | 0 | 0 | 0 | 0 | 7,983 |
| | | Edgerton | 0 | 0 | 0 | 0 | 1,945 |
| | | Edison | 0 | 0 | 0 | 0 | 452 |
| | | Elida | 0 | 0 | 0 | 0 | 1,897 |
| | | Elmwood Place | 0 | 0 | 0 | 0 | 2,461 |
| | | Elyria | 0 | 0 | 0 | 0 | 54,857 |
| | | Enon | 0 | 0 | 0 | 0 | 2,532 |
| | | Euclid | 0 | 0 | 0 | 0 | 46,871 |
| | | Fairborn | 0 | 0 | 0 | 0 | 32,451 |
| | | Fairfax | 0 | 0 | 0 | 0 | 1,847 |
| | | Fairfield | 0 | 0 | 0 | 0 | 42,414 |
| | | Fairlawn | 0 | 0 | 0 | 0 | 7,000 |
| | | Fayette | 0 | 0 | 0 | 0 | 1,281 |
| | | Forest | 0 | 0 | 0 | 0 | 1,444 |
| | | Forest Park | 0 | | | | 18,418 |
| | | Fort Recovery | 0 | 0 | 0 | 0 | 1,338 |
| | | Frazeysburg | 0 | 0 | 0 | 0 | 1,296 |
| | | Fredericktown | 0 | 0 | 0 | 0 | 2,480 |
| | | Gallipolis | 0 | 0 | 0 | 0 | 4,189 |
| | | Garfield Heights | 0 | 0 | 0 | 0 | 27,424 |
| | | Gates Mills | 0 | 0 | 0 | 0 | 2,254 |
| | | Geneva-on-the-Lake | 0 | 0 | 0 | 0 | 1,478 |
| | | Genoa | 0 | 0 | 0 | 0 | 2,270 |
| | | Georgetown | 0 | 0 | 0 | 0 | 3,405 |
| | | German Township, Clark County | 0 | 0 | 0 | | 7,186 |
| | | German Township, Montgomery County | 0 | 0 | 0 | 0 | 3,290 |
| | | Gibsonburg | 0 | 0 | 0 | 0 | 2,430 |
| | | Gilboa | | 0 | | | 167 |
| | | Girard | 0 | 0 | 0 | 0 | 9,982 |
| | | Glendale | 0 | 0 | 0 | 0 | 2,217 |
| | | Glenmont | | | 0 | 0 | 295 |
| | | Glenwillow | 0 | 0 | 0 | | 640 |
| | | Gnadenhutten | 0 | 0 | 0 | 0 | 1,283 |
| | | Golf Manor | 0 | 0 | 0 | 0 | 3,742 |
| | | Goshen Township, Clermont County | 0 | 0 | 0 | 0 | 16,564 |
| | | Goshen Township, Mahoning County | 0 | 0 | 0 | 0 | 3,429 |
| | | Grandview Heights | 0 | 0 | 0 | 0 | 6,265 |
| | | Granville | 0 | 0 | 0 | 0 | 5,414 |
| | | Gratis | | 0 | | 0 | 872 |
| | | Greenfield | 0 | 0 | 0 | 0 | 5,076 |
| | | Greenhills | 0 | 0 | 0 | 0 | 3,810 |
| | | Greenville | 0 | 0 | 0 | 0 | 12,908 |
| | | Greenwich | | 0 | 0 | | 1,500 |
| | | Grove City | 0 | 0 | 0 | 0 | 34,598 |
| | | Groveport | 0 | 0 | 0 | 0 | 5,409 |
| | | Harrisburg | | | 0 | | 314 |
| | | Haskins | | | 0 | 0 | 641 |
| | | Hebron | 0 | 0 | 0 | 0 | 2,161 |
| | | Hicksville | 0 | 0 | 0 | 0 | 3,383 |
| | | Highland | | 0 | 0 | | 291 |
| | | Highland Heights | 0 | | 0 | 0 | 8,580 |
| | | Highland Hills | 0 | 0 | 0 | 0 | 1,366 |
| | | Hillsboro | 0 | 0 | 0 | 0 | 6,688 |
| | | Hopedale | 0 | 0 | | | 961 |
| | | Hubbard | 0 | 0 | 0 | 0 | 7,625 |
| | | Hubbard Township | 0 | 0 | 0 | 0 | 5,649 |
| | | Hudson | 0 | 0 | 0 | 0 | 23,098 |
| | | Independence | 0 | 0 | 0 | 0 | 6,733 |
| | | Indian Hill | 0 | 0 | 0 | 0 | 6,047 |
| | | Ironton | 0 | 0 | 0 | 0 | 11,307 |
| | | Jackson Center | 0 | 0 | 0 | 0 | 1,450 |
| | | Jackson Township, Mahoning County | 0 | 0 | 0 | 0 | 2,257 |
| | | Jackson Township, Montgomery County | 0 | 0 | 0 | 0 | 3,844 |
| | | Jamestown | 0 | 0 | 0 | 0 | 1,855 |
| | | Jefferson | 0 | 0 | 0 | 0 | 3,399 |
| | | Jewett | 0 | 0 | 0 | 0 | 765 |
| | | Johnstown | 0 | 0 | 0 | 0 | 4,086 |
| | | Junction City | 0 | 0 | 0 | 0 | 843 |
| | | Kalida | 0 | | 0 | | 1,263 |

[1]Agencies published in this table indicated that no hate crimes occurred in their jurisdictions during the quarter(s) for which they submitted reports to the Hate Crime Statistics Program. Blanks indicate quarters for which agencies did not submit reports.

[2]Population figures are published only for the cities. The figures listed for the universities and colleges are student enrollment and were provided by the United States Department of Education for the 2008 school year, the most recent available. The enrollment figures include full-time and part-time students.

## Table 95. Hate Crime Zero Data Submitted per Quarter, by State and Agency, 2009—*Continued*

(Number.)

| State | Agency type | Agency name | Zero data per quarter[1] 1st quarter | 2nd quarter | 3rd quarter | 4th quarter | Population[2] |
|---|---|---|---|---|---|---|---|
| OHIO | | Kent | 0 | 0 | | 0 | 27,964 |
| | | Kenton | 0 | 0 | 0 | 0 | 8,021 |
| | | Kettering | 0 | 0 | 0 | 0 | 53,288 |
| | | Kirtland | 0 | 0 | 0 | 0 | 7,439 |
| | | Kirtland Hills | 0 | | | | 812 |
| | | Lake Township | 0 | 0 | 0 | 0 | 7,446 |
| | | Lakewood | 0 | 0 | 0 | 0 | 50,098 |
| | | Lawrence Township | 0 | 0 | 0 | 0 | 8,483 |
| | | Lebanon | 0 | 0 | 0 | 0 | 20,944 |
| | | Leipsic | 0 | 0 | 0 | 0 | 2,166 |
| | | Lexington | 0 | 0 | 0 | 0 | 4,086 |
| | | Liberty Township | 0 | 0 | 0 | 0 | 11,749 |
| | | Liverpool Township | 0 | 0 | 0 | 0 | 4,129 |
| | | Lockland | 0 | 0 | 0 | 0 | 3,450 |
| | | Logan | 0 | 0 | 0 | 0 | 7,489 |
| | | London | 0 | 0 | 0 | 0 | 9,679 |
| | | Lordstown | 0 | 0 | 0 | 0 | 3,509 |
| | | Loudonville | 0 | 0 | 0 | 0 | 3,083 |
| | | Louisville | 0 | 0 | 0 | 0 | 9,516 |
| | | Loveland | | 0 | 0 | 0 | 11,736 |
| | | Lowellville | 0 | 0 | 0 | 0 | 1,132 |
| | | Luckey | 0 | | 0 | 0 | 988 |
| | | Lynchburg | 0 | 0 | 0 | 0 | 1,396 |
| | | Lyndhurst | 0 | 0 | 0 | 0 | 13,702 |
| | | Madeira | 0 | 0 | 0 | 0 | 8,521 |
| | | Madison Township, Franklin County | 0 | 0 | 0 | 0 | 18,389 |
| | | Maineville | 0 | 0 | 0 | 0 | 1,050 |
| | | Manchester | 0 | 0 | 0 | 0 | 2,099 |
| | | Marblehead | 0 | 0 | 0 | 0 | 829 |
| | | Marietta | | 0 | 0 | 0 | 14,272 |
| | | Marion | 0 | 0 | 0 | 0 | 35,683 |
| | | Marion Township | 0 | 0 | 0 | | 2,942 |
| | | Marshallville | 0 | 0 | 0 | 0 | 808 |
| | | Martins Ferry | 0 | 0 | 0 | 0 | 6,609 |
| | | Mason | 0 | 0 | 0 | 0 | 30,624 |
| | | Massillon | 0 | | 0 | 0 | 32,736 |
| | | Mayfield Village | 0 | 0 | 0 | 0 | 3,089 |
| | | McArthur | 0 | 0 | 0 | 0 | 2,036 |
| | | McConnelsville | 0 | 0 | 0 | | 1,551 |
| | | Mechanicsburg | | | 0 | 0 | 1,694 |
| | | Medina Township | 0 | 0 | 0 | 0 | 9,023 |
| | | Mentor-on-the-Lake | 0 | 0 | 0 | 0 | 8,306 |
| | | Miamisburg | 0 | 0 | 0 | 0 | 19,819 |
| | | Middlefield | 0 | 0 | 0 | | 2,392 |
| | | Middleport | | 0 | 0 | 0 | 2,463 |
| | | Midvale | 0 | | | | 587 |
| | | Mifflin Township | | | 0 | 0 | 3,060 |
| | | Milford | 0 | 0 | 0 | 0 | 6,334 |
| | | Millersburg | 0 | 0 | 0 | 0 | 3,636 |
| | | Millersport | | 0 | | 0 | 928 |
| | | Milton Township | 0 | 0 | 0 | 0 | 2,827 |
| | | Monroe | 0 | 0 | 0 | 0 | 15,319 |
| | | Monroeville | 0 | 0 | 0 | 0 | 1,336 |
| | | Montgomery | 0 | 0 | 0 | 0 | 10,497 |
| | | Montpelier | 0 | 0 | 0 | 0 | 3,983 |
| | | Montville Township | 0 | 0 | 0 | 0 | 6,517 |
| | | Moreland Hills | | | 0 | | 3,039 |
| | | Mount Gilead | 0 | 0 | 0 | 0 | 3,593 |
| | | Mount Orab | 0 | 0 | 0 | 0 | 2,781 |
| | | Mount Pleasant | 0 | 0 | 0 | | 492 |
| | | Mount Sterling | 0 | 0 | 0 | 0 | 1,827 |
| | | Munroe Falls | 0 | 0 | 0 | 0 | 5,149 |
| | | Navarre | 0 | 0 | 0 | 0 | 1,892 |
| | | Nelsonville | 0 | 0 | 0 | 0 | 5,390 |
| | | New Albany | 0 | 0 | 0 | 0 | 7,546 |
| | | Newark | 0 | 0 | 0 | 0 | 47,338 |
| | | New Boston | 0 | 0 | 0 | 0 | 2,151 |
| | | New Bremen | 0 | 0 | 0 | | 3,087 |
| | | Newcomerstown | 0 | 0 | | | 3,882 |
| | | New Concord | 0 | 0 | 0 | 0 | 2,582 |
| | | New Franklin | 0 | 0 | 0 | 0 | 14,986 |
| | | New Lebanon | 0 | 0 | 0 | 0 | 4,085 |
| | | New Lexington | 0 | 0 | 0 | 0 | 4,569 |
| | | New London | 0 | 0 | 0 | 0 | 2,586 |
| | | New Madison | 0 | | | | 749 |
| | | New Middletown | 0 | 0 | 0 | 0 | 1,539 |
| | | New Paris | | 0 | | | 1,477 |
| | | New Philadelphia | 0 | 0 | 0 | 0 | 17,342 |
| | | New Richmond | 0 | 0 | 0 | 0 | 2,544 |
| | | New Straitsville | | 0 | 0 | 0 | 795 |
| | | Newton Falls | 0 | 0 | 0 | 0 | 4,603 |
| | | Newtonsville | | | | 0 | 539 |
| | | Newtown | 0 | 0 | 0 | 0 | 4,148 |
| | | New Vienna | 0 | 0 | 0 | 0 | 1,381 |
| | | New Waterford | 0 | 0 | 0 | 0 | 1,340 |
| | | North College Hill | 0 | 0 | 0 | 0 | 9,496 |
| | | Northfield | 0 | | | | 3,635 |
| | | North Olmsted | 0 | 0 | 0 | 0 | 31,025 |
| | | North Randall | | 0 | 0 | 0 | 822 |
| | | North Ridgeville | 0 | 0 | 0 | 0 | 28,875 |
| | | Northwood | 0 | 0 | 0 | 0 | 5,524 |
| | | Norwalk | 0 | 0 | 0 | 0 | 16,652 |
| | | Oak Hill | 0 | 0 | 0 | 0 | 1,606 |
| | | Oakwood, Paulding County | | 0 | 0 | 0 | 552 |
| | | Oberlin | | 0 | 0 | | 8,404 |
| | | Olmsted Falls | 0 | | | 0 | 8,183 |
| | | Ontario | 0 | | 0 | | 5,193 |
| | | Oregon | 0 | 0 | 0 | 0 | 18,872 |
| | | Orrville | 0 | 0 | 0 | 0 | 8,367 |
| | | Orwell | 0 | 0 | 0 | 0 | 1,466 |
| | | Ostrander | | | 0 | | 582 |
| | | Ottawa | 0 | | | | 4,390 |
| | | Ottawa Hills | 0 | 0 | 0 | 0 | 4,597 |
| | | Owensville | 0 | 0 | 0 | 0 | 850 |
| | | Oxford | 0 | | | | 22,995 |
| | | Oxford Township | 0 | 0 | 0 | 0 | 2,695 |
| | | Parma Heights | 0 | 0 | 0 | 0 | 19,559 |
| | | Pataskala | 0 | 0 | 0 | 0 | 12,967 |
| | | Paulding | 0 | 0 | 0 | 0 | 3,331 |
| | | Payne | 0 | 0 | 0 | 0 | 1,145 |
| | | Peebles | | 0 | 0 | 0 | 1,838 |
| | | Pemberville | 0 | 0 | 0 | 0 | 1,357 |
| | | Peninsula | 0 | 0 | 0 | 0 | 699 |
| | | Perry Township, Allen County | 0 | 0 | 0 | 0 | 3,580 |
| | | Perry Township, Columbiana County | 0 | 0 | 0 | 0 | 4,578 |
| | | Perry Township, Franklin County | 0 | 0 | 0 | 0 | 3,653 |
| | | Perry Township, Montgomery County | 0 | 0 | 0 | 0 | 3,829 |
| | | Perry Township, Stark County | 0 | 0 | 0 | | 28,005 |

[1]Agencies published in this table indicated that no hate crimes occurred in their jurisdictions during the quarter(s) for which they submitted reports to the Hate Crime Statistics Program. Blanks indicate quarters for which agencies did not submit reports.

[2]Population figures are published only for the cities. The figures listed for the universities and colleges are student enrollment and were provided by the United States Department of Education for the 2008 school year, the most recent available. The enrollment figures include full-time and part-time students.

## Table 95. Hate Crime Zero Data Submitted per Quarter, by State and Agency, 2009—*Continued*

(Number.)

| State | Agency type | Agency name | Zero data per quarter[1] 1st quarter | 2nd quarter | 3rd quarter | 4th quarter | Population[2] |
|---|---|---|---|---|---|---|---|
| OHIO | | Pierce Township | 0 | 0 | 0 | 0 | 11,177 |
| | | Plain City | 0 | 0 | 0 | 0 | 3,629 |
| | | Plymouth | 0 | | | | 1,796 |
| | | Poland Township | 0 | 0 | 0 | 0 | 11,014 |
| | | Poland Village | 0 | 0 | 0 | 0 | 2,640 |
| | | Pomeroy | | 0 | | 0 | 1,952 |
| | | Port Clinton | 0 | 0 | 0 | 0 | 6,108 |
| | | Powell | 0 | 0 | 0 | 0 | 13,869 |
| | | Powhatan Point | 0 | 0 | 0 | 0 | 1,647 |
| | | Ravenna | | | | 0 | 11,335 |
| | | Reading | 0 | 0 | 0 | 0 | 10,446 |
| | | Reminderville | 0 | | 0 | 0 | 2,799 |
| | | Republic | 0 | | | | 573 |
| | | Richland Township | | 0 | | 0 | 9,285 |
| | | Rio Grande | 0 | 0 | 0 | 0 | 866 |
| | | Riverside | 0 | 0 | 0 | 0 | 25,147 |
| | | Roaming Shores Village | 0 | 0 | 0 | 0 | 1,190 |
| | | Rockford | 0 | 0 | 0 | 0 | 1,103 |
| | | Rocky Ridge | 0 | 0 | 0 | | 383 |
| | | Roseville | 0 | 0 | 0 | 0 | 1,893 |
| | | Rossford | 0 | 0 | 0 | 0 | 6,401 |
| | | Ross Township | 0 | 0 | 0 | | 8,026 |
| | | Russells Point | 0 | 0 | 0 | 0 | 1,509 |
| | | Rutland | | | 0 | | 413 |
| | | Sabina | 0 | 0 | 0 | 0 | 2,783 |
| | | Saline Township | 0 | 0 | 0 | 0 | 1,331 |
| | | Sardinia | 0 | 0 | | 0 | 822 |
| | | Seaman | 0 | 0 | 0 | 0 | 1,076 |
| | | Sebring | 0 | 0 | 0 | 0 | 4,484 |
| | | Seven Hills | 0 | 0 | 0 | 0 | 11,565 |
| | | Seville | 0 | 0 | 0 | 0 | 2,419 |
| | | Sharon Township | 0 | 0 | 0 | 0 | 2,373 |
| | | Sharonville | 0 | 0 | 0 | 0 | 13,334 |
| | | Shawnee Hills | | 0 | | 0 | 593 |
| | | Sheffield Lake | 0 | 0 | 0 | 0 | 8,858 |
| | | Shelby | 0 | 0 | 0 | 0 | 9,256 |
| | | Shreve | | | | 0 | 1,487 |
| | | Silverton | 0 | 0 | 0 | 0 | 5,152 |
| | | Smithfield | | | 0 | 0 | 791 |
| | | Smithville | 0 | 0 | 0 | 0 | 1,294 |
| | | Somerset | 0 | 0 | 0 | 0 | 1,557 |
| | | South Bloomfield | 0 | 0 | 0 | 0 | 1,700 |
| | | South Charleston | 0 | 0 | 0 | 0 | 1,766 |
| | | South Point | | | 0 | | 4,011 |
| | | South Russell | 0 | 0 | 0 | 0 | 3,902 |
| | | South Solon | 0 | 0 | 0 | 0 | 385 |
| | | South Vienna | 0 | 0 | 0 | 0 | 448 |
| | | South Zanesville | 0 | 0 | 0 | 0 | 2,024 |
| | | Spencer | 0 | 0 | 0 | 0 | 828 |
| | | Spencerville | 0 | 0 | 0 | 0 | 2,152 |
| | | Springboro | 0 | 0 | 0 | 0 | 18,209 |
| | | Springfield Township, Hamilton County | 0 | 0 | 0 | 0 | 40,051 |
| | | Springfield Township, Mahoning County | 0 | 0 | 0 | 0 | 5,956 |
| | | Springfield Township, Summit County | 0 | 0 | 0 | 0 | 15,263 |
| | | St. Bernard | 0 | 0 | 0 | 0 | 4,596 |
| | | St. Clairsville | 0 | | | 0 | 5,045 |
| | | St. Clair Township | 0 | 0 | 0 | 0 | 7,596 |
| | | St. Henry | 0 | 0 | 0 | 0 | 2,421 |
| | | St. Paris | 0 | 0 | 0 | 0 | 1,960 |
| | | Strasburg | 0 | 0 | 0 | 0 | 2,719 |
| | | Struthers | 0 | 0 | | | 10,629 |
| | | Sugarcreek Township | 0 | 0 | 0 | 0 | 7,005 |
| | | Swanton | 0 | 0 | 0 | 0 | 3,676 |
| | | Sylvania Township | 0 | 0 | 0 | 0 | 26,142 |
| | | Thornville | 0 | 0 | 0 | | 1,196 |
| | | Timberlake | 0 | | | | 731 |
| | | Tipp City | 0 | 0 | 0 | 0 | 9,255 |
| | | Toronto | 0 | 0 | 0 | | 5,175 |
| | | Tremont City | 0 | 0 | 0 | | 341 |
| | | Twinsburg | | 0 | 0 | 0 | 17,432 |
| | | Uhrichsville | 0 | 0 | 0 | 0 | 5,501 |
| | | Union | 0 | 0 | 0 | 0 | 6,361 |
| | | Uniontown | 0 | 0 | 0 | 0 | 2,849 |
| | | Uniopolis | | 0 | | | 246 |
| | | Upper Sandusky | 0 | | | 0 | 6,343 |
| | | Urbana | 0 | 0 | 0 | 0 | 11,424 |
| | | Utica | 0 | 0 | 0 | 0 | 2,101 |
| | | Vandalia | | 0 | 0 | 0 | 14,070 |
| | | Village of Leesburg | 0 | 0 | 0 | 0 | 1,307 |
| | | Wadsworth | 0 | 0 | 0 | 0 | 20,943 |
| | | Waite Hill | | 0 | 0 | | 567 |
| | | Walbridge | 0 | 0 | 0 | 0 | 3,088 |
| | | Walton Hills | 0 | 0 | 0 | 0 | 2,265 |
| | | Wapakoneta | 0 | 0 | 0 | 0 | 9,427 |
| | | Warrensville Heights | 0 | 0 | 0 | 0 | 13,465 |
| | | Warren Township | 0 | 0 | 0 | 0 | 5,968 |
| | | Washington Court House | 0 | 0 | 0 | 0 | 13,659 |
| | | Washingtonville | 0 | 0 | 0 | | 738 |
| | | Waterville Township | 0 | 0 | 0 | 0 | 5,793 |
| | | Wauseon | 0 | 0 | 0 | 0 | 7,261 |
| | | Waverly | 0 | 0 | 0 | 0 | 4,437 |
| | | Wayne | | 0 | | | 856 |
| | | Waynesburg | 0 | 0 | 0 | 0 | 965 |
| | | Weathersfield | | 0 | 0 | 0 | 8,095 |
| | | Wellston | 0 | 0 | 0 | 0 | 5,923 |
| | | Wells Township | 0 | 0 | 0 | 0 | 2,817 |
| | | Wellsville | | | 0 | | 3,867 |
| | | West Alexandria | 0 | 0 | 0 | 0 | 1,289 |
| | | West Carrollton | 0 | 0 | 0 | 0 | 12,652 |
| | | West Elkton | | | 0 | | 172 |
| | | West Jefferson | 0 | 0 | 0 | 0 | 4,252 |
| | | West Lafayette | | 0 | 0 | 0 | 2,462 |
| | | Westlake | 0 | 0 | 0 | 0 | 30,413 |
| | | West Liberty | 0 | 0 | 0 | 0 | 1,720 |
| | | West Salem | 0 | 0 | 0 | 0 | 1,460 |
| | | West Union | 0 | 0 | 0 | 0 | 3,102 |
| | | Whitehall | 0 | 0 | 0 | 0 | 18,071 |
| | | Willard | 0 | 0 | 0 | 0 | 6,640 |
| | | Williamsburg | 0 | 0 | 0 | 0 | 2,385 |
| | | Windham | 0 | 0 | 0 | 0 | 2,715 |
| | | Wintersville | 0 | 0 | 0 | 0 | 3,873 |
| | | Woodlawn | 0 | 0 | 0 | 0 | 2,628 |
| | | Woodsfield | 0 | 0 | 0 | | 2,406 |
| | | Wooster | 0 | 0 | 0 | 0 | 26,318 |
| | | Wyoming | 0 | 0 | 0 | 0 | 8,364 |
| | Universities and Colleges | Bowling Green State University | 0 | 0 | 0 | 0 | 17,874 |
| | | Central State University | | | 0 | 0 | 2,171 |

[1]Agencies published in this table indicated that no hate crimes occurred in their jurisdictions during the quarter(s) for which they submitted reports to the Hate Crime Statistics Program. Blanks indicate quarters for which agencies did not submit reports.

[2]Population figures are published only for the cities. The figures listed for the universities and colleges are student enrollment and were provided by the United States Department of Education for the 2008 school year, the most recent available. The enrollment figures include full-time and part-time students.

## Table 95. Hate Crime Zero Data Submitted per Quarter, by State and Agency, 2009—*Continued*

(Number.)

| State | Agency type | Agency name | Zero data per quarter[1] | | | | Population[2] |
|---|---|---|---|---|---|---|---|
| | | | 1st quarter | 2nd quarter | 3rd quarter | 4th quarter | |
| OHIO | | Cleveland State University | 0 | 0 | 0 | 0 | 15,139 |
| | | College of Mount St. Joseph | 0 | 0 | 0 | 0 | 2,133 |
| | | Columbus State Community College | 0 | | 0 | 0 | 24,482 |
| | | Cuyahoga Community College | 0 | 0 | | 0 | 23,234 |
| | | Kent State University | 0 | 0 | 0 | 0 | 22,944 |
| | | Lakeland Community College | 0 | 0 | 0 | 0 | 9,017 |
| | | Marietta College | 0 | 0 | 0 | 0 | 1,606 |
| | | Miami University | 0 | 0 | 0 | 0 | 17,191 |
| | | Muskingum College | | | | 0 | 2,135 |
| | | Notre Dame College | 0 | 0 | 0 | 0 | 1,637 |
| | | Ohio State University, Marion | 0 | 0 | 0 | 0 | 1,673 |
| | | Ohio University | 0 | 0 | 0 | 0 | 21,369 |
| | | Otterbein College | | 0 | 0 | 0 | 3,131 |
| | | Sinclair Community College | 0 | 0 | 0 | 0 | 19,466 |
| | | University of Akron | 0 | 0 | 0 | 0 | 24,119 |
| | | University of Cincinnati | 0 | | | | 29,617 |
| | | University of Rio Grande | 0 | 0 | 0 | 0 | 1,967 |
| | | University of Toledo | 0 | | 0 | | 22,336 |
| | | Wilberforce University | 0 | | | | 785 |
| | | Youngstown State University | 0 | 0 | 0 | 0 | 13,704 |
| | Metropolitan Counties | Belmont | 0 | 0 | 0 | 0 | |
| | | Brown | 0 | 0 | 0 | 0 | |
| | | Carroll | 0 | 0 | 0 | 0 | |
| | | Clark | 0 | 0 | 0 | 0 | |
| | | Erie | 0 | 0 | 0 | 0 | |
| | | Fairfield | 0 | 0 | 0 | 0 | |
| | | Fulton | 0 | 0 | 0 | 0 | |
| | | Greene | 0 | 0 | 0 | 0 | |
| | | Hamilton | 0 | 0 | 0 | 0 | |
| | | Licking | 0 | 0 | 0 | 0 | |
| | | Lorain | 0 | 0 | 0 | 0 | |
| | | Medina | 0 | 0 | 0 | 0 | |
| | | Miami | 0 | 0 | 0 | 0 | |
| | | Morrow | 0 | 0 | 0 | 0 | |
| | | Pickaway | 0 | 0 | 0 | 0 | |
| | | Portage | 0 | 0 | 0 | 0 | |
| | | Preble | 0 | 0 | 0 | 0 | |
| | | Richland | 0 | 0 | 0 | 0 | |
| | | Trumbull | 0 | 0 | 0 | 0 | |
| | | Union | 0 | 0 | 0 | 0 | |
| | | Warren | 0 | 0 | 0 | 0 | |
| | | Washington | 0 | 0 | 0 | | |
| | | Wood | 0 | 0 | 0 | 0 | |
| | Nonmetropolitan Counties | Adams | 0 | 0 | 0 | 0 | |
| | | Ashland | 0 | 0 | 0 | 0 | |
| | | Athens | 0 | | | | |
| | | Auglaize | 0 | 0 | 0 | 0 | |
| | | Clinton | 0 | 0 | 0 | 0 | |
| | | Columbiana | 0 | 0 | 0 | 0 | |
| | | Crawford | 0 | 0 | 0 | 0 | |
| | | Darke | 0 | 0 | 0 | 0 | |
| | | Defiance | 0 | 0 | 0 | 0 | |
| | | Fayette | 0 | 0 | 0 | 0 | |
| | | Guernsey | 0 | 0 | 0 | 0 | |
| | | Hardin | 0 | 0 | 0 | 0 | |
| | | Harrison | 0 | 0 | 0 | 0 | |
| | | Henry | 0 | 0 | 0 | 0 | |
| | | Hocking | 0 | 0 | 0 | 0 | |
| | | Huron | 0 | 0 | 0 | 0 | |
| | | Jackson | 0 | 0 | | | |
| | | Logan | 0 | 0 | 0 | 0 | |
| | | Marion | 0 | 0 | 0 | 0 | |
| | | Meigs | 0 | 0 | 0 | 0 | |
| | | Monroe | 0 | 0 | 0 | 0 | |
| | | Morgan | 0 | 0 | 0 | 0 | |
| | | Muskingum | 0 | 0 | 0 | 0 | |
| | | Noble | 0 | 0 | 0 | | |
| | | Paulding | 0 | 0 | 0 | 0 | |
| | | Perry | 0 | 0 | 0 | 0 | |
| | | Pike | 0 | 0 | 0 | 0 | |
| | | Putnam | 0 | 0 | 0 | 0 | |
| | | Scioto | 0 | 0 | 0 | 0 | |
| | | Shelby | 0 | 0 | 0 | 0 | |
| | | Tuscarawas | 0 | 0 | 0 | 0 | |
| | | Van Wert | 0 | 0 | 0 | 0 | |
| | | Vinton | 0 | 0 | 0 | 0 | |
| | | Wayne | 0 | 0 | 0 | 0 | |
| | | Williams | 0 | 0 | | 0 | |
| | | Wyandot | 0 | 0 | 0 | 0 | |
| | State Police Agencies | Ohio State Highway Patrol | 0 | 0 | 0 | 0 | |
| | Other Agencies | Bureau of Criminal Identification and Investigation | 0 | 0 | 0 | | |
| | | Butler County Metroparks | 0 | 0 | | 0 | |
| | | Cedar Point | 0 | 0 | | | |
| | | Columbus and Franklin County Metropolitan Park District | 0 | 0 | 0 | | |
| | | Hamilton County Park District | 0 | 0 | 0 | 0 | |
| | | Lake Metroparks | 0 | 0 | 0 | 0 | |
| | | Licking County Park District | 0 | | | | |
| | | Lorain County Metropolitan Park District | 0 | 0 | 0 | 0 | |
| | | Port Columbus International Airport | 0 | 0 | 0 | 0 | |
| | | Toledo Metropolitan Park District | | 0 | 0 | | |
| OKLAHOMA | Cities | Achille | 0 | 0 | 0 | 0 | 537 |
| | | Allen | 0 | 0 | 0 | 0 | 998 |
| | | Alva | 0 | 0 | 0 | 0 | 4,805 |

[1]Agencies published in this table indicated that no hate crimes occurred in their jurisdictions during the quarter(s) for which they submitted reports to the Hate Crime Statistics Program. Blanks indicate quarters for which agencies did not submit reports.

[2]Population figures are published only for the cities. The figures listed for the universities and colleges are student enrollment and were provided by the United States Department of Education for the 2008 school year, the most recent available. The enrollment figures include full-time and part-time students.

## Table 95. Hate Crime Zero Data Submitted per Quarter, by State and Agency, 2009—*Continued*

(Number.)

| State | Agency type | Agency name | Zero data per quarter[1] | | | | Population[2] |
|---|---|---|---|---|---|---|---|
| | | | 1st quarter | 2nd quarter | 3rd quarter | 4th quarter | |
| **OKLAHOMA** | | Anadarko | 0 | 0 | 0 | 0 | 6,289 |
| | | Antlers | 0 | 0 | 0 | 0 | 2,478 |
| | | Apache | 0 | 0 | 0 | 0 | 1,528 |
| | | Ardmore | 0 | 0 | 0 | 0 | 24,933 |
| | | Arkoma | 0 | 0 | 0 | 0 | 2,175 |
| | | Atoka | 0 | 0 | 0 | 0 | 3,115 |
| | | Bartlesville | 0 | 0 | 0 | 0 | 36,045 |
| | | Beaver | 0 | 0 | 0 | 0 | 1,352 |
| | | Beggs | 0 | 0 | 0 | 0 | 1,354 |
| | | Bethany | 0 | 0 | 0 | 0 | 19,667 |
| | | Blackwell | 0 | 0 | 0 | 0 | 7,092 |
| | | Blanchard | 0 | 0 | 0 | 0 | 6,825 |
| | | Boise City | 0 | 0 | 0 | 0 | 1,158 |
| | | Boley | 0 | 0 | 0 | 0 | 1,083 |
| | | Bristow | 0 | 0 | 0 | 0 | 4,395 |
| | | Broken Bow | 0 | 0 | 0 | 0 | 4,136 |
| | | Caddo | 0 | 0 | 0 | 0 | 994 |
| | | Calera | 0 | 0 | 0 | 0 | 1,841 |
| | | Calumet | 0 | 0 | 0 | 0 | 532 |
| | | Caney | 0 | 0 | 0 | 0 | 214 |
| | | Carnegie | 0 | 0 | | 0 | 1,534 |
| | | Catoosa | 0 | 0 | 0 | 0 | 6,748 |
| | | Chandler | 0 | 0 | 0 | 0 | 2,820 |
| | | Checotah | 0 | 0 | 0 | 0 | 3,468 |
| | | Chelsea | 0 | 0 | 0 | 0 | 2,237 |
| | | Cherokee | 0 | 0 | 0 | 0 | 1,418 |
| | | Choctaw | 0 | 0 | 0 | 0 | 11,579 |
| | | Chouteau | 0 | 0 | 0 | 0 | 2,021 |
| | | Claremore | 0 | 0 | 0 | 0 | 17,635 |
| | | Clayton | 0 | 0 | 0 | 0 | 728 |
| | | Cleveland | 0 | 0 | 0 | 0 | 3,123 |
| | | Clinton | 0 | 0 | 0 | 0 | 8,761 |
| | | Coalgate | 0 | 0 | 0 | 0 | 1,861 |
| | | Colbert | 0 | 0 | 0 | 0 | 1,129 |
| | | Comanche | 0 | 0 | 0 | 0 | 1,519 |
| | | Cordell | 0 | 0 | 0 | 0 | 2,936 |
| | | Coweta | 0 | 0 | 0 | 0 | 9,282 |
| | | Crescent | 0 | 0 | 0 | 0 | 1,415 |
| | | Davenport | 0 | 0 | 0 | 0 | 873 |
| | | Davis | 0 | 0 | 0 | 0 | 2,640 |
| | | Del City | 0 | 0 | 0 | 0 | 22,060 |
| | | Dewar | 0 | 0 | 0 | 0 | 896 |
| | | Dewey | 0 | 0 | 0 | 0 | 3,324 |
| | | Dibble | 0 | 0 | 0 | 0 | 648 |
| | | Drumright | 0 | 0 | 0 | 0 | 2,881 |
| | | Duncan | 0 | 0 | 0 | 0 | 22,630 |
| | | Durant | 0 | 0 | 0 | 0 | 16,726 |
| | | Elk City | 0 | 0 | 0 | 0 | 11,408 |
| | | El Reno | 0 | 0 | 0 | 0 | 16,583 |
| | | Enid | 0 | 0 | 0 | 0 | 47,448 |
| | | Eufaula | 0 | 0 | 0 | 0 | 2,767 |
| | | Fairfax | 0 | 0 | 0 | 0 | 1,443 |
| | | Fairview | 0 | 0 | 0 | 0 | 2,503 |
| | | Fletcher | 0 | 0 | 0 | 0 | 1,084 |
| | | Forest Park | 0 | 0 | 0 | 0 | 1,190 |
| | | Fort Gibson | 0 | 0 | 0 | 0 | 4,404 |
| | | Frederick | 0 | 0 | 0 | 0 | 3,794 |
| | | Geary | 0 | 0 | 0 | 0 | 1,234 |
| | | Glenpool | 0 | 0 | 0 | 0 | 10,097 |
| | | Goodwell | 0 | 0 | 0 | 0 | 1,182 |
| | | Grandfield | 0 | 0 | 0 | 0 | 925 |
| | | Grove | 0 | 0 | 0 | 0 | 6,476 |
| | | Guthrie | 0 | 0 | 0 | 0 | 11,175 |
| | | Guymon | 0 | 0 | 0 | 0 | 10,721 |
| | | Haileyville | 0 | 0 | 0 | 0 | 905 |
| | | Harrah | 0 | 0 | 0 | 0 | 5,259 |
| | | Hartshorne | 0 | 0 | 0 | 0 | 2,077 |
| | | Haskell | 0 | 0 | 0 | 0 | 1,989 |
| | | Healdton | 0 | 0 | 0 | 0 | 2,782 |
| | | Heavener | 0 | 0 | 0 | 0 | 3,236 |
| | | Henryetta | 0 | 0 | 0 | 0 | 6,016 |
| | | Hinton | 0 | 0 | 0 | 0 | 2,129 |
| | | Hobart | 0 | 0 | 0 | 0 | 3,595 |
| | | Holdenville | 0 | 0 | 0 | 0 | 5,388 |
| | | Hollis | 0 | 0 | 0 | 0 | 1,931 |
| | | Hominy | 0 | 0 | 0 | 0 | 3,613 |
| | | Hooker | 0 | 0 | 0 | 0 | 1,715 |
| | | Howe | 0 | 0 | 0 | 0 | 718 |
| | | Hugo | 0 | 0 | 0 | 0 | 5,371 |
| | | Hulbert | 0 | 0 | 0 | 0 | 539 |
| | | Hydro | 0 | 0 | 0 | 0 | 1,004 |
| | | Idabel | 0 | 0 | 0 | 0 | 6,831 |
| | | Jay | 0 | 0 | 0 | 0 | 3,057 |
| | | Jenks | 0 | 0 | 0 | 0 | 16,438 |
| | | Jones | 0 | 0 | 0 | 0 | 2,723 |
| | | Kaw City | 0 | 0 | 0 | 0 | 367 |
| | | Kiefer | 0 | 0 | 0 | 0 | 1,646 |
| | | Kingfisher | 0 | 0 | 0 | 0 | 4,357 |
| | | Kingston | 0 | 0 | 0 | 0 | 1,599 |
| | | Kiowa | 0 | 0 | 0 | 0 | 706 |
| | | Krebs | 0 | 0 | 0 | 0 | 2,139 |
| | | Lexington | 0 | 0 | 0 | 0 | 2,117 |
| | | Lindsay | 0 | 0 | 0 | 0 | 2,913 |
| | | Locust Grove | 0 | 0 | 0 | 0 | 1,596 |
| | | Lone Grove | 0 | 0 | 0 | 0 | 5,356 |
| | | Luther | 0 | 0 | 0 | 0 | 1,147 |
| | | Madill | 0 | 0 | 0 | 0 | 3,808 |
| | | Mangum | 0 | 0 | 0 | 0 | 2,689 |
| | | Mannford | 0 | 0 | 0 | 0 | 2,878 |
| | | Marietta | 0 | 0 | 0 | 0 | 2,540 |
| | | Marlow | 0 | 0 | 0 | 0 | 4,601 |
| | | Maysville | 0 | 0 | 0 | 0 | 1,300 |
| | | McAlester | 0 | 0 | 0 | 0 | 18,459 |
| | | McLoud | 0 | 0 | 0 | 0 | 4,448 |
| | | Medicine Park | 0 | 0 | 0 | 0 | 379 |
| | | Meeker | 0 | 0 | 0 | 0 | 982 |
| | | Midwest City | 0 | 0 | 0 | 0 | 56,631 |
| | | Minco | 0 | 0 | 0 | 0 | 1,817 |
| | | Moore | 0 | 0 | 0 | 0 | 54,059 |
| | | Mooreland | 0 | 0 | 0 | 0 | 1,256 |
| | | Morris | 0 | 0 | 0 | 0 | 1,311 |
| | | Mountain View | 0 | 0 | 0 | 0 | 777 |
| | | Muldrow | 0 | 0 | 0 | 0 | 3,158 |
| | | Mustang | 0 | 0 | 0 | 0 | 18,314 |
| | | Newcastle | 0 | 0 | 0 | 0 | 7,474 |
| | | Newkirk | 0 | 0 | 0 | 0 | 2,112 |
| | | Nichols Hills | 0 | 0 | 0 | 0 | 4,031 |
| | | Nicoma Park | 0 | 0 | 0 | 0 | 2,398 |
| | | Noble | 0 | 0 | 0 | 0 | 5,875 |
| | | Nowata | 0 | 0 | 0 | 0 | 3,997 |
| | | Oilton | 0 | 0 | 0 | 0 | 1,125 |
| | | Okemah | 0 | 0 | 0 | 0 | 2,897 |
| | | Okmulgee | 0 | 0 | 0 | 0 | 12,595 |
| | | Oologah | 0 | 0 | 0 | 0 | 1,158 |
| | | Pauls Valley | 0 | 0 | 0 | 0 | 6,106 |
| | | Pawhuska | 0 | 0 | 0 | 0 | 3,403 |
| | | Pawnee | 0 | 0 | 0 | 0 | 2,140 |
| | | Perkins | 0 | 0 | 0 | 0 | 2,412 |
| | | Perry | 0 | 0 | 0 | 0 | 5,041 |
| | | Piedmont | 0 | 0 | 0 | 0 | 5,756 |
| | | Pocola | 0 | 0 | 0 | 0 | 4,518 |
| | | Porum | 0 | 0 | 0 | 0 | 736 |
| | | Poteau | 0 | 0 | 0 | 0 | 8,287 |
| | | Prague | 0 | 0 | 0 | 0 | 2,126 |
| | | Pryor | 0 | 0 | 0 | 0 | 9,345 |
| | | Purcell | 0 | 0 | 0 | 0 | 6,194 |
| | | Ringling | 0 | 0 | 0 | 0 | 1,035 |
| | | Roland | 0 | 0 | 0 | 0 | 3,453 |
| | | Rush Springs | 0 | 0 | 0 | 0 | 1,352 |
| | | Sapulpa | 0 | 0 | 0 | 0 | 21,288 |
| | | Sawyer | | | | 0 | 266 |
| | | Sayre | 0 | 0 | 0 | 0 | 4,413 |
| | | Seminole | 0 | 0 | 0 | 0 | 6,797 |
| | | Shawnee | 0 | 0 | 0 | 0 | 30,724 |
| | | Skiatook | 0 | 0 | 0 | 0 | 6,973 |
| | | Snyder | 0 | 0 | 0 | 0 | 1,365 |
| | | South Coffeyville | 0 | 0 | 0 | 0 | 787 |
| | | Spencer | 0 | 0 | 0 | 0 | 4,056 |
| | | Spiro | 0 | 0 | 0 | 0 | 2,334 |

[1]Agencies published in this table indicated that no hate crimes occurred in their jurisdictions during the quarter(s) for which they submitted reports to the Hate Crime Statistics Program. Blanks indicate quarters for which agencies did not submit reports.
[2]Population figures are published only for the cities. The figures listed for the universities and colleges are student enrollment and were provided by the United States Department of Education for the 2008 school year, the most recent available. The enrollment figures include full-time and part-time students.

## Table 95. Hate Crime Zero Data Submitted per Quarter, by State and Agency, 2009—*Continued*

(Number.)

| State | Agency type | Agency name | Zero data per quarter[1] 1st quarter | 2nd quarter | 3rd quarter | 4th quarter | Population[2] |
|---|---|---|---|---|---|---|---|
| OKLAHOMA | | Stigler | 0 | 0 | 0 | 0 | 2,876 |
| | | Stilwell | 0 | 0 | 0 | 0 | 3,519 |
| | | Stonewall | 0 | 0 | 0 | 0 | 496 |
| | | Stratford | 0 | 0 | 0 | 0 | 1,491 |
| | | Stringtown | 0 | 0 | 0 | 0 | 424 |
| | | Stroud | 0 | 0 | 0 | 0 | 2,721 |
| | | Sulphur | 0 | 0 | 0 | 0 | 4,844 |
| | | Tahlequah | 0 | 0 | 0 | 0 | 16,865 |
| | | Talihina | 0 | 0 | 0 | 0 | 1,237 |
| | | Tecumseh | 0 | 0 | 0 | 0 | 6,732 |
| | | The Village | 0 | 0 | 0 | 0 | 9,728 |
| | | Tishomingo | 0 | 0 | 0 | 0 | 3,151 |
| | | Tonkawa | 0 | 0 | 0 | 0 | 3,121 |
| | | Tryon | 0 | 0 | 0 | 0 | 448 |
| | | Tushka | 0 | 0 | 0 | 0 | 373 |
| | | Tuttle | 0 | 0 | 0 | 0 | 6,265 |
| | | Valliant | 0 | 0 | 0 | 0 | 740 |
| | | Verdigris | 0 | 0 | 0 | 0 | 3,126 |
| | | Vian | 0 | 0 | 0 | 0 | 1,447 |
| | | Vinita | 0 | 0 | 0 | 0 | 6,052 |
| | | Wagoner | 0 | 0 | 0 | 0 | 8,122 |
| | | Walters | 0 | 0 | 0 | 0 | 2,408 |
| | | Warner | 0 | 0 | 0 | 0 | 1,449 |
| | | Warr Acres | 0 | 0 | 0 | 0 | 9,394 |
| | | Washington | 0 | 0 | 0 | 0 | 555 |
| | | Watonga | 0 | 0 | 0 | 0 | 5,818 |
| | | Waukomis | 0 | 0 | 0 | 0 | 1,209 |
| | | Waurika | 0 | 0 | 0 | 0 | 1,802 |
| | | Waynoka | 0 | 0 | 0 | 0 | 892 |
| | | Weatherford | 0 | 0 | 0 | 0 | 10,224 |
| | | Weleetka | 0 | 0 | 0 | 0 | 917 |
| | | Westville | 0 | 0 | 0 | 0 | 1,643 |
| | | Wetumka | 0 | 0 | 0 | 0 | 1,400 |
| | | Wewoka | 0 | 0 | 0 | 0 | 3,289 |
| | | Wilburton | 0 | 0 | 0 | 0 | 2,885 |
| | | Wilson | 0 | 0 | 0 | 0 | 1,640 |
| | | Woodward | 0 | 0 | 0 | 0 | 12,355 |
| | | Wright City | 0 | 0 | 0 | 0 | 785 |
| | | Wynnewood | 0 | 0 | 0 | 0 | 2,280 |
| | | Yale | 0 | 0 | 0 | 0 | 1,359 |
| | | Yukon | 0 | 0 | 0 | 0 | 23,058 |
| | **Universities and Colleges** | Cameron University | 0 | 0 | 0 | 0 | 5,449 |
| | | East Central University | 0 | 0 | 0 | 0 | 4,361 |
| | | Murray State College | 0 | 0 | 0 | 0 | 2,379 |
| | | Northeastern Oklahoma A&M College | 0 | 0 | 0 | 0 | 1,807 |
| | | Northeastern State University: Broken Arrow[3] | 0 | 0 | 0 | 0 | |
| | | Tahlequah | 0 | 0 | 0 | 0 | 8,771 |
| | | Oklahoma State University: Main Campus | 0 | 0 | 0 | 0 | 22,995 |
| | | Okmulgee[3] | 0 | 0 | 0 | 0 | |
| | | Tulsa[3] | 0 | 0 | 0 | 0 | |
| | | Rogers State University | 0 | 0 | 0 | 0 | 3,913 |
| | | Seminole State College | 0 | 0 | 0 | 0 | 2,031 |
| | | Southeastern Oklahoma State University | 0 | 0 | 0 | 0 | 3,866 |
| | | Southwestern Oklahoma State University | 0 | 0 | 0 | 0 | 4,850 |
| | | Tulsa Community College | 0 | 0 | 0 | 0 | 18,325 |
| | | University of Oklahoma, Norman | 0 | 0 | 0 | 0 | 26,140 |
| | **Metropolitan Counties** | Canadian | 0 | 0 | 0 | 0 | |
| | | Comanche | 0 | 0 | 0 | 0 | |
| | | Grady | 0 | 0 | 0 | 0 | |
| | | Le Flore | 0 | 0 | 0 | 0 | |
| | | Lincoln | 0 | 0 | 0 | 0 | |
| | | McClain | 0 | 0 | 0 | 0 | |
| | | Oklahoma | 0 | 0 | 0 | 0 | |
| | | Okmulgee | 0 | 0 | 0 | 0 | |
| | | Osage | 0 | 0 | 0 | 0 | |
| | | Pawnee | 0 | 0 | 0 | 0 | |
| | | Rogers | 0 | 0 | 0 | 0 | |
| | | Sequoyah | 0 | 0 | 0 | 0 | |
| | | Wagoner | 0 | 0 | 0 | 0 | |
| | **Nonmetropolitan Counties** | Adair | 0 | 0 | 0 | 0 | |
| | | Alfalfa | 0 | 0 | 0 | 0 | |
| | | Atoka | 0 | 0 | 0 | 0 | |
| | | Beaver | 0 | 0 | 0 | 0 | |
| | | Beckham | 0 | 0 | 0 | 0 | |
| | | Blaine | 0 | 0 | 0 | 0 | |
| | | Bryan | 0 | 0 | 0 | 0 | |
| | | Caddo | 0 | 0 | 0 | 0 | |
| | | Carter | 0 | 0 | 0 | 0 | |
| | | Cherokee | 0 | 0 | 0 | 0 | |
| | | Choctaw | 0 | 0 | 0 | 0 | |
| | | Cimarron | 0 | 0 | 0 | 0 | |
| | | Coal | 0 | 0 | 0 | 0 | |
| | | Cotton | 0 | 0 | 0 | 0 | |
| | | Craig | 0 | 0 | 0 | 0 | |
| | | Custer | 0 | 0 | 0 | 0 | |
| | | Delaware | 0 | 0 | 0 | 0 | |
| | | Dewey | 0 | 0 | 0 | 0 | |
| | | Ellis | 0 | 0 | 0 | 0 | |
| | | Garfield | 0 | 0 | 0 | 0 | |
| | | Garvin | 0 | 0 | 0 | 0 | |
| | | Grant | 0 | 0 | 0 | 0 | |
| | | Greer | 0 | 0 | 0 | 0 | |
| | | Harmon | 0 | 0 | 0 | 0 | |
| | | Harper | 0 | 0 | 0 | 0 | |
| | | Haskell | 0 | 0 | 0 | 0 | |
| | | Hughes | 0 | 0 | 0 | 0 | |
| | | Jackson | 0 | 0 | 0 | 0 | |
| | | Jefferson | 0 | 0 | 0 | 0 | |
| | | Johnston | 0 | 0 | 0 | 0 | |
| | | Kay | 0 | 0 | 0 | 0 | |
| | | Kingfisher | 0 | 0 | 0 | 0 | |
| | | Kiowa | 0 | 0 | 0 | 0 | |
| | | Love | 0 | 0 | 0 | 0 | |
| | | Major | 0 | 0 | 0 | 0 | |
| | | Marshall | 0 | 0 | 0 | 0 | |
| | | Mayes | 0 | 0 | 0 | 0 | |
| | | McCurtain | 0 | 0 | 0 | 0 | |
| | | McIntosh | 0 | 0 | 0 | 0 | |
| | | Murray | 0 | 0 | 0 | 0 | |
| | | Muskogee | 0 | 0 | 0 | 0 | |
| | | Noble | 0 | 0 | 0 | 0 | |
| | | Nowata | 0 | 0 | 0 | 0 | |
| | | Okfuskee | 0 | 0 | 0 | 0 | |
| | | Ottawa | 0 | 0 | 0 | 0 | |
| | | Payne | 0 | 0 | 0 | 0 | |
| | | Pontotoc | 0 | 0 | 0 | 0 | |
| | | Pottawatomie | 0 | 0 | 0 | 0 | |
| | | Pushmataha | 0 | 0 | 0 | 0 | |
| | | Roger Mills | 0 | 0 | 0 | 0 | |
| | | Seminole | 0 | 0 | 0 | 0 | |
| | | Stephens | 0 | 0 | 0 | 0 | |
| | | Texas | 0 | 0 | 0 | 0 | |
| | | Tillman | 0 | 0 | 0 | 0 | |
| | | Washington | 0 | 0 | 0 | 0 | |

[1]Agencies published in this table indicated that no hate crimes occurred in their jurisdictions during the quarter(s) for which they submitted reports to the Hate Crime program. Blanks indicate quarters for which agencies did not submit reports.
[2]Population figures are published only for the cities. The figures listed for the universities and colleges are student enrollment and were provided by the United States Department of Education for the 2006 school year, the most recent available. The enrollment figures include full-time and part-time students.
[3]Student enrollment figures were not available.

## Table 95. Hate Crime Zero Data Submitted per Quarter, by State and Agency, 2009—*Continued*

(Number.)

| State | Agency type | Agency name | Zero data per quarter[1] 1st quarter | 2nd quarter | 3rd quarter | 4th quarter | Population[2] |
|---|---|---|---|---|---|---|---|
| | | Washita | 0 | 0 | 0 | 0 | |
| | | Woods | 0 | 0 | 0 | 0 | |
| | | Woodward | 0 | 0 | 0 | 0 | |
| | **Other Agencies** | Capitol Park Police | 0 | 0 | 0 | 0 | |
| | | Grand River Dam Authority, Lake Patrol | 0 | 0 | 0 | 0 | |
| | | Guymon Public Schools | 0 | 0 | 0 | 0 | |
| | | Jenks Public Schools | 0 | 0 | 0 | 0 | |
| | | Madill Public Schools | 0 | 0 | 0 | 0 | |
| | | McAlester Public Schools | 0 | 0 | 0 | 0 | |
| | | Norman Public Schools | 0 | 0 | 0 | 0 | |
| | | Putnam City Campus | 0 | 0 | 0 | 0 | |
| **OREGON** | **Cities** | Amity | 0 | 0 | 0 | 0 | 1,466 |
| | | Ashland | 0 | 0 | 0 | 0 | 21,611 |
| | | Aumsville | 0 | 0 | 0 | 0 | 3,673 |
| | | Aurora | 0 | 0 | 0 | 0 | 1,053 |
| | | Black Butte | 0 | 0 | 0 | 0 | |
| | | Carlton | 0 | 0 | 0 | 0 | 1,699 |
| | | Central Point | 0 | 0 | 0 | 0 | 16,971 |
| | | Dallas | 0 | 0 | 0 | 0 | 16,317 |
| | | Eagle Point | 0 | 0 | 0 | 0 | 8,787 |
| | | Gervais | 0 | 0 | 0 | 0 | 2,453 |
| | | Hubbard | 0 | 0 | 0 | 0 | 2,850 |
| | | Independence | 0 | 0 | 0 | 0 | 9,822 |
| | | Jacksonville | 0 | 0 | 0 | 0 | 2,177 |
| | | Keizer | 0 | 0 | 0 | 0 | 36,275 |
| | | Lincoln City | 0 | 0 | 0 | 0 | 8,121 |
| | | Manzanita | 0 | 0 | 0 | 0 | 624 |
| | | Monmouth | 0 | 0 | 0 | 0 | 9,836 |
| | | Mount Angel | 0 | 0 | 0 | 0 | 3,511 |
| | | Myrtle Creek | 0 | 0 | 0 | 0 | 3,489 |
| | | Newberg-Dundee | 0 | 0 | 0 | 0 | 26,669 |
| | | Phoenix | 0 | 0 | 0 | 0 | 4,429 |
| | | Pilot Rock | 0 | 0 | 0 | 0 | 1,512 |
| | | Redmond | 0 | 0 | 0 | 0 | 25,856 |
| | | Rogue River | 0 | 0 | 0 | 0 | 1,942 |
| | | Shady Cove | 0 | 0 | 0 | 0 | 2,647 |
| | | Stayton | 0 | 0 | 0 | 0 | 7,375 |
| | | Sunriver | 0 | 0 | 0 | 0 | |
| | | Sutherlin | 0 | 0 | 0 | 0 | 7,154 |
| | | Talent | 0 | 0 | 0 | 0 | 6,287 |
| | | Tillamook | 0 | 0 | 0 | 0 | 4,414 |
| | | Turner | 0 | 0 | 0 | 0 | 1,784 |
| | | Umatilla | 0 | 0 | 0 | 0 | 6,443 |
| | | Yamhill | 0 | 0 | 0 | 0 | 928 |
| | **Metropolitan Counties** | Deschutes | 0 | 0 | 0 | 0 | |
| | | Jackson | 0 | 0 | 0 | 0 | |
| | | Polk | 0 | 0 | 0 | 0 | |
| | | Yamhill | 0 | 0 | 0 | 0 | |
| | **Nonmetropolitan Counties** | Morrow | 0 | 0 | 0 | 0 | |
| | | Union | 0 | 0 | 0 | 0 | |
| | **Other Agencies** | Blue Mountain Enforcement Narcotics Team: Morrow County | 0 | 0 | 0 | 0 | |
| | | Umatilla County | 0 | 0 | 0 | 0 | |

| State | Agency type | Agency name | Zero data per quarter[1] 1st quarter | 2nd quarter | 3rd quarter | 4th quarter | Population[2] |
|---|---|---|---|---|---|---|---|
| **PENNSYLVANIA** | **Cities** | Adamstown | 0 | 0 | 0 | 0 | 1,572 |
| | | Adams Township, Butler County | 0 | 0 | 0 | 0 | 9,823 |
| | | Adams Township, Cambria County | 0 | 0 | 0 | 0 | 6,008 |
| | | Akron | 0 | 0 | 0 | 0 | 4,014 |
| | | Albion | 0 | 0 | 0 | 0 | 1,490 |
| | | Alburtis | 0 | 0 | 0 | 0 | 2,425 |
| | | Aldan | 0 | 0 | 0 | 0 | 4,229 |
| | | Aleppo Township | 0 | 0 | 0 | 0 | 1,271 |
| | | Aliquippa | 0 | 0 | 0 | 0 | 10,525 |
| | | Allegheny Township, Blair County | 0 | 0 | 0 | 0 | 6,845 |
| | | Allegheny Township, Westmoreland County | 0 | 0 | 0 | 0 | 8,199 |
| | | Allentown | 0 | 0 | 0 | 0 | 107,326 |
| | | Altoona | 0 | 0 | 0 | 0 | 45,793 |
| | | Ambler | 0 | 0 | 0 | 0 | 6,171 |
| | | Ambridge | 0 | 0 | 0 | 0 | 6,949 |
| | | Amity Township | 0 | 0 | 0 | 0 | 12,149 |
| | | Annville Township | 0 | 0 | 0 | 0 | 4,786 |
| | | Apollo | 0 | 0 | 0 | 0 | 1,619 |
| | | Archbald | 0 | 0 | 0 | 0 | 6,519 |
| | | Arnold | 0 | 0 | 0 | 0 | 5,165 |
| | | Ashland | 0 | 0 | 0 | 0 | 3,080 |
| | | Ashley | 0 | 0 | 0 | 0 | 2,642 |
| | | Ashville | 0 | 0 | 0 | 0 | 256 |
| | | Aspinwall | 0 | 0 | 0 | 0 | 2,678 |
| | | Aston Township | 0 | 0 | 0 | 0 | 16,886 |
| | | Atglen | 0 | 0 | 0 | 0 | 1,383 |
| | | Athens | 0 | 0 | 0 | 0 | 3,188 |
| | | Athens Township | 0 | 0 | 0 | 0 | 4,998 |
| | | Auburn | 0 | 0 | 0 | 0 | 795 |
| | | Austin | 0 | 0 | 0 | 0 | 556 |
| | | Avalon | 0 | 0 | 0 | 0 | 4,763 |
| | | Avoca | 0 | 0 | 0 | 0 | 2,637 |
| | | Avondale | 0 | 0 | 0 | 0 | 1,083 |
| | | Avonmore Boro | 0 | 0 | 0 | 0 | 754 |
| | | Baden | 0 | 0 | 0 | 0 | 3,978 |
| | | Baldwin Borough | 0 | 0 | 0 | 0 | 18,414 |
| | | Baldwin Township | 0 | 0 | 0 | 0 | 2,016 |
| | | Bally | 0 | 0 | 0 | 0 | 1,098 |
| | | Bangor | 0 | 0 | 0 | 0 | 5,249 |
| | | Barrett Township | 0 | 0 | 0 | 0 | 4,278 |
| | | Beaver | 0 | 0 | 0 | 0 | 4,330 |
| | | Beaver Falls | 0 | 0 | 0 | 0 | 8,967 |
| | | Beaver Meadows | 0 | 0 | 0 | 0 | 944 |
| | | Bedminster Township | 0 | 0 | 0 | 0 | 6,273 |
| | | Bell Acres | 0 | 0 | 0 | 0 | 1,384 |
| | | Bellefonte | 0 | 0 | 0 | 0 | 6,125 |
| | | Bellevue | 0 | 0 | 0 | 0 | 7,899 |
| | | Bellwood | 0 | 0 | 0 | 0 | 1,854 |
| | | Ben Avon | 0 | 0 | 0 | 0 | 1,730 |
| | | Ben Avon Heights | 0 | 0 | 0 | 0 | 356 |
| | | Bendersville | 0 | 0 | 0 | 0 | 604 |
| | | Benton Area | 0 | 0 | 0 | 0 | 2,001 |

[1]Agencies published in this table indicated that no hate crimes occurred in their jurisdictions during the quarter(s) for which they submitted reports to the Hate Crime Statistics Program. Blanks indicate quarters for which agencies did not submit reports.

[2]Population figures are published only for the cities. The figures listed for the universities and colleges are student enrollment and were provided by the United States Department of Education for the 2008 school year, the most recent available. The enrollment figures include full-time and part-time students.

## Table 95. Hate Crime Zero Data Submitted per Quarter, by State and Agency, 2009—*Continued*

(Number.)

| State | Agency type | Agency name | Zero data per quarter[1] | | | | Population[2] |
|---|---|---|---|---|---|---|---|
| | | | 1st quarter | 2nd quarter | 3rd quarter | 4th quarter | |
| **PENNSYLVANIA** | | Berks-Lehigh Regional | 0 | 0 | 0 | 0 | 30,216 |
| | | Berlin | 0 | 0 | 0 | 0 | 2,059 |
| | | Bern Township | 0 | 0 | 0 | 0 | 7,231 |
| | | Bernville | 0 | 0 | 0 | 0 | 878 |
| | | Berwick | 0 | 0 | 0 | 0 | 10,160 |
| | | Bessemer | 0 | 0 | 0 | 0 | 1,088 |
| | | Bethel Park | 0 | 0 | 0 | 0 | 31,354 |
| | | Bethel Township, Armstrong County | 0 | 0 | 0 | 0 | 1,198 |
| | | Bethel Township, Berks County | 0 | 0 | 0 | 0 | 4,521 |
| | | Bethel Township, Delaware County | 0 | 0 | 0 | 0 | 11,954 |
| | | Bethlehem | 0 | 0 | 0 | 0 | 72,349 |
| | | Bethlehem Township | 0 | 0 | 0 | 0 | 23,846 |
| | | Biglerville | 0 | 0 | 0 | 0 | 1,151 |
| | | Birdsboro | 0 | 0 | 0 | 0 | 5,178 |
| | | Birmingham Township | 0 | 0 | 0 | 0 | 4,257 |
| | | Blacklick Township | 0 | 0 | 0 | 0 | 2,053 |
| | | Blairsville | 0 | 0 | 0 | 0 | 3,346 |
| | | Blair Township | 0 | 0 | 0 | 0 | 4,712 |
| | | Blakely | 0 | 0 | 0 | 0 | 6,718 |
| | | Blawnox | 0 | 0 | 0 | 0 | 1,424 |
| | | Bloomsburg Town | 0 | 0 | 0 | 0 | 12,821 |
| | | Blythe Township | 0 | 0 | 0 | 0 | 905 |
| | | Bolivar | 0 | 0 | 0 | 0 | 460 |
| | | Boswell | 0 | 0 | 0 | 0 | 1,241 |
| | | Boyertown | 0 | 0 | 0 | 0 | 3,917 |
| | | Brackenridge | 0 | 0 | 0 | 0 | 3,195 |
| | | Braddock | 0 | 0 | 0 | 0 | 2,642 |
| | | Braddock Hills | 0 | 0 | 0 | 0 | 1,809 |
| | | Bradford | 0 | 0 | 0 | 0 | 8,312 |
| | | Bradford Township | 0 | 0 | 0 | 0 | 4,811 |
| | | Branch Township | 0 | 0 | 0 | 0 | 1,799 |
| | | Brecknock Township, Berks County | 0 | 0 | 0 | 0 | 4,949 |
| | | Brentwood | 0 | 0 | 0 | 0 | 9,426 |
| | | Briar Creek Township | 0 | 0 | 0 | 0 | 3,102 |
| | | Bridgeport | 0 | 0 | 0 | 0 | 4,347 |
| | | Bridgeville | 0 | 0 | 0 | 0 | 4,828 |
| | | Bridgewater | 0 | 0 | 0 | 0 | 877 |
| | | Brighton Township | 0 | 0 | 0 | 0 | 7,929 |
| | | Bristol | 0 | 0 | 0 | 0 | 9,602 |
| | | Bristol Township | 0 | 0 | 0 | 0 | 53,660 |
| | | Brockway | 0 | 0 | 0 | 0 | 2,044 |
| | | Brookhaven | 0 | 0 | 0 | 0 | 7,876 |
| | | Brookville | 0 | 0 | 0 | 0 | 3,968 |
| | | Brownsville | 0 | 0 | 0 | 0 | 2,613 |
| | | Bryn Athyn | 0 | 0 | 0 | 0 | 1,324 |
| | | Buckingham Township | 0 | 0 | 0 | 0 | 19,847 |
| | | Buffalo Township | 0 | 0 | 0 | 0 | 7,284 |
| | | Burgettstown | 0 | 0 | 0 | | 1,468 |
| | | Bushkill Township | 0 | 0 | 0 | 0 | 8,361 |
| | | Butler | 0 | 0 | 0 | 0 | 13,809 |
| | | Butler Township, Butler County | 0 | 0 | 0 | 0 | 16,514 |
| | | Butler Township, Luzerne County | 0 | 0 | 0 | 0 | 9,589 |
| | | Butler Township, Schuylkill County | 0 | 0 | 0 | 0 | 6,120 |
| | | Caernarvon Township, Berks County | 0 | 0 | 0 | 0 | 3,601 |
| | | California | 0 | 0 | 0 | 0 | 6,384 |
| | | Caln Township | 0 | 0 | 0 | 0 | 12,217 |
| | | Cambria Township | 0 | 0 | 0 | 0 | 6,164 |
| | | Cambridge Springs | 0 | 0 | 0 | 0 | 2,665 |
| | | Camp Hill | 0 | 0 | 0 | 0 | 7,351 |
| | | Canonsburg | 0 | 0 | 0 | 0 | 8,730 |
| | | Canton | 0 | 0 | 0 | 0 | 1,683 |
| | | Carbondale | 0 | 0 | 0 | 0 | 9,147 |
| | | Carlisle | 0 | 0 | 0 | 0 | 18,406 |
| | | Carmichaels | 0 | 0 | 0 | 0 | 517 |
| | | Carnegie | 0 | 0 | 0 | 0 | 7,871 |
| | | Carrolltown | 0 | 0 | 0 | 0 | 950 |
| | | Carroll Township, Washington County | 0 | 0 | 0 | 0 | 5,449 |
| | | Carroll Township, York County | 0 | 0 | 0 | 0 | 5,855 |
| | | Carroll Valley | 0 | 0 | 0 | 0 | 3,558 |
| | | Cass Township | 0 | 0 | 0 | 0 | 1,786 |
| | | Castle Shannon | 0 | 0 | 0 | 0 | 7,974 |
| | | Catasauqua | 0 | 0 | 0 | 0 | 6,555 |
| | | Catawissa | 0 | 0 | 0 | 0 | 1,533 |
| | | Cecil Township | 0 | 0 | 0 | 0 | 10,600 |
| | | Center Township | 0 | 0 | 0 | 0 | 11,666 |
| | | Centerville | 0 | 0 | 0 | 0 | 3,192 |
| | | Central Berks Regional | 0 | 0 | 0 | 0 | 7,525 |
| | | Chalfont | 0 | 0 | 0 | 0 | 4,191 |
| | | Chambersburg | 0 | 0 | 0 | 0 | 18,352 |
| | | Charleroi | 0 | 0 | 0 | 0 | 5,673 |
| | | Chartiers Township | 0 | 0 | 0 | 0 | 7,455 |
| | | Cheltenham Township | 0 | 0 | 0 | 0 | 35,760 |
| | | Cherry Tree | 0 | 0 | 0 | 0 | 411 |
| | | Chester | 0 | 0 | 0 | 0 | 36,529 |
| | | Chester Township | 0 | 0 | 0 | 0 | 4,431 |
| | | Cheswick | 0 | 0 | 0 | 0 | 1,725 |
| | | Chippewa Township | 0 | 0 | 0 | 0 | 9,789 |
| | | Christiana | 0 | 0 | 0 | 0 | 1,109 |
| | | Churchill | 0 | 0 | 0 | 0 | 3,222 |
| | | Clairton | 0 | 0 | 0 | 0 | 7,765 |
| | | Clarion | 0 | 0 | 0 | 0 | 5,170 |
| | | Clarks Summit | 0 | 0 | 0 | 0 | 6,490 |
| | | Claysville | 0 | 0 | 0 | 0 | 670 |
| | | Clay Township | 0 | 0 | 0 | 0 | 5,965 |
| | | Clearfield | 0 | 0 | 0 | 0 | 6,124 |
| | | Cleona | 0 | 0 | 0 | 0 | 2,118 |
| | | Clifford Township | 0 | | | | 2,459 |
| | | Clifton Heights | 0 | 0 | 0 | 0 | 6,516 |
| | | Coaldale | 0 | 0 | 0 | 0 | 2,104 |
| | | Coal Township | 0 | 0 | 0 | 0 | 10,194 |
| | | Coatesville | 0 | 0 | 0 | 0 | 11,711 |

[1]Agencies published in this table indicated that no hate crimes occurred in their jurisdictions during the quarter(s) for which they submitted reports to the Hate Crime Statistics Program. Blanks indicate quarters for which agencies did not submit reports.

[2]Population figures are published only for the cities. The figures listed for the universities and colleges are student enrollment and were provided by the United States Department of Education for the 2008 school year, the most recent available. The enrollment figures include full-time and part-time students.

## Table 95. Hate Crime Zero Data Submitted per Quarter, by State and Agency, 2009—*Continued*

(Number.)

| State | Agency type | Agency name | Zero data per quarter[1] 1st quarter | 2nd quarter | 3rd quarter | 4th quarter | Population[2] |
|---|---|---|---|---|---|---|---|
| PENNSYLVANIA | | Cochranton | 0 | 0 | 0 | 0 | 1,057 |
| | | Colebrookdale District | 0 | 0 | 0 | 0 | 6,413 |
| | | Collegeville | 0 | 0 | 0 | 0 | 5,066 |
| | | Collier Township | 0 | 0 | | 0 | 6,582 |
| | | Collingdale | 0 | 0 | 0 | 0 | 8,334 |
| | | Colonial Regional | 0 | 0 | 0 | 0 | 20,125 |
| | | Columbia | 0 | 0 | 0 | 0 | 10,001 |
| | | Conemaugh Township, Cambria County | 0 | 0 | 0 | 0 | 2,441 |
| | | Conemaugh Township, Somerset County | 0 | 0 | 0 | 0 | 7,194 |
| | | Conewago Township, Adams County | 0 | 0 | 0 | 0 | 6,130 |
| | | Conewango Township | 0 | 0 | 0 | 0 | 3,518 |
| | | Conneaut Lake Regional | 0 | 0 | 0 | 0 | 3,488 |
| | | Connellsville | 0 | 0 | 0 | 0 | 8,404 |
| | | Conoy Township | 0 | 0 | 0 | 0 | 3,348 |
| | | Conshohocken | 0 | 0 | 0 | 0 | 8,509 |
| | | Conway | 0 | 0 | 0 | 0 | 2,116 |
| | | Conyngham | 0 | 0 | 0 | 0 | 1,823 |
| | | Coopersburg | 0 | 0 | 0 | 0 | 2,560 |
| | | Coplay | 0 | 0 | 0 | 0 | 3,365 |
| | | Coraopolis | 0 | 0 | 0 | 0 | 5,552 |
| | | Cornwall | 0 | 0 | 0 | 0 | 3,501 |
| | | Corry | 0 | 0 | 0 | 0 | 6,253 |
| | | Coudersport | 0 | 0 | 0 | 0 | 2,346 |
| | | Covington Township | 0 | 0 | 0 | 0 | 2,203 |
| | | Crafton | 0 | 0 | 0 | 0 | 6,473 |
| | | Cranberry Township | 0 | 0 | 0 | 0 | 27,605 |
| | | Crescent Township | 0 | 0 | 0 | 0 | 2,790 |
| | | Cresson | 0 | 0 | 0 | 0 | 1,466 |
| | | Cresson Township | 0 | 0 | 0 | 0 | 4,539 |
| | | Croyle Township | 0 | 0 | 0 | 0 | 2,221 |
| | | Cumberland Township, Adams County | 0 | 0 | 0 | 0 | 6,357 |
| | | Cumberland Township, Greene County | 0 | 0 | | | 6,381 |
| | | Cumru Township | 0 | 0 | 0 | 0 | 17,607 |
| | | Curwensville | 0 | 0 | 0 | 0 | 2,443 |
| | | Dale | 0 | 0 | 0 | 0 | 1,343 |
| | | Dallas | 0 | 0 | 0 | 0 | 2,467 |
| | | Dallas Township | 0 | 0 | 0 | 0 | 8,908 |
| | | Dalton | 0 | 0 | 0 | 0 | 1,217 |
| | | Danville | 0 | 0 | 0 | 0 | 4,403 |
| | | Darby | 0 | 0 | 0 | 0 | 9,861 |
| | | Darby Township | 0 | 0 | 0 | 0 | 9,509 |
| | | Darlington Township | 0 | 0 | 0 | 0 | 1,999 |
| | | Decatur Township | 0 | 0 | 0 | 0 | 4,736 |
| | | Delaware Water Gap | 0 | 0 | 0 | 0 | 796 |
| | | Delmont | 0 | 0 | 0 | 0 | 2,409 |
| | | Denver | 0 | 0 | 0 | 0 | 3,684 |
| | | Derry | 0 | 0 | 0 | 0 | 2,753 |
| | | Derry Township, Dauphin County | 0 | 0 | 0 | 0 | 22,091 |
| | | Dickson City | 0 | 0 | 0 | 0 | 5,872 |
| | | Donegal Township | 0 | 0 | 0 | 0 | 2,601 |
| | | Donora | 0 | 0 | 0 | 0 | 5,221 |
| | | Dormont | 0 | 0 | 0 | 0 | 8,330 |
| | | Douglass Township, Berks County | 0 | 0 | 0 | 0 | 3,503 |
| | | Douglass Township, Montgomery County | 0 | 0 | 0 | 0 | 10,259 |
| | | Downingtown | 0 | 0 | 0 | 0 | 7,974 |
| | | Doylestown | 0 | 0 | 0 | 0 | 8,100 |
| | | Doylestown Township | 0 | 0 | 0 | 0 | 18,705 |
| | | Dublin Borough | 0 | 0 | 0 | 0 | 2,146 |
| | | Du Bois | 0 | 0 | 0 | 0 | 7,598 |
| | | Duboistown | 0 | 0 | 0 | 0 | 1,186 |
| | | Duncannon | 0 | 0 | | | 1,492 |
| | | Duncansville | 0 | 0 | 0 | 0 | 1,159 |
| | | Dunmore | 0 | 0 | 0 | 0 | 13,942 |
| | | Dunnstable Township | 0 | 0 | 0 | 0 | 990 |
| | | Dupont | 0 | 0 | 0 | 0 | 2,563 |
| | | Duquesne | 0 | 0 | 0 | 0 | 6,616 |
| | | Duryea | 0 | 0 | 0 | 0 | 4,305 |
| | | Earl Township | 0 | 0 | 0 | 0 | 7,202 |
| | | East Bangor | 0 | 0 | 0 | 0 | 1,129 |
| | | East Berlin | 0 | 0 | 0 | 0 | 1,432 |
| | | East Bethlehem Township | 0 | 0 | 0 | 0 | 2,332 |
| | | East Brandywine Township | 0 | 0 | 0 | 0 | 6,792 |
| | | East Buffalo Township | 0 | 0 | 0 | 0 | 5,916 |
| | | East Cocalico Township | 0 | 0 | 0 | 0 | 10,509 |
| | | East Conemaugh | 0 | 0 | 0 | 0 | 1,150 |
| | | East Coventry Township | 0 | 0 | 0 | 0 | 6,853 |
| | | East Deer Township | 0 | 0 | 0 | 0 | 1,318 |
| | | East Earl Township | 0 | 0 | 0 | 0 | 6,669 |
| | | Eastern Adams Regional | 0 | 0 | 0 | 0 | 9,948 |
| | | Eastern Pike Regional | 0 | 0 | 0 | 0 | 5,535 |
| | | East Fallowfield Township | 0 | 0 | 0 | 0 | 7,817 |
| | | East Franklin Township | 0 | 0 | 0 | 0 | 3,950 |
| | | East Hempfield Township | 0 | 0 | 0 | 0 | 23,680 |
| | | East Lampeter Township | 0 | 0 | 0 | 0 | 15,147 |
| | | East Lansdowne | 0 | 0 | 0 | 0 | 2,461 |
| | | East Marlborough Township | 0 | 0 | 0 | 0 | 8,219 |
| | | East McKeesport | 0 | 0 | 0 | 0 | 2,772 |

[1]Agencies published in this table indicated that no hate crimes occurred in their jurisdictions during the quarter(s) for which they submitted reports to the Hate Crime Statistics Program. Blanks indicate quarters for which agencies did not submit reports.

[2]Population figures are published only for the cities. The figures listed for the universities and colleges are student enrollment and were provided by the United States Department of Education for the 2008 school year, the most recent available. The enrollment figures include full-time and part-time students.

## Table 95. Hate Crime Zero Data Submitted per Quarter, by State and Agency, 2009—*Continued*

(Number.)

| State | Agency type | Agency name | Zero data per quarter[1] 1st quarter | 2nd quarter | 3rd quarter | 4th quarter | Population[2] |
|---|---|---|---|---|---|---|---|
| PENNSYLVANIA | | East Norriton Township | 0 | 0 | 0 | 0 | 13,627 |
| | | East Norwegian Township | 0 | 0 | 0 | 0 | 828 |
| | | Easton | 0 | 0 | 0 | 0 | 26,065 |
| | | East Pennsboro Township | 0 | 0 | 0 | 0 | 19,992 |
| | | East Penn Township | 0 | 0 | 0 | 0 | 2,750 |
| | | East Petersburg | 0 | 0 | 0 | 0 | 4,336 |
| | | East Pikeland Township | 0 | 0 | 0 | 0 | 6,940 |
| | | East Pittsburgh | 0 | 0 | 0 | 0 | 1,821 |
| | | East Rochester | 0 | 0 | 0 | 0 | 558 |
| | | East Taylor Township | 0 | 0 | 0 | 0 | 2,498 |
| | | Easttown Township | 0 | 0 | 0 | 0 | 10,549 |
| | | East Union Township | 0 | 0 | 0 | 0 | 1,423 |
| | | East Vincent Township | 0 | 0 | 0 | 0 | 6,589 |
| | | East Washington | 0 | 0 | 0 | 0 | 1,847 |
| | | East Whiteland Township | 0 | 0 | 0 | 0 | 10,790 |
| | | Ebensburg | 0 | 0 | 0 | 0 | 2,907 |
| | | Economy | 0 | 0 | 0 | 0 | 9,112 |
| | | Eddystone | 0 | 0 | 0 | 0 | 2,330 |
| | | Edgewood | 0 | 0 | 0 | 0 | 2,987 |
| | | Edgeworth | 0 | 0 | 0 | 0 | 1,575 |
| | | Edinboro | 0 | 0 | 0 | 0 | 6,625 |
| | | Edwardsville | 0 | 0 | 0 | 0 | 4,625 |
| | | Elizabeth | 0 | 0 | 0 | 0 | 1,445 |
| | | Elizabethtown | 0 | 0 | 0 | 0 | 12,090 |
| | | Elizabeth Township | 0 | 0 | 0 | 0 | 12,752 |
| | | Elkland | 0 | 0 | 0 | 0 | 1,651 |
| | | Elk Lick Township | 0 | 0 | | | 2,137 |
| | | Ellwood City | 0 | 0 | 0 | 0 | 7,889 |
| | | Emlenton Borough | 0 | 0 | 0 | 0 | 728 |
| | | Emmaus | 0 | 0 | 0 | 0 | 11,354 |
| | | Emporium | 0 | 0 | 0 | 0 | 2,176 |
| | | Emsworth | 0 | 0 | 0 | 0 | 2,354 |
| | | Ephrata | 0 | 0 | 0 | 0 | 13,059 |
| | | Ephrata Township | 0 | 0 | 0 | 0 | 9,666 |
| | | Erie | 0 | 0 | 0 | 0 | 103,837 |
| | | Etna | 0 | 0 | 0 | 0 | 3,523 |
| | | Evans City | 0 | 0 | 0 | 0 | 1,870 |
| | | Everett | 0 | 0 | 0 | 0 | 1,843 |
| | | Everson | 0 | 0 | 0 | 0 | 781 |
| | | Exeter | 0 | 0 | 0 | 0 | 5,899 |
| | | Exeter Township, Berks County | 0 | 0 | 0 | 0 | 27,355 |
| | | Exeter Township, Luzerne County | 0 | 0 | 0 | 0 | 2,519 |
| | | Fairchance | 0 | | | 0 | 2,037 |
| | | Fairfield | 0 | 0 | 0 | 0 | 512 |
| | | Fairview Township, Luzerne County | 0 | 0 | 0 | 0 | 4,301 |
| | | Fairview Township, York County | 0 | 0 | 0 | 0 | 17,114 |
| | | Fallowfield Township | 0 | 0 | 0 | 0 | 4,172 |
| | | Falls Township, Bucks County | 0 | 0 | 0 | 0 | 33,445 |
| | | Falls Township, Wyoming County | 0 | 0 | 0 | 0 | 1,955 |
| | | Fawn Township | 0 | 0 | 0 | 0 | 2,291 |
| | | Fayette City | 0 | 0 | 0 | 0 | 662 |
| | | Ferndale | 0 | 0 | 0 | 0 | 1,635 |
| | | Findlay Township | 0 | 0 | 0 | 0 | 5,045 |
| | | Fleetwood | 0 | 0 | 0 | 0 | 3,996 |
| | | Folcroft | 0 | 0 | 0 | 0 | 6,806 |
| | | Ford City | 0 | 0 | 0 | 0 | 3,150 |
| | | Forest City | 0 | 0 | 0 | 0 | 1,712 |
| | | Forest Hills | 0 | 0 | 0 | 0 | 6,179 |
| | | Forks Township | 0 | 0 | 0 | 0 | 15,173 |
| | | Forty Fort | 0 | 0 | 0 | 0 | 4,209 |
| | | Forward Township | 0 | 0 | 0 | 0 | 3,458 |
| | | Foster Township | 0 | 0 | 0 | 0 | 4,204 |
| | | Fountain Hill | 0 | 0 | 0 | 0 | 4,571 |
| | | Fox Chapel | 0 | 0 | 0 | 0 | 5,107 |
| | | Frackville | 0 | 0 | 0 | 0 | 4,098 |
| | | Franconia Township | 0 | 0 | 0 | 0 | 12,920 |
| | | Franklin | 0 | 0 | 0 | 0 | 6,608 |
| | | Franklin Park | 0 | 0 | 0 | 0 | 12,264 |
| | | Franklin Township, Beaver County | 0 | 0 | 0 | 0 | 4,282 |
| | | Franklin Township, Carbon County | 0 | 0 | 0 | 0 | 4,906 |
| | | Frazer Township | 0 | 0 | 0 | 0 | 1,196 |
| | | Freedom | 0 | 0 | 0 | 0 | 1,578 |
| | | Freedom Township | 0 | 0 | 0 | 0 | 3,171 |
| | | Freeland | 0 | 0 | 0 | 0 | 3,357 |
| | | Freemansburg | 0 | 0 | 0 | 0 | 2,037 |
| | | Freeport | 0 | 0 | 0 | 0 | 1,794 |
| | | Gaines Township | 0 | 0 | 0 | 0 | 564 |
| | | Galeton | 0 | 0 | 0 | 0 | 1,196 |
| | | Gallitzin | 0 | 0 | 0 | 0 | 1,855 |
| | | Gallitzin Township | 0 | 0 | 0 | 0 | 1,295 |
| | | Geistown | 0 | 0 | 0 | 0 | 2,331 |
| | | Gettysburg | 0 | 0 | 0 | 0 | 8,103 |
| | | Gilpin Township | 0 | 0 | 0 | | 2,509 |
| | | Girard | 0 | 0 | 0 | 0 | 2,904 |
| | | Glassport | 0 | 0 | 0 | 0 | 4,503 |
| | | Glenolden | 0 | 0 | 0 | 0 | 7,174 |
| | | Granville Township | 0 | 0 | 0 | 0 | 4,953 |
| | | Greencastle | 0 | 0 | 0 | 0 | 4,092 |
| | | Greenfield Township, Blair County | 0 | 0 | 0 | 0 | 3,709 |
| | | Greensburg | 0 | 0 | 0 | 0 | 15,183 |
| | | Green Tree | 0 | 0 | 0 | 0 | 4,295 |
| | | Greenville | 0 | 0 | 0 | 0 | 6,077 |
| | | Greenwood Township | 0 | 0 | 0 | 0 | 2,059 |
| | | Grove City | 0 | 0 | 0 | 0 | 7,684 |
| | | Halifax Regional | 0 | 0 | 0 | 0 | 829 |
| | | Hamburg | 0 | 0 | 0 | 0 | 4,222 |
| | | Hamiltonban Township | 0 | 0 | 0 | 0 | 2,777 |
| | | Hampden Township | 0 | 0 | 0 | 0 | 27,352 |
| | | Hampton Township | 0 | 0 | 0 | 0 | 17,183 |
| | | Hanover | 0 | 0 | 0 | 0 | 15,076 |

[1]Agencies published in this table indicated that no hate crimes occurred in their jurisdictions during the quarter(s) for which they submitted reports to the Hate Crime program. Blanks indicate quarters for which agencies did not submit reports.
[2]Population figures are published only for the cities. The figures listed for the universities and colleges are student enrollment and were provided by the United States Department of Education for the 2008 school year, the most recent available. The enrollment figures include full-time and part-time students.

## Table 95. Hate Crime Zero Data Submitted per Quarter, by State and Agency, 2009—*Continued*

(Number.)

| State | Agency type | Agency name | Zero data per quarter[1] | | | | Population[2] |
|---|---|---|---|---|---|---|---|
| | | | 1st quarter | 2nd quarter | 3rd quarter | 4th quarter | |
| PENNSYLVANIA | | Hanover Township, Luzerne County | 0 | 0 | 0 | 0 | 10,931 |
| | | Hanover Township, Washington County | 0 | 0 | 0 | 0 | 2,711 |
| | | Harleton | 0 | 0 | 0 | 0 | 263 |
| | | Harmar Township | 0 | 0 | 0 | 0 | 3,015 |
| | | Harmony Township | 0 | 0 | 0 | 0 | 3,029 |
| | | Harrison Township | 0 | 0 | 0 | 0 | 9,922 |
| | | Harrisville | 0 | 0 | 0 | 0 | 875 |
| | | Harveys Lake | 0 | 0 | 0 | 0 | 2,936 |
| | | Hastings | 0 | 0 | 0 | 0 | 1,285 |
| | | Hatboro | 0 | 0 | 0 | 0 | 7,096 |
| | | Hatfield Township | 0 | 0 | 0 | 0 | 20,037 |
| | | Haverford Township | 0 | 0 | 0 | 0 | 47,827 |
| | | Hawley | 0 | 0 | 0 | 0 | 1,298 |
| | | Hazleton | 0 | 0 | 0 | 0 | 21,569 |
| | | Hegins Township | 0 | 0 | | | 3,353 |
| | | Heidelberg | 0 | 0 | 0 | 0 | 1,135 |
| | | Heidelberg Township, Berks County | 0 | 0 | 0 | 0 | 1,768 |
| | | Heidelberg Township, Lebanon County | 0 | 0 | 0 | 0 | 4,192 |
| | | Hellam Township | 0 | 0 | 0 | 0 | 9,149 |
| | | Hellertown | 0 | 0 | 0 | 0 | 5,666 |
| | | Hemlock Township | 0 | 0 | 0 | 0 | 2,273 |
| | | Hempfield Township, Mercer County | 0 | 0 | 0 | 0 | 3,833 |
| | | Hermitage | 0 | 0 | 0 | 0 | 16,340 |
| | | Hickory Township | 0 | | 0 | 0 | 2,266 |
| | | Highland Township | 0 | 0 | 0 | 0 | 1,213 |
| | | Highspire | 0 | 0 | 0 | 0 | 2,594 |
| | | Hilltown Township | 0 | 0 | 0 | 0 | 13,602 |
| | | Hollidaysburg | 0 | 0 | 0 | 0 | 5,477 |
| | | Homer City | 0 | 0 | 0 | 0 | 1,697 |
| | | Homestead | 0 | 0 | 0 | 0 | 3,483 |
| | | Honesdale | 0 | 0 | 0 | 0 | 4,702 |
| | | Hooversville | 0 | 0 | 0 | 0 | 701 |
| | | Hop Bottom Borough | 0 | 0 | 0 | 0 | 301 |
| | | Hopewell Township | 0 | 0 | 0 | 0 | 12,297 |
| | | Horsham Township | 0 | 0 | 0 | 0 | 24,765 |
| | | Houston | 0 | 0 | 0 | 0 | 1,238 |
| | | Hughesville | 0 | 0 | 0 | 0 | 2,028 |
| | | Hulmeville | 0 | 0 | 0 | 0 | 871 |
| | | Hummelstown | 0 | 0 | 0 | 0 | 4,432 |
| | | Huntingdon | 0 | 0 | 0 | 0 | 6,742 |
| | | Independence Township, Beaver County | 0 | 0 | 0 | 0 | 2,666 |
| | | Indiana | 0 | 0 | 0 | 0 | 14,727 |
| | | Indiana Township | 0 | 0 | 0 | 0 | 7,059 |
| | | Industry | 0 | 0 | 0 | 0 | 1,775 |
| | | Ingram | 0 | 0 | 0 | 0 | 3,336 |
| | | Irwin | 0 | 0 | 0 | 0 | 4,017 |
| | | Ivyland | 0 | 0 | 0 | 0 | 853 |
| | | Jackson Township, Butler County | 0 | 0 | 0 | 0 | 3,720 |
| | | Jackson Township, Cambria County | 0 | 0 | 0 | 0 | 4,669 |
| | | Jackson Township, Luzerne County | 0 | 0 | 0 | 0 | 4,801 |
| | | Jamestown | 0 | 0 | 0 | 0 | 571 |
| | | Jeannette | 0 | 0 | 0 | 0 | 9,777 |
| | | Jefferson Hills Borough | 0 | 0 | 0 | 0 | 9,660 |
| | | Jefferson Township, Mercer County | 0 | 0 | 0 | 0 | 2,293 |
| | | Jenkins Township | 0 | 0 | 0 | 0 | 4,893 |
| | | Jenkintown | 0 | 0 | 0 | 0 | 4,280 |
| | | Jennerstown | 0 | 0 | 0 | 0 | 689 |
| | | Jermyn | 0 | 0 | 0 | 0 | 2,225 |
| | | Jersey Shore | 0 | 0 | 0 | 0 | 4,282 |
| | | Jessup | 0 | | | | 4,534 |
| | | Jim Thorpe | 0 | 0 | 0 | 0 | 4,870 |
| | | Johnsonburg | 0 | 0 | 0 | 0 | 2,645 |
| | | Juniata Valley Regional | 0 | 0 | 0 | 0 | 2,685 |
| | | Kane | 0 | 0 | 0 | 0 | 3,729 |
| | | Kennedy Township | 0 | 0 | 0 | | 9,656 |
| | | Kennett Square | 0 | 0 | 0 | 0 | 5,269 |
| | | Kennett Township | 0 | 0 | 0 | 0 | 7,951 |
| | | Kidder Township | 0 | 0 | 0 | 0 | 1,477 |
| | | Kilbuck Township | 0 | 0 | 0 | 0 | 652 |
| | | Kingston | 0 | 0 | 0 | 0 | 12,850 |
| | | Kingston Township | 0 | 0 | 0 | 0 | 7,038 |
| | | Kiskiminetas Township | 0 | 0 | 0 | 0 | 4,768 |
| | | Kittanning | 0 | 0 | 0 | 0 | 4,312 |
| | | Kline Township | 0 | 0 | 0 | 0 | 1,484 |
| | | Knox | 0 | 0 | 0 | | 1,089 |
| | | Koppel | 0 | 0 | 0 | 0 | 766 |
| | | Kulpmont | 0 | 0 | 0 | 0 | 2,740 |
| | | Kutztown | 0 | 0 | 0 | 0 | 5,107 |
| | | Laceyville | 0 | 0 | 0 | | 365 |
| | | Laflin Borough | 0 | 0 | 0 | 0 | 1,485 |
| | | Lake City | 0 | 0 | 0 | 0 | 2,880 |
| | | Lamar Township | 0 | 0 | 0 | 0 | 2,403 |
| | | Lancaster Township, Butler County | 0 | 0 | 0 | 0 | 2,578 |
| | | Lancaster Township, Lancaster County | 0 | 0 | 0 | 0 | 14,607 |
| | | Lanesboro | 0 | 0 | 0 | 0 | 547 |
| | | Langhorne Borough | 0 | 0 | 0 | 0 | 1,944 |
| | | Langhorne Manor | 0 | 0 | 0 | 0 | 1,058 |
| | | Lansdale | 0 | 0 | 0 | 0 | 15,466 |
| | | Lansdowne | 0 | 0 | 0 | 0 | 10,595 |
| | | Lansford | 0 | 0 | 0 | 0 | 4,122 |
| | | Larksville | 0 | 0 | 0 | 0 | 4,408 |
| | | Latimore Township | 0 | 0 | 0 | 0 | 2,867 |
| | | Latrobe | 0 | 0 | 0 | 0 | 8,281 |
| | | Laureldale | 0 | 0 | 0 | 0 | 3,734 |

[1]Agencies published in this table indicated that no hate crimes occurred in their jurisdictions during the quarter(s) for which they submitted reports to the Hate Crime Statistics Program. Blanks indicate quarters for which agencies did not submit reports.

[2]Population figures are published only for the cities. The figures listed for the universities and colleges are student enrollment and were provided by the United States Department of Education for the 2008 school year, the most recent available. The enrollment figures include full-time and part-time students.

## Table 95. Hate Crime Zero Data Submitted per Quarter, by State and Agency, 2009—*Continued*

(Number.)

| State | Agency type | Agency name | Zero data per quarter[1] | | | | Population[2] |
|---|---|---|---|---|---|---|---|
| | | | 1st quarter | 2nd quarter | 3rd quarter | 4th quarter | |
| **PENNSYLVANIA** | | Lawrence Park Township | 0 | 0 | 0 | 0 | 3,650 |
| | | Lawrence Township, Clearfield County | 0 | 0 | 0 | 0 | 7,436 |
| | | Lawrence Township, Tioga County | 0 | 0 | 0 | 0 | 1,680 |
| | | Lebanon | 0 | 0 | 0 | 0 | 24,061 |
| | | Leechburg | 0 | 0 | 0 | 0 | 2,194 |
| | | Leetsdale | 0 | 0 | 0 | 0 | 1,105 |
| | | Leet Township | 0 | 0 | 0 | 0 | 1,485 |
| | | Lehighton | 0 | 0 | 0 | 0 | 5,417 |
| | | Lehigh Township, Northampton County | 0 | 0 | 0 | 0 | 10,926 |
| | | Lehman Township | 0 | 0 | 0 | 0 | 3,324 |
| | | Lewisburg | 0 | 0 | 0 | 0 | 5,435 |
| | | Liberty | 0 | 0 | 0 | 0 | 2,412 |
| | | Liberty Township, Adams County | 0 | 0 | 0 | 0 | 1,303 |
| | | Liberty Township, Bedford County | 0 | 0 | 0 | | 1,440 |
| | | Ligonier | 0 | 0 | 0 | 0 | 1,589 |
| | | Ligonier Township | 0 | 0 | 0 | 0 | 6,709 |
| | | Limerick Township | 0 | 0 | 0 | 0 | 17,276 |
| | | Lincoln | 0 | 0 | 0 | 0 | 1,110 |
| | | Linesville | 0 | 0 | 0 | 0 | 1,084 |
| | | Lititz | 0 | 0 | 0 | 0 | 9,034 |
| | | Little Beaver Township | | 0 | 0 | 0 | 1,264 |
| | | Littlestown | 0 | 0 | 0 | 0 | 4,134 |
| | | Lock Haven | 0 | 0 | 0 | 0 | 8,477 |
| | | Locust Township | 0 | 0 | 0 | 0 | 2,536 |
| | | Logan Township | 0 | 0 | 0 | 0 | 12,185 |
| | | Loretto | 0 | 0 | 0 | 0 | 1,356 |
| | | Lower Allen Township | 0 | 0 | 0 | 0 | 17,471 |
| | | Lower Burrell | 0 | 0 | 0 | 0 | 12,032 |
| | | Lower Chichester Township | 0 | 0 | 0 | 0 | 3,424 |
| | | Lower Frederick Township | 0 | 0 | 0 | 0 | 4,813 |
| | | Lower Gwynedd Township | 0 | 0 | 0 | 0 | 11,433 |
| | | Lower Heidelberg Township | 0 | 0 | 0 | 0 | 5,470 |
| | | Lower Makefield Township | 0 | 0 | 0 | 0 | 32,111 |
| | | Lower Merion Township | 0 | 0 | 0 | 0 | 57,033 |
| | | Lower Milford Township | 0 | 0 | 0 | 0 | 3,915 |
| | | Lower Moreland Township | 0 | 0 | 0 | 0 | 12,807 |
| | | Lower Paxton Township | 0 | 0 | 0 | 0 | 45,534 |
| | | Lower Pottsgrove Township | 0 | 0 | 0 | 0 | 12,266 |
| | | Lower Providence Township | 0 | 0 | 0 | 0 | 26,271 |
| | | Lower Salford Township | 0 | 0 | 0 | 0 | 14,683 |
| | | Lower Saucon Township | 0 | 0 | 0 | 0 | 11,435 |
| | | Lower Southampton Township | 0 | 0 | 0 | 0 | 18,954 |
| | | Lower Swatara Township | 0 | 0 | 0 | 0 | 8,563 |
| | | Lower Windsor Township | 0 | 0 | 0 | 0 | 7,875 |
| | | Luzerne Township | 0 | 0 | 0 | 0 | 6,753 |
| | | Lykens | 0 | 0 | 0 | 0 | 1,839 |
| | | Macungie | 0 | 0 | 0 | 0 | 3,131 |
| | | Madison Township | 0 | 0 | 0 | 0 | 1,594 |
| | | Mahanoy City | 0 | 0 | 0 | 0 | 4,347 |
| | | Mahanoy Township | 0 | 0 | 0 | 0 | 3,780 |
| | | Mahoning Township, Carbon County | 0 | 0 | 0 | | 4,435 |
| | | Mahoning Township, Montour County | 0 | 0 | 0 | 0 | 4,238 |
| | | Main Township | 0 | 0 | 0 | 0 | 1,289 |
| | | Malvern | 0 | 0 | 0 | 0 | 3,102 |
| | | Manheim | 0 | 0 | 0 | 0 | 4,631 |
| | | Manheim Township | 0 | 0 | 0 | 0 | 36,582 |
| | | Manor | 0 | 0 | 0 | 0 | 2,927 |
| | | Manor Township, Armstrong County | 0 | 0 | 0 | 0 | 3,917 |
| | | Manor Township, Lancaster County | 0 | 0 | 0 | 0 | 19,812 |
| | | Mansfield | 0 | 0 | 0 | 0 | 3,152 |
| | | Marcus Hook | 0 | 0 | 0 | 0 | 2,219 |
| | | Marietta | 0 | 0 | 0 | 0 | 2,583 |
| | | Marion Center | 0 | 0 | | | 412 |
| | | Marion Township, Beaver County | 0 | 0 | 0 | 0 | 880 |
| | | Marion Township, Berks County | 0 | 0 | 0 | 0 | 1,782 |
| | | Marlborough Township | 0 | 0 | 0 | 0 | 3,283 |
| | | Marple Township | 0 | 0 | 0 | 0 | 23,407 |
| | | Mars | 0 | 0 | 0 | 0 | 1,643 |
| | | Martinsburg | 0 | 0 | 0 | 0 | 2,109 |
| | | Marysville | 0 | 0 | 0 | 0 | 2,439 |
| | | Masontown | 0 | 0 | 0 | 0 | 3,371 |
| | | Mayfield | 0 | 0 | 0 | 0 | 1,698 |
| | | McAdoo | 0 | 0 | 0 | 0 | 2,069 |
| | | McCandless | 0 | 0 | 0 | 0 | 27,119 |
| | | McDonald Borough | 0 | 0 | 0 | 0 | 2,103 |
| | | McKeesport | 0 | 0 | 0 | 0 | 21,932 |
| | | McKees Rocks | 0 | 0 | 0 | 0 | 5,956 |
| | | McSherrystown | 0 | 0 | 0 | 0 | 2,803 |
| | | Meadville | 0 | 0 | 0 | 0 | 13,186 |

[1]Agencies published in this table indicated that no hate crimes occurred in their jurisdictions during the quarter(s) for which they submitted reports to the Hate Crime Statistics Program. Blanks indicate quarters for which agencies did not submit reports.

[2]Population figures are published only for the cities. The figures listed for the universities and colleges are student enrollment and were provided by the United States Department of Education for the 2008 school year, the most recent available. The enrollment figures include full-time and part-time students.

# Table 95. Hate Crime Zero Data Submitted per Quarter, by State and Agency, 2009—*Continued*

(Number.)

| State | Agency type | Agency name | Zero data per quarter[1] 1st quarter | 2nd quarter | 3rd quarter | 4th quarter | Population[2] |
|---|---|---|---|---|---|---|---|
| PENNSYLVANIA | | Media | 0 | 0 | 0 | 0 | 5,381 |
| | | Mercer | 0 | 0 | 0 | 0 | 2,188 |
| | | Mercersburg | 0 | 0 | 0 | 0 | 1,589 |
| | | Meshoppen | 0 | 0 | 0 | 0 | 424 |
| | | Meyersdale | 0 | 0 | 0 | 0 | 2,252 |
| | | Middleburg | 0 | 0 | 0 | 0 | 1,321 |
| | | Middlesex Township, Butler County | 0 | 0 | 0 | 0 | 5,438 |
| | | Middlesex Township, Cumberland County | 0 | 0 | 0 | 0 | 6,920 |
| | | Middletown | 0 | 0 | 0 | 0 | 8,799 |
| | | Middletown Township | 0 | 0 | 0 | 0 | 46,978 |
| | | Midland | 0 | 0 | 0 | 0 | 2,817 |
| | | Midway | 0 | 0 | 0 | 0 | 918 |
| | | Mifflin | 0 | 0 | 0 | 0 | 603 |
| | | Mifflinburg | 0 | 0 | 0 | 0 | 3,509 |
| | | Mifflin County Regional | 0 | 0 | 0 | 0 | 26,265 |
| | | Mifflin Township | 0 | 0 | 0 | 0 | 2,249 |
| | | Milford | 0 | 0 | 0 | 0 | 2,904 |
| | | Millbourne | 0 | 0 | 0 | 0 | 901 |
| | | Millcreek Township, Erie County | 0 | 0 | 0 | 0 | 51,758 |
| | | Millcreek Township, Lebanon County | 0 | 0 | 0 | 0 | 3,210 |
| | | Millersburg | 0 | 0 | 0 | 0 | 2,449 |
| | | Millersville | 0 | 0 | 0 | 0 | 7,296 |
| | | Mill Hall | 0 | 0 | 0 | 0 | 1,469 |
| | | Millvale | 0 | 0 | 0 | 0 | 3,618 |
| | | Millville | 0 | 0 | 0 | 0 | 940 |
| | | Milton | 0 | 0 | 0 | 0 | 6,331 |
| | | Minersville | 0 | 0 | 0 | 0 | 4,187 |
| | | Mohnton | 0 | 0 | 0 | 0 | 3,081 |
| | | Monaca | 0 | 0 | 0 | 0 | 5,694 |
| | | Monessen | 0 | 0 | 0 | 0 | 7,958 |
| | | Monongahela | 0 | 0 | 0 | 0 | 4,387 |
| | | Monroeville | 0 | 0 | 0 | 0 | 27,462 |
| | | Montgomery | 0 | 0 | 0 | 0 | 5,184 |
| | | Montgomery Township | 0 | 0 | 0 | 0 | 24,360 |
| | | Montoursville | 0 | 0 | 0 | 0 | 4,536 |
| | | Montrose | 0 | 0 | 0 | 0 | 1,518 |
| | | Moon Township | 0 | 0 | 0 | 0 | 22,923 |
| | | Moore Township | 0 | 0 | 0 | 0 | 9,494 |
| | | Moosic | 0 | 0 | 0 | 0 | 5,779 |
| | | Morris-Cooper Regional | 0 | 0 | 0 | 0 | 5,625 |
| | | Morrisville | 0 | 0 | 0 | 0 | 9,547 |
| | | Morton | 0 | 0 | 0 | 0 | 2,625 |
| | | Moscow | 0 | 0 | 0 | 0 | 1,945 |
| | | Mount Carmel | 0 | 0 | 0 | 0 | 5,836 |
| | | Mount Carmel Township | 0 | 0 | 0 | 0 | 2,568 |
| | | Mount Gretna Borough | 0 | 0 | 0 | 0 | 233 |
| | | Mount Holly Springs | 0 | 0 | 0 | 0 | 1,907 |
| | | Mount Jewett | 0 | 0 | 0 | 0 | 987 |
| | | Mount Joy | 0 | 0 | 0 | 0 | 7,304 |
| | | Mount Lebanon | 0 | 0 | 0 | 0 | 30,106 |
| | | Mount Oliver | 0 | 0 | 0 | 0 | 3,621 |
| | | Mount Pleasant | 0 | 0 | 0 | 0 | 4,344 |
| | | Mount Pleasant Township | 0 | 0 | 0 | 0 | 3,633 |
| | | Mount Union | 0 | 0 | 0 | 0 | 2,327 |
| | | Muhlenberg Township | 0 | 0 | 0 | 0 | 18,767 |
| | | Muncy | 0 | 0 | 0 | 0 | 2,438 |
| | | Munhall | 0 | 0 | 0 | 0 | 11,090 |
| | | Murrysville | 0 | 0 | 0 | 0 | 19,563 |
| | | Myerstown | 0 | 0 | 0 | 0 | 3,115 |
| | | Nanticoke | 0 | 0 | 0 | 0 | 10,122 |
| | | Nanty Glo | | | | 0 | 2,766 |
| | | Narberth | 0 | 0 | 0 | 0 | 4,019 |
| | | Nazareth Area | 0 | 0 | 0 | 0 | 6,021 |
| | | Nelson Township | 0 | 0 | 0 | 0 | 562 |
| | | Nescopeck | 0 | 0 | 0 | 0 | 1,417 |
| | | Neshannock Township | 0 | 0 | 0 | 0 | 9,290 |
| | | Nesquehoning | 0 | 0 | 0 | 0 | 3,305 |
| | | Nether Providence Township | 0 | 0 | 0 | 0 | 13,123 |
| | | Neville Township | 0 | 0 | 0 | 0 | 1,114 |
| | | New Berlin | 0 | 0 | 0 | 0 | 815 |
| | | Newberry Township | 0 | 0 | 0 | 0 | 15,577 |
| | | New Bethlehem | 0 | 0 | 0 | 0 | 974 |
| | | New Brighton | 0 | 0 | 0 | 0 | 9,252 |
| | | New Britain | 0 | 0 | 0 | 0 | 2,255 |
| | | New Britain Township | 0 | 0 | 0 | 0 | 10,981 |
| | | New Castle | 0 | 0 | 0 | 0 | 23,994 |
| | | New Castle Township | 0 | 0 | 0 | 0 | 393 |
| | | New Cumberland | 0 | 0 | 0 | | 7,017 |
| | | New Florence | 0 | 0 | | | 720 |
| | | New Garden Township | 0 | 0 | 0 | 0 | 12,073 |
| | | New Hanover Township | 0 | 0 | 0 | 0 | 9,694 |
| | | New Holland | 0 | 0 | 0 | 0 | 5,158 |
| | | New Hope | 0 | 0 | 0 | 0 | 2,280 |
| | | New Kensington | 0 | 0 | 0 | 0 | 13,561 |
| | | New Philadelphia | 0 | 0 | 0 | 0 | 1,083 |
| | | Newport | 0 | 0 | 0 | 0 | 1,459 |
| | | Newport Township | 0 | 0 | 0 | 0 | 4,735 |
| | | New Sewickley Township | 0 | 0 | 0 | 0 | 7,591 |
| | | Newton Township | 0 | 0 | 0 | 0 | 2,774 |
| | | Newtown | 0 | 0 | 0 | 0 | 2,384 |
| | | Newtown Township, Bucks County | 0 | 0 | 0 | 0 | 19,327 |
| | | Newtown Township, Delaware County | 0 | 0 | 0 | 0 | 11,796 |
| | | Newville | 0 | 0 | 0 | 0 | 1,296 |
| | | New Wilmington | 0 | | | | 2,233 |
| | | Norristown | 0 | 0 | 0 | 0 | 31,909 |
| | | Northampton | 0 | 0 | 0 | 0 | 9,892 |
| | | Northampton Township | 0 | 0 | 0 | 0 | 40,813 |
| | | North Beaver | 0 | 0 | 0 | 0 | 3,981 |
| | | North Belle Vernon | 0 | 0 | 0 | 0 | 1,933 |
| | | North Braddock | 0 | 0 | 0 | 0 | 5,761 |
| | | North Buffalo | 0 | 0 | 0 | 0 | 2,781 |
| | | North Catasauqua | 0 | 0 | 0 | 0 | 2,837 |
| | | North Charleroi | 0 | 0 | 0 | 0 | 1,304 |

[1]Agencies published in this table indicated that no hate crimes occurred in their jurisdictions during the quarter(s) for which they submitted reports to the Hate Crime Statistics Program. Blanks indicate quarters for which agencies did not submit reports.

[2]Population figures are published only for the cities. The figures listed for the universities and colleges are student enrollment and were provided by the United States Department of Education for the 2008 school year, the most recent available. The enrollment figures include full-time and part-time students.

## Table 95. Hate Crime Zero Data Submitted per Quarter, by State and Agency, 2009—*Continued*

(Number.)

| State | Agency type | Agency name | Zero data per quarter[1] 1st quarter | 2nd quarter | 3rd quarter | 4th quarter | Population[2] |
|---|---|---|---|---|---|---|---|
| PENNSYLVANIA | | North Cornwall Township | 0 | 0 | 0 | 0 | 6,589 |
| | | North Coventry Township | 0 | 0 | 0 | 0 | 7,747 |
| | | North East, Erie County | 0 | 0 | 0 | 0 | 4,146 |
| | | Northeastern Regional | 0 | 0 | 0 | 0 | 11,264 |
| | | Northern Berks Regional | 0 | 0 | 0 | 0 | 12,590 |
| | | Northern Cambria Borough | 0 | 0 | 0 | 0 | 3,877 |
| | | Northern Regional | 0 | 0 | 0 | 0 | 28,544 |
| | | North Fayette Township | 0 | 0 | 0 | 0 | 13,147 |
| | | North Franklin Township | 0 | 0 | 0 | 0 | 4,619 |
| | | North Huntingdon Township | 0 | 0 | 0 | 0 | 29,516 |
| | | North Irwin | | | | 0 | 834 |
| | | North Lebanon Township | 0 | 0 | 0 | 0 | 10,987 |
| | | North Londonderry Township | 0 | 0 | 0 | 0 | 7,012 |
| | | North Middleton Township | 0 | 0 | 0 | 0 | 11,066 |
| | | North Sewickley Township | 0 | 0 | 0 | 0 | 5,615 |
| | | North Strabane Township | 0 | 0 | 0 | 0 | 12,647 |
| | | Northumberland | 0 | 0 | 0 | 0 | 3,491 |
| | | North Union Township | 0 | 0 | 0 | 0 | 1,257 |
| | | North Versailles Township | 0 | 0 | 0 | 0 | 12,112 |
| | | North Wales | 0 | 0 | 0 | 0 | 3,213 |
| | | Northwest Lancaster County Regional | 0 | 0 | 0 | 0 | 18,094 |
| | | Northwest Lawrence County Regional | 0 | 0 | 0 | 0 | 6,627 |
| | | Norwood | 0 | 0 | 0 | 0 | 5,752 |
| | | Oakdale | 0 | 0 | 0 | 0 | 1,423 |
| | | Oakland | 0 | 0 | 0 | 0 | 567 |
| | | Oakmont | 0 | 0 | 0 | 0 | 6,373 |
| | | O'Hara Township | 0 | 0 | 0 | 0 | 9,578 |
| | | Ohio Township | 0 | 0 | 0 | 0 | 4,166 |
| | | Ohioville | 0 | 0 | 0 | 0 | 3,599 |
| | | Oil City | 0 | 0 | 0 | 0 | 10,504 |
| | | Old Forge | 0 | 0 | 0 | 0 | 8,497 |
| | | Old Lycoming Township | 0 | 0 | 0 | 0 | 5,248 |
| | | Oley Township | 0 | 0 | 0 | 0 | 3,681 |
| | | Oliver Township | 0 | 0 | 0 | 0 | 2,064 |
| | | Olyphant | 0 | 0 | 0 | 0 | 4,953 |
| | | Orangeville Area | 0 | 0 | 0 | 0 | 1,637 |
| | | Orwigsburg | 0 | 0 | 0 | 0 | 2,966 |
| | | Osceola Township | 0 | 0 | 0 | 0 | 702 |
| | | Otto Eldred Regional | 0 | 0 | 0 | 0 | 2,430 |
| | | Overfield Township | 0 | 0 | 0 | 0 | 1,538 |
| | | Oxford | 0 | 0 | 0 | 0 | 4,696 |
| | | Paint | 0 | 0 | 0 | | 1,027 |
| | | Paint Township | 0 | 0 | 0 | 0 | 3,133 |
| | | Palmerton | 0 | 0 | 0 | 0 | 5,205 |
| | | Palmer Township | 0 | 0 | 0 | 0 | 20,742 |
| | | Palmyra | 0 | 0 | 0 | 0 | 6,987 |
| | | Parker | 0 | 0 | 0 | 0 | 742 |
| | | Parkesburg | 0 | 0 | 0 | 0 | 3,436 |
| | | Parkside | 0 | 0 | 0 | 0 | 2,166 |
| | | Parks Township | 0 | 0 | 0 | 0 | 2,574 |
| | | Patterson Area | 0 | 0 | 0 | 0 | 3,539 |
| | | Patton | 0 | 0 | 0 | 0 | 1,830 |
| | | Paxtang | 0 | 0 | 0 | 0 | 1,477 |
| | | Pen Argyl | 0 | 0 | 0 | 0 | 3,629 |
| | | Penbrook | 0 | 0 | 0 | 0 | 2,906 |
| | | Penn Hills | 0 | 0 | 0 | 0 | 43,755 |
| | | Pennridge Regional | 0 | 0 | 0 | 0 | 10,633 |
| | | Penn Township, Butler County | 0 | 0 | 0 | 0 | 5,142 |
| | | Penn Township, Lancaster County | 0 | 0 | 0 | 0 | 8,688 |
| | | Penn Township, Perry County | 0 | 0 | 0 | | 3,246 |
| | | Penn Township, Westmoreland County | 0 | 0 | 0 | 0 | 20,193 |
| | | Penn Township, York County | 0 | 0 | 0 | 0 | 15,959 |
| | | Pequea Township | 0 | 0 | 0 | 0 | 4,542 |
| | | Perkasie | 0 | 0 | 0 | 0 | 8,614 |
| | | Perryopolis | 0 | 0 | 0 | 0 | 1,707 |
| | | Peters Township | 0 | 0 | 0 | 0 | 20,540 |
| | | Phoenixville | 0 | 0 | 0 | 0 | 16,569 |
| | | Pine Creek Township | 0 | 0 | 0 | 0 | 3,199 |
| | | Pine Grove | 0 | 0 | 0 | 0 | 2,031 |
| | | Pitcairn | 0 | 0 | 0 | 0 | 3,308 |
| | | Pittston | 0 | 0 | 0 | 0 | 7,490 |
| | | Plainfield Township | 0 | 0 | 0 | 0 | 6,235 |
| | | Plains Township | 0 | 0 | 0 | 0 | 10,364 |
| | | Pleasant Hills | 0 | 0 | 0 | 0 | 7,684 |
| | | Plum | 0 | 0 | 0 | 0 | 26,118 |
| | | Plumstead Township | 0 | 0 | 0 | 0 | 11,811 |
| | | Plymouth Township, Montgomery County | 0 | 0 | 0 | 0 | 16,350 |
| | | Pocono Mountain Regional | 0 | 0 | 0 | 0 | 35,793 |
| | | Pocono Township | 0 | 0 | 0 | 0 | 11,295 |
| | | Point Marion | 0 | 0 | 0 | 0 | 1,238 |
| | | Point Township | 0 | 0 | 0 | 0 | 3,885 |
| | | Polk | 0 | 0 | 0 | 0 | 991 |
| | | Portage | 0 | 0 | 0 | 0 | 2,555 |
| | | Port Allegany | 0 | 0 | 0 | 0 | 2,173 |
| | | Port Carbon | 0 | 0 | 0 | 0 | 1,733 |
| | | Porter Township | 0 | 0 | 0 | 0 | 1,591 |
| | | Port Vue | 0 | 0 | 0 | 0 | 3,804 |
| | | Pottstown | 0 | 0 | 0 | 0 | 21,226 |
| | | Pottsville | 0 | 0 | 0 | 0 | 14,288 |
| | | Prospect Park | 0 | 0 | 0 | 0 | 6,351 |
| | | Punxsutawney | 0 | 0 | 0 | 0 | 5,910 |
| | | Pymatuning Township | 0 | 0 | 0 | 0 | 3,530 |

[1] Agencies published in this table indicated that no hate crimes occurred in their jurisdictions during the quarter(s) for which they submitted reports to the Hate Crime Statistics Program. Blanks indicate quarters for which agencies did not submit reports.

[2] Population figures are published only for the cities. The figures listed for the universities and colleges are student enrollment and were provided by the United States Department of Education for the 2008 school year, the most recent available. The enrollment figures include full-time and part-time students.

## Table 95. Hate Crime Zero Data Submitted per Quarter, by State and Agency, 2009—*Continued*

(Number.)

| State | Agency type | Agency name | Zero data per quarter[1] 1st quarter | 2nd quarter | 3rd quarter | 4th quarter | Population[2] |
|---|---|---|---|---|---|---|---|
| PENNSYLVANIA | | Quakertown | 0 | 0 | 0 | 0 | 8,612 |
| | | Quarryville | 0 | 0 | 0 | 0 | 2,163 |
| | | Raccoon Township | 0 | 0 | 0 | 0 | 3,199 |
| | | Radnor Township | 0 | 0 | 0 | 0 | 30,958 |
| | | Ralpho Township | 0 | 0 | 0 | 0 | 3,886 |
| | | Rankin | 0 | 0 | 0 | 0 | 2,087 |
| | | Redstone Township | 0 | 0 | 0 | 0 | 6,006 |
| | | Reilly Township | 0 | 0 | 0 | 0 | 826 |
| | | RESA Regional | 0 | 0 | 0 | 0 | 2,536 |
| | | Reserve Township | 0 | 0 | 0 | 0 | 3,497 |
| | | Reynoldsville | 0 | 0 | 0 | 0 | 2,535 |
| | | Rice Township | 0 | 0 | 0 | 0 | 3,055 |
| | | Richland | 0 | 0 | 0 | 0 | 1,490 |
| | | Richland Township, Bucks County | 0 | 0 | 0 | 0 | 12,914 |
| | | Richland Township, Cambria County | 0 | 0 | 0 | 0 | 12,275 |
| | | Ridgway | 0 | 0 | 0 | 0 | 4,046 |
| | | Ridley Park | 0 | 0 | 0 | 0 | 6,956 |
| | | Ridley Township | 0 | 0 | 0 | 0 | 29,767 |
| | | Ringtown | 0 | 0 | 0 | 0 | 756 |
| | | Riverside | 0 | 0 | 0 | 0 | 1,852 |
| | | Roaring Brook Township | 0 | 0 | 0 | 0 | 1,804 |
| | | Roaring Spring | 0 | 0 | 0 | 0 | 2,235 |
| | | Robesonia | 0 | 0 | 0 | 0 | 2,050 |
| | | Robeson Township | 0 | 0 | 0 | 0 | 7,682 |
| | | Robinson Township, Allegheny County | 0 | 0 | 0 | 0 | 13,534 |
| | | Robinson Township, Washington County | | | | 0 | 2,114 |
| | | Rochester | 0 | 0 | 0 | 0 | 3,626 |
| | | Rochester Township | 0 | 0 | 0 | 0 | 2,846 |
| | | Rockledge | 0 | 0 | 0 | 0 | 2,467 |
| | | Roseto | 0 | 0 | 0 | 0 | 1,642 |
| | | Rosslyn Farms | 0 | 0 | 0 | 0 | 419 |
| | | Ross Township | 0 | 0 | 0 | 0 | 30,340 |
| | | Rostraver Township | 0 | 0 | 0 | 0 | 11,621 |
| | | Royalton | 0 | 0 | 0 | 0 | 944 |
| | | Royersford | 0 | 0 | 0 | 0 | 4,368 |
| | | Rush Township | 0 | 0 | 0 | 0 | 3,724 |
| | | Ryan Township | 0 | 0 | 0 | 0 | 2,544 |
| | | Rye Township | 0 | 0 | 0 | 0 | 2,548 |
| | | Sadsbury Township, Chester County | 0 | 0 | 0 | 0 | 3,393 |
| | | Salem Township, Luzerne County | 0 | 0 | 0 | 0 | 4,075 |
| | | Salisbury Township | 0 | 0 | 0 | 0 | 14,068 |
| | | Saltsburg | 0 | 0 | 0 | 0 | 876 |
| | | Sandy Lake | 0 | 0 | 0 | 0 | 686 |
| | | Sandy Township | 0 | 0 | 0 | 0 | 11,577 |
| | | Sankertown | 0 | 0 | 0 | 0 | 649 |
| | | Saxonburg | 0 | 0 | 0 | 0 | 1,589 |
| | | Saxton | 0 | 0 | 0 | 0 | 758 |
| | | Sayre | 0 | 0 | 0 | 0 | 5,401 |
| | | Schuylkill Haven | 0 | 0 | 0 | 0 | 5,121 |
| | | Schuylkill Township, Chester County | 0 | 0 | 0 | 0 | 7,779 |
| | | Scottdale | 0 | 0 | 0 | 0 | 4,372 |
| | | Scott Township, Allegheny County | 0 | 0 | 0 | 0 | 15,732 |
| | | Scott Township, Columbia County | 0 | 0 | 0 | 0 | 5,062 |
| | | Scott Township, Lackawanna County | 0 | 0 | 0 | 0 | 4,892 |
| | | Scranton | 0 | 0 | 0 | 0 | 71,843 |
| | | Selinsgrove | 0 | 0 | 0 | 0 | 5,341 |
| | | Seven Springs | 0 | 0 | 0 | 0 | 116 |
| | | Seward | 0 | 0 | 0 | 0 | 448 |
| | | Sewickley | 0 | 0 | 0 | 0 | 4,045 |
| | | Sewickley Heights | 0 | 0 | 0 | 0 | 912 |
| | | Shaler Township | 0 | 0 | 0 | 0 | 27,750 |
| | | Shamokin | 0 | 0 | 0 | 0 | 7,301 |
| | | Shamokin Dam | 0 | 0 | 0 | 0 | 1,432 |
| | | Sharon | 0 | 0 | 0 | 0 | 14,721 |
| | | Sharon Hill | 0 | 0 | 0 | 0 | 5,291 |
| | | Sharpsburg | 0 | 0 | 0 | 0 | 3,229 |
| | | Sharpsville | 0 | 0 | 0 | 0 | 4,059 |
| | | Sheffield Township | 0 | 0 | 0 | 0 | 2,185 |
| | | Shenandoah | 0 | 0 | 0 | 0 | 5,107 |
| | | Shenango Township, Lawrence County | 0 | 0 | 0 | 0 | 7,614 |
| | | Shillington | 0 | 0 | 0 | 0 | 4,990 |
| | | Shinglehouse | 0 | 0 | 0 | 0 | 1,090 |
| | | Shippensburg | 0 | 0 | 0 | 0 | 5,577 |
| | | Shippingport | 0 | 0 | 0 | 0 | 217 |
| | | Shiremanstown | 0 | 0 | 0 | 0 | 1,458 |
| | | Shohola Township | 0 | 0 | 0 | 0 | 2,469 |
| | | Silver Lake Township | 0 | 0 | 0 | 0 | 1,723 |
| | | Silver Spring Township | 0 | 0 | 0 | 0 | 13,488 |
| | | Sinking Spring | 0 | 0 | 0 | 0 | 3,726 |
| | | Slatington | 0 | 0 | 0 | 0 | 4,401 |
| | | Slippery Rock | 0 | 0 | 0 | 0 | 3,069 |
| | | Smethport | 0 | 0 | 0 | 0 | 1,551 |
| | | Smithfield | 0 | 0 | 0 | | 798 |
| | | Smith Township | 0 | 0 | 0 | 0 | 4,467 |
| | | Solebury Township | 0 | 0 | 0 | 0 | 8,889 |
| | | Somerset | 0 | 0 | 0 | 0 | 6,316 |
| | | Souderton | 0 | 0 | 0 | 0 | 6,533 |
| | | South Abington Township | 0 | 0 | 0 | 0 | 9,663 |
| | | South Annville Township | 0 | 0 | 0 | | 3,226 |
| | | South Beaver Township | 0 | 0 | 0 | 0 | 2,827 |
| | | South Buffalo Township | 0 | 0 | 0 | 0 | 2,797 |
| | | South Centre Township | 0 | 0 | 0 | 0 | 1,903 |
| | | South Coatesville | 0 | 0 | 0 | 0 | 1,067 |
| | | South Connellsville Borough | 0 | 0 | 0 | 0 | 2,137 |

[1]Agencies published in this table indicated that no hate crimes occurred in their jurisdictions during the quarter(s) for which they submitted reports to the Hate Crime Statistics Program. Blanks indicate quarters for which agencies did not submit reports.

[2]Population figures are published only for the cities. The figures listed for the universities and colleges are student enrollment and were provided by the United States Department of Education for the 2008 school year, the most recent available. The enrollment figures include full-time and part-time students.

## Table 95. Hate Crime Zero Data Submitted per Quarter, by State and Agency, 2009—*Continued*

(Number.)

| State | Agency type | Agency name | Zero data per quarter[1] | | | | Population[2] |
|---|---|---|---|---|---|---|---|
| | | | 1st quarter | 2nd quarter | 3rd quarter | 4th quarter | |
| PENNSYLVANIA | | Southern Regional Lancaster County | 0 | 0 | 0 | 0 | 3,842 |
| | | Southern Regional York County | 0 | 0 | 0 | 0 | 10,027 |
| | | South Fayette Township | 0 | 0 | 0 | 0 | 13,304 |
| | | South Fork | 0 | 0 | 0 | 0 | 1,017 |
| | | South Greensburg | 0 | 0 | 0 | 0 | 2,210 |
| | | South Heidelberg Township | 0 | 0 | 0 | 0 | 7,409 |
| | | South Heights | 0 | 0 | 0 | 0 | 487 |
| | | South Lebanon Township | 0 | 0 | 0 | 0 | 8,732 |
| | | South Londonderry Township | 0 | 0 | 0 | 0 | 7,503 |
| | | South New Castle | 0 | 0 | 0 | 0 | 730 |
| | | South Park Township | 0 | 0 | 0 | 0 | 13,823 |
| | | South Pymatuning Township | 0 | | | | 2,779 |
| | | South Strabane Township | 0 | 0 | 0 | 0 | 8,807 |
| | | South Waverly | 0 | 0 | 0 | 0 | 962 |
| | | Southwestern Regional | 0 | 0 | 0 | 0 | 18,230 |
| | | Southwest Greensburg | 0 | 0 | 0 | 0 | 2,181 |
| | | Southwest Mercer County Regional | 0 | 0 | 0 | 0 | 11,096 |
| | | Southwest Regional | 0 | 0 | 0 | 0 | 2,842 |
| | | South Whitehall Township | 0 | 0 | 0 | 0 | 19,853 |
| | | South Williamsport | 0 | 0 | 0 | 0 | 5,976 |
| | | Spring City | 0 | 0 | 0 | 0 | 3,383 |
| | | Springdale Township | 0 | 0 | 0 | 0 | 1,632 |
| | | Springettsbury Township | 0 | 0 | 0 | 0 | 24,940 |
| | | Springfield Township, Bucks County | 0 | 0 | 0 | 0 | 5,079 |
| | | Springfield Township, Delaware County | 0 | 0 | 0 | 0 | 22,682 |
| | | Spring Garden Township | 0 | 0 | 0 | 0 | 12,154 |
| | | Spring Township, Berks County | 0 | 0 | 0 | 0 | 26,803 |
| | | Spring Township, Centre County | 0 | 0 | 0 | 0 | 7,083 |
| | | Spring Township, Snyder County | 0 | 0 | 0 | 0 | 1,547 |
| | | State College | 0 | 0 | 0 | 0 | 53,587 |
| | | St. Clair Boro | 0 | 0 | 0 | 0 | 2,960 |
| | | St. Clair Township | 0 | 0 | 0 | 0 | 1,329 |
| | | Steelton | 0 | 0 | 0 | 0 | 5,571 |
| | | Stewartstown | 0 | 0 | 0 | 0 | 2,024 |
| | | St. Marys City | 0 | 0 | 0 | 0 | 13,296 |
| | | Stockertown | 0 | 0 | 0 | 0 | 761 |
| | | Stoneboro | 0 | 0 | 0 | 0 | 1,006 |
| | | Stonycreek Township | 0 | 0 | 0 | 0 | 2,874 |
| | | Stowe Township | 0 | 0 | 0 | 0 | 6,032 |
| | | Strasburg | 0 | 0 | 0 | 0 | 2,774 |
| | | Stroud Area Regional | 0 | 0 | 0 | 0 | 34,763 |
| | | Sugarcreek | 0 | 0 | 0 | 0 | 4,931 |
| | | Sugarloaf Township, Luzerne County | 0 | 0 | 0 | 0 | 4,086 |
| | | Sugar Notch | 0 | 0 | 0 | 0 | 949 |
| | | Summerhill Township | 0 | 0 | 0 | 0 | 2,565 |
| | | Summit Hill | 0 | 0 | 0 | 0 | 2,954 |
| | | Summit Township | 0 | 0 | 0 | 0 | 2,234 |
| | | Sunbury | 0 | 0 | 0 | 0 | 9,737 |
| | | Susquehanna Depot | 0 | 0 | 0 | 0 | 1,547 |
| | | Susquehanna Regional | 0 | 0 | 0 | 0 | 7,177 |
| | | Susquehanna Township, Cambria County | 0 | | | | 2,031 |
| | | Susquehanna Township, Dauphin County | 0 | 0 | 0 | 0 | 23,181 |
| | | Sutersville | 0 | 0 | 0 | 0 | 582 |
| | | Swarthmore | 0 | 0 | 0 | 0 | 6,082 |
| | | Swatara Township | 0 | 0 | 0 | 0 | 22,426 |
| | | Sweden Township | 0 | | | | 708 |
| | | Swissvale | 0 | 0 | 0 | 0 | 8,674 |
| | | Swoyersville | 0 | 0 | 0 | 0 | 7,534 |
| | | Sykesville | 0 | 0 | 0 | | 1,163 |
| | | Tamaqua | 0 | 0 | 0 | 0 | 6,521 |
| | | Tarentum | 0 | 0 | 0 | 0 | 4,487 |
| | | Tatamy | 0 | 0 | 0 | 0 | 1,097 |
| | | Taylor | 0 | 0 | 0 | 0 | 6,118 |
| | | Telford | 0 | 0 | 0 | 0 | 4,590 |
| | | Terre Hill | 0 | 0 | 0 | 0 | 1,264 |
| | | Throop | 0 | 0 | 0 | 0 | 4,057 |
| | | Tidioute | 0 | 0 | 0 | 0 | 710 |
| | | Tilden Township | 0 | 0 | 0 | 0 | 3,825 |
| | | Tinicum Township, Bucks County | 0 | 0 | 0 | 0 | 4,201 |
| | | Tinicum Township, Delaware County | 0 | 0 | 0 | 0 | 4,178 |
| | | Tioga | 0 | 0 | 0 | 0 | 578 |
| | | Titusville | 0 | 0 | 0 | 0 | 5,735 |
| | | Towamencin Township | 0 | 0 | 0 | 0 | 17,619 |
| | | Towanda | 0 | 0 | 0 | 0 | 2,805 |
| | | Tower City | 0 | 0 | 0 | 0 | 1,310 |
| | | Trafford | 0 | 0 | 0 | 0 | 2,987 |
| | | Trainer | 0 | 0 | 0 | 0 | 1,824 |
| | | Tredyffrin Township | 0 | 0 | 0 | 0 | 28,915 |
| | | Troy | 0 | 0 | 0 | 0 | 1,451 |
| | | Tullytown | 0 | 0 | 0 | 0 | 1,948 |
| | | Tulpehocken Township | 0 | 0 | 0 | 0 | 3,570 |

[1]Agencies published in this table indicated that no hate crimes occurred in their jurisdictions during the quarter(s) for which they submitted reports to the Hate Crime program. Blanks indicate quarters for which agencies did not submit reports.

[2]Population figures are published only for the cities. The figures listed for the universities and colleges are student enrollment and were provided by the United States Department of Education for the 2008 school year, the most recent available. The enrollment figures include full-time and part-time students.

## Table 95. Hate Crime Zero Data Submitted per Quarter, by State and Agency, 2009—*Continued*

(Number.)

| State | Agency type | Agency name | Zero data per quarter[1] 1st quarter | 2nd quarter | 3rd quarter | 4th quarter | Population[2] |
|---|---|---|---|---|---|---|---|
| PENNSYLVANIA | | Tunkhannock | 0 | 0 | 0 | 0 | 1,759 |
| | | Tunkhannock Township, Wyoming County | 0 | 0 | 0 | 0 | 4,284 |
| | | Turtle Creek | 0 | 0 | 0 | 0 | 5,493 |
| | | Tyrone | 0 | 0 | 0 | 0 | 5,163 |
| | | Union City | 0 | 0 | 0 | 0 | 3,257 |
| | | Union Dale | 0 | 0 | 0 | 0 | 338 |
| | | Uniontown | 0 | 0 | 0 | 0 | 11,603 |
| | | Union Township, Lawrence County | 0 | 0 | 0 | 0 | 4,992 |
| | | Union Township, Schuylkill County | 0 | 0 | 0 | 0 | 1,335 |
| | | Upland | 0 | 0 | 0 | 0 | 2,852 |
| | | Upper Allen Township | 0 | 0 | 0 | 0 | 18,353 |
| | | Upper Burrell Township | 0 | 0 | 0 | 0 | 2,113 |
| | | Upper Chichester Township | 0 | 0 | 0 | 0 | 17,621 |
| | | Upper Darby Township | 0 | 0 | 0 | 0 | 78,088 |
| | | Upper Dublin Township | 0 | 0 | 0 | 0 | 25,904 |
| | | Upper Gwynedd Township | 0 | 0 | 0 | 0 | 16,234 |
| | | Upper Leacock Township | 0 | 0 | 0 | 0 | 8,617 |
| | | Upper Makefield Township | 0 | 0 | 0 | 0 | 8,630 |
| | | Upper Merion Township | 0 | 0 | 0 | 0 | 26,410 |
| | | Upper Moreland Township | 0 | 0 | 0 | 0 | 24,093 |
| | | Upper Nazareth Township | 0 | 0 | 0 | 0 | 6,026 |
| | | Upper Perkiomen | 0 | 0 | 0 | 0 | 6,372 |
| | | Upper Pottsgrove Township | 0 | 0 | 0 | 0 | 5,330 |
| | | Upper Providence Township, Delaware County | 0 | 0 | 0 | 0 | 11,131 |
| | | Upper Providence Township, Montgomery County | 0 | 0 | 0 | 0 | 20,048 |
| | | Upper Saucon Township | 0 | 0 | 0 | 0 | 15,182 |
| | | Upper Southampton Township | 0 | 0 | 0 | 0 | 15,192 |
| | | Upper St. Clair Township | 0 | 0 | 0 | 0 | 18,723 |
| | | Upper Uwchlan Township | 0 | 0 | 0 | 0 | 11,728 |
| | | Upper Yoder Township | 0 | 0 | 0 | 0 | 5,455 |
| | | Uwchlan Township | 0 | 0 | 0 | 0 | 18,869 |
| | | Valley Township | 0 | 0 | 0 | 0 | 6,869 |
| | | Vandergrift | 0 | 0 | 0 | 0 | 4,950 |
| | | Vandling | 0 | 0 | 0 | 0 | 696 |
| | | Vernon Township | 0 | 0 | 0 | 0 | 5,413 |
| | | Verona | 0 | 0 | 0 | 0 | 2,813 |
| | | Vintondale | 0 | 0 | 0 | 0 | 472 |
| | | Walker Township | 0 | 0 | 0 | 0 | 976 |
| | | Walnutport | 0 | 0 | 0 | 0 | 2,202 |
| | | Wampum | 0 | 0 | 0 | 0 | 617 |
| | | Warminster Township | 0 | 0 | 0 | 0 | 33,914 |
| | | Warren | 0 | 0 | 0 | 0 | 9,316 |
| | | Warrington Township | 0 | 0 | 0 | 0 | 23,417 |
| | | Warwick Township, Bucks County | 0 | 0 | 0 | 0 | 14,980 |
| | | Warwick Township, Lancaster County | 0 | 0 | 0 | 0 | 17,426 |
| | | Washington, Washington County | 0 | 0 | 0 | 0 | 14,709 |
| | | Washington Township, Fayette County | 0 | 0 | 0 | 0 | 4,126 |
| | | Washington Township, Franklin County | 0 | 0 | 0 | 0 | 12,201 |
| | | Washington Township, Northampton County | 0 | 0 | 0 | 0 | 4,932 |
| | | Washington Township, Westmoreland County | 0 | 0 | 0 | 0 | 7,347 |
| | | Watsontown | 0 | 0 | 0 | 0 | 2,086 |
| | | Waymart | 0 | 0 | 0 | 0 | 3,467 |
| | | Waynesboro | 0 | 0 | 0 | 0 | 9,985 |
| | | Waynesburg | 0 | 0 | 0 | 0 | 4,144 |
| | | Weatherly | 0 | 0 | 0 | 0 | 2,586 |
| | | Weissport | 0 | 0 | | | 423 |
| | | Wellsboro | 0 | 0 | 0 | 0 | 3,233 |
| | | Wernersville | 0 | 0 | 0 | 0 | 2,478 |
| | | Wesleyville | 0 | 0 | 0 | 0 | 3,267 |
| | | West Brandywine Township | 0 | 0 | 0 | 0 | 7,936 |
| | | West Brownsville | 0 | 0 | 0 | 0 | 1,015 |
| | | West Caln Township | 0 | 0 | 0 | 0 | 8,477 |
| | | West Carroll Township | 0 | 0 | 0 | 0 | 1,335 |
| | | West Chester | 0 | 0 | 0 | 0 | 18,366 |
| | | West Cocalico Township | 0 | 0 | 0 | 0 | 7,184 |
| | | West Conshohocken | 0 | 0 | 0 | 0 | 1,501 |
| | | West Cornwall Township | 0 | 0 | 0 | 0 | 2,005 |
| | | West Deer Township | 0 | 0 | 0 | 0 | 11,974 |
| | | West Earl Township | 0 | 0 | 0 | 0 | 7,779 |
| | | West Fallowfield Township | 0 | 0 | 0 | 0 | 2,603 |
| | | Westfield | 0 | 0 | 0 | 0 | 1,108 |

[1]Agencies published in this table indicated that no hate crimes occurred in their jurisdictions during the quarter(s) for which they submitted reports to the Hate Crime Statistics Program. Blanks indicate quarters for which agencies did not submit reports.

[2]Population figures are published only for the cities. The figures listed for the universities and colleges are student enrollment and were provided by the United States Department of Education for the 2008 school year, the most recent available. The enrollment figures include full-time and part-time students.

## Table 95. Hate Crime Zero Data Submitted per Quarter, by State and Agency, 2009—*Continued*

(Number.)

| State | Agency type | Agency name | Zero data per quarter[1] 1st quarter | 2nd quarter | 3rd quarter | 4th quarter | Population[2] |
|---|---|---|---|---|---|---|---|
| **PENNSYLVANIA** | | West Goshen Township | 0 | 0 | 0 | 0 | 21,262 |
| | | West Grove Borough | 0 | 0 | 0 | 0 | 2,773 |
| | | West Hazleton | 0 | 0 | 0 | 0 | 3,278 |
| | | West Hempfield Township | 0 | 0 | 0 | 0 | 16,179 |
| | | West Hills Regional | 0 | 0 | 0 | 0 | 10,568 |
| | | West Homestead | 0 | 0 | 0 | 0 | 1,977 |
| | | West Kittanning | 0 | 0 | 0 | 0 | 1,129 |
| | | West Lampeter Township | 0 | 0 | 0 | 0 | 15,819 |
| | | West Lebanon Township | 0 | 0 | 0 | 0 | 843 |
| | | West Mahanoy Township | 0 | 0 | 0 | 0 | 2,970 |
| | | West Manchester Township | 0 | 0 | 0 | 0 | 18,393 |
| | | West Manheim Township | 0 | 0 | 0 | 0 | 7,762 |
| | | West Mayfield Borough | 0 | 0 | 0 | 0 | 1,068 |
| | | West Mead Township | 0 | 0 | 0 | 0 | 5,047 |
| | | West Mifflin | 0 | 0 | 0 | 0 | 20,484 |
| | | West Newton | 0 | 0 | 0 | 0 | 2,824 |
| | | West Norriton Township | 0 | 0 | 0 | 0 | 14,488 |
| | | West Nottingham Township | 0 | 0 | 0 | 0 | 2,806 |
| | | West Penn Township | 0 | 0 | 0 | 0 | 4,343 |
| | | West Pikeland Township | 0 | 0 | 0 | 0 | 4,089 |
| | | West Pike Run | 0 | 0 | 0 | 0 | 1,829 |
| | | West Pittston | 0 | 0 | 0 | 0 | 4,901 |
| | | West Reading | 0 | 0 | 0 | 0 | 4,025 |
| | | West Sadsbury Township | 0 | 0 | 0 | 0 | 2,510 |
| | | West Salem Township | 0 | 0 | 0 | 0 | 3,324 |
| | | West Shore Regional | 0 | 0 | 0 | 0 | 6,568 |
| | | Westtown-East Goshen Regional | 0 | 0 | 0 | 0 | 31,830 |
| | | West View | 0 | 0 | 0 | 0 | 6,615 |
| | | West Vincent Township | 0 | 0 | 0 | 0 | 5,082 |
| | | West Whiteland Township | 0 | 0 | 0 | 0 | 18,397 |
| | | West Wyoming | 0 | 0 | 0 | 0 | 2,668 |
| | | West York | 0 | 0 | 0 | 0 | 4,183 |
| | | Whitaker Borough | 0 | 0 | 0 | 0 | 1,204 |
| | | Whitehall | 0 | 0 | 0 | 0 | 13,293 |
| | | Whitehall Township | 0 | 0 | 0 | 0 | 27,053 |
| | | White Haven Borough | 0 | 0 | 0 | 0 | 1,135 |
| | | Whitemarsh Township | 0 | 0 | 0 | 0 | 17,840 |
| | | White Oak | 0 | 0 | 0 | 0 | 7,958 |
| | | White Township | 0 | 0 | 0 | 0 | 1,298 |
| | | Whitpain Township | 0 | 0 | 0 | 0 | 18,829 |
| | | Wiconisco Township | 0 | 0 | 0 | 0 | 1,100 |
| | | Wilkes-Barre | 0 | 0 | 0 | 0 | 40,710 |
| | | Wilkes-Barre Township | 0 | 0 | 0 | 0 | 3,045 |
| | | Wilkinsburg | 0 | 0 | 0 | 0 | 17,351 |
| | | Wilkins Township | 0 | 0 | 0 | 0 | 6,146 |
| | | Williamsburg | 0 | 0 | 0 | 0 | 1,238 |
| | | Williamsport | 0 | 0 | 0 | 0 | 29,329 |
| | | Willistown Township | 0 | 0 | 0 | 0 | 10,838 |
| | | Wilson | 0 | 0 | 0 | 0 | 7,622 |
| | | Windber | 0 | 0 | 0 | 0 | 3,973 |
| | | Wind Gap | 0 | 0 | 0 | 0 | 2,782 |
| | | Womelsdorf | 0 | 0 | 0 | 0 | 2,811 |
| | | Woodward Township | 0 | 0 | 0 | 0 | 2,266 |
| | | Wrightsville | 0 | 0 | 0 | 0 | 2,234 |
| | | Wright Township | 0 | 0 | 0 | 0 | 5,920 |
| | | Wyoming | 0 | 0 | 0 | 0 | 2,972 |
| | | Wyomissing | 0 | 0 | 0 | 0 | 10,396 |
| | | Yardley | 0 | 0 | 0 | 0 | 2,491 |
| | | Yeadon | 0 | 0 | 0 | 0 | 11,325 |
| | | York | 0 | 0 | 0 | 0 | 39,970 |
| | | York Area Regional | 0 | 0 | 0 | 0 | 58,530 |
| | | Youngsville | 0 | 0 | 0 | 0 | 1,649 |
| | | Zelienople | 0 | 0 | 0 | 0 | 3,902 |
| | | Zerbe Township | 0 | 0 | 0 | 0 | 1,863 |
| | **Universities and Colleges** | Bloomsburg University | 0 | 0 | 0 | 0 | 8,855 |
| | | California University | 0 | 0 | 0 | 0 | 8,519 |
| | | Cheyney University | 0 | 0 | 0 | 0 | 1,488 |
| | | Clarion University | 0 | 0 | 0 | 0 | 7,100 |
| | | Dickinson College | 0 | 0 | 0 | 0 | 2,388 |
| | | East Stroudsburg University | 0 | 0 | 0 | 0 | 7,234 |
| | | Edinboro University | 0 | 0 | 0 | 0 | 7,671 |
| | | Elizabethtown College | 0 | 0 | 0 | 0 | 2,311 |
| | | Indiana University | 0 | 0 | 0 | 0 | 14,310 |
| | | Kutztown University | 0 | 0 | 0 | 0 | 10,393 |
| | | Lehigh University | 0 | 0 | 0 | 0 | 6,994 |
| | | Lock Haven University | 0 | 0 | 0 | 0 | 5,266 |
| | | Millersville University | 0 | 0 | 0 | 0 | 8,320 |
| | | Moravian College | 0 | 0 | 0 | 0 | 2,040 |
| | | Pennsylvania State University: | | | | | |
| | | Altoona | 0 | 0 | 0 | 0 | 4,013 |
| | | Beaver | 0 | 0 | 0 | 0 | 845 |
| | | Behrend | 0 | 0 | 0 | 0 | 4,334 |
| | | Berks | 0 | 0 | 0 | 0 | 2,800 |
| | | Harrisburg | 0 | 0 | 0 | 0 | 3,936 |
| | | Hazelton | 0 | 0 | 0 | 0 | 1,228 |
| | | McKeesport[3] | 0 | 0 | 0 | 0 | |
| | | Mont Alto | 0 | 0 | 0 | 0 | 1,189 |
| | | Shippensburg University | 0 | 0 | 0 | 0 | 7,942 |
| | | Slippery Rock University | 0 | 0 | 0 | 0 | 8,458 |

[1]Agencies published in this table indicated that no hate crimes occurred in their jurisdictions during the quarter(s) for which they submitted reports to the Hate Crime Statistics Program. Blanks indicate quarters for which agencies did not submit reports.
[2]Population figures are published only for the cities. The figures listed for the universities and colleges are student enrollment and were provided by the United States Department of Education for the 2008 school year, the most recent available. The enrollment figures include full-time and part-time students.
[3]Student enrollment figures were not available.

## Table 95. Hate Crime Zero Data Submitted per Quarter, by State and Agency, 2009—*Continued*

(Number.)

| State | Agency type | Agency name | Zero data per quarter[1] 1st quarter | 2nd quarter | 3rd quarter | 4th quarter | Population[2] |
|---|---|---|---|---|---|---|---|
| **PENNSYLVANIA** | | University of Pittsburgh: | | | | | |
| | | Bradford | 0 | 0 | 0 | 0 | 1,502 |
| | | Pittsburgh | 0 | 0 | 0 | 0 | 27,562 |
| | **Metropolitan Counties** | Allegheny | 0 | 0 | 0 | 0 | |
| | | Allegheny County Police Department | 0 | 0 | 0 | 0 | |
| | | Beaver | 0 | 0 | 0 | 0 | |
| | | Cumberland | 0 | 0 | 0 | 0 | |
| | | Erie | 0 | 0 | 0 | 0 | |
| | | Luzerne | 0 | 0 | 0 | 0 | |
| | | Lycoming | 0 | 0 | 0 | 0 | |
| | | Mercer | 0 | 0 | 0 | 0 | |
| | | Montgomery | 0 | 0 | 0 | 0 | |
| | | Northampton | 0 | 0 | | | |
| | | Pike | 0 | 0 | 0 | 0 | |
| | | Washington | 0 | 0 | 0 | 0 | |
| | | York | 0 | 0 | 0 | 0 | |
| | **Nonmetropolitan Counties** | Bradford | 0 | 0 | 0 | 0 | |
| | | Clarion | 0 | 0 | 0 | 0 | |
| | | Elk | 0 | 0 | 0 | 0 | |
| | | Franklin | 0 | 0 | 0 | 0 | |
| | | Greene | 0 | 0 | 0 | 0 | |
| | | Jefferson | 0 | 0 | 0 | 0 | |
| | | Snyder | 0 | 0 | 0 | 0 | |
| | | Tioga | 0 | 0 | 0 | 0 | |
| | **State Police Agencies** | State Police: | | | | | |
| | | Adams County | 0 | 0 | 0 | 0 | |
| | | Allegheny County | 0 | 0 | 0 | 0 | |
| | | Armstrong County | 0 | 0 | 0 | 0 | |
| | | Beaver County | 0 | 0 | 0 | 0 | |
| | | Bedford County | 0 | 0 | 0 | 0 | |
| | | Berks County | 0 | 0 | 0 | | |
| | | Blair County | 0 | 0 | 0 | 0 | |
| | | Bradford County | 0 | 0 | 0 | 0 | |
| | | Butler County | 0 | 0 | 0 | 0 | |
| | | Cambria County | 0 | 0 | 0 | 0 | |
| | | Cameron County | 0 | 0 | 0 | 0 | |
| | | Carbon County | 0 | 0 | 0 | 0 | |
| | | Centre County | 0 | 0 | 0 | 0 | |
| | | Clarion County | 0 | 0 | 0 | 0 | |
| | | Clearfield County | 0 | 0 | 0 | 0 | |
| | | Clinton County | 0 | 0 | 0 | 0 | |
| | | Columbia County | 0 | 0 | 0 | 0 | |
| | | Crawford County | 0 | 0 | 0 | 0 | |
| | | Cumberland County | 0 | 0 | 0 | 0 | |
| | | Delaware County | 0 | 0 | 0 | 0 | |
| | | Elizabethville | 0 | 0 | 0 | 0 | |
| | | Elk County | 0 | 0 | 0 | 0 | |
| | | Erie County | 0 | 0 | 0 | 0 | |
| | | Fayette County | 0 | 0 | 0 | 0 | |
| | | Franklin County | 0 | 0 | 0 | 0 | |
| | | Fulton County | 0 | 0 | 0 | 0 | |
| | | Gaming Enforcement | 0 | 0 | | | |
| | | Greene County | 0 | 0 | 0 | 0 | |
| | | Huntingdon County | 0 | 0 | 0 | 0 | |
| | | Indiana County | 0 | 0 | 0 | 0 | |
| | | Jefferson County | 0 | 0 | 0 | 0 | |
| | | Juniata County | 0 | 0 | 0 | 0 | |
| | | Lackawanna County | 0 | 0 | 0 | 0 | |
| | | Lancaster County | 0 | 0 | 0 | 0 | |
| | | Lawrence County | 0 | 0 | 0 | 0 | |
| | | Lebanon County | 0 | 0 | 0 | 0 | |
| | | Lehigh County | 0 | 0 | 0 | 0 | |
| | | Luzerne County | 0 | 0 | 0 | 0 | |
| | | Lycoming County | 0 | 0 | 0 | 0 | |
| | | McKean County | 0 | 0 | 0 | 0 | |
| | | Mercer County | 0 | 0 | 0 | 0 | |
| | | Mifflin County | 0 | 0 | 0 | 0 | |
| | | Monroe County | 0 | 0 | | 0 | |
| | | Montour County | 0 | 0 | 0 | 0 | |
| | | Northampton County | 0 | 0 | 0 | 0 | |
| | | Northumberland County | 0 | 0 | 0 | 0 | |
| | | Perry County | 0 | 0 | 0 | 0 | |
| | | Philadelphia County | 0 | 0 | 0 | 0 | |
| | | Pike County | 0 | 0 | 0 | 0 | |
| | | Potter County | 0 | 0 | 0 | 0 | |
| | | Schuylkill County | 0 | 0 | 0 | 0 | |
| | | Skippack | 0 | 0 | 0 | 0 | |
| | | Snyder County | 0 | 0 | 0 | 0 | |
| | | Somerset County | 0 | 0 | 0 | 0 | |
| | | Sullivan County | 0 | 0 | 0 | 0 | |
| | | Susquehanna County | 0 | 0 | 0 | 0 | |
| | | Tioga County | 0 | 0 | 0 | 0 | |
| | | Tionesta | 0 | 0 | 0 | 0 | |
| | | Union County | 0 | 0 | 0 | 0 | |
| | | Venango County | 0 | 0 | 0 | 0 | |
| | | Warren County | 0 | 0 | 0 | 0 | |
| | | Wayne County | 0 | 0 | 0 | 0 | |
| | | Wyoming County | 0 | 0 | 0 | 0 | |
| | | York County | 0 | 0 | 0 | 0 | |
| | | State Police, Bureau of Criminal Investigation: | | | | | |
| | | Adams County | 0 | 0 | 0 | 0 | |
| | | Allegheny County | 0 | 0 | 0 | 0 | |
| | | Armstrong County | 0 | 0 | 0 | 0 | |
| | | Beaver County | 0 | 0 | 0 | 0 | |
| | | Bedford County | 0 | 0 | 0 | 0 | |
| | | Berks County | 0 | 0 | 0 | 0 | |
| | | Blair County | 0 | 0 | 0 | 0 | |
| | | Bradford County | 0 | 0 | 0 | 0 | |
| | | Bucks County | 0 | 0 | 0 | 0 | |
| | | Butler County | 0 | 0 | 0 | 0 | |
| | | Cambria County | 0 | 0 | 0 | 0 | |
| | | Cameron County | 0 | 0 | 0 | 0 | |
| | | Carbon County | 0 | 0 | 0 | 0 | |
| | | Centre County | 0 | 0 | 0 | 0 | |
| | | Chester County | 0 | 0 | 0 | 0 | |
| | | Clarion County | 0 | 0 | 0 | 0 | |

[1]Agencies published in this table indicated that no hate crimes occurred in their jurisdictions during the quarter(s) for which they submitted reports to the Hate Crime Statistics Program. Blanks indicate quarters for which agencies did not submit reports.

[2]Population figures are published only for the cities. The figures listed for the universities and colleges are student enrollment and were provided by the United States Department of Education for the 2008 school year, the most recent available. The enrollment figures include full-time and part-time students.

## Table 95. Hate Crime Zero Data Submitted per Quarter, by State and Agency, 2009—*Continued*

(Number.)

| State | Agency type | Agency name | Zero data per quarter[1] 1st quarter | 2nd quarter | 3rd quarter | 4th quarter | Population[2] |
|---|---|---|---|---|---|---|---|
| PENNSYLVANIA | | Clearfield County | 0 | 0 | 0 | 0 | |
| | | Clinton County | 0 | 0 | 0 | 0 | |
| | | Columbia County | 0 | 0 | 0 | 0 | |
| | | Crawford County | 0 | 0 | 0 | 0 | |
| | | Cumberland County | 0 | 0 | 0 | 0 | |
| | | Dauphin County | 0 | 0 | | 0 | |
| | | Delaware County | 0 | 0 | 0 | 0 | |
| | | Elk County | 0 | 0 | 0 | 0 | |
| | | Erie County | 0 | 0 | 0 | 0 | |
| | | Fayette County | 0 | 0 | 0 | 0 | |
| | | Forest County | 0 | 0 | 0 | 0 | |
| | | Franklin County | 0 | 0 | 0 | 0 | |
| | | Fulton County | 0 | 0 | 0 | 0 | |
| | | Greene County | 0 | 0 | 0 | 0 | |
| | | Huntingdon County | 0 | 0 | 0 | 0 | |
| | | Indiana County | 0 | 0 | 0 | 0 | |
| | | Jefferson County | 0 | 0 | 0 | 0 | |
| | | Juniata County | 0 | 0 | 0 | 0 | |
| | | Lackawanna County | 0 | 0 | 0 | 0 | |
| | | Lancaster County | 0 | 0 | 0 | 0 | |
| | | Lawrence County | 0 | 0 | 0 | 0 | |
| | | Lebanon County | 0 | 0 | 0 | 0 | |
| | | Lehigh County | 0 | 0 | 0 | 0 | |
| | | Luzerne County | 0 | 0 | 0 | 0 | |
| | | Lycoming County | 0 | 0 | 0 | 0 | |
| | | McKean County | 0 | 0 | 0 | 0 | |
| | | Mercer County | 0 | 0 | 0 | 0 | |
| | | Mifflin County | 0 | 0 | 0 | 0 | |
| | | Monroe County | 0 | 0 | 0 | 0 | |
| | | Montgomery County | 0 | 0 | 0 | 0 | |
| | | Montour County | 0 | 0 | 0 | 0 | |
| | | Northampton County | 0 | 0 | 0 | 0 | |
| | | Northumberland County | 0 | 0 | 0 | 0 | |
| | | Perry County | 0 | 0 | 0 | 0 | |
| | | Philadelphia County | 0 | 0 | 0 | 0 | |
| | | Pike County | 0 | 0 | 0 | 0 | |
| | | Potter County | 0 | 0 | 0 | 0 | |
| | | Schuylkill County | 0 | 0 | 0 | 0 | |
| | | Snyder County | 0 | 0 | 0 | 0 | |
| | | Somerset County | 0 | 0 | 0 | 0 | |
| | | Sullivan County | 0 | 0 | 0 | 0 | |
| | | Susquehanna County | 0 | 0 | 0 | 0 | |
| | | Tioga County | 0 | 0 | 0 | 0 | |
| | | Union County | 0 | 0 | 0 | 0 | |
| | | Venango County | 0 | 0 | 0 | 0 | |
| | | Warren County | 0 | 0 | 0 | 0 | |
| | | Washington County | 0 | 0 | 0 | 0 | |
| | | Wayne County | 0 | 0 | 0 | 0 | |
| | | Westmoreland County | 0 | 0 | 0 | 0 | |
| | | Wyoming County | 0 | 0 | 0 | 0 | |
| | | York County | 0 | 0 | 0 | 0 | |
| | Other Agencies | Allegheny County Port Authority | 0 | 0 | 0 | 0 | |
| | | Altoona Hospital | 0 | 0 | 0 | 0 | |
| | | Bureau of Narcotics: Allegheny County | 0 | 0 | 0 | 0 | |
| | | Bedford County | 0 | 0 | 0 | 0 | |
| | | Berks County | 0 | 0 | 0 | 0 | |
| | | Blair County | 0 | 0 | 0 | 0 | |
| | | Bradford County | 0 | 0 | 0 | 0 | |
| | | Bucks County | 0 | 0 | 0 | 0 | |
| | | Cambria County | 0 | 0 | 0 | 0 | |
| | | Cameron County | 0 | 0 | 0 | 0 | |
| | | Carbon County | 0 | 0 | 0 | 0 | |
| | | Centre County | 0 | 0 | 0 | 0 | |
| | | Chester County | 0 | 0 | 0 | 0 | |
| | | Clearfield County | 0 | 0 | 0 | 0 | |
| | | Clinton County | 0 | 0 | 0 | 0 | |
| | | Columbia County | 0 | 0 | 0 | 0 | |
| | | Crawford County | 0 | 0 | 0 | 0 | |
| | | Delaware County | 0 | 0 | 0 | 0 | |
| | | Elk County | 0 | 0 | 0 | 0 | |
| | | Erie County | 0 | 0 | 0 | 0 | |
| | | Fayette County | 0 | 0 | 0 | 0 | |
| | | Forest County | 0 | 0 | 0 | 0 | |
| | | Greene County | 0 | 0 | 0 | 0 | |
| | | Huntingdon County | 0 | 0 | 0 | 0 | |
| | | Juniata County | 0 | 0 | 0 | 0 | |
| | | Lackawanna County | 0 | 0 | 0 | 0 | |
| | | Lehigh County | 0 | 0 | 0 | 0 | |
| | | Luzerne County | 0 | 0 | 0 | 0 | |
| | | Lycoming County | 0 | 0 | 0 | 0 | |
| | | McKean County | 0 | 0 | 0 | 0 | |
| | | Mifflin County | 0 | 0 | 0 | 0 | |
| | | Monroe County | 0 | 0 | 0 | 0 | |
| | | Montgomery County | 0 | 0 | 0 | 0 | |
| | | Montour County | 0 | 0 | 0 | 0 | |
| | | Northampton County | 0 | 0 | 0 | 0 | |
| | | Northumberland County | 0 | 0 | 0 | 0 | |
| | | Philadelphia County | 0 | 0 | 0 | 0 | |
| | | Pike County | 0 | 0 | 0 | 0 | |
| | | Potter County | 0 | 0 | 0 | 0 | |
| | | Schuylkill County | 0 | 0 | 0 | 0 | |
| | | Snyder County | 0 | 0 | 0 | 0 | |
| | | Somerset County | 0 | 0 | 0 | 0 | |
| | | Sullivan County | 0 | 0 | 0 | 0 | |
| | | Susquehanna County | 0 | 0 | 0 | 0 | |
| | | Tioga County | 0 | 0 | 0 | 0 | |
| | | Union County | 0 | 0 | 0 | 0 | |

[1]Agencies published in this table indicated that no hate crimes occurred in their jurisdictions during the quarter(s) for which they submitted reports to the Hate Crime Statistics Program. Blanks indicate quarters for which agencies did not submit reports.

[2]Population figures are published only for the cities. The figures listed for the universities and colleges are student enrollment and were provided by the United States Department of Education for the 2008 school year, the most recent available. The enrollment figures include full-time and part-time students.

## Table 95. Hate Crime Zero Data Submitted per Quarter, by State and Agency, 2009—*Continued*

(Number.)

| State | Agency type | Agency name | Zero data per quarter[1] | | | | Population[2] |
|---|---|---|---|---|---|---|---|
| | | | 1st quarter | 2nd quarter | 3rd quarter | 4th quarter | |
| PENNSYLVANIA | | Venango County | 0 | 0 | 0 | 0 | |
| | | Warren County | 0 | 0 | 0 | 0 | |
| | | Washington County | 0 | 0 | 0 | 0 | |
| | | Wayne County | 0 | 0 | 0 | 0 | |
| | | Westmoreland County | 0 | 0 | 0 | 0 | |
| | | Wyoming County | 0 | 0 | 0 | 0 | |
| | | County Detective: | | | | | |
| | | Berks County | 0 | 0 | 0 | 0 | |
| | | Bucks County | 0 | 0 | 0 | 0 | |
| | | Butler County | 0 | 0 | 0 | 0 | |
| | | Chester County | 0 | 0 | 0 | 0 | |
| | | Clarion County | 0 | 0 | 0 | 0 | |
| | | Clinton County | 0 | 0 | 0 | 0 | |
| | | Dauphin County | 0 | 0 | 0 | 0 | |
| | | Lackawanna County | 0 | | 0 | 0 | |
| | | Lebanon County | 0 | 0 | 0 | 0 | |
| | | Lehigh County | 0 | 0 | 0 | 0 | |
| | | Pike County | 0 | 0 | 0 | 0 | |
| | | Schuylkill County | 0 | 0 | 0 | 0 | |
| | | Westmoreland County | 0 | 0 | 0 | 0 | |
| | | York County | 0 | 0 | 0 | 0 | |
| | | Delaware County District Attorney, Criminal Investigation Division | 0 | 0 | 0 | 0 | |
| | | Delaware County Park | 0 | 0 | 0 | 0 | |
| | | Department of Environmental Resources | 0 | 0 | 0 | 0 | |
| | | Easton Area School District | 0 | 0 | 0 | 0 | |
| | | Fort Indiantown Gap | 0 | 0 | 0 | 0 | |
| | | Harrisburg International Airport | 0 | 0 | 0 | 0 | |
| | | State Capitol Police | 0 | 0 | 0 | 0 | |
| | | State Park Police: | | | | | |
| | | Pine Grove Furnace | 0 | 0 | 0 | 0 | |
| | | Presque Isle | 0 | | | | |
| | | Pymatuning | 0 | 0 | 0 | 0 | |
| | | Tyrone Area School District | 0 | 0 | 0 | 0 | |
| | | Uniontown Hospital | 0 | 0 | 0 | 0 | |
| | | Washington County Alternative Education | 0 | | 0 | | |
| | | Westmoreland County Park | 0 | 0 | 0 | 0 | |
| | | Wilkes-Barre Area School District | 0 | 0 | 0 | 0 | |
| RHODE ISLAND | Cities | Barrington | 0 | 0 | 0 | 0 | 16,353 |
| | | Bristol | 0 | 0 | 0 | 0 | 22,510 |
| | | Burrillville | 0 | 0 | 0 | 0 | 16,590 |
| | | Central Falls | 0 | 0 | 0 | 0 | 18,696 |
| | | Charlestown | 0 | 0 | 0 | 0 | 8,067 |
| | | Coventry | 0 | 0 | 0 | 0 | 34,837 |
| | | Cumberland | 0 | 0 | 0 | 0 | 34,546 |
| | | East Greenwich | 0 | 0 | 0 | 0 | 13,357 |
| | | Foster | 0 | 0 | 0 | 0 | 4,537 |
| | | Glocester | 0 | 0 | 0 | 0 | 10,583 |
| | | Hopkinton | 0 | 0 | 0 | 0 | 7,988 |
| | | Jamestown | 0 | 0 | 0 | 0 | 5,467 |
| | | Lincoln | 0 | 0 | 0 | 0 | 22,156 |
| | | Middletown | 0 | 0 | 0 | 0 | 16,009 |
| | | Narragansett | 0 | 0 | 0 | 0 | 16,476 |
| | | New Shoreham | 0 | 0 | 0 | 0 | 1,036 |
| | | North Kingstown | 0 | 0 | 0 | 0 | 26,615 |
| | | North Providence | 0 | 0 | 0 | 0 | 32,794 |
| | | Portsmouth | 0 | 0 | 0 | 0 | 16,913 |
| | | Richmond | 0 | 0 | 0 | 0 | 7,657 |
| | | Scituate | 0 | 0 | 0 | 0 | 10,894 |
| | | Tiverton | 0 | 0 | 0 | 0 | 14,944 |
| | | Warren | 0 | 0 | 0 | 0 | 10,990 |
| | | Westerly | 0 | 0 | 0 | 0 | 23,466 |
| | | West Greenwich | 0 | 0 | 0 | 0 | 6,540 |
| | | Woonsocket | 0 | 0 | 0 | 0 | 43,366 |
| | Universities and Colleges | Brown University | 0 | 0 | 0 | 0 | 8,318 |
| | State Police Agencies | Rhode Island State Police Headquarters | 0 | 0 | 0 | 0 | |
| | | State Police: | | | | | |
| | | Chepachet | 0 | 0 | 0 | 0 | |
| | | Hope Valley | 0 | 0 | 0 | 0 | |
| | | Lincoln | 0 | 0 | 0 | 0 | |
| | | Portsmouth | 0 | 0 | 0 | 0 | |
| | | Wickford | 0 | 0 | 0 | 0 | |
| | Other Agencies | Department of Environmental Management | 0 | 0 | 0 | 0 | |
| | | Rhode Island State Airport | 0 | 0 | 0 | 0 | |
| SOUTH CAROLINA | Cities | Abbeville | 0 | 0 | 0 | 0 | 5,514 |
| | | Aiken | 0 | 0 | 0 | 0 | 29,829 |
| | | Anderson | 0 | 0 | 0 | 0 | 27,144 |
| | | Andrews | 0 | 0 | 0 | 0 | 2,968 |
| | | Aynor | 0 | 0 | 0 | 0 | 642 |
| | | Bamberg | 0 | 0 | 0 | 0 | 3,401 |
| | | Barnwell | 0 | 0 | 0 | 0 | 4,766 |
| | | Batesburg-Leesville | 0 | 0 | 0 | 0 | 5,584 |
| | | Belton | 0 | 0 | 0 | 0 | 4,691 |
| | | Bennettsville | 0 | 0 | 0 | 0 | 8,956 |
| | | Bethune | 0 | | 0 | 0 | 372 |
| | | Bishopville | 0 | 0 | 0 | 0 | 3,880 |
| | | Blacksburg | 0 | 0 | 0 | 0 | 1,905 |
| | | Blackville | 0 | 0 | 0 | 0 | 2,823 |
| | | Bluffton | 0 | 0 | 0 | 0 | 12,557 |
| | | Briarcliffe Acres | 0 | 0 | 0 | 0 | 557 |
| | | Brunson | 0 | 0 | 0 | | 569 |
| | | Burnettown | 0 | 0 | 0 | 0 | 2,669 |
| | | Camden | 0 | 0 | 0 | 0 | 7,072 |
| | | Central | 0 | 0 | 0 | 0 | 4,154 |
| | | Chapin | 0 | 0 | 0 | 0 | 718 |
| | | Charleston | 0 | 0 | 0 | 0 | 113,681 |
| | | Cheraw | 0 | 0 | 0 | 0 | 5,411 |
| | | Chesnee | 0 | 0 | 0 | 0 | 1,084 |
| | | Chester | 0 | 0 | 0 | 0 | 5,999 |
| | | Chesterfield | 0 | 0 | 0 | 0 | 1,313 |
| | | Clemson | 0 | 0 | 0 | 0 | 13,147 |

[1] Agencies published in this table indicated that no hate crimes occurred in their jurisdictions during the quarter(s) for which they submitted reports to the Hate Crime Statistics Program. Blanks indicate quarters for which agencies did not submit reports.

[2] Population figures are published only for the cities. The figures listed for the universities and colleges are student enrollment and were provided by the United States Department of Education for the 2008 school year, the most recent available. The enrollment figures include full-time and part-time students.

## Table 95. Hate Crime Zero Data Submitted per Quarter, by State and Agency, 2009—*Continued*

(Number.)

| State | Agency type | Agency name | Zero data per quarter[1] | | | | Population[2] |
|---|---|---|---|---|---|---|---|
| | | | 1st quarter | 2nd quarter | 3rd quarter | 4th quarter | |
| **SOUTH CAROLINA** | | Clio | 0 | 0 | 0 | 0 | 715 |
| | | Conway | 0 | 0 | 0 | 0 | 16,295 |
| | | Cottageville | 0 | 0 | 0 | 0 | 674 |
| | | Coward | 0 | 0 | 0 | 0 | 679 |
| | | Darlington | 0 | 0 | 0 | 0 | 6,645 |
| | | Denmark | 0 | 0 | 0 | 0 | 2,972 |
| | | Dillon | 0 | 0 | 0 | 0 | 6,350 |
| | | Due West | 0 | 0 | 0 | 0 | 1,274 |
| | | Duncan | 0 | 0 | 0 | 0 | 3,141 |
| | | Easley | 0 | 0 | 0 | 0 | 20,589 |
| | | Edgefield | 0 | 0 | 0 | 0 | 4,415 |
| | | Edisto Beach | 0 | 0 | 0 | 0 | 726 |
| | | Ehrhardt | | 0 | | | 546 |
| | | Elgin | 0 | 0 | 0 | 0 | 1,294 |
| | | Elloree | 0 | 0 | 0 | 0 | 695 |
| | | Estill | 0 | 0 | 0 | 0 | 2,315 |
| | | Eutawville | 0 | 0 | 0 | 0 | 326 |
| | | Fairfax | 0 | 0 | 0 | 0 | 3,154 |
| | | Florence | 0 | 0 | 0 | 0 | 31,642 |
| | | Folly Beach | 0 | 0 | 0 | 0 | 2,445 |
| | | Fort Lawn | 0 | 0 | 0 | 0 | 804 |
| | | Fountain Inn | 0 | 0 | 0 | 0 | 7,944 |
| | | Gaffney | 0 | 0 | 0 | 0 | 13,223 |
| | | Georgetown | 0 | 0 | 0 | 0 | 8,450 |
| | | Great Falls | 0 | 0 | 0 | 0 | 2,027 |
| | | Greeleyville | 0 | 0 | 0 | 0 | 391 |
| | | Greenville | 0 | 0 | 0 | 0 | 60,355 |
| | | Greenwood | 0 | 0 | 0 | 0 | 22,551 |
| | | Greer | 0 | 0 | 0 | 0 | 25,463 |
| | | Hanahan | 0 | 0 | 0 | 0 | 16,460 |
| | | Hardeeville | 0 | 0 | 0 | 0 | 2,918 |
| | | Harleyville | 0 | 0 | 0 | 0 | 690 |
| | | Hemingway | 0 | 0 | 0 | 0 | 493 |
| | | Honea Path | 0 | 0 | 0 | 0 | 3,691 |
| | | Inman | 0 | 0 | 0 | 0 | 2,107 |
| | | Irmo | 0 | 0 | 0 | 0 | 11,738 |
| | | Isle of Palms | 0 | 0 | 0 | 0 | 4,690 |
| | | Iva | 0 | 0 | 0 | 0 | 1,205 |
| | | Jackson | 0 | 0 | 0 | 0 | 1,650 |
| | | Jamestown | 0 | 0 | 0 | 0 | 103 |
| | | Johnsonville | 0 | 0 | 0 | 0 | 1,496 |
| | | Johnston | 0 | 0 | 0 | 0 | 2,330 |
| | | Jonesville | 0 | 0 | 0 | 0 | 893 |
| | | Kingstree | 0 | 0 | 0 | 0 | 3,211 |
| | | Lake City | 0 | 0 | 0 | 0 | 6,687 |
| | | Lake View | 0 | 0 | 0 | 0 | 781 |
| | | Lancaster | 0 | 0 | 0 | 0 | 10,193 |
| | | Landrum | 0 | 0 | 0 | 0 | 2,630 |
| | | Lane | 0 | | | | 509 |
| | | Liberty | 0 | 0 | 0 | 0 | 3,070 |
| | | Lincolnville | 0 | 0 | | | 834 |
| | | Loris | 0 | 0 | 0 | 0 | 2,383 |
| | | Lyman | 0 | 0 | 0 | 0 | 2,890 |
| | | Lynchburg | 0 | 0 | 0 | 0 | 549 |
| | | Manning | 0 | 0 | 0 | 0 | 3,935 |
| | | Marion | 0 | 0 | 0 | 0 | 6,775 |
| | | Mayesville | 0 | | 0 | 0 | 1,002 |
| | | McBee | 0 | 0 | 0 | 0 | 705 |
| | | McColl | 0 | 0 | 0 | 0 | 2,288 |
| | | McCormick | 0 | 0 | 0 | 0 | 2,660 |
| | | Moncks Corner | 0 | 0 | 0 | 0 | 7,160 |
| | | Mullins | 0 | 0 | 0 | 0 | 4,683 |
| | | Myrtle Beach | 0 | 0 | 0 | 0 | 31,465 |
| | | Newberry | 0 | 0 | 0 | 0 | 10,952 |
| | | Nichols | | 0 | | 0 | 395 |
| | | Ninety Six | 0 | 0 | 0 | 0 | 1,920 |
| | | North | 0 | 0 | 0 | 0 | 772 |
| | | North Augusta | 0 | 0 | 0 | 0 | 21,066 |
| | | North Myrtle Beach | 0 | 0 | 0 | 0 | 16,413 |
| | | Norway | 0 | 0 | | | 365 |
| | | Orangeburg | 0 | 0 | 0 | 0 | 13,278 |
| | | Pamplico | 0 | 0 | 0 | 0 | 1,156 |
| | | Pawleys Island | 0 | | | | 141 |
| | | Pelion | 0 | 0 | 0 | 0 | 597 |
| | | Pickens | 0 | 0 | 0 | 0 | 3,024 |
| | | Pine Ridge | 0 | 0 | 0 | 0 | 2,007 |
| | | Port Royal | 0 | 0 | 0 | 0 | 11,282 |
| | | Prosperity | 0 | 0 | 0 | 0 | 1,065 |
| | | Ridgeland | 0 | 0 | 0 | 0 | 2,586 |
| | | Ridgeville | 0 | 0 | 0 | | 2,015 |
| | | Salem | 0 | 0 | 0 | 0 | 133 |
| | | Salley | 0 | 0 | 0 | 0 | 414 |
| | | Saluda | 0 | 0 | 0 | 0 | 2,894 |
| | | Santee | 0 | 0 | 0 | 0 | 715 |
| | | Scranton | 0 | 0 | 0 | 0 | 1,039 |
| | | Seneca | 0 | 0 | 0 | 0 | 8,074 |
| | | Simpsonville | 0 | 0 | 0 | 0 | 17,433 |
| | | Society Hill | 0 | 0 | 0 | 0 | 683 |
| | | South Congaree | 0 | 0 | 0 | 0 | 2,379 |
| | | Springfield | 0 | 0 | | | 480 |
| | | St. George | 0 | 0 | 0 | 0 | 2,127 |
| | | St. Matthews | 0 | 0 | 0 | 0 | 1,931 |
| | | St. Stephen | 0 | 0 | 0 | 0 | 1,778 |
| | | Sullivans Island | 0 | 0 | 0 | 0 | 1,866 |
| | | Summerton | 0 | 0 | 0 | 0 | 1,025 |
| | | Summerville | 0 | 0 | 0 | 0 | 47,507 |
| | | Sumter | 0 | 0 | 0 | 0 | 38,399 |
| | | Surfside Beach | 0 | 0 | 0 | 0 | 4,823 |
| | | Swansea | 0 | 0 | 0 | 0 | 805 |
| | | Tega Cay | 0 | 0 | 0 | 0 | 5,103 |
| | | Timmonsville | 0 | 0 | 0 | 0 | 2,380 |
| | | Travelers Rest | 0 | 0 | 0 | 0 | 4,574 |
| | | Turbeville | 0 | 0 | 0 | 0 | 705 |
| | | Union | 0 | 0 | 0 | 0 | 7,960 |
| | | Wagener | 0 | 0 | 0 | 0 | 876 |
| | | Walhalla | 0 | 0 | 0 | 0 | 3,551 |
| | | Walterboro | 0 | 0 | 0 | 0 | 5,825 |
| | | Ware Shoals | 0 | 0 | 0 | 0 | 2,346 |
| | | West Columbia | 0 | 0 | 0 | 0 | 13,982 |
| | | Westminster | 0 | 0 | 0 | 0 | 2,654 |
| | | West Union | 0 | 0 | 0 | 0 | 301 |
| | | Whitmire | 0 | 0 | 0 | 0 | 1,530 |
| | | Williamston | 0 | 0 | 0 | 0 | 3,983 |
| | | Williston | 0 | 0 | 0 | 0 | 3,178 |
| | | Winnsboro | 0 | 0 | 0 | 0 | 3,562 |
| | | Woodruff | 0 | 0 | 0 | 0 | 4,089 |
| | | Yemassee | 0 | 0 | 0 | 0 | 866 |
| | **Universities and Colleges** | Benedict College | 0 | 0 | 0 | 0 | 2,883 |
| | | Bob Jones University | 0 | 0 | 0 | 0 | 4,141 |
| | | Clemson University | 0 | 0 | 0 | 0 | 18,317 |
| | | College of Charleston | 0 | 0 | 0 | 0 | 11,367 |
| | | Columbia College | 0 | 0 | 0 | 0 | 1,445 |
| | | Denmark Technical College | | 0 | 0 | 0 | 2,277 |
| | | Erskine College | 0 | 0 | 0 | | 864 |
| | | Francis Marion University | 0 | 0 | 0 | 0 | 4,020 |
| | | Greenville Technical College | 0 | 0 | 0 | 0 | 14,414 |
| | | Lander University | 0 | 0 | 0 | 0 | 2,614 |
| | | Medical University of South Carolina | 0 | 0 | 0 | 0 | 2,528 |
| | | Midlands Technical College | 0 | 0 | 0 | 0 | 11,234 |
| | | Presbyterian College | 0 | 0 | | | 1,177 |
| | | South Carolina State University | 0 | 0 | 0 | 0 | 4,888 |

[1]Agencies published in this table indicated that no hate crimes occurred in their jurisdictions during the quarter(s) for which they submitted reports to the Hate Crime program. Blanks indicate quarters for which agencies did not submit reports.

[2]Population figures are published only for the cities. The figures listed for the universities and colleges are student enrollment and were provided by the United States Department of Education for the 2008 school year, the most recent available. The enrollment figures include full-time and part-time students.

# Table 95. Hate Crime Zero Data Submitted per Quarter, by State and Agency, 2009—*Continued*

(Number.)

| State | Agency type | Agency name | Zero data per quarter[1] | | | | Population[2] |
|---|---|---|---|---|---|---|---|
| | | | 1st quarter | 2nd quarter | 3rd quarter | 4th quarter | |
| SOUTH CAROLINA | | Spartanburg Methodist College | 0 | 0 | 0 | 0 | 750 |
| | | The Citadel | 0 | 0 | 0 | 0 | 3,328 |
| | | Trident Technical College | 0 | 0 | | | 12,763 |
| | | University of South Carolina: | | | | | |
| | | Aiken | 0 | 0 | 0 | 0 | 3,232 |
| | | Columbia | 0 | 0 | 0 | 0 | 27,488 |
| | | Upstate | 0 | | 0 | 0 | 5,063 |
| | | Winthrop University | 0 | 0 | 0 | 0 | 6,249 |
| | Metropolitan Counties | Calhoun | 0 | 0 | 0 | 0 | |
| | | Charleston | 0 | 0 | 0 | 0 | |
| | | Darlington | 0 | 0 | 0 | 0 | |
| | | Dorchester | 0 | 0 | 0 | 0 | |
| | | Edgefield | 0 | 0 | 0 | 0 | |
| | | Fairfield | 0 | 0 | 0 | 0 | |
| | | Florence | 0 | 0 | 0 | 0 | |
| | | Horry | 0 | 0 | 0 | 0 | |
| | | Kershaw | 0 | 0 | 0 | 0 | |
| | | Lexington | 0 | 0 | 0 | 0 | |
| | | Saluda | 0 | 0 | 0 | 0 | |
| | | Spartanburg | 0 | 0 | 0 | 0 | |
| | | Sumter | 0 | 0 | 0 | 0 | |
| | | York | 0 | 0 | 0 | 0 | |
| | Nonmetropolitan Counties | Allendale | 0 | 0 | 0 | 0 | |
| | | Bamberg | 0 | 0 | 0 | 0 | |
| | | Barnwell | 0 | 0 | 0 | 0 | |
| | | Beaufort | 0 | 0 | 0 | 0 | |
| | | Cherokee | 0 | 0 | 0 | 0 | |
| | | Lancaster | 0 | 0 | 0 | 0 | |
| | | Marion | 0 | 0 | 0 | 0 | |
| | | Marlboro | 0 | 0 | 0 | 0 | |
| | | McCormick | 0 | 0 | 0 | 0 | |
| | | Newberry | 0 | 0 | 0 | 0 | |
| | | Oconee | 0 | 0 | 0 | 0 | |
| | | Orangeburg | 0 | 0 | 0 | 0 | |
| | | Union | 0 | 0 | 0 | 0 | |
| | | Williamsburg | 0 | 0 | 0 | 0 | |
| | State Police Agencies | Highway Patrol: | | | | | |
| | | Abbeville County | 0 | 0 | 0 | 0 | |
| | | Aiken County | 0 | 0 | 0 | 0 | |
| | | Allendale County | 0 | 0 | 0 | 0 | |
| | | Anderson County | 0 | 0 | 0 | 0 | |
| | | Bamberg County | 0 | 0 | 0 | 0 | |
| | | Barnwell County | 0 | 0 | 0 | 0 | |
| | | Beaufort County | 0 | 0 | 0 | 0 | |
| | | Berkeley County | 0 | 0 | 0 | 0 | |
| | | Calhoun County | 0 | 0 | 0 | 0 | |
| | | Charleston County | 0 | 0 | 0 | 0 | |
| | | Cherokee County | 0 | 0 | 0 | 0 | |
| | | Chester County | 0 | 0 | 0 | 0 | |
| | | Chesterfield County | 0 | 0 | 0 | 0 | |
| | | Clarendon County | 0 | 0 | 0 | 0 | |
| | | Colleton County | 0 | 0 | 0 | 0 | |
| | | Darlington County | 0 | 0 | 0 | 0 | |
| | | Dillon County | 0 | 0 | 0 | 0 | |
| | | Dorchester County | 0 | 0 | 0 | 0 | |
| | | Edgefield County | 0 | 0 | 0 | 0 | |
| | | Fairfield County | 0 | 0 | 0 | 0 | |
| | | Florence County | 0 | 0 | 0 | 0 | |
| | | Georgetown County | 0 | 0 | 0 | 0 | |
| | | Greenville County | 0 | 0 | 0 | 0 | |
| | | Greenwood County | 0 | 0 | 0 | 0 | |
| | | Hampton County | 0 | 0 | 0 | 0 | |
| | | Horry County | 0 | 0 | 0 | 0 | |
| | | Jasper County | 0 | 0 | 0 | 0 | |
| | | Kershaw County | 0 | 0 | 0 | 0 | |
| | | Lancaster County | 0 | 0 | 0 | 0 | |
| | | Laurens County | 0 | 0 | 0 | 0 | |
| | | Lee County | 0 | 0 | 0 | 0 | |
| | | Lexington County | 0 | 0 | 0 | 0 | |
| | | Marion County | 0 | 0 | 0 | 0 | |
| | | Marlboro County | 0 | 0 | 0 | 0 | |
| | | McCormick County | 0 | 0 | 0 | 0 | |
| | | Newberry County | 0 | 0 | 0 | 0 | |
| | | Oconee County | 0 | 0 | 0 | 0 | |
| | | Orangeburg County | 0 | 0 | 0 | 0 | |
| | | Pickens County | 0 | 0 | 0 | 0 | |
| | | Richland County | 0 | 0 | 0 | 0 | |
| | | Saluda County | 0 | 0 | 0 | 0 | |
| | | Spartanburg County | 0 | 0 | 0 | 0 | |
| | | Sumter County | 0 | 0 | 0 | 0 | |
| | | Union County | 0 | 0 | 0 | 0 | |
| | | Williamsburg County | 0 | 0 | 0 | 0 | |
| | | York County | 0 | 0 | 0 | 0 | |
| | Other Agencies | Bureau of Protective Services | 0 | 0 | 0 | 0 | |
| | | Columbia Metropolitan Airport | 0 | 0 | 0 | 0 | |
| | | Department of Mental Health | 0 | 0 | 0 | 0 | |
| | | Department of Natural Resources: | | | | | |
| | | Abbeville County | 0 | 0 | 0 | 0 | |
| | | Aiken County | 0 | 0 | 0 | 0 | |
| | | Allendale County | 0 | 0 | 0 | 0 | |
| | | Anderson County | 0 | 0 | 0 | 0 | |

[1]Agencies published in this table indicated that no hate crimes occurred in their jurisdictions during the quarter(s) for which they submitted reports to the Hate Crime program. Blanks indicate quarters for which agencies did not submit reports.
[2]Population figures are published only for the cities. The figures listed for the universities and colleges are student enrollment and were provided by the United States Department of Education for the 2008 school year, the most recent available. The enrollment figures include full-time and part-time students.
[3]Student enrollment figures were not available.

**Table 95. Hate Crime Zero Data Submitted per Quarter, by State and Agency, 2009**—*Continued*

(Number.)

| State | Agency type | Agency name | Zero data per quarter[1] | | | | Population[2] |
|---|---|---|---|---|---|---|---|
| | | | 1st quarter | 2nd quarter | 3rd quarter | 4th quarter | |
| SOUTH-CAROLINA | | Bamberg County | 0 | 0 | 0 | 0 | |
| | | Barnwell County | 0 | 0 | 0 | 0 | |
| | | Beaufort County | 0 | 0 | 0 | 0 | |
| | | Berkeley County | 0 | 0 | 0 | 0 | |
| | | Calhoun County | 0 | 0 | 0 | 0 | |
| | | Charleston County | 0 | 0 | 0 | 0 | |
| | | Cherokee County | 0 | 0 | 0 | 0 | |
| | | Chester County | 0 | 0 | 0 | 0 | |
| | | Chesterfield County | 0 | 0 | 0 | 0 | |
| | | Clarendon County | 0 | 0 | 0 | 0 | |
| | | Colleton County | 0 | 0 | 0 | 0 | |
| | | Darlington County | 0 | 0 | 0 | 0 | |
| | | Dillon County | 0 | 0 | 0 | 0 | |
| | | Dorchester County | 0 | 0 | 0 | 0 | |
| | | Edgefield County | 0 | 0 | 0 | 0 | |
| | | Fairfield County | 0 | 0 | 0 | 0 | |
| | | Florence County | 0 | 0 | 0 | 0 | |
| | | Georgetown County | 0 | 0 | 0 | 0 | |
| | | Greenville County | 0 | 0 | 0 | 0 | |
| | | Greenwood County | 0 | 0 | 0 | 0 | |
| | | Hampton County | 0 | 0 | 0 | 0 | |
| | | Horry County | 0 | 0 | 0 | 0 | |
| | | Jasper County | 0 | 0 | 0 | 0 | |
| | | Kershaw County | 0 | 0 | 0 | 0 | |
| | | Lancaster County | 0 | 0 | 0 | 0 | |
| | | Laurens County | 0 | 0 | 0 | 0 | |
| | | Lee County | 0 | 0 | 0 | 0 | |
| | | Lexington County | 0 | 0 | 0 | 0 | |
| | | Marion County | 0 | 0 | 0 | 0 | |
| | | Marlboro County | 0 | 0 | 0 | 0 | |
| | | McCormick County | 0 | 0 | 0 | 0 | |
| | | Newberry County | 0 | 0 | 0 | 0 | |
| | | Oconee County | 0 | 0 | 0 | 0 | |
| | | Orangeburg County | 0 | 0 | 0 | 0 | |
| | | Pickens County | 0 | 0 | 0 | 0 | |
| | | Richland County | 0 | 0 | 0 | 0 | |
| | | Saluda County | 0 | 0 | 0 | 0 | |
| | | Spartanburg County | 0 | 0 | 0 | 0 | |
| | | Sumter County | 0 | 0 | 0 | 0 | |
| | | Union County | 0 | 0 | 0 | 0 | |
| | | Williamsburg County | 0 | 0 | 0 | 0 | |
| | | York County | 0 | 0 | 0 | 0 | |
| | | Employment Security Commission | 0 | 0 | 0 | 0 | |
| | | Forestry Commission: | | | | | |
| | | Abbeville County | 0 | 0 | 0 | 0 | |
| | | Aiken County | 0 | 0 | 0 | 0 | |
| | | Allendale County | 0 | 0 | 0 | 0 | |
| | | Anderson County | 0 | 0 | 0 | 0 | |
| | | Bamberg County | 0 | 0 | 0 | 0 | |
| | | Barnwell County | 0 | 0 | 0 | 0 | |
| | | Beaufort County | 0 | 0 | 0 | 0 | |
| | | Berkeley County | 0 | 0 | 0 | 0 | |
| | | Calhoun County | 0 | 0 | 0 | 0 | |
| | | Charleston County | 0 | 0 | 0 | 0 | |
| | | Cherokee County | 0 | 0 | 0 | 0 | |
| | | Chester County | 0 | 0 | 0 | 0 | |
| | | Chesterfield County | 0 | 0 | 0 | 0 | |
| | | Clarendon County | 0 | 0 | 0 | 0 | |
| | | Colleton County | 0 | 0 | 0 | 0 | |
| | | Darlington County | 0 | 0 | 0 | 0 | |
| | | Dillon County | 0 | 0 | 0 | 0 | |
| | | Dorchester County | 0 | 0 | 0 | 0 | |
| | | Edgefield County | 0 | 0 | 0 | 0 | |
| | | Fairfield County | 0 | 0 | 0 | 0 | |
| | | Florence County | 0 | 0 | 0 | 0 | |
| | | Georgetown County | 0 | 0 | 0 | 0 | |
| | | Greenville County | 0 | 0 | 0 | 0 | |
| | | Greenwood County | 0 | 0 | 0 | 0 | |
| | | Hampton County | 0 | 0 | 0 | 0 | |
| | | Horry County | 0 | 0 | 0 | 0 | |
| | | Jasper County | 0 | 0 | 0 | 0 | |
| | | Kershaw County | 0 | 0 | 0 | 0 | |
| | | Lancaster County | 0 | 0 | 0 | 0 | |
| | | Laurens County | 0 | 0 | 0 | 0 | |
| | | Lee County | 0 | 0 | 0 | 0 | |
| | | Lexington County | 0 | 0 | 0 | 0 | |
| | | Marion County | 0 | 0 | 0 | 0 | |
| | | Marlboro County | 0 | 0 | 0 | 0 | |
| | | McCormick County | 0 | 0 | 0 | 0 | |
| | | Newberry County | 0 | 0 | 0 | 0 | |
| | | Oconee County | 0 | 0 | 0 | 0 | |
| | | Orangeburg County | 0 | 0 | 0 | 0 | |
| | | Pickens County | 0 | 0 | 0 | 0 | |
| | | Richland County | 0 | 0 | 0 | 0 | |
| | | Saluda County | 0 | 0 | 0 | 0 | |

[1]Agencies published in this table indicated that no hate crimes occurred in their jurisdictions during the quarter(s) for which they submitted reports to the Hate Crime Statistics Program. Blanks indicate quarters for which agencies did not submit reports.

[2]Population figures are published only for the cities. The figures listed for the universities and colleges are student enrollment and were provided by the United States Department of Education for the 2008 school year, the most recent available. The enrollment figures include full-time and part-time students.

## Table 95. Hate Crime Zero Data Submitted per Quarter, by State and Agency, 2009—*Continued*

(Number.)

| State | Agency type | Agency name | Zero data per quarter[1] 1st quarter | 2nd quarter | 3rd quarter | 4th quarter | Population[2] |
|---|---|---|---|---|---|---|---|
| SOUTH CAROLINA | | Spartanburg County | 0 | 0 | 0 | 0 | |
| | | Sumter County | 0 | 0 | 0 | 0 | |
| | | Union County | 0 | 0 | 0 | 0 | |
| | | Williamsburg County | 0 | 0 | 0 | 0 | |
| | | York County | 0 | 0 | 0 | 0 | |
| | | Greenville-Spartanburg International Airport | 0 | 0 | 0 | 0 | |
| | | South Carolina Law Enforcement Division, Vehicle Crimes | 0 | 0 | 0 | 0 | |
| | | South Carolina Law Enforcement Division, Vice: | | | | | |
| | | Abbeville County | 0 | 0 | 0 | 0 | |
| | | Aiken County | 0 | 0 | 0 | 0 | |
| | | Allendale County | 0 | 0 | 0 | 0 | |
| | | Anderson County | 0 | 0 | 0 | 0 | |
| | | Bamberg County | 0 | 0 | 0 | 0 | |
| | | Barnwell County | 0 | 0 | 0 | 0 | |
| | | Beaufort County | 0 | 0 | 0 | 0 | |
| | | Berkeley County | 0 | 0 | 0 | 0 | |
| | | Calhoun County | 0 | 0 | 0 | 0 | |
| | | Charleston County | 0 | 0 | 0 | 0 | |
| | | Cherokee County | 0 | 0 | 0 | 0 | |
| | | Chester County | 0 | 0 | 0 | 0 | |
| | | Chesterfield County | 0 | 0 | 0 | 0 | |
| | | Clarendon County | 0 | 0 | 0 | 0 | |
| | | Colleton County | 0 | 0 | 0 | 0 | |
| | | Darlington County | 0 | 0 | 0 | 0 | |
| | | Dillon County | 0 | 0 | 0 | 0 | |
| | | Dorchester County | 0 | 0 | 0 | 0 | |
| | | Edgefield County | 0 | 0 | 0 | 0 | |
| | | Fairfield County | 0 | 0 | 0 | 0 | |
| | | Florence County | 0 | 0 | 0 | 0 | |
| | | Georgetown County | 0 | 0 | 0 | 0 | |
| | | Greenville County | 0 | 0 | 0 | 0 | |
| | | Greenwood County | 0 | 0 | 0 | 0 | |
| | | Hampton County | 0 | 0 | 0 | 0 | |
| | | Horry County | 0 | 0 | 0 | 0 | |
| | | Jasper County | 0 | 0 | 0 | 0 | |
| | | Kershaw County | 0 | 0 | 0 | 0 | |
| | | Lancaster County | 0 | 0 | 0 | 0 | |
| | | Laurens County | 0 | 0 | 0 | 0 | |
| | | Lee County | 0 | 0 | 0 | 0 | |
| | | Lexington County | 0 | 0 | 0 | 0 | |
| | | Marion County | 0 | 0 | 0 | 0 | |
| | | Marlboro County | 0 | 0 | 0 | 0 | |
| | | McCormick County | 0 | 0 | 0 | 0 | |
| | | Newberry County | 0 | 0 | 0 | 0 | |
| | | Oconee County | 0 | 0 | 0 | 0 | |
| | | Orangeburg County | 0 | 0 | 0 | 0 | |
| | | Pickens County | 0 | 0 | 0 | 0 | |
| | | Richland County | 0 | 0 | 0 | 0 | |
| | | Saluda County | 0 | 0 | 0 | 0 | |
| | | Spartanburg County | 0 | 0 | 0 | 0 | |
| | | Sumter County | 0 | 0 | 0 | 0 | |
| | | Union County | 0 | 0 | 0 | 0 | |
| | | Williamsburg County | 0 | 0 | 0 | 0 | |
| | | York County | 0 | 0 | 0 | 0 | |
| | | South Carolina School for the Deaf and Blind | 0 | 0 | 0 | 0 | |
| | | State Museum | | 0 | 0 | 0 | |
| | | State Ports Authority | 0 | 0 | 0 | 0 | |
| | | State Transport Police: | | | | | |
| | | Aiken County | 0 | 0 | 0 | 0 | |
| | | Allendale County | 0 | 0 | 0 | 0 | |
| | | Anderson County | 0 | 0 | 0 | 0 | |
| | | Bamberg County | 0 | 0 | 0 | 0 | |
| | | Barnwell County | 0 | 0 | 0 | 0 | |
| | | Beaufort County | 0 | 0 | 0 | 0 | |
| | | Berkeley County | 0 | 0 | 0 | 0 | |
| | | Charleston County | 0 | 0 | 0 | 0 | |
| | | Cherokee County | 0 | 0 | 0 | 0 | |
| | | Colleton County | 0 | 0 | 0 | 0 | |
| | | Darlington County | 0 | 0 | 0 | 0 | |
| | | Dillon County | 0 | 0 | 0 | 0 | |
| | | Dorchester County | 0 | 0 | 0 | 0 | |
| | | Edgefield County | 0 | 0 | 0 | 0 | |
| | | Fairfield County | 0 | 0 | 0 | 0 | |
| | | Florence County | 0 | 0 | 0 | 0 | |
| | | Georgetown County | 0 | 0 | 0 | 0 | |
| | | Greenville County | 0 | 0 | 0 | 0 | |
| | | Greenwood County | 0 | 0 | 0 | 0 | |
| | | Horry County | 0 | 0 | 0 | 0 | |
| | | Jasper County | 0 | 0 | 0 | 0 | |
| | | Kershaw County | 0 | 0 | 0 | 0 | |
| | | Laurens County | 0 | 0 | 0 | 0 | |
| | | Lee County | 0 | 0 | 0 | 0 | |

[1]Agencies published in this table indicated that no hate crimes occurred in their jurisdictions during the quarter(s) for which they submitted reports to the Hate Crime Statistics Program. Blanks indicate quarters for which agencies did not submit reports.

[2]Population figures are published only for the cities. The figures listed for the universities and colleges are student enrollment and were provided by the United States Department of Education for the 2008 school year, the most recent available. The enrollment figures include full-time and part-time students.

# Table 95. Hate Crime Zero Data Submitted per Quarter, by State and Agency, 2009—*Continued*

(Number.)

| State | Agency type | Agency name | Zero data per quarter[1] 1st quarter | 2nd quarter | 3rd quarter | 4th quarter | Population[2] |
|---|---|---|---|---|---|---|---|
| SOUTH CAROLINA | | Lexington County | 0 | 0 | 0 | 0 | |
| | | Marion County | 0 | 0 | 0 | 0 | |
| | | Marlboro County | 0 | 0 | 0 | 0 | |
| | | Newberry County | 0 | 0 | 0 | 0 | |
| | | Oconee County | 0 | 0 | 0 | 0 | |
| | | Orangeburg County | 0 | 0 | 0 | 0 | |
| | | Richland County | 0 | 0 | 0 | 0 | |
| | | Saluda County | | 0 | 0 | 0 | |
| | | Spartanburg County | 0 | 0 | 0 | 0 | |
| | | Sumter County | 0 | 0 | 0 | 0 | |
| | | Union County | 0 | 0 | 0 | 0 | |
| | | Williamsburg County | 0 | 0 | 0 | 0 | |
| | | York County | 0 | 0 | 0 | 0 | |
| | | United States Department of Energy, Savannah River Plant | 0 | 0 | 0 | 0 | |
| | | Whitten Center | 0 | 0 | 0 | 0 | |
| SOUTH DAKOTA | Cities | Aberdeen | 0 | 0 | 0 | 0 | 24,441 |
| | | Armour | 0 | 0 | 0 | 0 | 642 |
| | | Avon | 0 | 0 | 0 | 0 | 511 |
| | | Belle Fourche | 0 | 0 | 0 | 0 | 5,001 |
| | | Box Elder | 0 | 0 | 0 | 0 | 3,601 |
| | | Brandon | 0 | 0 | 0 | 0 | 9,195 |
| | | Brookings | 0 | 0 | 0 | 0 | 19,986 |
| | | Canton | 0 | 0 | 0 | 0 | 3,680 |
| | | Centerville | 0 | 0 | 0 | 0 | 837 |
| | | Chamberlain | 0 | 0 | 0 | 0 | 2,255 |
| | | Colman | 0 | 0 | 0 | 0 | 546 |
| | | Corsica | 0 | 0 | 0 | 0 | 563 |
| | | Deadwood | 0 | 0 | 0 | 0 | 1,273 |
| | | Eagle Butte | 0 | 0 | 0 | 0 | 927 |
| | | Estelline | 0 | 0 | 0 | 0 | 665 |
| | | Eureka | 0 | 0 | 0 | 0 | 921 |
| | | Faith | 0 | 0 | 0 | 0 | 436 |
| | | Flandreau | 0 | 0 | 0 | 0 | 2,206 |
| | | Freeman | 0 | 0 | 0 | 0 | 1,181 |
| | | Gettysburg | 0 | 0 | 0 | 0 | 1,031 |
| | | Hot Springs | 0 | 0 | 0 | 0 | 4,015 |
| | | Hoven | 0 | 0 | 0 | 0 | 384 |
| | | Irene | 0 | 0 | 0 | 0 | 401 |
| | | Jefferson | 0 | 0 | 0 | 0 | 600 |
| | | Kadoka | 0 | 0 | 0 | 0 | 628 |
| | | Kimball | | | | 0 | 687 |
| | | Lead | 0 | 0 | 0 | 0 | 2,878 |
| | | Lemmon | 0 | 0 | 0 | 0 | 1,164 |
| | | Lennox | 0 | 0 | 0 | 0 | 2,453 |
| | | Leola | 0 | 0 | 0 | 0 | 383 |
| | | Madison | 0 | 0 | 0 | 0 | 6,478 |
| | | Martin | 0 | 0 | 0 | 0 | 986 |
| | | Menno | 0 | 0 | 0 | 0 | 648 |
| | | Mitchell | 0 | 0 | 0 | 0 | 14,769 |
| | | Mobridge | 0 | 0 | 0 | 0 | 3,113 |
| | | North Sioux City | 0 | 0 | 0 | 0 | 2,547 |
| | | Parkston | 0 | 0 | 0 | 0 | 1,467 |
| | | Rosholt | 0 | 0 | 0 | 0 | 427 |
| | | Scotland | 0 | 0 | 0 | 0 | 780 |
| | | Selby | | | 0 | 0 | 638 |
| | | Sisseton | 0 | 0 | 0 | 0 | 2,437 |
| | | Springfield | 0 | 0 | 0 | 0 | 1,479 |
| | | Sturgis | 0 | 0 | 0 | 0 | 5,899 |
| | | Summerset | 0 | 0 | 0 | 0 | 442 |
| | | Tripp | 0 | 0 | 0 | 0 | 623 |
| | | Tyndall | 0 | 0 | 0 | 0 | 1,088 |
| | | Vermillion | 0 | 0 | 0 | 0 | 10,523 |
| | | Viborg | 0 | 0 | 0 | 0 | 768 |
| | | Wagner | 0 | 0 | 0 | 0 | 1,538 |
| | | Whitewood | 0 | 0 | 0 | 0 | 850 |
| | | Winner | 0 | 0 | 0 | 0 | 2,705 |
| | Universities and Colleges | South Dakota State University | 0 | 0 | 0 | 0 | 11,995 |
| | Metropolitan Counties | Lincoln | 0 | 0 | 0 | 0 | |
| | | McCook | 0 | 0 | 0 | 0 | |
| | | Meade | 0 | 0 | 0 | 0 | |
| | | Pennington | 0 | 0 | 0 | 0 | |
| | | Turner | 0 | 0 | 0 | 0 | |
| | | Union | 0 | 0 | 0 | 0 | |
| | Nonmetropolitan Counties | Aurora | 0 | 0 | 0 | 0 | |
| | | Beadle | 0 | 0 | 0 | 0 | |
| | | Bennett | 0 | 0 | 0 | 0 | |
| | | Bon Homme | 0 | 0 | 0 | 0 | |
| | | Brookings | 0 | 0 | 0 | 0 | |
| | | Brown | 0 | 0 | 0 | 0 | |
| | | Butte | 0 | 0 | 0 | 0 | |
| | | Campbell | 0 | 0 | 0 | 0 | |
| | | Charles Mix | 0 | 0 | 0 | 0 | |
| | | Clark | 0 | | | | |
| | | Clay | 0 | 0 | 0 | 0 | |
| | | Codington | 0 | 0 | 0 | 0 | |
| | | Corson | 0 | 0 | 0 | 0 | |
| | | Davison | 0 | 0 | 0 | 0 | |
| | | Deuel | 0 | 0 | 0 | 0 | |
| | | Dewey | 0 | 0 | 0 | 0 | |
| | | Douglas | 0 | 0 | 0 | 0 | |
| | | Edmunds | 0 | 0 | 0 | 0 | |
| | | Fall River | 0 | 0 | 0 | | |
| | | Faulk | 0 | 0 | 0 | 0 | |
| | | Hamlin | 0 | 0 | 0 | 0 | |
| | | Hand | 0 | 0 | 0 | 0 | |
| | | Hanson | 0 | 0 | 0 | 0 | |
| | | Harding | 0 | 0 | 0 | 0 | |
| | | Hughes | 0 | 0 | 0 | 0 | |
| | | Hutchinson | 0 | 0 | 0 | 0 | |
| | | Jerauld | 0 | 0 | 0 | 0 | |
| | | Lawrence | 0 | 0 | 0 | 0 | |
| | | Marshall | 0 | 0 | 0 | 0 | |
| | | McPherson | 0 | 0 | 0 | 0 | |
| | | Mellette | 0 | | | | |
| | | Moody | 0 | 0 | 0 | 0 | |
| | | Perkins | 0 | 0 | 0 | 0 | |
| | | Potter | 0 | 0 | 0 | 0 | |
| | | Roberts | 0 | 0 | 0 | 0 | |
| | | Sanborn | 0 | 0 | 0 | 0 | |
| | | Spink | 0 | 0 | 0 | 0 | |
| | | Stanley | 0 | 0 | 0 | 0 | |
| | | Sully | 0 | 0 | 0 | 0 | |
| | | Tripp | 0 | 0 | 0 | 0 | |
| | | Walworth | 0 | 0 | 0 | 0 | |
| | | Yankton | 0 | 0 | 0 | 0 | |
| | | Ziebach | 0 | 0 | 0 | 0 | |
| | Other Agencies | Division of Criminal Investigation | 0 | 0 | 0 | 0 | |
| TENNESSEE | Cities | Adamsville | 0 | 0 | 0 | 0 | 2,138 |
| | | Alamo | 0 | 0 | 0 | 0 | 2,307 |
| | | Alcoa | 0 | 0 | 0 | 0 | 8,681 |
| | | Alexandria | 0 | 0 | 0 | 0 | 879 |
| | | Algood | 0 | 0 | 0 | 0 | 3,430 |
| | | Ardmore | 0 | 0 | 0 | 0 | 1,172 |
| | | Ashland City | 0 | 0 | 0 | 0 | 4,695 |
| | | Athens | 0 | 0 | 0 | 0 | 14,388 |
| | | Atoka | 0 | 0 | 0 | 0 | 7,900 |
| | | Baileyton | 0 | 0 | 0 | 0 | 491 |

[1]Agencies published in this table indicated that no hate crimes occurred in their jurisdictions during the quarter(s) for which they submitted reports to the Hate Crime Statistics Program. Blanks indicate quarters for which agencies did not submit reports.

[2]Population figures are published only for the cities. The figures listed for the universities and colleges are student enrollment and were provided by the United States Department of Education for the 2008 school year, the most recent available. The enrollment figures include full-time and part-time students.

## Table 95. Hate Crime Zero Data Submitted per Quarter, by State and Agency, 2009—*Continued*

(Number.)

| State | Agency type | Agency name | Zero data per quarter[1] 1st quarter | 2nd quarter | 3rd quarter | 4th quarter | Population[2] |
|---|---|---|---|---|---|---|---|
| **TENNESSEE** | | Baneberry | 0 | 0 | 0 | 0 | 488 |
| | | Baxter | 0 | 0 | 0 | 0 | 1,422 |
| | | Bean Station | 0 | 0 | 0 | 0 | 3,072 |
| | | Belle Meade | 0 | 0 | 0 | 0 | 3,513 |
| | | Bells | 0 | 0 | 0 | 0 | 2,247 |
| | | Benton | 0 | 0 | 0 | 0 | 1,189 |
| | | Berry Hill | 0 | 0 | 0 | 0 | 822 |
| | | Bethel Springs | 0 | 0 | 0 | 0 | 777 |
| | | Big Sandy | 0 | 0 | 0 | 0 | 508 |
| | | Blaine | 0 | 0 | 0 | 0 | 1,770 |
| | | Bluff City | 0 | 0 | 0 | 0 | 1,664 |
| | | Bolivar | 0 | 0 | 0 | 0 | 5,627 |
| | | Brentwood | 0 | 0 | 0 | 0 | 37,479 |
| | | Brighton | 0 | 0 | 0 | 0 | 2,736 |
| | | Bristol | 0 | 0 | 0 | 0 | 25,859 |
| | | Brownsville | 0 | 0 | 0 | 0 | 10,267 |
| | | Bruceton | 0 | 0 | 0 | 0 | 1,439 |
| | | Burns | 0 | 0 | 0 | 0 | 1,401 |
| | | Calhoun | 0 | 0 | 0 | 0 | 526 |
| | | Camden | 0 | 0 | 0 | 0 | 3,640 |
| | | Carthage | 0 | 0 | 0 | 0 | 2,234 |
| | | Caryville | 0 | 0 | 0 | 0 | 2,400 |
| | | Celina | 0 | 0 | 0 | 0 | 1,332 |
| | | Centerville | 0 | 0 | 0 | 0 | 3,994 |
| | | Chapel Hill | 0 | 0 | 0 | 0 | 1,363 |
| | | Charleston | 0 | 0 | 0 | 0 | 668 |
| | | Church Hill | 0 | 0 | 0 | 0 | 6,864 |
| | | Clarksburg | 0 | 0 | 0 | 0 | 369 |
| | | Clifton | 0 | 0 | 0 | 0 | 2,694 |
| | | Clinton | 0 | 0 | 0 | 0 | 9,646 |
| | | Collegedale | 0 | 0 | 0 | 0 | 8,106 |
| | | Collierville | 0 | 0 | 0 | 0 | 39,973 |
| | | Collinwood | 0 | 0 | 0 | 0 | 1,011 |
| | | Columbia | 0 | 0 | 0 | 0 | 34,529 |
| | | Cookeville | 0 | 0 | 0 | 0 | 29,609 |
| | | Coopertown | 0 | 0 | 0 | 0 | 3,428 |
| | | Copperhill | 0 | 0 | 0 | 0 | 435 |
| | | Cornersville | 0 | 0 | 0 | 0 | 965 |
| | | Covington | 0 | 0 | 0 | 0 | 9,339 |
| | | Cowan | 0 | 0 | 0 | 0 | 1,710 |
| | | Cross Plains | 0 | 0 | 0 | 0 | 1,671 |
| | | Crump | 0 | 0 | 0 | 0 | 1,463 |
| | | Cumberland City | 0 | 0 | 0 | 0 | 328 |
| | | Cumberland Gap | 0 | 0 | 0 | 0 | 208 |
| | | Dandridge | 0 | 0 | 0 | 0 | 2,760 |
| | | Dayton | 0 | 0 | 0 | 0 | 6,799 |
| | | Decatur | 0 | 0 | 0 | 0 | 1,485 |
| | | Decaturville | 0 | 0 | 0 | 0 | 819 |
| | | Decherd | 0 | 0 | 0 | 0 | 2,112 |
| | | Dover | 0 | 0 | 0 | 0 | 1,633 |
| | | Dresden | 0 | 0 | 0 | 0 | 2,816 |
| | | Dyer | 0 | 0 | 0 | 0 | 2,415 |
| | | Dyersburg | 0 | 0 | 0 | 0 | 17,088 |
| | | East Ridge | 0 | 0 | 0 | 0 | 19,546 |
| | | Elkton | 0 | 0 | 0 | 0 | 593 |
| | | Englewood | 0 | 0 | 0 | 0 | 1,768 |
| | | Erin | 0 | 0 | 0 | 0 | 1,458 |
| | | Erwin | 0 | 0 | 0 | 0 | 5,798 |
| | | Estill Springs | 0 | 0 | 0 | 0 | 2,263 |
| | | Ethridge | 0 | 0 | 0 | 0 | 555 |
| | | Etowah | 0 | 0 | 0 | 0 | 3,787 |
| | | Fairview | 0 | 0 | 0 | 0 | 8,094 |
| | | Fayetteville | 0 | 0 | 0 | 0 | 7,184 |
| | | Friendship | 0 | 0 | 0 | 0 | 592 |
| | | Gadsden | 0 | 0 | 0 | 0 | 531 |
| | | Gainesboro | 0 | 0 | 0 | 0 | 841 |
| | | Gallatin | 0 | 0 | 0 | 0 | 30,102 |
| | | Gallaway | 0 | 0 | 0 | 0 | 694 |
| | | Gates | 0 | 0 | 0 | 0 | 846 |
| | | Gatlinburg | 0 | 0 | 0 | 0 | 5,862 |
| | | Germantown | 0 | 0 | 0 | 0 | 41,419 |
| | | Gibson | 0 | 0 | 0 | 0 | 400 |
| | | Gleason | 0 | 0 | 0 | 0 | 1,395 |
| | | Goodlettsville | 0 | 0 | 0 | 0 | 17,481 |
| | | Gordonsville | 0 | 0 | 0 | 0 | 1,319 |
| | | Grand Junction | 0 | 0 | 0 | 0 | 304 |
| | | Graysville | 0 | 0 | 0 | 0 | 1,430 |
| | | Greeneville | 0 | 0 | 0 | 0 | 15,446 |
| | | Greenfield | 0 | 0 | 0 | 0 | 2,022 |
| | | Halls | 0 | 0 | 0 | 0 | 2,178 |
| | | Harriman | 0 | 0 | 0 | 0 | 6,646 |
| | | Henderson | 0 | 0 | 0 | 0 | 6,483 |
| | | Henning | 0 | 0 | 0 | 0 | 1,270 |
| | | Henry | 0 | 0 | 0 | 0 | 549 |
| | | Hohenwald | 0 | 0 | 0 | 0 | 3,803 |
| | | Hollow Rock | 0 | 0 | 0 | 0 | 930 |
| | | Hornbeak | 0 | 0 | 0 | 0 | 414 |
| | | Huntingdon | 0 | 0 | 0 | 0 | 4,101 |
| | | Huntland | 0 | 0 | 0 | 0 | 861 |
| | | Jacksboro | 0 | 0 | 0 | 0 | 2,127 |
| | | Jackson | 0 | 0 | 0 | 0 | 63,530 |
| | | Jamestown | 0 | 0 | 0 | 0 | 1,927 |
| | | Jasper | 0 | 0 | 0 | 0 | 3,113 |
| | | Jefferson City | 0 | 0 | 0 | 0 | 8,188 |
| | | Jellico | 0 | 0 | 0 | 0 | 2,532 |
| | | Jonesborough | 0 | 0 | 0 | 0 | 5,351 |
| | | Kenton | 0 | 0 | 0 | 0 | 1,289 |
| | | Kimball | 0 | 0 | 0 | 0 | 1,411 |
| | | Kingston | 0 | 0 | 0 | 0 | 5,641 |
| | | Kingston Springs | 0 | 0 | 0 | 0 | 2,972 |
| | | Lafayette | 0 | 0 | 0 | 0 | 4,482 |
| | | La Follette | 0 | 0 | 0 | 0 | 8,218 |
| | | La Grange | 0 | 0 | 0 | 0 | 143 |
| | | Lake City | 0 | 0 | 0 | 0 | 1,843 |
| | | Lakewood | 0 | 0 | 0 | 0 | 2,624 |
| | | La Vergne | 0 | 0 | 0 | 0 | 31,620 |
| | | Lawrenceburg | 0 | 0 | 0 | 0 | 10,779 |
| | | Lenoir City | 0 | 0 | 0 | 0 | 8,147 |
| | | Lewisburg | 0 | 0 | 0 | 0 | 11,048 |
| | | Lookout Mountain | 0 | 0 | 0 | 0 | 1,853 |
| | | Loretto | 0 | 0 | 0 | 0 | 1,710 |
| | | Loudon | 0 | 0 | 0 | 0 | 4,959 |
| | | Lynnville | 0 | 0 | 0 | 0 | 337 |
| | | Madisonville | 0 | 0 | 0 | 0 | 4,800 |
| | | Manchester | 0 | 0 | 0 | 0 | 10,188 |
| | | Martin | 0 | 0 | 0 | 0 | 10,172 |
| | | Maryville | 0 | 0 | 0 | 0 | 27,641 |
| | | Mason | 0 | 0 | 0 | 0 | 1,248 |
| | | Maury City | 0 | 0 | 0 | 0 | 689 |
| | | Maynardville | 0 | 0 | 0 | 0 | 1,923 |
| | | McEwen | 0 | 0 | 0 | 0 | 1,671 |
| | | McKenzie | 0 | 0 | 0 | 0 | 5,362 |
| | | McMinnville | 0 | 0 | 0 | 0 | 13,318 |
| | | Medina | 0 | 0 | 0 | 0 | 2,342 |
| | | Middleton | 0 | 0 | 0 | 0 | 609 |
| | | Milan | 0 | 0 | 0 | 0 | 7,939 |
| | | Millersville | 0 | 0 | 0 | 0 | 6,387 |
| | | Millington | 0 | 0 | 0 | 0 | 10,137 |
| | | Minor Hill | 0 | 0 | 0 | 0 | 450 |
| | | Monteagle | 0 | 0 | 0 | 0 | 1,197 |
| | | Monterey | 0 | 0 | 0 | 0 | 2,943 |
| | | Morristown | 0 | 0 | 0 | 0 | 27,775 |
| | | Moscow | 0 | 0 | 0 | 0 | 558 |
| | | Mountain City | 0 | 0 | 0 | 0 | 2,398 |
| | | Mount Carmel | 0 | 0 | 0 | 0 | 5,538 |
| | | Mount Juliet | 0 | 0 | 0 | 0 | 22,778 |
| | | Mount Pleasant | 0 | 0 | 0 | 0 | 4,438 |
| | | Munford | 0 | 0 | 0 | 0 | 6,851 |
| | | Newbern | 0 | 0 | 0 | | 3,158 |
| | | New Hope | 0 | 0 | 0 | 0 | 1,049 |
| | | New Johnsonville | 0 | 0 | 0 | 0 | 1,959 |
| | | New Market | 0 | 0 | 0 | 0 | 1,330 |
| | | New Tazewell | 0 | 0 | 0 | 0 | 2,883 |
| | | Niota | 0 | 0 | 0 | 0 | 802 |
| | | Nolensville | 0 | 0 | 0 | 0 | 2,713 |

[1]Agencies published in this table indicated that no hate crimes occurred in their jurisdictions during the quarter(s) for which they submitted reports to the Hate Crime Statistics Program. Blanks indicate quarters for which agencies did not submit reports.

[2]Population figures are published only for the cities. The figures listed for the universities and colleges are student enrollment and were provided by the United States Department of Education for the 2008 school year, the most recent available. The enrollment figures include full-time and part-time students.

## Table 95. Hate Crime Zero Data Submitted per Quarter, by State and Agency, 2009—*Continued*

(Number.)

| State | Agency type | Agency name | Zero data per quarter[1] 1st quarter | 2nd quarter | 3rd quarter | 4th quarter | Population[2] |
|---|---|---|---|---|---|---|---|
| **TENNESSEE** | | Norris | 0 | 0 | 0 | 0 | 1,481 |
| | | Oakland | 0 | 0 | 0 | 0 | 5,792 |
| | | Oak Ridge | 0 | 0 | 0 | 0 | 27,718 |
| | | Obion | 0 | 0 | 0 | 0 | 1,063 |
| | | Oliver Springs | 0 | 0 | 0 | 0 | 3,329 |
| | | Oneida | 0 | 0 | 0 | 0 | 3,861 |
| | | Paris | 0 | 0 | 0 | 0 | 9,990 |
| | | Parsons | 0 | 0 | 0 | 0 | 2,338 |
| | | Petersburg | 0 | 0 | 0 | 0 | 606 |
| | | Pigeon Forge | 0 | 0 | 0 | 0 | 6,318 |
| | | Pikeville | 0 | 0 | 0 | 0 | 1,907 |
| | | Piperton | 0 | 0 | 0 | 0 | 1,297 |
| | | Pittman Center | 0 | 0 | 0 | 0 | 697 |
| | | Pleasant View | 0 | 0 | 0 | 0 | 4,232 |
| | | Portland | 0 | 0 | 0 | 0 | 11,476 |
| | | Powells Crossroads | 0 | 0 | 0 | 0 | 1,267 |
| | | Pulaski | 0 | 0 | 0 | 0 | 7,835 |
| | | Puryear | 0 | 0 | 0 | 0 | 676 |
| | | Red Bank | 0 | 0 | 0 | 0 | 11,488 |
| | | Red Boiling Springs | 0 | 0 | 0 | 0 | 1,116 |
| | | Ridgely | 0 | 0 | 0 | 0 | 1,496 |
| | | Ridgetop | 0 | 0 | 0 | 0 | 1,758 |
| | | Ripley | 0 | 0 | 0 | 0 | 7,616 |
| | | Rockwood | 0 | 0 | 0 | 0 | 5,553 |
| | | Rogersville | 0 | 0 | 0 | 0 | 4,357 |
| | | Rossville | 0 | 0 | 0 | 0 | 582 |
| | | Rutherford | 0 | 0 | 0 | 0 | 1,253 |
| | | Rutledge | 0 | 0 | 0 | 0 | 1,295 |
| | | Samburg | 0 | 0 | 0 | 0 | 248 |
| | | Scotts Hill | 0 | 0 | 0 | 0 | 925 |
| | | Selmer | 0 | 0 | 0 | 0 | 4,716 |
| | | Sharon | 0 | 0 | 0 | 0 | 908 |
| | | Shelbyville | 0 | 0 | 0 | 0 | 20,078 |
| | | Signal Mountain | 0 | 0 | 0 | 0 | 7,075 |
| | | Smithville | 0 | 0 | 0 | 0 | 4,435 |
| | | Sneedville | 0 | 0 | 0 | 0 | 1,308 |
| | | Soddy-Daisy | 0 | 0 | 0 | 0 | 12,624 |
| | | Somerville | 0 | 0 | 0 | 0 | 2,966 |
| | | South Carthage | 0 | 0 | 0 | 0 | 1,363 |
| | | South Fulton | 0 | 0 | 0 | 0 | 2,389 |
| | | South Pittsburg | 0 | 0 | 0 | 0 | 3,125 |
| | | Sparta | 0 | 0 | 0 | 0 | 4,976 |
| | | Spencer | 0 | 0 | 0 | 0 | 1,696 |
| | | Spring City | 0 | 0 | 0 | 0 | 2,021 |
| | | Springfield | 0 | 0 | 0 | 0 | 17,608 |
| | | St. Joseph | 0 | 0 | 0 | 0 | 859 |
| | | Surgoinsville | 0 | 0 | 0 | 0 | 1,830 |
| | | Sweetwater | 0 | 0 | 0 | 0 | 6,758 |
| | | Tazewell | 0 | 0 | 0 | 0 | 2,221 |
| | | Tellico Plains | 0 | 0 | 0 | 0 | 976 |
| | | Tiptonville | 0 | 0 | 0 | 0 | 3,978 |
| | | Toone | 0 | 0 | 0 | 0 | 349 |
| | | Townsend | 0 | 0 | 0 | 0 | 275 |
| | | Trenton | 0 | 0 | 0 | 0 | 4,499 |
| | | Trezevant | 0 | 0 | 0 | 0 | 878 |
| | | Trimble | 0 | 0 | 0 | 0 | 717 |
| | | Troy | 0 | 0 | 0 | 0 | 1,201 |
| | | Tullahoma | 0 | 0 | 0 | 0 | 18,636 |
| | | Tusculum | 0 | 0 | 0 | 0 | 2,309 |
| | | Vonore | 0 | 0 | 0 | 0 | 1,533 |
| | | Wartburg | 0 | 0 | 0 | 0 | 932 |
| | | Watertown | 0 | 0 | 0 | 0 | 1,425 |
| | | Waverly | 0 | 0 | 0 | 0 | 4,201 |
| | | Waynesboro | 0 | 0 | 0 | 0 | 2,130 |
| | | Westmoreland | 0 | 0 | 0 | 0 | 2,199 |
| | | White Bluff | 0 | 0 | 0 | 0 | 2,556 |
| | | White House | 0 | 0 | 0 | 0 | 10,385 |
| | | White Pine | 0 | 0 | 0 | 0 | 2,159 |
| | | Whiteville | 0 | 0 | 0 | 0 | 4,456 |
| | | Whitwell | 0 | 0 | 0 | 0 | 1,597 |
| | | Winchester | 0 | 0 | 0 | 0 | 7,919 |
| | | Winfield | 0 | 0 | 0 | 0 | 1,002 |
| | | Woodbury | 0 | 0 | 0 | 0 | 2,630 |
| | **Universities and Colleges** | Austin Peay State University | 0 | 0 | 0 | 0 | 9,401 |
| | | Christian Brothers University | 0 | 0 | 0 | 0 | 1,869 |
| | | East Tennessee State University | 0 | 0 | 0 | 0 | 13,646 |
| | | Middle Tennessee State University | 0 | 0 | 0 | 0 | 23,872 |
| | | Northeast State Technical Community College | 0 | 0 | 0 | 0 | 5,470 |
| | | Southwest Tennessee Community College | 0 | 0 | 0 | 0 | 11,427 |
| | | Tennessee State University | 0 | 0 | 0 | 0 | 8,254 |
| | | University of Tennessee: | | | | | |
| | | Martin | 0 | 0 | 0 | 0 | 7,574 |
| | | Memphis[3] | 0 | 0 | 0 | 0 | |
| | | Vanderbilt University | 0 | 0 | 0 | 0 | 12,093 |
| | | Volunteer State Community College | 0 | 0 | 0 | 0 | 7,241 |
| | **Metropolitan Counties** | Blount | 0 | 0 | 0 | 0 | |
| | | Cannon | 0 | 0 | 0 | 0 | |
| | | Carter | 0 | 0 | 0 | 0 | |
| | | Chester | 0 | 0 | 0 | 0 | |
| | | Fayette | 0 | 0 | 0 | 0 | |
| | | Grainger | 0 | 0 | 0 | 0 | |
| | | Hamblen | 0 | 0 | 0 | 0 | |
| | | Hartsville-Trousdale | 0 | 0 | 0 | 0 | |
| | | Hawkins | 0 | 0 | 0 | 0 | |
| | | Hickman | 0 | 0 | 0 | 0 | |
| | | Jefferson | 0 | 0 | 0 | 0 | |
| | | Macon | 0 | 0 | 0 | 0 | |
| | | Madison | 0 | 0 | 0 | 0 | |
| | | Marion | 0 | 0 | 0 | 0 | |
| | | Polk | 0 | 0 | 0 | 0 | |
| | | Robertson | 0 | 0 | 0 | 0 | |
| | | Sequatchie | 0 | 0 | 0 | 0 | |
| | | Smith | 0 | 0 | 0 | 0 | |
| | | Stewart | 0 | 0 | 0 | 0 | |
| | | Sumner | 0 | 0 | 0 | 0 | |
| | | Unicoi | 0 | 0 | 0 | 0 | |
| | | Union | 0 | 0 | 0 | 0 | |
| | | Williamson | 0 | 0 | 0 | 0 | |
| | | Wilson | 0 | 0 | 0 | 0 | |
| | **Nonmetropolitan Counties** | Bedford | 0 | 0 | 0 | 0 | |
| | | Benton | 0 | 0 | 0 | 0 | |
| | | Bledsoe | 0 | 0 | 0 | 0 | |
| | | Campbell | 0 | 0 | 0 | 0 | |
| | | Carroll | 0 | 0 | 0 | 0 | |
| | | Claiborne | 0 | 0 | 0 | 0 | |
| | | Clay | 0 | 0 | 0 | 0 | |
| | | Cocke | 0 | 0 | 0 | 0 | |
| | | Coffee | 0 | 0 | 0 | 0 | |
| | | Crockett | 0 | 0 | 0 | 0 | |
| | | Cumberland | 0 | 0 | 0 | 0 | |
| | | Decatur | 0 | 0 | 0 | 0 | |

[1]Agencies published in this table indicated that no hate crimes occurred in their jurisdictions during the quarter(s) for which they submitted reports to the Hate Crime Statistics Program. Blanks indicate quarters for which agencies did not submit reports.
[2]Population figures are published only for the cities. The figures listed for the universities and colleges are student enrollment and were provided by the United States Department of Education for the 2008 school year, the most recent available. The enrollment figures include full-time and part-time students.
[3]Student enrollment figures were not available.

## Table 95. Hate Crime Zero Data Submitted per Quarter, by State and Agency, 2009—*Continued*

(Number.)

| State | Agency type | Agency name | Zero data per quarter[1] | | | | Population[2] |
|---|---|---|---|---|---|---|---|
| | | | 1st quarter | 2nd quarter | 3rd quarter | 4th quarter | |
| **TENNESSEE** | | DeKalb | 0 | 0 | 0 | 0 | |
| | | Dyer | 0 | 0 | 0 | 0 | |
| | | Franklin | 0 | 0 | 0 | 0 | |
| | | Gibson | 0 | 0 | 0 | 0 | |
| | | Giles | 0 | 0 | 0 | 0 | |
| | | Greene | 0 | 0 | 0 | 0 | |
| | | Hancock | 0 | 0 | 0 | 0 | |
| | | Hardeman | 0 | 0 | 0 | 0 | |
| | | Haywood | 0 | 0 | 0 | 0 | |
| | | Henderson | 0 | 0 | 0 | 0 | |
| | | Henry | 0 | 0 | 0 | 0 | |
| | | Houston | 0 | 0 | 0 | 0 | |
| | | Humphreys | 0 | 0 | 0 | 0 | |
| | | Jackson | 0 | 0 | 0 | 0 | |
| | | Johnson | 0 | 0 | 0 | 0 | |
| | | Lake | 0 | 0 | 0 | 0 | |
| | | Lauderdale | 0 | 0 | 0 | 0 | |
| | | Lewis | 0 | 0 | 0 | 0 | |
| | | Lincoln | 0 | 0 | 0 | 0 | |
| | | Maury | 0 | 0 | 0 | 0 | |
| | | McMinn | 0 | 0 | 0 | 0 | |
| | | McNairy | 0 | 0 | 0 | 0 | |
| | | Meigs | 0 | 0 | 0 | 0 | |
| | | Moore | 0 | 0 | 0 | 0 | |
| | | Morgan | 0 | 0 | 0 | 0 | |
| | | Obion | 0 | 0 | 0 | 0 | |
| | | Overton | 0 | 0 | 0 | 0 | |
| | | Perry | 0 | 0 | 0 | 0 | |
| | | Pickett | 0 | 0 | 0 | 0 | |
| | | Putnam | 0 | 0 | 0 | 0 | |
| | | Rhea | 0 | 0 | 0 | 0 | |
| | | Roane | 0 | 0 | 0 | 0 | |
| | | Sevier | 0 | 0 | 0 | 0 | |
| | | Warren | 0 | 0 | 0 | 0 | |
| | | Wayne | 0 | 0 | 0 | 0 | |
| | | White | 0 | 0 | 0 | 0 | |
| | **Other Agencies** | Alcoholic Beverage Commission | 0 | 0 | 0 | 0 | |
| | | Chattanooga Housing Authority | 0 | 0 | 0 | 0 | |
| | | Chattanooga Metropolitan Airport | 0 | 0 | 0 | 0 | |
| | | Department of Correction, Internal Affairs | 0 | 0 | 0 | 0 | |
| | | Dickson Parks and Recreation | 0 | 0 | 0 | 0 | |
| | | Drug Task Force: | | | | | |
| | | 1st Judicial District | 0 | 0 | 0 | 0 | |
| | | 2nd Judicial District | 0 | 0 | 0 | 0 | |
| | | 3rd Judicial District | 0 | 0 | 0 | 0 | |
| | | 4th Judicial District | 0 | 0 | 0 | 0 | |
| | | 5th Judicial District | 0 | 0 | 0 | 0 | |
| | | 8th Judicial District | 0 | 0 | 0 | 0 | |
| | | 9th Judicial District | 0 | 0 | 0 | 0 | |
| | | 10th Judicial District | 0 | 0 | 0 | 0 | |
| | | 12th Judicial District | 0 | 0 | 0 | 0 | |
| | | 13th Judicial District | 0 | 0 | 0 | 0 | |
| | | 14th Judicial District | 0 | 0 | 0 | 0 | |
| | | 15th Judicial District | 0 | 0 | 0 | 0 | |
| | | 17th Judicial District | 0 | 0 | 0 | 0 | |
| | | 18th Judicial District | 0 | 0 | 0 | 0 | |
| | | 19th Judicial District | 0 | 0 | 0 | 0 | |
| | | 21st Judicial District | 0 | 0 | 0 | 0 | |
| | | 22nd Judicial District | 0 | 0 | 0 | 0 | |
| | | 23rd Judicial District | 0 | 0 | 0 | 0 | |
| | | 24th Judicial District | 0 | 0 | 0 | 0 | |
| | | 25th Judicial District | 0 | 0 | 0 | 0 | |
| | | 27th Judicial District | 0 | 0 | 0 | 0 | |
| | | 31st Judicial District | 0 | 0 | 0 | 0 | |
| | | Knoxville Metropolitan Airport | 0 | 0 | 0 | 0 | |
| | | Memphis International Airport | 0 | 0 | 0 | 0 | |
| | | Metropolitan Board of Parks and Recreation, Nashville-Davidson | 0 | 0 | 0 | 0 | |
| | | Nashville International Airport | 0 | 0 | 0 | 0 | |
| | | Smyrna/Rutherford County Airport Authority | 0 | 0 | 0 | 0 | |
| | | State Fire Marshal | 0 | 0 | 0 | 0 | |
| | | State Park Rangers: | | | | | |
| | | Bicentennial Capitol Mall | 0 | 0 | 0 | 0 | |
| | | Big Hill Pond | 0 | 0 | 0 | 0 | |
| | | Big Ridge | 0 | 0 | 0 | 0 | |
| | | Bledsoe Creek | 0 | 0 | 0 | 0 | |
| | | Booker T. Washington | 0 | 0 | 0 | 0 | |
| | | Burgess Falls Natural Area | 0 | 0 | 0 | 0 | |
| | | Cedars of Lebanon | 0 | 0 | 0 | 0 | |
| | | Chickasaw | 0 | 0 | 0 | 0 | |
| | | Cove Lake | 0 | 0 | 0 | 0 | |
| | | Cumberland Mountain | 0 | 0 | 0 | 0 | |
| | | Cumberland Trail | 0 | 0 | 0 | 0 | |
| | | David Crockett | 0 | 0 | 0 | 0 | |
| | | Davy Crockett Birthplace | 0 | 0 | 0 | 0 | |
| | | Dunbar Cave Natural Area | 0 | 0 | 0 | 0 | |
| | | Edgar Evins | 0 | 0 | 0 | 0 | |
| | | Fall Creek Falls | 0 | 0 | 0 | 0 | |
| | | Fort Loudon State Historic Park | 0 | 0 | 0 | 0 | |

[1]Agencies published in this table indicated that no hate crimes occurred in their jurisdictions during the quarter(s) for which they submitted reports to the Hate Crime Statistics Program. Blanks indicate quarters for which agencies did not submit reports.

[2]Population figures are published only for the cities. The figures listed for the universities and colleges are student enrollment and were provided by the United States Department of Education for the 2008 school year, the most recent available. The enrollment figures include full-time and part-time students.

## Table 95. Hate Crime Zero Data Submitted per Quarter, by State and Agency, 2009—*Continued*

(Number.)

| State | Agency type | Agency name | Zero data per quarter[1] | | | | Population[2] |
|---|---|---|---|---|---|---|---|
| | | | 1st quarter | 2nd quarter | 3rd quarter | 4th quarter | |
| TENNESSEE | | Fort Pillow State Historic Park | 0 | 0 | 0 | 0 | |
| | | Frozen Head Natural Area | 0 | 0 | 0 | 0 | |
| | | Harpeth Scenic Rivers | 0 | 0 | 0 | 0 | |
| | | Harrison Bay | 0 | 0 | 0 | 0 | |
| | | Henry Horton | 0 | 0 | 0 | 0 | |
| | | Hiwassee/ Ocoee State Scenic Rivers | 0 | 0 | 0 | 0 | |
| | | Indian Mountain | 0 | 0 | 0 | 0 | |
| | | Johnsonville State Historic Park | 0 | 0 | 0 | 0 | |
| | | Long Hunter | 0 | 0 | 0 | 0 | |
| | | Meeman-Shelby Forest | 0 | 0 | 0 | 0 | |
| | | Montgomery Bell | 0 | 0 | 0 | 0 | |
| | | Mousetail Landing | 0 | 0 | 0 | 0 | |
| | | Natchez Trace | 0 | 0 | 0 | 0 | |
| | | Nathan Bedford Forrest | 0 | 0 | 0 | 0 | |
| | | Norris Dam | 0 | 0 | 0 | 0 | |
| | | Old Stone Fort State Archaeological Park | 0 | 0 | 0 | 0 | |
| | | Panther Creek | 0 | 0 | 0 | 0 | |
| | | Paris Landing | 0 | 0 | 0 | 0 | |
| | | Pickett | 0 | 0 | 0 | 0 | |
| | | Pickwick Landing | 0 | 0 | 0 | 0 | |
| | | Pinson Mounds State Archaeological Park | 0 | 0 | 0 | 0 | |
| | | Radnor Lake Natural Area | 0 | 0 | 0 | 0 | |
| | | Red Clay State Historic Park | 0 | 0 | 0 | 0 | |
| | | Reelfoot Lake | 0 | 0 | 0 | 0 | |
| | | Roan Mountain | 0 | 0 | 0 | 0 | |
| | | Rock Island | 0 | 0 | 0 | 0 | |
| | | Sgt. Alvin C. York | 0 | 0 | 0 | 0 | |
| | | South Cumberland Recreation Area | 0 | 0 | 0 | 0 | |
| | | Standing Stone | 0 | 0 | 0 | 0 | |
| | | Sycamore Shoals State Historic Park | 0 | 0 | 0 | 0 | |
| | | Tim's Ford | 0 | 0 | 0 | 0 | |
| | | T.O. Fuller | 0 | 0 | 0 | 0 | |
| | | Warrior's Path | 0 | 0 | 0 | 0 | |
| | | TennCare Office of Inspector General | 0 | 0 | 0 | 0 | |
| | | Tennessee Department of Revenue, Special Investigations Unit | 0 | 0 | 0 | 0 | |
| | | Tri-Cities Regional Airport | 0 | 0 | 0 | 0 | |
| | | West Tennessee Violent Crime Task Force | 0 | 0 | 0 | 0 | |
| | | Wildlife Resources Agency: | | | | | |
| | | Region 1 | 0 | 0 | 0 | 0 | |
| | | Region 2 | 0 | 0 | 0 | 0 | |
| | | Region 3 | 0 | 0 | 0 | 0 | |
| | | Region 4 | 0 | 0 | 0 | 0 | |
| TEXAS | Cities | Abernathy | 0 | 0 | 0 | 0 | 2,721 |
| | | Abilene | 0 | 0 | 0 | 0 | 116,557 |
| | | Addison | 0 | 0 | 0 | 0 | 15,063 |
| | | Alamo | 0 | 0 | 0 | 0 | 16,810 |
| | | Alamo Heights | 0 | 0 | 0 | 0 | 7,378 |
| | | Alice | 0 | 0 | 0 | 0 | 19,886 |
| | | Alpine | 0 | 0 | 0 | 0 | 6,322 |
| | | Alto | 0 | 0 | 0 | 0 | 1,175 |
| | | Alton | 0 | 0 | 0 | 0 | 11,945 |
| | | Alvarado | 0 | 0 | 0 | 0 | 4,290 |
| | | Amarillo | 0 | 0 | 0 | 0 | 188,767 |
| | | Andrews | 0 | 0 | 0 | 0 | 10,209 |
| | | Angleton | 0 | 0 | 0 | 0 | 18,665 |
| | | Anna | 0 | 0 | 0 | 0 | 1,906 |
| | | Anson | 0 | 0 | 0 | 0 | 2,252 |
| | | Anthony | 0 | 0 | 0 | 0 | 4,401 |
| | | Aransas Pass | 0 | 0 | 0 | 0 | 8,885 |
| | | Arcola | 0 | 0 | 0 | 0 | 1,251 |
| | | Arlington | 0 | 0 | 0 | 0 | 379,104 |
| | | Arp | 0 | 0 | 0 | 0 | 969 |
| | | Athens | 0 | 0 | 0 | 0 | 12,402 |
| | | Atlanta | 0 | 0 | 0 | 0 | 5,444 |
| | | Azle | 0 | 0 | 0 | 0 | 11,555 |
| | | Baird | 0 | 0 | 0 | 0 | 1,677 |
| | | Balch Springs | 0 | 0 | 0 | 0 | 20,052 |
| | | Balcones Heights | 0 | 0 | 0 | 0 | 2,981 |
| | | Ballinger | 0 | 0 | 0 | 0 | 3,672 |
| | | Bangs | 0 | 0 | 0 | 0 | 1,561 |
| | | Bastrop | 0 | 0 | 0 | 0 | 8,792 |
| | | Bay City | 0 | 0 | 0 | 0 | 17,811 |
| | | Bayou Vista | 0 | 0 | 0 | 0 | 1,691 |
| | | Baytown | 0 | 0 | 0 | 0 | 70,764 |
| | | Bee Cave | 0 | 0 | 0 | 0 | 2,996 |
| | | Beeville | 0 | 0 | 0 | 0 | 12,642 |
| | | Bellaire | 0 | 0 | 0 | 0 | 18,492 |
| | | Bellville | 0 | 0 | 0 | 0 | 4,486 |
| | | Belton | 0 | 0 | 0 | 0 | 18,130 |
| | | Benbrook | 0 | 0 | 0 | 0 | 23,280 |
| | | Bertram | 0 | 0 | 0 | 0 | 1,444 |
| | | Beverly Hills | 0 | 0 | 0 | 0 | 2,040 |
| | | Big Sandy | 0 | 0 | 0 | 0 | 1,368 |
| | | Big Spring | 0 | 0 | 0 | 0 | 24,181 |
| | | Bishop | 0 | 0 | 0 | 0 | 3,122 |
| | | Blanco | 0 | 0 | 0 | 0 | 1,562 |
| | | Bloomburg | 0 | 0 | 0 | 0 | 359 |
| | | Blue Mound | 0 | 0 | 0 | 0 | 2,362 |
| | | Boerne | 0 | 0 | 0 | 0 | 10,835 |
| | | Bogata | 0 | 0 | 0 | 0 | 1,219 |
| | | Bonham | 0 | 0 | 0 | 0 | 10,735 |
| | | Borger | 0 | 0 | 0 | 0 | 12,516 |
| | | Bovina | | 0 | 0 | 0 | 1,680 |
| | | Bowie | 0 | 0 | 0 | 0 | 5,601 |
| | | Brady | 0 | 0 | 0 | 0 | 5,306 |
| | | Brazoria | 0 | 0 | 0 | 0 | 2,970 |
| | | Breckenridge | 0 | 0 | 0 | 0 | 5,610 |
| | | Bremond | 0 | 0 | 0 | 0 | 853 |
| | | Brenham | 0 | 0 | 0 | 0 | 15,415 |
| | | Bridge City | 0 | 0 | 0 | 0 | 8,587 |
| | | Bridgeport | 0 | 0 | 0 | 0 | 6,231 |
| | | Brookshire | 0 | 0 | 0 | 0 | 4,009 |
| | | Brookside Village | 0 | 0 | 0 | 0 | 1,987 |
| | | Brownfield | 0 | 0 | 0 | 0 | 8,893 |
| | | Brownsville | 0 | 0 | 0 | 0 | 179,491 |

[1]Agencies published in this table indicated that no hate crimes occurred in their jurisdictions during the quarter(s) for which they submitted reports to the Hate Crime program. Blanks indicate quarters for which agencies did not submit reports.

[2]Population figures are published only for the cities. The figures listed for the universities and colleges are student enrollment and were provided by the United States Department of Education for the 2008 school year, the most recent available. The enrollment figures include full-time and part-time students.

[3]Student enrollment figures were not available.

## Table 95. Hate Crime Zero Data Submitted per Quarter, by State and Agency, 2009—*Continued*

(Number.)

| State | Agency type | Agency name | Zero data per quarter[1] | | | | Population[2] |
|---|---|---|---|---|---|---|---|
| | | | 1st quarter | 2nd quarter | 3rd quarter | 4th quarter | |
| **TEXAS** | | Bruceville-Eddy | 0 | 0 | 0 | 0 | 1,544 |
| | | Bryan | 0 | 0 | 0 | 0 | 73,111 |
| | | Bullard | 0 | 0 | 0 | 0 | 1,909 |
| | | Bulverde | 0 | 0 | 0 | 0 | 4,704 |
| | | Burkburnett | 0 | 0 | 0 | 0 | 10,361 |
| | | Burnet | 0 | 0 | 0 | 0 | 6,105 |
| | | Cactus | 0 | 0 | 0 | 0 | 2,612 |
| | | Caddo Mills | 0 | 0 | 0 | 0 | 1,210 |
| | | Caldwell | 0 | 0 | 0 | 0 | 3,744 |
| | | Calvert | 0 | 0 | 0 | 0 | 1,351 |
| | | Cameron | 0 | 0 | 0 | 0 | 5,750 |
| | | Canton | 0 | 0 | 0 | 0 | 3,703 |
| | | Canyon | 0 | 0 | 0 | 0 | 14,781 |
| | | Carthage | 0 | 0 | 0 | 0 | 6,632 |
| | | Castle Hills | 0 | 0 | 0 | 0 | 4,206 |
| | | Castroville | 0 | 0 | 0 | 0 | 3,104 |
| | | Cedar Hill | 0 | 0 | 0 | 0 | 46,480 |
| | | Cedar Park | 0 | 0 | 0 | 0 | 68,464 |
| | | Celina | 0 | 0 | 0 | 0 | 6,017 |
| | | Center | 0 | 0 | 0 | 0 | 5,754 |
| | | Childress | 0 | 0 | 0 | 0 | 6,484 |
| | | Chillicothe | 0 | 0 | 0 | 0 | 676 |
| | | Cibolo | 0 | 0 | 0 | 0 | 17,291 |
| | | Cisco | 0 | 0 | 0 | 0 | 3,711 |
| | | Clarksville | 0 | 0 | 0 | 0 | 3,436 |
| | | Cleveland | 0 | 0 | 0 | 0 | 7,979 |
| | | Clifton | 0 | 0 | 0 | 0 | 3,567 |
| | | Clint | 0 | 0 | 0 | 0 | 971 |
| | | Clute | 0 | 0 | 0 | 0 | 10,803 |
| | | Clyde | 0 | 0 | 0 | 0 | 3,833 |
| | | Cockrell Hill | 0 | 0 | 0 | 0 | 4,254 |
| | | Coffee City | 0 | 0 | 0 | 0 | 209 |
| | | Coleman | 0 | 0 | 0 | 0 | 4,648 |
| | | College Station | 0 | 0 | 0 | 0 | 86,072 |
| | | Colleyville | 0 | 0 | 0 | 0 | 25,006 |
| | | Collinsville | 0 | 0 | 0 | 0 | 1,524 |
| | | Colorado City | 0 | 0 | 0 | 0 | 3,851 |
| | | Columbus | 0 | 0 | 0 | 0 | 3,886 |
| | | Comanche | 0 | 0 | 0 | 0 | 4,173 |
| | | Combes | 0 | 0 | 0 | 0 | 2,850 |
| | | Commerce | 0 | 0 | 0 | 0 | 9,427 |
| | | Conroe | 0 | 0 | 0 | 0 | 57,685 |
| | | Converse | 0 | 0 | 0 | 0 | 18,353 |
| | | Coppell | 0 | 0 | 0 | 0 | 39,465 |
| | | Copperas Cove | 0 | 0 | 0 | 0 | 30,793 |
| | | Corinth | 0 | 0 | 0 | 0 | 22,152 |
| | | Corrigan | 0 | 0 | 0 | 0 | 1,887 |
| | | Corsicana | 0 | 0 | 0 | 0 | 26,678 |
| | | Cottonwood Shores | 0 | 0 | 0 | 0 | 1,221 |
| | | Crandall | 0 | 0 | 0 | 0 | 3,983 |
| | | Crane | 0 | 0 | 0 | 0 | 3,199 |
| | | Crockett | 0 | 0 | 0 | 0 | 6,782 |
| | | Crowell | 0 | 0 | 0 | 0 | 935 |
| | | Crowley | 0 | 0 | 0 | 0 | 13,077 |
| | | Crystal City | 0 | 0 | 0 | 0 | 7,159 |
| | | Cuero | 0 | 0 | 0 | 0 | 6,401 |
| | | Daingerfield | 0 | 0 | 0 | 0 | 2,446 |
| | | Dalhart | 0 | 0 | 0 | 0 | 7,008 |
| | | Dalworthington Gardens | 0 | 0 | 0 | 0 | 2,437 |
| | | Danbury | 0 | 0 | 0 | 0 | 1,692 |
| | | Dayton | 0 | 0 | 0 | 0 | 7,461 |
| | | Decatur | 0 | 0 | 0 | 0 | 6,575 |
| | | Deer Park | 0 | 0 | 0 | 0 | 31,164 |
| | | De Kalb | 0 | 0 | 0 | 0 | 1,804 |
| | | De Leon | 0 | 0 | 0 | 0 | 2,325 |
| | | Denver City | 0 | 0 | 0 | 0 | 4,085 |
| | | DeSoto | 0 | 0 | 0 | 0 | 48,798 |
| | | Devine | 0 | 0 | 0 | 0 | 4,589 |
| | | Diboll | 0 | 0 | 0 | 0 | 5,545 |
| | | Dickinson | 0 | 0 | 0 | 0 | 17,975 |
| | | Dilley | 0 | 0 | 0 | 0 | 3,597 |
| | | Dimmitt | 0 | 0 | 0 | 0 | 3,636 |
| | | Donna | 0 | 0 | 0 | 0 | 17,323 |
| | | Double Oak | 0 | 0 | 0 | 0 | 3,426 |
| | | Driscoll | 0 | 0 | 0 | 0 | 800 |
| | | Dublin | 0 | 0 | 0 | 0 | 3,808 |
| | | Dumas | 0 | 0 | 0 | 0 | 13,933 |
| | | Duncanville | 0 | 0 | 0 | 0 | 36,115 |
| | | Eagle Lake | 0 | 0 | 0 | 0 | 3,681 |
| | | Eagle Pass | 0 | 0 | 0 | 0 | 27,147 |
| | | Early | 0 | 0 | 0 | 0 | 2,774 |
| | | Earth | | 0 | 0 | 0 | 990 |
| | | East Mountain | 0 | 0 | 0 | 0 | 633 |
| | | Edcouch | 0 | 0 | 0 | 0 | 4,771 |
| | | Eden | 0 | 0 | 0 | 0 | 2,362 |
| | | Edgewood | 0 | 0 | 0 | 0 | 1,452 |
| | | Edinburg | 0 | 0 | 0 | 0 | 74,611 |
| | | Edna | 0 | 0 | 0 | 0 | 5,792 |
| | | El Campo | 0 | 0 | 0 | 0 | 10,735 |
| | | Electra | 0 | 0 | 0 | 0 | 2,867 |
| | | Elgin | 0 | 0 | 0 | 0 | 10,524 |
| | | Elsa | 0 | 0 | 0 | 0 | 6,744 |
| | | Ennis | 0 | 0 | 0 | 0 | 19,887 |
| | | Euless | 0 | 0 | 0 | 0 | 53,339 |
| | | Everman | 0 | 0 | 0 | 0 | 5,767 |
| | | Fairfield | 0 | 0 | 0 | 0 | 3,677 |
| | | Fair Oaks Ranch | 0 | 0 | 0 | 0 | 6,565 |
| | | Falfurrias | 0 | 0 | 0 | 0 | 4,906 |
| | | Farmers Branch | 0 | 0 | 0 | 0 | 26,344 |
| | | Farmersville | 0 | 0 | 0 | 0 | 3,516 |
| | | Farwell | 0 | 0 | 0 | 0 | 1,240 |
| | | Ferris | 0 | 0 | 0 | 0 | 2,611 |
| | | Flatonia | 0 | 0 | 0 | 0 | 1,437 |
| | | Florence | 0 | 0 | 0 | 0 | 1,140 |
| | | Floresville | 0 | 0 | 0 | 0 | 7,859 |
| | | Flower Mound | 0 | 0 | 0 | 0 | 71,605 |
| | | Floydada | 0 | 0 | 0 | 0 | 2,999 |
| | | Forest Hill | 0 | 0 | 0 | 0 | 13,961 |
| | | Forney | 0 | 0 | 0 | 0 | 16,977 |
| | | Fort Stockton | 0 | 0 | 0 | 0 | 7,498 |
| | | Frankston | 0 | 0 | 0 | 0 | 1,237 |
| | | Fredericksburg | 0 | 0 | 0 | 0 | 11,339 |
| | | Freeport | 0 | 0 | 0 | 0 | 12,471 |
| | | Freer | 0 | 0 | 0 | 0 | 2,906 |
| | | Friendswood | 0 | 0 | 0 | 0 | 34,558 |
| | | Friona | 0 | 0 | 0 | 0 | 3,489 |
| | | Gainesville | 0 | 0 | 0 | 0 | 16,547 |
| | | Galena Park | 0 | 0 | 0 | 0 | 10,166 |
| | | Ganado | 0 | 0 | 0 | 0 | 1,833 |
| | | Gatesville | 0 | 0 | 0 | 0 | 15,198 |
| | | Georgetown | 0 | 0 | 0 | 0 | 52,555 |
| | | Giddings | 0 | 0 | 0 | 0 | 5,455 |
| | | Gilmer | 0 | 0 | 0 | 0 | 5,300 |
| | | Gladewater | 0 | 0 | 0 | 0 | 6,298 |
| | | Glenn Heights | 0 | 0 | 0 | 0 | 11,594 |
| | | Godley | 0 | 0 | 0 | 0 | 1,021 |
| | | Gonzales | 0 | 0 | 0 | 0 | 7,305 |
| | | Gorman | 0 | 0 | 0 | 0 | 1,230 |
| | | Graham | 0 | 0 | 0 | 0 | 8,455 |
| | | Granbury | 0 | 0 | 0 | 0 | 8,931 |
| | | Grand Prairie | 0 | 0 | 0 | 0 | 164,766 |
| | | Grand Saline | 0 | 0 | 0 | 0 | 3,187 |
| | | Granger | 0 | 0 | 0 | 0 | 1,371 |
| | | Granite Shoals | 0 | 0 | 0 | 0 | 2,877 |
| | | Grapeland | 0 | 0 | 0 | 0 | 1,373 |
| | | Grapevine | 0 | 0 | 0 | 0 | 51,427 |
| | | Gregory | 0 | 0 | 0 | 0 | 2,188 |
| | | Groesbeck | 0 | 0 | 0 | 0 | 4,279 |
| | | Groves | 0 | 0 | 0 | 0 | 14,255 |
| | | Gruver | | | 0 | 0 | 1,124 |
| | | Gun Barrel City | 0 | 0 | 0 | 0 | 6,057 |
| | | Hale Center | 0 | 0 | 0 | 0 | 2,102 |
| | | Hallettsville | 0 | 0 | 0 | 0 | 2,480 |
| | | Hallsville | 0 | 0 | 0 | 0 | 3,037 |
| | | Haltom City | 0 | 0 | 0 | 0 | 40,303 |

[1]Agencies published in this table indicated that no hate crimes occurred in their jurisdictions during the quarter(s) for which they submitted reports to the Hate Crime Statistics Program. Blanks indicate quarters for which agencies did not submit reports.

[2]Population figures are published only for the cities. The figures listed for the universities and colleges are student enrollment and were provided by the United States Department of Education for the 2008 school year, the most recent available. The enrollment figures include full-time and part-time students.

## Table 95. Hate Crime Zero Data Submitted per Quarter, by State and Agency, 2009—*Continued*

(Number.)

| State | Agency type | Agency name | Zero data per quarter[1] | | | | Population[2] |
|---|---|---|---|---|---|---|---|
| | | | 1st quarter | 2nd quarter | 3rd quarter | 4th quarter | |
| TEXAS | | Hamlin | 0 | 0 | 0 | 0 | 1,870 |
| | | Harker Heights | 0 | 0 | 0 | 0 | 26,468 |
| | | Haskell | 0 | 0 | 0 | 0 | 2,577 |
| | | Hawk Cove | 0 | 0 | 0 | 0 | 618 |
| | | Hawkins | 0 | 0 | 0 | 0 | 1,547 |
| | | Hawley | 0 | 0 | 0 | 0 | 569 |
| | | Hearne | 0 | 0 | 0 | 0 | 4,566 |
| | | Heath | 0 | 0 | 0 | 0 | 8,267 |
| | | Hedwig Village | 0 | 0 | 0 | 0 | 2,345 |
| | | Helotes | 0 | 0 | 0 | 0 | 8,176 |
| | | Hemphill | 0 | 0 | 0 | 0 | 1,018 |
| | | Hempstead | 0 | 0 | 0 | 0 | 7,763 |
| | | Henderson | 0 | 0 | 0 | 0 | 11,675 |
| | | Hereford | 0 | 0 | 0 | 0 | 14,495 |
| | | Hewitt | 0 | 0 | 0 | 0 | 13,853 |
| | | Hickory Creek | 0 | 0 | 0 | 0 | 4,032 |
| | | Hidalgo | 0 | 0 | 0 | 0 | 12,590 |
| | | Highland Park | 0 | 0 | 0 | 0 | 9,222 |
| | | Hill Country Village | 0 | 0 | 0 | 0 | 1,124 |
| | | Hillsboro | 0 | 0 | 0 | 0 | 9,002 |
| | | Hitchcock | 0 | 0 | 0 | 0 | 7,289 |
| | | Holland | 0 | 0 | 0 | 0 | 1,144 |
| | | Holliday | 0 | 0 | 0 | 0 | 1,809 |
| | | Hollywood Park | 0 | 0 | 0 | 0 | 3,345 |
| | | Hondo | 0 | 0 | 0 | 0 | 9,121 |
| | | Hooks | 0 | 0 | 0 | 0 | 2,953 |
| | | Horizon City | 0 | 0 | 0 | 0 | 14,408 |
| | | Horseshoe Bay | 0 | 0 | 0 | 0 | 2,487 |
| | | Howe | 0 | 0 | 0 | 0 | 2,717 |
| | | Hubbard | 0 | 0 | 0 | 0 | 1,770 |
| | | Hudson | 0 | 0 | 0 | 0 | 4,358 |
| | | Hudson Oaks | 0 | 0 | 0 | 0 | 2,123 |
| | | Humble | 0 | 0 | 0 | 0 | 14,934 |
| | | Huntington | 0 | 0 | 0 | 0 | 2,110 |
| | | Huntsville | 0 | 0 | 0 | 0 | 38,875 |
| | | Hurst | 0 | 0 | 0 | 0 | 38,801 |
| | | Hutchins | 0 | 0 | 0 | 0 | 3,129 |
| | | Hutto | 0 | 0 | 0 | 0 | 17,482 |
| | | Idalou | 0 | 0 | 0 | 0 | 2,114 |
| | | Ingleside | 0 | 0 | 0 | 0 | 9,004 |
| | | Ingram | 0 | 0 | 0 | 0 | 1,928 |
| | | Iowa Park | 0 | 0 | 0 | 0 | 6,256 |
| | | Irving | 0 | 0 | 0 | 0 | 202,447 |
| | | Italy | 0 | 0 | 0 | 0 | 2,161 |
| | | Itasca | 0 | 0 | 0 | 0 | 1,717 |
| | | Jacinto City | 0 | 0 | 0 | 0 | 9,883 |
| | | Jacksboro | 0 | 0 | 0 | 0 | 4,488 |
| | | Jacksonville | 0 | 0 | 0 | 0 | 14,424 |
| | | Jamaica Beach | 0 | 0 | 0 | 0 | 1,103 |
| | | Jarrell | 0 | 0 | 0 | 0 | 1,462 |
| | | Jasper | 0 | 0 | 0 | 0 | 7,319 |
| | | Jefferson | 0 | 0 | 0 | 0 | 1,908 |
| | | Jersey Village | 0 | 0 | 0 | 0 | 7,324 |
| | | Johnson City | 0 | 0 | 0 | 0 | 1,606 |
| | | Jones Creek | 0 | 0 | 0 | 0 | 2,100 |
| | | Jonestown | 0 | 0 | 0 | 0 | 2,533 |
| | | Joshua | 0 | 0 | 0 | 0 | 5,967 |
| | | Jourdanton | 0 | 0 | 0 | 0 | 4,382 |
| | | Junction | 0 | 0 | 0 | 0 | 2,546 |
| | | Karnes City | 0 | 0 | 0 | 0 | 3,326 |
| | | Katy | 0 | 0 | 0 | 0 | 14,166 |
| | | Kaufman | 0 | 0 | 0 | 0 | 9,073 |
| | | Keene | 0 | 0 | 0 | 0 | 6,452 |
| | | Keller | 0 | 0 | 0 | 0 | 40,421 |
| | | Kemah | 0 | 0 | 0 | 0 | 2,518 |
| | | Kemp | 0 | 0 | 0 | 0 | 1,355 |
| | | Kempner | 0 | 0 | 0 | 0 | 1,199 |
| | | Kenedy | 0 | 0 | 0 | 0 | 3,288 |
| | | Kennedale | 0 | 0 | 0 | 0 | 7,252 |
| | | Kerens | 0 | 0 | 0 | 0 | 1,824 |
| | | Kermit | 0 | 0 | 0 | 0 | 5,189 |
| | | Kerrville | 0 | 0 | 0 | 0 | 23,091 |
| | | Kingsville | 0 | 0 | 0 | 0 | 24,612 |
| | | Kirby | 0 | 0 | 0 | 0 | 8,599 |
| | | Kirbyville | 0 | 0 | 0 | 0 | 1,931 |
| | | Kountze | 0 | 0 | 0 | 0 | 2,177 |
| | | Kress | 0 | 0 | 0 | 0 | 761 |
| | | Kyle | 0 | 0 | 0 | 0 | 30,846 |
| | | Lacoste | 0 | 0 | 0 | | 1,424 |
| | | Lacy-Lakeview | 0 | 0 | 0 | 0 | 5,896 |
| | | La Feria | 0 | 0 | 0 | 0 | 7,042 |
| | | Lago Vista | 0 | 0 | 0 | 0 | 6,506 |
| | | La Grange | 0 | 0 | 0 | 0 | 4,733 |
| | | La Grulla | 0 | 0 | 0 | 0 | 1,867 |
| | | Laguna Vista | 0 | 0 | 0 | 0 | 4,291 |
| | | La Joya | 0 | 0 | 0 | 0 | 4,983 |
| | | Lakeside | 0 | 0 | 0 | 0 | 1,359 |
| | | Lakeview | 0 | 0 | 0 | 0 | 6,477 |
| | | Lakeway | 0 | 0 | 0 | 0 | 11,587 |
| | | Lake Worth | 0 | 0 | 0 | 0 | 4,832 |
| | | La Marque | 0 | 0 | 0 | 0 | 14,297 |
| | | Lamesa | 0 | 0 | 0 | 0 | 8,772 |
| | | Lampasas | 0 | 0 | 0 | 0 | 8,107 |
| | | Lancaster | 0 | 0 | 0 | 0 | 37,061 |
| | | Laredo | 0 | 0 | 0 | 0 | 226,944 |
| | | La Vernia | 0 | 0 | 0 | 0 | 1,252 |
| | | La Villa | 0 | 0 | 0 | 0 | 1,447 |
| | | Lavon | 0 | 0 | 0 | 0 | 426 |
| | | League City | 0 | 0 | 0 | 0 | 74,801 |
| | | Leon Valley | 0 | 0 | 0 | 0 | 10,390 |
| | | Levelland | 0 | 0 | 0 | 0 | 12,410 |
| | | Lewisville | 0 | 0 | 0 | 0 | 104,601 |
| | | Lexington | 0 | 0 | 0 | 0 | 1,241 |
| | | Liberty | 0 | 0 | 0 | 0 | 8,362 |
| | | Lindale | 0 | 0 | 0 | 0 | 4,910 |
| | | Linden | 0 | 0 | 0 | 0 | 2,116 |
| | | Little Elm | 0 | 0 | 0 | 0 | 30,392 |
| | | Littlefield | 0 | 0 | 0 | 0 | 5,871 |
| | | Live Oak | 0 | 0 | 0 | 0 | 13,677 |
| | | Livingston | 0 | 0 | 0 | 0 | 6,280 |
| | | Llano | 0 | 0 | 0 | 0 | 3,226 |
| | | Lockhart | 0 | 0 | 0 | 0 | 13,891 |
| | | Lockney | 0 | 0 | 0 | 0 | 1,631 |
| | | Lone Star | 0 | 0 | 0 | 0 | 1,584 |
| | | Lorena | 0 | 0 | 0 | 0 | 1,698 |
| | | Lorenzo | 0 | 0 | 0 | 0 | 1,166 |
| | | Los Fresnos | 0 | 0 | 0 | 0 | 5,657 |
| | | Lott | 0 | 0 | 0 | 0 | 670 |
| | | Lubbock | 0 | 0 | 0 | 0 | 222,884 |
| | | Lufkin | 0 | 0 | 0 | 0 | 34,668 |
| | | Luling | 0 | 0 | 0 | 0 | 5,499 |
| | | Lumberton | 0 | 0 | 0 | 0 | 10,530 |
| | | Lytle | 0 | 0 | 0 | 0 | 2,869 |
| | | Madisonville | 0 | 0 | 0 | 0 | 4,396 |
| | | Magnolia | 0 | 0 | 0 | 0 | 1,267 |
| | | Malakoff | 0 | 0 | 0 | 0 | 2,333 |
| | | Manor | 0 | 0 | 0 | 0 | 3,928 |
| | | Manvel | 0 | 0 | 0 | 0 | 6,570 |
| | | Marble Falls | 0 | 0 | 0 | 0 | 7,785 |
| | | Marfa | 0 | 0 | | | 1,836 |
| | | Marlin | 0 | 0 | 0 | 0 | 5,736 |
| | | Marshall | 0 | 0 | 0 | 0 | 23,791 |
| | | Mart | 0 | 0 | 0 | 0 | 2,433 |
| | | Martindale | 0 | 0 | 0 | 0 | 1,171 |
| | | Mathis | 0 | 0 | 0 | 0 | 5,286 |
| | | McAllen | 0 | 0 | 0 | 0 | 132,598 |
| | | McGregor | 0 | 0 | 0 | 0 | 4,909 |
| | | Meadows Place | 0 | 0 | 0 | 0 | 6,624 |
| | | Melissa | 0 | 0 | 0 | 0 | 4,859 |
| | | Memorial Villages | 0 | 0 | 0 | 0 | 12,024 |
| | | Memphis | 0 | 0 | 0 | 0 | 2,169 |
| | | Mercedes | 0 | 0 | 0 | 0 | 15,261 |
| | | Meridian | 0 | 0 | 0 | 0 | 1,495 |
| | | Merkel | 0 | 0 | 0 | 0 | 2,612 |
| | | Mesquite | 0 | 0 | 0 | 0 | 132,941 |
| | | Mexia | 0 | 0 | 0 | 0 | 6,545 |
| | | Midlothian | 0 | 0 | 0 | 0 | 17,718 |

[1]Agencies published in this table indicated that no hate crimes occurred in their jurisdictions during the quarter(s) for which they submitted reports to the Hate Crime Statistics Program. Blanks indicate quarters for which agencies did not submit reports.

[2]Population figures are published only for the cities. The figures listed for the universities and colleges are student enrollment and were provided by the United States Department of Education for the 2008 school year, the most recent available. The enrollment figures include full-time and part-time students.

## Table 95. Hate Crime Zero Data Submitted per Quarter, by State and Agency, 2009—*Continued*

(Number.)

| State | Agency type | Agency name | Zero data per quarter[1] 1st quarter | 2nd quarter | 3rd quarter | 4th quarter | Popu-lation[2] |
|---|---|---|---|---|---|---|---|
| TEXAS | | Milford | 0 | 0 | 0 | 0 | 754 |
| | | Mineola | 0 | 0 | 0 | 0 | 5,253 |
| | | Mission | 0 | 0 | 0 | 0 | 69,997 |
| | | Monahans | 0 | 0 | 0 | 0 | 6,489 |
| | | Mont Belvieu | 0 | 0 | 0 | 0 | 2,737 |
| | | Montgomery | 0 | 0 | 0 | 0 | 609 |
| | | Morgans Point Resort | 0 | 0 | 0 | 0 | 4,603 |
| | | Mount Pleasant | 0 | 0 | 0 | 0 | 15,111 |
| | | Muleshoe | 0 | 0 | 0 | 0 | 4,234 |
| | | Munday | 0 | 0 | 0 | 0 | 1,178 |
| | | Murphy | 0 | 0 | 0 | 0 | 17,459 |
| | | Mustang Ridge | 0 | 0 | 0 | 0 | 950 |
| | | Nacogdoches | 0 | 0 | 0 | 0 | 32,459 |
| | | Nash | 0 | 0 | 0 | 0 | 2,430 |
| | | Nassau Bay | 0 | 0 | 0 | 0 | 4,026 |
| | | Navasota | 0 | 0 | 0 | 0 | 7,647 |
| | | Nederland | 0 | 0 | 0 | 0 | 15,959 |
| | | Needville | 0 | 0 | 0 | 0 | 3,564 |
| | | New Boston | 0 | 0 | 0 | 0 | 4,642 |
| | | New Deal | 0 | 0 | 0 | 0 | 753 |
| | | Nixon | 0 | 0 | 0 | 0 | 2,188 |
| | | Nocona | 0 | 0 | 0 | 0 | 3,241 |
| | | Nolanville | 0 | 0 | 0 | 0 | 3,015 |
| | | Northlake | 0 | 0 | 0 | 0 | 2,260 |
| | | Oak Ridge | 0 | 0 | 0 | 0 | 249 |
| | | Oak Ridge North | 0 | 0 | 0 | 0 | 3,446 |
| | | O'Donnell | | | | 0 | 901 |
| | | Olmos Park | 0 | 0 | 0 | 0 | 2,309 |
| | | Olney | 0 | 0 | 0 | 0 | 3,220 |
| | | Olton | 0 | 0 | 0 | 0 | 2,137 |
| | | Onalaska | 0 | 0 | 0 | 0 | 1,452 |
| | | Orange | 0 | 0 | 0 | 0 | 19,366 |
| | | Orange Grove | 0 | 0 | 0 | 0 | 1,417 |
| | | Ovilla | 0 | 0 | 0 | 0 | 4,026 |
| | | Oyster Creek | 0 | 0 | 0 | 0 | 1,244 |
| | | Paducah | 0 | 0 | 0 | 0 | 1,234 |
| | | Palacios | 0 | 0 | 0 | 0 | 5,058 |
| | | Palestine | 0 | 0 | 0 | 0 | 18,477 |
| | | Palmer | 0 | 0 | 0 | 0 | 2,316 |
| | | Palmhurst | 0 | 0 | 0 | 0 | 5,002 |
| | | Palmview | 0 | 0 | 0 | 0 | 5,537 |
| | | Pampa | 0 | 0 | 0 | 0 | 17,345 |
| | | Panhandle | 0 | 0 | 0 | 0 | 2,474 |
| | | Pantego | 0 | 0 | 0 | 0 | 2,388 |
| | | Parker | 0 | 0 | 0 | 0 | 3,066 |
| | | Pearsall | 0 | 0 | 0 | 0 | 7,663 |
| | | Pecos | 0 | 0 | 0 | 0 | 7,643 |
| | | Pelican Bay | 0 | 0 | 0 | 0 | 1,626 |
| | | Penitas | 0 | 0 | 0 | 0 | 1,183 |
| | | Perryton | 0 | 0 | 0 | 0 | 8,365 |
| | | Pflugerville | 0 | 0 | 0 | 0 | 42,395 |
| | | Pharr | 0 | 0 | 0 | 0 | 67,628 |
| | | Pilot Point | 0 | 0 | 0 | 0 | 4,513 |
| | | Pinehurst | 0 | 0 | 0 | 0 | 2,151 |
| | | Pittsburg | 0 | 0 | 0 | 0 | 4,703 |
| | | Plainview | 0 | 0 | 0 | 0 | 21,227 |
| | | Pleasanton | 0 | 0 | 0 | 0 | 9,844 |
| | | Point Comfort | 0 | 0 | 0 | 0 | 706 |
| | | Ponder | 0 | 0 | 0 | 0 | 1,427 |
| | | Port Aransas | 0 | 0 | 0 | 0 | 3,896 |
| | | Port Arthur | 0 | 0 | 0 | 0 | 55,725 |
| | | Port Isabel | 0 | 0 | 0 | 0 | 5,322 |
| | | Portland | 0 | 0 | 0 | 0 | 16,675 |
| | | Port Lavaca | 0 | 0 | 0 | 0 | 11,375 |
| | | Port Neches | 0 | 0 | 0 | 0 | 12,501 |
| | | Poteet | 0 | 0 | 0 | 0 | 3,677 |
| | | Poth | 0 | 0 | 0 | 0 | 2,418 |
| | | Pottsboro | 0 | 0 | 0 | 0 | 2,162 |
| | | Premont | 0 | 0 | 0 | 0 | 2,791 |
| | | Presidio | 0 | 0 | 0 | 0 | 4,753 |
| | | Primera | 0 | 0 | 0 | 0 | 4,319 |
| | | Princeton | 0 | 0 | 0 | 0 | 6,519 |
| | | Progreso | 0 | 0 | 0 | 0 | 5,588 |
| | | Prosper | 0 | 0 | 0 | 0 | 8,005 |
| | | Queen City | 0 | 0 | 0 | 0 | 1,541 |
| | | Quinlan | 0 | 0 | 0 | 0 | 1,438 |
| | | Quitman | 0 | 0 | 0 | 0 | 2,254 |
| | | Ralls | 0 | 0 | 0 | 0 | 1,946 |
| | | Rancho Viejo | 0 | 0 | 0 | 0 | 1,854 |
| | | Ranger | 0 | 0 | 0 | 0 | 2,557 |
| | | Ransom Canyon | 0 | 0 | 0 | 0 | 1,125 |
| | | Raymondville | 0 | 0 | 0 | 0 | 9,502 |
| | | Red Oak | 0 | 0 | 0 | 0 | 9,852 |
| | | Refugio | 0 | 0 | 0 | 0 | 2,694 |
| | | Reno | 0 | 0 | 0 | 0 | 3,121 |
| | | Richardson | 0 | 0 | 0 | 0 | 102,675 |
| | | Richmond | 0 | 0 | 0 | 0 | 13,706 |
| | | Richwood | 0 | 0 | 0 | 0 | 3,502 |
| | | Riesel | 0 | 0 | 0 | 0 | 1,016 |
| | | Rio Grande City | 0 | 0 | 0 | 0 | 14,167 |
| | | Rising Star | 0 | 0 | 0 | 0 | 826 |
| | | River Oaks | 0 | 0 | 0 | 0 | 6,961 |
| | | Roanoke | 0 | 0 | 0 | 0 | 4,429 |
| | | Robinson | 0 | 0 | 0 | 0 | 10,642 |
| | | Robstown | 0 | 0 | 0 | 0 | 12,106 |
| | | Rockdale | 0 | 0 | 0 | 0 | 5,983 |
| | | Rockport | 0 | 0 | 0 | 0 | 10,026 |
| | | Rollingwood | 0 | 0 | 0 | 0 | 1,438 |
| | | Roma | 0 | 0 | 0 | 0 | 11,441 |
| | | Roman Forest | 0 | 0 | 0 | 0 | 4,219 |
| | | Ropesville | 0 | 0 | 0 | 0 | 508 |
| | | Roscoe | 0 | 0 | 0 | 0 | 1,260 |
| | | Rosebud | 0 | 0 | 0 | 0 | 1,320 |
| | | Rose City | 0 | 0 | 0 | 0 | 502 |
| | | Rosenberg | 0 | 0 | 0 | 0 | 34,838 |
| | | Rowlett | 0 | 0 | 0 | 0 | 57,119 |
| | | Royse City | 0 | 0 | 0 | 0 | 10,277 |
| | | Runaway Bay | 0 | 0 | 0 | 0 | 1,463 |
| | | Rusk | 0 | 0 | 0 | 0 | 5,330 |
| | | Sabinal | 0 | 0 | 0 | 0 | 1,625 |
| | | Sachse | 0 | 0 | 0 | 0 | 19,996 |
| | | Saginaw | 0 | 0 | 0 | 0 | 21,388 |
| | | Salado | 0 | 0 | 0 | 0 | 2,071 |
| | | San Angelo | 0 | 0 | 0 | 0 | 92,269 |
| | | San Augustine | 0 | 0 | 0 | 0 | 2,333 |
| | | San Benito | 0 | 0 | 0 | 0 | 25,176 |
| | | San Diego | 0 | 0 | 0 | 0 | 4,401 |
| | | San Felipe | 0 | 0 | 0 | 0 | 985 |
| | | Sanger | 0 | 0 | 0 | 0 | 8,209 |
| | | San Juan | 0 | 0 | 0 | 0 | 34,896 |
| | | San Marcos | 0 | 0 | 0 | 0 | 55,187 |
| | | San Saba | 0 | 0 | 0 | 0 | 2,481 |
| | | Sansom Park Village | 0 | 0 | 0 | 0 | 4,198 |
| | | Santa Anna | 0 | 0 | 0 | 0 | 1,010 |
| | | Santa Fe | 0 | 0 | 0 | 0 | 10,578 |
| | | Santa Rosa | 0 | 0 | 0 | 0 | 3,163 |
| | | Schertz | 0 | 0 | 0 | 0 | 31,984 |
| | | Schulenburg | 0 | 0 | 0 | 0 | 2,690 |
| | | Seabrook | 0 | 0 | 0 | 0 | 11,777 |
| | | Seadrift | 0 | 0 | 0 | 0 | 1,442 |
| | | Seagoville | 0 | 0 | 0 | 0 | 12,133 |
| | | Seagraves | 0 | 0 | 0 | 0 | 2,351 |
| | | Sealy | 0 | 0 | 0 | 0 | 6,383 |
| | | Seguin | 0 | 0 | 0 | 0 | 26,705 |
| | | Selma | 0 | 0 | 0 | 0 | 5,626 |
| | | Seminole | 0 | 0 | 0 | 0 | 6,149 |
| | | Seven Points | 0 | 0 | 0 | 0 | 1,328 |
| | | Seymour | 0 | 0 | 0 | 0 | 2,590 |
| | | Shallowater | 0 | 0 | 0 | 0 | 2,312 |
| | | Shamrock | 0 | 0 | 0 | 0 | 1,786 |
| | | Shavano Park | 0 | 0 | 0 | 0 | 3,332 |
| | | Shenandoah | 0 | 0 | 0 | 0 | 2,066 |
| | | Sherman | 0 | 0 | 0 | 0 | 38,414 |
| | | Silsbee | 0 | 0 | 0 | 0 | 6,923 |
| | | Sinton | 0 | 0 | 0 | 0 | 5,321 |

[1]Agencies published in this table indicated that no hate crimes occurred in their jurisdictions during the quarter(s) for which they submitted reports to the Hate Crime Statistics Program. Blanks indicate quarters for which agencies did not submit reports.
[2]Population figures are published only for the cities. The figures listed for the universities and colleges are student enrollment and were provided by the United States Department of Education for the 2008 school year, the most recent available. The enrollment figures include full-time and part-time students.

# Table 95. Hate Crime Zero Data Submitted per Quarter, by State and Agency, 2009—*Continued*

(Number.)

| State | Agency type | Agency name | Zero data per quarter[1] 1st quarter | 2nd quarter | 3rd quarter | 4th quarter | Population[2] |
|---|---|---|---|---|---|---|---|
| TEXAS | | Slaton | 0 | 0 | 0 | 0 | 5,770 |
| | | Smithville | 0 | 0 | 0 | 0 | 4,534 |
| | | Snyder | 0 | 0 | 0 | 0 | 10,376 |
| | | Socorro | 0 | 0 | 0 | 0 | 32,522 |
| | | Somerset | 0 | 0 | 0 | 0 | 1,874 |
| | | Somerville | 0 | 0 | 0 | 0 | 1,683 |
| | | Sonora | 0 | 0 | 0 | 0 | 3,054 |
| | | Sour Lake | 0 | 0 | 0 | 0 | 1,744 |
| | | South Houston | 0 | 0 | 0 | 0 | 16,410 |
| | | Southlake | 0 | 0 | 0 | 0 | 27,189 |
| | | South Padre Island | 0 | 0 | 0 | 0 | 2,884 |
| | | Southside Place | 0 | 0 | 0 | 0 | 1,680 |
| | | Spearman | 0 | 0 | 0 | 0 | 2,937 |
| | | Springtown | 0 | 0 | 0 | 0 | 3,274 |
| | | Spring Valley | 0 | 0 | 0 | 0 | 3,910 |
| | | Spur | 0 | 0 | 0 | 0 | 923 |
| | | Stafford | 0 | 0 | 0 | 0 | 19,990 |
| | | Stamford | 0 | 0 | 0 | 0 | 3,060 |
| | | Stanton | 0 | 0 | 0 | 0 | 2,193 |
| | | Stephenville | 0 | 0 | 0 | 0 | 17,151 |
| | | Stratford | 0 | 0 | 0 | 0 | 1,905 |
| | | Sudan | 0 | 0 | 0 | 0 | 973 |
| | | Sugar Land | 0 | 0 | 0 | 0 | 82,696 |
| | | Sullivan City | 0 | 0 | 0 | 0 | 4,485 |
| | | Sulphur Springs | 0 | 0 | 0 | 0 | 15,564 |
| | | Sunrise Beach Village | 0 | 0 | 0 | 0 | 758 |
| | | Sunset Valley | 0 | 0 | 0 | 0 | 903 |
| | | Surfside Beach | 0 | 0 | 0 | 0 | 896 |
| | | Sweeny | 0 | 0 | 0 | 0 | 3,612 |
| | | Taft | 0 | 0 | 0 | 0 | 3,331 |
| | | Tahoka | 0 | 0 | 0 | 0 | 2,479 |
| | | Tatum | 0 | 0 | 0 | 0 | 1,215 |
| | | Taylor | 0 | 0 | 0 | 0 | 16,394 |
| | | Teague | 0 | 0 | 0 | 0 | 4,754 |
| | | Temple | 0 | 0 | 0 | 0 | 60,243 |
| | | Terrell | 0 | 0 | 0 | 0 | 20,300 |
| | | Terrell Hills | 0 | 0 | 0 | 0 | 5,266 |
| | | Texarkana | 0 | 0 | 0 | 0 | 36,812 |
| | | The Colony | 0 | 0 | 0 | 0 | 44,448 |
| | | Thorndale | 0 | 0 | 0 | 0 | 1,313 |
| | | Thrall | 0 | 0 | 0 | 0 | 939 |
| | | Three Rivers | 0 | 0 | 0 | 0 | 1,655 |
| | | Tioga | 0 | 0 | 0 | 0 | 947 |
| | | Tolar | 0 | 0 | 0 | 0 | 704 |
| | | Tomball | 0 | 0 | 0 | 0 | 10,345 |
| | | Tom Bean | | | 0 | 0 | 1,039 |
| | | Tool | 0 | 0 | 0 | 0 | 2,457 |
| | | Trinity | 0 | 0 | 0 | 0 | 2,725 |
| | | Troy | 0 | 0 | 0 | 0 | 1,428 |
| | | Tulia | 0 | 0 | 0 | 0 | 4,535 |
| | | Tye | 0 | 0 | 0 | 0 | 1,138 |
| | | Tyler | 0 | 0 | 0 | 0 | 99,279 |
| | | Universal City | 0 | 0 | 0 | 0 | 18,821 |
| | | University Park | 0 | 0 | 0 | 0 | 25,026 |
| | | Uvalde | 0 | 0 | 0 | 0 | 16,171 |
| | | Valley View | 0 | 0 | 0 | 0 | 793 |
| | | Van | 0 | 0 | 0 | 0 | 2,603 |
| | | Van Alstyne | 0 | 0 | 0 | 0 | 3,013 |
| | | Vernon | 0 | 0 | 0 | 0 | 10,849 |
| | | Victoria | 0 | 0 | 0 | 0 | 62,788 |
| | | Waco | 0 | 0 | 0 | 0 | 125,098 |
| | | Waelder | 0 | 0 | 0 | 0 | 997 |
| | | Wake Village | 0 | 0 | 0 | 0 | 5,659 |
| | | Waller | 0 | 0 | 0 | 0 | 2,051 |
| | | Wallis | 0 | 0 | 0 | 0 | 1,343 |
| | | Watauga | 0 | 0 | 0 | 0 | 24,235 |
| | | Waxahachie | 0 | 0 | 0 | 0 | 29,576 |
| | | Webster | 0 | 0 | 0 | 0 | 10,868 |
| | | Weimar | 0 | 0 | 0 | 0 | 2,021 |
| | | Wells | 0 | 0 | 0 | 0 | 799 |
| | | Weslaco | 0 | 0 | 0 | 0 | 33,998 |
| | | West | 0 | 0 | 0 | 0 | 2,688 |
| | | West Columbia | 0 | 0 | 0 | 0 | 4,175 |
| | | West Lake Hills | 0 | 0 | 0 | 0 | 3,160 |
| | | West Orange | 0 | 0 | 0 | 0 | 3,803 |
| | | Westover Hills | 0 | 0 | 0 | 0 | 730 |
| | | West Tawakoni | 0 | 0 | 0 | 0 | 1,760 |
| | | West University Place | 0 | 0 | 0 | 0 | 15,736 |
| | | Westworth | 0 | 0 | 0 | 0 | 3,141 |
| | | Wharton | 0 | 0 | 0 | 0 | 9,137 |
| | | Whitehouse | 0 | 0 | 0 | 0 | 7,957 |
| | | White Oak | 0 | 0 | 0 | 0 | 6,377 |
| | | Whitesboro | 0 | 0 | 0 | 0 | 4,056 |
| | | White Settlement | 0 | 0 | 0 | 0 | 16,471 |
| | | Whitney | 0 | 0 | 0 | 0 | 2,076 |
| | | Willis | 0 | 0 | 0 | 0 | 4,325 |
| | | Willow Park | 0 | 0 | 0 | 0 | 4,755 |
| | | Wills Point | 0 | 0 | 0 | 0 | 3,839 |
| | | Wilmer | 0 | 0 | 0 | 0 | 3,594 |
| | | Windcrest | 0 | 0 | 0 | 0 | 5,386 |
| | | Wink | 0 | 0 | 0 | 0 | 907 |
| | | Winnsboro | 0 | 0 | 0 | 0 | 3,969 |
| | | Winters | 0 | 0 | 0 | 0 | 2,535 |
| | | Wolfe City | 0 | 0 | 0 | 0 | 1,640 |
| | | Wolfforth | 0 | 0 | 0 | 0 | 3,619 |
| | | Woodville | 0 | 0 | 0 | 0 | 2,266 |
| | | Woodway | 0 | 0 | 0 | 0 | 8,823 |
| | | Wortham | 0 | 0 | 0 | 0 | 1,090 |
| | | Wylie | 0 | 0 | 0 | 0 | 41,824 |
| | | Yoakum | 0 | 0 | 0 | 0 | 5,443 |
| | | Yorktown | 0 | 0 | 0 | 0 | 2,145 |
| | **Universities and Colleges** | Abilene Christian University | 0 | 0 | 0 | 0 | 4,669 |
| | | Alamo Community College District[3] | 0 | 0 | 0 | 0 | |
| | | Alvin Community College | 0 | 0 | 0 | 0 | 4,402 |
| | | Amarillo College | 0 | 0 | 0 | 0 | 10,224 |
| | | Angelo State University | 0 | 0 | 0 | 0 | 6,155 |
| | | Austin College | 0 | 0 | 0 | 0 | 1,298 |
| | | Baylor Health Care System[3] | 0 | 0 | 0 | 0 | |
| | | Baylor University, Waco | 0 | 0 | 0 | 0 | 14,541 |
| | | Blinn College | 0 | 0 | 0 | 0 | 15,608 |
| | | Brookhaven College | 0 | 0 | 0 | 0 | 11,173 |
| | | Central Texas College | 0 | 0 | 0 | 0 | 24,498 |
| | | College of the Mainland | 0 | 0 | 0 | 0 | 3,561 |
| | | Eastfield College | 0 | 0 | 0 | 0 | 10,501 |
| | | El Paso Community College | 0 | 0 | 0 | 0 | 25,818 |
| | | Hardin-Simmons University | 0 | 0 | 0 | 0 | 2,387 |
| | | Houston Baptist University | 0 | 0 | 0 | 0 | 2,564 |
| | | Lamar University, Beaumont | 0 | 0 | 0 | 0 | 13,465 |
| | | Laredo Community College | 0 | 0 | 0 | 0 | 8,256 |

[1]Agencies published in this table indicated that no hate crimes occurred in their jurisdictions during the quarter(s) for which they submitted reports to the Hate Crime Statistics Program. Blanks indicate quarters for which agencies did not submit reports.

[2]Population figures are published only for the cities. The figures listed for the universities and colleges are student enrollment and were provided by the United States Department of Education for the 2008 school year, the most recent available. The enrollment figures include full-time and part-time students.

[3]Student enrollment figures were not available.

## Table 95. Hate Crime Zero Data Submitted per Quarter, by State and Agency, 2009—*Continued*

(Number.)

| State | Agency type | Agency name | Zero data per quarter[1] 1st quarter | 2nd quarter | 3rd quarter | 4th quarter | Population[2] |
|---|---|---|---|---|---|---|---|
| TEXAS | | McLennan Community College | 0 | 0 | 0 | 0 | 7,884 |
| | | Midwestern State University | 0 | 0 | 0 | 0 | 6,093 |
| | | Mountain View College | 0 | 0 | 0 | 0 | 7,126 |
| | | North Lake College | 0 | 0 | 0 | 0 | 10,174 |
| | | Paris Junior College | 0 | 0 | 0 | 0 | 4,733 |
| | | Prairie View A&M University | 0 | 0 | 0 | 0 | 8,203 |
| | | Rice University | 0 | 0 | 0 | 0 | 5,357 |
| | | Southern Methodist University | 0 | 0 | 0 | 0 | 10,965 |
| | | South Plains College | 0 | 0 | 0 | 0 | 9,111 |
| | | Southwestern University | 0 | 0 | 0 | 0 | 1,270 |
| | | Stephen F. Austin State University | 0 | 0 | 0 | 0 | 12,000 |
| | | St. Mary's University | 0 | 0 | 0 | 0 | 3,889 |
| | | Sul Ross State University | 0 | 0 | 0 | 0 | 2,772 |
| | | Tarleton State University | 0 | 0 | 0 | 0 | 9,633 |
| | | Texas A&M International University | 0 | 0 | 0 | 0 | 5,856 |
| | | Texas A&M University: | | | | | |
| | | College Station | 0 | 0 | 0 | 0 | 48,039 |
| | | Commerce | 0 | 0 | 0 | 0 | 8,725 |
| | | Corpus Christi | 0 | 0 | 0 | 0 | 9,007 |
| | | Galveston | 0 | 0 | 0 | 0 | 1,612 |
| | | Kingsville | 0 | 0 | 0 | 0 | 7,133 |
| | | Texas Christian University | 0 | 0 | 0 | 0 | 8,696 |
| | | Texas Southern University | 0 | 0 | 0 | 0 | 9,102 |
| | | Texas State Technical College: | | | | | |
| | | Harlingen | 0 | 0 | 0 | 0 | 5,466 |
| | | Marshall | 0 | 0 | 0 | 0 | 946 |
| | | Waco | 0 | 0 | 0 | 0 | 5,093 |
| | | Texas State University, San Marcos | 0 | 0 | 0 | 0 | 29,105 |
| | | Texas Tech University, Lubbock | 0 | 0 | 0 | 0 | 28,422 |
| | | Texas Woman's University | 0 | 0 | 0 | 0 | 12,465 |
| | | Trinity University | 0 | 0 | 0 | 0 | 2,703 |
| | | Tyler Junior College | 0 | 0 | 0 | 0 | 9,928 |
| | | University of Houston: | | | | | |
| | | Central Campus | 0 | 0 | 0 | 0 | 36,104 |
| | | Clearlake | 0 | 0 | 0 | 0 | 7,658 |
| | | Downtown Campus | 0 | 0 | 0 | 0 | 12,283 |
| | | University of Mary Hardin-Baylor | 0 | 0 | 0 | 0 | 2,648 |

| State | Agency type | Agency name | Zero data per quarter[1] 1st quarter | 2nd quarter | 3rd quarter | 4th quarter | Population[2] |
|---|---|---|---|---|---|---|---|
| | | University of North Texas: | | | | | |
| | | Denton | 0 | 0 | 0 | 0 | 34,830 |
| | | Health Science Center | 0 | 0 | 0 | 0 | 1,225 |
| | | University of Texas: | | | | | |
| | | Arlington | 0 | 0 | 0 | 0 | 25,084 |
| | | Brownsville | 0 | 0 | 0 | 0 | 17,189 |
| | | Dallas | 0 | 0 | 0 | 0 | 14,913 |
| | | El Paso | 0 | 0 | 0 | 0 | 20,458 |
| | | Health Science Center, San Antonio | 0 | 0 | 0 | 0 | 3,093 |
| | | Health Science Center, Tyler[3] | 0 | 0 | 0 | 0 | |
| | | Houston[3] | 0 | 0 | 0 | 0 | |
| | | Medical Branch | 0 | 0 | 0 | 0 | 2,338 |
| | | Pan American | 0 | 0 | 0 | 0 | 17,534 |
| | | Permian Basin | 0 | 0 | 0 | 0 | 3,496 |
| | | San Antonio | 0 | 0 | 0 | 0 | 28,413 |
| | | Southwestern Medical School | 0 | 0 | 0 | 0 | 2,461 |
| | | Tyler | 0 | 0 | 0 | 0 | 6,117 |
| | | Western Texas College | 0 | 0 | 0 | 0 | 2,090 |
| | | West Texas A&M University | 0 | 0 | 0 | 0 | 7,535 |
| | **Metropolitan Counties** | Aransas | 0 | 0 | 0 | 0 | |
| | | Archer | 0 | 0 | 0 | 0 | |
| | | Armstrong | 0 | 0 | 0 | 0 | |
| | | Atascosa | 0 | 0 | 0 | 0 | |
| | | Austin | 0 | 0 | 0 | 0 | |
| | | Bandera | 0 | 0 | 0 | 0 | |
| | | Bastrop | 0 | 0 | 0 | 0 | |
| | | Bell | 0 | 0 | 0 | 0 | |
| | | Bexar | 0 | 0 | 0 | 0 | |
| | | Bowie | 0 | 0 | 0 | 0 | |
| | | Brazoria | 0 | 0 | 0 | 0 | |
| | | Brazos | 0 | 0 | 0 | 0 | |
| | | Burleson | 0 | 0 | 0 | 0 | |
| | | Caldwell | 0 | 0 | 0 | 0 | |
| | | Calhoun | 0 | 0 | 0 | 0 | |
| | | Callahan | 0 | 0 | 0 | 0 | |
| | | Cameron | 0 | 0 | 0 | 0 | |
| | | Carson | 0 | 0 | 0 | 0 | |
| | | Chambers | 0 | 0 | 0 | 0 | |
| | | Clay | 0 | 0 | 0 | 0 | |
| | | Collin | 0 | 0 | 0 | 0 | |
| | | Comal | 0 | 0 | 0 | 0 | |
| | | Coryell | 0 | 0 | 0 | 0 | |
| | | Crosby | 0 | 0 | 0 | 0 | |
| | | Dallas | 0 | 0 | 0 | 0 | |
| | | Delta | 0 | 0 | 0 | 0 | |
| | | Denton | 0 | 0 | 0 | 0 | |
| | | Ector | 0 | 0 | 0 | 0 | |
| | | Ellis | 0 | 0 | 0 | 0 | |
| | | El Paso | 0 | 0 | 0 | 0 | |
| | | Fort Bend | 0 | 0 | 0 | 0 | |
| | | Galveston | 0 | 0 | 0 | 0 | |
| | | Goliad | 0 | 0 | 0 | 0 | |
| | | Grayson | 0 | 0 | 0 | 0 | |
| | | Gregg | 0 | 0 | 0 | 0 | |
| | | Guadalupe | 0 | 0 | 0 | 0 | |
| | | Hardin | 0 | 0 | 0 | 0 | |
| | | Hays | 0 | 0 | 0 | 0 | |
| | | Hidalgo | 0 | 0 | 0 | 0 | |
| | | Hunt | 0 | 0 | 0 | 0 | |
| | | Irion | 0 | 0 | 0 | 0 | |
| | | Jefferson | 0 | 0 | 0 | 0 | |
| | | Johnson | 0 | 0 | 0 | 0 | |
| | | Jones | 0 | 0 | 0 | 0 | |

[1]Agencies published in this table indicated that no hate crimes occurred in their jurisdictions during the quarter(s) for which they submitted reports to the Hate Crime Statistics Program. Blanks indicate quarters for which agencies did not submit reports.

[2]Population figures are published only for the cities. The figures listed for the universities and colleges are student enrollment and were provided by the United States Department of Education for the 2008 school year, the most recent available. The enrollment figures include full-time and part-time students.

[3]Student enrollment figures were not available.

## Table 95. Hate Crime Zero Data Submitted per Quarter, by State and Agency, 2009—*Continued*

(Number.)

| State | Agency type | Agency name | Zero data per quarter[1] | | | | Population[2] |
|---|---|---|---|---|---|---|---|
| | | | 1st quarter | 2nd quarter | 3rd quarter | 4th quarter | |
| **TEXAS** | | Kaufman | 0 | 0 | 0 | 0 | |
| | | Kendall | 0 | 0 | 0 | 0 | |
| | | Lampasas | 0 | 0 | 0 | 0 | |
| | | Liberty | 0 | 0 | 0 | 0 | |
| | | McLennan | 0 | 0 | 0 | 0 | |
| | | Medina | 0 | 0 | 0 | 0 | |
| | | Midland | 0 | 0 | 0 | 0 | |
| | | Montgomery | 0 | 0 | 0 | 0 | |
| | | Nueces | 0 | 0 | 0 | 0 | |
| | | Orange | 0 | 0 | 0 | 0 | |
| | | Parker | 0 | 0 | 0 | 0 | |
| | | Potter | 0 | 0 | 0 | 0 | |
| | | Randall | 0 | 0 | 0 | 0 | |
| | | Robertson | 0 | 0 | 0 | 0 | |
| | | Rockwall | 0 | 0 | 0 | 0 | |
| | | Rusk | 0 | 0 | 0 | 0 | |
| | | San Jacinto | 0 | 0 | 0 | 0 | |
| | | San Patricio | 0 | 0 | 0 | 0 | |
| | | Smith | 0 | 0 | 0 | 0 | |
| | | Tarrant | 0 | 0 | 0 | 0 | |
| | | Taylor | 0 | 0 | 0 | 0 | |
| | | Tom Green | 0 | 0 | 0 | 0 | |
| | | Travis | 0 | 0 | 0 | 0 | |
| | | Upshur | 0 | 0 | 0 | 0 | |
| | | Victoria | 0 | 0 | 0 | 0 | |
| | | Waller | 0 | 0 | 0 | 0 | |
| | | Webb | 0 | 0 | 0 | 0 | |
| | | Wichita | 0 | 0 | 0 | 0 | |
| | | Williamson | 0 | 0 | 0 | 0 | |
| | | Wilson | 0 | 0 | 0 | 0 | |
| | | Wise | 0 | 0 | 0 | 0 | |
| | **Nonmetropolitan Counties** | Andrews | 0 | 0 | 0 | 0 | |
| | | Angelina | 0 | 0 | 0 | 0 | |
| | | Bailey | 0 | 0 | 0 | 0 | |
| | | Baylor | 0 | 0 | 0 | 0 | |
| | | Bee | 0 | 0 | 0 | 0 | |
| | | Blanco | 0 | 0 | 0 | 0 | |
| | | Borden | 0 | 0 | 0 | 0 | |
| | | Bosque | 0 | 0 | 0 | 0 | |
| | | Brewster | 0 | 0 | 0 | 0 | |
| | | Briscoe | 0 | 0 | 0 | 0 | |
| | | Brooks | 0 | 0 | 0 | 0 | |
| | | Brown | 0 | 0 | 0 | 0 | |
| | | Burnet | 0 | 0 | 0 | 0 | |
| | | Camp | 0 | 0 | 0 | 0 | |
| | | Cass | 0 | 0 | 0 | 0 | |
| | | Castro | 0 | 0 | 0 | 0 | |
| | | Childress | 0 | 0 | 0 | 0 | |
| | | Cochran | 0 | 0 | 0 | 0 | |
| | | Coke | 0 | 0 | 0 | 0 | |
| | | Coleman | 0 | 0 | 0 | 0 | |
| | | Collingsworth | 0 | 0 | 0 | 0 | |
| | | Comanche | 0 | 0 | 0 | 0 | |
| | | Concho | 0 | 0 | 0 | 0 | |
| | | Cooke | 0 | 0 | 0 | 0 | |
| | | Cottle | 0 | 0 | 0 | 0 | |
| | | Crane | 0 | 0 | 0 | 0 | |
| | | Crockett | 0 | 0 | | | |
| | | Culberson | 0 | 0 | 0 | 0 | |
| | | Dallam | 0 | 0 | 0 | 0 | |
| | | Dawson | 0 | 0 | 0 | 0 | |
| | | Deaf Smith | 0 | 0 | 0 | 0 | |
| | | Dewitt | 0 | 0 | 0 | 0 | |
| | | Dickens | 0 | 0 | 0 | 0 | |
| | | Dimmit | 0 | 0 | 0 | 0 | |
| | | Donley | 0 | 0 | 0 | 0 | |
| | | Duval | 0 | 0 | 0 | 0 | |
| | | Eastland | 0 | 0 | 0 | 0 | |
| | | Edwards | 0 | 0 | 0 | 0 | |
| | | Erath | 0 | 0 | 0 | 0 | |
| | | Falls | 0 | 0 | 0 | 0 | |
| | | Fannin | 0 | 0 | 0 | 0 | |
| | | Fayette | 0 | 0 | 0 | 0 | |
| | | Fisher | 0 | 0 | 0 | 0 | |
| | | Floyd | 0 | 0 | 0 | 0 | |
| | | Foard | 0 | 0 | 0 | 0 | |
| | | Franklin | 0 | 0 | 0 | 0 | |
| | | Freestone | 0 | 0 | 0 | 0 | |
| | | Frio | 0 | 0 | 0 | 0 | |
| | | Gaines | 0 | 0 | 0 | 0 | |
| | | Garza | 0 | 0 | 0 | 0 | |
| | | Gillespie | 0 | 0 | 0 | 0 | |
| | | Glasscock | 0 | 0 | 0 | 0 | |
| | | Gonzales | 0 | 0 | 0 | 0 | |
| | | Gray | 0 | 0 | 0 | 0 | |
| | | Grimes | 0 | 0 | 0 | 0 | |
| | | Hale | 0 | 0 | 0 | 0 | |
| | | Hall | 0 | 0 | 0 | 0 | |
| | | Hamilton | 0 | 0 | 0 | 0 | |
| | | Hansford | 0 | 0 | 0 | 0 | |
| | | Hardeman | 0 | 0 | 0 | 0 | |
| | | Harrison | 0 | 0 | 0 | 0 | |
| | | Hartley | 0 | 0 | 0 | 0 | |
| | | Haskell | 0 | 0 | 0 | 0 | |
| | | Hemphill | 0 | 0 | 0 | 0 | |
| | | Henderson | 0 | 0 | 0 | 0 | |
| | | Hill | 0 | 0 | 0 | 0 | |
| | | Hockley | 0 | 0 | 0 | 0 | |
| | | Hood | 0 | 0 | 0 | 0 | |
| | | Hopkins | 0 | 0 | 0 | 0 | |
| | | Houston | 0 | 0 | 0 | 0 | |
| | | Howard | 0 | 0 | 0 | 0 | |
| | | Hudspeth | 0 | 0 | 0 | 0 | |
| | | Hutchinson | 0 | 0 | 0 | 0 | |
| | | Jack | 0 | 0 | 0 | 0 | |
| | | Jackson | 0 | 0 | 0 | 0 | |
| | | Jasper | 0 | 0 | 0 | 0 | |
| | | Jeff Davis | 0 | 0 | 0 | 0 | |
| | | Jim Hogg | 0 | 0 | 0 | 0 | |
| | | Jim Wells | 0 | 0 | 0 | 0 | |
| | | Karnes | 0 | 0 | 0 | 0 | |
| | | Kenedy | 0 | 0 | 0 | 0 | |
| | | Kent | 0 | 0 | 0 | 0 | |
| | | Kerr | 0 | 0 | 0 | 0 | |
| | | Kimble | 0 | 0 | 0 | 0 | |
| | | King | 0 | 0 | 0 | 0 | |
| | | Kinney | 0 | 0 | 0 | 0 | |
| | | Kleberg | 0 | 0 | 0 | 0 | |
| | | Knox | 0 | 0 | 0 | 0 | |
| | | Lamar | 0 | 0 | 0 | 0 | |
| | | Lamb | 0 | 0 | 0 | 0 | |
| | | La Salle | 0 | 0 | 0 | 0 | |
| | | Lavaca | 0 | 0 | 0 | 0 | |
| | | Lee | 0 | 0 | 0 | 0 | |
| | | Leon | 0 | 0 | 0 | 0 | |
| | | Limestone | 0 | 0 | 0 | 0 | |
| | | Lipscomb | 0 | 0 | 0 | 0 | |
| | | Live Oak | 0 | 0 | 0 | 0 | |
| | | Llano | 0 | 0 | 0 | 0 | |
| | | Loving | 0 | 0 | 0 | 0 | |
| | | Lynn | 0 | 0 | 0 | 0 | |
| | | Madison | 0 | 0 | 0 | 0 | |
| | | Marion | 0 | 0 | 0 | 0 | |
| | | Martin | 0 | 0 | 0 | 0 | |
| | | Mason | 0 | 0 | 0 | 0 | |
| | | Matagorda | 0 | 0 | 0 | 0 | |
| | | Maverick | 0 | 0 | 0 | 0 | |
| | | McCulloch | 0 | 0 | 0 | 0 | |
| | | McMullen | 0 | 0 | 0 | 0 | |
| | | Menard | 0 | 0 | 0 | 0 | |
| | | Milam | 0 | 0 | 0 | 0 | |
| | | Mills | 0 | 0 | 0 | 0 | |
| | | Mitchell | 0 | 0 | 0 | 0 | |
| | | Montague | 0 | 0 | 0 | 0 | |
| | | Moore | 0 | 0 | 0 | 0 | |
| | | Morris | 0 | 0 | 0 | 0 | |
| | | Motley | 0 | 0 | 0 | 0 | |
| | | Nacogdoches | 0 | 0 | 0 | 0 | |

[1] Agencies published in this table indicated that no hate crimes occurred in their jurisdictions during the quarter(s) for which they submitted reports to the Hate Crime Statistics Program. Blanks indicate quarters for which agencies did not submit reports.

[2] Population figures are published only for the cities. The figures listed for the universities and colleges are student enrollment and were provided by the United States Department of Education for the 2008 school year, the most recent available. The enrollment figures include full-time and part-time students.

## Table 95. Hate Crime Zero Data Submitted per Quarter, by State and Agency, 2009—*Continued*

(Number.)

| State | Agency type | Agency name | Zero data per quarter[1] 1st quarter | 2nd quarter | 3rd quarter | 4th quarter | Population[2] |
|---|---|---|---|---|---|---|---|
| TEXAS | | Navarro | 0 | 0 | 0 | 0 | |
| | | Newton | 0 | 0 | 0 | 0 | |
| | | Nolan | 0 | 0 | 0 | 0 | |
| | | Ochiltree | 0 | 0 | 0 | 0 | |
| | | Oldham | 0 | 0 | 0 | 0 | |
| | | Palo Pinto | 0 | 0 | 0 | 0 | |
| | | Panola | 0 | 0 | 0 | 0 | |
| | | Parmer | 0 | 0 | 0 | 0 | |
| | | Pecos | 0 | 0 | 0 | 0 | |
| | | Polk | 0 | 0 | 0 | 0 | |
| | | Presidio | 0 | 0 | 0 | 0 | |
| | | Rains | 0 | 0 | 0 | 0 | |
| | | Reagan | 0 | 0 | 0 | 0 | |
| | | Real | 0 | 0 | 0 | 0 | |
| | | Red River | 0 | 0 | 0 | 0 | |
| | | Reeves | 0 | 0 | 0 | 0 | |
| | | Refugio | 0 | 0 | 0 | 0 | |
| | | Roberts | 0 | 0 | 0 | 0 | |
| | | Runnels | 0 | 0 | 0 | 0 | |
| | | Sabine | 0 | 0 | 0 | 0 | |
| | | San Augustine | 0 | 0 | 0 | 0 | |
| | | San Saba | 0 | 0 | 0 | 0 | |
| | | Schleicher | 0 | 0 | 0 | 0 | |
| | | Scurry | 0 | 0 | 0 | 0 | |
| | | Shackelford | 0 | 0 | 0 | 0 | |
| | | Shelby | 0 | 0 | 0 | 0 | |
| | | Sherman | 0 | 0 | 0 | 0 | |
| | | Somervell | 0 | 0 | 0 | 0 | |
| | | Starr | 0 | 0 | 0 | 0 | |
| | | Stephens | 0 | 0 | 0 | 0 | |
| | | Sterling | 0 | 0 | 0 | 0 | |
| | | Stonewall | 0 | 0 | 0 | 0 | |
| | | Sutton | 0 | 0 | 0 | 0 | |
| | | Swisher | 0 | 0 | 0 | 0 | |
| | | Terrell | 0 | 0 | 0 | 0 | |
| | | Terry | 0 | 0 | 0 | 0 | |
| | | Throckmorton | 0 | 0 | 0 | 0 | |
| | | Titus | 0 | 0 | 0 | 0 | |
| | | Trinity | 0 | 0 | 0 | 0 | |
| | | Tyler | 0 | 0 | 0 | 0 | |
| | | Upton | 0 | 0 | 0 | 0 | |
| | | Uvalde | 0 | 0 | 0 | 0 | |
| | | Val Verde | 0 | 0 | 0 | 0 | |
| | | Van Zandt | 0 | 0 | 0 | 0 | |
| | | Walker | 0 | 0 | 0 | 0 | |
| | | Ward | 0 | 0 | 0 | 0 | |
| | | Washington | 0 | 0 | 0 | 0 | |
| | | Wharton | 0 | 0 | 0 | 0 | |
| | | Wheeler | 0 | 0 | 0 | 0 | |
| | | Wilbarger | 0 | 0 | 0 | 0 | |
| | | Willacy | 0 | 0 | 0 | 0 | |
| | | Winkler | 0 | 0 | 0 | 0 | |
| | | Wood | 0 | 0 | 0 | 0 | |
| | | Yoakum | 0 | 0 | 0 | 0 | |
| | | Young | 0 | 0 | 0 | 0 | |
| | | Zapata | 0 | 0 | 0 | 0 | |
| | | Zavala | 0 | 0 | 0 | 0 | |
| | **Other Agencies** | Amarillo International Airport | 0 | 0 | 0 | 0 | |
| | | Dallas-Fort Worth International Airport | 0 | 0 | 0 | 0 | |
| | | Hospital District: | | | | | |
| | | Dallas County | 0 | 0 | 0 | 0 | |
| | | Tarrant County | 0 | 0 | 0 | 0 | |
| | | Houston Metropolitan Transit Authority | 0 | 0 | 0 | 0 | |

| State | Agency type | Agency name | Zero data per quarter[1] 1st quarter | 2nd quarter | 3rd quarter | 4th quarter | Population[2] |
|---|---|---|---|---|---|---|---|
| | | Independent School District: | | | | | |
| | | Aldine | 0 | 0 | 0 | 0 | |
| | | Alvin | 0 | 0 | 0 | 0 | |
| | | Angleton | 0 | 0 | 0 | 0 | |
| | | Austin | 0 | 0 | 0 | 0 | |
| | | Barbers Hill | 0 | 0 | 0 | 0 | |
| | | Bay City | 0 | 0 | 0 | 0 | |
| | | Cedar Hill | 0 | 0 | 0 | 0 | |
| | | Conroe | 0 | 0 | 0 | 0 | |
| | | Corpus Christi | 0 | 0 | 0 | 0 | |
| | | East Central | 0 | 0 | 0 | 0 | |
| | | Ector County | 0 | 0 | 0 | 0 | |
| | | El Paso | 0 | 0 | 0 | 0 | |
| | | Floresville | 0 | 0 | 0 | 0 | |
| | | Fort Bend | 0 | 0 | 0 | 0 | |
| | | Humble | 0 | 0 | 0 | 0 | |
| | | Judson | 0 | 0 | 0 | 0 | |
| | | Katy | 0 | 0 | 0 | 0 | |
| | | Kaufman | 0 | 0 | | | |
| | | Killeen | 0 | 0 | 0 | 0 | |
| | | Klein | 0 | 0 | 0 | 0 | |
| | | Mexia | 0 | 0 | 0 | 0 | |
| | | Midland | 0 | 0 | 0 | 0 | |
| | | North East | 0 | 0 | 0 | 0 | |
| | | Pasadena | 0 | 0 | 0 | 0 | |
| | | Pflugerville | 0 | 0 | 0 | 0 | |
| | | Raymondville | 0 | 0 | 0 | 0 | |
| | | Rio Grande City | 0 | 0 | 0 | 0 | |
| | | Socorro | 0 | 0 | 0 | 0 | |
| | | Spring | 0 | 0 | 0 | 0 | |
| | | Spring Branch | 0 | 0 | 0 | 0 | |
| | | Taft | 0 | 0 | 0 | 0 | |
| | | United | 0 | 0 | 0 | 0 | |
| UTAH | Cities | American Fork/Cedar Hills | 0 | 0 | 0 | 0 | 38,183 |
| | | Big Water | 0 | 0 | 0 | 0 | 403 |
| | | Blanding | 0 | 0 | 0 | 0 | 3,280 |
| | | Bountiful | 0 | 0 | 0 | 0 | 44,591 |
| | | Brian Head | 0 | 0 | 0 | 0 | 127 |
| | | Brigham City | 0 | 0 | 0 | 0 | 18,750 |
| | | Cedar City | 0 | 0 | 0 | 0 | 29,568 |
| | | Centerville | 0 | 0 | 0 | 0 | 15,763 |
| | | Clearfield | 0 | 0 | 0 | 0 | 27,913 |
| | | Clinton | 0 | 0 | 0 | 0 | 20,745 |
| | | Cottonwood Heights | 0 | 0 | 0 | 0 | 35,258 |
| | | Enoch | 0 | 0 | 0 | 0 | 5,263 |
| | | Grantsville | 0 | 0 | 0 | 0 | 9,402 |
| | | Harrisville | 0 | 0 | 0 | 0 | 6,367 |
| | | Heber | 0 | 0 | 0 | 0 | 10,068 |
| | | Helper | 0 | 0 | 0 | 0 | 1,852 |
| | | Hildale | 0 | 0 | 0 | 0 | 1,967 |
| | | Hurricane | 0 | 0 | 0 | 0 | 13,961 |
| | | Ivins | 0 | 0 | 0 | 0 | 8,294 |
| | | Kanab | 0 | 0 | 0 | 0 | 3,786 |
| | | Kaysville | 0 | 0 | 0 | 0 | 26,363 |
| | | La Verkin | 0 | 0 | 0 | 0 | 4,602 |
| | | Layton | 0 | 0 | 0 | 0 | 65,947 |
| | | Leeds | 0 | 0 | 0 | 0 | 774 |
| | | Lehi | 0 | 0 | 0 | 0 | 51,307 |
| | | Lindon | 0 | 0 | 0 | 0 | 10,666 |
| | | Logan | 0 | 0 | 0 | 0 | 49,105 |
| | | Lone Peak | 0 | 0 | 0 | 0 | 27,542 |
| | | Mapleton | 0 | 0 | 0 | 0 | 8,183 |
| | | Moab | 0 | 0 | 0 | 0 | 5,130 |
| | | Monticello | 0 | 0 | 0 | 0 | 2,015 |
| | | Mount Pleasant | 0 | 0 | 0 | 0 | 2,811 |
| | | Murray | 0 | 0 | 0 | 0 | 46,026 |
| | | Naples | 0 | 0 | 0 | 0 | 1,735 |
| | | Nephi | 0 | 0 | 0 | 0 | 5,459 |
| | | North Ogden | 0 | 0 | 0 | 0 | 17,897 |
| | | North Park | 0 | 0 | 0 | 0 | 12,739 |

[1]Agencies published in this table indicated that no hate crimes occurred in their jurisdictions during the quarter(s) for which they submitted reports to the Hate Crime Statistics Program. Blanks indicate quarters for which agencies did not submit reports.

[2]Population figures are published only for the cities. The figures listed for the universities and colleges are student enrollment and were provided by the United States Department of Education for the 2008 school year, the most recent available. The enrollment figures include full-time and part-time students.

## Table 95. Hate Crime Zero Data Submitted per Quarter, by State and Agency, 2009—*Continued*

(Number.)

| State | Agency type | Agency name | Zero data per quarter[1] 1st quarter | 2nd quarter | 3rd quarter | 4th quarter | Population[2] |
|---|---|---|---|---|---|---|---|
| **UTAH** | | North Salt Lake | 0 | 0 | 0 | 0 | 14,026 |
| | | Ogden | 0 | 0 | 0 | 0 | 83,016 |
| | | Park City | 0 | 0 | 0 | 0 | 7,998 |
| | | Parowan | 0 | 0 | 0 | 0 | 2,615 |
| | | Payson | 0 | 0 | 0 | 0 | 17,890 |
| | | Perry | 0 | 0 | 0 | 0 | 4,080 |
| | | Pleasant Grove | 0 | 0 | 0 | 0 | 35,016 |
| | | Pleasant View | 0 | 0 | 0 | 0 | 7,183 |
| | | Price | 0 | 0 | 0 | 0 | 7,957 |
| | | Richfield | 0 | 0 | 0 | 0 | 7,220 |
| | | Riverdale | 0 | 0 | 0 | 0 | 8,135 |
| | | Roosevelt | 0 | 0 | 0 | 0 | 5,088 |
| | | Roy | 0 | 0 | 0 | 0 | 35,761 |
| | | Salem | 0 | 0 | 0 | 0 | 6,635 |
| | | Salina | 0 | 0 | 0 | 0 | 2,403 |
| | | Santaquin/ Genola | 0 | 0 | 0 | 0 | 9,990 |
| | | Smithfield | 0 | 0 | 0 | 0 | 9,770 |
| | | South Ogden | 0 | 0 | 0 | 0 | 15,989 |
| | | Spanish Fork | 0 | 0 | 0 | 0 | 32,882 |
| | | Stockton | 0 | 0 | 0 | 0 | 588 |
| | | Sunset | 0 | 0 | 0 | 0 | 4,892 |
| | | Syracuse | 0 | 0 | 0 | 0 | 24,168 |
| | | Taylorsville City | 0 | 0 | 0 | 0 | 58,472 |
| | | Tremonton | 0 | 0 | 0 | 0 | 6,891 |
| | | Vernal | 0 | 0 | 0 | 0 | 8,769 |
| | | Washington | 0 | 0 | 0 | 0 | 19,183 |
| | | Wellington | 0 | 0 | 0 | 0 | 1,553 |
| | **Universities and Colleges** | Brigham Young University | 0 | 0 | 0 | 0 | 34,244 |
| | | College of Eastern Utah | 0 | 0 | 0 | 0 | 1,438 |
| | | Southern Utah University | 0 | 0 | 0 | 0 | 7,516 |
| | | University of Utah | 0 | 0 | 0 | 0 | 28,211 |
| | | Utah State University | 0 | 0 | 0 | 0 | 15,099 |
| | | Utah Valley University | 0 | 0 | 0 | 0 | 26,696 |
| | | Weber State University | 0 | 0 | 0 | 0 | 21,388 |
| | **Metropolitan Counties** | Cache | 0 | 0 | 0 | 0 | |
| | | Juab | 0 | 0 | 0 | 0 | |
| | | Morgan | 0 | 0 | 0 | 0 | |
| | | Summit | 0 | 0 | 0 | 0 | |
| | | Utah | 0 | 0 | 0 | 0 | |
| | | Weber | 0 | 0 | 0 | 0 | |
| | **Nonmetropolitan Counties** | Beaver | 0 | 0 | 0 | 0 | |
| | | Box Elder | 0 | 0 | 0 | 0 | |
| | | Carbon | 0 | 0 | 0 | 0 | |
| | | Daggett | 0 | 0 | 0 | 0 | |
| | | Duchesne | 0 | 0 | 0 | 0 | |
| | | Emery | 0 | 0 | 0 | 0 | |
| | | Grand | 0 | 0 | 0 | 0 | |
| | | Iron | 0 | 0 | 0 | 0 | |
| | | Kane | 0 | 0 | 0 | 0 | |
| | | Millard | 0 | 0 | 0 | 0 | |
| | | Rich | 0 | 0 | 0 | 0 | |
| | | San Juan | 0 | 0 | 0 | 0 | |
| | | Sevier | 0 | 0 | 0 | 0 | |
| | | Wasatch | 0 | 0 | 0 | 0 | |
| | | Wayne | 0 | 0 | 0 | 0 | |
| | **State Police Agencies** | Utah Highway Patrol | 0 | 0 | 0 | 0 | |
| | **Other Agencies** | Cache-Rich Drug Task Force | 0 | 0 | 0 | 0 | |
| | | Davis Metropolitan Narcotics Strike Force | 0 | 0 | 0 | 0 | |
| | | Parks and Recreation | 0 | 0 | 0 | 0 | |
| | | Utah County Attorney, Investigations Division | 0 | 0 | 0 | 0 | |
| | | Utah County Major Crime Task Force | 0 | 0 | 0 | 0 | |
| | | Wildlife Resources | 0 | 0 | 0 | 0 | |
| **VERMONT....** | **Cities** | Barre | 0 | 0 | 0 | 0 | 8,790 |
| | | Barre Town | 0 | 0 | 0 | 0 | 8,049 |
| | | Bellows Falls | 0 | 0 | 0 | 0 | 2,873 |
| | | Bennington | 0 | 0 | 0 | 0 | 15,026 |
| | | Berlin | 0 | 0 | 0 | 0 | 2,818 |
| | | Bradford | 0 | 0 | 0 | 0 | 820 |
| | | Brandon | 0 | 0 | 0 | 0 | 3,860 |
| | | Brattleboro | 0 | 0 | 0 | 0 | 11,438 |
| | | Brighton | 0 | 0 | 0 | 0 | 1,317 |
| | | Canaan | 0 | 0 | 0 | 0 | 1,085 |
| | | Castleton | 0 | 0 | 0 | 0 | 4,647 |
| | | Chester | 0 | 0 | 0 | 0 | 2,995 |
| | | Dover | 0 | 0 | 0 | 0 | 1,434 |
| | | Fair Haven | 0 | 0 | 0 | 0 | 2,923 |
| | | Hardwick | 0 | 0 | 0 | 0 | 3,209 |
| | | Hartford | 0 | 0 | 0 | 0 | 10,730 |
| | | Middlebury | 0 | 0 | 0 | 0 | 8,281 |
| | | Milton | 0 | 0 | 0 | 0 | 10,853 |
| | | Montpelier | 0 | 0 | 0 | 0 | 7,731 |
| | | Morristown | 0 | 0 | 0 | 0 | 5,606 |
| | | Newport | 0 | 0 | 0 | 0 | 5,163 |
| | | Northfield | 0 | 0 | 0 | 0 | 5,735 |
| | | Norwich | 0 | 0 | 0 | 0 | 3,519 |
| | | Randolph | 0 | 0 | 0 | 0 | 5,057 |
| | | Richmond | 0 | 0 | 0 | 0 | 4,167 |
| | | Rutland | 0 | 0 | 0 | 0 | 16,688 |
| | | Springfield | 0 | 0 | 0 | 0 | 8,551 |
| | | St. Albans | 0 | 0 | 0 | 0 | 7,207 |
| | | St. Johnsbury | 0 | 0 | 0 | 0 | 7,404 |
| | | Stowe | 0 | 0 | 0 | 0 | 4,984 |
| | | Swanton | 0 | 0 | 0 | 0 | 6,451 |
| | | Thetford | 0 | 0 | 0 | 0 | 2,797 |
| | | Vergennes | 0 | 0 | 0 | 0 | 2,658 |
| | | Vernon | 0 | 0 | 0 | | 2,024 |
| | | Waterbury | 0 | 0 | 0 | 0 | 5,399 |
| | | Weathersfield | 0 | 0 | 0 | 0 | 2,836 |
| | | Williston | 0 | 0 | 0 | 0 | 8,515 |
| | | Wilmington | 0 | 0 | 0 | 0 | 2,351 |
| | | Windsor | 0 | 0 | 0 | 0 | 3,585 |
| | | Winhall | 0 | 0 | 0 | 0 | 796 |
| | | Winooski | 0 | 0 | 0 | 0 | 6,401 |
| | **Metropolitan Counties** | Chittenden | 0 | 0 | 0 | 0 | |
| | | Franklin | 0 | 0 | 0 | 0 | |
| | | Grand Isle | 0 | 0 | 0 | 0 | |
| | **Nonmetropolitan Counties** | Addison | 0 | 0 | 0 | 0 | |
| | | Bennington | 0 | 0 | 0 | 0 | |
| | | Lamoille | 0 | 0 | 0 | 0 | |
| | | Orange | 0 | 0 | 0 | 0 | |
| | | Orleans | 0 | 0 | 0 | 0 | |

[1]Agencies published in this table indicated that no hate crimes occurred in their jurisdictions during the quarter(s) for which they submitted reports to the Hate Crime Statistics Program. Blanks indicate quarters for which agencies did not submit reports.

[2]Population figures are published only for the cities. The figures listed for the universities and colleges are student enrollment and were provided by the United States Department of Education for the 2008 school year, the most recent available. The enrollment figures include full-time and part-time students.

## Table 95. Hate Crime Zero Data Submitted per Quarter, by State and Agency, 2009—*Continued*

(Number.)

| State | Agency type | Agency name | Zero data per quarter[1] | | | | Population[2] |
|---|---|---|---|---|---|---|---|
| | | | 1st quarter | 2nd quarter | 3rd quarter | 4th quarter | |
| **VERMONT** | | Rutland | 0 | 0 | 0 | 0 | |
| | | Washington | 0 | 0 | 0 | 0 | |
| | | Windham | 0 | 0 | 0 | 0 | |
| | | Windsor | 0 | 0 | 0 | 0 | |
| | **State Police Agencies** | State Police: | | | | | |
| | | Bradford | 0 | 0 | 0 | 0 | |
| | | Brattleboro | 0 | 0 | 0 | 0 | |
| | | Derby | 0 | 0 | 0 | 0 | |
| | | New Haven | 0 | 0 | 0 | 0 | |
| | | Rockingham | 0 | 0 | 0 | 0 | |
| | | Royalton | 0 | 0 | 0 | 0 | |
| | | Rutland | 0 | 0 | 0 | 0 | |
| | | St. Johnsbury | 0 | 0 | 0 | 0 | |
| | | Williston | 0 | 0 | 0 | 0 | |
| | | Vermont State Police | 0 | 0 | 0 | 0 | |
| | | Vermont State Police Headquarters, Bureau of Criminal Investigations | 0 | 0 | 0 | 0 | |
| | **Other Agencies** | Attorney General | 0 | 0 | 0 | 0 | |
| | | Department of Motor Vehicles | 0 | 0 | 0 | 0 | |
| | | Fish and Wildlife Department, Law Enforcement Division | 0 | 0 | 0 | 0 | |
| **VIRGINIA** ..... | **Cities** | Abingdon | 0 | 0 | 0 | 0 | 8,034 |
| | | Altavista | 0 | 0 | 0 | 0 | 3,362 |
| | | Amherst | 0 | 0 | 0 | 0 | 2,216 |
| | | Appalachia | 0 | 0 | 0 | 0 | 1,729 |
| | | Ashland | 0 | 0 | 0 | 0 | 7,152 |
| | | Berryville | 0 | 0 | 0 | 0 | 3,187 |
| | | Big Stone Gap | 0 | 0 | 0 | 0 | 5,652 |
| | | Blacksburg | 0 | 0 | 0 | 0 | 42,047 |
| | | Blackstone | 0 | 0 | 0 | 0 | 3,568 |
| | | Bowling Green | 0 | 0 | 0 | 0 | 1,031 |
| | | Boykins | 0 | 0 | 0 | 0 | 599 |
| | | Bridgewater | 0 | 0 | 0 | 0 | 5,458 |
| | | Bristol | 0 | 0 | 0 | 0 | 17,502 |
| | | Broadway | 0 | 0 | 0 | 0 | 3,335 |
| | | Brookneal | 0 | 0 | 0 | 0 | 1,248 |
| | | Buena Vista | 0 | 0 | 0 | 0 | 6,509 |
| | | Burkeville | 0 | 0 | 0 | 0 | 470 |
| | | Cape Charles | 0 | 0 | 0 | 0 | 1,510 |
| | | Cedar Bluff | 0 | 0 | 0 | 0 | 1,039 |
| | | Chase City | 0 | 0 | 0 | 0 | 2,307 |
| | | Chatham | 0 | 0 | 0 | 0 | 1,543 |
| | | Chilhowie | 0 | 0 | 0 | 0 | 1,737 |
| | | Chincoteague | 0 | 0 | 0 | 0 | 4,293 |
| | | Clarksville | 0 | 0 | 0 | 0 | 1,251 |
| | | Clifton Forge | 0 | 0 | 0 | 0 | 3,895 |
| | | Clintwood | 0 | 0 | 0 | 0 | 1,517 |
| | | Coeburn | 0 | 0 | 0 | 0 | 1,974 |
| | | Crewe | 0 | 0 | 0 | 0 | 2,274 |
| | | Damascus | 0 | 0 | 0 | 0 | 1,081 |
| | | Dayton | 0 | 0 | 0 | 0 | 1,354 |
| | | Dublin | 0 | 0 | 0 | 0 | 2,180 |
| | | Dumfries | 0 | 0 | 0 | 0 | 4,792 |
| | | Edinburg | 0 | 0 | 0 | 0 | 903 |
| | | Elkton | 0 | 0 | 0 | 0 | 2,625 |
| | | Emporia | 0 | 0 | 0 | 0 | 5,662 |
| | | Exmore | 0 | 0 | 0 | 0 | 1,341 |
| | | Farmville | 0 | 0 | 0 | 0 | 7,462 |
| | | Franklin | 0 | 0 | 0 | 0 | 8,980 |
| | | Fries | 0 | 0 | 0 | 0 | 546 |
| | | Gate City | 0 | 0 | 0 | 0 | 2,037 |
| | | Glade Spring | 0 | 0 | 0 | 0 | 1,538 |
| | | Glasgow | 0 | 0 | 0 | 0 | 1,003 |
| | | Glen Lyn | 0 | 0 | 0 | 0 | 164 |
| | | Gordonsville | 0 | 0 | 0 | 0 | 1,720 |
| | | Gretna | 0 | 0 | 0 | 0 | 1,185 |
| | | Grottoes | 0 | 0 | 0 | 0 | 2,192 |
| | | Grundy | 0 | 0 | 0 | 0 | 947 |
| | | Halifax | 0 | 0 | 0 | 0 | 1,280 |
| | | Haymarket | 0 | 0 | 0 | 0 | 1,268 |
| | | Haysi | 0 | 0 | 0 | 0 | 308 |
| | | Herndon | 0 | 0 | 0 | 0 | 22,078 |
| | | Hillsville | 0 | 0 | 0 | 0 | 2,630 |
| | | Honaker | 0 | 0 | 0 | 0 | 1,438 |
| | | Hopewell | 0 | 0 | 0 | 0 | 23,324 |
| | | Hurt | 0 | 0 | 0 | 0 | 1,208 |
| | | Independence | 0 | 0 | 0 | 0 | 887 |
| | | Jonesville | 0 | 0 | 0 | 0 | 964 |
| | | Kenbridge | 0 | 0 | 0 | 0 | 1,273 |
| | | Kilmarnock | 0 | 0 | 0 | 0 | 1,287 |
| | | La Crosse | 0 | 0 | 0 | 0 | 586 |
| | | Lawrenceville | 0 | 0 | 0 | 0 | 1,342 |
| | | Lebanon | 0 | 0 | 0 | 0 | 3,186 |
| | | Lexington | 0 | 0 | 0 | 0 | 7,049 |
| | | Louisa | 0 | 0 | 0 | 0 | 1,583 |
| | | Luray | 0 | 0 | 0 | 0 | 4,840 |
| | | Martinsville | 0 | 0 | 0 | 0 | 14,509 |
| | | Middleburg | 0 | 0 | 0 | 0 | 979 |
| | | Middletown | 0 | 0 | 0 | 0 | 1,154 |
| | | Mount Jackson | 0 | 0 | 0 | 0 | 2,014 |
| | | Narrows | 0 | 0 | 0 | 0 | 2,151 |
| | | New Market | 0 | 0 | 0 | 0 | 1,865 |
| | | Norton | 0 | 0 | 0 | 0 | 3,697 |
| | | Occoquan | 0 | 0 | 0 | 0 | 824 |
| | | Onancock | 0 | 0 | 0 | 0 | 1,375 |
| | | Onley | 0 | 0 | 0 | 0 | 468 |
| | | Orange | 0 | 0 | 0 | 0 | 4,688 |
| | | Parksley | 0 | 0 | 0 | 0 | 785 |
| | | Pembroke | 0 | 0 | 0 | 0 | 1,166 |
| | | Pennington Gap | 0 | 0 | 0 | 0 | 1,721 |
| | | Petersburg | 0 | 0 | 0 | 0 | 32,966 |
| | | Pocahontas | 0 | 0 | 0 | 0 | 417 |
| | | Poquoson | 0 | 0 | 0 | 0 | 11,902 |
| | | Pound | 0 | 0 | 0 | 0 | 1,070 |
| | | Pulaski | 0 | 0 | 0 | 0 | 8,932 |
| | | Quantico | 0 | 0 | 0 | 0 | 614 |
| | | Radford | 0 | 0 | 0 | 0 | 16,216 |
| | | Remington | 0 | 0 | 0 | 0 | 678 |
| | | Rich Creek | 0 | 0 | 0 | 0 | 682 |
| | | Richlands | 0 | 0 | 0 | 0 | 3,983 |
| | | Rocky Mount | 0 | 0 | 0 | 0 | 4,536 |
| | | Rural Retreat | 0 | 0 | 0 | 0 | 1,346 |
| | | Saltville | 0 | 0 | 0 | 0 | 2,207 |
| | | Shenandoah | 0 | 0 | 0 | 0 | 1,856 |
| | | Smithfield | 0 | 0 | 0 | 0 | 7,115 |
| | | South Boston | 0 | 0 | 0 | 0 | 7,822 |
| | | South Hill | 0 | 0 | 0 | 0 | 4,558 |
| | | Stanley | 0 | 0 | 0 | 0 | 1,562 |
| | | Staunton | 0 | 0 | 0 | 0 | 24,072 |
| | | Stephens City | 0 | 0 | 0 | 0 | 1,505 |
| | | St. Paul | 0 | 0 | 0 | 0 | 963 |
| | | Strasburg | 0 | 0 | 0 | 0 | 4,405 |
| | | Tappahannock | 0 | 0 | 0 | 0 | 2,202 |
| | | Tazewell | 0 | 0 | 0 | 0 | 4,247 |
| | | Timberville | 0 | 0 | 0 | 0 | 1,714 |
| | | Victoria | 0 | 0 | 0 | 0 | 1,722 |
| | | Vienna | 0 | 0 | 0 | 0 | 14,946 |
| | | Vinton | 0 | 0 | 0 | 0 | 7,879 |
| | | Warrenton | 0 | 0 | 0 | 0 | 9,235 |
| | | Warsaw | 0 | 0 | 0 | 0 | 1,350 |
| | | Waverly | 0 | 0 | 0 | 0 | 2,142 |
| | | Weber City | 0 | 0 | 0 | 0 | 1,322 |
| | | West Point | 0 | 0 | 0 | 0 | 3,177 |
| | | White Stone | 0 | 0 | 0 | 0 | 336 |
| | | Williamsburg | 0 | 0 | 0 | 0 | 12,584 |

[1]Agencies published in this table indicated that no hate crimes occurred in their jurisdictions during the quarter(s) for which they submitted reports to the Hate Crime Statistics Program. Blanks indicate quarters for which agencies did not submit reports.

[2]Population figures are published only for the cities. The figures listed for the universities and colleges are student enrollment and were provided by the United States Department of Education for the 2008 school year, the most recent available. The enrollment figures include full-time and part-time students.

## Table 95. Hate Crime Zero Data Submitted per Quarter, by State and Agency, 2009—*Continued*

(Number.)

| State | Agency type | Agency name | Zero data per quarter[1] 1st quarter | 2nd quarter | 3rd quarter | 4th quarter | Population[2] |
|---|---|---|---|---|---|---|---|
| VIRGINIA | | Winchester | 0 | 0 | 0 | 0 | 26,252 |
| | | Wise | 0 | 0 | 0 | 0 | 3,226 |
| | | Woodstock | 0 | 0 | 0 | 0 | 4,315 |
| | | Wytheville | 0 | 0 | 0 | 0 | 8,336 |
| | Universities and Colleges | Christopher Newport University | 0 | 0 | 0 | 0 | 4,904 |
| | | Emory and Henry College | 0 | 0 | 0 | 0 | 1,015 |
| | | Ferrum College | 0 | 0 | 0 | 0 | 1,397 |
| | | James Madison University | 0 | 0 | 0 | 0 | 18,454 |
| | | J. Sargeant Reynolds Community College | | | 0 | 0 | 13,079 |
| | | Longwood University | 0 | 0 | 0 | 0 | 4,727 |
| | | Norfolk State University | 0 | 0 | 0 | 0 | 6,325 |
| | | Richard Bland College | | 0 | 0 | 0 | 1,634 |
| | | Thomas Nelson Community College | 0 | 0 | 0 | 0 | 10,557 |
| | | University of Mary Washington | | | | 0 | 5,084 |
| | | University of Richmond | 0 | 0 | 0 | 0 | 4,249 |
| | | University of Virginia's College at Wise | 0 | 0 | 0 | 0 | 1,964 |
| | | Virginia Commonwealth University | 0 | 0 | 0 | 0 | 32,044 |
| | | Virginia Military Institute | 0 | 0 | 0 | 0 | 1,428 |
| | | Virginia State University | 0 | 0 | 0 | 0 | 5,042 |
| | | Virginia Western Community College | 0 | 0 | 0 | 0 | 8,532 |
| | Metropolitan Counties | Appomattox | 0 | 0 | 0 | 0 | |
| | | Campbell | 0 | 0 | 0 | 0 | |
| | | Caroline | 0 | 0 | 0 | 0 | |
| | | Charles City | 0 | 0 | 0 | 0 | |
| | | Craig | 0 | 0 | 0 | 0 | |
| | | Fauquier | 0 | 0 | 0 | 0 | |
| | | Fluvanna | 0 | 0 | 0 | 0 | |
| | | Franklin | 0 | 0 | 0 | 0 | |
| | | Frederick | 0 | 0 | 0 | 0 | |
| | | Giles | 0 | 0 | 0 | 0 | |
| | | Gloucester | 0 | 0 | 0 | 0 | |
| | | Goochland | 0 | 0 | 0 | 0 | |
| | | Hanover | 0 | 0 | 0 | 0 | |
| | | Isle of Wight | 0 | 0 | 0 | 0 | |
| | | King William | 0 | 0 | 0 | 0 | |
| | | Louisa | 0 | 0 | 0 | 0 | |
| | | Mathews | 0 | 0 | 0 | 0 | |
| | | Montgomery | 0 | 0 | 0 | 0 | |
| | | Nelson | 0 | 0 | 0 | 0 | |
| | | Pittsylvania | 0 | 0 | 0 | 0 | |
| | | Powhatan | 0 | 0 | 0 | 0 | |
| | | Prince George County Police Department | 0 | 0 | 0 | 0 | |
| | | Pulaski | 0 | 0 | 0 | 0 | |
| | | Rockingham | 0 | 0 | 0 | 0 | |
| | | Scott | 0 | 0 | 0 | 0 | |
| | | Surry | 0 | 0 | 0 | 0 | |
| | | Sussex | 0 | 0 | 0 | 0 | |
| | | Washington | 0 | 0 | 0 | 0 | |
| | Nonmetropolitan Counties | Accomack | 0 | 0 | 0 | 0 | |
| | | Alleghany | 0 | 0 | 0 | 0 | |
| | | Bath | 0 | 0 | 0 | 0 | |
| | | Bland | 0 | 0 | 0 | 0 | |
| | | Brunswick | 0 | 0 | 0 | 0 | |
| | | Buchanan | 0 | 0 | 0 | 0 | |
| | | Buckingham | 0 | 0 | 0 | 0 | |
| | | Carroll | 0 | 0 | 0 | 0 | |
| | | Culpeper | 0 | 0 | 0 | 0 | |
| | | Dickenson | 0 | 0 | 0 | 0 | |
| | | Essex | 0 | 0 | 0 | 0 | |
| | | Floyd | 0 | 0 | 0 | 0 | |
| | | Grayson | 0 | 0 | 0 | 0 | |
| | | Greensville | 0 | 0 | 0 | 0 | |
| | | Halifax | 0 | 0 | 0 | 0 | |
| | | Henry | 0 | 0 | 0 | 0 | |
| | | Highland | 0 | 0 | 0 | 0 | |
| | | King George | 0 | 0 | 0 | 0 | |
| | | Lancaster | 0 | 0 | 0 | 0 | |
| | | Lee | 0 | 0 | 0 | 0 | |
| | | Lunenburg | 0 | 0 | 0 | 0 | |
| | | Madison | 0 | 0 | 0 | 0 | |
| | | Mecklenburg | 0 | 0 | 0 | 0 | |
| | | Middlesex | 0 | 0 | 0 | 0 | |
| | | Northampton | 0 | 0 | 0 | 0 | |
| | | Northumberland | 0 | 0 | 0 | 0 | |
| | | Nottoway | 0 | 0 | 0 | 0 | |
| | | Orange | 0 | 0 | 0 | 0 | |
| | | Page | 0 | 0 | 0 | 0 | |
| | | Patrick | 0 | 0 | 0 | 0 | |
| | | Prince Edward | 0 | 0 | 0 | 0 | |
| | | Rappahannock | 0 | 0 | 0 | 0 | |
| | | Richmond | 0 | 0 | 0 | 0 | |
| | | Rockbridge | 0 | 0 | 0 | 0 | |
| | | Russell | 0 | 0 | 0 | 0 | |
| | | Shenandoah | 0 | 0 | 0 | 0 | |
| | | Smyth | 0 | 0 | 0 | 0 | |
| | | Southampton | 0 | 0 | 0 | 0 | |
| | | Tazewell | 0 | 0 | 0 | 0 | |
| | | Westmoreland | 0 | 0 | 0 | 0 | |
| | | Wise | 0 | 0 | 0 | 0 | |
| | | Wythe | 0 | 0 | 0 | 0 | |
| | State Police Agencies | State Police: | | | | | |
| | | Accomack County | 0 | 0 | 0 | 0 | |
| | | Albemarle County | 0 | 0 | 0 | 0 | |
| | | Alexandria | 0 | 0 | 0 | 0 | |
| | | Alleghany County | 0 | 0 | 0 | 0 | |
| | | Amelia County | 0 | 0 | 0 | 0 | |
| | | Amherst County | 0 | 0 | 0 | 0 | |
| | | Appomattox County | 0 | 0 | 0 | 0 | |
| | | Augusta County | 0 | 0 | 0 | 0 | |
| | | Bath County | 0 | 0 | 0 | 0 | |
| | | Bedford | 0 | 0 | 0 | 0 | |
| | | Bedford County | 0 | 0 | 0 | 0 | |
| | | Bland County | 0 | 0 | 0 | 0 | |
| | | Botetourt County | 0 | 0 | 0 | 0 | |
| | | Bristol | 0 | 0 | 0 | 0 | |
| | | Brunswick County | 0 | 0 | 0 | 0 | |
| | | Buchanan County | 0 | 0 | 0 | 0 | |

[1]Agencies published in this table indicated that no hate crimes occurred in their jurisdictions during the quarter(s) for which they submitted reports to the Hate Crime Statistics Program. Blanks indicate quarters for which agencies did not submit reports.

[2]Population figures are published only for the cities. The figures listed for the universities and colleges are student enrollment and were provided by the United States Department of Education for the 2008 school year, the most recent available. The enrollment figures include full-time and part-time students.

## Table 95. Hate Crime Zero Data Submitted per Quarter, by State and Agency, 2009—*Continued*

(Number.)

| State | Agency type | Agency name | Zero data per quarter[1] 1st quarter | 2nd quarter | 3rd quarter | 4th quarter | Population[2] |
|---|---|---|---|---|---|---|---|
| **VIRGINIA** | | Buckingham County | 0 | 0 | 0 | 0 | |
| | | Buena Vista | 0 | 0 | 0 | 0 | |
| | | Campbell County | 0 | 0 | 0 | 0 | |
| | | Caroline County | 0 | 0 | 0 | 0 | |
| | | Carroll County | 0 | 0 | 0 | 0 | |
| | | Charles City County | 0 | 0 | | 0 | |
| | | Charlotte County | 0 | 0 | 0 | 0 | |
| | | Charlottesville | 0 | 0 | 0 | 0 | |
| | | Chesapeake | 0 | 0 | 0 | 0 | |
| | | Chesterfield County | 0 | 0 | 0 | 0 | |
| | | Clarke County | 0 | 0 | 0 | 0 | |
| | | Clifton Forge | 0 | 0 | 0 | 0 | |
| | | Colonial Heights | 0 | 0 | 0 | 0 | |
| | | Covington | 0 | 0 | 0 | 0 | |
| | | Craig County | 0 | 0 | 0 | 0 | |
| | | Culpeper County | 0 | 0 | 0 | 0 | |
| | | Cumberland County | 0 | 0 | 0 | 0 | |
| | | Danville | 0 | 0 | 0 | 0 | |
| | | Dickenson County | 0 | 0 | 0 | 0 | |
| | | Dinwiddie County | 0 | 0 | 0 | 0 | |
| | | Emporia | 0 | 0 | 0 | 0 | |
| | | Essex County | 0 | 0 | 0 | 0 | |
| | | Fairfax City | | | 0 | | |
| | | Fairfax County | 0 | 0 | 0 | 0 | |
| | | Falls Church | 0 | 0 | 0 | | |
| | | Fauquier County | 0 | 0 | 0 | 0 | |
| | | Floyd County | 0 | 0 | 0 | 0 | |
| | | Fluvanna County | 0 | 0 | 0 | 0 | |
| | | Franklin | 0 | 0 | 0 | 0 | |
| | | Franklin County | 0 | 0 | 0 | 0 | |
| | | Frederick County | 0 | 0 | 0 | 0 | |
| | | Fredericksburg | 0 | 0 | 0 | 0 | |
| | | Galax | 0 | 0 | 0 | 0 | |
| | | Giles County | 0 | 0 | 0 | 0 | |
| | | Gloucester County | 0 | 0 | 0 | 0 | |
| | | Goochland County | 0 | 0 | 0 | 0 | |
| | | Grayson County | 0 | 0 | 0 | 0 | |
| | | Greene County | 0 | 0 | 0 | 0 | |
| | | Greensville County | 0 | 0 | 0 | 0 | |
| | | Halifax County | 0 | 0 | 0 | 0 | |
| | | Hampton | 0 | 0 | 0 | 0 | |
| | | Hanover County | 0 | 0 | 0 | 0 | |
| | | Harrisonburg | 0 | 0 | 0 | 0 | |
| | | Henrico County | 0 | 0 | 0 | 0 | |
| | | Henry County | 0 | 0 | 0 | 0 | |
| | | Highland County | 0 | 0 | 0 | | |
| | | Hopewell | 0 | 0 | 0 | 0 | |
| | | Isle of Wight County | 0 | 0 | 0 | 0 | |
| | | James City County | 0 | 0 | 0 | 0 | |
| | | King and Queen County | 0 | 0 | | | |
| | | King George County | 0 | 0 | 0 | 0 | |
| | | King William County | 0 | 0 | 0 | 0 | |
| | | Lancaster County | 0 | 0 | 0 | 0 | |
| | | Lee County | 0 | 0 | 0 | 0 | |
| | | Lexington | 0 | 0 | 0 | 0 | |
| | | Loudoun County | 0 | 0 | 0 | 0 | |
| | | Louisa County | 0 | 0 | 0 | 0 | |
| | | Lunenburg County | 0 | 0 | 0 | 0 | |
| | | Lynchburg | 0 | 0 | 0 | 0 | |
| | | Madison County | 0 | 0 | 0 | 0 | |
| | | Manassas | 0 | 0 | 0 | 0 | |
| | | Manassas Park | 0 | | | | |
| | | Martinsville | 0 | 0 | 0 | 0 | |
| | | Mathews County | 0 | 0 | 0 | 0 | |
| | | Mecklenburg County | 0 | 0 | 0 | 0 | |
| | | Middlesex County | 0 | 0 | 0 | 0 | |
| | | Montgomery County | 0 | 0 | 0 | 0 | |
| | | Nelson County | 0 | 0 | 0 | 0 | |
| | | New Kent County | 0 | 0 | 0 | 0 | |
| | | Newport News | 0 | 0 | 0 | 0 | |
| | | Norfolk | 0 | 0 | 0 | 0 | |
| | | Northampton County | 0 | 0 | 0 | 0 | |
| | | Northumberland County | 0 | 0 | 0 | 0 | |
| | | Nottoway County | 0 | 0 | 0 | 0 | |
| | | Orange County | 0 | 0 | 0 | 0 | |
| | | Page County | 0 | 0 | 0 | 0 | |
| | | Patrick County | 0 | 0 | 0 | 0 | |
| | | Petersburg | 0 | 0 | 0 | 0 | |
| | | Pittsylvania County | 0 | 0 | 0 | 0 | |
| | | Poquoson | 0 | 0 | 0 | 0 | |
| | | Portsmouth | 0 | 0 | 0 | 0 | |
| | | Powhatan County | 0 | 0 | 0 | 0 | |
| | | Prince Edward County | 0 | 0 | 0 | 0 | |
| | | Prince George County | 0 | 0 | 0 | 0 | |
| | | Prince William County | 0 | 0 | 0 | 0 | |
| | | Pulaski County | 0 | 0 | 0 | 0 | |
| | | Radford | 0 | 0 | 0 | 0 | |
| | | Rappahannock County | 0 | 0 | 0 | 0 | |
| | | Richmond | 0 | 0 | 0 | 0 | |
| | | Richmond County | 0 | 0 | 0 | 0 | |
| | | Roanoke | 0 | 0 | 0 | 0 | |
| | | Roanoke County | 0 | 0 | 0 | 0 | |
| | | Rockbridge County | 0 | 0 | 0 | 0 | |
| | | Rockingham County | 0 | 0 | 0 | 0 | |
| | | Russell County | 0 | 0 | 0 | 0 | |
| | | Salem | 0 | 0 | 0 | 0 | |
| | | Scott County | 0 | 0 | 0 | 0 | |
| | | Shenandoah County | 0 | 0 | 0 | 0 | |
| | | Smyth County | 0 | 0 | 0 | 0 | |
| | | Southampton County | 0 | 0 | 0 | 0 | |

[1]Agencies published in this table indicated that no hate crimes occurred in their jurisdictions during the quarter(s) for which they submitted reports to the Hate Crime Statistics Program. Blanks indicate quarters for which agencies did not submit reports.

[2]Population figures are published only for the cities. The figures listed for the universities and colleges are student enrollment and were provided by the United States Department of Education for the 2008 school year, the most recent available. The enrollment figures include full-time and part-time students.

## Table 95. Hate Crime Zero Data Submitted per Quarter, by State and Agency, 2009—*Continued*

(Number.)

| State | Agency type | Agency name | Zero data per quarter[1] | | | | Population[2] |
|---|---|---|---|---|---|---|---|
| | | | 1st quarter | 2nd quarter | 3rd quarter | 4th quarter | |
| VIRGINIA | | Spotsylvania County | 0 | 0 | 0 | 0 | |
| | | Stafford County | 0 | 0 | 0 | 0 | |
| | | Staunton | 0 | 0 | 0 | | |
| | | Suffolk | 0 | 0 | 0 | 0 | |
| | | Surry County | 0 | 0 | 0 | 0 | |
| | | Sussex County | 0 | 0 | 0 | 0 | |
| | | Tazewell County | 0 | 0 | 0 | 0 | |
| | | Virginia Beach | 0 | 0 | 0 | 0 | |
| | | Warren County | 0 | 0 | 0 | 0 | |
| | | Washington County | 0 | 0 | 0 | 0 | |
| | | Waynesboro | 0 | 0 | 0 | 0 | |
| | | Westmoreland County | 0 | 0 | 0 | 0 | |
| | | Williamsburg | 0 | 0 | 0 | 0 | |
| | | Winchester | 0 | 0 | 0 | 0 | |
| | | Wise County | 0 | 0 | 0 | 0 | |
| | | Wythe County | 0 | 0 | 0 | 0 | |
| | | York County | 0 | 0 | 0 | 0 | |
| | Other Agencies | Alcoholic Beverage Control Commission | 0 | 0 | 0 | 0 | |
| | | Department of Conservation and Recreation | 0 | 0 | 0 | 0 | |
| | | Department of Motor Vehicles | 0 | 0 | 0 | 0 | |
| | | Norfolk Airport Authority | 0 | 0 | 0 | 0 | |
| | | Port Authority, Norfolk | 0 | 0 | 0 | 0 | |
| | | Reagan National Airport | 0 | 0 | 0 | 0 | |
| | | Richmond International Airport | 0 | 0 | 0 | 0 | |
| | | Southside Virginia Training Center | 0 | 0 | 0 | 0 | |
| | | Virginia State Capitol | 0 | 0 | 0 | 0 | |
| WASHINGTON | Cities | Aberdeen | 0 | 0 | 0 | 0 | 16,000 |
| | | Airway Heights | 0 | 0 | 0 | 0 | 5,384 |
| | | Algona | 0 | 0 | 0 | 0 | 2,763 |
| | | Anacortes | 0 | 0 | 0 | 0 | 17,063 |
| | | Arlington | 0 | 0 | 0 | 0 | 17,413 |
| | | Asotin | 0 | 0 | 0 | 0 | 1,133 |
| | | Bainbridge Island | 0 | 0 | 0 | 0 | 22,061 |
| | | Battle Ground | 0 | 0 | 0 | 0 | 17,865 |
| | | Bingen | 0 | 0 | 0 | 0 | 681 |
| | | Black Diamond | 0 | 0 | 0 | 0 | 4,007 |
| | | Blaine | 0 | 0 | 0 | 0 | 5,128 |
| | | Bonney Lake | 0 | 0 | 0 | 0 | 17,461 |
| | | Bothell | 0 | | 0 | 0 | 32,517 |
| | | Bremerton | 0 | 0 | 0 | 0 | 35,888 |
| | | Brewster | 0 | 0 | 0 | 0 | 2,076 |
| | | Brier | 0 | 0 | 0 | 0 | 6,340 |
| | | Buckley | 0 | 0 | 0 | 0 | 5,514 |
| | | Carnation | 0 | 0 | 0 | 0 | 1,806 |
| | | Castle Rock | 0 | 0 | 0 | 0 | 2,120 |
| | | Centralia | 0 | 0 | 0 | 0 | 15,811 |
| | | Chehalis | 0 | 0 | 0 | 0 | 7,397 |
| | | Chewelah | 0 | 0 | | 0 | 2,313 |
| | | Clarkston | 0 | 0 | 0 | 0 | 7,194 |
| | | Cle Elum | 0 | 0 | | 0 | 3,514 |
| | | Clyde Hill | 0 | 0 | 0 | 0 | 2,708 |
| | | Colfax | 0 | 0 | 0 | 0 | 2,744 |
| | | College Place | 0 | 0 | 0 | 0 | 9,106 |
| | | Colville | 0 | 0 | 0 | 0 | 4,919 |
| | | Connell | 0 | 0 | 0 | 0 | 3,214 |
| | | Cosmopolis | 0 | 0 | 0 | 0 | 1,669 |
| | | Coulee City | 0 | 0 | 0 | 0 | 636 |
| | | Coulee Dam | 0 | 0 | 0 | 0 | 1,051 |
| | | Coupeville | 0 | 0 | 0 | 0 | 1,907 |
| | | Covington | 0 | 0 | 0 | 0 | 18,619 |
| | | Des Moines | 0 | 0 | 0 | 0 | 28,667 |
| | | Dupont | 0 | 0 | 0 | 0 | 7,799 |
| | | Duvall | 0 | 0 | 0 | 0 | 6,150 |
| | | East Wenatchee | 0 | 0 | 0 | 0 | 12,355 |
| | | Eatonville | 0 | 0 | 0 | 0 | 2,512 |
| | | Edgewood | 0 | 0 | 0 | 0 | 9,778 |
| | | Ellensburg | 0 | 0 | 0 | 0 | 17,331 |
| | | Elma | 0 | 0 | 0 | 0 | 3,114 |
| | | Enumclaw | 0 | 0 | 0 | 0 | 10,640 |
| | | Ephrata | 0 | 0 | 0 | 0 | 7,399 |
| | | Everson | 0 | 0 | 0 | 0 | 2,210 |
| | | Ferndale | 0 | 0 | 0 | 0 | 11,669 |
| | | Fife | 0 | 0 | 0 | 0 | 8,622 |
| | | Fircrest | 0 | 0 | 0 | 0 | 6,251 |
| | | Forks | 0 | 0 | 0 | 0 | 3,276 |
| | | Garfield | | 0 | 0 | 0 | 614 |
| | | Gig Harbor | 0 | 0 | 0 | 0 | 7,059 |
| | | Goldendale | 0 | 0 | 0 | 0 | 3,733 |
| | | Grand Coulee | 0 | 0 | 0 | 0 | 1,924 |
| | | Grandview | 0 | 0 | 0 | 0 | 9,498 |
| | | Granger | 0 | 0 | 0 | 0 | 3,019 |
| | | Granite Falls | 0 | 0 | 0 | 0 | 3,180 |
| | | Hoquiam | 0 | 0 | 0 | 0 | 8,823 |
| | | Ilwaco | 0 | 0 | 0 | 0 | 991 |
| | | Issaquah | 0 | 0 | 0 | 0 | 25,019 |
| | | Kalama | 0 | 0 | 0 | 0 | 2,295 |
| | | Kenmore | 0 | 0 | 0 | 0 | 20,568 |
| | | Kent | 0 | 0 | 0 | 0 | 84,363 |
| | | Kettle Falls | 0 | | | | 1,430 |
| | | Kirkland | 0 | 0 | 0 | 0 | 47,565 |
| | | Kittitas | 0 | 0 | 0 | 0 | 1,246 |
| | | La Center | 0 | 0 | 0 | 0 | 2,660 |
| | | Lacey | 0 | 0 | 0 | | 41,915 |
| | | Lake Forest Park | 0 | 0 | 0 | 0 | 12,394 |
| | | Lake Stevens | 0 | 0 | 0 | 0 | 13,758 |
| | | Langley | 0 | 0 | 0 | 0 | 1,085 |
| | | Liberty Lake | 0 | 0 | 0 | 0 | 7,592 |
| | | Long Beach | 0 | 0 | 0 | 0 | 1,361 |
| | | Longview | 0 | 0 | 0 | 0 | 36,778 |
| | | Lynnwood | 0 | 0 | 0 | 0 | 33,544 |
| | | Marysville | 0 | 0 | 0 | 0 | 35,110 |
| | | McCleary | 0 | 0 | 0 | 0 | 1,616 |
| | | Medical Lake | 0 | | | | 4,820 |
| | | Medina | 0 | 0 | 0 | 0 | 3,634 |
| | | Mercer Island | 0 | 0 | 0 | 0 | 24,411 |
| | | Milton | 0 | 0 | 0 | 0 | 6,901 |
| | | Montesano | 0 | 0 | 0 | 0 | 3,633 |
| | | Morton | 0 | 0 | 0 | 0 | 1,090 |
| | | Moxee | 0 | 0 | 0 | 0 | 2,601 |
| | | Mukilteo | 0 | 0 | 0 | 0 | 21,057 |
| | | Newcastle | 0 | 0 | 0 | 0 | 10,138 |
| | | Normandy Park | 0 | 0 | 0 | 0 | 6,225 |
| | | North Bend | 0 | 0 | 0 | 0 | 4,618 |
| | | North Bonneville | 0 | 0 | | | 1,008 |
| | | Oakesdale | 0 | 0 | 0 | | 388 |
| | | Oak Harbor | 0 | 0 | 0 | 0 | 23,098 |
| | | Oakville | 0 | 0 | 0 | 0 | 727 |
| | | Ocean Shores | 0 | 0 | 0 | | 5,180 |
| | | Odessa | 0 | 0 | 0 | 0 | 913 |
| | | Omak | 0 | 0 | 0 | 0 | 4,697 |
| | | Oroville | 0 | 0 | 0 | 0 | 1,653 |
| | | Orting | 0 | 0 | 0 | 0 | 6,511 |
| | | Othello | 0 | 0 | 0 | 0 | 6,662 |
| | | Pacific | 0 | 0 | 0 | 0 | 6,102 |

[1] Agencies published in this table indicated that no hate crimes occurred in their jurisdictions during the quarter(s) for which they submitted reports to the Hate Crime Statistics Program. Blanks indicate quarters for which agencies did not submit reports.

[2] Population figures are published only for the cities. The figures listed for the universities and colleges are student enrollment and were provided by the United States Department of Education for the 2008 school year, the most recent available. The enrollment figures include full-time and part-time students.

## Table 95. Hate Crime Zero Data Submitted per Quarter, by State and Agency, 2009—*Continued*

(Number.)

| State | Agency type | Agency name | Zero data per quarter[1] 1st quarter | 2nd quarter | 3rd quarter | 4th quarter | Population[2] |
|---|---|---|---|---|---|---|---|
| WASHINGTON | | Palouse | 0 | 0 | 0 | 0 | 926 |
| | | Pe Ell | 0 | 0 | 0 | 0 | 681 |
| | | Port Angeles | 0 | 0 | 0 | 0 | 19,044 |
| | | Port Orchard | 0 | 0 | 0 | 0 | 7,973 |
| | | Port Townsend | 0 | 0 | 0 | 0 | 9,223 |
| | | Poulsbo | 0 | 0 | 0 | 0 | 8,271 |
| | | Prosser | 0 | 0 | 0 | 0 | 5,148 |
| | | Puyallup | 0 | 0 | 0 | 0 | 36,659 |
| | | Quincy | 0 | 0 | 0 | 0 | 5,977 |
| | | Rainier | 0 | 0 | 0 | 0 | 1,664 |
| | | Raymond | 0 | 0 | 0 | 0 | 2,853 |
| | | Reardan | 0 | 0 | 0 | 0 | 596 |
| | | Renton | 0 | 0 | 0 | 0 | 63,599 |
| | | Republic | 0 | 0 | 0 | 0 | 939 |
| | | Ridgefield | 0 | 0 | 0 | 0 | 4,681 |
| | | Ritzville | 0 | 0 | 0 | 0 | 1,736 |
| | | Roy | 0 | 0 | 0 | 0 | 809 |
| | | Royal City | 0 | 0 | 0 | 0 | 1,981 |
| | | Ruston | 0 | 0 | 0 | 0 | 733 |
| | | Sammamish | 0 | 0 | 0 | 0 | 40,837 |
| | | Sedro Woolley | 0 | 0 | 0 | 0 | 11,114 |
| | | Selah | 0 | 0 | 0 | 0 | 7,215 |
| | | Snohomish | 0 | 0 | 0 | 0 | 8,794 |
| | | Soap Lake | 0 | 0 | 0 | 0 | 1,838 |
| | | South Bend | 0 | 0 | 0 | 0 | 1,783 |
| | | Stanwood | 0 | 0 | 0 | 0 | 6,340 |
| | | Steilacoom | 0 | 0 | 0 | 0 | 6,061 |
| | | Sultan | 0 | 0 | 0 | 0 | 4,334 |
| | | Sumas | 0 | 0 | 0 | 0 | 1,265 |
| | | Sumner | 0 | 0 | 0 | 0 | 9,832 |
| | | Sunnyside | 0 | 0 | 0 | 0 | 15,040 |
| | | Tenino | 0 | 0 | 0 | 0 | 2,241 |
| | | Tieton | 0 | 0 | 0 | 0 | 1,161 |
| | | Toledo | 0 | 0 | 0 | 0 | 681 |
| | | Tonasket | 0 | 0 | 0 | 0 | 942 |
| | | Toppenish | 0 | 0 | 0 | 0 | 9,185 |
| | | Tumwater | 0 | 0 | 0 | 0 | 14,235 |
| | | Twisp | 0 | 0 | 0 | 0 | 896 |
| | | Union Gap | 0 | 0 | 0 | 0 | 5,707 |
| | | University Place | 0 | 0 | 0 | 0 | 30,385 |
| | | Wapato | 0 | 0 | 0 | 0 | 4,537 |
| | | Washougal | 0 | 0 | 0 | 0 | 14,182 |
| | | Wenatchee | 0 | 0 | 0 | 0 | 30,051 |
| | | Westport | 0 | 0 | 0 | 0 | 2,631 |
| | | West Richland | 0 | 0 | 0 | 0 | 11,162 |
| | | White Salmon | 0 | 0 | 0 | 0 | 2,434 |
| | | Wilbur | 0 | 0 | 0 | | 874 |
| | | Winlock | 0 | 0 | 0 | 0 | 1,254 |
| | | Woodinville | 0 | 0 | 0 | 0 | 11,417 |
| | | Woodland | 0 | 0 | 0 | 0 | 4,952 |
| | | Woodway | 0 | 0 | 0 | 0 | 1,157 |
| | | Yarrow Point | 0 | 0 | 0 | 0 | 1,081 |
| | | Yelm | 0 | 0 | 0 | 0 | 6,182 |
| | | Zillah | 0 | | 0 | 0 | 2,735 |
| | Universities and Colleges | Central Washington University | 0 | 0 | 0 | 0 | 10,662 |
| | | University of Washington | 0 | | | | 39,675 |
| | | Washington State University, Vancouver[3] | 0 | 0 | 0 | 0 | |
| | | Western Washington University | 0 | 0 | 0 | 0 | 14,620 |
| | Metropolitan Counties | Asotin | 0 | 0 | 0 | 0 | |
| | | Benton | 0 | 0 | 0 | 0 | |
| | | Chelan | 0 | 0 | 0 | 0 | |
| | | Cowlitz | 0 | 0 | 0 | 0 | |
| | | Douglas | 0 | 0 | 0 | 0 | |
| | | Franklin | 0 | 0 | 0 | 0 | |
| | | Skagit | 0 | 0 | 0 | 0 | |
| | | Skamania | 0 | 0 | 0 | 0 | |
| | | Whatcom | 0 | 0 | 0 | 0 | |
| | | Yakima | 0 | 0 | 0 | 0 | |
| | Nonmetropolitan Counties | Adams | 0 | 0 | 0 | 0 | |
| | | Clallam | 0 | 0 | 0 | 0 | |
| | | Columbia | 0 | 0 | 0 | 0 | |
| | | Ferry | 0 | 0 | 0 | 0 | |
| | | Grant | 0 | 0 | 0 | 0 | |
| | | Island | 0 | 0 | 0 | 0 | |
| | | Jefferson | 0 | 0 | 0 | 0 | |
| | | Kittitas | 0 | 0 | 0 | 0 | |
| | | Klickitat | 0 | 0 | 0 | 0 | |
| | | Lewis | 0 | 0 | 0 | 0 | |
| | | Lincoln | 0 | 0 | 0 | 0 | |
| | | Mason | 0 | 0 | | 0 | |
| | | Okanogan | 0 | | 0 | 0 | |
| | | Pacific | 0 | 0 | 0 | 0 | |
| | | Pend Oreille | 0 | 0 | 0 | 0 | |
| | | San Juan | 0 | 0 | 0 | 0 | |
| | | Stevens | 0 | 0 | 0 | 0 | |
| | | Wahkiakum | 0 | 0 | 0 | 0 | |
| | | Whitman | 0 | 0 | 0 | 0 | |
| | Tribal Agencies | Chehalis Tribal | 0 | 0 | 0 | 0 | |
| | | Colville Tribal | 0 | 0 | 0 | 0 | |
| | | Kalispel Tribal | 0 | 0 | 0 | 0 | |
| | | Lummi Tribal | 0 | 0 | 0 | 0 | |
| | | Nisqually Tribal | 0 | | | | |
| | | Nooksack Tribal | 0 | 0 | 0 | | |
| | | Puyallup Tribal | 0 | 0 | 0 | 0 | |
| | | Skokomish Tribal | 0 | 0 | 0 | 0 | |
| | | Spokane Tribal | 0 | 0 | 0 | 0 | |
| | | Swinomish Tribal | 0 | 0 | 0 | 0 | |
| | | Yakima Tribal | 0 | 0 | 0 | 0 | |
| | Other Agencies | Port of Seattle | 0 | 0 | | 0 | |
| | | State Insurance Commissioner, Special Investigations Unit | 0 | 0 | 0 | 0 | |
| WEST VIRGINIA ..... | Cities | Barboursville | 0 | 0 | 0 | 0 | 3,428 |
| | | Beckley | 0 | 0 | 0 | 0 | 16,777 |
| | | Belington | | | | 0 | 1,798 |
| | | Benwood | 0 | 0 | 0 | 0 | 1,416 |
| | | Bethany | 0 | | | | 968 |
| | | Bethlehem | 0 | 0 | 0 | 0 | 2,470 |
| | | Bluefield | 0 | 0 | 0 | 0 | 11,056 |
| | | Bridgeport | 0 | 0 | 0 | 0 | 7,982 |
| | | Cameron | 0 | 0 | 0 | 0 | 1,064 |
| | | Capon Bridge | 0 | | | | 279 |
| | | Ceredo | 0 | 0 | 0 | 0 | 1,575 |
| | | Chapmanville | 0 | 0 | 0 | 0 | 1,108 |
| | | Charleston | 0 | 0 | 0 | 0 | 49,976 |
| | | Charles Town | 0 | 0 | 0 | 0 | 5,005 |
| | | Chesapeake | 0 | | | | 1,532 |
| | | Clearview | 0 | 0 | 0 | 0 | 544 |
| | | Danville | 0 | | | | 531 |
| | | Dunbar | 0 | 0 | 0 | 0 | 7,614 |
| | | East Bank | | | | 0 | 883 |
| | | Elkins | 0 | 0 | 0 | 0 | 6,972 |
| | | Fairview | 0 | 0 | 0 | | 441 |
| | | Follansbee | 0 | 0 | 0 | 0 | 2,829 |
| | | Fort Gay | | | 0 | | 793 |
| | | Gauley Bridge | 0 | | | | 685 |
| | | Glen Dale | 0 | 0 | 0 | 0 | 1,380 |

[1]Agencies published in this table indicated that no hate crimes occurred in their jurisdictions during the quarter(s) for which they submitted reports to the Hate Crime Statistics Program. Blanks indicate quarters for which agencies did not submit reports.

[2]Population figures are published only for the cities. The figures listed for the universities and colleges are student enrollment and were provided by the United States Department of Education for the 2008 school year, the most recent available. The enrollment figures include full-time and part-time students.

[3]Student enrollment figures were not available.

## Table 95. Hate Crime Zero Data Submitted per Quarter, by State and Agency, 2009—*Continued*

(Number.)

| State | Agency type | Agency name | Zero data per quarter[1] 1st quarter | 2nd quarter | 3rd quarter | 4th quarter | Population[2] |
|---|---|---|---|---|---|---|---|
| **WASHING-TON** | | Glenville | 0 | 0 | 0 | 0 | 1,447 |
| | | Grafton | 0 | 0 | 0 | 0 | 5,297 |
| | | Granville | 0 | 0 | 0 | 0 | 816 |
| | | Hamlin | 0 | 0 | 0 | 0 | 1,100 |
| | | Harpers Ferry/ Bolivar | 0 | 0 | 0 | 0 | 1,369 |
| | | Harrisville | | 0 | 0 | 0 | 1,814 |
| | | Hinton | 0 | 0 | 0 | 0 | 2,498 |
| | | Hurricane | 0 | 0 | 0 | 0 | 6,435 |
| | | Kenova | 0 | 0 | 0 | 0 | 3,245 |
| | | Kermit | 0 | 0 | 0 | | 218 |
| | | Keyser | 0 | 0 | 0 | 0 | 5,217 |
| | | Kingwood | 0 | 0 | 0 | 0 | 2,949 |
| | | Lewisburg | 0 | 0 | 0 | 0 | 3,524 |
| | | Logan | 0 | 0 | 0 | 0 | 1,488 |
| | | Lumberport | 0 | | 0 | 0 | 970 |
| | | Mannington | 0 | 0 | 0 | | 2,075 |
| | | Marmet | 0 | 0 | 0 | 0 | 1,596 |
| | | Matewan | 0 | 0 | 0 | | 477 |
| | | Matoaka | 0 | 0 | 0 | 0 | 304 |
| | | Milton | | 0 | 0 | 0 | 2,420 |
| | | Monongah | 0 | 0 | 0 | 0 | 908 |
| | | Montgomery | 0 | 0 | 0 | 0 | 1,920 |
| | | Moorefield | 0 | 0 | 0 | 0 | 2,444 |
| | | Mullens | 0 | 0 | 0 | 0 | 1,565 |
| | | New Haven | 0 | 0 | 0 | 0 | 1,525 |
| | | Nitro | 0 | 0 | 0 | 0 | 6,770 |
| | | Northfork | 0 | 0 | 0 | | 411 |
| | | Nutter Fort | 0 | 0 | 0 | 0 | 1,628 |
| | | Oak Hill | 0 | 0 | 0 | 0 | 7,172 |
| | | Oceana | 0 | 0 | 0 | 0 | 1,397 |
| | | Paden City | 0 | 0 | 0 | 0 | 2,572 |
| | | Parkersburg | 0 | 0 | 0 | 0 | 31,419 |
| | | Paw Paw | 0 | 0 | 0 | | 485 |
| | | Philippi | 0 | 0 | 0 | 0 | 2,774 |
| | | Point Pleasant | 0 | 0 | 0 | 0 | 4,432 |
| | | Princeton | 0 | 0 | 0 | 0 | 6,248 |
| | | Ranson | 0 | 0 | 0 | 0 | 4,838 |
| | | Ravenswood | 0 | 0 | 0 | 0 | 3,925 |
| | | Ripley | 0 | 0 | 0 | 0 | 3,239 |
| | | Rivesville | 0 | 0 | 0 | | 905 |
| | | Ronceverte | 0 | 0 | 0 | 0 | 1,598 |
| | | Salem | 0 | 0 | 0 | 0 | 2,046 |
| | | Shepherdstown | 0 | 0 | 0 | 0 | 1,140 |
| | | Shinnston | 0 | 0 | 0 | 0 | 2,238 |
| | | Spencer | 0 | 0 | 0 | 0 | 2,136 |
| | | St. Albans | 0 | 0 | 0 | 0 | 10,938 |
| | | Stonewood | 0 | | 0 | 0 | 1,843 |
| | | Summersville | 0 | 0 | 0 | 0 | 3,305 |
| | | Vienna | 0 | 0 | 0 | 0 | 10,509 |
| | | Wardensville | 0 | 0 | 0 | 0 | 259 |
| | | Wayne | 0 | 0 | 0 | | 1,117 |
| | | Wellsburg | 0 | 0 | 0 | 0 | 2,561 |
| | | West Logan | 0 | 0 | 0 | 0 | 386 |
| | | Weston | 0 | 0 | 0 | 0 | 4,261 |
| | | Westover | 0 | 0 | | | 4,105 |
| | | West Union | 0 | 0 | 0 | 0 | 774 |
| | | White Sulphur Springs | 0 | 0 | 0 | 0 | 2,275 |
| | | Williamson | 0 | 0 | 0 | 0 | 3,018 |
| | | Williamstown | 0 | 0 | 0 | 0 | 2,981 |
| | | Winfield | 0 | 0 | | | 2,072 |
| | **Universities and Colleges** | Concord University | 0 | 0 | 0 | 0 | 2,812 |
| | | Fairmont State University | 0 | 0 | 0 | 0 | 4,547 |
| | | Potomac State College | 0 | 0 | 0 | 0 | 1,582 |
| | | Shepherd University | 0 | 0 | 0 | 0 | 4,185 |
| | | West Virginia State University | 0 | 0 | 0 | 0 | 3,003 |

| State | Agency type | Agency name | Zero data per quarter[1] 1st quarter | 2nd quarter | 3rd quarter | 4th quarter | Population[2] |
|---|---|---|---|---|---|---|---|
| | | West Virginia Tech | 0 | 0 | 0 | 0 | 1,224 |
| | | West Virginia University | 0 | 0 | 0 | 0 | 28,840 |
| | **Metropolitan Counties** | Boone | 0 | 0 | 0 | 0 | |
| | | Brooke | 0 | 0 | 0 | 0 | |
| | | Cabell | 0 | 0 | 0 | 0 | |
| | | Hampshire | 0 | 0 | 0 | 0 | |
| | | Hancock | 0 | 0 | 0 | 0 | |
| | | Marshall | 0 | 0 | 0 | 0 | |
| | | Mineral | 0 | 0 | 0 | 0 | |
| | | Morgan | 0 | 0 | 0 | 0 | |
| | | Ohio | 0 | 0 | 0 | 0 | |
| | | Pleasants | 0 | 0 | 0 | 0 | |
| | | Preston | 0 | 0 | 0 | 0 | |
| | | Putnam | 0 | 0 | 0 | 0 | |
| | | Wayne | 0 | 0 | 0 | 0 | |
| | | Wirt | 0 | 0 | 0 | 0 | |
| | | Wood | 0 | 0 | 0 | 0 | |
| | **Nonmetropolitan Counties** | Barbour | 0 | 0 | 0 | 0 | |
| | | Braxton | 0 | 0 | 0 | 0 | |
| | | Fayette | 0 | 0 | 0 | 0 | |
| | | Gilmer | 0 | 0 | 0 | 0 | |
| | | Grant | 0 | 0 | 0 | 0 | |
| | | Greenbrier | 0 | 0 | 0 | 0 | |
| | | Hardy | 0 | 0 | 0 | 0 | |
| | | Harrison | 0 | 0 | 0 | 0 | |
| | | Jackson | 0 | 0 | 0 | 0 | |
| | | Lewis | 0 | 0 | 0 | 0 | |
| | | Logan | 0 | 0 | 0 | 0 | |
| | | Marion | 0 | 0 | 0 | 0 | |
| | | Mason | 0 | 0 | 0 | 0 | |
| | | McDowell | 0 | 0 | 0 | 0 | |
| | | Mercer | 0 | 0 | 0 | 0 | |
| | | Mingo | 0 | 0 | 0 | 0 | |
| | | Monroe | 0 | 0 | 0 | 0 | |
| | | Nicholas | 0 | 0 | 0 | 0 | |
| | | Pocahontas | 0 | 0 | | | |
| | | Raleigh | 0 | 0 | 0 | 0 | |
| | | Randolph | 0 | 0 | 0 | 0 | |
| | | Ritchie | 0 | 0 | 0 | 0 | |
| | | Roane | 0 | | | | |
| | | Taylor | 0 | | | | |
| | | Tucker | 0 | 0 | | | |
| | | Tyler | 0 | 0 | 0 | 0 | |
| | | Wyoming | 0 | 0 | 0 | 0 | |
| | **State Police Agencies** | State Police: Beckley | 0 | 0 | 0 | 0 | |
| | | Berkeley Springs | 0 | 0 | 0 | 0 | |
| | | Bridgeport | 0 | 0 | 0 | 0 | |
| | | Buckeye | 0 | 0 | 0 | 0 | |
| | | Buckhannon | 0 | 0 | 0 | 0 | |
| | | Clay | 0 | 0 | 0 | 0 | |
| | | Danville | 0 | 0 | 0 | 0 | |
| | | Elizabeth | 0 | 0 | 0 | 0 | |
| | | Elkins | 0 | 0 | 0 | 0 | |
| | | Fairmont | 0 | 0 | 0 | 0 | |
| | | Franklin | 0 | 0 | 0 | 0 | |
| | | Gauley Bridge | 0 | 0 | 0 | 0 | |
| | | Gilbert | 0 | 0 | 0 | 0 | |
| | | Glenville | 0 | 0 | 0 | 0 | |
| | | Grafton | 0 | 0 | 0 | 0 | |
| | | Grantsville | 0 | 0 | 0 | 0 | |
| | | Hamlin | 0 | 0 | 0 | 0 | |
| | | Harrisville | 0 | 0 | 0 | 0 | |
| | | Hinton | 0 | 0 | 0 | 0 | |
| | | Hundred | 0 | 0 | 0 | 0 | |
| | | Huntington | 0 | 0 | 0 | 0 | |
| | | Jesse | 0 | 0 | 0 | 0 | |

[1]Agencies published in this table indicated that no hate crimes occurred in their jurisdictions during the quarter(s) for which they submitted reports to the Hate Crime Statistics Program. Blanks indicate quarters for which agencies did not submit reports.

[2]Population figures are published only for the cities. The figures listed for the universities and colleges are student enrollment and were provided by the United States Department of Education for the 2008 school year, the most recent available. The enrollment figures include full-time and part-time students.

## Table 95. Hate Crime Zero Data Submitted per Quarter, by State and Agency, 2009—*Continued*

(Number.)

| State | Agency type | Agency name | Zero data per quarter[1] 1st quarter | 2nd quarter | 3rd quarter | 4th quarter | Population[2] |
|---|---|---|---|---|---|---|---|
| **WASHINGTON** | | Kearneysville | 0 | 0 | 0 | 0 | |
| | | Keyser | 0 | 0 | 0 | 0 | |
| | | Kingwood | 0 | 0 | 0 | 0 | |
| | | Lewisburg | 0 | 0 | 0 | 0 | |
| | | Logan | 0 | 0 | 0 | 0 | |
| | | Martinsburg | 0 | 0 | 0 | 0 | |
| | | Moorefield | 0 | 0 | 0 | 0 | |
| | | Morgantown | 0 | 0 | 0 | 0 | |
| | | Moundsville | 0 | 0 | 0 | 0 | |
| | | New Cumberland | 0 | 0 | 0 | 0 | |
| | | Oak Hill | 0 | 0 | 0 | 0 | |
| | | Paden City | 0 | 0 | 0 | 0 | |
| | | Parkersburg | 0 | 0 | 0 | 0 | |
| | | Parsons | 0 | 0 | 0 | 0 | |
| | | Petersburg | 0 | 0 | 0 | 0 | |
| | | Philippi | 0 | 0 | 0 | 0 | |
| | | Point Pleasant | 0 | 0 | 0 | 0 | |
| | | Princeton | 0 | 0 | 0 | 0 | |
| | | Quincy | 0 | 0 | 0 | 0 | |
| | | Rainelle | 0 | 0 | 0 | 0 | |
| | | Richwood | 0 | 0 | 0 | 0 | |
| | | Ripley | 0 | 0 | 0 | 0 | |
| | | Romney | 0 | 0 | 0 | 0 | |
| | | South Charleston | 0 | 0 | 0 | 0 | |
| | | Spencer | 0 | 0 | 0 | 0 | |
| | | St. Marys | 0 | 0 | 0 | 0 | |
| | | Summersville | 0 | 0 | 0 | 0 | |
| | | Sutton | 0 | 0 | 0 | 0 | |
| | | Union | 0 | 0 | 0 | 0 | |
| | | Upperglade | 0 | 0 | 0 | 0 | |
| | | Wayne | 0 | 0 | 0 | 0 | |
| | | Welch | 0 | 0 | 0 | 0 | |
| | | Wellsburg | 0 | 0 | 0 | 0 | |
| | | Weston | 0 | 0 | 0 | 0 | |
| | | West Union | 0 | 0 | 0 | 0 | |
| | | Wheeling | 0 | 0 | 0 | 0 | |
| | | Whitesville | 0 | 0 | 0 | 0 | |
| | | Williamson | 0 | 0 | 0 | 0 | |
| | | Winfield | 0 | 0 | 0 | 0 | |
| | | State Police, Bureau of Criminal Investigation: | | | | | |
| | | Beckley | 0 | 0 | 0 | 0 | |
| | | Bluefield | 0 | 0 | 0 | 0 | |
| | | Buckhannon | 0 | 0 | 0 | 0 | |
| | | Charleston | 0 | 0 | 0 | 0 | |
| | | Fairmont | 0 | 0 | 0 | 0 | |
| | | Martinsburg | 0 | 0 | | | |
| | | State Police, Parkway Authority: | | | | | |
| | | Fayette County | 0 | 0 | 0 | 0 | |
| | | Kanawha County | 0 | 0 | 0 | 0 | |
| | | Mercer County | 0 | 0 | 0 | 0 | |
| | | Raleigh County | 0 | 0 | 0 | 0 | |
| | **Other Agencies** | Central West Virginia Drug Task Force | | | 0 | | |
| | | Division of Natural Resources: | | | | | |
| | | Barbour County | 0 | 0 | 0 | 0 | |
| | | Berkeley County | 0 | 0 | 0 | 0 | |
| | | Boone County | 0 | 0 | 0 | 0 | |
| | | Braxton County | 0 | 0 | 0 | 0 | |
| | | Brooke County | 0 | 0 | 0 | 0 | |
| | | Cabell County | 0 | 0 | 0 | 0 | |
| | | Calhoun County | 0 | 0 | 0 | 0 | |
| | | Clay County | 0 | 0 | 0 | 0 | |
| | | Doddridge County | | | | 0 | |
| | | Fayette County | 0 | 0 | 0 | 0 | |
| | | Gilmer County | 0 | 0 | 0 | 0 | |
| | | Grant County | 0 | 0 | 0 | 0 | |
| | | Greenbrier County | 0 | 0 | 0 | 0 | |
| | | Hampshire County | 0 | 0 | 0 | 0 | |
| | | Hancock County | 0 | 0 | 0 | 0 | |
| | | Hardy County | 0 | 0 | 0 | 0 | |
| | | Harrison County | 0 | 0 | 0 | 0 | |
| | | Jackson County | 0 | 0 | 0 | 0 | |
| | | Jefferson County | 0 | 0 | 0 | 0 | |
| | | Kanawha County | 0 | 0 | 0 | 0 | |
| | | Lewis County | 0 | 0 | 0 | 0 | |
| | | Lincoln County | 0 | 0 | 0 | 0 | |
| | | Logan County | 0 | 0 | 0 | 0 | |
| | | Marion County | 0 | 0 | 0 | 0 | |
| | | Marshall County | 0 | 0 | 0 | 0 | |
| | | Mason County | 0 | 0 | 0 | 0 | |
| | | McDowell County | 0 | 0 | 0 | 0 | |
| | | Mercer County | 0 | 0 | 0 | 0 | |
| | | Mineral County | 0 | 0 | 0 | 0 | |
| | | Mingo County | 0 | 0 | 0 | 0 | |
| | | Monongalia County | 0 | 0 | 0 | 0 | |
| | | Monroe County | 0 | 0 | 0 | 0 | |
| | | Morgan County | 0 | 0 | 0 | 0 | |
| | | Nicholas County | 0 | 0 | 0 | 0 | |
| | | Ohio County | 0 | 0 | 0 | 0 | |
| | | Pendleton County | 0 | 0 | 0 | 0 | |
| | | Pleasants County | 0 | 0 | 0 | 0 | |
| | | Pocahontas County | 0 | 0 | 0 | 0 | |
| | | Preston County | 0 | 0 | 0 | 0 | |
| | | Putnam County | 0 | 0 | 0 | 0 | |
| | | Raleigh County | 0 | 0 | 0 | 0 | |
| | | Randolph County | 0 | 0 | 0 | 0 | |
| | | Ritchie County | 0 | 0 | 0 | 0 | |
| | | Roane County | 0 | 0 | 0 | 0 | |
| | | Summers County | 0 | 0 | 0 | 0 | |
| | | Taylor County | 0 | 0 | 0 | 0 | |
| | | Tucker County | 0 | 0 | 0 | 0 | |
| | | Upshur County | 0 | 0 | 0 | 0 | |
| | | Wayne County | 0 | 0 | 0 | 0 | |
| | | Webster County | 0 | 0 | 0 | 0 | |
| | | Wetzel County | 0 | 0 | 0 | 0 | |
| | | Wirt County | 0 | 0 | 0 | 0 | |
| | | Wood County | 0 | 0 | 0 | 0 | |
| | | Wyoming County | 0 | 0 | 0 | 0 | |
| | | Eastern Panhandle Drug and Violent Crime Task Force | 0 | 0 | 0 | 0 | |
| | | Greenbrier County Drug and Violent Crime Task Force | 0 | 0 | 0 | 0 | |

[1]Agencies published in this table indicated that no hate crimes occurred in their jurisdictions during the quarter(s) for which they submitted reports to the Hate Crime Statistics Program. Blanks indicate quarters for which agencies did not submit reports.

[2]Population figures are published only for the cities. The figures listed for the universities and colleges are student enrollment and were provided by the United States Department of Education for the 2008 school year, the most recent available. The enrollment figures include full-time and part-time students.

# Table 95. Hate Crime Zero Data Submitted per Quarter, by State and Agency, 2009—*Continued*

(Number.)

| State | Agency type | Agency name | Zero data per quarter[1] | | | | Population[2] |
|---|---|---|---|---|---|---|---|
| | | | 1st quarter | 2nd quarter | 3rd quarter | 4th quarter | |
| WASHINGTON | | Hancock-Brooke-Weirton Drug Task Force | 0 | 0 | 0 | 0 | |
| | | Harrison County Drug and Violent Crime Task Force | 0 | 0 | 0 | 0 | |
| | | Huntington Drug and Violent Crime Task Force | 0 | 0 | 0 | 0 | |
| | | Kanawha County Parks and Recreation | | | | 0 | |
| | | Logan County Drug and Violent Crime Task Force | | 0 | 0 | 0 | |
| | | Metropolitan Drug Enforcement Network Team | 0 | 0 | 0 | 0 | |
| | | Mon Valley Drug Task Force | 0 | 0 | 0 | 0 | |
| | | Ohio Valley Drug and Violent Crime Task Force | 0 | 0 | 0 | 0 | |
| | | Parkersburg Narcotics and Violent Crime Task Force | 0 | 0 | 0 | 0 | |
| | | Potomac Highlands Drug and Violent Crime Task Force | 0 | 0 | 0 | 0 | |
| | | Three Rivers Drug and Violent Crime Task Force | 0 | 0 | 0 | 0 | |
| | | Tri-Lateral Drug Enforcement Network Team | 0 | | | | |
| WISCONSIN .. | Cities | Adams | 0 | 0 | 0 | 0 | 1,734 |
| | | Albany | 0 | 0 | 0 | 0 | 1,108 |
| | | Algoma | 0 | 0 | 0 | 0 | 3,091 |
| | | Altoona | 0 | 0 | 0 | 0 | 6,759 |
| | | Amery | 0 | 0 | 0 | 0 | 2,770 |
| | | Antigo | 0 | 0 | 0 | 0 | 7,849 |
| | | Arcadia | 0 | 0 | 0 | 0 | 2,312 |
| | | Ashland | 0 | 0 | 0 | 0 | 8,066 |
| | | Ashwaubenon | 0 | 0 | 0 | 0 | 17,197 |
| | | Athens | 0 | 0 | 0 | 0 | 1,029 |
| | | Avoca | 0 | 0 | 0 | 0 | 563 |
| | | Bangor | 0 | 0 | 0 | 0 | 1,405 |
| | | Baraboo | 0 | 0 | 0 | 0 | 11,302 |
| | | Barron | 0 | 0 | 0 | 0 | 3,104 |
| | | Bayfield | 0 | 0 | 0 | 0 | 566 |
| | | Beaver Dam | 0 | 0 | 0 | 0 | 15,116 |
| | | Belleville | 0 | 0 | 0 | 0 | 2,306 |
| | | Beloit | 0 | 0 | 0 | 0 | 36,197 |
| | | Beloit Town | 0 | 0 | 0 | 0 | 7,555 |
| | | Berlin | 0 | 0 | 0 | 0 | 4,965 |
| | | Big Bend | 0 | 0 | 0 | 0 | 1,334 |
| | | Black River Falls | 0 | 0 | 0 | 0 | 3,382 |
| | | Blair | 0 | 0 | 0 | 0 | 1,243 |
| | | Bloomer | 0 | 0 | 0 | 0 | 3,294 |
| | | Bloomfield | 0 | 0 | 0 | 0 | 5,087 |
| | | Boscobel | 0 | 0 | 0 | 0 | 3,198 |
| | | Brillion | 0 | 0 | 0 | 0 | 2,857 |
| | | Brodhead | 0 | 0 | 0 | 0 | 3,118 |
| | | Brookfield | 0 | 0 | 0 | 0 | 39,049 |
| | | Brookfield Township | 0 | 0 | 0 | 0 | 6,154 |
| | | Brown Deer | 0 | 0 | 0 | 0 | 11,671 |
| | | Burlington | 0 | 0 | 0 | 0 | 11,030 |
| | | Burlington Town | 0 | 0 | 0 | 0 | 6,671 |
| | | Butler | 0 | 0 | 0 | 0 | 1,759 |
| | | Caledonia | 0 | 0 | 0 | 0 | 24,291 |
| | | Campbellsport | 0 | 0 | 0 | 0 | 1,943 |
| | | Campbell Township | 0 | 0 | 0 | 0 | 4,551 |
| | | Cashton | 0 | 0 | 0 | 0 | 1,060 |
| | | Cedarburg | 0 | 0 | 0 | 0 | 11,092 |
| | | Chenequa | 0 | 0 | 0 | 0 | 591 |
| | | Chetek | 0 | 0 | 0 | 0 | 2,135 |
| | | Chilton | 0 | 0 | 0 | 0 | 3,563 |
| | | Chippewa Falls | 0 | 0 | 0 | 0 | 12,897 |
| | | Cleveland | 0 | 0 | 0 | 0 | 1,408 |
| | | Clinton | 0 | 0 | 0 | 0 | 3,298 |
| | | Clintonville | 0 | 0 | 0 | 0 | 4,235 |
| | | Colby-Abbotsford | 0 | 0 | 0 | 0 | 3,540 |
| | | Columbus | 0 | 0 | 0 | 0 | 5,162 |
| | | Combined Locks | 0 | 0 | 0 | 0 | 3,348 |
| | | Coon Valley | 0 | 0 | 0 | 0 | 747 |
| | | Cornell | 0 | 0 | 0 | 0 | 1,377 |
| | | Cottage Grove | 0 | 0 | 0 | 0 | 6,445 |
| | | Crandon | 0 | 0 | 0 | 0 | 1,801 |
| | | Cross Plains | 0 | 0 | 0 | 0 | 3,603 |
| | | Cuba City | 0 | 0 | 0 | 0 | 2,035 |
| | | Cudahy | 0 | 0 | 0 | 0 | 18,856 |
| | | Cumberland | 0 | 0 | 0 | 0 | 2,231 |
| | | Dane | 0 | 0 | 0 | 0 | 1,026 |
| | | Darien | 0 | 0 | 0 | 0 | 1,708 |
| | | Darlington | 0 | 0 | 0 | 0 | 2,191 |
| | | DeForest | 0 | 0 | 0 | 0 | 9,006 |
| | | Delafield | 0 | 0 | 0 | 0 | 6,821 |
| | | Delavan | 0 | 0 | 0 | 0 | 8,555 |
| | | Delavan Town | 0 | 0 | 0 | 0 | 4,521 |
| | | Denmark | 0 | 0 | 0 | 0 | 2,138 |
| | | De Pere | 0 | 0 | 0 | 0 | 25,288 |
| | | Dodgeville | 0 | 0 | 0 | 0 | 5,063 |
| | | Durand | 0 | 0 | 0 | 0 | 1,847 |
| | | Eagle River | 0 | 0 | 0 | 0 | 1,754 |
| | | Eagle Village | 0 | 0 | 0 | 0 | 1,836 |
| | | East Troy | 0 | 0 | 0 | 0 | 4,591 |
| | | Eau Claire | 0 | 0 | 0 | 0 | 65,802 |
| | | Edgar | 0 | 0 | 0 | 0 | 1,339 |
| | | Edgerton | 0 | 0 | 0 | 0 | 5,374 |
| | | Eleva | 0 | 0 | 0 | 0 | 637 |
| | | Elkhart Lake | 0 | 0 | 0 | 0 | 1,186 |
| | | Elkhorn | 0 | 0 | 0 | 0 | 9,480 |
| | | Elk Mound | 0 | 0 | 0 | 0 | 814 |
| | | Ellsworth | 0 | 0 | 0 | 0 | 3,119 |
| | | Elm Grove | 0 | 0 | 0 | 0 | 6,118 |
| | | Elroy | 0 | 0 | 0 | 0 | 1,471 |
| | | Evansville | 0 | 0 | 0 | 0 | 5,061 |
| | | Fall Creek | 0 | 0 | 0 | 0 | 1,280 |
| | | Fennimore | 0 | 0 | 0 | 0 | 2,306 |
| | | Fitchburg | 0 | 0 | 0 | 0 | 23,668 |
| | | Fontana | 0 | 0 | 0 | 0 | 1,957 |
| | | Fort Atkinson | 0 | 0 | 0 | 0 | 11,923 |
| | | Fountain City | 0 | 0 | 0 | 0 | 993 |
| | | Fox Lake | 0 | 0 | 0 | 0 | 1,461 |
| | | Fox Point | 0 | 0 | 0 | 0 | 6,797 |
| | | Fox Valley Metro | 0 | 0 | 0 | 0 | 17,428 |
| | | Franklin | 0 | 0 | 0 | 0 | 36,217 |
| | | Frederic | 0 | 0 | 0 | 0 | 1,190 |
| | | Freedom | 0 | 0 | 0 | 0 | 5,994 |
| | | Geneva Town | 0 | 0 | 0 | 0 | 4,174 |

[1]Agencies published in this table indicated that no hate crimes occurred in their jurisdictions during the quarter(s) for which they submitted reports to the Hate Crime Statistics Program. Blanks indicate quarters for which agencies did not submit reports.
[2]Population figures are published only for the cities. The figures listed for the universities and colleges are student enrollment and were provided by the United States Department of Education for the 2008 school year, the most recent available. The enrollment figures include full-time and part-time students.

## Table 95. Hate Crime Zero Data Submitted per Quarter, by State and Agency, 2009—*Continued*

(Number.)

| State | Agency type | Agency name | Zero data per quarter[1] | | | | Population[2] |
|---|---|---|---|---|---|---|---|
| | | | 1st quarter | 2nd quarter | 3rd quarter | 4th quarter | |
| **WISCONSIN** | | Genoa City | 0 | 0 | 0 | 0 | 2,994 |
| | | Germantown | 0 | 0 | 0 | 0 | 19,740 |
| | | Glendale | 0 | 0 | 0 | 0 | 12,956 |
| | | Grafton | 0 | 0 | 0 | 0 | 11,728 |
| | | Grand Chute | 0 | 0 | 0 | 0 | 21,079 |
| | | Grand Rapids | 0 | 0 | 0 | 0 | 7,347 |
| | | Grantsburg | 0 | 0 | 0 | 0 | 1,354 |
| | | Green Bay | 0 | 0 | 0 | 0 | 100,836 |
| | | Greendale | 0 | 0 | 0 | 0 | 13,937 |
| | | Greenfield | 0 | 0 | 0 | 0 | 36,148 |
| | | Green Lake | 0 | 0 | 0 | 0 | 1,092 |
| | | Hales Corners | 0 | 0 | 0 | 0 | 7,556 |
| | | Hartford | 0 | 0 | 0 | 0 | 14,207 |
| | | Hartland | 0 | 0 | 0 | 0 | 8,774 |
| | | Hayward | 0 | 0 | 0 | 0 | 2,365 |
| | | Hazel Green | 0 | 0 | 0 | 0 | 1,176 |
| | | Highland | 0 | 0 | 0 | 0 | 795 |
| | | Hillsboro | 0 | 0 | 0 | 0 | 1,350 |
| | | Hobart-Lawrence | 0 | 0 | 0 | 0 | 9,229 |
| | | Holmen | 0 | 0 | 0 | 0 | 8,769 |
| | | Horicon | 0 | 0 | 0 | 0 | 3,466 |
| | | Hortonville | 0 | 0 | 0 | 0 | 2,777 |
| | | Hurley | 0 | 0 | 0 | 0 | 1,514 |
| | | Independence | 0 | 0 | 0 | 0 | 1,208 |
| | | Iron Ridge | 0 | 0 | 0 | 0 | 975 |
| | | Jackson | 0 | 0 | 0 | 0 | 6,978 |
| | | Jefferson | 0 | 0 | 0 | 0 | 7,874 |
| | | Juneau | 0 | 0 | 0 | 0 | 2,615 |
| | | Kaukauna | 0 | 0 | 0 | 0 | 15,695 |
| | | Kendall | 0 | 0 | 0 | 0 | 461 |
| | | Kenosha | 0 | 0 | 0 | 0 | 97,657 |
| | | Kewaskum | 0 | 0 | 0 | 0 | 3,999 |
| | | Kiel | 0 | 0 | 0 | 0 | 3,600 |
| | | Kohler | 0 | 0 | 0 | 0 | 1,951 |
| | | Kronenwetter | 0 | 0 | 0 | 0 | 7,118 |
| | | La Crosse | 0 | 0 | 0 | 0 | 50,791 |
| | | Ladysmith | 0 | 0 | 0 | 0 | 3,279 |
| | | Lake Delton | 0 | 0 | 0 | 0 | 3,311 |
| | | Lake Geneva | 0 | 0 | 0 | 0 | 8,437 |
| | | Lake Hallie | 0 | 0 | 0 | 0 | 4,455 |
| | | Lake Mills | 0 | 0 | 0 | 0 | 5,639 |
| | | Lancaster | 0 | 0 | 0 | 0 | 3,904 |
| | | Lodi | 0 | 0 | 0 | 0 | 3,021 |
| | | Lomira | 0 | 0 | 0 | 0 | 2,344 |
| | | Maple Bluff | 0 | 0 | 0 | 0 | 1,354 |
| | | Marathon City | 0 | 0 | 0 | 0 | 1,527 |
| | | Marinette | 0 | 0 | 0 | 0 | 10,699 |
| | | Marion | 0 | 0 | 0 | 0 | 1,163 |
| | | Markesan | 0 | 0 | 0 | 0 | 1,270 |
| | | Marshall Village | 0 | 0 | 0 | 0 | 3,778 |
| | | Marshfield | 0 | 0 | 0 | | 18,205 |
| | | Mauston | 0 | 0 | 0 | 0 | 4,491 |
| | | Mayville | 0 | 0 | 0 | 0 | 5,107 |
| | | McFarland | 0 | 0 | 0 | 0 | 7,923 |
| | | Medford | 0 | 0 | 0 | 0 | 4,085 |
| | | Menasha | 0 | 0 | 0 | 0 | 16,651 |
| | | Menomonee Falls | 0 | 0 | 0 | 0 | 34,822 |
| | | Menomonie | 0 | 0 | 0 | 0 | 15,652 |
| | | Mequon | 0 | 0 | 0 | 0 | 23,688 |
| | | Middleton | 0 | 0 | 0 | 0 | 16,284 |
| | | Milton | 0 | 0 | 0 | 0 | 5,629 |
| | | Mineral Point | 0 | 0 | 0 | 0 | 2,446 |
| | | Minocqua | 0 | 0 | 0 | 0 | 4,749 |
| | | Mishicot | 0 | 0 | 0 | 0 | 1,380 |
| | | Mondovi | 0 | 0 | 0 | 0 | 2,553 |
| | | Monona | 0 | 0 | 0 | 0 | 7,814 |
| | | Monroe | 0 | 0 | 0 | 0 | 10,442 |
| | | Montello | 0 | 0 | 0 | 0 | 1,466 |
| | | Mosinee | 0 | 0 | 0 | 0 | 3,962 |
| | | Mount Horeb | 0 | 0 | 0 | 0 | 6,799 |
| | | Mount Pleasant | 0 | 0 | 0 | 0 | 26,985 |
| | | Mukwonago | 0 | 0 | 0 | 0 | 7,341 |
| | | Muskego | 0 | 0 | 0 | 0 | 23,440 |
| | | Neenah | 0 | 0 | 0 | 0 | 25,105 |
| | | Neillsville | 0 | 0 | 0 | 0 | 2,576 |
| | | Neshkoro | 0 | 0 | 0 | 0 | 438 |
| | | New Berlin | 0 | 0 | 0 | 0 | 38,686 |
| | | New Glarus | 0 | 0 | 0 | 0 | 2,065 |
| | | New Holstein | 0 | 0 | 0 | 0 | 3,150 |
| | | New Lisbon | 0 | 0 | 0 | 0 | 2,553 |
| | | New London | 0 | 0 | 0 | 0 | 6,702 |
| | | New Richmond | 0 | 0 | 0 | 0 | 8,486 |
| | | Niagara | 0 | 0 | 0 | 0 | 1,720 |
| | | North Fond du Lac | 0 | 0 | 0 | 0 | 5,271 |
| | | North Hudson | 0 | 0 | 0 | 0 | 3,869 |
| | | North Prairie | 0 | 0 | 0 | 0 | 2,111 |
| | | Oak Creek | 0 | 0 | 0 | 0 | 34,069 |
| | | Oconomowoc | 0 | 0 | 0 | 0 | 14,359 |
| | | Oconomowoc Town | 0 | 0 | 0 | 0 | 8,251 |
| | | Oconto | 0 | 0 | 0 | 0 | 4,278 |
| | | Oconto Falls | 0 | 0 | 0 | 0 | 2,582 |
| | | Omro | 0 | 0 | 0 | 0 | 3,446 |
| | | Onalaska | 0 | 0 | 0 | 0 | 16,998 |
| | | Oregon | 0 | 0 | 0 | 0 | 9,594 |
| | | Osceola | 0 | 0 | 0 | 0 | 2,754 |
| | | Oshkosh | 0 | 0 | 0 | 0 | 63,700 |
| | | Osseo | 0 | 0 | 0 | 0 | 1,624 |
| | | Oxford | 0 | 0 | 0 | 0 | 942 |
| | | Palmyra | 0 | 0 | 0 | 0 | 1,745 |
| | | Park Falls | 0 | 0 | 0 | 0 | 2,210 |
| | | Pepin | 0 | 0 | 0 | 0 | 912 |
| | | Peshtigo | 0 | 0 | 0 | 0 | 3,200 |
| | | Pewaukee | 0 | 0 | 0 | 0 | 12,631 |
| | | Pewaukee Village | 0 | 0 | 0 | 0 | 8,874 |
| | | Phillips | 0 | 0 | 0 | 0 | 1,377 |
| | | Plainfield | 0 | 0 | 0 | 0 | 883 |
| | | Platteville | 0 | 0 | 0 | 0 | 10,330 |
| | | Pleasant Prairie | 0 | 0 | 0 | 0 | 20,297 |
| | | Plover | 0 | 0 | 0 | 0 | 11,852 |
| | | Plymouth | 0 | 0 | 0 | 0 | 8,276 |
| | | Portage | 0 | 0 | 0 | 0 | 9,939 |
| | | Port Washington | 0 | 0 | 0 | 0 | 11,247 |
| | | Poynette | 0 | 0 | 0 | 0 | 2,577 |
| | | Prairie du Chien | 0 | 0 | 0 | 0 | 5,820 |
| | | Prescott | 0 | 0 | 0 | 0 | 4,039 |
| | | Princeton | 0 | 0 | 0 | 0 | 1,388 |
| | | Pulaski | 0 | 0 | 0 | 0 | 3,602 |
| | | Racine | 0 | 0 | 0 | 0 | 82,232 |
| | | Readstown | 0 | 0 | 0 | 0 | 385 |
| | | Reedsburg | 0 | 0 | 0 | 0 | 8,758 |
| | | Rice Lake | 0 | 0 | 0 | 0 | 8,247 |
| | | Richland Center | 0 | 0 | 0 | 0 | 5,040 |
| | | Ripon | 0 | 0 | 0 | 0 | 7,392 |
| | | River Hills | 0 | 0 | 0 | 0 | 1,660 |
| | | Rome Town | 0 | 0 | 0 | 0 | 2,997 |
| | | Rosendale | 0 | 0 | 0 | 0 | 1,033 |
| | | Rothschild | 0 | 0 | 0 | 0 | 5,052 |
| | | Sauk Prairie | 0 | 0 | 0 | 0 | 4,050 |
| | | Saukville | 0 | 0 | 0 | 0 | 4,301 |
| | | Seymour | 0 | 0 | 0 | 0 | 3,490 |
| | | Shawano | 0 | 0 | 0 | 0 | 8,706 |
| | | Sheboygan | 0 | 0 | 0 | 0 | 47,578 |
| | | Sheboygan Falls | 0 | 0 | 0 | 0 | 8,025 |
| | | Shorewood | 0 | 0 | 0 | 0 | 13,173 |
| | | Shorewood Hills | 0 | 0 | 0 | 0 | 1,675 |
| | | Silver Lake | 0 | 0 | 0 | 0 | 2,543 |
| | | Siren | 0 | 0 | 0 | 0 | 998 |
| | | Slinger | 0 | 0 | 0 | 0 | 4,757 |
| | | Somerset | 0 | 0 | 0 | 0 | 2,836 |

[1]Agencies published in this table indicated that no hate crimes occurred in their jurisdictions during the quarter(s) for which they submitted reports to the Hate Crime Statistics Program. Blanks indicate quarters for which agencies did not submit reports.

[2]Population figures are published only for the cities. The figures listed for the universities and colleges are student enrollment and were provided by the United States Department of Education for the 2008 school year, the most recent available. The enrollment figures include full-time and part-time students.

## Table 95. Hate Crime Zero Data Submitted per Quarter, by State and Agency, 2009—*Continued*

(Number.)

| State | Agency type | Agency name | Zero data per quarter[1] 1st quarter | 2nd quarter | 3rd quarter | 4th quarter | Population[2] |
|---|---|---|---|---|---|---|---|
| WISCONSIN | | South Milwaukee | 0 | 0 | 0 | 0 | 21,122 |
| | | Sparta | 0 | 0 | 0 | 0 | 8,836 |
| | | Spencer | 0 | 0 | 0 | 0 | 1,792 |
| | | Spooner | 0 | 0 | 0 | 0 | 2,653 |
| | | Spring Green | 0 | 0 | 0 | 0 | 1,503 |
| | | Stanley | 0 | 0 | 0 | 0 | 3,567 |
| | | St. Croix Falls | 0 | 0 | 0 | 0 | 2,163 |
| | | Stevens Point | 0 | 0 | 0 | 0 | 25,320 |
| | | St. Francis | 0 | 0 | 0 | 0 | 9,862 |
| | | Stoughton | 0 | 0 | 0 | 0 | 13,013 |
| | | Strum | 0 | 0 | 0 | 0 | 1,022 |
| | | Sturgeon Bay | 0 | 0 | 0 | 0 | 8,721 |
| | | Sturtevant | 0 | 0 | 0 | 0 | 7,120 |
| | | Summit | 0 | 0 | 0 | 0 | 5,055 |
| | | Sun Prairie | 0 | 0 | 0 | 0 | 29,324 |
| | | Superior | 0 | 0 | 0 | 0 | 26,098 |
| | | Theresa | 0 | 0 | 0 | 0 | 1,249 |
| | | Thiensville | 0 | 0 | 0 | 0 | 3,013 |
| | | Three Lakes | 0 | 0 | 0 | 0 | 2,251 |
| | | Tomah | 0 | 0 | 0 | 0 | 8,692 |
| | | Tomahawk | 0 | 0 | 0 | 0 | 3,684 |
| | | Town of East Troy | 0 | 0 | 0 | 0 | 3,970 |
| | | Town of Madison | 0 | 0 | 0 | 0 | 6,309 |
| | | Town of Menasha | 0 | 0 | 0 | 0 | 16,005 |
| | | Trempealeau | 0 | 0 | 0 | 0 | 1,529 |
| | | Twin Lakes | 0 | 0 | 0 | 0 | 5,809 |
| | | Two Rivers | 0 | 0 | 0 | 0 | 11,716 |
| | | Valders | 0 | 0 | 0 | 0 | 973 |
| | | Verona | 0 | 0 | 0 | 0 | 12,056 |
| | | Viroqua | 0 | 0 | 0 | 0 | 4,437 |
| | | Walworth | 0 | 0 | 0 | 0 | 2,738 |
| | | Washburn | 0 | 0 | 0 | 0 | 2,155 |
| | | Waterloo | 0 | 0 | 0 | 0 | 3,273 |
| | | Waukesha | 0 | 0 | | 0 | 68,248 |
| | | Waunakee | 0 | 0 | 0 | 0 | 11,569 |
| | | Waupaca | 0 | 0 | 0 | 0 | 5,837 |
| | | Waupun | 0 | 0 | 0 | 0 | 10,441 |
| | | Wausau | | 0 | 0 | 0 | 37,459 |
| | | Wautoma | 0 | 0 | 0 | 0 | 2,122 |
| | | Wauwatosa | 0 | 0 | 0 | 0 | 44,777 |
| | | West Allis | 0 | 0 | 0 | 0 | 59,240 |
| | | West Bend | 0 | 0 | 0 | 0 | 30,070 |
| | | Westby | 0 | 0 | 0 | 0 | 2,188 |
| | | Westfield | 0 | 0 | 0 | 0 | 1,174 |
| | | West Milwaukee | 0 | 0 | 0 | 0 | 4,008 |
| | | West Salem | 0 | 0 | 0 | 0 | 4,829 |
| | | Whitefish Bay | 0 | 0 | 0 | 0 | 13,527 |
| | | Whitehall | 0 | 0 | 0 | 0 | 1,593 |
| | | Whitewater | 0 | 0 | 0 | 0 | 14,380 |
| | | Williams Bay | 0 | 0 | 0 | 0 | 2,734 |
| | | Winneconne | 0 | 0 | 0 | 0 | 2,469 |
| | | Wisconsin Dells | 0 | 0 | 0 | 0 | 2,474 |
| | | Wisconsin Rapids | 0 | 0 | 0 | 0 | 17,020 |
| | | Woodruff | 0 | 0 | 0 | 0 | 1,895 |
| | **Universities and Colleges** | University of Wisconsin: | | | | | |
| | | Eau Claire | 0 | 0 | 0 | 0 | 11,140 |
| | | Green Bay | 0 | 0 | 0 | 0 | 6,286 |
| | | La Crosse | 0 | 0 | 0 | 0 | 9,880 |
| | | Madison | 0 | 0 | 0 | 0 | 41,620 |
| | | Milwaukee | 0 | 0 | 0 | 0 | 29,215 |
| | | Oshkosh | 0 | 0 | 0 | 0 | 12,753 |
| | | Parkside | 0 | 0 | 0 | 0 | 5,167 |
| | | Platteville | 0 | 0 | 0 | | 7,512 |
| | | Stevens Point | 0 | 0 | 0 | 0 | 9,163 |
| | | Stout | 0 | 0 | 0 | 0 | 8,839 |
| | | Superior | 0 | 0 | 0 | 0 | 2,689 |
| | **Metropolitan Counties** | Brown | 0 | 0 | 0 | 0 | |
| | | Calumet | 0 | 0 | 0 | 0 | |
| | | Chippewa | 0 | 0 | 0 | 0 | |
| | | Columbia | 0 | 0 | 0 | 0 | |
| | | Douglas | 0 | 0 | 0 | 0 | |
| | | Eau Claire | 0 | 0 | 0 | 0 | |
| | | Fond du Lac | 0 | 0 | 0 | 0 | |
| | | Iowa | 0 | 0 | 0 | 0 | |
| | | Kenosha | 0 | 0 | 0 | 0 | |
| | | Kewaunee | 0 | 0 | 0 | 0 | |
| | | Marathon | 0 | 0 | 0 | 0 | |
| | | Milwaukee | 0 | 0 | 0 | 0 | |
| | | Oconto | 0 | 0 | 0 | 0 | |
| | | Ozaukee | 0 | 0 | 0 | 0 | |
| | | Pierce | 0 | 0 | 0 | 0 | |
| | | Rock | 0 | 0 | 0 | 0 | |
| | | Sheboygan | 0 | 0 | 0 | 0 | |
| | | St. Croix | 0 | 0 | 0 | 0 | |
| | | Washington | | 0 | 0 | 0 | |
| | | Waukesha | 0 | 0 | 0 | 0 | |
| | | Winnebago | 0 | 0 | 0 | 0 | |
| | **Nonmetropolitan Counties** | Adams | 0 | 0 | 0 | 0 | |
| | | Ashland | 0 | 0 | 0 | 0 | |
| | | Barron | 0 | 0 | 0 | 0 | |
| | | Bayfield | 0 | 0 | 0 | 0 | |
| | | Buffalo | 0 | 0 | 0 | 0 | |
| | | Burnett | 0 | 0 | 0 | 0 | |
| | | Crawford | 0 | 0 | 0 | 0 | |
| | | Dodge | 0 | 0 | 0 | 0 | |
| | | Door | 0 | 0 | 0 | 0 | |
| | | Dunn | 0 | 0 | 0 | 0 | |
| | | Florence | 0 | 0 | 0 | 0 | |
| | | Forest | 0 | 0 | 0 | 0 | |
| | | Grant | 0 | 0 | 0 | 0 | |
| | | Green | 0 | 0 | 0 | 0 | |
| | | Green Lake | 0 | 0 | 0 | 0 | |
| | | Iron | 0 | 0 | 0 | 0 | |
| | | Jackson | 0 | 0 | 0 | 0 | |
| | | Jefferson | 0 | 0 | 0 | 0 | |
| | | Juneau | 0 | 0 | 0 | 0 | |
| | | Lafayette | 0 | 0 | 0 | 0 | |
| | | Langlade | 0 | 0 | 0 | 0 | |
| | | Lincoln | 0 | 0 | 0 | 0 | |
| | | Manitowoc | 0 | 0 | 0 | 0 | |
| | | Marinette | 0 | 0 | 0 | 0 | |
| | | Marquette | 0 | 0 | 0 | 0 | |
| | | Menominee | 0 | 0 | 0 | 0 | |
| | | Monroe | 0 | 0 | 0 | 0 | |
| | | Oneida | 0 | 0 | 0 | 0 | |
| | | Pepin | 0 | 0 | 0 | 0 | |
| | | Polk | 0 | 0 | 0 | 0 | |
| | | Portage | 0 | 0 | 0 | 0 | |
| | | Price | 0 | 0 | 0 | 0 | |
| | | Richland | 0 | 0 | 0 | 0 | |
| | | Rusk | 0 | 0 | 0 | 0 | |
| | | Sauk | 0 | 0 | 0 | 0 | |
| | | Sawyer | 0 | 0 | 0 | 0 | |
| | | Shawano | 0 | 0 | 0 | 0 | |
| | | Taylor | 0 | 0 | 0 | 0 | |
| | | Trempealeau | 0 | 0 | 0 | 0 | |
| | | Vernon | 0 | 0 | 0 | 0 | |
| | | Vilas | 0 | 0 | 0 | 0 | |
| | | Walworth | 0 | 0 | 0 | 0 | |
| | | Washburn | 0 | 0 | 0 | 0 | |
| | | Waupaca | 0 | 0 | 0 | 0 | |
| | | Waushara | 0 | 0 | 0 | 0 | |
| | | Wood | 0 | 0 | 0 | 0 | |
| | **Tribal Agencies** | Lac du Flambeau Tribal | 0 | 0 | 0 | 0 | |

[1]Agencies published in this table indicated that no hate crimes occurred in their jurisdictions during the quarter(s) for which they submitted reports to the Hate Crime Statistics Program. Blanks indicate quarters for which agencies did not submit reports.

[2]Population figures are published only for the cities. The figures listed for the universities and colleges are student enrollment and were provided by the United States Department of Education for the 2008 school year, the most recent available. The enrollment figures include full-time and part-time students.

## Table 95. Hate Crime Zero Data Submitted per Quarter, by State and Agency, 2009—*Continued*

(Number.)

| State | Agency type | Agency name | Zero data per quarter[1] | | | | Population[2] |
|---|---|---|---|---|---|---|---|
| | | | 1st quarter | 2nd quarter | 3rd quarter | 4th quarter | |
| **WISCONSIN** | | Menominee Tribal | 0 | 0 | 0 | 0 | |
| | | Oneida Tribal | 0 | 0 | 0 | 0 | |
| | **Other Agencies** | Capitol Police | 0 | 0 | 0 | 0 | |
| **WYOMING....** | **Cities** | Afton | 0 | 0 | 0 | 0 | 1,866 |
| | | Alpine | 0 | 0 | 0 | 0 | 845 |
| | | Basin | 0 | 0 | 0 | 0 | 1,243 |
| | | Buffalo | 0 | 0 | 0 | 0 | 4,945 |
| | | Casper | 0 | 0 | 0 | 0 | 54,550 |
| | | Cheyenne | 0 | 0 | 0 | 0 | 57,317 |
| | | Cody | 0 | 0 | 0 | 0 | 9,358 |
| | | Diamondville | 0 | 0 | 0 | 0 | 657 |
| | | Douglas | 0 | 0 | 0 | 0 | 6,049 |
| | | Evanston | 0 | 0 | 0 | 0 | 11,823 |
| | | Evansville | 0 | 0 | 0 | 0 | 2,408 |
| | | Glenrock | 0 | 0 | 0 | 0 | 2,443 |
| | | Greybull | 0 | 0 | 0 | 0 | 1,732 |
| | | Guernsey | 0 | 0 | 0 | 0 | 1,065 |
| | | Hanna | 0 | 0 | 0 | 0 | 866 |
| | | Kemmerer | 0 | 0 | 0 | 0 | 2,449 |
| | | Lander | 0 | 0 | 0 | 0 | 7,304 |
| | | Laramie | 0 | 0 | 0 | 0 | 27,730 |
| | | Lovell | 0 | 0 | 0 | 0 | 2,268 |
| | | Lusk | 0 | 0 | 0 | 0 | 1,485 |
| | | Mills | 0 | 0 | 0 | 0 | 3,177 |
| | | Moorcroft | 0 | 0 | 0 | 0 | 900 |
| | | Newcastle | 0 | 0 | 0 | 0 | 3,406 |
| | | Pine Bluffs | 0 | 0 | 0 | 0 | 1,155 |
| | | Powell | 0 | 0 | 0 | 0 | 5,540 |
| | | Rawlins | 0 | 0 | 0 | 0 | 8,716 |
| | | Rock Springs | 0 | 0 | 0 | 0 | 20,391 |
| | | Saratoga | 0 | 0 | 0 | 0 | 1,763 |
| | | Sheridan | 0 | 0 | 0 | 0 | 17,350 |
| | | Sundance | 0 | 0 | 0 | 0 | 1,264 |
| | | Thermopolis | 0 | 0 | 0 | 0 | 2,951 |
| | | Torrington | 0 | 0 | 0 | 0 | 5,486 |
| | | Wheatland | 0 | 0 | 0 | 0 | 3,273 |
| | | Worland | 0 | 0 | 0 | 0 | 4,926 |
| | **Universities and Colleges** | Sheridan College | 0 | 0 | 0 | 0 | 4,130 |
| | | University of Wyoming | 0 | 0 | 0 | 0 | 12,067 |
| | **Metropolitan Counties** | Laramie | 0 | 0 | 0 | 0 | |
| | | Natrona | 0 | 0 | 0 | 0 | |
| | **Nonmetropolitan Counties** | Albany | 0 | 0 | 0 | 0 | |
| | | Big Horn | 0 | 0 | 0 | 0 | |
| | | Campbell | 0 | 0 | 0 | 0 | |
| | | Carbon | 0 | 0 | 0 | 0 | |
| | | Converse | 0 | 0 | 0 | 0 | |
| | | Crook | 0 | 0 | 0 | 0 | |
| | | Fremont | 0 | 0 | 0 | 0 | |
| | | Goshen | 0 | 0 | 0 | 0 | |
| | | Hot Springs | 0 | 0 | 0 | 0 | |
| | | Johnson | 0 | 0 | 0 | 0 | |
| | | Lincoln | 0 | 0 | 0 | 0 | |
| | | Niobrara | 0 | 0 | 0 | 0 | |
| | | Park | 0 | 0 | 0 | 0 | |
| | | Platte | 0 | 0 | 0 | 0 | |
| | | Sheridan | 0 | 0 | 0 | 0 | |
| | | Sublette | 0 | 0 | 0 | 0 | |
| | | Sweetwater | 0 | 0 | 0 | 0 | |
| | | Teton | 0 | 0 | 0 | 0 | |
| | | Uinta | 0 | 0 | 0 | 0 | |
| | | Washakie | 0 | 0 | 0 | 0 | |
| | | Weston | 0 | 0 | 0 | 0 | |

[1]Agencies published in this table indicated that no hate crimes occurred in their jurisdictions during the quarter(s) for which they submitted reports to the Hate Crime Statistics Program. Blanks indicate quarters for which agencies did not submit reports.

[2]Population figures are published only for the cities. The figures listed for the universities and colleges are student enrollment and were provided by the United States Department of Education for the 2008 school year, the most recent available. The enrollment figures include full-time and part-time students.

# APPENDIXES

## APPENDIX I. METHODOLOGY

Submitting Uniform Crime Reporting (UCR) Program data to the Federal Bureau of Investigation (FBI) is a collective effort on the part of city, county, state, tribal, and federal law enforcement agencies to present a nationwide view of crime. Law enforcement agencies in 46 states and the District of Columbia voluntarily contribute crime data to the UCR Program through their respective state UCR Programs. For those states that do not have a state program, local agencies submit crime statistics directly to the FBI. The state UCR Programs function as liaisons between local agencies and the FBI. Many states have mandatory reporting requirements, and many state programs collect data beyond the scope of the UCR Program to address crime problems specific to their particular jurisdictions. In most cases, state programs also provide direct and frequent service to participating law enforcement agencies, make information readily available for statewide use, and help streamline the national program's operations.

### Criteria for State UCR Programs

The criteria established for state programs ensure consistency and comparability in the data submitted to the national program, as well as regular and timely reporting. These criteria are:

1. The state program must conform to the national UCR Program standards, definitions, and information required.
2. The state criminal justice agency must have a proven, effective, statewide program and have instituted acceptable quality control procedures.
3. The state crime reporting must cover a percentage of the population at least equal to that covered by the national UCR Program through direct reporting.
4. The state program must have adequate field staff assigned to conduct audits and to assist contributing agencies in record-keeping practices and crime-reporting procedures.
5. The state program must furnish the FBI with all of the detailed data regularly collected by the FBI from individual agencies that report to the state program in the form of duplicate returns, computer printouts, and/or appropriate electronic media.
6. The state program must have the proven capability (tested over a period of time) to supply all the statistical data required in time to meet publication deadlines of the national UCR Program.

### Data Completeness and Quality

The FBI, in order to fulfill its responsibilities in connection with the UCR Program, continues to edit and review individual agency reports for completeness and quality. National program staff members directly contact individual contributors within the state, when necessary, in connection with crime-reporting matters; staff members also coordinate such contact with the UCR Program. Upon request, they conduct training programs within the state on law enforcement record-keeping and crime-reporting procedures. The FBI conducts an audit of each state's UCR data collection procedures once every three years, in accordance with audit standards established by the federal government. Should circumstances develop in which the state program does not comply with the aforementioned requirements, the national program may institute a direct collection of Uniform Crime Reports from law enforcement agencies within the state.

### Reporting Procedures

**Offenses known and value of property**–Law enforcement agencies tabulate the number of Part I offenses brought to their attention based on records of all reports of crime received from victims, officers who discover infractions, or other sources, and submit them each month to the FBI either directly or through their state UCR Programs. Part I offenses include murder and nonnegligent manslaughter, forcible rape, robbery, aggravated assault, burglary, larceny-theft, motor vehicle theft, and arson. Law enforcement agencies also submit monthly to the FBI the value of property stolen and recovered in connection with the offenses and detailed information pertaining to criminal homicide.

**Unfounded offenses and clearances**—When, through investigation, an agency determines that complaints of crimes are unfounded or false, the agency eliminates that offense from its crime tally through an entry on the monthly report. The report also provides the total number of actual Part I offenses, the number of offenses cleared, and the number of clearances that involve only offenders under the age of 18. (Law enforcement can clear crimes in one of two ways: by the arrest of at least one person who is charged and turned over to the court for prosecution or by exceptional means—when some element beyond law enforcement's control precludes the arrest of a known offender.)

**Persons arrested—**In addition to reporting Part I offenses, law enforcement agencies provide monthly to the UCR Program data on the age, sex, and race of persons arrested for Part I and Part II offenses. Part II offenses encompass all crimes, except traffic violations, that are not classified as Part I offenses.

**Officers killed or assaulted—**Law enforcement agencies also report monthly to the UCR Program information regarding law enforcement officers killed or assaulted, and yearly, the number of full-time sworn and civilian law enforcement personnel employed as of October 31.

**Hate crimes—**At the end of each quarter, law enforcement agencies report summarized data on hate crimes, i.e., specific offenses that were motivated by an offender's bias against the perceived race, religion, ethnic/national origin, sexual orientation, or physical or mental disability of the victim. Those agencies participating in the UCR Program's National Incident-Based Reporting System (NIBRS) submit hate crime data monthly.

## Editing Procedures

The UCR Program thoroughly examines each report it receives for arithmetical accuracy and for deviations in crime data from month to month and from present to past years that may indicate errors. UCR staff members compare an agency's monthly reports with its previous submissions and with reports from similar agencies to identify any unusual fluctuations in the agency's crime count. Large variations in crime levels may indicate modified records procedures, incomplete reporting, or changes in the jurisdiction's geopolitical structure.

**Evaluation of trends**—Data reliability is a high priority of the FBI, which brings any deviations or arithmetical adjustments to the attention of state UCR Programs or the submitting agencies. Typically, FBI staff members study the monthly reports to evaluate periodic trends prepared for individual reporting units. Any significant increase or decrease becomes the subject of a special inquiry. Changes in crime reporting procedures or annexations that affect an agency's jurisdiction can influence the level of reported crime. When this occurs, the FBI excludes the figures for specific crime categories or totals, if necessary, from the trend tabulations.

**Training for contributors**—In addition to the evaluation of trends, the FBI provides training seminars and instructional materials on crime reporting procedures to assist contributors in complying with UCR standards. Throughout the country, the national program maintains liaison with state programs and law enforcement personnel and holds training sessions to explain the purpose of the program, the rules of uniform classification and scoring, and the methods of assembling the information for reporting. When an individual agency has specific problems in compiling its crime statistics and its remedial efforts are unsuccessful, personnel from the FBI's Criminal Justice Information Services Division may visit the contributor to aid in resolving the difficulties.

***UCR Handbook***—The national UCR Program publishes a Uniform Crime Reporting Handbook (revised 2004), which details procedures for classifying and scoring offenses and serves as the contributing agencies' basic resource for preparing reports. The national staff also produces letters to UCR contributors, State Program Bulletins, and UCR Newsletters as needed. These provide policy updates and new information, as well as clarification of reporting issues.

The final responsibility for data submissions rests with the individual contributing law enforcement agency. Although the FBI makes every effort through its editing procedures, training practices, and correspondence to ensure the validity of the data it receives, the accuracy of the statistics depends primarily on the adherence of each contributor to the established standards of reporting. Deviations from these established standards that cannot be resolved by the national UCR Program may be brought to the attention of the Criminal Justice Information Systems Committees of the International Association of Chiefs of Police and the National Sheriffs' Association.

## Population Estimation

For the 2009 population estimates used in this report, the FBI computed individual rates of growth from one year to the next for every city/town and county using 2000 decennial population counts and 2001 through 2008 population estimates from the U.S. Census Bureau. Each agency's rates of growth were averaged; that average was then applied and added to its 2008 Census population estimate to derive the agency's 2009 population estimate.

Population estimates for 2008 are based on the percent change in the state population from the U.S. Census Bureau's 2007 revised estimates and 2008 provisional estimates. Population estimates for 2005 are based on the percent change in the state population from the U.S. Census Bureau's 2004 revised estimates and 2005 provisional estimates. Population totals for 2000 are from the U.S. Census Bureau's 2000 decennial population counts.

## NIBRS Conversion

Thirty-one state programs are certified to provide their UCR data in the expanded National Incident-Based Reporting System (NIBRS) format. For presentation in this book, the NIBRS data were converted to the historical Summary Reporting System data. The UCR Program staff constructed the NIBRS database to allow for such conversion so that UCR's long-running time series could continue.

## Crime Trends

By showing fluctuations from year to year, trend statistics offer the data user an added perspective from which to study crime. Percent change tabulations in this publication are computed only for reporting agencies that provided comparable data for the periods under consideration. The FBI excludes from the trend calculations all figures except those received for common months from common agencies. Also excluded are unusual fluctuations of data that the FBI determines are the result of such variables as improved records procedures, annexations, etc.

## Caution to Users

Data users should exercise care in making any direct comparison between data in this publication and those in prior issues of Crime in the United States. Because of differing levels of participation from year to year and reporting problems that require the FBI to estimate crime counts for certain contributors, some data may not be comparable from year to year. In addition, this publication may contain updates to data provided in prior years' publications. For example, because of the receipt of additional data after the 2008 publication deadline, the 2008 Supplementary Homicide Report (SHR) data in last year's publication may not match the 2008 SHR data in this 2009 publication.

**2009 Arrest Data**

- Limited arrest data were received from Illinois. Arrest counts were received for Chicago and Rockford only.
- Except for the cities of Minneapolis and St. Paul, the Minnesota State UCR Program's guidelines for reporting forcible rape arrest counts do not comply with the national UCR Program's guidelines; i.e., Minnesota data include arrests made for forcible rapes of male victims. Therefore, the state forcible rape counts that are published include only the totals received from Minneapolis and St. Paul.
- For 2009, only arrest totals (with no age or gender breakdowns) are available for Florida. Therefore, Florida arrest totals are included only in Table 69, "Arrests by State, 2009."
- No 2009 arrest data were received from the District of Columbia's Metropolitan Police Department. The two agencies in the District of Columbia for which 12 months of arrest data were received, Metro Transit Police and the National Zoological Park, have no attributable population.
- No 2009 arrest data were received from the New York City Police Department. However, arrest totals for this agency were estimated by the national UCR Program and were included in Table 29 "Estimated Number of Arrests, United States, 2009."

**Offense Estimation**

Tables 1 through 5 and Table 7 of this publication contain statistics for the entire United States. Because not all law enforcement agencies provide data for complete reporting periods, the FBI includes estimated crime numbers in these presentations. The FBI estimates data for three areas: metropolitan statistical areas (MSAs), cities outside MSAs, and nonmetropolitan counties. The FBI computes estimates for participating agencies not providing 12 months of complete data. For agencies supplying 3 to 11 months of data, the national UCR Program estimates for the missing data by following a standard estimation procedure using the data provided by the agency. If an agency has supplied less than 3 months of data, the FBI computes estimates by using the known crime figures of similar areas within a state and assigning the same proportion of crime volumes to nonreporting agencies. The estimation process considers the following: population size covered by the agency; type of jurisdiction, e.g., police department versus sheriff's office; and geographic location.

**Estimation of State-Level Data**

In response to various circumstances, the FBI calculates estimated offense totals for certain states. For example, some states do not provide forcible rape figures in accordance with UCR guidelines. In addition, problems at the state level have, at times, resulted in no useable data. Also, the conversion of the National Incident-Based Reporting System (NIBRS) data to Summary data has contributed to the need for unique estimation procedures. A summary of state-specific and offense-specific estimation procedures can be found online at <http://www2.fbi.gov/ucr/cius2009/about/table_methodology.html>.

## APPENDIX II. DEFINITIONS

The Uniform Crime Reporting (UCR) Program divides offense into two groups. Contributing agencies submit information on the number of Part I offenses known to law enforcement; those offenses cleared by arrest or exceptional means; and the age, sex, and race of persons arrested for each of thse offenses. Contributors provide only arrest data for Part II offenses.

**Part I** offenses include murder, and nonnegligent manslaughter, forcible rape, robbery, aggravated assault, burglary, larceny-theft, motor vehicle theft, and arson.

**Violent crime** is composed of four offenses: murder and nonnegligent manslaughter, forcible rape, robbery, and aggravated assault. According to the UCR Program's definition, violent crimes involve force or threat of force.

**Criminal homicide**—a.) Murder and nonnegligent manslaughter: the willful (nonnegligent) killing of one human being by another. Deaths caused by negligence, attempts to kill, assaults to kill, suicides, and accidental deaths are excluded. The program classifies justifiable homicides separately and limits the definition to (1) the killing of a felon by a law enforcement officer in the line of duty; or (2) the killing of a felon, during the commission of a felony, by a private citizen. b.) Manslaughter by negligence: the killing of another person through gross negligence. Traffic fatalities are excluded.

**Forcible rape—**The carnal knowledge of a female forcibly and against her will. Assaults and attempts to commit rape by force or threat of force are also included. Statutory rape (no force used—female victim is under the age of consent) and other sex offenses are excluded. Sexual attacks on males are counted as aggravated assaults or sex offenses, depending on the circumstances and the extent of any injuries.

**Robbery—**The taking or attempted taking of anything of value from the care, custody, or control of a person or persons by force or threat of force or violence and/or by putting the victim in fear.

**Aggravated assault—**An unlawful attack by one person upon another for the purpose of inflicting severe or aggravated bodily injury. This type of assault usually is accompanied by the use of a weapon or by means likely to produce death or great bodily harm. Attempted aggravated assaults that involve the display of—or threat to use—a gun, knife, or other weapon is included in this crime category because serious personal injury would likely result if the assault were completed. When aggravated assault and larceny-theft occur together, the offense falls under the category of robbery. Simple assaults are excluded.

**Property crime** includes the offenses of burglary, larceny-theft, motor vehicle theft, and arson. The object of the theft-type offenses is the taking of money or property, but there is no force or threat of force against the victims. The property crime category includes arson because the offense involves the destruction of property; however, arson victims may be subjected to force.

**Burglary (breaking or entering)**—The unlawful entry of a structure to commit a felony or a theft. The use of force to gain entry need not have occurred. The UCR Program has three subclassifications for burglary: forcible entry, unlawful entry where no force is used, and attempted forcible entry. The UCR definition of "structure" includes, for example, apartment, barn, house trailer or houseboat when used as a permanent dwelling, office, railroad car (but not automobile), stable, and vessel (i.e., ship).

**Larceny-theft (except motor vehicle theft)**—The unlawful taking, carrying, leading, or riding away of property from the possession or constructive possession of another. Examples are thefts of bicycles or automobile accessories, shoplifting, pocket-picking, or the stealing of any property or article that is not taken by force and violence or by fraud. Attempted larcenies are included. Embezzlement, confidence games, forgery, worthless checks, and the like, are excluded.

**Motor vehicle theft**—The theft or attempted theft of a motor vehicle. It includes the stealing of automobiles, trucks, buses, motorcycles, snowmobiles, and the like. The taking of a motor vehicle for temporary use by persons having lawful access is excluded from this definition. A motor vehicle is self-propelled and runs on land surface and not on rails. Motorboats, construction equipment, airplanes, and farming equipment are specifically excluded from this category.

**Arson**—Any willful or malicious burning or attempt to burn, with or without intent to defraud, a dwelling house, public building, motor vehicle, aircraft, personal property of another, and the like. Limited data are available for arson because of limited participation and varying collection procedures by local law enforcement agencies. Arson statistics are included in trend, clearance, and arrest tables throughout *Crime in the United States*, but they are not included in any estimated volume data.

In addition to reporting Part I offenses, law enforcement agencies provide the UCR Program with monthly data on persons arrested for all crimes except traffic violations. These arrest data include the age, sex, and race of arrestees for both Part I and Part II offenses. **Part II** offenses encompass all crimes, except traffic violations, that are not classified as Part I offenses, including:

**Other assaults (simple)**—Assaults and attempted assaults which are not of an aggravated nature and do not result in serious injury to the victim.

**Forgery and counterfeiting**—The altering, copying, or imitating of something, without authority or right, with the intent to deceive or defraud by passing the copy or thing altered or imitated as that which is original or genuine; or the selling, buying, or possession of an altered, copied, or imitated thing with the intent to deceive or defraud. Attempts are included.

**Fraud**—The intentional perversion of the truth for the purpose of inducing another person or other entity in reliance upon it to part with something of value or to surrender a legal right. Fraudulent conversion and obtaining of money or property by false pretenses. Confidence games and bad checks, except forgeries and counterfeiting, are included.

**Embezzlement**—The unlawful misappropriation or misapplication by an offender to his/her own use or purpose of money, property, or some other thing of value entrusted to his/her care, custody, or control.

**Stolen property; buying, receiving, possessing**—Buying, receiving, possessing, selling, concealing, or transporting any property with the knowledge that it has been unlawfully taken, as by burglary, embezzlement, fraud, larceny, robbery, etc. Attempts are included.

**Vandalism**—To willfully or maliciously destroy, injure, disfigure, or deface any public or private property, real or personal, without the consent of the owner or person having custody or control by cutting, tearing, breaking, marking, painting, drawing, covering with filth, or any other such means as may be specified by local law. Attempts are included.

**Weapons; carrying, possessing, etc.**—The violation of laws or ordinances prohibiting the manufacture, sale, purchase, transportation, possession, concealment, or use of firearms, cutting instruments, explosives, incendiary devices, or other deadly weapons. Attempts are included.

**Prostitution and commercialized vice**—The unlawful promotion of or participation in sexual activities for profit, including attempts.

**Sex offenses (except forcible rape, prostitution, and commercialized vice)**—Statutory rape, offenses against chastity, common decency, morals, and the like. Attempts are included.

**Drug abuse violations**—The violation of laws prohibiting the production, distribution, and/or use of certain controlled substances. The unlawful cultivation, manufacture, distribution, sale, purchase, use, possession, transportation, or importation of any controlled drug or narcotic substance. Arrests for violations of state and local laws, specifically those relating to the unlawful possession, sale, use, growing, manufacturing, and making of narcotic drugs. The following drug categories are specified: opium or cocaine and their derivatives (morphine, heroin, codeine); marijuana; synthetic narcotics/manufactured narcotics that can cause true addiction (demerol, methadone); and dangerous nonnarcotic drugs (barbiturates, benzedrine).

**Gambling**—To unlawfully bet or wager money or something else of value; assist, promote, or operate a game of chance for money or some other stake; possess or transmit wagering information; manufacture, sell, purchase, possess, or transport gambling equipment, devices, or goods; or tamper with the outcome of a sporting event or contest to gain a gambling advantage.

**Offenses against the family and children**—Unlawful nonviolent acts by a family member (or legal guardian) that threaten the physical, mental, or economic well-being or morals of another family member and that are not classifiable as other offenses, such as assault or sex offenses. Attempts are included.

**Driving under the influence**—Driving or operating a motor vehicle or common carrier while mentally or physically impaired as the result of consuming an alcoholic beverage or using a drug or narcotic.

**Liquor laws**—The violation of state or local laws or ordinances prohibiting the manufacture, sale, purchase, transportation, possession, or use of alcoholic beverages, not including driving under the influence and drunkenness. Federal violations are excluded.

**Drunkenness**—To drink alcoholic beverages to the extent that one's mental faculties and physical coordination are substantially impaired. Excludes driving under the influence.

**Disorderly conduct**—Any behavior that tends to disturb the public peace or decorum, scandalize the community, or shock the public sense of morality.

**Vagrancy**—The violation of a court order, regulation, ordinance, or law requiring the withdrawal of persons from the streets or other specified areas; prohibiting persons from remaining in an area or place in an idle or aimless manner; or prohibiting persons from going from place to place without visible means of support.

**All other offenses**—All violations of state or local laws not specifically identified as Part I or Part II offenses, except traffic violations.

**Suspicion**—Arrested for no specific offense and released without formal charges being placed.

**Curfew and loitering laws (persons under 18 years of age)**—Violations by juveniles of local curfew or loitering ordinances.

**Runaways (persons under 18 years of age)**—Limited to juveniles taken into protective custody under the provisions of local statutes.

# APPENDIX III. GEOGRAPHIC AREA DEFINITIONS

The UCR Program collects crime data and supplemental information that make it possible to generate a variety of statistical compilations, including data presented by reporting areas. These statistics allow data users to analyze local crime data in conjunction with those for areas of similar geographic location or population size. The reporting areas that the UCR Program uses in its data breakdowns include community types, population groups, and regions and divisions. For community types, the UCR Program considers proximity to metropolitan areas using the designations created by the U.S. Office of Management and Budget (OMB). (Generally, sheriffs, county police, and state police report crimes within counties but outside of cities; local police report crimes within city limits.) The number of inhabitants living in a locale (based on the U.S. Census Bureau's figures) determines the population group into which the program places it. For its geographic breakdowns, the UCR Program divides the United States into regions, divisions, and states.

## Regions and Divisions

The map below illustrates the nine divisions that make up the four regions of the United States. The UCR Program uses this widely recognized geographic organization when compiling the nation's crime data. The regions and divisions are as follows:

***Northeast***

*New England*—Connecticut, Maine, Massachusetts, New Hampshire, Rhode Island, and Vermont

*Middle Atlantic*—New York, New Jersey, and Pennsylvania

***Midwest***

*East North Central*—Illinois, Indiana, Michigan, Ohio, and Wisconsin

*West North Central*—Iowa, Kansas, Minnesota, Missouri, Nebraska, North Dakota, and South Dakota

***South***

*South Atlantic*—Delaware, District of Columbia, Florida, Georgia, Maryland, North Carolina, South Carolina, Virginia, and West Virginia

*East South Central*—Alabama, Kentucky, Mississippi, and Tennessee

*West South Central*—Arkansas, Louisiana, Oklahoma, and Texas

***West***

*Mountain*—Arizona, Colorado, Idaho, Montana, Nevada, New Mexico, Utah, and Wyoming

*Pacific*—Alaska, California, Hawaii, Oregon, and Washington

## Community Types

To assist data users who wish to analyze and present uniform statistical data about metropolitan areas, the UCR Program uses reporting units that represent major population centers. The program compiles data for the following three types of communities:

**United States Regions and Divisions**

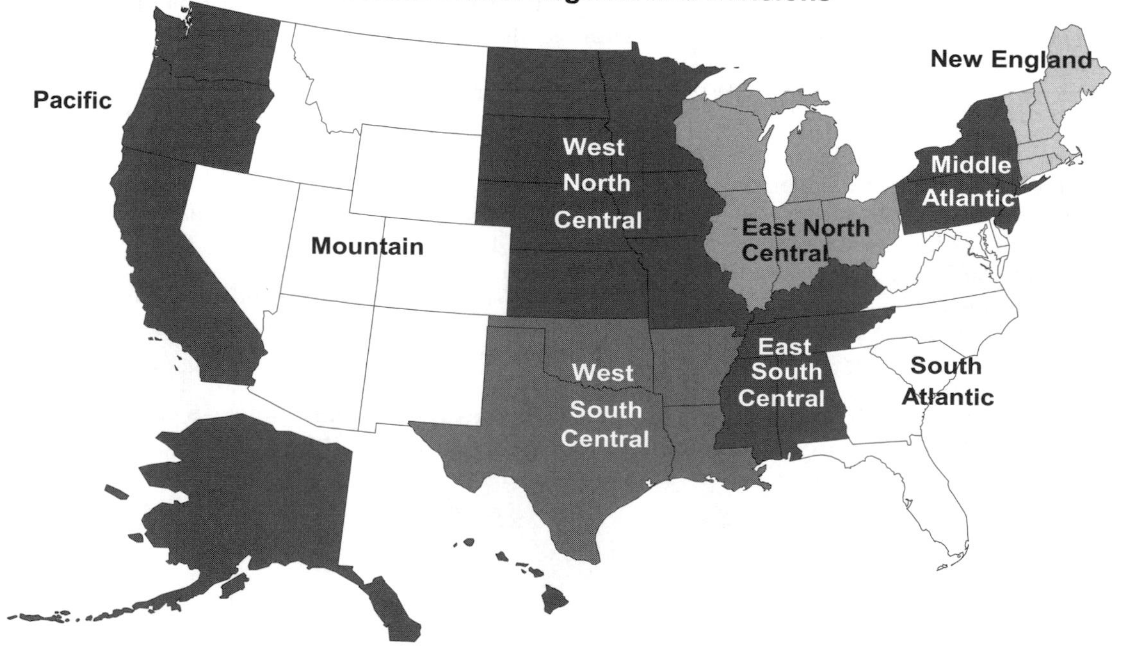

**Metropolitan statistical areas (MSAs)**—Each MSA contains a principal city or urbanized area with a population of at least 50,000 inhabitants. MSAs include the principal city, the county in which the city is located, and other adjacent counties that have a high degree of economic and social integration with the principal city and county (as defined by the OMB), which is measured through commuting. In the UCR Program, counties within an MSA are considered metropolitan counties. In addition, MSAs may cross state boundaries.

In 2009, approximately 83.6 percent of the Nation's population lived in MSAs. Some presentations in this publication refer to Metropolitan Divisions, which are subdivisions of an MSA that consists of a core with "a population of at least 2.5 million persons. A Metropolitan Division consists of one or more main/secondary counties that represent an employment center or centers, plus adjacent counties associated with the main county or counties through commuting ties," (*Federal Register* 65 [249]). Also, some tables reference suburban areas, which are subdivisions of MSAs that exclude the principal cities but include all the remaining cities (those having fewer than 50,000 inhabitants) and the unincorporated areas of the MSAs.

Because the elements that comprise MSAs, particularly the geographic compositions, are subject to change, the UCR Program discourages data users from making year-to-year comparisons of MSA data.

**Cities Outside MSAs**—Ordinarily, cities outside MSAs are incorporated areas. In 2009, cities outside MSAs made up 6.5 percent of the nation's population.

**Nonmetropolitan Counties Outside MSAs**—Most nonmetropolitan counties are composed of unincorporated areas. In 2009, 9.8 percent of the nation's population resided in nonmetropolitan counties.

Metropolitan and nonmetropolitan community types are further illustrated in the following table:

| Metropolitan | Nonmetropolitan |
|---|---|
| Principal cities (50,000+ inhabitants)<br>Suburban cities | Cities outside metropolitan areas |
| Metropolitan counties | Nonmetropolitan counties |

**Population Groups**

The UCR Program uses the following population group designations:

| Population Group | Political Label | Population Range |
|---|---|---|
| I | City | 250,000 or more |
| II | City | 100,000 to 249,999 |
| III | City | 50,000 to 99,999 |
| IV | City | 25,000 to 49,999 |
| V | City | 10,000 to 24,999 |
| VI | City[1] | Fewer than 10,000 |
| VIII (Nonmetropolitan county) | County[2] | N/A |
| IX (Metropolitan county) | County[2] | N/A |

[1]Includes universities and colleges to which no population is attributed.
[2]Includes state police agencies to which no population is attributed.

Individual law enforcement agencies are the source of UCR data. The number of agencies included in each population group may vary from year to year because of population growth, geopolitical consolidation, municipal incorporation, etc. In noncensus years, the UCR Program estimates population figures for individual jurisdictions. (A more comprehensive explanation of population estimations can be found in Appendix I.)

The categories below show the number of agencies contributing to the UCR Program within each population group for 2008:

| Population Group | Number of Agencies | Population Covered |
|---|---|---|
| I | 76 | 57,278,467 |
| II | 202 | 29,918,119 |
| III | 479 | 32,650,587 |
| IV | 866 | 29,691,658 |
| V | 1,918 | 30,367,808 |
| VI[1] | 9,321 | 26,459,228 |
| VIII (Nonmetropolitan county)[2] | 3,024 | 30,232,284 |
| IX (Metropolitan county)[2] | 2,099 | 70,408,399 |
| Total | 17,985 | 307,006,550 |

[1]Includes universities and colleges to which no population is attributed.
[2]Includes state police to which no population is attributed.

## APPENDIX IV. THE NATION'S TWO CRIME MEASURES

The Department of Justice administers two statistical programs to measure the magnitude, nature, and impact of crime in the nation: the Uniform Crime Reporting (UCR) Program and the National Crime Victimization Survey (NCVS). Each of these programs produces valuable information about aspects of the nation's crime problem. Because the UCR and NCVS programs are conducted for different purposes, use different methods, and focus on somewhat different aspects of crime, the information they produce together provides a more comprehensive panorama of the nation's crime problem than either could produce alone.

### Uniform Crime Reporting (UCR) Program

The UCR Program, administered by the Federal Bureau of Investigation (FBI), was created in 1929 and collects information on the following crimes reported to law enforcement authorities: murder and nonnegligent manslaughter, forcible rape, robbery, aggravated assault, burglary, larceny-theft, motor vehicle theft, and arson. Law enforcement agencies also report arrest data for 21 additional crime categories.

The UCR Program compiles data from monthly law enforcement reports and from individual crime incident records transmitted directly to the FBI or to centralized state agencies that report to the FBI. The program thoroughly examines each report it receives for reasonableness, accuracy, and deviations that may indicate errors. Large variations in crime levels may indicate modified records procedures, incomplete reporting, or changes in a jurisdiction's boundaries. To identify any unusual fluctuations in an agency's crime counts, the program compares monthly reports to previous submissions of the agency and to those for similar agencies.

The UCR Program presents crime counts for the Nation as a whole, as well as for regions, states, counties, cities, towns, tribal law enforcement, and colleges and universities. This permits studies among neighboring jurisdictions and among those with similar populations and other common characteristics.

The FBI annually publishes its findings in a preliminary release in the spring of the following calendar year, followed by a detailed annual report, *Crime in the United States*, issued in the fall. (The printed copy of *Crime in the United States* is now published by Bernan Press.) In addition to crime counts and trends, this report includes data on crimes cleared, persons arrested (age, sex, and race), law enforcement personnel (including the number of sworn officers killed or assaulted), and the characteristics of homicides (including age, sex, and race of victims and offenders; victim-offender relationships; weapons used; and circumstances surrounding the homicides). Other periodic reports are also available from the UCR Program.

The state and local law enforcement agencies participating in the UCR Program are continually converting to the more comprehensive and detailed National Incident-Based Reporting System (NIBRS). The NIBRS provides detailed information about each criminal incident in 22 broad categories of offenses.

The UCR Program presents crime counts for the nation as a whole, as well as for regions, states, counties, cities, towns, tribal law enforcement areas, and colleges and universities. This allows for studies among neighboring jurisdictions and among those with similar populations and other common characteristics.

### National Crime Victimization Survey

The NCVS, conducted by the Bureau of Justice Statistics (BJS), began in 1973. It provides a detailed picture of crime incidents, victims, and trends. After a substantial period of research, the BJS completed an intensive methodological redesign of the survey in 1993. It conducted this redesign to improve the questions used to uncover crime, update the survey methods, and broaden the scope of crimes measured. The redesigned survey collects detailed information on the frequency and nature of the crimes of rape, sexual assault, personal robbery, aggravated and simple assault, household burglary, theft, and motor vehicle theft. It does not measure homicide or commercial crimes (such as burglaries of stores).

Twice a year, Census Bureau personnel interview household members in a nationally representative sample of approximately 43,000 households (about 76,000 people). Approximately 150,000 interviews of individuals 12 years of age and over are conducted annually. Households stay in the sample for 3 years, and new households rotate into the sample on an ongoing basis.

The NCVS collects information on crimes suffered by individuals and households, whether or not those crimes were reported to law enforcement. It estimates the proportion of each crime type reported to law enforcement, and it summarizes the reasons that victims give for reporting or not reporting.

The survey provides information about victims (age, sex, race, ethnicity, marital status, income, and educational level); offenders (sex, race, approximate age, and victim-offender relationship); and crimes (time and place of occurrence, use of weapons, nature of injury, and economic consequences). Questions also cover victims' experiences with the criminal justice system, self-protective measures used by victims, and possible substance abuse by offenders. Supplements are added to the survey periodically to obtain detailed information on specific topics, such as school crime.

The BJS published the first data from the redesigned NCVS in a June 1995 bulletin. The publication of NCVS data includes *Criminal Victimization in the United States*, an annual report that covers the broad range of detailed information collected by the NCVS. The bureau also publishes detailed reports on topics such as crime against women, urban crime, and gun use in crime. The National Archive of Criminal Justice Data at the University of Michigan archives the NCVS data files to help researchers perform independent analyses.

## Comparing the UCR Program and the NCVS

Because the BJS designed the NCVS to complement the UCR Program, the two programs share many similarities. As much as their different collection methods permit, the two measure the same subset of serious crimes with the same definitions. Both programs cover rape, robbery, aggravated assault, burglary, theft, and motor vehicle theft; both define rape, robbery, theft, and motor vehicle theft virtually identically. (Although rape is defined analogously, the UCR Program measures the crime against women only, and the NCVS measures it against both sexes.)

There are also significant differences between the two programs. First, the two programs were created to serve different purposes. The UCR Program's primary objective is to provide a reliable set of criminal justice statistics for law enforcement administration, operation, and management. The BJS established the NCVS to provide previously unavailable information about crime (including crime not reported to police), victims, and offenders.

Second, the two programs measure an overlapping but nonidentical set of crimes. The NCVS includes crimes both reported and not reported to law enforcement. The NCVS excludes—but the UCR Program includes—homicide, arson, commercial crimes, and crimes committed against children under 12 years of age. The UCR Program captures crimes reported to law enforcement but collects only arrest data for simple assaults and sexual assaults other than forcible rape.

Third, because of methodology, the NCVS and UCR have different definitions of some crimes. For example, the UCR defines burglary as the unlawful entry or attempted entry of a structure to commit a felony or theft. The NCVS, not wanting to ask victims to ascertain offender motives, defines burglary as the entry or attempted entry of a residence by a person who had no right to be there.

Fourth, for property crimes (burglary, theft, and motor vehicle theft), the two programs calculate crime rates using different bases. The UCR Program rates for these crimes are per capita (number of crimes per 100,000 persons), whereas the NCVS rates for these crimes are per household (number of crimes per 1,000 households).

Because the number of households may not grow at the same annual rate as the total population, trend data for rates of property crimes measured by the two programs may not be comparable. In addition, some differences in the data from the two programs may result from sampling variation in the NCVS and from estimating for nonresponsiveness in the UCR Program.

The BJS derives the NCVS estimates from interviewing a sample and are, therefore, subject to a margin of error. The bureau uses rigorous statistical methods to calculate confidence intervals around all survey estimates, and describes trend data in the NCVS reports as genuine only if there is at least a 90-percent certainty that the measured changes are not the result of sampling variation. The UCR Program bases its data on the actual counts of offenses reported by law enforcement agencies. In some circumstances, the UCR Program estimates its data for nonparticipating agencies or those reporting partial data. Apparent discrepancies between statistics from the two programs can usually be accounted for by their definitional and procedural differences, or resolved by comparing NCVS sampling variations (confidence intervals) of crimes said to have been reported to police with UCR Program statistics.

For most types of crimes measured by both the UCR Program and the NCVS, analysts familiar with the programs can exclude those aspects of crime not common to both from analysis. Resulting long-term trend lines can be brought into close concordance. The impact of such adjustments is most striking for robbery, burglary, and motor vehicle theft, whose definitions most closely coincide.

With robbery, the BJS bases the NCVS victimization rates on only those robberies reported to the police. It is also possible to remove UCR Program robberies of commercial establishments, such as gas stations, convenience stores, and banks, from analysis. When users compare the resulting NCVS police-reported robbery rates and the UCR Program noncommercial robbery rates, the results reveal closely corresponding long-term trends.

## Conclusion

Each program has unique strengths. The UCR Program provides a measure of the number of crimes reported to law enforcement agencies throughout the country. The program's Supplementary Homicide Reports provide the most reliable, timely data on the extent and nature of homicides in the nation. The NCVS is the primary source of information on the characteristics of criminal victimization and on the number and types of crimes not reported to law enforcement authorities.

By understanding the strengths and limitations of each program, it is possible to use the UCR Program and NCVS to achieve a greater understanding of crime trends and the nature of crime in the United States. For example, changes in police procedures, shifting attitudes towards crime and police, and other societal changes can affect the extent to which people report and law enforcement agencies record crime. NCVS and UCR Program data can be used in concert to explore why trends in reported and police-recorded crime may differ.

# INDEX

# INDEX